Annotated Teacher's Edition

Prentice Hall

LITERATURE

Timeless Voices, Timeless Themes

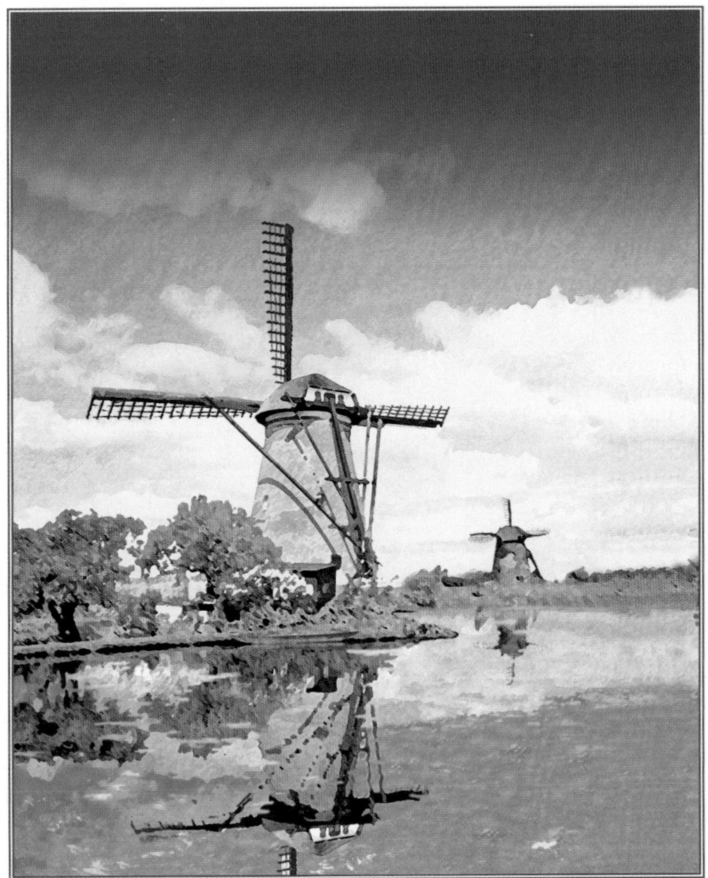

PLATINUM

PRENTICE HALL
Upper Saddle River, New Jersey
Needham, Massachusetts
Glenview, Illinois

ISBN 0-13-050427-0

2 3 4 5 6 7 8 9 10   03 02 01 00 99

Only Prentice Hall gives you an outstanding array of print and technology support, developed to let you customize easily to your teaching style and local or state curriculum.

Print components and Transparency Resources

- Student Edition
- Annotated Teacher's Edition
- Teaching Resources
    - Selection Support
    - Formal Assessment with Assessment Resources Software CD-ROM
    - Alternative Assessment
    - Beyond Literature
    - Strategies for Diverse Student Needs
    - Art Transparencies
    - Professional Development Library
        - Assess Student Work
        - Kick Off for Success
        - Putting Patterns to Work
        - Manage Instruction in the Block
    - Daily Language Practice
- *Resource Pro*® CD-ROM with Local Objectives Editor
    - Exclusive *Planning Express*® software with Local Objectives Editor
    - Instant access to all teaching resources
    - 100 additional selections per grade level
- Writer's Companion
- Grammar Practice Book
- Writing and Language Transparencies
- Fine Arts Posters
- Spanish Language Support

Plus...Technology Resources

- Assessment Resources Software CD-ROM
- *Got It!* Videotapes
- Interactive Student Tutorial CD-ROM
- Literature Companion Web Site
- *Looking at Literature* Videotapes
- *Looking at Literature* Videodiscs
- *Humanities* Videotapes
- Student Book on Audiocassettes
- *AuthorWorks* CD-ROM series
- *BBC Shakespeare* CD-ROM series
- *Writer's Solution Writing Lab* CD-ROM
- *Writer's Solution Language Lab* CD-RO
- *Writers at Work* Videotapes
- *Writers at Work* Videodiscs

print and technology resources

Introducing a Web site developed specifically for Prentice Hall Literature.

▲ Grade 9 components shown.

On-line Student Resources

- Current Events Writing Workshop keeps students up to date with two fully developed writing assignments, updated twice each year.
- Activities incorporate Internet resources for nearly every selection.
- Multiple-choice tests—scored-online—for every selection.
- Hot links provide instant access to sites supporting every selection.

On-line Teacher Resources

- Teachers can consult with colleagues through the Faculty Forum.
- Teaching links provide instant access to sites providing teaching support for every selection.

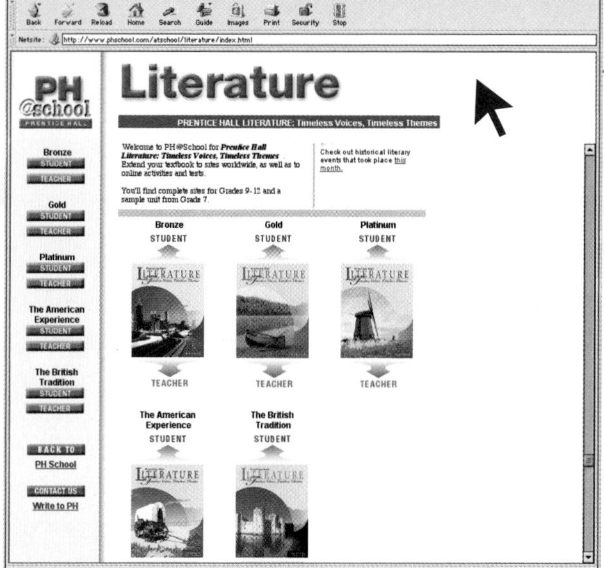

◀ Access a wide range of interactive tools at **www.phlit.phschool.com**

Outstanding blend of classic contemporary, and

Prentice Hall *Literature*:

Timeless Voices, Timeless Themes

combines an outstanding blend of time-tested classics, the finest contemporary literature, and inspirational literature to create a new enthusiasm for literature.

Classic literature opens your classroom to lives and cultures across time and place. From Homer to Mark Twain, we give you the classic literature that you love to teach.

inspirational literature

Contemporary literature is relevant to students' lives. Prentice Hall gives you the finest selections of today to engage your students and foster an appreciation of literature. Prentice Hall also offers an extensive sampling of real-world texts that help students build skills for success in both school and work.

Inspirational literature evokes in students the passion a writer feels for life and literature. In turn, students gain a sense of a living literature—writing that explores the immediate wonders and beauty of the world around them.

Unmatched skills instruction

ONLY **PRENTICE HALL**

- Teaches literary elements before, during, and after every selection.
- Integrates strategic reading instruction before, during, and after every selection, making the finest literature accessible to all students.
- Motivates students to read through real-world connections before, during, and after every selection.
- Teaches vocabulary-building strategies with every selection.
- Provides more writing and grammar instruction than any other literature program.
- Offers an Authors in Depth study for at least one key author for every unit.

Prepare and Engage

LESSON OBJECTIVES

1. **To develop vocabulary and word identification skills**
   - Latin Suffixes: *-ous-*
   - Using the Word Bank: Synonyms
   - Extending Word Study: Suffixes (ATE)
2. **To use a variety of reading strategies to comprehend a short story**
   - Connect Your Experience
   - Reading Strategy: Use Your Senses
   - Tips to Guide Reading (ATE)
   - Read to Discover Writing Models (ATE)
3. **To increase knowledge of other cultures and to connect common elements across cultures**
   - Connecting Themes Across Cultures (ATE)
4. **To express and support responses to the text**
   - Critical Thinking
   - Idea Bank: Suggestion Letter
   - Idea Bank: Essay
   - Idea Bank: Dramatic Reading
   - Speaking, Listening, and Viewing Mini-Lesson (ATE)
5. **To analyze literary elements**
   - Literary Focus: Setting
6. **To read in order to research self-selected and assigned topics**
   - Idea Bank: Research
   - Idea Bank: Visual Presentation
   - Idea Bank: Diagram
   - Viewing and Representing Mini-Lesson (ATE)
   - Idea Bank: Map
7. **To use recursive writing processes t[o] write a eulogy**
   - Guided Writing Lesson
8. **To increase knowledge of the rules [of] grammar and usage**
   - Build Grammar Skills: Punctuating Dialogue

Test Preparation

Reading Comprehension: Recognize Author's Point of View (ATE, p. 521) The teaching tips and sample test item in this workshop support the instruction and practice in the unit workshop: **Reading Comprehension: Recognize Author's Point of View and Purpose** (SE, p. 553)

520

Guide for Reading

Leslie Marmon Silko
(1948–)

Storytelling has been an important part of Leslie Marmon Silko's life practically from the day she was born. Raised on the Laguna Pueblo reservation in New Mexico, she grew up listening to tribal stories told by her great-grandmother and great-aunts. Drawing upon elements from the traditional tales she heard as a child, Silko has forged a successful career as a writer.

In her stories, novels, and poems, Silko explores what life is like for Native Americans in today's world. Many of her works, including "The Man Who Sends Rain Clouds," capture the contrast between traditional values and beliefs and the elements of modern-day life.

Featured in AUTHORS IN DEPTH Series

Mark Twain *(1835–*

Born Samuel Langhorne Clemens, this great American humorist grew up in the river town of Hannibal, Missouri. Though Twain traveled and lived all over the United States, it is the great Mississippi River that runs through the heart of his life and work.

As a young man, he learned the trade of the riverboat pilot and took his pen name from a sounding cry used on Mississippi stea[m]boats: 'By the mark—twain,' which means the wat[er] two fathoms deep. Although Twain worked as a pri[nter,] prospector, reporter, editor, and lecturer, writing wa[s his] true calling. He was the best-known and most succ[essful] author of his generation. Some of his most popular [works] include *Tom Sawyer*, *The Adventures of Huckleberr[y] Finn*, and *Life on the Mississippi*.

Guide for Reading

Leslie Marmon Silko
(1948–)

Storytelling has been an important part of Leslie Marmon Silko's life practically from the day she was born. Raised on the Laguna Pueblo reservation in New Mexico, she grew up listening to tribal stories told by her great-grandmother and great-aunts. Drawing upon elements from the traditional tales she heard as a child, Silko has forged a successful career as a writer.

In her stories, novels, and poems, Silko explores what life is like for Native Americans in today's world. Many of her works, including "The Man Who Sends Rain Clouds," capture the contrast between traditional values and beliefs and the elements of modern-day life.

Featured in AUTHORS IN DEPTH Series

Mark Twain *(1835–19*

Born Samuel Langhorne Clemens, this great American humorist grew up in the river town of Hannibal, Missouri. Though Twain traveled and lived all over the United States, it is the great Mississippi River that runs through the heart of his life and work.

As a young man, he learned the trade of the riverboat pilot and took his pen name from a sounding cry used on Mississippi steamboats: 'By the mark—twain,' which means the water i[s] two fathoms deep. Although Twain worked as a print[er,] prospector, reporter, editor, and lecturer, writing was h[is] true calling. He was the best-known and most success[ful] author of his generation. Some of his most popular w[orks] include *Tom Sawyer*, *The Adventures of Huckleberry Finn*, and *Life on the Mississippi*.

◆ Build Vocabulary

LATIN SUFFIXES: -ous

... appear in ... are many-syllabled words ending with the suffix *-ous*, from the Latin *-osus*, meaning "full of." For instance, *prodigious* combines *prodigy*, meaning "a marvel or wonder," with *-ous*; *prodigious* means "wonderful" or "amazing." In Twain's story, the word *prodigious* refers to a mistake. Fortunately for the reader, this prodigious mistake leads to a humorous story.

WORD BANK

Before you read, preview this list of words from the stories.

cloister
pagans
perverse
prodigious
deleterious
ominous
judicious
placidly
desultory

◆ Build Grammar Skills

PUNCTUATING DIALOGUE

Both of these stories rely heavily on dialogu[e—] conversation involving at least two speakers. Follow these rules for punctuating the dialogue:

- Use quotation marks before and after a speaker's exact words.
- Begin a new paragraph each time the speak[er] changes.
- Use commas to separate quotations from words that identify the speaker—no matte[r] where those words appear in the sentence. The comma always appears before the quo[ta]tion marks.
- When a paragraph ends while a character [is] still speaking, quotation marks do not appe[ar] at the end of that paragraph. However, they appear at the beginning of the new paragra[ph].

520 ◆ Short Stories

Build Vocabulary introduces a vocabulary-building strategy with every selection.

Reading Strategy provided before, during, and after every selection.

The Man to Send Rain Clouds
◆ The Invalid's Story ◆

Literature and Your Life

NECT YOUR EXPERIENCE
some time, everyone has to deal with the loss of a loved o e cope with this in different ways. They may try to preserve ved one's memory, or they may look to fulfill the person's last s. These stories present two very different sets of circum- es surrounding a person's death and others' responses to it.

ATIC FOCUS: FACING CONFLICTS
these stories reveal, dealing with death can involve working ifficult and sometimes unexpected issues and situations.

ackground for Understanding

URE
he Man to Send Rain Clouds" explores the traditions of the o Indians. The Pueblos have lived in the southwestern United for nearly 3,000 years. They first came into contact with Eu- ns when the Spanish arrived in the 1500's. During the twenti- entury, the Pueblos have incorporated many aspects of the

◆ Reading Strategy

YOUR SENSES
setting of each story gives your senses a real workout. As you read each one, **use your senses** to picture the setting and the characters in your mind.

Draw from your own expe- riences to see, hear, smell, taste, or feel what each author describes. For example, when Twain describes a piece of cheese with an overpowering odor, search your memory to recall when you've smelled especially pungent cheese, and try to re-create the sensation in your mind.

Interest Grabber Have students name movies that they've seen—one involving humor- ous treatment of the events surround- ing death and one involving reflections on the honor and respect arising from death. Discuss the ways that death can provoke such different responses. Tell students that the contrasting views of death in the movies parallel the views of death in these stories.

Connecting Themes Across Cultures

Each of these stories deals with death and survivors' reactions to it. In both cases, the survivors follow a set of rules dictated by their culture. Ask students to share their knowl- edge of mourning customs from their own culture or other cultures they know. For example, in Judaism, a body is usually buried within 24 hours of death, while in other religions, a

The Man to Send Rain Clouds
◆ The Invalid's Story ◆

Literature and Your Life

NNECT YOUR EXPERIENCE
t some time, everyone has to deal with the loss of a loved one. ple cope with this in different ways. They may try to preserve oved one's memory, or they may look to fulfill the person's last es. These stories present two very different sets of circum- ces surrounding a person's death and others' responses to it.

MATIC FOCUS: FACING CONFLICTS
s these stories reveal, dealing with death can involve working difficult and sometimes unexpected issues and situations.

Background for Understanding

TURE
The Man to Send Rain Clouds" explores the traditions of the blo Indians. The Pueblos have lived in the southwestern United es for nearly 3,000 years. They first came into contact with Eu- eans when the Spanish arrived in the 1500's. During the twenti- century, the Pueblos have incorporated many aspects of the strial world into their lives. Nevertheless, they have tried to ntain their ancient traditions and beliefs—including the view that ey keep themselves in harmony with the natural world, nature give them what they need, such as sufficient rainfall for their ps. The Pueblos' balancing of modern ways with their own cus- s and views provides the central conflict in Silko's story.

ournal Writing Jot down what you know about the ueblo ... cultures.

◆ Reading Strategy

USE YOUR SENSES
A dry wintry desert wait- ing for rain. A stifling boxcar with a smelly package. The setting of each story gives your senses a real workout. As you read each one, **use your senses** to picture the setting and the characters in your mind.

Draw from your own expe- riences to see, hear, smell, taste, or feel what each author describes. For example, when Twain describes a piece of cheese with an overpowering odor, search your memory to recall when you've smelled especially pungent cheese, and try to re-create the sensation in your mind.

Use a graphic organizer like this one to help you record key details appealing to each sense.

Sights	Sounds	Smells	Tastes	Physical Sensation

◆ Literary Focus

TING
...etting—the e and ... the setting simply vides a backdrop for the actions and characters. In other sto- —including these—the setting shapes the characters' actions. n addition to time and place, a story's setting includes the ural background against which the action takes place: the toms, ideas, values, and beliefs of the society in which it occurs. cultural background for "The Man to Send Rain Clouds" con- s of the customs and beliefs of the Pueblo people.

Guide for Reading ◆ 521

Customize for
Less Proficient Readers
Twain's long sentences may pose a problem for these students ... result, ... with them to break down some of the long sentences toward the beginning of the story. For example, show that the second sentence in the second paragraph includes a long series of details relating to the circumstances surrounding the narrator's discovery of his friend's death. Have students list each of the details separately; then show how they fit together.

Customize for
Pre-AP Students
Challenge students to retell Silko's story from Father Paul's or Louise's point of view and Twain's story from the expressman's point of view. Afterward, hold a group discussion to evaluate the presentations.

Customize for
English Language Learners
Help these students by clarifying con- fusing passages in the Twain story, such as "He gasped once or twice, then moved toward the cof—gun-box ..." or "... here he scrambled to his feet and broke a pane...." You might also help with words written in dialect, such as "How long has he *ben* dead?"

521

Customize for... notes in the Teacher's Edition offer strategies and tips for helping readers of all levels.

Literary Focus teaches literary elements before, during, and after every selection.

Motivation for today's students

ONLY PRENTICE HALL

- Makes the finest collection of classic and contemporary literature relevant to students.
- Engages students with *Literature and Your Life* sections before, during, and after every selection.
- Features *Connections to Today's World* that link high-interest contemporary selections to thematically related classic literature.
- Explores cross-curricular, career, community, and media connections in the *Beyond Literature* feature.
- Offers an outstanding array of videos, software, and technology to make literature accessible to today's multimedia generation.

CONNECTIONS TO TODAY'S WORLD

In April 1970, the three-man crew modern-day [illegible] embarked on a Odysseus, they set out with a spirit of anticipation and adventure. Their mission almost ended tragically, however, when an oxygen tank ruptured on board, but after several nerve-wracking days, the crew finally managed to return safely to Earth.

Jim Lovell, one of the astronauts on [illegible] co-authored [illegible] inspired a feature film. In this excerpt from the book, Lovell has just reported a gas leak to controllers on the ground.

From APOLLO 13

Jim Lovell and Jeffrey Kluger

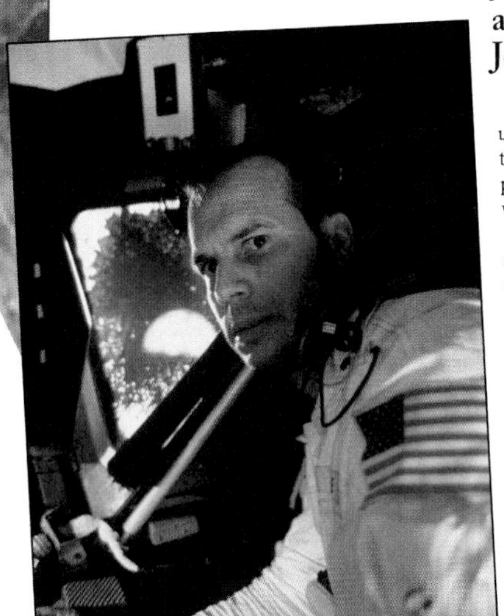

"It looks to me," Lovell told the ground uninflectedly, "that we are venting something." Then, for impact, and perhaps to persuade himself, he repeated "We are venting something into space."

"Roger," Lousma responded, in the mandatory matter-of-factness of the Capcom, "we copy your venting."

"It's a gas of some sort," Lovell said.

"Can you tell us anything about it? Where is it coming from?"

"It's coming out of window one right now, Jack," Lovell answered, offering only as much detail as his vantage point provided.

The understated report from the spacecraft tore through the control room like a bullet.

"Crew thinks they're venting something," Lousma said to the loop at large.

934 ◆ The Epic

▲

Connections to Today's World links classic literature to high-interest contemporary writings.

The Gift of the Magi

MODEL SELECTION

◆ Literature and Your Life

…CT YOUR EXPERIENCE … on your birthday gift. You open the box—and your spirits sink. Your gift is a lopsided sweater, made by an inexperienced knitter in your least favorite color. Hiding your disappointment, you thank the giver enthusiastically. After all, it's the thought that counts.

Gifts are sometimes less appropriate or more meaningful than they first appear. In this story, a husband and wife discover the unexpected problems and joys of giving gifts.

THEMATIC FOCUS: WORKING TOWARD A GOAL

As this story shows, a person may strive toward a goal with the best of intentions, only to find that his or her effort was misdirected. How can people redirect their efforts in such a situation?

Journal Writing In your journal, describe an incident—real or imagined—in which someone tried to do something nice but had his or her plans go awry. Explain what, if anything, the person did to fix problems resulting from his or her actions.

◆ Background for Understanding

ECONOMICS

When you read a story that was written more than ten years ago, you will find that prices or amounts of money seem ridiculously low. This is because the United States has experienced inflation over the years. Inflation is a continual increase in most or all major prices throughout an economy. Although the causes of inflation are hotly debated, the effects are clear: The purchasing power of a unit of currency goes down. In the story, which was written at the beginning of the twentieth century, $32 is a month's rent for Della and Jim. Today, $32 would not even pay for a night in an inexpensive motel.

…iterary Focus

…OT

The events in a story make up its **plot,** which is traditionally divided into five parts: *exposition, rising action, climax, falling action,* and *resolution.* The exposition provides background information and sets the scene for the conflict—a struggle between opposing people or forces that drives the action of the story. The introduction of the conflict marks the beginning of the rising action, in which the conflict intensifies until it reaches the high point, or climax, of the story. After the climax, the action falls to a resolution. The resolution shows how the situation turns out and ties up loose ends.

As you read the story, jot down events associated with the different parts of the plot on a diagram like this one.

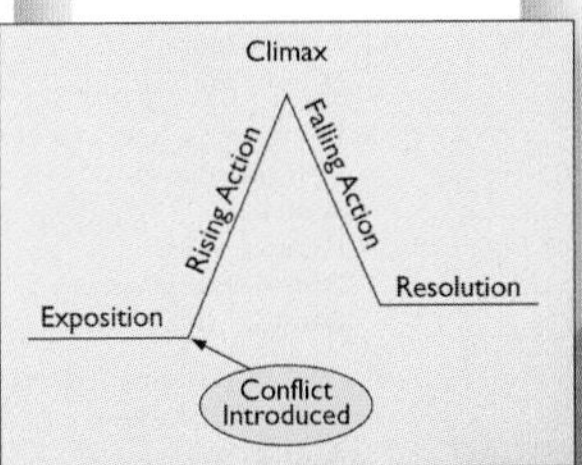

◀ **Literature and Your Life** sections before, during, and after every selection connect literature to students' lives.

A wide array of videos, software, and technology makes literature come alive for today's students. ▶

Assessment success

ONLY **PRENTICE HALL**

- Integrates standardized test preparation activities and strategies with every selection.
- Provides point-of-use test-taking strategies in the Teacher's Edition.
- Provides the most support and practice for national tests, such as the SAT and ACT, as well as state and local tests.
- Provides the most comprehensive array of print and technology to prepare students for standardized tests.

Test Practice Bank

Reading Comprehension

Context Clues and Prefixes/Suffixes

Read the passage, and then answer the questions that follow. Mark the letter of your answer on a bubble sheet if your teacher provides one; otherwise, number from 1 to 6 on a separate sheet of paper, and write the letter of the correct answer next to each number.

From the 1500's until the Marxist revolution of 1917, Russia was ruled by czars—iron-fisted emperors who held tight control over virtually every aspect of Russian life. To keep a close eye on local officials throughout Russia's vast landscape, the czars employed people in the position of inspector-general. The inspectors-general were charged to observe how local schools, courts, hospitals, and so on were functioning. Because the unhappy people were resentful of the czar's absolute authority, the inspecto... general public.

1 The word Marxist in this passage means—
A in support of the czars
B based on the ideas of Karl Marx
C opposed to the ideas of Karl Marx
D long and violent

2 In this passage, the term iron-fisted means—
A strict
B lazy
C reasonable
D ineffective

3 In this passage, the word charged means—
A attacked
B disappointed
C electrified
D ordered

See the Test Preparation Worksh... about word meanings.

Perseus

◆ *Literature and Your Life*

CONNECT YOUR EXPERIENCE
Some people love to rise to difficult occasions, while others prefer to keep their lives on an even keel. Perseus, the main character in this selection, is the first sort of person—the type who thrives on grappling with thorny problems. Which sort are you?

THEMATIC FOCUS: PUTTING OURSELVES TO THE TEST
Perseus' passage from one peril to the next might make you wonder what you would do if you suddenly found yourself in his sandals, faced with the choice between taking on a highly dangerous mission or being viewed with scorn. What alternatives might you have in such a tight spot?

◆ Background for Understanding

CULTURE
"Perseus" takes place in a mythological world populated by Greek gods and goddesses. The cast of Greek gods you will meet in Perseus' story includes Zeus, the chief god, who fathered a number of human children; Athena, goddess of war and wisdom; and Hermes, the messenger god (whom you may know by his Roman name Mercury).

Journal Writing Perseus' world is full of mythic beauty and horror that go beyond normal human experience. Write a physical description of a fantastic creature of your own invention—either beautiful or monstrous (or both).

◆ Literary Focus

HERO IN A MYTH
Start with a brave young man who loves his mother. Add some sympathetic gods and a terrible monster. You now have the makings of a **hero in a myth**—a character who performs amazing feats in a tale involving supernatural beings and fantastic events. The hero in a myth is often aided by magical elements. Nevertheless, the hero must exhibit admirable qualities such as courage, loyalty, and fairness. As you...

◆ Reading Strategy

PREDICT
"Perseus" begins with a prediction by an oracle (prophet) about a future event. When you read any work of literature, you too can **predict outcomes**—not by using supernatural powers, but by thinking about the world presented in the literature and about the logical consequences of the characters' actions. These factors help you narrow down many possible outcomes to the few most likely ones.

To help you predict outcomes in "Perseus," make a chart like this one.

Situation	Possible Outcome	Reasons for Prediction	Outcome

Guide for Reading ◆ *185*

Test Preparation Workshop

studen... order.

Before he could attack Medusa, Perseus had to receive help from Athena and Hermes. Later he delivered the Gorgon's head to the cruel Polydectes, but only after saving Andromeda on his way home.

Which of these actions happens last?

...meda.
...edusa.
A Perse... Polydectes the head of

...Perseus is aided by Athena and Hermes. Students can piece together the sequence of events by looking for words or phrases that signal time, like *before, later,* and *after.* Bringing the Gorgon's head to Polydectes happens *later* than the attack, and *after* the saving of Andromeda. It is the last of the events in the sequence, ...

▲

Standardized Test Practice Bank integrates standardized test format activities in the student edition.

Standardized Test Preparation Workshops at point-of-use in the Teacher's Edition help you plan for student assessment success.

A wide variety of print and technology assessment resources gives you flexible review and testing options.

Resource Pro® CD-ROM with Local Objectives Editor lets you customize your lessons by importing local or state objectives.

Resources for varying learning

ONLY **PRENTICE HALL**

- Recognizes diverse learning styles and provides appropriate teaching support.
- Features integrated reading support before, during, and after every selection.
- Provides *Customize for...* teacher notes that offer strategies for various student populations.
- Offers *Idea Bank* activities geared to all types of learners.
- Features *Interest Grabber* notes at the beginning of every selection.
- Provides selection support pages for students of all learning modalities.

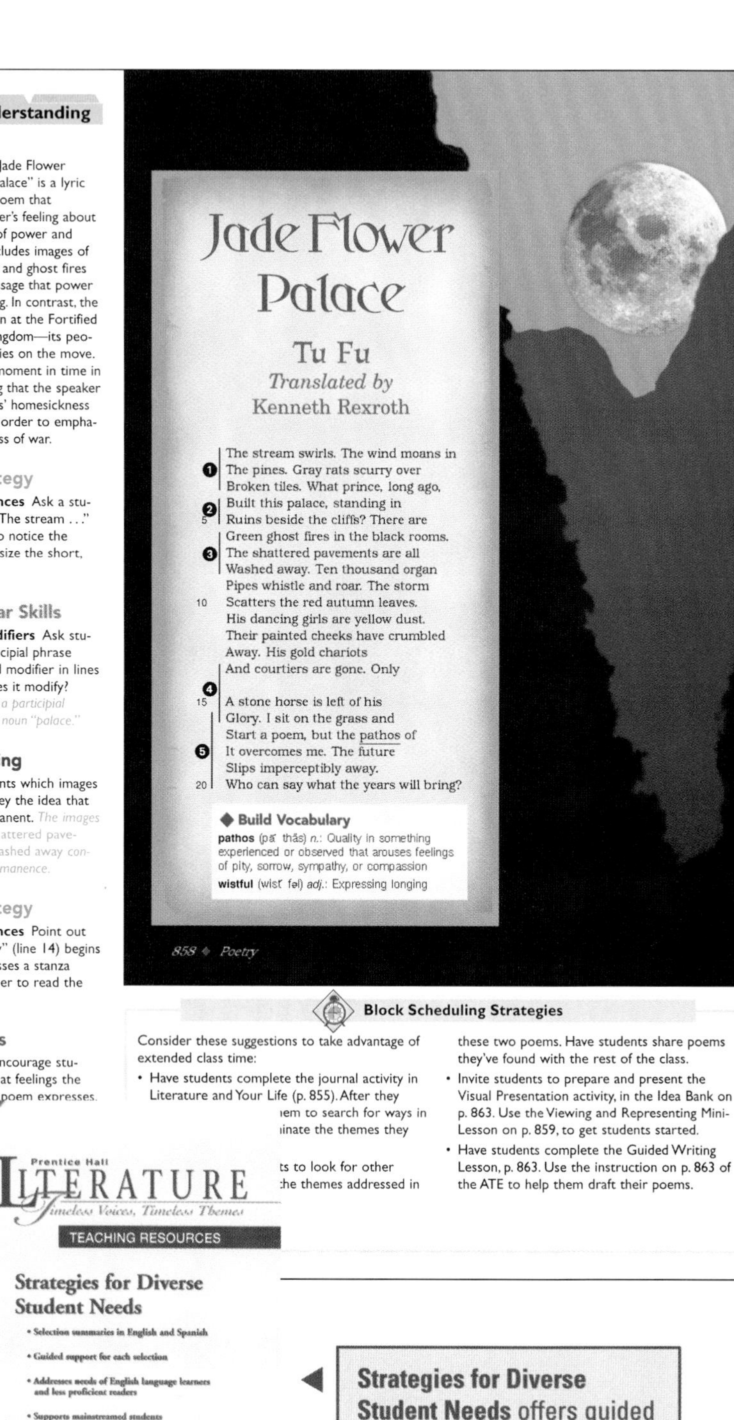

Strategies for Diverse Student Needs offers guided support for every selection.

styles and ability levels

Li Po

Translated by
Lin Yutang

The bright moon lifts from the Mountain of Heaven
In an infinite haze of cloud and sea,
And the wind, that has come a thousand miles, (6)
Beats at the Jade Pass[1] basements. . . .
China marches its men down Po-teng Road
While Tartar[2] troops peer across blue waters of the bay. . . . (7)
And since not one battle famous in history
Sent all its fighters back again,
The soldiers turn round, looking toward the border,
And think of home, with wistful eyes, (8)
And of those tonight in the upper chambers
Who toss and sigh and cannot rest.

1. **Jade Pass:** Gap in the Great Wall in northeastern China.
2. **Tartar** (tär′ tər): Tartars were nomadic tribes who originally lived in Mongolia, Manchuria, and Siberia. From A.D. 200 through 400, the Tartars were almost constantly at war with the Chinese. A thousand years later, under the leadership of Genghis Khan, the Tartars conquered China as well as a number of European and Asian countries.

◀ Critical Viewing Imagine this picture as a setting for "The Moon at the Fortified Pass." What might make the soldiers "wistful"? **[Analyze]** (9)

Jade Flower Palace/ The Moon at the Fortified Pass ◆ *859*

◆ Build Grammar Skills

(6) Adjectival Modifiers Challenge students to identify the adjectival modifiers for "haze" (line 2) and "wind" (line 3) and to state what type each is. *The prepositional phrase "of cloud and sea" modifies the noun "haze." The adjective clause "that has come a thousand miles" modifies the noun "wind."*

◆ Literary Focus

(7) Lyric Poetry Point out that since this is a lyric poem, its historical situation is described in only two lines. In a narrative poem, much more about the history of this conflict would have been explained. Ask students to describe the setting for this event. *Sample answer: The place is the Jade Pass, a fortified gap in the Great Wall in northeastern China. The setting is moonlit, hazy, windy, and far from home.*

◆ Critical Thinking

(8) Infer What descriptive words in this passage indicate the soldiers' feeling, and what is that feeling? *The phrases "looking toward the border," "And think of home," reflect the soldiers' feeling, which is one of homesickness.*

▶ Critical Viewing ◀

(9) Analyze *Suggested response: These aspects of the setting would make the soldiers*

Customize for
Gifted/Talented Students
These students might be interest... ...essing the theme an... form; for example, a journal entry, a brief musical interpretation, a painting, or a dance. Suggest that they begin by jotting down the theme, then decide which art form would best express the feelings they associate with that theme.

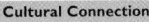

Cultural Connection

Community Gathering Places The speaker in Rosellen Brown's poem suggests that friends make life more enjoyable. Many communities and different cultures host events where people gather to share friendship and good times. Holiday activities, parades, block parties, town picnics, and concerts in the park are just a few types of gatherings that are sponsored by communities.

Challenge students to generate a list of places around the world where friends gather—they can research, as needed. In France, outdoor cafes are popular summertime gathering places; in Greece, the town square; in other locations it might be church or the community hall. What events or gathering places does your own community offer?

Discuss with them how community gathering places may have changed over time. What might have caused changes? Encourage them to consider the impact of technological advances such as cars, TV, air conditioning, and so forth. Ask them to speculate about future gathering places.

859

PRENTICE HALL
Interactive
Student Tutorial
Prentice Hall
LITERATURE
Timeless Voices, Timeless Themes
GOLD

A wide range of technology support appeals to varying learning styles.

Customize for... notes in the Teacher's Edition make it easy to tailor instruction to varying student populations.

The largest literature library

ONLY **PRENTICE HALL**

- Combines over 80 titles to give you the classic and contemporary fiction, nonfiction, and drama that you love to teach.
- Offers exclusive thematic anthologies.
- Provides you with all of the teaching resources you need to explore each title.

PLUS...

We give you a choice of over 8 million books, videos, audiotapes, and software through our partnership with barnesandnoble.com.

Choose the books that you want to teach!

available

WORLD WRITERS TODAY
THE BIBLE AS/IN LITERATURE
MULTICULTURAL VOICES
A SEPARATE PEACE
JOHNNY TREMAIN
LORD JIM
Joseph Conrad
A RAISIN IN THE SUN
THE CLAY MARBLE
CALL OF THE WILD
BY JACK LONDON
Workplace Writing
The Red Badge of Courage
Stephen Crane
A Midsummer Night's Dream
William Shakespeare
PRENTICE HALL LITERATURE LIBRARY

ONLY **PRENTICE HALL**

- Choose from over 8 million books, videos, audiotapes, and software—the world's largest selection.
- Find exactly the resources you want for you and your students.
- Take advantage of a bookstore that never closes.
- Visit www.phlit.phschool.com to find details on this exciting partnership.

The nation's leading literature program now comes with the world's largest bookstore.

that comes with a bookstore!

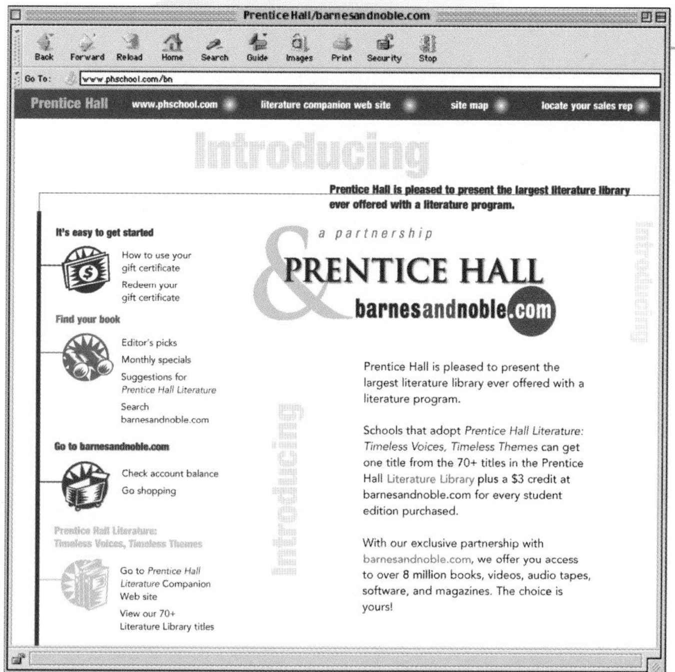

Exclusive partnership!

Prentice Hall is pleased to present the largest literature library ever offered with a literature program. With our exclusive partnership with barnesandnoble.com, we offer you access to over *8 million titles*. *We make it easy to get what you want.* Log on to www.phlit.phschool.com/bn and see how.

Key features help you find your book

- Editor's picks guide you to titles our editors enjoy and recommend.
- Bargain books help you shop and get the best deals.
- Suggestions for *Prentice Hall Literature* always correlate to the title you teach.
- Search barnesandnoble.com and choose from over 8 million books, videos, audio-tapes, and software.

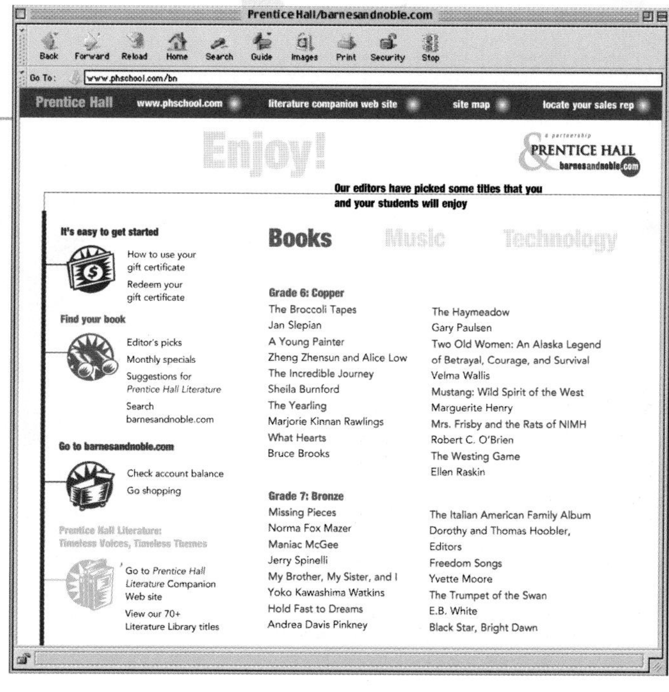

Outstanding array of technology resources

ONLY **PRENTICE HALL**

- Motivates students with a wide range of fully integrated technology.
- Makes teachers' planning easier with the groundbreaking *Resource Pro® CD-ROM with Local Objectives Editor.*
- Grabs students' attention with videos for each selection.
- Helps varying learning styles with selections on tape and video segments that hook students.
- Features the award-winning interactive writing instruction of *Writer's Solution.*
- Gives you a dedicated companion Web site at www.phlit.phschool.com to access a full-range of interactive, Internet-based activities.

Listening to Literature Audiocassettes bring literature to life and meet the diverse needs and learning styles of your students.

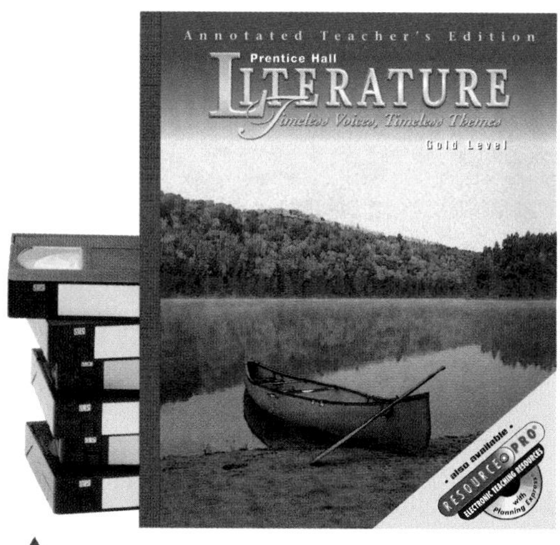

A wide array of **Video Series** are fully integrated into the textbook and feature point-of-use notes in the Teacher's Edition.

Resource Pro® with Local Objectives Editor CD-ROM gives you the tools to customize your lessons.

Writer's Solution, Prentice Hall's award-winning interactive writing instruction program, has been fully integrated into *Prentice Hall Literature: Timeless Voices, Timeless Themes.*

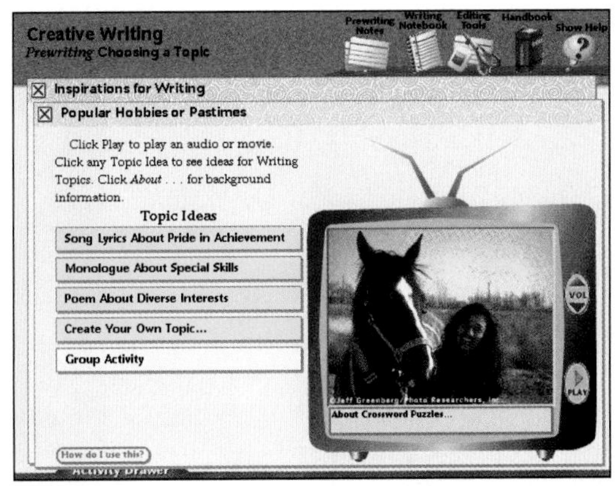

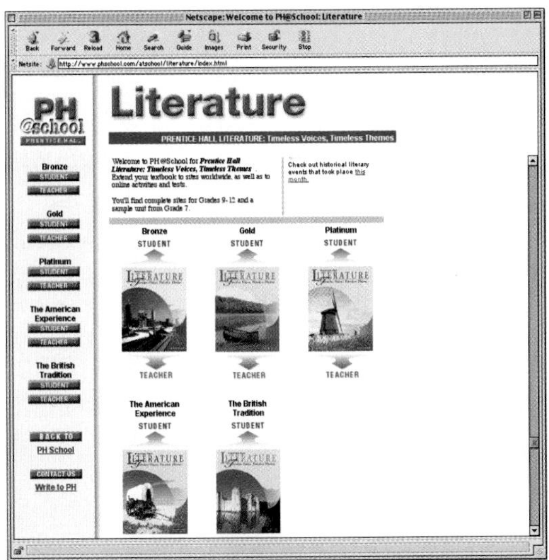

Internet Home Page, at www.phlit.phschool.com provides features that support *Prentice Hall Literature: Timeless Voices, Timeless Themes.*

Literature CD-ROM Library features multimedia presentations; hyperlinks to glossaries, indexes, and encyclopedias; and complete on-line testing; as just some of the outstanding features on these interactive CD-ROMs.

Formal Assessment CD-ROM allows you to gauge your students' ability levels and establish your own skills objectives.

Support for block scheduling

ONLY PRENTICE HALL

- Provides block scheduling lesson suggestions with every selection.
- Offers a full range of activities and workshops to create opportunities for in-depth exploration of a topic.
- Supports the use of a variety of instructional models.
- Encourages students to demonstrate their knowledge and understanding of concepts and content through alternative assessment.
- Features the award-winning *Resource Pro®* *with Planning Express® CD-ROM* to help you manage block scheduling lesson planning and manage resources.

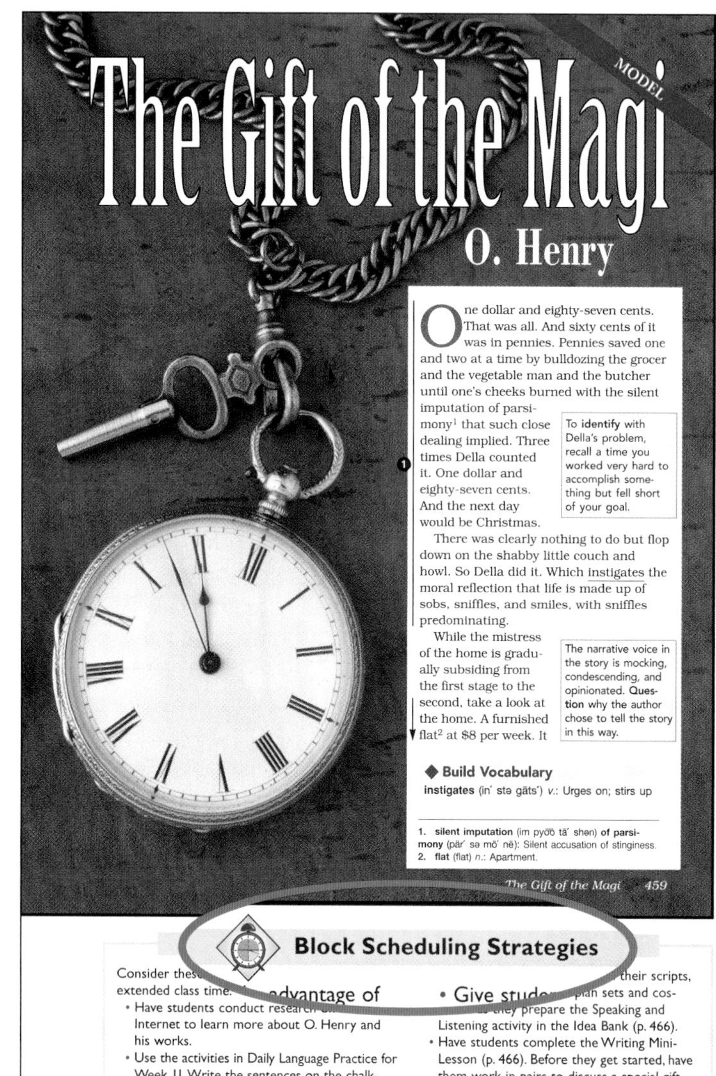

MODEL

The Gift of the Magi

O. Henry

One dollar and eighty-seven cents. That was all. And sixty cents of it was in pennies. Pennies saved one and two at a time by bulldozing the grocer and the vegetable man and the butcher until one's cheeks burned with the silent imputation of parsimony[1] that such close dealing implied. Three times Della counted it. One dollar and eighty-seven cents. And the next day would be Christmas.

There was clearly nothing to do but flop down on the shabby little couch and howl. So Della did it. Which instigates the moral reflection that life is made up of sobs, sniffles, and smiles, with sniffles predominating.

While the mistress of the home is gradually subsiding from the first stage to the second, take a look at the home. A furnished flat[2] at $8 per week. It

To **identify** with Della's problem, recall a time you worked very hard to accomplish something but fell short of your goal.

The narrative voice in the story is mocking, condescending, and opinionated. **Question** why the author chose to tell the story in this way.

◆ **Build Vocabulary**

instigates (in' stə gāts') *v.*: Urges on; stirs up

1. **silent imputation** (im pyōō tā' shən) **of parsimony** (pär' sə mō' nē): Silent accusation of stinginess.
2. **flat** (flat) *n.*: Apartment.

The Gift of the Magi 459

Develop Understan

One-Minute Insight This cla story of sacrifici love—and its ironic conseque has been a favorite for genera The narrative follows the acti a young woman named Della, wants to buy her husband a s Christmas gift but has virtually money. She solves her probler selling her hair, so that she ca a chain for her husband's poc watch. Ironically, her husband sold his pocket watch in orde buy her a special present—a s combs! The story's ironic endi likely to spur spirited discussi debate among your students a the wisdom—or foolishness— young couple, each of whom s fices a most-prized possessio the other.

Tips to Guide Readir

Shared Reading Tell studen the story is written from the p view of a narrator with a very tive voice. In order to establish tone of that voice for students, the first five paragraphs aloud t class.

◆ ***Literature and Your L***

Tell students that a gold pocke watch like this plays an impor part in this story. Ask student relate the importance of a fam heirloom like this one to their feelings about a favorite posse *Students may mention their own heirlooms, as well as souvenirs fr cial vacations or events, special g from relatives and friends, or thi have made themselves.*

Customize for *English Language Lear* These students may be confus the metaphorical use of the w *bulldozing.* Describe how a bul works and ask in what way a c tomer looking for a bargain m feel like a bulldozer.

◆ **Literary Focus**

❶ **Plot** Ask students what im tant background information t learn about Della and Jim in th few paragraphs of the story. *Th don't have much money; they ha scrimp to pay bills and save for*

Block Scheduling Strategies

Consider thes... extended class time... advantage of

- Have students conduct resea... Internet to learn more about O. Henry and his works.
- Use the activities in Daily Language Practice for Week 11. Write the sentences on the chalkboard and have students correct the errors.
- Students may work together in small groups to analyze the plot of "The Gift of the Magi" and answer the Literary Focus questions on p. 465.
- Give stude... their scripts, ...n sets and cos- ...they prepare the Speaking and Listening activity in the Idea Bank (p. 466).
- Have students complete the Writing Mini-Lesson (p. 466). Before they get started, have them work in pairs to discuss a special gift and why they liked it. As one partner talks, the other should ask questions to help the speaker think of ways to make the letter more personal.

▲

Block Scheduling Strategies give you point-of-use suggestions with every selection.

Resource Pro® with Planning Express® CD-ROM helps you manage lesson planning and resources.

PRENTICE HALL
professional educator's library

HOW·TO MANAGE INSTRUCTION IN THE BLOCK

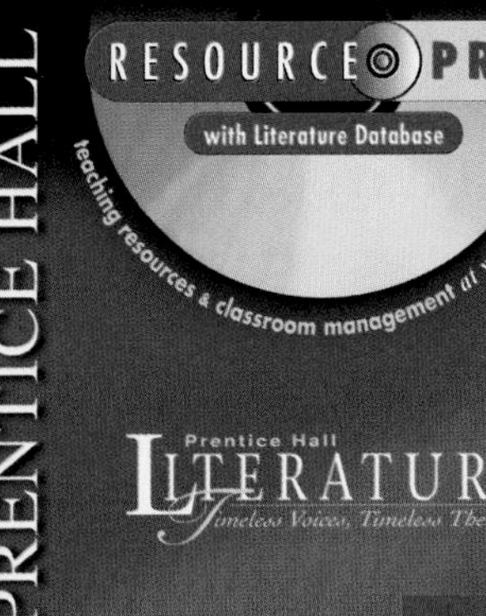

PRENTICE HALL
RESOURCE PRO®
with Literature Database
teaching resources & classroom management at your fingertips
Prentice Hall
LITERATURE
Timeless Voices, Timeless Themes
GOLD

THREE-PERSON JIGSA
(15 minutes)

Each student in a trio reads a separate page or a porti
longer selection. Then he or she teaches the main poi
two other members of their study group. Each then q
other members to make sure everyone know all parts

Can you identify three different related articles or chapter se
could assign in a three-person jigsaw?

THINK-PAIR-SHARE
(5-10 minutes)

After an explanation or demonstration, distribute ind
students, and ask them to think about what they hav
Have them write down three statements about it on
card and exchange their responses with a partner. Ha
whole class debrief on the topic. Ask for frequently m
ideas or terms.

Write your ideas for a Think-Pair-Share on a topic you have
about to teach.

EIGHT QUESTIONS FOR PLANNING LESSONS IN THE BLOCK

Before you begin to develop your lesson, ask yourself the following questions to help you focus on the content, skills, and students for whom you are designing the lesson.

1. In setting up this lesson, what can I do to develop a positive learning climate, one that demonstrates acceptance, comfort, and order?

2. What can I do to make the learning tasks clear? How will I help students to feel confident that they can do the work I will require of them?

3. What is the focus of this lesson? Will it require students to acquire new information, practice a skill, or both?
   - If they will acquire new information, how will I have them report out or show me what they have learned or understood?
   - If they will practice a new skill, how will they get feedback?

4. What strategies will I use to help students make meaning, organize information, or store/retrieve these ideas? How can I help students connect concepts and big ideas?

88 HOW TO MANAGE INSTRUCTION IN THE BLOCK

Teaching Resources give you guidance and support for managing time, adapting curriculum materials, and designing lessons.

Fast Facts Calendar

What happened on this day in . . .

The following list calls out important dates in literary history as well as other historical dates, which appear in italics. You may use this information as a quick enrichment activity to start classes or as the basis for students' writing assignments, research projects, collaborative work, or cross-curricular study.

January

1 1660 Samuel Pepys records the first entry in his Diary: "This morning (we lying lately in the garret) I rose, put on my suit with great skirts, having not lately worn any other clothes but them."

2 1920 Isaac Asimov is born in Petrovichi, Russia.

3 1882 Docking in New York City, Oscar Wilde is asked by customs officials if he has anything to declare. "Nothing but my genius," he replies.

4 1960 Albert Camus is killed in an automobile accident.

6 1840 Fanny Burney, Mme d'Arbley, dies in Bath, England, at age 87.

1878 Carl Sandburg, winner of Pulitzer Prizes in history (1940) and poetry (1951), is born in Galesburg, Illinois.

7 1841 Victor Hugo is elected to the Académie Française.

1903 Zora Neale Hurston is born in Eatonville, Florida.

8 1913 In London, Robert Frost and Ezra Pound meet for the first time at the opening of the Poetry Bookshop.

9 1946 Harlem Renaissance poet Countee Cullen dies in New York.

10 1845 Elizabeth Barrett and Robert Browning begin corresponding after she receives a note from him saying "I love you."

11 1928 Thomas Hardy dies at his home near Dorchester, England.

12 1876 Jack London is born in San Francisco, California.

13 1695 Jonathan Swift is ordained an Anglican priest.

14 1894 Inaugural issue of *Vogue* features two stories by Kate Chopin.

15 1846 Fyodor Dostoyevsky publishes his first novel at age 25.

17 1706 Benjamin Franklin is born in Boston, Massachusetts.

1860 Anton Chekhov is born in Taganrog, Russia.

23 1936 George Orwell writes: "I worshipped Kipling at 13, loathed him at 17, enjoyed him at 20, despised him at 25, and now again rather admire him."

27 1302 Dante Alighieri is expelled from Florence when a political group he opposes seizes control.

29 1963 Robert Frost dies in Boston, Massachusetts.

30 1935 Ezra Pound meets Benito Mussolini and reads aloud several lines from a draft of the *Cantos.* The dictator finds the reading entertaining.

February

1 1902 Langston Hughes is born in Joplin, Missouri.

2 1870 Mark Twain marries Olivia Langdon in Elmira, New York.

1922 On James Joyce's 40th birthday, *Ulysses* is published.

3 1874 Gertrude Stein is born in Allegheny, Pennsylvania. She will later boast: "I have been the creative mind of the century."

4 1818 At an evening at Leigh Hunt's, John Keats, Hunt, and Percy Bysshe Shelley vie with each other in composing sonnets on the subject of the Nile. Hunt's is deemed the best.

1938 Thorton Wilder's Pulitzer Prize-winning play *Our Town* opens.

7 1812 Lord Byron, in his first speech in the House of Lords, denounces a measure that would provide the death penalty for rebellious laborers.

1885 Sinclair Lewis, the first American to win the Nobel Prize for Literature (1930), is born in Sauk Centre, Minnesota.

9 1944 Alice Walker, winner of the 1983 Pulitzer Prize for Fiction for *The Color Purple,* is born.

10 1846 Edward Lear's *A Book of Nonsense* is published.

12 1959 On the 150th anniversary of Lincoln's birth, Carl Sandburg addresses a joint session of the United States Congress.

13 1974 Alexander Solzhenitsyn is expelled from the Soviet Union. He settles in the United States two years later.

16 1751 Thomas Gray anonymously publishes "Elegy Written in a Country Churchyard."

18 1931 Toni Morrison is born in Lorain, Ohio.

19 *1878 Thomas Alva Edison receives the first patent for a phonograph.*

1927 Carson McCullers is born in Columbus, Georgia.

20 1950 Dylan Thomas arrives in New York for his first series of American poetry readings.

23 1821 John Keats dies in Rome, Italy, of tuberculosis.

27 1807 Henry Wadsworth Longfellow is born in Portland, Maine.

1902 John Steinbeck is born in Salinas, California.

1934 N. Scott Momaday is born in Lawton, Oklahoma.

28 1916 Henry James dies in London. His last words are: "So here it is at last, the distinguished thing."

29 1960 James Thurber writes in the *New York Post* that "Humor is emotional chaos remembered in tranquillity."

March

1 1914 Ralph Ellison is born in Oklahoma City, Oklahoma.
2 1942 D. H. Lawrence dies of tuberculosis at age 45.
4 1916 Playwright Horton Foote is born. Foote goes on to write the Pulitzer Prize-winning play *The Young Man From Atlanta*.
1921 E. M. Forster (*A Passage to India*) sets out for India.
5 *1770 Five American colonists are killed in the Boston Massacre.*
6 1928 Gabriel García Márquez is born in Antarctica, Colombia. He wins the Nobel Prize for Literature in 1982.
7 1870 Thomas Hardy meets Emma Gifford, who will become his first wife. When she dies in 1912, Hardy leaves his desk calendar on her death date until his own death in 1928.
8 1941 Sherwood Anderson dies after eating a toothpick along with an hors d'oeuvre.
10 1948 Zelda Fitzgerald, wife of F. Scott Fitzgerald, dies in a fire at Highland Hospital.
11 1818 Mary Shelley's *Frankenstein* is published. It begins as a simple ghost story to entertain house guests, who encourage her to develop the story.
13 1818 John Keats writes to a friend: "I am sometimes so very skeptical as to think poetry is a mere Jack-o'-Lantern to whoever may chance to be struck with its brilliance."
1943 Stephen Vincent Benét dies of a heart attack at age 44.
14 *1841 David Livingstone arrives in Cape Town, South Africa, beginning a lifelong exploration of Africa's southern interior.*
16 1850 Nathaniel Hawthorne's *The Scarlet Letter* is published.
1904 James Joyce is awarded a bronze medal in a singing contest in Dublin. He immediately throws the medal in the river.
18 1932 John Updike, winner of the 1982 Pulitzer Prize for Fiction, is born in Shillington, Pennsylvania.
19 1842 As a publicity stunt for his play *Les Ressources de Quinola*, Honoré de Balzac starts a rumor that tickets are scarce. The plan backfires when his potential audience stays home upon hearing the news.
20 1828 Henrik Ibsen is born in Skien, Norway.
1852 Harriet Beecher Stowe's *Uncle Tom's Cabin* is published.
21 1843 Robert Southey, poet laurete, dies in Keswick, England.
23 1913 Jack London writes to Winston Churchill, Bernard Shaw, and H. G. Wells to ask what they are paid for their "stuff."
25 1811 Percy Bysshe Shelley is expelled from Oxford for refusing to admit writing *The Necessity of Atheism*.
26 1874 Robert Frost, winner of four Pulitzer Prizes for Poetry (1924, 1931, 1937, 1943), is born in San Francisco, California.
1892 Walt Whitman dies in Camden, New Jersey.
1911 Tennessee Williams is born in Columbus, Mississippi.
28 1775 Samuel Johnson says of poet Thomas Gray: "He was dull in company, dull in his closet, dull everywhere. He was dull in a new way, and that made people think him great."
29 1952 E. B. White writes to his daughter about *Charlotte's Web*: "Whether children will find anything amusing in it only time will tell."
31 1631 John Donne dies in London.
1914 Octavio Paz is born in Mexico City, Mexico.

April

1 1816 When the secretary of the Prince Regent asks her to write a "historical romance," Jane Austen responds: "I could not seriously sit down to write a serious romance under any other motive than to save my life."
2 1836 Charles Dickens and Catherine Hogarth are married in London.
1846 Nathaniel Hawthorne is appointed Surveyor of the Salem Custom House.
3 1783 Washington Irving is born in New York, New York.
4 1928 Maya Angelou is born in St. Louis, Missouri.
6 1327 Petrarch sees a beautiful woman in church. Smitten, he will write 366 poems to "Laura."
7 1770 William Wordsworth is born in Cumberland, England.
1889 Gabriela Mistral is born. She will be the first South American to win the Nobel Prize for Literature.
9 1821 Charles Baudelaire is born in Paris, France.
10 1925 F. Scott Fitzgerald's *The Great Gatsby* is published.
11 1914 Bernard Shaw's *Pygmalion* opens in London.
1931 Dorothy Parker steps down as drama critic for *The New Yorker*.
12 1709 Richard Steele publishes the first issue of *The Tatler*.
1861 Confederate guns fire on Fort Sumter, in Charleston Harbor, South Carolina, starting the American Civil War.
13 1845 Victor Hugo is made a peer of France, Vicomte Hugo.
1909 Eudora Welty is born in Jackson, Mississippi.
14 1828 Noah Webster's dictionary, 22 years in the making, is published.
15 1755 Samuel Johnson's *A Dictionary of the English Language* is published.
1947 Jackie Robinson, the first African American baseball player in the major leagues, plays his first game with the Brooklyn Dodgers.
16 1994 Ralph Ellison dies in New York.
17 1884 Isak Dinesen is born in Rungsted, Denmark.
1897 Thornton Wilder is born in Madison, Wisconsin.
18 *1774 On his Midnight Ride, Paul Revere warns colonists of a British attack.*
1958 A Federal Court decides that because Ezra Pound is insane, he cannot be held for treason and can be released from custody.
19 1824 George Gordon, Lord Byron, dies at age 36.
20 1859 The first volume of Charles Dickens's *A Tale of Two Cities* is published.
21 1910 Mark Twain dies in Redding, Connecticut.
23 1564 William Shakespeare is born in Stratford-upon-Avon, England.
1850 William Wordsworth dies in the Lake District.
24 1905 Robert Penn Warren is born in Guthrie, Kentucky.
25 1719 After several rejections, Daniel Defoe's *Robinson Crusoe* is published.
26 1914 Bernard Malamud is born in Brooklyn, New York.
27 1667 John Milton sells the copyright for *Paradise Lost* for 10 pounds to Samuel Simmons.
1945 Dramatist August Wilson is born in Pittsburgh, Pennsylvania.
1994 Nelson Mandela is elected president in the first election open to all races in South Africa.
28 1926 Harper Lee, author of *To Kill a Mockingbird* (1960), is born in Monroeville, Alabama.
30 1922 A. E. Housman dies at age 77.

May

1 1700 John Dryden dies in London.
1931 The Empire State Building opens in New York City.
2 1936 The manuscript of Edna St. Vincent Millay's *Conversation at Midnight* is destroyed in a hotel fire.
1945 Colette becomes the first female member of the Académie Goncourt, a literary honor.
3 *Under Milkwood,* by Dylan Thomas, is given its first American reading.
4 1940 Nora Joyce, wife of James Joyce, tells her husband: "Well, Jim, I haven't read any of your books, but I'll have to someday because they must be good considering how well they sell."
5 1902 Bret Harte dies in London at age 65.
1926 Sinclair Lewis declines the Pulitzer Prize, saying that such prizes tend to make writers "safe, polite, obedient, and sterile."
1927 Virginia Woolf publishes *To the Lighthouse*.
6 1862 Henry David Thoreau dies in Concord, Massachusetts.
1940 John Steinbeck's *The Grapes of Wrath* wins the Pulitzer Prize.
7 1812 Robert Browning is born in London.
1945 World War II ends in Europe.
10 *1869 The Transcontinental Railroad is completed.*
12 1812 Edward Lear is born in Highgate, England.
1828 Dante Gabriel Rossetti is born in London.
13 1906 Willa Cather becomes editor of *McClure's Magazine*.
14 1900 Hal Borland is born in Sterling, Colorado.
1931 Her coffee plantation a failure, Isak Dinesen leaves Africa. Five years later, *Out of Africa* makes her internationally famous.
15 1886 Emily Dickinson dies in Amherst, Massachusetts.
1890 Pulitzer Prize-winning author Katherine Anne Porter is born in Texas. She goes on to write *Ship of Fools*.
16 1763 James Boswell first meets Samuel Johnson. His biography of Johnson will be published 28 years later.
1836 Edgar Allan Poe marries his cousin, Virginia Clemm.
18 1593 After dramatist Christopher Marlow is falsely accused of heresy by his roommate, a warrant is issued for Marlowe's arrest.
19 1795 James Boswell, Dr. Johnson's biographer, dies in London.
1930 Lorraine Hansberry is born in Chicago, Illinois.
20 1845 Robert Browning pays his first visit to Elizabeth Barrett.
1932 Amelia Earhart begins her first solo flight across the Atlantic Ocean.
21 1688 Alexander Pope is born in London, England.
22 1859 Sir Arthur Conan Doyle is born in Edinburgh, Scotland.
1969 Langston Hughes dies in New York.
23 1839 Henry Wadsworth Longfellow says of Jane Austen: "Her writings are a capital picture of real life, with all the little wheels and machinery laid bare like a patent clock. But she explains and fills out too much."
25 1808 Ralph Waldo Emerson is born in Boston, Massachusetts.
1908 Theodore Roethke is born in Saginaw, Michigan.
26 735 The Venerable Bede dies at Jarrow.
27 1907 Rachel L. Carson is born in Springdale, Pennsylvania.
29 1906 T. H. White is born in Bombay, India.
1953 Sir Edmund Hillary and Nepalese mountaineer Tenzing Norgay make the first ascent of Mount Everest (29,028 feet).
30 1903 Countee Cullen is born in Louisville, Kentucky.
1909 The National Conference on the Negro convenes, which will lead to the founding of the NAACP.
31 1819 Walt Whitman is born in West Hills, Long Island.

June

1 1898 Bernard Shaw marries Charlotte Payne-Townsend.
2 1825 Emily Brontë leaves Cowan Bridge School, where officials have noted in her record: "Subsequent career—governess."
3 1936 Author Larry McMurtry is born in Texas. He goes go on to write the Pulitzer Prize-winning *Lonesome Dove*.
4 1962 William Faulkner's last novel, *The Reivers*, is published posthumously and wins the Pulitzer Prize for Fiction the following year.
5 1900 Stephen Crane dies of tuberculosis in Germany.
6 *1944 The D-Day invasion of France by Allied troops in World War II takes place.*
7 1899 Elizabeth Bowen is born in Dublin, Ireland.
8 1374 Chaucer is appointed Comptroller for the Customs and Subsidy of Wools at £10 a year.
9 1870 Charles Dickens dies at age 58.
11 1899 Kawabata Yasunari is born. In 1968, he is the first Japanese to win the Nobel Prize for Literature.
12 1929 Anne Frank is born in Frankfurt-am-Main, Germany.
13 1865 William Butler Yeats is born in Dublin, Ireland.
1894 Poet Mark Van Doren is born in Hope Park, Illinois.
15 *1215 King John of England signs the Magna Carta.*
16 1938 Joyce Carol Oates is born in Lockport, New York.
17 1719 Joseph Addison dies at age 47. He is buried in Westminster Abbey.
1914 John Hersey is born in Tientsin, China.
1917 Gwendolyn Brooks is born in Topeka, Kansas.
18 *1983 Sally Ride becomes the first American woman in space.*
21 1956 Playwright Arthur Miller refuses to betray his left-wing associates before the House Committee on Un-American Activities.
24 1842 Ambrose Bierce is born in Meigs County, Ohio.
1916 John Ciardi is born in Boston, Massachusetts.
25 1903 George Orwell is born in Motihari, India.
26 *1945 Fifty nations sign the charter of the United Nations in San Francisco.*
27 1872 Paul Laurence Dunbar is born in Dayton, Ohio.
1936 Lucille Clifton is born in Depew, New York.
28 1888 Robert Louis Stevenson leaves San Francisco on his first voyage to the South Seas.
1914 Archduke Francis Ferdinand is assassinated, touching off World War I.
29 1613 The Globe Theater catches fire and burns to the ground during a performance of Shakespeare's *Henry VIII*.
30 1911 Czeslaw Milosz, winner of the Nobel Prize for Literature, is born near Vilna, Lithuania.

July

1 *1997 Great Britain gives up control of Hong Kong to China.*
2 1961 Ernest Hemingway dies in Ketcham, Idaho.
3 1883 Franz Kafka is born in Prague, Czechoslovakia.
4 *1776 American Declaration of Independence is signed.*
1804 Nathaniel Hawthorne is born in Salem, Massachusetts.
1855 Walt Whitman prints the first edition of his *Leaves of Grass.*
5 1880 Bernard Shaw leaves his job with the Edison Telephone Company. He later said, "You must not suppose, because I am a man of letters, that I never tried to earn an honest living."
6 1895 O. Henry, trying to flee a charge of embezzlement, boards a train headed for New Orleans.
7 1535 Sir Thomas More is beheaded for refusing to acknowledge Henry VIII as supreme authority of the Church.
8 1822 Percy Bysshe Shelley is drowned while sailing off the coast of Italy.
9 1942 Anne Frank and her family go into hiding.
10 *1962 Telstar, the first communications satellite, transmits the first television pictures from the United States to Europe.*
11 1937 Dylan Thomas marries Caitlin Macnamara.
12 1904 Pablo Neruda is born in Parral, Chile.
14 *1789 The French Revolution begins in Paris.*
1904 Isaac Bashevis Singer is born in Radzymin, Poland.
1986 Jorge Luis Borges dies in Geneva, Switzerland.
16 1660 Even as he is being ordered into custody, Milton works on *Paradise Lost*, which he publishes 7 years later.
17 1886 Poet Gerard Manley Hopkins converts to Roman Catholicism.
18 1817 Jane Austen dies in Winchester, England.
19 *1848 The first U.S. women's rights convention in Seneca Falls, N.Y., begins, led by Lucretia Mott and Elizabeth Cady Stanton.*
20 1869 Mark Twain's *Innocents Abroad* is published.
1969 Neil Armstrong becomes the first person to set foot on the moon.
22 1898 Stephen Vincent Benét is born in Bethlehem, Pennsylvania.
23 1846 Thoreau is jailed for refusing to pay a $1 poll tax; this moves him to write *Civil Disobedience*.
25 1897 Jack London heads for the Klondike aboard the steamer *Umatilla*.
26 1892 Pearl S. Buck, winner of the 1932 Pulitzer Prize in fiction and the 1938 Nobel Prize in Literature, is born in Hillsboro, West Virginia.
29 1805 Statesman and writer Alexis de Tocqueville is born in Paris, France.
31 1703 After having written *The Shortest Way with Dissenters*, Daniel Defoe is forced to stand in the pillory in front of Temple Bar. He draws sympathetic crowds who pelt him with flowers instead of mud.

August

1 1819 Herman Melville is born in New York, New York.
2 1924 James Baldwin is born in New York, New York.
3 1887 Wartime poet Rupert Brooke is born in Warwickshire, England.
5 1850 Guy de Maupassant is born near Dieppe, France.
6 1637 Ben Jonson dies in London at the age of 65.
1809 Alfred, Lord Tennyson, poet laureate of England, is born in Lincolnshire, England.
7 1804 William Blake writes to William Hayley: "Money flies from me. Profit never ventures upon my threshold."
8 1884 Sara Teasdale is born in St. Louis, Missouri.
9 1842 Herman Melville escapes from a one-month captivity by South Sea Island cannibals.
10 1824 Charlotte Brontë is sent to Cowan Bridge School by her widowed father.
11 1921 Pulitzer Prize-winning author Alex Haley is born in Ithaca, New York.
12 1827 William Blake dies at age 70 in London.
14 1925 Journalist Russell Baker is born.
15 1771 Sir Walter Scott is born in Edinburgh, Scotland.
17 1917 Wilfred Owen and Siegfried Sassoon, both recuperating from battle fatigue at the Craiglockhart War Hospital, meet and form an intense friendship.
1930 Ted Hughes is born in West Yorkshire, England.
18 *1920 The Nineteenth Amendment, giving women the right to vote, is ratified.*
19 *1691 Six people are hanged in Salem Village, Massachusetts, for witchcraft.*
21 1762 Lady Wortley Montague dies. Her last words are: "It has all been very interesting."
22 1904 Kate Chopin dies in her hometown of St. Louis, Missouri.
1920 Ray Bradbury is born in Waukegan, Illinois.
23 1869 Edgar Lee Masters is born in Garnett, Kansas.
24 1847 Charlotte Brontë's *Jane Eyre* is sent to the publisher under the name Currer Bell.
25 1836 Bret Harte is born in Albany, New York.
26 1893 Jack London returns to San Francisco after spending eight months on a seal-hunting expedition aboard the *Sophia Sutherland*.
1914 Julio Cortázar is born in Brussels, Belgium.
27 1660 John Milton's books are burned in London after Milton, in his pamphlets, repeatedly attacks King Charles II.
28 *1963 Martin Luther King, Jr., delivers his "I have a dream" speech to more than 200,000 people in Washington, D.C.*
29 1809 Oliver Wendell Holmes is born in Cambridge, Massachusetts.
1962 Robert Frost leaves for a goodwill tour of the U.S.S.R., sponsored by the U.S. State Department.
30 1797 Mary Wollstonecraft Shelley, author of *Frankenstein*, is born in London.

September

2 *1945 Japan signs a peace treaty to end World War II.*
3 1849 Sarah Orne Jewett is born in South Berwick, Maine.
1962 E. E. Cummings dies in North Conway, New Hampshire.
4 1908 Richard Wright is born near Natchez, Mississippi.
6 1890 Joseph Conrad becomes master of the *Roi des Belges*, an experience he will draw upon later in his writing.
7 1892 John Greenleaf Whittier dies of a stroke in Hampton Falls, New Hampshire.
8 *1522 Ferdinand Magellan's crew arrives in Seville, Spain, becoming the first people to circumnavigate the globe.*
1947 Ann Beattie is born in Washington, D.C.
9 1828 Leo Tolstoy is born in Tula, a province of Russia.
10 1886 Poet H. D. (Hilda Doolittle) is born in Bethlehem, Pennsylvania.
11 1862 William Sidney Porter, later known as O. Henry, is born. He would spend a good portion of his life in Texas, and go on to write "The Gift of the Magi" and other short stories.
12 1846 Elizabeth Barrett and Robert Browning secretly marry.
13 1876 Sherwood Anderson is born in Camden, Ohio. F. Scott Fitzgerald would later describe him as "the possessor of a brilliant and almost inimitable prose style, and of scarcely any ideas at all."
14 *1814 British end bombardment of Fort McHenry, inspiring Francis Scott Key to write the words to "The Star-Spangled Banner."*
1851 James Fennimore Cooper dies in Cooperstown, New York.
16 1672 Anne Bradstreet dies in Andover, Massachusetts.
17 1883 William Carlos Williams, winner of the 1963 Pulitzer Prize for Poetry, is born in Rutherford, New Jersey.
18 1709 Samuel Johnson is born in Staffordshire, England.
19 1985 Italo Calvino dies in Siena, Italy.
20 1923 T. S. Eliot's *The Waste Land* receives scathing reviews in the *Times Literary Supplement.*
22 1598 Ben Jonson is indicted for manslaughter after killing another actor in a duel.
24 1896 F. Scott Fitzgerald is born in St. Paul, Minnesota.
25 1897 William Faulkner, winner of the 1949 Nobel Prize for Literature and of the 1955 and 1963 Pulitzer Prizes for Fiction, is born in New Albany, Mississippi.
26 1888 T. S. Eliot is born in St. Louis, Missouri.
28 1891 Herman Melville dies in New York, having never achieved literary recognition.
1909 Poet Stephen Spender is born in London.
29 1973 W. H. Auden dies in Vienna, Austria, at age 66.
30 1598 Edmund Spenser is appointed Sheriff of Cork, Ireland.
1937 Albert Camus writes: "It is in order to shine sooner that authors refuse to rewrite. Despicable. Begin again."

October

1 *1847 American astronomer Maria Mitchell records the first comet (Comet Mitchell) viewed by a telescope.*
2 1836 Charles Darwin returns from his voyage on H.M.S. *Beagle*.
1904 Graham Greene is born in Hertfordshire, England.
3 1895 Stephen Crane's *The Red Badge of Courage* is published.
1916 James Herriot is born in Sunderland, Scotland.
4 1910 Jack London buys nine plot outlines from Sinclair Lewis for $52.50.
6 1599 William Shakespeare's *Romeo and Juliet* is published.
7 1849 Edgar Allan Poe dies in Baltimore, Maryland. He is 40 years old.
8 1779 William Blake begins his studies at the Royal Academy.
9 1950 Edna St. Vincent Millay dies in Austerlitz, New York.
10 1935 George Gershwin's *Porgy and Bess*, the first American-theme opera, opens in New York City.
12 *1492 Columbus and crew arrive at the islands now known as the West Indies.*
1908 Ann Petry is born in Old Saybrook, Connecticut.
14 1888 Katherine Mansfield is born in Wellington, New Zealand.
15 1897 Stephen Crane and Joseph Conrad have lunch together, marking the start of a famous friendship.
17 1586 Sir Philip Sidney, fighting a war in Holland, dies of battle wounds at age 32.
1915 Arthur Miller is born in New York City.
19 1745 Jonathan Swift dies in Dublin, Ireland.
20 1854 Arthur Rimbaud is born in Charlesville, France.
21 1929 Ursula Le Guin is born in Berkeley, California.
22 1919 Doris Lessing is born in Kermanshah, Iran.
24 1923 Denise Levertov is born in Essex, England.
25 1400 Geoffrey Chaucer dies in London, possibly of the plague.
1498 Amerigo Vespucci returns to Cadiz, Spain, from the lands that will later be named after him, the Americas.
26 1880 In Hartford, Connecticut, Mark Twain remarks, "I don't mind what the opposition says of me, so long as they don't tell the truth."
27 1914 Dylan Thomas is born in Swansea, Wales.
28 *1886 The Statue of Liberty is dedicated to the United States by France.*
29 1618 Sir Walter Raleigh is executed in the Tower of London.
1929 The New York Stock Exchange crashes, signaling the start of a worldwide economic depression.
31 1795 John Keats is born in Finsbury Pavement, England.

November

1 1871 Stephen Crane is born in Newark, New Jersey.
1930 Ernest Hemingway breaks his arm in a car crash following a hunting trip with John Dos Passos.
2 1927 T. S. Eliot becomes a British subject.
4 1918 Wilfred Owen dies in France at age 25.
1948 T. S. Eliot receives the Nobel Prize for Literature.
5 1644 Samuel Pepys records in his *Diary* that *Macbeth* is "a pretty good play."
6 1315 Dante Alighieri is sentenced to death when he refuses to return to Florence following his exile. He dies of malaria in Ravenna six years later.
7 1913 Albert Camus is born in Mondoni, Algeria.
8 1674 John Milton dies in London at age 65.
9 1953 Dylan Thomas dies in New York City.
11 *1620 The Mayflower Compact is signed off Cape Cod, Massachusetts.*
12 1935 Theodore Roethke is hospitalized with delusions brought on by hypothermia after spending a night in the Michigan woods.
13 1797 Samuel Taylor Coleridge and William Wordsworth begin work on *The Rime of the Ancient Mariner*.
14 1851 Herman Melville's *Moby-Dick* is published.
15 1887 Marianne Moore, winner of the 1952 Pulitzer Prize for Poetry, is born in St. Louis, Missouri.
16 1849 Fyodor Doestoevsky is sentenced to death for his socialist activities. The sentence is later lessened to four-years' hard labor in Siberia.
18 *1805 The Lewis and Clark expedition reaches the Pacific Ocean and claims the Oregon region for the United States.*
1865 Mark Twain's "The Celebrated Jumping Frog of Calaveras County" appears in the *Saturday Press*.
19 *1863 Lincoln delivers the Gettysburg Address.*
21 1694 Voltaire is born in Paris, France.
1910 Leo Tolstoy dies en route to the Caucasus.
22 1621 John Donne is elected dean of St. Paul's Cathedral.
1916 Jack London dies in Santa Rosa, California.
24 1868 Scott Joplin, the "King of Ragtime" music, is born near Linden, Texas.
26 1862 On meeting Harriet Beecher Stowe, Abraham Lincoln comments: "So this is the little lady who made the big war."
27 1970 Fearing that he will not be allowed to return home, Alexander Solzhenitsyn writes that he cannot go to Stockholm, Sweden, to receive the Nobel Prize.
28 1757 William Blake is born in London, England.
29 *1929 Richard E. Byrd makes the first flight over the South Pole.*
30 1667 Jonathan Swift is born in Dublin, Ireland.
1835 Mark Twain (Samuel Longhorn Clemens) is born in Florida, Missouri.

December

1 1860 The first installment of Charles Dickens's *Great Expectations* is published.
1955 Rosa Parks is arrested for refusing to give up her seat on a bus in Montgomery, Alabama.
2 1793 Samuel Taylor Coleridge enlists in the Light Dragoons.
1867 Charles Dickens gives his first readings in New York City. The lines at the box office stretch for miles.
3 1857 Joseph Conrad is born in the Polish Ukraine, then under Russian rule.
5 1830 Christina Rossetti is born in London, England.
1934 Joan Didion is born in Sacramento, California.
6 1712 Joseph Addison and Richard Steele publish the last issue of *The Spectator*.
7 *1941 A surprise attack is launched on the American naval base at Pearl Harbor.*
9 1854 Alfred, Lord Tennyson, publishes "The Charge of the Light Brigade" six weeks after the Battle of Balaclava.
10 1830 Emily Dickinson is born in Amherst, Massachusetts.
11 1875 Robert Louis Stevenson says of Robert Browning's writing: "He floods acres of paper with brackets and inverted commas."
12 1889 Robert Browning dies in Venice, Italy.
13 1927 Poet James Wright is born in Martin's Ferry, Ohio.
14 1953 Marjorie Kinnan Rawlings dies in Saint Augustine, Florida.
15 *1790 The U.S. Bill of Rights takes effect.*
1936 George Orwell leaves England to help in the war effort in Spain.
16 *1773 The Boston Tea Party takes place.*
1775 Jane Austen is born in Hampshire, England.
1917 Arthur C. Clarke is born in Somerset, England.
17 1843 *A Christmas Carol*, by Charles Dickens, is published.
18 1870 Saki (H. H. Munro) is born in Burma.
19 1732 Ben Franklin publishes *Poor Richard's Almanack*, a best seller in colonial America.
20 1871 In the *Chicago Tribune,* Mark Twain compares himself with George Washington: "I have a higher and greater standard of principle. Washington could not lie. I *can* lie but I won't."
21 1767 The Newport, Rhode Island, *Mercury* publishes a poem by 13-year-old African American poet Phillis Wheatley.
22 1869 Edwin Arlington Robinson is born in Head Tide, Maine.
24 1881 Poet Juan Ramón Jiménez, winner of the 1956 Nobel Prize for Literature, is born in Andalusia, Spain.
25 1642 Isaac Newton is born in Lincolnshire, England.
26 1606 William Shakespeare's *King Lear* is performed at court.
1913 Ambrose Bierce, while serving in Pancho Villa's army, writes his last letter and is never heard from again.
29 *1845 U.S. President James K. Polk signs legislation making Texas the twenty-eighth state of the United States.*
30 1816 Percy Bysshe Shelley marries Mary Godwin.
1865 Rudyard Kipling is born in Bombay, India.
31 1900 Edward Everett Hale welcomes in the new century, presiding at a Boston civic ceremony.

Selection	Reading	Literary Elements/Forms	Vocabulary	Grammar
"Contents of the Dead Man's Pocket," Jack Finney, SE p. 2	Reading Level: Average • Literal Comp. Strategies, SE pp. 4, 19; TR Sel. Sup., pp. 3–4 • Model, SE pp. 5–18 • Sequence of Events, TR Str. for Diverse St. Needs, p. 1	Suspense, SE pp. 3, 19; TR Selection Support, p. 5	• Latin Word Roots: *-term-,* SE pp. 2, 19; TR Sel. Sup., p. 1 Word Bank: convoluted, p. 7; grimace, deftness, imperceptibly, p. 11; reveling, p. 13; interminable, p. 15	• Poss. *its* vs. Contract. *it's,* SE pp. 2, 19; TR Sel. Sup., p. 2 • WS Language Lab CD-ROM, Capitalization and Punctuation • WS Gram. Pr. Book, p. 110
"The Final Assault," Sir Edmund Hillary; "The Dream Comes True," Tenzing Norgay, SE p. 22	Reading Levels: Challenging, Challenging • Dist. Fact/Opinion, SE pp. 23, 42; TR Selection Support, p. 8 • Outline Main Idea/Supp. Det., TR Str. for Div. St. Needs, p. 2	• Author's Perspective, SE pp. 23, 42; TR Selection Support, p. 9 • Analyze Literary Criticism, ATE p. 35	• Latin Word Roots: *-voc-,* SE pp. 22, 42; TR Selection Support, p. 6 Word Bank: precipitous, discernible, belay, p. 28; encroaching, p. 31; undulations, p. 33; vociferous, p. 34	• Compound Predicates, SE pp. 22, 42; TR Sel. Support, p. 7 • WS Language Lab CD-ROM, Subject/Verb Agreement • WS Gram. Pr. Book, pp. 26–29
"The Monkey's Paw," W. W. Jacobs; "The Bridegroom," Alexander Pushkin, SE p. 44	Reading Levels: Avg., Avg. • Predict Outcomes, SE pp. 45, 58; TR Selection Support, p. 12 • Recognize Cause and Effect, TR Str. for Diverse St. Needs, p. 3	• Foreshadowing, SE pp. 45, 58; TR Selection Support, p. 13	• Latin Word Roots: *-cred-,* SE pp. 44, 58; TR Selection Support, p. 10 Word Bank: doughty, p. 46; maligned, credulity, p. 49; prosaic, avaricious, furtively, p. 50; fusillade, p. 53; foreboding, p. 54; tumult, p. 56	• Regular and Irregular Verb Forms, SE pp. 44, 58; TR Selection Support, p. 11 • WS Language Lab CD-ROM, Verb Tense • WS Gram. Pr. Book, pp. 67–69
from **A Walk to the Jetty, Jamaica Kincaid,** SE p. 60	Reading Level: Average • Draw Inferences, SE pp. 61, 69; TR Selection Support, p. 16 • Identify Characters, TR Str. for Diverse St. Needs, p. 4	• Flashback, SE pp. 61, 69; TR Selection Support, p. 17	• Latin Word Roots: *-stup-,* SE pp. 60, 69; TR Selection Support, p. 14 Word Bank: loomed, apprenticed, p. 62; raked, stupor, p. 68	• Clauses, SE pp. 60, 69; TR Selection Support, p. 15 • WS Gram. Pr. Book, pp. 51–58
"The Masque of the Red Death," Edgar Allan Poe, SE p. 76	Reading Level: Challenging • Context Clues, SE pp. 77, 84; TR Selection Support, p. 20 • Paraphrase, TR Str. for Diverse St. Needs, p. 5	• Symbols, SE pp. 77, 84; TR Selection Support, p. 21	• Latin Suffixes: *-tion,* SE pp. 76, 84; TR Selection Support, p. 18 Word Bank: august, p. 78; piquancy, arabesque, p. 81; cessation, disapprobation, habiliments, p. 82	• Subject-Verb Agreement, SE pp. 76, 84; TR Sel. Sup., p. 19 • WS Language Lab CD-ROM, Subject/Verb Agreement • WS Gram. Pr. Book, pp. 80–82
"Fear," Gabriela Mistral; "The street," Octavio Paz; "Spring and All," William Carlos Williams, SE p. 86	Reading Levels: Average, Challenging, Average • Form a Mental Image, SE pp. 87, 92; TR Se. Sup., p. 24 • Restate Poetry as Prose, TR Str. for Diverse St. Needs, p. 6	• Imagery, SE pp. 87, 92; TR Selection Support, p. 25	• Anglo-Saxon Suffixes: *-less,* SE pp. 86, 92; TR Selection Support, p. 22 Word Bank: contagious, lifeless, clarity, stark, profound, p. 91	• Pronouns and Antecedents, SE pp. 86, 92; TR Selection Support, p. 23 • WS Language Lab CD-ROM, Pronoun and Antecedent • WS Gram. Pr. Book, p. 83
"Two Friends," Guy de Maupassant; "Damon and Pythias," myth retold by William F. Russell, SE p. 94	Reading Levels: Average, Easy • Significant Details, SE pp. 95, 106; TR Sel. Sup., p. 28 • Identify Chain of Events, TR Str. for Diverse St. Needs, p. 7•	• Climax, SE pp. 95, 106; TR Selection Support, p. 29 • Analyze Literary Criticism, ATE p. 99	• Latin Word Roots: *-tain-,* SE pp. 94, 106; TR Selection Support, p. 26 Word Bank: ardent, vernal, p. 96; jauntiness, p. 98; dire, p. 102; detained, impediments, hindrances, annals, p. 104	• Appositives, SE pp. 94, 106; TR Selection Support, p. 27 • WS Language Lab CD-ROM, Commas • WS Gram. Pr. Book, p. 40

On the Edge

Writing	Speaking, Listening, and Viewing	Researching and Representing	Assessment	Technology
• Guided Writing Lesson: Scene From A Movie [Audience's Attention], SE p. 20 • Annotated Drawing, New Story Titles, Personal Credo, SE p. 20 • Epitaph, Advice Letter, Suspense, TR Alt. Assess., p. 1	• Role Play, School Speech, SE p. 20 • S/L/V Mini-Lesson: Speech, Role Play, ATE pp. 10, 15 • Ballad, TR Alt. Assess., p. 1	• Risks of Everyday Life, Changing Technology, SE p. 20 • Scrapbook, Proposal, TR Alt. Assess., p. 1 • Viewing/Representing Lesson: Annotated Drawing, ATE p. 11	• Sel. Test, TR Form. Assess., pp. 1–3; Assess. Res. Software • Drama Rubric [for Wr. Lesson], TR Alt. Assess., p. 112 • TR Alt. Assess., p. 1	• "The Contents of the Dead Man's Pocket," LL Audiocassettes • WS Writing Lab CD-ROM, Narration Tutorial; Wr. at Work Videodisc, Ch. 2
• Writing : Placards [Transitions to Show Time], SE p. 43 • Book Jacket, Art. on Everest, Mountain's Eye View, SE p. 43 • Letter, Intrapersonal Reflection, TR Alt. Assess., p. 2	• Advice for Future Climbers, Oral Report, SE p. 43 • S/L/V Mini-Lessons: Oral Report, Working with Others ATE p. 34, 36 • Debate, TR Alt. Assess., p. 2	• Everest Statistics, Video Game Design, SE p. 43 • Activity Log, Scale Drawing, Triptych, TR Alt. Assess., p. 2 • Research Skills Mini-Lesson: Article on Everest, ATE p. 31 • V/R Less.: Book Jacket, ATE p. 37	• Selection Test, TR Formal Assessment, pp. 4–6; Assess. Res. Software • Description Rubric [for Wr. Lesson], TR Alt. Assess., p. 100 • TR Alt. Assess., p. 2	• "The Final Assault," "The Dream Comes True," LL Audiocassettes • Looking at Lit., Ch. 1 • WS Writing Lab CD-ROM, Description Tutorial; Wr. at Work Videodisc, Ch. 1
• Writing: Prediction [Transitions to Show Cause/Effect], SE p. 59 • Newspaper Headlines, Warning Label, Proposal, SE p. 59 • Nonverbal Communication, Fateful Essay, Three Sensible Wishes, TR Alt. Assess., p. 3	• TV Interview, Dramatic Monologue, SE p. 59 • S/L/V Lessons: Being Tactful; TV Interview, ATE pp. 50, 54 • Wish Charade, TR Alt. Assess., p. 3	• A Monkey's Paw Poll, Poster Showing Fortuna, SE p. 59 • Dramatic Enactment, Missing Poster, TR Alt. Assess., p. 3	• Sel. Test, TR Form. Assess., pp. 7–9; Assess. Res. Software • Cause/Effect Rubric [for Wr. Lesson], TR Alt. Assess., p. 105 • TR Alt. Assess., p. 3	• "The Monkey's Paw," "The Bridegroom," LL Audiocassettes • WS Writing Lab CD-ROM, Narration Tutorial
• Guided Writing Lesson: How-to Manual [Clear Explanation of Procedures], SE p. 70 • Packing List, Letter of Intro., Desc. for the Internet, SE p. 70 • Letter, Intrapersonal Reflection, TR Alt. Assess., p. 4	• Telephone Interview, Persuasive Speech, SE p. 70 • S/L/V Mini-Lesson: Conducting an Interview, ATE p. 67 • Reality Check, TR Alt. Assess., p. 4	• The Statistics of a Decision, Map of Annie's Walk, SE p. 70 • Capital Tour, Climate Comparison, Farewell Snapshot, TR Alt. Assess., p. 4 • Viewing/Representing Lesson: Map of Anne's Walk, ATE p. 64	• Sel. Test, TR Form. Assess., pp. 10–12; Assess. Res. Software • How-To Process Rub. [for Wr. Lesson], TR Alt. Assess., p. 103 • TR Alt. Assess., p. 4	• from *A Walk to the Jetty,* LL Audiocassettes • WS Writing Lab CD-ROM, Exposition Tutorial; Wr. at Work Videodisc, Ch. 3
• Writing: Proposal [Demo the Benefits of an Idea], SE p. 85 • Invitation, Description of a Modern Masquerade, Report on the Black Plague, SE p. 85 • Story Summary, Personality Portrait, Pro-Con Argument, TR Alt. Assess., p. 5	• Press Conference, Radio Script, SE p. 85 • S/L/V Mini-Lesson: Radio Script, ATE p. 80	• Costume Design, Multimedia Presentation, SE p. 85 • Musical Score, Set Design, TR Alt. Assessment, p. 5	• Sel. Test, TR Form. Assess., pp. 13–15; Assess. Software • Persuasion Rubric [for Wr. Lesson], TR Alt. Assess., p. 105 • TR Alt. Assess., p. 5	• "The Masque of the Red Death," LL Audiocassettes • WS Writing Lab CD-ROM, Persuasion Tutorial; Wr. at Work Videodisc, Ch. 4
• Guided Writing: Anecdote [Cause-and-Effect], SE p. 93 • Letter, Poem, Short Story Based on a Poem, SE p. 93 • Desc., Journal Entry, Differing Persp., TR Alt. Assess., p. 6	• Oral Interpretation, Speech, SE p. 93 • S/L/V Mini-Lesson: Speech, ATE p. 90 • Color Report, Monologue, Letting Go, TR Alt. Assess., p. 6	• Scientific Diagram, Dance, SE p. 93 • Science Report: Quarantine, TR Alt. Assess., p. 6	• Sel. Test, TR Form. Assess., pp. 16–18; Assess. Software • Nar./Pers. Exp. Rub. [for Wr. Lesson], TR Alt. Assess., p. 96 • TR Alt. Assess., p. 6	• "Fear," "The street," Spring and All," LL Audiocassettes • WS Writing Lab CD-ROM, Narration
• Guided Writing: Ext. Definition [Examples], SE p. 107 • Epitaph, Yearbook Profiles, Officer's Report, SE p. 107 • Images, Comp/Cont Characters, Reflection, Letter/Ed., TR Alt. Assess., p. 7	• Role Play, Humorous Monologue, SE p. 107 • Speaking, Listening, and Viewing Mini-Lesson: Role Play, ATE p. 100 • Myth, TR Alt. Assess., p. 7	• Friendship Collage, Brochure, SE p. 107 • Report on Prussia, Song Lyrics, TR Alt. Assess., p. 7 • Research Skills Mini-Lesson: Research Criteria, ATE p. 102	• Sel. Test, TR Form. Assess., pp. 19–21; Assess. Software • Def./Classification Rub. [for Wr. Lesson], TR Alt. Assess., p. 99 • TR Alt. Assess., p. 7	• "Two Friends," "Damon and Pythias" LL Audiocassettes • WS Writing Lab CD-ROM, Exposition

Selection	Reading	Literary Elements/Forms	Vocabulary	Grammar
from **In Commemoration: One Million Volumes, Rudolfo A. Anaya,** SE p. 116	Reading Level: Average • Reading for Success: Interactive Strategies, SE pp. 118, 125; TR Sel. Sup., pp. 32–33 • Model, SE pp. 119–124 • Summarize, TR Str. for Diverse St. Needs, p. 8	• Author's Purpose, SE pp. 117, 125; TR Sel. Support, p. 34	• Latin Prefixes: *in-,* SE pp. 116, 125; TR Sel. Sup., p. 30 Word Bank: induced, p. 119; inherent, litany, dilapidated, satiated, p. 121; enthralls, labyrinth, p. 122; poignant, termination, p. 124	• Action Verbs and Linking Verbs, SE pp. 116, 125; TR Selection Support, p. 31 • WS Language Lab CD-ROM, Eight Parts of Speech • WS Gram. Pr. Book, p. 11
"How Much Land Does a Man Need?," Leo Tolstoy, SE p. 128	Reading Level: Average • Predict Based on Character Traits, SE pp. 129, 144; TR Selection Support, p. 37 • Identify Character Traits, TR Str. for Diverse St. Needs, p. 9	• Parable, SE pp. 129, 144; TR Selection Support, p. 38 • Analyze Lit. Crit., ATE p. 139	• Words In Context: Tech./ Multiple-Meaning Words, SE pp. 128, 144; TR Sel. Sup., p. 35 Word Bank: piqued, disparaged, p. 131; forbore, aggrieved, p. 133; sheaf, arable, fallow, p. 135	• Possessive Nouns, SE pp. 128, 144; TR Sel. Sup., p. 36 • WS Gram. Pr. Book, p. 110
"Success . . ." and **"I dwell . . . ," Emily Dickinson; "Uncoiling," Pat Mora; "Columbus," Vassar Miller,** SE p. 146	Reading Levels: Avg., Challenging, Challenging, Avg. • Draw Inferences, SE pp. 147, 152; TR Sel. Support, p. 41 • Explain Poetic Phrases, TR Str. for Diverse St. Needs, p. 10	• Stated and Implied Themes in Poetry, SE pp. 147, 152; TR Selection Support, p. 42	• Latin Prefixes: *im-,* SE pp. 146, 152; TR Sel. Sup., p. 39 Word Bank: impregnable, p. 149; thrall, vertigo, p. 151	• Subject/Verb Agree/, SE pp. 146, 152; TR Sel/ Sup/, p. 40 • WS Language Lab CD-ROM, Subject/Verb Agreement • WS Gram. Pr. Book, pp. 80–86
from **My Left Foot, Christy Brown,** SE p. 154	Reading Level: Average • Identify Author's Purp., SE pp. 155, 162; TR Sel. Sup., p. 45 • ID Main Idea/Sup. Details, TR Str. for Div. St. Needs, p. 11	• Significant Moment, SE pp. 155, 162; TR Sel. Sup., p. 46 •Analyze Film Crit., ATE p. 160	• Latin Word Roots: *-vol-*, SE pp. 154, 162; TR Sel. Sup., p. 43 Word Bank: impertinence, conviction, p. 157; inert, contention, p. 158; volition, taut, p. 160	• Active/Passive Voice, SE pp. 154, 162; TR Sel. Sup., p. 44 • WS Language Lab CD-ROM, Active and Passive Voice • WS Gram. Pr. Book, pp. 74–75
"A Visit to Grandmother," William Melvin Kelley, SE p. 164	Reading Level: Easy • Clarify, SE pp. 165, 175; TR Selection Support, p. 49 • Resp. to Characters' Actions, TR Str. for Div. St. Needs, p. 12	• Characterization, SE pp. 165, 175; TR Sel. Support, p. 50	• Lat. Word Origins: *ventured,* SE pp. 164, 175; TR Sel.Sup., p. 47 Word Bank: ventured, p. 167; indulgence, grimacing, p. 168; lacquered, p. 174	• Pronoun Case, SE pp. 164, 175; TR Sel. Sup., p. 48 • WS Language Lab CD-ROM, Pronoun Case • WS Gram. Pr. Book, pp. 76–79
"Mowing" and **"After Apple-Picking," Robert Frost; "Style"** and **"At Harvest-time," Maya Angelou,** SE p. 182	Reading Levels: Average, Average, Easy, Easy • Interpret, SE pp. 183, 190; TR Selection Support, p. 53 • Compare/Contrast Images, TR Str. for Diverse St. Needs, p. 13	• Tone, SE pp. 183, 190; TR Selection Support, p. 54	• Spelling vs. Pron: *-ough,* SE pp. 182, 190; TR Sel. Sup., p. 51 Word Bank: bough, trough, p. 187; manifestation, disparaging, judicious, gibe, admonition, immutable, potency, p. 188	• Participles as Adjectives, SE pp. 182, 190; TR Sel. Sup., p. 52 • WS Gram. Pr. Book, p. 41
"The Apple Tree," Katherine Mansfield, SE p. 192	Reading Level: Average • Question, SE pp. 193, 198; TR Selection Support, p. 57 • Readers' Theater, TR Str. for Diverse St. Needs, p. 14	• Allusion, SE pp. 193, 198; TR Selection Support, p. 58	• Greek, Roman Word Origins: Words From Myths, SE pp. 192, 198; TR Sel. Support, p. 55 Word Bank: paddocks, p. 195; exquisite, bouquet, jovial, p. 196	• Punctuation, SE pp. 192, 198; TR Select. Support, p. 56 • WS Language Lab CD-ROM, Semicolons, Colons, and Quotation Marks • WS Gram. Pr. Book, pp. 104–106
"Africa," David Diop; "Old Song;" The Analects, Confucius; "All," Bei Dao; "Also All," Shu Ting, SE p. 200,	Reading Levels: Chall., Avg., Avg., Chall., Chall. • Relate to What You Know, SE pp. 201, 208; TR Sel. Sup., p. 61 • Explain Comparisons TR Str. for Diverse St. Needs, p. 15	• Aphorisms, SE pp. 201, 208; TR Selection Support, p. 62	• Latin Suffixes:*-ment,* SE pp. 200, 208; TR Sel. Sup., p. 59 Word Bank: impetuous, p. 202; chastisements, p. 204; lamentation, p. 206	• Infinitives and Infinitive Phrases, SE pp. 200, 208; TR Selection Support, p. 60 • WS Gram. Pr. Book, p. 46

Striving for Success

Writing	Speaking, Listening, and Viewing	Researching and Representing	Assessment	Technology
• Writing: Reading Journal [Level of Formality], SE p. 126 • Library Dedication, Inform. Article, Directions, SE p. 126 • Article, Prediction, Travel Guide, TR Alt. Assess., p. 8	• Storytelling Perf., Library Panel Discussion, SE p. 126 • S/L/V Mini-Lesson: Storytelling Perf., ATE p. 122 • Cult. Rep., Tech. Report, Panel Disc., TR Alt. Assess., p. 8	• Library Poster, Library Survey, SE p. 126 • Display, TR Alt. Assess., p. 8	• Sel. Test, TR Form. Assess., pp. 26–28; Assess. Res. Software • Resp. to Lit. Rub. [for Wr. Lesson], TR Alt. Assess., p. 110 • TR Alt. Assess., p. 8	• from *In Commemoration: One Million Volumes,* LL Audiocassettes • Looking at Lit., Ch. 2 • WS Writing Lab CD-ROM Response to Literature
• Writing Lesson: Video Script [Clear Exp. of a Proc.], SE p. 145 • Newspaper Article, Land Advertisement, Parable, SE p. 145 • Personal Obstacle, Essay, TR Alt. Assess., p. 9	• Update the Story, Eulogy, SE p. 145 • S/L/V Mini-Lessons: Eulogy ATE p. 142 • Conversation With the Devil, TR Alt. Assess., p. 9	• Map of Russia, Scale Diagram of Pahom's Field, SE p. 145 • Land-Cost Graph, Contemp. Greed Tales, TR Alt. Assess., p. 9 • V/R Mini-Lesson: Map of Russia, ATE p. 141 • Research Skills Mini-Lesson: Questionaire, ATE p. 136	• Sel. Test, TR Form. Assess., pp. 29–31; Assess. Res. Software • Drama Rubric [for Wr. Lesson], TR Alt. Assess., p. 109 • TR Alt. Assess., p. 9	• "How Much Land Does a Man Need?," LL Audiocassettes • WS Writing Lab CD-ROM, Creative Writing Tutorial; Wr. at Work Videodisc, Ch. 8
• Writing Lesson: Subm. Letter [Elab. To Give Inform.], SE p. 153 • Letter to a Poet, Ad., Parody of a Poem, SE p. 153 • Achieve. Log, Personification, Thesis, Comp., Elegy, TR Alt. Assess., p. 10	• Informal Debate, Panel Discussion, SE p. 153 • S/L/V Mini-Lessons: Inf. Debate ATE p. 149	• Round Earth Demonstration, Oral Report, SE p. 153 • Wind Dance, Architectural Sketches, TR Alt. Assess., p. 10	• Sel. Test, TR Form. Assess., pp. 32–34; Assess. Res. Software • Business Letter Rubric [for Wr. Lesson], TR Alt. Assess., p. 113 • TR Alt. Assess., p. 10	• "Success. . .," "I dwell in . . .," "Uncoiling," "Columbus . . .," LL Audiocassettes • WS Writing Lab CD-ROM, Practical and Tech. Writing Tut.; Wr. at Work Videodisc, Ch. 8
• Writing: Pers. Nar. [Clear Exp. of Cause/Effects], SE p. 163 • Card, Movie Rev., Story From a Mother's POV, SE p. 163 • Task Breakdown, Art., Book Jacket, TR Alt. Assess., p. 11	• Role Play, Speech, SE p. 163 • S/L/V Mini-Lesson: Speech, ATE p. 157 • Persuasive Speech, TR Alt. Assess., p. 11	• Chart on CP, Christy Brown Timeline, SE p. 163 • Graphic Org., Bill of Rights, Art. Interp., TR Alt. Assess., p. 11 •Research Mini-Lesson: Chart on Cerebral Palsy, ATE p. 159	• Sel. Test, TR Form. Assess., pp. 35–37; Assess. Res. Software • Personal Narrative Rubric [for Wr. Lesson], TR Alt. Assess., p. 96 • TR Alt. Assess., p. 11	• from *My Left Foot,* LL Audiocassettes • WS Writing Lab CD-ROM, Narration Tutorial
• Writing: Firsthand Biography [Provide Ex.], SE p. 176 • Letter, Report., Alt. End., SE p. 176 • Express., Conflict Journ., Predict., First Chapt., TR Alt. Assess., p. 12	• Casting Discussion, Oral Anecdote, SE p. 176 • S/L/V Mini-Lesson: Casting Discussion, ATE p. 173 • Dinner Conversation, Debate, TR Alt. Assess., p. 12	• Conflict/Resolution Workshop, Cult. Comp. Chart, SE p. 176 • Family Tree Presentation, TR Alt. Assess., p. 12	• Sel. Test, TR Form. Assess., pp. 38-40; Assess. Res. Software • Personal Narrative Rubric [for Wr. Lesson], TR Alt. Assess., p. 96 • TR Alt. Assess., p. 12	• "A Visit to Grandmother," LL Audiocassettes • WS Writing Lab CD-ROM, Narration Tutorial
• Writing Lesson: App. Letter for a Summer Job [Support with Details], SE p. 191 • Description, Essay, Advice Column, SE p. 191 • Intrapersonal Reflection, Letter of Advice, Poem, Essay, TR Alt. Assess., p. 13	• Speech, Role Play, SE p. 191 • Speaking, Listening, and Viewing Mini-Lesson: Role Play, ATE p. 186 • Skits, TR Alt. Assess., p. 13	• Farming Update, Food Source, SE p. 191 • Career Perspectives, Poetry Collection, TR Alt. Assess., p. 13 •V/R/ Mini-Lesson: Timeline, ATE p. 187	• Sel. Test, TR Form. Assess., pp. 41–43; Assess. Res. Software • Résumé/Cover Letter Rub. [for Wr. Lesson], TR Alt. Assess., p. 114 • TR Alt. Assess., p. 13	• "Mowing," "After Apple-Picking," "Style, "At Harvest-time," LL Audiocassettes • WS Writing Lab CD-ROM, Practical Writing Tutorial • "The Apple Tree," LL Audiocassettes
• Writing: Retelling a Story [Show, Don't Tell], SE p. 199 •Story Sum., Pers. Nar., Alternative Ending, SE p. 199 • Analysis, Poem, Essay, TR Alt. Assess., p. 14	• Dram. Reading, Mono-logue From a Father's POV, SE p. 199 • S/L/V Mini-Lesson: Monologue, ATE p. 196 • Oral Report, TR Alt. Assess., p. 14	• Brochure, Map, SE p. 199 • Sci. Illust, Timeline, Cookbook, TR Alt. Assess., p. 14	• Sel. Test, TR Form. Assess., pp. 44-46; Assess. Res. Software • Fict. Narrative Rub. [for Wr. Lesson], TR Alt. Assess, p. 95 • TR Alt. Assess, p. 14	• WS Writing Lab CD-ROM, Narration Tutorial; Wr. at Work Videodisc, Ch. 2
• Writing Lesson: Calendar [Brevity/Clarity], SE p. 209 • Letter to an Author, Life Poem, Comp/Cont Poems SE p. 209 • Credo, Rebuttal, Journal, TR Alt. Assess., p. 15	• Oral Interpretation, Interview, SE p. 209 • S/L/V Mini-Lesson: Oral Interpretation, ATE p. 205 • Non-Western Music Rep., Aphorism Play List, TR Alt. Assess., p. 15	• Tiananmen Square Presentation, Collage, SE p. 209 • History Table, Relativity Map, TR Alt. Assess., p. 15	• Sel. Test, TR Form. Assess., pp. 47–49; Assess. Res. Software • Expression Rubric [for Wr. Lesson], TR Alt. Assess., p. 94 • TR Alt. Assess., p. 15	• "Africa," "Old Song," from *The Analects,* "All," "Also All," LL Audiocassettes • WS Writing Lab CD-ROM, Creative Writing Tutorial; Wr. at Work Videodisc, Ch. 6

Selection	Reading	Literary Elements/Forms	Vocabulary	Grammar
"Through the Tunnel," Doris Lessing, SE p. 218	Reading Level: Average • Reading for Success: Interactive Strategies, SE pp. 220, 229; TR Sel. Sup., pp. 65–66 • Model, SE pp. 221–228 • Form a Mental Image, TR Str. for Diverse St. Needs, p. 16	• Internal Conflict, SE pp. 219, 229; TR Sel. Sup., p. 67	• Latin Word Roots: *-lum-,* SE pp. 218, 229; TR Sel. Sup., p. 63 Word Bank: contrition, p. 221; promontories, luminous, supplication, p. 223; frond, p. 225; convulsive, p. 227; gout, p. 228	• Participial Phrases, SE pp. 218, 229; TR Sel. Sup., p. 64 • WS Gram. Pr. Book, p. 41
"The Dog That Bit People," James Thurber, SE p. 232	Reading Level: Average • Form Mental Images, SE pp. 233, 240; TR Sel. Sup., p. 70 • Break Down Sentences, TR Str. for Diverse St. Needs, p. 17	• Humorous Essay, SE pp. 233, 240; TR Sel. Sup., p. 71 •Analyze Lit. Crit., ATE p. 237	• Greek Prefixes: *epi-,* SE pp. 232, 240; TR Sel. Support,p. 68 Word Bank: incredulity, choleric, p. 235; irascible, jangle, p. 236; indignant, epitaph, p. 239	• Correct use of *like* and *as if,* SE pp. 232, 240; TR Selection Support, p. 69
"Conscientious Objector," Edna St. Vincent Millay; "A Man," Nina Cassian; "The Weary Blues," Langston Hughes; "Jazz Fantasia," Carl Sandburg, SE p. 242	Reading Levels: Challenging, Easy, Challenging, Challenging • Resp. to Images/Ideas, SE pp. 243, 248; TR Sel. Sup., p. 74 • Translate Music Terms, TR Str. for Diverse St. Needs, p. 18	• Tone, SE pp. 243, 248; TR Selection Support, p. 75	• Greek Word Roots: *-chol-,* SE pp. 242, 248; TR Sel. Sup., p. 72 Word Bank: reap, p. 245; pallor, melancholy, p. 246	• Use of *shall* and *will,* SE pp. 242, 248; TR Sel. Sup., p. 73
"Like the Sun," R.K. Narayan; "Tell all the Truth but tell it slant—," Emily Dickinson, SE p. 250	Reading Levels: Avg., Avg. • Analyze Causes/Effects, SE pp. 251, 255; TR Sel. Sup., p. 78 • Identify Chain of Events, TR Str. for Diverse St. Needs, p. 19	• Irony, SE pp. 251, 255; TR Selection Support, p. 79	• Latin Word Roots: *-gratis-,* SE pp. 250, 255; TR Sel. Sup., p. 76 Word Bank: essence, tempering, shirked, incessantly, ingratiating, stupefied, p. 253; scrutinized, p. 254	• Comparative and Superlative Forms, SE pp. 250, 255; TR Selection Support, p. 77 • WS Lang. Lab CD-ROM, Forms of Comparisons • WS Gram. Pr. Book, pp. 86–88
"Hearts and Hands, " O. Henry; "The Fish," Elizabeth Bishop, SE p. 262	Reading Levels: Easy, Easy • Predict Events, SE pp. 263, 268; TR Sel. Sup., p. 82 • Explain Comparisons, TR Str. for Diverse St. Needs, p. 20	• Surprise Ending, SE pp. 263, 268; TR Sel. Sup., p. 83 •Analyze Lit. Crit., ATE p. 265	• Latin Prefixes: *counter-,* SE pp. 262, 268; TR Sel. Sup., p. 80 Words: influx, forestalled, counterfeiting, sidled, p. 264; venerable, infested, sullen, p. 266	• Coordinate Adjectives, SE pp. 262, 268; TR Sel. Sup., p. 81
from **Desert Exile, Yoshiko Uchida; "Remarks Upon Signing a Proclamation . . .,"** SE p. 270	Reading Levels: Avg., Avg. • Background Knowledge, SE pp. 271, 280; TR S. Sup., p. 86 • Analyze Author's Purpose, TR Str. for Diverse St. Needs, p. 21	• Writer's Purpose, SE pp. 271, 280; TR Sel. Sup., p. 87	• Latin Word Roots: *-curs-,* SE pp. 270, 280; TR Sel. Sup., p. 84 Words: cursory, euphemism, p. 272; adept, destitute, unwieldy, communal, p. 275; conspicuous, p. 277; assuage, p. 278	• Adjective Clauses, SE pp. 270, 280; TR Sel. Sup., p. 85 • WS Gram. Pr. Book, p. 51
"The Cabuliwallah," Rabindranath Tagore, SE p. 282	Reading Level: Average • Engage Your Senses, SE pp. 283, 292; TR Sel. Sup., p. 90 • Identify Characters, TR Str. for Diverse St. Needs, p. 22	• Relationships Bet. Char., SE pp. 283, 292; TR Sel. Sup., p. 91	• Latin Word Roots: *-jud-,* SE pp. 282, 292; TR Sel. Sup., p. 88 Word Bank: precarious, impending, judicious, euphemism, imploring, p. 287; fettered, sordid, pervaded, p. 288	• Pronoun and Antecedent Agreement, SE pp. 282, 292; TR Selection Support, p. 89 • WS Language Lab CD-ROM, Pronouns and Antecedents • WS Gram. Pr. Book, p. 83

Clashing Forces

Writing	Speaking, Listening, and Viewing	Researching and Representing	Assessment	Technology
• Guided Writing: Brochure [Persuasive Tone], SE p. 230 • Water Safety Rules, Letter, Observation, SE p. 230 • Intrapersonal Reflection, Char. Analysis, TR Alt. Assess., p. 16	• Account of an Outdoor Adventure, Dialogue, SE p. 230 • S/L/V Mini-Lesson: Account of an Outdoor Adv., ATE p. 224	• Collage, Movie Score, SE p. 230 • Pro-Con Chart, Model, Susp. Diag., How-to Pamphlet, Body Inventory, TR Alt. Assess., p. 16 •Viewing/Representing Mini-Lesson: Collage., ATE p. 224	• Sel. Test, TR Form. Assess., pp. 54-56; Assess. Res. Software • Description Rubric [for Wr. Lesson], TR Alt. Assess., p. 97 • TR Alt. Assess., p. 16	• "Through the Tunnel," LL Audiocassettes • WS Writing Lab CD-ROM, Description Tutorial; Wr. at Work Videodisc, Ch. 1
• Guided Writing: Animal Anec. [Vivid Verbs], SE p. 241 • Description, News Story, Persuasive Letter, SE p. 241 • Desc., Police Report, Character Sketch, Intrapersonal Reflection, List, Limerick, Comparison, TR Alt. Assess., p. 17	• Pet Talk, Pantomime, SE p. 241 • S/L/V Mini-Lesson: Pet Talk, ATE p. 236	• Wanted Poster, Dog Breed Chart, SE p. 241	• Sel. Test, TR Form. Assess., pp. 57–59; Assess. Res. Software • Fict. Narrative Rubric [for Wr. Lesson], TR Alt. Assess., p. 95 • TR Alt. Assess., p. 17	• "The Dog That Bit People," LL Audiocassettes • WS Writing Lab CD-ROM, Narration Tutorial; Wr. at Work Videodisc, Ch. 2
• Guided Writing Lesson: Press Rel. [Approp. Lang.], SE p. 249 • Newspaper Headlines, Interview, Song Lyrics, SE p. 249 • Jazz Report, C.O. Report, Death Report, TR Alt. Assess., p. 18	• Music Panel, Dramatic Reading, SE p. 249 • S/L/V Mini-Lesson: Dramatic Reading, ATE p. 245 • Population Analysis, Presentation, TR Alt. Assess., p. 18	• Graphic Design, Music Timeline, SE p. 249 • Essay, Drawing/Painting, TR Alt. Assess., p. 18	• Sel. Test, TR Form. Assess., pp. 60–62; Assess. Res. Software • Persuasion Rubric [for Wr. Lesson], TR Alt. Assess., p. 105 • TR Alt. Assess., p. 18	• "Conscientious Objector," "A Man," "The Weary Blues," "Jazz Fantasia," LL Audio • WS Writing Lab CD-ROM, Persuasion Tutorial; Wr. at Work Videodisc, Ch. 4 • Lit. CD-ROMs, Reading Poetry
• Guided Writing: Rev. of a Song [Sup. Details], SE p. 256 • Advice Column, Guidelines, Fairy Tale, SE p. 256 • Reflection, Comp., Essay, Day of Truth, TR Alt. Assess., p. 19	• Oral Argument, Debate, SE p. 256 • Children's Lesson, TR Alt. Assess., p. 19	• Res. Songs, Map, SE p. 256 • Fictional Town, Truth Study, TR Alt. Assess., p. 19	• Sel. Test, TR Form. Assess., pp. 63–65; Assess. Res. Software • Eval/Review Rubric [for Wr. Lesson], TR Alt. Assess., p. 104 • TR Alt. Assess., p. 19	• "Like the Sun," "Tell all the Truth but tell it slant—," LL Audiocassettes • Looking at Lit., Ch. 3 • WS Writing Lab CD-ROM, Response to Literature Tutorial
• Guided Writing: Letter to the Editor [Elaboration], SE p. 269 • Monologue, Opening Scene, Speech, SE p. 269 • Remembrances, Poem, Continuation, TR Alt. Assess., p. 20	• Casting Discussion, Sound Effects Tape, SE p. 269 • Drama, Oral Report, TR Alt. Assess., p. 20	• Money Chart, Opening Credits, SE p. 269 • Anatomical Drawing, Hist. Invest., TR Alt. Assess., p. 20	• Sel. Test, TR Form. Assess., pp. 66–68; Assess. Res. Software • Persuasion Rubric [for Wr. Lesson], TR Alt. Assess., p. 105 • TR Alt. Assess., p. 20	• "Hearts and Hands," "The Fish," LL Audiocassettes • WS Writing Lab CD-ROM, Persuasion Tutorial • Lit. CD-ROMs, How to Read and Understand Poetry
• Guided Writing: WRA Camp Report [Accuracy], SE p. 281 • Letter to a Friend, Monologue, Dear Editor, SE p. 281 • Rules of Conduct, Speech Writing, Nonfiction Organization, TR Alt. Assess., p. 21	• Lawyer's Argument, Oral Interpretation, SE p. 281 • S/L/V Mini-Lesson: Lawyer's Argument, ATE p. 275 • S/L/V Mini-Lesson: Resolving Conflicts, ATE p. 276 • Debate, TR Alt. Assess., p. 21	Interview, Meet the Press, SE p. 281 • Stamp design, Public Recognition, Photo Montage, TR Alt. Assess., p. 21 • Research: Text Org., ATE p. 274	• Sel. Test, TR Form. Assess., pp. 69-71; Assess. Res. Software • Research Report Rub. [for Lesson], TR Alt. Assess. p. 106 • TR Alt. Assess., p. 21	• from *Desert Exile,* "Remarks Upon Signing a Proclamation . . .," LL Audiocassettes • WS Writing Lab CD-ROM, Research. Tutorial; Wr. at Work Videodisc, Ch. 5
• Desc., Character's Journ. Entry, Letter to the Embassy, SE p. 293 • Guided Writing: Firsthand Biography [Logical Org.], SE p. 293 • Diary Entry, Letter From Prison, TR Alt. Assess., p. 22	• Courtroom Speech, Oral Interpretation, SE p. 293 • Mini-Lesson: Courtroom Speech, ATE p. 289 • Oral Presentation, Wedding Music, TR Alt. Assess., p. 22	• Timeline, Sketch, SE p. 293 • Sensory Detail Web, Comp/Cont Chart, Mixed-Media Portrait, TR Alt. Assess., p. 96 • Research Skills Mini-Lesson: Using Notecards, ATE p. 287	• Sel. Test, TR Form. Assess., pp. 72–74; Assess. Res. Software • Nar./Pers. Exp. Rub. [for Wr. Lesson], TR Alt. Assess., p. 96 • TR Alt. Assess., p. 22	• "The Cabuliwallah," LL Audio • Looking at Lit., Ch. 3 • WS Writing Lab CD-ROM, Narration Tutorial

Selection	Reading	Literary Elements/Forms	Vocabulary	Grammar
from **Speak, Memory, Vladimir Nabokov,** SE p. 302	• Reading Level: Average • Reading for Success: Strategies for Reading Critically, SE pp. 304, 309; TR Selection Support, pp. 94–95 • Model, SE pp. 305–308 • Simplifying Word Order, TR Str. for Diverse St. Needs, p. 23	• Personal Narrative, SE pp. 303, 309; TR Sel. Sup., p. 96 • Analyze Lit. Rev., ATE p. 306	• Latin Prefixes: *pro-,* SE pp. 302, 309; TR Sel. Sup., p. 92 Word Bank: procession, p. 305; proficiency, laborious, portentously, limpid, p. 306	• Dashes, SE pp. 302, 309; TR Selection Support, p. 93 • WS Gram. Pr. Book, p. 107
"With All Flags Flying," Anne Tyler, SE p. 312	• Reading Level: Easy • Evaluate a Character's Decision, SE pp. 313, 322; TR Selection Support, p. 99 • Classify Descriptive Details, TR Str. for Diverse St. Needs, p. 24	• Characters as Symb., SE pp. 313, 322; TR Sel. Sup., p. 100	• Greek Prefixes: *mono-,* SE pp. 312, 322; TR Sel. Sup., p. 97 Word Bank: appurtenances, conspicuous, p. 316; doddering, monosyllabic, p. 319	• Past Participial Phrases, SE pp. 312, 322; TR Sel. Sup., p. 98 • WS Gram. Pr. Book, p. 41
"The Bridge," Leopold Staff; "The Old Stoic," Emily Brontë; "I Am Not One of Those . . . ," Anna Akhmatova; "Speech During the Invasion of Constantinople," Empress Theodora, SE p. 324	• Reading Levels: Average, Challenging, Challenging, Average • Author's Perspective, SE pp. 325, 331; TR Selection Support, p. 103 • Interpret Poetic Images, TR Str. for Diverse St. Needs, p. 25	• Dramatic Situation, SE pp. 325, 331; TR Sel. Sup., p. 104	• Latin Word Roots: *-dom-,* SE pp. 324, 331; TR Sel. Sup., p. 101 Word Bank: implore, p. 327; timorous, indomitable, p. 329	• Negatives and Double Negatives, SE pp. 324, 331; TR Selection Support, p. 102 • WS Gram. Pr. Book, p. 90
"The Good Deed," Pearl S. Buck, SE p. 338	• Reading Level: Average • Draw Inferences, SE pp. 339, 354; TR Selection Support, p. 107 • Respond to Characters' Actions, TR Str. for Diverse St. Needs, p. 26	• Static/Dynamic Char., SE pp. 339, 354; TR Sel. Sup., p. 108 • Analyze Lit. Crit., ATE p. 347	• Latin Word Roots: *-pel-,* SE pp. 338, 354; TR Sel. Sup., p. 105 Word Bank: contemplatively, p. 341; revere, compelled, p. 342; abashed, p. 344; repressed, indignantly, p. 346; assailed, p. 348; expedition, conferred, p. 350	• Adverb Clauses, SE pp. 338, 354; TR Sel. Sup., p. 106 • WS Language Lab CD-ROM, Problems with Modifiers and Varying Sentence Structure • WS Gram. Pr. Book, p. 52
"Thoughts of Hanoi," Nguyen Thi Vinh; "Pride," Dahlia Ravikovitch; "Auto Wreck," Karl Shapiro; "Before the Law," Franz Kafka, SE p. 362	• Reading Levels: Challenging, Easy, Average, Challenging • Evaluate a Writer's Message, SE pp. 363, 370; TR Selection Support, p. 111 • Identify Key Ideas, TR Str. for Diverse St. Needs, p. 27	• Theme, SE pp. 363, 370; TR Selection Support, p. 112	• Latin Word Roots: *-sat-,* SE pp. 362, 370; TR Sel. Sup., p. 109 Word Bank: deranged, convalescents, banal, expedient, p. 367; importunity, contemplation, insatiable, p. 369	• Present Participial Phrases, SE pp. 362, 370; TR Selection Support, p. 110 • WS Language Lab CD-ROM, Misplaced Modifiers • WS Gram. Pr. Book, pp. 41–43

Turning Points

Writing	Speaking, Listening, and Viewing	Researching and Representing	Assessment	Technology
• Guided Writing: Mem. of a Milestone [Sens. Det.], SE p. 310 • On-line Message, Children's Story, Author's World, SE p. 310 • Letter, Personal Narrative, TR Alt. Assess., p. 23	• Memory Exchange, Oral Presentation, SE p. 310 • Speaking, Listening, and Viewing Mini-Lesson: Oral Presentation, ATE p. 307 • Oral Reading, TR Alt. Assess., p. 23	• Multimedia Presentation, Illustration, SE p. 310 • Book Cover, Book List, Reading Statistics, Landscape at Dusk, TR Alt. Assess., p. 23	• Selection Test, TR Formal Assessment, pp. 79-81; Assess. Res. Software • Narrative Based on Personal Experience Rubric [for Wr. Lesson], TR Alt. Assess., p. 96 • TR Alt. Assess., p. 23	• from *Speak, Memory,* LL Audiocassettes • WS Writing Lab CD-ROM, Narration Tutorial; Wr. at Work Videodisc, Ch. 2
• Guided Writing: Dialogue [Appropriate Language for Purpose], SE p. 323 • Essay on Growing Old, Letter, Alternative Ending, SE p. 323 • Scrapbook, Old Age Plan, Business Memo, TR Alt. Assess., p. 24	• Soundtrack, Debate, SE p. 323 • Speaking, Listening, and Viewing Mini-Lesson: Debate, ATE p. 317 • Dialogue, One-Act Play, TR Alt. Assess., p. 24	• Volunteer at a Nursing Home, Service for the Elderly, SE p. 323 • Population Projection, Advertisement, TR Alt. Assess., p. 24 • Research Skills Mini-Lesson: Oral Research, ATE p. 315	• Selection Test, TR Formal Assessment, pp. 82–84; Assess. Res. Software • Drama Rubric [for Wr. Lesson], TR Alt. Assess., p. 109 • TR Alt. Assess., p. 24	• "With All Flags Flying," LL Audiocassettes • WS Writing Lab CD-ROM, Creative Writing Tutorial; Wr. at Work Videodisc, Ch. 6
• Guided Writing Lesson: Poem [Fig. Lang.], SE p. 332 • Sum., News Commentary, Comp/Cont Essay, SE p. 332 • Letter., Rep. on Russia, Jour. Ent., TR Alt. Assess., p. 25	• Speech, Role Play, SE p. 332 • Speaking, Listening, and Viewing Mini-Lesson: Speech, ATE p. 328 • Top Five List, Presentation—A Nation Surrounded, TR Alt. Assess., p. 25	• Timeline, Collage, SE p. 332 • Travel Brochure—Ancient Rome, Drama—The Empress Rises, TR Alt. Assess., p. 25	• Selection Test, TR Formal Assessment, pp. 85–87; Assess. Res. Software • Poetry Rubric [for Wr. Lesson], TR Alt. Assess., p. 108 • TR Alt. Assess., p. 25	• "The Bridge," "The Old Stoic," "I Am Not One of Those Who Left the Land," "Speech During the Invasion of Constantinople," LL Audiocassettes • WS Writing Lab CD-ROM, Creative Writing Tutorial; Wr. at Work Videodisc, Ch. 6
• Guided Writing: Award Speech [Main Impression], SE p. 355 • Letters, Story Segment, Newsletter, SE p. 355 • Good Deeds, Reflections on Home, Sequel, Personal Essay, TR Alt. Assess., p. 26	• Unrehearsed Speech, Radio Interview, SE p. 355 • Speaking, Listening, and Viewing Mini-Lesson: Radio Interview, ATE p. 348 • Dramatic Monologue, TR Alt. Assess., p. 26	• Multimedia Presentation, Timeline, SE p. 355 • Presentation, Day of Good Deeds, TR Alt. Assess., p. 26 • Research Skills Mini-Lesson: Reader's Guide to Periodical Literature, ATE p. 351 • Viewing and Representing Mini-Lesson: Timeline, ATE p. 352	• Selection Test, TR Formal Assessment, pp. 88–90; Assess. Res. Software • Classification Rubric [for Wr. Lesson], TR Alt. Assess., p. 99 • TR Alt. Assess., p. 26	• "The Good Deed," LL Audiocassettes • WS Writing Lab CD-ROM, Exposition Tutorial; Wr. at Work Videodisc, Ch. 3
• Guided Writing: Letter to the Editor [Elab. to Make Writing Personal], SE p. 371 • Interview, Visitor's Guide, Allegory, SE p. 371 • Thoughts on Friendship, Comp/Cont, Alternative Theme, TR Alt. Assess., p. 27	• Telephone Conversation, Improvisational Skit, SE p. 371 • Speaking, Listening, and Viewing Mini-Lesson: Improvisational Skit, ATE p. 369 • Interpretive Reading, TR Alt. Assess., p. 27	• Two Maps, Auto Safety Presentation, SE p. 371 • Choreography, Artistic Representation, "First on the Scene" Pamphlet, TR Alt. Assess., p. 27 • Viewing and Representing Mini-Lesson: Visual Representation of Tone, ATE p. 366	• Selection Test, TR Formal Assess., pp. 91–93; Assess. Res. Software • Persuasion Rubric [for Wr. Lesson], TR Alt. Assess., p. 105 • TR Alt. Assess., p. 27	• "Thoughts of Hanoi," "Pride," "Auto Wreck," "Before the Law," LL Audiocassettes • Looking at Lit., Ch. 4 • WS Writing Lab CD-ROM, Persuasion

Selection	Reading	Literary Elements/Forms	Vocabulary	Grammar
"The Widow and the Parrot," Virginia Woolf, SE p. 380	Reading Level: Easy • Reading for Success: Strategies for Reading Fiction, SE pp. 382, 391; TR Selection Support, pp. 115–116 • Model, SE pp. 383–390 • Identify Predictions, TR Str. for Diverse St. Needs, p. 28	• Motivation, SE pp. 381, 391; TR Selection Support, p. 117 • Analyze Literary Crtiticism, ATE p. 388	• Related Words: Forms of *sagacity,* SE pp. 380, 391; TR Selection Support, p. 113 Words: ford, dilapidated, p. 385; sovereigns, sagacity, p. 389	• Correct Use of Adjectives and Adverbs, SE pp. 380, 391; TR Selection Support, p. 114 • WS Language Lab CD-ROM, Eight Parts of Speech • WS Gram. Pr. Book, p. 19
"Civil Peace," Chinua Achebe, SE p. 394	Reading Level: Challenging • Prior Background Knowledge, SE pp. 395, 402; TR Selection Support, p. 120 • Understand Dialect, TR Str. for Diverse St. Needs, p. 29	• Key Statement, SE pp. 395, 402; TR Sel. Support, p. 121	• Latin Word Roots: *-reput-* Disreputable, SE pp. 394, 402; TR Selection Support, p. 118 Word Bank: inestimable, disreputable, amenable, p. 396; edifice, destitute, p. 398; imperious, p. 399; commiserate, p. 400	• Past and Past Perfect Tenses, SE pp. 394, 402; TR Selection Support, p. 119 • WS Language Lab CD-ROM, Verb Tense • WS Gram. Pr. Book, pp. 67–71
"The Bean Eaters," Gwendolyn Brooks; "How to React to Familiar Faces," Umberto Eco, SE p. 404	Reading Levels: Easy, Easy • Resp. to Connotations, SE pp. 405, 410; TR Sel. Sup., p. 124 • Compare/Contrast Images, TR Str. for Diverse St. Needs, p. 30	• Tone, SE pp. 405, 410; TR Selection Support, p. 125	• Latin Word Roots: *-ami-,* SE pp. 404, 410; TR Sel. Sup., p. 122 Word Bank: expound, syndrome, amiably, protagonist, p. 409	• Pronoun Agreement With an Indefinite Antecedent, SE pp. 404, 410; TR Sel. Sup., p. 123 • WS Language Lab CD-ROM, Pronouns and Antecedents • WS Gram. Pr. Book, p. 83
"A Picture From the Past: Emily Dickinson," Reynolds Price; "What Makes a Degas a Degas?" Richard Mühlberger, SE p. 412	Reading Levels: Avg., Avg. • Rel. Text and Pictures, SE pp. 413, 419; TR Sel. Sup., p. 128 • Question Author's Purpose, TR Str. for Div. St. Needs, p. 31	• Analytical Essay, SE pp. 413, 419; TR Sel. Support, p. 129	• Latin Word Roots: *-cent-,* SE pp. 412, 419; TR Sel.Sup., p. 126 Word Bank: titanic, centenarian, austere, p. 415; lacquered, p. 417	• Compound Sentences, SE pp. 412, 419; TR Selection Support, p. 127 • WS Language Lab CD-ROM, Varying Sentence Structure • WS Gram. Pr. Book, pp. 120–121
"The Orphan Boy and the Elk Dog," Blackfeet myth, SE p. 426	Reading Level: Average • Identify With a Character, SE pp. 427, 436; TR Selection Support, p. 132 • Prepare a Reader's Theater, TR Str. for Div. St. Needs, p. 32	• Myth, SE pp. 427, 436; TR Selection Support, p. 133	• Word Groups: Homographs, SE pp. 426, 436; TR Sel. Sup., p. 130 Word Bank: refuse, p. 429; surpassed, p. 431; emanating, relish, p. 432; stifle, p. 434	• Commonly Confused Words: *accept* and *except,* SE pp. 426, 436; TR Selection Support, p. 131
"The Street of the Cañon," Josephina Niggli, SE p. 438	Reading Level: Easy • Predict, SE pp. 439, 446; TR Selection Support, p. 136 • Use a Chain of Events Org., TR Str. for Div. St. Needs, p. 33	• Point of View, SE pp. 439, 446; TR Selection Support, p. 137	• Anglo-Saxon Suffixes: *-ly,* SE pp. 438, 446; TR Sel. Sup., p. 134 Word Bank: officious, mottled, p. 441; nonchalantly, audaciously, imperiously, plausibility, p. 443	• Commas in a Series, SE pp. 438, 446; TR Sel. Support, p. 135 • WS Lang. Lab CD-ROM, Commas • WS Gram. Pr. Book, pp. 99–101
"A Storm in the Mountains," Alexander Solzhenitsyn; "In the Orchard," Henrik Ibsen; "A Tree Telling of Orpheus," Denise Levertov, SE p. 448	Reading Levels: Average, Average, Challenging • Engage the Senses, SE pp. 449, 458; TR Sel. Sup., p. 140 • Form a Mental Image, TR Str. for Diverse St. Needs, p. 34	• Speaker, SE pp. 449, 458; TR Selection Support, p. 141 • Analyze Lit. Crit., ATE p. 454	• Borrowed Words: Latin Terms, SE pp. 448, 458; TR Sel. Sup., p. 138 Word Bank: terra firma, p. 450; sultry, p. 451; asunder, p. 456	• Correct use of *like* and *as,* SE pp. 448, 458; TR Sel. Sup., p. 139

Expanding Horizons

Writing	Speaking, Listening, and Viewing	Researching and Representing	Assessment	Technology
• Guided Writing Lesson: Will [Logical Organization], SE p. 392 • Character Sketch, Review, Health Report, SE p. 392 • Report, POV Study, Essay, Proposal, TR Alt. Assess., p. 28	• Animal Behavior Video, Dialogue Between Person and Pet, SE p. 392 • S/L/V Mini-Lessons: Debate, ATE p. 385, Dialogue Between Person and Pet, ATE p. 389 • Role Play, TR Alt. Assess., p. 28	• Conversion Chart, Area Map, SE p. 392 • Plot Diagram, Animal Behavior Chart, TR Alt. Assess., p. 28 •Viewing and Representing: Video Summary, ATE p. 385	• Sel. Test, TR Form. Assess., pp. 98–100; Assess. Res. Software • Classification Rubric [for Wr. Lesson], TR Alt. Assess., p. 99 • TR Alt. Assess., p. 28	• "The Widow and the Parrot," LL Audiocassettes • Looking at Lit., Ch. 5 • WS Writing Lab CD-ROM, Exposition Tutorial; Wr. at Work Videodisc, Ch. 3
• Guided Writing Lesson: Annot. Map [Brevity/Clarity], SE p. 403 • Interview, Art., Poem, SE p. 403 • Pamphlet, Letter, Documentary, Cultural Sketch, Observation, TR Alt. Assess., p. 29	• Reworking a Dialogue Collage, SE p. 403 • S/L/VMini-Lesson: Reworking a Dialogue, ATE p. 398	• Proverbs Presentation, Scenic Sketches, SE p. 403 • Comparison-Contrast Chart, Timeline, TR Alt. Assess., p. 29	• Sel. Test, TR Form. Assess., pp. 101–103; Assess. Res. Software • Definition/Classification Rub. [for Wr. Lesson], TR Alt. Assess., p. 99 • TR Alt. Assess., p. 29	• "Civil Peace," LL Audiocassettes • WS Writing Lab CD-ROM, Exposition Tutorial
• Writing: Intro. of Talk-Show Guest [Aud. Knowledge], SE p. 411 • Interview, Dialogue, Techno-Reaction, SE p. 411 • Eulogy, Narrative, Letter, Contract, TR Alt. Assess., p. 30	• Perform and Evaluate, Debate, SE p. 411 • S/L/V Mini-Lesson: Debate, ATE p. 408 • Monologue, Interview and Article, TR Alt. Assess., p. 30	• Drawing, Celebrity Home Page, SE p. 411	• Sel. Test, TR Form. Assess., pp. 104–106; Assess. Res. Software • Description Rubric [for Wr. Lesson], TR Alt. Assess., p. 97 • TR Alt. Assess., p. 30	• "The Bean Eaters," "How to React to Familiar Faces," LL Audiocassettes • WS Writing Lab CD-ROM, Description Tutorial; Wr. at Work Videodisc, Ch. 1
• Guided Writing: Placard [Antic. of Questions], SE p. 420 • Exhibit Promotion, Photo Essay, Art Analysis, SE p. 420 • Poem, Jour. Entry, Portrait Nar., Tour Guide, TR Alt. Assess., p. 31	• Poetry Reading, Art Narration, SE p. 420 • Mini-Lesson: Art Narration, ATE p. 417	• Painting and Poetry Exhibit, Art Exchange, SE p. 420 • Daguerrotype History, Painting, Analysis, TR Alt. Assess., p. 31	• Sel. Test, TR Form. Assess., pp. 107–109; Assess. Res. Software • Classification Rubric [for Wr. Lesson], TR Alt. Assess., p. 99 • TR Alt. Assess., p. 31	• "A Picture From the Past: Emily Dickinson," "What Makes a Degas a Degas?" LL Audio • WS Writing Lab CD-ROM, Exposition Tutorial; Wr. at Work Videodisc, Ch. 3
• Guided Writing: Retelling of a Myth [Clear Beginning, Middle, and End], SE p. 437 • Speech, Dialogue, Description of a Mystery Animal, SE p. 437 • Journal, Reflection, Myth, Story, TR Alt. Assess., p. 32	• Debate, Retell a Myth, SE p. 437 • S/L/V Mini-Lesson: Debate, ATE p. 434 • Animals and People, TR Alt. Assess., p. 32	• Animal Population Graph, Storyboard Mural, SE p. 437 • Mythical Board Game, Map, TR Alt. Assess., p. 32 • V/R Mini-Lesson: Storyboard Mural, ATE p. 428 • Res: Source List, ATE p. 430	• Sel. Test, TR Form. Assess., pp. 110–112; Assess. Res. Software • Fict. Narrative Rubric [for Wr. Lesson], TR Alt. Assess., p. 95 • TR Alt. Assess., p. 32	• "The Orphan Boy and the Elk Dog," LL Audiocassettes • WS Writing Lab CD-ROM, Narration Tutorial; Wr. at Work Videodisc, Ch. 2
• Guided Writing Lesson: Song [Connotation], SE p. 447 • Postcard, Legend, Compare and Contrast, SE p. 447 • Suspense, Celebration Scene, Alternate Ending, Essay, TR Alt. Assess., p. 33	• Dialogue, Debate, SE p. 447 • S/L/V Mini-Lesson: Dialogue, ATE p. 444 • Interview, TR Alt. Assess., p. 33	• Sketch, Photo Essay, SE p. 447 • Social Dance, Conflict Resolution, TR Alt. Assess., p. 33	• Sel. Test, TR Form. Assess., pp. 113–115; Assess. Res. Software • Poetry Rubric [for Wr. Lesson], TR Alt. Assess., p. 108 • TR Alt. Assess., p. 33	• "The Street of the Cañon," LL Audiocassettes • WS Writing Lab CD-ROM, Creative Writing Tutorial; Wr. at Work Videodisc, Ch. 6
• Guided Writing Lesson: Monologue [Grab Readers' Attention], SE p. 459 • Description, Film Treatment, Biographical Sketch, SE p. 459 • Journal, Rebuttal, TR Alt. Assess., p. 34	• Video or Audio, Interview, SE p. 459 • S/L/V Mini-Lesson: Interview, ATE p. 451 • Instrumentation Report, TR Alt. Assess., p. 34	• Presentation of Ancient Inst., Multimedia Project, SE p. 459 • Poster, Drawing, Accomp., Interp. Dance, TR Alt. Assess., p. 34 • Research Skills Mini-Lesson: Writing Source Cards, ATE p. 453	• Sel. Test, TR Form. Assess., pp. 116–118; Assess. Res. Software • Fict. Narrative Rubric [for Wr. Lesson], TR Alt. Assess., p. 95 • TR Alt. Assess., p. 34	• "A Storm in the Mountains," "In the Orchard," "A Tree Telling of Orpheus," LL Audiocassettes • WS Writing Lab CD-ROM, Narration Tutorial

Program Planner Unit 6

Selection	Reading	Literary Elements/Forms	Vocabulary	Grammar
"The Open Window," Saki, SE p. 468	Reading Level: Average • Reading for Success: Strategies for Constructing Meaning, SE pp. 470, 475; TR Selection Support, pp. 144–145 • Model, SE pp. 471–474 • Identifying Story Elements, TR Str. for Diverse St. Needs, p. 35	• Plot Structure, SE pp. 469, 475; TR Selection Support, p. 146	• Word Origins: Words From Names, SE pp. 468, 475; TR Selection Support, p. 142 Word Bank: delusion, p. 472; iminent, mackintosh, pariah, p. 474	• Placement of *only* and *just,* SE pp. 468, 475; TR Sel. Sup., p. 143 • WS Language Lab CD-ROM, Misplaced Modifiers Lesson • WS Gram. Pr. Book, pp. 61–63
"Leiningen Versus the Ants," Carl Stephenson, SE p. 478	Reading Level: Average • Make Predictions Based on Plot Details, SE pp. 479, 496; TR Selection Support, p. 149 • Identifying Chain of Events, TR Str. for Diverse St. Needs, p. 36	• Conflict, SE pp. 479, 496; TR Selection Support, p. 150	• Borrowed Words: Latin Plural Forms, SE pp. 478, 496; TR Selection Support, p. 147 Word Bank: peons, p. 483; flout, weir, p. 485; provender, p. 487; alluvium, fomentations, p. 495	• Correct Use of Apostrophes, SE pp. 478, 496; TR Selection Support, p. 148 • WS Gram. Pr. Book, pp. 110–111
"By the Waters of Babylon," Stephen Vincent Benét, SE p. 498	Reading Level: Challenging • Draw Conclusions, SE pp. 499, 510; TR Sel. Sup., p. 153 • Sequence Events, TR Str. for Diverse St. Needs, p. 37	• First-Person POV, SE pp. 499, 510; TR Sel Sup, p. 154	• Word Groups: Conjunctive Adverbs, SE pp. 498, 510; TR Selection Support, p. 151 Word Bank: purified, p. 500; bowels, p. 503; moreover, nevertheless, p. 506	• Subordination, SE pp. 498, 510; TR Sel. Sup., p. 152 • WS Gram. Pr. Book, pp. 51–52
"A Problem," Anton Chekhov; "Luck," Mark Twain, SE p. 512	Reading Levels: Average, Average • Draw Inferences About Character, SE pp. 513, 525; TR Selection Support, p. 157 • Analyze Character's Behavior, TR Str. for Div. St. Needs, p. 38	• Static and Dynamic Characters, SE pp. 513, 525; TR Selection Support, p. 158 • Analyze Literary Criticism, ATE p. 517	• Latin Word Roots: *-ver-,* SE pp. 512, 525; TR Sel. Sup., p. 155 Words: taciturn, rheumatic, p. 515; vestibule, p. 519; zenith, countenance, veracity, p. 520; guileless, prodigious, sublimity, p. 522	• Restrictive and Nonrestrictive Adjective Clauses, SE pp. 512, 525; TR Selection Support, p. 156
"There Will Come Soft Rains," Ray Bradbury; "The Garden of Stubborn Cats," Italo Calvino, SE p. 532	Reading Levels: Average, Average • Clarify, SE pp. 533, 548; TR Selection Support, p. 161 • Form a Mental Image, TR Str. for Diverse St. Needs, p. 39	• Setting, SE pp. 533, 548; TR Selection Support, p. 162 • Analyze Literary Criticism, ATE p. 535	• Word Origins: Words From Myths, SE pp. 532, 548; TR Selection Support, p. 159 Word Bank: warrens, p. 535; titanic, paranoia, tremulous, p. 536; psychopathic, p. 539; supernal, itinerary, p. 541; transoms, rank, p. 543; scrimmage, p. 545; indigence, p. 546	• Commonly Confused Words: *lie* and *lay,* SE pp. 532, 548; TR Selection Support, p. 160 • WS Gram. Pr. Book, p. 91
"The Princess and All the Kingdom," Pär Lagerkvist; "The Censors," Luisa Valenzuela, SE p. 550	Reading Levels: Easy, Average • Challenge the Writer's Message, SE pp. 551, 558; TR Selection Support, p. 165 • Identify Key Ideas, TR Str. for Diverse St. Needs, p. 40	• Universal Themes, SE pp. 551, 558; TR Selection Support, p. 166	• Latin Word Roots: *-ultra-,* SE pp. 550, 558; TR Sel. Sup., p. 163 Word Bank: ardent, venerable, sordid, p. 553; ulterior, staidness, p. 556	• *Who* and *Whom* in Adjective Clauses, SE pp. 550, 558; TR Selection Support, p. 164 • WS Language Lab CD-ROM, Pronoun Case • WS Gram. Pr. Book, p. 79

Short Stories

Writing	Speaking, Listening, and Viewing	Researching and Representing	Assessment	Technology
• Guided Writing Lesson: Study Notes: Summary [Transitions That Show Time], SE p. 476 • Letter, Diary, Story, SE p. 476 • Lists, Description, Tall Tale, Personal Essay, TR Alt. Assess., p. 35	• Tape Recording, Storytelling, SE p. 476 • S/L/V Mini-Lesson: Storytelling, ATE p. 472 • Role Play, Poem of Introduction, TR Alt. Assess., p. 35	• Music, Comic Strip, SE p. 476 • Vacation Plan, TR Alt. Assess., p. 35	• Sel. Test, TR Form. Assess., pp. 123–125; Assess. Res. Software • Summary Rubric [for Wr. Lesson], TR Alt. Assess., p. 98 • TR Alt. Assess., p. 35	• "The Open Widow," LL Audiocassettes • WS Writing Lab CD-ROM, Exposition Tutorial
• Guided Writing: Movie Scene [Climax and Res.], SE p. 497 • Letter to the Editor, Change the Disaster, News Report, SE p. 497 • Natural Medicine, Point of View, Bias Analysis, Special Effects, Action Plan, TR Alt. Assess., p. 36	• Motivational Speech, Watch the Movie, SE p. 497 • S/L/V Mini-Lesson: Motivational Speech, ATE p. 482 • Tall Tale, TR Alt. Assess., p. 36	• Map of the Plantation, Pests and Pals, SE p. 497 • Research: Steps to Conduct Research, ATE p. 485 • V/R Mini-Lesson: Map of the Plantation, ATE p. 491 • Character Wheel, TR Alt. Assess., p. 36	• Sel. Test, TR Form. Assess., pp. 126–128; Assess. Res. Software • Drama Rubric [for Wr. Lesson], TR Alt. Assess., p. 109 • TR Alt. Assess., p. 36	• "Leiningen Versus the Ants," LL Audiocassettes • WS Writing Lab CD-ROM, Creative Writing Tutorial
• Guided Writing: Description From Another Vantage Point [Consistent POV], SE p. 511 • Postcard, Publicity Release, Poem, SE p. 511 • Wilderness Survival Kit, Intrapersonal Reflection, Hypotheses, TR Alt. Assess., p. 37	• Radio Interview, Oral Presentation, SE p. 511 • S/L/V Mini-Lessons: Radio Inter., Oral Present., ATE pp. 502, 506 • Storytelling, TR Alt. Assess., p. 37	• Tourism Poster, Storyboard, SE p. 511 • Travel Plan, Chart, Story Graph, TR Alt. Assess., p. 37	• Sel. Test, TR Form. Assess., pp. 129–131; Assess. Res. Software • Description Rubric [for Wr. Lesson], TR Alt. Assess., p. 97 • TR Alt. Assess., p. 37	• "By the Waters of Babylon," LL Audiocassettes • WS Writing Lab CD-ROM, Description Tutorial; Wr. at Work Videodisc, Ch. 1
• Writing: Telephone Conversation [Realistic Dialogue], SE p. 526 • Invitation, Journal Entry, Story Ending, SE p. 526 • Reflection, Def., Comp/Cont, Biography, TR Alt. Assess., p. 38	• Monologue, Period Presentation, SE p. 526 • S/L/V Mini-Lesson: Roundtable Discussion, ATE p. 518 • Judgment, TR Alt. Assess., p. 38	• Roundtable Discussion, Multimedia Biography, SE p. 526 • V/R Mini-Lesson: Using Text Organizers, ATE p. 522 • Portrait, Song for Sasha, TR Alt. Assess., p. 38	• Sel. Test, TR Form. Assess., pp. 132–134; Assess. Res. Software • Drama Rubric [for Wr. Lesson], TR Alt. Assess., p. 109 • TR Alt. Assess., p. 38	• "A Problem," "Luck," LL Audiocassettes • WS Writing Lab CD-ROM, Creative Writing Tutorial; Wr. at Work Videodisc, Ch. 2
• Writing: Ad for a New Technology [Consider the Knowledge Level of Your Aud.], SE p. 549 • Schedule, Speculation, Science Fiction Story, SE p. 549 • Cat Journ., TR Alt. Assess., p. 39	• Inanimate Dialogue, Persuasive Argument, SE p. 549 • S/L/V Mini-Lessons: Inanimate Dialogue, Persuasive Argument, ATE pp. 544, 538, • Debate, Technology Report, TR Alt. Assess., p. 39	• Painting Presentation, Floor Plan, SE p. 549 • V/R Mini-Lesson: Floor Plan, ATE p. 543 • City Plan, Time Capsule, Sounds of a Day, Population Graph, TR Alt. Assess., p. 39	• Sel. Test, TR Form. Assess., pp. 135–137; Assess. Res. Software • Persuasion Rubric [for Wr. Lesson], TR Alt. Assess., p. 105 • TR Alt. Assess., p. 39	• "There Will Come Soft Rains," "The Garden of Stubborn Cats," LL Audiocassettes • Looking at Lit., Ch. 6 • WS Writing Lab CD-ROM, Persuasion Tutorial; Wr. at Work Videodisc, Ch. 4
• Guided Writing: Letter to an Elected Official [Format], SE p. 559 • Letter to Juan, The Censor, Princess With a Point of View, SE p. 559 • Sequel, Building Design, Front-Page Story, TR Alt. Assess., p. 40	• Debate, Improvised Speech, SE p. 559 • S/L/V Mini-Lesson: Improvised Speech, ATE p. 553 • Monologue, TR Alt. Assess., p. 40	• Music Collection, Internet Research, SE p. 559 • Flow Chart, Informational Poster, Children's Fairy Tale, TR Alt. Assess., p. 40	• Sel. Test, TR Form. Assess., pp. 138–140; Assess. Res. Software • Persuasion Rubric [for Wr. Lesson], TR Alt. Assess., p. 105 • TR Alt. Assess., p. 40	• "The Princess and All the Kingdom," "The Censors," LL Audiocassettes • WS Writing Lab CD-ROM, Persuasion Tutorial; Wr. at Work Videodisc, Ch. 4

Selection	Reading	Literary Elements/Forms	Vocabulary	Grammar
"The Marginal World," Rachel Carson, SE p. 568	Reading Level: Average • Reading for Success: Strategies for Reading Nonfict., SE pp. 570, 577; TR Sel. Sup., pp. 169–170 • Model, SE pp. 571–576 • ID Main Idea/Sup. Details, TR Str. for Diverse St. Needs, p. 41	• Expository Essay, SE pp. 569, 577; TR Selection Support, p. 171	• Latin Suffixes: *-able,* SE pp. 568, 577; TR Sel. Sup., p. 167 Words: mutable, p. 571; ephemeral, p. 572; primeval, essence, marginal, p. 575; subjectively, manifestations, cosmic, p. 576	• Linking Verbs and Subject Complements, SE pp. 568, 577; TR Selection Support, p. 168 • WS Language Lab CD-ROM, Eight Parts of Speech • WS Gram. Pr. Book, p. 33
from **The Way to Rainy Mountain, N. Scott Momaday; "The One Great Heart," Alexander Solzhenitsyn; "Keep Memory Alive," Elie Wiesel,** SE p. 580	Reading Levels: Average, Challenging, Challenging • Analyze the Author's Purpose, SE pp. 581, 592; TR Selection Support, p. 174 • Summarize Main Idea, TR Str. for Diverse St. Needs, p. 42	• Reflective and Persuasive Essays, SE pp. 581, 592; TR Selection Support, p. 175 • Analyze Literary Criticism, ATE p. 589	• Related Words: Forms of *Reciprocity,* SE pp. 580, 592; TR Selection Support, p. 171 Word Bank: engender, tenuous, p. 585; reciprocity, p. 587; assimilate, inexorably, oratory, p. 588; transcends, p. 591	• Capitalization of Proper Nouns and Adjectives, SE pp. 580, 592; TR Selection Support, p. 172 • WS Language Lab CD-ROM, Problems with Capitalization • WS Gram. Pr. Book, pp. 93–94
"A Child's Christmas in Wales," Dylan Thomas; "Marian Anderson: Famous Concert Singer," Langston Hughes, SE p. 594	Reading Levels: Average, Average • Recognize the Author's Attitude, SE pp. 595, 606; TR Selection Support, p. 178 • Question Author's Purpose, TR Str. for Diverse St. Needs, p. 43	• Biography and Autobiography, SE pp. 595, 606; TR Selection Support, p. 179	• Word Groups: Musical Words, SE pp. 594, 606; TR Selection Support, p. 176 Word Bank: sidle, prey, wallowed, p. 597; crocheted, p. 598; brittle, trod, forlorn, p. 601; arias, staunch, p. 603; repertoire, p. 605	• Restrictive and Nonrestrictive Appositives, SE pp. 594, 606; TR Selection Support, p. 177 • WS Language Lab CD-ROM, Commas • WS Gram. Pr. Book, p. 40
"Flood," Annie Dillard, SE p. 608	Reading Level: Average • Recognize Facts and Impressions, SE pp. 609, 617; TR Selection Support, p. 182 • Classify Descriptive Details, TR Str. for Diverse St. Needs, p. 44	• Descriptive Essay, SE pp. 609, 617; TR Selection Support, p. 183	• Latin Prefixes: *mal-,* SE pp. 608, 617; TR Selection Support, p. 180 Word Bank: obliterates, opacity, usurped, p. 612; mauled, malevolent, repressed, p. 614	• Subject/Verb Agreement, SE pp. 608, 617; TR Se. Sup., p. 181 • WS Language Lab CD-ROM, Subject/Verb Agreement • WS Gram. Pr. Book, pp. 80–82
"Star Wars: A Trip to a Far Galaxy That's Fun and Funny . . . ," Vincent Canby; "Star Wars: Breakthrough Film Still Has the Force," Roger Ebert, SE p. 624	Reading Levels: Average, Easy • Identify Evidence, SE pp. 625, 634; TR Selection Support, p. 186 • Recognizing Allusions, TR Str. for Diverse St. Needs, p. 45	• Critical Review, SE pp. 625, 634; TR Selection Support, p. 187 • Analyze Film Reviewers, ATE p. 631	• Connotations, SE pp. 624, 634; TR Selection Support, p. 184 Words: apotheosis, eclectic, facetiousness, adroit, p. 627; piously, condescension, p. 628; watershed, synthesis, p. 629; fastidious, p. 631; effete, laconic, p. 633	• Parenthetical Interrupters, SE pp. 624, 634; TR Selection Support, p. 185 • WS Language Lab CD-ROM, Commas • WS Gram. Pr. Book, pp. 99–101
"Mothers and Daughters," Tillie Olsen and Estelle Jussim, SE p. 636	Reading Level: Average • Reading Strategy: Interpret Pictures, SE pp. 637, 644; TR Selection Support, p. 190 • Summarize Observations, TR Str. for Diverse St. Needs, p. 46	• Visual Essay, SE pp. 637, 644; TR Selection Support, p. 191	• Related Words: Words Describing Color, SE pp. 636, 644; TR Selection Support, p. 188 Word Bank: hue, sullenness, rapture, p. 639; fervor, p. 640; implicit, p. 642	• Semicolons in a Series, SE pp. 636, 644; TR Sel. Sup., p. 189 • WS Language Lab CD-ROM, Semicolons, Colons, and Quotation Marks • WS Gram. Pr. Book, pp. 102–103
"Imitating Nature's Mineral Artistry," Paul O'Neil; "Work That Counts," Ernesto Ruelas Inzunza, SE p. 646	Reading Levels: Challenging, Easy • Relate Diagrams to Text, SE pp. 647, 654; TR Sel. Support, p. 194 • Translate Technical Terms, TR Str. for Diverse St. Needs, p. 47	• Technical Article, SE pp. 647, 654; TR Selection Support, p. 195	• Greek Prefixes: *syn-,* SE pp. 646, 654; TR Sel. Support, p. 192 Word Bank: synthetic, constituents, synthesized, metamorphosis, p. 649; divulge, saturated, fortuitous, vigilance, p. 650; myriad, topography, p. 652	• Varied Sentence Beginnings: Adverb Phrases, SE pp. 646, 654; TR Selection Support, p. 193 • WS Language Lab CD-ROM, Varying Sentence Structure • WS Gram. Pr. Book, pp. 121–123

Nonfiction

Writing	Speaking, Listening, and Viewing	Researching and Representing	Assessment	Technology
• Guided Writing Lesson: Proposal for a Documentary [Transitions], SE p. 578 • Letter, Nature Report, Essay, SE p. 578 • Bibliography, Cause/Effect Essay, Nature Essay, TR Alt. Assess., p. 41	• Poetry Reading, Photo Essay, SE p. 578 • S/L/V Mini-Lesson: Poetry Reading, ATE p. 573 • Dialogue, Ocean Music, TR Alt. Assess., p. 41	• Art Exhibit, The Living Sea, SE p. 578 • Audubon Exhibit, Comp/Cont/ Chart, TR Alt. Assess., p. 41 • Research: Researching Specific Information, ATE p. 574	• Sel. Test, TR Form. Assess., pp. 145–147; Assess. Res. Software • Description Rubric [for Wr. Lesson], TR Alt. Assess., p. 97 • TR Alt. Assess., p. 41	• "The Marginal World," LL Audiocassettes • WS Writing Lab CD-ROM, Description Tutorial
• Guided Writing Lesson: Speech [Emphasis], SE p. 593 • Letter, Report, Creation Myth, SE p. 593 • Reflective Essay, Transcript, Letter of Recommendation, Article, TR Alt. Assess., p. 42	• Persuasive Speech, Reviewing a Movie, Reading, SE p. 593 • S/L/V Mini-Lesson: Persuasive Speech, ATE p. 588 • Public Service Announcement, Oral Report, TR Alt. Assess., p. 42	• Native American Dances, Writers-in-Prison, SE p. 593 • American Scenes, TR Alt. Assess., p. 42	• Sel. Test, TR Form. Assess., pp. 148–150; Assess. Res. Software • Persuasion Rubric [for Wr. Lesson], TR Alt. Assess., p. 105 • TR Alt. Assess., p. 42	• from *The Way to Rainy Mountain,* "The One Great Heart," "Keep Memory Alive," LL Audio • Looking at Lit., Ch. 7 • WS Writing Lab CD-ROM, Persuasion Tutorial
• Guided Writing: Letter to Yourself in 20 Years [Log. Org.], SE p. 607 • Holiday, Memory, Biography, SE p. 607 • List, Journal, Letter, Review, TR Alt. Assess., p. 43	• Visual Presentation, Marian Anderson Recording, SE p. 607 • S/L/V Mini-Lesson: Analyzing a Marian Anderson Performance, ATE p. 603 • Dramatic Readings, TR Alt. Assess., p. 43	• Greeting Card, Multimedia Presentation, SE p. 607 • Children's Production, Music Study, TR Alt. Assess., p. 43 • V/R Mini-Lesson: Multimedia Presentation, ATE p. 601	• Sel. Test, TR Form. Assess., pp. 151–153; Assess. Res. Software • Fict. Narrative Rubric [for Wr. Lesson], TR Alt. Assess., p. 95 • TR Alt. Assess., p. 43	• "A Child's Christmas in Wales," "Marian Anderson: Famous Concert Singer," LL Audiocassettes • WS Writing Lab CD-ROM, Nar. Tut.; Wr. at Work Videodisc, Ch. 2
• Guided Writing: Radio Call-In Trans. [Sensory Lang.], SE p. 618 • Descriptive Paragraph, Storm Journal, Fable, SE p. 618 • Description, Journal, Essay, Description, TR Alt. Assess., p. 44	• Storm Report, Talk-Show Interview, SE p. 618 • S/L/V Mini-Lesson: Storm Report, ATE p. 613 • Poem, TR Alt. Assess., p. 44	• Hurricane Chart, Food-Chain Presentation, SE p. 618 • Storm Study, Painting, TR Alt. Assess., p. 44 • Research Skills Mini-Lesson: Research Specific Information, ATE p. 611	• Sel. Test, TR Form. Assess., pp. 154–156; Assess. Res. Software • Description Rubric [for Wr. Lesson], TR Alt. Assess., p. 97 • TR Alt. Assess., p. 44	• "Flood," LL Audiocassettes • WS Writing Lab CD-ROM, Description Tutorial
• Guided Writing Lesson: Movie Review [Examples], SE p. 635 • Press Release, Speech, Interview, SE p. 635 • Reference Search, TR Alt. Assess., p. 45	• Star Wars Recording, Skit, SE p. 635 • S/L/V Mini-Lesson: Star Wars Recording, Skit, ATE pp. 627, 630 • Debate, Play List, TR Alt. Assess., p. 45	• Movie Collage, Science-Fiction Exhibit, SE p. 635 • Review Critique, Wanted Poster, Box Office Graph, Scene Re-enactment, TR Alt. Assess., p. 45	• Sel. Test, TR Form. Assess., pp. 157–159; Assess. Res. Software • Evaluation/Review Rubric [for Wr. Lesson], TR Alt. Assess., p. 104 • TR Alt. Assess., p. 45	• "Star Wars: A Trip to a Far Galaxy That's Fun and Funny . . .," "Star Wars: Breakthrough Film Still Has the Force," LL Audiocassettes • WS Writing Lab CD-ROM, Response to Literature Tuto-rial; Wr. at Work Videodisc, Ch. 7
• Guided Writing: Intro. to an Art Exhibit [Elaboration], SE p. 645 • Descriptive Paragraph, Interview, Poem, SE p. 645 • Letter, Advice Column, Meta-phor, Intrapersonal Reflection, TR Alt. Assess., p. 46	• Award Panel, Dramatic Reading, SE p. 645 • S/L/V Mini-Lesson: Award Panel, ATE p. 641	• Parent-and-Child Encyc., Parent-and-Child Video, SE p. 645 • Mood Palette, Soundtrack, Dance, TR Alt. Assess., p. 46 • V/R Mini-Lesson: Parent-Child Video, ATE p. 642	• Sel. Test, TR Form. Assess., pp. 160–162; Assess. Res. Software • Definition/Classification Rubric [for Wr. Lesson], TR Alt. Assessment, p. 99 • TR Alt. Assess., p. 46	• "Mothers & Daughters," LL Audiocassettes • WS Writing Lab CD-ROM, Exposition Tutorial
• Guided Writing: Product Description [Precise Details], SE p. 655 • Persuasive Letter, Essay, Technical Article, SE p. 655 • Dream Job, Outline, TR Alt. Assess., p. 47	• Bird Shapes, Oral Demonstration, SE p. 655 • S/L/V Mini-Lesson: Oral Demonstration, ATE p. 651 • Diagram Analysis, Career Profile, Interview, TR Alt. Assess., p. 47	• Conservation Update, Diamond Weighing, SE p. 655 • Diamond Sources, Heat Pictograph, TR Alt. Assess., p. 47	• Sel. Test, TR Form. Assess., pp. 163–165; Assess. Res. Software • Description Rubric [for Wr. Lesson], TR Alt. Assess., p. 97 • TR Alt. Assess., p. 47	• "Imitating Nature's Mineral Artistry," "Work That Counts," LL Audiocassettes • WS Writing Lab CD-ROM, Description Tutorial; Wr. at Work Videodisc, Ch. 1

Program Planner

Unit 8

Selection	Reading	Literary Elements/Forms	Vocabulary	Grammar
Antigone, Prologue Through Scene 2, Sophocles, SE p. 668	Reading Level: Average • Question the Characters' Motives, SE pp. 669, 683; TR Selection Support, p. 198 • Write Headlines, TR Str. for Diverse St. Needs, p. 48	• Protagonist and Antagonist, SE pp. 669, 683; TR Sel. Sup., p. 199 • Analyze Literary Criticism, ATE p. 672	• Latin Prefixes: *trans-*, SE pp. 668, 683; TR Sel. Sup., p. 196 Word Bank: sated, p. 674; anarchists, sententiously, p. 676; sultry, p. 678; transcends, p. 682	• Coordinating Conjunctions, SE pp. 668, 683; TR Selection Support, p. 197 • WS Language Lab CD-ROM, Eight Parts of Speech • WS Gram. Pr. Book, pp. 22, 120
Antigone, Scenes 3 Through 5, Sophocles, SE p. 684	Reading Level: Average • Identify With a Character, SE pp. 684, 699; TR Sel. Sup., p. 202 • Paraphrase Dialogue, TR Str. for Diverse St. Needs, p. 49	• Tragic Character, SE pp. 684, 699; TR Selection Support, p. 203	• Greek Word Roots: *-chor-*, SE pp. 684, 699; TR Sel. Sup., p. 200 Word Bank: deference, p. 685; vile, p. 686; piety, blasphemy, p. 688; lamentation, p. 690; chorister, p. 694	• Pronoun Case in Incomplete Clauses, SE pp. 684, 699; TR Selection Support, p. 201 • WS Language Lab CD-ROM, Special Problems with Agreement
The Tragedy of Julius Caesar, Act I, William Shakespeare, p. 710	Reading Level: Challenging • Use Text Aids, SE pp. 711, 731; TR Selection Support, p. 206 • Predict Events, TR Str. for Diverse St. Needs, p. 50	• Exposition in Drama, SE pp. 711, 731; TR Sel. Sup., p. 207 • Analyze Literary Criticism, ATE p. 725	• Related Words: Forms of *Portent,* SE pp. 711, 731; TR Selection Support, p. 204 Word Bank: replication, p. 715; spare, p. 721; infirmity, p. 724; surly, portentous, prodigious, p. 727	• The Subjunctive Mood, SE pp. 711, 731; TR Sel. Sup., p. 205
The Tragedy of Julius Caesar, Act II, William Shakespeare, p. 732	Reading Level:Challenging • Read Blank Verse, SE pp. 732, 749; TR Selection Support, p. 210 • Analyze Characters, TR Str. for Diverse St. Needs, p. 51	• Blank Verse, SE pp. 732, 749; TR Selection Support, p. 211	• Latin Word Roots: *-spir-*, SE pp. 732, 749; TR Sel. Sup., p. 208 Word Bank: augmented, entreated, conspiracy, p. 735; resolution, p. 736; exploit, p. 742; imminent, p. 744	• Commonly Confused Words: *affect* and *effect,* SE pp. 732, 749; TR Sel. Sup., p. 209
The Tragedy of Julius Caesar, Act III, William Shakespeare, p. 750	Reading Level: Challenging • Paraphrase, SE pp. 750, 771; TR Selection Support, p. 214 • Recognize Cause and Effect, TR Str. for Diverse St. Needs, p. 52	• Dramatic Speeches, SE pp. 750, 771; TR Sel. Sup., p. 215 • Analyze Literary Criticism: Mark Anthony's Speech, ATE p. 766	• Latin Word Roots: *-ora-*, SE pp. 750, 771; TR Sel. Sup., p. 212 Word Bank: suit, p. 751; spurn, confounded, mutiny, p. 753; malice, p. 756; oration, discourse, p. 758; vile, p. 761	• Parallel Structure, SE pp. 750, 771; TR Selection Support, p. 213 • WS Gram. Pr. Book, p. 64
The Tragedy of Julius Caesar, Act IV, William Shakespeare, p. 772	Reading Level: Challenging • Read Between the Lines, SE pp. 772, 787; TR Sel. Sup., p. 218 • Prepare a Readers' Theater, TR Str. for Diverse St. Needs, p. 53	• Conflict in Drama, SE pp. 772, 787; TR Selection Support, p. 219	• Greek Word Roots: *-phil-*, SE pp. 772, 787; TR Sel. Sup., p. 216 Word Bank: legacies, slanderous, p. 773; covert, p. 775; chastisement, p. 777; philosophy, p. 781	• Noun Clauses, SE pp. 772, 787; TR Selection Support, p. 217 • WS Gram. Pr. Book, p. 53
The Tragedy of Julius Caesar, Act V, William Shakespeare, p. 788	Reading Level: Challenging • Identify Cause and Effect, SE pp. 788, 802; TR Sel. Sup., p. 222 • Use a Story Map Organizer, TR Str. for Diverse St. Needs, p. 54	• Tragedy, SE pp. 788, 802; TR Selection Support, p. 223	• Anglo-Saxon Prefixes: *mis-*, SE pp. 788, 802; TR Sel. Sup., p. 220 Word Bank: presage, ensign, consorted, demeanor, p. 793; disconsolate, p. 795; misconstrued, p. 796; envy, p. 801	• Words of Direct Address, SE pp. 788, 802; TR Selection Support, p. 221

Drama

Writing	Speaking, Listening, and Viewing	Researching and Representing	Assessment	Technology
• Newspaper Art., Letter, SE p. 683 • Interpersonal Reflection, Modern Reworking, Gender-Role Analysis, TR Alt. Assess., p. 48	• Readers Theater, SE p. 683 • S/L/V Mini-Lesson: Readers' Theater, ATE p. 677	• Character Wheels, Playbill, Pro-Con Chart, Song, TR Alt. Assess., p. 48	• Selection Test, TR Formal Assessment, pp. 170–172; Assess. Res. Software • TR Alt. Assess., p. 48	• *Antigone,* Prol.–Sc. 2, LL Audiocassettes • Looking at Lit., Ch. 8 • WS Language Lab CD-ROM, Eight Parts of Speech Tutorial
• Guided Writing Lesson: Scene of Conflict [Format], SE p. 700 • Introduction, Final Speech, Editorial, SE p. 700 • Diary Entry, Alternative Ending, TR Alt. Assess., p. 49	• Mock Trial, Film Response, SE p. 700 • S/L/V Mini-Lesson: Mock Trial, ATE p. 691 • Debate, Charades, TR Alt. Assess., p. 49	• Multimedia Presentation, SE p. 700 • Plot Diag., Sympathy Ratings, Set Design, TR Alt. Assess., p. 49 • Research Mini-Lesson: Select a Specific Topic, ATE p. 688 • V/R Mini-Lesson: Multimedia Presentation, ATE p. 694	• Selection Test, TR Formal Assessment, pp. 173–175; Assess. Res. Software • Drama Rubric [for Wr. Lesson], TR Alt. Assess., p. 109 • TR Alt. Assess., p. 49	• *Antigone,* Sc. 3–5, LL Audiocassettes • WS Writing Lab CD-ROM, Creative Writing Tutorial
• Journal Entry, Speech, SE p. 731 • Film Review, Character Sketches, TR Alt. Assess., p. 50	• Roman Symbols, SE p. 731 • S/L/V Mini-Lesson: Enacting an Improvised Scene, ATE p. 723	• Political Cartoon, Biography, Stage Directions, Tour Brochure, Billboard, TR Alt. Assess., p. 50 • V/R Mini-Lesson: Visual Images, ATE p.726	• Selection Test, TR Formal Assessment, pp. 176–178; Assess. Res. Software • TR Alt. Assess., p. 50	• *The Tragedy of Julius Caesar, Act I,* LL Audiocassettes • Lit. CD-ROMs: How to Read and Understand Drama
• Editorial, Monologue, SE p. 749 • Correspondence, Journal Entry, Comparison, TR Alt. Assess., p. 51	• Debate, SE p. 749 • S/L/V Mini-Lesson: Debate, ATE p. 746 • Assassination Report, TR Alt. Assess., p. 51	• Map of Rome, Bill of Rights, Drawing, TR Alt. Assess., p. 51 • Research Mini-Lesson: Hist. Background, ATE p. 735	• Selection Test, TR Formal Assessment, pp. 179–181; Assess. Res. Software • TR Alt. Assess., p. 51	• *The Tragedy of Julius Caesar, Act II,* LL Audiocassettes • Lit. CD-ROMs: How to Read and Understand Drama
• Obituary, Reaction to Speeches, SE p. 771 • Outline, Motivation, Script, TR Alt. Assess., p. 52	• Background Music, SE p. 771 • S/L/V Mini-Lesson: Background Music, ATE p. 754 • Oration, Public Address, TR Alt. Assess., p. 52	• Magazine Cover, Survey, TR Alt. Assess., p. 52	• Selection Test, TR Formal Assessment, pp. 182–184; Assess. Res. Software • TR Alt. Assess., p. 52	• *The Tragedy of Julius Caesar, Act III,* LL Audiocassettes • Lit. CD-ROMs: The Time, Life, and Works of Shakespeare
• Character Profile, Rewrite a Scene, SE p. 787 • Letter, Journal Entry, Ghost Story, Personal Essay, TR Alt. Assess., p. 53	• Presentation, SE p. 787 • S/L/V Mini-Lesson: Musical Score, ATE p. 777 • Scene, TR Alt. Assess., p. 53	• Tragic Hero Poem or Essay, Map, TR Alt. Assess., p. 53	• Selection Test, TR Formal Assessment, pp. 185–187; Assess. Res. Software • TR Alt. Assess., p. 53	• *The Tragedy of Julius Caesar, Act IV,* LL Audiocassettes • Lit. CD-ROMs: The Time, Life, and Works of Shakespeare
• Guided Writing Lesson: Speech [Connotation], SE p. 803 • Epitaph, Response, Take a Side, SE p. 803 • Character Description, Journal Entry, Speech, Newspaper Article, TR Alt. Assess., p. 54	• Sound Effects, View a Play, SE p. 803 • S/L/V Mini-Lessons: Respond to Shakespearean English, Sound Effects, ATE pp. 794, 797 • Dramatic Monologue, TR Alt. Assess., p. 54	• Model of the Globe, Elizabethan Faire, SE p. 803 • Constitution, Poster, TR Alt. Assess., p. 54 • Viewing and Representing Mini-Lesson: [TK], ATE p. 791 • Research Skills Mini-Lesson: Elizabethan Faire, ATE p. 796	• Selection Test, TR Formal Assessment, pp. 188–190; Assess. Res. Software • Persuasion Rubric [for Wr. Lesson], TR Alt. Assess., p. 105 • TR Alt. Assess., p. 54	• *The Tragedy of Julius Caesar, Act V,* LL Audiocassettes • Lit. CD-ROMs: The Time, Life, and Works of Shakespeare

Selection	Reading	Literary Elements/Forms	Vocabulary	Grammar
"The Stolen Child," W. B. Yeats, SE p. 812	Reading Level: Average • Reading for Success: Strat. for Reading Poetry, SE pp. 814, 819; TR Sel. Sup., pp. 226–227 • Model, SE pp. 815–816 • Restate Poetry as Prose, TR Str. for Diverse St. Needs, p. 55	• Atmosphere, SE pp. 813, 819; TR Selection Support, p. 228	• Words With Multiple Meanings, SE pp. 812, 819; TR Selection Support, p. 224 Word Bank: herons, glosses, p. 815; slumbering, p. 816	• WS Language Lab CD-ROM, Special Problems in Agreement • WS Gram. Pr. Book, p. 121
"In Flanders Fields," J. McCrae; "The Kraken," Alfred, Lord Tennyson; "Reapers," J. Toomer; "Meeting at Night," R. Browning; "Prayer of First Dancers," Navajo, SE p. 822	Reading Levels: Avg., Chall., Avg., Chall., Easy • Listen, SE pp. 823, 830; TR Selection Support, p. 231 • Identify Key Ideas, TR Str. for Diverse St. Needs, p. 56	• Musical Devices, SE pp. 823, 830; TR Selection Support, p. 232	• Latin Prefixes: *mil-,* SE pp. 822, 830; TR Sel. Sup., p. 229 Word Bank: abysmal, millenni-al, p. 825	• Concrete/Abstract Nouns, SE pp. 822, 830; TR Sel. Sup., p. 230 • WS Language Lab CD-ROM, Types of Nouns • WS Gram. Pr. Book, pp. 5–6
"The Wind—tapped like a tired Man," E. Dickinson; "A Pace Like That," Y. Amichai; "Metaphor," E. Merriam; "Right Hand," P. Fried, SE p. 832	Reading Levels: Average, Challenging, Easy, Average • Paraphrase, SE pp. 833, 839; TR Selection Support, p. 235 • Recognize Similes, TR Str. for Diverse St. Needs, p. 57	• Figurative Language, SE pp. 833, 839; TR Selection Support, p. 236 •Analyze Literary Criticism, ATE p. 835	• Latin Word Roots: *-tac-,* SE pp. 832, 839; TR Sel. Sup., p. 233 Word Bank: countenance, tremulous, flurriedly, p. 834; decipher, p. 835; taciturn, elo-quent, guttural, diffused, gar-rulity, p. 838	• Elliptical Clauses, SE pp. 832, 839; TR Selection Support, p. 234
"La Belle Dame sans Merci," J. Keats; "Danny Deever," R. Kipling, SE p. 846	Reading Levels: Average, Average • Identify the Speaker, SE pp. 847, 852; TR Sel. Sup., p. 239 • Prepare a Readers' Theater, TR Str. for Diverse St. Needs, p. 58	• Narrative and Dramatic Poetry, SE pp. 847, 852; TR Selection Support, p. 240	• Word Roots: *-journ-,* SE pp. 846, 852; TR Sel. Sup., p. 237 Word Bank: sedge, thrall, sojourn, p. 849; whimpers, quickstep, p. 850	• Hyphens, SE pp. 846, 852; TR Selection Support, p. 238 • WS Gram. Pr. Book, p. 109
"The Guitar," F. García Lorca; "Making a Fist," N. S. Nye; "Jade Flower Palace," Tu Fu; "The Moon at the Fortified Pass," Li Po; "What Are Friends For," R. Brown; "Some Like Poetry," W. Szymborska, SE p. 854	Reading Levels: Avg., Easy, Chall., Chall., Easy, Avg. • Read in Sentences, SE pp. 855, 862; TR Sel. Sup., p. 243 • Recognize Unusual Comp., TR Str. for Diverse St. Needs, p. 59	• Lyric Poetry, SE pp. 855, 862; TR Selection Support, p. 244	• Greek Word Roots: *-path-,* SE pp. 854, 862; TR Sel. Sup., p. 241 Word Bank: monotonously, p. 856; pathos, wistful, p. 858	• Adjectival Modifiers, SE pp. 854, 862; TR Sel. Support, p. 242 • WS Gram. Pr. Book, p. 51
Sonnet 18, W. Shakespeare; "The Waking," T. Roethke; Tanka, Ki no Tsurayuki & Priest Jakuren; Haiku, Bashō & Issa, SE p. 864	Reading Levels: Chall., Easy, Chall., Chall., Easy, Avg. • Envision the Imagery, SE pp. 865, 870; TR Sel. Sup., p. 247 • Identify Sensory Words, TR Str. for Diverse St. Needs, p. 60	• Poetic Forms, SE pp. 865, 870; TR Selection Support, p. 248 • Analyze Literary Criticism, ATE p. 867	• Related Words: Forms of *Temperate,* SE pp. 864, 870; TR Selection Support, p. 245 Word Bank: temperate, p. 866• Inverted Word Order, SE pp. 812, 819; TR Sel. Support, p. 225	• Noun Clauses, SE pp. 864, 870; TR Selection Support, p. 246 • WS Language Lab CD-ROM, Varying Sentence Structure • WS Gram. Pr. Book, p. 53

Poetry

Writing	Speaking, Listening, and Viewing	Researching and Representing	Assessment	Technology
• Guided Writing Lesson: Crime Report [Clear, Consistent Purpose], SE p. 820 • Journal Entry, Editorial, Alternate Chorus, SE p. 820 • Fairy Tale, Rebuttal, TR Alt. Assess., p. 55	• Reading World Literature, Folk Music, SE p. 820 • S/L/V Mini-Lesson: Folk Music, ATE p. 817 • Rebuttal, Folktale, TR Alt. Assess., p. 55	• Irish Writers Timeline, Encyclopedia of Folklore, SE p. 820 • Irish Music, Sketch, Panel Discussion, TR Alt. Assess., p. 55	• Sel. Test, TR Form. Assess., pp. 195–197; Assess. Res. Software • Tech. Desc./ Explan. Rub. [for Wr. Lesson], TR Alt. Assess., p. 115 • TR Alt. Assess., p. 55	• "The Stolen Child," LL Audio • Lit. CD-ROMs: How to Read and Understand Poetry; Feature 2 • WS Writing Lab CD-ROM, Pract. Writing; Wr. at Work Videodisc, Ch. 8
• Guided Writing Lesson: Proposal for a Poetry Anthology [Specific Examples], SE p. 831 • Letter to Editor, City Chant, Musical Devices, SE p. 831 • Journal Entry, Description, Onomatopoeia Poem, "Meeting at Night" Scene, TR Alt. Assess., p. 56	• Visual Presentation, Oral Report, SE p. 831 • S/L/V Mini-Lesson: Oral Report, ATE p. 826 • "Prayer of First Dancers" Listening to Poems, TR Alt. Assess., p. 56	• Creatures Across Cultures, World War I, SE p. 831 • Viewing and Representing Mini-Lesson: Creatures Across Cultures, ATE p. 825 • Myth, TR Alt. Assess., p. 56	• Sel. Test, TR Form. Assess., pp. 198–200; Assess. Res. Software • Description Rubric [for Wr. Lesson], TR Alt. Assess., p. 97 • TR Alt. Assess., p. 56	• "In Flanders Fields," "The Kraken," "Reapers," "Meeting at Night," "Prayer of First Dancers," LL Audiocassettes • Looking at Lit., Ch. 9 • WS Writing Lab CD-ROM, Description Tutorial • Lit. CD-ROMs: How to Read and Understand Poetry; Features 8 and 10
• Guided Writing Lesson: Character Creation [Consistent Focus], SE p. 840 • Most Admired, Perfect Day Directions, Metaphor Poem, SE p. 840 • Morning Description, Biographical Poem, Personification Poem, Personal Essay, TR Alt. Assess., p. 57	• Wind Interview, Dialogue, SE p. 840 • S/L/V Mini-Lesson: Dialogue, ATE p. 837 • Discussion, Presentation, TR Alt. Assess., p. 57	• Visual Biography, Hurricane Statistics, SE p. 840 • Illustration, TR Alt. Assess., p. 57	• Sel. Test, TR Form. Assess., pp. 201–203; Assess. Res. Software • Description Rubric [for Wr. Lesson], TR Alt. Assess., p. 97 • TR Alt. Assess., p. 57	• "The Wind—tapped like a tired Man," "A Pace Like That," "Metaphor," "Right Hand," LL Audiocassettes • WS Writing Lab CD-ROM, Description Tutorial
• Guided Writing Lesson: News Bulletin Based on Poem [Climax and Resolution], SE p. 853 • Diary Entry, Letter to the Knight, Mock Narrative, SE p. 853 • Journal Entry, Eulogy, Comp., TR Alt. Assess., p. 58	• Oral Reading, Story in Music, SE p. 853 • S/L/V Mini-Lesson: Story in Music, ATE p. 850 • Oral Report, Debate, TR Alt. Assess., p. 58	• Dialect Chart, Art, SE p. 853 • Sound Track, Rank Chart, TR Alt. Assess., p. 58	• Sel. Test, TR Form. Assess., pp. 204–206; Assess. Res. Software • Summary Rubric [for Wr. Lesson], TR Alt. Assess., p. 98 • TR Alt. Assess., p. 58	• "La Belle Dame sans Merci," "Danny Deever," LL Audiocassettes • WS Writing Lab CD-ROM, Narration Tutorial • Lit. CD-ROMs: How to Read and Understand Poetry; Feature 4
• Remembrance, Statement Poem, Story, SE p. 863 • Guided Writing: Lyric Poem [Setting and Mood], SE p. 863 • Letter, Intrapersonal Response, Hypothesis, TR Alt. Assess., p. 59	• Reading to Music, Visual Presentation, SE p. 863 • S/L/V Mini-Lesson: Newscast, ATE p. 859	• Painting/Drawing, Profile of a People, SE p. 863 • Cluster Diagram, Advice Booklet, Mood Graph, Interpretive Dance, TR Alt. Assess., p. 59 •V/R Mini-Lesson: Visual Presentation, ATE p. 857	• Sel. Test, TR Form. Assess., pp. 207–209; Assess. Res. Software • Poetry Rubric [for Wr. Lesson], TR Alt. Assess., p. 108 • TR Alt. Assess., p. 59	• "The Guitar," "Making a Fist," "Jade Flower Palace," "The Moon at the Fortified Pass," "What Are Friends For," "Some Like Poetry," LL Audiocassettes • WS Writing Lab CD-ROM, Creative Writing Tutorial; Wr. at Work Videodisc, Ch. 6
• Villanelle Opener, Haiku, Essay, SE p. 871 • Guided Writing: Consumer Report of Poetic Forms [Grab Readers' Attention], SE p. 871 • Paraphrase, Debate, Trans., TR Alt. Assess., p. 60	• Rhyme Scheme, Viewing Poets Corner, SE p. 871 • S/L/V Mini-Lesson: Poetry Reading, ATE p. 867 • Clapping, TR Alt. Assess., p. 60	• Oral Report, Japanese Poetry, SE p. 871 • Venn Diagram, Concentration, Snapshots, TR Alt. Assess., p. 60 •Research Skills Mini-Lesson: Locate Appropriate Information, ATE p. 868	• Sel. Test, TR Form. Assess., pp. 210–212; Assess. Res. Software • Comp/Cont and Tech. Desc./ Explan. Rubrics [for Wr. Lesson] TR Alt. Assess., pp. 103, 115 • TR Alt. Assess., p. 60	• Sonnet 18, "The Waking," Tanka, Haiku, LL Audiocassettes • Lit. CD-ROMs: How to Read and Understand Poetry; Feature 10 • WS Writing Lab CD-ROM, Exposition Tutorial

Program Planner

Selection	Reading	Literary Elements/Forms	Vocabulary	Grammar
from **Don Quixote, Miguel de Cervantes,** SE p. 882	Reading Level: Average • Compare and Contrast, SE pp. 883, 890; TR Selection Support, p. 251 • Selection, SE pp. 884–889 • Analyze Characters' Behavior, TR Str. for Diverse St. Needs, p. 61	• Parody, SE pp. 883, 890; TR Selection Support, p. 252	• Latin Word Roots: *-son-*, SE pp. 882, 890; TR Selection Support, p. 249 Word Bank: lucidity, adulation, interminable, p. 885; affable, sallying, requisite, sonorous, veracious, vanquish, extolled, p. 886	• Gerunds and Gerund Phrases, SE pp. 882, 890; TR Selection Support, p. 250 • WS Gram. Pr. Book, pp. 44–45
"Morte d'Arthur," Alfred, Lord Tennyson; "Arthur Becomes King of Britain," T. H. White, SE p. 892	Reading Levels: Challenging, Average • Recognize an Author's Attitude, SE pp. 893, 915; TR Selection Support, p. 255 • Paraphrase Dialogue, TR Str. for Diverse St. Needs, p. 62	• Legend, SE pp. 893, 915; TR Selection Support, p. 256 • Analyze Literary Criticism, ATE p. 899	• Latin Suffixes: *-ous,* SE pp. 892, 915; TR Selection Support, p. 253 Word Bank: lamentation, p. 900; swarthy, p. 902; stickler, p. 904; sumptuous, p. 909; palfrey, p. 911	• Subjunctive Mood, SE pp. 892, 915; TR Selection Support, p. 254
"Rama's Initiation" from the **Ramayana, R. K. Narayan,** SE p. 922	Reading Level: Challenging • Draw Inferences About Culture, SE pp. 923, 930; TR Selection Support, p. 259 • Identify Epic Elements, TR Str. for Diverse St. Needs, p. 63	• The Epic Hero, SE pp. 923, 930; TR Selection Support, p. 260	• Latin Word Roots: *-min-,* SE pp. 922, 930; TR Selection Support, p. 257 Word Bank: austerities, decrepitude, sublime, august, p. 925; secular, obeisance, exuberance, diminutive, p. 927; esoteric, p. 928	• Restrictive and Nonrestrictive Appositives, SE pp. 922, 930; TR Selection Support, p. 258 • WS Language Lab CD-ROM, Commas • WS Gram. Pr. Book, p. 40
from Sundiata: An Epic of Old Mali, D. T. Niane, SE p. 932	Reading Level: Average • Storyteller's Purpose, SE pp. 933, 940; TR Selection Support, p. 263 • Connect with Hero's Conflict, TR Str. for Diverse St. Needs, p. 64	• Epic Conflict, SE pp. 933, 940; TR Selection Support, p. 264	• Latin Word Roots: *-firm-,* SE pp. 932, 940; TR Selection Support, p. 261 Word Bank: fathom, taciturn, malicious, infirmity, innuendo, diabolical, estranged, p. 935; affront, p. 939	• Sentence Variety, SE pp. 932, 940; TR Selection Support, p. 262 • WS Language Lab CD-ROM, Varying Sentence Structure and Varying Sentence Length • WS Gram. Pr. Book, pp. 121–123

Epics and Legends

Writing	Speaking, Listening, and Viewing	Researching and Representing	Assessment	Technology
• Guided Writing Lesson: Sketch of a Comic Hero [Clear and Logical Organization], SE p. 891 • Definition of a Hero, Don Quixote in America, Create a Scene, SE p. 891 • Postcard From Sancho, Continuation, Want Ad for a Squire, TR Alt. Assess., p. 61	• Role Play, Musical Drama , SE p. 891 • Speaking, Listening, and Viewing Mini-Lesson: Role Play, ATE p. 888 • Technology Report, Committee Meeting, TR Alt. Assess., p. 61	• Cartoon, Visual Essay, SE p. 891 • Media List, Casting Call, TR Alt. Assess., p. 61	• Selection Test, TR Formal Assessment, pp. 217-219; Assess. Res. Software • Description Rubric [for Wr. Lesson], TR Alt. Assess., p. 97 • TR Alt. Assess., p. 61	• from *Don Quixote,* LL Audiocassettes • WS Writing Lab CD-ROM, Description Tutorial; Wr. at Work Videodisc, Ch. 1
• Guided Writing Lesson: Letter of Recommendation [Clear and Consistent Purpose], SE p. 916 • List, Epic Essay, Local Legends, SE p. 916 • Thoughts on Destiny, Book Review, Modern-Day Arthur, TR Alt. Assess., p. 62	• Music, Oral Report, SE p. 916 • Speaking, Listening, and Viewing Mini-Lesson: Oral Reading, ATE p. 896 • Social History, Dramatization, TR Alt. Assess., p. 62	• Art, Feudalism Chart, SE p. 916 • Compare and Contrast, Travel Brochure, TR Alt. Assess., p. 62 • Viewing and Representing Mini-Lesson: Feudalism Chart, ATE p. 907 •Research Skills Mini-Lesson: Evaluating Sources, ATE p. 911	• Selection Test, TR Formal Assessment, pp. 220–222; Assess. Res. Software • Business Letter/Memo Rubric [for Wr. Lesson], TR Alt. Assess., p. 113 • TR Alt. Assess,, p. 62	• "Morte d'Arthur," "Arthur Becomes King of Britain," LL Audiocassettes • Looking at Lit., Ch. 10 • WS Writing Lab CD-ROM, Practical and Technical Writing Tutorial
• Guided Writing Lesson: Script Treatment Proposal [Appropriate Language for Your Purpose], SE p. 931 • Letter, Personal Narrative, Opening Argument, SE p. 931 • Letter, Skills Description, Sequel, Mentor, TR Alt. Assess., p. 63	• Oral Tales, Poster, SE p. 931 • Speaking, Listening, and Viewing Mini-Lesson: Oral Tales, ATE p. 925 • Mantra, Pantomime, TR Alt. Assess., p. 63	• Painting, Dance, SE p. 931 • Comparison-Contrast Chart, TR Alt. Assess., p. 63	• Selection Test, TR Formal Assessment, pp. 223–225; Assess. Res. Software • Description Rubric [for Wr. Lesson], TR Alt. Assess., p. 97 • TR Alt. Assess., p. 63	• "Rama's Initiation" from the *Ramayana,* LL Audiocassettes • WS Writing Lab CD-ROM, Description Tutorial
• Guided Writing Lesson: Storytelling Notes [Audience Knowledge], SE p. 941 • News Article, Writing in the Heroic Tradition, Critical Evaluation, SE p. 941 • Reflection, Legacy List, Short Story, Personal Essay, TR Alt. Assess., p. 64	• Oral Tales, Role Play, SE p. 941 • Speaking, Listening, and Viewing Mini-Lesson: Oral Tales, ATE p. 938 • Reading of Sundiata, TR Alt. Assess., p. 64	• Documentary, Herb Research, SE p. 941 • Hero Mural, Wildlife Map, TR Alt. Assess., p. 64 • Viewing and Representing Mini-Lesson: Herbal Chart, ATE p. 936	• Selection Test, TR Formal Assessment, pp. 226–228; Assess. Res. Software • Fictional Narrative Rubric [for Wr. Lesson], TR Alt. Assess., p. 95 • TR Alt. Assess., p. 64	• from *Sundiata: An Epic of Old Mali,* LL Audiocassettes • WS Writing Lab CD-ROM, Narration Tutorial; Wr. at Work Videodisc, Ch. 2

Skills Workshops

Unit	Writing Process Workshops	Applying Language Skills	Student Success Workshops	Speaking, Listening, and Viewing Workshops	Test Preparation Workshops
On the Edge	How-to Instructions, p. 71 Problem-and-Solution Essay, p. 108	Transitions to Show Time; Pronouns and Antecedents, pp. 72, 73 Sentence Fragments; Coordination and Subor-dination, pp. 109,110	Vocabulary Development: Researching Word Origins, p. 74 Real-World Reading: Evaluating Persuasive Texts, p. 111	Presenting a Literary Interpretation, p. 112	Reading Comprehension: Using Context Clues to Determine Word Meaning, p. 113
Striving for Success	User's Manual, p. 177 Timed-Test Essay, p. 210	Exact Nouns; Subject-Verb Agreement, pp. 178,179 Standard and Informal English; Placement of Modifiers, pp. 211, 212	Real-World Reading: Using Text Organizers, p. 180 Vocabulary Development: Using Reference Materials, p. 213	Job Interview, p. 214	Reading Comprehension: Recognize Facts and Details; Sequence, p. 215
Clashing Forces	Editorial, p. 257 Position Paper, p. 294	Active/Passive Voice; Load-ed Words, pp. 258, 259 Unity and Coherence; Appositives, pp. 295, 296	Vocabulary Development: Analogies, p. 260 Real-World Reading: Establishing a Purpose for Reading, p. 297	Expressing Disagreement, p. 298	Reading Comprehension: Stated and Implied Main Ideas, p. 299
Turning Points	Description, p. 333 Reflective Essay, p. 372	Figurative Language; Pre-cise Nouns, pp. 334, 335 Misplaced and Dangling Modifiers; Vivid Adjectives and Adverbs, pp. 373, 374	Real-World Reading: Read-ing a Newspaper, p. 336 Real-World Reading: Constructing Graphic Organizers, p. 375	Following Oral Directions, p. 376	Reading Comprehension: Recognizing Cause and Effect; Predicting Outcomes, p. 377
Expanding Horizons	Oral Presentation of Research, p. 421 Firsthand Biography, p. 460	Direct and Indirect Quo-tations; Varying Sentence Structure, pp. 422, 423 Quotation Marks; Vivid Verbs, pp. 461, 462	Research Skills: Evaluating Sources of Information, p. 424 Real-World Reading: Monitoring Reading Strategies, p. 463	Producing a Visual Representation, p. 464	Reading Comprehension: Interpret Graphic Aids; Evaluate and Make Judgments, p. 465
Short Stories	Short Story, p. 527 Persuasive Essay, p. 560	Verb Tense; Proper Nouns, pp. 528, 529 Types of Sentences; Parallel Structure, pp. 561, 562	Study Skills: Using Study Strategies, p. 530 Literary Response: Defending Your Response or Interpretation, p. 563	Evaluating Performance Techniques, p. 564	Critical Reading: Recognize Forms of Propaganda; Distinguish Between Fact and Nonfact, p. 565
Nonfiction	Comparison-and-Contrast Essay, p. 619 Responding to Literature in an Essay Test, p. 656	Commas; Forms of Comparison, pp. 620, 621 Eliminating Unnecessary Words; Infinitives and Infinitive Phrases, pp. 657, 658	Real-World Reading: Evaluating Information Sources, p. 622 Real-World Reading: Analyzing Text Structures, p. 659	Analyze a Media Presentation, p. 660	Reading Comprehension: Comparing and Contrasting Texts; Analyzing Literary Language, p. 661
Drama	Video Script, p. 701 Critical Evaluation, p. 804	Spoken and Written Language; Punctuating Words of Direct Address, pp. 702, 703 Quotation Marks and Underlining; Capitaliza-tion, pp. 805, 806	Research Skills: Locating Databases and Information on the Internet, p. 704 Research Skills: Conducting a Research Project, p. 807	Performing a Dramatic Scene, p. 808	Reading Comprehension: Characteristics of Text, p. 809
Poetry	Literary Analysis, p. 841 Narrative Poem, p. 872	Run-on Sentences; Adjec-tive Clauses, pp. 842, 843 Punctuating Poetry; Problems With Modifiers, pp. 873, 874	Vocabulary Development: Connotation and Denotation, p. 844 Real-World Reading: Analyzing Characteristics of Text, p. 875	Presenting a Nonverbal Interpretation, p. 876	Critical Reading: Analyzing an Author's Meaning and Style, p. 877
Epics and Legends	Research Paper, p. 917 Multimedia Presentation, p. 946	Topic Sentence and Support; Citing Sources, pp. 918, 919 Semicolons and Colons; Concise Language, pp. 947, 948	Real-World Reading: Reading Silently With Comprehension, p. 920 Real-World Reading: Reading a Map, p. 949	Telling a Story, p. 950	Writing Skills: Strategy, Organization, and Style, p. 951

Prentice Hall

LITERATURE

Timeless Voices, Timeless Themes

PLATINUM

PRENTICE HALL
Upper Saddle River, New Jersey
Needham, Massachusetts
Glenview, Illinois

ISBN 0-13-050288-X
1 2 3 4 5 6 7 8 9 10   03 02 01 00 99

PRENTICE HALL

ACKNOWLEDGMENTS

Grateful acknowledgment is made to the following for permission to reprint copyrighted material:

Rudolfo Anaya "In Commemoration: One Million Volumes" by Rudolfo Anaya, from *A Million Stars: The Millionth Acquisition for the University of New Mexico General Library*, edited by Connie Capers Thorsen (Albuquerque: The University of New Mexico General Library, 1981). Reprinted by permission of the author.

Aperture Foundation, Inc. "Mothers and Daughters" from *Mothers and Daughters* by Tillie Olsen with Julie Olsen Edwards and Estelle Jussim. Copyright © 1987 by Aperture Foundations, Inc.

Bancroft Library Excerpt from *Desert Exile: The Uprooting of a Japanese-American Family* by Yoshiko Uchida. Copyright © 1982 by Yoshiko Uchida. Reprinted courtesy of the Bancroft Library, University of California, Berkeley.

Elizabeth Barnett, Literary Executor of the Estate of Norma Millay Ellis "Conscientious Objector" by Edna St. Vincent Millay, from *Collected Poems,* HarperCollins. Copyright © 1934, 1962 by Edna St. Vincent Millay and Norma Millay Ellis. All rights reserved. Reprinted by permission of Elizabeth Barnett, literary executor.

Susan Bergholz Literary Services, and Henry Dunow Literary Agency "The Censors" by Luisa Valenzuela. Copyright 1976 by Luisa Valenzuela, renewed 1988. Translation copyright © 1982 by David Unger, first published in *Short Stories,* ed. Howe, David Godine. Translation reprinted by permission of Susan Bergholz Literary Services, New York, underlying rights by Henry Dunow Literary Agency. All rights reserved.

Nguyen Ngoc Bich "Thoughts of Hanoi" by Nguyen Thi Vinh from *A Thousand Years of Vietnamese Poetry,* edited by Nguyen Ngoc Bich. Copyright 1962, 1967, 1968, 1969, 1970, 1971, 1974 by The Asia Society and Nguyen Ngoc Bich. Reprinted by permission of Nguyen Ngoc Bich.

(Acknowledgments continue on p. 1040.)

Copper

Bronze

Silver

Gold

Platinum

The American Experience

The British Tradition

World Masterpieces

Program Authors

The program authors guided the direction and philosophy of *Prentice Hall Literature, Timeless Voices, Timeless Themes*. Working with the development team, they contributed to the pedagogical integrity of the program and to its relevance for today's teachers and students.

Reading Specialist

Linda Ellis teaches reading and language arts methods courses at Stephen F. Austin State University and for five years has sponsored the school's Student Reading Council.

Reading Specialist

Jacqueline Parten Gerla teaches reading education classes at The University of Texas at Tyler and has received numerous teaching awards.

Writing Specialist

Joyce Armstrong Carroll has taught every grade level in her forty years in the profession. She is co-director of the New Jersey Writing Project, serving as a consultant in all aspects of the language arts.

Writing Specialist

Edward E. Wilson, a former editor of English, is co-director of the New Jersey Writing Project, working as a writing/reading/literature consultant for school districts nationwide.

Language Specialist

Richard Lederer, who taught for twenty-seven years, is the author of such best-selling titles as *Anguished English* and *Pun & Games*. He writes a syndicated column, "Looking at Language," and hosts a weekly radio show, *A Way With Words*.

Assessment Specialist

Argelia Arizpe Guadarrama, secondary curriculum coordinator in the Pharr-San Juan-Alamo Independent School District, is also the program developer for English as a Second Language and at-risk students.

Assessment Specialist

Peggy Leeman, in addition to teaching full time and handling administrative duties, is an adjunct English professor at Dallas County Community College and a consultant to the College Board for Advanced Placement English.

Speaking, Listening, Viewing, & Representing Specialist

Jocelyn Chadwick-Joshua, Director of American Studies at the Dallas Institute of Humanities and Culture, is a teacher, lecturer, author, and consultant to school districts.

Contributing Writers

Carol Domblewski
Former English Instructor
Suffolk University, Regis College, Virginia Polytechnic Institute

Meish Goldish
Former English Teacher
Teaneck High School
Teaneck, New Jersey

Emily Hutchinson
Former English Teacher
Los Angeles Unified School District
Los Angeles, California

Lois Markham
Former English Teacher
Fort Lee High School
Fort Lee, New Jersey

Eileen Oshinsky
Former ESL Teacher
New York City Public Schools
Brooklyn, New York

Diane Tasca
Former Literature and Writing Instructor
University of Illinois
Urbana, Illinois

Program Advisors

The program advisors provided ongoing input throughout the development of *Prentice Hall Literature: Timeless Voices, Timeless Themes*. Their valuable insights ensure that the perspectives of the teachers throughout the country are represented within this literature series.

Diane Cappillo
Language Arts Department Chair
Barbara Goleman Senior High School
Miami, Florida

Anita Clay
English Instructor
Gateway Institute of Technology
St. Louis, Missouri

Nancy M. Fahner
Language Arts Instructor
Charlotte High School
Charlotte, Michigan

Terri Fields
Language Arts and Communication Arts Teacher, Author
Sunnyslope High School
Phoenix, Arizona

V. Pauline Hodges
Teacher and Educational Consultant
Forgan High School
Forgan, Oklahoma

Jennifer Huntress
Secondary Language Arts Coordinator
Putnam City Schools
Oklahoma City, Oklahoma

Angelique McMath Jordan
English Teacher
Dunwoody High School
Dunwoody, Georgia

Nancy L. Monroe
English and Speed Reading Teacher
Bolton High School
Alexandria, Louisiana

Rosemary A. Naab
English Chairperson
Ryan High School
Archdiocese of Philadelphia
Philadelphia, Pennsylvania

Ann Okamura
English Teacher
Laguna Creek High School
Elk Grove, California

Jonathan L. Schatz
English Teacher/Team Leader
Tappan Zee High School
Orangeburg, New York

John Scott
English Teacher
Hampton High School
Hampton, Virginia

Ken Spurlock
Assistant Principal
Boone County High School
Florence, Kentucky

Multicultural Review Board

Clara M. Chu
Assistant Professor, Department of Library and Information Science
UCLA
Los Angeles, California

Nora A. Little Light Bird
Bilingual Project Director
Lodge Grass Public Schools
Lodge Grass, Montana

K. Tsianina Lomawaima
Associate Professor, American Indian Studies
University of Arizona
Tucson, Arizona

Larry L. Martin
Chair of History, Geography, and International Studies
Coppin State College
Baltimore, Maryland

Sunita Sunder Mukhi
Program Associate, Cultural Programs Division, Asia Society
New York, New York

Julio Noboa Polanco
Professor, Department of Teaching
The University of Northern Iowa, San Antonio Center
San Antonio, Texas

Alfredo Samone
Educational Consultant
Region 4, Education Service Center
Houston, Texas

A. J. Williams-Meyers
Professor, Black Studies Department
SUNY-College at New Paltz
New Paltz, New York

Unit 1

Looking at Literary Forms

On the Edge

Looking at Universal Themes

Unit 2

Striving for Success

Unit 3

Looking at Universal Themes

Clashing Forces

Looking at Universal Themes

Unit 4

Turning Points

Unit 5

Looking at Universal Themes

Expanding Horizons

Looking at Literary Forms

Unit 6

Short Stories

Unit 7

Looking at Literary Forms

Nonfiction

Looking at Literary Forms

Unit 8

Drama

Unit 9

Looking at Literary Forms

Poetry

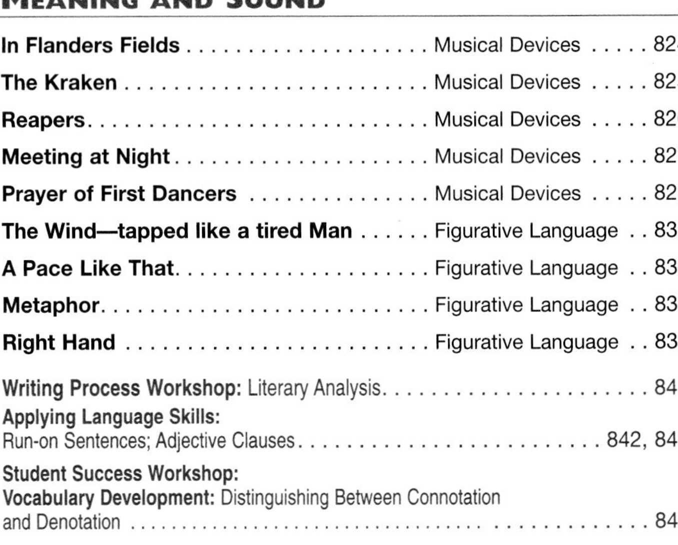

PART I: MEANING AND SOUND

Poetry

PART 2: STRUCTURE

Unit 10

Looking at Literary Forms

Epics and Legends

Additional Readings and Resources

Analyzing Real-World Texts

Literature in Translation: Paired Readings in English and Spanish

Complete Contents by Genre

Short Stories

Poetry

Complete Contents by Genre

POETRY (CONTINUED)

Complete Contents by Genre

Drama

Nonfiction

Essays and Articles

Biographies and Autobiographies

Letters

Speeches

Visual Essays/Workplace Writing

Other Media

Complete Contents by Genre

Epics, Legends, and Myths

Complete Contents by Theme

Legacies

Man, the Myth Maker

Bible as Lit.

To the Future

From the Past

Complete Contents by Theme

The Natural World

Expanding Horizons

Choices and Consequences

Turning Points

Complete Contents by Theme

Catcher

Turning Points

Farewell to Manzanar?

Of Mice + Men

Striving for Success

Lord of the Flies

Clashing Forces

Inherit the Wind

Imp. of Being Ernest - where?

Complete Contents by Theme

Black Boy / Color of Water

On the Edge

Literature from Around the World*

Literature From Around the World*

**Does not include selections from the United States and England*

Planning Instruction and Assessment

Unit Objectives

1. To read selections in different genres that develop the theme of Unit 1, "On the Edge"
2. To apply a variety of reading strategies, particularly literal comprehension strategies, appropriate for reading these selections
3. To analyze literary elements
4. To use a variety of strategies to read unfamiliar words and to build vocabulary
5. To learn elements of grammar, usage, and style
6. To use recursive writing processes to write in a variety of forms
7. To express and support responses to various types of texts
8. To prepare, organize, and present literary interpretations

Meeting the Objectives With each selection, you will find instructional material and portfolio opportunities through which students can meet these objectives. Further, you will find additional practice pages for reading strategies, literary elements, vocabulary, and grammar in the ***Selection Support*** booklet in the ***Teaching Resources*** box.

Test Preparation

The end of unit workshop, **Use Context Clues to Determine Word Meanings** (SE, p. 113), is supported by teaching tips and a sample test item in the ATE workshop with each selection grouping.

- **Use Context Clues to Determine Word Meanings** (ATE, pp. 3, 23, 45, 61, 77, 87)
- **Analogies** (ATE, p. 95)

The following additional workshops in the ATE give teaching tips and a sample test item for applying the skill taught in the Student Success Workshops:

- **Researching Word Origins** (ATE, p. 74)
- **Evaluating Persuasive Texts** (ATE, p. 111)

Guardrail/Ocean, Woody Gwyn

Humanities: Art

Guardrail/Ocean by Woody Gwyn.

Born in west Texas, Gwyn frequently combines natural vistas with highways, road signs, underpasses, and other symptoms of humanity's encroachment on the natural world. His earlier works tended to comment ironically on such human invasions of nature; however, his later paintings are less ironic and create formal and thematic connections between nature and the artifices of humanity. In *Guardrail/Ocean,* a kind of balance has been achieved between the natural and nonnatural: The curve of the rail and the road harmonize with the serenity of the ocean. The vertical posts on the rail, however, menacingly suggest teeth biting into the land, the weathered rust marks on the guardrail suggest that nature is claiming it, making it as moral as any living creature.

Have your students link the art to the theme of Unit 1, "On the Edge," by answering this question: If you were standing at this guardrail on the edge between highway and sea, what emotions would you feel, and why? *They might feel frightened by the danger of the situation.*

UNIT 1

On the Edge

Your heart pounds, your brow perspires, your stomach is in knots—like riding a rollercoaster, reading suspenseful literature can be nerve-wracking, even frightening, but always exciting. The stories, poems, and essays you are about to read in this unit will take you to the edge—and beyond. You'll hang perilously from a narrow ledge, travel to the top of the world, and be greeted by Death's terrifying messenger. By the end, you'll feel as if you've gone along on the most dangerous but delightfully daring ride of your life!

Assessing Student Progress

Tools that are available to measure the degree to which students meet the unit objectives are listed here.

Informal Assessment

The questions on the Guide for Responding sections are a first level of response to the concepts and skills presented with the selection. Students' responses are a brief, informal measure of their grasp of the material. Their responses on this level can indicate where further instruction and practice are needed. You may then follow up with the practice pages in the ***Selection Support*** booklet.

You will find literature and reading guides in the ***Alternative Assessment*** booklet, which you may give students on an individual basis for informal assessment of their performance.

Formal Assessment

In the ***Formal Assessment*** booklet, you will find selection tests and a unit test.

Selection Tests The selection tests measure comprehension and skills acquisition for each selection or group of selections.

Unit Test The unit test, which calls on students to read a passage of literature they have not previously seen, applies the unit skills on a broader level. The Critical Reading section measures Unit Objectives 1, 2, and 3. The Vocabulary and Grammar section measures Objectives 4 and 5. The Essay section measures Objectives 1 and 6. Both the Critical Reading and the Grammar sections use formats similar to those found on many standardized tests.

Alternative Assessment

Portfolios As you review individual pieces or the collected work in students' portfolios, you will find assessment sheets available in the portfolio section of the ***Alternative Assessment*** booklet.

Scoring Rubrics You will find scoring rubrics for writing modes in the ***Alternative Assessment*** booklet. You can apply these to Guided Writing Lessons and to Writing Process Workshop lessons.

Speaking, Listening, and Viewing The ***Alternative Assessment*** booklet contains assessment sheets for speaking, listening, and viewing activities.

Learning Modalities The ***Alternative Assessment*** booklet contains activities that appeal to different learning styles. You may use these as an alternative measurement of students' growth.

Prepare and Engage

LESSON OBJECTIVES

1. **To develop vocabulary and word identification skills**
   - Latin Word Roots: *-term-*
   - Using the Word Bank: Synonyms
   - Extending Word Study: Use Context Clues (ATE)
2. **To use a variety of reading strategies to comprehend a short story**
   - Connect Your Experience
   - Reading for Success: Interactive Reading Strategies
   - Tips to Guide Reading: Recall (ATE)
   - Read to Appreciate Author's Craft (ATE)
   - Idea Bank: New Titles for the Story
3. **To increase knowledge of other cultures and to connect common elements across cultures**
   - Connecting Themes Across Cultures (ATE)
   - Cultural Connection: The 50's (ATE)
4. **To express and support responses to the text**
   - Critical Thinking
   - Idea Bank: Personal Credo
   - Viewing and Representing Mini-Lesson: Annotated Drawing (ATE)
5. **To analyze literary elements**
   - Literary Focus: Suspense
6. **To read in order to research self-selected and assigned topics**
   - Idea Bank: Changing Technology
7. **To speak clearly and effectively for a specific audience and purpose**
   - Speaking, Listening, and Viewing Mini-Lesson: School Speech
   - Speaking, Listening, and Viewing Mini-Lesson: Role Play
8. **To use recursive writing processes to write a screenplay**
   - Guided Writing Lesson
9. **To increase knowledge of the rules of grammar and usage**
   - Build Grammar Skills: Possessive *Its* vs. Contraction *It's*

Test Preparation

Reading Comprehension: Using Context Clues to Determine Word Meanings (ATE, p. 3) The teaching tips and sample test item in this workshop support the instruction and practice in the unit workshop:

Reading Comprehension: Using Context Clues to Determine Word Meanings (SE, p. 113)

Guide for Reading

Jack Finney *(1911–1995)*

Jack Finney combines fantastic events and realistic characters in his fascinating, and sometimes frightening, tales.

Finney's short story "The Body Snatchers" inspired the popular horror film **The Invasion of the Body Snatchers.**

A Brilliant Beginning In 1946, Finney worked for an advertising agency and dreamed of becoming a writer. He began to realize his dream when he entered his first short story in a contest sponsored by a magazine—and won! Not long afterward, Finney took his wife and two children to Marin County, California, and started to concentrate more seriously on writing.

Impossible Links With the Past He continued to combine real and imaginary details in his fiction, often writing about time travel. In many of his tales, the hero escapes from the present into a simpler and calmer time in the past. For example, his novel *Time and Again* is about a man who participates in an experiment to travel back to the nineteenth century. Once there, he falls in love with a woman and chooses to spend his life with her in the nineteenth century.

Finney's concern with time, and escaping from it, is reflected in the titles of some of his works: "About Time" (1986) and *From Time to Time,* the long-awaited sequel to *Time and Again.*

"Contents of the Dead Man's Pocket" is not about time travel. However, it does show how a single step can take a man out of his ordinary life and into another dimension.

◆ Build Vocabulary

LATIN WORD ROOTS: *-term-*

In this story, a character describes a series of movie previews as *interminable*. The Latin root *-term-* means "end," and as you probably know, the prefix *in-* means "not" or "without." You can combine these meanings to figure out that *interminable* means "without end" or "seemingly endless."

WORD BANK

As you read "Contents of the Dead Man's Pocket," you will encounter the words on this list. Each word is defined on the page where it first appears. Preview the list before you read and look for another *-term-* word in the story: *determined.*

convoluted
grimace
deftness
imperceptibly
reveling
interminable

◆ Build Grammar Skills

POSSESSIVE *ITS* VS. CONTRACTION *IT'S*

In "Contents of the Dead Man's Pocket," you will see both *it's* and *its*—two forms of the pronoun *it* that are sometimes confused:

Contraction: It's just that I hate you to miss this movie . . .

Possessive: He . . . stared at the yellow paper . . . hoping he could follow its course to the street . . .

It's is a **contraction,** an abbreviation for *it is*. As in other contractions, the apostrophe replaces a missing letter; here, the letter replaced is *i*.

Its is the **possessive** form of the pronoun *it,* showing that something belongs to the noun for which the pronoun stands. That noun is *paper* in the example from the story.

Prentice Hall Literature Program Resources

REINFORCE / RETEACH / EXTEND

Selection Support Pages
Build Vocabulary: Word Roots: *-term-*, p. 1
Build Grammar Skills: Possessive *Its* vs. Contraction *It's*, p. 2
Reading for Success: Literal Comprehension Strategies, pp. 3–4
Literary Focus: Suspense, p. 5

Strategies for Diverse Student Needs, p. 5

Formal Assessment Selection Test, pp. 1–3; Assessment Resources Software

Alternative Assessment, p. 5

Resource Pro CD-ROM

Listening to Literature Audiocassettes

Contents of the Dead Man's Pocket

MODEL SELECTION

◆ Literature and Your Life

Connect Your Experience

Living means taking chances—not foolish ones, as your teachers and parents correctly warn against. However, even crossing the street means taking a small chance. You constantly take all kinds of everyday risks, such as trying out for a team, approaching someone you like, and making an effort to succeed in school. This story is about a man who takes a more dramatic and foolish risk, based on a moment's impulse.

Journal Writing In your journal, briefly list some everyday risks you have taken. Remember that they shouldn't involve life-threatening situations. Anything you do that can fail involves a risk.

Thematic Focus: On the Edge

The central character in this story risks everything for what he has written on a sheet of paper. A single step takes him to the edge of death and forces him to ask: What is really important in life?

◆ Background for Understanding

Culture

Not only will this story take you out on the edge; it will also take you back in time to the 1950's. In the mid-twentieth century, there were no photocopiers or computers, and most people still worked on typewriters or laboriously wrote things out in longhand. As a result, a single document was often unique. Losing it meant losing it forever.

Documents may have been one-of-a-kind in the 1950's, but time seemed to stretch out. For example, movies were often double features, combining two major films with previews and cartoons and lasting four or five hours.

These facts about the 1950's may seem unrelated, but they both add to the tension of the story.

◆ Literary Focus

Suspense

Another word for the tension and nervous uncertainty that some stories can create is **suspense.** This feeling keeps you wondering about the outcome of events, guessing, and turning pages. Often the uncertainty comes from a dangerous choice that you must live through with a character.

In this story, for example, a man wonders whether to pursue a piece of paper onto a narrow building ledge high above the street. Notice how Finney forces you to ponder this choice with the character, make it, and then experience the consequences.

Test Preparation Workshop

Reading Comprehension: Using Context Clues to Determine Word Meanings Standardized tests often require that students be able to use sentence context clues to determine the best meaning of selected words from a passage of reading. Use the following sample question.

"As the door opening narrowed, the current of warm air from the hallway, channeled through this smaller opening now, suddenly rushed past him with accelerated force."

In this sentence, <u>channeled</u> means—

A tumbled
B widened
C called
D sent

Have students read the sentence containing the underlined word and then carefully examine each answer choice. *A* can be eliminated because the sentence is about air; *B* can be eliminated because the opening is narrowed, not widened; and *C* does not relate to air. Students should be able to see that by systematically eliminating the words that do not fit the context of the sentence, they can select *D* as the best answer.

Interest Grabber Write the following passages from the story on the chalkboard:

"For an instant he hung suspended between balance and falling, his fingertips pressed onto the quarter-inch wood strips."

"Quite realistically, he knew that he would fall; no one could stay out here on this ledge for four hours."

"All they'd find in his pockets would be the yellow sheet."

Have students try to piece together what the story is about based on these quotations. Then have them predict how the story might turn out.

Connecting Themes Across Cultures

As they read this story set in the 50's, have students identify similarities and differences that the character might face if the setting of the story were changed to modern day.

Tips to Guide Reading

Recall When students reach the suspenseful point in the story where Tom is perched on the ledge of the building, have them recall as many details as they can about how and why he got there. After recalling those details, have students reread to help them locate further details.

Customize for *Less Proficient Readers*
By summarizing at the end of each page, students can review important details of the plot and fit them into their picture of what is happening.

Customize for *Pre-AP Students*
Have students create a story map or chart that identifies the story's exposition, rising action, climax, and resolution. Have them analyze how Finney structures his plot to build suspense.

Customize for *English Language Learners*
Breaking down confusing sentences will help students literally comprehend the story. Remind students that the *subject* of a sentence is the noun that tells what or whom the sentence is about, and the *predicate* of a sentence always includes a verb that tells what the subject does or is.

Reading for Success

The Reading for Success page in each unit presents a set of problem-solving procedures to help readers understand authors' words and ideas on multiple levels. Good readers develop a bank of strategies from which they can draw as needed.

Unit 1 introduces strategies for literal comprehension. It is important for students to understand a work on its literal level before they apply higher-level critical thinking strategies. These strategies for literal comprehension give readers an approach for attacking text on a surface level—understanding, vocabulary, sentence structure, and sometimes complex language.

These strategies for literal comprehension are modeled with "Contents of the Dead Man's Pocket." An example of the thinking process involved in applying one of these strategies is shown in each green box.

How to Use the Reading for Success Pages

- Introduce the literal comprehension strategies, presenting each as a problem-solving procedure. Be sure students understand what each strategy involves and under what circumstances to apply it.
- Before students read the story, have them preview it, looking at the annotations in the green boxes that model the strategies.
- To reinforce these strategies after students have read "Contents . . . ," have students do the Reading for Success page in ***Selection Support*** (pp. 9–10). These pages gives students an opportunity to read a selection and practice strategies for literal comprehension by writing their own annotations.

Reading for Success

Literal Comprehension Strategies

With any piece of literature—from fiction to poetry—your first goal in reading is to understand what the writer is saying. Some writers have a clear, direct style that is easy to understand, but others may write in a way that is less clear. However, there are strategies you can apply to help you understand even complex writing.

Reread or read ahead.

- Reread a sentence or a paragraph to find the connections among the words.
- Read ahead—a word or detail you don't understand may become clear further on.

Use context clues.

Context refers to the words, phrases, and sentences that surround a word. Look for clues in the context to help you figure out the meaning of an unknown word. For example, you might be unfamiliar with the word *muffled* in the following sentence from "Contents of the Dead Man's Pocket."

> Her voice was *muffled*, and he knew her head and shoulders were in the bedroom closet.

The context clue that "her head and shoulders were in the bedroom closet" suggests the reason that her voice was muffled, that is, "quieted" or "softened and blurred."

Analyze or break down confusing sentences.

- Read sentences in logical sections, not word by word.
- Determine the subject of each sentence (what the sentence is about). Then read to see what the rest of the sentence says about the subject.

Restate for understanding.

- Paraphrase, or restate a sentence or a paragraph in your own words.
- Summarize at appropriate points; review and state the main ideas or points of what has happened. Notice story details that seem to be important. Try to fit them into your picture of what is happening.

As you read the following story by Jack Finney, look at the notes in the boxes. These notes demonstrate how to apply these strategies to a work of literature.

Reading Strategies: Support and Reinforcement

Appropriate Reading Strategies Students are given a reading strategy to apply when reading each selection. In those selections where surface language may be challenging, students are given one of these literal comprehension strategies.

Reading Prompts To encourage application of the given reading strategy, there are occasional prompts, within green boxes, at appropriate and significant points.

In addition, there are red boxes prompting application of the Literary Focus concept and maroon boxes prompting students to connect with their lives.

Using the Boxed Annotations and Prompts

The material in the green, red, and maroon boxes along the sides of selections is intended to help students apply the literary element and the reading strategy and to make a connection with their lives.

You may use the boxed material in several ways:

- Have students pause when they come to a box and respond to its prompt before they continue reading.
- Urge students to read through the selection ignoring the boxes. After they have read the selection completely, they may go back and review the selection, responding to the prompts.

Contents of the Dead Man's Pocket

Jack Finney

MODEL

At the little living-room desk Tom Benecke rolled two sheets of flimsy[1] and a heavier top sheet, carbon paper sandwiched between them, into his portable. Interoffice Memo, the top sheet was headed, and he typed tomorrow's date just below this; then he glanced at a creased yellow sheet, covered with his own handwriting, beside the typewriter. "Hot in here," he muttered to himself. Then, from the short hallway at his back, he heard the muffled clang of wire coat hangers in the bedroom closet, and at this reminder of what his wife was doing he thought: Hot, no—guilty conscience.

Read ahead and use context to determine that several words in this paragraph—*flimsy, carbon paper,* and *portable*—are connected to typing.

He got up, shoving his hands into the back pockets of his gray wash slacks, stepped to the living-room window beside the desk and stood breathing on the glass, watching the expanding circle of mist, staring down through the autumn night at Lexington Avenue, eleven stories below. He was a tall, lean, dark-haired young man in a pullover sweater, who looked as though he had played not football, probably, but basketball in college. Now he placed the heels of his hands against the top edge of the lower window frame and shoved upward. But as usual the window didn't budge, and he had to lower his hands and then shoot them hard upward to jolt the window open a few inches. He dusted his hands, muttering.

But still he didn't begin his work. He crossed the room to the hallway entrance and, leaning against the doorjamb, hands shoved into his back pockets again, he called, "Clare?" When his wife answered, he said, "Sure you don't mind going alone?"

▲ Critical Viewing How does this photograph suggest suspense and danger? **[Interpret]**

1. **flimsy** (flim′ zē) *n.*: Thin typing paper for making carbon copies.

Develop Understanding

One-Minute Insight This suspenseful story captures what happens when a character, Tom Benecke, stays home to work on a business proposal while his wife goes to the movies alone. Clearly, Tom's ambition to get ahead is his top priority. However, when events lead Tom to a harrowing experience on the ledge of his apartment building, he is forced to reexamine his life and reshape his outlook. The suspenseful events in this story convey the message that sometimes people have to be pushed into a crisis in order to sort out their true priorities.

❶ **Clarification** Point out that the word *portable* refers to a portable typewriter, one that is small and lightweight enough to be carried. You might add that, although lighter in weight than standard typewriters, portable typewriters are generally heavier than portable computers.

◆ Literary Focus

❷ **Suspense** Ask students why the writer might point out this detail about the window so early in the story. *Students may guess that the stuck window will be a crucial element in building the story's suspense. Skilled readers may suggest that it is an example of foreshadowing.*

▶Critical Viewing◀

❸ **Interpret** *Students may suggest that the dark sky, feeling of isolation, and towering heights combine to create a feeling of suspense and danger.*

Customize for *Gifted/Talented Students*

Suggest that students use the plot of Finney's story to write a screenplay. Encourage them to study Finney's visual effects created with words that would be essential aspects of a screenplay. Students might benefit from locating and viewing other film versions of Finney's writing.

Block Scheduling Strategies

Consider these suggestions to take advantage of extended class time:

- Suggest that students preview the story's annotations in the green boxes. Then have them read the story. If you wish to give them further practice with literal comprehension reading strategies, have them do the follow-up in ***Selection Support*** (pp. 3–4).
- Pair students to answer the Critical Thinking questions on p. 19. Then have them share their responses with the entire class.
- Have students complete the journal activity in Literature and Your Life on p. 3. After students read the story, have them compare their risks with those of Tom Benecke.
- Have partners prepare and perform the Role Play, p. 20.
- Guide students to complete the Guided Writing Lesson on p. 20. First, students can create and complete a graphic organizer such as a flowchart or plot web to help them organize the events.

◆ Build Grammar Skills

❶ Possessive *Its* vs. Contraction *It's* Have students decide whether "it's" in Clare's dialogue is a possessive or contraction, and why. *Students should recognize that "it's" is a contraction standing for it is and that the apostrophe represents the missing letter i. Also, "it's" could not be a possessive pronoun, because no noun follows it.*

◆ Literary Focus

❷ Suspense Point out that this is where the author starts to build suspense. Ask students what details, combined with what they already know, start to build suspense. *We know that the paper is important to Tom. He needs it for the work he was planning to do. The suspense starts when the reader wonders "What will he do without the paper?" or "Will he try to get the paper?"*

Customize for Logical/Mathematical Learners

Ask these students to explain how the force of the warm and cold air currents would draw the paper from the room to the outside. Students may wish to use diagrams, charts, or other graphic organizers to demonstrate this effect.

Customize for Less Proficient Readers

Draw students' attention to the extra space that appears between two paragraphs toward the middle of the first column. Explain that in this way, authors often break up their stories or indicate shifts or pauses in the action. Encourage students to use these breaks to pause and check their understanding by summarizing what has happened in the preceding section.

"No." Her voice was muffled, and he knew her head and shoulders were in the bedroom closet. Then the tap of her high heels sounded on the wood floor and she appeared at the end of the little hallway, wearing a slip, both hands raised to one ear, clipping on an earring. She smiled at him—a slender, very pretty girl with light brown, almost blonde, hair—her prettiness emphasized by the pleasant nature that showed in her face. "It's just
❶ that I hate you to miss this movie; you want to see it too."

"Yeah, I know." He ran his fingers through his hair. "Got to get this done though."

She nodded, accepting this. Then, glancing at the desk across the living room, she said, "You work too much, though, Tom—and too hard."

He smiled. "You won't mind though, will you, when the money comes rolling in and I'm known as the Boy Wizard of Wholesale Groceries?"

"I guess not." She smiled and turned back toward the bedroom.

Tom sat at his desk again; then a few moments later Clare appeared, dressed and ready to leave. "Just after seven," she said. "I can make the beginning of the first feature."

He walked to the front-door closet to help her on with her coat. He kissed her then and, for an instant, holding her close, smelling the perfume she had used, he was tempted to go with her; it was not actually true that he had to work tonight, though he very much wanted to. This was his own project, unannounced as yet in his office, and it could be postponed. But then they won't see it till Monday, he thought once again, and if I give it to the boss tomorrow he might read it over the weekend . . . "Have a good time," he said aloud. He opened the door for her, feeling the air from the building hallway, smelling faintly of floor wax, stream gently past his face.

He watched her walk down the hall, flicked a hand in response as she waved, and then he started to close the door, but it resisted for a moment. As the door opening narrowed, the current of warm air from the hallway, channeled through this smaller opening now, suddenly rushed past him with accelerated force. Behind him he heard the slap of the window curtains against the wall and the sound of paper fluttering from his desk, and he had to push to close the door.

> **Analyze** this sentence to identify the chronological order of events: First Tom waves to his wife. Then he starts to close the door. The door resists.

Turning, he saw a sheet of white paper drifting to the floor in a series of arcs, and another sheet, yellow, moving toward the window, caught in the dying current flowing through the narrow opening. As he watched, the paper struck the bottom edge of the window and hung there for an instant, plastered against the glass and wood. Then as the moving air stilled completely the curtains swinging back from the wall to hang free again, he saw the yellow sheet drop to the window ledge and slide over out of sight.

He ran across the room, grasped the bottom edge of the window and tugged, staring through the glass. He saw the yellow sheet, dimly now in the darkness outside, lying on the ornamental ledge a yard below the window. Even as he watched, it was ❷ moving, scraping slowly along the ledge, pushed by the breeze that pressed steadily against the building wall. He heaved on the window with all his strength and it shot open with a bang, the window weight rattling in the casing. But the paper was past

Cultural Connection

The 50's This story takes place during the era of the 50's. Tom uses a typewriter and carbon paper to prepare a statistical report for his employer, instead of a powerful computer and laser printer. The 50's was an era of rapid technological change and economic growth. The United States had just participated in a war, so this era that included bomb shelters and fears of nuclear war. Black-and-white TV screens carried programs such as *The Mickey Mouse Club, I Love Lucy, Dragnet, Superman,* and *The Twilight Zone.* Variety shows, quiz shows, comedies, and westerns dominated viewers' choices. Students may need to be reminded that cable and satellite dish reception did not make numerous stations available. Rabbit-ear television antennas captured snowy reception of two or three stations—nonetheless, viewers were thrilled by the choices available to them.

Women wore pony tails, flared skirts with petticoats, and seamed nylons. Men's hair was slicked down. Teenagers partied at sock hops in the school gymnasium. Children played with toys made of the new miracle material—plastic. Lego building blocks, hula hoops, Silly Putty, and coonskin caps became popular during the 50's. Have students discuss the following:

- Realizing the technological advances of our computer-driven, electronic era, would you enjoy living in the 50's? Why or why not?
- How would Tom change his research and reporting styles if the story had a current setting?

his reach and, leaning out into the night, he watched it scud steadily along the ledge to the south, half plastered against the building wall. Above the muffled sound of the street traffic far below, he could hear the dry scrape of its movement, like a leaf on the pavement.

The living room of the next apartment to the south projected a yard or more farther out toward the street than this one; because of this the Beneckes paid seven and a half dollars less rent than their neighbors. And now the yellow sheet, sliding along the stone ledge, nearly invisible in the night, was stopped by the projecting blank wall of the next apartment. It lay motionless, then, in the corner formed by the two walls—a good five yards away, pressed firmly against the ornate corner ornament of the ledge, by the breeze that moved past Tom Benecke's face

He knelt at the window and stared at the yellow paper for a full minute or more, waiting for it to move, to slide off the ledge and fall, hoping he could follow its course to the street, and then hurry down in the elevator and retrieve it. But it didn't move, and then he saw that the paper was caught firmly between a projection of the convoluted corner ornament and the ledge. He thought about the poker from the fireplace, then the broom, then the mop—discarding each thought as it occurred to him. There was nothing in the apartment long enough to reach that paper.

It was hard for him to understand that he actually had to abandon it—it was ridiculous—and he began to curse. Of all the papers on his desk, why did it have to be this one in particular! On four long Saturday afternoons he had stood in supermarkets counting the people who passed certain displays, and the results were scribbled on that yellow sheet. From stacks of trade publications, gone over page by page in snatched half hours at work and during evenings at home, he had copied facts, quotations, and figures onto that sheet. **3** And he had carried it with him to the Public Library on Fifth Avenue, where he'd spent a dozen lunch hours and early evenings adding more. All were needed to support and lend authority to his idea for a new grocery-store display method; without them his idea was a mere opinion. And there they all lay, in his own improvised shorthand—countless hours of work—out there on the ledge. **4**

Summarize the four sentences beginning with "On four long Saturday afternoons." The results of hours of work are written on the paper. Without the paper, Tom cannot present his idea to his boss.

For many seconds he believed he was going to abandon the yellow sheet, that there was nothing else to do. The work could be duplicated. But it would take two months, and the time to present this idea was now, for use in the spring displays. He struck his fist on the window ledge. Then he shrugged. Even though his plan were adopted, he told himself, it wouldn't bring him a raise in pay—not immediately, anyway, or as a direct result. It **5** won't bring me a promotion either, he argued—not of itself.

But just the same, and he couldn't escape the thought, this and other independent projects, some already done and others planned for the future, would gradually mark him out from the score of other young men in

◆ Build Vocabulary

convoluted (kän′ və lo͞ot′ id) *adj.*: Intricate; twisted

◆ Critical Thinking

3 Infer Ask students: How has Tom been spending his free time? What does this imply about his attitude toward life? *Tom has been compiling statistics and doing research during his free time. His attitude toward life seems to be that one should apply oneself relentlessly in order to get ahead.*

Comprehension Check ☑

4 What is on this yellow paper? How is it written? *The yellow paper contains Tom's plan, he is developing, with all the supporting information that he has been researching for months.*

◆ Literary Focus

5 Suspense Ask students how Tom's indecision builds suspense. *As Tom reviews all his work, what it means to him, and what the loss of it would mean, the reader wonders what action he will take.*

Customize for *Gifted/Talented Students*

Encourage students to analyze Tom's dismay over the loss of the important paper. Have students predict what they think Tom will do and suggest alternative and perhaps safer problem-solving strategies he might choose.

Customize for *Logical/Mathematical Learners*

Interested students may wish to duplicate Tom's research at a local store. Suggest that they select a display and count the number and type of shoppers who stop to look. Groups of students may wish to work together to tabulate their results and compile them in a shopping habits survey. Encourage a discussion of how statistical data can be manipulated and studied to obtain differing results.

Beyond the Classroom

Career Connection

Retailing and Marketing In this story, Tom Benecke compiles facts and figures to create a more efficient grocery-store display. Retailers maximize sales through a variety of methods. For example, grocery retailers place "impulse purchase" items such as candy bars and magazines in checkout aisles where customers wait in line. Some companies have people hand out free samples of their products in grocery stores. Let students know that people who specialize in marketing plan and implement these selling strategies. Companies that sell everything from books to cars use marketing strategies, though smaller companies may hire consulting marketing firms rather than maintaining staff in their own marketing departments.

Students can compare special displays at retailers to discover what makes sales presentations effective. If they think a career in marketing would interest them, have them research the preparation required for an entry-level position.

Community Connection

Architecture Point out the architectural details that prove important to the plot—ornate corner ornaments and the narrow ledge. The height of the apartment buildings in New York City also contributes to the story's suspense. Ask students to note architectural details that distinguish the buildings in their area, such as tile roofs or weathered siding. Students can speculate how events in this story might differ if the story were set in their community.

◆ Critical Thinking

❶ **Draw Conclusions** Ask students: Why is getting the paper back so important to Tom? *The paper is crucial because it can help him distinguish himself from all the other young men in the company.*

◆ Reading for Success

❷ **Use Context Clues** Have students use context clues to infer the meaning of *infinite* in this sentence. *The context clues are the situation itself ("he brought out his other leg") and the word* care. *Tom is doing something very dangerous, so he would be taking extremely great care. Students might be able to infer that* infinite *means "boundless" or "limitless," but* extremely great *or* very great *will unlock the meaning of the sentence.*

Customize for *Visual/Spatial Learners*

Have visual/spatial learners set up a demonstration or explanation for the class of the difficulty of walking on a ledge that's only twelve inches wide.

Customize for *Musical/Rhythmic Learners*

Suggest that interested students listen to the background music that is used for suspenseful television programs or movies. Ask them to analyze how and why the music contributes to the effectiveness of the filming and acting. Have them work in small groups to locate music that they believe might enhance a reading or screenplay of the short story and play it for the class. They may wish to have a volunteer read a selected portion as they play the music.

his company. They were the way to change from a name on the payroll to a name in the minds of the company
❶ officials. They were the beginning of the long, long climb to where he was determined to be, at the very top. And he knew he was going out there in the darkness, after the yellow sheet fifteen feet beyond his reach.

By a kind of instinct, he instantly began making his intention acceptable to himself by laughing at it. The mental picture of himself sidling along the ledge outside was absurd—it was actually comical—and he smiled. He imagined himself describing it; it would make a good story at the office and, it occurred to him, would add a special interest and importance to his memorandum, which would do it no harm at all.

> **The context clue** that Tom would be out on the ledge indicates that *sidling* probably describes the way he would move—sideways and very slowly.

To simply go out and get his paper was an easy task—he could be back here with it in less than two minutes—and he knew he wasn't deceiving himself. The ledge, he saw, measuring it with his eye, was about as wide as the length of his shoe, and perfectly flat. And every fifth row of brick in the face of the building, he remembered—leaning out, he verified this—was indented half an inch, enough for the tips of his fingers, enough to maintain balance easily. It occurred to him that if this ledge and wall were only a yard aboveground—as he knelt at the window staring out, this thought was the final confirmation of his intention—he could move along the ledge indefinitely.

> **Break down** the sentence beginning with "It occurred to him." Read it without the words set off by dashes. Then reread it to include the interrupting thought.

On a sudden impulse, he got to his feet, walked to the front closet and took out an old tweed jacket; it would be cold outside. He put it on and buttoned it as he crossed the room rapidly toward the open window. In the back of his mind he knew he'd better hurry and get this over with before he thought too much, and at the window he didn't allow himself to hesitate.

He swung a leg over the sill, then felt for and found the ledge a yard below the window with his foot. Gripping the bottom of the window frame very tightly and carefully, he slowly ducked his head under it, feeling on his face the sudden change from the warm air of the room to the chill outside. With infinite care he brought out
his other leg, his mind concentrating ❷
on what he was doing. Then he slowly stood erect. Most of the putty, dried out and brittle, had dropped off the bottom edging of the window frame, he found, and the flat wooden edging provided a good gripping surface, a half inch or more deep, for the tips of his fingers.

Now, balanced easily and firmly, he stood on the ledge outside in the slight, chill breeze, eleven stories above the street, staring into his own lighted apartment, odd and different-seeming now.

First his right hand, then his left, he carefully shifted his fingertip grip from the puttyless window edging to an indented row of bricks directly to his right. It was hard to take the first shuffling sideways step then—to make himself move—and the fear stirred in his stomach, but he did it, again by not allowing himself time to think. And now—with his chest, stomach, and the left side of his face pressed against the rough cold brick—his lighted apartment was suddenly

Beyond the Classroom

Career Connection

Physical Education At the beginning of the story, the author notes that Tom "looked as though he had played not football, probably, but basketball in college" (see p. 5). From this, we can infer that Tom is athletic with a tall, thin build. His college experience as a basketball player would likely have helped him develop the equilibrium he needed to maintain his balance on the narrow ledge. In addition, he would have the training to remain somewhat calm in tense situations.

Tom has not made his career in sports, but many young men and women who are interested in sports and are gifted athletes pursue careers in physical education. Have students interested in careers in sports consider this option and the possible jobs that are available, including teaching physically challenged classes. Students can interview a physical education teacher at your school to find out how she or he prepared for this career. Encourage students to report to the class what they have learned.

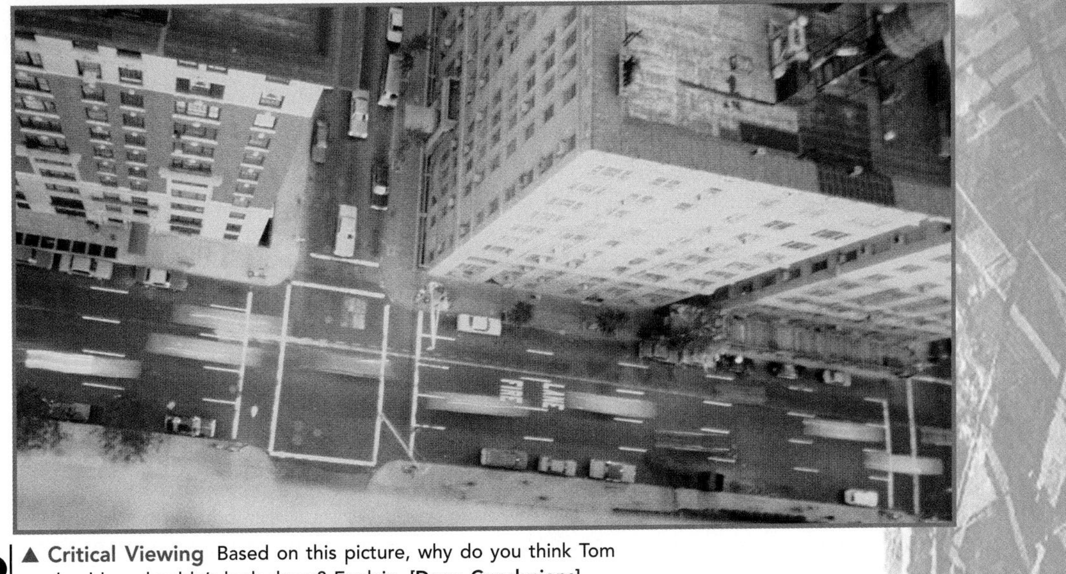

3 ▲ **Critical Viewing** Based on this picture, why do you think Tom should or shouldn't look down? Explain. **[Draw Conclusions]**

gone, and it was much darker out here than he had thought.

Without pause he continued—right foot, left foot, right foot, left—his shoe soles shuffling and scraping along the rough stone, never lifting from it, fingers sliding along the exposed edging of brick. He moved on the balls of his feet, heels lifted slightly; the ledge was not quite as wide as he'd expected. But leaning slightly inward toward the face of the building and pressed against it, he could feel his balance firm and secure, and moving along the ledge was quite as easy as he had thought it would be. He could hear the buttons of his jacket scraping steadily along the rough bricks and feel them catch momentarily, tugging a little, at each mortared crack. He simply did not permit himself to look down, though the compulsion to do so never left him; nor did he allow himself actually to think. Mechanically—right foot, left foot, over and again—he shuffled along crabwise, watching the projecting wall ahead loom steadily closer . . .

Context clues can help you figure out the meaning of *compulsion*. Because Tom will not permit himself to look down, you can figure out that "compulsion to do so" means he wants to. His fear and the danger are clues that the word *compulsion* conveys some intensity.

Then he reached it, and, at the corner—he'd decided how he was going to pick up the paper—he lifted his right foot and placed it carefully on the ledge that ran along the projecting wall at a right angle to the ledge on which his other foot rested. And now, facing the building, he stood in the corner formed by the two walls, one foot on the ledging of each, a hand on the shoulder-high indentation of each wall. His forehead was pressed directly into the corner against the cold bricks, and now he carefully lowered first one hand, then the other, perhaps a foot farther down, to the next indentation in the rows of bricks.

Very slowly, sliding his forehead down the trough of the brick corner and bending his knees, he lowered his body toward the paper lying between

▶Critical Viewing◀

3 Draw Conclusions *Students may suggest that looking down makes Tom feel scared and panicky. Responses should focus on the height of the buildings and the dizzying view of the street below.*

Customize for
Pre-AP Students

Have more advanced readers explain why the author includes scenes like this, showing Tom as confident and ignoring the danger of the situation. *By minimizing the suspense now, the author increases his opportunity to build the suspense to greater peaks later in the story.*

Customize for
Visual/Spatial Learners

Encourage these students to use the photograph on this page to help them visualize what Tom is experiencing. Have them consider what the photograph adds to the details that Finney provides in his story. How does viewing the photograph compare with envisioning the situation while reading? *Students may respond that viewing the photograph evokes a more powerful response in them because it calls to mind experiences in which they looked down from a great height.*

Humanities: Photography

Capturing the Moment Have students consider how photographs like this one can capture a scene or a moment in time in a way that motion video cannot. While video captures action over a period of time, a photograph preserves a single moment and draws viewers into the scene. This scene sparks individual connections and associations. Encourage students to study the details of this photograph and to use their personal observations and reactions to help them answer the following questions:

1. How might viewing video footage of this scene differ from viewing the photograph? *Encourage students to explain their answers.*
2. What might you notice in the video that you don't notice in the photograph? *Students may note that they would get a stronger sense of motion from viewing the video.*
3. What do you notice in the photograph that you would probably miss in the video? *Students may respond that they would not notice specific cars in the video.*

◆ Literature and Your Life

Draw students' attention to the risk Tom is taking. Ask if they think the risk is worth the reward if he succeeds. What about if he fails? Parallel Tom's experience here to some of the less dangerous risks that students have taken.

◆ Reading for Success

1 Restate for Understanding At this point, have students summarize the story from the beginning to the point at which Tom retrieves the paper. Encourage them to include all important details to form a picture of what has happened. Ask students to predict what will happen, now that Tom appears to have achieved his goal.

◆ Critical Thinking

2 Analyze Have students analyze how Tom's emotions in this scene may affect his ability to get off the ledge safely. *Students may say that Tom's panic might make him fall. When he was feeling more confident, he didn't have these problems.*

Customize for *Less Proficient Readers*

Be sure students understand that the author is speaking figuratively, not literally, at the bottom of the first column, when he describes the "instantaneous explosion of absolute terror" that Tom experiences. Only Tom can hear the "explosion" that roars through his head. There is no actual explosion.

his outstretched feet. Again he lowered his fingerholds another foot and bent his knees still more, thigh muscles taut, his forehead sliding and bumping down the brick V. Half squatting now, he dropped his left hand to the next indentation and then slowly reached with his right hand toward the paper between his feet.

He couldn't quite touch it, and his knees now were pressed against the wall; he could bend them no farther. But by ducking his head another inch lower, the top of his head now pressed against the bricks, he lowered his
1 right shoulder and his fingers had the paper by a corner, pulling it loose. At the same instant he saw, between his legs and far below, Lexington Avenue stretched out for miles ahead.

Read ahead. In the next paragraph, Tom's mental picture of himself makes clear how dangerous his physical position is.

He saw, in that instant, the Loew's theater sign, blocks ahead past Fiftieth Street; the miles of traffic signals, all green now; the lights of cars and street lamps; countless neon signs; and the moving black dots of people. And a violent instantaneous explosion of absolute terror roared through him. For a motionless instant he saw himself externally—bent practically double, balanced on this narrow ledge, nearly half his body projecting out above the street far below—and he began to tremble violently, panic flaring through his mind and muscles, and he felt the blood rush from the surface of his skin.

In the fractional moment before horror paralyzed him, as he stared between his legs at that terrible length of street far beneath him, a fragment of his mind raised his body in a spasmodic jerk to an upright position again, but so violently that his head scraped hard against the wall, bouncing off it, and his body swayed outward to the knife edge of balance, and he very nearly plunged backward and fell. Then he was leaning far into the corner again, squeezing and pushing into it, not only his face but his chest and stomach, his back arching; and his fingertips clung with all the pressure of his pulling arms to the shoulder-high half-inch indentation in the bricks.

He was more than trembling now; his whole body was racked with a violent shuddering beyond control, his eyes squeezed so tightly shut it was painful, though he was past awareness of that. His teeth were exposed in a frozen grimace, the strength draining like water from his knees and calves. It was extremely likely, he knew, that he would faint, to slump down along 2
the wall, his face scraping, and then drop backward, a limp weight, out into nothing. And to save his life he concentrated on holding onto consciousness, drawing deliberate deep breaths of cold air into his lungs, fighting to keep his senses aware.

Then he knew that he would not faint, but he could neither stop shaking nor open his eyes. He stood where he was, breathing deeply, trying to hold back the terror of the glimpse he had had of what lay below him; and he knew he had made a mistake in not making himself stare down at the street, getting used to it and accepting it, when he had first stepped out onto the ledge.

It was impossible to walk back. He simply could not do it. He couldn't bring himself to make the slightest movement. The strength

Paraphrase this paragraph about what has happened to Tom: Tom didn't prepare himself for how high up he would be, so when he accidentally looked down at the street, he became so frightened that he couldn't move. 3

Speaking, Listening, and Viewing Mini-Lesson

School Speech: Critical Listening

This mini-lesson extends the Speaking, Listening, and Viewing activity in the Idea Bank on p. 20.

Introduce Point out that when they are listening to persuasive speeches, students should pay close attention in order to carefully evaluate the ideas and arguments the speaker presents. A combination of their own personal knowledge of the topic and how well the speaker presents and supports his or her points will provide a critical basis.

Develop Before students listen to the school speech, give them these guidelines to follow:

1. Identify the speaker's main idea. Focus on the introduction and conclusion of the speech, where the speaker's main idea is often stated or restated.
2. Look for clear organization, logical reasoning, and evidence that support the speaker's main points.
3. Keep an open mind.
4. Summarize the speaker's main points.

Apply Have students apply these criteria as they listen critically to the speeches that their classmates make.

Assess Students should be able to answer the following:

1. What was the speaker's main idea, and how well did he or she support it?
2. How was the speech organized, and how did that organization affect my understanding of the speech?
3. What important new idea or attitude did I take away from the speech?

was gone from his legs; his shivering hands—numb, cold and desperately rigid—had lost all deftness; his easy
3 ability to move and balance was gone. Within a step or two, if he tried to move, he knew that he would stumble clumsily and fall.

Seconds passed, with the chill faint wind pressing the side of his face, and he could hear the toned-down volume of the street traffic far beneath him. Again and again it slowed and then stopped, almost to silence; then presently, even this high, he would hear the click of the traffic signals and the subdued roar of the cars starting up again. During a lull in the street sounds, he called out. Then he was shouting "*Help!*" so loudly it rasped his throat. But he felt the steady pressure of the wind, moving between his face and the blank wall, snatch up his cries as he uttered them, and he knew they must sound directionless and distant. And he remembered how habitually, here in New York, he himself heard and ignored shouts in the night. If anyone heard him, there was no sign of it, and presently Tom Benecke knew he had to try moving; there was nothing else he could do.

Eyes squeezed shut, he watched scenes in his mind like scraps of motion-picture film—he could not stop them. He saw himself stumbling suddenly sideways as he crept along the ledge and saw his upper body arc outward, arms flailing. He saw a dangling shoestring caught between the ledge and the sole of his other shoe, saw a foot start to move, to be stopped with a jerk, and felt his balance leaving him. He saw himself falling with a terrible speed as his body revolved in the air, knees clutched tight to his chest, eyes squeezed shut, moaning softly.

Out of utter necessity, knowing that any of these thoughts might be reality in the very next seconds, he was slowly able to shut his mind against every thought but what he now began to do. With fear-soaked slowness, he slid his left foot an inch or two toward his own impossibly distant window. Then he slid the fingers of his shivering left hand a corresponding distance. For a moment he could not bring himself to lift his right foot from one ledge to the other; then he did it, and became aware of the harsh exhalation of air from his throat and realized that he was panting. As his right hand, then, began to slide along the brick edging, he was astonished to feel the yellow paper pressed to the bricks underneath his stiff fingers, and he uttered a terrible, abrupt bark that might have been a laugh or a moan. He opened his mouth and took the paper in his teeth, pulling it out from under his fingers.

By a kind of trick—by concentrating his entire mind on first his left foot, then his left hand, then the other foot, then the other hand—he was able to move, almost imperceptibly, trembling steadily, very nearly without thought. But he could feel the terrible strength of the pent-up horror on just the other side of the flimsy barrier he had erected in his mind; and he knew that if it broke through he would lose this thin artificial control of his body.

During one slow step he tried keeping his eyes closed; it made him feel

◆ Build Vocabulary

grimace (gri´ məs) *n.*: Twisted facial expression

deftness (deft´ nis) *n.*: Skillfulness

imperceptibly (im pər sep´ tə blē) *adv.*: In such a slight way as to be almost unnoticeable

◆ Critical Thinking

3 Analyze Have students analyze Tom in terms of his response to the pressure he feels here. *Some students may realize that the pressure Tom is under has caused him to feel paralyzed; they may take his loss of control as a normal response to a dangerous situation. Other students may think that a stronger character would be able to master his body's response to terror.*

Customize for *Interpersonal Learners*

Invite interpersonal learners, students who communicate especially well with other people, to explain what they might say to Tom to calm him in this situation.

Read to Appreciate Author's Craft

Finney's short story is an excellent example of a suspenseful writing style. Help students appreciate the author's craft and skill at creating suspense and excitement in the plot. Suggest that they note words that enhance the white-knuckled, tense atmosphere of Tom's attempt to retrieve his important paper. Have students jot down their observations for future reference in their own writing.

Listening to Literature Audiocassettes To reinforce the terror of Tom's situation, you may wish to play the audiocassette recording of this portion of Finney's story as students follow along in their texts.

Viewing and Representing Mini-Lesson

Annotated Drawing

This mini-lesson supports the Annotated Drawing writing activity in the Idea Bank on p. 20.

Introduce Point out to students that authors use words to verbally describe a scene so that the reader can "see" the picture. In a similar creative and communicative mode, visual artists use visual tools to portray their perceptions of reality to viewers.

Develop Have students reread the description of the building ledge and take careful notes on the author's details.

Apply Have students create a visual representation of the ledge. Using the notes they took to help them plan their representations, they might choose to use materials such as cardboard, posterboard, or boxes to create a three-dimensional representation. Alternatively, they can draw representations of the building and the narrow ledge. Have students write accompanying notes that list the details they used from the story.

Assess Create a class display of students' visual representations. Assess their work based on effective use of the story's details.

▶Critical Viewing◀

❶ **Connect** *The tall buildings emphasize the fact that he has no means of reaching the ground.*

◆Build Grammar Skills

❷ **Possessive *Its* vs. Contraction *It's*** Have students explain how they know that *its* is a possessive pronoun rather than a contraction. Then ask students to identify the noun that the possessive pronoun *its* stands for. *Students should be able to tell that its is not a contraction because it has no apostrophe. The pronoun stands for the noun* apartment *and shows that the apartment possesses something—"unbelievable security."*

Customize for
Visual/Spatial Learners
Encourage these students to use this photograph to help them appreciate what Tom is picturing in his mind. You may even want to have them contrast this photograph with the one on p. 9 to make it easier for them to understand what Finney describes at the end of this page. Ask: If they were in Tom's place, how would the contrast between the two scenes affect them? *Students may respond that the contrast would cause them to be overcome with panic or a sense of despair.*

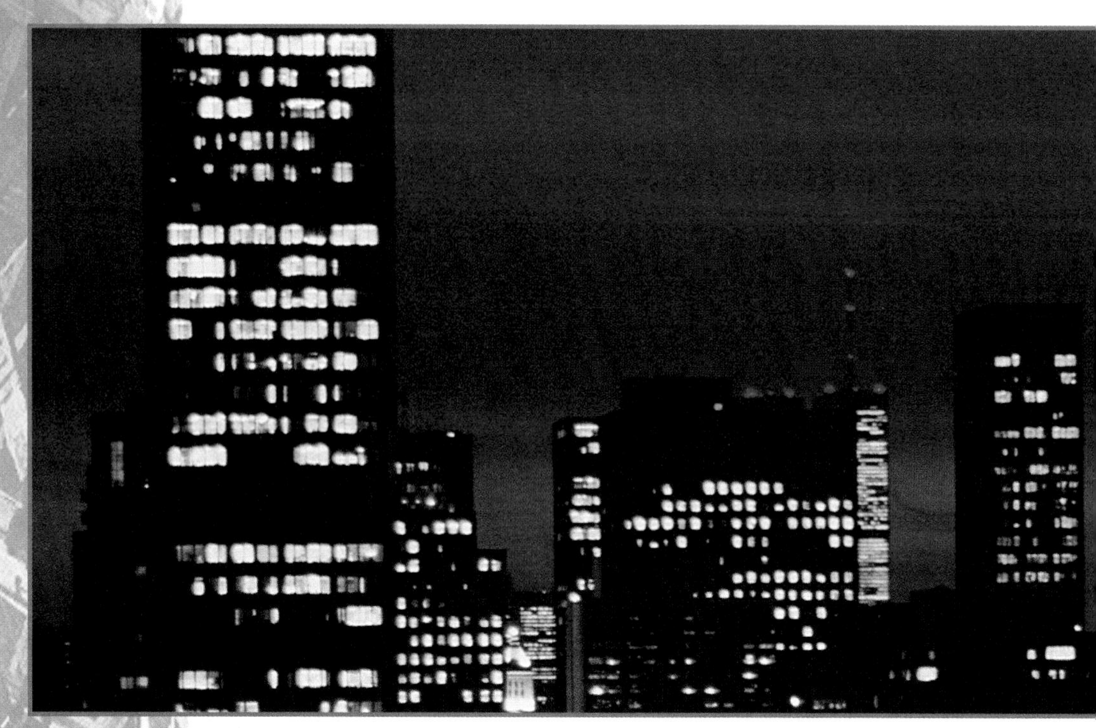

❶ ▲ Critical Viewing In what ways does this picture help you appreciate Tom's feelings on the ledge? **[Connect]**

safer, shutting him off a little from the fearful reality of where he was. Then a sudden rush of giddiness swept over him and he had to open his eyes wide, staring sideways at the cold rough brick and angled lines of mortar, his cheek tight against the building. He kept his eyes open then, knowing that if he once let them flick outward, to stare for an instant at the lighted windows across the street, he would be past help.

He didn't know how many dozens of tiny sidling steps he had taken, his chest, belly, and face pressed to the wall; but he knew the slender hold he was keeping on his mind and body was going to break. He had a sudden mental picture of his apartment on just the other side of this wall—warm, ❷ cheerful, incredibly spacious. And he saw himself striding through it, lying down on the floor on his back, arms spread wide, reveling in its unbelievable security. ❷ The impossible remoteness of this utter safety, the contrast between it and where he now stood, was more than he could bear. And the barrier broke then, and the fear of the awful height he stood on coursed through his nerves and muscles.

> **Context clues** help you understand the full meaning of *striding*. Because Tom is envisioning a relief from what he is experiencing, *striding* is probably walking fast and confidently, or the opposite of the careful, cautious movement he is using on the ledge.

A fraction of his mind knew he was going to fall, and he began taking rapid blind steps with no feeling of what he was doing, sidling with a ❸

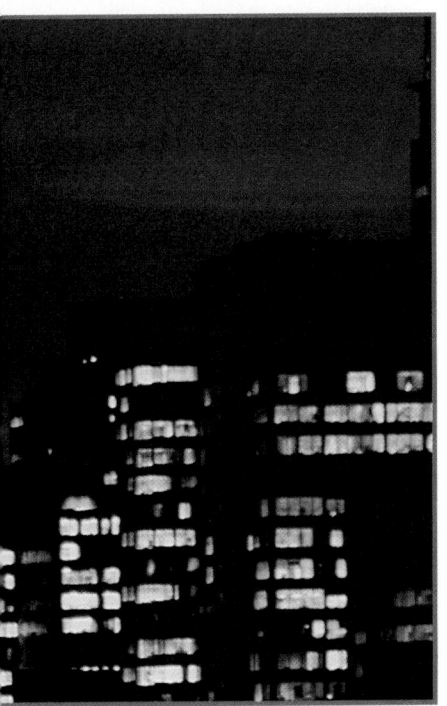

clumsy desperate swiftness, fingers scrabbling along the brick, almost
3 hopelessly resigned to the sudden backward pull and swift motion outward and down. Then his moving left hand slid onto not brick but sheer emptiness, an impossible gap in the face of the wall, and he stumbled.

His right foot smashed into his left anklebone; he staggered sideways, began falling, and the claw of his hand cracked against glass and wood, slid down it, and his fingertips were pressed hard on the puttyless edging of his window. His right hand smacked gropingly beside it as he fell
4 to his knees; and, under the full weight and direct downward pull of his sagging body, the open window dropped shudderingly in its frame till it closed and his wrists struck the sill 4
and were jarred off.

For a single moment he knelt, knee bones against stone on the very edge of the ledge, body swaying and touching nowhere else, fighting for balance. Then he lost it, his shoulders plunging backward, and he flung his arms forward, his hands smashing against the window casing on either side; and—his body moving backward—his fingers clutched the narrow wood stripping of the upper pane.

For an instant he hung suspended between balance and falling, his fingertips pressed onto the quarter-inch wood strips. Then, with utmost delicacy, with a focused concentration of all his senses, he increased even further the strain on his fingertips hooked to these slim edgings of wood. Elbows slowly bending, he began to draw the full weight of his upper body forward, knowing that the instant his fingers slipped off these quarter-inch strips he'd plunge backward and be falling. Elbows imperceptibly bending, body shaking with the strain, the sweat starting from his forehead in great sudden drops, he pulled, his entire being and thought concentrated in his fingertips. Then suddenly, the strain slackened and ended, his chest touching the window sill, and he was kneeling on the ledge, his forehead pressed to the glass of the closed window.

Dropping his palms to the sill, he stared into his living room—at the red-brown davenport[2] across the room, and a magazine he had left there; at the pictures on the walls and the gray rug; the entrance to the hallway; and at his papers, typewriter and desk, not two feet from his nose. All was as he had left it—this was past all belief—only a few minutes before.

◆ Build Vocabulary

reveling (rev´ əl iŋ) *v.*: Taking great pleasure

2. **davenport** (dav´ ən pôrt) *n.*: Couch.

◆ Reading for Success

3 Analyze or Break Down Confusing Sentences Have students break down this long sentence into logical parts. Lead them to identify both subjects and predicates of this compound sentence. Then have them tell what Tom knew, how he reacted to what he knew, and to what Tom was "almost hopelessly resigned." *Students might break down the sentence as follows: "A fraction of his mind knew he was going to fall,/and he began taking rapid blind steps with no feeling of what he was doing,/sidling with a clumsy desperate swiftness,/fingers scrabbling along the brick,/almost hopelessly resigned to the sudden backward pull and swift motion outward and down." The first complete subject and predicate are "A fraction of his mind" and "knew he was going to fall"; the second complete subject and predicate are "he" and "began taking rapid blind steps with no feeling of what he was doing." Tom was almost hopelessly resigned to the fact that he will fall. The remaining phrases are all modifiers describing his actions and feelings.*

◆ Literary Focus

4 Suspense Have students explain how this incident increases the story's tension and builds suspense. *Just when Tom appears to be safe, his avenue of escape—the window—is slammed shut. Further, Tom's "wrists struck the sill and were jarred off," suggesting that he will plunge off the ledge to his death.*

Workplace Skills Mini-Lesson

Concentration

Introduce the Concept Ask students to identify the personal qualities that help Tom through his ordeal on the ledge. What does Tom tell himself to do each time he feels he may fall? Guide students to appreciate Tom's power of concentration despite the distractions of general fear and concern for his life. Tom's ability to concentrate on the task at hand and filter out anything that would distract him enables him to think clearly and make decisions that may save his life.

Develop Background Ask students when concentration is important in their lives and activities. For example, what distractions do they filter out in order to concentrate on homework or studying for a test? How does concentration help them to perform in sports or music?

Although some tasks may require less concentration, students should understand that the ability to concentrate is important for virtually all jobs, including students' part-time or summer jobs.

Apply the Information Have students give themselves concentration tests. They should set aside one hour to concentrate fully on a book, a job, a basketball game, etc. Afterward, have them list the distractions they encountered and/or avoided.

Assess the Outcome In groups, have students talk about their concentration tests and evaluate their own powers of concentration. Have them list the personal strategies they used for canceling out distractions and focusing on the task at hand.

Comprehension Check ☑

❶ What is Tom's dilemma now? *Although he has the paper he wants, he can't get back into his apartment.*

◆ Critical Thinking

❷ **Analyze** What do Tom's actions reveal about his state of mind now? *Although Tom is still trapped out on the ledge, he's feeling that he's probably out of danger. He is not feeling the urgency and fear that he felt moments ago.*

◆ Literary Focus

❸ **Suspense** Point out that when Tom gets the paper, the suspense eases a little. Ask how the author brings up the suspense level again. *He sets up a situation that makes the reader wonder how and if Tom will get back into his apartment.*

Customize for *English Language Learners*

These students might have difficulty following the details in this passage. Suggest that they visualize each essential action the author describes: Tom takes the half dollar from his pocket; he strikes the pane with the half dollar; the pane doesn't break. Tom lifts his leg onto the ledge; he unties his shoelace; he takes off his shoe; he draws his arm back and hits the glass with his shoe. The glass doesn't break, so he puts his shoe back on.

Extending Word Study

Use Context Clues Have students discuss words that may be unfamiliar to them, such as *giddiness* and *angled.* After they explore the context clues that are available, have students use the dictionary to determine the precise meanings of the words. Suggest that students write the unfamiliar words on index cards and keep the cards in a pack for further study and review.

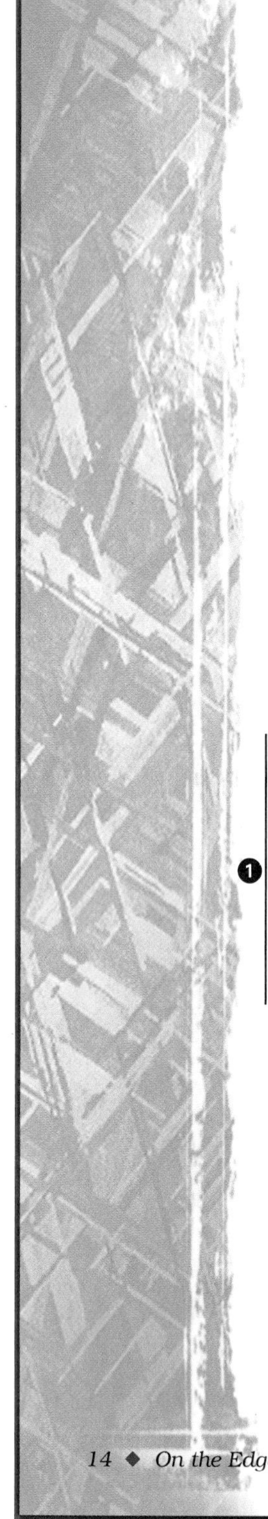

His head moved, and in faint reflection from the glass before him he saw the yellow paper clenched in his front teeth. Lifting a hand from the sill he took it from his mouth; the moistened corner parted from the paper, and he spat it out.

For a moment, in the light from the living room, he stared wonderingly at the yellow sheet in his hand and then crushed it into the side pocket of his jacket.

He couldn't open the window. It had been pulled not completely closed, but its lower edge was below the level of the outside sill; there was no room to get his fingers underneath it. Between the upper sash and the lower was a gap not wide enough—reaching up, he tried—to get his fingers into; he couldn't push it open. The upper window panel, he knew from long experience, was impossible to move, frozen tight with dried paint.

Very carefully observing his balance, the fingertips of his left hand again hooked to the narrow stripping of the window casing, he drew back
❶ his right hand, palm facing the glass, and then struck the glass with the heel of his hand.

His arm rebounded from the pane, his body tottering, and he knew he didn't dare strike a harder blow.

But in the security and relief of his new position, he simply smiled; with only a sheet of glass between him and the room just before him, it was not possible that there wasn't a way past it. Eyes narrowing, he thought for a few moments about what to do. Then his eyes widened, for nothing occurred to him. But still he felt calm: the trembling, he realized, had stopped. At the back of his mind there still lay the thought that once he was again in his home, he could give release to his feelings. He actually *would* lie on the floor, rolling, clenching tufts of the rug in his hands. He would literally run across the room, free to move as he liked, jumping on the floor, testing and reveling in its absolute security, letting the relief flood through him, draining the fear from his mind and body. His yearning for this was astonishingly intense, and somehow he understood that he had better keep this feeling at bay.

He took a half dollar from his pocket and struck it against the pane, but without any hope that the glass would break and with very little disappointment when it did not. After a few moments of thought he drew his leg up onto the ledge and picked loose the knot of his shoelace. He slipped off the shoe and, holding it across the
instep, drew back his arm as far as he ❷
dared and struck the leather heel against the glass. The pane rattled, but he knew he'd been a long way from breaking it. His foot was cold and he slipped the shoe back on. He shouted again experimentally, and then once more, but there was no answer.

The realization suddenly struck him that he might have to wait here till Clare came home, and for a moment the thought was funny. He could see Clare opening the front door, withdrawing her key from the lock, closing the door behind her, and then glancing up to see him crouched on the other side of the
window. He could see her rush across ❸
the room, face astounded and frightened, and hear himself shouting instructions: "Never mind how I got here! Just open the wind—" She couldn't open it, he remembered, she'd never been able to; she'd always had to call him. She'd have to get the building superintendent or a neighbor, and he pictured himself smiling and answering their questions as he

3 climbed in. "I just wanted to get a breath of fresh air, so—"

He couldn't possibly wait here till Clare came home. It was the second feature she'd wanted to see, and she'd left in time to see the first. She'd be 4 another three hours or—He glanced at his watch; Clare had been gone eight minutes. It wasn't possible, but only eight minutes ago he had kissed his wife goodbye. She wasn't even at the theater yet!

It would be four hours before she could possibly be home, and he tried to picture himself kneeling out here, fingertips hooked to these narrow strippings, while first one movie, preceded by a slow listing of credits, began, developed, reached its climax 5 and then finally ended. There'd be a newsreel next, maybe, and then an animated cartoon, and then <u>interminable</u> scenes from coming pictures. And then, once more, the beginning of a full-length picture—while all the time he hung out here in the night.

He might possibly get to his feet, but he was afraid to try. Already his legs were cramped, his thigh muscles tired; his knees hurt, his feet felt numb and his hands were stiff. He couldn't possibly stay out here for four hours, or anywhere near it. Long before that his legs and arms would give out; he would be forced to try changing his position often—stiffly, clumsily, his coordination and strength gone—and he would fall. Quite realistically, he knew that he would fall; no one could stay out here on this ledge for four hours.

> **Analyze** the structure of this sentence to identify the cause and effect. The effect is that he will fall. The beginning of the sentence explains that his movements will cause him to fall. The words set off by dashes describe his movements.

A dozen windows in the apartment building across the street were lighted. Looking over his shoulder, he could see the top of a man's head behind the newspaper he was reading; in another window he saw the blue-gray flicker of a television screen. No more than twenty-odd yards from his back were scores of people, and if just one of them would walk idly to his 6 window and glance out. . . . For some moments he stared over his shoulder at the lighted rectangles, waiting. But no one appeared. The man reading his paper turned a page and then continued his reading. A figure passed another of the windows and was immediately gone.

In the inside pocket of his jacket he found a little sheaf of papers, and he pulled one out and looked at it in the light from the living room. It was an old letter, an advertisement of some sort; his name and address, in purple ink, were on a label pasted to the envelope. Gripping one end of the envelope in his teeth, he twisted it into a tight curl. From his shirt pocket he brought out a book of matches. He didn't dare let go the casing with both hands, but, with the twist of paper in his teeth, he opened the matchbook with his free hand; then he bent one of the matches in two without tearing it from the folder, its red-tipped end now touching the striking surface. 7 With his thumb, he rubbed the red tip across the striking area.

He did it again, then again, and still again, pressing harder each time, and the match suddenly flared, burning his thumb. But he kept it alight, cupping the matchbook in his hand and shielding it with his body. He held the flame to the paper in his

◆ Build Vocabulary

interminable (in tur′ mi nə bəl) *adj.*: Seemingly endless

◆ Critical Thinking

4 Synthesize Remind students that Jack Finney's stories are famous for their concern with time. Have students analyze how the author makes eight minutes seem like hours. Then have them analyze the effect of the time distortion here. *Finney makes a short time seem endless by describing every single detail of Tom's actions and every thought that goes through his mind. Students may say that Finney distorts time to create suspense. It seems that readers will never find out what happens to Tom in the end.*

5 Clarification Point out that a "newsreel" was a short motion picture presenting current events, similar to today's TV news. Although regular TV broadcasts began in 1939, very few people had TV sets at that time. It was not until 1952, when the FCC announced a plan for more than 2,000 TV stations, that sales of televisions soared and the TV news began to replace newsreels.

◆ Reading for Success

6 Use Context Clues Ask students to identify the "lighted rectangles" in this passage. Point out that often the meaning of an unclear word or phrase is found right in the sentence. Have them find a word that could correspond to "lighted rectangles." *Students should be able to identify the "lighted rectangles" as windows of apartment buildings, using the context clue "window."*

◆ Build Grammar Skills

7 Possessive *Its* vs. Contraction *It's* Ask students whether *its* is a possessive pronoun or a contraction. Direct them to give reasons for their response. *Its is a possessive pronoun. The "red-tipped end" belongs to "it," the match.*

Speaking, Listening, and Viewing Mini-Lesson

Role Play

This mini-lesson supports the Speaking, Listening, and Viewing activity in the Idea Bank on p. 20.

Introduce Explain that role-playing requires assuming a character's personality in order to interpret his or her behavior.

Develop Before students begin, have them explore ways to make their skits realistic:

1. Analyze their characters' personalities and behaviors.
2. Vary the expression in their voices to convey their characters' personalities.
3. Use body language to reveal characters.
4. Listen to each other—as Tom and Clare would.

Apply Students should rehearse the meeting between Tom and Clare, using these guidelines. They can then present their role-played meetings to the class.

Assess Audience members can write a brief review of each role play. In their reviews, they should assess the following aspects of the role plays:

1. How true to personality each character seemed.
2. How effectively each student used body language in his or her role.
3. The pace and style of each student's delivery.
4. How real the two characters seem.

◆ Critical Thinking

1 Connect Ask students why no one would be able to identify Tom's body. Then have students link Tom's realization here with his earlier career goals. *There is nothing on Tom to identify him—only the paper with the cryptic notes. Tom begins to realize the emptiness of his driving ambition; he doesn't want to be defined only by his career.*

◆ Reading for Success

2 Reread or Read Ahead At this point, encourage students to reread to understand why Tom feels that his life has been wasted. They should go back to the beginning of the story to remind themselves of how important the yellow paper was to Tom; then contrast his feelings now.

◆ Critical Thinking

3 Interpret What does the phrase *"contents of the dead man's pockets"* signify for Tom now? *He puts the emphasis on* dead man, *and realizes that if he did die, his life would have been wasted because he didn't enjoy what he had while he was alive.*

mouth till it caught. Then he snuffed out the match flame with his thumb and forefinger, careless of the burn, and replaced the book in his pocket. Taking the paper twist in his hand, he held it flame down, watching the flame crawl up the paper, till it flared bright. Then he held it behind him over the street, moving it from side to side, watching it over his shoulder, the flame flickering and guttering in the wind.

There were three letters in his pocket and he lighted each of them, holding each till the flame touched his hand and then dropping it to the street below. At one point, watching over his shoulder while the last of the letters burned, he saw the man across the street put down his paper and stand—even seeming, to Tom, to glance toward his window. But when he moved, it was only to walk across the room and disappear from sight.

There were a dozen coins in Tom Benecke's pocket and he dropped them, three or four at a time. But if they struck anyone, or if anyone noticed their falling, no one connected them with their source, and no one glanced upward.

His arms had begun to tremble from the steady strain of clinging to this narrow perch, and he did not know what to do now and was terribly frightened. Clinging to the window stripping with one hand, he again searched his pockets. But now—he had left his wallet on his dresser when he'd changed clothes—there was nothing left but the yellow sheet. It occurred to him irrelevantly that his death on the sidewalk below would be an eternal mystery; the window closed —why, how, and from where could he have fallen? No one would be able to
1 identify his body for a time, either—
the thought was somehow unbearable and increased his fear. All they'd find in his pockets would be the yellow sheet. *Contents of the dead man's pockets, he thought, one sheet of paper bearing penciled notations—incomprehensible.*

Paraphrase the two sentences beginning with "All they'd find" to understand a central point in the story: As Tom imagines his death, he realizes that the only thing people will find in his pockets is a meaningless scrap of paper. 1

He understood fully that he might actually be going to die; his arms, maintaining his balance on the ledge, were trembling steadily now. And it occurred to him then with all the force of a revelation that, if he fell, all he was ever going to have out of life he would then, abruptly, have had. Nothing, then, could ever be changed; and nothing more—no least experience or pleasure—could ever be added to his life. He wished, then, that he had not allowed his wife to go off by herself 2
tonight—and on similar nights. He thought of all the evenings he had spent away from her, working; and he regretted them. He thought wonderingly of his fierce ambition and of the direction his life had taken; he thought of the hours he'd spent by himself, filling the yellow sheet that had brought him out here. *Contents of the dead man's* pockets, he thought with sudden fierce anger, *a wasted life.* 3

He was simply not going to cling here till he slipped and fell; he told himself that now. There was one last thing he could try; he had been aware of it for some moments, refusing to think about it, but now he faced it. Kneeling here on the ledge, the fingertips of one hand pressed to the narrow strip of wood, he could, he knew, draw his other hand back a yard perhaps, fist clenched tight, doing it very slowly till he sensed the outer limit of

Reteach

Students who have difficulty following the story's events and how they contribute to the suspense of the writing may benefit from rereading for understanding—a Reading for Success strategy. Have students stop reading after the first paragraph on p. 14 and restate what has happened so far. Suggest that they reread sections of text, as necessary, to clarify details.

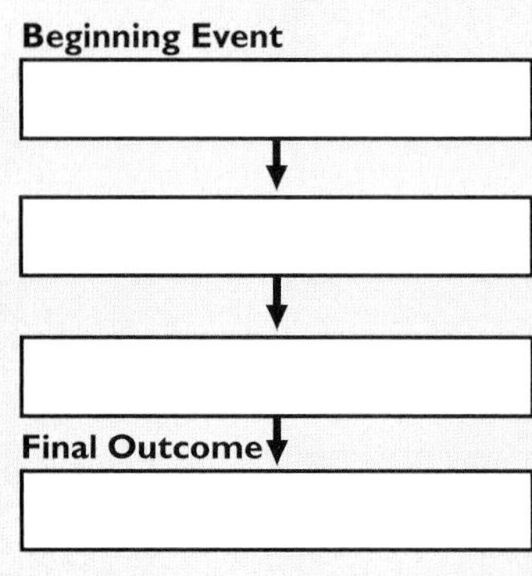

Then have students draw and complete a series-of-events chain, adding as many event boxes as they find are necessary to describe the story's events. The first box should be the story's initial event, and each successive box should detail important events. As students continue reading the story, have them continue adding boxes until they read the final outcome, or conclusion, of the story.

balance, then, as hard as he was able from the distance, he could drive his fist forward against the glass. If it broke, his fist smashing through, he was safe; he might cut himself badly, and probably would, but with his arm inside the room, he would be secure. But if the glass did not break, the rebound, flinging his arm back, would topple him off the ledge. He was certain of that.

He tested his plan. The fingers of his left hand clawlike on the little stripping, he drew back his other fist until his body began teetering backward. But he had no leverage now—he could feel that there would be no force to his swing—and he moved his fist slowly forward till he rocked forward on his knees again and could sense that his swing would carry its greatest force. Glancing down, however, measuring the distance from his fist to the glass, he saw that it was less than two feet.

It occurred to him that he could raise his arm over his head, to bring it down against the glass. But, experimenting in slow motion, he knew it would be an awkward blow without the force of a driving punch, and not nearly enough to break the glass.

Facing the window, he had to drive a blow from the shoulder, he knew now, at a distance of less than two feet; and he did not know whether it would break through the heavy glass. It might; he could picture it happening, he could feel it in the nerves of his arm. And it might not; he could feel that too—feel his fist striking this glass and being instantaneously flung back by the unbreaking pane, feel the fingers of his other hand breaking loose, nails scraping along the casing as he fell.

He waited, arm drawn back, fist balled, but in no hurry to strike; this pause, he knew, might be an extension of his life. And to live even a few seconds longer, he felt, even out here on this ledge in the night, was infinitely better than to die a moment earlier than he had to. His arm grew tired, and he brought it down and rested it.

Then he knew that it was time to make the attempt. He could not kneel here hesitating indefinitely till he lost all courage to act, waiting till he slipped off the ledge. Again he drew back his arm, knowing this time that he would not bring it down till he struck. His elbow protruding over Lexington Avenue far below, the fingers of his other hand pressed down bloodlessly tight against the narrow stripping, he waited, feeling the sick tenseness and terrible excitement building. It grew and swelled toward the moment of action, his nerves tautening. He thought of Clare—just a wordless, yearning thought—and then drew his arm back just a bit more, fist so tight his fingers pained him, and knowing he was going to do it. Then with full power, with every last scrap of strength he could bring to bear, he shot his arm forward toward the glass, and he said, *"Clare!"*

He heard the sound, felt the blow, felt himself falling forward, and his hand closed on the living-room curtains, the shards and fragments of glass showering onto the floor. And then, kneeling there on the ledge, an arm thrust into the room up to the shoulder, he began picking away the protruding slivers and great wedges of glass from the window frame, tossing them in onto the rug. And, as he grasped the edges of the empty window frame and climbed into his home, he was grinning in triumph.

He did not lie down on the floor or run through the apartment, as he had promised himself; even in the first few

◆ Reading for Success

❹ Restate for Understanding Invite students to paraphrase this passage to clarify its meaning. Remind students that *paraphrase* means restating in their own words. *Paraphrases should include Tom's effort to figure out a way to achieve the greatest power from his swing. Example paraphrase: Because of Tom's position, he knew he would not be able to swing his fist far enough to break the window. He tried it out and saw that he was right—he had only two feet to swing his fist.*

Customize for *Bodily/Kinesthetic Learners* Students who process information through motion may wish to pantomime this scene for classmates. Encourage students to use their posture, stance, and facial expressions to convey Tom's tension and fear.

Customize for *Musical/Rhythmic Learners* Students comfortable with oral interpretation can read this passage aloud to the class, using tone, pitch, and volume to capture the tension and suspense.

Art Transparency After students have read and discussed "Contents of the Dead Man's Pocket," display Art Transparency 19. Invite students to comment upon details in Frida Kahlo's still life, *¡Qué bonita es la vida, cuando nos da de sus riquezas! (How Beautiful Life Is When It Gives Us Riches!)*, and to discuss the meaning of its title. Ask students how Tom Benecke, the "dead man" of Finney's story, changed his ideas about the riches" of life as a result of his experience. Students may enjoy writing or talking about the things they consider to be the "riches" of life, as well.

Cross-Curricular Connection: Social Studies

The History of Physics Tom realizes that he has only one way to save his life—he must break the glass in the window. Tom weighs his chances of successfully punching through the glass without having the rebound fling his arm back and topple him off the ledge.

In his calculations, Tom is dealing with the science of *physics*, which concerns itself with the fundamental elements of the universe, the forces they exert on each other, and the results produced by these forces.

The ancient Babylonians, Egyptians, and early Meso-Americans observed the motions of the planets. The Greek mathematician Archimedes designed devices to deal with force and motion, such as the lever. It was not until 1665, however, that English mathematician Sir Isaac Newton stated the principles of mechanics. The subsequent development of physics owes much to Newton's laws of motion. Have interested students research how Newton's laws of motion, notably the second and third, affect Tom's chances of success.

◆ Critical Thinking

1 Draw Conclusions Judging from Tom's actions, what does the piece of paper mean to him now? *Tom has realized what's really important in his life and what's not. The piece of paper and what it represented now mean little to him.*

◆ Critical Thinking

2 Synthesize Challenge students to explain why Tom immediately went to find his wife. *Tom realizes that he has wasted too much of his life in isolation and, perhaps, in vanity because of his fierce ambition.*

Customize for
Pre-AP Students
Have students discuss with a group how Tom's climb to retrieve the paper symbolizes his career goals. *Tom must climb across the face of the building just as he is trying to climb the "ladder of success." As he risks his life to climb along the ledge, he risks his happiness and possibly his marriage by his determination to climb the "corporate ladder."*

Reinforce and Extend

Answers

◆ Literature and Your Life

Reader's Response Students may say that they agreed with Tom's choice to stay at home and work, but disagreed with his choice to go out on the ledge.

Thematic Focus Students may say that by taking risks and succeeding, they learn more about what's important to them.

Check Your Comprehension

1. Tom goes out on the ledge to retrieve a paper that was blown out by the wind.
2. Tom creeps up to the paper, retrieves it, creeps back, falls against the window and accidentally forces it shut, sets letters on fire to attract attention, and finally breaks the window.
3. Clare had been gone for eight minutes.
4. He breaks the window.
5. Tom laughs when the yellow paper soars out the window again.

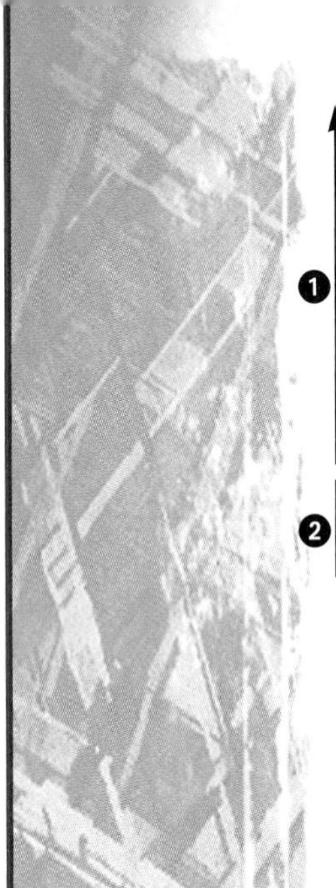

moments it seemed to him natural and normal that he should be where he was. He simply turned to his desk, pulled the crumpled yellow sheet from his pocket and laid it down where it had been, smoothing it out; then he absently laid a pencil across it to weight it down. He shook his head wonderingly, and turned to walk toward the closet. **1**

2 There he got out his topcoat and hat and, without waiting to put them on, opened the front door and stepped out, to go find his wife. He turned to pull the door closed and the warm air from the hall rushed through the narrow opening again. As he saw the yellow paper, the pencil flying, scooped off the desk and, unimpeded by the glassless window, sail out into the night and out of his life, Tom Benecke burst into laughter and then closed the door behind him. **2**

The meaning of *unimpeded* is implied by **context clues** in the rest of the sentence.

Guide for Responding

◆ Literature and Your Life

Reader's Response At what points in the story did you agree with Tom's choices? When did you disagree with his choices?

Thematic Focus Not all risks are as dramatic or dangerous as the risk Tom took. How do everyday risks, like trying out for a team or auditioning for a play, help you understand what's important to you?

Check Your Comprehension

1. Why does Tom go out on the ledge?
2. Briefly summarize what Tom does on the ledge before he manages to get back in.
3. About how much time elapses from Clare's departure to when Tom is kneeling on the ledge, trying to break the window?
4. How does Tom succeed in getting back into his apartment?
5. What event causes Tom to laugh at the end of the story?

Beyond Literature

Math Connection

Statistics in Business Tom Benecke collects statistics to support his idea for a new grocery-store display method. Statistics play an important role in countless businesses. Collecting data through surveys and samples and then analyzing the data is essential to everything from test marketing a new cola to creating a safer automobile for the public. Economists and meteorologists use statistical techniques to predict future economic and weather conditions. How do statistics help to ensure the success of a product?

Beyond the Selection

FURTHER READING

Other Works by Jack Finney
5 Against the House
The Body Snatchers
Time and Again

Other Works About Risk Taking
Greek myths: *Phaethon, Daedalus and Icarus, Prometheus*
Kon Tiki, Thor Heyerdahl

We suggest that you preview these works before recommending them to students.

INTERNET

You and your students may find additional information about Jack Finney on the Internet. We suggest the following site: **http://www.catch22.com/~espana/SFAuthors/SFF/Finney,Jack.html**

Please be aware, however, that the site may have changed from the time we published this information. We *strongly recommend* that you preview the site before you send students to it.

Guide for Responding *(continued)*

◆ Critical Thinking

INTERPRET

1. Why does Tom risk his life for a piece of paper? **[Draw Conclusions]**

2. Give three examples of how Tom's thoughts and feelings affect his ability to get off the ledge. **[Analyze]**

3. Contrast Tom's attitude toward life at the beginning of the story with his attitude at the end. **[Compare and Contrast]**

APPLY

4. What changes, if any, will Tom make in his life as a result of this experience? Explain. **[Apply]**

EXTEND

5. In the end, Tom regrets risking his life for his job. (a) In what kinds of jobs is it routine to risk one's life? (b) Why are some people attracted to these jobs? **[Career Link]**

◆ Reading for Success

LITERAL COMPREHENSION STRATEGIES

Review the reading strategies and the notes showing how to understand what a writer is saying. Then apply the strategies to answer the following.

1. Paraphrase the paragraph that begins "His right foot smashed" on page 13.

2. Analyze, or break down, the sentence that begins "Then, with utmost delicacy" on page 13.

3. Use context clues to identify the meaning of *incomprehensible* on page 16.

◆ Literary Focus

SUSPENSE

In this story, Finney creates the feeling of uncertainty called **suspense** by keeping you guessing whether Tom will fall.

1. Find a passage describing Tom's thoughts and actions on the ledge and explain how Finney keeps you uncertain about the outcome.

2. How does the suspense in the story make you feel closer to Tom?

3. Why does the suspense make you more likely to think about what is really important in life?

◆ Build Vocabulary

USING THE LATIN ROOT *-term-*

Knowing that the Latin root *-term-* means "end," answer the following questions in your notebook.

1. When do you hand in a *term* paper?

2. How would you *terminate* a conversation?

3. Why did Tom's time on the ledge seem *interminable*?

4. How was Tom's decision nearly a *terminal* one?

USING THE WORD BANK: Synonyms

On your paper, write the word whose meaning is closest to the meaning of the word from the Word Bank.

1. convoluted: (a) boisterous, (b) twisted, (c) greedy

2. grimace: (a) sneer, (b) buffoon, (c) sadness

3. deftness: (a) foolishness, (b) clumsiness, (c) skill

4. imperceptibly: (a) obviously, (b) visually, (c) unnoticeably

5. reveling: (a) mourning, (b) enjoying, (c) showing

◆ Build Grammar Skills

POSSESSIVE *ITS* VS. CONTRACTION *IT'S*

Two forms of the pronoun *it* that are sometimes confused are the **possessive** *its,* meaning "belonging to it," and the **contraction** *it's,* which stands for "it is."

Practice On your paper, rewrite each sentence using *its* or *it's*.

1. (Its, It's) amazing that there was ever a time when people did not own computers.

2. "(Its, It's) cold out here!" Tom exclaimed as he stepped out onto the ledge.

3. A pigeon landed on the ledge and turned (its, it's) back on Tom.

4. Tom saw the paper and could hear the muffled scrape of (its, it's) movement along the ledge.

5. Tom's wife saw the paper but did not understand (its, it's) significance.

Writing Application Write a brief description of the behavior of a pet or another animal. Use both *its* and *it's* in your description.

Answers

◆ Critical Thinking

1. The paper contains information that represents a chance to advance in his workplace.
2. Tom's worrying and fretting cause his legs to cramp, trembling to overtake his body, and strength to leave his limbs.
3. At the beginning of the story, Tom thinks getting ahead is the most important thing in life, while at the end he comes to realize that his relationship with his wife is more important.
4. Students might say that Tom will not spend all his time working at getting ahead and will devote more time to what he really values.
5. (a) Police officers, firefighters, and rescue workers are some who routinely risk their lives. (b) Perhaps they feel the rewards of saving lives justify the risk; perhaps they like performing heroic acts.

◆ Reading for Success

1. Tom stumbled, and in using the window to break his fall, he pulled the window shut.
2. Tom is the subject of the sentence. "He increased even further the strain on his fingertips" (he pressed harder) is the predicate.
3. "Penciled notations" is a context clue that points to the meaning of *incomprehensible*—not clear.

◆ Literary Focus

1. The passage on page 14, beginning with "The realization . . .," lets the reader know that Clare will not be home any time soon to help Tom off the ledge.
2. Tom's fear makes him vulnerable and more human.
3. The suspense has a way of compressing time to make you look at life with a special clarity.

◆ Build Vocabulary

Using the Latin Root *-term-*

1. You hand in a term paper at the end of a term.
2. You would terminate a conversation by ending it.
3. Tom's time on the ledge seemed as if it would never end.
4. Tom's life could have ended with one misstep.

Using the Word Bank

1. b 2. a 3. c 4. c 5. b

◆ Build Grammar Skills

1. It's; 2. It's; 3. its; 4. its; 5. its

Grammar Reinforcement

For additional instruction and practice, use the lesson in the **Language Lab CD-ROM** on punctuation and the page on apostrophes (p. 110) in the *Writer's Solution Grammar Practice Book.*

Idea Bank

Following are suggestions for matching Idea Bank topics with your students' performance levels and learning modalities:

Customizing for
Performance Levels

Less Advanced Students: 1, 4, 6
Average Students: 2, 4, 7
Pre-AP Students: 3, 5

Customizing for
Learning Modalities

Visual/Spatial: 1, 6
Verbal/Linguistic: 4, 5
Logical/Mathematical: 7

Guided Writing Lesson

Elaboration Strategy To help students improve the opening shots of their scenes, divide them into pairs for a say back once they have written their first drafts. The "screenwriter" should read the description of his first camera shot while his partner, the "director," listens and visualizes the scene. The director should keep in mind that the opening shot in a movie is like the introductory sentence in a piece of writing—it must grab the viewer's attention with an exciting image or event. As the screenwriter reads his work aloud a second time, the director jots down answers to these questions:

- What did I like?
- What did I want to know more about?

The director then says these ideas back to the screenwriter to assist with elaborating on his opening shot.

For more prewriting, elaboration, and revision strategies, see *Prentice Hall Writing and Grammar.*

Writers at Work Videodisc

Have students view the videodisc segment (Ch. 2) featuring Maxine Hong Kingston to spark discussion of narrative writing, mood and atmosphere.

Play frames 11644 to 20980

Writing Lab CD-ROM

Have students complete the tutorial on Narration. Follow these steps:

1. Have students use the Word Bins activities to gather details of setting and character.
2. Have students draft on computer.
3. Have them use the Self-Evaluation Checklist for revision help.

Build Your Portfolio

Idea Bank

Writing

1. **Annotated Drawing** Using details from the story, draw the ledge on which Tom is caught. Then write brief notes on the drawing that explain Tom's movements away from and back to the window. **[Art Link]**

2. **New Titles for the Story** Choose three possible titles for the story, in addition to "Contents of the Dead Man's Pocket." Describe the pluses and minuses of each choice.

3. **Personal Credo** This story may have led you to reconsider what's important to you in life. Write a credo, a statement that summarizes what you believe or value most.

Speaking, Listening, and Viewing

4. **Role Play** Suppose that Tom runs into Clare as he's walking out the door at the story's end. With a partner, role-play a dialogue between Tom and Clare. Have Tom explain what has happened, and have Clare respond. **[Performing Arts Link]**

5. **School Speech** Prepare a speech for your classmates in which you warn them about the dangers of making sudden decisions to do physically risky things. **[Performing Arts Link]**

Researching and Representing

6. **Risks of Everyday Life** Going out on a ledge is foolish, but you face more common risks everyday. Design a poster that presents tips for minimizing a risk such as a sports injury. **[Art Link]**

7. **Changing Technology** Create a timeline that shows when photocopiers and personal computers were introduced to the market and how quickly they caught on. **[Science Link; Art Link]**

Online Activity www.phlit.phschool.com

Guided Writing Lesson

Cliffhanger Scene From a Movie

Tom's sidling dance across the ledge is as suspenseful as any movie's cliffhanger scene. Write your own "cliffhanger" with a dangerous setting that includes one or more characters, sound effects, and dialogue. To make your scene successful, grab viewers' attention and keep them involved in the action.

Writing Skills Focus: Grab and Hold Your Audience's Attention

Whether you write a cliffhanger scene, a story, or a how-to essay, it's important to grab and hold your audience's attention. Finney grabs your attention before you even start reading with the title of his story: "Contents of the Dead Man's Pocket." Although the story itself begins with a very ordinary moment, the title keeps you wondering when a crime or accident will occur.

At the beginning of your scene, you can hook your audience with an exciting image or event.

Prewriting Choose a setting or situation that will keep viewers on the edge of their seats. Examples: a high-speed train derailment, a person hanging from a ledge fifty stories up, or a jumbo jet that is about to crash.

Drafting The filmmaker Alfred Hitchcock once said that an audience will never forgive you if you endanger a star's life for a period of time and then let him or her die. Be sure that your star is rescued in the end.

Revising In reviewing your scene, add camera shots that heighten the uncertainty and suspense. For example, as someone clings to a ledge, zoom in on his or her whitening knuckles. Then move the camera back for a shot that shows exactly what could happen if the person let go.

✓ ASSESSMENT OPTIONS

Formal Assessment, Selection Test, pp. 1–3, and Assessment Resources Software. The selection test is designed so that it can be easily customized to the performance levels of your students.

Alternative Assessment, p. 1, includes options for less advanced students, more advanced students, interpersonal learners, musical/rhythmic learners, verbal/linguistic learners, and visual/spatial learners.

PORTFOLIO ASSESSMENT

Use the following rubrics in the ***Alternative Assessment*** booklet to assess student writing:
Annotated Drawing: Process Explanation Rubric, p. 100
New Titles for the Story: Description Rubric, p. 97
Credo: Summary Rubric, p. 97
Guided Writing Lesson: Drama Rubric, p. 109

Part 1 *Daring Decisions*

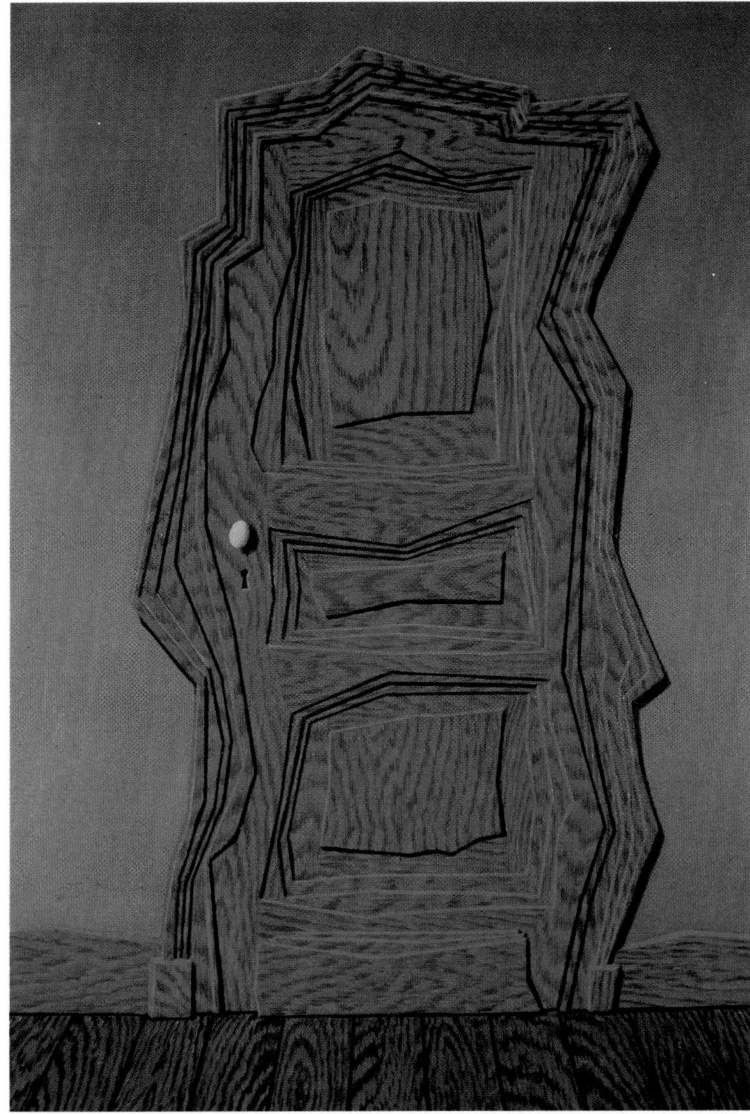

Le Modele Vivant, Rene Magritte, Christie's Images

One-Minute Planning Guide

The selections in this section encompass a wide range of suspenseful and challenging situations in which people make daring decisions or deal with the result of them. In "The Final Assault" Edmund Hillary gives his view of the decisions he and Tenzing Norgay faced in their push to the summit of Mt. Everest. In "The Dream Comes True" Norgay describes his reflections on the experience. The selections are paired with an excerpt from Jon Krakauer's *Into Thin Air*, an account of the 1996 disaster on Everest. "The Monkey's Paw" is a classic tale of horror that describes what happens when people decide not to heed a mysterious warning. "The Bridegroom" is a narrative poem that tells the tale of a bride-to-be's horrible dream and what it reveals. Part 1 ends with Jamaica Kincaid's "A Walk to the Jetty." This selection describes the anxiety a young girl feels as she walks for the last time down the streets of her town on the island of Antigua.

Customize for
Varying Student Needs

When assigning the selections in Part 1, keep in mind the following factors:

"The Final Assault"; "The Dream Comes True"

- Together, a long selection (17 pp.)
- The prose is dense in places and filled with technical terms

"The Monkey's Paw"

- A brief short story that should be of high interest to most students

"The Bridegroom"

- Elements of 19-century Russian culture may need further explaining

from "A Walk to the Jetty"

- Contains long paragraphs that may give less proficient readers trouble

Humanities: Art

Le Modele Vivant by René Magritte.

Belgian painter René Magritte (1898–1967) was one of the leading artists of the Surrealist movement in the early twentieth century. Arising from the period's awakening of interest in the human unconscious, Surrealist art combined elements of realism and fantasy in an attempt to explore the mysteries of the unconscious. Surrealist artists like Magritte created dreamlike images to startle the viewer and express the irrational side of human experience. Magritte was drawn to the surreal, and his paintings of the mysterious, bizarre, and inexplicable were often rendered in a concretely detailed style.

Le Modele Vivant (The Living Model), with its wavy door and baseboard, seems to offer a portal to a warped world in which normally inanimate objects are, to say the least, bent into strange shapes and, given the title, perhaps are not inanimate at all. Help students notice that the floorboards are not wavy; it is as if this wall represents the intersection between our everyday, normal world and a new dimension.

Have your students link the painting to the theme of Part 1, "Daring Decisions," by answering the following question.

If you were following someone through this door, what questions would cross your mind as you decided whether or not to open it?

Sample answers: Why is the door wavy? Is it alive? Who or what is on the other side? Will I be stepping into another dimension? Is it dangerous?

Prepare and Engage

LESSON OBJECTIVES

1. **To develop vocabulary and word identification skills**
   - Latin Word Roots: *-voc-*
   - Using the Word Bank: Synonyms
   - Extending Word Study: Use Reference Material (ATE)
2. **To use a variety of reading strategies to comprehend nonfiction narratives**
   - Connect Your Experience
   - Reading Strategy: Distinguish Fact From Opinion
   - Tips to Guide Reading: Skimming (ATE)
   - Read to Be Informed (ATE)
   - Idea Bank: Mountain's Eye View
3. **To increase knowledge of other cultures and to connect common elements across cultures**
   - Connecting Themes Across Cultures (ATE)
   - Cultural Connection: Sherpas (ATE)
4. **To express and support responses to the text**
   - Critical Thinking
   - Analyze Literary Criticism (ATE)
5. **To analyze literary elements**
   - Literary Focus: Author's Perspective
6. **To read in order to research self-selected and assigned topics**
   - Research Mini-Lesson: Article on Everest (ATE)
   - Idea Bank: Everest Statistics
   - Idea Bank: Oral Report
7. **To plan, prepare, organize, and present literary interpretations**
   - Viewing and Representing Mini-Lesson: Book Jacket (ATE)
   - Idea Bank: Video Design
8. **To use recursive writing processes to write a brief summary**
   - Guided Writing Lesson
9. **To increase knowledge of the rules of grammar and usage**
   - Build Grammar Skills: Compound Predicates

Test Preparation

Reading Comprehension: Using Context Clues to Determine Word Meanings (ATE, p. 23) The teaching tips and sample test item in this workshop support the instruction and practice in the unit workshop:

Reading Comprehension: Using Context Clues to Determine Word Meanings (SE, p. 113)

Guide for Reading

Sir Edmund Hillary *(1919–)*

Few people can claim they have stood on top of the world—and only one man can claim to have been there first. That person is Sir Edmund Hillary. Although he shares the glory of his achievement with climbing partner Tenzing Norgay, Hillary was the first person to reach the summit of Mount Everest in Nepal, 29,028 feet above sea level—the highest spot on Earth.

Hillary has said of himself, "I've moved from being a child who dreamed a lot and read a lot of books about adventure, to actually getting involved in things like mountaineering, and then becoming a reasonably competent mountaineer. . . ." These are humble words for a man who has climbed the Swiss Alps and conquered eleven different peaks of over 20,000 feet in the Himalayas of Tibet and Nepal.

Tenzing Norgay *(1914–1986)*

At 11:30 on the morning of May 29, 1953, Tenzing Norgay changed the course of his destiny—and began a journey toward international fame. At that moment, he and Edmund Hillary stood on the summit of Mount Everest in Nepal—a place where no man or woman had ever stood before and where few have stood since!

Norgay was born into a family of Sherpa farmers—Nepalese people of Tibetan descent. Norgay started guiding climbers at the age of fourteen. In 1953, he joined a Mount Everest expedition led by Sir John Hunt. Although all the other members of the expedition eventually turned back, Norgay and Hillary struggled on and fulfilled their dream of being the first men ever to reach the summit.

◆ Build Vocabulary

LATIN WORD ROOTS: *-voc-*

Edmund Hillary recalls that upon reaching the summit of Mount Everest, he felt "a satisfaction less *vociferous* but more powerful than [he] had ever felt on a mountain top before." *Vociferous* contains the Latin word root *-voc-*, which means "speak" or "say." The meaning of the root seems to indicate that something that is *vociferous* speaks out. This meaning is close to the actual definition, which is "loud or noisy in making one's feelings known." It is understandable that Hillary and Norgay would be too tired for a *vociferous* celebration after climbing over 29,000 feet!

WORD BANK

Before you read, preview this list of words from the selections.

precipitous
discernible
belay
encroaching
undulations
vociferous

◆ Build Grammar Skills

COMPOUND PREDICATES

A **compound predicate** consists of two or more verbs or verb phrases (a main verb plus a helping verb) that share the same subject. Compound predicates enable the writer to include a lot of action in a single sentence without having to repeat the subject. In the following example from "The Final Assault," Hillary links two related climbing actions by using a compound predicate to combine them in a single sentence.

s v v
I swung my ice axe and started chipping a line of steps upward . . .

As you read "The Final Assault" and "The Dream Comes True," notice the authors' frequent use of compound predicates to describe related or sequential actions.

Prentice Hall Literature Program Resources

REINFORCE / RETEACH / EXTEND

Selection Support Pages
Build Vocabulary: Word Roots: *-voc-*, p. 6
Build Grammar Skills: Compound Predicates, p. 7
Reading Strategy: Distinguish Fact From Opinion, p. 8
Literary Focus: Author's Perspective, p. 9

Strategies for Diverse Student Needs, p. 2

Beyond Literature
Cross-Curricular Connection: Physical Education, p. 2

Formal Assessment Selection Test, pp. 4–6; Assessment Resources Software

Alternative Assessment, p. 2

Resource Pro CD-ROM

Listening to Literature Audiocassettes

The Final Assault ◆ The Dream Comes True

◆ Literature and Your Life

Connect Your Experience

Whether you are training to improve your race time or studying to get an *A* on your final exam, you may have to convince yourself that your goal is worth the effort required to reach it. When Hillary doubted his ability to reach the top of Everest, he said to himself, "Ed, my boy, this is Everest—you've got to push it a bit."

Thematic Focus: Daring Decisions

As you read these two men's accounts of the dangers they faced in their quest to stand on the highest point on the planet, you may ask yourself, "Where do I find what it takes to reach the top?"

Journal Writing Describe a time when you had to struggle to achieve a goal or complete a task. How did you keep yourself motivated to make the effort required to meet the goal?

◆ Background for Understanding

Math

The temperature on the day of Hillary and Norgay's historic achievement—twenty degrees *below zero*—was colder than anything you have probably experienced. Read the graph to contrast the temperature with others that may be more familiar to you.

Think about the ways the extreme temperature would make Hillary's and Norgay's climb more difficult.

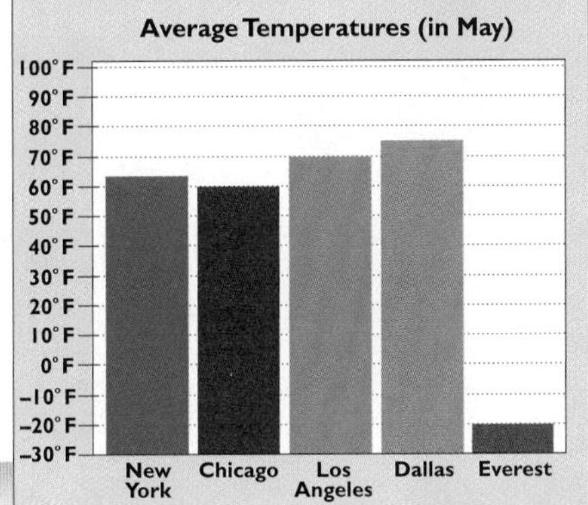

◆ Literary Focus

Author's Perspective

When you read a novel, a poem, a magazine, or even a newspaper article, you get the point of view of one person: the author. How the author views and interprets the events that he or she sees, hears, or experiences personally is the **author's perspective**. In these two accounts of the ascent of Everest, each man's report is influenced by his own beliefs and assumptions. To identify each author's perspective, pay close attention to the details and events they choose to present and the descriptive words they use.

◆ Reading Strategy

Distinguish Fact From Opinion

Many people have died attempting to reach the summit of Everest. That's a **fact**—a statement that can be proved true or false by evidence. Mountain climbing is an exciting sport. That's an **opinion**—a statement that can be *supported* by facts but is not itself a fact.

When you read works of nonfiction, determine whether the author's statements are facts or opinions by asking yourself, "Can this statement be proved true or false by evidence?" If the answer is yes, the statement is a fact; if no, it is an opinion.

By distinguishing fact from opinion, you can form your own opinions and understanding of an event or idea, rather than simply accepting what the author wants you to believe. As you read, use a chart like the one below to separate facts from opinions in these accounts.

Facts	Opinions

A great way to engage your students' interest and help them appreciate the enormity of Hillary and Norgay's accomplishment is to play a segment of the TV film adaptation of Jon Krakauer's book, *Into Thin Air* (available on videotape), depicting a tragic climbing expedition on Mt. Everest You may want to choose a segment toward the end of the film, when the members of the party are trapped on top of the mountain by a violent storm. Have students discuss what the film reveals about the dangers of climbing Everest. Then have them imagine what it might have been like to have been one of the first people to climb the mountain. Tell them that they are about to find out.

Connecting Themes Across Cultures

Historically, people from all over the world have been intrigued and challenged by Mt. Everest. Have students research the nationalities of climbers and guides who have launched expeditions to climb Mt. Everest through the years. Have them analyze how climbers coming from various cultures differ or share the desire to face danger and challenge.

Customize for
Less Proficient Readers
Help less proficient readers understand that these two narratives describe the same journey as seen through the eyes of two different people. Students may benefit from noting the opinions each writer expresses about his experiences.

Customize for
Pre-AP Students
Encourage students to compare and contrast the two perspectives offered in the narratives. Urge them to make inferences about the personalities of the writers based on the details each includes, excludes, or emphasizes.

Customize for
Gifted/Talented Students
Have students generate a list of relevant and interesting questions to research the rigors of mountain climbing—oxygen deprivation, subzero temperatures—and how these impact successful climbs.

Test Preparation Workshop

Reading Comprehension: Using Context Clues to Determine Word Meanings Students taking the SAT test will encounter vocabulary questions based on sentences or reading passages that will require them to use context clues to select the best answer. To give students practice using context clues, use the following sample test item.

The sentence contains a blank which indicates that something has been omitted. Choose the word that, inserted in the sentence, best fits the meaning of the sentence as a whole.

"The pleasure of this safe belay after all the uncertainty below was like a _______ to a condemned man."

A reproach **C** reprimand
B reprisal **D** reprieve

Suggest that students apply an elimination strategy to make the correct selection. Have students read the sentence several times, inserting each word in turn until they decide that D is the best choice. Caution students not to be misled by the similar spellings of the answer choices.

Develop Understanding

One-Minute Insight No two people perceive the same experience alike, as these narratives clearly illustrate. In telling the story of the first successful climb to the summit of Mt. Everest, Sir Edmund Hillary focuses on his achievement and the difficulties his guide experienced. His guide, Tenzing Norgay, provides his perspective in "The Dream Comes True" (see p. 36). The differences in perspectives will give students both a full interpretation of the climb and a glimpse into the characters of the two climbers.

Tips to Guide Reading

Skimming Suggest that students skim through Krakaur's and Norgay's accounts of the climbing expedition and locate confusing or unfamiliar vocabulary words in the passages. As they note a word, have them jot it down and look it up so that when they begin reading they will not be confused by difficult or unfamiliar words.

Extending Word Study

Use Reference Materials Have students use the dictionary, the Internet, or a book about mountain climbing to determine the precise meaning and use of words included in these passages. For example, students may wish to look up easy words, such as *ice axe* or *pick* that become specific to mountain climbing when used in context.

Customize for English Language Learners

English language learners (and other students as well) might be unfamiliar with words relating to mountain climbing. Help these students define words such as *crampons, cornice, summit,* and *precipice.*

Block Scheduling Strategies

Consider these suggestions to take advantage of extended class time:

- Have students work in groups to discuss the Thematic Focus question in Literature and Your Life on p. 23. Groups can list character traits as well as outside resources, and then compare their lists with other class lists.
- After students have read the two narratives, encourage them to debate their responses to the two narratives from the Reader's Response in Literature and Your Life on p. 41. Students who prefer Hillary's account can present their reasons, and those who like Norgay's version can give their reasons.
- Have students work in pairs to complete and discuss the Critical Thinking questions on pp. 35 and 41.
- Suggest that students work in groups of three to write their Articles on Everest in the Idea Bank on p. 43. One student can write an editorial, one can write a news article, and one can write a profile of the climbers.

The Final Assault

from High Adventure

Edmund Hillary

I watched our support party disappear down the ridge and then turned to examine our campsite more closely. It wasn't really much of a place. Above us was a rock cliff—black and craggy, but at least devoid of loose stones to fall on us. From the foot of the cliff a little snow slope ran at an easy angle for eight or nine feet to the top of the steep and exposed South Face of the mountain. This little slope was to be our campsite. It was certainly far from flat and it was going to need a lot of work on it before we could possibly pitch a tent. We carefully moved all the gear to one side and then set to work with our ice axes to remove the surface snow off a reasonably large area. Ten inches down, we struck rock, and after an hour's hard work we had cleared an area about eight feet long and six feet wide. The slope underneath was made up of stones and rubble all firmly glued together with ice. This was much harder going. With the picks on our ice axes we chopped away at the slope, prizing out the separate stones and scraping away the rubble. But our progress was very slow. We weren't using any oxygen at all, but we found we could work very hard indeed for periods of ten minutes or so. Then we'd have to stop and have a short rest. With the debris we chopped out of the slope we tried to build up the platform on the downhill side, but almost invariably saw it collapse and go roaring down over the bluffs below. At times we were buffeted[1] by wind and snow, yet we worked doggedly on, knowing that our tent was our only 

1. **buffeted** (buf' it əd) *v.*: Beaten back as by repeated blows.

◀ **Critical Viewing** What can you conclude about Hillary based on his desire to conquer mountains like these? **[Draw Conclusions]** ❷

❶ **Clarification** Explain to students that at very high elevations, there is less oxygen than humans are used to. This can make it difficult to perform, both mentally and physically. You may wish to encourage students who have had experiences at high altitudes to share how they were affected by the thinness of the air. They may note that the altitude made them feel light-headed, short of breath, even sick to their stomachs.

▶Critical Viewing◀

❷ **Draw Conclusions** *Students may conclude that since Everest is very high and looks very dangerous, Hillary must be an adventurer who seeks challenges and danger. They may also observe that Hillary must be extremely brave to attempt to climb such a mountain.*

Read to Be Informed

These first-person selections introduce specific vocabulary and present a great deal of information about mountain climbing in general and the dangers of attempting to climb Mount Everest specifically. Students may wish to set a purpose for their reading to discover information and be informed. Additionally, students may wish to jot down notes, detailing information that they learn while reading the selections.

Customize for *Visual/Spatial Learners*

Visual/spatial learners can best comprehend these narratives if they continue to look at the photographs provided with the selections. The photographs of the mountains provide a visual reinforcement of the details of the struggles and achievement that the writers describe.

Humanities: Photography

Dramatic Photography This dramatic photograph shows part of the Himalayas—the mountain range that includes Mt. Everest. The photograph presents both the majesty and the menace of the mountains. The awesome spectacle suggests both why humans want to conquer these mountain peaks and the formidable challenge required to do so. Encourage students to study the mountains, and then use these questions for discussion.

1. What can you conclude about the weather in these mountains from the photograph? *It is cold, stormy, and changeable.*
2. What effect does the play of light and shadow in the photograph have? *It makes the mountains look both threatening and beautiful.*
3. What feelings does this photo evoke? *Answers may include fear, awe, or appreciation for the tremendous beauty of this jagged peak.*

◆ Build Grammar Skills

1 Compound Predicates Have students identify the two verbs in the compound predicate and discuss the effect the compound predicate has on the narrative. *The two verbs are crawled and stood; the compound predicate links the actions and helps show how difficult movement was.*

◆ Critical Thinking

2 Infer Ask students: What does this passage reveal about the importance of oxygen at these heights? *It shows that oxygen is vital to the climbers' physical and mental endurance; without sufficient oxygen, humans can't perform as well as they normally would.*

◆ Literary Focus

3 Author's Perspective The author speaks commendably about Norgay and describes Norgay's movements as he saw them.

▶Critical Viewing◀

4 Analyze *Because the mountain is much steeper closer to the summit (and therefore more arduous for climbers), it is necessary for Camps 8 and 9 to be spaced closer together than Camps 3 and 4, which are on a less steep part of the mountain. In addition, students may note that the air is much thinner toward the top, making it difficult for climbers to travel even short distances.*

Customize for
Visual/Spatial Learners
Have students study the photographs of the Himalayan Mountains that are included in the book. They may wish to extend their research on the Internet or in library resources. Choosing an art medium of their choice, students may enjoy planning and creating a three-dimensional re-creation of Mount Everest.

chance of survival against the rigors of the night.

1 At 6:30 A.M. we crawled slowly out of the tent and stood on our little ledge. Already the upper part of the mountain was bathed in sunlight. It looked warm and inviting, but our ledge was dark and cold. We lifted our oxygen onto our backs and slowly connected up the tubes to our face masks. My thirty-pound load seemed to crush me downward and stifled all enthusiasm, but when I turned on the oxygen 2 and breathed it deeply, the burden seemed to lighten and the old urge to get to grips with the mountain came back. We strapped on our crampons[2] and tied on our nylon rope, grasped our ice axes, and were ready to go.

2. **crampons** (kram′ pənz) *n.*: Pair of spiked iron plates fastened on climbers' shoes to prevent slipping.

I looked at the way ahead. From our tent very steep slopes covered with deep powder snow led up to a prominent snow shoulder on the southeast ridge about a hundred feet above our heads. The slopes were in the shade and breaking trail was going to be cold work. Still a little worried about my boots, I asked Tenzing to lead off. Always willing to do his share, and more than his share if necessary, Tenzing scrambled past me and tackled the slope. With powerful thrusts of his legs he

◆ Literary Focus Which details in this paragraph suggest that it is told from Hillary's perspective?

▼ Critical Viewing Why do you think Camps 8 and 9 are so close together compared with Camps 3 and 4? **[Analyze]** 4

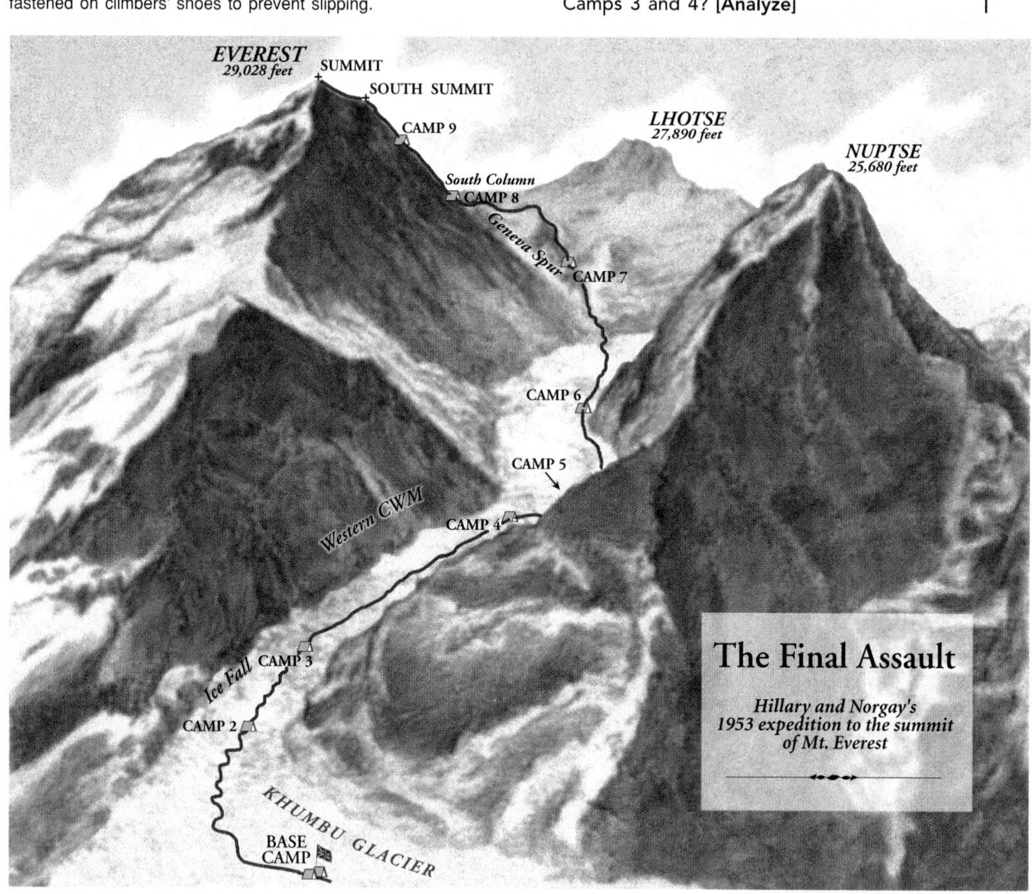

The Final Assault

Hillary and Norgay's 1953 expedition to the summit of Mt. Everest

Humanities: Photography

Enhanced Photography This enhanced photograph visually represents the heights of the mountains and the locations of the camps Hillary and Norgay made as they ascended Mt. Everest. You may want to point out that the enhancement of this photo, going beyond the beauty of the landscape, creates the visual effect of a map or diagram. Use these questions for discussion:

1. What can you learn from this map that you could not learn from an ordinary photograph? *This map shows the relative heights of the three mountains, the shape and terrain of the three mountains, and the route the climbers took.*
2. Why did the climbers follow such a circuitous route to the summit? *They had to find a safe and accessible route to ascend the mountain.*
3. What features does this map have that other maps you've seen do not share? *Students may note that the map has a three-dimensional quality and is very colorful and lifelike.*

forced his way up in knee-deep snow. I gathered in the rope and followed along behind him.

We were climbing out over the tremendous South Face of the mountain and below us snow chutes and rock ribs plummeted thousands of feet down to the Western Cwm.[3] Starting in the morning straight on to exposed climbing is always trying on the nerves and this was no exception. In imagination I could feel my heavy load dragging me backward down the great slopes below; I seemed clumsy and unstable and my breath was hurried and uneven. But Tenzing was pursuing an irresistible course up the slope and I didn't have time to think too much. My muscles soon warmed up to their work, my nerves relaxed, and I dropped into the old climbing rhythm and followed steadily up his tracks. As we gained a little height we moved into the rays of the sun, and although we could feel no appreciable warmth, we were greatly encouraged by its presence. Taking no rests, Tenzing plowed his way up through the deep snow and led out onto the snow shoulder. We were now at a height of 28,000 feet. Towering directly above our heads was the South Summit—steep and formidable. And to the right were the enormous cornices of the summit ridge. We still had a long way to go.

Ahead of us the ridge was sharp and narrow but rose at an easy angle. I felt warm and strong now, so took over the lead. First I investigated the ridge with my ice ax. On the sharp crest of the ridge and on the right-hand side loose powder snow was lying dangerously over hard ice. Any attempt to climb on this would only produce an unpleasant slide down toward the Kangshung Glacier. But the left-hand slope was better—it was still rather steep, but it had a firm surface of wind-blown powder snow into which our crampons would bite readily.

Taking every care, I moved along onto the left-hand side of the ridge. Everything seemed perfectly safe. With increased confidence I took another step. Next moment I was almost thrown off balance as the wind crust suddenly gave way and I sank through it up to my knee. It took me a little while to regain my breath. Then I gradually pulled my leg out of the hole. I was almost upright again when the wind crust under the other foot gave way and I sank back with both legs enveloped in soft loose snow to the knees. It was the mountaineer's curse—breakable crust. I forced my way along. Sometimes for a few careful steps I was on the surface, but usually the crust would break at the critical moment and I'd be up to my knees again. Though it was tiring and exasperating work, I felt I had plenty of strength in reserve. For half an hour I continued on in this uncomfortable fashion, with the violent balancing movement I was having to make completely destroying rhythm and breath. It was a great relief when the snow condition improved and I was able to stay on the surface. I still kept down on the steep slopes on the left of the ridge, but plunged ahead and climbed steadily upward. I came over a small crest and saw in front of me a tiny hollow on the ridge. And in this hollow lay two oxygen bottles almost completely covered with snow. It was Evans and Bourdillon's[4] dump.

I rushed forward into the hollow and knelt beside them. Wrenching one of the bottles out of its frozen bed, I wiped the snow off its dial—it showed a thousand pounds pressure—it was nearly a third full of oxygen. I checked the other—it was the same. This was great news. It meant that the oxygen we were carrying on our backs only had to get us back to these bottles instead of right down to the South Col. It gave us more than another hour of endurance. I explained this to Tenzing through my oxygen mask. I don't think he understood, but he realized I was pleased about something and nodded enthusiastically. (6)

◆ **Reading Strategy** Is it a fact or Hillary's opinion that Norgay did not understand Hillary's explanation? (7)

I led off again. I knew there was plenty of hard work ahead and Tenzing could save his energies for that. The ridge climbed on upward rather more steeply now and then broadened (8)

3. **Western Cwm** (ko͞om) *n.*: Steep, hollow hole in Everest's mountainside, made by glacial erosion.

4. **Evans and Bourdillon:** Mountain climbers who attempted unsuccessfully to ascend Mount Everest in 1951.

◆ Reading Strategy

5 Distinguish Fact From Opinion Ask students to identify the opinion in this passage and to explain how it is proven faulty. *"Everything seemed perfectly safe"; a moment later, Hillary faces danger.*

◆ Build Grammar Skills

6 Compound Predicates Have students identify the verbs in this compound predicate and explain the impact of the compound predicate on the narrative. *The verbs are* rushed *and* knelt; *the compound predicate helps show the speed with which Hillary moves to his important find—the oxygen bottles.*

◆ Reading Strategy

7 Distinguish Fact From Opinion Students should recognize that it is Hillary's opinion; there is no factual evidence to indicate Norgay doesn't understand. Additionally, the clue word *think* indicates Hillary is venturing an opinion.

Comprehension Check ☑

8 How does Hillary reveal that he is in charge of the expedition in this passage? *He makes the decision to lead and plans to reserve Norgay's strength—it is not a mutual decision.*

Cross-Curricular Connection: Science

Glaciers Point out the author's mention, on this page, of an "unpleasant slide down toward the Kangshung Glacier." Have students visually locate the Khumbu Glacier on p. 26. Explain that a glacier is a huge ice mass that actually moves, flowing very slowly—less than 1 foot per day. Glaciers form in very high mountains, such as the Himalayas. Low temperatures cause large amounts of snow to build up and turn into ice, up to 10,000 feet thick. The glacier shown on p. 26 is a *valley glacier*—a long, narrow "river" of ice that fills a high mountain valley.

Glaciers begin to form when more snow falls during the winter than melts and evaporates in summer. The excess snow gradually builds up in layers. Its increasing weight compresses the snow underneath into dense crystals of ice. The ice becomes so thick and heavy that the pull of gravity causes it to move downhill, while more ice layers continue to form at the top.

Glaciers can be seen in the United States in Alaska, on Mt. Rainier in Washington, and in Glacier National Park in Montana.

◆ Reading Strategy

1 Distinguish Fact From Opinion Ask students to explain why part of this statement is a fact and part of it is an opinion. *It is Hillary's opinion that the steepness of the slope is "appalling." That the South Summit of the mountain was 400 feet above them is a fact that could probably be proven.*

◆ Literary Focus

2 Author's Purpose What does Hillary reveal about the relationship between himself and Norgay? *Hillary is in charge; he determines what should be done and when, and he judges Norgay's efforts.*

Listening to Literature Audiocassettes You may wish to play the audiocassette at this point in the narrative. Suspense is mounting as the danger gets more intense; listening to the audiocassette can help students feel the sense of urgency and an awareness of the increasing danger.

Customize for
Less Proficient Readers
To check understanding, have these students pause at the end of the first paragraph on this page—before the paragraph beginning, "Ahead of us was a really formidable problem . . ." —to summarize what has happened up to this point. Then have them make predictions about what will happen as the story progresses. Encourage them to jot down their predictions and then revise them as they continue reading.

out and shot up at a sharp angle to the foot of the enormous slope running up to the South Summit. I crossed over onto the right-hand side of the ridge and found the snow was firm there. I started chipping a long line of steps up to the foot of the great slope. Here we stamped out a platform for ourselves and I checked our oxygen. Everything seemed to be going well. I had a little more oxygen left than Tenzing, which meant I was obtaining a slightly lower flow rate from my set, but it wasn't enough to matter and there was nothing I could do about it anyway.

Ahead of us was a really formidable problem and I stood in my steps and looked at it. Rising from our feet was an enormous slope slanting steeply down onto the precipitous East Face of Everest and climbing up with appalling steepness to the South Summit of the mountain 400 feet above us. The left-hand side of the slope was a most unsavory mixture of steep loose rock and snow, which my New Zealand training immediately regarded with grave suspicion, but which in actual fact the rock-climbing Britons, Evans and Bourdillon, had ascended in much trepidation when on the first assault. The only other route was up the snow itself, and still fairly discernible here and there were traces of the track made by the first assault party, who had come down it in preference to their line of ascent up the rocks. The snow route it was for us! There looked to be some tough work ahead, and as Tenzing had been taking it easy for a while I hardheartedly waved him through. With his first six steps I realized that the work was going to be much harder than I had thought. His first two steps were on top of the snow, the third was up to his ankles, and by the sixth he was up to his hips. But almost lying against the steep slope, he drove himself onward, plowing a track directly upward. Even following in his steps was hard work, for the loose snow refused to pack into safe steps. After a long and valiant spell he was plainly in need of a rest, so I took over.

Immediately I realized that we were on dangerous ground. On this very steep slope the snow was soft and deep with little coherence. My ice ax shaft sank into it without any support and we had no form of a belay. The only factor that made it at all possible to progress was a thin crust of frozen snow which tied the whole slope together. But this crust was a poor support. I was forcing my way upward, plunging deep steps through it, when suddenly with a dull breaking noise an area of crust all around me about six feet in diameter broke off into large sections and slid with me back through three or four steps. And then I stopped; but the crust, gathering speed, slithered on out of sight. It was a nasty shock. My whole training told me that the slope was exceedingly dangerous, but at the same time I

◆ Build Vocabulary

precipitous (prē sip′ ə təs) *adj.*: Steep

discernible (di zurn′ i bəl′) *adj.*: Recognizable; noticeable

belay (bi lā′) *n.*: Rope support

Beyond the Classroom

Community Connection

Outdoor Challenges Not many communities boast a 29,000-foot mountain to climb, but many do have physical endurance sites and activities, such as mountains, rivers, rock walls, caves, hiking trails, and so on. Cities, too, can offer similar challenges in sports centers, parks and outlying areas.

Ask students to name outdoor activities that the natural world in your community offers to its citizens. Encourage them to share stories of challenges they, themselves, have undertaken. Have them compare their feelings of accomplishment and success with Hillary's and Norgay's.

Interested students may wish to research challenging outdoor jobs and activities available in your community. They may locate clubs or organizations that travel together, have guest speakers, or lectures on outdoor topics. Others may note that photography of outdoor events is a challenge in itself. Guides, instructors, writers, and photographers all participate in the challenging adventures available in the outdoors.

was saying to myself, "Ed, my boy, this is Everest—you've got to push it a bit harder!" My solar plexus was tight with fear as I plowed on. Halfway up I stopped, exhausted. I could look down 10,000 feet between my legs and I have never felt more insecure. Anxiously I waved Tenzing up to me.

"What do you think of it, Tenzing?" And the immediate response, "Very bad, very dangerous!" "Do you think we should go on?" and there came the familiar reply that never helped you much but never let you down: "Just as you wish!" I waved him on to take a turn at leading. Changing the lead much more frequently now, we made our unhappy way upward, sometimes sliding back and wiping out half a dozen steps and never feeling confident that at any moment the whole slope might not avalanche. In the hope of some sort of a belay we traversed a little toward the rocks but found no help in their smooth holdless surface. We plunged on upward. And then I noticed that, a little above us, the left-hand rock ridge turned into snow and the snow looked firm and safe. Laboriously and carefully we climbed across some steep rock and I sank my ice ax shaft into the snow of the ridge. It went firm and hard. The pleasure of this safe belay after all the uncertainty below was like a reprieve to a condemned man.

Strength flowed into my limbs and I could feel my tense nerves and muscles relaxing. I swung my ice ax at the slope and started chipping a line of steps upward—it was very steep but seemed so gloriously safe. Tenzing, an inexpert but enthusiastic step cutter, took a turn and chopped a haphazard line of steps up another pitch. We were making fast time now and the slope was starting to ease off. Tenzing gallantly waved me through and with a growing feeling of excitement I cramponed up some firm slopes to the rounded top of the South Summit. It was only 9 A.M.

◆ **Literary Focus**
How might Hillary's assessment of Norgay's climbing skills differ from Norgay's perspective? ❺

With intense interest I looked at the vital ridge leading to the summit—the ridge about which Evans and Bourdillon had made such gloomy forecasts. At first glance it was an exceedingly impressive and indeed a frightening sight. In the narrow crest of this ridge, the basic rock of the mountain had a thin capping of snow and ice—ice that reached out over the East Face in enormous cornices,[5] overhanging and treacherous, and only waiting for the careless foot of the mountaineer to break off and crash

5. **cornices** (kôr′ nis əs) *n.*: Layers of ice and snow projecting over the top of a ridge.

Cross-Curricular Connection: Geography

The Himalayan Mountains Explain to students that the Himalayan Mountains were formed 27 to 70 million years ago, when two continental plates crashed together. The mountain system extends for about 1,500 miles through Pakistan, India, China, Nepal, Sikkim, Bhutan, and Tibet. The Himalayas are some of the highest mountains in the world. Many of the mountain passes are covered with snow most of the year and completely impassable. In fact, in Sanskrit, the word *Himalaya* means "Snowy Range." Because of the difficult terrain, few roads for vehicles exist, and transportation is largely on foot. In places, the mountains are as much as 200 miles wide. It is not difficult to understand why much of the area is uninhabited. The mountain system is still relatively young and suffers frequent earthquakes.

Have students locate the Himalayan Mountains on a world map or a map of Asia. Encourage them to find photographs of these mountains in library reference books, travel magazines, or on the Internet.

◆ *Literature and Your Life*

Toward the beginning of this page, Hillary remarks, "I could look down 10,000 feet between my legs and I have never felt more insecure." Draw students' attention to Hillary's observations. Then have them share their own experiences with heights. For example, they may have been to the top of a skyscraper, or they may have had experiences of their own on tall mountains. How did their reactions compare with Hillary's? *Students may respond that, like Hillary, they experienced fear when they looked down from a great height.* Considering their reactions to heights, would they ever consider climbing a tall mountain? Why or why not? *Many students may respond that they would have no desire to climb a tall mountain such as Everest.*

◆ Literary Focus

❸ **Author's Perspective** Ask students to describe how Hillary views Mt. Everest. What does this reveal about his character? *He sees Everest as a challenge and as something he can control. He is adventurous and confident.*

◆ Critical Thinking

❹ **Draw Conclusions** Ask students why they think Hillary asked Norgay's opinion of the situation. Does he like the answer Norgay gives? *He wanted to verify his own feelings of fear and anxiety. He liked the answer because it allowed him to make the decision.*

◆ Literary Focus

❺ **Author's Perspective** Norgay probably considers himself as good a step cutter as anyone else.

Customize for
Visual/Spatial Learners
Interested students may wish to research the location of mountains that climbers enjoy and frequently challenge. Have students list the frequently climbed mountains and then locate them on a world map. They may wish to analyze the information to determine if certain areas of the world are more challenging to mountain climbers.

◆ Critical Thinking

1 Make Judgments Have students determine whether the difference in the amount of oxygen the two men had left was significant. *The amount was not significant; Norgay had a little less than Hillary.*

◆ Reading Strategy

2 Distinguish Fact From Opinion It is Hillary's opinion that the ledge is safe. Although he forms this opinion on the basis of his mountain-climbing experience, it is not a fact that can be proven.

Customize for *Logical/Mathematical Learners*
Have these students work out the mathematical equations on this page. Exactly how long will the oxygen last the climbers?

Customize for *Less Proficient Readers*
Less proficient readers might need help understanding why Hillary was so excited at this point in the narrative. Explain that the hard, crystalline snow was strong enough to support steps that he could cut, easing the ascent.

10,000 feet into the Kangshung Glacier. And from the cornices the snow dropped steeply to the left to merge with the enormous rock bluffs which towered 8,000 feet above the Western Cwm. It was impressive all right! But as I looked, my fears started to lift a little. Surely I could see a route there? For this snow slope on the left, although very steep and exposed, was practically continuous for the first half of the ridge, although in places the great cornices reached hungrily across. If we could make a route along that snow slope we could go quite a distance at least.

With a feeling almost of relief I set to work with my ice ax and cut a platform for myself just down off the top of the South Summit. Tenzing did the same, and then we removed our oxygen sets and sat down. The day was still remarkably fine and we felt no discomfort through our thick layers of clothing from either wind or cold. We had a drink out of Tenzing's water bottle and then I checked our oxygen supplies. Tenzing's bottle was practically
1 exhausted, but mine still had a little in it. As well as this we each had a full bottle. I decided that the difficulties ahead would demand as light a weight on our backs as possible, so determined to use only the full bottles. I removed Tenzing's empty bottle and my nearly empty one and laid them in the snow. With particular care I connected up our last bottles and tested to see that they were working efficiently. The needles on the dials were steady on 3,300 pounds per square inch pressure—they were very full bottles, holding just over 800 liters of oxygen each. At 3 liters a minute we consumed 180 liters an hour, and this meant a total endurance of nearly 4 1/2 hours. This didn't seem much for the problems ahead, but I was determined if necessary to cut down to 2 liters a minute for the homeward trip.

I was greatly encouraged to find how, even at 28,700 feet and with no oxygen, I could work out slowly but clearly the problems of mental arithmetic that the oxygen supply demanded. A correct answer was imperative—any mistake could well mean a trip with no return. But we had no time to waste. I stood up and took a series of photographs in every direction, then thrust my camera back to its warm home inside my clothing. I heaved my now pleasantly light oxygen load onto my back and connected up my tubes. I did the same for Tenzing and we were ready to go. I asked Tenzing to belay me and then with a growing air of excitement I cut a broad and safe line of steps down to the snow saddle below the South Summit. I wanted an easy route when we came back up here weak and tired. Tenzing came down the steps and joined me and then belayed[6] once again.

I moved along onto the steep snow slope on the left side of the ridge. With the first blow of my ice ax my excitement increased. The snow—to my astonishment—was crystalline and hard. A couple of rhythmical blows of the ice ax produced a step that was big enough even for our oversize high-altitude boots. But best of all, the steps were strong and safe. A little conscious of the great drops beneath me, I chopped a line of steps for the full length of the rope—forty feet—and then forced the shaft of my ice ax firmly into the snow. It made a fine belay and I looped the rope around it. I waved to Tenzing to join me, and as he moved slowly and carefully along the steps I took in the rope as I went on cutting steps. It was exhilarating work—the summit ridge of Everest, the crisp snow, and the smooth, easy blows of the ice ax all combined to make me feel a greater sense of power than I had ever felt at great altitudes before. I went on cutting for rope length after rope length.

We were now approaching a point where one of the great cornices was encroaching onto our slope. We'd have to go down to the rocks to avoid it. I cut a line of steps steeply down the slope to a small ledge on top of the rocks. There wasn't much room, but it made a reasonably safe stance. I waved to Tenzing to join me. As he came down to me I realized there was something wrong with him. I had been so absorbed in the technical problems of the ridge that I hadn't thought much about Tenzing

> **◆ Reading Strategy**
> Is it a fact or an opinion that the ledge is "safe"? 2

6. **belayed** (bi lād′) *v.*: Supported by a rope.

except for a vague feeling that he seemed to move along the steps with unnecessary slowness. But now it was quite obvious that he was not only moving extremely slowly but was breathing quickly and with difficulty and was in considerable distress. I immediately suspected his oxygen set and helped him down onto the ledge so that I could examine it. The first thing I noticed was that from the outlet of his face mask there were hanging some long icicles. I looked at it more closely and found that the outlet tube—about two inches in diameter—was almost completely blocked up with ice. This was preventing Tenzing from exhaling freely and must have made it extremely unpleasant for him. Fortunately the outlet tube was made of rubber, and by manipulating this with my hand I was able to release all of the ice and let it fall out. The valves started operating and Tenzing was given immediate relief. Just as a check I examined my own set and found that it, too, had partly frozen up in the outlet tube, but not sufficiently to have affected me a great deal. I removed the ice out of it without a great deal of trouble. Automatically I looked at our pressure gauges—just over 2,900 pounds (2,900 pounds was just over 700 liters; 180 into 700 was about 4)—we had nearly four hours' endurance left. That meant we weren't going badly.

4 ▲ **Critical Viewing** What feelings are revealed in the expressions on Hillary's and Norgay's faces? **[Interpret]**

I looked at the route ahead. This next piece wasn't going to be easy. Our rock ledge was perched right on top of the enormous bluff running down into the Western Cwm. In fact, almost under my feet, I could see the dirty patch on the floor of the cwm which I knew was Camp IV. In a sudden urge to escape our isolation I waved and shouted, then as suddenly stopped as I realized my foolishness. Against the vast expanse of Everest, 8,000 feet above them, we'd be quite invisible to the best binoculars. I turned back to the problem ahead. The rock was far too steep to attempt to drop down and go around this pitch. The only thing to do was to try and shuffle along the ledge and cut handholds in the bulging ice that was trying to push me off it. Held on a tight rope by Tenzing, I cut a few handholds and then thrust my ice ax as hard as I could into the solid snow and ice. Using this to take my weight, I moved quickly along the ledge. It proved easier than I had anticipated. A few more handholds, another quick swing across them, and I was able to cut a line of steps up onto a safe slope and chop out a roomy terrace from which to belay Tenzing as he climbed up to me. 5

We were now fast approaching the most formidable obstacle on the ridge—a great rock step. This step had always been visible in aerial photographs and in 1951 on the Everest

◆ Build Vocabulary

encroaching (en krōch′ iŋ) *v.*: Trespassing or intruding

3 Clarification Point out that as Hillary and Norgay breathed through the tubes, the cold made the moisture in their breath freeze inside the tube, blocking their airways.

▶Critical Viewing◀

4 Interpret Students might indicate that Norgay's expression is of "delight," as Hillary indicated, while Hillary's expression is more subdued, but proud, as he also indicated.

◆ Build Grammar Skills

5 Compound Predicates Have students identify the two verbs in the main clause of this sentence. Ask them why Hillary performed these two actions. *The verbs are waved and shouted; he suddenly realized how completely alone he and Tenzing were.*

Customize for *Visual/Spatial Learners*

Have these students use this photograph, which shows the two climbers after their success on Everest, to help them picture Hillary and Norgay and to enhance their appreciation of the characters of the two climbers. Have them compare the expressions on Norgay's and Hillary's faces. Which of them looks more at ease? Why? *Norgay looks more relaxed, perhaps because his feelings about conquering Everest are more straightforward.* Ask: Do the two men look as if they are friends? Explain. *Answers should touch on the awkwardness of their body language and the fact that they are not looking at each other.*

Research Skills Mini-Lesson

Article on Everest

This mini-lesson supports the Writing activity in the Idea Bank on p. 43.

Introduce Because newspapers are often used for primary research, remind students that writing a newspaper article requires responsible and accurate interview and research techniques.

Develop Have students analyze several current newspaper articles and review the concept that they need to cover the *Who, What, When, Where, Why,* and *How* questions in their writing. Have them write down at least one interesting and relevant question they wish to research for each W topic.

Apply To make it easier to locate needed information and organize their notes, as students conduct their research have them use the text organizers Hillary employs in his writing—an overview at the beginning, times, and altitudes reached. As they write, remind students to cover the facts accurately and completely.

Assess Use the Research Report/Paper Scoring Rubric, p. 106, in ***Alternative Assessment*** to assess students' articles.

▶Critical Viewing◀

❶ **Analyze** *The sheer sides and the steepness suggest the difficulties of the climb; the border of clouds suggests the dangers of lack of oxygen.*

❷ **Clarification** Explain that the climbers' protective clothing is important because, even though the weather on Everest is good, the temperature is very low and the wind is strong, blowing ice at dangerously high speeds. The clothing provides warmth and protection from eye and skin damage.

◆ *Literature and Your Life*

❸ Students' answers will vary but should note Hillary's anxiety and desperation and focus on the various manifestations of fear when faced with a challenge, and the ability to overcome that fear.

Customize for *Visual/Spatial Learners*

Encourage these students to study the details of the photograph on this page and to use them to enhance their appreciation for the challenges that Hillary and Norgay faced as they completed their ascent. Draw their attention to the steepness of the face. Ask: How does the photograph help to illustrate the dangers that the two climbers faced? *Students should note such features as the steep cliffs and the snow and ice.*

❶ ▲ **Critical Viewing** What elements in this photograph suggest the dangers of climbing? **[Analyze]**

Reconnaissance we had seen it quite clearly with glasses from Thyangboche. We had always thought of it as the obstacle on the ridge which could well spell defeat. I cut a line of steps across the last snow slope and then commenced traversing[7] over a steep rock slab that led to the foot of the great step. The holds were small and hard to see and I brushed my snow glasses away from my eyes. Immediately I was ❷ blinded by a bitter wind sweeping across the ridge and laden with particles of ice. I hastily replaced my glasses and blinked away the ice and tears until I could see again. But it made me realize how efficient was our clothing in protecting us from the rigors of even a fine day at 29,000 feet. Still half-blinded, I climbed across the slab and then dropped down into a tiny snow hollow at the foot the step. And here Tenzing slowly joined me.

I looked anxiously up at the rocks. Planted squarely across the ridge in a vertical bluff, they looked extremely difficult, and I knew that our strength and ability to climb steep rock at this altitude would be severely limited. I examined the route out to the left. By dropping fifty or a hundred feet over steep slabs, we might be able to get around the bottom of the bluff, but there was no indication that we'd be able to climb back onto the ridge again. And to lose any height now might be fatal. Search as I could, I was unable to see an easy route up to the step or in fact any route at all. Finally, in desperation, I examined the right-hand end of the bluff. Attached to this and overhanging the precipitous East Face was a large cornice. This

> ◆ *Literature and Your Life*
> Compare Hillary's feelings of anxiety and fear with your own when faced with a difficult challenge. ❸

7. **traversing** (trə vurs′ iŋ) *v.*: Crossing.

Humanities: Photography

Photographic Perspective This photograph shows the peaks of the highest Himalayan mountains above a layer of clouds. The photographer's perspective presents a view that emphasizes the height of the peaks and presents a strong reminder of the difficulties and dangers of the problems associated with reduced oxygen at such altitudes. Encourage students to think about what it might be like to be perched on one of the peaks shown in this photograph. Then use these questions for discussion:

1. How does the photograph emphasize the height of the mountains? *By showing the clouds below the peaks, which makes it seem as if the mountains reach into the sky.*
2. Imagine mountain climbing above the cloud line. How might you feel? *Students may say they'd feel courageous, scared, proud, disoriented, or anxious.*
3. What makes photographs of mountain peaks beautiful and captivating? *Students may note that photographs can capture scenes that few people can witness firsthand.*

cornice, in preparation for its inevitable crash down the mountainside, had started to lose its grip on the rock and a long narrow vertical crack had been formed between the rock and the ice. The crack was large enough to take the human frame, and though it offered little security it was at least a route. I quickly made up my mind—Tenzing had an excellent belay and we must be near the top—it was worth a try.

Before attempting the pitch I produced my camera once again. I had no confidence that I would be able to climb this crack and with a surge of competitive pride which unfortunately afflicts even mountaineers I determined to have proof that at least we had reached a good deal higher than the South Summit. I took a few photographs and then made another rapid check of the oxygen—2,500 pounds pressure (2,550 from 3,300 leaves 750; 750 is about 2/9; 2/9 off 800 liters leaves about 600 liters; 600 divided by 180 is nearly 3 1/2. Three and a half hours to go. I examined Tenzing's belay to make sure it was a good one and then slowly crawled inside the crack.

In front of me was the rock wall, vertical but with a few promising holds. Behind me was the ice wall of the cornice, glittering and hard but cracked and there. I took a hold on the rock in front and then jammed one of my crampons hard into the ice behind. Leaning back with my oxygen set on the ice, I slowly levered myself upward. Searching feverishly with my spare boot, I found a tiny ledge on the rock and took some of the weight off my other leg. Leaning back on the cornice, I fought to regain my breath. Constantly at the back of my mind was the fear that the cornice might break off, and my nerves were taut with suspense. But slowly I forced my way up—wriggling and jamming and using every little hold. In one place I managed to force my ice ax into a crack in the ice, and this gave me the necessary purchase to get over a holdless stretch. And then I found a solid foothold in a hollow in the ice and next moment I was reaching over the top of the rock and pulling myself to safety. The rope came tight—its forty feet had been barely enough.

I lay on the little rock ledge panting furiously. Gradually it dawned on me that I was up the step and I felt a glow of pride and determination that completely subdued my temporary feeling of weakness. For the first time on the whole expedition I really knew I was going to get to the top. "It will have to be pretty tough to stop us now" was my thought. But I couldn't entirely ignore the feeling of astonishment and wonder that I'd been able to get up such a difficulty at 29,000 feet even with oxygen. 4

When I was breathing more evenly I stood and, leaning over the edge, waved to Tenzing to come up. He moved into the crack and I gathered in the rope and took some of his weight. Then he, in turn, commenced to struggle and jam and force his way up until I was able to pull him to safety—gasping for breath. We rested for a moment. Above us the ridge continued on as before—enormous overhanging cornices on the right and steep snow slopes on the left running down to the rock bluffs. But the angle of the snow slopes was easing off. I went on chipping a line of steps, but thought it safe enough for us to move together in order to save time. The ridge rose up in a great series of snakelike undulations which bore away to the right, each one concealing the next. I had no idea where the top was. I'd cut a line of steps around the side of one undulation and another would come into view. We were getting desperately tired now and Tenzing was going very slowly. I'd been cutting steps for almost two hours and my back and arms were starting to tire. I tried cramponing along the slope without cutting steps, but my feet slipped uncomfortably down the slope. I went on cutting. We seemed to have been going for a very long time and my confidence was fast evaporating. Bump followed bump with maddening regularity. A patch of shingle barred our way and I climbed

> **◆ Literary Focus**
> Which details in this paragraph reveal that it is told from Hillary's perspective? 5

6

◆ Build Vocabulary

undulations (un′ dyo͞o lā′ shənz) *n.*: Waves

Customize for *Logical/Mathematical Learners*
Have these students determine exactly how much time the climbers have left, assuming they have two ninths of 800 liters of oxygen remaining. *They had 3.4 hours left.*

◆ Reading Strategy

4 Distinguish Fact From Opinion Ask students if Hillary really knows that he will get to the top. *He does not know; this is just his opinion.*

◆ Literary Focus

5 Author's Perspective The description is entirely from Hillary's point of view, and he describes things as he would have seen them.

◆ Critical Thinking

6 Infer Ask students to infer what the climbers are experiencing from Hillary's description of Norgay's movements. *They are approaching exhaustion; Norgay's slow movements hint that he is very tired and perhaps low on oxygen.*

Speaking, Listening, and Viewing Mini-Lesson

Oral Report

This mini-lesson supports the Speaking, Listening, and Viewing activity in the Idea Bank on p. 43.

Introduce Remind students that, like a written report, an oral report needs a central idea that is clear from the beginning. The central idea should be supported by details that are logically organized. Have students brainstorm for aspects of mountain climbing, drawing on the narratives for report ideas such as climbing on ice and the use of oxygen.

Develop Encourage students to use library materials such as encyclopedias, reference books , and periodicals to find information. They should take notes and outline the information. Those students who would be uncomfortable delivering a report from an outline can write out their reports.

Apply Encourage students to make use of visual aids such as maps, charts, or photos, to add or enhance details and engage their listeners' interest. When they have prepared and practiced, have students present their reports to the class.

Assess Have students assess their own and others' reports in terms of (a) the organization of the information and (b) how well the central idea was presented and supported. You might have students use the Self and Peer Assessment sheets for a speech, pp. 117 and 118 in ***Alternative Assessment.***

◆ Literary Focus

❶ **Author's Perspective** Have students compare how Hillary describes his own feelings and those of Norgay at achieving the summit. *He describes his own feelings as those of powerful satisfaction, and says that Norgay felt sheer delight.*

Reinforce and Extend

Answers

◆ *Literature and Your Life*

Reader's Response: Some students will answer that they felt happy and relieved for Hillary and Norgay.

Thematic Focus: The character traits needed to face a difficult challenge are determination, dedication, hard work, discipline, and courage.

☑ Check Your Comprehension

1. Hillary and Norgay woke from their tents, waded through knee-deep snow, and struggled up the mountain. They paused at times to catch their breath and adjust their oxygen masks. They took turns plowing the trail and helped each other reach the summit.
2. They found oxygen masks from an earlier expedition. It is a helpful discovery because Norgay's oxygen level was low.
3. They reach the summit at 11:30 A.M.

◆ Critical Thinking

1. Some students might infer that Hillary thinks his partner's skills were inferior to his own.
2. Some students might suggest that Hillary exaggerated Norgay's distress in order to look like the stronger and more competent climber.
3. Even though Hillary and Norgay were from different backgrounds, they both shared a love of mountain climbing, a respect for Everest, and a desire to reach the summit.

Guide for Responding

◆ *Literature and Your Life*

Reader's Response How did you feel when Hillary and Norgay finally reached the summit of Everest? Explain your reaction.

Thematic Focus Norgay and Hillary possessed certain qualities that helped them reach the top. What character traits are needed to face a difficult challenge?

Group Discussion As a group, discuss why people are so interested in conquering mountains, raging rivers, and other wilderness challenges. Also, discuss whether or not you would try to climb to the summit of a mountain and why you would or would not.

☑ Check Your Comprehension

1. Summarize the events leading up to the reaching of the summit on the final day of climbing.
2. What does Hillary find in the snow? Why is it such a helpful discovery?
3. At what time do Hillary and Norgay reach the summit?

◆ Critical Thinking

INTERPRET

1. Why does Hillary continually mention the progress and condition of his partner? **[Infer]**
2. Do you think Norgay's oxygen situation was as critical as Hillary made it seem? Explain your answer. **[Make a Judgment]**

APPLY

3. After reading about the effort and energy required to conquer Everest, why do you think two men from such different backgrounds are able to help each other succeed? **[Speculate]**

dully up it and started cutting steps around another bump. And then I realized that this was the last bump, for ahead of me the ridge dropped steeply away in a great corniced curve, and out in the distance I could see the pastel shades and fleecy clouds of the highlands of Tibet.

To my right a slender snow ridge climbed up to a snowy dome about forty feet above our heads. But all the way along the ridge the thought had haunted me that the summit might be the crest of a cornice. It was too late to take risks now. I asked Tenzing to belay me strongly and I started cutting a cautious line of steps up the ridge. Peering from side to side and thrusting with my ice ax, I tried to discover a possible cornice, but everything seemed solid and firm. I waved Tenzing up to me. A few more whacks of the ice ax, a few very weary steps, and we were on the summit of Everest.

It was 11:30 A.M. My first sensation was one of relief—relief that the long grind was over; that the summit had been reached before our oxygen supplies had dropped to a critical level; and relief that in the end the mountain had been kind to us in having a pleasantly rounded cone for its summit instead of a fearsome and unapproachable cornice. But mixed with the relief was a vague sense of astonishment that I could have been the lucky one to attain the ambition of so many brave and determined climbers. It seemed difficult at first to grasp that we'd got there. I was too tired and too conscious of the long way down to safety really to feel any great elation. But as the fact of our success thrust itself more clearly into my mind I felt a quiet glow of satisfaction spread through my body—a satisfaction less vociferous but more powerful than I had ever felt on a mountaintop before. I turned and looked at Tenzing. Even beneath his oxygen mask and the icicles hanging from his hair I could see his infectious grin of sheer delight.

◆ Build Vocabulary

vociferous (vō sif´ ər əs) *adj.*: Loud; noisy

Cultural Connection

Sherpas Explain to students that the Sherpas are a distinct ethnic group of Nepal, who live mainly in the Himalayan Mountains. They live in the northeast part of Nepal in the high valleys. Because they are accustomed to high altitudes, they are popular as climbing guides or porters. In addition, many Sherpas make a living growing potatoes, wheat, and barley and herding goats, yaks, and sheep. A yak is a breed of oxen that is adapted to survival in the high altitudes of the Himalayas.

Many historians believe that the Sherpas immigrated to Nepal from Tibet. They continue to follow some of the customs and dress of their Tibetan forefathers and neighbors—their language is a Tibetan dialect, and they practice Lamaism, which is a form of Buddhism found in Tibet.

Some students may recall having seen a television advertisement highlighting the capabilities of the Internet in which a Sherpa advertises his service through his own Web site.

Connections to Today's World

In April 1996, writer and climber Jon Krakauer signed on as a client of an Everest expedition to report on the growing commercialization of Everest. As he horrifyingly discovered, climbing in the Himalayas is just as dangerous today as it was in Hillary's and Norgay's day.

from Into Thin Air

Jon Krakauer

Straddling the top of the world, one foot in Tibet and the other in Nepal, I cleared the ice from my oxygen mask, hunched a shoulder against the wind, and stared absently at the vast sweep of earth below. I understood on some dim, detached level that it was a spectacular sight. I'd been fantasizing about this moment, and the release of emotion that would accompany it, for many months. But now that I was finally here, standing on the summit of Mount Everest, I just couldn't summon the energy to care.

It was the afternoon of May 10. I hadn't slept in 57 hours. The only food I'd been able to force down over the preceding three days was a bowl of Ramen soup and a handful of peanut M&M's. Weeks of violent coughing had left me with two separated ribs, making it excruciatingly painful to breathe. Twenty-nine thousand twenty-eight feet up in the troposphere, there was so little oxygen reaching my brain that my mental capacity was that of a slow child. Under the circumstances, I was incapable of feeling anything but cold and tired.

* * *

I snapped four quick photos of Harris and Bourkeev [two guides] striking summit poses, and then turned and started down. My watch read 1:17 P.M. All told, I'd spent less than five minutes on the roof of the world.

After a few steps, I paused to take another photo, this one looking down the Southeast Ridge, the route we had ascended. Training my lens on a pair of climbers approaching the summit, I saw something that until this moment had escaped my attention. To the south, where the sky had been perfectly clear just an hour earlier, a blanket of clouds now hid Pumori, Ama Dablam, and the other lesser peaks surrounding Everest.

Days later—after six bodies had been found, after the search for two others had been abandoned, after surgeons had amputated the gangrenous right hand of my teammate Beck Weathers—people would ask why, if the weather had begun to deteriorate, had climbers on the upper mountain not heeded the signs? Why did veteran Himalayan guides keep moving upward, leading a gaggle of amateurs, each of whom had paid as much as $65,000 to be ushered safely up Everest, into an apparent death trap?

* * *

Climbers, as a species, are simply not distinguished by an excess of common sense. And that holds especially true for Everest climbers: When presented with a chance to reach the planet's highest summit, people are surprisingly quick to abandon prudence altogether.

Compare and contrast Krakauer's expedition to Hillary and Norgay's.

Connections to Today's World

Journalist Jon Krakauer was one of the survivors of a disastrous attempt on Everest in May 1996. He published his account of that trip in *Into Thin Air*. In these passages from his account of the tragic expedition, students will see that although technology and human knowledge may have advanced in the forty-three years between Hillary and Norgay's historic climb and Krakauer's expedition, the beautiful Mt. Everest remains as formidable—and as dangerous—as ever.

Reading this segment will help students to appreciate the enormity of Hillary and Norgay's accomplishment and stir debate about whether people who are not professional climbers should attempt to climb a peak as challenging as Everest. In addition, the segment should help enhance students' appreciation for the awesome power of nature. To ensure that students grasp this fact, make sure that they understand that the climbers were killed as a result of an incredibly violent and unforgiving storm that appeared virtually without warning.

Customize for *Pre-AP Students*

Encourage these students to extend their exploration of the dangers of Mt. Everest by reading the rest of Krakauer's book and sharing their reactions with the rest of the class.

Answer

In Krakauer's expedition, there were more climbers in the party, and the mortality rate was higher. Students might recognize that, unlike Hillary and Norgay's expedition, his was a commercial expedition involving amateurs.

Analyze Literary Criticism

In a letter to the editor of *Outside* magazine dated July 31, 1996, Anatoli Boukreev from Almaty, Kazakhstan criticizes Jon Krakauer's account, "Into Thin Air."

"While I have respect for Mr. Krakauer, share some of his opinions about high altitude guiding, and believe he did everything within his power to assist fellow climbers on that tragic day on Everest, I believe his lack of proximity to certain events and his limited experience at high altitude may have gotten in the way of his ability to objectively evaluate the events of summit day. My decision and actions were based upon more than twenty years of high altitude climbing experience."

Read Boukreev's evaluation of Krakauer's account of the fateful climb on Mt. Everest to the students. Then discuss his statements by asking students questions such as these:

1. Why do accounts of climbing Mt. Everest contain different assessments of the dangers and challenges? *Each climber analyzes the difficulties based on his or her own climbing experience and background.*
2. Do you agree with Boukreev that Krakauer was not experienced enough to offer an authoritative opinion? Why or why not? *Students may agree that Krakauer wasn't an expert climber without enough knowledge.*

Develop Understanding

One-Minute Insight In this narrative, Tenzing Norgay presents his perspective of the ascent of Everest and defends his competence in response to Hillary's account. Norgay also focuses on the mountain itself. His perspective provides a balance to Hillary's account.

◆ Literary Focus

❶ **Author's Perspective** Ask students what perspective Norgay brings to the conquering of Mt. Everest. *Tenzing presents a focus on the mountain as a force; he also is responding to Hillary's account.*

◆ Reading Strategy

❷ **Distinguish Fact From Opinion** This is Norgay's opinion of what Hillary has said. In fact, Norgay even directly states that he is presenting an opinion.

▶Critical Viewing◀

❸ **Infer** *The photo was probably taken at the end of the adventure; the men look tired and weathered. At the same time, however, they look as if they are relieved and have a sense of accomplishment.*

Art Transparency To help introduce this account of the historic conquest of Everest, have students brainstorm for challenges that cannot be met without great physical effort. Then display Art Transparency 3 and explain how Joan Brown met a physical challenge in her Alcatraz swim. After reading the selection, interested students might enjoy writing a prose or poetic account of a challenging situation that they have conquered or hope to conquer in the future.

The Dream Comes True *from* The Tiger of the Snows

Tenzing Norgay

Written in collaboration with James Ramsey Ullman

▲ Critical Viewing Do you think this photo was taken at the beginning or end of the climb? Explain. **[Infer]** ❸

From the south summit we first had to go down a little. Then up, up, up. All the time the danger was that the snow would slip, or that we would get too far out on a cornice that would then break away; so we moved just one at a time, taking turns going ahead, while the second one wrapped the rope around his ax and fixed the ax in the snow as an anchor. The weather was still fine. We were not too tired. But every so often, as had happened all the way, we would have trouble breathing and have to stop and clear away the ice that kept forming in the tubes of our oxygen sets. ❶ In regard to this, I must say in all honesty that I do not think Hillary is quite fair in the story he later told, indicating that I had more trouble than he with breathing and that without his help I might have been in serious difficulty. In my opinion our difficulties were the same—and luckily never too great—and we each helped and were helped by the other in equal measure.

❷ ◆ Reading Strategy Is this statement a fact or an opinion?

Anyhow, after each short stop we kept going, twisting always higher along the ridge between the cornices and the precipices. And at last we came to what might be the last big obstacle below the top. This was a cliff of rock rising straight up out of the ridge and blocking it off, and we had already known about it from aerial photographs and from seeing it through binoculars from Thyangboche.[1] Now it was a question of how to get over or around it, and we could find only one possible way. This was along a steep, narrow gap between one side of the rock and the inner

1. **Thyangboche** (tän bō´ chā): Village in Nepal.

Speaking, Listening, and Viewing Mini-Lesson

Working With Others

Introduce Point all that all workplaces, from construction sites to offices to Mt. Everest, depend upon successful working relationships. Discuss whether students think Hillary and Norgay had problems in their working relationship.

Develop Have students explore ways to establish and enhance working relationships. Encourage them to consider goals and how to achieve them:

- good communication
- clearly defined working roles
- ability to compromise
- ability to solve problems

Apply Students can work in groups to develop a handbook for successful work relationships. Have them include problems that might arise between workers and some methods to resolve them.

Assess Have groups exchange their handbooks and evaluate the suggested ways to handle work-related problems. They should consider the effectiveness of the proposed communication and compromise strategies and problem-solving ideas.

l Viewing What qualities do you think Norgay needed
le climbers through mountains like these? **[Speculate]** 

side of an adjoining cornice, and Hillary, now going first, worked his way up it, slowly and carefully, to a sort of platform above. While climbing, he had to press backwards with his feet against the cornice, and I belayed him from below as strongly as I could, for there was great danger of the ice giving way. Luckily, however, it did not. Hillary got up safely to the top of the rock and then held the rope while I came after.

Here again I must be honest and say that I do not feel his account, as told in *The Conquest of Everest*, is wholly accurate. For one thing, he has written that this gap up the rock wall was about forty feet high, but in my judgment it was little more than fifteen. Also, he gives the impression that it was only he who really climbed it on his own, and that he then practically pulled me, so that I "finally collapsed exhausted at the top, like a giant fish when it has just been hauled from the sea after a terrible struggle." Since then I have heard plenty about that "fish," and I admit I do not like it. For it is the plain truth that no one pulled or hauled me up the gap. I climbed it myself, just as Hillary had done; and if he was protecting me with the rope while I was doing it, this was no more than I had done for him. In speaking of this I must make one thing very plain. Hillary is my friend. He is a fine climber and a fine man, and I am proud to have gone with him to the top of Everest. But I do feel that in his story of our final climb he is not quite fair to me;

◆ **Literary Focus** How does Norgay's perspective differ from Hillary's? ❺

❻

▶Critical Viewing◀

❹ **Speculate** *Answers should mention Norgay's love and respect for the mountain helped him. He also needed knowledge of the mountain, weather, and climbing techniques, and he needed the ability to "read" the mountain.*

◆ Literary Focus

❺ **Author's Perspective** *Norgay feels that the rock wall was smaller than Hillary thought. He also believed that his climbing was as energetic as Hillary's.*

◆ Critical Thinking

❻ **Make Judgments** Ask students which version of the story they believe: Hillary's or Norgay's. Have them give reasons for their responses. *Some students may believe Hillary because he has little reason to lie; others may feel Norgay is truthful because Hillary may have been trying to make himself look heroic.*

Customize for
Less Proficient Readers
To help these students appreciate the contrasts between Hillary's and Norgay's views of the events, encourage them to record the points of view of the two men in a reader's log. They may even want to create a two-column chart—one column for Norgay's views and one column for Hillary's.

Customize for
Visual/Spatial Learners
The photograph on this page dramatically captures the steepness and jaggedness of the peak of Everest. Encourage these students to look carefully at the details of the photograph and to keep in mind these details as they read Norgay's account. They may even find it helpful to flip back to this photograph when they reach later points in Norgay's account.

Viewing and Representing Mini-Lesson

Book Jacket
This lesson supports the Writing activity in the Idea Bank on p. 43.

Introduce Book jackets, their illustrations, and information are important to the marketing and sales of a book. Information appearing on the book jacket must be accurately researched and attractively presented.

Develop Have students locate and study several book-jacket designs, analyzing the details on them and deciding what elements to include in their own designs:

- Author biography
- Short synopsis or highlights of the book
- Photographs

Apply Students will need appropriate information from the library, Internet, or their textbooks to distill the most important and effective information. Have them write the book-jacket copy and design visual elements for their book jackets.

Assess Have students display their book jackets and have the class evaluate each cover for thoroughness of research and creativity.

◆ *Literature and Your Life*

❶ *Answers might focus on feelings of hurt and anger and methods of bringing the truth to light.*

▶Critical Viewing◀

❷ **Infer** *Answers might mention feelings of accomplishment, awe, exhaustion, excitement, and fear.*

◆ Build Grammar Skills

❸ **Compound Predicates** Have students identify the compound predicate in this sentence. "I pick up two small stones and put them in my pocket." *The verbs are pick and put.*

Customize for
Less Proficient Readers
Draw these students' attention to the last sentence—"We were partners."—in the first paragraph. Point out that this sentence sums up one of the key points of Norgay's account. Urge students to look carefully for other sentences that appear at the beginnings or ends of paragraphs and seem to sum up main ideas. Tell students that looking closely at opening and closing sentences is an effective reading strategy to help them improve comprehension.

that all the way through he indicates that when things went well it was his doing and when things went badly it was mine. For this is simply not true. Nowhere do I make the suggestion that I could have climbed Everest by myself; and I do not think Hillary should suggest that he could have, or that I could not have done it without his help. All the way up and down we helped, and were helped by, each other—and that was the way it should be. But we were not leader and led. We were partners.

❶ ◆ *Literature and Your Life*
How would you respond to false accusations or rumors that were being spread about you?

On top of the rock cliff we rested again. Certainly, after the climb up the gap we were both a bit breathless, but after some slow pulls at the oxygen I am feeling fine. I look up; the top is very close now; and my heart thumps with excitement and joy. Then we are on our way again. Climbing again. There are

▲ **Critical Viewing** Describe how Hillary and Norgay must have felt as they looked ahead and back from this point. **[Infer]** ❷

still the cornices on our right and the precipice on our left, but the ridge is now less steep. It is only a row of snowy humps, one beyond the other, one higher than the other. But we are still afraid of the cornices and, instead of following the ridge all the way, cut over to the left, where there is now a long snow slope above the precipice. About a hundred feet below the top we come to the highest bare rocks. There is enough almost level space here for two tents, and I wonder if men will ever camp in this place, so near the summit of the earth. I pick up two small stones and put them in my pocket to bring back to the world below. Then the rocks, too, are beneath us. We are back among the snowy humps. They are curving off to the right, and each time we pass one I wonder, "Is the next the last one? Is the ❸

Humanities: Photography

Nepal: Mt. Everest by Paul Keel.

This photograph shows the peak of Everest from partway up the slope. Use these questions for discussion:

1. Why do you think the photographer chose to position the photo so that Mt. Everest is in that particular spot? *Mt. Everest is in front so it looks even bigger, and by showing the other peaks, the photographer allows the viewer to compare its size.*
2. How does Mt. Everest's peak compare with the other peaks in the photograph? *It is higher and more jagged, giving it a more imposing or threatening appearance.*

next the last?" Finally we reach a place where we can see past the humps, and beyond them is the great open sky and brown plains. We are looking down the far side of the mountain upon Tibet. Ahead of us now is only one more hump—the last hump. It is not a pinnacle. The way to it is an easy snow slope, wide enough for two men to go side by side. About thirty feet away we stop for a minute and look up. Then we go on. . . .

I have thought much about what I will say now: of how Hillary and I reached the summit of Everest. Later, when we came down from the mountain, there was much foolish talk about who got there first. Some said it was I, some Hillary. Some that only one of us got there—or neither. Still others that one of us had to drag the other up. All this was nonsense. And in Katmandu,[2] to put a stop to such talk Hillary and I signed a statement in which we said, "we reached the summit almost together." We hoped this would be the end of it. But it was not the end. People kept on asking questions and making up stories. They pointed to the "almost" and said, "What does that mean?" Mountaineers understand that there is no sense to such a question; that when two men are on the same rope they are *together*, and that is all there is to it. But other people did not understand. In India and Nepal, I am sorry to say, there has been great pressure on me to say that I reached the summit before Hillary. And all over the world I am asked, "Who got there first? Who got there first?"

> ◆ **Literary Focus**
> Which details indicate that the account is told from Norgay's perspective?

Again I say: it is a foolish question. The answer means nothing. And yet it is a question that has been asked so often—that has caused so much talk and doubt and misunderstanding—that I feel, after long thought, that the answer must be given. As will be clear, it is not for my own sake that I give it. Nor is it for Hillary's. It is for the sake of Everest—the prestige of Everest—and for the generations who will come after us. "Why," they will say, "should there be a mystery to this thing? Is there something to be ashamed of? To be hidden? Why can we not know the truth?" . . . Very well: now they will know the truth. Everest is too great, too precious, for anything but the truth. ❺

A little below the summit Hillary and I stopped. We looked up. Then we went on. The rope that joined us was thirty feet long, but I held most of it in loops in my hand, so that there was only about six feet between us. I was not thinking of "first" and "second." I did not say to myself, "There is a golden apple up there. I will push Hillary aside and run for it." We went on slowly, steadily. And then we were there. Hillary stepped on top first. And I stepped up after him.

So there it is: the answer to the "great mystery." And if, after all the talk and argument, the answer seems quiet and simple, I can only say that that is as it should be. Many of my own people, I know, will be disappointed at it. They have given a great and false importance to the idea that it must be I who was "first." These people have been good and wonderful to me, and I owe them much. But I owe more to Everest—and to the truth. If it is a discredit to me that I was a step behind Hillary, then I must live with that discredit. But I do not think it was that. Nor do I think that, in the end, it will bring discredit on me that I tell the story. Over and over again I have asked myself, "What will future generations think of us if we allow the facts of our achievement to stay shrouded in mystery? Will they not feel ashamed of us—two comrades in life and death—who have something to hide from the world?" And each time I asked it the answer was the same: "Only the truth is good enough for the future. Only the truth is good enough for Everest." ❻

Now the truth is told. And I am ready to be judged by it.

We stepped up. We were there. The dream had come true. . . .

What we did first was what all climbers do when they reach the top of their mountain. We shook hands. But this was not enough for Everest. I waved my arms in the air and then threw them around Hillary, and we thumped each other on the back until, even with the

2. **Katmandu** (kät′män do͞o′): Capital of Nepal.

◆ Literary Focus

❹ Author's Perspective *This account of who reached the top of Everest first describes Norgay's thoughts on the matter and reflects Norgay's feelings about the mountain.*

◆ Critical Thinking

❺ Draw Conclusions Ask students why Norgay feels it is important to tell the truth about what happened at the summit. *He respects the mountain and feels its greatness deserves a truthful account.*

◆ Literary Focus

❻ Author's Perspective Have students summarize Norgay's view of the issue. *Norgay states that Hillary stepped first on the peak of Everest. He feels that it's important that everyone know the truth, regardless of how people will receive it.*

Beyond the Classroom

Career Connection

Guides Tenzing Norgay worked as a guide for mountain climbers in the Himalayas. He was suited for the work because he knew the mountains and their dangers and was accustomed to living at high altitudes. Many people who love the outdoors hold jobs as guides in the United States. Some take people on adventurous treks, such as river rafting, rock climbing, or sailing. Others lead hunting or fishing parties in wilderness areas. Still others conduct nature walks, pointing out wildflowers, birds, and trees. Interested students can research what a guide needs to know and what training would benefit a guide. They can explore the organizations that employ guides, such as the National Park Service and private and local organizations, and learn what each type of organization requires of its guides.

▶Critical Viewing◀

❶ **Connect** *Answers should mention the photograph is particularly dramatic, with the peaks highlighted in the sun; in this sense, it might reflect the climbers' sense of triumph.*

◆ Literary Focus

❷ **Author's Perspective** How do Norgay's feelings about Everest as described here compare with Hillary's feelings? *Norgay feels that the mountain is almost a living thing, to be loved and respected, while Hillary treats it as a challenge to be conquered.*

❸ **Clarification** Explain to students that Norgay feels the Indian or Nepalese flag should have been highest because the mountain itself—located on the border of Nepal and Tibet, just north of India—is more important than those who climbed it.

Customize for
Visual/Spatial Learners
Students who learn best through visual aids might benefit from looking back at the map on page 26 and noting the landmarks that Norgay describes. Have them locate the Khumbu Glacier, the South Column, and the peaks of Lhotse and Nuptse.

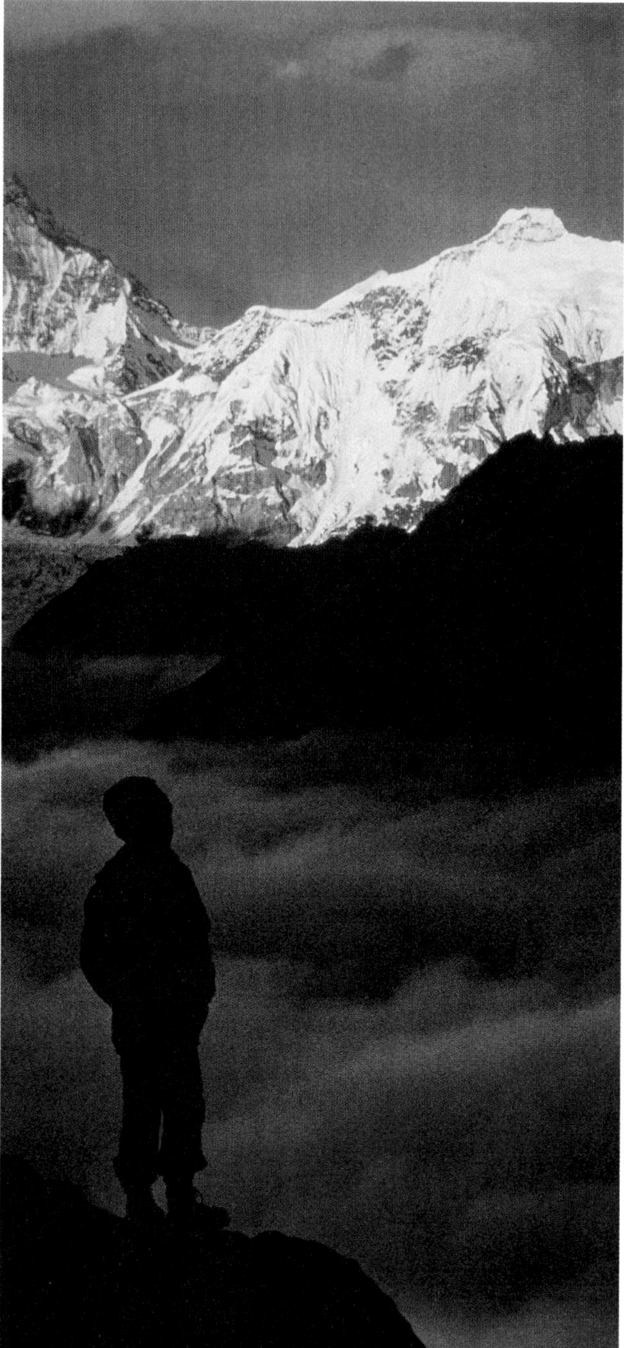

◀ **Critical Viewing** How does this image reflect the climbers' triumph? **[Connect]** ❶

oxygen, we were almost breathless. Then we looked around. It was eleven-thirty in the morning, the sun was shining, and the sky was the deepest blue I have ever seen. Only a gentle breeze was blowing, coming from the direction of Tibet, and the plume of snow that always blows from Everest's summit was very small. Looking down the far side of the mountain, I could see all the familiar landmarks from the earlier expeditions: the Rongbuk Monastery, the town of Shekar Dzong, the Kharta Valley, the Rongbuk and East Rongbuk Glaciers, the North Col, the place near the northeast ridge where we had made Camp Six in 1938. Then, turning, I looked down the long way we ourselves had come: past the south summit, the long ridge, the South Col; onto the Western Cwm, the icefall, the Khumbu Glacier; all the way down to Thyangboche and on to the valleys and hills of my homeland.

Beyond them, and around us on every side, were the great Himalayas, stretching away through Nepal and Tibet. For the closer peaks—giants like Lhotse, Nuptse and Makalu—you now had to look sharply downward to see their summits. And farther away, the whole sweep of the greatest range on earth—even Kangchenjunga[3] itself—seemed only like little bumps under the spreading sky. It was such a sight as I had never

3. **Kangchenjunga** (kän′ chən jo͝on′ gə): Third highest mountain in the world, lies near Mount Everest.

Reteach

Students may have difficulty differentiating between opinion and fact when confronting two accounts of the same event. Point out that Hillary and Norgay would have tried to portray themselves and their abilities in the best possible light. Students may find it helpful to understand the difference between fact and opinion if they find details in both accounts that agree. Have students draw a Venn diagram. In one circle, students will label and list details as told by Hillary, on the other, details related by Norgay. Have them analyze the details that are found where the two circles overlap. Because these details are agreed upon by both authors, they are more likely to be facts.

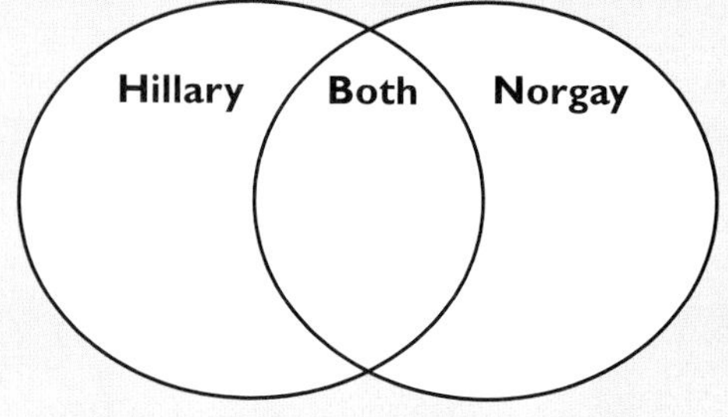

seen before and would never see again:
wild, wonderful and terrible. But terror
was not what I felt. I loved the mountains too well for that. I loved Everest too
well. At that great moment for which I
had waited all my life my mountain did
not seem to me a lifeless thing of rock
and ice, but warm and friendly and liv-
2 ing. She was a mother hen, and the
other mountains were chicks under her
wings. I too, I felt, had only to spread my
own wings to cover and shelter the brood
that I loved.

We turned off our oxygen. Even there on top of the world it was possible to live without it, so long as we were not exerting ourselves. We cleared away the ice that had formed on our masks, and I popped a bit of sweet into my mouth. Then we replaced the masks. But we did not turn on the oxygen again until we were ready to leave the top. Hillary took out his camera, which he had been carrying under his clothing to keep it from freezing, and I unwound the four flags from around my ax. They were tied together on a string, which was fastened to the blade of the ax, and now I held the ax up and Hillary took my picture. Actually he took three, and I think it was lucky, in those difficult conditions, that one came out so well. The order of the flags from top to bottom was United Nations, British, Nepalese, Indian; and the same sort of people who have made
trouble in other ways have tried to find
political meaning in this too. All I can
say is that on Everest I was not thinking
3 about politics. If I had been, I suppose I
would have put the Indian or Nepalese
flag highest—though that in itself would
have been a bad problem for me. As it is, I am glad that the U.N. flag was on top. For I like to think that our victory was not only for ourselves—not only for our own nations—but for all men everywhere.

Guide for Responding

◆ Literature and Your Life

Reader's Response Whose account of climbing Everest was more appealing to you—Hillary's or Norgay's? Why?

Thematic Focus Hillary and Norgay spent many years preparing themselves mentally and physically for the climb of their lives. Discuss ways in which you prepare yourself—mentally and physically—for a challenging task.

Role Play With a partner, take turns role-playing a conversation with Tenzing Norgay. Ask him questions about his preparation and attitude and how they helped him conquer Everest. Also, ask his advice on how you can prepare yourself for challenges you face.

☑ Check Your Comprehension

1. What qualities does Norgay possess that helped contribute to his success?
2. Who does Norgay say reached the summit first?
3. What do Norgay and Hillary do when they reach the top of Everest?

◆ Critical Thinking

INTERPRET

1. Why is Norgay so bothered by the comparison Hillary makes between Norgay and a "giant fish"? **[Connect]**
2. (a)Why do you think Norgay is so concerned with the "prestige of Everest"? (b) What does he mean by "Everest and the truth"? **[Analyze]**

EVALUATE

3. Norgay calls Hillary his friend at the beginning of this excerpt. Do you think that was a sincere compliment? Why or why not? **[Evaluate]**

COMPARE LITERARY WORKS

4. Based on the content of each text, compare and contrast Hillary's and Norgay's purposes for writing. **[Compare and Contrast]**

Reinforce and Extend

Answers

◆ Literature and Your Life

Reader's Response Some students might think Hillary's was more appealing because it was more detailed about the climb itself. Others might prefer Norgay's.

Thematic Focus Some students might say they prepare themselves for a challenge by working out and getting into shape or by studying, if their challenge is some kind of test.

☑ Check Your Comprehension

1. He possesses determination, courage, patriotism, and a great love for Everest.
2. Norgay said that Hillary stepped up first.
3. They shake hands, pat each other on the back, and then remove their oxygen.

◆ Critical Thinking

1. One acceptable answer is Norgay is so upset because he considered himself Hillary's equal climbing partner.
2. (a) He is concerned with the "prestige of Everest" because he grew up in the foothills of Everest and wants to preserve its mystique. (b) He wants the truth to be known about who stepped up first to put an end to the questions and also to assert that it is an insignificant matter.
3. Some students might suggest that Norgay believed Hillary to be his friend and that is why he was so hurt by his account of Everest.
4. Both men want to relate the story of the expedition. Hillary seems to want to proclaim his achievement, while Norgay seems to focus on his individual perspective on events.

Beyond the Selection

FURTHER READING

Other Works by Hillary and Norgay

High Adventure, Sir Edmund Hillary
After Everest, Tenzing Norgay

Other Works About Reaching the Top

The Shining Mountain: Two Men on Changabang's West Wall, Peter Boardman
The Spirit of St. Louis, Charles A. Lindbergh
Into Thin Air, Jon Krakauer

We suggest that you preview these works before recommending them to students.

INTERNET

You and your students may find additional information about these authors and Mt. Everest on the Internet. We suggest the following sites. Please be aware, however, that sites may have changed from the time we published this information. For wonderful photographs and a guide to what it feels like to climb Mt. Everest, go to **http://www. 1997everest.com/**

We *strongly recommend* that you preview the site before you send students to it.

Answers

◆ Reading Strategy

1. Hillary states a fact that he found oxygen tanks and an opinion that Norgay was in distress during the climb. Norgay states the fact that Hillary was the first to reach the summit and the opinion that it is not important who reached the top first.
2. It is an opinion because it cannot be proven.
3. The two men have different accounts of whether or not Norgay was in distress as he climbed and on whether or not they were equal partners.

◆ Literary Focus

1. Hillary's account includes these details: Norgay was an "inexpert step cutter"; Norgay was in "considerable distress" toward the end of the climb; Norgay had no idea why finding the oxygen tanks is positive.
2. Norgay's account includes (1) that he and Hillary were equal partners and that Hillary could not have climbed Everest alone; (2) that it is not important who reached the summit first; it was still a joint effort.
3. Hillary's excitement is more controlled and internal, while Norgay shows more joy.
4. Someone who was not involved would have a broader perspective—perhaps focusing on the challenge of the environment rather than on either climber's views.

◆ Build Vocabulary

Using the Latin Root *-voc-*

1. vocal: of or pertaining to the voice
2. vocabulary: the words a person knows and uses
3. vocalist: singer

Using the Word Bank

1. b 2. a 3. a 4. c 5. b 6. c

Guide for Responding *(continued)*

◆ Reading Strategy

Distinguish Fact From Opinion

Norgay and Hillary include many **facts**—statements that can be proven—in their accounts of the climb up Everest. They also include their **opinions**, statements that can be supported but not proved. For instance, Norgay supports his statement that Hillary was not quite fair with examples from Hillary's writing. However, since the statement cannot be proved true or false by evidence, it is an opinion.

1. Identify one fact and one opinion that each climber states about the other.
2. Hillary calls Norgay "an inexpert but enthusiastic step cutter." Explain whether this statement is a fact or an opinion.
3. List two examples of the writers' different opinions about the same events.

◆ Literary Focus

Author's Perspective

Like most nonfiction works, "The Final Assault" and "The Dream Comes True" are each told from one **author's perspective**—the presentation of events that reflects the author's personal outlook and recollection of the experience. For example, from Hillary's perspective, Norgay often struggled and needed Hillary's help during their ascent of Everest. However, from Norgay's perspective, the climbers helped each other equally.

1. List three details in the account told from Hillary's perspective that are not included in the account told from Norgay's perspective.
2. List two details in the account told from Norgay's perspective that are not included in the account told from Hillary's perspective.
3. Compare the two writers' perspectives on the final moment of the climb—reaching the summit.
4. In what ways might an account of Hillary and Norgay's expedition written by someone who was not involved in the expedition be different from these first-person accounts?

◆ Build Vocabulary

Using the Latin Root *-voc-*

The Latin root *-voc-* means "speak" or "say." Define each of these words. Explain how the definition of each word is related to "speaking" or "saying."

1. vocal **2.** vocabulary **3.** vocalist

Using the Word Bank: Synonyms

Write the letter of the word that is the best synonym, or closest meaning, of the first word.

1. precipitous: (a) rainy, (b) steep, (c) noisy
2. discernible: (a) visible, (b) agreeable, (c) ornery
3. belay: (a) support, (b) hindrance, (c) alcove
4. encroaching: (a) growing, (b) helping, (c) invading
5. undulations: (a) holes, (b) waves, (c) shivers
6. vociferous: (a) timid, (b) uneventful, (c) loud

◆ Build Grammar Skills

Compound Predicates

A **compound predicate** consists of two or more verbs or verb phrases that share the same subject and are joined by a conjunction.

Practice On your paper, copy the following sentences. Then write *S* over each subject and *V* over each verb in the compound predicates.

1. Hillary chipped away at ice, secured his rope support, and hoisted himself up to the next level.
2. Making their way up the mountain, they sometimes slid back, sometimes changed leads, and always hoped they would conquer Everest.
3. Norgay checked his oxygen level, paused to adjust his backpack, and then trudged on.

Writing Application Combine the following sentences, using compound predicates.

1. Hillary and Norgay cleared away ice and rocks. They pitched a tent. They prepared their gear for the following day.
2. Hillary waited for Norgay to catch his breath. He also helped him secure his oxygen mask. Then Hillary paved a trail for Norgay to follow.

◆ Build Grammar Skills

1. *Subject:* Hillary; *verbs:* chipped, secured, hoisted
2. *Subject:* they; *verbs:* slid, changed, hoped
3. *Subject:* Norgay; *verbs:* checked, paused, trudged

Writing Application

1. Hillary and Norgay cleared away ice and rocks, pitched their tent, and prepared their gear for the following day.
2. Hillary waited for Norgay to catch his breath, helped him secure his oxygen mask, and paved a trail for Norgay to follow.

Grammar Reinforcement

For additional instruction and practice, use the lesson in the **Language Lab CD-ROM** on Subject and Verb Agreement and the pages on Subjects and Verbs (pp. 26–29) in the *Writer's Solution Grammar Practice Book.*

Build Your Portfolio

Idea Bank

Writing

1. **Book Jacket** Write a summary for the back-cover of either Hillary's or Norgay's book. Highlight a gripping scene or suspenseful moment to entice your readers to read the book.

2. **Article on Everest** Write a newspaper article about the first successful Everest climb based on what you learned from Hillary's and Norgay's accounts. Include an attention-grabbing headline.

3. **Mountain's Eye View** Write a description of what you think the world looks like from the top of Everest based on the descriptions you read about in the selections.

Speaking, Listening, and Viewing

4. **Advice for Future Climbers** Drawing from the details in one or both of the selections, prepare a brief talk in which you provide advice to aspiring climbers. Present your talk to the class.

5. **Oral Report** Using information in these selections and facts that you gather through research, prepare and present a brief oral report on an aspect of mountain climbing. **[Science Link]**

Researching and Representing

6. **Everest Statistics** Create a chart illustrating some statistics related to Mount Everest. For example, how many people have attempted to climb it, and how many have succeeded? How many have died trying? **[Math Link]**

7. **Video Game Design** Design the graphics for a video game based on this story. Present your ideas in a series of sketches. Show what the game screens will look like, how the players will move, and where the hazards will be. **[Art Link]**

Online Activity www.phlit.phschool.com

Guided Writing Lesson

Hall-of-Fame Placards

Choose your favorite sport—it doesn't have to be mountain climbing—and write **placards**—display cards that briefly describe a player's achievements, statistics, and accomplishment—for your favorite players. The following tip will help you indicate the time order of events.

Writing Skills Focus: Transitions to Show Time

When writing your placards, use **transitions to show time.** Transitional words that show time include *first, next, finally, before, after, later,* and *at the same time.*

Tenzing Norgay uses transitions to show what happened first and next as he recalls his famous climb:

> From the south summit we *first* had to go down a little. *Then* up, up, up.

As you draft, use transitions to show the order of events and achievements you jotted down in prewriting. Check for clear transitions when you revise.

Prewriting Begin by making individual lists for each athlete, recording his or her statistics, achievements, and any interesting anecdotes you may discover. Choose only the most significant statistics and facts and arrange them in time order.

Drafting As you draft each placard, be sure to write your facts and statistics using transitions to show time. For example, you might start by saying "First ___?___ did ___?___. Then ___?___. Finally ___?___ capped his career off with ___?___."

Revising Have a friend read your placards and see if the time relations are clear. If not, you may need to insert transitions where your readers may get confused.

ASSESSMENT OPTIONS

Formal Assessment, Selection Test, pp. 4–6, and Assessment Resources Software. The selection test is designed so that it can be easily customized to the performance levels of your students.

Alternative Assessment, p. 2, includes options for less advanced students, Pre-AP Students, logical/mathematical learners, visual/spatial learners, bodily/kinesthetic learners, and intrapersonal learners.

PORTFOLIO ASSESSMENT

Use the following rubrics in the ***Alternative Assessment*** booklet to assess student writing:
Book Jacket: Process Summary Rubric, p. 98
Article on Everest: Description Rubric, p. 97
Mountain's Eye View: Description Rubric, p. 97
Guided Writing Lesson: Description Rubric, p. 97

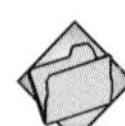

Idea Bank

Following are suggestions for matching Idea Bank topics with your students' performance levels and learning modalities:

Customizing for *Performance Levels*
Less Advanced Students: 1, 4,
Average Students: 2, 4, 6, 7
Pre-AP Students: 3, 5

Customizing for *Learning Modalities*
Visual/Spatial: 3, 6, 7
Verbal/Linguistic: 4, 5
Logical/Mathematical: 6

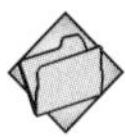

Guided Writing Lesson

Revision Strategy Explain to students that transition words help readers find their way through writing just as signposts help travelers find their way along roads. After they have written their placards, have students reenter their writing and highlight every transition word they used. Next, have them write these words in order on a clean sheet of paper. They should make sure the transition words appear in a logical chronological order and make the appropriate revisions if they do not. They should also be sure that there are no major gaps in time between two transition words. If there are, students should consider whether signposts would be helpful to readers in these parts of their writing and insert them where they deem necessary.

For more prewriting, elaboration, and revision strategies, see *Prentice Hall Writing and Grammar.*

Writers at Work Videodisc
Have students view the videodisc segment (Ch. 1) featuring Colleen McElroy to see some techniques for descriptive writing. Have students discuss the points McElroy makes about the elements of good description.

Play frames 335 to 9140

Writing Lab CD-ROM
Have students complete the tutorial on Description. Follow these steps:

1. Have students browse through the word bin for character trait words to use on their placards.
2. Have students draft on computer.
3. Invite pairs of students to answer the questions of a peer evaluation checklist to help them evaluate each other's placards.

Prepare and Engage

LESSON OBJECTIVES

1. **To develop vocabulary and word identification skills**
   - Latin Word Roots *-cred-*
   - Using the Word Banks: Synonyms
   - Extending Word Study: Use Text Organizers (ATE)
2. **To use a variety of reading strategies to comprehend a short story**
   - Connect Your Experience
   - Reading Strategy: Predict Outcomes
   - Tips to Guide Reading: Use Text Organizers (ATE)
   - Read to Be Entertained (ATE)
   - Idea Bank: Newspaper Headlines
   - Idea Bank: Warning Label
3. **To increase knowledge of other cultures and to connect common elements across cultures**
   - Connecting Themes Across Cultures (ATE)
4. **To express and support responses to the text**
   - Critical Thinking
   - Idea Bank: Paw Proposal
5. **To analyze literary elements**
   - Literary Focus: Foreshadowing
6. **To read in order to research self-selected and assigned topics**
   - Questions for Research
   - Idea Bank: Poster Showing Fortunes
7. **To plan, prepare, organize, and present literary interpretations**
   - Speaking, Listening, and Viewing Mini-Lesson: Television Interview (ATE)
   - Idea Bank: Dramatic Monologue
8. **To use recursive writing processes to write a prediction**
   - Guided Writing Lesson
9. **To increase knowledge of the rules of grammar and usage**
   - Build Grammar Skills: Regular and Irregular Verbs

Test Preparation

Reading Comprehension: Using Context Clues to Determine Word Meanings (ATE, p. 45) The teaching tips and sample test item in this workshop support the instruction and practice in the unit workshop:

Reading Comprehension: Using Context Clues to Determine Word Meanings (SE, p. 113)

Guide for Reading

W. W. Jacobs *(1863–1943)*

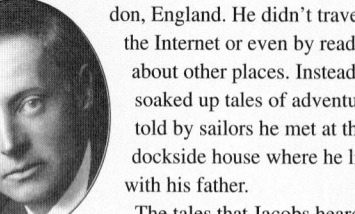

As a boy, W. W. Jacobs traveled around the world without ever leaving his home in London, England. He didn't travel via the Internet or even by reading about other places. Instead, he soaked up tales of adventure told by sailors he met at the dockside house where he lived with his father.

The tales that Jacobs heard as a child shaped the stories he wrote as an adult—stories in which everyday life is disrupted by strange and fantastic events.

"The Monkey's Paw" is his most famous tale of suspense and the supernatural. First published in 1902, it was made into a successful one-act play a year later.

One reason for the story's popularity is that it hardly seems like a story that someone wrote. It is more like an age-old tale made up by no one in particular and told around a campfire at night.

Alexander Pushkin *(1799–1837)*

This father of modern Russian literature is more like an adventurous teenager than a settled "father." Although born into the nobility, he had great sympathy for poor Russian peasants and criticized the absolute power and corruption of the government. His dangerous opinions and friendships got him banished to a remote part of Russia and later to his family's estate.

In literature, too, he was a rebel. His poems express his democratic ideas and draw on themes from folklore, the oral literature of the people. "The Bridegroom," for example, is like a literary version of a song passed on by word of mouth.

Pushkin's own death was like an incident from a folk tale or ballad. Resettled in the capital city of St. Petersburg, he was as hotheaded as ever and died after being wounded in a duel.

◆ Build Vocabulary

LATIN WORD ROOTS: *-cred-*

In "The Monkey's Paw," a character smiles "shamefacedly at his own credulity." The meaning of the Latin word root *-cred-* is "believe"; *credulity* means "a tendency to believe something too quickly."

doughty
maligned
credulity
prosaic
avaricious
furtively
fusillade
foreboding
tumult

WORD BANK

As you read these selections, you will encounter the words on this list. Each word is defined on the page where it first appears. Preview the list before you read.

◆ Build Grammar Skills

REGULAR AND IRREGULAR VERB FORMS

A verb has four basic forms known as principal parts: the present (also known as the infinitive), the present participle, the past, and the past participle. All verbs form the present participle by adding *-ing* to the present form. **Regular** verbs form their past and past participles by adding *-d* or *-ed* to the present form. Other verbs are **irregular**; they form their past and past participles in some other way.

Regular: . . . the fire *burned* brightly

Irregular: . . . *said* Mr. White, the old man *rose* . . .

It is important to know the irregular forms so that you can use them correctly.

Prentice Hall Literature Program Resources

REINFORCE / RETEACH / EXTEND

Selection Support
Build Vocabulary: Word Roots: *-cred-*, p. 10
Build Grammar Skills: Regular and Irregular Verb Forms, p. 11
Reading Strategy: Predict Outcomes, p. 12
Literary Focus: Foreshadowing, p. 13

Strategies for Diverse Student Needs, p. 3.

Beyond Literature
Cross-Curricular Connection: Community Action, p. 3

Formal Assessment Selection Test, pp. 7–9; Assessment Resources Software

Alternative Assessment, p. 3

Writing and Language Transparencies
Daily Language Practice Week 2, p. 113

Resource Pro CD-ROM

Listening to Literature Audiocassettes

The Monkey's Paw ◆ The Bridegroom

◆ *Literature and Your Life*

Connect Your Experience

Fate, chance, and *luck* are words that hint at mysterious forces out of your control. Your team, for example, might seem fated to win a championship, as if the outcome were determined beforehand.

By contrast, the words *choice, will,* and *determination* suggest that you can control the outcome of events. If you're losing in any situation, the answer is to get determined, figure out the problems, and make some choices.

The characters in this story and poem believe that they *can* choose the future. You'll soon see whether or not they get the future they choose.

Journal Writing Describe a situation whose outcome seemed to be decided by fate, luck, or chance. Then describe a situation that you influenced through your own choices.

Thematic Focus: Daring Decisions

This story and poem will help you think about the power you have to influence events.

◆ Background for Understanding

Culture

The concept of fate—a force that determines the outcome of events before they occur—plays a key role in "The Monkey's Paw." Ancient peoples sometimes worshiped fate in the form of one or more goddesses. The ancient Greeks, for example, pictured fate as three goddesses, weavers of human destiny: Clotho (klō´ thō), who spun the thread of life; Lachesis (lak´ i sis), who measured it out; and Atropos (a´ trə päs), who cut it.

◆ Literary Focus

Foreshadowing

Writers determine the outcome of *all* the events in the fictional worlds they create. They keep you interested in what will happen by giving you hints, called **foreshadowing**, of future events. If you find these hints, you'll have the fun of almost knowing what the future will bring.

To find the foreshadowing in "The Monkey's Paw," listen more carefully than the White family does to the sergeant major's tale. In reading "The Bridegroom," find clues to future events in Natasha's changing reactions to her suitor.

◆ Reading Strategy

Predict Outcomes

You can use a writer's hints at future events to **predict outcomes** or to make educated guesses about what will happen in a story or poem. Your predictions will keep you involved in the world the author creates as you read on to see whether you were correct.

In predicting the outcome of "The Monkey's Paw," remember that warnings sometimes turn out to be true—even if characters disregard them. To figure out what will happen in "The Bridegroom," think about who is coming to Natasha's wedding. One guest is a clue to her plans.

As you read, jot down predictions in a chart like this one. Note predictions in one column and the actual outcome in the other.

Predictions	Actual Outcome

Engage your students' attention by writing these story details on the chalkboard:

Who: An elderly man and wife and their son.

Where: An isolated house near a factory.

What: A guest carries a monkey's paw in his pocket.

Invite volunteers to tell impromptu scary stories using and embellishing these details.

You could try the same with these details from "The Bridegroom":
Who: A young, unmarried woman.
Where: A village in Russia years ago.
What: A mysterious bridegroom comes to claim the young woman.

Connecting Themes Across Cultures

Many cultures past and present believe in the concept of fate, which plays a role in "Monkey's Paw." Discuss how a belief in fate might affect decisions and choices made by people from varying cultures.

Customize for
Less Proficient Readers

To help less proficient readers with the selection, have them follow along in their text as they listen to the recording. Have students work in pairs to try to make sense of the selections by questioning reasons for characters' words and actions.

Listening to Literature Audiocassettes

Customize for
Pre-AP Students

As students read "The Monkey's Paw," have them consider the question, "Could this story have really happened?" Have small groups discuss and explain their responses.

Customize for
Gifted/Talented Students

Invite students to imagine they are directing a movie version of "The Monkey's Paw," or "The Bridegroom." Have them work in a group to discuss which moments of foreshadowing they consider most important and how they might capture those moments on film.

Test Preparation Workshop

Reading Comprehension: Using Context Clues to Determine Word Meanings Students preparing to take standardized tests need practice using context clues to determine the meanings of words that appear in a reading passage. Have students read the description of the soldier's visit and storytelling on pp. 48–49, and then give the following practice test item.

The word which best captures the meaning of <u>enthralled</u> is—

A bored
B captivated
C envious
D surprised

Suggest that students analyze each word as it applies to the context of the selection. The members of the family were not *bored, envious,* or *surprised* by their visitor's stories as much as they were charmed and entertained by him. Discuss with students that *captivated* captures the charm and entertainment that he exudes, so the answer that provides the best meaning for *enthralled* is B.

Develop Understanding

One-Minute Insight "The Monkey's Paw" is a chilling version of the "three-wishes" tale told the world over. Like many renditions of the tale, it offers lessons in morality, but it distinguishes itself from other three-wishes tales through its aura of terror and suspense. Students will be taken on an emotional roller-coaster ride as the Whites are pushed to the brink of desperation, trying to reverse their wish and bring their son back from the dead.

Tips to Guide Reading

Use Text Organizers The author uses roman numerals as a text organizer in the story. Suggest that students stop reading at each roman numeral and summarize the foreshadowing details they have encountered up to that point. Have them use these details to make predictions about the remainder of the story.

1 Clarification Explain that "Hark at the wind" is a British phrase meaning "listen to the wind." Remind students that the author was British. Then point out that the story is set in England around 1900 and that students will encounter other British words and phrases throughout.

◆ Reading Strategy

2 Predict Outcomes Elicit responses like the following: *The gloomy setting suggests that something unpleasant may happen. The eerie isolation of the Whites' house further hints that the family may become cut off from society or parted from one another.*

◆ Critical Thinking

3 Infer Ask what the meaning behind the knowing glance between the mother and son is. *They are acknowledging that the mother has just humored Mr. White because he was set off by his failure to win at chess.*

Customize for
English Language Learners
The long dialogue scene that opens the story offers an opportunity for developing oral reading skills. Organize groups of three to read the scene aloud. Include at least one native speaker in each group.

The Monkey's Paw

W. W. Jacobs

I

Without, the night was cold and wet, but in the small parlor of Laburnam Villa the blinds were drawn and the fire burned brightly. Father and son were at chess, the former, who possessed ideas about the game involving radical changes, putting his king into such sharp and unnecessary perils that it even provoked comment from the white-haired old lady knitting placidly by the fire.

1 "Hark at the wind," said Mr. White, who, having seen a fatal mistake after it was too late, was amiably desirous of preventing his son from seeing it.

"I'm listening," said the latter, grimly surveying the board as he stretched out his hand. "Check."[1]

I should hardly think that he'd come tonight," said his father, with his hand poised over the board.

"Mate,"[2] replied the son.

"That's the worst of living so far out," bawled Mr. White, with sudden and unlooked-for violence; "of all the beastly, slushy, out-of-the-way places to live in, this is the worst. Pathway's a bog, and the road's a torrent. I don't know what people are thinking about. I suppose because only two houses on the road are let, they think it doesn't matter."

2 ◆ **Reading Strategy** What predictions can you make about this story based on the gloomy setting?

"Never mind, dear," said his wife, soothingly; "perhaps you'll win the next one."

3 Mr. White looked up sharply, just in time to intercept a knowing glance between mother and son. The words died away on his lips, and he hid a guilty grin in his thin gray beard. 3

"There he is," said Herbert White, as the gate banged to loudly and heavy footsteps came toward the door.

The old man rose with hospitable haste, and opening the door, was heard condoling with the new arrival. The new arrival also condoled with himself, so that Mrs. White said, "Tut, tut!" and coughed gently as her husband entered the room, followed by a tall, burly man, beady of eye and rubicund of visage.[3] 4

"Sergeant Major Morris," he said, introducing him.

The sergeant major shook hands, and taking the proffered seat by the fire, watched contentedly while his host got out tumblers and stood a small copper kettle on the fire.

At the third glass his eyes got brighter, and he began to talk, the little family circle regarding with eager interest this visitor from distant parts, as he squared his broad shoulders in the chair and spoke of wild scenes and doughty deeds; of wars and plagues and strange peoples.

"Twenty-one years of it," said Mr. White, nodding at his wife and son. "When he went away he was a slip of a youth in the warehouse. Now look at him."

"He don't look to have taken much harm," said Mrs. White, politely.

"I'd like to go to India myself," said the old man, "just to look round a bit, you know." 5

"Better where you are," said the sergeant major, shaking his head. He put down the empty glass, and sighing softly, shook it again.

1. **check** *n.*: Chess move that threatens to capture the king.
2. **mate** *n.*: Checkmate, a chess move in which the king is captured and the game is over.

3. **rubicund** (ro͞o′ bi kund′) **of visage** (viz′ ij) *adj.*: Having a red complexion.

◆ **Build Vocabulary**
doughty (dout′ ē) *adj.*: Brave; valiant

Block Scheduling Strategies

Consider these suggestions to take advantage of extended class time:

- After students have completed the journal activity in Literature and Your Life and read the Background for Understanding on p. 45 of their books, have a brief class discussion about the concept of fate. Elicit opinions about the role of fate in our lives.
- Use the Daily Language Practice sentences for Week 2, on page 118 of ***Writing and Language Transparencies.***
- Encourage interested students to locate British words and phrases in the story and provide their American English equivalents. Examples include: "at chess," "hark at the wind," "only two houses on the road are let," and so on.
- Challenge motivated students to explore the Internet for Web sites, researching information about classic horror stories. Ask your Internet researchers to share what they've learned with the class. Encourage them to find and present a range of information.

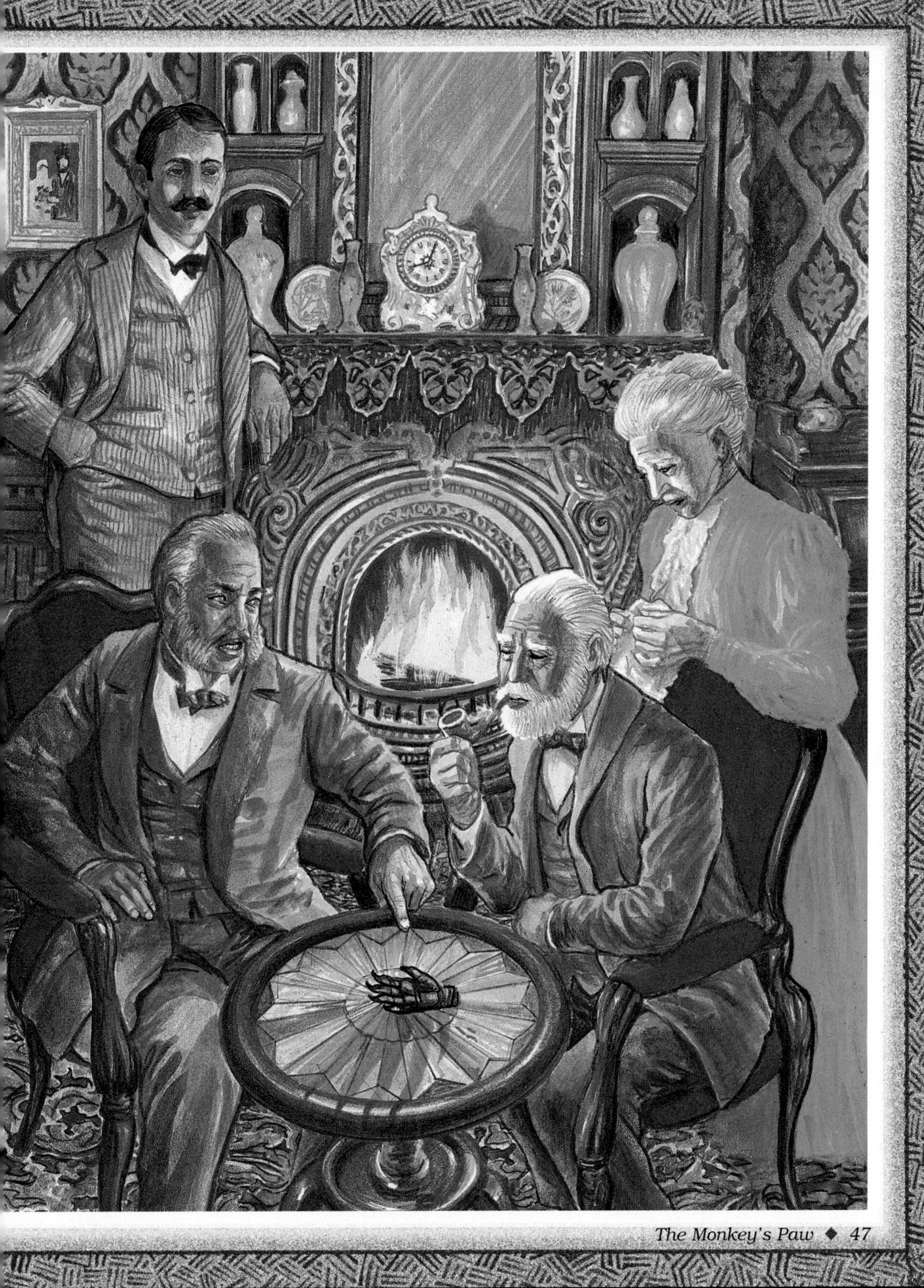

The Monkey's Paw ◆ 47

◆ Critical Thinking

❹ **Draw Conclusions** "Tut" is a sound made by sucking in breath and is an expression of disapproval or disbelief. Ask students: What is Mrs. White expressing disapproval about? *She's probably expressing disapproval that the new arrival is complaining about the weather and road conditions to an unnecessary degree.*

❺ **Clarification** India was a colony of Great Britain from the late 1770's to 1947. See the Cross-Curricular Connection on page 48.

Customize for *Musical/Rhythmic Learners*

Numerous sounds and noises echo through "The Monkey's Paw"—from the wind at the beginning of the story to Mrs. White's "long loud wail of disappointment" at the end. Invite your musical/rhythmic learners to notice these as they read, imagining how they might create sound effects to accompany an oral reading of the story.

Read to Be Entertained

Students will enjoy reading "The Monkey's Paw" to be entertained by Jacobs's use of foreshadowing to provide a sinister sense of danger and suspense.

Customize for *Verbal/Linguistic Learners*

Encourage students to note that the number three is prevalent in tales from all over the world. Whether it is three wishes, three bears, or three musketeers, the number three seems to have a special significance in stories from various cultures. You may wish to have students work in groups to research examples of threes found in stories or beliefs from various parts of the world. One group may wish to explore stories from Africa while another investigates stories from Asia.

Cultural Connection

Cultural Connection

The theme of wishing comes up again and again in the folklore of different cultures. One common variation features characters who have three wishes and who use them so foolishly that in the end their lives do not change for the better. In a Jewish folk tale from Eastern Europe, a man is helped by a magical wishing ring, but he nearly dies when he reveals its existence to others. An Ancient Chinese tale tells of the mother of heaven who tries to grant everyone's wishes, but who only causes more problems.

Proverbs, like folk tales, about wishing also reveal something of the culture from which they come. The French, for example, have the following saying: "After the act, wishing is in vain." The Italians say, "With wishing comes grieving." The Chinese warn, "Be careful what you wish for; you may get it."

Interested students might want to locate other folk tales about wishing. Have them speculate about why wishing is a universal theme—commonly found in folk tales and other types of fiction, TV programs, film, and even in news stories.

❶ **Clarification** A fakir is someone who is believed to be able to cast spells and work wonders.

◆ Literary Focus

❷ **Foreshadowing** Ask students: How does this warning about fate foreshadow a possible disaster? *Sergeant Major Morris's words are a clear warning that interfering with fate by making wishes on the monkey's paw will bring unhappiness or misfortune.*

◆ Literature and Your Life

❸ Ask students to jot down what they would do with the three wishes. Encourage them to keep their lists and to look them over later in their reading to see if they would change them.

Extending Word Study

Have students locate the word *fakirs* at the top of the page. Suggest that they keep reading until they locate a context clue that explains the term. Students should be encouraged not to use only context clues, however, but to also use the dictionary or glossary to expand their understanding of the word meaning and to determine the correct pronunciation. Ask students to use the pronunciation guide to decide whether or not the word is pronounced the same as *faker*, someone who fakes.

Customize for *Less Proficient Readers*

Draw these students' attention to Sergeant Major Morris's warnings about the monkey's paw. Lead them to see that this is a key detail that they should consider when making predictions about the story's outcome.

"I should like to see those old temples and ❶ fakirs and jugglers," said the old man. "What was that you started telling me the other day about a monkey's paw or something, Morris?"

"Nothing," said the soldier, hastily. "Leastways nothing worth hearing."

"Monkey's paw?" said Mrs. White, curiously.

"Well, it's just a bit of what you might call magic, perhaps," said the sergeant major, offhandedly.

His three listeners leaned forward eagerly. The visitor absent-mindedly put his empty glass to his lips and then set it down again. His host filled it for him.

"To look at," said the sergeant major, fumbling in his pocket, "it's just an ordinary little paw, dried to a mummy."

He took something out of his pocket and proffered it. Mrs. White drew back with a grimace, but her son, taking it, examined it curiously.

"And what is there special about it?" inquired Mr. White as he took it from his son, and having examined it, placed it upon the table.

"It had a spell put on it by an old fakir," said the sergeant major, "a very holy man."

❷ "He wanted to show that fate ruled people's lives, and that those who interfered with it did so to their sorrow. He put a spell on it so that three separate men could each have three wishes from it."

His manner was so impressive that his hearers were conscious that their light laughter jarred somewhat.

"Well, why don't you have three, sir?" said Herbert White, cleverly.

The soldier regarded him in the way that middle age is wont to regard presumptuous youth. "I have," he said, quietly, and his blotchy face whitened.

"And did you really have the three wishes granted?" asked Mrs. White.

"I did," said the sergeant major, and his glass tapped against his strong teeth.

"And has anybody else wished?" persisted the old lady.

"The first man had his three wishes, yes," was the reply; "I don't know what the first two were, but the third was for death. That's how I got the paw."

His tones were so grave that a hush fell upon the group.

"If you've had your three wishes, it's no good to you now, then, Morris," said the old man at last. "What do you keep it for?"

The soldier shook his head. "Fancy, I suppose," he said, slowly. "I did have some idea of selling it, but I don't think I will. It has caused enough mischief already. Besides, people won't buy. They think it's a fairy tale, some of them, and those who do think anything of it want to try it first and pay me afterward."

"If you could have another three wishes," said the old man, eyeing him keenly, "would you have them?"

> ◆ **Literature and Your Life** ❸
> How would you change the future if you could have three wishes?

"I don't know, said the other. "I don't know."

He took the paw, and dangling it between his forefinger and thumb, suddenly threw it upon the fire. White, with a slight cry, stooped down and snatched it off.

"Better let it burn," said the soldier, solemnly.

"If you don't want it, Morris," said the other, "give it to me."

"I won't," said his friend doggedly. "I threw it on the fire. If you keep it, don't blame me for what happens. Pitch it on the fire again, like a sensible man."

The other shook his head and examined his new possession closely. "How do you do it?" he inquired.

"Hold it up in your right hand and wish aloud," said the sergeant major, "but I warn you of the consequences."

"Sounds like the *Arabian Nights*,"[4] said Mrs. White, as she rose and began to set the supper. "Don't you think you might wish for four pairs of hands for me?"

Her husband drew the talisman from his pocket, and then all three burst into laughter

4. ***Arabian Nights***: Collection of stories from the ancient Near East.

Cross-Curricular Connection: Social Studies

India as a Colony From the late 1700's until it became an independent nation in 1947, India was a colony of Great Britain. Because India's culture was so different from that of England, the English had a great fascination with India. During the colonial period, many British government officials and soldiers—like Sergeant Major Morris in "The Monkey's Paw"—lived and worked in India. Through letters and visits back home, these officials and soldiers passed on information—and misinformation—about India to their fellow British citizens. Before long, India became a symbol of the mysterious and exotic. Its reputation for mystery and magic is suggested in "The Monkey's Paw" when Mr. White says, "I should like to see those old temples and fakirs and jugglers." Have students discuss the connection between India's reputation and the Whites' fascination with and belief in the monkey's paw.

Interested students might want to look into films that visually represent India and its history as a colony.

as the sergeant major, with a look of alarm on his face, caught him by the arm. "If you must wish," he said, gruffly, "wish for something sensible."

Mr. White dropped it back in his pocket, and placing chairs, motioned his friend to the table. In the business of supper the talisman was partly forgotten, and afterward the three sat listening in an enthralled fashion to a second installment of the soldier's adventures in India.

"If the tale about the monkey's paw is not more truthful than those he has been telling us," said Herbert, as the door closed behind their guest, just in time for him to catch the last train, "we shan't make much out of it."

"Did you give him anything for it, Father?" inquired Mrs. White, regarding her husband closely.

"A trifle," said he, coloring slightly. "He didn't want it, but I made him take it. And he pressed me again to throw it away."

"Likely," said Herbert, with pretended horror. "Why, we're going to be rich, and famous and happy. Wish to be an emperor, Father, to begin with; then you can't be bossed around."

He darted round the table, pursued by the maligned Mrs. White armed with an antimacassar.[5]

Mr. White took the paw from his pocket and eyed it dubiously. "I don't know what to wish for, and that's a fact," he said, slowly. "It seems to me I've got all I want."

"If you only cleared the house, you'd be quite happy, wouldn't you?" said Herbert, with his hand on his shoulder. "Well, wish for two hundred pounds,[6] then; that'll just do it."

His father, smiling shamefacedly at his own credulity, held up the talisman, as his son, with a solemn face somewhat marred by a wink at his mother, sat down at the piano and struck a few impressive chords.

"I wish for two hundred pounds," said the old man distinctly.

A fine crash from the piano greeted the words, interrupted by a shuddering cry from the old man. His wife and son ran toward him.

"It moved," he cried, with a glance of disgust at the object as it lay on the floor. "As I wished it twisted in my hand like a snake."

"Well, I don't see the money," said his son as he picked it up and placed it on the table, "and I bet I never shall."

"It must have been your fancy, Father," said his wife, regarding him anxiously.

He shook his head. "Never mind, though; there's no harm done, but it gave me a shock all the same."

They sat down by the fire again while the two men finished their pipes. Outside, the wind was higher than ever, and the old man started nervously at the sound of a door banging upstairs. A silence unusual and depressing settled upon all three, which lasted until the old couple rose to retire for the night.

"I expect you'll find the cash tied up in a big bag in the middle of your bed," said Herbert, as he bade them good night, "and something horrible squatting up on top of the wardrobe watching you as you pocket your ill-gotten gains."

Herbert sat alone in the darkness, gazing at the dying fire, and seeing faces in it. The last face was so horrible and so simian[7] that he gazed at it in amazement. It got so vivid that, with a little uneasy laugh, he felt on the table for a glass containing a little water to throw over it. His hand grasped the monkey's paw, and with a little shiver he wiped his hand on his coat and went up to bed.

◆ Literary Focus
How is the crash of the piano immediately following Mr. White's wish a foreshadowing of what might happen? 6

7

5. **antimacassar** (an´ ti mə kas´ ər) *n.*: Small cover on the arms or back of a chair or sofa to prevent soiling.
6. **pounds** *n.*: English money.

7. **simian** *adj.*: Monkeylike.

◆ Build Vocabulary

maligned (mə līnd´) *adj.*: Spoken ill of

credulity (krə do͞o´ lə tē) *n.*: Tendency to believe too readily

◆ Reading Strategy

4 Predict Outcomes Ask students: Do you agree with Herbert's prediction that the monkey's paw will bring wealth, fame, and happiness? Why or why not? *Herbert's prediction may be right because the sergeant major probably exaggerated about the dangers of the monkey's paw in the same way he stretched the truth in his other tales. Or: Herbert's prediction is mistaken; his hopefulness has blinded him to the dangers of the monkey's paw.*

◆ Reading Strategy

5 Predict Outcomes Ask students what they predict Mr. White will wish for. *Students should use what they know about Mr. White and human nature in general to speculate about what he will wish for. Possible answers include: long life, a new house in a pleasant setting, more money, and travel.*

◆ Literary Focus

6 Foreshadowing Elicit responses such as the following: *The crash is emotionally jarring, suggesting that something bad will happen. The crash is also surprising, hinting that the outcome of the wish may be a surprise even to the one making the wish.*

◆ Literary Focus

7 Foreshadowing Ask: What might Herbert's vision of the monkey face in the fire foreshadow? *The horrible monkey face that frightens Herbert might foreshadow the way the monkey's paw wishes will later terrify the wisher.*

Beyond the Classroom

Career Connection

Armed Services In this tale, Sergeant Major Morris is a soldier who has served in the British armed forces in India. The formal and informal education Morris gained by traveling the world in service to his country may make him the worldliest and wisest character in the story.

Have students research the armed services of the U. S. and the career and educational opportunities they offer. Encourage students to investigate the recruiting offices in your area. Ask these students to share their findings with the class.

Community Connection

Streets and Highways Remind students that Mr. White complains about the conditions of the roads that lead to his house: "Pathway's a bog, and the road's a torrent." Invite students to imagine they work for the department of streets and highways in your area. What problems and dangerous conditions can they identify? How can these conditions be improved? Encourage students to find out how local authorities ordinarily maintain roads and what they plan to do about the problems students have identified.

◆ Critical Thinking

1 Analyze Ask students: What does this exchange among the three family members reveal about each one? *Mrs. White shows common sense. Herbert appears to be carefree and a little silly. Mr. White is gullible and hopes, almost blindly, that the monkey's paw will work.*

◆ Literary Focus

2 Foreshadowing Point out that Mrs. White's remark referring to Herbert's remarks at dinner is an ironic foreshadowing. Ask students what it might foreshadow. *Some students may be able to guess that Herbert won't be home for dinner as the wish is fulfilled.* If they are unable to see that outcome at this point, have them look back to this statement after they have completed reading this section.

◆ Reading Strategy

3 Predict Outcomes Possible answers from students include: *The stranger has bad news of some sort—perhaps about Sergeant Major Morris, Herbert, the monkey's paw, the Whites' house, or the money wished for.*

II

In the brightness of the wintry sun next morning as it streamed over the breakfast table Herbert laughed at his fears. There was an air of prosaic wholesomeness about the room which it had lacked on the previous night, and the dirty, shriveled little paw was pitched on the sideboard with a carelessness which betokened no great belief in its virtues.

"I suppose all old soldiers are the same," said Mrs. White. "The idea of our listening to such nonsense! How could wishes be granted in these days? And if they could, how could two hundred pounds hurt you, Father?"

1 "Might drop on his head from the sky," said the frivolous Herbert.

"Morris said the things happened so naturally," said his father, "that you might if you so wished attribute it to coincidence."

"Well, don't break into the money before I come back," said Herbert, as he rose from the table. "I'm afraid it'll turn you into a mean, avaricious man, and we shall have to disown you."

His mother laughed, and following him to the door, watched him down the road, and, returning to the breakfast table, was very happy at the expense of her husband's credulity. All of which did not prevent her from scurrying to the door at the postman's knock, nor prevent her from referring somewhat shortly to retired sergeant majors of bibulous habits when she found that the post brought a tailor's bill.

2 "Herbert will have some more of his funny remarks, I expect, when he comes home," she said, as they sat at dinner.

"I dare say," said Mr. White, "but for all that, the thing moved in my hand; that I'll swear to."

"You thought it did," said the old lady soothingly.

"I say it did," replied the other. "There was no thought about it; I had just—What's the matter?"

His wife made no reply. She was watching the mysterious movements of a man outside, who, peering in an undecided fashion at the house, appeared to be trying to make up his mind to enter. In mental connection with the two hundred pounds, she noticed that the stranger was well dressed, and wore a silk hat of glossy newness. Three times he paused at the gate, and then walked on again. The fourth time he stood with his hand upon it, and then with sudden resolution flung it open and walked up the path. Mrs. White at the same moment placed her hands behind her, and hurriedly unfastening the strings of her apron, put that useful article of apparel beneath the cushion of her chair.

She brought the stranger, who seemed ill at ease, into the room. He gazed at her furtively, and listened in a preoccupied fashion as the old lady apologized for the appearance of the room, and her husband's coat, a garment which he usually reserved for the garden. She then waited patiently for him to broach his business, but he was at first strangely silent.

> **◆ Reading Strategy**
> Predict why the stranger has come calling on the Whites.

"I—was asked to call," he said at last, and stooped and picked a piece of cotton from his trousers. "I come from 'Maw and Meggins.'"

The old lady started. "Is anything the matter?" she asked, breathlessly. "Has anything happened to Herbert? What is it? What is it?"

Her husband interposed. "There, there, mother," he said, hastily. "Sit down, and don't jump to conclusions. You've not brought bad news, I'm sure, sir," and he eyed the other wistfully.

"I'm sorry—" began the visitor.

"Is he hurt?" demanded the mother, wildly.

The visitor bowed in assent. "Badly hurt," he said quietly, "but he is not in any pain."

"Oh, thank God!" said the old woman, clasping her hands. "Thank God for that! Thank—"

She broke off suddenly as the sinister meaning of the assurance dawned upon her and she saw the awful confirmation of her fears in the

◆ Build Vocabulary

prosaic (prō zā´ ik) *adj.*: Commonplace; ordinary
avaricious (av´ ə rish´ əs) *adj.*: Greedy for riches
furtively (fur´ tiv lē) *adv.*: Secretly; stealthily

Speaking, Listening, and Viewing Mini-Lesson

Being Tactful

Introduce Remind students that tact is the ability to appreciate the delicacy of a situation and to do or say the most suitable thing. Invite a volunteer to read aloud the passage from "The Monkey's Paw" on page 50 that begins "She brought the stranger" and ends at the bottom of the page. Have them discuss whether or not the stranger showed tact in the way he announced the bad news.

Develop Through discussion, guide students to list situations in which tact might be important and appropriate approaches to each situation.

- When delivering negative criticism, also stress the positive of a situation.
- Deliver bad news in a sensitive and delicate way.

Apply Ask students how they would use tact to deal with the following situation: A classmate is not contributing to a team project in which all students will receive the same grade. Form small groups to discuss the situation, and come up with a tactful solution.

Assess Use these questions to evaluate students' tactful solutions: Did they try to gain cooperation from the student without hurting his or her feelings? Did they make sure the student knew that his or her contribution would be valued?

other's averted face. She caught her breath, and turning to her husband, laid her trembling old hand upon his. There was a long silence.

"He was caught in the machinery," said the visitor at length, in a low voice.

"Caught in the machinery," repeated Mr. White, in a dazed fashion, "yes."

He sat staring blankly out at the window, and taking his wife's hand between his own, pressed it as he had been wont to do in their old courting days nearly forty years before.

"He was the only one left to us," he said, turning gently to the visitor. "It is hard."

The other coughed, and, rising, walked slowly to the window. "The firm wished me to convey their sincere sympathy with you in your great loss," he said, without looking round. "I beg that you will understand I am only their servant and merely obeying orders."

There was no reply; the old woman's face was white, her eyes staring, and her breath inaudible; on the husband's face was a look such as his friend the sergeant might have carried into his first action.

"I was to say that Maw and Meggins disclaim all responsibility," continued the other. "They admit no liability at all, but in consideration of your son's services they wish to present you with a certain sum as compensation."

Mr. White dropped his wife's hand, and rising to his feet, gazed with a look of horror at his visitor. His dry lips shaped the words, "How much?"

"Two hundred pounds," was the answer.

Unconscious of his wife's shriek, the old man smiled faintly, put out his hands like a sightless man, and dropped, a senseless heap, to the floor.

III

In the huge new cemetery, some two miles distant, the old people buried their dead, and came back to a house steeped in shadow and silence. It was all over so quickly that at first they could hardly realize it, and remained in a state of expectation as though of something else to happen—something else which was to lighten this load, too heavy for old hearts to bear.

But the days passed, and expectation gave place to resignation—the hopeless resignation of the old, sometimes miscalled apathy. Sometimes they hardly exchanged a word, for now they had nothing to talk about, and their days were long to weariness. ❺

It was about a week after that the old man, waking suddenly in the night, stretched out his hand and found himself alone. The room was in darkness, and the sound of subdued weeping came from the window. He raised himself in bed and listened.

"Come back," he said, tenderly. "You will be cold."

"It is colder for my son," said the old woman, and wept afresh.

The sound of her sobs died away on his ears. The bed was warm, and his eyes heavy with sleep. He dozed fitfully, and then slept until a sudden wild cry from his wife awoke him with a start. ❻

"The paw!" she cried wildly. "The monkey's paw!"

He started up in alarm. "Where? Where is it? What's the matter?"

She came stumbling across the room toward him. "I want it," she said quietly. "You've not destroyed it?"

"It's in the parlor, on the bracket," he replied, marveling. "Why?"

She cried and laughed together, and bending over, kissed his cheek.

◆ Reading Strategy

❹ Predict Outcomes Ask students to review the predictions they had made about the stranger's news. How close did they come to predicting correctly, and on what did they base their predictions? *Some students may say they predicted the bad news would be about Herbert because Herbert was the only family member missing and because his mother had already alluded to his return.*

◆ Literature and Your Life

❺ Ask students: After seeing Mr. White's wish come true in a horrible way, would you change your three wishes? How? *Students might revise their wishes to make them more inconsequential or say they would rather not wish at all.*

◆ Build Grammar Skills

❻ Regular and Irregular Verb Forms Have students identify the three verbs in this sentence. Ask students: What is the present tense of each verb? Which of the verbs is regular in form, and which are irregular? *dozed/doze—regular; slept/sleep—irregular; awoke/awake—irregular*

Reteach

Some students may need additional practice using foreshadowing clues to predict outcomes in the plot. After reading the entire story of "The Monkey's Paw," have students draw a sunburst diagram.

In the centers of their diagrams, have the students list the final outcome of the story. Then have them skim the story, looking for details that were hints or clues to what the final result would be and write them on each arm.

Students should find it easier to locate these details as they reread because they know the final outcome and know what to look for. For additional practice, suggest that students apply the same strategy to "The Bridegroom." Discuss whether it was easier or more difficult to make predictions with a short story or ballad.

◆ Literary Focus

1 Foreshadowing Elicit such responses as the following: *Because the result of the first wish was so disastrous, it seems likely that the results of the other wishes might be just as bad or worse. Or the following wishes might be more wisely made and successful now that the Whites know the danger of the monkey's paw.*

◆ Critical Thinking

2 Compare and Contrast Ask students: How have Mr. and Mrs. White's attitudes toward the monkey's paw changed since Sergeant Major Morris first introduced them to it? *Mrs. White now desperately believes in it, as Mr. White originally did; and Mr. White no longer wants to have anything to do with it.*

◆ Critical Thinking

3 Analyze What in this description creates suspense? *Suspense is created as the reader wonders whether wishing on the monkey's paw again can really bring Herbert back, and if he comes back, in what kind of condition he will be. Readers also wonder if Mr. White will really make the wish.*

◆ Critical Thinking

4 Infer Why would Mr. White be afraid of his wife? *He seems to fear her almost unnatural obsession with wishing on the monkey's paw as a way to bring their son back. He's afraid of what might really happen.*

◆ Critical Thinking

5 Analyze Ask students to identify the words and details that create suspense in these paragraphs. *The following words or details contribute to the suspense: their silent expectant waiting and the ticking of the clock and other sounds; Mr. White's going downstairs in the dark; the knock on the door and its repetition.*

Listening to Literature Audiocassettes To help students appreciate the final horrifying effects in the story, play the audiocassette from the paragraph that begins "Neither spoke, but lay silently listening to the ticking of the clock" to the end.

"I only just thought of it," she said hysterically. "Why didn't I think of it before? Why didn't *you* think of it?"

"Think of what?" he questioned.

"The other two wishes," she replied rapidly. "We've only had one."

"Was not that enough?" he demanded, fiercely.

"No," she cried triumphantly; "we'll have one more. Go down and get it quickly, and wish our boy alive again."

> **◆ Literary Focus**
> How might the outcome of the first wish foreshadow that of the other two wishes?

1 The man sat up in bed and flung the bedclothes from his quaking limbs. "You are mad!" he cried, aghast.

"Get it," she panted; "get it quickly, and wish—Oh, my boy, my boy!"

Her husband struck a match and lit the candle. "Get back to bed," he said unsteadily. "You
2 don't know what you are saying."

"We had the first wish granted," said the old woman feverishly; "why not the second?"

"A coincidence," stammered the old man.

"Go and get it and wish," cried his wife, quivering with excitement.

The old man turned and regarded her, and his voice shook. "He has been dead ten days, and besides he—I would not tell you else, but—I could only recognize him by his clothing. If he was too terrible for you to see then, how now?"

"Bring him back," cried the old woman, and dragged him toward the door. "Do you think I fear the child I have nursed?"

He went down in the darkness, and felt his way to the parlor, and then to the mantelpiece. The talisman was in its place, and a horrible fear that the unspoken wish might bring his mutilated son before him ere he could escape from the room seized upon him, and he caught
3 his breath as he found that he had lost the direction of the door. His brow cold with sweat, he felt his way round the table, and groped along the wall until he found himself in the small passage with the unwholesome thing in his hand.

Even his wife's face seemed changed as he entered the room. It was white and expectant,
and to his fears seemed to have an unnatural 4
look upon it. He was afraid of her.

"*Wish!*" she cried, in a strong voice.

"It is foolish and wicked," he faltered.

"*Wish!*" repeated his wife.

He raised his hand. "I wish my son alive again."

The talisman fell to the floor, and he regarded it fearfully. Then he sank trembling into a chair as the old woman, with burning eyes, walked to the window and raised the blind.

He sat until he was chilled with the cold, glancing occasionally at the figure of the old woman peering through the window. The candle-end, which had burned below the rim of the china candlestick, was throwing pulsating shadows on the ceiling and walls, until, with a flicker larger than the rest, it expired. The old man, with an unspeakable sense of relief at the failure of the talisman, crept back to his bed, and a minute or two afterward the old woman came silently and apathetically beside him.

Neither spoke, but lay silently listening to the ticking of the clock. A stair creaked, and a squeaky mouse scurried noisily through the wall. The darkness was oppressive, and after lying for some time screwing up his courage, he took the box of matches, and striking one, went downstairs for a candle.

At the foot of the stairs the match went out, and he paused to strike another; and at the same moment a knock so quiet and stealthy as to be scarcely audible, sounded on the front door.

The matches fell from his hand and spilled in the passage. He stood motionless, his breath suspended until the knock was repeated. Then he turned and fled swiftly back to his room, and closed the door behind him. A third knock sounded through the house.

"*What's that?*" cried the old woman, starting up.

"A rat," said the old man in shaking tones—"a rat. It passed me on the stairs."

His wife sat up in bed listening. A loud knock resounded through the house.

"It's Herbert!" she screamed. "It's Herbert!"

Beyond the Selection

FURTHER READING

Other Works by W. W. Jacobs

The Lady of the Barge (collection in which "The Monkey's Paw" first appeared)
Short Cruises
Sailor's Knots

Other Works With the Theme of the Power of Wishes

"Gift of the Magi," O. Henry
"The Necklace," Guy de Maupassant
"The Third Wish," Joan Aiken

She ran to the door, but her husband was before her, and catching her by the arm, held her tightly.

"What are you going to do?" he whispered hoarsely.

"It's my boy; it's Herbert!" she cried, struggling mechanically. "I forgot it was two miles away. What are you holding me for? Let go. I must open the door."

"Don't let it in," cried the old man, trembling.

"You're afraid of your own son," she cried struggling. "Let me go. I'm coming Herbert; I'm coming."

There was another knock, and another. The old woman with a sudden wrench broke free and ran from the room. Her husband followed to the landing, and called after her appealingly as she hurried downstairs. He heard the chain rattle back and the bottom bolt drawn slowly and stiffly from the socket. Then the old woman's voice, strained and panting.

"The bolt," she cried, loudly. "Come down. I can't reach it."

But her husband was on his hands and knees groping wildly on the floor in search of the paw. If he could only find it before the thing outside got in. A perfect fusillade of knocks reverberated through the house, and he heard the scraping of a chair as his wife put it down in the passage against the door. He heard the creaking of the bolt as it came slowly back, and at the same moment he found the monkey's paw, and frantically breathed his third and last wish.

The knocking ceased suddenly, although the echoes of it were still in the house. He heard the chair drawn back and the door opened. A cold wind rushed up the staircase, and a long loud wail of disappointment and misery from **7** his wife gave him courage to run down to her side, and then to the gate beyond. The street lamp flickering opposite shone on a quiet and deserted road.

◆ Build Vocabulary

fusillade (fyo͞o´ sə läd´) *n.*: Something that is like the rapid firing of many firearms

Guide for Responding

◆ Literature and Your Life

Reader's Response What was the most frightening moment of the story? Why?

Thematic Focus Contrast the wishes made by the Whites with wishes that you work to fulfill. In what way are both these types of wishes daring?

Check Your Comprehension

1. Summarize the story that the sergeant major tells the Whites.
2. In what way is Mr. White's first wish fulfilled?
3. Describe Mr. White's next two wishes and how they are fulfilled.
4. How does the story end?

◆ Critical Thinking

INTERPRET

1. How does the opening setting of the cold, wet night and the warm, cozy fire set the mood? **[Analyze]**
2. Contrast the reactions of mother, father, and son to the paw as the story progresses. **[Compare and Contrast]**
3. Would things have turned out better if Mr. and Mrs. White had phrased the second wish more carefully? Explain. **[Infer]**
4. What do the events of the story seem to indicate about "fate"? **[Draw Conclusions]**

APPLY

5. After reading the story, what would you do if you were granted three wishes? Why? **[Speculate]**

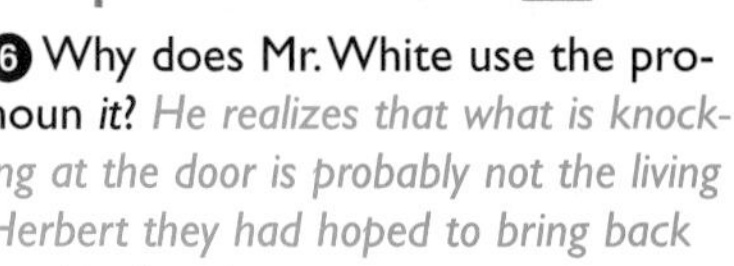

Comprehension Check

6 Why does Mr. White use the pronoun *it*? *He realizes that what is knocking at the door is probably not the living Herbert they had hoped to bring back but his decaying corpse.*

◆ Reading Strategy

7 Predict Outcomes Point out the unsettling end of the story. Ask students if they were surprised by the conclusion. Why or why not? *Those who were surprised may cite the gloomy inevitability of the story—especially after the first wish is made. Others may be surprised because, like the Whites, they did not consider the open-ended possibilities of the wishes.*

Reinforce and Extend

Answers

◆ Literature and Your Life

Reader's Response Students might respond that the most frightening moment was when there was a knock at the door the second time. It could have been the mutilated Herbert.

Thematic Focus The kind of wishes the Whites made are dreamy and unrealistic, while wishes that you work to fulfill, such as becoming a doctor, can be fulfilled through application and luck.

Check Your Comprehension

1. The fakir put the spell on the monkey's paw to show people that fate ruled their lives.
2. He receives 200 pounds as compensation for Herbert's fatal accident on the job.
3. Mr. White's second wish is for his son to be alive again, which results in a knocking at the door. His third wish is to undo his second wish, and the knocking stops.
4. Mr. White joins his wife on the empty street.

◆ Critical Thinking

1. This is a typical setting of a suspenseful, frightening story; it sets up a mood of foreboding.
2. At first, Mr. White believes in it, Mrs. White is dubious, and Herbert cynical. Later, Mrs. White is desperate to believe in the paw's power to return her son, and Mr. White doesn't want anything to do with it
3. If they had wished for Herbert to come back as he was before the accident, the story might have turned out better.
4. The events indicate that fate is powerful and should not be tampered with.
5. Students might indicate that after reading the story, they would wish more carefully, such as wishing for their favorite dinner.

Develop Understanding

One-Minute Insight "The Bridegroom" is a variation on the familiar folk motif of a worthy young person standing up to declare independence and becoming heroic by doing so. It raises questions about fate, wishes, and particularly about making choices for yourself.

◆ Reading Strategy

❶ **Predict Outcomes** Ask students to predict what Natasha will tell her parents in response to their questions. *Natasha might tell her parents that she ran away to be by herself or to meet a boyfriend. She might also say she was abducted. Or she might say nothing at all.*

◆ Literary Focus

❷ **Foreshadowing** Have students explain what the word *foreboding* suggests about the events that will follow. *The word foreboding means "an omen or prediction of coming evil"; the parents' fear of the future is a powerful clue that there will be trouble ahead.*

◆ Critical Thinking

❸ **Analyze Characters** Ask students: What does Natasha's silence say about her? *Natasha's silence suggests that she is strong, independent, and perhaps considerate of her parents' feelings, not wishing to hurt them, or that there is something she feels she cannot tell them.*

The Bridegroom

Alexander Pushkin

Translated by D. M. Thomas

For three days Natasha,
The merchant's daughter,
Was missing. The third night,
She ran in, distraught.
❶ Her father and mother
Plied her with questions.
She did not hear them,
She could hardly breathe.

❷ Stricken with foreboding
They pleaded, got angry,
But still she was silent;
At last they gave up.
Natasha's cheeks regained
Their rosy color.
And cheerfully again
She sat with her sisters.

Once at the shingle-gate
She sat with her friends
—And a swift troika[1]
Flashed by before them;
A handsome young man
Stood driving the horses;
Snow and mud went flying,
Splashing the girls.

He gazed as he flew past,
And Natasha gazed.
He flew on. Natasha froze.
Headlong she ran home.
"It was he! It was he!"
She cried. "I know it!
I recognized him! Papa,
Mama, save me from him!"

Full of grief and fear,
They shake their heads, sighing.
Her father says: "My child,
Tell me everything.
If someone has harmed you,
Tell us . . . even a hint."
She weeps again and
Her lips remain sealed. ❸

The next morning, the old
Matchmaking woman
Unexpectedly calls and
Sings the girl's praises;
Says to the father: "You
Have the goods and I
A buyer for them:
A handsome young man.

"He bows low to no one,
He lives like a lord
With no debts nor worries;

1. **troika** (troi´ kə) *n.*: Russian carriage or sleigh drawn by a specially trained team of three horses abreast.

◆ Build Vocabulary

foreboding (fôr bōd´ iŋ) *n.*: Feeling that something bad will happen

Speaking, Listening, and Viewing Mini-Lesson

Television Interview

This mini-lesson supports the Speaking, Listening, and Viewing activity in the Idea Bank on p. 59.

Introduce Have students review television interviews they've seen and identify the purpose, procedures, and other details that they remember.

Develop Suggest that students prepare their role-playing interviews with the following points in mind:

Good interview questions
- often begin with the words *who, what, where, when, why,* and *how*
- are short and to the point

A good interviewer
- listens attentively without interjecting personal opinions
- does not ask overly personal questions
- asks for further clarification if necessary
- respects the interviewee

A good interviewee
- answers questions directly and generously
- responds to the main point of the question

Apply When students feel prepared, have them conduct their role-played interviews for the class.

Assess Evaluate the interviews with these questions: Were the interview questions appropriate and concise? Did the interviewer exhibit good listening skills? Were the interviewee's responses focused?

The Lights of Marriage, Marc Chagall, Kunsthaus, Zurich

▲ **Critical Viewing** What might you infer about Natasha's marriage based on this painting? **[Infer]** 5

He's rich and he's generous,
Says he will give his bride,
On their wedding-day,
A fox-fur coat, a pearl,
Gold rings, brocaded[2] dresses.

"Yesterday, out driving,
He saw your Natasha;
Shall we shake hands
4 And get her to church?"
The woman starts to eat
A pie, and talks in riddles,
While the poor girl
Does not know where to look.

"Agreed," says her father;
"Go in happiness
To the altar, Natasha;
It's dull for you here;
A swallow should not spend
All its time singing,
It's time for you to build
A nest for your children."

Natasha leaned against
The wall and tried
To speak—but found herself
Sobbing; she was shuddering
And laughing. The matchmaker
Poured out a cup of water,

2. **brocaded** (brō kād′ əd) *adj.*: Woven, raised design in a cloth.

◆ Literature and Your Life

4 Encourage students to think about how they would feel if others made major life decisions for them.

▶Critical Viewing◀

5 **Infer** *The strange, surrealistic quality of the painting suggests that Natasha's marriage will be less than perfect. Students may also note the distracted, disturbed look of the bride, who, like Natasha, seems to have more than a simple wedding on her mind.*

Customize for
Visual/Spatial Learners
Encourage these students to take some time to study the details in the Chagall painting either before or after they read the poem. Then have them note ways in which the painting adds to or changes their impressions of the poem. Urge them to share their observations with classmates.

Customize for
Less Proficient Readers
To help these students follow the story that Pushkin presents, instruct them to read the poem in sentences, rather than pausing at the end of each line. In addition, you may want to encourage them to pause at the end of each stanza, to summarize the events and details that it presents.

Humanities: Art

The Lights of Marriage by Marc Chagall.

This painting by Marc Chagall (1887–1985) depicts a wedding scene that is suggestive of the wedding scene described in "The Bridegroom."

Chagall was born in Russia and educated as a painter in Paris. His paintings are distinguished by deeply colored landscapes in which people, objects, and animals fly and float in dreamlike fantasy. His work is associated with Surrealism and Cubism, two schools of painting that gave the world new, nonrealistic ways of looking at itself.

Use these questions for discussion:

1. How is the mood of the painting similar to the mood of Natasha's wedding? *Just as the painting creates a mysterious tension in the viewer with its unexplained human and animal figures flying about, so Natasha's wedding is unsettling to the guests and the reader with its vivid description of a mysterious, violent dream and its melodramatic revelation and conclusion.*
2. Natasha is the focus of the story. Who is the focus of the painting? Provide evidence to support your answer. *The bride is the focus of the painting, too. The painter accomplishes this by placing the bride in the center of the painting and by using light and detail to draw our eye to the bride.*

◆ Reading Strategy

❶ Predict Outcomes Challenge students to think about *why* Natasha suddenly becomes calm. Then ask them what her new state suggests about the events to come. *Natasha becomes calm because she realizes she has no choice and will just go through with the wedding; however she suddenly hatches a plan to get out of the marriage, and that plan will unfold in the events to come.*

◆ Critical Thinking

❷ Infer Ask students: Why does Natasha choose to tell about the dream at this moment and not at an earlier time? *Telling the dream is probably part of a plan Natasha has devised, which no one else knows about.*

◆ Literary Focus

❸ Predict Outcomes Have students read this description of the men's behavior that continues on page 57. Ask how the men's behavior can help them predict what will happen. *The men's uncivilized behavior and dishonoring of religious symbols suggest that they do not live by any rules and may therefore perform some sort of evil deed.*

Customize for
Musical/Rhythmic Learners
Interested students may wish to locate the music or a recording of a ballad or song that tells a story such as "The Bridegroom" and either perform or play it for students in the class. To further expand the activity, students may be interested in locating poems or ballads that have been set to music.

Gave her some to drink,
Splashed some in her face.

Her parents are distressed.
Then Natasha recovered,
❶ And calmly she said:
"Your will be done. Call
My bridegroom to the feast,
Bake loaves for the whole world,
Brew sweet mead[3] and call
The law to the feast."

"Of course, Natasha, angel!
You know we'd give our lives
To make you happy!"
They bake and they brew;
The worthy guests come,
The bride is led to the feast,
Her maids sing and weep;
Then horses and a sledge[4]

With the groom—and all sit.
The glasses ring and clatter,
The toasting-cup is passed

From hand to hand in tumult,
The guests are drunk.

BRIDEGROOM
"Friends, why is my fair bride
Sad, why is she not
Feasting and serving?"

The bride answers the groom:
"I will tell you why
As best I can. My soul
❷ Knows no rest, day and night
I weep; an evil dream
Oppresses me." Her father
Says: "My dear child, tell us
What your dream is."

"I dreamed," she says, "that I
Went into a forest,
It was late and dark;

The moon was faintly
Shining behind a cloud;
I strayed from the path;
Nothing stirred except
The tops of the pine-trees.

"And suddenly, as if
I was awake, I saw
A hut. I approach the hut
And knock at the door
—Silence. A prayer on my lips
I open the door and enter.
A candle burns. All
Is silver and gold."

BRIDEGROOM
"What is bad about that?
It promises wealth."

BRIDE
"Wait, sir, I've not finished.
Silently I gazed
On the silver and gold,
The cloths, the rugs, the silks,
From Novgorod,[5] and I
Was lost in wonder.

"Then I heard a shout
And a clatter of hoofs . . .
Someone has driven up
To the porch. Quickly
I slammed the door and hid
Behind the stove. Now
I hear many voices . . .
Twelve young men come in,

"And with them is a girl,
Pure and beautiful.
They've taken no notice ❸
Of the ikons,[6] they sit

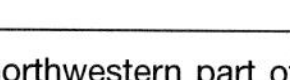

3. **mead** (mēd) *n.*: Drink made of fermented honey and water.
4. **sledge** *n.*: Sleigh.

5. **Novgorod**: City in the northwestern part of Russia.
6. **ikons** (ī känz′) *n.*: Images of Jesus, Mary, a saint, or another sacred Christian religious figure.

◆ Build Vocabulary

tumult (to͞o′ mult) *n.*: Noisy commotion

Beyond the Selection

FURTHER READING

Other Works by Alexander Pushkin
Southern Verse Tales (series of which "The Bridegroom" is a selection)
The Captain's Daughter (novel)

Other Works About the Power to Influence Events
"The Finish of Patsy Barnes," Paul Laurence Dunbar
"Flowers for Algernon," Daniel Keyes

We suggest that you preview these works before recommending them to students.

INTERNET
For more information on Alexander Pushkin, we suggest the following site. Please be aware, however, that this site may have changed from the time we published this information.
http://www.dailybruin.ucla.edu/EMStaff/jchen/pushkin/htm
You may also find related information on the work of Alexander Pushkin and W. W. Jacobs on the Internet. We *strongly recommend* that you preview the sites before you send students to them.

To the table without
Praying or taking off
Their hats. At the head,
The eldest brother,
At his right, the youngest;
At his left, the girl.
Shouts, laughs, drunken clamor . . . "

BRIDEGROOM
"That betokens merriment."

BRIDE
"Wait, sir, I've not finished.
The drunken din goes on
And grows louder still.
Only the girl is sad.

"She sits silent, neither
Eating nor drinking;
But sheds tears in plenty;
The eldest brother
Takes his knife and, whistling,
Sharpens it; seizing her by
The hair he kills her
And cuts off her right hand."

"Why," says the groom, "this
Is nonsense! Believe me,
My love, your dream is not evil."
She looks him in the eyes.
"And from whose hand
Does this ring come?"
The bride said. The whole throng
Rose in the silence.

With a clatter the ring
Falls, and rolls along
The floor. The groom blanches,
Trembles. Confusion . . .
"Seize him!" the law commands.
He's bound, judged, put to death.
Natasha is famous!
Our song at an end.

Guide for Responding

◆ Literature and Your Life

Reader's Response Do you admire Natasha? Why or why not?

Thematic Focus What does the poem suggest about the power of choice versus that of chance or fate?

Questions for Research Name another song or ballad that, like "The Bridegroom," tells a story. Then write one or more questions you could research about the song or ballad.

☑ Check Your Comprehension

1. What unexplained event occurs at the very beginning of the poem?
2. What upsets Natasha when she's sitting with her friends at the gate?
3. Describe her changing reactions to the marriage.
4. Summarize the events of the wedding.

◆ Critical Thinking

Interpret

1. Where was Natasha during the three days she was missing? **[Infer]**
2. Why does she refuse to reveal where she was to her parents? **[Analyze]**
3. What accounts for her changing reactions to the marriage? **[Infer]**
4. Do you think Natasha had the "evil" dream she describes? Explain. **[Interpret]**
5. How does Natasha's behavior at the beginning of the poem contrast with her behavior at the end? **[Compare and Contrast]**
6. Why does Natasha become famous? **[Draw Conclusions]**

Evaluate

7. Is the title of the poem effective in grabbing your attention and hinting at the poem's story? Explain. **[Criticize]**

Compare Literary Works

8. Compare and contrast the authors' use of fate as a theme in the story and the ballad. **[Compare and Contrast]**

2. She probably felt she couldn't tell them because they probably would not believe she witnessed a murder, or she didn't want to upset them.
3. Possibly she felt resigned and felt that she would be safe in confronting the bridegroom as a murderer with all of her family and friends surrounding her.
4. Probably not; she probably used the dream rather than make an outright accusation.
5. At the beginning of the poem, Natasha is terrified and timid, by the end, she bravely confronts the murderer.
6. She becomes famous because her bravery led to the arrest of a murderer.
7. Students might say the simplicity of the title hints at something much more complex and ominous.
8. Students might recognize that although arranged marriages are not common in our country today, they do occur in other cultures—the story might be more likely to happen in another culture.

◆ Literary Focus

4 Foreshadowing Ask students what the repetition of this line suggests about events to follow. *The repetition of this line demonstrates Natasha's strength and determination and foreshadows her ultimate victory.*

◆ Literature and Your Life

5 Natasha took a risk, which resulted in her achieving fame. Encourage students to think about a risk they have taken and how the situation turned out. Did the risk accomplish what they had hoped? How do they feel when they look back at the risk-taking behavior now?

Reinforce and Extend

Answers

◆ Literature and Your Life

Reader's Response Many students will say that they admire Natasha's independence and resourcefulness in carrying through her plan to expose the bridegroom.

Thematic Focus Students may say that the poem suggests that the power of choice can sometimes be stronger than the power of fate.

Questions for Research Students might look for information on recording artists such as Bob Dylan, Joni Mitchell, or Peter, Paul and Mary in the library or on the Internet. Have them use the ballad songs that these performers recorded to generate questions to research.

☑ Check Your Comprehension

1. Natasha disappears for three days.
2. She sees a man drive by in a carriage, whom she recognizes as the man she witnessed murdering a woman as 12 brothers looked on.
3. At first she is upset, then she resigns herself to the marriage.
4. She tells the guests at the wedding that she had a horrible dream, and as the dream unfolds, she reveals the killer to be her husband.

◆ Critical Thinking

1. She had gone into the forest, and when it became late and dark, she entered a cottage. When people came, she hid behind the stove and probably witnessed the murder she later describes.

Answers

◆ Reading Strategy

1. Her sudden decision to have the wedding probably coincides with her plan to expose the murderer; she probably refuses food or drink for fear of being poisoned; her tale of the evil dream predicts her exposure of the murderer.
2. (1) The sergeant major doesn't want to talk about the paw. (2) The sergeant wanted to burn the paw. (3) Herbert sees a simian face in the fire.

◆ Literary Focus

1. It foreshadows Herbert's horrible death.
2. It is an example of foreshadowing because of its ironic truth: It is because of his death that the money is received.
3. Her reaction of terror indicated she knew him or something about him, and that knowledge foreshadows the events to come.
4. It foreshadows her intent to reveal the murderer and the eventual arrest of the bridegroom.

◆ Build Vocabulary

Using the Latin Root *-cred-*

1. *incredible*—unbelievable;
2. *credible*—capable of being believed;
3. *credentials*—qualifications that make a person believable;
4. *credulity*—a disposition to believe too readily;
5. *credit*—belief in the truth of someone or something

Using the Word Bank

1. c 2. b 3. a 4. c 5. a 6. b 7. a 8. c

◆ Build Grammar Skills

1. seen; 2. became; 3. known; 4. saw; 5. knew

Grammar Reinforcement

For additional instruction and practice, use the lesson in the **Language Lab CD-ROM** on Verb Tenses and the pages on Verb Tenses (pp. 67–69) in the *Writer's Solution Grammar Practice Book*.

Guide for Responding *(continued)*

◆ Reading Strategy

Predict Outcomes

Reading in "The Bridegroom" that Natasha invites "the whole world" and "the law" to her wedding, you may wonder why she singles out someone who enforces the law. This clue helps you **predict the outcome** of the story because it suggests that Natasha plans to capture a criminal.

1. Explain how each of these other details helps you predict the outcome of "The Bridegroom": Natasha's sudden decision to have the wedding; her refusal to eat and drink at the wedding; and her tale of "an evil dream."

2. List three clues from "The Monkey's Paw" that suggest the paw will bring sorrow to the Whites. Give reasons for your choices.

◆ Literary Focus

Foreshadowing

In the story and the poem, hints at future events, called **foreshadowing**, give you glimpses of what will happen that make you want to find out more. Sometimes these hints give a general sense of what will come. Other times, they can be linked to specific occurrences, although you may not understand the connection until much later.

For example, in "The Monkey's Paw," Herbert says that "something horrible squatting up on top of the wardrobe" will watch his father pocket the wished-for money. This hint suggests that frightening events are in store but leaves you guessing about what they are. Later you find out that Herbert's image also foreshadows something specific.

1. What exactly does the horrible squatting thing foreshadow?

2. Why is Herbert's statement that he'll never see the money an example of foreshadowing?

3. In "The Bridegroom," why is Natasha's first reaction to the "handsome young man" an example of foreshadowing?

4. Natasha invites "the law" to her wedding. What specific later event does this invitation foreshadow?

◆ Build Vocabulary

Using the Latin Root *-cred-*

Knowing that the Latin root *-cred-* means "to believe," use a form of the word *believe* in defining each of these words:

1. incredible **3.** credentials **5.** credit (noun)
2. credible **4.** credulity

Using the Word Bank: Synonyms

On your paper, write the word whose meaning is closest to that of the first word:

1. doughty: (a) exhausted, (b) sarcastic, (c) brave
2. maligned: (a) flattered, (b) slandered, (c) underlined
3. credulity: (a) gullibility, (b) disbelief, (c) futility
4. prosaic: (a) unusual, (b) essential, (c) ordinary
5. avaricious: (a) greedy, (b) generous, (c) stubborn
6. fusillade: (a) handful, (b) barrage, (c) shot
7. foreboding: (a) forewarning, (b) hindsight, (c) unawareness
8. tumult: (a) boredom, (b) order, (c) commotion

◆ Build Grammar Skills

Regular and Irregular Verbs

Irregular verbs, like the ones in the following chart, form their past and past participles in a variety of ways.

Practice Choose a form of the given irregular verb to complete the sentences.

Present	Past	Past Participle
know	knew	known
see	saw	seen
become	became	become

1. The sergeant major had __?__ what happened to people who used the monkey's paw. (see)
2. Mr. White __?__ fascinated with the monkey's paw. (become)
3. The Whites could not have __?__ the terrible result of their wishes. (know)
4. Natasha __?__ a sight that terrified her. (see)
5. Natasha's tale revealed what she __?__. (know)

Build Your Portfolio

Idea Bank

Writing

1. Newspaper Headlines For each selection, write two headlines that would entice people to read the sensational story. An example of such a headline might be "Bridegroom in Big Trouble."

2. Warning Label Write a warning label for the monkey's paw. Caution users to wish carefully and include a list of possible consequences for those who do not heed your warning.

3. Paw Proposal The Whites have given you the monkey's paw. Write a persuasive letter to a government leader suggesting how the paw could be used for the public good. **[Social Studies Link]**

Speaking, Listening, and Viewing

4. Television Interview With a partner, role-play an interview between Natasha from "The Bridegroom" and a television reporter. Focus on Natasha's three-day absence and her plans for confronting the criminal. **[Media Link]**

5. Dramatic Monologue Imagine the bridegroom in prison, awaiting execution. Write and perform a dramatic monologue for him, a speech he gives to a silent listener explaining *his* side of the story. **[Performing Arts Link]**

Researching and Representing

6. A Monkey's Paw Poll List ten possible wishes, ranging from such things as a shopping spree at the mall to a new school library. Use the list as a class survey and record your results on a bar graph or a pie chart. **[Math Link]**

7. Poster Showing Fortuna Research Fortuna, the ancient goddess of fortune. Then create a poster illustrating what you've learned about her. **[Social Studies Link; Art Link]**

Online Activity www.phlit.phschool.com

Guided Writing Lesson

Yearbook Prediction

Choose a wish you have for your own future. Then write a yearbook prediction for yourself based on this wish. Show the cause-and-effect relationships that would be involved in making your wish a reality.

Writing Skills Focus: Transitions to Show Cause and Effect

You'll need to use **transitions to show cause and effect**—words and phrases that show how one thing brings about another—when writing a how-to essay, a prediction, or a short story. Such transitions include words like *because, as a result,* and *consequently.* Jacobs uses one of these words in "The Monkey's Paw" to show how a situation influences people's thoughts:

transition — cause
"I suppose *because* only two houses on the road
effect
are let, they think it doesn't matter."

Prewriting Make an imaginary timeline showing how today's interests and abilities can lead you step by step to tomorrow's opportunities. In addition, list cause-and-effect transition words you can draw on as you draft and revise your prediction.

Drafting Refer to your cause-and-effect word list as you write, using transitions to show how one event brings about another.

Revising Reread your prediction and add transitions to clarify any vague cause-and-effect relationships. Also, be sure you've used the correct forms of any irregular verbs.

For more on regular and irregular verb forms, see Build Grammar Skills on pages 44 and 58.

Idea Bank

Following are suggestions for matching Idea Bank topics with your students' performance levels and learning modalities:

Customizing for Performance Levels

Less Advanced Students: 1, 4
Average Students: 2, 4, 6, 7
Pre-AP Students: 3, 5

Customizing for Learning Modalities

Visual/Spatial: 7
Verbal/Linguistic: 4,5
Logical/Mathematical: 6
Interpersonal: 4

Guided Writing Lesson

Prewriting Strategy To access memories that may contain interesting writing topics, encourage students to draw small illustrations to accompany the events on their timelines. As they draw, students should be open to the memories sparked by recreating events visually. Often topics are difficult to put into words, and drawing can help unlock interesting details that will later find their way into written accounts. After completing their illustrated timelines, students should examine their work and pinpoint the event that most "tugs at them." This event can be explored as a topic for their yearbook prediction.

For more prewriting, elaboration, and revision strategies, see *Prentice Hall Writing and Grammar.*

Writing Lab CD-ROM

Have students complete the tutorial on Narration. Follow these steps:

1. Have students use the Storyline Diagram to help them develop their plots.
2. Have students draft on computer.
3. Have students use the Self-Evaluation Checklist to help them revise.

ASSESSMENT OPTIONS

Formal Assessment, Selection Test, pp. 7–9, and Assessment Resources Software. The selection test is designed so that it can be easily customized to the performance levels of your students.

Alternative Assessment, p. 3, includes options for less advanced students, Pre-AP Students, verbal/linguistic learners, logical/mathematical learners, bodily/kinesthetic learners, interpersonal learners, and visual/spatial learners.

PORTFOLIO ASSESSMENT

Use the following rubrics in the ***Alternative Assessment*** booklet to assess student writing:
Newspaper Headlines: Summary Rubric, p. 98
Warning Label: Process Explanation Rubric, p. 100
Paw Proposal: Persuasion Rubric, p. 105
Guided Writing Lesson: Cause-and-Effect Rubric, p. 102

Prepare and Engage

LESSON OBJECTIVES

1. **To develop vocabulary and word identification skills**
   - Latin Word Roots: *-stup-*
   - Using the Word Bank: Context Clues
   - Extending Word Study: Use Reference Material (ATE)
2. **To use a variety of reading strategies to comprehend a short story**
   - Connect Your Experience
   - Reading Strategy: Draw Inferences
   - Tips to Guide Reading: Sustained Reading (ATE)
   - Read to Appreciate the Author's Craft (ATE)
   - Idea Bank: Letter of Introduction
3. **To increase knowledge of other cultures and to connect common elements across cultures**
   - Connecting Themes Across Cultures (ATE)
4. **To express and support responses to the text**
   - Critical Thinking
5. **To analyze literary elements**
   - Literary Focus: Flashback
6. **To read in order to research self-selected and assigned topics**
   - Idea Bank: Description of Antigua for the Internet
7. **To speak clearly and effectively for a specific audience and purpose**
   - Speaking, Listening, and Viewing Mini-Lesson: Conducting a Telephone Interview
   - Idea Bank: Persuasive Speech
8. **To plan, prepare, organize, and present literary interpretations**
   - Viewing and Representing Mini-Lesson: A Map of Annie's Walk (ATE)
9. **To use recursive writing processes to write a how-to manual**
   - Guided Writing Lesson
10. **To increase knowledge of the rules of grammar and usage**
    - Build Grammar Skills: Clauses

Test Preparation

Reading Comprehension: Using Context Clues to Determine Word Meanings (ATE, p. 61) The teaching tips and sample test item in this workshop support the instruction and practice in the unit workshop:

Reading Comprehension: Using Context Clues to Determine Word Meanings (SE, p. 113)

Guide for Reading

Jamaica Kincaid *(1949–)*

Imagine leaving everyone and everything that is familiar to you and moving to a foreign country on your own. That is exactly what this writer did.

At the age of sixteen, Jamaica Kincaid set off into the unknown.

She left her home in Antigua to take a job caring for the children of a family in New York.

A Changing Family Situation She was born Elaine Potter Richardson on the West Indian island of Antigua. Although she grew up in a home without electricity or running water, Kincaid's early childhood was a happy one because of her deep connection with her mother. As a teen however, she yearned for a life of her own.

She moved to America, held a series of unskilled jobs, and made an unsuccessful attempt to get a college degree. Despite setbacks, she entered the New York publishing world and soon was writing articles for teen magazines. She also adopted the pen name Jamaica Kincaid, a symbol of her new, independent self.

Literary Success Jamaica Kincaid has won acclaim for her autobiographical novels *Annie John* and *Lucy*. These works focus on the complex relationship between a mother and daughter and how it changes, sometimes painfully.

"A Walk to the Jetty" is the conclusion to *Annie John*. It describes the narrator's last walk through her childhood world, as she prepares to leave her native island.

◆ Build Vocabulary

LATIN WORD ROOTS: *-stup-*

In "A Walk to the Jetty," the main character shakes herself as if waking herself "out of a *stupor*." The word *stupor* contains the Latin root *-stup-*, which means "to be stunned or amazed." Knowing this meaning, you can figure out that *stupor* means "a state in which the mind is stunned."

WORD BANK

As you read the excerpt from "A Walk to the Jetty," you will encounter the words on this list. Each word is defined on the page where it first appears. Preview the list before you read.

loomed
apprenticed
raked
stupor

◆ Build Grammar Skills

CLAUSES

Clauses are groups of words with both a subject and a verb. An **independent clause** can stand by itself as a sentence, and a sentence can contain more than one independent clause. A **subordinate clause** cannot stand alone. It must be linked with an independent clause to form a sentence.

Kincaid uses both types of clauses:

subordinate clause (s, v): When we were all on board, | independent clause (s, v): the launch headed out to sea.

Prentice Hall Literature Program Resources

REINFORCE / RETEACH / EXTEND

Selection Support Pages
Build Vocabulary: Word Roots: *-stup-*, p. 14
Build Grammar Skills: Clauses, p. 15
Literary Focus: Flashback, p. 17
Reading Strategy: Make Inferences, p. 16

Strategies for Diverse Student Needs, p. 4

Beyond Literature
Cross-Curricular Connection: Social Studies. p. 4

Formal Assessment Selection Test, pp. 10–12; Assessment Resources Software

Alternative Assessment, p. 4

Resource Pro CD-ROM

Listening to Literature Audiocassettes

from A Walk to the Jetty

◆ Literature and Your Life

Connect Your Experience

One day you might move away from home to go to college, join the military, or live on your own. Preparing to leave, you may be flooded with memories. A little keepsake may recall a store that your family often visited. A battered volleyball may remind you of a field where you played with friends.

The teenage girl in this story is about to leave her island home, and her walk to the harbor is along a road of bittersweet memories.

Journal Writing Jot down some of the things you would miss most if you were leaving home.

Thematic Focus: Daring Decisions

On the verge of being an adult, the young woman in this story leaves her home and says goodbye to her childhood self.

◆ Reading Strategy

Draw Inferences

As you read a story, you can **draw inferences**—reach conclusions—about characters based on their speech, thoughts, and actions. These inferences help you better understand who the characters are and why they behave as they do.

In "A Walk to the Jetty," characters' present actions and flashbacks can serve as evidence in the text for inferences you draw. At the beginning of the story, for example, a flashback shows you how proud Annie's mother was when her five-year-old daughter went on an errand alone. From this detail, you can infer that Annie and her mother were very close.

◆ Background for Understanding

History

Antigua is the island home that Annie John, the main character in this story, is leaving. It is also the place where the author herself grew up. Antigua became a British colony in the seventeenth century and won its independence in 1981. As a result of the long-term British presence on the island, Antiguans speak English, use the British monetary system, and play British games such as cricket.

Early on, the British discovered that the island's tropical climate was ideal for growing sugar cane. Until 1834 when they abolished slavery, the British brought enslaved Africans to work on the island's sugar plantations. Most Antiguans, like Annie John and the author herself, are descendants of these Africans.

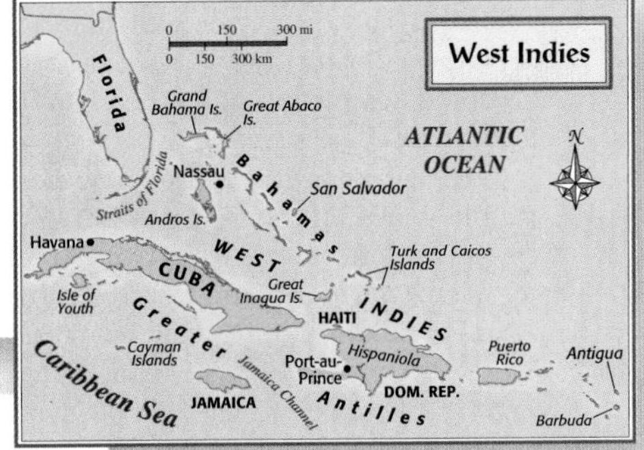

◆ Literary Focus

Flashback

A **flashback** is a section of a literary work that interrupts the sequence of events to relate an event from an earlier time. Writers often use flashbacks to show what motivates a character or to reveal something about a character's past in a dramatic way.

In this story, you learn about Annie John's childhood through a series of flashbacks triggered by familiar sights as she walks through town. These flashbacks hint at the reasons for Annie's departure.

Interest Grabber Invite students to picture themselves in the following situation: They are 16 years old and they are leaving their family to begin life in another country. Help students to generate a class list of the feelings that might surround these circumstances, such as fear of the unknown, excitement, and a sense of insecurity. Generate a brief discussion about ways students could help themselves overcome fears and maximize the positive aspects of this situation. Tell the class that Annie John had this experience as a teenager, and she shares her thoughts and feelings in this selection.

Connecting Themes Across Cultures

Suggest that students list historical occasions such as the Pilgrims coming to America, when people left their homes and traveled far away from friends and family. Challenge students to imagine what it must be like to make such a daring choice.

Tips to Guide Reading

Sustained Reading To lead students into a period of sustained reading, you may wish to read the first page of the selection out loud as an introduction. Invite students to continue to read to the end of the selection before pausing to answer the Guide for Responding questions.

Customize for *Less Proficient Readers*

Help students recognize flashbacks. Before they read, explain cues which may signal an earlier time, such as: "I was five years old. . . ."

Customize for *Pre-AP Students*

Students skilled at drawing inferences can model this process for others. Ask students to watch for details in the story that hint at Annie's relationship with her mother and father.

Customize for *Gifted/Talented Students*

Challenge students to write a second chapter to Annie's story. Suggest that they reread the selection to be certain that they accurately portray what might happen next on her journey.

Test Preparation Workshop

Reading Comprehension: Use Context Clues to Determine Word Meanings Students taking the SAT test may be required to determine the best meaning of a vocabulary word from the context of a reading passage. Use the following sample question.

"She boiled my milk to purify it before I was allowed to drink it."

Which of the following represents the best meaning of the word purify as it is used in this sentence?

A to free from guilt
B to ceremoniously clean
C to cleanse
D to purge

Discuss with students that they should carefully read each answer choice to make the best selection, as more than one choice may answer the question. Milk would not be considered guilty; boiling milk is not ceremoniously cleaning, so *A* and *B* are incorrect. While *D* may seem to be a good choice, *C* is closer in meaning to the action of sterilizing milk by boiling, therefore *C* is a better choice.

Develop Understanding

One-Minute Insight Fear, excitement, nostalgia, resentment, confusion, regret—this autobiographical story captures all the complex emotions a young adult can feel when taking the first tentative steps toward independence. For Annie John, the emotions associated with leaving home are complicated by her conflicted relationship with her mother and her island home, as well as her need to rise above the low expectations for girls in her culture. Students will find much to identify with in this poignant leaving-home story.

❶ **Clarification** Point out that some ports are too shallow to accommodate large ships, so passengers must be ferried out to the ships in deep water.

◆ *Literature and Your Life*

❷ Have students write in their journals about a time they were in the company of their parent(s) or guardian(s). Have them analyze how this feeling is connected to a growing sense of independence.

◆ Reading Strategy

❸ **Infer** Students may say that Miss Dulcie's treatment of Annie shows a lack of respect for the girl's feelings and intelligence. The woman's low expectations for Annie and her critical, fault-finding attitude may have been typical of the way adults treated Annie.

◆ Critical Thinking

❹ **Interpret** Ask what the narrator means by "the dustheap of my life." *The narrator considers the experiences with Miss Dulcie as something to be discarded—in "the dustheap."*

Customize for
English Language Learners
Students from the West Indies can share their knowledge of these islands. Other immigrants may be unfamiliar with the Britishisms *chemist* (druggist, pharmacist), *cricket* (a game with some resemblance to baseball), and *sixpence* (a unit of money). Use the footnotes in the story to clarify these terms before students read.

from A Walk to the Jetty

from Annie John

Jamaica Kincaid

My mother had arranged with a stevedore[1] to take my trunk to the jetty ahead of me. At ten o'clock on the dot, I was dressed, and we set off for
❶ the jetty. An hour after that, I would board
a launch that would take me out to sea, where I then would board the ship. Starting out, as if for old time's sake and without giving it a thought, we lined up in the old way: I walking between my mother and my
❷ father. I loomed way above my father and
could see the top of his head. We must have made a strange sight: a grown girl all dressed up in the middle of a morning, in the middle of the week, walking in step in the middle between her two parents, for people we didn't know stared at us. It was all of half an hour's walk from our house to the jetty, but I was passing through most of the years of my life. We passed by the house where Miss Dulcie, the seamstress that I had been apprenticed to for a time, lived, and just as I was passing by, a wave of bad feeling for her came over me, because I suddenly remembered that the months I spent with her all she had me do was sweep the floor, which was always full of threads and pins and needles, and I never seemed to sweep it clean enough to please her. Then she would send me to the store to buy buttons or thread, though I was only allowed to do this if I was given a sample of the button or thread, and then she would find fault even though they were an exact match of the samples she had given me. And all the while she said to me, "A girl like you will never learn to sew properly, you know." At the time, I don't suppose I minded it, because it was customary to treat the first-year apprentice with such scorn, but now I placed
on the dustheap of my life Miss Dulcie and ❹
everything that I had had to do with her.

> ◆ **Reading Strategy**
> How does this first reminiscence of childhood help you infer why Annie might be leaving the island?

1. **stevedore** (stē′ və dôr) *n.*: Person whose job is loading and unloading ships.

◆ **Build Vocabulary**

loomed (lo͞omd) *v.*: Appeared in a large or threatening form

apprenticed (ə pren′ tist) *v.*: Assigned to work a specified length of time in a craft or trade in return for instruction

Block Scheduling Strategies

Consider these suggestions to take advantage of extended class time:

- Introduce the reading strategy. You may wish to use the Reading Strategy page from ***Selection Support*** (p. 16) to give students practice in making inferences before they read the story.
- After students have read the selection, facilitate (or choose a student to facilitate) a panel discussion on the role of girls and women in Antigua versus the United States. Encourage West Indian students to lend their expertise to the discussion.
- Give students the Cross-Curricular Connection, from ***Beyond Literature*** (p. 4). Have them do the map activity to build background on Antigua.
- Have students complete the Guided Writing Lesson on p. 70. First they can meet in small groups to brainstorm for ideas and procedures to include in their manual. Then each person can choose one procedure to break down into steps.
- Encourage students to research information about Antigua and the West Indies on the Internet.

San Antonio de Oriente (detail), José Antonio Velásquez, Museum of Modern Art of Latin America, Washington, D.C.

5 ▲ **Critical Viewing** In what ways does this picture evoke a small-town feel? **[Interpret]**

▶Critical Viewing◀

5 Interpret *Students may say that the photograph conveys a small-town feel because it depicts a landscape with few buildings, people, or vehicles; the town is surrounded by nature; and the church seems to be the focus of the town.*

Read to Appreciate Author's Craft

Have students analyze Kincaid's use of flashbacks to appreciate her creation of Annie. Discuss writing elements, such as first-person point of view, that make Annie an interesting character.

Extending Word Study

Dictionary Suggest that students preview the Build Vocabulary and numbered words defined in the text before beginning to read. After they finish, have them look up each word in the dictionary and compare the precise definition given in the text to the choices in the dictionary.

Customize for *Bodily/Kinesthetic Learners*

To help these students infer Annie's feelings, have them role-play one of the flashbacks or the final scene in which Annie boards the ship and says good-bye to her parents. After the role-plays, have students tell what emotions they think each character in the scene was feeling.

Customize for *Visual/Spatial Learners*

Encourage these students to use the painting on this page to help them envision the story's setting. Have them note the colorfulness of the landscape that is depicted, and draw their attention to the many flowers. Point out that the lush vegetation is typical of a tropical landscape.

Humanities: Art

San Antonio de Oriente (detail) by José Antonio Velásquez.

This painting depicts a quiet Honduran village in a setting similar to the one Jamaica Kincaid—and her character Annie John—decided to leave.

The primitivist painter José Antonio Velásquez has painted many pictures depicting San Antonio de Oriente, a small town in the Latin American country of Honduras. His paintings allow viewers to identify the charming and humble reality of Honduran small towns—and of small towns the world over. In this painting, the rhythmic patterns of the tiles, flowers, and stone walls are offset by the smooth, solid planes of the white walls of the buildings and the colorful wash hung on a line in the foreground. Encourage students to study the painting and then use these questions for discussion.

1. What mood, or feeling, does the painting convey to you? *Responses may range from peaceful, quiet, serene, unhurried, and relaxing to lazy and boring.*
2. Why might a young person who grew up in such a setting choose to leave it as he or she reaches adulthood? *Responses may include a desire for a more exciting, busy life; desire for economic opportunities available only in metropolitan areas; desire to be in touch with technological progress and popular culture; desire to meet a wider variety of people.*

◆ Literary Focus

1 Flashback Students may mention the three pennies, the little basket, the freshly ironed yellow dress printed with acrobats, the smell of Annie's mother's talcum powder, the scene on the can of talcum powder, the name of the talcum powder, her mother's tears of pride and joy at Annie's return, her being swooped up in her mother's arms, and her mother's proud words at Annie's accomplishments.

◆ Critical Thinking

2 Analyze Ask students what this vivid memory suggests about Annie's childhood relationship with her mother. *Students may say that Annie and her mother had a close, affectionate relationship, that Annie's mother was proud of her young daughter's growing independence, and that her mother's pride in her meant a great deal to Annie.*

◆ Build Grammar Skills

3 Clauses Have students identify the independent and subordinate clauses in the two sentences beginning "Once, when she had mumps" and "I don't know how." *Once I went to visit her against my mother's wishes—independent; when she had mumps—subordinate; we sat on her bed and ate the cure of roasted, buttered sweet potatoes—independent; that had been placed on her swollen jaw—subordinate; I don't know how—independent; my mother found out about it—subordinate; I don't know how—independent; she put an end to our friendship—independent.*

◆ Literature and Your Life

4 Ask students if they can remember an instance when, like Annie John, they argued with their parent(s) over an article of clothing. What are some reasons parents and children argue over clothing? *Students might say that parents' ideas about clothes don't often match theirs. Parents might perceive their children's independent taste in clothing as a sign they are growing away from them; parents sometimes disagree with or don't understand the important role clothes play in gaining social acceptance.*

We were soon on the road that I had taken to school, to church, to Sunday school, to choir practice, to Brownie meetings, to Girl Guide meetings, to meet a friend. I was five years old when I first walked on this road unaccompanied by someone to hold my hand. My mother had placed three pennies in my little basket, which was a duplicate of her bigger basket, and sent me to the chemist's shop to buy a pennyworth of senna leaves, a pennyworth of eucalyptus leaves, and a pennyworth of camphor.[2] She then instructed me on what side of the road to walk, where to make a turn, where to cross, how to look carefully before I crossed, and if I met anyone that I knew to politely pass greetings and keep on my way. I was wearing a freshly ironed yellow dress that had printed on it scenes of acrobats flying through the air and swinging on a trapeze. I had just had a bath, and after it, instead of powdering me with my baby-smelling talcum powder, my mother had, as a special favor, let me use her own talcum powder, which smelled quite perfumy and came in a can that had painted on it people going out to dinner in nineteenth-century London and was called Mazie. How it pleased me to walk out the door and bend my head down to sniff at myself and see that I smelled just like my mother. I went to the chemist's shop, and he had to come from behind the counter and bend down to hear what it was that I wanted to buy, my voice was so little and timid then. I went back just the way I had come, and when I walked into the yard and presented my basket with its three packages to my mother, her eyes filled with tears and she swooped me up and held me high in the air and said that I was wonderful and good and that there would never be anybody better. If I had just conquered Persia, she couldn't have been more proud of me.

> **◆ Literary Focus**
> 1 What details in this flashback help you to picture in your mind Annie's first walk?

We passed by our church—the church in which I had been christened and received[3] and had sung in the junior choir. We passed by a house in which a girl I used to like and was sure I couldn't live without had lived. Once, when she had mumps, I went to visit her against my mother's wishes, and we sat on her bed and ate the cure of roasted, buttered sweet potatoes that had been placed on her swollen jaws, held there by a piece of white cloth. I don't know how, but my mother found out about it, and I don't know how, but she put an end to our friendship. Shortly after, the girl moved with her family across the sea to somewhere else. We passed the doll store, where I would go with my mother when I was little and point out the doll I wanted that year for Christmas. We passed the store where I bought the much-fought-over shoes I wore to church to be received in. We passed the bank. On my sixth birthday, I was given, among other things, the present of a sixpence.[4] My mother and I then went to this bank, and with the sixpence I opened my own savings account. I was given a little gray book with my name in big letters on it, and in the balance column it said "6d." Every Saturday morning after that, I was given a sixpence—later a shilling, and later a two-and-sixpence piece—and I would take it to the bank for deposit. I had never been allowed to withdraw even a farthing from my bank account until just a few weeks before I was to leave; then the whole account was closed out, and I received from the bank the sum of six pounds ten shillings and two and a half pence.

2. **chemist's shop . . . camphor** (kam´ fər): The first phrase is a British term for a pharmacy. The items mentioned are small amounts of plant matter to be used in remedies.

3. **received** *v.*: Accepted into the congregation as a mature Christian.

4. **sixpence** *n.*: A monetary unit in the British commonwealth, worth six pennies (not of the same value as the pennies in United States currency). A shilling is worth two sixpence, a two-and-sixpence is two and one-half shillings, that is, two shillings and one sixpence. A pound is worth twenty shillings. A farthing is a "fourthing": one fourth of a penny.

Viewing and Representing Mini-Lesson

Map of Annie's Walk

This mini-lesson supports the Researching and Representing activity on p. 70 of the Idea Bank.

Introduce Have students look at a variety of maps in the atlas or a social studies text book and study the way the details are presented and how the map legend is constructed.

Develop Suggest that students quickly skim the selection and take careful notes of the details of Annie's walk that the author mentions. Some students may wish to add further details to the list from their own imagination.

Apply Using their notes, have students create a map of Annie's neighborhood and the walk to the jetty. Some students may wish to draw a stylized map that uses art materials and is colorful; others may wish to create a detailed line drawing map; they might use magazine photographs as illustrations. If they wish, students may create a three-dimensional representation of Annie's walk.

Assess Have students display their maps in the classroom. Assess students' projects based on completeness and accurate details, how well directions were followed, and creativity.

We passed the office of the doctor who told my mother three times that I did not need glasses, that if my eyes were feeling weak a glass of carrot juice a day would make them strong again. This happened when I was eight. And so every day at recess I would run to my school gate and meet my mother, who was waiting for me with a glass of juice from carrots she had just grated and then squeezed, and I would drink it and then run back to meet my chums. I knew there was nothing at all wrong with my eyes, but I had recently read a story in *The Schoolgirl's Own Annual* in which the heroine, a girl a few years older than I was then, cut such a figure to my mind with the way she was always adjusting her small, round, horn-rimmed glasses that I felt I must have a pair exactly like them. When it became clear that I didn't need glasses, I began to complain about the glare of the sun being too much for my eyes, and I walked around with my hands shielding them—especially in my mother's presence. My mother then bought for me a pair of sunglasses with the exact horn-rimmed frames I wanted, and how I enjoyed the gestures of blowing on the lenses, wiping them with the hem of my uniform, adjusting the glasses when they slipped down my nose, and just removing them from their case and putting them on. In three weeks, I grew tired of them and they found a nice resting place in a drawer, along with some other things that at one time or another I couldn't live without.

We passed the store that sold only grooming aids, all imported from England. This store had in it a large porcelain dog—white, with black spots all over and a red ribbon of satin tied around its neck. The dog sat in front of a white porcelain bowl that was always filled with fresh water, and it sat in such a way that it looked as if it had just taken a long drink. When I was a small child, I would ask my mother, if ever we were near this store, to please take me to see the dog, and I would stand in front of it, bent over slightly, my hands resting on my knees, and stare at it and stare at it. I

Port de la Saline, Haiti, Lois Mailou Jones

▲ Critical Viewing The people in this painting are setting out on unique adventures. Explain how you can be surrounded by people sharing a similar experience and yet still be alone. **[Analyze]**

◆ Critical Thinking

5 Evaluate Ask students what this episode about the carrot juice and Annie's demand for glasses reveals about the personalities of Annie and her mother and their relationship. *Students may say that the episode shows that Annie is imaginative, impressionable, determined, and changeable. Her mother seems devoted to Annie's needs and desires and is eager to please her when possible.*

▶Critical Viewing◀

6 Analyze *Students may say that an experience such as setting out on an adventure can arouse feelings such as fear of the unknown or sadness at leaving loved ones. These feelings can cause people to withdraw into their own memories of the past or their fantasies about the future, rather than relating to people sharing their current experience.*

Customize for
Less Proficient Readers
Check these students' comprehension by having them summarize the events leading up to this point in the story. Then encourage them to make predictions about how the story will turn out. Urge them to record their predictions, and revise them as they proceed through the story.

Customize for
Gifted/Talented Students
Students may be interested in studying the emigration patterns of the population of the islands of Antigua and Barbados in recent years. In the 1980's, for example, 17 percent legally emigrated to North America. Many of those leaving were young professionals. Have students speculate about what effects a tiny island nation might experience when a number of young people trained in professions leave.

Humanities: Art

Port de la Saline, Haiti, by Lois Mailou Jones.

Lois Mailou Jones was born in Boston in 1905. She has enjoyed a consistently successful career as a painter, teacher, book illustrator, and textile designer. In 1945, James Lane, then curator of painting at the National Gallery of Art in Washington, D.C., said of Jones's work, "It is all, in the best sense of the word, happy art."

This painting depicts a busy wharf in the Caribbean island nation of Haiti. Its vivid primary colors and repeated angular forms suggest a busy, bustling place. The geometric shapes of the clouds, sails, and foreground objects speak of the artist's ties to the style of Cubism and fascination with African textile patterns. The port suggests a connection with other parts of the world, a connection that Annie John is about to make.

1. How does the mood of this scene compare to that of the art on p. 61? *The mood of this piece is bustling, vibrant, and exciting, unlike the calm mood of the earlier work.*
2. What feelings might a child growing up in an otherwise serene island have about visiting the island's busy harbor? *It might seem exciting or frightening; seeing boats arrive from faraway places might evoke curiosity and eagerness to see those places.*

◆ Reading Strategy

1 Infer Students may say that the library was important to Annie because it was important to her mother, and she wanted to be close to her mother and be like her mother. They may also say that the books in the library allowed the curious girl a view of a wider world outside her island home and that she was a young person with a vivid imagination who loved books.

2 Clarification Make sure students understand that a jetty is a platform or other structure projecting out into a harbor to influence the current or tide or protect a harbor or shoreline. A jetty may connect to a wharf, where boats can pull alongside to pick up or discharge passengers and cargo.

◆ Critical Thinking

3 Interpret Ask how the narrator's description of physical sensations suggests an emotional state. *The increased heartbeat and open mouth reflect her nervousness and anticipation.*

◆ Critical Thinking

4 Compare and Contrast Have students compare and contrast Annie's childhood feelings about being in her father's company with those feelings she has expressed about being in her mother's company. *As a child, Annie felt very intimate with her mother and comfortable sharing the experiences and feelings of her mother's world. In contrast, she finds her father's conversation difficult to understand and identify with because it is not "personal."*

◆ Literary Focus

5 Flashback In what specific way is this flashback relevant to the action on the jetty now? *Students might say that the fact that this childhood fear returns as she is about to leave home is significant because now—as then—she fears her uncertain, unknown future.*

thought this dog more beautiful and more real than any actual dog I had ever seen or any actual dog I would ever see. I must have outgrown my interest in the dog, for when it disappeared I never asked what became of it. We passed the library, and if there was anything on this walk that I might have wept over leaving, this most surely would have been the thing. My mother had been a member of the library long before I was born. And since she took me everywhere with her when I was quite little, when she went to the library she took me along there, too. I would sit in her lap very quietly as she read books that she did not want to take home with her. I could not read the words yet, but just the way they looked on the page was interesting to me. Once, a book she was reading had a large picture of a man in it, and when I asked her who he was she told me that he was Louis Pasteur[5] and that the book was about his life. It stuck in my mind, because she said it was because of him that she boiled my milk to purify it before I was allowed to drink it, that it was his idea, and that that was why the process was called pasteurization. One of the things I had put away in my mother's old trunk in which she kept all my childhood things was my library card. At that moment, I owed sevenpence in overdue fees.

> ◆ Reading Strategy
> 1 Infer why the library is such an important part of Annie's childhood.

As I passed by all these places, it was as if I were in a dream, for I didn't notice the people coming and going in and out of them, I didn't feel my feet touch ground, I didn't even feel my own body—I just saw these places as if they were hanging in the air, not having top or bottom, and as if I had gone in and out of them all in the same moment. The sun was bright; the sky was blue and just above my head. We then arrived at the jetty. 2

5. **Louis Pasteur** (Pas tʉr´) (1822–1895): The French chemist and bacteriologist who developed the process (pasteurization) for using heat to kill disease-causing bacteria in milk.

My heart now beat fast, and no matter how hard I tried, I couldn't keep my mouth from falling open and my nostrils from spreading to the ends of my face. 3 My old fear of slipping between the boards of the jetty and falling into the dark-green water where the dark-green eels lived came over me. When my father's stomach started to go bad, the doctor had recommended a walk every evening right after he ate his dinner. Sometimes he would take me with him. When he took me with him, we usually went to the jetty, and there he would sit and talk to the night watchman about cricket[6] or some other thing that didn't interest me, because it was not personal; they didn't talk about their wives, or their children, or their parents, or about any of their likes and dislikes. They talked about things in such a strange way, and I didn't see what they found funny, but sometimes they made each other laugh so much that their guffaws would bound out to sea and send back an echo. I was always sorry when we got to the jetty and saw that the night watchman on duty was the one he enjoyed speaking to; it was like being locked up in a book filled with numbers and diagrams and what-ifs. 4 For the thing about not being able to understand and enjoy what they were saying was I had nothing to take my mind off my fear of slipping in between the boards of the jetty. 5

Now, too, I had nothing to take my mind off what was happening to me. My mother and my father—I was leaving them forever. My home on an island—I was leaving it forever. What to make of everything? I felt a familiar hollow space inside. I felt I was being held down against my will. I felt I was burning up from head to toe. I felt that someone was tearing me up into little pieces and soon I would be able to see all the little pieces as they floated out into nothing in the deep blue sea. I didn't know whether to laugh or cry. I could see that it would be

6. **cricket** *n.*: A British game, similar to baseball, but played with a flat bat and eleven players on each team.

Reteach

Some students may experience difficulty following the story because the author's use of flashbacks seems to disrupt the chronological order and flow of the story. Students may find it helpful to use a timeline to organize story events. Have them design a timeline on a piece of paper, using a straight edge to draw a line. Then guide students as they reread the story and find details to place on the timeline as starting and ending points—they can place other events in relation to these points. If the author does not specify a date or Annie's age in the text, students must be prepared to make an educated guess as to where events should be placed on the timeline. For example, at the beginning of the story Annie says she is a "grown girl." Students may need to reread carefully to see if the author ever says how old Annie is when she leaves home. Have students discuss in small groups the author's details that indicate how they should create their timelines.

better not to think too clearly about any one thing. The launch was being made ready to take me, along with some other passengers, out to the ship that was anchored in the sea. My father paid our fares, and we joined a line of people waiting to board. My mother checked my bag to make sure that I had my passport, the money she had given me, and a sheet of paper placed between some pages in my Bible on which were written the names of the relatives—people I had not known existed—with whom I would live in England. Across from the jetty was a wharf, and some stevedores were loading and unloading barges. I don't know why seeing that struck me so, but suddenly a wave of strong feeling came over me, and my heart swelled with a great gladness as the words "I shall never see this again" spilled out inside me. But then, just as quickly, my heart shriveled up and the words "I shall never see this again" stabbed at me. I don't know what stopped me from falling in a heap at my parents' feet.

When we were all on board, the launch headed out to sea. Away from the jetty, the water became the customary blue, and the launch left a wide path in it that looked like a road. I passed by sounds and smells that were so familiar that I had long ago stopped paying any attention to them. But now here they were, and the ever-present "I shall never see this again" bobbed up and down inside me. There was the sound of the seagull diving down into the water and coming up with something silverish in its mouth. There was the smell of the sea and the sight of small pieces of rubbish floating around in it. There were boats filled with fishermen coming in early. There was the sound of their voices as they shouted greetings to each other. There was the hot sun, there was the blue sea, there was the blue sky. Not very far away, there was the white sand of the shore, with the run-down houses all crowded in next to each other, for in some places only poor people lived near the shore. I was seated in the launch between my parents, and when I realized that I was gripping their hands tightly I glanced quickly to see if they were looking at me with scorn, for I felt sure that they must have known of my never-see-this-again feelings. But instead my father kissed me on the forehead and my mother kissed me on the mouth, and they both gave over their hands to me, so that I could grip them as much as I wanted. I was on the verge of feeling that it had all been a mistake, but I remembered that I wasn't a child anymore, and that now when I made up my mind about something I had to see it through. At that moment, we came to the ship, and that was that.

The goodbyes had to be quick, the captain said. My mother introduced herself to him and then introduced me. She told him to keep an eye on me, for I had never gone this far away from home on my own. She gave him a letter to pass on to the captain of the next ship that I would board in Barbados.[7] They walked me to my cabin, a small space that I would share with someone else—a woman I did not know. I had never before slept in a room with someone I did not know. My father kissed me goodbye and told me to be good and to write home often. After he said this, he looked at me, then looked at the floor and swung his left foot, then looked at me again. I could see that he wanted to say something else, something that he had never said to me before, but then he just turned and walked away. My mother said, "Well," and then she threw her arms around me. Big tears streamed down her face, and it must have been that—for I could not bear to see my mother cry—which started me crying, too. She then tightened

> **◆ Reading Strategy**
> What can you infer about Annie's relationship with her mother based on the fact that she cannot breathe because her mother squeezes her so tightly?

7. **Barbados** (bär bā′ dōs): The easternmost island in the West Indies; southeast of Antigua.

◆ Critical Thinking

6 Interpret Ask students why the words "I shall never see this again" first cause Annie's heart to swell with gladness and then shrivel up? *She has mixed emotions about leaving the people and places she knows. She longs for wider experience and opportunities, but she loves much of her past and fears her uncertain future.*

◆ Critical Thinking

7 Analyze Ask students how Annie's parents surprise her on the launch. What does this scene suggest about Annie's relationship with her parents? *She expects them to note her weakness, but instead they kiss her and offer their hands to her. Annie discovers how much her parents love her and how much she depends on them.*

◆ Critical Thinking

8 Analyze What do you think Annie's father wanted to say to her that he had never said before? *He wanted to say he loved her.*

◆ Reading Strategy

9 Make Inferences *Students may say Annie feels her mother is overprotective, holding her back from her own life.*

Customize for
Intrapersonal Learners
As Annie walks to the jetty, she passes community landmarks that remind her of her childhood. Every community has such landmarks. Suggest that students consider the landmarks in their own community such as buildings, parks, or monuments. Then have them consider "personal landmarks" similar to what Annie recalls in the story. Have each student write a description of his or her personal landmarks, explaining their importance.

Speaking, Listening, and Viewing Mini-Lesson

Conducting a Telephone Interview

This mini-lesson supports the Speaking, Listening, and Viewing activity in the Idea Bank on p. 70.

Introduce Tell students that an interview is an opportunity to ask a knowledgeable person a series of focused questions. An interview is an excellent way to gather first-hand, practical information.

Develop Help students prepare for their interview by giving them these pointers:

- Students should develop a list of specific questions to ask. What particular concerns do they have about traveling on their own?
- Students should be prepared to ask follow-up questions.
- Encourage students to take notes or tape the interview.

Apply Help groups of students to locate a travel agent to interview. Have them schedule their telephone interview for a time that is convenient for the travel agent and then carry out the telephone interview. As the interviewee answers their questions, they should take notes. Have them share the information they received with the class.

Assess Evaluate the success of the interviews with these questions: (1) What valuable tips for traveling did they gain? (2) What important information did follow-up questions elicit? (3) What did they learn about conducting an interview?

◆ Critical Thinking

1 Support Ask students how this last image reinforces one of the themes of the selection. *The image reinforces her growing separation from her mother.*

Reinforce and Extend

Answers

◆ *Literature and Your Life*

Reader's Response Students may admire Annie for leaving home because she was looking to better herself.

Thematic Focus Students may suggest pursuing a new interest or forging new friendships.

☑ **Check Your Comprehension**

1. The places that remind Annie of her childhood are Miss Dulcie's house, the chemist's shop, the church, the doll store, the bank, the doctor's office, and the store that sold grooming aids.
2. Miss Dulcie's house conjures up her unhappy days as a seamstress's apprentice; the chemist's shop makes her think of her first walk alone; the church calls up her christening and the choir; the doll store makes her think of her Christmas dolls; the bank brings back memories of opening her savings account; the doctor's office makes her recall her longing for eyeglasses; the grooming store makes her think of the porcelain dog in the window.
3. Annie has mixed feelings about leaving home. She is happy to be independent, but at the same time, sad to leave home.
4. Annie's mother clutches Annie tightly and sobs during the farewell. Annie's father looks as if he has something important to say, then walks away.

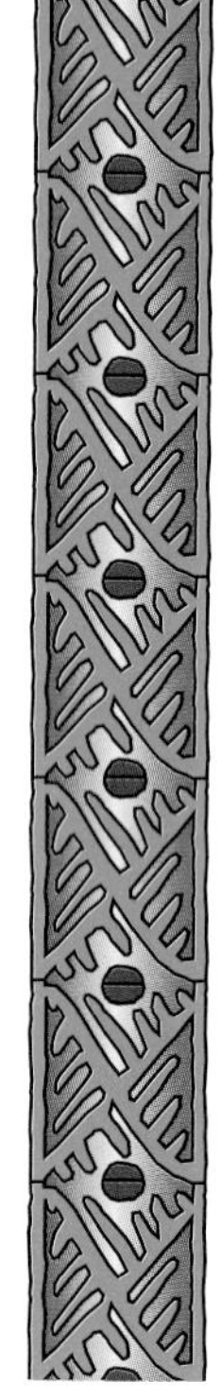

her arms around me and held me to her close, so that I felt that I couldn't breathe. With that, my tears dried up and I was suddenly on my guard. "What does she want now?" I said to myself. Still holding me close to her, she said, in a voice that raked across my skin, "It doesn't matter what you do or where you go, I'll always be your mother and this will always be your home."

I dragged myself away from her and backed off a little, and then I shook myself, as if to wake myself out of a stupor. We looked at each other for a long time with smiles on our faces, but I know the opposite of that was in my heart. As if responding to some invisible cue, we both said, at the very same moment, "Well." Then my mother turned around and walked out the cabin door. I stood there for I don't know how long, and then I remembered that it was customary to stand on deck and wave to your relatives who were returning to shore. From the deck, I could not see my father, but I could see my mother facing the ship, her eyes searching to pick me out. I removed from my bag a red cotton handkerchief that she had earlier given me for this purpose, and I waved it wildly in the air. Recognizing me immediately, she waved back just as wildly, and we continued to do this until she became just a dot in the matchbox-size launch swallowed up in the big blue sea.

I went back to my cabin and lay down on my berth. Everything trembled as if it had a spring at its very center. I could hear the small waves lap-lapping around the ship. They made an unexpected sound, as if a vessel filled with liquid had been placed on its side and now was slowly emptying out.

◆ Build Vocabulary

raked (rākd) *v.*: Scratched or scraped, as with a rake

stupor (sto͞o′ per) *n.*: Mental dullness, as if drugged

Guide for Responding

◆ *Literature and Your Life*

Reader's Response Do you admire Annie for leaving home? Why or why not?

Thematic Focus There are many quieter ways of showing independence than a dramatic departure from home. Tell about a quiet way in which you have shown greater maturity and independence.

Timeline On a timeline showing the next five years, indicate some of the steps you will take to achieve an important goal.

☑ **Check Your Comprehension**

1. Identify four of the places that remind Annie of episodes from her childhood.
2. Briefly summarize the memory that each of these places calls up.
3. What are Annie's feelings about leaving home?
4. Describe how her mother and father say goodbye.

Beyond Literature

Geography Connection

The Landscape and Climate of Antigua White sand beaches, spectacular coral reefs, and an average temperature of 80 degrees make Antigua a popular vacation spot. There are 365 beaches on Antigua—one for each day of the year! Antigua is about 14 miles long and 11 miles wide, covering 108 square miles. With an average rainfall of only 40 inches per year, Antigua is one of the sunniest eastern Caribbean islands. While this is welcome news for tourists, for the people who live on Antigua year-round, droughts can be devastating to their property and livelihood. Why do you think islands are such popular tourist spots?

Beyond the Selection

FURTHER READING

Other Works by Jamaica Kincaid

Annie John, Lucy, The Autobiography of My Mother

Other Works About Growing Up and Leaving Home

The Beggar Maid and Other Stories, Alice Munro

Black Ice, Lorene Cary

I Know Why the Caged Bird Sings, Maya Angelou

We suggest that you preview these works before recommending them to students.

INTERNET

For more information on Jamaica Kincaid, we suggest that you and your students visit the following site on the Internet. Please be aware, however, that sites may have changed from the time we published this information. **http://www.Salon1999.com./05/ features/ kincaid.html**

We *strongly recommend* that you preview the site before you send students to it.

Guide for Responding (continued)

◆ Critical Thinking

Interpret

1. In what way is Annie walking through time as well as through space? **[Infer]**

2. Why does Annie reexperience her old fear of falling through the boards of the jetty? **[Infer]**

3. Compare Annie's relationship with her father with the one she has with her mother. **[Compare and Contrast]**

4. Describe Annie's response to leaving the island. **[Interpret]**

Apply

5. Will Annie be successful in her new life? Why or why not? **[Hypothesize]**

Extend

6. Although Annie disliked it, an apprentice situation could have advantages. Name three trades that could be best learned this way. **[Career Link]**

◆ Reading Strategy

Draw Inferences

Annie's mother hugs Annie so tightly that she can hardly breathe. From this painful embrace and Annie's response to it, you can **infer** that Annie sometimes feels trapped by her mother.

From the following text details, draw inferences about Annie's relationship with her father.

1. His conversation with the watchman didn't interest her "because it was not personal."

2. As they part, he wants "to say . . . something he had never said . . . before," but then he walks away.

◆ Literary Focus

Flashback

This story is told mainly through **flashbacks,** journeys back into time. These flashbacks help you understand how Annie developed, but their precise details also make the past come alive.

1. Find two other flashbacks and explain how the author uses precise details to make them vivid.

2. What do the flashbacks suggest about Annie's reasons for leaving home?

◆ Build Vocabulary

Using the Latin Root *-stup-*

Knowing that *-stup-* means "to be stunned or amazed," choose the letter of the best synonym for each of the numbered words containing *-stup-*.

1. stupefy: (a) entertain, (b) numb, (c) revive

2. stupendous: (a) astonishing, (b) excessive, (c) ridiculous

3. stupefaction: (a) alertness, (b) satisfaction, (c) bewilderment

Using the Word Bank: Sentence Completions

On your paper, complete each sentence with the most appropriate word from the Word Bank:

1. Annie had been __?__ to a rude and stern seamstress.

2. Annie __?__ above her father and could see the top of his head.

3. Annie complained that her mother's voice __?__ across her skin.

4. For a moment, staring at her mother, Annie was in a __?__.

◆ Build Grammar Skills

Clauses

A **clause** is a group of words that contains both a subject and a verb. An **independent clause** can stand alone as a sentence, but a **subordinate clause** cannot.

Practice Identify the independent and subordinate clauses in these sentences from the story.

1. If I had just conquered Persia, she couldn't have been more proud of me.

2. We passed the bank.

3. We then arrived at the jetty.

4. My father paid our fares, and we joined a line of people waiting to board.

5. She told him to keep an eye on me, for I had never gone this far away from home on my own.

Writing Application Write a paragraph describing places that are special to you. Include at least three sentences that contain subordinate clauses.

Answers

◆ Critical Thinking

1. As she walks, Annie is going back to scenes from her childhood and forward to a new life.
2. Annie's fear reflects her apprehension about leaving home.
3. Annie's relationship with her father is constrained, while the relationship with her mother is affectionate and mutually dependent.
4. Her response to leaving home is bittersweet; she's torn between the need to strike out on her own and her attachment to childhood experiences.
5. Some students will say that although luck will play a role in Annie's future, her determination and curiosity will serve her well in her new life.
6. Examples of trades in which people could benefit from an apprenticeship include electrician, carpenter, hair stylist, salesperson.

◆ Reading Strategy

1. Since Annie responds to the personal, you can infer her relationship with her father is remote.
2. You can infer that this lost opportunity to make a connection leaves both Annie and her father feeling sad; the incident reinforces their communication difficulties.

◆ Literary Focus

1. Possible flashbacks include the apprenticeship with Miss Dulcie, brought alive by details such as sweeping needles off the floor, and Annie's walk to the chemist, brought alive by details such as the smell of her mother's talcum powder and Annie's dress with acrobats on it.
2. Some students will say the flashbacks suggest that Annie was overprotected and that her life in Antigua had its limitations; therefore, she wanted to leave home.

◆ Build Grammar Skills

1. If I had just conquered Persia—*subordinate*; she couldn't have been more proud of me—*independent*
2. We passed the bank—*independent*
3. We then arrived at the jetty—*independent*
4. My father paid our fares—*independent*; we joined a line of people waiting to board—*independent*
5. She told him to keep an eye on me—*independent*; I had never gone this far away from home on my own—*independent*

Grammar Reinforcement

For additional instruction and practice, use the lesson in the **Language Lab CD-ROM** on clauses and use the pages on clauses (pp. 51–58) in the *Writer's Solution Grammar Practice Book.*

◆ Build Vocabulary

Using the Word Root *-stup-*

1. b 2. a 3. c

Using the Word Bank

1. apprenticed; 2. loomed; 3. raked; 4. stupor

Idea Bank

Following are suggestions for matching Idea Bank topics with your students' performance levels and learning modalities:

Customizing for
Performance Levels
Less Advanced Students: 1, 4
Average Students: 2, 5, 7
Pre-AP Students: 3, 6

Customizing for
Learning Modalities
Visual/Spatial: 7
Verbal/Linguistic: 4, 5
Logical/Mathematical: 6
Interpersonal: 4

Guided Writing Lesson

Revision Strategy Have groups of 4 or 5 meet for tri-fold conferences after they complete their first drafts.

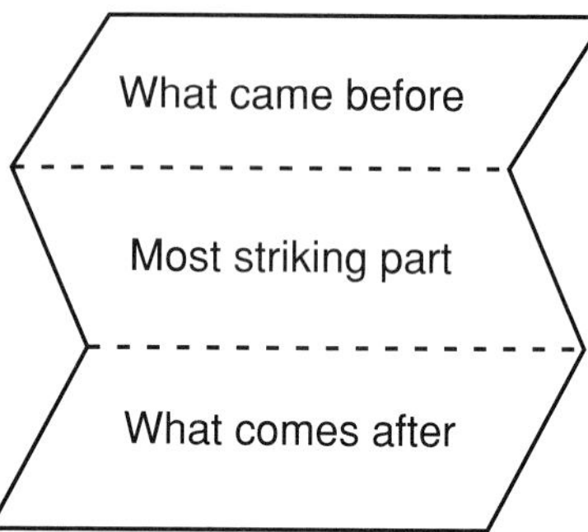

One group member reads his or her piece twice. After the second reading, listeners write in the center third of their papers what struck them most about the writing. In the top third, they write what came before the part in the center section, and in the bottom, what came after it.

Play frames 22803 to 32243

Writers at Work Videodisc
Have students view the videodisc segment (Ch. 3) featuring Rudolfo Anaya to hear what Anaya says about commitment to a subject.

Writing Lab CD-ROM
Have students follow these steps for the tutorial on Expository Writing:

1. Students can view a video clip to learn more about how to write how-to instructions.
2. Invite students to complete a notecard activity to enter details for their how-to manual.
3. Have students draft on computer.
4. Have students use the Revision Checker for transition words.

Build Your Portfolio

Idea Bank

Writing

1. **Annie's Packing List** Create a list of items that Annie might have packed for her journey to England.
2. **Letter of Introduction** As Annie John, write a letter of introduction to an English family or business, offering a brief biography and a description of your skills. **[Career Link]**
3. **Description of Antigua for the Internet** Write a description of Antigua for an Internet Home Page. Describe Antigua's attractions so that Internet surfers will want to visit the island. **[Media Link; Social Studies Link]**

Speaking, Listening, and Viewing

4. **Telephone Interview** Like Annie John, you may soon be making a trip on your own. Interview a local travel agent by phone to learn some of the dos and don'ts for the teenage traveler.
5. **Persuasive Speech** One way in which teenagers can travel abroad is to participate in exchange programs. Write a persuasive speech that convinces listeners that your school should participate in such a program. **[Social Studies Link]**

Researching and Representing

6. **The Statistics of a Decision** Create a chart that shows the numbers of high-school graduates who move out of state to pursue education or job opportunities. **[Social Studies Link; Math Link]**
7. **Map of Annie's Walk** Using details from the story and your own imagination, create a map showing Annie's walk to the jetty. Include all the landmarks mentioned in the story. **[Art Link]**

Online Activity www.phlit.phschool.com

Guided Writing Lesson

How-to Manual for New Students

Write a how-to manual for new students in your school. Include tips, advice, and amusing anecdotes. As you cover everything from lunchroom behavior to test taking, be sure to explain clearly any procedures new students must follow.

Writing Skills Focus: Clear Explanation of Procedures

Problem-solution essays and informative speeches also require a clear explanation of procedures. Even short stories may contain such explanations, as this example from "A Walk to the Jetty" proves.

Model From the Story

My mother . . . instructed me on what side of the road to walk, where to make a turn, where to cross, how to look carefully before I crossed, and if I met anyone that I knew to politely pass greetings and keep on my way.

Your explanation won't be designed for a five-year-old, but like this one it will contain all the necessary details. Also, you can develop your explanation at every stage of the writing process.

Prewriting Brainstorm for items to include in your how-to manual. Then identify the items you will actually include. After identifying the procedures you'll explain, break them down into steps.

Drafting Begin by drafting the most important procedures and explain them as clearly as possible. For example, don't just say, "Join a team." Give the steps involved in trying out for a team.

Revising Have a classmate read your explanations of procedures and determine whether or not they're clear and concise. Where appropriate, add or clarify steps in a procedure to ensure that your manual will be useful to a newcomer.

✓ ASSESSMENT OPTIONS

Formal Assessment, Selection Test, pp. 10–12, and Assessment Resources Software. The selection test is designed so that it can be easily customized to the performance levels of your students.

Alternative Assessment, p. 4, includes options for less advanced students, Pre-AP Students, logical/mathematical learners, verbal/linguistic learners, and visual/spatial learners.

PORTFOLIO ASSESSMENT
Use the following rubrics in the ***Alternative Assessment*** booklet to assess student writing:
Annie's Packing List: Definition/Classification Rubric, p. 99
Letter of Introduction: Résumé/Cover Letter Rubric, p. 114
Description of Antigua for the Internet: Description Rubric, p. 97
Guided Writing Lesson: How-to/Process Explanation Rubric, p. 100

Writing Process Workshop

How-to Instructions

How-to instructions explain the steps involved in doing a particular activity or process. Write a set of instructions for something you know how to do—for example, hit a baseball or install a new game on your computer. Your instructions will help your readers perform the process—even if they are unfamiliar with it.

The following skills, introduced in this section's Guided Writing Lessons, will help you write clear how-to instructions.

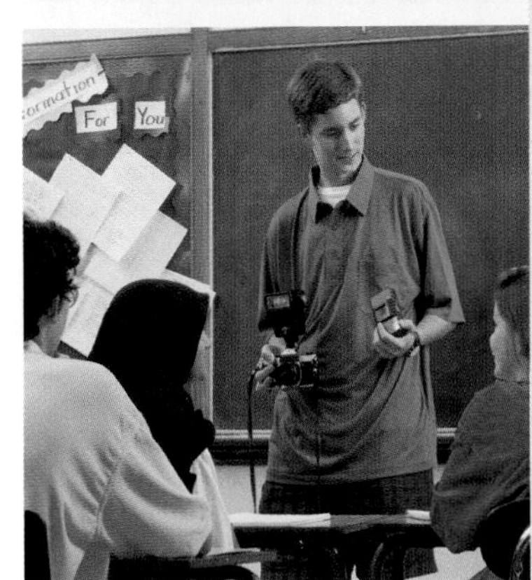

Writing Skills Focus

- **Give a clear explanation** of the procedures involved. Start by writing down the most important procedures and then explaining the steps within each procedure. (See p. 70.)
- **Use transitions to show time.** Words such as *first, next,* and *finally* will make the sequence of steps that you are describing more logical. (See p. 43.)
- **Use transitions to show cause-and-effect relationships.** Words and phrases such as *as a result, because,* and *in order to* will let the reader clearly understand how one action will bring about another. (See p. 57.)

Edmund Hillary uses these skills as he describes the laborious ascent up Mt. Everest.

Model From Literature

from "The Final Assault" by Edmund Hillary

I took a hold on the rock in front ① and then jammed one of my crampons into the hard ice behind. Leaning back with my oxygen set on the ice, I slowly levered myself upward. ② Searching feverishly with my spare boot, I found a tiny ledge on the rock and took some of the weight off of my other leg. I slowly forced my way up—wriggling and jamming and using every little hold. In one place I managed to force my ice axe into a crack in the ice, ③ and this gave me the necessary purchase to get over a holdless stretch.

① The phrase *and then* indicates a transition in time that makes the sequence easier to follow.

② Hillary clearly explains the steps involved in his struggle up the rock wall.

③ This sentence describes a clear cause-and-effect relationship.

Beyond the Classroom

Career Connection

Written Instructions Tell students that they will frequently come across written instructions for completing a task and may someday be asked to write such instructions themselves. Careers that may involve such a task range from a technical writer who writes instruction manuals to a person working at a foundation or for a member of Congress, writing instructions that tell how to change people's attitude on a particular subject.

Have students think of how-to instructions they've come across that strike them as poorly or expertly written, such as computer hardware or mechanical assembly instructions. Invite them to describe the problems with weak real-life examples and to suggest ways to improve them. You may want to suggest that they "stand in the shoes" of a person who might be reading and trying to use the instructions to spot weaknesses and determine what improvements would be helpful.

Prepare and Engage

LESSON OBJECTIVES

1. To use recursive writing processes to write how-to instructions.
2. To recognize and use transitions to show time
3. To use pronouns and antecedents appropriately

You may distribute copies of the Scoring Rubric for How-to/Process Explanation (p. 101) in ***Alternative Assessment*** to make students aware before they begin of the criteria on which they will be evaluated. See the suggestions on page 73 for ways you can customize the rubric for this workshop.

Writers at Work Videodisc

To introduce students to the key elements and show them how Rudolfo Anaya uses them in his expository writing, play the videodisc segment on Exposition (Ch. 2). Have students discuss what Anaya says about commitment to his subject.

Play frames 22803 to 32243

Writing Lab CD-ROM

If your students have access to computers, you may want to have them work on the tutorial on Exposition to complete all or part of their how-to instructions. Follow these steps:

1. Have students review the interactive model of how-to instructions.
2. Suggest that students see examples of broad and narrowed topics to help them narrow their own topics.
3. Have students draft on computer.
4. Suggest students use a revision checker for transition words.
5. Have students use the proofreading checklist to proofread their drafts for spelling, usage, and mechanical errors.

Develop Student Writing

Prewriting Strategy

To help students choose a topic, you might suggest that they think about unusual activities that might be fun for others to learn, and jot them down on separate slips of paper. Have students place their topics in a bin. Other students then pick topics at random.

How to play bagpipes

How to draw a cartoon

How to care for an iguana

Customize for
Less Proficient Writers
Students may benefit from using a transition word bin, listing any transition words they might use, before they begin to draft.

Customize for
Pre-AP Students
Challenge students to use a topic that is new to them. Doing so will enhance their research skills, vocabulary, and general knowledge.

Grammar Reinforcement

Writing Lab CD-ROM
The Gathering Details section of the tutorial on Exposition includes the screen Identifying Important Details. Have students consult this screen to help streamline their instructions and weed out unnecessary information.

Elaboration

After students draft their how-to instructions, have them jot down the specific steps and key ideas that they used on notecards. They can evaluate the organization they used, and rearrange the cards for clarity. Once they have decided that their organization is clear, they can look for places where transition words will enhance the clarity of their how-to instructions.

APPLYING LANGUAGE SKILLS: Transitions to Show Time

Transition words that show time will make the sequence of steps that you are describing obvious.

Transition Words:

first	second	next
last	then	finally
after	before	soon
third	fourth	later
after a while		following
simultaneously		
at the same time		

Practice On your paper, add transition words to show time to the following passage.

Crack two eggs in a bowl. Whip the eggs. Pour into a preheated frying pan. Turn over the eggs with a spatula.

Writing Application As you draft your how-to instructions, use transition words to show time in order to make the sequence of steps you are describing logical.

Writer's Solution Connection
Writing Lab

To help you narrow your topic, see the screen entitled Focusing Your Topic. You'll find it in the Writing Lab tutorial on Exposition.

Prewriting

Choose a Topic Think about a skill or activity that interests you, that you know well, and that is complicated to the extent that a person could not learn it simply by watching. It could be a hobby, such as building model airplanes or origami. You can also choose one of the topics below.

Topic Ideas

- Setting up an aquarium
- Skateboarding
- Collecting crystals
- Starting a vegetable garden
- Training a pet to perform a trick

Focus Your Topic Once you've chosen your topic, make sure you'll be able to give complete instructions within the planned length of your paper. The example below shows how one student narrowed his topic.

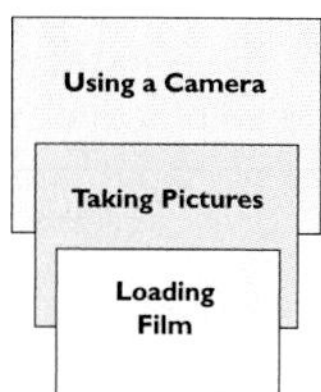

Organize Details in Categories Make lists of details for each of the following: materials, safety factors, steps in the process.

Drafting

Make Your Writing Clear and Brief As you write, assume that readers know little or nothing about your topic. Write your explanation in easy-to-understand terms. Avoid using specialized vocabulary that readers might not understand. Show how one step or event leads to another by using transition words to indicate the cause-and-effect relationships.

Anticipate Problems At some time, you may have encountered problems doing the activity you're now explaining. If you had a problem, there's a good chance others will as well. Mention possible problems that the reader may have, and show how to solve them.

Applying Language Skills

Transitions to Show Time

Remind students that transitions such as *first, next,* and *finally* are especially important in how-to instructions. They not only make the instructions flow more smoothly but are crucial for a proper understanding.

Answers

1. *First,* crack two eggs in a bowl. *Next,* whip the eggs, *then* pour into a preheated frying pan. *Last,* turn over the eggs with a spatula.

Grammar Reinforcement

For additional instruction and practice, have students complete the **Language Lab CD-ROM** lesson on Unity and Coherence in Paragraphs.

Revising

Use a Checklist Review the Writing Skills Focus on p. 71. Use the items as a checklist to evaluate and revise your observation.

- ▶ Have I given a clear explanation of the procedures involved?
  Include any steps you may have forgotten to mention in the first draft.
- ▶ Have I used transitions to show cause-and-effect relationships?
  Add words or phrases such as because, as a result, consequently, *and so on, to make the relationships between cause and effect clear to the reader.*
- ▶ Have I used transitions to show time?
  Add words such as first, simultaneously, at the same time, *and so on, to describe a logical sequence of events.*

REVISION MODEL
Fixing a Flat Tire

First let all the air out of the tire. ① Then remove the entire tire from the bicycle. Separate the tire from the rim, revealing the tube inside. ② Next, using a dull knife or a spoon, take the tube out of the metal rim and reinflate it. Place the tube in a pan of water and gently squeeze. ③ ~~Keep your hair out of the water.~~ Look for tiny bubbles on the tube. When you see them, you've found the puncture.

① The writer adds an important step in the process, using a transition to show time order.
② The writer adds a transition word.
③ The writer deletes an unnecessary sentence.

Publishing and Presenting

Demonstration Hold a demonstration of your how-to instructions. Here are some tips for presenting your writing.

- ▶ Create charts or diagrams to aid your presentation.
- ▶ Use index cards to keep your information organized and handy.
- ▶ Print out finished copies of your instructions so your listeners can refer to them during your presentation.
- ▶ Leave time for questions.

APPLYING LANGUAGE SKILLS: Pronouns

Pronouns—words that take the place of nouns—help writers avoid repeating the same nouns over and over. For a pronoun to make sense, however, its antecedent—the noun or nouns it replaces—must be clear. All personal pronouns, such as *he, she, it, they,* and *we,* must have clear antecedents.

Example:

Make sure that your oxygen tank (antecedent) has all of its (pronoun) valves working properly.

Practice On your paper, circle the pronoun and its antecedent.

1. Edmund Hillary stopped to check his oxygen.
2. Make sure that your partner has both of his or her hands on the ice axe.

Writing Application Review your how-to instructions, and make sure that all of the pronouns have clear antecedents.

Writer's Solution Connection
Language Lab

For more practice with pronouns, complete the Language Lab lesson on Pronouns and Antecedents.

Revision Strategy

Before students reenter their writing, have them work with peer editors to review their how-to instructions. Tell the peer reviewers to offer specific, concrete suggestions for improvement rather than general criticism.

Prentice Hall Writing and Grammar For more prewriting, elaboration, and revision strategies, see *Prentice Hall Writing and Grammar.*

Publishing

If students choose not to share their instructions, have them ask themselves these questions to help them reflect on the assignment:

- What parts did I enjoy the most? The least?
- What did this writing experience teach me about the topic? What else would I like to learn about it?

Reinforce and Extend

Applying Language Skills

Answers

1. Edmund Hillary stopped to check his oxygen. Pronoun: *his.* Antecedent: *Edmund Hillary.*
2. Make sure that your partner has both of his or her hands on the ice axe. Pronouns: *his, her.* Antecedent: *partner.*

Grammar Reinforcement

For additional instruction and practice, have students complete the **Language Lab CD-ROM** lessons on Pronouns and Antecedents or Pronoun Case and the practice pages in the *Writer's Solution Grammar Practice Book* (pp. 76–79).

ASSESSMENT

PORTFOLIO ASSESSMENT
Use the rubric on How-to/Process Explanation in the ***Alternative Assessment*** booklet (p. 100) to assess students' writing. Add these criteria to customize the rubric to this assignment.

	4	3	2	1
Transitional Words	Transitions to show time and cause-effect relationships are used effectively.	Transitions to show time and cause-effect relationships are used.	Transition words are few.	Transition words are almost completely absent.
Pronouns	There are no mistakes with pronoun case. All antecedents are clear.	There are minor mistakes with pronoun case and antecedents.	There are noticeable mistakes with pronoun case, as well as misplaced and dangling modifiers.	There are frequent mistakes with pronoun case as well as numerous misplaced and dangling modifiers.

Prepare and Engage

LESSON OBJECTIVES

- To use reference materials to research word origins as an aid to understanding meanings

Apply the Strategies

In addition to reviewing the information about abbreviations that is explained in students' books, you may wish to review the guide(s) to the use of the dictionary that are found in the dictionary or dictionaries that students have available to them.

Answers

Possible answers:

1. Students should realize that they can combine what they find about the Greek word *xenos*—referring to something unknown—with what they already know (or can research) about the word *phobia*—from the Greek word *phobos*—to understand that *xenophobia* means "fear of the unknown."
2. The origin of the suffix *-ment* is from the Latin word *mentum.* Four words that share this suffix, which means "a result or product," might include *achievement* (a result of achieving); *attachment* (a product of attaching something); *announcement* (a product of announcing something); and *fragment* (a result of breaking something—also from the Latin word *frangere,* meaning "break").
3. *Lexicography* means "the act or work of writing or compiling a dictionary"; lexico means "of words"; *-logy* means "the study of," so *lexicology* would mean "the study of dictionaries, or words."

Student Success Workshop

Vocabulary Development: Researching Word Origins

Strategies for Success

When you research a word's origins, you learn the word's history. Knowing a word's origins can also make the word easier to spell, remember, define, and use. It can even help you figure out how different words are related: If you know that the word *humble* comes from the Latin word *humilis,* meaning "lowly," you can use it to help you guess the meaning of *humility.*

English has often borrowed whole words from other languages. For example, the word *pajama* is borrowed from Hindi—a language spoken in India. Other English words contain prefixes, suffixes, and roots borrowed from other languages. The prefix *pyro-* is one example. It is a Greek term meaning "fire."

Use Reference Materials There are many resources to research a word's origins: dictionaries, the glossary of a textbook, and the Internet. On the Internet, search for *references* first; next, the key words *dictionary* or *word origins;* then, a specific word. At the library, try an etymological dictionary (of word origins).

Learn the Abbreviations When you research word origins in a dictionary, information may be abbreviated something like this:

> **canyon** . . . *n.* [AmSp *cañón* < Sp, a pipe, tube, gorge < *caño,* a tube < L *canna,* a reed: see CANE]

Symbols and the abbreviations for different languages are listed and explained in the introductory pages of a dictionary. The symbol "<" means "from." It tells you that the word has come into English from another language—or, over time, from more than one language. The example of *canyon* reveals that this word came from the American Spanish word *cañón,* which developed from the older Spanish word *caño,* which had developed from the Latin word *canna,* meaning "a reed."

Apply the Strategies

A dictionary gives you information on the origins of whole words, prefixes, and suffixes. These activities will give you practice in researching the origins of some prefixes, suffixes, and word roots:

1. Look at the origins of the word *xenon.* How might knowing the meaning of the prefix *xeno-* help you understand the word *xenophobia?*

   > **xenon** . . . *n.* [ModL < Gr, neut. of *xenos,* foreign, a stranger: so named (1898) by Sir William RAMSAY & M. W. Travers (see KRYPTON), as the hitherto unknown inert gas]

2. Find out the origins of the suffix *-ment.* Write down four words that share this suffix and its meaning.
3. Look up the meaning of the word *lexicography* and its prefix, *lexico-.* Then find the meaning of the suffix *-logy.* Use this information to guess what *lexicology* means.

Knowing word origins can come in handy:

- When you visit a science museum
- To understand the puns in a Shakespeare play
- To figure out a word you've never read before
- When you visit a country with an unfamiliar language

Test Preparation Workshop

Vocabulary: Word Origins

The verbal section of the SAT test contains questions that are based on sentence completions. Students will be able to answer some of those by applying their knowledge of word origins. For some words, their knowledge of foreign languages, especially those related to Latin, will prove helpful. For instance, they may know the meaning of *blanch,* "to make white; take color out of," based on their knowledge of the French word for white, *blanc,* or the Spanish word *blanco.* Give students the following test question for practice.

The source for the ancient city's ________ is the mountain snowfall.

A plumbous **C** refrigerant
B aqueduct **D** generator

Students who know the Spanish word for water, *agua,* may note that *aqueduct* contains a similar word root, *aque,* from the Latin word *aqua,* meaning "water." Melted snow might be a water source, and an *aqueduct,* answer B, carries water from a distance. Knowing that the word origin of *duct* is "to lead" will further help them know that an *aqueduct* "leads" water from a distant source.

Part 2 *Dangerous Destinies*

Untitled, Rob Day/SIS

One-Minute Planning Guide

This section's selections emphasize the dangers, real and imagined, in our destinies. In "The Masque of the Red Death," destiny takes the form of a horrible plague to which the sequestered nobles of Middle Ages Europe find they are not immune. The "fear" described in the poem of the same name is a fear of not raising a daughter well. The fear in the poem "The street" is the fear of following and being followed by a nameless, faceless foe. The poem "Spring and All," meanwhile, describes the delicate rebirth of the natural world in a cold, harsh environment. The danger in "Two Friends" is very real indeed—the Prussian soldiers who patrol the outskirts of Paris during the Franco-Prussian War. The two friends who encounter this danger find it has fatal consequences. The section ends on a positive note, in "Damon and Pythias." This retelling of the classical Greek myth tells how two friends are able to evade death through their unswerving loyalty to each other.

Customize for *Varying Student Needs*

When assigning the selections in this part to your students, keep in mind the following factors:

"The Masque of the Red Death"

- A classic short story whose nineteenth-century prose may be challenging, especially for less proficient readers
- The macabre subject matter will appeal to students.

"Fear"; The street"; "Spring and All"

- Three short poems
- Vivid imagery and short stanzas make these poems accessible to students

"Two Friends"

- A medium-length short story (6 pp.) with a shocking ending

"Damon and Pythias"

- A very brief selection (3 pp.)
- Simple vocabulary and style make it accessible to most students

Humanities: Art

Untitled by Rob Day.

Born and raised in Indiana, and staunchly committed to staying there, Rob Day has become an extremely successful illustrator of magazine and newspaper articles, having created works for such publications as *Sports Illustrated, Business Week,* and *Rolling Stone.* Day began to draw as a small child and first thought of a career in art under the encouragement of his junior-high-school art teacher. After graduating from the Herron School of Art, he began to submit his work to publishers. His combination of a dreamlike tone and realistic style won him almost instantaneous success as a graphic illustrator.

Have your students link the painting to the theme of Part 2, "Dangerous Destinies," by making up a story idea to explain how the man got there. *Sample answers: The man climbed up from below but has reached a point where he cannot go any higher; the man fell from his business class seat in an airplane and slid down the cliff to this spot.*

Prepare and Engage

LESSON OBJECTIVES

1. **To develop vocabulary and word identification skills**
   - Latin Suffixes: *-tion*
   - Using the Word Bank: Context Clues
   - Extending Word Study: Word Choice (ATE)
2. **To use a variety of reading strategies to comprehend a short story**
   - Connect Your Experience
   - Reading Strategy: Context Clues
   - Tips to Guide Reading: Recall (ATE)
   - Read to Appreciate Author's Craft (ATE)
   - Idea Bank: Description of a Modern Masquerade
3. **To increase knowledge of other cultures and to connect common elements across cultures**
   - Connecting Themes Across Cultures (ATE)
   - Cultural Connections: Masques (ATE)
4. **To express and support responses to the text**
   - Critical Thinking
   - Idea Bank: Invitation to the Prince's Masquerade
5. **To analyze literary elements**
   - Literary Focus: Symbols
6. **To read in order to research self-selected and assigned topics**
   - Idea Bank: Report on the Black Plague
7. **To plan, prepare, organize, and present literary interpretations**
   - Speaking, Listening, and Viewing Mini-Lesson: Radio Script
   - Idea Bank: Multimedia Presentation
   - Idea Bank: Press Conference
8. **To use recursive writing processes to write a proposal**
   - Guided Writing Lesson
9. **To increase knowledge of the rules of grammar and usage**
   - Build Grammar Skills: Subject-Verb Agreement

Test Preparation

Reading Comprehension: Using Context Clues to Determine Word Meanings (ATE, p. 77) The teaching tips and sample test item in this workshop support the instruction and practice in the unit workshop:

Reading Comprehension: Using Context Clues to Determine Word Meanings (SE, p. 113)

Guide for Reading

Featured in AUTHORS IN DEPTH Series

Edgar Allan Poe

(1809–1849)

The early American author Edgar Allan Poe died childless, but today he is credited with numerous literary grandchildren and great-grandchildren.

> ***Included among Poe's literary "descendants" are Stephen King and Sir Arthur Conan Doyle.***

In fact, as the author who set the standards for the modern horror story and detective story, Poe has influenced literally thousands of writers.

A Troubled Childhood Poe was born in Boston, Massachusetts, to a family of impoverished traveling actors. Within a year, his father had deserted the family and his mother had died.

Young Edgar was raised, but never formally adopted, by Mr. and Mrs. John Allan of Richmond, Virginia. As he grew up, Poe got into conflicts with his adoptive father. In 1827, for example, Poe had to withdraw from the University of Virginia because of gambling debts that Allan refused to pay.

Success and Failure and Success In 1833, Poe entered a group of stories and a poem in a Baltimore literary contest. One of the stories, "MS. Found in a Bottle," won the fiction prize.

Although Poe's stories and poems continued to win recognition, his writing did not bring him financial success. In 1849, two years after the death of his beloved wife, Virginia, Poe died poor and alone.

Today the works of this solitary figure—stories like "The Tell-Tale Heart" and poems like "The Raven"—attract crowds of readers. You can join Poe's enormous "family" too as you enter the frightening but fascinating world of "The Masque of the Red Death."

◆ Build Vocabulary

LATIN SUFFIXES: *-tion*

At one point in the story, there comes "an uneasy *cessation* of all things"—all activity ceases. The word *cessation* is built on *cease* with the Latin suffix *-tion*, which means "the act of." Therefore, the word *cessation* literally means "the act of ceasing."

The suffix *-tion* makes a noun of the word to which it is added. It is a very common suffix. The Word Bank also contains the word *disapprobation*, which means "the act of disapprobating," or disapproving.

WORD BANK

Before you read, preview this list of words from the selection.

august
piquancy
arabesque
cessation
disapprobation
habiliments

◆ Build Grammar Skills

SUBJECT-VERB AGREEMENT

A verb must **agree** with its subject in number (singular or plural), even when the subject comes after the verb, rather than before it.

In describing the palace in this story, Poe often lists details in sentences beginning with *there* followed by the verb *is* or *was* (singular) or *are* or *were* (plural). Notice how the verb agrees with the subject that follows it:

Singular Subject and Verb:

There was (v) a sharp turn (s) at every twenty yards . . .

Plural Subject and Verb:

There were (v) arabesque figures (s) . . .

Prentice Hall Literature Program Resources

REINFORCE / RETEACH / EXTEND

Selection Support Pages
Build Vocabulary: Suffixes: *-tion*, p. 18
Build Grammar Skills: Subject-Verb Agreement, p. 19
Reading Strategy: Context Clues, p. 20
Literary Focus: Symbols, p. 21

Strategies for Diverse Student Needs, p. 5

Beyond Literature
Cross-Curricular Connection: Science, p. 5

Formal Assessment Selection Test, pp. 13–15; Assessment Resources Software

Alternative Assessment, p. 5

Writing and Language Transparencies
Daily Language Practice, Weeks 8 and 9, pp. 119 and 120

Resource Pro CD-ROM

Listening to Literature Audiocassettes

The Masque of the Red Death

◆ Literature and Your Life

CONNECT YOUR EXPERIENCE

Some celebrities go to great lengths to shield themselves from the world, building elaborate homes with grounds protected by gates and guards. Inside these compounds, they can create a fantasy world filled with every luxury money can buy.

Like one of these celebrities, the prince in this story builds a palace where he can live out all his fantasies and escape from the sufferings of his subjects and the disease that ravages his country.

Journal Writing As a celebrity, plan what you would include in your magnificent dream house.

THEMATIC FOCUS: DANGEROUS DESTINIES

As you read about Prince Prospero's attempt to escape from the "Red Death," ask yourself: Can money and power buy safety?

◆ Background for Understanding

HISTORY

It seemed that no one was safe in medieval Europe. In the 1300's and 1400's, a plague known as the Black Death swept across the continent, killing 25 million people. Most of the afflicted died within three to five days after the first symptoms appeared. Again, in 1665, an outbreak of the plague ravaged the city of London.

For Poe and others living in the early nineteenth century, these outbreaks were a haunting historical memory. In addition, diseases like influenza, cholera, and typhoid were an ever-present threat. The "Red Death" is a plague Poe invented for his story, but it is based on historical and timeless fear.

◆ Literary Focus

SYMBOLS

If you wanted to create a **symbol** for the disease Poe calls the "Red Death"—a person, place, event, or thing that represented it—you might describe a skeleton in a red cape. Writers often use concrete symbols like this to help readers understand the meaning of a general idea, like "disease" or "safety."

Poe's story is filled with symbols. The prince, his fantastic masquerade ball, the plague raging in the kingdom—all these things seem to stand for more than the things themselves. Ask yourself what they could mean.

◆ Reading Strategy

CONTEXT CLUES

If you were to attend a masquerade, you'd use **context clues**—hints from things nearby, such as people's voices and actions—to figure out who the masked partygoers were. In a similar way, you can figure out the meanings of unfamiliar words by using context clues in surrounding sentences.

As you read the story, identify context clues to define unfamiliar words. Look at the example from the following passage:

> . . . All these and security were within. Without was the Red Death.
>
> It was toward the close of the fifth or sixth month of his *seclusion*, and while the pestilence raged most furious abroad . . .

Unfamiliar word: *seclusion*
Words similar in meaning: *within*
Words opposite in meaning: *without*
Probable meaning of *seclusion:* *Keeping inside, hiding*

Test Preparation Workshop

Reading Comprehension: Using Context Clues to Determine Word Meanings Some standardized tests require students to choose the appropriate meaning of multiple-meaning words by using context clues. Use the following sample question.

Ask students to read Edgar Allan Poe's description of Prince Prospero on p. 78–79.

In this passage, the word eccentric means —

A not in the center
B not concentric
C deviating from a circular form
D unusual or irregular

Discuss with students that *A, B,* and *C* do not describe a person, or a person's behavior. By process of elimination, students will be able to determine the best answer is *D*. If students have difficulty using context clues to determine that Prince Prospero was slightly unusual in his behavior, suggest that they check the dictionary for various meanings of the word and synonyms.

Have students imagine themselves in this situation: They are living in Europe in the 1300's. A plague called the Black Death threatens the lives of millions. They have been invited to embark on a plague-free ship until the epidemic dies out. However, some members of their families and many of their friends are not invited. How would they handle this dilemma?

Use students' comments as a springboard to discuss the plague and Poe's use of it. In Poe's story, the Black Death becomes the Red Death.

Tips to Guide Reading

The rich descriptions used in "The Masque of the Red Death" provide an opportunity for students to recall details. Have students stop at the end of the description of the apartments on p. 80 and recall as many details as possible. You may wish to repeat the exercise and have students recall details that describe the party scene.

Customize for
Less Proficient Readers
To help readers deal with the sophisticated vocabulary in this story, guide them to locate and determine the meaning of unfamiliar words from context clues as they read.

Customize for
Pre-AP Students
Suggest that students summarize and evaluate the plot of this selection and write a short newspaper account of the party given by the Prince.

Customize for
Gifted/Talented Students
In an allegorical story, the characters, setting, and events are intended to have a meaning independent of the surface story—analyzed entirely on a symbolic level. For example, the palace may symbolize the entire world. Challenge students to determine the symbolic lesson about life being taught in this tale.

Develop Understanding

One-Minute Insight In addition to being a chilling horror story, this selection is a brilliant portrayal of the vanity of the rich and powerful and their illusions of invulnerability. Prince Prospero, the main character, believes he can save himself and a select few from the plague that is menacing the rest of society. In the story's climax, Prospero learns that wealth and privilege will not spare him from the grip of death.

◆ Reading Strategy

1 Context Clues Ask students to explain how the sequence "seizure, progress and termination" is a context clue that can help them figure out the meaning of *termination*. Encourage them to then define *termination*. *Because the sequence refers to a deadly disease,* seizure *would mean the beginning of the disease,* progress *would refer to the stages of the disease from beginning to end, and* termination, *coming last in the sequence, would mean the end of the disease.*

◆ Critical Thinking

2 Deduce Ask students: What kind of person is Prince Prospero? How does Poe play on Prospero's name? *The prince is wealthy, happy, and not particularly concerned about the pestilence devastating his land. His name suggests "prosperity."*

◆ Literary Focus

3 Symbol Students should take into account details that suggest how carefully the prince planned the wall to make sure it was strong and would protect him from the disease outside: "gates of iron," "welded bolts." Their reasoning should lead them to conclude the following: *The wall represents the efforts of the rich and powerful to shield themselves from the dangers faced by ordinary people.*

◆ Critical Thinking

4 Interpret Ask students: From the courtiers' point of view, why was it folly to grieve or to think? *They felt that since there was nothing they could do about the Red Death, there was nothing to be gained from grieving for those who lost their lives to it.*

The Masque[1] of the Red Death

Edgar Allan Poe

The "Red Death" had long devastated the country. No pestilence had ever been so fatal, or so hideous. Blood was its Avatar[2] and its seal—the redness and the horror of blood. There were sharp pains, and sudden dizziness, and then profuse bleeding at the pores, with dissolution. The scarlet stains upon the body and especially upon the face of the victim, were the pest ban which shut him out from the aid and from the sympathy of his fellow men. And the whole **1** seizure, progress and termination of the disease, were the incidents of half an hour.

2 But the Prince Prospero was happy and dauntless and sagacious. When his dominions were half depopulated, he summoned to his presence a thousand hale and lighthearted friends from among the knights and dames of his court, and with these retired to the deep seclusion of one of his castellated abbeys.[3] This was an extensive and magnificent structure, the creation of the prince's own eccentric yet august taste. A strong and lofty wall girdled it in. This wall had gates of iron. The courtiers, having entered, brought furnaces and massy[4] hammers and welded the bolts. They resolved to leave means neither of ingress or egress[5] to the sudden impulses of despair or frenzy from within. The abbey was amply provisioned. With such precautions the courtiers might bid defiance to contagion. The external world could take care of itself. In the meantime it was folly to grieve, or to think. **4** The prince had provided all the appliances of

◆ **Literary Focus** What could the wall symbolize? **3**

1. **masque** (mask) *n.*: Costume ball or masquerade theme.
2. **Avatar** (av´ ə tär) *n.*: Symbol or manifestation of an unseen force.
3. **castellated** (kas´ tə lā´ tid) **abbeys** (ab´ ez): Monasteries or convents with castlelike towers.
4. **massy** (mas´ ē) *adj.*: Massive or large.
5. **ingress** (in´ gres) or **egress** (ē´ gres): Entering or leaving.

◆ Build Vocabulary

august (ô gust´) *adj.*: Imposing and magnificent

Block Scheduling Strategies

Consider these suggestions to take advantage of extended class time:

- Have students complete the journal activity in Literature and Your Life (p. 77) and read their entries aloud to the class.
- Introduce the reading strategy. To give students practice, have them do the Reading Strategy page (p. 20) in ***Selection Support.***
- Use the Daily Language Practice sentences for Weeks 8 and 9, in the Teaching Resources and in the ***Writing and Language Transparencies.***
- Interested students can use a computer program or grid paper to design a layout of the floor plan in Prince Prospero's castle.
- Set aside class time for students to perform the radio script they write for the Speaking, Listening, and Viewing activity or share their multimedia presentation (both on p. 85).
- Have students complete the Writing Mini-Lesson on page 85. While some students draft and revise the proposal, others can sketch designs of the symbol and choose the best one.

pleasure. There were buffoons, there were improvisatori,[6] there were ballet dancers, there were musicians, there was Beauty, there was wine. All these and security were within. Without was the "Red Death."

It was toward the close of the fifth or sixth month of his seclusion, and while the pestilence raged most furiously abroad, that the Prince Prospero entertained his thousand friends at a masked ball of the most unusual magnificence.

It was a voluptuous scene, that masquerade. But first let me tell of the rooms in which it was held. There were seven—an imperial suite. In many palaces, however, such suites form a long and straight vista, while the folding doors slide back nearly to the walls on either hand, so that the view of the whole extent is scarcely impeded. Here the case was very different; as might have been expected from the duke's love of the bizarre. The apartments were so irregularly disposed that the vision embraced but little more than one at a time. There was a sharp turn at every twenty or thirty yards, and at each turn a novel effect. To the right and left, in the middle of each wall, a tall and narrow Gothic window looked out upon a closed corridor which pursued the windings of the suite. These windows were of stained glass whose color varied in accordance with the prevailing hue of the decorations of the chamber into which it opened. That at the eastern extremity was hung, for example, in blue—and vividly blue were its windows. The second chamber was purple in its ornaments and tapestries, and here the panes were purple. The third was green throughout, and so were the casements. The fourth was furnished and lighted 9
with orange—the fifth with white—the sixth with violet. The seventh apartment was closely shrouded in black velvet tapestries that hung all over the ceiling and down the

6. **improvisatori** (im′ prə vē zə tôr ē) *n.:* Poets who improvise, or create verses without previous thought.

Beyond the Classroom

Career Connection

Architecture/Construction Visual/spatial learners who were able to imagine the castle chambers in this story may be interested in a career in architecture or construction. Encourage students to visit the architecture department of a nearby college or university to learn more about preparing for careers in this field. Let students know that architects and construction workers often work side by side. Invite students to interview a construction worker about his or her job or visit a building under construction.

Community Connection

Containing Contagious Diseases The prince seeks to isolate himself and his friends from the Red Death. Have students contact your local Red Cross or public health hotline to get information on what contagious diseases are of concern to health-care workers in your community. Have them find out what preventive measures are recommended to stop the spread of the disease.

◆ Literary Focus

5 Symbols Have students discuss the different kinds of people whom Prospero has invited to the security of the abbey. Collectively, whom do they represent? *Prospero's guests include two categories of people: his friends, who are knights and ladies, and a variety of people to entertain them and provide for their needs. They represent the privileged class.*

◆ Build Grammar Skills

6 Subject-Verb Agreement Call students' attention to the series of clauses beginning "there were" and "there was." Have them explain why some clauses use the verb *was* and some use *were*. *The singular verb* was *agrees with the singular subjects "Beauty" and "wine." The plural verb* were *agrees with the plural subjects "buffoons," "improvisatori," "ballet dancers," and "musicians."*

◆ Literary Focus

7 Symbols Point out that the number seven is often considered significant. Lead students to see that seven apartments may represent the seven deadly sins: pride, lust, envy, anger, covetousness, gluttony, and sloth. These sins might be related to the pleasures of the masked ball.

◆ Reading Strategy

8 Context Clues Have students infer the meaning of the word *impeded* from the context of the sentence. *When rooms are lined up in sequence and the doors between them slide back to the walls, a person's view is not impeded, that is, "interfered with" or "slowed down."*

◆ Literary Focus

9 Symbols Engage students in a discussion of the symbolism of colors. Ask what the color of each apartment might mean. *Possible responses: Blue represents water, coolness, wisdom and the intellect, and the sky. Purple seems to be a color of royalty, and therefore suggests power. Green, associated with nature, often symbolizes growth and life. Orange may suggest midday—the high noon of existence, the harvest, or fire and destruction. White generally symbolizes purity. Violet symbolizes memory or knowledge, sorrow and mourning. Black generally represents gloom and death.*

◆ Literary Focus

1 Symbols Ask students what the black room with blood-red window panes might represent. *This room probably represents death.*

◆ Critical Thinking

2 Analyze Have students describe the lighting in the rooms—especially the last room. What effect does the lighting have on the guests? What feeling or quality does Poe create in this passage? *The only light comes from fires opposite each window, which produce glare and "gaudy and fantastic appearances." The light in the last room reflects off blood-red panes, and the effect is "ghastly in the extreme." Poe creates feelings of horror as the surroundings take on a fantastic, nightmarish quality.*

◆ Literary Focus

3 Symbols Ask students what the clock represents. *The clock represents time; specifically, the limited time remaining in their lives. As it strikes each hour, it serves as a reminder and a warning that death is always near.*

◆ *Literature and Your Life*

4 Students may say the prince's revel reminds them of today's celebrity parties because it takes place in a lavish setting in which exotic entertainment is provided. They may add that most celebrities probably do not try to create such ghastly effects.

◆ Critical Thinking

5 Speculate Why does Poe try to create doubt in the reader's mind about whether the prince is sane? *He wants to keep the reader on edge about what exactly is going on and what will happen next.*

Read to
Appreciate Author's Craft

Students should be encouraged to read to appreciate Poe's imagery and choice of colorful, rich, and descriptive words to describe the palace and party given by Prince Prospero.

Extending Word Study

Word Choice Challenge students to make a list of Poe's word choices that add to the richness of his storytelling.

walls, falling in heavy folds upon a carpet of the same material and hue. But in this chamber only, the color of the
1 windows failed to correspond with the decorations. The panes here were scarlet—a deep blood color. Now in no one of the seven apartments was there any lamp or candelabrum amid the profusion of golden ornaments that lay scattered to and fro or depended from the roof. There was no light of any kind emanating from lamp or candle within the suite of chambers. But in the corridors that followed the suite, there stood, opposite to each window, a heavy tripod, bearing a brazier[7] of fire that projected its rays through the tinted glass and so glaringly illumined the room. And thus were produced a mul-
2 titude of gaudy and fantastic appearances. But in the western or black chamber the effect of the firelight that streamed upon the dark hangings through the blood-tinted panes, was ghastly in the extreme, and produced so wild a look upon the countenances of those who entered, that there were few of the company bold enough to set foot within its precincts at all.

It was in this apartment, also, that there stood against the western wall a gigantic clock of ebony. Its pendulum swung to and fro with a dull, heavy, monotonous clang; and when the minute-hand made the circuit of the face, and the hour was to be stricken, there came from the brazen lungs of the clock a sound which was clear and loud and deep and exceedingly musi-
3 cal, but of so peculiar a note and emphasis that, at each lapse of an hour, the musicians of the orchestra were constrained to pause, momentarily, in their performance, to hearken to the sound; and thus the waltzers perforce ceased their evolutions; and there was a brief disconcert of the whole gay company; and, while the chimes of the clock yet rang, it was observed that the giddiest grew pale, and the more aged and sedate passed their hands over their brows as if in confused reverie or meditation. But when the echoes had fully ceased, a light laughter at once pervaded the assembly; the musicians looked at each other and smiled as if at their own nervousness and folly, and made whispering vows, each to the other, that the next chiming of the clock should produce in them no similar emotion; and then, after the lapse of sixty minutes, (which embrace three thousand and six hundred seconds of the Time that flies), there came yet another chiming of the clock, and then were the same disconcert and tremulousness and meditation as before.

> ◆ *Literature and Your Life*
>
> Connect the prince's revel with what you've read and heard about celebrity parties of today.

But, in spite of these things, it was a gay and magnificent revel. The tastes of the duke were peculiar. He had a fine eye for colors and effects. He disregarded the decora[8] of mere fashion. His plans were bold and fiery, and his conceptions glowed with barbaric luster. There are some who would have
thought him mad. His followers felt that he was 5

7. **brazier** (brā′ zhər) *n.*: Metal pan or bowl to hold burning coals or charcoal.

8. **decora** (də kôr′ ə) *n.*: Requirements of good taste.

Speaking, Listening, and Viewing Mini-Lesson

Radio Script

This mini-lesson supports the Speaking, Listening, and Viewing activity in the Idea Bank on p. 85.

Introduce Remind students that radio listeners can hear but not see the action being dramatized. Writers of radio scripts must provide sound effects as well as dialogue.

Develop Give students these pointers for writing their scripts:

- In a radio script, each character's name or NARRATOR is written in capital letters, followed by a colon and the speaker's exact words.
- Directions for sound effects and character's tone of voice are written in brackets. For example, ["Sound of running footsteps"]

Apply Have students work in small groups to write scripts. Some students may work specifically on dialogue, while others prepare sound and music for their radio performances.

Assess You may use the Scoring Rubric for Drama (p. 110) in the ***Alternative Assessment*** booklet.

not. It was necessary to hear and see and touch him to be *sure* that he was not.

He had directed, in great part, the movable embellishments of the seven chambers, upon occasion of this great fête; and it was his own guiding taste which had given character to the masqueraders. Be sure they were grotesque. There were much glare and glitter and piquancy and phantasm—much of what has been since seen in *Hernani*.[9] There were arabesque figures with unsuited limbs and appointments. There were delirious fancies such as the madman fashions. There was much of the beautiful, much of the wanton, much of the bizarre, something of the terrible, and not a little of that which might have excited disgust. To and fro in the seven chambers there stalked, in fact, a multitude of dreams. And these—the dreams—writhed in and about, taking hue from the rooms, and causing the wild music of the orchestra to seem as the echo of their steps. And, anon, there strikes the ebony clock which stands in the hall of the velvet. And then, for a moment, all is still, and all is silent save the voice of the clock. The dreams are stiff-frozen as they stand. But the echoes of the chime die away—they have endured but an instant—and a light, half-subdued laughter floats after them as they depart. And now again the music swells, and the dreams live, and writhe to and fro more merrily than ever, taking hue from the many-tinted windows through which stream the rays from the tripods. But to the chamber which lies most westwardly of the seven, there are now none of the maskers who venture; for the night is waning away; and there flows a ruddier light through the blood-colored panes; and the blackness of the sable drapery appalls; and to him whose foot falls upon the sable carpet, there comes from the near clock of ebony a muffled peal more solemnly emphatic than any which reaches *their* ears who

◆ **Reading Strategy**
Read ahead to find *tinted,* a context clue that will help you determine the meaning of *hue.*

9. ***Hernani:*** Extravagant drama by the French author Victor Hugo.

◆ Build Vocabulary

piquancy (pē´ kən sē) *n.*: Pleasantly sharp quality
arabesque (ar´ ə besk´) *adj.*: Elaborately designed

◆ Build Grammar Skills

6 Subject-Verb Agreement Have students justify the use of the verb *were* in these three sentences. *Each sentence has a plural subject requiring a plural verb. The first sentence has a compound subject:* glare, glitter, *and* piquancy. *The subject of the second sentence is the word* figures. *The subject of the third is* fancies.

◆ Reading Strategy

7 Context Clues Students will find both *hue* and *tinted* further in this column and recognize that *hue* refers to color.

◆ Critical Thinking

8 Infer Ask students what the striking of the ebony clock might foreshadow. Have them explain their responses. *Students should grasp that the striking of the clock foreshadows the death of the dancers. Reasoning leading to this inference should include the color of the clock (ebony, or black), the color of the room (black velvet), and the silence as the clock is striking.*

Customize for *Pre-AP Students*

Ask students: What could be the significance of the clock's "muffled peal"? What might the clock be trying to "say"? *Lead students to suggest that the sound of the clock is a warning to the dancers, who persist in their decadent revels while the common people are suffering and dying.*

Humanities: Music

Several classical composers have written orchestral works with a mood of horror or the fantastic. Portions of these works might make good music for a performance of a radio script based on the story. Encourage students to listen to recordings of the following works to find music for the dance at the Prince's ball:

Hector Berlioz, *Symphonie Fantastique,* Opus 14
Paul Dukas, *The Sorcerer's Apprentice*
Igor Stravinsky, *Le Sacre du Printemps*

Students might also consider movie soundtracks, such as John Williams's score for the movie *Dracula.*

Cultural Connection

Point out to students that the word *masque* comes from the Italian word *maschera,* used to describe any covering for the face. *Masque* is also used to describe a form of drama, based on allegorical themes, common in Renaissance England, as well as masquerade balls and other court entertainments.

Explain to your students that wearing masks is an ancient practice. Greek and Roman actors wore masks to conceal their identity as well as to direct their voice toward the stage. Masks are also used in Japanese Noh plays and in a popular Italian dramatic form known as the pantomime. Ask students what the purpose of wearing a mask might be. Does it give the actor more freedom of expression? What are some of the limitations of wearing a mask?

In Poe's timeless world, party-goers dress up in costumes and masks. Poe describes the abbey as grotesque and strangely imaginary. After students have read the story, ask them what such a place might stand for. Is Poe's description satiric? To what extent do the prince's abbey and the masque come to stand for the imagination itself?

▶Critical Viewing◀

❶ Analyze The story has a mood of horror and ghastliness. The same mood is conveyed through the eerie images of death in the painting. The faces are contorted in ghastly expressions of suffering or glee.

◆ Literary Focus

❷ Symbols Details that indicate that the uninvited guest represents death include the fact that the figure is shrouded like a corpse and that it wears a mask that resembles a stiffened corpse. His clothes are dabbled in blood, and his face is marked with the red markings of the Red Death.

◆ Reading Strategy

❸ Context Clues Have students use context clues to figure out the meaning of the words *visage* and *countenance*. *Both are synonyms for the word face. The contexts "mask concealed the visage" and "resemble the countenance of" suggest the meanings.*

❹ Clarify Make sure students understand that the word *convulsed* means "taken over by a violent, uncontrollable contraction of the muscles, shaken or agitated with spasms."

Humanities: Art

Les Masques et la Mort (Masks and Death), 1897, by James Ensor.

This piece of art depicts frightening masks reminiscent of those in Poe's story.

James Ensor (1860–1949) was a Belgian artist who found inspiration in the fantastic and morbid literature of Poe. Although Ensor did not name his work for a Poe story, it is not difficult to surmise that "The Masque of the Red Death" inspired it.

1. What details in the facial expressions of the masks make them especially horrifying? *Students should cite the hollow eyes, the misshapen mouths, and the contorted expressions.*
2. The title of the painting, "Les Masques et la Mort," is French for "Masks and Death." Why is Death smiling in the painting, whereas the masks all have contorted faces. *Students might say that no mask can compete with death—Death knows it will have "the last laugh."*

indulge in the more remote gaieties of the other apartments.

But these other apartments were densely crowded, and in them beat feverishly the heart of life. And the revel went whirlingly on, until at length there commenced the sounding of midnight upon the clock. And then the music ceased, as I have told; and the evolutions of the waltzers were quieted; and there was an uneasy cessation of all things as before. But now there were twelve strokes to be sounded by the bell of the clock; and thus it happened, perhaps, that more of thought crept, with more of time, into the meditations of the thoughtful among those who reveled. And thus, too, it happened, perhaps, that before the last echoes of the last chime had utterly sunk into silence, there were many individuals in the crowd who had found leisure to become aware of the presence of a masked figure which had arrested the attention of no single individual before. And the rumor of this new presence having spread itself whisperingly around, there arose at length from the whole company a buzz, or murmur, expressive of disapprobation and surprise—then, finally, of terror, of horror, and of disgust.

Les Masques et la Mort 1897, © Estate of James Ensor/VAGA, New York, 1993

▲ ❶ Critical Viewing How is the mood of "The Masque of the Red Death" reflected in the details in this painting? **[Analyze]**

In an assembly of phantasms such as I have painted, it may well be supposed that no ordinary appearance could have excited such sensation. In truth the masquerade license of the night was nearly unlimited; but the figure in question had out-Heroded Herod,[10] and gone beyond the bounds of even the prince's indefinite decorum. There are chords in the hearts of the most reckless which cannot be touched without emotion. Even with the utterly lost, to whom life and death are equally jests, there are matters of which no jest can be made. The whole company, indeed, seemed now deeply to feel that in the costume and bearing of the stranger neither wit nor propriety existed. The figure was tall and gaunt, and shrouded from head to foot in the habiliments of the grave. The mask which concealed the visage was made so nearly to resemble the countenance of a stiffened corpse that the closest scrutiny must have had difficulty in detecting the cheat. And yet all this might have been endured, if not approved, by the mad revelers around. But the mummer[11] had gone so far as to assume the type of the Red Death. His vesture was dabbled in *blood*—and his broad brow, with all the features of the face, was besprinkled with the scarlet horror.

◆ Literary Focus What details in the following description help you understand the symbolism of the new guest?

When the eyes of Prince Prospero fell upon this spectral image (which with a slow and solemn movement, as if more fully to sustain its role, stalked to and fro among the waltzers) he was seen to be convulsed, in the first moment ❹

10. **out-Heroded Herod:** Behaved excessively, just as King Herod did. In the Bible, Herod slaughtered innocent babies, hoping to kill Jesus.

11. **mummer** *n.*: Masked and costumed person who acts out pantomimes.

◆ Build Vocabulary

cessation (se sā´ shən) *n.*: Stopping, either forever or for some time

disapprobation (dis ap´ rə bā´ shən) *n.*: Disapproval

habiliments (hə bil´ ə mənts) *n.*: Clothing

Reteach

Understanding the symbolism Poe uses in "The Masque of the Red Death" will be a difficult concept for some students to grasp. Suggest that students draw a two-column chart on a piece of paper, labeling one column "Story Detail" and the other column "Symbolism."

Story Detail	Symbolism

Have students reread the information about symbols provided in the Literary Focus on p. 77 and in the Guide for Responding on p. 84. As a class, discuss these examples. Have students add the symbols discussed to the top of their chart in the appropriate column. Then, challenge students to reread the story, specifically looking for and evaluating story details that may denote symbolism, and determine what they might mean. When students have completed their charts, have them meet in small groups to discuss and defend the choices they have included in their chart.

with a strong shudder either of terror or distaste; but, in the next, his brow reddened with rage.

"Who dares?" he demanded hoarsely of the courtiers who stood near him—"who dares insult us with this blasphemous mockery? Seize him and unmask him—that we may know whom we have to hang at sunrise, from the battlements!"

It was in the eastern or blue chamber in which stood the Prince Prospero as he uttered these words. They rang throughout the seven rooms loudly and clearly—for the prince was a bold and robust man, and the music had become hushed at the waving of his hand.

It was in the blue room where stood the prince, with a group of pale courtiers by his side. At first, as he spoke, there was a slight rushing movement of this group in the direction of the intruder, who at the moment was also near at hand, and now, with deliberate and stately step, made closer approach to the speaker. But from a certain nameless awe with which the mad assumptions of the mummer had inspired the whole party, there were found none who put forth hand to seize him; so that, unimpeded, he passed within a yard of the prince's person; and, while the vast assembly, as if with one impulse, shrank from the centers of the rooms to the walls, he made his way uninterruptedly, but with the same solemn and measured step which had distinguished him from the first, through the blue chamber to the purple—through the purple to the green—through the green to the orange—through this again to the white—and even thence to the violet, ere a decided movement had been made to arrest him. It was then, however, that the Prince Prospero, maddening with rage and the shame of his own momentary cowardice, rushed hurriedly through the six chambers, while none followed him on account of a deadly terror that had seized upon all. He bore aloft a drawn dagger, and had approached, in rapid impetuosity, to within three or four feet of the retreating figure, when the latter, having attained the extremity of the velvet apartment, turned suddenly and confronted his pursuer. There was a sharp cry—and the dagger dropped gleaming upon the sable carpet, upon which, instantly afterwards, fell prostrate in death the Prince Prospero. Then, summoning the wild courage of despair, a throng of the revelers at once threw themselves into the black apartment, and, seizing the mummer, whose tall figure stood erect and motionless within the shadow of the ebony clock, gasped in unutterable horror at finding the grave cerements[12] and corpselike mask which they handled with so violent a rudeness, untenanted by any tangible form.

And now was acknowledged the presence of the Red Death. He had come like a thief in the night. And one by one dropped the revelers in the blood-bedewed halls of their revel, and died each in the despairing posture of his fall. And the life of the ebony clock went out with that of the last of the gay. And the flames of the tripods expired. ❻ And Darkness and Decay and the Red Death held illimitable dominion over all. ❼

12. **cerements** (ser′ ə mənts) *n.*: Wrappings or shroud.

Guide for Responding

◆ *Literature and Your Life*

Reader's Response Would you have liked Prince Prospero as a friend? Why or why not?

Thematic Focus What, if anything, is admirable about the prince's attempt to escape from his destiny? Give reasons for your answer.

Sketch Do a quick drawing of the symbolic stranger who crashes Prince Prospero's masquerade.

☑ Check Your Comprehension

1. Why do Prince Prospero and his followers retreat to one of his abbeys?
2. Briefly describe the series of rooms in which the prince entertains his guests.
3. Describe the uninvited guest.
4. Summarize the events that follow the uninvited guest's arrival.

◆ Critical Thinking

❺ **Interpret** Point out to students that the uninvited guest is able to pass "unimpeded" through the party. Ask how this fact helps convey the meaning of the story. *Like the uninvited guest, contagious disease is unstoppable and does not spare victims on the basis of their social status.*

◆ Literary Focus

❻ **Symbols** Ask students which symbols in these two lines represent death. *Symbols of death include the stopping of the clock and the extinguishing of the flames.*

◆ Critical Thinking

❼ **Evaluate** Ask students what makes this final statement so effective. *The statement makes clear that Death, with Darkness and Decay, is the ruler in the end. Try as they might, humans have no influence over Death.*

Reinforce and Extend

Answers

◆ *Literature and Your Life*

Reader's Response Some students might say they would like to be his friend because he is a reveler and very imaginative.

Thematic Focus Some students might say that Prospero's attempt to escape his destiny is admirable because he tries to resist fate.

☑ Check Your Comprehension

1. They retreat to the palace to try to hide from the Red Death.
2. Answers should include that there were seven rooms, all situated at different angles, and that they were of different colors and contained different decorations and windows.
3. The uninvited stranger is "tall and gaunt," wrapped in "habiliments of the grave," and wearing a mask that resembled a corpse.
4. Prince Prospero convulses when he sees the uninvited guest. He later pursues the uninvited guest with a knife through the chambers. The uninvited guest kills Prospero; the revelers unmask the guest and find he is the Red Death.

Beyond the Selection

FURTHER READING

Other Works by Edgar Allan Poe
"The Pit and the Pendulum"
"The Cask of Amontillado"
"The Raven"

Other Works With the Theme of Searching for Safety
"An Occurrence at Owl Creek Bridge," Ambrose Bierce

We suggest that you preview these works before recommending them to your students.

INTERNET

For more information on Edgar Allan Poe and his work, we suggest the following sites on the Internet. Please be aware, however, that sites may have changed from the time we published this information.

http://www.cais.com/webweave/poe. html
http://www.comnet.ca/~forrest/index.html

We *strongly recommend* that you preview the sites before you send students to them.

Answers

◆ Critical Thinking

1. Outside the palace there is death and despair. Inside the palace there is life and merriment. However, outside the abbey, there is no frantic denial of suffering and dying; inside there is total denial.
2. He is concerned only with himself and his well-being; he seems to think he's invincible.
3. He conveys the message that no one, no matter how privileged or grand, can vanquish death.
4. Students might suggest that the old-fashioned language adds an air of distant formality.
5. Most students will probably feel that Poe would agree with the quotation.

◆ Reading Strategy

Students should explain that because they know that *tinted* means "colored," they can infer from context that *hue* is a synonym for *color.*

◆ Literary Focus

1. The uninvited guest—Unstoppable disease and death
2. The clock—Passing time that brings death
3. The prince's abbey—An illusion of safety

◆ Build Vocabulary

Using the Suffix *-tion*

1. *decoration*—the quality of being decorated
2. *creation*—the act of creating
3. *desperation*—the state of being desperate
4. *termination*—the act of ending

Using the Word Bank

1. They perceived him as august.
2. The costumes were arabesque.
3. The uninvited guest wore habiliments.
4. The food had the quality of piquancy.
5. He viewed those who didn't enjoy his ball with disapprobation.
6. When the clock struck the hour there was a cessation of life.

◆ Build Grammar Skills

1. plague; was
2. costumes, music, dancing; were
3. windows; are
4. people; are
5. way; isn't

Guide for Responding *(continued)*

◆ Critical Thinking

Interpret

1. Contrast life outside the prince's abbey with life inside it. **[Compare and Contrast]**
2. Why does the prince think he'll be able to escape the plague? **[Infer]**
3. What message does Poe convey through the prince's unsuccessful battle with the intruder? **[Interpret]**

Evaluate

4. Does Poe's old-fashioned language add to the chilling mood and dreamlike atmosphere of the tale? Why or why not? **[Criticize]**

Apply

5. An Italian writer declared, "Every tiny part of us cries out against the idea of dying, and hopes to live forever." How would Poe have responded to this quotation? **[Hypothesize]**

◆ Reading Strategy

Context Clues

Context clues—hints in the surrounding passage—can help you figure out the meaning of unfamiliar words in the story.

Explain how the context clues give hints to the meaning of the italicized word: "These windows were of stained glass whose color varied in accordance with the prevailing *hue* of the decorations . . ."

◆ Literary Focus

Symbols

Many people, places, and objects in Poe's tale are **symbols** that stand for more than themselves, adding layers of meaning to the story. On your paper, connect the symbol in Column A with the idea it symbolizes in Column B.

Column A	Column B
1. The uninvited guest	a. An illusion of safety
2. The clock	b. Unstoppable disease and death
3. The prince's abbey	c. Passing time that brings death

◆ Build Vocabulary

Using the Latin Suffix *-tion*

Use the meaning of the Latin suffix *-tion* ("act or quality of") to define each of these words:

1. decoration
2. creation
3. desperation
4. termination

Using the Word Bank: Word Choice

On your paper, answer each question with a sentence that contains a word from the Word Bank. (Use each word once.)

1. How did the guests perceive the prince?
2. Describe the guests' costumes.
3. What was the uninvited guest wearing?
4. Describe the food that was probably served at the ball.
5. How did the prince view anyone who didn't enjoy his ball?
6. What happened when the clock struck the hour?

◆ Build Grammar Skills

Subject and Verb Agreement

Poe emphasizes things rather than actions by beginning sentences with *there*, reversing subject and verb, and using forms of the verb *be*: *is, was* (singular); *are, were* (plural).

When you begin sentences with *there*, remember that the **verb** must agree with the subject that follows it.

Practice Identify the subject in each sentence, then choose the verb that agrees with it.

1. There (was, were) a horrible plague devastating the kingdom.
2. There (was, were) costumes, music, and dancing at the masque.
3. There (is, are) beautiful windows of stained glass in the abbey.
4. There (is, are) people in every room but the last
5. There (isn't, aren't) any way to escape the uninvited guest.

Grammar Reinforcement

For additional instruction and practice, use the lesson in the **Language Lab CD-ROM** on Subject and Verb Agreement and the pages on Subject and Verb Agreement (pp. 80–82) in the *Writer's Solution Grammar Practice Book*.

Build Your Portfolio

Idea Bank

Writing

1. **Invitation to the Prince's Masquerade** Write and design an invitation to Prince Prospero's masquerade. Style the invitation in keeping with the party as Poe describes it. **[Art Link]**

2. **Description of a Modern Masquerade** Prince Prospero was inventive, but he didn't have the benefit of modern technology. Describe the party he could have thrown with up-to-date lighting and sound equipment.

3. **Report on the Black Plague** Research and report on the Black Plague that threatened Europe in the fourteenth century. Include the symptoms of the disease, the speed with which it spread, and its effect on society. **[Social Studies Link; Science Link]**

Speaking, Listening, and Viewing

4. **Press Conference** With a small group, role-play a press conference in which reporters ask the prince about the masquerade and the plague. **[Social Studies Link]**

5. **Radio Script** Write and perform a radio script for a scene from "The Masque of the Red Death." Include dialogue and sound effects. **[Media Link; Performing Arts Link]**

Researching and Representing

6. **Costume Design** Sketch out a costume you could wear to Prince Prospero's masquerade, indicating colors and fabrics. **[Art Link]**

7. **Multimedia Presentation** Give a multimedia presentation on an event that involves masks and costumes, like the Venice carnival. If possible, include slides and sound effects. **[Art Link; Social Studies Link]**

Online Activity www.phlit.phschool.com

Guided Writing Lesson

Proposal for a Team Symbol

In "The Masque of the Red Death," Poe's symbols stress the dark side of life. However, you see symbols every day that communicate a positive message about a group, an idea, a product, or a team. Keeping these in mind, propose a symbol for a school athletic team or for a professional team.

Writing Skills Focus: Demonstrate the Benefits of an Idea

Make your proposal convincing by demonstrating the benefits of your idea. Here, for example, are some benefits of using a lightning bolt as a team symbol:

- It will inspire the team with a sense of power.
- It will increase team pride.
- It will make a striking visual image on team jerseys.

After listing such benefits, support them by explaining *how* the lightning bolt will inspire the team, *why* it will boost pride, and *why* a strong visual image is important.

Prewriting Create a chart with several benefits categories, such as inspiration for team, inspiration for fans, and visual appeal. After choosing a symbol, note on the chart how it will benefit the team in each category.

Drafting Begin your proposal with a vivid description of the symbol. Then, referring to the chart you created, explain specifically how the symbol will benefit the team.

Revising Read your draft as if you were on the panel evaluating the pluses and minuses of the proposed symbol. If there are not enough pluses, you may want to include additional benefits that the symbol will bring.

✓ ASSESSMENT OPTIONS

Formal Assessment, Selection Test, pp. 13–15, and Assessment Resources Software. The selection test is designed so that it can be easily customized to the performance levels of your students.

Alternative Assessment, p. 5, includes options for less advanced students, more advanced students, musical/rhythmic learners, visual/spatial learners, and logical/mathematical learners.

PORTFOLIO ASSESSMENT

Use the following rubrics in the ***Alternative Assessment*** booklet to assess student writing:
Invitation to the Prince's Masquerade: Expression Rubric, p. 94
Description of a Modern Masquerade: Description Rubric, p. 97
Report on the Black Plague: Research Report Rubric, p. 106

Idea Bank

Customizing for *Performance Levels*

Following are suggestions for matching Idea Bank topics with your students' performance levels:
Less Advanced Students: 1, 6
Average Students: 2, 4, 5, 7
More Advanced Students: 3

Customizing for *Learning Modalities*

Following are suggestions for matching Idea Bank topics with your students' learning modalities:
Visual/Spatial: 1, 6, 7
Verbal/Linguistic: 4, 5, 7
Logical/Mathematical: 3

Guided Writing Lesson

Prewriting Strategy

Before they write, students can use listing to come up with an idea for their team symbol. At the top of a piece of paper, each student should write the words "team symbol" and brainstorm a list of terms and ideas they associate with those words. After you call time, students should stop writing and look over their lists. They should choose one or more of the terms they generated to use as prompts for their next lists. Repeat the exercise a few times, and then guide students to examine the items they wrote and the connections between them. Students can then freewrite about one of these ideas to develop it further or, if they feel ready, they can begin to write.

Writers at Work Videodisc

Have students view the videodisc segment (Ch. 4) featuring Sayu Bhojwani to see and hear some tips on how to interest readers in a subject. Have students discuss what Bhojwani says about how persuasive writing differs from other forms of writing.

Play frames 33643 to 43235

Writing Lab CD-ROM

Have students complete the tutorial on Persuasive Writing. Follow these steps:

1. Have students use the Note Cards activity to gather details.
2. Have students draft on computer.
3. Have students use the Self-Evaluation Checklist to help them revise.

Prepare and Engage

LESSON OBJECTIVES

1. To develop vocabulary and word identification skills
- Anglo-Saxon Suffixes: *-less*
- Using the Word Bank: Analogies
- Build Vocabulary: Suffixes: *-less*

2. To use a variety of reading strategies to comprehend poems
- Connect Your Experience
- Tips to Guide Reading: Scanning
- Reading Strategy: Form a Mental Image
- Read to Be Entertained (ATE)

3. To express and support responses to the text
- Critical Thinking
- Idea Bank: Letter to a Poet
- Idea Bank: Short Story Based on a Poem

4. To analyze literary elements
- Literary Focus: Imagery

5. To read in order to research self-selected and assigned topics
- Idea Bank: Scientific Diagram

6. To plan, prepare, organize, and present literary interpretations
- Speaking, Viewing, and Listening Mini-Lesson: Oral Interpretation
- Idea Bank: Speech

7. To use recursive writing processes to write an anecdote
- Guided Writing Lesson

8. To increase knowledge of the rules of grammar and usage
- Build Grammar Skills: Pronouns and Antecedents

Test Preparation

Reading Comprehension: Using Context Clues to Determine Word Meanings (ATE, p. 87) The teaching tips and sample test item in this workshop support the instruction and practice in the unit workshop:

Reading Comprehension: Using Context Clues to Determine Word Meanings (SE, p. 113)

Guide for Reading

Gabriela Mistral *(1889–1957)*

Most fifteen-year-olds do not have full-time jobs, but at fifteen, Gabriela Mistral (gä brē ā´ lä mē sträl´) was a full-time grade-school teacher in her native Chile. When Mistral (whose real name is Lucila Godoy Alcayaga) began publishing her poetry, she tried a variety of pen names, eventually settling on Gabriela Mistral.

In 1945, Mistral became the first woman poet and the first Latin American to receive the Nobel Prize for Literature.

Octavio Paz *(1914–1998)*

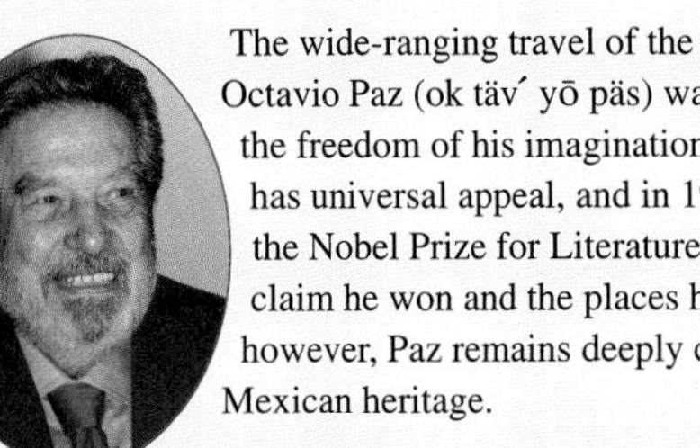

The wide-ranging travel of the Mexican poet Octavio Paz (ok täv´ yō päs) was matched by the freedom of his imagination. Paz's poetry has universal appeal, and in 1990 he received the Nobel Prize for Literature. For all the acclaim he won and the places he traveled, however, Paz remains deeply committed to his Mexican heritage.

William Carlos Williams *(1883–1963)*

Most people would agree that being a doctor is a full-time job. William Carlos Williams was both a doctor and a poet. When asked how he managed his double career, he replied that he treated his patients like poems and his poems like patients.

Williams believed that Americans should write about the details in the world around them. That's why the road in "Spring and All" describes a local route that he often took to see patients.

◆ Build Vocabulary

ANGLO-SAXON SUFFIXES: *-less*

Williams describes early spring as "lifeless." Knowing that the suffix *-less* means "without," you can figure out that *lifeless* means "without life."

WORD BANK

As you read the poems, you will encounter the words on this list. Each word is defined on the page where it first appears. Preview the list before you read. Also, look for other words with the suffix *-less*, like *leafless* and *doorless*.

contagious
lifeless
clarity
stark
profound

◆ Build Grammar Skills

PRONOUNS AND ANTECEDENTS

A pronoun's **antecedent** is the noun or pronoun to which it refers. An antecedent can come before or after the pronoun, can be in another sentence, and might be more than one word. In poetry, an antecedent may be on a different line, as in the following example from "The street":

antecedent
Someone behind me also stepping on
pronoun
stones, leaves:/if I slow down, *he* slows

As you read "Fear," however, you'll notice that the pronoun *them* has no antecedent. Think about why the poet leaves it out.

Prentice Hall Literature Program Resources

REINFORCE / RETEACH / EXTEND

Selection Support Pages
Build Vocabulary: Suffixes: *-less*, p. 22
Build Grammar Skills: Pronouns and Antecedents, p. 23
Reading Strategy: Form a Mental Image, p. 24
Literary Focus: Imagery, p. 25

Strategies for Diverse Student Needs, p. 6

Beyond Literature
Humanities Connection: Fine Art for "Spring and All," p. 6

Formal Assessment Selection Test, pp. 16–18

Alternative Assessment, p. 6

Writing and Language Transparencies, Writing Process Model 3: Personal Narrative, pp. 17–23

Resource Pro CD-ROM

Listening to Literature Audiocassettes

Fear ◆ The street ◆ Spring and All

◆ Literature and Your Life

CONNECT YOUR EXPERIENCE

As you grow older, you face new and sometimes difficult experiences. You may have to overcome your shyness to make a presentation to the class, or you may have to sacrifice time with friends to work at an after-school job. Without experiences like these, however, you'd remain the same person throughout your life—never changing, never growing.

Like you, the subjects in these poems must face difficult and frightening challenges.

THEMATIC FOCUS: DANGEROUS DESTINIES

These selections about challenges and change raise the question "What kind of courage does it take to live in an uncertain world?"

Journal Writing In the center of a sunburst diagram like the one shown, note a challenge you are facing. Along the rays projecting from it, briefly describe the rewards and difficulties associated with this challenge.

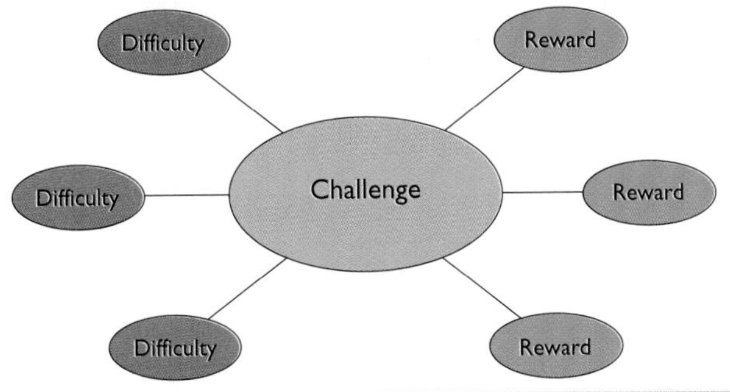

◆ Background for Understanding

LITERATURE

Translators face an especially difficult challenge; they must carry the meaning of a poem or story from one language to another. This job is difficult because a word in one language can often be translated by several possible words in another.

For example, the word *niña* in the Spanish original of Mistral's poem "Fear" could be translated as "child" or "little girl." Those translating "Fear" must make many such choices. As a result, different translators may write different versions of a poem or story.

◆ Literary Focus

IMAGERY

No matter what language they speak, people can all understand the language of the senses. For that reason, the element of a poem that is often easiest to appreciate is its **imagery**, the descriptive language that re-creates sensory experiences.

You can begin to enter the world each poem describes by identifying its imagery. In reading "Spring and All," for example, notice the sensory language the poet uses to describe the sky, the earth, and the plants of early spring.

◆ Reading Strategy

FORM A MENTAL IMAGE

Reading a poem is like having a conversation. As you hear someone speak, you often **form a mental image,** a picture in your mind, of what that person is saying. In the same way, you can picture in your mind what these poets are saying.

Enter the mysterious world of "The street," for example, by forming an image of the "dark and doorless" street that Paz describes. Glimpse the speaker in the "blackness" as he stumbles, falls, and rises.

Test Preparation Workshop

Reading Comprehension: Using Context Clues to Determine Word Meanings When students take standardized tests, they need to be prepared to use context clues to select the best word from a list of choices to complete a sentence. Ask students to read lines 1–10 of "Spring and All" on p. 90, and then use the following sample test item.

In lines 1–10, waste most nearly means—

A uselessly spend
B destroy
C uninhabited land
D gradually diminish

Although the meanings in answers *A, B,* and *D* are definitions of the word *waste*, help students determine that answer *C* is best because context clues indicate (a) the word is used as a noun, and (b) "broad, muddy fields" are probably not inhabited.

To demonstrate a test-taking strategy, do not give students the answer choices until they have used context clues and answered the item on their own. They can see which answer from the list most closely fits their own. This strategy may avoid confusion from "distractor" answer choices.

Interest Grabber Present students with magazine pictures that might inspire the feelings suggested by these poems: parting of people, which might suggest abandonment; a desolate street at night that would arouse fear; and the burst of new life that is spring. Encourage students to share their impressions of these pictures. Then explain that, like pictures, the images in poems bring forth responses and make ideas concrete. As they read the three poems, invite students to open their minds and look for ways in which one thing is transformed into another through the power of imagery.

Tips to Guide Reading

Scanning Introduce each poem individually and discuss the images presented as students scan the poems. If students wish, they may use flags to mark difficult passages they will encounter as they read the poems.

Customize for
Less Proficient Readers
Poems often pose challenges. Have students, in small groups, use difficult passages to practice reading strategies such as paraphrasing and breaking down long passages.

Customize for
Pre-AP Students
Have each student select one of the poems and analyze whether it would make a good song. Have students describe the kind of music that would enhance the poems' imagery and rhythms.

Customize for
Gifted/Talented Students
Suggest that students locate a poem written in a foreign language that they may be studying. Challenge them to translate part of the poem into English, with the help of a bilingual dictionary. Have students discuss reasons why poetry may be particularly difficult to translate from one language to another.

Customize for
English Language Learners
Two of these poems are translations of poems by Latin American poets. Invite students to select and translate a passage of one of the poems into their own language and share it with the class in an oral reading.

Develop Understanding

One-Minute Insight Although diverse in style and subject matter, these poems have one thing in common: Each explores a significant challenge or uncertainty that people face in life. In "Fear," a mother worries that her little girl might grow apart from her. In "The street," a man struggles with basic questions such as: Who am I? Where am I going?

◆ Literary Focus

❶ **Imagery** What imagery does the poet use in these lines? How does it add to the poem's ideas? *Imagery includes "swallow," "straw bed," "nest in the eaves." Students may say that the imagery emphasizes the idea that the speaker does not want her little girl to be away from her; the imagery conjures up a vivid picture.*

◆ Critical Thinking

❷ **Infer** Based on these lines, what inferences can you make about the speaker's fears and hopes? *The speaker fears that her little girl may not always be so close; she hopes that her little girl will always be able to express her joy freely.*

◆ Build Grammar Skills

❸ **Pronouns and Antecedents** Have students identify the noun from the preceding stanza to which the pronoun *her* refers. *girl*

▶Critical Viewing◀

❹ **Draw Conclusions** *Students will probably connect the fear of the woman in the painting to that of the speaker in the poem. Based on the evidence that the mother in the painting appears worried and is clinging to her child, students might conclude she fears the dangers of the world and wants to protect her child.*

◆ Literary Focus

❺ **Imagery** Lead students to identify specific images in this passage, such as "long and silent street," "dry leaves," and "someone behind me also stepping." Encourage them to comment on the senses that these images appeal to, as well as the overall impression they create. *The images appeal to the senses of sight, hearing, and touch. Students may say that the overall impression is one of being lost.*

Fear

Gabriela Mistral
Translated by Doris Dana

I don't want them to turn
my little girl into a swallow.
She would fly far away into the sky
❶ and never fly again to my straw bed,
or she would nest in the eaves[1]
where I could not comb her hair.
I don't want them to turn
my little girl into a swallow.

I don't want them to make
my little girl a princess.
❷ In tiny golden slippers
how could she play on the meadow?
And when night came, no longer
would she sleep at my side.
I don't want them to make
my little girl a princess.

❸ And even less do I want them
one day to make her queen.
They would put her on a throne
where I could not go to see her.
And when nighttime came
I could never rock her . . .
I don't want them to make
my little girl a queen!

1. **eaves** (ēvz) *n.*: The lower edge or edges of a roof, usually projecting beyond the sides of a building.

▲ Critical Viewing What might the mother in this painting fear? Explain your answer. **[Draw Conclusions]** ❹

Block Scheduling Strategies

Consider these suggestions to take advantage of extended class time:

- Have students meet in small groups to discuss the question in the Thematic Focus section of Literature and Your Life on p. 87. Then have compare the ideas charted on their sunburst diagrams.
- Direct pairs of students to brainstorm for a list of images that they think evoke fear. After discussing the significance of the images on their lists, students can compare them with some of the images that call up fear in these poems, such as "a long and silent street."
- Have students listen to the poems on audiocassette. Then guide them to practice and present oral interpretations of the poems, as suggested in the Speaking, Listening, and Viewing activities in the Idea Bank on p. 93.
- Have students complete the Guided Writing Lesson on p. 93. As a prewriting activity, invite volunteers to share interesting or amusing anecdotes about challenges they have faced.

The street

Octavio Paz
Translated by ***Muriel Rukeyser***

A long and silent street.
I walk in blackness and I stumble and fall
and rise, and I walk blind, my feet
stepping on silent stones and dry leaves.
Someone behind me also stepping on
stones, leaves:
if I slow down, he slows;
if I run, he runs, I turn: nobody.

❻ Everything dark and doorless.
Turning and turning among these corners
which lead forever to the street
where nobody waits for, nobody follows me,
where I pursue a man who stumbles
and rises and says when he sees me: nobody.

Guide for Responding

◆ Literature and Your Life

Reader's Response Did you want to comfort the speakers in these poems? Why or why not?

Thematic Focus Briefly describe the challenges that each speaker faces.

☑ Check Your Comprehension

1. Who is the speaker in "Fear"?
2. Describe three fears the speaker has.
3. What happens in the first stanza of "The street"? The second?

◆ Critical Thinking

INTERPRET

1. Find three details that give "Fear" the quality of a fairy tale and explain your choices. **[Support]**
2. In "Fear" what is the common element in each of the fears the speaker expresses? **[Draw Conclusions]**
3. Show how there are two speakers in "The street" and explain who they are. **[Interpret]**
4. In what ways does "The street" resemble a nightmare? **[Compare and Contrast]**
5. Compare and contrast the fears of the speaker in "Fear" with the fears expressed in "The street." **[Compare and Contrast]**

APPLY

6. Describe a situation that could lead up to the speech in "Fear." For example, how might the mother's speech be a response to fairy tales she has just told her daughter? **[Hypothesize]**

EXTEND

7. Mistral begins the first two stanzas of "Fear" with the words "I don't want." Imagine that you are Mistral. Name two other things you don't want. **[Relate]**

◆ Build Vocabulary

❻ **Suffixes: *-less*** Ask students to identify the word that contains the suffix *-less,* and tell its meaning. *The word doorless means "without doors."*

◆ Reading Strategy

❼ **Form a Mental Image** Have students form a mental image in response to these words and explain what their image suggests about the poem's larger meaning? *Students may compare the image of "turning and turning among these corners" to being caught in a maze, suggesting that the poem deals with feelings of entrapment.*

Reinforce and Extend

Answers

◆ Literature and Your Life

Reader's Response Some students may want to comfort the speakers with whom they sympathize.

Thematic Focus The mother in "Fear" faces the challenge of guarding her little girl from the world's dangers; the speaker of "The street" faces the challenge of discovering his identity.

☑ Check Your Comprehension

1. The speaker is a mother.
2. She fears her daughter turn into a swallow, a princess, and a queen.
3. In the first stanza the speaker walks blindly down a street, hears someone, but turns to see no one. In the second stanza the speaker pursues a phantom who is himself.

◆ Critical Thinking

1. Details include a princess, golden slippers, a queen, and a throne; all are associated with fairy tales involving royalty, such as *Cinderella.*
2. The common element is that the daughter will become independent.
3. The two speakers are the man who is being pursued and the pursuer—actually one person.
4. "The street" is like a nightmare because it shows being trapped in a circular situation.
5. Students may mention that both poems evoke fears of being alone and finding one's own identity.
6. Students might describe a situation in which the mother imagines her daughter swept away by romance.
7. Suggestions should follow the central idea of the mother fearing her daughter's separation from her.

Humanities: Art

Woman With Child by Pablo Picasso.

Both highly imaginative and prolific, Pablo Picasso (1881–1973) contributed inestimably to the development of modern art in the twentieth century. Picasso was born in Malaga, Spain, and began painting seriously at the age of fourteen. A master of both realistic and abstract styles, he explored such deeply human themes as love, war, and loneliness. His interpretations of these themes were sometimes tender and sometimes confrontational.

Use these questions for discussion:

1. How would you describe the feelings that the mother shows for her child in both the painting and the poem? *Students may describe her feelings as loving, caring, or protective.*
2. What details in the painting suggest that—like the speaker in the poem—the woman has fears and worries regarding her child? *Students may point out the far-off look in her eyes and the protective hand she has placed on the child's shoulder.*

In "Spring and All," the speaker finds that birth and renewal may be as difficult as they are joyous.

◆ Literary Focus

❶ **Imagery** Which images do students find particularly powerful in these opening lines? How would they describe the overall scene that these images create? *Some students may cite images such as "cold wind," "waste of broad muddy fields," and "standing water," which paint a picture of a cold, stagnant, unwelcoming spot. Others may find the image of the "contagious hospital" powerful because it is surprising and somewhat mysterious at this point.*

◆ Build Grammar Skills

❷ **Pronouns and Antecedents** Point out the pronouns *they* and *them*. Remind students that antecedents of pronouns sometimes follow the pronouns, as is the case with these. Have students find the noun(s) to which these pronouns refer. The antecedent *is* the objects, *including* the grass *and* the wildcarrot leaf, *in lines 21–23.*

◆ Reading Strategy

❸ **Form a Mental Image** Point out the image of the "stiff curl of wildcarrot leaf." What other images does this bring to mind? What ideas about spring does it suggest? *Students may think of a tightly coiled spring—which is full of tension and potential energy, just as the season spring is. The might also suggest a spiral design.*

▶Critical Viewing◀

❹ **Connect** *Students who feel the artist shares Williams's vision may point out that both the poem and the art communicate the two-sided nature of spring; Williams contrasts of lifelessness and reawakening, while the artist combines subdued colors with traditional symbols.*

Read to Be Entertained

Poetry provides an excellent opportunity for students to read to be entertained by the author's use of language, imagery, and rhythms. To further appreciate the literary melodies found in poetry, have students listen to the recording.

Listening to Literature Audiocassettes

Spring and All

William Carlos Williams

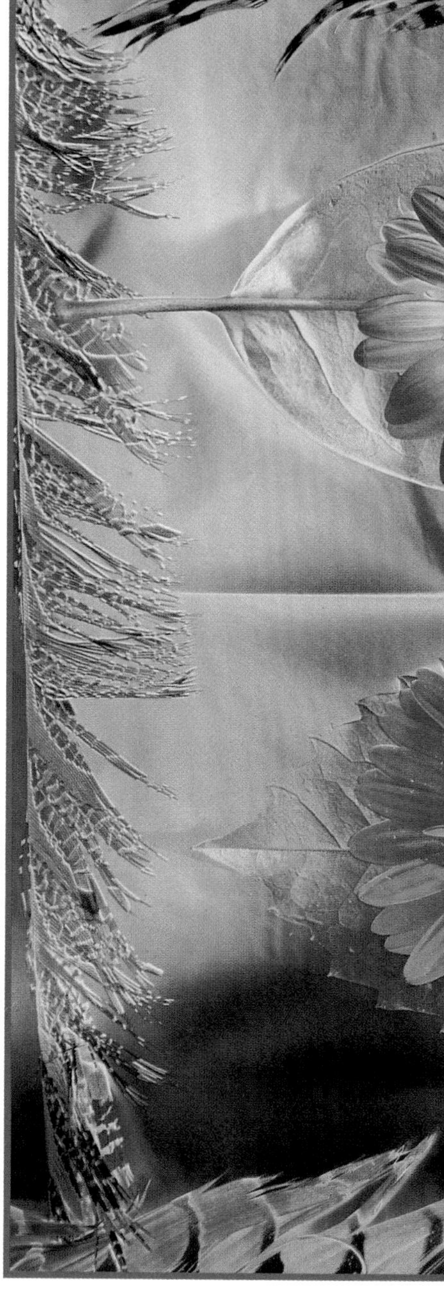

By the road to the contagious hospital
under the surge of the blue
mottled clouds driven from the
northeast—a cold wind. Beyond, the
waste of broad, muddy fields
brown with dried weeds, standing and fallen

❶ patches of standing water
the scattering of tall trees

All along the road the reddish
purplish, forked, upstanding, twiggy
stuff of bushes and small trees
with dead, brown leaves under them
leafless vines—

Lifeless in appearance, sluggish
dazed spring approaches—

❷ They enter the new world naked,
cold, uncertain of all
save that they enter. All about them
the cold, familiar wind—

❸ Now the grass, tomorrow
the stiff curl of wildcarrot leaf
One by one objects are defined—
It quickens: clarity, outline of leaf

But now the stark dignity of
entrance—Still, the profound change
has come upon them: rooted, they
grip down and begin to awaken

❹ ▶ **Critical Viewing** Do you think this artist shares Williams's vision of spring? Support your answer. **[Connect]**

Speaking, Listening, and Viewing Mini-Lesson

Oral Interpretation

This mini-lesson supports the Speaking, Listening, and Viewing activity in the Idea Bank on p. 93.

Introduce Oral readings of poetry provide an excellent opportunity for students to analyze the melodies of literary language.

Develop Have students discuss the elements they need to consider when preparing a poem for an oral reading:

- vary tone of voice
- vary the speed
- stress certain words
- observe punctuation marks

Apply Students should select one of the poems and practice reading it aloud. They may wish to practice reading it in front of a mirror. Suggest that students also work with a partner to practice their presentation and make suggestions for improvement.

Assess Have students perform their oral reading for the entire class. Have members of the class use the Peer Assessment: Oral Interpretation in **Alternative Assessments**, p. 119.

Untitled, David Gaz

Guide for Responding

◆ Literature and Your Life

Reader's Response How do the images in this poem compare to your images of spring?

Thematic Focus What details in lines 16–19 suggest that birth can be a dangerous destiny? Explain.

Sketch Make a quick line drawing of an image you like in this poem.

☑ Check Your Comprehension

1. What does the speaker see in the sky and on the earth?
2. Summarize the speaker's description of the approach of spring.

◆ Critical Thinking

INTERPRET

1. Why do you think the poet sets a spring scene near a hospital? **[Infer]**
2. Pointing to words like *defined, clarity,* and *awaken*, explain what the coming of spring means to this poet. **[Interpret]**

APPLY

3. How might this poet describe another season like fall or winter? **[Hypothesize]**

◆ Build Vocabulary

contagious (kən tā′ jəs) *adj.*: Spread by direct or indirect contact

lifeless (līf′ lis) *adj.*: Without life

clarity (klar′ ə tē) *n.*: The quality or condition of being clear

stark (stärk) *adj.*: Bare; plain

profound (prō found′) *adj.*: Deep

Reinforce and Extend

Answers

◆ Literature and Your Life

Reader's Response If students live in a place with definite seasonal cycles they may mention such signs of spring as crocuses budding or rain storms.

Thematic Focus Students should mention "naked," "cold," and "uncertain of all." These images suggest the vulnerability of the newborn.

☑ Check Your Comprehension

1. He sees mottled clouds in the sky and muddy fields, dry weeds, patches of standing water, and leafless vines on Earth.
2. The speaker notices new grass growing and wildcarrot leaf as nature grows clearer.

◆ Critical Thinking

1. A plant faces danger trying to survive, just as patients may struggle to survive in a hospital.
2. Spring is an awakening because it is a time of rebirth and renewal for plants, trees, and nature.
3. One acceptable response is that fall is a time of nature shrinking and folding in on itself and winter is a time of harshness.

Beyond the Selection

FURTHER READING

Other Works by the Featured Poets

Tenderness, Gabriela Mistral (collection of poems)
A Draft of Shadows and Other Poems, Paz
Spring and All, William Carlos Williams

Other Works With the Theme of Struggling With Uncertainty

"Prayer for my Daughter," William Butler Yeats
"The Road Not Taken," Robert Frost

We suggest that you preview these works before recommending them to students.

INTERNET

You may find more information on these poets and their work on the Internet. We suggest the following sites. Please be aware that sites may have changed from the time we published this information. For more on Mistral, go to **http://www.netsrq.com/~dbois/mistral.htm/** For more on Williams, go to **http://www.charm.net/~brooklyn/People/WilliamCarlosWilliams.html/**

We *strongly recommend* that you preview the sites before you send students to them.

◆ Reading Strategy

1. Students may say they formed a mental image of footsteps, the sound of breathing or whispers, or a shadowy figure in pursuit.
2. The little girl can be pictured as a swallow, a princess, and a queen.
3. The road is bleak, colorless, and lifeless.

◆ Build Grammar Skills

1. with dead brown leaves under them. (bushes and small trees)
2. if I slow down, he slows (someone)
3. and rises and says when he sees me: nobody (a man)
4. She would fly far away into the sky (girl or my little girl)
5. And even less do I want them/ one day to make her a queen. (girl or my little girl)

◆ Literary Focus

1. (a) Students will probably cite lines 1–6 because *cold wind* evokes the sense of touch and *the blue mottled clouds* and *muddy fields brown with dry weeds* call upon sight and touch (dry). (b) The description in this passage seems to imply the danger that spring will never come to enliven the dead scene.
2. Possible imagery includes the daughter being turned into a swallow and flying off and the daughter's long hair being combed by her mother.
3. Possible answer is the imagery of rooted plants gripping down and beginning to "awaken" in "Spring and All."

◆ Build Vocabulary

Using the Suffix *-less*

1. a 2. b 3. c 4. c

Using the Word Bank

1. contagious; 2. clarity; 3. lifeless; 4. profound; 5. stark

Grammar Reinforcement

For additional instruction and practice, use the lesson in the **Language Lab CD-ROM** on Pronoun Usage and the pages on Pronoun and Antecedent Agreement (p. 83) in the *Writer's Solution Grammar Practice Book.*

Guide for Responding *(continued)*

◆ Reading Strategy

Form a Mental Image

If you **form a mental image** of the scene in "The street," you can better experience the speaker's fear. You'll "hear" the silence, "walk blind" through the "blackness," and feel the footsteps on the "stones and dry leaves."

1. As you read "The street," what mental image did you form of the "Someone" who pursues the speaker?
2. Describe three different ways you can picture the little girl in "Fear."
3. Briefly describe your mental image of "the road to the contagious hospital" in "Spring and All."

◆ Build Grammar Skills

Pronouns and Antecedents

In "Fear" the speaker refers several times to *them*, a pronoun without an antecedent. By leaving out the antecedent, the poet creates a sense of mystery about *them*. Similarly, in "Spring and All," the pronoun *It* in line 23 doesn't have a clear antecedent and mysteriously refers to all of nature's rebirth. In your own writing, however, you'll want every pronoun to refer clearly to an antecedent.

An **antecedent** is a noun or pronoun to which a pronoun refers.

Practice Copy these lines from the poems. Find the underlined pronoun's antecedent in the poem and then write it next to the line you've copied.

1. with dead, brown leaves under <u>them</u> ("Spring and All," line 12)
2. if I slow down, <u>he</u> slows ("The street," line 7)
3. and rises and says when <u>he</u> sees me: nobody. ("The street," line 13)
4. <u>She</u> would fly far away into the sky ("Fear," line 3)
5. And even less do I want them/one day to make <u>her</u> a queen. ("Fear," lines 17 and 18)

◆ Literary Focus

Imagery

These poets use **imagery**—language that describes sensory experiences—to enhance your appreciation of the dangers and difficulties they describe. In "Spring and All," for example, words that appeal to the sense of touch—"naked,/cold"; "grip down"—stress the difficulty of nature's rebirth in spring.

1. (a) Find a passage in "Spring and All" that describes experiences of both touch and sight.
(b) Explain how this passage helps you appreciate the danger or uncertainty of spring.
2. Explain how two sensory descriptions in "Fear" help you understand the speaker's anxiety about losing her daughter.
3. Which sensory description in these poems creates the most vivid image of a struggle? Explain.

◆ Build Vocabulary

Using the Anglo-Saxon Suffix *-less*

Knowing that the suffix *-less* means "without," choose the letter of the word that is the best antonym, or opposite, of the first word.

1. odorless: (a) fragrant, (b) scentless, (c) pale
2. restless: (a) excited, (b) relaxed, (c) upset
3. speechless: (a) wordless, (b) mute, (c) talkative
4. sleepless: (a) alert, (b) annoyed, (c) drowsy

Using the Word Bank: Analogies

On your paper, write the word from the Word Bank that will make the relationship between the second pair of words similar to the relationship between the first pair. Use each word only once.

1. Sickly is to ill as infectious is to ___?___.
2. Darkness is to gloom as clearness is to ___?___.
3. Alive is to lively as dead is to ___?___.
4. Shallow is to superficial as deep is to ___?___.
5. Costumed is to naked as adorned is to ___?___.

Reteach

Some students may need help recognizing, appreciating, and enjoying literary imagery in poems. Have them select one of the poems to analyze in depth for descriptive words that appeal to the senses. To help organize their ideas, have students use a five-column chart.

Smell	Taste	Touch	Sound	Sight

In "The Street," Paz describes the street vividly—"I walk in blackness and I stumble and fall and rise, and I walk blind, my feet stepping on silent stones and dry leaves." *Blackness* and *blind* would be charted in the "Sight" column, *dry leaves* might be charted under "Sound," "Smell," and/or "Sight." As students identify imagery in the poems, urge them to think about and appreciate the actual images created by the words. Continue helping them appreciate the imagery so that their enjoyment of the poetry's visual impact will increase.

Build Your Portfolio

Idea Bank

Writing

1. Letter to a Poet Respond to one of the poems by writing a letter to the poet. Tell how the poem made you feel and which images helped you share the experience the poet describes.

2. Poem Write your own poem about a struggle or challenge using imagery that will help your readers share the experience.

3. Short Story Based on a Poem Turn one of these poems into a short story. Expand on the situation in the poem by showing, for example, why the man in "The street" is running or how the speaker in "Fear" brings up her daughter.

Speaking, Listening, and Viewing

4. Oral Interpretation Practice reading one of these poems aloud. Experiment with using your tone of voice, reading speed, and word emphasis to express your interpretation. Then read the poem for the class. **[Performing Arts Link]**

5. Speech The speaker in "Spring and All" vividly describes the drama of early spring. Write a speech in which you emphasize the drama and uncertainty of another season. Then deliver your speech to the class. **[Performing Arts Link]**

Researching and Representing

6. Scientific Diagram The speaker in "Spring and All" describes the rebirth of plants in spring as a struggle. Create a scientific diagram showing what happens to a plant in late winter and early spring. **[Science Link; Art Link]**

7. Dance Create a two-person dance that communicates the action and mood of "The street." With a partner, practice and perform your dance for the class. **[Performing Arts Link]**

Online Activity www.phlit.phschool.com

Guided Writing Lesson

Anecdote About a Challenge

Draw on your own experience to tell an **anecdote**—an interesting or amusing story—about a challenge. The following tip will help you clarify the cause-and-effect relationships in your anecdote.

Writing Skills Focus: Cause-and-Effect Relationships

Whether you're writing an anecdote, a remembrance, or a problem-and-solution essay, you must show how one event or condition (the cause) brings about another (the effect). Even a poem like "The street" describes cause-and-effect relationships:

Cause: Dark street
Effect: Speaker stumbles
Cause: Speaker stumbles
Effect: Speaker falls

In planning, writing, and revising your anecdote, show the cause-and-effect relationships among events.

Prewriting To find a topic for an anecdote, think about a mistake you have made, like showing up at the wrong time for an appointment. Jot down some amusing consequences that resulted from the error.

Drafting You can create humor in your account by showing how silly causes lead to ridiculous effects at an ever-quickening pace.

Revising In reviewing your draft, clarify any cause-and-effect relationships that are unclear by using words like *as a result, consequently,* and *because.* Also, be sure that each pronoun you use has an easily identifiable antecedent.

For more on pronouns and antecedents, see Build Grammar Skills on pages 86 and 92.

Idea Bank

Following are suggestions for matching Idea Bank topics with your students' performance levels and learning modalities:

Customizing for *Performance Levels*
Less Advanced Students: 1, 4
Average Students: 2, 4, 5, 7
More Advanced Students: 3, 6

Customizing for *Learning Modalities*
Visual/Spatial: 6
Verbal/Linguistic: 4, 5, 7
Logical/Mathematical: 6
Bodily/Kinesthetic: 7

Guided Writing Lesson

Prewriting Strategy
Once they have decided on an anecdote to write about, ask students to draw a story map that describes it. Each part of the story should be illustrated in the order in which it occurred, and students should leave a blank space between illustrations. After they have finished drawing, ask students to write the appropriate cause-and-effect words, such as consequently, as a result, or because, in each space. These words should explain the nature of the relationship of each part of the story to the next. This will help students break down the anecdote and understand the role that each part played in the story as a whole.

For more prewriting, elaboration, and revision strategies, see *Prentice Hall Writing and Grammar.*

Writing Lab CD-ROM
Have students complete the tutorial on Narration. Follow these steps:

1. Encourage students to use a Storyline Diagram to help them develop their plots.
2. Have students draft on computer.
3. Have students use the Revision Checkers to help them revise.

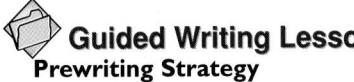

ASSESSMENT OPTIONS

Formal Assessment, Selection Test, pp. 16–18, and Assessment Resources Software. The selection test is designed so that it can be easily customized to the performance levels of your students. ***Alternative Assessment,*** p. 6, includes options for less advanced students, more advanced students, visual/spatial learners, verbal/linguistic learners, intrapersonal and bodily/kinesthetic learners.

PORTFOLIO ASSESSMENT
Use the following rubrics in the ***Alternative Assessment*** booklet to assess student writing:
Letter to a Poet: Expression Rubric, p. 94
Poem: Poetry Rubric, p. 108
Short Story Based on a Poem: Fiction Narrative Rubric, p. 95

Prepare and Engage

LESSON OBJECTIVES

1. **To develop vocabulary and word identification skills**
   - Latin Word Roots: *-tain-*
   - Using the Word Bank: Antonyms
   - Extending Word Study: Use Reference Materials
2. **To use a variety of reading strategies to comprehend a story and a myth**
   - Connect Your Experience
   - Reading Strategy: Significant Details
   - Tips to Guide Reading: Sustained Reading (ATE)
   - Read to Be Entertained (ATE)
   - Idea Bank: Friendship Collage
3. **To increase knowledge of other cultures and to connect common elements across cultures**
   - Connecting Themes Across Cultures (ATE)
4. **To express and support responses to the text**
   - Critical Thinking
   - Analyze Literary Criticism (ATE)
   - Idea Bank: Report of the Prussian Officer
   - Idea Bank: Brochure for a Friendship Film Festival
5. **To analyze literary elements**
   - Literary Focus: Climax
6. **To read in order to research self-selected and assigned topics**
   - Research Skills Mini-Lesson: Research Criteria (ATE)
7. **To plan, prepare, organize, and present literary interpretations**
   - Speaking, Listening, and Viewing Mini-Lesson: Role Play
   - Idea Bank: Humorous Monologue
8. **To use recursive writing processes to write a definition**
   - Guided Writing Lesson
9. **To increase knowledge of the rules of grammar and usage**
   - Build Grammar Skills: Appositives

Test Preparation

Reading Comprehension: Context Clues and Analogies (ATE, p. 95) The teaching tips and sample test item in this workshop support the instruction and practice in the unit workshop:

Reading Comprehension: Using Context Clues to Determine Word Meanings (SE, p. 113)

Guide for Reading

Guy de Maupassant

(1850–1893)

The modern short stories of Guy de Maupassant (gē də mō pä sän′) are filled with fascinating details of nineteenth-century life. Forces such as a person's family, surroundings, physical makeup, and personality determine the outcome of events.

Born into an aristocratic family, Maupassant was apparently destined for success. As a young man, he was a talented writer and won the attention of famous authors. Soon he was famous in his own right.

Then, as he might have described it in one of his own stories, his weaknesses caught up with him. Troubled by health problems, he died in his early forties. Yet he left a "fortune" to every future reader: 300 short stories.

About Myths

"Damon and Pythias" is a myth—a fictional story about gods or heroes. Myths may be ancient imaginary stories, but they attempt to explain real phenomena. They answer the most basic questions about the world and the human heart: How did this mountain come to be? Why is this flower purple? Who were the truest friends that ever lived? We read myths today because they offer timeless answers to timeless questions.

William F. Russell ***(1945–   )***

William F. Russell has retold this and many other myths so that modern readers can appreciate their universal messages. He is also the author of a widely read newspaper column on education.

◆ Build Vocabulary

LATIN WORD ROOTS: *-tain-*

In "Damon and Pythias," Pythias is "detained far longer in his task than he had imagined." Knowing that Pythias has not returned and that the Latin root *-tain-* means "to hold," you can figure out that *detained* means "held back."

WORD BANK

As you read "Damon and Pythias" and "Two Friends," you will encounter these words. Each word is defined on the page where it first appears. Preview the list before you read.

ardent
vernal
jauntiness
dire
detained
impediments
hindrances
annals

◆ Build Grammar Skills

APPOSITIVES

Maupassant gives details about characters by using **appositives**—nouns or noun phrases that are placed near another noun or pronoun to explain it:

> . . . M. Morissot, *watchmaker by trade but local militiaman for the time being*, stopped short . . .

The italicized appositive quickly explains both Morissot's usual trade and his military duties during the war. If Maupassant had provided these details in a separate sentence, he would have slowed down the pace of his story. Instead, he includes the appositive, separating it by commas because it is not essential to the meaning.

Prentice Hall Literature Program Resources

REINFORCE / RETEACH / EXTEND

Selection Support Pages
Build Vocabulary: Word Roots: *-tain-*, p. 26
Build Grammar Skills: Appositives, p. 27
Reading Strategy: Significant Details, p. 28
Literary Focus: Climax, p. 29

Strategies for Diverse Student Needs, p. 7

Beyond Literature
Cross-Curricular Connection: Social Studies: *Rules of Warfare*, p. 7

Art Transparencies 11 and 12, pp. 47–53

Formal Assessment Selection Test, pp. 19–21; Assessment Resources Software

Alternative Assessment, p. 7

Writing and Language Transparencies
Writing Process Model 4: Extended Definition, pp. 25–28

Resource Pro CD-ROM

Listening to Literature Audiocassettes

Two Friends ◆ Damon and Pythias

◆ *Literature and Your Life*

Connect Your Experience

Mathematics says that if you share something with another person, you each have less than the total amount. Friendship proves this statement wrong. If you share a dream, a joke, or a story with a friend, it increases in value—and you both get to keep it.

"Damon and Pythias" and "Two Friends" show the value of friendship. They also show how life can test friendship.

Journal Writing Jot down some of the qualities that you look for in a friend. Then tell why each of these qualities is important to you.

Thematic Focus: Dangerous Destinies

In this ancient myth and modern short story, friends get into dangerous situations. As the tension mounts, you may wonder whether the friendship—and the friends—will survive.

◆ Background for Understanding

Culture

Stories about friends appear not only in books. The ancient Greeks placed such a high value on friendship that they saw it written in the sky. They imagined the legendary friends and brothers Castor and Pollux as stars and included them in the constellation we call Gemini ("the twins").

Look for these ancient friends in today's night sky, close to the Big Dipper.

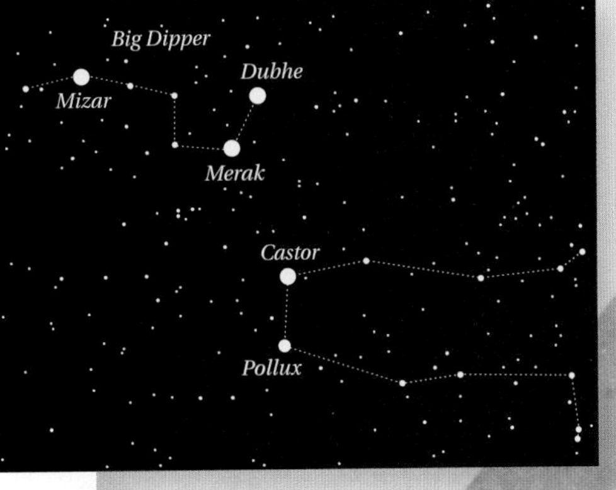

◆ Literary Focus

Climax

The **climax** of a story is the point at which the tension is greatest. It is also the point at which the outcome is about to be revealed. In some stories, the tension increases gradually, leading to a climax that you know is coming. In other stories, the climax arrives suddenly and unexpectedly.

"Damon and Pythias" and "Two Friends" show two different ways of building toward a climax. As you read each tale, decide whether the moment of greatest tension is expected or is unexpected.

◆ Reading Strategy

Significant Details

Significant details in a story often hint at how events may turn out. Sometimes these details describe character traits—human qualities that help to determine the outcome of events. Other times, these details are events in the world that surround the characters.

As you read "Damon and Pythias," jot down details about the characters themselves; then ask yourself how these details might influence what happens. For "Two Friends," notice significant details in the surroundings, even if they seem to be off in the distance. Then consider how things that were distant may suddenly become all too close.

Interest Grabber To capture students' interest, ask them to name and discuss a Hall of Fame with which they are familiar, such as a sports or rock-and-roll Hall of Fame. Elicit a list of the personal qualities of people elected to these Halls of Fame. Then have them imagine a Friendship Hall of Fame that honors the world's closest and noblest friendships. What special qualities would a Friendship Hall of Fame honor? Let students know that both of the stories in this selection pay tribute to unique friendships.

Connecting Themes Across Cultures

Friendship is a universal theme. Ask students to think about how friends and friendships have been challenged and tested all over the world.

Customize for
Less Proficient Readers

The early part of the narrative in "Two Friends" moves back and forth in time. Help students identify the flashbacks by calling their attention to such signal phrases as "some days" and "on a spring morning."

Customize for
Pre-AP Students

Challenge students to compare and contrast Russell's direct storytelling style with de Maupassant's indirectness. For example, they might contrast the ways in which Dionysius and the Prussian officer, both cruel characters, are described and revealed.

Customize for
Gifted/Talented Students

After students finish reading the stories, invite them to select one and write a different ending. Remind them to review the details from the story so that their rewritten conclusion makes sense and is probable.

Customize for
English Language Learners

To help these students with challenging vocabulary, particularly in Maupassant's descriptions of nature, pair them with native speakers. The partners can work together to use context clues to determine the meanings of such words as *ruddy, gilded,* and *draught.*

Test Preparation Workshop

Reading Comprehension: Analogies When taking the SAT test, students will be asked to make analogy choices. To give them practice using the context of the words being compared in an analogy, use this sample item.

Read the related pair of words followed by the choices. Select the pair from the choices that best expresses a similar relationship.

RUDDY : CHEEKS

A azure : sky
B cinnamon : nutmeg
C crimson : lake
D snow : winter

In order to understand the relationship, students must determine the meaning of *ruddy* from the context clues in the analogy: *ruddy* is a color that a person's cheeks may be. Then they can analyze the choices to see which is most similar in relationship. Students should determine that choice *A* has the closest meaning because it describes a color that the sky may be. Point out to students that when answering analogy questions on the SAT test, they will not have access to the context clues of a sentence or paragraph, but must use the context of the analogous relationship.

Develop Understanding

One-Minute Insight

In this story, Morissot (mô' rē sō) and Sauvage (sō' vazh) try to conduct their friendship in a business-as-usual manner against the backdrop of the Franco-Prussian War. War perplexes and disgusts these two characters, and they wish only to recapture the simple pleasures they shared before war changed their lives. When they are captured by the enemy, they must choose between honor and survival. Students will probably recall times in which their own friendships have been challenged by self-interest.

Tips to Guide Reading

Sustained Reading To introduce a session of sustained reading, the teacher may wish to present the selection "Two Friends" by reading and discussing the introduction found on p. 96. After the discussion, suggest that students read without stopping to see what happens in the short story.

◆ Critical Thinking

❶ **Infer** What inferences can you make about the narrator's attitude toward the Franco-Prussian War based on this opening description? The narrator seems more concerned with the suffering that it caused—evidenced particularly by his mention of the sparrows—than with the issues it was fought to determine.

◆ Build Grammar Skills

❷ **Appositives** Have students identify the appositive in this sentence. The appositive is a riverside acquaintance. What noun does this appositive explain? It is in apposition to M. Sauvage.

◆ Build Grammar Skills

❸ **Appositives** Point out that this sentence is unusual in that it contains three appositives. Have students identify the noun that *M. Sauvage,* the first of these appositives, explains. The appositives all explain man. Then have them identify the remaining two appositives that provide information about M. Sauvage. The remaining appositives are a haberdasher and another ardent fisherman.

Two Friends

Guy de Maupassant

Translated by Gordon R. Silber

The following story is set during the Franco-Prussian War. Beginning on July 19, 1870, the war had resulted from the Prussian prime minister Otto von Bismarck's belief that a war with France would strengthen the bond between the German states, along with French emperor Napoleon III's feeling that a successful conflict with Prussia would help him to gain support among the French people. As it turned out, the French army was no match for the German forces. After a series of victories, one of which ended in the capture of Napoleon III, the German army established a blockade around Paris on September 19, 1870. Led by a provisional government, Paris managed to hold out until January 28, 1871, though the city's inhabitants were plagued by famine and a sense of hopelessness. As Maupassant's story begins, the city is on the verge of surrender.

❶ Paris was blockaded, starved, in its death agony. Sparrows were becoming scarcer and scarcer on the rooftops and the sewers were being depopulated. One ate whatever one could get.

As he was strolling sadly along the outer boulevard one bright January morning, his hands in his trousers pockets and his stomach empty, M.[1] Morissot, watchmaker by trade but local militiaman for the time being, stopped short before a fellow militiaman whom he recognized as a friend. It was M. Sauvage, a riverside acquaintance. ❷

Every Sunday, before the war, Morissot left at dawn, a bamboo pole in his hand, a tin box on his back. He would take the Argenteuil railroad, get off at Colombes, and walk to Marante Island. As soon as he arrived at this ideal spot he would start to fish; he fished until nightfall.

Every Sunday he would meet a stout, jovial little man, M. Sauvage, a haberdasher[2] in Rue Notre-Dame-de-Lorette, another ardent fisherman. ❸ Often they spent half a day side by side, line in hand and feet dangling above the current. Inevitably they had struck up a friendship.

Some days they did not speak. Sometimes they did; but they understood one another admirably without saying anything because they had similar tastes and responded to their surroundings in exactly the same way.

On a spring morning, toward ten o'clock, when the young sun was drawing up from the tranquil stream wisps of haze which floated off in the direction of the current and was pouring down its vernal warmth on the backs of the two fanatical anglers,[3] Morissot would sometimes say to

◆ Build Vocabulary

ardent (ärd´ ənt) *adj.*: Intensely enthusiastic or devoted

vernal (vurn´ əl) *adj.*: Springlike

1. **M.:** Abbreviation for *Monsieur* (mə syö´), or "Mister" or "Sir" (French).
2. **haberdasher** (hab´ ər dash´ ər) *n.*: Person who is in the business of selling men's clothing.
3. **anglers** (an´ glərz) *n.*: People who fish.

Block Scheduling Strategies

Consider these suggestions to take advantage of extended class time:

- Use the Interest Grabber note on this page to introduce the subject of friendship. Then have students complete the journal activity in Literature and Your Life on p. 95.
- Introduce the literary element, climax. To reinforce this concept, have students answer the Literary Focus questions on p. 106 after they read, and follow up with the Literary Focus page in ***Selection Support*** (p. 29).
- Ask students to work in pairs to complete the Critical Thinking questions on pp. 101 and 105.
- As preparation for creating a brochure for a friendship film festival (see p. 107), have pairs of students come up with a list of movies that have treated friendship in a special way. Next to each entry, they should jot down the message about friendship that the movie presented.
- Have students look for concrete examples in "Two Friends" and "Damon and Pythias," then complete the Guided Writing Lesson on p. 107.

The Anglers, Georges Seurat, Musée National d'Art Moderne, Troyes, France

his neighbor, "Nice, isn't it?" and M. Sauvage would answer, "There's nothing like it." And that was enough for them to understand and appreciate each other.

◆ *Literature and Your Life*

4 Does their friendship remind you of one of your own friendships?

On an autumn afternoon, when the sky, reddened by the setting sun, cast reflections of its scarlet clouds on the water, made the whole river crimson, lighted up the horizon, made the two friends look as ruddy as fire, and gilded the trees which were already brown and beginning to tremble with a wintery shiver, M. Sauvage would look at Morissot with a smile and say, "Fine sight!" And Morissot, awed, would answer, "It's better than the city, isn't it?" without taking his eyes from his float.

5 As soon as they recognized one another they shook hands energetically, touched at meeting under such changed circumstances. M. Sauvage, with a sigh, grumbled, "What goings-on!" Morissot groaned dismally, "And what weather! This is the first fine day of the year." 5

▲ **Critical Viewing** Compare this painting with the description in the story of an autumn afternoon. **[Compare and Contrast]** 6

The sky was, in fact, blue and brilliant.

They started to walk side by side, absent-minded and sad. Morissot went on, "And fishing! Ah! Nothing but a pleasant memory."

"When'll we get back to it?" asked M. Sauvage.

They went into a little café and had an absinthe,[4] then resumed their stroll along the sidewalks.

Morissot stopped suddenly, "How about another, eh?" M. Sauvage agreed, "If you want." And they entered another wine shop.

On leaving they felt giddy, muddled, as one does after drinking on an empty stomach. It was mild. A caressing breeze touched

4. **absinthe** (ab´ sinth) *n.*: Type of liqueur.

◆ *Literature and Your Life*

4 Sauvage and Morissot communicate with each other easily and naturally; as they enjoy the beautiful sunset, they are able to share their responses without having to say much. Students may describe similar experiences they have had while enjoying a sight in nature, a movie, or a sports event with a friend.

◆ Critical Thinking

5 **Infer** What does this exchange reveal about the two friends' attitude toward the war? *Students may point out that both regret the way it has disrupted normal life. They may also note that, while the war has affected both men, they do not seem to feel completely overwhelmed by it at this point in the story.*

▶Critical Viewing◀

6 **Compare and Contrast** *Students may describe the mood of the painting as peaceful, calm, or idyllic. The two men are sitting together companionably, as do Morissot and Sauvage in the story, exchanging few words.*

Read to Interpret

Reading to enjoy and interpret significant details is a valid purpose to set for reading. "Two Friends" and "Damon and Pythias" both explore the nature of friendship, and the author's use of details enhances this purpose for reading.

Customize for *Less Proficient Readers*

Make sure that these students have read the background information on page 96 and that they are aware that Morissot and Sauvage have been kept from their fishing expeditions by the war. Have them consider why the war might prevent them from engaging in leisure activities such as fishing. *They should recognize that if the two men were to go fishing, they would be in extreme danger because enemy forces surround the city.*

Humanities: Art

The Anglers, 1883, by Georges Seurat.

This oil painting captures the idyllic pleasures of a fishing trip.

French artist Georges Seurat (1859–1891) was a contemporary of Guy de Maupassant. Many of Seurat's works, including *The Anglers,* were heavily influenced by impressionism—a style of painting that used loose brush strokes and dabs of rich color to capture fleeting moments in nature and everyday life.

Use these questions for discussion:

1. In this painting, Seurat uses light and color to convey a special mood. What words might you use to describe the light in this painting and the mood it helps to convey? *Possible response: The light on the pond is soft and shimmering, presenting a contrast to the shadowy figures of the fishermen. The light conveys a mood of tranquillity.*
2. How does the picture that de Maupassant "paints" add to your understanding of the two friends? *Students may respond that it helps readers understand the love of nature and fishing that they share.*

◆ Critical Thinking

❶ **Infer** Have students discuss what leads the two men to decide to go fishing again. Is it a wise decision? *They have been discussing their pleasant memories of fishing. After several drinks, their desire to fish overcomes their concern about the circumstances. Students may suggest that it's not a wise decision, because of the blockade by the Prussian soldiers.*

Comprehension Check ☑

❷ Why would the two men need a pass to travel to the island? *The area is under the control of the French army, which is monitoring all comings and goings as a security measure.*

▶Critical Viewing◀

❸ **Draw Conclusions** S*ome students may say that the painting was selected because it evokes the normal, peaceful times that the friends are trying to recapture by going on their fishing trip. Others may say that the trees and land in the painting are reminiscent of the "bare cherry trees" and "colorless fields" that Morissot and Sauvage see; in this respect, the painting evokes the eerie stillness of the wartime landscape.*

◆ Reading Strategy

❹ **Significant Details** Elicit the following responses: *Apparently, the people who live in the area have fled; this suggests that an attack by the Prussians is a very real possibility.*

Customize for
Visual/Spatial Learners

Encourage these students to use the painting on this page to help them visualize the story's foreign setting—which may seem incredibly remote to them. Have them note the ways in which the countryside in the painting differs from the area in which they live. Then have them look for details in the painting that add to the details provided in the story. Encourage them to share their observations with classmates.

Les Maisons Cabassud à la Ville D'Avray, Camille Corot

their faces.

The warm air completed what the absinthe had begun. M. Sauvage stopped. "Suppose we went?"

"Went where?"

"Fishing, of course."

"But where?"

❶ "Why, on our island. The French outposts are near Colombes. I know Colonel Dumoulin; they'll let us pass without any trouble."

Morissot trembled with eagerness: "Done! I'm with you." And they went off to get their tackle.

❷ An hour later they were walking side by side on the highway. They reached the villa which the Colonel occupied. He smiled at their request and gave his consent to their whim. They started off again, armed with a pass.

Soon they passed the outposts, went through the abandoned village of Colombes, and reached the edge of the little vineyards which slope toward the Seine. It was about eleven.

Opposite, the village of Argenteuil seemed dead. The heights of Orgemont and Sannois dominated the whole countryside. The broad plain which stretches as far as Nanterre was empty, absolutely empty, with its bare cherry trees and its colorless fields.

Pointing up to the heights, M. Sauvage

▲ **Critical Viewing** This painting does not suggest the horror or hardships of war. What aspects of this story does it illustrate? **[Draw Conclusions]** ❸

◆ **Reading Strategy** What significant details suggest the possible danger of this setting? ❹

◆ **Build Vocabulary**

jauntiness (jônt′ ē nis) *n.:* Carefree attitude

Humanities: Art

Les Maisons Cabassud à la Ville d'Avray (The Cabassud Houses in the Town of Avray) by Camille Corot.

During his long, distinguished career, French artist Camille Corot (1796–1875) became known primarily as a landscape painter. Classically trained, Corot traveled throughout Europe, painting pastures, mountainsides, and villages. His early landscapes were rendered in a highly detailed and highly realistic style. Later, he adopted the softer, more romantic style represented by *Les Maisons Cabassud.*

Use these questions for discussion:

1. What elements in the painting convey a sense of harmony and peacefulness? *Students may point to the harmony between the color of the ground and the earthy colors of the buildings and to the small, unhurried human figures.*
2. Like Morissot and Sauvage, Corot—also a Parisian—was drawn to rural places. What do students think city-dwellers find most appealing about the country? *Responses may include the opportunity to observe nature; the slower pace of life.*

murmured, "The Prussians are up there!" And a feeling of uneasiness paralyzed the two friends as they faced this deserted region.

"The Prussians!" They had never seen any, but for months they had felt their presence—around Paris, ruining France, pillaging, massacring, starving the country, invisible and all-powerful. And a kind of superstitious terror was superimposed on the hatred which they felt for this unknown and victorious people.

Morissot stammered, "Say, suppose we met some of them?"

His Parisian jauntiness coming to the surface in spite of everything, M. Sauvage answered, "We'll offer them some fish."

But they hesitated to venture into the country, frightened by the silence all about them.

Finally M. Sauvage pulled himself together: "Come on! On our way! But let's go carefully." And they climbed over into a vineyard, bent double, crawling, taking advantage of the vines to conceal themselves, watching, listening.

A stretch of bare ground had to be crossed to reach the edge of the river. They began to run, and when they reached the bank they plunged down among the dry reeds.

Morissot glued his ear to the ground and listened for sounds of anyone walking in the vicinity. He heard nothing. They were indeed alone, all alone.

Reassured, they started to fish.

Opposite them Marante Island, deserted, hid them from the other bank. The little building which had housed a restaurant was shut up and looked as if it had been abandoned for years.

M. Sauvage caught the first gudgeon.[5] Morissot got the second, and from then on they pulled in their lines every minute or
5 two with a silvery little fish squirming on the end, a truly miraculous draught.

Skillfully they slipped the fish into a sack made of fine net which they had hung in the water at their feet. And happiness pervaded their whole being, the happiness which seizes upon you when you regain a 5
cherished pleasure of which you have long been deprived.

The good sun was pouring down its warmth on their backs. They heard nothing more; they no longer thought about anything at all; they forgot about the rest of the world—they were fishing!

But suddenly a dull sound which seemed to come from under ground made the earth tremble. The cannon were beginning.

Morissot turned and saw, over the bank to the left, the great silhouette of Mount Valérien wearing a white plume on 6
its brow, powdersmoke which it had just spit out.

And almost at once a second puff of smoke rolled from the summit, and a few seconds after the roar still another explosion was heard.

> **◆ Reading Strategy** Which details about the mountain may be significant, and why? 7

Then more followed, and time after time the mountain belched forth death-dealing breath, breathed out milky-white vapor which rose slowly in the calm sky and formed a cloud above the summit.

M. Sauvage shrugged his shoulders. "There they go again," he said.

As he sat anxiously watching his float bob up and down, Morissot was suddenly seized by the wrath which a peace-loving man will feel toward madmen who fight, and grumbled, "Folks sure are stupid to kill one another like that."

M. Sauvage answered, "They're worse than animals."

And Morissot, who had just pulled in a bleak, went on, "And to think that it will always be like this as long as there are governments."

M. Sauvage stopped him: "The Republic[6] wouldn't have declared war—"

5. **gudgeon** (guj´ ən) *n.*: Small European freshwater fish.

6. **The Republic:** The provisional republican government that assumed control when Napoleon III was captured by the Prussians.

◆ Critical Thinking

5 Analyze Encourage students to comment on this description of the pleasures of fishing. How does this passage help the reader understand de Maupassant's attitude toward war? *Elicit the following responses: Through this tender description, the author suggests that everyday life and its simple pleasures are precious. By vividly reminding us of these pleasures, the author makes the miseries of war seem even more painful.*

◆ Build Grammar Skills

6 Appositives Have students identify the appositive in this sentence along with the noun that it explains. *appositive: powdersmoke which it had just spit out; noun: plume*

◆ Reading Strategy

7 Significant Details Students may say that the cannon fire smoke coming from the mountain suggests that the war will intrude on the friends' peaceful day.

Customize for *Logical/Mathematical Learners*

Have these students choose one of the stories and design a flowchart or other graphic that displays significant details and their relationship to the climax.

Analyze Literary Criticism

As a noted French writer in the realm of world literature, Guy de Maupassant has written many widely enjoyed short stories. Arthur Symons says of his writing: "His appeal is genuine, and his skill, of its kind incontestable. He attracts as certain men do, by a warm and blunt plausibility. He is so frank, and seems so broad; and is so skillful, and seems so living. All the exterior heat of life is in his work; and this exterior heat gives a more immediate illusion of what we call real life..." Share this analysis of de Maupassant's work with students. Then have them use the following questions to discuss whether or not they agree with Symon's analysis:

1. After reading "Two Friends" do you agree that Guy de Maupassant's writing is genuinely appealing? *Students may answer the writer made them care about the characters.*
2. What details does de Maupassant use to reflect real life in his description of the two men? *Possible response: His fishing descriptions seem real.*
3. Would you recommend this story to a friend? Why or why not? *Some students might recommend the story because of its ending; others may say they wouldn't recommend it because they didn't like the author's style or characterizations.*

◆ Literary Focus

❶ **Climax** Do students think that this passage signals the beginning of the story's climax? Why or why not? *Possible responses: Yes—whereas earlier details hinted at danger, the danger becomes very concrete at this moment. Now that Sauvage and Morissot have been captured, the story's outcome is about to be revealed.*

◆ Literary Focus

❷ **Climax** Students should note that the officer informs the friends in a cold, matter-of-fact manner that they will die in five minutes if they do not reveal the password. The chilling quality of this news adds to the urgency and suddenness of the climax.

◆ Reading Strategy

❸ **Significant Details** Point out that the detail about the cannon fire has appeared twice before. Have students compare and contrast the effect that the detail has here with its effect earlier in the story. *Possible responses: Earlier, the "thunder" acted as a reminder of the war and of surrounding danger. Here it heightens the tension of the story's climax; it emphasizes that the war has caught up with Morissot and Sauvage.*

Comprehension Check ☑

❹ Why does the officer take each of the men aside? *He thinks that each is more likely to give up the password if his friend isn't present; in this way, he is trying to break down the friends' sense of honor and loyalty.*

Customize for *Pre-AP Students*

As students read "Two Friends" they may become interested in the territory that used to be called Prussia. Encourage students to prepare a list of relevant questions to find out more about this subject. For example, they may wish to locate a historic map of Prussia in an encyclopedia or other reference source to find out what still-famous city was the kingdom's capital. (Berlin was the capital.) They may choose to formulate questions to research the Franco-Prussian War or the formation of the country of Germany.

Morissot interrupted: "Under kings you have war abroad; under the Republic you have war at home."

And they started a leisurely discussion, unraveling great political problems with the sane reasonableness of easygoing, limited individuals, and found themselves in agreement on the point that men would never be free. And Mount Valérien thundered unceasingly, demolishing French homes with its cannon, crushing out lives, putting an end to the dreams which many had dreamt, the joys which many had been waiting for, the happiness which many had hoped for, planting in wives' hearts, in maidens' hearts, in mothers' hearts, over there, in other lands, sufferings which would never end.

"That's life for you," opined M. Sauvage.

"You'd better say 'That's death for you,'" laughed Morissot.

❶ But they shuddered in terror when they realized that someone had just come up behind them, and looking around they saw four men standing almost at their elbows, four tall men, armed and bearded, dressed like liveried[7] servants, with flat caps on their heads, pointing rifles at them.

The two fish lines dropped from their hands and floated off down stream.

In a few seconds they were seized, trussed up, carried off, thrown into a rowboat and taken over to the island.

And behind the building which they had thought deserted they saw a score of German soldiers.

A kind of hairy giant who was seated astride a chair smoking a porcelain pipe asked them in excellent French: "Well, gentlemen, have you had good fishing?"

Then a soldier put down at the officer's feet the sack full of fish which he had carefully brought along. The Prussian smiled: "Aha! I see that it didn't go badly. But we have to talk about another little matter. Listen to me and don't get excited.

"As far as I am concerned, you are two spies sent to keep an eye on me. I catch you and I shoot you. You were pretending to fish in order to conceal your business. You have fallen into my hands, so much the worse for you. War is like that.

"But—since you came out past the outposts you have, of course, the password to return. Tell me that password and I will pardon you."

The two friends, side by side, pale, kept silent. A slight nervous trembling shook their hands.

The officer went on: "No one will ever know. You will go back placidly. The secret will disappear with you. If you refuse, it is immediate death. Choose."

They stood motionless, mouths shut.

> ◆ **Literary Focus** How does the officer's calm manner add to the tension?

The Prussian quietly went on, stretching out his hand toward the stream: "Remember that within five minutes you will be at the bottom of that river. Within five minutes! You have relatives, of course?" ❷

Mount Valérien kept thundering. ❸

The two fishermen stood silent. The German gave orders in his own language. Then he moved his chair so as not to be near the prisoners and twelve men took their places, twenty paces distant, rifles grounded.

The officer went on: "I give you one minute, not two seconds more."

Then he rose suddenly, approached the two Frenchmen, took Morissot by the arm, dragged him aside, whispered to him, "Quick, the password? Your friend won't know. I'll pretend to relent." ❹

Morissot answered not a word.

The Prussian drew M. Sauvage aside and put the same question.

M. Sauvage did not answer.

They stood side by side again.

And the officer began to give commands. The soldiers raised their rifles.

Then Morissot's glance happened to fall on the sack full of gudgeons which was lying on the grass a few steps away.

---

7. **liveried** (liv′ ər ēd) *adj.*: Uniformed.

Speaking, Listening, and Viewing Mini-Lesson

Role Play

This mini-lesson supports the Speaking, Listening, and Viewing activity in the Idea Bank on p. 107.

Introduce Point out that in a role play students will step into the shoes of characters and carry on with dialogue and behavior—it is important that they be true to those characters.

Develop Before students begin their role-playing, have them explore and discuss the characters' states of mind at this crucial moment. Lead students to consider:

- Would the two men be completely certain of their choice, or would they feel some doubt?
- What reasons would they have for revealing the password? What reasons would they have for refusing?

Apply Have pairs of students develop and practice their role-play conversations and then perform them for the class.

Assess Evaluate the conversations based on the following criterion: Were the ideas expressed true to the characters?

A ray of sunshine made the little heap of still squirming fish gleam. And he almost weakened. In spite of his efforts his eyes filled with tears.

He stammered, "Farewell, Monsieur
5 Sauvage."

M. Sauvage answered, "Farewell, Monsieur Morissot."

They shook hands, trembling from head to foot with a shudder which they could not control.

The officer shouted, "Fire!"

The twelve shots rang out together.

M. Sauvage fell straight forward, like a log. Morissot, who was taller, tottered, half turned, and fell crosswise on top of his comrade, face up, as the blood spurted from his torn shirt.

The German gave more orders.

His men scattered, then returned with rope and stones which they tied to the dead men's feet. Then they carried them to the bank.

Mount Valérien continued to roar, its summit hidden now in a mountainous cloud of smoke.

Two soldiers took Morissot by the head and the feet, two others seized M. Sauvage. They swung the bodies for a moment then let go. They described an arc and plunged into the river feet first, for the weights made them seem to be standing upright.

There was a splash, the water trembled, then grew calm, while tiny wavelets spread to both shores.

A little blood remained on the surface.

The officer, still calm, said in a low voice: "Now the fish will have their turn."

And he went back to the house.

And all at once he caught sight of the
sack of gudgeons in the grass. He picked it 6
up, looked at it, smiled, shouted, "Wilhelm!" 7

A soldier in a white apron ran out. And the Prussian threw him the catch of the two and said: "Fry these little animals right away while they are still alive. They will be delicious."

Then he lighted his pipe again.

Guide for Responding

◆ Literature and Your Life

Reader's Response Were you shocked by the outcome of the story? Why or why not?

Thematic Focus In this story, is it friendship itself that leads the two men into danger and finally to death? Explain.

Farewell Note As Morissot or Sauvage, write a brief farewell note to your family before you are executed.

☑ Check Your Comprehension

1. How does the wartime situation in Paris affect the Sunday habits of Morissot and Sauvage?
2. How do they succeed for a while in defying the war?
3. What surprise do they encounter?
4. How does a final choice they have to make lead to the end of the story?

◆ Critical Thinking

INTERPRET

1. What causes the two friends to try fishing again? **[Infer]**
2. (a) Find two details of the men's journey to the island that might give readers an uneasy feeling. (b) Explain your choices. **[Infer]**
3. What message does Maupassant convey by showing how war breaks in on the peacefulness of fishing? **[Synthesize]**

EVALUATE

4. Is it effective to end the story with the Prussian officer's order to cook the fish? Explain. In answering, consider what this detail does or does not add to the central idea of the story. **[Assess]**

APPLY

5. What does this story suggest about the effects of modern warfare on everyday life? **[Generalize]**

◆ Critical Thinking

1. Giddiness from the wine and the warm weather tempts them to try fishing again.
2. (a) Students might cite the emptiness of the landscape and the abandoned restaurant building. (b) Both these details suggest people had left the area because it is dangerous.
3. A possible answer is that simple, daily pleasures cannot be taken for granted; war destroys citizens' right to relax.
4. One acceptable answer is that the incident reinforces the shocking nature of events, and also emphasizes the activity of fishing at the heart of the story.
5. The story shows that even the simplest human activities become prohibited in times of war.

◆ Critical Thinking

5 Analyze Ask students how they would characterize the two men's behavior in their final moments. *Possible response: Even in the face of death, the men remained true to their friendship; neither betrays the other.*

◆ Critical Thinking

6 Identify Character Traits What traits do the Prussian officer's words and actions reveal? Is his behavior here consistent with his behavior earlier in the story? *Responses may include: The officer is clearly unaffected by the deaths he himself ordered and thus shows himself to be callous and cold-blooded. His behavior is consistent with the cold-blooded way in which he treated Morissot and Sauvage when they were captured.*

7 Enrichment Help students to see the irony of this sequence of events. The two friends, who were going to eat their fish, will presumably now be eaten by fish. Meanwhile the Prussian officer, who has had the two friends executed (as they trembled and squirmed like fish), has now given orders to have the fish fried while they are still alive. Students can note the parallels between the fate of the two men and the fate of the fish.

Reinforce and Extend

Answers

◆ Literature and Your Life

Reader's Response Some students might say they did not expect the two friends to die for the honor of their country after discussing the folly of war.

Thematic Focus It is not the friendship itself, but the sense of honor of each man.

☑ Check Your Comprehension

1. They have to forgo fishing because of the war.
2. They decide to go fishing at their old spot despite the war.
3. They encounter cannon fire and soldiers with rifles upon them.
4. Their decision to keep the password to themselves leads to their execution.

Develop Understanding

One-Minute Insight In the myth "Damon and Pythias," two friends prove that they are willing to lay down their lives for each other. Students may be challenged to apply the standards of loyalty brought out in these stories to their own friendships.

◆ Reading Strategy

❶ **Significant Details** The author stresses the friends' unwavering trust and their belief in each other's honesty.

◆ Build Grammar Skills

❷ **Appositives** Have students identify the appositive in this sentence as well as the noun that it explains. *The word Dionysius is in apposition to the noun tyrant.*

◆ Critical Thinking

❸ **Infer** What inferences can students make about Pythias based on this passage? *Possible responses: He is loyal to his family as well as his friends; he places the needs of others above his own.*

▶Critical Viewing◀

❹ **Infer** *Inferences may include the following: Damon, the figure whose hands are tied, is loyal, brave, and noble; these traits are revealed by his willingness to die for his friend. Pythias, the figure who is stepping forward, is equally loyal, brave, and noble; these traits are revealed by his willingness to be put to death in order to save Damon.*

Extending Word Study

Use Reference Materials Students will find when they use a glossary or text-note definition of a word that it describes a precise meaning and usage for the context of that specific text and does not give all the possible meanings of the word. For example, ask students to look up each word in the Build Vocabulary box on p. 104 in the dictionary. Have them note the dictionary meanings of the words that are not specific to this selection and thus not given in the text definition.

Damon and Pythias

Retold by William F. Russell, Ed.D.

Damon and Pythias were two noble young men who lived on the island of Sicily in a city called Syracuse. They were such close companions and were so devoted to each other that all the people of the city admired them as the highest examples of true friendship. Each trusted the other so completely that nobody could ever have persuaded one that the other had been unfaithful or dishonest, even if that had been the case.

> ◆ Reading Strategy
> ❶ What details of the friendship are stressed?

Now it happened that Syracuse was, at that time, ruled by a famous tyrant named Dionysius, who had gained the throne for himself through treachery, and who from then on flaunted his power by behaving cruelly to his own subjects and to all strangers and enemies who were so unfortunate as to fall into his clutches. ❷ This tyrant, Dionysius, was so unjustly cruel that once, when he awoke from a restless sleep during which he dreamt that a certain man in the town had attempted to kill him, he immediately had that man put to death.

It happened that Pythias had, quite unjustly, been accused by Dionysius of trying to overthrow him, and for this supposed crime of treason Pythias was sentenced by the king to die. ❸ Try as he might, Pythias could not prove his innocence to the king's satisfaction, and so, all hope now lost, the noble youth asked only for a few days' freedom so that he could settle his business affairs and see to it that his relatives would be cared for after he was executed. Dionysius, the hardhearted tyrant, however, would not believe Pythias's promise to return and would not allow him to leave unless he left behind him a hostage, someone who would be put to death in his place if he should fail to return within the stated time.

Pythias immediately thought of his friend Damon, and he unhesitatingly sent for him in this hour of dire necessity, never thinking for a moment that his trusty

◆ Build Vocabulary

dire (dīr) *adj.*: Calling for quick action; urgent

▶ Critical Viewing What does this picture reveal about the characters of Damon and Pythias? **[Infer]** ❹

Research Skills Mini-Lesson

Research Criteria

This mini-lesson supports the Epitaph writing activity in the Idea Bank on p. 107.

Introduce Discuss with students that an epitaph is the words engraved on a tombstone or plaque in a cemetery or mortuary. Often the words in an epitaph tell something unique about the person, the dates they lived, and give a complete name.

Develop To write an appropriate epitaph for Damon and Pythias, students need to generate relevant questions for research. Questions such as these will elicit the information they may require:

- When did the person(s) live and die?
- What did the person(s) do that was noteworthy?
- What is the person's complete name?

Apply Suggest that students use library resource materials or the Internet to find answers to their questions and then write the epitaph. They may wish to use poster board, special lettering, and appropriate decoration to illustrate the epitaph.

Assess Have students display their epitaphs in class and as a group evaluate how well they asked and answered relevant research questions.

Damon and Pythias

Customize for
Visual/Spatial Learners

Because this engraving directly illustrates a scene from the myth, it provides an excellent opportunity for visual/spatial learners to utilize their ability to absorb visual details to enhance their understanding of the story. Have them carefully study the details of the engraving and consider how the depiction of the events and the characters compares to the way in which they envision them as they read the selection. Encourage them to share their observations with classmates.

Customize for
Bodily/Kinesthetic Learners

Ask these students to describe the body language of Damon, Pythias, and Dionysius in this picture and how—in each case—that body language communicates what a character is feeling. *Possible answers: Damon is leaning toward his friend and his eyes express his relief, although not surprise, that Pythias has returned; Pythias' sense of urgency is conveyed through his outstretched hand, as well as his flowing hair and robe, which indicate his speed; Dionysius appears shocked.*

Humanities: Art

Damon and Pythias (engraving), artist unknown.

An engraving is a picture printed from an image that has been cut into a metal plate. This engraving illustrates the climactic moment in which Pythias appears to save Damon, to the surprise of the tyrant Dionysius and the cheers of the crowd.

Use these questions for discussion:

1. Call students' attention to the artist's use of diagonals. Have them identify various diagonal elements in the composition. *Elements include the executioner's arm and sword; the upper half of Damon's body; the outstretched arms of Pythias, Dionysius, and the spectator in the lower left corner; the line that extends from the executioner's shoulder to Pythias' robe.*
2. What effect do all these diagonals create? In what way is this effect appropriate for the climax of the story? *Students may say that the lines convey movement and action; the climax is the point at which the action is most intense.*

◆ Critical Thinking

1 Infer What does Damon's reply to the king reveal? What does it suggest about the outcome of the story? *He is sincere in the commitment he made to his friend. At this point it seems inevitable that one of the two friends will be put to death.*

◆ Build Vocabulary

2 Word Roots: *-tain-* Ask students to explain the relationship between the meaning of the word *detained* and the meaning of the word root *-tain-*. *Detained means "kept in custody." The meaning of the word root -tain- is "hold." To keep someone is custody is to hold him or her in custody.*

◆ Literary Focus

3 Climax Possible responses: The details add to the suspense because although the reader might trust Pythias' loyalty to his friend, it begins to look like he will not be able to fulfill his promise and Damon will be put to death—a very disappointing climax to the story.

companion would refuse his request. Nor did he, for Damon hastened straightaway to the palace—much to the amazement of King Dionysius—and gladly offered to be held hostage for his friend, in spite of the dangerous condition that had been attached to this favor. Therefore, Pythias was permitted to settle his earthly affairs before departing to the Land of the Shades,[1] while Damon remained behind in the dungeon, the captive of the tyrant Dionysius.

After Pythias had been released. Dionysius asked Damon if he did not feel afraid, for Pythias might very well take advantage of the opportunity he had been given and simply not return at all, and then he, Damon, would be executed in his place. But Damon replied at once with a willing smile: "There is no need for me to feel afraid, O King, since I have perfect faith in the word of my true friend, and I know that **1** he will certainly return before the appointed time—unless, of course, he dies or is held captive by some evil force. Even so, even should the noble Pythias be captured and held against his will, it would be an honor for me to die in his place."

Such devotion and perfect faith as this was unheard of to the friendless tyrant; still, though he could not help admiring the true nobility of his captive, he nevertheless determined that Damon should certainly be put to death should Pythias not return by the appointed time.

And, as the Fates would have it, by a strange turn of events, Pythias was **2** detained far longer in his task than he had imagined. Though he never for a single minute intended to evade the sentence of death to which he had been so unjustly committed, Pythias met with several accidents and unavoidable delays. Now his time was running out and he had yet to overcome the many impediments that had been placed in his path. At last he succeeded in clearing away all the hindrances, and he sped back the many miles to the palace of the king, his heart almost bursting with grief and fear that he might arrive too late.

> **◆ Literary Focus**
> How do these details add to the tension of the climax? **3**

Meanwhile, when the last day of the allotted time arrived, Dionysius commanded that the place of execution should be readied at once, since he was still ruthlessly determined that if one of his victims escaped him, the other should not. And so, entering the chamber in which Damon was confined, he began to utter words of sarcastic pity for the "foolish faith," as he termed it, that the young man of Syracuse had in his friend.

In reply, however, Damon merely smiled, since, in spite of the fact that the eleventh hour had already arrived, he still believed that his lifelong companion would not fail him. Even when, a short time later, he was actually led out to the site of his execution, his serenity remained the same.

Great excitement stirred the crowd that had gathered to witness the execution, for all the people had heard of the bargain that had been struck between the two friends.

1. **Land of the Shades:** Mythical place where people go when they die.

◆ Build Vocabulary

detained (dē tānd′) *v.*: Kept in custody

impediments (im ped′ ə mәntz) *n.*: Something standing in the way of something else

hindrances (hin′ drәns әz) *n.*: People or things in the way; obstacles

annals (an′ әlz) *n.*: Historical records or chronicles; history

Beyond the Selection

FURTHER READING

Other Works by the Featured Authors

"The Necklace," Guy de Maupassant
"The Piece of String," Guy de Maupassant
Classic Myths to Read Aloud, William F. Russell

Other Works With the Theme of Tests of Friendship

"A Child's Heart," Herman Hesse
A Separate Peace, John Knowles

We suggest that you preview these works before recommending them to students.

INTERNET

You and your students may find additional information about Guy de Maupassant on the Internet. We suggest the following site. Please be aware, however, that the site may have changed from the time we published this information.

To access stories by Guy de Maupassant in English, go to **http://lib.univ-fcomte.fr/PEOPLE/selva/Maupassant.html**

We *strongly recommend* that you preview the site before you send students to it.

There was much sobbing and cries of sympathy were heard all around as the captive was brought out, though he himself somehow retained complete composure even at this moment of darkest danger.

Presently the excitement grew more intense still as a swift runner could be seen approaching the palace courtyard at an astonishing speed, and wild shrieks of relief and joy went up as Pythias, breathless and exhausted, rushed headlong through the crowd and flung himself into the arms of his beloved friend, sobbing with relief that he had, by the grace of the gods, arrived in time to save Damon's life.

4 This final exhibition of devoted love and faithfulness was more than even the stony heart of Dionysius, the tyrant, could resist. As the throng of spectators melted into tears at the companions' embrace, the king approached the pair and declared that Pythias was hereby pardoned and his death sentence canceled. In addition, he begged the pair to allow him to become their friend, to try to be as much a friend to them both as they had shown each other to be.

> ◆ *Literature and Your Life*
> When have you observed that friendship can be contagious?

5 Thus did the two friends of Syracuse, by the faithful love they bore to each other, conquer the hard heart of a tyrant king, and in the annals of true friendship there are no more honored names than those of Damon and Pythias—for no person can do more than be willing to lay down his life for the sake of his friend.

Guide for Responding

◆ Literature and Your Life

Reader's Response At what point in the story were you most nervous about the return of Pythias? Explain.

Thematic Focus You may not have risked your life for a friend, as Damon does in this tale. However, you've probably helped friends who were in danger of failing a test, not making a team, or doing the wrong thing in a social situation. Choose one such incident and tell how you came through for your friend.

☑ Check Your Comprehension

1. As the story begins, what reputations do Damon, Pythias, and Dionysius have in Syracuse?
2. What are the events leading up to the execution scene at the end?
3. How does the outcome of the story affect the king?

◆ Critical Thinking

INTERPRET

1. Give two examples of how Damon and Pythias are "noble" in ways other than their birth. **[Infer]**
2. Compare and contrast Dionysius's behavior at the beginning and end of the story. **[Compare and Contrast]**
3. Why isn't Damon afraid as he waits for Pythias? **[Infer]**
4. What universal message does this myth teach? **[Interpret]**

EVALUATE

5. Remembering what you know about tyrants—both ancient and modern—decide whether the king's change of heart is realistic. **[Evaluate]**

APPLY

6. Could a friendship like the one between Damon and Pythias exist in our own times? Why or why not? **[Relate]**

◆ Critical Thinking

4 Relate Ask students if they think that modern readers share the admiration that the tyrant and the crowd show for Damon and Pythias. If so, what does this demonstrate about the meaning of friendship? *Students may say that people today can appreciate the two friends as much as the ancient Greeks did—showing that trust and loyalty are still the essentials of true friendship.*

◆ Literature and Your Life

5 Some students might say that observing the warmth and closeness of a particular relationship has inspired them to want to join that friendship or give and get more out of a growing friendship of their own.

Reinforce and Extend

Answers

◆ Literature and Your Life

Reader's Response Students will probably cite the point at which "he had yet to overcome the many impediments that had been placed in his path."

Thematic Focus Example incidents should show how students gave advice or provided the practical help that made a difference in their friend's life

☑ Check Your Comprehension

1. Damon and Pythias had the reputation of being noble and loyal, while Dionysius was considered treacherous and power hungry.
2. Pythias needs Damon's help while he goes to settle his affairs before he is executed. Damon stays in his cell to guarantee his return.
3. Dionysius is so touched by the unselfishness of the two friends that he spares Pythias' life.

◆ Critical Thinking

1. Possible examples: Pythias' willingness to die although he had been wrongly accused; Damon's readiness to die in his friend's place; Pythias' return to his own execution.
2. Dionysius' behavior at the beginning of the story is cold-blooded and cruel, while at the end he acts justly because he has been warmed by the friendship of Pythias and Damon.
3. Damon isn't afraid while he waits for Pythias, because he has faith that his friend will return.
4. One acceptable response is that you should always stand by your friends.
5. Students may answer that it is not realistic; tyrants usually do not have sudden changes of heart.
6. Students might say that the dramatic events that tested Pythias and Damon's friendship are not likely to occur in daily life today, but that in times of war there might be similar circumstances.

Answers

◆ Reading Strategy

1. The powdersmoke indicates cannon fire nearby.
2. They both detest war and fighting and have expressed moral values.
3. Damon is probably happy to have his loyalty to Pythias tested.

◆ Literary Focus

1. The climax occurs when the friends are shot after refusing to betray each other; the conflict and suspense are resolved.
2. Hints include needing a pass to enter the war zone; the abandoned landscape and buildings on the way to the river; smoke from cannon fire. A reader might overlook these hints because they are woven into the story.
3. The climax comes when Pythias returns just in time and the king spares the friends' lives.
4. Some students might find surprising climaxes exciting; others will find expected climaxes satisfying.

◆ Build Vocabulary

Using the Root *-tain-*

1. *contain*—to be able to hold
2. *retain*—to hold in one's possession
3. *maintain*—to carry on

Using the Word Bank

1. b 2. c 3. c 4. b 5. a 6. c 7. a

◆ Build Grammar Skills

Practice

1. Damon and Pythias
2. a shy man
3. a man of honor

Writing Application

1. This tyrant, Dionysius, was so unjustly cruel that he had many men put to death.
2. However, Dionysius, a hardhearted tyrant, would not believe Pythias' promise.
3. Morissot, a watchman by trade but a local militiaman for the time being, stopped short before a fellow militiaman.

Grammar Reinforcement

For additional instruction and practice, use the lesson in the **Language Lab CD-ROM** on Commas—and the pages on appositives and appositive phrases in the *Writer's Solution Grammar Practice Book* (p. 40).

Guide for Responding *(continued)*

◆ Reading Strategy

SIGNIFICANT DETAILS

Paying close attention to the **significant details** in these stories helps you guess the fate of characters. Among the most important details in the two selections are the descriptions of the friendship of Damon and Pythias in the myth and background details of the war in "Two Friends." Because Damon and Pythias are so "devoted," their friendship is more likely to survive a test. In "Two Friends," however, the strange "silence all about" Morissot and Sauvage near the river suggests that they may not survive their little outing.

1. In "Two Friends," what is significant about the "powdersmoke" that Morissot and Sauvage see on the mountain?
2. What details about the two men in "Two Friends" might lead you to believe that they will not betray each other?
3. How is Damon's gladness about being a "hostage" a significant detail?

◆ Literary Focus

CLIMAX

"Damon and Pythias" builds up to its **climax**—the moment of greatest tension—like an imaginary drumroll that gets louder and louder. Detail after detail, from the imprisoning of Damon to the delay of Pythias, add to this drumroll as the expected climax approaches.

In "Two Friends," however, the climax comes unexpectedly. The drumming of cannon seems part of the background, a noise in a faraway war that does not concern the friends. Suddenly, the distant war comes close, in the form of a Prussian officer with the power of life and death.

1. What is the climax in "Two Friends"? Give reasons for your answer.
2. In "Two Friends," Maupassant hints at the climax even though it arrives with a shocking suddenness. Find three of these hints; then tell why a reader might overlook them.
3. Identify the climax in "Damon and Pythias" and explain your choice.
4. Which type of climax do you prefer—expected or unexpected? Why?

◆ Build Vocabulary

USING THE LATIN ROOT *-tain-*

Knowing that the Latin root *-tain-* means "to hold," write definitions for the following words:

1. contain **2.** retain **3.** maintain

USING THE WORD BANK: Antonyms

On your paper, write the letter of the word that is the antonym—opposite in meaning—of the first word:

1. dire: (a) urgent, (b) unimportant, (c) alive
2. detained: (a) restrained, (b) studied, (c) released
3. impediments: (a) footwear, (b) obstacles, (c) supports
4. hindrances: (a) fronts, (b) aids, (c) lances
5. ardent: (a) indifferent, (b) confident, (c) intent
6. vernal: (a) mild, (b) angry, (c) wintry
7. jauntiness: (a) seriousness, (b) lightheartedness, (c) reluctance

◆ Build Grammar Skills

APPOSITIVES

By including information in appositives, the authors of "Damon and Pythias" and "Two Friends" avoid putting each new fact in a separate sentence.

Appositives are nouns or noun phrases placed near another noun or pronoun to explain it.

Practice Identify the appositives in the following sentences.

1. The faithful friends Damon and Pythias won over the tyrant.
2. Morissot, a shy man, grew bolder as he drank absinthe.
3. The Prussian officer, a man of honor, insisted on executing the friends.

Writing Application Combine each pair of sentences by using appositives.

1. This tyrant was so unjustly cruel that he had many men put to death. This tyrant was named Dionysius.
2. Dionysius, however, would not believe Pythias' promise. Dionysius was a hardhearted tyrant.
3. Morissot stopped short before a fellow militiaman. Morissot was a watchmaker by trade but local militiaman for the time being.

Reteach

By drawing a "picture" of the action in the story, students may be better able to understand the rising action and the climax. Have them draw a large triangle on a piece of paper.

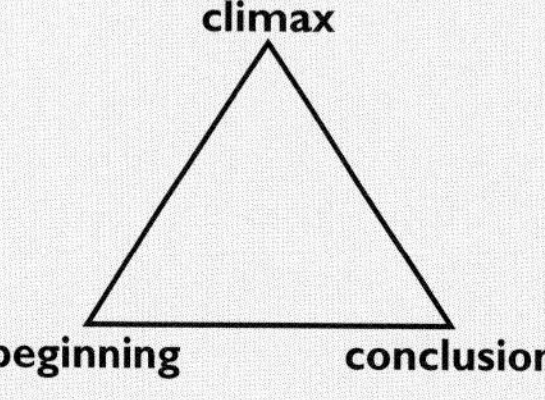

Have students choose one of the stories they read and skim to review its events. Below the triangle they have drawn, have them list the main characters. At the triangle's bottom left point, they should list the story's beginning events. Along the left side of the triangle, have them list the details of the rising action—the events leading to the climax. At the top point of the triangle, have them describe the climax, or turning point. Down the right side of the triangle, they can list events that lead to the conclusion.

Build Your Portfolio

Idea Bank

Writing

1. Epitaph for Damon and Pythias Write a few words to be carved into a stone that will stand above the graves of Damon and Pythias. **[Art Link]**

2. Yearbook Profiles Write yearbook profiles for yourself and a good friend. Include information about your accomplishments and preferences.

3. Report of the Prussian Officer As the Prussian officer in "Two Friends," write a report for your superior on the execution of Morissot and Sauvage. Include such details as where you discovered them, what they were doing, and why you had them shot. **[Social Studies Link]**

Speaking, Listening, and Viewing

4. Role Play With a partner, role-play a conversation between the two friends in Maupassant's story, discussing whether or not you should give away the password. **[Performing Arts Link]**

5. Humorous Monologue Write and deliver a funny speech about a friend. Purposely exaggerate your friend's ordinary experiences, pretending that they're dangerous adventures. **[Performing Arts Link]**

Researching and Representing

6. Friendship Collage Create a collage of pictures from magazines, ticket stubs, photographs, and other items that "illustrate" an adventure you've had with a friend. **[Art Link]**

7. Brochure for a Friendship Film Festival Choose three movies about friendship to be included in a brochure for a "Friendship Film Festival." Create a brochure describing why each film is included in the festival. **[Media Link]**

Online Activity www.phlit.phschool.com

Guided Writing Lesson

Extended Definition of Friendship

Use your own ideas and feelings as well as events in "Damon and Pythias" and "Two Friends" to write an extended definition of friendship. Unlike a dry dictionary definition, your extended definition will illustrate your ideas with concrete examples of friends and their behavior from your own experience, literature, the movies, and television.

Writing Skills Focus: Concrete Examples

Use **concrete examples** to support your ideas when writing an extended definition, a problem-and-solution essay, or an editorial. Such examples even help to make a short story more vivid. Maupassant, for example, begins "Two Friends" with a general statement and then brings it to life with two concrete examples:

Model From the Story

Paris was blockaded, starved, in its death agony. *Sparrows were becoming scarcer and scarcer on the rooftops* and *the sewers were being depopulated.*

Jot down concrete examples of friendship as you plan your extended definition, and refer to them as you draft and revise it.

Prewriting Start with a two-column chart. In the left column, write general ideas about friendship. In the right column, describe a concrete example that supports each idea.

Drafting Use the left column of your chart to write a general definition of friendship. Then choose the best examples from the right column to make that definition more vivid.

Revising Illustrate each general point you make about friendship with a concrete example. Where necessary, describe the actions that show what friends do for each other and how they express their devotion.

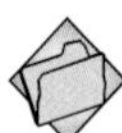

Idea Bank

Following are suggestions for matching Idea Bank topics with your students' performance levels and learning modalities:

Customizing for *Performance Levels*

Less Advanced Students: 1, 6
Average Students: 2, 4, 5, 7
More Advanced Students: 3

Customizing for *Learning Modalities*

Visual/Spatial: 1, 6
Verbal/Linguistic: 4, 5, 7

Guided Writing Lesson

Elaboration Strategy Distribute 4 or 5 notecards to each student. On their first cards, students should write their general definitions of friendship. On their other cards, they should write specific elements of their general definitions. Then students should re-enter their writing and find concrete examples they used to illustrate this part of their definitions and write them on the back of their cards. Students should fill out cards for each part of their definitions: general ideas on the front, concrete examples on the back.

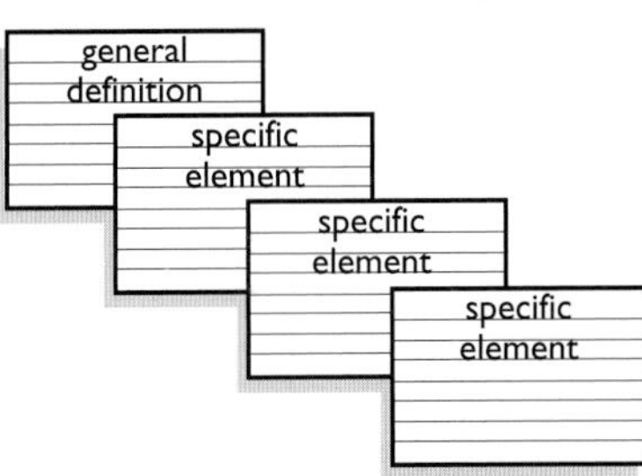

Students will know which parts of their definitions need elaboration by examining which of their notecards lack concrete details and examples.

For more prewriting, elaboration, and revision strategies, see *Prentice Hall Writing and Grammar.*

Writing Lab CD-ROM

Have students complete the tutorial on Expositon. Follow these steps:

1. Have them look at the audio-annotated model organized by order of importance.
2. Ask them to complete a note card activity to help them organize their ideas.
3. Have students draft on computer.
4. Encourage students to use the Self-Evaluation Checklist to help them revise.

✓ ASSESSMENT OPTIONS

Formal Assessment, Selection Test, pp. 19–21, and Assessment Resources Software. The selection test is designed so that it can be easily customized to the performance levels of your students.

Alternative Assessment, p. 7, includes options for less advanced students, more advanced students, verbal/linguistic learners, logical/mathematical learners, visual/spatial learners, and musical/rhythmic learners.

PORTFOLIO ASSESSMENT

Use the following rubrics in the ***Alternative Assessment*** booklet to assess student writing:
Epitaph for Damon and Pythias: Expression Rubric, p. 94
Yearbook Profiles: Narrative Based on Personal Experience Rubric, p. 96
Report of the Prussian Officer: Summary Rubric, p. 98

Prepare and Engage

LESSON OBJECTIVES

1. To use recursive writing processes to write a problem-and-solution essay
2. To recognize and avoid sentence fragments
3. To use subordinate clauses appropriately

You may want to distribute the scoring rubric for Problem-Solution (p. 102 in ***Alternative Assessment***) to make students aware before they begin of the criteria on which they will be evaluated. See the suggestions on page 110 for how you can customize the rubric for this workshop.

Writers at Work Videodisc
To introduce students to the key elements and show them how Rudolfo Anaya uses them in his expository writing, play the videodisc segment on Exposition (Ch. 2). Have students discuss what Anaya says about the way he gets his ideas across.

Play frames 22803 to 32243

Writing Lab CD-ROM
You may want to have students use the tutorial on Exposition to complete all or part of their problem-and-solution essays. Follow these steps:

1. Have students review the interactive model of a problem-and-solution essay.
2. Suggest that students complete the self-interview activity to find out what problems or issues are important to them.
3. Have students draft on computer.
4. Suggest students use a revision checker for unity and coherence.
5. Have students use the revision checker for homophones.

Problem-and-Solution Essay Writing Process Workshop

Air pollution . . . information overload . . . can't concentrate on schoolwork . . . Everywhere you turn, there are problems! What can you do about it? One thing you can do is write a **problem-and-solution essay.** In a problem-and-solution essay, you identify a problem, then lay out a plan for solving that problem. In the course of the essay, you explain the strategy for solving the problem, as well as the steps required to solve it. For this type of essay to work, it's important that a solution to the problem exists.

The following skills, introduced in this section's Guided Writing Lessons, will help you write an effective problem-and-solution essay.

Writing Skills Focus

- As you explain your solution, **show the benefits of your proposal.** Few will be willing to accept your proposed solution to the problem if they do not know the benefits of it. (See p. 85.)
- Every problem has both a cause and an effect. Make sure you clearly **show cause-and-effect relationships**—how one event or condition brings about another. (See p. 93.)

James Thurber puts these skills to humorous use as he explains how his family tried to deal with a troublesome dog.

MODEL FROM LITERATURE

from "The Dog That Bit People" by James Thurber

. . . Muggs used to spend practically all of his time outdoors. . . . ① It was hard to get him to come in and as a result the garbage man, the iceman, and the laundry man wouldn't come near the house. ② We had to haul the garbage down to the corner, take the laundry out and bring it back, and meet the iceman a block from home. After this had gone on for some time ③ we hit on an ingenious arrangement for getting the dog in the house . . . Thunder frightened him out of his senses . . . So we fixed up a thunder machine [to scare him inside.] ④

① Here, the writer reveals his particular problem: The biting dog won't come inside.
② Further details emphasize the importance of the problem.
③ The writer signals that a solution to the problem is coming.
④ The solution to the problem is given here: a thunder machine.

Beyond the Classroom

Career Connection

Solving Problems as a Career Students should have little difficulty thinking of problems to write about in their essays. Remind them that no matter what career they eventually choose, they will be confronted with problems either directly and indirectly and be required to offer plausible solutions to them.

Suggest to politically inclined students that they think of problems that are frequently in the news, such as poverty and welfare. Scientifically minded students may be inclined to tackle problems such as pollution or ozone depletion. Suggest to mathematically inclined students that they look at the business section of a newspaper to find articles about business or financial problems for which they might suggest solutions.

Discuss with students that large-scale problems may actually be a series or group of smaller problems to be solved—you may wish to offer the example of pollution and its breakdown of problems in the areas of air, water, and so forth.

Prewriting

Choose an Interesting Topic Choose a problem that interests you and about which you have an opinion. If you're having trouble thinking of one, use a problems-and-solutions chart like the one below to help you.

Problems	Solutions
overdevelopment	zoning restrictions
pollution	recycling
elderly	retirement communities
loneliness	friends
obesity	exercise and a good diet

Focus Decide whether your problem is too broad to explain a solution in the time and space you are given. If your problem has too many parts or aspects to it, decide on just one part to examine. For example, instead of discussing all the problems associated with illiteracy, discuss illiteracy in your community and how your school could do its part in setting up tutoring programs.

Drafting

Show the Benefits of Your Proposed Solution As you draft your proposed solution, show your readers why your suggestions are the most logical or beneficial. Explain how the steps you recommend will lead to a solution of the problem, and emphasize the positive effects of solving the problem.

Show Cause-and-Effect Relationships People are more likely to follow your advice if you show how their actions will bring about these positive effects. Make the cause-and-effect relationships clear in your proposed solution.

> People often ask me how to lose weight. I used to give them detailed explanations about calories and the body's ability to use fuel. Now I give a simple answer—to lose weight, eat less and exercise more.

Here the writer has clearly identified the causes (eating less, exercising more) and the effect (losing weight).

APPLYING LANGUAGE SKILLS: Sentence Fragments

A sentence fragment lacks a subject or a verb or simply does not express a complete thought. Always try to express your ideas in complete sentences, which contain a subject and a verb and express a complete thought.

Sentence Fragment:

While almost everyone likes to eat sweets.

Complete Sentence:

While almost everyone likes to eat sweets, you need to eat healthy foods to stay slim.

Practice On your paper, rewrite the following fragments as complete sentences.

1. Because our rivers are polluted.
2. Exercising on a daily basis.

Writing Application Check your problem-and-solution essay to make sure that all of your sentences are complete.

Writer's Solution Connection
Language Lab

For more practice on fixing sentence fragments, complete the Language Lab lesson on Run-on Sentences and Fragments.

Develop Student Writing

Prewriting Strategy

Once students select a problem about which to write, suggest that they use cubing to consider all aspects before they begin to write.

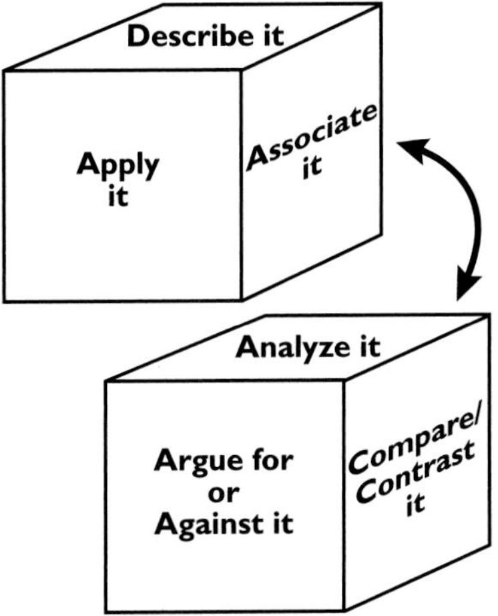

Customize for
Englsih Language Learners

Encourage students to think about a problem with which they are familiar in their native country. They will feel more confident writing about something they know better than other students. Help them with vocabulary for the topic they choose.

Customize for
Pre-AP Students

Challenge students to write about an issue that they will have to research, such as a major political, scientific, or social issue.

Writing Lab CD-ROM

Have students review the Tips on Gathering Details and Conducting Library Research screens in the Gathering Details section of the Writing Lab tutorial on Exposition.

Elaboration Strategy

Encourage students to draft their problem-and-solution essay in a single sitting, without pausing to labor over single words or grammatical errors. Once students have completed a draft, they can go back into their work and make extensive revisions.

Applying Language Skills

Sentence Fragments Remind students that while they may speak in fragments, they are unacceptable for a piece of formal writing.

Answers

Possible Responses:

1. Because our rivers are polluted, we must not swim or fish in them.
2. Exercising on a daily basis not only builds muscles and strengthens your heart; it also significantly reduces stress.

Grammar Reinforcement

For additional instruction and practice, have students complete the **Language Lab CD-ROM** lesson on Fragments and Run-on Sentences and the practice p. 59 in the *Writer's Solution Grammar Practice Book*.

Revision Strategy

Before students reenter their writing, it may help for them to reading their essays aloud in order to hear stiff language, overused words, choppy sentences, disjointed paragraphs, or other errors. This approach works well for partners. The peer editor can read a draft aloud as the writer listens for spots where revisions are needed; roles can be reversed.

Prentice Hall Writing and Grammar For more prewriting, elaboration, and revision strategies, see *Prentice Hall Writing and Grammar.*

Publishing

In addition to publishing on-line, some students may want to present their essays orally. Arrange for a time and place for students to give oral presentations of their essays. Have them post a notice on a bulletin board inviting people to attend the reading.

Reinforce and Extend

Applying Language Skills

Answers

1. Grapefruits help you lose weight <u>because they speed up your metabolism and also contain lots of water.</u>
2. <u>Although it may at first be difficult to maintain,</u> a healthy diet has many benefits.

Grammar Reinforcement

For additional instruction and practice, have students complete the **Language Lab CD-ROM** lesson on Varying Sentence Structure and the practice p. 121 in the *Writer's Solution Grammar Practice Book.*

Applying Language Skills: Subordination

Use subordination to vary your sentences. Subordinating conjunctions such as *because, since, while,* and *though* link a subordinate clause (a clause of less importance) to a main clause.

Example: subordinate clause

<u>Because we have an addiction to junk food,</u> many of us find it difficult to lose weight.

Practice On your paper, underline the subordinate clauses in the following sentences.

1. Grapefruits help you to lose weight because they speed up your metabolism and also contain lots of water.
2. Although it may at first be difficult to maintain, a healthy diet has many benefits.

Writing Application Review your essay. Look for places where subordinate clauses would make your sentence structure more interesting.

Writer's Solution Connection Writing Lab

For more tips on how to be a peer reviewer, look at the tips for peer reviewers in the Writing Lab tutorial on Exposition.

Revising

Use a Checklist Make sure that the following are true for your paper.

- Your opening sentences lead logically into your topic.
- You identify a problem and suggest a solution.
- You clearly show the relationships between causes and effects. Your instructions show how the reader's actions can bring about a desired effect.
- Your essay grabs and keeps the reader's interest.

Use a Peer Reviewer A classmate can often point out weaknesses that you may have missed. Ask one of your classmates to read your paper and comment on it.

If you are the peer reviewer, make sure that you offer your criticism in a positive way. This will ensure that your comments are put to good use instead of causing resentment.

Negative Comment	Positive Comment
This is totally unorganized!	Reorganize your points so that the reader can follow them more easily.

Revision Model

① Because

^We don't think about how our actions affect the future^. ^Many of us don't do our part to conserve natural resources.

② If gasoline use and air pollution will be reduced

^People ~~should~~ drive in carpools^.

① The writer combines two sentences by making one a subordinate clause. The subordinating conjunction *because* clarifies the cause-and-effect relationship.

② The writer adds details that show the benefits of his suggestion.

Publishing

Publish Your Paper On-Line No matter what your topic is, there's bound to be a site related to it on the World Wide Web. Consult with an experienced Internet user to post your paper on the appropriate Web site.

ASSESSMENT

PORTFOLIO ASSESSMENT

Use the rubric on Description in ***Problem-Solution*** (p. 97) to assess students' writing. Add these criteria to customize the rubric to this assignment.

	4	3	2	1
Sentence Fragments	There are no sentence fragments or run-on sentences.	There are one or two sentence fragments or run-on sentences.	There are noticeable sentence fragments or run-on sentences.	There are so many sentence fragments or run-on sentences that understanding of the piece is impaired.
Subordination	The essay contains a perfect mix of sentence structures including subordinate clauses.	The essay contains different sentence structures and subordination.	The essay could clearly use more subordination and/or sentence variety.	Subordination and sentence variety are nonexistent; grammar is atrocious and shows an utter lack of effort.

Student Success Workshop

Real-World Reading Skills — Evaluating Persuasive Texts

Strategies for Success

"Buy the sneakers worn by pros!" "Elect the candidate who's working for *you!*" "Support a worthy cause: Give generously!" A persuasive message can be delivered in many ways, but its goal is the same: to persuade you to think or to do something. The following guidelines will help you identify persuasive messages and evaluate the techniques they use:

Identify Persuasive Techniques Look for persuasive techniques. Does the text state facts, or does it deceptively state things that only *sound* like facts? Does the text use logical reasoning or evidence to support ideas or opinions, or might its reasoning be faulty? The following techniques, common in persuasive writing, may be used to mislead you:

- ▶ Using enticing slogans or images to get the reader or viewer to buy a product
- ▶ Promising desirable outcomes
- ▶ Seeming to appeal to the reader's intellect or sense of reason, but in fact appealing to his or her emotions

Evaluate the Message and the Technique
Since persuasive texts often promise outcomes and appeal to your emotions, you must evaluate them on the basis of your needs and on what you believe to be the facts.

As you evaluate an advertisement, ask yourself:

- ▶ Does the message make valid statements or misleading claims?
- ▶ Is the message based on logic and facts or on statements of opinion?
- ▶ Is this message one that I am willing to be persuaded by?

Apply the Strategies

Evaluate the ad below:

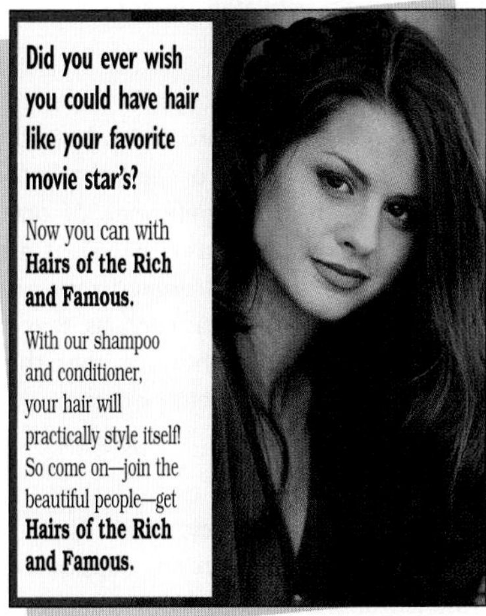

Did you ever wish you could have hair like your favorite movie star's?
Now you can with Hairs of the Rich and Famous.
With our shampoo and conditioner, your hair will practically style itself! So come on—join the beautiful people—get Hairs of the Rich and Famous.

1. What claim is made in this advertisement?
2. How does the ad attempt to influence you?
3. Does the ad support its claims? If so, how?
4. Would you buy this product after evaluating the ad? Explain.

It's important to evaluate persuasive texts like these:

- ▶ Advertisements for health or safety products (*e.g.,* smoke alarms, water purifiers, vitamins)
- ▶ Fund-raising letters (for charitable organizations or political campaigns)
- ▶ Advertisements promising a service (*e.g.,* cheapest telephone rates, Internet access, health care)

Prepare and Engage

LESSON OBJECTIVES

- To recognize logical, deceptive, and/or faulty modes of persuasion in texts

Apply the Strategies

Customize for
Interpersonal Learners
Have pairs or small groups of students examine advertisements in magazines that they enjoy reading and evaluate the persuasive techniques that the advertisements use. Students might focus on different ads for similar products to determine the varying messages and techniques employed. Encourage students to assess which ads they feel are most effective, and why.

Answers

1. The ad claims that the product will make anyone's hair look like a movie star's.
2. The ad attempts to influence the reader by suggesting that looking like a movie star is only a matter of one's hair care products, and uses an enticing image to persuade the reader.
3. The ad does not attempt to support its claims.
4. Possible answers: No, I would not buy this product, because its claims are not supported by facts.

Test Preparation Workshop

Evaluating Persuasive Texts
Evaluating the techniques and logic behind persuasive texts will help students with test items on standardized tests. Explain to students that once they identify the messages in a persuasive text, they can make generalizations about them. Have students return to the ad and then give them the following question.

Which statement best describes the message in the ad?
A Dreams will come true with this shampoo.
B Users will become movie stars.
C Your favorite movie star uses this shampoo.
D Users will look like movie stars if they use this shampoo.

Lead students to recognize that D is the best answer, because it most accurately describes the ad's message, which says nothing about dreams, makes no claims about movie stars using the product, and does not suggest that the product will make anyone a movie star. It does indicate, however, that users will look beautiful and/or rich and famous, implying that they can be like movie stars.

Prepare and Engage

LESSON OBJECTIVES

- To present a valid literary interpretation for an audience

Customize for
English Language Learners
Students who are uncomfortable with English may be shy about saying "no" for fear of offending the other person or feeling inadequate about their language use. Remind these students that their lack of English ability is not indicative of any deficiency.

Apply the Strategies

Answers

1. Possible responses include trying to persuade the other students to consider the consequences of their actions. If the students still persist, the lone student might explain to friends that he or she is not obligated to give a reason for refusing to go along, and that if they respect him or her as a person, they will respect his or her decision.
2. A good way to deal with phone solicitors is to politely say something to the effect of "I'm sorry, but I can't do that now," and repeat it as necessary.
3. If a student is shy about revealing a fact that can be embarrassing to teenagers—say, that he or she is frightened by scary movies—he or she can make a general comment such as "I'm not crazy about that kind of movie," which gets the point across without revealing any personal details.

Speaking, Listening, and Viewing Workshop

Presenting a Literary Interpretation

No one else has had all the same experiences as you. Because every reader has a unique perspective, readers often have different interpretations of the same literary work. Your interpretation might give your listeners a new way of understanding a text. The following strategies will help you present a literary interpretation:

Choose a Topic First, you'll need a topic. Avoid one that's too broad, such as the themes of Shakespeare's plays, or one that's too narrow, such as the significance of one line spoken by a minor character. Select an idea about the literary work which may not be obvious to every reader, such as that the tone of the poem is melancholy or that the novel's main character is modeled on the author or that the essay's humor is expressed through figurative language.

Use Supporting Evidence The main ideas of a valid interpretation are supported with evidence and examples from the text. For example, suppose that you have chosen to interpret Gerard Manley Hopkins's use of personification in "The Wreck of the *Deutschland,*" a poem about an 1875 shipwreck. Among other lines, you might focus on these:

Hope had grown gray hairs,
Hope had mourning on. . . .

You might point out that instead of simply stating that the situation was hopeless, the poet invites the reader to imagine the *feeling* of hopelessness—by personifying hope as an aging person, grieving. However, a valid interpretation could not argue that the poet has personified hope as an aging woman, because there is no evidence to support that idea in the text.

Organize Whether you read directly from a written essay or refer to notes or an outline, your interpretation should be presented in an organized, logical way. Practicing your presentation beforehand will help you feel confident.

Plan Consider where you'll present your literary interpretation, how much time you'll have, and who your audience will be. Will you have ten minutes to speak to a small group of classmates, sitting in a circle? You may also want to prepare beforehand for any questions from your audience.

Present To hold your audience's attention, show enthusiasm for your topic from the start. Make eye contact with your audience and speak clearly. Visual aids, such as transparencies or photocopies that you hand out, may also help to keep your listeners interested.

Apply the Strategies

Present a valid literary interpretation. The text you choose to interpret can be from this unit.

1. Choose a short story with a strong main character. Present an interpretation of what motivated the main character's actions.
2. Select a biographical text. Present your interpretation of how events in the person's life prepared him or her to achieve a major accomplishment.

Beyond the Classroom

Workplace Skills
Presenting an Idea Making a presentation is common in the work arena. Whether employees are making a formal presentation to a client, sharing an idea or suggestion at a staff meeting, or are meeting with a supervisor to discuss wages, a presentation should be focused, planned, and give solid evidence to support ideas.

Have students brainstorm for specific workplace situations that might involve giving a presentation. List their ideas on the board. Then have students determine what strategies they might use to give an effective presentation for each situation. Suggest that students work in pairs to select and role-play one of the situations, trading roles as presenter and listener.

Test Preparation Workshop

Reading Comprehension

Using Context Clues to Determine Word Meanings

Strategies for Success

The reading sections of standardized tests often require you to understand multiple-meaning words and specialized and technical terms. Use these strategies to answer test questions with the help of context clues:

Multiple-Meaning Words The context in which a multiple-meaning word appears can help you determine which definition applies. Find words that suggest the word's part of speech and connotation. Look at the following example:

> Shayla always assumed she would go to Springfield State with Amy, one of her best friends. But her application was denied. Then Shayla got a letter from a private college in a city 2,000 miles away. The letter informed her that she had been accepted for matriculation. Shayla knew she should jump at the opportunity—it was a noteworthy college in a beautiful location, but she would be far from home.

1 What is the best meaning for *private?*

A soldier in the army **C** secluded; isolated
B not publicly owned **D** dreary

Look at the context in which *private* appears. Answer **D** can be eliminated, since she said the location is beautiful. Because the passage has nothing to do with soldiers or the army, and *private* is used as an adjective and not a noun, **A** is wrong. **C** is also incorrect: If the college is in a city, it must not be secluded or isolated. Also consider Shayla's assumption that she would attend a state, or publicly owned, college with her friend. Answer **B** is the correct choice.

Specialized and Technical Terms Context clues can also help you determine the meaning of specialized or technical terms—terms used only in a particular context.

2 Use context to determine which of the following might be the meaning of matriculation:

A refusal **C** humiliation
B test **D** admission; registration

Answer **C** can be eliminated because the context words "opportunity" and "noteworthy" are positive, and Shayla seems honored. The context does not support **B** because the passage implies that Shayla is being offered an opportunity, not a test. Shayla considers attending the private college, so **A** can be eliminated. **D** must be correct.

Apply the Strategies

Read the following sample text, and answer the questions below.

> Before the Articles of Confederation could become law, each state had to ratify them. By 1779, only the state of Maryland had not voted in favor of the articles. During colonial times, seven states had received charters granting them control of western lands. Maryland, one of six states that had not received western territory from Great Britain, wanted all western lands turned over to the federal government.

1 Which word best defines *charters* as it is used in the passage?

A legal documents giving privileges
B letters from the government
C contracts to rent land
D documents creating institutions

2 In the passage, the word *ratify* means

A ignore **C** approve
B enjoy **D** reject

Correlations to Standardized Test

The reading comprehension skills reviewed in this Workshop correspond to the following standardized test section:
ACT Reading

Test Preparation

Each ATE workshop in Unit 1 supports the instruction here by providing teaching suggestions and a sample test item:
Use Context Clues to Determine Word Meanings (ATE, pp. 3, 23, 45, 61, 77, 87)
Analogies (ATE, p. 95)

LESSON OBJECTIVES

- To rely on context to determine meanings of words and phrases such as figurative language, idioms, multiple-meaning words, and technical vocabulary

Answers

1. (A) legal documents giving privileges
2. (C) approve

Test-Taking Tip

Try Out Answer Choices Explain to students that when they answer vocabulary questions on standardized tests, the items will be in a multiple-choice format. Many of these items will be one- or two-blank vocabulary questions. Other vocabulary questions may ask about the meaning of a word as it is used in a reading passage—students should be aware that this type of context question is not likely to use the most common meaning of the word.

When answering vocabulary-in-context or vocabulary questions, one strategy for determining the best answer is to substitute each answer choice for the tested word where it appears in the sentence. For example, when looking for the word closest in meaning to *ratify* in a text passage, substituting each answer choice for *ratify* in the passage would indicate that *ignore, enjoy,* and *reject* are incorrect, and that the correct answer is *approve.* Similarly, trying each word or pair of words in the blanks of sentences will often allow students to clearly see which answer is best in the context in which it is being used.

Planning Instruction and Assessment

Unit Objectives

1. To read selections in different genres that develop the theme of Unit 2, "Striving for Success"
2. To apply a variety of reading strategies, particularly interactive reading strategies, appropriate for reading these selections
3. To analyze literary elements
4. To use a variety of strategies to read unfamiliar words and to build vocabulary
5. To learn elements of grammar, usage, and style
6. To use recursive writing processes to write in a variety of forms
7. To express and support responses to various types of texts
8. To prepare, organize, and present literary interpretations

Meeting the Objectives With each selection, you will find instructional material and portfolio opportunities through which students can meet these objectives. Further, you will find additional practice pages for reading strategies, literary elements, vocabulary, and grammar in the ***Selection Support*** booklet in the ***Teaching Resources*** box.

Test Preparation

The unit workshop, **Reading Comprehension: Recognize Facts, Details, and Sequence** (SE, p. 215), is supported by teaching tips and a sample test item in the ATE workshop with each selection grouping.

- **Facts and Details** (ATE, pp. 117, 183)
- **Details** (ATE, pp. 155, 165, 201)
- **Facts, Details, and Sequence** (ATE, pp. 129)
- **Sequence** (ATE, pp. 147, 193)

The following additional workshops in the ATE give teaching tips for applying the skill taught in the Student Success Workshop:

- **Reading Comprehension: Using Text Organizers** (ATE, p. 180)
- **Reading Comprehension: Note Special Wording** (ATE, p. 215)

Steps to the Steps, Brad Holland

Humanities: Art

Steps to the Steps by Brad Holland.

In his early twenties, Brad Holland began writing and drawing for underground newspapers; he has since created covers for such mainstream publications as *The New Yorker, Newsweek,* and *U.S. News and World Report.* In 1981 Holland designed a U.S. postage stamp of Chief Crazy Horse and also produced a 10-by-30-foot mural for the United Nations Building in New York.

1. Imagine that the man on the steps already has climbed a long way. How do you think he feels about seeing the next set of steps? *Possible answers: He might feel discouraged that he is facing a much greater challenge; he might feel proud of having gotten so far; he might be thinking about how to climb these tall steps.*
2. Imagine that the steps you see represent stages on the way to success in a field such as science, athletics, or the performing arts. What would be at the very top of the steps? *Possible answers: For science, it might be the cure for cancer; for athletics, it might be a world championship or Olympic gold medal; for performing arts, it might be an Oscar or critical acclaim.*

Striving for Success

You will strive to reach many goals in life—getting your driver's license, graduating from high school, establishing a successful career, starting a family—and along the way you may have to overcome many obstacles. Let these poems, stories, and essays inspire you to strive for success and accomplish your goals. Share the determination and fear, the disappointment and hope of people from a wide variety of times and places.

Assessing Student Progress

Tools that are available to measure the degree to which students meet the unit objectives are listed here.

Informal Assessment

The questions on the Guide for Responding sections are a first level of response to the concepts and skills presented with the selection. Students' responses are a brief informal measure of their grasp of the material. Their responses on this level can indicate where further instruction and practice are needed. You may then follow up with the practice pages in the ***Selection Support*** booklet.

You will find literature and reading guides in the ***Alternative Assessment*** booklet, which you may give students on an individual basis for informal assessment of their performance.

Formal Assessment

In the ***Formal Assessment*** booklet, you will find selection tests and a unit test.

Selection Tests The selection tests measure comprehension and skills acquisition for each selection or group of selections.

Unit Test The unit test applies the unit skills on a broader level. The Critical Reading section measures Unit Objectives 1, 2, and 3. The Vocabulary and Grammar section measures Objectives 4 and 5. The Essay section measures Objectives 1 and 6.

Alternative Assessment

Portfolios As you review individual pieces or the collected work in students' portfolios, you will find assessment sheets available in the portfolio section of the ***Alternative Assessment*** booklet.

Scoring Rubrics You will find scoring rubrics for writing modes in the ***Alternative Assessment*** booklet. You can apply these to Guided Writing Lessons and to Writing Process Workshop lessons.

Speaking, Listening, and Viewing The ***Alternative Assessment*** booklet contains assessment sheets for speaking and listening activities.

Learning Modalities The ***Alternative Assessment*** booklet contains activities that appeal to different learning styles. You may use these too as an alternative measurement of students' growth.

Prepare and Engage

LESSON OBJECTIVES

1. **To develop vocabulary and word identification skills**
   - Latin Prefixes: *in-*
   - Using the Word Bank: Elaboration
   - Extending Word Study: Latin Prefix *in-*
2. **To use a variety of reading strategies to comprehend the author's purpose for writing an essay**
   - Connect Your Experience 7B
   - Reading for Success: Interactive Reading Strategies
   - Tips to Guide Reading: Recall (ATE)
   - Read to Appreciate Author's Craft (ATE)
3. **To increase knowledge of other cultures and to connect common elements across cultures**
   - Connecting Themes Across Cultures (ATE)
4. **To express and support responses to the text**
   - Critical Thinking
   - Idea Bank: Library Dedication
5. **To analyze literary elements**
   - Literary Focus: Author's Purpose
6. **To read to do research on a self-selected or an assigned topic**
   - Idea Bank: Informational Article
   - Idea Bank: Library Panel Discussion
   - Idea Bank: Directions
   - Idea Bank: Library Survey
7. **To plan, prepare, organize, and present literary interpretations**
   - Idea Bank: Library Panel Discussion
   - Idea Bank: Library Poster
   - Speaking, Listening, and Viewing Mini-Lesson: Storytelling Performance
8. **To use recursive writing processes to keep a journal**
   - Guided Writing Lesson
9. **To increase knowledge of the rules of grammar and usage**
   - Build Grammar Skills: Action Verbs and Linking Verbs

Test Preparation

Reading Comprehension: Recognize Facts and Details (ATE, p. 117) The teaching tips and sample test item in this workshop support the instruction and practice in the the unit workshop:

Reading Comprehension: Recognize Facts, Details, and Sequence (SE, p. 215)

Guide for Reading

Rudolfo Anaya *(1937–)*

The deep blue sky stretching as far as the eye can see to the horizon . . . the dry, red soil dotted with patches of brown grass and green cacti . . . the sweet smell of sagebrush wafting in the air. . . . This is New Mexico, the land that Rudolfo Anaya has called home his entire life, the land that has nurtured his imagination and given birth to his stories.

The Wisdom of the *Cuentos*

Anaya was born in the rural village of Pastura in 1937. His poems, short stories, novels, and articles reflect his Mexican American heritage. As a child, Anaya listened to the *cuentos* of his people—stories that had been passed down from generation to generation. Listening to these *cuentos* set Anaya's imagination on fire, and he knew he wanted to be a writer. Anaya feels a strong connection with the past in his personal life and in his work as a writer. He says, "The oral tradition of telling stories was part of my culture."

> *The old legends and the myths of the people, the whispers of the blood draw us to our past.*

Bless Me, Ultima In 1972, while he was a high-school English teacher, Anaya wrote *Bless Me, Ultima,* a coming-of-age novel set in New Mexico. The book received immediate praise and has sold over 300,000 copies. Anaya later became a professor of writing and literature at the University of New Mexico. In 1993, he retired so he could write full time. He says, "Writing novels seems to be the medium which allows me to bring together all the questions I ask about life."

◆ Build Vocabulary

LATIN PREFIXES: *in-*

When Rudolfo Anaya was a child, ancient tales *induced* him to become a writer. His love for these stories was *inherent.* You will encounter the words *induced* and *inherent* in this essay. The Latin prefix *in-* can mean "not" or "into." In both these words, the prefix *in-* means "into." *Induced* means "led into" or "caused." The prefix *in-* also contributes to the definition of *inherent,* which means "inborn."

WORD BANK

Before you read, preview this list of words from the essay.

induced
inherent
litany
dilapidated
satiated
enthralls
labyrinth
poignant
fomentation

◆ Build Grammar Skills

ACTION VERBS AND LINKING VERBS

The two main categories of verbs are **action verbs** (verbs that express physical or mental action) and **linking verbs** (verbs that express a state of being and tell what the subject is by linking it to one or more words that further describe or identify it).

In "One Million Volumes," Anaya describes a memory of his grandfather with an action verb:

> Then he would *whisper* his favorite riddle.

The action verb *whisper* expresses a physical action and creates a vivid sensory image.

Linking verbs connect the subject with other words that describe or identify it:

> I *was* fortunate.

The adjective *fortunate* describes the subject, *I,* and is linked to it by the linking verb *was.*

Prentice Hall Literature Program Resources

REINFORCE / RETEACH / EXTEND

Selection Support Pages
Build Vocabulary: Prefixes, *in-*, p. 30
Build Grammar Skills: Action and Linking Verbs, p. 31
Reading for Success: Interactive Reading, pp. 32–33
Literary Focus: Author's Purpose, p. 34

Strategies for Diverse Student Needs, p. 8

Beyond Literature
Community Connection: The Library, p. 8

Formal Assessment Selection Test, pp. 26–28; Assessment Resources Software

Alternative Assessment, p. 8

Writing and Language Transparencies
Writing Process Model 8: Interpreting a Work of Literature, pp. 53–59

Resource Pro CD-ROM

Listening to Literature Audiocassettes

from *In Commemoration:* One Million Volumes

MODEL SELECTION

◆ Literature and Your Life

CONNECT YOUR EXPERIENCE

Do you remember when you were a child and you turned ten years old? Remember how it felt to be in "double digits"? At the time, it may have seemed like a significant milestone. Three years later, you were finally in "the teens." Throughout our lives, we remember specific dates, events, and numbers. They act as markers of progress, showing us how far we've come and giving us an opportunity to reflect what we've learned. In this essay Rudolfo Anaya celebrates his university's library for reaching the one-millionth book mark. He uses the milestone as an occasion to reflect on the importance of libraries, books, and words in general.

THEMATIC FOCUS: STRIVING FOR SUCCESS

In his essay, Anaya not only honors his university's library but explains how the words and ideas housed in libraries have helped him reach goals in his life. Ask yourself how his vision of a library compares with your own.

Journal Writing Anaya describes a library as "a warm place that reflects the needs and aspirations of the people." List ten titles (of real books or books you would like to see written) that would reflect your needs and aspirations.

◆ Literary Focus

AUTHOR'S PURPOSE

The **author's purpose** is his or her reason for writing. For example, Anaya's general purpose is to share ideas. Other general purposes include persuading readers or explaining how to do something. Determine Anaya's specific purpose by noticing the kinds of details he includes, the direct statements he makes, and his attitude toward his subject.

◆ Background for Understanding

MATH

When Anaya entered the University of New Mexico's library for the first time, he was astounded at the size of it compared with his neighborhood library. There are other libraries even larger, containing more books than any person could read in a lifetime. Use this graph to get a sense of the size of several well-known libraries. These vast collections house, as Anaya marvels, "Books on every imaginable subject, in every field, a history of the thought of the world . . . the collective memory of all mankind at my fingertips."

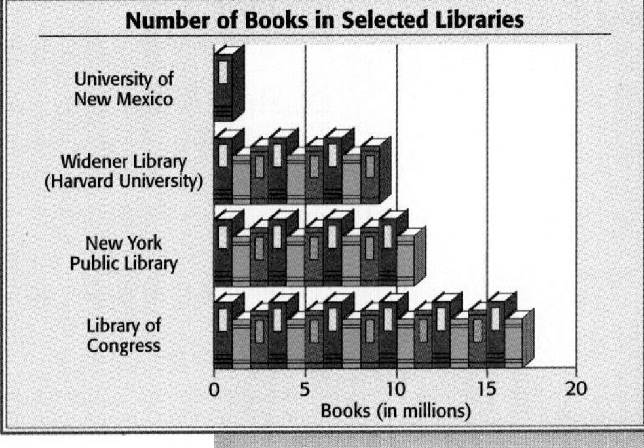

Test Preparation Workshop

Reading Comprehension: Recognize Facts and Details Standardized tests often require students to recognize facts, details, and sequence while reading. Use this sample test item to give students practice with details that are central to the purpose of a text.

In the summer evenings when I was a child, we, all the children of the neighborhood, sat outside under the stars and listened to the stories of the old ones, *los viejitos*. The stories of the old people taught us to wonder and imagine. Their *adivinanzas* [riddles] induced the stirring of our first questioning, our early learning.

What did the children learn from the old ones?

A How to tell stories
B The answers to riddles
C To wonder, imagine, and question
D The number of stars in the sky

Help students notice that the word *taught* in the passage is a clue to what was learned, so the answer is C.

Interest Grabber Ask students to take out a piece of paper and write down the first things that come to mind when you say "library." Guide them to think about *everything* associated with a library, not just books and computers. What do the rooms of the library look like; with whom do students usually go to the library; what do they do there? What mood does a library call up for them? After volunteers share their writing, encourage students to compare their impressions of libraries with those of Rudolfo Anaya as they read this selection.

Connecting Themes Across Cultures

Let students know that the Argentine writer, Jorge Luis Borges (1899–1986), also wrote a speech in honor of the library in his native city, Buenos Aires. In "Blindness," from the collection *Seven Nights*, Borges describes being appointed director of the National Library—just when he was losing his eye sight to an illness. Initiate a class discussion about the importance of libraries in all cultures.

Customize for *Less Proficient Readers*

Anaya does not directly state his purpose for writing—to celebrate the acquisition of the University of New Mexico Library's millionth book—at the outset of his essay. Make sure students understand the milestone that has inspired Anaya to write this essay. Ask them to look for references to this event as they read the essay.

Customize for *Pre-AP Students*

Have students analyze how Anaya achieves links between his topic, the million books in the library, and de-tails such as the million stars and the cuentos. Have students consider whether they think the author connects these elements successfully, and if so—why, if not—why not?

Customize for *Gifted/Talented Students*

Have students brainstorm for ways to design or construct a model representing one million, showing why it is used as a "magic" number.

Reading for Success

The Reading for Success page in each unit presents a set of problem-solving procedures to help readers understand authors' words and ideas on multiple levels. Good readers develop a bank of strategies from which they can draw as needed.

Unit 2 introduces strategies for interactive reading. Interactive strategies get students actively involved in their reading. The process of interacting with text while reading is an important factor in students' constructing of meaning from the text.

These strategies for interactive reading are modeled with "One Million Volumes." An example of the thinking process involved in applying one of these strategies is shown in each green box.

How to Use the Reading for Success Page

- Introduce the interactive reading strategies, presenting each as a means of enhancing the reading experience for maximum retention and enjoyment. Be sure students understand what each strategy involves and under what circumstances to apply it.
- Before students read the essay, have them preview it, looking at the annotations in the green boxes that model the strategies.
- To reinforce these strategies after students have read "One Million Volumes," have students do the Reading for Success pages in ***Selection Support,*** pp. 32–33. This activity gives students an opportunity to read a selection and practice interactive reading strategies by writing their own annotations.

Reading for Success

Interactive Reading Strategies

You wouldn't stand in front of a video game and just watch it like a movie, would you? Of course not! Video games are interactive—your choices affect the way the game turns out. Like a video game, reading is also interactive. It's a process by which you get involved with the ideas, images, events, and information presented in the text. The more involved you are, the richer your understanding is.

Apply the following strategies to interact with what you read:

Establish a purpose for reading.

Decide *why* you are reading a piece. You may read for enjoyment, for information, or to discover new ideas. For example, Anaya's essay can help you look at libraries in a new way. Set a purpose to discover a new perspective on libraries; then look for details that help you achieve this purpose.

Use your prior background knowledge.

Keep in mind what you already know—in this case, what you know about libraries. Use that knowledge to make connections with what the author is saying. You may find details in the text that confirm opinions you already have, as well as details that change your opinions.

Question.

Don't accept everything you read at face value. Ask yourself questions about why certain information is included or how a fact or idea fits in with what you've already read. Look for answers to your questions as you read on. Questioning will help you recognize the relationships between ideas and form your own opinion about the work.

Clarify details and information.

Clear up any parts of the work that you don't understand. The best way to do this is to read ahead for more information or read back to review what you've already learned. Another technique is to represent information visually. For instance, you can clarify Anaya's picture of the ideal library by making a cluster diagram to jot down key words that describe his feelings and opinions.

Summarize.

At appropriate places, review and state the main points of the author. Notice details that seem important. Try to fit them into your picture of what the author is saying.

As you read "One Million Volumes," look at the notes in the boxes. These notes demonstrate how to apply the above strategies to a work of literature.

Reading Strategies: Support and Reinforcement

Appropriate Reading Strategies Students are given a reading strategy to apply in reading each selection. In appropriate selections, students are given an interactive reading strategy. In other selections a strategy is suggested that is appropriate to the selection.

Reading Prompts To encourage application of the given reading strategy, there are occasional prompts, within green boxes, at appropriate and significant points.

In addition, there are red boxes prompting application of the Literary Focus concept and maroon boxes prompting students to connect with their lives.

Using the Boxed Annotations and Prompts

The material in the green, red, and maroon boxes along the sides of selections is intended to help students apply the literary element and the reading strategy and to make a connection with their lives.

You may use the boxed material in these ways:

- Have students pause when they come to a box and respond to its prompt before they continue reading.
- Urge students to read through the selection ignoring the boxes. After they have read the selection completely, they may go back and review the selection, responding to the prompts.

MODEL

from In Commemoration: ONE MILLION VOLUMES

Rudolfo A. Anaya

A million volumes.

A magic number.

A million books to read, to look at, to hold in one's hand, to learn, to dream. . . .

I have always known there were at least a million stars. In the summer evenings when I was a child, we, all the children of the neighborhood, sat outside under the stars and listened to the stories of the old ones, los viejitos.[1] The stories of the old people taught us to wonder and imagine. Their adivinanzas[2] induced the stirring of our first questioning, our early learning.

> **Clarify** the Spanish phrases by reading ahead and looking at the footnotes.

I remember my grandfather raising his hand and pointing to the swirl of the Milky Way which swept over us. Then he would whisper his favorite riddle:

Hay un hombre con tanto dinero
Que no lo puede contar
Una mujer con una sábana tan grande
Que no la puede doblar.

There is a man with so much money
He cannot count it
A woman with a bedspread so large
She cannot fold it

We knew the million stars were the coins of the Lord, and the heavens were the bedspread of his mother, and in our minds the sky was a million miles wide. A hundred million. Infinite. Stuff for the imagination. And what was more important, the teachings of the old ones made us see that we were bound to the infinity of that cosmic dance of life which swept around us. Their teachings created in us a thirst for knowledge. Can this library with its million volumes bestow that same inspiration? ❷

I was fortunate to have had those old and

1. **los viejitos** (lôs´ byā hē´ tôs)
2. **adivinanzas** (a thē vē nan´ sas) *n.*: Riddles.

◆ **Build Vocabulary**

induced (in do͞ost´) *v.*: Caused

Develop Understanding

One-Minute Insight When the University of New Mexico Library acquires its one millionth book, Rudolfo Anaya uses the occasion to reflect upon the great importance of libraries as places that stimulate and nurture free thought. What makes this essay especially unique is that Anaya draws a connection between books and the many people and stories that opened his childhood mind to the natural and intellectual world.

Tips to Guide Reading

Recall Encourage students to keep their purpose for reading clearly in mind as they read the selection. After they finish reading, have them individually, or as a group, list all the details they remember.

◆ Reading for Success

❶ **Question** Ask students what question they are asking themselves at this point in the essay. Suggest they keep their questions in mind until they are answered. *Students may say they are wondering how the author will connect the two ideas he has raised so far: books and the stories and riddles of los viejitos.*

◆ Reading for Success

❷ **Establish a Purpose for Reading** Have students set a preliminary purpose for reading. Let them know they may add to or revise this purpose later. *For now, students' purpose is to find out how the author will answer this question.*

Block Scheduling Strategies

Consider these suggestions to take advantage of extended class time:

- Have students complete the journal activity under Literature and Your Life on p. 117. As a class, make a list of the books chosen. Under each title, have a volunteer write the type of book—such as adventure story or how-to book—as well as its specific purpose—for example, to entertain. Then invite students to discuss how books help us meet our needs.
- With students, read Literary Focus: Author's Purpose on p. 117. Let them know that Anaya's general purpose was to share ideas with his audience—people assembled to celebrate the acquisition of a library's one millionth volume. Lead a discussion with students about how audience affects a writer's purpose. Have them suggest how Anaya's purpose might have changed to adjust to these audiences. For instance for a group of primary school children, Anaya might have stressed humor or entertainment in his purpose; for a group of people who never used libraries, Anaya's purpose would probably be persuasive. Have students suggest other audiences/purposes for Anaya's essay.
- Have students work in groups to answer the Critical Thinking questions on p. 125.
- Encourage students to begin their Reading Journals on p. 126 before they read the essay. They can continue them afterward.

◆ Critical Thinking

1 Infer Ask students what Anaya means by the "power inherent in each volume." *The stories of the old people had the power to inspire and teach; books have that same power.*

◆ Build Grammar Skills

2 Action and Linking Verbs Have students identify the action verbs and the linking verbs in this sentence. Action verbs: *spoke, came;* linking verbs: *were, were.*

▶ Critical Viewing ◀

3 Interpret *The painting suggests that books have the power to open the universe to readers.*

◆ Reading for Success

4 Use Your Prior Background Knowledge Ask students if Anaya's grandfather's statement about books confirms an opinion they already held, and why or why not. *Students may say they have already thought about the power of words and relate an event they experienced or observed that shows the power of words.*

Read to Appreciate Author's Craft

Rudolfo Anaya carries on the story-telling skills of his grandfather in his writing. He illustrates the power of words to spur the imagination by describing how he responded to both stories and books as a child. Just as los viejitos introduced him to the communal memory of his people, the library offers the collective memory of mankind in its books.

Insight From Pat Mora

Pat Mora offers the following insight. "When Rudy Anaya and I spend time together, we soon begin to discuss the importance of books in the lives of young people. He and I know how important books and libraries have been in our lives, how we are writers because we were and are readers.

The selection moves back and forth so respectfully between the oral and written tradition. Anaya's life and writing value both. Are your students aware of story-telling traditions in their families? Might they document some?"

wise viejitos as guides into the world of nature and knowledge. They taught me with their stories; they taught me the magic of words. Now the words lie captured in
1 ink, but the magic is still there, the power inherent in each volume. Now with book in hand we can participate in the wisdom of mankind.

Each person moves from innocence through rites of passage into the knowledge of the world, and so I entered the world of school in search of the magic in the words. The sounds were no longer the soft sounds of Spanish which my
2 grandfather spoke; the words were in English, and with each new awareness came my first steps toward a million volumes. I, who was used to reading my oraciones en español[3] while I sat in the kitchen and answered the litany to the slap of my mother's tortillas,[4] I now stumbled from sound to word to groups of words, head throbbing, painfully aware that each new sound took me deeper into the maze of the new language. Oh, how I clutched the hands of my new guides then!

Learn, my mother encouraged me, learn. Be as wise as your grandfather. He could speak many languages. He could speak to the birds and the animals of the field.

Yes, I remember the cuentos[5] of my grandfather, the stories of the people. Words are a way, he said, they hold joy, and they are a deadly 4
power if misused. I clung to each syllable which lisped from his tobacco-stained lips. That was the winter the snow came, he would say, it piled high and we lost many sheep and cattle, and the trees groaned and broke with its weight. I looked across the llano[6] and saw the raging blizzard, the awful destruction of that winter which was imbedded in our people's mind.

And the following summer, he would say, the grass of the llano grew so high we

Question how the *cuentos* connect to Anaya's message about libraries. As you read on, you will find that one connection is the power of words to inspire.

3 ▲ **Critical Viewing** What does the painting on this page suggest about the power of books? **[Interpret]**

3. **oraciones en español** (ô ra syôn´ ās en es pa nyōl´): Spanish for "prayers in Spanish."
4. **tortillas** (tôr tē´ yəs) *n.*: Thin, flat, round cakes of unleavened cornmeal.
5. **cuentos** (kwen´ tôs) *n.*: Stories.
6. **llano** (ya´ nō) *n.*: Plain.

Orion, 1984, Martin Wong, Exit Art Gallery, New York

Humanities: Art

Orion, 1984, by Martin Wong.

Martin Wong (1946–), a self-taught painter, was originally inspired by San Francisco's neighborhood graffiti art. He now lives in New York City and is well-known for his stark paintings of urban struggles. Several motifs regularly occur in Wong's paintings, including gold picture frames and constellations in a night sky—*Orion* features both of these. The frame containing the constellation is circular, perhaps suggesting the mystical and infinite qualities of the geometric shape. The stack of books gives reference to Orion.

You might read aloud the inscription around the painting or have a student do so.

1. Suppose Anaya had quoted Wong's inscription. How might he connect that quotation to his own ideas about books and stories? *He might say that stories are so powerful, the mythical Orion means more to us than some real-life conquerors.*
2. What is similar about the way Anaya and Wong see books? *Both see that books inspire us to appreciate and connect to natural wonders, such as stars and constellations.*

couldn't see the top of the sheep. And I would look and see what was once clean and pure and green. I could see a million sheep and the pastores[7] caring for them, as I now care for the million words that pasture in my mind.

5 But a million books? How can we see a million books? I don't mean just the books lining the shelves here at the University of New Mexico Library, not just the fine worn covers, the intriguing titles; how can we see the worlds that lie waiting in each book? A million worlds. A million million worlds. And the beauty of it is that each world is related to the next, as was taught to us by the old ones. Perhaps it is easier for a child to see. Perhaps it is easier for a child to ask: How many stars are there in the sky? How many leaves in the trees of the river? How many blades of grass in the llano? How many dreams in a night of dreams?

6 So I worked my way into the world of books, but here is the paradox, a book at once quenches the thirst of the imagination and ignites new fires. I learned that as I visited the library of my childhood, the Santa Rosa Library. It was only a dusty room in those days, a room sitting atop the town's fire department, which was comprised of one dilapidated fire truck used by the town's volunteers only in the direst emergencies. 7 But in that small room I found my shelter and retreat. If there were a hundred books there we were fortunate, but to me there were a million volumes. I trembled in awe when I first entered that library, because I realized that if the books held as much magic as the words of the old ones, then indeed this was a room full of power.

> **Question** what this paradox means. How can something quench thirst *and* start fires? As you continue to read, you will discover that books quenched Anaya's thirst for knowledge but lit the fires of curiosity.

Miss Pansy, the librarian, became my new guide. She fed me books as any mother would nurture her child. She brought me book after book, and I consumed them all. Saturday afternoons disappeared as the time of day dissolved into the time of distant worlds. In a world that occupied most of my other schoolmates with games, I took the time to read. I was a librarian's dream. My tattered library card was my ticket into the same worlds my grandfather had known, worlds of magic that fed the imagination.

> You can **summarize** Anaya's Saturday afternoon in the following way: He read all day, lost track of time, then, at the end of the day, he raced home across the river that used to frighten him.

8 Late in the afternoon, when I was satiated with reading, when I could no longer hold in my soul the characters that crowded there, I heard the call of the llano, the real world of my father's ranchito, the solid, warm world of my mother's kitchen. Then to the surprise and bewilderment of Miss Pansy, I

7. **pastores** (pas tō´ rās) *n.*: Shepherds.

◆ Build Vocabulary

inherent (in hir´ ənt) *adj.*: Inborn; existing in naturally and inseparably

litany (lit´ ən ē) *n.*: Series of responsive religious readings

dilapidated (di lap´ ə dā´ tid) *adj.*: Broken down

satiated (sā´ shē ā tid) *adj.*: Having had enough; full

◆ Literary Focus

5 Author's Purpose Ask students how this passage serves Anaya's purpose in this essay—to communicate to readers how books can inspire readers. Have them cite the phrase that encapsulates his purpose. *The phrase that captures his purpose is "the worlds that lie waiting in each book."*

◆ Critical Thinking

6 Relate Ask students for other examples of something that "quenches the thirst of the imagination and ignites new fires." *Students might say that this is true of most activities you enjoy, such as listening to a favorite kind of music, exchanging anecdotes with friends, or even playing a sport.*

◆ Build Grammar Skills

7 Action and Linking Verbs Have students identify the action verbs and the linking verbs in these two sentences. Have them explain how each kind of verb functions in the sentence. *Action verb:* found; *linking verbs:* were, were. *In both cases,* were *links the subject of the verb to something that further describes it.* Found *in this sentence, expresses both mental and physical action.*

◆ Literature and Your Life

8 Invite students to relate their own experiences with being lost in an imaginary world and then coming back into the real world. In what kinds of experiences do they tend to get most absorbed? *Students might cite reading, playing music, listening to an involved anecdote, watching movies or videotapes, playing video games, or being involved in an individual sport such as running.*

Customize for Logical/Mathematical Learners

On the board, write the figures for one million, a hundred million, and a "million million." Invite students to think of logical items that might be indicated by these numbers, such as a million books, a million dollars, a hundred million people, a million million stars. Encourage interested students to make graphs, like the one shown on p. 117 of their books, comparing other large collections.

Reteach

Students who have trouble following the connection Anaya makes between stars, stories, and books may benefit by questioning ideas as they read. Encourage them to create two-column charts to track Anaya's ideas. As they read, students can fill in their charts. When they come to an idea that they find hard to understand, they can write a question about that passage in the left-hand column. As students continue to read, they can look for an answers to their questions. When they have finished reading, discuss with them how the essay provided answers to their questions.

My Question	Answer found in selection
What do stars have to do with library books?	*The infinite number of stars inspires the viewer's imagination, just as the million books in the library can inspire a person's thirst for knowledge.*

◆ Critical Thinking

❶ Speculate Anaya says that the word *freedom* must reflect what a library's collection is all about. Invite students to analyze that statement further by speculating about the collection of a library in a society that exercises censorship. *Students might say the collection would be smaller, would reflect the political views of one group, would not contain books that expressed views contrary to those that the group held.*

◆ Critical Thinking

❷ Connect Ask students how preserving and using the literature of other cultures can help preserve and regenerate one's own culture. *Students may say that by becoming aware of how other people see things, we become more aware of the views of our own cultures. Students may also point out that many cultures deal with universal issues, so that learning about another culture may reinforce one's own beliefs.*

◆ Reading for Success

❸ Question With students, question why Anaya is telling about this part of his childhood in this essay. Is it relevant? *Students may point out that the author is trying to show the ways in which libraries are exciting places, and that reading and writing can be connected to real-world values such as friendship, love, and even earning money.*

Extending Word Study

Latin Prefix *in-* Have students study the word *insanity*, using the dictionary if necessary. What is the meaning of the prefix *in-* in this word? What is the antonym of *insanity*? Then have them look at the word *inform*. What is the meaning of the prefix *in-* in this word?

would rush out and race down the streets of our town, books tucked under my shirt, in my pockets, clutched tightly to my breast. Mad with the insanity of books, I would cross the river to get home, shouting my crazy challenge even at la Llorona,[8] and that poor spirit of so many frightening cuentos would wither and withdraw. She was no match for me.

> These ideas will help you achieve your **purpose** for reading this essay—to discover a new perspective on libraries.

Those of you who have felt the same exhilaration from reading—or from love—will know about what I'm speaking. Alas, the people of the town could only shake their heads and pity my mother. At least one of her sons was a bit touched. Perhaps they were right, for few will trade a snug reality to float on words to other worlds.

And now there are a million volumes for us to read here at the University of New Mexico Library. Books on every imaginable subject, in every field, a history of the
❶ thought of the world which we must keep free of censorship, because we treasure our freedoms. It is the word *freedom* which eventually must reflect what this collection, or the collection of any library, is all about. We know that as we preserve and use the literature of all cultures, we preserve and regenerate our own. The old ones knew and taught me this. They eagerly read the few
❷ newspapers that were available. They kept their diaries, they wrote décimas[9] and cuentos, and they survived on their oral stories and traditions.

8. **la Llorona** (la yô rô´ na): Spirit of many stories, famous for shouting and crying for her lost love.
9. **décimas** (dā´ sē mas) *n.*: Ten-line stanzas.

Another time, another library. I entered Albuquerque[10] High School Library prepared to study, because that's where we spent our study time. For better or for worse, I received my first contracts as a writer there. It was a place where budding lovers spent most of their time writing notes to each other, and when my friends who didn't have the gift of words ❸
found out I could turn a phrase I quickly had all the business I could do. I wrote poetic love notes for a dime apiece and thus worked my way through high school. And there were fringe benefits, because the young women knew very well who was writing the sweet words, and many a heart I was supposed to capture fell in love with me. And so, a library is also a place where love begins.

> Use your **prior knowledge** to connect your own experience with libraries to Anaya's high-school library experiences.

A library should be the heart of a city. With its storehouse of knowledge, it liberates, informs, teaches, and enthralls. A library indeed should be the cultural center of any city. Amidst the bustle of work and commerce, the great libraries of the world have provided a sanctuary where scholars and common man alike come to enlarge and clarify knowledge, to read and reflect in quiet solitude.

10. **Albuquerque** (al´ bə kʉr´ kē): City in central New Mexico.

◆ Build Vocabulary

enthralls (en thrôlz´) *v.*: Captivates; fascinates

labyrinth (lab´ ə rinth) *n.*: Maze

Speaking, Listening, and Viewing Mini-Lesson

Storytelling Performance

This mini-lesson supports the Speaking, Listening, and Viewing activity in the Idea Bank on p. 126.

Introduce Let students know that when people perform stories, they use a range of acting techniques to bring the story to life. Have students recall situations in which they enjoyed listening to someone perform a story.

Develop With students, list the qualities that make an effective storytelling performance. The list should include knowing the story well, using different voices for different characters, facial and vocal expression, humor, pacing, and gestures.

Apply Have students work in pairs to develop and rehearse their stories. If possible, have them perform for younger children, the class or other groups.

Assess Encourage students to discuss their story-telling experiences as a class. Did the story-teller seem to know the story well? Were the stories well-paced? Did students use facial, bodily, and vocal expression to the story's advantage? Why or why not? You may wish to have students use the Peer Assessment forms for Oral Interpretation or Dramatic Performance in ***Alternative Assessment*** (pp. 120, 121).

I knew a place like this, I spent many hours in the old library on Central Avenue and Edith Street. But my world was growing, and quite by accident I wandered up the hill to enroll in the University of New Mexico. And what a surprise lay in store for me. The libraries of my childhood paled in comparison to this new wealth of books housed in
4 Zimmerman Library. Here there were stack after stack of books, and ample space and time to wander aimlessly in this labyrinth of new frontiers.

I had known the communal memory of my people through the newspapers and few books my grandfather read to me and through the rich oral tradition handed down by the old ones; now I discovered the collective memory of all mankind at my fingertips. I had only to reach for the books that laid all history bare. Here I could converse with the writers from every culture on earth, old and new, and at the same time I began my personal
6 odyssey, which would add a few books to the collection which 6
in 1981 would come to house a million volumes.

Those were exciting times. Around me swirled the busy world of the university, in many respects an alien world. 7 Like many fellow undergraduates, I sought refuge in the library. My haven during those student university years was the reading room of the west wing of the old library. There I found peace. The carved vigas[11] decorating the ceiling, the solid wooden tables and chairs and the warm adobe color of the stucco were things with which I was familiar. There I felt comfortable. 8 With books scattered around me, I could read and doze and dream. I took my breaks in the warm sun of the portal, where I ate my tortilla sandwiches, which I carried in my brown paper bag. There, with friends, I sipped coffee as we talked of changing the world and exchanged idealistic dreams.

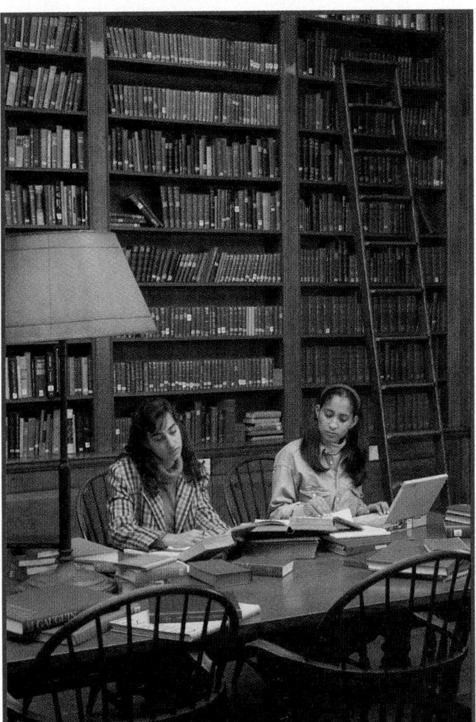

▲ 5 **Critical Viewing** How do you think the two women in this photograph feel about libraries? **[Infer]**

11. **vigas** (bē´ gas) *n.*: Roof beams.

◆ Literary Focus

4 Author's Purpose Ask students how recalling experiences with libraries of increasing size helps fulfill Anaya's purpose in writing this essay. *Students may say that Anaya is showing that by finding ever-larger libraries, he is demonstrating that his world is also becoming larger and more exciting. They might cite details such as "stack after stack of books" and "ample space and time to wander . . ."*

▶Critical Viewing◀

5 Infer *Students might cite the women's facial expressions and body language to infer that they are studious, that they are comfortable working in the library. Students might further surmise that the two are used to libraries and that they enjoy and respect them.*

◆ Reading for Success

6 Use Your Prior Background Knowledge Ask students to use their prior knowledge to explain Anaya's reference to his "personal odyssey, which would add a few books to the collection." *Students should point out that because they know Anaya has written books they can assume the books he added to the collection were ones he had written.*

◆ Reading for Success

7 Summarize Invite students to summarize the different experiences with libraries that Anaya has recounted so far. *Summaries should include that as a child Anaya learned about the world from the oral tradition of his grandfather and other elders, that he loved the tiny town library, that his high school library was a social center for him, and that the university library was a thrilling new place.*

◆ Build Grammar Skills

8 Action and Linking Verbs Invite students to tell whether the verb *felt* is an action or a linking verb here and to explain their answers. *The verb is a linking verb, because it describes the author's state of being. The word was could be substituted for the word felt.*

Beyond the Classroom

Career Connection

Library Science In this essay, Anaya describes a number of different kinds of libraries: his one-room local library, his high school library, and the huge university library that eventually acquires one million volumes. Each of these types of libraries has a system for ordering and cataloging books, so that library patrons can find what they were looking for, or so the librarian can help visitors find a particular book or piece of information.

A trained, professional librarian learns different systems of cataloging books, such as the Dewey Decimal system (used in most small libraries) and the Library of Congress system (used in most larger libraries)—both manually and in electronic database format. Most libraries offer materials besides books: audio- and videotapes, CDs, electronic resources, and the computers by which to access electronic files. Invite students to interview a school, community, or university librarian to find out about library ordering systems, the various skills and duties of a librarian, and the education and training necessary to become a librarian.

◆ Critical Thinking

❶ **Compare** What elements are shared by the village *resolana* and the library? *Both are places where people meet and pass on knowledge. The library provides an ongoing "conversation" about anything one finds of interest.*

Reinforce and Extend

Customize for
Less Proficient Readers
Invite students to review the essay, looking for three answers that Anaya offers for the question "Why are libraries important?" *Sample answers: "because they connect us to our culture," "they stimulate our imaginations," "they are places of love," "they are havens and places of refuge," "they help make us free," and "they are places of debate and research."*

Answers

◆ *Literature and Your Life*

Reader's Response Encourage students to think of nonfiction as well as fiction. Guide them toward discussion of new ideas and insights gained from reading.

Thematic Focus Students might say that libraries help people by providing access to a wide range of literature and research material. They might also mention library programs such as literacy and children's programs. Many libraries also provide access to the Internet.

☑ Check Your Comprehension

1. Anaya compares a million books to stars, worlds, leaves, blades of grass, and dreams.
2. Anaya's interest in learning was ignited by the stories of the old ones that he listened to as a child.
3. He learned to love reading as a child in the Santa Rosa library.
4. The old ones preserved and regenerated their culture through cuentos, the stories of the people.
5. Anaya's memories include visiting the Santa Rosa library atop the city's fire department, and its librarian, Miss Pansy; writing love notes on behalf of his friends at his high school library; seeking refuge in the Zimmerman Library at the University of New Mexico.

You can **summarize** Anaya's essay with the following points: Anaya's love of words comes from a rich storytelling tradition; his love of stories, books, and learning grew in libraries; he sees libraries as havens, gathering places, and storehouses of knowledge.

That is a rich and pleasant time in my memory. No matter how far across the world I find myself in the future, how deep in the creation of worlds with words, I shall keep the simple and poignant memories of those days. The sun set golden on the ocher walls, and the green pine trees and the blue spruce, sacred trees to our people, whispered in the breeze. I remembered my grandfather meeting with the old men of the village in the ❶ resolana[12] of one of the men's homes, or against the wall of the church on Sundays, and I remembered the things they said. Later, alone, dreaming against the sun-warmed wall of the library, I continued that discourse in my mind. ❶

Yes, the library is a place where people should gather. It is a place for research, reading, and for the quiet fomentation of ideas, but because it houses the collective memory of our race, it should also be a place where present issues are discussed and debated and researched in order for us to gain the knowledge and insight to create a better future. The library should be a warm place that reflects the needs and aspirations of the people.

12. **resolana** (rā sô la´ na) *n.*: Place for enjoying the sun.

◆ Build Vocabulary

poignant (pɔin´ yənt) *adj.*: Emotionally moving

fomentation (fō men tā´ shən) *n.*: Incitement; a stirring up

Guide for Responding

◆ *Literature and Your Life*

Reader's Response Anaya appeals to people who have "felt the same exhilaration from reading" as he has felt. What reading has exhilarated you? Why?

Thematic Focus In his essay, Anaya describes how libraries help individuals and societies to succeed by being places where "scholars and common man alike come to enlarge and clarify knowledge, to read and reflect in quiet solitude." How would you describe how libraries help people?

Activity Create a floor plan of your vision of the perfect library. Make the sections different sizes and label them—sports, history, poetry—to show what you think should be the largest sections.

☑ Check Your Comprehension

1. Name three things that Anaya compares to "a million volumes."
2. What ignited Anaya's passion for learning?
3. How and when did Anaya come to love words and reading?
4. How did the "old ones" of Anaya's childhood preserve and regenerate their culture?
5. Summarize three of Anaya's library memories.

Beyond the Selection

FURTHER READING

Other Works by Rudolfo Anaya
Bless Me, Ultima
Heart of Aztlan
Tortuga

Other Works With the Theme of Striving for Success
Crystal, Walter Dean Myers
To Be Young, Gifted, and Black, Lorraine Hansberry

We suggest that you preview these works before recommending them to students.

INTERNET

You and your students may find additional information about Rudolfo Anaya on the Internet. We suggest the following site. Please be aware, however, that the site may have changed from the time we published this information.

For information about Rudolfo Anaya, go to **http://www.unm.edu/~wrtgsw/anaya.html**

We *strongly recommend* that you preview this and related sites before you send students to them.

Guide for Responding (continued)

◆ Critical Thinking

Interpret

1. What does Anaya mean when he says that "a book at once quenches the thirst of the imagination and ignites new fires"? **[Interpret]**

2. Why does Anaya associate libraries with freedom? **[Connect]**

3. In what ways do books and reading help preserve a culture? **[Draw Conclusions]**

Apply

4. Anaya says that a library should "reflect the needs and aspirations of the people." What specific needs and aspirations do you think your library should reflect? **[Relate]**

Extend

5. List three works of literature that inspired you or helped you reach a goal, and explain how they did so. **[Literature Link]**

◆ Reading for Success

Interactive Reading Strategies

Review the reading strategies and notes showing how to read interactively. Then apply those strategies to answer the following questions.

1. Explain how Anaya's feelings about the stories of the old people reinforce the message of his essay.

2. List one question you asked yourself while reading and explain how you answered it.

◆ Literary Focus

Author's Purpose

Anaya wrote this essay as a speech to be delivered on the occasion of a library's acquiring its one-millionth volume. In general, this **author's purpose**—his reason for writing—is to share his ideas with the group that has gathered to celebrate the event. The information he presents helps him achieve his specific purpose of acknowledging the importance of libraries in linking the wisdom of the past to the goals of the future.

1. Identify two details that Anaya includes to illustrate how libraries can help children.

2. Find one direct statement that helped you recognize Anaya's specific purpose.

◆ Build Vocabulary

Using the Latin Prefix *in-*

In your notebook, write an antonym for each word below that begins with the Latin prefix *in-*, meaning "in" or "into."

1. inhale **2.** include **3.** internal

Using the Word Bank: Elaboration

In your notebook, describe what each of the following would be like.

1. dilapidated car
2. meal that left you satiated
3. book that enthralls
4. poem like a litany
5. fomentation of ideas
6. poignant movie scene
7. inherent quality of cats
8. labyrinth of hallways
9. speech that induces sleep

◆ Build Grammar Skills

Action Verbs and Linking Verbs

Common linking verbs include the following: *become, seem, appear, feel, look, taste, smell, sound, stay, remain, grow,* and *be* (including the forms *am, is, are, was,* and *were*). Some of these can also be used as action verbs. If you can replace the verb with a form of *be* and the sentence still makes sense, the verb is probably a linking verb.

Action verbs express physical or mental action. **Linking verbs** express a state of being and tell what the subject is by linking it to one or more words that further describe or identify it.

Practice Copy each of the following sentences in your notebook. Underline the verbs. Then identify the verb as an action verb *(V)* or a linking verb *(LV)*.

1. Anaya feels exhilarated by the power of words.
2. The people of his village told him stories.
3. His love for stories grew in the library.
4. In college, he grew eager to learn even more.
5. He delivered this speech at his alma mater.

Answers

◆ Critical Thinking

1. In books, we find the answers to the questions that intrigue us. We also find new ideas that spark our curiosity.
2. Anaya associates libraries with freedom because libraries represent ideas from many points of view in their uncensored collections.
3. Books are the written record of a culture. They transcend barriers of time and space and keep the thoughts and customs of a culture alive.
4. The library might reflect the need to know more about culture and heritage, practical skills, and career opportunity information. It might reflect aspirations to improve oneself or become a professional or skilled worker.
5. Selections in Units 1 and 2 that students might suggest include: "The Final Assault," "The Dream Comes True," "from My Left Foot," "Mowing," and "After Apple-Picking."

◆ Reading for Success

1. Both the stories of the old people and libraries serve to preserve culture and heritage. They both value the power of the word.
2. A possible response is that students questioned how Anaya would connect his childhood memories to his love for books; when they read on, they found the connections and went back in the text to confirm them.

◆ Literary Focus

1. Libraries can help children by providing refuge and introducing them to the power of stories.
2. A sample direct statement is "Now with book in hand we can participate in the wisdom of mankind."

◆ Build Vocabulary

Using the Latin Prefix *in-*

1. exhale; 2. exclude; 3. external

Using the Word Bank

1. A dilapidated car would be a broken down car.
2. A meal that left you satiated would leave you full.
3. A book that enthralls you is a book that captivates or fascinates you.
4. A poem like a litany would be one with a series of repetitive responses.
5. A fomentation of ideas is like a stirring up of ideas.
6. A poignant movie scene is an emotionally moving one.
7. An inherent quality of cats is their inborn grace.
8. A labyrinth of hallways is like a maze of hallways.
9. A speech that induces sleep is a speech that causes someone to sleep.

◆ Build Grammar Skills

1. Anaya <u>feels</u> exhilarated by the power of words. (LV)
2. The people of his village <u>told</u> him stories. (V)
3. His love for stories <u>grew</u> in the library. (V)
4. In college, he <u>grew</u> eager to learn even more. (LV)
5. He <u>delivered</u> this speech at his alma mater. (V)

Grammar Reinforcement

For additional instruction and practice, use the lesson in the **Language Lab CD-ROM** on Eight Parts of Speech and the page on Action Verbs and Linking Verbs (p. 11) in the *Writer's Solution Grammar Practice Book*.

Idea Bank

Following are suggestions for matching Idea Bank topics with your students' performance levels and learning modalities:

Customizing for
Performance Levels
Less Advanced Students: 1, 4, 6
Average Students: 2, 5, 7
Pre-AP Students: 3

Customizing for
Learning Modalities
Visual/Spatial: 6
Logical/Mathematical: 3, 7
Bodily/Kinesthetic: 4
Verbal/Linguistic: 2, 4, 5

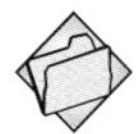

Guided Writing Lesson

Prewriting Strategy Help students differentiate between a diary they might keep at home and a journal they keep at school, encourage them to brainstorm about the meanings of these terms. Write *diary* on the board, and ask students to suggest ideas they associate with it; do the same with *reading journal.* After students have expressed their ideas, discuss differences between these two forms. Students should use their reading journals to explore interesting topics in their reading rather than to record intimacies or list everyday events.

Writing and Language Transparencies Use Writing Process Model 8: Interpreting a Work of Literature (pp. 53–59) to provide pointers on responding to literature.

Writers at Work Videodisc
Have students view the videodisc segment (Ch. 7) featuring Miguel Algarín to spark a class discussion on the importance of responding to works of literature.

Play frames 22209 to 31154

Writing Lab CD-ROM
Have students complete the tutorial on Response to Literature. Follow these steps:

1. Direct students to use the Sunburst Diagram to organize details.
2. Have them use an Evaluation Word Bin for precise modifiers.
3. Have them get a video tip from Miguel Algarín on revising a draft.

Build Your Portfolio

Idea Bank

Writing

1. **Library Dedication** Based on the ideas Anaya has shared and your own opinions, write a brief statement, to be read at the dedication of a newly opened library, about the value of libraries.
2. **Informational Article** Find out what resources (besides books) and activities are available to the public at your local library. Present your findings in a brief article for your school or local newspaper. **[Community Link]**
3. **Directions** Write step-by-step directions for how to use a technological tool, such as a CD-ROM guide to periodicals or an electronic card catalog. **[Technology Link]**

Speaking, Listening, and Viewing

4. **Storytelling Performance** Choose a story you liked when you were a child. Practice telling it aloud with expression, using gestures and facial expressions. If possible, perform your story for a group of young children. **[Performing Arts Link]**
5. **Library Panel Discussion** Have a group discussion in which each group member gives reasons why his or her favorite books should be included in the school library. Present your reasons to the class.

Researching and Representing

6. **Library Poster** Libraries frequently display posters that promote the benefits of reading. Create your own reading promotion poster. Display the poster in your classroom.
7. **Library Survey** Ask your school librarian what percentage of the school's library books are fiction, nonfiction, poetry, and drama. Represent the percentages on a chart or graph. **[Math Link]**

Online Activity www.phlit.phschool.com

Guided Writing Lesson

Reading Journal

One way to explore the ideas you find in books is to respond to them in writing. For one week, keep a **reading journal**—a record of your thoughts and feelings about what you read and how the issues or topics apply to your life. The following tips will help you record your ideas in the most appropriate style.

Writing Skills Focus: Level of Formality

Whether you're writing a letter to a company, a report for school, or a journal entry, take time to consider the **level of formality** you should use.

Because you are the audience for your journal, you want to capture your thoughts in your own natural voice. For a journal, it is appropriate to use informal English—the "everyday" English that we speak. Feel free to use contractions and slang—but the standard rules of grammar, punctuation, and spelling still apply.

Use informal English to capture the natural sound of speech in your journal.

Prewriting While you are reading, keep your journal handy so you can jot down your reactions to specific passages and ideas. Sketch characters and settings and record quotations you want to remember.

Drafting Write each full entry as if you were speaking to a friend. Expand your notes into full sentences written in the language and informal style of your everyday speech. Explain why you do or do not like or agree with what you read.

Revising In a personal journal, you don't need to revise as extensively as you would if someone else were going to read it. You may want to look over your entries, however, and add a few more details or reword a sentence to better express your thoughts.

✓ ASSESSMENT OPTIONS

Formal Assessment, Selection Test, pp. 26–28, and Assessment Resources Software. The selection test is designed so that it can be easily customized to the performance levels of your students.

Alternative Assessment, p. 8, includes options for less advanced students, Pre-AP Students, logical/mathematical learners, verbal/linguistic learners, interpersonal learners, and visual/spatial learners.

PORTFOLIO ASSESSMENT
Use the following rubrics in the ***Alternative Assessment*** booklet to assess student writing:
Library Dedication: Persuasion Rubric, p. 105
Informational Article: Explanation Rubric, p. 115
Directions: How-to Explanation Rubric, p. 100

PART 1 *Overcoming Obstacles*

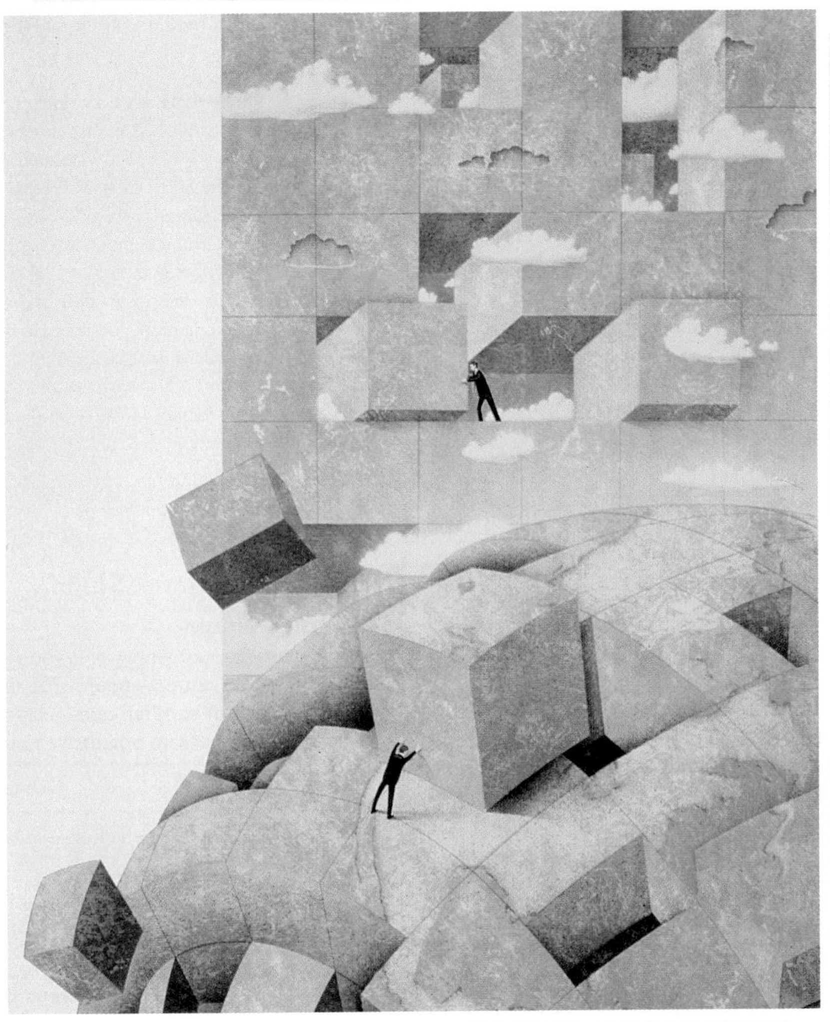

Earth and Sky Puzzle, Curtis Parker/SIS

One-Minute Planning Guide

The selections in this section deal with people's trying to overcome obstacles. In "How Much Land Does a Man Need?" a Russian farmer assumes that the obstacle is his lack of land, though he finds out too late it is his own greed. The poems "Success is counted sweetest," "I dwell in Possibility—," "Uncoiling," and "Columbus Dying" deal with success and failure. In the excerpt from *My Left Foot,* Christy Brown overcomes the obstacles of his cerebral palsy and the attitudes of others. In "A Visit to Grandmother," a man must overcome what he perceives to be his mother's unequal treatment of him and a sibling.

Customize for
Varying Student Needs

When assigning the selections in this part to students, keep in mind the following factors:

"How Much Land Does a Man Need?"
- A longer selection (13 pp.)
- Less proficient readers may need to read in sections

"Success is counted sweetest," "I dwell in Possibility—," "Uncoiling," "Columbus Dying"
- Four brief poems

from *My Left Foot*
- Connection to popular film will interest students

"A Visit to Grandmother"
- Story will be accessible to most students

Humanities: Art

Earth and Sky Puzzle by Curtis Parker.

Parker, who operated his own design studio before becoming a commercial artist, is known as a "thinking person's illustrator." He uses acrylic paints to create images with appealing textures that engage the viewer in intriguing visual puzzles that recall the works of M. C. Escher.

Earth and Sky Puzzle combines recognizable concrete images with abstract geometric ones. Help students notice the way the painting resembles a three-dimensional puzzle. Encourage them to speculate what the completed puzzle should look like as well as to speculate about where the various loose pieces might belong.

Help students link the painting to the theme of Part 1, "Overcoming Obstacles," with the following questions:

1. What do you think the figures in this painting are trying to do? *Possible answers: They are trying to put the pieces of the puzzle together so that they form the earth and sky; they are trying to move the pieces of the puzzle around to change the appearance of earth and sky.*
2. What particular obstacles do the various figures have to deal with? *Possible answers: They have to move pieces larger than themselves; they have to figure out where the pieces go; the pieces might fall out of the sky and off of the earth; the figures could lose their footing and fall.*

Prepare and Engage

LESSON OBJECTIVES

1. To develop vocabulary and word identification skills
- Words in Context: Technical and Multiple-Meaning Words
- Using the Word Bank: Sentence Completions
- Extending Word Study: Word Origins (ATE)

2. To use a variety of reading strategies to read and comprehend a short story
- Connect Your Experience
- Reading Strategy: Predict Based on Character Traits
- Tips to Guide Reading: Sustained Reading (ATE)
- Read to Interpret (ATE)

3. To increase knowledge of other cultures and to connect common elements across cultures
- Connecting Themes Across Cultures (ATE)
- Cultural Connections

4. To express and support responses to the text
- Critical Thinking
- Analyze Literary Criticism (ATE)
- Idea Bank: Newspaper Article

5. To analyze literary elements
- Literary Focus: Parable
- Idea Bank: Parable

6. To read in order to research self-selected and assigned topics
- Idea Bank: Land Advertisement
- Viewing and Representing Mini-Lesson: Map of Russia (ATE)
- Research Skills Mini-Lesson: Questionnaire (ATE)

7. To plan, prepare, organize, and present literary interpretations
- Idea Bank: Update the Story
- Speaking, Listening, and Viewing Mini-Lesson: Eulogy (ATE)

8. To use recursive writing processes to write a video script
- Guided Writing Lesson

9. To increase knowledge of the rules of grammar and usage
- Build Grammar Skills: Possessive Nouns

Guide for Reading

Leo Tolstoy *(1828–1910)*

Leo Tolstoy is remembered almost as much for his unusual lifestyle as he is for his literary achievements.

Tolstoy's life reads like a Cinderella story in reverse. He was born rich and died poor.

After inheriting the wealth and power of his family's estate at the age of nineteen, he opened a school for peasant children and tried somewhat unsuccessfully to improve the lives of the serfs who were bound to the estate.

One Wife, Two Masterpieces, Thirteen Children When he was thirty-four, Tolstoy married an intelligent, headstrong woman named Sonya Baers. She energetically supported his writing, copying by hand his long, nearly indecipherable manuscript for the mammoth novel *War and Peace* nine times, by candlelight, so that it could be sent to publishers. At the same time, she found time to manage Tolstoy's estate and raise thirteen children.

Tolstoy's other masterpiece is *Anna Karenina*, a tragic love story. While working on the novel, Tolstoy began to question the meaning of life and the inevitability of death.

A Personal Crisis After *Anna Karenina* was published in installments from 1875 to 1877, Tolstoy suffered a spiritual crisis. He created his own religion, took up shoemaking, became a vegetarian, and stopped drinking and smoking. He handed over the copyrights to all of his works produced before 1881 to his wife and attempted to be as self-sufficient as possible. He often wore peasant's clothes and worked in the fields. His actions placed a great strain on his marriage and eventually forced him to leave home. In 1910, he died at an obscure railroad station.

◆ Build Vocabulary

WORDS IN CONTEXT: TECHNICAL AND MULTIPLE-MEANING WORDS

As the title of Tolstoy's story suggests, many of the words you will encounter in this story are farming terms. Some of these words, such as *fallow*, which means "not cultivated," can be used in other contexts as well. *Fallow* can refer to land left uncultivated or, for example, to a mind that is inactive.

WORD BANK

As you read you will encounter the words on this list. Each word is defined on the page where it first appears. Preview the list before you read, and look for more farming terms, such as *sowed,* that can have other implications in other contexts.

piqued
disparaged
forbore
aggrieved
sheaf
arable
fallow

◆ Build Grammar Skills

POSSESSIVE NOUNS

In this story about owning land, you will see many **possessive nouns**—nouns that show ownership, belonging, or another close relationship. The chart shows how to form possessive nouns.

Rules for Possessive Forms of Nouns	Examples
To form the possessive of singular nouns, add an apostrophe and s.	• Pahom's field • sun's rays
To form the possessive of plural nouns that end in s, just add an apostrophe.	• peasants' complaints • three days' work
To form the possessive of plural nouns that do not end in s, add an apostrophe and s.	• women's conversation • people's land

Notice other examples of these possessive forms of nouns in Tolstoy's story.

Test Preparation

Reading Comprehension: Recognize Facts, Details, and Sequence (ATE, p. 129) The teaching tips and sample test item in this workshop support the instruction and practice in the unit workshop:

Reading Comprehension: Recognize Facts, Details, and Sequence (SE, p. 215)

Prentice Hall Literature Program Resources

REINFORCE / RETEACH / EXTEND

Selection Support Pages
Build Vocabulary: Using Words in Other Contexts, p. 35
Build Grammar Skills: Possessive Nouns, p. 36
Reading Strategy: Predict Based on Character Traits, p. 37
Literary Focus: Parable, p. 38

Strategies for Diverse Student Needs, p. 9

Beyond Literature
Cross-Curricular Connection: Social Studies, p. 9

Formal Assessment Selection Test, pp. 29–31; Assessment Resources Software

Alternative Assessment, p. 9

Resource Pro CD-ROM

Listening to Literature Audiocassettes

How Much Land Does a Man Need?

◆ Literature and Your Life

CONNECT YOUR EXPERIENCE

Just one more . . . just a little longer . . . just a little farther—almost everyone has used one of these phrases at one time or another. For instance, you yourself have probably felt that you could have done better on that last test if you had had just a little longer!

The events in this Russian tale illustrate the universal truth that "a little more" is *never* enough.

THEMATIC FOCUS: OVERCOMING OBSTACLES

Tolstoy's story illustrates the old proverb, "The more you have, the more you want." As you read this story, ask yourself, How much is enough?

◆ Background for Understanding

HISTORY

From the sixteenth century to the mid-nineteenth century, Russian peasants were bound by law to work land they could rent but not own. They grew food they couldn't eat, cultivated crops they couldn't sell, and worked to exhaustion to make a profit for the landowner. Peasants could be bought and sold with the land they lived on. This story is set after the laws had been changed to allow ordinary people to own land. Because of the old laws, however, land is more than just property. Land ownership represents the ability to control one's own destiny.

It is not a coincidence that Tolstoy uses land to explore the question "How much is enough?" He uses an image that was close to the heart of every Russian.

◆ Literary Focus

PARABLE

Tolstoy's story is not simply a tale about land. It is a **parable**, a simple, brief narrative that teaches a lesson by using characters and events to stand for abstract ideas or moral principles.

This parable focuses on Pahom, a Russian peasant who feels that all his problems would be solved if he had enough land. Through Pahom's actions, the story explores the question "How much land is enough land?" Think about the lesson that this parable teaches, a lesson concerning the difference between *need* and *greed*.

◆ Reading Strategy

PREDICT BASED ON CHARACTER TRAITS

When you read stories that teach a lesson, you can usually **predict** the outcome before you actually read what happens. In such stories, casual remarks and small details are filled with meaning and hint at future events. Clouds on the horizon can foretell a thunderstorm; a minor dispute between neighbors can foreshadow a bitter feud.

In "How Much Land Does a Man Need?" the peasant Pahom's wife says to her wealthier sister, "Though you often earn more than you need, you're very likely to lose all you have." This statement hints at the lesson to come. Pahom's response to the conversation between the two women reveals character traits that will help you predict how he will act in the story.

Capture students' attention by showing a range of consumer product ads from a magazine aimed at young people. Point to ads for clothes, jewelry, sports or computer equipment. Generate a brief discussion with these questions: Does advertising lead us to buy more than we need? Let students know that Tolstoy asked these same questions in his time, as they will see when they read his parable about a peasant's quest for more and more land.

Connecting Themes Across Cultures

Have students brainstorm for similar parables on the subject of greed, such as the Greek myth of Pandora's box or Aesop's fable, "The Fox and the Grapes."

Customize for
Less Proficient Readers

Have these students pause after they read each numbered section of the story and summarize its main idea before continuing.

Customize for
Pre-AP Students

Suggest that students meet in a group to compare and contrast Tolstoy's style in this parable with the writing style of other works they have recently read. Encourage them to discover the relationship between an author's style and the central message of the story. Of the works they analyze, students should select a story style that best fits its message and, in their journals, explain their choice.

Customize for
English Language Learners

Before students read, choose some longer sentences and model the process of breaking a sentence into its main subject and verb to determine its basic meaning. Ask "Whom or what is this sentence about? What is happening to that subject?"

Test Preparation Workshop

Reading Comprehension:
Recognize Facts, Details, and Sequence

Have students look for details central to the purpose of this sample passage describing Pahom's feelings about the first plot of land he buys.

> The grass that grew and the flowers that bloomed there seemed to him unlike any that grew elsewhere. Formerly, when he had passed by that land, it had appeared the same as any other land, but now it seemed quite different.

Which statement best sums up the main idea of the passage?

A Pahom had never noticed the land before.

B Pahom planted unusual flowers on his land.

C Pahom has worked to make the grass grow better than before.

D Pahom sees the land differently now that he owns it.

Guide students to assess accuracy in the statements—answers *A–C* do not represent accurate statements. Students should see that *D* is accurate and sums up the main idea.

Develop Understanding

One-Minute Insight This parable illuminates Tolstoy's sentiments about the perils of private ownership. A peasant named Pahom seeks to acquire more and more land. He rejects the advantages of cooperative ownership and finds fault with each new land acquisition until, far from his home, he at last dies in a final, desperate grasp for even more land.

Tolstoy would have approved of the peasants' owning the land jointly. It is owning private property, this story tells us, that encourages individual greed.

Tips to Guide Reading

Sustained Reading Encourage students to read the story all the way through in one sitting. Suggest that they use sticky notes to mark any passage that contains confusing ideas or vocabulary they don't know. Reading further may clarify points. If not, students can return to their marked pages and ask questions during class discussion on the reading.

▶Critical Viewing◀

❶ **Speculate** *Students are likely to suggest that the peasants want to gain more control over their lives so they won't be beholden to landowners, that they want to feel a pride in ownership, that they generally want to improve their prospects for the future and to be able to provide better for their material needs.*

Customize for *Logical/Mathematical Learners*

Pahom's land acquisition grows by leaps and bounds. Have these students create a diagram or graph showing how his holdings increase as the story progresses.

How Much *Land* Does a Man Need?

Leo Tolstoy

Translated by Louise and Aylmer Maude

Rest During the Harvest, Alexander Morosov, Tretyakov Gallery, Moscow, Russia

❶ ▲ Critical Viewing Why do you think people like the peasants in this picture place great importance on owning land? **[Speculate]**

130 ◆ *Striving for Success*

Humanities: Art

Rest During the Harvest (detail) by Alexander Morosov.

This painting depicts peasants taking a break from their labor. It might be set in the region of Bryansk, a province of Russia from which the painter Alexander Morosov comes. Encourage students to study the details of the painting and what they show about its setting and characters. Then use these questions for discussion:

1. What might the people in this picture have in common? *They are tied to working a landowner's farm; they are all members of the peasant class.*
2. What are some advantages and disadvantages of tending land that you do not own? *Possible advantages: You aren't burdened with the responsibility of ownership; freedom to enjoy simple pleasures. Possible disadvantages: There is no opportunity to better yourself and no incentive to do well.*

1

An elder sister came to visit her younger sister in the country. The elder was married to a shopkeeper in town, the younger to a peasant in the village. As the sisters sat over their tea talking, the elder began to boast of the advantages of town life, saying how comfortably they lived there, how well they dressed, what fine clothes her children wore, what good things they ate and drank, and how she went to the theater, promenades,[1] and entertainments. ❷

The younger sister was piqued, and in turn disparaged the life of a shopkeeper, and stood up for that of a peasant.

"I wouldn't change my way of life for yours," said she. "We may live roughly, but at least we're free from worry. You live in better style than we do, but though you often earn more than you need, you're very likely to lose all you have. You know the proverb, 'Loss and gain are brothers twain.'[2] It often happens that people who're wealthy one day are begging their bread the next. Our way is safer. Though a peasant's life is not a rich one, it's long. We'll never grow rich, but we'll always have enough to eat." ❸

1. **promenades** (präm´ ə nädz) *n.*: Balls or formal dances.
2. **twain** (twān) *n.*: Two.

◆ Build Vocabulary

piqued (pēkt) *v.*: Offended

disparaged (di spar´ ijd) *v.*: Spoke slightly of; belittled

The elder sister said sneeringly:

"Enough? Yes, if you like to share with the pigs and the calves! What do you know of elegance or manners! However much your good man may slave, you'll die as you live—in a dung heap—and your children the same."

"Well, what of that?" replied the younger sister. "Of course our work is rough and hard. But on the other hand, it's sure, and we need not bow to anyone. But you, in your towns, are surrounded by temptations; today all may be right, but tomorrow the Evil One may tempt your husband with cards, wine, or women, and all will go to ruin. Don't such things happen often enough?"

Pahom, the master of the house, was lying on the top of the stove and he listened to the women's chatter.

"It is perfectly true," thought he. "Busy as we are from childhood tilling mother earth, we peasants have no time to let any nonsense settle in our heads. Our only trouble is that we haven't land enough. If I had plenty of land, I shouldn't fear the Devil himself!" ❹

The women finished their tea, chatted a while about dress, and then cleared away the tea things and lay down to sleep.

But the Devil had been sitting behind the stove and had heard all that had been said. He was pleased that the peasant's wife had led her husband into boasting and that he had said that if he had plenty of land he would not fear the Devil himself.

"All right," thought the Devil. "We'll have a tussle. I'll give you land ❺

◆ Background for Understanding

❷ **History** Explain to students that the disparity between town and country living was far greater in Tolstoy's day than it is today. A shopkeeper's wife, although not rich, was in an entirely different class from a peasant's wife, and had access to many more luxuries.

◆ Critical Thinking

❸ **Relate** Ask students to identify other works or tales they know in which a character expresses this sentiment. *Many students will refer to the fable of "The Town Mouse and the Country Mouse," although other works may have a similar theme.*

◆ Reading Strategy

❹ **Predict Based on Character Traits** Ask students how Pahom tempts fate in his thoughts. Have them predict what will happen, keeping in mind that this is a parable, not a realistic story. *He challenges the Devil by saying that if he had plenty of land, he wouldn't fear him. Students may predict that the Devil will soon appear in the story.*

◆ Literature and Your Life

❺ Have students explain how their own experiences with the concept that the more you have the more you want helps them predict how Pahom will react to the land he is about to get. *Most students will recognize that the story will not end with Pahom being satisfied.*

Block Scheduling Strategies

Consider these suggestions to take advantage of extended class time:

- After students have read Build Vocabulary on p. 128, ask them to record in their journals all the land-related words they find in the selection. In pairs, students can discuss the meanings of these words. Suggest that students add to the list as they come across land-related words in their other reading.
- For additional background, have students do the Social Studies Connection page in ***Beyond Literature*** (p. 9), which explains the revolutionary movement among the peasants in Russia in Tolstoy's time.
- Students might enjoy researching Tolstoy on the Internet before reading the story.
- As you review the information in Background for Understanding on p. 129, discuss what students already know about the history of nineteenth-century Russia from their social studies and history classes.
- Have students complete the Guided Writing Lesson on p. 145. Before they write, discuss the setting of the parable: Where does it take place? What is the land like? When does it take place? How do people probably dress? How do they travel?

◆ Literary Focus

❶ **Parable** Ask students: Who is the focus of this parable? What does he want? *Pahom is the main character, and he wants more land.*

◆ Critical Thinking

❷ **Interpret** Ask students: Who is the "Evil One" and why would the Evil One "sow discord" among the peasants? *Students might say that the Evil One is the Devil himself, or another peasant struck by the devil (perhaps Pahom himself), and that the Evil One would want to divide the peasants and plant the seed for future problems over the land.*

◆ Critical Thinking

❸ **Draw Conclusions** How can you tell that Pahom's first land purchase is a sacrifice for him? *He has to be frugal, sell things, borrow, and use up his savings to make the down payment.*

◆ Reading Strategy

❹ **Predict Based on Character Traits** Students should have observed that Pahom is ambitious and prone toward discontent; they should predict Pahom will not be happy now.

Customize for *Logical/Mathematical Learners*

❺ Encourage these students to relate Pahom's loan to modern day mortgages or bank loans. Lead them to recognize that he pays off his loan in half the time agreed. Ask students what this tells them about Pahom's ambition. *Pahom's paying off the loan so quickly indicates that he is focused on material wealth, and that his goal is to move forward, not to stay in his current position.*

❶ enough; and by means of the land I'll get you into my power."

2

Close to the village there lived a lady, a small landowner who had an estate of about three hundred acres. She had always lived on good terms with the peasants until she engaged as her manager an old soldier, who took to burdening the people with fines. However careful Pahom tried to be, it happened again and again that now a horse of his got among the lady's oats, now a cow strayed into her garden, now his calves found their way into her meadows—and he always had to pay a fine.

Pahom paid up, but grumbled, and, going home in a temper, was rough with his family. All through that summer Pahom had much trouble because of this manager, and he was actually glad when winter came and the cattle had to be stabled. Though he grudged the fodder when they could no longer graze on the pasture land, at least he was free from anxiety about them.

In the winter the news got about that the lady was going to sell her land and that the keeper of the inn on the high road was bargaining for it. When the peasants heard this they were very much alarmed.

"Well," thought they, "if the innkeeper gets the land, he'll worry us with fines worse than the lady's manager. We all depend on that estate."

So the peasants went on behalf of their village council and asked the lady not to sell the land to the innkeeper, offering her a better price for it themselves. The lady agreed to let them have it. Then the peasants tried to arrange for the village council to buy the whole estate, so that it might be held by them all in common. They met twice to dis- ❷
cuss it, but could not settle the matter; the Evil One sowed discord among them and they could not agree. So they decided to buy the land individually, each according to his means; and the lady agreed to this plan as she had to the other. ❷

Presently Pahom heard that a neighbor of his was buying fifty acres, and that the lady had consented to accept one half in cash and to wait a year for the other half. Pahom felt envious.

"Look at that," thought he, "the land is all being sold, and I'll get none of it." So he spoke to his wife.

"Other people are buying," said he, "and we must also buy twenty acres or so. Life is becoming impossible. That manager is simply crushing us with his fines."

So they put their heads together and considered how they could manage to buy it. They had one hundred rubles[3] laid by. They sold a colt and one half of their bees, hired out one of their sons as a farmhand and took his wages in advance, borrowed the rest from a brother-in-law, and so scraped together half the purchase money. ❸

> **◆ Reading Strategy**
> Based on what you know about Pahom's character, predict whether he will be happy now. ❹

Having done this, Pahom chose a farm of forty acres, some of it wooded, and went to the lady to bargain for it. They came to an agreement, and he shook hands with her upon it and paid her a deposit in advance. Then they went to town and signed the deeds, he paying half the price down, and undertaking to pay the remainder within two years. ❺

So now Pahom had land of his own. He borrowed seed and sowed it on the land he had bought. The harvest was a

3. **rubles** (ro͞o′ bəlz) *n.*: Russian money.

Cultural Connection

Councilperson The village council before which the peasants appear in this story is much like village, town, and city councils today. In the United States, councilmen and councilwomen are elected officials. Although being a councilperson can be a full-time position in smaller municipalities, they usually hold other jobs as well.

Suggest that students learn who their city or town council members are. Encourage students to contact the office of one or more of the council members, and if possible, interview someone there about how to become a member of the council, what the council does, and recent decisions of the council.

good one, and within a year he had man-
5 aged to pay off his debts both to the lady and to his brother-in-law. So he became a landowner, plowing and sowing his own land, making hay on his own land, cutting his own trees, and feeding his cattle on his own pasture. When he went out to plow his fields, or to look at his growing corn, or at his grass meadows, his heart would fill with joy. The grass that grew and the flowers that bloomed there seemed to him unlike any that grew elsewhere. Formerly, when he had passed by that land, it had appeared the same as
6 any other land, but now it seemed quite different.

3

So Pahom was well contented, and everything would have been right if the neighboring peasants would only not have trespassed on his wheatfields and meadows. He appealed to them most civilly, but they still went on: now the herdsmen would let the village cows stray into his meadows, then horses from the night pasture would get among his corn. Pahom turned them out again and again, and forgave their owners, and for a long time he forbore to prosecute anyone. But at last he lost patience and complained to the District Court. He knew it was the peasants' want of land, and no evil intent on their part, that caused the trouble, but he thought:

"I can't go on overlooking it, or they'll destroy all I have. They must be taught a lesson."

So he had them up, gave them one les-
7 son, and then another, and two or three of the peasants were fined. After a time Pahom's neighbors began to bear him a grudge for this, and would now and then let their cattle onto his land on purpose. One peasant even got into Pahom's wood at night and cut down five young lime trees for their bark. Pahom, passing through the wood one day, noticed something white. He came nearer and saw the stripped trunks lying on the ground, and close by stood the stumps where the trees had been. Pahom was furious.

"If he'd only cut one here and there it would have been bad enough," thought Pahom, "but the rascal has actually cut down a whole clump. If I could only find out who did this, I'd get even with him."

He racked his brains as to who it could be. Finally he decided: "It must be Simon—no one else could have done it." So he went to Simon's homestead to have a look around, but he found nothing and only had an angry scene. However, he now felt more certain than ever that Simon had done it, and he lodged a complaint. Simon was summoned. The case 8
was tried, and retried, and at the end of it all Simon was acquitted, there being no evidence against him. Pahom felt still more aggrieved, and let his anger loose upon the Elders and the Judges.

"You let thieves grease your palms," said he. "If you were honest folk yourselves you wouldn't let a thief go free."

So Pahom quarreled with the judges and with his neighbors. Threats to burn his hut began to be uttered. So though Pahom had more land, his place in the community was much worse than before.

About this time a rumor got about that many people were moving to new parts.

> **◆ Literary Focus**
> How do Pahom's experiences begin to teach a lesson about greed? 9

"There's no need for me to leave my land," thought Pahom. "But some of the others may leave our village and then

◆ Build Vocabulary

forbore (fôr bôr′) *v.*: Refrained from

aggrieved (ə grēvd′) *v.*: Wronged

◆ Critical Thinking

6 Infer Why does Pahom see this familiar land differently now? *The land is now Pahom's property, so he looks at it differently. Students may say he thinks it looks more beautiful, bigger, more important, and so on. Some might infer that Pahom is beginning to identify himself with his property.*

◆ Build Grammar Skills

7 Possessive Nouns Ask students to identify three uses of possessive nouns in this passage. Then ask: Which of the possessive nouns is plural? *The possessive nouns are peasants' and Pahom's (used twice). Peasants' is plural; therefore, the apostrophe follows the s.*

◆ Critical Thinking

8 Compare and Contrast Ask students how Pahom's thoughts and actions have changed now that he is a landowner. How did Pahom feel when he himself was accused of trespassing and fined? *Before Pahom became a landowner, his sympathies were with the peasants. When he was fined, he was angry and went home in a temper. Now he takes measures to accuse and fine a peasant for trespassing.*

◆ Literary Focus

9 Parable At this point in the parable Pahom alienates himself from his community. The parable is showing us that greed can cause people to sacrifice their humanity or community feeling.

Read to Interpret

Tolstoy's purpose in writing this parable is to teach a moral lesson. Encourage students to look for clues in Pahom's actions that show how he is changing from his initial happiness at owning land to feeling possessive about his property. Ask students to consider whether Pahom's growing greed is inevitable, as the parable indicates, or if he could realize his mistake before it's too late.

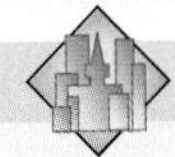

Beyond the Classroom

Community Connection

Mortgages Pahom buys his 40-acre farm by scraping together half the purchase price and agreeing to pay the remainder within 2 years. Today, most home buyers apply to a local bank for a *mortgage*. The buyer pays a certain amount of the total asking price upfront—for example, 10 or 15 percent, and the bank lends the buyer the money for the rest of the payment—to be repaid to the bank with interest over a period of years (longer than Pahom's 2-year period.

Have students inquire at local banks or lending agencies about current interest rates for loans to purchase real estate. Have them find out the total cost of a specified mortgage—say, $50,000 or $100,000—over several time periods, including 25, 30, and 40 years. Students may be interested in finding out how amortization rates are calculated, discovering the incremental benefits of repaying a loan in a shorter period of time. They may find a graphic representation useful to compare the various lengths of repayment time.

◆ Build Vocabulary

1 Words in Context: Technical and Multiple-Meaning Words Point out the word *sheaf,* which means "a bundle of cut stalks of grain." Explain that the word may be used to refer to a variety of items that are bundled together. Ask: What would a *sheaf* of paper look like? *It would be a stack of paper bound together.*

◆ *Literature and Your Life*

2 Students may reveal that they get angry or upset. Or they may take a more philosophical attitude and reason that they will not miss out on the next good thing.

◆ Critical Thinking

3 Evaluate The use of communal land is typical of many agrarian societies. Usually, a section of land was set aside on which everyone in a village might graze cattle or plant a garden. Ask students to briefly evaluate the pros and cons of such a system. *Some students might say the system is a good one because it is equitable, allows everyone to be productive, and fosters self-esteem; others might argue the system is rigid and does not allow people to get ahead on their own or to be independent.*

4 Clarification The phrase *stood treat to the Elders* involves a rare connotation for *treat*—"negotiation." This meaning for the word *treat* is related to the word *treaty.* Ask: What did Pahom do when he "stood treat"? *He negotiated with the chiefs of the village.*

Extending Word Study

Word Origins Invite students to look up the origins of *sheaf, arable,* and *fallow* in the dictionary. Have them predict whether these agricultural words all come from the same language.

there'd be more room for us. I'd take over their land myself and make my estates somewhat bigger. I could then live more at ease. As it is, I'm still too cramped to be comfortable."

One day Pahom was sitting at home when a peasant, passing through the village, happened to drop in. He was allowed to stay the night, and supper was given him. Pahom had a talk with this peasant and asked him where he came from. The stranger answered that he came from beyond the Volga,[4] where he had been working. One word led to another, and the man went on to say that many people were settling in those parts. He told how some people from his village had settled there. They had joined the community there and had had twenty-five acres per man granted them. The land was so good, he said, that the rye
1 sown on it grew as high as a horse, and so thick that five cuts of a sickle made a sheaf. One peasant, he said, had brought nothing with him but his bare hands, and now he had six horses and two cows of his own.

2 ◆ *Literature and Your Life*

How do you react when you feel you're missing out on a good thing?

Pahom's heart kindled with desire.

"Why should I suffer in this narrow hole, if one can live so well elsewhere?" he thought. "I'll sell my land and my homestead here, and with the money I'll start afresh over there and get everything new. In this crowded place one is always having trouble. But I must first go and find out all about it myself."

Toward summer he got ready and started out. He went down the Volga on a steamer to Samara,[5] then walked another three hundred miles on foot, and at last reached the place. It was just as the stranger had said. The peasants had plenty of land: every man had twenty-five acres of communal land
given him for his use, and anyone who 3
had money could buy, besides, at a ruble and a half an acre, as much good freehold land[6] as he wanted.

Having found out all he wished to know, Pahom returned home as autumn came on, and began selling off his belongings. He sold his land at a profit, sold his homestead and all his cattle, and withdrew from membership in the village. He only waited till the spring, and then started with his family for the new settlement.

4

As soon as Pahom and his family reached their new abode, he applied for admission into the council of a large village. He stood treat to the Elders and obtained the necessary documents. Five
shares of communal land were given him 4
for his own and his sons' use: that is to say—125 acres (not all together, but in different fields) besides the use of the communal pasture. Pahom put up the buildings he needed and bought cattle. Of the communal land alone he had three times as much as at his former home, and the land was good wheat land. He was ten times better off than he had been. He had plenty of arable land and pasturage, and could keep as many head of cattle as he liked.

At first, in the bustle of building and settling down, Pahom was pleased with it all, but when he got used to it he began to think that even here he hadn't enough land. The first year he sowed wheat on his share of the communal land and had

4. **Volga** (väl′ gə): The major river in western Russia.
5. **Samara** (Sə ma′ rə): City in eastern Russia.

6. **freehold land:** Privately owned land that the owner can lease to others for a fee.

Cross-Curricular Connection: Science

Crop Rotation The practices of rotating crops and of sowing wheat for one or two years and then allowing the field to lie fallow until it is covered with grass have a scientific justification. Certain crops, such as wheat and corn, leach nutrients from soil. Other crops, such as alfalfa or soybeans, can reconstitute the soil, making it ready for planting grain again. By rotating crops from year to year, farmers can increase the productivity of their cropland. Sometimes farmers let the land "rest," so they do not plant it, and let it just lie fallow.

Students might like to speculate on how greed might make a farmer sacrifice productivity over time. If a farmer were shortsighted and planted grain year after year in hopes of making the best profit, eventually the grain crop would fail because the soil would be barren.

Cornfield at Ewell, c. 1846 (detail), William Holman Hunt, Tate Gallery, London

a good crop. He wanted to go on sowing wheat, but had not enough communal land for the purpose, and what he had already used was not available, for in those parts wheat is sown only on virgin soil or on fallow land. It is sown for one
5 or two years, and then the land lies fallow till it is again overgrown with steppe grass. There were many who wanted such land, and there was not enough for all, so that people quarreled about it. Those who were better off wanted it for

▲ **Critical Viewing** What might be going through the mind of the person tending to this land? **[Speculate]** 6

growing wheat, and those who were poor
wanted it to let to dealers, so that they 5
might raise money to pay their taxes. Pahom wanted to sow more wheat, so he rented land from a dealer for a year. He sowed much wheat and had a fine crop, but the land was too far from the village—the wheat had to be carted more
than ten miles. After a time Pahom 7
noticed that some peasant dealers were 8
living on separate farms and were growing wealthy, and he thought:

"If I were to buy some freehold land and have a homestead on it, it would be a different thing altogether. Then it

◆ Build Vocabulary

sheaf (shēf) *n.*: Bundle of grain

arable (ar′ ə bəl) *adj.*: Suitable for growing crops

fallow (fal′ ō) *adj.*: Plowed, but not planted

Customize for *English Language Learners*

5 Use simpler language to explain this passage. Words like *sowing* (planting) *virgin* (unplanted) and *let* (rent) may cause confusion because English language learners may not have encountered these words in the context in which they are used here.

▶Critical Viewing◀

6 **Speculate** Students' answers may include the following: *He may be overwhelmed by the work he has to do, or he may feel pride in the success of the crop he has produced.*

◆ Literary Focus

7 **Parable** Ask students to relate the story so far to this proverb: "The grass is always greener on the other side of the fence." *Even when he has a lot of land and a fine crop, Pahom is not satisfied. Here, his problem is that the wheat is too far from town. He thinks there's a better way to do his farming.*

Customize for *Less Proficient Readers*

8 These readers may have difficulty distinguishing between the land Pahom now holds and freehold land. However, they should be able to identify the main idea of this passage: Once again, Pahom thinks others are doing better than he is and thinks he needs more land.

Humanities: Art

Cornfield at Ewell (detail), c. 1846, by William Holman Hunt.

This landscape depicts a large field of grain similar to those Pahom would have cultivated in Russia. The artist, William Holman Hunt, was a member of the Pre-Raphaelite Brotherhood in England, a group of artists and poets who held to Renaissance standards and ideals in art. They strove to portray nature in a way that demonstrated both its detail and its simplicity. Use these questions for discussion:

1. What quality does this field have that might appeal to Pahom? *Students might mention its vastness or its potential productivity.*
2. Do you think this is an appropriate illustration for this story? Explain. *Students may say that its content—a lone man in vast expanse of land—suits the story well.*

◆ Reading Strategy

❶ **Predict Based on Character Traits** Students may say that Pahom is never satisfied and that he is stubborn—traits that will clearly lead him to a fall.

Customize for *Less Proficient Readers*

❷ Length and unusual idioms may make this sentence particularly difficult to comprehend. Ask a volunteer to paraphrase it. *In the third year, Pahom and a dealer rented some land from some peasants. They had already plowed it up, but the peasants argued with them and took them to court, so all their work was wasted.*

◆ Build Grammar Skills

❸ **Possessive Nouns** Students may not realize that phrases such as *one hundred rubles' worth* are possessive. Point out that the phrase could also be expressed as "the worth of one hundred rubles." Then have volunteers write the following phrases on the board, punctuating them correctly: *ten dollars' worth, a lifetime's worth, seven weeks' worth.*

◆ Literary Focus

❹ **Parable** As Pahom's actions indicate, one of the lessons this story teaches is that the more people have, the more they want. Ask students to agree or disagree with this view. *Some students may agree, and cite examples. Others may disagree, not having a basis for seeing the statement as true.*

❺ **Enrichment** The Bashkirs live "far away" from Pahom's present home, but their land is still in Europe, not Asia. Pahom is moving eastward (somewhat like America's westward-moving pioneers) in search of cheaper and more abundant land.

would all be fine and close together."

The question of buying freehold land recurred to him again and again.

He went on in the same way for three years, renting land and sowing wheat. The seasons turned out well and the crops were good, so that he began to lay by money. He might have gone on living contentedly, but he grew tired of having to rent other people's land every year and having to scramble for it. Wherever there was good land to be had, the peasants would rush for it and it was taken up at once, so that unless you were sharp about it, you got none. It happened in the third year that he and a dealer together rented a piece of pasture land from some peasants, and they had already plowed it up, when there was some dispute and the peasants went to law about it, and things fell out so that the labor was all lost.

> ◆ Reading Strategy
> What can you predict about Pahom's future decisions?

"If it were my own land," thought Pahom, "I should be independent, and there wouldn't be all this unpleasantness."

So Pahom began looking out for land which he could buy, and he came across a peasant who had bought thirteen hundred acres, but having got into difficulties was willing to sell again cheap. Pahom bargained and haggled with him, and at last they settled the price at fifteen hundred rubles, part in cash and part to be paid later. They had all but clinched the matter when a passing dealer happened to stop at Pahom's one day to get feed for his horses. He drank tea with Pahom, and they had a talk. The dealer said that he was just returning from the land of the Bashkirs,[7] far away, where he had bought thirteen thousand acres of land, all for a thousand rubles. Pahom questioned him further, and the dealer said:

"All one has to do is to make friends with the chiefs. I gave away about one hundred rubles' worth of silk robes and carpets, besides a case of tea, and I gave wine to those who would drink it; and I got the land for less than three kopecks[8] an acre." And he showed Pahom the title deed, saying:

"The land lies near a river, and the whole steppe is virgin soil."

Pahom plied him with questions, and the dealer said:

"There's more land there than you could cover if you walked a year, and it all belongs to the Bashkirs. They're as simple as sheep, and land can be got almost for nothing."

"There, now," thought Pahom, "with my one thousand rubles, why should I get only thirteen hundred acres, and saddle myself with a debt besides? If I take it out there, I can get more than ten times as much for my money."

5

Pahom inquired how to get to the place, and as soon as the grain dealer had left him, he prepared to go there himself. He left his wife to look after the homestead, and started on his journey, taking his hired man with him. They stopped at a town on their way and bought a case of tea, some wine, and other presents, as the grain dealer had advised.

On and on they went until they had gone more than three hundred miles, and on the seventh day they came to a place where the Bashkirs had pitched their round tents. It was all just as the dealer had said. The people lived on the

7. **Bashkirs** (bash kirz′): Nomadic people who live in the plains of southwestern Russia.

8. **kopecks** (kō′ peks) *n.*: Russian money, equal to one hundredth of a ruble.

Research Skills Mini-Lesson

Questionnaire

This mini-lesson supports the Questions for Research activity in the Guide for Responding on p. 143.

Introduce Discuss with students that a questionnaire is a list a questions designed to elicit responses from a group of people to determine their ideas about a particular issue. The responses can be analyzed to draw conclusions on a given subject. Have students bring in questionnaires from magazines or direct mail campaigns to use as models for their questionnaire on happiness.

Develop Ask students to consider what they want to learn about people's views on happiness. What questions will elicit this information from the people that they question? How should they phrase the questions—should the responses be yes/no, multiple choice, or short answer.

Apply Have students work together to write questionnaires to find out people's responses to the subject of happiness. Encourage students to interview other students throughout the school, or another population's response they are curious about, such as teachers or those at home. Then have students present their findings to the class.

Assess Students' questionnaires should contain questions that can be answered in a reasonable fashion. Their reports should describe the findings in a clear manner.

The Hay Harvest, Boris Kustodiev, St. Petersburg, Russia

6 ▲ Critical Viewing Based on this painting, what do you learn about the responsibility of owning a lot of land? **[Interpret]**

steppe,[9] by a river, in felt-covered tents. They neither tilled the ground nor ate bread. Their cattle and horses grazed in herds on the steppe. The colts were tethered behind the tents, and the mares were driven to them twice a day. The mares were milked, and from the milk kumiss[10] was made. It was the women who prepared the kumiss, and they also
7 made cheese. As far as the men were concerned, drinking kumiss and tea, eating mutton, and playing on their pipes was all they cared about. They were all stout and merry, and all the summer long they never thought of doing any work. They were quite ignorant, and knew no Russian, but were good-natured enough. 7

As soon as they saw Pahom, they came out of their tents and gathered around the visitor. An interpreter was found, and Pahom told them he had come about some land. The Bashkirs seemed very glad; they took Pahom and led him into one of the best tents, where they made him sit on some down cushions placed on a carpet, while they sat around him. They gave him some tea 8 9

9. steppe (step) *n.*: High grassland of central Asia.
10. kumiss (ko͞o´ mis) *n.*: Mare's milk that has been fermented and is used as a drink.

▶Critical Viewing◀

6 Interpret *Students may say that owning a lot of land involves the responsibility and work of maintaining it and keeping it productive. To do so, an owner may need to employ other people.*

◆Critical Thinking

7 Infer Let students know the Bashkirs are nomads, people traveling from place to place in search of food, water, and grazing land. Based on this passage, ask students what might be Pahom's opinion about the Bashkir men. *Students will probably say that because Pahom places such value on land ownership he does not respect the men.*

8 Clarification Tell students that Pahom needs an interpreter because the Bashkirs, who are a Muslim people, speak a Turkic language.

◆Critical Thinking

9 Infer Ask students what inferences they can make about Bashkir culture, based on details in this passage and in earlier passages. *The Bashkirs are probably a nomadic people, since they don't live in tents or place much importance on land ownership. They are probably a peaceful people, since they welcome Pahom without hostility. Based on their treatment of Pahom—bringing him to one of the best tents and giving him cushions and tea, they probably place great importance on hospitality, even to strangers.*

Customize for
Visual/Spatial Learners
These students might enjoy looking at a topographical map of Russia to get a sense of the vast distances Pahom covered in his quest for land. Ask them to find some of the points of reference in the story: the Volga, the Samara, and the plains or steppes of southwestern Russia.

Humanities: Art

The Hay Harvest by Boris Kustodiev.

Boris Kustodiev (1878–1933) is not well known today, but in his day he was famous for his brightly colored paintings of country and small-town life. Popular in the Soviet Union in the early twentieth century, Kustodiev's paintings celebrated Soviet ideals.

The Russian peasants harvesting hay in this painting are like those that Tolstoy might have seen in the countryside where he lived. Call students' attention to the color and tone of this painting, and then use these questions for discussion:

1. Does this painting have a joyous or a somber mood? Which specific part of the story would it best illustrate? *The line of the path and the river give the painting a feeling of lively, joyous motion. The women seem happy working the land together. The painting depicts what life could have been like for Pahom and the other peasants if they had bought land together.*
2. What does this painting tell you about the life of a peasant in Russia? *It indicates that life involved hard work but perhaps that community feeling was strong.*

Listening to Literature Audiocassettes The conversation between Pahom and the Bashkirs demonstrates Pahom's obsessive nature and is a good point at which to introduce the audiocassette recording of this selection. Play this section of the selection to the whole class and then have them read through to the end.

Comprehension Check

❶ Why might these nomads find Pahom's request amusing? *Nomads do not own land in the traditional sense; they simply use what they find and move on.*

❷ **Clarification** Make sure that students understand that a deed is a legal document that grants title for a piece of land to the deed holder. When Pahom says this will "make it secure," he means that it will protect him from other people's claims on the land.

❸ **Clarification** Tell students that in earlier times very few people in tribes such as the Bashkirs could write. They might have a single *scribe,* or person with writing skills, to take care of all their written tasks.

Reteach

To help students predict Pahom's actions based on his character traits, share this cause and effect chart. Have them fill in the effects to show what happens to Pahom each time he acquires more land.

Cause	Effect
The lady landowner near the village sells Pahom twenty acres.	He quarrels with his neighbors because they trespass on his land.
Pahom buys 125 acres in a new settlement beyond the Volga.	
Pahom tries to acquire land from the Bashkirs.	

and kumiss, and had a sheep killed, and gave him mutton to eat. Pahom took presents out of his cart and distributed them among the Bashkirs, and divided the tea amongst them. The Bashkirs were delighted. They talked a great deal among themselves and then told the interpreter what to say.

"They wish to tell you," said the interpreter, "that they like you and that it's our custom to do all we can to please a guest and to repay him for his gifts. You have given us presents, now tell us which of the things we possess please you best, that we may present them to you."

"What pleases me best here," answered Pahom, "is your land. Our land is crowded and the soil is worn out, but you have plenty of land, and it is good land. I never saw the likes of it."

❶ The interpreter told the Bashkirs what Pahom had said. They talked among themselves for a while. Pahom could not understand what they were saying, but saw that they were much amused and heard them shout and laugh. Then they were silent and looked at Pahom while the interpreter said:

"They wish me to tell you that in return for your presents they will gladly give you as much land as you want. You have only to point it out with your hand and it is yours."

The Bashkirs talked again for a while and began to dispute. Pahom asked what they were disputing about, and the interpreter told him that some of them thought they ought to ask their chief about the land and not act in his absence, while others thought there was no need to wait for his return.

6

While the Bashkirs were disputing, a man in a large fox-fur cap appeared on the scene. They all became silent and rose to their feet. The interpreter said: "This is our chief himself."

Pahom immediately fetched the best dressing gown and five pounds of tea, and offered these to the chief. The chief accepted them and seated himself in the place of honor. The Bashkirs at once began telling him something. The chief listened for a while, then made a sign with his head for them to be silent, and addressing himself to Pahom, said in Russian:

"Well, so be it. Choose whatever piece of land you like; we have plenty of it."

"How can I take as much as I like?" thought Pahom. "I must get a deed to make it secure, or else they may say: 'It is yours,' and afterward may take it away again."

"Thank you for your kind words," he said aloud. "You have much land, and I only want a little. But I should like to be sure which portion is mine. Could it not be measured and made over to me? Life and death are in God's hands. You good people give it to me, but your children might wish to take it back again." ❷

"You are quite right," said the chief. "We will make it over to you."

"I heard that a dealer had been here," continued Pahom, "and that you gave him a little land, too, and signed title deeds to that effect. I should like to have it done in the same way."

The chief understood.

"Yes," replied, he, "that can be done quite easily. We have a scribe, and we will go to town with you and have the deed properly sealed." ❸

"And what will be the price?" asked Pahom.

"Our price is always the same: one thousand rubles a day."

Pahom did not understand.

"A day? What measure is that? How many acres would that be?"

Beyond the Classroom

Career Connection

Interpreting ESL Students may not have considered that their bilingual skills may be useful in the workplace. Point out the role of the interpreter in this story—he listens to both sides and translates what the people are saying and is equally fluent in Russian and the language of the Bashkirs.

Have students identify skills that a good interpreter should have, such as facility with languages, tact, good listening skills, good speaking skills, and so on.

Then have students work in pairs to decide what kinds of businesses or services might use interpreters and for what reasons. Are there any local businesses or individuals who might hire a student as an interpreter? What special kind of training or specific preparation might be required for interpreting? Ask them to formulate their ideas as lists to present to the class. Write new ideas on the board as they are mentioned. Point out the variety of places where bilingual students might use their skills as interpreters.

"We do not know how to reckon it out," said the chief. "We sell it by the day. As much as you can go around on your feet in a day is yours, and the price is one thousand rubles a day."

Pahom was surprised.

4 "But in a day you can get around a large tract of land," he said.

The chief laughed.

"It will all be yours!" said he. "But there is one condition: If you don't return on the same day to the spot whence you started, your money is lost."

"But how am I to mark the way that I have gone?"

"Why, we shall go to any spot you like and stay there. You must start from that spot and make your round, taking a spade with you. Wherever you think necessary, make a mark. At every turning, dig a hole and pile up the turf; then
5 afterward we will go around with a plow from hole to hole. You may make as large a circuit as you please, but before the sun sets you must return to the place you started from. All the land you cover will be yours."

Pahom was delighted. It was decided to start early next morning. They talked a while, and after drinking some more kumiss and eating some more mutton, they had tea again, and then the night came on. They gave Pahom a featherbed to sleep on, and the Bashkirs dispersed for the night, promising to assemble the next morning at daybreak and ride out before sunrise to the appointed spot.

7

Pahom lay on the featherbed, but could not sleep. He kept thinking about the land.

"What a large tract I'll mark off!" thought he, "I can easily do thirty-five
6 miles in a day. The days are long now, and within a circuit of thirty-five miles what a lot of land there will be! I'll sell the poorer land or let it to peasants, but I'll pick out the best and farm it myself. I'll buy two ox teams and hire two more laborers. About a hundred and fifty acres shall be plowland, and I'll pasture cattle on the rest."

Pahom lay awake all night and dozed off only just before dawn. Hardly were his eyes closed when he had a dream. He thought he was lying in that same tent and heard somebody chuckling outside. He wondered who it could be, and rose and went out, and he saw the Bashkir chief sitting in front of the tent holding his sides and rolling about with laughter. Going nearer to the chief, Pahom asked: "What are you laughing at?" But he saw that it was no longer the chief but the grain dealer who had recently stopped at his house and had told him about the land. Just as Pahom was going to ask: "Have you been here long?" he saw that it was not the dealer, but the peasant who had come up from the Volga long ago, to Pahom's old home. Then he saw that it was not the peasant either, but the Devil himself with hoofs and horns, sitting there and chuckling, and before him lay a man, prostrate on the ground, barefooted, with only trousers and a shirt on. And Pahom dreamed that he looked more attentively to see what sort of man it was lying there, and he saw that the man was dead, and that it was himself. Horror-struck, he awoke.

> ◆ **Reading Strategy**
> How does this dream help you predict what will happen? 7

"What things one dreams about!" thought he.

Looking around he saw through the open door that the dawn was breaking.

"It's time to wake them up," thought he. "We ought to be starting."

He got up, roused his man (who was sleeping in his cart), bade him harness,

◆ Reading Strategy

4 Predict Based on Character Traits Have students recall Pahom's behavior thus far and predict how he will proceed as he measures his land according to the Bashkirs' rules. *He will probably be greedy and try to obtain as much as he can.*

◆ Build Vocabulary

5 Words in Context: Technical and Multiple-Meaning Words Have students use context clues to infer the meaning of the word *turf*. *Turf refers to a clump of sod or dirt.* Explain that *turf* may also be used casually to mean a piece of territory claimed by a person or group. Ask: How are these two meanings of *turf* related? *Both have to do with land.*

6 Enrichment Thirty-five miles is a very long distance to walk in one day. Tell students that if Pahom does walk that far—forming a square with 8.75 miles on each side—he will acquire 76.5 square miles of land, or 48,960 acres.

◆ Reading Strategy

7 Predict Based on Character Traits Elicit the following: *Pahom's dream foreshadows his death; the presence of the Devil seems to indicate that Pahom's greed will lead to his destruction.*

Customize for
Gifted/Talented Students
Invite students to choose scenes from the story to role play, such as the conversation between the two sisters, Pahom's quarrel with the Judges, or Pahom among the Bashkirs. Have students explain how the scene they choose reveals important character traits of the people involved.

Analyze Literary Criticism

The critic Edward Garnett, writing in 1903, claims that Tolstoy's greatness comes from his "hunger for spiritual truth," which leads him to "penetrate into the secret thought and emotion of men of all grades of society." Garnett goes on to say that Tolstoy never flinches from "his exploration of the dark world of man's . . . incessant self-deception."

Share Garnett's evaluation of Tolstoy with students. Discuss with them whether his statements apply to "How Much Land Does a Man Need?" Have students respond to the following questions:

1. How does Tolstoy's parable show his "hunger for spiritual truth"? *Students should explore Tolstoy's approach to man's desires and behaviors.*
2. How does Tolstoy "penetrate into the secret" thoughts and emotions of Pahom? *Possible response: Tolstoy details Pahom's desire for land.*
3. How does Tolstoy explore and reveal Pahom's "self-deception"? *Students may recognize how Pahom's desire and goal for land ultimately leads him to his downfall.*

▶Critical Viewing◀

❶ **Connect** Elicit the following: *The photograph shows a vast expanse of land that seems never to end. The endless quality reflects the theme of never having enough. There will always be more land to acquire.*

❷ **Analyze** Ask students what is revealed by the Bashkirs' ability to remain in the same spot for an entire day. Do they think that Pahom would be able to do this? Why or why not? *Suggested response: The Bashkirs are patient and don't seem overly concerned with material things. Pahom would probably not be able to do this. He is impatient and eager to do work that he sees as gainful.*

◆ Literature and Your Life

❸ Students might say that they feel excited and overwhelmed or that they can feel greed building up inside them. Some students may add that because they can have as much as they want, their desire decreases.

Customize for *English Language Learners*
A few idioms on this page may need clarification for English language learners. Have native English speakers assist their classmates by restating the following in their own words: *It's high time* and *Dawn was beginning to kindle*. The phrases mean *the time has come* and *the sky was turning the color of fire*.

Customize for *Less Proficient Readers*
Before they begin reading this page, tell students to note when Pahom turns the three corners to form the sides of his new property. This will help them keep track of his progress.

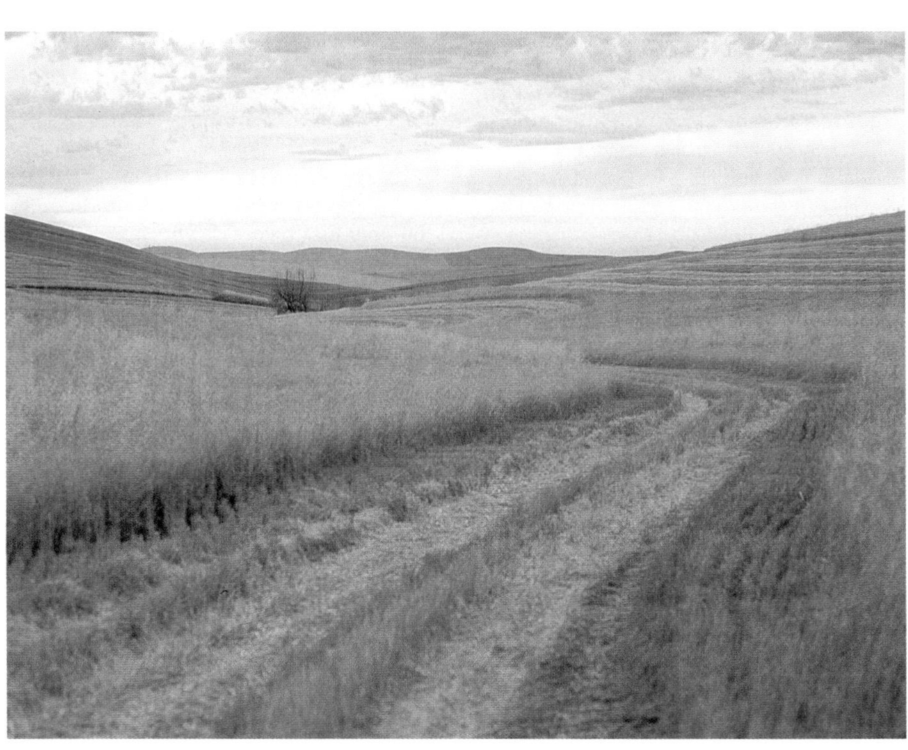

❶ ▲ Critical Viewing How does the setting in this picture relate to the theme of this parable? **[Connect]**

❷ and went to call the Bashkirs.

"It's time to go to the steppe to measure the land," he said.

The Bashkirs rose and assembled, and the chief came, too. Then they began drinking kumiss again, and offered Pahom some tea, but he would not wait.

"If we are to go, let's go. It's high time," said he.

8

The Bashkirs got ready and they all started; some mounted on horses and some in carts. Pahom drove in his own small cart with his servant and took a spade with him. When they reached the steppe, the red dawn was beginning to kindle. They ascended a hillock (called by the Bashkirs a shikhan) and, dismounting from their carts and their horses, gathered in one spot. The chief came up to Pahom and, stretching out his arm toward the plain:

"See," said he, "all this, as far as your eye can reach, is ours. You may have any part of it you like."

Pahom's eyes glistened: it was all virgin soil, as flat as the palm of your hand, as black as the seed of a poppy, and in the hollows different kinds of grasses grew breast-high.

◆ *Literature and Your Life*
How do you feel when someone offers you as much as you want of something? ❸

Humanities: Photography

Road in Field by D. Brookover.

This photograph of a road winding away in a field of grain illustrates the principle of *linear perspective*. To create the illusion of three-dimensionality, objects appear smaller as they recede into the distance, and lines that seem parallel actually converge at a vanishing point on the horizon. This vision of land as far as the eye can see would have tempted Pahom.

1. How do you think this scene would have made Pahom feel? *Students may say he would have become excited at the prospect of trying to buy this land, or they might say he would have felt envy because he did not own it.*
2. How would you react to owning such a vast tract of land? *Some students may think they would enjoy the feeling of ownership; others may think life would be lonely.*

The chief took off his fox-fur cap, placed it on the ground, and said:

"This will be the mark. Start from here, and return here again. All the land you go around shall be yours."

4 Pahom took out his money and put it on the cap. Then he took off his outer coat, remaining in his sleeveless undercoat. He unfastened his girdle and tied it tight below his stomach, put a little bag of bread into the breast of his coat, and, tying a flask of water to his girdle,[11] he drew up the tops of his boots, took the spade from his man, and stood ready to start. He considered for some moments which way he had better go—it was tempting everywhere.

"No matter," he concluded, "I'll go toward the rising sun."

He turned his face to the east, stretched himself, and waited for the sun to appear above the rim.

"I must lose no time," he thought, "and it's easier walking while it's still cool."

The sun's rays had hardly flashed above the horizon when Pahom, carrying the spade over his shoulder, went down into the steppe.

Pahom started walking neither slowly nor quickly. After having gone a thousand yards he stopped, dug a hole, and placed pieces of turf one on another to make it more visible. Then he went on; and now that he had walked off his stiffness he quickened his pace. After a while he dug another hole.

Pahom looked back. The hillock could be distinctly seen in the sunlight, with the people on it, and the glittering iron rims of the cartwheels. At a rough guess Pahom concluded that he had walked three miles. It was growing warmer; he took off his undercoat, slung it across his shoulder, and went on again. It had grown quite warm now; he looked at the sun—it was time to think of breakfast.

"The first shift is done, but there are four in a day, and it's too soon yet to turn. But I'll just take off my boots," said he to himself.

He sat down, took off his boots, stuck them into his girdle, and went on. It was easy walking now.

"I'll go on for another three miles," thought he, "and then turn to the left. This spot is so fine that it would be a pity to lose it. The further one goes, the better the land seems." 5

He went straight on for a while, and when he looked around, the hillock was scarcely visible and the people on it looked like black ants, and he could just see something glistening there in the sun.

"Ah," thought Pahom, "I have gone far enough in this direction; it's time to turn. Besides, I'm in a regular sweat, and very thirsty."

He stopped, dug a large hole, and heaped up pieces of turf. Next he untied his flask, had a drink, and then turned sharply to the left. He went on and on; the grass was high, and it was very hot. 6

Pahom began to grow tired: he looked at the sun and saw that it was noon.

"Well," he thought, "I must have a rest."

He sat down, and ate some bread and drank some water; but he did not lie down, thinking that if he did he might fall asleep. After sitting a little while, he went on again. At first he walked easily; the food had strengthened him; but it had become terribly hot and he felt sleepy. Still he went on, thinking: "An hour to suffer, a lifetime to live." 7

He went a long way in this direction also, and was about to turn to the left again, when he perceived a damp hollow:

11. **girdle** (gurd´ əl) *n.*: Belt or sash.

◆ Critical Thinking

4 Infer Ask students how they think Pahom is feeling at this point in the story. How can they tell? *Pahom is feeling optimistic. He is ready to go, and starts out in the direction of the rising sun—a symbol for hope. They might also say he is feeling greedy, "it was tempting everywhere."*

◆ Literary Focus

5 Connect Have students contemplate how this passage relates to the message that Tolstoy is trying to convey. *The passage conveys Pahom's inability to restrain his greed.*

Comprehension Check ☑

6 To make sure students understand that Pahom is following the instructions he was given by the chief, ask them why Pahom digs a hole and heaps up pieces of turf. *That is how the chief told him to mark his turnings.*

◆ Critical Thinking

7 Infer Have students discuss how Pahom's observation might foreshadow the outcome of the story. *Suggested response: The comment "a lifetime to live" is an ironic foreshadowing because Pahom is not going to live to enjoy the land.*

Viewing and Representing Mini-Lesson

This mini-lesson supports the Map of Russia Project in the Idea Bank on p. 145.

Introduce Have students read the Beyond Literature History Connection on p. 143 to learn about the history of Russia and the Soviet Union. As a result of historical events, the borders of Russia appear differently on maps that were created and printed after 1991.

Develop Pahom moves east across the southern part of Russia, from the European side to the Asian side of the country. Students may want to identify the story's places and areas, such as the Volga River, Samara, and the steppes.

Apply As students create their maps, they may choose to combine physical and political elements, showing cities as well as mountains and rivers, for example. This will allow for a visual representation that shows both the people and geography of Russia.

Assess Students may be evaluated on their research efforts, the accuracy of their maps, and their appropriate use of visual elements.

◆ Reading Strategy

❶ **Predict Based on Character Traits** Students will probably predict that, based on his character and past actions in this parable, Pahom will try to include more land.

◆ Literary Focus

❷ **Parable** Pahom now sees the error of his ways, but he is still unable to stop. Ask: Has Pahom learned a lesson from this experience? How do you know? *Students will probably say that Pahom has not learned a lesson. Although he now recognizes that his greed has made him foolish and hasty, he is not yet willing to make the necessary sacrifices to save himself. He is trying to beat the odds to make it back on time to claim his land.*

◆ Critical Thinking

❸ **Infer** Have students discuss what the Bashkirs would be likely to think of Pahom's actions. *Suggested response: They probably think he's very foolish. Most likely they don't understand why owning this land is so important to him.*

Customize for
Pre-AP Students
Have students consider why the author causes his main character to suffer the way he does. *This is a moralistic parable, and the author wants to underscore Pahom's fall in grasping for more than he needs.*

❶ ◆ **Reading Strategy** Based on Pahom's character, predict whether he will try to include any more land.

"It would be a pity to leave that out," he thought. "Flax would do well there." So he went on past the hollow and dug a hole on the other side of it before he made a sharp turn. Pahom looked toward the hillock. The heat made the air hazy: it seemed to be quivering, and through the haze the people on the hillock could scarcely be seen.

"Ah," thought Pahom, "I have made the sides too long; I must make this one shorter." And he went along the third side, stepping faster. He looked at the sun: it was nearly halfway to the horizon, and he had not yet done two miles of the third side of the square. He was still ten miles from the goal.

"No," he thought, "though it will make my land lopsided, I must hurry back in a straight line now. I might go too far, and as it is I have a great deal of land."

So Pahom hurriedly dug a hole and turned straight toward the hillock.

9

Pahom went straight toward the hillock, but he now walked with difficulty. He was exhausted from the heat, his bare feet were cut and bruised, and his legs began to fail. He longed to rest, but it was impossible if he meant to get back before sunset. The sun waits for no man, and it was sinking lower and lower.

"Oh, Lord," he thought, "if only I have not blundered trying for too much! What if I am too late?"

He looked toward the hillock and at the sun. He was still far from his goal, and the sun was already near the rim of the sky.

Pahom walked on and on; it was very hard walking, but he went quicker and quicker. He pressed on, but was still far from the place. He began running, threw away his coat, his boots, his flask, and his cap, and kept only the spade which he used as a support.

"What am I to do?" he thought again. "I've grasped too much and ruined the whole affair. I can't get there before the sun sets."

And this fear made him still more breathless. Pahom kept on running; his trousers stuck to him, and his mouth was parched. His breast was working like a blacksmith's bellows, his heart was beating like a hammer, and his legs were giving way as if they did not belong to him. Pahom was seized with terror lest he should die of the strain. ❷

Though afraid of death, he could not stop.

"After having run all that way they will call me a fool if I stop now," thought he.

And he ran on and on, and drew near and heard the Bashkirs yelling and shouting to him, and their cries inflamed his heart still more. He gathered his last strength and ran on. ❸

The sun was close to the rim of the sky and, cloaked in mist, looked large, and red as blood. Now, yes, now, it was about to set! The sun was quite low, but he was also quite near his goal. Pahom could already see the people on the hillock waving their arms to make him hurry. He could see the fox-fur cap on the ground and the money in it, and the chief sitting on the ground holding his sides. And Pahom remembered his dream.

"There's plenty of land," thought he, "but will God let me live on it? I have lost my life, I have lost my life! Never will I reach that spot!"

Pahom looked at the sun, which had reached the earth: one side of it had already disappeared. With all his remaining strength he rushed on, bending his body forward so that his legs could hardly follow fast enough to keep

Speaking, Listening, and Viewing Mini-Lesson

Eulogy
This mini-lesson supports the Speaking, Listening, and Viewing activity in the Idea Bank on p. 145.

Introduce Explain that a eulogy is a tribute that is often read aloud or spoken at a funeral by someone who knew the deceased well.

Develop Remind students that a eulogy positively celebrates the life of the deceased. Encourage students to:

- work in pairs to brainstorm for positive things to say about Pahom.
- point out that Pahom's example provided a lesson from which others can learn.
- recall an incident that particularly illustrates an aspect of Pahom's personality.

Apply Have students work individually to write eulogies for Pahom. Suggest that, with partners, they practice delivering their eulogies before presenting them to the class.

Assess Evaluate students' eulogies based on content and delivery. Did the eulogy include examples that illustrated Pahom's personality? Was it delivered in language and tone appropriate to the occasion? Alternatively, have students use the Peer Assessment: Speaker/Speech form, p. 121, in ***Alternative Assessment*** to guide them as they listen to and evaluate one another's speeches.

him from falling. Just as he reached the hillock it suddenly grew dark. He looked up—the sun had already set!

He gave a cry: "All my labor has been in vain," thought he, and was about to stop, but he heard the Bashkirs still shouting and remembered that though to him, from below, the sun seemed to have set, they on the hillock could still see it. He took a long breath and ran up the hillock. It was still light there. He reached the top and saw the cap. Before it sat the chief, laughing and holding his sides. Again Pahom remembered his dream, and he uttered a cry: his legs gave way beneath him, he fell forward and reached the cap with his hands.

"Ah, that's a fine fellow!" exclaimed the chief. "He has gained much land!"

Pahom's servant came running up and tried to raise him, but he saw that blood was flowing from his mouth. Pahom was dead.

◆ Literary Focus What lesson do you learn from Pahom's experiences? 4

The Bashkirs clicked their tongues to show their pity.

His servant picked up the spade and dug a grave long enough for Pahom to lie in, and buried him in it.

Six feet from his head to his toes was all he needed. 5

Guide for Responding

◆ Literature and Your Life

Reader's Response Do you sympathize with Pahom? Why or why not?

Thematic Focus Ultimately, Pahom pays for "success" with his life. What price are you willing to pay for success?

Questions for Research Like Pahom, many people find themselves always wanting something *more* to make them happy. With a group of classmates, write a questionnaire that could be used to interview people about happiness.

☑ Check Your Comprehension

1. What does Pahom believe is the only trouble that peasants face?
2. How does Pahom come to buy his first parcel of land?
3. List three problems Pahom experiences as he increases his land holdings.
4. How do the Bashkirs determine how much land a man can own?
5. Briefly summarize what happens on the last day of Pahom's life.

Beyond Literature

History Connection

Russia in the Twentieth Century In 1922, Russia became part of the newly established Union of Soviet Socialist Republics (USSR), better known as the Soviet Union. The Soviet Union initially consisted of four republics, with the Russian Republic being the strongest and most influential one. The Soviet Union gained further territory after World War II, under Joseph Stalin's rule. Increasing disillusionment with communism and demands for greater freedoms led to the eventual defeat of Communist party rule and the dissolution of the Soviet Union in 1991. Throughout the Soviet era and the years that followed, Russia has remained a highly agricultural society, like the one depicted in the story. Conduct research to find out how Russia is adapting to a changing economic climate in an increasingly industrial and technological world.

◆ Literary Focus

4 Parable *Students may say they learned the lesson that greed does not bring satisfaction, and that it can lead a person to isolation and even tragedy.*

◆ Critical Thinking

5 Analyze Remind students that irony is a literary technique that involves amusing contradictions. Ask students why this ending is ironic. *It is ironic because Pahom desired more and more land, and yet it took so little land to lay him to rest.*

Enrichment Tolstoy's story echoes the biblical parable of the rich fool (Luke 12:16–20). You may wish to share this parable with the class, and have students discuss the parallels between it and Tolstoy's story.

Reinforce and Extend

Answers

◆ Literature and Your Life

Reader's Response Some students might sympathize with Pahom for having lost a sense of community during his quest for more land; others might feel he deserves his fate.

Thematic Focus Possible responses include sacrificing material things or missing out on certain pleasurable activities.

Questions for Research Use the Research Skills Mini-Lesson on p. 136 of the ATE to help students generate questions.

☑ Check Your Comprehension

1. Pahom believes the only trouble that peasants face is that they don't have enough land.
2. He buys forty acres from the landlady by paying her a deposit and undertaking to pay the remainder within two years.
3. Peasants keep trespassing on his land, someone cuts down five young lime trees, his land is too far from the town market, he can't grow wheat on fallow fields.
4. A man can own as much land as he can walk around in one day. The price for one day's walk is one thousand rubles.
5. In his greed, Pahom walks so far he cannot get back in time to own the land. Although he arrives before sunset, he dies from the effort.

Beyond the Selection

FURTHER READING

Other Works by Leo Tolstoy

"The Death of Ivan Ilyich"
"Master and Man"

Other Works With the Theme of Greed

A Christmas Carol, Charles Dickens
The story of King Midas, Greek myth

We suggest that you preview these works before recommending them to your students.

INTERNET

Students can learn more about the author and his work at the following Web sites. Please be aware that sites may have changed from the time we published this information.

http://www. he.net/~works/tolstoy/life.html
http://www.ece. arizona.edu/~melcher/moscow/tolstoy.html

We *strongly recommend* that you preview sites before sending students to them.

Answers

◆ Critical Thinking

1. At first he's grateful for it, but then he begins to resent peasants trespassing on his land. At the same time, he grows greedy for more land.
2. Pahom believes in deeds and the exclusive rights of ownership, while the nomadic Bashkirs believe in communal sharing of the land.
3. The last sentence answers the title question by saying a man needs only enough land in which to be buried.
4. Some students will say many people are tempted by greed and would behave as Pahom did; others would say that most people have more control over themselves.
5. (a) Students may suggest characters from myths or fairy tales, such as King Midas or the farmer whose goose laid golden eggs. (b) These characters usually lose everything.

◆ Reading Strategy

1. He quickens his pace to cover more ground; he takes off his boots to walk more comfortably; he goes past a hollow and digs a hole on the other side of it even though he should have turned.
2. Students may find the ending satisfying in that it points up the futility of Pahom's ambitions.

◆ Literary Focus

1. The lesson is that greed does not end in satisfaction.
2. A possible response is that "How Much Land Does a Man Need?" could be used to teach humility and to illustrate the futility of living a materialistic existence.

◆ Build Vocabulary

Using Words in Other Contexts

1. sheaf; 2. fallow

Using the Word Bank

1. arable; 2. disparaged; 3. aggrieved; 4. piqued

◆ Build Grammar Skills

1. Pahom's heart kindled with desire.
2. He gave away about a hundred rubles' worth of silk robes and carpets.
3. It was the Bashkirs' custom to sell land by the day.
4. The chief's real identity is revealed at the end of the story.

Guide for Responding (continued)

◆ Critical Thinking

Interpret

1. How and why does Pahom's attitude toward his first plot of land change? **[Analyze]**

2. How do Pahom's and the Bashkirs' attitudes toward landownership differ? **[Compare and Contrast]**

3. How does the last sentence in the story reflect the message that answers the title question? **[Connect]**

Evaluate

4. Explain whether you think that most people would behave as Pahom does if they were put in his situation. **[Make a Judgment]**

Extend

5. (a) Name one other character you know from literature who, like Pahom, is never satisfied with what he or she has. (b) What happens to this character? **[Literature Link]**

◆ Reading Strategy

Predict Based on Character Traits

Based on Pahom's greed, you were probably able to **predict**—make an educated guess—that he would try to wrestle a large parcel of land from the Bashkirs.

1. Identify two things Pahom said or did that helped you predict he would try to take more land than he should have taken from the Bashkirs.

2. Did you predict the story's ending? Did you find it satisfying? Surprising? Explain.

◆ Literary Focus

Parable

Tolstoy's story of ownership and greed is classified as a **parable,** a type of short story that teaches a lesson.

1. What is the lesson that Tolstoy's parable teaches?

2. Parables are often used as a means of moral instruction. How might "How Much Land Does a Man Need?" be used for this purpose?

◆ Build Vocabulary

Using Words in Context

Words that have very specific meanings in one context often have a broader meaning in a broader context. For instance, in the context of land cultivation, *sheaf* refers to a bundle of grain stalks. In a broader context, *sheaf* is also used to describe any collection of things gathered together—such as a *sheaf* of paper.

Choose a word from the Word Bank to complete each sentence.

1. The landowner stormed into the house, holding a __?__ of bills in his hand.

2. His mind has gone __?__ ; he hasn't read a book in a month.

Using the Word Bank: Sentence Completions

Choose the word from the Word Bank that best fits each sentence. Write the complete sentence in your notebook.

1. Although the area used to be a desert, irrigation made the land __?__.

2. Pahom's sister-in-law __?__ the country ways.

3. The __?__ peasants complained to the landowner.

4. Pahom was __?__ by his neighbor's inconsiderate behavior.

◆ Build Grammar Skills

Possessive Nouns

The **possessive** form of a noun or pronoun shows ownership, belonging, or another close relationship.

Practice Copy the following sentences in your notebook, using the possessive form of the noun in parentheses.

1. (Pahom) heart kindled with desire.

2. He gave away about one hundred (rubles) worth of silk robes and carpets.

3. It was the (Bashkirs) custom to sell land by the day.

4. The (chief) real identity is revealed at the end of the story.

Grammar Reinforcement

For additional instruction and practice, use the page on Apostrophes (p. 110) in the *Writer's Solution Grammar Practice Book.*

Build Your Portfolio

Idea Bank

Writing

1. **Newspaper Article** Write a news article that reports the events leading up to Pahom's death. You may include quotations from other characters who knew or met Pahom. **[Career Link]**
2. **Land Advertisement** Write an advertisement for a piece of property or a building near your home. Focus on good points, such as beautiful views or access to schools. **[Career Link]**
3. **Parable** Using "How Much Land Does a Man Need?" as a model, write a contemporary parable. Choose a lesson you think would help people today. Teach your lesson by focusing on the actions of one or two main characters.

Speaking, Listening, and Viewing

4. **Update the Story** With a small group, improvise a scene from an updated version of this story. Perform your scene for the class. **[Performing Arts Link]**
5. **Eulogy** Prepare a eulogy—a speech about a person who has died—for Pahom. Look back at the story to recall some facts about his life. Deliver your eulogy to the class.

Researching and Representing

6. **Map of Russia** Make a map of modern Russia. On the map, label the various geographic regions and the peoples—including the Bashkirs—who live in each region. **[Social Studies Link]**
7. **Scale Diagram of Pahom's Field** Create a scale diagram that shows the dimensions of Pahom's field. Use one-half inch to represent a mile. You may need to convert some measurements from the story into miles before you create your diagram. **[Math Link]**

Online Activity www.phlit.phschool.com

Guided Writing Lesson

Video Script

Have you ever read a story and thought, "That would make a great movie"? Now's your chance to try your hand at making one. Choose any of parts one through nine from "How Much Land Does a Man Need?" and write a **video script** for that part. The following tip will ensure that your video turns out as you envision it.

Writing Skills Focus: Clear Explanation of Procedure

A good video script gives a **clear explanation** of everything that will be seen and heard. If you want the camera to show a scene moving from left to right, state those directions clearly. Explain how you see settings, action, sounds, music, and spoken words working together. The following technical terms will help you explain your ideas clearly.

long shot: view from a distance, showing one or more people and the background
close-up: shot of a single person or object
pan: move the camera across the scene
zoom: adjust from a long shot to a close-up using a single lens
cut: move directly from one shot to another
audio dub: sound added to the video
voice-over: comment or narration by an unseen person

Prewriting Create a storyboard—a rough sketch of each scene in your video. Then decide how you will make the visual transition from one image to another.

Drafting Describe what will be heard as well as what will be seen. Use technical terms to explain clearly how the parts of the video script work together.

Revising Compare your draft with your storyboards. If your script does not have a clear explanation of each shot you mapped out, add the necessary instructions.

ASSESSMENT OPTIONS

Formal Assessment, Selection Test, pp. 29–31, and Assessment Resources Software. The selection test is designed so that it can be easily customized to the performance levels of your students.

Alternative Assessment, p. 9, includes options for less advanced students, Pre-AP Students, logical/mathematical learners, verbal/linguistic learners, bodily/kinesthetic learners, and visual/spatial learners.

PORTFOLIO ASSESSMENT

Use the following rubrics in the ***Alternative Assessment*** booklet to assess student writing:
Newspaper Article: Summary Rubric, p. 98
Land Advertisement: Persuasion Rubric, p. 105
Parable: Expression Rubric, p. 94

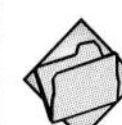

Idea Bank

Following are suggestions for matching Idea Bank topics with your students' performance levels and learning modalities:

Customizing for *Performance Levels*
Less Advanced Students: 2, 4
Average Students: 1, 5, 6
Pre-AP Students: 3, 7

Customizing for *Learning Modalities*
Visual/Spatial: 6, 7
Logical/Mathematical: 7
Verbal/Linguistic: 3, 4, 5

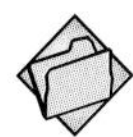

Guided Writing Lesson

Elaboration Strategy Students will feel more comfortable using technical film terms and writing stage directions if they see a model of a movie script first. If possible, find a copy of a professional movie script and read it over with students, discussing the techniques used by the screenwriter. If you have more than one movie script, read sections of both and guide students to compare and contrast the styles of the screenwriters. Help them to understand how much detail is necessary when describing settings, camera angles, and other non-verbal storytelling techniques used in a script.

For more prewriting, elaboration, and revision strategies, see *Prentice Hall Writing and Grammar.*

Writers at Work Videodisc

Have students view the videodisc segment (Ch. 8) featuring Larry Cataldo to hear some tips for writing clear explanations. Have students discuss how these tips can be applied to writing their video scripts.

Play frames 37727 to 39423

Writing Lab CD-ROM

Have students complete the tutorial on Creative Writing. Follow these steps:

1. Tell students to use the Story Line Diagram to map out plot elements.
2. Encourage them to view examples of dialogue in an audio-annotated Writing Model.
3. Allow time for drafting on the computer.
4. Direct students to complete the Peer Evaluation Checklists for drama.

Prepare and Engage

LESSON OBJECTIVES

1. **To develop vocabulary and word identification skills**
   - Latin Prefixes: *im-*
   - Using the Word Bank: True or False?
   - Extending Word Study: Determine Meanings (ATE)
2. **To use a variety of reading strategies to comprehend a poem**
   - Connect Your Experience
   - Reading Strategy: Draw Inferences
   - Tips to Guide Reading: Whisper Reading (ATE)
   - Read to Appreciate Author's Craft (ATE)
3. **To express and support responses to the poems**
   - Critical Thinking
   - Idea Bank: Advertisement
4. **To analyze literary elements**
   - Literary Focus: Stated and Implied Themes in Poetry
   - Idea Bank: Letter to a Poet
5. **To read in order to research self-selected and assigned topics**
   - Idea Bank: Oral Report
   - Speaking, Listening, and Viewing Mini-Lesson: Informal Debate
6. **To plan, prepare, organize, and present literary interpretations**
   - Idea Bank: Parody of a Poem
   - Idea Bank: Panel Discussion
7. **To use recursive writing processes to write a submission letter**
   - Guided Writing Lesson
8. **To increase knowledge of the rules of grammar and usage**
   - Build Grammar Skills: Subject and Verb Agreement

Test Preparation

Reading Comprehension: Sequence (ATE, p. 147) The teaching tips and sample test item in this workshop support the instruction and practice in the unit workshop:

Reading Comprehension: Recognize Facts, Details, and Sequence (SE, p. 215)

Guide for Reading

Emily Dickinson *(1830–1886)*

Like secret messages in a time capsule, many of Emily Dickinson's poems remained undiscovered and unread by the public during her lifetime. She wrote 1,775 poems, yet only seven were published—anonymously—before she died. Today, however, she is generally regarded as one of the greatest American poets.

Although she lived her life in virtual isolation, she explored the world through her poetry. The extent of Dickinson's talent was not widely recognized until 1955, when a complete, unedited edition of her poems was published.

Featured in AUTHORS IN DEPTH Series

Pat Mora *(1942–)*

Pat Mora is fascinated by borders. She herself was born and raised in El Paso, near the border that separates Mexico and the United States. During her childhood, she sometimes felt that living on the United States side of the border separated her not just from Mexico, but from her Mexican heritage and culture.

As an adult, Mora encourages today's young people to cross borders, feeling pride in their heritage but also appreciating cultural diversity. Her own Mexican American background is an important influence on her writing.

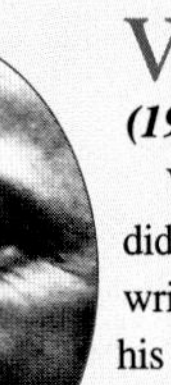

Vassar Miller *(1924–)*

Vassar Miller's father probably did not realize he was creating a world-class writer when he brought home a typewriter from his office! Yet his daughter—who typed her first poems on that secondhand typewriter—was once nominated for a Pulitzer Prize and was inducted into the Texas Women's Hall of Fame in 1997. Miller has had cerebral palsy since birth. The faith and courage that have helped her face her physical challenges are apparent in her work. In addition to books of her own poetry, she has published *Despite This Flesh,* an anthology of poetry and stories about the disabled.

◆ Build Vocabulary

LATIN PREFIXES: *im-*

In "I dwell in Possibility—", Emily Dickinson uses the word *impregnable*. *Impregnable* begins with the Latin prefix *im-* (a variation of *in-*), which usually means "not." The meaning of *impregnable* is "not conquerable" or "not able to be captured."

WORD BANK

As you read these poems, you will encounter the words on this list. Each word is defined on the page where it first appears. Preview the list before you read.

impregnable
thrall
vertigo

◆ Build Grammar Skills

SUBJECT AND VERB AGREEMENT

Although poetry is different from other forms of writing, some basic rules still apply. One of these rules is **subject and verb agreement**—using a verb form that agrees in number (singular or plural) with its subject. Notice how the verbs change form in these examples:

Singular: A river *leaps*. She *sighs*.

Plural: Rivers *leap*. They *sigh*.

In each of these poems, notice that the verbs agree with their subjects.

Prentice Hall Literature Program Resources

REINFORCE / RETEACH / EXTEND

Selection Support Pages
Build Vocabulary: Prefixes: *im-*, p. 39
Build Grammar Skills: Subject/Verb Agreement, p. 40
Reading Strategy: Make Inferences, p. 41
Literary Focus: Stated and Implied Theme, p. 42

Strategies for Diverse Student Needs, p. 10

Beyond Literature Humanities Connection: Impressionist Art, p. 10

Formal Assessment Selection Test, pp. 32–34;
Assessment Resources Software

Alternative Assessment, p. 10 lesson plan

Resource Pro CD-ROM

Writing and Language Transparencies, Writing Process Model 9: Business Letter, pp. 61–64

Listening to Literature Audiocassettes

Success is counted sweetest ◆ I dwell in Possibility— ◆ Uncoiling ◆ Columbus Dying

◆ Literature and Your Life

Connect Your Experience

Every day, you make judgments about your experiences: worth it or not worth it, success or failure. Like you, the three poets in this group explore the positive and negative feelings that accompany the big and small struggles in life.

Thematic Focus: Overcoming Obstacles

The speakers in these four poems describe facing and overcoming obstacles. Each poem, however, may suggest to you a unique answer to the question, "What does it take to succeed?"

Journal Writing In the center of a response wheel like the one shown, write a success you have recently had. In the outer sections of the circle, record the feelings you had as you worked to overcome obstacles to that success.

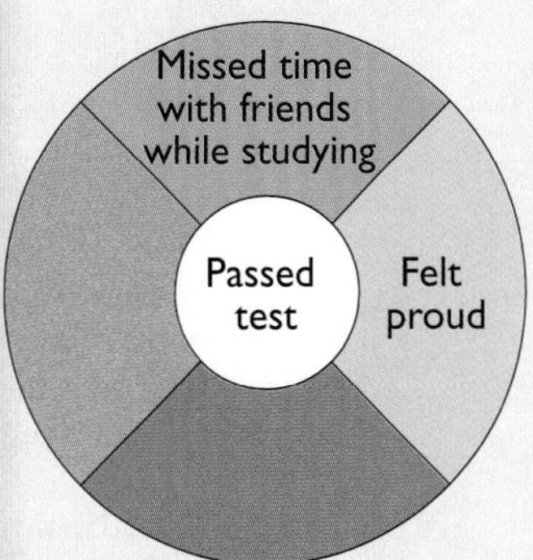

◆ Background for Understanding

Literature

A person sprawled across a couch tells you he is relaxed without saying a word. Poems, too, can communicate through "body language." Some poems "sprawl" across the page, while others "sit" properly.

In a traditional poem, lines are grouped into stanzas, and new lines always begin at the left margin. In other poems, the shape of the poem on the page suggests an action, object, or idea. Three poems in this group have a traditional appearance. One, however, "Uncoiling," may surprise you with the way its appearance reflects the action named in the title.

◆ Literary Focus

Stated and Implied Themes in Poetry

Poems, like most works of literature, convey a **theme**—a central idea, concern, or message about life. In some poems, the theme is directly **stated.** In other poems, the theme is **implied**—the message is suggested, not stated. An implied theme may be revealed through events, the actions of a character, a speaker's words and attitude, or the details a poet chooses to include.

One of these Emily Dickinson poems has a stated theme: "Success is counted sweetest / By those who ne'er succeed." You must figure out the implied themes of the other poems in this group.

◆ Reading Strategy

Draw Inferences

Like a letter from a friend, a poem brings you a message. To get the message, you may need to **draw inferences**—reach conclusions based on evidence. You can infer the message of a poem, when it is not stated, from specific details and images.

For example, when you begin reading "Columbus Dying," you will encounter images of sick, starving sailors. From these images you can infer that this poem is not about the glory of Columbus's voyage. Use the other images and details in these poems to draw inferences about their meanings.

Read aloud or write on the chalkboard the first two lines of Dickinson's first poem, "Success is counted sweetest/By those who ne'er succeed." Ask students to imagine that this is a motto written on a T-shirt or a bumper sticker. After discussing the meaning of these lines—that success is most glorified when it is most elusive—ask students if they agree or disagree with the motto, and why. You might also ask them for their own definitions of success. Let them know that each of these poems focuses on an aspect of success students may not have considered before.

Customize for
Less Proficient Readers and English Language Learners

To ensure literal comprehension, review the "story" of each poem with students. Have them read each poem, then tell a partner, in their own words, what is happening in the poem.

Customize for
Pre-AP Students

Invite Pre-AP Students to compare the different styles and poetic devices that the three poets use. For example, they might compare Emily Dickinson's and Vassar Miller's use of rhyme, or Vassar Miller's and Pat Mora's use of imagery.

Customize for
Gifted/Talented Students

Encourage students to read the poems aloud several times, focusing on how slight differences in stress, tone of voice, or rhythm can bring out different nuances of feeling and meaning in the poems.

Tips to Guide Reading

Sustained Reading Encourage students to whisper read the poems. Listen in to record miscues caused by line breaks. Remind them to follow punctuation as they read.

Test Preparation Workshop

Reading Comprehension:
Sequence The SAT test requires students to answer questions that are based on the logical flow of ideas. Point out to students that a few key introductory and transitional words reveal sequence and logic, such as *after, until, yet,* and *but.* Have students read "Uncoiling" by Pat Mora on p. 150. Then use this sample question to give students practice in recognizing logic and sequence in a test question.

The women comfort the children with lullabies while the wind is ________.

A blowing **C** whirring
B howling **D** spewing

Students should identify line 14 in the poem to as thee point at which the women are singing lullabies. Further guide them to find the key word *until,* which indicates that the lullabies comfort the children while the wind is B howling. Remind students to review all of the answers choices before choosing the best answer—in this case, all of the answers will complete the sentence, however, *howling* is accurate in the context of the entire sentence.

Develop Understanding

One-Minute Insight Emily Dickinson takes an ironic view of success. In "Success is counted sweetest," success is fully understood only by those to whom it is denied. In "I dwell in Possibility—," the poet paints a picture of a recluse who has attained no worldly trappings of success, yet feels successful. These poems should encourage students to look at success from a more psychological and personal perspective.

◆ Literary Focus

❶ **Stated and Implied Theme** Ask students if these two lines reveal a stated or an implied theme, and to tell the theme in their own words. *It is a stated theme. A possible rewording is, "People who don't succeed are the ones who best know how sweet success can be."*

◆ Build Grammar Skills

❷ **Subject and Verb Agreement** Ask students to identify the subject and verb in this sentence and explain why the two agree in number. *The subject is success and the verb is is. The singular subject requires the singular form of the verb.*

❸ **Clarification** Point out that "purple" is the color of victory, that "Host" means a large number (in this case, of soldiers), and that taking "the Flag" is what a victorious troop does in battle.

◆ Reading Strategy

❹ **Make Inferences** Ask students what the image "forbidden ear" suggests about the dying soldier, and how this image contributes to the meaning of the poem. *Students may say that "forbidden ear" suggests that the soldier is not permitted to know victory. It is an image that makes his sense of defeat all the harsher.*

▶Critical Viewing◀

❺ **Analyze** *Some may think that a person who owns a house with a garden like this must be successful. Students who notice the transparent figure sitting on the bench may see the sitting figure as dwelling "in possibility." The scene around her may be a possibility in her imagination.*

Success is counted sweetest

Emily Dickinson

❶ Success is counted sweetest
❷ By those who ne'er succeed.
To comprehend a nectar[1]
Requires sorest need.

❸ Not one of all the purple Host
Who took the Flag today
Can tell the definition
So clear of Victory

As he defeated—dying—
On whose forbidden ear
The distant strains of triumph
Burst agonized and clear! ❹

1. **nectar** (nek´ tər) *n.*: Something delicious to drink.

The Terrace at Meric, 1867, Frédéric Bazille, Cincinnati Museum of Art

▲ Critical Viewing What details in this painting suggest success or possibility? **[Analyze]** ❺

Block Scheduling Strategies

Consider these suggestions to take advantage of extended class time:

- Introduce the prefix *im-*, then use the Build Vocabulary page in ***Selection Support*** (p. 39).
- Direct students to read and complete the activity on Impressionist Art. In small groups, they can discuss their ideas about Impressionism. They might also enjoy comparing and contrasting this style of painting to the poet's use of language in these selections.
- Let students work in small groups to answer the Critical Thinking questions on pp. 149 and 151.
- Encourage students to work in small groups to prepare for the informal debate in the Speaking, Listening, and Viewing activity on p. 153. Suggest they brainstorm for a list of examples from life, literature, or the movies that prove or disprove the wisdom of the two lines from "Success is counted sweetest." Alternatively, teach the mini-lesson on p. 149 of the ATE.
- To assess their understanding of the poems, have students take the multiple-choice portion of the Selection Test, ***Formal Assessment,*** p. 32. You may wish to assign the test essay for homework.

I dwell in Possibility—

Emily Dickinson

I dwell in Possibility—
A fairer House than Prose—
More numerous of Windows—
Superior—for Doors—

Of Chambers as the Cedars—
Impregnable of Eye—
And for an Everlasting Roof—
The Gambrels[1] of the Sky—

Of Visiters[2]—the fairest—
For Occupation—This—
❻ The spreading wide my narrow Hands
To gather Paradise—

◆ **Build Vocabulary**

Impregnable (im preg´ nə bəl) *adj.*: Unconquerable; not able to be captured

1. **Gambrels:** Angled windows.
2. **Visiters:** Visitors.

Guide for Responding

◆ Literature and Your Life

Reader's Response With whom would you most like to share these poems? Why?

Thematic Focus Dickinson overcomes the obstacles of the "ordinary" world by using her imagination. Why do you think imagination is such a powerful positive force?

Journal Writing Make a list of ways in which imagination enriches your everyday experiences.

☑ Check Your Comprehension

1. To whom does success seem most sweet?
2. What thing does Dickinson use to represent "Possibility"?

◆ Critical Thinking

INTERPRET

1. Why does success seem sweeter to someone who has not achieved it? **[Interpret]**
2. Explain how the gesture the poet described in the last two lines of "I dwell in Possibility—" illustrates the statement she makes in the first two lines. **[Connect]**

EVALUATE

3. How much influence do you think imagination has on your approach to life? Decide whether Dickinson overstates the importance of imagination. **[Assess]**

APPLY

4. Which poem do you find easier to relate to your own life? Why? **[Relate]**

◆ Critical Thinking

❻ **Interpret** Invite students to explain the meaning of these lines. *Students might say that while the actual scope of the speaker's life is narrow, the workings of her imagination make her experience seem broad.*

Read to Appreciate Author's Craft

Have students note that Dickinson uses only dashes as punctuation. How does this create a feeling of "Possibility" in the poem?

Extending Word Study

Dictionary Have students determine the meanings of "fairer" and fairest" either by context or by looking in a dictionary.

Reinforce and Extend

Answers

◆ Literature and Your Life

Reader's Response Encourage students to describe the personalities of the individual they identify.

Thematic Focus Students may suggest that imagination allows people to envision positive outcomes.

☑ Check Your Comprehension

1. Success seems most sweet to people who do not succeed.
2. Dickinson uses a house with many windows and doors to represent possibility.

◆ Critical Thinking

1. Success seems sweeter to people who haven't achieved it because they build it up in their minds.
2. By spreading wide her narrow hands to gather Paradise, the speaker is confirming the ideas stated in the first two lines; her "real" world is small but her "possible" world is large.
3. Some students will say their imaginations help them create things or imagine their futures; others might say that Dickinson's emphasis on the life of the imagination promotes unsociable behavior.
4. Students who strive to succeed might choose "Success is counted sweetest," while students who tend toward introspection might choose "I dwell in Possibility—."

Speaking, Listening, and Viewing Mini-Lesson

Informal Debate

This mini-lesson supports the Speaking, Listening, and Viewing activity in the Idea Bank on p. 153.

Introduce Informal debates have fewer rules than formal ones. However, students still should represent their ideas clearly, support them with solid examples, and listen to others' opinions.

Develop As a class, review the literal meaning of Dickenson's assertion. Ask students for examples of people who try for success, but have not yet succeeded, such as an athlete who loses a race.

Discuss the pros and cons of success. For instance, success may bring more responsibility and higher expectations; or, success inspires feelings of satisfaction, accomplishment, and "sweetness."

Apply Groups of students can develop specific and relevant examples for the side they are supporting; then conduct their informal debates.

Assess Discuss the insights students gained on success. You may also wish to have students use the Listening Self-Assessment form, p. 124 in the ***Alternative Assessment*** booklet.

Develop Understanding

These poems represent the dark side of success. Pat Mora's tornado "successfully" destroys all in its path; Vassar Miller shows that in succeeding, Columbus lost his faith in the meaning of life.

◆ Reading Strategy

❶ **Make Inferences** Ask students for clues that the poem is about a tornado. *Students may say a tornado blows branches and is characterized by dark clouds and lightning.*

◆ Build Grammar Skills

❷ **Subject and Verb Agreement** Have students identify the subject and verb in this stanza. *The subject (plural) is* boulders; *the verb is* retreat.

◆ Literary Focus

❸ **Stated and Implied Theme** Have students identify the poem's theme and explain how it is revealed. *The theme is destruction, revealed by the images of frightened women and the tornado blowing itself out into "sound."*

◆ Critical Thinking

❹ **Analyze** Ask students to describe the poem's shape and how it relates to the meaning. *Students will probably point out that the poem is shaped like a tornado, extending the meaning.*

▶ Critical Viewing ◀

❺ **Compare** *Both portray a destructive tornado; the photo shows only the tornado; the poem shows the tornado's effects on human beings.*

Insight From Pat Mora

Pat Mora offers the following insight.

"Students occasionally ask why I keep writing about the desert, and I ask myself the question too. In writing my family memoir, *House of Houses,* I became more aware of my fascination with the desert, family, and Mexican American culture

In both prose and poetry, I've written about the sounds and sights of a good desert storm, good for me, anyway, the beauty of that wildness. The blank page is like that vast landscape for me. I'm trying to create the storm for you on the page. Notice the power of line breaks."

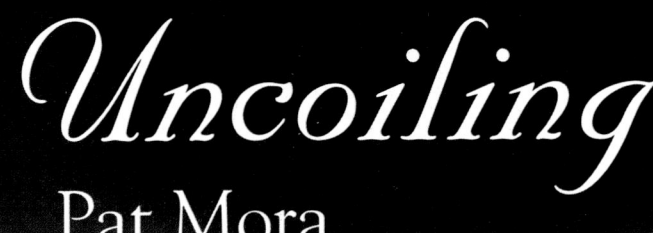

Uncoiling

Pat Mora

❶
With thorns, she scratches
on my window, tosses her hair dark with rain,
snares lightning, cholla,[1] hawks, butterfly
swarms in the tangles.

She sighs clouds,
head thrown back, eyes closed, roars
and rivers leap,

❷
boulders retreat like crabs
into themselves.

She spews gusts and thunder,
spooks pale women who scurry to
lock doors, windows
when her tumbleweed skirt starts its spin.

They sing lace lullabies
❸ so their children won't hear
❹ her uncoiling
through her lips, howling
leaves off trees, flesh
off bones, until she becomes

sound, spins herself
to sleep, sand stinging her ankles,
whirring into her raw skin like stars.

1. **cholla** (chōl´ yä) *n.*: Spiny shrub found in the southwestern United States and Mexico.

▲ Critical Viewing Compare the mood of this photograph with the mood of Mora's poem. **[Compare]** ❺

Cross-Curricular Connection: Science

Most tornadoes form between a layer of cool, dry air from the north and warm, humid air from the south. Warm air naturally rises, while cool air sinks. When the warm air rises, more warm air rushes in to replace it, causing winds. The inrushing air also rises. If the warm air rises very rapidly, it may begin to rotate. The rotating air then forms into the funnel shape of a tornado. In the United States, tornadoes are most common in the Midwest in the spring months.

Invite students to do research on tornadoes as well as on related storms: monsoons, cyclones, and hurricanes. Interested students might find out what causes the different storms, why they occur in some places and not others, what type of damage they may cause, and how people take precautions against them. Students can share their information with the class by presenting oral reports. Encourage students to bring in photographs, drawings, and other visual aids.

Columbus Dying

Vassar Miller

His men in fever, scabs, and hunger pains—
He found a world and put to scorn his scorners.
Yet having learned the living sea contains
No dragons gnawing on drowned sailors' brains, ❻
He missed the angels guarding the four corners,
And begged that he be buried with his chains.
In token that he'd sworn to serve as thrall
His vision of men creeping to and fro,
Gum-footed flies glued to a spinning ball. ❼
Whether they tumble off earth's edge or crawl
Till dropped dead in their tracks from vertigo,
He deemed would make no difference at all.

◆ **Build Vocabulary**

thrall (thrôl) *n.*: Servant; slave

vertigo (vʉr′ ti gō) *n.*: Dizzy, confused state of mind

Guide for Responding

◆ *Literature and Your Life*

Reader's Response How do you feel after reading these poems? Explain.

Thematic Focus As Columbus does in the poem, you may sometimes question whether a particular goal is as important as you originally thought it was. How do you decide when the price is too high?

☑ Check Your Comprehension

1. Identify three outcomes of the wind's actions in "Uncoiling."
2. What happened to the sailors on Columbus's ship?
3. According to the poem, what were Columbus's achievements?

◆ Critical Thinking

INTERPRET

1. Explain how the shape of the poem "Uncoiling" reflects the title. **[Connect]**
2. Describe Columbus's attitude toward his own achievements. **[Interpret]**

EVALUATE

3. How convincing do you find this portrait of Columbus? Why? **[Assess]**

COMPARE LITERARY WORKS

4. Compare and contrast the themes of these four poems. **[Compare and Contrast]**

Art Transparency Before students read Miller's poem, display Art transparency 10. Discuss the scene, emphasizing its busy excitement. Ask students to share what they may know of the explorers who set sail from western Europe, leading them to a brief discussion of Christopher Columbus. After students read "Columbus Dying," display the transparency again, and invite students to speculate about how Miller's disillusioned speaker might have responded to the exuberant scene.

❻ **Clarify** Explain that Columbus found there were no monsters in the sea, but he also discovered there were no angels guarding the world's four corners, as people used to believe.

◆ Critical Thinking

❼ **Interpret** Work with the class to understand the poet's meaning. What makes no difference? *Columbus no longer cares whether the world is flat (tumbling off the edge) or round (dropping from motion sickness).*

Reinforce and Extend

Answers

◆ *Literature and Your Life*

Reader's Response Students may feel sad because of the poems' destruction and human disappointment.

Thematic Focus The price may be too high when find they are trying to get something they no longer want.

☑ **Check Your Comprehension**

1. The boulders "retreat like crabs"; women lock doors and windows and sing lullabies to their children; leaves fall off trees and "flesh off bones" (people are killed).
2. They get sick, starve, or drown.
3. He found a world and put to scorn his scorners.

◆ **Critical Thinking**

1. The shape resembles a spiral.
2. Columbus is scornful of his achievement and finds it meaningless.
3. Some students may not believe that Columbus despaired as much as the poem portrays.
4. "Success" and "Columbus" explore success and failure; "Uncoiling," and "Possibility" share a theme of viewing the world through the imagination.

Beyond the Selection

FURTHER READING

Other Works by the Poets

"The Soul Selects Her Own Society," Emily Dickinson

Borders, Pat Mora

Wage War on Silence, Vassar Miller

Other Works About Striving for Success

My Name Is Asher Lev, Chaim Potok

Tell Me if the Lovers Are Losers, Cynthia Voight

We suggest that you preview these works before recommending them to students.

INTERNET

Students may visit the following Web sites for information about the poets and their poems. Addresses may have changed since we published this information.

Emily Dickinson: **http://english.cla.umn.edu/ Course web/1017/Emily dickinson/home**

Pat Mora: **http:/www.herald.com/liv_art/ books/docs/023698.htm**

We *strongly recommend* that you preview sites before you send students to them.

Answers

◆ Reading Strategy

1. The images "forbidden ear," "distant strains of triumph," and "burst agonized" lead the reader to infer that the speaker's sympathy is with the loser.
2. You can infer that the speaker equates her imaginary world with paradise.
3. You can infer that he finds his conception of the world as round to be comical.
4. The speaker might think the pale women are nervous or easily timid.

◆ Literary Focus

1. (a) Possible restatement: People envy and glorify success when they themselves are not successful. (b) The battle images make the theme clearer because the contrast between success and failure is so distinct.
2. (a) The theme of "Uncoiling" is destruction; of "I dwell in Possibility—," the joys of the imagination. (b) Students might say that in each poem, the poet uses images and events (e.g., "gather Paradise"; "howling/leaves off trees, flesh/off bones") from which the reader can infer the theme.

◆ Build Vocabulary

Using the Prefix *im-*

1. impassable—not passable
2. immobile—not mobile or not able to move
3. impossible—not possible
4. impatient—not patient

Using the Word Bank

1. true; 2. false; 3. false

◆ Build Grammar Skills

Practice

1. The rooms of "Possibility" have many windows. (rooms—plural)
2. Columbus's men are tired and hungry. (men—plural)
3. The wind stings my face. (wind—singular)
4. The people who fail are the ones who know how sweet success is. (people—plural)
5. The women scurry back to their houses. (women—plural)

Guide for Responding *(continued)*

◆ Reading Strategy

Draw Inferences

By **drawing inferences**—reaching conclusions based on evidence—you can interpret the rich meaning in each line of these poems. The image of the wind roaring with her head thrown back in "Uncoiling," for instance, suggests freedom and awesome power. From positive images like this one, you can infer that the speaker's fear of the force of the wind is mixed with admiration for it.

1. What images help you infer the speaker's sympathy for the loser in "Success is counted sweetest"?
2. The word "Paradise" is used in the last line of "I dwell in Possibility—." What can you infer from this word about the speaker's thoughts about imagination?
3. In "Columbus Dying," people are described as "Gum-footed flies glued to a spinning ball." What does this image help you infer about Columbus's ambition to prove the Earth is not flat?
4. What inference can you draw about the speaker's opinion of the "pale women" in "Uncoiling," based on her description of their actions?

◆ Literary Focus

Stated and Implied Themes in Poetry

The **theme**—the central idea or concern—is partly stated in the title of "Success is counted sweetest." You have to explore a little further to discover the **implied theme** of "Columbus Dying." Columbus's indifference to his own achievements, described in the last lines, suggests that the poem's message is that his success came at too high a price.

1. The theme of "Success is counted sweetest" is stated. (a) Restate it in your own words. (b) Explain how the battle images help make the theme clearer.
2. (a) What is the implied theme of "Uncoiling" and "I dwell in Possibility—"? (b) Explain how specific details, characters, events, or actions helped you determine the theme of each poem.

◆ Build Vocabulary

Using the Latin Prefix *im-*

The Latin prefix *im-* (a variation of the prefix *in-*) usually means "not." On your paper, explain how the meaning "not" works into the definition of each word.

1. impassable **3.** impossible
2. immobile **4.** impatient

Using the Word Bank: True or False?

Copy the following sentences in your notebook. Next to each, write *true* or *false*.

1. A king would most likely want his castle to be *impregnable*.
2. Most people would jump at the chance to become a *thrall*.
3. A person with *vertigo* would make an especially good tight-rope walker.

◆ Build Grammar Skills

Subject and Verb Agreement

These poets play with the appearances and structures of their poems. Dickinson sprinkles her poems with dashes; Mora spreads the words out on the page to create the shape of a whirlwind. All verbs, however, agree with their subjects.

Subject-verb agreement: A verb changes form to agree in number (singular or plural) with its subject.

Practice Write the following sentences on your paper. Label the subject as singular or plural, and choose the correct verb form to complete the sentence.

1. The rooms of "Possibility" (has, have) many windows.
2. Columbus's men (is, are) tired and hungry.
3. The wind (stings, sting) my face.
4. The people who fail (is, are) the ones who know how sweet success is.
5. The women (scurries, scurry) back to their houses.

Grammar Reinforcement

For additional instruction and practice, use the lesson in the **Language Lab CD-ROM** on Subject-Verb Agreement and the pages on agreement (pp. 80–86) in the *Writer's Solution Grammar Practice Book*.

Reteach

Help students draw inferences by exploring specific images in the poems. Ask students to choose an image they like, such as "boulders retreat like crabs," then describe what picture and feeling it brings to mind.

Build Your Portfolio

Idea Bank

Writing

1. **Letter to a Poet** Write a letter to one of these poets, responding to the theme of her poem. Explain whether you agree or disagree with her message and why.
2. **Advertisement** Write publisher's advertisement that highlights the qualities of one of these poems. **[Career Link]**
3. **Parody of a Poem** Choose one of the poems in this group and write a parody of it: an imitation that exaggerates its language, images, or theme.

Speaking, Listening, and Viewing

4. **Informal Debate** In a small group, debate the assertion "Success is counted sweetest / By those who ne'er succeed." Use situations from life, literature, or the movies to demonstrate the truth or falsehood of the poem's theme.
5. **Panel Discussion** Role-play a panel discussion that might take place among the three poets in this group. Have someone act as a moderator leading a discussion about the nature of success.

Researching and Representing

6. **Round Earth Demonstration** Columbus's voyage changed the way people view the world. Create a model that demonstrates something we now know about Earth; for instance, that the sun appears to rise and set because Earth rotates. Demonstrate your model in class. **[Science Link]**
7. **Oral Report** Prepare an oral report about the living conditions on Columbus's ships. Use visual aids, such as diagrams or charts, to illustrate some of your explanations. Present your report to the class. **[Social Studies Link]**

Online Activity www.phlit.phschool.com

Guided Writing Lesson

Submission Letter

When poets or other writers send their work to a magazine or journal, they usually accompany it with a **submission letter** explaining why the work is appropriate for the particular publication. As one of the poets in this group, write a submission letter that would accompany one of these poems. The following hints will help you explain in detail why the editor should publish your work.

Writing Skills Focus: Elaboration to Give Information

Use **elaboration**—details and examples—to give the editor more information about you and your work. For example, don't just say your poem will interest readers; point out a striking image or idea from the poem.

Prewriting Brainstorm for a list of reasons you think the poem should be published. Avoid vague words like *nice* and *good.* They don't give enough information to distinguish your poem from any other.

Drafting Organize the letter around the main points you have identified. Elaborate on each point by quoting from your work or describing a section of it.

Revising Review your letter and identify the example or detail that elaborates on each point you wish to make. If you come across a point that does not have an example or detail, elaborate on the point by adding one.

Proofread your work and check especially for subject-verb agreement.

For more on subject and verb agreement, see Build Grammar Skills on pp. 146 and 152.

ASSESSMENT OPTIONS

Formal Assessment, Selection Test, pp. 32–34, and Assessment Resources Software. The selection test is designed so that it can be easily customized to the performance levels of your students.

Alternative Assessment, p. 10, includes options for less advanced students, Pre-AP Students, bodily/kinesthetic learners, musical/rhythmic learners, visual/spatial learners, logical/mathematical learners, and verbal/linguistic learners.

PORTFOLIO ASSESSMENT

Use the following rubrics in the ***Alternative Assessment*** booklet to assess student writing:
Letter to a Poet: Response to Literature Rubric, p. 113
Advertisement: Poetry Rubric, p. 108
Parody of a Poem: Poetry Rubric, p. 111

Idea Bank

Following are suggestions for matching Idea Bank topics with your students' performance levels and learning modalities:

Customizing for *Performance Levels*
Less Advanced Students: 1, 4
Average Students: 2, 5,
Pre-AP Students: 3, 6, 7

Customizing for *Learning Modalities*
Visual/Spatial: 6, 7
Verbal/Linguistic: 3, 4, 5, 7

Guided Writing Lesson

Elaboration Strategy To evaluate the effectiveness of concrete examples they used, ask students to use a chart like the one below. As students evaluate the examples they chose, they might try to explain exactly how the example illustrates the point—if they can't come up with clear answers, it is likely that their examples do not illustrate the point well. In these cases, encourage students to reenter their poems and choose different examples to include in their letters.

Point	Example Used to Illustrate Point	Evaluation of Example

Writers at Work Videodisc

Have students view the videodisc segment (Ch. 8) featuring Larry Cataldo to spark a class discussion on various applications of practical writing.

Chapter 8

Writing Lab CD-ROM

Have students complete the tutorial on Practical Writing. Follow these steps:

1. Direct students to look at audio-annotated examples of writings for different audiences.
2. Have them use an outliner to help organize their points.
3. Encourage them to use the interactive subject and verb agreement instruction in Proofreading.

Prepare and Engage

LESSON OBJECTIVES

1. **To develop vocabulary and word identification skills**
   - Latin Word Roots: *-vol-*
   - Using the Word Bank: Connotations
   - Extending Word Study: Context (ATE)
2. **To use a variety of reading strategies to read and comprehend a personal narrative**
   - Connect Your Experience
   - Reading Strategy: Identify Author's Purpose
   - Tips to Guide Reading: Sustained Reading (ATE)
   - Read to Be Informed (ATE)
3. **To express and support responses to the text**
   - Critical Thinking
   - Idea Bank: Mother's Day Card
   - Idea Bank: Story From the Mother's Point of View
   - Analyze Film Criticism (ATE)
4. **To analyze literary elements**
   - Literary Focus: Significant Moment
   - Idea Bank: Movie Review
5. **To read in order to research self-selected and assigned topics**
   - Idea Bank: Christy Brown Timeline
   - Research Skills Mini-Lesson: Chart on Cerebral Palsy
   - Questions for Research
6. **To plan, prepare, organize, and present literary interpretations**
   - Idea Bank: Role Play
   - Speaking, Listening, and Viewing Mini-Lesson: Speech
7. **To use recursive writing processes to write a personal narrative**
   - Guided Writing Lesson
8. **To increase knowledge of the rules of grammar and usage**
   - Build Grammar Skills: Active and Passive Voice

Test Preparation

Reading Comprehension: Recognize Details (ATE, p. 155) The teaching tips and sample test item in this workshop support the instruction and practice in the unit workshop:

Reading Comprehension: Recognize Facts, Details, and Sequence (SE, p. 215)

Guide for Reading

Christy Brown *(1932–1981)*

He was trapped in a body that he could not control, surrounded by people but unbearably alone. These problems would crush most adults, but Christy Brown faced and overcame these obstacles when he was only a child.

The tenth of twenty-two children, Christy Brown was born in Dublin, Ireland, in 1932. His father was a bricklayer, a profession that usually—but not always—brought in enough money to support the family. When money was scarce, his mother often took odd jobs in addition to raising the children.

A Difficult Birth, a Difficult Life Born with cerebral palsy, Brown had no control over most of his limbs, could not talk, and had to be fed by hand. Many people assumed he was mentally retarded until one day he grabbed a piece of chalk with his left foot and scrawled the letter *A*. This action proved his intelligence and changed his life completely.

Christy Brown recalls, "I was tormented, revolted at the very thought that I had been made different—cruelly different—from other people."

> ***". . . I was soon to realize that it was this very affliction . . . that was to bring a strange beauty into my life."***

His Left Foot When he was ten years old, he started to paint, also with his left foot. He later grew tired of painting and started to write. He wrote the manuscript for *My Left Foot* with a pencil that he held with his left big toe. Later, he taught himself to type and wrote the novel *Down All the Days,* which became a bestseller in Ireland. He also wrote three more novels and a collection of poetry. In 1989, his life became the basis for the popular and critically acclaimed film *My Left Foot,* which introduced the rest of the world to this incredible man.

◆ Build Vocabulary

LATIN WORD ROOTS: *-vol-*

A dramatic moment in *My Left Foot* occurs when the author's left foot, apparently by its own volition, grabs a piece of chalk out of his sister's hand. The root of *volition* is *-vol-*, which comes from Latin and means "wish" or "will." *Volition* is "the act of using the will": Brown's foot apparently grabs the piece of chalk by its own free will.

WORD BANK

As you read you will encounter the words in the boxed list. Each word is defined on the page where it first appears. Preview the list before you read. Look for other words in the story, such as *involuntary,* that have the root *-vol-*.

- impertinence
- conviction
- inert
- contention
- volition
- taut

◆ Build Grammar Skills

ACTIVE AND PASSIVE VOICE

A verb is in the **active voice** when the subject of the sentence performs the action. A verb is in the **passive voice** when the action is performed on the subject. When the performer of an action is not known or is not important, the writer uses the passive voice.

Christy Brown uses both the active and passive voice in his narrative.

Active Voice: Mother *decided* there and then to take matters into her own hands.

Passive Voice: In a moment, everything *was* changed.

Brown uses the active voice more than the passive. Notice how this creates a sense of action and purpose in his narrative.

Prentice Hall Literature Program Resources

REINFORCE / RETEACH / EXTEND

Selection Support Pages
Build Vocabulary: Word Roots: *-vol-*, p. 43
Build Grammar Skills: Active and Passive Voice, p. 44
Reading Strategy: Author's Purpose, p. 45
Literary Focus: Significant Moment, p. 46

Strategies for Diverse Student Needs, p. 11

Beyond Literature
Community Connection: Accommodating the Physically Challenged, p. 11

Formal Assessment Selection Test, pp. 35–37; Assessment Resources Software

Alternative Assessment, p. 11

Writing and Language Transparencies
Writing Process Model 3: Personal Narrative, pp. 17–23

Resource Pro CD-ROM

Listening to Literature Audiocassettes

from My Left Foot

◆ Literature and Your Life

Connect Your Experience

Suppose you were kept after school every day for five years. Every day you would watch your friends run off to participate in sports, work at after-school jobs, or just sit around and talk to one another while you remained trapped in the detention classroom.

If you can imagine these five years of detention, you can begin to understand how Christy Brown might have felt. Able to think and feel emotions just like everyone else, Brown was trapped inside a body he couldn't control.

Thematic Focus: Overcoming Obstacles

This inspiring account of Christy Brown's first step in dealing with an enormous personal challenge may lead you to ask yourself, "What qualities must a person have to overcome great obstacles?"

Journal Writing List people you know or have seen in the news who have met great personal challenges. For each person, list a quality that has helped him or her achieve success.

◆ Background for Understanding

Science

Christy Brown was born with a disorder known as cerebral palsy. People who suffer from cerebral palsy have difficulty controlling their limbs, facial expressions, or both. The condition may be barely noticeable or extremely severe, as in Christy Brown's case. While some people with the condition are mentally retarded, others, such as Christy Brown, have average or above-average intelligence.

◆ Literary Focus

Significant Moment

If someone asked you to describe every moment of yesterday, you probably couldn't do it. Not every moment seems important. When you read a nonfiction account, the writer usually focuses on a **significant moment**—a moment that is a turning point, or a moment of discovery.

In this excerpt from his autobiography, Christy Brown describes the moment when he proved to his family that his physical disability had not affected his brain. In a single moment, Brown demonstrated his intelligence and changed the course of his life forever.

◆ Reading Strategy

Identify Author's Purpose

When you speak, you usually have a reason. Maybe you want to share information, make someone laugh, or express a new idea you've had. When an author writes, he or she has a **purpose,** a reason for writing. This purpose might be to influence you to take a position on an issue, to act in a certain way, or to make you laugh or think. The purpose shapes the writer's choice of language and use of details. Notice the details that Christy Brown chooses to tell you. Determine his purpose for writing his autobiography.

Test Preparation Workshop

Reading Comprehension:
Recognize Details Standardized tests often require students to answer questions based on the details of reading passages. After students read the excerpt from *My Left Foot,* use this sample.

Which important event occurred first?

A Christy grasped his mother's hair after she read to him.

B Christy's mother decided to treat him on the same plane as the other children.

C Christy showed an interest in his toes.

D Christy wrote an "A" with a piece of chalk held in his left foot.

The best approach to answering this question is to go back to the passage and look for the details that support or contradict each choice—in this case, answer B. When practicing for tests, students should find the details that prove their answer choice is correct. When taking tests, however, they may have to rely on what they remember.

Invite students to share what they know about Christopher Reeve and Stephen Hawkings. Explain that the actor Reeve, known for his role as Superman before his spinal cord injury, and the physicist and author Hawkings are both, in different ways, "locked" in their bodies. Yet both have found unique and resourceful ways of accomplishing their goals. While being productive in their fields, they have also served as models of what physically challenged people can accomplish. Ask students what personal qualities and attitudes they think are necessary for a physically challenged person to find and utilize his or her hidden resources. Let them know that in the narrative they are about to read, Christy Brown discovers such resources in himself.

Tips to Guide Reading

Sustained Reading Have students read the selection in one sitting, using sticky notes to mark questions or "tricky spots" they want to return to during class discussion

Customize for
Less Proficient Readers
Tell students that Brown considered *My Left Foot* to be "too sentimental, too corny," compared with his other books. Have them isolate phrases or sentences that might support or contradict Brown's opinion of his own writing in this selection.

Customize for
Pre-AP Students
Encourage students to examine the details of Brown's early life, as his mother realizes he has a problem, tries to get help, then takes her own course of action.

Customize for
English Language Learners
Brown adds to many of his sentences many phrase and clause modifiers that make them difficult for English language learners and less proficient readers. Work with these students to isolate the modifiers so that they can grasp the basic meaning of the sentences.

Develop Understanding

One-Minute Insight This personal narrative proves inspirational on two levels. It shows how the love and faith of Christy Brown's mother enhanced his development. Her faith was fully justified by Christy himself, a boy—and then a man—who determined he must be taken seriously. Through the nurturing atmosphere his mother created and his own drive to express himself truthfully, Christy overcame the limits of his cerebral palsy to become an artist and a writer of merit. Students may recognize aspects of his story in the lives of people they know.

◆ Build Grammar Skills

1 Active and Passive Voice Point out that Brown begins this narrative with a verb in the passive voice: "I *was born* . . ." Ask students to explain why the passive is appropriate in this context, and why the active voice would not be appropriate. *The passive voice is used when the performer of the action is either not known or not important. In this sentence, the subject of the sentence, "I," is the focal point, not Christy's mother. The emphasis of the sentence would be on the mother if the sentence had been written, "My mother gave birth to me . . ."—a less effective choice.*

2 Clarification Students might be confused by the word *steel* in the phrase "leaving thirteen steel to hold the family fort." Tell them that *steel* means "strong" in this context.

Extending Word Study

Context Encourage students to determine the meaning of *twine* in the second column, above, by relying on context. Then, using a dictionary, have them verify the meaning, in this context, and generate a list of synonyms for each meaning of the word.

Customize for
Gifted/Talented Students
Suggest that students pay particular attention to how Brown learns to write, as described on pp. 160 and 161. Students might demonstrate the technique.

from My Left Foot

Christy Brown

1 I was born in the Rotunda Hospital on June 5th, 1932. There were nine children before me and twelve after me, so I myself belong to the middle group. Out of this total of twenty-two, seventeen lived, but four died in in-
2 fancy, leaving thirteen steel to hold the family fort.

Mine was a difficult birth, I am told. Both mother and son almost died. A whole army of relations queued up[1] outside the hospital until the small hours of the morning, waiting for news and praying furiously that it would be good.

After my birth mother was sent to recuperate for some weeks and I was kept in the hospital while she was away. I remained there for some time, without name, for I wasn't baptized until my mother was well enough to bring me to church.

It was mother who first saw that there was something wrong with me. I was about four months old at the time. She noticed that my head had a habit of falling backward whenever she tried to feed me. She attempted to correct this by placing her hand on the back of my neck to keep it steady. But when she took it away back it would drop again. That was the first warning sign. Then she became aware of other defects as I got older. She saw that my hands were clenched nearly all of the time and were inclined to twine behind my back; my mouth couldn't grasp the teat of the bottle because even at that early age my jaws would either lock together tightly, so that it was impossible for her to open them, or they would suddenly become limp and fall loose, dragging my whole mouth to one side.[2] At six months I could not sit up without having a mountain of pillows around me; at twelve months it was the same.

1. **queued** (kyo͞od) **up:** Joined a line of people.

2. **my hands . . . dragging my whole mouth to one side:** Characteristic behavior of a person with severe cerebral palsy, a condition sometimes caused by lack of oxygen to the brain during birth. It often occurs as a result of a difficult childbirth.

Block Scheduling Strategies

Consider these suggestions to take advantage of extended class time:

- Have students read the Background for Understanding. Encourage them to exchange ideas about ways in which people can cope with the limitations imposed by cerebral palsy. (Students may wish to visit the Web site of the United Cerebral Palsy Association at http://www.ucpa.org/)
- To prepare students to answer the Literary Focus questions in Guide for Responding, have them gather in small groups to discuss the characteristics of a significant moment. Give students copies of the Literary Focus practice page in ***Selection Support,*** p. 46, for reinforcement.
- Using, Christy Brown's personal narrative as a model, have students work on their personal narratives (Guided Writing Lesson on p. 163).

Very worried by this, mother told my father her fears, and they decided to seek medical advice without any further delay. I was a little over a year old when they began to take me to hospitals and clinics, convinced that there was something definitely wrong with me, something which they could not understand or name, but which was very real and disturbing.

Almost every doctor who saw and examined me labeled me a very interesting but also a hopeless case. Many told mother very gently that I was mentally defective and would remain so. That was a hard blow to a young mother who had already reared five healthy children. The doctors were so very sure of themselves that mother's faith in me seemed almost an impertinence. They assured her that nothing could be done for me.

> ◆ **Reading Strategy**
> What do you think is Brown's **purpose** in focusing so strongly on his mother's belief that he was not hopeless?

She refused to accept this truth, the inevitable truth—as it then seemed—that I was beyond cure, beyond saving, even beyond hope. She could not and would not believe that I was an imbecile, as the doctors told her. She had nothing in the world to go by, not a scrap of evidence to support her conviction that, though my body was crippled, my mind was not. In spite of all the doctors and specialists told her, she would not agree. I don't believe she knew why—she just knew without feeling the smallest shade of doubt.

Finding that the doctors could not help in any way beyond telling her not to place her trust in me, or, in other words, to forget I was a human creature, rather to regard me as just something to be fed and washed and then put away again, mother decided there and then to take matters into her own hands. I was *her* child, and therefore part of the family. No matter how dull and incapable I might grow up to be, she was determined to treat me on the same plane as the others, and not as the "queer one" in the back room who was never spoken of when there were visitors present.

That was a momentous decision as far as my future life was concerned. It meant that I would always have my mother on my side to help me fight all the battles that were to come, and to inspire me with new strength when I

> ◆ **Build Vocabulary**
> **impertinence** (im purt´ ən əns) *n.*: Inappropriate, rude action
> **conviction** (kən vik´ shən) *n.*: Strong belief

▲ **Critical Viewing** Look at this still from the movie *My Left Foot.* Describe the feelings the actress playing Christy's mother is showing in her expression. **[Interpret]** 6

◆ Build Grammar Skills

3 Active and Passive Voice Ask students to analyze the use of active and passive voice in the sentence, "They assured her that nothing could be done for me." *"Assured" is in the active voice; they—the doctors—are the performers of the action. "Could be done" is passive voice; the performer of the action is unknown or not specified.*

◆ Reading Strategy

4 Identify Author's Purpose Elicit from students that even though it seems that the doctors are right, Christy wants his readers to know the extent of his mother's faith in him. His purpose is probably both to emphasize her strong and loving nature and also to begin to show how she would influence his development.

◆ Critical Thinking

5 Draw Conclusions Ask students: Why do the doctors want Brown's mother to forget that he is a human creature? *Students should realize that according to the thinking about cerebral palsy and its effects at the time, people with this disease were thought to be incapable of just about all levels of human functioning. It was also incorrectly assumed that mental function was minimal in all cases; the doctor thought he was acting in Christy's mother's best interest by encouraging her not to work on her son's development.*

▶Critical Viewing◀

6 Interpret *Christy's mother's position behind Christy symbolizes that she "stands behind" him, or supports him. Her facial expression shows pride in her son and happiness for him.*

Speaking, Listening, and Viewing Mini-Lesson

Speech

This mini-lesson supports the Speaking, Listening, and Viewing activity in the Idea Bank on p. 163.

Introduce Speeches convey emotion through the voice, face, and body.

Develop As students prepare their speeches, have them consider these issues:

- Christy's audience is his family.
- Christy is 5 years old. Most 5-year-olds can speak fluently, but their vocabulary and the complexity of their sentences are limited.
- Christy is intelligent. He has been observing and thinking even though he hasn't been speaking.

Apply Students should plan and write their speeches, expressing what they think Christy's main message would be.

Assess Have students use the Peer Assessment: Speaker/Speech form on p. 121 of the ***Alternative Assessment*** booklet to help them evaluate how well one another's speeches express the importance and emotion of this significant moment in Christy's life.

Develop Understanding

◆ Reading Strategy

❶ **Author's Purpose** Ask how this detail serves Brown's purpose in creating an inspiring portrait of his mother. *It is even more difficult to maintain faith and hope without the support of one's friends and relatives.*

◆ Literary Focus

❷ **Significant Moment** Ask students how the author starts here to build toward the significant moment of the narrative—the moment in which he will prove that his mother was right. *Students should grasp that by saying that his mother "was so successful," Brown is preparing the reader for the significant moment.*

◆ Reading Strategy

❸ **Identify Author's Purpose** Ask students what they think is the author's purpose in describing how unappealing he must have been as a young child. *Including these details underscores his mother's strength, love, and faith. She never let Christy's disabilities shake her confidence.*

◆ Build Vocabulary

❹ **Word Roots: *-vol-*** Point out the adverb *involuntarily*. Ask students how knowing the meaning of the root *-vol-* can help determine the meaning of the word. *If both the word root -vol- and the prefix in- are familiar, the meaning of the word—"without willing," or "unintentionally"—can be deduced.*

◆ Literary Focus

❺ **Significant Moment** *Students should recognize that Mrs. Brown is beginning to wonder if they might be right.*

Customize for
Pre-AP Students
Encourage students to examine the conflict between the doctors' advice to Brown's mother and the action she decided to take. Invite them to write a journal entry that the mother might have written after seeing the doctors.

was almost beaten. But it wasn't easy for her
❶ because now the relatives and friends had decided otherwise. They contended that I should be taken kindly, sympathetically, but not seriously. That would be a mistake. "For your own sake," they told her, "don't look to this boy as you would to the others; it would only break your heart in the end." Luckily for me, mother and father held out against the lot of them. But mother wasn't content just to say
❷ that I was not an idiot, she set out to prove it, not because of any rigid sense of duty, but out of love. That is why she was so successful.

At this time she had the five other children to look after besides the "difficult one," though as yet it was not by any means a full house. They were my brothers, Jim, Tony and Paddy, and my two sisters, Lily and Mona, all of them very young, just a year or so between each of them, so that they were almost exactly like steps of stairs.

Four years rolled by and I was now five, and still as helpless as a newly-born baby. While my father was out at bricklaying earning our bread and butter for us, mother was slowly, patiently pulling down the wall, brick by brick, that seemed to thrust itself between me and the other children, slowly, patiently penetrating beyond the thick curtain that hung over my mind, separating it from theirs. It was hard, heart-breaking work, for often all she got from me in return was a vague smile and perhaps a faint gurgle. I could not speak or even mumble, nor could I sit up without support on my own, let alone take steps. But I wasn't inert or motionless. I
❸ seemed, indeed, to be convulsed with movement, wild, stiff, snakelike movement that never left me, except in sleep. My fingers twisted and twitched continually, my arms twined backwards and would often shoot out suddenly this way and that, and my head lolled and sagged sideways. I was a queer, crooked little fellow.

Mother tells me how one day she had been sitting with me for hours in an upstairs room, showing me pictures out of a great big storybook that I had got from Santa Claus last Christmas and telling me the names of different animals and flowers that were in them, trying without success to get me to repeat them. This had gone on for hours while she talked and laughed with me. Then at the end of it she leaned over me and said gently into my ear:

"Did you like it, Chris? Did you like the bears and the monkeys and all the lovely flowers? Nod your head for yes, like a good boy."

But I could make no sign that I had understood her. Her face was bent over mine hopefully. Suddenly, involuntarily, my queer hand reached up and grasped one of the dark curls that fell in a thick cluster about her neck. Gently she loosened the clenched fingers, though some dark strands were still clutched between them.

Then she turned away from my curious stare and left the room, crying. The door closed behind her. It all seemed hopeless. It looked as though there was some justification for my relatives' contention that I was an idiot and beyond help.

> **◆ Literary Focus**
> What is the significance of this moment?

They now spoke of an institution.

"Never!" said my mother almost fiercely, when this was suggested to her. "I know my boy is not an idiot. It is his body that is shattered, not his mind. I'm sure of that."

Sure? Yet inwardly, she prayed God would give her some proof of her faith. She knew it

◆ Build Vocabulary

inert (i nurt´) *adj.*: Lacking the power to move; inactive

contention (kən ten´ shən) *n.*: Statement that one argues for

Beyond the Classroom

Career Connection

Developmental Psychology Christy's mother suspected that something was wrong with her son when he was 4 months old. Infants and children develop in predictable stages, conquering one developmental task before moving on to another.

Developmental psychologists study children's development in such areas as expressing needs appropriately, reasoning ability, and language acquisition. Have students gather information about child development stages and developmental psychologists, making a chart with their findings.

Community Connection

Parking Spaces Laws require that public parking spaces be provided, clearly marked and reserved for people who are designated as physically challenged. Students might survey a busy parking lot and investigate questions such as these:

- How many spaces are set aside? What percent?
- Are the spaces used? by cars with permits?
- Are the spaces located near ramps?
- In what other ways do public spaces provide for the needs of the physically challenged?

was one thing to believe but quite another thing to prove.

I was now five, and still I showed no real sign of intelligence. I showed no apparent interest in things except with my toes—more especially those of my left foot. Although my natural habits were clean I could not aid myself, but in this respect my father took care of me. I used to lie on my back all the time in the kitchen or, on bright warm days, out in the garden, a little bundle of crooked muscles and twisted nerves, surrounded by a family that loved me and hoped for me and that made me part of their own warmth and humanity. I was lonely, imprisoned in a world of my own, unable to communicate with others, cut off, separated from them as though a glass wall stood between my existence and theirs, thrusting me beyond the sphere of their lives and activities. I longed to run about and play with the rest, but I was unable to break loose from my bondage.

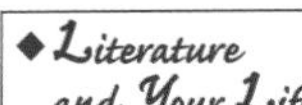

Literature and Your Life How would you feel if you were unable to communicate with your family or friends? 7

Then, suddenly, it happened! In a moment everything was changed, my future life molded into a definite shape, my mother's faith in me rewarded and her secret fear changed into open triumph. 8

It happened so quickly, so simply after all

▼ **Critical Viewing** This scene from the movie shows Christy as an adult with his mother. How does this picture reinforce what you have learned about them in the narrative? **[Connect]** 9

◆ Critical Thinking

6 Speculate In what ways did the fact that Christy Brown was part of a loving, caring family help him? *Possible response: His physical needs were attended to and he received attention. He was therefore able to focus his mind and spirit on finding a way to communicate.*

◆ Literature and Your Life

7 *Accept all reasonable responses. Students are likely to say that they would feel lonely, frustrated, and isolated.*

◆ Literary Focus

8 Significant Moment Ask students how Brown indicates that he is about to reveal the significant moment. *Brown's assertion that ". . . in a moment everything was changed indicates the importance of what is about to happen.*

▶Critical Viewing◀

9 Connect *Students should recognize the mood, or feeling, of the photograph as caring, compassionate, or loving. The mother's hand on her son's face and the proximity of their heads indicates closeness and caring.*

Customize for
English Language Learners

Use visual images from advertisements, art books, and posters to show students concrete examples of what is meant by figurative language. Discuss the images, then ask students to explain some of the images in Brown's narrative. *The images all highlight Brown's sense of isolation.*

Reteach

Tell students that they can better approach a nonfiction work if they understand why the author wrote it. To help them identify author's purposes, they can look for clues like these:

Clue	Purpose
Silly or exaggerated situations	to entertain
Advice to believe or to do something	to persuade
Facts or explanations	to inform
Description of a person's good qualities	to inspire

Point out to students that Brown's descriptions of his mother's actions are a clue to his purpose. Discuss with them why he might write about her, eliciting answers that indicate his purpose to be paying respect, informing others about her strength and courage, or showing his gratefulness to her.

Research Skills Mini-Lesson

Chart on Cerebral Palsy

This mini-lesson supports the Project activity in the Idea Bank on p. 163.

Introduce Discuss with students the different ways that research findings can be presented to others, including written and oral reports, speeches, multimedia presentations, charts and graphs, and models. Point out that when the goal is to provide an audience with a means of comparing and contrasting statistics and other hard data, visuals such as charts and graphs are often successful as communication tools.

Develop Students can work in groups to research cerebral palsy, referring to library resources, and the Internet to find out about the symptoms and causes of the disorder, as well as statistics on people who have it.

Apply Each group should brainstorm to develop the best way to display the information on a chart.

Assess Have students share their charts with the class. Discuss which presentations provide the information in clear and useful manners, examining what aspects achieve this goal.

Develop Understanding

◆ Literary Focus

❶ **Significant Moment** Point out the description of the weather and the setting. Ask students: Why does Brown describe the scene in such precise descriptive detail? *Possible responses: Because this was such a significant moment in his life, Brown wants the reader to know that he, as the silent child, was actually aware of all that was going on around him. Also, Brown, as the adult writer, wants to set the stage and draw out the suspense as the reader awaits the significant happening.*

❷ **Listening to Literature** This would be a good point at which to play the audiocassette recording. Students can hear the description of the significant moment along with the significance of the title.

Listening to Literature Audiocassettes

❸ **Clarification** Some students, especially ESL Students, might be confused by the use of the word *impolitely* in reference to Christy's taking the chalk out of his sister's hand. Tell students that Brown uses the word to inject humor into a tension-filled situation. No one was concerned with manners in the midst of such a significant event.

Comprehension Check ☑

❹ Why does the mother stop walking? *She was not in the room when Christy took the chalk, but as soon as she enters the room she realizes something important has happened because everyone is quiet and staring at Christy.*

the years of waiting and uncertainty, that I can see and feel the whole scene as if it had happened last week. ❶ It was the afternoon of a cold, gray December day. The streets outside glistened with snow; the white sparkling flakes stuck and melted on the window-panes and hung on the boughs of the trees like molten silver. The wind howled dismally, whipping up little whirling columns of snow that rose and fell at every fresh gust. And over all, the dull, murky sky stretched like a dark canopy, a vast infinity of grayness.

Inside, all the family were gathered round the big kitchen fire that lit up the little room with a warm glow and made giant shadows dance on the walls and ceiling.

In a corner Mona and Paddy were sitting huddled together, a few torn school primers[3] before them. They were writing down little sums on to an old chipped slate, using a bright piece of yellow chalk. I was close to them, propped up by a few pillows against the wall, watching.

It was the chalk that attracted me so much. It was a long, slender stick of vivid yellow. I had never seen anything like it before, and it showed up so well against the black surface of the slate that I was fascinated by it as much as if it had been a stick of gold.

❷ Suddenly, I wanted desperately to do what my sister was doing. Then—without thinking or knowing exactly what I was doing, I reached out and took the stick of chalk out of my sister's hand—*with my left foot.*

I do not know why I used my left foot to do this. It is a puzzle to many people as well as to myself, for, although I had displayed a curious interest in my toes at an early age, I had never attempted before this to use either of my feet in any way. They could have been as useless to me as were my hands. ❸ That day, however, my left foot, apparently by its own volition, reached out and very impolitely took the chalk out of my sister's hand.

I held it tightly between my toes, and, acting on an impulse, made a wild sort of scribble with it on the slate. Next moment I stopped, a bit dazed, surprised, looking down at the stick of yellow chalk stuck between my toes, not knowing what to do with it next, hardly knowing how it got there. Then I looked up and became aware that everyone had stopped talking and was staring at me silently. Nobody stirred. Mona, her black curls framing her chubby little face, stared at me with great big eyes and open mouth. Across the open hearth,[4] his face lit by flames, sat my father, leaning forward, hands outspread on his knees, his shoulders tense. I felt the sweat break out on my forehead.

My mother came in from the pantry with a steaming pot in her hand. She stopped midway between the table and the fire, feeling the tension flowing through the room. ❹ She followed their stare and saw me, in the corner. Her eyes looked from my face down to my foot, with the chalk gripped between my toes. She put down the pot.

Then she crossed over to me and knelt down beside me, as she had done so many times before.

"I'll show you what to do with it, Chris," she said, very slowly and in a queer, jerky way, her face flushed as if with some inner excitement.

Taking another piece of chalk from Mona, she hesitated, then very deliberately drew, on the floor in front of me, the single letter "A."

"Copy that," she said, looking steadily at me. "Copy it, Christy."

I couldn't.

I looked about me, looked around at the

◆ Build Vocabulary

volition (vō lish′ ən) *n.*: The act of using the will

taut (tôt) *adj.*: High-strung; tense

3. **primers** (prim′ ərz): Small books for teaching young children reading, writing, and arithmetic.

4. **hearth:** Fireplace.

Analyze Film Criticism

The film critic Roger Ebert writes about the movie *My Left Foot:* "I am trying to imagine what it would be like to write this review with my left foot. Quite seriously. I imagine it would be a great nuisance—unless, of course, it was the only part of my body over which I had control. If that were the case I would thank God that there was still some avenue down which I could communicate with the world."

Read Ebert's comments about Christy Brown's physical challenge to students. Encourage them to write a journal entry on whether this is an appropriate way to begin a review of the film about Brown's life. Have them consider whether Brown might have felt about Ebert's statement. On what point are Ebert and Brown in agreement? *Students should recognize that Ebert and Brown acknowledge the importance of a means of communication.*

faces that were turned toward me, tense, excited faces that were at that moment frozen, immobile, eager, waiting for a miracle in their midst.

The stillness was profound. The room was full of flame and shadow that danced before my eyes and lulled my taut nerves into a sort of waking sleep. I could hear the sound of the water-tap dripping in the pantry, the loud ticking of the clock on the mantelshelf, and the soft hiss and crackle of the logs on the open hearth.

I tried again. I put out my foot and made a wild jerking stab with the chalk which produced a very crooked line and nothing more. Mother held the slate steady for me.

"Try again, Chris," she whispered in my ear. "Again."

I did. I stiffened my body and put my left foot out again, for the third time. I drew one side of the letter. I drew half the other side. Then the stick of chalk broke and I was left with a stump. I wanted to fling it away and give up. Then I felt my mother's hand on my shoulder. I tried once more. Out went my foot. I shook, I sweated and strained every muscle. My hands were so tightly clenched that my fingernails bit into the flesh. I set my teeth so hard that I nearly pierced my lower lip. Everything in the room swam till the faces around me were mere patches of white. But—I drew it—*the letter "A."* There it was on the floor before me. Shaky, with awkward, wobbly sides and a very uneven center line. But it *was* the letter "A." I looked up. I saw my mother's face for a moment, tears on her cheeks. Then my father stooped down and hoisted me on to his shoulder. 5

> **◆ Literary Focus** Why is the outcome of this event so significant? 6

I had done it! It had started—the thing that was to give my mind its chance of expressing itself. True, I couldn't speak with my lips, but now I would speak through something more lasting than spoken words—written words.

That one letter, scrawled on the floor with a broken bit of yellow chalk gripped between my toes, was my road to a new world, my key to mental freedom. It was to provide a source of relaxation to the tense, taut thing that was me, which panted for expression behind a twisted mouth.

Guide for Responding

◆ Literature and Your Life

Reader's Response Which person do you admire most in this selection? Why?

Thematic Focus What qualities enabled Christy Brown—and his mother—to overcome his isolation?

Questions for Research What one question relevant to this selection could you research?

☑ Check Your Comprehension

1. What were the first signs that there was something wrong with Christy?
2. What was the doctors' conclusion about Christy's case?
3. How does Christy's mother respond to the doctors' diagnosis?
4. How did Christy's brothers and sisters treat him?
5. What did Christy do that changed other people's impression of him?

◆ Critical Thinking

5 Speculate Point out that Christy does not succeed immediately in copying the letter "A." Ask students to speculate about what Christy was feeling during this event, and why. *Students may speculate that Christy felt extremely tense as he tried to provide evidence of his intelligence. He was probably aware that this was his one chance to prove himself. If he failed, he would not gain his family's serious attention again.*

◆ Literary Focus

6 Significant Moment Students should recognize the following: *This is the first time anyone in the family knows for sure that Christy can learn and that his cerebral palsy does not affect him mentally. It means he has a future.*

Reinforce and Extend

Answers

◆ Literature and Your Life

Reader's Response Some students might admire Christy because his determination and talent caused him to override his physical limitation; others might say his mother because her patience and faith were an inspiration.

Thematic Focus Responses include determination, the ability to stand up against popular opinion, optimism, and courage.

Questions for Research Suggest that students identify the first question that comes to mind after reading the excerpt from *My Left Foot*.

☑ Check Your Comprehension

1. Christy could not hold his head up when he should have been able to; his hands were clenched all the time; he could not control his jaw movements; he could not sit up.
2. The doctors concluded Christy's case was hopeless.
3. Christy's mother ignores the doctors' advice. She takes matters into her own hands.
4. Christy's brothers and sisters treated him sympathetically, but they did not take him seriously.
5. He used his left foot to write the letter "A" on a slate.

Beyond the Selection

FURTHER READING

Other Works by Christy Brown

Down All the Days (novel)

Come Softly to My Wake: The Poems of Christy Brown

Other Works With the Theme of Facing Personal Challenge

The Miracle Worker, William Gibson

Flowers for Algernon, Daniel Keyes

We suggest that you preview these works before recommending them to students.

INTERNET

Students may find additional information about *My Left Foot* at the following site. Please be aware, however, that sites may have changed since the time we published this information.

For reviews of the film *My Left Foot* and links to resources about cerebral palsy, go to: **http://curry.edschool.virginia.edu/go/cise/ose/information/film/left/html**

We *strongly recommend* that you preview this and related sites before you send students to them.

Answers

◆ Critical Thinking

1. He was frustrated.
2. Possible answers include the obstacle of being labeled a hopeless case; the disregard of most of his family; his mother's attention to the competing demands of his brothers and sisters.
3. He was able to convince people that he had intelligence.
4. Examples will probably center on others not recognizing the strengths, talents, and abilities of people who are in some way physically challenged.
5. Mrs. Brown's belief in her son contributed in a major way to Christy's ability to flourish.

◆ Reading Strategy

1. Mrs. Brown overcame these obstacles: (1) doctors' hopeless prognoses for Christy; (2) friends and relatives' opinion that he should be institutionalized; (3) the demands of a large family without financial resources.
2. Possible statements include: "mother decided there and then to take matters into her own hands"; "It meant that I would always have my mother to inspire me with new strength when I was almost beaten."
3. Students' answers might acknowledge that the excerpt from *My Left Foot* reveals Christy's profound indebtedness to his mother and the courageous way in which she raised him.

◆ Literary Focus

1. Details leading up to the significant moment include Mrs. Brown's blind conviction in her son's mental abilities and Christy's own frustration at not being able to signal that he understood his mother.
2. Three details that emphasize the significant moment are (1) Mrs. Brown asking Christy to copy her letter "A"; (2) the stillness in the room as everyone watched; (3) Christy's tremendous concentration—his tightly clenched hands, the room swimming.

Guide for Responding *(continued)*

◆ Critical Thinking

INTERPRET

1. Explain how Christy feels about being unable to respond to his mother's questions. **[Infer]**

2. List two obstacles in addition to his physical disability that Christy has to overcome. **[Infer]**

3. Explain the significance of the incident with the chalk. **[Draw Conclusions]**

APPLY

4. Describe another situation in which a physically challenged person has had to deal with the ignorance or misunderstanding of others. **[Synthesize]**

EVALUATE

5. How did Christy's mother's belief in her son affect Christy's life? **[Evaluate]**

◆ Reading Strategy

IDENTIFY AUTHOR'S PURPOSE

Christy Brown uses language and includes details that best accomplish his **purpose,** his reason for writing. For instance, the many examples he includes of his mother's refusal to give up on him support his purpose to inspire—her strength in the face of obstacles is an example of courage and perseverance.

1. List three obstacles that Brown's mother overcomes.

2. Identify a direct statement in which Brown expresses his mother's strength.

3. In your own words, describe the impact Brown's mother had on his life.

◆ Literary Focus

SIGNIFICANT MOMENT

When Christy Brown drew the letter *A,* his life was instantly transformed. He builds toward this **significant moment,** the moment of discovery, throughout his narrative.

1. Identify two details in the early part of the narrative that indicate the deep significance of this moment in the author's life.

2. List three specific details that Brown includes to give emphasis to this moment.

◆ Build Vocabulary

USING THE LATIN ROOT *-vol-*

Knowing that the root of *volition* is *-vol-,* which means "wish" or "will," write the following items in your notebook and fill in the blanks.

1. Volition: act of using one's __?__

2. Volunteer: person who is __?__ to help

3. Benevolent: __?__ to do good

USING THE WORD BANK: Connotations

On your paper, respond to the following items:

1. An *inert* ingredient is (a) important, (b) strong, (c) inactive.

2. A *taut* rope is (a) tight, (b) loose, (c) uncut.

3. A person with strong *convictions* (a) gives up easily, (b) stands by her beliefs, (c) is intelligent.

4. What response would an *impertinent* person most likely get from others? (a) attraction, (b) boredom, (c) anger

5. Who would most likely make a *contention?* (a) a doctor, (b) a lawyer, (c) a minister

◆ Build Grammar Skills

ACTIVE AND PASSIVE VOICE

A verb is in the **active voice** when the subject of the sentence performs the action. A verb is in the **passive voice** when the action is performed on the subject.

Practice Determine whether the verb or verbs in the following sentences are in the active or passive voice.

1. After my birth, mother was sent home to recuperate for some weeks, and I was kept in the hospital.

2. I reached out and took the stick of chalk out of my sister's hand.

Writing Application Rewrite the following sentences in your notebook. Change each sentence from the passive voice to the active voice.

1. The room was filled with noise.

2. The piece of chalk was taken out of my hands by mother.

3. I was called a hopeless case by doctors.

162 ◆ Striving for Success

◆ Build Vocabulary

Using the Word Root *-vol-*

1. will; 2. willing; 3. wishing

Using the Word Bank

1. c 2. a 3. b 4. c 5. b

◆ Build Grammar Skills

Practice

1. passive; 2. active

Writing Application

1. Noise filled the room.
2. Mother took the piece of chalk out of my hands.
3. Doctors called me a hopeless case.

Grammar Reinforcement

For additional instruction and practice, use the lesson in the **Language Lab CD-ROM** on Active and Passive Voice and the pages on Active and Passive Voice (pp. 74–75) in the *Writer's Solution Grammar Practice Book.*

Build Your Portfolio

Idea Bank

Writing

1. Mother's Day Card Write a Mother's Day card from Christy to his mother, acknowledging all she has done for him.

2. Movie Review Watch the film *My Left Foot* and write a review of it. In your review, discuss how well the film portrays the incident you have just read about. **[Media Link; Performing Arts Link]**

3. Story From the Mother's Point of View Most of the events in this section of Christy Brown's autobiography also concern his mother. Rewrite this chapter of Brown's autobiography from the point of view of Christy's mother.

Speaking, Listening, and Viewing

4. Role Play Role-play a conversation between one of Christy's doctors and Christy's mother. Base your words and actions on what you've learned in the story. **[Performing Arts Link]**

5. Speech Suppose that Christy could clearly express his thoughts and feelings after writing the *A*. Improvise a speech that, under these circumstances, he might have spoken to his family. **[Performing Arts Link]**

Researching and Representing

6. Chart on Cerebral Palsy Create a poster with an awareness chart that outlines the symptoms and causes of cerebral palsy and the number of people in the United States who have it. **[Science Link; Art Link]**

7. Christy Brown Timeline Research other significant moments in Christy Brown's life. Create a timeline that shows these events in chronological order.

Online Activity www.phlit.phschool.com

Guided Writing Lesson

Personal Narrative

Choose a memorable moment from your own life and write a **personal narrative** about it, letting your feelings about events shape the way you tell your story. These tips will help you show why these events were significant:

Writing Skills Focus: Clear Explanation of Causes and Effects

A clear explanation of causes and effects is important in personal narratives, process explanations, and test essays. Such an explanation of causes and effects involves showing how one event or condition brings about another.

Notice, for example, how Christy Brown clearly demonstrates the cause-and-effect relationship between his mother's decision to treat him normally and his own sense of strength.

Prewriting Once you have identified the events to be included in your narrative, map out the relationship between them visually.

Drafting Refer to your prewriting notes to make sure you are connecting related events. Use terms like *because, consequently, as a result,* and *so* to show cause-and-effect relationships.

Revising Have a partner read your draft. Ask him or her to identify any places where you have not clearly established the cause-and-effect relationship between events. If necessary, add the words and phrases that will clarify the relationship. Also, clarify cause-and-effect links by changing the passive voice to the active voice.

For more on the active and passive voice, see Build Grammar Skills on pp. 154 and 162.

✓ ASSESSMENT OPTIONS

Formal Assessment, Selection Test, pp. 35–37, and Assessment Resources Software. The selection test is designed so that it can be easily customized to the performance levels of your students.

Alternative Assessment, p. 11, includes options for less advanced students, Pre-AP Students, visual/spatial learners, interpersonal and verbal/linguistic learners.

PORTFOLIO ASSESSMENT

Use the following rubrics in the ***Alternative Assessment*** booklet to assess student writing:
Mother's Day Card: Description Rubric, p. 100
Movie Review: Evaluation/Review Rubric, p. 107
Story From the Mother's Point of View: Fiction Narrative Rubric, p. 98

Idea Bank

Following are suggestions for matching Idea Bank topics with your students' performance levels and learning modalities:

Customizing for *Performance Levels*

Less Advanced Students: 1, 4
Average Students: 2, 5, 6
Pre-AP Students: 3, 7

Customizing for *Learning Modalities*

Visual/Spatial: 2, 6
Verbal/Linguistic: 3, 4, 5
Logical/Mathematical: 7
Bodily/Kinesthetic: 2

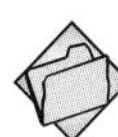

Guided Writing Lesson

Revision Strategy In order to help students evaluate their use of cause-and-effect words, divide them into pairs once they have completed their first drafts. Ask them to exchange papers and read their partners' work. Then, guide students to list the events that occur in their partners' papers. After each event, and in a different color ink, they should explain the way it is caused by the previous event. If the reader cannot do this, it is possible that the link is not clear. The writer should consider using cause-and-effect words or simply rephrasing cause-and-effect explanations at these points.

For more prewriting, elaboration, and revision strategies, see *Prentice Hall Writing and Grammar.*

Writing and Language Transparencies Use Writing Model 3: Personal Narrative (pp. 17–23) to help students shape their personal narratives.

Writing Lab CD-ROM

Have students complete the tutorial on Narration. Follow these steps:

1. Have students use the Inspirations for Narration to help them choose a topic for their personal narratives.
2. Have them read tips for peer revision to help them work productively with a peer reviewer.
3. Suggest that students use tips for publishing to get pointers for publishing in print or online.

Prepare and Engage

LESSON OBJECTIVES

1. **To develop vocabulary and word identification skills**
   - Latin Word Origins: *ventured*
   - Using the Word Bank: Context
   - Extending Word Study: Idioms (ATE)
2. **To use a variety of reading strategies to read and comprehend a story**
   - Connect Your Experience
   - Reading Strategy: Clarify
   - Tips to Guide Reading: Sustained Reading (ATE)
   - Read to Appreciate Author's Craft (ATE)
   - Idea Bank: News Report
3. **To increase knowledge of other cultures and to connect common elements across cultures**
   - Cultural Connection (ATE)
4. **To express and support responses to the text**
   - Critical Thinking
   - Idea Bank: Alternative Ending
5. **To analyze literary elements**
   - Literary Focus: Characterization
   - Idea Bank: Letter to Charles's Mother
6. **To read in order to research self-selected and assigned topics**
   - Idea Bank: Cultural Comparisons Chart
   - Questions for Research
7. **To speak clearly and effectively for a specific audience and purpose**
   - Idea Bank: Oral Anecdote
   - Speaking, Listening, and Viewing Mini-Lesson: Casting Discussion
8. **To use recursive writing processes to write a firsthand biography**
   - Guided Writing Lesson
9. **To increase knowledge of the rules of grammar and usage**
   - Build Grammar Skills: Pronoun Case

Test Preparation

Reading Comprehension: Recognize Details (ATE, p. 165) The teaching tips and sample test item in this workshop support the instruction and practice in the unit workshop:

Reading Comprehension: Recognize Facts, Details, and Sequence (SE, p. 215)

Guide for Reading

William Melvin Kelley

(1937–   )

Some people think they have all the answers. William Melvin Kelley, on the other hand, is a man of questions. He says, "I am not a sociologist or a politician or a spokesman. Such people try to give answers. A writer, I think, should ask questions."

Marching to His Own Beat Kelley's questions about his own life have rarely found their answers in conformity. The title of his first book—*A Different Drummer*—reflects his belief in the importance of individuality. The title is based on the words of the nineteenth-century philosopher Henry David Thoreau, who said, "If a man does not keep pace with his companions, perhaps it is because he hears a different drummer. Let him step to the music which he hears, however measured or far away."

A Question of Individuals Kelley's stories focus on the problems of individual characters, some of them black.

"A Visit to Grandmother" focuses on an age-old problem—a conflict between parent and child.

In this story, Kelley shows the drama of one family's search for answers to questions about pain in the past and acceptance in the present.

◆ Build Vocabulary

LATIN WORD ORIGINS: *ventured*

In this story, you will encounter the word *ventured*. Its similarity to the word *adventure* is no coincidence; both words come from the Latin *aventura*, which means "a happening." An adventure is usually a happening that involves some risk or excitement; *ventured* means taking a risk.

Tracing the origins of words often helps you understand the meaning of unfamiliar words by revealing their relationships to words you already know.

WORD BANK

As you read, you will encounter the words in this list. Each word is defined on the page where it first appears. Preview this list of words from the story.

ventured
indulgence
grimacing
lacquered

◆ Build Grammar Skills

PRONOUN CASE

William Melvin Kelley, like other writers, uses pronouns to avoid unnecessary repetition in his writing. His writing is clear because he uses the correct form of a pronoun, depending on its use in the sentence.

Pronoun case refers to the different forms that a pronoun takes to indicate its function in a sentence.

Subjective case pronouns—*I, we, you, she, it, they*—are used when the pronoun performs the action or renames the subject.

She let him go . . .

The objective case—*me, us, you, him, he, it, they*—is used when the pronoun receives the action of the verb or is the object of a preposition.

I swapped *him* for that old chair.

Prentice Hall Literature Program Resources

REINFORCE / RETEACH / EXTEND

Selection Support Pages
Build Vocabulary: Word Origins: *ventured*, p. 57
Build Grammar Skills: Pronoun Case, p. 48
Reading Strategy: Clarify, p. 49
Literary Focus: Characterization, p. 50

Strategies for Diverse Student Needs, p. 12

Beyond Literature
Career Connection: Performing Arts, p. 12

Formal Assessment Selection Test, pp. 38–40; Assessment Resources Software

Alternative Assessment, p. 11

Writing and Language Transparencies
Writing Process Model 2: Biographical Profile, pp. 13–16

Resource Pro CD-ROM

Listening to Literature Audiocassettes

A Visit to Grandmother

◆ Literature and Your Life

CONNECT YOUR EXPERIENCE

It doesn't matter whether a family has two members or ten—misunderstandings are common. Disagreements can be healthy, however, when they lead people to work out their differences. Through a confrontation, the family members in "A Visit to Grandmother" gain a better understanding of one another.

Journal Writing Use a Venn diagram like the one shown to explore both sides of a misunderstanding you've had with a friend or family member. Use the center area to show areas of agreement that helped you reach a common ground.

My Side | My Brother's Side

He bothers my friends and me.
He never leaves us alone.
We both like football.
He wants to hang out with us.
He says we never include him.

Common ground: We can share some activities like football games; other times he'll leave us alone.

THEMATIC FOCUS: OVERCOMING OBSTACLES

The events in this story may help you answer the question, "What happens when people don't communicate with one another?"

◆ Background for Understanding

CULTURE

In "A Visit to Grandmother," one character sweet-talks his mother into taking a hair-raising ride with a wild horse and a borrowed buggy. Today, a character might suggest a spin around the block in a new car, but in the late 1920's the automobile was just beginning its conquest of the American road. In parts of the rural South, where this story takes place, the horse and buggy was not just transportation; it was as much of a status symbol as a convertible or a hot rod.

◆ Literary Focus

CHARACTERIZATION

Sometimes writers use **direct characterization**, directly telling you about the character's personality. More frequently, a writer uses **indirect characterization**, revealing personality traits through the character's thoughts, words, and actions, and through other characters' comments. Kelley uses indirect characterization to show one character's kindness: "When people ventured timidly into his office, it took only a few words from him to make them relax, and even laugh."

Notice the other thoughts, actions, and reactions, as well as the direct statements, that bring the characters in this story to life.

◆ Reading Strategy

CLARIFY

To avoid misunderstandings when you read, **clarify**—check your understanding of—any parts of the story you don't understand. The best way to do this is to read ahead for more information or read back to review what you have already learned. For example, you might want to review details of the setting, clarify the relationships among the characters, or look back at the details of a key event.

One technique you can use to help you clarify relationships among characters and events is to represent the relationships visually.

As you meet the members of the Dunford family, you may want to sketch out a rough family tree, to clarify how the characters are related to one another, or a timeline that clarifies the order of events in the family's past.

Test Preparation Workshop

Reading Comprehension: Recognize Details Standardized tests, such as the SAT test, require students to identify details in order to determine the best answers to questions. Use this sample question to teach students how to recognize details that are central to the purpose of the text.

> Mae and Chig asked questions; the old lady answered; Aunt Rose directed the discussion, steering the old lady onto the best stories. Chig's father laughed from time to time; Uncle Hiram ate.

Which family member is least interested in the discussion?

A Mae
B Chig's father
C Rose
D Hiram

Help students review the details of the passage to see that D is the correct answer because Uncle Hiram is simply eating and is not involved in the discussion.

When taking tests with reading questions, suggest that students read the questions first to get a sense of what to look for in their reading.

Ask students to name a book they've read or TV show or film they've seen that dealt with a problem between a parent or guardian and a teenager. Encourage students to share their thoughts about the book or show and to explain how the conflict did—or didn't—get resolved. Did students agree with the resolution? Point out that some parent-child conflicts reach on into adulthood, when the "child" already has children of his or her own. Tell students that this kind of conflict is at the heart of "A Visit to Grandmother."

Connecting Themes Across Cultures

Discuss the universal theme of overcoming obstacles. Encourage students to suggest obstacles that present themselves to certain groups of people and not others.

Customize for *Less Proficient Readers*

Less proficient readers might have difficulty with the dialect in which some of the dialogue in this selection is written. Having them listen to the recording of the story as they follow the text will aid their comprehension.

Listening to Literature Audiocassettes

Customize for *Pre-AP Students*

Suggest that students select a section of the story and rewrite it to reflect the point of view of the grandmother. Advise them to use the characterizations presented in the story, but as seen from the grandmother's first-person perspective.

Customize for *English Language Learners*

Point out that the dialogue is written as informal speech and is often not standard English. Assist these students in restating these ideas in standard English.

Develop Understanding

One-Minute Insight This story shows how old grievances and tensions within a family can survive through the years, affecting even the most capable and accomplished people. Dr. Charles Dunford has achieved much in his life and has applied his intelligence, determination, and empathy to serve others. Yet even as an adult, he is not exempt from the emotional burdens of sibling rivalry and feelings of rejection. When his bitter feelings finally emerge, the result is a shock to his family, including his admiring son.

Customize for *Visual/Spatial Learners*
Have these students preview the illustrations on pp. 166, 169, and 172. Ask them what expectations these pictures create about the characters and their way of life.

Tips to Guide Reading

Sustained Reading Encourage students to read silently for a sustained period of time. If necessary, have them use sticky notes to mark places they may want to clarify by rereading.

A Visit to Grandmother

William Melvin Kelley

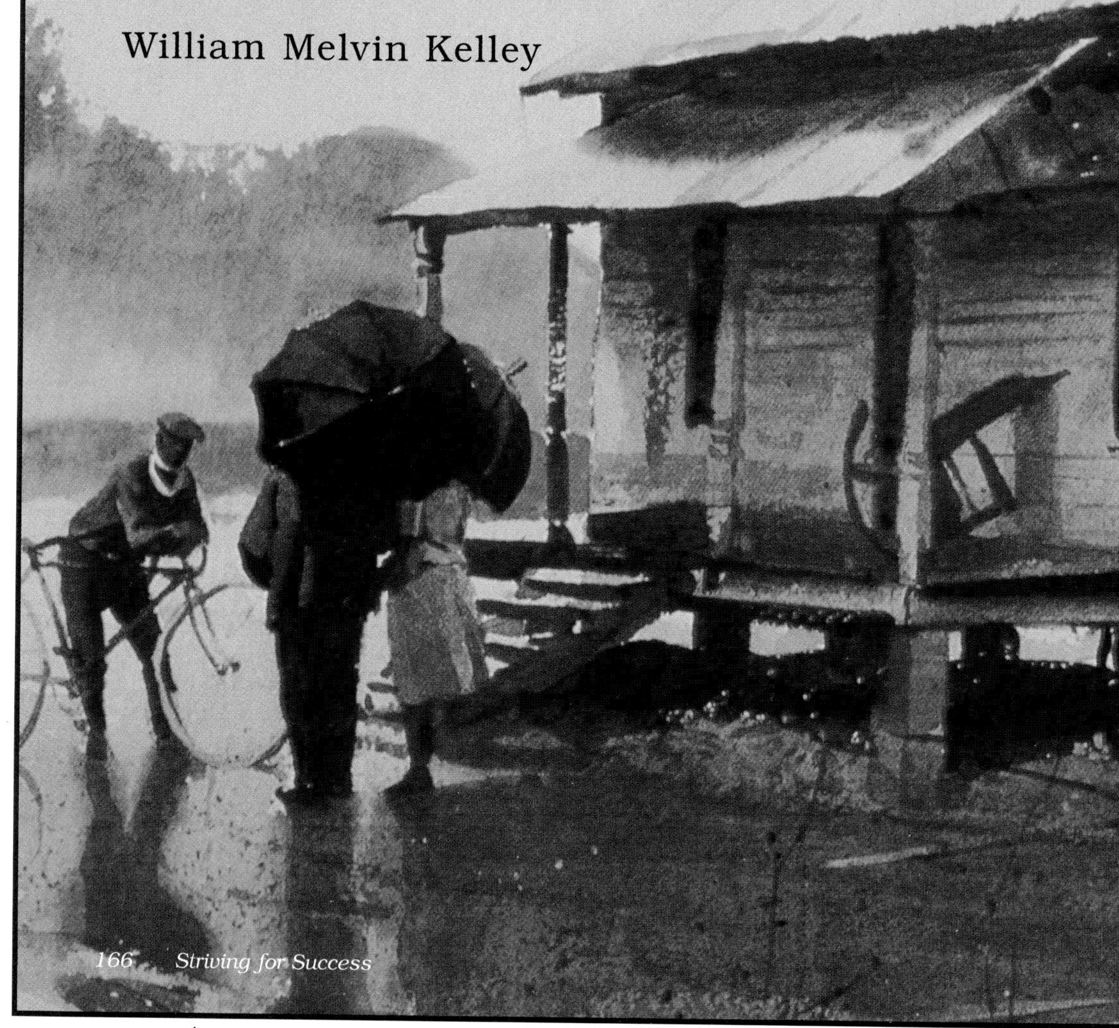

Block Scheduling Strategies

Consider these suggestions to take advantage of extended class time:

- Have students listen to all or part of the selection on audiocassette, and discuss the characters of the grandmother and Dr. Dunford, based on what they hear as well as what they have read.
- Give students practice with correct pronoun case by having them do the Build Grammar Skills exercise on p. 175, and the Build Grammar Skills page from ***Selection Support,*** p. 48.
- Introduce students to direct and indirect characterization with the Literary Focus information on p. 165. They might also complete the Literary Focus page from ***Selection Support*** for reinforcement.
- To structure classtime, have students break out into "four corners," based on whether they strongly agree, agree, disagree, or strongly disagree with Charles's decision to leave home. Have each group discuss and prepare a statement to present to the rest of the class.
- Help students to complete the Alternate Ending to the story in the Idea Bank on p. 176. Before they begin, ask them to make a comparison chart on which they note thoughts, words, and actions that reveal each brother's personality traits.
- Direct students to complete the Guided Writing Lesson on p. 176, using the instructional material in the ATE. Before students start writing, guide them through the drafts in the Writing Process Model 2: Biographical Profile (pp. 13–16).

Springtime Rain, 1975, Ogden M. Pleissner

Chig knew something was wrong the instant his father kissed her. He had always known his father to be the warmest of men, a man so kind that when people ventured timidly into his office, it took only a few words from him to make them relax, and even laugh. Doctor Charles Dunford cared about people. ❶

But when he had bent to kiss the old lady's black face, something new and almost ugly had come into his eyes: fear, uncertainty, sadness, and perhaps even hatred.

Ten days before in New York, Chig's father had decided suddenly he wanted to go to Nashville to attend his college class reunion, twenty years out. Both Chig's brother and sister, Peter and Connie, were packing for camp and besides were too young for such an affair. But Chig was seventeen, had nothing to do that summer, and his father asked if he would like to go along. His father had given him additional reasons: "All my running buddies got their diplomas and were snapped up by them crafty young gals, and had kids within a year—now all those kids, some of them gals, are your age."

The reunion had lasted a week. As they packed for home, his father, in a far too offhand way, had suggested they visit Chig's grandmother. "We this close. We might as well drop in on her and my brothers." ❷

So, instead of going north, they had gone farther south, had just entered her house. And Chig had a suspicion now that the reunion had

◆ Build Vocabulary

ventured (ven′ chərd) *v.*: Took a risk

◀ **Critical Viewing** Describe this setting as if you are speaking to someone who has never seen it. **[Analyze]** 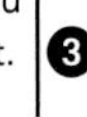

◆ Literary Focus

❶ Characterization Ask students to find examples of both indirect and direct characterization in this paragraph. Have them explain the examples they choose. Chig's thoughts about his father's kindness and ability to set people at ease are examples of indirect characterization. The author then uses direct characterization to tell that Dr. Dunford cared about people.

◆ Critical Thinking

❷ **Infer** Ask students: What do the words "in a far too offhand way" suggest? *These words suggest that Dr. Dunford was not really being offhand—that he had planned to make this visit all along; his announcement to his son sounds rehearsed.*

▶Critical Viewing◀

❸ **Analyze** *Elicit responses such as the following: The setting is bleak; there is a humble tin-roofed house on a post foundation situated on a barren piece of land. Smoke comes from the chimney, indicating that people are at home. The figure on the bicycle might be visiting and the people huddled under the umbrella might be members of the household.*

Humanities: Art

Springtime Rain, 1975, Ogden M. Pleissner.

Ogden Pleissner was as comfortable in New York City as he was in rural settings such as the one shown here. He traveled to Europe when he worked for the War Department during World War II, sketching battle scenes quickly and under dangerous conditions.

In addition to capturing the "essence" of a scene, Pleissner is known as a superb draftsman. He shows this skill in the balanced composition and perfect perspective of his work. The form and emotion of his human figures is also admired by many critics.

Have students analyze the painting on this page, looking for evidence of these strengths in Pleissner's work. Use these questions for discussion:

1. Why do you think Pleissner paints the scene from an angle, rather than head-on? *The angle gives a more immediate, realistic feel to the scene, as if the viewer is entering the scene. In addition, the angle of the building adds depth and balance to the composition.*
2. How does Pleissner make the people seem realistic and capture their human qualities? *Students may not that the postures of the people, and their placement outside the building make it seem as if they have been caught in a candid, unguarded moment.*

◆ Literary Focus

1 Characterization Dr. Dunford's refusal to discuss members of his family suggests negative feelings about them.

2 Clarification Point out that when Dr. Dunford was growing up segregation was a fact of life in the South. Public education facilities for African Americans were inferior in quality and far less available than those for white students.

◆ Critical Thinking

3 Infer Ask students what they can infer about Chig's grandmother from these lines. *Students will probably say they can infer that Chig's grandmother's eyesight is extremely poor or that she is nearly blind.*

◆ Reading Strategy

4 Clarify Ask students how they can clarify the relationship between Dr. Dunford and his mother. *Readers can look back to find that Dr. Dunford left home at an early age and that he was reluctant to tell his son they were going to visit his mother. They can use these details and the fact that the mother never hears from Charles to conclude that something is amiss between them.*

◆ Critical Thinking

5 Infer Ask students why they think Dr. Dunford's voice cracks. *Students may answer that he is showing the strain of a difficult moment, that even though he has had a troubled relationship with his mother, it is still important to him that she meet his son, of whom he is proud.*

---

been only an excuse to drive south, that his father had been heading to this house all the time.

His father had never talked much about his family, with the exception of his brother, GL, who seemed part con man, part practical joker and part Don Juan;[1] he had spoken of GL with the kind of indulgence he would have shown a cute, but ill-behaved and potentially dangerous, five-year-old.

1 **◆ Literary Focus** What does this detail indirectly reveal about Chig's father's feelings?

Chig's father had left home when he was fifteen. When asked why,

2 he would answer: "I wanted to go to school. They didn't have a Negro high school at home, so I went up to Knoxville and lived with a cousin and went to school."

They had been met at the door by Aunt Rose, GL's wife, and ushered into the living room. The old lady had looked up from her seat by the window. Aunt Rose stood between the visitors.

3 The old lady eyed his father. "Rose, who that? Rose?" She squinted. She looked like a doll, made of black straw, the wrinkles in her face running in one direction like the head of a broom. Her hair was white and coarse and grew out straight from her head. Her eyes were brown—the whites, too, seemed light brown—and were hidden behind thick glasses, which remained somehow on a tiny nose. "That Hiram?" That was another of his father's brothers. "No, it ain't Hiram; too big for Hiram." She turned then to Chig. "Now that man, he look like Eleanor, Charles's wife, but Charles wouldn't

4 never send my grandson to see me. I never even hear from Charles." She stopped again.

"It Charles, Mama. That who it is." Aunt Rose, between them, led them closer. "It Charles come all the way from New York to see you, and brung little Charles with him."

The old lady stared up at them. "Charles? Rose, that really Charles?" She turned away, and reached for a handkerchief in the pocket of her clean, ironed, flowered housecoat, and wiped her eyes. "God have mercy, Charles." She spread her arms up to him, and he bent down and kissed her cheek. That was when Chig saw his face, grimacing. She hugged him; Chig watched the muscles in her arms as they tightened around his father's neck. She half rose out of her chair. "How are you, son?"

Chig could not hear his father's answer.

She let him go, and fell back into her chair, grabbing the arms. Her hands were as dark as the wood, and seemed to become part of it. "Now, who that standing there? Who that man?"

"That's one of your grandsons, Mama." His father's voice cracked. "Charles Dunford, junior. You saw him once, when he was a baby, in Chicago. He's grown now." 5

"I can see that, boy!" She looked at Chig squarely. "Come here, son, and kiss me once." He did. "What they call you? Charles too?"

"No, ma'am, they call me Chig."

She smiled. She had all her teeth, but they were too perfect to be her own. "That's good. Can't have two boys answering to Charles in the same house. Won't nobody at all come. So you that little boy. You don't remember me, do

His father had never talked much about his family . . .

◆ Build Vocabulary

indulgence (in dul′ jəns) *n.*: Leniency; forgiveness

grimacing (grim′ əs iŋ) *v.*: Making a twisted or distorted facial expression

1. **Don Juan** (dän′ wän′): An idle, immoral nobleman who enjoyed a great appeal for women.

Cultural Connection

Notable African American Colleges

Because of the official segregation that existed during the early part of the twentieth century, Chig's father had to leave the South to get a high school education. He returned south, however, for his college education, probably to attend one of the several noted colleges set up for the higher education of African American students.

Morehouse College is a small liberal arts college that has such renowned alumni as Dr. Martin Luther King, Jr., Olympic athlete Edwin Moses, filmmaker Spike Lee, and a number of congressmen and federal judges.

Other African American colleges include Spelman College in Atlanta, Georgia, Howard University in Washington, D.C., and Booker T. Washington's alma mater, Hampton University in Hampton, Virginia.

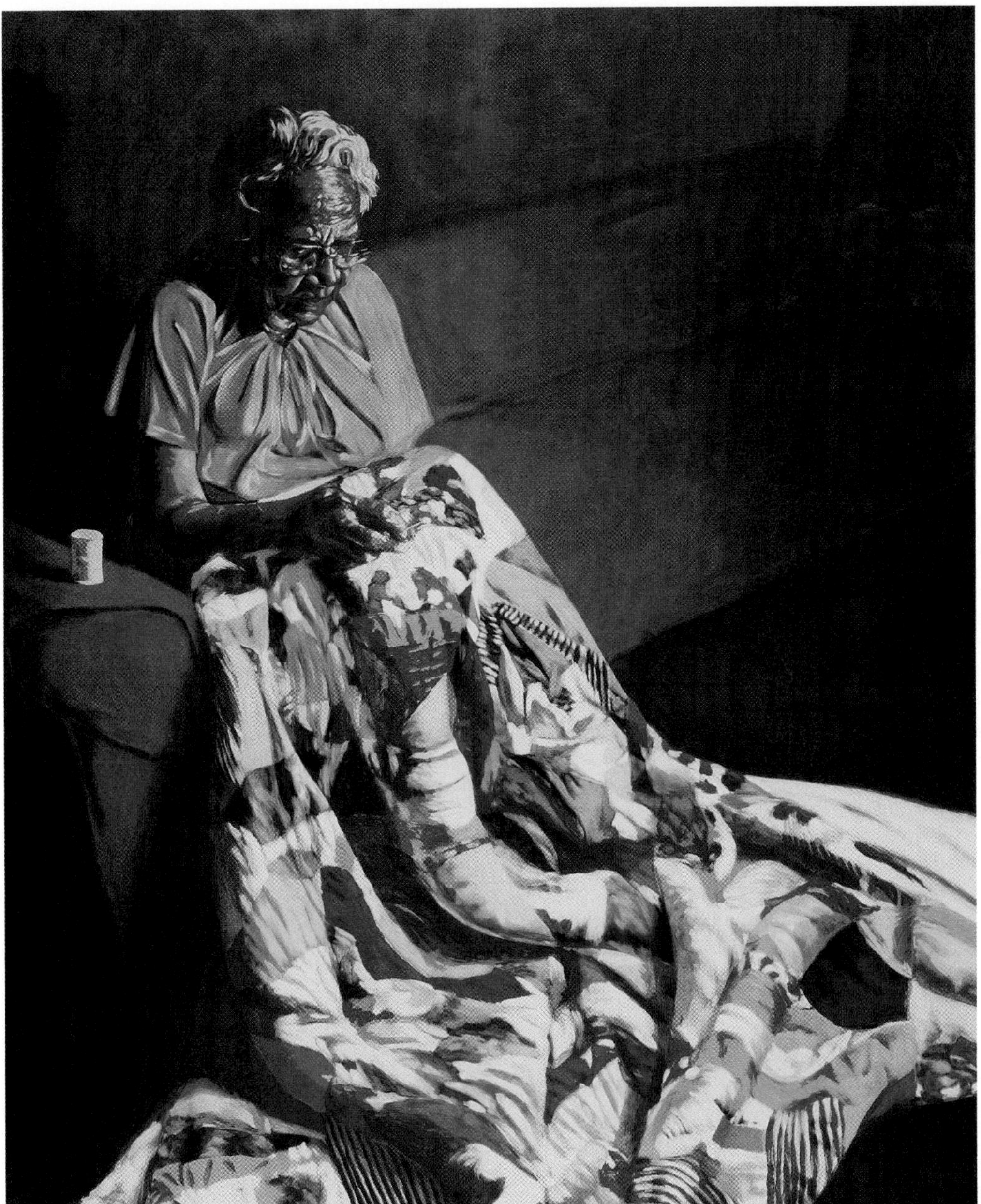

▲ **Critical Viewing** Compare and contrast the woman in this picture with Chig's grandmother. **[Compare and Contrast]** ❻

▶Critical Viewing◀

❻ **Compare and Contrast** Elicit responses such as the following: *Although the woman in the painting is an elderly African American woman, like the grandmother in the story, she looks different from Charles's mother. Her hair is more manageable and, most significant, her eyesight is good enough to enable her to do needlework.*

Read to Appreciate Author's Craft

Direct students' attention to the way the author reveals important details, especially about character traits, as the story progresses. The reader begins to understand what is happening to Charles at the same time that Chig is learning about his father's history with his family.

Customize for *Visual/Spatial Learners*

Encourage these students to describe in detail how their mental images of the grandmother contrast with the woman in the picture. Then ask them to use what they know about the grandmother to explore these two characters further. Eyesight allowing, would the grandmother in the story be likely to quilt? Why or why not?

Listening to Literature Audiocassettes Play the recording of this portion of the story to help students appreciate the sound and flavor of the dialect. Explain to students that although we use standard English for formal speaking and writing, people generally use a more colloquial English for conversations with friends and family. This informal speech varies from region to region. In this story, characters use a Southern dialect. Ask students to listen, and then to explain what the dialect adds to the story. *The dialect makes the characters seem more like real people from a real place.*

Humanities: Art

Strong Steady Hands by Alonzo Adams.

This serigraph—a print made by the silkscreen process—shows an African American woman working on an elaborate quilt.

Alonzo Adams was born in Harlem in New York City in 1961. As a painter, he specializes in capturing everyday scenes associated with contemporary black life. Students might be interested to know that Bill Cosby, the Rev. Jesse Jackson, Maya Angelou, and former Senator Bill Bradley all own works by Adams.

1. What personal quality might the woman in the picture share with the grandmother in the story? *Students may say that the woman in the painting shows strength and patience in being able to finish a difficult task. The grandmother in the story shows strength when she tells Chig she doesn't need help.*
2. How would the painting be different without the quilt? *Students might say that the quilt is what makes the painting beautiful. Without it, the painting would be dark and dull.*

Develop Understanding

◆ Reading Strategy

❶ **Clarify** *The phrase "those boys" implies that Hiram is another of Mama's sons. For verification, students can also look back at the following passage on page 168: "'That Hiram?' That was another of his father's brothers."*

◆ Literary Focus

❷ **Characterization** Ask students how the grandmother's own words characterize her in this passage. *Students may say that she shows herself to be strong or tough.*

◆ Critical Thinking

❸ **Infer** Ask students what they infer from the observation that Dr. Dunford's wife would sit and not speak for long periods. *Students may answer that Dr. Dunford's wife is calm and can focus on a task.*

◆ Reading Strategy

❹ **Clarify** Ask students to think back to what they know of Dr. Dunford's character and suggest why this situation might be especially difficult for him. *Students may answer that it must be very difficult for Dr. Dunford—a successful and independent professional—to feel reduced to a child in his mother's presence.*

◆ Literary Focus

❺ **Characterization** Ask students to give their ideas about GL's character, based on what they have read about him. *Students may say that GL seems unpredictable and immature on the one hand, but charming and fun-filled on the other.*

Extending Word Study

Idioms Ask students what the word *footloose* means. Invite them to speculate on how this word developed. Then have them look in the dictionary to confirm the definition and find the origin of the word.

you. I used to take you to church in Chicago, and you'd get up and hop in time to the music. You studying to be a preacher?"

"No, ma'am. I don't think so. I might be a lawyer."

"You'll be an honest one, won't you?"

"I'll try."

"Trying ain't enough! You be honest, you hear? Promise me. You be honest like your daddy."

"All right. I promise."

"Good. Rose, where's GL at? Where's that thief? He gone again?"

"I don't know, Mama." Aunt Rose looked embarrassed. "He say he was going by the store. He'll be back."

❶ "Well, then where's Hiram? You call up those boys, and get them over here—now! You got enough to eat? Let me go see." She started to get up. Chig reached out his hand. She shook him off. ❷ "What they tell you about me, Chig? They tell you I'm all laid up? Don't believe it. They don't know nothing about old ladies. When I want help, I'll let you know. Only time I'll need help getting anywheres is when I dies and they lift me into the ground."

> ◆ **Reading Strategy**
> What clues help you clarify who Grandma is talking about?

She was standing now, her back and shoulders straight. She came only to Chig's chest. She squinted up at him. "You eat much? Your daddy ate like two men."

"Yes, ma'am."

❸ "That's good. That means you ain't nervous. Your mama, she ain't nervous. I remember that. In Chicago, she'd sit down by a window all afternoon and never say nothing, just knit." She smiled. "Let me see what we got to eat."

"I'll do that, Mama." Aunt Rose spoke softly. "You haven't seen Charles in a long time. You sit and talk."

The old lady squinted at her. "You can do the cooking if you promise it ain't because you think I can't."

Aunt Rose chuckled. "I know you can do it, Mama."

"All right. I'll just sit and talk a spell." She sat again and arranged her skirt around her short legs.

❹ Chig did most of the talking, told all about himself before she asked. His father spoke only when he was spoken to, and then, only one word at a time, as if by coming back home, he had become a small boy again, sitting in the parlor while his mother spoke with her guests.

When Uncle Hiram and Mae, his wife, came they sat down to eat. Chig did not have to ask about Uncle GL's absence; Aunt Rose volunteered an explanation: "Can't never tell where the man is at. One Thursday morning he left here and next thing we knew, he was calling from Chicago, saying he went up to see Joe Louis[2] fight. He'll be here though; he ain't as young and footloose as he used to be." ❺ Chig's father had mentioned driving down that GL was about five years older than he was, nearly fifty.

Uncle Hiram was somewhat smaller than Chig's father; his short-cropped kinky hair was half gray, half black. One spot, just off his forehead, was totally white. Later, Chig found out it had been that way since he was twenty. Mae (Chig could not bring himself to call her Aunt) was a good deal younger than Hiram, pretty enough so that Chig would have looked at her twice on the street. She was a honey-colored woman, with long eyelashes. She was wearing a white sheath.

At dinner, Chig and his father sat on one side, opposite Uncle Hiram and Mae; his grandmother and Aunt Rose sat at the ends. The food was good; there was a lot and Chig ate a lot. All through the meal, they talked about the family as it had been thirty years before, and particularly about the young GL. Mae and Chig asked questions; the old lady answered; Aunt Rose directed the discussion, steering the old lady onto the best stories; Chig's father laughed from time to time; Uncle Hiram ate.

"Why don't you tell them about the horse, Mama?" Aunt Rose, over Chig's weak protest,

2. **Joe Louis**: U.S. boxer (1914–1981) and the world heavyweight champion from 1937 to 1949.

Cross-Curricular Connection: History

Segregation Dr. Dunford tells Chig that he left his hometown at fifteen because there was no high school for African American students. In 1896, the Supreme Court made a ruling in the case of *Plessy v. Ferguson* that segregation did not violate the constitutional rights of African Americans, provided that schools and other facilities were separate but equal. Despite this stipulation, schools and other public facilities for the segregated races were separate but *un*equal. In some cases, small towns did not even have high schools for African Americans.

Plessy v. Ferguson was overturned by the landmark 1954 Supreme Court decision, *Brown v. the Board of Education*, where the court ruled that all school segregation was unconstitutional. This eliminated school segregation by law. However, segregated school systems and their inequities stayed in place in much of the country for many years afterward.

was spooning mashed potatoes onto his plate. "There now, Chig."

"I'm trying to think." The old lady was holding her fork halfway to her mouth, looking at them over her glasses. "Oh, you talking about that crazy horse GL brung home that time."

"That's right, Mama." Aunt Rose nodded and slid another slice of white meat on Chig's plate.

Mae started to giggle. "Oh, I've heard this. This is funny, Chig."

The old lady put down her fork and began: Well, GL went out of the house one day with an old, no-good chair I wanted him to take over to the church for a bazaar, and he met up with this man who'd just brung in some horses from out West. Now, I reckon you can expect one swindler to be in every town, but you don't rightly think there'll be two, and God forbid they should ever meet—but they did, GL and his chair, this man and his horses. Well, I wished I'd-a been there; there must-a been some mighty high-powered talking going on. That man with his horses, he told GL them horses was half-Arab, half-Indian, and GL told that man the chair was an antique he'd stole from some rich white folks. So they swapped. Well, I was a-looking out the window and seen GL dragging this animal to the house. It looked pretty gentle and its eyes was most closed and its feet was shuffling.

"GL, where'd you get that thing?" I says.

"I swapped him for that old chair, Mama," he says. "And made myself a bargain. This is even better than Papa's horse."

Well, I'm a-looking at this horse and noticing how he be looking more and more wide awake every minute, sort of warming up like a teakettle until, I swears to you, that horse is blowing steam out its nose.

His father spoke only when he was spoken to, and then, only one word at a time.

"Come on, Mama," GL says, "come on and I'll take you for a ride." Now George, my husband, God rest his tired soul, he'd brung home this white folks' buggy which had a busted wheel and fixed it and was to take it back that day and GL says: "Come on, Mama, we'll use this fine buggy and take us a ride."

"GL," I says, "no, we ain't. Them white folks'll burn us alive if we use their buggy. You just take that horse right on back." You see, I was sure that boy'd come by that animal ungainly.

"Mama, I can't take him back," GL says.

"Why not?" I says.

"Because I don't rightly know where that man is at," GL says.

"Oh," I says. "Well, then I reckon we stuck with it." And I turned around to go back into the house because it was getting late, near dinner time, and I was cooking for ten.

"Mama," GL says to my back. "Mama, ain't you coming for a ride with me?"

"Go on, boy. You ain't getting me inside kicking range of that animal." I was eying that beast and it was boiling hotter all the time. I reckon maybe that man had drugged it. "That horse is wild, GL," I says.

"No, he ain't. He ain't. That man say he is buggy and saddle broke and as sweet as the inside of a apple."

My oldest girl, Essie, had-a come out on the porch and she says: "Go on, Mama. I'll cook. You ain't been out the house in weeks."

"Sure, come on, Mama," GL says. "There ain't nothing to be fidgety about. This horse is gentle as a rose petal." And just then that animal snorts so hard it sets up a little dust storm around its feet.

"Yes, Mama," Essie says, "you can see he gentle." Well, I looked at Essie and then at that

◆ Literary Focus

6 Characterization Ask students: What can you tell about GL from the fact that the family loves to tell stories about him? *Even though GL is still thought of as naughty, everyone is fond of him and finds him entertaining and charming.*

◆ Critical Thinking

7 Draw Conclusions Ask students what this exchange between Mama and GL might lead them to believe about GL and how he got the horse. What details point to their conclusion? *Students will probably conclude that GL either got the horse by deception or stole it. Mama's assertion that GL had "come by that horse ungainly" leads to this conclusion. Also, the fact that GL says he doesn't know where the man is indicates he either swindled him or is lying altogether and stole the horse.*

Comprehension Check ☑

8 What does Grandmother suspect has been done to the horse, and for what purpose? *She thinks it was given a sedative to quiet it, but it actually has not been broken.*

Listening to Literature Audiocassettes Play the recording of this portion of the story either before students read or as they read along. Discuss with students the elements that add to the interest and excitement of listening to this story. *Elements include the comments and interruptions from family members, the dialogue the mother uses as she tells the tale, and the mother's side comments about the action.*

Beyond the Classroom

Life and Workplace Skills

The difference between GL and Chig's father demonstrates the difference between someone who thinks ahead and someone who doesn't. Although GL is charming and funny, he doesn't appear to have set any goals for his life. Chig's father, on the other hand, set goals for his education and followed through on them in spite of the obstacle of segregation. Tell students that planning ahead and setting goals are important skills in life and in the workplace. Part of thinking ahead is considering all the possible outcomes in a situation, not just the ones you would like to have happen. Allow time for students to work in small groups and brainstorm for possible outcomes to GL's taking his mother out for a buggy ride. Have groups share their answers, then suggest how they would have approached the situation by thinking ahead or planning for potential problems.

After students have analyzed GL's situation, have them identify goals of their own and use the same strategies to explore the possible outcomes and necessary steps.

▶Critical Viewing◀

1 Connect *The title, "Spring Fever," emphasizes the "released" feeling that is evoked in this picture by people coming out of doors, the horse outside, and the bright green plant in the foreground.*

◆ Build Grammar Skills

2 Pronoun Case Have students determine whether the word *me* in this sentence is objective or subjective case. Ask them to explain their answers. *Students should know that* me *is objective because it receives the action of the verb* made.

◆ Literary Focus

3 Characterization Ask students what this part of the story shows about GL. *Students may say that GL, despite his mischievous nature, is charming and knows how to use his charm to win affection.*

Reteach

Call students' attention to the last sentence of the first paragraph of the story on p. 167. Tell them that it is a direct statement about the character, Charles, and therefore, an example of *direct characterization.* Then have them read the first sentence of the next paragraph on that page, and tell them that it is an example of *indirect characterization.* Encourage students to skim the rest of the story, helping them to locate examples of indirect characterization. Discuss with them how the author uses indirect characterization to reveal more and more information about Charles—some personality traits are expressed through Chig's thoughts and realizations; others are shown by Charles's words and actions. Encourage students to make a list of quotations from the story that lets the reader understand Charles.

Spring Fever, 1978 From the Profile Part I: The Twenties series (Mecklenburg County), Collage on board,

1 ▲ **Critical Viewing** How does the title of this painting contribute to the mood it evokes? **[Connect]**

horse because I didn't think we could be looking at the same animal. I should-a figured how Essie's eyes ain't never been so good.

"Come on, Mama," GL says.

"All right," I says. So I stood on the porch and watched GL hitching that horse up to the white folks' buggy. For a while there, the animal was pretty quiet, pawing a little, but not much. And I was feeling a little better about riding with GL behind that crazy-looking horse. I could see how GL was happy I was going with him. He was scurrying around that animal
2 buckling buckles and strapping straps, all the time smiling, and that made me feel good.

Then he was finished, and I must say, that horse looked mighty fine hitched to that buggy and I knew anybody what climbed up there would look pretty good too. GL came around and stood at the bottom of the steps, and took off his hat and bowed and said: "Madam," and reached out his hand to me and I was feeling real elegant like a fine lady. He helped me up to the seat and then got up beside me and we moved out down our alley. And I remember how black folks come out on their porches and shook their heads, saying: "Lord now, will you look at Eva Dunford, the fine lady! Don't she look good sitting up there!" And I pretended not to hear and sat up straight and proud.

We rode on through the center of town, up Market Street, and all the way out where Hiram is living now, which in them days was all woods, there not being even a farm in sight and that's when that horse must-a first realized

Humanities: Art

Spring Fever, 1978, by Romare Bearden.

Bearden (1912?–1988) was one of the most accomplished artists of his time. Born in Charlotte, North Carolina, he grew up in New York City, where his mother was a newspaper editor. Many of the African American artists of the Harlem Renaissance visited his home. For some time Bearden painted in an abstract, cubist style, but he greatest artistic success came when he shifted to collage in the 1960's. Despite the strong abstract element in *Spring Fever,* Bearden manages to make the people and horses seem alive.

1. How do you feel when you look at *Spring Fever*? How did Bearden create the mood of the work? *The mood seems to be rather relaxed and quiet. Bearden creates this mood by the colors, particularly the purple of the sky, and by the stillness of the figures.*
2. Explain in what ways this art reflects the characters or setting of "A Visit to Grandmother." *The figures in the scene might represent Grandmother and one of her sons, but the scene depicted seems much more calm than any of the scenes in this story.*

he weren't at all broke or tame or maybe thought he was back out West again, and started to gallop.

"GL," I says, "now you ain't joking with your mama, is you? Because if you is, I'll strap you purple if I live through this."

Well, GL was pulling on the reins with all his meager strength, and yelling, "Whoa, you. Say now, whoa!" He turned to me just long enough to say, "I ain't fooling with you, Mama. Honest!"

I reckon that animal weren't too satisfied with the road, because it made a sharp right turn just then, down into a gulley and struck out across a hilly meadow. "Mama," GL yells. "Mama, do something!"

I didn't know what to do, but I figured I had to do something...

I didn't know what to do, but I figured I had to do something so I stood up, hopped down onto the horse's back and pulled it to a stop. Don't ask me how I did that; I reckon it was that I was a mother and my baby asked me to do something, is all.

> ◆ **Literary Focus**
> What does this paragraph reveal about the relationship between Grandma and GL?

"Well, we walked that animal all the way home; sometimes I had to club it over the nose with my fist to make it come, but we made it, GL and me. You remember how tired we was, Charles?"

"I wasn't here at the time." Chig turned to his father and found his face completely blank, without even a trace of a smile or a laugh.

"Well, of course you was, son. That happened in . . . in . . . it was a hot summer that year and—"

"I left here in June of that year. You wrote me about it."

The old lady stared past Chig at him. They all turned to him; Uncle Hiram looked up from his plate.

"Then you don't remember how we all laughed?"

"No, I don't, Mama. And I probably wouldn't have laughed. I don't think it was funny." They were staring into each other's eyes.

"Why not, Charles?"

"Because in the first place, the horse was gained by fraud. And in the second place, both of you might have been seriously injured or even killed." He broke off their stare and spoke to himself more than to any of them: "And if I'd done it, you would've beaten me good for it."

"Pardon?" The old lady had not heard him; only Chig had heard.

Chig's father sat up straight as if preparing to debate. "I said that if I had done it, if I had done just exactly what GL did, you would have beaten me good for it, Mama." He was looking at her again. 5

"Why you say that, son?" She was leaning toward him.

"Don't you know? Tell the truth. It can't hurt me now." His voice cracked, but only once. "If GL and I did something wrong, you'd beat me first and then be too tired to beat him. At dinner, he'd always get seconds and I wouldn't. You'd do things with him, like ride in that buggy, but if I wanted you to do something with me, you were always too busy." He paused and considered whether to say what he finally did say: "I cried when I left here. Nobody loved me, Mama. I cried all the way up to Knoxville. That was the last time I ever cried in my life."

"Oh, Charles." She started to get up, to come around the table to him.

He stopped her. "It's too late."

"But you don't understand."

"What don't I understand? I understood

◆ Literary Focus

4 Characterization Elicit responses such as the following: *She refers to GL as her baby. She still saw him as an immature child in need of protection, and was willing to risk injury to save him.*

◆ Reading Strategy

5 Clarify Point out that we are finally about to find out what is really bothering Charles. Suggest they look back in the story for places where the author suggests that Charles has a troubled relationship with his mother. Then have them read a bit further to understand the source of the trouble. *Students will soon clarify that Charles was jealous of his brother because he thought their mother favored him.*

Customize for *Bodily Kinesthetic Learners*

Allow time for students to sit in a group, simulating the arrangement of family members around the dinner table. Have group members read the parts, noting the facial expressions and gestures they might use as they act out this scene. Ask students why they use these movements. *Students might scowl, pound the table, stand, or cover their faces with their hands. Encourage students to identify the emotion behind each of these expressions and gestures.*

Customize for *Gifted/Talented Students*

Students can dramatize the family situation by simulating the arrangement of family members around the dinner table. Have students read the story, taking on the roles of the characters, noting the facial expressions and gestures they might use in this scene. Ask students why they use the movements, expressions, and vocal inflections that they do. *Students might scowl, pound the table, stand, or cover their faces with their hands. Encourage students to identify the emotion behind each of these expressions and gestures.*

Speaking, Listening, and Viewing Mini-Lesson

Casting Discussion

This mini-lesson supports the Speaking, Listening, and Viewing activity in the Idea Bank on p. 176.

Introduce Talk with students about how actors are chosen for a film. First casting directors meet to talk about how the characters should look and behave. They can then choose appropriate actors. Explain that the class will form small groups to discuss casting a movie based on the story.

Develop The groups should jot down their thoughts about each character. Encourage students to draw upon the mental images they formed as they read the story.

Apply Using their notes, the group can choose actors they have seen in films and TV who best fit the roles as they conceive them. They should give reasons for each casting decision they propose.

Assess The groups can compare their cast lists and share the reasoning for their choices. Have students assess how imagining real actors in the parts of the characters affects their appreciation of the story.

◆ Critical Thinking

❶ **Make Judgments** Ask students if they find this explanation reasonable. Have them back up their opinions with evidence from the story. *Some students may cite the story about the horse as evidence that the mother really did love GL better. Some may cite her remarks about Charles's honesty as evidence that she loved both her sons equally, but for different reasons.*

◆ Critical Thinking

❷ **Make Judgments** Ask students if they think Charles's accusation is true. *Some students may believe that it is true; others may think Charles is now voicing childish fears and jealousies that had another basis.*

◆ Literary Focus

❸ **Characterization** Charles's words and abrupt departure from the table reveal the depth of his sense of rejection, even after the passage of thirty years.

Reinforce and Extend

Answers

◆ *Literature and Your Life*

Reader's Response Some students might sympathize with the grandmother because she is now the object of her son's withheld anger. Others may sympathize with Charles for his unfair treatment as a child, or with Chig, who has been dragged into the conflict.

Thematic Focus Communication difficulties can lead family members to grow remote from one another, to get into trouble, or to become deceitful.

Questions for Research Students may suggest questions regarding issues such as anger, disappointment, misunderstanding, and expectations.

☑ Check Your Comprehension

1. He says they are close by so they may as well visit her.
2. He went to Knoxville so he could attend high school.
3. He is silent and unamused.
4. She said she gave all of them what they needed most.
5. GL arrives immediately after the confrontation.

---

then; I understand now."

Tears now traveled down the lines in her face, but when she spoke, her voice was clear.

❶ "I thought you knew. I had ten children. I had to give all of them what they needed most." She nodded. "I paid more mind to GL. I had to. GL could-a ended up swinging if I hadn't. But you was smarter. You was more growed up than GL when you was five and he was ten, and I tried to show you that by letting you do what you wanted to do."

❷ "That's not true, Mama. You know it. GL was light-skinned and had good hair and looked almost white and you loved him for that."

"Charles, no. No, son. I didn't love any one of you more than any other."

"That can't be true." His father was standing now, his fists clenched tight. "Admit it, Mama . . . please!" Chig looked at him, shocked; the man was actually crying.

"It may not-a been right what I done, but I ain't no liar." Chig knew she did not really understand what had happened, what he wanted of her. "I'm not lying to you, Charles."

Chig's father had gone pale. He spoke very softly. "You're about thirty years too late, Mama." He bolted from the table. Silverware and dishes rang and jumped. Chig heard him hurrying up to their room.

> **◆ Literary Focus**
> What do Charles's actions reveal indirectly about him?

They sat in silence for awhile and then heard a key in the front door. A man with a new, lacquered straw hat came in. He was wearing brown and white two-tone shoes with very pointed toes and a white summer suit. "Say now! Man! I heard my brother was in town. Where he at? Where that rascal?"

He stood in the doorway, smiling broadly, an engaging, open, friendly smile, the innocent smile of a five-year-old.

◆ Build Vocabulary

lacquered (lak′ ərd) *adj.*: Coated with varnish made from shellac or resin

Guide for Responding

◆ *Literature and Your Life*

Reader's Response With which character in the story do you sympathize? Explain.

Thematic Focus When family members do not communicate, small misunderstandings can grow into big problems. What are some of the other possible effects of not discussing problems as they arise?

Questions for Research What questions could you ask a professional family counselor about common communication issues among family members?

☑ Check Your Comprehension

1. What is the reason Chig's father, Charles, gives for visiting Chig's grandmother?
2. What reason does Charles give for leaving home when he was fifteen?
3. How does Charles react to Mama's story about the horse?
4. How does Mama explain the different ways she treated her children?
5. Who arrives immediately after the confrontation between Charles and his mother?

Beyond the Selection

FURTHER READING

Other Works by William Melvin Kelley

A Different Drummer

Dancers on the Shore (stories)

Other Works About Families

Barrio Boy, Ernesto Galarza

My Father Sits in the Dark, Jerome Weidman

We suggest that you preview these works before recommending them to students.

INTERNET

You and your students may find additional information about William Melvin Kelley on the Internet. Sites may have changed since we published this information.

To read a review of Kelley's novel *A Drop of Patience*, go to **http://www.wwnorton.com/ecco/884601.htm**

We *strongly recommend* that you preview this and related sites before you send students to them.

Guide for Responding (continued)

◆ Critical Thinking

INTERPRET

1. Describe Charles's attitude toward GL. **[Interpret]**
2. Give two reasons that Charles has not visited his mother in so long. **[Analyze]**
3. What has drawn Charles back to his mother now? **[Infer]**
4. What do you think Charles's relationship with his mother will be like in the future? **[Draw Conclusions]**

APPLY

5. Identify two ways to clear up misunderstandings. **[Apply]**

EXTEND

6. Describe the qualities you think are important in a person whose career involves guiding other people to communicate and resolve their differences. **[Career Link]**

◆ Reading Strategy

CLARIFY

You may have felt confused by the force of Charles's emotions until you were able to **clarify** the reasons for his feelings.

1. Explain how you clarified two ideas or relationships that were not at first clear to you.
2. How you would help someone clarify the problem Charles has with his mother and brother?

◆ Literary Focus

CHARACTERIZATION

Kelley uses **direct characterization** when he states, "Doctor Charles Dunford cared about people." With **indirect characterization**, the author allows you to discover what a character is like through the dialogue and action of the character or through other characters' comments.

1. Explain three things you learned about GL indirectly.
2. Identify one thing you learned about a character through direct characterization and one thing you learned through indirect characterization.

◆ Build Vocabulary

RESEARCHING WORD ORIGINS

Use a dictionary to look up the origins of the following words. Then explain how each pair is related in meaning.

1. navigate, navy
2. pose, position
3. material, matter

USING THE WORD BANK: Context

Read each book title below. On your paper, write the word from the Word Bank that you would most expect to find in that book.

1. *A History of Japanese Enamels*
2. *Smile! Dr. Bill's Guide to Being Happy*
3. *The Church in Europe, A.D. 984–1517*
4. *Business Risks in the Twenty-first Century*

◆ Build Grammar Skills

PRONOUN CASE

The **subjective case** is used when a pronoun is the subject or renames the subject. The **objective case** is used when the pronoun is a direct object or the object of a preposition.

Practice Copy the following sentences in your notebook. Replace the noun or nouns in parentheses with the correct form of a pronoun.

1. Charles had never talked much about (Charles's) family.
2. (Charles) spoke very softly.
3. (Grandmother) had to give all of (the children in the family) what they needed most.
4. (Mae, Grandma, and Chig) sat down to supper.

Writing Application Rewrite the following passage, correcting the pronoun usage errors. Continue the passage with two more sentences that contain pronouns.

Charles felt that his mother loved GL more than he. Him and GL were very different. I would have felt bad if it happened to I.

Answers

◆ Critical Thinking

1. Charles is indulgent of GL but does not seem to respect him.
2. Charles has not visited his mother because he has been busy developing his career and raising his family. A second reason is that he has harbored resentment towards her.
3. Students might say Charles's mother is getting older and even though Charles feels anger toward her, he probably wants to see her again and clear the air.
4. Perhaps Charles and his mother will come to some sort of understanding and reestablish contact.
5. Possible ways to clear up misunderstandings include (1) paying particular attention to the other person's point of view and (2) finding a compromise between two positions.
6. A person who guides others in conflict resolution should be objective, empathetic, and tactful.

◆ Reading Strategy

1. Students' examples should indicate that they clarified information by looking back to review details of setting, characterization, or key events; looking ahead for more information; creating a family tree or timeline to keep track of characters and events.
2. Students might suggest they would highlight past events that contributed to the problem, such as Charles being beaten when his brother was not.

◆ Literary Focus

1. Possible responses are: (1) GL has a love of mischief; (2) he is irresponsible; (3) he knows how to charm and manipulate his mother.
2. Students might say they learned that Charles cared about people through direct characterization. They learned through indirect characterization—such as Charles grimacing when he kisses his mother—that Charles harbors resentment towards his mother.

◆ Build Vocabulary

Using Word Origins

1. *navigate* and *navy* derive from the Latin *navigāre*—to manage a ship.
2. *pose* and *position* derive from the Latin *pōnere*—to place.
3. *material* and *matter* derive from the Latin *materia*—matter.

Using the Word Bank

1. lacquered; 2. grimacing; 3. indulgence; 4. ventured

◆ Build Grammar Skills

Practice

1. Charles had never talked much about his family.
2. He spoke very softly.
3. She had to give all of them what they needed most.
4. They sat down to supper.

Writing Application

Charles felt that his mother loved GL more than him. He and GL were very different. I would have felt bad if it happened to me.

Grammar Reinforcement

For additional instruction and practice, use the lesson in the **Language Lab CD-ROM** on Pronoun case and the pages on the Cases of Pronouns (pp. 76–79) in the *Writer's Solution Grammar Practice Book*.

Idea Bank

Following are suggestions for matching Idea Bank topics with your students' performance levels and learning modalities:

Customizing for
Performance Levels
Less Advanced Students: 1, 4
Average Students: 2, 5, 6
Pre-AP Students: 3, 7

Customizing for
Learning Modalities
Logical/Mathematical: 7
Verbal/Linguistic: 2, 4, 5
Interpersonal: 4, 6

Guided Writing Lesson

Prewriting Strategy Students can use looping to focus their ideas for their firsthand biographies. Have students freewrite for five minutes about their subjects. Next, guide them to search their results for the "center of gravity" in the writing—the part that holds some attraction or promise that it would be worth writing about. Have them circle the center of gravity and then use it as the prompt for their next freewrite. Repeat the exercise until students have sufficiently honed their ideas. Finally, suggest that students mine the material they generated in these freewrites when looking for concrete details, anecdotes, or examples they can use to illustrate their ideas.

For more prewriting, elaboration, and revision strategies, see *Prentice Hall Writing and Grammar.*

Writing and Language Transparencies Use Writing Process Model 2: Biographical Profile (pp. 13–16) to help students draft and revise their firsthand biographies.

Writing Lab CD-ROM
Have students complete the tutorial on Narration. Follow these steps:

1. Encourage students to view video tips on narrative elements.
2. Use the word bins to help them select transition words that communicate relationships.
3. Use a proofreading checklist to locate possible errors in their drafts.

Build Your Portfolio

Idea Bank

Writing

1. **Letter to Charles's Mother** Put yourself in Charles's place and write a letter to Mama about your feelings. Base your letter on what you know about Charles from the story.
2. **News Report** Write a news report about the incident with the horse from the objective point of view of a newspaper reporter. Base your report on the facts you learn from the story.
3. **Alternative Ending** This story ends abruptly after Charles rushes from the table. Write an alternative ending to the story that has Charles staying to meet his brother.

Speaking, Listening, and Viewing

4. **Casting Discussion** With a group of classmates, choose actors to play the roles in a movie version of this story. Present and explain your recommendations to the class. **[Media Link]**
5. **Oral Anecdote** Choose a humorous or exciting incident from your own life as the subject of an anecdote—a brief story—and practice telling it aloud. Present your anecdote to the class.

Researching and Representing

6. **Conflict-Resolution Workshop** Plan activities for a conflict-resolution workshop that could teach people like Charles and his mother strategies for working out their differences. Lead a small group of classmates through one activity.
7. **Cultural Comparisons Chart** Create a chart that compares how family members relate to one another in three different world cultures. Address issues such as interaction with extended family, activities families share, and responsibilities of children and adults. **[Social Studies Link]**

Online Activity **www.phlit.phschool.com**

Guided Writing Lesson

Firsthand Biography

Flip through a mental scrapbook of the individuals who have played special roles in your life and have influenced your understanding of yourself and the world around you. These people might include relatives, friends, teachers, or other adults whom you admire. Choose one of these people and write a firsthand biography—a true story about the life or an important episode in the life of a person with whom you have had direct experiences. Include personal insights that show the close relationship between you and your subject. The following tips will explain how to highlight the significance of the events you include.

Writing Skills Focus: Provide Examples

Provide examples of events or actions that demonstrate the qualities of your subject and capture your relationship with him or her. For example, if you wish to point out that your subject is compassionate, you might include a description of a time when he or she worked in a food kitchen to feed the homeless. Use transitions such as *for example* and *for instance* to introduce your examples.

Prewriting Write your subject's name on a sheet of paper. Around the person's name, write down the words and phrases that capture his or her significant characteristics. Around each of the characteristics, jot down examples.

Drafting For each characteristic you want to highlight, include at least one example that demonstrates that quality in your subject. Use words that show the connection between the characteristic and the example.

Revising Review your firsthand biography and add examples of events or actions that will clarify the points you want to make about the subject.

ASSESSMENT OPTIONS

Formal Assessment, Selection Test, pp. 38–40, and Assessment Resources Software. The selection test is designed so that it can be easily customized to the performance levels of your students.

Alternative Assessment, p. 12, includes options for less advanced students, Pre-AP Students, verbal/linguistic learners, bodily/kinesthetic learners, logical/mathematical learners, and visual/ spatial learners.

PORTFOLIO ASSESSMENT
Use the following rubrics in the ***Alternative Assessment*** booklet to assess student writing:
Letter to Charles's Mother: Description Rubric, p. 97
News Report: Evaluation/Review Rubric, p. 104
Alternative Ending: Summary Rubric, p. 98

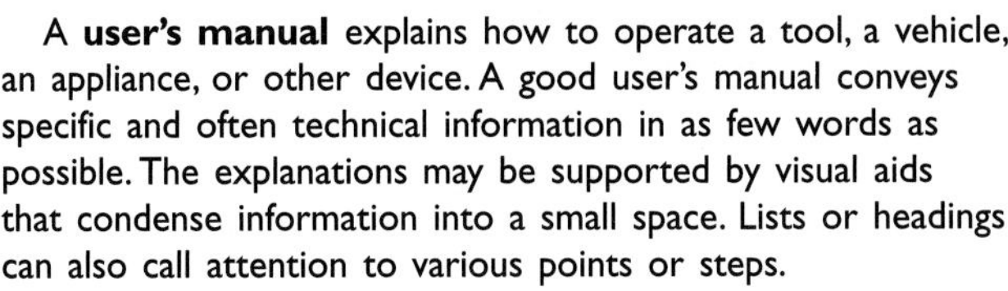

Writing Process Workshop

User's Manual

A **user's manual** explains how to operate a tool, a vehicle, an appliance, or other device. A good user's manual conveys specific and often technical information in as few words as possible. The explanations may be supported by visual aids that condense information into a small space. Lists or headings can also call attention to various points or steps.

The following skills, introduced in this section's Guided Writing Lessons, will help you write a user's manual about any product.

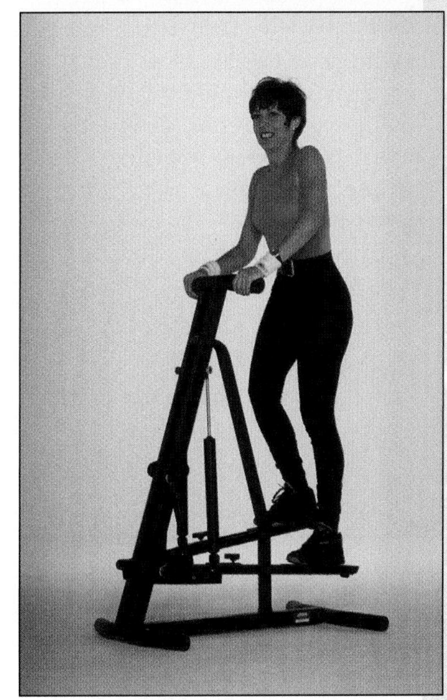

Writing Skills Focus

- **Give a clear explanation** of any procedures involved. A well-written user's manual is one in which directions are easy to follow. (See p. 145.)
- **Elaborate on certain steps** to give more information. Provide details that tell why or how the step is performed. Give examples when appropriate. (See p. 153.)
- **Clearly explain each cause and effect**—show how one action or condition brings about another. (See p. 163.)
- **Use transition words,** such as *first* or *next,* to describe the required sequence.

The following user's manual for the StairWalker 2000™ exercise machine demonstrates these skills.

Model

① Before you start using your new Stair-Walker 2000™, first adjust the steps to fit your height. Next ② set resistance and speed to your desired settings.

Refer to the chart below to find the proper resistance setting, speed, and length of time for your workouts:

Goal	Resistance	Avg. Speed	Time ③
Max. Fat Burn	1, 2, 3	90 steps per min.	30 min.
Max. Tone	4, 5, 6	80 steps per min.	20–30 min.
Max. Strength	7, 8	90 steps per min.	10–20 min.

BURNING FAT: If you exercise at a low resistance setting for a sustained period of time, you will burn fat. ④

① These sentences explain the procedure for the user to follow.

② Transition words such as *before, first,* and *next* clarify the order of steps in the procedure.

③ This chart elaborates on setting resistance and speed. It also presents a great deal of information in a small space.

④ Here the writer clearly shows a cause-and-effect relationship.

Prepare and Engage

LESSON OBJECTIVES

- To use recursive writing processes to write a user's manual
- To recognize and use exact nouns
- To demonstrate control over subject-verb agreement

You may want to distribute the Scoring Rubric for Technical Description/Explanation in ***Alternative Assessment*** (p. 116) to alert students to the criteria on which they will be evaluated. See the suggestions on p. 179 for customizing the rubric for this workshop.

Refer students to the Writing Handbook, p. 965, for instruction in the writing process, and p. 969 for further information on practical and technical writing.

Writers at Work Videodisc

To introduce students to the key elements and show them how auto mechanic Larry Cataldo uses technical writing in his work, play the videodisc segment on Practical and Technical Writing (Ch. 8).
Have students discuss what Cataldo says about the kind of writing he does at work.

Play frames 33166 to 42350

Writing Lab CD-ROM

If your students have access to computers, you may want to have them work on the tutorial on Practical and Technical Writing to complete all or part of their user's manuals. Follow these steps:

1. Have students review the interactive model of a user's manual.
2. Have students draft on computer.
3. Suggest that students consult the screen on formatting technical writing.

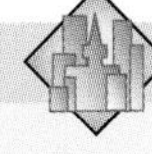

Beyond the Classroom

Workplace Skills

Technical Writing Regardless of what they do in their lives, students are likely to find themselves relying frequently on practical and technical writing, both as a writer and as a reader. Filling out a form, writing a memo, reading a user's manual for a recently bought product, and writing a job-application letter are all examples of practical and technical writing that they are all likely to engage in using or creating at some point in their lives.

Discuss with students their experiences with reading and following the information found in user's manuals, or other guides. What made it easy (or difficult) to use? Was all of the necessary information included? Was there too much explanation about anything? Would more of a certain type of information have been helpful?

Point out that the end user of technical writing may not have any prior information on the topic or experience in trying to complete a series of steps. Successful technical writing requires the writer to put him- or herself in the shoes of someone who knows nothing about the topic in order to adequately provide information.

Develop Student Writing

Prewriting Strategy

The most important guideline to follow when writing a user's manual is to know enough about the topic to be able to explain it clearly. Help students think about topics they are qualified to write about by using sentence stubs. On the board, write "I am knowledgeable about . . ." or "Something I am good at is . . ." and ask students to complete the sentences with as many ideas as they can generate. Then, suggest that they use one of these ideas as their topic.

Customize for
English Language Learners
Students learning English may not know the vocabulary related to their topics. Once they have chosen a topic, make a list of the words they are likely to need to describe it.

Customize for
Pre-AP Students
Challenge students to select a topic that they know little about and will have to research in order to explain.

Elaboration Strategy

Students may benefit from writing process components or steps on notecards. They can then arrange the cards in the order they think is best —chronologically, spatially, or in order of importance. They may discover details that should be included, as well as some that can be omitted.

Writing Lab CD-ROM
The Gathering Details section of the tutorial on Practical and Technical Writing includes a screen on using visual aids. Students can consult this screen to work with and incorporate visual aids such as charts and pictures.

Drafting

Visual aids are useful tools to include in user's manuals; they also can be writing tools. Students can sketch the object or process they want to explain—remind them that they are not drawing for art, but for writing: their goal is not to make a visually attractive drawing but one that is highly detailed. Encourage students to refer to their drawings as they write. Details may serve as visual cues about the steps they need to include in their explanations.

Applying Language Skills: Exact Nouns

Make your explanation as clear as possible by using exact nouns. An exact noun is the most specific or precise noun for the given situation.

Vague Nouns:
Using a tool, unscrew the thing on the front of your VCR.

Exact Nouns:
Using a Phillips screwdriver, unscrew the aluminum cover on the control panel of your VCR.

Practice On your paper, replace the vague nouns with exact nouns in the following sentence.

To turn on your device, first plug the thing into the nearest spot on your wall and turn the round object.

Writing Application As you draft your user's manual, use exact nouns to help your reader precisely visualize the steps.

Writer's Solution Connection
Writing Lab

To help you choose a topic for your user's manual, refer to the following activity in the Writing Lab tutorial on Practical/Technical Writing: Using Phrases to Find a Topic.

Prewriting

Choose a Topic Ideas for a user's manual may stem from recreational activities or from items in the classroom or home. For instance, creating guidelines for a personal fitness program or describing how to use an electronic device are great topics for a user's manual. Choose a topic that you find interesting or relevant.

Use different combinations of these words and phrases to spark an idea for writing a user's manual.

Combinations	
Making	a bird feeder
Building	a guitar
Programming	an answering machine
Maintaining	a remote control device
Using	a fish tank

Is Your Topic Too Broad? Make sure that your topic is narrow enough to cover in a short paper. Below, see how one student narrowed his topic.

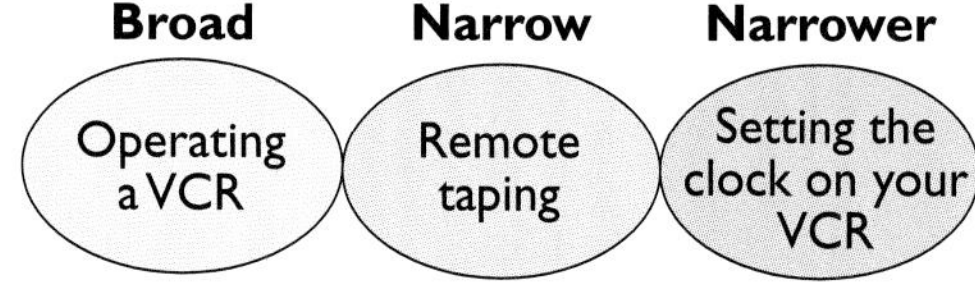

Drafting

Choose the Right Format Headings, lists, and charts can make your user's manual clear, concise, and effective. For example, a list will call out separate points in a direct and easy-to-read way. You can incorporate these features in your first draft or add them while revising.

Create Visual Aids Visual aids can be an important part of a user's manual. They can convey significant information in only a few words. Look over your draft to see where a visual aid will fit. If you use a visual aid, consider labeling parts.

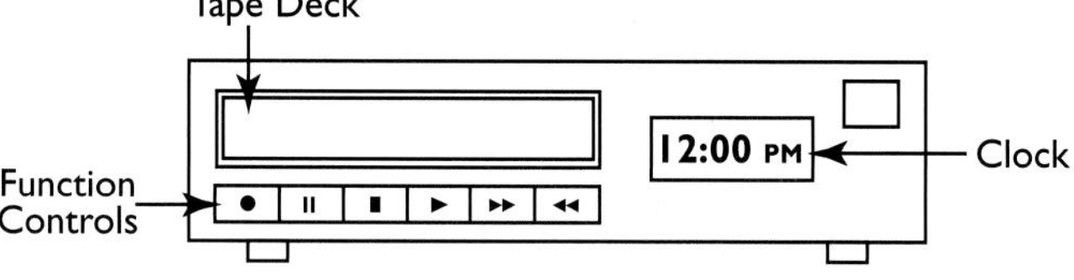

Applying Language Skills

Exact Nouns Explain to students that precise language is important in technical writing because an imprecise or vague word can make it impossible to follow directions properly.

Answer

Possible response:
To turn on your DVD player, first plug the AC cord into the nearest wall outlet, and turn the large round dial on the front right marked "ON/VOL."

Revising

Test Your Manual The most important aspect of your user's manual is to describe accurately the steps to perform a function. Precisely follow the steps you have outlined, and see whether they work. Add information you may have left out.

Use a Checklist Refer again to the Writing Skills Focus on p. 177, and use those and the following items as a checklist to evaluate and revise your user's manual.

- Have you given a clear explanation of the procedure?
  Fill in any details you may have forgotten when you drafted the manual.
- Have you elaborated on your information?
  Add a picture or graph to make your manual easier to understand.
- Have you clearly explained causes and effects?
  Make sure you demonstrate the effect of each action.
- Have you used transition words?
  Add words such as first, next, *and* finally *in places where they will clarify the steps you describe.*

Revision Model

Press the "action" button on the ~~thing you hold in your hand~~. ① remote control.

② Next, press ~~Press~~ the "down" arrow until the word "clock" is highlighted.

③ This will put the VCR in "clock" mode. Now you're ready to set the clock.

① The writer replaces a vague term with an exact noun.
② The writer adds a transition word.
③ The writer adds an explanation of cause and effect.

Publishing

Demonstration Booth A demonstration booth will allow you to showcase your talent as a writer, as well as your talent for assembling visuals and products in a creative way.

- Get permission from your teacher or librarian to set up a booth.
- Inside the booth, display a finished copy of your user's manual.
- Post charts, diagrams, and other visuals on the wall of the booth.
- If possible, include a working model so that visitors can actually follow your instructions.

Applying Language Skills: Subject and Verb Agreement

Make sure that all your verbs agree in number with their subjects. Number means that a word is either singular or plural. Verbs change form to agree with their subjects. A subject and verb agree when both are singular or both are plural.

Incorrect:
The action button control all the programming functions.

Correct:
The action button controls all the programming functions.

Practice On your paper, make the verb agree with the subject in the following sentences.

1. The dial on each of the meters inform you of your progress.
2. Many people who have a stairwalker exercises every day.

Writing Application Review your user's manual to make sure that all subjects and verbs agree in number.

Writer's Solution Connection
Language Lab

For more practice with subject and verb agreement, complete the Language Lab lesson on Agreement in Number.

Revision Strategy

Have students work with peer editors to revise their work. Have the peer editor read the user's manual and judge whether he or she can adequately understand its contents. Make sure that peer editors offer constructive comments rather than just general criticism.

Publishing

Tell students that even if they do not wish to share their user's manuals with a wider audience at this time, they should keep them for reference and possibly to incorporate into a longer piece of writing at a later time.

Reinforce and Extend

Applying Language Skills

Subject and Verb Agreement
Explain to students that the number of the subject determines the number of the verb, not the other way around.

Answers

1. The dial on each of the meters informs you of your progress.
2. Many people who have a stairwalker exercise every day.

Grammar Reinforcement

For additional instruction and practice, have students complete the **Language Lab CD-ROM** lesson on Subject-Verb Agreement and the practice pp. 80–82 in the *Writer's Solution Grammar Practice Book.*

✓ ASSESSMENT		4	3	2	1
PORTFOLIO ASSESSMENT Use the rubric on Technical Description/Explanation in the ***Alternative Assessment*** booklet (p. 115) to assess the students' writing. Add these criteria to customize the rubric to this assignment.	**Exact Nouns**	All nouns are exact and the best noun for each situation.	Most nouns are exact and descriptive.	There are both exact nouns and vague nouns that should be replaced	Most nouns are vague and provide little description.
	Subject-Verb Agreement	All verbs agree with their subjects; grammar is flawless.	Almost all verbs agree with their subjects; grammar is good.	Subject-verb agreement is acceptable, but there are noticeable errors.	Numerous errors in subject-verb agreement render the piece difficult to understand and read.

Prepare and Engage

LESSON OBJECTIVES

- To use reference material to research specific information
- To use text organizers to locate and categorize information
- To evaluate information sources and their appropriateness for varied needs

Customize for
Less Proficient Readers
Students will be familiar with reading to find specific information from their social studies and history assignments. Point out that such critical reading skills will serve them well in any kind of reading and/or analyzing, for instance business reports, to itemized bills and tax forms.

Apply the Strategies

Have students scan the entire sample so that they know what to expect. This should become a habit for reading such texts. Then have them read the selection as many times as necessary to acquire a full understanding of it.

Answers

Possible responses:

1. The Indus Valley is located in the region known as South Asia or the subcontinent of India. The first sentence of the section, entitled Geography: The Indian Subcontinent, reveals this information
2. The three major zones are the well-watered northern plain, the dry triangular Deccan plateau, and the coastal plains on either side of the Deccan. "Three regions" are the key words that indicate the section in which to find this information.
3. The monsoons bring rain that is needed to water crops, affecting whether famine occurs for the Indian people. "The monsoons" are the key words that indicate the section in which to find this information.
4. Early Civilization in China would be the appropriate section in which to look for information about rulers of northern China in 1027 B.C.

Student Success Workshop

Real-World Reading Skills

Using Text Organizers to Find Information

Strategies for Success

Your social studies homework requires you to answer questions about cities of the Indus Valley. You have your social studies book; now you just have to find the specific information you need to answer the questions. Use the strategies that follow to find specific information in a textbook or other reference.

Use the Table of Contents and the Index The table of contents may list a topic that is broader than your specific needs, but it will get you close. For example, information about the Indus Valley might be listed in the chapter entitled "Early Civilizations in India and China." An index lists very specific topics. For example, if you know the names of one of the cities, you could look it up in the index and find the exact page on which information about that city appears.

Scan Subheads and Key Words Scan the pages for subheads or key words that refer, or are related to, your topic. For example, if you want to find the location of the Indus Valley, scan the subheads until you find one that refers to geography or neighboring countries.

Early Civilizations in India and China

Chapter Outline
1. Cities of the Indus Valley
2. Kingdoms of the Ganges
3. Early Civilization in China

Cities of the Indus Valley
In 1922, archaeologists made a startling discovery. While digging in the Indus River valley, they unearthed bricks, small statues, and other artifacts. They soon realized that they had uncovered a "lost civilization." They had found the cities of the Indus Valley.

Geography: The Indian Subcontinent
The Indus Valley is located in the region known as South Asia or the subcontinent of India. The Indian subcontinent is a huge, wedge-shaped peninsula extending into the Indian Ocean. Towering snow-covered mountain ranges arc across the northern border of the subcontinent.

Three regions. The Indian subcontinent is divided into three major zones. They are the well-watered northern plain, the dry triangular Deccan plateau, and the coastal plains on either side of the Deccan.

The monsoons. Today, as in the past, a defining feature of Indian life is the monsoon. In late May or early June, the wet summer monsoon blows from the southwest. These winds pick up moisture over the Indian Ocean and then drench the land with daily downpours. Each year, people welcome the rain that is desperately needed to water the crops. If the rains are late, famine and starvation may occur.

Apply the Strategies

Scan the information in the sample textbook page to the left to answer these questions.

1. Where is the Indus Valley located? Which words helped you find this information?
2. Describe the three major zones of the Indian subcontinent. Which words helped you find the section with this information?
3. Describe how the monsoon affects Indian life. How did you find this information?
4. In which section of this chapter would you begin looking for information about rulers of northern China in 1027 B.C.?

You may also read for specific information
- Newspapers and magazines
- Almanacs
- Encyclopedias

Test Preparation Workshop

Reading Comprehension: Using Text Organizers Students probably will not encounter standardized questions that ask them specifically to use text organizers. However, some standardized tests will require them to read passages that may be broken into sections that may or may not be numbered. Questions based on this type of passage will be more accessible to students if, as they refer back to the passage while answering questions, they use the sections and any identifying features such as numbering to locate and categorize information.

Students might mark important sections, sentences or words, identifying key words and assigning subheads for reference as they answer questions. They may even want to jot short, summarizing notes in the margin for quick reference to key sentences or paragraphs. Caution students, however, not to mark too much—they want to be able to create and use their text organizers quickly. Time spent marking might be better used to evaluate answer choices, and if they have marked or written too much, they won't be able to locate specific information they need.

PART 2 *Reaching a Goal*

Untitled, Bart Forbes

One-Minute Planning Guide

The selections in this section are about striving for goals. "Mowing," and "After Apple Picking," deal with concrete physical goals. In "Style," and "At Harvesttime," Maya Angelou describes principles toward which all people should strive. In "The Apple Tree," the father's goal is to harvest the fruit of a beautiful apple tree, but finds that the apples are not what he expected. The poem "Africa" figuratively describes the struggle for liberty, while "Biko" describes the fatal consequences of one man who struggled for liberty. The African "Old Song" and the selections from *The Analects* offer advice for living successfully. The Chinese poems "All" and "Also All" describe the despair and subsequent hope after the Tiananmen Square massacre.

Customize for *Varying Student Needs*

When assigning the selections in this part to your students, keep in mind the following factors:

"Mowing"; "After Apple Picking"
- Two poems from a well-known, high-interest author

"Style"; "At Harvesttime"
- Two very short essays
- Well-known author

"The Apple Tree"
- A brief story with easy vocabulary and an accessible plot

"Africa"; "Old Song"; "Biko"; from *The Analects;* "All"; "Also All"
- "Biko" has connection to popular song and artist (Peter Gabriel)

"All" and "Also All" have connection to social studies (Tiananmen Square)

Humanities: Art

Untitled by Bart Forbes.

Bart Forbes has created posters and prints and has designed over twenty commemorative postage stamps, including the 1988 Olympic stamps, as well as the Lou Gehrig and Jesse Owens stamps. Forbes was appointed the official artist of the 1988 Olympics in Seoul, Korea.

Encourage students to notice the warm colors, somewhat unexpected in a painting of a snowy scene. Realistically, they might be reflections of the sunset; however, the strongest red tones in the center of the skier's chest might suggest the pumping of his heart.

Help students link the painting to the theme of Part 2, Reaching a Goal, by answering the following questions:

1. What do you think this skier is feeling? *Possible answers: He is feeling nervous about the success of his jump; he is proud, knowing he has jumped farther than ever.*
2. How do you think the painter feels about the goal of achieving a perfect ski jump? *The painter shows that he values this goal highly in the following details: the skier's disciplined posture; the Olympic insignia on his chest, indicating the highest level of competition; the beautiful natural backdrop against which the skier seems to fly like a bird; the pleasing combination of warm earth tones and the cool slate blues.*

Prepare and Engage

LESSON OBJECTIVES

1. To develop vocabulary and word identification skills
- Spelling vs. Pronunciation: *-ough*
- Using the Word Bank: Synonyms
- Extending Word Study: Context (ATE)

2. To use a variety of reading strategies to read and comprehend poetry and prose
- Connect Your Experience
- Reading Strategy: Interpret
- Tips to Guide Reading: Whisper Reading (ATE)
- Read to Appreciate Author's Craft (ATE)

3. To increase knowledge of other cultures and to connect common elements across cultures
- Connecting Themes Across Cultures (ATE)

4. To express and support responses to the text
- Critical Thinking
- Idea Bank: Advice Column

5. To analyze literary elements
- Literary Focus: Tone
- Idea Bank: Essay

6. To read to do research on a self-selected or an assigned topic
- Idea Bank: Food Source
- Viewing and Representing: Farming Update

7. To plan, prepare, organize, and present literary interpretations
- Idea Bank: Speech
- Speaking, Listening, and Viewing Mini-Lesson: Role Play

8. To use recursive writing processes to write an application letter
- Guided Writing Lesson

9. To increase knowledge of the rules of grammar and usage
- Build Grammar Skills: Participles as Adjectives

Test Preparation

Reading Comprehension: Recognize Facts and Details (ATE, p. 183) The teaching tips and sample test item in this workshop support the instruction and practice in the unit workshop:

Reading Comprehension: Recognize Facts, Details, and Sequence (SE, p. 215)

Guide for Reading

Robert Frost *(1874–1963)*

Frost was born in San Francisco but moved to New England, his family's original home, when he was eleven. In his youth, he worked as a farmer, editor, and schoolteacher, absorbing the ebb and flow of New England life that would form the themes of many of his poems.

In 1912, Frost moved to England, where he met the famous poets Ezra Pound and William Butler Yeats. Encouraged by their praise, he published his first volume of poetry, entitled *A Boy's Will*, in 1913. Frost went on to become one of the most successful and prolific poets the country has ever known, winning numerous awards, including four Pulitzer Prizes.

Maya Angelou *(1928–)*

Maya Angelou was born Marguerite Johnson in St. Louis, Missouri. She and her older brother were raised by their grandmother in Stamps, Arkansas. She records the experiences of her childhood in her autobiography, *I Know Why the Caged Bird Sings.*

In her adult life, she achieved success as a singer and actress, a civil rights worker, and a writer of nonfiction, fiction, poetry, and plays. "Style" and "At Harvesttime" are from *Wouldn't Take Nothin' for My Journey Now*, a collection of essays in which she shares her reflections on life.

◆ Build Vocabulary

SPELLING VS. PRONUNCIATION: *-ough*

In "After Apple-Picking," Robert Frost notices that there may be a few "Apples [he] didn't pick upon some bough." If you don't know the pronunciation of *bough*, you learn it as soon as you read the next line: it rhymes with *now*. Further down, Frost ends another line with the word *trough*, which rhymes with *off* three lines up. Still other words ending in *-ough* have an o͞o sound—*through*, for example. Think of other words that end in *-ough*. How do you pronounce them?

WORD BANK

Before you read, preview this list of words from the poems and essays.

- bough
- trough
- manifestation
- disparaging
- judicious
- admonition
- immutable
- potency

◆ Build Grammar Skills

PARTICIPLES AS ADJECTIVES

As Robert Frost describes cutting the long grass in "Mowing," he mentions his "long scythe whispering to the ground." If your teacher asked you to assign a part of speech to each word in that phrase, what would you put for *whispering*? If you answered participle, you'd be correct.

A **participle** is a word formed from a verb that modifies a noun or a pronoun. Participles fit into two groups: present or past. Present participles always end in *-ing*. Past participles usually end in *-ed* or *-d*, but they may also have irregular endings, such as *-t* and *-en*.

Present: . . . from the *drinking* trough

Past: *Magnified* apples appear . . .

Notice how participles add detail to these poems and essays.

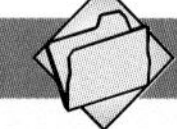

Prentice Hall Literature Program Resources

REINFORCE / RETEACH / EXTEND

Selection Support Pages
Build Vocabulary: Spelling vs. Pronunciation: *-ough*, p. 51
Build Grammar Skills: Participles as Adjectives, p. 52
Reading Strategy: Interpret, p. 53
Literary Focus: Tone, p. 54

Strategies for Diverse Student Needs, p. 13

Beyond Literature
Career Connection: Farming, p. 13

Formal Assessment Selection Test, pp. 41–43; Assessment Resources Software

Alternative Assessment, p. 13

Writing and Language Transparencies
Writing Process Model 9: Business Letter, pp. 61–64

Resource Pro CD-ROM

Listening to Literature Audiocassettes

Mowing ◆ After Apple-Picking
Style ◆ At Harvesttime

◆ Literature and Your Life

Connect Your Experience

When you plant a marigold seed, you don't expect a daisy to sprout, do you? In life, as in gardening, what you put into an experience usually affects what you get out of it. The poems and essays in this group remind you that success requires effort.

Journal Writing Write down your recollection of a particularly difficult job that, when finished, gave you a great deal of satisfaction.

Thematic Focus: Reaching a Goal

The ideas explored in these poems and essays will help you consider the question, "How do my attitudes and actions affect my chances for success?"

◆ Background for Understanding

Culture

Most of Robert Frost's poems take place among the rolling pastures, dark woods, and clear streams of rural New England. Life in New England is affected to a great extent by the ebb and flow of the four seasons. Winters in New England last from mid-November to early April and are marked by long nights and snowy days. Spring is damp and cool, with misty mornings. Summer days are long and hot, but the nights are often comfortable. Autumn, however, is when New England shows its true colors. Autumn is harvest time, time to go to work picking apples amid an array of brilliant red and orange and yellow leaves falling all around.

◆ Literary Focus

Tone

When the speaker in "Mowing" talks about "the earnest love that laid the swale in rows," he shows a respectful attitude toward his work. The attitude of the speaker or author toward his or her subject is known as the **tone** of a literary work. The tone may be, among other things, serious or casual, distant or personal, angry or humorous. You can determine the tone of a work by looking carefully at the writer's choice of words.

◆ Reading Strategy

Interpret

These poems and essays contain distinct images. In "Mowing," we see the image of a sharp blade slicing through the long grass. In "After Apple-Picking," we are presented with an image of "ten thousand thousand" apples. Writers use images such as these to create a mood, or feeling, and to convey the underlying meaning.

As a reader, part of your job is to **interpret** these images, to understand what the images represent and how they contribute to the work's mood or meaning. For instance, in "Mowing," the image of the lone whispering scythe creates a mood of solitude and tranquillity and captures the rhythm and progress of outdoor work. Think about the images you encounter in these works. What associations do the images call to mind? What feelings or emotions do the images spark? What are the speakers' attitudes toward the images? What point or message do the writers convey beyond the literal words? Answering these questions will help you interpret the images and delve into their underlying meanings.

Test Preparation Workshop

Reading Comprehension: Recognize Facts and Details Students may find that reading a poem calls for more careful attention to detail than reading prose. Questions on standardized tests assess recognition of facts and details that are central to the purpose of the text. Practicing this skill with a poem will offer students a chance to prepare to answer test questions that require them to recognize facts and details within a reading passage. Have students read "Mowing," then write this sample test question on the board.

The scythe's whispering relates to—

A the gift of idle hours
B making hay
C fairy tales
D a bright green snake

Students should reread, or skim the poem to review its details. They should recognize that all of the answer choices represent details in the poem, but *A, C,* and *D* do not relate to the central idea of mowing. Eliminating these answers, students can determine the correct answer to be B.

To prepare students to read the poems and essays, write on the chalkboard: "You reap what you sow." If necessary, clarify for students that *reap* means "to obtain a result" and *sow* means "to scatter seed for growing." Have them discuss both the literal and figurative meanings of this sentence. Then apply it directly to students' lives, using a two-column chart on the chalkboard. Label the left column *Sow* and write "works in a video store" and "misses three play rehearsals." Label the right column *Reap* and write "earns money for a computer" and "forgets lines on stage." Lead students to see the relationship between "reaping" and "sowing." After students have added examples to the list, tell them to keep this saying in mind as they read these selections.

Customize for
Less Proficient Readers

The Frost poems include some long sentences. Pair these students with stronger readers who can help them break down and paraphrase some of the more complicated sentences to grasp their literal meaning.

Customize for
Pre-AP Students

Introduce the term *explication of text* to students telling them that it refers to the analysis of a literary work in great detail, explaining the underlying meaning as a whole. Have them write an explication of one of the Frost poems in the selection. (For those studying French, you might add that the term comes originally from the French *explication de texte.*)

Customize for
English Language Learners

Listening to the recordings and following along in their books will help students grasp the sense of the poems.

Listening to Literature Audiocassettes

Customize for
Gifted/Talented Students

Have students plan choral readings of the poems. They should determine the rhythm of lines and the words or syllables to be stressed as they prepare.

Develop Understanding

Both these poems celebrate "the sweetest dream that labor knows" by focusing on the physicality of mowing and of harvesting. In "Mowing" the scythe with which the speaker mows seems itself to be a sentient being, whispering and communicating with the land. In "After Apple-Picking" the reader feels the exhaustion of the speaker who has just worked hard to harvest apples before the long winter sets in.

◆ Critical Thinking

❶ **Infer** Ask students why the personified scythe "whispered and did not speak." *Students might say that if the scythe was commenting to the ground about "the lack of sound," it was being respectful of that silence by whispering instead of talking aloud.*

◆ Reading Strategy

❷ **Interpret** Ask students what they think the scythe whispered. Tell them to consider lines 9 and 10 and line 13 for their interpretations. *Based on previous lines, some students may say that the scythe was simply whispering about its work, or loving its work. Accept all reasonable responses.*

Connecting Themes Across Cultures

Have students brainstorm to think of myths and stories of other cultures that involve agricultural tasks such as mowing or harvesting. Ask students which author they have studied in this unit might appreciate "Mowing." *Students may recognize that the theme of the poem might appeal to Tolstoy.*

Mowing

Robert Frost

There was never a sound beside the wood but one,
And that was my long scythe[1] whispering to the ground.
What was it it whispered? I knew not well myself;
Perhaps it was something about the heat of the sun,
Something, perhaps, about the lack of sound—
And that was why it whispered and did not speak. 
It was no dream of the gift of idle hours,
Or easy gold at the hand of fay[2] or elf:
Anything more than the truth would have seemed too weak
To the earnest love that laid the swale[3] in rows,
Not without feeble-pointed spikes of flowers
(Pale orchises),[4] and scared a bright green snake.
The fact is the sweetest dream that labor knows.
My long scythe whispered and left the hay to make. ❷

1. **scythe** (sīth) *n.*: Slightly curved blade at the end of a long handle, used for cutting grass.
2. **fay** (fā) *n.*: Fairy.
3. **swale** (swāl) *n.*: Low-lying marshland.
4. **orchises** (ôr´ kis iz) *n.*: Orchids.

Block Scheduling Strategies

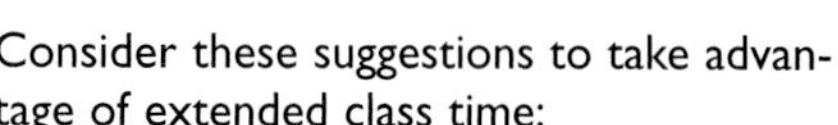

Consider these suggestions to take advantage of extended class time:

- Before students add examples to the chalkboard chart for the Interest Grabber activity on p. 183, have them gather in groups to exchange thoughts. Remind them that when a person reaps, he or she plants a seed, and that to sow means to obtain results from that planting. Tell them that the examples on the board shows a logical relationship between "reaping" and "sowing."
- Have students listen to the four selections on audiocassette; then have students read them to themselves or to partners.
- Introduce the concept of tone. Students may read about it in Literary Focus on page 183 and then answer the questions on page 190. You may follow up with Literary Focus page in ***Selection Support*** (p. 54).
- Ask students to write about their attitudes toward work in their journals. After they have read the Frost poems, have them write a quick response comparing their attitudes to those of the speakers.
- Suggest that students work in small groups on the Build Grammar Skills section on page 190 and the practice page from ***Selection Support*** (p. 52).
- Direct students to choose one of the writing activities from the Idea Bank on p. 191.

The Mowers, Sir George Clausen, Usher Art Gallery, Lincoln, Great Britain/The Bridgeman Art Library, London

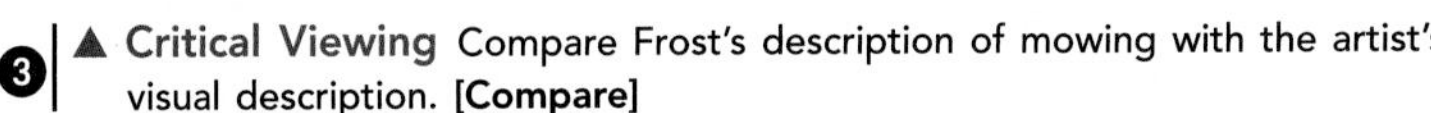

3 ▲ Critical Viewing Compare Frost's description of mowing with the artist's visual description. **[Compare]**

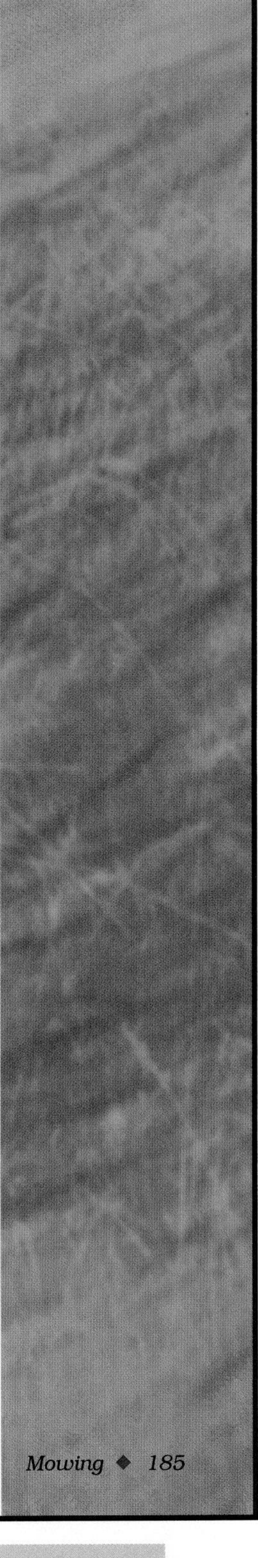

▶Critical Viewing◀

3 Compare *Students may respond that in the poem, the mower is solitary, but Clausen's painting shows several men working together. The action of mowing with a scythe is depicted in both. The trees in the background could be the wood beside the "swale" in the poem. Some students may say that the mood in both is tranquil, and the figures in the painting seem to be "listening" to the whisperings of their scythes.*

Customize for *Visual/Spatial Learners*

You might wish to have these students relate the movement of the clothes of the men in the foreground of *The Mowers* to that of the painting as a whole. *Students should observe how the curves of the men's flowing clothes echo the curves or diagonals of the scythe's handle, the grass, and the bending trees and grass.*

Tips to Guide Reading

Whisper Reading Encourage students to whisper read the poems. Listen for their attention to punctuation and phrasing, correcting mistakes when necessary.

Read to Appreciate Author's Craft

Invite students to look for a pattern in the end rhymes of "Mowing" and "After Apple-Picking." How do the rhymes affect the rhythm when students read the poems aloud?

Humanities: Art

The Mowers by Sir George Clausen.

Sir George Clausen (1852–1944) was an English painter who liked to paint landscapes and bucolic scenes. In this painting, workers mow a peaceful meadow, much like the one in Frost's poem.

Use these questions for discussion:

1. Looking carefully at the motion of the mowers, describe the sound you think the scythe makes. *The scythe probably makes a swishing or whispering sound as it moves through the grass.*
2. Jean-François Millet and Vincent Van Gogh are among many artists who have painted laborers mowing or sowing. Why do you think this is an appealing painting subject? *Students might say that the subject allows painters to show human anatomy in motion or that artists might paint laborers as a way that pays homage to the importance of honest physical labor.*

◆ Literary Focus

❶ Tone Ask students to describe the tone in the opening of this poem. *The detailed description of work partly done and the long sentences suggest a tone of weariness. This tone is reinforced by the speaker's statement that he or she is done with apple picking now.*

◆ Reading Strategy

❷ Interpret Ask students what lines 9–13 tell them about the weather. *The weather is getting cold. The temperature has dropped below 32 degrees—the "pane of glass" in the drinking trough that morning was actually a sheet of ice.*

◆ Build Grammar Skills

❸ Participles as Adjectives Have students identify the participial phrase in line 20 and identify the noun phrase it modifies. *The participial phrase is showing clear and the noun phrase it modifies is fleck of russet.*

◆ Critical Thinking

❹ Infer Ask students to explain the inference they make here. *The speaker has been working so long, and feels so overworked that he continues to hear the sounds of the apples even after the work is done.*

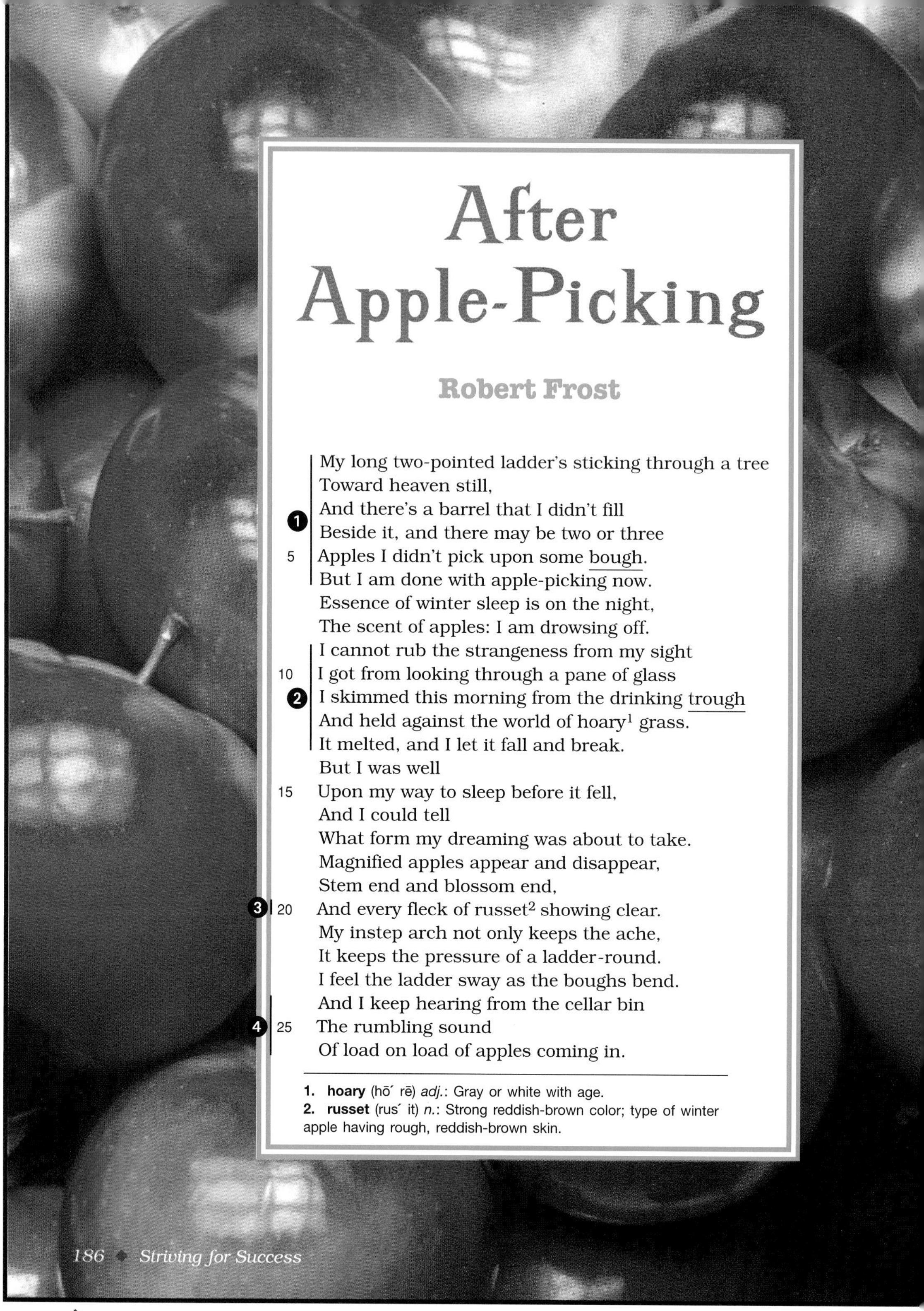

After Apple-Picking

Robert Frost

My long two-pointed ladder's sticking through a tree
Toward heaven still,
And there's a barrel that I didn't fill
❶ Beside it, and there may be two or three
Apples I didn't pick upon some bough.
But I am done with apple-picking now.
Essence of winter sleep is on the night,
The scent of apples: I am drowsing off.
I cannot rub the strangeness from my sight
I got from looking through a pane of glass
❷ I skimmed this morning from the drinking trough
And held against the world of hoary[1] grass.
It melted, and I let it fall and break.
But I was well
Upon my way to sleep before it fell,
And I could tell
What form my dreaming was about to take.
Magnified apples appear and disappear,
Stem end and blossom end,
❸ And every fleck of russet[2] showing clear.
My instep arch not only keeps the ache,
It keeps the pressure of a ladder-round.
I feel the ladder sway as the boughs bend.
And I keep hearing from the cellar bin
❹ The rumbling sound
Of load on load of apples coming in.

1. **hoary** (hō´ rē) *adj.*: Gray or white with age.
2. **russet** (rus´ it) *n.*: Strong reddish-brown color; type of winter apple having rough, reddish-brown skin.

Speaking, Listening, and Viewing Mini-Lesson

Role Play

This mini-lesson supports the Speaking, Listening, and Viewing activity in the Idea Bank on p. 191.

Introduce the Concept Remind students that the speakers in both poems are involved in hard, physical labor, and both probably have strong feelings about their work.

Develop Background To role-play the speakers, students will need to have a sense of each speaker. Have students discuss the attitude of each speaker. Lead them to realize that the speaker in "Mowing" seems more content than the one in "After Apple-Picking" who might be too tired to appreciate all that he has accomplished.

Apply the Information Students can work with a partner, each taking the role of one of the speakers, to work out a realistic conversation. You might suggest that they practice the conversation until they feel comfortable. Then they can present the conversations before the class.

Assess the Outcome Have students evaluate each pair's performance by answering the following questions:

1. Did each student faithfully represent the personality of his or her speaker?
2. Did each student communicate his or her speaker's thoughts clearly?

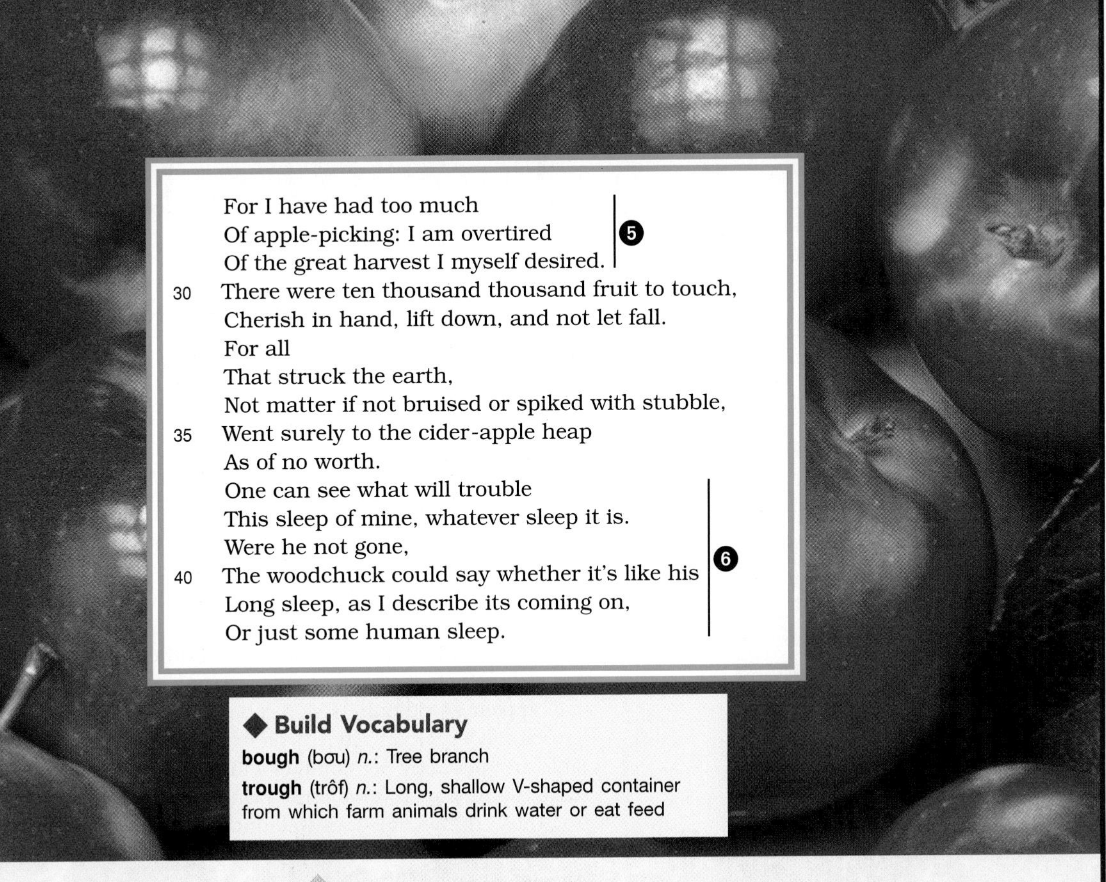

For I have had too much
Of apple-picking: I am overtired
Of the great harvest I myself desired.
There were ten thousand thousand fruit to touch,
Cherish in hand, lift down, and not let fall.
For all
That struck the earth,
Not matter if not bruised or spiked with stubble,
Went surely to the cider-apple heap
As of no worth.
One can see what will trouble
This sleep of mine, whatever sleep it is.
Were he not gone,
The woodchuck could say whether it's like his
Long sleep, as I describe its coming on,
Or just some human sleep.

◆ Build Vocabulary

bough (bou) *n.*: Tree branch

trough (trôf) *n.*: Long, shallow V-shaped container from which farm animals drink water or eat feed

Guide for Responding

◆ Literature and Your Life

Reader's Response What personal experiences do these poems call to mind?

Thematic Focus Why do you think it is sometimes hard for people to stop thinking about a job they've just completed?

☑ Check Your Comprehension

1. In "Mowing," what is the one sound the speaker hears?
2. What does the speaker of "Mowing" say is "the sweetest dream that labor knows"?
3. (a) In "After Apple-Picking," what pictures flash through the speaker's mind as he drifts off to sleep? (b) What sensations does he feel? (c) What does he hear?

◆ Critical Thinking

INTERPRET

1. Why is the setting of "Mowing" important? **[Support]**
2. (a) In "After Apple-Picking," how would you describe the speaker's condition? (b) What is the cause of his condition? **[Deduce]**

APPLY

3. How do the feelings a person experiences after completing a physical task, such as picking apples, compare with those one experiences after completing a mental task, such as homework? **[Distinguish]**

EXTEND

4. What are some of the advantages and disadvantages of jobs that require working outdoors? **[Career Link]**

Viewing and Representing Mini-Lesson

Farming Update

This mini-lesson supports the Project activity in the Idea Bank on p. 191.

Introduce the Concept In "After Apple-Picking" the poet refers to the work of picking apples by hand. While some agricultural tasks have to be done by hand, many jobs have been changed by technology.

Develop Background Students can research to learn more about the way farmers work. They may want to look at how haying, harvesting, and milking, for example, have changed in the past one hundred years.

Apply the Information Once students have gathered the information, they can determine a style to illustrate their timelines and show the dates of technological developments, as well as how the methods work.

Assess the Outcome The timelines can be evaluated on the accuracy and clarity of the information and on the inventiveness of the design.

◆ Critical Thinking

5 Infer Ask students what they can determine about the speaker from his words in lines 27–29. *A possible response is that the speaker might be a person who "bites off more than he can chew"—realizes he has taken on more than he can accomplish.*

◆ Literary Focus

6 Tone Have students describe the speaker's tone in these lines. *The tone seems to reflect what the speaker is saying; it communicates a feeling of profound tiredness.*

Reinforce and Extend

Answers

◆ Literature and Your Life

Reader's Response Students might recall a particular time in which they exerted themselves in physical labor.

Thematic Focus A possible response is that when people get involved in consuming work it is hard to leave it behind.

☑ Check Your Comprehension

1. He hears his scythe "whispering to the ground."
2. The simple "fact" of work being done is the sweetest dream that labor knows.
3. (a) Magnified apples appear and disappear; (b) his instep aches; he feels the ladder-round pressure; (c) he hears apples rumbling into the cellar bin.

◆ Critical Thinking

1. The setting is important because the silence of the wood and the work that is being done there are central to the meaning of the poem.
2. (a) The speaker is spent and exhausted; (b) He feels this way because he has worked very hard to help harvest apples.
3. Responses may include: a physical task might cause bodily pain or exhaustion while a mental task does not; someone could feel satisfied or energized after a physical task and stimulated after a mental task.
4. Advantages include physical movement and enjoyment of good weather; disadvantages include exposure to rain and snow or possibly dangerous conditions.

Develop Understanding

One-Minute Insight "Style" and "At Harvesttime" examine and expand upon the theme of the saying "You reap what you sow." Angelou says that those who cultivate and remain true to their unique styles can successfully deal with most situations in life.

◆ Build Grammar Skills

1 Participles as Adjectives There are two participles in this sentence. Have students identify them. *developed; accomplished* Ask students which participle is used as an adjective. *The participle accomplished is an adjective; it modifies the noun teacher. The other participle is part of the verb phrase "can be developed."*

◆ Literary Focus

2 Tone Ask students: What is the tone of this passage? *Responses suggest that the tone is serious because the author is teaching the reader something she considers important; others may suggest that the tone is humorous because the image of a robin with peacock feathers is funny.*

Extending Word Study

Context After students have read "Style," suggest that they reread the text to determine the meaning of *style*. Encourage them to define *style* in their own words, based on what they've learned from the context of the selection.

STYLE

MAYA ANGELOU

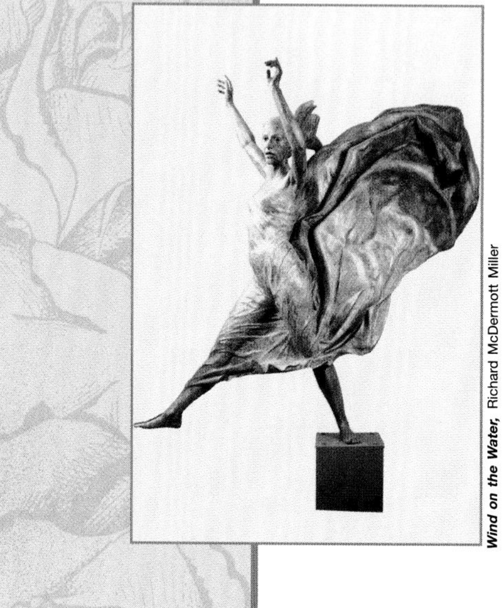

Wind on the Water, Richard McDermott Miller

Content is of great importance, but we must not underrate the value of style. That is, attention must be paid to not only what is said but how it is said; to what we wear, as well as how we wear it. In fact, we should be aware of all we do and of how we do all that we do.

Manners and a respect for style can be developed if one is eager and has an accomplished teacher. On the other hand, any observant person can acquire the same results without a teacher simply by carefully watching the steady march of the human parade.

Never try to take the manners of another as your own, for the theft will be immediately evident and the thief will appear as ridiculous as a robin with peacock feathers hastily stuck on. Style is as unique and nontransferable and perfectly personal as a fingerprint. It is wise to take the time to develop one's own way of being, increasing those things one does well and eliminating the elements in one's character which can hinder and diminish the good personality.

Any person who has charm and some confidence can move in and through societies ranging from the most privileged to the most needy. Style allows the person to appear neither inferior in one location nor superior in the other. Good manners and tolerance, which are the highest manifestation of style, can often transform disaster into good fortune. Many people utter insults or disparaging remarks without thinking, but a wise or stylish person takes the time to consider the positive as well as negative possibilities in each situation. The judicious response to a gibe can disarm the rude person, removing the power to injure.

This is not another admonition to turn the other cheek, although I do think that that can be an effective ploy on certain occasions. Rather, this is an encouragement to meet adverse situations with the intent and style to control them. Falling into an entanglement with brutes will usually result in nothing more conclusive than a stimulated nervous system and an upset digestive tract.

◆ Build Vocabulary

manifestation (man′ ə fes tā′ shən) *n.*: Something that is made clear or plainly revealed

disparaging (di spar′ ij iŋ) *adj.*: Belittling; showing contempt for

judicious (jo͞o dish′ əs) *adj.*: Showing good judgment; wise and careful

gibe (jīb) *v.*: Jeer; taunt

admonition (ad′ mə nish′ ən) *n.*: Warning; mild reprimand

immutable (im myo͞ot′ ə bəl) *adj.*: Unchangeable

potency (pōt′ ən sē) *n.*: Power

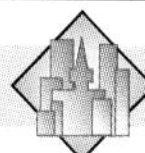

Beyond the Classroom

Career Connection

Landscape Architecture Many high school students earn money from the land by mowing lawns, raking leaves, shoveling snow, and so on. An interest in mowing can lead to a career in landscape architecture. A landscape architect may design anything from a backyard garden to the grounds of a corporate park. Have students investigate what a landscape architect does and the qualifications necessary to become one. Suggest that they present their research in a report with pictures, if possible.

Community Connection

Local Growing Apples, referred to in "After Apple-Picking" and tomatoes, in "Harvesttime," are hardy crops that grow in many areas of the U. S. Have students consider the following questions and then make an illustrated chart showing crops grown in the regions in which they live.

- Do apples grow in your region? If so, where, and what kinds of apples?
- Is other produce grown in your region? If so, which fruits and vegetables? If produce isn't grown in your region, where does it come from?

AT HARVESTTIME

MAYA ANGELOU

There is an <u>immutable</u> life principle with which many people will quarrel.

Although nature has proven season in and season out that if the thing that is planted bears at all, it will yield ❸ more of itself, there are those who seem certain that if they plant tomato seeds, at harvesttime they can reap ❹ onions.

Too many times for comfort I have expected to reap good when I know I have sown evil. My lame excuse is that I have not always known that actions can only reproduce themselves, or rather, I have not always allowed myself to be aware of that knowledge. Now, after years of observation and enough courage to admit what I have observed, I try to plant peace if I do not want discord; to plant loyalty and honesty if I want to avoid betrayal and lies.

Of course, there is no absolute assurance that those things I plant will always fall upon arable land and will take root and grow, nor can I know if another cultivator did not leave contrary seeds before I arrived. I do know, however, that if I leave little to chance, if I am careful about the kinds of seeds I plant, about their <u>potency</u> and nature, I can, within reason, trust my expectations.

Guide for Responding

◆ Literature and Your Life

Reader's Response With whom would you like to share these essays? Why?

☑ Check Your Comprehension

1. In "At Harvesttime," what does Maya Angelou suggest is a life principle that cannot be changed?
2. Why does Angelou say she sometimes expected to "reap good when [she] sowed evil"?
3. In the essay "Style," what two qualities are identified as the greatest proof of style?

◆ Critical Thinking

INTERPRET

1. Explain the meaning of the title "At Harvesttime." **[Interpret]**
2. In what ways can style help you achieve success? **[Analyze]**

COMPARE LITERARY WORKS

3. Compare and contrast the tone of Frost's poem and Angelou's essays. **[Compare and Contrast]**

◆ Build Vocabulary

❸ Spelling vs. Pronunciation: *-ough* Point out the word *although*. Remind students that *although* is an example of a word that ends in *-ough* but is pronounced differently from either *trough* or *plough*.

◆ Reading Strategy

❹ Interpret Angelou talks of planting tomato seeds and reaping onions. Ask: What is Angelou suggesting by using these images? *Some people have unrealistic expectations about the effects their present actions will have in the future.*

Reinforce and Extend

Answers

◆ Literature and Your Life

Reader's Response Students might name a friend or relative who they think would benefit from the advice in the essay.

☑ Check Your Comprehension

1. A thing that is planted yields more of itself.
2. She didn't recognize that actions reproduce themselves.
3. The greatest proof of style is good manners and tolerance.

◆ Critical Thinking

1. The essay focuses on the effect of people's actions, a concept similar to the "reap and sow" of harvest time.
2. If you behave with style, as Angelou defines it, you will be successful in your interactions with people.
3. Students may say that the speaker in each of Frost's poems has a respectful attitude toward work and nature. The speaker has a serious, yet satisfied attitude. The speaker in Angelou's selections has a lecturing tone, as if she wants to share what she's learned from experience.

Beyond the Selection

FURTHER READING

Other Works by Robert Frost

"The Road Not Taken"
"Stopping by Woods on a Snowy Evening"
"Birches"

Other Works by Maya Angelou

I Know Why the Caged Bird Sings
I Shall Not Be Moved
Wouldn't Take Nothing for My Journey Now

We suggest that you preview these works before recommending them to students.

INTERNET

Students may learn more about these poets at the following Web sites. Please be aware that sites may have changed since we published this information.

For Frost quotations, go to **http:/www. chesco.com/artman/frost.html**

For more information about Maya Angelou, go to **http://ucaswww.mem.uc.edu/worldfest/MayaPage.html**

We *strongly recommend* that you preview this and related sites before you send students to them.

Answers

◆ Reading Strategy

1. (a) He respects his work. (b) Students may be influenced to interpret the poem as a celebration of work.
2. (a) The speaker is exhausted. (b) Students may interpret the poem as one which takes a realistic look at the difficulty of labor.
3. The images reinforce Angelou's point about the relationship between actions and consequences.
4. Students might mention the image of the robin with peacock feathers to represent someone trying to imitate another's style.

◆ Literary Focus

1. (a) The tone is respectful. (b) The words "earnest love" and "sweetest dream that labor knows" convey that respect.
2. (a) Students may say that the tone is one of exhaustion. (b) The tone is communicated by "I am drowsing off," "My instep arch . . . keeps the ache," "sleep."
3. Students might find the tone of these essays to be either preachy or wise.

◆ Build Vocabulary

Using *-ough*
1. b 2. c 3. a

Using the Word Bank
1. admonition; 2. potency; 3. immutable; 4. judicious; 5. manifestation; 6. disparaging; 7. bough; 8. trough

◆ Build Grammar Skills

Practice
1. whispering; 2. rumbling; 3. accomplished; 4. disparaging; 5. stimulated

Writing Application
Sample answers:
1. picked; 2. exhausted; 3. bending; 4. fallen; 5. experienced

Grammar Reinforcement

For additional instruction and practice, use the lesson on Participial, Gerund, and Infinitive Phrases (pp. 264–265) in the *Sourcebook* and the page on participles and participial phrases (p. 41) in the *Writer's Solution Grammar Practice Book.*

Guide for Responding *(continued)*

◆ Reading Strategy

INTERPRET

Writers like Robert Frost and Maya Angelou use images to create a feeling and convey meaning. You can **interpret** these images by examining the feelings and attitudes associated with them.

1. (a) How does the speaker in "Mowing" feel about his work? (b) How do his feelings affect your interpretations of the poem?
2. (a) How does the speaker in "After Apple-Picking" feel at the end of the day? (b) How do his feelings affect your interpretations of the poem?
3. How do the images of planting and harvesting help you understand the message in "At Harvesttime"?
4. What images would you use to communicate the message of "Style" to someone who hasn't read it?

◆ Literary Focus

TONE

The words that a writer uses convey a specific **tone**—the speaker's or author's attitude toward the subject. Often, the tone is an important clue to the work's meaning.

1. (a) How would you describe the tone of "Mowing"? (b) What words and phrases are most helpful in determining this tone?
2. (a) What is the tone of "After Apple-Picking"? (b) What words convey this tone?
3. What word would you use to describe the tone of the essays "At Harvesttime" and "Style"?

Beyond Literature

Career Connection

Careers in Agriculture Career opportunities in agriculture are available around the world in such diverse areas as science, business, and education. Scientists and engineers work together to improve methods and machinery. Business people buy and sell crops and other agricultural products. Educators teach methods of protecting crops and livestock from disease. What kind of career in agriculture might interest you most?

◆ Build Vocabulary

USING *-ough*

Match the word from Column A to the rhyming word in Column B.

Column A	Column B
1. bough	**a.** dough
2. trough	**b.** plough
3. though	**c.** cough

USING THE WORD BANK: Synonyms

On your paper, write a synonym from the Word Bank for each numbered word.

1. warning	**5.** evidence
2. power	**6.** critical
3. unchangeable	**7.** branch
4. wise	**8.** tub

◆ Build Grammar Skills

PARTICIPLES

A **participle** is a verb form that can modify a noun or pronoun. Frost uses participles to add details that bring his images to life. Participles fall into two categories: present (always end in *-ing*) and past (usually end in *-ed* but may have an irregular ending).

Practice In your notebook, write the participle that modifies the following words from "Mowing," "After Apple-Picking," and "Style."

1. scythe ("Mowing": line 2)
2. sound ("After Apple-Picking": line 25)
3. teacher ("Style": paragraph 2)
4. remarks ("Style": paragraph 4)
5. nervous system ("Style": paragraph 5)

Writing Application Add a participle to each sentence to modify the noun in italics.

1. The *apples* are thrown on the cider heap.
2. The *worker* cannot stop thinking about the harvest.
3. The *branches* almost touch the ground.
4. The *fruit* fills the bin.
5. The *men* work faster than the boys.

Reteach

Tone, as a literary term, may be vague to some students. Provide a stack of magazines for students to find a picture that they can categorize for each of the following: serious, casual, distant, personal, angry or humorous. Then guide them to brainstorm for lists of words that could be used to describe each picture. Tell students that each of the pictures has a "tone," and just as the visual aspects of the pictures convey a serious or humorous tone the word lists they generated can convey that same tone.

Then help students better understand Maya Angelou's tone in "Style," by calling attention to her choice of words. In the third paragraph, she writes that a person who tries to "take the manners of another" will look as "ridiculous as a robin with peacock feathers hastily stuck on." Discuss how this image indicates a negative attitude toward imitating another person's outward appearance.

Help students list three other examples of Angelou's word choice that indicate her attitude toward style. What conclusion can they draw about how she feels about being honest with oneself?

Build Your Portfolio

Idea Bank

Writing Description

1. Description Write a paragraph describing a job that gives you satisfaction. Include details that will help your readers share the experience.

2. Essay The speakers in "Mowing" and "After Apple-Picking" are at two different stages of work. Write a brief essay in which you contrast the feelings and attitudes of the two speakers.

3. Advice Column "At Harvesttime" and "Style" offer good advice for people of any age. Write an advice column with at least two letters from readers asking advice on situations related to Angelou's ideas. Use the ideas in the selections as a basis for answering the letters.

Speaking, Listening, and Viewing

4. Speech Practice reading one of the selections as a speech. Experiment with pauses, volume, and tone of voice. Deliver your "speech" to the class.

5. Role Play With a partner, role-play a conversation between the speakers in "At Harvesttime" and "After Apple-Picking." Have them compare the nature of their work and their reactions to it.

Researching and Representing

6. Farming Update Technology has dramatically changed the way farmers work. Create a timeline that shows the impact of technology on a specific area of agriculture during the past ten decades. **[Technology Link]**

7. Food Source Choose one of your favorite foods and find out what work is involved in producing it. Discover how it travels, what happens to it, and what it's combined with before it reaches your table. Present your findings to the class. **[Science Link]**

Online Activity www.phlit.phschool.com

Guided Writing Lesson

Application Letter for a Summer Job

In his poems, Robert Frost talks about what it's like to work outside. If you've never had a job where you've worked in nature, a summer job might be a good place to start. Write a letter of application for a summer job in the great outdoors. The following tips will help you support your claim that you are qualified for the job.

Writing Skills Focus: Support With Details

A prospective employer will not hire you just because you *say* you can do the job. You will have to **support** your claim with details. For example, if you claim to work well with children, support your claim with details, such as your two years of babysitting experience and the fact that you have two younger brothers.

Brainstorm for details before you begin writing, and incorporate them in your draft. As you revise, make sure you have used enough details to support your points.

Prewriting First, identify the qualities that are required for the job. Then, brainstorm for details that show you have these qualities.

Drafting Organize your letter so that each of your points is supported clearly. One way to organize is to begin each paragraph with a general statement and then support the statement with details in the body of the paragraph.

Revising Ask a partner to read your letter and identify any claims you have not supported. Add details to support these areas.

ASSESSMENT OPTIONS

Formal Assessment, Selection Test, pp. 41–43, and Assessment Resources Software. The selection test is designed so that it can be easily customized to the performance levels of your students.

Alternative Assessment, p.13, includes options for less advanced students, Pre-AP Students, verbal/linguistic learners, interpersonal learners, visual/spatial learners, and bodily/kinesthetic learners.

PORTFOLIO ASSESSMENT

Use the following rubrics in the ***Alternative Assessment*** booklet to assess student writing:
Description: Description Rubric, p. 97
Essay: Comparison and Contrast Rubric, p. 103
Advice Column: Expression Rubric, p. 94

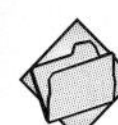

Idea Bank

Following are suggestions for matching Idea Bank topics with your students' performance levels and learning modalities:

Customizing for *Performance Levels*

Less Advanced Students: 1, 5
Average Students: 2, 3, 4, 6
Pre-AP Students: 7

Customizing for *Learning Modalities*

Visual/Spatial: 6
Interpersonal: 3
Verbal/Linguistic: 4, 5

Guided Writing Lesson

Prewriting Strategy Help students think of details to support their claims by having them perform mock job interviews with their classmates. Divide the class into pairs, assigning on partner the role of "interviewer" and other "interviewee." The interviewer should ask questions that the real interviewer might ask in this situation, and her partner should make her answers as realistic as possible. Remind the interviewer to employ basic interviewing techniques, such as asking open-ended questions and getting the interviewee talking. This will get students thinking about what prospective employers will be looking for, and they can address these points in their letters.

For more prewriting, elaboration, and revision strategies, see *Prentice Hall Writing and Grammar.*

Writing and Language Transparencies Use Writing Process Model 9: Business Letter, pp 61–64, to guide students through annotated drafts of a business letter.

Writing Lab CD-ROM

Have students complete the tutorial on Practical Writing. Follow these steps:

1. Have them use a details checklist to help them include appropriate supporting details in their application letter.
2. Encourage them to use the revision checker for vague language to help them determine if their language is concrete enough.

Prepare and Engage

LESSON OBJECTIVES

1. To develop vocabulary and word identification skills
- Word Origins: Words From Greek and Roman Myths
- Using the Word Bank: Synonyms
- Extending Word Study: Multiple Meaning Words (ATE)

2. To use a variety of reading strategies to read and comprehend a story
- Connect Your Experience
- Reading Strategy: Question
- Tips to Guide Reading: Recall Information (ATE)
- Read to Appreciate Author's Craft (ATE)
- Idea Bank: Summary of the Story • Idea Bank: Alternative Ending

3. To increase knowledge of other cultures and to connect common elements across cultures
- Connecting Themes Across Cultures (ATE)

4. To express and support responses to the text
- Critical Thinking

5. To analyze literary elements
- Literary Focus: Allusion

6. To read in order to research self-selected and assigned topics
- Idea Bank: Travel Brochure

7. To plan, prepare, organize, and present literary interpretations
- Idea Bank: Map
- Idea Bank: Dramatic Reading
- Speaking, Listening, and Viewing Mini-Lesson: Monologue From Father's Point of View

8. To use recursive writing processes to retell a story
- Guided Writing Lesson

9. To increase knowledge of the rules of grammar and usage
- Build Grammar Skills: Punctuation of Dialogue

Test Preparation

Reading Comprehension: Recognize Sequence (ATE, p. 193) The teaching tips and sample test item in this workshop support the instruction and practice in the unit workshop:

Reading Comprehension: Recognize Facts, Details, and Sequence (SE, p. 215)

Guide for Reading

Katherine Mansfield
(1888–1923)

Today, short stories are one of the most popular and respected forms of writing. However, one hundred years ago, plays, poetry, and novels were considered the highest forms of literary expression. One of the authors who helped increase our appreciation of the short story was Katherine Mansfield.

Mansfield is credited by critics for helping to refine and advance the art of the short story.

From the Edge to the Center Mansfield was born in Wellington, the capital of New Zealand. Believing that Wellington was too remote a place for someone with literary aspirations, Mansfield moved to London while still in her teens.

Although London was a vibrant literary center that was home to many of the world's finest writers, it seemed cold and impersonal to Mansfield. Her sense of disillusionment with life in London is reflected in her early stories.

From Death, Inspiration In 1915, she received a sudden shock. Her brother, a soldier in the British army, died in the trenches in World War I. This tragic event led Mansfield to the conclusion that she had neglected her roots, and she began to write stories, including "The Apple Tree," based on her childhood in New Zealand.

Tragically, Mansfield's life was cut short by disease. After contracting tuberculosis, she spent her last few years in and out of clinics and hospitals in France and Italy before the disease claimed her life in 1923.

◆ Build Vocabulary

WORD ORIGINS: WORDS FROM GREEK AND ROMAN MYTHS

Myths are fictional tales that explain the actions of gods or the causes of natural phenomena. Many English words come from Greek and Roman myths. For example, the word *jovial,* which appears in this story, comes from the name Jove, another name for Jupiter, the ruler of the Roman gods. The planet Jupiter is named for him, and it was once believed that people born under the sign of Jupiter (Jove) were playful and merry. The word *jovial* describes these qualities: a jovial mood; a jovial man.

WORD BANK

Before you read, preview this list of words from the story.

paddocks
exquisite
bouquet
jovial

◆ Build Grammar Skills

PUNCTUATION OF DIALOGUE

Mansfield uses **dialogue**—conversation between characters—to bring her characters to life and advance the action of her story. You will notice that she follows these rules for formatting and **punctuating** the dialogue:

- A speaker's exact words are enclosed in quotation marks.
- Commas separate quotations from words that identify the speaker. The comma always appears before the quotation mark.
- A new paragraph begins each time the speaker changes.
- When a paragraph ends while a character is still speaking, quotation marks *do not* appear at the end of that paragraph. However, quotation marks do appear at the beginning of the new paragraph.

Prentice Hall Literature Program Resources

REINFORCE / RETEACH / EXTEND

Selection Support Pages
Build Vocabulary: Words From Myths, p. 55
Build Grammar Skills: Punctuating Dialogue, p. 56
Reading Strategy: Question, p. 57
Literary Focus: Allusion, p. 58

Strategies for Diverse Student Needs, p. 14

Beyond Literature
Cross-Curricular Connection: Plant Science, p. 14

Formal Assessment Selection Test, pp. 44–46; Assessment Resources Software

Alternative Assessment, p. 14

Resource Pro CD-ROM

Listening to Literature Audiocassettes

The Apple Tree

◆ Literature and Your Life

Connect Your Experience

If you've ever spent a long time waiting in anticipation of something, then you know how the characters in "The Apple Tree" feel. Based on your own experiences, try to predict whether the anticipated event will live up to the characters' expectations.

Journal Writing Think of something for which you spent a long time waiting. In your journal, write about whether the outcome was worth the wait.

Thematic Focus: Reaching a Goal

As you read this story of a man and his children's painful, mouth-watering anticipation, you may ask yourself, What things in life are worth waiting for?

◆ Background for Understanding

Literature

In this story, a man discovers a special apple tree he has never noticed in his orchard before. He tells his children that eating the fruit of this tree is forbidden. "The Apple Tree" is only one of a vast number of literary works inspired by biblical stories.

This story may sound familiar. It is a variation of the biblical account of Adam and Eve. The Bible relates that Adam and Eve were forbidden by God to eat the fruit (traditionally represented as an apple) of a tree in the center of the garden. Adam and Eve *do* eat the fruit, and they are consequently banished from the Garden of Eden.

◆ Literary Focus

Allusion

Katherine Mansfield's reference to the forbidden tree is an **allusion**, a reference to a well-known person, place, event, literary work, or work of art. Writers most frequently make allusions to the Bible, Greek or Roman mythology, or Shakespeare's plays, but they may also allude to current events, popular culture, or other fields of interest to readers. Recognizing allusions will help you better understand and appreciate literature, because allusions often add layers of meaning to passages or events in a literary work.

◆ Reading Strategy

Question

Writers almost never spell out the significance of each detail or each character's actions. Instead, it's left up to the reader to ask questions and to look for answers. When you **question** as you read, you ask yourself about the meaning of events, character's actions, and key details. Why does a character act the way he or she does? Does a specific detail of the setting have an underlying meaning?

Keep your questions in mind as you read ahead. Try to piece together details that will enable you to answer them. For example, you might gather information about a character's background that will help you answer a question about his or her behavior.

Apple Plenty, 1970, Herbert Shuptrine

Test Preparation Workshop

Reading Comprehension: Recognize Sequence Many standarized tests contain reading comprehension questions that require students to recognize sequential order in a reading passage. Have students read "The Apple Tree." Then use this sample question to give students practice in identifying correct sequential order.

Choose the item that contains the correct order of events in the story.

A The visitor praises the apples; the children eat them secretly; Father is disappointed.

B The visitor praises the apples; the children are forbidden to touch them; Father and the children find the apples taste delicious.

C The visitor praises the apples; the children are forbidden to touch them; Father and the children find the apples taste terrible.

D The children are forbidden to eat the apples; Father and the children find the apples taste terrible; Father laughs about the tree.

Help students recognize that C is the correct sequence of events.

To capture students' interest, draw two simple signs on the chalkboard: "Private: Keep Out" and "Authorized Personnel Only." Encourage students to exchange information about where and when they have encountered such signs. Ask: What did you imagine was behind the signs? Did you ever find out? What is the effect of making something "off-limits" or forbidden? After discussing the effect of classifying something as "forbidden," tell students that "The Apple Tree" centers on a "forbidden" fruit—the apple. Students will have a chance to compare their own reactions to forbidden situations to those of the characters in this story.

Customize for
Less Proficient Readers

On the surface this is a very simple story. Work with these students to help them understand the building of the theme as the story progresses. They might pause after each page, for example, and summarize its most important idea before continuing.

Customize for
Pre-AP Students

Invite Pre-AP Students to read other stories that center on something forbidden, such as the stories of Pandora from Greek mythology or the story of Bluebeard. Have them analyze how something forbidden affects each main character.

Customize for
English Language Learners

Explain to students that they will encounter the idiom "Don't bolt it" (footnote 5) in the story. *Bolt* literally means "a sudden dash." "Don't bolt it" means "don't eat your food in a sudden dash." These students will also benefit from reading along as they listen to the recording.

Listening to Literature Audiocassettes

Customize for
Gifted/Talented Students

Have students role play a private conversation between the children after they have been told to stay away from the apple tree. Role-plays should stress how the admonition makes each character feel.

Develop Understanding

One-Minute Insight

On its literal level, this is the story of how anticipation is rewarded—literally—with bitter disappointment. The children's disappointment at how terrible the "magnificent" apple tastes is matched only by their desire to shield their father from disappointment. Read as an "Adam-and-Eve" story, the children, as the biblical characters, ultimately find that the forbidden fruit is bitter. Even though the children in this story have permission to taste the fruit, they are driven like Adam and Eve from the innocence of childhood as they witness the foolishness of their respected father.

Humanities: Art

Orchard With Flowering Fruit Trees, Springtime, Pontoise, 1877, by Camille Pissarro.

This painting captures the delicate light and colors of springtime, reminiscent of the season of anticipation in which the characters in this story await the fruit of an apple tree.

Camille Pissarro (1830–1903) was a French impressionist painter, the only painter to exhibit in all eight of the Impressionist group exhibitions of 1874 to 1886. Landscapes, often with peasant figures, were his main subjects. The blossoms on the fruit trees in this painting radiate light and illuminate the orchard. As Mansfield's story focuses in on a fleeting event in everyday life, this painting captures a spring day—one of nature's fleeting moments.

After reading the first page of the story, students can discuss the following questions:

1. From the details in the painting and the title of the selection, what can you predict about this story? *Students may say that the plot will revolve around an apple tree; that there is something special or mysterious about a particular tree.*
2. How is the orchard in the picture different from the second orchard described in the story? *The orchard in the story is more remote than the one in the picture—there would probably be no building or buildings in sight. Also, the grass in the picture is not as long as the grass described in the story.*

Block Scheduling Strategies

Consider these suggestions to take advantage of extended class time:

- Have students read the Background for Understanding. Elaborate on the story as necessary for your class.
- Focus on the literary concept of allusion. Ask students to recall allusions in their recent reading. For example, did they read a review of a film that alluded to another film, or a work of literature? Did they understand the allusion? If so, how did the allusion affect or change their understanding of what they read? Use the Literary Focus page on Allusions in ***Selection Support*** (p. 58).
- Have students work with a partner to develop responses to the Critical Thinking questions.
- Encourage students to share orally the stories they have retold in the Guided Writing Lesson.
- Have students complete the multiple-choice portion of the Selection Test (p. 44) in the ***Formal Assessment*** booklet. You may wish to assign the test essay as homework.

The Apple Tree

Katherine Mansfield

There were two orchards belonging to the old house. One, that we called the "wild" orchard, lay beyond the vegetable garden; it was planted with bitter cherries and damsons[1] and transparent yellow plums. For some reason it lay under a cloud; we never played there, we did not even trouble to pick up the fallen fruit; and there, every Monday morning, to the round open space in the middle, the servant girl and the washerwoman carried the wet linen—Grandmother's night-dresses, Father's striped shirts, the hired man's cotton trousers and the servant girl's "dreadfully vulgar" salmon-pink flannelette drawers jigged and slapped in horrid familiarity. But the other orchard, far away and hidden from the house, lay at the foot of a little hill and stretched right over to the edge of the paddocks—to the clumps of wattles[2] bobbing yellow in the bright sun and the blue gums with their streaming sickle-shaped leaves. There, under the fruit trees, the grass grew so thick and coarse that it tangled and knotted in your shoes as you walked, and even on the hottest day it was damp to touch when you stopped and parted it this way and that, looking for windfalls—the apples marked with a bird's beak, the big bruised pears, the quinces,[3] so good to eat with a pinch of salt, but so delicious to smell that you could not bite for sniffing. . . . 2

One year the orchard had its Forbidden Tree. It was an apple tree discovered by Father and a friend during an after-dinner prowl one Sunday afternoon.

◆ Literary Focus What allusion does the author make here? 3

1. **damsons** (dam´ zənz) *n.*: Small purple plums.

2. **wattles** (wät´ əlz) *n.*: Small flowering trees.

3. **quinces** (kwins´ iz) *n.*: Hard greenish-yellow apple-shaped fruit.

1 ◀ Critical Viewing What season is shown in this picture? What details reveal the season? [Deduce]

◆ **Build Vocabulary**

paddocks (pad´ əks) *n.*: Small enclosed fields

▶Critical Viewing◀

1 Deduce Elicit from students the following response: *It is probably spring. The picture shows budding trees.*

◆ Reading Strategy

2 Question Suggest to students that they ask themselves this question as they read: What makes this second orchard appealing to the storyteller? *It is hidden, grassy, cool, and more remote than the "wild" orchard.*

◆ Literary Focus

3 Allusion The allusion is to the tree of knowledge in the Garden of Eden in the biblical story in Genesis 2–3.

Customize for *Less Proficient Readers*

You may wish to preview the footnotes to familiarize students with the terms that describe specific types of shrubs and apples. Show students that context clues can also help them to determine the general meaning of these references. After discussing the footnotes, tell students that as they encounter these terms in their reading, it is not necessary for them to interrupt their reading to consult the footnote, as long as they remember the general idea of the reference.

Customize for *English Language Learners*

Use the pictures with the story, and other appropriate visuals, to help students appreciate the descriptions they read.

Tips to Guide Reading

Recall After students have finished reading the story, ask them to tell what they remember. Write a list on the board as students make suggestions.

Read to Appreciate Author's Craft

Encourage students to notice how the author reveals Father's personality traits as the story progresses.

Extending Word Study

Multiple-Meaning Words Encourage students to determine the meaning of *windfall* from context. Then ask them if they are aware of another meaning of the word. If necessary, have students look up *windfall* in the dictionary.

Humanities: Art

Apple Plenty by Herbert Shuptrine.

The basket of ripe apples, nestled in the autumn grass, suggests the bounty of apples. Such a heart-warming picture is probably what Father in this story expects from his tree. Have students examine the way in which the basket of apples is presented to the viewer, and discuss these questions:

1. How does its central position in the painting reflect the importance placed on the "rare" apple tree in the English farmer's life? *The central position suggests the focus that Father places on the apples while he is anticipating their harvest.*
2. Are these apples a fair representation of the crimson apples which the narrator describes in the story? *On the outside these apples match the narrator's description; however, the insides of these are probably sweet and crisp, not like the apples in this story.*
3. If students were to pick a theme for this picture, what would it be—harvest time, abandonment, nature's bounty, or what other theme? *Students might justify any of the suggested themes or supply another. Request reasons for their choices.*

◆ Critical Thinking

❶ **Infer** Why does the father act as if he knows what the visitor is talking about? *The father does not want to appear to be ignorant, especially in front of his children.*

◆ Build Grammar Skills

❷ **Punctuate Dialogue** Ask students to explain why the quotation marks and commas appear where they do in this sentence. Have them explain why a new paragraph begins with the word, "They're." *The quotation marks enclose what the characters are actually saying; the commas separate the dialogue from words that identify the speaker; the new paragraph indicates that the speaker has changed.*

◆ Reading Strategy

❸ **Question** Ask students: Why does the father issue this warning? How will answering this question help you to understand the story? *Students may say that the father issues the warning because he now thinks the tree is valuable. By answering this question, students can predict that the father's new conception of the tree will affect future events.*

◆ Literature and Your Life

❹ Point out that sometimes taking a particular walk or route becomes a custom for people. Ask: Do you have a customary route? What is special about it and its landmarks? *Students can describe the routes they take to get to special places and the associations they make with landmarks along the way.*

◆ Reading Strategy

❺ **Question** The father feels that the unique qualities he has discovered in the apple tree reflect on his own character; he takes pride in the tree as if it were his personal accomplishment.

◆ Critical Thinking

❻ **Infer** Ask students: Why do you think Bogey stood with his scratched knees pressed together and his hands behind his back? *Students may say he is trying to hide his scratched knees from his father, and trying to imitate his father, who also stands with his hands behind his back.*

"Great Scott!" said the friend, lighting upon it with every appearance of admiring astonishment: "Isn't that a—?" And a rich, splendid name settled like an unknown bird on the tree.

❶ "Yes, I believe it is," said Father lightly. He knew nothing whatever about the names of fruit trees.

"Great Scott!" said the friend again: "They're wonderful apples. Nothing like 'em—and you're going to have a tiptop crop. Marvelous apples! You can't beat 'em!"

❷ "No, they're very fine—very fine," said Father carelessly, but looking upon the tree with new and lively interest.

"They're rare—they're very rare. Hardly ever see 'em in England nowadays," said the visitor and set a seal on Father's delight. For Father was a self-made man and the price he had to pay for everything was so huge and so painful that nothing rang so sweet to him as to hear his purchase praised. He was young and sensitive still. He still wondered whether in the deepest sense he got his money's worth. He still had hours when he walked up and down in the moonlight half deciding to "chuck this confounded rushing to the office every day—and clear out—clear out once and for all." And now to discover that he'd a valuable apple tree thrown in with the orchard—an apple tree that this Johnny from England positively envied!

❸ "Don't touch that tree! Do you hear me, children!" said he, bland and firm; and when the guest had gone, with quite another voice and manner:

"If I catch either of you touching those apples you shall not only go to bed—you shall each have a good sound whipping." Which merely added to its magnificence.

Every Sunday morning after church Father, with Bogey and me tailing after, walked through the flower garden, down the violet path, past the lace-bark tree, past the white rose and syringa[4] bushes, and down the hill to the orchard. ❹ The apple tree seemed to have been miraculously warned of its high honor, standing apart from its fellows, bending a little under its rich clusters, fluttering its polished leaves, important and exquisite before Father's awful eye. His heart swelled to the sight—we knew his heart swelled. He put his hands behind his back and screwed up his eyes in the way he had. ❺ There it stood—the accidental thing—the thing that no one had been aware of when the hard bargain was driven. It hadn't been counted in, hadn't in a way been paid for. If the house had been burned to the ground at that time it would have meant less to him than the destruction of his tree. And how we played up to him, Bogey and I,—Bogey with his scratched knees pressed together, ❻ his hands behind his back, too, and a round cap on his head with "H.M.S. Thunderbolt" printed across it.

> **◆ Reading Strategy**
> Question why the father is so excited about the apple tree.

The apples turned from pale green to yellow; then they had deep pink stripes painted on them, and then the pink melted all over the yellow, reddened, and spread into a fine clear crimson.

At last the day came when Father took out of his waistcoat pocket a little pearl penknife. He reached up. Very slowly and very carefully he picked two apples growing on a bough.

"Why, they're warm," cried Father in amazement. "They're wonderful apples!

◆ Build Vocabulary

exquisite (eks´ kwi zit) *adj.*: Delicately beautiful
bouquet (bo͞o kā´) *n.*: Fragrance
jovial (jō´ vē əl) *adj.*: Full of good humor

4. **syringa** (sə riŋ´ gə) *n.*: Hardy shrub with tiny, fragrant flowers, also known as lilac.

Speaking, Listening, and Viewing Mini-Lesson

Monologue From Father's Point of View
This mini-lesson supports the Speaking, Listening, and Viewing activity in the Idea Bank on p. 199.

Introduce the Concept Remind students that in a monologue—a speech made by one person—a character reveals his or her truest feelings. Students should give the father the opportunity to tell events as he sees them.

Develop Background Students can brainstorm for a list of characteristics that describe the father and then decide which part of the story they want to relate from his point of view. He might think of ways to impress the visitor, how the fruit will taste, or how he feels at the end of the story.

Apply the Information Have students create their monologues with the father's character traits in mind. Suggest that they put themselves in his place and imagine his thoughts and feelings.

Assess the Outcome Have students use the Peer Assessment: Speech (p. 119) of the ***Alternative Assessment*** booklet to help them evaluate each others' and their own monologues.

Tiptop! Marvelous!" he echoed. He rolled them over in his hands.

"Look at that!" he said. "Not a spot—not a blemish!" And he walked through the orchard with Bogey and me stumbling after, to a tree stump under the wattles. We sat, one on either side of Father. He laid one apple down, opened the penknife and neatly and beautifully cut the other in half.

"Look at that!" he exclaimed.

"Father!" we cried, dutiful but really enthusiastic, too. For the lovely red color had bitten right through the white flesh of the apple; it was pink to the shiny black pips lying so justly in their scaly pods. It looked as though the apple had been dipped in wine.

"Never seen *that* before," said Father. "You won't find an apple like that in a hurry!" He put it to his nose and pronounced an unfamiliar word. "Bouquet. What a bouquet!" And then he handed to Bogey one half, to me the other.

"Don't *bolt* it!"[5] said he. It was agony to give even so much away. I knew it, while I took mine humbly and humbly Bogey took his.

Then he divided the second with the same neat beautiful little cut of the pearl knife.

I kept my eyes on Bogey. Together we took a bite. Our mouths were full of a floury stuff, a hard, faintly bitter skin—a horrible taste of something dry. . . .

"Well?" asked Father, very jovial. He had 7 cut his two halves into quarters and was taking out the little pods. "Well?"

Bogey and I stared at each other, chewing desperately. In that second of chewing and swallowing a long silent conversation passed between us—and a strange meaning smile. We swallowed. We edged near Father, just touching him. 8

"Perfect," we lied. "Perfect—Father! Simply lovely!" 9

But it was no use. Father spat his out and never went near the apple tree again.

5. **Don't bolt it:** Don't eat it all in one bite.

Guide for Responding

◆ Literature and Your Life

Reader's Response Were you surprised by the ending? Why or why not?

Thematic Focus Why do you think that eagerly anticipated events so often fail to live up to people's expectations?

Group Discussion With a small group, discuss why the children mislead their father about the taste of the apple. What would each of you have done in that situation? Why?

☑ Check Your Comprehension

1. What does the friend from England tell the father about the apple tree?
2. How does the father treat the tree after his friend's revelation?
3. Describe the apples' appearance.
4. Explain how the apples' taste compares with the characters' expectations.

◆ Build Vocabulary

7 Words From Myths Ask students to reread the Build Vocabulary feature on page 192 and explain in their own words how the word *jovial* applies to Father. *Students should say that people born under the sign of Jupiter (Jove) were considered to be merry, or jovial.*

◆ Critical Thinking

8 Interpret Ask: How could a long conversation take place in a second? *When people who know each other well communicate silently, by facial expressions or body language, they can say a great deal in a very short time.*

◆ Critical Thinking

9 Relate Ask students if they would have lied if they had been in the children's situation. Why or why not? *Some students will say that they would have lied to protect their father's pride. Others might say they would not have lied because their father was soon to find out the truth—the apple tasted bad and the tree was not a valuable one.*

Reinforce and Extend

Answers

◆ Literature and Your Life

Reader's Response Some students might say they were surprised by the ending because they thought the tree would in fact prove valuable; others will say they expected the apple to prove the father's fallibility.

Thematic Focus Students might say that people often end up disappointed because they attach too much importance to anticipated events.

☑ Check Your Comprehension

1. He tells him it is a rare apple tree and that it will bear wonderful fruit.
2. He treats the tree as a precious thing.
3. The apples are crimson and flawless, and they are pink to the core.
4. The characters expected the apples to taste wonderful, but they tasted floury and bitter.

Beyond the Selection

FURTHER READING

Other Works by Katherine Mansfield

"The Dolls' House"

"Her First Ball"

The Garden Party: Katherine Mansfield's New Zealand Stories—Stories illustrated with color plates by New Zealand artists

We suggest that you preview these works before recommending them to students.

INTERNET

Students may find additional information about the Katherine Mansfield on the Internet. Please be aware that sites may have changed from the time we published this information:

http://www.buffnet.net./~starmist/kmansfld/kmansfld.htm

http://www.futurenet.co.uk/Penguin/Books/01401888000.html

We *strongly recommend* that you preview these sites before you send students to them.

Answers

◆ Critical Thinking

1. He is easily convinced because he does not know anything about apple trees and is all too ready to believe he has a special one.
2. The first hint was probably the color inside the apple.
3. The children are afraid to disappoint and humiliate their father.
4. They learn not to build up expectations so high, particularly on the basis of someone else's opinion.
5. The need for approval might cause people to use poor judgment in attaching value to some things.
6. Students might suggest the jobs of politician or salesperson.

◆ Reading Strategy

1. Students' main question might be: Why is it so important to the father to have something rare and valuable?
2. Students might observe that the father needs the approval of others, including his children.

◆ Literary Focus

1. The story mentions the Forbidden Tree, an allusion to tree of knowledge; father cautions the children not to touch "that tree"—an allusion to God's forbidding Adam and Eve to eat from the tree of knowledge.
2. The tree in the biblical story represents worldly experience. In this story the tree stands for the value or prestige people seek.
3. By comparing the children with Adam and Eve, students can better understand the children's loss of innocence at the end.

◆ Build Vocabulary

Using Words From Myths

1. c 2. a 3. b

Using the Word Bank

1. c 2. b 3. a 4. a

◆ Build Grammar Skills

Practice

"Great Scott!" said the friend, lighting upon it with every appearance of admiring astonishment: "Isn't that a—?" And a rich splendid name settled like an unknown bird on the tree.

"Yes, I believe it is," said Father lightly. He knew nothing whatever about the names of fruit trees.

Guide for Responding *(continued)*

◆ Critical Thinking

INTERPRET

1. Why is the father so easily convinced by his friend that the tree produces wonderful apples? **[Infer]**

2. What are the first hints that the taste of the apples might not live up to expectations? **[Infer]**

3. Why do the children mislead their father about the taste of the apple? **[Infer]**

4. What lesson do the father and the children learn? **[Draw Conclusions]**

APPLY

5. How do image and public approval play a role in determining the worth of some of the things we value? **[Apply]**

EXTEND

6. What are some careers in which public opinion influences how a person performs his or her job? **[Career Link]**

◆ Reading Strategy

QUESTION

After you've finished reading a literary work, reflect on the **questions** that came to mind as you read. Answer any unresolved questions by piecing together details from the work and, if necessary, going back into the text.

1. What is the main question that came to mind about the father's behavior?

2. After reading the story, how would you answer that question?

◆ Literary Focus

ALLUSION

In "The Apple Tree," Katherine Mansfield makes an **allusion** to the biblical story of Adam and Eve.

1. Point out two references in "The Apple Tree" to the biblical story.

2. How does "The Apple Tree" differ from the biblical story?

3. How does knowing the biblical story of Adam and Eve increase your understanding and appreciation of "The Apple Tree"?

◆ Build Vocabulary

USING WORDS FROM GREEK AND ROMAN MYTHS

Use the clues below to match each word with the letter of its definition.

Clues From Greek Mythology

Pan: minor god who lived in wild places and sometimes frightened travelers

Chaos: formless confusion that existed before the Earth or the gods appeared

Lethe: river of forgetfulness that separates the worlds of the living and the dead

1. lethal ___?___ **a.** completely confused and disordered

2. chaotic ___?___ **b.** sudden, hysterical fear

3. panic ___?___ **c.** deadly

USING THE WORD BANK: Synonyms

On your paper, write the word or phrase whose meaning is closest to that of the first word:

1. jovial: (a) simple, (b) wealthy, (c) merry

2. paddock: (a) marsh, (b) pasture, (c) grove

3. exquisite: (a) superb, (b) favorable, (c) fragrant

4. bouquet: (a) smell, (b) collection, (c) roses

◆ Build Grammar Skills

PUNCTUATION OF DIALOGUE

You can picture Mansfield's characters interacting with one another because of her extensive use of **dialogue**—characters' conversations written as if quoted word for word.

Practice Copy the following passage from "The Apple Tree" and punctuate it correctly.

Great Scott! said the friend, lighting upon it with every appearance of admiring astonishment: Isn't that a—? And a rich, splendid name settled like an unknown bird on the tree. Yes, I believe it is, said Father lightly. He knew nothing whatever about the names of fruit trees.

Writing Application Re-create a recent conversation that you've had with a friend or family member in a brief passage of written dialogue. Punctuate your passage correctly.

Grammar Reinforcement

For additional instruction and practice, use the pages on Quotation Marks and Direct Quotations (pp. 104–106) in the *Writer's Solution Grammar Practice Book.*

Reteach

Help students understand the author's use of allusions by recognizing their own use of allusions in everyday conversation. For example, students may refer to characters from popular TV shows, lines from current movies, or lyrics from songs. Invite students to brainstorm to make a list of allusions they may make in conversation. Then have them write a dialogue in which people make allusions.

Build Your Portfolio

Idea Bank

Writing

1. Summary of the Story Write a summary of "The Apple Tree" to appear in *Short Story Digest* magazine. Keep the summary as brief as possible, but include all the key events from the story.

2. Personal Narrative Recall a time when an anticipated event didn't live up to your expectations. Then write a personal narrative in which you re-create the experience and tell what you learned from it.

3. Alternative Ending Write an alternative ending to the story in which you explore the possibility of what might have happened had the apples tasted better.

Speaking, Listening, and Viewing

4. Dramatic Reading With three classmates, give a dramatic reading of "The Apple Tree" in front of your classmates. Have one person be the narrator, one the father, one the father's friend, and one the boy. **[Performing Arts Link]**

5. Monologue From Father's Point of View Prepare a monologue in which you tell the story from the father's point of view. Show his anticipation and disappointment. Perform your monologue for the class. **[Performing Arts Link]**

Researching and Representing

6. Travel Brochure Make a travel brochure for New Zealand, Mansfield's native land. Include text and pictures that give information about geography, culture, and climate. **[Social Studies Link]**

7. Map Use details from the story and your imagination to create a map of the father's property. Show the locations of the two orchards and of the "Forbidden Tree." **[Social Studies Link]**

Online Activity www.phlit.phschool.com

Guided Writing Lesson

Retelling a Story

On one level, "The Apple Tree" is a retelling of the biblical story of Adam and Eve from the Bible. Choose a story that you can retell. It can be from any number of sources: the Bible, classical mythology, even current events. Retell the story, giving it a new setting or other unique twist.

Writing Skills Focus: Show, Don't Tell

Add interest to your story by **showing** readers your setting and characters rather than simply telling about them. Katherine Mansfield doesn't say the apple is beautiful, she shows its beauty with specific details.

> . . . the lovely red color had bitten right through the white flesh of the apple; it was pink to the shiny black pips lying so justly in their scaly pods. It looked as though the apple had been dipped in wine.

Prewriting Make your retelling unique. For example, you may want to recast *Romeo and Juliet* in modern times in your community. Then list the key elements of the work or event you're adapting.

Drafting Organize events in a logical order; time order is probably best. Present the key elements of the original work in a way that readers will recognize. Also, use dialogue as much as possible to make your characters come alive.

Revising After you've finished your draft, put it aside for a day or two. Then review it with a critical eye. Add descriptive details for characters that show (rather than tell) what you want readers to know.

✓ ASSESSMENT OPTIONS

Formal Assessment, Selection Test, pp. 44–46, and Assessment Resources Software. The selection test is designed so that it can be easily customized to the performance levels of your students.

Alternative Assessment, p. 14, includes options for less advanced students, Pre-AP Students, verbal/linguistic learners, intrapersonal learners, and interpersonal learners.

PORTFOLIO ASSESSMENT

Use the following rubrics in the ***Alternative Assessment*** booklet to assess student writing:
Summary of the Story: Summary Rubric, p. 98
Personal Narrative: Personal Narration Rubric, p. 96
Alternative Ending: Fiction Narrative Rubric, p. 95

Idea Bank

Following are suggestions for matching Idea Bank topics with your students' performance levels and learning modalities:

Customizing for *Performance Levels*

Less Advanced Students: 1, 4
Average Students: 2, 6
More Advanced Students: 3, 5, 7

Customizing for *Learning Modalities*

Visual/Spatial: 6, 7
Bodily/Kinesthetic: 4
Verbal/Linguistic: 4, 5

Guided Writing Lesson

Prewriting Strategy One way of retelling a story is to transform it into a different genre. For example, a short story could be cast as a newspaper report, or a character from a novel might tell his or her story in a letter. Once students have come up with a story they wish to retell, divide them into small groups for shaping conferences. Each student should share his or her story with the group. The listeners should think about different forms the story might take, and then group members should share their ideas. This will give the writer a number of ideas to think about, but ultimately, he or she will have to make a decision about which form seems the most sensible and intriguing.

For more prewriting, elaboration, and revision strategies, see *Prentice Hall Writing and Grammar.*

Writers at Work Videodisc

Have students view the videodisc segment (Ch. 2) featuring Maxine Hong Kingston. Use it as a springboard for a class discussion on narrative writing. Have students discuss what Kingston says about how a story can shape itself into a narrative.

Play frames 14659 to 15676

Writing Lab CD-ROM

Have students complete the tutorial on Narration. Follow these steps:

1. Have students get video tips on narrative elements to see how such elements can work together to create an effective story.
2. Suggest that students use interactive tips on ending a narrative.

Prepare and Engage

LESSON OBJECTIVES

1. To develop vocabulary and word identification skills
- Latin Suffixes: *-ment*
- Using the Word Bank: Antonyms
- Extending Word Study: Context (ATE)

2. To use a variety of reading strategies to read and comprehend
- Connect Your Experience
- Reading Strategy: Relate to What You Know
- Tips to Guide Reading: Sustained Reading (ATE)
- Read to Be Informed (ATE)

3. To increase knowledge of other cultures and to connect common elements across cultures
- Connect Your Experience

4. To express and support responses to the text
- Critical Thinking
- Idea Bank: Comparing and Contrasting Poems
- Idea Bank: Letter to an Author

5. To analyze literary elements
- Literary Focus: Aphorisms

6. To read in order to research self-selected and assigned topics
- Idea Bank: Interview
- Idea Bank: Tiananmen Square Presentation
- Idea Bank: Collage

7. To plan, prepare, organize, and present literary interpretations
- Speaking, Listening, and Viewing Mini-Lesson: Oral Interpretation

8. To use recursive writing processes to write an aphorism calendar
- Guided Writing Lesson

9. To increase knowledge of the rules of grammar and usage
- Build Grammar Skills: Infinitives and Infinitive Phrases

Test Preparation

Reading Comprehension: Recognize Details (ATE, p. 201) The teaching tips and sample test item in this workshop support the instruction and practice in the unit workshop:

Reading Comprehension: Recognize Facts, Details, and Sequence (SE, p. 215)

Guide for Reading

David Diop *(1927–1960)*

David Diop published only one volume of poetry before his life was tragically cut short in a plane crash. That one book, *Hammerblows*, reflects Diop's rejection of colonialism in Africa.

Diop was born in France, but his roots were in the region that became the West African nation of Senegal. His poem "Africa" captures the power and dignity of a continent struggling against oppression.

Confucius *(551?–479? B.C.)*

One man's ideas have influenced the pattern of Chinese life for more than two thousand years. That man is Confucius, a scholar from Shandong province in northeast China. In all his teachings, Confucius emphasized the importance of moral conduct.

Confucius' moral teachings have had a profound impact on Chinese life and have influenced the lives of many people in a number of other countries as well.

Bei Dao *(1949–)*

Born two months before the founding of the People's Republic of China in October 1949, Bei Dao seemed destined for a successful government career. However, he dropped out of school and joined the Red Guards, a movement of teenagers seeking to revitalize the Chinese Revolution. When he became disillusioned with the violent tactics of this movement, he turned to writing poetry. Soon his poems, including "All," became rallying cries for those who wanted China to become more democratic. He has lived outside China since 1989, when Chinese leaders ordered the massacre of protesting students in Tiananmen Square.

Shu Ting *(1952–)*

As a teenager, Shu Ting was forced by political events to leave Beijing and live in a small peasant village. She gained fame as a poet while still in her twenties. She won China's National Poetry Award in 1981 and 1983.

200 ◆ *Striving for Success*

◆ Build Vocabulary

LATIN SUFFIXES: *-ment*

In the excerpt from *The Analects*, you will encounter the word *chastisements*. The Latin suffix *-ment* can help you figure out that this word is the noun form of the verb *chastise*, which means "punish." *Chastisements*, then, are "punishments."

WORD BANK

Before you read, preview this list of words from the selections. As you read, look for other words—like *treatment* and *improvement*—that end with *-ment*.

impetuous
chastisements
lamentation

◆ Build Grammar Skills

INFINITIVES AND INFINITIVE PHRASES

An **infinitive** is the base form of a verb, usually preceded by *to*; it can be used as a noun, an adjective, or an adverb. An **infinitive phrase** is an infinitive with modifiers or complements (words that complete the meaning of the verb), all acting together as a single part of speech.

The following line from "Old Song" contains two infinitive phrases: *To be alive* is a noun; it is the subject of the sentence. *To hear this song* is an adverb modifying *alive*.

To be alive to hear this song is a victory.

Prentice Hall Literature Program Resources

REINFORCE / RETEACH / EXTEND

Selection Support Pages
Build Vocabulary: Suffixes: *-ment*, p. 59
Build Grammar Skills: Infinitives and Infinitive Phrases, p. 60
Reading Strategy: Relate to What You Know, p. 61
Literary Focus: Aphorisms, p. 62

Strategies for Diverse Student Needs, p. 15

Beyond Literature
Multicultural Connection: "Words to the Wise," p. 15

Formal Assessment Selection Test, pp. 47–49; Assessment Resources Software

Alternative Assessment, p. 15

Writing and Language Transparencies
Herringbone Organizer, p. 75

Resource Pro CD-ROM

Listening to Literature Audiocassettes

Africa ◆ Old Song
from The Analects ◆ All ◆ Also All

◆ Literature and Your Life

Connect Your Experience

Advice—you can't escape it. You get it from teachers, parents, and friends—even from talk show hosts. People love to tell you what you should do or think. Authors are no different. They want to communicate what they have learned about life.

These writers may not give you the same advice, but that's understandable because they come from different places and eras. Think about what they say and suggest about life's goals.

Thematic Focus: Reaching a Goal

Each of these works offers a different answer to the question, "How do we measure the success of a life?"

Journal Writing Make a cluster diagram to map out what you think are the ingredients of a successful life.

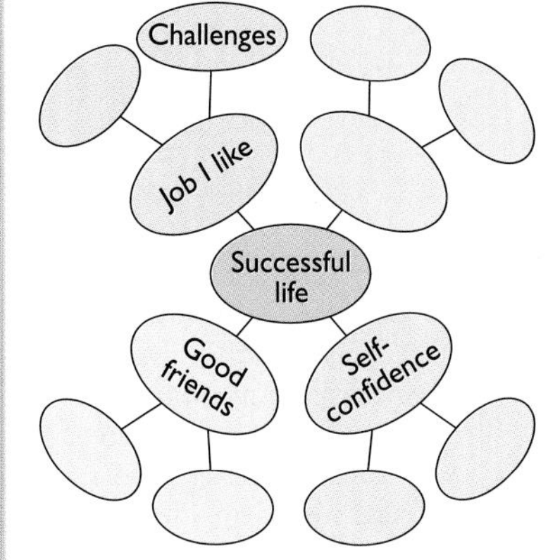

◆ Background for Understanding

Culture

If success is measured by time, "Old Song" and the sayings of Confucius are a success. These works have survived for thousands of years, passed down from generation to generation.

Many African societies did not preserve their wisdom and stories on paper. Instead, they developed a rich oral tradition. In each village, elders passed on wisdom in the form of sayings, stories, and poems like "Old Song."

No writings from Confucius' own hand exist today. *The Analects*, or collected sayings of Confucius, were also preserved orally and compiled in writing long after his death.

◆ Literary Focus

Aphorisms

The ideas of Confucius have endured partly because they were expressed as **aphorisms**—brief sayings that express a basic truth. Many cultures pass on truths in the form of aphorisms, like gifts handed from one generation to another.

All the literature selections in this group contain aphorisms. Look for these brief sayings. Then read them thoughtfully, as if you were slowly unwrapping a gift sent to you across many miles or years.

◆ Reading Strategy

Relate to What You Know

The best way to judge advice is to think about how it applies to your own situation. The best way to understand a writer's words is by **relating** them to what you know—finding something in your own experience that helps you understand and evaluate them.

These selections come from distant parts of the globe, Africa and China. When you first read them, you may think, "Interesting, but what does this have to do with me?" Look closely, and you'll discover that their themes are universal. Consider their messages about survival, hope, dignity, and morality. Then apply these messages to your own experience.

To draw students into this group of selections, tell them about the Tiananmen Square massacre in 1989. A large group of Chinese students gathered in Tiananmen Square in Beijing, China, to protest harsh, repressive government tactics. They wanted more freedom, including freedom of speech, a right which is protected, for example, by our United States Constitution. In response to the protest, the Chinese government gunned down citizens in Tiananmen Square. Hundreds of young people were killed. With the class, compare and contrast protest movements students have heard of in the United States and elsewhere. Tell them that poems by Bei Dao and Shu Ting in this group pertain to political protest in China. The other pieces also deal with political and social issues.

Connecting Themes Across Cultures

Ask students to suggest sayings or advice that they frequently hear at home or from adults with whom they come in contact. Discuss how these repeated words are being handed down to another generation. Invite them to speculate as to whether they, in turn, will hand down any of these sayings.

Customize for
Less Proficient Readers and English Language Learners

To help ensure their understanding of the poems, encourage students to work with partners to paraphrase the lines of poetry as they read.

Customize for
Pre-AP Students

Encourage these students to analyze the imagery in David Diop's poem, "Africa." What is the "young and sturdy tree," the "white and faded flowers," the "fruits" that "grow to have/The bitter taste of liberty"? Why is the taste of liberty bitter?

Customize for
Gifted/Talented Students

As they read, students can create a Venn diagram or chart to compare and contrast the writers' ideas about success.

Test Preparation Workshop

Reading Comprehension:
Recognize Details Critical reading questions, as found on the SAT test, require students to recognize and use details in order to select the best answer. This sample test item will help students practice using details to select the best answer.

> The Master said, A young man's duty is to behave well to his parents at home and to his elders abroad, to be cautious in giving promises and punctual in keeping them, to have kindly feelings towards everyone. . . .

The author's purpose in listing the details in this passage may be to teach young people to—

A stay at home
B respect other people
C always make promises
D always arrive on time

Guide students to identify the main idea of the passage as "a young man's duty." They can identify the answer choice which best represents details that are central to the main idea as B.

Develop Understanding

One-Minute Insight These writings offer a range of valuable insights intended to guide, caution, inspire, and ignite. The poem by David Diop searches for roots and renewal; the traditional song offers quiet, steady strength; the sayings of Confucius provide sound advice. Whereas the poem by Bei Dao reflects resignation, the poem by Shu Ting responds by offering hope. Voices from ancient times unite with contemporary voices to reflect on life's struggles and its triumphs.

◆ Reading Strategy

1 Relate to What You Know Ask students to think about people in their families. Did their ancestors have to overcome hardship or oppression? How did their ancestors' struggle for success affect students' lives? *Students can share family stories or write in their journals about how they have been influenced by their past.*

◆ Critical Thinking

2 Infer Ask students if the speaker is praising or criticizing Africa. How do they know? *The speaker is criticizing Africa for saying "yes" to oppression for so long. The speaker uses images reminiscent of slavery ("the trembling back striped red") to chide Africa for its submissiveness.*

◆ Critical Thinking

3 Infer Ask students: Who is the solemn answering voice? Why does it call the speaker "child"? *Students may think the solemn voice is the speaker's mother, the spirit of Africa, the spirit of the speaker's ancestors. All these could appropriately call the speaker "child."*

▶Critical Viewing◀

4 Synthesize *The painting shows Africans working together, and "Africa" says that African people will work together, "with patience and stubbornness." The painting shows people handing fish to each other. "Old Song" celebrates traditions that are handed down from one generation to the next.*

Africa

David Diop

Translated by Ulli Beier

to my Mother

Africa my Africa
Africa of proud warriors in the ancestral
savannahs[1]
Africa my grandmother sings of
Beside her distant river
1 I have never seen you
But my gaze is full of your blood
Your black blood spilt over the fields
The blood of your sweat
The sweat of your toil
The toil of slavery
The slavery of your children
Africa, tell me Africa,
Are you the back that bends
Lies down under the weight of humbleness?
2 The trembling back striped red
That says yes to the sjambok[2] on the roads
of noon?
Solemnly a voice answers me
"Impetuous child, that young and sturdy tree
That tree that grows
There splendidly alone among white and
faded flowers
3 Is Africa, your Africa. It puts forth new
shoots
With patience and stubbornness puts forth
new shoots
Slowly its fruits grow to have
The bitter taste of liberty."

1. **savannahs** (sə vä´ nəz) *n.*: Tropical grassland containing scattered trees.
2. **sjambok** (jam´ bôk) *n.*: Whip.

◆ Build Vocabulary

impetuous (im pech´ o͞o əs) *adj.*: Impulsive; passionate

▲ **Critical Viewing** Discuss how this painting reflects the thoughts conveyed in both poems. **[Synthesize]** 4

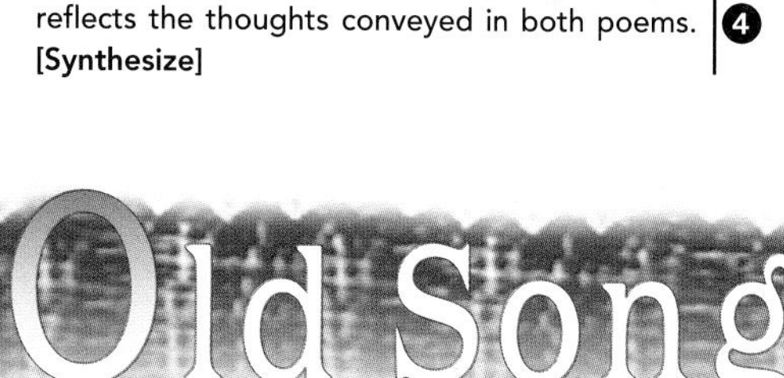

traditional

Do not seek too much fame,
but do not seek obscurity.
Be proud.
But do not remind the world of your deeds.
Excel when you must,
but do not excel the world.
Many heroes are not yet born,
many have already died.
To be alive to hear this song is a victory.

Block Scheduling Strategies

Consider these suggestions to take advantage of extended class time:

- Ask students to provide specific examples of how a teenager in today's world could live in accordance with the advice in "Old Song." Students could respond through a class discussion or in their journals.
- Let students work in small groups to answer Critical Thinking questions on pp. 203 and 205.
- Together with students, read Background for Understanding on p. 201. Lead a brief discussion in which students compare and contrast the qualities of orally based literature, such as "Old Song" and the analects of Confucius, with those of original written literature.
- Have students make a cluster diagram, like the one shown on p. 201, as a journal activity about a successful life.

Connections to Today's World

Until the 1990's, the right to vote and equal access to schools and public facilities were denied to South Africa's black majority.

However, mounting international pressure helped bring an end to **apartheid**—South Africa's system of forced segregation. Among the many voices to speak out against apartheid were musicians such as Peter Gabriel, who wrote the following song of tribute to Stephen Biko, a pioneer in the struggle against apartheid. Biko was killed by police in 1977.

1. Like poetry, song lyrics use a variety of sound devices, such as rhyme and repetition, to create a rhythmical effect and emphasize meaning. Explain how Gabriel uses rhyme and repetition in "Biko."
2. Look at lines 17–20. (a) In what way do they resemble an aphorism? (b) Explain what they mean in terms of the struggle for justice.
3. Explain how the last line of Bei Dao's poem—"every death reverberates forever"—is similar in meaning to lines 17–20 of this song.

Biko

Peter Gabriel

September '77
Port Elizabeth weather fine
It was business as usual
In police room 619
Oh Biko, Biko, because Biko
Oh Biko, Biko, because Biko
Yihla Moja, Yihla Moja
—The man is dead

When I try to sleep at night
I can only dream in red
The outside world is black and white
With only one colour dead
Oh Biko, Biko, because Biko
Oh Biko, Biko, because Biko
Yihla Moja, Yihla Moja
—The man is dead

You can blow out a candle
But you can't blow out a fire
Once the flames begin to catch
The wind will blow it higher
Oh Biko, Biko, because Biko
Yihla Moja, Yihla Moja
—The man is dead

And the eyes of the world are
watching now
watching now

Guide for Responding

◆ Literature and Your Life

Reader's Response Which poem did you find more powerful? Why?

Thematic Focus These poems suggest that success can rise out of failure. Explain why you agree or disagree.

☑ **Check Your Comprehension**

1. What question does the speaker of "Africa" ask?
2. What advice about fame is found in "Old Song"?

◆ Critical Thinking

Interpret

1. What troubles the speaker of "Africa" and causes him to ask his question? **[Infer]**
2. Explain the meaning of the final line of "Africa." **[Interpret]**

Evaluate

3. Which of these poems has the more hopeful message? Explain. **[Make a Judgment]**

Connections to Today's World

More About the Author The work Peter Gabriel did with African musicians in producing the film *Biko* inspired him to launch the World of Music, Arts, and Dance (WOMAD), an organization dedicated to preserving traditional arts through performances, education, special projects, and recordings.

Thematic Focus

More than twenty years after his violent death, Stephen Biko's commitment to the principles of justice and equality are still inspiring generations of young people.

Answers

1. Rhyme and repetition emphasize Biko's name and give the song a chantlike quality.
2. (a) These lines express a basic truth in a pithy way. (b) As the struggle for justice gains more supporters, it feeds on itself and gets stronger.
3. Both the lines in the poem and the lines in the song indicate that actions have consequences.

Reinforce and Extend

Answers

◆ Literature and Your Life

Reader's Response Some students might cite "Africa" because of its strong tone; others might prefer the quiet power of "Old Song."

Thematic Focus Students may say that failure can cause determined people to strive harder for success.

☑ **Check Your Comprehension**

1. The speaker of "Africa" asks if the country is meant to be treated as a slave.
2. Do not seek too much fame, but don't seek to be unknown, either.

◆ Critical Thinking

1. The speaker is troubled that Africa has martyred itself by accepting the oppression of its people.
2. "The bitter taste of liberty" means that liberty is won at human cost.
3. "Old Song" has the more hopeful message, because it celebrates living in an honest, humble way.

Cross-Curricular Connection: Social Studies

West Africa David Diop's poem speaks of the oppression African people have suffered under colonial rule and apartheid governmental systems. The following historical background about West Africa, the location of Diop's homeland, Senegal, will enrich students' reading experience:

In the late 1800's, the French government looked to Africa as a potential source of much-needed land, resources, and human power. As French colonial rule spread, the African people were subjugated and exploited. Colonial rule has slowly been replaced by independence, but French dominance in many West African countries is still evident, and economic and educational opportunities are still far from equal. The people of post-colonial Africa remain faced with the challenge of overcoming the legacy of exploitation and re-establishing their cultural identities.

Have students discuss how the hardships of regaining independence are reflected in Diop's poem and what Confucius might have said about French rule on the rich continent of Africa.

Tips to Guide Reading

Sustained Reading Encourage students to read the selection by Confucius in one sitting, making notes of passages that they want to reread for better comprehension.

◆ Critical Thinking

❶ **Generalize** Judging from these lines, ask students to indicate if Confucius advocates humility, ambitiousness, or greed in human relations, and to explain their response. *He advocates humility; it takes a sense of humility to "remain unsoured even though one's merits are unrecognized."*

◆ Literary Focus

❷ **Aphorisms** Have students use modern language to express this idea—"to have kindly feelings towards everyone but seek the intimacy of the Good"—as an aphorism. *Sample response: Treat everyone respectfully, but pursue the most worthy as friends.*

◆ Critical Thinking

❸ **Analyze Cause and Effect** Ask: According to Confucius, what kind of leadership will have the best results, and why? *Confucius advocates using moral leadership and being consistent in order to govern most effectively. He indicates that this approach to leadership will increase people's self-respect and make them more governable.*

▶ Critical Viewing ◀

❹ **Deduce** *His elaborate and rich-looking clothing, his venerable beard, and all suggest a respected position. Students might also suggest that the decorations on the clothing, and perhaps even some of the items of clothing, have symbolic significance.*

Extending Word Study

Context Ask students to write a definition of *homage* based on context clues in the reading.

from *The Analects*
Confucius

Translated by Arthur Waley

The Master[1] said, To learn and at due times to repeat what one has learnt, is that not after all[2] a pleasure? That friends should come to one from afar, is this not after all delightful? To remain unsoured even though one's merits are unrecognized by others, is that not after all what is expected of a gentleman? ❶

The Master said, A young man's duty is to behave well to his parents at home and to his elders abroad, to be cautious in giving promises and punctual in keeping them, to have kindly feelings towards everyone, but seek the intimacy of the Good. ❷ If, when all that is done, he has any energy to spare, then let him study the polite arts.[3]

The Master said, (the good man) does not grieve that other people do not recognize his merits. His only anxiety is lest he should fail to recognize theirs.

The Master said, He who rules by moral force is like the pole-star,[4] which remains in its place while all the lesser stars do homage to it.

The Master said, If out of three hundred Songs[5] I had to take one phrase to cover all my teaching, I would say, "Let there be no evil in your thoughts."

The Master said, Govern the people by regulations, keep order among them by chastisements, and they will flee from you, and lose all self-respect. Govern them by moral force, keep order among them by ritual, and they will keep their self-respect and come to you of their own accord. ❸

1. **The Master:** Confucius.
2. **after all:** Even though one does not hold public office.
3. **the polite arts:** Such activities as reciting from *The Book of Songs*, practicing archery, and learning proper behavior.
4. **pole-star:** Polaris, the North Star.
5. **three hundred Songs:** Poems in *The Book of Songs*.

▲ **Critical Viewing** What clues in this picture indicate that Confucius held a respected position in his society? **[Deduce]** ❹

◆ Build Vocabulary

chastisements (chas tiz´ mintz) *n.*: Punishments

Workplace Skills Mini-Lesson

Setting and Meeting Goals

Introduce the Concept Discuss the idea that success in any area almost always hinges on setting and meeting goals. Reaching goals requires dedication and discipline, whether you are determined to improve your backhand or help people to achieve equality.

Develop Background Have students recall the advice in *The Analects* of Confucius. Suggest that they jot down a list of possible ways to apply the wisdom of Confucius to everyday achievement.

Apply the Information Using their list of ideas, students can write up a set of goals that they wish to achieve. What steps will they take to ensure success? How can they use Confucius' teachings to inspire them when the going gets tough? Encourage students to put their ideas in a chart that shows a step-by-step plan for success.

Assess the Outcome Have students share their charts. Discuss which goals are realistic, and guide students to find ways to revise unrealistic goals so that they can be met successfully.

Meng Wu Po[6] asked about the treatment of parents. The Master said, Behave in such a way that your father and mother have no anxiety about you, except concerning your health.

The Master said, A gentleman can see a question from all sides without bias. The small man is biased and can see a question only from one side.

The Master said, Yu[7] shall I teach you what knowledge is? When you know a thing, to recognize that you know it, and when you do not know a thing, to recognize that you do not know it. That is knowledge.

The Master said, High office filled by men of narrow views, ritual performed without reverence, the forms of mourning observed without grief—these are things I cannot bear to see!

The Master said, In the presence of a good man, think all the time how you may learn to equal him. In the presence of a bad man, turn your gaze within!

The Master said, In old days a man kept a hold on his words, fearing the disgrace that would ensue should he himself fail to keep pace with them.

The Master said, A gentleman covets the reputation of being slow in word but prompt in deed.

The Master said, In old days men studied for the sake of self-improvement; nowadays men study in order to impress other people.

The Master said, A gentleman is ashamed to let his words outrun his deeds.

The Master said, He who will not worry about what is far off will soon find something worse than worry close at hand.

The Master said, To demand much from oneself and little from others is the way (for a ruler) to banish discontent. 7

6. **Meng Wu Po** (muŋ wo͞o bō): The son of one of Confucius' disciples.
7. **Yu** (yo͞o): Tzu-lu, one of Confucius' disciples.

Guide for Responding

◆ Literature and Your Life

Reader's Response If you had lived in China during the time of Confucius, do you think you would have been drawn to him and his ideas? Explain.

Thematic Focus According to Confucius, what attributes make a successful leader?

Group Discussion With a group, discuss how well some leaders of today fit Confucius' model of a successful leader.

☑ Check Your Comprehension

1. How does Confucius believe people should behave toward their parents?
2. What does Confucius believe knowledge is?

◆ Critical Thinking

INTERPRET

1. What does Confucius mean when he says that a ruler should govern by "moral force"? **[Interpret]**
2. Give two examples from these passages that show that Confucius attaches great importance to humility. **[Support]**

APPLY

3. Which of Confucius' ideas do you think you could apply to your own life? Explain. **[Apply]**

EXTEND

4. Which of Confucius' ideas do you think today's politicians should practice to gain more respect from voters? **[Social Studies Link]**

Speaking, Listening, and Viewing Mini-Lesson

Oral Interpretation

This mini-lesson supports the Speaking, Listening, and Viewing activity in the Idea Bank on p. 209.

Introduce the Concept Have students choose one of the poems for an oral presentation. Remind them that oral interpretation means reading it in a way that expresses its meaning.

Develop Background Students should paraphrase each line to ensure understanding of the text. Then they can discuss with partners how their readings can convey the poets' meanings.

Have students create a "script," adding notes to remind themselves how to read each line.

Apply the Information Students should practice their poems before presenting them.

Assess the Outcome Have students discuss what they discovered about the poems as they prepared their own presentations and listened to those of their classmates. What made presentations especially effective? Students might use the Peer Assessment page for Oral Interpretation (p. 120) in ***Alternative Assessment.***

5 Clarification Be sure students understand that Confucius, the Master, is teaching a group of students. Have them identify Meng Wu Po as being one of the students participating in the discussion.

◆ Reading Strategy

6 Relate to What You Know How do students apply this aphorism in their own lives? *Encourage them to suggest compromise measures that will allow them some freedom and reassure parents at the same time.*

◆ Build Grammar Skills

7 Infinitive and Infinitive Phrases Have students identify the infinitives in the paragraph and name their function in the sentence. *The infinitives are* to demand *(subject) and* to banish *(adjective).*

Reinforce and Extend

Answers

◆ Literature and Your Life

Reader's Response Some students may say they would have been drawn to Confucius and his ideas because he showed basic wisdom and serenity.

Thematic Focus A successful leader is one who governs by modeling moral standards.

☑ Check Your Comprehension

1. Young people should behave well toward their parents.
2. Knowledge is recognizing that you know a thing and recognizing that you do not know a thing.

◆ Critical Thinking

1. Governing by moral force means governing by strong moral principles, not through force.
2. Examples could be Confucius' definition of knowledge and his idea that a person should not grieve if his merits are not recognized.
3. Possible response: I could treat everyone with respect while choosing my friends with care.
4. Students will probably cite Confucius' idea about governing with moral force.

Develop Understanding

▶Critical Viewing◀

1 Speculate *Students may suggest that they hope to find inspiration or a sense of personal balance. Or, they hope to gain a sense of humility.*

◆ Reading Strategy

2 Relate to What You Know Have students write in their journals about a time when a person might feel so sad that "all joys [seemed] grave." What keeps a person going in such circumstances? *Students can write about insights and methods for continuing to move forward.*

◆ Literature and Your Life

3 Have students discuss what advice Bei Dao would give to someone striving for success. *Students can share their ideas; based on the content of the poem, Bei Dao's advice is likely to be cautionary.*

Read to Be Informed

Have students work in groups and brainstorm to discover what goals Bei Dao and Shu Ting have in these poems.

Art Transparency Introduce these paired poems by displaying Art Transparency 17. Use Delta by Paul Giovanopoulos as a springboard to discuss how there may be multiple ways of looking at an object, a person, a problem, and so on. Leave the transparency on the overhead as students read and discuss the point and counterpoint of "All" and "Also All." To extend the discussion, you might organize an informal panel discussion in which participants offer counterpoints to other poems.

Old Trees by Cold Waterfall, 1470–1559, Wen Zhengming, The Los Angeles County Museum of Art

1 ▲ **Critical Viewing** What might these people be hoping to find in this natural setting? **[Speculate]**

All

Bei Dao

Translated by Donald Finkel and Xueliang Chen

All is fated,
all cloudy,

all an endless beginning,
all a search for what vanishes,

all joys grave,
all griefs tearless, 2

every speech a repetition,
every meeting a first encounter,

all love buried in the heart,
all history prisoned in a dream,

all hope hedged with doubt,
all faith drowned in lamentation. 3

Every explosion heralds an instant of stillness,
every death reverberates forever.

◆ Build Vocabulary

lamentation (la mən tā′ shən) *n.*: Act of crying out in grief; wailing

Humanities: Art

Old Trees by Cold Waterfall by Wen Zhengming.

Chinese landscape painting follows an orderly set of rules in keeping with the teachings of Confucius. Mountains, streams, rocks, and trees are delicately executed with only minimal brush strokes to convey mood, atmosphere, and distance; human figures are kept small to reinforce the grandeur of nature.

Wen Zhengming (1470–1559) was a Ming dynasty painter who was revered as the ideal scholar-artist. After a career as a government official and a historian, he decided to abandon his city position. He retired to the country, and for the last thirty years of his life devoted himself to painting, poetry, and calligraphy.

Have students look at the painting and discuss the following questions:

1. Suppose Confucius is the teacher depicted in this painting. What might he be telling his pupil? *Encourage students to use details of the painting,* The Analects, *and their imaginations to create aphorisms.*
2. Why would the Master in the painting choose to conduct his "lesson" outdoors? *Students may say the Master teaches outdoors to use objects in nature and natural phenomena to support his ideas.*

Also All

In answer to Bei Dao's "All"

Shu Ting

Translated by Donald Finkel and Jinsheng Yi

Not all trees are felled by storms.
Not every seed finds barren soil.
❹ Not all the wings of dream are broken,
nor is all affection doomed
to wither in a desolate heart.

No, not all is as you say.

Not all flames consume themselves,
shedding no light on other lives.
Not all stars announce the night
and never dawn. Not every song
will drift past every ear and heart.

No, not all is as you say.

Not every cry for help is silenced,
nor every loss beyond recall.
Not every chasm spells disaster.
Not only the weak will be brought
to their knees,
nor every soul be trodden under.

It won't all end in tears and blood.
Today is heavy with tomorrow—
the future was planted yesterday.
❺ Hope is a burden all of us shoulder
though we might stumble under the load.

Guide for Responding

◆ Literature and Your Life

Reader's Response If you could ask either of these poets a question, what would you ask? Why?

Thematic Focus Judging from these poems, do you think either of these poets believes in striving to overcome obstacles? Explain.

☑ Check Your Comprehension

1. Summarize what the poet says in "All."
2. Summarize the speaker's view of life in "Also All."

◆ Critical Thinking

INTERPRET

1. What effect does the repetition have on the feeling that "All" calls up? **[Analyze]**
2. Explain how the last two lines of "All" suggest the possibility of hope. **[Interpret]**
3. List three details in "Also All" that indicate Shu Ting's optimism is difficult to maintain. **[Analyze]**

APPLY

4. Bei Dao's poem "All" is a response to political events in China. What events in American news today might inspire someone to write a poem like this? Explain. **[Hypothesize]**
5. Describe a situation in which a person—either someone you know or someone in the news—showed courage and perseverance when all hope seemed lost. **[Relate]**

EXTEND

6. "Also All" was written in response to Bei Dao's poem "All." (a) What is Shu Ting's interpretation of the poem she is answering? (b) Explain how lines 19 and 20 express her disagreement with "All." **[Literature Link]**

◆ Build Grammar Skills

❹ Infinitives and Infinitive Phrases Have students identify the infinitive phrase in the stanza and its part of speech and function in the sentence. *The infinitive phrase is* to wither in a desolate heart. *It serves as a noun, the complement of the participle* doomed.

◆ Critical Thinking

❺ Compare and Contrast Have students contrast what Shu Ting says to what Bei Dao says. *Bei Dao says that life is hopeless; Shu Ting disagrees. She says, "Hope is a burden all of us shoulder."*

Reinforce and Extend

Answers

◆ Literature and Your Life

Reader's Response Students might say they would ask Bei Dao why he is so pessimistic, because they don't agree with his world view.

Thematic Focus Students may say that Shu Ting probably believes in striving to overcome obstacles because she has a positive attitude.

☑ Check Your Comprehension

1. Sorrow overwhelms joy.
2. There is reason to have hope for the future.

◆ Critical Thinking

1. The repetition seems to emphasize the feeling of doom in this poem.
2. The last two lines seem to suggest it is everyone's responsibility to keep up hope.
3. She calls today "heavy"; she calls hope "a burden"; she indicates that sometimes we will stumble (or fail to keep up hope).
4. Possible examples are news of epidemics or wars.
5. Appropriate examples will show how the person's optimism and determination helped him or her to overcome the obstacles.
6. (a) Shu Ting interprets the poem she is answering as one that expresses complete desolation; (b) The two lines indicate that the lessons we learn accumulate through the years.

Beyond the Selection

FURTHER READING

"Vultures," David Diop
"The Renegade," David Diop
Old Snow, Bei Dao

Related Works

"Never Tell Me Again," Francis Bebey
"To David Diop," Paulin Joachim
Cry Freedom (film about Stephen Biko)

We suggest that you preview these works before recommending them to students.

INTERNET

For more information about Diop go to **http://www.uflib.ufl.edu/hss/africana/diop.html**

For information on Stephen Biko, go to **http://www.usnews.com/usnews/issue/10wrbr.htm**

To read an interview with Bei Dao, go to **http://philo.ucdavis.edu/~txie/faculty/faculty.htm**

Please be aware that sites may have changed from the time we published this information. We *strongly recommend* that you preview these sites before you send students to them.

Answers

◆ Reading Strategy

1. Students' comparisons might highlight the wise tone of the advice from both sources.
2. Possible response: I "turned my gaze within" by examining my own character when I met someone I didn't respect.
3. Students might say that mood plays a major role in people's attitudes, thus one day they may feel as the poet does in "All," and another day adapt the attitude expressed in "Also All."

◆ Literary Focus

1. Because aphorisms express a lot in a few words, they are more memorable than longer explanations.
2. The basic truth that it is important to be humble is expressed in both Confucius' sayings and in the poem "Old Song."
3. Example aphorism: Past mistakes can be turned to future triumphs.

◆ Build Vocabulary

Using the Suffix *-ment*

1. statement; 2. replacement; 3. commandment; 4. assignment

Using the Word Bank

1. b 2. c 3. a

◆ Build Grammar Skills

Practice

1. To learn and at due times to repeat what one has learnt, is that not after all a pleasure?
2. To remain unsoured even though one's merits are unrecognized by others, is that not after all what is expected of a gentleman?
3. The Master said, A young man's duty is to behave well to his parents and to his elders abroad, to be cautious in giving promises and punctual in keeping them, to have kindly feelings towards everyone, but [to] seek the intimacy of the Good.

Grammar Reinforcement

For additional instruction and practice, use the page on Infinitives and Infinitive Phrases (p. 46) in the *Writer's Solution Grammar Practice Book.*

Guide for Responding (continued)

◆ Reading Strategy

RELATE TO WHAT YOU KNOW

Relating what these writers say to your own experience will help you to find meaning in their work.

1. Compare the advice in "Old Song" with some advice you have received from an older relative or friend.
2. Describe an experience in your life in which one of Confucius' principles was illustrated.
3. Explain how one person might be able to experience the feelings expressed in both "All" and "Also All."

◆ Literary Focus

APHORISMS

The authors of these pieces use **aphorisms**—brief sayings that illustrate a basic truth.

1. How do aphorisms illustrate the expression "Less is more"?
2. Identify one basic truth expressed in both the sayings of Confucius and "Old Song."
3. Write your own aphorism that expresses a basic truth found in "Also All."

Beyond Literature

Cultural Connection

The Colonization of Africa Europeans began colonizing Africa in the late 1700's. By 1914, only Ethiopia and Liberia remained independent from European control. As World War II ended, independence movements gained strength in Africa. Today, Africa is a continent of more than fifty independent nations. The legacy of colonialism, however, lives on. New national boundaries, established in the 1950's and 1960's, were artificial creations of colonial powers. They bound in many rival ethnic groups. In addition, many new nations are small. These nations have difficulty meeting the economic needs of their people. Find out more about the effects of colonialism in Africa and in other parts of the world. Create a chart to display in your classroom.

◆ Build Vocabulary

USING THE LATIN SUFFIX *-ment*

The suffix *-ment* indicates the noun form of the word to which it is attached. Use the suffix *-ment* to create a noun for each of the following examples:

1. To state your opinion is to make a ___?___.
2. You replace something with a ___?___.
3. A ruler commands with a ___?___.
4. A teacher assigns an ___?___.

USING THE WORD BANK: Antonyms

In your notebook, write the antonym for each word from the Word Bank:

1. impetuous: (a) lively, (b) careful, (c) wise
2. lamentation: (a) despair, (b) interest, (c) rejoicing
3. chastisements: (a) rewards, (b) orders, (c) duties

◆ Build Grammar Skills

INFINITIVES AND INFINITIVE PHRASES

Writers of aphorisms, like Confucius, often use infinitives to express universal ideas. The infinitive form gives the action being described a timeless flavor.

Infinitives, which are the base forms of verbs and usually begin with the word *to*, can be used as nouns, adjectives, or adverbs. **Infinitive phrases** include an infinitive with its modifiers and complements (words that complete the meaning of the verb), all acting as a single part of speech.

Practice Copy each sentence in your notebook. Underline the infinitives or the infinitive phrases.

1. To learn and at due times to repeat what one has learnt, is that not after all a pleasure?
2. To remain unsoured even though one's merits are unrecognized by others, is that not after all what is expected of a gentleman?
3. The Master said, A young man's duty is to behave well to his parents at home and to his elders abroad, to be cautious in giving promises and punctual in keeping them, to have kindly feelings towards everyone, but seek the intimacy of the Good.

Reteach

Help students relate what they know to the poems "All" and "Also All" with a two-column chart.

Resignation	Hope

Have students choose a line from "All," such as "all cloudy," and say what it means in their own words. Make notes of what they say in the first column. Then have students choose a line from "Also All" that offers hope, such as "Not all the wings of dream are broken." In the second column write this line in students' own words. Continue to fill in the chart with ideas of resignation and hope, encouraging students to use their own words. Invite students to suggest what they think conventional wisdom says about these two emotions.

Build Your Portfolio

Idea Bank

Writing

1. **Letter to an Author** Write a letter to an author from this group. In your letter, explain why you agree or disagree with his or her ideas.
2. **Life Poem** Each writer expresses his or her view of life. Write a poem in which you express your view of life. Use images and examples from your own experience to express your ideas.
3. **Comparing and Contrasting Poems** Shu Ting wrote "Also All" as a rebuttal to Bei Dao's "All." Write a short essay in which you evaluate which poem makes a better case.

Speaking, Listening, and Viewing

4. **Oral Interpretation** Practice reading one of these works aloud. Vary the tone and speed of your voice for emphasis. Perform your reading for the class. **[Performing Arts Link]**
5. **Interview** With a partner, role-play an interview with one of the writers in this group. Develop questions about the author's views and experiences. Base your answers on what you've learned from their works and biographies.

Researching and Representing

6. **Tiananmen Square Presentation** "All" and "Also All" are responses to political events in China during the 1980's. In April 1989, students took over Tiananmen Square. Find out more about this event and give a presentation on it for your class. **[Social Studies Link]**
7. **Collage** Assemble a number of images with words from one of these works at the center. Find images in newspapers, magazines, and personal photos that reflect the ideas expressed. Display your collage in the classroom. **[Art Link]**

Online Activity www.phlit.phschool.com

Guided Writing Lesson

Aphorism Calendar

Aphorisms are meant to be useful in daily life. What better way to make them a part of your daily life than by putting them in a calendar? Create your own aphorism calendar by making up one brief saying for each month of the year. The following tips will help you state your ideas concisely.

Writing Skills Focus: Brevity and Clarity

Like written directions and essays on tests, aphorisms are best when they are **brief and clear**. In the following example, Confucius clearly states a basic principle of conduct in just two sentences:

> The Master said, A gentleman can see a question from all sides without bias. The small man is biased and can see a question only from one side.

This aphorism can be easily remembered and understood. As you plan, draft, and revise your calendar, use the fewest words possible to convey your ideas clearly.

Prewriting Brainstorm for single words that name qualities you admire in a person. Then briefly describe examples of each quality in action.

Drafting Refer to your prewriting notes as an inspiration for your twelve aphorisms. For example, you might write, "Courage is ___?___" and then use your description of someone's courageous action to help fill in the blank. Convey as much information as you can in few words.

Revising Revise each aphorism and eliminate any words that do not add to the meaning. However, ask a classmate to read your abbreviated sayings, and determine whether or not they are clear.

ASSESSMENT OPTIONS

Formal Assessment, Selection Test, pp. 47–49, and Assessment Resources Software. The selection test is designed so that it can be easily customized to the performance levels of your students.

Alternative Assessment, p. 15, includes options for less advanced students, Pre-AP Students, logical/mathematical learners, visual/spatial learners, musical/rhythmic learners, interpersonal learners, intrapersonal learners, and verbal/linguistic learners.

PORTFOLIO ASSESSMENT
Use the following rubrics in the ***Alternative Assessment*** booklet to assess student writing:
Letter to an Author: Expression Rubric, p. 94
Life Poem: Poetry Rubric, p. 108
Comparing and Contrasting Poems: Comparison and Contrast Rubric, p. 103

Idea Bank

Following are suggestions for matching Idea Bank topics with your students' performance levels and learning modalities:

Customizing for Performance Levels
Less Advanced Students: 1, 4
Average Students: 2, 5, 7
Pre-AP Students: 3, 6

Customizing for Learning Modalities
Visual/Spatial: 7
Bodily/Kinesthetic: 4
Verbal/Linguistic: 4, 5
Logical/Mathematical: 3

Guided Writing Lesson

Revision Strategy Like poetry, aphorisms are best when the writer makes the most of each word. To help students become more economical with their language, have them reenter their writing and circle any term that is an abstraction; in other words, any term that does not say something concrete. Students should then ask themselves two questions about each circled word:

- Is this word necessary?
- Is there a more concrete or less vague way of saying the same thing?

Students will then be ready to revise their work with the goals of clarity and brevity in mind.

For more prewriting, elaboration, and revision strategies, see *Prentice Hall Writing and Grammar.*

Writers at Work Videodisc
Have students view the videodisc segment (Ch. 6) featuring Naomi Shihab Nye to get them thinking about how aphorisms, like other forms of creative writing, can inspire people.

Play frames 11043 to 20512

Writing Lab CD-ROM
Have students complete the tutorial on Creative Writing. Follow these steps:

1. Have them consult a word bin to help them select vivid words expressing emotions.
2. Encourage them to view video tips for peer editors and then work with a peer to revise their aphorisms for clarity.

Prepare and Engage

LESSON OBJECTIVES

- To use recursive writing processes to write an essay
- To use standard and informal English
- To correctly place modifiers

You may want to distribute a scoring rubric for a timed-test essay (see page 212) to make students aware before they begin of the criteria on which they will be evaluated.

Refer students to the Writing Handbook, p. 965, for guidance in the writing process.

Grammar Reinforcement

You might give students the following pages from the *Writer's Solution Grammar Practice Book:*
p. 148: Preparing Answers to Essay Exams
p. 167: Reading and Test-Taking Skills
p. 168: Test-Taking Skills

Writing Lab CD-ROM
If your students have access to computers, you may want to have them work on the tutorial on Practical and Technical Writing to complete parts of their timed-test essays. Follow these steps:

1. Have students review the interactive model of a timed-test essay.
2. Have students use an outliner to organize their essays.
3. Have students draft on computer.
4. Suggest that students consult the screen on revising a timed-test essay.

Timed-Test Essay Writing Process Workshop

Tests are one way to measure how successfully you have learned something. A timed-test essay is an essay on a test that you must complete within a certain time limit.

The following skills, introduced in this section's Guided Writing Lessons, will help you write an effective test essay when you have time limits.

Writing Skills Focus

- **Support your ideas with details.** For instance, if you say "Every citizen over 21 has a responsibility to vote," say *why* as well. (See p. 191.)
- **Show, don't tell,** the features or qualities of your topic. Offer examples, summarize events, or cite facts. (See p. 199.)
- **Be brief and clear.** Since your time is limited, say only what is essential to cover your topic. (See p. 209.)

The following excerpt, from an essay about the importance of keeping beaches public, shows these skills.

Model

Beaches—whose waters, sands, dunes, and cliffs constantly change with the tides and the weather—are among our most inspiring landscapes. As such, they should never be private property. ① We are most likely to treasure and preserve them if we know they belong to us all.

As citizens of the planet, everyone should have the right to explore any tidepool, swim in any surf, or run on any sandy shore. Private ownership of beaches denies these rights and pleasures to all but a privileged few. ② This is unfair.

In addition, private beach ownership often results in destructive development of land closest to the sea. ③ Development may cause erosion of dunes or cliffs, pollution, and disturbance or destruction of wildlife habitats.

① The writer gets to the point in the first paragraph.
② Here, the writer supports his main idea with details and elaboration.
③ This brief, clear paragraph offers another assertion and example.

Beyond the Classroom

Workplace Skills

Working with a Deadline Point out to students that working under the pressure of a deadline is nearly as common in the "real" world as it is in school. Even if they never take another test after they leave high school or college, students may be called upon to compose a piece of writing or to perform some other task under pressure—on a job application or as part of a job itself. Organizing and elucidating one's thoughts quickly and clearly is a valuable benefit they will receive from the agonizing hours writing timed-test essays.

The best way to accurately plan one's time to perform tasks is to monitor the time it takes to complete a similar task when there isn't a deadline. Suggest that students structure a timeframe for one of their homework assignments once a week. When the time limit they have set is up, they can evaluate how much of the assignment they were able to complete and how they could have used the time more efficiently. Of course, they will want to thoroughly complete their homework, but encourage them to apply what they learn from the experience and try to increase efficiency.

Prewriting

Know Your Purpose and Your Audience Usually on an essay test, the topic is assigned to you. Make sure that you know exactly what the question requires you to write, so you won't get off track. Unless the instructions say otherwise, assume that you are expected to write in a formal way to an interested and objective audience.

Plan Your Time Imagine that you have twenty minutes to complete your essay. Quickly plan out your time. Allow a few minutes to gather and organize your thoughts, a large block of time to draft your essay, and a few minutes to revise.

Plan the Points You Will Elaborate Make a list of the main ideas you will introduce in your essay. Under each main idea, note the supporting details you will offer to convince your audience that your reasoning is sensible. Arrange your points in a logical sequence. This outline will prevent you from wasting time on irrelevant details and reorganization.

For practice, choose one of the following topics:

Topic Choices

1. In an essay addressed to parents and teachers, describe both sides of a particular issue, such as a school rule that is controversial. Take a stand and defend it.
2. Write an aphorism or a statement that you think communicates a valuable message about success. In a letter to the editor, explain the message and tell how you consider it relevant to a real-life situation.

Drafting

Get Started As soon as you've organized your main ideas and details, begin drafting. Use an objective tone. Present your main idea in the introduction of your essay.

Support Your Points In the body of your essay, state and develop your ideas. Each paragraph should either directly or indirectly support your main idea. Within each paragraph, make sure that each supporting sentence either directly or indirectly supports the topic sentence of the paragraph.

Conclude Finish your essay with a conclusion, in which you restate your main idea or make a general observation about it.

Applying Language Skills: Standard and Informal English

A timed-test essay should be written in standard English. Standard English uses an objective tone and correct usage, contains no slang, avoids contractions, and often uses long sentences with varied structures.

Informal English:

The Japanese are totally crazy about baseball.

Standard English:

Baseball is extremely popular in Japan.

Practice On your paper, rewrite the following passage in standard English.

Some people are grossed out by sushi, but they're crazy! It totally rules.

Writing Application Check your essay to make sure that it is written in standard English and follows the guidelines given above.

Writer's Solution Connection Writing Lab

For more help on writing a timed-test essay, see Drafting a Timed-Test Essay in the Writing Lab tutorial on Practical/Technical Writing.

Applying Language Skills

Standard and Informal English Explain to students that they should use standard, formal English when writing a timed-test essay. They should avoid informal phrases, contractions, and above all, slang.

Suggested Answer

Although some people find sushi hard to stomach, I disagree. I find it quite delicious.

Grammar Reinforcement

For additional instruction and practice, have students complete practice p. 66, The Varieties of English, in the *Writer's Solution Grammar Practice Book.*

Develop Student Writing

Prewriting Strategy

Students do not have much time to devote to prewriting on a timed-test essay. A quick and effective way to get their thoughts flowing is wet-ink writing. Suggest that students write the essay question at the top of their paper and then take two minutes to write continuously and freely about the issue. They should not pay attention to grammar, and they should never stop writing. Next, instruct them to examine the material they've generated and circle any ideas they wish to elaborate on. The goal of this exercise is to start generating ideas, which they can organize when they begin to write their essay.

Customize for *English Language Learners*

Vocabulary will be the biggest hurdle facing these students. Since they will not have time to consult a dictionary, encourage students to use simple language with which they are familiar. They should not spend too much time on grammar and spelling, but should not ignore it altogether either.

Writing Lab CD-ROM

The Organizing Details and Information section of the tutorial on Practical and Technical Writing includes a screen on organizing a timed-test essay. Have students consult this screen to help them learn how to organize their essays quickly and efficiently.

Elaboration Strategy

Writers can strengthen their essays by explaining their own opinions and by discrediting those of their opponents. Have students think about someone frequently disagrees with them, and ask themselves how this person would respond to the essay question. Encourage them to utilize this opposing opinion in their essays, and to explain the ways in which it is not as strong as his own opinion.

Students should draft their timed-test essays in a single sitting, without pausing to labor over a single word or to correct a grammatical error. Once students have completed a draft, they may have a brief opportunity to go back into their work and make revisions.

Revision Strategy

Have students reenter their writing to make sure that they begin and end with powerful, well-stated ideas. They want to hook the reader and to leave him with a strong impression as well. Suggest that students quickly look over their introductions and conclusions, underlining any words that are abstract or vague. Have them replace these words with more concrete, lively writing.

Writing Lab CD-ROM

The proofreading checklist in the Proofreading section of the tutorial on Practical and Technical Writing will help students quickly check their essays.

Publishing

Tell students that even if they do not wish to share their essays at this time, they might want to hold on to them and use them as reference for later writing projects.

Reinforce and Extend

Applying Language Skills

Placement of Modifiers Remind students that correctly placed modifiers are vital not only for stylistic reasons but also for a clear meaning. Misplaced or dangling modifiers can damage an otherwise perfect essay.

Answer

Each year, millions of Americans between the ages of seventeen and sixty-six enter blood centers to donate blood.

Grammar Reinforcement

Writing Lab CD-ROM

For additional instruction and practice, have students complete the **Language Lab CD-ROM** lesson on Problems With Modifiers.

Applying Language Skills: Placement of Modifiers

Make sure that all of your modifiers—your adjectives, adverbs, and modifying phrases—are in the proper place in each sentence.

Misplaced Modifier:

A red cross on a white field became the symbol of the Red Cross, which was a reversal of the Swiss flag.

Correctly Placed Modifier:

A red cross on a white field, which borrowed the image but reversed the colors of the Swiss flag, became the symbol of the Red Cross.

Practice On your paper, rewrite the following sentence so that the modifying phrase is in the proper place.

Each year, millions of Americans enter blood centers between the ages of 17 and 66 to donate blood.

Writing Application Review your essay, and make sure that all of your modifiers are correctly placed.

Writer's Solution Connection
Language Lab

For more practice with placement of modifiers, complete the Language Lab lesson on Misplaced Modifiers.

Revising

Check Quickly Because time is limited during this type of essay, you'll have only a few moments in which to review and polish your writing. Look through the tips that follow, and use them as a guide to revise your essay.

- ▶ Reread the essay question to make sure you've addressed it.
- ▶ Skim the introduction and conclusion to make sure you haven't drifted from your original topic.
- ▶ Make sure your ideas are logical and well organized. Review the points you've made. Add supporting details where needed. Delete irrelevant information.
- ▶ Make sure that you use standard English in your essay. Take out any slang terms and any unnecessary contractions. Check your spelling and grammar.

Revision Model

The computer industry is extremely important to the economy of California, our ① most populous ~~biggest~~ state. ② ~~I love playing Myst on my computer, but I've never been able to figure out how to get past the final stage.~~ ③ The companies of "Silicon Valley" alone employ more than 20,000 people.

① The student made this sentence more accurate.
② The student deleted this irrelevant sentence.
③ The student added this example to back up her assertion in the first sentence.

Publishing

Share Your Paper Because the information in timed-test essays is organized and compact, the essays are good records of what you've learned about effective writing. Here are some ideas for sharing your work.

- ▶ Start a portfolio of essays.
- ▶ Use the essay as the basis for a research paper.
- ▶ Ask your teacher for feedback and ways to improve your writing on future tests.

✓ ASSESSMENT		4	3	2	1
PORTFOLIO ASSESSMENT Use the general rubric in the ***Alternative Assessment*** booklet (p. 93) to assess the students' writing. Add these criteria to customize the rubric to this assignment.	**Organization**	The writing is clearly and consistently organized. All assertions are backed up by facts or examples.	The writing is clearly organized. Most assertions are backed up by facts or examples.	The writing has some organization, but needs improvement. Assertions need more evidence to back them up.	The writing is completely unorganized. Assertions have no support.
	Grammar, Usage, Spelling, and Mechanics	There are few or no errors. Word choice is appropriate for subject and audience.	There are minor errors. Word choice is usually appropriate for subject and audience. There are some precise details.	There are numerous errors. Word choice may be inappropriate for subject and audience. Verbs are vague.	Numerous errors hinder comprehension. Word choice shows little understanding of subject or audience.

Student Success Workshop

Vocabulary Development

Using Reference Materials for Vocabulary Development

Strategies for Success

When you're faced with an unfamiliar word, you can be resourceful. A dictionary is always a good place to begin researching definitions, but don't stop there. The Internet, the glossary of a book, and a thesaurus are all good resources to use to find the meaning of a word you don't know. Here are some strategies you can use to make the most of these valuable resources:

Use a Dictionary A dictionary will give you a word's exact meaning. It also provides information about the word's origins. Consider the word *nonplus*. The dictionary will tell you that the word is a noun, that it comes from Latin, and that it means "confusion" or "bewilderment."

Consult a Glossary Sometimes words related to the subject of a book are defined in a glossary at the back of the book. For example, if you saw the word *behest* while reading a medieval story, you might find it listed in the glossary. The glossary might explain that *behest* is a noun that means "promise."

Try a Thesaurus If you look up a word in a thesaurus, you'll find synonyms (words with similar meanings) and antonyms (words whose meaning is the opposite). Some thesauruses also include examples of how to use the word. Here's a sample thesaurus entry for the word *capricious:* adj., fickle, undecided, irresponsible, erratic: *a capricious man.* Ant. (opposite meanings) certain, serious.

Go Online The Internet provides a diversity of information. On the 'Net, you'll find word definitions and even whole articles about a term. For example, if you saw a news headline with the term *corporate welfare* in it, you could look up this term on the Internet, find out its meaning, and even read detailed articles about it.

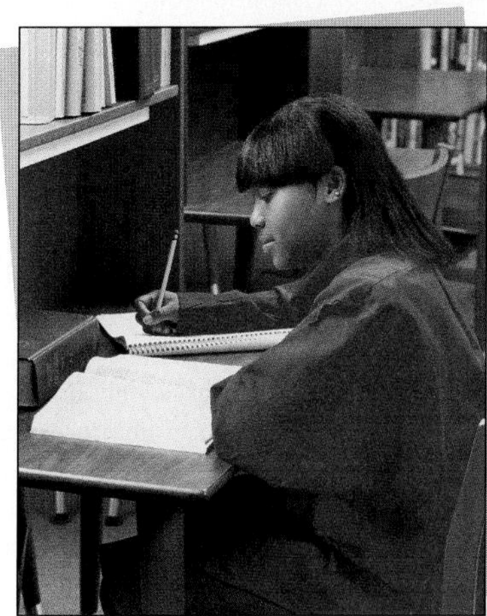

Apply the Strategies

Using the reference materials suggested, look up the following words and terms. Write down the meaning of each word or term, and use each in a sentence.

1. pithy (use a thesaurus)
2. invidious (use a dictionary)
3. Northern Lights (use the Internet)
4. ineffable (use a thesaurus)
5. jet lag (use the Internet)

Reference materials can help you define and use new words in these situations:

- Learning a new computer program
- Reading or writing a poem
- Researching a topic

Test Preparation Workshop

Vocabulary: Using Reference Materials for Vocabulary Development

Vocabulary development will help students on standardized tests. Using reference materials, such as a thesaurus, students will become familiar with synonyms, which will help them to determine meanings of some tested words, such as the following.

The view from the top of the mountain was indescribable.

Which of the following is closest in meaning to indescribable?

A objectionable **C** heartfelt
B confused **D** inexpressible

Suggest that, for this type of vocabulary question, students check all of the answer choices, substituting each word for indescribable in the sentence. They should conclude that D is the best answer. Students may also be able to draw on their knowledge of synonyms—gained from using a thesaurus in their reading and writing—to decide on the correct answer because *inexpressible* is a synonym for *indescribable*.

Prepare and Engage

LESSON OBJECTIVES

- To use reference material such as a glossary dictionary, thesaurus, and available technology to determine precise meanings and usage
- To use text organizers to locate and categorize information
- To evaluate information sources and their appropriateness for varied needs

Customize for
Visual/Spatial Learners

To help these students recognize which reference material they might use, and why, have them create a visual organizer. Encourage students to chart the different reference materials, what information they include, and in what situations they might be used. Invite students to compare the visual organizers they create.

Apply the Strategies

Answers

Possible answers might include:

1. Pithy: concise yet essential. The lawyer's pithy account of the three-year struggle was received well by the jury.
2. Invidious: causing or intending ill will or a slight. Comparisons between software products are often seen as invidious by their makers.
3. Northern Lights: flashing, brilliant lights seen in extreme northern regions. Seeing the Northern Lights was one of the highlights of our trip to Alaska.
4. Ineffable: indescribable or unspeakable. The quiet and beauty of the filled me with an ineffable sense of peace.
5. Jet lag: the physical and psychological disturbances caused by air travel across time zones. After his return to Illinois from Australia, Ted suffered from jet lag for three days.

Prepare and Engage

LESSON OBJECTIVES

- To listen attentively
- To use the conventions of oral language effectively
- To respond to questions clearly and effectively
- To ask clear questions to gain information and clarify understanding

Remind students that interviewing for a job is one thing that all of them will almost certainly have to do at least one time in their lives, and probably many times. Since a job interview can often determine the course of a person's career, its importance should not be underestimated.

Apply the Strategies

In addition to the strategies listed, tell students that they should learn the interviewer's full name and title before they leave and write a brief thank-you note to the interviewer as soon as they get home.

Answers

1. Important traits to display at such an interview would be technical expertise and the ability to work with others.
2. Important traits to show at such an interview would be cheerfulness and organizational ability.
3. Important traits to show at such an interview would be cheerfulness, enthusiasm, and responsibility.

Speaking, Listening, and Viewing Workshop — Job Interview

If you haven't done so already, you may soon apply for your first job and go on your first job interview. Whether you're looking for an after-school job, a summer job, or your first full-time job, the impression you make during your job interview will determine whether you are offered the position.

Make a Good Impression First impressions are important. Create a good one by arriving on time and being dressed appropriately. During the interview, be aware of the nonverbal messages you send through body language, eye contact, and gestures. Maintain eye contact with your interviewer; don't look around the room as if you're uninterested or avoiding answering questions. Positive body language, such as a firm handshake and good posture, will suggest that you are self-assured, confident, and capable. Speak clearly and loudly enough, and avoid using slang or clichés.

Strategies for a Successful Job Interview

If you want to make a good impression during your interview, remember these strategies:

- Arrive on time and dressed neatly
- Speak clearly, confidently, and positively about yourself and what you will bring to your new position
- Take your time answering questions, to make sure you answer completely
- Ask questions about the position to show your interest in the company

Throughout, listen attentively to your interviewer. Answer the questions asked, and listen for cues about what is important. You might use these cues to ask follow-up questions.

Apply the Strategies

With a partner, role-play these situations. Using the tips above, make a good impression at the following job interviews:

1. An interview at a local television show to help with teleprompting, set construction, and setting up camera equipment.
2. An interview at a doctor's office for administrative work.
3. An interview for a position as a baby sitter.

Test Preparation Workshop

Reading Comprehension

Recognize Facts, Details, and Sequence

Strategies for Success

The reading sections of standardized tests often require you to understand the facts and details that support the main idea in a variety of written texts. The test may also require you to arrange the events in a passage in sequence. Use the following strategies:

Recognize Facts and Details Before you can recognize supporting facts and details, you must identify the main idea. Then, if the passage is nonfiction, look for facts that elaborate on the main idea. If the passage is fictional, identify details that relate to what the passage is about. Look at this sample passage and the questions:

In 1921, Atlanta, Texas, native Bessie Coleman became the first American woman to receive an international pilot's license from the Federation Aeronautique Internationale in France. As an African American woman, Bessie Coleman had to overcome numerous obstacles to attain her goal.

Coleman attended college in Oklahoma after completing high school, but could afford only one term. She moved to Chicago and earned a certificate as a manicurist. Her applications to flight schools in the United States were turned down; racial and gender barriers were formidable at the time. With the financial help of a benefactor, she was accepted to flight school in France. After receiving her license, she presented flying exhibitions in the United States. Coleman's pioneering role in aviation has been honored and cited in innumerable ways.

1 Why did Coleman go to flight school in France?

A She could not afford schools in the United States.

B She wanted a license from France.

C Her applications to flight schools in the United States had been turned down.

D She had only one term of college.

Answers **A** and **B** are not facts that are stated in the passage, so they can be eliminated. **D** does not relate to the main idea. **C** is the correct answer because it is a fact that elaborates on the main idea of the passage.

Arrange Events in Sequential Order Determining the sequence of events in a passage is another way to identify supporting ideas. Words that signal time—*first, next, after,* and *finally*—can help you recognize the sequence, but they can be misleading. To answer a question like the following, review the passage and create a mental chart of the sequence of events.

2 Which of these did Coleman do first?

A She earned a certificate as a manicurist.

B She attended college in Oklahoma.

C She presented flying exhibitions.

D She received a pilot's license.

The items follow this sequence: **B, A, D, C.** Answer **B** is correct.

Apply the Strategies

Answer the following questions about the sample passage.

1 Which of the following was not an obstacle to Bessie Coleman's becoming a pilot?

A She was African American.

B She was a woman.

C She needed a college degree.

D She didn't have the money.

2 When did Coleman apply to flight school?

A After she graduated from college.

B After she graduated from high school.

C After she earned a certificate as a manicurist.

D After she presented flying exhibitions.

Correlations to Standardized Tests

The reading comprehension skills reviewed in this workshop correspond to the following standardized test section:

ACT Reading

Test Preparation

Each ATE workshop in Unit 2 supports the instruction here by providing teaching suggestions and a sample test item:

- **Facts and Details** (ATE, pp. 117, 183)
- **Details** (ATE, pp. 155, 165, 201)
- **Facts, Details, and Sequence** (ATE, p. 129)
- **Sequence** (ATE, pp. 147, 193)

LESSON OBJECTIVES

- To analyze text structures such as compare and contrast, cause and effect, and chronological ordering for how they influence the understanding
- To produce summaries of texts by identifying main ideas and their supporting details

Answers

1. (C) She needed a college degree.
2. (C) After she earned a certificate as a manicurist.

Test-Taking Tip

Note Special Wording Explain to students that many standardized tests use special wording in test items. When the word *not* appears in a test item, it signals that the correct answer will most likely be one that does not agree with what the passage has been about. By paying attention to when the word *not* appears in a question, students will know to look for an answer that does not correspond to what they have read in the passage. For example, the first question about the reading passage that students are expected to answer on this page asks students to identify which answer was not an obstacle to Bessie Coleman's becoming a pilot. Since the passage clearly states that being both African American and a woman were obstacles for Coleman, students can eliminate *A* and *B*. The passage explains that Coleman found financial help, but it does not indicate that she needed a college degree, which means that *C* is the correct answer.

Planning Instruction and Assessment

Unit Objectives

1. To read selections in different genres that develop the theme of Clashing Forces
2. To apply a variety of reading strategies, particularly literal comprehension strategies, appropriate for reading these selections
3. To analyze literary elements
4. To use a variety of strategies to read unfamiliar words and to build vocabulary
5. To learn elements of grammar, usage, and style
6. To use recursive writing processes to write in a variety of forms
7. To express and support responses to various types of texts
8. To prepare, organize, and present literary interpretations

Meeting the Objectives

With each selection, you will find instructional material and portfolio opportunities through which students can meet these objectives. Further, you will find additional practice pages for reading strategies, literary elements, vocabulary, and grammar in the ***Selection Support*** booklet in the ***Teaching Resources*** box.

The Deluge, 1920, Winifred Knights, Tate Gallery, London, Great Britain

Humanities: Art

The Deluge by Winifred Knights.

Ask students to define *deluge*, and then encourage them to identify details in this art that depict a flood *(the half-submerged houses; the men waist-deep in water; the girl being pulled out of the water)*. Help students see that the people's stylized postures give the art an abstract, formal quality. It is as if the artist is depicting a ballet about a flood, rather than real people fleeing real floodwaters.

1. Does the abstract quality of the painting add to or detract from the sense of the people's struggle? Why? *Sample answers: The abstract quality adds to the sense of the people's struggle because it focuses on the bodies straining to escape; the abstract quality detracts from the struggle because it creates grace and order, like a dance.*
2. Invent some circumstances for one of the people portrayed—who he or she is, who or what is being left behind, what hopes and fears the person experiences. *Sample answer: The man pulling the little girl up is her father, working with her mother to save their child; he had thought she was with them, but she fell behind and almost got swept away in the water.*

Clashing Forces

There are many clashing forces in life—good versus evil, right versus wrong, man versus nature. The stories, poems, and essays you're about to read share one common theme: They all deal with the clashing forces that we encounter in life. Turn the page to see how real people and fictional characters respond to—and often overcome—obstacles and injustices.

Assessing Student Progress

The following tools are available to measure the degree to which students meet the unit objectives:

Informal Assessment

The questions on the Guide for Responding sections are a first level of response to the concepts and skills presented with the selection. Students' responses are a brief informal measure of their grasp of the material. Their responses on this level can indicate where further instruction and practice are needed. You may then follow up with the practice pages in the ***Selection Support*** booklet.

You will find literature and reading guides in the ***Alternative Assessment*** booklet, which you may give students on an individual basis for informal assessment of their performance.

Formal Assessment

In the ***Formal Assessment*** booklet, you will find selection tests and a unit test.

Selection Tests The selection tests measure comprehension and skills acquisition for each selection or group of selections.

Unit Test The unit test, which calls on students to read a passage of literature they have not previously seen, applies the unit skills on a broader level. The Critical Reading section measures Unit Objectives 1, 2, and 3. The Vocabulary and Grammar section measures Objectives 4 and 5. The Essay section measures Objectives 1 and 6. Both the Critical Reading and Vocabulary and Grammar sections use formats similar to those found on many standardized tests, including the SAT measures Objectives 4 and 5. The Essay section measures Objectives 1 and 6.

Alternative Assessment

Portfolios As you review individual pieces or the collected work in students' portfolios, you will find assessment sheets available in the portfolio section of the ***Alternative Assessment*** booklet.

Scoring Rubrics You will find scoring rubrics for writing modes in the ***Alternative Assessment*** booklet. You can apply these to Guided Writing Lessons and to Writing Process Workshop lessons.

Speaking and Listening The ***Alternative Assessment*** booklet contains assessment sheets for speaking and listening activities.

Learning Modalities The ***Alternative Assessment*** booklet contains activities that appeal to different learning styles. You may use these as an alternative measurement of students' growth.

Prepare and Engage

LESSON OBJECTIVES

1. **To develop vocabulary and word identification skills**
   - Latin Word Roots: *-lum-*
   - Using the Word Bank: Synonyms
   - Extending Word Study: Wide Reading (ATE)
2. **To use a variety of reading strategies to comprehend a short story**
   - Connect Your Experience
   - Reading for Success: Interactive Reading Strategies
   - Tips to Guide Reading: Establish a Purpose for Reading (ATE)
   - Read to Be Entertained (ATE)
3. **To increase knowledge of other cultures and to connect common elements across cultures**
   - Connecting Themes Across Cultures (ATE)
4. **To express and support responses to the text**
   - Critical Thinking
   - Idea Bank: Observation
5. **To analyze literary elements (can vary)**
   - Literary Focus: Internal Conflict
   - Idea Bank: Letter
6. **To read in order to research self-selected and assigned topic**
   - Idea Bank: Water Safety Rules
   - Questions for Research
7. **To plan, prepare, organize, and present literary interpretations**
   - Idea Bank: Dialogue
   - Idea Bank: Movie Score
   - Idea Bank: Account of an Outdoor Adventure
   - Viewing and Representing Mini-Lesson: Collage
8. **To use recursive writing processes to write a travel brochure**
   - Guided Writing Lesson
9. **To increase knowledge of the rules of grammar and usage**
   - Build Grammar Skills: Participial Phrases

Test Preparation

Reading Comprehension: Stated and Implied Main Ideas (ATE, p. 219) The teaching tips and sample test item in this workshop support the instruction and practice in the unit workshop:
Reading Comprehension: Stated and Implied Main Ideas (SE, p. 299)

Guide for Reading

Doris Lessing *(1919–)*

Some writers shy away from controversy; Doris Lessing, however, seems to invite it. When her novel *The Golden Notebook* appeared in 1962, she was accused of being a "man-hater" because of the resentment and anger toward men that some of her female characters expressed. Lessing has also written about the conflicts between cultures, focusing especially on the conflicts between Europeans and Africans.

Growing up in Africa Doris May Taylor was born on October 22, 1919, in Persia (now Iran). In 1925, enticed by the prospect of getting rich by farming maize, her father moved the family to the colony of Rhodesia (now Zimbabwe) in southern Africa. There, Lessing began to observe how, under colonialism, Europeans displaced Africans from their land and ignored their traditions.

From Outcast to Hero In 1949, Lessing published her first novel, *The Grass Is Singing*. In this and her later novels, Lessing highlights the injustices suffered by black Africans at the hands of white colonials. Her strong views provoked a strong reaction.

In 1956, Lessing was declared a "prohibited alien" by the governments of Southern Rhodesia and South Africa.

Ironically, when apartheid ended in South Africa in 1995, she was welcomed back as a hero—for writing about the very topics for which she was banished earlier.

A Different Kind of Conflict In this story, Lessing doesn't write about the conflicts between men and women or between cultures. Instead, she describes the struggle going on in the mind of a boy.

◆ Build Vocabulary

Latin Word Roots: *-lum-*

In this story, you will encounter the word *luminous*. The word root *-lum-* comes from the Latin *lumen*, meaning "light." Knowing this root can help you figure out that words that contain the root *-lum-* are related to light. *Luminous* means "giving off light."

Word Bank

As you read this story, you will encounter the words on this list. Each word is defined on the page where it first appears. Preview the list before you read.

contrition
promontories
luminous
supplication
frond
convulsive
gout

◆ Build Grammar Skills

Participial Phrases

"Going to the shore on the first morning of the vacation, the young English boy stopped at a turning of the path . . ." So begins "Through the Tunnel"—with a participial phrase. A **participial phrase** consists of a participle (a verb form ending in *-ing*, *-ed*, or an irregular ending) plus any other words that go with it. Participial phrases function as adjectives.

The participial phrase "Going to the shore on the first morning of the vacation," beginning with the present participle *going*, acts as an adjective modifying "boy." Lessing varies her sentence structure and creates vivid pictures of the characters and setting in this story by using participial phrases.

Prentice Hall Literature Program Resources

REINFORCE / RETEACH / EXTEND

Selection Support Pages
Build Vocabulary: The Word Root *-lum-*, p. 63
Build Grammar Skills: Participial Phrases, p. 64
Reading for Success: Interactive Reading Strategies, p. 65
Literary Focus: Internal Conflict, p. 67

Writing and Language Transparencies
Herringbone Organizer, p. 75–77

Strategies for Diverse Student Needs, p. 16

Beyond Literature
Cross-Curricular Connection: Physical Education, p. 16

Formal Assessment Selection Test, pp. 54–56; Assessment Resources Software

Alternative Assessment, p. 16

Resource Pro CD-ROM

Listening to Literature Audiocassettes

MODEL SELECTION

Through the Tunnel

◆ Literature and Your Life

CONNECT YOUR EXPERIENCE

When you set personal goals, you challenge yourself, push yourself to see just how far you can go. Whether or not you succeed, you learn something about yourself. The boy in Lessing's story gives himself a physical challenge that requires all his courage to meet.

Journal Writing Write about a challenge you have successfully met—either physical, emotional, or intellectual. List the steps you took to accomplish your goal.

THEMATIC FOCUS: CLASHING FORCES

In this story, a boy chooses to take on an underwater challenge despite his inner fear of failure. How do you think success or failure to meet a challenge changes a person?

◆ Background for Understanding

SCIENCE

Oxygen, which your body needs on a regular basis, is an important, but relatively small, part of the air you breathe. Depriving the brain of oxygen can quickly cause dizziness and, if prolonged, brain damage. However, you don't usually have to think about breathing. Special cells, called chemoreceptors, sense the oxygen and carbon dioxide levels in your blood. These cells then send out signals that quicken or slow the rate of breathing as necessary.

Jerry, the young boy in this story, deprives his body of oxygen, pushing the limit of how long he can hold his breath. His self-testing makes for interesting reading, but it is not something you should imitate.

◆ Literary Focus

INTERNAL CONFLICT

The personal challenge that Jerry, the character in "Through the Tunnel," sets for himself involves an **internal conflict**—a struggle within a character over opposing feelings, beliefs, or needs. Jerry's struggle with his opposing feelings about this enormous and frightening challenge he faces results in a gripping story.

Use a graphic organizer like the one shown to identify Jerry' s conflicting feelings.

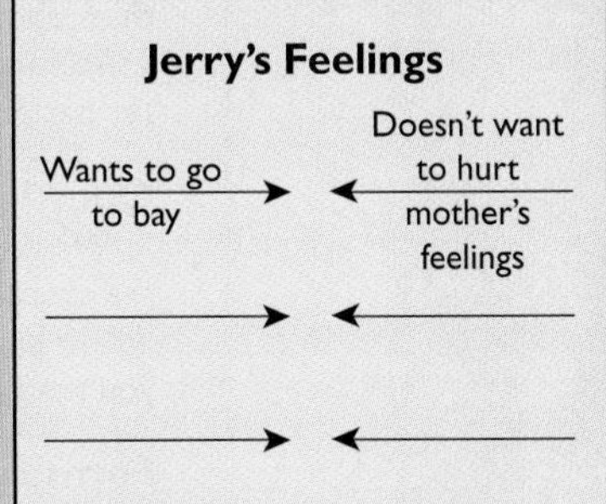

How much oxygen is in the air you breathe?

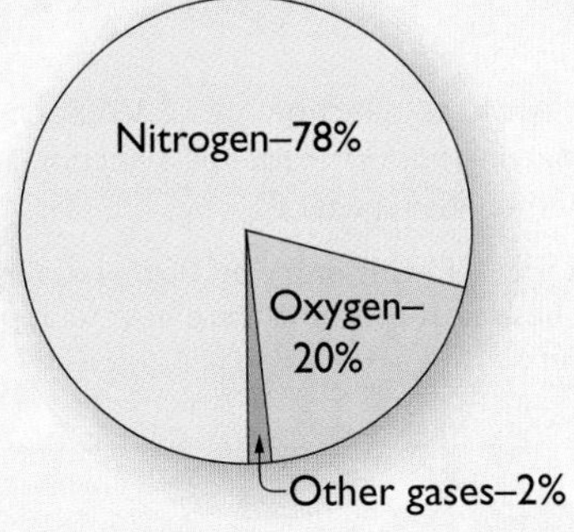

Give students an opportunity to relate to the way time seems to expand during Jerry's physical ordeal. Have them close their eyes; tell them to keep their eyes closed and raise their hands when they think 2 minutes have passed. Most students will raise their hands before the time has elapsed. Point out that a boy in this story will spend that much time in a dark, frightening place, holding his breath and facing a great physical challenge, affecting his perception of time.

Connecting Themes Across Cultures

Discuss with students whether Jerry may decide to take on the underwater challenge because he is trying to prove himself as a foreign visitor.

Tips to Guide Reading

Set a Purpose As a purpose for reading, suggest that students read to discover why the story is titled "The Tunnel."

Customize for *Less Proficient Readers*

As an aid to literal comprehension, have students use the Reading for Success strategy, Form Mental Images, pausing frequently while reading to form images in their minds of what is happening in the story.

Customize for *Pre-AP Students*

Have students pay particular attention to the subtle details of characterization in the selection. Suggest that they pause at intervals while reading to ask themselves questions concerning Jerry's and his mother's motivations.

Customize for *Gifted/Talented Students*

Have students work in groups to create different endings for the story. Remind them to use details from the original story as prompts so that their new conclusion is logical.

Customize for *English Language Learners*

Guide students to use the story's art to help them picture the setting and action.

Test Preparation Workshop

Reading Comprehension: Stated and Implied Main Ideas Many standardized tests require that students be skilled at recognizing and understanding main ideas of a reading passage. Ask students to read the entire paragraph that begins, "On the edge of a small cape . . ." at the bottom of p. 222. Then have them answer the following sample question.

Which of the following best expresses the main idea of this paragraph?

A The English boy wanted to be friends.
B The boys were all good swimmers.
C Swimming on the small cape was dangerous.
D The beach was rocky.

Encourage students to carefully analyze each of the answer choices. They should decide if the answer states a supporting detail from the paragraph or if it expresses the paragraph's main idea. Answers *B, C,* and *D* represent accurate details from the passage, but the best expression of the main idea is *A*—Jerry desperately wanted to be friends and not to swim alone.

Reading for Success

The Reading for Success page in each unit presents a set of problem-solving procedures to help readers understand authors' words and ideas on multiple levels. Good readers develop a bank of strategies from which they can draw as needed.

Unit 3 introduces strategies for interactive reading. Interacting with the text helps readers make meaning from a work in the context of their own experience, knowledge, and ideas. These strategies for interactive reading give students an approach for becoming involved with the text by envisioning details, considering the significance of events, and responding to characters, events, and ideas.

These strategies for interactive reading are modeled with "Through the Tunnel." Each green box shows an example of the thinking process involved in applying one of these strategies.

How to Use the Reading for Success Page

- Introduce the interactive reading strategies, presenting each as a problem-solving procedure. Be sure students understand what each strategy involves and under what circumstances to apply it.
- Before students read the story, have them preview it, looking at the annotations in the green boxes that model the strategies.
- To reinforce these strategies after students have read "Through the Tunnel," have students do the Reading for Success page in ***Selection Support,*** p. 65. This page gives students an opportunity to read a selection and practice strategies for interactive reading by writing their own annotations.

Reading for Success

Interactive Reading Strategies

Reading is interactive. When you interact with the words on each page, you can really feel the sights and sounds of new worlds. Otherwise, if you just sit back and passively look at the words, it's like going on a field trip and never getting off the bus!

When you read, apply the following strategies to help you interact with the text:

Predict.
What do you think will happen? Why? Look for hints in the story that seem to suggest a certain outcome. As you read on, you will see whether your predictions are correct.

Use your prior background knowledge.
No matter how different a character, subject matter, opinion, or situation is from what you are familiar with, chances are you will be able to relate to certain aspects of the character or experience. If a character goes to the beach, think about a trip to the beach you may have taken. This technique will give you a mental picture of what is happening and help you relate to the character better.

Question.
What questions come to mind as you are reading? For example, why do the characters act as they do? What causes events to happen? Why does the writer include certain information? Look for answers to your questions as you read.

Form mental images.
Use details from the selection you are reading to create pictures in your mind. As you read along, change your picture as the story unfolds and your understanding grows. If you find yourself confused, try to state your confusion. Use your visualization to clarify whatever hasn't been clear to you.

Respond.
Think about what the selection means. What does it say to you? What feelings does it evoke in you? What has the selection added to your understanding of people and of life in general?

As you read the following story by Doris Lessing, look at the notes along the margins. These notes demonstrate how to apply these strategies to a work of literature.

Reading Strategies: Support and Reinforcement

Appropriate Reading Strategies Students are given a reading strategy to apply in reading each selection. In selections where students' understanding will be especially enhanced by making connections to their own experiences and knowledge, one of these interactive reading strategies is suggested. In other selections, a strategy is suggested that is appropriate to the selection.

Reading Prompts To encourage application of the given reading strategy, there are occasional prompts, within green boxes, at appropriate and significant points.

In addition, there are red boxes prompting application of the Literary Focus concept and maroon boxes prompting students to connect with their lives.

Using the Boxed Annotations and Prompts The material in the green, red, and maroon boxes along the sides of selections is intended to help students apply the literary element and the reading strategy and to make a connection with their lives.

You may use the boxed material in several ways:

- Have students pause when they come to a box and respond to its prompt before they continue reading.
- After students have read the selection completely, they can review the selection in groups, discussing their responses to the prompts.

MODEL

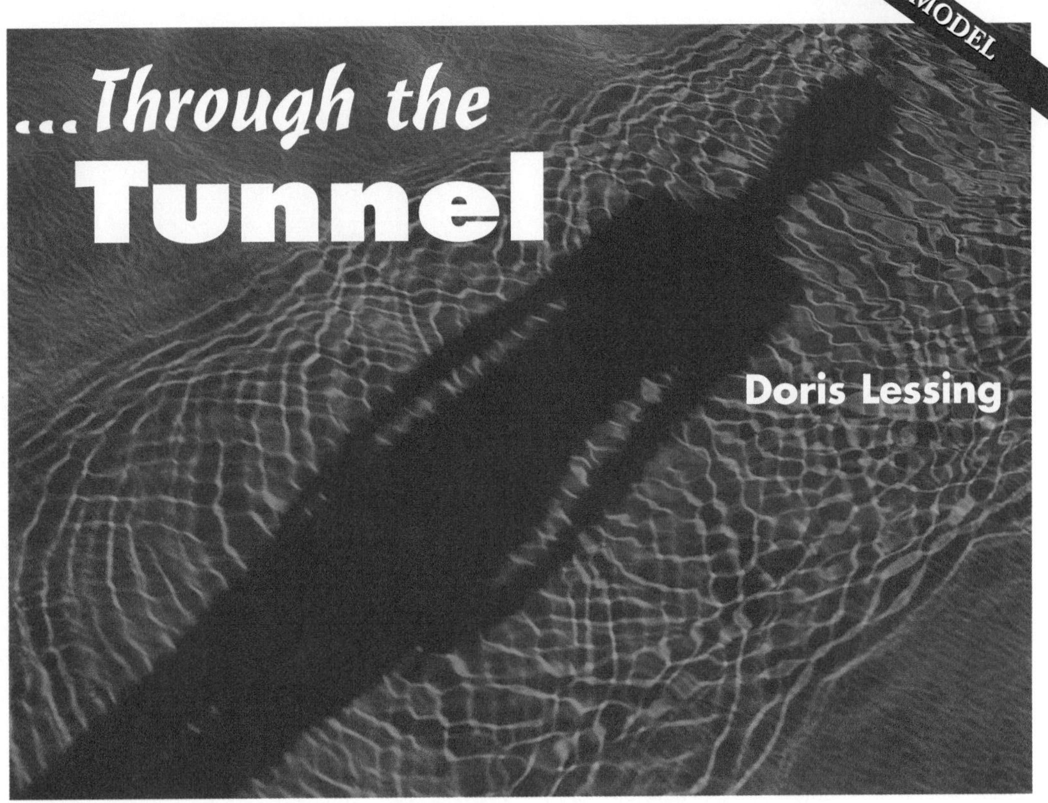

▲ Critical Viewing How does the use of shadows and light affect the mood of this photograph? **[Analyze]**

Going to the shore on the first morning of the vacation, the young English boy stopped at a turning of the path and looked down at a wild and rocky bay, and then over to the crowded beach he knew so well from other years. His mother walked on in front of him, carrying a bright striped bag in one hand. Her other arm, swinging loose, was very white in the sun. The boy watched that white, naked arm, and turned his eyes, which had a frown behind them, toward the bay and back again to his mother. When she felt he was not with her, she swung around. "Oh, there you are, Jerry!" she said. She looked impatient, then smiled. "Why, darling, would you rather not come with me? Would you rather—" She frowned, conscientiously worrying over what amusements he might secretly be longing for, which she had been too busy or too careless to imagine. He was very familiar with that anxious, apologetic smile. Contrition sent him running after her. ❸ And yet, as he ran, he looked back over his shoulder at the wild bay; and all morning, as he played on the safe beach, ❹

This detail helps you **predict** that something will happen at the bay.

◆ **Build Vocabulary**

contrition (kən trish′ ən) *n.*: Feeling of remorse for having done something wrong

Block Scheduling Strategies

Consider these suggestions to take advantage of extended class time:

- Have students preview the work in small groups, focusing on the visuals and answering the Critical Viewing questions on pp. 221 and 225.
- Introduce the Reading for Success strategies. As students read, have them notice the annotations that model the strategies. Then have students apply the interactive reading strategies by completing the Reading for Success page in ***Selection Support,*** p. 65.
- After all students have read the story, have them break into groups to explore the group discussion suggestion on p. 228.
- Complete the Literary Focus on p. 229 as a class. Then have students work independently to complete the Literary Focus page on Internal Conflict in ***Selection Support,*** p. 67.
- Use the Viewing and Representing Mini-Lesson (p. 224) to support the Researching and Representing activity on p. 230.

Develop Understanding

One-Minute Insight In "Through the Tunnel," Doris Lessing establishes a level of tension that increases with every heart-pounding moment. The story reaches beyond suspense, however, to make profound points about a boy's conflict between love for his mother and desire for independence. For the boy, making the perilous journey through a dark underwater tunnel and breaking through to the light on the other end is an important rite of passage that helps him reconcile these two forces.

▶Critical Viewing◀

❶ **Analyze** *Some students may suggest that the highlighted ripples on the water seem to be ensnaring the shaded human figure in a tangled web. Some may say the dark shaded figure, contrasted with the bright blue water, creates an air of mystery.*

Reading for Success

❷ **Form Mental Images** Ask a volunteer to read this first sentence aloud while the other students concentrate on picturing the setting. Ask students to describe the setting in their own words. *Suggested response: There is a path going down a hill to the beach. If you look down on one side you see a typical ocean beach, crowded with swimmers and sunbathers. If you look down on the other side you see a bay. It is wild and rocky, and totally deserted.*

◆Build Grammar Skills

❸ **Participial Phrases** Have students review the participial phrase "conscientiously worrying over what amusements he might secretly be longing for." Ask what noun the phrase modifies (*she*). Point out that the relationship between the phrase and the noun it modifies clarifies the significance of the information in the phrase.

Reading for Success

❹ **Predict** Have students speculate about what will come of the boy's interest in the "wild bay." *Students will probably say that the boy will return to the bay; some may say that something bad will happen when he does, based on the description of the bay as "wild," in contrast to "the safe beach."*

◆ Literary Focus

❶ **Internal Conflict** Ask students to identify the opposing feelings with which Jerry and his mother are struggling. *Jerry wants to go to the bay but doesn't want to worry his mother or leave her alone. Jerry's mother wants Jerry to be safe, but she doesn't want to baby him or hold him back.*

Reading for Success

❷ **Form Mental Images** Ask students which details help them imagine the scene. What details do they add to their mental pictures? *Students can identify details such as red-brown rocks, bluish green fringed with white, and inlets of rough, sharp rocks; they may add details such as the feel of wind or sunshine or the sound of the water.*

▶Critical Viewing◀

❸ **Compare and Contrast** *Students may say that the beach in the painting is less crowded than the one in the story. They may add more people and a woman sitting on a yellow towel or wearing a yellow bathing suit, sitting under an orange beach umbrella. They might also add the ocean and waves.*

◆ Build Grammar Skills

❹ **Participial Phrases** Have students identify the participial phrase that modifies *he* in this sentence. Ask what information the phrase adds to the sentence. *The phrase is "relieved at being sure she was there." The phrase provides information about the boy's conflicted feelings about his mother: He wants independence, but he wants to be close to his mother as well.*

Art Transparency Display Art Transparency 3 after students have read and discussed "Through the Tunnel." Invite student comments, focusing in particular upon the painting within the painting. Ask students how the painting reminds them of the goal that Jerry sets for himself in the story. You might challenge students to role-play a conversation in which Jerry and the woman compare their challenging swims.

he was thinking of it.

Next morning, when it was time for the routine of swimming and sunbathing, his mother said, "Are you tired of the usual beach, Jerry? Would you like to go somewhere else?"

> **Use your prior knowledge** by relating Jerry's reaction to a time when you've hidden your feelings to avoid hurting someone else's feelings.

"Oh, no!" he said quickly, smiling at her out of that unfailing impulse of contrition—a sort of chivalry. Yet, walking down the path with her, he blurted out, "I'd like to go and have a look at those rocks down there."

She gave the idea her attention. It was a wild-looking place, and there was no one there; but she said, "Of course, Jerry. When you've had enough, come to the big beach. Or just go straight back to the villa, if you like." She ❶ walked away, that bare arm, now slightly reddened from yesterday's sun, swinging. And he almost ran after her again, feeling it unbearable that she should go by herself, but he did not.

She was thinking, Of course he's old enough to be safe without me. Have I been keeping him too close? He mustn't feel he ought to be with me. I must be careful.

He was an only child, eleven years old. She was a widow. She was determined to be neither possessive nor lacking in devotion. She went worrying off to her beach.

As for Jerry, once he saw that his mother had gained her beach, he began the steep descent to the bay. From where he was, high up among red-brown rocks, it was a scoop of moving bluish green fringed with white. As he went lower, he saw that it spread among small promontories and inlets of rough, sharp rock, and the crisping, lapping surface showed stains of purple and darker blue. Finally, as he ran sliding and scraping down the last few yards, he saw an edge of white surf and the shallow, luminous movement of water over white sand, and,

> ❷ Use these sensory details—sharp rocks, vivid blue sea, and the sound of water—to **form a mental image** of this beautiful, isolated place.

▲ **Critical Viewing** Compare the details of this painting with the way you envisioned the "big beach" in the story. **[Compare and Contrast]** ❸

beyond that, a solid, heavy blue.

He ran straight into the water and began swimming. He was a good swimmer. He went out fast over the gleaming sand, over a middle region where rocks lay like discolored monsters under the surface, and then he was in the real sea—a warm sea where irregular cold currents from the deep water shocked his limbs.

When he was so far out that he could look back not only on the little bay but past the promontory that was between it and the big beach, he floated on the buoyant surface and looked for his mother. There she was, a speck of yellow under an umbrella that looked like a slice of orange peel. He swam back to shore, relieved at being sure she was there, but all at once very lonely. ❹

On the edge of a small cape that marked the

Humanities: Art

The Beach Treat by Suzanne Nagler.

Suzanne Nagler's painting of a beach scene is, in some ways, similar to the description of the beach in the story. Even the artist's use of childlike primary colors emphasizes the safe, peaceful quality of this place.

Have students study the painting, its details, and qualities. Then use the following questions for discussion:

1. What details in the painting give an impression of safety and tranquillity? *Possible observations the following: the building that could be a home or a life guard station gives a sense of permanence; phone lines link the remoteness of the beach to the rest of the world.*
2. What important element of a beach scene is missing in this painting? Why do you think the artist omitted it? *Encourage students to note that the ocean is missing. Suggest that the vastness and the motion of the sea would not contribute to the feelings of stability and calm of the beach scene.*

The Beach Treat (detail), Suzanne Nagler

side of the bay away from the promontory was a loose scatter of rocks. Above them, some boys were stripping off their clothes. They came running, naked, down to the rocks. The English boy swam toward them, but kept his distance at a stone's throw. They were of that coast; all of them were burned smooth dark brown and speaking a language he did not understand. To be with them, of them, was a craving that filled his whole body. He swam a little closer; they turned and watched him with narrowed, alert dark eyes. Then one smiled and waved. It was enough. In a minute, he had swum in and was on the rocks beside them, smiling with a desperate, nervous supplication. They shouted cheerful greetings at him; and then, as he preserved his nervous, uncomprehending smile, they understood that he was a foreigner strayed from his own beach, and they proceeded to forget him. But he was happy. He was with them.

They began diving again and again from a high point into a well of blue sea between rough, pointed rocks. After they had dived and come up, they swam around, hauled themselves up, and waited their turn to dive again. They were big boys—men, to Jerry. He dived, and they watched him; and when he swam around to take his place, they made way for him. He felt he was accepted and he dived again, carefully, proud of himself. ❺

Soon the biggest of the boys poised himself, shot down into the water, and did not come up. The others stood about, watching. Jerry, after waiting for the sleek brown head to appear, let out a yell of warning; they looked at him idly and turned their eyes back toward the water. ❻ After a long time, the boy came up on the other side of a big dark rock, letting the air out of his lungs in a sputtering gasp and a shout of triumph. Immediately the rest of them dived in. One moment, the morning seemed full of chattering boys; the next, the air and the surface of the water were empty. But through the heavy blue, dark shapes could be seen moving and groping.

Jerry dived, shot past the school of underwater swimmers, saw a black wall of rock looming at him, touched it, and bobbed up at once to the surface, where the wall was a low barrier he could see across. There was no one visible; under him, in the water, the dim shapes of the swimmers had disappeared. Then one, and then another of the boys came up on the far side of the barrier of rock, and he understood that they had swum through some gap or hole in it. He plunged down again. He could see nothing through the stinging salt water but the blank rock. When he came up the boys were all on the diving rock, preparing to attempt the feat again. And now, in a panic of

◆ Build Vocabulary

promontories (präm′ ən tôr′ ēz) *n.*: High places extending out over a body of water

luminous (lo͞o′ mə nəs) *adj.*: Giving off light

supplication (sup′ lə kā′ shən) *n.*: The act of asking humbly and earnestly

◆ Literary Focus

❺ Internal Conflict Point out to students that Jerry's interaction with these older boys highlights his desire to grow up and be independent of his mother. Tell students to notice how Jerry's actions in the next few paragraphs highlight his childlike side.

Reading for Success

❻ Question Wonder with students why the author includes this information. Jerry is feeling accepted by the boys. How do they feel about him? *The fact that the boys "looked at him idly and turned their eyes back toward the water" implies that they do not, in fact, accept Jerry. They are behaving indifferently, at best—possibly even in a hostile manner.*

Read to Be Entertained

Students should be encouraged to remember that reading for pleasure and entertainment is a valid purpose to set for reading.

Extending Word Study

Increase Vocabulary As students read widely for pleasure and enjoyment, their vocabulary expands. Ask them to skim through the selection and list words and phrases that describe the beach and ocean such as: wild and rocky bay. If they do not know the precise meaning of a word and cannot determine the meaning from the context, suggest that they look up the precise meaning in the dictionary.

Customize for *English Language Learners*

Help English language learners list words to identify the range of emotions that Jerry experiences during his encounter with the boys, such as *nervous, happy, accepted, proud, worried, surprised,* and *confused.*

Customize for *Verbal/Linguistic Learners*

Suggest that interested students find out more about sea caves and how they are formed. They can expand their research to include cave study—speleology, and cave exploration—spelunking. Have students share their research information with the class in the form of written reports.

Workplace Skills Mini-Lesson

Setting and Meeting Goals

Introduce Jerry sets a goal for himself and then challenges himself to meet it. Setting personal goals and finding systematic ways to meet them are essential life and workplace skills. Students' goals might include improving a grade in a particular subject or earning a spot on a team. Job-related goals might include improving keyboard skills or learning to use a digital camera.

Develop Ask students to identify goals they might set for themselves. Point out to that many goals are actually the final product of a set of smaller goals. Use the Herringbone graphic organizer transparency, ***Writing and Language Transparencies,*** pp. 75–77, to model how one of the student-suggested goals might be broken down into smaller goals or steps.

Apply Distribute copies of the Herringbone organizer for students to identify the steps of goals.

Assess Evaluate how well students identify the sequence or combination of events or skills that will lead to their goals. Pairs of students can evaluate each other on how well they identify the steps required to meet the stated goals.

Reading for Success

❶ Question Ask students how they would have responded to Jerry if they had been one of the big boys. What would they think about his actions, and how would they react? *Responses may range from wanting to ignore Jerry to feeling sorry for him, to trying to include him.*

Reading for Success

❷ Use Your Prior Background Knowledge Ask students how fear, anticipation, and other strong emotions affect their perception of time. Based on their experiences, do students think the older boys are underwater a dangerously long time or does Jerry only perceive the time to be too long? *Students will probably say that strong emotions can make time seem to pass more quickly or more slowly. For this reason, Jerry probably feels as if the older boys are under water a longer time than they actually are.*

◆ Critical Thinking

❸ Compare and Contrast Have students compare Jerry's attitude toward his mother in this passage with his treatment of her earlier. *Students may say that Jerry is acting selfishly and childishly. Because he has been hurt, he is now obsessed with his own needs and feelings, whereas before he was thoughtful of hers.*

◆ Reading Strategy

❹ Form Mental Images Encourage students to form a mental image based on this passage. Then ask them to identify the words that helped them form their images. *Sample answers: "shining white sand, rippled firm and hard," "two grayish shapes," "dart forward, swerve off," "the water sparkled as if sequins were dropping through it," "like swimming in flaked silver."*

failure, he yelled up, in English, "Look at me! Look!" and he began splashing and kicking in the water like a foolish dog.

They looked down gravely, frowning. He knew the frown. At moments of failure, when he clowned to claim his mother's attention, it was with just this grave, embarrassed inspection that she rewarded him.

> Question why Jerry might be acting this way. Is he trying to get attention?

❶ Through his hot shame, feeling the pleading grin on his face like a scar that he could never remove, he looked up at the group of big brown boys on the rock and shouted, *"Bonjour! Merci! Au revoir! Monsieur, monsieur!"*[1] while he hooked his fingers round his ears and waggled them.

Water surged into his mouth; he choked, sank, came up. The rock, lately weighted with boys, seemed to rear up out of the water as their weight was removed. They were flying down past him, now, into the water; the air was full of falling bodies. Then the rock was empty in the hot sunlight. He counted one, two, three. . . .

At fifty, he was terrified. They must all be drowning beneath him, in the watery caves of the rock! At a hundred, he stared around him at the empty hillside, wondering if he should yell for help. He counted faster, faster, to hurry them up, to bring them to the surface quickly, ❷ to drown them quickly—anything rather than the terror of counting on and on into the blue emptiness of the morning. And then, at a hundred and sixty, the water beyond the rock was full of boys blowing like brown whales. They swam back to the shore without a look at him.

He climbed back to the diving rock and sat down, feeling the hot roughness of it under his thighs. The boys were gathering up their bits of clothing and running off along the shore to another promontory. They were leaving to get away from him. He cried openly, fists in his eyes. There was no one to see him, and he cried himself out.

> Think about how you would **respond** to this situation.

1. **Bonjour! . . . monsieur!** (bōn zhōōr . . . mə syö'): Babbling of commonly known French words: "Hello! Thank you! Goodbye! Sir, sir!"

It seemed to him that a long time had passed, and he swam out to where he could see his mother. Yes, she was still there, a yellow spot under an orange umbrella. He swam back to the big rock, climbed up, and dived into the blue pool among the fanged and angry boulders. Down he went, until he touched the wall of rock again. But the salt was so painful in his eyes that he could not see.

> Use these sensory details to **form a mental image** of how difficult it is to swim in this place.

He came to the surface, swam to shore and went back to the villa to wait for his mother. Soon she walked slowly up the path, swinging her striped bag, the flushed, naked arm dangling beside her. "I want some swimming goggles," he panted, defiant and beseeching.

She gave him a patient, inquisitive look as she said casually, "Well, of course, darling."

But now, now, now! He must have them this minute, and no other time. He nagged and pestered until she went with him to a shop. As soon as she had bought the goggles, he grabbed them from her hand as if she were going to claim them for herself, and was off, running down the steep path to the bay.

Jerry swam out to the big barrier rock, adjusted the goggles, and dived. The impact of the water broke the rubber-enclosed vacuum, and the goggles came loose. He understood that he must swim down to the base of the rock from the surface of the water. He fixed the goggles tight and firm, filled his lungs, and floated, face down, on the water. Now he could see. It was as if he had eyes of a different kind—fish eyes that showed everything clear and delicate and wavering in the bright water.

Under him, six or seven feet down, was a floor of perfectly clean, shining white sand, rippled firm and hard by the tides. Two grayish shapes steered there, like long, rounded pieces of wood or slate. They were fish. He saw them nose toward each other, poise motionless, make a dart forward, swerve off, and come around again. It was like a water dance. A few inches above them the water sparkled as if

Viewing and Representing Mini-Lesson

Collage

This mini-lesson supports the Researching and Representing activity on p. 230 in the Idea Bank.

Introduce Explain to students that a collage is a work of art composed of a grouping of images, often relating to a theme. Collage images can be created from found objects such as: sand, sea shells, and fabric, or art materials such as: tissue paper, cardboard, or bits of stone, crayon, and chalk.

Develop Have students reread the story, skimming for details that describe the setting of the beach and the ocean. They will probably find it helpful to take notes on the details.

Apply Have students use their list of story details as a basis to compose a collage that represents the setting of the shore described by the author. They may add drawings or paintings to the collage if they wish.

Assess Ask students to display their collage beach representation in the classroom. Assess their work based on how well they used artistic creativity to capture the setting the author created with words.

▲ Critical Viewing How do you think this diver feels? **[Speculate]**

sequins were dropping through it. Fish again—myriads of minute fish, the length of his fingernail, were drifting through the water, and in a moment he could feel the innumerable tiny touches of them against his limbs. It was like swimming in flaked silver. The great rock the big boys had swum through rose sheer out of the white sand—black, tufted lightly with greenish weed. He could see no gap in it. He swam down to its base.

Again and again he rose, took a big chestful of air, and went down. Again and again he groped over the surface of the rock, feeling it, almost hugging it in the desperate need to find the entrance. And then, once, while he was clinging to the black wall, his knees came up and he shot his feet out forward and they met no obstacle. He had found the hole.

This discovery will help you **predict** that upcoming plot events will be related to the tunnel.

He gained the surface, clambered about the stones that littered the barrier rock until he found a big one, and, with this in his arms, let himself down over the side of the rock. He dropped, with the weight, straight to the sandy floor. Clinging tight to the anchor of stone, he lay on his side and looked in under the dark shelf at the place where his feet had gone. He could see the hole. It was an irregular, dark gap; but he could not see deep into it. He let go of his anchor, clung with his hands to the edges of the hole, and tried to push himself in.

He got his head in, found his shoulders jammed, moved them in sidewise, and was inside as far as his waist. He could see nothing ahead. Something soft and clammy touched his mouth; he saw a dark frond moving against the grayish rock, and panic filled him. He thought of octopuses, of clinging weed. He pushed himself out backward and caught a glimpse, as he retreated, of a harmless tentacle of seaweed drifting in the mouth of the tunnel. But it was enough. He reached the sunlight, swam to shore, and lay on the diving rock. He looked down into the blue well of water. He knew he must find his way through that cave, or hole, or tunnel, and out the other side.

First, he thought, he must learn to control his breathing. He let himself down into the water with another big stone in his arms, so that he could lie effortlessly on the bottom of the sea. He counted. One, two, three. He counted steadily. He could hear the movement of blood in his chest. Fifty-one, fifty-two. . . . His chest was hurting. He let go of the rock and went up into the air. He saw that the sun was low. He rushed to the villa and found his mother at her supper. She said only "Did you enjoy yourself?" and he said "Yes." 6

All night the boy dreamed of the water-filled cave in the rock, and as soon as breakfast was over he went to the bay.

◆ Build Vocabulary

frond (fränd) *n.*: Leaflike shoot of seaweed

▶Critical Viewing◀

5 Speculate As students respond to the question, have them discuss the mental preparation and concentration required to perform any difficult physical feat. Discuss also the effect of the artist's setting the diver against a vast expanse of sea and sky. *Students may suggest that the diver feels exhilarated and free, proud and triumphant. Others may speculate that the diver feels isolated and fearful. Many students will suggest a combination of fear and excitement.*

Customize for *Visual/Spatial Learners*

Have visual/spatial learners use the details of the tunnel description to create a diagram or sketch of the underwater scene.

◆ Literature and Your Life

6 Have students discuss Jerry's resolve to find his way through the tunnel, the steps he decides to take, and the goals he sets for himself. Have students share physical goals that they have set for themselves, such as learning a skill or training for a sport. How are their approaches to goal-setting similar to Jerry's? How are they different?

Humanities: Art

The Diver by Dennis Angel.

Dennis Angel received a Master of Fine Arts degree from Indiana University, Bloomington, in 1988. He has taught at several universities and has exhibited his paintings all over the United States.

In this painting, the scene is fantastic, but the grace and daring of the diver are very real. By blurring the distinction between sea and sky, the artist places the focus on the diver and the dive, capturing the moments when the diver hangs in midair before success or failure is determined.

Use the following questions for discussion:

1. Is this a realistic scene or a fantasy scene? *The scene is fantastic. The diver seems to hang in midair; the pool seems to be set in the middle of nowhere; the diver's position is more like a bird's than a person's.*
2. What does the diver in the painting have in common with Jerry in the story? *Both are executing a feat of daring; both are about to pass through a dark, mysterious opening under the water; perhaps neither one knows if he or she will succeed or even survive.*

❶ **Clarification** Explain that water pressure increases as a person dives deeper. The increased pressure can cause small blood vessels in the nose to burst and cause nosebleeds.

◆ Literary Focus

❷ **Internal Conflict** Ask students to describe the emotional extremes that Jerry is experiencing. Why is he waiting? Why does the author call his persistence "unchildlike"? Challenge students to compare Jerry's "unchildlike" behavior now with his behavior when he asked his mother to buy the swim goggles. To what do they attribute this change? *Jerry feels ready to try swimming through the tunnel but is forcing himself to wait with "controlled impatience." He is waiting because he wants to be certain he will succeed. His persistence is unchildlike because most children do not exhibit this much self-control. Jerry is acting in a much more mature way now. His new goal may be helping him to grow up.*

◆ Build Grammar Skills

❸ **Participial Phrases** Have students identify the participial phrase that modifies *words.* Ask students what purpose the phrase serves. *The participial phrase is "authorized by the clock." Its purpose is to show that Jerry could hold his breath for exactly two minutes—not approximately.*

◆ Critical Thinking

❹ **Make a Judgment** Have students discuss the pros and cons of Jerry's decision. *Pros include a sense of accomplishment, pride in overcoming fear, meeting a goal. Cons include potential failure, injury, or death.*

That night, his nose bled badly. For hours he had been underwater, learning to hold his
❶ breath, and now he felt weak and dizzy. His mother said, "I shouldn't overdo things, darling, if I were you."

That day and the next, Jerry exercised his lungs as if everything, the whole of his life, all that he would become, depended upon it. Again his nose bled at night, and his mother insisted on his coming with her the next day. It was a torment to him to waste a day of his careful self-training, but he stayed with her on that other beach, which now seemed a place for small children, a place where his mother might lie safe in the sun. It was not his beach.

He did not ask for permission, on the following day, to go to his beach. He went, before his mother could consider the complicated rights and wrongs of the matter. A day's rest, he discovered, had improved his count by ten. The big boys had made the passage while he counted a hundred and sixty. He had been counting fast, in his fright. Probably now, if he tried, he could get through that long tunnel,
❷ but he was not going to try yet. A curious, most unchildlike persistence, a controlled impatience, made him wait. In the meantime, he lay underwater on the white sand, littered now by stones he had brought down from the upper air, and studied the entrance to the tunnel. He knew every jut and corner of it, as far as it was possible to see. It was as if he already felt its sharpness about his shoulders.

He sat by the clock in the villa, when his mother was not near, and checked his time. He was incredulous and then proud to find he could hold his breath without strain for two minutes. The words "two minutes," authorized
❸ by the clock, brought close the adventure that was so necessary to him.

In another four days, his mother said casually one morning, they must go home. On the day before they left, he would do it. He would do it if it killed him, he said defiantly to himself. But two days before they were to leave—a day of triumph when he increased his count by fifteen—his nose bled so badly that he turned dizzy and had to lie limply over the big rock like a bit of seaweed, watching the thick red blood flow onto the rock and trickle slowly down to the sea. He was frightened. Supposing he turned dizzy in the tunnel? Supposing he died there, trapped? Supposing—his head went around, in the hot sun, and he almost gave up. He thought he would return to the house and lie down, and next summer, perhaps, when he had another year's growth in him—*then* he would go through the hole.

> The next paragraph provides the answer to the **question** of whether or not Jerry will go through the tunnel.

But even after he had made the decision, or thought he had, he found himself sitting up on the rock and looking down into the water; and he knew that now, this moment, when his nose had only just stopped bleeding, when his head was still sore and throbbing—this was the moment when he would try. If he did not do it now, he never would. He was trembling with fear that he would not go; and he was trembling with horror at that long, long tunnel under the rock, under the sea. Even in the open
sunlight, the barrier rock seemed very wide ❹
and very heavy; tons of rock pressed down on where he would go. If he died there, he would lie until one day—perhaps not before next year—those big boys would swim into it and find it blocked.

He put on his goggles, fitted them tight, tested the vacuum. His hands were shaking. Then he chose the biggest stone he could carry and slipped over the edge of the rock until half of him was in the cool, enclosing water and half in the hot sun. He looked up once at the empty sky, filled his lungs once, twice, and then sank fast to the bottom with the stone. He let it go and began to count. He took the edges of the hole in his hands and drew himself into it, wriggling his shoulders in sidewise as he remembered he must, kicking himself along with his feet.

Soon he was clear inside. He was in a small rockbound hole filled with yellowish-gray water. The water was pushing him up against the ❺
roof. The roof was sharp and pained his back. He pulled himself along with his hands—fast,

Reteach

One of the interactive reading strategies modeled with this selection is predicting outcomes. For additional practice with this strategy have students draw two columns on a piece of paper with the headings Prediction and Outcome. Ask students to reread the story—stopping at the bottom of each page to make a prediction about what they think might happen next. Have them write their prediction in the first column. When they reach the bottom of the next page, ask them to stop reading again. Have them determine whether they have enough information to write the proper outcome in the second column. At this point, they should make a second prediction. Students can follow this procedure throughout the entire selection, stopping at the bottom of each page to make a prediction and fill in the outcomes as they occur. After reading, have students review their chart to determine how many correct predictions they were able to make.

fast—and used his legs as levers. His head knocked against something; a sharp pain dizzied him. Fifty, fifty-one, fifty-two. . . . He was without light, and the water seemed to press upon him with the weight of rock. Seventy-one, seventy-two. . . . There was no strain on his lungs. He felt like an inflated balloon, his lungs were so light and easy, but his head was pulsing.

He was being continually pressed against the sharp roof, which felt slimy as well as sharp. Again he thought of octopuses, and wondered if the tunnel might be filled with weed that could tangle him. He gave himself a panicky, convulsive kick forward, ducked his head, and swam. His feet and hands moved freely, as if in open water. The hole must have widened out. He thought he must be swimming fast, and he was frightened of banging his head if the tunnel narrowed.

A hundred, a hundred and one. . . . The water paled. Victory filled him. His lungs were beginning to hurt. A few more strokes and he would be out. He was counting wildly; he said a hundred and fifteen, and then, a long time later, a hundred and fifteen again. The water was a clear jewel-green all around him. Then he saw, above his head, a crack running up through the rock. Sunlight was falling through it, showing the clean, dark rock of the tunnel, a single mussel shell, and darkness ahead.

He was at the end of what he could do. He looked up at the crack as if it were filled with air and not water, as if he could put his mouth to it to draw in air. A hundred and fifteen, he heard himself say inside his head—but he had said that long ago. He must go on into the blackness ahead, or he would drown. His head was swelling, his lungs cracking. A hundred and fifteen, a hundred and fifteen pounded through his head, and he feebly clutched at rocks in the dark, pulling himself forward, leaving the brief space of sunlit water behind. He felt he was dying. He was no longer quite conscious. He struggled on in the darkness between lapses into unconsciousness. An immense, swelling pain filled his head, and then the darkness cracked with an explosion of green light. His hands, groping forward, met nothing; and his feet, kicking back, propelled him out into the open sea. 9

He drifted to the surface, his face turned up to the air. He was gasping like a fish. He felt he

Coast Scene, Isles of Shoals, 1901, Childe Hassam, The Metropolitan Museum of Art

▲ **Critical Viewing** Does this picture make you think of Jerry's beach or his mother's? Explain. **[Compare and Contrast]** 8

◆ Build Vocabulary

convulsive (kən vul′ siv) *adj.*: Marked by an involuntary muscular contraction

Reading for Success

5 Use Your Prior Background Knowledge Even though students are not likely to have had an experience like Jerry's, many will have prior knowledge of what it is like to be in a situation that requires courage and some daring. Based on their experience, ask students to explain some of the emotions Jerry might be feeling. *Students might say that Jerry feels excited and determined but scared.*

Reading for Success

6 Question Guide students to question why Lessing made them think Jerry was nearly out of the tunnel, then surprised them by letting them know they—and Jerry—were wrong. *Students should grasp that this is a technique for building tension, increasing suspense, building to a climax.*

Reading for Success

7 Question Ask students if they think there is any chance that the author will let her main character die at the end of the story. If not, lead them to question where the suspense comes from in this passage. *Students should grasp that the suspense comes from identifying with the character. Jerry himself doesn't know if he will make it through the tunnel, and the reader shares Jerry's suspense.*

▶Critical Viewing◀

8 Compare and Contrast *The beach seems more like Jerry's beach—the scene is wild and isolated, surrounded by rocks and rough places. In contrast, Jerry's mother's beach is a stretch of smooth sand dotted with people.*

◆ Build Grammar Skills

9 Participial Phrases Have students identify the participial phrases that modify *hands* and *feet* in the sentence. *The phrase groping forward modifies hands; kicking back modifies feet*

Customize for *Body/Kinesthetic Learners*

Suggest to students that the Reading for Success strategy, Form Mental Images, can apply not only to visual images but to body-and-movement images as well. For example, for the underwater scenes, students can not only picture the scene visually, but "feel" it as well—as if they, themselves, were swimming in the tunnel.

Humanities: Art

Coast Scene, Isles of Shoals, 1901, by Childe Hassam.

American-born Childe Hassam established himself as a key figure in the French Impressionist movement of the late nineteenth century. His goal as a painter was to capture sunlight and its effect on the landscape. His paintings are noted for their sparkling radiance.

In this painting, the sunlit rocks look inviting and the sea appears to be calm, but the dark recesses of the churning water meeting the rocks in the foreground add an element of danger to the scene, while the deep blue of the water underscores the mystery of what is unseen.

Have students study the painting and then discuss the following question:

From which rock in the painting might the boys have dived? Which rock could be the one with the underwater tunnel? *Encourage students to support answers with details from the painting.*

◆ Literary Focus

❶ Internal Conflict Ask students how this sentence is one indication of how Jerry's internal conflict has been resolved. *The fact that Jerry no longer wants or needs the approval of the older boys indicates a newfound independence and maturity.*

Reinforce and Extend

Use the ***Beyond Literature*** Cross-Curricular page on Physical Education (p. 16) to help students relate Jerry's physical challenge to a high-interest topic.

Answers

◆ *Literature and Your Life*

Reader's Response While many students may feel that Jerry's experience has helped him mature and become more independent, others may point out that he should not have taken on a challenge that could have cost him his life.

Thematic Focus Jerry has matured, learned patience, and achieved a measure of independence.

Questions for Research Suggest that students use Internet resources to find answers to their relevant questions.

☑ Check Your Comprehension

1. While Jerry's mother is concerned for his safety, she is also worried that she may be overprotective.
2. (a) Jerry's encounter with the local boys begins well; they seem to accept him because he is able to dive along with them. When he begins clowning immaturely, they move on to get away from him. (b) Jerry is devastated by the change in the boys' attitude. His determination to do what they do is strengthened by their rejection.
3. Jerry prepares by getting goggles, checking the cave opening, and practicing holding his breath.
4. The tunnel is smaller than he thought, and much longer. When he thinks he has reached the end, he discovers he is only seeing light through a crack in the cave. Just when he thinks he can't go any further, he finally emerges into the open sea and pulls himself to safety on the big rock.
5. He sits quietly alone for a while and then goes back to the villa.

would sink now and drown; he could not swim the few feet back to the rock. Then he was clutching it and pulling himself up on to it. He lay face down, gasping. He could see nothing but a red-veined, clotted dark. His eyes must have burst, he thought; they were full of blood. He tore off his goggles and a gout of blood went into the sea. His nose was bleeding, and the blood had filled the goggles.

He scooped up handfuls of water from the cool, salty sea, to splash on his face, and did not know whether it was blood or salt water he tasted. After a time, his heart quieted, his eyes cleared, and he sat up. He could see the local boys diving and playing half a mile away. He
❶ did not want them. He wanted nothing but to get back home and lie down.

In a short while, Jerry swam to shore and climbed slowly up the path to the villa. He flung himself on his bed and slept, waking at the sound of feet on the path outside. His mother was coming back. He rushed to the bathroom, thinking she must not see his face with bloodstains, or tearstains, on it. He came out of the bathroom and met her as she walked into the villa, smiling, her eyes lighting up.

"Have a nice morning?" she asked, laying her hand on his warm brown shoulder a moment.

"Oh, yes, thank you," he said.

"You look a bit pale." And then, sharp and anxious, "How did you bang your head?"

"Oh, just banged it," he told her.

She looked at him closely. He was strained; his eyes were glazed-looking. She was worried. And then she said to herself, Oh, don't fuss! Nothing can happen. He can swim like a fish.

They sat down to lunch together.

"Mummy," he said, "I can stay under water for two minutes—three minutes, at least." It came bursting out of him.

"Can you, darling?" she said. "Well, I shouldn't overdo it. I don't think you ought to swim any more today."

She was ready for a battle of wills, but he gave in at once. It was no longer of the least importance to go to the bay.

◆ Build Vocabulary

gout (gout) *n.*: Spurt; splash; glob

Guide for Responding

◆ *Literature and Your Life*

Reader's Response Do you think Jerry's victory is worth the pain and risks entailed? Why or why not?

Thematic Focus How has Jerry changed as a result of his success?

Questions for Research Select a sport (such as scuba diving) and make a list of questions about the sport that could be researched. Discuss what resources you could use to research each question.

☑ Check Your Comprehension

1. What concerns does Jerry's mother have about raising him?
2. (a) Describe Jerry's encounter with the local boys. (b) What effect does it have on him?
3. How does Jerry prepare for his task?
4. Briefly summarize how Jerry finally swims through the tunnel.
5. What happens after Jerry passes the test he sets for himself?

Beyond the Selection

FURTHER READING

Other Works by Doris Lessing

"No Witchcraft for Sale" (1964)

Going Home—nonfiction (1968)

Other Works on the Theme of Clashing Forces

Red Badge of Courage, Stephen Crane

Diary of a Young Girl, Anne Frank

We suggest that you preview these works before recommending them to students.

INTERNET

Please be aware that sites may have changed since we published this information. Students can find out more about Doris Lessing at the following Web site: **http://tile.net/lessing/index.html**

Students can find out more about caves and cave diving at the following Web site: **http://www. caves.org/~cds**

We *strongly recommend* that you preview these sites before sending students to them.

Guide for Responding *(continued)*

◆ Critical Thinking

INTERPRET

1. (a) Describe Jerry's relationship with his mother at the beginning of the story. (b) How does it change by the story's end? Support your answer with examples. **[Analyze]**
2. What must Jerry prove to himself by swimming through the tunnel? **[Infer]**
3. At the end of the story, why is going to the bay "no longer of the least importance" to Jerry? **[Draw Conclusions]**

APPLY

4. Why do many young people set up situations in which they test themselves, as Jerry does? Give examples. **[Speculate]**

EXTEND

5. What jobs require people to meet physical challenges on a regular basis? What are the rewards of some of these jobs? **[Career Link]**

◆ Reading for Success

INTERACTIVE READING STRATEGIES

Review the reading strategies and notes showing how to read interactively. Then apply those strategies to answer the following questions.

1. What hints enable you to predict when Jerry will make his attempt?
2. What words help you form a mental image of Jerry's passage through the tunnel?
3. What does Jerry's experience with the tunnel tell you about the nature of growing up?

◆ Literary Focus

INTERNAL CONFLICT

A conflict involves a struggle between opposing forces. An **internal conflict** involves a character in conflict with himself. Jerry's internal conflict begins as he experiences "a craving that filled his whole body" to be one of the local boys who swim through the tunnel.

1. What are the two opposing forces in the internal conflict?
2. How does the physical challenge make the internal conflict more exciting?

◆ Build Vocabulary

USING THE LATIN ROOT *-lum-*

Knowing that the Latin root *-lum-* means light, define the *-lum-* words that appear in the following sentences.

1. The astronomer observed the *luminous* planet.
2. The torches *illuminate* the cave passage.
3. The scientist studied the *luminosity* of the star.
4. The great scientist is considered a *luminary* of our time.

USING THE WORD BANK: Synonyms

On your paper, write the word from the Word Bank that is the best synonym for each of the following words.

1. spurt
2. shining
3. ridges
4. remorse
5. leaf
6. begging
7. shaking violently

◆ Build Grammar Skills

PARTICIPIAL PHRASES

Doris Lessing uses a variety of sentence elements to keep "Through the Tunnel" moving as swiftly as Jerry through the underwater cave. One element she uses frequently is the participial phrase.

A **participial phrase** consists of a present or past participle (a verb form ending in *-ing, -ed,* or an irregular ending) and any other words that go with it. Participles function as adjectives.

Practice Copy the following sentences in your notebook. Underline each participial phrase and circle the noun it modifies. Each participial phrase begins with a present participle.

1. His mother walked on in front of him, carrying a bright striped bag.
2. Her other arm, swinging loose, was very white in the sun.
3. The boy came up, letting the air out of his lungs.
4. Walking down the path with her, he blurted out, "I'd like to go and have a look at those rocks."

Answers

◆ Critical Thinking 10B TAAS 2–5

1. (a) Jerry's relationship with his mother is close, but in some ways suffocating. (b) By the end of the story, Jerry doesn't feel it is necessary to challenge his mother to prove his independence.
2. Jerry originally wants to prove that he can do what the older boys do. His goal in the end, however, is to prove that he can overcome his own fear.
3. Jerry has proved to himself that he has courage and strength.
4. Students may suggest that, like Jerry, young people feel the need to do something that proves they are strong, mature, or "cool." Some examples may be positive, such as learning to drive or overcoming stage fright to try out for a play. Encourage students to distinguish between healthy and unhealthy challenges.
5. Jobs such as firefighter, construction worker, police officer, and soldier in the armed forces require people to meet physical challenges in the course of their work. Rewards include the satisfaction of meeting a physical challenge, working outdoors, and using strength to help others.

Reading for Success 7B, 7C, 7G TAAS 3–5

1. Jerry's mother's announcement that they will leave in four days is one hint that Jerry will soon make his attempt. Another hint is the internal debate that Jerry has with himself.
2. The words yellowish-gray water, blackness, darkness, and jewel-green help readers form a mental image of what Jerry sees. Sharp pain, inflated balloon, head pulsing, slimy, lungs cracking, and feebly clutching are words that help readers form a mental image of what Jerry feels.
3. Students may say that like Jerry's experience in the tunnel, growing up sometimes involves fear, pain, disappointment, and struggle.

◆ Literary Focus 11F

1. The two main forces in Jerry's internal conflict are his fear and his desire to accomplish his goal.
2. Jerry's internal conflict is intensified for readers by the knowledge that some of the dangers he fears are real possibilities.

◆ Build Vocabulary

Using the Root *-lum-* 6C, 6D

1. shining
2. light up, fill with light
3. light, quality of light
4. shining person, a star

Using the Word Bank 6F

1. gout; 2. luminous; 3. promontories; 4. contrition; 5. frond; 6. supplication; 7. convulsive

◆ Build Grammar Skills 3C

1. *Carrying a bright striped bag* modifies *mother.*
2. *Swinging loose* modifies *arm.*
3. *Letting the air out of his lungs* modifies *boy.*
4. *Walking down the path* modifies *he.*

Grammar Reinforcement

For additional instruction and practice, use the *Writer's Solution Grammar Practice Book* page on Participles and Participial Phrases, p. 41.

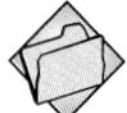

Idea Bank

Following are suggestions for matching the Idea Bank topics with your students' performance levels and learning modalities:

Customizing for
Performance Levels
Less Advanced Students: 1, 5, 6
Average Students: 2, 4, 5, 7
More Advanced: 3, 7

Customizing for
Learning Modalities
Kinesthetic: 1, 4, 6
Visual/Spatial: 6
Verbal/Linguistic: 2, 3, 5
Musical/Rhythmic: 7

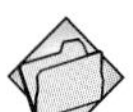

Guided Writing Lesson

Prewriting Strategy Students can use listing to pinpoint the qualities of their travel destination that they want to highlight. Ask each student to write their travel destination on the top of a piece of paper. For the next few minutes, have them write down all of the words, ideas, and experiences they associate with this place. Then, guide them to review their lists and circle the ideas that would be most appealing and persuasive to the reader of a travel brochure.

For more prewriting, elaboration, and revision strategies, see *Prentice Hall Writing and Grammar.*

Writing Lab CD-ROM

Have students complete the tutorial on Description. Follow these steps:

1. Encourage students to preview the criteria for a travel brochure.
2. Suggest that they use the audio-annotated model of a travel brochure.
3. Have students draft on the computer.
4. Tell them to use the Proofreading guidelines for checking for misplaced modifiers.

Build Your Portfolio

Idea Bank

Writing

1. **Water Safety Rules** Jerry is lucky to have survived the dangers of his underwater challenge. Write a list of water safety rules that wiser swimmers should follow. **[Physical Education Link]**
2. **Letter** As Jerry, write a letter to one of your friends at home, describing your accomplishment. Describe your thoughts and feelings before, during, and after your swim.
3. **Observation** Jerry first wants to swim through the tunnel in order to win acceptance from the local boys. Using your own experience, write an observation showing how peer pressure affects people's actions and decisions.

Speaking, Listening, and Viewing

4. **Account of an Outdoor Adventure** Give an oral presentation about an outdoor adventure you have had or would like to experience. Use visuals or props to enliven your presentation.
5. **Dialogue** Imagine that another boy has discovered Jerry's plan and wants to talk him out of it. Role-play the dialogue that might take place between the two boys. **[Performing Arts Link]**

Researching and Representing

6. **Collage** Doris Lessing uses vivid words to describe the setting of this story. Create your own vivid image of the setting in the form of a collage. Incorporate a variety of artistic media and found objects, such as sand, fabric, and shells. **[Art Link]**
7. **Movie Score** Use songs you know to create a musical score for a film version of this story. Choose different songs for different scenes. Play your choices for the class. **[Music Link]**

Online Activity www.phlit.phschool.com

Guided Writing Lesson

Travel Brochure

Choose a vacation place that you have visited or would like to visit and write a travel brochure about it. Packing a lot of information into a small space, use descriptions and colorful images to attract tourists. Provide specific details about things to do and sights to see. The following tip will help you convince readers that your destination is a worthwhile place to visit.

Writing Skills Focus: Persuasive Tone

Persuasive essays use a **persuasive tone**—they take a positive attitude toward the ideas and actions they want readers to accept. Here's how you can achieve a persuasive tone:

- Use words that appeal to readers' senses: *soft, tropical breezes.*
- Convey your own enthusiasm for activities: *a fun-filled afternoon of shopping.*
- Stress the benefits of a place or a plan: *For only a few dollars more, you can . . .*

Prewriting Consider what your readers may desire in a travel destination. Depending on the place you choose, you may want to highlight physical beauty, comfort, historical interest, or activities.

Drafting As you write, introduce your main points with phrases that create appealing images ("Leave the world behind . . .") or compelling reasons ("It's worth an extra day just to . . ."). Don't expect your readers to accept your claims at face value. Support each point you make with details and examples.

Revising Ask a partner to read your brochure to see if he or she would like to visit the place you describe. If not, add descriptions or details that would help persuade your partner to visit the place.

✓ ASSESSMENT OPTIONS

Formal Assessment, Selection Test, pp. 54–56, and Assessment Resources Software. The selection test is designed so that it can be easily customized to the ability levels of your students.

Alternative Assessment, p. 16, includes options for less advanced students, Pre-AP Students, logical/mathematical learners and bodily/ kinesthetic learners.

PORTFOLIO ASSESSMENT

Use the following rubrics in the ***Alternative Assessment*** booklet to assess students' writing:
Water Safety Rules: How-to/Process Explanation Rubric, p. 100
Letter: Expression Rubric, p. 94
Observation: Cause-and-Effect Rubric, p. 102
Guided Writing Lesson: Description Rubric, p. 97

PART 1 *Personal Challenges*

Woman Dragging Key to Keyhole, Brad Holland

One-Minute Planning Guide

The selections in Part 1 offer a variety of perspectives on personal challenges. "The Dog That Bit People" chronicles the humorous challenges of owning a problem dog. In "Conscientious Objector" and "A Man" the speakers describe a positive approach to dealing with choices and challenges. "The Weary Blues" and "Jazz Fantasia" show how music can inspire an individual. "Like the Sun" is a humorous perspective on the challenge of telling the truth, while "Tell all the Truth but tell it slant—" deals with the same theme in a more serious tone.

Customize for *Varying Student Needs*

When assigning the selections in this part to your students, keep in mind the following factors:

"The Dog That Bit People"
- A high-interest short story

"Conscientious Objector"
- Contains allusions with which some students may need help

"A Man"
- A short poem with easy-to-understand symbolism

"The Weary Blues" and "Jazz Fantasia"
- Poems that use dialect and slang

"Like the Sun"
- Vocabulary is more difficult than in other selections
- Terms specific to Indian culture will need to be explained

"Tell all the Truth but tell it slant—"
- A short poem

Humanities: Art

Woman Dragging Key to Keyhole by Brad Holland.

Brad Holland has been a professional artist since the age of 17. He has since created covers for such mainstream publications as *The New Yorker*, *Newsweek*, *The Atlantic Monthly*, and *U.S. News and World Report.*

Call students' attention to the very realistic way in which the artist has painted the key, down to the discolorations and rubbed spots on the metal. Invite them to contrast such details with the other, less representational aspects of the painting—the mysterious looming dark space, the fact that the key is as large as the woman but nowhere near a match for the size of that mysterious keyhole, the sketchiness of the area where the woman stands, the way the woman herself is faceless and almost blends into the keyhole.

Help students link the painting to the theme of Part 1, Personal Challenges, by answering the following questions:

1. What might the huge, dark space of the keyhole represent? *The keyhole might represent the unknown future or a problem the woman has to face.*
2. What might the artist be suggesting by making the key the woman drags very large but still much smaller than the keyhole? *The artist might be suggesting that we have resources to deal with our problems, but the problem often seems—and sometimes is—greater than our resources.*

Prepare and Engage

LESSON OBJECTIVES

1. **To develop vocabulary and word identification skills**
   - Greek Prefixes: *epi-*
   - Using the Word Bank: Synonyms
   - Extending Word Study: Use Reference Materials (ATE)
2. **To use a variety of reading strategies to comprehend a humorous essay**
   - Connect Your Experience
   - Reading Strategy: Form Mental Images
   - Tips to Guide Reading: Sustained Reading (ATE)
   - Read to Be Entertained (ATE)
   - Idea Bank: Lost Dog Description
   - Idea Bank: News Story
3. **To increase knowledge of other cultures and to connect common elements across cultures**
   - Connecting Themes Across Cultures (ATE)
4. **To express and support responses to the text**
   - Critical Thinking
   - Analyze Literary Criticism (ATE)
5. **To analyze literary elements**
   - Literary Focus: Humorous Essay
   - Idea Bank: Persuasive Letter to Mother
6. **To read in order to research self-selected and assigned topics**
   - Idea Bank: Dog Breed Chart
7. **To plan, prepare, organize, and present literary interpretations**
   - Idea Bank: Pantomime
   - Idea Bank: Wanted Poster
   - Speaking, Viewing, and Listening Mini-Lesson: Pet Talk
8. **To use recursive writing processes to write an animal anecdote**
   - Guided Writing Lesson
9. **To increase knowledge of the rules of grammar and usage**
   - Build Grammar Skills: Correct use of *like* and *as if*

Test Preparation

Reading Comprehension: Stated and Implied Main Ideas (ATE, p. 233) The teaching tips and sample test item in this workshop support the instruction and practice in the unit workshop:
Reading Comprehension: Stated and Implied Main Ideas (SE, p. 299)

Guide for Reading

James Thurber *(1894–1961)*

From Carol Burnett to Jerry Seinfeld, today's popular comedians make millions of people laugh by finding the humor in everyday life. Writer James Thurber helped lay the groundwork for this kind of comedy back in the 1920's.

> ***Thurber made people laugh by poking fun at pesky pets, stressed-out spouses, and misplaced valuables.***

From Clerk to Cartoonist

Thurber was born in Columbus, Ohio. He never completed college, leaving to become a clerk in the U.S. State Department. Soon, however, Thurber turned to writing and cartooning. Much of his early work appeared in *The New Yorker*. His cartoons of frightened men, menacing women, wicked children, and silent, observing animals delighted readers across the country.

Whimsical Style Thurber's whimsical, comedic style fills his autobiography, *My Life and Hard Times* (1933), with laughter and comic richness. In "The Dog That Bit People," which comes from this book, Thurber creates a likeable but hysterical character who also happens to be a dog.

Although Thurber left *The New Yorker* staff in 1933, he remained a leading contributor. In 1940, failing eyesight forced him to decrease his drawing. By 1952, when he became almost totally blind, he had to give it up altogether. He still continued, however, to contribute articles to numerous magazines.

Other works by James Thurber include *Fables for Our Time* (1940), *The Male Animal* (1941), and "The Secret Life of Walter Mitty."

◆ Build Vocabulary

GREEK PREFIXES: *epi-*

In this selection, you will encounter the word *epitaph*. The Greek prefix *epi-* can mean "upon," "outside," "among," or "above." Knowing this definition gives you a clue to the meaning of *epitaph*—an inscription on a tomb or gravestone.

incredulity
choleric
irascible
jangle
indignant
epitaph

WORD BANK

As you read this essay, you will encounter the words on this list. Each word is defined on the page where it first appears. Preview the list before you read.

◆ Build Grammar Skills

CORRECT USE OF *LIKE* AND *AS IF*

Even though he writes in an informal style, Thurber follows the rules of good usage, including using ***like*** and ***as if*** correctly. Although it's a common mistake, *like* cannot be used in place of *as if*.

Like is used to introduce a prepositional phrase—a preposition and a noun or pronoun.

Muggs could read him *like* a book.

As if is used to introduce a subordinate clause—a group of words that contains a subject and a verb but cannot stand alone as a sentence.

He always acted *as if* he thought I wasn't one of the family.

Prentice Hall Literature Program Resources

REINFORCE / RETEACH / EXTEND

Selection Support Pages
Build Vocabulary: The Prefix *epi-*, p. 68
Build Grammar Skills: *Like* and *As If*, p. 69
Reading Strategy: Form Mental Images, p. 70
Literary Focus: Humorous Essay, p. 71

Strategies for Diverse Student Needs, p. 17

Beyond Literature
Career Connection: Humor Columnist, p. 17

Formal Assessment Selection Test, pp. 57–58; Assessment Resources Software

Alternative Assessment, p. 17

Resource Pro CD-ROM

Listening to Literature Audiocassettes

The Dog That Bit People

◆ Literature and Your Life

Connect Your Experience

You may not think of yourself as a comedian—but you've probably made people laugh! In some way, we are all comedians. We all share stories and experiences with friends or relatives, exaggerating details to get a bigger laugh from our audience.

By giving a little twist of the ridiculous to your stories, you are following in the footsteps of comic writers like James Thurber. In this essay, he makes an irritable family pet into an unforgettable character.

Journal Writing Jot down several amusing real-life situations that, although they were not funny at the time, would make amusing stories.

Thematic Focus: Personal Challenges

In "The Dog That Bit People," James Thurber uses humor to lighten the seriousness of having a "challenging" pet. What does his essay reveal about the use of humor to help ease a conflict?

◆ Reading Strategy

Form Mental Images

All comic writers are cartoonists, whether or not they draw. They create humorous images with words. As you read, you **form mental images** of the funny situations they describe.

Don't just read this essay as words on the page. Think of it as a verbal cartoon. Picture the expressions on people's faces. See the dog chewing up the morning paper. By the end of this essay, you will have created a mental comic book.

◆ Background for Understanding

Art

James Thurber enjoyed a dual career as a writer and a cartoonist. Indeed, the lines of his drawings, as you can see, are as whimsical as the lines of his prose.

Thurber created nearly 500 cartoons—sketchy scribbles of men, women, children, and animals, especially dogs. People related to these cartoons. They felt as if they *knew* Thurber's overworked guy at the office or his angry woman filing a complaint with the police department.

In "The Dog That Bit People," James Thurber's cartoons combine with his prose to depict Muggs and his long list of "victims."

Lots of People Reported Our Dog to the Police, James Thurber

◆ Literary Focus

Humorous Essay

A **humorous essay** is a nonfiction composition that presents the author's thoughts on a subject in an amusing way. This lighthearted approach is intended to make the reader laugh.

A writer may create humor in an essay by describing a ridiculous situation in a serious way or by using exaggeration. Thurber uses anecdotes—brief stories about an event—to create humor in his essay about the vicious dog Muggs.

Test Preparation Workshop

Reading Comprehension: Stated and Implied Main Ideas As students prepare for the SAT or ACT tests, they should review strategies for determining main ideas. Ask students to read the first paragraph of "The Dog That Bit People" on p. 234.

What is the best title for this passage?

A Garage Men Hate Dogs
B Carefully Groomed Poodles
C Dogs Bring Pleasure
D Terrier Births Puppy on the Street

As students study the answer choices with which they are presented, remind them that main idea questions on standardized tests often have general answers. Students can probably arrive at the best answer to the question by using the process of elimination to rule out answers that are too specific, or only partly true. By analyzing the choices, they should be able to determine that *A, B,* and *D* are specific details from the paragraph. Answer *C* is the most general and therefore the best choice for a passage title (or main idea).

Interest Grabber Have students brainstorm for a list of their favorite animated and live comedy shows. Ask students to describe the type of humor in each show and to identify some of the techniques used to achieve the humor. Students might suggest such elements as exaggeration, sight gags, and word play. Guide students to present specific examples from each show. Then have students use the title and the introductory illustrations to predict how Thurber will create humor in this essay.

Tips to Guide Reading

Sustained Reading Use an amusing manner to read the first page of Thurber's essay aloud to students. Challenge them to continue with this humorous approach to the essay as they silently read it without stopping.

Customize for *Less Proficient Readers*
Guide less proficient readers in identifying the individual ideas expressed in some of Thurber's longer, more complex sentences.

Customize for *Pre-AP Students*
Ask students to retell the story from a different point of view. For example, have students use Muggs as the narrator. Then have students compare their retelling to Thurber's and analyze the effect of Thurber's choices of narrator and point of view on the essay's humor.

Customize for *English Language Learners*
Students may recognize some words but not understand them as they are used in this narrative. Help students clarify the meaning in context of words such as *miniature* (small dog), *garage* (repair shop), *good side* (in favor), and *humor* (attitude).

Customize for *Gifted/Talented Students*
Suggest that students work together in small groups to evaluate Thurber's problems with Muggs's behavior, composing a list of possible solutions that Thurber might wish to try.

Develop Understanding

One-Minute Insight Thurber uses exaggeration and contrast to achieve humor in this series of bad-dog anecdotes, but this master comic has other tricks up his sleeve as well. In addition, he uses understatement, irony, absurdity, and digression to keep his readers chuckling. Thurber's wry anecdotes will help students see that humor is a combination of keen observation of details and a unique style of reporting those details.

◆ Literary Focus

1 Humorous Essay Ask students how Thurber creates humor in this portion of the essay. *He creates humor through exaggeration, claiming that Muggs gave him more trouble than fifty-five or more other dogs. Then Thurber digresses with long, involved sentences in which each detail increases the absurdity of the situation.*

◆ Reading Strategy

2 Form Mental Images Have students visualize the scene described in this passage and invite them to verbalize what is funny about the mental images they form. *Lead students to grasp that the humor in this description comes from the absurdity of the mental image and the juxtaposition of images. The sight of a person holding a fancy green parasol over a poodle wearing a bib is unusual enough, but the humor is heightened when Thurber adds the tough garage men.*

◆ Literature and Your Life

3 Lead a discussion of why it can sometimes be helpful to laugh at oneself. Elicit from students examples of how the embarrassment or aggravation of certain situations can be alleviated with humor.

Customize for
Less Proficient Readers
Help students identify the three related ideas expressed in the opening sentence: (1) Thurber has had a lot of dogs. (2) Most of Thurber's dogs have given him more pleasure than trouble. (3) The Airedale named Muggs gave him more trouble than pleasure.

The Dog That Bit People

James Thurber

1 Probably no one man should have as many dogs in his life as I have had, but there was more pleasure than distress in them for me except in the case of an Airedale[1] named Muggs. He gave me more trouble than all the other fifty-four or-five put together, although my moment of keenest embarrassment was the time a Scotch terrier named Jeannie, who had just had six puppies in the clothes closet of a fourth floor apartment in New York, had the unexpected seventh and last at the corner of Eleventh Street and Fifth Avenue during a walk she had insisted on taking. Then, too, there was the prize winning French poodle, a great big black poodle—none of your little, untroublesome white miniatures—who got sick riding in the rumble seat[2] of a car with me on her way to the 2 Greenwich Dog Show. She had a red rubber bib tucked around her throat and, since a rain storm came up when we were halfway through the Bronx, I had to hold over her a small green umbrella, really more of a parasol. The rain beat down fearfully and suddenly the driver of the car drove into a big garage, filled with mechanics. 3 It happened so quickly that I forgot to put the umbrella down and I will always remember, with sickening distress, the look of incredulity mixed with hatred that came over the face of the particular hardened garage man that came over to see what we wanted, when he took a look at me and the poodle. All garage men, and people of that intolerant stripe, hate poodles with their curious hair

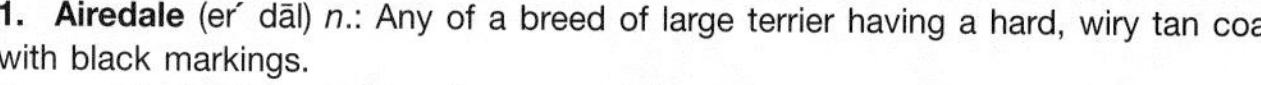

1. **Airedale** (er´ dāl) *n.*: Any of a breed of large terrier having a hard, wiry tan coat with black markings.
2. **rumble seat:** In some earlier automobiles, an open seat in the rear, behind the roofed seat, which could be folded shut when not in use.

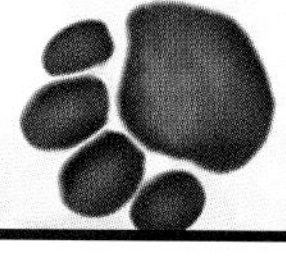

Block Scheduling Strategies

Consider these suggestions to take advantage of extended class time:

- Introduce the selection by playing a portion of the essay on the Listening to Literature audiocassette.
- Introduce the Build Grammar Skills topic—the correct use of *like* and *as if* (p. 232). After students have completed the exercise on p. 240, pairs of students can create dialogues showing how to use *like* and *as if* correctly.
- Have Pre-AP students work together to identify examples of irony, understatement, and digression while average students identify examples of exaggeration. Meanwhile, work with less proficient readers and ESL students to break down sentences and complete ***Strategies for Diverse Student Needs***, p. 17.
- Discussion groups can share their answers to the Reader's Response and Thematic Focus portions of the Guide for Responding, p. 239.

Nobody Knew Exactly What Was the Matter with Him

Nobody Knew Exactly What Was the Matter With Him, James Thurber

cut, especially the pom-poms that you got to leave on their hips if you expect the dogs to win a prize.

But the Airedale, as I have said, was the worst of all my dogs. He really wasn't my dog, as a matter of fact: I came home from a vacation one summer to find that my brother Roy had bought him while I was away. A big, burly, choleric dog, he always acted as if he thought I wasn't one of the family. There was a slight advantage in being one of the family, for he didn't bite the family as often as he bit strangers. Still, in the years that we had him he bit everybody but mother, and he made a pass at her once but missed. That was during the month when we suddenly had mice, and Muggs refused to do anything about them. Nobody ever had mice exactly like the mice we had that month. They acted like pet mice, almost like mice somebody had trained. They were so friendly that one night when mother entertained at dinner the Friraliras, a club she and my father had belonged to for twenty years, she put down a lot of little dishes with food in them on the pantry floor so that the mice would be satisfied with that and wouldn't come into the dining room. Muggs stayed out in the pantry with the mice, lying on the floor,

◆ Build Vocabulary

incredulity (in′ krə do͞o′ lə tē) *n.*: Unwillingness or inability to believe

choleric (käl′ ər ik) *adj.*: Quick-tempered

Humanities: Art

Nobody Knew Exactly What Was the Matter With Him, 1933, by James Thurber.

Thurber is well known for his sketches of sad-faced animals and frustrated humans trying to deal with zany situations. This cartoon of Muggs is typical of his cartoon style. It derives its humor from the dog's human facial expression and body position. Use these questions for discussion:

1. How does Thurber accentuate the human qualities that the dog seems to possess? *The furrowed brow and frowning mouth give the dog a human facial expression; the way the dog is resting his head on his paws is a pose more likely to be seen in a human than a dog.*
2. What effect does the dog's posture create? *The posture reinforces the impression of the dog's belligerent attitude.*
3. What can you infer about the dog's personality from this sketch? *The dog looks irritable and uncooperative.*

◆ Literary Focus

4 Humorous Essay Ask students what is funny about this passage. *The author explains a ridiculous situation in a serious way, "... he didn't bite the family as often as he bit strangers." He makes it sounds as if it were acceptable for Muggs to bite the family because he did it less often.*

◆ Literary Focus

5 Humorous Essay Call students' attention to the shift in topic. Ask students to identify the effects of this shift. *Thurber shifts from Muggs's biting people to Muggs's reaction to mice. Thurber's moving quickly from one topic to another allows him to build the humor, adding one ridiculous detail on top of another. In addition, the statement "That was during the month when we suddenly had mice..." gives a personal, conversational feel to the essay, as if Thurber is telling the story in person.*

◆ Reading Strategy

6 Form Mental Images Have students share the mental images they formed from this passage. *Students should envision a foul-tempered dog muttering like a woebegone child, surrounded by a "party" of mice eating from little dishes on the floor.*

Read to Be Entertained

Thurber's humorous essay provides an excellent opportunity for students to read to be entertained and amused.

Extending Word Study

Thesaurus Ask students to skim through the first two pages of the selection and list the descriptive, colorful words that Thurber uses. For example, they might list: white miniatures, red rubber bib, and parasol. Next to each word on the list, have students use a thesaurus to write a phrase that has a similar meaning.

◆ Literary Focus

❶ **Humorous Essay** Students should mention that the exaggerated tameness of the mice highlights Muggs's unwillingness to do anything to help his human family. Thurber is strengthening the humorous impression that the household is run for Muggs's convenience.

◆ Critical Thinking

❷ **Making Inferences** Ask students what they can infer from this detail. *Readers can infer that Thurber's mother felt affection for Muggs, because she made excuses for him. Her feelings are probably the reason the family doesn't get rid of Muggs.*

◆ Literary Focus

❸ **Humorous Essay** Ask students what effect Thurber achieves by including details such as the exact location where Major Moberly fired at Muggs or the Congressman's astrological sign. *Including precise, realistic details in this absurd anecdote makes it sound serious—and therefore, even funnier.*

◆ Build Grammar Skills

❹ ***Like* and *As If*** Have students explain why Thurber uses the word *like* rather than the phrase *as if* here. Challenge them to change the sentence so that *as if* would be correct. *Thurber uses* like *to introduce the prepositional phrase* "like a book." As *if could introduce the subordinate clause* "as if he were a book," *if the sentence were rewritten.*

◆ Reading Strategy

❺ **Form Mental Images** Students should identify these words and details: the modifiers *moodily, brass, vicious,* precise nouns *grapefruit, leap, fire screen,* and participial phrases *scattering dishes, spilling the coffee.*

◆ Critical Thinking

❻ **Draw Conclusions** Ask students: Why is Mother forever defending Muggs? *Based on the information in this paragraph and inferences they have made earlier in the essay, students should conclude that Mother defends Muggs's behavior because she loves him.*

◆ Literary Focus
❶ Explain how the exaggeration of the mice adds humor to this scene.

growling to himself—not at the mice, but about all the people in the next room that he would have liked to get at. Mother slipped out into the pantry once to see how everything was going. Everything was going fine. It made her so mad to see Muggs lying there, oblivious of the mice—they came running up to her—that she slapped him and he slashed at her, but didn't make it. He was sorry immediately, mother said. He was always sorry, she said, after he bit someone, but we could not understand how she figured this out. He didn't act sorry.

Mother used to send a box of candy every
❷ Christmas to the people the Airedale bit. The list finally contained forty or more names. Nobody could understand why we didn't get rid of the dog. I didn't understand it very well myself, but we didn't get rid of him. I think that one or two people tried to poison Muggs—he acted poisoned once in a while—and old Major Moberly fired at him once with his service revolver near the Seneca Hotel in East Broad Street—but Muggs lived to be almost eleven years old and even when he could hardly get around he bit a
❸ Congressman who had called to see my father on business. My mother had never liked the Congressman—she said the signs of his horoscope showed he couldn't be trusted (he was Saturn with the moon in Virgo)—but she sent him a box of candy that Christmas. He sent it right back, probably because he suspected it was trick candy. Mother persuaded herself it was all for the best that the dog had bitten him, even though father lost an important business association because of it. "I wouldn't be associ-
❹ ated with such a man," mother said, "Muggs could read him like a book."

We used to take turns feeding Muggs to be on his good side, but that didn't always work. He was never in a very good humor, even after a meal. Nobody knew exactly what was the matter with him, but whatever it was it made him irascible, especially in the mornings. Roy never felt very well in the morning, either, especially before breakfast, and once when he came downstairs and found that Muggs had moodily chewed up the morning paper he hit him in the face with a grapefruit and then jumped up on the dining room table, scattering dishes and silverware and spilling the coffee. Muggs' first free leap carried him all the way across the table and into a brass fire screen in front of the gas grate but he was back on his feet in a moment and in the end he got Roy and gave him a pretty vicious bite in the leg. Then he was all over it; he never bit anyone more than once at a time. Mother always mentioned that as an argument in his favor; she said he had a quick temper but that he didn't hold a grudge. She was forever defending him. I think she liked him because he wasn't well. "He's not strong," she would say, pityingly, but that was inaccurate; he may not have been well but he was terribly strong.

◆ Reading Strategy
Identify the details that help you form a mental picture of this scene.

One time my mother went to the Chittenden Hotel to call on a woman mental healer who was lecturing in Columbus on the subject of "Harmonious Vibrations." She wanted to find out if it was possible to get harmonious vibrations into a dog. "He's a large tan-colored Airedale," mother explained. The woman said that she had never treated a dog but she advised my mother to hold the thought that he did not bite and would not bite. Mother was holding the thought the very next morning when Muggs got

◆ Build Vocabulary

irascible (i ras´ ə bəl) *adj.*: Easily angered; quick-tempered

jangle (jaŋ´ gəl) *n.*: Discord; harsh sounds

Speaking, Listening, and Viewing Mini-Lesson

Pet Talk

This mini-lesson supports the Speaking, Listening, and Viewing activity in the Idea Bank on p. 241.

Introduce Students will prepare a radio talk show in which listeners call in with questions about their pets and a panel answers the questions. Their radio show will be assessed on the accuracy and clarity of their answers.

Develop Guide students toward resources that will help them find accurate answers to their questions. Suggest that they look for information on the Internet, interview veterinarians and animal trainers if possible.

Apply Based on what they discover through research, students may wish to modify or add questions. Tell students to prepare a script that gives the order of questions and to make sure that the panel is well prepared to answer the questions agreed upon.

Assess Assess the radio show based on evidence of research, accuracy of information, and clarity of presentation.

Muggs at His Meals Was an Unusual Sight, James Thurber

the iceman but she blamed that slip-up on the iceman. "If you didn't think he would bite you, he wouldn't," mother told him. He stomped out of the house in a terrible jangle of vibrations.

One morning when Muggs bit me slightly, more or less in passing, I reached down and grabbed his short stumpy tail and hoisted him into the air. It was a foolhardy thing to do and the last time I saw my mother, about six months ago, she said she didn't know what possessed me. I don't either, except that I was pretty mad. As long as I held the dog off the floor by his tail he couldn't get at me, but he twisted and jerked so, snarling all the time, that I realized I couldn't hold him that way very long. I carried him to the kitchen and flung him onto the floor and shut the door on him just as he crashed against it. But I forgot about the backstairs. Muggs went up the backstairs and down the frontstairs and had me cornered in the living room. I managed to get up onto 9
the mantelpiece above the fireplace, but it gave way and came down with a tremendous crash throwing a large marble clock, several vases, and myself heavily to the floor. Muggs was so alarmed by the racket that when I picked myself up he had disappeared. We couldn't find him anywhere, although we whistled and

Analyze Literary Criticism

In his review of Harrison Kinney's biography of James Thurber, Robert David Sullivan states: "James Thurber is a survivor. In bookstores today, he holds on while the humor section is overrun by Letterman, Seinfeld, and other TV Guide cover models. . . . Thurber and his drawings of meek husbands and sympathetic bloodhounds still occupy a few lonely inches of shelf space. . . . The style of writing may be casual, but it's not easy. Even the punctuation is perfect; it's impossible to read Thurber without falling into the inflections and pauses that he intended." Share this description of Thurber's humorous writing style with students. Then, have students discuss whether or not they agree with the statements.

1. Do you think Thurber's humor will survive for years to come? Why or why not? *Students will probably recognize that Thurber's humor has a timeless quality for some people because of its universal themes.*
2. Find an example of Thurber's punctuation that is used to indicate a desired pause in reading. *Students may identify colons, semicolons, and em dashes that indicate readers' pauses.*

7 Clarification Explain that in the early part of the twentieth century, people kept their food cold in an "icebox" rather than an electric refrigerator. Icemen delivered blocks of ice that were placed in the icebox.

◆ Literary Focus

8 Humorous Essay Call students' attention to the contrast between the result Thurber's mother expects and the result she gets. Explain that this kind of irony is frequently used in humorous essays.

◆ Literature and Your Life

9 Ask students how they think Thurber was feeling when he had this experience. Why do they think he is able to tell it as a humorous anecdote now? *Most students will say that Thurber felt a mixture of fear and anger when he had the experience, but that the fact that he didn't get hurt badly after all and the time that has passed have enabled him to take a humorous view of the event.*

Humanities: Art

Muggs at His Meals, 1933, by James Thurber.

This cartoon shows Muggs eating his dinner at a table, as described in the essay. Through simple lines and basic forms, Thurber captures the essence of the humorous situation. The dog's turned head and annoyed expression hint that a confrontation is about to occur.

Use these questions for discussion:

1. What does Muggs's posture suggest about his personality? *Muggs is guarding his food. His posture conveys his combative personality.*
2. How does this picture support what you've learned about Muggs from reading the essay? *The essay indicates that the family made special accommodations for Muggs because of his irritable personality. The picture shows him eating at a table, probably another special accommodation the family has made.*

◆ Literary Focus

❶ **Humorous Essay** Elicit responses that note the following: *The discrepancy between the dog's vicious attack and Mother's unrealistic explanation play on the reader's sense of the absurd—an important ingredient in a sense of humor.*

◆ Critical Thinking

❷ **Make Inferences** Ask students how they explain Mother's treatment of Muggs in this anecdote. *In Mother's eyes, Muggs can do no wrong. She defends Muggs because she sees him as misunderstood; she overindulges him by rewarding bad behavior. She treats him in much the way an overindulgent mother treats a spoiled child.*

◆ Literary Focus

❸ **Humorous Essay** Ask students to explain how this anecdote adds humor to the essay. *This anecdote highlights the ridiculousness of the way the family treats Muggs by viewing their behavior through an outsider's eyes. Second, exaggeration makes Uncle Horatio a humorous character. His outburst is all the more ridiculous because he wants to "do battle" with a dog.*

Customize for Bodily/Kinesthetic Learners

Have these students hold a bag of books or some other heavy object at arm's length to help them appreciate the difficulty Thurber has keeping the dog off the floor.

Reteach

Writers, such as Thurber, often use exaggeration to create images that provide readers with mental pictures. Discuss the appeal of visual humor and slapstick comedy with students. Then have them identify images of visual humor such as Thurber holding a snarling dog by the tail.

Have students make a chart with the headings: Image and Sense. As they identify a mental image description, have them enter it into the chart and then label the sense.

image	sense
snarling dog	*sight; sound*

shouted, until old Mrs. Detweiler called after dinner that night. Muggs had bitten her once, in the leg, and she came into the living room only after we assured her that Muggs had run away. She had just seated herself when, with a great growling and scratching of claws, Muggs emerged from under a davenport[3] where he had been quietly hiding all the time, and bit her again. Mother examined the bite and put arnica[4] on it and told Mrs. Detweiler that it was only a bruise. "He just bumped you," she said. But Mrs. Detweiler left the house in a nasty state of mind.

> ◆ **Literary Focus** ❶
> How does this anecdote highlight the ridiculousness of Mother's defense of Muggs?

Lots of people reported our Airedale to the police but my father held a municipal office at the time and was on friendly terms with the police. Even so, the cops had been out a couple of times—once when Muggs bit Mrs. Rufus Sturtevant and again when he bit Lieutenant-Governor Malloy—but mother told them that it hadn't been Muggs' fault but the fault of the people who were bitten. "When he starts for them, they scream," she explained, "and that excites him." ❷ The cops suggested that it might be a good idea to tie the dog up, but mother said that it mortified him to be tied up and that he wouldn't eat when he was tied up.

Muggs at his meals was an unusual sight. Because of the fact that if you reached toward the floor he would bite you, we usually put his food plate on top of an old kitchen table with a bench alongside the table. Muggs would stand on the bench and eat. I remember that my mother's Uncle Horatio, who boasted that he was the third man up Missionary Ridge,[5] was splutteringly indignant when he found out that we fed the dog on a table because we were afraid to put his plate on the floor. He said he wasn't afraid of any dog that ever lived and that he would put the dog's plate on the floor if we would give it to him. Roy said that if Uncle Horatio had fed Muggs on the ground just before the battle he would have been the first man up Missionary Ridge. Uncle Horatio was furious. "Bring him in! Bring him in now!" he shouted. "I'll feed the—on the floor!" Roy was all for giving him a chance, but my father wouldn't hear of it. He said that Muggs had already been fed. "I'll feed him again!" bawled Uncle Horatio. We had quite a time quieting him.

In his last year Muggs used to spend practically all of his time outdoors. He didn't like to stay in the house for some reason or other—perhaps it held too many unpleasant memories for him. Anyway, it was hard to get him to come in and as a result the garbage man, the iceman, and the laundryman wouldn't come near the house. We had to haul the garbage down to the corner, take the laundry out and bring it back, and meet the iceman a block from home. After this had gone on for some time we hit on an ingenious arrangement for getting the dog in the house so that we could lock him up while the gas meter was read, and so on. Muggs was afraid of only one thing, an electrical storm. Thunder and lightning frightened him out of his senses (I think he thought a storm had broken the day the mantelpiece fell). He would rush into the house and hide under a bed or in a clothes closet. So we fixed up a thunder machine out of a long narrow piece of sheet iron with a wooden handle on one end. Mother would shake this vigorously when she wanted to get Muggs into the house. It made an excellent imitation of thunder, but I suppose it was the most roundabout system for

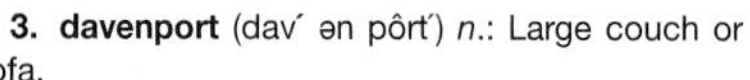

3. **davenport** (dav´ ən pôrt´) *n.*: Large couch or sofa.
4. **arnica** (är´ ni kə) *n.*: Preparation made from certain plants, once used for treating sprains, bruises, and so forth.

5. **Missionary Ridge:** Hill south of Chattanooga, Tennessee, that was the site of a Civil War battle.

Cross-Curricular Connection: Social Studies

Dogs and People Generally considered the first domesticated animals, dogs have coexisted with humans as pets and working partners through the ages in nearly all cultures. Originally, there were only a few species of *Canis familiaris*; through selective breeding, nearly 150 breeds exist today. The smallest dogs weigh less than two pounds; the largest ones tip the scales at over 200 pounds.

In addition to providing companionship, dogs fulfill many other functions today. For example, dogs often work with police officers on patrol duty. Some breeds of dogs, such as collies, are herders; huskies draw transport sleds in the Arctic; others, notably golden retrievers, aid the visually impaired and hearing impaired.

Have students work in small groups to discuss the care and training of dogs kept as family pets. Students should consider proper food, bedding, exercise, training, grooming, and affectionate care. Have them consider how they would cope with the problems of owning a dog like Muggs.

running a household that was ever devised. It took a lot out of mother.

A few months before Muggs died, he got to "seeing things." He would rise slowly from the floor, growling low, and stalk stiff-legged and menacing toward nothing at all. Sometimes the Thing would be just a little to the right or left of a visitor. Once a Fuller Brush salesman got hysterics. Muggs came wandering into the room like Hamlet[6] following his father's ghost. His eyes were fixed on a spot just to the left of the Fuller Brush man, who stood it until Muggs was about three slow, creeping paces from him. Then he shouted. Muggs wavered on past him into the hallway grumbling to himself but the Fuller man went on shouting. I think mother had to throw a pan of cold water on him before he stopped. That was the way she used to stop us boys when we got into fights.

Muggs died quite suddenly one night. Mother wanted to bury him in the family lot under a marble stone with some such inscription as "Flights of angels sing thee to thy rest" 5 but we persuaded her it was against the law. In the end we just put up a smooth board above his grave along a lonely road. On the board I wrote with an indelible pencil "Cave Canem."[7] Mother was quite pleased with the simple classic dignity of the old Latin epitaph.

6. **Hamlet:** The tragic hero of the play *Hamlet* by William Shakespeare. Hamlet follows his father's ghost and learns that his father, a Danish king, had been murdered by Hamlet's uncle Claudius.

7. **Cave Canem** (kä' vä kä' nəm): Latin for "Beware the dog."

◆ Build Vocabulary

indignant (in dig' nənt) *adj.*: Feeling or expressing anger or scorn, especially at an injustice

epitaph (ep' ə taf) *n.*: Inscription on a tomb or gravestone

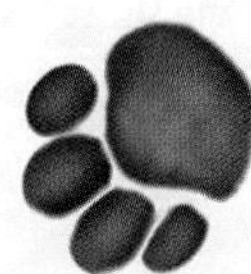

Guide for Responding

◆ Literature and Your Life

Reader's Response Which one of Muggs's escapades did you find most amusing? Why?

Thematic Focus James Thurber uses humor to lighten the seriousness of his dog's behavioral problems. Tell about an incident in which you used humor to ease a conflict or lighten a moment in your life.

Questions for Research If you were to conduct research on James Thurber, to what questions about him would you like to find answers?

☑ Check Your Comprehension

1. Who is the only person in Thurber's family never bitten by Muggs?
2. Briefly summarize the anecdote about Muggs and the mice.
3. Describe Thurber's "foolhardy" experience with Muggs.
4. Describe how Muggs eats his meals. Why does he eat this way?
5. Tell what Muggs does in his last year.

◆ Literary Focus

4 Humorous Essay Ask students what is funny about comparing Muggs to Hamlet. *Lead students to see the humor in comparing a dog to a tragic hero. As a result of the incongruity in the comparison, the mental image the scene evokes is quite ridiculous.*

5 Clarification Tell students that the lines, "... Good-night, sweet prince,/And flights of angels sing thee to thy rest!" is from the last act of *Hamlet*, spoken by Hamlet's friend as Hamlet dies.

Answers

◆ Literature and Your Life

Reader's Response Possible answers include: Muggs's attack on Roy, Muggs's manner of eating, Muggs's attack on Thurber, and Muggs's reaction to the "storm machine."

Thematic Focus Refer students to the notes they jotted down in the journal writing activity they completed before reading the selection (p. 233).

Questions for Research Help students formulate interesting and relevant questions that they can use in their research about James Thurber such as: When did he begin writing?

☑ Check Your Comprehension

1. Muggs never bit Mother.
2. During a dinner party, Muggs was locked in the pantry. His unwillingness to guard against mice frustrated Mother to the point where she slapped him. As a result, Muggs made his only attempt to bite Mother, but he missed.
3. Thurber foolishly grabbed Muggs by the tail in anger, then realized that he couldn't let him go without getting bitten. When released, Muggs chased Thurber onto a mantelpiece which came crashing down, frightening Muggs away.
4. Muggs eats at a table because the family is afraid he will bite them if they set his food on the floor.
5. During his last year, Muggs stalks imaginary things.

Beyond the Selection

FURTHER READING

Other Works by James Thurber

The Owl in the Attic and Other Perplexities
The Middle-Aged Man on the Flying Trapeze

Other Works About Animals and Conflict

Whitefang, Jack London
"Growltiger's Last Stand," T. S. Eliot

We suggest that you preview these works before recommending them to your students.

INTERNET

Students can read excerpts from Thurber's *Fables for Our Time* at the following Internet address. (Please be aware that sites may have changed since we published this information.)

http://www.escape.com/~tansal/Authors/Thurber/index.htm

We *strongly recommend* that you preview this site before sending students to it.

Guide for Responding (continued)

◆ Critical Thinking

INTERPRET

1. Describe the portrait of Muggs that Thurber creates. **[Infer]**

2. How do different family members react to the dog? **[Compare and Contrast]**

3. Why doesn't the family get rid of Muggs? **[Draw Conclusions]**

EVALUATE

4. Choose one of Thurber's stories about Muggs and rate how well Thurber conveys its humor. **[Evaluate]**

APPLY

5. Thurber describes an aspect of his home life in a humorous way. What other aspects of daily life could be the subject of a humorous essay? **[Relate]**

◆ Reading Strategy

FORM MENTAL IMAGES

The details in Thurber's story help you **form mental images**—pictures in your mind—of Muggs and his escapades. You "see" the fear in the eyes of Mrs. Detweiler, "hear" the clash of the sheet iron that scares Muggs, and "feel" sharp teeth biting at your leg.

1. What details help you form a mental image of Roy's reaction to the chewed up newspaper? Explain.

2. Find three details that help you picture Muggs.

3. Which mental picture inspired by this essay is most vivid? Why?

◆ Literary Focus

HUMOROUS ESSAY

In his **humorous essay,** Thurber transforms everyday events into an amusing series of stories. He conveys humor by exaggerating actions and reactions and by treating silly things seriously. For example, he exaggerates Uncle Horatio's response to Muggs's eating habits to create a ridiculous picture of a "heroic" uncle defying a ferocious dog.

1. Explain how Thurber uses exaggeration to make his readers laugh.

2. Show how Thurber creates humor by treating a silly situation as if it were serious.

◆ Build Vocabulary

USING THE GREEK PREFIX *epi-*

The Greek prefix *epi-* can mean "upon," "outside," "over," or "among." Explain how one or another of these meanings contributes to the definition of each of these words:

1. epitaph
2. epidermis
3. epicenter
4. epidemic
5. epilogue

USING THE WORD BANK: Synonyms

In your notebook, write a word from Column B next to its synonym from Column A.

Column A	Column B
1. irascible	**a.** disbelief
2. indignant	**b.** cranky
3. choleric	**c.** upset
4. incredulity	**d.** hot-headed
5. epitaph	**e.** vibration
6. jangle	**f.** inscription

◆ Build Grammar Skills

CORRECT USE OF *LIKE* AND *AS IF*

Thurber avoids the common usage error of using ***like*** in place of ***as if.*** As a preposition, *like* can be combined with a noun or pronoun to make a comparison. *As if* is used to introduce a subordinate clause (a group of words that contains a subject and a verb but cannot stand alone as a sentence).

Practice Complete the following sentences using *like* or *as if*.

1. Muggs behaved __?__ he had been abused as a puppy.

2. Mother treated Muggs __?__ a member of the family.

3. When Muggs chewed up the paper, Roy reacted __?__ he had destroyed a rare manuscript.

4. Thurber thought Muggs was __?__ a spoiled child.

5. Readers feel __?__ they know Muggs and his family.

Answers

◆ Critical Thinking

1. Muggs is a cranky, temperamental, spoiled dog.
2. Thurber tolerates Muggs, his brother Roy is less patient with Muggs, Uncle Horatio is aggressively disapproving of Muggs, Mother is loving and forgiving toward Muggs.
3. The family probably doesn't get rid of Muggs because Mother loves him.
4. Students should include specific examples of exaggeration, contrast, or describing something ridiculous in a serious way. Some students may suggest additional details that Thurber could have included to enhance the humor.
5. Students might suggest that school scheduling problems, vacations, or an outing with friends could be subjects for a humorous anecdote.

◆ Reading Strategy

1. Details include the grapefruit, the scattered dishes and silverware, and the crashing fire screen.
2. Details include *large*, *tan-colored*, *stumpy tail*, and *stiff-legged*.
3. Students should support their answers with examples of specific nouns, modifiers, vivid verbs, or phrases that provide the details that help them form a mental image.

◆ Literary Focus

1. Thurber's exaggerations include the reaction of the garage men to the poodle and the reactions of Roy and Uncle Horatio to Muggs's behavior. Through exaggeration he creates verbal caricatures, making the facts bigger than life to make them funnier.
2. Thurber describes the family's method for getting Muggs into the house as if he were explaining an ordinary household routine. Explaining this ridiculous activity in a serious, matter-of-fact way highlights just how ridiculous the activity is.

◆ Build Vocabulary

Using the Prefix *epi-*

1. An epitaph is written *upon* a tombstone.
2. The epidermis covers *over* a body.
3. The epicenter is the spot on the earth's surface directly *above* the origin of an earthquake.
4. An epidemic is a disease the spreads quickly *among* many individuals.
5. An epilogue is added *on* to the rest of a play or novel.

Using the Word Bank

1. b or d
2. c
3. b or d
4. a
5. f
6. e

◆ Build Grammar Skills

1. as if
2. like
3. as if
4. like
5. as if

Build Your Portfolio

Idea Bank

Writing

1. **Lost Dog Description** Imagine that Muggs is your dog and you have lost him. Write a description of him for a poster to help get him back.
2. **News Story** Write a news article about the neighborhood's quest to put a stop to Muggs's menacing ways. Answer the five standard "W" questions (*who, what, when, where,* and *why*) in your news story. **[Career Link]**
3. **Persuasive Letter to Mother** Write a letter to Mother persuading her to send Muggs for obedience training. Remind her of his past attacks and present her with success stories of pets who have attended obedience school.

Speaking, Listening, and Viewing

4. **Pet Talk** With a group, create a radio show called *Pet Talk*. Have some group members "call in" problems about pets and have others give advice. **[Media Link; Performing Arts Link]**
5. **Pantomime** Using only hand gestures, facial expressions, and exaggerated physical reactions, present a scene from this essay to your classmates that will bring to life the humor and absurdity of the situation. Afterward, write and answer questions from your audience about your interpretation. **[Performing Arts Link]**

Researching and Representing

6. **Wanted Poster** Create a "wanted" poster that features Muggs's "mug" as your subject. State Muggs's crime, physical features, and notable characteristics. **[Art Link]**
7. **Dog Breed Chart** Research the traits of several different dog breeds. Then create a chart that illustrates the characteristics of each breed. **[Science Link]**

Online Activity www.phlit.phschool.com

Guided Writing Lesson

Animal Anecdote

Like Thurber, many people find humor in the behavior of animals. Write an **anecdote**—a brief account about a humorous or strange event—about an animal you've known or observed. The following tips will help you bring the situation to life.

Writing Skills Focus: Vivid Verbs

Vivid verbs will add humor to your anecdote by creating specific pictures in the minds of your readers. Notice, for example, how Thurber uses vivid verbs in this description: "I reached down and grabbed his short stumpy tail and hoisted him into the air." Yet this passage would have fallen flat if Thurber had merely written "I picked up the dog."

Incorporate vivid verbs into all the phases of your writing.

Prewriting Brainstorm for a variety of vivid verbs to describe your animal's traits and actions. For instance, *run* can be expressed more specifically as *gallop, sprint, flee, scurry,* and *dash.* Outline the sequence of events in your anecdote and jot down notes about the characters you want to include.

Drafting Exaggerate physical features and personality traits with very specific and lively verbs. Thurber exaggerates his uncle's anger by saying he "bawled" rather than "yelled."

Revising Have a partner read your anecdote and point out places where more detail would help him or her form a mental picture. Add detail by replacing general verbs with more vivid ones. Also, in describing your animal and its actions, make sure you have used *like* and *as if* correctly.

For more on *like* and *as if,* see Build Grammar Skills on pp. 232 and 240.

ASSESSMENT OPTIONS

Formal Assessment, Selection Test, pp. 57–58, and Assessment Resources Software. The selection test is designed so that it can be easily customized to the ability levels of your students.

Alternative Assessment, p. 17, includes options for Pre-AP Students, less advanced students, logical/mathematical learners, visual/spatial learners, verbal/linguistic learners, and musical/rhythmic learners.

PORTFOLIO ASSESSMENT

Use the following rubrics in the ***Alternative Assessment*** booklet to assess student writing:
Lost Dog Description: Description Rubric, p. 97
New Story: Fictional Narrative Rubric, p. 95
Persuasive Letter to Mother: Persuasion Rubric, p. 105
Guided Writing Lesson: Fictional Narrative Rubric, p. 95

Idea Bank

Customizing for *Performance Levels*

Following are suggestions for matching the Idea Bank topics with your students' ability levels:
Less Advanced: 1, 5, 6
Average: 2, 4, 5, 6, 7
More Advanced: 3, 4, 7

Customizing for *Learning Modalities*

Following are suggestions for matching Idea Bank topics with your students' learning modalities:
Interpersonal: 4
Verbal/Linguistic: 1, 2, 3, 4
Bodily/Kinesthetic: 5
Visual/Spatial: 6, 7

Guided Writing Lesson

Revision Strategy Help students to replace lifeless verbs with more vivid and precise ones by encouraging them to reenter their first drafts and circle every verb they used. Have each student write these verbs on a clean sheet of paper. Then, ask them to come up with three synonyms for each verb. Finally, have students compare each verb with its synonyms and decide whether any of the synonyms would work better than the original verbs to make the writing vivid and meaningful. If so, they should replace all the verbs that need improvement.

Writers at Work Videodisc

Have students view the videodisc segment (Ch. 2) featuring writer Maxine Hong Kingston talking about the importance of setting, dialogue, and atmosphere. Point out to students that these elements can be used to enhance the humor of their anecdotes.

Play frames 18612 to 19873

Writing Lab CD-ROM

Have students complete the tutorial on Narration. Follow these steps.

1. Use the Character Traits Word Bins to develop character
2. Have students use the Audio-annotated Literary Models in the Drafting section to consider ways of organizing their anecdotes.
3. Encourage students to use the Self-evaluation checklist before submitting their completed anecdotes.

Develop Understanding

LESSON OBJECTIVES

1. **To develop vocabulary and word identification skills**
   - Greek Word Roots: *-chol-*
   - Using the Word Bank: Analogies
   - Extending Word Study: Context Clues (ATE)
2. **To use a variety of reading strategies to comprehend poems**
   - Connect Your Experience
   - Reading Strategy: Respond to Images and Ideas
   - Tips to Guide Reading: Sustained Reading (ATE)
   - Read to Appreciate Writer's Craft (ATE)
   - Idea Bank: Newspaper Headlines
3. **To increase knowledge of other cultures and to connect common elements across cultures**
   - Background for Understanding
   - Beyond Literature: Music Connection
4. **To express and support responses to the text**
   - Critical Thinking
5. **To analyze literary elements**
   - Literary Focus: Tone
   - Idea Bank: Interview
6. **To read in order to research self-selected and assigned topics**
   - Idea Bank: Music Timeline
7. **To plan, prepare, organize, and present literary interpretations**
   - Idea Bank: Music Panel
   - Speaking, Listening, and Viewing Mini-Lesson: Dramatic Reading (ATE)
8. **To use recursive writing processes to write a Press Release for a Favorite CD**
   - Guided Writing Lesson
9. **To increase knowledge of the rules of grammar and usage**
   - Build Grammar Skills: Use of *shall* and *will*

Test Preparation

Reading Comprehension: Stated and Implied Main Ideas of Poetry (ATE, p. 243) The teaching tips and sample test item in this workshop support the instruction and practice in the the unit workshop: **Reading Comprehension: Stated and Implied Main Ideas** (SE, p. 299)

Guide for Reading

Nina Cassian *(1924–)*

Poet Nina Cassian is from Romania. She studied music at the Bucharest Conservatory of Music in Romania and is a past Romanian State Prize Poet Laureate. Today she lives and works in New York City.

Edna St. Vincent Millay *(1892–1950)*

Actress, popular poet, foreign correspondent, and isolated writer—all these words describe Edna St. Vincent Millay, yet none describes her completely. She wrote and spoke her mind on controversial issues from women's rights to political freedom. Her opinions brought her public praise and public scorn. She retired from public life in 1925, moved to a farm, and wrote lyrical poems until her death.

Langston Hughes *(1901–1967)*

Langston Hughes makes music with words the way a blues musician plays notes on the saxophone. About poetry, he said: "It is the human soul entire, squeezed like a lemon or lime, drop by drop, into atomic words." Hughes read both Walt Whitman and Carl Sandburg as a high-school student, and he was especially influenced by Carl Sandburg's "Jazz Fantasia," published in 1919.

Carl Sandburg *(1876–1960)*

Carl Sandburg once said that some poetry was perfect only in form, "all dressed up with nowhere to go." The poetry of Carl Sandburg may have been dressed only in blue jeans, but it went everywhere and spoke in the voice of everyday people. That same voice came through in this poet's Pulitzer Prize-winning biography of Abraham Lincoln.

◆ Build Vocabulary

GREEK WORD ROOTS: *-chol-*

In "The Weary Blues," we hear a voice with a *melancholy* tone. The Greek word root *-chol-* refers to bile, a digestive fluid that was once believed to be one of the four "humors," or bodily fluids governing health and disposition. *Melancholy,* which literally means "black bile," supposedly caused depression and irritability. It's easy to understand how *melancholy* came to mean "sad" or "depressed."

WORD BANK

As you read these poems, you will encounter the words on this list. Each word is defined on the page where it first appears. Preview the list before you read.

reap
pallor
melancholy

◆ Build Grammar Skills

USE OF *SHALL* AND *WILL*

When Millay writes, "I shall die, but that is all that I shall do for Death," *shall* gives special emphasis to the speaker's determination to avoid assisting Death.

At one time **shall** was used when expressing future actions in the first person (*I, we*) and *will* for the second (*you*) and third person (*he, she, it, they*). Today **will** is the accepted form for first, second, and third person future and *shall* is used—as Millay does—to emphasize determination or indicate that something *must* happen.

Notice how these poets choose to use *shall* or *will* in their poems, depending on whether or not they want to create emphasis.

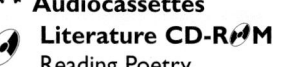

Prentice Hall Literature Program Resources

REINFORCE / RETEACH / EXTEND

Selection Support Pages
Build Vocabulary: The Word Root *-chol-*, p. 72
Build Grammar Skills: Use of *Shall* and *Will*, p. 73
Reading Strategy: Respond to Images and Ideas, p. 74
Literary Focus: Tone, p. 75

Strategies for Diverse Student Needs, p. 18

Beyond Literature
Cross-Curricular Connection: Music, p. 18

Formal Assessment Selection Test, pp. 60–62;
Assessment Resources Software

Alternative Assessment, p. 18

Resource Pro CD-ROM

Listening to Literature Audiocassettes

Literature CD-ROM
Reading Poetry

Conscientious Objector ◆ A Man
The Weary Blues ◆ Jazz Fantasia

◆ Literature and Your Life

CONNECT YOUR EXPERIENCE

You're walking along and you hear your favorite song through the open window of a passing car. Most likely, it influences how you feel and what you're thinking. Music of any kind can call forth an emotional response. The sounds, rhythms, and lyrics stir memories and call up feelings.

Two of these poems focus specifically on types of music, but all the poets express their ideas through the music of words.

Journal Writing Write a few sentences explaining how one of your favorite songs inspires you to face life's challenges.

THEMATIC FOCUS: PERSONAL CHALLENGES

Music helps two of the speakers in these poems to face life's challenges by lifting their spirits. Music is just one answer to the question, "Where do we find the strength to face challenges?"

◆ Background for Understanding

MUSIC

Two of these poems deal with specific musical forms. The music called the blues originated as folk music of African Americans. Early blues was characterized by mournful vocals and repetitive lyrics that told a story. Instruments, particularly guitars, were added to imitate and accompany the vocalists.

Jazz, which developed from blues, has been called the only art form to originate in the United States. Both Hughes and Sandburg capture the spontaneity and originality of these distinctly American forms of music.

◆ Literary Focus

TONE

A singer's attitude affects your response to a song. Similarly, your response to poems is influenced by the **tone** of the poem, the attitude the poet takes toward the poem's subject. In song or in conversation, a person conveys a certain attitude mainly through tone of voice. Usually, poets can't speak their poems for you. They must convey attitudes by choosing precise words and specific images.

In reading these poems, look for the words that communicate the poet's attitude. Sandburg, for example, conveys the power of jazz with vivid verbs like *sob* and *batter*.

◆ Reading Strategy

RESPOND TO IMAGES AND IDEAS

Whether you're discussing the great lyrics on your favorite CD or which poems you like and dislike, you are sharing a response. When you **respond to images and ideas** in poetry, you are reacting to the sensory descriptions and thoughts in a poem.

As you read these poems, respond to them with your whole self—your mind, your heart, and your senses. You don't need to be an expert on jazz, for example, to respond to Sandburg's instruction to jazz musicians:

"Moan like an autumn wind high in the lonesome treetops, . . ."

Just hear the "autumn wind" and remember what it's like to be lonesome.

Tell students that a conscientious objector is a person who, for reasons of conscience, refuses to take part in warfare. Then play the Listening to Literature audiocassette recording "Conscientious Objector." Tell students to listen for the examples Millay offers of ways that some people collaborate with death. Then ask students to suggest examples from recent history and current events. Point out the poems in this group are affirmations of life and hopefulness. Tell students to look for the way each poet celebrates life.

Tips to Guide Reading

Sustained Reading Before reading, introduce the poem by pointing out and discussing the title, the author's style, or difficult vocabulary. After students have silently read the poem, have volunteers read out loud.

Extending Word Study

Context Clues Have students use the context of the poem to identify the meaning of unfamiliar words such as: whereabouts, and password.

Customize for
Less Proficient Readers
Before reading, encourage students to preview the questions on p. 245 and p. 247 to give students a focus around which to organize the details of each poem.

Customize for
Pre-AP Students
Have students analyze the poems to determine which poem uses: metaphor "A Man", personification "Conscientious Objector", onomatopoeia "Jazz Fantasia" and rhythm and rhyme "The Weary Blues".

Customize for
Gifted/Talented Students
Ask students to select one of the poems and describe what it might be like if it was set to music or drawn as a painting.

Customize for
English Language Learners
Help these students understand the dialect and musical expressions in "The Weary Blues" and "Jazz Fantasia."

Test Preparation Workshop

Reading Comprehension: Implied Main Ideas of Poetry On many standardized tests, students will be asked to identify the main idea of a selection. To help prepare students to do this, have them read "The Man" on p. 245, and use the following sample question.

What is the author's main point in this poem?

A The narrator of the poem is afraid to live.
B The narrator cannot play the piano.
C The narrator will not clap his hands.
D The narrator wants to live life enthusiastically.

Understanding the implied main idea in a poem may be challenging to some students. As a strategy, students may wish to summarize the central thought in their own words before they read the answers choices for the test question. Using this strategy will help students realize that *A, B,* and *C* are details of the narrator's loss, not the main idea. Answer *D* is the best answer choice, because in lines 15–16, the narrator sets himself a goal to make up for his loss by trying twice as hard.

Develop Understanding

One-Minute Insight In "Conscientious Objector," the proud, determined speaker refuses to cooperate in any way—passive or active—with the forces of death. Through allusions and figurative language, Millay communicates a timeless portrait of an individual who accepts that evil forces exist in the world, but refuses to surrender to them.

◆ Literary Focus

❶ Tone Ask students to identify the ways that the poet immediately establishes a serious, determined tone. *The directness of the statement and the use of the word shall give the opening line a serious tone, as if the speaker is making a proclamation.*

◆ Build Grammar Skills

❷ Use of *Shall* and *Will* Point out the emphasis the poet creates by using the word *shall.*

❸ Clarification Cuba, an island country in the West Indies, has a long history of struggle for independence and social reform. In the early part of the twentieth century the government's lack of interest in the plight of the lower classes led to violent uprisings. The Balkans are located in the southeast corner of Europe. Throughout history, this region has been plagued with ethnic conflicts and political dispute. The bloody Balkan wars at the beginning of the twentieth century and the high tension prior to World War I earned the area the name "the powder keg of Europe."

◆ Reading Strategy

❹ Respond to Images and Ideas Ask students how these images communicate the poet's message about death. *These images suggest that the poet associates fear and oppression with death.*

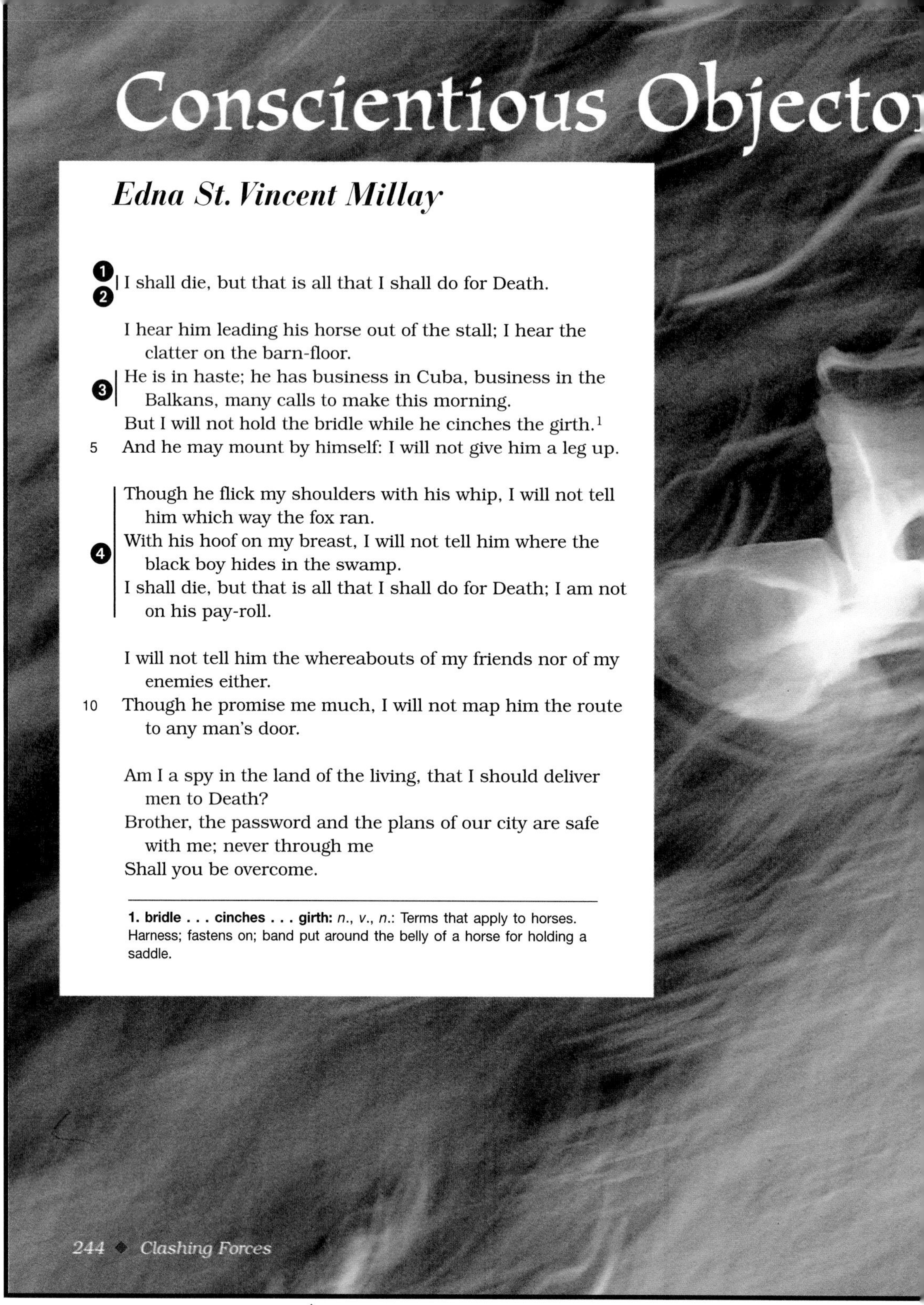

Conscientious Objector

Edna St. Vincent Millay

❶❷ I shall die, but that is all that I shall do for Death.

I hear him leading his horse out of the stall; I hear the clatter on the barn-floor.
❸ He is in haste; he has business in Cuba, business in the Balkans, many calls to make this morning.
But I will not hold the bridle while he cinches the girth.[1]
And he may mount by himself: I will not give him a leg up.

❹ Though he flick my shoulders with his whip, I will not tell him which way the fox ran.
With his hoof on my breast, I will not tell him where the black boy hides in the swamp.
I shall die, but that is all that I shall do for Death; I am not on his pay-roll.

I will not tell him the whereabouts of my friends nor of my enemies either.
Though he promise me much, I will not map him the route to any man's door.

Am I a spy in the land of the living, that I should deliver men to Death?
Brother, the password and the plans of our city are safe with me; never through me
Shall you be overcome.

---

1. **bridle . . . cinches . . . girth:** *n., v., n.*: Terms that apply to horses. Harness; fastens on; band put around the belly of a horse for holding a saddle.

Block Scheduling Strategies

Consider these suggestions to take advantage of extended class time:

- Have students share their explanations from the Journal Writing activity (p. 243) about how songs inspire people to face life's challenges. Ask students to identify some specific images and ideas from songs that they find inspiring.
- Introduce the literary concept of tone. Have students read about tone on p. 243 and answer the questions on p. 248 Use the Literature CD-ROM Reading Poetry feature 5, to prepare students to read these works.
- As a class, discuss the Music Connection, p. 248, and complete the activity on listening to the blues. Allow students to complete the Cross-Curricular page on which students complete a comparison and contrast chart on jazz and the blues, ***Beyond Literature,*** p. 18.
- Have students work in small groups to discuss the Reading Strategy questions (p. 248), discussing the poems' ideas and images.
- Assign specific research tasks to individual students and combine their findings to complete the Music Timeline activity, p. 249, as a class.

A Man

Nina Cassian

Translated by Roy MacGregor-Hastie

While fighting for his country, he lost an arm
and was suddenly afraid:
"From now on, I shall only be able to do
things by halves.
I shall reap half a harvest.

I shall be able to play either the tune
or the accompaniment on the piano,
but never both parts together.
I shall be able to bang with only one fist
on doors, and worst of all
I shall only be able to half hold
my love close to me.
There will be things I cannot do at all,
5 applaud for example,
at shows where everyone applauds."

From that moment on, he set himself to do
everything with twice as much enthusiasm.
And where the arm had been torn away
a wing grew.

◆ **Build Vocabulary**

reap (rēp) *v.*: Gather

6 ▲ **Critical Viewing** What details in this picture reflect the sentiments of the man in these poems? **[Support]**

Guide for Responding

◆ Literature and Your Life

Reader's Response How do you think the speakers of these poems would feel about each other?

Thematic Focus Challenges call forth emotional responses from these speakers. What are some other responses people have to challenges?

☑ Check Your Comprehension

1. What happened to the man in "A Man" when he was "fighting for his country"?
2. In "Conscientious Objector," what are two things the speaker will not do?

◆ Critical Thinking

INTERPRET

1. Why do you think the poet chooses the image of a wing to end "A Man"? **[Interpret]**
2. Why do you think the speaker in "Conscientious Objector" will not tell the whereabouts even of enemies? **[Speculate]**

APPLY

3. In what ways can ordinary people refuse to "cooperate with Death" in their day-to-day lives? **[Relate]**

EXTEND

4. What qualities are important for physical therapists or counselors who work with the physically challenged? **[Career Link]**

Develop Understanding

One-Minute Insight Through a vivid image that students will easily connect with freedom and upward motion, Cassian conveys the power of an individual's attitude.

5 Respond to Images and Ideas Discuss how the inability to applaud isolates the speaker more than the other adjustments he mentions. *The speaker is able to participate to some degree in other activities but there is no way to applaud partially.*

▶Critical Viewing◀

6 Support *The upward flight of the bird reflects the freedom of the speaker in "Conscientious Objector" and the hopefulness of the man at the end of Nina Cassian's poem. The wind or air currents pushing against the bird suggest that freedom and hopefulness require effort.*

Reinforce and Extend

Answers

Reader's Response Students may suggest that the speakers would admire each other's determination and optimism.

Thematic Focus Some people are intimidated by challenges, some are inspired by them.

☑ Check Your Comprehension

1. The man lost an arm.
2. The speaker will not help Death prepare for his journey. The speaker will not betray friends or enemies. Some students may give more literal answers from the poem, such as holding the bridle, or telling where the fox ran.

◆ Critical Thinking

1. The image of a wing ends the poem on an upbeat note.
2. Death is a greater enemy.
3. People can refuse to cooperate with Death in their everyday lives by avoiding unhealthy practices and substances, by not accepting injustice or cruelty, and by being aware of world events.
4. Optimism, determination, patience, and compassion are important qualities for a person working with the physically challenged.

Speaking, Listening, and Viewing Mini-Lesson

Dramatic Reading

This mini-lesson supports the Speaking, Listening, and Viewing activity in the Idea Bank on p. 249.

Introduce Introduce the term *oral interpretation,* emphasizing that a reader's interpretation of a poem is communicated by her or his own ideas as portrayed by a performance. Refer students to the Speaking and Listening Handbook, p. 100, for more information on oral interpretation.

Develop Have students copy the poems they choose into their notebooks. They may find it helpful to leave space between each line in which to make notes about their interpretation and performance instructions to themselves. Encourage them to evaluate the poet's use of punctuation in making decisions about performance. Guide them in marking their "scripts" to indicate words to be stressed, places to pause, and sections to read more emphatically or softly.

Apply Have students practice their performances with partners and then deliver their oral interpretations to the class.

Assess Use the Oral Interpretation peer assessment page in ***Alternative Assessment***, p. 119.

One-Minute Insight Hughes captures the languid repetition and syncopation of the blues by using long sentences punctuated with shorter ones. The repeated ō and o͞o sounds echo the crooning of a blues singer. Like a story within a story, the poem conveys the "blues" of the life of a blues musician.

◆ Reading Strategy

❶ Respond to Images and Ideas Ask students what they see, hear, and feel based on this section. *Students may say they hear soft, slow singing and piano music. They may see an African American man singing and swaying in the dim light.*

◆ Literary Focus

❷ Tone Ask students which words convey a melancholy tone. Why do they think the poet chose this tone for this poem? *Words that convey a melancholy tone include* poor piano, moan, rickety stool, *and* sad raggy tune. *The melancholy tone echoes the melancholy tone of the blues music that is the subject of the poem.*

▶Critical Viewing◀

❸ Infer *The relaxed poses and smiling faces of the people, and the prominence of the instruments indicate that these musicians enjoy playing the blues.*

Read to Appreciate a Writer's Craft

Reading poetry gives students an excellent opportunity to appreciate an author's craft and skill in using words and phrases. Suggest that students make a list of the author's words that are most descriptive.

Art Transparency As students discuss these two poems, have them explain why they think each speaker praises the music that he describes—both types of music have humble or folk origins. Display Art Transparency 8, and discuss how the painting shows average "folk" enjoying and responding to music. Interested students may want to write a story that links the painting with one of the poems. Alternatively, they may attempt a poem or reflective essay in which they explore their own feelings about a particular type of music.

The Weary Blues

Langston Hughes

Solo/Interval, 1987, Romare Bearden, collage on board, 11" x 14", © 1997

❶
Droning a drowsy syncopated[1] tune,
Rocking back and forth to a mellow croon,
I heard a Negro play.
Down on Lenox Avenue the other night
By the pale dull pallor of an old gas light
He did a lazy sway. . . .
He did a lazy sway. . . .
To the tune o' those Weary Blues.
With his ebony hands on each ivory key
He made that poor piano moan with melody.
O Blues!
❷
Swaying to and fro on his rickety stool
He played that sad raggy tune like a musical fool.
Sweet Blues!
Coming from a black man's soul.
O Blues!
In a deep song voice with a melancholy tone
I heard that Negro sing, that old piano moan—
"Ain't got nobody in all this world,
Ain't got nobody but ma self.
I's gwine to quit ma frownin'
And put ma troubles on the shelf."
Thump, thump, thump, went his foot on the floor.
He played a few chords then he sang some more—
"I got the Weary Blues
And I can't be satisfied.
Got the Weary Blues
And can't be satisfied—
I ain't happy no mo'
And I wish that I had died."
And far into the night he crooned that tune.
The stars went out and so did the moon.
The singer stopped playing and went to bed
While the Weary Blues echoed through his head.
He slept like a rock or a man that's dead.

1. **syncopated** (siŋ´ kə pā´ tid) *adj.*: With rhythm shifted stressing beats that are ordinarily weak.

◀ Critical Viewing How can you tell that these musicians enjoy playing the blues? **[Infer]** ❸

◆ Build Vocabulary

pallor (pal´ ər) *n.*: Lack of color; unnatural paleness

melancholy (mel´ ən käl´ ē) *adj.*: Sad and depressed

Humanities: Art

Solo/Interval, 1987, by Romare Bearden.

Although he was born more than a decade after Langston Hughes, Romare Bearden (1912–1988), like Hughes and the writers and artists of the Harlem Renaissance, focuses on themes from African American life and culture. Many of his works, including *Solo/Interval*, are collages, combinations of paper, magazine cutouts, paint, and photographs. Bearden received the National Medal of Arts in 1987.

Use the following question for discussion: Why is collage a good technique to employ in depicting a jazz man? *Both collage and jazz allow the artist a certain amount of freedom and room to improvise. Like music, collage combines individual parts to create a unified composition.*

Jazz Fantasia

Carl Sandburg

Drum on your drums, batter on your banjoes,
sob on the long cool winding saxophones.
Go to it, O jazzmen.

❹

Sling your knuckles on the bottoms of the happy
tin pans, let your trombones ooze, and go husha-
husha-hush with the slippery sand-paper.

Moan like an autumn wind high in the lonesome treetops,
moan soft like you wanted somebody terrible, cry like a
racing car slipping away from a motorcycle cop,
bang-bang! you jazzmen, bang altogether drums, traps,
banjoes, horns, tin cans—make two people fight on the
top of a stairway and scratch each other's eyes in a
clinch[1] tumbling down the stairs.

Can[2] the rough stuff . . . now a Mississippi steamboat
pushes up the night river with a hoo-hoo-hoo-oo . . . and
the green lanterns calling to the high soft stars . . . a red
moon rides on the humps of the low river hills . . . go to it,
O jazzmen.

1. **clinch** (klinch) *n.*: Slang for embrace.
2. **can:** Slang for stop.

Autumn Lamp (Guitar player), 1983, Romare Bearden, From the Mecklenburg Autumn Series, Oil with collage, 40" x 31", Private collection, ©1997 Romare Bearden Foundation/Licensed by VAGA, New York, New York

Critical Viewing Compare and contrast the musicians in the paintings by Romare Bearden on these pages. **[Compare and Contrast]** ❺

Guide for Responding

◆ Literature and Your Life

Reader's Response Would you rather listen to the music described in "The Weary Blues" or in "Jazz Fantasia"? Why?

Thematic Focus Both these poems describe a musical "attitude," or mood. How does attitude affect the way people face challenges?

☑ Check Your Comprehension

1. What kind of music does Sandburg describe?
2. What kind of music does Hughes describe?

◆ Critical Thinking

INTERPRET

1. Using Sandburg's images as a source of information, write a brief definition of jazz. **[Interpret]**
2. Describe the personality of the piano player and singer in "The Weary Blues." **[Draw Conclusions]**

COMPARE LITERARY WORKS

3. Compare and contrast how well each poet captures the feeling of the music he describes. Support your answer with examples from the poems. **[Evaluate]**

Develop Understanding

One-Minute Insight Sandburg combines slang and musical expressions to create a unique, jumpy rhythm that echoes the energetic rhythms of jazz.

◆ Literary Focus

❹ **Tone** Which words and expressions indicate Sandburg's attitude toward his subject? *Expressive words such as* drum, batter, sob, sling, *and* ooze *indicate Sandburg's enjoyment of the sounds of the music.*

▶Critical Viewing◀

❺ **Compare and Contrast** The trumpet player is more elegantly dressed, the colors in his clothes are varied and jewel-like. The guitar player is dressed casually; in his picture, most of the color is primary colors (yellow and blue, which occasionally overlap to make green).

Reinforce and Extend

Answers

◆ Literature and Your Life

Reader's Response Some students may prefer the relaxed, bittersweet music described by Hughes while others may lean toward the energetic variations described by Sandburg.

Thematic Focus Students will probably respond that a positive attitude helps people meet challenges more effectively than if they approach a challenge with a negative attitude.

☑ Check Your Comprehension

1. Sandburg describes jazz.
2. Hughes describes the blues.

◆ Critical Thinking

1. Jazz is a mix of instruments played with energy and passion.
2. The piano player/singer is a talented persistent man who is resigned to a difficult life.
3. Students may say that Hughes captures the feeling of the blues in the varied line lengths, the melancholy words, and the images of the singer swaying and crooning. Sandburg expresses the sound of jazz with onomatopoeic words like husha-husha, and hoo-hoo-

Beyond the Selection

FURTHER READING

Other Works by the Poets

Call Yourself Alive?, Nina Cassian
Selected Poems of Langston Hughes
Selected Poems of Edna St. Vincent Millay
The Complete Poems of Carl Sandburg

RELATED WORKS

Moment's Notice: Jazz in Poetry and Prose, edited by Art Lange and Nathaniel Mackey

We suggest that you preview these works before recommending them to students.

INTERNET

Students can find out more about the poets featured in this section at the following Web sites. Please be aware that sites may have changed since we published this information.

Hughes: **http://ie.uwindsor.ca/jazz/hughes. html**
Millay: **http://www.millaycolony.org/ednabio. html**
Sandburg: **http://www.lis.uiuc.edu/ ~roberts/ carlpage.htm**

We *strongly recommend* that you preview these sites before sending students to them.

◆ Reading Strategy

1. Some students will respond most to the image of the wing. Some may respond to the individual examples of fears expressed by the man.
2. Most students will probably think that "A Man" expresses the most upbeat ideas and that "Jazz Fantasia" has the most upbeat images of music and enjoyment.
3. Students should include in their answers reasons based on the rhythms and instruments mentioned in the poems.

◆ Literary Focus

1. The wing suggests that the man will "fly," that he will rise above his difficulties.
2. "The Weary Blues" has a relaxed, easygoing tone. Details include the swaying of the musician, the repetition of words and sounds, and words like *droning* and *drowsy*.
3. Some words that indicate the tone of "Jazz Fantasia" include *sob, happy, moan, tumbling*.

Beyond Literature

Music Connection Students can use the Comparison and Contrast Organizer in ***Writing and Language Transparencies***, p. 95, to find similarities and differences for the Beyond Literature activity on this page.

◆ Build Vocabulary

Greek Word Roots: *-chol-*

1. A choleric person is quick-tempered and has a negative outlook.
2. Melancholy is a sad feeling or mood.
3. Cholera is related to physical health; it is an intestinal disease.
4. Too much cholesterol can cause physical health problems.
5. Choler is anger, believed in the past to be caused by too much bile in the system.

Using the Word Bank

1. reap; 2. melancholy; 3. pallor

◆ Build Grammar Skills

1. shall
2. will
3. shall
4. will
5. shall

Guide for Responding (continued)

◆ Reading Strategy

Respond to Images and Ideas

Your own experience and knowledge influence the way you **respond to the images and ideas** in these poems. In "A Man," the image of a wing may call up a sense of freedom or possibility.

1. To which image in "A Man" do you respond most strongly? Why?
2. Which poem did you feel had the most upbeat images and ideas? Explain.
3. Do the descriptions in "Jazz Fantasia" and "The Weary Blues" make you want to listen to these forms of music? Why or why not?

◆ Literary Focus

Tone

Tone—a speaker's attitude toward the subject—helps convey a poem's meaning and creates an effect on the reader. For instance, the speaker's attitude in "Conscientious Objector" is dignified. This gives the poem a serious, purposeful tone.

1. What image helps to convey the positive tone of "A Man"? Explain.
2. Describe the tone of "The Weary Blues." Support your answer with details from the poem.
3. Identify three words that indicate the tone of "Jazz Fantasia." Explain.

Beyond Literature

Music Connection

The Blues Now one of the most recognizable types of music worldwide, the music known as the blues has come a long way from its roots along the rural back byways of the Mississippi Delta. It has influenced musical forms as varied as jazz, rock-and-roll, rhythm and blues, and soul music.

Activity Listen to a blues recording by B. B. King, such as "The Thrill Is Gone," and compare it to a selection of your favorite music. Create a chart showing similarities and differences in lyrics, types of instruments, and tempo.

◆ Build Vocabulary

Using the Greek Root *-chol-*

Using your knowledge of the Greek root *-chol-* (and a dictionary if necessary), explain how each of the following words containing the root *-chol-* relates to physical health, outlook, or mood.

1. choleric
2. melancholy
3. cholera
4. cholesterol
5. choler

Using the Word Bank: Analogies

For each of the following word analogies, notice that the second word of the first pair is a characteristic or result of the first word. In your notebook, write the word from the Word Bank that best completes the second word pair.

1. *Spring* is to *plant* as *autumn* is to __?__.
2. *Good luck* is to *joy* as *bad luck* is to __?__.
3. *Happiness* is to *smile* as *sickness* is to __?__.

◆ Build Grammar Skills

Use of Shall and Will

At one time, **shall** was used to express future actions in the first person. **Will** was used for the second and third person. Today, the difference between *shall* and *will* is no longer a question of correct usage but a question of emphasis. *Shall* indicates determination or compulsion.

Practice Copy the following sentences in your notebook. Complete each sentence with *shall* or *will* and explain why you made your choice.

1. They (will, shall) never surrender.
2. Mary (will, shall) call you later.
3. I (will, shall) never harm a living creature.
4. She (will, shall) meet us at the store.
5. Her inspiring words (will, shall) not soon be forgotten.

Reteach

Poetry is often challenging for students to read, understand, and enjoy. Formulating a response to the images and ideas in the poem will enhance comprehension and reading pleasure. Students reading poetry will form a very personal response to lines, phrases, and images the author uses. The work might please the student, frighten, anger, or bore. Remind students that they may connect the poem with a personal experience or memory. They may agree or disagree with the author's point of view. For practice in responding to images and ideas, have students fold a piece of paper in half lengthwise. On the first folded half, have them select and write a line or phrase of one of the poems. On the second half, have them list their response. For example, if students wrote the line, "Sundays too my father got up early" on the first side, they would respond to the phrase with their own memories of Sunday activities on the second.

Build Your Portfolio

Idea Bank

Writing

1. **Newspaper Headlines** Write a headline for each poem in this group that expresses the main idea of the poem and grabs the reader's interest. For instance, the headline for "A Man" might read "Hope Helps Man Grow Wing."
2. **Interview** Write an interview with the speaker of one of these poems. Base your questions on your response to the poem; base the speaker's response on the tone and content of the poem.
3. **Song Lyrics** Sandburg and Hughes write about music that helps them and others face some of life's challenges. Write song lyrics about a challenge you have faced. **[Music Link]**

Speaking, Listening, and Viewing

4. **Music Panel** With a small group, listen to a variety of songs and nonvocal pieces. (Group members may each choose one for the group to hear.) After listening, discuss what you liked or disliked about each of the pieces. Create a chart recording your responses. **[Music Link]**
5. **Dramatic Reading** Prepare a dramatic reading of one of these poems. Decide how you will use volume and tempo to help you express the tone of the poem. **[Performing Arts Link]**

Researching and Representing

6. **Graphic Design** Design a CD cover for the music described in "The Weary Blues" or "Jazz Fantasia." You can either sketch your design or write out the description. **[Art Link]**
7. **Music Timeline** Create a music timeline that indicates a major event in each of the past ten decades and the music that was popular at the time. **[Music Link]**

Online Activity www.phlit.phschool.com

Guided Writing Lesson

Press Release for a Favorite CD

Certain lines and phrases in Carl Sandburg's "Jazz Fantasia" could be used in a brief promotional statement (a press release) for a jazz CD. Write a **press release** for your favorite CD, explaining what the music is, who created it, why it's good, and when the CD will be available. The following tips will help you choose the right language to communicate with your readers.

Writing Skills Focus: Appropriate Language for the Audience

In almost every type of writing, including press releases and position papers, you must use **appropriate language for the audience.** You can assume, for example, that your readers probably know something about the style of music or the group featured on the CD. Their interest in the music means they have a basic vocabulary they share with others interested in this type of music. In "The Weary Blues," Hughes includes words like *syncopated, croon,* and *ivory key* that would be clear to any lover of the blues.

Before you begin writing, think about the words and phrases you usually use when you talk about the music you are describing. Keep them in mind as you draft and revise.

Prewriting Discuss the CD with a partner who shares your enthusiasm for it. As you speak, jot down expressions and words you use to describe what you like about the music and the musicians.

Drafting Write as if you were convincing a friend to buy this CD. Use the words and phrases that you jotted down before you began writing.

Revising Show your press release to several people. Ask them what catches their interest most and if it appears early enough in the press release. If not, consider moving it to the first paragraph.

ASSESSMENT OPTIONS

Formal Assessment, Selection Test, pp. 60–61, and Assessment Resources Software.

Alternative Assessment, p. 18, includes options for less advanced students, more advanced students, musical/rhythmic learners, interpersonal learners, visual/spatial learners, and verbal/linguistic learners.

PORTFOLIO ASSESSMENT

Use the following rubrics in the ***Alternative Assessment*** booklet to assess student writing and activities:

Song Lyrics: Expression Rubric, p. 94
Dramatic Reading: Poetry Rubric, p. 108
Guided Writing Lesson: Persuasion Rubric, p. 105

Idea Bank

Following are suggestions for matching the Idea Bank topics with your students' performance levels and learning modalities:

Customizing for *Performance Levels*
Less Advanced: 1, 4, 6
Average: 2, 4, 5, 6, 7
More Advanced: 3, 4, 5, 7

Customizing for *Learning Modalities*
Musical/Rhythmic: 4, 5
Verbal/Linguistic: 5
Visual/Spatial: 6, 7
Mathematical/Logical: 4, 7

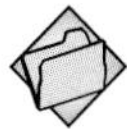

Guided Writing Lesson

Elaboration Strategy It can be difficult to describe art or music without sounding vague. Students can find concrete, thoughtful ways to describe their CDs with the cubing strategy. After completing a thorough analysis, they will be ready to write about it.

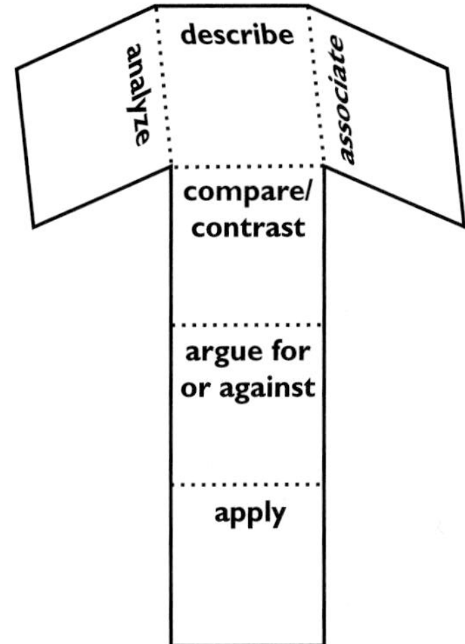

Writer's at Work Videodisc

Play the videodisc segment featuring Sayu Bhojwani, who writes promotional pieces for the Asia Society.

Play frames 33643 to 43235

Writing Lab CD-ROM

Have students complete the following steps in the tutorial on Persuasion.

1. In the prewriting section, use the audio-annotated models that demonstrate appropriate language.
2. Use the cluster diagram to organize main idea and details.
3. The publishing and presenting section gives tips for presenting ads.

Prepare and Engage

LESSON OBJECTIVES

1. **To develop vocabulary and word identification skills**
   - Latin Word Roots: *-gratis-*
   - Using the Word Bank: Sentence Completions
   - Extending Word Study: Increase Vocabulary (ATE)
2. **To use a variety of reading strategies to comprehend a short story and a poem**
   - Connect Your Experience
   - Reading Strategy: Analyze Causes and Effects
   - Tips to Guide Reading: Preview (ATE)
   - Read to Be Entertained (ATE)
3. **To increase knowledge of other cultures and to connect common elements across cultures**
   - Background for Understanding
4. **To express and support responses to the text**
   - Critical Thinking
   - Idea Bank: Guidelines
   - Idea Bank: Fairy Tale
   - Idea Bank: Oral Argument
5. **To analyze literary elements**
   - Literary Focus: Irony
6. **To read in order to research self-selected and assigned topics**
   - Idea Bank: Research Songs
   - Idea Bank: Map
7. **To speak clearly and effectively for a specific audience and purpose**
   - Idea Bank: Debate
8. **To use recursive writing processes to write a review of a song**
   - Guided Writing Lesson
9. **To increase knowledge of the rules of grammar and usage**
   - Build Grammar Skills: Comparative and Superlative Forms

Test Preparation

Reading Comprehension: Stated and Implied Main Ideas (ATE, p. 251) The teaching tips and sample test item in this workshop support the instruction and practice in the unit workshop:
Reading Comprehension: Stated and Implied Main Ideas (SE, p. 299)

Guide for Reading

R. K. Narayan (1906–)

If the Indian writer R. K. Narayan lived in your city or town, he might turn it on its head to create an imaginary place full of characters that would make you smile in recognition.

Narayan's own town, Mysore, probably served as the basis for his fictional town of Malgudi, a place full of eccentric characters who find themselves in peculiar situations.

Imaginary Town Writers sometimes devise special settings for the cast of characters that pass through their books, and Narayan has done this with Malgudi. "Malgudi was an earth-shaking discovery for me, because I had no mind for facts and things like that, which would be necessary in writing about . . . any real place." Narayan's fictional south Indian town of Malgudi has seen so many changes and human dramas that it almost seems like a character itself.

Narayan's Languages R. K. Narayan, whose initials stand for Rasipuram Kirshnaswamy, speaks both the Indian language Tamii and English—but he writes all his fiction in English. As a child, he was also taught traditional Indian melodies and prayers in Sanskrit. As an adult, Narayan went on to translate from Sanskrit the ancient Indian epic *Mahabharata*, a poem consisting of more than 90,000 pairs of rhyming lines!

Literary Forms R. K. Narayan has written extensively in several forms: novels, short stories, essays, and travel books among them.

If you want to find out more about the life of R. K. Narayan, you might be interested in reading his memoir, *My Days*.

His best-known novels include *Swami and Friends* (1935), *The English Teacher* (1945), and *The Painter of Signs* (1976).

◆ Build Vocabulary

LATIN WORD ROOTS: *-gratis-*

In "Like the Sun," you will learn that Sekhar's boss behaves in an ingratiating way. Knowing that the word root *-gratis-* comes from a Latin word meaning "pleasing" or "a favor," you can figure out that being *ingratiating* means "trying to please."

WORD BANK

As you read "Like the Sun," you will encounter the words on this list. Each word is defined on the page where it first appears. Preview the list before you read, and identify any words that are already familiar to you. In your notebook, write what you think they mean.

essence
tempering
shirked
incessantly
ingratiating
stupefied
scrutinized

◆ Build Grammar Skills

COMPARATIVE AND SUPERLATIVE FORMS

When writers compare two things, they use the **comparative form** of an adjective. To compare more than two things, they use the **superlative form**.

Comparative Form: No judge delivering a sentence felt *more pained* and *hopeless*.

In comparing a story character with one other person, the author uses the comparative form of the adjectives *pained* and *hopeless*. The comparative of these adjectives is formed by using *more* with them.

Superlative Form: Sekhar felt the *greatest* pity for him.

The author implies that of all the pity there is to feel, the character Sekhar feels the most. Therefore, the author uses *greatest*, the superlative form of the adjective *great*.

Prentice Hall Literature Program Resources

REINFORCE / RETEACH / EXTEND

Selection Support Pages
Build Vocabulary: The Word Root *-gratis-*, p. 76
Build Grammar Skills: Comparative and Superlative Forms, p. 77
Reading Strategy: Consequences of Actions, p. 78
Literary Focus: Irony, p. 79

Strategies for Diverse Student Needs, p. 19

Beyond Literature
Cross-Curricular Connection: Science, p. 19

Formal Assessment Selection Test, pp. 63–65; Assessment Resources Software

Alternative Assessment, p. 19

Writing and Language Transparencies
Cause and Effect Graphic Organizer, p. 99

Resource Pro CD-ROM

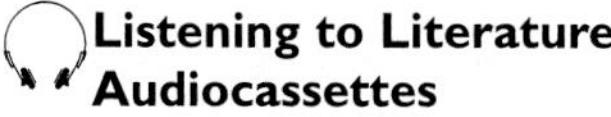

Listening to Literature Audiocassettes

Looking at Literature Videodisc

Like the Sun
◆ Tell all the Truth but tell it slant— ◆

◆ Literature and Your Life

CONNECT YOUR EXPERIENCE

Your closest friend just gave a less-than-impressive performance in the class play and asks for your honest response. Do you reveal your true opinion or do you spare your friend's feelings?

You're not alone with this dilemma. The matter of whether to tell the whole, unvarnished truth has troubled people throughout the ages. Follow Sekhar, the main character in this story, as he decides how to deal with the truth—at least for a day.

Journal Writing Briefly note what might happen if everyone told the truth all the time.

THEMATIC FOCUS: PERSONAL CHALLENGES

In different ways, Narayan's story and Dickinson's poem both pose this challenging question: Is it better to tell the absolute truth or to modify it for the sake of getting along with others?

◆ Background for Understanding

MUSIC

"Like the Sun" features the performance of a song, and this is not surprising, because song is at the root of south Indian music. The headmaster in the story sings an alapana—the introductory section of a piece of music—and then goes on to sing a song written by Thyagaraja (1767–1847), a composer who strongly influenced the music of south India. The region's biggest music festival, in fact, is named after Thyagaraja.

You'll notice, too, that the headmaster sings to the accompaniment of a drum and a violin. The violin is widely used in southern Indian music, and percussion instruments include the double-headed drum known as *mridangam* and the *ghatam*, a clay pot that the player may sometimes toss into the air.

◆ Literary Focus

IRONY

Irony is the literary technique that involves surprising, interesting, or amusing contradictions at work. These differences can result from clashes between what a character believes and what is actually the case. Irony might also result from clashes between what a character expects to happen and what actually happens.

By focusing on the clash between the main character's ideals and the real situation, you'll understand the irony of this tale.

◆ Reading Strategy

ANALYZE CAUSES AND EFFECTS

In life, you must experience directly the **effects** of your actions—the results of what you do. The advantage of reading a story, however, is that you can sit safe and sound in a chair and analyze the causes and effects in someone else's experience.

"Like the Sun" is a perfect story with which to analyze the relationship between causes and effects. Sekhar makes an important decision right off, a decision that just seems to invite consequences. Filling out a graphic organizer like the following will help you connect Sekhar's actions and their results.

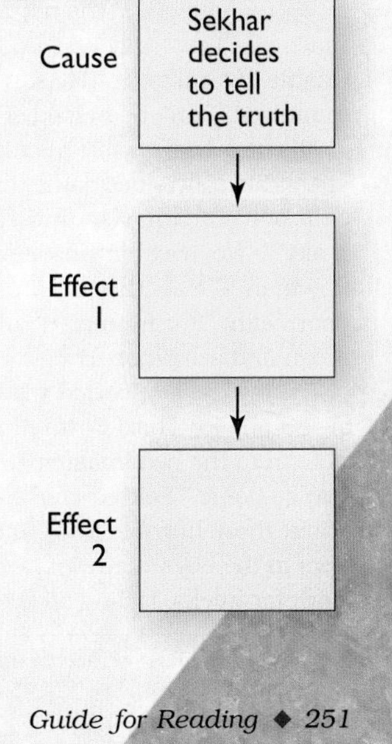

Test Preparation Workshop

Stated and Implied Main Ideas

For practice in identifying main ideas and their supporting details, use the following sample question:

Read the first two paragraphs of "Like the Sun" on p. 252.

What is the main idea of these paragraphs?

A Telling the truth is easy.
B Telling lies is easy.
C Telling the truth is like looking at the sun.
D Human beings are dazed by looking at the sun.

In order to select the best answer choice, suggest that students paraphrase the paragraph in a sentence or two, using their own words. This strategy will help them differentiate between the central idea and supporting details and incorrect choices. Lead students to notice that the author does not imply either answer *A* or *B* in the passage. *D* is a supporting detail from the paragraph. By process of elimination, students will find that *C* is the best answer from the choices given.

On the chalkboard, write the words "absolute truth." Ask students what they consider to be absolute truth. Then lead the class in a discussion of whether it is possible or desirable to tell the absolute truth at all times. Then, read aloud the first paragraph of "Like the Sun." Tell students that this story will allow them to watch—as if on hidden video—the adventures of a man who decides to tell what he considers the absolute truth for one full day.

Tips to Guide Reading

Skimming Before reading, have students skim the text to preview the material. To guide student's reading, point out unfamiliar vocabulary, difficult-to-pronounce names, and reading strategy prompts.

Read to Be Entertained

Students should be encouraged to read world literature for pleasure and entertainment.

Customize for *Less Proficient Readers*

To help students understand the story's irony, have them complete a chart like this one as they read:

	What Sekhar expects	What happens
1.		
2.		

Customize for *Pre-AP Students*

Invite these students to discuss Narayan's style with partners or in a group. Suggest that they pay particular attention to his use of figurative language.

Customize for *Gifted/Talented Students*

Have groups of students work together to select one of the situations Sekhar encounters to role-play for the class. Suggest that they extend the dialogue to explore the character's feelings and responses.

Customize for *English Language Learners*

Preview the Build Vocabulary boxes and footnotes with students and substitute simpler terms as needed.

Develop Understanding

One-Minute Insight When Sekhar decides to tell the whole truth for one day, he hurts his wife's feelings, alienates a colleague, and insults his headmaster. Through the experiences of the main character in this story, Narayan explores the question of whether it is possible or wise to tell the unvarnished truth at all times.

◆ Reading Strategy

❶ Consequences of Actions
Elicit the following: *Students should note that Sekhar's decision to be candid has made his wife feel bad.*

◆ Critical Thinking

❷ Infer What can students infer from Sekhar's procrastination? *Sekhar's procrastination indicates that he tries to avoid or put off unpleasant tasks. This would seem to indicate that if telling the absolute truth becomes unpleasant, he will be unable to continue for long.*

◆ Literature and Your Life

❸ Students might have been asked to comment on a friend's performance in an athletic event or concert. Ask them how they responded to what they considered a poor performance. *Guide students to distinguish between examples of constructive criticism, hurtful criticism, and tempered truth.*

◆ Critical Thinking

❹ Analyze Have students analyze why, at this point in the story, Narayan has the headmaster tell Sekhar that he has spent a fortune on his music. *The headmaster's remark shows how important his music is to him and how difficult it will be for Sekhar to be critical.*

Like the Sun

R. K. Narayan

Truth, Sekhar reflected, is like the sun. I suppose no human being can ever look it straight in the face without blinking or being dazed. He realized that, morning till night, the essence of human relationships consisted in tempering truth so that it might not shock. This day he set apart as a unique day—at least one day in the year we must give and take absolute Truth whatever may happen. Otherwise life is not worth living. The day ahead seemed to him full of possibilities. He told no one of his experiment. It was a quiet resolve, a secret pact between him and eternity.

The very first test came while his wife served him his morning meal. He showed hesitation over a titbit, which she had thought was her culinary[1] masterpiece. She asked, "Why, isn't it good?" At other times he would have said, considering her feelings in the matter, "I feel full up, that's all." But today he said, "It isn't good. I'm unable to swallow it." He saw her wince and said to himself, Can't be helped. Truth is like the sun.

> **◆ Reading Strategy** ❶ What is the first consequence of Sekhar's "pact" with "eternity"?

His next trial was in the common room when one of his colleagues came up and said, "Did you hear of the death of so-and-so? Don't you think it a pity?" "No," Sekhar answered. "He was such a fine man—" the other began. But Sekhar cut him short with: "Far from it. He always struck me as a mean and selfish brute."

❷ During the last period when he was teaching geography for Third Form A, Sekhar received a note from the headmaster: "Please see me before you go home." Sekhar said to himself: It must be about these horrible test papers. A hundred papers in the boys' scrawls; he had shirked this work for weeks, feeling all the time as if a sword were hanging over his head.

The bell rang, and the boys burst out of the class.

Sekhar paused for a moment outside the headmaster's room to button up his coat; that was another subject the headmaster always sermonized about.

He stepped in with a very polite "Good evening, sir."

The headmaster looked up at him in a very friendly manner and asked, "Are you free this evening?"

Sekhar replied, "Just some outing which I have promised the children at home—"

"Well, you can take them out another day. Come home with me now."

"Oh. . . yes, sir, certainly. . ." And then he added timidly, "anything special, sir?"

"Yes," replied the headmaster, smiling to himself. . . "You didn't know my weakness for music?"

"Oh, yes, sir. . ."

"I've been learning and practicing secretly, and now I want you to hear me this evening. I've engaged a drummer and a violinist to accompany me—this is the first time I'm doing it full-dress,[2] and I want your opinion. I know it will be valuable."

Sekhar's taste in music was well known. He was one of the most dreaded music critics in the town. But he never anticipated his musical inclinations would lead him to this trial. . . . "Rather a surprise for you, isn't it?" asked the headmaster. "I've spent a fortune on it behind closed doors. . . ." They started for the headmaster's house. "God hasn't given me a child, but at least let him not deny me the consolation of music," the headmaster said, pathetically, as they walked. He incessantly chattered about music: how he began one day out of sheer boredom; how his teacher at

1. **culinary** (kyōō´ lə ner´ ē) *adj.*: Having to do with cooking or the kitchen.

2. **full-dress:** Complete in every respect.

Block Scheduling Strategies

Consider these suggestions to take advantage of extended class time:

- Allow time for students to complete the journal activity in Literature and Your Life (p. 251) before introducing the "Interest Grabber" discussion (p. 251).
- Expand on the Background provided on page 251 by using the Looking at Literature Videodisc, Chapter 3, which features Indian music and dance.

Play frames 11043 to 20512

- Introduce the literary concept of irony. As a class, complete the Literary Focus page on irony in ***Selection Support***, p. 79. After reading the story, students can work independently or in small groups to answer the Literary Focus questions on p. 255.
- Model the action-consequence chart like the one on p. 251, or use the Cause and Effect Graphic Organizer in ***Writing and Language Transparencies***, p. 99.
- To prepare students for the Guided Writing Lesson (p. 256), allow them to bring in examples of songs to play for their classmates as possible topics for reviews. Lead a class discussion on what elements students might consider in their reviews. Then have students complete the Guided Writing Lesson.

▲ Critical Viewing Describe the personality the artist has given the sun. **[Interpret]**

rst laughed at him and then gave him hope; ow his ambition in life was to forget himself in nusic.

At home the headmaster proved very ngratiating. He sat Sekhar on a red silk carpet, et before him several dishes of delicacies, and ıssed over him as if he were a son-in-law of the ouse. He even said, "Well, you must listen with a ee mind. Don't worry about these test papers."

◆ Build Vocabulary

essence (es´ əns) *n.*: The crucial element or basis

tempering (tem´ pə riŋ) *adj.*: Modifying or adjusting

shirked (shûrkt) *v.*: Neglected or avoided

incessantly (in ses´ ənt lē) *adv.*: Endlessly; constantly

ingratiating (in grā´ shē āt´ iŋ) *adj.*: Bringing into favor

stupefied (stōō´ pə fid´) *adj.*: Dazed; stunned

He added half humorously, "I will give you a week's time."

"Make it ten days, sir," Sekhar pleaded.

"All right, granted," the headmaster said generously. Sekhar felt really relieved now—he would attack them at the rate of ten a day and get rid of the nuisance.

The headmaster lighted incense sticks. "Just to create the right atmosphere," he explained. A drummer and a violinist, already seated on a Rangoon mat, were waiting for him. The headmaster sat down between them like a professional at a concert, cleared his throat and began an alapana,[3] and paused to ask, "Isn't it good Kalyani?"[4] Sekhar pretended not to have heard the question. The headmaster went on to sing a full song composed by Thyagaraja and followed it with two more. All the time the headmaster was singing, Sekhar went on commenting within himself, He croaks like a dozen frogs. He is bellowing like a buffalo. Now he sounds like loose window shutters in a storm.

The incense sticks burnt low. Sekhar's head throbbed with the medley of sounds that had assailed his eardrums for a couple of hours now. He felt half stupefied. The headmaster had gone nearly hoarse, when he paused to ask, "Shall I go on?" Sekhar replied, "Please don't, sir; I think this will do. . . ." The headmaster looked stunned. His face was beaded with perspiration. Sekhar felt the greatest pity for him. But he felt he could not help ❼ it. No judge delivering a sentence felt more pained and helpless. Sekhar noticed that the headmaster's wife peeped in from the kitchen, with eager curiosity. The drummer and the violinist put away their burdens with an air of relief. The headmaster removed his spectacles, mopped his brow, and asked, "Now, come out with your opinion."

"Can't I give it tomorrow, sir?" Sekhar asked tentatively.

"No. I want it immediately—your frank opinion. Was it good?"

"No, sir. . ." Sekhar replied.

"Oh! . . . Is there any use continuing my

3. alapana: Improvisational Indian music in the classical style.

4. Kalyani: Traditional Indian folk songs.

▶Critical Viewing◀

❺ **Interpret** The arched eyebrows and big eyes suggest that this sun is observant and watchful. The smile suggests that the sun is amused by what it sees. Suggest to students that the sun's expression reflects that of a detached observer who might be chuckling at poor Sekhar's misadventures with the truth.

◆ Critical Thinking

❻ **Predict** Discuss how the headmaster is making a huge fuss over Sekhar. Ask students what they predict will happen. Will the headmaster's playing be good or bad? If bad, what will Sekhar say, after being treated so well? How will the headmaster react? *Some may predict he will criticize the headmaster's playing, making the headmaster angry; others may think the headmaster will accept Sekhar's criticism without anger; still others may predict that Sekhar will not tell the truth.*

◆ Build Grammar Skills

❼ **Comparative and Superlative Forms** Ask students to identify the comparative and superlative forms in this section and explain why each is used. *The comparative form is "more pained." It is used because Sekhar is being compared to only one other person. The superlative form is "greatest." It is used because this pity is being compared to all the other pity it would be possible to feel.*

Extending Word Study

Vocabulary Cards As they read *Like the Sun,* have students write words that are unfamiliar to them on index cards—one word per card. After they finish reading, have students use dictionaries look up and define the words. Suggest that they keep the cards rubber banded together, adding to them as they read new selections and find new vocabulary. Encourage students to refer back to their cards, as they encounter word used in new context. They might also review the cards occasionally to establish their increased vocabulary.

Reteach

Analyzing cause and effect, as well as linking several causes or effects, is a difficult reading strategy for some students to master. In order to reteach the concept, have students consider the idea of doing poorly on a test at school. As a group have students discuss whether doing poorly is a cause or an effect. To visually portray the concept, have students write doing poorly on a test in the middle of a piece of paper and draw a box around it. Since doing poorly on a test would be caused by not studying, have students write not studying above it in a box. An effect of doing poorly on a test, however, would be getting a low grade in the class, and then perhaps not qualifying for college scholarships, which could be written in boxes following the original box. Help students realize that one cause may result in more than one consequence, and sometimes more than one cause sets off a chain of consequences. Discuss with students that reading a literature selection and analyzing cause and effect follows the same process.

❶ **Enrichment** Discuss with students how Emily Dickinson's poem captures in verse a theme very similar to the one Narayan expresses in "Like the Sun."

◆ Literary Focus

❷ **Irony** At the beginning of the story, Sekhar felt a day of telling the truth was "full of possibilities." In contrast, by the end of the day, his truth telling appears to have destroyed his possibilities.

◆ Reading Strategy

❸ **Identify Consequences of Actions** Ask students to identify the positive and negative consequences of Sekhar's truth telling so far. Were any outcomes positive? *Sekhar's actions have hurt and angered his wife, upset a colleague, made Sekhar uncomfortable, and hurt the headmaster's feelings. Some students may point out that Sekhar won't have to keep eating the food he doesn't like and the headmaster won't keep wasting money on music lessons.*

Reinforce and Extend

Answers

◆ *Literature and Your Life*

Reader's Response Students will probably reply that telling the absolute truth all day would be difficult and uncomfortable.

Thematic Focus A person might become concerned that he or she was bending the truth more and more, or a person might tell the truth all day if protecting someone else's feelings would lead to larger problems later.

☑ Check Your Comprehension

1. He decided to tell the absolute truth for one complete day.
2. The headmaster wanted to get Sekhar's opinion of his music.
3. Sekhar decided that of all the consequences he might have suffered, grading 100 test papers in one day was not that bad.
4. She compares the truth to light.

Tell all the Truth but tell it slant—

Emily Dickinson

❶

Tell all the Truth but tell it slant—
Success in Circuit lies
Too bright for our infirm Delight
The Truth's superb surprise
As Lightning to the Children eased
With explanation kind
The Truth must dazzle gradually
Or every man be blind—

lessons?"

"Absolutely none, sir. . ." Sekhar said with his voice trembling. He felt very unhappy that he could not speak more soothingly. Truth, he reflected, required as much strength to give as to receive.

❷ **◆ Literary Focus** Notice the clash between Sekhar's noble view and the situation to which it has brought him.

All the way home he felt worried. He felt that his official life was not going to be smooth sailing hereafter. There were questions of increment and confirmation[5] and so on, all depending upon the headmaster's goodwill. All kinds of worries seemed to be in store for him. . . . Did not Harischandra[6] lose his throne, wife, child, because he would speak nothing less than the absolute Truth whatever happened?

At home his wife served him with a sullen face. He knew she was still angry with him for his remark of the morning. Two casualties for today, Sekhar said to himself. If I practice it for a week, I don't think I shall have a single friend left.

He received a call from the headmaster in his classroom next day. He went up apprehensively.

"Your suggestion was useful. I have paid off the music master. No one would tell me the truth about my music all these days. Why such antics at my age! Thank you. By the way, what about those test papers?"

"You gave me ten days, sir, for correcting them."

"Oh, I've reconsidered it. I must positively have them here tomorrow. . . ." A hundred papers in a day! That meant all night's sitting up! "Give me a couple of days, sir . . ."

"No. I must have them tomorrow morning. And remember, every paper must be thoroughly scrutinized."

"Yes, sir," Sekhar said, feeling that sitting up all night with a hundred test papers was a small price to pay for the luxury of practicing Truth.

◆ Build Vocabulary

scrutinized (skro͞ot´ ən īzd´) *v.*: Looked at carefully; examined closely

5. **increment and confirmation:** Salary increase and job security.
6. **Harishchandra** (hə rish chən´ drə): Legendary Hindu king who was the subject of many Indian stories. His name has come to symbolize truth and integrity.

Guide for Responding

◆ *Literature and Your Life*

Reader's Response Would you find telling the truth all day, as Sekhar does in this story, to be pleasurable? Why, or why not?

Thematic Focus Give a reason why a person might set himself or herself the personal challenge of telling the absolute truth for one day.

☑ Check Your Comprehension

1. What experiment did Sekhar set for himself at the beginning of the story?
2. For what reason did the headmaster want to meet with Sekhar?
3. What was Sekhar's response to having to grade 100 test papers in a day?
4. What comparison does Dickinson use to describe Truth?

Beyond the Selection

FURTHER READING

Other Works by R. K. Narayan

A Horse and Two Goats (stories)
An Astrologer's Day and Other Stories
Malgudi Days
Malgudi Landscapes: The Best of R. K. Narayan

Other Works With the Theme of Clashing Forces

"By Any Other Name," Santha Rama Rau
"Street Cries," Sarojini Naidu

We suggest that you preview these works before recommending them to students.

INTERNET

Please be aware that sites may have changed since we published this information.

For a profile of R. K. Narayan and a list of his books, students can visit the following Internet address: **http://www.cis,upenn. edu/~anoop/narayan/narayan.html**

We *strongly recommend* that you preview this site before sending students to it.

Guide for Responding *(continued)*

◆ Critical Thinking

INTERPRET

1. What effect does the headmaster's remark that he has spent a fortune on his music have on the story? **[Analyze]**

2. The phrase "luxury of practicing Truth" appears at the end of the story. How can truth be a luxury? **[Interpret]**

EVALUATE

3. Was Sekhar brave or foolish to tell the truth all day? Why? **[Make a Judgment]**

APPLY

4. Describe a situation in which you might "temper the truth." **[Interpret]**

◆ Reading Strategy

ANALYZE CAUSES AND EFFECTS

This story is somewhat unusual in that all its key events are so clearly the **effects** of a single decision: Sekhar's vow to tell the truth all day.

1. Identify two consequences that follow as a result of Sekhar's truthfulness about the headmaster's performance.

2. In describing the effects of his vow, Sekhar calls them "casualties." Why?

3. Is Sekhar right in predicting that if he keeps telling the truth, he won't have a single friend left? Why or why not?

◆ Literary Focus

IRONY

The central **irony** in this story is the clash between Sekhar's idealistic expectations and what actually occurs. For example, telling the absolute truth, as Sekhar vows to do, seems to be a noble goal. However, this vow leads to bad feelings. At breakfast, Sekhar's wife winces when he criticizes her cooking. The contrast between noble intention and disappointing effect is what creates irony.

1. What do you think Sekhar believes might happen as a result of his poor review of the headmaster's performance?

2. What is ironic about the headmaster's actual reaction to the criticism?

◆ Build Vocabulary

USING THE LATIN ROOT ***-gratis-***

Use your knowledge of the root *-gratis-*, which means "pleasing" or "a favor," to define these words.

1. grateful
2. gratitude
3. ingrate
4. gratis
5. gratuitous

USING THE WORD BANK: Sentence Completions

Write the paragraph on your paper and fill in the blanks with words from the Word Bank. Use each word just once.

The __?__ of Sekhar's vow was to tell the truth. This one day at least, he was not in favor of __?__ truth to protect people's feelings. __?__ throughout the day, he __?__ no opportunity of telling his wife and colleagues exactly what he thought. As they __?__ Sekhar's behavior, many of his colleagues were __?__. They expected Sekhar to be more __?__.

◆ Build Grammar Skills

COMPARATIVE AND SUPERLATIVE FORMS

Almost all one-syllable adjectives and some two-syllable adjectives use *-er* to form the **comparative** and *-est* to form the **superlative**. Many adjectives of two or more syllables use the words *more* or *most*, respectively, for comparative and superlative forms.

Practice In your notebook, write the correct form of the adjective from the choices given in parentheses.

1. Sekhar didn't say whether he liked one of the headmaster's songs (better, best) than the other.

2. If Sekhar had told the headmaster his music was the (more fine, most fine, finer, finest) he'd ever heard, the story would have had a different ending.

3. Sekhar would have told a (more temperate, most temperate, temperater, temperatest) truth the next day.

Writing Application Write a paragraph in which you compare Sekhar and the headmaster. Use at least two each of the comparative and the superlative forms of adjectives.

Answers

◆ Critical Thinking

1. The headmaster's remark gives some justification for Sekhar to tell him the absolute truth.
2. If the price of something is more than a person can afford, the person considers that thing a luxury. Sekhar's experiences show that the price of telling the truth can be high.
3. Students should base their answers on the range of Sekhar's experiences not just on one or two.
4. Situations might include ones in which another person's feelings might be hurt without any constructive effect or situations in which telling the absolute truth would cause harm.

◆ Reading Strategy

1. The headmaster quits his music lessons and Sekhar must correct the papers overnight instead of within ten days.
2. Most of the consequences were negative.
3. Based on people's reactions to the truth, Sekhar is probably correct. Even when hearing the truth is constructive, people often resent the person who tells it to them.

◆ Literary Focus

1. Sekhar thinks he will be fired or demoted.
2. While Sekhar fears the headmaster will be angry, the headmaster actually appreciates that someone has stopped him from wasting his money. In another ironic twist, however, his gratitude does not extend to allowing Sekhar the extra time for the test papers.

◆ Build Vocabulary

Using the Root *-gratis-*

1. Grateful is thankful for a favor.
2. Gratitude is the feeling of thankfulness you have when someone does you a favor.
3. An ingrate is someone who does not appreciate a favor.
4. Something done gratis is done as a favor.
5. Something that is gratuitous is extra—outside what is required—thrown in as a favor.

Using the Word Bank

The essence of Sekhar's vow was to tell the truth. This one day at least, he was not in favor of tempering the truth to protect people's feelings. Incessantly through the day, he shirked no opportunity of telling his wife and colleagues exactly what he thought. As they scrutinized Sekhar's behavior, many of his colleagues were stupefied. They expected Sekhar to be more ingratiating.

◆ Build Grammar Skills

1. better; 2. finest;
3. more temperate

Grammar Reinforcement

For additional instruction and practice, use the lesson in the **Language Lab CD-ROM** on Forms of Comparison. For more practice, use the Recognizing Degrees of Comparison and Using Comparative and Superlative Degrees pages in the *Writer's Solution Grammar Practice Book*, pp. 86 and 88.

Idea Bank

Following are suggestions for matching the Idea Bank topics with your students' performance levels and learning modalities:

Customizing for
Performance Levels

Less Advanced: 1, 5
Average: 2, 4, 7
More Advanced: 3, 4, 6, 7

Customizing for
Learning Modalities

Interpersonal: 4, 5
Verbal/Linguistic: 4, 5, 6
Musical/Rhythmic: 6
Visual/Spatial: 7

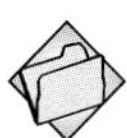

Guided Writing Lesson

Revision Strategy Dividing students into small groups for a say back can help them figure out where they need to add supporting details to their reviews. The reader shares his paper with the group while the others listen. After the second reading, the listeners write down the answer to the question "What did I want to know more about?" Then the listeners say their answers back to the reader. This strategy alerts the reader to the places in his text that are lacking in information or details.

For more prewriting, elaboration, and revision strategies, see *Prentice Hall Writing and Grammar.*

Writing Lab CD-ROM

Have students complete the Response to Literature tutorial. Follow these steps:

1. Tell students to use the Topic Web to organize subtopics and details that relate to their response to the song.
2. Encourage them to use the Evaluation Word Bins to choose suitable and precise adjectives and adverbs.
3. Have students draft on computer.
4. Suggest that they use the Language Variety Checker to find places to revise and eliminate repeated words.

Build Your Portfolio

Idea Bank

Writing

1. **Advice Column** Write an advice column response to tenth-grader Dara. Should Dara tell her friend, who can't carry a tune, not to try out for the school musical? Give reasons for your answer.
2. **Guidelines** You and your classmates will be exchanging ideas and editing one another's papers throughout the year. Write a set of guidelines for telling the truth in a useful, constructive way.
3. **Fairy Tale** Write a fairy tale about a teenager who must tell the truth in every situation. Set your fairy tale in ancient or modern times.

Speaking, Listening, and Viewing

4. **Oral Argument** Suppose that Sekhar was fired for telling the truth. As his attorney, prepare and deliver an oral argument summing up why he has been unfairly treated and why he should be rehired. **[Social Studies Link]**
5. **Debate** With a small group, debate the question of whether it is better to reveal the truth fully in social interactions or to soften it in some way. **[Social Studies Link; Performing Arts Link]**

Researching and Representing

6. **Research Songs** The term *Kalyani* refers to traditional Indian folk songs. Using text and musical resources at the library or via the Internet, find out more about Kalyani and present your findings to the class. If possible, play a recording of Kalyani. **[Music Link]**
7. **Map** Draw a map of southern India that shows Madras, where Narayan was born, and Mysore, which served as the basis for Narayan's fictional Malgudi. **[Social Studies Link]**

Online Activity www.phlit.phschool.com

Guided Writing Lesson

Review of a Song

Sekhar had to give an oral review of his headmaster's song. In writing, a **review** is an article giving a critical evaluation of a work of art. Use your knowledge of music to write a review of a song. Address your review to readers of a popular music magazine and win their confidence by clearly supporting your opinions with reasons.

Writing Skills Focus: Supporting Details

When writing a review, a research paper, or an editorial, use **supporting details**—facts, statistics, examples, or reasons—to persuade readers that your assertions are true.

Suppose, for example, that you write this topic sentence: "The lyrics of the song have particular meaning for teenagers living in the city." Your readers are going to ask themselves why this is the case. To answer that question, you can provide a supporting detail: "The lyrics of the song focus on what it feels like to be alone on a crowded city street."

Prewriting Create an outline for your review. For each paragraph, come up with a topic sentence and at least two supporting details to back it up.

I. Paragraph topic sentence
   A. Supporting detail
   B. Supporting detail

Drafting Your details should support the point in your topic sentence by clarifying, explaining, or giving an example.

Revising Show your review to a friend or writing partner. Ask whether your supporting details fit with their topic sentences. If any supporting details seem unclear, rewrite them to establish a clear connection to the main idea of your paragraph.

✓ ASSESSMENT OPTIONS

Formal Assessment, Selection Test, pp. 63–65, and Assessment Resources Software. The selection test is designed so that it can be easily customized to the ability levels of your students.

Alternative Assessment, p. 19, includes options for less advanced students, Pre-AP Students, verbal/linguistic learners, visual/spatial learners, logical/mathematical learners, interpersonal learners, and bodily/kinesthetic learners.

PORTFOLIO ASSESSMENT

Use the following rubrics in the ***Alternative Assessment*** booklet to evaluate student writing

Advice Column: Problem Solution Rubric, p. 101
Guidelines: Process Explanation, p. 100
Fairy Tale Fictional Narrative Rubric, p. 95
Guided Writing Lesson: Evaluation/Review Rubric, p. 104

Writing Process Workshop

Editorial

Where there is conflict, there are opinions. Like people, publications have their own opinions on issues. An **editorial** is a piece of persuasive writing, found in newspapers and magazines, that is written by the editor or editors of the publication about a current issue. In an editorial, the writer states the publication's viewpoint and tries to persuade readers to agree with it.

Write an editorial stating your viewpoint on an issue. The following skills, introduced in this section's Guided Writing Lessons, will help you write an effective editorial.

Writing Skills Focus

- **Use the appropriate language** for your audience. If your readers will be your classmates, use vocabulary that will be familiar to them. (See p. 249.)
- **Use supporting details** to back up any assertions that you make. (See p. 256.)
- **Use a persuasive tone.** Use words that appeal to the readers' senses, convey enthusiasm for your idea, and stress the idea's benefits. (See p. 230.)
- **Use vivid verbs.** These will create specific pictures in your readers' minds. (See p. 241.)

The following editorial uses these skills to convince readers of the importance of teaching typing in school.

Writing Model

We are alarmed ① that despite America's continuing move toward electronic communication, many American schools today do not teach typing.

It is ② incomprehensible that our educational establishment spends billions of dollars to purchase computers, yet does not teach students how to type quickly so they can obtain the maximum benefit from these machines. Our schools require driver education so that students will drive ③ safely, but many do not teach typing so their students will work more efficiently at computers and be much better prepared for college and the work world.④

① *Alarmed is a vivid verb that sets an urgent tone for the editorial.*

② *Words such as incomprehensible set a persuasive tone by showing the writer's strong feelings about the issue.*

③ *Here the writer uses a supporting detail to back up his argument.*

④ *The writer uses language that doesn't talk down to readers or insult their intelligence.*

Prepare and Engage

LESSON OBJECTIVES

- To use recursive processes to write an editorial
- To recognize and avoid loaded words
- To recognize and use active and passive voice appropriately

You may want to distribute the scoring rubric for Persuasion in ***Alternative Assessment*** (p. 105) to make students aware before they begin of the criteria on which they will be evaluated. See the suggestion on page 259 for additional points with which to customize the rubric for this workshop assignment.

Writers at Work Videodisc
To introduce students to the key elements of persuasive writing and show them how Sayu Bhojwani of the Asia Society in New York City incorporates them into her fund-raising writing, play the videodisc segment on Persuasion (Ch. 4).

Play frames 3 to 9933

Writing Lab CD-ROM
If your students have access to computers, you may want to have them work on the tutorial on Persuasion to complete all or part of their editorials. Follow these steps:

1. Have students review the interactive model of an editorial.
2. Suggest students use an Issue Wheel to help find an appropriate topic.
3. Have students draft on computer.
4. Suggest that students use a Transition Word Bin.
5. Have students complete the Proofreading checklist.

Connection to Literature To see examples of persuasive essays that share many of the characteristics of an editorial, refer students to Alexander Solzhenitsyn's Nobel Lecture (p. 587) and Elie Wiesel's "Keep Memory Alive" (p. 590).

Beyond the Classroom

Career Connection

Journalism Tell students interested in journalism or current events that they may someday be called upon or wish to write an editorial. To write a good editorial, it is important to keep aware of current events and know what the issues of concern to the public are. Suggest that students survey the OpEd (Opinions and Editorial) pages of several newspapers to determine what types of issues and topics are covered. In addition, they may want to look for the issues addressed by editorials in printed news magazines or television news magazine programs. You might point out that reading the same editorial column in a newspaper over a period of time will provide an understanding of that journalist's general "take" on current events and issues.

Encourage interested students to research the variety of jobs available in the field of journalism. Have them make a chart showing the educational requirements, starting salaries, and job responsibilities for each position.

Develop Student Writing

Prewriting Strategy

Encourage students to clarify their thoughts on their topic by writing a dialogue. Dialogue is a natural strategy for this assignment, as people dialogue daily about the types of controversial issues that students will be writing about in their editorials. Have them write a conversation that two people might have about the topic, and recommend that they choose two people with opposing opinions. This will help students to see the issue from more than one perspective, and will force them to construct sound ways of expressing their own opinions.

Writing Lab CD-ROM
The Considering Audience and Purpose section of the tutorial on Persuasion contains the screen Getting the Opposition on Your Side. Students can consult this screen to sharpen their persuasive techniques before they begin drafting.

Elaboration Strategy

Make sure students understand the facts about their topics so they can write valid and well-informed opinions. Encourage them to use the reporter's formula to gather as much information as possible about the issue at hand. Have them answer the standard journalistic questions regarding their topics: who? what? where? when? why? how? Students can use the information they gather to inform and support their opinions.

Applying Language Skills: Active and Passive Voice

Excessive use of the **passive voice** makes writing flat, wordy, and hard to follow. The **active voice** is generally more lively, concise, and easier to understand.

Passive Voice:
Citizens are endangered by the current condition of our town's streets.

Active Voice:
The current condition of our town's streets endangers our citizens.

Practice On your paper, rewrite the following sentences in the active voice.

1. Midwestern farmlands were devastated by the 1996 floods.
2. Crops were destroyed by the flood waters.

Writing Application As you draft your editorial, use active-voice verbs to keep your writing lively and easy to read.

Writer's Solution Connection
Language Lab

For more practice with active-voice verbs, complete the Language Lab lesson on Active and Passive Voice.

Prewriting

Choose a Topic A good way to choose a topic for an editorial is to sit with a group of classmates and brainstorm for a list of important issues in your community or school. Some people's opinions might be focused on crime; others', on pollution. Jot down notes as group members express their ideas, and refer to your notes for topics for your editorial.

Is Your Topic Too Broad? You can't effectively cover a large issue in a short piece of persuasive writing. Consider all the things you want to say about your topic. Do you think you can deal adequately with all the different parts of your topic? If not, narrow your topic so that you can focus on a more specific aspect of it.

Narrowing Your Topic

Broad	Narrow	Narrower
Sports	Funding for high-school sports	Men's and women's sports should receive equal funds
Politics	Presidential elections	Presidents should be elected for a single six-year term

Drafting

Avoid Faulty Logic As you write, avoid the following types of faulty logic and unreasonable statements:

Overgeneralization: Nobody likes the present lunch menu.
Improved: The cafeteria staff has heard dozens of complaints about the lunch menu this month.

Circular reasoning: Movies are popular because many people attend them.
Improved: Movies are popular because people love to be entertained by good stories.

Bandwagon appeal: All of the most attractive people exercise regularly.
Improved: People who exercise regularly improve their strength and stamina.

Either/Or arguments: Either we adopt a curfew, or the gangs will run wild.
Improved: If we don't adopt a curfew, it will be harder to keep our neighborhood safe and manageable.

Applying Language Skills
Active and Passive Voice
Explain to students that the active voice should be used in almost all situations. In general, the only appropriate use of the passive voice in persuasive writing is if the actor is clearly unknown or less important than the act itself.

Answers
1. The 1996 floods devastated midwestern farmlands.
2. The flood waters destroyed crops.

Grammar Reinforcement

For additional instruction and practice, have students complete the **Language Lab CD-ROM** lesson on Active and Passive Voice and practice page 74 in the *Writer's Solution Grammar Practice Book.*

Revising

Use a Checklist Review the Writing Skills Focus on p. 257, and use the points as a checklist to evaluate and revise your editorial.

- ▶ Have you used language appropriate for your audience?
  Define any difficult terms or use more sophisticated language if appropriate.
- ▶ Have you used supporting details?
  Back up each assertion with a fact or detail that supports it.
- ▶ Have you used a persuasive tone?
  Convey a sense of enthusiasm or urgency regarding your idea or position.
- ▶ Have you used vivid verbs?
  Replace any general verbs with vivid ones that will help your readers picture what you are trying to say.

Revision Model

We ~~should~~ ① must make shops accessible to people with disabilities. Not only ~~is it proper jurisprudence~~ ② does the law require it, but so does common sense. ③ People with disabilities need food, clothing, and personal items just as everyone else does.

① The word *must* is more persuasive than *should*.
② The writer replaces an unnecessarily difficult term with a simpler, more direct one.
③ The writer adds this supporting detail.

Proofreading

Use a Proofreading Checklist ✔

✔ Make sure you have no spelling or punctuation errors.
✔ Correct run-on sentences or sentence fragments.
✔ Replace the passive voice with the active voice.
✔ Eliminate loaded words.

Publishing

Send a Letter to the Editor By adding an introduction and changing a few words, you can turn your editorial into a letter to the editor. After you turn your editorial into a letter to the editor, mail it to the editor of your school or local newspaper.

Applying Language Skills: "Loaded" Words

Avoid "loaded" words—words with strong connotations—that will influence your readers' judgment by appealing to their fears or prejudices rather than their good sense.

Loaded Word:
Unfortunately, in England soccer attracts a rowdy audience.

Unbiased:
English police frequently have to break up fights among members of the audience at soccer matches.

Practice On your paper, rewrite the following sentence, removing any loaded words.

Security should bounce the punks from the stadium.

Writing Application Review your editorial to make sure you have eliminated loaded words.

Writer's Solution Connection Writing Lab

To learn more about loaded language, see the section on Drafting in the Persuasion tutorial in the Writing Lab.

Revision Strategy

Small groups of students can use a summarizing activity once they have completed their first drafts. Writers should read their pieces aloud, pause, and then read again. During the second reading, listeners should focus on what they think is the main idea:

1. Main ideas can be single sentences.
2. One word can express the main idea.

Listeners should then share their summaries with the group. This will give writers a sense of whether they communicated their main ideas effectively.

Writing Lab CD-ROM
The Proofreading section of the tutorial on Persuasion contains the screen About Active and Passive Voice. Have students consult this screen to make sure they have used active-voice verbs where appropriate.

Publishing

Students should be encouraged to keep their editorials as an example of persuasive writing.

Reinforce and Extend

Applying Language Skills

"Loaded" Words Remind students that loaded words attempt to manipulate feelings, fears, or prejudices rather than persuade by reason and logic.

Answer
Possible response:
Security should eject rowdy fans from the stadium.

Grammar Reinforcement

For additional practice, have students complete the practice page 74 on Active and Passive Voice in the *Writer's Solution Grammar Practice Book.*

✓ Assessment

PORTFOLIO ASSESSMENT
Use the rubric on Persuasion in the ***Alternative Assessment*** booklet (p. 105) to assess students' writing. Add these criteria to customize the rubric to this assignment.

	4	3	2	1
Active Voice	Verbs are in the active voice except in cases where the passive is clearly acceptable.	Most verbs are in the active voice.	Most verbs are in the active voice, but there are some improper passive-voice verbs.	A large number of passive-voice verbs make the piece tedious to read.
Loaded Words	The editorial contains no inappropriate loaded words. The argument uses reason, not emotional appeals.	The editorial avoids loaded words; the argument appeals to the reader's reason rather than emotions.	The editorial contains many loaded words; the argument appeals more to emotions than to reason.	The editorial is fraught with loaded words; the argument appeals primarily to the reader's emotions.

Prepare and Engage

LESSON OBJECTIVES
- To expand vocabulary through reading, listening, and discussing
- To read and understand analogies

Customize for
English Language Learners
Use the six numbered examples to guide students in making oral statements that incorporate each completed pair. Their statements should tell about related meanings. Here, for example, are possible statements for the first analogy: A light bulb is inside a lamp; a light bulb is part of a lamp; a light bulb is an essential part of a lamp. Encourage students to make their statements specific. Then, they can apply the relationship they've identified to the incomplete analogy.

Apply the Strategies

Answers

1. b (lead)
2. a (fins)
3. c (one)
4. c (silk)
5. a (ice cream)
6. a (desk)

Student Success Workshop

Vocabulary Development

Reading and Understanding Analogies

Strategies for Success

When a writer points out similarities between two things that seem different, he or she is drawing an **analogy.** For example, the following sentence draws an analogy: *Mustard goes with hot dogs as syrup goes with pancakes.* It points out that the relationship between mustard and hot dogs is logically parallel to the relationship between syrup and pancakes. Good analogies make careful distinctions between word meanings and show a logical, parallel relationship between two things or two pairs of things.

You may come across analogies as you read various types of texts or when taking a test.

How to Read a Word Analogy The type of analogy often found on tests is called a **word analogy.** Word analogies are usually phrased like this example: *An orange is to a watermelon as a lily is to a daffodil.* The same word analogy may be written this way:

orange : watermelon :: lily : daffodil.

Think About the Logic Logic is the basis of all analogies. A language test might ask you to choose a word to complete a word analogy. To choose the correct word, your challenge is to figure out the logical relationship between the parallel pairs of words. For example, both pairs of words might be synonyms, or antonyms, or things of the same kind, or they might have another type of relationship.

Suppose that in the following test problem you had to choose one of three words to complete this analogy:

orange : watermelon :: ___?___ : daffodil

(a) apple (b) baseball (c) lily

First, you would think about the logical relationship between the first pair of words and the meanings of the words in the incomplete analogy. Oranges and watermelons are both fruits—things of the same kind. Looking at the words *apple, baseball,* and *lily,* you can see that only the word *lily* can be paired with *daffodil* to make two things of the same kind.

Apply the Strategies

Practice your analogy comprehension skills by completing the following sentences.

1. A light bulb is to a lamp as ___?___ is to a pencil.
   a. paper b. lead c. pen
2. Wings are to eagles as ___?___ are to salmon.
   a. fins b. scales c. gills
3. a is to d as ___?___ is to four.
   a. two b. three c. one
4. Gold : silver :: ___?___ : satin
   a. cotton b. thread c. silk
5. milkshake : ___?___ :: cake : flour
   a. ice cream b. straw c. french fries
6. sofa : living room :: ___?___ : classroom
   a. desk b. pencil c. chalkboard

✔ *Understanding analogies can make a difference in these situations:*
- ▶ Explaining how to fix something
- ▶ Telling jokes and understanding them

Test Preparation Workshop

Vocabulary:
Understanding Word Relationships The SAT test requires students to understand analogies in order to answer questions. Point out to students that once they know how to identify the relationship between one pair of words in an analogy, they can use that knowledge to complete the other pair of words in the analogy. Knowledge of synonyms, antonyms, homonyms and awareness of attributes, part/whole, function, class-example, cause-effect and so forth can be applied.

Write the following sample on the board.

cool : warm :: high : _______

A altitude
B low
C temperature
D ground

Students should easily recognize the opposite relationship of *cool* and *warm.* However, they must apply that relationship to select the best answer. Caution them that all of the answer choices relate to *high* in some fashion, but B is the only word that achieves the same relationship as the first pair of words in the analogy.

PART 2 # Struggling for Justice

Hands, Gerald Bustomante/Stock Illustration Source

One-Minute Planning Guide

The selections in Part 2 deal with people and groups struggling for personal and public justice. "Hearts and Hands" and "The Fish" will help students see how compassion is a form of justice. The excerpt from "Desert Exile" and Gerald Ford's "Remarks Upon Signing a Proclamation Concerning Japanese American Internment During World War II" give a personal and a public perspective on basic human rights. "The Cabuliwallah" is a bittersweet story that shows how time can be the cruelest thief of all. This theme is reinforced in the Connections to Today's World feature, "Yesterday."

Customize for
Varying Student Needs

When assigning the selections in this part to your students, keep in mind the following factors:

"Hearts and Hands"
- A very short short story

"The Fish"
- An easy-to-understand poem
- Some students may need assistance with vocabulary

from "Desert Exile" and "Remarks Upon Signing a Proclamation"
- Students will need to understand context of selections before reading

"The Cabuliwallah "
- A long short story
- Cultural references may need to be explained
- Vocabulary is more difficult than in other selections

"Yesterday"
- High-interest song lyrics connecting theme to music

Humanities: Art

Hands by Gerald Bustomante.

Ask students to count how many hands or near-complete hands (as opposed to just fingertips) are in the artwork and to tally how many of those hands are right versus left hands. *There are eighteen hands: six right hands, twelve left hands*

Help students link the artwork to the theme of Part 2, Struggling for Justice, by answering the following questions:

1. Do you think the hands are cooperating with one another or opposing one another, and why? Sample answer: *Students who see the hands as cooperating might point to the way the fingers are outstretched, as opposed to clenched in fists, as well as the fact that many of the hands overlap. Students who see the hands as opposing one another might note that none of the hands grasps another and the outstretched fingers could be regarded as pushing other hands away or reaching for something the other hands want.*
2. Give this work a different title, one using the word *hands* to make some comment about society or human nature. *Sample answer: "Helping Hands"; "The Right Hand Doesn't Know What the Left Hand Is Doing"; "Many Hands Make Light Work."*

Prepare and Engage

LESSON OBJECTIVES

1. **To develop vocabulary and word identification skills**
   - Latin Prefixes: *counter-*
   - Using the Word Bank: Sentence Completions
2. **To use a variety of reading strategies to comprehend a short story and a poem**
   - Connect Your Experience
   - Reading Strategy: Predict Events
   - Tips to Guide Reading: Sustained Reading (ATE)
   - Read to Discover Models for Writing (ATE)
3. **To express and support responses to the text**
   - Critical Thinking
   - Analyze Literary Criticism (ATE)
   - Idea Bank: Opening Scene
4. **To analyze literary elements**
   - Literary Focus: Surprise Ending
5. **To read in order to research self-selected and assigned topics**
   - Idea Bank: Money Chart
6. **To speak clearly and effectively for a specific audience and purpose**
   - Idea Bank: Casting Discussion
7. **To plan, prepare, organize, and present literary interpretations**
   - Idea Bank: Monologue
   - Idea Bank: Sound Effects Tape
8. **To use recursive writing processes to write persuasively**
   - Guided Writing Lesson
   - Idea Bank: Speech
9. **To increase knowledge of the rules of grammar and usage**
   - Build Grammar Skills: Coordinate Adjectives

Test Preparation

Reading Comprehension: Stated and Implied Main Ideas (ATE, p. 263) The teaching tips and sample test item in this workshop support the instruction and practice in the unit workshop:
Reading Comprehension: Stated and Implied Main Ideas (SE, p. 299)

Guide for Reading

O. Henry *(1862–1910)*

A criminal turned storyteller, O. Henry (real name: William Sydney Porter) stole the show when it came to surprise endings.

William Sydney Porter was born in Greensboro, North Carolina. He had the amazing ability to identify with the common man, but his own life was anything but ordinary. He moved to Texas at the age of twenty-four and tried a number of unrelated jobs, including ranch hand, cartoonist, and bank teller. While working as a bank teller, he was accused (and eventually convicted) of embezzling funds. In prison, he took up writing short stories under the now famous pen name O. Henry.

Elizabeth Bishop *(1911–1979)*

A childhood friend of Elizabeth Bishop once said, "We all knew with no doubt whatsoever that she was a genius." Based on Bishop's accomplishments, it's hard to argue with her friend's assessment.

Bishop was born and raised in Massachusetts, but she loved to travel and spent many years living in Brazil. In 1945, she entered a poetry contest along with 800 other contestants—and she won! As a result, her first book, *North and South,* was published. "The Fish" was one of the poems in that first book.

By the time she died, Bishop had won virtually every poetry prize in the United States at least once, including the Pulitzer in 1956.

◆ Build Vocabulary

LATIN PREFIXES: *counter-*

One of the characters in "Hearts and Hands" is being taken to prison for counterfeiting. *Counterfeiting* begins with the Latin prefix *counter-*, which means "in opposition." *Counterfeiting* (in this story, making fake money) means making something that is "in opposition" to what it seems—an imitation made to deceive.

WORD BANK

As you read this story, you will encounter the words on this list. Each word is defined on the page where it first appears. Preview the list before you read. Identify any words you think you know already.

influx
forestalled
counterfeiting
sidled
venerable
infested
sullen

◆ Build Grammar Skills

COORDINATE ADJECTIVES

Writers use adjectives to describe characters, settings, and images. When they use **coordinate adjectives**—two or more adjectives of equal rank that separately modify the same noun—the adjectives are separated by commas.

The order of coordinate adjectives can be changed without altering the meaning of the sentence or sounding incorrect. For example, when O. Henry describes a character's voice as "full, sweet, and deliberate," he could have arranged the adjectives in any order—the adjectives are coordinate.

In Bishop's description of the "five old pieces of fish-line" in a fish's jaw, on the other hand, the adjectives "five" and "old" are not coordinate—their order cannot be reversed. A comma is not used between adjectives that are not coordinate.

Prentice Hall Literature Program Resources

REINFORCE / RETEACH / EXTEND

Selection Support Pages
Build Vocabulary: The Prefix *counter-*, p. 80
Build Grammar Skills: Coordinate Adjectives, p. 81
Reading Strategy: Predict Story Events, p. 82
Literary Focus: Surprise Ending, p. 83

Strategies for Diverse Student Needs, p. 20

Beyond Literature
Community Connection: Random Acts of Kindness, p. 20

Formal Assessment Selection Test, pp. 66–68; Assessment Resources Software

Alternative Assessment, p. 20

Writing and Language Transparencies
Writing Process Model 9, Business Letter, pp. 61–64

Literature CD-ROM

Resource Pro CD-ROM

Listening to Literature Audiocassettes

◆ Literature and Your Life

CONNECT YOUR EXPERIENCE

When your best friend tells you a sad story about a difficult time he or she is going through, you probably don't respond by telling your latest success story. It's easy to feel sympathy for a friend—but compassion isn't limited to people we know. When there are news reports of an abandoned animal or a lost child, people from all over the country respond with calls to help or donations of money. Even if you can't help personally, you feel compassion for the sufferer.

Journal Writing Write about a compassionate act that you have witnessed or heard about.

THEMATIC FOCUS: STRUGGLING FOR JUSTICE

The actions of the characters in this story and this poem may surprise you. Their compassion offers a unique answer to the question, "What is 'justice'?"

◆ Background for Understanding

THE STORY BEHIND THE STORY

It's no surprise if you feel compassion for the prisoner when you read "Hearts and Hands." O. Henry deliberately creates sympathy for the prisoner—perhaps because he had been one himself.

While working as a bank teller, William Sydney Porter (later to be known as O. Henry) was accused of embezzling funds. He denied the accusations and fled to Honduras. A year later, he returned to Texas to visit his sick wife and was arrested. He spent three years in a penitentiary in Columbus, Ohio. The story "Hearts and Hands" may have been inspired by his own journey to prison.

◆ Literary Focus

SURPRISE ENDING

Sometimes you can predict the ending of a story while you are reading it. At other times, you can't guess how the story will be resolved, but the ending seems in all ways the logical outcome of the events. Some stories have **surprise endings**—twists at the end that you did not expect. Authors build up to surprise endings by misleading you. No matter how surprising an ending is, however, it must be believable. Therefore, the author plants clues throughout that lead to the final outcome.

Pay attention to the details in the story and the poem that hint at the unexpected, but logical, outcomes.

◆ Reading Strategy

PREDICT EVENTS

You can predict whether or not it will rain by looking at the sky. You can **predict events** in literature in much the same way—you make an educated guess based on what you know about the characters, the situation, and the text structure of a story or narrative poem (which tells a story).

No matter how logical your predictions, you may need to revise them. Just as a new cloud in an otherwise clear sky might change your prediction about the weather, new circumstances introduced by the author may lead you to change your predictions about literary events.

Use a chart like the one shown to record and check your predictions.

Prediction	Reason	Actual Outcome

Test Preparation Workshop

Reading Comprehension: Stated and Implied Main Ideas Students will encounter questions on standardized tests that will test their ability to find the main idea of a selection and determine the details that best support the main idea. Give students the following sample test question for practice based on the first paragraph of "Hearts and Hands" on p. 264.

What is the main idea of this paragraph?

A The woman is an experienced traveler.
B The train is crowded.
C The woman is wealthy.
D The travelers have little in common.

When reading the answer choices, students may feel that none of the ideas expresses the main idea of the paragraph. Remind students that they are not looking for details when reading to find the main idea, they are looking for the central idea. Answers *A*, *B*, and *C* are details from the paragraph, but *D* expresses the implied main idea—the handcuffed men have very little in common with a wealthy young woman.

Interest Grabber Show video of magicians such as Siegfried and Roy or David Copperfield performing an illusion in which something or someone is exchanged for another. (If you have any amateur magicians in your class, invite them to perform an illusion live for the class.) Lead students to see that an illusion is like a surprise ending. When the curtain is whisked away, you see a person where a tiger used to be, or a quarter appears from behind your ear when you expect it to be in the magician's hand. Tell students that the selections they are about to read are like magic tricks. When the writers "whisk away the curtain" to reveal the ending, readers may not see what they expect to see.

Tips to Guide Reading

Sustained Reading In order to enjoy O. Henry's surprise ending, encourage students to use sustained reading when they read the selection.

Customize for ***Less Proficient Readers***
Have students pause frequently to review important details and visualize the action of the story. Ask them to make predictions based on their review and visualization and them guide them to verbalize details that support their predictions.

Customize for ***Pre-AP Students***
Have students speculate about the reasons behind characters' actions. As students read, have them take notes for a "character history" that explains how each character develops the personality described in the story.

Customize for ***Gifted/Talented Students***
Encourage students to put a different twist on O. Henry's story by retelling the story with a new and different ending.

Customize for ***English Language Learners***
Ask students to find the punctuation that will help them identify complete sentences in the poem. Then assist students in restating the sentences in simpler terms.

Develop Understanding

One-Minute Insight "Hearts and Hands" tells the story of a brief encounter between three characters on a train. Through dialogue, O. Henry hints at a past conflict between one young man and the young woman. At the end of the story, we realize that the real conflict, which is not between the young man and the young woman, is very much in the present, and that what characters say doesn't always reveal who they are.

◆ Build Grammar Skills

❶ **Coordinate Adjectives** Have students explain why O. Henry doesn't separate the adjectives "two" and "young" with commas yet does separate the adjectives "bold" and "frank" with commas. *The first pair are not coordinate, so their order cannot be switched without losing meaning. ("Young two men" doesn't make sense.) The second pair, in contrast, are coordinate, so they are separated by commas ("frank, bold countenance" still makes sense).*

◆ Reading Strategy

❷ **Predict Events** Guide students to recognize that Easton's embarrassment is a clue that there is something he doesn't want the young woman to know. Students' predictions can springboard from this inference.

◆ Build Vocabulary

❸ **The Prefix *counter-*** In context, most students will probably identify counterfeiting as creating fake money. Discuss the way in which counterfeit money is "in opposition" to real money.

◆ Critical Thinking

❹ **Draw Conclusions** Based on this conversation, have students draw conclusions about the past relationship of Easton and Miss Fairchild. *The conversation suggests that at one time, Easton was interested in Miss Fairchild romantically, but that he was without money and status and thought she preferred an ambassador (who probably had money).*

Hearts and Hands

O. HENRY

At Denver there was an influx of passengers into the coaches on the eastbound B. & M. express. In one coach there sat a very pretty young woman dressed in elegant taste and surrounded by all the luxurious comforts of an experienced traveler. Among the newcomers were ❶ two young men, one of handsome presence with a bold, frank countenance and manner; the other a ruffled, glum-faced person, heavily built and roughly dressed. The two were handcuffed together.

As they passed down the aisle of the coach the only vacant seat offered was a reversed one facing the attractive young woman. Here the linked couple seated themselves. The young woman's glance fell upon them with a distant, swift disinterest; then with a lovely smile brightening her countenance and a tender pink tingeing her rounded cheeks, she held out a little gray-gloved hand. When she spoke her voice, full, sweet, and deliberate, proclaimed that its owner was accustomed to speak and be heard.

"Well, Mr. Easton, if you *will* make me speak first, I suppose I must. Don't you ever recognize old friends when you meet them in the West?"

> ◆ **Reading Strategy**
> ❷ What prediction do you make based on Easton's embarrassment?

The younger man roused himself sharply at the sound of her voice, seemed to struggle with a slight embarrassment which he threw off instantly, and then clasped her fingers with his left hand.

"It's Miss Fairchild," he said, with a smile. "I'll ask you to excuse the other hand; it's otherwise engaged just at present."

He slightly raised his right hand, bound at the wrist by the shining "bracelet" to the left one of his companion. The glad look in the girl's eyes slowly changed to a bewildered horror. The glow faded from her cheeks. Her lips parted in a vague, relaxing distress. Easton, with a little laugh, as if amused, was about to speak again when the other forestalled him. The glum-faced man had been watching the girl's countenance with veiled glances from his keen, shrewd eyes.

"You'll excuse me for speaking, miss, but I see you're acquainted with the marshal here. If you'll ask him to speak a word for me when we get to the pen he'll do it, and it'll make things easier for me there. He's taking me to Leavenworth prison. It's seven years for counterfeiting."

"Oh!" said the girl, with a deep breath and returning color. "So that is what you are doing out here? A marshal!"

"My dear Miss Fairchild," said Easton, calmly, "I had to do something. Money has a way of taking wings unto itself, and you know it takes money to keep step with our crowd in Washington. I saw this opening in the West, and—well, a marshalship isn't quite as high a position as that of ambassador, but—"

"The ambassador," said the girl, warmly,

> ◆ **Build Vocabulary**
> **influx** (in´ fluks) *n.*: A coming in
> **forestalled** (fôr stôld´) *v.*: Prevented by having done something ahead of time
> **counterfeiting** (koun´ tər fit´ iŋ) *v.*: Making imitation money to pass off as real money
> **sidled** (sī´ dəld) *v.*: Moved sideways

Block Scheduling Strategies

Consider these suggestions to take advantage of extended class time:

- Use the Community Connection page on Random Acts of Kindness in the ***Beyond Literature*** booklet, p. 20. This activity can supplement the Literature and Your Life journal writing activity (p. 263).
- Preview the vocabulary list on p. 262 as a class. Ask volunteers to identify words they think they know and share definitions. Guide students to check the accuracy of each definition by looking at the Build Vocabulary box on the page where the word appears.
- Introduce the Reading Strategy, and model the use of the chart on p. 263 for predicting events and checking predictions. You may use the Grid Organizer in the ***Writing and Language Transparencies,*** p. 79, to demonstrate.
- Link "Hearts and Hands" to math skills by having small groups of students work in class to complete the Money Chart project on p. 269.
- Have students complete the Guided Writing Lesson (p. 269), perhaps using a tape recorder during the interview.

"doesn't call any more. He needn't ever have done so. You ought to know that. And so now you are one of these dashing Western heroes, and you ride and shoot and go into all kinds of dangers. That's different from the Washington life. You have been missed from the old crowd."

The girl's eyes, fascinated, went back, widening a little, to rest upon the glittering handcuffs.

"Don't you worry about them, miss," said the other man. "All marshals handcuff themselves to their prisoners to keep them from getting away. Mr. Easton knows his business."

"Will we see you again soon in Washington?" asked the girl.

"Not soon, I think," said Easton. "My butterfly days are over, I fear."

"I love the West," said the girl irrelevantly. Her eyes were shining softly. She looked away out the car window. She began to speak truly and simply, without the gloss of style and manner: "Mamma and I spent the summer in Denver. She went home a week ago because father was slightly ill. I could live and be happy in the West. I think the air here agrees with me. Money isn't everything. But people always misunderstand things and remain stupid—"

"Say, Mr. Marshal," growled the glum-faced man. "This isn't quite fair. Haven't had a smoke all day. Haven't you talked long enough? Take me in the smoker now, won't you? I'm half dead for a pipe."

The bound travelers rose to their feet, Easton with the same slow smile on his face.

"I can't deny a petition for tobacco," he said lightly. "It's the one friend of the unfortunate. Goodbye, Miss Fairchild. Duty calls, you know." He held out his hand for a farewell.

"It's too bad you are not going East," she said, reclothing herself with manner and style. "But you must go on to Leavenworth, I suppose?"

"Yes," said Easton. "I must go on to Leavenworth."

The two men sidled down the aisle into the smoker.

The two passengers in a seat nearby had heard most of the conversation. Said one of them: "That marshal's a good sort of chap. Some of these Western fellows are all right."

"Pretty young to hold an office like that, isn't he?" asked the other.

"Young!" exclaimed the first speaker, "why— Oh! didn't you catch on? Say—did you ever know an officer to handcuff a prisoner to his *right* hand?" 5

Guide for Responding

◆ Literature and Your Life

Reader's Response Would you have bailed Mr. Easton out of his uncomfortable situation? Explain.

Thematic Focus How does the marshal's compassionate act broaden the definition of justice?

☑ Check Your Comprehension

1. Why did the two handcuffed men sit across from Miss Fairchild?
2. How do Miss Fairchild and Mr. Easton know each other?

◆ Critical Thinking

INTERPRET

1. Why does the marshal deceive Miss Fairchild? **[Speculate]**
2. Explain what role "hearts" and "hands" play. **[Analyze]**

EXTEND

3. Do you think compassion is a necessary quality for a person who works in law enforcement or the justice system? Why or why not? **[Career Link]**

Analyze Literary Criticism

In her review of O. Henry's short stories, Toni Shiffman says: "If you thought of him only as a writer of funny stories, which he surely was, you would miss much of the wonder this man created. His gift for language was ingenious . . . . He wrote of real people, with real problems, but he brought such tender understanding to his portraits of life, and such verbal gymnastics to his manner of expression, that any story of his can be read now, a century later, and still summon your innermost tender spot." Share this review of O. Henry's writing with the students. Then discuss with students whether or not they agree with Shiffman's assessment of his work. Have students consider questions such as they following:

1. Will O. Henry's writing be of interest to readers years from now? Why or why not? *Students may say that people will always enjoy a surprise ending; or they may think that his stories will be outdated.*
2. In the story, "Hearts and Hands," find examples of the characters he described in the story as "real people, with real problems." *Possible response: Mr. Easton, who is being taken to prison, and is embarrassed that Miss Fairchild will know.*

◆ Literary Focus

5 Surprise Ending Have students review the story and identify other clues that Easton is a prisoner and not a marshal. *When Easton first meets Miss Fairchild he is embarrassed; his explanation of the handcuffs is interrupted by the other man; Easton indicates that he will not return to Washington by saying "My butterfly days are over, I fear"; Easton says, "I must go on to Leavenworth."*

Read to Discover Models for Writing

O. Henry is known for his surprise endings and his descriptive writing style, which gives students excellent models to use for their own writing.

Reinforce and Extend

Answers

◆ Literature and Your Life

Reader's Response Encourage students to include in their reasons a response to Mr. Easton's character based on details in the story.

Thematic Focus Lead students to recognize that the marshal's emotional and compassionate justice is separate from the civil justice he administers. The marshal's compassionate actions indicate that he doesn't feel that humiliation in front of an old friend is a just part of Easton's punishment for his crime.

◆ Critical Thinking

1. The marshal doesn't want to humiliate Easton in front of an old friend.
2. The marshal has a big heart that allows him to understand what might be in Easton's heart. This knowledge leads him to conceal the real reason that their hands are cuffed together.
3. Many students will say that compassion is necessary for a balanced sense of justice; others may feel that it would prevent someone from punishing the guilty.

Develop Understanding

One-Minute Insight At the opening of this poem, the conflict seems to be resolved—the fish is caught. As the poem continues, the speaker reveals an internal conflict that leads to an outcome readers may not expect.

◆ Critical Thinking

❶ **Infer** Ask students what they can infer about the fish from details such as "ancient wallpaper" and "stained and lost through age." *The fish is very old. He has survived what appears to be a difficult life.*

◆ Reading Strategy

❷ **Predict Events** Encourage students to predict what the speaker will do with the fish. *This section indicates that the speaker is thinking about filleting the fish. Some students may interpret this passage as the speaker's reflection on the fish's living organs, and that this reflection will lead to feeling compassion for the fish.*

◆ Critical Thinking

❸ **Make Inferences** Ask students why Bishop wants the reader to know that the fish didn't return the speaker's stare. How might this make the speaker feel? *Students may say that the fish doesn't care about being caught and is not interested in the speaker at all. This might make the speaker feel unimportant.*

◆ Build Grammar Skills

❹ **Coordinate Adjectives** Ask students why Bishop puts commas between the adjectives "grim, wet, and weaponlike" but not between "five old." *The first three adjectives are coordinate. The second pair are not coordinate (their order cannot be switched without losing their meaning).*

◆ Reading Strategy

❺ **Predict Events** Have students make a logical guess about the poem's outcome. *Students might guess that the speaker will let the fish go because she feels compassion for the pain it has suffered in the past or respect for the fish who has eluded being caught so many times.*

I caught a tremendous fish
and held him beside the boat
half out of water, with my hook
fast in a corner of his mouth.
He didn't fight.
He hadn't fought at all.
He hung a grunting weight,
battered and venerable
and homely. Here and there
his brown skin hung in strips
like ancient wallpaper,
❶ and its pattern of darker brown
was like wallpaper:
shapes like full-blown roses
stained and lost through age.
He was speckled with barnacles,
fine rosettes of lime,
and infested
with tiny white sea-lice,
and underneath two or three
rags of green weed hung down.
While his gills were breathing in
the terrible oxygen
—the frightening gills,
fresh and crisp with blood,
that can cut so badly—
I thought of the coarse white flesh
packed in like feathers,
❷ the big bones and the little bones,
the dramatic reds and blacks
of his shiny entrails,[1]
and the pink swim-bladder[2] ❷
like a big peony.
I looked into his eyes
which were far larger than mine
but shallower, and yellowed,
the irises backed and packed
with tarnished tinfoil ❸
seen through the lenses
of old scratched isinglass.[3]
They shifted a little, but not
to return my stare.
—It was more like the tipping
of an object toward the light.
I admired his sullen face,
the mechanism of his jaw,
and then I saw
that from his lower lip
—if you could call it a lip— ❹
grim, wet, and weaponlike, ❺
hung five old pieces of fish-line,

1. **entrails** (en´ trālz) *n.*: Intestines; guts.

2. **swim-bladder:** Gas-filled sac that keeps a fish from sinking.

3. **isinglass** (ī´ zin glas´) *n.*: Semitransparent substance obtained from fish bladders and sometimes used for windows.

◆ Build Vocabulary

venerable (ven´ ər ə bəl) *adj.*: Worthy of respect or reverence by reason of age, character, or position

infested (in fest´ id) *adj.*: Overrun by

sullen (sul´ ən) *adj.*: Gloomy; sad

Reteach

Using the reading strategy of prediction is an important tool students can use to enhance their reading pleasure. Point out to students that making a correct prediction on an O. Henry short story will be a challenge to any reader because he delights in surprise endings. To help students who find the concept difficult, suggest that they think of a weather forecaster who must stand in front of the television audience every day and predict the weather. Have students brainstorm clues or weather signs that a forecaster might use to predict a blizzard. In a similar way, an author uses verbal clues or signals that foretell events or the conclusion of a story. Have students fold a piece of paper in half lengthwise to make two columns. Suggest that they select either the short story or the poem and reread, analyzing each line to see if it contains a clue. If they believe it does, have them write it in the first column. As they finish rereading, have them analyze each clue again and put a check mark in the second column if it supported their predictions.

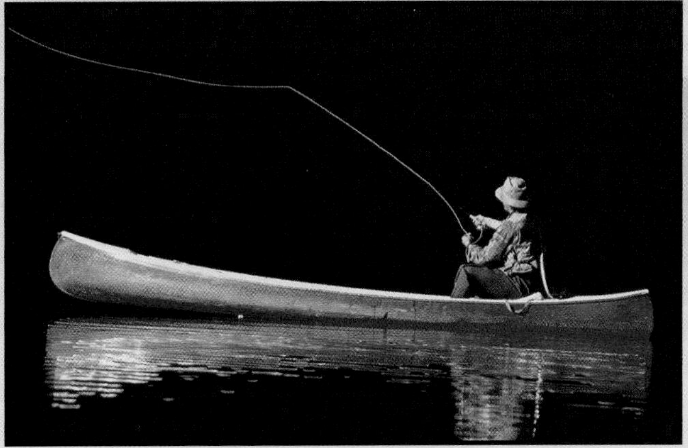

▲ Critical Viewing Based on this picture, why do you think many people enjoy fishing? [Draw Conclusions] ❼

or four and a wire leader
with the swivel still attached,
with all their five big hooks
grown firmly in his mouth.
A green line, frayed at the end
where he broke it, two heavier
lines
and a fine black thread
still crimped from the strain and
snap
when it broke and he got away.
Like medals with their ribbons
frayed and wavering,
a five-haired beard of wisdom
trailing from his aching jaw.
I stared and stared
❻ and victory filled up
the little rented boat,
from the pool of bilge[4]
where oil had spread a rainbow
around the rusted engine
to the bailer rusted orange,
the sun-cracked thwarts,[5]
the oarlocks on their strings,
the gunnels[6]—until everything
was rainbow, rainbow, rainbow!
And I let the fish go.

4. **bilge** (bilj) *n.*: Dirty water in the bottom of a boat.

5. **thwarts** (*th*wôrts) *n.*: Rowers' seats lying across a boat.

6. **gunnels** (gun′ əlz) *n.*: Upper edges of the sides of a boat.

Guide for Responding

◆ *Literature and Your Life*

Reader's Response Would you have let the fish go? Explain.

Thematic Focus How do the fish's past conflicts affect the speaker?

☑ Check Your Comprehension

1. What does the speaker find in the lower lip of the fish?
2. Explain what the speaker does with the fish.

◆ Critical Thinking

INTERPRET

1. Why didn't the fish fight against being caught? **[Infer]**

APPLY

2. Explain how compassion can be a sign of strength. **[Relate]**

COMPARE LITERARY WORKS

3. Compare and contrast what O. Henry's story and Bishop's poem suggest about the nature of compassion. **[Compare and Contrast]**

Beyond the Selection

FURTHER READING

Other Works by O. Henry

The Four Million (short stories)

The Gentle Grafter (short stories)

Other Works by Elizabeth Bishop

North and South (poems)

Other Works About Clashing Forces

"After Twenty Years," O. Henry

"The Old Man and the Sea," Ernest Hemingway

We suggest that you preview these works before recommending them to students.

INTERNET

Students can learn more about O. Henry at the following Web site: **http://www.ci.austin.tx.us/parks/ohenry.htm**

For a look into O. Henry's life, students can visit **http://www.dcr.state.nc.us/NC/NCSITES/GREENSBO/O_HENRY.HTM**

We *strongly suggest* that you preview these Web sites before sending students to them. Please be aware that addresses may have changed since this information was published.

◆ Critical Thinking

❻ **Interpret** Ask students what the poet means by "victory filled up the little boat." To whose victory does she refer—the speaker's or the fish's? *Students may say that the victory is the fish's because it has so many "medals" and battle scars. Some may say that the speaker feels victorious, having caught such a venerable fish.*

▶Critical Viewing◀

❼ **Draw Conclusions** *Students may say that it looks quiet and peaceful on the lake, or that the man looks relaxed.*

Reinforce and Extend

Literature CD-ROMs
Use the **Literature CD-ROM** *How to Read Poetry,* Feature 6, to expose students to other poems that explore the themes of moral choices.

Answers

◆ *Literature and Your Life*

Reader's Response Some students may feel that, like the speaker, they would have felt admiration for the fish and released it. Others may say they would not release it, feeling that the fish is an even more valuable "prize" because it has eluded so many other anglers.

Thematic Focus Because the fish has successfully survived so many battles, the speaker doesn't feel it would be fair to end his life by being caught.

☑ Check Your Comprehension

1. The speaker finds four or five pieces of fish line and five hooks in the fish's jaw.
2. The speaker holds the fish up and examines him, then releases him.

◆ Critical Thinking

1. The fish may not have fought against getting caught because he was old and tired, or because he realized the hopelessness of his situation.
2. A person who shows compassion is strong enough not to have to prove his or her strength.
3. Students may feel that catching the fish in the first place is contrary to the concept of compassion. Others may see the speaker's change of heart as a perfect example of compassion.

Answers

◆ Reading Strategy

1. The way the young woman brightens up helps you predict that the young woman knows one of the men.
2. Mr. Easton's reaction confirms the past acquaintance between the young woman and Mr. Easton. In addition, it indicates that he is worried about what she thinks of him.
3. Mr. Easton's embarrassment and ironic way of speaking are clues that can help you predict that Mr. Easton is not who he seems to be.
4. Some students will have predicted that the speaker would take the fish home as a prize, or to eat it. Other students may have predicted the actual outcome of the fish's release.

◆ Literary Focus

1. Until very near the end of the story, it seems as if Mr. Easton and Miss Fairchild may renew their relationship.
2. Students should identify the specific detail that gave them the final clue to Easton's identity.
3. Mr. Easton's embarrassment, his comment that money takes wing, and his easy acceptance of the "prisoner's" request to leave the car are clues that he is not really the marshal.
4. Students should explain how details from the poem led to their realization that the speaker would release the fish.
5. The rough appearance and manner of Mr. Easton's companion contribute to the surprise when it is revealed that he is the marshal. The excitement the speaker feels at having caught the fish contributes to the surprise when the speaker releases the fish.

◆ Build Vocabulary

Using the Prefix *counter-*

1. Counterclockwise is the opposite direction from the way a clock moves.
2. Counterproductive is the opposite of productive, or constructive, action.
3. A counterbalance is a weight or force placed in opposition so that it balances another weight.
4. Counterpoint is something (often a melody or an argument) set up to contrast or be opposite to another thing.

Guide for Responding (continued)

◆ Reading Strategy

Predict Events

Many stories and narrative poems seem to follow a logical pattern that helps you **predict events**—that is, to make educated guesses about what will happen. In "Hearts and Hands," for instance, when the two handcuffed men board the train, you can predict that they will somehow become involved with the young woman. As you learn more about the characters and the situation, you can make more specific, and usually more accurate, predictions.

1. In "Hearts and Hands," what prediction can you make based on the young woman's reaction when she sees the two men?
2. How does Mr. Easton's reaction to the young woman affect your prediction?
3. Why might you expect that Mr. Easton and the other man are not exactly who they claim to be?
4. In "The Fish," what did you predict the speaker would do after catching the fish? Why?

◆ Literary Focus

Surprise Ending

Literature, like life, can sometimes surprise you. A **surprise ending** is an unexpected twist at the end of a story or a narrative poem. O. Henry is known for his surprise endings, and many readers try to outsmart him by looking for his clues to the real ending. In "Hearts and Hands," the fact that Mr. Easton has the handcuff on his right hand is one such clue. Elizabeth Bishop also gives a surprising twist to the end of her poem by having the speaker do the opposite of what you would expect.

1. What ending are you led to expect as you read "Hearts and Hands"?
2. At what point in the story did you realize that Mr. Easton was not the marshal?
3. Point out at least three things in Mr. Easton's words and behavior that provide clues to the real ending.
4. At what point did you first suspect that the speaker in "The Fish" would release the catch?
5. What quality or personality trait contributed to the surprise ending in the story and the poem?

◆ Build Vocabulary

Using the Latin Prefix *counter-*

Knowing that the Latin prefix *counter-* means "in opposition," explain how *opposite* contributes to the meaning of each of the following words.

1. counterclockwise **3.** counterbalance
2. counterproductive **4.** counterpoint

Using the Word Bank: Sentence Completions

Choose the best word from the Word Bank to complete each sentence.

1. The fish was __?__ with lice.
2. The marshal __?__ an embarrassing situation.
3. The prisoner __?__ toward the door.
4. An __?__ of people hid them from view.
5. The __?__ man never looked up.
6. O. Henry's crime was embezzlement, not __?__.

◆ Build Grammar Skills

Coordinate Adjectives

The order of coordinate adjectives can be reversed without changing the meaning of the description or sounding awkward. O. Henry uses coordinate adjectives when he describes Mr. Easton's "*bold, frank* countenance."

Coordinate adjectives are adjectives of equ rank that separately modify a noun.

Practice Copy the following sentences in your notebook. Put commas between any coordinate adjectives.

1. The embarrassed young man didn't speak.
2. The thoughtful compassionate marshal helped him out.
3. The ugly battered fish didn't fight.
4. The little rented boat was full of rainbows.

Writing Application Use coordinate adjectives to add details to each of the following sentences.

1. The train pulled out of the station.
2. The woman looked at the men.
3. The marshal and the prisoner walked away.

268 ◆ Clashing Forces

Using the Word Bank

1. infested; 2. forestalled;
3. sidled; 4. influx;
5. sullen; 6. counterfeiting

◆ Build Grammar Skills

Practice

1. The embarrassed young man didn't speak. *no change*
2. The thoughtful, compassionate marshal helped him out.
3. The ugly, battered fish didn't fight.
4. The little rented boat was full of rainbows. *no change*

Writing Application

Suggested answers:

1. The *fast, powerful* train pulled out of the *noisy, crowded* station.
2. The *pleasant, gentle* woman looked at the two *scruffy, ragged* men.
3. The *thoughtful, compassionate* marshal and the *angry, sullen* prisoner walked away.

Build Your Portfolio

Idea Bank

Writing

1. **Monologue** Write a brief monologue—a speech to be delivered by a single character—in which the marshal explains why he pretended to be the criminal. **[Performing Arts Link]**

2. **Opening Scene** Write an opening scene for a sequel to "Hearts and Hands" in which Mr. Easton and Miss Fairchild meet after Mr. Easton is released from prison.

3. **Speech** Write a speech expressing where you stand on the issue of whether to preserve natural areas for recreation (such as fishing and boating) or to develop them for industry and housing. **[Science Link]**

Speaking, Listening, and Viewing

4. **Casting Discussion** With a group, discuss actors who could play the roles in "Hearts and Hands." Reach a consensus and present your recommendations and reasons to the class.

5. **Sound-Effects Tape** Create a sound-effects tape to accompany a dramatic reading of "The Fish." Experiment with ways of creating the sound of a boat rocking in the water, a fishing line being reeled, and a fish slipping back into the water.

Researching and Representing

6. **Money Chart** O. Henry's counterfeiting character created fake money—money that had no value. Create a chart that shows the value of a U.S. dollar compared with the value of the currency of two other countries. Write a brief explanation to go with your chart. **[Math Link; Social Studies Link]**

7. **Opening Credits** Create a set of images that you would show behind the opening credits of a movie of "Hearts and Hands." Choose images that will set the scene for the events that follow.

Online Activity www.phlit.phschool.com

Guided Writing Lesson

Letter to the Editor

Many compassionate acts—such as those of the marshal and the speaker in "The Fish"—go unnoticed or unacknowledged. Write a letter to the editor of your local newspaper about a person in your community that you feel deserves to be acknowledged for his or her compassion or charitable deeds. The following tips will help you create a convincing portrait of the person you wish to acknowledge.

Writing Skills Focus: Elaboration

Don't just *say* that the subject of your letter deserves recognition for a compassionate act—*prove it!* **Elaborate** with details, examples, and facts to support your claim. Describe the actions that led you to choose this person as the subject of your letter. If appropriate, offer statistics, such as number of hours of volunteer work. The more specific and factual you are, the more compelling your letter will be. Look for ways to elaborate as you draft and revise.

Prewriting Interview the person you are writing about or talk to people who know your subject. Personal conversations will allow you to ask questions and obtain more detailed information about the person.

Drafting Organize your letter around several key points. As you draft, include the details you've discovered to support each of the points you make.

Revising Reread your draft and identify at least one fact, example, or detail that supports each main point. If you cannot identify at least one detail supporting each main point, add a detail or example that elaborates on your general statement.

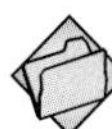

Idea Bank

Following are suggestions for matching Idea Bank topics with your students' performance levels and learning modalities.

Customizing for *Performance Levels*

Less Advanced: 1, 4, 7
Average: 2, 4, 5, 6, 7
More Advanced: 3, 5, 6

Customizing for *Learning Modalities*

Interpersonal: 4
Intrapersonal: 6, 7
Mathematical/Logical: 6

Guided Writing Lesson

Elaboration Strategy Guide students to strengthen their letters to the editor by elaborating with details, examples, and facts that support their claim. Use the **SEE** technique: making a **S**tatement, **E**xtending the statement, and **E**laborating on the statement. Model the **SEE** technique with the following example:
Statement: Mrs. Dobson is a compassionate person.
Extension: She delivers meals to homebound people.
Elaboration: Mrs. Dobson discusses homebound people's favorite TV shows with them when she delivers their meals.

For more prewriting, elaboration, and revision strategies, see *Prentice Hall Writing and Grammar.*

Writing and Language Transparencies Use Writing Process Model 9: Business Letter pp. 61–64, to model the format and writing of a business letter.

Writing Lab CD-ROM
Have students complete the tutorial on Persuasion to help them write a convincing letter to the editor. Follow these steps:

1. Use the Cluster Diagram to brainstorm for details about the person and his or her compassionate act.
2. Use the Note Cards activity to experiment with different ways of organizing information about the subject.
3. Draft on the computer.
4. Use the interactive Self-Evaluation Checklist to judge the effectiveness of the letter.

✓ ASSESSMENT OPTIONS

Formal Assessment, Selection Test, pp. 66–67, and on Assessment Resources Software. The selection test is designed so that it can be easily customized to the ability levels of your students. ***Alternative Assessment,*** p. 20, includes options for less advanced students, Pre-AP Students, visual/spatial learners, verbal/linguistic learners, and logical/mathematical learners.

PORTFOLIO ASSESSMENT
Use the following rubrics in the ***Alternative Assessment*** booklet to assess students' writing
Monologue: Expression Rubric, p. 94
Opening Scene: Drama Rubric, p. 107
Speech: Persuasion Rubric, p. 105
Guided Writing Lesson: Persuasion Rubric, p. 105 and Business Letter Rubric, p. 113

Prepare and Engage

LESSON OBJECTIVES

1. **To develop vocabulary and word identification skills**
   - Latin Word Roots: *-curs-*
   - Using the Word Bank: Context
   - Extending Word Study: Context Clues
2. **To use a variety of reading strategies to comprehend a narrative and a speech**
   - Connect Your Experience
   - Reading Strategy: Background Knowledge
   - Tips to Guide Reading: Background Information (ATE)
   - Read to Be Informed (ATE)
3. **To increase knowledge of other cultures and to connect common elements across cultures**
   - Connecting Themes Across Cultures (ATE)
   - Cultural Connection (ATE)
   - Background for Understanding
4. **To express and support responses to the text**
   - Critical Thinking
   - Idea Bank: Letter to a Friend
5. **To analyze literary elements**
   - Literary Focus: Writer's Purpose
   - Idea Bank: Monologue
   - Idea Bank: Dear Editor
6. **To read in order to research self-selected and assigned topics**
   - Research Skills Mini-Lesson: Use Text Organizers (ATE)
   - Idea Bank: Interview
7. **To plan, prepare, organize, and present literary interpretations**
   - Speaking, Listening, and Viewing Mini-Lesson: Lawyer's Argument
   - Idea Bank: Oral Interpretation
8. **To use recursive writing processes to write a research report**
   - Guided Writing Lesson
9. **To increase knowledge of the rules of grammar and usage**
   - Build Grammar Skills: Adjective Clauses

Test Preparation

Reading Comprehension: Stated and Implied Main Ideas (ATE, p. 271) The teaching tips and sample test item in this workshop support the instruction and practice in the unit workshop:
Reading Comprehension: Stated and Implied Main Ideas (SE, p. 453)

Guide for Reading

Yoshiko Uchida *(1921–1992)*

There was nothing unusual about Yoshiko Uchida's life until she and her family had to give up their comfortable home in Berkeley, California, and move into a stable.

In 1941, while Uchida was a student at the University of California, Japan attacked the United States naval base at Pearl Harbor. Under mounting political pressure, President Franklin Roosevelt ordered all Japanese Americans placed in camps administered by the Wartime Relocation Agency (WRA). Uchida and her family were taken first to Tanforan Racetrack near San Francisco, where they actually lived in a stable, and then to a camp in Utah.

After her release, Uchida went on to attend Smith College and became a teacher and an award-winning author of more than thirty books. In this excerpt from her book *Desert Exile: The Uprooting of a Japanese-American Family* Uchida tells how her family coped with life in a WRA camp.

Gerald Ford *(1913–)*

As a young man, Gerald Ford turned down the chance to play professional football for the Detroit Lions and the Green Bay Packers, choosing instead to study law at Yale University.

Ford graduated from Yale Law School in 1941. He practiced law briefly but soon entered politics, serving in the House of Representatives for nearly twenty-five years.

In 1973, Ford replaced the resigning vice president, Spiro Agnew. When President Nixon resigned his office eight months later, Ford became the first president of the United States who had not been elected either president or vice president.

In 1976—more than thirty years after World War II ended—President Ford issued a public apology for the way Japanese Americans had been treated by their government.

◆ Build Vocabulary

Latin Word Roots: *-curs-*

In Uchida's narrative, you learn that she and her family receive a *cursory* medical check. Knowing that the word root *-curs-* comes from the Latin word meaning "to run," you may be able to guess that *cursory* means "run through rapidly and without care."

Word Bank

As you read this story, you will encounter the words on this list. Each word is defined on the page where it first appears. Preview the list before you read.

cursory
euphemism
adept
destitute
unwieldy
communal
conspicuous
assuage

◆ Build Grammar Skills

Adjective Clauses

Uchida makes her writing concise and varied by using **adjective clauses**—groups of words that contain a subject and verb, modify a noun or pronoun, and begin with *who, that, what, whom,* or *which.*

For example, in the following sentence, Uchida tells us that friends found them and that these friends had arrived earlier. She makes one of these ideas an adjective clause that begins with *who* and modifies *friends:*

> Fortunately, some friends *who had arrived earlier* found us. . . .

Look for other adjective clauses in Uchida's narrative and in Ford's speech, and notice that they add information to sentences in an economical way.

Prentice Hall Literature Program Resources

REINFORCE / RETEACH / EXTEND

Selection Support Pages
Build Vocabulary: Word Roots: *-curs-*, p. 84
Build Grammar Skills: Adjective Clauses, p. 85
Reading Strategy: Prior Knowledge, p. 86
Literary Focus: Writer's Purpose, p. 87

Strategies for Diverse Student Needs, p. 21

Beyond Literature Media Connection: Japanese American Internment, p. 21

Formal Assessment Selection Test, pp. 69–71; Assessment Resources Software

Alternative Assessment, p. 21

Writing and Language Transparencies
Outline, p. 103
Context Chart, p. 107

Resource Pro CD-ROM

Listening to Literature Audiocassettes

◆ from Desert Exile ◆
Remarks Upon Signing a Proclamation . . .

◆ Literature and Your Life

CONNECT YOUR EXPERIENCE

Although it's unfair, people often judge by appearances rather than actions. Some people may form their opinion of you based on what they think of your clothes, your hairstyle, or some other aspect of your physical appearance. As this narrative and speech demonstrate, in 1942, thousands of Americans were judged by their appearance. They were wrongly imprisoned simply because they "looked like the enemy."

Journal Writing Describe a situation in which you were judged by your appearance instead of by your actions.

THEMATIC FOCUS: STRUGGLING FOR JUSTICE

In this account, you read about innocent people who became political prisoners. Why do you think President Ford's public apology was such an important moment in our nation's history?

◆ Background for Understanding

HISTORY

During the 1940's, many Japanese Americans were imprisoned in camps run by the Wartime Relocation Agency (WRA). As this graph shows, two thirds of those imprisoned in 1942 were United States citizens. (About 33,000 Japanese Americans volunteered for the armed forces and fought courageously.) Many others had lived in the United States for years but had been barred from becoming citizens by a 1924 federal law.

After the war, the Japanese American Citizens League struggled to have the government pay the former prisoners for their lost property. In 1988, Congress finally agreed to pay the surviving Japanese Americans $1.25 billion for their losses.

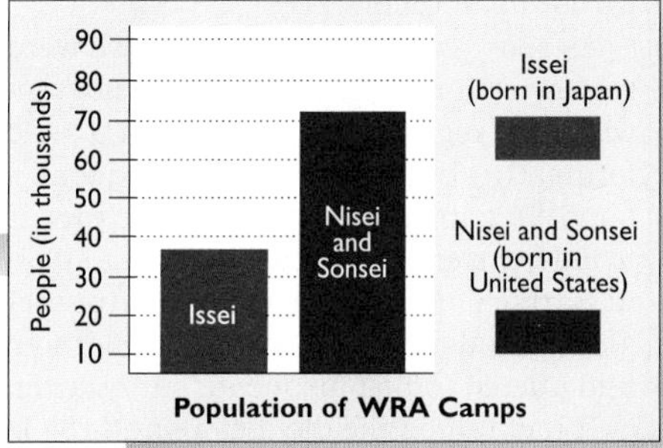

Population of WRA Camps

◆ Literary Focus

WRITER'S PURPOSE

Writers often have **purposes**—reasons for writing—such as these: to entertain, to inform, or to persuade. The purpose or combination of purposes for any work affects the writer's choice of details and writing style. Uchida wants to inform readers about the WRA camps, so she includes details of day-to-day life in the camps. President Ford's purpose is to acknowledge officially that an injustice was done to Japanese Americans. He uses formal language appropriate for a historic speech.

◆ Reading Strategy

BACKGROUND KNOWLEDGE

Whether you're reading a story about a young person like yourself or a narrative about an event in history, you can use **prior background knowledge**—what you already know about the subject—to help you understand what you are reading.

As you read Uchida's narrative and Ford's speech, make connections between what each author is saying and your own experience. You will also need to keep in mind the background information about WRA camps during World War II. You may find details in the narrative and the speech that confirm opinions you already have, as well as details that change your opinions.

Ask students to imagine the following situation: One day you are ordered out of your home and school and told you must go and live in a camp with other people whose families came originally from the same country as yours. Your parents have to leave their jobs, and you have to leave your home, school, and friends to live in a place that is crowded and uncomfortable. It's like being in prison. Have them tell how they respond to this situation. After discussion, make sure students know that the United States Government actually forced thousands of Japanese Americans into internment camps during World War II. Have students discuss whether a similar situation could ever arise in the United States today.

Connecting Themes Across Cultures

Have students suggest examples of other political injustices around the world that have been found during times of war.

Tips to Guide Reading

Background Information Before students begin reading, background knowledge. Then, have students read the selection and monitor their own use of the strategy.

Customize for
Less Proficient Readers

Less proficient readers might benefit from using their prior knowledge about the thoughts and feelings of teenagers. Suggest that they pause after reading each paragraph and consider how they would feel if they were in the writer's position.

Customize for
Pre-AP Students

Ask students to analyze and discuss why Uchida wanted to write about such a devastating event as the internment of her family. Have them consider how writing about the event may have helped the author deal with it emotionally.

Test Preparation Workshop

Reading Comprehension: Stated and Implied Main Ideas

As students prepare to take the SAT and ACT tests they should review the process of finding the author's main idea. An author's purpose is to express a main idea and support it with details, secondary ideas, facts, and examples. For practice, have students read Gerald Ford's proclamation on p. 279, and answer the following sample question:

The primary purpose of the passage is to—

A Celebrate February 19 as an important date in American history
B Remind all American citizens to value liberty
C Point out that Japanese Americans have contributed greatly to our nation's well-being
D Abolish an obsolete document

As a strategy, suggest that students reread to find the most important sentence of the speech: President Ford reminded all citizens of the value of liberty and freedom at the same time he explained and ended a tragic situation in American history. Using this strategy, student will find that B is the best answer.

Develop Understanding

One-Minute Insight This narrative describes one family's experiences in one of the Japanese American internment camps of the 1940's. The speech following the narrative is an apology for the treatment of Japanese Americans in these camps. Read together, they give a personal and a public perspective on an episode in American history.

◆ Literary Focus

❶ **Writer's Purpose** Have students note that in this passage Uchida begins to fulfill her purpose to inform readers about what happened to Japanese Americans during World War II. Ask them to list the details they learn in the first two paragraphs. *The internees were transported by bus; there were hundreds of people in the camp; they were fenced in; they were bored; they were not treated with respect, they had to live in a barrack.*

◆ Critical Thinking

❷ **Analyze** Have students determine what these details about the writer's mother tell them about her character. *She is a traditional, conservative woman who believes in proper manners and does not adapt well to change.*

◆ Reading Strategy

❸ **Background Knowledge** Have students refer to the graph on p. 271 to get a sense of the total number of people who were in WRA camps across the country.

Customize for
English Language Learners
Students may be confused by the dual references to *apartment* and *stall* and other euphemisms that are used in Uchida's description of the camps. Encourage them to ask about these words and discuss with them the nature of using different terms for the same thing.

from Desert Exile:

The Uprooting of a Japanese-American Family

Yoshiko Uchida

As the bus pulled up to the grandstand, I could see hundreds of Japanese Americans jammed along the fence that lined the track. These people had arrived a few days earlier and were now watching for the arrival of friends or had come to while away the empty hours that had suddenly been thrust upon them.

❶ As soon as we got off the bus, we were directed to an area beneath the grandstand where we registered and filled out a series of forms. Our baggage was inspected for contraband,[1] a cursory medical check made, and our living quarters assigned. We were to be housed in Barrack 16, Apartment 40. Fortunately, some friends who had arrived earlier found us and offered to help us locate our quarters.

It had rained the day before and the hundreds of people who had trampled on the track had turned it into a miserable mass of slippery mud. We made our way on it carefully, helping my mother who was dressed just as she would have been to go to church. She wore a hat, gloves, her good coat, and her Sunday shoes, because she would not have thought of venturing outside our house dressed in any other way.

Everywhere there were black tar-papered barracks[2] that had been hastily erected to ❸ house the 8,000 Japanese Americans of the area who had been uprooted from their homes. Barrack 16, however, was not among them, and we couldn't find it until we had traveled

1. **contraband** (kän′ trə band′) *n.*: Smuggled goods.

2. **barracks** (bar′ əks) *n.*: Large, plain, often temporary housing.

◆ Build Vocabulary

cursory (kur′ sə rē) *adj.*: Superficial; done rapidly with little attention to detail

euphemism (yōō′ fə miz′ əm) *n.*: Word or phrase substituted for a more offensive word or phrase

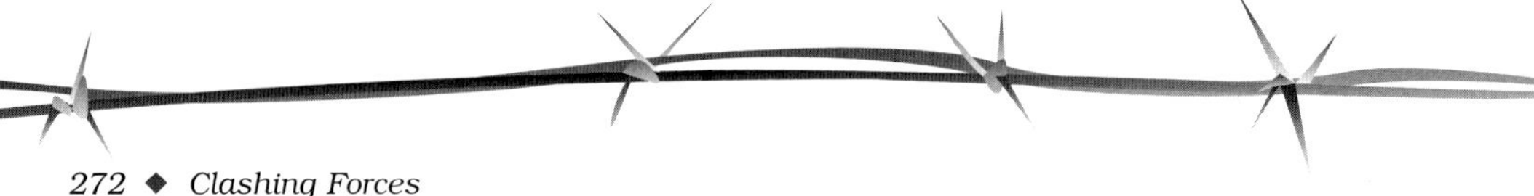

Block Scheduling Strategies

Consider these suggestions to take advantage of extended class time:

- Introduce the Reading Strategy and the Background for Understanding on p. 271. With the class, discuss additional facts about World War II and Japanese-American internment. Follow up by having students complete the Cross-Curricular Connection page in ***Beyond Literature,*** p. 21.
- Use the Context Chart in ***Writing and Language Transparencies,*** p. 107. As a class, complete a Context Chart for each selection to set them in their respective historical and cultural contexts.
- Allow time for students to work in groups to discuss each writer's purpose and to complete the Literary Focus page on Writer's Purpose in ***Selection Support,*** p. 87.
- Before students complete the Guided Writing Lesson (p. 281) in class, provide instruction on citing sources and using an outline to organize their information. Use the Outline in ***Writing and Language Transparencies,*** p. 103, to model the making of an outline.

half the length of the track and gone beyond it to the northern rim of the racetrack compound.

Finally one of our friends called out, "There it is, beyond that row of eucalyptus trees." Barrack 16 was not a barrack at all, but a long stable raised a few feet off the ground with a broad ramp the horses had used to reach their stalls. Each stall was now numbered, and ours was number 40. That the stalls should have been called "apartments" was a euphemism so ludicrous it was comical.

When we reached stall number 40, we pushed open the narrow door and looked uneasily into the vacant darkness. The stall was about ten by twenty feet and empty except for three folded Army cots lying on the floor. Dust, dirt, and wood shavings covered the linoleum that had been laid over manure-covered boards, the smell of horses hung in the air, and the whitened corpses of many insects still clung to the hastily white-washed walls. 4

▲ **Critical Viewing** This photograph shows Japanese Americans in a WRA camp. What do you think will be some of the hardships of life in such a camp? **[Interpret]** 5

High on either side of the entrance were two small windows which were our only source of daylight. The stall was divided into two sections by Dutch doors[3] worn down by teeth marks, and each stall in the stable was separated from the adjoining one only by rough partitions that stopped a foot short of the sloping roof. The space, while perhaps a good source of ventilation for the horses, deprived us of all but visual privacy, and we couldn't even

3. **Dutch doors:** Doors split across the middle so the top and bottom halves can be opened separately.

◆ Literary Focus

4 Writer's Purpose What purpose do these details help Uchida fulfill? *These details help Uchida achieve her purpose of informing readers about the deplorable conditions of the camps.*

▶Critical Viewing◀

5 Interpret *Based on the lines of people shown in the picture and the desolate setting, students may interpret that waiting for food and supplies, overcrowding, and boredom will be some of the hardships faced at the camp.*

Read to Be Informed

Students may find that they do not know very much of the history of Japanese internment camps in the United States during World War II. Reading to gain information is a valuable purpose to set for reading.

Extending Word Study

Context Clues In addition to the Build Vocabulary words, students may need help with additional terms such as: ludicrous, and ventilation. Suggest that students use context clues to determine the meaning and then check the precise meaning in the dictionary.

Customize for *Gifted/Talented Students*

Have students consider how they would have felt if they were in the camp with Uchida and her family. Ask them to write a description of how they believe they might have felt and how they might have behaved—whether the same or differently than the characters in the selection did.

Customize for *Visual/Spatial Learners*

Encourage students to create diagrams or sketches that will help them visualize the setup of the stalls in which the internees are expected to live.

Cultural Connection

Japanese Houses Explain to students that the arrangement of traditional Japanese homes stresses space, light, simplicity, and harmony of form. The rooms are divided by sliding screens made of wood and paper or glass. The floors are covered by *tatami,* woven grass mats. Bedding is hidden in closets during the day, and furniture is minimal. Often a home includes an alcove with a flower arrangement and a hanging scroll. Discuss with students why people used to this sort of home would find the internment camps especially difficult to bear. Call their attention to the contrast between the simple, spacious elegance of a traditional Japanese home and the crowded squalor of the stalls would make living in the stalls an especially difficult adjustment.

Have interested students research information and locate pictures of Japanese architecture and home decor. Suggest that they use resources in the library or on the Internet and prepare a report or display of pictures to share with others in the class.

◆ Reading Strategy

❶ Background Knowledge Based on what they know about the reasons for the internment, why do students think the internees were brought in before everything was prepared? *As public sentiment against the Japanese Americans increased, pressure to move them into the camps faster probably led to many being brought to inadequately prepared facilities.*

◆ Literary Focus

❷ Writer's Purpose Guide students to see that Uchida includes these details to communicate the feelings of the internees about the conditions they endured.

▶Critical Viewing◀

❸ Analyze *Call students' attention to the tags on each of the people in this picture. Elicit from students that the people's individual identity has been reduced to a name or number on a tag.*

◆ Literature and Your Life

❹ Ask students how they would react in this situation. *Students may respond to the depressing setting, to the unsanitary serving methods, or to the unappetizing menu.*

◆ Critical Thinking

❺ Infer What effect do the details of the living conditions have on the internees? *Suggested response: Their living conditions have so depressed the internees that they cannot even make polite small talk.*

be sure of that because of the crevices and knotholes in the dividing walls.

Because our friends had already spent a day as residents of Tanforan, they had become adept at scrounging for necessities. One found a broom and swept the floor for us. Two of the boys went to the barracks where mattresses were being issued, stuffed the ticking with straw themselves, and came back with three for our cots.

❶ Nothing in the camp was ready. Everything was only half-finished. I wondered how much the nation's security would have been threatened had the Army permitted us to remain in our homes a few more days until the camps were adequately prepared for occupancy by families.

By the time we had cleaned out the stall and set up the cots, it was time for supper. Somehow, in all the confusion, we had not had lunch, so I was eager to get to the main mess hall,[4] which was located beneath the grandstand.

The sun was going down as we started along the muddy track, and a cold, piercing wind swept in from the bay. When we arrived, there were six long weaving lines of people waiting to get into the mess hall. We took our place at the end of one of them, each of us clutching a plate and silverware borrowed from friends who had already received their baggage.

❷ **◆ Literary Focus** What is Uchida's purpose in revealing her feelings about standing in the line?

Shivering in the cold, we pressed close together trying to shield Mama from the wind. As we stood in what seemed a breadline for the destitute, I felt degraded, humiliated, and overwhelmed with a longing for home. And I saw the unutterable sadness on my mother's face.

4. **mess hall:** Room or building where a group regularly meets for meals.

▲ **Critical Viewing** What detail in this picture indicates that people in WRA camps were not viewed as individuals? **[Analyze]** ❸

This was only the first of many lines we were to endure, and we soon discovered that waiting in line was as inevitable a part of Tanforan as the north wind that swept in from the bay stirring up all the dust and litter of the camp.

Once we got inside the gloomy cavernous mess hall, I saw hundreds of people eating at wooden picnic tables, while those who had already eaten were shuffling aimlessly over the wet cement floor. When I reached the serving table and held out my plate, a cook reached into a dishpan full of canned sausages and dropped two onto my plate with his fingers. Another man gave me a boiled potato and a piece of butterless bread.

With 5,000 people to be fed, there were few unoccupied tables, so we separated from our friends and shared a table with an elderly man and a young family with two crying babies. No one at the table spoke to us, and even Mama could seem to find no friendly word to offer as she normally would have done. We tried to eat, but the food wouldn't go down.

"Let's get out of here," my sister suggested. We decided it would be better to go back to

Research Skills Mini-Lesson

Use Text Organizers

This mini-lesson supports the Dear Editor writing activity in the Idea Bank on p. 281.

Introduce Discuss with students that a well-written letter to the editor should make its points clearly. In order to persuade newspaper readers, the letter also needs to contain well-researched facts to support the writer's opinion.

Develop In order to use facts in their letter, students need to locate information about the time period about which they are writing. Using text organizers such as headings to locate and categorize information will aid students in their research. Have students list general research topic headings such as: Japanese Americans, 1942, World War II, and Wartime Relocation Agency. Point out to students that they may more topics and headings to use to find information as they further develop their research.

Apply Have students use their list of topics and locate headings in research materials. Guide them to evaluate the information to determine which kinds of facts are most convincing when cited in persuasive writing. When students are confident that they have enough factual information to back up their opinion, have them write their letters.

Assess Compile the letters in a booklet and have students take turns reading and evaluating the letter's logical and persuasive qualities and the facts presented. You also may wish to use the Persuasion scoring rubric, p. 105 in ***Alternative Assessment.***

our barrack than to linger in the depressing confusion of the mess hall. It had grown dark by now and since Tanforan had no lights for nighttime occupancy, we had to pick our way carefully down the slippery track.

Once back in our stall, we found it no less depressing, for there was only a single electric light bulb dangling from the ceiling, and a one-inch crevice at the top of the north wall admitted a steady draft of the cold night air. We sat huddled on our cots, bundled in our coats, too cold and miserable even to talk. My sister and I worried about Mama, for she wasn't strong and had recently been troubled with neuralgia,[5] which could easily be aggravated by the cold. She in turn was worrying about us, and of course we all worried and wondered about Papa.

Suddenly we heard the sound of a truck stopping outside.

"Hey, Uchida! Apartment 40!" a boy shouted.

I rushed to the door and found the baggage boys trying to heave our enormous "camp bundle" over the railing that fronted our stall.

"What ya got in here anyway?" they shouted good-naturedly as they struggled with the unwieldy bundle. "It's the biggest thing we got on our truck!"

I grinned, embarrassed, but I could hardly wait to get out our belongings. My sister and I fumbled to undo all the knots we had tied into the rope around our bundle that morning and eagerly pulled out the familiar objects from home.

We unpacked our blankets, pillows, sheets, tea kettle, and, most welcome of all, our electric hot plate. I ran to the nearest washroom to fill the kettle with water, while Mama and Kay made up the Army cots with our bedding. Once we hooked up the hot plate and put the kettle on to boil, we felt better. We sat close to its warmth, holding our hands toward it as though it were our fireplace at home.

Before long some friends came by to see us, bringing with them the only gift they had—a box of dried prunes. Even the day before, we wouldn't have given the prunes a second glance, but now they were as welcome as the boxes of Maskey's chocolate my father used to bring home from San Francisco. 7

Mama managed to make some tea for our friends, and we sat around our steaming kettle, munching gratefully on our prunes. We spent much of the evening talking about food and the lack of it, a concern that grew obsessive over the next few weeks, when we were constantly hungry.

Our stable consisted of twenty-five stalls facing north which were back to back with an equal number facing south, so we were surrounded on three sides. Living in our stable were an assortment of people—mostly small family units—that included an artist, my father's barber and his wife, a dentist and his wife, an elderly retired couple, a group of Kibei bachelors (Japanese born in the United States but educated in Japan), an insurance salesman and his wife, and a widow with two daughters. To say that we all became intimately acquainted would be an understatement. It was, in fact, communal living, with semi-private cubicles provided only for sleeping.

◆ ***Literature and Your Life***

Discuss how you would feel if faced with the same uprooting and imprisonment that these teens dealt with. 8

5. **neuralgia** (no͞o ral′ jə) *n.:* Pain along the path of a nerve.

◆ **Build Vocabulary**

adept (ə dept′) *adj.:* Expert; highly skilled

destitute (des′ tə to͞ot) *n.:* Those living in poverty

unwieldy (un wēl′ dē) *adj.:* Hard to manage because of shape or weight

communal (käm yo͞o′ nəl) *adj.:* Shared by the community

◆ Critical Thinking

6 Draw Conclusions Based on what they have learned and inferred so far, ask students to draw conclusions about the effect that imprisonment has on the mother's physical and emotional state. *Physically, she might suffer from cold and exhaustion. Emotionally, the worry and crude conditions might depress her.*

◆ Reading Strategy

7 Prior Knowledge Ask students to think about the effects of hunger on people. Why did the writer compare the prunes they received to chocolate? *The food that Tanforan offered was so bad, and the Uchidas were so hungry, that the prunes were a real treat to them.*

◆ *Literature and Your Life*

8 Most answers will focus on feelings of confusion, anger, depression, and fear students might experience.

Customize for
Interpersonal Learners

Remind students that people in the camp community helped the Uchidas, making furniture and putting up shelves. Point out that volunteering is a way to help others in local communities. Have interested students list different jobs such as: helping older people, cleaning up public areas, and tutoring. In addition to helping others, volunteers gain valuable leadership experience and learn job skills. Students may wish to find out about local volunteer opportunities and find a way to participate.

Speaking, Listening, and Viewing Mini-Lesson

Lawyer's Argument

This mini-lesson supports the Speaking, Listening, and Viewing activity in the Idea Bank on p. 281.

Introduce the Concept As a class, discuss what happened to the Uchida family and others like them. Elicit from students why they think it should not have happened.

Develop Background Encourage students to read Amendments 5 and 14 to the United States Constitution to discover exactly which of the Japanese Americans' rights were violated. Students can use this information to support their defense arguments. Students might also focus on the conditions of the internment camps and the Japanese American's loss of jobs, homes, and lifestyles.

Apply the Information Have students integrate background information they have read in their books, and that they may have researched, into their arguments. Encourage students to practice their arguments before giving them for the group.

Assess the Outcome Encourage students to evaluate one another's arguments using the Peer Assessment Speaker/Speech Guide in ***Alternative Assessment,*** p. 118.

◆ Literary Focus

❶ **Writer's Purpose** Ask students why they think the wrier included this statement about family life. *She wanted to show that internment had an effect on families as well as on individuals.*

▶Critical Viewing◀

❷ **Draw Conclusions** *The small overnight cases that the people in the picture carry indicate that they did not have time to gather many belongings. The worried expressions on the faces of the people in line and the impatient expressions on the faces of the soldiers are another indication that these people are moving in a hurry.*

◆ Critical Thinking

❸ **Relate** Encourage students to think about how difficult circumstances can lead to friendship. *Students may recall friends they made during the difficult first weeks of starting a new school or while at camp, or learning the ropes of an after-school job.*

◆ Critical Thinking

❹ **Make Judgments** Ask students why the army didn't provide privacy for the Japanese Americans. *Students may say that the Army was used to housing soldiers or because of prejudice against Japanese Americans the Army didn't want to make them comfortable. Some students may observe that the larger a group becomes, the more difficult it is to accommodate the need for privacy.*

▲ **Critical Viewing** What details indicate that these people were forced to leave their homes in a hurry? **[Draw Conclusions]**

Our neighbors on one side spent much of their time playing cards, and at all hours of the day we could hear the sound of cards being shuffled and money changing hands. Our other
❶ neighbors had a teenage son who spent most of the day with his friends, coming home to his stall at night only after his parents were asleep. Family life began to show signs of strain almost immediately, not only in the next stall but throughout the entire camp.

One Sunday our neighbor's son fell asleep in the rear of his stall with the door bolted from inside. When his parents came home from church, no amount of shouting or banging on the door could awaken the boy.

"Our stupid son has locked us out," they explained, coming to us for help.

I climbed up on my cot and considered pouring water on him over the partition, for I knew he slept just on the other side of it. Instead I dangled a broom over the partition and poked and prodded with it, shouting, "Wake up! Wake up!" until the boy finally bestirred himself and let his parents in. We became good friends with our neighbors after that.

About one hundred feet from our stable were two latrines and two washrooms for our section of camp, one each for men and women. The latrines were crude wooden structures containing eight toilets, separated by partitions, but having no doors. The washrooms were divided into two sections. In the front section was a

Workplace Skills Mini-Lesson

Resolving Conflicts

Introduce The ability to resolve conflicts was an important skill in the internment camps. It is an important skill in the workplace as well.

Develop Have students identify and discuss workplace conflicts, such as scheduling mixups, interaction with angry customers, and disagreements over responsibilities. Discuss resolution strategies such as the following:

- Communicate feelings and needs clearly and calmly.
- Listen to the other person and restate your understanding of what he or she said.
- Be willing to compromise and consider other viewpoints.

Apply Have students role-play each conflict situation using the skills discussed to bring the conflicts to resolution.

Assess Encourage students to evaluate one another's resolutions. Ask them to consider if any of their solutions would have helped the families in the internment camp.

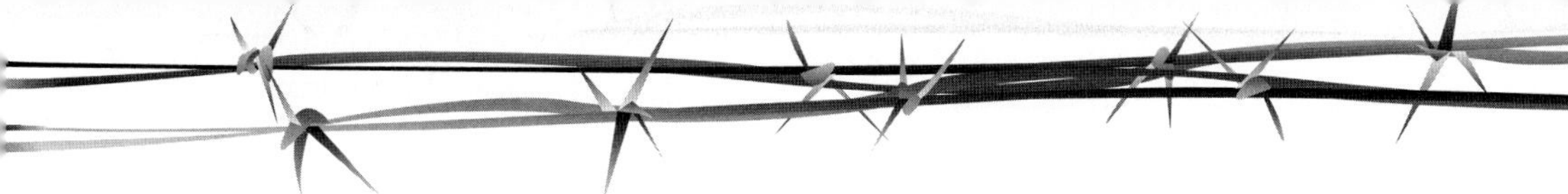

long tin trough spaced with spigots of hot and cold water where we washed our faces and brushed our teeth. To the rear were eight showers, also separated by partitions but lacking doors or curtains. The showers were difficult to adjust and we either got scalded by torrents of hot water or shocked by an icy blast of cold. Most of the Issei[6] were unaccustomed to showers, having known the luxury of soaking in deep pine-scented tubs during their years in Japan, and found the showers virtually impossible to use.

Our card-playing neighbor scoured the camp for a container that might serve as a tub, and eventually found a large wooden barrel. She rolled it to the showers, filled it with warm water, and then climbed in for a pleasant and leisurely soak. The greatest compliment she could offer anyone was the use of her private tub.

The lack of privacy in the latrines and showers was an embarrassing hardship especially for the older women, and many would take newspapers to hold over their faces or squares of cloth to tack up for their own private curtain. The Army, obviously ill-equipped to build living quarters for women and children, had made no attempt to introduce even the most common of life's civilities into these camps for us.

During the first few weeks of camp life everything was erratic and in short supply. Hot water appeared only sporadically, and the minute it was available, everyone ran for the showers or the laundry. We had to be clever and quick just to keep clean, and my sister and I often walked a mile to the other end of the camp where hot water was in better supply, in order to boost our morale with a hot shower.

Even toilet paper was at a premium, for new rolls would disappear as soon as they were placed in the latrines. The shock of the evacuation compounded by the short supply of every necessity brought out the baser instincts of the internees,[7] and there was little inclination for anyone to feel responsible for anyone else. In the early days, at least, it was everyone for himself or herself. ❼

One morning I saw some women emptying bed pans into the troughs where we washed our faces. The sight was enough to turn my stomach, and my mother quickly made several large signs in Japanese cautioning people against such unsanitary practices. We posted them in conspicuous spots in the washroom and hoped for the best. ❽

Across from the latrines was a double barrack, one containing laundry tubs and the other equipped with clotheslines and ironing boards. Because there were so many families with young children, the laundry tubs were in constant use. The hot water was often gone by 9:00 A.M., and many women got up at 3:00 and 4:00 in the morning to do their wash, all of which, including sheets, had to be done entirely by hand.

We found it difficult to get to the laundry by 9:00 A.M., and by then every tub was taken and there were long lines of people with bags of dirty laundry waiting behind each one. When we finally got to a tub, there was no more hot water. Then we would leave my mother to hold the tub while my sister and I rushed to the washroom where there was a better supply and carried back bucketfuls of hot water as everyone else learned to do. By the time we had ❾

6. **Issei:** Japanese who emigrated to the United States after 1907. They were not granted citizenship until 1952.

7. **internees** (in´ turn´ ēz´) *n.*: Prisoners, especially during wartime.

◆ **Build Vocabulary**

conspicuous (kən spik´ yo͞o əs) *adj.*: Easy to see

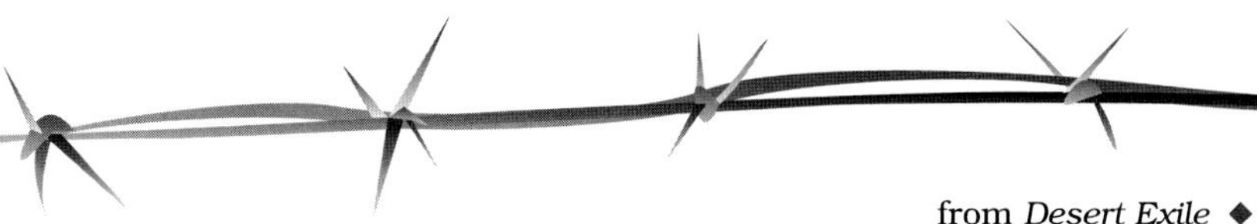

❺ **Clarification** Tell students that *Issei* refers to Japanese people who were born in Japan. Refer students to the graph on page 271 to clarify that almost twice as many internees were born in the United States (*Nisei* and *Sonsei*) as were born in Japan.

◆ Literary Focus

❻ **Writer's Purpose** Point out that Uchida highlights the poor conditions of the camp by concentrating on basic needs to which most people can relate: food, privacy, and cleanliness.

◆ Critical Thinking

❼ **Make a Judgment** Ask students whether they agree that difficult conditions bring out the worst in people. *Some students may say that difficult conditions bring out the best in people, as evidenced by examples of cooperation and kindness Uchida has offered earlier in the narrative. Other students may say that the toilet paper example illustrates that difficult situations bring out the worst in people. Encourage students to offer examples from current events and literature as well as citing examples from the story.*

◆ Build Grammar Skills

❽ **Adjective Clauses** Have students locate the adjective clause in this sentence. How does the clause add to the impact of the statement? *The adjective clause is "where we washed our faces"; it modifies troughs. The clause makes the emptying of the bedpans more horrifying.*

◆ Literature and Your Life

❾ Have students compare the Uchidas' laundry with the way students' families do their laundry. Whether students have washers in their own homes and apartments or go to the Laundromat, most will agree that they do not face the same difficulties as the Uchidas in getting their laundry done.

Cross-Curricular Connection: Social Studies

Wartime Relocation Agency Camps In the early 1940's, most Japanese Americans lived on the West Coast or in Hawaii. Many of those on the West Coast were successful farmers or business people. For years, they had faced prejudice, in part because of their success.

After Pearl Harbor, many people on the West Coast questioned the loyalty of Japanese Americans. Japanese Americans, they said, might act as spies and help Japan invade the United States. No evidence of disloyalty existed. Nonetheless, President Roosevelt agreed to move Japanese Americans to inland camps set up by the Wartime Relocation Agency. Approximately 120,000 Japanese Americans were forced to sell their homes and businesses at great loss.

Years later, Americans began to recognize the injustice that had been done to Japanese Americans. Congress reviewed the government's wartime policy toward Japanese Americans. Lawmakers admitted that they could not right the wrong that had been done. They did, however, approve a payment of $20,000 dollars to every survivor of the camps.

◆ Literary Focus

❶ Writer's Purpose Ask students for what purpose Uchida may have included this information about her non-Japanese friends. *She may have wanted readers to know that the government's distrust of Japanese Americans was not shared by all non-Japanese.*

◆ Literature and Your Life

❷ Point out to students that Uchida is citing as luxuries conditions and food items that students probably take for granted such as soap for washing dishes and an occasional lettuce salad for dinner.

◆ Reading Strategy

❸ Prior Knowledge Students have already learned that if the internees don't rush around they are likely to miss out on something.

◆ Critical Thinking

❹ Analyze Have these students consider why the Uchidas' friends helped them in the camp. Why were they not giving in to their basic instincts? *Students may suggest that difficult situations such as the Uchidas' are complex—they bring out people's baser instincts and also their more noble ones. The same person who ran to be first in line at the mess hall may give someone else part of her or his meal a few minutes later.*

◆ Critical Thinking

❺ Make Inferences Have students consider why the Uchidas worked so hard to make their dreadful "apartment" comfortable and homelike. *The more like home they could make their stall, the more "normal" they would feel and the less unbearable it would be to endure the harsh conditions at the camp.*

finally hung our laundry on lines outside our stall, we were too exhausted to do much else for the rest of the day.

For four days after our arrival we continued to go to the main mess hall for all our meals. My sister and I usually missed breakfast because we were assigned to the early shift and we simply couldn't get there by 7:00 A.M. Dinner was at 4:45 P.M., which was a terrible hour, but not a major problem, as we were always hungry. Meals were uniformly bad and skimpy, with an abundance of starches such as beans and bread. I wrote to my non-Japanese friends in Berkeley shamelessly asking them to send ❶ us food, and they obliged with large cartons of cookies, nuts, dried fruit, and jams.

We looked forward with much anticipation to the opening of a half dozen smaller mess halls located throughout the camp. But when ours finally opened, we discovered that the preparation of smaller quantities had absolutely no effect on the quality of the food. We went eagerly to our new mess hall only to be confronted at our first meal with chili con carne, corn, and butterless bread. To assuage our disappointment, a friend and I went to the main mess hall which was still in operation, to see if it had anything better. Much to our amazement and delight, we found small lettuce salads, the first fresh vegetables we had seen in many days. We ate ravenously and exercised enormous self-❷ control not to go back for second and third helpings.

The food improved gradually, and by the time we left Tanforan five months later, we had fried chicken and ice cream for Sunday dinner. By July tubs of soapy water were installed at the mess hall exits so we could wash our plates and utensils on the way out. Being slow eaters, however, we usually found the dishwater tepid and dirty by the time we reached the tubs, and we often rewashed our dishes in the washroom.

Most internees got into the habit of rushing for everything. They ran to the mess halls to be first in line, they dashed inside for the best tables and then rushed through their meals to get to the washtubs before the suds ran out. The three of us, however, seemed to be at the end of every line that formed and somehow never managed to be first for anything.

> **◆ Reading Strategy**
> How does your prior knowledge about the harsh living conditions in the camps help explain why internees might be constantly rushing around?

One of the first things we all did at Tanforan was to make our living quarters as comfortable as possible. A pile of scrap lumber in one corner of camp melted away like snow on a hot day as residents salvaged whatever they could to make shelves and crude pieces of furniture to supplement the Army cots. They also made ingenious containers for carrying their dishes to the mess halls, with handles and lids that grew more and more elaborate in a sort of unspoken competition.

Because of my father's absence, our friends helped us in camp, just as they had in Berkeley, and we relied on them to put up shelves and build a crude table and two benches for us. We put our new camp furniture in the front half of our stall, which was our "living room," and put our three cots in the dark windowless rear section, which we promptly dubbed "the dungeon." We ordered some print fabric by mail and sewed curtains by hand to hang at our windows and to cover our shelves. Each new addition to our stall made it seem a little more like home.

One afternoon about a week after we had arrived at Tanforan, a messenger from the administration building appeared with a telegram for us. It was from my father, telling us he had been released on parole from Montana and would be able to join us soon in camp. Papa was coming home. The wonderful news had come like an unexpected gift, but even as we hugged each other in joy, we didn't quite dare believe it until we actually saw him. . . .

◆ Build Vocabulary

assuage (ə swāj′) *v.*: Calm; pacify

Reteach

Guide students to review the reading strategy of using background knowledge to help them understand and make connections with the text. When a writer's purpose is to inform or persuade a reader, background knowledge provides a means to evaluate and analyze the credibility of the writer. In order to make use of this strategy, it may be possible helpful for students to use an organizer chart. Suggest that students fill in the first and second columns of a KWL chart and then reread Uchida's narrative and fill in details on the third column.

Topic

What I **K**now	What I **W**ant to Know	What I **L**earned

Students can assess what they already know, with what they want to know and finally what they learn they from the author's information.

Remarks Upon Signing a Proclamation Concerning Japanese American Internment During World War II

Gerald Ford February 19, 1976

February 19 is the anniversary of a very, very sad day in American history. It was on that date in 1942 that Executive Order 9066 was issued resulting in the uprooting of many, many loyal Americans. Over 100,000 persons of Japanese ancestry were removed from their homes, detained in special camps, and eventually relocated.

We now know what we should have known then—not only was that evacuation wrong but Japanese Americans were and are loyal Americans. On the battlefield and at home the names of Japanese Americans have been and continue to be written in America's history for the sacrifices and the contributions they have made to the well-being and to the security of this, our common Nation.

Executive Order 9066 ceased to be effective at the end of World War II. Because there was no formal statement of its termination, there remains some concern among Japanese Americans that there yet may be some life in that obsolete document. The proclamation [4417] that I am signing here today should remove all doubt on that matter.

I call upon the American people to affirm with me the unhyphenated American promise that we have learned from the tragedy of that long ago experience—forever to treasure liberty and justice for each individual American and resolve that this kind of error shall never be made again.

Guide for Responding

◆ Literature and Your Life

Reader's Response Were you surprised by Uchida's description of life in the camp? Tell why or why not.

Thematic Focus What forces came into conflict in the creation of WRA camps?

Questions for Research If you were giving an oral report on the internment of Japanese Americans during World War II, what questions do you think your audience would want your report to answer?

☑ Check Your Comprehension

1. What was "Barrack 16"?
2. How did one of the Uchidas' neighbors cope with the lack of bathtubs at Tanforan?
3. Why did President Ford choose February 19 to give his speech and to sign Proclamation 4417?
4. What did Proclamation 4417 do?

◆ Critical Thinking

INTERPRET

1. Is the camp prepared for the arrival of prisoners when the Uchidas arrive? Explain. **[Draw Conclusions]**
2. Why do you think Executive Order 9066 was never formally revoked? **[Speculate]**

EVALUATE

3. President Ford describes the imprisonment of Japanese Americans as an "error." Does that seem accurate to you? Why or why not? **[Assess]**

EXTEND

4. What do the conditions at the camp suggest about the government's attitude toward Japanese Americans? Do you think other groups would have been treated the same way? **[Social Studies Link]**

Beyond the Selection

FURTHER READING

Other Works by Yoshiko Uchida

The Sea of Gold and Other Tales from Japan
Journey to Topaz
Journey Home

Other Works About Clashing Forces

Voices from the Camps, Larry Dane Brimner
We Were Not Like Other People, Ephriam Sevela

We suggest that you preview these works before recommending them to your students.

INTERNET

Students can read the introduction to Yoshiko Uchida's short story, "The Bracelet" at the following address: **http://www.mca.com/putnam/ books/bracelet_ph/book.html**

Please be aware that the address may have changed since this information was published. We *strongly recommend* that you preview the site before sending students to it.

◆ Literary Focus

❻ Writer's Purpose How does this sentence help establish the purpose of Ford's speech? *By calling it a sad day, Ford indicates that his purpose is to acknowledge the wrong that has been done.*

Reinforce and Extend

Answers

◆ Literature and Your Life

Reader's Response Encourage students to identify the specific reasons why they were or were not surprised.

Thematic Focus Fear and prejudice came into conflict with the basic human rights of Japanese Americans.

Questions for Research Have students decide what relevant questions they wish to research by skimming through the story and reviewing the facts and details that are presented.

☑ Check Your Comprehension

1. Barrack 16 was a stable that had been minimally modified to provide shelter for the internees.
2. The neighbor scrounged around for an empty barrel and filled it with water from the showers.
3. February 19 is the anniversary of the signing of the executive order that resulted in Japanese American internment.
4. It publicly acknowledged the injustice of internment and formally terminated Executive Order 9066.

◆ Critical Thinking

1. The camp is not prepared as evidenced by the overcrowded conditions, and the shortage of supplies.
2. Students may suggest that Executive Order 9066 was never revoked because people assumed that internment would not be enforced again.
3. Most students will respond based on whether or not they think the word *error* is strong enough.
4. The conditions suggest that the government did not view the Japanese Americans as citizens or individuals. Although the United States was also at war with Germany and Italy, German Americans and Italian Americans were not treated as traitors.

Answers

◆ Reading Strategy

1. Students may draw on the information presented in Background for Understanding, p. 271, from movies, plays, or novels on the subject, as well as from what they may have learned in social studies classes or at home.
2. Students will probably say they thought of examples of conditions in the camp as described by Uchida while they read Ford's speech.
3. Some students may say that the narrative gave them a deeper understanding of the conditions in the camps. Others may say that the speech helped them realize some of the underlying reasons people reacted as they did.

◆ Build Vocabulary

Using the Root *-curs-*

1. a 2. c 3. b

Using the Word Bank

1. A euphemism used for the WRA centers is "camps."
2. In order to get what they needed, the prisoners needed to be skillful, or adept, at scrounging.
3. A destitute, or poverty stricken, person might steal or beg to assuage, or calm, his or her hunger.
4. The Uchidas would not have brought unwieldy furniture to camp because it would have been difficult to transport.
5. A difficult adjustment to communal living is learning to deal with less privacy than one would have living in a private residence.
6. A thief wouldn't want to be conspicuous because he or she wouldn't want to be noticed while committing a crime.

◆ Literary Focus

1. The stalls are dirty, drafty, and not very private. The meals are not healthful or plentiful, the hot water for washing dishes and bathing is scarce.
2. History books would probably not contain details about how the internees dealt with the lack of privacy, or the feelings of frustration and humiliation.
3. The formal, dignified style of Ford's speech indicates the importance of the issue and the official nature of the acknowledgment.
4. The number of the executive order, the number of the proclamation, and the formal request to the public would probably not be found in a personal account. Students may explain that these details would not help the writer of a personal account communicate the day-to-day experience of living in one of the camps.

◆ Build Grammar Skills

1. The clause "who had trampled on the track" modifies people.
2. The clause "which were our only source of daylight" modifies windows.
3. The clause "that I am signing here today" modifies proclamation.

Writing Application

Suggested answers:

1. Uchida, who experienced life in the camp firsthand, wrote about WRA camps.
2. Ford's speech, which he made in 1976, acknowledged a government mistake.
3. Uchida described the food that was served in the mess hall.

Grammar Reinforcement

For additional instruction and practice, use the *Writer's Solution Grammar Practice Book* page on adjective clauses, p. 51.

Guide for Responding (continued)

◆ Reading Strategy

Background Knowledge

Your **prior background knowledge**—what you already knew about WRA camps—may have influenced your understanding of and reaction to this narrative and speech. What you read may also have influenced what you thought you knew about the subject.

1. What did you know about WRA camps before you read the excerpt from "Desert Exile"?
2. What did you learn in one of these pieces that you thought about while you read the other?
3. Explain how your ideas about WRA camps did or did not change as a result of reading these two works.

◆ Build Vocabulary

Using the Latin Root *-curs-*

Knowing that the Latin word root *-curs-* means "to run," match each word in Column A with its description in Column B.

Column A	Column B
1. cursory	a. quickly done
2. cursor	b. handwriting in which the letters run together
3. cursive	c. movable light that runs across a computer screen

Using the Word Bank: Context

Answer the following questions in your notebook.

1. What is a *euphemism* used for the WRA centers?
2. Why did the prisoners become *adept* at scrounging necessities?
3. What might a *destitute* person do to *assuage* his or her hunger?
4. Would the Uchidas bring *unwieldy* furniture to the camp?
5. What do you think would be the most difficult adjustment to *communal* living?
6. Why wouldn't a thief want to be *conspicuous?*

◆ Literary Focus

Writer's Purpose

Ford and Uchida both write about the WRA camps, but each writer's **purpose**—reason for writing—was different. Uchida's purpose is to create a personal record of her experience to help others understand what it was like to live in the camp. Ford's purpose was to create a historical record acknowledging the injustice of the camps.

1. Identify three details in the excerpt from "Desert Exile" that give you a personal glimpse of life inside the camp.
2. Identify one detail in Uchida's narrative that you would not find in a history book.
3. Explain how the style of Ford's speech helps him accomplish his purpose.
4. Identify one detail that Ford includes for the sake of history that would not be included in a personal account. Explain your choice.

◆ Build Grammar Skills

Adjective Clauses

An **adjective clause** is a group of words that contains a subject and a verb, modifies a noun or pronoun, and begins with a word like *who, that,* or *which.*

Practice Copy the following sentences in your notebook. Underline the adjective clause in each. Draw an arrow from the clause to the noun it modifies.

1. People who had trampled on the track had turned it into a slippery mess.
2. On either side of the entrance were two small windows which were our only source of daylight.
3. The proclamation that I am signing here today should remove all doubt.

Writing Application In your notebook, combine each pair of sentences by turning one of them into an adjective clause.

1. Uchida wrote about WRA camps. Uchida experienced life in the camp firsthand.
2. Ford's speech was made in 1976. Ford's speech acknowledged a government mistake.
3. Uchida described the food. The food was served in the mess hall.

Build Your Portfolio

Idea Bank

Writing

1. **Letter to a Friend** As Uchida, write a letter to one of your friends back in Berkeley describing conditions in the camp and your feelings about being there.
2. **Monologue** Write a brief monologue in which a guard at one of the camps tells how he or she feels about the imprisonment of innocent people.
3. **Dear Editor** Imagine that you are a teenager in 1942. Write a letter to the editor in which you express your views on the imprisonment of Japanese Americans.

Speaking, Listening, and Viewing

4. **Lawyer's Argument** As a lawyer during World War II, prepare an argument you could present in court to defend a Japanese American family against unlawful imprisonment. Then perform your defense for the class. **[Social Studies Link; Performing Arts Link]**
5. **Oral Interpretation** Pretend that you are President Ford and rehearse his 1976 speech. Then give the speech in class. Afterwards, explain why you delivered the speech as you did.

Researching and Representing

6. **Interview** Interview someone who lived during World War II, or read another firsthand account of someone's wartime experiences. Share what you learn in an oral presentation to your class.
7. **Meet the Press** After a president gives a speech, reporters often have the chance to ask questions. Act out the press conference that might have taken place after President Ford's speech. **[Social Studies Link; Performing Arts Link]**

Online Activity www.phlit.phschool.com

Guided Writing Lesson

WRA Camp Report

Yoshiko Uchida describes only one of the many places where Japanese Americans were held. Write a **research report** that describes conditions at other WRA camps during World War II.

Writing Skills Focus: Accuracy

When you use facts to support a point in a research report, on a test, or in a position paper, **accuracy** is essential. Often you'll find more than one version of the facts and have to decide which one is more likely to be correct. President Ford says

> Over 100,000 persons of Japanese ancestry were removed from their homes, detained in special camps, and eventually relocated.

The Japanese American Citizens League says the total was closer to 120,000.

It is important to cite several sources in order to ensure accuracy in your research paper. Be accurate in your notetaking as well as your writing. When you revise, check facts again.

Prewriting Use books about World War II to compile facts and figures about the many WRA centers set up for Japanese Americans during the war. Refer to several sources to ensure the accuracy of your facts.

Drafting As you draft, include specific details you learned from your research about the other WRA camps and explain how they compare with Uchida's description. Don't include any facts you are unable to verify.

Revising As you revise your report, double-check all facts and figures mentioned in your draft with your original notes. If necessary, qualify statements with words like *approximately, nearly,* and *more than.*

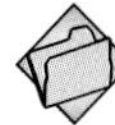

Idea Bank

Following are suggestions for matching Idea Bank topics with your students' performance levels and learning modalities:

Customizing for *Performance Levels*

Less Advanced: 1, 5, 7
Average: 2, 4, 7
More Advanced: 3, 5, 6

Customizing for *Learning Modalities*

Verbal/Linguistic: 4, 5, 6
Interpersonal: 6, 7
Bodily/Kinesthetic: 4, 7

Guided Writing Lesson

Prewriting Strategy

Students can use the Reporter's formula to organize their research and compile their facts and figures in order to ensure accuracy in their writing. Distribute six 5-by-8-inch index cards to each student to generate detailed research questions based on the standard journalistic approach to gathering information. Students can use the information on the cards to verify the accuracy of their writing when they are ready to revise their reports.

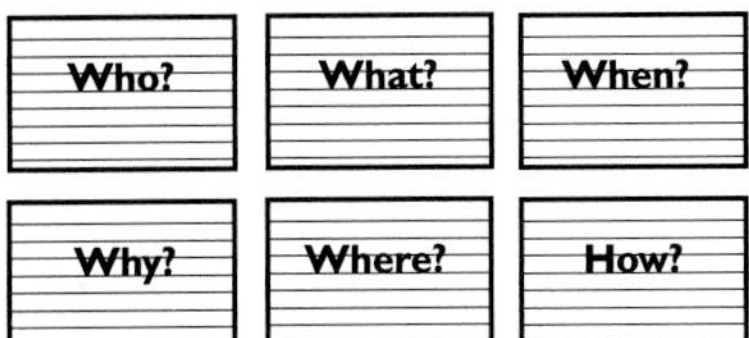

Writers at Work Videodisc

Use the Research Writing segment (Ch. 5) of the videodisc in which N. Scott Momaday discusses his research techniques.

Play frames 3 to 9933

Writing Lab CD-ROM

Have students complete the Research tutorial. Follow these steps:

1. Complete the Audience Profile activity.
2. Use the interactive KWL chart to focus research needs.
3. Use the Timeline to organize information on the computer.
4. Draft on the computer.
5. Review the audio-annotated student models before revising your report.

ASSESSMENT OPTIONS

Formal Assessment, Selection Test, pp. 69–70, and in Assessment Resources Software.

Alternative Assessment, p. 21, includes options for less advanced students, Pre-AP Students, verbal/linguistic learners, visual/spatial learners, and logical/mathematical learners.

PORTFOLIO ASSESSMENT

Use the following rubrics to assess student writing and activities.

Letter to a Friend: Expressive Writing Rubric, p. 94
Monologue: Drama Rubric, p. 109
Dear Editor: Business Letter Rubric, p. 113
Guided Writing Lesson: Research Report Rubric, p. 106

Prepare and Engage

LESSON OBJECTIVES

1. **To develop vocabulary and word identification skills**
   - Latin Word Roots: *-jud-*
   - Using the Word Bank: Antonyms
   - Extending Word Study: Context Clues
2. **To use a variety of reading strategies to comprehend a short story**
   - Connect Your Experience
   - Reading Strategy: Engage Your Senses
   - Tips to Guide Reading: Recall (ATE)
   - Read to Be Entertained (ATE)
   - Idea Bank: Description
3. **To increase knowledge of other cultures and to connect common elements across cultures**
   - Connecting Themes Across Cultures (ATE)
   - Cultural Connection (ATE)
   - Background for Understanding
4. **To express and support responses to the text**
   - Critical Thinking
   - Idea Bank: Character's Journal Entry
5. **To analyze literary elements**
   - Literary Focus: Relationships Between Characters
6. **To read in order to research self-selected and assigned topics**
   - Idea Bank: Timeline
   - Idea Bank: Letter to the Embassy
   - Research Skills Mini-Lesson
7. **To plan, prepare, organize, and present literary interpretations**
   - Idea Bank: Oral Interpretation
   - Speaking, Viewing, and Listening Mini-Lesson: Courtroom Speech
   - Viewing and Representing Mini-Lesson: Sketch
8. **To use recursive writing processes to write a firsthand biography**
   - Guided Writing Lesson
9. **To increase knowledge of the rules of grammar and usage**
   - Build Grammar Skills: Pronoun and Antecedent Agreement

Test Preparation

Reading Comprehension: Stated and Implied Main Ideas (ATE, p. 283) The teaching tips and sample test item in this workshop support the instruction and practice in the unit workshop:
Reading Comprehension: Stated and Implied Main Ideas (SE, p. 299)

Guide for Reading

Rabindranath Tagore

(1861–1941)

Rabindranath Tagore spent his life fighting for India's independence—but his weapon was a pen, not a sword or a gun. Six years after his death, Tagore's dream came true: India won its independence.

A Man of Many Talents Tagore was a very diverse man. He was a poet, short-story writer, novelist, playwright, philosopher, and an accomplished painter and composer. He composed more than 4,000 songs, including India's national anthem.

A Man of Principles Tagore was deeply disturbed by the poverty and other hardships faced by millions of Indians. He was also troubled by the British army's use of force to suppress any type of protest by the Indian people. (Britain ruled India at the time.) He took action in response to the problems he saw.

Tagore turned down a knighthood as a protest against the injustices of British rule in India.

Although Tagore died in 1941 at the age of 80, his work continues to grow in popularity throughout the world. In honor of his work as a writer, Tagore received the Nobel Prize for Literature in 1913. He was the first Indian to win this award.

◆ Build Vocabulary

Latin Word Roots: *-jud-*

In this selection, you will encounter the word *judicious.* The Latin word root *-jud-,* which means "judge," gives you a clue that *judicious* means "showing good judgment," or "common sense."

Word Bank

As you read "The Cabuliwallah," you will encounter the words on this list. Each word is defined on the page where it first appears. Preview the list before you read. With a partner, explain the meanings of any words you think you already know.

precarious
impending
judicious
euphemism
imploring
fettered
sordid
pervaded

◆ Build Grammar Skills

Pronoun and Antecedent Agreement

Pronouns help writers avoid repeating the same nouns over and over. For a pronoun to make sense, however, it must **agree** with its **antecedent** (the noun or pronoun it replaces) in **number** (singular or plural) and **gender** (masculine, feminine, or neuter).

Notice the pronouns in these examples:

> ... the two *friends* so far apart in age would subside into *their* old language and *their* old jokes ...

(The plural pronoun *their* refers to the plural antecedent *friends.*)

> I cannot tell what my *daughter's* feelings were at the sight of this *man,* but *she* began to call *him* loudly.

(The singular feminine pronoun *she* refers to the singular feminine noun *daughter;* the singular masculine pronoun *him* refers to the singular masculine noun *man.*)

Prentice Hall Literature Program Resources

REINFORCE / RETEACH / EXTEND

Selection Support Pages
Build Vocabulary: Word Roots: *-jud-*, p. 88
Build Grammar Skills: Pronoun-Antecedent Agreement, p. 89
Reading Strategy: Engage Your Senses, p. 90
Literary Focus: Character Relationships, p. 91

Strategies for Diverse Student Needs, p. 22

Beyond Literature
Multicultural Connection: Wedding Customs, p. 22

Formal Assessment Selection Test, pp. 72–74; Assessment Resources Software

Alternative Assessment, p. 22

Writing and Language Transparencies
Writing Process Model 2: Biographical Profile, p. 13

Resource Pro CD-ROM

Listening to Literature Audiocassettes

The Cabuliwallah

◆ Literature and Your Life

Connect Your Experience

Your memory records people from your past like snapshots in a scrapbook. When you don't see or hear from someone for a long time, that person becomes "frozen" on the film of your memory. A childhood friend who moved away remains five years old in your mind, although he or she would be attending high school now.

The main character in this story experiences a conflict created by such a "time freeze."

Journal Writing Describe someone you used to know who is "frozen" on the film of your memory. What do you think that person is like now?

Thematic Focus: Struggling for Justice

In this story, clashing forces send a man to prison, separating him from his family and friends for eight years. You may find yourself questioning whether his punishment fits his crime.

◆ Background for Understanding

Culture

The Cabuliwallah in this story is a kind of traveling salesman. The Indian word *wallah* means "salesman"; the *Cabuli*wallah is the "salesman from Cabul" (Kabul, the capital of Afghanistan).

People travel from their homes to live and work temporarily in other countries for a variety of reasons. Frequently, these "guest workers" come to a country with greater economic opportunities, working hard and living poorly so they can send money to loved ones at home. The Cabuliwallah travels from Afghanistan to India, returning home once a year to visit his wife and daughter.

◆ Literary Focus

Relationships Between Characters

You can learn a lot about a person by the company he or she keeps. Similarly, in a short story you can learn a lot by examining the **relationships between characters**—the interactions and feelings that pass between the people in the story. For instance, in "The Cabuliwallah" a little girl grows up and grows away from her childhood friend who has been gone for eight years. The changes in the way she responds to him reveal important changes in her character.

◆ Reading Strategy

Engage Your Senses

People say "a picture is worth a thousand words," but pictures show you only how something looks. You can't *hear* a picture of a bell or *taste* a picture of an orange. When you read a short story, **engage your senses**—use the details of sight, sound, taste, smell, and touch to fully experience the richness of the characters and the setting. For example, when Tagore describes the sound of his daughter's laughter and the feel of sunshine on his face, draw on your own memories to try to experience these sensations yourself.

Use a sensory details chart to record the variety of sensory details that bring this story to life.

Sight	Sound	Touch	Taste	Smell
	Daughter's laughter	Sunshine on his face		

Play a recording of the Beatles song "Yesterday," featured in the Connections to Today's World, page 288. Ask students what they think the lyrics say about the nature of relationships. Then direct students' attention to the song lyrics and the questions on p. 288 and the picture on p. 289. Lead a discussion in which students discuss ways people and relationships change. Tell students that "The Cabuliwallah" provides another perspective on the changing nature of relationships.

Connecting Themes Across Cultures

Cultures from around the world have varying systems of justice. Challenge students to compare various cultures and how they punish criminals.

Tips to Guide Reading

Recall Students may find it helpful when reading a selection of world literature in which the names and words may be unfamiliar, to stop periodically as they read to recall information.

Customize for *Less Proficient Readers*

To help less proficient readers understand the story, encourage them to make a chart showing the relationships among these characters: the narrator and his daughter, the narrator and the Cabuliwallah, Mini (the daughter) and the Cabuliwallah, and so on. They can note how the relationships change as the story progresses.

Customize for *Pre-AP Students*

Pre-AP Students might enjoy noting how the sensory descriptions in the story give a sense of a culture that is different from their own. What sensory details reflect the culture of the narrator?

Customize for *Gifted/Talented Students*

Challenge students to analyze whether or not they think this story would make a good movie. Have them outline the plot, list the characters, review the dialogue, and the setting to decide whether the story would become an interesting screenplay.

Test Preparation Workshop

Reading Comprehension: Stated and Implied Main Ideas

To help students prepare for standardized tests, review the identification of stated or implied main ideas. Ask students to read the first paragraph of the world literature selection "The Cabuliwallah" on p. 284 and then answer the following sample question

What is the main idea of this passage?

A Mini talks too much.

B Mini's father enjoys her conversations.

C Mini's mother does not enjoy her constant chatter.

D Silence is unnatural for Mini.

Students may find making a choice easier if they first summarize the passage in their own words. This will help them differentiate between details and the main idea. *A, C,* and *D* are details that support the main idea which is Mini's father's enjoyment of her constant chattering. *B* best states the main idea of the passage.

Develop Understanding

One-Minute Insight This short story is set in India and describes a culture and customs very different from the culture in the United States. However, it treats themes that are universal: the love of fathers for their daughters, and the ways that relationships change as people change. In the beginning of the story, the narrator considers the Cabuliwallah very different from himself, but by the story's end, he realized that the similarities between them are more important than the differences.

◆ Literary Focus

❶ **Relationships Between Characters** Have students describe the relationship between father and daughter at the beginning of the story as open, communicative, and comfortable.

❷ **Enrichment** Explain to students that, while the official language of India is Hindi, only about half the people speak it. In fact, there are fourteen major languages, more than 150 minor ones, and more than 700 dialects spoken in India. The most widely spoken language has two different alphabets. Written one way, it is called Hindi, and written the other way, it is called Urdu. Bengali, Gujariti, Kashmiri, and Punjabi are only a few of the other languages spoken in India. Most people who live in the same state speak the same language.

◆ Reading Strategy

❸ **Engage Your Senses** To what senses does the writer appeal in these lines? *The writer appeals to the senses of sight and hearing.*

▶Critical Viewing◀

❹ **Connect** *The busy, chaotic scene reflects the feeling of energy in the author's description of Mini. The scene suggests the lively variety that might draw a child of Mini's temperament to look out the window.*

The Cabuliwallah

Rabindranath Tagore

Translated From the Bengali Language

❶ Mini, my five-year-old daughter, cannot live without chattering. I really believe that in all her life she has not wasted one minute in silence. Her mother is often vexed at this and would stop her prattle, but I do not. To see Mini quiet is unnatural, and I cannot bear it for long. Because of this, our conversations are always lively.

One morning, for instance, when I was in the midst of the seventeenth chapter of my new novel, Mini stole into the room and, putting her hand into mine, said: "Father! Ramdayal the doorkeeper calls a crow a krow! He doesn't know anything, does he?"

❷ Before I could explain the language differences in this country, she was on the trace of another subject. "What do you think, Father? Shola says there is an elephant in the clouds, blowing water out of his trunk, and that is why it rains!"

The child had seated herself at my feet near the table and was playing softly, drumming on her knees. I was hard at work on my seventeenth chapter, where Pratap Singh, the hero, had just caught Kanchanlata, the heroine, in his arms and was about to escape with her by the third-story window of the castle, when all of a sudden Mini left her play and ran to the window, crying "A Cabuliwallah! a Cabuliwallah!" Sure enough, in the street below was a Cabuliwallah passing slowly along. ❸ He wore the loose, soiled clothing of his people, and a tall turban; there was a bag on his back, and he carried boxes of grapes in his hand.

I cannot tell what my daughter's feelings were at the sight of this man, but she began to call him loudly. Ah, I thought, he will come in, and my seventeenth chapter will never be

❹ **Critical Viewing** How does this market scene reflect the mood at the beginning of "The Cabuliwallah"? **[Connect]** ▶

Block Scheduling Strategies

Consider these suggestions to take advantage of extended class time:

- Use the Journal Activity from Literature and Your Life on p. 283 as a lead-in to introduce the Literary Focus, Relationships Between Characters. Point out to students that like real people, as characters grow and change, so do their relationships with others.
- Use the Cultural Connection on the Caste System (p. 285) and the Cross-Curricular Connection on Afghanistan and Britain (p. 286) for additional background.
- Use the ***Beyond Literature*** feature, p. 291, to expand students' understanding of the story's setting and develop their map-reading skills.
- Allow time for students to meet in groups and discuss the Connections to Today's World feature on p. 288.
- Have the class work in groups to create the Timeline from the Idea Bank on p. 293.

Read to Be Entertained

When reading world literature, students may wish to set a reading purpose to be entertained by the author's choice of words and setting.

Extending Word Study

Context Clues As an introduction to the selection, have students preview the targeted vocabulary words and definitions. Suggest that they jot down any of the words that are unfamiliar. As they encounter them in the selection, note how the author uses the word in context.

Customize for *Visual/Spatial Learners*

Have these students describe the sounds that might accompany the scene in this photograph. Encourage students to add details of sight, sound, touch, taste, and smell to their sensory details chart, based on what they see in the photograph.

Descriptions may include shouting voices, music, and the sounds of wagons and motor vehicles.

Customize for *English Language Learners*

Students might benefit from listing and defining words that refer to items from the narrator's culture, such as *turban*, *bamboo*, and *sari*.

Cultural Connection

The Caste System Explain to students that the caste system is a class system in Hindu society. The top caste is the *Brahman*, or priest, caste. Below that are the *Kshatriyas*, or warriors, the *Vaisyas*, who are merchants and bankers, and the *Sudras*, artisans and laborers. Each of these broad divisions has many subdivisions—perhaps as many as 3,000 in all. There are also the untouchables, people in the lowest social group. The caste system was abolished in India in 1950, but discrimination against the untouchables is still a problem. Tell students that Tagore's own caste was *pirali brahman*—one of the brahman castes. Suggest that interested students use research materials in the library or on the internet to find out more about the class system found in Hindu society. Have them make a list of headings or topics that will help them locate information.

◆ Literary Focus

❶ **Relationships Between Characters** Ask students why Mini decides to make friends with the Cabuliwallah. *She has found an adult who will listen to her and isn't too busy to spend time with her.*

◆ Critical Thinking

❷ **Make Inferences** Why is Mini's mother shocked that Mini took money from the Cabuliwallah? *Mini's mother does not understand the relationship between Mini and the Cabuliwallah. Also, the Cabuliwallah is from a lower and poorer class than Mini's.*

◆ Critical Thinking

❸ **Speculate** Ask students to offer reasons why the Cabuliwallah enjoys talking to Mini so much. *Some students may say that, because the Cabuliwallah travels all the time, he has no friends and is lonely. Other students may suggest that the Cabuliwallah likes children or that spending time with Mini allows him to laugh and be silly.*

Customize for *Less Proficient Readers*

❹ Students who have trouble identifying the relationships between characters should examine the exchange about the elephant to understand the relationship between the Cabuliwallah and Mini. The private joke emphasizes that these two have found in each other a quality they do not find in other people.

finished! At this exact moment the Cabuliwallah turned and looked up at the child. When she saw this, she was overcome by terror, fled to her mother's protection, and disappeared. She had a blind belief that inside the bag which the big man carried were two or three children like herself. Meanwhile, the peddler entered my doorway and greeted me with a smiling face.

So precarious was the position of my hero and my heroine that my first impulse was to stop and buy something, especially since Mini had called to the man. I made some small purchases, and a conversation began about Abdurrahman, the Russians, the English, and the frontier policy.[1]

As he was about to leave, he asked: "And where is the little girl, sir?"

I, thinking that Mini must get rid of her false fear, had her brought out. She stood by my chair, watching the Cabuliwallah and his bag. He offered her nuts and raisins, but she would not be tempted and only clung closer to me, with all her doubts increased. This was their first meeting.

❶ One morning, however, not many days later, as I was leaving the house, I was startled to find Mini seated on a bench by the door, laughing and talking with the great Cabuliwallah at her feet. In all her life, it appeared, my small daughter had never found so patient a listener, except for her father. Already the corner of her little sari[2] was stuffed with almonds and raisins, gifts from her visitor. "Why did you give her those?" I said and, taking out an eight-anna piece,[3] handed it to him. The man accepted the money without delay, and slipped it into his pocket.

❷ Alas, on my return an hour later, I found the unfortunate coin had made twice its own worth of trouble. The Cabuliwallah had given it to Mini, and her mother, seeing the bright round object, had pounced on the child with: "Where did you get that eight-anna piece?"

"The Cabuliwallah gave it to me," said Mini cheerfully.

"The Cabuliwallah gave it to you!" cried her mother much shocked. "O Mini! how could you take it from him?"

Entering at this moment, I saved her from impending disaster and proceeded to make my own inquiries. I found that it was not the first or the second time the two had met. The Cabuliwallah had overcome the child's first terror by a judicious bribery of nuts and almonds, and the two were now great friends.

They had many quaint jokes which afforded them a great deal of amusement. Seated in front of him, and looking with all her tiny dignity on his gigantic frame, Mini would ripple her face with laughter and begin "O Cabuliwallah! Cabuliwallah! what have you got in your bag?"

He would reply in the nasal accents of a mountaineer: "An elephant!" Not much cause for merriment, perhaps, but how they both enjoyed their joke! And for me, this child's talk with a grown-up man always had in it something strangely fascinating.

Then the Cabuliwallah, not to be caught behind, would take his turn with: "Well, little one, and when are you going to the father-in-law's house?"[4]

Now most small Bengali[5] maidens have heard long ago about the father-in-law's house, but we, being a little modern, had kept these things from our child, and at this question Mini must have been a trifle bewildered. But she would not show it and with instant composure replied: "Are you going there?"

Among men of the Cabuliwallah's class, however, it is well-known that the words "father-in-law's house" have a double meaning. It is a euphemism for jail, the place where we are well cared for at no expense. The sturdy peddler

1. **Abdurrahman . . . policy:** Political issues between Great Britain and Afghanistan at the time of the story.
2. **sari** (sä´ rē) *n.*: Garment worn by a Hindu woman, which consists of a long piece of cloth worn wrapped around the body, with one end forming an ankle-length skirt and the other end draped over one shoulder and, sometimes, around the head.
3. **eight-anna piece**: Coin formerly used in India.
4. **father-in-law's house:** An expression meaning "getting married."
5. **Bengali:** Of or from Bengal, a region of eastern India and, now, Bangladesh.

Cross-Curricular Connection: Social Studies

Afghanistan and Britain Explain to students that Afghanistan became a united state in 1747. In the 1800's, Britain wanted to protect India, which it controlled, from the Russians, but Afghanistan wanted the British off their frontier. Afghanistan engaged in two wars with the British, one in 1839 and one in 1878. In 1893 Shah Abdur Rahman Khan negotiated a treaty defining the boundary between Afghanistan and Pakistan, and an uneasy peace was maintained until World War I. In 1919, there was a third Afghan War, and with the treaty following it, the British gave up their interests in Afghanistan. Point out that the story takes place during the rule of Abdur Rahman; ask students what the narrator and the Cabuliwallah would have discussed.

would take my daughter's question in this sense. "Ah," he would say, shaking his fist at an invisible policeman, "I will thrash my father-in-law!" Hearing this, and picturing the poor, uncomfortable relative, Mini would go into peals of laughter, joined by her formidable friend.

These were autumn mornings, the time of year when kings of old went forth to conquest; and I, never stirring from my corner in Calcutta,[6] would let my mind wander over the whole world. At the very name of another country, my heart would go out to it, and at the sight of a foreigner in the streets, I would fall to weaving a network of dreams: the mountains, the glens,[7] the forests of his distant homeland with a cottage in its setting, and the free and independent life of faraway wilds. Perhaps these scenes of travel pass in my imagination all the more vividly because I lead a vegetable existence such that a call to travel would fall upon me like a thunderbolt. In the presence of this Cabuliwallah I was immediately transported to the foot of mountains, with narrow defiles[8] twisting in and out amongst their towering, arid peaks. I could see the string of camels bearing merchandise, and the company of turbaned merchants carrying queer old firearms, and some of their spears down toward the plains. I could see—but at this point Mini's mother would intervene, imploring me to "beware of that man."

> ◆ **Reading Strategy**
> To which sense or senses does this paragraph appeal?

Unfortunately Mini's mother is a very timid lady. Whenever she hears a noise in the street or sees people coming toward the house, she always jumps to the conclusion that they are either thieves, drunkards, snakes, tigers, malaria, cockroaches, caterpillars, or an English sailor. Even after all these years of experience, she is not able to overcome her terror. Thus she was full of doubts about the Cabuliwallah and used to beg me to keep a watchful eye on him.

I tried to gently laugh her fear away, but then she would turn on me seriously and ask solemn questions.

Were children never kidnapped?

Was it, then, not true that there was slavery in Cabul?

Was it so very absurd that this big man should be able to carry off a tiny child?

I told her that, though not impossible, it was highly improbable. But this was not enough, and her dread persisted. As her suspicion was unfounded, however, it did not seem right to forbid the man to come to the house, and his familiarity went unchecked.

Once a year, in the middle of January, Rahmun the Cabuliwallah was in the habit of returning to his country, and as the time approached, he would be very busy going from house to house collecting his debts. This year, however, he always found time to come and see Mini. It would have seemed to an outsider that there was some conspiracy between them, for when he could not come in the morning, he would appear in the evening. ❻

Even to me it was a little startling now and then, to suddenly surprise this tall, loose-garmented man of bags in the corner of a dark room; but when Mini would run in, smiling, with her "O Cabuliwallah! Cabuliwallah!" and the two friends so far apart in age would subside into their old language and their old jokes, I felt reassured. ❼

> ◆ **Literary Focus**
> What does this sentence suggest about the father's feelings toward the Cabuliwallah?

One morning, a few days

6. **Calcutta:** Large city in eastern India.
7. **glens** (glenz) *n.*: Valleys.
8. **defiles** (de fils´) *n.*: Deep, narrow mountain passes.

◆ Build Vocabulary

precarious (prē ker´ ē əs) *adj.*: Dangerously lacking in security or stability

impending (im pen´ diŋ) *adj.*: About to happen

judicious (jo͞o dish´ əs) *adj.*: Exhibiting sound judgment or common sense

euphemism (yo͞o´ fə miz´ əm) *n.*: Word or phrase substituted for a more offensive word or phrase

imploring (im plôr´ iŋ) *v.*: Asking or begging

◆ Reading Strategy

❺ **Engage Your Senses** *The descriptions in this paragraph appeal mainly to the sense of sight.*

◆ Build Grammar Skills

❻ **Pronoun-Antecedent Agreement** Have students identify the pronouns and their antecedents in this passage. *"His" and "he" refer to Rahmun the Cabuliwallah. "Them" refers to the Cabuliwallah (he) and Mini.*

◆ Literary Focus

❼ **Relationships Between Characters** Mini's father seems fond of the Cabuliwallah and intrigued by him, but also a little nervous and mistrustful of his strangeness.

Customize for *Interpersonal Learners*

The Cabuliwallah is a salesperson similar to those who were once common even in the United States—those who sold goods door-to-door. Today, many salespeople work in stores or offices. Ask groups of students to work together to list the kinds of personality traits and skills that a good salesperson needs to possess or develop.

Customize for *English Language Learners*

Use pictures from magazines, social studies textbooks, and encyclopedias to give these students a visual reference for "narrow defiles twisting," "towering, arid peaks," and "turbaned merchants."

Research Skills Mini-Lesson

Locating Resources

This mini-lesson supports the Oral Interpretation activity in the Idea Bank on p. 293.

Introduce The oral interpretation requires that students find a story from Indian mythology.

Develop Locating an Indian mythology story to use for their interpretation may be challenging. As a class, brainstorm for a list of places to start such as the library or on the Internet. Point out that during their search, students may need to begin with the broad topic of "Indian Mythology," and then narrow the topic and search for a specific story or author. As they search, they may be led to additional topics or research venues.

Apply Divide the class into small groups to search for appropriate stories. Have students make a detailed list of where they look, the topics they use, the additional resources they find, and the locations that were most helpful.

Assess After students have completed their research, as a class compile a list of research suggestions and tips. Discuss whether looking at the library or on the Internet was faster and which was more helpful.

Connections to Today's World

Thematic Focus Like the speaker in the song, by the end of the story, the Cabuliwallah and Mini's father will both feel that time has passed quickly and changed an important relationship in their lives. The Beatles themselves are an example of how people change and grow apart over time. Due to artistic, business, and personal differences the musicians began experimenting with independent projects in the late 1960's. Although "Yesterday" was ultimately recorded as a Beatles song, it was originally recorded by Paul McCartney alone. In 1970, the group broke up and the band members moved on to perform as soloists or to lead other groups.

Answer

Mini's father might sing this song as an expression of his sadness over losing his "little girl," and the change in Mini's attitude from the easy closeness of a child to the awkward distance of a young woman about to become married. The Cabuliwallah might sing the song about Mini for the same reasons, or he might sing it about his own daughter.

◆ Reading Strategy

1 Engage Your Senses Ask students to which senses this description appeals. What impression does it give the reader? *The contrast between the chill in the air and the warmth of the sun appeals to the sense of touch.*

Customize for
Musical/Rhythmic Learners
Interested students may wish to locate a recording of "Yesterday" performed by the Beatles and listen to it in a small group or play it for the entire class. Have them discuss how the music, vocalists, and accompaniment enhances the written lyrics they have read on the page.

Customize for
Logical/Mathematical Learners
Have interested students use the map on p. 291 or an atlas to appreciate just how far the Cabuliwallah was from his home and family during his imprisonment and while he worked as a fruit seller.

CONNECTIONS TO TODAY'S WORLD

The Cabuliwallah and Mini's father both discover that the passage of time changes relationships. This theme of changing relationships is common in songs as well as in literature. The song "Yesterday" by The Beatles deals with this theme.

The Beatles—George Harrison, John Lennon, Paul McCartney, and Ringo Starr—burst onto the American music scene in 1962 with their hit "Love Me Do." Although their early musical style was influenced by such American rock artists as Chuck Berry, Buddy Holly, and the Everly Brothers, the Beatles gave a new direction to rock-and-roll in the middle and late sixties. Earlier rock music was based mostly on rhythm—a strong beat—but The Beatles emphasized melody, complex chord progressions, and imaginative and meaningful lyrics. The Beatles also incorporated Indian instruments into some of their music. This ballad, from their later years, is one of their most popular.

YESTERDAY

Paul McCartney

Yesterday, all my troubles seemed so far away
Now it looks as though they're here to stay
Oh, I believe in yesterday

Suddenly, I'm not half the man I used to be
There's a shadow hanging over me
Oh, yesterday came suddenly

Why she had to go I don't know, she wouldn't say
I said something wrong, now I long for yesterday

Yesterday, love was such an easy game to play
Now I need a place to hide away
Oh, I believe in yesterday

Why she had to go I don't know, she wouldn't say
I said something wrong, now I long for yesterday

Yesterday, love was such and easy game to play
Now I need a place to hide away
Oh, I believe in yesterday.

1. If this song were sung by a character in "The Cabuliwallah," with who would sing it? Explain.
2. How does the mood of the song compare and contrast with the mood of the story?

before he had made up his mind to go, I was correcting my proof sheets[9] in my study. It was chilly weather. Through the window the rays of
1 the sun touched my feet, and the slight warmth was very welcome. It was almost eight o'clock, and the early pedestrians were returning home with their heads covered. All at once I heard an uproar in the street and, looking out, saw Rahmun bound and being led away between two policemen, followed by a crowd of curious boys. There were bloodstains on the clothes of the Cabuliwallah, and one of the policemen carried a knife. Hurrying out, I stopped them and inquired what it all meant. Partly from one, partly from another, I gathered that a certain neighbor had owed the peddler something for a

9. **proof sheets:** Copies of a typeset manuscript on which changes or corrections are made by the author or an editor.

◆ Build Vocabulary

fettered (fet′ ərd) *adj.*: Restrained, as with a chain
sordid (sôr′ did) *adj.*: Filthy or dirty
pervaded (pər vād′ id) *v.*: Spread throughout; filled

Viewing and Representing Mini-Lesson

Sketch
This mini-lesson supports the Researching and Representing project on p. 293.
Introduce Point out to students that authors use words much as an artist uses pencil, ink, or chalk to capture a portrait of a person.
Develop Suggest that students carefully reread the author's description of Cabuliwallah at the beginning of the story. As they skim for details, suggest that they make a list of the words the author uses.
Apply Have students use their list of details to create a visual representation of the Cabuliwallah as they believe the author intended him to look. They may use any art medium they choose. They may wish to focus on his face, or do a portrait of his entire body including his clothing.
Assess Have students display their sketches for the class to view. Assess students' work based on the number of details they were able to use from the story and how effectively they were able to use them in their representation.

Rampuri shawl[10] but had falsely denied having bought it, and that in the course of the quarrel Rahmun had struck him. Now, in the heat of his excitement, the prisoner began calling his enemy all sorts of names. Suddenly, from a verandah of my house my little Mini appeared, with her usual exclamation: "O Cabuliwallah! Cabuliwallah!" Rahmun's face lighted up as he turned to her. He had no bag under his arm today, so she could not discuss the elephant with him. She at once therefore proceeded to the next question: "Are you going to the father-in-law's house?" Rahmun laughed and said: "Just where I am going, little one!" Then seeing that the reply did not amuse the child, he held up his fettered hands. "Ah," he said, "I would have thrashed that old father-in-law, but my hands are bound!"

On a charge of murderous assault, Rahmun was sentenced to many years of imprisonment.

Time passed, and he was forgotten. The accustomed work in the accustomed place was ours, and the thought of the once free mountaineer spending his years in prison seldom occurred to us. Even my lighthearted Mini, I am ashamed to say, forgot her old friend. New companions filled her life. As she grew older, she spent more of her time with girls, so much in fact that she came no more to her father's room. I was scarcely on speaking terms with her.

Many years passed. It was autumn once again, and we had made arrangements for Mini's marriage; it was to take place during the Puja holidays.[11] With the goddess Durga returning to her seasonal home in Mount Kailas, the light of our home was also to depart, leaving our house in shadows.

The morning was bright. After the rains, there was a sense of cleanness in the air, and the rays of the sun looked like pure gold; so bright that they radiated even to the sordid brick walls of our Calcutta lanes. Since early dawn, the wedding pipes had been sounding, and at each beat my own heart throbbed. The wailing tune, Bhairavi,[12] seemed to intensify my pain at the approaching separation. My Mini was to be married tonight. ❸

From early morning, noise and bustle pervaded the house. In the courtyard the canopy had to be slung on its bamboo poles; the tinkling chandeliers should be hung in

10. **Rampuri shawl:** Shawl from Rampur, India. Such shawls are the finest in India because of the quality of the fabric.

11. **Puja holidays:** Great Hindu festival (also called Durgapuja) that honors Durga, a war goddess. It is a time for family reunions and other gatherings, as well as religious ceremonies.

12. **Bhairavi** (bī′ rə vē): The name of a particular tune. It is a happy piece of music and is associated with joyous events.

▶ Critical Viewing What details of this man's appearance do you think five-year-old Mini would notice? **[Speculate]**

◆ Reading Strategy

❷ Relationships Between Characters Ask students how Mini's relationship with her father has changed. Why has their relationship changed so much? *Mini has grown up and has her own friends to talk to now. She is no longer interested in getting and keeping her father's attention.*

◆ Literary Focus

❸ Relationships Between Characters Have students describe the narrator's feelings for his daughter. Have they changed over time? *He loves her as deeply as he did when she was a child; he considers her the light of his home; he feels pain over the impending separation.*

▶Critical Viewing◀

❹ Speculate *The man's long white beard and baggy, soiled clothes would probably seem strange and interesting to five-year old Mini.*

Customize for
Interpersonal Learners
Ask these students to share with the class details of celebrations they have helped prepare. These students can lead a class discussion on how these details can help readers understand the preparations for Mini's wedding.

Speaking, Listening, and Viewing Mini-Lesson

Courtroom Speech
This mini-lesson supports the Speaking, Listening, and Viewing activity in the Idea Bank on p. 293.

Introduce the Concept Have students discuss the Cabuliwallah's crime. Of what, exactly, is he accused? Is he guilty? Is the punishment fair or too severe?

Develop Background Students can use information about the Cabuliwallah's background and character traits as the basis for their defense. Have them consider these points as they prepare:

- Why did the Cabuliwallah assault the customer?
- Were there extenuating circumstances?
- Is the Cabuliwallah a violent man or a criminal? How do you know?

Apply the Information Students can use this information to prepare their speeches. Have them give the speeches to the rest of the class.

Assess the Outcome The class can act as a jury and decide on the fate of the Cabuliwallah after the speeches have been given. Encourage them to give reasons for their decision.

◆ Literary Focus

❶ **Relationships Between Characters** Encourage students to notice that time and events have changed the Cabuliwallah's appearance and manner and Mini's father's reaction to him.

◆ Literary Focus

❷ **Relationships Between Characters** Discuss with students the reasons that Mini will probably not respond to the Cabuliwallah in the same way she did when she was a child. *She has become more quiet and reserved even with her father and she will no longer be influenced by jokes and treats. As a young woman, she will probably pay more attention to appearances than she did as a child.*

◆ *Literature and Your Life*

❸ Guide students to recognize that while appearances change over time, the types of details people notice also change as they get older. For this reason, a person may seem different than students remember due to changes in themselves as well as in the person.

Customize for Musical/Rhythmic Learners

Interested students may wish to find out more about the "wedding pipes" mentioned by the narrator as a part of the Indian wedding ceremony. Suggest that students explore the various styles of music that have developed in India over the years and if possible share examples with the class.

Reteach

Remind students that when they read a short story, they are given an opportunity for a brief period of time to live the life of another person—another character. At the same time, they also have the opportunity to react to other characters in the story. Reteach the literary focus for this selection which targets relationships between characters for students who have difficulty understanding the concept.

each room and verandah; there was great hurry and excitement. I was sitting in my study, looking through the accounts, when someone entered, saluting respectfully, and stood before me. It was Rahmun the Cabuliwallah, and at first I did not recognize him. He had no bag, nor the long hair, nor the same vigor that he used to have. But he smiled, and I knew him again.

❶ "When did you come, Rahmun?" I asked him.

"Last evening," he said, "I was released from jail."

The words struck harsh upon my ears. I had never talked with anyone who had wounded his fellowman, and my heart shrank when I realized this, for I felt that the day would have been better omened if he had not turned up.

"There are ceremonies going on," I said, "and I am busy. Could you perhaps come another day?"

At once he turned to go; but as he reached the door, he hesitated and said: "May I not see the little one, sir, for a moment?" It was his belief that Mini was still the same. He had pic-
❷ tured her running to him as she used to do, calling "O Cabuliwallah! Cabuliwallah!" He had imagined that they would laugh and talk together, just as in the past. In fact, in memory of those former days he had brought, carefully wrapped up in paper, a few almonds and raisins and grapes, somehow obtained from a countryman—his own little fund was gone.

I said again: "There is a ceremony in the house, and you will not be able to see anyone today."

The man's face fell. He looked wistfully at me for a moment, said "Good morning," and went out.

I felt a little sorry, and would have called him back, but saw that he was returning of his own accord. He came close up to me, holding out his offerings, and said: "I brought these few things, sir, for the little one. Will you give them to her?"

I took them and was going to pay him, but he caught my hand and said: "You are very kind, sir! Keep me in your recollection; do not offer me money! You have a little girl; I too have one like her in my own home. I thought of my own and brought fruits to your child, not to make a profit for myself."

Saying this, he put his hand inside his big loose robe and brought out a small dirty piece of paper. With great care he unfolded this and smoothed it out with both hands on my table. It bore the impression of a little hand, not a photograph, not a drawing. The impression of an ink-smeared hand laid flat on the paper. This touch of his own little daughter had been always on his heart, as he had come year after year to Calcutta to sell his wares in the streets.

Tears came to my eyes. I forgot that he was a poor Cabuli fruit seller, while I was—but no, was I more than he? He was also a father.

That impression of the hand of his little Parbati in her distant mountain home reminded me of my own little Mini, and I immediately sent for her from the inner apartment. Many excuses were raised, but I would not listen. Clad in the red silk of her wedding day, with the sandal paste[13] on her forehead, and adorned as a young bride, Mini came and stood bashfully before me.

> ◆ *Literature and Your Life*
>
> Discuss a time when you saw someone after many years who did not look as you remembered.

The Cabuliwallah was staggered at the sight of her. There was no hope of reviving their old friendship. At last he smiled and said: "Little one, are you going to your father-in-law's house?"

But Mini now understood the meaning of the word "father-in-law," and she could not reply to him as in the past. She flushed at the question and stood before him with her bride's face looking down.

I remembered the day when the Cabuliwallah and my Mini first met, and I felt sad. When she had gone, Rahmun heaved a deep sigh and sat down on the floor. The idea had suddenly come to him that his daughter also must have grown up during this long time, and that he

13. **sandal paste:** Paste made from sandalwood sawdust mixed with water and used as a liquid makeup that gives the skin a paler appearance.

Cultural Connection

Afghan Dress Explain that in the cities nowadays, most Afghans wear western clothing. However, in the villages, they still dress as they did in the Cabuliwallah's time. The men wear long shirts over baggy pants. In the summer they wear cotton shawls, while in the winter they wear heavy coats called *chapans*. Most wear turbans wound around caps, or in cold weather a lambskin cap. The women wear long dresses with long sleeves over baggy pants. Their ankle bands can be beautifully embroidered. Most wear the *chador*, a cloth draped over the hair. In public, until 1959, women wore a *chaderi*, a long garment that covered them completely. Point out which of these garments the man in the photo on p. 289 is wearing, and which the Cabuliwallah might have worn. Suggest that interested students generate a list of questions that will help them locate information to find out more about the kinds of clothing worn and what the styles look like.

would have to make friends with her all over again. Surely he would not find her as he used to know her; besides, what might have happened to her in these eight years?

The marriage pipes sounded, and the mild autumn sun streamed around us. But Rahmun sat in the little Calcutta lane and saw before him the barren mountains of Afghanistan.

I took out a bank note and gave it to him, saying: "Go back to your own daughter, Rahmun, in your own country, and may the happiness of your meeting bring good fortune to my child!"

After giving this gift, I had to eliminate some of the festivities. I could not have the electric lights, nor the military band, and the ladies of the house were saddened. But to me the wedding feast was brighter because of the thought that in a distant land a long-lost father met again with his only child. ❹

Beyond Literature

Social Studies Connection

India and Its People India is the second largest country in the world in population. In fact, nearly one out of every six people in the world lives in India! A country of vast differences, India's land includes a desert, jungles, broad plains, the tallest mountain system in the world, and one of the world's rainiest areas. The map shows the diversity of physical features in India. The people of India belong to many different ethnic groups, religions, and caste systems—or social classes. They speak sixteen major languages and more than 1,000 minor languages and dialects.

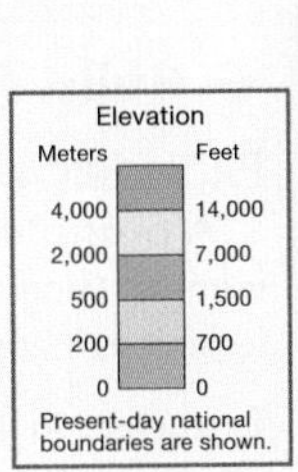

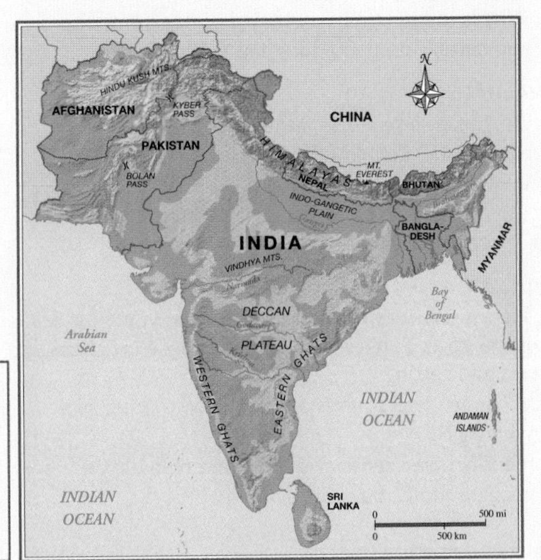

Guide for Responding

◆ Literature and Your Life

Reader's Response With which character do you identify most? Why?

Thematic Focus The Cabuliwallah loses eight years of his life and eight years of his daughter's life. His experiences may have led you to question the justice of his situation.

☑ Check Your Comprehension

1. What is Mini's relationship with her mother? With her father?
2. Why is Mini afraid of the Cabuliwallah at first?
3. What are the two meanings of "the father-in-law's house"?
4. What is Mini's father's final act of kindness and justice to Rahmun the Cabuliwallah?

◆ Literary Focus

❹ Relationships Between Characters Ask students how the relationship between the narrator and the Cabuliwallah has changed. *The narrator and the Cabuliwallah are both fathers and are sharing the feelings of loss. This shared feeling brings the two men closer than they were before.*

Beyond Literature

India and Its People Help students locate the Cabuliwallah's home of Afghanistan, and the physical features (such as mountains and rivers) that he would have dealt with as he traveled back and forth. Ask students why, before he was arrested, he would travel home once a year. *His love for his family is probably what led him to make the difficult trip home once a year as well.*

Reinforce and Extend

Answers

◆ Literature and Your Life

Reader's Response Students should include in their answers specific examples of character's experiences and traits to which they relate.

Thematic Focus Many students may feel that because of the emotional cost and the extenuating circumstances of his crime, the Cabuliwallah's punishment was too harsh.

☑ Check Your Comprehension

1. As a child, Mini has a practical relationship with her mother; her mother takes care of her and makes the rules. Mini's relationship with her father is more relaxed; he enjoys listening to her prattle.
2. Mini is at first afraid of the Cabuliwallah because she has heard frightening tales about him.
3. Father-in-law's house has a literal meaning of getting married and moving into the house of your husband's parents. It has a figurative meaning of going to jail.
4. Mini's father's final act of kindness and justice is to give Rahmun some of the wedding money so that the Cabuliwallah can return to his own daughter.

Beyond the Selection

FURTHER READING

Other Works by Rabindranath Tagore

A Poet's Tale
The Hungry Stones and Other Stories
Glimpses of Bengal

Other Works With the Theme of Clashing Forces

Letters from the Inside, John Marsden
Somewhere in the Darkness, Walter Dean Myers

We recommend that you preview these titles before suggesting them to students.

INTERNET

A collection of Tagore's poems is available at the following Internet address: **http://www.genius.net/indolink/poetry/tgorPref.html**

For conversations between Tagore and Einstein and H. G. Wells, visit **http://www.c.s.brockport.edu/~smitra/tagore.html**

Please be aware that the addresses may have changed since this information was published. We *strongly recommend* that you preview the sites before sending students to them.

Answers
◆ Critical Thinking

1. (a) Mini and the Cabuliwallah develop a close relationship; they both enjoy laughing with and talking to each other. (b) Each gets attention from the other that they do not get from other people.
2. Mini has become more reserved and self-conscious in the years of the Cabuliwallah's absence.
3. Mini feels awkward because she cannot interact with the Cabuliwallah on the level that she used to do.
4. It is sometimes awkward to see someone you haven't seen in a long time because interests and attitudes that you once had in common may have changed.
5. Students should explain their answers with details from the story such as the extenuating circumstances of the Cabuliwallah's crime, the feelings Mini's father has for his daughter, and the sadness Rahmun feels at being separated from his daughter.

◆ Reading Strategy

1. The childlike chattering and the musical laughter are two sounds students might associate with Mini as a little girl.
2. Sensory details that help students imagine the Cabuliwallah include the sight of his loose, soiled clothing, his tall turban, the taste of the grapes he carries and the fruits and nuts he brings to Mini, and the sound of his nasal voice telling jokes to Mini.

◆ Literary Focus

1. (a) Mini's relationship with the Cabuliwallah before he is arrested is comfortable and merry. (b) Her reaction to him on her wedding day is awkward and uncomfortable.
2. Mini's relationship with her father has changed in that she used to share every thought that entered her head with him; now she has some private thoughts.
3. Mini's father is able to relate his own feelings and experiences as a father to the pain the Cabuliwallah must feel at being separated from his own daughter.

Guide for Responding *(continued)*

◆ Critical Thinking

INTERPRET

1. (a) Why do Mini and the Cabuliwallah develop such a close relationship? (b) What does each gain from the other? **[Infer]**

2. In what ways do you think Mini has changed in the eight years of the Cabuliwallah's absence? **[Speculate]**

3. Why do you think Mini acts so reserved with the Cabuliwallah when she sees him again? **[Hypothesize]**

APPLY

4. Why is it sometimes awkward to see someone you haven't seen in a long time? **[Relate]**

EVALUATE

5. Do you believe Mini's father acted appropriately toward the Cabuliwallah at the end of the story? Why or why not? **[Make a Judgment]**

◆ Reading Strategy

ENGAGE YOUR SENSES

Tagore provides many details to help you **engage your senses** to fully experience his characters and setting.

1. What are two sounds associated with Mini as a young girl?

2. Identify three sensory details that helped you imagine the Cabuliwallah.

◆ Literary Focus

RELATIONSHIPS BETWEEN CHARACTERS

Important changes in the characters of Mini and her father are revealed in their **relationships** to each other and to the Cabuliwallah.

1. (a) Describe Mini's relationship with the Cabuliwallah before he is arrested. (b) Describe her reaction to him when he returns on her wedding day.

2. Explain how Mini's relationship with her father has changed.

3. Why does Mini's father feel such a close relationship to the Cabuliwallah at the end of the story?

◆ Build Vocabulary

USING THE LATIN ROOT *-jud-*

Knowing that the Latin word root *-jud-* means "judge," match the word in Column A with its definition in Column B.

Column A	Column B
1. judicial	**a.** a judgment or opinion formed before the facts are known
2. prejudice	**b.** showing sound judgment
3. judicious	**c.** belonging to or related to judges and law courts

USING THE WORD BANK: Antonyms

In your notebook, match each numbered word from the Word Bank to the letter of its antonym, the word most opposite in meaning.

1. sordid	**a.** safe
2. imploring	**b.** distant
3. precarious	**c.** clean
4. impending	**d.** blunt statement
5. euphemism	**e.** refusing
6. fettered	**f.** free
7. pervaded	**g.** emptied

◆ Build Grammar Skills

PRONOUN AND ANTECEDENT AGREEMENT

A **pronoun** must agree with its **antecedent** in number (singular or plural) and gender (masculine, feminine, or neuter).

Practice In your notebook, copy the following sentences from the story. Circle each pronoun and draw an arrow to its antecedent. Then label each pronoun as masculine, feminine, or neuter and as singular or plural.

1. Mini, my five-year-old daughter, cannot live without chattering. I really believe that in all her life she has not wasted one minute in silence.

2. The man accepted the money without delay, and slipped it into his pocket.

3. Whenever Mini's mother sees people in the street, she thinks they are thieves.

◆ Build Vocabulary

Using the Root *-jud-*

1. c 2. a 3. b

Using the Word Bank

1. d 2. f 3. b 4. c 5. e
6. a 7. h 8. g 9. i

◆ Build Grammar Skills

1. "Her" and "she" refer to Mini (feminine singular).
2. "His" refers to "man" (masculine singular); "it" refers to "money" (neuter).
3. "She" refers to Mini's mother (feminine singular); "they" refers to "people" (plural).

Grammar Reinforcement

For additional instruction and practice, use the **Language Lab CD-ROM** lesson on Pronouns and Antecedents. You can also use the *Writer's Solution Grammar Practice Book* page on Pronoun and Antecedent Agreement, p. 83.

Build Your Portfolio

Idea Bank

Writing

1. Description Describe a place that could be the setting for a short story about an episode from your childhood. Include sensory details that will help your readers experience the setting.

2. Character's Journal Entry As the Cabuliwallah, write a journal entry that expresses your thoughts and feelings about the events of the wedding day.

3. Letter to the Embassy Write a letter to the Indian embassy requesting information about the history and culture of the country. Use a business-letter format. **[Social Studies Link]**

Speaking, Listening, and Viewing

4. Courtroom Speech As the Cabuliwallah's lawyer, give a speech recommending that the Cabuliwallah be given a light sentence for his crime. In your speech, refer to the circumstances of his life and the character traits you have discovered in the story.

5. Oral Interpretation Find a story from Indian mythology. Practice reading the story aloud, using an expressive voice. Then read the story to the class. **[Performing Arts Link]**

Researching and Representing

6. Timeline Create a timeline that shows key events in India's fight for independence. Illustrate your timeline with copies of photos from magazines, newspapers, or books. **[Social Studies Link; Media Link]**

7. Sketch Using any medium (pencil, ink, or paint), draw what you think the Cabuliwallah looks like at the beginning of the story. **[Art Link]**

Online Activity www.phlit.phschool.com

Guided Writing Lesson

Firsthand Biography

Tagore describes his characters so well that readers almost feel as if they've met them in person! Write a firsthand biography of someone you do know. A **firsthand biography** tells about the life of a person with whom the writer is personally acquainted. This close relationship allows for personal insights that are not found in biographies based solely on research. The following tips will help you create a biography that reads smoothly and carries the reader along from idea to idea.

Writing Skills Focus: Logical Organization

Your firsthand biography should have a logical, consistent overall **order**. Chronological order (time order) and order of importance are both good choices for a firsthand biography.

If you want to tell the events in the order in which they happened, use chronological order. Begin with events from the subject's childhood and work your way up to the present day.

If you want to stress what you think are the person's most important qualities, arrange the details you include around each important quality you want to illustrate. Present the details in order of importance.

Prewriting Talk with the subject of your biography. Ask him or her to identify some significant events. Take careful notes during your discussion. Then arrange your notes into an outline.

Drafting Add details to the bare bones of your biography. Where you include the details depends on the kind of organization you choose.

Revising Compare your draft with your outline to ensure that you've used a consistent organization. In addition, look for places where you can add transitions to make the organization more clear.

ASSESSMENT OPTIONS

Formal Assessment, Selection Test, pp. 72–73, and Assessment Resources Software. The selection test is designed so that it can be easily customized to the ability levels of your students. ***Alternative Assessment,*** p. 22, includes options for less advanced students, Pre-AP Students, visual/spatial learners, logical/mathematical learners, and verbal/linguistic learners.

PORTFOLIO ASSESSMENT

Use the following rubrics in ***Alternative Assessment*** to assess student writing:
Description: Description Rubric, p. 97
Character's Journal Entry: Expressive Writing Rubric, p. 94
Letter to the Embassy: Business Letter Rubric, p. 113
Guided Writing Lesson: Narrative Based on Personal Experience Rubric, p. 96

Idea Bank

Customizing for
Learning Modalities

Following are suggestions for matching Idea Bank topics with your students' learning modalities:
Verbal/Linguistic: 4, 5
Logical/Mathematical: 6
Visual/Spatial: 6, 7

Customizing for
Performance Levels

Following are suggestions for matching the Idea Bank topics with your students' ability levels:
Less Advanced: 1, 5, 7
Average: 2, 4, 6, 7
More Advanced: 3, 4, 6

Guided Writing Lesson

Prewriting Strategy After students have identified the events will cover in their biographies, have them create sequence charts to determine the chronological order. Distribute four-feet-long sheets of butcher paper or cash register tape to each student. Have them reenter the events and represent them on the paper. Encourage them to write, draw, cut out suitable pictures, use symbols, ord a combination of media, textures, and words. Then have students share their sequence charts in small groups before using them as a basis to write their biographies.

For more prewriting, elaboration, and revision strategies, see *Prentice Hall Writing and Grammar.*

Writing Lab CD-ROM

The tutorial on Narration will help students create their firsthand biography. Have them follow these steps:

1. Use the Character Trait and Sensory Details word bins to gather details with which they can describe their subject and the setting.
2. Use the Chain of Events Organizer to map the sequence of events in the firsthand biography.
3. Draft on the computer.
4. Use the Transitions Word Checker and Revision Checkers for passive voice, language variety, sentence openers, and sentence length.

Prepare and Engage

LESSON OBJECTIVES

- To use recursive writing processes to write a position paper
- To write with unity and coherence
- To recognize and use appositives appropriately

You may want to distribute the scoring rubric for Persuasion (p. 105 in ***Alternative Assessment***) to make students aware before they begin of the criteria on which they will be evaluated. See the suggestions on page 296 for ways to customize the rubric for this workshop.

Writers at Work Videodisc

To introduce students to the key elements of persuasive writing and show them how Sayu Bhojwani uses them in her writing, play the videodisc segment on Persuasion (Ch. 4). Have students discuss the ways in which persuasive writing differs from other writing.

Play frames 33643 to 43235

Writing Lab CD-ROM

If your students have access to computers, you may want to have them work on the tutorial on Persuasion to complete all or part of their position papers. Follow these steps:

1. Have students review the interactive model of a position paper.
2. Suggest that students complete the Interviewing Yourself activity to find out what problems or issues are important to them.
3. Have students draft on computers.
4. Suggest students use a revision checker for sentence openers.
5. Have students use the revision checker for double comparisons.

Position Paper

Writing Process Workshop

If you had a strong opinion about a controversial issue, you'd want to let others know about it. One way to do this is to write a **position paper**. In a position paper, the writer attempts to persuade the reader to accept his or her viewpoint on a controversial issue. In many cases, position papers are written for an audience, such as a town council, with the power to shape policy related to the issue.

Write a position paper on an issue that's important to you. The following skills, introduced in this section's Guided Writing Lessons, will help you write a persuasive position paper.

Writing Skills Focus

- **Elaborate** with details, examples, and facts to support your claims. The more specific and factual your argument is, the more compelling it will be. (See p. 269.)
- **Use a logical organization** for your paper. Order of importance, cause and effect, pro and con, and comparison and contrast are all good methods of organization. (See p. 293.)
- **Be accurate.** Use care in expressing your ideas—avoid words like *all* and *never* unless you know they are true. (See p. 281.)

The following excerpt uses these skills to argue a point persuasively: Youths need more training to drive safely.

Model

New drivers under the age of twenty-one should be required to take at least thirty hours of formal driver training. ① Drivers age twenty-one and under make up less than 10 percent of the driving population, yet they represent nearly 20 percent of Americans killed in auto accidents.

A study by the University of North Carolina's Highway Safety Research Center ② suggests that a major reason so many young people are involved in accidents is that they are inadequately prepared . . .

① The writer uses statistics to support her position.

② The writer cites a reliable source of information to back up her example.

Cross-Curricular Connection: Social Studies

Current Events Point out that current events provide a wealth of controversial issues that students may plumb for their position papers. A perusal through a week's worth of daily papers or a few issues of a national newsmagazine should reveal any number of social issues they may want to tackle. In addition, they may want to use television or radio news programs and Web sites that present the news as a source of current events and issues. Remind students that writing papers that require them to set down their viewpoints on paper will help them clarify their ideas as they logically think through their own views on an issue.

The ability to establish a viewpoint will help them in the future whether or not they write more position papers. For instance, voting requires people to be clear about their views on the capabilities of candidates and about propositions.

Prewriting

Choose Your Topic You'll find many ideas for a position paper in newspapers and magazines. Scan the contents of a newspaper or magazine. Do any issues or current events especially engage your interests or emotions? What issues make you want to write to a government official or other leader? Jot down your reactions to various stories or photographs. Then review your notes and choose a topic. Write your topic as a statement of your position.

Know Your Audience Knowing the identity of the audience you're trying to persuade is essential. Use the following questions to help identify your audience.

- Who is your audience? Your peers? Teachers? Experts on the topic?
- How old are the people in your audience? Are they younger than, older than, or the same age as you?
- What is your audience's view on the position you'll argue? If it's an opposing view, what counterarguments can you devise?
- What parts of your subject might especially interest your audience? How can you make these parts stand out?

As you draft your position paper, you can make your points address the concerns of the audience you've identified.

Drafting

Distinguish Fact From Opinion Facts are statements that can be proven true by research or direct observation. Opinions are statements of belief that can be supported, but not proven, with facts. As you draft, use facts from your research to support your opinions. Notice how the following facts support opinions:

Opinions	Facts
This is a responsible newspaper.	This newspaper won a Pulitzer Prize.
Americans eat too much fat.	The average American diet is 40 percent fat.
We need more pet shelters.	Last year, more than 600 stray animals were destroyed because shelters had no room for them.

Applying Language Skills: Unity and Coherence

Good writing has **unity** (it focuses on one thought at a time) and **coherence** (the ideas are arranged in an orderly fashion).

Not Unified or Coherent:
Jazz, pop, and rock are all legitimate forms of music. Sting is my favorite musician. I don't think the Grammy Awards always go to the best musicians, however…

Unified and Coherent:
Although they have their critics, the Grammy Awards today honor a spectrum of musical talent far broader than they did when they originated in 1959. For example . . .

Writing Application Check your essay to make sure that you focus on a single topic and that your ideas within the essay are coherently arranged.

Writer's Solution Connection
Writing Lab

To help you choose a topic, refer to the Inspirations for Persuasion in the Writing Lab tutorial on Persuasion.

Develop Student Writing

Prewriting Strategy

Have students hone their perspectives on their chosen topics by cubing. They should write something for each of the following perspectives.

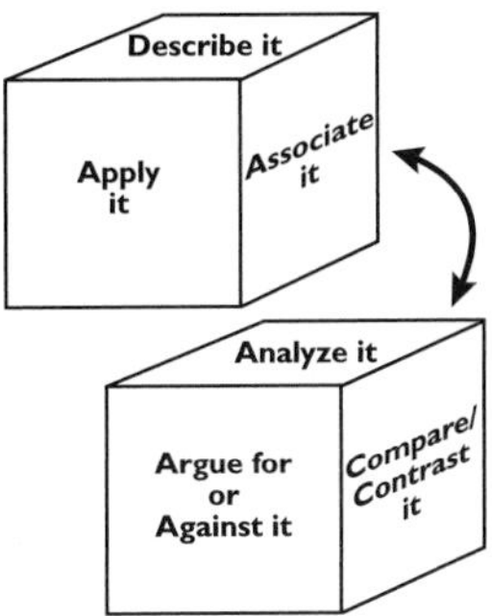

After students write to all 6 perspectives, they may choose to focus on one or several, blur more than one together, or omit one that seems weak.

Customize for
English Language Learners
Discuss issues with which these students may be familiar—perhaps relating to challenges they encounter with English as their second language. Help them determine the appropriate audience for their persuasion.

Writing Lab CD-ROM
To help them conduct research for their position papers, have students consult the screen Detecting Bias in Sources in the Organizing Details section of the tutorial on Persuasion.

Elaboration Strategy

As students begin drafting, they may find it useful to use the **SEE** technique: Making a **S**tatement, **E**xtending the statement, and **E**laborating on the statement. Model the **SEE** technique with the following example of a well-supported opinion:

Statement: This is a responsible newspaper.
Extension: This responsible newspaper covers a wide range of current events.
Elaboration: This Pulitzer Prize-winning newspaper covers a wide range of current events responsibly.

Applying Language Skills

Unity and Coherence
Explain to students that it is important that a unified and coherent essay present an argument more effectively.

Grammar Reinforcement

For additional instruction and practice, have students complete the **Language Lab CD-ROM** lesson on Unity and Coherence.

Revision Strategy

In their writing, students can circle each use of the pronoun *I* and mark out the adverb *very*. Discuss ways to make persuasive arguments stronger: take the emphasis away from personal opinions and focusing on facts; *very* is an intensifier, but a more precise word is often stronger.

Prentice Hall Writing and Grammar For more prewriting, elaboration, and revision strategies, see *Prentice Hall Writing and Grammar.*

Writing Lab CD-ROM
The Persuasion Word Bin in the Revising and Editing section of the tutorial on Persuasion will help students add the right persuasive and transitional words to their drafts.

Publishing

Encourage students to send their papers to a policy maker. For more information, consult Prentice Hall on the World Wide Web at **http://www.phschool.com.**

Reinforce and Extend

Applying Language Skills

Appositives Explain to students that appositives always explain nouns. They are useful when the writer wants to add or clarify information without using too many words.

Answers

1. Mahmoud
2. the most dangerous accidents

Grammar Reinforcement

For additional instruction and practice, have students complete practice page 40 on Appositives and Appositive Phrases in the *Writer's Solution Grammar Practice Book.*

Applying Language Skills: Appositives

An **appositive** is a noun or pronoun placed near another noun or pronoun to identify or provide more information about it.

My main mode of transportation, my car, is not very reliable.

Here, *my car* identifies the writer's main mode of transportation.

Use appositives to add details and specifics to your position paper. For example, don't just say "drivers under twenty-one," say "drivers under twenty-one, *the majority of drivers in our state,* account for . . ."

Practice On your paper, identify the appositives in the following sentences.

1. My friend Mahmoud was born in Cairo.
2. Head-on collisions, the most dangerous accidents, are on the rise.

Writing Application Review your position paper, adding appositives where they would strengthen your writing.

Writer's Solution Connection
Language Lab

For more practice with appositives, complete the Language Lab lesson on Varying Sentence Structure.

Revising

Use a Self-Evaluation Checklist Review your draft and answer the following questions about it.

- Do you elaborate on assertions with facts and statistics? *Add facts where necessary to make your argument more compelling.*
- Are your researched facts and statistics accurate? *Check with at least two sources to make sure that the integrity of your information cannot be challenged.*
- Is your organization coherent? *Make sure that your paragraphs and sentences within each paragraph follow a logical and easy-to-understand organizational plan.*
- Have you checked your spelling and grammar?

Revision Model

① In countries where formal driver education is mandated, teen driver fatalities are significantly lower.
^For any driver under 21, formal driver education should be required. In addition, there should be a lower limit of the number of points, from the current ~~10~~ ② 12, a driver is allowed to collect before his or her license is suspended.

① The writer strengthens her argument with a fact that supports her position.

② The writer changes this inaccurate information.

Publishing

Deliver a Persuasive Speech One way to publish your position paper is by presenting it as a speech. Use these tips to guide you as you present your speech:

- Practice several times on your own.
- Mark places that you want to emphasize.
- Speak slowly and clearly.
- Allow your voice to rise and fall naturally.
- Speak loudly enough to be heard.
- Look directly at your audience or the camera.

✓ ASSESSMENT

PORTFOLIO ASSESSMENT
Use the rubric on Persuasion in the ***Alternative Assessment*** booklet (p. 105) to assess the students' writing. Add these criteria to customize the rubric to this assignment.

	4	3	2	1
Elaboration	The writer elaborates all important claims with specific facts, details, or examples.	The writer elaborates most important claims with facts, details, or examples.	The writer elaborates some claims with facts and examples, but stronger support is needed.	The writer provides little or no details, facts, or examples to support any of his or her claims.
Unity and Coherence	The paper has a clear thesis statement, which each paragraph directly supports. Transitions are used effectively.	The paper has a thesis statement that is supported by most of the body paragraphs. Transitions are used.	Thesis statement is unclear. Body paragraphs provide some support. Better transitions are needed.	The paper has no thesis statement. Body paragraphs provide scant support. Transitions are lacking.

Student Success Workshop

Real-World Reading Skills

Establishing a Purpose for Reading

Strategies for Success

Reading without a purpose is like starting a car trip without knowing your destination—you might get lost if you don't know where you want to go. If you can read with a purpose, you are more likely to get what you want from a text, and you might even save time. Even if you just want to relax and read a novel, you still need to know your purpose—to enjoy what you're reading.

Establish Your Purpose Ask yourself whether your purpose for reading is to enjoy, to discover, to interpret, to analyze, to evaluate, to compare and contrast, to do research, or to do something else. If you decide what aspect of a work most interests you, it will be easier to stay focused as you read. For example, your purpose for reading an article on African lions could be to learn about how lions hunt. But if you haven't decided your purpose for reading the article, you might get lost in the author's wide-ranging information and conclusions.

You Can Have More Than One Often, you'll have more than one purpose for reading. For example, you may want to read a particular poet's works for the sheer enjoyment you experience when you read them; you may also want to read them in order to analyze the poet's use of imagery so you can write about it in a paper.

Here are some situations in which it's helpful to establish a purpose for reading:

- Looking through a travel guide
- Searching the Internet
- Reading a cookbook

Apply the Strategies

Write a sentence explaining what purpose (or purposes) you might have for reading each of the following texts:

1. Computer software manual
2. Newspaper article about new recycling laws
3. Poem entitled "Electric Blue Skies"
4. Science-fiction novel *Foundation's Edge* by Isaac Asimov
5. Biography of Eleanor Roosevelt
6. Movie review entitled "*Underwater Voyage* Sinks Off the Screen"
7. Article about black holes in an astronomy magazine
8. Latest *Garfield* comic strip
9. Shakespeare's play *The Merchant of Venice*
10. Encyclopedia article on the Nile River

Prepare and Engage

LESSON OBJECTIVES

- To establish a purpose for reading such as to discover, interpret, and enjoy
- To read to be entertained, to appreciate a writer's craft, to be informed, to take action, and to discover models to use in one's own writing

Customize for ***Less Advanced Students***

In order to make concepts concrete, provide an array of reading materials. Have students look over each item and tell why a person might read it. Questions like these can help students identify likely purposes:

- Why might someone read a newspaper article with this headline?
- Why might someone explore this true story of a baseball player's life?
- Why might someone read this automotive repair manual?

Apply the Strategies

Answers

Possible answers:

I might read . . .

1. . . . a computer software manual to discover how to set up a spreadsheet.
2. . . . the news article to discover how the new recycling rules affect me.
3. . . . the poem "Electric Blue Skies" to discover what the title means, to enjoy the poet's use of language, and to interpret ideas.
4. . . . a science-fiction novel to enjoy the imaginative descriptions and to interpret the author's ideas about the universe.
5. . . . the biography to discover facts about Eleanor Roosevelt's life benefit from her example.
6. . . . the movie review to discover why the reviewer thinks it "sinks" and to evaluate this opinion.
7. . . . an astronomy article to discover facts about quasars for a report.
8. . . . a comic strip to laugh.
9. . . . a play by Shakespeare to discover who the characters are and to enjoy hearing the speeches.
10. . . . the encyclopedia article to discover general information about the Nile for a report on Egypt.

Test Preparation Workshop

Establishing a Purpose for Reading Discuss the kinds of reading materials that often appear on standardized tests: science articles, selections from fictional works, biographical articles, poems, and more. Often, test directions indicate a purpose for reading the selection—to discover main ideas, to interpret the author's message, to discover what characters do and why, and so on. Establishing a purpose that fits the genre will help students stay focused, read at an appropriate rate, and find answers they need.

Present students with the following situation.

You are asked to read a science article and answer several questions that follow. What will be your purpose for reading?

A To be entertained
B To be informed
C To be persuaded
D All of the above

Help students to see that answer B is correct, as they will need to be informed about what they've read in order to answer follow-up questions.

Prepare and Engage

LESSON OBJECTIVES

- To use effective verbal and nonverbal strategies to express an opinion
- Present logical claims and arguments to support an argument
- Use appropriate appeals to support an argument

Explain to students that just as being persuasive without being pushy is an important social skill, so is being able to disagree without being disagreeable. Not having this ability can turn minor disagreements into major problems. Tell students that because being a "team player" has become increasingly important in today's business world, being able to express disagreement in a constructive manner is a critical aspect of that skill.

Customize for
English Language Learners
Fear of exposing a language difficulty or shyness about their command of English may make these students hesitant to express disagreement. Emphasize that because body language and tone are just as important as the actual words spoken when expressing disagreement, students can work on these aspects of the skill independently of improving their English.

Apply the Strategies

As students role-play, explain to them that body language and tone of voice are as important as what they actually say.

Answer
Possible response:
For all three examples, students should concentrate on keeping calm while remaining assertive, not insulting the other, and not getting angry.

Speaking, Listening, and Viewing Workshop — Expressing Disagreement

You are not always going to agree with other people's opinions and suggestions, but it is up to you to decide when to express your disagreement. Sometimes, expressing disagreement can cause tension between you and the person with whom you are disagreeing. It's important to learn how to express disagreement constructively and in a way that will not alienate others.

Present Your Case If you disagree with a person's comments, opinions, or actions, express your disagreement in a way that makes your position known without offending or upsetting others. Suppose your friends think that the legal driving age should be changed from sixteen or seventeen to fourteen. You feel, however, that fourteen-year-olds lack the maturity needed for such an awesome responsibility, and furthermore, you know plenty of sixteen- and seventeen-year-olds who aren't mature enough to drive. In expressing your disagreement, present your position in a calm, clear voice. Arguing with people will only cause them to defend their own position more firmly, and they will fail to see your point.

Express Disagreement Successfully To express your disagreement in an intelligent and effective way, follow these strategies:

- Think about how you look and sound. Use a clear, respectful tone, while remaining assertive. Do not raise your voice or get upset when expressing disagreement. Doing so will only cause tension between you and the person with whom you are disagreeing.
- Present specific reasons why you disagree.
- Offer evidence, if available, to support your position. For example, if you believe the legal driving age should be raised, you could cite the statistic that drivers age twenty-one and under make up less than 10 percent of the driving population, yet they represent nearly 20 percent of Americans killed in auto accidents.

Apply the Strategies

With a partner, role-play these situations. Express your disagreement clearly and constructively:

1. You and your best friend disagree over what movie to see. How would you express your disagreement?
2. Your sister borrows your clothes without asking you first and sees nothing wrong with doing so. What would you say to her to express your disagreement with her actions?
3. One person in your science lab makes decisions and plans projects without consulting the rest of the group. What would you say to this person to get him or her to listen to input from the rest of the group?

Beyond the Classroom

Workplace Skills

Teamwork Many jobs require workers to participate in a group, or work as a team. The skills of speaking, listening, and cooperating with other are building blocks for successful teamwork. In any group situation, disagreement is inevitable.

Have students brainstorm for a list of careers in which group work, and therefore positive resolution of disagreements, are inevitable. Students may suggest careers such as a construction crew whose workers rely on each other for assistance and safety, medical teams who work together to provide health care, restaurant staff who prepare and serve food, and assembly line workers who each complete parts of a larger task.

Divide students into groups and have each group focus on one of the listed careers. Ask groups to identify the "team players," and their roles and responsibilities. In addition, have each group discuss and summarize what they think makes a team of workers in that field successful, including how they think disagreements are expressed and resolved. Have the groups present their summaries to the class.

Test Preparation Workshop

Reading Comprehension — Stated and Implied Main Ideas

Strategies for Success

The reading sections of both national and Texas standardized tests require you to read a passage to understand a stated or implied main idea. The following strategies can help:

Identify the Stated Main Idea Look for a topic sentence that states what the passage is about. Recognizing supporting details will help you identify the stated main idea. For example, suppose you were asked to find a stated main idea in this passage:

> Minerals are essential to good health. They control the body's water balance and act as parts of hormones, enzymes, and vitamins. Eating a variety of foods will help ensure that the body receives enough minerals.
>
> An overabundance of certain minerals, however, can lead to serious health problems. Most people get more sodium than they need. An adult's body requires only 500 milligrams of sodium a day.

What is the stated main idea of the second paragraph?

A We need 500 milligrams of sodium a day.
B Too much of certain minerals can be harmful.
C Too much sodium can be harmful.
D Minerals are essential to good health.

Answer **A** is a supporting detail. Answer **C** is a detail not stated in the paragraph. Answer **D** is an idea from the first paragraph. Answer **B**, which summarizes the main idea, is correct.

Identify the Implied Main Idea An implied main idea is one that is not stated directly in the text. Summarizing the author's points can help you identify an implied main idea. For example, in the passage about minerals, what is the implied main idea of the first paragraph?

A The body needs minerals.
B Minerals control the body's water balance.
C Although the body needs minerals, too many of certain minerals can be harmful.
D Eating many different foods will give the body the minerals it needs to stay healthy.

Answer **A** is only part of the main idea. Answer **B** is a supporting detail. Answer **C** is a detail from the second paragraph. Answer **D**, which combines and summarizes the ideas in the first paragraph, is the correct answer.

Apply the Strategies

Read the following passage from a newspaper editorial, and answer the questions that follow.

> The critics of the proposed recycling initiative are concerned that recycling plastic and aluminum containers will create more work for citizens who already recycle glass and newspaper. While this notion is true, it misses a more important point.
>
> By recycling plastic and aluminum we will reduce the waste in our landfill. Most important, the initiative will better the planet. Isn't that worth the extra time?

1 What is the stated main idea of the first paragraph?

A Recycling plastic and aluminum containers will create more work for citizens.
B The critics miss a more important point.
C The initiative will improve our lives.
D Citizens already recycle glass and paper.

2 What is the implied main idea of the passage?

A Citizens can extend the life of the landfill.
B A compromise must be found.
C Recycling plastic and aluminum containers is worth the time it takes.
D Plastic and aluminum harm our planet.

Correlations to Standardized Tests

The reading comprehension skills reviewed in this workshop correspond to the following standardized test section:

ACT Reading

Test Preparation

Each ATE workshop in Unit 3 supports the instruction here by providing teaching suggestions and a sample test item:

- **Stated and Implied Main Ideas** pp. 219, 233, 243, 251, 263, 271, 283

LESSON OBJECTIVES

- To identify main ideas and their supporting details

Answers

1. (B) The critics miss a more important point.
2. (C) Recycling plastic and aluminum containers is worth the time it takes.

Test-Taking Tip

Read Every Word of the Question

Emphasize that questions on multiple choice tests are carefully worded. The test developers have tried to give exact information so that the test taker knows how to answer the question.

Have students reread the two questions at the end of this workshop. Ask what words are especially important in each question (stated, implied) and why test takers should notice those words. Students may realize that if they are asked to find a stated main idea, they should try to match the wording of the answer choice to words in the passage. If they are asked to find an implied main idea, they can eliminate any answer choice that has an exact wording match with the passage.

Planning Instruction and Assessment

Unit Objectives

1. To read selections in different genres that develop the theme of Unit 4, "Turning Points"
2. To apply a variety of reading strategies, particularly literal comprehension strategies, appropriate for reading these selections
3. To analyze literary elements
4. To use a variety of strategies to read unfamiliar words and to build vocabulary
5. To learn elements of grammar, usage, and style
6. To use recursive writing processes to write in a variety of forms
7. To express and support responses to various types of texts
8. To prepare, organize, and present literary interpretations

Meeting the Objectives With each selection, you will find instructional material and portfolio opportunities through which students can meet these objectives. Further, you will find additional practice pages for reading strategies, literary elements, vocabulary, and grammar in the ***Selection Support*** booklet in the ***Teaching Resources*** box.

Test Preparation

The end-of-unit workshop, **Recognizing Cause and Effect and Predicting Outcomes** (SE, p. 377), is supported by teaching tips and a sample test item in the ATE workshop with each selection grouping.

- **Recognizing Cause and Effect** (ATE, pp. 303, 313, 339)
- **Predicting Outcomes** (ATE, pp. 325, 363)

The following additional workshops in the ATE give teaching tips and a sample test item for applying the skill taught in the Student Success Workshops:

- **Analyzing Newspapers** (ATE, p. 336)
- **Constructing Graphic Organizers** (ATE, p. 375)

Summer Breeze, Alice Dalton Brown, Fischbach Gallery, New York

Humanities: Art

Summer Breeze, 1995, by Alice Dalton Brown.

Alice Dalton Brown has made a specialty of painting Victorian houses, usually in summer (like the house suggested in *Summer Breeze*), experimenting with different lighting and times of day. Use *Summer Breeze* to help students develop a sense of the way a painter incorporates mood and formal design elements into an apparently realistic picture. Have your students link the art to the theme of Unit 4, "Turning Points."

1. What mood does the painting create? Cite details that support your answer. *Most students will say that the painting creates a hopeful mood because of the sunny sky, the breeze blowing, the delicate room, and the summery landscape; students may sense an ominous mood because of the eerie shadows and the emptiness of the room.*
2. What details in the painting suggest a change or turning point to you? *Students will probably mention the breeze blowing in the window, suggesting a change in weather. Some may also suggest that the bareness of the room makes it look as if someone has just moved out or is about to move in.*

Turning Points

Turning points can be exciting and frightening. Windows of opportunity open briefly and life-changing decisions must be made. Stories, poems, and essays can show you how some people approach these fateful moments. Share the anticipation and anxiety of the writers and characters in this unit as they deal with the chances and challenges that change their lives.

◆ 301

Assessing Student Progress

The following tools are available to measure the degree to which students meet the unit objectives:

Informal Assessment

The questions on the Guide for Responding sections are a first level of response to the concepts and skills presented with the selection. Students' responses are a brief informal measure of their grasp of the material. Their responses on this level can indicate where further instruction and practice are needed. You may then follow up with the practice pages in the ***Selection Support*** booklet.

You will find literature and reading guides in the ***Alternative Assessment*** booklet, which you may give students on an individual basis for informal assessment of their performance.

Formal Assessment

In the ***Formal Assessment*** booklet, you will find selection tests and a unit test.

Selection Tests The selection tests measure comprehension and skills acquisition for each selection or group of selections.

Unit Test The unit test, which calls on students to read a passage of literature they have not previously seen, applies the unit skills on a broader level. The Critical Reading section measures Unit Objectives 1, 2, and 3. The Vocabulary and Grammar section measures Objectives 4 and 5. The Essay section measures Objectives 1 and 6.

Both the Critical Reading and the Vocabulary and Grammar sections use formats similar to those found on many standardized tests, including the SAT.

Alternative Assessment

Portfolios As you review individual pieces or the collected work in students' portfolios, you will find assessment sheets available in the portfolio section of the ***Alternative Assessment*** booklet.

Scoring Rubrics You will find scoring rubrics for writing modes in the ***Alternative Assessment*** booklet. You can apply these to Guided Writing Lessons and to Writing Process Workshop lessons.

Speaking, Listening, and Viewing The ***Alternative Assessment*** booklet contains assessment sheets for speaking, listening, and viewing activities.

Learning Modalities The ***Alternative Assessment*** contains activities that appeal to different learning styles. You may use these as an alternative measurement of students' growth.

Prepare and Engage

LESSON OBJECTIVES

1. **To develop vocabulary and word identification skills**
   - Latin Prefixes: *pro-*
   - Using the Word Bank: Sentence Completions
   - Extending Word Study: Context Clues
2. **To use a variety of reading strategies to comprehend a personal narrative**
   - Connect Your Experience
   - Reading for Success: Strategies for Reading Critically
   - Tips to Guide Reading: Sustained Reading (ATE)
   - Read to Discover Models for Writing (ATE)
3. **To increase knowledge of other cultures and to connect common elements across cultures**
   - Connecting Themes Across Cultures (ATE)
   - Background for Understanding
4. **To express and support responses to the text**
   - Critical Thinking
   - Idea Bank: On-line Message
   - Idea Bank: Children's Story
   - Analyze Literary Review (ATE)
5. **To analyze literary elements**
   - Literary Focus: Personal Narrative
6. **To read in order to research self-selected and assigned topics**
   - Idea Bank: The Author's World
   - Idea Bank: Multimedia Presentation
   - Questions for Research
7. **To plan, prepare, organize, and present literary interpretations**
   - Idea Bank: Illustration
   - Speaking, Listening, and Viewing Mini-Lesson: Oral Presentation
8. **To use recursive writing processes to write a narrative with sensory details**
   - Guided Writing Lesson
9. **To increase knowledge of the rules of grammar and usage**
   - Build Grammar Skills: Dashes

Test Preparation

Reading Comprehension: Recognizing Cause and Effect (ATE, p. 303) The teaching tips and sample test item in this workshop support the instruction and practice in the unit workshop:

Reading Comprehension: Recognizing Cause and Effect; Predicting Outcomes (SE, p. 377)

Guide for Reading

Vladimir Nabokov (1899–1977)

Besides being a novelist, a poet, and a translator, Russian-born Vladimir Nabokov was a passionate butterfly collector. Some critics have said that Nabokov, who wrote in both Russian and English, treated words like butterflies: each a rare, colorful specimen pinned to the page.

Early Success Nabokov was born into an upper-class but politically liberal Russian family from St. Petersburg. He quickly became, in his own words, "a perfectly normal trilingual child." His languages were Russian, French, and English. By the time he was fifteen years old, he had published his first volume of Russian verse.

Early Tragedy The Russian Revolution of 1917 drove the Nabokovs into exile, and Vladimir finished his education at an English university. There, in 1922, he learned the tragic news that his father had been assassinated while shielding another man at a political gathering. Nabokov's great affection for his father and equally great feeling of loss are evident in his autobiography.

From Exile to Citizenship Nabokov spent years in Europe, living away from his native Russia. In 1940, he had to flee Hitler's Germany. He moved his wife and young son to the United States, where he taught at various universities. In 1945, he became a citizen of this country.

Literary Achievements From his early teens until his death, Nabokov was a committed writer. His carefully constructed and playful novels include *Bend Sinister* (1947), *Pnin* (1957), and *Ada* (1969). He also won acclaim for his autobiography, *Speak, Memory* (1967), whose title shows the importance of memory for this writer. Not only words but memories were the rare, fluttering specimens of this literary butterfly collector.

◆ Build Vocabulary

LATIN PREFIXES: *pro-*

In this personal narrative, you will encounter the word *procession*. Knowing that the Latin prefix *pro-* often means "before in place or time" or "moving forward," you can figure out the part that it plays in the word *procession*, which means "a number of persons or things moving forward."

WORD BANK

As you read this excerpt from *Speak, Memory*, you will encounter the words on this list. Work together with a group of classmates to write sentences containing as many of the words as you can. If necessary, use a dictionary to help you.

procession
proficiency
laborious
portentously
limpid

◆ Build Grammar Skills

DASHES

Throughout this selection, Nabokov uses **dashes**—punctuation marks that create longer pauses than commas do. Used in pairs, dashes separate material that would interrupt the flow of the thought:

> The kind of Russian family to which I belonged—a kind now extinct—had, among other virtues . . .

Used singly, dashes can announce an example or definition or can signal an abrupt change of mood:

> Summer *soomerki*—the lovely Russian word for dusk.

For Nabokov, dashes—and the information they set off—are like little notes with further background. They help him explain and bring you in to the lost world of his childhood.

Prentice Hall Literature Program Resources

REINFORCE / RETEACH / EXTEND

Selection Support Pages
Build Vocabulary: Prefixes: *pro-*, p. 92
Build Grammar Skills: Dashes, p. 93
Reading for Success: Reading Critically, pp. 94–95
Literary Focus: Personal Narrative, p. 96

Strategies for Diverse Student Needs, p. 23

Beyond Literature
Cross-Curricular Connection: Geography, p. 23

Formal Assessment Selection Test, pp. 79–81; Assessment Resources Software.

Alternative Assessment, p. 23

Writing and Language Transparencies
Writing Process Model 3: Personal Narrative, pp. 17–23

Resource Pro CD-ROM

Listening to Literature Audiocassettes

from Speak, Memory

◆ Literature and Your Life

CONNECT YOUR EXPERIENCE

Just think, no two people have read the exact same books, articles, and stories in their lifetime. The special combination of books you have read contributes uniquely to your personality.

In this section of his autobiography, Nabokov fondly recalls his first reading experiences—he learned to read English before Russian, his native language!

Journal Writing Jot down some impressions of your first reading experiences.

THEMATIC FOCUS: TURNING POINTS

Learning to read is a turning point in most people's lives. This narrative asks (and gives one answer to) the question: How does what you read affect your life?

◆ Background for Understanding

THE STORY BEHIND THE STORY

People write in order to preserve what might otherwise be lost. Nabokov's autobiography preserves the upper-class life with loving parents that was snatched from him by the Russian Revolution of 1917. (In this picture, you see Vladimir, age seven, with his beloved father.)

Nabokov was a teenager when his family was forced to leave Russia. From the graced life of his childhood, he took a few belongings and countless vivid memories—some of which he shares in this excerpt from his autobiography. The life he lost became the life he could never forget.

◆ Literary Focus

PERSONAL NARRATIVE

This episode from a larger autobiography of Vladimir Nabokov's life is a **personal narrative**—a true story about a memorable person, event, or situation in the writer's life. Writers tell such narratives from the first-person point of view. They also hint at or state directly the meaning of this chapter in their lives. In his narrative, Nabokov captures memories of childhood reading just as he netted butterflies. He closes in on some fluttering early impressions, traps them, pins them down, and examines them in a clear light.

Use a graphic organizer like the one shown to jot down details that help you share Nabokov's memories.

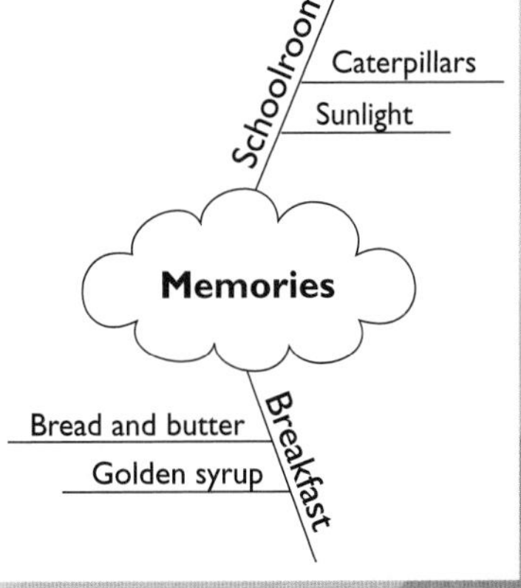

Interest Grabber Ask students why some memories are so vivid they stand out, while others just fade away. Invite students to share their ideas on what makes a particular memory last—its dramatic qualities, its emotional power, or some completely mysterious quality. Let them know that in this excerpt from Nabokov's autobiography, *Speak, Memory,* the author "listened" as his memory "spoke," bringing forth some unforgettable images and impressions from his early reading and his childhood in Russia.

Connecting Themes Across Cultures

Point out that Nabokov and his family consider it necessary to speak English as well as Russian. Members of language groups in smaller countries usually learn several languages to communicate with people in larger, more populous countries.

Tips to Guide Reading

Sustained Reading Have students read the selection without stopping in order to appreciate elements of personal narrative, such as imagery.

Customize for *Less Proficient Readers*
Less proficient readers may be confused by the way the author jumps from one memory to another. Encourage students to summarize each memory and consider the author's purpose for including it.

Customize for *Pre-AP Students*
Have students analyze Nabokov's use of syntax, such as in the sentence "Pleasant was the decreasing weight of the English collapsible tub. . . ." In their journals, they can note how syntax affects style in this piece.

Customize for *English Language Learners*
Much of the power of Nabokov's writing results from the powerful and appropriate adjectives he uses to describe simple events. Have students identify adjectives they don't understand and discuss them with proficient speakers for clarification.

Test Preparation Workshop

Reading Comprehension: Recognizing Cause and Effect Standardized tests require students to perceive relationships and recognize outcomes in texts. Use the following sample item to help students recognize implied cause-and-effect relationships that may be central to the purpose of the text.

> Another time they went on a bicycle journey and were captured by cannibals; our unsuspecting travelers had been quenching their thirst at a palm-fringed pool when the tom-toms sounded. Over the shoulder of my past I admire again the crucial picture: the Golliwogg, still on his knees by the pool but no longer drinking: his hair stands on end and the normal black of his face has changed to a weird ashen hue.

Why has the Golliwogg's face changed colors?
A The water in the pool is poisonous.
B He has seen a cannibal.
C The tom-toms are played by cannibals.
D Golliwoggs are always changing colors.

There is no evidence to support *A*, *B*, or *D*. The cause of the Golliwogg's reaction is knowledge and fear of the unseen, so *C* is the correct answer.

Reading for Success

The Reading for Success page in each unit presents a set of problem-solving procedures to help readers understand authors' words and ideas on multiple levels. Good readers develop a bank of strategies from which they can draw as needed.

Unit 4 introduces strategies for reading critically. These strategies give readers an approach for examining text on a critical level. By using these strategies as they read, students will gain a higher-level understanding and appreciation of the selection.

These strategies for reading critically are modeled with the excerpt from *Speak, Memory.* Each green box shows an example of the thinking process involved in applying one of these strategies.

How to Use the Reading for Success Page

- Introduce the strategies for reading critically, presenting each as a problem-solving procedure. Be sure students understand what each strategy involves and under what circumstances to apply it.
- Before students read the story, have them preview it, looking at the annotations in the green boxes that model the strategies.
- To reinforce these strategies after students have read the excerpt from *Speak, Memory,* have students do the Reading for Success pages in ***Selection Support,*** pp. 94–95. This activity gives students an opportunity to read a selection and practice strategies for reading critically by writing their own annotations.

Reading for Success

Strategies for Reading Critically

When you read a work that presents an individual's perspective or ideas on a subject, it is a good idea to read the work critically. Examine and question the writer's ideas. Evaluate the information the writer includes (or doesn't include) as support, and form a judgment about the content and quality of the work. Here are specific strategies to help you read critically:

Recognize the author's purpose.

The author's purpose is his or her reason for writing, such as to inform or to persuade. An author might have more than one purpose. In a personal narrative, for example, an author might want to inform *and* entertain.

Writers sometimes express a particular bias—a point of view influenced by their experience. It's important to be aware of any factors that might bias a writer's opinion. For example, Nabokov's aristocratic background certainly influenced his attitude toward the Russian Revolution.

Distinguish fact from opinion.

A fact is information that can be proved true or false. An opinion cannot be proved true or false. Nabokov's statement that he "learned to read English before . . . Russian" is a fact. However, when he describes children's book characters as "wan-faced, big-limbed, silent nitwits," he's expressing an opinion.

Some forms of literature, including personal narratives, contain both fact and opinion. However, it's always important to be able to tell the two apart.

Evaluate the writer's credibility.

Evaluating credibility involves making a critical judgment about an author's trustworthiness as a source of information. Ask questions like these:

- Does the writer present facts that are true or seem to be true?
- Does the writer support opinions with sound reasons?
- Does the writer's background or experience qualify him or her to make such a statement?
- How might the writer's motivation, or reason for writing, affect his or her credibility?

Judge the writer's work.

As you judge the work in its totality, ask yourself questions like these:

- Do the statements follow logically?
- Is the material clearly organized?
- Are the writer's points interesting and well supported?

As you read this excerpt from *Speak, Memory* by Vladimir Nabokov, look at the notes in the boxes. These notes demonstrate how to apply these strategies to a work of literature.

Reading Strategies: Support and Reinforcement

Appropriate Reading Strategies Students are given a reading strategy to apply in reading each selection in this unit. As appropriate, students are given a critical reading strategy. In other selections a strategy is suggested that is appropriate to the selection.

Reading Prompts To encourage application of the given reading strategy, there are occasional prompts, within green boxes, at appropriate and significant points.

In addition, there are red boxes prompting application of the Literary Focus concept and maroon boxes prompting students to connect with their lives.

Using the Boxed Annotations and Prompts

The material in the green, red, and maroon boxes along the sides of selections is intended to help students apply the literary element and the reading strategy and to make a connection with their lives.

You may use the boxed material in these ways:

- Have students pause when they come to a box and respond to its prompt before they continue reading.
- Urge students to read through the selection ignoring the boxes. After they have read the selection completely, they may go back and review the selection, responding to the prompts.

MODEL

from Speak, Memory

Vladimir Nabokov

1

❶ The kind of Russian family to which I belonged—a kind now extinct—had, among other virtues, a traditional leaning toward the comfortable products of Anglo-Saxon civilization. Pears' Soap, tar-black when dry, topaz-like when held to the light between wet fingers, took care of one's morning bath. Pleasant was the decreasing weight of the English collapsible tub when it was made to protrude a rubber underlip and disgorge its frothy contents into the slop pail. "We could not improve the cream, so we improved the tube," said the English toothpaste. At breakfast, Golden Syrup imported from London would entwist with its glowing coils the revolving spoon from ❷ which enough of it had slithered onto a piece of Russian bread and butter. All sorts of snug, mellow things came in a steady procession from the English Shop on Nevski Avenue: fruitcakes, smelling salts, playing cards, picture puzzles, striped blazers, talcum-white tennis balls.

> These details show that Nabokov came from an aristocratic background, which helps explain his **bias** about the characters in his books.

I learned to read English before I could read Russian. My first English friends were four simple souls in my grammar—Ben, Dan, Sam and Ned. There used to be a great deal of fuss about their identities and whereabouts—"Who is Ben?" "He is Dan," "Sam is in bed," and so on. Although it all remained rather stiff and patchy (the compiler was handicapped by having to employ—for the initial lessons, at least—words of not more than three letters), my imagination somehow managed to obtain the necessary data. Wan-faced, big-limbed, silent nitwits, proud in the possession of certain tools ("Ben has an axe"), they now drift with a slow-motioned slouch across the remotest backdrop of memory; and, akin to the mad alphabet of an optician's chart, the grammar-book lettering looms again before me. ❸

> It is a **fact** that Nabokov learned to read English before he could read Russian, but it was Nabokov's **opinion** that the text of his grammar book was "stiff and patchy."

The schoolroom was drenched with sunlight. In a sweating glass jar, several spiny

◆ Build Vocabulary

procession (prō sesh′ ən) *n.*: Number of persons or things moving forward in an orderly or formal way

Develop Understanding

One-Minute Insight

In this excerpt from *Speak, Memory*, Vladimir Nabokov blends memories, sensory impressions, and historical facts to create a unique autobiographical reflection. The excerpt focuses primarily on Nabokov's early memories of books—those his mother read to him and those he first learned to read on his own. These experiences had a profound effect on Nabokov, helping to develop an enduring love for language.

◆ Reading for Success

❶ **Distinguish Fact From Opinion** Ask students to identify the detail in this opening sentence that is the author's opinion. *It is an opinion that the "traditional leaning toward the comfortable products of Anglo-Saxon civilization" is a virtue.*

◆ Reading for Success

❷ **Judge the Writer's Work** Ask students what criteria they would use to judge this passage. *Students might point out such elements as the language and choice of details as well as the use of sensory images, such as "glowing coils," or vivid verbs, such as "slithered." They might also point to the author's use of syntax—or arrangement of sentence parts—as a criteria for judging the passage.*

◆ Reading for Success

❸ **Evaluate Writer's Statements** Have students explain whether the writer's background qualifies him to judge the writing in his grammar as "stiff and patchy." *Yes; the writer is a respected author who even as a child would probably be a good judge of writing as "stiff and patchy."*

Block Scheduling Strategies

Consider these suggestions to take advantage of extended class time:

- Have students read The Story Behind the Story in Background for Understanding on p. 303. Let students know that the Nabokov family was forced into exile because Nabokov's father was a liberal politician who opposed the Bolshevik government that came into power in 1917.
- Introduce the Critical Reading Strategies. Discuss the kinds of reading situations that call for critical reading. Encourage students to review the annotations that model the strategies. To give students more practice, you can follow up with the Reading for Success pages in ***Selection Support,*** pp. 94–95.
- Have students work in groups to answer the Critical Thinking questions on p. 309. When they finish, they might compare and discuss their suggestions for books or stories Nabokov might have enjoyed as a child.
- Direct students to complete the Guided Writing Lesson, p. 310. Before students write, guide them through the drafts in the Writing Process Model 3: Personal Narrative, pp. 17–23.

Customize for *Gifted/Talented Students*

Have students examine Nabokov's use of dashes in his writing. Ask them to suggest how he uses this punctuation style to communicate ideas. Then encourage them to compare his use with that of other writers' use of dashes. You might have them begin by looking at the Emily Dickinson poems in this book.

▶Critical Viewing◀

❶ **Connect** *Students might say the boy's finger in the air might indicate he is discovering something in his reading that pleases him and that his smile indicates that pleasure.*

◆Build Vocabulary

❷ **The Prefix *pro-*** Call students' attention to the definition of the word *proficiency*. Ask them to explain how the concept of "before in place or time" might contribute to the definition of the word. *Expertise in a field of study or in a skill requires a knowledge acquired before addressing the issue. Someone who has expertise has learned a lot about a subject before encountering a question about it.*

◆Critical Thinking

❸ **Distinguish** Ask students to notice the difference between the prefix *pro-* and the first three letters of the word *portentously*. Tell students that these two word beginnings are often confused with each other, resulting in misspelled words. *Encourage students to make lists of words that begin with* pro- *and* por-. *Some words that begin with* pro- *include* pronounce, produce, program, proponent. *Words that begin with* por- *include* porous, portent, *and* portion.

◆Reading for Success

❹ **Recognize Author's Purpose and Bias** Ask: In what way does this passage reflect Nabokov's bias? *His ironic use of the phrase "happy days" reflects his bitterness about the Revolution.*

Read to Discover Models for Writing

As students respond to Nabokov's memories of his youth, suggest that they think of some moments in their own pasts that they often remember. They might use these memories later for their own writing—for instance, a narrative about a memory on p. 310 or a reflective essay on pp. 372–374.

caterpillars were feeding on nettle[1] leaves (and ejecting interesting, barrel-shaped pellets of olive-green grass). The oilcloth that covered the round table smelled of glue. Miss Clayton smelled of Miss Clayton. Fantastically, gloriously, the blood-colored alcohol of the outside thermometer had risen to 24° Réaumur (86° Fahrenheit) in the shade. Through the window one could see kerchiefed peasant girls weeding a garden path on their hands and knees or gently raking the sun-mottled sand. (The happy days when they would be cleaning streets and digging canals for the State were still beyond the horizon.) Golden orioles in the greenery emitted their four brilliant notes: dee-del-dee-O! ❹

Ned lumbered past the window in a fair impersonation of the gardener's mate Ivan (who was to become in 1918 a member of the local Soviet). On later pages longer words appeared; and at the very end of the

▲ **Critical Viewing** What details in this picture reflect the feelings Nabokov associates with reading? **[Connect]** ❶

1. **nettle** (net′ əl) *n.*: Any of various other stinging or spiny plants.

◆ Build Vocabulary

proficiency (prō fish′ ən sē) *n.*: Expertise

❷ **laborious** (lə bôr′ ē əs) *adj.*: Involving or calling for much hard work; difficult

❸ **portentously** (pôr ten′ təs lē) *adv.*: Ominously; scarily

limpid (lim′ pid) *adj.*: Perfectly clear; transparent

Analyze Literary Review

A perceptive—and entertaining—review of *Speak, Memory* was written by Vladimir Nabokov himself in 1950, but it remained unpublished until 1998 when it appeared in *The New Yorker Magazine*. Writing of his own book, he said, "Nabokov's method is to explore the remotest regions of his past life for what may be termed thematic trails or currents. Once found, this or that theme is followed up through the years." Read this evaluation that Nabokov wrote of his own work to students. Then discuss with them whether it is appropriate for an author to review his own work. Further discuss how successfully they think he has explored his early life for themes. Have students write a journal entry in which they answer the following question:

> Can you identify any themes in this excerpt from *Speak, Memory* that the author may develop further? *Possible responses: learning languages; the impact of people; living in Russia, and so forth.*

Students can use the response that they write as a starting point for The Author's World or the Illustration in the Idea Bank on p. 310.

Here, the **author's purpose** is to emphasize the profound effect learning to read had on him as a child and how it has continued with him throughout adulthood.

brown, inkstained volume, a real, sensible story unfolded its adult sentences ("One day Ted said to Ann: Let us—"), the little reader's ultimate triumph and reward. I was
5 thrilled by the thought that some day I might attain such proficiency. The magic has endured, and whenever a grammar book comes my way, I instantly turn to the last page to enjoy a forbidden glimpse of the laborious student's future, of that promised land where, at last, words are meant to mean what they mean.

2

Summer *soomerki*—the lovely Russian word for dusk. Time: a dim point in the first decade of this unpopular century. Place: latitude[2] 59° north from your equator, longitude[3] 100° east from my writing hand. The day would take hours to fade,
6 and everything—sky, tall flowers, still water—would be kept in a state of infinite vesperal[4] suspense, deepened rather than resolved by the doleful moo of a cow in a distant meadow or by the still more moving cry that came from some bird beyond the lower course of the river, where the vast expanse of a misty-blue sphagnum[5] bog, because of its mystery and remoteness, the Rukavishnikov children had baptized America.

In the drawing room of our country house, before going to bed, I would often be read to in English by my mother. As she came to a particularly dramatic passage, where the hero was about to encounter some strange, perhaps fatal danger, her voice would slow down, her words would be spaced portentously, and before turning the page
7 she would place upon it her hand, with its familiar pigeon-blood ruby and diamond ring (within the limpid facets of which, had I been a better crystal-gazer, I might have seen a room, people, lights, trees in the rain—a whole period of émigré life for which that ring was to pay).

Evaluate Nabokov's description and feeling about the "lovely" summer dusk: His supporting details create a soft, warm, and satisfying time of day that ended with his mother reading to him.

8 There were tales about knights whose terrific but wonderfully aseptic[6] wounds were bathed by damsels in grottoes.[7] From a windswept clifftop, a medieval maiden with flying hair and a youth in hose gazed at the round Isles of the Blessed. In "Misunderstood," the fate of Humphrey used to bring a more specialized lump to one's throat than anything in Dickens or Daudet[8] (great devisers of lumps), while a shamelessly allegorical story, "Beyond the Blue Mountains," dealing with two pairs of little travelers—good Clover and Cowslip, bad Buttercup and Daisy—contained enough exciting details to make one forget its "message."

Nabokov expresses the **opinion** that stories about knights were better than the works he read by Dickens or Daudet.

There were also those large, flat, glossy picture books. I particularly liked the blue-coated, red-trousered, coal-black

2. **latitude** (lat´ ə to͞od) *n.*: Angular distance, measured in degrees, north or south from the equator.
3. **longitude** (län´ jə to͞od) *n.*: Distance east or west on the Earth's surface, measured as an arc of the equator.
4. **vesperal** (ves´ pər əl) *adj.*: Eveninglike.
5. **sphagnum** (sfag´ nəm) *n.*: Highly absorbent, spongelike, grayish peat mosses found in bogs.
6. **aseptic** (ā sep´ tik) *adj.*: Free from or keeping away disease-producing microorganisms.
7. **grottoes** (grät´ ōz) *n.*: Caves.
8. **Dickens** (dik´ ənz) **or Daudet** (dō dä´): Charles Dickens and Alphonse Daudet, nineteenth-century novelists who sympathized with common people.

◆ Critical Thinking

5 Analyze Cause and Effect Ask students how the writer's understanding of the sentences in his grammar book affected his life. *His excitement at understanding and at the thought that someday he too might write may have pushed him toward his career as a writer.*

◆ Build Grammar Skills

6 Dashes Ask students to explain the purpose the dashes in this passage serve. Why did the author use them? *They set off words that specify the term everything, thereby completing the author's description of the Russian dusk. The dashes signal to the reader that it is necessary to pause when reading this clarifying information.*

◆ Reading for Success

7 Judge the Writer's Work Ask students to determine if the two parts of this statement—the part about his mother's ringed hand and the part about émigré life—have a logical connection. *Students should recognize that the author is saying that the ring his mother wore was later sold to pay for their life in exile. Although it may not appear so at first, the two thoughts are logically connected.*

◆ Critical Thinking

8 Connect Ask students how this memory reflects Nabokov's statement that his type of family is "extinct." *Just as the chivalrous knights and maidens of his tales no longer exist, so his family and its habits are no more.*

Extending Word Study

Context Clues Have students explain words such as *compiler*, *allegorical*, and *articulations* by using context clues and then the dictionary to determine meanings and usage.

Speaking, Listening, and Viewing Mini-Lesson

Oral Presentation

This mini-lesson supports the Speaking, Listening, and Viewing activity in the Idea Bank on p. 310.

Introduce Have students think of a book that had meaning for them when they were younger. Remind them to think about the book's characters, language, and illustrations.

Develop Encourage students to make a list of the elements of the book that most affected them, and why. For example:

1. Most memorable character: funny grandmother who gives advice to all the kids in the neighborhood
2. Language—no compound or complex sentences created a strange, lulling rhythm
3. Tone—moralistic, but humorous, too

Apply Working from their notes, students can present the book to the class. Remind them to use sensory details, as Nabokov does, so their audience will "see" the book.

Assess Students can use the following questions as criteria to evaluate one another's presentations:

1. What did the presenter like most—and least—about the book?
2. Did descriptions appeal to the senses?
3. Was the presentation clearly organized, with transitions between points?

Alternatively, you may wish to have students use the Peer Assessment: Speech form, p. 117 in the ***Alternative Assessment*** booklet.

◆ Literary Focus

1 Personal Narrative Ask students how Nabokov links the stories he reads with details from his life in this passage. What effect does the link have on the narrative? *He associates the frightened expression on the face of Sarah, a book character, with the expressions of little girls he encountered at children's parties, making the narrative all the more personal.*

◆ Critical Thinking

2 Draw Conclusions Ask students why they think the writer had been envious of the solo balloonist. *He wanted to be part of the soloist's adventure, even though it was dangerous.*

Reinforce and Extend

Answers

◆ Literature and Your Life

Reader's Response Students' comparisons should consider such elements as characterization, language and illustration styles, and tone.

Thematic Focus Being able to read opens up possibilities.

Questions for Research Students may suggest questions such as "When did you first read?" "Who was the first character you remember reading about?" and "What was the first event you remember reading about?"

☑ Check Your Comprehension

1. The author's first friends were Ben, Dan, Sam, and Ned—children's book characters.
2. The author's impressions were that his friends were "wan-faced, big-limbed, silent nitwits."
3. The author turns to the last page of a grammar because he wants to see what the future will hold for the student who reads it.
4. The author remembers "the Golliwog and his harem" for their funny clothes and their adventurous spirits and merrymaking.

Reteach

For students who need further assistance in grasping the features and conventions of a personal narrative, urge them to find parallels in their own childhood memories. For more guidance, you may wish to refer them to ***Strategies for Diverse Student Needs,*** p. 23.

Golliwogg, with underclothes buttons for eyes, and his meager harem of five wooden dolls. By the illegal method of cutting themselves frocks out of the American flag (Peg taking the motherly stripes, Sarah Jane the pretty stars) two of the dolls acquired a certain soft femininity, once their neutral articulations had been clothed. The Twins (Meg and Weg) and the Midget remained stark naked and, consequently, sexless.

We see them in the dead of night stealing out of doors to sling snowballs at one another until the chimes of a remote clock ("But Hark!" comments the rhymed text) send them back to their toybox in the nursery. A rude jack-in-the-box shoots out, frightening my lovely Sarah, and that picture I heartily disliked because it reminded me of children's parties at which this or that graceful little girl, who had bewitched me, happened to pinch her finger
1 or hurt her knee, and would forthwith expand into a purple-faced goblin, all wrinkles and bawling mouth. Another time they went on a bicycle journey and were captured by cannibals; our unsuspecting travelers had been quenching their thirst at a palm-fringed pool when the tom-toms sounded. Over the shoulder of my past I admire again the crucial picture: the Golliwogg, still on his knees by the pool but no longer drinking; his hair stands on end and the normal black of his face has changed to a weird ashen hue. There was also the motorcar book (Sarah Jane, always my favorite, sporting a long green veil), with the usual sequel—crutches and bandaged heads.

And, yes—the airship. Yards and yards of yellow silk went to make it, and an additional tiny balloon was provided for the sole use of the fortunate Midget. At the immense altitude to which the ship reached, the aeronauts huddled together for warmth while the lost little soloist, still the object of my intense envy notwithstanding his plight, 2
drifted into an abyss of frost and stars—alone.

Judge whether Nabokov has successfully presented the pleasure and satisfaction of his learning to read.

Guide for Responding

◆ Literature and Your Life

Reader's Response Compare the earliest books and stories you read with those that Nabokov read as a boy.

Thematic Focus Explain why learning to read might be considered a turning point.

Questions for Research Suppose that you are conducting a survey to research people's earliest reading experiences. What questions will you ask?

☑ Check Your Comprehension

1. Who were the author's "first English friends," and where did they come from?
2. What were the author's impressions of his first English friends?
3. Why does the author now always turn to the last page of a "grammar" (student's first reader)?
4. Summarize the author's impressions of the "Golliwog and his harem."

Beyond the Selection

FURTHER READING

Other Works by Vladimir Nabokov

Pnin (novel)
Nabokov's Dozen (short stories)
Glory (novel)

Other Works With the Theme of Turning Points

My Life, Helen Keller
Up From Slavery, Frederick Douglass
Out of Africa, Isak Dinesen

We suggest that you preview these works before recommending them to students.

INTERNET

Your students can find information about Nabokov at the following site. Please be aware that sites may have changed since we published this information.

http://www.libraries.psu.edu/iasweb/nabokov/hsintro.html

We *strongly recommend* that you preview the site before you send students to it.

Guide for Responding (continued)

◆ Critical Thinking

Interpret

1. Why does Nabokov say the kind of family to which he belonged is "now extinct"? **[Speculate]**
2. What does Nabokov intend for you to know about his mother's ruby and diamond ring? **[Draw Conclusions]**
3. Nabokov was strongly affected by the books of his childhood. Support this statement with evidence from the selection. **[Support]**
4. What was the author's purpose in writing these particular impressions of his childhood? **[Infer]**

Apply

5. Recommend a book or story that you think Nabokov would have liked. Give reasons for your recommendation. **[Apply]**

Extend

6. What are some reasons that people would use products imported from another country, as the Nabokovs did? **[Social Studies Link]**

◆ Reading For Success

Strategies for Reading Critically

Apply the strategies and the notes showing how to read critically to answer the following questions.

1. Give an example of an opinion from this essay and explain how you know it's an opinion.
2. Explain how Nabokov's first sentence reflects the bias of an upper-class Russian.
3. What do you think was the author's purpose in recording these impressions of his early reading?

◆ Literary Focus

Personal Narrative

Nabokov's essay is a **personal narrative**—a true story drawn from his own life and told in the first person.

1. How does the first sentence indicate that this work is a personal narrative?
2. Find two details that help you see the characters Ben, Dan, Sam, and Ned.
3. Show how Nabokov appeals to every sense except taste in his description of the schoolroom.

◆ Build Vocabulary

Using the Latin Prefix *pro-*

In the following words, the Latin prefix *pro-* means "before in place or time" or "moving forward." Match each *pro-* word with the correct definition.

1. proceed	**a.** drive forward
2. projection	**b.** something read before a drama
3. prologue	**c.** go forward
4. propel	**d.** a look ahead

Using the Word Bank: Sentence Completions

On your paper, fill in the blanks with words from the Word Bank. Use each word only once.

Nabokov offers a __?__ of sensory details, rendered with __?__. The author is accurate without being __?__. You can almost see the __?__ facets of his mother's jewels and hear how she __?__ lowers her voice.

◆ Build Grammar Skills

Dashes

As Nabokov introduces you to his childhood world, he uses **dashes** to set off interrupting or clarifying phrases, to show an unfinished thought, and to introduce a final word that changes or emphasizes thought.

Practice In your notebook, write the following sentences, adding two dashes where necessary to set off interrupting phrases or sentences, or one dash to signal a clarification or shift in thought.

1. A biography of Nabokov the first major one in years shows the relationship between his life and work.
2. You can read about Nabokov his life, work, and travels in reference sources on world authors.
3. Nabokov spent many years in France and Germany impoverished.
4. Everyone knows Nabokov's favorite hobby butterfly collecting.
5. Nabokov not popular with all readers is greatly respected by those who call themselves his fans.

Answers

◆ Critical Thinking

1. The economy and government in Russia at the time Nabokov was writing were very different from those of his childhood.
2. He intends for you to know that she sold the ring to support the family in exile.
3. Students may cite the very fact that Nabokov remembered the names Ben, Dan, Sam, and Ned, or that he was attached to the character Sarah Jane from a series picture book.
4. Nabokov might have wanted to preserve recollections from a life that is "now extinct."
5. Students should support their recommendations with details they observed about Nabokov's character or his reading taste.
6. Students might observe that some countries import products they don't have the resources to produce, or they might say that consumers like to try goods that come from different cultures.

◆ Reading for Success

1. An example might be "Summer *soomerki*—the lovely Russian word for dusk." It can't be proven that this is a lovely word.
2. To say that a taste for products of Anglo-Saxon civilization is a virtue implies that those products are superior—a cultural bias.
3. His purpose might have been to entertain and to share memories with which readers could identify.

◆ Literary Focus

1. The first sentence uses the first-person point of view.
2. Possible details include that these characters were proud in their possession of tools, that they were silent and "dim-witted."
3. "Drenched with sunlight" appeals to both sight and touch; the oilcloth smelling of glue appeals to smell; the chirps of the golden orioles appeals to sound.

◆ Build Vocabulary

Using the Prefix *pro-*

1. c 2. d 3. b 4. a

Using the Word Bank

Nabokov offers a procession of sensory details rendered with proficiency. The author is accurate without being laborious. You can almost see the limpid facets of his mother's jewels and hear how she portentously lowers her voice.

◆ Build Grammar Skills

Practice

1. A biography of Nabokov—the first major one in years—shows the relationship between his life and work.
2. You can read about Nabokov—his life, work, and travels—in reference sources on world authors.
3. Nabokov spent many years in France and Germany—impoverished.
4. Everyone knows Nabokov's favorite hobby—butterfly collecting.
5. Nabokov—not popular with all readers—is greatly respected by those who call themselves his fans.

Grammar Reinforcement

For additional instruction and practice, use the lesson in the **Language Lab CD-ROM** on mechanics and the page on Dashes and Parentheses, p. 107 in the *Writer's Solution Grammar Practice Book.*

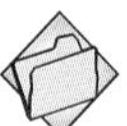

Idea Bank 10B, 13A, 13B, 18A, 18C

Following are suggestions for matching Idea Bank topics with your students' performance levels and learning modalities:

Customizing for
Performance Levels
Less Advanced Students: 1, 4
Average Students: 2, 5, 7
More Advanced Students: 3, 6

Customizing for
Learning Modalities
Visual/Spatial: 7
Bodily/Kinesthetic: 4
Verbal/Linguistic: 4, 5
Logical/Mathematical: 3

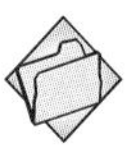

Guided Writing Lesson 1A–1C

Prewriting Strategy To gather sensory details for their narratives, have students use webbing, writing their memories on a sun diagram.

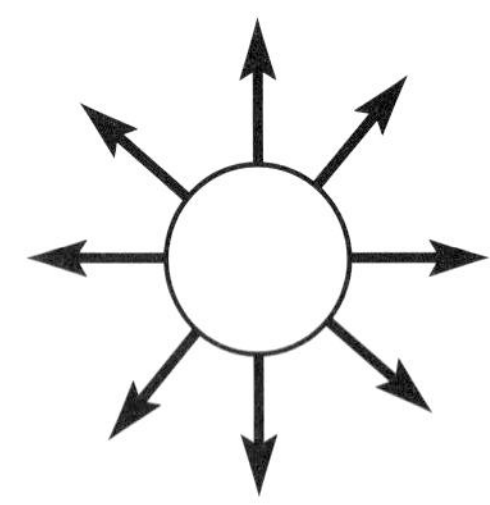

The central memories go in the centers. The sun's rays explore sensory associations, experiences, and moods. After students tap into their memories, they might reenter their webs in search of writing patterns.

Writing and Language Transparencies Writing Process Model 3: Personal Narrative offers tips for narrative drafting (pp. 17–23).

Writers at Work Videodisc
Have students view the videodisc segment for Chapter 2 in which Maxine Hong Kingston talks about

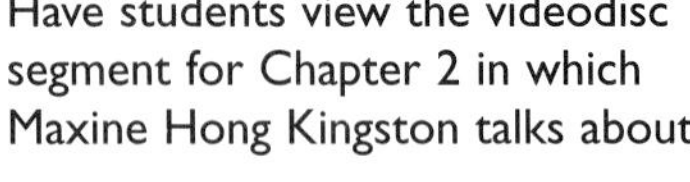

Play frames 18612 to 19873

developing narrative elements.

Writing Lab CD-ROM
Have students complete the tutorial on Narration, using these steps:

1. Have students consult an audio-annotated slide show on drafting.
2. Suggest that students use Word Bins to select sensory words.

Build Your Portfolio

Idea Bank

Writing

1. On-line Message Write a message about this excerpt from Nabokov's *Speak, Memory* to send to an on-line reader's circle. Tell why you liked or disliked it. Support your opinion.

2. Children's Story Make up characters like Nabokov's Golliwog and friends and write a story about them that children would enjoy reading.

3. The Author's World Write a description of the world Nabokov lost when he left Russia as a teenager. Use details from *Speak, Memory*, as well as from an encyclopedia and books on early twentieth-century Russia. **[Social Studies Link]**

Speaking, Listening, and Viewing

4. Memory Exchange In a small group, exchange stories about some of your most important achievements as young children—for example, learning to read, swim, or travel by yourself. Record your stories on tape or tell them to the class. **[Performing Arts Link]**

5. Oral Presentation Give a presentation to your class on a children's book that meant a great deal to you. Following Nabokov's example, describe the characters and events of the book so that your listeners will "see" them. **[Art Link]**

Researching and Representing

6. Multimedia Presentation Using film clips, recordings, pictures from books, and quotations from authors, research and report on the Russian Revolution of 1917. **[Social Studies Link]**

7. Illustration Choose one of Nabokov's detailed descriptions and illustrate it with a drawing or painting. **[Art Link]**

Online Activity www.phlit.phschool.com

Guided Writing Lesson

Memory of a Milestone

Nabokov describes how he learned to read English. Choose a milestone (significant event) from your life and write a **narrative** about your memory of it. You might describe learning to swim, moving to a new home, or graduating from school. Tell readers not only what happened, but why it was important. Help them understand its importance by using sensory details to make events come alive.

Writing Skills Focus: Sensory Details

Sensory details—details that appeal to the senses—are important in stories, personal narratives, and descriptions of all kinds. Nabokov begins his personal narrative with details that appeal both to the eye and to the sense of touch:

> Pears' Soap, tar-black when dry, topaz-like when held to the light between wet fingers, took care of one's morning bath.

The sensory details help you experience this long-lost bath as he did himself. Even before you draft your narrative, begin gathering sensory details you can use.

Prewriting In gathering sensory details, pay special attention to the often neglected senses of smell, touch, and taste.

Drafting Sometimes you can suggest how important a milestone was by showing someone else's reaction to it. For example, you might show how catching your first fish won you the respect of your brothers and sisters.

Revising Ask a classmate whether it's clear why the event was a milestone. If not, add sensory details to make the description more vivid or include a statement explaining the importance of what happened.

✓ ASSESSMENT OPTIONS

Formal Assessment, Selection Test, pp. 79–81, and Assessment Resources Software. The selection test is designed so that it can be easily customized to the performance levels of your students. ***Alternative Assessment,*** p. 23, includes options for less advanced students, more advanced students, verbal/linguistic learners, logical/mathematical learners, bodily/kinesthetic learners, and visual/spatial learners.

PORTFOLIO ASSESSMENT
Use the following rubrics in the ***Alternative Assessment*** booklet to assess student writing:
On-line Message: Expression Rubric, p. 94
Children's Story: Fiction Narrative Rubric, p. 95
The Author's World: Description Rubric, p. 97

PART 1 *Working It Out*

Untitled, David Wilcox, The Newborn Group

One-Minute Planning Guide

The characters in these selections work through problems. The main character in "With All Flags Flying" is an 82-year-old man who decides to move into a nursing home. In "The Bridge," the speaker describes his indecision and fear about a treacherous crossing. Emily Brontë's narrator in "The Old Stoic" asks for the courage to endure her final days. The tone of Anna Akhmatova's "I Am Not One of Those Who Left the Land" is one of defiance and victory after surviving the Russian Revolution's violence. The part ends with Roman Empress Theodora's rousing "Speech During the Invasion of Constantinople," in which she exhorts her timid husband and advisors to stay in Constantinople and fight rather than live in exile.

Customize for *Varying Student Needs*

When assigning the selections in this part to your students, keep in mind the following factors:

"With All Flags Flying"
- A medium-length short story (7 pp.)

"The Bridge"; The Old Stoic"; "I Am Not One of Those Who Left the Land"
- Three very short poems

Speech During the Invasion of Constantinople
- A short speech
- Will be accessible to students

Art Transparency As you introduce Part 1, display Art Transparency 18. Have students comment upon the details in Lee's quilt—in particular, the Statue of Liberty and the railroad workers—and discuss the meaning of the title, *Liberty Is Gold.* As students read Part 1, challenge them to explain the role of liberty in each selection.

Humanities: Art

Untitled by David Wilcox.

Born in 1943 in Kansas City, Missouri, David Wilcox has created illustrations for magazines, movie posters, and book covers, and his clients include a number of corporations and mainstream publications.

Encourage students to describe what seems to be going on in the painting. Once they have established the representational circumstances of the painting, have them look at its formal elements: the fact that the empty spot in the bridge lines up with the mountain peak in the distance, dividing the picture into right and left halves. Encourage them to notice the unrealistic landscape—the small, lollipop-like trees, the succession of hills—as well as other unrealistic touches, such as the facelessness of the people and the fact that they are doing heavy manual labor in what appear to be business clothes.

Help students link the art to the theme of Part 1, "Working It Out," by answering the following questions:

1. Normally, people building a bridge would not be dressed in suits. The clothing hints that the bridge-building here is meant as a metaphor. What might it stand for? *Possible answers include working to make a better society or cooperating to accomplish a goal in the business world.*
2. Does the group appear to be cooperating successfully? What tensions might be present among them? *Most students will feel that the group is cooperating; possible tensions might arise from the fact that three men are pulling, while only one is pushing.*

Prepare and Engage

LESSON OBJECTIVES

1. **To develop vocabulary and word identification skills**
   - Greek Prefixes: *mono-*
   - Using the Word Bank: Antonyms
   - Extending Word Study: Word Origins
2. **To use a variety of reading strategies to comprehend a short story**
   - Connect Your Experience
   - Reading Strategy: Evaluate a Character's Decision
   - Tips to Guide Reading: Paired Reading (ATE)
   - Idea Bank: Letter from Mr. Carpenter
   - Idea Bank: Alternative Ending
3. **To increase knowledge of other cultures and to connect common elements across cultures**
   - Connecting Themes Across Cultures (ATE)
   - Background for Understanding
4. **To express and support responses to the text**
   - Critical Thinking
5. **To analyze literary elements**
   - Literary Focus: Characters as Symbols
6. **To plan, prepare, organize, and present literary interpretations**
   - Idea Bank: Soundtrack
   - Speaking, Listening, and Viewing: Debate
7. **To read in order to research self-selected and assigned topics**
   - Questions for Research
   - Research Skills Mini-Lesson: Oral Research
8. **To use recursive writing processes to write a dialogue**
   - Guided Writing Lesson
9. **To increase knowledge of the rules of grammar and usage**
   - Build Grammar Skills: Past Participial Phrases

Test Preparation

Reading Comprehension: Recognizing Cause and Effect (ATE, p. 313) The teaching tips and sample test item in this workshop support the instruction and practice in the unit workshop: **Reading Comprehension: Recognizing Cause and Effect; Predicting Outcomes** (SE, p. 377)

Guide for Reading

Anne Tyler (1941–)

At an age when most people are thinking about prom dates and getting their driver's licenses, Anne Tyler was already in college, majoring in Russian.

Tyler began her college career at age sixteen and graduated at nineteen!

Early Achiever Born in Minneapolis, Minnesota, Anne Tyler moved frequently with her family during childhood. She lived in many communities in the South and the Midwest. After attending Duke University, she went on to do graduate work in Russian studies at Columbia University. Tyler wrote her first novel, *If Morning Ever Comes*, at the age of twenty-two and has been writing full time since 1965.

In her works, Tyler draws heavily from her personal experiences. Many of her stories and novels, including "With All Flags Flying," are set in Baltimore, Maryland, where she has lived since 1967. The characters and events in her work are often drawn from her encounters with real people and from her daily observations.

Acclaim and Awards Anne Tyler's tales about the lives of ordinary people have won her widespread critical acclaim. Tyler is a member of the American Academy and Institute of Arts and Letters and the recipient of the 1988 Pulitzer Prize for her novel *Breathing Lessons*. Many of her novels, including *Dinner at the Homesick Restaurant* (1982), *The Accidental Tourist* (1985), and *Saint Maybe* (1991), have been bestsellers.

◆ Build Vocabulary

Greek Prefixes: *mono–*

In this story, an old man gives *monosyllabic* answers to his granddaughter's questions. The Greek prefix *mono-* means "one." A *monosyllabic* word, therefore, is a word with one syllable. The main character answers his granddaughter in words of one syllable.

Word Bank

As you read, you will encounter the words on this list. Each word is defined on the page where it first appears. Preview the list before you read.

appurtenances
conspicuous
doddering
monosyllabic

◆ Build Grammar Skills

Past Participial Phrases

In this story, Anne Tyler incorporates detailed information into many of her sentences using participial phrases formed with past participles. A past participle is a form of a verb that usually ends in *-ed* but may also have an irregular ending such as *-t* or *-en*. A **past participial phrase** consists of a past participle and its modifiers and complements. Participles and participial phrases act as adjectives. In this sentence, the italicized participial phrase modifies the noun *weeds:*

"The bank was covered with small, crawling weeds, *planted especially by young men with scientific training in how to prevent soil erosion.*"

Prentice Hall Literature Program Resources

REINFORCE / RETEACH / EXTEND

Selection Support Pages
Build Vocabulary Worksheet: Prefixes: *mono-*, p. 97
Build Grammar Skills: Past Participial Phrases, p. 98
Reading Strategy: Judge a Character's Decision, p. 99
Literary Focus: Characters as Symbols, p. 100

Strategies for Diverse Student Needs, p. 24

Beyond Literature
Community Connection: Caring for the Elderly, p. 24

Formal Assessment Selection Test, pp. 82–84; Assessment Resources Software

Alternative Assessment, p. 24

Resource Pro CD-ROM

Listening to Literature Audiocassettes

With All Flags Flying

◆ *Literature and Your Life*

Connect Your Experience

At each stage in your life, you have to make decisions. Some decisions, like choosing between spending your money on clothes or on a movie, have minimal consequences. Occasionally, you have to make a more significant and difficult decision, such as choosing a college. This story focuses on one character's life-changing decision.

Journal Writing Jot down your memories of some tough decisions you've made. On what did you base these decisions?

Thematic Focus: Working It Out

This selection shows how one man works out his own answer to the question, "Where am I going?"

◆ Background for Understanding

Culture

As life expectancies rise, the question of how the elderly are cared for in a society becomes an increasingly important issue. In many societies around the world, elderly adults do not have to decide where to live when they can no longer care for themselves because they already live in an extended family that tends to their needs. For example, in some countries in Africa and Asia, it is common to have three or even four generations of one family living under the same roof. In Japan it is traditionally the duty of the oldest son to care for his parents. Most older American parents, however, do not live with their adult children. When an elderly family member can no longer live alone, life-changing decisions must be made.

◆ Literary Focus

Characters as Symbols

Sometimes the characters in a story are just that: characters, and nothing else. Other times, writers use **characters as symbols**—that is, a character represents an idea, belief, or feeling. You can figure out whether a character symbolizes something by looking for especially strong character traits or a remarkably consistent pattern of behavior. For example, if a particular character always has a cheerful outlook despite repeated tragedies, that character may represent optimism.

Examine the individual characters in "With All Flags Flying" and think about what some of them might represent.

◆ Reading Strategy

Evaluate a Character's Decision

In this story, Mr. Carpenter, the main character, makes a decision that will change his entire life. As you read this story, **evaluate the main character's decision.** Using the facts at hand, assess whether the decision he makes is the best one.

To evaluate a decision fairly, you have to look at it from many angles. Consider what would have happened had the character acted differently. Look to see what other options may have been available. Try to find out the character's motive—why does he or she act in this way? What were the reasons behind his or her action? The answers to these questions will help you make an informed evaluation of the character's decision.

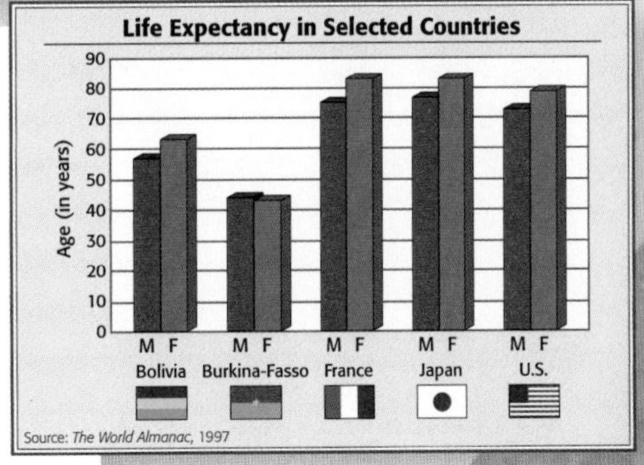

Source: *The World Almanac*, 1997

Interest Grabber Ask students to imagine themselves at the following ages: twenty, thirty, forty, sixty, eighty. What will they look like? What will they be doing? To whom would they be close? Focus students' attention on the age of eighty. What are some problems people face at that age? What do students hope for themselves? Suggest that they base their ideas on an older person they know or have known. Anne Tyler's story ponders some of these same questions. Like most good fiction, it both comes up with answers and poses more questions.

Connecting Themes Across Cultures

The United States is not the only country where the elderly often live separately from their children and grandchildren. Have students research the kinds of senior residences that exist in countries other than the United States. There have been such establishments for the elderly in Northern Europe for centuries.

Customize for
Less Proficient Readers

To help students attach symbolic meanings to some of the characters in the story, have them make a chart like this one, and fill it in as they read:

Name of Character:

His/Her Belief:

His/Her Feelings:

His/Her Pattern of Behavior:

After studying their charts, students can write the main quality the character symbolizes.

Customize for
Pre-Ap Students

Have students examine small symbols in the story, such as the motorcycle or the contents of the brown bag, that stand for aspects of Mr. Carpenter's character.

Customize for
English Language Learners

Words and references in this story, which will be culturally familiar to many students, may challenge these students. An "old folks' home" would be unknown to students from Asian or Latin American countries. "Fig Newtons" and "teeny-bopper" may also require explanation.

Test Preparation Workshop

Reading Comprehension: Recognizing Cause and Effect The Critical Reading sections of the SAT test require students to read a passage and answer questions on the basis of what is stated or implied in that passage. Students can use the following sample item to recognize the cause of Mr. Carpenter's behavior.

He walked two blocks daily, fighting off the weakness. He shelled peas for Clara and mended little household articles, which gave him an excuse to sit. Nobody noticed how he arranged to climb the stairs only once a day, at bedtime. When he had empty time he chose a chair without rockers, one that would not be a symbol of age and weariness and lack of work.

What is the cause of Mr. Carpenter's behavior?

A He wants to appear helpful.
B He likes household chores.
C He wishes to conceal the effects of age.
D He fears being seen as lazy.

All of the answers are contributing reasons for Mr. Carpenter's behavior and therefore answer the question. However, *C* is the main underlying cause because of Mr. Carpenter's attitude about his age.

Develop Understanding

One-Minute Insight

By choosing to live in an old-age home rather than with his daughter, Mr. Carpenter asserts his will and maintains his independence. While some readers may think Mr. Carpenter pays too high a price by giving up the opportunity to end his life in the midst of his loving family, others will applaud his determination to chart his own course. Mr. Carpenter's body may be weakening, but his determination to be his own master emerges in this story as undiminished.

Tips to Guide Reading

Paired Reading Have pairs of students read the story aloud to one another, using the breaks in printed text as signals to alternate readers and listeners. Encourage them to follow the main character's train of thought. Have pairs discuss the character of Mr. Carpenter, making inferences and generalizations to evaluate his decision.

Humanities: Art

Route 6, Eastham, 1941, by Edward Hopper.

The painting depicts a farm from across a highway. The absence of human and animal figures, along with the scale of the houses in relation to the road and sky, evokes a feeling of remoteness, emptiness, or loneliness.

Edward Hopper (1882–1967) was an American painter born in Nyack, New York. Hopper lived in New York City and worked as a commercial artist and illustrator for many years before he concentrated fully on painting after he was forty.

1. How does the painting help you understand how the old man has been living? *Students may notice the isolation of the house and outbuildings, as well as the highway.*
2. Compare the painting with the description of the old man's house in this story. *In the story, the house is very small, with only two rooms. The rest of the farm has been sold. In the painting, the large farmhouse and outbuildings are intact. Still, students should recognize the painting reflects the mood of the story.*

Route 6, Eastham, 1941, Edward Hopper, Sheldon Swope Art Museum, Terre Haute, Indiana

1 ▲ Critical Viewing What details in this painting suggest that this story will deal with changes? **[Analyze]**

Block Scheduling Strategies

Consider these suggestions to take advantage of extended class time:

- Together with students, read the Background for Understanding on p. 313 and look at the Life Expectancy chart. Invite students to speculate about reasons for the difference in life expectancies between countries and between men and women.
- Introduce the concept of characters as symbols. Review symbols; then have students read the Literary Focus on p. 313. After students have read the story, guide them through the Literary Focus questions on p. 322. You may follow up with the Literary Focus page in ***Selection Support,*** p. 100.
- Have students get together in small groups to discuss the Critical Thinking questions on p. 320.
- Have students complete the Guided Writing Lesson (p. 323). Invite pairs of students to act out their dialogues.

With All Flags Flying

2

Anne Tyler

Weakness was what got him in the end. He had been expecting something more definite—chest pains, a stroke, arthritis—but it was only weakness that put a finish to his living alone. A numbness in
3 his head, an airy feeling when he walked. A wateriness in his bones that made it an effort to pick up his coffee cup in the morning. He waited some days for it to go away, but it never did. And meanwhile the dust piled up in corners; the refrigerator wheezed and creaked for want of defrosting. Weeds grew around his rosebushes.

He was awake and dressed at six o'clock on a Saturday morning, with the patchwork quilt pulled up neatly over the mattress. From the kitchen cabinet he took a hunk of bread and two Fig Newtons, which he dropped into a paper bag. He was wearing a brown suit that he had bought on sale in 1944, a white T-shirt and copper-toed work boots. These and his other set of under-
4 wear, which he put in the paper bag along with a razor, were all the clothes he took with him. Then he rolled down the top of the bag and stuck it under his arm, and stood in the middle of the kitchen staring around him for a moment.

The house had only two rooms, but he owned it—the last scrap of the farm that he had sold off years ago. It

Route 6, Eastham (detail), Edward Hopper, Sheldon Swope Art Museum, Terre Haute, Indiana

▶Critical Viewing◀

❶ Analyze *The road itself suggests the idea of change ahead. The color of the grass and trees suggests that the season is changing from summer to fall.*

◆Critical Thinking

❷ Infer What inference can students make about the author's attitude toward her characters? *Students can infer from the valiant nature of the title that the author feels her characters—or at least one of them—is brave and daring.*

◆Critical Thinking

❸ Apply Clarify for students that this character is growing older and no longer has the strength or energy to take care of his home. Ask: What are the options that are open to a person in this character's physical condition? *Some options are hiring a care-giver, moving in with family, forming a collective-living situation with other elderly people, or moving to a nursing home.*

◆Critical Thinking

❹ Interpret Ask students how they would characterize a person who would leave home with so few possessions. *Students may say the man must be eccentric, or simply not interested in material possessions.*

Customize for
Gifted/Talented Students
Have students improvise a conversation between Clara and her father in which Clara convinces the old man to stay with her, rather than go to the old folks' home.

Research Skills Mini-Lesson

Oral Research This mini-lesson will help develop students' oral research skills.

Introduce Tell students that as they conduct oral research for an assignment, using a tape record will allow them to review information as they complete their assignments and also save their research for future use.

Develop Demonstrate and discuss appropriate recording technique. Students should:

- Always ask their subjects for permission to record interviews and discussions.
- Position the recorder so that it captures the voices of the interviewer and the person being interviewed.
- Label tapes with the date and time of the interview.

Tell students that expert use of the recorder will put interviewees at ease. Too much attention to the recorder can make people uneasy and inhibit them from talking freely. Later, students can transcribe the tapes by listening to brief excerpts in the sequence and writing or entering into a computer those passages they wish to use.

Apply Have students work in pairs to practice interviewing.

Assess Evaluate students on their application of the points you discussed as a class. In addition, you may wish to have students use the experience to assess themselves with the Self-Assessment: Speaking and Listening Progress form, p. 122, in the ***Alternative Assessment*** booklet.

◆ Critical Thinking

❶ **Infer** Ask students why the man didn't mind having "a thousand appurtenances" when he had a wife and children, but now considers even his few possessions too much. *Lead students to see that the man is giving up his grasp on life. "Worldly" possessions symbolize ties to the world, which he is preparing to leave behind. On a more literal level, students might also suggest that the man is overwhelmed by the prospect of caring for so many things.*

▶Critical Viewing◀

❷ **Infer** *Students might judge from the man's expression that he was feeling calm, but perhaps also sad and resigned.*

◆ Build Grammar Skills

❸ **Past Participial Phrases** Have students identify the past participial phrase in this sentence. Have them name the participle and the noun the phrase modifies. *The past participial phrase is "clenched tight upon the paper bag." The past participle in the phrase is "clenched." The phrase modifies the noun "fingers."*

◆ Reading Strategy

❹ **Judge a Character's Decision** By now, students should have an idea of where Mr. Carpenter is going—either to a nursing home or to stay with a relative. Ask: If this man considers this his "last free day," why is he leaving his home? *Students should grasp that the man has accepted that he no longer has the strength to take care of himself.*

Customize for
English Language Learners
Students may have trouble with the homophones in this story. Team them with native speakers who can help clarify the two meanings of words on this page such as *suit, bank, buckled, stretches, limp, temples.* Be sure they understand the correct meaning in the given context and other possible meanings.

stood in a hollow of dying trees beside a superhighway in Baltimore County. All it held was a few sticks of furniture, a change of clothes, a skillet and a set of dishes. Also odds and ends, which disturbed him. If his inventory were complete, he would have to include six clothespins, a salt and a pepper shaker, a broken-toothed comb, a cheap ballpoint pen—oh, on and on, past logical numbers. Why should he be so cluttered? He was eighty-two years old.
He had grown from an infant owning nothing to a family man with a wife, five children, everyday and Sunday china
❶ and a thousand appurtenances, down at last to solitary old age and the bare essentials again, but not bare enough to suit him. Only what he needed surrounded him. Was it possible he needed so much?

Now he had the brown paper bag; that was all. It was the one satisfaction in a day he had been dreading for years.

He left the house without another glance, heading up the steep bank toward the superhighway. The bank was covered with small, crawling weeds planted especially by young men with scientific training in how to prevent soil erosion. Twice his knees buckled. He had to sit and rest, bracing himself against the slope of the bank. The scientific weeds, seen from close up, looked straggly and gnarled. He sifted dry earth through his fingers without thinking, concentrating only on steadying his breath and calming the twitching muscles in his legs.

Once on the superhighway, which was fairly level, he could walk for longer stretches of time. He kept his head down and his fingers clenched tight upon the paper bag, which was growing limp and damp now. Sweat rolled down the back of his neck, fell in drops from his temples. When he had been walking maybe half an hour he had to sit down again for a rest. A black motorcycle buzzed up from behind and stopped a few feet away from him. The driver was young and shabby, with hair so long that it drizzled out beneath the back of his helmet.

"Give you a lift, if you like," he said. "You going somewhere?"

"Just into Baltimore."

"Hop on."

He shifted the paper bag to the space beneath his arm, put on the white helmet he was handed and climbed on behind the driver. For safety he took a clutch of the boy's shirt, tightly at first and then more loosely when he saw there was no danger. Except for the helmet, he was perfectly comfortable. He felt his face cooling and stiffening in the wind, his body learning to lean gracefully with the tilt of the motorcycle as it swooped from lane to lane. It was a fine way to spend his last free day.

Half an hour later they were on the outskirts of Baltimore, stopped at the first traffic light.

❷ ▲ **Critical Viewing** How do you think this man was feeling when this picture was taken? **[Infer]**

◆ Build Vocabulary

appurtenances (ə purt′ ən əns əz) *n.*: Accessories

conspicuous (kən spik′ yo͞o əs) *adj.*: Attracting attention by being unexpected

Humanities: Photography

Resident of Valle Verde Retirement Home
by Bill Aron.

The photographic portrait on this page shows an elderly man sitting on a chair with a lamp in the background. In the lines of the man's face and body, the artist has captured the passivity and acceptance that sometimes comes with old age.

Use the following questions for discussion:

1. How would you compare the man in this picture with your mental image of Mr. Carpenter? *Students can share their ideas about how the man in this picture is the same as or different from their image of Mr. Carpenter. They might say the man in the picture seems more complaisant than they imagine Mr. Carpenter to be—he has a mild or pleasant facial expression that students might not associate with the story character.*
2. Which details in the portrait make you think that the man may be experiencing the same weakness that the old man in the story is feeling? *Students may cite the man's position in the chair, the way he holds his head, the position of his hands.*

The boy turned his head and shouted, "Whereabouts did you plan on going?"

> ◆ **Literary Focus**
> What might the boy on the motorcycle symbolize?

"I'm visiting my daughter, on Belvedere near Charles Street."

"I'll drop you off, then," the boy said. "I'm passing right by there."

The light changed, the motor roared. Now that they were in traffic, he felt more conspicuous, but not in a bad way. People in their automobiles seemed sealed in, overprotected; men in large trucks must envy the way the motorcycle looped in and out, hornetlike, stripped to the bare essentials of a motor and two wheels. By tugs at the boy's shirt and single words shouted into the wind he directed him to his daughter's house, but he was sorry to have the ride over so quickly.

His daughter had married a salesman and lived in a plain, square stone house that the old man approved of. There were sneakers and a football in the front yard, signs of a large, happy family. A bicycle lay in the driveway. The motorcycle stopped just inches from it. "Here we are," the boy said.

"Well, I surely do thank you."

He climbed off, fearing for one second that his legs would give way beneath him and spoil everything that had gone before. But no, they held steady. He took off the helmet and handed it to the boy, who waved and roared off. It was a really magnificent roar, ear-dazzling. He turned toward the house, beaming in spite of himself, with his head feeling cool and light now that the helmet was gone. And there was his daughter on the front porch, laughing. "Daddy, what on *earth*?" she said. "Have you turned into a teeny-bopper?" Whatever that was. She came rushing down the steps to hug him—a plump, happy-looking woman in an apron. She was getting on toward fifty now. Her hands were like her mother's, swollen and veined. Gray had started dusting her hair.

"You never *told* us," she said. "Did you ride all this way on a motorcycle? Oh, why didn't you find a telephone and call? I would have come. How long can you stay for?"

"Now . . . " he said, starting toward the house. He was thinking of the best way to put it. "I came to a decision. I won't be living alone any more. I want to go to an old folks' home. That's what I *want*," he said, stopping on the grass so she would be sure to get it clear. "I don't want to live with you—I want an old folks' home." Then he was afraid he had worded it too strongly. "It's nice *visiting* you, of course," he said. **6**

"Why, Daddy, you know we always asked you to come and live with us."

"I know that, but I decided on an old folks' home."

"We couldn't do that. We won't even talk about it."

"Clara, my mind is made up."

Then in the doorway a new thought hit her, and she suddenly turned around. "Are you sick?" she said. "You always said you would live alone as long as health allowed."

"I'm not up to that any more," he said.

"What is it? Are you having some kind of pain?"

"I just decided, that's all," he said. "What I *will* rely on you for is the arrangements with the home. I know it's a trouble."

"We'll talk about that later," Clara said. And she firmed the corners of her mouth exactly the way her mother used to do when she hadn't won an argument but wasn't planning to lose it yet either. **7**

In the kitchen he had a glass of milk, good and cold, and the hunk of bread and the two Fig Newtons from his paper bag. Clara wanted to make him a big breakfast, but there was no sense wasting what he had brought. He munched on the dry bread and washed it down with milk, meanwhile staring at the Fig Newtons, which lay on the smoothed-out bag. They were the worse for their ride—squashed and pathetic looking, the edges worn down and crumbling. They seemed to have come from somewhere long ago and far away. **8** "Here, now, we've got cookies I baked only yesterday," Clara said; but he said, "No, no," and ate the Fig Newtons, whose warmth on his tongue filled him with a vague, sad feeling deeper than

◆ Literary Focus

5 Characters as Symbols *The motorcyclist represents freedom, a sense of reckless abandon, or energy.*

◆ Reading Strategy

6 Judge a Character's Decision Have students discuss whether the old man seems to have thought his decision through carefully. *He seems to have anticipated his daughter's objections, and his determination suggests that his decision was well thought out.*

◆ Critical Thinking

7 Analyze Ask students why they think that Tyler included this reference to Clara's mother. *Students might say that the reference to Clara's mother—Mr. Carpenter's deceased wife—was meant to evoke Mr. Carpenter's younger days, and perhaps remind the reader that it might be difficult for Mr. Carpenter to see his wife reflected in his daughter.*

◆ Build Grammar Skills

8 Past Participial Phrases Have students identify the two past participial phrases in this sentence. Which nouns or pronouns do they modify? Which past participle is irregular? *The two past participial phrases are "squashed and pathetic looking," which modifies the pronoun "they" (the Fig Newtons), and "worn down and crumbling," which modifies the noun "edges." "Worn" is irregular.*

Read to Appreciate Author's Craft

Anne Tyler is appreciated for her gentle, seemingly non-obtrusive development of characters. The cumulative effect of small details of behavior and the thoughts that accompany them works especially well in novels, where she has time and space to develop characters further. Discuss with students how Tyler, for the purposes of a short story, limits her characterization of Mr. Carpenter to essential personality details. Readers learn only a few facts about his long life, but much about his character.

Speaking, Listening, and Viewing Mini-Lesson

Debate

This mini-lesson supports the Speaking, Listening, and Viewing activity in the Idea Bank on p. 323.

Introduce Briefly explain the rules of formal debate (or refer students to the entry on Debate in the Speaking and Listening Handbook). Two teams take turns arguing the "pro" and "con" sides of the statement: *Mr. Carpenter made the right decision.* Team members express opinions, supported by facts and details. Then team members "rebut," or argue against, their opponents' points.

Develop Have team members develop their arguments about the old man's decision, taking into account other options he could have taken.

Apply Assign a time frame for students to make their first arguments. Follow with a shorter time for rebuttals. Remind students to pace themselves and to include strong, well-supported points.

Assess Have students evaluate the debate: Were opinions presented clearly? Were they supported with facts and real-life examples? Were rebuttal arguments strong and to the point?

◆ Literary Focus

1 Characters as Symbols Encourage students to speculate about the qualities Francie represents in this story, and in particular in Mr. Carpenter's life. *Students might suggest she represents honesty, openness, and innocence.*

◆ Reading Strategy

2 Judge a Character's Decision Ask why students think he has rejected the idea of living with family members. *Students may say he does not want to be taken care of like a child; he does not want to be a burden.*

◆ Reading Strategy

3 Judge a Character's Decision *Students should respond that in addition to considering moving into a nursing home, he could have lived with any one of his children.*

◆ Critical Thinking

4 Infer Ask students: What kind of impression is the old man trying to make on his daughter and her family? Why is he working so hard to make this impression? *The old man wants to make the impression that he is still in control of his life. He does not want to be taken care of by his family. He doesn't want to be a burden to them, but more important, he wants to remain independent in his own eyes. He is holding on to his pride and dignity.*

Extending Word Study

Word Origins Have students research the word origins of *urgency* and *impress*. For each word, have them list several related words with the same word origins.

homesickness. "In my house," he said, "I left things a little messy. I hate to ask it of you, but I didn't manage to straighten up any."

"Don't even think about it," Clara said. "I'll take out a suitcase tomorrow and clean everything up. I'll bring it all back."

"I don't want it. Take it to the poor people."

"Don't want any of it? But, Daddy—"

He didn't try explaining it to her. He finished his lunch in silence and then let her lead him upstairs to the guest room.

Clara had five boys and a girl, the oldest twenty. During the morning as they passed one by one through the house on their way to other places, they heard of his arrival and trooped up to see him. They were fine children, all of them, but it was the girl he enjoyed the most. Francie. She was only thirteen, too young yet to know how to hide what she felt. And what she felt was always about love, it seemed: whom she just loved, who she hoped loved her back.
1 Who was just a darling. Had thirteen-year-olds been so aware of love in the old days? He didn't know and didn't care; all he had to do with Francie was sit smiling in an armchair and listen. There was a new boy in the neighborhood who walked his English sheepdog past her yard every morning, looking toward her house. Was it because of her, or did the dog just like to go that way? When he telephoned her brother Donnie, was he hoping for her to answer? And when she did answer, did he want her to talk a minute or hand the receiver straight to Donnie? But what would she say to him, anyway? Oh, all her questions had to do with where she might find love, and everything she said made the old man wince and love her more. She left in the middle of a sentence, knocking against a doorknob as she flew from the room, an unlovable-looking tangle of blond hair and braces and scrapes and Band-Aids. After she was gone the room seemed too empty, as if she had accidentally torn part of it away in her flight.

Getting into an old folks' home was hard. Not only because of lack of good homes, high expenses, waiting lists; it was harder yet to talk his family into letting him go. His son-in-law argued with him every evening, his round, kind face anxious and questioning across the supper table. "Is it that you think you're not welcome here? You are, you know. You were one of the reasons we bought this big house." His grandchildren when they talked to him had a kind of urgency in their voices, as if they were trying to impress him with their acceptance of him. His other daughters called long distance from all across the country and begged him to come to them if he wouldn't stay with Clara. They had room, or they would make room; he had no idea what homes for the aged were like these days. To all of them he gave the same answer: "I've made my decision." He was proud of them for asking, though. All his children had turned out so well, every last one of them. They were good, strong women with happy families, and they had never given him a moment's worry. He was luckier than he had a right to be. He had felt lucky all his life, dangerously lucky, cursed by luck; it had seemed some disaster must be waiting to even things up. But the luck had held. When his wife died it was at a late age, sparing her the pain she would have had to face, and his life had continued in its steady, reasonable pattern with no more sorrow than any other man's. His final lot was to weaken, to crumble and to die—only a secret disaster, not the one he had been expecting.

> **◆ Reading Strategy** Evaluate the man's options.

He walked two blocks daily, fighting off the weakness. He shelled peas for Clara and mended little household articles, which gave him an excuse to sit. Nobody noticed how he arranged to climb the stairs only once a day, at bedtime. When he had empty time he chose a chair without rockers, one that would not be a symbol of age and weariness and lack of work. He rose every morning at six and stayed in his room a full hour, giving his legs enough warning to face the day ahead. Never once did he disgrace himself by falling down in front of people. He dropped nothing more important than a spoon or a fork.

Workplace Skills Mini-Lesson

Making Decisions

Introduce Making good decisions requires the ability to assess a situation from different angles. This is an important workplace skill for most jobs.

Develop Discuss with students jobs they have now or might have in the future. Ask them what sorts of decisions are required by these jobs. How does knowing the parameters of a particular work situation help with good decision-making on the job?

Apply the Information Present the following hypothetical situation: If your boss told you that in six months you could move from the job of stocking CDs to the job of selling them, what information would you want to know? Students may suggest questions they would ask, such as: What skills would I need for the new position? How could I acquire those skills? What would be the difference in pay and working hours? What other opportunities might be available to me?

Assess the Outcome Have students share their decision-making questions. Discuss which questions are the most helpful and why, and any further questions that would help them make an informed decision.

Meanwhile the wheels were turning; his name was on a waiting list. Not that that meant anything, Clara said. "When it comes right down to driving you out there, I just won't let you go," she told him. "But I'm hoping you won't carry things that far. Daddy, won't you put a stop to this foolishness?"

He hardly listened. He had chosen long ago what kind of old age he would have; everyone does. Most, he thought, were weak, and chose to be loved at any cost. He had seen women turn soft and sad, anxious to please, and had watched with pity and impatience their losing battles. And he had once known a schoolteacher, no weakling at all, who said straight out that when she grew old she would finally eat all she wanted and grow fat without worry. He admired that—a simple plan, dependent on no one. "I'll sit in an armchair," she had said, "with a lady's magazine in my lap and a box of homemade fudge on the lampstand. I'll get as fat as I like and nobody will give a hang." The schoolteacher was thin and pale, with a kind of stooped, sloping figure that was popular at the time. He had lost track of her long ago, but he liked to think that she had kept her word. He imagined her fifty years later, cozy and fat in a puffy chair, with one hand moving constantly between her mouth and the candy plate. If she had died young or changed her mind or put off her eating till another decade, he didn't want to hear about it.

He had chosen independence. Nothing else had even occurred to him. He had lived to himself, existed on less money than his family would ever guess, raised his own vegetables and refused all gifts but an occasional tin of coffee. **7** And now he would sign himself into the old folks' home and enter on his own two feet, relying only on the impersonal care of nurses and cleaning women. He could have chosen to die alone of neglect, but for his daughters that **8** would have been a burden too—a different kind of burden, much worse. He was sensible enough to see that.

Stairway, Edward Hopper, Whitney Museum of American Art

5 ▲ Critical Viewing Explain how this picture symbolizes choice. **[Analyze]**

Meanwhile, all he had to do was to look as busy as possible in a chair without rockers and hold fast against his family. Oh, they gave him no peace. Some of their attacks were obvious—the arguments with his son-in-law over the supper table—and some were subtle; you had to be on your guard every minute for those. Francie, for instance, asking him questions about what she called the "olden days." Inviting him to sink unnoticing into doddering reminiscence. "Did I see Granny ever? I don't remember her. Did she like me? What kind of person was she?" He stood his ground, gave monosyllabic answers. **9** It was easier than he had expected. For him, middle age tempted up more memories. Nowadays events had telescoped. The separate agonies and worries—the long, hard births of each of his children, the youngest daughter's

◆ **Build Vocabulary**

doddering (däd′ ər iŋ) *adj.*: Shaky, tottering, or senile

monosyllabic (mon′ ō si lab′ ik) *adj.*: Having only one syllable

▶Critical Viewing◀

5 Analyze *Students should recognize that an open door symbolizes choice, or the opening of opportunities.*

◆ Literary Focus

6 Characters as Symbols Ask students to imagine that the school teacher had changed her plan. How would that affect her status as a symbol for Mr. Carpenter? *She would no longer be a symbol for the independent-mindedness of old age.*

◆ *Literature and Your Life*

7 Ask students how choosing independence and resolving to do things on your own can be a difficult decision. Encourage students to apply the discussion to their own lives. *Students might say that making decisions about independence is difficult because others may want you to do something else.*

◆ Critical Thinking

8 Interpret Ask students: Why would dying alone of neglect create a burden for the old man's daughters? Why would it be "much worse" for them than his spending his last days in a nursing home? *Dying alone of neglect would be a burden for the man's daughters because they would feel guilty. It would be an emotional burden that would last all their lives.*

◆ Build Vocabulary

9 Prefixes: *mono-* Point out the vocabulary word *monosyllabic*. Ask students to suggest possible monosyllabic answers Mr. Carpenter could have given to his granddaughter's questions. Remind them to keep in mind the meaning of the prefix *mono-*, one. *Possible responses: no, yes, yeah, sure, fine, sweet, smart, good*

Humanities: Art

Stairway by Edward Hopper.

This painting by the American realist painter Edward Hopper (1882–1967) shows the interior of a room, uncluttered by furnishings or possessions. Hopper painted rural, urban, and suburban American scenes. He portrayed with simple honesty the beauty and the ugliness of everyday surroundings. He took the mundane and the ordinary and turned them into something unforgettable.

Have students examine the interior in the painting and then discuss these questions:

1. Why would this interior appeal to the old man in the story? *Students may say that he would feel comfortable in the stark room because it is tidy and devoid of "appurtenances."*
2. How does the room make you feel? *Some students may say the room is peaceful and serene because it is uncluttered; others will find it sterile or impersonal. They will want to add things—a lamp, pictures, books, a chair—to make it warmer and homier.*
3. How would the addition of people to the room change the mood of the painting? *Students may say that people would give the room more "life." If possible, show them a picture of Hopper's Nighthawks to show that, sometimes, the addition of people creates an even lonelier mood.*

◆ Reading Strategy

❶ Judge a Character's Decision Ask students how they feel about the man's apparent disregard for his daughter's feelings. Under what conditions might they support a decision that hurts another person's feelings? *Students may wish the old man would change his mind and stay with Clara for a "happy ending," but they might also recognize that even though he is temporarily hurting his daughter's feelings, he is mastering his own fate, a choice that under certain circumstances justifies hurting someone else's feelings.*

◆ Critical Thinking

❷ Infer Why does the old man insist on giving all the answers himself? *He wants to show the world and himself that he is independent. He wants to be respected and to maintain his self-respect.*

◆ Build Grammar Skills

❸ Past Participial Phrases Have students identify the past participial phrases and the words they modify in the paragraph. *The phrases are "deadened by carpeting," which modifies "corridor," and "flooded with sunlight," which modifies "room."*

◆ Critical Thinking

❹ Interpret Ask students: In what way is Mr. Carpenter being "generous"? What victory has he "won"? *He knows that his daughter feels hurt because her father will not accept anything from her. He is being generous by letting her know he will accept her help now. His victory is his success in asserting his will over the objections of his children.*

chronic childhood earaches, his wife's last illness—were smoothed now into a single, summing-up sentence: He was a widowed farmer with five daughters, all married, twenty grandchildren and three great-grandchildren. "Your grandmother was a fine woman," he told Francie; "just fine." Then he shut up.

Francie, not knowing that she had been spared, sulked and peeled a strip of sunburned skin from her nose.

Clara cried all the way to the home. She was the one who was driving; it made him nervous. One of her hands on the steering wheel held a balled-up tissue, which she had stopped using. She let tears run unchecked down her face and drove jerkily with a great deal of brake-slamming and gear-gnashing.

"Clara, I wish you wouldn't take on so," he told her. "There's no need to be sad over *me*."

❶ "I'm not sad so much as mad," Clara said. "I feel like this is something you're doing *to* me, just throwing away what I give. Oh, why do you have to be so stubborn? It's still not too late to change your mind."

The old man kept silent. On his right sat Francie, chewing a thumbnail and scowling out the window, her usual self except for the unexplainable presence of her other hand in his, tight as wire. Periodically she muttered a number: she was counting red convertibles, and had been for days. When she reached a hundred, the next boy she saw would be her true love.

He figured that was probably the reason she had come on this trip—a greater exposure to red convertibles.

Whatever happened to DeSotos?[1] Didn't there use to be a car called a roadster?[2]

They parked in the U-shaped driveway in front of the home, under the shade of a poplar tree. If he had had his way, he would have arrived by motorcycle, but he made the best of it—picked up his underwear sack from between his feet, climbed the front steps ramrod-straight. They were met by a smiling woman in blue who had to check his name on a file and ask more questions. He made sure to give all the answers himself, overriding Clara when necessary. Meanwhile Francie spun on one squeaky sneaker heel and examined the hall, a cavernous, polished square with old-fashioned parlors on either side of it. A few old people were on the plush couches, and a nurse sat idle beside a lady in a wheelchair.

They went up a creaking elevator to the second floor and down a long, dark corridor deadened by carpeting. The lady in blue, still carrying a sheaf of files, knocked at number 213. Then she flung the door open on a narrow green room flooded with sunlight.

"Mr. Pond," she said, "this is Mr. Carpenter. I hope you'll get on well together."

Mr. Pond was one of those men who run to fat and baldness in old age. He sat in a rocking chair with a gilt-edged Bible on his knees.

"How-do," he said. "Mighty nice to meet you."

They shook hands cautiously, with the women ringing them like mothers asking their children to play nicely with each other. "Ordinarily I sleep in the bed by the window," said Mr. Pond, "but I don't hold it in much importance. You can take your pick."

"Anything will do," the old man said.

Clara was dry-eyed now. She looked frightened.

"You'd best be getting on back now," he told her. "Don't you worry about me. I'll let you know," he said, suddenly generous now that he had won, "if there is anything I need."

Clara nodded and kissed his cheek. Francie kept her face turned away, but she hugged him tightly, and then she looked up at him as she stepped back. Her eyebrows were tilted as if she were about to ask him one of her questions. Was it her the boy with the sheepdog came for? Did he care when she answered the telephone?

They left, shutting the door with a gentle click. The old man made a great business out of settling his underwear and razor in a bureau drawer, smoothing out the paper bag and folding it, placing it in the next drawer down.

"Didn't bring much," said Mr. Pond, one

---

1. **DeSotos** (də sō′ tōz): Models of a car in the 1950's.
2. **roadster** (rōd′ stər) *n.*: Early sportscar with an open cab.

Reteach

To emphasize the importance of judging the main character's decision, students might use a Problem/Solution Organizer. Discuss the main character's problem, or his decision, with students, encouraging them to consider the problem from several perspectives. Depending upon the amount of reteaching help that students need, help them identify the goals, alternatives, pros and cons, and reasons that Mr. Carpenter indicates in this story. Encourage them to put themselves in the places of Mr. Carpenter and his daughter to help understand the situation.

Problem	Goal(s)
Mr. Carpenter has grown old.	

Alternatives	Pros (+) and Cons (–)
	+
	–
	+
	–

Decision(s)	Reason(s)

thumb marking his page in the Bible.

"I don't need much."

"Go on—take the bed by the window. You'll feel better after awhile."

"I *wanted* to come," the old man said.

"That there window is a front one. If you look out, you can see your folks leave."

He slid between the bed and the window and looked out. No reason not to. Clara and Francie were just climbing into the car, the sun lacquering the tops of their heads. Clara was blowing her nose with a dot of tissue.

"*Now* they cry," said Mr. Pond, although he had not risen to look out himself. "Later they'll buy themselves a milkshake to celebrate."

"I wanted to come. I made them bring me."

"And so they did. *I* didn't want to come. My son wanted to put me here—his wife was expecting. And so he did. It all works out the same in the end."

"Well, I could have stayed with one of my daughters," the old man said. "But I'm not like some I have known. Hanging around making burdens of themselves, hoping to be loved. Not me."

"If you don't care about being loved," said Mr. Pond, "how come it would bother you to be a burden?"

Then he opened the Bible again, at the place where his thumb had been all the time and went back to reading.

The old man sat on the edge of the bed, watching the tail of Clara's car flash as sharp and hard as a jewel around the bend of the road. Then, with nobody to watch that mattered, he let his shoulders slump and eased himself out of his suit coat, which he folded over the foot of the bed. He slid his suspenders down and let them dangle at his waist. He took off his copper-toed work boots and set them on the floor neatly side by side. And although it was only noon, he lay down full-length on top of the bedspread. Whiskery lines ran across the plaster of the ceiling high above him. There was a cracking sound in the mattress when he moved; it must be covered with something waterproof.

The tiredness in his head was as vague and restless as anger; the weakness in his knees made him feel as if he had just finished some exhausting exercise. He lay watching the plaster cracks settle themselves into pictures, listening to the silent, neuter voice in his mind form the words he had grown accustomed to hearing now: Let me not give in at the end. Let me continue gracefully till the moment of my defeat. Let Lollie Simpson be alive somewhere even as I lie on my bed; let her be eating homemade fudge in an overstuffed armchair and growing fatter and fatter. 6

Guide for Responding

◆ Literature and Your Life

Reader's Response What do you think will be most important to you in your old age? Explain.

Thematic Focus The onset of old age marks a turning point in any person's life. What are some concrete things that a person can do to maintain his or her dignity through this difficult stage?

Questions for Research If you were asked to write a news feature on some aspect of aging—such as claims that it can be slowed by regular exercise or meditation—what questions would you be interested in answering?

☑ Check Your Comprehension

1. Why does Mr. Carpenter decide not to live alone anymore?
2. How does he plan to live the rest of his life?
3. How does Mr. Carpenter's family feel about his plan?
4. What obstacles does Mr. Carpenter encounter?
5. Explain whether Mr. Carpenter is able to carry out his plan.

Beyond the Selection

FURTHER READING

Other Works by Anne Tyler

Ladder of Years

Dinner at the Homesick Restaurant

Searching for Caleb

Related Works

Cold Sassy Tree, Olive Burns

"You Are Old, Father William," Lewis Carroll

We suggest that you preview these works before recommending them to students.

INTERNET

Your students can find more information on the Internet. We suggest the following sites. Please be aware, however, that sites may have changed from the time we published this information.

For more information on Anne Tyler, visit **http:// www.randomhouse.com/vintage/read/ladder/ladder.html** or **http://web.aacpl.lib.md. us/dsakers/tylera.htm**

We *strongly recommend* that you preview the sites before you send students to them.

◆ Literary Focus

5 Characters as Symbols Ask students to explain what Mr. Pond might represent in the story, and to give reasons for their answers. *Students may say that Mr. Pond represents the bitterness that can sometimes come with old age. Because he feels unloved and rejected, he assumes that everyone else feels the same.*

◆ Critical Thinking

6 Interpret Ask students why Mr. Carpenter hopes that Lollie Simpson is alive and growing fat from eating fudge. *Although exhausted, he is proud of his victory. He wishes the same victory to others: that, until they die, they will make their own choices and live by their own decisions.*

Reinforce and Extend

Answers

◆ Literature and Your Life

Reader's Response Students might say that, like Mr. Carpenter in Tyler's story, independence will be important to them. They might also cite good health, financial security, and the capacity to enjoy life.

Thematic Focus Students might recognize the importance of planning ahead and keeping informed about options in order to make a well-considered and independent decision.

Questions for Research Students should be encouraged to pose questions that are truly relevant to the problems of aging, such as how views of the elderly might be more enlightened and how the diseases of age might be cured.

☑ Check Your Comprehension

1. He feels he's too weak to take care of himself and his home.
2. He plans to go to an old age home.
3. His family is unhappy about his plan; they want to take care of him.
4. It is hard to get into the old age home, and it is hard for Mr. Carpenter to talk his family into letting him go.
5. Mr. Carpenter is able to carry out his plan by overriding his family's objections and not allowing himself to get too comfortable in their home.

Answers

◆ Critical Thinking

1. Mr. Carpenter wants only the most essential possessions. He reflects on having needed so much—two sets of china and a "thousand appurtenances"—when he was younger.
2. He loves his family and does not want to burden them; he also wants to be his own master.
3. Mr. Carpenter is relieved; Mr. Pond is bitter.
4. Students might interpret the title "With All Flags Flying" to represent Mr. Carpenter's victory in determining his own fate.
5. Responses might cover a spectrum: Our society does well by providing Social Security and other benefits for the elderly, but does not encourage enough respect for the elderly.
6. Students might say they learned that it is important to be faithful to your principles up to the end of your life.

◆ Reading Strategy

1. He does not want to burden his family; he wants to maintain his dignity.
2. He could have lived with any one of his daughters and their families, or he could have lived alone—neglecting himself.
3. Some students will sympathize with Mr. Carpenter's need to claim his psychological independence; others will wish he had stayed in the more personal atmosphere of family.

◆ Literary Focus

1. Clara represents security, conventionality, a sense of responsibility, and generosity.
2. Lollie Simpson represents willful and joyful independence.
3. Mr. Pond represents bitterness and loneliness.

◆ Build Vocabulary

Using the Greek Prefix *mono-*

1. c 2. b 3. a

Using the Word Bank

1. c 2. d 3. a 4. b

Guide for Responding *(continued)*

◆ Critical Thinking

INTERPRET

1. Using examples from the story, describe Mr. Carpenter's attitude about material possessions. **[Analyze]**

2. Why is Mr. Carpenter so determined not to move in with his daughter and her family? **[Infer]**

3. How does Mr. Carpenter's attitude about the nursing home compare with Mr. Pond's? **[Compare and Contrast]**

4. What is the significance of the story's title? **[Draw Conclusions]**

EVALUATE

5. How well do you think our society cares for the elderly? Explain. **[Evaluate]**

APPLY

6. What can you learn from this story that might help you at some point in your life? **[Apply]**

◆ Reading Strategy

EVALUATE A CHARACTER'S DECISION

When you **evaluate a character's decision,** such as Mr. Carpenter's decision to enter the nursing home, consider the reasons for the decision, the alternatives, and the consequences of the decision.

1. What are the reasons for Mr. Carpenter's decision?

2. What other options were available to him?

3. Do you think Mr. Carpenter made the right decision? Explain.

◆ Literary Focus

CHARACTERS AS SYMBOLS

Writers often get their message across by using **characters as symbols.** For instance, Tyler uses Mr. Carpenter to represent *all* elderly people who fear the loss of dignity and independence.

What do you think each of the following characters represents?

1. Clara

2. Lollie Simpson (the teacher)

3. Mr. Pond

◆ Build Vocabulary

USING THE GREEK PREFIX ***mono–***

Knowing that the Greek prefix *mono-* means "one," match each word from Column A with its definition in Column B.

Column A	Column B
1. monopoly	**a.** Having no variety
2. monocle	**b.** Eyeglass for one eye only
3. monotonous	**c.** Exclusive control over a commodity or service

USING THE WORD BANK: Antonyms

On your paper, match each word with the word most nearly opposite in meaning.

1. appurtenances	**a.** firm
2. conspicuous	**b.** long-winded
3. doddering	**c.** necessities
4. monosyllabic	**d.** hidden

◆ Build Grammar Skills

PAST PARTICIPIAL PHRASES

Anne Tyler uses past participial phrases to pack her sentences full of details about Mr. Carpenter, his family, and his surroundings.

A **past participial phrase** consists of a past participle along with its modifiers and complements.

Practice Copy the following sentences in your notebook. Underline each participial phrase and circle the noun it modifies.

1. The scientific weeds, seen from close up, looked straggly and gnarled.

2. They were on the outskirts of Baltimore, stopped at a red light.

3. Men in large trucks must envy the way the motorcycle looped in and out, hornetlike, stripped to the bare essentials of a motor and two wheels.

4. By tugs at the boy's shirt and single words shouted into the wind he directed him.

◆ Build Grammar Skills

Practice

1. The scientific weeds, seen from close up, looked straggly and gnarled. (modifies weeds)
2. They were on the outskirts of Baltimore, stopped at a red light. (modifies They)
3. Men in large trucks must envy the way the motorcycle looped in and out, hornetlike, stripped to the bare essentials of a motor and two wheels. (modifies motorcycle)
4. By tugs at the boy's shirt and single words shouted into the wind he directed him. (modifies words)

Grammar Reinforcement

For additional instruction and practice, use the page on Participles and Participial Phrases, p. 41, in the *Writer's Solution Grammar Practice Book*.

Build Your Portfolio

Idea Bank

Writing

1. Essay on Growing Old What kinds of activities would you like to do when you're old? Write a brief description on how you would ideally spend your "autumn years."

2. Letter From Mr. Carpenter Pretend that you are Mr. Carpenter and you've just moved into the nursing home. Write a letter to your family, explaining in detail your reasons for moving.

3. Alternative Ending What do you think the story would be like if Mr. Carpenter had decided to live with his daughter? Write an alternative ending exploring this possibility.

Speaking, Listening, and Viewing

4. Soundtrack Create a soundtrack for a dramatic adaptation of the story. Make a mix tape of songs that relate to various themes of the story. Indicate where in the story each song would appear. **[Music Link]**

5. Debate Against another team, debate whether Mr. Carpenter made the best decision in entering the nursing home. Use examples from the story and your knowledge of real life to back up any points or generalizations you make.

Researching and Representing

6. Volunteer at a Nursing Home Volunteer to help in a local nursing home or retirement home for a day. Compare what you learned about the people in the home with what your classmates observed about the people they met. **[Community Link]**

7. Service for the Elderly With a group of classmates, outline a plan for providing a service for the elderly. Include how you intend to provide the service and what the estimated cost might be.

Online Activity www.phlit.phschool.com

Guided Writing Lesson

Dialogue With an Older Person

A crucial part of any story is good dialogue. In "With All Flags Flying," there are a number of dialogues between Mr. Carpenter, the main character, and people who are younger than he is. Using these examples from the story as inspiration, write a **dialogue** involving an older person and someone younger, possibly the older person's son or daughter. You can either use two of the characters from the story or make up two of your own.

Writing Skills Focus: Appropriate Language for Purpose

One purpose of dialogue is to bring characters to life. Use **appropriate language for your purpose**—make sure the words and phrases you use are consistent with the age and personality of the character. For example, when Mr. Carpenter says, "Well, I surely do thank you," his courteously formal speech pattern is consistent with the character Tyler has created.

Prewriting First, come up with a topic for your dialogue. Focus on an important decision in the older person's life. Then brainstorm for a list of expressions that an older person might use—or talk to an older person and jot down the phrases that he or she says. These phrases will make your dialogue sound more realistic.

Drafting As you write your dialogue, strive to make the speech as natural as possible. Remember that most people use contractions and speak informally in conversation. Copy these natural speech patterns in your dialogue.

Revising Read your draft aloud—if possible, with another person. Does the dialogue sound realistic? Sometimes changing just a few words will fix it. Use language that is consistent and accurately reflects how a person of that age would speak.

✓ ASSESSMENT OPTIONS

Formal Assessment, Selection Test, pp. 82–84, and Assessment Resources Software. The selection test is designed so that it can be easily customized to the performance levels of your students.

Alternative Assessment, p. 24, includes options for less advanced students, more advanced students, visual/spatial and bodily/kinesthetic learners.

PORTFOLIO ASSESSMENT

Use the following rubrics in the ***Alternative Assessment*** booklet to assess student writing:
Essay on Growing Old: Description Rubric, p. 97
Letter From Mr. Carpenter: Problem/Solution Rubric, p. 101
Alternative Ending: Fiction Narrative Rubric, p. 95

Idea Bank

Following are suggestions for matching Idea Bank topics with your students' performance levels and learning modalities:

Customizing for *Performance Levels*
Less Advanced Students: 1, 6
Average Students: 2, 4
More Advanced Students: 3, 5, 7

Customizing for *Learning Modalities*
Musical/Rhythmic: 4
Interpersonal: 6
Verbal/Linguistic: 4, 5
Logical/Mathematical: 7

Guided Writing Lesson

Revision Strategy Before students use ratiocination with their dialogues, encourage them to spend a day "eavesdropping" on the conversations they encounter in their lives. Ask them to key into the different ways that people communicate—from hallway conversations to discussions at home. Discuss with them ways to capture the essence of everyday communication, such as interruptions, nonverbal responses, and phrases that trail off. Then invite them to reenter their writing and implement techniques for making dialogue sound realistic.

For more prewriting, elaboration, and revision strategies, see *Prentice Hall Writing and Grammar.*

Writers at Work Videodisc
Have students view the videodisc segment for Chapter 6 in which Naomi Shihab Nye talks about drafting. Discuss with students the reasons why she likes to "begin quickly."

Play frames 14950 to 17080

Writing Lab CD-ROM
Have students complete the tutorial on Creative Writing. Follow these steps:

1. Have students use interactive tips on purpose to get advice on techniques that can help them tailor their language to their purpose in their dialogues.
2. Direct students to view the video tips for peer editors to learn the benefits of revising their dialogues with a peer.

Prepare and Engage

LESSON OBJECTIVES

1. **To develop vocabulary and word identification skills**
   - Latin Word Roots: *-dom-*
   - Using the Word Bank: Analogies
   - Extending Word Study: Antonyms
2. **To use a variety of reading strategies to comprehend poems and a speech**
   - Connect Your Experience
   - Reading Strategy: Author's Perspective
   - Tips to Guide Reading: Speculate (ATE)
   - Read to Discover Models for Writing (ATE)
   - Idea Bank: Summaries
3. **To increase knowledge of other cultures and to connect common elements across cultures**
   - Connecting Themes Across Cultures (ATE)
   - Background for Understanding
   - Beyond Literature: Byzantine Empire
4. **To express and support responses to the text**
   - Critical Thinking
   - Idea Bank: News Commentary
   - Idea Bank: Comparison-and-Contrast Essay
5. **To analyze literary elements**
   - Literary Focus: Dramatic Situation
6. **To read in order to research self-selected and assigned topics**
   - Idea Bank: Timeline
7. **To plan, prepare, organize, and present literary interpretations**
   - Idea Bank: Collage
   - Idea Bank: Role Play
   - Speaking, Listening, and Viewing Mini-Lesson: Speech
8. **To use recursive writing processes to write poetry with figurative language**
   - Guided Writing Lesson
9. **To increase knowledge of the rules of grammar and usage**
   - Build Grammar Skills: Negatives

Test Preparation

Reading Comprehension: Predicting Outcomes (ATE, p. 325) The teaching tips and sample test item in this workshop support the instruction and practice in the unit workshop:

Reading Comprehension: Recognizing Cause and Effect; Predicting Outcomes (SE, p. 377)

Guide for Reading

Leopold Staff *(1878–1957)*

Leopold Staff loved the quiet moments of life: marveling at the beauty of nature or musing on the glories of long-past civilizations. The miracle of Staff's poetry is that he kept true to those concerns despite the times in which he lived. Poland was a major battleground during both World War I and World War II, yet during that same period Staff and a group of other poets revitalized Polish literature.

Emily Brontë *(1818–1848)*

Featured in AUTHORS IN DEPTH Series

To have one famous writer in a family is unusual, but having three is extraordinary! The Brontë sisters—Emily, Charlotte, and Ann—were all successful novelists. They grew up in Yorkshire, England, in a landscape of bleak, windswept hills. When Emily was eighteen years old, she and her two sisters published a book of their poems. Just two years later, they each published novels. Emily's was *Wuthering Heights,* a classic story of love and revenge.

Anna Akhmatova *(1889–1966)*

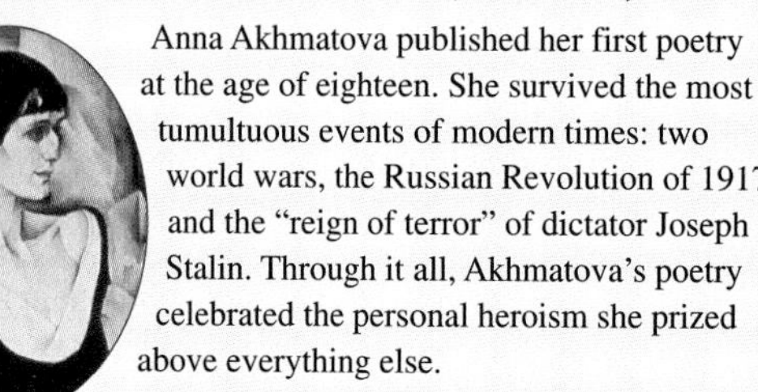

Anna Akhmatova published her first poetry at the age of eighteen. She survived the most tumultuous events of modern times: two world wars, the Russian Revolution of 1917, and the "reign of terror" of dictator Joseph Stalin. Through it all, Akhmatova's poetry celebrated the personal heroism she prized above everything else.

Empress Theodora *(c. 502–548)*

Theodora and her husband, the emperor Justinian, ruled the eastern Roman empire early in the sixth century. She is mostly remembered for a single action: When a rebellion broke out against her and her husband, she persuaded her husband to defend their palace in Constantinople, rather than try to escape.

◆ Build Vocabulary

LATIN WORD ROOTS: *-dom-*

The time: A.D. 532. The place: Rome, the emperor's palace. The main character: The *indomitable* Empress Theodora. The word *indomitable* contains the Latin root *-dom-*, which means "to rule." Add the prefix *in-*, meaning "not," and you might guess that the meaning of *indomitable* is "unrulable," which is close to the actual meaning "not easily defeated."

WORD BANK

Before you read, preview this list of words from the selections.

implore
timorous
indomitable

◆ Build Grammar Skills

NEGATIVES AND DOUBLE NEGATIVES

The Roman empress Theodora cries out in her speech, ". . . may I never see the day when those who meet me do not call me empress." In this dramatic request, she uses two **negatives**—words or word parts that deny or mean "no." In former times, two negatives may have been used to make a point emphatically, but today it is incorrect to use a **double negative**—two negatives that express the same "no." For instance, it would be incorrect to say ". . . may I *not never* see the day . . ."

Prentice Hall Literature Program Resources

REINFORCE / RETEACH / EXTEND

Selection Support Pages
Build Vocabulary: Word Roots: *-dom-*, p. 101
Build Grammar Skills: Negatives and Double Negatives, p. 102
Reading Strategy: Author's Perspective, p. 103
Literary Focus: Dramatic Situation, p. 104

Strategies for Diverse Student Needs, p. 25
Beyond Literature
Humanities Connection: What Is Courage? p. 25
Formal Assessment Selection Test, pp. 85–87; Assessment Resources Software.

Alternative Assessment, p. 25
Resource Pro CD-ROM
Listening to Literature Audiocassettes

The Bridge ◆ The Old Stoic ◆ I Am Not One of Those Who Left the Land ◆ Speech During the Invasion of Constantinople

◆ Literature and Your Life

Connect Your Experience

Life is filled with situations in which we're forced to make tough decisions. It might involve something as simple as deciding to try out for the school play despite having terrible stage fright. In the following selections, however, you'll encounter characters who show the courage to make decisions that could be a matter of life or death.

Journal Writing Jot down your memories about the toughest decision you've faced. What was the outcome?

Thematic Focus: Working It Out

These selections may set you thinking about decisions you've made or fears you've overcome.

◆ Background for Understanding

History

In 532, citizens of the eastern Roman empire rebelled against Emperor Justinian and Empress Theodora. When rebels stormed the castle, Theodora encouraged her husband to face their attackers rather than flee. As it turned out, Justinian and Theodora survived.

Fourteen centuries later, in the early 1900's, Russia was torn by civil war. Many Russians emigrated to Germany and France. The poet Anna Akhmatova, however, refused to go, even after her husband was executed and her son put in jail.

◆ Literary Focus

Dramatic Situation

The life-and-death conditions under which Empress Theodora makes her speech create a gripping backdrop for her impassioned words. This **dramatic situation**—the circumstances and conflicts that form the focal point of a literary work—provides a context that helps you understand the full significance of Theodora's words.

The dramatic situation of Akhmatova's poem arises from the circumstances of the civil war in Russia. Due to food shortages, riots, strikes, and political oppression, many of Akhmatova's friends and neighbors fled the country. The dramatic situation gives you a framework in which you can appreciate the courage of her decision.

◆ Reading Strategy

Author's Perspective

If you've just lost a game, the account you give will be very different from the story told by the winner. The details that are included in a piece of literature depend on the **author's perspective**—his or her outlook on the subject.

Often, writers hint at or directly reveal their perspective. For example, Akhmatova indicates her perspective in the opening lines of her poem:

> I am not one of those who
> left the land/to the mercy
> of its enemies.

In other cases, however, it is left up to the reader to determine the author's perspective by looking closely at the use of words to see what attitude the words convey. To fully understand an author's perspective, it is sometimes necessary to go beyond the text and gather information about the historical or social context in which the work was written.

Write on the chalkboard the following words: *money, love, fame, freedom, power.* Ask students why they think these are "big" themes—ones that have attracted writers from ancient to present times. Lead students to see that although each of these goals is desirable, each can lead to conflict or test people. Ask students to suggest some negative and positive results that might come from attaining each goal listed on the board. Tell students that the writers of these pieces highlight rewards and conflicts connected to these universal themes.

Connecting Themes Across Cultures

Three of these selections deal with decisions people in other countries and times made during war or rebellion. Have students identify conflicts in which the United States has been involved and how American civilians behaved and reacted.

Customize for
Less Proficient Readers

Help students with difficult vocabulary before they read. Define words such as *esteem* and *endure* in "The Old Stoic"; *fragile* and *wavered* in "The Bridge"; *felon* and *wormwood* in "I Am Not One . . ."; and *convention* in "Speech During the Invasion of Constantinople."

Customize for
Pre-AP Students

Point out that poetry often reflects the poet's deep feelings. Invite students to think of some incident or turning point in their own lives that still causes them to have a strong emotional response. Challenge them to use this emotion in a controlled way to write a brief poem about it.

Customize for
English Language Learners

Students learning English may be confused by the word order and sentence structure in the first two poems. For "The Old Stoic," work with them to rephrase the lines with inverted word order (Riches I hold in light esteem; *I hold riches in light esteem.*) For "The Bridge," help them rephrase the first sentence so that "That I would cross that bridge" immediately follows "I didn't believe."

Test Preparation Workshop

Reading Comprehension: Predicting Outcomes When taking standardized tests, students may be asked to use text evidence and experience to draw inferences such as conclusions, generalizations, and predictions. Use this sample test question to give students practice predicting outcomes.

> I didn't believe,
> Standing on the bank of a river
> Which was wide and swift,
> That I would cross that bridge
> Plaited from thin, fragile reeds
> Fastened with bast.

From this passage you may predict that the speaker—

A will drown
B has crossed the bridge
C will build another bridge
D regrets not crossing the bridge

Guide students to understand that the speaker hasn't drowned (he's written the poem); there's no evidence to suggest he'll build another bridge; the tone of the poem, "I didn't believe..." suggests success, so the speaker doesn't have regrets. Therefore, *B* is the correct answer to the question.

Develop Understanding

One-Minute Insight

"The Bridge" metaphorically describes the anxiety and fear associated with life's risks and changes. Staff had to cross the bridge of the dangers and difficulties of wartime Poland, but people of any time can relate his theme to changes in their own lives.

◆ Literary Focus

❶ Dramatic Situation Ask students to describe the dramatic situation that forms the framework for the poem. *The speaker is recalling standing on the bank of a wide, dangerous river, trying to muster the courage to cross a bridge that looks as if it might not hold him.*

◆ Literature and Your Life

❷ Turning Points Ask students if they have ever faced a situation that, similar to the bridge in this poem, seemed like a difficult and dangerous crossing to a new life. *Answers should focus on the idea of change as a bridge.*

◆ Reading Strategy

❸ Author's Perspective Ask students how the author's perspective changes from the beginning to the end of the poem. *At the beginning of the poem, the perspective is that of a person trying to muster the courage to take an important step in life. At the end, the perspective is that of a person who has taken the step successfully, but, as before, still sees the step as being difficult and dangerous.*

Read to Discover Models for Writing

Point out to students that the poems on these pages differ in form. Staff's poem is in free verse, while Brontë's has a simple rhyme scheme and alternating lines of four and three feet of iambs. Encourage students to decide which approach works best for their own poems about turning points.

The Bridge

Leopold Staff

I didn't believe,
Standing on the bank of a river
❶ Which was wide and swift,
That I would cross that bridge
❷ Plaited[1] from thin, fragile reeds
Fastened with bast.[2]
I walked delicately as a butterfly
And heavily as an elephant,
I walked surely as a dancer
And wavered like a blind man.
I didn't believe that I would cross that bridge,
❸ And now that I am standing on the other side,
I don't believe I crossed it.

1. **plaited** (plāt′ əd) *adj.*: Braided; woven.
2. **bast** (bast) *n.*: Inner bark of trees.

Block Scheduling Strategies

Consider these suggestions to take advantage of extended class time:

- Introduce the concept of author's perspective with the Reading Strategy on p. 325. After students have read these selections, they can answer the Reading Strategy questions on p. 331. If you wish, you can follow up with the Reading Strategy practice, p. 103, in ***Selection Support.***
- Have students explore the idea of courage with the ***Beyond Literature*** activity on p. 25.
- Have students work in pairs to complete the Role Play activity in the Idea Bank on p. 332. If possible, have them tape record or videotape their role-playing.
- Encourage students to complete the Guided Writing Lesson on p. 332. Before they write their poems, have them work in pairs to create mental images using figurative language.
- Use Activity 7, p. 25, in ***Alternative Assessment,*** Presentation—A Nation Surrounded.

The Old Stoic

Emily Brontë

◀ Critical Viewing In what ways does this woman's expression suggest courage? [Analyze] ❹

Riches I hold in light esteem,
And love I laugh to scorn;
And lust of fame was but a dream
That vanished with the morn:

And if I pray, the only prayer
That moves my lips for me
Is, "Leave the heart that now I bear,
And give me liberty!" ❺

Yes, as my swift days near their goal, ❻
'Tis all that I implore—
Through life and death a chainless soul,
With courage to endure. ❼

◆ Build Vocabulary

implore (im plôr′) *v.*: Plead; ask for earnestly

In "The Old Stoic," Brontë celebrates the freedom of facing the future unafraid. Her wish is not for material wealth or for fame but for internal courage and a strong life spirit.

▶Critical Viewing◀

❹ **Analyze** *Possible response: Her gaze is steady, and her expression is one of determination.*

◆ Critical Thinking

❺ **Interpret** Ask students why the speaker doesn't think fame is important. *By calling "lust of fame" a ". . . dream/That vanished with the morn," she means that fame is something to dream about briefly, not a lasting value.*

◆ Reading Strategy

❻ **Author's Perspective** Have students analyze this line to determine the author's perspective. Ask how the speaker's main points in this poem might have been different if she had written from a different perspective. *By "as my swift days near their goal," the speaker means, "as I grow older and nearer to the end of my life." The speaker is writing from a perspective of growing older. Perhaps a speaker writing from the perspective of youth would value riches, fame, and love more than this speaker.*

◆ Critical Thinking

❼ **Draw Conclusions** Ask students to name the two things the speaker thinks are most important. *The speaker thinks freedom and courage are the most important things.*

Extending Word Study

Antonyms Point out to students that *esteem* and *scorn* are antonyms. Have students think of three other pairs of antonyms, such as *value* and *reject.* Have them use a thesaurus.

Customize for
English Language Learners
Students may have difficulty with the following expressions: "but a dream" (only a dream), "laugh to scorn" (laugh at), "'Tis all that I implore" (It is all I ask). Before students read, you may want to explain these expressions to them.

Beyond the Classroom

Community Connection
Volunteering With the Elderly The speaker of Emily Brontë's "The Old Stoic," an elderly woman, has lived long enough to know what she values in life. Explain to students that older people's perspective on values is bound to differ from young people's. Suggest that they spend some time at a retirement community, senior center, or other setting where elderly people gather. Students might like to put together an oral history project in which several elderly people identify the most important values in their lives and tell how they came to embrace these values. Help students focus their oral history questions:

1. Use Emily Brontë's poem "The Old Stoic" with interviewees and ask if they agree that independence and courage are important values. How did they come to their views?
2. Encourage interview subjects to identify three guiding principles in their lives and to talk about why those principles are important.

Students can record their interviews and compile them into a class oral history presentation—they might choose an oral or visual format.

One-Minute Insight Akhmatova's poem illustrates how poets often use their art as a means of political expression. In this poem, Akhmatova suggests that in times of trouble, securing personal safety is not worth sacrificing national identity. She feels those who stay and face the dangers will emerge on the other side with fewer regrets and more pride than those who left their country in its time of need.

◆ Background for Understanding

❶ **History** Help students understand this reference by telling them that many of the upper classes in Russia became exiles in countries such as England and France to avoid execution by the Revolutionary forces. Ask: Who are the "enemies" the speaker refers to in line 2? *The speaker thinks the Revolutionaries were enemies of Russia.*

◆ Literary Focus

❷ **Dramatic Situation** Ask students to explain the "murk of conflagration" to which the poet refers. *It is the horror of revolution and its aftermath, which resulted in the deaths of thousands and the destruction of a way of life.*

◆ Reading Strategy

❸ **Author's Perspective** Have students explain what the poet, from the perspective of an anti-Revolutionary, thinks will happen to those who engineered the Revolution. *She says "the reckoning will be made"; she feels that the Revolution is temporary and those responsible will be punished.*

▶Critical Viewing◀

❹ **Speculate** *Students may note the expressions of anger and distress on the people's faces and recognize that they are trying to get away from something upsetting.*

I Am Not One of Those Who Left the Land

Anna Akhmatova
Translated by Stanley Kunitz

❶ I am not one of those who left the land
to the mercy of its enemies.
Their flattery leaves me cold,
my songs are not for them to praise.

But I pity the exile's lot.
Like a felon, like a man half-dead,
dark is your path, wanderer;
wormwood infects your foreign bread.

But here, in the murk of conflagration,[1]
❷ where scarcely a friend is left to know,
we, the survivors, do not flinch
from anything, not from a single blow.

❸ Surely the reckoning will be made
after the passing of this cloud.
We are the people without tears,
straighter than you . . . more proud . . .

1. **conflagration** (kän′ flə grā′ shən) *n.*: Destructive fire.

❹ ▼ Critical Viewing Why do you think these people are on this train? **[Speculate]**

Speaking, Listening, and Viewing Mini-Lesson

Speech

This mini-lesson supports the Speaking, Listening, and Viewing activity in the Idea Bank on p. 332.

Introduce Have students review the elements of a successful speech: strong points, or opinions; support for the opinions; body language and vocal intonation to emphasize the strongest points.

Develop Before students begin writing their speeches, have them consider these questions:

- Why does Theodora say it is intolerable for a ruler to be a fugitive? Is this true?
- What can realistically be accomplished by staying?
- How far do a ruler's responsibilities extend?

Apply Students can prepare speeches that address the questions in Develop Background, or they can argue other points related to Theodora's position. Give students an opportunity to practice their speeches before presenting them to the class.

Assess Have students use the Peer Assessment form: Speech, p. 118, in the ***Alternative Assessment*** booklet to evaluate the effectiveness of their classmates' speeches.

Speech During the Invasion of Constantinople

Empress Theodora

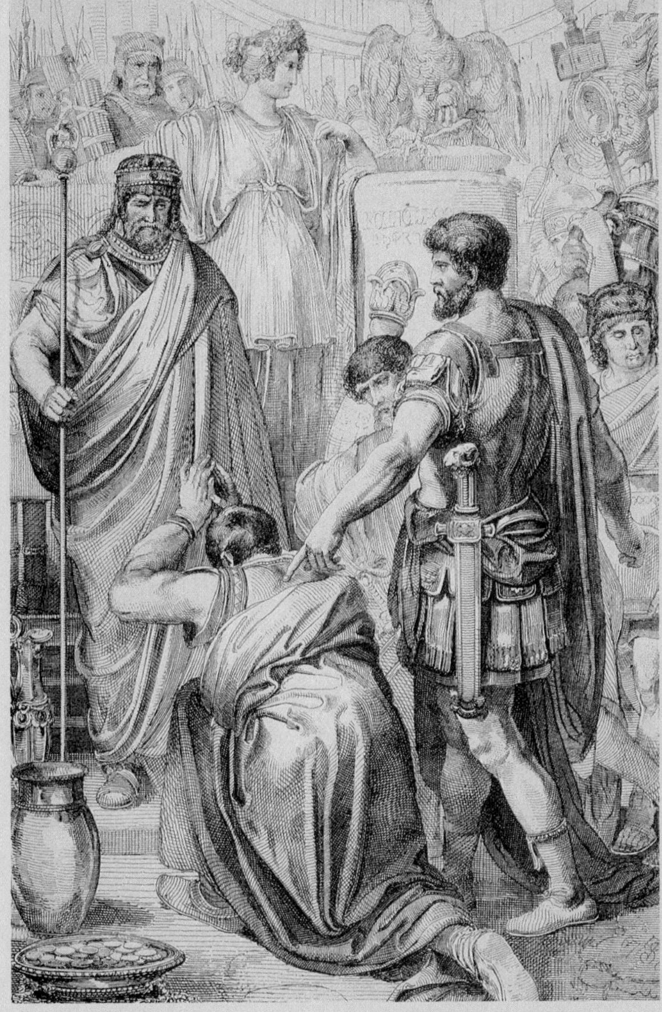

5 ▲ Critical Viewing This picture shows a strong, triumphant Theodora. Identify details in the speech that reflect these qualities. **[Connect]**

In his collection of historical speeches, Lend Me Your Ears, *William Safire wrote the following introduction to Empress Theodora's inspirational words.*

Roman Emperor Justinian, on January 18 of the year 532, was certain he was about to be overthrown by rebel leader Hypatius and killed. A fast galley waited at the palace's private harbor to take him and Empress Theodora to safety in Thrace. His timorous advisers persuaded him that the rebellion could not be stopped and that the way out for the imperial couple was flight. As the panicky leader made for the door, the indomitable empress rose from her throne and delivered a brief speech that kept her husband in Rome and led to the slaughter of the rebels. 6

◆ Build Vocabulary

timorous (tim´ ər es) *adj.*: Full of fear; timid

indomitable (in däm´ it ə bəl) *adj.*: Not easily defeated

One-Minute Insight This inspirational speech by Empress Theodora expresses a universal theme, based on specific historical circumstances. Faced with almost certain death at the hands of invaders, Theodora halts the panicky evacuation of government leaders with her proud words. Her speech carries a message of courage and integrity that applies far beyond the historical events that prompted it.

▶Critical Viewing◀

5 Connect *Possible responses: Although the Empress Theodora stands in the background of the picture, she assumes a confident, authoritative pose. While others seem to be responding to dramatic events, the empress seems to represent reasoned calm and wisdom.*

◆ Background for Understanding

6 History Explain to students that Theodora's speech was given during a riot staged by two political groups called the Blues and the Greens. These groups disagreed on religious beliefs and on Justinian's political appointments. They set up a new emperor who might have overthrown Justinian's empire if it had not been for Theodora's speech.

Tips to Guide Reading

Speculate Have students read the selection silently and then encourage them to speculate about Theodora's perspective. Guide students to see that although she displays considerable courage, she also has certain beliefs about her status is life.

Humanities: Art

Illustration for Speech During the Invasion of Constantinople.

In this piece of art, the Emperor Justinian is receiving a supplicant. Behind him stands the Empress Theodora. Discuss these questions:

1. The artist has chosen to make the figures in the foreground darker than those in the background. What effect does this have? *Students may say that the figures in front are more detailed and darker, but the eye is drawn to the contrast of the background where Theodora appears.*
2. How is Theodora's speech different from the way she is portrayed in the picture? *In the picture, she is seen behind Justinian; whereas, reading the speech, the reader may picture her alone or in the foreground of a scene—a more prominent position.*
3. Do you think the illustration represents Theodora truthfully? *Possible answer: Yes; though she is placed behind the throne, she very possibly was a "power behind the throne"—one whose influence was subtle but great.*

◆ Literary Focus

❶ Dramatic Situation To what dramatic situation is Theodora referring when she says "the present occasion" and "extreme danger"? *She is referring to the riot and attempted takeover of the government.*

◆ Reading Strategy

❷ Author's Perspective How is the author's perspective reflected here? *The author implies that she believes it would be better to die than to give up the empire.*

Reinforce and Extend

Answers

◆ *Literature and Your Life*

Reader's Response Students may answer this question by relating the concerns of the poems—the value of riches, fame, courage, freedom, and love—to incidents from their own lives.

Thematic Focus Turning points call upon people to make decisions that might have great consequences for their own and other lives; this requires courage.

Check Your Comprehension

1. The speaker is surprised that he has crossed the bridge.
2. The speaker values independence and courage.
3. The speaker thinks those who fled Russia acted in a cowardly and faithless manner.
4. She has a matter-of-fact view of death: "It is impossible for a person . . . not to die."

◆ Critical Thinking

1. The speaker knows the bridge is fragile and doesn't seem to think himself capable of the necessary maneuvers to cross it successfully.
2. As the speaker has grown older she has seen that love and fame are elusive.
3. Many students will recognize that staying to live in difficult circumstances is the more courageous choice because it involves standing up for one's principles.
4. Possible response: Stand up for what you believe in, even if you risk unpopularity.

❶ My lords, the present occasion is too serious to allow me to follow the convention that a woman should not speak in a man's council. Those whose interests are threatened by extreme danger should think only of the wisest course of action, not of conventions.

In my opinion, flight is not the right course, even if it should bring us to safety. It is impossible for a person, having been born into this world, not to die; but for one who has reigned it ❷ is intolerable to be a fugitive. May I never be deprived of this purple robe, and may I never see the day when those who meet me do not call me empress.

If you wish to save yourself, my lord, there is no difficulty. We are rich; over there is the sea, and yonder are the ships. Yet reflect for a moment whether, when you have once escaped to a place of security, you would not gladly exchange such safety for death. As for me, I agree with the adage that the royal purple is the noblest shroud.

Beyond Literature

Social Studies Connection

Byzantine Empire At the height of its power in the fifth century A.D., the Byzantine empire (also known as the East Roman empire) included parts of southern and eastern Europe, as well as parts of northern Africa and the Middle East. Christianity, Greek culture, and Roman customs flourished in the empire, which served as a link between ancient and modern European civilization. From A.D. 527 to 565, the Byzantine empire was ruled by Emperor Justinian.

Activity Use an encyclopedia to find the extent of Justinian's empire. On a copy of a contemporary world map, indicate the areas he ruled.

Guide for Responding

◆ *Literature and Your Life*

Reader's Response What personal experiences do these works call to mind?

Thematic Focus Why is courage required at turning points?

Check Your Comprehension

1. What surprises the speaker in "The Bridge"?
2. What does the speaker in "The Old Stoic" value?
3. In "I Am Not One of Those . . . ," what is the speaker's attitude toward those who fled Russia?
4. How does the Empress Theodora feel about dying?

◆ Critical Thinking

INTERPRET

1. Why doesn't the speaker in "The Bridge" think he can cross the bridge? **[Speculate]**
2. Why doesn't the speaker in "The Old Stoic" care for love and fame? **[Infer]**

EVALUATE

3. Do you think it is more courageous to face the dangers of traveling across a continent and an ocean or to stay and live in difficult and dangerous circumstances? **[Apply]**

COMPARE LITERARY WORKS

4. Compare and contrast the advice you think the speaker of each poem would give to you and your friends. **[Compare and Contrast]**

Beyond the Selection

FURTHER READING

Other Works by the Authors

Wuthering Heights, Emily Brontë
Wyklina, Leopold Staff
Requiem, Anna Akhmatova

Other Works About Turning Points

Cry the Beloved Country, Alan Paton
Children of the Fox, Jill Paton Walsh

We suggest that you preview these works before recommending them to students.

INTERNET

Students can visit the following Web sites for information. Please be aware that sites may have changed since we published this information.

For Emily Brontë go to **http://www.buckinghamgate.com/events/features/emily/emily.html**

For Anna Akhmatova go to **http://www.odessit.com/namegal/english/ahmatova.htm**

We *strongly recommend* that you preview the sites before you send students to them.

Guide for Responding (continued)

◆ Reading Strategy

Author's Perspective

Understanding the historical context of Anna Akhmatova's poem "I Am Not One of Those Who Left the Land" helps you identify the **author's perspective**—the viewpoint from which the poem is written. An author's perspective affects the details that are included in the work, as well as the way an event or idea is presented. For instance, Akhmatova's reference to the wormwood in foreign bread reflects her deep love for her country as well as her disapproval of those who would leave.

1. Leopold Staff lived through some of the most devastating events in history. What details in Staff's poem indicate that he has lived through dangerous times?
2. Empress Theodora's speech is made from the perspective of royalty. What details are included that might not be included in a speech by one of the common people during the invasion?
3. Identify two details in Akhmatova's poem that indicate she opposes the rulers of her country.

◆ Literary Focus

Dramatic Situation

The **dramatic situation**—the circumstances and events that provide the context of a work of literature—of Akhmatova's poem is the turmoil of civil war in Russia. For Empress Theodora's speech, the dramatic situation is the rebellion that threatens the lives of the empress and her husband.

1. Theodora makes her speech just as she and Justinian are about to board a ship and sail to Thrace. How does this detail add to the drama of her remarks?
2. Akhmatova stayed in Russia in the "murk of conflagration" while others fled. How do the circumstances surrounding her decision make her situation more dramatic?
3. Leopold Staff's poem was written in the aftermath of the tremendous devastation that Poland suffered during World War II. How does knowing this affect your understanding of the poem?

◆ Build Vocabulary

Using the Latin Root *-dom-*

Fill in the blanks to complete the meanings of these words that include the Latin root *-dom-*, meaning "to rule."

1. domineer: __?__ in a harsh or arrogant way
2. domain: the area that is __?__
3. dominant: __?__ over another

Using the Word Bank: Analogies

On your paper, complete the following word pairs with words from the Word Bank.

1. Courageous is to hero as __?__ is to ruler.
2. Devour is to eat as __?__ is to ask.
3. Enraged is to joyful as __?__ is to brave.

◆ Build Grammar Skills

Negatives and Double Negatives

Negatives are words or word parts that deny or mean "no." Some examples of negatives include *no, not* (and contractions with *n't*), *never, none, nobody, no one, nothing, nowhere, neither, barely, scarcely,* and *hardly*. Using a **double negative**—two negative words where only one is needed—is incorrect.

Practice Identify which of the following sentences use double negatives and which use negatives correctly. Correct the double negatives you identify.

1. Although Empress Theodora did not leave, she was not killed during the rebellion.
2. Staff's poem tells of a man who didn't believe he could never get across a bridge.
3. Hardly none of Akhmatova's friends remained in Russia.
4. Brontë does not care for riches and she does not care for fame.

Writing Application In your notebook, rewrite each of these sentences using only one negative.

1. Those who meet me don't never call me empress.
2. Scarcely no friends are left to know.
3. We do not flinch from nothing.
4. I didn't believe in nothing.
5. She wasn't scared of no one.

◆ Build Grammar Skills

Practice

1. correct
2. incorrect: Staff's poem tells of a man who didn't believe he could ever get across a bridge.
3. incorrect. Hardly any of Akhmatova's friends remained in Russia.
4. correct

Writing Application

1. Those who meet me don't ever call me empress.
2. Scarcely any friends are left to know.
3. We do not flinch from anything.
4. I didn't believe in anything.
5. She wasn't scared of anyone.

Grammar Reinforcement

For additional instruction and practice, use the lesson in the **Language Lab CD-ROM** on avoiding double negatives, and p. 90 on Negative Sentences in the *Writer's Solution Grammar Practice Book*.

Answers

◆ Reading Strategy

1. This poem suggests that he lived through difficult times by referring to the river (his life) as "wide and swift," and by describing the way to cross it (get through his life) as "fragile." Sometimes he had to "walk delicately" or "waver."
2. The empress refers to herself as "one who has reigned." She says "we are rich" and alludes to the adage that "the royal purple is the noblest shroud." All these details relate to her perspective as an empress.
3. The first detail is that she speaks up against the convention of "not speaking in a man's council." Another detail is her assertion that one who reigns cannot be a fugitive.

◆ Literary Focus

1. The timing of the empress's remarks make them all the more dramatic; it is late to suggest an altogether contrary course of action.
2. The circumstances surrounding Akhmatova's decision show that she has taken the least popular—and therefore more dramatic—course of action.
3. Knowing that Staff lived through events that devastated Poland makes his survival all the more dramatic.

◆ Build Vocabulary

Using the Root *-dom-*

1. Rule; 2. ruled; 3. ruling

Using the Word Bank

1. indomitable; 2. implore; 3. timorous

Reteach

To help students understand the author's perspective, discuss a sports event, in which there are supporters of two different players or teams. Point out that accounts of a football or basketball game will differ when told by supporters of different teams. A consideration of how umpires' or referees' calls vary may help students consider the perspective authors may have when they write.

Idea Bank

Following are suggestions for matching Idea Bank topics with your students' performance levels and learning modalities:

Customizing for
Performance Levels
Less Advanced Students: 1, 7
Average Students: 2, 4, 6
More Advanced Students: 3, 5

Customizing for
Learning Modalities
Visual/Spatial: 6, 7
Interpersonal: 5
Verbal/Linguistic: 2, 4, 5

Guided Writing Lesson

Prewriting Strategy Lead students to figurative language for their poetry by inviting them to draw what they think or feel about their turning points. Drawing will enable students to create visual metaphors that they then can translate into words. Tell students that they are not trying to create art by drawing—instead they can draw to find visual images that shows their experiences.

For more prewriting, elaboration, and revision strategies, see *Prentice Hall Writing and Grammar.*

Writers at Work Videodisc
Have students view the videodisc segment for Ch. 6 in which Naomi Shihab Nye talks about gathering details for creative writing. Discuss with student what Nye means when she says that poetry isn't "primarily a mental experience."

Play frames 20514 to 20978

Writing Lab CD-ROM
Have students complete the tutorial on Creative Writing with these steps:

1. Have students use Word Bins for poetry to help them choose sensory words and rhyming words for their poems.
2. Suggest that students consult interactive instruction on poetic structures. Here they can learn the meanings of *couplet, tercet, quatrain, cinquain, sestet, heptastich, octave, sonnet,* and *haiku.* Suggest that students might try writing their poems about a turning point in one of these forms.

Build Your Portfolio

Idea Bank

Writing

1. **Summaries** Write a summary of each of these works that captures the key details.
2. **News Commentary** Write a commentary that a newscaster might give following Empress Theodora's speech. Summarize what she said and discuss the impact that the speech may have.
3. **Comparison-and-Contrast Essay** Write an essay in which you compare and contrast Anna Akhmatova's poem with Empress Theodora's speech. Look at similarities and differences in the attitudes of the speakers, the situations they face, and the character traits they exhibit.

Speaking, Listening, and Viewing

4. **Speech** Give a short speech in which you answer Empress Theodora and try to persuade Emperor Justinian and his aides that the wiser course of action is to board the ship and sail to safety in Thrace. Deliver your speech to the class. **[Performing Arts Link]**
5. **Role Play** Role-play a conversation between Akhmatova and someone who chose to leave Russia. Use what you learn in the poem and in the background on p. 325 as the basis for the discussion.

Researching and Representing

6. **Timeline** Several of these works are written in response to specific historical events. Using information gathered through research, create a timeline that captures the events surrounding one of these works. **[Social Studies Link]**
7. **Collage** Create a collage of visual images, quotations, and found objects that captures the ideas expressed in one of these works. **[Art Link]**

Online Activity www.phlit.phschool.com

Guided Writing Lesson

Poem About a Turning Point

Each of these works captures the thoughts of a person making a choice—facing a turning point. Write a **poem** about a turning point in your own life. You might write about a social or political issue that affects your life (as Akhmatova does), or you might write about a personal choice. Use the following tip to help you communicate your ideas.

**Writing Skills Focus:
Figurative Language**

Words such as *happy* or *sad* and other abstract language—language that refers to things that cannot be experienced with the senses—can mean something different to every person. By connecting abstract words to concrete images, however, you can help readers identify with what you're describing. The best way to do this is to use **figurative language**—writing not meant to be interpreted literally. For example, Leopold Staff uses figurative language when he describes a period of life as a fragile bridge. The specific type of figurative language that Staff uses is a **metaphor**—a comparison in which one thing is described as another. You can also use **similes**—comparisons between dissimilar things using the word *like* or *as.*

Prewriting Choose the experience on which you will focus. Then brainstorm for a list of images you can use to help capture your feelings associated with the experience.

Drafting Don't overload your poem with a wide variety of images. Choose a small number that are related, and use them as the focus of your poem.

Revising Read your poem to a friend. Get feedback about how you can improve the wording or strengthen the images in your poem.

ASSESSMENT OPTIONS

Formal Assessment, Selection Test, pp. 85–87, and Assessment Resources Software. The selection test is designed so that it can be easily customized to the performance levels of your students.
Alternative Assessment, p. 25, includes options for less advanced students, more advanced students, intrapersonal learners, verbal/linguistic learners, bodily/kinesthetic learners, interpersonal learners, and visual/spatial learners.

PORTFOLIO ASSESSMENT
Use the following rubrics in the ***Alternative Assessment*** booklet to assess student writing:
Summaries: Summary Rubric, p. 98
News Commentary: Summary Rubric, p. 98
Compare-and-Contrast Essay: Comparison and Contrast Rubric, p. 103

Writing Process Workshop

Description

Much of the pleasure we take in the world around us comes through our senses. We observe the beauties of nature, listen to music, enjoy the feel of comfortable clothing, and taste and smell our favorite foods. **Description** is writing that captures the sensory pleasures in the world using precise details to show the way something looks, tastes, smells, sounds, or feels. Effective description re-creates a scene or an image so that readers can perceive it for themselves.

The following skills, introduced in this section's Guided Writing Lessons, will help you write an effective descriptive essay.

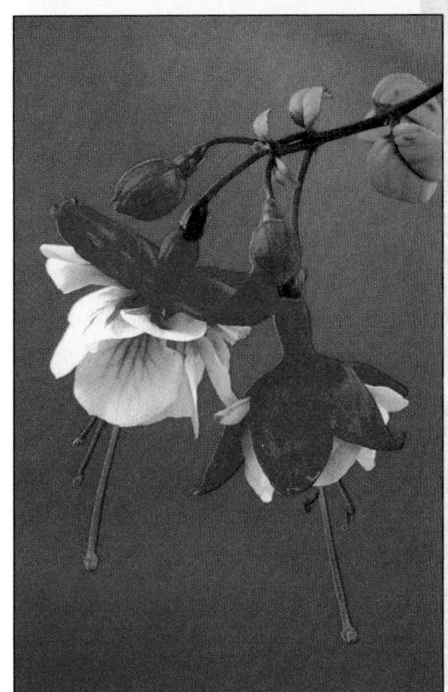

Writing Skills Focus

- **Use sensory details**—words that appeal to the five senses. (See p. 310.)
- **Use appropriate language** for your purpose. (See p. 323.)
- **Use figurative language** such as metaphors, similes, or personification. (See p. 332.)
- **Make abstract terms concrete.** Connect abstract terms, such as *delicate* or *powerful,* to concrete images, such as a *butterfly* or a *freight train.*

Anne Tyler uses these skills to describe one man's experience with old age.

Model From Literature

from "With All Flags Flying" by Anne Tyler

① Weakness was what got him in the end. He had been expecting something more definite—chest pains, a stroke, arthritis—but it was only weakness that put a finish to his living alone. ② A numbness in his head, an airy feeling when he walked. ③ A wateriness in his bones that made it an effort to pick up his coffee cup in the morning. He waited some days for it to go away, but it never did. And meanwhile the dust piled up in the corners; the refrigerator wheezed and creaked ④ for want of defrosting. Weeds grew around his rosebushes.

① *The author's language is simple and direct, appropriate for a short story.*

② *Numbness appeals to the sense of touch.*

③ *The writer connects the abstract term weakness to the concrete images of air and water.*

④ *The words wheezed and creaked appeal to the sense of hearing.*

Prepare and Engage

Lesson Objectives

1. To use recursive writing processes to write a description
2. To recognize and use figurative language
3. To recognize and use precise nouns

You may want to distribute the scoring rubric for Description (p. 97 in ***Alternative Assessment***) to inform students before they begin of the criteria on which they will be evaluated. See the suggestions on page 335 for additional points with which you can customize the rubric for this workshop.

Writers at Work Videodisc

To introduce students to the key elements of description and show how author Colleen McElroy uses them in her writing, play the videodisc segment on Description (Ch. 1). Have students discuss what McElroy says about what makes a description a good one.

Play frames 335 to 9140

Writing Lab CD-ROM

If your students have access to computers, you may want to have them work on the tutorial on Description to complete all or part of their descriptions. Follow these steps:

1. Have students review the Inspirations for Description to choose a topic.
2. Have students draft on the computer.
3. Suggest students use Word Bins while revising to make their descriptions more vivid.

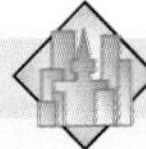

Beyond the Classroom

Career Connection

Descriptive Writing Tell students that some people in the world of work may routinely write descriptively during their jobs. Students can find examples of descriptive writing in print advertisements, travel brochures, and detailed descriptions of salsas and cheeses at the supermarket. Have students discuss what descriptive pieces catch their attention and why, as well as what common features, such as vivid nouns and verbs, they may notice in different descriptions.

Provide students with magazines for them to look for examples of descriptive writing. Print ads will offer a wealth of descriptions, but encourage them to look for articles that describe items, travel, and so forth with figurative language as well. When each student feels that he or she has found one or more good example of descriptive writing, hold a class discussion in which students offer examples of what they found in their search. Then have students write their own brief samples of "professional" descriptive writing.

Develop Student Writing

Prewriting Strategy

Once students have decided on a topic, you might want to tell them to make a chart with the five senses and then list any sensory words or details that come to mind pertaining to their topic. They can refer to the list while drafting.

You might have them use the grid organizer, which you can find in the ***Writing and Language Transparencies,*** pp. 79–81, to create a sensory language chart.

Customize for English Language Learners

Students may find description more manageable if they describe something they can see, rather than describing something from memory. You might suggest that they bring in something to describe, or you might use one of the art transparencies, such as Art Transparency 12 or 20 in ***Art Transparencies,*** pp. 51 and 83.

Customize for Pre-AP Students

Challenge students to describe something from a professional's point of view. For example, a student might describe the last inning of a championship baseball game from the point of view of the home plate umpire.

Writing Lab CD-ROM

Sensory, Color, Places, and Character Trait word bins in the Gathering Details section of the tutorial on Description contain exhaustive lists of words. Students should consult these lists to help them find the most descriptive words and phrases for their topics.

Elaboration Strategy

Guide students to elaborate on their descriptions by using the **SEE** technique: Making a **S**tatement, **E**xtending the statement, and **E**laborating on the statement. Model the **SEE** technique with the following example:
Statement: Nabokov learned to read English.
Extension: Nabokov learned to read English before he could read Russian.
Elaboration: Nabokov was thrilled to learn to read English, although it was before he could read Russian.

Applying Language Skills: Figurative Language

Figurative language is not meant to be taken literally; it's usually used to state or imply a comparison of two unlike things.

Simile:
The taxi moved like a python through the evening traffic.

Metaphor:
In the evening traffic, the taxi was a slithering python.

Personification:
The taxi moved in and out of traffic, cleverly weaving a fabric in the night.

Practice On your paper, add figurative language to the following passage.

It was a hot day. The sun shone brightly. The riverbed was dry. I walked slowly down the road.

Writing Application Use figurative language to make your descriptive essay more vivid.

Writer's Solution Connection Writing Lab

For more examples of topics for descriptive writing, see the Inspirations for Description in the Description tutorial in the Writing Lab.

Prewriting

Choose a Topic Choose a topic that you find interesting enough to describe in detail. Memorable people, remarkable places, unusual events, and intriguing objects or ideas all make great topics for description. Use the following chart to help you choose a topic.

If you're considering...	Then try this ...
A remarkable place	Think about cities, regions, or countries you've visited or would like to visit.
A memorable person	Make a list of five distinct groups of people; for example, Sports Heroes or People From Mythology. Write down people for each category, and choose one.
An idea description	Consider subjects that interest you at school.

Consider Your Purpose How do you want your description to affect the people who read it? Your purpose will shape your tone, word choice, and details. For example, if your purpose is to encourage people to visit a place, you'll want to provide attractive details and use positively charged words and phrases, such as *breathtaking views* or *pleasant climate year-round.* On the other hand, if your purpose is to describe a trip that you didn't enjoy, you will focus on unpleasant details and use words and phrases with negative connotations, such as *dismal, gloomy weather,* or *surly, abusive waiters.*

Drafting

Organize Your Draft Choose the right method of organization for your topic. You may choose **chronological order** and place details in the order in which they happened in time. If you use chronological order, include transitional terms, such as *before, next,* and *a few minutes later.*

If you use **spatial order,** you place details as they appear in some physical relationship to one another. To make spatial order clear, use directional terms, such as *next to, in the center,* or *on the right.*

If you present ideas in **order of importance,** you place details from most important to least important or vice versa.

Applying Language Skills

Figurative Language Tell students that figurative language will enliven their descriptions, making them more fun to read and more memorable.

Suggested Answer

The day was so hot the tar on the roads bubbled and dripped like molten lava. The sun was a spotlight focused on me. The dry riverbed shrank further behind its dusty stones. Like a desert tortoise, I slowly ambled down the road.

Grammar Reinforcement

For additional instruction and practice, have students complete the **Language Lab CD-ROM** lesson on Figurative Language.

Revising

Have a Peer Review Your Work Team up with a classmate to review each other's work. Ask your peer reviewer to read your description once straight through to get a general impression. Then, he or she should read it a second time and jot down notes indicating what is strong about the description, pointing out areas that need clarification and offering constructive criticism with specific suggestions for improvement. Use the following questions to guide your peer reviewer:

- What is the central impression of the description? Does the language contribute to the impression?
- Is the description vivid? Where can I add sensory details or precise nouns?
- Where can I use figurative language to make comparisons more vivid?
- Is the imagery effective? How can I improve these details to make them more vivid or interesting?

Revision Model

I save everything. Nothing ever goes into the garbage without my rapt contemplation over whether or not I am throwing away something meaningful. My drawers ^① overflow ~~are filled to the brim~~ with ~~junk~~ ② ticket stubs, playbills, old letters, and photographs that would be worthless to anybody else. I am a ^③ packrat, storing up memories like food for the cold winter. ~~saver, a collector of memories.~~

① The writer adds the precise word *overflow.*
② These sensory details clarify the vague term *junk.*
③ The writer adds a metaphor and a simile to compare himself to an image of a creature famous for saving things.

Publishing

- **Create a Class Anthology** Working with classmates, gather your writings into a book of descriptions. Include a cover, title, and table of contents. Artistically talented students might also add illustrations.
- **Post Your Work On-Line** The Internet has many sites where you can post your writing. For a list of sites that publish student work, visit Prentice Hall at http://www.phschool.com.

Applying Language Skills: Precise Nouns

Vague or general nouns will make your description less effective and more difficult for your readers to envision. Use **precise nouns** to give your readers a vivid and accurate picture of what you are describing.

Vague Nouns:
building, food, animal, ballplayer

More Specific Nouns:
library, pasta, reptile, shortstop

Precise Nouns:
Ridgewood Public Library, ziti, crocodile, Derek Jeter

Practice Replace the vague nouns with precise ones in the following sentences.

1. I bought my friend a piece of colored jewelry with an animal on it.
2. A vehicle passed the place where the man stood.

Writing Application Review your description. Replace any vague nouns with precise ones.

Writer's Solution Connection
Language Lab
For more practice with precise nouns, complete the Language Lab lesson on Exact Nouns.

Revision Strategy

Have students reenter their writing and highlight each detail. Then ask them to review each detail—is it a sensory detail? does it provide vivid imagery? Encourage them to look for abstract images that can be converted to concrete terms.

Prentice Hall Writing and Grammar For more prewriting, elaboration, and revision strategies, see *Prentice Hall Writing and Grammar.*

Publishing

In addition to the suggestions presented in the Student Edition, students may also wish to read their descriptions aloud to background music. Students who do not wish to share their descriptions with other students should be encouraged to save them for future reference.

Reinforce and Extend

Applying Language Skills

Precise Nouns Tell students that using precise nouns is especially important in a description. Rather than loading up and weighing down their descriptions with adjectives and adverbs, they should concentrate on using the most precise nouns to describe people, places, things, and ideas.

Suggested Answers

1. I bought Amy a silver necklace with a lizard on it.
2. A bus passed the corner where the construction worker stood.

Grammar Reinforcement

For additional instruction and practice, have students complete the **Language Lab CD-ROM** lesson on Writing With Nouns and Verbs.

✓ ASSESSMENT		4	3	2	1
PORTFOLIO ASSESSMENT Use the rubric on Description in ***Alternative Assessment*** (p. 97) to assess students' writing. Add these criteria to customize the rubric to this assignment.	**Figurative Language**	The description uses figurative language effectively.	The description contains some figurative language.	There is little figurative language, but the description could use more.	There is no figurative language.
	Precise Nouns	All nouns are both precise and well chosen for each situation.	Most nouns are precise.	There are some precise nouns but also a number of vague nouns. Adjectives are overused.	Most nouns are vague and nondescriptive, and/or the piece is weighed down by too many adjectives.

Prepare and Engage

LESSON OBJECTIVES

- To read extensively and intensively for different purposes: to be entertained, to appreciate a writer's craft, to be informed, to take action, and to discover models to use in one's own writing
- To read extensively and intensively in varied sources such as diaries, journals, textbooks, maps, newspapers, letters, speeches, memoranda, electronic texts, and other media

Customize for
Pre-AP Students

Have students watch the national TV news, choose a story of interest, and take notes on the information provided. They then locate the same story in a print newspaper. Have students compare and contrast the treatment in both sources. What might be a reason to choose the newspaper instead of television? What might be a reason to choose an Internet news source?

Answers

Possible answers:

1. The letter to the editor should have a clearly stated opinion with logical support.
2. The one-paragraph summary should be brief. The main idea is stated in a topic sentence, and only the most important supporting details are in the other sentences.
3. The local news story can have the same "5 Ws and an H" (who, what, where, when, why, and how) organization as the model students have found.
4. The opinion paragraph should include a clearly stated opinion, with supporting examples and quotations from the sports article.
5. The expository paragraph should begin with a topic sentence stating the most important idea about the new business.

Student Success Workshop

Real-World Reading Skills — Reading a Newspaper

Strategies for Success

Many things you read are made up of one type of writing and cover just one topic. For instance, a biography is nonfiction writing about one person's life, and a novel tells a story about fictional characters. A newspaper, on the other hand, contains various topics and types of writing. In some newspapers, you can read articles about everything from sports to computers. You can get information from news and feature articles, classified ads, calendars of events, and the weather report. You can get opinions from editorials, interpretations from news analyses, and entertainment from comics and crossword puzzles. Here are some strategies for making the most of your newspaper reading:

Learn the Paper's Contents If a newspaper contains so much information, how can you know where to begin reading it? Start by learning how the newspaper is organized and what subject matter it contains.

- ▶ Read the index to find page numbers for specific sections and articles.
- ▶ Skim sections to see what they contain.
- ▶ Pull out the sections that interest you.
- ▶ Read the headlines. Then read the articles or other types of text that interest you.

INDEX

World/Nation, **A**	Broadway Revisited, **D6**
Space Station Scare, **A9**	Travel, **E**
Metro, **B**	Leisure Spurs: Vacations on Horseback, **E3**
Local Taxes Rebuild Schools, **B5**	Real Estate, **F**
Business, **C**	Local House Bargains, **F2**
Virtual Merger: Internet Giant Grows, **C12**	Classified Ads, **G**
Arts and Entertainment, **D**	Help Wanted, **G3**

Know What You Want Few people read the whole paper. Most people read a few articles and locate information they need. Knowing what you're looking for can help you use a newspaper effectively. Are you looking for information about a national or an international event? Try the front page. Do you want to know about a fire that occurred in town last night? Try the front page of the city (or "Metro") section. Do you want to find out who won a game? Look in the Sports section.

Apply the Strategies

Try out your newspaper reading skills with one or more of these exercises:

1. Read an editorial. Write a letter to the editor responding to it.
2. Read a front-page story. In a paragraph, summarize its main ideas.
3. Choose a local news story. Use it as a model for writing one of your own.
4. After reading a sports article, explain why you do or don't consider it well written.
5. Read an article about a new business. Then write a paragraph describing what you've learned about it.

✔ *Here are some reasons for reading a newspaper:*

- ▶ *Learning about recent scientific discoveries*
- ▶ *Finding the weather forecast*
- ▶ *Hunting for a job in the classified ads*
- ▶ *Reading different points of view about current events*

Test Preparation Workshop

Analyzing Newspapers

Emphasize that test questions about newspaper text and information that is found on standardized tests may ask about many things, from interpreting a weather map to evaluating the ideas in an editorial. Students should recognize that the best way to prepare for such test items is to read newspapers regularly.

Display the following question, and have students refer to the sample index entries:

In which section of this newspaper would you find stock market listings?

A Section A　　**C** Section C
B Section B　　**D** Section D

Have students tell why C is the correct answer.

Encourage exploration of a newspaper. Display the business section stock tables of a metropolitan newspaper. Students may name a major corporation, look for its listing, and then use the key and column headings to interpret the numerical data. Extend the exploration by having students suggest other categories of information found in the business section, the travel section, the entertainment section, and so on.

Part 2 *Fateful Moments*

Man Catching Shooting Sun, James Endicott, Stock Illustration Source, Inc.

One-Minute Planning Guide

The selections in this part show people dealing with important or fateful moments and events that shape their lives. In Pearl S. Buck's "The Good Deed," an elderly Chinese woman finds new worth for herself by arranging a meeting between two younger people. Frank Deford's article "The Greatest Ever" lists the men he considers the fifty greatest basketball players of all time, as well as the qualities that make them special. Michael Jordan gives his own take on what it means to be the greatest in "Rare Air: Michael on Michael." The author of "Thoughts of Hanoi" remembers her city before it was destroyed by war, while in "Pride," the poet discusses how pride can lead to a point at which a person cracks like a rock. "Auto Wreck" describes the horrifying moments after an auto accident. The section ends with "Before the Law," Franz Kafka's description of the futility of trying to alter fate.

Customize for *Varying Student Needs*

When assigning the selections in this part to your students, keep in mind the following factors:

"The Good Deed"

- A longer story (14 pp.)
- Its subject matter may be unfamiliar to many students

"The Greatest Ever"; "Rare Air"

- Very brief, high-interest topic and author
- Accessible to most students

"Thoughts of Hanoi"; "Pride"; "Auto Wreck"

- Diverse subject matter will be of interest

"Before the Law"

- Difficult vocabulary and sentence structure will be challenging for many students

Humanities: Art

Man Catching Shooting Sun by James Endicott.

Born in 1946, James Endicott has been a freelance illustrator all his adult life.

Have students establish the surface premise of the art: A man standing on a high, narrow promontory, with a paper or banner streaming from his right hand, appears to be reaching his left hand to catch the most colorful of the many stars shooting in the sky. Help students to recognize the fantasy elements in the painting, the most striking of which is the man catching the shooting star; others include the sheer quantity of simultaneously shooting stars; the flat, cut-out quality of the man; the strangely curvy promontory on which he stands; the mysterious item that streams from his right hand.

Help students link the artwork to the theme of Part 2, "Fateful Moments," by answering the following questions:

1. Does the art suggest whether it is good or bad to catch a shooting star, and what elements in the picture lead you to think so? *Most students will say that the art suggests it is a good thing to catch the shooting star, since the man has safely reached a high place and catches the star gracefully. The star itself seems to be something special—more colorful than the others.*
2. What "fateful" event might catching a shooting star represent? *Sample answers: It might suggest unexpected success in a long pursuit or reaching for an ultimately unattainable dream.*

Prepare and Engage

LESSON OBJECTIVES

1. **To develop vocabulary and word identification skills**
   - Latin Word Roots: *-pel-*
   - Using the Word Bank: Definitions
   - Extending Word Study: Connotations (ATE)
2. **To use a variety of reading strategies to comprehend a personal narrative**
   - Connect Your Experience
   - Reading Strategy: Draw Inferences
   - Tips to Guide Reading: Sustained Reading (ATE)
   - Read to Be Informed (ATE)
3. **To increase knowledge of other cultures and to connect common elements across cultures**
   - Connecting Themes Across Cultures (ATE)
   - Cultural Connection (ATE)
   - Background for Understanding
4. **To express and support responses to the text**
   - Critical Thinking
   - Idea Bank: Letters
   - Idea Bank: Story Segment
   - Analyze Literary Criticism (ATE)
5. **To analyze literary elements**
   - Literary Focus: Character
6. **To read in order to research self-selected and assigned topics**
   - Research Skills Mini-Lesson: Readers' Guide to Periodicals
7. **To plan, prepare, organize, and present literary interpretations**
   - Idea Bank: Multimedia Presentation
   - Viewing and Representing: Timeline
8. **To speak clearly and effectively for specific audience and purpose**
   - Idea Bank: Unrehearsed Speech
   - Speaking, Listening, and Viewing : Radio Interview
9. **To use recursive writing processes to write a speech**
   - Guided Writing Lesson
10. **To increase knowledge of the rules of grammar and usage**
    - Build Grammar Skills: Adverb Clauses

Test Preparation

Reading Comprehension: Recognizing Cause and Effect (ATE, p. 339) The teaching tips and sample test item in this workshop support the instruction and practice in the unit workshop: **Reading Comprehension: Recognizing Cause and Effect; Predicting Outcomes** (SE, p. 377)

Guide for Reading

Pearl S. Buck *(1892–1973)*

Pearl Buck's novel *The Good Earth* not only won her a Pulitzer Prize, but also earned her $50,000 for the movie rights (which was a record sum at the time). In addition, the female lead in *The Good Earth* won an Academy Award for best actress.

Living in Two Worlds Most of Buck's work, including the novel *The Good Earth* and the story "The Good Deed," focuses on China, its people, and its traditions. Although Buck was born to American parents in West Virginia, she spent most of her first forty years in China. Her father was a missionary in the Chinese countryside, and she and her sister grew up speaking both Chinese and English and playing with Chinese friends.

Buck married an American who taught at the university in Nanking, and she became an English teacher in local high schools. Because of circumstances in China and her personal life, she began spending extended periods of time in the United States.

Life as a Writer By the late 1930's, Chinese politics as well as an impending divorce from her husband brought Pearl Buck back to the United States permanently. She decided to support herself and her daughter by writing, and her first book was published to some acclaim. Her next book, *The Good Earth,* made her an overnight success. It also influenced American thinking about China and Chinese culture, erasing many old, untrue stereotypes. In 1938, Buck became the first woman to win the Nobel Prize for Literature.

◆ Build Vocabulary

LATIN WORD ROOTS: *-pel-*

As recently as fifty years ago, young men and women in China had their spouses chosen for them by their elders. Whether or not they loved the other person, they were *compelled* to marry that person. The verb *compel* includes the root *-pel-*, which means "drive" or "push." The Latin root *-pel-* helps you determine that the word *compel* means "to push to do something." The idea of being compelled to marry someone is an important factor in this story.

WORD BANK

As you read this story, you will encounter the words on this list. Each word is defined on the page where it first appears. Preview the list before you read.

contemplatively
revere
compelled
abashed
repressed
indignantly
assailed
expedition
conferred

◆ Build Grammar Skills

ADVERB CLAUSES

An **adverb clause** is a subordinate clause—a group of words that contains a subject and a verb but cannot stand by itself as a complete sentence—that modifies a verb, an adjective, or an adverb. Adverb clauses clarify information in other clauses by telling *where, when, why, how, to what extent,* or *under what conditions* actions occur. Adverb clauses are introduced by subordinating conjunctions such as *when, whenever, where, although, because, since, if, as,* and *while.*

main clause / adv. clause

She took up that magazine | when her daughter-in-law came in . . .

In this example from "The Good Deed," the adverb clause clarifies *when* the old woman took up the magazine.

Prentice Hall Literature Program Resources

REINFORCE / RETEACH / EXTEND

Selection Support Pages
Build Vocabulary: Word Roots: *-pel-*, p. 105
Build Grammar Skills: Adverb Clauses, p. 106
Reading Strategy: Make Inferences About Character, p. 107
Literary Focus: Static and Dynamic Characters, p. 108

Strategies for Diverse Student Needs, p. 26

Beyond Literature
Multicultural Connection: Dating Customs, p. 26

Formal Assessment Selection Test, pp. 88–90; Assessment Resources Software

Alternative Assessment, p. 26

Resource Pro CD-ROM

Listening to Literature Audiocassettes

The Good Deed

◆ Literature and Your Life

Connect Your Experience

Starting a new school, joining a new club, moving to a new neighborhood—you might feel uncertainty in any of these situations. Just imagine how uncertain Mrs. Pan, the central character in this story, must feel after moving away from China late in her life to live with her son in New York City.

Thematic Focus: Fateful Moments

For Mrs. Pan, moving to New York City is a major turning point that opens the door to a new life. As you read, you may find yourself thinking about how moving to a distant place would change your life.

Journal Writing Mrs. Pan eventually makes adjustments that help her enjoy her new life. Make a list of ways that you can help yourself deal with a new situation and even enjoy the experience.

◆ Background for Understanding

Culture

In "The Good Deed," an elderly Chinese woman tries to arrange a marriage between two young Chinese Americans. Arranged marriages have been a tradition in China as well as in many other countries. Parents choose their children's spouse; then they engage in negotiations with the parents of the prospective bride or groom. In modern China, many young people choose marriage partners based on common interests and mutual attraction, but arranged marriages still do take place, especially in the countryside.

◆ Literary Focus

Static and Dynamic Characters

Adjusting to life in a new home is likely to bring about important changes in a character. These experiences help the person to change and grow. A character that changes during the course of a literary work is known as a **dynamic character**. The changes dynamic characters undergo affect their attitudes and beliefs. A **static character** does not change.

Notice the changes in the characters—especially in Mrs. Pan—in "The Good Deed." Think about how the change helps her grow.

◆ Reading Strategy

Draw Inferences

Writers rarely announce that a character is changing or state directly that a character is happy or sad. Instead, you must **draw inferences**—logical assumptions—about the characters based on what they say and how they act. For example, young Mr. Pan saves his money and risks his life to help his mother escape from the dangers she faces in China to come to live safely with him. Buck never writes the words "Mr. Pan loves his mother," but based on the evidence, you can infer that he does.

Use a graphic organizer like the one shown below to record your observations and draw inferences about the characters.

Words	Actions
	Mr. Pan risks his life to help his mother escape from China.

Inference
Mr. Pan loves his mother.

Test Preparation Workshop

Reading Comprehension: Recognizing Cause and Effect

Students need to recognize cause and effect for the reading comprehension section of the ACT test. Tell them that as they tackle test questions, it is best to go back and look for specific details that support the best answers. Use this sample.

> She was a decent, plain, good girl and, left to herself, Mrs. Pan could predict, nothing at all would happen. She would wither away like a dying flower. Old Mrs. Pan forgot herself and for the first time since she had been hurried away from the village without even being allowed to stop and see that the salted cabbage, drying on ropes across the big courtyard, was brought in for the winter.

Mrs. Pan forgets herself because—

A she is unhappy about the girl's looks
B she can think only of the salted cabbage
C she regrets hasty departures
D she is thinking about someone else

Guide students to see that the passage focuses on Mrs. Pan's reaction to the girl (the cause), and that the effect of her interest is *D*, to forget herself.

Discuss with students informal match-making. What do they think of "blind dates"? Are people who try to "fix up" others doing a good deed, or interfering in other people's lives? Encourage students to consider the pros and cons of such arrangements. Also encourage them to keep an open mind as they read about the custom of matchmaking—practiced in China and other cultures from ancient times—carried forward in this story by an old woman who finds herself settled in a new land.

Connecting Themes Across Cultures

Lead students to notice that old Mrs. Pan will not compromise her Chinese cultural values in her new country. She is able to keep them because she lives in a Chinese enclave in the United States. Have students brainstorm for situations in which Americans abroad would be able to maintain their ways and customs in a foreign country.

Customize for
Less Proficient Readers

Less proficient readers may have a hard time sustaining their reading efforts through the length of this story. Also, certain details, such as the many views of marriage expressed along the way, may puzzle them. Break the story into sections and assign by sections. Thus, students can find success in completing smaller reading tasks. Have them summarize the plot as they complete each section.

Customize for
Pre-AP Students

Encourage students to gather information on Chinese culture and political history as they read. Have them find out in greater detail the political events that caused old Mrs. Pan to emigrate to the United States.

Customize for
English Language Learners

Suggest that students listen to the recording of the story as they follow in their texts. Have them place sticky notes on words that they don't understand so that after they listen, they can return to those words for clarification.

Develop Understanding

One-Minute Insight Through her good deed, the old woman in this story joins the traditional to the modern. When her son brings her from China to New York, Mrs. Pan at first feels profoundly homesick. Her spirits lift, however, once she discovers and sets a purpose for herself: to arrange a satisfactory marriage for Lili Yang, the only young person who has taken the time to speak to Mrs. Pan in her own language. The matchmaking effort proves successful not only for the young people involved but, also for Mrs. Pan, who discovers she can make a mark in her newly adopted country without abandoning the ways of her cherished homeland.

Comprehension Check ☑

❶ What has Mr. Pan done to help his mother? Why did he take this action? *He brought her from China to New York. Her life was in danger because of political changes in China.*

◆ Reading Strategy

❷ **Make Inferences About Character** What do the words Mrs. Pan tells her son reveal about her feelings and thoughts? *Some students may say that Mrs. Pan's words reveal how acutely homesick and unhappy she is. Others may say that they reveal her stubbornness or resentment—she suggests she would rather die than live in New York.*

▶Critical Viewing◀

❸ **Connect** *Students might say that judging by the women's traditional style of dress, they seem closer to old Mrs. Pan's experience than to her son's.*

The Good Deed

Pearl S. Buck

❶ Mr. Pan was worried about his mother. He had been worried about her when she was in China, and now he was worried about her in New York, although he had thought that once he got her out of his ancestral village in the province of Szechuen and safely away from the local bullies, who took over when the distant government fell, his anxieties would be ended. To this end he had risked his own life and paid out large sums of sound American money, and he felt that day when he saw her on the wharf, a tiny, dazed little old woman, in a lavender silk coat and black skirt, that now they would live happily together, he and his wife, their four small children and his beloved mother, in the huge safety of the American city.

It soon became clear, however, that safety was not enough for old Mrs. Pan. She did not even appreciate the fact, which he repeated again and again, that had she remained in the village, she would now have been dead, because she was the widow of the large landowner who had been his father and therefore deserved death in the eyes of the rowdies in power.

Old Mrs. Pan listened to this without reply, but her eyes, looking very large in her small withered face, were haunted with homesickness.

❷ "There are many things worse than death, especially at my age," she replied at last, when again her son reminded her of her good fortune in being where she was.

He became impassioned when she said this. He struck his breast with his clenched fists and he shouted, "Could I have forgiven myself if I had allowed you to die? Would the ghost of my father have given me rest?"

"I doubt his ghost would have traveled over such a wide sea," she replied. "That man was

❸ ▶ Critical Viewing Do these women seem closer to Mr. Pan's experience or to his mother's? **[Connect]**

Block Scheduling Strategies

Consider these suggestions to take advantage of extended class time:

- Have students complete the journal activity in Literature and Your Life (p. 339). Then have them meet in small groups to discuss their lists.
- Introduce and reinforce the Build Grammar Skills lesson on pp. 338 and 354 by leading a brief discussion on the function of adverb clauses—to provide more information and add specificity to sentences. Then encourage students to find further examples of adverb clauses in the story and in their own pieces of writing.
- Ask small groups of students to select portions of the story to act out. Then have them listen to the selection on audiocassette so that they can model their portrayals of the characters on the readers' portrayals.
- Introduce the concept of static and dynamic characters. Have them read the Literary Focus on p. 339. After reading have them answer the Literary Focus questions on page 354. You may follow up with the Literary Focus page on Dynamic Character in ***Selection Support,*** p. 108.
- Have students work in discussion groups to answer the Critical Thinking questions on p. 354.
- Have students complete the Guided Writing Lesson on p. 355, using notecards for an elaboration strategy.

◆ Reading Strategy

❹ Make Inferences About Character What can students tell about Mrs. Pan from her remarks about the water? *Responses may include these: She finds it difficult to let go of her memories; because she feels that she does not belong in New York, nothing there seems right to her.*

◆ Build Grammar Skills

❺ Adverb Clauses Have students identify the two adverb clauses in this sentence and tell what words or phrases these adverb clauses modify. *"When they were in the same room with her" modifies* watched *and "when they were gone" modifies* glad.

Mother and Daughter: Leaf from a Manchu family album, Unidentified artist, The Metropolitan Museum of Art

always afraid of the water."

Yet there was nothing that Mr. Pan and his wife did not try to do for his mother in order to make her happy. They prepared the food that she had once enjoyed, but she was now beyond the age of pleasure in food, and she had no appetite. She touched one dish and another with the ends of her ivory chopsticks,[1] which she had brought with her from her home, and she thanked them prettily. "It is all good," she said, "but the water is not the same as our village water; it tastes of metal and not of earth, and so the flavor is not the same. Please allow the children to eat it." ❹

She was afraid of the children. They went to an American school and they spoke English very well and Chinese very badly, and since she could speak no English, it distressed her to hear her own language maltreated by their careless tongues. For a time she tried to coax them to a few lessons, or she told them stories, to which they were too busy to listen. Instead they preferred to look at the moving pictures in the box that stood on a table in the living room. She gave them up finally and merely watched them contemplatively when they were in the same room with her and was glad when they were gone. ❺ She liked her son's wife. She did not understand how there could be a Chinese woman who had never been in China, but such her son's wife was. When her son was away, she could not say to her daughter-in-law, "Do you remember how the willows grew over the

1. **ivory chopsticks:** Thin pair of sticks used as eating utensils.

◆ Build Vocabulary

contemplatively (kən tem′ plā tiv lē) *adv.:* In a thoughtful or studious way

Read to Be Informed

Whatever critics may have thought of Pearl Buck's writing, no one argued with her knowledge of China and its customs. She could not only speak Chinese, but she could think Chinese as well. Point out how Buck turns a custom, arranged marriage, which most Americans view with some hostility, into a rather charming and acceptable idea. She doesn't plead for it or promote it, but she places it in a cultural context that she knew well.

Customize for *Less Proficient Readers*

Since much of this story reflects Mrs. Pan's perspective, students may have difficulty with some of the descriptions. Guide students to understand that the moving pictures in the box describes a television, and that a Chinese woman who had never been to China is a woman of Chinese heritage who was brought up in America.

Customize for *Visual/Spatial Learners*

Have these students devise a graphic organizer that they can use to note changes in Mrs. Pan, a dynamic character. Invite the students to share their finished charts with the class.

Humanities: Art

Mother and Daughter, Leaf from a Manchu family album.

Manchu warriors frequently invaded China in the 1600's. They conquered northern China in 1644 and remained the ruling dynasty in China until 1912.

In the illustration, the Manchu mother and daughter are posed in a stiff and formal manner. While Mrs. Pan in "The Good Deed" lives in the United States in modern times, she clings to the traditional formal ways of her native China.

1. What might the similarity between mother and daughter indicate about the old Manchu culture? Would Mrs. Pan approve or disapprove of this cultural trait? *Children were expected to emulate their parents rather than develop their own individual styles. Mrs. Pan would have approved.*
2. Is Lili more like the daughter in the illustration, or a modern American daughter? Explain. *Lili is an independent young woman, yet she respects traditional Chinese culture.*

◆ Critical Thinking

❶ **Interpret** Ask students: What do you think Mr. Pan means when he says that the children were not taught as he was in China? Why is this difficult for Mrs. Pan to accept? *Mr. Pan seems to be making an excuse for lax discipline, implying that Americans don't value the kind of discipline he had. To Mrs. Pan, children's lack of obedience is unimaginable and unacceptable.*

◆ Critical Thinking

❷ **Infer** Point out that feeling lonely and useless is the most difficult aspect of Mrs. Pan's new life. Based on this information, what can students assume about the life she left behind in China? *Students should infer that Mrs. Pan's life was busy and productive.*

◆ Literature and Your Life

❸ Ask students if they think they might have feelings similar to Mrs. Pan's if they moved to a distant place. If so, in what ways? *Some students may say that they would miss their friends, neighbors, and community. Others may say that, like Mrs. Pan, they would miss the ease and independence that come with knowing how things are done in a familiar place.*

◆ Reading Strategy

❹ **Make Inferences About Character** What inference can students make about Mr. Pan from this conversation? *Inferences may include that he cares deeply about his mother's well-being and that he has a sensitive understanding of her needs.*

◆ Critical Thinking

❺ **Interpret** Ask students what point they think the author is making. *Students should note that Mrs. Pan and her daughter-in-law react very differently to what is probably an American fashion magazine, revealing that their tastes reflect cultural differences.*

gate?" For her son's wife had no such memories. She had grown up here in the city and she did not even hear its noise. At the same time, though she was so foreign, she was very kind to the old lady, and she spoke to her always in a gentle voice, however she might shout at the children, who were often disobedient.

The disobedience of the children was another grief to old Mrs. Pan. She did not understand how it was that four children could all be disobedient, for this meant that they had never been taught to obey their parents and revere their elders, which are the first lessons a child should learn.

"How is it," she once asked her son, "that the children do not know how to obey?"

❶ Mr. Pan had laughed, though uncomfortably. "Here in America the children are not taught as we were in China," he explained.

"But my grandchildren are Chinese nevertheless," old Mrs. Pan said in some astonishment.

"They are always with Americans," Mr. Pan explained. "It is very difficult to teach them."

Old Mrs. Pan did not understand, for Chinese and Americans are different beings, one on the west side of the sea and one on the east, and the sea is always between. Therefore, why should they not continue to live apart even in the same city? She felt in her heart that the children should be kept at home and taught those things which must be learned, but she said nothing. She felt lonely and there was no one who understood the things she felt and she was quite use- ❷
less. That was the most difficult thing: She was
❸ of no use here. She could not even remember which spout the hot water came from and which brought the cold. Sometimes she turned on one and then the other, until her son's wife came in briskly and said, "Let me, Mother."

So she gave up and sat uselessly all day, not by the window, because the machines and the many people frightened her. She sat where she could not see out; she looked at a few books, and day by day she grew thinner and thinner until Mr. Pan was concerned beyond endurance.

One day he said to his wife, "Sophia, we must
❹ do something for my mother. There is no use in saving her from death in our village if she dies here in the city. Do you see how thin her hands are?"

"I have seen," his good young wife said. "But what can we do?"

"Is there no woman you know who can speak Chinese with her?" Mr. Pan asked. "She needs to have someone to whom she can talk about the village and all the things she knows. She cannot talk to you because you can only speak English, and I am too busy making our living to sit and listen to her."

Young Mrs. Pan considered. "I have a friend," she said at last, "a schoolmate whose family compelled her to speak Chinese. Now she is a social worker here in the city. She visits families in Chinatown and this is her work. I will call her up and ask her to spend some time here so that our old mother can be happy enough to eat again."

"Do so," Mr. Pan said.

That very morning, when Mr. Pan was gone, young Mrs. Pan made the call and found her friend, Lili Yang, and she explained everything to her.

"We are really in very much trouble," she said finally. "His mother is thinner every day, and she is so afraid she will die here. She has made us promise that we will not bury her in foreign soil but will send her coffin back to the ancestral village. We have promised, but can we keep this promise, Lili? Yet I am so afraid, because I think she will die, and Billy will think he must keep his promise and he will try to take the coffin back and then he will be killed. Please help us, Lili."

Lili Yang promised and within a few days she came to the apartment and young Mrs. Pan led her into the inner room, which was old Mrs. Pan's room and where she always sat, wrapped in her satin coat and holding a magazine at whose pictures she did not care to look. She took up that magazine when her daughter-in-law came in, because she did not want to hurt her feelings, but the pictures frightened her. The

◆ Build Vocabulary

revere (ri vir′) *v.*: Regard with deep respect and love

compelled (kəm peld′) *v.*: Forced to do something

Cross-Curricular Connection: Social Studies

China's Political Climate "The Good Deed" is set against a backdrop of decades of political instability, civil war, and revolution in China.

In 1912, China's last emperor gave up his throne following a prolonged popular uprising. Over the years that followed, the new Nationalist party government was besieged by troubles as foreign powers, provincial war-lords, and a growing Communist movement all struggled to gain control of all or parts of the country. Finally, in 1949, Communist forces drove Nationalist forces from power. It is during the years immediately after this Communist takeover—while the party was consolidating its control over China—that Mrs. Pan fled China to join her son in the U. S.

- Challenge students to find a detail in the story (other than references to the political situation in China) that helps establish when it is set.
- Have students research leaders and their roles in the history of 20th-century China: Sun Yat-sen; Chiang Kai-shek; Mao Zedong.
- Encourage students to gather information on current political and economic conditions in China and report their findings to the class.

women looked bold and evil, their bosoms bare, and sometimes they wore only a little silk stuff over their legs and this shocked her. She wondered that her son's wife would put such a magazine into her hands, but she did not ask questions. There would have been no end to them had she once begun, and the ways of foreigners did not interest her. Most of the time she sat silent and still, her head sunk on her breast, dreaming of the village, the big house there where she and her husband had lived together with his parents and where their children were born. She knew that the village had fallen into the hands of their enemies and that strangers lived in the house, but she hoped even so that the land was tilled.[2] All that she remembered was the way it had been when she was a young woman and before the evil had come to pass.

She heard now her daughter-in-law's voice, "Mother, this is a friend. She is Miss Lili Yang. She has come to see you."

Old Mrs. Pan remembered her manners. She tried to rise but Lili took her hands and begged her to keep seated.

"You must not rise to one so much younger," she exclaimed.

Old Mrs. Pan lifted her head. "You speak such good Chinese!"

"I was taught by my parents," Lili said. She sat down on a chair near the old lady.

Mrs. Pan leaned forward and put her hand on Lili's knee. "Have you been in our own country?" she asked eagerly.

Lili shook her head. "This is my sorrow. I have not and I want to know about it. I have come here to listen to you tell me."

"Excuse me," young Mrs. Pan said, "I must prepare the dinner for the family."

She knew that the village had fallen into the hands of their enemies . . .

She slipped away so that the two could be alone and old Mrs. Pan looked after her sadly. "She never wishes to hear; she is always busy."

"You must remember in this country we have no servants," Lili reminded her gently.

"Yes," old Mrs. Pan said, "and why not? I have told my son it is not fitting to have my daughter-in-law cooking and washing in the kitchen. We should have at least three servants: one for me, one for the children and one to clean and cook. At home we had many more but here we have only a few rooms."

Lili did not try to explain. "Everything is different here and let us not talk about it," she said. "Let us talk about your home and the village. I want to know how it looks and what goes on there."

Old Mrs. Pan was delighted. She smoothed the gray satin of her coat as it lay on her knees and she began.

"You must know that our village lies in a wide valley from which the mountains rise as sharply as tiger's teeth." ❼

"Is it so?" Lili said, making a voice of wonder.

"It is, and the village is not a small one. On the contrary, the walls encircle more than one thousand souls, all of whom are relatives of our family."

"A large family," Lili said.

"It is," old Mrs. Pan said, "and my son's father was the head of it. We lived in a house with seventy rooms. It was in the midst of the village. We had gardens in the courtyards. My own garden contained also a pool wherein are aged goldfish, very fat. I fed them millet[3] and they knew me." ❽

"How amusing." Lili saw with pleasure that the old lady's cheeks were faintly pink and that her large beautiful eyes were beginning to shine and glow. "And how many years did you live there, Ancient One?"

2. **tilled** (tild) *v.*: Plowed and fertilized to be ready for planting.

3. **millet** (mil′ it) *n.*: Food grain.

◆ Reading Strategy

❻ Make Inferences About Character What inferences can students make about Lili, based on her first words to Mrs. Pan? *Suggested responses: She is respectful and courteous; she has an understanding of Chinese customs.*

◆ Literary Focus

❼ Static and Dynamic Characters Ask students whether they think Mrs. Pan shows signs of change in this part of her conversation with Lili. *Some students may say yes—whereas Mrs. Pan was unhappy and listless before, she is now delighted and animated; others may say no—her delight in talking about her village shows that she continues to have more interest in her old life than in her new one.*

◆ Critical Thinking

❽ Infer Ask: What does this description reveal about Mrs. Pan and her life in China? How does it help you to understand her character? *Suggested response: The description reveals that Mrs. Pan and her family lived a wealthy and comfortable life. Knowing what she has lost makes it easier to understand her difficulty in and her resistance to adjusting to life in the United States*

Customize for *English Language Learners*

Remind students that Lili and Mrs. Pan are supposed to be speaking in Chinese. "Ancient One" is Buck's translation of a respectful title that someone like Lili would have used when addressing the elderly woman.

Customize for *Gifted/Talented Students*

Have these students try telling the story from Lili Yang's point of view. They can begin the story from the moment Sophia Pan engages her to help old Mrs. Pan. Encourage them to imagine Lili's professional attitude toward helping out a depressed old woman. Then they can describe her meeting with Mrs. Pan from Lili's viewpoint.

Cross-Curricular Connection: Social Studies/Geography

China's Geography and Population Ask students the following "trick" question: "Is China the world's largest country? Vote yes or no." After students have voted, explain that either answer could be considered correct, depending on what is meant by "largest." With a population of over one billion, China is the largest country in terms of population. In terms of land area, it is the third largest, after Russia and Canada. Follow up by pointing out references to places within China in the story. These include *Szechuen,* the province where Mrs. Pan's ancestral village is located, *Shantung,* the province that is the ancestral home of the Lim family, and the cities of *Canton, Hangchow,* and *Soochow.* Have students locate each of these places on a map of China.

You might help students find the cities by providing these hints: Canton is near the southern coast of China; Hangchow and Soochow are near the city of Shanghai.

◆ Reading Strategy

1 Make Inferences About Character From her remark "I cannot be responsible for what other persons do, but I must be responsible for my own kind," students can infer that Mrs. Pan is responsible, lives by her sense of morality, and is community-minded.

◆ Literary Focus

2 Static and Dynamic Characters Ask: Do Mrs. Pan's words signal a change in her attitude or behavior? Why or why not? *Students may say that there is a change; she is taking action rather than withdrawing from life; she is taking an interest in something other than her past; she is now at least admitting to the reality of living in a foreign country.*

◆ Critical Thinking

3 Compare and Contrast Have students use this passage to compare and contrast Mrs. Pan's view of Chinese customs and traditions with Lili's view. *Students may point out that Mrs. Pan has an absolute belief in the customs; Lili seems sympathetic to the customs and the values they represent, but she also accepts that things are done differently in the United States.*

Customize for *Pre-AP Students*

Have Pre-AP students look back over the story to find examples of details or events related from one character's point of view. *Possibilities include "moving pictures in a box"—a television set from Mrs. Pan's point of view—and "bullies" and "rowdies"—those in power in China from Mr. Pan's point of view.*

"I went there as a bride. I was seventeen." She looked at Lili, questioning, "How old are you?"

Lili smiled, somewhat ashamed, "I am twenty-seven."

Mrs. Pan was shocked. "Twenty-seven? But my son's wife called you Miss."

"I am not married," Lili confessed.

Mrs. Pan was instantly concerned. "How is this?" she asked. "Are your parents dead?"

"They are dead," Lili said, "but it is not their fault that I am not married."

Old Mrs. Pan would not agree to this. She shook her head with decision. "It is the duty of the parents to arrange the marriage of the children. When death approached, they should have attended to this for you. Now who is left to perform the task? Have you brothers?"

"No," Lili said, "I am an only child. But please don't worry yourself, Madame Pan. I am earning my own living and there are many young women like me in this country."

1 Old Mrs. Pan was dignified about this. "I cannot be responsible for what other persons do, but I must be responsible for my own kind," she declared. "Allow me to know the names of the suitable persons who can arrange your marriage. I will stand in the place of
2 your mother. We are all in a foreign country now and we must keep together and the old must help the young in these important matters."

> ◆ Reading Strategy
> What do Mrs. Pan's words reveal about her character?

Lili was kind and she knew that Mrs. Pan meant kindness. "Dear Madame Pan," she said. "Marriage in America is very different from marriage in China. Here the young people choose their own mates."

"Why do you not choose, then?" Mrs. Pan said with some spirit.

Lili Yang looked abashed. "Perhaps it would be better for me to say that only the young men choose. It is they who must ask the young women."

"What do the young women do?" Mrs. Pan inquired.

"They wait," Lili confessed.

"And if they are not asked?"

"They continue to wait," Lili said gently.

"How long?" Mrs. Pan demanded.

"As long as they live."

Old Mrs. Pan was profoundly shocked. "Do you tell me that there is no person who arranges such matters when it is necessary?"

"Such an arrangement is not thought of here," Lili told her.

"And they allow their women to remain unmarried?" Mrs. Pan exclaimed. "Are there also sons who do not marry?"

"Here men do not marry unless they wish to do so."

Mrs. Pan was even more shocked. "How can this be?" she asked. "Of course, men will not marry unless they are compelled to do so to provide grandchildren for the family. It is necessary to make laws and create customs so that a man who will not marry is denounced as an unfilial[4] son and one who does not fulfill his duty to his ancestors."

3 "Here the ancestors are forgotten and parents are not important," Lili said unwillingly.

"What a country is this," Mrs. Pan exclaimed. "How can such a country endure?"

Lili did not reply. Old Mrs. Pan had unknowingly touched upon a wound in her heart. No man had ever asked her to marry him. Yet above all else she would like to be married and to have children. She was a good social worker, and the head of the Children's Bureau sometimes told her that he would not know what to do without her and she must never leave them, for then there would be no one to serve the people in Chinatown. She did not wish to leave except to be married, but how could she find a husband? She looked down at her hands, clasped in her lap, and thought that if she had been in her own country, if her father had not come here as a young man and married here, she would have been in China and by now the mother of many children. Instead what would

4. **unfilial** (un fil′ ē əl) *adj.*: Without the devotion of a son or daughter.

◆ Build Vocabulary

abashed (ə bashd′) *adj.*: Embarrassed

Beyond the Classroom

Career Connection

Social Work The character Lili Yang in this story is a social worker, and she works for the city's Children's Bureau; she serves the people of Chinatown by visiting families who need help.

The type of work that Lili does is known as casework, and her field is known as family and child welfare. Caseworkers in this field may help families obtain financial assistance or medical care. They may also counsel people on family issues such as child care, education, and adoption.

Have students gather more information about social work. Some students might report on other settings, such as hospitals, retirement communities, and homeless shelters that employ social workers. Others might contact a school of social work for information about higher education and career opportunities in this field.

become of her? She would grow older and older, and twenty-seven was already old, and at last hope must die. She knew several American girls quite well; they liked her, and she knew that they faced the same fate. They, too, were waiting. They tried very hard; they went in summer to hotels and in winter to ski lodges, where men gathered and were at leisure enough to think about them, and in confidence they told one another of their efforts. They compared their experiences and they asked anxious questions. "Do you think men like talkative women or quiet ones?" "Do you think men like lipstick or none?" Such questions they asked of one another and who could answer them? If a girl succeeded in winning a proposal from a man, then all the other girls envied her and asked her special questions and immediately she became someone above them all, a successful woman. The job which had once been so valuable then became worthless and it was given away easily and gladly. But how could she explain this to old Mrs. Pan?

Meanwhile Mrs. Pan had been studying Lili's face carefully and with thought. This was not a pretty girl. Her face was too flat, and her mouth was large. She looked like a girl from Canton and not from Hangchow or Soochow. But she had nice skin, and her eyes, though small, were kind. She was the sort of girl, Mrs. Pan could see, who would make an excellent wife and a good mother, but certainly she was one for whom a marriage must be arranged. She was a decent, plain, good girl and, left to herself, Mrs. Pan could predict, nothing at all would happen. She would wither away like a dying flower.

Old Mrs. Pan forgot herself and for the first time since she had been hurried away from the village without even being allowed to stop and see that the salted cabbage, drying on ropes across the big courtyard, was brought in for the winter. She had been compelled to leave it there and she had often thought of it with regret. She could have brought some with her had she known it was not to be had here. But there it was, and it was only one thing among others that she had left undone. Many people depended upon her and she had left them, because her son compelled her, and she was not used to this idleness that was killing her day by day.

Now as she looked at Lili's kind, ugly face it occurred to her that here there was something she could do. She could find a husband for this good girl, and it would be counted for merit when she went to heaven. A good deed is a good deed, whether one is in China or in America, for the same heaven stretches above all. 5

> *Yes, she grieved in the secret places of her heart . . .*

She patted Lili's clasped hands. "Do not grieve anymore," she said tenderly. "I will arrange everything."

"I am not grieving," Lili said.

"Of course, you are," Mrs. Pan retorted. "I see you are a true woman, and women grieve when they are not wed so that they can have children. You are grieving for your children."

Lili could not deny it. She would have been ashamed to confess to any other person except this old Chinese lady who might have been her grandmother. She bent her head and bit her lip; she let a tear or two fall upon her hands. Then she nodded. Yes, she grieved in the secret places of her heart, in the darkness of the lonely nights, when she thought of the empty future of her life. 6

"Do not grieve," old Mrs. Pan was saying, "I will arrange it; I will do it."

It was so comforting a murmur that Lili could not bear it. She said, "I came to comfort you, but it is you who comfort me." Then she got up and

4 Clarification Point out that Canton, Hangchow, and Soochow are all major cities in China.

◆ Critical Thinking

5 Interpret Encourage students to paraphrase Mrs. Pan's observation about a good deed. Then have them comment on its significance. *Paraphrases should resemble this: Helping others is important, no matter where you live; kindness is universally recognized. Students may note that, for the first time, Mrs. Pan sees a common thread in American and Chinese life. They may also note that Mrs. Pan's observation is reflected in the story's title.*

◆ Build Grammar Skills

6 Adverb Clauses Have students identify the adverb clause that appears in this sentence. Also have them identify the word that it modifies. *The adverb phrase is "when she thought of the empty future of her life." It modifies the verb grieved.*

Extending Word Study

Connotations Call students' attention to the word *confidence* in the first paragraph on the page. Ask them what confidence means and discuss varying definitions of the word. Point out that the connotation of the *confidence* in this context is that trust exists. Have students locate and explore the connotations of other words on this page, such as *arranged,* and *killing.* After they have had a chance to consider these words, hold a class discussion in which you guide them to completely understand the difference between the connotative and denotative meanings of these words. You may wish to extend this vocabulary study throughout the rest of the story.

Workplace Skills Mini-Lesson

Sensitivity to Others

This mini-lesson is designed to help students explore the value of interpersonal skills, including sensitivity to others, in the work setting.

Introduce Have students briefly discuss some ways in which Lili shows sensitivity and empathy toward Mrs. Pan when she is with her. Point out that "people skills" are important in her job as a social worker.

Develop Lead students to see that sensitivity to others is essential in any job that deals directly with people. Have students brainstorm for examples of summer or part-time jobs that fit this description (such as camp counselor and supermarket cashier). Then have them discuss how sensitivity to others might come into play in these roles.

Apply Have pairs of students role-play a situation in which they show sensitivity as part of an everyday work situation. Alternatively, they could role-play another interaction between Lili Yang and Mrs. Pan that demonstrates the positive results of showing sensitivity.

Assess In a class discussion, have students share what they learned as a result of their role-playing.

◆ Literary Focus

❶ Static and Dynamic Characters Have students explain the reason behind the change in Mrs. Pan. Elicit the following response: *She now feels that she has a purpose in life.*

❷ Clarify Help students to understand Mrs. Pan's remarks to her son about arranged marriages by letting them know that arrangements were taken very seriously; go-betweens were sometimes involved, and the bride's and groom's entire families played important roles. Suggest that students review earlier parts of the story to gather more facts and details about traditionally arranged marriages.

◆ Critical Thinking

❸ Infer What does the fact that Mr. Pan and Sophia fell in love but then allowed their marriage to be arranged indicate about them and their attitude toward traditional Chinese culture? *Suggested response: It shows that they respected their elders and traditional customs.*

Customize for
English Language Learners
Suggest that these students listen to the audiocassette as they follow in their texts. Have them use sticky notes to mark the words they don't understand and, after the recording, clarify those words for them. Students who are fluent in Chinese dialects might want to translate simple sentences or passages for the class.

went out of the room quickly because she did not want to sob aloud. She was unseen, for young Mrs. Pan had gone to market and the children were at school, and Lili went away telling herself that it was all absurd, that an old woman from the middle of China who could not speak a word of English would not be able to change this American world, even for her.

Old Mrs. Pan could scarcely wait for her son to come home at noon. She declined to join the family at the table, saying that she must speak to her son first.

❶ When he came in, he saw at once that she was changed. She held up her head and she spoke to him sharply when he came into the room, as though it was her house and not his in which they now were.

"Let the children eat first," she commanded, "I shall need time to talk with you and I am not hungry."

He repressed his inclination to tell her that he was hungry and that he must get back to the office. Something in her look made it impossible for him to be disobedient to her. He went away and gave the children direction and then returned.

"Yes, my mother," he said, seating himself on a small and uncomfortable chair.

Then she related to him with much detail and repetition what had happened that morning; she declared with indignation that she had never before heard of a country where no marriages were arranged for the young, leaving to them the most important event of their lives and that at a time when their judgment was still unripe, and a mistake could bring disaster upon the whole family.

❷ "Your own marriage," she reminded him, "was arranged by your father with great care, two families knowing each other well. Even though you and my daughter-in-law were distant in this country, yet we met her parents through a suitable go-between, and her uncle here stood in her father's place, and your father's friend in place of your father, and so it was all done according to custom though so far away."

❸ Mr. Pan did not have the heart to tell his mother that he and his wife Sophia had fallen in love first, and then, out of kindness to their elders, had allowed the marriage to be arranged for them as though they were not in love, and as though, indeed, they did not know each other. They were both young people of heart, and although it would have been much easier to be married in the American fashion, they considered their elders.

"What has all this to do with us now, my mother?" he asked.

"This is what is to do," she replied with spirit. "A nice, ugly girl of our own people came here today to see me. She is twenty-seven years old and she is not married. What will become of her?"

"Do you mean Lili Yang?" her son asked.

"I do," she replied. "When I heard that she has no way of being married because, according to the custom of this country, she must wait for a man to ask her—"

Old Mrs. Pan broke off and gazed at her son with horrified eyes.

"What now?" he asked.

"Suppose the only man who asks is one who is not at all suitable?"

"It is quite possible that it often happens thus," her son said, trying not to laugh.

"Then she has no choice," old Mrs. Pan said indignantly. "She can only remain unmarried or accept one who is unsuitable."

"Here she has no choice," Mr. Pan agreed, "unless she is very pretty, my mother, when several men may ask and then she has choice." It was on the tip of his tongue to tell how at least six young men had proposed to his Sophia, thereby distressing him continually until he was finally chosen, but he thought better of it. Would it not be very hard to explain so much to his old mother, and could she understand? He doubted it. Nevertheless, he felt it necessary at least to make one point.

"Something must be said for the man also, my mother. Sometimes he asks a girl who will not have him, because she chooses another,

◆ Build Vocabulary

repressed (ri presd′) *v.:* Held back or restrained

indignantly (in dig′ nənt lē) *adv.:* Feeling anger as a reaction to ungratefulness

Cross-Curricular Connection: Social Studies

Arranged Marriages Throughout history, in many cultures, the practice of arranging marriages has enabled families or countries to create advantageous social, economic, or political ties. Rulers often arranged marriages between their sons and daughters and the relative of a rival nation. In this way, they hoped to ensure peaceful relations between the two countries.

Arranged marriage is not a practice restricted to royalty. As Mrs. Pan explains in this story, arranged marriages were once common in China. Although today many young people choose whom they will marry, parents still might arrange a marriage; this practice is more common in rural areas. In Japan, also, arranged marriages were more common in the past than they are today, but some marriages are still arranged. In some cases, the bride and groom might not even meet before the wedding. In India, marriages are usually arranged by the parents, but the young person has the right to reject any arrangement. As the Pans discuss in this story, there are advantages and disadvantages to both arranged marriages and allowing young people to choose whom they will marry.

and then his sufferings are intense. Unless he wishes to remain unmarried he must ask a second girl, who is not the first one. Here also is some injustice."

Old Mrs. Pan listened to this attentively and then declared, "It is all barbarous.[5] Certainly it is very embarrassing to be compelled to speak of these matters, man and woman, face to face. They should be spared; others should speak for them."

She considered for a few seconds and then she said with fresh indignation, "And what woman can change the appearance her ancestors have given her? Because she is not pretty is she less a woman? Are not her feelings like any woman's; is it not her right to have husband and home and children? It is well-known that men have no wisdom in such matters; they believe that a woman's face is all she has, forgetting that everything else is the same. They gather about the pretty woman, who is surfeited with them,[6] and leave alone the good woman. And I do not know why heaven has created ugly women always good but so it is, whether here or in our own country, but what man is wise enough to know that? Therefore his wife should be chosen for him, so that the family is not burdened with his follies."

Mr. Pan allowed all this to be said and then he inquired, "What is on your mind, my mother?"

Old Mrs. Pan leaned toward him and lifted her forefinger. "This is what I command you to do for me, my son. I myself will find a husband for this good girl of our people. She is helpless and alone. But I know no one; I am a stranger, and I must depend upon you. In your business there must be young men. Inquire of them and see who stands for them, so that we can arrange a meeting between them and me; I will stand for the girl's mother. I promised it."

Now Mr. Pan laughed heartily. "Oh, my mother!" he cried. "You are too kind, but it cannot be done. They would laugh at me, and do you believe that Lili Yang herself would like such an arrangement? I think she would not. She has been an American too long." ❺

Old Mrs. Pan would not yield, however, and in the end he was compelled to promise that he would see what he could do. Upon this promise she consented to eat her meal, and he led her out, her right hand resting upon his left wrist. The children were gone and they had a quiet meal together, and after it she said she felt that she would sleep. This was good news, for she had not slept well since she came, and young Mrs. Pan led her into the bedroom and helped her to lie down and placed a thin quilt over her.

. . . he saw at once that she was changed.

When young Mrs. Pan went back to the small dining room where her husband waited to tell her what his mother had said, she listened thoughtfully.

"It is absurd," her husband said, "but what shall we do to satisfy my mother? She sees it as a good deed if she can find a husband for Lili Yang."

Here his wife surprised him. "I can see some good in it myself," she declared. "I have often felt for Lili. It is a problem, and our mother is right to see it as such. It is not only Lili—it is a problem here for all young women, especially if they are not pretty." She looked quizzically at her husband for a moment and then said, "I too used to worry when I was very young, lest I should not find a husband for myself. It is a great burden for a young woman. It would be nice to have someone else arrange the matter." ❻

5. **barbarous** (bär′ bə rəs) *adj.*: Uncivilized.

6. **is surfeited** (sur′ fit əd) **with them:** Has had enough of them.

Comprehension Check ☑

❹ Have students summarize the argument against American-style marriages that Mrs. Pan makes here. *She argues that men make the mistake of valuing women's looks over their inner qualities; in her view, such "follies" lead to unsound marriages.*

◆ Critical Thinking

❺ **Evaluate** Ask students whether they agree or disagree with Mr. Pan's opinion that Lili would not appreciate an arranged meeting. Encourage them to support their responses. *Students who agree may cite the reason Mr. Pan himself gives—"She has been in America too long." Those who disagree may cite the fact that earlier in the story, Lili was deeply moved by Mrs. Pan's talk of marriage and tradition.*

◆ Reading Strategy

❻ **Make Inferences About Character** Ask students what they can tell about the young Mrs. Pan from her remarks. *Students will probably infer from her remarks that Mrs. Pan is sensitive and empathetic; she can reach beyond her own circumstance to imagine the experience of someone else and judge it unfair.*

Customize for
Less Proficient Readers

Mrs. Pan uses a formal speech pattern and choice of words that may challenge less proficient readers. Assist these students in previewing some of the words on this page that are not commonly used in conversation. Use the footnotes to clarify *barbarous* and *surfeited.* Discuss with students synonyms for words like *compelled, inquire, follies.* You may wish to follow up by having students role-play or summarize the conversation in their own words.

Analyze Literary Criticism

Pearl Buck has always been considered a controversial author. Most critics think that her reputation as a writer will always rest on *The Good Earth* and that she never wrote anything else that equaled it. When she won the Nobel Prize in 1938, many critics were outraged that she beat out such writers as John Steinbeck and Ernest Hemingway (both of whom won in subsequent years).

Much of Buck's later fiction was written for women's magazines, and it has been described as "drippingly romantic." Buck said of her own writing, "The truth is I never write with a sense of mission or to accomplish any purpose whatever except the revelation of human character through a life situation." One of her critics wrote that "her weaknesses as a novelist included didacticism, sentimentalism, and an inability to control her energy long enough to explore deeply, revise, and improve."

Summarize Buck's evaluation of her work and that of her critics for students and have them discuss the contrasting views. Do they agree with Buck's assessment of her writing or not?

1. Do you find "The Good Deed" reveals human character through a life situation? *Students who appreciate Mrs. Pan's character traits and behavior will probably say yes. Students who do not relate to the circumstances of the story will probably say no.*
2. Would you think that this is one of Buck's better stories? Why? *Students may recognize that this story does not fit the description of "drippingly romantic."*

◆ Critical Thinking

❶ **Compare and Contrast** Have students analyze this passage and describe how marriage is the same and different in China and in the United States. *Responses may include this: Unhappy or unsuccessful marriages exist in both places, but in the United States such marriages frequently end in divorce.*

▶Critical Viewing◀

❷ **Compare** *Students may say that, like the stores they are used to, this one draws customers in with an attractive and colorful display of items.*

◆ Literary Focus

❸ **Static and Dynamic Characters** *For the first time, old Mrs. Pan is making a change in her behavior; by opening the curtains to the outside world, she is exhibiting curiosity about her new environment.*

▲ **Critical Viewing** How would you compare this Chinese store with the stores in which you shop? **[Compare]** ❷

❶ "Remember," he told her, "how often in the old country the wrong men are arranged for and how often the young men leave home because they do not like the wives their parents choose for them."

"Well, so do they here," she said pertly. "Divorce, divorce, divorce!"

"Come, come," he told her. "It is not so bad."

"It is very bad for women," she insisted. "When there is divorce here, then she is thrown out of the family. The ties are broken. But in the old country, it is the man who leaves home and the woman stays on, for she is still the daughter-in-law and her children will belong to the family, and however far away the man wants to go, she has her place and she is safe."

Mr. Pan looked at his watch. "It is late and I must go to the office."

"Oh, your office," young Mrs. Pan said in an uppish[7] voice, "what would you do without it?"

They did not know it but their voices roused old Mrs. Pan in the bedroom, and she opened her eyes. She could not understand what they said for they spoke in English, but she understood that there was an argument. She sat up on the bed to listen, then she heard the door slam and she knew her son was gone. She was about to lie down again when it occurred to her that it would be interesting to look out of the window to the street and see what young men there were coming to and from. One did not choose men from the street, of course, but still she could see what their looks were.

She got up and tidied her hair and tottered on her small feet over to the window and opening the curtains a little she gazed into the street really for the first time since she came.

◆ **Literary Focus** How do Mrs. Pan's actions indicate the beginning of a change in her character?

◆ Build Vocabulary

assailed (ə sāld′) *v.:* Attacked physically

7. **uppish:** Haughty or arrogant.

Speaking, Listening, and Viewing Mini-Lesson

Radio Interview

This mini-lesson supports the Speaking, Listening, and Viewing activity in the Idea Bank on p. 355.

Introduce Point out to students that it is beginning to be apparent that, despite the original impression that readers may have gotten, Mrs. Pan is a dynamic character, capable of changing to accommodate new circumstances. Have students suggest why old Mrs. Pan would make a particularly good subject for a radio interview.

Develop Before students prepare their interviews, suggest that they consider two kinds of questions—general questions to make the interviewee comfortable and queries designed to gain in-depth responses. Specifically, the interviewer will need to do the following:

- Start the interview by asking a few basic questions, such as "Why did you come to this country?"
- Ask questions that follow up on interesting aspects of Mrs. Pan's story.

Apply Have students prepare, practice, and complete their interviews. Encourage them to ask questions they have formulated and ones that come naturally to mind as the interview progresses.

Assess Have students evaluate their own and their classmates' interviews according to the following criteria: How effectively did the interviewer probe Mrs. Pan for interesting and fresh information? How well did the interviewer listen to and follow up on Mrs. Pan's responses?

She was pleased to see many Chinese men, some of them young. It was still not late, and they loitered in the sunshine before going back to work, talking and laughing and looking happy. It was interesting to her to watch them, keeping in mind Lili Yang and thinking to herself that it might be this one or that one, although still one did not choose men from the street. She stood so long that at last she became tired and she pulled a small chair to the window and kept looking through the parted curtain.

Here her daughter-in-law saw her a little later, when she opened the door to see if her mother-in-law was awake, but she did not speak. She looked at the little satin-clad figure, and went away again, wondering why it was that the old lady found it pleasant today to look out of the window when every other day she had refused the same pleasure.

It became a pastime for old Mrs. Pan to look out of the window every day from then on. Gradually she came to know some of the young men, not by name but by their faces and by the way they walked by her window, never, of course looking up at her, until one day a certain young man did look up and smile. It was a warm day, and she had asked that the window be opened, which until now she had not allowed, for fear she might be assailed by the foreign winds and made ill. Today, however, was near to summer, she felt the room airless and she longed for freshness.

After this the young man habitually smiled when he passed or nodded his head. She was too old to have it mean anything but courtesy and so bit by bit she allowed herself to make a gesture of her hand in return. It was evident that he belonged in a china shop across the narrow street. She watched him go in and come out; she watched him stand at the door in his shirt sleeves on a fine day and talk and laugh, showing, as she observed, strong white teeth set off by two gold ones. Evidently he made money. She did not believe he was married, for she saw an old man who must be his father, who smoked a water pipe, and now and then an elderly woman, perhaps his mother, and a younger brother, but there was no young woman.

She began after some weeks of watching to fix upon this young man as a husband for Lili. But who could be the go-between except her own son?

She confided her plans one night to him, and, as always, he listened to her with courtesy and concealed amusement. "But the young man, my mother, is the son of Mr. Lim, who is the richest man on our street."

"That is nothing against him," she declared.

"No, but he will not submit to an arrangement, my mother. He is a college graduate. He is only spending the summer at home in the shop to help his father." ❻

"Lili Yang has also been to school."

"I know, my mother, but, you see, the young man will want to choose his own wife, and it will not be someone who looks like Lili Yang. It will be someone who—"

He broke off and made a gesture which suggested curled hair, a fine figure and an air. Mrs. Pan watched him with disgust. "You are like all these other men, though you are my son," she said and dismissed him sternly.

Nevertheless, she thought over what he had said when she went back to the window. The young man was standing on the street picking his fine teeth and laughing at friends who passed, the sun shining on his glistening black hair. It was true he did not look at all obedient; it was perhaps true that he was no more wise than other men and so saw only what a girl's face was. She wished that she could speak to him, but that, of course, was impossible. Unless—

She drew in a long breath. Unless she went downstairs and out into that street and crossed it and entered the shop, pretending that she came to buy something! If she did this, she could speak to him. ❼ But what would she say, and who would help her cross the street? She did not want to tell her son or her son's wife, for they would suspect her and laugh. They teased her often even now about her purpose, and Lili was so embarrassed by their laughter that she did not want to come anymore.

Old Mrs. Pan reflected on the difficulty of her position as a lady in a barbarous and strange country. Then she thought of her eldest grandson, Johnnie. On Saturday, when her son was at ❽

◆ Literary Focus

❹ Static and Dynamic Characters Encourage students to compare the detail about Mrs. Pan's longing for fresh air with the earlier detail about her dislike of the water in New York. In what way do these details, considered together, reveal a change in Mrs. Pan? *Earlier, she rejected anything that did not remind her of home; now she seems more in harmony with her new surroundings.*

◆ Reading Strategy

❺ Make Inferences About Character Point out that Mrs. Pan makes inferences about the young man she has been watching. Have students identify these inferences as well as the "evidence" Mrs. Pan used to make them. *Mrs. Pan infers that the young man has money and that he is unmarried. The evidence she uses is his gold teeth and the fact that no one resembling a wife dropped by to see him.*

◆ Critical Thinking

❻ Analyze Cause and Effect Ask students to explain the basis upon which Mr. Pan assumes that Mr. Lim will not submit to an arranged marriage. *Students should recognize that Mr. Pan assumes that because Mr. Lim has a bright future and is eligible he has no reason to submit to an arranged marriage.*

◆ Critical Thinking

❼ Analyze Why is the thought of going downstairs and out into the street so terrifying to Mrs. Pan? *Suggested response: She is still afraid of her new environment and of the way people behave.*

◆ Critical Thinking

❽ Connect Have students summarize some of the reasons Mrs. Pan has for calling this country "barbarous." *She feels that people are undisciplined, unmannered, and ignorant of the proper ways of doing things.*

Beyond the Classroom

Career Connection

Retail Sales Like the young man in the story, some students may wish to consider jobs in retail sales. Sales people are required to dress neatly and be well-groomed. Some types of sales requires specialized training and knowledge, but good communication skills and the ability to deal with all kinds of people are probably the most important assets in any retail position. Math skills are also helpful in most retail sales jobs.

Retail positions are available in a wide variety of areas. Automobiles, clothing, food, and electronics are just a few retail areas. Salespeople sometimes advance to the position of manager. A manager needs patience and good organizational skills. Students should be aware that a high school diploma and further education in retailing and merchandising will further a career in sales. Students who think they might enjoy retail work can talk to salespeople about their responsibilities

◆ Literary Focus

❶ Static and Dynamic Characters *Mrs. Pan's plan to venture outside marks a significant change in her behavior and attitude. She is overcoming her fear and suspicions as well as her earlier feelings of "uselessness."*

◆ Build Grammar Skills

❷ Adverb Clauses Have students find two adverb clauses in this sentence and tell how they add to the sentence. *The clauses are* because he was a man *and* because she was not ill. *Both answer the question why.*

◆ Critical Thinking

❸ Compare and Contrast What qualities do young Mr. Lim and Lili share? *They are courteous and respectful toward Mrs. Pan.*

Comprehension Check ☑

❹ Ask students to explain why Mrs. Pan is glad that Mr. Lim is "not too handsome." *This makes him a better match for Lili, who is not beautiful.*

◆ Critical Thinking

❺ Compare Ask students what similarities they see between the way Mrs. Pan responds to young Mr. Lim and way she responded to Lili. *Students may note that she is comfortable talking about her past, as well as her feelings about living in a strange new place.*

◆ Critical Thinking

❻ Evaluate Ask students if they agree or disagree with Mrs. Pan's major points in this passage, and to explain why. *Many students will disagree that "beauty in a woman made virtue unlikely" and that plain women are grateful to their husbands for marrying them; some might state that Mrs. Pan's point of view is sexist, although it emerges from her cultural background.*

Customize for *Bodily/Kinesthetic Learners*

Ask these students to identify some physical reactions to stress. These may include trembling, increased heart rate, and sweaty palms. Tell students to relate Mrs. Pan's adventure to some challenge they have faced that produced these physical reactions. For Mrs. Pan, crossing the street to go to the shop was a feat of daring.

> **◆ Literary Focus**
> How is this event an example of what happens to a dynamic character?

❶ his office and her son's wife was at the market, she could coax Johnnie to lead her across the street to the china shop; she would pay him some money, and in the shop she would say he was looking for two bowls to match some that had been broken. It would be an expedition, but she might speak to the young man and tell him—what should she tell him? That must first be planned.

This was only Thursday and she had only two days to prepare. She was very restless during those two days, and she could not eat. Mr. Pan spoke of a doctor whom she indignantly refused ❷ to see, because he was a man and also because she was not ill. But Saturday came at last and everything came about as she planned. Her son went away, and then her son's wife, and she crept downstairs with much effort to the sidewalk where her grandson was playing marbles and beckoned him to her. The child was terrified to see her there and came at once, and she pressed a coin into his palm and pointed across the street with her cane.

"Lead me there," she commanded and, shutting her eyes tightly, she put her hand on his shoulder and allowed him to lead her to the shop. Then to her dismay he left her and ran back to play and she stood wavering on the threshold, feeling dizzy, and the young man saw her and came hurrying toward her. To her joy he spoke good Chinese, and the words fell sweetly upon her old ears.

"Ancient One, Ancient One," he chided[8] her ❸ kindly. "Come in and sit down. It is too much for you."

He led her inside the cool, dark shop and she sat down on a bamboo chair.

"I came to look for two bowls," she said faintly.

"Tell me the pattern and I will get them for you," he said. "Are they blue willow pattern or the thousand flowers?"

"Thousand flowers," she said in the same faint voice, "but I do not wish to disturb you."

"I am here to be disturbed," he replied with the utmost courtesy.

He brought out some bowls and set them on a small table before her and she fell to talking with him. He was very pleasant; his rather large face was shining with kindness and he laughed easily. Now that she saw him close, she was glad to notice that he was not too handsome; his nose and mouth were big, and he had big hands and feet. ❹

"You look like a countryman," she said. "Where is your ancestral home?"

"It is in the province of Shantung," he replied, "and there are not many of us here."

"That explains why you are so tall," she said. "These people from Canton are small. We of Szechuen are also big and our language is yours. I cannot understand the people of Canton."

From this they fell to talking of their own country, which he had never seen, and she told him about the village and how her son's father had left it many years ago to do business here in this foreign country and how he had sent for their son and then how she had been compelled to flee because the country was in fragments and torn between many leaders. When she had told this much, she found herself telling him how difficult it was to live here and how strange the city was to her and how she would never have looked out of the window had it not been for the sake of Lili Yang.

"Who is Lili Yang?" he asked.

Old Mrs. Pan did not answer him directly. That would not have been suitable. One does not speak of a reputable young woman to any man, not even one as good as this one. Instead she began a long speech about the virtues of young women who were not pretty, and how beauty in a woman made virtue unlikely, and how a woman not beautiful was always grateful to her husband and did not consider that she had done him a favor by the marriage, but rather that it was he who conferred the favor, so that she served him

8. **chided** (chīd′ əd) *v.:* Gently scolded.

◆ Build Vocabulary

expedition (eks′ pə dish′ ən) *n.:* Journey or voyage for a definite purpose

conferred (kən furd′) *v.:* Granted or bestowed

Cultural Connection

Community Connection

Resources for Recent Immigrants Ask students to suppose that old Mrs. Pan lives in your community. After a period of adjustment, she wishes to learn to speak English and to discover more about the practical aspects of life in her new country and community.

Encourage students to consult resources such as the library, community newspapers, and the Internet to find out the names and specific services of some local organizations and institutions that might assist recent immigrants like Mrs. Pan.

You might also have students find out if any of the local services provide volunteer opportunities. For example, does a local English language program have a need for tutors? Suggest that students write detailed descriptions of any volunteer opportunities they learn about and post their descriptions in your classroom or another area of your school.

Invite students with volunteer experience in this type of setting and/or those that try out the volunteer opportunities they researched to share their experiences with the rest of the class.

far better than she could have done were she beautiful.

To all this the young man listened, his small eyes twinkling with laughter.

"I take it that this Lili Yang is not beautiful," he said.

Old Mrs. Pan looked astonished. "I did not say so," she replied with spirit. "I will not say she is beautiful and I will not say she is ugly. What is beautiful to one is not so to another. Suppose you see her sometime for yourself, and then we will discuss it."

"Discuss what?" he demanded.

"Whether she is beautiful."

Suddenly she felt that she had come to a point and that she had better go home. It was enough for the first visit. She chose two bowls and paid for them and while he wrapped them up she waited in silence, for to say too much is worse than to say too little.

When the bowls were wrapped, the young man said courteously, "Let me lead you across the street, Ancient One."

So, putting her right hand on his left wrist, she let him lead her across and this time she did not shut her eyes, and she came home again feeling that she had been a long way and had accomplished much. When her daughter-in-law came home she said quite easily, "I went across the street and bought these two bowls."

Young Mrs. Pan opened her eyes wide. "My mother, how could you go alone?"

"I did not go alone," old Mrs. Pan said tranquilly. "My grandson led me across and young Mr. Lim brought me back."

Each had spoken in her own language with helpful gestures.

Young Mrs. Pan was astonished and she said no more until her husband came home, when she told him. He laughed a great deal and said, "Do not interfere with our old one. She is enjoying herself. It is good for her."

But all the time he knew what his mother was doing and he joined in it without her knowledge. That is to say, he telephoned the same afternoon from his office to Miss Lili Yang, and when she answered, he said, "Please come and see my old mother again. She asks after you every day. Your visit did her much good."

Lili Yang promised, not for today but for a week hence, and when Mr. Pan went home he told his mother carelessly, as though it were nothing, that Lili Yang had called him up to say she was coming again next week.

Old Mrs. Pan heard this with secret excitement. She had not gone out again, but every day young Mr. Lim nodded to her and smiled, and once he sent her a small gift of fresh ginger root. She made up her mind slowly but she made it up well. When Lili Yang came again, she would ask her to take her to the china shop, pretending that she wanted to buy something, and she would introduce the two to each other; that much she would do. It was too much, but, after all, these were modern times, and this was a barbarous country, where it did not matter greatly whether the old customs were kept or not. The important thing was to find a husband for Lili, who was already twenty-seven years old. 9

> *. . . these were modern times, and this was a barbarous country . . .*

So it all came about, and when Lili walked into her room the next week, while the fine weather still held, old Mrs. Pan greeted her with smiles. She seized Lili's small hand and noticed that the hand was very soft and pretty, as the hands of most plain-faced girls are, the gods being kind to such women and giving them pretty bodies when they see that ancestors have not bestowed pretty faces. 10

"Do not take off your foreign hat," she told Lili. "I wish to go across the street to that shop and

◆ Literary Focus

7 Static and Dynamic Characters Ask students to explain in specific terms why the following detail reveals that Mrs. Pan is a dynamic character: "this time she did not shut her eyes." *A possible response is that by opening her eyes to the world around her Mrs. Pan shows that her attitude about her new home is beginning to change; she is becoming more open and curious. This significant change in attitude marks her as a dynamic character.*

◆ Build Grammar Skills

8 Adverb Clauses Point out the two adverb clauses in this sentence. Help students see that the adverb clause *until her husband came home* modifies *said* and that the adverb clause *when she told him* modifies *came*, the verb in the first adverb clause. Both adverb clauses answer the question *when*.

◆ Literary Focus

9 Static and Dynamic Characters Have students explain the change in Mrs. Pan that this passage reveals. *Students should note her new willingness to adjust to modern times and a "barbarous country"; that is, she is adjusting her ways in response to her new situation.*

◆ Build Grammar Skills

10 Adverb Clauses Ask students to identify the adverb clauses in this sentence. *The clauses are* as the hands of most plain-faced girls are *and* when they see that the ancestors ... Also have students identify the word that each clause modifies. *The first clause modifies* soft and pretty; *the second clause modifies the participle* giving.

Research Skills Mini-Lesson

Readers' Guide to Periodical Literature

This mini-lesson supports the Researching and Representing activity on p. 355.

Introduce Tell students that when they conduct research for an assignment such as a multimedia presentation, they will probably find themselves using the *Readers' Guide to Periodical Literature* as a resource for current information. Many students will already be familiar with this resource (or something similar) that makes it possible to locate magazine articles on specific topics.

Develop For more than 90 years, the *Readers' Guide* has been the resource to turn to for locating articles in a wide range of popular publications. The guide provides references to articles in 240 publications. Borrow a copy of the print form of the guide from the library and encourage students to acquaint themselves with both the subject indexes and the title indexes. The *Readers' Guide to Periodical Literature* is also available in database form, and many libraries are able to provide this resource.

Apply Ask students to identify two subjects and one title for a search. Have them create a short bibliography of the periodical articles they find and decide which articles to review. They will be limited to the library's periodical subscriptions; however, encourage them to investigate whether the library has an interlibrary loan relationship with an institution that does subscribe to the periodical.

Assess Evaluate students on their ability to locate articles in diverse periodicals that really are relevant to their topics.

◆ Critical Thinking

❶ **Analyze** Ask students: What is ironic about this passage? *Suggested response: Lili is unaware of Mrs. Pan's real reason for wanting to go to the shop, which is to have Lili meet young Mr. Lim.*

◆ Reading Strategy

❷ **Make Inferences About Character** Lili blushes in response to young Mr. Lim's gallant compliment and frank gaze. From this, students may infer that she is feeling shy and nervous.

▶Critical Viewing◀

❸ **Speculate** *Students might imagine that these two people, like Mr. Lim and Mrs. Pan in a previous scene, are talking about their own country.*

◆ Critical Thinking

❹ **Infer** Ask students why Mrs. Pan is so cautious when talking about marriage. *Students may infer that she is wary of customs in this country and doesn't know if Mr. Lim will be open to her matchmaking plan.*

buy some dishes as a gift for my son's wife. She is very kind to me."

❶ Lili Yang was pleased to see the old lady so changed and cheerful and in all innocence she agreed and they went across the street and into the shop. Today there were customers, and old Mr. Lim was there too, as well as his son. He was a tall, withered man, and he wore a small beard under his chin. When he saw old Mrs. Pan he stopped what he was doing and brought her a chair to sit upon while she waited. As soon as his customer was gone, he introduced himself, saying that he knew her son.

"My son has told me of your honored visit last week," he said. "Please come inside and have some tea. I will have my son bring the dishes, and you can look at them in quiet. It is too noisy here."

She accepted his courtesy, and in a few minutes young Mr. Lim came back to the inner room with the dishes while a servant brought tea.

Old Mrs. Pan did not introduce Lili Yang, for it was not well to embarrass a woman, but young Mr. Lim boldly introduced himself, in English.

"Are you Miss Lili Yang?" he asked. "I am James Lim."

"How did you know my name?" Lili asked, astonished.

"I have met you before, not face to face, but through Mrs. Pan," he said, his small eyes twinkling. "She has told me more about you than she knows."

Lili blushed. "Mrs. Pan is so old-fashioned," she murmured. "You must not believe her."

"I shall only believe what I see for myself," he said gallantly. He looked at her frankly and Lili kept blushing. Old Mrs. Pan had not done her justice, he thought. The young woman had a nice, round face, the sort of face he liked. She was shy, and he liked that also. It was something new.

❷ ◆ **Reading Strategy** What can you infer about Lili from the way she acts?

Meanwhile old Mrs. Pan watched all this with amazement. So this was the way it was: The young man began speaking immediately, and the young woman blushed. She wished that she knew what they were saying but perhaps it was better that she did not know.

▲ **Critical Viewing** What do you think these people are saying? **[Speculate]** ❸

She turned to old Mr. Lim, who was sitting across the square table sipping tea. At least here she could do her duty. "I hear your son is not married," she said in a tentative way.

"Not yet," Mr. Lim said. "He wants first to finish learning how to be a Western doctor."

"How old is he?" Mrs. Pan inquired.

"He is twenty-eight. It is very old but he did not make up his mind for some years, and the learning is long."

"Miss Lili Yang is twenty-seven," Mrs. Pan said in the same tentative voice.

Viewing and Representing Mini-Lesson

Timeline

This mini-lesson supports the Researching and Representing activity in the Idea Bank on p. 355.

Introduce Have students reread the story and decide what elements of the story are most important. They might choose to identify those moments when characters change significantly or the meetings of various characters. They might simply chart the chronology of the story.

Develop After students decide which features they want on their timelines, point out that they might want to add colors to the various entries to distinguish among them or highlight particular happenings with color or an icon they develop.

Apply Provide paper, straight edges, colored pencils, or whatever materials students think they will need. Encourage students to make sure that events or features of similar importance receive the same visual treatment.

Assess Evaluate students' timelines on originality of concept and visual presentation. Make sure that the elements students have chosen for their timelines are of a similar nature or distinguished visually if they are not.

The young people were still talking in English and not listening to them. Lili was telling James Lim about her work and about old Mrs. Pan. She was not blushing anymore; she had forgotten, it seemed, that he was a young man and she a young woman. Suddenly she stopped and blushed again. A woman was supposed to let a man talk about himself, not about her.

"Tell me about your work," she said. "I wanted to be a doctor, too, but it cost too much."

"I can't tell you here," he said. "There are customers waiting in the shop and it will take a long time. Let me come to see you, may I? I could come on Sunday when the shop is closed. Or we could take a ride on one of the riverboats. Will you? The weather is so fine."

"I have never been on a riverboat," she said. "It would be delightful."

She forgot her work and remembered that he was a young man and that she was a young woman. She liked his big face and the way his black hair fell back from his forehead and she knew that a day on the river could be a day in heaven.

The customers were getting impatient. They began to call out and he got up. "Next Sunday," he said in a low voice. "Let's start early. I'll be at the wharf at nine o'clock."

"We do not know each other," she said, reluctant and yet eager. Would he think she was too eager?

He laughed. "You see my respectable father, and I know old Mrs. Pan very well. Let them guarantee us." ❺

He hurried away, and old Mrs. Pan said immediately to Lili, "I have chosen these four dishes. Please take them and have them wrapped. Then we will go home."

Lili obeyed, and when she was gone, old Mrs. Pan leaned toward old Mr. Lim.

"I wanted to get her out of the way," she said in a low and important voice. "Now, while she is gone, what do you say? Shall we arrange a match? We do not need a go-between. I stand as her mother, let us say, and you are his father. We must have their horoscopes read, of course, but just between us, it looks as though it is suitable, does it not?"

Mr. Lim wagged his head. "If you recommend her, Honorable Old Lady, why not?"

Why not, indeed? After all, things were not so different here, after all.

"What day is convenient for you?" she asked.

"Shall we say Sunday?" old Mr. Lim suggested.

"Why not?" she replied. "All days are good, when one performs a good deed, and what is better than to arrange a marriage?"

"Nothing is better," old Mr. Lim agreed. "Of all good deeds under heaven, it is the best."

They fell silent, both pleased with themselves, while they waited.

Guide for Responding

◆ Literature and Your Life

Reader's Response How do you think this experience will affect Mrs. Pan's life in the United States in the future?

Thematic Focus What, for you, is the most fateful moment in this story about Mrs. Pan? Why?

Group Discussion With a few other students, discuss ways in which the experience of a new immigrant student in your school could be made easier and more comfortable. List your ideas and share them with the other groups in the class.

☑ Check Your Comprehension

1. In the beginning of the story, why can't Mrs. Pan sleep or eat properly?
2. What important idea does Mrs. Pan come up with when she meets Lili Yang?
3. What are two reasons why Mrs. Pan goes to the shop across the street?
4. What is the outcome of Mrs. Pan's visits to the shop across the street?

◆ Critical Thinking

❺ Interpret How does the date that Mr. Lim proposes represent a blend of old and new ways? *Students should note that young Mr. Lim reminds Lili that they have the older people's blessing. They should also note that it is equally true that the date was arranged in the old, traditional way and that the young people, who were truly interested in each other, arranged it on their own.*

Reinforce and Extend

Answers

◆ Literature and Your Life

Reader's Response Students might answer that the successful matchmaking experience might open doors for Mrs. Pan, making her more outgoing and happy.

Thematic Focus Possible fateful moments include these: She first decides to make a match for Lili, she spots Mr. Lim; she pulls back the curtain; she ventures across the street.

☑ Check Your Comprehension

1. She is homesick.
2. She gets the idea of making a marriage match for Lili.
3. She came to buy two bowls and to see young Mr. Lim for herself.
4. Ultimately young Mr. Lim and Lili meet and arrange to go out on a date.

Reteach

For students who seem uncertain about the changes that have occurred in Mrs. Pan, refer back to the graphic organizer on p. 339 of their books. Encourage them to skim the story again for additional information. Then discuss with them how the words and actions provide a basis for them to draw inferences. Remind them that they must use their own experience to understand the words and action they observe. For further instruction, you may wish to use p. 26 in ***Strategies for Diverse Student Needs.***

Beyond the Selection

FURTHER READING

Other Works by Pearl S. Buck

The Good Earth
Dragon Seed
China as I See It

Other Works With the Theme of Moving to a New Place

Yellow Raft in Blue Water, Michael Dorris
Giants of the Earth, Ole Rolvaag

We suggest that you preview these works before recommending them to students.

INTERNET

The Internet provides an excellent opportunity for students to learn more about Pearl S. Buck and her work. Encourage students to visit the following Web site for information. Please be aware, however, that the site may have changed from the time we published this information.

http://www.cup.org/Books/conn/pearl.html

We *strongly recommend* that you preview the site before you send students to it.

Answers

◆ Critical Thinking

1. She feels displaced and useless in her new country. Her depression causes her to eat and sleep poorly.
2. Lili and Mrs. Pan both respect their heritage; Lili is more modern.
3. She can discuss her old country and both men show traditional respect for her.
4. Choosing one's own mate clashes with the custom of arranged marriages. Both cultures respect family bonds.
5. Students might say it is important to combine old and new ways—for example, reading classic literature but also using the Internet.
6. Students might think people should be free to choose their own partners; they may think that arranged marriages for religious or economic purposes are appropriate.

◆ Reading Strategy

1. Young Mrs. Pan is kind, respectful, and to some extent, traditional.
2. Lili is empathetic and sensitive and is respectful of her elders.
3. (a) They are interested in each other. (b) They plan a date.

◆ Literary Focus

1. Old Mr. Lim and young Mrs. Pan are static characters: their behavior and attitudes do not change.
2. She leaves the apartment and cheers up.
3. At the beginning of the story she is depressed, homesick, and unwilling to adapt; by the end she is more open and optimistic and has begun to reach out to others.

◆ Build Vocabulary

Using the Latin Root *-pel-*

1. c 2. b 3. a

Using the Word Bank

1. *Contemplatively*—thoughtfully; *contemptuously*—scornfully
2. *Compel*—force to do something; *ask*—to make a request
3. *Abashed*—embarrassed; *ashamed*—disgraced
4. *Repressed*—held back; *impressed*—affected the mind favorably
5. *Revere*—regard with deep respect; *respect*—admire or honor
6. *Indignantly*—angrily reacting to something that is not right; *insistently*—demandingly
7. *Assail*—to attack physically; *assist*—to help
8. *Conferred*—granted or bestowed; *inferred*—made logical assumptions

◆ Build Grammar Skills

Practice

1. Mrs. Pan (worried) <u>because Lili was not married.</u>
2. Mr. Pan (listened) <u>when his mother revealed her plan.</u>
3. Mrs. Pan (watched) <u>while they talked.</u>

Writing Application

Sample sentences:

1. Mrs. Pan decided to cross the street when she saw the young Mr. Lim.
2. Mrs. Pan's daughter-in-law spoke slowly to Mrs. Pan because she wanted to be clearly understood.
3. Young Mr. Lim met Lili Yang after Mrs. Pan made certain arrangements.

Grammar Reinforcement

For additional instruction and practice, use the lesson in the **Language Lab CD-ROM** on Varying Sentence Structure, and page 52 on Adverb Clauses in the *Writer's Solution Grammar Practice Book.*

Guide for Responding *(continued)*

◆ Critical Thinking

INTERPRET

1. Identify the causes of old Mrs. Pan's depression. How does her depression affect her physical health? **[Analyze]**
2. In what ways are Lili and Mrs. Pan similar? How are they different? **[Compare and Contrast]**
3. Why does Mrs. Pan enjoy her conversations with old Mr. Lim and his son? **[Draw a Conclusion]**
4. In what ways does the story reveal a clash of cultures? In what ways does it reveal similarities between cultures? **[Deduce]**

APPLY

5. Do you think it is important for people to hold on to the old as well as the new? Use details from life to support your answer. **[Apply]**

EVALUATE

6. In what situations, if any, would arranged marriages be appropriate in modern American society? Explain. **[Make a Judgment]**

◆ Reading Strategy

DRAW INFERENCES

You can learn a lot about characters by **drawing inferences**—logical assumptions—about them based on their words, thoughts, and actions.

1. What can you infer about young Mrs. Pan based on the fact that old Mrs. Pan likes her?
2. What can you infer about Lili based on her treatment of Mrs. Pan?
3. (a) What inferences can you make about Lili's and Mr. Lim's feelings about each other? (b) On what did you base your inferences?

◆ Literary Focus

STATIC AND DYNAMIC CHARACTERS

Mrs. Pan is a **dynamic character**, a character who changes during the course of a literary work. **Static characters** do not change.

1. Identify two static characters in this story. Explain.
2. What actions does Mrs. Pan take that show you she is changing?
3. How is Mrs. Pan's character different at the end of the story from her character at the beginning?

◆ Build Vocabulary

USING THE LATIN ROOT *-pel-*

Knowing that the Latin root *-pel-* means "to drive" or "to push," match each word that contains the root with its definition.

1. repel	**a.** drive forward
2. expel	**b.** drive out
3. propel	**c.** push away

USING THE WORD BANK: Definitions

Explain the difference between the following pairs of words.

1. contemplatively, contemptuously
2. expedition, expedite
3. abashed, ashamed
4. repressed, impressed
5. revere, respect
6. indignantly, insistently
7. assail, assist
8. conferred, inferred

◆ Build Grammar Skills

ADVERB CLAUSES

Pearl S. Buck frequently uses adverb clauses to tell *where, when, why, how, to what extent,* or *under what conditions* the actions in the story occur.

An **adverb clause** is a subordinate clause—a group of words that contain a subject and a ver but cannot stand alone—that modifie a verb, an adjective or an adverb.

Practice Copy the following sentences into your notebook. Underline the adverb clause and circle the word it modifies.

1. Mrs. Pan worried because Lili was not married.
2. Mr. Pan listened when his mother revealed her plan.
3. Mrs. Pan watched while they talked.

Writing Application Add one or more adverb clauses to make each sentence more specific and informative.

1. Mrs. Pan decided to cross the street.
2. Mrs. Pan's daughter-in-law spoke slowly to Mrs. Pan.
3. Young Mr. Lim met Lili Yang.

Build Your Portfolio

Idea Bank

Writing

1. Letters Write two letters from old Mrs. Pan to a friend who still lives in China. In the first letter, tell how you felt when you first arrived in the United States. In the second letter, explain how you felt after introducing Lili and James.

2. Story Segment Write a continuation of this story, telling of another adventure in which Mrs. Pan adjusts to an aspect of life in the United States.

3. Newsletter Create a newsletter that tells about events and services that would help a recent immigrant, like Mrs. Pan, to adjust to life in your community. **[Social Studies Link]**

Speaking, Listening, and Viewing

4. Unrehearsed Speech When James asks Mrs. Pan about Lili Yang, she launches into an unrehearsed speech. Have a partner ask your opinion on an issue and speak for a full minute on the topic.

5. Radio Interview Imagine that old Mrs. Pan is interviewed for a radio program about the experiences of recent immigrants. With a partner, develop questions and responses. Perform your interview for the class. **[Performing Arts Link]**

Researching and Representing

6. Multimedia Presentation Give a multimedia presentation that focuses on Chinese culture and traditions. Include in your presentation art, photos, maps, music, and, if possible, food. **[Social Studies Link]**

7. Timeline Create a timeline of the events in "The Good Deed." You may choose to represent the events as a series of quotations from the story, as illustrations, or in some other way.

Online Activity www.phlit.phschool.com

Guided Writing Lesson

Award Speech on a Character

Any number of characters from "The Good Deed" could win a community award for helping others in their Chinese American community in New York City. Write a brief **speech** introducing a story character to whom you would give an award. In your speech, identify the award, the character, and the reasons he or she is receiving the award. The following tips will help you create a clear picture of your award winner.

Writing Skills Focus: Create a Main Impression

Create a main impression that makes clear to your audience why the character is winning an award. First identify a quality—such as kindness, determination, or courage—that you would like your audience to recognize in the character. Then support this impression by sharing appropriate accomplishments, anecdotes, and insights.

Prewriting After you have decided on a character and an award, brainstorm for a list of qualities that relate to the award. Choose the quality you feel is strongest in the character and list accomplishments and experiences that demonstrate this quality.

Drafting You don't have to begin your speech by identifying your character. You may want to start building the impression first, naming the award, and then revealing the name of your character. However you choose to organize your speech, be sure to include details that are related only to the award and contribute to your main impression.

Revising Ask a partner to read your draft and identify the main impression he or she has of the character after reading your speech of introduction. Ask your partner how you can strengthen the main impression you want to create.

ASSESSMENT OPTIONS

Formal Assessment, Selection Test, pp. 88–90, and Assessment Resources Software. The selection test is designed so that it can be easily customized to the performance levels of your students.

Alternative Assessment, p. 26, includes options for less advanced students, more advanced students, verbal/linguistic learners, visual/spatial learners, logical/mathematical learners, and bodily/kinesthetic learners.

PORTFOLIO ASSESSMENT

Use the following rubrics in the ***Alternative Assessment*** booklet to assess student writing:
Letters: Comparison and Contrast Rubric, p. 103
Story Segment: Fiction Narrative Rubric p. 95
Newsletter: Technical Description Rubric, p. 115

Idea Bank

Following are suggestions for matching Idea Bank topics with your students' performance levels and learning modalities:

Customizing for *Performance Levels*
Less Advanced Students: 1, 7
Average Students: 2, 4, 6
More Advanced Students: 3, 5

Customizing for *Learning Modalities*
Visual/Spatial: 6, 7
Interpersonal: 5
Verbal/Linguistic: 4, 5
Logical/Mathematical: 7

Guided Writing Lesson

Elaboration Strategy Give each student 5 notecards to develop his or her speech. As they brainstorm for award-winning qualities, they can write each quality on a card. Then as they prepare to draft their speeches they can elaborate on the qualities on the corresponding cards and determine which of the qualities are strongest for their speeches.

For more prewriting, elaboration, and revision strategies, see *Prentice Hall Writing and Grammar.*

Writers at Work Videodisc
Students can hear Rudolfo Anaya talk about keeping an audience in mind on the videodisc segment for Ch. 3.

Play frames 23159 to 33243

Writing Lab CD-ROM
Have students complete the tutorial on Exposition. Follow these steps:

1. Have students use the cluster diagram tool to help them identify the main impression they want to create about their character.
2. Suggest that students use the revision checker for language variety

Prepare and Engage

LESSON OBJECTIVES

1. **To increase knowledge of other cultures and to connect common elements across cultures**
   - Connecting Themes Across Cultures (ATE)
2. **To express and support responses to the text**
   - Thematic Connection
3. **To read in order to research self-selected and assigned topics**
   - Idea Bank: Hall-of-Fame Placard
   - Idea Bank: Fitness Is Fundamental
4. **To plan, prepare, organize, and present literary interpretations**
   - Idea Bank: Sports Poem
5. **To speak clearly and effectively for a specific audience and purpose**
   - Speaking, Listening, and Viewing Mini-Lesson: Television Interview
   - Idea Bank: Virtual Reality One on One

Thematic Connection

Fateful Moments Have students identify the fateful moment in "The Good Deed," and compare it to the first Knicks' game. *The fateful moment occurs when Mrs. Pan helps Lili. Both events have far-reaching consequences: Mrs. Pan's match probably leads to marriage for Lili and a renewed sense of purpose for herself; the first Knicks' game leads to great success for the NBA.*

◆ Background for Understanding

Professional basketball debuted in 1896, when a group of players charged admission to cover the cost of renting a court in Trenton, New Jersey. From the proceeds, each player got $15; the captain got a bonus of $1!

Connecting Themes Across Cultures

Basketball has recently challenged baseball as the "national sport" of the U. S. Baseball, however, still reflects the American emphasis on diversity, excellence, and competition, and height is not an issue. Have students research other countries that have sports with which the country is identified. For instance, in Pakistan, much attention is given to badminton.

Connections to Today's World

NBA at Fifty: The Greatest Ever
Frank Deford

from Rare Air
Michael Jordan

Thematic Connection

Fateful Moments

Often we don't know a moment is fateful until after it occurs. For example, no one could have imagined how successful the National Basketball Association (NBA) would become when the first game between the New York Knicks tipped off on November 1, 1946.

Today, an NBA ticket is one of the hottest tickets in town! In celebration of fifty successful years, the NBA announced a list of the "50 Greatest Players," identifying the biggest superstars from 1947 to 1997.

The following selections capture some results of that fateful moment when the first NBA game was held. In "NBA at Fifty: The Greatest Ever," sportswriter Frank Deford introduces you to fifty basketball superstars who have each created their share of unforgettable moments. The excerpt from *Rare Air* gives an insight from one of those players, Michael Jordan.

The Birth of the NBA

The first professional basketball league was the six-team National League, formed in 1898. Other leagues, including the National Basketball League (NBL) and the Basketball Association of America (BAA), were formed in the 1930's and 1940's. However, it wasn't until November 1946 that the first NBA game was played. Today, basketball's popularity is at an all-time high. Superstars of the 1980's and 1990's—like Michael Jordan, Larry Bird, Magic Johnson, and Shaquille O'Neal—sent attendance and television ratings soaring into the record books. Individually and collectively, the fifty players on this list are all responsible for turning basketball into one of the most popular professional and recreational sports in the world.

FRANK DEFORD (1938–)

Frank Deford has been voted "Sportswriter of the Year" six times! This Baltimore native has written for *Sports Illustrated*, *Newsweek*, National Public Radio and ESPN Radio. Deford is also the author of eleven books—including his famous football novel *Everybody's All-American*, which was made into a movie.

MICHAEL JORDAN (1963–)

Amazingly, basketball superstar Michael Jordan was cut from his high-school team in his sophomore year! Jordan made the high-school team in his junior year and quickly became its star player. Today, Jordan has established himself as one of the greatest basketball players of all time. He has led his team to numerous NBA championships and has won many individual awards, including Most Valuable Player of the Year and Defensive Player of the Year.

NBA at Fifty: The Greatest Ever

Frank Deford

Sports is perhaps the only entertainment where we actually expect the best to be succeeded by someone better. If you suggested that anyone today could surpass Beethoven, or Shakespeare, or Caruso or Michelangelo, you'd be laughed at. But we accept it that athletes are always improving—and, of all sports, basketball seems to advance the most dramatically.

In that sense, basketball is like modern technology or science. But, in fact, it is quite the reverse. It is *not* improved technique which primarily makes for improved basketball players.

Rather, the best players—the stars on this list of the 50 greatest players in NBA history—are originals. They are unique and idiosyncratic.

Perhaps it's not fair to compare other sports, but, really, Mark McGwire swings for a home run pretty much exactly like Babe Ruth did 70 years ago. And John Elway throws a pass in the same magic way as Johnny Unitas or Sammy Baugh.

But the best basketball players seem to have invented themselves. The first time I saw big George Mikan, when I was a boy, or when I saw Elgin Baylor turning a horizontal move into a vertical one, or when I saw Earl Monroe yo-yoing at a little black college called Winston-Salem State, I just instinctively recognized that what I was seeing was seminal and pure. For lack of a better word . . . yes, it

The Fifty Greatest Players In NBA History 1947–1997

Kareem Abdul-Jabbar	Karl Malone
Nate Archibald	Moses Malone
Paul Arizin	Pete Maravich
Charles Barkley	Kevin McHale
Rick Barry	George Mikan
Elgin Baylor	Earl Monroe
Dave Bing	Hakeem Olajuwon
Larry Bird	Shaquille O'Neal
Wilt Chamberlain	Robert Parish
Bob Cousy	Bob Pettit
Dave Cowens	Scottie Pippen
Billy Cunningham	Willis Reed
Dave DeBusschere	Oscar Robertson
Clyde Drexler	David Robinson
Julius Erving	Bill Russell
Patrick Ewing	Dolph Schayes
Walt Frazier	Bill Sharman
George Gervin	John Stockton
Hal Greer	Isiah Thomas
John Havlicek	Nate Thurmond
Elvin Hayes	Wes Unseld
Earvin Johnson	Bill Walton
Sam Jones	Jerry West
Michael Jordan	Lenny Wilkens
Jerry Lucas	James Worthy

To capture students' interest, ask them to suppose they are putting together a basketball team that they hope will go all the way to the top. What qualities would they look for in individual players? Invite students to rank ten qualities they think a professional athlete should have, from most to least important. Here are some qualities to consider: *strong character, good attitude, individuality, intelligence, focus, speed, shooting ability, discipline, ball handling skills,* and *team spirit.* Let students know that in reading these essays they will have the opportunity to see what a major sportswriter and a basketball superstar think are the most winning qualities in a player.

Develop Understanding

◆ Critical Thinking

1 Compare and Contrast Have students summarize the difference Deford finds between the best basketball players and the best football and baseball players. *He finds the best basketball players to be unique, while the best football and baseball players do not distinguish themselves through their unique or individual styles.*

Customize for ***English Language Learners***
Some of these students may not be familiar with the basketball jargon sprinkled throughout these essays. Help them to "translate" terms such as *yo-yoing* (moving from one position to another repeatedly) and *get to the hole* (get to an opening in the other team's defensive formation).

Customize for ***Pre-AP Students***
Challenge learners to evaluate the *tone* of Deford's essay. Help students first isolate terms such as *blessed by God, superiority,* and *majesty* to identify Deford's worshipful tone. Ask students to consider whether Deford's reverent tone fits his subject matter, and why or why not.

Beyond the Classroom

Career Connection

Sportswriter In addition to writing articles and books on sports, Deford is a sports analyst on the radio.

Have interested students gather information about the requirements for a career as a sportswriter or sportscaster. Students can start by locating the biographies of famous sportswriters and sportscasters. They can also request catalogues from colleges and universities that have journalism programs.

Community Connection

Sports Areas Most communities have an area designated for sports, whether the area is a high-school gym, a park with a baseball diamond and basketball hoops, or a major sports arena that is the home of a professional team. Encourage students to visit their local sports areas and jot down their best and worst features. Students can later gather in small groups to compare their lists and make recommendations for how their sports areas could be improved.

◆ Critical Thinking

1 Infer Ask students to explain why Deford would recognize the best moves of the players he mentions even if he could not see their features. *He would recognize their best moves because each of them has a particularly individual style of play.*

2 Clarification Although he does not like having attention called to it, Michael Jordan is well-known for sticking out his tongue in concentration. Discuss with students that Deford is making the point that details like this are not as apparent in sports such as football or hockey, in which players' heads and often faces are covered with helmets or face guards. Deford also says that basketball players "perform so close to us." Discuss with students how television brings players of all sports closer to the spectators.

◆ Critical Thinking

3 Assess Ask students to weigh the importance of a single player or participant in any sport or group effort. Do students agree with Deford's assertion that in basketball, particularly, one player can be extraordinarily important? *Some students may agree, based on the statistic he cites; others may feel that in all team sports, victories and defeats are a group responsibility.*

▶ Critical Viewing ◀

4 Analyze *Details students might mention include Larry Bird's unique dribbling style and Shaquille O'Neal's look of concentration.*

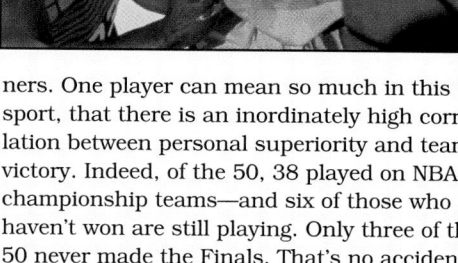

CONNECTIONS TO TODAY'S WORLD

was genius.

And most all of the 50 players selected are, in the Latin, *sui generis*—one of a kind. Put most of them in silhouette, and tell them to put on their best move, and I will recognize them. That's The Big O, that's Dr. J, that's
1 Kareem, that's Magic, that's Larry. It may be 30 years later, and while much of the sport may have improved altogether, nobody yet can put a shot softly off the glass like Sam Jones did. Trust me.

But, of course, it is not just their moves that distinguish the basketball elite. We feel like we know basketball players, for they perform so close to us. They have faces, not uniforms.
2 They have expressions, not numbers. We even know one tongue! There are 50 *people* on this list. Fifty friends.

3 Most of them can also be identified as winners. One player can mean so much in this sport, that there is an inordinately high corr lation between personal superiority and tean victory. Indeed, of the 50, 38 played on NBA championship teams—and six of those who haven't won are still playing. Only three of th 50 never made the Finals. That's no acciden

The 50 are blessed by God with talent anc possessed of their own desire and discipline. They are intelligent, most all of them and as extraordinary as they are, they know how to subjugate their own skill to their team.

But above all, to each his own special maje —which is why I think of these 50 more as artists than as athletes.

◀ **Critical Viewing** What details in these pictures of Larry Bird and Shaquille O'Neal show that the have the qualities Deford describes? **[Analyze]**

Speaking, Listening, and Viewing Mini-Lesson

Television Interview

This mini-lesson supports the Speaking, Listening, and Viewing activity in the Idea Bank on p. 361.

Introduce The key to a successful interview is preparation. An interviewer should have a basic understanding of the subject's field; he or she should brush up on special terms or issues related to that field; he or she should have a list of prepared questions.

Develop Before students stage their interviews, have them prepare questions using these guidelines:

- Questions that can't be answered with *yes* or *no* get better responses. These questions often begin with *who, what, when, where, why,* or *how.*
- Be prepared to ask follow-up questions to clarify confusing points or get more detail.
- Keep an audience's knowledge level in mind.

Apply Have students use these guidelines as they conduct their interviews. Remind them to make sure the subject is finished speaking before asking the next question or commenting on a response.

Assess Have students evaluate each other's interviews by answering these questions: How well suited were questions to audience knowledge level? How well prepared was the interviewer?

FROM Rare Air:

Michael on Michael

Michael Jordan

I always felt I could shoot. When I came out of college everyone said, "He can't shoot the jumper." I never had to. I could penetrate zones in college. And teams played me one-on-one at North Carolina. They never double-teamed me. I always had a quick enough first step to get to the hole. I never looked to be aggressive offensively in college because I was playing in a system and I was learning the game. ❺

That was the education I got from Dean Smith. Coming out of high school, I had all the ability in the world but I didn't know the game. Dean taught me the game, when to apply speed, how to use your quickness, when to use that first step, or how to apply certain skills in certain situations. I gained all that knowledge so that when I got to the pros, it was just a matter of applying the information. ❻

A lot of people say Dean Smith held me to under 20 points a game.

▲ **Critical Viewing** What do you think is going through the mind of the person trying to guard Michael Jordan in this photograph? **[Speculate]** ❼

◆ Critical Thinking

❺ Clarify Encourage students to use context clues to try to clarify these technical terms. Ask students what resources they might use to check their assumptions. *Students might use a book on basketball, a related site on the Internet, or they might ask a fellow student or a family member who follows basketball.* Then ask students who are particularly knowledgeable about basketball and its terminology to define the following terms for the class: *shoot the jumper; penetrate zones; double-teamed me.*

◆ Critical Thinking

❻ Compare and Contrast Have students compare Jordan's athleticism before and after his work with Dean Smith. *Before his work with Smith, Jordan was talented but unformed; after Smith, Jordan was able to combine his talent with the concrete skills Smith taught him to become a much better athlete.*

▶Critical Viewing◀

❼ Speculate *Students might suggest that the guard is probably unhappy and frustrated because Jordan is outmaneuvering him.*

Enrichment In January 1999, Michael Jordan announced his retirement from the NBA. At that time, he was celebrated by NBA Comissioner David Stern as "the greatest" to ever play the game. Jordan retired while still a champion. In fact, his last shot on an NBA court won the Chicago Bulls their sixth championship with Jordan.

Cross-Curricular Connection: Physical Education

The History of Basketball

James Naismith, a physical education instructor at what is now Springfield College, invented the game of basketball in 1891. He created the game to provide a challenging team sport that could be played indoors during the winter months. The first game was played with a soccer ball, and players tried to shoot the ball into a peach basket attached to the gym's balcony railing, about ten feet above the floor. The original rules were first published in the school's newspaper in 1892. The game quickly became popular, and some modifications followed: Metal hoops were replaced with net bags in 1893 and larger basketballs replaced the soccer balls; the backboard was added in 1894; bottomless nets were introduced in 1913.

The first intercollegiate basketball game using five-man teams was played between the University of Chicago and the University of Iowa. The game was played in Iowa City, Iowa, on January 16, 1896. The University of Chicago defeated the University of Iowa, with a score of 15–12.

◆ Critical Thinking

❶ **Evaluate** Michael Jordan claims that ability is the least important requirement for success as a professional basketball player. Have students debate this issue, relating their opinions now to the ranking they prepared in the beginning of this lesson.

◆ Critical Thinking

❷ **Interpret** Ask: What do you think Jordan means when he uses the word *heart* in this sentence? *Interpretations might include these: He means generosity toward himself and other players; he means to be focused, or to have your whole heart in what you're doing; he means a strong enough love of the game to carry him through tough situations.*

▶ Critical Viewing ◀

❸ **Connect** Students might suggest the following: *Jordan looks highly focused, he's looking directly at the ball; a viewer can conclude that he has his whole heart in what he is doing.*

Customize for
Bodily/Kinesthetic Learners
Invite the basketball players in your class to demonstrate some basic basketball moves and explain what makes them so difficult to master.

CONNECTIONS TO TODAY'S WORLD

Dean Smith gave me the knowledge to score 37 points a game and that's something people don't understand.

• • • •

If I was looking for players I would want around me, I'd look for quickness, heart, and strong fundamentals.
❶ Ability comes last. If you've got a good mind for the game, you can overcome the lack of ability in certain areas.

Look at Larry Bird. He's a prime example. He was slow. He couldn't jump that well. He had good hands, good ball handling and shooting skills. But he was very smart. He could outthink his opponents and he had a big heart.

Heart is probably the
❷ biggest key to success in basketball at this level. There are a lot of players who pass through the NBA with the ability, but they don't have the heart or the intelligence to get the job done. That's the divider, always has been.

Give me four guys of average ability with strong fundamentals and big hearts and I'll take my chances every time. Big games come down to those two things. The team that executes is usually the team that reaches inside for that little extra. I want those kinds of guys with me.

▲ Critical Viewing How does this picture of Michael Jordan show what it means to have heart? **[Connect]**

Cross-Curricular Connection: Social Studies

The Making of a Basketball How is a basketball made? An official NBA ball starts with a piece of top-grade cowhide, prepared by a tanning process (a process that turns cowhide into leather) that goes back to the days of cave-dwellers. The hide is then imprinted with tiny pebbles to give it the right texture. The inner part of the ball is created from a molded form wound with 6,890 feet of glue-coated nylon thread. The leather covering is glued to the inner part and then put under 140 pounds of pressure to force out any air bubbles. A finished regulation ball must measure between $29\frac{1}{2}$ and $29\frac{7}{8}$ inches around. It is inflated to an air pressure of $7\frac{1}{2}$ to $8\frac{1}{2}$ pounds per square inch. Official NBA balls are "highly guarded": if they end up in the stands, spectators are not allowed to take them home!

- Discuss with students why it might be important for all teams to play with a special, regulation ball.
- Have students who play basketball compare the balls they play with to the official NBA basketball.

Thematic Connection

TURNING POINTS

Basketball has come a long way since its early days of soccer balls and peach baskets. The creation of the NBA marked a turning point in the popularity of basketball because it introduced the world to this little-known sport. Since the establishment of the NBA, the league has grown immensely in popularity, and basketball is rapidly becoming the most popular sport in the world.

1. How does breaking a scoring or most-games-played record serve as a turning point in basketball history?
2. Frank Deford states that in sports, people "expect the best to be succeeded by someone better." Do you agree with this statement, or do you believe that some records will never be broken?
3. What do the fateful moments in a basketball game have in common with the fateful moments in a short story or novel?

Idea Bank

Writing

1. **Hall-of-Fame Placard** Imagine that you work for a sports hall of fame, and write a description of your favorite athlete to appear beside his or her picture. In your placards, include vivid descriptive details that capture the players' contributions to the game.
2. **Sports Poem** A number of memorable poems, stories, and novels have been written about sports. Write a poem about your favorite sport or athlete.
3. **Fitness Is Fundamental** All the athletes mentioned in Deford's article had to train vigorously to be in top physical condition. Write a brief report in which you stress the value of a regular exercise routine. **[Science Link]**

Speaking, Listening, and Viewing

4. **Television Interview** Work with a partner to stage an interview with a famous athlete. One of you should assume the role of reporter and the other should take on the role of the athlete. Ask and answer questions that you've always wanted to ask the athlete. Present your interview to your classmates. **[Performing Arts Link]**

Researching and Representing

5. **Virtual Reality One on One** Imagine that you can create your ideal virtual reality video game that enables players to go one on one with their favorite basketball player. Describe the computer graphics, sound effects, and details of your game. If possible, provide sketches of what the screen will look like. **[Art Link]**

Online Activity www.phlit.phschool.com

Reinforce and Extend

Answers

Thematic Connection

1. Breaking a scoring record is a turning point because it sets a new benchmark for success; breaking a most-games-played record represents a turning point in the career of the player by marking the length and success of his or her career.
2. Some students may agree with this statement because better training and equipment, as well as sports psychology, are factors that contribute to ever-greater accomplishments; students who disagree might say that an athlete's capacity is finite, that perhaps people just have the perception that current athletes are better than past ones.
3. In both a basketball game and in a short story, fateful moments affect consequences. For example, in Buck's story, Mrs. Pan's decision to make a match resulted in a major change in Lili's life. Likewise, in basketball, a fateful moment like missing a key shot in a close game could result in the loss of the game.

Idea Bank

Customizing for
Performance Levels

Following are suggestions for matching Idea Bank topics with your students' performance levels:

Less Advanced Students: 1
Average Students: 2, 3, 4
More Advanced Students: 5

Beyond the Selection

FURTHER READING

Other Work by Frank Deford

Alex: The Life of a Child

Other Works About Turning Points in Sports

I Am Third by Gale Sayers
Comeback Stars of Pro Sports by Nathan Aaseng
Shoeless Joe by W. P. Kinsella
Hoops by Walter Dean Myers

We suggest that you preview these works before recommending them to students.

INTERNET

Students can learn more at the following Web sites. Please be aware, however, that these sites may have changed from the time we published this information.

For background about Deford and his thoughts on sports and sportswriters today, go to: **http://bon. boulder.co.us/campuspress/Deford.html**

For information about Jordan, go to: **http//www. evansville.net/~lhess/Jordan23.html**

We *strongly recommend* that you preview the sites before you send students to them.

Prepare and Engage

LESSON OBJECTIVES

1. **To develop vocabulary and word identification skills**
   - Latin Word Roots: *-sat-*
   - Using the Word Bank: Context
   - Extending Word Study: Connotations (ATE)
2. **To use a variety of reading strategies to comprehend a personal narrative**
   - Connect Your Experience
   - Reading Strategy: Evaluate a Writer's Message
   - Read to Be Entertained (ATE)
3. **To increase knowledge of other cultures and to connect common elements across cultures**
   - Connecting Themes Across Cultures (ATE)
   - Background for Understanding
   - The Geography of Viet Nam
4. **To express and support responses to the text**
   - Critical Thinking
   - Idea Bank: Interview
5. **To analyze literary elements**
   - Literary Focus: Theme
   - Viewing and Representing Mini-Lesson: Visual Representation of Tone
6. **To read in order to research self-selected and assigned topics**
   - Idea Bank: Visitor's Guide
   - Idea Bank: Two Maps
   - Idea Bank: Auto Safety Presentation
7. **To plan, prepare, organize, and present literary interpretations**
   - Idea Bank: Allegory
   - Speaking, Listening, and Viewing: Improvisational Skit
   - Idea Bank: Telephone Conversation
8. **To use recursive writing processes to write persuasively using elaboration**
   - Guided Writing Lesson
9. **To increase knowledge of the rules of grammar and usage**
   - Build Grammar Skills: Present Participial Phrases

Test Preparation

Reading Comprehension: Predicting Outcomes (ATE, p. 363) The teaching tips and sample test item in this workshop support the instruction and practice in the unit workshop:

Reading Comprehension: Recognizing Cause and Effect; Predicting Outcomes (SE, p. 377)

Guide for Reading

Nguyen Thi Vinh *(1924–)*

A prominent writer in Saigon (Vietnam) before the Communist takeover in 1975, Nguyen Thi Vinh has written novels, poems, and short stories, as well as being an editor and a publishing executive. Her collection *The Poetry of Nguyen Thi Vinh* was published in 1973. She remained in Vietnam for eight years after the fall of Saigon, but then joined her family in Norway, as a refugee.

Dahlia Ravikovitch *(1936–)*

The intensely personal poems of this Israeli author also use images of history, religion, and mythology. A native of Tel Aviv, Dahlia Ravikovitch has translated the poetry of William Butler Yeats and T. S. Eliot. In turn, two of her books, *Dress of Fire* and *The Window*, have been translated into English.

Karl Shapiro *(1913–)*

American poet Karl Shapiro has been a college professor, a critic, and an editor, as well as a Pulitzer Prize–winning poet. Shapiro has said that he would like to see the elimination "of the line between poetry and prose." The harsh realism of "Auto Wreck" reflects Shapiro's preferred poetic style.

Franz Kafka *(1883–1924)*

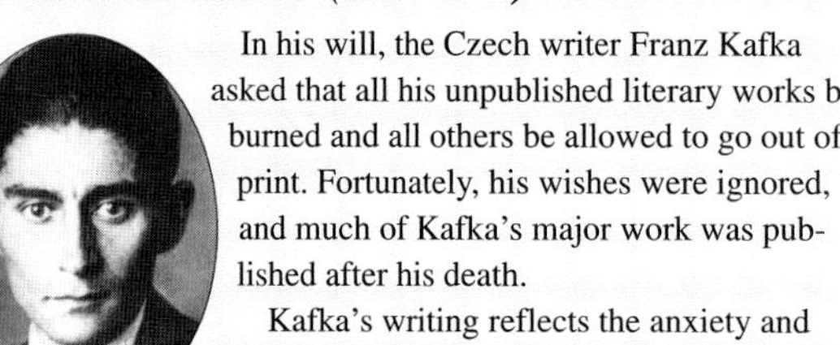

In his will, the Czech writer Franz Kafka asked that all his unpublished literary works be burned and all others be allowed to go out of print. Fortunately, his wishes were ignored, and much of Kafka's major work was published after his death.

Kafka's writing reflects the anxiety and alienation that has pervaded much of twentieth-century society. "Before the Law" is an allegory—a narrative in which the actions of characters represent abstract ideas and moral principles.

◆ Build Vocabulary

LATIN WORD ROOTS: *-sat-*

Have you ever wanted something so badly that you kept asking and asking for it? You might say that your desire was *insatiable*. *Insatiable* has as its root *-sat-* and comes from the Latin *satiare* meaning "to fill entirely." An *insatiable* desire, curiosity, or appetite, therefore, is one that cannot be filled.

WORD BANK

Before you read, preview this list of words from the selections.

deranged
convalescents
banal
expedient
importunity
contemplation
insatiable

◆ Build Grammar Skills

PRESENT PARTICIPIAL PHRASES

A **present participial phrase** consists of a present participle—a verb form ending in *-ing*—plus any other words that go with it. Participial phrases function as adjectives.

Nguyen Thi Vihn writes these lines in "Thoughts of Hanoi":

jubilant voices of children
stumbling through the alphabet,

The participial phrase *stumbling through the alphabet* modifies *children*. It identifies *what kind* of children.

Notice other participial phrases that these writers use to add detail to their work.

Prentice Hall Literature Program Resources

REINFORCE / RETEACH / EXTEND

Selection Support Pages
Build Vocabulary: Word Roots: *-sat-*, p. 109
Build Grammar Skills: Present Participial Phrases, p. 110
Reading Strategy: Evaluate a Writer's Message, p. 111
Literary Focus: Theme, p. 112

Strategies for Diverse Student Needs, p. 27

Beyond Literature
Community Connection: Emergency Medical Technician, p. 27

Formal Assessment Selection Test, pp. 91–93; Assessment Resources Software

Alternative Assessment, p. 27

Resource Pro CD-ROM

Listening to Literature Audiocassettes

Thoughts of Hanoi ◆ Pride
Auto Wreck ◆ Before the Law

◆ Literature and Your Life

Connect Your Experience

If you could control all the events that affect your life, you'd win every game and pass every test. Sometimes, however, life throws a curve ball: Your team forfeits the game because half the players have the flu, or the science test includes a section of questions you weren't expecting. These selections show how people respond to circumstances that are (or seem to be) beyond their control.

Thematic Focus: Fateful Moments

These selections show how specific events become fateful moments that change a person's life forever. The different ways the speakers deal with these events may lead you to examine how you respond to events that seem to be out of your control.

Journal Writing Jot down ideas for adjusting to circumstances you cannot change, taking action on circumstances you can change, and knowing the difference between the two.

◆ Background for Understanding

Vietnam

Nguyen Thi Vinh writes about her home country, Vietnam, which was torn apart by a long and bloody war that lasted from just after the end of World War II until 1974. A 1954 treaty led to the division of the country into South Vietnam, which was supported by the United States, and North Vietnam, which was controlled by a Communist government. With support from the North Vietnamese, guerrillas called Viet Cong fought to overthrow South Vietnam. To support South Vietnam, the United States sent hundreds of thousands of troops to Vietnam. Ultimately, however, the Americans withdrew. In 1974, the North Vietnamese routed the South Vietnamese army, and in 1976 Hanoi became the capital of Vietnam.

◆ Literary Focus

Theme

The **theme** of a work is its central meaning—the comment the writer is making about human life and values. For example, the central message of "Pride" is that just as a hidden crack in a rock can eventually cause the rock to crumble, so a hidden hurt or problem in a person can eventually cause the person to "crack." By writing about how weather and other conditions cause rocks to crack, Ravikovitch communicates an insight about people without directly stating it.

◆ Reading Strategy

Evaluate a Writer's Message

You walk out of a movie theater discussing the movie you just saw with your friends. As you evaluate it, you consider a variety of questions. Did the movie have a point? Did the plot make sense? You can examine literature in a similar way. You **evaluate a writer's message** by first identifying the message and then judging whether the message is valid—that is, whether it makes sense and is well supported. You can evaluate a message without necessarily agreeing or disagreeing with it.

In the poem "Pride," Dahlia Ravikovitch communicates a message about how difficulties and troubles affect people. Your evaluation of her message will rate how well you think she communicates and supports her message. Identify the message in each of the other selections. Then use a graphic organizer like the one shown to help you evaluate the message.

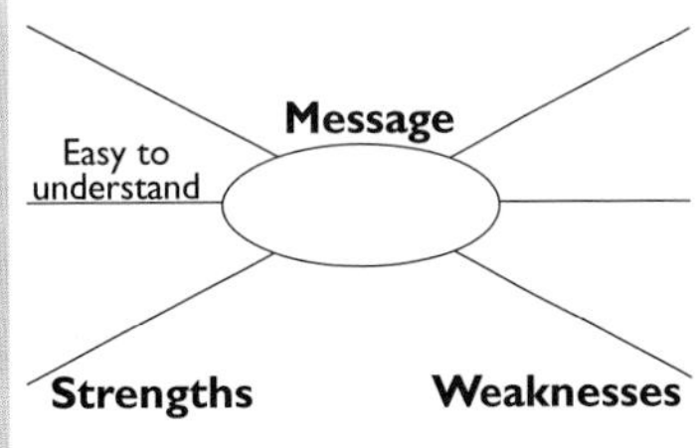

Test Preparation Workshop

Reading Comprehension: Predicting Outcomes The SAT test presents short selections for students to read, followed by multiple-choice questions that test a variety of reading skills. Use the following passage to prepare students to predict outcomes.

Since the gate stands open, as usual, and the doorkeeper steps to one side, the man stoops to peer through the gateway into the interior. Observing that, the doorkeeper laughs and says: "If you are so drawn to it, just try to go in despite my veto. But take note: I am powerful. And I am only the least of the doorkeepers. From hall to hall there is one doorkeeper after another, each more powerful than the last."

Information provided in the passage would lead you to predict that the man—

A will try to get in
B will never get in
C is not interested
D should give up

Lead students to understand that, based on the information provided in this passage about the unlimited doorkeepers, they can predict that *A*, the man probably will never get in.

Interest Grabber Display pictures with bold headlines from newspapers and magazines, depicting the effects of natural disasters, wars, or accidents. Help students recognize that the media uses pictures like these because they grab attention—encouraging people to buy the publication. Lead a discussion about why people's attention is captured by tragic or frightening scenes. Then, guide students to recognize that traumatic events can be turning points for those involved and for those who witness them—either live or through the media. These events have such a deep emotional effect upon people that they are forever changed. Suggest that they keep this in mind as they read the pieces.

Connecting Themes Across Cultures

The fateful moments in these selections deal with life and death. Encourage students to consider moments that are less dramatic but may influence one's life in a profound way. In some countries, such as China and France, performance on a written examination can determine one's future profession, income, and position in life. Have students consider the importance of tests such as the SAT and discuss the impact of testing in their own lives and those of young people in other countries.

Customize for *Less Proficient Readers and English Language Learners*

Students may have difficulty distinguishing between the *subject* and *theme* in each work. Explain that the *subject* tells what the piece is about; the *theme* expresses the central idea the author wants to get across. Have students fill in the chart for each work:

	Title	Subject	Theme
1			
2			
3			
4			

Customize for *Pre-AP Students*

"Before the Law" is the only prose piece in this selection. Challenge students to retell the story in verse and compare the result with the original.

Develop Understanding

One-Minute Insight "Thoughts of Hanoi" looks at the deep and conflicted feelings associated with having a peacetime friend who has become a wartime enemy.

❶ **Clarification** Explain that, as in the Civil War in the United States, in the Vietnam War, the North and the South fought against each other; countrymen fought against each other. Ask: What is the frontier of hatred? *It is the imaginary line dividing North Vietnam from South Vietnam, making enemies of countrymen.*

◆ Critical Thinking

❷ **Infer** Who is the speaker of the poem? To whom is the speaker addressing the poem? Why does the speaker call the person Brother? *The speaker of the poem is a Vietnamese person who has left Vietnam because of the war. The poem is addressed to a Vietnamese person living in Vietnam. The person is called Brother because the two are countrymen, although one has left.*

Thoughts of Hanoi

Nguyen Thi Vinh

Translated by Nguyen Ngoc Bich With Burton Raffel and W. S. Merwin

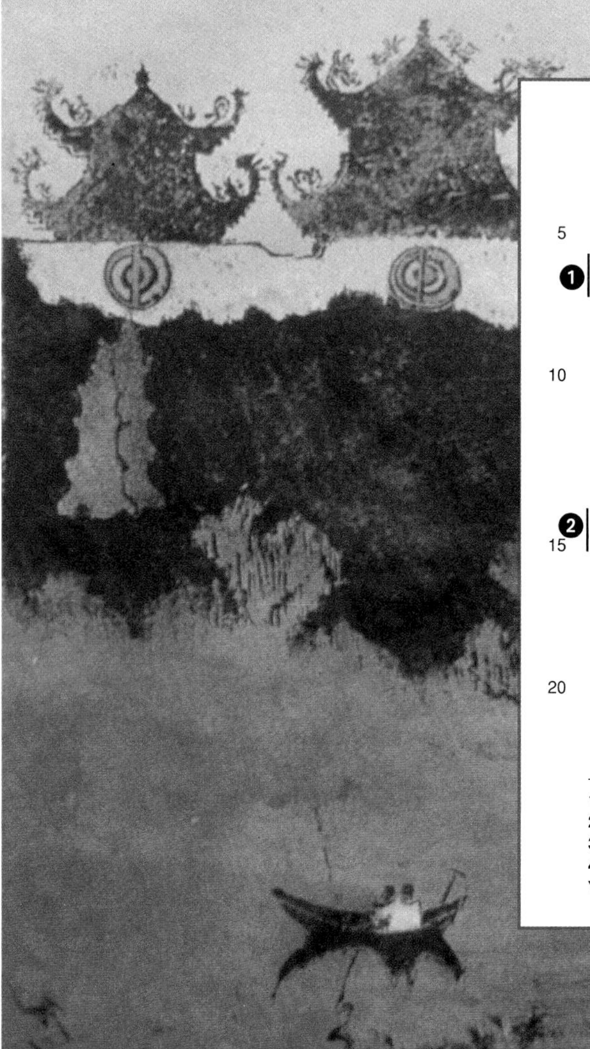

Peacefulness, Tran Nguyen Dan, Indochina Arts Project

The night is deep and chill
as in early autumn. Pitchblack,
it thickens after each lightning flash.
I dream of Hanoi:
Co-ngu[1] Road
❶ ten years of separation
the way back sliced by a frontier of hatred.
I want to bury the past
to burn the future
still I yearn
still I fear
those endless nights
waiting for dawn.

❷ Brother,
how is Hang Dao[2] now?
How is Ngoc Son[3] temple?
Do the trains still run
each day from Hanoi
to the neighboring towns?
To Bac-ninh, Cam-giang, Yen-bai,[4]
the small villages, islands
of brown thatch in a lush green sea?

1. **Co-ngu** (cô gōō)
2. **Hang Dao** (häŋ dou)
3. **Ngoc Son** (nōk sōn)
4. **Bac-ninh** (bäk nin), **Cam-giang** (cäm giäŋ), **Yen-bai** (ēŋ bī)

Block Scheduling Strategies

Consider these suggestions to take advantage of extended class time:

- Before students read, introduce the concept of theme. After they have read, guide students through the Literary Focus questions. Help them to understand that in all of these works the theme is not directly stated, but that the poet or writer uses images, symbols, or figurative language to communicate his or her ideas. Encourage students to look at these devices as clues to the work's underlying theme.
- Have students listen to the works on audiocassette. Guide them to explain how hearing the selections, especially the poems, added to their appreciation of the author's craft.
- Encourage students to research Kafka on the Internet either before or after they read. They can access the Internet site listed on p. 369.
- Have students work through the Guided Writing Lesson (p. 371). Suggest they consult an almanac or newspapers for the latest statistics on car accidents.

The girls
bright eyes
ruddy cheeks
four-piece dresses
raven-bill scarves
sowing harvesting
spinning weaving
all year round,
the boys
plowing
transplanting
in the fields
in their shops
running across
the meadow at evening
to fly kites
and sing alternating songs.

Stainless blue sky,
jubilant voices of children
stumbling through the alphabet,
village graybeards strolling to the temple,
grandmothers basking in twilight sun,
chewing betel leaves
while the children run—

Brother,
how is all that now? ❸
Or is it obsolete?
Are you like me,
reliving the past,
imagining the future?
Do you count me as a friend
or am I the enemy in your eyes?
Brother, I am afraid
that one day I'll be with the March-North Army ❹
meeting you on your way to the South.
I might be the one to shoot you then
or you me
but please
not with hatred.
For don't you remember how it was,
you and I in school together,
plotting our lives together?
Those roots go deep!

Brother, we are men,
conscious of more
than material needs.
How can this happen to us ❺
my friend
my foe?

Guide for Responding

◆ Literature and Your Life

Reader's Response Explain a situation in which someone you thought of as a "foe" became a friend.

Thematic Focus What are some turning points that could change friends into enemies or enemies into friends?

☑ Check Your Comprehension

1. What is probably the speaker's hometown?
2. What does the speaker remember the "village graybeards" doing?

◆ Critical Thinking

INTERPRET

1. Why would the speaker wonder if the daily life he describes is now obsolete? **[Analyze]**

EVALUATE

2. Do you think it's possible to shoot someone "not with hatred" in war? Explain. **[Make a Judgment]**

EXTEND

3. How might the situation described in the poem compare with others in history? Explain. **[Social Studies Link]**

Cross-Curricular Connection: Social Studies

Hanoi Located in the north on the Red River, Hanoi is the capital of Vietnam. Originally called Long Bien, the city was founded in the sixth century and briefly served as the country's capital. It became the capital again in the eleventh century. In 1883, the French renamed the city Hanoi and fourteen years later made it the seat of the French Indochina government. When Vietnam was divided in 1954, Hanoi became the capital of North Vietnam. From 1965 to 1972, Hanoi was the target of frequent bombings. Although most of Hanoi was destroyed, the Vietnamese rebuilt the city and it again became the capital when the country was reunited in 1976.

Knowing these facts, have students discuss why the poet Nguyen Thi Vinh selected Hanoi rather than another Vietnamese city as the subject of her poem.

◆ Critical Thinking

❸ Analyze Cause and Effect Have students analyze the causes and effects of the changes Vietnam experienced, as alluded to in the lines 48–49. *War and foreign influence have changed the traditional way of life.*

Comprehension Check ☑

❹ Ask students what the speaker is afraid of. *The speaker fears that one day he/she will have to kill a fellow countryman because of war within Vietnam.*

◆ Reading Strategy

❺ Evaluate a Writer's Message Have students explain how this stanza relates to the writer's message. *The writer's message concerns the war's focus on land and power. The writer suggests that friendship and family are what really matter.*

Reinforce and Extend

Answers

◆ Literature and Your Life

Reader's Response Students might describe a time when a miscommunication was cleared up and an enemy became a friend.

Thematic Focus Turning points that could change enemies into friends include coming to an enemy's aid when he or she is in trouble or discovering a mutual interest. Turning points that could change friends into enemies include an act of betrayal, such as breaking a confidence.

☑ Check Your Comprehension

1. Hanoi is probably the speaker's hometown.
2. The speaker remembers them strolling to the temple.

◆ Critical Thinking

1. As a result of the war, so much has changed that the daily life he describes could be obsolete.
2. Students might say that it is possible to shoot someone "not without hatred" because a soldier might feel he or she is fighting for a cause, not against a person.
3. Students might cite other wars or clashes between groups that divide people who had been peaceful among themselves.

Develop Understanding

One-Minute Insight The tone of these two poems shows that turning points can come upon one slowly ("Pride") or with a terrible and stunning suddenness ("Auto Wreck").

◆ Critical Thinking

1 Interpret Have students explain what the author means by pride in this passage. *The poet means the kind of pride that makes people hide their painful feelings; that makes people stop themselves from crying because they are ashamed to show weakness.*

◆ Critical Thinking

2 Deduce Ask students what the seal represents in the poem. *The seal stands for the last straw; not necessarily the worst thing that happens to a person, but the one that completes the crack that was there all along.*

◆ Critical Thinking

3 Infer Ask students to infer how the rocks in this poem are like people. *Students might suggest that with people, as with rocks, a crack that starts out small can turn into a complete break under pressure.*

Extending Word Study

Connotations Have students use the context of the poem to identify the connotations of *sickly, richest,* and *occult* as positive, negative, or neutral. Then have them use a dictionary to determine the precise meanings of these words in this context.

Customize for *Visual/Spatial Learners*

These pieces are rich in imagery. Invite pairs of these students to choose and describe an image to a partner. The partners can add visual details to further enrich the image. Partners can then exchange roles, with one describing a scene and the other adding details.

Pride

Dahlia Ravikovitch

Translated by Chana Bloch and Ariel Bloch

I tell you, even rocks crack,
and not because of age.
For years they lie on their backs
in the heat and the cold,
so many years,
it almost seems peaceful.
(1) They don't move, so the cracks stay hidden.
A kind of pride.
Years pass over them, waiting.
Whoever is going to shatter them
hasn't come yet.
And so the moss flourishes, the seaweed
whips around,
the sea pushes through and rolls back—
the rocks seem motionless.
(2) Till a little seal comes to rub against them,
comes and goes away.
And suddenly the rock has an open wound.
(3) I told you, when rocks break, it happens by surprise.
And people, too.

Viewing and Representing Mini-Lesson

Visual Representation of Tone

This mini-lesson extends the concept of the poems' tone on these pages.

Introduce Discuss with students how writers choose words to convey a tone. In the case of "Pride" and "Auto Wreck," the poets' tone indicates the impact of two different turning points.

Develop Have students work in pairs to develop a visual representation of tone for one or both of the poems. Guide them to evaluate the word choices of the poems and determine what visual elements they might use to represent the same tone—color, line, composition, or arrangement of elements.

Apply Provide students with art media such as paint, markers, or colored chalk. Have them create a visual representation of tone for the poems.

Assess Have students show their tone representations to the class and explain their choice of medium and representation. Evaluate students on their explanations rather than on the artistic quality of their work.

Auto Wreck

Karl Shapiro

Its quick soft silver bell beating, beating,
And down the dark one ruby flare
Pulsing out red light like an artery,
4 The ambulance at top speed floating down
Past beacons and illuminated clocks
Wings in a heavy curve, dips down,
And brakes speed, entering the crowd.
The doors leap open, emptying light;
Stretchers are laid out, the mangled lifted
And stowed into the little hospital.
Then the bell, breaking the hush, tolls once,
And the ambulance with its terrible cargo
Rocking, slightly rocking, moves away,
As the doors, an afterthought, are closed.

We are deranged, walking among the cops
Who sweep glass and are large and composed.
5 One is still making notes under the light.
One with a bucket douches ponds of blood
Into the street and gutter.
One hangs lanterns on the wrecks that cling,
Empty husks of locusts, to iron poles.

Our throats were tight as tourniquets,[1]
Our feet were bound with splints, but now,
Like convalescents intimate and gauche,[2] 6
We speak through sickly smiles and warn
With the stubborn saw of common sense,
The grim joke and the banal resolution.
The traffic moves around with care,
But we remain, touching a wound
That opens to our richest horror.
Already old, the question Who shall die?
Becomes unspoken Who is innocent?
For death in war is done by hands;
Suicide has cause and stillbirth, logic;
And cancer, simple as a flower, blooms.
But this invites the occult mind,
Cancels our physics with a sneer,
And spatters all we knew of denouement[3]
Across the expedient and wicked stones.

◆ Build Vocabulary

deranged (də rānjd′) *adj.*: Unsettled

convalescents (kän′ və les′ ənts) *n.*: People who are recovering from illness

banal (bā′ nəl) *adj.*: Dull or stale because of overuse

expedient (ek spē′ dē′ ənt) *adj.*: Convenient

1. **tourniquets** (tʉr′ nə ketz) *n.*: Bandages to stop bleeding by compressing a blood vessel.
2. **gauche** (gōsh) *adj.*: Awkward.
3. **denouement** (dā′ nü män′) *n.*: Outcome or the end.

◆ Build Grammar Skill

4 Present Participial Phrases Have students identify the two present participial phrases and the noun they both modify. *The present participial phrases are* pulsing out red light *and* floating down. *They both modify* ambulance.

◆ Reading Strategy

5 Evaluate a Writer's Message Have students identify the message in this passage, say how well Shapiro communicates that message, and give reasons to support their answer. *Possible response: The poet is showing the calm and professional detachment of the police officers and contrasting it with the "deranged" reaction of the "we" of the poem. Shapiro communicates his message well because he uses strong images to convey the police officer's composure.*

◆ Critical Thinking

6 Interpret Ask students why they think the poet compares the spectators to convalescents. *Students might suggest the shock of the accident has made the spectators feel that they are recovering from a life-threatening illness.*

Read to Be Entertained

Kafka is known for the surreal, sinister settings of his fiction. His novels deal with people trapped in ambiguous, dream-like situations that they usually try, unsuccessfully, to escape. A feeling of mystery and frustration pervades both *The Trial* and *The Castle.* Inform interested students that the remarkable thing is that the clarity and beauty of Kafka's prose enable the reader to enjoy the frustrations and insights of his characters. "Before the Law" provides a good glimpse of Kafka's style.

Customize for *Less Proficient Readers*

Complex sentence structure makes the first seven lines of this poem particularly difficult. Have students find the subject (ambulance) and complete predicate with three verbs (wings in a heavy curve, dips down, and brakes speed) in these opening lines.

Beyond the Classroom

Career Connection

Paramedic Behind the scenes of "Auto Wreck," paramedics were probably hard at work, trying to save lives and administer emergency care as the ambulance sped to the hospital. These specialized paramedics, known as emergency medical technicians, or EMTs, are at the pulse of emergency medicine; their efforts have saved thousands of lives. Let students know that the term *paramedic* originated during the Korean War. Military medical technicians were parachuted into locations where they were urgently needed—a paramedic was a medical corpsman who was also a trained parachutist.

Have interested students gather more information about paramedics. Some students might report on the different kinds of paramedics, such as physicians' assistants, EMTs, and veterinary technicians. Other students might contact a college or vocational program to find out specifically what is required to train for and be successful in these fields.

Develop Understanding

One-Minute Insight This parable describes the frustration and lost opportunity of a man waiting his turn to be allowed through a door. Students can read this on several levels, recognizing the message that sometimes a person must trigger a turning point through his or her own action rather than waiting for something to happen.

▶Critical Viewing◀

❶ **Analyze** *Students might observe that the figure, viewed from behind, seems without identity; the long shadow cast by the building gives the scene a forlorn look; and the starkness of the scene in general suggests isolation.*

◆Critical Thinking

❷ **Speculate** Ask students: What might happen if the man goes through the gateway? *Students may say he will meet even greater obstacles than the first doorkeeper; he may find what he is seeking from the Law; he may never find justice; he may even be killed.*

Reteach

Finding the theme of a work may challenge students who have difficulty understanding the actual text of the literature. Students might benefit from a question-and-answer session about the works' events and their meanings. Help students fill in a chart for one or more of the works that details what each is about.

Title:	
Event	What it Means

Once a student comprehends the text thoroughly, he or she will probably "get" the themes of the three poems. The message of the Kafka piece is ambiguous. Encourage students to decide what the theme is for themselves.

Enigma of the Hour, 1912, Giorgio de Chirico, Coll. Mattioli, Milan, Italy© Foundation Giorgio de Chirico/Licensed by VAGA, New York, NY

◀ Critical View... What details ... picture on th... indicate a se... isolation? [An...

Before the Law

Franz Kafka

Translated by Willa and Edwin Muir

Before the Law stands a doorkeeper. To this doorkeeper there comes a man from the country and prays for admittance to the Law. But the doorkeeper says that he cannot grant admittance at the moment. The man thinks it over and then asks if he will be allowed in later. "It is possible," says the doorkeeper, "but not at the moment." Since the gate stands open, as usual, and the doorkeeper steps to one side, the man stoops to peer through the gateway into the interior. Observing that, the doorkeeper laughs and says: "If you are so drawn to it, just try to go in despite my veto.[1] But take note: I am powerful. And I am only the least of the doorkeepers. From hall to hall there is one doorkeeper after another, each more powerful than the last. The third doorkeeper is already so terrible that even I cannot bear to look at him." These are difficulties the man from the country has not expected; the Law, he thinks, should surely be accessible at all times and to everyone, but as he now takes a closer look at the doorkeeper in his fur coat, with his big sharp nose and long, thin, black Tartar[2] beard, he decides that it is better to wait

1. **veto** (vē´ tō) *n.*: An order prohibiting some proposed or intended act.
2. **Tartar** (tär´ tər): Member of a Turkic people living in a region of European Russia.

Humanities: Art

Enigma of the Hour, 1912, by Giorgio de Chirico.

In this painting, a figure stands before a facade of arches with the face of a clock above. The identity of the figure, the place, the historical period, and the significance of the clock are all unclear.

Giorgio de Chirico was an Italian painter, born in Greece in 1888. Chirico's earlier paintings communicate a sense of reality very different from ordinary experience, and for that reason he is considered a forerunner of the Surrealist movement of the early 1920's.

Use the following questions for discussion:

1. How does the mood of this painting reflect the mood of Kafka's story? *Both are mysterious. The people and places in both are outside of ordinary reality. Both invite speculation and interpretation.*
2. How can you connect the clock in the painting to the theme of the story? *Students may say the clock may reflect the idea that time runs out for the man in the story.*

until he gets permission to enter. The doorkeeper gives him a stool and lets him sit down at one side of the door. There he sits for days and years. He makes many attempts to be admitted, and wearies the doorkeeper by his importunity. The doorkeeper frequently has little interviews with him, asking him questions about his home and many other things, but the questions are put indifferently, as great lords put them, and always finish with the statement that he cannot be let in yet. The man, who has furnished himself with many things for his journey, sacrifices all he has, however valuable, to bribe the doorkeeper. The doorkeeper accepts everything, but always with the remark: "I am only taking it to keep you from thinking you have omitted anything." During these many years the man fixes his attention almost continuously on the doorkeeper. He forgets the other doorkeepers, and this one seems to him the sole obstacle preventing access to the Law. He curses his bad luck, in his early years boldly and loudly; later, as he grows old, he only grumbles to himself. He becomes childish, and since in his yearlong contemplation of the doorkeeper he has come to know even the fleas in his fur collar, he begs the fleas as well to help him and to change the doorkeeper's mind. At length his eyesight begins to fail, and he does not know whether the world is really darker or whether his eyes are only deceiving him. Yet in his darkness he is now aware of a radiance that streams inextinguishable from the gateway of the Law. Now he has not very long to live. Before he dies, all his experiences in these long years gather themselves in his head to one point, a question he has not yet asked the doorkeeper. He waves him nearer, since he can no longer raise his stiffening body. The doorkeeper has to bend low toward him, for the difference in height between them has altered much to the man's disadvantage. "What do you want to know now?" asks the doorkeeper; "you are insatiable." "Everyone strives to reach the Law," says the man, "so how does it happen that for all these many years no one but myself has ever begged for admittance?" The doorkeeper recognizes that the man has reached his end, and, to let his failing senses catch the words, roars in his ear: "No one else could ever be admitted here, since this gate was made only for you. I am now going to shut it." 4

> ◆ **Reading Strategy**
> What do you think the message of this piece is?

◆ Build Vocabulary

importunity (im′ pôr to͞on′ i tē) *n.*: Persistence in requesting or demanding

contemplation (kän′ tem plā′ shən) *n.*: Thoughtful inspection; study

insatiable (in sā′ shə bəl) *adj.*: Cannot be satisfied; constantly wanting more

Guide for Responding

◆ Literature and Your Life

Reader's Response Suggest another title that you think would fit one of these selections.

Thematic Focus What do these works say about turning points?

☑ Check Your Comprehension

1. In "Pride," what causes the rocks to crack?
2. What questions does the speaker of "Auto Wreck" ask?
3. Why has no one else begged admittance to the Law in "Before the Law"?

◆ Critical Thinking

INTERPRET

1. What does the seal represent in "Pride"? **[Apply]**

APPLY

2. Do you agree with the speaker in "Auto Wreck" that some forms of death seem to have a purpose? **[Apply]**

COMPARE LITERARY WORKS

3. Compare these works to other stories or poems you have read that treat the theme of love, pride, or justice. **[Comparison and Contrast]**

◆ Critical Thinking

3 Interpret Ask students to explain why the doorkeeper gives this response after he accepts the bribes. *Students will probably recognize that the doorkeeper is serving himself, and really won't do anything.*

◆ Reading Strategy

4 Evaluate a Writer's Message *Possible responses: A person who sits and waits for justice to come to him will never obtain it. The person who demands justice, who is not afraid to stand up for his rights, may have a chance.*

Reinforce and Extend

Answers

◆ Literature and Your Life

Reader's Response Sample alternative titles are "The Final Blow" ("Pride"); "Shock" ("Auto Wreck"); "The Gatekeeper and the Man" ("Before the Law").

Thematic Focus Together, these works suggest that turning points can be subtle, as in "Pride," or sudden and violent, as in "Auto Wreck."

☑ Check Your Comprehension

1. A seal rubs up against them.
2. The speaker asks, "Who shall die?" "Who is innocent?"
3. The gate was made only for the man.

◆ Critical Thinking

1. Possible responses: the seal represents the "last straw" that causes a person to crack.
2. Possible responses: Yes, sometimes people die for a cause or to end suffering; or no, all death is random.
3. Students should compare works in terms of content and tone.

Speaking, Listening, and Viewing Mini-Lesson

Improvisational Skit

This mini-lesson supports the Speaking, Listening, and Viewing activity in the Idea Bank on p. 371.

Introduce Let students know that in an improvisation actors are called upon to act out a situation with no rehearsal and little or no planning. Therefore, they need to be spontaneous.

Develop Before students perform their improvisational skits, present these guidelines:

- Respond in character to what the other person says and does.
- Use gestures, expressions, posture, and movement to reveal *who* you are, *what* you are doing, and *where* you are.
- Relax and focus on the activity.

Apply Give partners 5 minutes to quickly plan their approach. Then have them improvise a skit.

Assess Have students evaluate their own performances in terms of how effectively they communicated the situation between the man and the gatekeeper and how effectively they created an impression of the characters.

Answers

◆ Reading Strategy

1. Events like auto accidents defy logic and order.
2. Encourage students to support their answers with reasons.
3. Most students will feel that the message is clearly communicated.

◆ Literary Focus

1. Example: Individual friendships can be destroyed by political divisions.
2. The message is communicated through images: the rock (pride) and the seal (final pressure).
3. He uses the images "pulsing out red light like an artery," "throats tight as tourniquets."
4. Sample response: "frustrated." The feeling suggests that Kafka's theme relates to futility.

◆ Build Vocabulary

Using the Latin Root *-sat-*

1. fill; 2. fill; 3. fully

Using the Word Bank

Example sentences:

1. The salesperson called over and over, showing *importunity*.
2. He sat in deep *contemplation*.
3. She has an *insatiable* appetite.
4. Bob's thoughts became *deranged*.
5. The *convalescents* healed.
6. His observations are *banal*.
7. This method is *expedient*.

◆ Build Grammar Skills

Practice

1. . . . (flare,) Pulsing out a red light
2. (doors,) emptying light
3. (We,) walking among the cops
4. Observing that, (doorkeeper)
5. (graybeards,) strolling to the temple

Writing Application

1. Sitting at the gate, the man cannot enter.
2. The gatekeeper guards the gate, keeping the man out.
3. Waiting a long time, the man grew old.

Grammar Reinforcement

For additional instruction and practice, use the lessons in the **Language Lab CD-ROM** on Misplaced Modifiers, and pp. 41–43 on Participles and Participial Phrases in the *Writer's Solution Grammar Practice Book.*

Guide for Responding *(continued)*

◆ Reading Strategy

EVALUATE A WRITER'S MESSAGE

You **evaluate a writer's message** by identifying the message, rating its validity, and examining the examples and support the writer offers.

For example, in "Thoughts of Hanoi" the questions the speaker asks are a clue that the message of the work deals with change. As you read, examine the details and examples to evaluate the message.

1. Identify the message in "Auto Wreck."
2. Explain whether you think the message in "Pride" is valid.
3. How clearly does Thi Vinh communicate her message in "Thoughts of Hanoi"? Give reasons to support your opinion.

◆ Literary Focus

THEME

The **theme** of a work is its central meaning—the comment the writer is making about human life and values.

1. In your own words, state the theme of "Thoughts of Hanoi."
2. Explain how Ravikovitch communicates the theme of "Pride" without directly stating it.
3. What images does Shapiro use to communicate his theme in "Auto Wreck"?
4. What word would you use to describe the feeling you get after reading "Before the Law"? How does this feeling give you a clue to Kafka's theme?

Beyond Literature

Social Studies Connection

The Geography of Vietnam A tropical country in Southeast Asia, Vietnam extends south from China in a long, narrow S-curve. North and Central Vietnam are mountainous regions interspersed with coastal lowlands, while South Vietnam lies very close to sea level.

Activity On a map of Vietnam locate the major cities of Hanoi and Ho Chi Minh City, the Mekong and Red River Deltas, and the Annamite mountain range.

◆ Build Vocabulary

USING THE LATIN ROOT *-sat-*

On your paper, complete the meanings of these words that include the root *-sat-*.

1. satisfy: __?__ one's needs or expectations
2. satiate: to completely __?__
3. saturate: to cause to be soaked __?__

USING THE WORD BANK: Context

On your paper, write sentences using the words from the Word Bank as directed.

1. Describe an action, using the word *importunity.*
2. Describe a library, using the word *contemplation.*
3. Describe a person, using the word *insatiable.*
4. Describe a character, using the word *deranged.*
5. Use the word *convalescents* in a sentence about a hospital.
6. Use the word *banal* in a sentence from a book review.
7. Use the word *expedient* in an advertisement.

◆ Build Grammar Skills

PRESENT PARTICIPIAL PHRASES

A **present participial phrase** consists of a present participle (a verb form ending in *-ing*) plus any other words that go with it. Participial phrases function as adjectives in sentences.

Practice Copy the following examples on to your paper. Underline the present participial phrase and circle the word it modifies.

1. . . . one ruby flare/Pulsing out a red light . . .
2. The doors leap open, emptying light;
3. We are deranged, walking among the cops
4. Observing that, the doorkeeper laughs . . .
5. . . . village graybeards strolling to the temple,

Writing Application Combine each pair of sentences by making one of them a present participial phrase.

1. The man sits at the gate. The man cannot enter.
2. The gatekeeper guards the gate. The gatekeeper keeps the man out.
3. The man grew old. The man waited a long time.

Beyond the Selection

FURTHER READING

Other Works by the Authors

Metamorphosis by Franz Kafka
The Dome of Sunday by Karl Shapiro
Two Sisters by Nguyen Thi Vinh

Other Works About Turning Points

Ethan Frome, Edith Wharton
The Joy Luck Club, Amy Tan

We suggest that you preview these works before recommending them to students.

INTERNET

To learn more about Franz Kafka, go to:
http//www.levity.com/corduroy/kafka.htm

To access an interview with Karl Shapiro, go to:
http://www.wilmington.net/arts/ poets

For other works by Vietnamese women, go to:
http://globetrotter.berkeley.edu/Global Gender/sea.lit.html

Please be aware sites may have changed since we published this information.

We *strongly recommend* that you preview the sites before you send students to them.

Build Your Portfolio

Idea Bank

Writing

1. **Interview** Prepare a list of interview questions for Nguyen Thi Vinh. Focus six or eight questions around the author's life before and after the Vietnam War.
2. **Visitor's Guide** Research Kafka's birthplace in Prague, capital of the Czech Republic. Write a one-page visitor's guide highlighting the interesting aspects of the famous writer's home.
3. **Allegory** Write an allegory—a narrative in which the actions of characters represent abstract ideas or moral principles. First decide upon your message, then develop characters and a plot.

Speaking, Listening, and Viewing

4. **Telephone Conversation** Suppose you are the "you" in "Thoughts of Hanoi." Call the poem's speaker and answer his last question.
5. **Improvisational Skit** With a partner, perform an improvisational skit—a skit without preparation—based on a conversation between the man and the gatekeeper from "Before the Law." Make your skit humorous. Afterwards, explain your reasons for performing it as you did.

Researching and Representing

6. **Two Maps** On a computer or by hand, create two maps of Vietnam—one before the Communist takeover in 1974 and one after it. For both maps, label capital cities. **[Social Studies Link; Art Link; Technology Link]**
7. **Auto Safety Presentation** "Auto Wreck" introduces us to the grim realities of car crashes. Create a chart or other visual aid that shows some of the important auto safety legislation your state has passed since you were born.

Online Activity www.phlit.phschool.com

Guided Writing Lesson

Letter to the Editor

Write a **letter to the editor** of the local paper expressing your concerns about an issue such as auto safety. Your letter will give statistics and pose several recommendations on how people can reduce the likelihood of being in an auto accident. However, you don't want your letter to be all blunt statistics and cold, hard facts. The following tip will help you give your writing that personal touch.

Writing Skills Focus: Elaboration to Make Writing Personal

Make a connection with your audience by providing personal examples. For instance, if you make the point that not enough people wear their seat belts for local trips, you can elaborate by adding that you almost made this mistake when you were riding with your uncle—and later you were sure glad he made you buckle up when he slammed on the brakes to avoid hitting a raccoon. Use examples from your own experience sparingly and only when they really "drive" home your point.

Prewriting Go to the library, use the Internet, or call your local police precinct to find out where you can get the latest statistics on car accidents. Jot down your ideas about personal experiences that illustrate the same point as the statistics.

Drafting Choose the most dramatic personal anecdotes to include with your draft. Support the points you make with these anecdotes by citing the statistics that show your experience is not unique.

Revising Reread your draft. Look for places where you can elaborate with a personal anecdote or a human interest story that will make your point more immediate for your audience.

ASSESSMENT OPTIONS

Formal Assessment, Selection Test, pp. 91–93, and Assessment Resources Software. The selection test is designed so that it can be easily customized to the performance levels of your students.

Alternative Assessment, p. 27, includes options for less advanced students, more advanced students, musical/rhythmic learners, bodily/kinesthetic learners, visual/spatial learners, interpersonal learners, and logical/mathematical learners.

PORTFOLIO ASSESSMENT

Use the following rubrics in the ***Alternative Assessment*** booklet to assess student writing:
Interview: Response to Literature Rubric, p. 110
Visitor's Guide: Description Rubric p. 97
Allegory: Fiction Narrative Rubric, p. 95

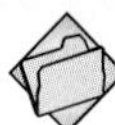

Idea Bank

Following are suggestions for matching Idea Bank topics with your students' performance levels and learning modalities:

Customizing for *Performance Levels*
Less Advanced Students: 1, 4
Average Students: 2, 5
More Advanced Students: 3, 6, 7

Customizing for *Learning Modalities*
Visual/Spatial: 6, 7
Interpersonal: 4
Verbal/Linguistic: 4, 5
Logical/Mathematical: 7

Guided Writing Lesson

Elaboration Strategy Discuss with students that the persuasive power of a personal anecdote relies on the factual details that support it. Have them list two or three personal anecdotes related to their topic on the left side of a piece of paper. Then, as they research the facts, they can list the information on the right side of the paper. When their research is complete, students can connect the information to the anecdotes and use the personal anecdote that is best supported by facts and statistics.

For more prewriting, elaboration, and revision strategies, see *Prentice Hall Writing and Grammar.*

Writers at Work Videodisc
Have students view the videodisc segment for Ch. 8 in which Larry Cataldo discusses techniques he uses to organize ideas. Ask students how they can apply his techniques. Discuss with students which of Cataldo's techniques for capturing an audience would work best for their award speech, and why.

Play frames 23159 to 33243

Writing Lab CD-ROM
Have students complete the tutorial on Practical Writing. Follow these steps:

1. Have students use the notecard activity to help them arrange their points and examples in order of importance.
2. Suggest that students use the transition word checker to highlight transition words so they can see whether they have shown relationships that indicate logical order.

Prepare and Engage

LESSON OBJECTIVES

1. To use recursive writing processes to write a reflective essay
2. To recognize and avoid misplaced and dangling modifiers
3. To recognize vivid adjectives and adverbs

You may want to distribute the scoring rubric for Narrative Based on Personal Experience (p. 96 in ***Alternative Assessment***) to make students aware of the criteria on which their work will be evaluated. For suggestions on how you can customize the rubric, see p. 374.

Writers at Work Videodisc

If you encourage students to use description in their position papers, you might show them how Colleen McElroy uses descriptive elements in her writing. Play the videodisc segment on Description (Ch. 1). Have students discuss how McElroy draws on her own images to call forth images for readers.

Play frames 335 to 10062

Writing Lab CD-ROM

If your students have access to computers, you may want to have them work on the tutorial on Description if they are including description in their reflective essays. Follow these steps:

1. Have students review the interactive model of a reflective essay.
2. Have students listen to tips from authors for writing for different audiences.
3. Have students draft on computer.
4. Suggest students review the screen on Making Point of View Consistent.

Reflective Essay Writing Process Workshop

A **reflective essay** describes your thoughts and feelings about a person, place, or memorable event. It may be anchored in a specific moment in the past, but it can also be a reflection upon an event or trend that you notice in the present. An effective reflective essay uses vivid details and figurative language to capture not only physical appearances but also your emotional responses.

The following skills, introduced in this section's Guided Writing Lesson, will help you write an effective reflective essay.

Writing Skills Focus

- **Create a main impression** that you would like to instill in the reader of your reflective essay. For example, if you would like to establish a sentimental mood, use words and phrases such as, *as I fondly remember.* (See p. 355.)
- **Elaborate to make your writing personal.** For instance, if you say that summer is your favorite season, give an example of something that happened one particular summer. (See p. 369.)
- **Record your final insight** by stating the effect this memory had on you and what you learned or discovered from it.

The following excerpt from "Speak, Memory" shows how Vladimir Nabokov uses these skills.

Model From Literature

from "Speak, Memory" by Vladimir Nabokov

Summer *soomerki*—the lovely Russian word for dusk. ① Time: a dim point in the first decade of this unpopular century. Place: latitude 59° north from your equator, longitude 100° east from my writing hand. The day would take hours to fade, and everything—sky, tall flowers, still water—would be kept in a state of infinite vesperal suspense, deepened rather than resolved by the doleful moo of a cow in a distant meadow ② or by the still more moving cry that came from some bird beyond the lower course of the river.

① *The phrase lovely Russian word for dusk gives the essay a personal, reflective tone.*

② *The writer elaborates on how much he loved the summers of his youth by giving concrete examples of the sights and sounds of those remote summer evenings.*

Cross-Curricular Connection: Art

Art Transparency Just as a painting uses imagery to capture a particular scene or moment in time, so a reflective essay uses words to accomplish the same task. Point out to students that, just as an artist brings his or her own feelings, thoughts, and responses to bear on the visual representation of an object, so will their own feelings, thoughts, and responses affect their representation of an event as presented in a reflective essay.

For a concrete example of this concept, place Art Transparency 17 on an overhead projector. Point out to students that the art shows a variety of interpretations of what is recognizably the same shape. The triangle is shown in a fragmented way, in a fluid way, in a colorful way, in a crisp, clear way, and also with blurred edges. Discuss with students the feelings that might lead to different interpretations and representations of an event.

Prewriting

Choose Your Topic: What Triggers a Memory? Does the smell of burning leaves or perfume or nutmeg recall an experience that you had years ago? Does hearing an "oldie" on the radio remind you of an incident from your childhood? Focus on different sensory stimuli that you encounter in the world around you, and jot down past experiences that these tastes, smells, sounds, sights, and physical sensations bring to mind. Then choose one experience on which you can reflect in your essay.

Use a Word Bin As you gather details for your reflective essay, think about how you want to portray your subject. What kinds of words will you use to describe it? How will you describe its color or the way it sounds? Make a list of words that describe how your subject looks, sounds, feels, tastes, and smells, but also include words that conjure feelings and suggest opinions. The following word bin shows examples of various sensory words.

Sensory Words

Sight	Sound	Smell	Taste	Touch
sunny	musical	flowery	spicy	smooth
glistening	humming	pungent	salty	knotted
glowing	whining	musty	zesty	wet
murky	melodic	ripe	bitter	sandy

Drafting

Create a Main Impression As you draft your reflective essay, focus on conveying a particular impression of your topic. Include enough sensory details to support your main impression. Study the following example:

Topic: A fireworks display from a July 4th celebration when I was younger

Main Impression: The fireworks display was an unforgettable presentation of energy, excitement, and color.

Include: Descriptions of vibrant colors, the sounds of the fireworks exploding, the smells of popcorn and cotton candy, the feel of the wet grass or hard pavement under your feet, the joy of witnessing this grand historical event.

Applying Language Skills: Misplaced and Dangling Modifiers

Misplaced modifiers (phrases or clauses placed so that they seem to modify something other than what they are meant to modify) and **dangling modifiers** (modifying phrases that don't really modify anything) make your writing confusing.

Misplaced Modifier:
My house is on Cedar Avenue, which has a huge red front door.

Corrected:
My house, which has a huge red front door, is on Cedar Avenue.

Practice Rewrite the sentences, correcting misplaced or dangling modifiers.

1. Watching the sunset, dusk was beautiful.
2. He realized the mistake he had made after a few minutes.

Writing Application Correct any misplaced or dangling modifiers in your essay.

Writer's Solution Connection Writing Lab

For more on sensory words, use the Sensory Language Word Bin in the Drafting section of the Writing Lab tutorial on Description.

Develop Understanding

Prewriting Strategy

Students may benefit from using a topic web to narrow their topics. Have them list their broad topic at the top of the web and divide that topic into two or more subtopics. Then have them divide those subtopics further into subtopics. This should help them find a narrowed topic for their essays.

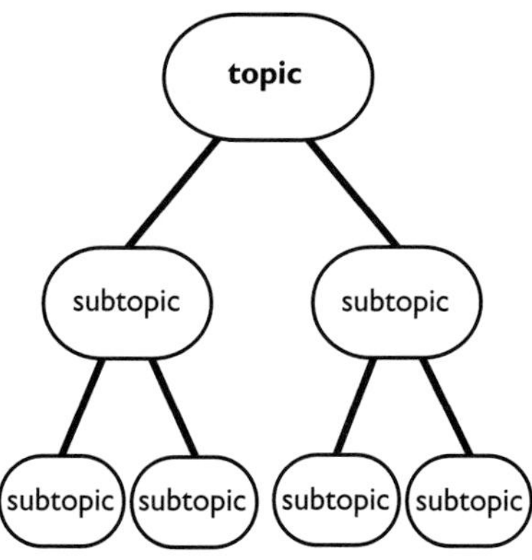

Customize for *Pre-AP Students*

Challenge students to present their reflective essays in creative ways, such as in copy for a newspaper, or as information that a witness to a crime might give to a police officer.

Writing Lab CD-ROM

The Drafting section of the tutorial on Description contains Sensory, Colors, Places, and Character Traits word bins. Have students consult these lists of words before or while they draft to make their essays more descriptive and concise.

Elaboration

As students begin elaborating on their topics, remind them that a reflective essay is personal in nature and has a beginning, a middle, and an end. Although the inherent nature of reflection is a memory—something from one's past—students might want to use flashbacks to elaborate on their memories.

Connect to Literature You might have students look again at the excerpt from *Speak Memory* by Vladimir Nabokov on p. 305, which is a reflective essay.

Applying Language Skills

Misplaced and Dangling Modifiers Explain to students that they should be extra careful about misplaced and dangling modifiers in their reflective essays, since they will probably be using a lot of modifiers in their pieces.

Answers

Possible responses:

1. Watching the sunset, *I thought* dusk was beautiful.
2. *After a few minutes,* he realized the mistake he had made.

Grammar Reinforcement

For additional instruction and practice, have students complete the **Language Lab CD-ROM** lesson on Problems With Modifiers, and practice p. 61 on Misplaced and Dangling Modifiers in the *Writer's Solution Grammar Practice Book.*

Revision Strategy

Have students team up with peer editors as they revise. Have the peer editors use these guidelines:

- Does the essay have a vivid and memorable mood?
- Is the writing personal and detailed?
- Is there a clear insight that the writer gained from the experience?

Writing Lab CD-ROM

The revising and editing section of the tutorial on Description contains the following strategies for self-revision:

- A video of author Colleen McElroy's thoughts on revising.
- Revision checkers for vague adjectives and sentence length.
- Audio-annotated instruction of a first and revised draft.

Publishing

Encourage students to save their essays for possible incorporation into a longer work.

Prentice Hall Writing and Grammar For more prewriting, elaboration, and revision strategies, see *Prentice Hall Writing and Grammar.*

Reinforce and Extend

Applying Language Skills

Suggested Answer

Last spring was delightful. The flowers were radiantly blooming and the weather was balmy.

Grammar Reinforcement

For additional instruction and practice, have students complete Choosing Precise Words, p. 116 in the *Writer's Solution Grammar Practice Book.*

Applying Language Skills: Vivid Adjectives and Adverbs

Avoid vague adjectives whose meanings have become imprecise or unclear. Instead, use **vivid adjectives and adverbs**. These will make your writing more colorful and interesting to read.

Vague:

Our Sunday brunch is great. My mom's good bread tastes good.

Vivid:

Our Sunday brunch is eagerly awaited. My mom's home-baked bread tastes heavenly.

Practice On your paper, replace the vague adjectives and adverbs in the following sentence with vivid ones.

Last spring was really nice. The flowers were pretty and the weather was fine.

Writing Application Review your reflective essay and replace any vague adjectives and adverbs with vivid ones.

Writer's Solution Connection Language Lab

For more practice with vivid adjectives and adverbs, complete the Language Lab lesson on Vivid Adjectives and Adverbs.

Revising

Revise With a Fresh Mind After you've finished drafting your reflective essay, put it aside for a while before revising it. It's best to approach your writing with a fresh mind; you're more likely to see areas where you can make improvements. You might also try reading your essay aloud. Hearing your writing can help you pinpoint aspects that need revising.

Proofreading

Use a Proofreading Checklist Make sure you can answer yes to each of the following questions:

- ▶ Have you spelled all words correctly?
- ▶ Have you used contractions correctly?
- ▶ Have you corrected misplaced or dangling modifiers?
- ▶ Have you used words that appeal to the five senses to evoke vivid images?
- ▶ Have you avoided run-on sentences and sentence fragments?

Revision Model

When autumn leaves begin to fall, my mind ① sadly returns to my favorite summer spot: the beach in the early morning. ② There, I used to set my blanket down in the cool sand and listen to the waves crashing against the shore. I can still hear the seagulls calling to each other, and if I close my eyes, I can sometimes smell the salty air.

① The writer adds the word *sadly* to convey an impression of longing and loss.

② The writer adds this sentence to elaborate on why the beach is such a memorable place to her.

Publishing

Read Your Description Aloud to Background Music Choose music that would go best with your essay, and play it as you read your essay aloud.

Bulletin Board Display With classmates, post your reflective essays on a bulletin board. Decide on a theme for the board, as well as a visual organization plan that will make the essays appealing.

✓ ASSESSMENT

PORTFOLIO ASSESSMENT Use this rubric to assess the students' writing.

	4	3	2	1
Modifiers	All modifiers are vivid and precise. There are no misplaced or dangling modifiers.	Most modifiers are vivid and precise. No misplaced or dangling modifiers.	Many modifiers are vague and could be improved. Misplaced or dangling modifiers are noticeable.	Most modifiers are vague. Incorrect placement of modifiers impairs understanding.
Impression	The essay creates a vivid, personal mood for the reader; the impression the subject left on the writer is clear.	The piece has a definite mood. The writing has a personal touch.	The essay's mood could be better defined. The writer elaborates some, but the topic needs more development.	There is no distinct mood and little or no elaboration that tells why the subject is important to the writer.

Student Success Workshop

Real-World Reading Skills

Constructing Graphic Organizers

Strategies for Success

You may have heard that a picture is worth a thousand words. This is often true in reading. Visual tools called **graphic organizers** can help you understand a text more fully. Graphic organizers can take several forms: charts, graphs, or diagrams. These tools help you to arrange complex information so that you can understand it clearly. If you use graphic organizers such as charts or graphs in your own writing, you can help readers better understand your ideas.

Decide What Information to Express Graphically Consider what parts of the text might be expressed on a chart, graph, or diagram. For instance, maybe you want to show what two story characters have in common or chart three possible outcomes of a character's actions. Or you might want to compare and contrast the percentages of people who own mountain bikes and racing bikes.

Decide Which Type of Graphic Organizer to Use Knowing which type of graphic organizer to use will help you to express the text's information or ideas effectively. For instance, a simple two-column chart is best for a side-by-side comparison of information. A Venn diagram—two overlapping circles showing different and shared elements or characteristics—is best if you are dealing with both differences and similarities.

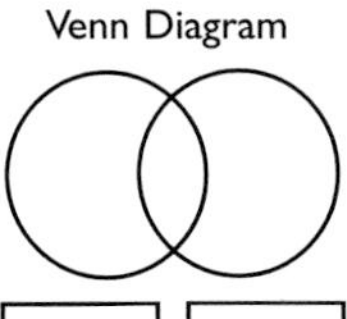
Venn Diagram

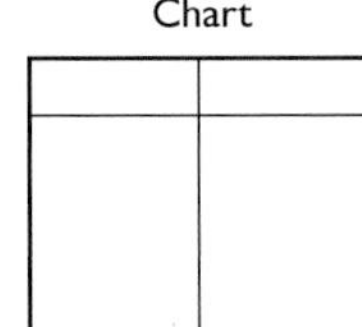
Chart

Apply the Strategies

Read the following paragraphs and follow the instructions:

Football has recently replaced baseball as America's favorite sport. Not only is football popular in America, it has caught on in Canada, too. Canada even has its own league. American football is run by the NFL, or National Football League. In Canada, football is dominated by the CFL, or Canadian Football League.

The NFL is made up of 30 teams from across the United States. The CFL has only 16 teams. While the NFL plays from September to January, the CFL's season runs from August to November. The grand prize in American football is to win the Super Bowl in late January. For Canadian football players, the ultimate achievement is to win the Grey Cup, a competition played in mid-November.

1. What information can a graphic organizer help you to understand better?
2. Using either a Venn diagram or a chart, represent the information visually. Give reasons, based on the text and structure, for choosing the graphic organizer you did.
3. Give examples of other graphic organizers that could also represent the information in this selection.

Test Preparation Workshop

Constructing Graphic Organizers Many standardized tests have sections in which students are asked to interpret information presented in a graphic organizer. Creating their own graphic organizers while reading a test passage can also help students focus on main ideas, and analyze text structures such as compare/contrast, cause and effect, and chronological ordering.

Have students use the Venn Diagram or chart they prepared for this workshop to answer a question such as the following:

During which months does the NFL's season overlap with the CFL's season?

A August to October

B September to November

C October to January

D None of the above

Help students use their own graphic organizers to determine that answer B is correct. Encourage them to develop and consider additional questions that can be answered from their graphic organizers.

Prepare and Engage

LESSON OBJECTIVES

- To construct images such as graphic organizers based on text descriptions and text structures
- To analyze text structures such as compare and contrast, cause and effect, and chronological ordering for how they influence understanding

Apply the Strategies

Customize for
Verbal/Linguistic Learners

Outlining and listing may be the most effective organizing methods for verbal learners. Encourage such students to test the helpfulness of visual tools—and to spend time examining the maps, charts, diagrams, and graphs that they might prefer only to glance at when reading. They can find examples of informational graphics in newspapers, magazines, and textbooks. Discuss their findings: Which drawings are easy to understand? Can drawings make the information easier to understand than the text alone?

Answers

1. Facts and numbers are often easier to compare and contrast in a graphic organizer. Graphic organizers can point out patterns of information.
2. Students who choose the Venn diagram may note that the Canadian and American football leagues have shared characteristics to list in the overlapping section of the Venn diagram. (For example, both leagues are popular, have a playing season, and end their seasons with a grand prize.) Students who choose the two-column chart may point out that the paragraphs focus on differences between the leagues, such as number of teams, playing season, and prizes.
3. Students will have their own arrangements to highlight CFL/NFL comparisons and contrasts. One possibility is a grid in which shared characteristics are listed as category headings and differing details are listed under the headings.

Prepare and Engage

LESSON OBJECTIVES

- To listen attentively, interpret, and clarify understanding

Tell students that receiving oral directions to a place is something that they will have to do in countless situations over the course of their lives. Listening carefully the first time to acquire the necessary details is a vital and often-ignored communication skill.

Customize for
Visual/Spatial Learners

Remind these students that they can use line drawings and simple pictures as part of their notes. In taking notes on how to get from one place to another, these students may benefit from using line drawings to show where to turn and to identify important landmarks. Arrows, circles, and stars can also help these learners to highlight the most significant parts of the directions.

Apply the Strategies

In order to facilitate the role-playing, you might have students brainstorm for directional terms and phrases that will make directions accessible and provide a basis for asking questions to clarify.

Speaking, Listening, and Viewing Workshop

When a new friend gives you directions to her house over the phone or a teacher gives you instructions before a test, you're getting directions orally. Oral directions are more critical than written ones because you have only one chance to get them right.

Listen Up The most important thing to remember when receiving oral directions is to listen carefully. Focus on hearing and remembering important details. If you are unclear on any part of the directions, ask for that portion of the directions to be repeated. Otherwise, when you actually carry out the directions, you may find yourself lost or confused.

Repeat What You Hear Repeat the directions to the person who gave them. Doing so will ensure that you have heard the directions carefully.

Tips for Listening to Oral Directions

Getting correct directions is the first step in ensuring that you arrive at your destination or achieve your goal. When listening to oral directions, keep these points in mind:

- Listen attentively and carefully.
- Repeat what you have heard.
- If steps must be followed in a certain order, be sure you understand that order.
- Ask questions to clarify any part of the oral directions that are confusing or unclear.
- Take notes as the person gives the directions; *do not* rely on your memory.
- If you are getting directions to a place, ask for visual identification markers to locate key points along the way.

Apply the Strategies

With a partner, role-play these situations:

1. Take turns giving each other oral directions on how to get from one part of your school to another. After you have followed the directions, discuss with your partner how successful each of you was in both giving and receiving oral directions.
2. Dictate directions to a place that both you and your partner know. Do not identify the place. Have your partner mentally follow your directions and identify the place.

Test Preparation Workshop

Reading Comprehension

Recognizing Cause and Effect; Predicting Outcomes

Strategies for Success

The reading sections of standardized tests often require you to read a passage to understand cause-and-effect relationships. The test may also require you to predict future actions and outcomes. Use the following strategies to answer test questions on these skills:

Recognize Causes and Effects A cause is an event that makes something else happen, and an effect is the result that happens. In a passage on a test, you may find words and phrases that hint at cause-and-effect relationships, such as *because* and *as a result.* To recognize cause-and-effect relationships, ask yourself: "What happened? What was the result? What caused this occurrence?"

You might be asked to recognize the cause-and-effect relationships in a passage such as this:

> Last month's ski trip was a flop. Only eight of our thirty members came. Some had no transportation. Others had prior holiday commitments. In addition, the cost of the trip was more than most members could pay. We need to work together to address these concerns before scheduling the next trip.

1 What effect did the holidays have on the trip?
A Some members had no transportation.
B Some members couldn't afford to go.
C The trip's organizers had not planned well.
D Some members had other holiday plans.

Answers **A** and **B** refer to causes of low attendance on the trip. Answer **C** does not explain why the holidays had an effect on who could go on the trip. Answer **D** is correct because it explains how the holidays prevented some people from participating.

Predict Actions and Outcomes Use what you know from the text and your own experience to predict probable future actions and outcomes. Ask yourself, "What might happen next?"

2 What can you predict about the next ski trip?
A The cost will still be too high for most.
B The trip will be planned more carefully.
C The trip will be another failure.
D The planners will disagree on where to go.

Answers **A**, **C**, and **D** are incorrect because the passage suggests that the organizers are aware of the problems and want to address them. Answer **B** is the correct answer.

Apply the Strategies

Read the following passage, and answer the questions that follow.

> Gina and Phoebe had planned to study together for tomorrow's algebra exam, as they often did. They had agreed to meet at the library at six-thirty. But as Gina was leaving the house, her mother fell and hurt her arm. Gina had to rush her to the hospital. By the time she could call Phoebe, it was past her bedtime. Although it wasn't her fault that she missed their appointment, Gina was worried that Phoebe would be angry with her.

1 Why didn't Gina meet Phoebe at the library?
A Gina forgot that they had planned to meet.
B Gina's mother hurt her arm.
C Gina took her mother to the hospital.
D It was past closing time at the library.

2 How might Phoebe react to Gina's explanation?
A She will doubt Gina's story.
B She will pretend to be understanding, but will actually feel angry or hurt.
C She will never study with Gina again.
D She will probably be understanding.

Correlations to Standardized Tests

The reading comprehension skills reviewed in this Workshop correspond to the following standardized test section:
ACT Reading

Test Preparation

Each ATE workshop in Unit 4 supports the instruction here by providing teaching suggestions and a sample test item:
Recognizing Cause and Effect
(ATE, pp. 303, 313, 339)
Predicting Outcomes
(ATE, p. 325, 363)

LESSON OBJECTIVES

- To analyze text structures such as compare and contrast, cause and effect, and chronological ordering for how they influence understanding
- To draw inferences such as conclusions, generalizations, and predictions and support them with text evidence and experience

Answers

1. (C) Gina took her mother to the hospital.
2. (D) She will probably be understanding.

Test-Taking Tip

Read All Answer Choices Explain that students sometimes lower their scores on a multiple-choice test because they respond too quickly to an answer choice that seems right. Urge students to read through all the answer choices, thinking about each one, even if the first or second answer seems correct. Differences among the answers can be subtle, and another answer choice may be better.

Have students reread question 1 at the end of the workshop. Point out that answer *B* is technically correct—Gina missed her library appointment because her mother hurt her arm. Ask students why reading the other answer choices is a good strategy. They should note that choice *C* is clearly the better answer, since it states a more direct cause of Gina's missed appointment.

Planning Instruction and Assessment

Unit Objectives

1. To read selections in different genres that develop the theme of Expanding Horizons
2. To apply a variety of reading strategies, particularly Strategies for Reading Fiction, appropriate for reading these selections
3. To analyze literary elements
4. To use a variety of strategies to read unfamiliar words and to build vocabulary
5. To learn elements of grammar and style
6. To use recursive writing processes to write in a variety of forms
7. To express and support responses to various types of texts
8. To prepare, organize, and present literary interpretations

Meeting the Objectives

With each selection, you will find instructional material and portfolio opportunities through which students can meet these objectives. Further, you will find additional practice pages for reading strategies, literary elements, vocabulary, and grammar in the ***Selection Support*** booklet in the ***Teaching Resources*** box.

Test Preparation

The unit workshop **Reading Comprehension: Evaluate and Make Judgments** (SE, p. 465), is supported by teaching tips and a sample test item in the ATE workshop with each selection grouping.

- **Reading Comprehension: Evaluate and Make Judgments** (ATE, pp. 381, 395, 405, 413, 427, 439, 449)

The following additional workshops in the ATE give teaching tips and a sample test item for applying the skill taught in the Student Success Workshop:

- **Reading Comprehension: Distinguish Fact from Nonfact** (ATE, p. 424)
- **Reading Comprehension: Understand Specialized or Technical Terms** (ATE, p. 463)

Torn in Transit, John Haberle, Brandywine River Museum

Humanities: Art

Torn in Transit by John Haberle, 1890–95.

Help students examine the multiple levels of meaning of this painting. Ask students about the title; it refers to the tickets shown and to the package, whose torn edges are seen around the perimeter of the landscape. The painting might be interpreted as a comment on the way human traffic tends to despoil nature; the work might also be interpreted as expressing the opposite idea—that nature cannot be tidily contained, despite human efforts to do so.

Help students link the artwork to the theme of Unit 5, "Expanding Horizons," by answering the following question:

1. Has the painter made the landscape seem an intimidating or an inviting place, and how? *Most students will probably say that the landscape seems inviting because it is so beautiful; some students might find the mountains challenging and the water potentially treacherous.*

UNIT 5

Expanding Horizons

New places, new ideas, new friends—every new experience expands your horizons. Your world becomes larger when you consider new ways of seeing and doing. Through the stories, poems, and essays in this unit, you will travel from Nigeria to England, meeting a kindly old widow, celebrities, and a band of thieves. Your horizons will expand with a variety of new experiences and interesting people.

Assessing Student Progress

The following tools are available to measure the degree to which students meet the unit objectives:

Informal Assessment

The questions on the Guide for Responding sections are a first level of response to the concepts and skills presented with the selection. Students' responses are a brief informal measure of their grasp of the material. Their responses on this level can indicate where further instruction and practice are needed. You may then follow up with the practice pages in the ***Selection Support*** booklet.

You will find literature and reading guides in the ***Alternative Assessment*** booklet, which you may give students on an individual basis for informal assessment of their performance.

Formal Assessment

In the ***Formal Assessment*** booklet, you will find selection tests and part tests.

Selection Tests The selection tests measure comprehension and skills acquisition for each selection or group of selections.

Part Tests Each part test, which calls on students to read a passage of literature they have not previously seen, applies the unit skills on a broader level. The Critical Reading section measures Unit Objectives 1, 2, and 3. The Vocabulary and Grammar section measures Objectives 4 and 5. The Essay section measures Objectives 1 and 6. Both the Critical Reading and Vocabulary and Grammar section use formats similar to those found on many standardized tests, including the SAT.

Alternative Assessment

Portfolios As you review individual pieces or the collected work in students' portfolios, you will find assessment sheets available in the portfolio section of the ***Alternative Assessment*** booklet.

Scoring Rubrics You will find scoring rubrics for writing modes in the ***Alternative Assessment*** booklet. You can apply these to Guided Writing Lessons and to Writing Process Workshop lessons.

Speaking, Listening, and Viewing The ***Alternative Assessment*** booklet contains assessment sheets for speaking, listening, and viewing activities.

Learning Modalities The ***Alternative Assessment*** booklet contains activities that appeal to different learning styles. You may use these as an alternative measurement of students' growth.

Prepare and Engage

LESSON OBJECTIVES

1. **To develop vocabulary and word identification skills**
   - Related Words: Forms of *sagacity*
   - Using the Word Bank: Context
   - Extending Word Study: Synonyms
2. **To use a variety of reading strategies to comprehend a personal narrative**
   - Connect Your Experience
   - Reading for Success: Strategies for Reading Fiction
   - Tips to Guide Reading
   - Read to Appreciate Author's Craft
3. **To increase knowledge of other cultures and to connect common elements across cultures**
   - Connecting Themes Across Cultures (ATE)
4. **To express and support responses to the text**
   - Critical Thinking
   - Idea Bank: Char. Sketch
   - Idea Bank: Review
   - Idea Bank: Area Map
   - Analyze Literary Criticism
5. **To analyze literary elements**
   - Literary Focus: Motivation
6. **To read in order to research self-selected and assigned topics**
   - Idea Bank: Health Report
   - Questions for Research
   - Idea Bank: Video
   - Viewing and Representing Mini-Lesson
7. **To plan, prepare, organize, and present literary interpretations**
   - Idea Bank: Dialogue
   - Speaking, Listening, and Viewing Mini-Lesson
8. **To use recursive writing processes to write a last will and testament**
   - Guided Writing Lesson
9. **To increase knowledge of the rules of grammar and usage**
   - Build Grammar Skills: Adjectives and Adverbs

Test Preparation

Reading Comprehension: Evaluate and Make Judgments (ATE, p. 381) The teaching tips and sample test item in this workshop support the instruction and practice in the unit workshop: **Reading Comprehension: Interpret Graphic Aids; Evaluate and Make Judgments** (SE, p. 465)

Guide for Reading

Virginia Woolf *(1882–1941)*

Breaking free from her prim and proper upbringing, Virginia Woolf overcame sexism and stereotypes to become one of the most influential shapers of contemporary modern fiction.

Virginia Woolf (born Virginia Stephen) was brought up in a family of old-fashioned Victorians. Her father, Leslie Stephen, saw to it that his daughter grew up surrounded by books. He also introduced her to a number of writers in person. By the age of twenty-three, Virginia began contributing reviews to the Literary Supplement of *The Times of London.*

Meeting of the Minds In 1912, Virginia married Leonard Woolf, author and social reformer, with whom she founded the Hogarth Press. Their house in London became an informal meeting place for some of the more important thinkers of the era, including writers E. M. Forster and Katherine Mansfield, art critic Roger Fry, and economist John Maynard Keynes.

A Matter of Principle Virginia Woolf's intellectual and privileged social background allowed her liberal beliefs to flourish. She resented the sexism and corruption of English universities and other aspects of male-dominated Victorian England.

Virginia Woolf's sensitivity to the abuse of women's rights led to her refusal of honorary degrees from several universities.

Stream of Novels After her first two novels, Woolf began to experiment with "stream of consciousness," a narrative technique that presents thoughts as if they are coming directly from a character's mind. Woolf continued to refine her fluid, inward-looking style in the novels *Mrs. Dalloway* (1925), *To the Lighthouse* (1927), and *The Waves* (1931). Unlike many of her works, "The Widow and the Parrot" has a traditional narrative form.

◆ Build Vocabulary

RELATED WORDS: FORMS OF *SAGACITY*

In this story, you will encounter an unusual parrot—a parrot of great sagacity. *Sagacity* and its related words come from the Latin word *sagax,* which means "keen" or "acute." *Sagacity* means "wisdom," or "keen judgment." A *sage* is a person who has keen judgment—a wise person. *Sagacious,* on the other hand, describes a person or thing, such as a decision that shows good judgment.

WORD BANK

As you read, you will encounter the words on this list. Each word is defined on the page where it first appears. Preview the list before you read.

ford
dilapidated
sovereigns
sagacity

◆ Build Grammar Skills

CORRECT USE OF ADJECTIVES AND ADVERBS

Do not confuse the use of **adjectives** and **adverbs.** Remember that adjectives modify nouns and adverbs modify verbs, adjectives, and other adverbs. A common mistake is the use of an adjective to modify a verb, whereas an adverb is correct.

Notice the correct use of the adjective *slow* and the adverb *slowly* in these sentences from "The Widow and the Parrot."

. . . her progress was very *slow* indeed.

(The predicate adjective *slow* modifies the subject *progress.*)

At the best of times she walked *slowly.*

(The adverb *slowly* modifies the verb *walked.* The adjective *slow* would be incorrect here.)

Prentice Hall Literature Program Resources

REINFORCE / RETEACH / EXTEND

Selection Support Pages
Build Vocabulary: Forms of *sagacity,* p. 113
Build Grammar Skills: Correct Use of Adjectives and Adverbs, p. 114
Reading for Success: Strategies for Reading Fiction, pp. 115–116
Literary Focus: Motivation, p. 117

Strategies for Diverse Student Needs, p. 28
Beyond Literature, Career Connection: Veterinary Science, p. 28
Formal Assessment
Selection Test, pp. 98–100

Alternative Assessment, p. 28
Resource Pro CD-ROM
Listening to Literature Audiocassettes

The Widow and the Parrot

MODEL SELECTION

◆ Literature and Your Life

Connect Your Experience

If you've ever had a pet, you know that the bond between people and animals can be a strong one. The woman in this story has a strong connection with animals. Her kindness and devotion to animals change her life for the better.

Journal Writing Describe a time when it seemed that your pet was trying to tell you something or communicate something to you. For example, you may have a pet who reminds you of feeding times by scratching at the pantry at the same time every day. If you've never had a pet, describe an unusual exchange between a person and an animal that you witnessed on television or at a zoo.

Thematic Focus: Expanding Horizons

The woman and the parrot in this story communicate as if the parrot were human. As you read this story, ask yourself what animals can teach us.

◆ Background for Understanding

Language

You wouldn't expect to understand someone who speaks a language you don't know, but you would probably expect to understand someone who speaks English. You might be surprised to find that someone who speaks American English might, in fact, have difficulty understanding some words and expressions in British English.

In "The Widow and the Parrot," Mrs. Gage mentions *pounds sterling* and *solicitors*. Although an American might think of *pounds* as weight and *solicitors* as salespeople, a resident of Great Britain thinks of *pounds* as British money (shown below) and *solicitors* as lawyers.

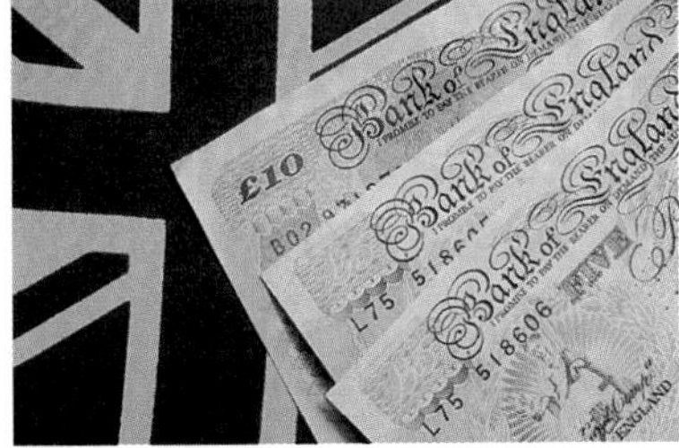

◆ Literary Focus

Motivation

Detectives in mystery stories are always looking for the motive for a crime. However, you don't have to be a detective to want to know a character's **motivation**—the reason for his or her actions or words. Understanding why characters act as they do will help you understand story events. For instance, in "The Widow and the Parrot," a rich old man leaves all his wealth to a sister he hasn't seen in years. This action is understandable when you consider the man's possible motive: He may have been sorry that he didn't help her during his lifetime.

Use a chart like the one shown here to explore the motives behind the actions of the characters in this story.

Motive
Sorrow that he hasn't been in touch

Action
Leaves money to sister

Action

Action

Interest Grabber Ask students what they would do if they suddenly learned they had won or inherited a million dollars. Would they continue their lives much as they are living them now? Would they make any significant changes? What would they buy? Would they give any money away? After discussing what students would do if they received such an unexpected piece of good fortune, tell them they are about to read a story about a poor person who is told she inherits a large fortune.

Connecting Themes Across Cultures

Stories about parrots might be said to constitute a genre. There are parrot stories in every country where parrots live. Parrots are prized for the beauty of their plumage, but it is their gift for mimicking human speech that makes them so interesting. Discuss with student stories about parrots in other cultures.

Customize for
Less Proficient Readers
These students can benefit from breaking the plot of the story into scenes. Have students work together to list the scenes in the story that advance the plot, as if in a play version of the story.

Customize for
Pre-AP Students
Tell students that Mrs. Gage is an unusual character for Virginia Woolf—most of Woolf's characters are upper-class intellectuals. As they read, have these students appraise the author's attitude toward Mrs. Gage and consider why Woolf might have created this particular character to be the heroine of her story.

Customize for
Visual/Spatial Learners
As they read the story, have students graph and label the main character's highs and lows. Reviewing the graph will help students recall the plot of the story.

Test Preparation Workshop

Reading Comprehension
Evaluate and Make Judgments Standardized tests often require students to be able to make judgments based upon evidence from passages. Use the following sample test item to help students practice this skill:

> Although lame and rather shortsighted Mrs. Gage was doing her best to mend a pair of clogs, for she had only a few shillings a week to live on. As she hammered at the clog, the postman opened the door and threw a letter into her lap.

The author provides evidence that the postman's act was—

A rude
B considerate
C offhand
D facetious

Help students to see that by tossing the letter into a lame woman's lap he was being considerate, B.

Reading for Success

The Reading for Success page in each unit presents a set of problem-solving procedures to help readers understand authors' words and ideas on multiple levels. Good readers develop a bank of strategies from which they can draw as needed.

Unit 5 focuses on strategies for reading fiction. For students to enjoy a work of fiction it is important to apply strategies that will enhance their understanding and appreciation of an author's craft.

These strategies for reading fiction are modeled with "The Widow and the Parrot." Each green box shows an example of the thinking process involved in applying one of these strategies.

How to Use the Reading for Success Page

- Introduce the strategies, presenting each as a problem solving procedure. Be sure students understand what each strategy involves and under what circumstances to apply it.
- Before students read the story, have them preview it, looking at the annotations in the green boxes that model the strategies.
- To reinforce these strategies after students have read "The Widow and the Parrot," have students do the Reading for Success pages in ***Selection Support,*** pp. 115–116. This activity gives students an opportunity to read a selection and practice the strategies for reading fiction by writing their own annotations.

Reading for Success

Strategies for Reading Fiction

Suppose you could visit a new and exciting place each week—you can if you read works of fiction! Reading fiction allows you to explore unfamiliar places and unusual worlds.

Just as mapping out a strategy for a vacation helps ensure a pleasant trip, applying effective strategies as you read fiction helps you understand and enjoy what you are reading. When you read fiction, use the following strategies:

Predict what will happen or what the author will say.

As you read, ask yourself what might happen. You may base a prediction on your own experience in a similar situation or on information that has been provided in the text. Continue to make predictions as you read.

Identify with a character or the situation.

Identify with a character or the situation in your reading. Put yourself in the place of the character and experience his or her thoughts, feelings, and so on. Ask yourself how you would handle the situation.

Envision the setting and the action.

Use details from the story to create a picture in your mind, as if you were watching the story unfold on the big screen. For example, see the house that your character lives in. Is it big or small? How is it decorated? As you read along, envision the action and revise the images in your mind as events unfold.

Draw inferences.

Writers don't always tell you everything directly. You have to make inferences to arrive at ideas that writers suggest but don't say. You make an inference by considering the details that the writer includes or doesn't include. Sometimes it's also helpful to "read between the lines"—to look beyond the literal meaning of the words to obtain a full picture of what the author means.

Draw conclusions.

A conclusion is a general statement that you can make and explain by reasons or that you can support with details from the text. A series of inferences can lead you to a conclusion.

Respond.

Think about what the story means. What feelings does it evoke in you? What has the story added to your understanding of people and of life in general?

As you read the following story by Virginia Woolf, look at the notes in the boxes. These notes demonstrate how to apply these strategies to a work of fiction.

Reading Strategies: Support and Reinforcement

Appropriate Reading Strategies Students are given a reading strategy to apply in reading each selection. For example, students may be asked to identify with a character or situation in a selection where character is central to the story.

Reading Prompts To encourage application of the given reading strategy, there are occasional prompts, within green boxes, at appropriate and significant points. In addition, there are red boxes prompting application of the Literary Focus concept and maroon boxes prompting students to connect with their lives.

Using the Boxed Annotations and Prompts

The material in the green, red, and maroon boxes along the sides of selections is intended to help students apply the literary element and the reading strategy and to make a connection with their lives.

You may use the boxed material in these ways:

- Have students pause when they come to a box and respond to its prompt before they continue reading.
- Urge students to read through the selection ignoring the boxes. After they have read the selection completely, they may go back and review the selection, responding to the prompts.

MODEL

The Widow and the Parrot

Virginia Woolf

Some fifty years ago Mrs. Gage, an elderly widow, was sitting in her cottage in a village called Spilsby in Yorkshire. Although lame and rather shortsighted she was doing her best to mend a pair of clogs, for she had only a few shillings a week to live on. As she hammered at the clog, the postman opened the door and threw a letter into her lap. ❷

It bore the address "Messrs. Stagg and Beetle, 67 High Street, Lewes, Sussex."

Mrs. Gage opened it and read:

"Dear Madam: We have the honor to inform you of the death of your brother Mr. Joseph Brand."

"Lawk a mussy," said Mrs. Gage. "Old brother Joseph gone at last!" ❸

"He has left you his entire property," the letter went on, "which consists of a dwelling house, stable, cucumber frames, mangles, wheelbarrows, etc., etc., in the village of Rodmell, near Lewes. He also bequeaths to you his entire fortune; Viz: £3,000. (three thousand pounds[1]) sterling."

You might **predict** that there will be obstacles to Mrs. Gage's getting this inheritance.

▲ Critical Viewing What role might a parrot like this one play in the story? **[Predict]**

1. **three thousand pounds:** This amount of British money was worth about $15,000 at the time of the story.

Develop Understanding

One-Minute Insight Kindly old Mrs. Gage gains an inheritance from her brother, but the miserly old man hides it where it cannot be found. After a series of apparent disasters, Mrs. Gage's kindness to her brother's beloved parrot leads her to discover the missing fortune. The story ends happily, as the heroine's goodness to animals is rewarded with her finding the inheritance.

▶Critical Viewing◀

❶ **Predict** Students may note that the title implies that a parrot will be a main character in the story.

◆ Reading for Success

❷ **Predict What Will Happen** Point out this introduction to Mrs. Gage. Ask: What do you know about Mrs. Gage so far? What makes you think the letter is important? *She is old, lame, and poor. The appearance of the letter at the end of the first paragraph indicates that it will influence the plot in an important way.*

❸ **Clarification** The phrase "lawk a mussy" is a dialect form of "Lord have mercy." Ask: What does the author's use of this phrase tell you about the character? *Her speech indicates that she is not from the upper class and is probably not very well educated.*

Customize for *English Language Learners*

An occasional "Briticism" or archaic term such as "sovereign" or "half a crown" in the story may pose problems for these students. Explain these unfamiliar expressions as needed. Guide students to determine meanings of expressions such as "wealth of the Indies" from context.

Block Scheduling Strategies

Consider these suggestions to take advantage of extended class time:

- Have students complete the journal activity in Literature and Your Life (p. 381) and discuss their entries with the class.
- Introduce the Reading for Success strategies for reading fiction. As they read, encourage students to look at the annotations that model the strategies. For more practice, give them the Reading for Success pages in ***Selection Support***, pp. 115–116.
- As you review the information in Background for Understanding (p. 381), have students mention any other British expressions with which they are familiar; for example, *boot* for trunk of a car, *pram* for baby carriage, *flat* for apartment, and *lorry* for truck.
- Have students work in small groups to discuss their answers to the Critical Thinking Questions (p. 391).
- Before students complete the Guided Writing Lesson (p. 392), have them brainstorm for a list of story characters who might leave money, property, or advice in a will. Students may select from the class list or use ideas of their own as they prepare their last will and testament.

◆ Critical Thinking

❶ **Make Inferences** Ask students: What does the fact that Mrs. Gage is devoted to animals even though she is poor tell you about her personality? *That she would sacrifice for her dog shows that she has a kind, unselfish nature. Some students, however, may say that some people who are devoted to animals do not show the same concern for fellow humans. Students should be encouraged to read on to find if this is true of Mrs. Gage or not.*

◆ Reading for Success

❷ **Envision the Setting** This description shows very clearly what the ford was like. Have students describe the ford in their own words. *Students may say that it is a shallow, rocky path across the wide river.*

◆ Reading for Success

❸ **Draw Conclusions** Ask students to think back to the beginning of the story when they learn that Mrs. Gage is devoted to her dog. Have them combine what they learned about Mrs. Gage's personality with this description of her with the parrot and draw a conclusion about her personality. *It should now be evident that she is a kind, sensitive person.*

◆ Critical Thinking

❹ **Identify Character Traits** Ask students: Would you say Mrs. Gage is an optimist or a pessimist? Why? *She is an optimist; even though part of her inheritance has come to nothing, she is able to focus on the other part.*

Read to Appreciate Author's Craft

Virginia Woolf was a sophisticated writer, acquainted with the works of many writers. In this story, Woolf experiments with conventions of folk stories and oral tradition. Have students identify some of these conventions as they read. They might point out Woolf's use of dialect and the importance of a parrot. Students may also note the repetition of the line "Mrs. Gage, as I have already said, was lame in her right leg" to approximate an oral rendering.

Mrs. Gage almost fell into the fire with joy. She had not seen her brother for many years, and, as he did not even acknowledge the Christmas card which she sent him every year, she thought that his miserly habits, well known to her from childhood, made him grudge even a penny stamp for a reply.

But now it had all turned out to her advantage. With three thousand pounds, to say nothing of house, etc., etc., she and her family could live in great luxury for ever.

She determined that she must visit Rodmell at once. The village clergyman, the Rev. Samuel Tallboys, lent her two pound ten, to pay her fare, and by next day all preparations for her journey were complete. The most important of these was the care of her dog Shag during her absence, for in spite of her poverty she was devoted to animals, and often went short herself rather than stint her dog of his bone. ❶

She reached Lewes late on Tuesday night. In those days, I must tell you, there was no bridge over the river at Southease, nor had the road to Newhaven yet been made. To reach Rodmell it was necessary to cross the river Ouse by a ford, traces of which still exist, but this could only be attempted at low tide, when the stones on the riverbed appeared above the water. ❷ Mr. Stacey, the farmer, was going to Rodmell in his cart, and he kindly offered to take Mrs. Gage with him. They reached Rodmell about nine o'clock on a November night and Mr. Stacey obligingly pointed out to Mrs. Gage the house at the end of the village which had been left her by her brother. Mrs. Gage knocked at the door. There was no answer. She knocked again. A very strange high voice shrieked out "Not at home." She was so much taken aback that if she had not heard footsteps coming she would have run away. However, the door was opened by an old village woman, by name Mrs. Ford.

"Who was that shrieking out 'Not at home'?" said Mrs. Gage.

"Drat the bird!" said Mrs. Ford very peevishly, pointing to a large gray parrot. "He almost screams my head off. There he sits all day humped up on his perch like a monument screeching 'Not at home' if ever you go near his perch." He was a very handsome bird, as Mrs. Gage could see; but his feathers were sadly neglected. "Perhaps he is unhappy, or he may be hungry," she said. But Mrs. Ford said it was temper merely; he was a seaman's parrot and had learnt his language in the east. However, she added, Mr. Joseph was very fond of him, had called him James; and, it was said, talked to him as if he were a rational being. Mrs. Ford soon left. Mrs. Gage at once went to her box and fetched some sugar which she had with her and offered it to the parrot, saying in a very kind tone that she meant him no harm, but was his old master's sister, come to take possession of the house, and she would see to it that he was as happy as a bird could be. ❸ Taking a lantern she next went round the house to see what sort of property her brother had left her. It was a bitter disappointment. There were holes in all the carpets. The bottoms of the chairs had fallen out. Rats ran along the mantelpiece. There were large toadstools growing through the kitchen floor. ❹ There was not a stick of furniture worth seven pence halfpenny; and Mrs. Gage only cheered herself by thinking of the three thousand pounds that lay safe and snug in Lewes Bank.

She determined to set off to Lewes next day in order to claim her money from

You can **infer** that Joseph, despite his miserliness, seemed to be good to his parrot.

You might **predict** that Mrs. Gage's kindness to the parrot will have a positive effect.

Details such as the holes in the carpets and the rats on the floor help you **envision** the house.

Cross-Curricular Connection: Science

Mrs. Gage found toadstools growing through the kitchen floor. Point out to students that toadstools are inedible forms of mushrooms. These are fungi consisting of two parts: a mycelium (stem) and a fruiting body (the umbrella-shaped top). Mushrooms vary greatly in size and color, rising from about ¾ of an inch to about 15 inches in height and ranging from whites and yellows to blue, violet, green, red, and black. Many species of mushroom live on decaying matter, although some live on living organisms such as trees and plants. In some instances the mushroom causes no harm to its host; however, many such growths are parasitic and will destroy the host plant.

Ask students what the presence of toadstools indicates about the house Mrs. Gage has inherited. *Students should note that the toadstools are feeding on the decaying matter of the floor of the house.* Suggest that interested students research species of mushroom that can be described as toadstools.

Messrs. Stagg and Beetle the solicitors,[2] and then to return home as quick as she could. Mr. Stacey, who was going in to market with some fine Berkshire pigs, again offered to take her with him, and told her some terrible stories of young people who had been drowned through trying to cross the river at high tide, as they drove. A great disappointment was in store for the poor old woman directly she got in to Mr. Stagg's office.

"Pray take a seat, Madam," he said, looking very solemn and grunting slightly. "The fact is," he went on, "that you must prepare to face some very disagreeable news. Since I wrote to you I have gone carefully through Mr. Brand's papers. I regret to say that I can find no trace whatever of the three thousand pounds. Mr. Beetle, my partner, went himself to Rodmell and searched the premises with the utmost care. He found absolutely nothing—no gold, silver, or valuables of any kind—except a fine gray parrot which I advise you to sell for whatever he will fetch. His language, Benjamin Beetle said, is very extreme. But that is neither here nor there. I much fear you have had your journey for nothing. The premises are dilapidated; and of course our expenses are considerable." Here he stopped, and Mrs. Gage well knew that he wished her to go. She was almost crazy with disappointment. Not only had she borrowed two pound ten from the Rev. Samuel Tallboys, but she would return home absolutely empty handed, for the parrot James would have to be sold to pay her fare. It was raining hard, but Mr. Stagg did not press her to stay, and she was too beside herself with sorrow to care what she did. In spite of the rain she started to walk back to Rodmell across the meadows.

> Because you know Mrs. Gage's feelings and expectations, you can **identify** with her great disappointment.

Mrs. Gage, as I have already said, was lame in her right leg. At the best of times she walked slowly, and now, what with her disappointment and the mud on the bank, her progress was very slow indeed. As she plodded along, the day grew darker and darker, until it was as much as she could do to keep on the raised path by the river side. You might have heard her grumbling as she walked, and complaining of her crafty brother Joseph, who had put her to all this trouble "Express," she said, "to plague me. He was always a cruel little boy when we were children," she went on. "He liked worrying the poor insects, and I've known him trim a hairy caterpillar with a pair of scissors before my very eyes. He was such a miserly varmint too. He used to hide his pocket money in a tree, and if anyone gave him a piece of iced cake for tea, he cut the sugar off and kept it for his supper. I make no doubt he's all aflame at this very moment in fire, but what's the comfort of that to me?" she asked, and indeed it was very little comfort, for she ran slap into a great cow which was coming along the bank, and rolled over and over in the mud. 6 7

> You can **predict** that Mrs. Gage will be overcome by obstacles or that something unforeseen will happen to turn events around.

She picked herself up as best she could and trudged on again. It seemed to her that she had been walking for hours. It was now pitch dark and she could scarcely see her own hand before her nose. Suddenly she bethought her of Farmer Stacey's words about the ford. "Lawk a mussy," she said, "however shall I find my way across? If the tide's in, I shall step into deep water and be swept out to sea in a jiffy! Many's the couple that been drowned here; to say nothing of horses, carts, herds of cattle, and stacks of hay."

Indeed what with the dark and the mud she had got herself into a pretty pickle. She could

2. **solicitors:** British legal representatives.

◆ Build Vocabulary

ford (fôrd) *n.*: Shallow place in a stream or river, where people can cross

dilapidated (di lap´ ə dāt´ id) *adj.*: Fallen into a shabby and neglected state

Customize for
Less Proficient Readers
Have volunteers summarize Mr. Stagg's remarks to Mrs. Gage. *It appears that the three thousand pounds Mrs. Gage expected are nowhere to be found. The only thing of worth she has inherited is the parrot.*

◆ Reading for Success

5 Identify With a Character or the Situation Have students think about times when they have been so disappointed that they didn't care what they did. Ask: Why does your identification with Mrs. Gage's despair make you want to read on? *Students may say that they hope that something good will happen to her.*

◆ Build Grammar Skills

6 Correct Use of Adjectives and Adverbs Ask students to identify and explain Mrs. Gage's grammar error in this passage. What part of speech is *express*? Which word does it modify? Which word should she have used instead? *Mrs. Gage has used the adjective* express *to modify the verb* put*. She should have used the adverb* expressly.

◆ Critical Thinking

7 Compare and Contrast Have students compare and contrast Mrs. Gage and her brother Joseph as children. How did Mrs. Gage, as a child, feel about her brother's treatment of insects? Would Mrs. Gage have been cruel to any animal? Would she have been miserly or generous? *From what readers already know and from the words "worrying," "poor," and "before my very eyes," readers should know that Mrs. Gage disapproved of her brother's treatment of insects. While Joseph was miserly with his pocket money, readers can assume that Mrs. Gage was generous, based on their knowledge that she has done with less food herself in order to feed her dog.*

Viewing and Representing Mini-Lesson

Video Summary

This mini-lesson supports the first Speaking, Listening, and Viewing activity in the Idea Bank on p. 392.

Introduce Remind students that a summary of any material must include an accurate accounting of its main idea and supporting details. Have volunteers revise this definition for a video. A video summary should have a description of the visuals and the narration. Remind students to include only the details the listeners will need to understand the key features of the video. The summary should recall some of the interest or excitement that the video provides.

Develop Once students obtain videos from libraries, video stores, or home collections, consider having students work in pairs. It might be good idea to pair visual/spatial learners with verbal/linguistic learners, and have them work together on the summary. One student can make notes about the visual elements while the other focuses on the narration.

Apply Have students combine their notes to create a summary of the video. Students can then share the information they learned.

Assess Assess each summary according to the students' ability to convey the main idea of the video they studied.

◆ Reading for Success

❶ Predict What Will Happen or What the Author Will Say Mrs. Gage's fate appears bleak indeed. Ask students: Based on your experience reading similar stories, you would most likely predict that Mrs. Gage will neither drown nor freeze to death. Why? *Students may say that she seems to be a good woman, and they doubt whether the author will allow her to die without some reward for her goodness. They may also say that she is the main character, and if she dies, the story will end pointlessly.*

◆ Build Vocabulary

❷ Related Words: Forms of *Sagacity* Like *sagacity, monstrosity* is a noun with an *-ity* ending. Have students identify the forms of *monstrosity* that parallel *sagacious* and *sage*. *The words are monstrous and monster.*

◆ Reading for Success

❸ Draw Conclusions Have students identify the hints in previous paragraphs that lead them to conclude that the mysterious light is not a comet but Mrs. Gage's burning house. *The village of Rodmell was lit up, the light shot up into the sky, the brother's house was described as being "at the end of the village."*

Customize for
Gifted/Talented Students
Although they might deny it, people often feel pleasure over the misfortunes of others. For example, call students' attention to the sentence "A small boy in his nightgown came capering up to her and cried out, 'Come and see old Joseph Brand's house ablaze!'" Have students look for other examples of this in the story. Then suggest that they think of similar moments that could be turned into short stories.

hardly see the river itself, let alone tell whether she had reached the ford or not. No lights were visible anywhere, for, as you may be aware, there is no cottage or house on that side of the river nearer than Asheham House, lately the seat of Mr. Leonard Woolf. It seemed that there was nothing for it but to sit down and wait for the morning. But at her age, with the rheumatics in her system, she might well die of cold. On the other hand, if she tried to cross the river it was almost certain that she would be drowned. So miserable was her state that she would gladly have changed places with one of the cows in the field. No more wretched old woman could have been found in the whole county of Sussex; standing on the river bank, not knowing whether to sit or to swim, or merely to roll over in the grass, wet though it was, and sleep or freeze to death, as her fate decided. ❶

> You can **infer** that, in her disappointment and in the face of these obstacles, Mrs. Gage has given up hope.

At that moment a wonderful thing happened. An enormous light shot up into the sky, like a gigantic torch, lighting up every blade of grass, and showing her the ford not twenty yards away. It was low tide, and the crossing would be an easy matter if only the light did not go out before she had got over.

> You can **identify** with Mrs. Gage's feeling of relief.

❷ "It must be a comet or some such wonderful monstrosity," she said as she hobbled across. She could see the village of Rodmell brilliantly lit up in front of her.

"Bless and save us!" she cried out. "There's a house on fire—thanks be to the Lord"—for she reckoned that it would take some minutes at least to burn a house down, and in that time she would be well on her way to the village.

"It's an ill wind that blows nobody any good," she said as she hobbled along the Roman road. Sure enough, she could see every inch of the way, and was almost in the village street when for the first time it struck her: "Perhaps it's my own house that's blazing to cinders before my very eyes!"

She was perfectly right.

A small boy in his nightgown came capering up to her and cried out, "Come and see old Joseph Brand's house ablaze!"

Cross-Curricular Connection: Geography

Students may be surprised that a river can be affected by tides. The river Ouse flows into the North Sea to the east of England at a bay called The Wash. For many miles upstream, the ocean tides control the river's depth. Similarly, in New York State, the mouth of the Hudson River, where it empties into the Atlantic Ocean, is east of New York City. The Hudson is tidal—and salty—for more than 20 miles north of its mouth.

A name for the part of a river whose waters mix with ocean water is *estuary*.

Explain to students that tides are controlled primarily by the gravitational pull of the moon. At any time of day, there are always two points on Earth that are at high tide: the point directly facing the moon and the point facing directly away from the moon.

▲ Critical Viewing How do you think Mrs. Gage felt at seeing a sight like this and learning that it was her own house? **[Infer]**

All the villagers were standing in a ring round the house handing buckets of water which were filled from the well in Monk's house kitchen, and throwing them on the flames. But the fire had got a strong hold, and just as Mrs. Gage arrived, the roof fell in.

"Has anybody saved the parrot?" she cried.

"Be thankful you're not inside yourself, Madam," said the Rev. James Hawkesford, the clergyman. "Do not worry for the dumb creatures. I make no doubt the parrot was mercifully suffocated on his perch."

But Mrs. Gage was determined to see for herself. She had to be held back by the village people, who remarked (5) that she must be crazy to hazard her life for a bird.

"Poor old woman," said Mrs. Ford, "she has lost all her property, save one old wooden box, with her night things in it. No doubt we should be crazed in her place too."

So saying, Mrs. Ford took Mrs. Gage by the hand and led her off to her own cottage, where she was to sleep the night. The fire was now extinguished, and everybody went home to bed. But poor Mrs. Gage could not sleep. She tossed and tumbled thinking of her miserable state, and wondering how she could get back to Yorkshire and pay the Rev. Samuel Tallboys the money she owed him. At the same time she was even more grieved to think of the fate of the poor parrot James. She had taken a liking to the bird, and thought that he must have an affectionate heart to mourn so deeply for the death of old Joseph Brand, who had never (6) done a kindness to any human creature. It was a terrible death for an innocent bird, she thought; and if only she had been in time, she would have risked her own life to save his.

She was lying in bed thinking these thoughts when a slight tap at the window made her start. The tap was repeated three times over. Mrs. Gage got out of bed as quickly as she could and went to the window. There, to her utmost surprise, sitting on the window ledge, was an enormous parrot. The rain had stopped and it was a fine moonlight night. She was greatly alarmed at first, but soon recognized the gray parrot,

▶Critical Viewing◀

4 Infer Have students answer the question by identifying with Mrs. Gage—putting themselves in her shoes: *She probably felt even worse to know that now every last bit of her inheritance was gone.*

◆Critical Thinking

5 Compare and Contrast Ask: What does Mrs. Gage's reaction to the fire tell you about her character? How does her reaction compare with those of the people around her? *Mrs. Gage thinks only of the parrot because she cares about animals. The people around her think she's mad to care about the bird, because if the house were theirs, they would think only of their own safety.*

◆Reading for Success

6 Respond Have volunteers tell how they feel about this thought by Mrs. Gage. Do they believe her? *Students will probably say that they believe Mrs. Gage is sincere and that they respect her for her caring nature.*

Tips to Guide Reading

Shared Reading Have a student read the last paragraph on this page ("She was lying . . .") or read it aloud yourself. Help students to see that at this point the action has become slightly less plausible. Suggest that this is characteristic of a folktale. Ask students to predict what might happen next, and then let them continue to read silently.

Extending Word Study

Synonyms Have students use a dictionary or thesaurus to find synonyms for the words *uncanny, hobbled,* and *prized.* In each case have students compare and contrast the connotations of the words they've located. Then, ask students to analyze Woolf's decision to use the word she did, rather than the synonyms students have found.

Beyond the Classroom

Career Connection

Clergy The Reverends James Hawkesford and Samuel Tallboys play a part in this story because clergymen played an important part in the life of the English community in the nineteenth century. In many communities today, clergy play an important role in social services such as teaching children, providing food for the poor, counseling those in trouble, and so on. Discuss with students any special services that are provided in your community by members of the clergy.

Community Connection

Volunteer Fire Department In small villages at the time when this story is set, fires were generally put out by an army of neighbors working together with the tools they had at hand. Today, many small communities that cannot afford a full-time fire department rely on volunteers to answer the call "Fire!" Have students find out whether their community has a paid fire department, a volunteer fire department, or a combination of the two.

◆ Reading for Success

❶ Envision the Setting and the Action Have students close their eyes and imagine the parrot's actions as a volunteer reads this sentence aloud. Ask students to identify how the author makes the parrot's actions come alive. *She uses specific action verbs and descriptive phrases.*

◆ Literary Focus

❷ Motivation Have students consider what they know about Mrs. Gage's character. Ask: What motivates Mrs. Gage to follow the parrot? *She likes the animal and thinks he's intelligent; she treats him with as much respect as she would a human being. She may be motivated by her respect for him or by simple curiosity.*

◆ Build Grammar Skills

❸ Correct Use of Adjectives and Adverbs The author uses adverbs throughout the story to make the action clear. Have students identify the adverbs that end in *-ly* in these sentences and tell which verbs they modify. What would happen if the adverbs were omitted? *Soothingly modifies "said"; violently modifies "repeated." Without these modifiers, the way Mrs. Gage spoke and the way the bird acted would be less clear.*

◆ Reading for Success

❹ Make Inferences Previously, Mrs. Gage did not understand what the bird meant by his squawking. Why does Mrs. Gage now understand the parrot? *She has paid close attention to his actions, which seem to have some logic to them.*

> You can **infer** that the writer has respect for the intelligence of animals.

James, and was overcome with joy at his escape. She opened the window, stroked his head several times, and told him to come in. The parrot replied by gently shaking his head from side to side, then flew to the ground, walked away a few steps, looked back as if to see whether Mrs. Gage were coming, and then returned to the window sill, where she stood in amazement. ❶

"The creature has more meaning in its acts than we humans know," she said to herself. "Very well, James," she said aloud, talking to him as though he were a human being, "I'll take your word for it. Only wait a moment while I make myself decent."

❷ So saying she pinned on a large apron, crept as lightly as possible downstairs, and let herself out without rousing Mrs. Ford.

The parrot James was evidently satisfied. He now hopped briskly a few yards ahead of her in the direction of the burnt house. Mrs. Gage followed as fast as she could. The parrot hopped, as if he knew his way perfectly, round to the back of the house, where the kitchen had originally been. Nothing now remained of it except the brick floor, which was still dripping with the water which had been thrown to put out the fire. Mrs. Gage stood still in amazement while James hopped about, pecking here and there, as if he were testing the bricks with his beak. It was a very uncanny sight, and had not Mrs. Gage been in the habit of living with animals, she would have lost her head, very likely, and hobbled back home. But stranger things yet were to happen. All this time the parrot had not said a word. He suddenly got into a state of the greatest excitement, fluttering his wings, tapping the floor repeatedly with his beak, and crying so shrilly, "Not at home! Not at home!" that Mrs. Gage feared that the whole village would be roused.

> Judging from the way Woolf has described Joseph, you can probably **predict** what's under the bricks.

"Don't take on so, James; you'll hurt yourself," she said soothingly. But he repeated his attack on the bricks more violently than ever. ❸

"Whatever can be the meaning of it?" said Mrs. Gage, looking carefully at the kitchen floor. The moonlight was bright enough to show her a slight unevenness in the laying of the bricks, as if they had been taken up and then relaid not quite flat with the others. She had fastened her apron with a large safety pin, and she now prized this pin between the bricks and found that they were only loosely laid together. Very soon she had taken one up in her hands. No sooner had she done this than the parrot hopped onto the brick next to it, and, tapping it smartly with his beak, cried, "Not at home!" which Mrs. Gage understood to mean that she was to move it. ❹ So they went on taking up the bricks in the moonlight until they had laid bare a space some six feet by four and a half. This the parrot seemed to think was enough. But what was to be done next?

Analyze Literary Criticism

Point out to students that Virginia Woolf's fame is based not only on her voluminous writing and her central position in the Bloomsbury Group, but on her feminism as well.

Woolf's essay "A Room of One's Own" has been described as an "icon of feminism" by her nephew and biographer, literary critic Quentin Bell. Woolf believed that women in general were held back by lack of educational opportunities. She also had great faith in the writing abilities of women, including her own. Although "The Widow and the Parrot" cannot be counted as one of Woolf's more feminist works, have students discuss how this aspect of Woolf's character may have affected the story. Then have them write a journal entry in which they answer the following question:

In what ways is Mrs. Gage an extraordinary woman? Do you find her believable as a character? *Students should mention Mrs. Gage's remarkable bravery in walking from Lewes to Rodmell at night as well as her conscientious treatment of the parrot. Students may find Mrs. Gage, if not the parrot, a believable character.*

Mrs. Gage now rested, and determined to be guided entirely by the behavior of the parrot James. She was not allowed to rest for long. After scratching about in the sandy foundations for a few minutes, as you may have seen a hen scratch in the sand with her claws, he unearthed what at first looked like a round lump of yellowish stone. His excitement became so intense that Mrs. Gage now went to his help. To her amazement she found that the whole space which they had uncovered was packed with long rolls of these round yellow stones, so neatly laid together that it was quite a job to move them. But what could they be? And for what purpose had they been hidden here? It was not until they had removed the entire layer on the top, and next a piece of oilcloth which lay beneath them, that a most miraculous sight was displayed before their eyes—there, in row after row, beautifully polished, and shining brightly in the moonlight, were thousands of brand new sovereigns!

This, then, was the miser's hiding place; and he had made sure that no one would detect it by taking two extraordinary precautions. In the first place, as was proved later, he had built a kitchen range over the spot where his treasure lay hid, so that unless the fire had destroyed it, no one could have guessed its existence; and secondly he had coated the top layer of sovereigns with some sticky substance, then rolled them in the earth, so that if by any chance one had been laid bare no one would have suspected that it was anything but a pebble such as you may see for yourself any day in the garden. Thus, it was only by the extraordinary coincidence of the fire and the parrot's sagacity that old Joseph's craft was defeated.

From the parrot's actions, you can **infer** that he wants to help Mrs. Gage.

Mrs. Gage and the parrot now worked hard and removed the whole hoard—which numbered three thousand pieces, neither more nor less—placing them in her apron which was spread upon the ground. As the three thousandth coin was placed on the top of the pile, the parrot flew up into the air in triumph and alighted very gently on the top of Mrs. Gage's head. It was in this fashion that they returned to Mrs. Ford's cottage, at a very slow pace, for Mrs. Gage was lame, as I have said, and now she was almost weighted to the ground by the contents of her apron. But she reached her room without anyone knowing of her visit to the ruined house.

Next day she returned to Yorkshire. Mr. Stacey once more drove her into Lewes and was rather surprised to find how heavy Mrs. Gage's wooden box had become. But he was a quiet sort of man, and merely concluded that the kind people of Rodmell had given her a few odds and ends to console her for the dreadful

◆ Build Vocabulary

sovereigns (säv´ rənz) *n.*: British gold coins worth one pound each

sagacity (sə gas´ ə tē) *n.*: Wisdom

Customize for *Logical/Mathematical Learners*

Have students calculate the area required to lay out the three thousand coins under the floor. Approximately how deep would coins need to be stacked to fit in the 6-by-4½-foot space if each sovereign were 1 inch in diameter? *The area of 3,888 square inches would permit 1-inch coins to be laid out in a single layer with space to spare.*

◆ Literary Focus

5 Motivation Ask students to speculate on the motivation that led Mrs. Gage's brother to hide the coins. *He may have been too miserly to let anyone know he had the money and too mistrustful to leave it where it might be stolen.*

6 Clarification The word *craft* has a variety of meanings; among them are "skill," "trickery," and "occupation." Have students explain how they know which of those three meanings is intended here. *"Trickery" is the intended meaning; the old man was crafty, or devious, not artistically skilled or employed.*

Reteach

If students need further assistance in analyzing behavior or inferring motives to discern a character's motivation, encourage them to apply examples from their own lives. Suggest that they think of some moment when the reason for a personal act was other than the stated—or obvious—one. For more guidance, you may wish to refer students to p. 28 in ***Strategies for Diverse Student Needs***.

Speaking, Listening, and Viewing Mini-Lesson

Dialogue Between Person and Pet

This mini-lesson supports the second Speaking, Listening, and Viewing activity in the Idea Bank on p. 392.

Introduce Ask students who have or know pets what they wish they could ask their animal friends, if pets could only speak. Invite them to pair up and role-play a conversation between Mrs. Gage and James the parrot.

Develop Before students begin their conversations, have them brainstorm for what the parrot might have to say and how Mrs. Gage would answer him. Have them consider these questions:

- What would James have to say about his life with Joseph?
- How would James explain the fire?
- How would James feel about Joseph's death?
- How would James feel about Mrs. Gage?

Apply With this background, students should be able to let their imaginations guide them in improvised conversations between Mrs. Gage and James the parrot.

Assess Have students discuss how this activity enriched their appreciation of the story. You may want to have students use the Peer Assessment: Dramatic Performance page in ***Alternative Assessment***, p. 120, to assess this activity.

◆ Reading for Success

❶ **Respond** Ask students how this ending makes them feel, and why. Do they think that good people are rewarded in real life, or only in fiction? *Students may say that they like the ending because Mrs. Gage is rewarded for being good and kind. Opinions may vary as to whether or not the ending is realistic.*

◆ Literary Focus

❷ **Motivation** Have students consider what they know about Mrs. Gage's character and hypothesize about why she might have kept this story secret until she was on her deathbed. *Mrs. Gage was not the sort of person to try to impress others with her wealth. She probably wanted to live as simply as before without a lot of fuss being made over her.*

Reinforce and Extend

Answers

◆ Literature and Your Life

Reader's Response Students should list their responses in order of importance.

Thematic Focus Students may wish to discuss whether the goodness and kindness had a cause-and-effect relationship to the outcome.

Questions for Research Students' questions should distinguish between people who expected to inherit large sums and those, like Mrs. Gage, who are surprised by inheritances.

☑ Check Your Comprehension

1. Mrs. Gage is living in poverty, so the news of inherited wealth was good news indeed.
2. The house is worthless and the promised inheritance is not to be found.
3. Mrs. Gage faces the obstacles of fatigue and darkness, plus the danger of drowning in the river.
4. The burning of the house prompts Mrs. Gage's concern for the parrot's fate; the parrot leads her to the buried treasure.
5. Mrs. Gage believes that the parrot's actions were her reward for her kindness to animals.

loss of all her property in the fire. Out of sheer goodness of heart Mr. Stacey offered to buy the parrot off her for half a crown; but Mrs. Gage refused his offer with such indignation, saying that she would not sell the bird for all the wealth of the Indies, that he concluded that the old woman had been crazed by her troubles.

❶ It now only remains to be said that Mrs. Gage got back to Spilsby in safety; took her black box to the Bank; and lived with James the parrot and her dog Shag in great comfort and happiness to a very great age.

❷ It was not till she lay on her deathbed that she told the clergyman (the son of the Rev. Samuel Tallboys) the whole story, adding that she was quite sure that the house had been burnt on purpose by the parrot James, who, being aware of her danger on the river bank, flew into the scullery, and upset the oil stove which was keeping some scraps warm for her dinner. By this act, he not only saved her from drowning, but brought to light the three thousand pounds, which could have been found in no other manner. Such, she said, is the reward of kindness to animals.

> You can **respond** to a general statement like the one Mrs. Gage makes about kindness to animals by agreeing or disagreeing with it.

The clergyman thought that she was wandering in her mind. But it is certain that the very moment the breath was out of her body, James the parrot shrieked out, "Not at home! Not at home!" and fell off his perch stone dead. The dog Shag had died some years previously.

Visitors to Rodmell may still see the ruins of the house, which was burnt down fifty years ago, and it is commonly said that if you visit it in the moonlight you may hear a parrot tapping with his beak upon the brick floor, while others have seen an old woman sitting there in a white apron.

Guide for Responding

◆ Literature and Your Life

Reader's Response What would you do with a $15,000 inheritance?

Thematic Focus Mrs. Gage's life was forever changed because of her goodness and kindness. What good quality in you or someone you know has brought about a positive change in your life?

Questions for Research Mrs. Gage continued to lead a simple, unselfish life, even after inheriting a large sum of money. If you were to conduct research on how a majority of people have used large sums of inherited money, what questions would you hope to answer?

☑ Check Your Comprehension

1. Why is the news Mrs. Gage receives at the beginning of the story so welcome?
2. In what two ways does the inheritance from her brother prove disappointing?
3. What obstacles does Mrs. Gage face as she returns to Rodmell from Mr. Stagg's office?
4. Summarize the series of events that reverses Mrs. Gage's fortune.
5. At the end of the story, to what does Mrs. Gage attribute her good fortune?

Beyond the Selection

FURTHER READING

Other Works by Virginia Woolf

A Room of One's Own

Haunted House and Other Short Stories

Other Works About Communication With Animals

Shiloh, Phyllis Reynolds Naylor

When Elephants Weep, Susan McCarthy and Jeffrey Moussaieff Masson

We suggest that you preview these works before recommending them to students.

INTERNET

Biographical information about Virginia Woolf can be found at **http://www.biography.com/biography/read/reviews/vwoolf.html**

A useful list of links to other sites related to Virginia Woolf is at **http://199.185.130.85/orlando/woolf.html**

Please be aware, however, that sites may have changed from the time we published this information. We *strongly recommend* that you preview the sites before you send students to them.

Guide for Responding (continued)

◆ Critical Thinking

INTERPRET

1. How does Mrs. Gage show her concern for animals? **[Analyze]**
2. What can you infer about Mrs. Gage's relationship with her brother based on her comments about his will? **[Infer]**
3. Describe Mrs. Gage's personality. Support your answer with examples from the story. **[Support]**

EVALUATE

4. Do you think Mrs. Gage's good fortune is a reward, or is it merely a coincidence? Explain your answer. **[Make a Judgment]**

APPLY

5. Are there more benefits or disadvantages to elderly people having pets? Explain. **[Generalize]**

◆ Reading for Success

STRATEGIES FOR READING FICTION

Review the reading strategies and notes showing how to read fiction. Then apply those strategies to answer the following questions.

1. What predictions did you make about Mrs. Gage's inheritance? Which predictions did you change before you reached the end of the story?
2. What words does the author use to help you envision the unfolding action?
3. What can you infer about Joseph from the measures he took to hide his fortune?
4. Relate two scenes in the story in which you particularly identified with Mrs. Gage. Explain why.

◆ Literary Focus

MOTIVATION

A character's **motivation** is the reason for his or her actions or words. Identifying characters' motives will help you understand story events.

1. What motivates Mrs. Gage to be kind to the parrot?
2. Why do you think the parrot helps Mrs. Gage?
3. Using examples from the story, explain how a character's motivation may bring about unexpected results.

◆ Build Vocabulary

USING FORMS OF *SAGACITY*

On your paper, write sentences that indicate that you understand these forms of the word *sagacity*.

1. Describe a decision that shows sagacity.
2. Identify a sagacious person you know.
3. Offer a piece of sage advice.

USING THE WORD BANK: Context

On your paper, answer the following questions.

1. If you ford a river, do you cross it on a bridge?
2. Would most people want to move into a dilapidated house?
3. Where might you be if you reached into your pocket and pulled out a sovereign?
4. People of what professions are known for their sagacity?

◆ Build Grammar Skills

CORRECT USE OF ADJECTIVES AND ADVERBS

Do not confuse **adjectives** and **adverbs.** Use adjectives to modify nouns, and use adverbs to modify verbs, adjectives, and other adverbs.

Practice Copy the following sentences on your paper, completing each with the correct adjective or adverb. Circle the word it modifies and label that word's part of speech.

1. He was a very handsome bird, but his feathers were (sad, sadly) neglected.
2. "Drat that bird," said Mrs. Ford (peevish, peevishly).
3. Mrs. Gage walked (slow, slowly) across the fields.
4. The parrot, James, hopped (brisk, briskly) a few yards ahead of her towards the burnt house.
5. His excitement became so (intense, intensely) that Mrs. Gage now went to his help.

Writing Application Write several sentences in which you correctly use the following adjectives and adverbs: *quick, quickly; safe, safely.*

◆ Critical Thinking

1. She arranges care for her dog and feeds the neglected parrot.
2. Mrs. Gage has been ill treated by her brother but has nevertheless extended her hand in friendship.
3. Students should note her kindness to animals, her acceptance of her circumstances, and her refusal to lay blame on others.
4. Students may see the bequeathed inheritance as penance by Mrs. Gage's brother for his evil ways and thereby support the idea of the good fortune as a reward.
5. Students may cite studies that have shown how pets enhance the lives of the elderly by providing companionship and help.

◆ Reading for Success

1. Students who predicted that the inheritance was fake will have revised their predictions; those who predicted it was legitimate had their predictions confirmed.
2. The ford in Mrs. Gage's rocky road is described as follows: "the stones of the riverbed appeared above the water"; the house is seen by lantern light as having "holes in all the carpets"; "bottoms of all the chairs . . . fallen out"; "large toadstools growing through the kitchen floor."
3. Joseph is so miserly that he hid his fortune so thoroughly that it would take the destruction of his house to discover it.
4. Students may identify with her elation at hearing the good news of her inheritance as well as with her resignation when it seems that she has been the victim of a hoax. They may also relate to her concern for the parrot, her fears at being alone on a dark journey, and her courage in trusting the parrot to lead her to an interesting discovery.

◆ Literary Focus

1. Mrs. Gage feels sorry for the parrot.
2. The parrot recognizes Mrs. Gage's kindness and repays her in kind.
3. Students may cite Mrs. Gage's trust in the parrot as bringing the unexpected consequence of discovering the fortune.

◆ Build Vocabulary

Using Forms of *Sagacity*

1. Students may say that avoiding substance abuse shows sagacity.
2. Students may name a teacher, a parent or relative, or a wise neighbor.
3. Accept reasonable responses.

Using the Word Bank

1. No; 2. No
3. You would most likely be in Great Britain.
4. Teachers and professors, counselors and psychiatrists are known for their sagacity.

◆ Build Grammar Skills

1. sadly; 2. peevishly;
3. slowly; 4. briskly;
5. intense

Grammar Reinforcement

For additional instruction and practice, use the lesson in the **Language Lab CD-ROM** on the Eight Parts of Speech and the practice page Adjective or Adverb? in the *Writer's Solution Grammar Practice Book*, p. 19.

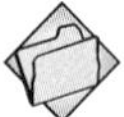

Idea Bank

Customizing for *Performance Levels*

Following are suggestions for matching Idea Bank topics with your students' performance levels:

Less Advanced Students: 1, 4, 7
Average Students: 2, 4, 6
More Advanced: 3, 5

Customizing for *Learning Modalities*

Following are suggestions for matching Idea Bank topics with your students' learning modalities:

Verbal/Linguistic: 2, 4, 5
Logical/Mathematical: 5,6
Visual/Spatial: 5,7

Guided Writing Lesson

Revision Strategy Have students reenter their writing to check its organization. Encourage students to assign each item in the will a specific color and then highlight all details relating to the item. This color coding will serve two purposes. First, it will show whether students have supplied enough detail for every item in the will. Second, it will reveal any errors in organization. Look at this example from Humpty Dumpty's will:

> I should never have been on the wall to start with. I leave my shell to future eggs so they can learn from my error. I leave my financial empire to the King's emergency services. The King's horses and men should be better prepared to deal with such accidents as mine.

For more prewriting, elaboration, and revision strategies, see *Prentice Hall Writing and Grammar*.

Writers at Work Videodisc

Have students view the videodisc segment (Ch. 3) featuring Rudolfo Anaya for more on organizing material.

Play frames 28660 to 29650

Writing Lab CD-ROM

Have students complete the tutorial on Exposition. Follow these steps:

1. Have students use the interactive instruction on gathering details.
2. Students may draft on computer.
3. Suggest that students use the revision checker for language variety in revising their last will and testament.

Build Your Portfolio

Idea Bank

Writing Ideas

1. **Character Sketch** The parrot in this story has a unique and strong personality. Write a character sketch of an animal you would use as a character in a short story.
2. **Review** Imagine that you have been assigned to create a "Best Short Stories" Home Page on the Internet. Write a brief review of "The Widow and the Parrot" that will make Web-surfers want to read the story. **[Technology Link]**
3. **Health Report** Studies have shown that owning a pet can reduce stress. Do research to find specific information about the relationship between pets and stress reduction. Write a brief report explaining your findings. **[Science Link]**

Speaking, Listening, and Viewing

4. **Animal Behavior Video** Some people believe that much can be learned from the study of animal behavior. At the library, find a video that focuses on animal behavior, such as that of parrots or myna birds. Watch the video, and present a summary to your class.
5. **Dialogue Between Person and Pet** With a partner, take turns playing the roles of James and Mrs. Gage. Allow James to say everything he's wanted to say to Mrs. Gage.

Researching and Representing

6. **Conversion Chart** Suppose you inherited 3,000 pounds—you'd want to know how that translated into dollars! Create a conversion chart showing pounds sterling to dollars. **[Math Link]**
7. **Area Map** Create a map of the setting of this story—where you envision the house, village, and river. Base your map on the details provided in the story. **[Art Link; Social Studies Link]**

Online Activity www.phlit.phschool.com

Guided Writing Lesson

Last Will and Testament

Readers learn about Mrs. Ford's brother, in part, from the contents of his will and the possessions he leaves behind when he dies. Write a revealing **last will and testament** for a character from another fictional work. List possessions that indicate what was important to the character. Use the following tip to help you organize your character's last will and testament:

Writing Skills Focus: Logical Organization

Your character's last will and testament will flow more smoothly and be easier to understand if you use a **logical organization**—an arrangement that shows clear relationships among ideas. For example, you might choose order of importance and present the most important details first, followed by the less significant ones. If you choose part-to-whole organization, arrange your details into categories, such as money, property, and advice.

Prewriting Before you begin drafting your character's last will and testament, jot down your ideas on note cards. Write a single thought on each card. Then, experiment with different ways of grouping your ideas until you find the most logical organization.

Drafting Begin your character's last will and testament by stating his or her overall wishes. Then, present the details of the character's will—specifically, what should go to whom. Follow a consistent organization throughout the will and testament.

Revising As you revise your character's last will and testament, be sure that you have used a logical organization. Read over your draft to be sure that every item was addressed in detail. Add transitions if necessary to show how ideas are related.

✓ ASSESSMENT OPTIONS

Formal Assessment, Selection Test, pp. 98–100, and Assessment Resources Software. The selection test is designed so that it can be easily customized to the performance levels of your students.

Alternative Assessment, p. 28, includes options for less advanced students, more advanced students, logical/mathematical learners, intrapersonal learners, verbal/linguistic learners, bodily/kinesthetic learners, and interpersonal learners.

PORTFOLIO ASSESSMENT

Use the following rubrics in the ***Alternative Assessment*** booklet to assess student writing:
Character Sketch: Description Rubric, p. 97
Review: Evaluation/Review Rubric, p. 104
Health Report: Research Report/Paper Rubric, p. 106
Guided Writing Lesson: Expression Rubric, p. 94

PART 1 *A World of People*

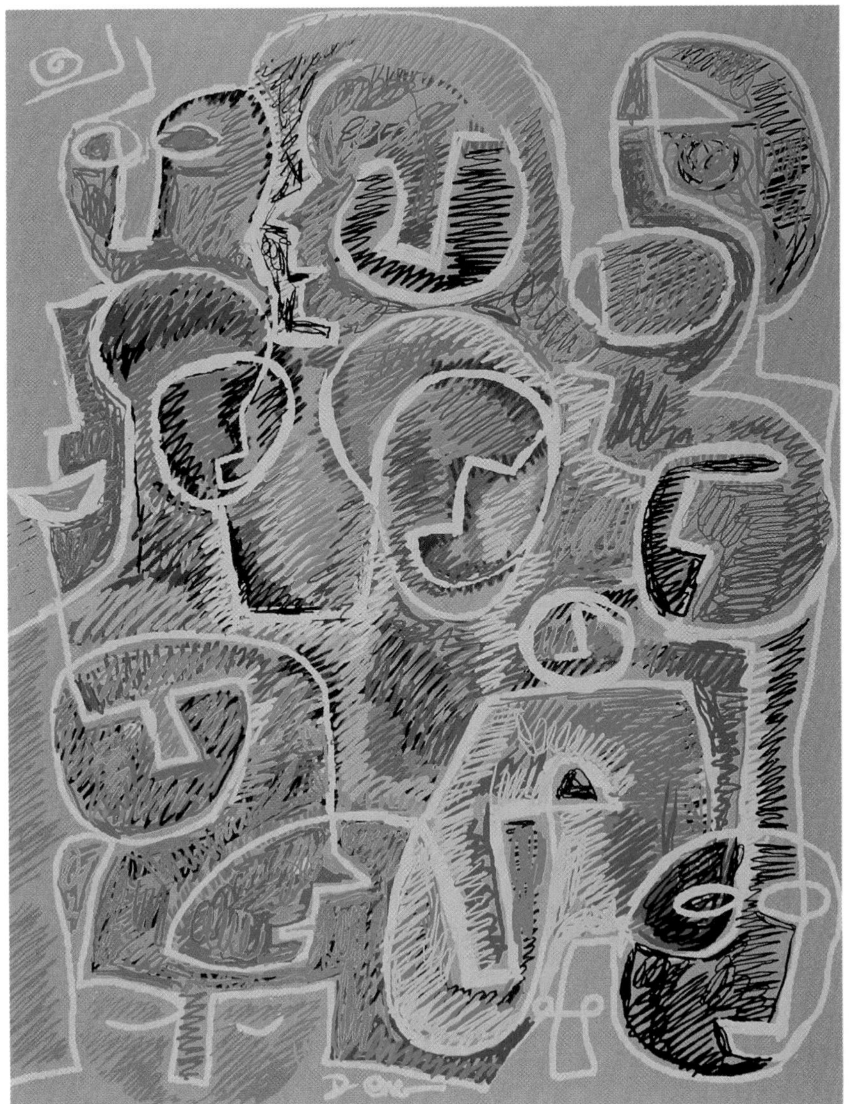

Mingling, Diana Ong

One-Minute Planning Guide

The selections in this part show the variety of people and situations from around the world. The section opens with Chinua Achebe's "Civil Peace," a short story about a man who is robbed during the Biafran War in Nigeria. "The Bean Eaters" is a poem that describes the monotonous lives of faceless, nameless characters, while Paul Simon's "Old Friends" explores how friendships expand our horizons. Umberto Eco's "How to React to Familiar Faces" talks about the disorienting feeling that comes with seeing a famous person. Finally, "A Picture from the Past: Emily Dickinson," and "What Makes a Degas a Degas?" discuss the role photographs and paintings have in opening up new worlds for us.

Customize for
Varying Student Needs

When assigning the selections in this part to your students, keep in mind the following factors:

"Civil Peace"

- Contains dialect that may be difficult for some students to understand

"The Bean Eaters"

- Short poem by a well-known writer
- Vocabulary accessible to all ability levels

"Old Friends"

- Popular music by a contemporary artist

"How to React to Familiar Faces"

- High interest topic of celebrities
- Appealing to interpersonal learners

"A Picture from the Past: Emily Dickinson"; "What Makes a Degas a Degas?"

- Very short nonfiction
- Appealing to visual/spatial learners

Humanities: Art

Mingling by Diana Ong.

Encourage students to enumerate as many kinds of "mingling" as they can see in this painting—for example, the mingling of colors, the overlapping of heads, the blending of heads and upper bodies, and so on. Discuss the artist's technique of using white to outline and define spaces which are filled in with multi-colored scribbled lines. Encourage students to talk about how color influences the mood of the painting. You might explain that some color analysts say that shades of yellow are associated with optimism.

Help students link the artwork to the theme of this section, "A World of People," by answering the following questions:

1. How does the artist emphasize what people have in common? How does she emphasize their differences? *She emphasizes what people share by using the same scribbling technique and the same combinations of colors for all the heads. She emphasizes their differences by boldly defining heads and features.*
2. Imagine that this work were untitled, and that you were asked to provide a title with the word "people" in it. What would you come up with? *Sample answers: People Talking; People Face to Face; People Who Need People; Too Many People? How Do People Get Along?*

Prepare and Engage

LESSON OBJECTIVES

1. **To develop vocabulary and word identification skills**
   - Latin Word Roots: *-reput-*
   - Using the Word Bank: Context
   - Extending Word Study: Word Forms
2. **To use a variety of reading strategies to comprehend a personal narrative**
   - Connect Your Experience
   - Reading Strategy: Prior Knowledge
   - Tips to Guide Reading
   - Read to Take Action
3. **To increase knowledge of other cultures and to connect common elements across cultures**
   - Connecting Themes Across Cultures (ATE)
4. **To express and support responses to the text**
   - Critical Thinking
   - Idea Bank: News Interview
   - Idea Bank: Human-Interest Article
   - Idea Bank: Poem
5. **To analyze literary elements**
   - Literary Focus: Key Statements
6. **To read in order to research self-selected and assigned topics**
   - Idea Bank: Proverbs Presentation
7. **To plan, prepare, organize, and present literary interpretations**
   - Idea Bank: Collage
   - Idea Bank: Rework Dialogue
   - Speaking, Listening and Viewing Mini-Lesson: Dialogue
8. **To use recursive writing processes to write an annotated map**
   - Guided Writing Lesson
9. **To increase knowledge of the rules of grammar and usage**
   - Build Grammar Skills: Past and Past Perfect Tense

Test Preparation

Reading Comprehension: Evaluate and Make Judgments (ATE, p. 395) The teaching tips and sample test in this workshop support the instruction and practice in the unit workshop.

Reading Comprehension: Interpret Graphic Aids; Evaluate and Make Judgments (SE, p. 465)

Guide for Reading

Chinua Achebe *(1930–)*

During civil war in his homeland of Nigeria, Chinua Achebe (chin wä´ ə cheb´ ā) survived the bombing of his house. He fled the town, leaving behind a book in press at the publishing company he had formed with his friend, poet Christopher Okigbo. That book was *How the Leopard Got His Claws,* Achebe's parable about Nigeria. Okigbo died in the war, and when Achebe returned, the Citadel Press was demolished. There remained only one copy of the proofs of the book, which someone had managed to save.

Early Life Born in the Ibo village of Ogibi, Nigeria, Achebe was brought up with both the traditional values of the Ibo people as well as Western values. He believes that stories are a way to preserve the traditional values that are so important to him.

"Stories are not just meant to make people smile . . . our life depends on them."

Achebe has also been influenced by his experiences with war and its aftermath.

Professional Life Achebe has directed a radio station, taught in universities, and involved himself in local Nigerian politics as a diplomat. His greatest success, however, has been as a novelist. His novels, including *Things Fall Apart* (1958) and *Anthills of the Savannah* (1988), convey the tragic history of tribal Africa's encounter with European power.

◆ Build Vocabulary

LATIN WORD ROOTS: *-reput-*

You can increase your vocabulary by learning that many words contain the same word root. For example, in this story, you will encounter the word *disreputable,* which means "not respectable" and refers to the filthy clothes that one character wears. Using other forms of *disreputable,* you might describe a disreputable person as someone who has a bad *reputation,* a person of ill *repute,* or someone who has fallen into *disrepute.* The words *reputation, repute, disrepute,* and *disreputable* are all related because they contain the Latin word root *-reput-.*

WORD BANK

As you read this story, you will encounter the words on this list. Each word is defined on the page where it first appears. Preview the list before you read.

inestimable
disreputable
amenable
edifice
destitute
imperious
commiserate

◆ Build Grammar Skills

PAST AND PAST PERFECT TENSES

The **past tense** of a verb indicates that an action took place prior to the present.

The **past perfect tense** indicates a past action that was completed before another action that took place in the past. It is formed with *had* and the past participle of a verb (the form ending in *-ed* or an irregular ending such as *-n* or *-t*).

In the following sentence from the story, the past perfect *had started* indicates that the water began running before the other past actions.

past / past

. . . he . . . *bought* fresh palm-wine which he *mixed*

past perfect

. . . with the water which *had* recently *started* running again . . .

Notice other places in the story where Achebe uses the past and past perfect tenses to indicate the relationship between past events.

Prentice Hall Literature Program Resources

REINFORCE / RETEACH / EXTEND

Selection Support Pages
Build Vocabulary: Related Words: Forms of *Disreputable*, p. 118
Build Grammar Skills: Past and Past Perfect Tenses, p. 119
Reading Strategy: Prior Knowledge, p. 120
Literary Focus: Key Statement, p. 121

Strategies for Diverse Student Needs, p. 29

Beyond Literature
Cross-Curricular Connection: Geography, p. 29

Formal Assessment
Selection Test, pp. 101–103

Alternative Assessment, p. 29

Writing and Language Transparencies
Herringbone Organizer, p. 76

Resource Pro CD-ROM

Listening to Literature Audiocassettes

Civil Peace

◆ Literature and Your Life

Connect Your Experience

Different factors, such as your outlook or your circumstances, influence the way you respond to a loss: If you lose the last five dollars you had for this month, your reaction will probably be stronger than if you lose five dollars the day before you get paid for your after-school job.

The main character in this story faces several difficulties and losses more serious than five dollars, yet he tries to keep a positive attitude.

Journal Writing What strategies do you use to keep a positive attitude?

Thematic Focus: A World of People

The changes in the world of the main character broaden his horizons, but they also create difficulty. His experiences may lead you to ask yourself, "How do I deal with the difficulties of change?"

◆ Background for Understanding

History

In the late 1800's, the British annexed lands in west Africa, eventually setting up the colony of Nigeria. Local rulers resisted British domination, and in 1960, Nigeria finally achieved independence.

Religious, economic, and ethnic divisions flared after independence. The Ibo in the southeast felt that the Muslim Huasa-Fulani of the north dominated Nigeria. The Ibo seceded from Nigeria, setting up the independent Republic of Biafra. A brutal civil war followed, and in 1970, a defeated Biafra rejoined Nigeria. "Civil Peace" takes place in the aftermath of this civil war.

◆ Literary Focus

Key Statement

Just as a key unlocks a door, **key statements** unlock the meaning of a story. Key statements often go beyond the events of a particular story and point to a general truth about life. Chinua Achebe uses repetition to emphasize one key statement in "Civil Peace." Such key statements can help you unlock the meaning behind the tale. Use a graphic organizer like the one shown to identify and explore the meaning of key statements in "Civil Peace."

◆ Reading Strategy

Prior Background Knowledge

When a story takes you to another country or introduces you to unfamiliar people and places, you may feel the need for a "guide." Your **prior knowledge**—what you already know and can relate to—can guide you in understanding the new experiences and ideas.

In "Civil Peace," Achebe tells about a man in a particular historical situation—a man returning home after the civil war in Nigeria. Even if you have not lived through a war, you can use your prior knowledge of coping with loss and gain to understand the man's experiences.

Key Statement	Possible Meaning
Happy survival!	

Test Preparation Workshop

Reading Comprehension: Evaluate and Make Judgments

Standardized tests often require students to evaluate and make judgments. Use the following sample test item to teach this reading comprehension skill.

He was normally a heavy sleeper but that night he heard all the neighborhood noises die down one after another. Even the night watchman who knocked the hour on some metal somewhere in the distance had fallen after knocking one o'clock. That must have been the last thought in Jonathan's mind before he was finally carried away himself.

Which of the following statements is supported by the evidence in the passage?

A The night watchman slept at midnight.
B Jonathan tried to keep himself awake.
C Jonathan had trouble sleeping that night.
D The neighborhood was very noisy

The details in the passage prove *A, B,* and *D* wrong. *C* is the correct response.

Interest Grabber Play a video segment from a documentary or show pictures of a disaster area after such events as a flood, an earthquake, or a war. Ask students: What would be their first concerns if they found themselves in such a disaster area? Have students make a list of the first steps they would take. After students have compiled a list, tell them to read the story and find out how the characters in the story dealt with a similar disaster.

Connecting Themes Across Cultures

This story deals with a man living in a post-civil war society. Have students identify countries with ongoing civil disorder. Then, discuss the effects these troubles have had on civilians.

Customize for
Less Proficient Readers
Suggest to these students that, as they read, they make a list of the things that Jonathan Iwegbu considers a "miracle." Such a list can help them understand the main character's outlook on life.

Customize for
Pre-AP Students
Have these students consider the following question as they read: Besides a positive outlook, what other character traits does Jonathan Iwegbu possess? Have students jot down notes for a character description of Jonathan.

Customize for
English Language Learners
This story contains unfamiliar vocabulary, unexpected phrasing, and difficult dialect. To help these students, have them follow along in their text as they listen to the recording of the selection. Pause the recording after particularly puzzling passages and explain the meanings of the passages written in dialect.

Listening to Literature Audiocassettes

Customize for
Intrapersonal Learners
Have these students keep a "reflective journal" as they read the story. Encourage them to write their thoughts and feelings each time Jonathan Iwegbu states, "Nothing puzzles God."

Develop Understanding

One-Minute Insight "If life gives you lemons, make lemonade." This expression sums up the main character's ability to make the best of the difficult situations thrust upon him by a chaotic, lawless post-civil war society. Having survived with most of his family intact, Jonathan Iwegbu realizes that flexibility is the key to success. If one business doesn't work, another one might. Even when thieves threaten his family and steal his money, Jonathan shows that a positive mental attitude helps one to adapt to change and loss.

Tips to Guide Reading

Set a Purpose for Reading Suspenseful stories hold readers' interest because the author purposely creates curiosity and describes events in such a way that tension is created. Ask students to look for elements that create suspense. After sustained reading, discuss students' findings and ask students to determine whether the author has built suspense successfully.

◆ Literary Focus

1 Key Statement Ask students what they think the greeting "Happy survival" means and why it is used. Then have students predict, on the basis of this opening paragraph, whether or not Jonathan will have a "happy survival." *"Happy survival" is the equivalent of our "hello" or, "hi." It is used because people were so happy to have survived the war. This optimistic key statement sets the tone for the rest of the story, in which Jonathan looks at the positive aspect of all situations. Students may predict a happy survival for Jonathan.*

◆ Critical Thinking

2 Identify Character Traits Ask students what they have learned about Jonathan from the opening paragraph. *He has a positive attitude, recognizes the important things in life, and also delights in the less important things.*

Civil Peace

Chinua Achebe

1 Jonathan Iwegbu counted himself extraordinarily lucky. "Happy survival!" meant so much more to him than just a current fashion of greeting old friends in the first hazy days of peace. It went deep to his heart. He had come out of the war with five inestimable blessings—his head, his wife Maria's head and the heads of three out of their four children. As a bonus he also had his old bicycle—a miracle too but naturally not to be compared to the safety of five human heads.

2 The bicycle had a little history of its own. One day at the height of the war it was commandeered "for urgent military action." Hard as its loss would have been to him he would still have let it go without a thought had he not had some doubts about the genuineness of the officer. It wasn't his disreputable rags, nor the toes peeping out of one blue and one brown canvas shoe, nor yet the two stars of his rank done obviously in a hurry in biro,[1] that troubled Jonathan; many good and heroic soldiers looked the same or worse. It was rather a certain lack of grip and firmness in

3 his manner. So Jonathan, suspecting he might

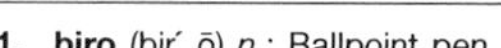

1. **biro** (bir´ ō) *n.*: Ballpoint pen.

◆ Build Vocabulary

inestimable (in es´ tə mə bəl) *adj.*: Priceless; beyond measure

disreputable (dis rep´ yoo tə bəl) *adj.*: Not respectable

amenable (ə mē´ nə bəl) *adj.*: Responsive; open

Block Scheduling Strategies

Consider these suggestions to take advantage of extended class time:

- Have students preview the story by reading Beyond Literature on p. 401. Then have them complete the Cross-Curricular Connection: Geography page in ***Beyond the Literature***, p. 29, to learn about the setting of the story.
- Students may also benefit from researching the history of Nigeria before reading the selection to give them a better understanding of the story's setting. Suggest that they look for maps and atlases in encyclopedias or on the Internet.
- After students have read the selection, have them listen to the part of the audiocassette recording that contains the scene with the thieves. Discuss how listening to the dialogue affects their understanding of what the thief and his accomplices are demanding.
- Since the dialect in the story may present difficulties, have students work with partners on Speaking, Listening, and Viewing: Reworking a Dialogue (p. 403). Invite several pairs of students to present their interpretations to the class.

◀ Critical Viewing Why would a bicycle be important to Jonathan, who lives in a landscape like the one shown? **[Infer]** 4

be amenable to influence, rummaged in his raffia bag and produced the two pounds with which he had been going to buy firewood which his wife, Maria, retailed to camp officials for extra stock-fish and corn meal, and got his bicycle back. That night he buried it in the little clearing in the bush where the dead of the camp, including his own youngest son, were buried. When he dug it up again a year later after the surrender all it needed was a little palm-oil greasing. "Nothing puzzles God," he said in wonder. 5

He put it to immediate use as a taxi and accumulated a small pile of Biafran[2] money

2. **Biafran** (bē äf′ rən) *adj.*: From the east part of the Gulf of Guinea on the west coast of Africa.

3 Clarification This sentence about the bicycle may be confusing to students. Explain that Jonathan had money with which he was planning to buy firewood. He planned to give the firewood to his wife, who would exchange it for stock-fish and corn meal from camp officials. Instead, he used the money to "persuade" the soldier not to confiscate his bicycle. Point out that the "camp" is a refugee camp for Biafrans who had fled their homes.

▶Critical Viewing◀

4 Infer Students may observe that the landscape appears vast and rugged. As there are no automobiles visible, animals and bicycles would be the most likely forms of transportation.

◆ Literary Focus

5 Key Statement This is the first of several times that Jonathan says, "Nothing puzzles God." Ask students what they think he means by this statement. *Students may suggest that the statement means that people don't always have to understand the reason why something happens. Some may extend their interpretation to suggest that, as Jonathan does, people should accept that there probably is a reason for everything, even when we don't understand it or recognize it.*

Customize for *Gifted/Talented Students*

Have these students compose their own proverbs that have the same meaning as "Nothing puzzles God" and then brainstorm for other proverbs and sayings that mean the same thing.

Workplace Skills Mini-Lesson

Positive Attitude

This mini-lesson supports the value of developing a positive attitude.

Introduce Have students discuss the effect Jonathan's positive attitude has on his life.

Develop Students who work at part-time jobs might have noticed that co-workers (or even they themselves) often complain about their jobs. Discuss how excessive complaining can make a situation seem worse than it is, while concentrating on positive aspects can make the same situation seem better.

Apply Share these negative thoughts with students. Have them determine how to make them more positive:

- My job pays only $4.75 an hour.
- They make me sweep the floor when I'm not working at a register.
- We have to wear nerdy-looking uniforms instead of our own clothes.

Have students suggest how they might apply positive thinking to real-life situations.

Assess Assess students' ability to apply the skill by the number and quality of suggestions they make. Ask students to explain why a positive attitude would be beneficial in the situations they suggest.

◆ Critical Thinking

❶ Identify Character Traits Ask students: What does Jonathan's starting a taxi service tell you about his attitude toward life? *Students should recognize that Jonathan has a positive attitude, is ambitious, and is resourceful because he uses what little he has to make a better life for himself and his family.*

◆ Critical Thinking

❷ Identify Character Traits Ask students: What is Jonathan's attitude toward the condition of his home? How might someone else react when faced with the same situation? *His attitude is positive; he is both grateful and happy that the house is salvageable. Responses regarding other possible reactions might indicate that some people would be angry, upset, or discouraged about the missing doors and windows and the damaged roof.*

◆ Build Grammar Skills

❸ Past and Past Perfect Tenses Have students identify the past tense and past perfect tense verbs in this sentence. Ask them to explain the use of the past perfect tense. *Past:* took, bought, mixed, opened; *past perfect:* had started; *the water "had recently started running" before any of the other past actions occurred.*

◆ Critical Thinking

❹ Infer Draw attention to the contrast between the other ex-miners and Jonathan. Why might some of these ex-miners have no place to go? Why aren't they as resourceful as Jonathan? *Their homes were probably destroyed in the war; they may not be as resourceful as Jonathan, but even if they were, it would be harder for them to start up in business because they have no homes. Jonathan is well-off compared to these men.*

ferrying camp officials and their families across the four-mile stretch to the nearest tarred road. His standard charge per trip was six pounds and those who had the money were only glad to be rid of some of it in this way. At the end of a ❶ fortnight[3] he had made a small fortune of one hundred and fifteen pounds.

Then he made the journey to Enugu and found another miracle waiting for him. It was unbelievable. He rubbed his eyes and looked again and it was still standing there before him. But, needless to say, even that monumental blessing must be accounted also totally inferior to the five heads in the family. This newest miracle was his little house in Ogui Overside. Indeed nothing puzzles God! Only two houses away a huge concrete edifice some wealthy contractor had put up just before the war was a ❷ mountain of rubble. And here was Jonathan's little zinc house of no regrets built with mud blocks quite intact! Of course the doors and windows were missing and five sheets off the roof. But what was that? And anyhow he had returned to Enugu early enough to pick up bits of old zinc and wood and soggy sheets of cardboard lying around the neighborhood before thousands more came out of their forest holes looking for the same things. He got a destitute carpenter with one old hammer, a blunt plane and a few bent and rusty nails in his tool bag to turn this assortment of wood, paper and metal into door and window shutters for five Nigerian shillings or fifty Biafran pounds. He paid the pounds, and moved in with his overjoyed family carrying five heads on their shoulders.

His children picked mangoes near the military cemetery and sold them to soldiers' wives for a few pennies—real pennies this time—and his wife started making breakfast akara balls[4] for neighbors in a hurry to start life again. With his family earnings he took his bicycle to the villages around and bought fresh palm-wine which he mixed generously in his rooms with the water which had recently started running again in the public tap down the road, and opened up a bar for soldiers and other lucky people with good money.

At first he went daily, then every other day and finally once a week, to the offices of the Coal Corporation where he used to be a miner, to find out what was what. The only thing he did find out in the end was that that little house of his was even a greater blessing than he had thought. Some of his fellow ex-miners who had nowhere to return at the end of the day's waiting just slept outside the doors of the offices and cooked what meal they could scrounge together in Bournvita tins. As the weeks lengthened and still nobody could say what was what Jonathan discontinued his weekly visits altogether and faced his palm-wine bar.

But nothing puzzles God. Came the day of the windfall when after five days of endless scuffles in queues[5] and counterqueues in the sun outside the Treasury he had twenty pounds counted into his palms as ex-gratia[6] award for the rebel money he had turned in. It was like Christmas for him and for many others like him when the payments began. They called it (since few could manage its proper official name) *egg-rasher*.

> **◆ Literary Focus**
> How does the key statement that begins this paragraph capture the spirit of Jonathan's attitude toward good and bad events?

As soon as the pound notes were placed in his palm Jonathan simply closed it tight over them and buried fist and money inside his trouser pocket. He had to be extra careful because he had seen a man a couple of days earlier collapse into near-madness in an instant before that oceanic crowd because no sooner had he got his twenty pounds than some heartless ruffian picked it off him. Though it was not

3. **fortnight** (fôrt´ nīt) *n.*: Two weeks.
4. **akara** (ə kär´ ə) **balls:** Balls made of cooked yams.
5. **queues** (kyo͞oz) *n.*: Lines.
6. **ex gratia** (eks grä´ shē ə): As a favor.

◆ Build Vocabulary

edifice (ed´ i fis) *n.*: Building

destitute (des´ tə to͞ot´) *adj.*: Poverty stricken; in great need

Speaking, Listening, and Viewing Mini-Lesson

Reworking a Dialogue
This mini-lesson supports the Speaking, Listening, and Viewing activity in the Idea Bank on p. 403.

Introduce the Concept Remind students that there are many regional dialects of English even within the United States. For example, depending on where they live, people may refer to soft drinks as *soda, tonic,* or *pop*.

Develop Background Have students discuss why the dialect in the story might be difficult to understand. Lead students to recognize these points:

- Some words and phrases are unfamiliar.
- The word order in the sentence does not follow the normal English pattern.

Apply the Information Remind students that they can use context to figure out the meanings of words and sentences. Reading aloud can help, as well. Have students work in pairs to rewrite the dialogue.

Assess the Outcome Have students read their dialogues to the class. Encourage listeners to evaluate the dialogues on the basis of how well they made sense within the context of the story. Students may use the Peer Assessment: Dramatic Performance page in ***Alternative Assessment***, p. 120.

right that a man in such an extremity of agony should be blamed yet many in the queues that day were able to remark quietly at the victim's carelessness, especially after he pulled out the innards of his pocket and revealed a hole in it big enough to pass a thief's head. But of course he had insisted that the money had been in the other pocket, pulling it out too to show its comparative wholeness. So one had to be careful.

Jonathan soon transferred the money to his left hand and pocket so as to leave his right free for shaking hands should the need arise, though by fixing his gaze at such an elevation as to miss all approaching human faces he made sure that the need did not arise, until he got home.

He was normally a heavy sleeper but that night he heard all the neighborhood noises die down one after another. Even the night watchman who knocked the hour on some metal somewhere in the distance had fallen silent after knocking one o'clock. That must have been the last thought in Jonathan's mind before he was finally carried away himself. He couldn't have been gone for long, though, when he was violently awakened again.

"Who is knocking?" whispered his wife lying beside him on the floor.

"I don't know," he whispered back breathlessly.

The second time the knocking came it was so loud and imperious that the rickety old door could have fallen down.

"Who is knocking?" he asked them, his voice parched and trembling.

"Na tief-man and him people," came the cool reply. "Make you hopen de door."[7] This was followed by the heaviest knocking of all.

Maria was the first to raise the alarm, then he followed and all their children.

▲ Critical Viewing What is the effect of this extreme close-up photo? **[Interpret]** 

◆ Reading Strategy
How does your prior knowledge of anxiety help you understand Jonathan's experience here?

◆ Build Vocabulary

imperious (im pir′ ē əs) *adj.*: Commanding; powerful

7. **"Na tief-man . . . hopen de door":** The man is speaking a dialect of English that includes some word forms and grammar of his own language. He is saying, "I am not a thief with my accomplices. Open the door." As you read the rest of the story, read aloud when characters speak this way and try to figure out what they are saying.

◆ Literary Focus

❺ Key Statement Jonathan is resilient, undaunted by setbacks; he accepts the good and the bad; he believes that all is for the good, even if human beings cannot see the reasons.

◆ Build Grammar Skills

❻ Past and Past Perfect Tenses Have students identify the past form of the verb *have* and past perfect form of the verb *turn* in this passage. Ask them to explain the use of the past perfect. *Past:* had; *past perfect:* had turned (in); *Jonathan had turned in the rebel money before receiving the twenty pounds "ex-gratia."*

❼ Clarification Be sure students recognize that "egg-rasher" is the Nigerians' pronunciation of "ex-gratia."

Listening to Literature Audiocassettes

❽ Because of the difficult dialect in the passage that follows, this is a good time to play the audiocassette recording. The inflections of the speakers' voices can help students understand the meaning of the dialogue.

◆ Reading Strategy

❾ Prior Knowledge Students should recognize that anxiety can cause behavioral changes and sleeplessness. Jonathan does not look at people on the way home and even when he is safe at home, he has difficulty falling asleep.

▶Critical Viewing◀

❿ Interpret Students may suggest that the close-up forces the viewer to look at the man's expression and share in his feelings.

Read to Take Action

Tell students that such works as the novel *Things Fall Apart* and this story are intended not only to inform and entertain readers, but to warn them of what happens when people are not vigilant in the pursuit of justice. Have students discuss whether this story gives them incentive to help people who are legally or financially disadvantaged.

Beyond the Classroom

Career Connection

Law Enforcement Lawlessness and chaos often characterize a society in the aftermath of war. As they read on, students will see that restoration of law enforcement by ethical and well-trained law-enforcement officers is necessary for life to go on in any reasonable, orderly way.

Students interested in a career in law enforcement can do research to find out what kind of background is necessary to become an officer of the law. Some questions students might consider include the following:

- How does one apply to become a police officer?
- Is a college education necessary?
- How does one become a detective or an FBI agent?

❶ **Clarification** If students seem confused by this passage, tell them that the Iwegbu family has neither a telephone nor a sophisticated security system. This is the family's way of calling for help.

❷ **Clarification** Point out that the leader is saying "We'll help you a little. Now, everybody!" Then the thieves, imitating the previous chant of the Iwegbu family, all call for the police and neighbors, to show how little they are impressed by the Iwegbus' calls for help.

◆ Critical Thinking

❸ **Make Inferences** Ask students if they think it is normal for thieves to have so little fear of apprehension and punishment that they would make fun of a threat to call soldiers and police. What is the cause of this strange situation? *Students should understand that chaos and lawlessness often follow war. In a peaceful society, an active police force is a deterrent to crime.*

◆ Critical Thinking

❹ **Interpret** Point out that the thief says that the civil war is over; now "civil peace." Ask: What is ironic about the thief's statement? *The civil war was between two political entities. Now that the war is over, people expect to live in peace, but instead, the people are now faced with a new threat from their fellow citizens.*

Comprehension Check ☑

❺ What reason does the thief give for stealing Jonathan's money? *The thief says perhaps Jonathan does not have plenty of money but he and his cohorts themselves have none; therefore, Jonathan should give them his money.*

Extending Word Study

Word Forms Have students extend the Related Words activity in Build Vocabulary by learning other forms of the word *continuously*. Each form is related to the verb *continue*, and there are many of them. You may wish to help students distinguish between *continuous*, which means "going on or extending without interruption or break," and *continual*, which means "happening over and over again" or "repeated often."

"Police-o! Thieves-o! Neighbors-o! Police-o! We are lost! We are dead! Neighbors, are you asleep? Wake up! Police-o!"

❶ This went on for a long time and then stopped suddenly. Perhaps they had scared the thief away. There was total silence. But only for a short while.

"You done finish?" asked the voice outside. "Make we help you small. Oya, everybody!"

❷ *"Police-o! Tief-man-so! Neighbors-o! we done loss-o! Police-o! . . ."*

There were at least five other voices besides the leader's.

Jonathan and his family were now completely paralyzed by terror. Maria and the children sobbed inaudibly like lost souls. Jonathan groaned continuously.

The silence that followed the thieves' alarm vibrated horribly. Jonathan all but begged their leader to speak again and be done with it.

"My frien," said he at long last, "we don try our best for call dem but I tink say dem all done sleep-o . . . So wetin we go do now? Sometaim you wan call soja? Or you wan make we call ❸ dem for you? Soja better pass police. No be so?"

"Na so!" replied his men. Jonathan thought he heard even more voices now than before and groaned heavily. His legs were sagging under him and his throat felt like sandpaper.

"My frien, why you no de talk again. I de ask you say you wan make we call soja?"

"No."

"Awrighto. Now make we talk business. We no be bad tief. We no like for make trouble. ❹ Trouble done finish. War done finish and all the katakata wey de for inside. No Civil War again. This time na Civil Peace. No be so?"

"Na so!" answered the horrible chorus.

"What do you want from me? I am a poor man. Everything I had went with this war. Why do you come to me? You know people who have money. We . . ."

"Awright! We know say you no get plenty money. But we sef no get even anini. So derefore make you open dis window and give us one hundred pound and we go commot. Orderwise we de come for inside now to show you guitar-boy like dis . . ."

A volley of automatic fire rang through the sky. Maria and the children began to weep aloud again.

"Ah, missisi de cry again. No need for dat. We done talk say we na good tief. We just take our small money and go nwayorly. No molest. Abi we de molest?"

"At all!" sang the chorus.

"My friends," began Jonathan hoarsely. "I hear what you say and I thank you. If I had one hundred pounds . . ."

"Lookia my frien, no be play we come play for your house. If we make mistake and step for inside you no go like am-o. So derefore . . ."

"To God who made me; if you come inside and find one hundred pounds, take it and shoot me and shoot my wife and children. I swear to God. The only money I have in this life is this twenty-pounds *egg-rasher* they gave me today . . ."

"Ok. Time de go. Make you open dis window and bring the twenty pound. We go manage am like dat."

There were now loud murmurs of dissent among the chorus: "Na lie de man de lie; e get plenty money . . . Make we go inside and search properly well . . . Wetin be twenty pound? . . ."

"Shurrup!" rang the leader's voice like a lone shot in the sky and silenced the murmuring at once. "Are you dere? Bring the money quick!"

"I am coming," said Jonathan fumbling in the darkness with the key of the small wooden box he kept by his side on the mat.

At the first sign of light as neighbors and others assembled to commiserate with him he was already strapping his five-gallon demijohn[8] to his bicycle carrier and his wife, sweating in the open fire, was turning over akara balls in a

◆ Build Vocabulary

commiserate (kə miz′ ər āt′) *v.*: Sympathize; share suffering

8. **demijohn** (dem′ i jän′) *n.*: Large bottle.

Cross-Curricular Connection: Science

The story mentions palm oil, which Jonathan uses to grease his bicycle, and palm wine, which he sells at his bar. Explain that palms are important in tropical regions, such as Nigeria, because they provide people with food, clothing, and building materials. There are more than 2,600 different kinds of palm trees throughout the world, varying greatly in size and the kind of flowers, leaves, and fruits they produce. Widely used food products made from palm trees include dried coconut meat, soap, salad oils, margarine, dates, and sago, a starch taken from palm trunks. Other palm products include baskets and chair bottoms, woven from strips of palm leaves, and furniture made from the stems of the rattan palm.

Have interested students find out more about palm trees and their products. After students have collected their information, reserve some time for them to share with the class what they discovered.

wide clay bowl of boiling oil. In the corner his eldest son was rinsing out dregs of yesterday's palm-wine from old beer bottles.

"I count it as nothing," he told his sympathizers, his eyes on the rope he was tying. "What is *egg-rasher*? Did I depend on it last week? Or is it greater than other things that went with the war? I say, let *egg-rasher* perish in the flames! Let it go where everything else has gone. Nothing puzzles God." 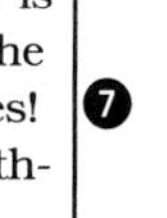

Beyond Literature

Cultural Connection

Changing Boundaries in Africa

In 1945, four European powers—Britain, France, Belgium, and Portugal—controlled almost all of Africa. However, a great liberation took place in Africa following World War II. Slowly at first, and then with increasing speed, the peoples of Africa regained their independence.

Activity In the struggle for independence, some nations, like Nigeria, have experienced internal difficulties. Using library or Internet sources, research and compare the cultural changes that have occurred in two or more African nations since they regained independence.

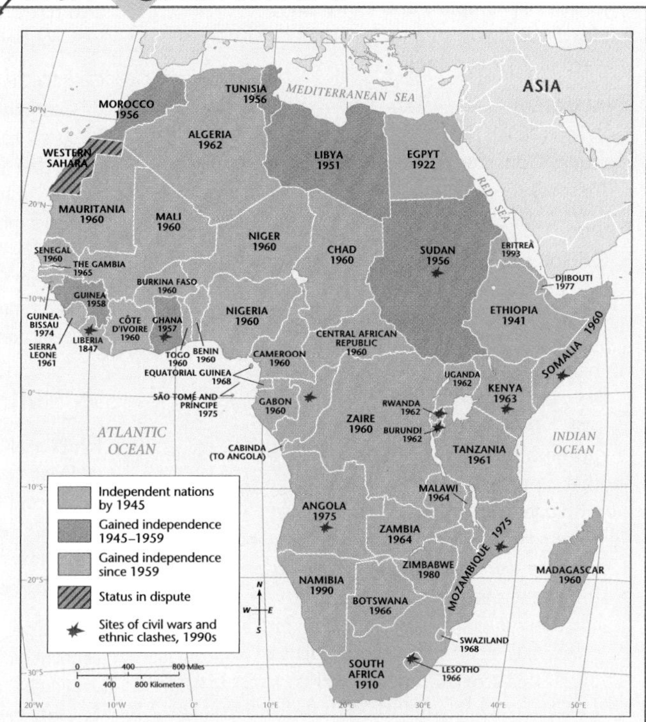

Guide for Responding

◆ Literature and Your Life

Reader's Response In what ways do you identify with Jonathan? Explain.

Thematic Focus Did reading about Jonathan's experiences make you feel more or less connected to people in Nigeria? Explain.

☑ Check Your Comprehension

1. What does Jonathan Iwegbu count as his greatest blessings? For what else is he grateful?
2. How does Jonathan earn money?
3. How do Jonathan and his family behave after their money is stolen?

Beyond the Selection

FURTHER READING

Other Works by Chinua Achebe

Things Fall Apart

Christmas in Biafra, and Other Poems

Girls at War

Other Works With the Theme of the Difficulties of Change

Two Moons In August, Martha Brooks

Daniel's Story, Carol Matas

We suggest that you preview these works before recommending them to students.

INTERNET

For more Nigerian proverbs translated by Chinua Achebe, suggest that students go to http://www. **bemorecreative.com/one/890.htm**

Please be aware, however, that sites may have changed from the time we published this information. We *strongly recommend* that you preview the sites before you send students to them.

Customize for Pre-AP Students

Have these students summarize the conversation between the thief and Jonathan. *Summaries should include the following: The thief wants Jonathan's money; Jonathan and his family call for help; the thieves mimic their calls; the thief threatens to harm the family; Jonathan admits that he has twenty pounds; the thief decides to take it against the wishes of his companions.*

◆ Critical Thinking

❻ Analyze Ask students why they think the thief decides to take the twenty pounds and leave Jonathan alone. Why doesn't he agree with his companions that they should go in and look for more money? *Students may think the thief's attitude toward life is ironically similar to Jonathan's: he will take what he gets and be satisfied. Others may conjecture that the thief doesn't want to get into a situation where he would hurt or kill anyone.*

◆ Critical Thinking

❼ Interpret Ask students to explain Jonathan's reaction. *Although he did not want the money to be stolen, Jonathan can put it out of his mind because he knows that he and his family will survive without it. He assumes that there is a reason for what happened, so he doesn't have to worry about it himself.*

Reinforce and Extend

Answers

◆ Literature and Your Life

Reader's Response Students may admire his positive attitude and his sense of priorities.

Thematic Focus Students should relate to the successes and failures of the characters in the story and compare them to those they feel in their own time and place.

☑ Check Your Comprehension

1. Above all he is thankful that his family has survived in the midst of chaos. He is also grateful that his bicycle was salvaged from the war.
2. Jonathan uses his bicycle as a taxi; then he uses it to supply a palm-wine business in his home.
3. They return to their businesses as if nothing has happened.

Answers

◆ Critical Thinking

1. The war destroyed people's homes and possessions and killed people, including one of Jonathan's children.
2. The thief feels he can just take what he wants; Jonathan knows how to create what he wants by working for it.
3. Jonathan is optimistic, trusting, and peaceful.
4. The peace between Jonathan and the thieves is achieved with civility, without resorting to violence.
5. Students may argue that rich people have so much they can easily accept the loss of some of their possessions. Others may say that although poor people may be accustomed to loss, they may value what little they have and grieve for its loss.

◆ Reading Strategy

1. Students may cite such sayings as "A penny saved is a penny earned" or "Never put off 'til tomorrow what you can do today."
2. Most students will admit that they may become upset by setbacks more easily than Jonathan is.

◆ Literary Focus

1. This key statement reflects Jonathan's optimism and happiness in just being alive.
2. The proverb states the philosophy that underlies Jonathan's trust that all will work out for the best.

◆ Build Vocabulary

Using Forms of *Disreputable*

1. reputed; reputation; disreputable

Using the Word Bank

1. edifice; 2. imperious; 3. commiserate; 4. amenable; 5. destitute; 6. inestimable

◆ Build Grammar Skills

1. past perfect tense: had put; past tense: was
2. past perfect tense: had returned; past tense: came
3. past tense: was; past perfect tense: had thought
4. past tense: pulled, revealed; past perfect tense: had insisted, had been
5. past tense: went, stopped; past perfect tense: had scared

Guide for Responding *(continued)*

◆ Critical Thinking

Interpret

1. How did the war affect the lives of people like Jonathan? **[Infer]**

2. Compare and contrast the attitude toward money of the leader of the thieves with that of Jonathan. **[Compare and Contrast]**

3. How would you sum up Jonathan's attitude toward life? **[Interpret]**

Evaluate

4. Why is "Civil Peace" an appropriate title for this story? Consider the meanings of the word *civil.* **[Assess]**

Apply

5. Do you think it is easier for a poor person or a rich person to accept the loss of material possessions? Explain your answer. **[Generalize]**

◆ Reading Strategy

Prior Knowledge

Although this story takes place after a civil war in another country, your **prior knowledge** about dealing with unexpected events can help you understand the main character's experiences and reactions.

1. Jonathan frequently quotes a proverb as a reaction to events in his life. What proverbs or sayings do you use to respond to events in your life?

2. Jonathan experiences several turns of fortune during this story. Compare and contrast his reactions to his changing luck with the way you respond to life's ups and downs.

◆ Literary Focus

Key Statements

Chinua Achebe makes use of a proverb that has been important in Ibo life. This proverb also acts as a **key statement** that throws light on the central meaning of his story.

1. What does the key statement, "Happy survival!" reveal about Jonathan's values?

2. Why do you think the proverb "Nothing puzzles God" is repeated in the story? How does it help reveal the story's message about life?

◆ Build Vocabulary

Using the Latin Root *-reput-*

Write the sentences below in your notebook and fill in the blanks with *disreputable, reputation,* or *reputed.*

Jonathan is __?__ to be a careful man. He also has a __?__ for honesty. Unfortunately, he was robbed by some __?__ men.

Using the Word Bank: Context

Copy the following book titles in your notebook. Next to each title, write the word from the Word Bank that you would expect to find in the book.

1. *The Architecture of Frank Lloyd Wright*

2. *Kings and Queens of the World*

3. *Sharing Your Pain*

4. *Getting Others to Agree*

5. *The Causes of Poverty*

6. *Jewels and Gemstones*

◆ Build Grammar Skills

Past and Past Perfect Tenses

Past tense indicates an action or condition that began and ended at a given time in the past. **Past perfect tense** (formed with *had* plus a past participle) shows an action or condition that was completed when another past action began.

Practice In your notebook, copy each of these sentences. Circle the past tense verbs and underline the verbs in the past perfect tense.

1. Only two houses away a huge concrete edifice some wealthy contractor had put up before the war was a mountain of rubble.

2. . . . he had returned to Enugu early enough . . . before thousands more came out of their forest holes . . .

3. . . . that little house of his was even a greater blessing than he had thought.

4. . . . he pulled out the innards of his pocket and revealed a hole in it. . . . But of course he had insisted that the money had been in the other pocket . . .

5. This went on for a long time and then stopped suddenly. Perhaps they had scared the thief away.

Grammar Reinforcement

For additional instruction and practice, use the lesson in the **Language Lab CD-ROM** on Verb Tense and the pages on tenses of verbs, pp. 67–71 in the *Writer's Solution Grammar Practice Book*.

Reteach

Students who have difficulty with accessing prior knowledge may benefit from using a graphic organizer. Encourage students to write passages from the selection in the first box and in the same position in the second box, incidents or thoughts from their own lives. By isolating the passage and the personal experience, students can make connections and understand new ideas.

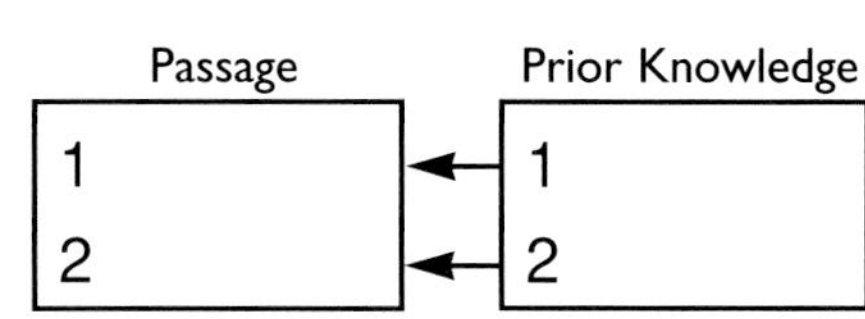

Build Your Portfolio

Idea Bank

Writing

1. **News Interview** Create a list of five interview questions a reporter covering the aftermath of the civil war might ask Jonathan. Based on details in the story, write Jonathan's answers to the questions. **[Social Studies Link]**
2. **Human-Interest Article** Use the events described in the story to write a human-interest article about one family's experiences after the civil war.
3. **Poem** Write a short poem expressing some thoughts or feelings that the story "Civil Peace" evoked in you.

Speaking, Listening, and Viewing

4. **Reworking a Dialogue** Rewrite the dialogue between the thieves and Jonathan in language that is familiar to you. With a partner, read the dialogue aloud. **[Performing Arts Link]**
5. **Multimedia Collage** Create a collage composed of magazine pictures, your own artwork, poems, music or musical lyrics, and words, which shows your interpretation of the proverb "Nothing puzzles God." If possible, create and share your multimedia collage on a computer. **[Art Link]**

Researching and Representing

6. **Proverbs Presentation** With a panel of "experts," collect some proverbs and sayings. Present the origins and applications of each, and speculate on why the saying has survived the test of time.
7. **Scenic Sketches** Sketch the settings for several scenes of a movie version of "Civil Peace." Possible scenes to include are Jonathan's home, the road to Enugu, and the outside of the Treasury. **[Art Link]**

Online Activity www.phlit.phschool.com

Guided Writing Lesson

Annotated Map of Nigeria

The setting of this story is Nigeria, a country of great diversity and political and social change. Conduct research and create an **annotated map** of Nigeria to instruct readers about significant features of the country's landscape, ethnic diversity, and types of industry. The annotations you write will give essential information about each aspect of Nigeria you decide to include. The following tip will help you in preparing your annotations.

Writing Skills Focus: Brevity and Clarity

When you need to convey a great deal of information in a small space, **brevity and clarity** (being brief and being clear) are especially important. Bulleted lists, numbered sentences, and charts are a few ways you can communicate important information in a small space. Annotations that you write in sentence form should be brief and to the point.

Prewriting Brainstorm for a list of questions you could research to help someone better understand the story. For instance, researching the question *In which regions do different ethnic groups live?* might give insight into the causes and boundaries of the civil war.

Drafting Put numbers on the map to locate the area to which each annotation refers. Then write your annotations. Try to avoid making the map too crowded, but include the facts that will be most helpful to readers.

Revising Look back at the biography of Achebe and the story. See if there is any information that you could present that would further enhance reading. Review each of your annotations to make sure they are not only short but clear.

✓ ASSESSMENT OPTIONS

Formal Assessment, Selection Test, pp. 101–103, and Assessment Resources Software. The selection test is designed so that it can be easily customized to the performance levels of your students.

Alternative Assessment, p. 29, includes options for less advanced students, more advanced students, bodily/kinesthetic learners, intrapersonal learners, logical/mathematical learners, and verbal/linguistic learners.

PORTFOLIO ASSESSMENT

Use the following rubrics in the ***Alternative Assessment*** booklet to assess student writing:
News Interview: Expression Rubric, p. 94
Human-Interest Article: Fictional Narrative Rubric, p. 95
Poem: Poetry Rubric, p. 108
Guided Writing Lesson: Technical Description/ Explanation Rubric, p. 115

Idea Bank

Following are suggestions for matching the Idea Bank topics with your students' performance levels and learning Modalities:

Customizing for *Performance Levels*
Less Advanced Students: 1, 5, 6
Average Students: 2, 4, 7
More Advanced Students: 3, 5

Customizing for *Learning Modalities*
Verbal/Linguistic: 1, 2, 3, 4, 5
Visual/Spatial: 6, 7

Guided Writing Lesson

Prewriting Strategy Help students brainstorm for their list of topics to generate annotations. When listing, students actually will generate several lists. Using the general topic of Nigeria, they can quickly write associations based on Achebe's story. This initial list can provide prompts for additional lists.

TOPIC ___________

Guide students to use the ideas generated on their lists to begin their research.

Writing and Language Transparencies Students may use the Herringbone Organizer, p. 76, to list and organize the information for their annotated maps before making labels on the map.

Writing Lab CD-ROM
Have students complete the tutorial on Exposition. Follow these steps:

1. Students can use the Questionnaire to help them gather details for their annotated maps.
2. Students may work in pairs to use the interactive instruction on conducting library research.
3. Have students draft their annotations on computer.
4. Students can use the guidelines for sharing reports with a group when presenting their annotated maps.

Prepare and Engage

LESSON OBJECTIVES

1. To develop vocabulary and word identification skills
- Latin Word Roots: *-ami-*
- Using the Word Bank: Context
- Reading Strategy: Respond to Connotations
- Extending Word Study: Portmanteau Words

2. To use a variety of reading strategies to comprehend a personal narrative
- Connect Your Experience
- Tips to Guide Reading

3. To increase knowledge of other cultures and to connect common elements across cultures
- Connecting Themes Across Cultures (ATE)

4. To express and support responses to the text
- Critical Thinking
- Idea Bank: Fan Magazine Interview
- Idea Bank: Dialogue
- Idea Bank: Techno-Reaction
- Idea Bank: Celebrity Home Page
- Idea Bank: Debate
- Speaking, Listening, and Viewing Mini-Lesson: Debate

5. To analyze literary elements
- Literary Focus: Tone

6. To plan, prepare, organize, and present literary interpretations
- Idea Bank: Drawing
- Idea Bank: Perform and Evaluate

7. To use recursive writing processes to write an introduction
- Guided Writing Lesson

8. To increase knowledge of the rules of grammar and usage
- Build Grammar Skills: Pronoun Agreement

Test Preparation

Reading Comprehension: Evaluate and Make Judgments (ATE, p. 405) The teaching tips and sample test item in this workshop support the instruction and practice in the unit workshop: **Reading Comprehension: Interpret Graphic Aids; Evaluate and Make Judgments** (SE, p. 465)

Guide for Reading

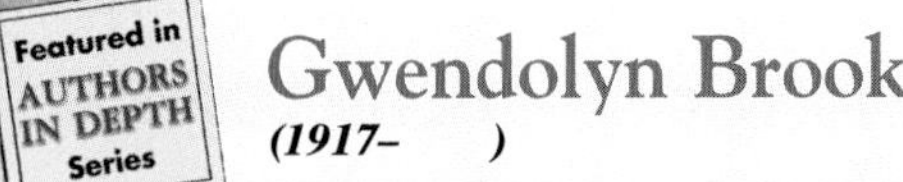

Featured in AUTHORS IN DEPTH Series

Gwendolyn Brooks (1917–)

If there is such a thing as a "born writer," Gwendolyn Brooks must be one. She began to write at age seven and published her first poem, "Eventide," at the age of seventeen.

In many of her poems, Brooks explores the struggles and dreams of African Americans. She won the Pulitzer Prize (the first African American to do so) for her 1949 collection of poetry, *Annie Allen.* She has received numerous other honors, including the title Poet Laureate of Illinois (1968) and an appointment as poetry consultant to the Library of Congress (1985–1986).

Umberto Eco (1932–)

Umberto Eco's personal library is larger than some school libraries—holding more than 30,000 volumes! His extensive library is just one indication of the Italian author's strong interest in all forms of communication. At the University of Bologna in Italy he teaches Semiotics, the study of communication through signs and symbols. He is also an avid follower of the information revolution taking place on the Internet. Eco achieved an international audience with his 1981 novel, *The Name of the Rose,* a suspenseful tale of murder in a Benedictine monastery.

◆ Build Vocabulary

LATIN WORD ROOTS: *-ami-*

In "How to React to Familiar Faces" you will encounter the word *amiably,* meaning "in a friendly way." The Latin word root *-ami-,* meaning "friend," appears in the French word for friend (*ami*) and in the Spanish words for friend (*amigo, amiga*). In English, *-ami-* is the root of several words related to friendship, such as *amiably, amenable, amity,* and *amicable.*

WORD BANK

As you read this poem and essay, you will encounter the words on this list. Each word is defined on the page where it first appears. Preview the list before you read.

expound
syndrome
amiably
protagonist

◆ Build Grammar Skills

PRONOUN AGREEMENT WITH AN INDEFINITE ANTECEDENT

A pronoun's **antecedent** is the noun or pronoun to which the pronoun refers. A pronoun must agree in number (singular or plural) and gender (feminine or masculine) with its antecedent. Sometimes the gender or the number of the antecedent may not be known. For instance, in his essay, Eco says:

> . . .we don't speak of *this person* in a loud voice when *he* or *she* can overhear.

Because the antecedent, *this person,* is singular but of unknown gender, Eco use the singular *he* or *she* to refer to the antecedent.

A common mistake is to use the word *they* in this situation; however, *they* is plural, so it does not agree with the singular antecedent.

Prentice Hall Literature Program Resources

REINFORCE / RETEACH / EXTEND

Selection Support Pages
Build Vocabulary: Word Roots: *-ami-,* p. 122
Build Grammar Skills: Pronoun Agreement with Indefinite Antecedent, p. 123
Reading Strategy: Respond to Connotations, p. 124
Literary Focus: Tone, p. 125

Strategies for Diverse Student Needs, p. 30
Beyond Literature Art of Portraiture, p. 30
Formal Assessment Selection Test, pp. 104–106; Assessment Resources Software
Alternative Assessment, p. 30

Writing and Language Transparencies Writing Process Model 2, Biographical Profile, pp. 13–16, Art Transparency 1
Resource Pro CD-ROM
Listening to Literature Audiocassettes

◆ The Bean Eaters ◆
How to React to Familiar Faces

◆ Literature and Your Life

Connect Your Experience

Although you've never met your favorite movie actor, chances are you know his or her age, likes and dislikes, and hobbies. With television and film delivering people into our living rooms, it's easy to feel as if you know celebrities. This poem and essay provide a contrast between the very public life of famous people and the very personal details of ordinary people who might live near you.

Thematic Focus: A World of People

These selections give you a glimpse of famous people and anonymous lives. Both the people you know and those who enter your life through books and film can expand your horizons.

Journal Writing Jot down details about a famous or not-so-famous person who has made a favorable impression on you.

◆ Background for Understanding

Entertainment

Umberto Eco was born in 1932, so the entertainment names he's familiar with may not be familiar to you. Then again, they might be. The following information identifies the people to whom Eco refers in his essay.

The film actor Anthony Quinn was born in Chihuahua, Mexico, in 1916. After years of being stereotyped in such roles as a Mexican bandit and an Indian warrior, Quinn eventually achieved international fame, winning two Academy Awards. Charlton Heston is an American actor. Johnny Carson was the host of *The Tonight Show* for thirty years, until 1992. Oprah Winfrey has been one of the most successful talk-show hosts in history.

Journal Writing Think about a character—from a book, movie, or television show—that you feel you really know. Describe the character's qualities that seem most familiar to you.

◆ Literary Focus

Tone

Each of these literary selections has a distinct **tone**—that is, an attitude toward its readers and its subject matter. A writer's tone may be formal or informal, friendly or distant, personal or impersonal. For example, Eco's tone is lighthearted and amusing. His attitude toward his subject and his readers is good-natured.

◆ Reading Strategy

Respond to Connotations

When you see a familiar face, you respond based on the associations you have with that person. In a similar way, you **respond** to connotations (associations that go beyond a word's literal definition) based on your personal experience. For example, in reading "The Bean Eaters," you probably create an image in your mind of the two people—what they look like and what they are wearing. The title "The Bean Eaters" refers literally to people who eat beans. Yet the phrase connotes simplicity and poverty.

Be prepared to take some words in literary works beyond their everyday meanings; these words tap you on the shoulder as if to say, "Hey, don't I remind you of something else?"

Anthony Quinn

People Magazine... Us ... The Tonight Show ... Brainstorm with students to name some of the many magazines and TV shows that focus on celebrities. Discuss with students the fascination people have for these subjects. Ask them why "ordinary people" are less likely to be subject to media attention. Tell them that the selections they will read offer some interesting insights on this topic.

Connecting Themes Across Cultures

Umberto Eco's academic specialty, semiotics—the study of communication through signs and symbols— is becoming increasingly important as the use of computers and the World Wide Web expands to all cultures. Have students brainstorm for symbols that everyone around the world already understands and suggest some that will become known worldwide.

Customize for
Less Proficient Readers

Less proficient readers may need extra help in identifying the distinct tone of each piece. Help students by highlighting specific passages for them to consider. Ask such guiding questions as: Is the attitude expressed here light-hearted or serious? Joyous or sad? Formal or informal?

Customize for
Pre-AP Students

Encourage these students to compare aspects of the two selections and distinguish between Eco's tone and that of Gwendolyn Brooks. Also have them consider any common thread of theme or style that runs through each one.

Customize for
Interpersonal Learners

Have these students evaluate the attitude toward people that each of the authors expresses. Suggest that they work with partners to role-play an interview with Brooks and Eco to demonstrate these attitudes to classmates.

Test Preparation Workshop

Reading Comprehension:
Evaluate and Make Judgments Standardized test often require students to evaluate and make judgments. Use the following sample test item to help students evaluate a poet's word choice.

They eat beans mostly, this old yellow pair.
Dinner is a casual affair.
Plain chipware on a plain and creaking wood,
Tin flatware.

The poet's choice of items used by the couple indicates that the use of the word *casual* may be ironic and that the couple is probably—

A vegetarian
B tired
C hungry
D poor

By noting the quality of the objects that the poet describes—chipped earthenware and tin utensils—students should recognize that the couple is poor and that D is the correct answer.

Develop Understanding

One-Minute Insight These selections explore the lives of people, both ordinary and extraordinary, and how we view them. Poet Gwendolyn Brooks vividly evokes the texture of everyday lives and helps us glimpse the sensitive realities that lie beneath surface images.

◆ Reading Strategy

❶ Respond to Connotations Encourage students to comment on the connotations of "this old yellow pair." Students may say that the description of their skin color as yellow evokes the quality of wear and age. One meaning of yellow is "changed to a yellowish color as by age, as old paper."

◆ Critical Thinking

❷ Interpret Ask students what two aspects of the people's lives Brooks contrasts in these lines. Also have students comment on the larger meaning of this contrast. *Brooks contrasts the pair's ordinary, day-to-day existence with the accumulated richness of their lives; she shows that these seemingly ordinary lives are full of complexity and meaning.*

◆ Literary Focus

❸ Tone Ask students to describe the tone of the poem. Encourage them to cite specific phrases or images that support their responses. *Students may describe the tone as sympathetic, straightforward, and slightly sad or bittersweet.*

▶ Critical Viewing ◀

❹ Analyze *The plain plate and fork are serviceable and practical; the beans are common and everyday.*

Extending Word Study

Portmanteau Words The word *chipware* is a portmanteau word—a word that combines two other words in form and meaning. Brooks made up this one. Have students decide what words Brooks combined (chipped and earthenware) and then brainstorm for a list of other portmanteau words that are in the dictionary, such as smog (smoke + fog) or postmark (postal + marking).

The Bean Eaters

Gwendolyn Brooks

They eat beans mostly, this old yellow pair.
Dinner is a casual affair.
❶ Plain chipware on a plain and creaking wood,
Tin flatware.

Two who are Mostly Good.
Two who have lived their day,
But keep on putting on their clothes
And putting things away.
❷

❸ And remembering . . .
Remembering, with twinklings and twinges,
As they lean over the beans in their rented back room
that is full of beads and receipts and dolls
and cloths, tobacco crumbs, vases and fringes.

❹ ▲ Critical Viewing In what ways do these pictures suggest the simplicity of the old couple's lives? [Analyze]

Block Scheduling Strategies

Consider these suggestions to take advantage of extended class time:

- Play a recording of Paul Simon's song, "Old Friends." Have students read the lyrics and answer the questions in the Connections to Today's World on p. 407.
- Have students complete the activities on Tone on page 410 and the Literary Focus page in ***Selection Support,*** p. 125.
- Use Art Transparency 1 to introduce "How to React to Familiar Faces." You might have students do one of the optional activities accompanying the transparency.
- Have students complete the page on the Art of Portraiture in ***Beyond Literature,*** p. 30, and compare their responses to the portrait of Anthony Quinn on page 408.
- Students may work in discussion groups to identify and explore words and images that have powerful connotations in the works in this section. Then have students answer the Reading Strategy questions (p. 410).

Old Friends

Paul Simon

Old Friends,
Old Friends
Sat on their park bench
Like bookends.
A newspaper blown through the grass
Falls on the round toes
Of the high shoes
Of the Old Friends.

Old Friends,
Winter companions,
The old men
Lost in their overcoats,
Waiting for the sunset.
The sounds of the city,
Sifting through the trees,
Settle like dust
On the shoulders
Of the old friends.

Connections to Today's World

In the late 1960's, singer/songwriter Paul Simon recorded this song with Art Garfunkel, who was his partner at that time. In this song, Paul Simon looks at the friendship of anonymous elderly people. Like the couple in "The Bean Eaters," these old friends show how our everyday relationships expand the horizons of our world.

Can you imagine us
Years from today,
Sharing a park bench quietly?
How terribly strange
To be seventy.

Old Friends,
Memory brushes the same years.
Silently sharing the same fears. . . .

1. Describe the qualities of the friendship shown in these lyrics.
2. Based on the thoughts he expresses here, how much importance do you think celebrity Paul Simon places on fame?

Guide for Responding

◆ Literature and Your Life

Reader's Response If you could meet the people in "The Bean Eaters," what would you ask them about their memories?

Thematic Focus In what ways do people like the pair in "The Bean Eaters" enrich the world?

☑ Check Your Comprehension

1. Who is the subject of "The Bean Eaters"?
2. How do they spend most of their time?

◆ Critical Thinking

INTERPRET

1. Identify two details that indicate the couple in the poem are not rich. **[Deduce]**
2. Which details lead you to believe that they share many memories? Explain. **[Draw Conclusions]**

APPLY

3. Do you think the people in this poem are happy? Explain. **[Hypothesize]**

☑ Check Your Comprehension

1. The subject is an old couple who live together in a rented room.
2. They spend their time reminiscing about people, places, and things from their past.

◆ Critical Thinking

1. Details that indicate the old pair's poverty include "plain and creaking wood" and "rented back room."
2. The phrase "twinklings and twinges" suggests that the pair share many memories.
3. They are happy enough to care for themselves and share their memories with each other.

Connections to Today's World

About the Author Paul Simon wrote and recorded such hits as "Kodachrome" and "Still Crazy After All These Years." During the 1980's, he explored international styles and rhythms. His musical experimentation resulted in two highly successful albums: *Graceland,* on which he collaborated with several black South African musicians, and *Rhythms of the Saints,* on which he collaborated with some of Brazil's leading musicians. Simon collaborated with Derek Walcott on the 1997 Broadway musical *The Capeman.*

Thematic Connection

Have students compare the importance of memories in the song and the poem, "The Bean Eaters." *The role is similar. In "The Bean Eaters," the two people have "lived their day." In the song, the two friends sit passively while life goes on around them. Their memories are "all that's left."*

Tips to Guide Reading

Silent Reading Brooks creates poetry by choosing to omit words, as well as choosing to include them. As students read silently, have them evaluate the words she has chosen and judge whether they think she included enough to convey her meaning.

◆ Critical Thinking

Compare and Contrast Ask students: How is the tone of "Old Friends" similar to or different from that of "The Bean Eaters"? *Students may say that the tone is similar—it is sympathetic and somewhat melancholy.*

Answers to Connections to Today's World

1. The friends are seventy years old, quiet, thoughtful, and fearful.
2. He places little importance on fame.

Reinforce and Extend

Answers

◆ Literature and Your Life

Reader's Response Students might ask them about their work, their friends and family, and their hobbies.

Thematic Focus They have stores of memories that others will appreciate when they are shared.

Develop Understanding

Author and social critic Umberto Eco humorously analyzes the effects of the media on the way people react to celebrities. In a lighthearted tone, he raises questions on a serious theme.

Art Transparency Place Art Transparency 1, *Bauhaus Stairway,* on the overhead projector. As students look at the art, have them discuss the issue of familiarity and anonymity among people.

◆ Literary Focus

❶ **Tone** Have students describe the tone of this passage. Encourage them to cite specific phrases or offer explanations in support of their descriptions. *Students may describe the tone as humorous. They may note comic exaggerations when he writes, "It was too late to flee"; and "I might as well make the first move."*

▶Critical Viewing◀

❷ **Hypothesize** Students may say he is reacting to a greeting from an acquaintance or a fan; his expression seems pleased.

◆ *Literature and Your Life*

❸ Ask students if they agree with Eco's statement. If not, why not?

Customize for
English Language Learners
You might use this essay as an opportunity for students to share knowledge and ideas about popular culture. Students of different cultures might inform classmates about the familiar faces in the popular cultures of their countries.

How to React to Familiar Faces

▲ **Critical Viewing** This photograph is of the movie star Anthony Quinn. What do you think he is reacting to in this picture? **[Hypothesize]**

Umberto Eco

A few months ago, as I was strolling in New York, I saw, at a distance, a man I knew very well heading in my direction. The trouble was that I couldn't remember his name or where I had met him. This is one of those sensations you encounter especially when, in a foreign city, you run into someone you met back home, or vice versa. A face out of context creates confusion. Still, that face was so familiar that, I felt, I should certainly stop, greet him, converse; perhaps he would immediately respond, "My dear Umberto, how are you?" or "Were you able to do that thing you were telling me
❶ about?" And I would be at a total loss. It was too late to flee. He was still looking at the opposite side of the street, but now he was beginning to turn his eyes towards me. I might as well make the first move; I would wave and then, from his voice, his first remarks, I would try to guess his identity.

We were now only a few feet from each other, I was just about to break into a broad, radiant smile, when suddenly I recognized him. It was Anthony Quinn. Naturally, I had never met him in my life, nor he me. In a thousandth of a second I was able to check myself, and I walked past him, my eyes staring into space.

Afterwards, reflecting on this incident, I realized how totally normal it was. Once before, in a restaurant, I had glimpsed Charlton Heston and had felt an impulse to say hello. These faces inhabit our memory; watching the screen we spend so many hours with them that they are as familiar to us as our relatives', even more so. You can be a student of mass communication, debate the effects of reality, or the confusion between the real and the imagined, and expound the way some people fall permanently into this confusion; but still you are not immune to the syndrome. And there is worse.

I have received confidences from people who

Speaking, Listening, and Viewing Mini-Lesson

Debate
This mini-lesson supports the Speaking, Listening, and Viewing activity in the Idea Bank on p. 411.

Introduce Point out that in a debate, two teams present opposing viewpoints on a subject. The teams then take turns "rebutting," or arguing against, their opponents' views.

Develop Before students debate, encourage them to think about both sides of the question. For example, present these statements:

- Celebrities owe their success to the public—they should do all they can to please fans.
- Most celebrities owe their success to hard work in a certain field, such as acting or sports—they shouldn't have to give up their privacy to please fans.

Apply Opposing teams can develop arguments to support their side. Then they can present their positions in debate format.

Assess After the debate, assess students on their ability to present arguments that were clear, focused, and persuasive.

appearing fairly frequently on TV, have been subjected to the mass media over a certain period of time. I'm not talking about Johnny Carson or Oprah Winfrey, but public figures, experts who have participated in panel discussions often enough to become recognizable. All of them complain of the same disagreeable experience. Now, as a rule, when we see someone we don't know personally, we don't stare into his or her face at length, we don't point out the person to the friend at our side, we don't speak of this person in a loud voice when he or she can overhear. Such behavior would be rude, even—if carried too far—aggressive. But the same people who would never point to a customer at a counter and remark to a friend that the man is wearing a smart tie behave quite differently with famous faces.

My guinea pigs insist that, at a newsstand, in the tobacconist's, as they are boarding a train or entering a restaurant toilet, they encounter others who, among themselves, say aloud, "Look there's X." "Are you sure?" "Of course I'm sure. It's X, I tell you." And they continue their conversation amiably, while X hears them, and they don't care if he hears them: it's as if he didn't exist.

Such people are confused by the fact that a protagonist of the mass media's imaginary world should abruptly enter real life, but at the same time they behave in the presence of the real person as if he still belonged to the world of images, as if he were on a screen, or in a weekly picture magazine. As if they were speaking in his absence.

I might as well have grabbed Anthony Quinn by the lapel, dragged him to a phone booth, and called a friend to say, "Talk about coincidence! I've run into Anthony Quinn. And you know something? He seems real!" (After which I would throw Quinn aside and go on about my business.)

The mass media first convinced us that the imaginary was real, and now they are convincing us that the real is imaginary; and the more reality the TV screen shows us, the more cinematic our everyday world becomes. ❺

◆ Build Vocabulary

expound (eks pound′) *v.*: Explain in detail

syndrome (sin′ drōm) *n.*: Group of signs that occur together and may form a pattern

amiably (ā′ mē ə blē) *adv.*: In a cheerful, friendly way

protagonist (prō tag′ ə nist′) *n.*: Main character; person who plays a leading part

Guide for Responding

◆ Literature and Your Life

Reader's Response Do you react to celebrities in the way Umberto describes? Explain.

Thematic Focus Which celebrities interest you? Why?

☑ Check Your Comprehension

1. What celebrity does the author see in New York?
2. What reaction does Eco say most people have to celebrities?
3. Why does Eco say people react as they do?

◆ Critical Thinking

INTERPRET

1. How do you think Eco feels about the way people react to celebrities? **[Interpret]**
2. Explain how the title of the essay relates to its message. **[Connect]**
3. Explain Eco's understanding of the role the media plays in our reaction to and attitude toward famous people. **[Analyze]**

APPLY

4. Based on Eco's observations, do you think you would like to be famous? Why or why not? **[Relate]**

Beyond the Selection

FURTHER READING

Other Works by the Authors

Annie Allen, Gwendolyn Brooks
The Name of the Rose, Umberto Eco

Other Works About Individuals

Working, Studs Terkel
"Richard Cory," Edwin Arlington Robinson
Our Town, Thornton Wilder

We suggest that you preview these works before recommending them to students.

INTERNET

Students can use the Internet to learn more about the writers Gwendolyn Brooks:
http://www.wilmington.net/arts/poets/brooks.html
Umberto Eco:
http://www1.geocites.com/Athens/6642/index.html
Paul Simon:
http://www.connix.com/~rdrie/Frames/simon/history.html

Please be aware, that sites may have changed since we published this information. We *strongly recommend* that you preview the sites before you send students to them.

◆ Reading Strategy

❹ Respond to Connotations Ask students why Eco cites the names Johnny Carson and Oprah Winfrey here. How do the connotations that these names carry help him make his point? *Eco is contrasting people who are somewhat recognizable with those who are truly famous; both Carson and Winfrey have instantly recognizable names and faces because of their remarkable television success.*

◆ Literary Focus

❺ Tone Encourage students to contrast the tone of this paragraph with the tone of the previous one. Then have them discuss the purpose that this variation in tone serves. *Elicit the following: The tone of this paragraph is more serious and philosophical than that of the previous one; Eco uses humorous anecdotes and scenarios to illustrate a serious point about the effect of the mass media in the modern world.*

Reinforce and Extend

Answers

◆ Literature and Your Life

Reader's Response Students may share anecdotes about their reactions to celebrities.

Thematic Focus Students should provide reasons for their interest in celebrities.

☑ Check Your Comprehension

1. He sees Anthony Quinn.
2. People view them as familiar objects.
3. Eco observes that the mass media has convinced us that the people on screen are imaginary, not real.

◆ Critical Thinking

1. Eco disapproves of treating celebrities—or any people—as objects.
2. Eco's title suggests a set of instructions, implying that people don't know how to react to familiar faces.
3. In the last paragraph of the essay Eco indicates that in bringing celebrities into our intimate lives the media has distorted our way of relating to strangers.
4. Students may respond that they would prefer to live private lives.

Guide for Responding (continued)

◆ Reading Strategy

RESPOND TO CONNOTATIONS

You might find yourself relating more to one of these selections than to another. Your personal experience and the associations you have with particular words influence your response to the images and connotations in each selection.

1. Keeping in mind the subject of "The Bean Eaters," what is the connotation of "plain chipware" and "tin flatware"?
2. (a) How do you respond to the words "twinklings" and "twinges" in "The Bean Eaters"? (b) What do you think the poet was trying to convey with each of these words?
3. To which image in "How to React to Familiar Faces" do you respond most strongly? What connotations create the image for you?

◆ Build Vocabulary

USING THE LATIN ROOT *-ami-*

Knowing that the root *-ami-* means "friend," respond to the following questions in your notebook.

1. Would a person approach you amiably wearing a smile or a frown?
2. You've just finished meeting with the principal, and you parted amicably. Write the last two things you might have said to each other.
3. Write one suggestion for fostering amity between students and teachers.
4. Explain why you would or would not be amenable to shorter vacations.

USING THE WORD BANK: Context

On your paper, respond to the following items.

1. What kind of person might expound on the importance of reading?
2. Name a person to whom you usually respond amiably.
3. Describe the protagonist in your favorite movie or book.
4. Describe a humorous syndrome that might affect students early on a Monday morning.

◆ Literary Focus

TONE

The **tone** of a literary work is the writer's attitude toward the readers and toward the subject. In the poem "The Bean Eaters," Gwendolyn Brooks presents you with two people in a room. Her tone is as intimate as her subject matter, but some readers will find it lonely, too. In his social commentary "How to React to Familiar Faces," Eco's purpose is to reveal a common human behavior, and his tone is suitably objective. It is also a bit wry, or humorous.

1. (a) How do you think Brooks feels about the people in her poem "The Bean Eaters"? (b) List two details that help you identify her attitude toward the people.
2. Find two statements in "How to React to Familiar Faces" that reflect a humorous tone.
3. Compare and contrast the tone of "The Bean Eaters" with the tone of "How to React to Familiar Faces."

◆ Build Grammar Skills

PRONOUN AGREEMENT WITH AN INDEFINITE ANTECEDENT

Singular pronouns must be used to refer to **indefinite antecedents** such as *someone, anyone,* and *everybody.* If the gender is unknown, it's best to use a combination of two singular personal pronouns such as *he or she* or *his or her.* When words like *all* or *several* are antecedents, they require a plural word to refer to them.

Practice In your notebook, write the pronoun that agrees with its indefinite antecedent in each of the following sentences:

1. Anyone who wants a seat to hear Gwendolyn Brooks read should buy (their, his, her, his or her) ticket early.
2. Several could have reserved (their, his or her) seats earlier.
3. One person thought (he, she, they, he or she) would have to stand for the reading.
4. All who called ahead had seats, and (they, he or she, he, she) were grateful.

Answers

◆ Reading Strategy

1. The connotation is simplicity.
2. (a) They alliteratively suggest the pleasures and pain of memory. (b) The poet suggests the two extremes of memory—the positive and negative aspects.
3. Encourage students to explain whether the connotations affected their response in a positive or negative manner.

◆ Build Vocabulary

Latin Word Roots *-ami-*

1. An amiable approach would be accompanied by a smile.
2. You might have said, "Thanks for meeting with me" and "I appreciate your interest."
3. Students may suggest good communication.
4. Some students may be willing to accept shorter vacations if they occur at more frequent intervals. Others may argue that they need a long vacation to rest from the pressure of academic work.

Using the Word Bank

1. A bibliophile may expound on the importance of reading.
2. You usually act amiably to your parents and friends.
3. Descriptions should include personality traits as well as physical details.
4. Students may find it humorous that they all need a "wake-up" activity in order to pay attention on Monday mornings.

◆ Literary Focus

1. (a) Brooks appears to be warmly sympathetic to the couple. (b) Phrases that reflect her attitude include *casual, Mostly Good,* and *remembering with twinklings and twinges.*
2. A humorous tone is reflected in statements such as "It was too late to flee," and "My guinea pigs insist that. . . ."
3. Brooks reveals a positive and empathetic attitude toward people often disparaged; Eco pokes fun at those who dehumanize the celebrities of mass media.

◆ Build Grammar Skills

1. Anyone . . . should buy his or her . . . .
2. Several could have reserved their. . . .
3. One person thought he or she. . . .
4. All . . . had seats, and they. . . .

Grammar Reinforcement

For additional instruction and practice, use the lesson in the **Language Lab CD-ROM** on Pronouns and Antecedents and the page on Pronoun and Antecedent Agreement, p. 83 in the *Writer's Solution Grammar Practice Book.*

Reteach

To reteach the reading strategy, respond to connotations, use ***Strategies for Diverse Student Needs,*** p. 30.

Build Your Portfolio

Idea Bank

Writing

1. **Fan Magazine Interview** Write five questions you would ask your favorite celebrity in an interview. Write an answer to one of the questions, as if you were the celebrity.

2. **Dialogue** Write a brief dialogue that might occur between the man and the woman in the poem "The Bean Eaters."

3. **Techno-Reaction** Write your reaction to some effect of technology, such as doing business on the World Wide Web or making friends on Internet chat lines. **[Technology Link]**

Speaking, Listening, and Viewing

4. **Perform and Evaluate** With a group, enact a scene in which several teenagers recognize their favorite music star somewhere near them in public. When you are in the "audience," evaluate how true to life each group's scene is. **[Performing Arts Link]**

5. **Debate** Divide into teams to debate this statement: Publicity is part of the "job" of being a celebrity. Support your position with sound reasoning. **[Social Studies Link]**

Researching and Representing

6. **Drawing** Using the medium of your choice (color pencils, markers, charcoal), draw a picture of the room and couple described in "The Bean Eaters." Try to capture the tone of the poem in your drawing. **[Art Link]**

7. **Celebrity Home Page** Design a home page for one of the celebrities Eco mentions in his nonfiction piece. Choose visuals and suggest topics and links. **[Technology Link]**

Online Activity www.phlit.phschool.com

Guided Writing Lesson

Introduction of Talk-Show Guest

Although celebrities are usually well known to the public, talk-show hosts often introduce them in a way that builds up audience interest. Do some research and write an **introduction** for a celebrity guest you would like to interview on a talk show. Keep your audience in mind as you prepare your introduction.

Writing Skills Focus: Audience Knowledge

Finding details about your celebrity that haven't already been published or broadcast may be difficult. Your audience will probably already know a great deal about the guest, so conduct your research in the hope of finding details that show the person in a light the audience doesn't normally view him or her.

For example, if your guest is a movie actor, listing all of his or her movies will probably not add to **audience knowledge.** Instead, name just one or two recent projects, then focus on an anecdote that will draw audience attention to an aspect of the celebrity's personality that isn't usually considered.

Prewriting Focus on listing details that will build interest in the aspect that you want to highlight. For instance, if you want to show how hardworking a movie actor is, you might plan to include details about the difficult conditions during the making of his or her last movie, such as filming during the hurricane season or sixteen-hour filming sessions.

Drafting Keep your introduction brief. Include just enough details to heighten your audience's interest and draw them into the interview that will follow.

Revising Read your draft aloud to a partner. Ask him or her to identify the most and least interesting details. Revise your draft based on your partner's suggestions.

✓ ASSESSMENT OPTIONS

Formal Assessment, Selection Test, pp. 104–106, and Assessment Resources Software. The selection test is designed so that it can be easily customized to the performance levels of your students.

Alternative Assessment, p. 30, includes options for less advanced students, more advanced students, intrapersonal learners, verbal/linguistic learners, and interpersonal learners.

PORTFOLIO ASSESSMENT

Use the following rubrics in the ***Alternative Assessment*** booklet to assess student writing:
Fan Magazine Interview: Fictional Narrative Rubric, p. 95
Dialogue: Fictional Narrative Rubric, p. 95
Techno-Reaction: Expression Rubric, p. 94
Guided Writing Lesson: Description Rubric, p. 97

Idea Bank

Following are suggestions for matching the Idea Bank topics with your students' performance levels and learning modalities:

Customizing for *Performance Levels*
Less Advanced Students: 1, 4, 6
Average Students: 2, 4, 7
More Advanced Students: 3, 5

Customizing for *Learning Modalities*
Verbal/Linguistic: 1, 2, 4, 5
Visual/Spatial: 3, 6, 7
Bodily/Kinesthetic: 4

Guided Writing Lesson

Prewriting Strategy Help students brainstorm about their celebrity by filling out a web like the one below. After students have completed the web, encourage them to use a colored pencil to circle any information that they believe their audience may not know. Students may then choose to focus on these details in the introduction.

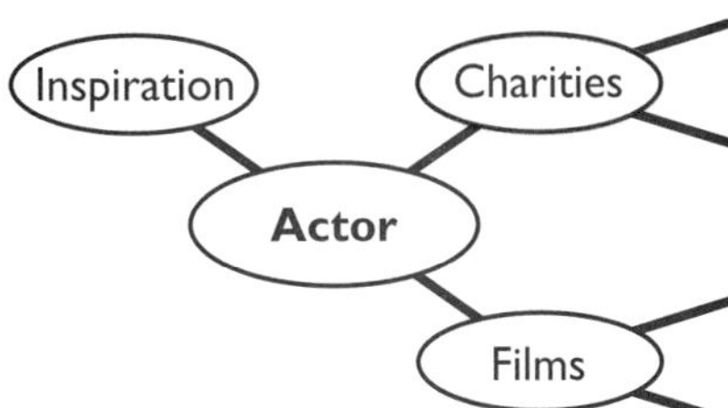

For more prewriting, elaboration, and revision strategies, see *Prentice Hall Writing and Grammar.*

Writing and Language Transparencies You may use the Writing Process Model 2 for a Biographical Profile, pp. 13–16, to guide students through the process of writing biographical information about a person.

Writing Lab CD-ROM
Have students complete the tutorial on Description. Follow these steps:

1. Students can use the Annotated Writing Models to learn how audience affects a writer's choice of language and details.
2. Have students use the interactive instruction on creating a main impression.
3. Students can use the Peer Evaluation Checklist to help them revise their work.

Prepare and Engage

LESSON OBJECTIVES

1. **To develop vocabulary and word identification skills**
   - Latin Word Roots: *-cent-*
   - Using the Word Bank: Sentence Completion
   - Extending Word Study: Dictionary
2. **To use a variety of reading strategies to comprehend a personal narrative**
   - Connect Your Experience
   - Reading Strategy: Relate Text and Pictures
   - Tips to Guide Reading: Shared Reading
   - Read to Discover Models for Writing
3. **To increase knowledge of other cultures and to connect common elements across cultures**
   - Connecting Themes Across Cultures (ATE)
4. **To express and support responses to the text**
   - Critical Thinking
   - Idea Bank: Exhibit Promotion
   - Idea Bank: Painting and Poetry Exhibit
   - Idea Bank: Art Narration
5. **To analyze literary elements**
   - Literary Focus: Analytical Essay
   - Idea Bank: Poetry Reading
   - Idea Bank: Art Analysis
6. **To read in order to research self-selected and assigned topics**
   - Idea Bank: Photo Essay
   - Idea Bank: Art Exchange
8. **To use recursive writing processes to write a museum placard**
   - Guided Writing Lesson
9. **To increase knowledge of the rules of grammar and usage**
   - Build Grammar Skills: Compound Sentences

Test Preparation

Reading Comprehension: Evaluate and Make Judgments (ATE, p. 413) The teaching tips and sample test item in this workshop support the instruction and practice in the unit workshop: **Reading Comprehension: Interpret Graphic Aids; Evaluate and Make Judgments** (SE, p. 465)

Guide for Reading

Reynolds Price *(1933–)*

American author Reynolds Price "photographs" his characters with words. He is known for his talent for characterization, creating people that readers feel they have known all their lives. Most of his characters are drawn from the North Carolina cotton country where Price was raised.

Although best known for his novels—including *A Long and Happy Life* and *A Generous Man*, as well as his short stories—Price works in a variety of genres. He has published essays, poetry, and a memoir in addition to his fiction works.

In this essay, Reynolds Price uses his keen perception of characters to analyze the character of the very private American author Emily Dickinson.

Richard Mühlberger *(1938–)*

You're most likely to find Richard Mühlberger's nonfiction in museum shops. In his book *What Makes a Degas a Degas?* he makes the work of a famous French artist understandable to the ordinary reader and viewer. In this essay, he analyzes two works of the nineteenth-century French painter Edgar Degas. Many of Degas's paintings show scenes that might have been captured by a hidden camera. They depict people in unguarded moments and sometimes show them in awkward positions. Degas studied art in both Paris and Italy. He intended to become a painter of historical scenes, but he soon turned to modern subjects. He became part of an artistic movement known as Impressionism, whose followers focused on capturing a momentary glimpse of a subject.

◆ Build Vocabulary

LATIN WORD ROOTS: *-cent-*

Have you ever seen a *centenarian*? That's not some kind of monster with the head of a man and the body of a horse, but a person who is at least one hundred years old. An important clue to the meaning of the word *centenarian* is the Latin word root *-cent-*, which means "hundred." What other words can you think of that contain the root *-cent-*?

WORD BANK

Before you read, preview this list of words from the essays. Several of the words may already be familiar to you. Discuss the words with a partner, and jot down what you think the words mean.

titanic
centenarian
austere
lacquered

◆ Build Grammar Skills

COMPOUND SENTENCES

Both Reynolds Price and Richard Mühlberger use compound sentences to provide information about their subjects. A **compound sentence** consists of two or more equally important, or coordinate, independent clauses. (An independent clause is a group of words with a subject and a verb that can stand alone as a sentence.) The clauses may be joined by a coordinating conjunction such as *and, but,* or *or,* or by a semicolon (;). Look at these examples:

> Subscribers to the Opéra were allowed backstage in the theater, *and* some took advantage of this access to pester dancers.
>
> The Impressionists painted out of doors; Degas preferred working in his studio.

Prentice Hall Literature Program Resources

REINFORCE / RETEACH / EXTEND

Selection Support Pages
Build Vocabulary: Word Roots: *-cent-*, p. 126
Build Grammar Skills: Compound Sentences, p. 127
Reading Strategy: Relate Text and Pictures, p. 128
Literary Focus: Analytical Essay, p. 129

Strategies for Diverse Student Needs, p. 31

Beyond Literature
Humanities Connection: Art and Photography, p. 31

Formal Assessment Selection Test, pp. 107–109; Assessment Resources Software

Alternative Assessment, p. 31

Writing and Language Transparencies
Grid organizer, p. 80; Cubing organizer, p. 88

Resource Pro CD-ROM

Listening to Literature Audiocassettes

A Picture From the Past: Emily Dickinson
◆ What Makes a Degas a Degas? ◆

◆ Literature and Your Life

Connect Your Experience

Your eye doctor tests your vision by having you read an eye chart, but a hidden picture puzzle like the one on this page tests how much you really *see*. Look carefully at this picture to find the young woman *and* the old woman. (Hint: The young woman's ear is the old woman's eye.) To find the hidden pictures, you have to do more than just look, you have to notice details that might not be immediately apparent. The authors of these two essays will help you notice the "hidden" details in a photograph and in two pieces of art.

Journal Writing In your journal, describe another activity that requires you to see, not just to look.

Thematic Focus: A World of People

Looking at things in a new way can expand your horizons. These two essays will help you analyze pictures and see the significance of details you might otherwise have overlooked.

◆ Background for Understanding

Humanities

Think about photographs that have caught your eye in a magazine, newspaper, or exhibit. In addition to the pleasure they bring or the curiosity they satisfy, photographs help us learn about people from different places, at different points in time. Far-off people and places can appear right before our eyes.

Paintings also have the power to transport viewers to distant places and to earlier periods in history. In fact, paintings and other works of art provide our only visual records of what life was like in the centuries before photography was invented in the 1830's.

◆ Literary Focus

Analytical Essay

Finding out how something works (or why it has stopped working) often involves taking the thing apart. A mechanic working on a car engine will take out parts of the engine to examine them and make sure they are working together properly. In an **analytical essay,** the author breaks down a large idea into parts, helping the reader to understand how the parts fit together and what they mean as a whole. The authors of these two essays analyze pictures. By focusing on details, they will increase your appreciation of the whole picture.

◆ Reading Strategy

Relate Text and Pictures

Movies have dialogue and comic strips often have captions. Sometimes, visual images and words are meant to go together. Together, they communicate a meaning that neither can convey alone.

Relate the text to the pictures in these essays: pause to look at the images and notice the details being described and interpreted. Compare the writers' interpretations of each image with your own impressions.

For instance, in the essay "A Picture From the Past: Emily Dickinson," the author presents a detailed analysis of a specific photograph, and the essay about Degas includes a detailed description of two of his paintings. The authors' insights enhance your appreciation of what you see.

Use the picture on page 413 to generate discussion on the difference between looking and seeing. Ask students to suggest reasons that people's eyes can be fooled. Explain that people's expectations affect their perceptions. Have students preview the pictures, jotting down details they notice. Tell students that the essays that analyze the pictures may help readers notice details they did not expect to see.

Connecting Themes Across Cultures

Edgar Degas was interested in painting the details of everyday life rather than depicting historic moments and painting portraits of the wealthy. Have students brainstorm for examples of great art work showing everyday life in other cultures and periods. They might mention Egyptian tomb paintings or the paintings of Mexican Diego Rivera.

Customize for
Less Proficient Readers
These essays require readers to move between pictures and text. Encourage these students to use a placeholder—a finger or the eraser tip of a pencil—to keep their place in the text.

Customize for
Gifted/Talented Students
Reynolds Price describes Emily Dickinson in great detail. After students have read both essays, challenge them to describe one of the Degas dancers in the style of Price.

Customize for
English Language Learners
Preview the pictures with these students, having students describe in their own words what they see. Guide students as they read the essays to locate the portions of the picture being described.

Customize for
Visual/Spatial Learners
Have these students preview the art on pages 414, 417, and 418. Before they begin reading, have them jot down what they believe are the important aspects of the pictures. Encourage them to compare their notes with the points in the essays.

Test Preparation Workshop

Reading Comprehension: Evaluate and Make Judgments
Standardized tests require students to make judgments based on evidence from the text. Use the following sample test item to help students practice this skill:

> The results of Degas's experiments could have been executed much more quickly had he used pastels instead of oils. What Degas wanted, however was to make paint look spontaneous. This was part of his lifelong quest: to make viewers feel that they were right there, beside him.

The evidence in this passage suggests that the writer—

A approved of Degas's technique
B understood the qualities of oil paints
C did not study Degas's ideas
D conducted the same experiments as Degas.

Help students see that, although the writer seems very knowledgeable about Degas, there is no evidence to support answers *A, C,* or *D.* The correct response is *B.*

Develop Understanding

One-Minute Insight In this essay, Reynolds Price describes an image of Emily Dickinson and speculates on what the image reveals about the poet's personality and life. His analysis of the image raises questions about perceptions and appearances.

Tips to Guide Reading

Shared Reading Both of these selections have dense prose, full of ideas and descriptions. Select passages that are especially likely to challenge students. Read these parts of the texts together and analyze them for meaning. Have the students continue reading silently.

◆ Build Vocabulary

❶ Word Roots: *-cent-* Have students identify the word that has the root *-cent-*. The word is century. Ask: How is the root meaning reflected in the meaning of the word *century*? How can knowing the meaning of the root help you determine the meaning of the word? *-Cent- means hundred; there are one hundred years in a century.*

◆ Critical Thinking

❷ Make Judgments Ask students if they can tell whether this negative physical description of the subject of the photograph is an indication of the author's feelings about her. How can they find out? *Students should note that reading ahead will answer this question.*

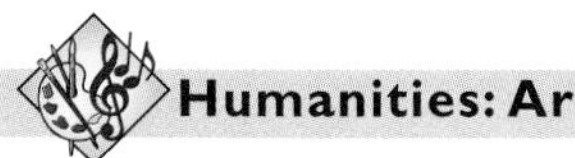

Humanities: Art

Emily Dickinson, daguerreotype, 1847 or 1848.

The first popular method of photography was daguerreotype, a process named for Louis J. M. Daguerre, the Frenchman who perfected it in 1837. Daguerreotypes required subjects to remain still for a long period of time, resulting in the formal style seen in this image of Emily Dickinson. Ask: Why might Emily Dickinson have chosen to have a book in the picture? *The book draws attention to the literary aspect of her life.*

A Picture From the Past: Emily Dickinson

Reynolds Price

Sorting the effects of an ancient aunt, in the wake of her death in the family homeplace or a merciless cell in an old-folks corral, you still might find such a picture and a face. The table drawers of middle-class America were once stuffed with them. No name, no date, no indication of why it's been saved to turn up now like a pebble from Mars in the glare of our world, where pictures of faces assail us at every glance and turn—assaulted children, the baffled old, the sleek in-betweeners.

A daguerreotype[1] the size of a
❶ calling card, hazed with the passage
of more than a century; yet for all the immobility forced on the hapless sitter by a primitive process, it rides as lightly in your hand as a fragment of undoubted life, still pulsing.
A homely girl with oddly dead eyes, set too far apart and flat as the eyes
❷ of a stunned fish in your stagnant bowl—or could she be warming to the verge of a blush and a big-
toothed smile? A lopsided face, big-
❸ ger on her right; a skewed part in the dark horsehair above the high forehead, unmatched eyebrows, a

▲ **Critical Viewing** What can you infer about Emily Dickinson based on this photograph? **[Infer]**

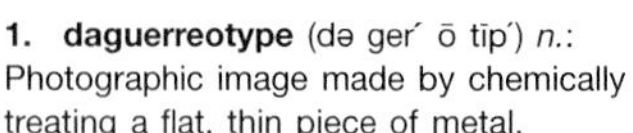

1. **daguerreotype** (də ger′ ō tip′) *n.*: Photographic image made by chemically treating a flat, thin piece of metal.

Block Scheduling Strategies

Consider these suggestions to take advantage of extended class time:

- Have students discuss the hidden picture puzzle on p. 413. Then have them complete the journal activity and talk over their ideas before they read the essays.
- Introduce the Literary Focus on p. 413. When students have read the selections they can answer the Literary Focus questions on p. 419. You may also use the page on Analytical Essay in ***Selection Support,*** p. 129.
- Have students apply the Reading Strategy, Relate Text to Pictures, as they read. Then have them work in small groups to complete the Reading Strategy activity on p. 419. Suggest each group appoint a Presenter to share the group's responses with the other groups.
- Give students the opportunity to research pieces of art before they begin the Guided Writing Lesson on p. 420. After they have chosen the art, encourage them to anticipate and list questions others might have.

fleshy nose, unpainted bruised lips, an ample chin and a tall strong neck.

The hair, the ribbon around the neck, the sensible rough-knuckled hands and the complicated clinging dress date her to the midst of the 19th century. She's lasted somewhere between 16 and 20 years. Will she die shortly after this moment—consumption or childbirth—or will she endure through titanic throes and the ambush of pleasure to be your great-great-grandmother, say, or the maiden great-aunt your father remembers as a centenarian in his boyhood, a smuggler of priceless news to children—the secrets of solitude in the heart of the family but only on the rim, the watchful outrider?

5 None of those—no prior known option. Once this closely held girlhood ended, and the path ahead found no one waiting, she mastered solitude patiently as any rogue lioness, though she haunted her home's back room and kitchen (a sensible cook). Through the chilling or broiling hours in her upstairs room with the white door ajar on a chattering mother, an austere father, a loyal, silly sister, she wrote 1,800 lyrics—some clear as hill water, some dark as oak gall—that stand her yet, with no rival but Whitman,[2] at the head of our poetry: maiden aunt after all, our own Cassandra,[3] presiding mother of all this staggering nation still spooked as cubs by the mere glimpse of loneliness, that steady diet she ate by the hour all her lean years. 6

◆ Build Vocabulary

titanic (tī tan′ ik) *adj.*: Huge and powerful

centenarian (sen′ tə ner′ ē ən) *n.*: Person who is at least one hundred years old

austere (ô stir′) *adj.*: Severe; stern

2. **Whitman:** Walt Whitman (1819–1892). Recognized as one of the most gifted American poets. Both he and Dickinson wrote poetry that was different from the standard poetry of their times.

3. **Cassandra:** In Greek mythology, Cassandra was a prophetess whose predictions were always correct but never believed. Her name is used to refer to any prophet of doom.

Guide for Responding

◆ Literature and Your Life

Reader's Response What detail in the essay or photograph did you find most surprising?

Thematic Focus How do you enlarge your world by thinking about someone you "know" only from a photograph?

☑ Check Your Comprehension

1. To what does Price compare old pictures?
2. Describe Dickinson's appearance.

◆ Critical Thinking

INTERPRET

1. How do you think Price feels about Dickinson? Explain. **[Infer]**
2. What is the main impression Price gives of Dickinson? Support your answer with details. **[Synthesize]**

APPLY

3. How much do you think people judge you by your appearance? **[Relate]**

EVALUATE

4. How well do you think Price interprets the picture of Emily Dickinson? **[Make a Judgment]**

◆ Reading Strategy

3 Relate Text and Pictures Have students look at the photograph on p. 414 to check the authors details. Ask if they would see the photograph in the same way if they hadn't read the author's interpretation. *Students should note that the author uses details to back up his point that the subject is "homely." If they see the subject differently, they should use the same details to back up their own views.*

◆ Literary Focus

4 Analytical Essay Have students explain how the specific points the author brings out contribute to the overall effect of the photograph. *Students may say that the details make them see the photograph in a new way; it may give them more to think about when they look at the photograph.*

Comprehension Check ☑

5 Ask students to rephrase "*None of those*—no prior known option" and "the path ahead found no one waiting." *None of the suggested possibilities in the previous paragraph actually happened to Dickinson; she did not find someone with whom to share her life.*

◆ Critical Thinking

6 Analyze Have students review the physical descriptions of Dickinson and discuss why the author emphasized Dickinson's homeliness when he considers her a giant of American literature. *The description makes his assessment of Dickinson as a literary leader more effective by contrast.*

Customize for *Pre-AP Students*

Have these students analyze the line "this staggering nation still spooked as cubs by the mere glimpse of loneliness." Does it refer to the United States at Dickinson's time or ours?

Reinforce and Extend

Answers

◆ Literature and Your Life

Reader's Response Students may remark at how unflattering the details are in Price's description of Dickinson.

Thematic Focus Using the imagination enlarges a person's world.

☑ Check Your Comprehension

1. He compares them to a pebble from Mars.
2. She is plain, homely, and awkward-looking.

◆ Critical Thinking

1. Price admires her work and finds it astounding that such a homely person could create such art.
2. Price focuses on Dickinson's loneliness both as a consequence of her homeliness and a source of her sensitivity.
3. Students will probably feel appearance plays a strong part in how they are perceived by others.
4. Price accurately describes the picture, although he may exaggerate the negative qualities of Dickinson's features.

Develop Understanding

One-Minute Insight In this essay, Richard Mühlberger analyzes Edgar Degas's painting style and points out the techniques he used to bring immediacy and the illusion of reality to his work.

◆ Reading Strategy

❶ Relate Text and Pictures Have students match each detail in this passage with details in the painting. Ask: Would you describe the painting in the same way or differently? *Students' descriptions would probably be similar to the author's.*

◆ Critical Thinking

❷ Compare and Contrast Ask students: How would you compare and contrast the way Mühlberger describes this painting with the way Price describes the photograph of Emily Dickinson? *Students should note that Mühlberger's description is much more objective.*

◆ Literary Focus

❸ Analytical Essay Ask students: How can reading an analysis of a work of art affect your perception of the work? *Students should note that the analysis brings out details in the painting that viewers might not notice. Noticing such details can enrich a viewer's experience of the painting.*

Customize for Logical/Mathematical Learners
Have these students make a chart to compare and contrast the two paintings by Degas. They may use the Grid organizer in ***Writing and Language Transparencies,*** p. 80.

Read to Discover Models for Writing
Students wishing to write about art should notice the knowledge and skills that Richard Mühlberger brings to this piece. He describes the art accurately; he understands the techniques involved in painting; he knows the historical context of the work; and he knows about the lives of the artist and his contemporaries.

What Makes a DEGAS a DEGAS?

Richard Mühlberger

DANCERS, PINK AND GREEN

Degas's famous ballet paintings witness his enthusiasm for dance and his intimacy with the private backstage areas of the Paris Opéra, the huge complex where the ballet made its home. He was equally familiar with the theater's more public boxes and stalls, where he watched many performances. During his lifetime, he produced about fifteen hundred drawings, prints, pastels, and oil paintings with ballet themes.

In *Dancers, Pink and Green,* each ballerina is caught in a characteristic pose as she waits to go on the stage. One stretches and flexes her foot. Another secures her hair, while
❶ a third is almost hidden. The fourth dancer, who looks at her
❷ shoulder strap as she adjusts it, holds a pose that was a favorite of the artist and one he used in many paintings. An upright beam separates her from the fifth ballerina, who also turns her head but in the opposite direction, full of anticipation. Above her in the distance are the box seats, which Degas
❸ simplified into a stack of six red and orange rectangles along the edge of the canvas. The vertical beam the ballerina is touching extends to the top and the bottom of the painting. The multicolored vertical shapes behind the dancers represent a large, painted landscape used as a backdrop for one of the dances. It will provide an immaterial, dreamworld quality to the performance, as it does to the painting.

> **WHAT MAKES A DEGAS A DEGAS?**
> Notice the following techniques as you look at the paintings by Degas:
> - As if viewing it from above, Degas tipped the stage upward to keep figures from blocking one another.
> - Degas used patches of brilliant color to increase the feeling of movement.
> - Degas cut figures off at the edge of the canvas, creating a candid effect.
> - Degas used large, open spaces to move the eye deep into the picture.

Subscribers to the Opéra were allowed backstage in the theater, and some took advantage of this access to pester dancers. On the far side of the tall wood column is the partial silhouette of a large man in a top hat. He seems to be trying to keep out of the way, but his protruding profile overlaps a ballerina. None of the dancers pay attention to him. They also ignore one another, for this scene represents the tense moments just before the curtain rises.

Degas discovered that with oil paints he could achieve the same fresh feeling conveyed with pastels. Although this painting took the same amount of time to finish as many of his others and was designed and executed in his studio, Degas wanted to make it look as though it had been executed quickly, backstage. To do this, he imitated the marks of a charcoal pencil with his brush, making narrow black lines that edge the dancers' bodies and costumes. Next, he used

Humanities: Art

Dancers, Pink and Green by Edgar Degas.

Hillaire Germain Edgar Degas (1834–1917) was born in Paris of wealthy parents. He spent much time in Italy studying painters of the Italian Renaissance. Back in France, he came under the influence of the Impressionist movement and, influenced by painters Gustave Courbet and Edouard Manet, began to concentrate on scenes from everyday life.

This piece of art is one of Degas's many paintings of ballet dancers. Most of Degas's ballet pictures were painted from the early 1870's to the early 1880's. Degas tried to capture the idea that ballet is work; sometimes dancers look tired or bored. In this painting, the body positions of the dancers reflect strength and energy as well as grace and delicacy.

Use this question for discussion:

If you had read the essay but never seen the painting, would you imagine it as it is or differently? Explain. *Students should make specific references to details in the art.*

▲ Critical Viewing Which of Degas's techniques can you identify in this painting? [Apply]

his own innovation of simulating the matte finish of pastels by taking the sheen out of oil paint, then filling in the sketchy "charcoal" outlines of his figures with a limited range of colors. The colors he used for the dancers extend to the floor and the background. The technique gives the impression that he applied the colors hastily while standing in the wings watching the dancers get ready.

The results of Degas's experiments could have been executed much more quickly had he used pastels instead of oils. What Degas wanted, however, was to make paint look spontaneous. This was part of his lifelong quest: to make viewers feel that they were right there, beside him.

Carriage at the Races

Paul Valpinçon was Degas's best friend in school and remained close to the artist all his life. 7 Degas was a frequent visitor to his country house in Normandy, the northwest region of France, a long journey from Paris. Degas thought that the Normandy countryside was "exactly like England," and the beautiful horse farms there inspired him to paint equestrian subjects. 8 During a visit in 1869, however, Degas found horses secondary to Paul Valpinçon's infant son, Henri. This becomes apparent by looking at the painting *Carriage at the Races.*

At first, Degas's composition seems lopsided. In one corner are the largest and darkest objects, a pair of horses and a carriage. Against the lacquered body of the carriage, the creamy white tones of the passengers stand out. They are framed by the dark colors rather than overwhelmed by them.

◆ Build Vocabulary

lacquered (lak´ ərd) *adj.*: Covered in tough, adherent varnish

►Critical Viewing◄

4 Apply Students should list the view from above that keep figures from blocking one another, the patches of color that suggest movement, the cutoff figure at right, and the pole that obstructs the dancer in the center.

◆ Critical Thinking

5 Connect Ideas Ask students to identify elements in the essay that support this statement. *Students might include the poses of the dancers, the presence of the man with the top hat, and Degas's painting technique.*

◆ Critical Thinking

6 Identify Character Traits Ask: What does the final paragraph tell you about Degas? *He was an innovator; he looked for new ways to achieve a desired effect.*

◆ Build Grammar Skills

7 Compound Sentences Ask students to explain whether this is a compound sentence. *This sentence has a compound predicate, but it is not a compound sentence because it has only one subject— "Paul Valpinçon."*

◆ Build Grammar Skills

8 Compound Sentences Have students identify the parts of this compound sentence: the two independent clauses, and the subject of each clause. *The subjects of the independent clauses in this compound sentence are "Degas" and "horse farms."*

Extending Word Study

Dictionary Point out that *equestrian* and *equine* refer to horses. Have students look up the following animal-related words in a dictionary: *bovine, canine, porcine, hircine, feline.* Encourage students to continue the list, adding more animal adjectives they know.

Speaking, Listening, and Viewing Mini-Lesson

Art Narration

This mini-lesson supports the second Speaking, Listening, and Viewing activity in the Idea Bank on p. 420.

Introduce Tell students that they will use their imaginations to invent a story about a scene evoked by a work of art. Point out that pictures, as well as words, can tell a story.

Develop Before students begin their story, have them think about what makes an interesting story. Lead them to consider these points:

- The story can be told by a narrator who is viewing the scene or in the first person by one of the people in the painting.
- The story may focus on one or more "main characters."
- A plot that has a conflict to be resolved will make the story more interesting.

Apply As students plan and develop their stories, have them try to incorporate as many of the painting's details as they can. When they present their story, remind them to show a picture of the painting and to speak clearly and expressively.

Assess Students can evaluate the narrations on the basis of how well they correlate with the art, as well as on how well they are performed. Use the Peer Assessment: Dramatic Performance page in ***Alternative Assessment,*** p. 120, to evaluate the narrations.

◆ Reading Strategy

❶ **Relate Text and Pictures** As students read this passage, have them identify each detail in the painting. Ask them which elements of the composition the essay helped them to notice. *Students may mention the lopsided first impression the painting makes, the pair of horses and the carriage in one corner, the creamy white tones of the passengers standing out against the dark body of the carriage.*

◆ Literary Focus

❷ **Analytical Essay** Have students locate, in the essay, the larger idea that the details in this passage support. *The larger idea is, "Degas found horses secondary to Paul Valpinçon's infant son, Henri." The details in this passage demonstrate how Degas made the baby the center of attention.*

▶Critical Viewing◀

❸ **Interpret** The painting focuses on a family in a carriage, with an infant at the center, shaded from the bright sunlight by a white umbrella. A team of horses seems to be moving the carriage off the canvas to the right.

◆ Critical Thinking

❹ **Support** Have students identify Mühlberger's support, in this section of the essay, for his point that Degas wanted his paintings to be intimate, immediate, and realistic. *Degas showed only part of the horses and carriage in the painting.*

Reteach

Encourage students who have difficulties relating the texts to the pictures in these selections to look at other illustrations in the unit with simpler texts, such as "The Street of the Canon." For more guidance, you may wish to refer them to p. 31 in ***Strategies for Diverse Student Needs***.

Degas placed a cream-colored umbrella in the middle of the painting above some of the figures in the carriage. Near it, balanced on the back of the driver's seat, is a
❶ black bulldog. Paul
❷ Valpinçon himself is the driver. Both Paul and the dog are gazing at the baby, who lies in the shade of the umbrella. With pink, dimpled knees, Henri, not yet a year old, sprawls on the lap of his nurse while his mother looks on.

Carriage at the Races, Edgar Degas, Museum of Fine Arts, Boston

▲ **Critical Viewing** Describe this painting to someone who has not seen it. **[Interpret]**

Ideas From the Exotic, Old, and New

Degas always enjoyed looking at art. One of the thrills of his school years was being allowed to inspect the great paintings in the collection of Paul Valpinçon's father. Throughout his life, the artist drew inspiration from the masterpieces in the Louvre in Paris, one of the greatest museums in the world. He also found ideas in Japanese prints. They were considered cheap, disposable souvenirs in Japan, but were treasured by artists and others in the West as highly original, fascinating works of art. Photographs, then newly invented, also suggested to Degas ways of varying his paintings. He eventually became an enthusiastic photographer himself.

In *Carriage at the Races*, the way in which the horses and carriage are cut off recalls figures in photographs and Japanese prints. For Degas, showing only part of a subject made his paintings more intimate, immediate, and realistic. He wanted viewers to see the scene as if they were actually there.

Guide for Responding

◆ Literature and Your Life

Reader's Response Would you like to see more of the work of Edgar Degas? Why or why not?

Thematic Focus How can the work of artists like Degas expand our view of the world?

☑ Check Your Comprehension

1. What kinds of scenes did Degas paint?
2. What kind of effect did Degas hope to achieve in his paintings?

◆ Critical Thinking

INTERPRET

1. In his later years, Degas took up photography. What qualities in his paintings suggest he might have been a good photographer? **[Infer]**

APPLY

2. Which of the two paintings better illustrates the points Mühlberger makes about Degas's work? Why? **[Make a Judgment]**

COMPARE LITERARY WORKS

3. Compare and contrast the ways in which Price and Mühlberger use the illustrations in their articles. **[Compare and Contrast]**

Reinforce and Extend

Answers

◆ Literature and Your Life

Reader's Response Students should support their opinions with specific reasons.

Thematic Focus Degas brings into focus people in situations not usually open to public view.

☑ Check Your Comprehension

1. Degas painted performers in candid, "off-camera" moments.
2. He hoped to achieve an immediacy and intimacy with his subjects.

◆ Critical Thinking

1. Degas was a follower in imitating the effects of pastel artists and photographers; he was a leader in creating similar effects in oils.
2. *Dancers, Pink and Green* illustrates the candid immediacy of Degas's art. *Carriage at the Races* appears more posed.
3. Degas knows how to line up his subjects to create a pleasing effect. This quality also creates an effective photograph.

Guide for Responding (continued)

◆ Reading Strategy

RELATE TEXT AND PICTURES

To fully understand these essays, you need to **relate the text to the pictures** the writers describe. For example, when Richard Mühlberger describes how Degas outlines the figures with imitation charcoal pencil lines, you should be able to look at the painting of the dancers and actually see the effect of this technique.

1. Explain whether you think Price's conclusions about Dickinson are supported by the details in the photograph.
2. In "What Makes a Degas a Degas?" Mühlberger describes characteristics of Degas's work. Identify details from the paintings that illustrate three of these characteristics.

◆ Literary Focus

ANALYTICAL ESSAYS

In an **analytical essay,** an author breaks a big idea down into its smaller pieces. The authors of these two essays focus point by point on the details of pictures. In doing so, they give you a broader understanding of the whole image.

1. (a) On which details of Emily Dickinson's appearance does Price focus? (b) What personality traits does he relate to these details?
2. (a) What does Mühlberger say is Degas's lifelong quest? (b) What techniques does Mühlberger identify that helped Degas achieve his goal?

Beyond Literature

Humanities Connection

Degas and the Impressionists Although Edgar Degas is considered one of the Impressionist painters, he did not share their enthusiasm for light and color. Instead, he focused on composition, drawing, and form. He created many sculptures to study form and body movement. These "practice works" made Degas one of the most important sculptors in modern times. Find pictures of some of Degas's sculptures, and compare them with his paintings.

◆ Build Vocabulary

USING THE LATIN ROOT *-cent-*

Knowing that the root *-cent-* means "hundred," match each word with its definition.

1. centigrade
2. century
3. centennial
4. centimeter

a. hundredth anniversary
b. one one-hundredth of a meter
c. period of one hundred years
d. temperature scale in which one hundred degrees represents the boiling point of water

USING THE WORD BANK: Sentence Completions

Complete each of the numbered items by writing a word from the Word Bank on your paper.

1. Judges are often __?__.
2. Critics might use the word __?__ to describe a huge new blockbuster movie.
3. You might find a __?__ item in a fine gift shop.
4. The __?__ remembered historic events we had only read about.

◆ Build Grammar Skills

COMPOUND SENTENCES

In these essays, the authors convey a great deal of information in **compound sentences**—sentences that consist of two or more equally important independent clauses.

Practice Combine each pair of sentences into a compound sentence. Use a coordinating conjunction or semicolon to join them.

1. Emily Dickinson lived a lonely life. She produced more than 1,800 poems.
2. Her picture raises questions. It gives only a glimpse of her personality.

Writing Application Rewrite the following paragraph, combining independent clauses into compound sentences.

Degas enjoyed looking at art. He drew his inspirations from the masterpieces in the Louvre. He found ideas in Japanese art, too. The prints he admired were considered cheap disposable souvenirs in Japan. They were treasured by Degas and other artists in the West.

Answers

◆ Reading Strategy

1. Price's interpretation is supported by details from the picture, but it is not the only interpretation.
2. In *Dancers, Pink and Green* Degas's candid style is revealed in the cutoff figure whose back is to the viewer; his spontaneous quality is captured in the unsynchronized movements of the dancers. *Carriage at the Races* captures Degas's photographic style.

◆ Literary Focus

1. (a) Price describes Dickinson's wide-set eyes, strong neck, large chin, and rough hands. (b) He relates them to strength and solitude.
2. (a) Degas's quest is to place the viewer in immediate contact with his subject. (b) Elements of Degas's paintings that contribute to its effect of spontaneity are the matte finish and limited range of colors of his oils, and his choice of off-center composition.

◆ Build Vocabulary

Latin Word Roots *-cent-*
1. d 2. c 3. a 4. b

Using the Word Bank
1. austere; 2. titanic;
3. lacquered; 4. centenarian

◆ Build Grammar Skills

Sample sentences:

1. Emily Dickinson lived a lonely life, but she produced more than 1,800 poems.
2. Her picture raises questions, and it gives only a glimpse of her personality.

Writing Application
Degas enjoyed looking at art, and he drew inspiration from the masterpieces in the Louvre. He found ideas in Japanese art too, but the prints he admired were considered cheap, disposable souvenirs in Japan. They were treasured by Degas and other artists in the West.

Grammar Reinforcement

For additional instruction and practice, use the pages on Sentence Combining and Varying Your Sentences, pp. 120–121 in the *Writer's Solution Grammar Practice Book.*

Beyond the Selection

FURTHER READING

Other Works by the Authors
Good Hearts, Reynolds Price
What Makes a Raphael a Raphael? Richard Mühlberger

Other Works With the Theme of Seeing, Not Just Looking
Hidden Pictures, Linda Bolton
That's the Way I See It, David Hockney

We suggest that you preview these works before recommending them to students.

INTERNET

For information about Emily Dickinson students can visit the following Web site:
http://www.gis.net/~mtf/related.htm

To see more paintings by Degas, suggest students visit
http://who.inet.jpmorgan:com/CorpInfo/Perspectives/Degas/1-Degas_frames.html

Please be aware that sites may have changed since we published this information. We *strongly recommend* that you preview the sites before you send students to them.

Idea Bank

Following are suggestions for matching Idea Bank topics with your students' performance levels and learning modalities:

Customizing for
Performance Levels
Less Advanced Students: 1, 5, 6
Average Students: 2, 5, 7
More Advanced Students: 3, 4

Customizing for
Learning Modalities
Visual/Spatial: 1, 2, 3, 6, 7
Verbal/Linguistic: 4, 5

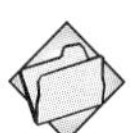

Guided Writing Lesson

Prewriting Strategy Use a pentad to help students focus the information of their placards. Have them draw a five-pointed star; at each point they can write questions that viewers might have.

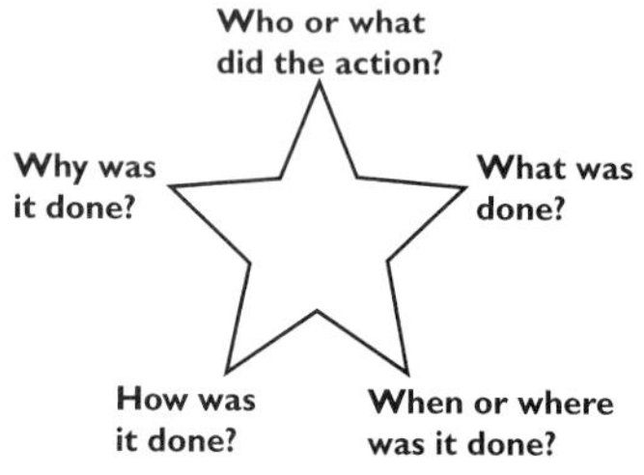

Who or what did the action?
What was done?
When or where was it done?
How was it done?
Why was it done?

Then students can focus on one question, freewriting to answer it.

For more prewriting, elaboration, and revision instruction, see *Prentice Hall Writing and Grammar.*

Writing and Language Transparencies Students may use the Cubing organizer, p. 88, to brainstorm for more information.

Writers at Work Videodisc
Have students view the videodisc segment (Ch. 3) to hear Rudolfo Anaya's views on expository writing.

Play frames 22803 to 32243

Writing Lab CD-ROM
Have students complete the tutorial on Exposition. Follow these steps:

1. Students can use the Cluster Diagram to help organize details..
2. Have students draft on computer.
3. Students may use the Interactive Self-Evaluation Checklists to help them revise their placards.

Build Your Portfolio

Idea Bank

Writing

1. **Exhibit Promotion** Write a paragraph to appear on a poster promoting an exhibit of Edgar Degas's work. Include details that raise audience interest and give highlights of the exhibit. **[Art Link]**
2. **Photo Essay** Put together a series of photographs that provide insights into your personality or the personality of someone close to you. Write a caption for each photograph.
3. **Art Analysis** Choose another painting or photograph of a person and analyze it using one of these essays as your model. **[Art Link]**

Speaking, Listening, and Viewing

4. **Poetry Reading** The best way to learn about Emily Dickinson is through her poetry. Find one or more Dickinson poems to read aloud to the class. Then lead a discussion about what each poem reveals about her.
5. **Art Narration** Choose a painting that you like by Degas. From the images in the painting, make up a story about what might have been happening at the time it was painted. Display a reproduction of the painting and tell the story aloud to the class. **[Performing Arts Link]**

Researching and Representing

6. **Painting and Poetry Exhibit** Find an Emily Dickinson poem you like and create a drawing, painting, or collage to accompany it. Display your artwork with the poem. **[Art Link]**
7. **Art Exchange** With a small group, organize an art exhibit of famous paintings, with each group member selecting one entry. Display the paintings and hold a question-and-answer session in which your group explains its choices.

Online Activity www.phlit.phschool.com

Guided Writing Lesson

Museum Placard

Write a **placard**—a small informational card—that might be displayed beside a favorite painting or sculpture in a museum. Conduct research to find basic information about the painting, such as the date, title, and painter. Write a few sentences that would help a reader appreciate the images and ideas that inspired or influenced the artist.

Writing Skills Focus: Anticipation of Questions

The information that you provide on your placard will influence the way people view the work of art. By **anticipating questions** that viewers might ask, you can decide what information to include. For instance, someone viewing *Dancers, Pink and Green* might wonder where Degas got his inspiration. Therefore, on a placard for this painting, you might mention that he went to the Opéra regularly in order to observe and sketch the dancers. However, you probably wouldn't mention that Degas had brothers who lived in New Orleans, because that doesn't answer any questions about the painting.

Prewriting Choose a piece of art you like. Then brainstorm for a list of questions viewers might have. Choose one or two questions to answer that will give the most insight into the painting or sculpture.

Drafting The basic information, such as title, date, and artist, should be easy for the viewer to locate. Write this information clearly at the top of the placard. Then write a short paragraph including other interesting facts about the work.

Revising Exchange your placard with a partner. Ask your partner if the information is clearly presented. Revise where necessary to clarify.

✓ ASSESSMENT OPTIONS

Formal Assessment, Selection Test, pp. 107–109, and Assessment Resources Software. The selection test is designed so that it can be easily customized to the performance levels of your students.

Alternative Assessment, p. 31, includes options for less advanced students, more advanced students, verbal/linguistic learners, visual/spatial learners, and logical/mathematical learners.

PORTFOLIO ASSESSMENT
Use the following rubrics in the ***Alternative Assessment*** booklet to assess student writing:
Exhibit Promotion: Persuasion Rubric, p. 105
Photo Essay: Expression Rubric, p. 94
Art Analysis: Evaluation/Review Rubric, p. 104
Guided Writing Lesson: Description Rubric, p. 97

Writing Process Workshop

Oral Presentation of Research

One way to make a research paper come alive is to give an **oral presentation of your research.** Giving an oral presentation is much like teaching a class: You'll be educating your listeners about what you've discovered through your research.

The following skills, introduced in this section's Guided Writing Lessons, will help you prepare and give an effective oral presentation of your research.

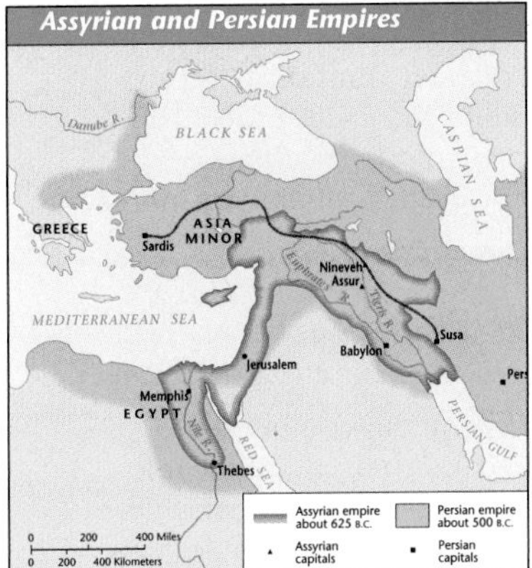

Writing Skills Focus

- **Use logical organization.** Organizations such as order of importance, chronological, and compare/contrast will help your listeners follow your report. (See p. 392.)
- **Anticipate questions** that your listeners will have about your topic. (See p. 420.)
- **Consider audience knowledge.** Think about what the audience might know about your topic, and try to teach them something new. (See p. 411.)
- **Be brief and clear.** Stick to the main topic so that your listeners' interest and attention don't wander. (See p. 403.)
- **Use visual aids,** such as maps, graphs, and photos.

In the following passage from a presentation about the Assyrian empire, the speaker uses these skills.

Model

After Ashurbanipal died in 631 B.C., internal troubles broke out, and the Assyrian empire declined and failed. Babylonia became independent and in 626 B.C. established its eleventh and last dynasty, called the Chaldean dynasty. ① By 615 B.C. all of the Sumer and Akkad had been liberated and the Medes had invaded Assyria and marched to Nineveh. ② By the end of 612 B.C., Assyria's enemies had destroyed its three main cities, shown on the map: ③ Ashur, the religious hub; Nineveh, the administrative center; and Nimrud, the military headquarters. ④

① The speaker uses clear, chronological organization.

② The speaker is brief and keeps to the point.

③ The speaker uses a map to illustrate his subject.

④ By further explaining the significance of the three main cities, the speaker both anticipates a listener's question and teaches the audience something new.

Prepare and Engage

Lesson Objectives

1. To use recursive writing processes to write an oral presentation of research
2. To write in complete sentences, varying the types, and to use appropriately punctuated independent and dependent clauses
3. To proofread for punctuation errors related to direct and indirect quotations.

You may want to distribute the scoring rubric for Research Report/Paper (p. 106 in ***Alternative Assessment***) to make students aware before they begin of the criteria on which they will be evaluated. See the suggestions on page 423 for customizing the rubric for this workshop.

Refer students to the Writing Handbook, page 965, for instruction in the writing process, and page 968 for further information on research writing.

Writing Lab CD-ROM

If your students have access to computers, you may want to have them work on the tutorial on Research to complete all or part of their oral presentations of research. Follow these steps:

1. Students can use the Research Paper Topic Bin to select a topic.
2. Review the Video tips from writers on audience.
3. Have students draft on computer.
4. Suggest students use the interactive instruction on improving content.
5. Use the tips on presenting work orally.

Beyond the Classroom

Career Connection

Presentations Tell students that giving an oral presentation of research they have conducted is a common practice in the business and professional world. For example, analysts frequently give oral reports on companies or industries they have been studying. Consultants give presentations to companies in order to solicit their business and as a part of their work. Politicians give presentations in order to sway voters to agree with them on an issue, while lawyers and lobbyists give presentations to those same politicians in order to sway *them* to vote a particular way. Teachers give oral presentations to their classes every day.

Develop Student Writing

Prewriting Strategy

To help students plan visual aids, have them use a web like the one shown. With their topic in a center circle, students can list potential visual aids. Encourage students to list as many sources as possible, as some ideas may prove impossible.

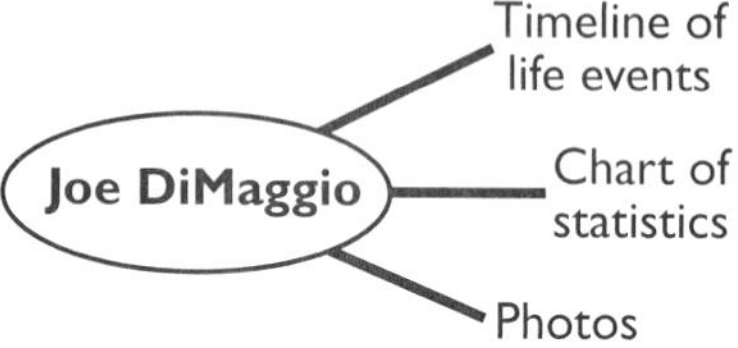

Customize for
English Language Learners
Once these students have chosen a topic, have them analyze it in terms of *Who? What? Where? When?* and, if appropriate, *Why?* and *How?* Answers to these questions can form the outline for the presentation. Students might also benefit from using the Cubing organizer, which is available in ***Writing and Language Transparencies,*** pp. 87–90.

Customize for
Pre-AP Students
Challenge these students to give an oral presentation on a historical figure whom they do not admire, or on a controversial event, or on an event that had a negative impact on society.

Writing Lab CD-ROM

The Considering Audience and Purpose section of the tutorial on Research Writing helps students tailor their work to different purposes and audiences. Have students consult these screens to help focus their presentations on a specific audience.

Elaboration Strategy

Encourage students to refer to their outline or notes as they draft their oral presentations of research. Remind them to keep their audience and purpose in mind. Have them pay particular attention to writing a strong introduction and following up with an effective conclusion. Once students have completed a draft, they can go back and make revisions.

Applying Language Skills: Direct and Indirect Quotations

A **direct quotation** represents the exact speech of a person. The words are enclosed in quotation marks.

Direct Quotation:
The secretary general said, "Unchecked population growth is an environmental time bomb."

An indirect quotation reports the general meaning of a person's words and does not require quotation marks.

Indirect Quotation:
The secretary general said that rapid population growth is a serious problem.

Writing Application Vary your use of direct and indirect quotations in your presentation. Quote directly when the speaker's words are especially powerful. Use indirect quotations to lend weight to general information.

Writer's Solution Connection
Writing Lab

For more help finding a topic, see Choosing a Topic: Inspirations for Research. You'll find it in the Writing Lab tutorial on Research Writing.

Prewriting

Choose a Topic Choose a topic that you find interesting and for which there is adequate source information. The following suggestions may help you if you're having trouble thinking of a topic.

Topic Ideas

- **Oral Report on a Southeast Asian Country** With a combined population of more than 452 million people, the ten nations that make up Southeast Asia offer a wealth of information. Choose one nation, conduct research, and prepare a report on an aspect of its history or culture.
- **The Environment** Choose a process or practice that aims to protect the environment, such as building jetties to prevent beach erosion, and evaluate whether or not such a process is effective.
- **Current Events** Choose a topic that has been in the news lately. Prepare a report that informs the audience of the important aspects of the topic, and then make your own comments about it.

Find Reliable Sources It's extremely important that the information in your research report be accurate. There are numerous sources of reliable and current information. (See the Research Handbook, p. 1029, for suggestions.) It's also important to evaluate your sources. (For strategies to evaluate sources, see p. 424.) Use at least three sources to find information.

Plan Visual Aids When you're giving an oral presentation, you'll feel more comfortable referring to visual aids, and your audience will probably grasp your points better. Consider using any of the following:

- **Maps** can clarify historical information.
- **Graphs** can represent changes over time.
- **Diagrams** can show the relationship of parts to a whole.
- **Charts** can help show comparison/contrast relationships.

Drafting

Use Note Cards Draft your presentation based on notes from your research. Writing out your presentation will ensure that you include all necessary information and that you organize it in a way that's easy to follow.

Applying Language Skills

Direct and Indirect Quotations
Tell students that using direct quotations will enliven their oral presentations by making them more direct and personal, and will also lend the reports an air of authority.

Grammar Reinforcement

For additional instruction and practice, have students complete the **Language Lab CD-ROM** lesson on Semicolons, Colons, and Quotation Marks and practice page 104 on Quotation Marks and Direct Quotations in the *Writer's Solution Grammar Practice Book.*

Revising

Read Your Work Aloud After you've finished drafting, read your presentation aloud. Listen for movement from one point to another. Make sure your important ideas are emphasized and do not get lost in your presentation. Revise any parts that do not flow naturally. Also, organize your research notes in an order that will be easy for you to refer to during the presentation, or prepare a set of brief notes, based on your draft, to guide you as you give your presentation. Your notes will serve as cues for visual aids and reminders of quotations you plan to use.

Do a Dry Run Before your presentation, rehearse in front of family members or a friend, before a video camera, or in front of a mirror. This will help you improve your speaking form and calm any jitters you may have about speaking in front of others.

Revision Model

Since the introduction of CD technology ① in 1983, the music industry has increased sales ~~quite a bit~~ ② 100 million dollars annually. The new technology created consumer demand in nearly every category ③ —from classical to jazz, rock, and rap. The instant popularity of CDs created a revolution in how music is delivered.

① This date answers a potential question from the audience.

② The writer replaced this vague term with an exact figure from her research.

③ These examples help define "every category."

Publishing

Give Your Oral Presentation Refer to your note cards as you make your presentation, but be as familiar as possible with your draft so that your presentation will be credible and engaging.

- When you speak, **vary the sentence structure** to include a mix of simple, compound, and complex sentences.
- **Refer to your visual aids** to support your findings and maintain audience interest.
- **Speak loudly** enough so that everyone can hear you.
- **Be prepared** to answer questions at the end of the report.

Applying Language Skills: Varying Sentence Structure

If your sentences are all simple sentences of the same length, your report will be very monotonous. **Vary your sentence structure** in order to make your presentation more interesting.

Same Sentence Structure:
Lacrosse was originally a Native American game. It was played on the east coast. Games were violent. They often lasted two or more days.

Varied Sentence Structure:
Lacrosse was originally a Native American game played on the east coast. Games, which were sometimes violent, often lasted two or more days.

Writing Application Review your report before you present it. Make sure that your sentence structure is varied. If it is not, add transitions and subordinate clauses to make the sentences more interesting.

Writer's Solution Connection
Language Lab

For more practice with sentence structures, complete the Language Lab lesson on Varying Sentence Structure.

Revision Strategy

Have students do a dry run of their presentations with peer reviewers before they present them to the class. Giving a practice presentation will reveal rough spots that need revising. Peer reviewers should offer concrete suggestions and constructive criticism.

Prentice Hall Writing and Grammar For more instruction on prewriting, elaboration, and revision, see *Prentice Hall Writing and Grammar.*

Publishing

Before giving their oral presentations, suggest that students practice them at least once in front of family members or on videotape.

Reinforce and Extend

Applying Language Skills

Varying Sentence Structure
Though students will probably consult notecards as they give their presentations, they should be reminded to vary their sentences as they speak. Using only simple sentences or one type of sentence will probably bore the audience.

For additional instruction and practice, have students complete the **Language Lab CD-ROM** lesson on Varying Sentence Structure and the practice p. 121 on Varying Your Sentences in the *Writer's Solution Grammar Practice Book.*

✓ Assessment

Portfolio Assessment		4	3	2	1
Use the rubric on Research Report/Paper in the ***Alternative Assessment*** booklet (p. 106) to assess the students' writing. Add these criteria to customize the rubric to this assignment.	**Research**	The research is thorough and accurate and explores the topic fully.	The research is accurate, and explores the topic adequately.	Research lacks sufficient depth and may be questionable in one or two instances.	Research is clearly inadequate; accuracy is suspect.
	Presentation	Student speaks clearly, using appropriate vocal expression to keep audience interested. Visuals are compelling and augment the report.	Student speaks loudly and clearly enough to be understood. Visuals are used.	Student should speak louder or more clearly, and/or vary vocal expression to retain interest. Visuals are inadequate or irrelevant.	Student is unable to be heard. Visuals are not used or not related to the subject matter.

Prepare and Engage

LESSON OBJECTIVES

- To analyze information in order to evaluate and make judgments
- To evaluate the credibility of information sources

With the wealth of information available for research, including the Internet, it becomes ever more important to scrutinize that information closely and evaluate its appropriateness for writing purposes. Students should be urged to validate the information they find by looking for supporting information in other sources.

Apply the Strategies

Answers

1. The *Washington Post* article would be preferable, since it is specifically about the relationship between cats and people.
2. The *Washington Post* article would be preferable because the topic is closer to that of the research paper and it is much newer, so the research would be more current.
3. The title *Cat Fancy* suggests a relationship between cats and people, so that book would be preferable.

Student Success Workshop

Research Skills — Evaluating Sources of Information

Strategies for Success

Research is a major part of writing a report. (See the Research Handbook, beginning on p. 1029, for suggestions about sources of information.) As you undertake your research, you may find yourself poring through books, magazines, encyclopedias, and other materials that may have information on your topic. Before you plunge into writing, evaluate your sources of information to determine which resources will provide the best information.

Consider the Source Before choosing a source, investigate the author of the text. Is he or she an expert on the subject? Look in the book for biographical information that tells the author's qualifications.

Consider the Date Check to see when a book was published. (You can usually find the date on the page following the title page.) The information in older works might be outdated, especially if the subjects are science or social studies. For example, if you were researching information on Germany today and used a book from 1987, it would refer to East Germany and West Germany, but it would not include information about the reunification of Germany since the Berlin Wall came down in 1989. The information would not be current.

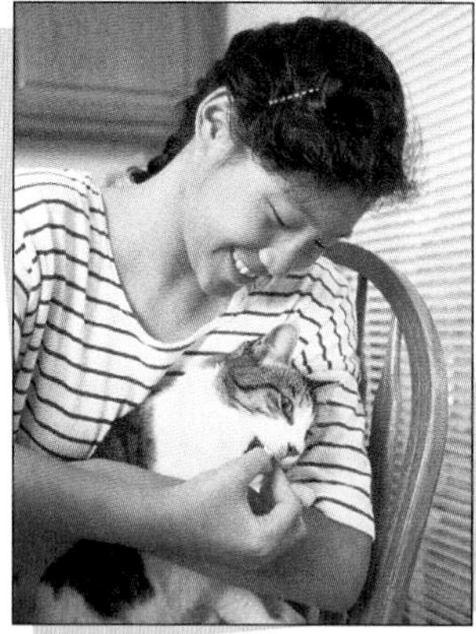

Apply the Strategies

You are writing a research paper on the relationship between cats and their owners. Look at the sources available to you as you answer the questions that follow:

The World Book Encyclopedia, Volume C, © 1998

Cats: Creatures of Wonder, by Lori Rigby, © 1960 by Roan Publishing

"New Research on Cat–People Connection," *The Washington Post*, February 5, 1998

"Cats Have Feelings Too," *Milford Daily News*, November 8, 1975

Cat Fancy by Dr. R. Gonzales, © 1998 by Prentice Hall

1. Which would you prefer to use—the encyclopedia or *The Washington Post* article? Why?
2. Which of the two newspapers would you prefer to use? Why?
3. Which of the two books would you prefer to use? Why?

Here are other situations in which it is helpful to evaluate sources of information:

- Reading newspaper editorials
- Investigating a rumor
- Reading two articles on the same topic

Test Preparation Workshop

Reading Comprehension: Distinguish Between Fact and Nonfact

Standardized tests require students to distinguish between fact and opinion in a variety of written texts. Use this sample test item to give students practice with the skill.

> The latest round of proposed price increases seems unjustified given that neither the quality nor the range of service has increased. Frankly, the monthly charges of $15.98 are already outrageous.

Which of the following is a FACT expressed in the passage?

A A price increase is unjustified.
B The monthly charge is $15.98.
C The quality of service is poor.
D The range of service is poor.

Point out that while each sentence can be found in the passage, only B is a fact.

Part 2 A Larger World

Waiting for Will, 1986, Janet Fish

One-Minute Planning Guide

The selections in Part 2 describe the adventures and thoughts of people from across cultures and across generations. "The Orphan Boy and the Elk Dog" tells how the Blackfeet got horses. "The Street of the Cañon," set in a small village in old Mexico, tells about young woman's encounter with a mysterious stranger. Alexander Solzhenitsyn's essay "A Storm in the Mountains" vividly describes a terrifying storm that swamped the author and his companions in the Caucasus mountains. Henrik Ibsen's poem "In the Orchard," describes nature at its most calm and pastoral. The section ends with Denise Levertov's poem "A Tree Telling of Orpheus," which describes the ancient Greek musician's beautiful music from the point of view of one of the trees persuaded to uproot itself and dance.

Customize for
Varying Student Needs

When assigning the selections in this part to your students, keep in mind the following factors:

"The Orphan Boy and the Elk Dog"
- Subject matter may be remote for some students

"The Street of the Cañon"
- A medium-length short story
- Accessible to all ability levels

"A Storm in the Mountains"; "In the Orchard"
- Two short selections
- Language is more difficult than that in other selections

"A Tree Telling of Orpheus"
- A longer narrative poem
- An echo of a classical Greek myth

Humanities: Art

Waiting for Will, 1986, by Janet Fish.

Born in 1938, New Englander Janet Fish hails from several generations of artists. She is known for her bright, glowing paintings; although her subjects are usually still lifes, her paintings seem to be full of movement.

Direct students' attention to the contrast between the foreground and background in *Waiting for Will*. The foreground is full of pattern and color, mostly warm golds and roses, with a few contrasting blue and green notes. The cool blues and greens take over completely in the background, and the whole painting is almost neatly divided into two horizontal halves by the yellow railing.

Help students link the artwork to the theme of this part, "A Larger World," by answering the following questions:

1. This painting has two definite halves: the table in the foreground, and the green and blue landscape in the background. What is the atmosphere of each? *The foreground, with its clutter and bright colors has a warm, inviting, cheerful atmosphere; the landscape, with its cool colors and cloudy sky, has a dreamy, pensive atmosphere.*
2. Why might the person in this painting have turned away from the table to gaze at the hills? *Sample answer: The woman, who might be the artist, might be thinking about "Will," or waiting for inspiration.*

Prepare and Engage

LESSON OBJECTIVES

1. To develop vocabulary and word identification skills
- Word Groups: Homographs
- Using the Word Bank: Synonyms and Antonyms
- Build Grammar Skills: Commonly Confused Words: *Accept* and *Except*

2. To use a variety of reading strategies to comprehend a personal narrative
- Connect Your Experience
- Reading Strategy: Identify with a Character
- Tips to Guide Reading
- Read to Be Entertained

3. To increase knowledge of other cultures and to connect common elements across cultures
- Connecting Themes Across Cultures (ATE)

4. To express and support responses to the text
- Critical Thinking
- Idea Bank: Speech
- Idea Bank: Dialogue
- Idea Bank: Storyboard Mural
- Viewing and Representing Mini-Lesson
- Idea Bank: Debate
- Speaking, Listening, and Viewing Mini-Lesson

5. To analyze literary elements
- Literary Focus: Myth

6. To read in order to research self-selected and assigned topics
- Idea Bank: Population Graph
- Research Skills Mini-Lesson

6. To plan, prepare, organize, and present literary interpretations
- Idea Bank: Animal Description
- Idea Bank: Retell a Myth

7. To use recursive writing processes to retell a myth
- Guided Writing Lesson

Test Preparation

Reading Strategy: Evaluate and Make Judgments (ATE, p. 427) The teaching tips and sample text item in this workshop support the instruction and practice in the unit workshop:

Reading Comprehension: Interpret Graphic Aids; Evaluate and Make Judgments (SE, p. 465)

Guide for Reading

Blackfeet

The Blackfeet are one of the many Native American nations that have lived on the Great Plains of North America. Like other Plains Indians, the Blackfeet had no horses before the 1600's. Once they discovered these strange creatures, however, they quickly recognized their value.

The Shoshone (another group of Plains Indians) had herds of horses before the Blackfeet did. One daring Blackfeet, who may have been the inspiration for the "orphan boy" in this myth, slipped into a Shoshone camp with his companions, untied four horses, and led them away. To the amazed Blackfeet, these animals looked like elk-sized dogs.

In time, the Blackfeet became skillful riders. Because they could travel farther and faster than before, they raised fewer crops and hunted more. They made larger tipis because the strong horses could easily pull the folded tipis from one encampment to the next. Slowly, horses transformed the Blackfeet way of life.

Today, the Blackfeet live on reservations in Montana and in Canada. (Those in Canada usually go by the name Black*foot.*) Although they are no longer a nomadic people following buffalo, traditional stories like "The Orphan Boy and the Elk Dog" reflect the importance of the horse to their culture.

◆ Build Vocabulary

WORD GROUPS: HOMOGRAPHS

In this story you will meet an orphan boy who is forced to eat things he finds in the *refuse* heaps. *Refuse* is a **homograph**—a word with the same spelling as another but with a different meaning and pronunciation. For example, *refuse* (ref´ yo͞oz) in this myth is a noun meaning "garbage." *Refuse* (ri fyo͞oz´) is a verb that means "to reject."

When you encounter a homograph such as *refuse,* the context in which it appears will give you clues to its meaning. Use a dictionary, if necessary, to confirm the correct pronunciation.

WORD BANK

Before you read, preview this list of words from the myth.

refuse
surpassed
emanating
relish
stifle

◆ Build Grammar Skills

COMMONLY CONFUSED WORDS: *ACCEPT* AND *EXCEPT*

In this Blackfeet myth, you will encounter the words ***accept*** and ***except.*** These words are often confused because they have a similar spelling and sound. *Accept* is a verb meaning "to receive" or "to agree with." *Except* is usually a preposition meaning "not including," but it is sometimes a verb meaning "to leave out."

Notice the correct use of *accept* and *except* in these sentences from "The Orphan Boy and the Elk Dog":

"*Accept* these wonderful Elk Dogs as my gift."

. . . no one *except* his grandfather knew where and for what purpose.

Prentice Hall Literature Program Resources

REINFORCE / RETEACH / EXTEND

Selection Support Pages
Build Vocabulary: Word Groups: Homographs, p. 130
Build Grammar Skills: Commonly Confused Words: *accept* and *except,* p. 131
Reading Strategy: Identify with a Character, p. 132
Literary Focus: Myth, p. 133

Strategies for Diverse Student Needs, p. 32

Beyond Literature Cultural Connection: The Role of the Horse, p. 32

Formal Assessment Selection Test, pp. 110–113; Assessment Resources Software

Alternative Assessment, p. 32

Writing and Language Transparencies Story Map, pp. 83–86

Resource Pro CD-ROM

Listening to Literature Audiocassettes

The Orphan Boy and the Elk Dog

◆ Literature and Your Life

CONNECT YOUR EXPERIENCE

When you need to go somewhere, you have many choices about how you will travel. Depending on where you're going, you might take a bus, a car, a train, or an airplane. Without cars and buses, suburbs probably wouldn't exist, and malls would never have developed if people couldn't get to them easily or often enough to keep so many stores in business. Transportation influences the way people live. Big changes in transportation mean big changes in lifestyle.

THEMATIC FOCUS: A LARGER WORLD

As a new form of transportation, horses changed the Blackfeet world! Thinking about the impact of horses on Blackfeet society may start you wondering, "How does modern transportation make my world larger or smaller?"

Journal Writing Explain how your life would be different without a particular form of transportation—such as cars.

◆ Reading Strategy

IDENTIFY WITH A CHARACTER

The main character in this story dives into a pond and discovers a fantastic world beneath the surface. One way you can dive into a work of literature is to **identify with a character**—put yourself in the character's place and share his or her thoughts, feelings, problems, adventures, and so on.

In "The Orphan Boy and the Elk Dog," you will travel with an outcast Native American boy who becomes a triumphant hero. You will experience his difficulties and his successes. Throughout the story, think about what you might say, do, or think in his situation.

◆ Background for Understanding

HISTORY

At one time, most Plains Indians were farmers who lived in semi-permanent villages. They sent out hunting parties that pursued buffalo and other animals—on foot. Agriculture, however, was their main source of food.

During the 1600's, the Plains Indians' way of life changed. The Indians captured and tamed wild horses descended from herds the Spanish had brought to the Americas. On horseback, the Indians could travel farther and faster. Hunting replaced farming as the Plains Indians became better hunters. They moved often to follow the herds of buffalo. Large tipis and other belongings could easily be carried on a travois—a sledge pulled by a horse.

Following the Buffalo Run, Charles M. Russell, Amon Carter Museum, Fort Worth, Texas

◆ Literary Focus

MYTH

Myths are traditional stories passed down from generation to generation, characteristically involving immortal beings. Myths attempt to explain natural phenomena, the origin of humans or the universe, the customs or institutions of a people, or events beyond people's control. Indirectly, myths teach the values and ideals of a culture.

"The Orphan Boy and the Elk Dog" is a myth that offers an explanation of how the Blackfeet came to have horses.

Interest Grabber Read the following passage aloud to students:

"... he boldly jumped into the water. To his surprise, he found it did not make him wet, that it parted before him, that he could breathe and see."

Ask students to tell from what kind of story they think this excerpt comes. On the chalkboard, list the qualities they might expect to find in such a story. *Possible responses: magic, adventure, symbolic meaning.*

Connecting Themes Across Cultures

The introduction of horses into Native American culture had negative as well as positive effects. Many groups became migratory and lost the incentive and ability to farm and grow essential crops. The use of horses also increased warfare between rival groups and created general insecurity. Have students brainstorm for examples in other cultures of "advances in transportation" that have had undesired results.

Customize for
Less Proficient Readers
Suggest that students imagine the myth as a movie and divide it into scenes, jotting down a brief summary of what happens in each scene.

Customize for
Pre-AP Students
Invite students to point out story elements that this myth has in common with other myths or traditional tales they have read; for example, an underwater world ("The Little Mermaid"), a quest with difficult obstacles to overcome (the Grail legends), increasingly bigger obstacles ("The Tinder Box"), magical objects ("Aladdin"), an order to "never look back" (Orpheus, Lot).

Customize for
English Language Learners
Have these students preview the Check Your Comprehension questions on page 435 before they read and answer them as they read. Suggest they look for key words in the text to find answers, and avoid getting stuck on unfamiliar words.

Test Preparation Workshop

Reading Comprehension:
Evaluate and Make Judgments Standardized tests like TAAS require students to evaluate the evidence in a passage in order to make judgments. Use the following sample test item to review this strategy with students.

He grew up into a fine young hunter, tall and good-looking in the quilled buckskin outfit the chief's wife made for him. He helped his grandfather in everything and became a staff for Good Running to lean on.

The passage provides evidence that—

A The boy described has disappointed his family.
B The culture described values hunting skills.
C The boy described is unhappy in his life.
D The culture described is technologically advanced.

Guide students to see that responses *A, C,* and *D* cannot be supported by the passage. *B* is the correct response.

Develop Understanding

So important were horses to the Plains Indians, that the explanation for how these animals came into their possession is an integral part of their cultural history. According to this myth, a young man who had been an outcast went on a dangerous quest to prove himself to his people and to prove his own self-worth. By a feat of courage and daring, and aided by magic, he returned with horses, or "Elk Dogs," which changed and improved the lives of his people. This myth, in addition to explaining an important aspect of life for the Blackfeet, conveys important cultural values through the relationship of the young man to the old chief who adopted him: courage, respect for elders, generosity, and compassion.

▶Critical Viewing◀

❶ **Draw Conclusions** The Native American man may be standing sentry, watching for threats of attack; or he may be hunting, searching for game.

Customize for
Visual/Spatial Learners
Have these students infer what the story may be about from the image of the young man and horse in the painting. *Students may infer that the story will be about Indians and horses in a beautiful natural setting.*

Humanities: Art

The Color of Sun by Howard Terpning.

This painting shows a young Plains Indian brave riding a horse with bow and arrow strapped behind. The horse nuzzles the spring flowers as the brave scans the horizon. The horse's piebald coloring serves as effective camouflage against the dappled woodland background.

Use this question for discussion: Based on the composition of the painting, how did the artist make the youth look brave and heroic? *The young man and his horse take up most of the canvas; the horse and rider appear arrested in a moment of calm, awaiting action.*

The Color of Sun, Howard Terpning, The Greenwich Workshop, Inc.

▲ **Critical Viewing** What do you think this Native American man is seeing or searching for? **[Draw Conclusions]** ❶

Viewing and Representing Mini-Lesson

Storyboard Mural

This Mini-Lesson supports the project in the Idea Bank on p. 437.

Introduce the Concept Tell students that, like a comic strip, a storyboard usually consists of sequential illustrations. Captions beneath each image explain the action.

Develop Background Lead students to identify the main events in "The Orphan Boy and the Elk Dog" and limit them to the minimum number of individual scenes needed to represent the story. As students create the mural, have them reconsider events that do not add to an understanding of the story. In a good mural, less is often more.

Apply the Information Have students consider how best to give the events pictorial interest. Invite students to use art materials of their choice to illustrate the scenes for the mural.

Assess the Outcome Have students display their mural. Discuss how the scenes convey the story, what they add to the story, and what has been lost. Evaluate students' work on how well they have chosen their scenes and their representational creativity.

The Orphan Boy and the Elk Dog

Native American (Blackfeet)

In the days when people had only dogs to carry their bundles, two orphan children, a boy and his sister, were having a hard time. The boy was deaf, and because he could not understand what people said, they thought him foolish and dull-witted. Even his relatives wanted nothing to do with him. The name he had been given at birth, while his parents still lived, was Long Arrow. Now he was like a beaten, mangy dog, the kind who hungrily roams outside a camp, circling it from afar, smelling the good meat boiling in the kettles but never coming close for fear of being kicked. Only his sister, who was bright and beautiful, loved him.

Then the sister was adopted by a family from another camp, people who were attracted by her good looks and pleasing ways. Though they wanted her for a daughter, they certainly did not want the awkward, stupid boy. And so they took away the only person who cared about him, and the orphan boy was left to fend for himself. He lived on scraps thrown to the dogs and things he found on the refuse heaps. He dressed in remnants of skins and frayed robes discarded by the poorest people. At night he bedded down in a grass-lined dugout, like an animal in its den.

Eventually the game was hunted out near the camp that the boy regarded as his, and the people decided to move. The lodges were taken down, belongings were packed into rawhide bags and put on dog travois, and the village departed. "Stay here," they told the boy. "We don't want your kind coming with us."

For two or three days the boy fed on scraps the people had left behind, but he knew he would starve if he stayed. He had to join his people, whether they liked it or not. He followed their tracks, frantic that he would lose them, and crying at the same time. Soon the sweat was running down his skinny body. As he was stumbling, running, panting, something suddenly snapped in his left ear with a sound like a small crack, and a wormlike substance came out of that ear. All at once on his left side he could hear birdsongs for the first time. He took this wormlike thing in his left hand and hurried on. Then there was a snap in his right ear and a wormlike thing came out of it, and on his right side he could hear the rushing waters of a stream. His hearing was restored! And it was razor-sharp—he could make out the rustling of a tiny mouse in dry leaves a good

◆ **Reading Strategy** Identify with Long Arrow by thinking of times in your life when you felt excluded. ❹

❺

◆ **Build Vocabulary**

refuse (ref´ yo͞oz) *n.*: Anything thrown away as useless

◆ Critical Thinking

❷ **Compare and Contrast** Point out that like all myths, this story takes place in a far-off time. Have students compare and contrast the way deaf people are treated in modern society. *Students may say that modern society also discriminates against the physically challenged, but they should note that many steps have been taken to end discrimination.*

◆ Build Vocabulary

❸ **Homographs** Ask students to identify the part of speech for the word *close* in this sentence. Then have them think of a homograph and its part of speech. *In this sentence,* close *is an adverb modifying coming.* Close *can also be a verb when pronounced differently and serving a different function in a sentence.*

◆ Reading Strategy

❹ **Identify With a Character** Students may say that although they have not been as cruelly abandoned as Long Arrow, they understand what it feels like to be rejected and can generalize from that experience.

Comprehension Check ☑

❺ What is happening to Long Arrow's ear? *A blockage is falling out, enabling him to hear. Some may think the event is realistic, others magical.*

Tips to Guide Reading

Sustained Reading The increasingly fantastic nature of this myth is part of the pleasure of reading it. When a student stops, the atmosphere of wonderment is interrupted. Read students Long Arrow's first encounter with water spirits and continue on, expressing curiosity about the mystery. This will demonstrate the value of a sustained pace of reading.

Block Scheduling Strategies

Consider these suggestions to take advantage of extended class time:

- Build background with the ***Beyond the Literature*** page, Cultural Connection: The Role of the Horse in Different Cultures, p. 32.
- Introduce the concept of Myth by reading with students the Literary Focus paragraph on p. 427. After students have read the selection, have them answer the Literary Focus questions on p. 436 and complete the page on Myth in ***Selection Support***, p. 133.
- Students may listen to all or part of the myth on audiocassette. Reminding students that myths were originally oral tales, invite them to compare and contrast the experience of hearing the myth with that of reading it.
- Have students work on the Critical Thinking questions (p. 436) in small discussion groups.
- Encourage students to form pairs or small groups to select and work on a project from the Idea Bank on p. 437.
- Have students complete the Guided Writing Lesson (p. 437). Before they prewrite individually, have groups brainstorm for myths they know. Then have students use the Story map organizer in ***Writing and Language Transparencies***, p. 84, to plan their myth.

Listening to Literature Audiocassettes The entrance of the chief, and his later discussions with his wife and with Long Arrow on this page and page 431 make dramatic listening. Invite students to discuss how the oral reading helps define the three characters for them.

◆ Literary Focus

1 Myth Students may say that the sharpness of his hearing gives him a kind of super-power; or, that the experience of having been magically healed of a disability sets him off as special.

◆ Reading Strategy

2 Identify With a Character Ask students to imagine how they would feel if they had to catch up all at once with what their peers had learned long ago. (ESL Students may in fact feel that way.) Discuss whether this is easy or hard for Long Arrow, and how students relate to his achievement.

◆ Build Grammar Skills

3 Commonly Confused Words Referring to the phrase, "Good Running's wife accepted him," ask students whether Good Running's wife took Long Arrow in or left him out. *She took him in.* Ask them to name the similar-sounding word that would mean that she left him out. *Excepted*

◆ Critical Thinking

4 Analyze Character Ask students how Long Arrow's ambition to do something special is connected to his unusual early life. *Because he was once ostracized, he now feels he must prove his worth both to those who ostracized him and to himself.*

distance away. The orphan boy laughed and was happy for the first time in his life. With renewed courage he followed the trail his people had made.

In the meantime the village had settled into its new place. Men were already out hunting. Thus the boy came upon Good Running, a kindly old chief, butchering a fat buffalo cow he had just killed. When the chief saw the boy, he said to himself, "Here comes that poor good-for-nothing boy. It was wrong to abandon him." To the boy Good Running said "Rest here, grandson, you're sweaty and covered with dust. Here, have some tripe."[1]

◆ Literary Focus
1 How might the events in the preceding paragraph contribute to Long Arrow's eventual hero status?

The boy wolfed down the meat. He was not used to hearing and talking yet, but his eyes were alert and Good Running also noticed a change in his manner. "This boy," the chief said to himself, "is neither stupid nor crazy." He gave the orphan a piece of the hump meat, then a piece of liver, then a piece of raw kidney, and at last the very best kind of meat—a slice of tongue. The more the old man looked at the boy, the more he liked him. On the spur of the moment he said, "Grandson, I'm going to adopt you; there's a place for you in my tipi. And I'm going to make you into a good hunter and warrior." The boy wept, this time for joy. Good Running said, "They called you a stupid, crazy boy, but now that I think of it, the name you were given at birth is Long Arrow. I'll see that people call you by your right name. Now come along."

> He grew up into a fine young hunter, tall and good-looking in the quilled buckskin outfit the chief's wife made for him.

The chief's wife was not pleased. "Why do you put this burden on me," she said, "bringing into our lodge this good-for-nothing, this slow-witted crazy boy? Maybe you're a little slow-witted and crazy yourself!"

"Woman, keep talking like that and I'll beat you! This boy isn't slow or crazy; he's a good boy, and I have taken him for my grandson. Look—he's barefooted. Hurry up, and make a pair of moccasins for him, and if you don't do it well I'll take a stick to you."

Good Running's wife grumbled but did as she was told. Her husband was a kind man, but when aroused, his anger was great.

So a new life began for Long Arrow. He had to learn to speak and to understand well, and to catch up on all the things a boy should know. He was a fast learner and soon surpassed other boys his age in knowledge and skills. At last even Good Running's wife accepted him. 3

He grew up into a fine young hunter, tall and good-looking in the quilled buckskin outfit the chief's wife made for him. He helped his grandfather in everything and became a staff for Good Running to lean on. But he was lonely, for most people in the camp could not forget that Long Arrow had once been an outcast. "Grandfather," he said one day, "I want to do something to make you proud and show people that you were wise to adopt me. What can I do?"

Good Running answered, "Someday you will be a chief and do great things."

"But what's a great thing I could do now, Grandfather?"

The chief thought for a long time. "Maybe I shouldn't tell you this," he said. "I love you and don't want to lose you. But on winter nights, men talk of powerful spirit people living

1. **tripe** (trīp) *n.*: Part of the stomach of an ox or cow when used as food.

Research Skills Mini-Lesson

Working Source List

Introduce Tell students doing library research that the step that follows selection of a topic for research is to prepare a working source list, a list of all the available sources that they intend to use to research a project, such as a paper.

Develop Explain that they make a working source list by consulting a card catalog or library database, indexes to periodical literature, and other reference works, depending upon the research project. Advise them not to choose a topic that is too broad but to make sure it is not too obscure either. Suggest that they should have at least five sources. If students cannot find enough information on their topics, suggest that they change their topics to ones that they can adequately research in their libraries.

Apply Have students go the school library or local public library to prepare their lists. Try to stagger the assignments so that the library will not be overwhelmed with students using the same resources.

Assess Evaluate the working source lists according to the following criteria:
- Did the student choose a manageable topic?
- Did he or she demonstrate an ability to use library facilities?
- Are their sources actually relevant and useful for their projects?

at the bottom of a faraway lake. Down in that lake the spirit people keep mystery animals who do their work for them. These animals are larger than a great elk, but they carry the burdens of the spirit people like dogs. So they're called Pono-Kamita—Elk Dogs. They are said to be swift, strong, gentle, and beautiful beyond imagination. Every fourth generation, one of our young warriors has gone to find these spirit folk and bring back an Elk Dog for us. But none of our brave young men has ever returned."

◆ **Reading Strategy**
Why might people want to do great deeds for those they love?

Crow Lodge of Twenty-five Buffalo Skins, George Catlin, National Museum of American Art, Washington, D.C.

▲ **Critical Viewing** What do you imagine life might be like living in such a vulnerable setting? **[Infer]** ❽

"Grandfather, I'm not afraid. I'll go and find the Elk Dog."

"Grandson, first learn to be a man. Learn the right prayers and ceremonies. Be brave. Be generous and open-handed. Pity the old and the fatherless, and let the holy men of the tribe find a medicine for you which will protect you on your dangerous journey. We will begin by purifying you in the sweat bath."

So Long Arrow was purified with the white steam of the sweat lodge. He was taught how to use the pipe, and how to pray to the Great Mystery Power. The tribe's holy men gave him a medicine and made for him a shield with designs on it to ward off danger.

Then one morning, without telling anybody, Good Running loaded his best travois dog with all the things Long Arrow would need for traveling. The chief gave him his medicine, his shield, and his own fine bow and, just as the sun came up, went with his grandson to the edge of the camp to purify him with sweet-smelling cedar smoke. Long Arrow left unheard and unseen by anyone else. After a while some people noticed that he was gone, but no one except his grandfather knew where and for what purpose.

Following Good Running's advice, Long Arrow wandered southward. On the fourth day of his journey he came to a small pond, where a strange man was standing as if waiting for him. "Why have you come here?" the stranger asked.

"I have come to find the mysterious Elk Dog."

"Ah, there I cannot help you," said the man, who was the spirit of the pond. "But if you travel further south, four-times-four days, you might chance upon a bigger lake and there meet one of my uncles. Possibly he might talk to you; then again, he might not. That's all I can tell you." ❾

Long Arrow thanked the man, who went down to the bottom of the pond, where he lived.

Long Arrow wandered on, walking for long hours and taking little time for rest. Through deep canyons and over high mountains he went, wearing out his moccasins and enduring

◆ Build Vocabulary

surpassed (sər past′) *v.*: Went beyond; excelled

◆ Reading Strategy

❺ **Identify With a Character** Students might conclude that people want to give benefits to people they love, or, that people want to merit being loved in return.

◆ Critical Thinking

❻ **Analyze** In the conversation between Long Arrow and Good Running, several qualities of a Blackfeet hero are stated or implied. Ask students to point them out. *Qualities include fearlessness, knowledge of prayers and ceremonies, generosity, pity for the weak, respect for the elders of the tribe.*

◆ Build Grammar Skills

❼ **Homographs** Ask students to differentiate the two words that are spelled *bow* but pronounced differently. *A noun referring to a weapon that shoots arrows, and a verb meaning "to bend at the waist."* Note that *bow*, meaning a kind of knot, is not a homograph with *bow*, meaning a weapon that shoots arrows, since they are pronounced identically.

▶Critical Viewing◀

❽ **Infer** *Accept a variety of answers, such as "exciting," "adventurous," "dangerous," "mobile," "free."*

Customize for
Less Proficient Readers
❾ Ask students how many days Long Arrow must travel further south. *Sixteen.* Help students recognize the repeated pattern of Long Arrow's journey: four days to one lake, then four-times-four (four squared) days to another lake.

Humanities: Art

Crow Lodge of Twenty-five Buffalo Skins, 1832–1833, by George Catlin.

This painting documents a domestic scene centered on the tipi. The Crow are a Plains hunting people who lived along the Yellowstone River. They call themselves *Absaroka,* or "bird people."

George Catlin (1796–1872) was an American painter famous for his portrayal of Native Americans. From 1830 to 1836 he lived among Native Americans, recording their lives in a colorful, realistic style. After unsuccessful attempts to sell his paintings, he traveled to England and France in 1839 with more than 500 paintings and a group of Native Americans. Abroad, he found the success he sought.

Use these questions for discussion:

1. What elements of the myth can you find in this painting? *The tipi, dog, weapons, man and woman working are all mentioned in the myth.*
2. How would life in a tipi differ from your life? *Among reasonable responses is that camping out in a tipi provides a closeness to nature that isn't possible in a house or an apartment building.*

◆ Critical Thinking

1 Analyze Ask students how Long Arrow's encounter with the tall spirit man helps Long Arrow. *Students may say that it boosts his self-esteem to be accepted by a powerful spirit who rejects most other humans.*

▶Critical Viewing◀

2 Interpret *The thin outlines and modulated tones of the horses and the landscape give the animals a mystical, shimmery quality like the "gamboling," "wonderful" animals of the myth.*

◆ Critical Thinking

3 Interpret Ask students how Long Arrow's early life might have prepared him to withstand his journey. *As a child, he had to fend for himself, including sleeping alone in the open and scavenging for food.*

Read to Be Entertained

"The Orphan Boy and the Elk Dog" is a myth that explains how the Blackfeet came to have horses. Stories like this one were regarded with great reverence and there were strict observances in the telling of them. The season for telling myths was the winter, when people stayed inside for warmth and protection. It was considered inappropriate, and even sacrilegious, to tell these stories in the summer. The myths also served as entertainment for the long nights of winter, when dancing and powwows were impossible. To fully enjoy the story, students should be encouraged to imagine they are hearing it told by someone they respect a great deal, surrounded by other listeners who feel the same way. The supernatural events are exciting to visualize, but they are secondary to the admirable bravery and good sense of the hero.

▲ Critical Viewing What mood or feeling does the artist invoke through his use of subtle color and shadow? How is this feeling conveyed in the story? **[Interpret]**

cold and heat, hunger and thirst.

Finally Long Arrow approached a big lake surrounded by steep pine-covered hills. There he came face to face with a tall man, fierce and scowling and twice the height of most humans. This stranger carried a long lance with a heavy spearpoint made of shining flint. "Young one," he growled, "why did you come here?"

"I came to find the mysterious Elk Dog."

The stranger, who was the spirit of the lake, stuck his face right into Long Arrow's and shook his mighty lance. "Little one, aren't you afraid of me?" he snarled.

"No, I am not," answered Long Arrow, smiling.

The tall spirit man gave a hideous grin, which was his way of being friendly. "I like small humans who aren't afraid," he said, "but I can't help you. Perhaps our grandfather will take the trouble to listen to you. More likely he won't. Walk south for four-times-four days, and maybe you'll find him. But probably you won't." With that the tall spirit turned his back on Long Arrow and went to the bottom of the lake, where he lived.

Long Arrow walked on for another four-times-four days, sleeping and resting little. By now he staggered and stumbled in his weakness, and his dog was not much better off. At last he came to the biggest lake he had ever seen, surrounded by towering snow-capped peaks and waterfalls of ice. This time there was nobody to receive him. As a matter of fact, there seemed to be no living thing around. "This must be the Great Mystery Lake," thought Long Arrow. Exhausted, he fell down

◆ Build Vocabulary

emanating (em´ ə nāt´ iŋ) *v.*: Coming forth

relish (rel´ ish) *n.*: Pleasure and enjoyment

Humanities: Art

Wild Horses at Play, 1834–1837, by George Catlin.

This landscape painting shows a herd of horses gamboling on the prairie in the foreground, overseen by the mountain peak in the middle of the canvas. Large areas of uninterrupted land and sky give the painting a feeling of open space and freedom.

Tell students that "wild" horses in North America, sometimes called mustangs, are actually the escaped descendants of domesticated horses brought by the Spanish in the 1500's. True wild horses had become extinct on this continent thousands of years earlier.

Use these questions for discussion:

1. If, like Long Arrow's people, you had never seen a horse before, what might you think of these animals? *It would be reasonable to think of them as a kind of large dog or elk-like animal.*
2. Which scene in the myth could this painting illustrate? *The painting could illustrate the scene in which Long Arrow first sees the Elk Dogs.*

upon the shortgrass meadow by the lake, fell down among the wild flowers, and went to sleep with his tired dog curled up at his feet.

When Long Arrow awoke, the sun was already high. He opened his eyes and saw a beautiful child standing before him, a boy in a dazzling white buckskin robe decorated with porcupine quills of many colors. The boy said, "We have been expecting you for a long time. My grandfather invites you to his lodge. Follow me."

Telling his dog to wait, Long Arrow took his medicine shield and his grandfather's bow and went with the wonderful child. They came to the edge of the lake. The spirit boy pointed to the water and said, "My grandfather's lodge is down there. Come." The child turned himself into a kingfisher and dove straight to the bottom.

Afraid, Long Arrow thought, "How can I follow him and not be drowned?" But then he said to himself, "I knew all the time that this would not be easy. In setting out to find the Elk Dog, I already threw my life away." And he boldly jumped into the water. To his surprise, he found it did not make him wet, that it parted before him, that he could breathe and see. He touched the lake's sandy bottom. It sloped down, down toward a center point.

> ... some strange animals, unlike any the young man had ever seen, were galloping and gamboling ...

Long Arrow descended this slope until he came to a small flat valley. In the middle of it stood a large tipi of tanned buffalo hide. The images of two strange animals were drawn on it in sacred vermilion[2] paint. A kingfisher perched high on the top of the tipi flew down and turned again into the beautiful boy, who said, "Welcome. Enter my grandfather's lodge."

> **◆ Literary Focus**
> Keep in mind Long Arrow's bravery in this scene, as it will be rewarded later.

Long Arrow followed the spirit boy inside. In the back at the seat of honor sat a black-robed old man with flowing white hair and such power emanating from him that Long Arrow felt himself in the presence of a truly Great One. The holy man welcomed Long Arrow and offered him food. The man's wife came in bringing dishes of buffalo hump, liver, tongues, delicious chunks of deer meat, the roasted flesh of strange, tasty water birds, and meat pounded together with berries, chokecherries, and kidney fat. Famished after his long journey, Long Arrow ate with relish. Yet he still looked around to admire the furnishings of the tipi, the painted inner curtain, the many medicine shields, wonderfully wrought weapons, shirts and robes decorated with porcupine quills in rainbow colors, beautifully painted rawhide containers filled with wonderful things, and much else that dazzled him.

After Long Arrow had stilled his hunger, the old spirit chief filled the pipe and passed it to his guest. They smoked, praying silently. After a while the old man said, "Some came before you from time to time, but they were always afraid of the deep
water, and so they went away with empty 7
hands. But you, grandson, were brave enough to plunge in, and therefore you are chosen to receive a wonderful gift to carry back to your people. Now, go outside with my grandson."

The beautiful boy took Long Arrow to a meadow on which some strange animals, unlike any the young man had ever seen, were
galloping and gamboling, neighing and nicker- 8
ing. They were truly wonderful to look at, with 9
their glossy coats fine as a maiden's hair, their long manes and tails streaming in the wind.

2. **vermilion** (vər mil′ yən) *n.*: Bright red.

◆ Build Vocabulary

4 Homographs Point out the word *dove* in this sentence. Have students pronounce it and identify its part of speech. Then ask them to name a homograph for *dove*. Dove *is a verb; a homograph is the noun, "dove," a bird.*

◆ Literary Focus

5 Myth Ask students what personal quality allows Long Arrow to enter the lake. Then ask what external phenomenon helps Long Arrow. *The personal quality is courage; the external phenomenon is magic.*

6 Clarification A kingfisher is a bird usually found in the tropics or subtropics. It is brightly colored, with a crested head and a long powerful beak. There are several varieties—the American varieties are fishing birds, while some other varieties live in forests.

◆ Reading Strategy

7 Identify With a Character
Invite students to imagine how they would feel in Long Arrow's situation. *They would probably feel proud, happy, excited.*

Comprehension Check ☑

8 What kind of animal is it? *It is the horse.*

◆ Build Vocabulary

9 Homographs Have students note the word *wind* in this sentence and identify its part of speech. Then ask them to name a differently pronounced word that is spelled "wind." Wind, *in this sentence, is a noun. The homograph* wind *is a verb meaning to twist or turn.*

Workplace Skills Mini-Lesson

Following a Procedure

Introduce In making his journey, Long Arrow listened to, remembered, and followed several procedures: when his grandfather gave him advice, when the stranger at the pond directed him to the lake, when the tall spirit directed him to another lake, and when the old spirit chief gave him gifts and instructed him on how to catch the Elk Dogs. Have students reread the relevant passages and summarize the procedures Long Arrow followed.

Develop Ask students to think of procedures they must follow either at a job, at a recreational activity, or in a school activity. Have students write a list of steps for performing one such procedure.

Apply Have students work in pairs, each partner reciting his or her procedures list to the other. The partner then repeats the steps of the procedure from memory. Partners should then switch roles and repeat the process.

Assess Ask students to assess how well they and their partners recalled the procedures step by step.

◆ Build Vocabulary

❶ Homographs Ask students which homograph is used here, the noun meaning "garbage" or the verb meaning "to reject." *It is the verb.*

◆ Build Grammar Skills

❷ Commonly Confused Words Ask students to choose the correct word to fill in the blank in the following sentence: He could not (accept, except) such as lavish gift.

Customize for *Pre-AP Students*

Point out the repeated use of the number four in this myth: Long Arrow travels four days, then four times four days, then stays under the lake four days. Invite students to discuss the purpose of this motif. *Accept reasonable answers: four might have a mystical meaning in Blackfeet culture; the repetition lends unity to the myth.*

◆ Literary Focus

❸ Myth Students should note the presence of magical helpers, the encounter with a powerful spirit, the granting of magical aids to the hero, and the hero's successful return from a quest.

Customize for *Pre-AP Students*

Ask students where else in literature or myth they have seen the command not to look back. *The story of Lot's wife in Genesis, and the Greek myth of Orpheus and Eurydice.*

Now rearing, now nuzzling, they looked at Long Arrow with gentle eyes which belied their fiery appearance.

"At last," thought Long Arrow, "here they are before my own eyes, the Pono-Kamita, the Elk Dogs!"

"Watch me," said the mystery boy, "so that you learn to do what I am doing." Gracefully and without effort, the boy swung himself onto the back of a jet-black Elk Dog with a high, arched neck. Larger than any elk Long Arrow had ever come across, the animal carried the boy all over the meadow swiftly as the wind. Then the boy returned, jumped off his mount, and said, "Now you try it." A little timidly Long Arrow climbed up on the beautiful Elk Dog's back. Seemingly regarding him as feather-light, it took off like a flying arrow. The young man felt himself soaring through the air as a bird does, and experienced a happiness greater even than the joy he had felt when Good Running had adopted him as a grandson.

When they had finished riding the Elk Dogs, the spirit boy said to Long Arrow, "Young hunter from the land above the waters, I want you to have what you have come for. Listen to me. You may have noticed that my grandfather wears a black medicine robe as long as a woman's dress, and that he is always trying to hide his feet. Try to get a glimpse of them, for if ❶ you do, he can refuse you nothing. He will then tell you to ask him for a gift, and you must ask for these three things: his rainbow-colored quilled belt, his black medicine robe, and a herd of these animals which you seem to like."

Long Arrow thanked him and vowed to follow his advice. For four days the young man stayed in the spirit chief's lodge, where he ate well and often went out riding on the Elk Dogs. But try as he would, he could never get a look at the old man's feet. The spirit chief always kept them carefully covered. Then on the morning of the fourth day, the old one was walking out of the tipi when his medicine robe caught in the entrance flap. As the robe opened, Long Arrow caught a glimpse of a leg and one foot. He was awed to see that it was not a human limb at all, but the glossy leg and firm hoof of an Elk Dog! He could not stifle a cry of surprise, and the old man looked over his shoulder and saw that his leg and hoof were exposed. The chief seemed a little embarrassed, but shrugged and said, "I tried to hide this, but you must have been fated to see it. Look, both of my feet are those of an Elk Dog. You may as well ask me for a gift. Don't be timid; tell me what you want."

Long Arrow spoke boldly: "I want three things: your belt of rainbow colors, your black medicine robe, and your herd of Elk Dogs."

"Well, so you're really not timid at all!" said the old man. "You ask for a lot, and I'll give it to you, except that you cannot have all my Elk Dogs; I'll give you half of them. Now I must tell you that my black medicine robe and my many-colored belt have Elk Dog magic in them. Always wear the robe when you try to catch Elk Dogs; then they can't get away from you. On quiet nights, if you listen closely to the belt, you will hear the Elk Dog dance song and Elk Dog prayers. You must learn them. And I will give you one more magic gift: this long rope woven from the hair of a white buffalo bull. With it you will never fail to catch whichever Elk Dog you want."

> **◆ Literary Focus**
> What elements does this myth have in common with other myths you've read?

The spirit chief presented him with the gifts and said, "Now you must leave. At first the Elk Dogs will not follow you. Keep the medicine robe and the magic belt on at all times, and walk for four days toward the north. Never look back—always look to the north. On the fourth day the Elk Dogs will come up beside you on the left. Still don't look back. But after they have overtaken you, catch one with the rope of white buffalo hair and ride him home. Don't lose the black robe, or you will lose the Elk Dogs and never catch them again."

Long Arrow listened carefully so that he would remember. Then the old spirit chief had

◆ Build Vocabulary

stifle (stī′ fəl) *v.*: Hold back

Speaking, Listening, and Viewing Mini-Lesson

Debate

This Mini-Lesson supports the first Speaking, Listening, and Viewing activity in the Idea Bank on p. 437.

Introduce Debates were an important feature in the political life of many Native American peoples. Remind students that in debating they do not necessarily have to argue for the side with which they agree. They should plan their arguments based on facts and details from the story and form their arguments to anticipate the arguments of the other side. Refer students to the Speaking and Listening Handbook, p. 978, for more information on Debate.

Develop Form teams of two or three students. Before they debate, have teams reread the myth and takes notes on any points they feel might bear on Long Arrow's potential as a chief. They should then make an outline of their arguments and anticipated counter-arguments.

Apply After rehearsing their arguments, have students debate Long Arrow's fitness as chief.

Assess Evaluate the debates according to the following criteria:

1. Were the arguments clear and well-supported?
2. Were the counter-arguments reasonable and well expressed?
3. Which team was more convincing in its presentation?

his wife make up a big pack of food, almost too heavy for Long Arrow to carry, and the young man took leave of his generous spirit host. The mysterious boy once again turned himself into a kingfisher and led Long Arrow to the surface of the lake, where his faithful dog greeted him joyfully. Long Arrow fed the dog, put his pack of food on the travois, and started walking north.

On the fourth day the Elk Dogs came up on his left side, as the spirit chief had foretold. Long Arrow snared the black one with the arched neck to ride, and he caught another to carry the pack of food. They galloped swiftly on, the dog barking at the big Elk Dogs' heels.

When Long Arrow arrived at last in his village, the people were afraid and hid. They did not recognize him astride his beautiful Elk Dog but took him for a monster, half man and half animal. Long Arrow kept calling, "Grandfather Good Running, it's your grandson. I've come back bringing Elk Dogs!"

Recognizing the voice, Good Running came out of hiding and wept for joy, because he had given Long Arrow up for lost. Then all the others emerged from their hiding places to admire the wonderful new animals.

Long Arrow said, "My grandfather and grandmother who adopted me, I can never repay you for your kindness. Accept these wonderful Elk Dogs as my gift. Now we no longer need to be humble footsloggers, because these animals will carry us swiftly everywhere we want to go. Now buffalo hunting will be easy. Now our tipis will be larger, our possessions will be greater, because an Elk Dog travois can carry a load ten times bigger than that of a dog. Take them, my grandparents. I shall keep for myself only this black male and this black female, which will grow into a fine herd."

"You have indeed done something great, grandson," said Good Running, and he spoke true. The people became the bold riders of the Plains and soon could hardly imagine how they had existed without these wonderful animals.

After some time Good Running, rich and honored by all, said to Long Arrow, "Grandson, lead us to the Great Mystery Lake so we can camp by its shores. Let's visit the spirit chief and the wondrous boy; maybe they will give us more of their power and magic gifts."

Long Arrow led the people southward and again found the Great Mystery Lake. But the waters would no longer part for him, nor would any of the kingfishers they saw turn into a boy. Nor, gazing down into the crystal-clear water, could they discover people, Elk Dogs, or a tipi. There was nothing in the lake but a few fish. ❺

Guide for Responding

◆ Literature and Your Life

Reader's Response Would you have wanted to travel with Long Arrow? Why or why not?

Thematic Focus Long Arrow brought back a great gift to his people, which changed the way they lived. Who in the last one hundred years do you think has given modern American society a gift that has changed some aspect of how many people live?

☑ Check Your Comprehension

1. Why do the villagers shun Long Arrow at the beginning of the story?
2. Who takes pity on Long Arrow and why?
3. Why is the chief reluctant to tell Long Arrow about the Elk Dogs?
4. Summarize Long Arrow's journey to and from the Great Mystery Lake.

◆ Reading Strategy

❹ Identify With a Character Ask students how they would feel if they were Long Arrow, returning home with his horses. *They would probably feel triumphant, finally accepted as valuable by the whole tribe.*

◆ Literary Focus

❺ Myth Have students explain how this paragraph conveys the qualities of a myth. *Students may say that a myth helps to explain how something real came to be; once the reality has been created, the magic that created it ceases to function.*

Reinforce and Extend

Answers

◆ Literature and Your Life

Reader's Response Adventurous students could respond to the journey as to an exciting wilderness trek.

Thematic Focus Students may identify an inventor, such as Thomas Edison, a political or social force, such as Dr. Martin Luther King, Jr., or an artist, writer, or musician.

☑ Check Your Comprehension

1. Long Arrow is disabled by his inability to hear, and people think he is stupid.
2. The old chief, Good Running, adopts the boy.
3. He doesn't want to lose the boy to a dangerous quest.
4. Summaries should include the purification of the sweat lodge, the spirit of the pond, the spirit of the lake, the boy of the Great Mystery Lake, the Great One of the underwater lodge, and the gift of the Elk Dogs, followed by the return north with the Elk Dogs.

Beyond the Selection

FURTHER READING

Other Native American Myths

American Indian Myths and Legends, edited by Richard Erdoes and Alfonso Ortiz

The Winged Serpent: American Indian Prose and Poetry, edited by Margot Astrov

They Dance in the Sky: Native American Star Myths, Jean Guard Monroe and Ray A. Williamson

Other Works About Transportation Expanding Our Horizons

The Spirit of St. Louis, Charles A. Lindbergh

The Right Stuff, Tom Wolfe

Life on the Mississippi, Mark Twain

We suggest that you preview these works before recommending them to students.

INTERNET

You and your students may visit the following Web sites for more information about the Blackfeet **http://users.aol.com/Donh523/navapage/blackfee.htm** **http://itrc29.itrc.umt.edu/indianinfo/blackfeet.htm**

Please be aware, however, that sites may have changed from the time we published this information. We *strongly recommend* that you preview the sites before you send students to them.

Answers

◆ Critical Thinking

1. Courage and determination keep Long Arrow on his quest.
2. Long Arrow discovers his own strength and identity.
3. Most students will say the use of horses for the tribe is the greatest benefit; others may say that the tribe's acceptance of Long Arrow is the greatest benefit.
4. Special educational facilities and technological equipment to enhance auditory capabilities are available for the hearing-impaired today.

◆ Reading Strategy

1. Students should consider whether they have the courage to set out on an unknown path.
2. He must have felt proud and happy.

◆ Literary Focus

1. Long Arrow endures extreme hardships on his journey and experiences magical powers in his descent to the underwater lodge of the Elk Dog. These qualities make him seem "larger than life."
2. The Blackfeet use steam sweat baths and cedar smoke for purification; they have a holy man who dispenses medicine; they revere the horse or Elk Dog.

◆ Build Vocabulary

Word Groups: Homographs

1. I refuse to accept your criticism. She placed her garbage in the refuse container.
2. I am content to read at the beach. What is the content of that jar?
3. He stood in the entrance to the tipi, brooding. Puzzles and mysteries entrance my brother for hours on end.
4. Bow to your elders to show respect. String your bow tight to shoot your arrow straight.

Using the Word Bank

1. S 2. S 3. A 4. A 5. S

◆ Build Grammar Skills

1. accept; 2. accepted; 3. except; 4. except; 5. accepted

Guide for Responding *(continued)*

◆ Critical Thinking

Interpret

1. What qualities help Long Arrow overcome the obstacles he faces during his journey? **[Infer]**
2. Long Arrow's journey was beneficial to his people because he brought back horses. In what ways was his journey beneficial to himself as an individual? **[Analyze]**

Evaluate

3. What do you think is the most important result of Long Arrow's journey? Why? **[Assess]**

Apply

4. The people of Long Arrow's village made no accommodation for Long Arrow's disability at the beginning of the story. In what ways does our society make accommodations for physical disabilities? In what ways can we improve? **[Relate]**

◆ Reading Strategy

Identify With a Character

In reading "The Orphan Boy and the Elk Dog," you **identify** with Long Arrow. That means you share his experiences and feelings. As you do, you consider what you would have done and felt in his place.

1. If you were Long Arrow, would you have undertaken the journey to find the Elk Dogs? Why or why not?
2. How do you think Long Arrow felt when he returned with the Elk Dogs?

◆ Literary Focus

Myth

Myths are ancient stories that generally involve immortal or "larger-than-life" characters. These stories explain the mysteries of nature or the customs of a people. Often, details in a myth reveal the values and customs of the culture.

1. What qualities make Long Arrow seem "larger than life"?
2. Identify three details about Blackfeet culture that are revealed in this myth.

◆ Build Vocabulary

Using Homographs

On your paper, write two sentences for each homograph, showing its two different meanings.

1. refuse
2. content
3. entrance
4. bow

Using the Word Bank: Synonyms or Antonyms?

On your paper, write *S* if the pair of words are synonyms and *A* if the pair are antonyms.

1. refuse, garbage
2. surpassed, exceeded
3. emanating, suppressing
4. relish, loathe
5. stifle, smother

◆ Build Grammar Skills

Commonly Confused Words: *Accept* and *Except*

Accept is a verb meaning "to receive" or "to agree with." ***Except*** is a preposition meaning "not including," but it is sometimes a verb meaning "to leave out." These words are commonly confused, because although they have different meanings, they have a similar look and sound.

Practice Choose the word that correctly completes each sentence.

1. Will you (accept, except) these moccasins?
2. He (accepted, excepted) a ride on an Elk Dog.
3. All (accept, except) Long Arrow returned.
4. The holy man looked normal (accept, except) for his leg and foot.
5. The holy man offered gifts, and Long Arrow (accepted, excepted) them.

Writing Application Write a single sentence in which you use both *accept* and *except* correctly.

Reteach

Students who find it difficult to identify with a character may benefit from a visual aid. Before you offer the help of a graphic organizer, you might want to remind these students that, to fully understand literary characters, they must read with their hearts as well as their heads. When they identify with a character, they experience that character's joy and sorrows as they would their own. Also suggest that students compare the situations in which characters find themselves with similar situations from their own lives.

Use this cluster diagram to help students identify with a character.

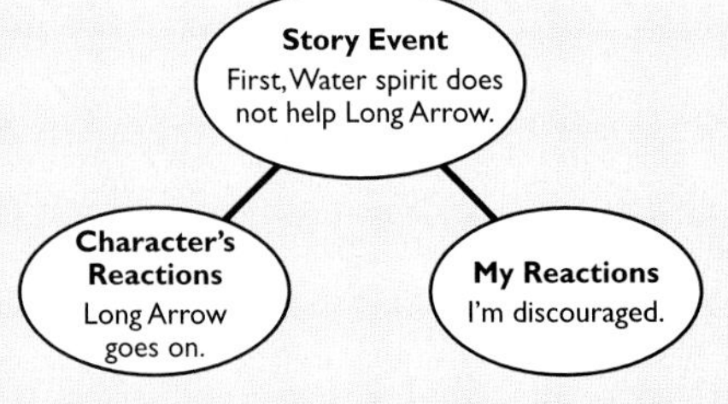
Story Event
First, Water spirit does not help Long Arrow.
Character's Reactions
Long Arrow goes on.
My Reactions
I'm discouraged.

Build Your Portfolio

Idea Bank

Writing

1. **Speech** Write a brief statement that Long Arrow might make to the villagers when he returns with the Elk Dogs.
2. **Dialogue** Write a dialogue that might occur between Long Arrow and the Chief when they reach the Great Mystery Lake at the end of the myth and discover only fish in the lake.
3. **Animal Description** Horses were at first such a mystery to the Blackfeet that they could describe them only by using words for familiar animals. Describe an animal as if you had never seen it before and didn't know its name. Compare its features with those of other animals. **[Science Link]**

Speaking, Listening, and Viewing

4. **Debate** With other students, debate whether or not Long Arrow will make a good chief. Support your view with story details.
5. **Retell a Myth** Retell this myth in your own words. Use tone of voice, facial expressions, and body language to make your telling exciting. Watch and listen to how each person's retelling differs. **[Performing Arts Link]**

Researching and Representing

6. **Animal Population Graph** Buffalo were important to the Blackfeet, but their numbers have declined since the late nineteenth century. Create a bar graph that shows the changes in the buffalo population in the United States since 1850. **[Math Link; Science Link]**
7. **Storyboard Mural** Create a mural of scenes that show the major events of "The Orphan Boy" in order. Look at the illustrations that accompany the myth to get ideas for color and style. **[Art Link]**

Online Activity www.phlit.phschool.com

Guided Writing Lesson

Retelling a Myth

"The Orphan Boy and the Elk Dog" has been retold many times over many generations. When you **retell a myth**, you use your own words and style to tell a tale that already exists.

Think of a myth you already know and retell it in your own words. The following tip will help you organize the events of the myth.

Writing Skills Focus: Clear Beginning, Middle, and End

A myth, like any other good story, needs a **clear beginning, middle,** and **end** in order to make sense. In the beginning of your retelling, include important details about the setting. When and where does it take place? Introduce the main characters, then the conflict or problem that the characters face. In the middle, as the tale develops, present events in a logical order, such as time order. As you bring the tale to a close, tell how the conflict is worked out.

Prewriting Create a story map to organize the retelling of your myth. Include these categories: title, setting, character names and descriptions, conflict description, and events that develop and resolve the conflict.

Drafting Use your story map to write a clear beginning, logical development for the middle, and an effective end. Inject your retelling with clear, lively language. To do this, use active verbs and specific nouns.

Revising Read your draft to a small group of classmates. See whether they can summarize your story correctly. If there are places where group members become confused, add details or transitional words to indicate the connections among events.

✓ ASSESSMENT OPTIONS

Formal Assessment, Selection Test, pp. 110–112, and Assessment Resources Software. The selection test is designed so that it can be easily customized to the performance levels of your students.

Alternative Assessment, p. 32, includes options for less advanced students, move advanced students, verbal/linguistic learners, visual/spatial learners, and logical/mathematical learners.

PORTFOLIO ASSESSMENT

Use the following rubrics in the ***Alternative Assessment*** booklet to assess student writing:
Speech: Expression Rubric, p. 94
Dialogue: Fictional Narrative Rubric, p. 95
Description of a Mystery Animal: Description Rubric, p. 97
Guided Writing Lesson: Fictional Narrative Rubric, p. 95

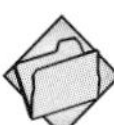

Idea Bank

Following are suggestions for matching Idea Bank topics with your students' performance levels and learning modalities:

Customizing for *Performance Levels*
Less Advanced Students: 1, 5, 7
Average Students: 2, 4, 6
More Advanced Students: 3, 4, 6

Customizing for *Learning Modalities*
Visual/Spatial: 3, 6, 7
Verbal/Linguistic: 1, 4, 5
Logical/Mathematical: 6

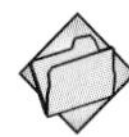

Guided Writing Lesson

Prewriting Strategy To help students give their retellings an exciting, suspenseful flavor, ask students to identify an adventure or frightening brush with danger that they've had. Encourage them to brainstorm for a list of words about these experiences. Students can choose words from their lists to transfer into their retellings.

scared — heart pounding
sweaty — Run!

For more prewriting, elaboration, and revision strategies, see *Prentice Hall Writing and Grammar.*

Writing and Language Transparencies Students may use the Story Map, pp. 83–86, to organize their retelling of a myth.

Writers at Work Videodisc
Have students view the videodisc segment (Ch. 2) featuring Maxine Hong Kingston to see how she develops narrative elements.

Play frames 18612 to 19873

Writing Lab CD-ROM
Have students complete the tutorial on Narration. Follow these steps:

1. Students may use the Photo Storyboard activity to suggest a story line.
2. Have students draft on computer.
3. Suggest that students use the homophone checker in revising their work.

Prepare and Engage

LESSON OBJECTIVES

1. **To develop vocabulary and word identification skills**
   - Anglo-Saxon Suffixes: *-ly*
   - Using the Word Bank: Context
   - Extending Word Study: Connotations
2. **To use a variety of reading strategies to comprehend a personal narrative**
   - Connect Your Experience
   - Reading Strategy: Predict Story Events
   - Tips to Guide Reading
   - Read to Appreciate Author's Craft
3. **To increase knowledge of other cultures and to connect common elements across cultures**
   - Connecting Themes Across Cultures (ATE)
   - Background for Understanding
4. **To express and support responses to the text**
   - Critical Thinking
   - Idea Bank: Sketch
   - Idea Bank: Compare and Contrast
   - Idea Bank: Dialogue
   - Speaking, Listening and Viewing Mini-Lesson
   - Idea Bank: Debate
5. **To analyze literary elements**
   - Literary Focus: Point of View
6. **To read in order to research self-selected and assigned topics**
   - Idea Bank: Photo Essay
6. **To plan, prepare, organize, and present literary interpretations**
   - Idea Bank: Postcard
   - Idea Bank: Legend
7. **To use recursive writing processes to write a song for a moment in the story**
   - Guided Writing Lesson
8. **To increase knowledge of the rules of grammar and usage**
   - Build Grammar Skills: Commas in Series

Test Preparation

Reading Strategy: Evaluate and Make Judgments (ATE, p. 439)
The teaching tips and sample test item in this workshop support the instruction and practice in the unit workshop:
Reading Comprehension: Interpret Graphic Aids; Evaluate and Make Judgments (SE, p. 465)

Guide for Reading

Josephina Niggli

(1910–1983)

When Josephina Niggli was just a child, she and her family fled their native Mexico to escape the turmoil of the Mexican Revolution. They settled in San Antonio, Texas, where Niggli grew up.

From Texas to Hollywood Niggli was educated at home until she reached high school. Her first book of poems was published shortly after her high-school graduation. After college, she began writing and producing plays, and later, movie scripts.

Niggli spent two years in Hollywood as a screen-writer.

Niggli's background in drama served her well in her prose works. Her dialogue is believable, and her skill at describing a setting enables the reader to picture the scene as if it were on stage.

Cultural Influences Although she left Mexico at a young age, Niggli carried the richness of her Mexican culture with her to the United States. In 1945, she published *Mexican Village,* a collection of ten stories, all set in the Sabinas Valley of northern Mexico. In these stories, she shows a talent for capturing the local color—the details of life in this valley.

Daring Heroes As a child, she heard exciting stories of the fearless heroes Pancho Villa and Emiliano Zapata, who fought for reform during the Mexican Revolution. Pepe Gonzalez, the main character in "The Street of Cañon," exhibits the same daring, romantic nature as these daring, romantic figures.

◆ Build Vocabulary

ANGLO-SAXON SUFFIXES: *-ly*

The Anglo-Saxon suffix *-ly* is one of the most common in English. Most, but not all, words that end in *-ly* are adverbs. An adverb is a word that modifies a verb, adjective, or another adverb. Josephina Niggli uses adverbs to make her writing more descriptive. When one of her characters *nonchalantly* enters a room, for instance, you can picture the person's walk as he tries to enter the room without being noticed.

WORD BANK

As you read "The Street of the Cañon," you will encounter the words on this list. Each word is defined on the page where it first appears. Preview the list before you read.

officious
mottled
nonchalantly
audaciously
imperiously
plausibility

◆ Build Grammar Skills

COMMAS IN A SERIES

A **comma** can make a big difference in the clarity of your writing. Separating three or more items in a series is one way that commas make writing clear.

> . . . the air was hot with the too-sweet perfume of gardenias, tuberoses, and the pungent scent of close-packed humanity.

In this sentence, commas separate the three details that describe what the room is hot with. Notice that Niggli uses a comma before the coordinating conjunction *and,* which joins the last two items.

If the items in the series are already separated by conjunctions (such as *and* or *or*), commas are not necessary.

> There were yellow cheese *and* white cheese *and* curded cheese from cow's milk.

Prentice Hall Literature Program Resources

REINFORCE / RETEACH / EXTEND

Selection Support Pages
Build Vocabulary: Suffixes: *-ly*, p. 134
Build Grammar Skills: Commas in a Series, p. 135
Reading Strategy: Predict, p. 136
Literary Focus: Point of View, p. 137

Strategies for Diverse Student Needs, p. 33

Beyond Literature
Community Connection, p. 33

Formal Assessment Selection Test, pp. 113–115; Assessment Resources Software

Alternative Assessment, p. 33

Writing and Language Transparencies
Analysis Map, pp. 71–73

Resource Pro CD-ROM

Listening to Literature Audiocassettes

The Street of the Cañon

◆ Literature and Your Life

Connect Your Experience

Celebrations acknowledge significant occasions. Some celebrations, such as a Fourth of July picnic or a town parade, are public. Others, such as a wedding or birthday party, are personal. In this story, a young woman named Sarita celebrates her birthday. The celebration has elements of a public event, however, as Sarita's father throws a fiesta to which the whole town is invited.

Journal Writing Describe the last celebration you attended, and tell what made it special.

Thematic Focus: A Larger World

Celebrations sometimes unite you with other cultural groups who honor the same event or person. How does celebrating with others enlarge your world?

◆ Background for Understanding

Culture

Courtship and marriage customs play an important role in this story. In Mexico, there have been different traditional marriage customs, depending on the region. In some regions, a young man seeking to marry must still ask permission of the young woman's family elders. In some regions, the parents still arrange a match. Marriages typically take place within the community. In the town of San Juan Iglesias, the Mexican village in which this story is set, "to walk around the plaza with a girl" is a sign of engagement.

◆ Literary Focus

Point of View

Imagine a kind of microscope that allows you to see someone's thoughts and feelings. Actually, writers give you this kind of look into fictional characters' minds. They do it through **point of view** in a story—the vantage point from which the story is told. The point of view determines what you as a reader know.

When a story is told from a **third-person** point of view, it is told by a narrator who is not a story character but who reveals the thoughts and feelings of one main character. If the third-person point of view is all-knowing, or **omniscient**, the narrator knows and reveals the thoughts and feelings of more than one character. This is the point of view of "The Street of the Cañon." Niggli allows us to peek into the minds of several characters, and she reveals some details that even the characters don't know!

◆ Reading Strategy

Predict

Your baseball team is up against a team whose best players are injured. You can probably predict that your team will win. You can **predict** story events in much the same way—you make an educated guess based on what the text reveals about the characters and the situation, and based on what you know from experience.

No matter how logical your predictions, however, you may need to revise them as new information is revealed. If the injured players from the other team were suddenly able to play, you might reconsider your prediction. Similarly, new circumstances introduced by the author may lead you to change your predictions about story events.

Use a chart like the one shown to keep track of your predictions and how they change as you read this story.

Question	Clues	Prediction
Who is the stranger?		
What does he have tightly clutched to his side?		
Why is he going to San Juan Iglesias?		
Why would the townspeople turn on him if they recognized him?		

Set up the following situation for students: You are at a dance with all your friends from school. A mysterious stranger enters and proceeds to mix with the group, even dancing with the most popular girl in the class. Ask students: What would your reaction be to this stranger? How would he be treated by most of the students at the dance?

Tell students that the story they will read includes a situation similar to this one. Have them look for clues that will enable them to identify the mysterious stranger and understand why he has come to the dance.

Connecting Themes Across Cultures

Most celebrations are associated with specific cultures or religions. People commemorate national leaders, such as George Washington in the United States, and events, such as Bastille Day in France. They celebrate religious days such as Easter, Ramadan, or the three anniversaries of the Buddha's life. Have students brainstorm for celebrations that cross cultural, national, and religious boundaries and include all people.

Customize for
Less Proficient Readers

In addition to having students predict story events, have them jot down key details that confirm or help them revise their predictions as they read. Doing so will help students keep track of important information that unfolds in bits and pieces within the story.

Customize for
Pre-AP Students

Niggli's stories are known for their vivid creation of a region and its culture as well as for their exciting plots. Have these students appraise her use of folk sayings and other details that paint a lifelike picture of one Mexican village.

Customize for
Visual/Spatial Learners

Have students create a chart that relates key details to the manner in which they were revealed—that is, through the narrator, dialogue, or a character's thoughts. Students can then present their charts to the class.

Test Preparation Workshop

Reading Comprehension: Evaluate and Make Judgments Standardized tests require students to make judgments based on evidence in given passages. Use this sample test item to help students practice this skill.

The man in the doorway, while trying to appear at ease, was carefully examining every smiling face. If just one person recognized him, the room would turn on him like a den of snarling mountain cats, but so far all the laughter-dancing eyes were friendly.

The evidence in the passage indicates that the man in the doorway—

A is a coward
B is not expected
C is really a dog
D is looking for someone

Help students to understand that the author is emphasizing that the man is not expected, *B*. He is searching the faces not because he is looking for someone, *D*, but because he fears recognition. His uneasiness does not indicate cowardice, *A*. The correct response is *B*.

Develop Understanding

One-Minute Insight Josephina Niggli uses changing perspectives to full advantage in this tale of intrigue, local color, and local legend. The story's omniscient narrator sets the scene: A stranger makes his way to Sarita Calderon's eighteenth-birthday celebration, carrying a mysterious package. Gradually, pieces of the puzzle—in the forms of conversations, glimpses into the stranger's and Sarita's thoughts, and further insights from the narrator—come together. It becomes clear that the stranger is Pepe Gonzalez—a notoriously daring young "devil" from a rival town. What remains intriguingly unclear, however, are Pepe's intentions toward Sarita—does he charm his way into her heart because he genuinely wishes to marry her, or is winning her affection merely another daring adventure on his part?

◆ Critical Thinking

❶ **Analyze** Call students' attention to the details the author uses to describe the man's movements. What can students tell about him based on this description? *Responses may include that he has something to hide or that he has a secret purpose.*

◆ Build Vocabulary

❷ **Suffixes: *-ly*** Point out the suffix *-ly* in the word tightly. Ask: What part of speech is this word? *It is an adverb.* What word does it modify? *It modifies the verb* clutched.

Customize for
Gifted/Talented Students
The story of an uninvited mystery-man at a party may seem overly familiar to these students. Have them prepare a short parody of the story.

The Street of the Cañon

from Mexican Village

Josephina Niggli

▲ Critical Viewing What time period do you think this painting depicts? What details suggest the time period? **[Infer]**

It was May, the flowering thorn was sweet in the air, and the village of San Juan Iglesias in the Valley of the Three Marys was celebrating. The long dark streets were empty because all of the people, from the lowest-paid cowboy to the mayor, were helping Don Roméo Calderón celebrate his daughter's eighteenth birthday.

On the other side of the town, where the Cañon Road led across the mountains to the Sabinas Valley, a tall slender man, a package clutched
❶ tightly against his side, slipped from shadow to
❷ shadow. Once a dog barked, and the man's black suit merged into the blackness of a wall. But no voice called out, and after a moment he slid into the narrow, dirt-packed street again.

The moonlight touched his shoulder and spilled across his narrow hips. He was young, no more than twenty-five, and his black curly head was bare. He walked swiftly along, heading always for the distant sound of guitar and flute. If he met anyone now, who could say from which direction he had come? He might be a trader from Monterrey, or a buyer of cow's milk from farther north in the Valley of the Three Marys. Who would guess that an Hidalgo[1] man dared to walk alone in the moonlit streets of San Juan Iglesias?

Carefully adjusting his flat package so that it was not too prominent, he squared his shoulders and walked jauntily across the street to the laughter-filled house. Little boys packed in the doorway made way for him, smiling and nodding to him. The long, narrow room with the orchestra at one end was filled with

1. **Hidalgo** (ē dal´ gō) *adj.*: Nearby village.

Block Scheduling Strategies

Consider these suggestions to take advantage of extended class time:

- Use the Daily Language Practice for Week 6, which is based on "The Street of the Cañon," p. 117 in ***Writing and Language Transparencies.***
- Students may work with a partner to complete a Prediction Chart like the one on p. 439 as they read. Have pairs compare their charts with other pairs when they have finished reading the story.
- Introduce the Literary Focus, Point of View, by reading with students the paragraphs on p. 439. Have students preview the Literary Focus questions on p. 446 before they read. After they have read the story they may work in groups to answer the questions and do the page on Point of View in ***Selection Support,*** p. 137.
- To help students understand the context of the story, have students work in groups to complete the activity page in ***Beyond Literature:*** Community Connection: Social Dancing, p. 33.
- Have students complete the Guided Writing Lesson (p. 447). Before students get started, have them review the story to find and discuss words within it that have rich connotations. You may wish to have them use the Analysis Map, p. 72 in ***Writing and Language Transparencies,*** to analyze the connotations of words.

(detail), Gentilz, The Alamo Library

whirling dancers. Rigid-backed chaperones were gossiping together, seated in their straight chairs against the plaster walls. Over the scene was the yellow glow of kerosene lanterns, and the air was hot with the too-sweet perfume of gardenias, tuberoses, and the pungent scent of close-packed humanity. 5

The man in the doorway, while trying to appear at ease, was carefully examining every smiling face. If just one person recognized him, the room would turn on him like a den of snarling mountain cats, but so far all the laughter-dancing eyes were friendly. 6

Suddenly a plump, officious little man, his round cheeks glistening with perspiration, pushed his way through the crowd. His voice, many times too large for his small body, boomed at the man in the doorway. "Welcome, stranger, welcome to our house." Thrusting his arm through the stranger's, and almost dislodging the package, he started to lead the way through the maze of dancers. "Come and drink a toast to my daughter—to my beautiful Sarita. She is eighteen this night."

In the square patio the gentle breeze ruffled the pink and white oleander bushes. A long table set up on sawhorses held loaves of flaky crusted French bread, stacks of thin, delicate tortillas, plates of barbecued beef, and long red rolls of spicy sausages. But most of all there were cheeses, for the Three Marys was a cheese-eating valley. There were yellow cheese and white cheese and curded cheese from cow's milk. There was even a flat white cake of goat cheese from distant Linares, a delicacy too expensive for any but feast days.

To set off this feast were bottles of beer floating in ice-filled tin tubs, and another table was covered with bottles of mescal, of tequila, of maguey wine.

Don Roméo Calderón thrust a glass of tequila into the stranger's hand. "Drink, friend, to the prettiest girl in San Juan. As pretty as my fine fighting cocks, she is. On her wedding day she takes to her man, and may she find him soon, the best fighter in my flock. Drink deep, friend. Even the rivers flow with wine."

The Hidalgo man laughed and raised his glass high. "May the earth be always fertile beneath her feet."

Someone called to Don Roméo that more guests were arriving, and with a final delighted pat on the stranger's shoulder, the little man scurried away. As the young fellow smiled after his retreating host, his eyes caught and held another pair of eyes—laughing black eyes set in a young girl's face. The last time he had seen that face it had been white and tense with rage, and the lips clenched tight to prevent an outgushing stream of angry words. That had been in February, and she had worn a white lace shawl over her hair. Now it was May, and a gardenia was a splash of white in the glossy dark braids. The moonlight had mottled his face that February night, and he knew that she did not recognize him. He grinned impudently back at her, and her eyes widened, then slid sideways to one of the chaperones. The fan in her small hand snapped shut. She tapped its parchment tip against her mouth and slipped away to join the dancing couples in the front room. The gestures of a fan translate into a coded language on the frontier. The stranger raised one eyebrow as he 7 8

◆ Build Vocabulary

officious (ə fish′ əs) *adj.*: Overly ready to serve

mottled (mät′ əld) *adj.*: Marked with spots of different shades

Humanities: Art

Fandango (detail), by Theodore Gentilz.

The paintings of the renowned Texas artist Theodore Gentilz (1819–1906) can be seen at the Alamo and Witte museums in San Antonio, Texas. In this painting, the artist captures the drama and color of a Spanish *baile,* or festive dance.

Use these questions for discussion:

1. In addition to the partygoers' costumes, what details in the painting suggest that this celebration takes place in a past era? *Students may cite the candlelight in the room and the old-fashioned dance being performed, in which a man holds a candle in one hand and his partner's hand in the other.*
2. What details in the story suggest that the party that the stranger attends takes place in the not-too-recent past? *Details include the kerosene lamps that light Don Romeo's house; the presence of chaperones; and the importance of traditional social customs, such as walking around the plaza to announce an engagement.*

▶Critical Viewing◀

❸ **Infer** Students may say that based on the partygoers' elaborate, old-fashioned costumes, the painting depicts a time about a hundred years ago.

◆ Literary Focus

❹ **Point of View** Ask students to explain how this passage illustrates the third-person point of view. *Students should observe that Niggli lets us in on the mysterious man's thoughts as he makes his way through the village.*

◆ *Literature and Your Life*

❺ Have students compare the celebration described here to those they have attended or heard about. *Students may describe weddings or other celebrations they have attended that, like the celebration in the story, featured musicians, guests of all ages, and lively, festive atmospheres.*

◆ Reading Strategy

❻ **Predict** Encourage students to make predictions about the reasons the guests might have for turning on the stranger. *Students should note that there is some sort of hostility between the two towns.*

◆ Reading Strategy

❼ **Predict** Ask students whether the information in this passage affects the predictions they made about the reasons for the grudge between the two towns. In what way? *Students should note that they can now revise their predictions—an event in which Sarita was in some way involved had something to do with the hostilities.*

◆ Build Vocabulary

❽ **Suffixes: *-ly*** Point out the suffix *-ly* in *impudently.* Ask students what part of speech this word is and what word it modifies. *It is an adverb; it modifies* grinned. You might also ask which word in the Word Bank is close in meaning to *impudently*. *The word is* audaciously.

Extending Word Study

Connotations Have students distinguish between the following pairs of words: *impudently/audaciously, officious/efficient, nonchalantly/carelessly.* Discuss the connotative power of each of these words.

Comprehension Check ☑

❶ What is the meaning of Sarita's gesture? *She wants the stranger to follow her to the front room, where the dancing is taking place.*

◆ Critical Thinking

❷ **Infer** What inferences can students make about the stranger's personality from the way he behaves toward the old lady and from her reaction to him? *He is a smooth, suave character; he knows how to charm people to get his way.*

◆ Reading Strategy

❸ **Predict** Students should note that the song that the stranger requested is associated with the town of Hidalgo. Predictions may include these: The stranger plans to reveal that he is from Hidalgo; he plans to shock the guests.

Read to Appreciate Author's Craft

Stories about uninvited guests showing up at parties have always been popular. These scenes were a common device in romantic poems and novels of the early 1800's. Students may be familiar with "Lochinvar" by Sir Walter Scott and "The Masque of the Red Death" by Edgar Allen Poe. Ask students to make note of the ways that Josephina Niggli breathes life into this device. *[Students should notice her use of changing perspectives, her colorful descriptions, and her careful attention to local customs and traditions. Others may point out the unusual detail of the remarkable cheese, which may be—and may not be—intended as humorous. Finally, some students may cite the mystery of Pepe Gonzalez's motives for risking his life to attend Sarita Calderon's birthday party. At the end of the story, the reader is left to guess what they are.]*

Tips to Guide Reading

Silent Reading Have students monitor their own prediction-making in this story by encouraging the use of a graphic organizer like the one on p. 439.

interpreted the signal.

❶ But he did not move toward her at once. Instead, he inched slowly back against the table. No one was behind him, and his hands quickly unfastened the package he had been guarding so long. Then he nonchalantly walked into the front room.

The girl was sitting close to a chaperone. As he came up to her he swerved slightly toward the bushy-browed old lady.

"Your servant, señora. I kiss your hands and feet."

The chaperone stared at him in astonishment. Such fine manners were not common to the town of San Juan Iglesias.

"Eh, you're a stranger," she said. "I thought so."

"But a stranger no longer, señora, now that I have met you." He bent over her, so close she ❷ could smell the faint fragrance of talcum on his freshly shaven cheek.

"Will you dance the *parada* with me?"

This request startled her eyes into popping open beneath the heavy brows. "So, my young rooster, would you flirt with me, and I old enough to be your grandmother?"

"Can you show me a prettier woman to flirt with in the Valley of the Three Marys?" he asked audaciously.

She grinned at him and turned toward the girl at her side. "This young fool wants to meet you, my child."

The girl blushed to the roots of her hair and shyly lowered her white lids. The old woman laughed aloud.

"Go out and dance, the two of you. A man clever enough to pat the sheep has a right to play with the lamb."

The next moment they had joined the circle of dancers and Sarita was trying to control her laughter.

"She is the worst dragon in San Juan. And how easily you won her!"

"What is a dragon," he asked imperiously, "when I longed to dance with you?"

"Ay," she retorted, "you have a quick tongue. I think you are a dangerous man."

In answer he drew her closer to him, and turned her toward the orchestra. As he reached the chief violinist he called out, "Play the *Virgencita*, 'The Shy Young Maiden.'"

The violinist's mouth opened in soundless surprise. The girl in his arms said sharply, "You heard him, the *Borachita*, 'The Little Drunken Girl.'"

With a relieved grin, the violinist tapped his music stand with his bow, and the music swung into the sad farewell of a man to his sweetheart:

> *Farewell, my little drunken one,*
> *I must go to the capital*
> *To serve the master*
> *Who makes me weep for my return.*

The stranger frowned down at her. "Is this a joke, señorita?" he asked coldly.

"No," she whispered, looking about her quickly to see if the incident had been observed. "But the *Virgencita* is the favorite song of Hidalgo, a village on the other side of the mountains in the next valley. The people of Hidalgo and San Juan Iglesias do not speak."

◆ **Reading Strategy** Make a prediction about the stranger, based on his actions.

"That is a stupid thing," said the man from Hidalgo as he swung her around in a large turn. "Is not music free as air? Why should one town own the rights to a song?"

The girl shuddered slightly. "Those people from Hidalgo—they are wicked monsters. Can you guess what they did not six months since?"

The man started to point out that the space of time from February to May was three months, but he thought it better not to appear too wise. "Did these Hidalgo monsters frighten you, señorita? If they did, I personally will kill them all."

She moved closer against him and tilted her face until her mouth was close to his ear. "They

Cross-Curricular Connection: Social Studies

Mexican Revolution The history of early twentieth-century Mexico is marked by political turbulence as well as legendary exploits. As noted in the Guide for Reading, Josephina Niggli and her family fled the country shortly after the Mexican Revolution of 1910; years later, as a writer, Niggli would be inspired by the colorful stories she had heard about two famous rebel leaders, Pancho Villa and Emiliano Zapata.

Villa and Zapata were leaders of two of the revolutionary bands that formed across Mexico to bring down the dictatorship of General Porfirio Diaz. In the years that followed, each led one of the many rival factions that opposed the presidents who assumed power in the wake of the Revolution. Zapata, an Indian, demanded more far-reaching land reforms. Villa became the notorious leader of a band of outlaws. Have students research more about Villa, Zapata, and the Mexican Revolution.

attempted to steal the bones of Don Rómolo Balderas."

"Is it possible?" He made his eyes grow round and his lips purse up in disdain. "Surely not that! Why, all the world knows that Don Rómolo Balderas was the greatest historian in the entire Republic. Every school child reads his books. Wise men from Quintana Roo to the Río Bravo bow their heads in admiration to his name. What a wicked thing to do!" He hoped his virtuous tone was not too virtuous for plausibility, but she did not seem to notice.

"It is true! In the night they came. Three devils!"

"Young devils, I hope."

"Young or old, who cares? They were devils. The blacksmith surprised them even as they were opening the grave. He raised such a shout that all of San Juan rushed to his aid, for they were fighting, I can tell you. Especially one of them—their leader."

"And who was he?"

"You have heard of him doubtless. A proper wild one named Pepe Gonzalez."

"And what happened to them?"

"They had horses and got away, but one, I think, was hurt."

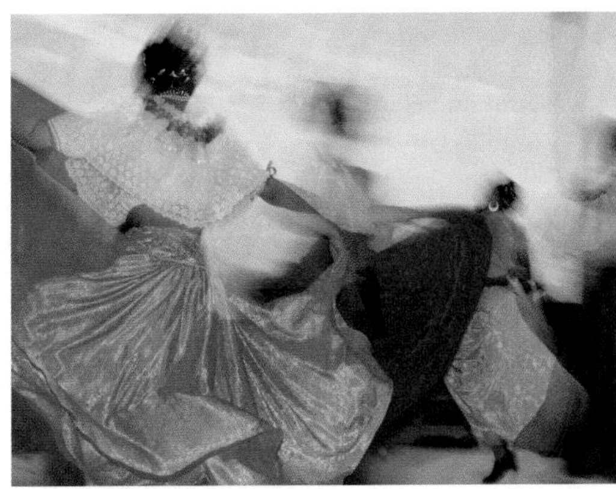

▲ Critical Viewing How do the style and arrangement of figures in this photograph suggest a celebration? [Analyze] 8

The Hidalgo man twisted his mouth remembering how Rubén the candymaker had ridden across the whitewashed line high on the cañon trail that marked the division between the Three Marys' and the Sabinas' sides of the mountains, and then had fallen in a faint from his saddle because his left arm was broken. There was no candy in Hidalgo for six weeks, and the entire Sabinas Valley resented that broken arm as fiercely as did Rubén. 7

◆ **Literary Focus**
What clues do the stranger's memories provide about his identity? 6

The stranger tightened his arm in reflexed anger about Sarita's waist as she said, "All the world knows that the men of Hidalgo are sons of the mountain witches."

"But even devils are shy of disturbing the honored dead," he said gravely.

"'Don Rómolo was born in our village,' Hidalgo says. 'His bones belong to us.' Well, anyone in the valley can tell you he died in San Juan Iglesias, and here his bones will stay! Is that not proper? Is that not right?" 9

To keep from answering, he guided her through an intricate dance pattern that led them past the patio door. Over her head he could see two men and a woman staring with amazement at the open package on the table.

His eyes on the patio, he asked blandly, "You say the leader was one Pepe Gonzalez? The name seems to have a familiar sound."

"But naturally. He has a talent." She tossed her head and stepped away from him as the music stopped. It was a dance of two *paradas*. He

◆ **Build Vocabulary**

nonchalantly (nän´ shə länt´ lē) *adv.*: Casually; indifferently

audaciously (ô dā´ shəs lē) *adv.*: In a bold manner

imperiously (im pir´ ē əs lē) *adv.*: Arrogantly

plausibility (plô´ zə bil´ ə tē) *n.*: Believability

Comprehension Check ☑

4 What is the cause of the conflict between the towns of Hidalgo and San Juan Iglesias? *Men from Hidalgo attempted to steal the remains of a national hero buried in San Juan Iglesias.*

◆ Reading Strategy

5 **Predict** Have students compare their predictions with the information revealed here.

◆ Literary Focus

6 **Point of View** Students may say the stranger's thoughts reveal that he knows a great deal about the notorious act Sarita is about to describe. Perhaps he is one of the "wicked monsters" to whom she refers.

◆ Literary Focus

7 **Point of View** What clues about the stranger's identity can students gather from his thoughts? *Students should point out that his memory of the incident confirms that he was there. They may conclude that there is a strong possibility that he is Pepe Gonzalez—the leader of the three-man raiding party.*

▶Critical Viewing◀

8 **Analyze** *Students may say that the movement captured in the photo vividly conveys both dancing and joy.*

◆ Critical Thinking

9 **Analyze** Ask students to explain what is clever about the stranger's response. *He manages to present the point of view of the people of Hidalgo without giving away his identity; he continues to win Sarita's confidence while planning some sort of surprise.*

Insight From Pat Mora

Pat Mora notes, "As Dr. María Herrera-Sobek states in her introductory essay to *Mexican Village*, Niggli is an interesting example of the complex issues of identity. Her parents were Scandinavian Americans who moved to Mexico. We sometimes forget that the terms *bilingual* and *bicultural* can apply to people living in Mexico from the States or other countries since Mexico also has a diverse population not only of indigenous groups but of Blacks and Jews and Arabs and Chinese. Even members of the same family can define their nationality and culture differently."

Cross-Curricular Connection: Social Studies

Mexican Geography The story's narrator and characters make several references to well-known places in Mexico. These references provide a good opportunity for students to learn more about the country's geography.

Read each of the following passages aloud. Challenge students to use the hints you provide to find each place on a map. (Be sure that the maps have indexes that provide coordinates that students can use to locate states, cities, and towns.)

- "... who could say from which direction he had come? He might be a trader from Monterrey... ." (*Hint:* Monterrey is a large city in northern Mexico.)
- "Ask the people of Chihuahua, of Sonora. Ask the man on the bridge at Laredo, or the man in his boat at Tampico. . . ." (*Hints:* Chihuahua and Tampico are cities; Sonora is a state; *Laredo* refers to *Nuevo Laredo,* a city with a famous bridge that crosses the Rio Bravo.)

◆ Reading Strategy

❶ **Predict** Have students predict what is in the package, which is now open on the table. Ask them to connect the package with the conversation between Sarita and the stranger. *Students should note that the stranger is probably Pepe Gonzalez—the daring and colorful character who led the attempt to recover Don Rómolo's bones. Some students may connect the placement of the package to the "talent for doing the impossible" mentioned in the conversation.*

◆ Critical Thinking

❷ **Speculate** Point out that both Sarita and the stranger know that "to walk around the plaza with a girl means a wedding." Have students speculate on the stranger's motives for asking Sarita to do so with him. *Some students may say that the stranger—Pepe Gonzalez—fell in love with Sarita when he saw her three months ago and has returned to court her in a characteristically bold way. Others may say that he is toying with her affections as part of a plan to get even with the people of San Juan Iglesias.*

◆ Build Grammar Skills

❸ **Commas in a Series** Have students identify the sentence that contains three items in a series. *The sentence contains these three items: Such flavor, such texture, such whiteness.* How are the items punctuated? *They are separated by commas.*

◆ Reading Strategy

❹ **Predict** Students should note that the content of the package has been discovered; the stranger has probably left because he does not want to be identified and caught.

slipped his hand through her arm and guided her into place in the large oval of parading couples. Twice around the room and the orchestra would play again.

"A talent?" he prompted.

❶ "For doing the impossible. When all the world says a thing cannot be done, he does it to prove the world wrong. Why, he climbed to the top of the Prow, and not even the long vanished Joaquín Castillo had ever climbed that mountain before. And this same Pepe caught a mountain lion with nothing to aid him but a rope and his two bare hands."

"He doesn't sound such a bad friend," protested the stranger, slipping his arm around her waist as the music began to play the merry song of the soap bubbles:

Pretty bubbles of a thousand colors
That ride on the wind
And break as swiftly
As a lover's heart.

The events in the patio were claiming his attention. Little by little he edged her closer to the door. The group at the table had considerably enlarged. There was a low murmur of excitement from the crowd.

"What has happened?" asked Sarita, attracted by the noise.

"There seems to be something wrong at the table," he answered, while trying to peer over the heads of the people in front of him. Realizing that this might be the last moment of peace he would have that evening, he bent toward her.

"If I come back on Sunday, will you walk around the plaza with me?"

She was startled into exclaiming, "Ay, no! "

"Please. Just once around."

❷ "And you think I'd walk more than once with you, señor, even if you were no stranger? In San Juan Iglesias, to walk around the plaza with a girl means a wedding."

"Ha, and you think that is common to San Juan alone? Even the devils of Hidalgo respect that law." He added hastily at her puzzled upward glance. "And so they do in all the villages." To cover his lapse he said softly, "I don't even know your name."

A mischievous grin crinkled the corners of her eyes. "Nor do I know yours, señor. Strangers do not often walk the streets of San Juan."

Before he could answer, the chattering in the patio swelled to louder proportions. Don Roméo's voice lay on top, like thick cream on milk. "I tell you it is a jewel of a cheese. Such flavor, such texture, such whiteness. It is a jewel of a cheese."

"What has happened?" Sarita asked of a woman at her elbow.

"A fine goat's cheese appeared as if by magic on the table. No one knows where it came from."

"Probably an extra one from Linares," snorted a fat bald man on the right.

"Linares never made such a cheese as this," said the woman decisively.

"Silence!" roared Don Roméo. "Old Tio[2] Daniel would speak a word to us."

A great hand of silence closed down over the mouths of the people. The girl was standing on tiptoe trying vainly to see what was happening. She was hardly aware of the stranger's whispering voice although she remembered the words that he said. "Sunday night—once around the plaza."

She did not realize that he had moved away, leaving a gap that was quickly filled by the blacksmith.

Old Tío Daniel's voice was a shrill squeak, and his thin, stringy neck jutted forth from his body like a turtle's from its shell. "This is no cheese from Linares," he said with authority, his mouth sucking in over his toothless gums between his sentences. "Years ago, when the great Don Rómolo Balderas was still alive, we had such ❺

> ◆ **Reading Strategy** Predict why the stranger has left.

2. **Tio** (tē´ ō): Spanish for uncle

Speaking, Listening, and Viewing Mini-Lesson

Dialogue

This mini-lesson supports the first Speaking, Listening, and Viewing activity in the Idea Bank on p. 447.

Introduce Remind students that, by the end of the story, Sarita learns that the stranger who had asked her to walk around the plaza was actually the notorious Pepe Gonzalez. The dialogue, or conversation between the two characters, will pick up where the story ends.

Develop Before students prepare their dialogues, have them explore and discuss the following:

- How might knowing Pepe's true identity affect Sarita's feelings and attitude toward him?
- What were Pepe's real intentions regarding Sarita? Had he really fallen in love with her, or was he only trying to live up to his reputation for "doing the impossible" by courting her?

Apply Once students have decided on answers to both of these questions, they can plan to act out what might happen next between Pepe and Sarita.

Assess After each performance, ask: Was the dialogue true to the story? Did it effectively reveal the characters' thoughts and feelings? Students may use the Peer Assessment: Dramatic Performance page in ***Alternative Assessment,*** p. 120, to evaluate the dialogues.

cheese as this—ay, in those days we had it. But after he died and was buried in our own sainted ground, as was right and proper . . ."

"Yes, yes," muttered voices in the crowd. He glared at the interruption. As soon as there was silence again, he continued:

"After he died, we had it no more. Shall I tell you why?"

"Tell us, Tío Daniel," said the voices humbly.

"Because it is made in Hidalgo!"

The sound of a waterfall, the sound of a wind in a narrow cañon, and the sound of an angry crowd are much the same. There were no distinct words, but the sound was enough.

"Are you certain, Tío?" boomed Don Roméo.

"As certain as I am that a donkey has long ears. The people of Hidalgo have been famous for generations for making cheese like this—especially that wicked one, that owner of a cheese factory, Timotéo Gonzalez, father to Pepe, the wild one, whom we have good cause to remember."

"We do, we do," came the sigh of assurance.

"But on the whole northern frontier there are no vats like his to produce so fine a product. Ask the people of Chihuahua, of Sonora. Ask the man on the bridge at Laredo, or the man in his boat at Tampico, '*Hola*, friend, who makes the finest goat cheese?' And the answer will always be the same, 'Don Timotéo of Hidalgo.'"

It was the blacksmith who asked the great question. "Then where did that cheese come from, and we haters of Hidalgo these ten long years?"

No voice said, "The stranger," but with one fluid movement every head in the patio turned toward the girl in the doorway. She also turned, her eyes wide with something that she realized to her own amazement was more apprehension than anger.

But the stranger was not in the room. When the angry, muttering men pushed through to the street, the stranger was not on the plaza. He was not anywhere in sight. A few of the more religious crossed themselves for fear that the Devil had walked in their midst. "Who was he?" one voice asked another. But Sarita, who was meekly listening to a lecture from Don Roméo on the propriety of dancing with strangers, did not have to ask. She had a strong suspicion that she had danced that night within the circling arm of Pepe Gonzalez.

> ◆ **Literary Focus** Why do you think the author reveals the stranger's identity through the thoughts of Sarita? ❼

Guide for Responding

◆ *Literature and Your Life*

Reader's Response Based on this excerpt, would you like to read more of *Mexican Village?* Why or why not?

Thematic Focus In this story, a family celebration expands a young girl's horizons by showing her that people are not always who they seem to be. How can participating in town and family celebrations expand your horizons?

☑ Check Your Comprehension

1. What kind of welcome does Pepe Gonzalez receive?
2. What two things does Pepe set out to do at the party?
3. What outrageous deed had men from Hidalgo attempted in San Juan Iglesias three months previously?
4. What causes an uproar among the guests?

Beyond the Selection

FURTHER READING

Other Works by Josephina Niggli

Mexican Village
Mexican Folk Plays
This is Villa!
A Miracle for Mexico

Other Works About Cultural Heritage

I Dream a World, Brian Lanker
Talking Leaves, Craig Lesley, ed.

We suggest that you preview these works before recommending them to students.

INTERNET

For an essay on teaching Chicano literature that includes a discussion of Niggli's work, go to **http://www.georgetown.edu/tamlit/essays/chicano.html**

For a timeline of Chicano culture and history, go to **http://www.pbs.org.chicano/19211940.html**

Please be aware, however, that sites may have changed from the time we published this information. We *strongly recommend* that you preview the sites before you send students to them.

◆ Reading Strategy

❺ **Predict** Point out that this conversation reveals what was in the package. Have students compare this information with their predictions.

◆ Build Grammar Skills

❻ **Commas in a Series** Have students identify the items in a series in this sentence. *The items are the sounds of a waterfall, a wind in a narrow cañon, and an angry crowd.*

◆ Literary Focus

❼ **Point of View** Responses may include: Sarita's thoughts of the stranger are associated with the memory of their dance together—this leaves readers with a romantic and dashing image of him. Also, Sarita does not know the stranger's motives and intentions—by revealing the stranger's identity through her thoughts, the author can leave these aspects of his character somewhat uncertain and mysterious.

Art Transparency After students have read the story, display Art Transparency16. Discuss the artist's ability to blend reality and illusion. Have students comment on Pepe Gonzalez's use of illusion as he deals with the people of San Juan Iglesias.

Reinforce and Extend

Answers

◆ *Literature and Your Life*

Reader's Response Students should give reasons for their opinion.

Thematic Focus Students may observe that these events provide the opportunity to meet new people and learn about how others live.

☑ Check Your Comprehension

1. He is warmly welcomed as a stranger.
2. He sets out to deliver the cheese and dance with Sarita.
3. They had attempted to dig up the grave of Don Rómolo Balderas and steal his bones.
4. The discovery of the goat cheese from Hidalgo causes the uproar.

Reteach

To reteach this selection, see p.33 in ***Strategies for Diverse Student Needs.***

Answers

◆ Critical Thinking

1. His behavior suggests that he has something to hide.
2. He is bold, humorous, caring, and just.
3. Gonzalez wants to remind the people of San Juan Iglesias of the fine quality of the Hidalgo cheese, to upset the festivities by infiltrating as a spy, and to prove again that he has accomplished the impossible.
4. Gonzalez saw the festivities as an opportunity to prove himself and a challenge to his enemies.
5. The relationship has the potential to heal the rift between the two communities; it also has the potential to bring disaster to them. Students should support their speculations with specific reasons.

◆ Reading Strategy

1. Students may have suspected that he meant to do harm to the festivities.
2. They could predict his identity from the direction he was taking on the Street of the Cañon and from his hiding in the shadows.
3. His charm and pleasure at the festivities suggested that he was not there to harm anyone.

◆ Literary Focus

1. The stranger knows that her viewpoint on the proper location of Don Rómolo's grave differs from his.
2. Sarita is thinking about her feelings for the stranger who she has now learned is her enemy.
3. Niggli may want readers to see that the potential for healing the rift between two warring towns lies in personal relationships.

◆ Build Vocabulary

Anglo-Saxon Suffixes *-ly*

1. generously; 2. timidly;
3. confidently

Using the Word Bank

1. Pepe Gonzalez behaves audaciously.
2. A cheetah's coat is mottled.
3. You would act nonchalantly if you saw someone was embarrassed and didn't want to make them feel worse.
4. Advertisements gain plausibility by including testimonials and statistics that support their claims.
5. Officious people are unpleasant to work with because they behave as if they know everything but they don't.
6. Pepe and perhaps Don Roméo act imperiously in the story.

◆ Build Grammar Skills

1. A table held loaves of bread, stacks of tortillas, and plates of beef.
2. Sarita nodded, smiled, and turned away.
3. The sound of a waterfall, the sound of a wind in a narrow cañon, and the sound of an angry crowd are much the same.

Grammar Reinforcement

For additional instruction and practice, use the lesson in the **Language Lab CD-ROM** on Commas and the pages on commas, pp. 99–101 in the *Writer's Solution Grammar Practice Book*.

Guide for Responding (continued)

◆ Critical Thinking

Interpret

1. What does Pepe Gonzalez's caution in arriving in the village suggest about his motives? **[Draw Conclusions]**
2. Describe Gonzalez's personality. **[Infer]**
3. Give three reasons Pepe Gonzalez might have had for leaving the cheese. **[Infer]**

Evaluate

4. Do you think Pepe Gonzalez was wise to go to Sarita's party when doing so posed such a great danger to him? Explain. **[Make a Judgment]**

Apply

5. What do you think will happen now between Pepe and Sarita and between the two villages? Give your reasons for making those predictions. **[Speculate]**

◆ Reading Strategy

Predict

Review the story and your process of **making predictions.** Evaluate the reasons you made certain predictions and whether you revised them when new information was revealed.

1. What predictions did you make about the stranger when he first arrived?
2. What details helped you predict his identity?
3. What details led you to revise, or at least reconsider, a prediction?

◆ Literary Focus

Point of View

A story told from a **third-person point of view** is told by an outside observer. "The Street of the Cañon" is told in third-person omniscient point of view—the narrator, who is all knowing, allows readers to know the thoughts and feelings of more than one character.

1. What are the stranger's thoughts when Sarita talks about the people of Hidalgo?
2. What is Sarita thinking at the end of the story?
3. Why do you think Niggli wants readers to know the thoughts and feelings of both Sarita and Pepe Gonzalez?

◆ Build Vocabulary

Using the Anglo-Saxon Suffix *-ly*

Add *-ly* to the following words to make them adverbs. Then, on your paper, complete the following sentences with one of the adverbs you created.

confident timid generous

1. She gave __?__, keeping hardly any for herself.
2. The nervous men entered the room __?__.
3. The champ smiled __?__ at his weaker opponent.

Using the Word Bank: Context

In your notebook, write your response to each of the numbered items.

1. Which character from the story behaves audaciously?
2. Name an animal whose coat is mottled.
3. Describe a situation in which you would try to act nonchalantly.
4. What types of details give an advertisement plausibility?
5. Would you want to work with an officious person? Why or why not?
6. Which character or characters from the story behave imperiously?

◆ Build Grammar Skills

Commas in a Series

When you list three or more items in a series, separate them with commas to make your meaning clear. A series may be a series of words, a series of phrases, or a series of clauses.

Practice In your notebook, copy the following sentences. Insert commas to separate each of the items in the series.

1. A table held loaves of bread stacks of tortillas and plates of beef.
2. Sarita nodded smiled and turned away.
3. The sound of a waterfall the sound of a wind in a narrow cañon and the sound of an angry crowd are much the same.

Writing Application In a paragraph or two, describe a celebration you've attended. Include at least two series. Punctuate the series.

Build Your Portfolio

Idea Bank

Writing

1. Postcard Write a postcard home to your family describing your recent visit to San Juan Iglesias. Use sensory details to help your family envision the town.

2. Legend Pepe Gonzalez's feats quickly became legendary among the people of San Juan Iglesias. Write a legend about a person who performed a heroic feat. Base your legend on a news story you read or something impressive done by a friend.

3. Compare and Contrast In an essay, compare and contrast Pepe Gonzalez with another hero you know—real or fictional. Present readers with specific examples of the legends and feats surrounding your hero.

Speaking, Listening, and Viewing

4. Dialogue With a partner, take turns speaking as Sarita and Pepe when they meet in the plaza now that Sarita is aware of Pepe's identity.

5. Debate Break into two teams to debate the question from the story, "Is not music free as air?" Develop your arguments around current issues related to the censorship and rating of music.

Researching and Representing

6. Sketch Choose your favorite scene in the story and illustrate it. In your illustration, try to convey the same sense of mystery that Niggli creates in her writing. **[Art Link]**

7. Photo Essay Collect photographs of Mexico from travel magazines and brochures. Organize your photos around a theme or a message. Arrange the photos and display them.

Online Activity www.phlit.phschool.com

Guided Writing Lesson

Song for a Moment in the Story

Music is an important part of the celebration in this story. Imagine that you are a playwright who wants to turn this story into a musical. Select a moment in the story and write the **lyrics** to a song that will be sung in your musical.

As you plan and write the song lyrics, keep these points in mind:

Writing Skills Focus: Connotation

All writers, whether consciously or unconsciously, select words to convey a certain message or elicit a particular feeling or emotion. A word's **connotation** is the set of associations that the word calls to mind. For example, most people would prefer a "vintage automobile" to a "used car." A word's connotation can be positive, negative, or neutral.

Prewriting Reread the story, keeping an eye out for scenes that would be suitable for a song. For example, you might identify the opening scene or the scene where Sarita and Pepe dance. After you've selected a scene for your song, think about whether you want your scene to be happy, sad, or funny. Then jot down words that elicit the specific connotations that you are trying to convey.

Drafting As you write the lyrics to your song, capture the actions and mood of the moment in the story. Include some of the words you jotted down.

Revising Reread your draft. Make sure you've used words with connotations that will stir in your audience the feelings you desire. If necessary, add details that strengthen the song's connection with the actions and mood of the moment in the story.

✓ ASSESSMENT OPTIONS

Formal Assessment, Selection Test, pp. 113–115, and Assessment Resources Software. The selection test is designed so that it can be easily customized to the performance levels of your students.

Alternative Assessment, p. 33, includes options for less advanced students, more advanced students, bodily/kinesthetic learners, musical/rhythmic learners, verbal/linguistic learners, logical/mathematical learners and interpersonal learners.

PORTFOLIO ASSESSMENT
Use the following rubrics in the ***Alternative Assessment*** booklet to assess student writing:
Postcard: Expression Rubric, p. 94
Legend: Fictional Narrative Rubric, p. 95
Compare and Contrast: Comparison/Contrast Rubric, p. 103
Guided Writing Lesson: Poetry Rubric, p. 108

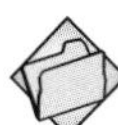

Idea Bank

Following are suggestions for matching Idea Bank topics with your students' performance levels and learning modalities:

Customizing for
Performance Levels
Less Advanced Students: 1, 4, 7
Average Students: 2, 4, 6
More Advanced Students: 3, 5

Customizing for
Learning Modalities
Visual/Spatial: 6, 7
Verbal/Linguistic: 1, 2, 3, 4, 5
Logical/Mathematical: 5

Guided Writing Lesson

Revising Strategy Help students use strong verbs in their poetry. Have them reenter their writing, circling all "to be" verbs with a colored pen or pencil. When students have located all the "to be" verbs, they should determine the best places to use or omit them and replace them with strong, active verbs.

I (am) dancing,
I (am) whirling
I see you across the room.

For more prewriting, elaboration, and revision strategies, see *Prentice Hall Writing and Grammar.*

Writing and Language Transparencies Have students use the Analysis Map, p. 72, to analyze the connotations of words to use in their song.

Writers at Work Videodisc
Have students view the videodisc segment (Ch. 6) featuring Naomi Shihab Nye to see how she finds ideas for creative writing.

Play frames 13046 to 14935

Writing Lab CD-ROM
Have students complete the tutorial on Creative Writing. Follow these steps:

1. Students can use the Poetry Topic Wheel to find words and images.
2. Have students use the Audio-annotated Writing Models for poetry.
3. Students can draft on computer.

Prepare and Engage

LESSON OBJECTIVES

1. To develop vocabulary and word identification skills
- Borrowed Words: Latin Terms
- Using the Word Bank: Context
- Extending Word Study: Word Forms

2. To use a variety of reading strategies to comprehend a personal narrative
- Connect Your Experience
- Reading Strategy: Engage Your Senses
- Tips to Guide Reading
- Read to Be Entertained

3. To increase knowledge of other cultures and to connect common elements across cultures
- Connecting Themes Across Cultures (ATE)

4. To express and support responses to the text
- Critical Thinking
- Idea Bank: Film Treatment
- Analyze Literary Criticism

5. To analyze literary elements
- Literary Focus: Speaker

6. To read in order to research self-selected and assigned topics
- Idea Bank: Presentation of Ancient Instrument
- Idea Bank: Multimedia Project
- Research Skills Mini-lesson

7. To plan, prepare, organize, and present literary interpretations
- Idea Bank: Interview
- Speaking, Listening and Viewing Mini-Lesson

8. To use recursive writing processes to write a monologue
- Guided Writing Lesson

9. To increase knowledge of the rules of grammar and usage
- Build Grammar Skills: Correct Use of *Like* and *As*

Test Preparation

Reading Comprehension: Evaluate and Make Judgments (ATE, p. 449) The teaching tips and sample test item in this workshop support the instruction and practice in the unit workshop:

Reading Comprehension: Interpret Graphic Aids; Evaluate and Make Judgments (SE, p. 465)

Guide for Reading

Alexander Solzhenitsyn *(1918–)*

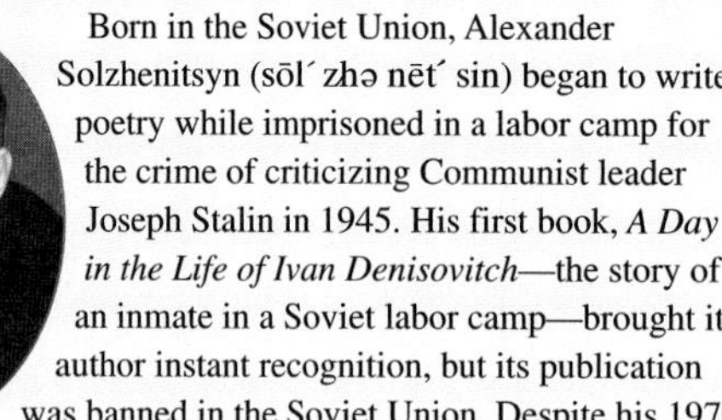

Born in the Soviet Union, Alexander Solzhenitsyn (sōl′ zhə nēt′ sin) began to write poetry while imprisoned in a labor camp for the crime of criticizing Communist leader Joseph Stalin in 1945. His first book, *A Day in the Life of Ivan Denisovitch*—the story of an inmate in a Soviet labor camp—brought its author instant recognition, but its publication was banned in the Soviet Union. Despite his 1970 Nobel Prize for Literature, Solzhenitsyn was tried for treason and exiled after the publication in Paris of parts of *The Gulag Archipelago*. Only since 1991 has his work been available to the people of his homeland.

Henrik Ibsen *(1828–1906)*

It all started with poetry for Henrik Ibsen. Isolated on a small farm near the port town of Skien, Norway, young Henrik turned for solace to writing poetry. His first successful play, *Brand*, was in fact originally written as a narrative poem. It was his plays, however, that made him famous. His emphasis on character rather than the predictable plots that were popular at the time resulted in realistic plays such as *A Doll's House* and *Hedda Gabler*.

Denise Levertov *(1923–1998)*

When Denise Levertov moved to the United States from England in 1948, she became associated with the Black Mountain School, an experimental community of writers, painters, musicians, and dancers that thrived from 1933 to 1956. The Black Mountain poets, Levertov among them, began to change the rigid view of how a poem should read and look. Levertov published a great many volumes of poetry, including *Relearning the Alphabet,* the 1966 collection in which "A Tree Telling of Orpheus" first appeared.

◆ Build Vocabulary

BORROWED WORDS: LATIN TERMS

When Alexander Solzhenitsyn describes the terror of being caught in a violent thunderstorm while in the mountains, he mentions that, for only a second, he and his companions felt as if they were on *terra firma*. *Terra firma* (which means "solid earth") is one of many Latin phrases that have found their way unchanged into modern English.

WORD BANK

Before you read, preview this list of words from the selections.

terra firma
sultry
asunder

◆ Build Grammar Skills

CORRECT USE OF *LIKE* AND *AS*

A common usage error is to use *like* when we mean *as*.

Like, a preposition meaning "similar to" introduces a prepositional phrase—a preposition and a noun or pronoun.

> *Like* the arrows of Sabaoth, the lightning flashes . . .

As, a subordinating conjunction, introduces a subordinate clause—a group of words that contains a subject and a verb but that cannot stand alone as a sentence.

> . . . we forgot to be afraid of the lightning, the thunder, and the downpour, just *as* [not *like*] a droplet in the ocean has no fear of a hurricane.

Prentice Hall Literature Program Resources

REINFORCE / RETEACH / EXTEND

Selection Support Pages
Build Vocabulary: Latin Terms, p. 138
Build Grammar Skills: *Like* and *As,* p. 139
Reading Strategy: Engage the Senses, p. 140
Literary Focus: Speaker, p. 141

Strategies for Diverse Student Needs, p. 34

Beyond Literature
Career Connection: Meteorology, p. 34

Formal Assessment Selection Test, pp. 116–118; Assessment Resources Software

Alternative Assessment, p. 34

Writing and Language Transparencies
Writing Process Model 1, Reflective Essay, pp. 5–11

Resource Pro CD-ROM

Listening to Literature Audiocassettes

A Storm in the Mountains ◆ In the Orchard ◆ A Tree Telling of Orpheus ◆

◆ Literature and Your Life

Connect Your Experience

You dim the lights, put on your headphones, and pop in your favorite CD. That's it—you're taken to a place all its own, beyond the pressures of the daily world, a place that seems to be music itself.

The selections in this group show the transforming powers of nature and music. Connect with the sensations described and imagine what it feels like to be in the place the poet is writing about.

Thematic Focus: A Larger World

As you explore the beauties and the power of nature through these selections, you will expand your view of the natural world.

Journal Writing Write three sentences describing the last time you paused to examine something in nature. What was it, and how did it make you feel?

◆ Background for Understanding

Literature

"A Tree Telling of Orpheus" is Denise Levertov's interpretation of the classic Orpheus myth. Orpheus' skill on the lyre (an ancient stringed instrument) was so great and his voice was so beautiful that trees were said to uproot themselves and follow him, rivers stopped flowing to listen to him, and wild beasts were made gentle by his music. In her *Mythology,* Edith Hamilton quotes one of the great Roman writers:

> In the deep still woods upon the Thracian mountains
> Orpheus with his singing lyre led the trees,
> Led the wild beasts of the wilderness.

◆ Literary Focus

Speaker

Each of these selections has a **speaker,** the imaginary voice assumed by the writer of a work. The speaker is the character—the poet, person, animal, or object—who says the work.

These selections present a range of speakers, each with a distinct personality. To enrich your understanding of what is being said, consider who might be speaking in each of these works and what you can tell about each speaker.

◆ Reading Strategy

Engage the Senses

To fully appreciate poems with sensory images, you need to **engage your senses** as you read. This means allowing the poem to speak not just to your mind, but to your eyes, ears, and senses of touch, taste, and smell. For example, when the speaker of "In the Orchard" says "Brothers! there is better music / In the singing of the birds," he is counting on your sense of hearing (and your memory) to re-create the sound of that singing so you can experience and be moved by the image.

To help you engage your senses as you read, construct a chart, like the one below, of the five senses. Fill in as many sensory details as you can.

	"Storm"	"Orchard"	"Tree"
Sight			
Sound			
Smell			
Taste			
Touch			

Test Preparation Workshop

Reading Comprehension: Evaluate and Make Judgments

Standardized tests require students to make judgments based on the evidence provided in a text. Use this sample test item to demonstrate how to practice the skill.

> As for us, we forgot to be afraid of the lightning, the thunder, and the downpour, just as a droplet in the ocean has no fear of a hurricane. Insignificant yet grateful, we became part of this world—a primal world in creation before our eyes.

Using the passage, fill in the blank in the sentence with the most appropriate word.

The evidence in this passage suggests that the speaker is—

A terrified
B exhausted
C awestruck
D careless

Help students to see that *C* is true and that *A, B,* and *D* cannot be supported by the passage.

Read aloud the following passage from Alexander Solzhenitsyn's "A Storm in the Mountains": "It caught us one pitch-black night at the foot of the pass. We crawled out of our tents and ran for shelter as it came towards us over the ridge." Ask students to conjecture about what "It" might be. List students' responses on the chalkboard. Tell them that the passage describes a storm in the mountains. Then have students brainstorm to make a list of comparisons they might use for different kinds of weather. *Responses may include a lamb, a dervish, a windbag, and so on.* Tell them that each of the selections they will read views nature as an entity with a life and voice of its own.

Connecting Themes Across Cultures

Denise Levertov's "A Tree Telling of Orpheus" is one of many retellings or interpretations of this timeless myth. Most of the myths about arts in the Western tradition originated in Greece. Have students identify myths from other traditions that explain the origins of the arts.

Customize for *Gifted/Talented Students*

The writers in the section have all used literature to explore social issues: political oppression (Solzhenitsyn), equality for women (Ibsen), and world peace (Levertov). Have these students compile an anthology of poetry and other writings that explore social issues or current events that have particular meaning for them.

Customize for *English Language Learners*

Use context clues and pictures to help these students determine the meaning of unfamiliar vocabulary such as *serpentine, primal, warblers, fruitage, sapling,* and *felled.*

Customize for *Visual/Spatial Learners*

Encourage visual/spatial learners to picture the landscapes suggested by the descriptive language in one of the works in this selection and draw or collect photographs that illustrate them. They may use details they list in the sensory details chart on p. 449.

Develop Understanding

One-Minute Insight The selections in this group explore different aspects of nature. In "A Storm in the Mountains," Solzhenitsyn describes a raging storm so overwhelming that individuals surrender to it, transcending their fear to feel at one with the powerful phenomenon—and with all of nature.

◆ Literary Focus

1 Speaker Ask students what information is revealed about the speaker in this first paragraph. *Readers can tell that the speaker is camping outdoors in a tent, and that he or she is not alone, since the plural pronouns* we, us, *and* our *are used.*

◆ Critical Thinking

2 Interpret Have students rephrase this sentence to express, in their own words, what the speaker sees. If they are not sure, have them read the next paragraph before answering. *The speaker is seeing tall trees and mountain peaks illuminated only for a split second when a bolt of lightning flashes.*

◆ Reading Strategy

3 Engage the Senses Ask students which senses they engage in reading this passage. *The thunder engages the sense of hearing; the lightning flashes engage the sense of sight.*

◆ Build Grammar Skills

4 Correct Use of *Like* and *As* Ask students why *like* is used here rather than *as*. *"Like a living thing" is a prepositional phrase, not a subordinate clause with a subject and verb.*

◆ Build Grammar Skills

5 Correct Use of *Like* and *As* Have students identify the subordinate clause in this passage. Ask them to find the subordinating conjunction. Then ask why *as* is used here instead of *like*. *The subordinate clause is "just as a droplet in the ocean has no fear of a hurricane." The subordinating conjunction is as.*

Connecting to Real World Texts
To connect this selection to a science text, see "Lightning and Thunder" on p. 959 of this book.

A Storm in the Mountains

Alexander Solzhenitsyn
Translated by Michael Glenny

1 It caught us one pitch-black night at the foot of the pass. We crawled out of our tents and ran for shelter as it came towards us over the ridge.

Everything was black—no peaks, no valleys, no horizon to be seen, only the searing flashes of lightning separating darkness from light, and the gigantic peaks of Belaya-Kaya and Djuguturlyuchat[1] looming up out of the night. 2 The huge black pine trees around us seemed as high as the mountains themselves. For a split second we felt ourselves on terra firma; then once more everything would be plunged into darkness and chaos.

The lightning moved on, brilliant light alternating with pitch blackness, flashing white, then pink, then violet, the mountains and pines always springing back in the same place, their hugeness filling us with awe; yet when they disappeared we could not believe that they had ever existed.

3 The voice of the thunder filled the gorge, drowning the ceaseless roar of the rivers. Like the arrows of Sabaoth,[2] the lightning flashes rained down on the peaks, then split up into 4 serpentine streams as though bursting into spray against the rock face, or striking and then shattering like a living thing.

As for us, we forgot to be afraid of the lightning, 5 the thunder, and the downpour, just as a droplet in the ocean has no fear of a hurricane. Insignificant yet grateful, we became part of this world—a primal world in creation before our eyes.

1. **Belaya-Kaya** (bye lī´ə kī´ə) **and Djuguturlyuchat** (djo͞o go͞o to͝or lyo͞o´ chət): Russian mountains.
2. **Sabaoth** (sab´ ā äth´): Biblical word for "armies."

◆ Build Vocabulary

terra firma (ter´ ə fur´ mə): Latin for "solid earth."

Block Scheduling Strategies

Consider these suggestions to take advantage of extended class time:

- Have students listen to the audiocassette "A Storm in the Mountains," focusing on how the tension builds throughout and then releases in the last paragraph.
- To have students engage their senses as they read, refer them to the Reading Strategy explained on p. 449. Have them complete a sensory image chart like the one on p. 449.
- Have students work in groups to answer the Reading Strategy questions on p. 458.
- Introduce the concept of speaker. As students read, have them consider who the speaker is in each selection. You may follow up with the Literary Focus: Speaker page in ***Selection Support,*** p. 141.
- Have students complete the Guided Writing Lesson on p. 459. Before they get started, have a class discussion about the authors' use of sensory details. Suggest students use sensory details in their monologues.

In the Orchard

Henrik Ibsen

Translated by Sir Edmund Gosse

In the sunny orchard closes,[1]
 While the warblers sing and swing,
(6) Care not whether blustering Autumn
 Break the promises of Spring!
Rose and white, the apple blossom
 Hides you from the sultry sky—
(7) Let it flutter, blown and scatter'd,
 On the meadows by-and-by!

Will you ask about the fruitage
 In the season of the flowers?
Will you murmur, will you question,
 Count the run of weary hours?
(8) Will you let the scarecrow clapping
 Drown all happy sounds and words?
Brothers! there is better music
 In the singing of the birds.

From your heavy-laden garden
 Will you hunt the mellow thrush;
(9) He will play you for protection
 With his crown-song's liquid rush.
O but you will win the bargain,
 Though your fruit be spare and late,
For remember Time is flying (10)
 And will shut the garden gate.

With my living, with my singing,
 I will tear the hedges down.
Sweep the grass and heap the blossom!
 Let it shrivel, pale and brown!
Swing the wicket![2] Sheep and cattle,
 Let them graze among the best!
I broke off the flowers; what matter
 Who may revel with the rest?

1. **closes:** Enclosed place, as a farmyard.
2. **wicket:** Small door or gate.

◆ Build Vocabulary

sultry (sul′ trē) *adj.*: Oppressively hot and moist; sweltering

▲ **Critical Viewing** Explain how the photograph on this page suggests the speaker's sense of celebration. **[Connect]** (11)

One-Minute Insight Ibsen uses the seasons spring and autumn as symbols of youth and old age—and ultimately, death. His poem urges readers to enjoy the budding blossoms of spring without thinking about the withered leaves of fall.

◆ Literary Focus

(6) Speaker Point out to students that the first stanza of the poem is an imperative sentence. What is the speaker telling readers not to do? What does this tell about the speaker? *The speaker is telling readers not to let thoughts of autumn ruin their enjoyment of spring; in other words, not to let worrying about the future spoil enjoyment of the present. The speaker is someone who feels qualified to give advice about life—perhaps an older person or a philosopher.*

◆ Reading Strategy

(7) Engage the Senses Have students identify the sense engaged by these lines. *These lines engage the sense of sight.*

◆ Critical Thinking

(8) Interpret Ask students to identify in this passage symbols of spring and symbols of autumn or late summer. *Symbols of spring are "flowers" and "singing of the birds"; symbols of autumn/late summer are "fruitage" and "scarecrow."*

◆ Reading Strategy

(9) Engage the Senses Ask students to identify the lines in this stanza that engage the sense of hearing. *"He will play you for protection/With his crown-song's liquid rush."*

◆ Critical Thinking

(10) Interpret Ask students: What does the garden represent? What happens when the gate is shut? *The garden represents life, youth, happiness; death shuts the gate when life has ended.*

▶Critical Viewing◀

(11) Connect *The lavish profusion of daffodils and apple blossoms suggests the speaker's message to celebrate life in its fullness.*

Speaking, Listening, and Viewing Mini-Lesson

Interview

This mini-lesson supports the second Speaking, Listening, and Viewing activity in the Idea Bank on p. 459.

Introduce Establish that a good interviewer avoids questions that can be answered by "yes" or "no." The best questions begin with "Who," "What," "Where," "When," "Why," and "How."

Develop Students can re-read "A Storm in the Mountains," putting themselves in the speaker's place. As they plan the questions and answers, suggest they consider questions like the following:

Who was there when the storm broke out? What did they do? What did they see? How did they feel?

Apply Have partners work together to create questions and answers and then stage the interview for the class.

Assess Have students use p. 118 in ***Alternative Assessment,*** Peer Assessment: Speaker/Speech.

Denise Levertov uses the point of view of a tree to describe the stirrings of the emotions created by the music of nature. Through a metaphor based on ancient mythology she presents an enchanted view of nature.

◆ Literary Focus

1 Speaker Have students read this passage and identify the speaker of the poem. *The speaker is a tree, as indicated by the words, "the leaves of my brothers remained outstretched. . . ."*

◆ Reading Strategy

2 Engage the Senses Ask students: Which of your senses is engaged by these lines? Which words appeal to this sense? *The words and phrases "tingle," "fire," and "drying and curling" appeal to the sense of touch.*

◆ Build Grammar Skills

3 Correct Use of *Like* and *As* Point out the two uses of the word *like* in this passage and ask students to explain its function. *"Like the beaked face of a bird" and "like a flower's" are prepositional phrases. Like correctly functions as a preposition in these situations.*

4 Clarification Point out that the tree sees Orpheus with his lyre. Explain that in Greek mythology, Orpheus was the son of Oeagrus, the king of Thrace, and Calliope, the muse of epic poetry. Apollo, the god of the sun and also the god of music, gave Orpheus a lyre, and the music he played on it could enchant wild beasts and make trees and rocks dance.

◆ Critical Thinking

5 Analyze Ask students: What is the speaker describing? Why do you think Levertov chose to describe it in this way? What is the ripple? *The words, "From this,/when he touched it, and from his voice/. . . came the ripple" let the reader know the speaker is describing a stringed musical instrument (a lyre). "Some cut branch" and "strands of a vine" refer to the frame and strings of the instrument. Levertov is describing the instrument as it might be seen from the point of view of a tree. The "ripple" is music.*

A Tree Telling of Orpheus

Denise Levertov

White dawn. Stillness.   When the rippling began
    I took it for sea-wind, coming to our valley with rumors
1   of salt, of treeless horizons. But the white fog
didn't stir; the leaves of my brothers remained outstretched,
unmoving.
        Yet the rippling drew nearer—and then
2 my own outermost branches began to tingle, almost as if
fire had been lit below them, too close, and their twig-tips
were drying and curling.
                Yet I was not afraid, only
                deeply alert.

I was the first to see him, for I grew
        out on the pasture slope, beyond the forest.
He was a man, it seemed: the two
moving stems, the short trunk, the two
arm-branches, flexible, each with five leafless
                        twigs at their ends,
and the head that's crowned by brown or gold grass,
3 bearing a face not like the beaked face of a bird,
        more like a flower's.
                He carried a burden made of
some cut branch bent while it was green,
4 strands of a vine tight-stretched across it. From this,
5 when he touched it, and from his voice
which unlike the wind's voice had no need of our
leaves and branches to complete its sound,
                        came the ripple,
But it was now no longer a ripple (he had come near and
stopped in my first shadow) it was a wave that bathed me
            as if rain
                rose from below and around me
            instead of falling.
And what I felt was no longer a dry tingling:

▲ **Critical Viewing** 6 What details in this photo indicate the dance described in the poem? **[Analyze]**

Cultural Connection

Greek Mythology Tell students the story of Orpheus.

After the death of his young wife Eurydice, Orpheus did what no other mortal had ever done—he descended to the underworld and, by charming Hades, the lord of the dead, with his enchanting music, convinced him to allow Eurydice to return to the world of the living. Orpheus was permitted to lead Eurydice out of the underworld, but was not to look back at her. Because he was so eager to make sure Eurydice was behind him, he looked back a moment too soon, and she was lost forever.

Grief stricken, Orpheus wandered through the wild country of Thrace, always playing his lyre, the rocks and trees his only companions. When a band of Maenads (followers of Dionysus, god of wine in Greek mythology) became frenzied by his music, they killed Orpheus and flung his head into a river. The Muses buried Orpheus' body at the foot of Mount Olympus, but his head and his lyre were carried across the sea.

A Tree Telling of Orpheus ◆ 453

▶Critical Viewing◀

6 Analyze Students may point out features of the tree that reflect movement, such as the sinewy look of the trunk and the graceful, arm-like lines of the branches.

Customize for
Less Proficient Readers
Have these students make a list of words that describe the tree's feelings as they are revealed in the poem. They may then organize these words in a flow chart to indicate the changes as they evolve in the poem.

Customize for
Visual/Spatial Learners
These students may benefit from creating a story board for the poem, chronicling the scenes in the tree's "story."

Humanities

Photography:
Photographs of trees illustrate this poem. Students can identify details of the photographs that evoke the shape or movement of a dancing human body. For example, the photograph on this page can help them picture the trees in motion.

Use the following question for discussion: What features of these trees in the photograph give them the appearance of movement and life? *Students can describe the curve of the branches, the interplay of light and shadow, and the contrasting textures.*

Research Skills Mini-Lesson

Writing Source Cards

Introduce Explain to students that source cards are usually three-by-five-inch index cards used to record the identifying information from books, pamphlets, articles, and other sources. For extensive research, source cards are the most convenient way to record this information. Tell students that the cards enable them to relocate sources more easily when they need to review information. Second, they provide all the necessary information to prepare a list of resources later.

Develop Distribute a variety of books, magazines, videos, and encyclopedia volumes to the students. Explain that different sources are recorded in different ways. For example, source cards for books are not filled out like those for films. Use a reference or writing text to provide different examples.

Apply Distribute index cards. Have each student prepare one source card. They can share sources if necessary. Make sure that they work in pencil so that they can make changes, if necessary. You may extend this lesson by having each student prepare cards for several different types of sources.

Assess Evaluate the source cards by making sure that students have recorded all the requisite information according to the forms you have provided.

◆ Build Grammar Skills

❶ Correct Use of *Like* and *As* Have students identify the subordinate clause introduced by the conjunction *as*. *The clause is "as he sang."*

◆ Reading Strategy

❷ Engage the Senses Ask students: How does the poet blend two senses in these lines? *Levertov blends the sense of touch with the sense of hearing by mentioning the tree's bark (skin) and music in the same stanza.*

Customize for *Gifted/Talented Students*

Levertov offers a detailed description of Orpheus. Have these students prepare a list of details on which they would rely if they were to create a painting of Orpheus. You might also ask students to add details Levertov omitted, basing their responses on the mood and tone of the poem.

Customize for *Pre-AP Students*

The form of Levertov's poem varies from section to section, but some of the sections have recognizable meter and form. Have these students analyze the poems for patterns of meter and form and then relate them to meaning.

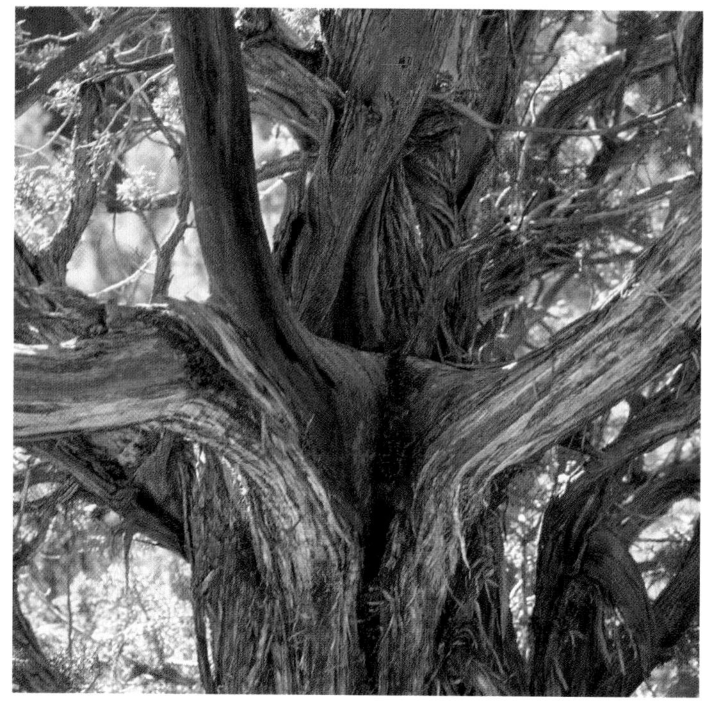

❶ I seemed to be singing as he sang, I seemed to know
what the lark knows; all my sap
was mounting towards the sun that by now
had risen, the mist was rising, the grass
was drying, yet my roots felt music moisten them
deep under earth.

He came still closer, leaned on my trunk:
❷ the bark thrilled like a leaf still-folded.
Music! There was no twig of me not
trembling with joy and fear.

Then as he sang
it was no longer sounds only that made the music:
he spoke, and as no tree listens I listened, and language
came into my roots
out of the earth,
into my bark
out of the air,
into the pores of my greenest shoots
gently as dew
and there was no word he sang but I knew its meaning.

Analyze Literary Criticism

Denise Levertov was part of a group of writers and poets affiliated with the experimental Black Mountain College in North Carolina. Levertov became associated with the group in 1948. These poets developed a poetic form known as projective verse that was supposed to bring back the oral aspects of poetry to modern poetry writing. The leader of the group, Charles Olson, promoted a verse form that depended on the individual poet's breath rhythm to determine the poem's form. According to Olson, the emphasis should be placed on the syllable and not prescribed verse forms. This produced poems with varied spaces and unusual groupings of type on the page.

"A Tree Telling of Orpheus" may have been written during Levertov's involvement with the Black Mountain poets, when she was under the influence of Charles Olson. Have students read the poem and write answers to the following questions in their journals.

1. What evidence can you find to support the idea that Levertov was placing emphasis on the syllable and not on prescribed verse forms? *Students should note that there is no set meter or rhyme.*
2. Does the form of the poem seem natural or artificial to you? *Students should support their responses.*

He told of journeys,
of where sun and moon go while we stand in dark,
of an earth-journey he dreamed he would take some day ❸
deeper than roots . . .
He told of the dreams of man, wars, passions, griefs,
and I, a tree, understood words—ah, it seemed
my thick bark would split like a sapling's that
grew too fast in the spring ❹
when a late frost wounds it.

Fire he sang,
that trees fear, and I, a tree, rejoiced in its flames.
New buds broke forth from me though it was full summer. ❺
As though his lyre[1] (now I knew its name)
were both frost and fire, its chords flamed
up to the crown of me.
I was seed again.
I was fern in the swamp.
I was coal.

And at the heart of my wood
(so close I was to becoming man or a god)
there was a kind of silence, a kind of sickness,
something akin to what men call boredom,
something ❻
(the poem descended a scale, a stream over stones)
that gives to a candle a coldness
in the midst of its burning, he said.

It was then,
when in the blaze of his power that
reached me and changed me
I thought I should fall my length,
that the singer began
to leave me. Slowly
moved from my noon shadow
to open light,
words leaping and dancing over his shoulders
back to me
rivery sweep of lyre-tones becoming
slowly again
ripple.
And I
in terror ↓

1. **lyre** (lir) *n.*: Small stringed instrument of the harp family, used by the ancient Greeks to accompany singers.

❸ **Clarification** Explain that these lines refer to Orpheus' journey to the underworld to rescue his wife Eurydice.

◆ Build Grammar Skills

❹ **Correct Use of *Like* and *As*** Have students explain why *like* is used here. *"Like a sapling's" is a prepositional phrase; like is a preposition.*

◆ Reading Strategy

❺ **Engage the Senses** Ask students how these lines blend the senses of hearing and touch. *The words "Fire he sang" blends the heat of fire with the music of a song; "its chords flamed/up to the crown of me" blends the music of chords with the heat of a flame.*

Customize for *Musical/Rhythmic Learners*

❻ Point out the lines that refer to a descending scale. Have these students explain the effect of this image in describing the "kind of sickness" called boredom. *Students may observe that descending musical scales create a negative effect, while rising scales create a lively, upbeat effect.*

Tips to Guide Reading

Silent Reading Encourage students to read silently, using sticky notes or bookmarks. Students can note tricky spots in the text or questions that the text provokes. After all students have done this exercise, have students work in pairs or small groups to discuss their interpretations, reactions, or questions.

Cultural Connection

Music History When students think of music, they may focus on their favorite CDs or Top 40 radio station without considering how powerful a force music can be. Music plays a central role in cultures worldwide and may be used to educate and inspire as well as to entertain.

For example, music was seen as a powerful tool during the French revolution. Agents of the new regime traveled through the countryside, teaching schoolchildren short, patriotic tunes that were easy to sing. When huge groups gathered in the streets for political rallies, there was no public address system; the politicians relied on the singing of the children to spread the word and tap emotions to sway the population.

Hymns, chants, folk songs, work songs, lullabies, and nursery rhymes have all been used to pass along information, share ideas, teach morals, define political ideology, and forge cultural ties.

Invite students to explore the power of music in "A Tree Telling of Orpheus" and the role it has played in their own lives. Have them consider these questions: What songs do they all know? What songs explore the history they share? How do these songs shape the way they see the world?

Comprehension Check ☑

❶ Ask what the speaker is moved to do, inspired by Orpheus' music. *The tree uproots itself to follow Orpheus and is joined by the other trees of the forest.*

◆ Reading Strategy

❷ **Engage the Senses** Point out how, once again, Levertov blends the senses of touch and hearing. Ask students: Which parts of this passage engage the sense of touch? Which engage the sense of hearing? *References to pain, to wrenching, tearing, and pulling engage the sense of touch. "But the music! The music reached us" engages the sense of hearing.*

◆ Literature and Your Life

❸ Ask students to connect their own lives to the poem by thinking of music that makes them feel like dancing, or at least tapping a foot and moving to the rhythm.

◆ Literary Focus

❹ **Speaker** Ask students to estimate how old the speaker of the poem is. How can they tell from this passage? *Orpheus led the trees to a grassy knoll. When he left them there, they took root, creating what is now an "ancient grove," implying that the tree is now very old, or ancient.*

Extending Word Study

Word Forms Call students' attention to the word *wept,* which is the past tense and past participle of *weep*. Have students look in the dictionary to find these forms of the verbs *leap, kneel, deal, sleep,* and *creep*. How do they vary? *Word forms are* leapt, knelt, dealt, slept, *and* crept. *Students should note that in these irregular verbs there is no unifying pattern. Some keep a double vowel; others do not.*

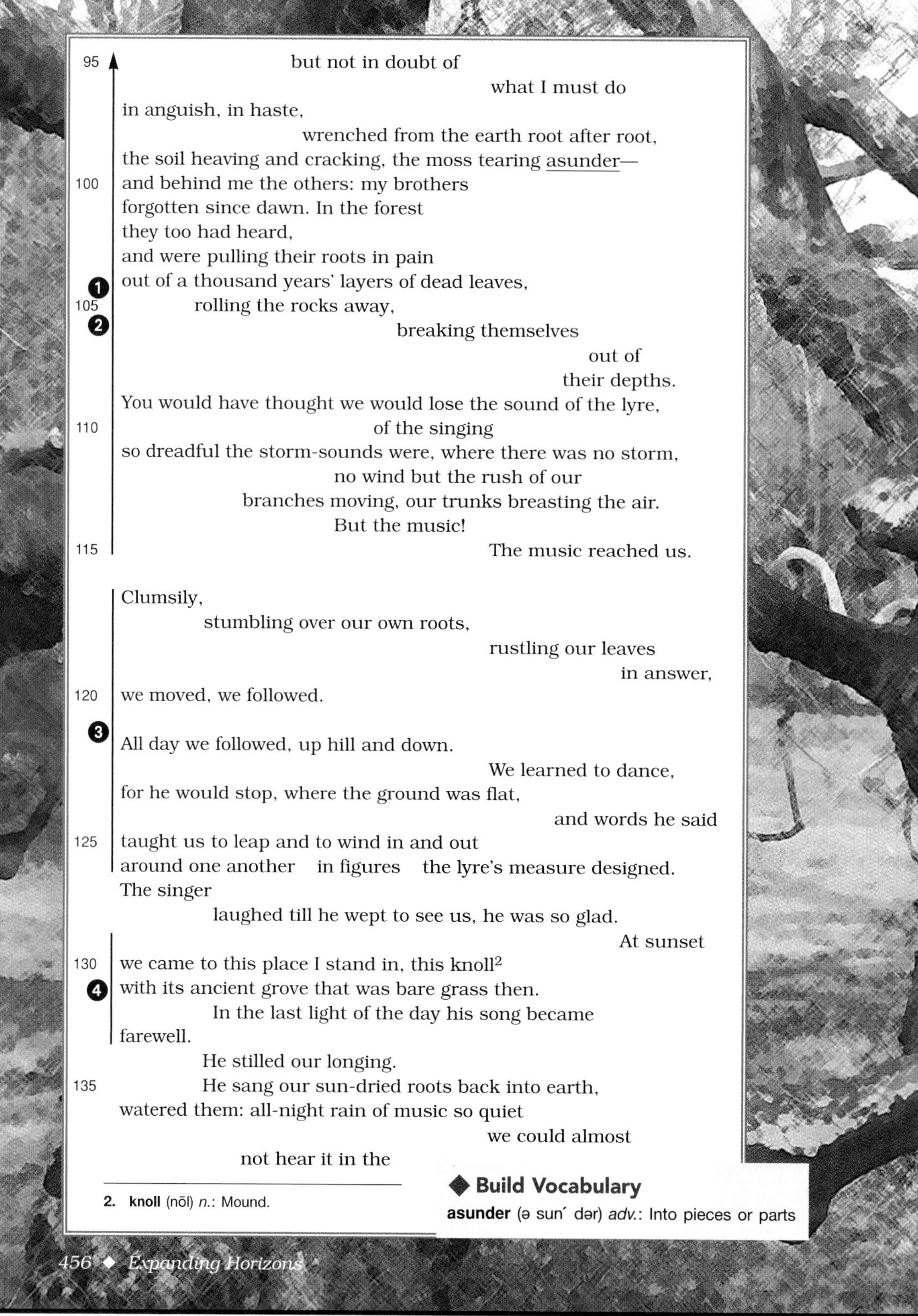

but not in doubt of
what I must do
in anguish, in haste,
wrenched from the earth root after root,
the soil heaving and cracking, the moss tearing asunder—
and behind me the others: my brothers
forgotten since dawn. In the forest
they too had heard,
and were pulling their roots in pain
out of a thousand years' layers of dead leaves,
rolling the rocks away,
breaking themselves
out of
their depths.
You would have thought we would lose the sound of the lyre,
of the singing
so dreadful the storm-sounds were, where there was no storm,
no wind but the rush of our
branches moving, our trunks breasting the air.
But the music!
The music reached us.

Clumsily,
stumbling over our own roots,
rustling our leaves
in answer,
we moved, we followed.

All day we followed, up hill and down.
We learned to dance,
for he would stop, where the ground was flat,
and words he said
taught us to leap and to wind in and out
around one another in figures the lyre's measure designed.
The singer
laughed till he wept to see us, he was so glad.
At sunset
we came to this place I stand in, this knoll[2]
with its ancient grove that was bare grass then.
In the last light of the day his song became
farewell.
He stilled our longing.
He sang our sun-dried roots back into earth,
watered them: all-night rain of music so quiet
we could almost
not hear it in the

2. **knoll** (nōl) *n.*: Mound.

◆ Build Vocabulary

asunder (ə sun′ dər) *adv.*: Into pieces or parts

Beyond the Selection

FURTHER READING

Other Work by the Authors

One Day in the Life of Ivan Denisovitch, Alexander Solzhenitsyn
The First Circle, Alexander Solzhenitsyn
A Doll's House, Henrik Ibsen
Peer Gynt, Henrik Ibsen
The Cold Spring, and Other Poems, Denise Levertov
Footprints, Denise Levertov

Other Works About the Beauty and Power of Nature

Pilgrim at Tinker Creek, Annie Dillard
The Sea Around Us, Rachel Carson
"Birches," Robert Frost
"Ode to the West Wind," Percy Bysshe Shelley
"To Autumn," John Keats

We suggest that you preview these works before recommending them to students.

moonless dark.
By dawn he was gone.
We have stood here since,
in our new life.
We have waited.
He does not return.
It is said he made his earth-journey, and lost
what he sought.
It is said they felled him
and cut up his limbs for firewood. ❺
And it is said
his head still sang and was swept out to sea singing.
Perhaps he will not return.
But what we have lived
comes back to us.
We see more.
We feel, as our rings increase,
something that lifts our branches, that stretches our furthest
leaf-tips
further.
The wind, the birds,
do not sound poorer but clearer,
recalling our agony, and the way we danced.
The music!

Guide for Responding

◆ Literature and Your Life

Reader's Response Which selection gives you the most unexpected view of nature? Explain.

Thematic Focus How do these views of nature broaden the way you look at the natural world?

☑ Check Your Comprehension

1. Describe the setting of "A Storm in the Mountains."
2. In which season is "In the Orchard" set? How do you know?
3. By what power does Orpheus lead the trees?
4. What does the tree say happens to Orpheus?

◆ Critical Thinking

INTERPRET

1. Why does the speaker in "A Storm . . ." feel on terra firma for only a split second? **[Interpret]**
2. Explain the significance of the scarecrow in the second stanza of "In the Orchard." **[Interpret]**
3. How well does Ibsen's use of sensory images communicate the meaning of "In the Orchard"? **[Assess]**
4. What details in "A Tree . . ." indicate that Orpheus is making music? **[Synthesize]**
5. What lasting effect does Orpheus have on the trees? **[Infer]**

COMPARE LITERARY WORKS

6. Explain which of these poems might best be used in a public-service announcement about protecting the environment. **[Compare and Contrast]**

Beyond the Selection

INTERNET

Students can explore the following Web sites to learn more about the writers and their work:
Solzhenitsyn: **http://www.empirenet.com/~rdaeley/authors/solzhenitsyn.html**
Ibsen: **http://odin.edp.no/ud/nornytt/ibsen.html**
Levertov: **http://www.keplers.com/theme16.shtml**

The following Web sites are for further exploration of the Orpheus myth: **http://cdr.stanford. edu/PENS/pandp/vonkrogh/5704.html** **http://cdr.stanford.edu/PENS/pandp/lam/10451.html**

Please be aware, however, that sites may have changed from the time we published this information. We *strongly recommend* that you preview the sites before you send students to them.

❺ **Clarification** Explain that Orpheus' "earth-journey" was his journey to the underworld to rescue Eurydice; the rest of the passage refers to Orpheus' death, according to the myth, at the hands of the Maenads, or Bacchantes.

Reinforce and Extend

Answers

◆ Literature and Your Life

Reader's Response Students may say that "A Tree Telling of Orpheus" is the most unusual in its combination of mythology and a tree speaking. Others may say that the personified "Storm in the Mountains" is the more unusual.

Thematic Focus Viewing a subject from different perspectives broadens your understanding of it.

☑ Check Your Comprehension

1. The setting is the foot of a mountain pass, or the narrow valley between high-peaked mountains.
2. "In the Orchard" is set in spring, when the apple trees are in blossom.
3. Orpheus leads the tree by the power of his singing and playing on his lute.
4. He was killed and his head was swept out to sea, singing.

◆ Critical Thinking

1. Only when the lightning illuminates his surroundings does he experience the earth beneath him.
2. The scarecrow is an image of the coming winter, the end of the fruiting season and also death.
3. Most students will feel the images effectively convey the meaning of growth and death.
4. The references to voice and singing indicate that Orpheus is making music.
5. The trees are more alive than they were before they heard the music.
6. Students may cite any of the poems to argue for preserving nature.

Answers

◆ Reading Strategy

1. They call upon sight and touch.
2. The image of time flying and shutting the gate underscores the "seize the day" theme.
3. The image of the coldness in the candle (a combination of touch and sight) effectively suggests the lifelessness of the sickness of boredom, from which Orpheus' song has rescued the grove of trees.

◆ Build Vocabulary

Using Latin Terms

1. ad hoc; 2. caveat emptor; 3. de facto; 4. status quo

Using the Word Bank

1. High humidity and temperatures in the region will produce sultry weather for the next few days.
2. The tremor split highways and buildings asunder.
3. View the magnificent volcano from terra firma in our earthquake-proof lodge.

◆ Literary Focus

1. The speaker is addressing a gardener or worker in an orchard who is concerned with the produce rather than the beauty of the garden.
2. The speaker could be the poet or the wind, as in "With my living, with my singing" and "I broke off the flowers. . . ."
3. The image of a tree so moved as to uproot itself and dance is a dramatic metaphor for the power of passion.

◆ Build Grammar Skills

1. as; 2. like; 3. like; 4. as; 5. as

Writing Application

1. The leaves ripple in the wind as waves do in the ocean.
2. Orpheus' trees move to the sound of his music as teenagers flock to a rock concert.

Guide for Responding (continued)

◆ Reading Strategy

Engage Your Senses

Sensory details in a poem or a description allow you to enter a work completely. **Engaging your senses** as you read helps you to experience the work's sights, sounds, smells, textures, and tastes. For example, images such as "a wave that bathed me/as if rain/rose from below and around me" from "A Tree Telling of Orpheus" draw upon your sense of touch to coax you into experiencing the sensation just as the tree did.

1. What two senses do Solzhenitsyn's words "the searing flashes of lightning" call upon?

2. Which image in "In the Orchard" made you most "sense the meaning" of the poem, and why?

3. From your chart, choose a sensory detail from the poem "A Tree Telling of Orpheus," and explain why it is important to the poem.

◆ Build Vocabulary Skills

Using Latin Terms

The following list gives some Latin terms, and their English definitions, that have found their way, unchanged, into English. Fill in the blanks below with the correct Latin term.

ad hoc: for a specific purpose
caveat emptor: let the buyer beware
status quo: the existing state of things
de facto: in reality

1. The school board assembled a(an) __?__ committee to handle budget issues.

2. A good slogan for those who purchase items from street vendors might be __?__.

3. Though Kim was editor of the school paper, everyone knew that Ms. Lao was the __?__ editor.

4. The rest of the group decided it would be easier to maintain the __?__

Using the Word Bank: Context

On your paper, respond to the numbered sentences using words from the Word Bank.

1. Write a weather forecast using the word *sultry*.

2. Use the word *asunder* to describe the effects of an earthquake.

3. Use the term *terra firma* in a passage from a travel journal.

◆ Literary Focus

Speaker

Even with no conversation, poems can sometimes seem like a dialogue between the **speaker,** or voice telling the poem, and the person (or thing) being addressed. Often a poet chooses to speak directly to you, the reader, but sometimes he or she will speak to a character or object in the poem.

1. Whom is the speaker addressing in "In the Orchard"? Give evidence from the poem to support your answer.

2. Among the following, who is the most likely speaker of "In the Orchard"—a tree, the wind, the poet, a song? Explain your choice.

3. For what reason might Levertov have had a tree be the speaker of "A Tree Telling of Orpheus"?

◆ Build Grammar Skills

Correct Use of *Like* and *As*

Both ***like*** and ***as*** can be used in making comparisons. When writing, use *like* as the preposition in a prepositional phrase that compares one thing with another. Do not use *like* as a conjunction to introduce a subordinate clause (a group of words that contains a subject and a verb but cannot stand alone as a sentence).

Practice Write these sentences in your notebook, replacing the blanks with *like* or *as*.

1. . . . my own outermost branches began to tingle, almost __?__ if/fire had been lit below them . . .

2. . . . the bark thrilled __?__ a leaf still-folded.

3. . . . it seemed my thick bark would split __?__ a sapling's . . .

4. . . . into the pores of my greenest shoots/ gently __?__ dew . . .

5. The poet wrote __?__ a tree would speak.

Writing Application On your paper, follow the directions to write a sentence for each numbered item. Use the word indicated in parentheses.

1. Compare the way the wind moves with the way the ocean moves. (as)

2. Compare Orpheus' effect on the trees with the way people react to music stars today. (like)

Reteach

Many students have difficulty making the distinction between the author who is writing a work of literature and the speaker, the imaginary voice assumed by the writer or the poet. Remind them that sometimes the speaker is the poet; other times the speaker is a character created by the poet. Have students use Levertov's poem to make a list of tree parts in the poem and the human equivalent of what the tree describes. For example, the tree's sap is its blood. What is the tree talking about when it says "at the heart of my wood"? Levertov's feat of personification in creating a speaker/tree should give students plenty of examples.

Speaker/Tree	Human Equivalent
Sap	Blood
Roots	Feet
Bark	
New buds	

Build Your Portfolio

Idea Bank

Writing

1. **Description** From the point of view of a third-person observer, write a description of a tree in a severe storm. Use strong images to engage your readers' senses.

2. **Film Treatment** You are pitching a three-scene film based on the myth of Orpheus to a film producer. Describe what will happen in each scene.

3. **Biographical Sketch** Write a biographical sketch on Russian writer Alexander Solzhenitsyn.

Speaking, Listening, and Viewing

4. **Video or Audio** At the library, look up a video or audio recording of or about Solzhenitsyn's life or work. Share it with the class. **[Social Studies Link]**

5. **Interview** With a partner, role-play a television interview with the speaker of "A Storm in the Mountains." **[Performing Arts Link]**

Researching and Representing

6. **Presentation of Ancient Instrument** The lyre that Orpheus plays is one of the world's most ancient stringed instruments. Create a diagram that shows the construction of a lyre. If possible, find recordings of lyre music to play for the class. **[Social Studies Link; Music Link]**

7. **Multimedia Project** The Black Mountain School, which Denise Levertov attended, had an exceptional influence on the development of the arts in America. Gather materials—audio- and videotapes, poems, photos—and give a multimedia presentation about this school. **[Art Link]**

Online Activity www.phlit.phschool.com

Guided Writing Lesson

Monologue Spoken by a Plant or an Animal

A **monologue** is a speech delivered by one person, without interruption from other people. A monologue may be spoken in the presence of others and may or may not reveal what the speaker really thinks or feels. "A Tree Telling of Orpheus" could be read as the monologue of a tree. Open your imagination and write a monologue from the perspective of a plant or an animal.

Writing Skills Focus: Grab Readers' Attention

Don't bury your most stylish line or interesting fact deep within your monologue. Your audience might walk out before you get to it! **Grab** their **attention** with a strong, controversial statement, a joke, or an exceptionally curious fact. Here's the beginning of a monologue spoken by a queen ant to its worker ants:

> You pay homage to me every hour of your miserable, sniveling lives, but do you think my life is a bed of roses?

This disagreeable speaker immediately raises a question in your mind: Why is her life not a "bed of roses"?

Prewriting Establish a speaker and a situation. After all, your plant or animal must speak *about* something. Decide what the speaker wants to say about the situation, and jot down main points or key phrases.

Drafting In the monologue, your speaker will respond to a situation in its life; it should do so with emotion. Through its emotion, your speaker will communicate its personality and attitude to the audience.

Revising Ask a classmate whether the beginning of your monologue is attention-grabbing, if the "voice" of your speaker is consistent throughout, and if the speaker's emotion is communicated. If necessary, go back and revise to strengthen these areas.

Idea Bank

Following are suggestions for matching Idea Bank topics with your students' performance levels and learning modalities:

Customizing for *Performance Levels*
Less Advanced Students: 1, 5, 7
Average Students: 2, 4, 6
More Advanced Students: 3, 4, 6

Customizing for *Learning Modalities*
Visual/Spatial: 1, 2, 7
Verbal/Linguistic: 3, 4, 5
Musical/Rhythmic: 6

Guided Writing Lesson

Revising Strategy Have students reenter their writing and use a colored pen or pencil to underline ideas and emotions that are not consistent with the voice of their speakers. Then have them return to the main points and key phrases they jotted down during prewriting. Encourage them to draw on ideas they did not use or extend the voice that emerged to revise the items they marked. Use the sample below to model this strategy:

Finally, I am being treated! Lo, the glorious water in its shiny watering can! My ~~anger~~ bubbles. Behold, the fabulous misting that sets my itchy leaves at rest!
excitement

For more prewriting, elaboration, and revision strategies, see *Prentice Hall Writing and Grammar.*

Writing and Language Transparencies Use the Writing Process Model 1: Reflective Essay to guide students' writing.

Writing Lab CD-ROM
Have students complete the tutorial on Creative Writing. Follow these steps:
1. Encourage students to use the word bin featuring words that describe emotional responses.
2. Allow time for students to draft on the computer.
3. Tell students to review the tips for peer reviewing.
4. Suggest that students use the Guidelines for Publishing and Presenting to help them plan a presentation of their monologue.

✓ ASSESSMENT OPTIONS

Formal Assessment, Selection Test, pp. 116–118, and Assessment Resources Software. The selection test is designed so that it can be easily customized to the performance levels of your students.

Alternative Assessment, p. 34, includes options for less advanced students, more advanced students, visual/spatial learners, musical/rhythmic learners, interpersonal learners, and bodily/kinesthetic learners.

PORTFOLIO ASSESSMENT
Use the following rubrics in the ***Alternative Assessment*** booklet to assess student writing:
Description: Description Rubric, p. 97
Film Treatment: Summary Rubric, p. 98
Biographical Sketch: Description Rubric, p. 97
Guided Writing Lesson: Fictional Narrative Rubric, p. 95

Prepare and Engage

LESSON OBJECTIVES

1. To use recursive writing processes to write a firsthand biography
2. To recognize and use quotation marks and vivid verbs

You may want to create a scoring rubric for a firsthand biography using the General Rubric, p. 93 in ***Alternative Assessment,*** to make students aware before they begin of the criteria on which they will be evaluated. You may include the additional points outlined on p. 462.

Refer students to the Writing Handbook, p. 965, for instruction in the writing process, and p. 967 for further information on narration.

Writing Lab CD-ROM

If your students have access to computers, you may want to have them work on the tutorial on Narration to complete all or part of their firsthand biographies. Follow these steps:

1. Have students review the interactive model of a firsthand biography.
2. Students can look at the examples written for different audiences.
3. Have students draft on the computer.
4. Suggest students use the language variety checker.
5. Have students review the Proofreading Checklist.

Firsthand Biography — Writing Process Workshop

In this unit, you've met some interesting characters—both fictional and real—from dashing Pepe Gonzalez to the famous Anthony Quinn. Choose someone you know, and write a **firsthand biography** of him or her. A firsthand biography is a narrative about a person—the subject—with whom you have had direct experience. A firsthand biography can be about the entire life of the subject or it may focus on an important episode or period in the subject's life. Your relationship with your subject should give you insights not found in biographies based solely on research.

The following skills, introduced in this section's Guided Writing Lessons, will help you write an interesting firsthand biography.

Writing Skills Focus

- **Grab your reader's attention** at the beginning with a startling quotation or interesting anecdote. (See p. 459.)
- Like other stories, a biography should have a **beginning, middle,** and **end.** (See p. 437.)
- **Choose words with appropriate connotations**. For example, when describing a person, the word *skinny* has a different connotation from the word *lean*.(See p. 447.)

The following excerpt from Truman Capote's *A Christmas Story* illustrates these skills.

MODEL FROM LITERATURE

from *A Christmas Memory* by Truman Capote

She is wearing tennis shoes and a shapeless gray sweater over a summery calico dress. She is small and sprightly, like a bantam hen; but due to a long youthful illness her shoulders are pitifully hunched ①. Her face is remarkable—not unlike Lincoln's, craggy like that, and tinted by the sun and wind; but it is delicate too, finely boned, and her eyes are sherry-colored and timid. "Oh my," she exclaims, her breath smoking the windowpane, "it's fruitcake weather!"

The person to whom she is speaking is myself. I am seven; she is sixty-something. We are each other's best friend. ②

① *The connotation of the phrase pitifully hunched creates sympathy by conjuring up the image of a frail, old woman.*

② *When the writer says that "We are each other's best friend," he grabs the reader's attention, since the ages of the two are so far apart.*

Cross-Curricular Connection: Social Studies

Students can use their firsthand biographies to explore larger social issues as well. For example, if a student is writing about a friend from South Africa, he or she might also discuss apartheid and how it affected the subject's life. Closer to home, if a student is writing about an adult who happened to have lost his or her job recently, the student may wish to explore briefly such issues as corporate downsizing or factory closings caused by the changing American economy.

Prewriting

Choose a Topic Think about a person whom you admire. It might be a close friend, a student or teacher you admire, a favorite relative, or someone who has done something interesting. Make a list of several possibilities, and then consider which one you know best. Choose that person as the subject of your firsthand biography.

Consider Your Audience Before you begin to write, think about the people for whom you are writing. Consider your audience's interests and background, and make sure your details and language are appropriate for such an audience. The following checklist will help you define your audience:

- ▶ Who are your readers—classmates, relatives, or a teacher?
- ▶ How much does your audience know about your subject?
- ▶ Is your audience familiar with words or phrases that your subject may use or have used?
- ▶ If you wish to convey a message, how do you think your readers will feel about it?

Drafting

Reveal Your Subject You can reveal important aspects of your subject's personality or life either directly or indirectly. When you reveal the character of your subject directly, you openly state the personality traits of the subject. To reveal your subject's character indirectly, present his or her own thoughts, words, or actions. Use direct quotations and vivid verbs to reveal your character's personality more effectively. Look at the following two examples:

Direct

Tom is a very competitive person. He always wants to have the highest score. He is rude to anyone who scores higher than he does.

Indirect

Last week I ran into Tom at the mall. My smile of greeting froze on my face when he said, "Hey Brad! What's the big idea? Since when did you become the brilliant math student? How did you get a better score than I did?" I had expected Tom to be upset. He's been known to sulk for days if he doesn't get the highest score on an exam.

APPLYING LANGUAGE SKILLS: Quotation Marks

You'll probably want to use **quotations** in your firsthand biography. Make sure that you punctuate all of your direct quotations correctly.

- Use quotation marks to set off the exact words of a speaker.
- Place commas and periods inside final quotation marks.
- Start a new paragraph when the speaker changes.

Practice On your paper, punctuate the following dialogue correctly.

I can't believe Mike isn't here yet said Frank. Me neither, replied Bob. He was supposed to be here an hour ago. Where could he be? You got me, answered Frank.

Writing Application Include direct quotations in your firsthand biography. Punctuate them correctly.

Writer's Solution Connection Language Lab

For more practice with quotation marks, complete the Language Lab lesson on Quotation Marks, Colons, and Semicolons.

Develop Student Writing

Prewriting Strategy

Remind students that a good biography will offer anecdotes, not just adjectives. Once students have decided on a subject, have them use an organizer like the one shown here. Students can make a statement about their subject in the center box. Then, on the spokes, students should jot down incidents or examples that support the main idea.

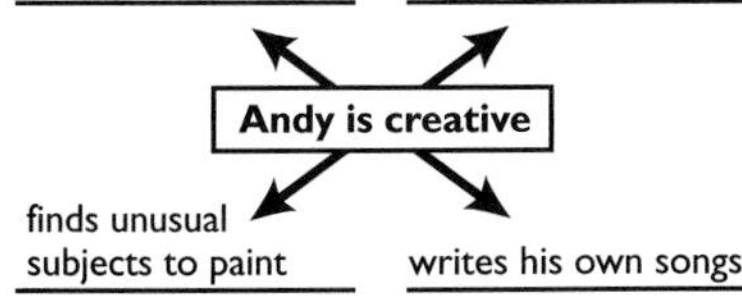
Andy is creative
finds unusual subjects to paint
writes his own songs

Customize for
English Language Learners

Because these students may have trouble with verb tenses, encourage them to write their firsthand biography in the historical present. This will make the task more manageable as well as make their writing more immediate.

Writing Lab CD-ROM

The Character Trait Word Bin in the Developing Narrative Elements section of the tutorial on Narration will help students find words to describe their subject.

Elaboration Strategy

Encourage students to begin their drafts of their firsthand biographies with a colorful image or anecdote to set the tone of their narrative. Then have them organize the details about the person in a meaningful way as they draft. They should consider which point will make an effective ending and build toward it. Once students have completed a draft, they can reenter and revise to make their biographies more interesting.

Applying Language Skills

Quotation Marks

Remind students that their firsthand biographies will be much more immediate and lively if they use direct quotations. Make sure they know how to punctuate those quotations correctly.

Answers

"I can't believe Mike isn't here yet," said Frank. "Me neither," replied Bob. "He was supposed to be here an hour ago. Where could he be?" "You got me," answered Frank.

For additional instruction and practice, have students complete the **Language Lab CD-ROM** lesson on Semicolons, Colons, and Quotation Marks and practice pp. 104–105 on punctuating quotations in the *Writer's Solution Grammar Practice Book*.

Revision Strategy

Writing Lab CD-ROM
The Revising and Editing section of the tutorial on Narration contains the following screens to help students revise their firsthand biographies:

- Character trait word bin
- Using details of setting to enhance mood
- Transition word bin

Prentice Hall Writing and Grammar For more prewriting, elaboration, and revision instruction, see *Prentice Hall Writing and Grammar.*

Publishing

In addition to the publishing suggestions, students may also wish to consider publishing in a student newspaper or national literary magazine that publishes student writing. For more information, visit Prentice Hall on the World Wide Web at **http://www.phschool.com.**

Reinforce and Extend

Applying Language Skills

Answers:
Possible response:
Last week the temperature *skyrocketed* to 95°. The morning sun *shone* brightly as John *rode* to my house on his bike.

Grammar Reinforcement

For additional instruction and practice, have students complete the **Language Lab CD-ROM** lesson on Choosing Words: Writing With Nouns and Verbs.

APPLYING LANGUAGE SKILLS: Vivid Verbs

Good writers use **vivid verbs** to make their writing clear and precise. A vivid verb describes an action in a strong, exact manner.

Vague Verbs:

Rows of books and trophies are on John's shelves. Posters are on his wall. On his desk is a small totem-pole.

Vivid Verbs:

Rows of books and trophies clutter John's shelves. Posters decorate his wall. On his desk stands a small totem pole.

Practice On your paper, replace the vague verbs in the following sentence with vivid ones.

The weather was hot last week. The morning sun was bright as John came up to my house on his bike.

Writing Application Review your firsthand biography and replace vague, weak verbs with vivid ones.

Writer's Solution Connection Writing Lab

To see more ideas for publishing your firsthand biography, refer to Publishing and Presenting in the Writing Lab tutorial on Narration.

Revising

Read Your Firsthand Biography Aloud A good revising technique is to read your work aloud. If you find parts difficult to read aloud, chances are a reader will also have trouble reading and understanding it. Work on making those areas smooth and clear.

Proofreading

Use a Proofreading Checklist Use the following checklist to make sure your draft is free of errors in grammar, spelling, and punctuation:

- ▶ Have you punctuated all dialogue correctly?
- ▶ Does each sentence end with the appropriate punctuation?
- ▶ Have you spelled all words correctly, including homophones such as *your* and *you're*?
- ▶ If you're using a computer, did you check that you didn't accidentally substitute one small word for another, such as *and* for *an* or *of* for *or*?

REVISION MODEL

① "Belay on! Climb when ready!" ② those words, ③ stared ③ stepped

When I heard Lynn shout I took a big gulp, ~~looked~~ up at the rope snaking into the distance above me, and ~~moved~~ out onto the blank rock face.

① The writer adds this direct quotation to make the situation more lifelike.
② This addition is needed to clarify the connection to the direct quotation.
③ The writer replaces these vague verbs with vivid ones.

Publishing

Publish On-Line On-line magazines, Usenet news groups, and electronic bulletin boards are just a few of the options for publishing your writing on the World Wide Web. For more information, consult Prentice Hall on the Web at http://www.phschool.com.

ASSESSMENT		4	3	2	1
PORTFOLIO ASSESSMENT Use the following criteria to assess students' firsthand biographies.	**Organization**	The biography has a clear beginning, middle, and end. It contains relevant personal thoughts and insights.	The biography has a beginning, middle, and end. It contains personal thoughts and insights.	The biography lacks a clear beginning or end. It contains personal comment but may require more elaboration.	The biography lacks both a narrative structure and personal comments.
	Elements of Narration	The biography is compelling. Transitions make the order clear; the writer uses the first-person point of view consistently.	The biography is interesting. Transitions are used, though they may be repetitive. The writer uses the first-person point of view.	The biography is readable. More transitions are needed; point of view may shift from first- to third-person.	The biography is confusing and difficult to read. Transitions are lacking; point of view continually shifts.

Student Success Workshop

Real-World Reading Skills

Monitoring Reading Strategies

Strategies for Success

In your reading, you will sometimes come across a passage that you find confusing or complex. Don't let this discourage you. Instead, get in the habit of using different reading strategies. Certain strategies help you to break down and review what you've read, so that a text makes more sense. Be alert to the strategies you use, and when one doesn't work, try another.

Reread After reading the entire text for the main ideas, go back and carefully read it again. This time, look at titles and section headings. Pay more attention to details. Notice punctuation. See what you can figure out about the work's organization. Read footnotes and captions, and study illustrations that might clarify the text.

Ask Questions As you read, write down any questions that come to mind. This will help you piece together answers and will help you gain a better understanding of what you've read. In some cases, the answers to your questions may be in the material you're reading. In other cases, you may need to conduct research to find the answers you need.

Use Resources Resources both within the text and outside it can help you make sense of a difficult work. A book or an article may contain an introduction, a bibliography of other sources, or a glossary. If you need to consult outside sources for information, you can find them at the library or on the Internet. For example, if you were reading about an event taking place in a European country, you could consult an encyclopedia or a Web site for that country to find out more about it. Using resources can make reading easier and more rewarding.

Apply the Strategies

Read this excerpt from an article, using the strategies on this page to monitor your reading. Then answer the questions that follow.

Robotics: Japanese Researchers Look to the Twenty-First Century

Robotics Assembly Lines Advance

Since the 1970's, the Japanese have been leaders in making and using robotic structures to increase productivity on assembly lines at car manufacturing plants. Robots have been used for jobs that are dangerous or for which there is a shortage of workers. Today, Japanese scientists are working to design robots that are even more helpful.

Computer-Aided Manufacturing

In the field of CAD/CAM[1], scientists are attempting to design a new robotic structure that will not only create such devices as integrated circuits, but will perform even more intricate work. In their attempt to refine CIM[2] processes, they will create increasingly autonomous robots. These robots will be equipped with vision and touch senses and will be able to share learned data.

1. **CAD/CAM:** Computer-aided design; Computer-aided manufacturing.
2. **CIM:** Computer-integrated manufacturing.

1. When you reread the article, what do you notice about the way information is organized? What are the main ideas?
2. Write down questions that come to mind.
3. With your questions, review the article. Are answers to any of your questions within the article? Does the author provide any resources to help answer your questions?
4. List two outside resources that might help you to understand this article better.

Test Preparation Workshop

Understand Specialized or Technical Terms Standardized tests require students to analyze reading passages that may contain specialized or technical terms. Point out that test takers can still answer comprehension questions correctly, even if they do not know the meaning of every term and sentence in the passage. Use this sample test item to show students how to use context clues:

> Although you did not break any laws, the fact that you took advantage of credulous and vulnerable people is certainly unethical.

The word credulous in this passage means—

A sharply vindictive
B amazingly clever
C unassumingly shy
D easily convinced

Help students to see that clue words and phrases like *unethical,* and *took advantage* suggest the people were tricked. The best response is D.

Prepare and Engage

LESSON OBJECTIVES

- To monitor one's own reading strategies and make modifications
- To use strategies such as rereading, using resources, and questioning

Customize for *Interpersonal Learners*

Provide a challenging content-area selection so that student partners can practice applying self-monitoring strategies. Students read part or all of the selection silently and then take turns thinking aloud about the main ideas, essential terms, and any points of confusion. Partners work together to apply fix-up strategies of rereading, asking questions, and using resources.

Apply the Strategies

Answers

1. Information about Japanese work in robotics is split into two paragraphs; the subheadings give the topic of each paragraph. The first main idea is that the Japanese have been leaders in the use of robotics in manufacturing. The second main idea is that scientists are developing robots that will do intricate work with less dependence on people.
2. What are some examples of the "intricate work" robots may do? Are the Japanese still in the forefront of robotics research?
3. One example of intricate work is building integrated circuits, though the article says there is work of greater intricacy. Further research is needed to fully answer that question and the question about today's robotics researchers.
4. An Internet search engine might lead to useful Web sites in response to the key words "Robotics research." The same key words used with an online periodicals index could lead to recent articles in magazines and newspapers.

Prepare and Engage

LESSON OBJECTIVES

1. To recognize and analyze the effects of media
2. To communicate with a video message

Customize for
Musical/Rhythmic Learners
Encourage students to choose a medium for their message in which they can incorporate audio. How will they combine sound and images to make their message appealing and effective?

Apply the Strategies

Answers

1. Students' plan for a documentary should include an early decision about audience and a reason for choosing the subject.
2. Once partners have decided on a topic for the book, they should familiarize themselves with popular books for the target age group.
3. In making their own plan, students can list the attributes of an effective Web site—for example, inventive use of original images, clear layout, ease of navigation, and useful links.
4. Animated greeting cards sent electronically are one possibility; paper cards are another. Emphasize that paper cards combine typography and art in all sorts of ways. Encourage students to aim for something out of the ordinary.
5. Point out that a parody works well if the original work seems to take itself too seriously

Speaking, Listening, and Viewing Workshop

Producing a Visual Representation

Visual representations—including photographs, television ads and programs, films, news reports, paintings, book and magazine illustrations, and Internet Web pages—all communicate messages visually. Some combine images and text. If several images and phrases from a TV documentary on Cambodia come to mind when you think of that country, that documentary has influenced your idea of a part of the world. What you see in visual representations often shapes your perception of reality. When you have a chance to produce your own visual representation to express an idea to an audience, the following strategies will help:

Decide on Your Message Before you can decide what type of visual representation to produce, you need to be clear about your reason for producing it. Ask yourself these questions:

- What do I want to say?
- To what audience do I want to direct my message?

For example, you might want to tell a group of friends what you learned about the architecture of a neighborhood across town.

Decide on Your Medium Think about the variety of media forms you could use to get your message across. Your representation of the architecture across town might be produced as a video, a poster combining words and images, a three-dimensional model, a series of photographs or drawings with or without captions, or a series of linked Web pages. You decide.

Plan It Out Depending on the form you choose, you will need a plan for creating your product. For example, to produce a video, you might begin by making a list of scenes to include. Next, you might make a storyboard: a series of "thumbnail" drawings showing the sequence of film shots. Then you could use the storyboard as a guide for shooting the video.

Create Your Product The creative process is the most fulfilling—and sometimes the most challenging—part of producing a visual representation. Keep your plan and your message in mind, and follow it!

Be Your Own Best Critic Once you have completed your product, take time to reflect on it critically. Imagine that you are a member of your audience. What does the finished product say to you? Is your product's message the same as the one you intended to communicate? If you find that your product needs revision, you'll need to return to the creative process.

Apply the Strategies

Use what you've learned about producing a visual representation to create one or more of the following media products:

1. Produce a five-minute documentary about a family member or friend.
2. With a partner, create an illustrated children's book.
3. Design an Internet Home Page for yourself or a Web site to promote a service or product.
4. Create a holiday greeting card.
5. Produce a parody of a commercial or a music video.

Beyond the Classroom

Career Connection

Commercial illustrators, graphic designers, Web designers, photographers—careers in the visual arts take many forms. How many jobs can students list? One library source is the *Occupational Outlook Handbook,* published by the U.S. Department of Labor. It is also available at the Web site of the Bureau of Labor Statistics at: **www.bls.gov**

Once students have generated a list of careers related to visual arts, they may choose a career to focus on and, if possible, an interview subject.

Possible questions to explore:

- What are the special skills and educational requirements needed for success?
- What are the working conditions, opportunities for advancement, and salary range?
- What advice would a person with a career in the visual arts offer students?

Have students share their feelings with the class.

Test Preparation Workshop

Reading Comprehension — Interpret Graphic Aids; Evaluate and Make Judgments

Strategies for Success

The reading sections of standardized tests often require you to interpret graphs, charts, diagrams, and tables. The test may also require you to evaluate and make judgments. Use the following strategies:

Interpret Information in Visual Form
Graphs, charts, diagrams, and tables are all devices for organizing and presenting information visually. To interpret graphic aids, read titles, labels, captions, and keys. Look for a caption that summarizes or explains the information shown. For example, you might be asked to interpret the information in a bar graph such as this:

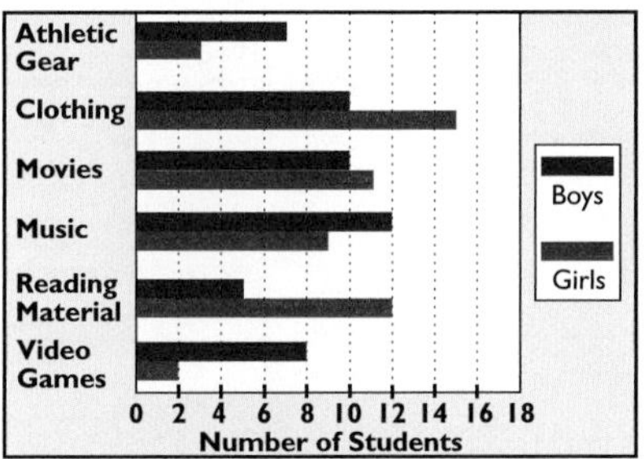

The bar graph shows the results of a poll regarding student spending habits. Thirty-one students, 17 girls and 14 boys, were asked which categories they spent money on in the last month. The poll shows we spent the most on clothing, movies, and music.

1 In which category do the spending habits of girls and boys differ most?
A clothing **C** reading materials
B video games **D** athletic gear

To answer, refer to the chart and subtract the smaller number from the larger number for each category. You'll find that **C** is correct.

Evaluate and Make Judgments After reading a passage, you may be asked to evaluate the information and make a judgment about it. Read each choice carefully, and refer to the information in the passage. The question that follows asks you to evaluate and make a judgment about the bar graph and passage about student spending habits:

2 Based on information in the bar graph and the passage, which of these statements is true?
A Girls spent the most money on clothing.
B Boys and girls spent nearly the same on movies.
C Many more boys than girls bought music.
D Most boys spent money on athletic gear.

Answer **A** is incorrect because the survey does not indicate how much students spent. The difference between the numbers of boys and girls who spent money on music is only 3, so **C** is incorrect. **D** is incorrect because only half the boys in the class spent money on athletic gear. **B** is the correct answer: About the same number of boys and girls spent money on movies.

Apply the Strategies

Refer again to the bar graph and sample passage, and answer the following questions:

1 In which category are the spending habits of girls and boys most alike?
A music **C** movies
B athletic gear **D** reading

2 The bar graph and passage offer evidence that
A more students in the class spent time reading than watching videos.
B a minority of boys in the class spent money on clothes.
C boys are more athletic than girls.
D most girls have no interest in videos.

Correlations to Standardized Tests

The reading comprehension skills reviewed in this Workshop correspond to the following standardized test section:

ACT Reading

Test Preparation

Each ATE workshop in Unit 5 supports the instruction here by providing teaching suggestions and a sample test item:

- **Evaluate and Make Judgments** (ATE, pp. 381, 395, 405, 413, 427, 439, 449)

LESSON OBJECTIVES

- To draw conclusions and make inferences
- To interpret and use graphic aids in order to locate and categorize information

Answers

1. C (movies)
2. B (a minority of boys in the class spent money on clothes.)

Test-Taking Tip

Look for Labels
Emphasize the importance of reading titles, captions, and all labels in graphic aids. Point out that an incorrect answer choice may be based on the misreading of numerical data, so test takers must pay close attention to the numerical values in graphs. Does each section, bar, or line represent whole numbers, for example? Should the numbers be multiplied by hundreds or thousands? Are the values given in fractions or percentages? The answers to such questions will lead test takers to correct answers on the test.

Have students tell what the bars in the workshop graph represent. *They represent whole numbers.* How would the graph differ if the bars represented percentages? *Instead of standing for the number of respondents, a bar would represent the proportion of respondents. The bars would show what percentage of 17 girls and 14 boys spent money in the listed category.*

Planning Instruction and Assessment

Unit Objectives

1. To read short stories that illustrate different elements of the genre
2. To apply a variety of reading strategies, particularly strategies for constructing meaning, appropriate for reading these selections
3. To analyze literary elements
4. To use a variety of strategies to read unfamiliar words and to build vocabulary
5. To learn elements of grammar, usage, and style
6. To use recursive writing processes to write in a variety of forms
7. To prepare, organize, and present literary interpretations

Meeting the Objectives With each selection, you will find instructional material and portfolio opportunities through which students can meet these objectives. Further, you will find additional practice pages for reading strategies, literary elements, vocabulary, and grammar in the ***Selection Support*** booklet in the ***Teaching Resources*** box.

Test Preparation

The end-of-unit workshop **Recognize Forms of Propaganda; Distinguish Between Fact and Nonfact** (SE, p. 565), is supported by teaching tips and a sample test item in the ATE workshop with each selection grouping.

- **Recognize Forms of Propaganda** (ATE, p. 513)
- **Distinguish Between Fact and Nonfact** (ATE, pp. 469, 479, 499, 533, 551)

The following additional workshops in the ATE give teaching tips and a sample test item for applying the skill taught in the Student Success Workshops:

- **Identify the Main Idea** (ATE, p. 530)
- **Evaluate and Make Judgments** (ATE, p. 563)

Final Departure, Lisa Learner

Humanities: Art

Final Departure by Lisa Learner.

Help students establish the literal reality portrayed in this artwork. It shows a terminal, probably a platform for boarding trains or buses, covered by a barrel roof that lets in the sunlight. The artist draws a great deal of attention to the structure of the building and has chosen an unusual perspective, from the steps going up to the platform.

Help students link the artwork to the focus of Unit 6, "The Short Story," by answering the following questions:

1. In what ways might reading a story be like boarding a train, bus, or plane? *The story takes us to new places; it has its own direction; it presents many images.*
2. Why would a train or bus station or an airport be a good place to set the beginning of a story? *A terminal is full of many different individuals, each with a strong reason for being there; it can be a setting for homecomings and leave-takings; it also is a large area with many potentially mysterious spaces, as shown here.*

Short Stories

As long as people have had language, they have had stories—stories of the hunt, stories of battles, stories of romance, mystery, and adventure. There are no limits to the places short stories can take you. In a realistic short story, you might share the experiences of someone like yourself, while in a science-fiction short story, you might travel to a future world. No matter where you go or whom you meet, however, you can be sure your brief encounter will enrich your life.

Assessing Student Progress

The following tools are available to measure the degree to which students meet the unit objectives:

Informal Assessment

The questions on the Guide for Responding sections are a first level of response to the concepts and skills presented with the selection. Students' responses are a brief informal measure of their grasp of the material. Their responses on this level can indicate where further instruction and practice are needed. You may then follow up with the practice pages in the ***Selection Support*** booklet.

You will find literature and reading guides in the ***Alternative Assessment*** booklet, which you may give students on an individual basis for informal assessment of their performance.

Formal Assessment

In the ***Formal Assessment*** booklet, you will find selection tests and part tests.

Selection Tests The selection tests measure comprehension and skills acquisition for each selection or group of selections.

Part Tests Each part test, which calls on students to read a passage of literature they have not previously seen, applies the unit skills on a broader level. The Critical Reading section measures Unit Objectives 1, 2, and 3. The Vocabulary and Grammar section measures Objectives 4 and 5. The Essay section measures Objectives 1 and 6. Both the Critical Reading and Vocabulary and Grammar sections use formats similar to those found on many standardized tests, including the SAT.

Alternative Assessment

Portfolios As you review individual pieces or the collected work in students' portfolios, you will find assessment sheets available in the portfolio section of the ***Alternative Assessment*** booklet.

Scoring Rubrics You will find scoring rubrics for writing modes in the ***Alternative Assessment*** booklet. You can apply these to Writing Mini-Lessons and to Writing Process Workshop lessons.

Speaking, Listening, and Viewing The ***Alternative Assessment*** booklet contains assessment sheets for speaking, listening, and viewing activities.

Learning Modalities The ***Alternative Assessment*** booklet contains activities that appeal to different learning styles. You may use these as an alternative measurement of students' growth.

Prepare and Engage

LESSON OBJECTIVES

1. **To develop vocabulary and word identification skills**
   - Word Origins: Words From Names
   - Using the Word Bank: Word Choice
   - Extending Word Study: Expand Vocabulary (ATE)
2. **To use a variety of reading strategies to comprehend a short story**
   - Connect Your Experience
   - Reading for Success: Strategies for Constructing Meaning
   - Tips to Guide Reading (ATE)
   - Read to Be Entertained (ATE)
3. **To increase knowledge of other cultures and to connect common elements across cultures**
   - Connecting Themes Across Cultures (ATE)
   - Background for Understanding
4. **To express and support responses to the text**
   - Critical Thinking
   - Idea Bank: Letter
   - Idea Bank: Diary
   - Idea Bank: Story
   - Idea Bank: Comic Strip
5. **To analyze literary elements**
   - Literary Focus: Plot Structure
6. **To plan, prepare, organize, and present literary interpretations**
   - Idea Bank: Tape Recording
   - Idea Bank: Storytelling
   - Speaking, Listening, and Viewing
   - Idea Bank: Music
7. **To use recursive writing processes to write Study Notes: Summary**
   - Guided Writing Lesson
8. **To increase knowledge of the rules of grammar and usage**
   - Build Grammar Skills: Placement of *Only* and *Just*

Test Preparation

Critical Reading: Distinguish Between Fact and Nonfact (ATE, p. 469) The teaching tips and sample test item in this workshop support the instruction and practice in the unit workshop:

Critical Reading: Recognize Forms of Propaganda; Distinguish Between Fact and Nonfact (SE, p. 565)

Guide for Reading

Saki *(1870–1916)*

Long before celebrities of today started using single names, the writer Saki made his one name famous. Saki is the pen name of Hector Hugh Munro, born to British parents in Akyab, Burma (now Myanmar), which was a British colony at that time.

A Struggle to Survive When Saki was born, a doctor told his parents that their son had little chance of reaching adulthood. Although he did live, his mother died when he was only two years old. He was sent to England to be raised by two aunts and his grandmother. Saki based many of the characters in his work on family members, particularly his two aunts.

Throughout his life, Saki was plagued with illnesses. At the age of twenty-three, he returned to Burma to join the military police, but only one year later contracted a severe case of malaria that forced him to return to England. There, he began his writing career, penning political satires for several newspapers.

Stories With a Twist Although Saki began by writing nonfiction, he is most famous for his fiction, especially his short stories. These tales, including "The Open Window," are noted for both their wit and humor as well as for their surprise endings. Curiously, the story of Saki's own life ends with an ironic twist. After surviving childhood diseases and a bout with malaria, Saki was killed at the age of forty-five by a sniper's bullet during World War I.

◆ Build Vocabulary

WORD ORIGINS: WORDS FROM NAMES

One of the characters in "The Open Window" carries a white mackintosh, or waterproof raincoat, over his shoulder. *Mackintosh* is a word that derives from the name of an actual person— Charles *Macintosh* (1766–1843), a Scottish chemist who invented waterproof clothing by soaking layers of cloth in rubber.

WORD BANK

As you read, you will encounter the words on this list. Each word is defined on the page where it first appears. Preview the list before you read.

delusion
imminent
mackintosh
pariah

◆ Build Grammar Skills

PLACEMENT OF *ONLY* AND *JUST*

Certain modifiers, such as *only* and *just,* should be placed immediately before the words they modify. If they are not, the intended meaning may be unclear. In the following example from the story, notice the placement of *only*.

> . . . he was conscious that his hostess was giving him *only* a fragment of her attention . . .

In this example, *only* modifies *a fragment.* If you change the placement of *only,* the meaning of the sentence changes:

> He was conscious that his hostess was giving *only* him a fragment of her attention . . .

Now, *only* modifies *him* and gives the sentence an entirely new meaning.

Prentice Hall Literature Program Resources

REINFORCE / RETEACH / EXTEND

Selection Support Pages
Build Vocabulary: Word Origins: Words From Names, p. 142
Build Grammar Skills: Placement of *Only* and *Just,* p. 143
Reading for Success: Strategies for Constructing Meaning, p. 144
Literary Focus: Plot Structure, p. 146

Strategies for Diverse Student Needs, p. 35

Beyond Literature Career Connection: Letter of Recommendation, p. 35

Formal Assessment Selection Test, pp. 123–125; Assessment Resources Software

Alternative Assessment, p. 35

Writing and Language Transparencies Outline Organizer, pp. 103–106

Resource Pro CD-ROM

Listening to Literature Audiocassettes

The Open Window

MODEL SELECTION

◆ Literature and Your Life

CONNECT YOUR EXPERIENCE

The popularity of horror movies indicates that many people enjoy fictional stories that shock, frighten, or surprise. Not everyone enjoys a terrifying tale, however. For some, stories of romance or humor are more entertaining. In "The Open Window," two characters have very different feelings about the same tale: It horrifies one yet amuses the other.

Journal Writing Make a list of your five favorite stories and your five favorite movies. Look for a pattern in the types of entertainment you enjoy.

THEMATIC FOCUS: DANGEROUS DESTINIES

Imagination plays an important role in the destinies of the characters in this story. The events in this story may lead you to wonder whether a person's imagination can be too vivid!

◆ Literary Focus

PLOT STRUCTURE

Plot is the sequence of events that make up a story. The plot usually begins with an exposition, which introduces the setting, characters, and basic situation. An inciting incident often introduces the story's central conflict, or problem. The conflict then develops in the rising action until it reaches a high point of interest or suspense—the climax. The climax is followed by the resolution of the conflict or the end of the story. Use a plot diagram, like the one shown here, to note the plot elements of "The Open Window."

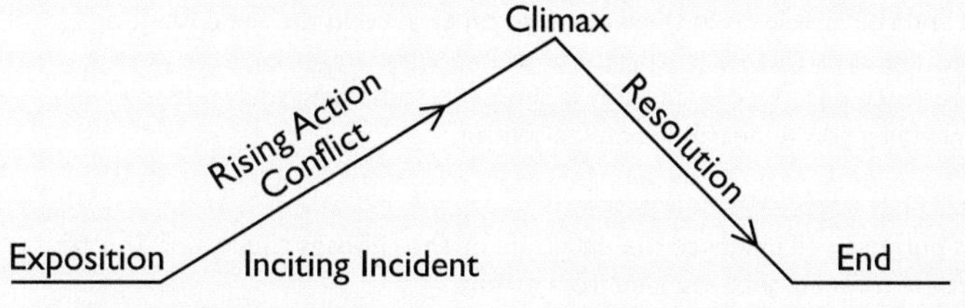

◆ Background for Understanding

CULTURE

During the time that this story is set—around the beginning of the twentieth century—people with money and land enjoyed a life of leisure in which social connections were very important. A person was judged as much on his or her acquaintances and family background as on his or her personality and accomplishments. To make new acquaintances, people often presented themselves through letters of introduction—a kind of social letter of recommendation. Mr. Nuttel, a character in this story, arrives at the country home of a "friend of a friend" with just such a letter.

Test Preparation Workshop

Critical Reading: Distinguish Between Fact and Nonfact

Standardized tests such as ACT and SAT require students to distinguish between facts and nonfacts in order to understand the writer's message. To help students prepare, introduce this sample test item.

Saki's award-winning tales are noted for their surprise endings. Curiously, the story of Saki's own life ends with an ironic twist. After surviving childhood diseases and a bout of malaria, he was killed at the age of forty-five by a sniper's bullet.

Which of the following is an OPINION expressed in the passage?

A Saki's tales have won awards.
B Saki died at age forty-five.
C Saki was killed by a bullet.
D Saki's death was ironic.

Point out that each statement can be found in the passage. However, only D states an opinion. Each other answer can be proven.

Draw students into the selection by reading the following passage from the story aloud:

The child was staring out through the open window with dazed horror in her eyes. In a chill shock of nameless fear Framton swung around in his seat and looked in the same direction.

Have students discuss what kind of story they would expect this quotation to come from. *Students may respond: a horror story; a ghost story.* Tell them to read "The Open Window" to find out.

Connecting Themes Across Cultures

Have students read the Background for Understanding, which underscores the society in which the story is set. After they have read "The Open Window," have students analyze ways in which the action might change if the setting of the story were changed to modern day.

Tips to Guide Reading

Sustained Reading As students read a world literature selection, it is helpful if they read with understanding for a sustained period of time. Encourage students to take special note of the details of setting to help them become absorbed into Saki's characters' world.

Customize for *Less Proficient Readers*

Because of the dialogue and short paragraphs, this selection is ideal for oral reading. Have students form a Read Around Circle in which students all take turns reading a paragraph.

Customize for *Pre-AP Students*

Tell students that Saki's stories are known for their surprise endings. As students read, have them take notes to help them predict the ending.

Customize for *English Language Learners*

Help these students paraphrase sections of dialogue that are peppered with unfamiliar "Britishisms" such as *rectory, moor,* and *bound.*

Reading for Success

The Reading for Success page in each unit presents a set of problem-solving procedures to help readers understand authors' words and ideas on multiple levels. Good readers develop a bank of strategies from which they can draw as needed.

Unit 6 introduces strategies for constructing meaning. It is important for students to go beyond the literal comprehension level in order to apply higher-level critical thinking strategies. These strategies for constructing meaning help readers achieve a higher level of reading comprehension—making inferences, drawing conclusions, interpreting information and identifying relationships, and recognizing an author's purpose.

These strategies for constructing meaning are modeled with "The Open Window." Each green box shows an example of the thinking process involved in applying one of these strategies.

How to Use the Reading for Success Page

- Introduce the strategies for constructing meaning, presenting each as a problem-solving procedure. Be sure students understand what each strategy involves and under what circumstances to apply it.
- Before students read the story, have them preview it, looking at the annotations in the green boxes that model the strategies.
- To reinforce these strategies after students have read "The Open Window," have students do the Reading for Success pages in ***Selection Support,*** pp. 144–145. These pages give students an opportunity to read a selection and practice these strategies by writing their own annotations.

Reading for Success

Strategies for Constructing Meaning

In order to understand a piece of writing fully, you must do more than simply comprehend the writer's words. You have to go a step further and put the words and ideas together in your own mind. Why did the author write it? What idea does he or she want to convey? What does the work mean to you? In looking for answers to questions like these, you construct the meaning that the work has for you.

Use these strategies to help you construct meaning:

Draw inferences.

Writers don't always tell you everything directly. You have to draw inferences to arrive at ideas that writers suggest but don't say. You draw an inference by considering the details that the writer includes or doesn't include. Sometimes it's also helpful to "read between the lines." This means looking beyond the literal meaning of the words to obtain a full understanding of what the author means.

Draw conclusions.

A conclusion is a general statement that you can make and explain by reasons or that you can support with details from the text. A series of inferences can lead you to a conclusion.

Interpret the information.

Interpret, or explain the meaning or significance of, what you read. When you interpret, you also explain the importance of what the author is saying.

Identify relationships in the text.

Identify the various relationships in the story. For example, look for the causes and effects of important actions, keep clear in your mind the sequence of events, and identify which events are of greater or lesser importance. This will help you get the "nuts and bolts" of the story down and let you devote your energy to more challenging tasks, such as finding out the theme.

Compare and contrast the ideas.

Compare and contrast ideas in the work with other ideas in the same work or with ideas that are already familiar to you. For example, you might look for ways in which an experience described in an essay is similar to something you've done or different from anything you've heard of or experienced.

Recognize the writer's purpose.

A writer's purpose will influence the details he or she chooses to present. This factor can affect the meaning that you take from a work.

As you read "The Open Window," look at the notes in the boxes. These notes demonstrate how to apply these strategies to a piece of literature.

Reading Strategies: Support and Reinforcement

Appropriate Reading Strategies Students are given a reading strategy to apply in reading each selection. For example, students will be asked to draw conclusions in a selection where a writer has an implied message. In other selections a strategy is suggested that is appropriate to the selection.

Reading Prompts To encourage application of the given reading strategy, there are occasional prompts, within green boxes, at appropriate and significant points.

In addition, there are red boxes prompting application of the Literary Focus concept and maroon boxes prompting students to connect with their lives.

Using the Boxed Annotations and Prompts

The material in the green, red, and maroon boxes along the sides of selections is intended to help students apply the literary element and the reading strategy and to make a connection with their lives. You may use the boxed material in several ways:

- Have students pause when they come to a box and respond to its prompt before they continue reading.
- Urge students to read through the selection ignoring the boxes. After they have read the selection completely, they may go back and review the selection, responding to the prompts.

Nelli Kabel, Gari Melchers

The Open Window

Saki

1 "My aunt will be down presently, Mr. Nuttel," said a very self-possessed young lady of fifteen; "in the meantime you must try and put up with me."

Framton Nuttel endeavored to say the correct something that should duly flatter the niece of the moment without unduly discounting the aunt that was to come. I  Privately he doubted more than ever whether these formal visits on a succession of total strangers would do much towards helping the nerve cure which he was supposed to be undergoing.

"I know how it will

The details in this passage **identify** Mr. Nuttel's reason for being here. During the time in which this story is set, a common prescription for a "nervous condition" was rest and clean country air.

2 ▲ Critical Viewing Based on her posture, expression, and surroundings, what is your impression of the girl in the painting? **[Infer]**

Develop Understanding

One-Minute Insight

This story celebrates the power a good storyteller can have over a susceptible audience. Fifteen-year-old Vera is bright, poised, and imaginative—with a wry sense of humor. When she meets the nervous Mr. Nuttel, she quickly determines he is the perfect victim and plays a little joke on him, with spectacular results. She tells Nuttel a story so tragic and convincing that she has him believing in ghosts—and seeing them as well. When faced with explaining the man's odd behavior to her aunt, she invents an equally bizarre story, making her aunt the next unsuspecting victim.

◆ Critical Thinking

1 Interpret Ask students: What do you know about Vera and Framton after reading this passage? *Vera's words and the author's description of her indicate that she is self-assured and talkative. Framton Nuttel appears is a worrier, unsure of himself and uncomfortable in social situations.*

▶Critical Viewing◀

2 Infer *From her posture and facial expression, the young woman in the painting appears poised and in command of the situation; her clothing and surroundings—artwork and freshly cut flowers—suggest wealth.*

Humanities: Art

Nellie Kabel by Gari Melchers.

Gari Melchers (1860–1932) was an American painter who focused on human figures and faces. His best known work is a portrait of President Theodore Roosevelt, painted in 1906.

Use these questions for discussion:

1. Would you imagine the young woman in the painting to be shy or self-confident? Which of her features helped you form your opinion? *The subject of the painting seems confident. Her straightforward gaze and her relaxed, open posture create this impression.*
2. When you learn more about Vera, decide if you think this painting is a good illustration for the story and explain why. *The subject appears to have character traits similar to Vera's—self-confidence and a mischievous streak.*

Block Scheduling Strategies

Consider these suggestions to take advantage of extended class time:

- Begin by introducing the Reading for Success strategies for Constructing Meaning. After students have read the story, have them work in small groups to complete the Reading for Success activity on p. 475. For more practice, give students the Reading for Success pages in ***Selection Support,*** pp. 144–145.
- Use the Daily Language Practice activities for Week 10, based on "The Open Window," p. 121 in ***Writing and Language Transparencies.***
- Direct students to the plot diagram on p. 469. Suggest that as they read "The Open Window" they look for and identify the plot elements noted on the diagram. You may wish to give them the Story Map blackline master in ***Writing and Language Transparencies,*** p. 84.
- Have students meet in discussion groups to answer the Critical Thinking questions (p. 475).
- Have students work together on one of the projects in the Idea Bank on p. 476.

◆ Reading for Success

❶ **Make Inferences** Draw students' attention to Framton's remembered conversation with his sister. Ask: What does this conversation tell you about Framton Nuttel? *Since his sister believed that he would never attempt to meet people on his own, Framton is probably an introvert with a passive personality.*

◆ Reading for Success

❷ **Interpret the Information** Ask students: Might you interpret Vera's questions in some way other than mere polite conversation? *The choice of the word* pursued, *rather than* asked, *suggests that Vera might be probing for information about what Framton knows and does not know about local people and her aunt.*

❸ **Clarification** In order for Vera's story to make sense, students need to understand that a French window is really a door with glass panes—a door that people can use to walk in and out of a room or house.

◆ Reading for Success

❹ **Make Inferences** Ask students what earlier clue lets the careful reader infer that the story might not be true. Give them a moment to look back over the text to find the clue. *The clue that the story might not be true is the earlier mention of "masculine habitation." If the aunt is a widow and her brothers are dead, men would probably not be living in the house.*

Read to Be Entertained

When reading from the realm of world literature, encourage students to be entertained by the author's use of cultural observations. Ask students to point out those aspects of the story which make it entertaining.

Extending Word Study

Expand Vocabulary Reading vocabulary will increase if students monitor their understanding of words from another country or another culture. Challenge students to list words found in the selection that are specific to the setting, such as *bog*, and *marsh*. Students can use reference materials to find precise meanings of words that are unfamiliar.

be," his sister had said when he was preparing to migrate to this rural retreat; "you will bury yourself down there and not speak to a living soul, and your nerves will be worse than ever ❶ from moping. I shall just give you letters of introduction to all the people I know there. Some of them, as far as I can remember, were quite nice."

Framton wondered whether Mrs. Sappleton, the lady to whom he was presenting one of the letters of introduction, came into the nice division.

"Do you know many of the people round here?" asked the niece, when she judged that they had had sufficient silent communion.

"Hardly a soul," said Framton. "My sister was staying here, at the rectory, you know, ❷ some four years ago, and she gave me letters of introduction to some of the people here."

He made the last statement in a tone of distinct regret.

"Then you know practically nothing about my aunt?" pursued the self-possessed young lady.

"Only her name and address," admitted the caller. He was wondering whether Mrs. Sappleton was in the married or widowed state. An undefinable something about the room seemed to suggest masculine habitation.

> When the author says that "something about the room seemed to suggest masculine habitation," you can **infer** that men live there.

"Her great tragedy happened just three years ago," said the child; "that would be since your sister's time."

"Her tragedy?" asked Framton; somehow in this restful country spot tragedies seemed out of place.

"You may wonder why we keep that window ❸ wide open on an October afternoon," said the niece, indicating a large French window that opened on to a lawn.

"It is quite warm for the time of the year," said Framton; "but has that window got anything to do with the tragedy?"

"Out through that window, three years ago to a day, her husband and her two young brothers went off for their day's shooting. They never came back. In crossing the moor to their favorite snipe-shooting ground[1] they were all three engulfed in a treacherous piece of bog. It had been that dreadful wet summer, you know and places that were safe in other years gave way suddenly without warning. Their bodies were never recovered. That was the dreadful part of it." Here the child's voice lost its self-possessed note and became falteringly human. "Poor aunt always thinks that they will come back some day, they and the little brown spaniel that was lost with them, and walk in at that window just as they used to do. That is why the window is kept open every evening till it is quite dusk. Poor dear aunt, she has often told me how they went out, her husband with his white waterproof coat over his arm, and Ronnie, her youngest brother, singing, 'Bertie, why do you bound?' as he always did to tease her, because she said it got on her nerves. Do you know, sometimes on still, quiet evenings like this, I almost get a creepy feeling that they will walk in through that window—"

She broke off with a little shudder. It was a relief to Framton when the aunt bustled into the room with a whirl of apologies for being late in making her appearance.

"I hope Vera has been amusing you?" she said.

"She has been very interesting," said Framton.

"I hope you don't mind the open window," said Mrs. Sappleton briskly; "my husband and brothers will be home directly from shooting, and they always come in this way. They've been out for snipe in the marshes today, so they'll make a fine mess over my poor carpets. So like you menfolk, isn't it?"

She rattled on cheerfully about the shooting and the scarcity of birds, and the prospects for duck in the winter. To Framton, it was all

◆ Build Vocabulary

delusion (di lo͞o′ zhən) *n.*: False belief held in spite of evidence to the contrary

1. **snipe-shooting ground:** Area for hunting snipe—wading birds who live chiefly in marshy places and have long, flexible bills.

Speaking, Listening, and Viewing Mini-Lesson

Storytelling

This mini-lesson supports the Speaking, Listening, and Viewing activity in the Idea Bank on p. 476.

Introduce Vera is an engaging storyteller. Have students discuss what she does to make her stories sound believable.

Develop Have students discuss what Vera does to make her stories sound believable. Then, review the following points about successful storytelling:

Details in a story should interest the audience.

- A story should be vivid enough to create "mind pictures" for the audience.
- A storyteller should use pauses and facial expressions to help get meaning across.

Apply Using these hints about storytelling, students should plan their stories and then practice their delivery.

Assess Have students assess their own stories and on the basis of how convincing or believable they are. To evaluate the presentations, students may use the page for Self-Assessment: Speech (p. 117) in ***Alternative Assessment.***

The Hunters, Gari Melchers, Private collection

▲ **Critical Viewing** How is this picture similar to and different from the scene Vera describes? **[Compare and Contrast]** 6

purely horrible. He made a desperate but only partially successful effort to turn the talk on to a less ghastly topic; he was conscious that his hostess was giving him only a fragment of her attention, and her eyes were constantly straying past him to the open window and the lawn beyond. It was certainly an unfortunate coincidence that he should have paid his visit on this tragic anniversary.

"The doctors agree in ordering me complete rest, an absence of mental excitement, and avoidance of anything in the nature of violent physical exercise," announced Framton, who labored under the tolerably wide-spread delusion that total strangers and chance acquaintances are hungry for the least detail of one's ailments and infirmities, their cause and cure. "On the matter of diet they are not so much in agreement," he continued.

"No?" said Mrs. Sappleton, in a voice which ↓

◆ Reading for Success

5 Compare and Contrast Ideas

Now that students have met Vera's aunt, Mrs. Sappleton, ask: How does your view of Mrs. Sappleton compare or contrast with what Vera has told Framton about her? *Students should recognize that the facts in Mrs. Sappleton's hunting story agree with Vera's story; but in speaking to Framton earlier, Vera referred sympathetically to her "poor" aunt. Mrs. Sappleton does not seem to fit that description, with her brisk, cheerful tone ("She rattled on cheerfully . . .") and her offhand mention of the "menfolk."*

▶Critical Viewing◀

6 Compare and Contrast

Students should recognize that Mr. Nuttel essentially sees the scene that Vera described to him in her story—the hunters with their guns and dogs. In the story, there was one more hunter and only one dog. Also, it is winter rather than fall in the painting, and the white coat is not shown.

Customize for
Gifted/Talented Students

Challenge students to create a story sequel. Remind them to use the details from the plot and characterizations so that the sequel makes sense.

Humanities: Art

The Hunters by Gari Melchers.

Julius Gari Melchers (1860–1932) was born in Detroit, Michigan. The scene Vera describes to Framton is quite similar to this one. By using sharply contrasting colors and letting the figures occupy the central foreground, the artist creates as vivid and striking a visual scene as Vera creates a verbal one.

Use these questions for discussion:

1. How does the artist draw your attention to the men and the animals? *The men and the animals are delineated with bold colors. The colors of the background are muted grays and off-white.*
2. Imagine how Framton would feel if he saw this scene from the window at this point in the story. What would he do or say? *Students may conjecture that he would scream, run out of the house, or have a nervous breakdown.*

Reteach

For students who need additional instruction understanding the parts of plot, review the concept by describing the plot of a movie your students will know. Tell students that most films introduce a conflict in the first half-hour, spend the next hour developing the problem, reach a climax, and then spend 10 to 15 minutes wrapping up loose ends. Show students how to map the parts of the plot onto a diagram like the one shown here. Identify the conflict and then indicate the details that show rising and falling action. To extend the activity, place students in small groups to analyze the plot of a movie or television sitcom they have seen. Encourage students to use a diagram like the one you have modeled.

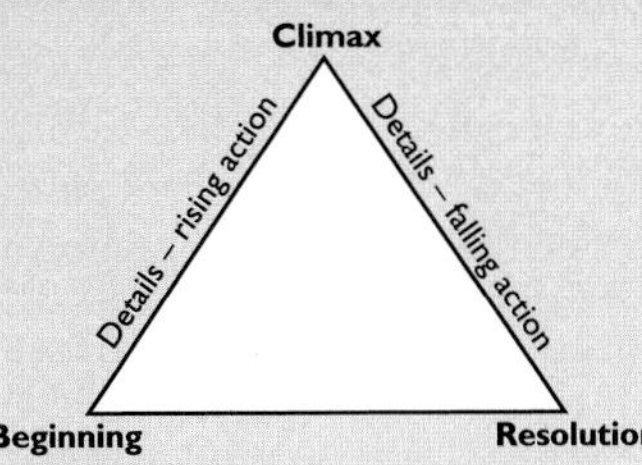

Listening to Literature Audiocassettes Play the audiocassette so that students can hear the climax of the story.

◆ Build Grammar Skills

❶ **Placement of *Only* and *Just*** Ask students where else the "only" could be placed without changing the meaning of the sentence. *It could be placed after* yawn *to modify the prepositional phrase* at the last moment.

◆ Reading for Success

❷ **Recognize the Writer's Purpose** Ask: Why does the writer include the detail, "don't they look as if they were muddy up to the eyes"? *The phrase recalls Vera's description of how the men died in a bog.*

◆ Reading for Success

❸ **Draw Conclusions** Ask: What can you conclude from Framton's behavior? *He believes Vera's story.*

◆ Reading for Success

❹ **Identify Relationships in Text** Ask students to identify the relationship between this story of Vera's and the one she told Framton. *This story suggests Vera doesn't have evil intentions but just likes to amuse herself in this way.*

Reinforce and Extend

Answers

◆ *Literature and Your Life*

Reader's Response Students might say Nuttel would simply express horror at what he thought to be ghosts.

Thematic Focus Students who share Vera's sense of humor might answer yes; those who feel Vera acted cruelly may answer no.

Check Your Comprehension

1. (a) Nuttel is living in the country to calm a nervous condition. (b) He is visiting the Sappletons at his sister's suggestion.
2. Vera says that her aunt expects her dead husband and brothers to return through the window.
3. Three men who fit Vera's descriptions come in through the window. Nuttel thinks they are ghosts.
4. She says that Nuttel told her that, due to a horrifying experience in India, he is terrified of dogs.

---

❶ You can **interpret** Mrs. Sappleton's yawn to mean she is bored.

only replaced a yawn at the last moment. Then she suddenly brightened into alert attention—but not to what Framton was saying.

❷ "Here they are at last!" she cried. "Just in time for tea, and don't they look as if they were muddy up to the eyes!"

Framton shivered slightly and turned towards the niece with a look intended to convey sympathetic comprehension. The child was staring out through the open window with dazed horror in her eyes. In a chill shock of nameless fear Framton swung round in his seat and looked in the same direction.

In the deepening twilight three figures were walking across the lawn towards the window; they all carried guns under their arms, and one of them was additionally burdened with a white coat hung over his shoulders. A tired brown spaniel kept close at their heels. Noiselessly they neared the house, and then a hoarse young voice chanted out of the dusk: "I said, Bertie, why do you bound?"

Framton grabbed wildly at his stick and hat; the hall door, the gravel drive, and the front gate were dimly noted stages in his headlong retreat. A cyclist coming along the road had to run into the hedge to avoid imminent collision.

"Here we are, my dear," said the bearer of the white mackintosh, coming in through the window; "fairly muddy, but most of it's dry. Who was that who bolted out as we came up?"

"A most extraordinary man, a Mr. Nuttel," said Mrs. Sappleton; "could only talk about his illnesses, and dashed off without a word of goodbye or apology when you arrived. One would think he had seen a ghost."

"I expect it was the spaniel," said the niece calmly; "he told me he had a horror of dogs. He was once hunted into a cemetery somewhere on the banks of the Ganges[2] by a pack of pariah dogs, and had to spend the night in a newly dug grave with the creatures snarling and grinning and foaming just above him. Enough to make anyone lose their nerve."

Vera's made-up story gives you a final clue from which you can **draw the conclusion** that her story about her uncle and cousins was false.

Romance at short notice was her specialty.

◆ Build Vocabulary

imminent (im´ ən ənt) *adj.*: Likely to happen soon; threatening

mackintosh (mak´ in täsh´) *n.*: Waterproof raincoat

pariah (pə rī´ ə) *adj.*: Despised; outcast

2. **Ganges** (gan´ jēz): River in northern India and Bangladesh.

Guide for Responding

◆ *Literature and Your Life*

Reader's Response If you were Mr. Nuttel, what would you have said to Vera as the men came through the window?

Thematic Focus Would you ever tell such a tale to a newcomer? Why or why not?

Activity Based on what you know about Nuttel, write a letter of introduction for him. You may wish to write the letter as Nuttel's sister.

☑ Check Your Comprehension

1. (a) For what reason is Framton Nuttel living in the country? (b) Why is he visiting the Sappletons?
2. How does Vera explain the open window?
3. Explain what causes Nuttel to rush from the house so suddenly.
4. How does Vera explain Nuttel's departure?

Beyond the Selection

FURTHER READING

Other Works by Saki

"The Interlopers"
"The Square Egg"

Other Works With the Theme of Imagination

"The Catbird Seat," James Thurber
"The Veldt," Ray Bradbury

We suggest that you preview these works before recommending them to students.

INTERNET

You can find additional information about Saki on the Internet. We suggest the following sites:

For a biography of Saki, go to **http://www.crl.com/%7Esubir/saki/bio.html**

For a bibliography of Saki's works, go to **http://www.crl.com/~subir/saki/bib.html**

Please be aware, however, that sites may have changed since we published this information. We *strongly recommend* that you preview the sites before you send students to them.

Guide for Responding *(continued)*

◆ Critical Thinking

Interpret

1. Contrast the personalities of Framton and Vera. What personality traits of Framton make him susceptible to her story? **[Contrast]**

2. At what point could you begin to suspect that Vera is telling a story? Give evidence from the story that shows her intent. **[Deduce]**

3. Explain how this story can be thought of as having a double ending. **[Interpret]**

4. Saki concludes the story with the statement "Romance at short notice was her specialty." Explain the meaning of romance. **[Interpret]**

Evaluate

5. Do you think the story's ending is effective? Why or why not? **[Criticize]**

Apply

6. Explain how a person's expectations can lead him or her to misunderstand or misinterpret obvious facts. **[Generalize]**

◆ Reading for Success

Strategies for Constructing Meaning

Review the reading strategies and notes showing how to construct meaning from what you read. Then apply the strategies to answer the following.

1. What is the effect of combining Mr. Nuttel's condition with Vera's mischievous nature?

2. What details and clues lead you to conclude that Vera's tale is fiction and not reality?

3. What can you infer about Vera's character from the way she treats Mr. Nuttel?

◆ Literary Focus

Plot Structure

The **plot structure** is the sequence of a story's events.

1. What are two events that lead up to the climax of the story?

2. What is the climax of the story?

3. What are two events that lead to the resolution, or end of the story?

◆ Build Vocabulary

Using Words From Names

English contains some words that derive from the name of a person. On your paper, match the following words with the definition and description of the person from whose name they derive.

1. boycott	**a.** a nonconformist; from a Texas rancher who refused to brand his cattle
2. draconian	**b.** to protest by refusing to use; from a nineteenth-century Irish land agent who refused to lower his rents
3. maverick	**c.** someone who willfully destroys property; from a Germanic tribe from the Dark Ages of Europe
4. vandal	**d.** severe; from a harsh Athenian lawgiver

Using the Word Bank: Word Choice

On your paper, write the word from the Word Bank described in each sentence.

1. This would be handy in the rain.

2. Nobody wants to be one of these.

3. This keeps you from seeing reality.

4. If you drive recklessly, having an accident is this.

◆ Build Grammar Skills

Placement of *Only* and *Just*

The placement of modifying words can affect the meaning of a sentence. For example, when the placement of the word ***just*** or ***only*** is changed, the meaning of a sentence changes.

Practice In your notebook, explain how the different placement of the word *just* or *only* changes the meaning of the following sentences.

1. (a) Mr. Nuttel could *only* talk about his illnesses.
(b) Mr. Nuttel could talk about *only* his illnesses.

2. (a) I shall give *just* you letters of introduction to all the people I know there.
(b) I shall give you *just* letters of introduction to all the people I know there.

Answers
◆ Critical Thinking

1. Framton is introverted, timid, and humorless; Vera is extroverted, self-confident, and mischievous. Framton's self-consciousness and self-absorption prevent him from correctly assessing the situation. His negative nature may lead him to expect the worst to happen.
2. Students might note that Vera begins her story after determining that Framton knows nothing about her aunt. She deliberately seeks to determine this fact so that her made-up story will not be detected.
3. One ending is the culmination of the story Vera tells Framton; the other is the beginning of the story she weaves about Framton for the benefit of her aunt.
4. In the context of the story, the word romance means an imaginative or whimsical tale. Vera can whip up such a tale on the spur of the moment.
5. Students may respond positively to the irony of the story's ending. They should support their opinions with reasons.
6. Students may cite experiences of their own when they misunderstood or misinterpreted a situation based on their own preconceived notions or expectations.

◆ Reading for Success

1. Students may find the contrast accentuates the qualities of each character. Nuttel is so wrapped up in his own self that he is an easy target for a practical joke.
2. Students may cite that Mrs. Sappleton's cheerfulness seems to contradict Vera's description of her tragedy. The final clue that the men are not ghosts is when one of them speaks in a casual way.
3. Suggested response: Vera is mischievous and considers others to be fair targets for her practical jokes.

◆ Literary Focus

1. Mrs. Sappleton says, "Here they are at last"; Framton sees the three men walking across the lawn.
2. The climax occurs when Framton runs from the house.
3. Mr. Sappleton asks about Framton; Vera begins her story about Framton.

◆ Build Vocabulary

Using Words From Names

1. b. 2. d 3. a 4. c

Using the Word Bank

1. mackintosh; 2. pariah; 3. delusion; 4. imminent

◆ Build Grammar Skills

Answers should be similar to these:

1. (a) All Mr. Nuttel could do about his illnesses was talk about them. (b) *His* illnesses were all Mr. Nuttel could talk about.
2. (a) You are the only person to whom I shall give letters of introduction. (b) All I shall give you are letters of introduction.

Grammar Reinforcement

For additional instruction and practice, use the lesson in the **Language Lab CD-ROM** on Misplaced Modifiers and the pages on Misplaced and Dangling Modifiers, pp. 61–63, in the *Writer's Solution Grammar Practice Book*.

Idea Bank

Customizing for
Performance Levels

Following are suggestions for matching Idea Bank topics with your students' performance levels:
Less Advanced Students: 1, 4, 6
Average Students: 2, 4, 7
More Advanced Students: 3, 5

Customizing for
Learning Modalities

Following are suggestions for matching Idea Bank topics with your students' learning modalities:
Verbal/Linguistic: 1, 2, 3, 4, 5
Musical/Rhythmic: 6
Visual/Spatial: 7
Interpersonal: 5

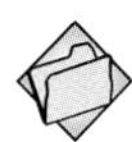

Guided Writing Lesson

Revision Strategy Have students reenter their writing to identify places where additional transitions that show time could illustrate the relationships between events. Students can use highlighter markers to identify each specific event in their summaries. Then, guide them to assess the relationships that they have shown between events in their drafts. Encourage them to consider additional or different transition words to make the relationships clearer as they revise their writing.

For more prewriting, elaboration, and revision instruction, see *Prentice Hall Writing and Grammar.*

Writing and Language Transparencies Have students use the Outline organizer, pp. 103–106, to organize their summaries.

Writing Lab CD-ROM
Have students complete the tutorial on Exposition. Follow these steps:

1. Students can use the timeline to arrange details of their summary chronologically.
2. Use the computer for drafting.
3. Have students use the interactive Self-Evaluation checklist for summaries.

Allow approximately 60 minutes of class time to complete these steps.

Build Your Portfolio

Idea Bank

Writing

1. **Letter** As Mr. Nuttel, write a letter to your sister. Tell her what happened at Mrs. Sappleton's.
2. **Diary** Write a diary entry from Vera's point of view, describing Nuttel's reactions to her trick.
3. **Story** Vera invents stories that contain factual information. Write another story that Vera might tell about the open window if the story were set in your city or town. Include factual information about life where you live.

Speaking, Listening, and Viewing

4. **Tape Recording** With classmates, record a reading of this story. In your recording, experiment with different tones (sarcastic, sincere, surprised, regretful, and so on) as you read the dialogue. Discuss how the different tones affect the story's meaning.
5. **Storytelling** Practice telling the tale that Vera tells. Use the details Vera provides, and add some of your own that make the story seem more real. Use pauses and facial expressions to make your telling believable. Tell the story to the class. Afterwards, invite the class to analyze what your facial expressions added to the story.

Researching and Representing

6. **Music** Find music that would be appropriate background for one scene in the story. Play the music for the class while you read the scene. Then explain why you chose it. **[Music Link]**
7. **Comic Strip** Illustrate key moments from the story in comic-strip form. Show characters' thoughts as well as their words. **[Art Link]**

Online Activity www.phlit.phschool.com

Guided Writing Lesson

Study Notes: Summary

When you **summarize**, you condense something longer into a few sentences or a paragraph. Vera's story about the open window is, in a sense, a summary of what could have been a longer, more detailed story. When writing a summary of a short story, you should include the key events of the story's plot. As you plan and write your summary, keep this point in mind:

Writing Skills Focus: Transitions That Show Time

When summarizing, it's important to indicate which events happened before others. **Transitions that show time** order include *first, then, next, afterward, at that time, before, earlier, immediately, in the past, later, now, soon, when,* and so on. These words indicate how one event is related to another in time.

Prewriting Reread "The Open Window." As you read, jot down the key events in the order in which they occur and the people involved. If you made a plot map earlier, you can use that to help you. At this stage, you can simply make a list of the events on a plot map, timeline, or in outline form.

Drafting Using the diagram you created, draft a summary of the story. Develop each key event into a sentence or two. Use transitional words to show readers the relationships between the events as they occurred over time.

Revising Reread your draft. Make sure you captured all the key events and people in your summary. Add any important details you may have forgotten, as well as transitional words and phrases that show time order. If you have used the modifiers *only* and *just,* check that they are placed correctly. For more on the placement of *only* and *just,* see pp. 468 and 475.

✓ ASSESSMENT OPTIONS

Formal Assessment, Selection Test, pp. 123–125, and Assessment Resources Software. The selection test is designed so that it can be easily customized to the performance levels of your students.
Alternative Assessment, p. 35, includes options for less advanced students, more advanced students, verbal/linguistic learners, visual/spatial learners, bodily/kinesthetic learners, and musical/rhythmic learners.

PORTFOLIO ASSESSMENT
Use the following rubrics in ***Alternative Assessment*** to assess student writing:
Letter: Expression Rubric, p. 94
Diary: Description Rubric, p. 97
Story: Fictional Narrative Rubric, p. 95
Guided Writing Lesson: Summary Rubric, p. 98

Part 1 Plot, Character, and Point of View

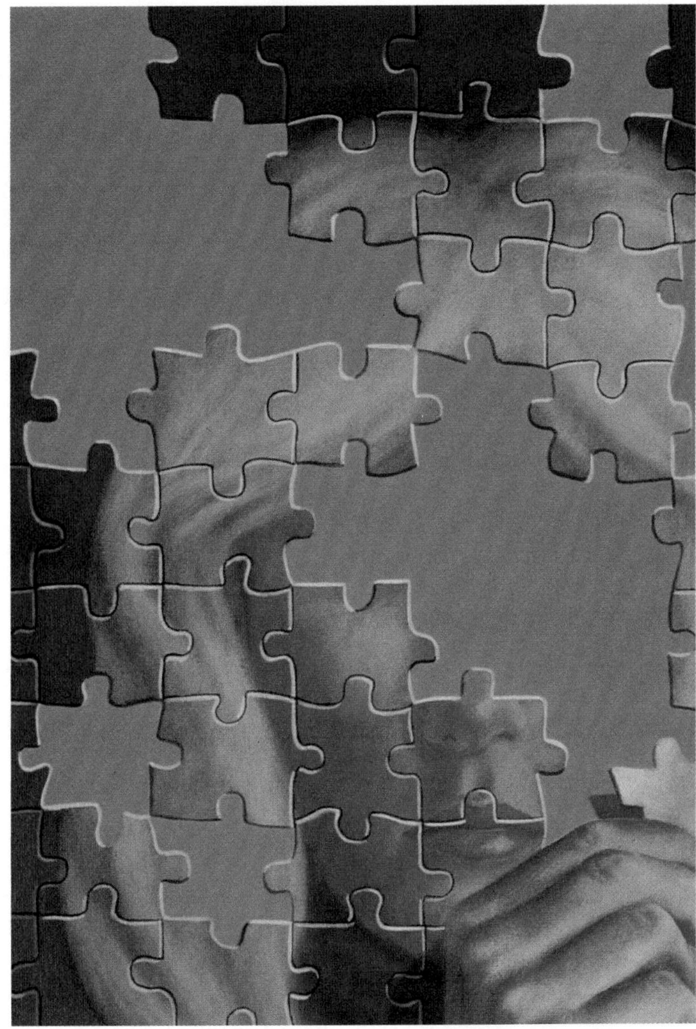

Abstract Puzzle of Woman Assembling Self,
Paul Micich

One-Minute Planning Guide

The selections in this part are stories that have strong elements of plot, character, and point of view. The section opens with Carl Stephenson's "Leiningen and the Ants," a short story about a man whose intelligence and will are pitted against an infestation of killer ants. "By the Waters of Babylon" is Stephen Vincent Benét's poetic story told from the viewpoint of a future dweller on our planet. Anton Chekhov's "A Problem" and Mark Twain's "Luck" reveal the peculiarities of memorable characters.

Customize for *Varying Student Needs*

When assigning the selections in this part to your students, keep in mind the following factors:

"Leiningen and the Ants"
- Contains violence in the struggle of man against nature.
- High interest for visual/spatial learners.

"By the Waters of Babylon"
- Students need to follow clues carefully to unravel the mystery of the story.

"A Problem"
- Through conversations, subtle qualities of character and issues are revealed.

"Luck"
- Difficult reading, but highly humorous satire.
- Some stilted language, used for comic effect.

Humanities: Art

Abstract Puzzle of Woman Assembling Self by Paul Micich.

Ask students to explain what they see here in light of the title of the artwork. They should notice that the puzzle is incomplete; encourage them to describe what is most clear, what is partly clear, and what is missing from the puzzle.

Help students link the artwork to the focus of Part 1—Plot, Character, Point of View—by answering the following questions:

1. The eyes are thought to be the feature that most reveals the inner person. What explanations can you give for the fact that all the woman's features are at least partly visible except for her eyes? *If the woman is "assembling herself," the inner person, as shown in her eyes, may be the part of her that remains most mysterious or difficult to see. She might be unwilling to reveal that part of herself, or she may not know herself well enough to have "assembled" that part yet.*
2. In what way is the woman gradually assembling herself doing the same thing a writer of stories does? *A story writer creates characters out of details that are gradually revealed to an audience.*

Prepare and Engage

LESSON OBJECTIVES

1. **To develop vocabulary and word identification skills**
   - Latin Plural Forms
   - Using the Word Bank: Analogies
   - Extending Word Study: Word Origins (ATE)
2. **To use a variety of reading strategies to comprehend a short story**
   - Connect Your Experience
   - Reading Strategy: Predict
   - Tips to Guide Reading: (ATE)
   - Read to Appreciate an Author's Craft (ATE)
3. **To increase knowledge of other cultures and to connect common elements across cultures**
   - Connecting Themes Across Cultures (ATE)
   - Cultural Connection (ATE)
4. **To express and support responses to the text**
   - Critical Thinking
   - Idea Bank: News Report
   - Idea Bank: Map
   - Viewing and Representing Mini-Lesson (ATE)
5. **To analyze literary elements**
   - Literary Focus: Conflict
   - Idea Bank: Change the Disaster
6. **To read in order to research self selected and assigned topics**
   - Idea Bank: Pests and Pals
   - Research Skills Mini-Lesson (ATE)
7. **To plan, prepare, organize, and present literary interpretations**
   - Idea Bank: Speech
8. **To use recursive writing processes to write a movie scene**
   - Guided Writing Lesson
9. **To increase knowledge of the rules of grammar and usage**
   - Build Grammar Skills: Apostrophes

Test Preparation

Critical Reading: Distinguish Between Fact and Nonfact (ATE, p. 479) The teaching tips and sample test item in this work-shop support the instruction and practice in the unit workshop:

Critical Reading: Recognize Forms of Propaganda; Distinguish Between Fact and Nonfact (SE, p. 565)

Guide for Reading

Carl Stephenson *(1886–1954)*

Although Carl Stephenson was born and lived his entire life in Germany, he vividly captures the torrid atmosphere and raw wilderness of the jungles of Brazil in "Leiningen Versus the Ants." This short story has been widely read and included in numerous anthologies since it was first published in *Esquire* magazine in 1938. It was also adapted for a radio program entitled "Suspense," starring Vincent Price, and made into a film entitled "The Naked Jungle," starring Charlton Heston as Leiningen.

Shying away from the spotlight, Stephenson insisted that "Leiningen Versus the Ants" be the only story of his to be published during his lifetime.

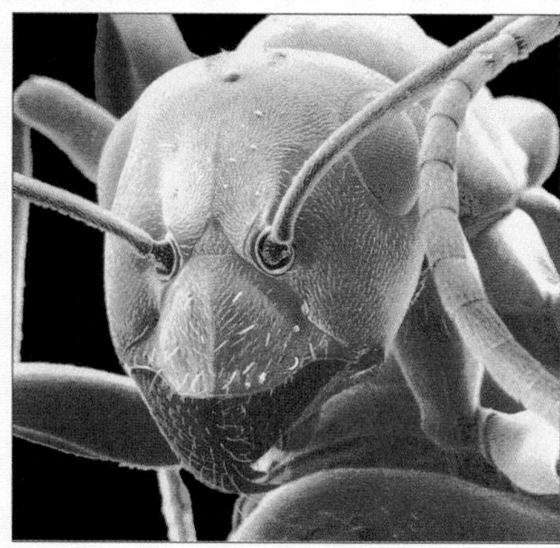

◆ Build Vocabulary

Borrowed Words: Latin Plural Forms

As a group of ants are swept down a river in this story, the author refers to them as "an *alluvium* of ants." *Alluvium* is a word borrowed from Latin that means "material, such as sand or gravel, swept along by water." Because *alluvium* comes directly from Latin, it retains its Latin plural form: *alluvia.* There are other borrowed words in English that behave the same way: *data* is the Latin plural form of *datum.* When you use *data,* therefore, you are always referring to more than one *datum.*

Word Bank

As you read "Leiningen Versus the Ants," you will encounter the words on this list. Each word is defined on the page where it first appears. Preview the list before you read.

peons
flout
weir
provender
alluvium
fomentations

◆ Build Grammar Skills

Correct Use of Apostrophes

While reading "Leiningen Versus the Ants," you'll see several instances where the author uses apostrophes. An **apostrophe** (') is a punctuation mark used to show possession and contraction.

Apostrophes are used to form possessives as follows: To make a singular noun possessive, an apostrophe and *s* are added: *Leiningen's* word.

To make a plural noun possessive, an apostrophe is added after the *s*: *Indians'* trust.

When apostrophes are used to form contractions, the apostrophe indicates where letters are omitted. In the following example, the apostrophe indicates that the *i* from *is* has been omitted.

... *there's* no reason ...

Apostrophes are *not* used to form plurals:

ten *miles* wide

nothing but *ants*

Prentice Hall Literature Program Resources

REINFORCE / RETEACH / EXTEND

Selection Support Pages
Build Vocabulary: Borrowed Words, p. 147
Build Grammar Skills: Correct Use of Apostrophes, p. 148
Reading Strategy: Predict Based on Plot Details, p. 149
Literary Focus: Conflict, p. 150

Strategies for Diverse Student Needs, p. 36

Beyond Literature Cross-Curricular Connection: Science, p. 36

Formal Assessment Selection Test, pp. 126–128; Assessment Resource Software

Alternative Assessment, p. 36

Writing and Language Transparencies
Story Map, pp. 83–86

Resource Pro CD-ROM

Listening to Literature Audiocassettes

Leiningen Versus the Ants

◆ Literature and Your Life

Connect Your Experience

Nature can be a terrifying enemy. Hurricanes, tornadoes, and violent thunderstorms are just a few of the natural phenomena that can do serious damage. Compare these familiar catastrophes with the one that the main character in this story, Leiningen, faces.

Journal Writing Imagine you have just learned that your community is in the path of a tornado or hurricane. What would you do? Write about steps you and your neighbors would take to avert disaster.

Thematic Focus: Personal Challenges

Leiningen uses a variety of tactics to try to overcome a seemingly invincible foe. What do you think are the most important attributes a person needs to succeed against overpowering odds?

◆ Background for Understanding

Science

Scientists divide the army ants that invade Stephenson's story into two groups. *Legionary ants* live in South America, while *driver ants* haunt the jungles of central Africa. Army ant colonies may have anywhere from ten thousand to more than one million members. The colonies travel across the land in narrow columns, killing anything unlucky enough to get in their path—usually other insects, but occasionally small mammals or lizards. A colony usually hunts for a few weeks, then rests for a few weeks, often clinging together in one giant mass. Imagine stumbling upon *that* while taking a stroll!

◆ Literary Focus

Conflict

A story almost always contains a **conflict**—a struggle between opposing forces. The conflict can be internal or external. An **internal conflict** takes place within a character, as he or she struggles with opposing feelings, beliefs, or needs. An **external conflict** occurs between two or more characters or between a character and a natural force. The main character in this story faces an external conflict as he struggles to protect his home from an onslaught of army ants.

◆ Reading Strategy

Make Predictions Based on Plot Details

You're watching the latest thriller when the main character hears a noise outside. As she steps into the darkness you think "No!" Based on what has already happened in the story, and the formula that movies like this seem to follow, you can **predict** that something scary is about to happen.

Stories, too, follow a pattern that helps you predict what is going to happen. Your predictions may be based on details or evidence in the story, as well as on what you know from your own experience.

As this story opens, we learn that an army of flesh-eating ants is headed toward the main character's plantation. Because there would be no story without a problem, you can predict that the ants will get close enough to be a real threat to the plantation. Details revealed in the story will enable you to make more specific predictions. Keep track of your predictions with a chart like the one shown.

Prediction	Reason	Outcome

Ask students if they have seen horror movies in which the "monster" was an insect or insects. If they were making such a movie, which insect would they choose to be the monster? *Students may cite spiders, locusts, cockroaches, etc.*

Point out that the story they are about to read, "Leiningen Versus the Ants," first published in 1938, was made into a horror movie entitled "The Naked Jungle," starring Charlton Heston, a famous movie star. Have students speculate about the kind of ant that would be the more dramatic in the film—a monster ant or a giant mass of small, deadly ants.

Connecting Themes Across Cultures

Challenge students to analyze the story to see what changes would need to be made to the plot and action to set the story in a more familiar environment and setting instead of the jungles of Brazil.

Tips to Guide Reading

Buddy Reading Suggest that students read this selection with a partner, noting both the questions the text raises as well as the elements that raise the suspense level of this exciting story.

Customize for
Less Proficient Readers

Have these students complete the prediction chart (p. 479) as they read. Suggest that they pause at intervals during the story to check the predictions they have made and revise the predictions, if necessary.

Customize for
Pre-AP Students

These students can be challenged to think about the internal conflict that Leiningen faces throughout the story, in addition to the external one. What forces are at war in him? Which force wins?

Test Preparation Workshop

Critical Reading: Distinguish Between Fact and Nonfact

Students preparing to take standardized tests need to be able to distinguish fact from opinion. A fact can be verified or proved, and an opinion cannot. Use this sample test item to reinforce the concept.

> The vivid descriptions and exciting action in the story inspired movie makers to create a film. The film version starring Charlton Heston was released in 1954 with the unusual title *The Naked Jungle*.

Which of the following is a FACT stated in the passage?

A The description in the story is vivid.
B The movie was released in 1954.
C The action in the story is exciting.
D The movie's title is unusual.

Remind students that adjectives such as *exciting, vivid*, or *unusual* state one person's opinion and cannot be proven. Only *B* is a fact which could be proven.

Develop Understanding

One-Minute Insight "Leiningen Versus the Ants" is a story in the long tradition of "man against nature" fiction. Leiningen is convinced that his superior intelligence will enable him to win the war against the voracious army of ants that attacks his plantation. He has planned long and carefully, but the battle insects prove to be persistent and resourceful. In the end, human intelligence and courage win out—but not by much. Leiningen shows bravado at the finale, but he has also learned humility in the face of nature's devastating threats.

Customize for *Visual/Spatial Learners*
Direct these students to infer from the photograph what the story may be about. *Students may say that there will be giant ants in the story.*

Customize for *English Language Leraners*
To help students who are unfamiliar with English expression, you may wish to paraphrase idiomatic expressions such as: "decent of you" *kind of you*; "give me the tip" *warn me*; and "do a bunk" *evacuate or leave*. Have students preview the story with a partner, discussing such phrases before beginning to read.

Leiningen Versus the Ants

Carl Stephenson

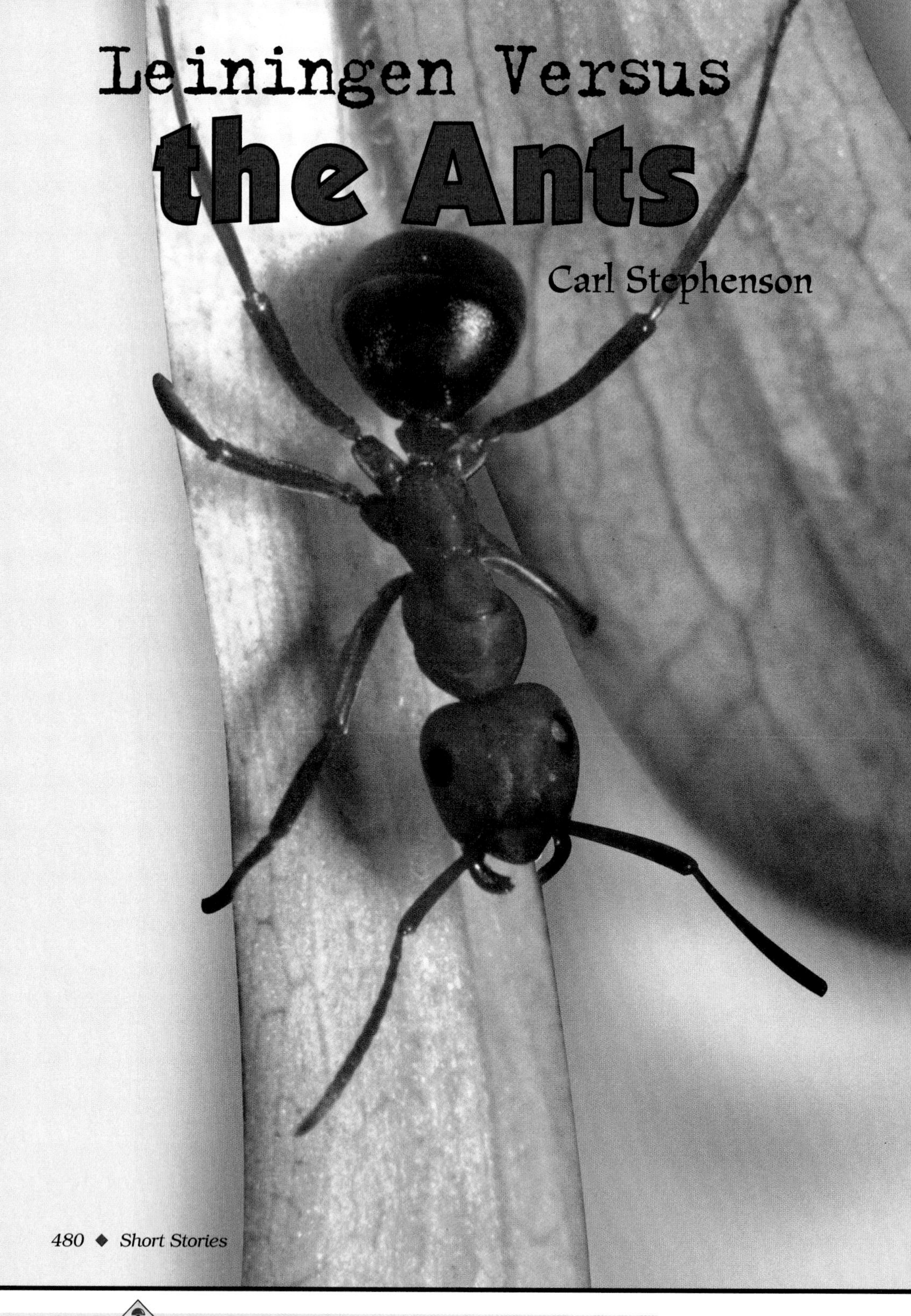

Block Scheduling Strategies

Consider these suggestions to take advantage of extended class time:

- Build background with the Cross-Curricular Connection: Science page in ***Beyond Literature***, p. 36.
- Have students work in pairs to complete the Journal Activity in Literature and Your Life on p. 479. Pairs can form groups to discuss their disaster plans.
- Introduce the Reading Strategy, Predict Based on Plot Details. As students read, encourage them to watch for details in the story that help readers predict the outcome. Suggest they complete a chart such as the one on p. 479 as they read.
- Use the Literary Focus paragraph on p. 479 to introduce the concept of conflict in a story, referring to familiar stories to clarify the distinction between internal and external conflict. After reading, have students answer the Literary Focus questions on p. 496 and follow up with the Literary Focus: Conflict page in ***Selection Support***, p. 150.
- Interested students can do further research into the habits of army ants discussed in Background for Understanding on p. 479. Encourage them to present their findings to the class.
- Have students work in groups to complete the Disaster Relief project in Build Your Portfolio on p. 497. If their area has been involved in a disaster, they might wish to focus specifically on that event.

"Unless they alter their course, and there's no reason why they should, they'll reach your plantation in two days at the latest."

Leiningen sucked placidly at a cigar about the size of a corn cob and for a few seconds gazed without answering at the agitated District Commissioner. Then he took the cigar from his lips and leaned slightly forward. With his bristling gray hair, bulky nose, and lucid eyes, he had the look of an aging and shabby eagle.

"Decent of you," he murmured, "paddling all this way just to give me the tip. But you're pulling my leg, of course, when you say I must do a bunk. Why, even a herd of saurians[1] couldn't drive me from this plantation of mine."

The Brazilian official threw up lean and lanky arms and clawed the air with wildly distended fingers. "Leiningen!" he shouted, "you're insane! They're not creatures you can fight—they're an elemental—an 'act of God'! Ten miles long, two miles wide—ants, nothing but ants! And every single one of them a fiend from hell; before you can spit three times they'll eat a full-grown buffalo to the bones. I tell you if you don't clear out at once there'll be nothing left of you but a skeleton picked as clean as your own plantation."

Leiningen grinned. "Act of God, my eye! Anyway, I'm not going to run for it just because an elemental's on the way. And don't think I'm the kind of fathead who tries to fend off lightning with his fists, either. I use my intelligence, old man. With me, the brain isn't a second blind gut;[2] I know what it's there for. When I began this model farm and plantation three years ago, I took into account all that could conceivably happen to it. And now I'm ready for anything and everything—including your ants."

The Brazilian rose heavily to his feet. "I've done my best," he gasped. "Your obstinacy endangers not only yourself, but the lives of your four hundred workers. You don't know these ants!"

1. **saurians** (sôr′ ē ənz) *n.*: Lizardlike animals.
2. **blind gut:** Reference to the appendix, which may have no function.

Leiningen accompanied him down to the river, where the government launch was moored. The vessel cast off. As it moved downstream, the exclamation mark neared the rail and began waving arms frantically. Long after the launch had disappeared round the bend, Leiningen thought he could still hear that dimming, imploring voice. "You don't know them, I tell you! *You don't know them!*"

But the reported enemy was by no means unfamiliar to the planter. Before he started work on his settlement, he had lived long enough in the country to see for himself the fearful devastations sometimes wrought by these ravenous insects in their campaigns for food. But since then he had planned measures of defense accordingly, and these, he was convinced, were in every way adequate to withstand the approaching peril.

Moreover, during his three years as planter, Leiningen had met and defeated drought, flood, plague, and all other "acts of God" which had come against him—unlike his fellow settlers in the district, who had made little or no resistance. This unbroken success he attributed solely to the observance of his lifelong motto: *The human brain needs only to become fully aware of its powers to conquer even the elements.* Dullards reeled senselessly and aimlessly into the abyss; cranks, however brilliant, lost their heads when circumstances suddenly altered or accelerated and ran into stone walls; sluggards drifted with the current until they were caught in whirlpools and dragged under. But such disasters, Leiningen contended, merely strengthened his argument that intelligence, directed aright, invariably makes man the master of his fate. ❸

Yes, Leiningen had always known how to grapple with life. Even here, in this Brazilian wilderness, his brain had triumphed over every difficulty and danger it had so far encountered. First he had vanquished primal forces by cunning and organization, then he had enlisted the resources of modern science to increase miraculously the yield of his plantation. And now he was sure he would prove more than a match for the "irresistible" ants.

◆ Reading Strategy

❶ Predict Based on Plot Details Ask students to use information from the title and the opening photograph to predict what the speaker is describing. *He is describing the movement of vicious ants.*

◆ Critical Thinking

❷ Infer Have students determine what they can tell about Leiningen's personality, based on his response to the official. *He is proud and very self-assured.*

◆ Critical Thinking

❸ Make a Judgment Ask students if they think Leiningen is correct when he says that the human brain can conquer the elements. *Sample answers: No; the elements cannot always be predicted and can foil even the best-laid plans. Yes; the human intellect is powerful when used wisely.*

Read to Appreciate Author's Craft

Students will enjoy reading this selection to appreciate the author's skill in crafting a suspenseful story with an exciting plot. Suggest that they take notes on the author's use of suspense in the climax of the plot as a model for their own writing.

Extending Word Study

Word Origins Many words used in the selection are commonly used British English words, including the following:

- *petrol* gas
- *blighters* mean or contemptible creatures or people
- *torches* flashlights

Suggest that students make a three column chart for their study of such words. As they read the selection, students can note the word in the first column and its context in the second. In the third column, students can write their own estimation of the word's meaning. Later, suggest that students use a good dictionary to confirm their impressions.

Cross-Curricular Connection: Geography

Brazil Point out to students that the landscape of Brazil, where "Leiningen Versus the Ants" is set, is varied. In the Northeast Region is a coastal plain and high plateaus. The Central and Southern Plateau Region is fertile and includes large coffee plantations. The Amazon Region is located in the North, and includes tropical rain forests and mountains. Most of the inhabitants of Brazil live in the plateaus, where the cities of São Paulo and Rio de Janeiro are located.

Give students the opportunity to look at a map of Brazil that shows geographical features and have them decide in what region the story probably takes place and what is probably grown on the plantation. *coffee* If possible, provide pictures from an Atlas or geography text that show coffee plantations in the Southern Plateau Region.

As students read the story, have them notice clues to the geographical features and animal and plant life of this region of Brazil.

◆ Critical Thinking

❶ Draw Conclusions Ask students what aspect of Leiningen's character makes his workers trust him so completely. *His utter self-confidence gives the workers confidence in him.*

◆ Reading Strategy

❷ Predict Based on Plot Details The ants must be very fierce to frighten the animals into a stampede.

◆ Literary Focus

❸ Conflict Have students identify the type of conflict in these paragraphs and name the two opposing sides. *The conflict is external, between the ants and the people of the plantation.*

◆ Reading Strategy

❹ Predict Based on Plot Details Ask students if they agree with Leiningen's opinion that the petrol would be impassable. *Sample answer: No; Leiningen appears overconfident and will probably underestimate the ants.*

Customize for
Visual/Spatial Learners
Visual/spatial learners might plot out a map of the plantation that shows the advance of the ants as the story progresses.

That same evening however, Leiningen assembled his workers. He had no intention of waiting till the news reached their ears from other sources. Most of them had been born in the district; the cry, "The ants are coming!" was to them an imperative signal for instant, panic-stricken flight, a spring for life itself. But so great was the Indians' trust in Leiningen, in Leiningen's word, and in Leiningen's wisdom, that they received his curt tidings, and his orders for the imminent struggle, with the calm-
❶ ness with which they were given. They waited, unafraid, alert, as if for the beginning of a new game or hunt which he had just described to them. The ants were indeed mighty, but not so mighty as the boss. Let them come!

They came at noon the second day. Their approach was announced by the wild unrest of the horses, scarcely controllable now either in stall or under rider, scenting from afar a vapor instinct with horror.

> ◆ **Reading Strategy**
> ❷ What can you predict about the ants based on the behavior of the animals?

It was announced by a stampede of animals, timid and savage, hurtling past each other; jaguars and pumas flashing by nimble stags of the pampas;[3] bulky tapirs, no longer hunters, themselves hunted, outpacing fleet kinkajous; maddened herds of cattle, heads lowered, nostrils snorting, rushing through tribes of loping monkeys, chattering in a dementia[4] of terror; then followed the creeping and springing denizens of bush and steppe, big and little rodents, snakes, and lizards.

Pell-mell the rabble swarmed down the hill to the plantation, scattered right and left before the barrier of the water-filled ditch, then sped onwards to the river, where, again hindered, they fled along its banks out of sight.

This water-filled ditch was one of the defense measures which Leiningen had long since prepared against the advent of the ants. It encompassed three sides of the plantation like a huge horseshoe. Twelve feet across, but not very deep, when dry it could hardly be described as an obstacle to either man or beast. But the ends of the "horseshoe" ran into the river which formed the northern boundary, and fourth side, of the plantation. And at the end nearer the house and outbuildings in the middle of the plantation, Leiningen had constructed a dam by means of which water from the river could be diverted into the ditch.

So now, by opening the dam, he was able to fling an imposing girdle of water, a huge quadrilateral with the river as its base, completely around the plantation, like the moat encircling a medieval city. Unless the ants were clever enough to build rafts, they had no hope of reaching the plantation, Leiningen concluded.

The twelve-foot water ditch seemed to afford in itself all the security needed. But while awaiting the arrival of the ants, Leiningen made a further improvement. The western section of the ditch ran along the edge of a tamarind wood,[5] and the branches of some great trees reached over the water. Leiningen now had them lopped so that ants could not descend from them within the "moat."

The women and children, then the herds of cattle, were escorted by peons on rafts over the river, to remain on the other side in absolute safety until the plunderers had departed. Leiningen gave this instruction, not because he believed the noncombatants were in any danger, but in order to avoid hampering the efficiency of the defenders.

Finally, he made a careful inspection of the "inner moat"—a smaller ditch lined with concrete, which extended around the hill on which stood the ranch house, barns, stables, and other buildings. Into this concrete ditch emptied the inflow pipes from three great petrol[6] tanks. If by some miracle the ants managed to cross the water and reach the plantation, this "rampart of petrol" would be an absolutely impassable protection for the besieged and their dwellings and stock. Such, at least, was Leiningen's opinion.

He stationed his men at irregular distances

3. **pampas** (pam´ pəz) *n.*: South American grassland.
4. **dementia** (di men´ shə) *n.*: Insanity or madness.
5. **tamarind** (tam´ ə rind) **wood:** Grove of leafy trees found in the tropics.
6. **petrol** (pet´ rəl) *adj.*: Gasoline.

Speaking, Listening, and Viewing Mini-Lesson

Motivational Speech

This mini-lesson supports the Speaking, Listening, and Viewing activity in the Idea Bank on p. 497.

Introduce Like an advertisement or a pep talk, a motivational speech encourages a group of people to act in a certain way. The speaker should use strong persuasive language, as well as facial expressions and body language to support his or her ideas.

Develop Ask students to identify the persuasive language Leiningen uses to motivate his workers. Use these questions:

- What character traits do the workers admire in Leiningen?
- What emotions does Leiningen appeal to as he addresses the workers?
- What words does he use to inspire trust?
- How does Leiningen address potential critics?

Apply As students plan their speeches, encourage them to use tactics similar to Leiningen's. You may choose to ask students to underline the specific words they have chosen to inspire their audience.

Assess Students can base their evaluations of their classmates' speeches on the strength of their persuasive language. Students might also use Peer Assessment: Speaker/Speech in ***Alternative Assessment,*** p. 118.

along the water ditch, the first line of defense. Then he lay down in his hammock and puffed drowsily away at his pipe until a peon came with the report that the ants had been observed far away in the south.

Leiningen mounted his horse, which at the feel of its master seemed to forget its uneasiness, and rode leisurely in the direction of the threatening offensive. The southern stretch of ditch—the upper side of the quadrilateral—was nearly three miles long; from its center one could survey the entire countryside. This was destined to be the scene of the outbreak of war between Leiningen's brain and twenty square miles of life-destroying ants.

It was a sight one could never forget. Over the range of hills, as far as eye could see, crept a darkening hem, ever longer and broader, until the shadow spread across the slope from east to west, then downward, downward, uncannily swift, and all the green herbage of that wide vista was being mown as by a giant sickle, leaving only the vast moving shadow, extending, deepening, and moving rapidly nearer. 6

When Leiningen's men, behind their barrier of water, perceived the approach of the long-expected foe, they gave vent to their suspense in screams and imprecations. But as the distance began to lessen between the "sons of hell" and the water ditch, they relapsed into silence. Before the advance of that awe-inspiring throng, their belief in the powers of the boss began to steadily dwindle.

Even Leiningen himself, who had ridden up just in time to restore their loss of heart by a display of unshakable calm, even he could not free himself from a qualm of malaise. Yonder were thousands of millions of voracious jaws bearing down upon him and only a suddenly

◆ **Build Vocabulary**

peons (pē´ änz) *n.*: Laborers

▼ **Critical Viewing** What does this picture suggest will happen to those who get too close to the ants? **[Draw Conclusions]** 7

◆ Literary Focus

5 Conflict Have students find the phrase in this passage that states the conflict of the story. *Students should cite "war between Leiningen's brain and twenty square miles of life-destroying ants."*

◆ Reading Strategy

6 Predict Based on Plot Details Ask students: What do you predict will happen when the ants reach the plantation? Will Leiningen's lines of defense hold, or will the ants get through them? Explain. *Students should predict, based on prior experience with reading stories, that the ants will get through Leiningen's defenses—otherwise, there would be no story.*

▶Critical Viewing◀

7 Draw Conclusions *The covered body of the dead man suggests that the ants will kill whatever they attack.*

Beyond the Classroom

Career Connection:

Wildlife Management Explain to students that a wildlife manager is someone employed by a state, federal, or private agency to manage animals in a specific area. A wildlife manager's responsibilities might include taking a census to find what animals inhabit an area, restocking game fish and birds, controlling animal diseases, and providing favorable environments for animals by planting trees and controlling harmful species. A career in wildlife management requires at least a bachelor's degree and demands strenuous outdoor work.

Ask students how a wildlife manager might have helped Leiningen. *Students may respond that Leiningen has assumed a role as wildlife manager in making plans to protect his plantation. Some may also point out that the District Commissioner supplied a warning that a wildlife manager may have issued.*

◆ Literary Focus

❶ Conflict The conflict in the story has grown in Leiningen's mind. Ask students what, in his opinion, he is fighting now. *He equates the ants with evil and rational thought with good; he sees the impending fight as a struggle between good and evil.*

◆ Literary Focus

❷ Conflict Have students identify the kind of conflict they find in this passage. What conflict is beginning to stir within Leiningen and the workers? *They are beginning to struggle with doubt and fear.*

◆ Reading Strategy

❸ Predict Based on Plot Details Ask: Do you believe that the ants will withdraw from the plantation? *Sample response: No; the ants are too determined and too numerous. They will find another way to attack. Once again, students should use their prior experience with stories to know that if the ants withdrew now, there would be no point to the story. Even the title proclaims that a fight is necessary.*

◆ Critical Thinking

❹ Make a Judgment Ask students whether they think the ants are making an intelligent choice to ford the ditch or are simply operating instinctively. *Some students may say the ants are acting intelligently, sacrificing the few so the many can reach the plantation.*

insignificant, narrow ditch lay between him and his men and being gnawed to the bones "before you can spit three times."

Hadn't his brain for once taken on more than it could manage? If the blighters decided to rush the ditch, fill it to the brim with their corpses, there'd still be more than enough to
❶ destroy every trace of that cranium of his. The planter's chin jutted; they hadn't got him yet, and he'd see to it they never would. While he could think at all, he'd flout both death and the devil.

The hostile army was approaching in perfect formation; no human battalions, however well drilled, could ever hope to rival the precision of that advance. Along a front that moved forward as uniformly as a straight line, the ants drew nearer and nearer to the water ditch. Then, when they learned through their scouts the nature of the obstacle, the two outlying wings of the army detached themselves from the main body and marched down the western and eastern sides of the ditch.

This surrounding maneuver took rather more than an hour to accomplish; no doubt the ants expected that at some point they would find a crossing.

During this outflanking movement by the wings, the army on the center and southern front remained still. The besieged were therefore able to contemplate at their leisure the thumb-long, reddish-black, long-legged insects; some of the Indians believed they could see, too, intent on them, the brilliant, cold eyes, and the razor-edged mandibles,[7] of this host of infinity.

It is not easy for the average person to imagine that an animal, not to mention an insect, can *think*. But now both the brain of Leiningen and the brains of the Indians began to stir with
❷ the unpleasant foreboding that inside every single one of that deluge of insects dwelled a thought. And that thought was: Ditch or no ditch, we'll get to your flesh!

Not until four o'clock did the wings reach the "horseshoe" ends of the ditch, only to find these ran into the great river. Through some kind of secret telegraphy, the report must then have flashed very swiftly indeed along the entire enemy line. And Leiningen, riding—no longer casually—along his side of the ditch, noticed by energetic and widespread movements of troops that for some unknown reason the news of the check had its greatest effect on the southern front, where the main army was massed. Perhaps the failure to find a way over the ditch was persuading the ants to withdraw from the plantation in search of spoils more easily attainable.

An immense flood of ants, about a hundred yards in width, was pouring in a glimmering black cataract down the far slope of the ditch. Many thousands were already drowning in the sluggish creeping flow, but they were followed by troop after troop, who clambered over their sinking comrades, and then themselves served as dying bridges to the reserves hurrying on in their rear.

Shoals of ants were being carried away by the current into the middle of the ditch, where gradually they broke asunder and then, exhausted by their struggles, vanished below the surface. Nevertheless, the wavering, floundering hundred-yard front was remorselessly if slowly advancing toward the besieged on the other bank. Leiningen had been wrong when he supposed the enemy would first have to fill the ditch with their bodies before they could cross: instead, they merely needed to act as stepping-stones, as they swam and sank, to the hordes ever pressing onwards from behind.

Near Leiningen a few mounted herdsmen awaited his orders. He sent one to the weir—the river must be dammed more strongly to increase the speed and power of the water coursing through the ditch.

A second peon was dispatched to the outhouses to bring spades and petrol sprinklers. A third rode away to summon to the zone of the offensive all the men, except the observation posts, on the nearby sections of the ditch, which were not yet actively threatened.

The ants were getting across far more quickly than Leiningen would have deemed possible. Impelled by the mighty cascade behind them, they struggled nearer and nearer to the inner

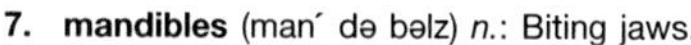

7. **mandibles** (man′ də bəlz) *n.*: Biting jaws.

Cultural Connection

Insect Plagues One of the most common themes of insect plagues in world folklore is that of the locust, a small type of grasshopper swarms, eating all vegetation in its path. Plagues of locusts are mentioned in the Bible and by the ancient Greeks, who thought the little insects were mythological monsters. Special ceremonies to drive away the feared locusts exist in Dahomey (West Africa), India, and Syria, where the people simply make as much noise as possible to deter an oncoming swarm. The locust is also a symbol of death and destruction for many Native Americans, especially among the Yurok and Wiyot groups.

Have students explore other plagues that appear in the folk literature and history of different cultures or in such works as the Bible.

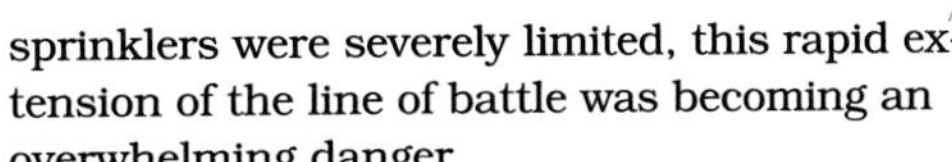

bank. The momentum of the attack was so great that neither the tardy flow of the stream nor its downward pull could exert its proper force; and into the gap left by every submerging insect, hastened forward a dozen more.

When reinforcements reached Leiningen, the invaders were halfway over. The planter had to admit to himself that it was only by a stroke of luck for him that the ants were attempting the crossing on a relatively short front: had they assaulted simultaneously along the entire length of the ditch, the outlook for the defenders would have been black indeed.

Even as it was, it could hardly be described as rosy, though the planter seemed quite unaware that death in a gruesome form was drawing closer and closer. As the war between his brain and the "act of God" reached its climax, the very shadow of annihilation began to pale to Leiningen, who now felt like a champion in a new Olympic game, a gigantic and thrilling contest, from which he was determined to emerge victor. Such, indeed, was his aura of confidence that the Indians forgot their fear of the peril only a yard or two away; under the planter's supervision, they began fervidly digging up to the edge of the bank and throwing clods of earth and spadefuls of sand into the midst of the hostile fleet.

The petrol sprinklers, hitherto used to destroy pests and blights on the plantation, were also brought into action. Streams of evil-reeking oil now soared and fell over an enemy already in disorder through the bombardment of earth and sand.

The ants responded to these vigorous and successful measures of defense by further developments of their offensive. Entire clumps of huddling insects began to roll down the opposite bank into the water. At the same time, Leiningen noticed that the ants were now attacking along an ever-widening front. As the numbers both of his men and his petrol sprinklers were severely limited, this rapid extension of the line of battle was becoming an overwhelming danger.

To add to his difficulties, the very clods of earth they flung into that black floating carpet often whirled fragments toward the defenders' side, and here and there dark ribbons were already mounting the inner bank. True, wherever a man saw these they could still be driven back into the water by spadefuls of earth or jets of petrol. But the file of defenders was too sparse and scattered to hold off at all points these landing parties, and though the peons toiled like mad men, their plight became momently more perilous.

One man struck with his spade at an enemy clump, did not draw it back quickly enough from the water; in a trice the wooden haft swarmed with upward scurrying insects. With a curse, he dropped the spade into the ditch; too late, they were already on his body. They lost no time; wherever they encountered bare flesh they bit deeply; a few, bigger than the rest, carried in their hindquarters a sting which injected a burning and paralyzing venom. Screaming, frantic with pain, the peon danced and twirled like a dervish.[8]

Realizing that another such casualty, yes, perhaps this alone, might plunge his men into confusion and destroy their morale, Leiningen roared in a bellow louder than the yells of the victim: "Into the petrol, idiot! Douse your paws in the petrol!" The dervish ceased his pirouette as if transfixed, then tore off his shirt and plunged his arm and the ants hanging to it up to the shoulder in one of the large open tins of petrol. But even then the fierce mandibles did not slacken; another peon had to help him squash and detach each separate insect.

Distracted by the episode, some defenders had turned away from the ditch. And now

◆ *Literature and Your Life*
How do Leiningen's observations about morale in an emergency apply to less drastic situations? 6

◆ **Build Vocabulary**
flout (flout) *v.*: Show open contempt
weir (wēr) *n.*: Low dam

8. **dervish** (dər′ vish) *n.*: One who performs a ritual Muslim whirling dance.

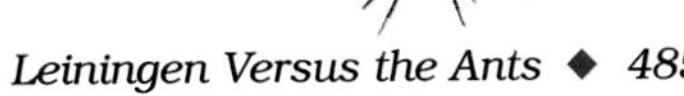

◆ Critical Thinking

5 Analyze Character Ask students what Leiningen's new attitude tells them about his character. *He is unwilling or unable to consider defeat, is highly competitive, and is blinded by his own determination. He sees life as a game.*

◆ *Literature and Your Life*

6 *Students will recognize the importance of morale in sports teamwork as well as in firefighting and disaster rescue operations.*

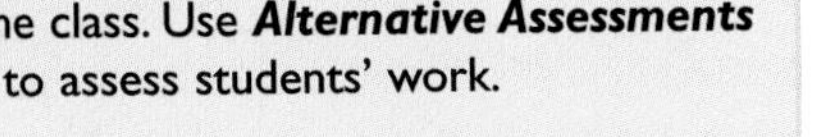

Research Skills Mini-Lesson

Steps to Conduct Research

This mini-lesson supports the Pests and Pals Researching and Representing project in the Idea Bank on p. 497.

Introduce When conducting a research project, it is important that students first determine their research priorities. They must narrow the scope of their topic and determine what kind and how much information they need in order to find facts and draw appropriate conclusions.

Develop Advise students to complete these pre-research steps:

- narrow a topic to allow effective research
- make a list of relevant and researchable questions
- decide what sources might yield the best results

Apply After students have developed a research plan, encourage them to take action. Remind students that they may need to revise their plans based on the availability of information. Have them decide on a format to report their conclusions and information such as: a chart, report, oral presentation, or multimedia representation. In addition to reporting on their findings, ask students to share information about their search. Students may benefit from the research experiences of their classmates.

Assess Have students share their findings with the class. Use ***Alternative Assessments*** p. 106 to assess students' work.

◆ Reading Strategy

❶ **Predict Based on Plot Details** Ask students if they predict that the ants or Leiningen will win the struggle. On what do they base their predictions? *Students may use this sentence to predict that Leiningen will win the struggle: "But then such an onlooker would have reckoned only by what he saw . . . and not by the unseen activity that can go on in a man's brain." The author is implying that Leiningen's reasoning ability will help him defeat the ants.*

▶Critical Viewing◀

❷ **Speculate** *Suggested response: The men may be looking at and discussing a place where the ants could breach their defenses.*

cries of fury, a thudding of spades, and a wild trampling to and fro, showed that the ants had made full use of the interval, though luckily only a few had managed to get across. The men set to work again desperately with the barrage of earth and sand. Meanwhile an old Indian, who acted as medicine man to the plantation workers, gave the bitten peon a drink he had prepared some hours before, which, he claimed, possessed the virtue of dissolving and weakening ants' venom.

❶ Leiningen surveyed his position. A dispassionate observer would have estimated the odds against him at a thousand to one. But then such an onlooker would have reckoned only by what he saw—the advance of myriad battalions of ants against the futile efforts of a few defenders—and not by the unseen activity that can go on in a man's brain.

For Leiningen had not erred when he decided he would fight elemental with elemental. The water in the ditch was beginning to rise; the stronger damming of the river was making itself apparent.

Visibly the swiftness and power of the masses of water increased, swirling into quicker and quicker movement its living black surface, dispersing its pattern, carrying away more and more of it on the hastening current.

Victory had been snatched from the very jaws of defeat. With a hysterical shout of joy, the peons feverishly intensified their bombardment of earth clods and sand.

And now the wide cataract down the opposite bank was thinning and ceasing, as if the ants were becoming aware that they could not

▼ **Critical Viewing** What do you think Leiningen and his assistant are discussing here? **[Speculate]**

Cultural Connection

Medicine Men Medicine men, or shamans, have been found in cultures all over the world. These powerful men were believed to communicate with the spirit world. People believed that they helped make hunts successful and they foresaw the future. Above all, medicine men were healers. They assisted at births and deaths, and in many cultures they were the only doctors available. Their knowledge of local medicinal plants made it possible for them to treat many injuries and illnesses successfully. Have students consider how the Brazilian medicine man's knowledge might help Leiningen.

Interested students may wish to explore the kinds of alternative medicines and therapies that are available throughout the world. They may wish to find out more about legal restrictions that the United States places on experimental or alternative healing methods and the kinds of safeguards that are in place such as the Food and Drug Administration.

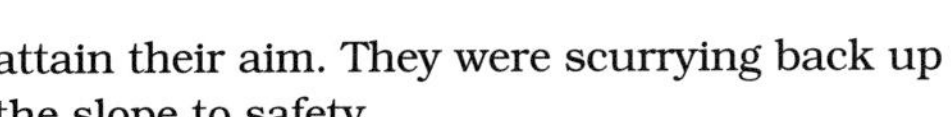

attain their aim. They were scurrying back up the slope to safety.

All the troops so far hurled into the ditch had been sacrificed in vain. Drowned and floundering insects eddied in thousands along the flow, while Indians running on the bank destroyed every swimmer that reached the side.

Not until the ditch curved toward the east did the scattered ranks assemble again in a coherent mass. And now, exhausted and half-numbed, they were in no condition to ascend the bank. Fusillades of clods drove them round the bend toward the mouth of the ditch and then into the river, wherein they vanished without leaving a trace.

The news ran swiftly along the entire chain of outposts, and soon a long scattered line of laughing men could be seen hastening along the ditch toward the scene of victory.

For once they seemed to have lost all their native reserve, for it was in wild abandon now they celebrated the triumph—as if there were no longer thousands of millions of merciless, cold and hungry eyes watching them from the opposite bank, watching and waiting.

The sun sank behind the rim of the tamarind wood and twilight deepened into night. It was not only hoped but expected that the ants would remain quiet until dawn. But to defeat any forlorn attempt at a crossing, the flow of water through the ditch was powerfully increased by opening the dam still further.

In spite of this impregnable barrier, Leiningen was not yet altogether convinced that the ants would not venture another surprise attack. He ordered his men to camp along the bank overnight. He also detailed parties of them to patrol the ditch in two of his motor cars and ceaselessly to illuminate the surface of the water with headlights and electric torches.

After having taken all the precautions he deemed necessary, the farmer ate his supper with considerable appetite and went to bed. His slumbers were in no wise disturbed by the memory of the waiting, live, twenty square miles.

Dawn found a thoroughly refreshed and active Leiningen riding along the edge of the ditch. The planter saw before him a motionless and unaltered throng of besiegers. He studied the wide belt of water between them and the plantation, and for a moment almost regretted that the fight had ended so soon and so simply. In the comforting, matter-of-fact light of morning, it seemed to him now that the ants hadn't the ghost of a chance to cross the ditch. Even if they plunged headlong into it on all three fronts at once, the force of the now powerful current would inevitably sweep them away. He had got quite a thrill out of the fight—a pity it was already over. ❹

He rode along the eastern and southern sections of the ditch and found everything in order. He reached the western section, opposite the tamarind wood, and here, contrary to the other battle fronts, he found the enemy very busy indeed. The trunks and branches of the trees and the creepers of the lianas,[9] on the far bank of the ditch, fairly swarmed with industrious insects. But instead of eating the leaves there and then, they were merely gnawing through the stalks, so that a thick green shower fell steadily to the ground. ❺

No doubt they were victualing columns sent out to obtain provender for the rest of the army. The discovery did not surprise Leiningen. He did not need to be told that ants are intelligent, that certain species even use others as milch cows, watchdogs, and slaves. He was well aware of their power of adaptation, their sense of discipline, their marvelous talent for organization. ❻

His belief that a foray to supply the army was in progress was strengthened when he saw the leaves that fell to the ground being dragged to the troops waiting outside the wood. Then all at once he realized the aim that rain of green was intended to serve.

9. **lianas** (lē a′ nəz) *n.*: Climbing vines found in the tropics.

◆ **Build Vocabulary**

provender (präv′ ən dər) *n.*: Food

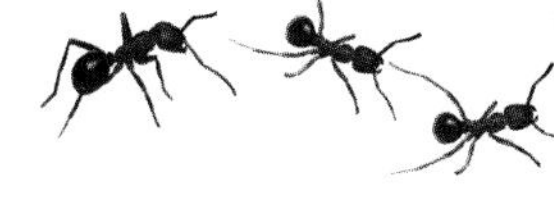

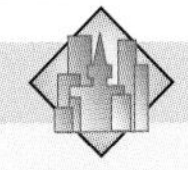

◆ Reading Strategy

❸ **Predict Based on Plot Details** Ask students if they think the men have really vanquished the ants. *Sample answer: No; the ants will regroup and try another strategy. Students can use their experience with other stories to know that if the ants were vanquished at this point, the story would be over.*

◆ Reading Strategy

❹ **Predict Based on Plot Details** Have students think of a way the ants might cross the wide belt of water. *Sample answer: They could cross on a raft or a bridge of debris. Accept any reasonable predictions.*

◆ Critical Thinking

❺ **Draw Conclusions** What do students think the ants plan to do with the creepers of the lianas? Are the ants acting intelligently or simply using instinct? *They plan to use them to float across the water. It seems that the ants are now matching their ingenuity and intelligence against Leiningen's.*

◆ Background for Understanding

❻ **Science** Explain to students that army ants, like other ants, live in highly structured societies. Each colony has a queen, whose job is to reproduce, and legions of workers that perform the various tasks that are necessary to maintain the colony. Although real army ants are not quite as destructive as the author portrays, they are well-organized, carnivorous creatures that can cause great damage.

Beyond the Classroom

Community Connection

Insect Threats Many communities face threats from insects—though, unlike Leiningen's ants, they are rarely threats to the inhabitants' lives. Some midwestern areas live through periodic infestations of locusts. Fruit-growing communities have pests that eat fruit. Many areas are infested with tent caterpillars or gypsy moths, or suffer from disease-carrying ticks or mosquitoes. Have students look into the insect pests that bother their community to find out how they threaten the area and what can be done to control them. Alternatively, students may wish to find out more about the effects of pests and insects on farming, available pesticide controls, and the resulting environmental concerns. Suggest that students find out the areas of our country that place restrictions on importation of fruits, vegetables and live plants to help control insect threats to the local crops.

◆ Critical Thinking

❶ **Connect** Have students connect Macbeth's fate to the fate suggested for Leiningen. *Macbeth misinterpreted a prophecy and believed he was invulnerable; Leiningen's belief in the invulnerability of his fortifications is about to be tested.*

◆ Critical Thinking

❷ **Infer** Ask students what Leiningen's curiosity about the stag reveals about him. *He is a bit cold-blooded, and he has very little fear. He is also curious.*

◆ Literary Focus

❸ **Conflict** The ants will probably find a way to ride out the water surges and cross the ditch. It is still too soon in the story for the ants to be finally defeated.

Customize for *Pre-AP Students*

Students can be challenged to note how Leiningen's attitude toward the ants has changed. Point out that now his battle has taken on the epic proportions of a struggle between good and evil, and he has cast himself as the proponent of good. Have students discuss evidence for this change and why it has occurred.

Customize for *Gifted/Talented Students*

Encourage these students to find words in the narrative that set the tone and pace of the action. *Students may note the writer uses such words as* quivering, toiling, ominous, rustled, galloped, blinded, *and* reeled. Ask students to suggest music that might match the mood these words convey.

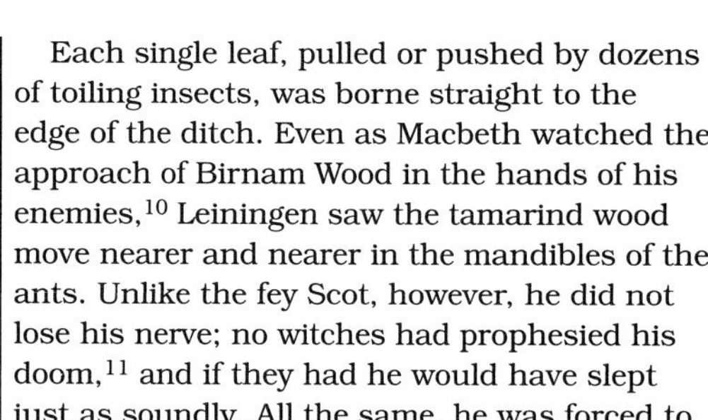

❶ Each single leaf, pulled or pushed by dozens of toiling insects, was borne straight to the edge of the ditch. Even as Macbeth watched the approach of Birnam Wood in the hands of his enemies,[10] Leiningen saw the tamarind wood move nearer and nearer in the mandibles of the ants. Unlike the fey Scot, however, he did not lose his nerve; no witches had prophesied his doom,[11] and if they had he would have slept just as soundly. All the same, he was forced to admit to himself that the situation was now far more ominous than that of the day before.

He had thought it impossible for the ants to build rafts for themselves—well, here they were, coming in thousands, more than enough to bridge the ditch. Leaves after leaves rustled down the slope to the water, where the current drew them away from the bank and carried them into midstream. And every single leaf carried several ants. This time the farmer did not trust to the alacrity of his messengers. He galloped away, leaning from his saddle and yelling orders as he rushed past outpost after outpost: "Bring petrol pumps to the southwest front! Issue spades to every man along the line facing the wood!" And arrived at the eastern and southern sections, he dispatched every man except the observation posts to the menaced west.

Then, as he rode past the stretch where the ants had failed to cross the day before, he witnessed a brief but impressive scene. Down the slope of the distant hill there came toward him a singular being, writhing rather than running, an animal-like blackened statue with a shapeless head and four quivering feet that knuckled under almost ceaselessly. When the creature reached the far bank of the ditch and collapsed opposite Leiningen, he recognized it as a pampas stag, covered over and over with ants.

It had strayed near the zone of the army. As usual, they had attacked its eyes first. Blinded, it had reeled in the madness of hideous torment straight into the ranks of its persecutors, and now the beast swayed to and fro in its death agony.

With a shot from his rifle Leiningen put it out of its misery. Then he pulled out his watch. He hadn't a second to lose, but for life itself he could not have denied his curiosity the satisfaction of knowing how long the ants would take—for personal reasons, so to speak. After six minutes the white polished bones alone remained. That's how he himself would look before you can—Leiningen spat once, and put spurs to his horse.

The sporting zest with which the excitement of the novel contest had inspired him the day before had now vanished; in its place was a cold and violent purpose. He would send these vermin back to the hell where they belonged, somehow, anyhow. Yes, but how was indeed the question; as things stood at present it looked as if the devils would raze him and his men from the earth instead. He had underestimated the might of the enemy; he really would have to bestir himself if he hoped to outwit them.

The biggest danger now, he decided, was the point where the western section of the ditch curved southward. And arrived there, he found his worst expectations justified. The very power of the current had huddled the leaves and their crews of ants so close together at the bend that the bridge was almost ready.

True, streams of petrol and clumps of earth still prevented a landing. But the number of floating leaves was increasing ever more swiftly. It could not be long now before a stretch of water a mile in length was decked by a green pontoon over which the ants could rush in millions.

Leiningen galloped to the weir. The damming of the river was controlled by a wheel on its bank. The planter ordered the man at the wheel first to lower the water in the ditch almost to vanishing point, next to wait a moment, then suddenly to

> **◆ Literary Focus**
> Predict whether this strategy will be successful.

10. **Macbeth . . . enemies:** In William Shakespeare's play *Macbeth*, soldiers carried boughs from Birnam Wood to hide behind as they attacked a castle.
11. **fey** (fā) **Scot . . . doom:** "Fey Scot" refers to Macbeth, whose death was foretold by three witches.

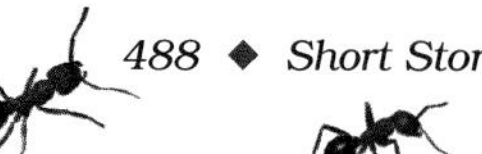

Cross-Curricular Connection: Social Studies

Farming in Brazil Explain to students that the interior of Brazil is a harsh region, with scarce grazing land and poor soil. Farmers there raise small crops of beans, corn, and cotton. On the coastal plains of the Northeast, there are cacao bean, sugar cane, and tobacco farms. In the Central and Southern Plateaus, where Leiningen's plantation is probably located, coffee is the largest crop. Farmers also grow potatoes, sugar cane, rice, and wheat.

Challenge interested students to use reference materials to discover further information about farming practices in Brazil and the climate and the types of crops grown there. Alternatively, students may wish to select a different topic to research such as worldwide plantation farming practices throughout history, for example, tobacco plantations in the South before the Civil War.

let the river in again. This maneuver of lowering and raising the surface, of decreasing then increasing the flow of water through the ditch, was to be repeated over and over again until further notice.

This tactic was at first successful. The water in the ditch sank, and with it the film of leaves. The green fleet nearly reached the bed and the troops on the far bank swarmed down the slope to it. Then a violent flow of water at the original depth raced through the ditch, overwhelming leaves and ants, and sweeping them along.

This intermittent rapid flushing prevented just in time the almost completed fording of the ditch. But it also flung here and there squads of the enemy vanguard simultaneously up the inner bank. These seemed to know their duty only too well, and lost no time accomplishing it. The air rang with the curses of bitten Indians. They had removed their shirts and pants to detect the quicker the upward-hastening insects; when they saw one, they crushed it; and fortunately the onslaught as yet was only by skirmishers.

Again and again, the water sank and rose, carrying leaves and drowned ants away with it. It lowered once more nearly to its bed; but this time the exhausted defenders waited in vain for the flush of destruction. Leiningen sensed disaster; something must have gone wrong with the machinery of the dam. Then a sweating peon tore up to him:

"They're over!"

While the besieged were concentrating upon the defense of the stretch opposite the wood, the seemingly unaffected line beyond the wood had become the theater of decisive action. Here the defenders' front was sparse and scattered; everyone who could be spared had hurried away to the south.

Just as the man at the weir had lowered the water almost to the bed of the ditch, the ants on a wide front began another attempt at a direct crossing like that of the preceding day. Into the emptied bed poured an irresistible throng. Rushing across the ditch, they attained the inner bank before the Indians fully grasped the situation. Their frantic screams dumbfounded the man at the weir. Before he could direct the river anew into the safeguarding bed he saw himself surrounded by raging ants. He ran like the others, ran for his life. 4

When Leiningen heard this, he knew the plantation was doomed. He wasted no time bemoaning the inevitable. For as long as there was the slightest chance of success, he had stood his ground; and now any further resistance was both useless and dangerous. He fired three revolver shots into the air—the prearranged signal for his men to retreat instantly within the "inner moat." Then he rode toward the ranch house.

This was two miles from the point of invasion. There was therefore time enough to prepare the second line of defense against the advent of the ants. Of the three great petrol cisterns near the house, one had already been half emptied by the constant withdrawals needed for the pumps during the fight at the water ditch. The remaining petrol in it was now drawn off through underground pipes into the concrete trench which encircled the ranch house and its outbuildings.

And there, drifting in twos and threes, Leiningen's men reached him. Most of them were obviously trying to preserve an air of calm and indifference, belied, however, by their restless glances and knitted brows. One could see their belief in a favorable outcome of the struggle was already considerably shaken.

The planter called his peons around him.

"Well, lads," he began, "we've lost the first round. But we'll smash the beggars yet, don't you worry. Anyone who thinks otherwise can draw his pay here and now and push off. There are rafts enough and to spare on the river and plenty of time still to reach 'em." 5

Not a man stirred.

Leiningen acknowledged his silent vote of confidence with a laugh that was half a grunt. "That's the stuff, lads. Too bad if you'd missed the rest of the show, eh? Well, the fun won't start till morning. Once these blighters turn

◆ Critical Thinking

4 Draw Conclusions Ask students what the workers now realize about their situation. *They can now see that they are in mortal danger, a fact that their faith in Leiningen has kept them from knowing.*

◆ Build Grammar Skills

5 Correct Use of Apostrophes Have students identify the words in these paragraphs that use apostrophes. Ask them whether the apostrophes indicate contractions or possessives; for the contractions, have them state the words that have been joined or shortened. *They are all contractions: we've for "we have," we'll for "we will," 'em for "them," and that's for "that is."*

Customize for *Less Proficient Readers*

These students may benefit from having Leiningen's plan outlined to them. Explain that there are two lines of defense for the plantation, and that the men have had to retreat from the first line. The second line is much nearer to the house; retreating there means that the ants will destroy the crops grown on the plantation.

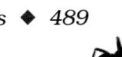

◆ Literary Focus

❶ Conflict Ask students how Leiningen is able to resolve the inner conflict that had disturbed him earlier. *He has worked out a plan and is once again confident in the power of his mind to defeat the ants.*

◆ Reading Strategy

❷ Predict Based on Plot Details Ask students what they think Leiningen has planned for the ants. *Suggested answer: His calm demeanor indicates he has a resourceful plan. Knowing that the petrol is highly flammable may lead students to guess that he is planning to burn them.*

tail, there'll be plenty of work for everyone and higher wages all round. And now run along and get something to eat; you've earned it all right."

In the excitement of the fight the greater part of the day had passed without the men once pausing to snatch a bite. Now that the ants were for the time being out of sight, and the "wall of petrol" gave a stronger feeling of security, hungry stomachs began to assert their claims.

The bridges over the concrete ditch were removed. Here and there solitary ants had reached the ditch; they gazed at the petrol meditatively, then scurried back again. Apparently they had little interest at the moment for what lay beyond the evil-reeking barrier, the abundant spoils of the plantation were the main attraction. Soon the trees, shrubs and beds for miles around were hulled with ants zealously gobbling the yield of long weary months of strenuous toil.

As twilight began to fall, a cordon of ants marched around the petrol trench, but as yet made no move toward its brink. Leiningen posted sentries with headlights and electric torches, then withdrew to his office, and began to reckon up his losses. He estimated these as large, but, in comparison with his bank balance, by no means unbearable. He worked out in some detail a scheme of intensive cultivation ❶ which would enable him, before very long, to more than compensate himself for the damage now being wrought to his crops. It was with a contented mind that he finally betook himself to bed where he slept deeply until dawn, undisturbed by any thought that next day little more might be left of him than a glistening skeleton.

He rose with the sun and went out on the flat roof of his house. And a scene like one from Dante[12] lay around him; for miles in every direction there was nothing but a black, glittering multitude, a multitude of rested, sated, but nonetheless voracious ants; yes, look as far as one might, one could see nothing but that rustling black throng, except in the north, where the great river drew a boundary they could not hope to pass. But even the high stone breakwater, along the bank of the river, which Leiningen had built as a defense against inundations, was, like the paths, the shorn trees and shrubs, the ground itself, black with ants.

So their greed was not glutted in razing that vast plantation? Not by a long chalk; they were all the more eager now on a rich and certain booty—four hundred men, numerous horses, and bursting granaries.

At first it seemed that the petrol trench would serve its purpose. The besiegers sensed the peril of swimming it, and made no move to plunge blindly over its brink. Instead they devised a better maneuver; they began to collect shreds of bark, twigs and dried leaves and dropped these into the petrol. Everything green, which could have been similarly used, had long since been eaten. After a time, though, a long procession could be seen bringing from the west the tamarind leaves used as rafts the day before.

Since the petrol, unlike the water in the outer ditch, was perfectly still, the refuse stayed where it was thrown. It was several hours before the ants succeeded in covering an appreciable part of the surface. At length, however, they were ready to proceed to a direct attack.

Their storm troops swarmed down the concrete side, scrambled over the supporting surface of twigs and leaves, and impelled these over the few remaining streaks of open petrol until they reached the other side. Then they began to climb up this to make straight for the helpless garrison.

During the entire offensive, the planter sat peacefully, watching them with interest, but not stirring a muscle. Moreover, he had ordered his men not to disturb in any way whatever the advancing horde. So they squatted listlessly along the bank of the ditch and waited for a sign from the boss.

The petrol was now covered with ants. A few had climbed the inner concrete wall and were scurrying toward the defenders.

12. **Dante** (dan´ tā): Italian poet (1265–1321) who wrote *The Divine Comedy*, describing the horrors of hell.

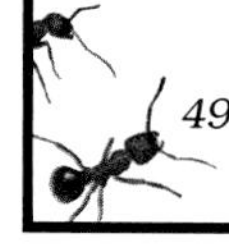

Beyond the Classroom

Career Connection

Workplace Leadership Point out to students that showing leadership in the workplace can help them achieve their goals. Invite students to describe a workplace situation in which they would be required to show leadership qualities. Have them consider these questions:

- What qualities does a leader need?
- How can a leader promote confidence in his or her workers?
- What aspects of a situation does a leader need to consider?

With their answers to these questions, students can create a realistic workplace situation in which they could identify leadership qualities. Have them write down their situations.

Students can exchange their written situations and judge the qualities and actions their classmates have outlined. As a final discussion, they can note which of the qualities they have chosen are qualities Leiningen possesses, and whether they, as leaders, would have made the choices Leiningen made.

"Everyone back from the ditch!" roared Leiningen. The men rushed away, without the slightest idea of his plan. He stooped forward and cautiously dropped into the ditch a stone which split the floating carpet and its living freight, to reveal a gleaming patch of petrol. A match spurted, sank down to the oily surface—Leiningen sprang back; in a flash a towering rampart of fire encompassed the garrison.

This spectacular and instant repulse threw the Indians into ecstasy. They applauded, yelled and stamped. Had it not been for the awe in which they held their boss, they would infallibly have carried him shoulder high.

It was some time before the petrol burned down to the bed of the ditch, and the wall of smoke and flame began to lower. The ants had retreated in a wide circle from the devastation, and innumerable charred fragments along the outer bank showed that the flames had spread from the holocaust in the ditch well into the ranks beyond, where they had wrought havoc far and wide.

Yet the perseverance of the ants was by no means broken; indeed, each setback seemed only to whet it. The concrete cooled, the flicker of the dying flames wavered and vanished, petrol from the second tank poured into the trench—and the ants marched forward anew to the attack.

The foregoing scene repeated itself in every detail, except that on this occasion less time was needed to bridge the ditch, for the petrol was now already filmed by a layer of ash. Once again they withdrew; once again petrol flowed into the ditch. Would the creatures never learn that their self-sacrifice was utterly senseless? It really was senseless, wasn't it? Yes, of course it was senseless—provided the defenders had an *unlimited* supply of petrol.

When Leiningen reached this stage of reasoning, he felt for the first time since the arrival of the ants that his confidence was deserting him. His skin began to creep; he loosened his collar. Once the devils were over the trench there wasn't a chance for him and his men. What a prospect, to be eaten alive like that!

For the third time the flames immolated the attacking troops, and burned down to extinction. Yet the ants were coming on again as if nothing had happened. And meanwhile Leiningen had made a discovery that chilled him to the bone—petrol was no longer flowing into the ditch. Something must be blocking the outflow pipe of the third and last cistern—a snake or a dead rat? Whatever it was, the ants could be held off no longer, unless petrol could by some method be led from the cistern into the ditch.

Then Leiningen remembered that in an outhouse nearby were two old disused fire engines. The peons dragged them out of the shed, connected their pumps to the cistern, uncoiled and laid the hose. They were just in time to aim a stream of petrol at a column of ants that had already crossed and drive them back down the incline into the ditch. Once more an oily girdle surrounded the garrison, once more it was possible to hold the position—for the moment.

It was obvious, however, that this last resource meant only the postponement of defeat and death. A few of the peons fell on their knees and began to pray; others, shrieking insanely, fired their revolvers at the black, advancing masses, as if they felt their despair was pitiful enough to sway fate itself to mercy.

◆ **Literary Focus** What other elements besides ants influence the external conflict? ❺

At length, two of the men's nerves broke: Leiningen saw a naked Indian leap over the north side of the petrol trench, quickly followed by a second. They sprinted with incredible speed toward the river. But their fleetness did not save them; long before they could attain the rafts, the enemy covered their bodies from head to foot.

In the agony of their torment, both sprang blindly into the wide river, where enemies no less sinister awaited them. Wild screams of mortal anguish informed the breathless onlookers that crocodiles and sword-toothed piranhas were no less ravenous than ants, and

◆ Critical Thinking

❸ **Draw Conclusions** Ask students how the Indians feel about Leiningen, and why. *They respect him, admire him, and think of him as almost superhuman. His calmness and determination makes him seem powerful.*

◆ Literary Focus

❹ **Conflict** Ask: What effect does the conflict with Leiningen seem to have on the ants? *It appears to make them more determined to advance—just as it makes Leiningen more determined to halt them.*

◆ Literary Focus

❺ **Conflict** Students may cite the presence of crocodiles and piranhas in the water, rendering the water unusable for refuge. The dwindling supply of petrol also influences the external conflict.

Viewing and Representing Mini-Lesson

Map of the Plantation

This mini-lesson supports the Researching and Representing project in the Idea Bank on p. 497.

Introduce Maps are an invaluable tool in war conditions. They can alert soldiers to the relative location of structures and to unusual elements of the terrain. Stephenson provides detailed descriptions of the advance of the ants on Leiningen's plantation.

Develop Suggest that students consult maps in an atlas, an encyclopedia, a social studies text, or a news magazine to decide what kinds of symbols they wish to use in their representation. Students may find it helpful to look at a strategic defense map used in battle descriptions.

Apply Have students skim through the selection, taking careful notes about the structure of the plantation and the march of the ants. Students can use these notes to create their maps. Remind students to give the map a title and to include a legend explaining any symbols they have used.

Assess Allow students to display their work for the class to critique. Have students decide whether story details were accurately and completely explained and represented on the map.

◆ Critical Thinking

❶ Analyze Character Ask students why they think Leiningen is able to keep developing new ideas to repel the ants. *He has trained himself to analyze a situation carefully and thoroughly. His mind keeps working logically, and he never panics, even in an emergency.*

◆ Build Grammar Skills

❷ Correct Use of Apostrophes Have students note the words that are contractions in this paragraph and tell what words were joined to make each one. *The contractions are* I'm *for "I am,"* That'll *for "that will," and* I've *for "I have."*

◆ Critical Thinking

❸ Make a Judgment Ask students what Leiningen's elaborate preparations reveal about him. *He is thorough and thinks things through, and he plans to survive his trip to the dam.*

even nimbler in reaching their prey.

In spite of this bloody warning, more and more men showed they were making up their minds to run the blockade. Anything, even a fight midstream against alligators, seemed better than powerlessly waiting for death to come and slowly consume their living bodies.

Leiningen flogged his brain till it reeled. Was there nothing on earth could sweep this devils' spawn back into the hell from which it came?

Then out of the inferno of his bewilderment
❶ rose a terrifying inspiration. Yes, one hope remained, and one alone. It might be possible to dam the great river completely, so that its waters would fill not only the water ditch but overflow into the entire gigantic "saucer" of land in which lay the plantation.

The far bank of the river was too high for the waters to escape that way. The stone breakwater ran between the river and the plantation; its only gaps occurred where the "horseshoe" ends of the water ditch passed into the river. So its waters would not only be forced to inundate into the plantation, they would also be held there by the breakwater until they rose to its own high level. In half an hour, perhaps even earlier, the plantation and its hostile army of occupation would be flooded.

The ranch house and outbuildings stood upon rising ground. Their foundations were higher than the breakwater, so the flood would not reach them. And any remaining ants trying to ascend the slope could be repulsed by petrol.

It was possible—yes, if one could only get to the dam! A distance of nearly two miles lay between the ranch house and the weir—two miles of ants. Those two peons had managed only a fifth of that distance at the cost of their lives. Was there an Indian daring enough after that to run the gauntlet five times as far? Hardly likely; and if there were, his prospect of getting back was almost nil.

No, there was only one thing for it, he'd have to make the attempt himself; he might just as well be running as sitting still, anyway, when the ants finally got him. Besides, there *was* a bit of a chance. Perhaps the ants weren't so almighty, after all; perhaps he had allowed the mass suggestion of that evil black throng to hypnotize him, just as a snake fascinates and overpowers.

The ants were building their bridges. Leiningen got up on a chair. "Hey, lads, listen to me!" he cried. Slowly and listlessly, from all sides of the trench, the men began to shuffle toward him, the apathy of death already stamped on their faces.

"Listen, lads!" he shouted. "You're frightened of those beggars, but I'm proud of you. There's still a chance to save our lives—by flooding the plantation from the river. Now one of you might manage to get as far as the weir—but he'd never come back. Well, I'm not going to let you try it; if I did, I'd be worse than one of those ants. No, I called the tune, and now I'm going to pay the piper.

"The moment I'm over the ditch, set fire to the petrol. That'll allow time for the flood to do
the trick. Then all you have to do is to wait ❷
here all snug and quiet till I'm back. Yes, I'm coming back, trust me"—he grinned—"when I've finished my slimming cure."

He pulled on high leather boots, drew heavy gauntlets over his hands, and stuffed the spaces between breeches and boots, gauntlets and arms, shirt and neck, with rags soaked in petrol. With close-fitting mosquito goggles he shielded his eyes, knowing too well the ants' dodge of first robbing their victim of sight. Finally, he plugged his nostrils and ears with cottonwool, and let the peons drench his clothes with petrol.

He was about to set off when the old Indian medicine man came up to him; he had a wondrous salve, he said, prepared from a species of chafer[13] whose odor was intolerable to ants. Yes, this odor protected these chafers from the attacks of even the most murderous ants. The Indian smeared the boss's boots, his gauntlets, and his face over and over with the extract.

Leiningen then remembered the paralyzing
effect of ants' venom, and the Indian gave him ❸
a gourd full of the medicine he had administered to the bitten peon at the water ditch.

---

13. chafer (chāf′ ər) *n.*: Insect that feeds on plants.

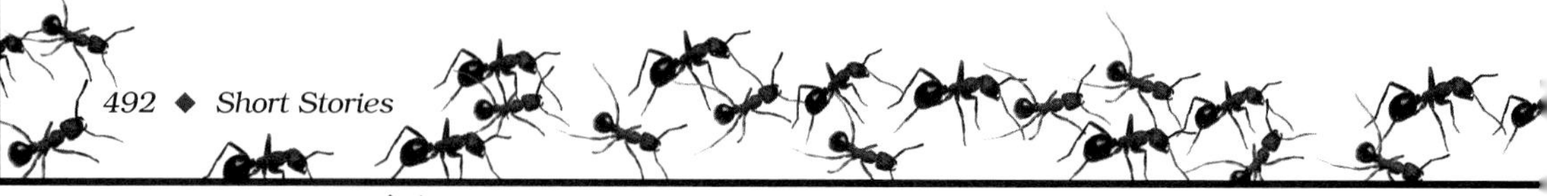

Cross-Curricular Connection: Science

Animals of Brazilian Rivers Point out that the largest river in Brazil is the Amazon, which is home to a vast number of species of animals. Other rivers in the area would support the same wildlife, which includes the small but vicious piranha, which will attack any animal in the water; electric eels; giant anacondas; crocodiles; and freshwater stingrays. There are other less fearsome animals as well, such as the pirarucu, reputed to be the best and biggest freshwater fish in the world, and the giant catfish. Ask students why in "Leiningen Versus the Ants" only the dangerous river inhabitants are mentioned. *Students should observe that only the dangerous animals contribute to the conflict in the story.*

▲ **Critical Viewing** Imagine yourself in this situation. What would you need to do to survive? **[Connect]**

The planter drank it down without noticing its bitter taste; his mind was already at the weir.

He started off toward the northwest corner of the trench. With a bound he was over—and among the ants.

The beleaguered garrison had no opportunity to watch Leiningen's race against death. The ants were climbing the inner bank again—the lurid ring of petrol blazed aloft. For the fourth time that day the reflection from the fire shone on the sweating faces of the imprisoned men, and on the reddish-black cuirasses[14] of their oppressors. The red and blue, dark-edged flames leaped vividly now, celebrating what? The funeral pyre of the four hundred, or of the hosts of destruction? 5

Leiningen ran. He ran in long, equal strides, with only one thought, one sensation, in his being—he *must* get through. He dodged all trees and shrubs; except for the split seconds his soles touched the ground, the ants should have no opportunity to alight on him. That they

14. **cuirasses** (kwi ras´ əz) *n.*: Body armor; here, the ants' outer bodies.

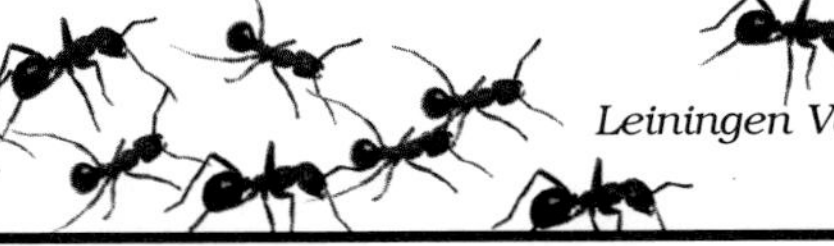

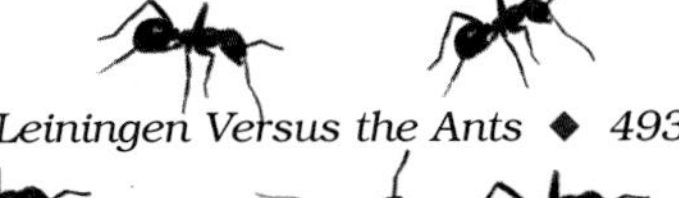

Listening to Literature Audiocassettes This may be a good time to play the recording of "Leiningen Versus the Ants," since the suspense and action in the story are building to a climax.

▶Critical Viewing◀

❹ **Connect** *Students may say you would need to keep moving, cover your skin as completely as possible, and get to safety quickly.*

❺ **Clarification** Make sure students understand that the "four hundred" are the people on the plantation, while the "hosts of destruction" are the ants.

Cross-Curricular Connection: Health

Poisonous Animal Bites Point out to students that Leiningen's ants aren't the only animals with poisonous, or even fatal, bites. Spiders such as the black widow, tarantula, or brown spider can administer dangerous or even fatal bites. Mosquitoes can transmit diseases such as malaria and dengue fever that, if untreated, can kill. Some ticks transmit Lyme disease; bee stings, if the victim is allergic to them, can result in shock and death. Rattlesnakes and copperheads can kill with their venomous bites. Even mammals such as raccoons, skunks, and bats can transmit rabies, an infectious disease that is fatal, if untreated. Remind students that these animals present relatively minor threats because they do not travel in huge packs, as the ants do.

◆ Reading Strategy

❶ Predict Based on Plot Details Have students predict whether they think Leiningen will die at this point. *Suggested answer: No. Based on what we know of his determination, he will triumph over his own weakness.*

◆ Critical Thinking

❷ Draw Conclusions Ask students why they think Leiningen was able to rise again and go on. Until now, he has relied on his intellect. What is he relying on now? *When Leiningen recalls the horrifying death of the deer, his instinct for survival forces him to get to his feet and continue.*

would get to him soon, despite the salve on his boots, the petrol on his clothes, he realized only too well, but he knew even more surely that he must, and that he would, get to the weir.

Apparently the salve was some use after all: not until he had reached halfway did he feel ants under his clothes, and a few on his face. Mechanically, in his stride, he struck at them, scarcely conscious of their bites. He saw he was drawing appreciably nearer the weir—the distance grew less and less—sank to five hundred—three—two—hundred yards.

Then he was at the weir and gripping the ant-hulled wheel. Hardly had he seized it when a horde of infuriated ants flowed over his hands, arms, and shoulders. He started the wheel—before it turned once on its axis the swarm covered his face. Leiningen strained like a madman, his lips pressed tight; if he opened them to draw breath . . .

He turned and turned; slowly the dam lowered until it reached the bed of the river. Already the water was overflowing the ditch. Another minute, and the river was pouring through the nearby gap in the breakwater. The flooding of the plantation had begun.

Leiningen let go the wheel. Now, for the first time, he realized he was coated from head to foot with a layer of ants. In spite of the petrol, his clothes were full of them, several had got to his body or were clinging to his face. Now that he had completed his task, he felt the smart raging over his flesh from the bites of sawing and piercing insects.

Frantic with pain, he almost plunged into the river. To be ripped and slashed to shreds by piranhas? Already he was running the return journey, knocking ants from his gloves and jacket, brushing them from his bloodied face, squashing them to death under his clothes.

One of the creatures bit him just below the rim of his goggles; he managed to tear it away, but the agony of the bite and its etching acid drilled into the eye nerves; he saw now through circles of fire into a milky mist, then he ran for a time almost blinded, knowing that if he once tripped and fell. . . . The old Indian's brew didn't seem much good; it weakened the poison a bit, but didn't get rid of it. His heart pounded as if it would burst; blood roared in his ears; a giant's fist battered his lungs.

Then he could see again, but the burning girdle of petrol appeared infinitely far away; he could not last half that distance. Swift-changing pictures flashed through his head, episodes in his life, while in another part of his brain a cool and impartial onlooker informed this ant-blurred, gasping, exhausted bundle named Leiningen that such a rushing panorama of scenes from one's past is seen only in the moment before death.

A stone in the path . . . too weak to avoid it . . . the planter stumbled and collapsed. He tried to rise . . . he must be pinned under a rock . . . it was impossible . . . the slightest movement was impossible. . . .

Then all at once he saw, starkly clear and huge, and, right before his eyes, furred with ants, towering and swaying in its death agony, the pampas stag. In six minutes—gnawed to the bones. He *couldn't* die like that! And something outside him seemed to drag him to his feet. He tottered. He began to stagger forward again.

Through the blazing ring hurtled an apparition which, as soon as it reached the ground on the inner side, fell full length and did not move. Leiningen, at the moment he made that leap through the flames, lost consciousness for the first time in his life. As he lay there, with glazing eyes and lacerated face, he appeared a man returned from the grave. The peons rushed to him, stripped off his clothes, tore away the ants from a body that seemed almost one open wound; in some places the bones were showing. They carried him into the ranch house.

As the curtain of flames lowered, one could see in place of the illimitable host of ants an extensive vista of water. The thwarted river had swept over the plantation, carrying with it the entire army. The water had collected and mounted in the great "saucer," while the ants had in vain attempted to reach the hill on which stood the ranch house. The girdle of flames held them back.

Reteach

To help students who have difficulty understanding the man vs. nature conflict of this story, model the use of an organizer like the one shown here. For each side, have students add more descriptive words that show the conflict. Once students have finished reading, ask them to use the web to evaluate the story's outcome. Which parts of Leiningen's personality helped him succeed? Which description of the ants made them such a fearsome competitor? Have students circle their answers and defend their responses.

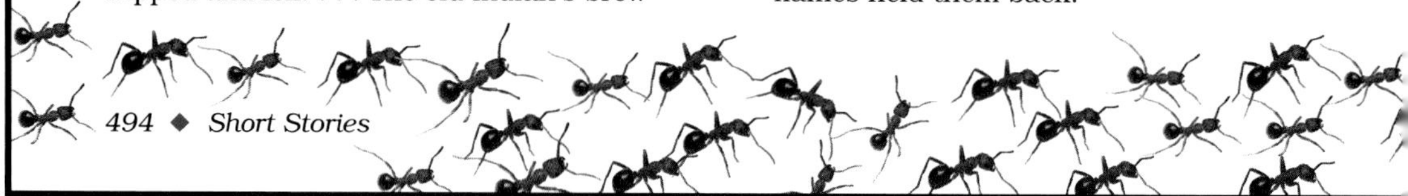

And so, imprisoned between water and fire, they had been delivered into the annihilation that was their god. And near the farther mouth of the water ditch, where the stone mole had its second gap, the ocean swept the lost battalions into the river, to vanish forever.

The ring of fire dwindled as the water mounted to the petrol trench and quenched the dimming flames. The inundation rose higher and higher: because its outflow was impeded by the timber and underbrush it had carried along with it, its surface required some time to reach the top of the high stone breakwater and discharge over it the rest of the shattered army.

It swelled over ant-stippled shrubs and bushes, until it washed against the foot of the knoll whereon the besieged had taken refuge. For a while an alluvium of ants tried again and again to attain the dry land, only to be repulsed by streams of petrol back into the merciless flood.

Leiningen lay on his bed, his body swathed from head to foot in bandages. With fomentations and salves, they had managed to stop the bleeding, and had dressed his many wounds. Now they thronged around him, one question in every face. Would he recover? "He won't die," said the old man who had bandaged him, "if he doesn't want to."

The planter opened his eyes. "Everything in order?" he asked.

"They're gone," said his nurse. He held out to his master a gourd full of a powerful sleeping-draft. Leiningen gulped it down.

"I told you I'd come back," he murmured, "even if I am a bit streamlined."

◆ Build Vocabulary

alluvium (ə lōō′ vē əm) *n.*: Material such as sand or gravel deposited by moving water

fomentations (fō′ mən tā′ shənz) *n.*: Applications of warm, moist substances in the treatment of an injury

Beyond Literature

Media Connection

The Naked Jungle The vivid descriptions and exciting action in "Leiningen Versus the Ants" inspired movie makers at Paramount Pictures to create a film based on Stephenson's short story. The film version, starring Charlton Heston, was released in 1954 with the title *The Naked Jungle.* The photos you see in the story are stills from the movie. Screenwriters Ranald MacDouggall, Ben Maddow, and Philip Yordan expanded the cast of characters, adding a wife for Leiningen and increasing the roles of two plantation workers. They also added several more "close calls" to the plot. Why do you think the screenwriters made some of these changes? What changes might you make if you were doing a movie version of this story?

Guide for Responding

◆ Literature and Your Life

Reader's Response Put yourself in Leiningen's place. What would you have done differently? Why?

Thematic Focus What attributes do you think helped Leiningen overcome the ants? Why?

☑ Check Your Comprehension

1. What threat do the ants pose to Leiningen?
2. At what point in the story does it first seem that Leiningen has snatched victory "from the very jaws of defeat"? How do the ants recover?
3. How does Leiningen finally defeat the ants?

◆ Literary Focus

❸ Conflict Leiningen has won the battle. Suggest to students that in most conflicts, the winner pays a price for victory. Ask students: What has been the price of Leiningen's victory? Was the victory worth the price? *He has sacrificed several lives and lost much of the plantation. Some students may think the victory was not worth the price, since if Leiningen and his people had evacuated in the first place, all lives would have been saved. Others will think that it was worth the price to prove that the human mind and spirit can triumph over anything.*

Reinforce and Extend

Answers

◆ Literature and Your Life

Reader's Response Students may say they would have been less confident that they could save themselves in the conflict with the ants.

Thematic Focus Students may cite Leiningen's determination and ingenuity. Without determination, he would have given up; without ingenuity he would have been defeated.

☑ Check Your Comprehension

1. The ants threaten to destroy his plantation and kill him and his workers.
2. It first appears that Leiningen will defeat the ants when they can't find a way to cross the moat. However, the ants create "rafts" to ferry themselves across.
3. He lowers the dam to allow the river to flood the plantation. The flood waters of the river carry away the ants.

Beyond the Selection

FURTHER READING

Other Works With the Theme of Clashing Forces

Hour of the Wolf, Patricia Calvert
"The Most Dangerous Game," Richard Connell
Hatchet, Gary Paulsen
"The Open Boat," Stephen Crane
Lost in the Barrens, Farley Mowat
The Old Man and the Sea, Ernest Hemingway
Kon Tiki, Thor Heyerdahl

We suggest that you preview these works before recommending them to students.

INTERNET

You and your students may not find information about Carl Stephenson on the Internet, as "Leiningen Versus the Ants" is his only published work. Students who are interested in discovering more about ants and how they live can visit the following Web site:
http://science.coe.4wf.edu/SH/curr/insects/ants.htm

Please be aware that the site may have changed since we published this information. We *strongly recommend* that you preview the site.

Develop Understanding

Answers

◆ Critical Thinking

1. It is his nature to fight back rather than surrender; he enjoys the challenge to his intelligence and ingenuity; he has worked very hard to build his plantation.
2. (a) The qualities that equip Leiningen to fight the ants include intelligence, courage, self-confidence, determination, and experience. (b) His self-confidence leads him to put the lives of others in danger.
3. The ants use each other as bridges and cut leaves to make rafts. Overall, they demonstrate an ability to adapt, discipline, and organize.
4. Leiningen's instinct for survival forces him up when he sees the stag eaten by the ants.
5. Some students may say that Leiningen was justified because the plantation was the peons' home, too, and the peons did not stand a chance out in the open against the ants. Others may think that he was wrong to risk the lives of others to satisfy his own need for victory.
6. Students who have read stories or novels set in wartime featuring disaster situations may have titles to suggest.

◆ Reading Strategy

1. Leiningen's resolve not to die as the stag does suggests a resolve that won't be defeated.
2. Some may say that making predictions increases the suspense of a story by keeping readers guessing whether their predictions will prove valid. Others may enjoy a mental duel with the author as they try to discover his or her intentions.

◆ Literary Focus

1. The two opposing forces are Leiningen and the ants.
2. Leiningen's internal conflict is between his fear of the ants and his determination to defeat them.
3. The peons experience an internal conflict between their loyalty to and dependence on Leiningen and their desire to flee the plantation.

Guide for Responding *(continued)*

◆ Critical Thinking

Interpret

1. Why do you think Leiningen is so determined to stay and fight the ants? **[Infer]**

2. (a)What qualities do you think make Leiningen well equipped to fight the ants? (b)What qualities might make him dangerous to others? **[Analyze]**

3. What behavior of the ants makes them appear to be intelligent beings? **[Interpret]**

4. After Leiningen stumbles and falls on the way back from the river, is it his intellect that forces him to get up or his natural instinct? Explain. **[Distinguish]**

Evaluate

5. By staying to fight the ants, Leiningen risks others' lives as well as his own. Do you think he was justified? Why or why not? **[Make a Judgment]**

Extend

6. What other examples from literature can you recall in which a character has to make a decision upon which others' lives depend? Compare them with this tale. **[Literature Link]**

◆ Reading Strategy

Make Predictions Based on Plot Details

As the plot of an action-filled story like this develops, you continue to **make predictions** based on new details.

1. What hints in the text suggest how the war against the ants will end?

2. How can making predictions increase your enjoyment of a story?

◆ Literary Focus

Conflict

The **conflicts** in this tale are both **internal**—within a character—and **external**—between a character and an outside force.

1. What are the two opposing forces in the external conflict?

2. What is Leiningen's internal conflict?

3. Which characters besides Leiningen experience an internal conflict? What is that conflict?

◆ Build Vocabulary

Using Latin Plural Forms

Some words in English, such as *alluvium,* that are borrowed from Latin retain their Latin plural forms. Words from Latin change endings as follows to form plurals:

-um becomes *-a*
-us becomes *-i*
-a becomes *-ae*

On your paper, write the plural forms of each of the following words.

1. datum **3.** focus **5.** octopus
2. curriculum **4.** medium **6.** antenna

Using the Word Bank: Analogies

On your paper, complete the following analogies using the words from the Word Bank. Fill in the blank with the word that best completes each comparison.

1. *Water* is to *plants* as __?__ is to *ants.*
2. *Ignore* is to *rule* as __?__ is to *law.*
3. *Bandage* is to *cut* as __?__ is to *river.*
4. *Sawdust* is to *chainsaw* as __?__ is to *current.*
5. *Employee* is to *manager* as __?__ is to *master.*
6. *Detergent* is to *clothing* as __?__ is to *injury.*

◆ Build Grammar Skills

Correct Use of Apostrophes

Apostrophes are used to form possessives and contractions. They are not used to form plurals. To make a singular noun possessive, add an apostrophe and an *s*. To make a plural noun possessive, add an apostrophe after the *s* or, if the plural does not end in *s,* add an apostrophe and an *s*.

Practice Copy the following sentences on your paper, and add apostrophes in the proper places.

1. Finally, two of the mens nerves broke.
2. Here the defenders front was sparse.
3. "Well, lads," he began, "theres no shame in leaving."
4. Hadnt his brain for once taken on more than it could manage?
5. The workers watched, thinking, "Hes not going to make it."
6. Leiningens bandages covered the ants damage.

◆ Build Vocabulary

Latin Plural Forms

1. data; 2. curricula; 3. foci; 4. media; 5. octopi; 6. antennae

Using the Word Bank

1. provender; 2. flout; 3. weir; 4. alluvium; 5. peon; 6. fomentations

◆ Build Grammar Skills

1. Finally, two of the men's nerves broke.
2. Here the defenders' front was sparse.
3. "Well, lads," he began, "there's no shame in leaving."
4. Hadn't his brain for once taken on more than it could manage?
5. The workers watched, thinking, "He's not going to make it."
6. Leiningen's bandages covered the ants' damage.

Grammar Reinforcement

For additional instruction and practice, use pp. 110–111 on Apostrophes in the *Writer's Solution Grammar Practice Book.*

Build Your Portfolio

Idea Bank

Writing

1. **Letter to the Editor** Leiningen is not able to defeat the ants single-handedly. Think of a situation in which people you know have tried to solve a problem together. Describe their actions in a letter to the editor of your local paper.
2. **Change the Disaster** How would the story be different if Leiningen's foe were a volcano rather than ants? Write a brief summary of the story as it would change if you change the enemy.
3. **News Report** Imagine that you are a reporter covering Leiningen's war against the ants. Write the story in 250 words or less.

Speaking, Listening, and Viewing

4. **Motivational Speech** Review the motivational tactics Leiningen uses on his workers. Then develop your own speech to raise morale and inspire courage in the frightened peons.
5. **Watch the Movie** As a class, watch the videotape of the 1954 film "The Naked Jungle." Discuss whether your favorite scenes in the movie were the same as your favorite episodes in the story, and why.

Researching and Representing

6. **Map of the Plantation** Based on Stephenson's description, draw a map of Leiningen's plantation. On your map, use symbols and lines to show the measures of defense taken and the distance the ants advanced at each stage. **[Art Link]**
7. **Pests and Pals** Do some research, or contact environmental groups or agencies, to find out about insect pests and helpers. For example, you might find out how some insects are used instead of pesticides in modern agriculture. **[Science Link]**

Online Activity www.phlit.phschool.com

Guided Writing Lesson

New Movie Scene

Carl Stephenson's tale of terror has all the ingredients of a blockbuster movie: exotic locale, heroic main character, terrifying villain. Write a script for a new movie scene of the final action-packed moment—the climax and resolution—of the thriller.

Write a screenplay of the scene with dialogue and a description of the actors' movements. Also include camera angles and other directions to the film crew.

Writing Skills Focus: Climax and Resolution

The conflict is the central part of the plot of any story. Your conflict should be both believable and serious enough so that a solution is not readily apparent. Following the **climax,** or high point of the conflict, the **resolution** shows how the problems and tension are worked out. Make sure that your resolution ties up any "loose ends" of the plot.

Prewriting Reread the end of the story, jotting down crucial actions and words of the story's high point. Brainstorm for visual details that will add to the suspense of the climax.

Drafting Begin your scene with a striking image that will capture the mood you want to portray. For example, a close-up of Leiningen's face followed by a shot of the millions of ants he must soon face will establish a mood of suspense. Refer to your notes as you draft the scene to remind yourself of details that will translate into vivid on-screen images.

Revising Reread your draft, pretending that you are an actor who will use the screenplay. Would you understand everything you must do based only on the screenplay? Fill in any gaps in the action, dialogue, and directions.

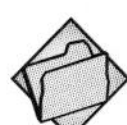

Idea Bank

Customizing for
Performance Levels

Following are suggestions for matching Idea Bank topics with your students' performance levels:
Less Advanced Students: 1, 6, 7
Average Students: 2, 4, 6
More Advanced Students: 3, 4, 5

Customizing for
Learning Modalities

Following are suggestions for matching Idea Bank topics with your students' learning modalities:
Verbal/Linguistic: 1, 2, 3, 4, 5
Visual/Spatial: 6
Logical/Mathematical: 6

Guided Writing Lesson

Prewriting Strategy Have students use a trifold like the one shown here to be sure they have set the stage for their scenes, created tension, and resolved the conflict. Students write or draw the image they use to capture the mood on the the first fold. On the second fold, they write the conflict and how it will climax. On the third fold, they indicate the resolution. Encourage students to refer to their trifolds as they draft and revise their scenes.

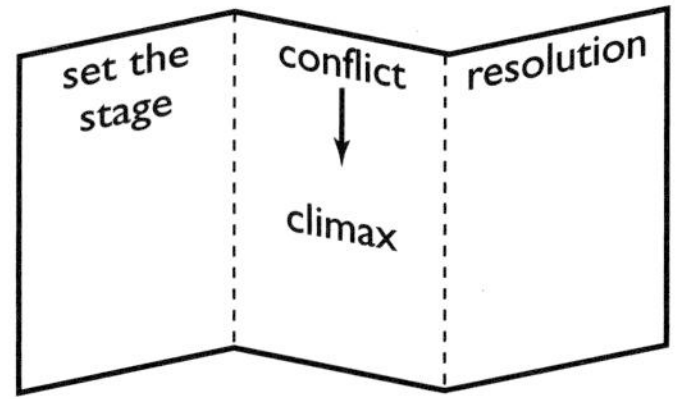

For more prewriting, elaboration, and revision instruction, see *Prentice Hall Writing and Grammar.*

Writing and Language Transparencies Have students use the Story Map, p. 84, to help organize the details for their movie scripts.

Writing Lab CD-ROM
Have students complete the tutorial on Creative Writing. Follow these steps:
1. Students can use the interactive tips on purpose to learn about techniques that can help them.
2. Have students draft on computer.
3. Students can use the proofreading checklist for drama to revise.

ASSESSMENT OPTIONS

Formal Assessment, Selection Test, pp. 126–128, and Assessment Resources Software. The selection test is designed so that it can be easily customized to the performance levels of your students.

Alternative Assessment, p. 36, includes options for less advanced students, more advanced students, bodily/kinesthetic learners, verbal/linguistic learners, visual/spatial learners, and logical/mathematic learners.

PORTFOLIO ASSESSMENT
Use the following rubrics in ***Alternative Assessment*** to assess student writing:
Letter to the Editor: Persuasion Rubric, p. 105
Change the Disaster: Summary Rubric, p. 98
News Report: Research/Report Rubric, p. 106
Guided Writing Lesson: Drama Rubric, p. 109

Prepare and Engage

LESSON OBJECTIVES

1. **To develop vocabulary and word identification skills**
   - Word Groups: Conjunctive Adverbs
   - Using the Word Bank: Context
   - Extending Word Study: Use Reference Materials (ATE)
2. **To use a variety of reading strategies to comprehend a story**
   - Connect Your Experience
   - Reading Strategy: Draw Conclusions
   - Tips to Guide Reading: (ATE)
   - Read to Take Action (ATE)
3. **To increase knowledge of other cultures and to connect common elements across cultures**
   - Connecting Themes Across Cultures (ATE)
   - Beyond Literature
4. **To express and support responses to the text**
   - Critical Thinking
   - Idea Bank: Postcard
   - Idea Bank: Publicity Release
   - Idea Bank: Poem
5. **To analyze literary elements**
   - Literary Focus: First-Person Point of View
6. **To read in order to research self-selected and assigned topics**
   - Idea Bank: Oral Presentation
   - Idea Bank: Tourism Poster
   - Idea Bank: Oral Presentation
7. **To plan, prepare, organize, and present literary interpretations**
   - Idea Bank: Radio Interview
   - Idea Bank: Storyboard
8. **To use recursive writing processes to write a description from another vantage point**
   - Guided Writing Lesson
9. **To increase knowledge of the rules of grammar and usage**
   - Build Grammar Skills: Subordination

Test Preparation

Critical Reading: Distinguish Between Fact and Nonfact (ATE, p. 499) The teaching tips and sample test item in this workshop support the instruction and practice in the unit workshop:

Critical Reading: Recognize Forms of Propaganda; Distinguish Between Fact and Nonfact (SE, p. 565)

Guide for Reading

Stephen Vincent Benét

(1898–1943)

When a clock strikes thirteen, you can expect strange things to happen. "By the Waters of Babylon" first appeared in a story collection by Stephen Vincent Benét with just that title—*Thirteen O'Clock* (1937).

Proud American Born in Bethlehem, Pennsylvania, Benét grew up listening to his father's evening poetry readings. As a young man, he took time off from his studies at Yale University to serve in the State Department during World War I. (His poor eyesight prevented him from serving in the army.) Much of Benét's work centers on American history and the establishment of American ideals.

A Poet at Heart Benét considered himself a poet first and foremost. His interest in American history and folklore, in addition to his interest in the ballad form, influenced his epic poem, *John Brown's Body,* which won a Pulitzer Prize in 1929. (He was awarded another Pulitzer, after his death, for the first part of an unfinished American epic, *Western Star.*)

Though he preferred poetry, Benét also achieved success writing short stories. His best-known short story, "The Devil and Daniel Webster," was the basis for a play, an opera, and a motion picture.

"By the Waters of Babylon" actually began as a poem, which Benét then transformed into a short story called "The Place of the Gods." He later changed the title while preparing *Thirteen O'Clock* for publication.

◆ Build Vocabulary

WORD GROUPS: CONJUNCTIVE ADVERBS

In this story, the main character encounters a dog "as big as a wolf." He lists a number of reasons for not killing the dog, and he ends by saying "*Moreover,* night was falling." *Moreover* is a special type of adverb called a conjunctive adverb. **Conjunctive adverbs** show a relationship between ideas and often connect independent clauses. *Moreover* indicates that the idea that follows (night was falling) is in addition to what has come before. Other conjunctive adverbs include *nevertheless, finally, therefore,* and *however.*

WORD BANK

Preview this list of words from the story. Look for familiar word parts and discuss with a partner which ones can help you determine the meaning of the whole word.

purified
bowels
moreover
nevertheless

◆ Build Grammar Skills

SUBORDINATION

Subordination is the process by which writers connect two unequal but related ideas in a complex sentence. The subordinate (less important) idea limits, develops, describes, or adds meaning to the main idea. For instance, in the following sentence from the story, the subordinate (adverb) clause clarifies under what circumstances the idea in the main clause occurs.

> We do not even say its name *though we know its name.*

The less important idea is introduced with the subordinate conjunction *though.* Other words that indicate the relationship between main clauses and subordinate clauses include subordinating conjunctions like *after, because, while, unless, when, if,* and *than,* as well as relative pronouns like *who, which,* and *that.*

Prentice Hall Literature Program Resources

REINFORCE / RETEACH / EXTEND

Selection Support Pages: Build Vocabulary: Word Groups, p. 151
Build Grammar Skills: Subordination, p. 152
Reading Strategy: Draw Conclusions, p. 153
Literary Focus: First-Person Point of View, p. 154

Strategies for Diverse Students Needs, p. 37

Beyond Literature Cross-Curricular Connection: Social Studies, p. 37

Formal Assessment Selection Test, pp. 129–131; Assessment Resources Software

Alternative Assessment, p. 37

Writing and Language Transparencies Comparison and Contrast Organizer, pp. 95–97

Resource Pro CD-ROM

Listening to Literature Audiocassettes

By the Waters of Babylon

◆ Literature and Your Life

CONNECT YOUR EXPERIENCE

The crumbling buildings you see when you look at pictures of ancient civilizations were once schools, theaters, and places of business. As they do today, people of the past worked, learned, and socialized. Someday in the future, people may look at the ruins of the buildings of today and try to imagine the kind of people who lived here.

Journal Writing Describe a public building in your neighborhood that would tell a good story of your community to future generations.

THEMATIC FOCUS: TO THE FUTURE

The main character in "By the Waters of Babylon" explores the ruins of a once mighty civilization. This story raises the question, "What story will our society tell to the future?"

◆ Background for Understanding

LITERATURE

The title "By the Waters of Babylon" is an allusion to Psalm 137 in the Bible, in which the Israelites, held captive in Babylon, wept over their lost homeland, Zion.

> By the rivers of Babylon, there we sat down, yea, we wept, when we remembered Zion . . .

When you read "By the Waters of Babylon," consider how these lines from the psalm relate to the story.

◆ Literary Focus

FIRST-PERSON POINT OF VIEW

The information you receive when you hear or read a story is influenced by the point of view of the storyteller. **Point of view** is the position or perspective from which the events of a story are seen. When the author uses **first-person** point of view, the narrator is a character who participates in the events and tells the story using the first-person pronoun *I* to refer to himself or herself. The reader "sees" the events of the story through the eyes and mind of this first-person narrator.

The "I" in "By the Waters of Babylon" is John, who introduces himself in the following way: "I am the son of a priest. I have been in the Dead Places near us . . . at first, I was afraid." Because John tells the story, you see, feel, and know only what John sees, feels, and knows.

◆ Reading Strategy

DRAW CONCLUSIONS

When an author gives you details about settings, events, and characters, you use those details along with your logic to **draw conclusions** about what is happening, where it's happening, and why. Sometimes an author creates a sense of mystery by presenting only a few details at a time. As each new detail is revealed, you combine it with others to draw conclusions.

At the beginning of "By the Waters of Babylon," the narrator presents these mysterious details:

> It is forbidden to go to any of the Dead Places except to search for metal . . . It is forbidden to cross the great river and look upon the place that was the Place of the Gods . . . it is there that there are the ashes of the Great Burning.

As the story continues, you will learn more details that will help you draw conclusions about the Dead Places, why it is forbidden to go there, and what events led to the Great Burning.

Ask students to imagine that they are exploring an empty building and they come upon the following scene:

> "He was sitting in his chair, by the window . . . and, for the first moment, I thought he was alive. Then I saw the skin on the back of his hand—it was like dry leather."

Ask students to tell what their reaction would be to this discovery. Then tell students that the narrator of this story relates his adventures as he explores a place where danger and other frightening discoveries like this one lie in wait.

Connecting Themes Across Cultures

As students read a futuristic story that describes a ruined culture from long ago, they can compare and contrast the culture of the future and the lessons they have learned, to our modern day culture. Ask students to recall stories of ancient cultures and what these stories have told about the people who lived in the past.

Tips to Guide Reading

Buddy Reading Present this story's setting as a mystery to be solved. Encourage students to work in pairs, reading and taking notes as they problem-solve to identify the surprising setting.

Customize for
Less Proficient Readers

Have these students keep lists of clues that help answer the questions: Who are the gods in the story? Where is the "Place of the Gods"? As more clues accumulate, they can begin to draw conclusions.

Customize for
Pre-AP Students

The author of this story gives his narrator a style of speech meant to sound more primitive than contemporary English. To analyze this style, have students rewrite short passages of John's monologue in a more contemporary style and compare their rewritten passages with the original.

Test Preparation Workshop

Critical Reading:
Distinguish Between Fact and Nonfact

Standardized tests require students to distinguish fact and nonfact in a variety of texts. Use the following sample test item to give students practice in the critical reading skill.

> Born in Bethlehem, Pennsylvania, Benét grew up listening to his father's evening poetry readings. As a young man, he took time off from his rigorous studies at Yale to serve in the State Department during World War I. (His poor eyesight prevented him from serving in the army.)

Which of the following is an OPINION expressed in the passage?

A His poor eyesight prevented him from serving in the army.
B His father read poetry nightly.
C His studies at Yale were rigorous.
D Benét became a leading poet.

Guide students to see that *A* and *B* can be proven, and that *D* is not supported by the passage. *C* is the correct response.

Develop Understanding

One-Minute Insight John's people are the survivors of our own civilization after it is destroyed in a war. They know little of that civilization, and call its ruins "Places of the Gods." John's hunger for knowledge drives him to enter the forbidden ruins and learn the secrets of the "gods." John, the son of a priest, will reveal what he has learned. Will his people embark on a path toward their own destruction—or avoid the mistakes of the past? The story is a warning that unless we use technology wisely, we may destroy civilization.

◆ Reading Strategy

1 Draw Conclusions Ask students: What are the "Dead Places"? What was the "Great Burning"? Who are the gods? *Students might guess that the "Dead Places" are houses that contain dead people, that the Great Burning was a great explosion, and that the gods are people from a former civilization. Accept all reasonable answers.*

◆ Build Vocabulary

2 Conjunctive Adverbs Ask students to identify the conjunctive adverb in this sentence and explain the relationship between the ideas it connects. *The adverb nevertheless contrasts the idea that the narrator touched the metal with the idea that his brothers would not have touched it.*

Customize for *English Language Learners*
Alert these students that, in this story, the character tells his story using language that is neither standard English nor modern colloquial speech. Students should take notes as they read and list phrases or references that need explanation. Pause at the end of a page or a section to explain the confusing passages.

By the Waters of Babylon

Stephen Vincent Benét

The north and the west and the south are good hunting ground, but it is forbidden to go east. It is forbidden to go to any of the Dead Places except to search for metal, and then he who touches the metal must be a priest or the son of a priest. Afterwards, both the man and the metal must be purified! These are the rules and the laws: they are well made.
1 It is forbidden to cross the great river and look upon the place that was the Place of the Gods—this is most strictly forbidden. We do not even say its name though we know its name. It is there that spirits live, and demons—it is there that there are the ashes of the Great Burning. These things are forbidden—they have been forbidden since the beginning of time.

My father is a priest; I am the son of a priest. I have been in the Dead Places near us, with my father—at first, I was afraid. When my father went into the house to search for the metal, I stood by the door and my heart felt small and weak. It was a dead man's house, a spirit house. It did not have the smell of man, though there were old bones in a corner. But it is not fitting that a priest's son should show fear. I looked at the bones in the shadow and kept my voice still.

Then my father came out with the metal —a good, strong piece. He looked at me with both eyes but I had not run away. He gave me the metal to hold—I took it and did not die. So he knew that I was truly his son and would be a priest in my time. That was when I was very young—nevertheless, my brothers would not have done it, though they are good hunters. After that, they gave me the good piece of meat and the warm corner by the fire. My father watched over me—he was glad that I should be a priest. But when I boasted or wept without a reason, he punished me more strictly than my brothers. That was right.

After a time, I myself was allowed to go into the dead houses and search for metal. So I learned the ways of those houses—and if I saw bones, I was no longer afraid. The bones are light and old—sometimes they will fall into dust if you touch them. But that is a great sin.

I was taught the chants and the spells—I was taught how to stop the running of blood from a wound and many secrets. A priest must know many secrets—that was what my father said. If the hunters think we do all things by chants and spells, they may believe so—it does not hurt them. I was taught how to read in the

◆ Build Vocabulary
purified (pyoor´ ə fīd) *v.*: Cleansed; made pure.

▶ **Critical Viewing** How does this picture of a city fit into your ideas of a future world? **[Relate]**

Block Scheduling Strategies

Consider these suggestions to take advantage of extended class time:

- Introduce the Reading Strategy, Draw Conclusions, on p. 499. Encourage students to note the details in the story that help them draw conclusions about facts the author does not directly reveal.
- After students have read the first few paragraphs of the story, direct their attention to the concept of the first-person point of view. Have them read the Literary Focus on p. 499.
- After students have read the story, they can work in pairs to answer the Literary Focus questions on p. 510. For more practice, follow up with the Literary Focus page in ***Selection Support,*** p. 154.
- Have students work in groups on the Community Connection activity in ***Beyond Literature*** on p. 509. Creating a visitors' guide for community landmarks will help students connect their own experience with Benét's story.

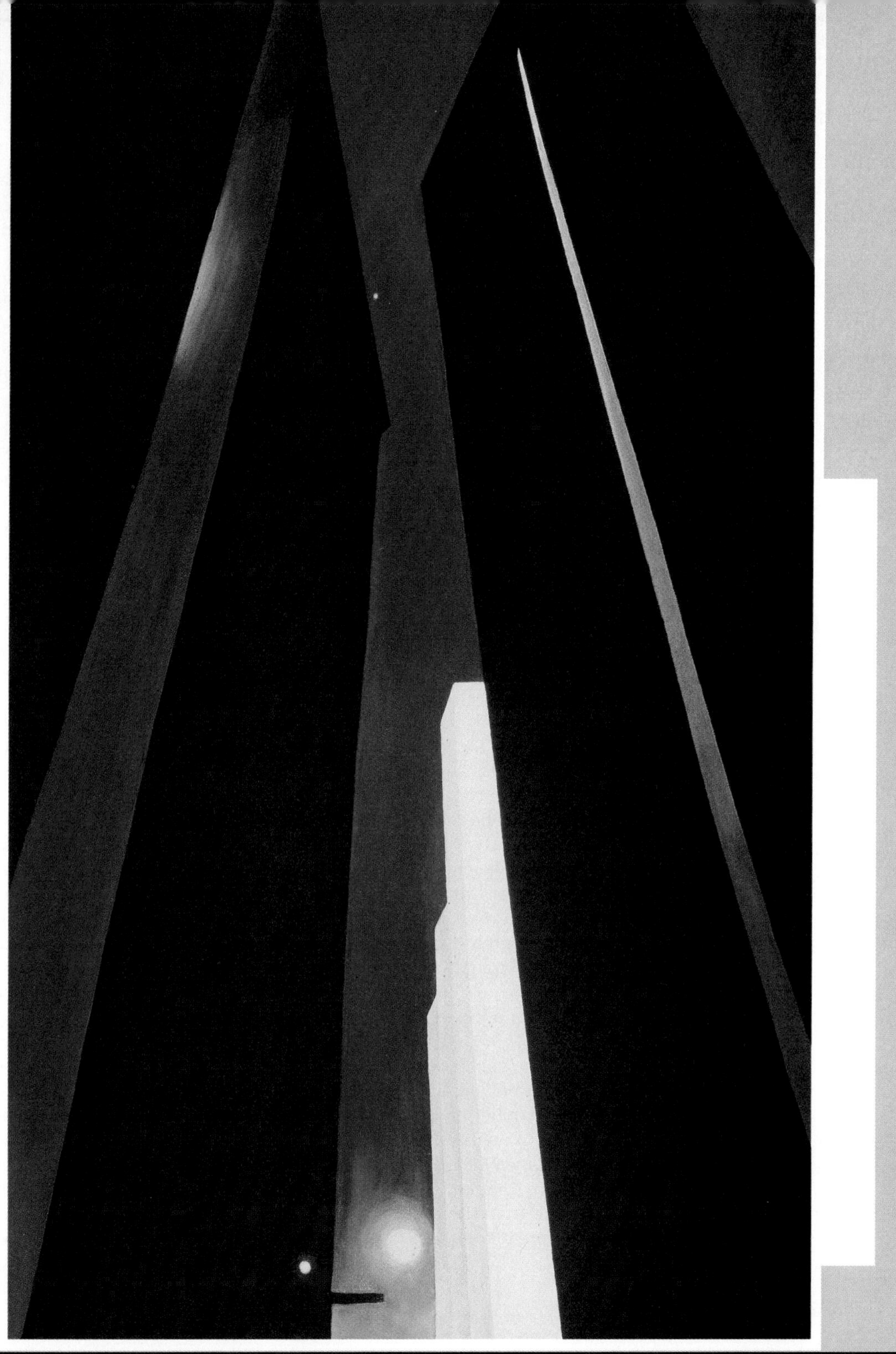

City Night, Georgia O'Keeffe, Minneapolis Institute of Art

◆ Build Grammar Skills

3 Subordination Ask students to identify the main and subordinate clauses in this sentence. Have them explain how the subordinate limits the idea in the main clause. *The main clause is "he punished me more strictly than my brothers." The subordinate clause is "when I boasted or wept without a reason." The subordinate clause tells under what circumstances his father punished him.*

◆ Reading Strategy

4 Draw Conclusions Ask students what they can conclude about the narrator's people. *Students can conclude that these people are primitive; only the priests know simple first aid techniques, and only people of the priestly class learn how to read.*

Read to Take Action

Bradbury's story describes a fallen culture. Ask students to make inferences about the reasons the culture has died. What action does Bradbury seem to advocate for readers of today?

Extending Word Study

Use Reference Materials Challenge students to use reference materials to determine precise meaning as they encounter unfamiliar words, or words that are used in an unfamiliar manner in the selection. For example, ask students to determine the meaning of *ruins, anteroom,* or *baying*.

As an ongoing study habit, and an excellent preparation method for vocabulary items on standardized tests, suggest that students keep an index card file of unfamiliar words that they have encountered in their reading and school work. Have them write one word on each card along with the definition, and periodically review the words to expand their vocabulary.

Humanities: Art

City Night, 1926, by Georgia O'Keeffe.

Georgia O'Keeffe (1887–1986) is considered one of the foremost twentieth-century American artists. The greater part of her life and work is associated with the American Southwest, particularly New Mexico. However, this painting of towering monolithic skyscrapers illuminated by the moon is typical of O'Keeffe's cityscapes, as it features a geometric design with no human figures.

1. What clue does this painting give you about the forbidden "Place of the Gods"? *The painting, "City Night," could be a clue that the "Place of the Gods" is really a city.*
2. How does the mood of the painting reflect the mood of the beginning of the story? *Students may say that the beginning of the story is mysterious because so much is left unexplained—Place of the Gods, Dead Places, the Great Burning. The painting reflects this mood because it, too, looks mysterious and eerie.*

◆ Build Grammar Skills

❶ Subordination Ask students to identify the main and subordinate clauses in this sentence. Ask: What information does the subordinate idea add to the main idea? *The main clause begins, "I came to my father and said. . . ." The subordinate clause is "When I was a man at last." The subordinate clause answers the question "When?"*

◆ Reading Strategy

❷ Draw Conclusions Ask students what they think the narrator's intentions may be, based on this passage. Ask: Which words lead you to draw your conclusion? *While the narrator agrees with his father, the words, ". . . it was my voice that spoke and not my spirit," may lead students to believe that he intends to explore the forbidden places.*

◆ Critical Thinking

❸ Infer Ask students: What does the father mean by dreams that "eat you up"? Why will the boy become a great priest if he is not eaten up by his dreams? *By dreams that "eat you up," the father might mean dreams that are too big for the boy because they become obsessions and lead him into danger. If he is not eaten up by his dreams, the boy will become a great priest because he will return from his journey with new and powerful knowledge that he will use for the good of his people.*

Customize for
Pre-AP Students
As they read, encourage these students to think about the inner qualities that make John a person of destiny in his community. Suggest they note their thoughts in their journals.

I went fasting, as is the law. My body hurt but not my heart. When the dawn came, I was out of sight. . . .

old books and how to make the old writings—that was hard and took a long time. My knowledge made me happy—it was like a fire in my heart. Most of all, I liked to hear of the Old Days and the stories of the gods. I asked myself many questions that I could not answer, but it was good to ask them. At night, I would lie awake and listen to the wind—it seemed to me that it was the voice of the gods as they flew through the air.

We are not ignorant like the Forest People—our women spin wool on the wheel, our priests wear a white robe. We do not eat grubs from the tree, we have not forgotten the old writings, although they are hard to understand. Nevertheless, my knowledge and my lack of knowledge burned in me—I wished to know more. When I was a man at ❶ last, I came to my father and said, "It is time for me to go on my journey. Give me your leave."

He looked at me for a long time, stroking his beard, then he said at last, "Yes. It is time." That night, in the house of the priesthood, I asked for and received purification. My body hurt but my spirit was a cool stone. It was my father himself who questioned me about my dreams.

He bade me look into the smoke of the fire and see—I saw and told what I saw. It was what I have always seen—a river, and, beyond it, a great Dead Place and in it the gods walking. I have always thought about that. His eyes were stern when I told him—he was no longer my father but a priest. He said, "This is a strong dream."

"It is mine," I said, while the smoke waved and my head felt light. They were singing the Star song in the outer chamber and it was like the buzzing of bees in my head.

He asked me how the gods were dressed and I told him how they were dressed. We know how they were dressed from the book, but I saw them as if they were before me. When I had finished, he threw the sticks three times and studied them as they fell.

"This is a very strong dream," he said. "It may eat you up."

"I am not afraid," I said and looked at him with both eyes. My voice sounded thin in my ears but that was because of the smoke.

He touched me on the breast and the forehead. He gave me the bow and the three arrows.

"Take them," he said. "It is forbidden to travel east. It is forbidden to cross the river. It is forbidden to go to the Place of the Gods. All these things are forbidden."

"All these things are forbidden," I said, but it was my voice that spoke and not my spirit. He looked at me again.

"My son," he said. "Once I had young dreams. If your dreams do not eat you up, you may be a great priest. If they eat ❸ you, you are still my son. Now go on your journey."

I went fasting, as is the law. My body hurt but not my heart. When the dawn came, I was out of sight of the village. I prayed and purified myself, waiting for a sign. The sign was an eagle. It flew east.

Sometimes signs are sent by bad spirits. I waited again on the flat rock, fasting, taking no food. I was very still—I could feel the sky above me and the earth beneath. I waited till the sun was beginning to sink. Then three deer passed in the valley, going east—they did not wind me or see me. There was a white fawn with them—a very great sign.

I followed them, at a distance, waiting for what would happen. My heart was troubled about going east, yet I knew that I must go. My head hummed with my fasting—I did not even see the panther spring upon the white fawn. But, before I knew it, the bow was in my hand. I shouted and the panther lifted his head from the fawn. It is not easy to kill a panther with one arrow but the arrow

Speaking, Listening, and Viewing Mini-Lesson

Radio Interview
This mini-lesson supports the Speaking, Listening, and Viewing activity in the Idea Bank on p. 511.

Introduce In a radio interview, a professional interviewer asks a guest questions, the answers to which will be of interest to listeners.

Develop Ask students to describe radio interviews they have heard. What makes a radio interview interesting? In preparing, their interviews with John, students might consider these points:

- Interview questions that elicit the most interesting answers begin with *Who, What, Where, When, Why,* and *How.* These questions are least likely to be answered by "yes" or "no."
- John may not want to reveal certain information to his people.
- John might have a particular message he wants to deliver to his people.

Apply In pairs, have students draft five to ten questions and answers. Encourage students to rehearse their interviews before performing them for the class or recording them on audiocassette.

Assess Have students evaluate their own interviews on the basis of how well the interviewer was able to elicit answers other than "yes" or "no" answers. Use the Self-Assessment: Speech page in ***Alternative Assessment***, p. 117.

went through his eye and into his brain. He died as he tried to spring—he rolled over, tearing at the ground. Then I knew I was meant to go east—I knew that was my journey. When the night came, I made my fire and roasted meat.

It is eight suns' journey to the east and a man passes by many Dead Places. The Forest People are afraid of them but I am not. Once I made my fire on the edge of a Dead Place at night and, next morning, in the dead house, I found a good knife, little rusted. That was small to what came afterward, but it made my heart feel big. Always when I looked for game, it was in front of my arrow, and twice I passed hunting parties of the Forest People without their knowing. So I knew my magic was strong and my journey clean, in spite of the law.

> ◆ ***Literature and Your Life***
> How is the knife John finds similar to the kinds of things we study to learn about ancient civilizations?

Toward the setting of the eighth sun, I came to the banks of the great river. It was half-a-day's journey after I had left the god-road—we do not use the god-roads now for they are falling apart into great blocks of stone, and the forest is safer going. A long way off, I had seen the water through trees but the trees were thick. At last, I came out upon an open place at the top of a cliff. There was the great river below, like a giant in the sun. It is very long, very wide. It could eat all the streams we know and still be thirsty. Its name is Ou-dis-sun, the Sacred, the Long. No man of my tribe had seen it, not even my father, the priest. It was magic and I prayed.

Then I raised my eyes and looked south. It was there, the Place of the Gods.

How can I tell what it was like—you do not know. It was there, in the red light, and they were too big to be houses. It was there with the red light upon it, mighty and ruined. I knew that in another moment the gods would see me. I covered my eyes with my hands and crept back into the forest. 6

Surely, that was enough to do, and live. Surely it was enough to spend the night upon the cliff. The Forest People themselves do not come near. Yet, all through the night, I knew that I should have to cross the river and walk in the places of the gods, although the gods ate me up. My magic did not help me at all and yet there was a fire in my bowels, a fire in my mind. When the sun rose, I thought, "My journey has been clean. Now I will go home from my journey." But, even as I thought so, I knew I could not. If I went to the place of the gods, I would surely die, but, if I did not go, I could never be at peace with my spirit again. It is better to lose one's life than one's spirit, if one is a priest and the son of a priest. 7

Nevertheless, as I made the raft, the tears ran out of my eyes. The Forest People could have killed me without fight, if they had come upon me then, but they did not come. 8 When the raft was made, I said the sayings for the dead and painted myself for death. My heart was cold as a frog and my knees like water, but the burning in my mind would not let me have peace. As I pushed the raft from the shore, I began my death song—I had the right. It was a fine song.

"I am John, son of John," I sang.
"My people are the Hill People.
They are the men.
I go into the Dead Places but I am not slain.
I take the metal from the Dead Places

> ◆ **Build Vocabulary**
> **bowels** (bou´ əlz) *n.*: Intestines; guts

The Forest People could have killed me without fight, if they had come upon me then, but they did not come.

◆ ***Literature and Your Life***

4 Students might mention that the knife is an artifact—an object that would tell someone who found it some facts about the civilization that produced it, for example: they had the technology to manufacture the item; they ate food that needed to be cut with a sharp blade.

◆ **Reading Strategy**

5 Draw Conclusions Have students add the name of the river to the clues they have already gathered to help them draw a conclusion about where the story takes place. Can they think of any river in the United States whose name sounds like *Ou-dis-sun* when pronounced quickly? *Some students may recognize that "Ou-dis-sun" sounds like Hudson, the great river that flows past Manhattan Island.*

◆ **Reading Strategy**

6 Draw Conclusions Ask students to identify the red light. Have them add details in the passage to information they have already noted to draw a conclusion about the Place of the Gods. What is it? *The red light is the sunset. Students should be able to conclude that the Place of the Gods is a city that was destroyed in a war.*

◆ **Literary Focus**

7 First-Person Point of View Direct students' attention to this passage. Write on the chalkboard: "If I went to the place of the gods, I would surely die. . . ." Ask students to rephrase these words as they would be spoken by a third-person narrator and contrast their version with the original. *The passage could be rephrased as, "John thought that if he went to the place of the gods, he would surely die." John speaks from the point of view of a person who really fears that he might die.*

◆ **Build Vocabulary Skills**

8 Conjunctive Adverbs Ask students to identify the conjunctive adverb in this sentence and to explain the relationship between the two ideas it connects. *The conjunctive adverb is* Nevertheless. *It contrasts the narrator's courage in the preceding paragraph with his fear of death as he makes the raft.*

Cross-Curricular Connection: Geography

The Hudson River The Hudson—which John calls "Ou-dis-sun"—is a major waterway. It originates in New York's Adirondack Mountains and flows 315 miles (510 km), emptying into New York Bay and the Atlantic Ocean at New York City. It is navigable by ocean-going vessels as far north as Albany. The New York State Barge Canal links the river to the Great Lakes. Among the points of interest on the Hudson are the United States Military Academy at West Point and Sing Sing Prison on the lower east bank.

The beauty of the Hudson inspired the famous Hudson River school of nineteenth-century American painters. One of the river's most beautiful and imposing landmarks is the Palisades, a line of sheer cliffs on the west bank of the lower Hudson that rise as high as 550 feet (165 m). It is from these cliffs that John first sees the Place of the Dead.

Have students discuss how his first glimpse of the feared Place of the Dead from such a vantage point might have affected John.

Customize for *Musical/Rhythmic Learners*

Have these students characterize this "song" of John. *Students may observe that John's song, with its repeated cry of "E-yah," suggests a Native American song. The author may be suggesting that John's people are similar to members of early Native American groups.*

◆ Reading Strategy

1 Draw Conclusions John has described "god roads" as made of stone and in disrepair. He sees god roads that spanned the river, but now hang down like "broken vines" (cables). God roads must be paved roads and bridges.

◆ Critical Thinking

2 Infer Ask students: After learning that the ground does not burn forever and that the island is not covered with fogs and enchantments, what might John start thinking about the other tales he has heard? How could these thoughts make John a better priest? *John might start to think that other tales are not true either. John can be a better priest by dispelling some of the fears that prevented his people from exploring the places of the gods.*

◆ Reading Strategy

3 Draw Conclusions Have students add the information in this passage to other clues in the story to draw a conclusion (or confirm a conclusion already drawn) about the "high towers of the gods" and about the gods themselves. Who were they? *Many students will put the information together to conclude that the high towers are skyscrapers; John is in a big city after it has been destroyed, perhaps by war ("The Great Burning"). The gods are really the people who lived there.*

Never have I been so alone . . . There was no strength in my knowledge anymore . . .

but I am not blasted.
I travel upon the god-roads and am not afraid. E-yah! I have killed the panther, I have killed the fawn!
E-yah! I have come to the great river. No man has come there before.
It is forbidden to go east, but I have gone, forbidden to go on the great river, but I am there.
Open your hearts, you spirits, and hear my song.
Now I go to the Place of the Gods, I shall not return.
My body is painted for death and my limbs weak, but my heart is big as I go to the Place of the Gods!"

All the same, when I came to the Place of the Gods, I was afraid, afraid. The current of the great river is very strong—it gripped my raft with its hands. That was magic, for the river itself is wide and calm. I could feel evil spirits about me, in the bright morning; I could feel their breath on my neck as I was swept down the stream. Never have I been so much alone—I tried to think of my knowledge, but it was a squirrel's heap of winter nuts. There was no strength in my knowledge any more, and I felt small and naked as a new-hatched bird—alone upon the great river, the servant of the gods.

1 Yet, after a while, my eyes were opened and I saw. I saw both banks of the river—I saw that once there had been god-roads across it, though now they were broken and fallen like broken vines. Very great they were, and wonderful and broken—broken in the time of the Great Burning when the fire fell out of the sky. And always the current took me nearer to the Place of the Gods, and the huge ruins rose before my eyes.

> ◆ **Reading Strategy** Put John's description together with the other things he's seen and found to draw a conclusion about the "god roads."

I do not know the customs of rivers—we are the People of the Hills. I tried to guide my raft with the pole but it spun around. I thought the river meant to take me past the Place of the Gods and out into the Bitter Water of the legends. I grew angry then—my heart felt strong. I said aloud, "I am a priest and the son of a priest!" The gods heard me—they showed me how to paddle with the pole on one side of the raft. The current changed itself—I drew near to the Place of the Gods.

When I was very near, my raft struck and turned over. I can swim in our lakes—I swam to the shore. There was a great spike of rusted metal sticking out into the river—I hauled myself up upon it and sat there, panting. I had saved my bow and two arrows and the knife I found in the Dead Place but that was all. My raft went whirling downstream toward the Bitter Water. I looked after it, and thought if it had trod me under, at least I would be safely dead. Nevertheless, when I had dried my bow-string and restrung it, I walked forward to the Place of the Gods.

It felt like ground underfoot; it did not burn me. It is not true what some of the tales say, that the ground there burns forever, for I have been there. Here and there were the marks and stains of the Great Burning, on the ruins, that is true. But they were old marks and old stains. It is not true either, what some of our priests say, that it is an island covered with fogs and enchantments. It is not. It is a great Dead Place—greater than any Dead Place we know. Everywhere in it there are god-roads, though most are cracked and broken. Everywhere there are the ruins of the high

Cultural Connection

Manhattan The Dead Place that John explores is the ruins of Manhattan in New York City. Many people think of Manhattan and New York City as one and the same, though the city has four other boroughs—the Bronx, Brooklyn, Queens, and Staten Island. However, Manhattan remains the cultural and commercial heart of the city. The 1990 census estimated Manhattan's population at almost 1,500,000, with a population density of about 67,615 per square mile (26,097 per sq. km.).

Manhattan is a world capital for theater, music, and the other arts. The shops, such as those along Fifth Avenue, are equally renowned. It is a financial capital, as well; the New York Stock Exchange, on Wall Street, is among the most important of such institutions.

Discuss with students the effect of having Manhattan serve as the location of the Place of the Gods in this selection. A great urban center is now in ruins.

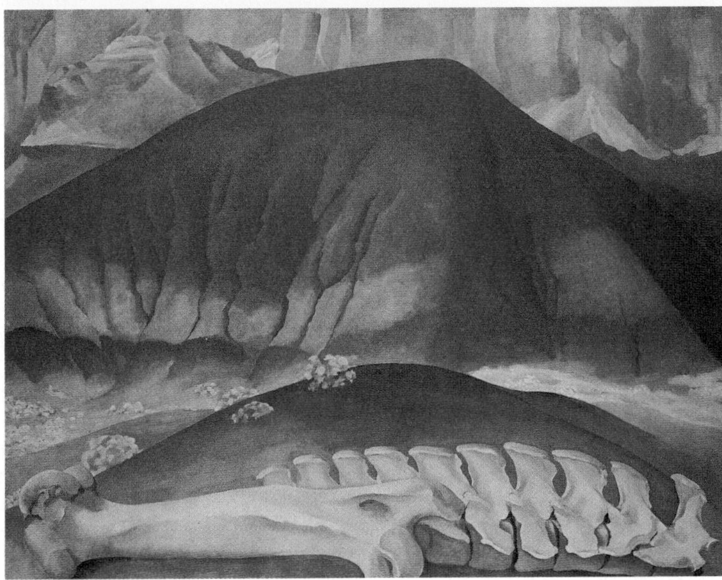

Red Hills and Bones, Georgia O'Keeffe, Philadelphia Museum of Art, The Alfred Stieglitz Collection

◀ Critical Viewing What details in this painting indicate lifelessness? **[Analyze]** 8

towers of the gods.

How shall I tell what I saw? I went carefully, my strung bow in my hand, my skin ready for danger. There should have been the wailings of spirits and the shrieks of demons, but there were not. It was very silent and sunny where I had landed—the wind and the rain and the birds that drop seeds had done their work—the grass grew in the cracks of the broken stone. It is a fair island—no wonder the gods built there. If I had come there, a god, I also would have built.

How shall I tell what I saw? The towers are not all broken—here and there one still stands, like a great tree in a forest, and the birds nest high. But the towers themselves look blind, for the gods are gone. I saw a fish-hawk, catching fish in the river. I saw a little dance of white butterflies over a great heap of broken stones and columns. I went there and looked about me—there was a carved stone with cut-letters, broken in half. I can read letters but I could not understand these. They said UBTREAS. There was also the shattered image of a man or a god. It had been made of white stone and he wore his hair tied back like a woman's. His name was ASHING, as I read on the cracked half of a stone. I thought it wise to pray to ASHING, though I do not know that god.

How shall I tell what I saw? There was no smell of man left, on stone or metal. Nor were there many trees in that wilderness of stone. There are many pigeons, nesting and dropping in the towers—the gods must have loved them, or, perhaps, they used them for sacrifices. There are wild cats that roam the god-roads, green-eyed, unafraid of man. At night they wail like demons but they are not demons. The wild dogs are more dangerous, for they hunt in a pack, but them I did not meet till later. Everywhere there are the carved stones carved with magical numbers or words. 9

I went North—I did not try to hide myself. When a god or a demon saw me, then I would die, but meanwhile I was no longer afraid. My hunger for knowledge burned in me—there was so much that I could not understand. After awhile, I knew that my belly was hungry. I could have hunted for my meat, but I did not hunt. It is known that the gods did not hunt as we do—they got their food from enchanted boxes and jars. 10 Sometimes these are still found in the Dead Places—once, when I was a child and foolish, I opened such a jar and tasted it and

◆ Reading Strategy

4 Draw Conclusions Ask students: What information in this passage can help you begin to draw a conclusion about the name of the city? *The information that the city is built on a "fair island" may help some students conclude that John is on Manhattan Island in New York City.*

◆ Build Grammar Skills

5 Subordination Ask students to identify the main and subordinate clauses in this sentence and to explain how the subordinate clause qualifies the main clause. *The main clause is, "I also would have built"; the subordinate clause is "If I had come there, a god." The subordinate clause clarifies the circumstances under which the idea in the main clause would have occurred.*

◆ Critical Thinking

6 Synthesize Ask students to decide whether this story takes place in the present, past, or future. How do they know? *Great buildings have been destroyed, but John's people do not know how to build these things. Therefore, the story must take place in the future after a more advanced civilization has been destroyed.*

Comprehension Check ☑

7 Explain that "UBTREAS" refers to the Manhattan Subtreasury Building and the statue is of George Washington.

▶Critical Viewing◀

8 Analyze *Details indicating lifelessness include the bones, the dry landscape, and the red clay with no plants growing in it.*

◆ Reading Strategy

9 Draw Conclusions Ask students to explain where the wild cats and dogs most likely came from. *The dogs and cats are probably descendants of pets kept by residents of what became the Dead Place.*

◆ Literary Focus

10 First-Person Point of View Have students observe the effect of the point of view on the passage. *Students may say that the author adds a dimension of humor when John observes that our food came not from hunting but "from enchanted boxes and jars."*

Humanities: Art

Red Hills and Bones, 1941, by Georgia O'Keeffe.

In 1929, Georgia O'Keeffe first visited New Mexico, and lived there from 1949 on. From her first visit, she made increasing use of southwestern motifs in her work. Animal bones were frequent subjects, as in *Red Hills and Bones.* O'Keeffe's attention to detail makes the painting seem realistic, but the subject matter and perspective gives a surreal quality.

Use these questions for discussion:

1. Do you think this is an appropriate illustration for the story? *Students may say that the painting gives the impression of a "dead place," even though it is of a desert rather than a city.*
2. How would you describe the mood of the painting? How does the artist create that mood? *Students may say the mood is lonely, desolate, eerie. The artist creates this mood by using only earth tones, and including no human or animal figures.*

❶ **Clarification** Explain that John is in Grand Central Terminal in New York City. The ceiling of the main concourse there is painted with stars forming well-known constellations. The tunnels are subway tunnels. This information confirms that John is in Manhattan.

◆ **Reading Strategy**

❷ **Draw Conclusions** Ask students to use what they already know from experience along with this description to draw a conclusion about the kind of place where John found the food and drink. What might the drink have been? *Students may say that John found food and drink in an old market, and that the drink probably contained alcohol.*

◆ **Reading Strategy**

❸ **Draw Conclusions** Have students explain where John finds himself in this passage. *He is on an upper floor of an apartment building, in a hallway between the elevator door and a door to an apartment.*

I had long gone past what was forbidden, and I entered the likeliest towers . . .

found the food sweet. But my father found out and punished me for it strictly, for, often, that food is death. Now, though, I had long gone past what was forbidden, and I entered the likeliest towers, looking for the food of the gods.

I found it at last in the ruins of a great temple in the mid-city. A mighty temple it must have been, for the roof was painted like the sky at night with its stars—that ❶ much I could see, though the colors were faint and dim. It went down into great caves and tunnels—perhaps they kept their slaves there. But when I started to climb down, I heard the squeaking of rats, so I did not go—rats are unclean, and there must have been many tribes of them, from the squeaking. But near there, I found food, in the heart of a ruin, behind a door that still opened. I ate only the fruits from the jars— ❷ they had a very sweet taste. There was drink, too, in bottles of glass—the drink of the gods was strong and made my head swim. After I had eaten and drunk, I slept on the top of a stone, my bow at my side.

When I woke, the sun was low. Looking down from where I lay, I saw a dog sitting on his haunches. His tongue was hanging out of his mouth; he looked as if he were laughing. He was a big dog, with a gray-brown coat, as big as a wolf. I sprang up and shouted at him but he did not move—he just sat there as if he were laughing. I did not like that. When I reached for a stone to throw, he moved swiftly out of the way of the stone. He was not afraid of me; he looked at me as if I were meat. No doubt I could have killed him with an arrow, but I did not know if there were others. Moreover, night was falling.

I looked about me—not far away there was a great, broken god-road, leading North. The towers were high enough, but not so high, and while many of the dead-houses were wrecked, there were some that stood. I went toward this god-road, keeping to the heights of the ruins, while the dog followed. When I had reached the god-road, I saw that there were others behind him. If I had slept later, they would have come upon me asleep and torn out my throat. As it was they were sure enough of me; they did not hurry. When I went into the dead-house, they kept watch at the entrance—doubtless they thought they would have a fine hunt. But a dog cannot open a door and I knew, from the books, that the gods did not like to live on the ground but on high.

I had just found a door I could open when the dogs decided to rush. Ha! They were surprised when I shut the door in their faces—it was a good door, of strong metal. I could hear their foolish baying beyond it, but I did not stop to answer them. I was in darkness—I found stairs and climbed. There were many stairs, turning around till my head was dizzy. At the top was another door—I found the knob and opened it. I was in a long small chamber—on one side of it was a bronze door that could not be opened, for it had no handle. Perhaps there was a magic word to open it, but I did not have the word. I turned to the door in the opposite side of the wall. The lock of it was broken and I opened it and went in.

Within, there was a place of great riches. The god who lived there must have been a powerful god. The first room was a small anteroom—I waited there for some time, telling the spirits of the place that I came in peace and not as a robber. When it seemed to me that they had had time to hear me, I

◆ **Build Vocabulary**

moreover (môr ō´ vər) *adv.*: In addition to; further

nevertheless (nev´ ər thə les´) *adv.*: In spite of that; however

Speaking, Listening, and Viewing Mini-Lesson

Oral Presentation

This mini-lesson supports the Speaking, Listening, and Viewing activity in the Idea Bank on p. 511.

Introduce With the class, discuss techniques for making an oral presentation interesting. Include such techniques as beginning with an interest-grabbing sentence, using lively, vivid language, and using visual aids.

Develop Once students have topics, they should check to see that their reports answer these questions:

- When and where did the culture flourish?
- What artifacts of the civilization have been found?
- What do we know of how these people lived?
- What connection exists between their culture and ours?

Apply Before presenting their reports to the class, students can pair off and practice, using their partners' suggestions to polish their delivery and clarify the material, if necessary.

Assess Have students evaluate the presentations for accuracy of content and effectiveness of presentation. Use the Peer Assessment: Speaker/Speech page in ***Alternative Assessment,*** p. 118.

went on. Ah, what riches! Few, even, of the windows had been broken—it was all as it had been. The great windows that looked over the city had not been broken at all though they were dusty and streaked with many years. There were coverings on the floors, the colors not greatly faded, and the chairs were soft and deep. There were pictures upon the walls, very strange, very wonderful—I remember one of a bunch of flowers in a jar—if you came close to it, you could see nothing but bits of color, but if you stood away from it, the flowers might have been picked yesterday. It made my heart feel strange to look at this picture—and to look at the figure of a bird, in some hard clay, on a table and see it so like our birds. Everywhere there were books and writings, many in tongues that I could not read. The god who lived there must have been a wise god and full of knowledge. I felt I had right there, as I sought knowledge also.

Nevertheless, it was strange. There was a washing-place but no water—perhaps the gods washed in air. There was a cooking-place but no wood, and though there was a machine to cook food, there was no place to put fire in it. Nor were there candles or lamps—there were things that looked like lamps but they had neither oil nor wick. All these things were magic, but I touched them and lived—the magic had gone out of them. Let me tell one thing to show. In the washing-place, a thing said "Hot" but it was not hot to the touch—another thing said "Cold" but it was not cold. This must have been a strong magic but the magic was gone. I do not understand—they had ways I wish that I knew.

It was close and dry and dusty in their house of the gods. I have said the magic was gone but that is not true—it had gone from the magic things but it had not gone from the place. I felt the spirits about me, weighing upon me. Nor had I ever slept in a Dead Place before—and yet, tonight, I must sleep there. When I thought of it, my tongue felt dry in my throat, in spite of my wish for knowledge. Almost I would have gone down again and faced the dogs, but I did not.

I had not gone through all the rooms when the darkness fell. When it fell, I went back to the big room looking over the city and made fire. There was a place to make fire and a box with wood in it, though I do not think they cooked there. I wrapped myself in a floor-covering and slept in front of the fire—I was very tired.

Now I tell what is very strong magic. I woke in the midst of the night. When I woke, the fire had gone out and I was cold. It seemed to me that all around me there were whisperings and voices. I closed my eyes to shut them out. **6** Some will say that I slept again, but I do not think that I slept. I could feel the spirits drawing my spirit out of my body as a fish is drawn on a line. Why should I lie about it? I am a priest and the son of a priest. If there are spirits, as they say, in the small Dead Places near us, what spirits must there not be in that great Place of the Gods? And would not they wish to speak? After such long years? I know that I felt myself drawn as a fish is drawn on a line. I had stepped out of my body—I could see my body asleep in front of the cold fire, but it was not I. I was drawn to look out upon the city of the gods. **7**

> **◆ Literary Focus**
> How does the first-person point of view affect this description? What questions do you have about John's situation?

It should have been dark, for it was night, but it was not dark. Everywhere there were lights—lines of light—circles and blurs of light—ten thousand torches would not have been the same. The sky itself was alight—you could barely see the stars for the glow in the sky. I thought to myself "This is strong magic" and trembled. There was a roaring in my ears like the rushing of rivers. Then my eyes grew used to the light and my ears to the sound. I knew that I was seeing the city as it had been when the gods were alive.

◆ Literary Focus

4 First-Person Point of View
Invite students to discuss how a third-person narrator would describe this room. Why does the author have John describe it in this way? *A third-person narrator might say, "The carpets on the floors" instead of "coverings on the floors"; "The people who lived there," rather than "The god who lived there." John, however, speaks from the point of view of someone who has never seen carpeted floors and who still believes that the people of the city were gods. The description lets us see ourselves from John's point of view.*

◆ Literary Focus

5 First-Person Point of View
Ask students: What is the effect of the first-person point of view in this paragraph? *John describes modern appliances—a sink, a stove, lamps—from the point of view of a person who cannot see how they work. He explains everything he does not understand by "magic."*

◆ Build Grammar Skills

6 Subordination Ask students to identify the main and subordinate clauses in this sentence. Have them explain how the subordinate clause adds meaning to the main idea. *The main clause is "It seemed to me"; the subordinate clause is, "that all around me there were whisperings and voices." The subordinate clause adds meaning by answering the question "what?"*

◆ Literary Focus

7 First-Person Point of View
The author uses the first-person point of view to describe what is real to him but only imagined by the character. John imagines what the city once looked like when it was alive with light and sound.

Workplace Skills Mini-Lesson

Intellectual Curiosity

Introduce John's intellectual curiosity is so strong that not even fear of death can keep him from exploring the unknown.

Develop Have small groups of students work together to list career fields in which such intellectual curiosity would be a strong asset. *Students may list science, history, or journalism.* Then have students explain why curiosity is an asset to each field. *It could lead a historian to unearth evidence that sheds new light on the past. Writers might develop new ways of expressing thoughts and feelings.*

Apply Have students research jobs requiring intellectual curiosity. The research could take the form of interviews, surveys, explorations, or observations. Students should decide on a format that best explains their research, such as a chart, a report, or a multimedia display.

Assess To assess projects, have students display them for the class. Use ***Alternative Assessment*** materials on p. 106.

Comprehension Check ☑

❶ Make sure students understand that John is having a vision of the city as it was before it was destroyed.

◆ Critical Thinking

❷ **Interpret** Ask students what John thought would have happened if the "gods" had not destroyed themselves by war. Do students agree? *John says, ". . . their wisdom could not but grow until all was peace." John thinks that, if given the chance, the "gods" would have used their wisdom to ensure world peace. Whether or not students agree, they should back up their opinions with facts.*

◆ Critical Thinking

❸ **Synthesize** Ask students how John's vision can be interpreted as a warning. *John's vision is a warning that war can end in annihilation. (While the description sounds like a nuclear attack, the first atom bomb was not exploded until 1945. Benét would have been referring to massive bombing.)*

◆ Critical Thinking

❹ **Infer** Ask students why they think John weeps. *Students may say that he weeps over the loss of life, or over the idea that such a miraculous and beautiful place could be destroyed by the same knowledge that had built it in the first place.*

◆ Critical Thinking

❺ **Analyze** Ask students to tell why this passage is ironic. *John sees the "magic" as being wonderful. He doesn't yet comprehend that it was the "magic" that caused the destruction.*

That was a sight indeed—yes, that was a sight: I could not have seen it in the body—my body would have died. Everywhere went the gods, on foot and in chariots—there were gods beyond number and counting
❶ and their chariots blocked the streets. They had turned night to day for their pleasure—they did not sleep with the sun. The noise of their coming and going was the noise of many waters. It was magic what they could do—it was magic what they did.

I looked out of another window—the great vines of their bridges were mended and the god-roads went East and West. Restless, restless, were the gods and always in motion! They burrowed tunnels under rivers—they flew in the air. With unbelievable tools they did giant works—no part of the earth was safe from them, for, if they wished for a thing, they summoned it from the other side of the world. And always, as they labored and rested, as they feasted and made love, there was a drum in their ears—the pulse of the giant city, beating and beating like a man's heart.

Were they happy? What is happiness to the gods? They were great, they were mighty, they were wonderful and terrible. As I looked upon them and their magic, I felt like a child—but a little more, it seemed to me, and they would pull down the moon
❷ from the sky. I saw them with wisdom beyond wisdom and knowledge beyond knowledge. And yet not all they did was well done—even I could see that—and yet their wisdom could not but grow until all was peace.

Then I saw their fate come upon them and that was terrible past speech. It came upon them as they walked the streets of their city. I have been in the fights with the Forest People—I have seen men die. But
❸ this was not like that. When gods war with gods, they use weapons we do not know. It was fire falling out of the sky and a mist that poisoned. It was the time of the Great Burning and the Destruction. They ran about like ants in the streets of their city—poor gods, poor gods! Then the towers began to fall. A few escaped—yes, a few. The legends tell it. But, even after the city had become a Dead Place, for many years the poison was still in the ground. I saw it happen, I saw the last of them die. It was darkness over the broken city, and I wept.

All this, I saw. I saw it as I have told it, though not in the body. When I woke in the morning, I was hungry, but I did not think first of my hunger, for my heart was perplexed and confused. I knew the reason for the Dead Places but I did not see why it had happened. It seemed to me it should not have happened, with all the magic they had. I went through the house looking for an answer. There was so much in the house I could not understand—and yet I am a priest and the son of a priest. It was like being on one side of the great river, at night, with no light to show the way.

Then I saw the dead god. He was sitting in his chair, by the window, in a room I had not entered before and, for the first moment, I thought that he was alive. Then I saw the skin on the back of his hand—it was like dry leather. The room was shut, hot and dry—no doubt that had kept him as he was. At first I was afraid to approach him—then the fear left me. He was sitting looking out over the city—he was dressed in the clothes of the gods. His age was neither young nor old—I could not tell his age. But there was wisdom in his face and great sadness. You could see that he would have not run away. He had sat at his window, watching his city die—then he himself had died. But it is better to lose one's life than one's spirit—and you could see from the face that his spirit had not been lost. I knew, that, if I touched him, he would fall into dust—and yet, there was something unconquered in the face.

That is all of my story, for then I knew he was a man—I knew then that they had been men, neither gods nor demons. It is a great knowledge, hard to tell and believe. They were men—they went a dark road, but they

Reteach

Some students may need extra help understanding point of view. When a story is told from first-person point of view, readers only know details that the narrator knows. To help students realize the difference a point of view makes, suggest that they think about the story as if it were a movie. Although John doesn't know about the dogs, the viewer might have glimpses of them jumping at the door. Ask students to make a Venn diagram. Together, list details in one circle that only John, the narrator knows. This would include how he feels and what he thinks. In the second circle, list details that only a viewer watching the action from the outside might know. Any details that would be known by both are placed in the intersection.

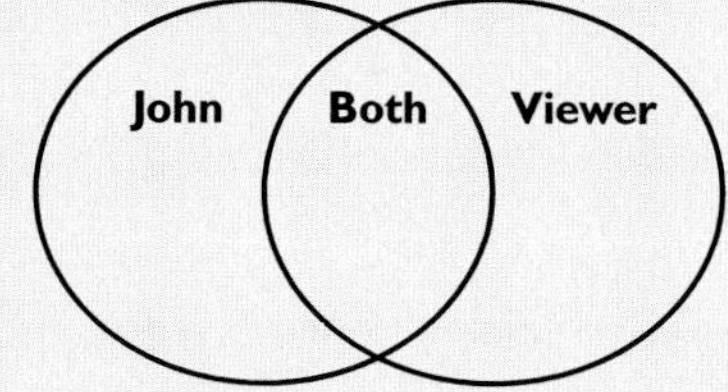

were men. I had no fear after that—I had no fear going home, though twice I fought off the dogs and once I was hunted for two days by the Forest People. When I saw my father again, I prayed and was purified. He touched my lips and my breast, he said, "You went away a boy. You come back a man and a priest." I said, "Father, they were men! I have been in the Place of the Gods and seen it! Now slay me, if it is the law—but still I know they were men."

He looked at me out of both eyes. He said, "The law is not always the same shape—you have done what you have done. I could not have done it in my time but you come after me. Tell!"

I told and he listened. After that, I wished to tell all the people but he showed me otherwise. He said, "Truth is a hard deer to hunt. If you eat too much truth at once, you may die of the truth. It was not idly that our fathers forbade the Dead Places." He was right—it is better the truth should come little by little. I have learned that, being a priest. Perhaps, in the old days, they ate knowledge too fast.

Nevertheless, we make a beginning. It is not for the metal alone we go to the Dead Places now—there are the books and the writings. They are hard to learn. And the magic tools are broken—but we can look at them and wonder. At least, we make a beginning. And, when I am chief priest we shall go beyond the great river. We shall go to the Place of the Gods—the place newyork—not one man but a company. We shall look for the images of the gods and find the god ASHING and the others—the gods Lincoln and Biltmore[1] and Moses.[2] But they were men who built the city, not gods or demons. They were men. I remember the dead man's face. They were men who were here before us. We must build again. ❼

1. **Biltmore:** A hotel in New York City.
2. **Moses:** Robert Moses, former New York City municipal official who oversaw many large construction projects.

Beyond Literature

Cultural Connection

Landmarks and Monuments In this story, John encounters the Subtreasury building and a statue of George Washington—two landmarks in New York City. Most cities have special places, buildings, or statues. For example, Athens has the Parthenon, Beijing has the Great Hall of the People, and Rio de Janeiro has its Monument to Christ the Redeemer. Such landmarks reflect strong cultural values and traditions.

Activity Identify one such landmark and research its origins and history, asking what it reflects about the broader culture in which it is found.

Guide for Responding

◆ *Literature and Your Life*

Reader's Response John's father says, "Perhaps, in the old days, they ate knowledge too fast." In your opinion, does our society "eat knowledge too fast"? Explain your answer.

Thematic Focus What warning is Benét giving about the future?

☑ Check Your Comprehension

1. Why does John set out on his journey? Why is John's journey unusual?
2. Describe three things John sees in the Place of the Gods.

◆ Critical Thinking

❻ Make a Judgment Ask students: When John's father says, "If you eat too much truth at once, you may die of the truth," to which truth is he referring? In what ways did the gods eat too much truth at once? *Students may say that the people in the destroyed city acquired too much knowledge of science and technology before acquiring the wisdom to know how to use it properly—for making life better, rather than for war and destruction.*

◆ Critical Thinking

❼ Speculate Ask students: How will John's people's lives change when John is their chief priest? Will they eventually destroy themselves, or will they learn a lesson from the ruined city? *John's people's lives will change radically if he follows through with his plan to "build again." Their religion will change, and they will acquire knowledge that will change their view of the world. If John's wisdom prevails they will not make the same mistakes that led to the destruction of "the place new york."*

Beyond Literature Students may contact bureaus of tourism to obtain information about specific areas or locales.

Reinforce and Extend

Answers

◆ *Literature and Your Life*

Reader's Response Students' responses might distinguish between knowledge and wisdom. When wisdom does not lead to knowledge, destruction can follow.

Thematic Focus Benét's story warns that advanced technology can be used for destructive as well as constructive purposes.

☑ Check Your Comprehension

1. John goes on his journey as a rite of passage to manhood. His journey is unusual because he discovers secrets that will change his society.
2. John sees statues and fragments of ruined buildings, such as the Subtreasury Building; he sees the living quarters of one of the "gods"; he also sees a vision of the city when it was alive.

Beyond the Selection

FURTHER READING

Other Works on the Theme of Ruined Civilizations

"Ozymandias," Percy Bysshe Shelley
The Planet of the Apes, Pierre Boulle
"The Stars Look Down," Isaac Asimov

We suggest that you preview these works before recommending them to students.

INTERNET

The Internet provides many sites where interested students can find out more about Stephen Vincent Benét and his work. One Web site that provides several examples of his poetry can be found at: **http://ftp.lexmark.com/data/poem/benet01.html**

Please be aware, however, that sites may have changed from the time we published this information. We *strongly recommend* that you preview the site before you send students to it.

Guide for Responding (continued)

◆ Critical Thinking

Interpret

1. What significance does the journey have for John and his people? **[Draw Conclusions]**

2. Explain why John's father wants to keep secret what John has learned about the Place of the Gods. **[Speculate]**

3. Explain the title of this story. Why is it appropriate that this story would appear in a collection called *Thirteen O'Clock?* **[Connect]**

Apply

4. How do you think John's people can best avoid repeating the mistakes that led to the destruction of civilization in the past? **[Solve]**

Extend

5. What other places do you know that are ruins of a past civilization? What do you imagine life in those places was like ? **[Social Studies Link]**

◆ Reading Strategy

Draw Conclusions

You **draw conclusions** based on facts and details given in a story. When John describes the "god-roads" that are fallen and broken like vines, you can put this detail together with the other facts you have learned to draw the conclusion that he is looking at the ruins of suspension bridges.

1. What is the Great Burning? Why and how did it happen?

2. What is the Place of the Gods? What details led you to your conclusion?

◆ Literary Focus

First-Person Point of View

In a story told from the **first-person point of view,** the narrator tells what he or she thinks, feels, and observes. The narrator's attitudes and experiences shape the story. In turn, the readers' view of what happens, and why, is shaped by the narrator's perspective.

1. Identify two ways that the first-person point of view adds to the mystery of this story.

2. What does the narrator reveal about his feelings toward the past?

◆ Build Vocabulary

Using Conjunctive Adverbs

Conjunctive adverbs are words like *moreover, nevertheless,* and *therefore* that act as conjunctions. They act as adverbs in the clauses in which they appear, but they also link clauses or sentences and clarify the relation between them. On your paper, copy the following sentences, completing them with one of these conjunctive adverbs: *nevertheless, therefore,* or *moreover.*

1. Our life raft was sinking; ___?___, we donned our life vests.

2. The elders had forbidden me to enter the Place of the Gods; ___?___, curiosity pushed me onward.

3. I needed to find shelter soon: night was falling; ___?___, the wolves would soon be out.

Using the Word Bank: Context

On your paper, answer the following questions using the words from the Word Bank.

1. Which would be referred to as the *bowels* of a city: the streets, subways, or skyscrapers?

2. What is an example of something you can buy that has been *purified?*

◆ Build Grammar Skills

Subordination

Writers use **subordination** when they connect unequal but related ideas in a complex sentence. The subordinate (less important) idea limits, develops, describes, or adds meaning to the main idea.

Practice Copy the following sentences in your notebook. Underline the subordinate clause, and explain why it is less important than the idea in the main clause.

1. It was my father himself who questioned me about my dreams.

2. . . . he who touches the metal must be a priest or the son of a priest.

3. When my father went into the house to search for the metal, I stood by the door . . .

4. John entered the building because the dogs were chasing him.

5. After he ate and drank, he went to sleep.

◆ Critical Thinking

1. For John, the journey means becoming a man. For his people it is an opportunity to build again.
2. John's father wants the truth to be revealed gradually.
3. The title refers to Psalm 137, in which the Israelites, captured by the Babylonians, weep for their lost homeland. It is appropriate for this story to appear in a collection called *Thirteen O'Clock* because that hour, like the events in this story, has not yet occurred.
4. Some students might say that avoidance may occur by not eating knowledge so fast. Others may say that people always repeat the mistakes of the past.
5. Students may cite ancient Egypt, Greece, Rome, Machu Picchu, or other past civilizations. Encourage students to research these civilizations.

◆ Reading Strategy

1. The Great Burning was the destruction of the city by bombs during a war.
2. The Place of the Gods is New York City after its destruction. Clues include the river's name, Ou-dis-sun; broken signs with names like the Subtreasury Building; and, the reference to "the place new york."

◆ Literary Focus

1. The first-person point of view allows the reader to explore the mysterious ruins as John does. It also allows the reader to see over John's shoulder, because the details enable readers to solve the mystery before John does.
2. The narrator reveals that he thinks the people of the past were great, but that they made mistakes that ended in their destruction.

◆ Build Vocabulary

Word Groups: Conjunctive Adverbs

1. Our life raft was sinking; therefore, we donned our life vests.
2. The elders had forbidden me to enter the Place of the Gods; nevertheless, curiosity pushed me onward.
3. I needed to find shelter soon: night was falling; moreover, the wolves would soon be out.

Using the Word Bank

1. The subways are the *bowels* of a city.
2. Water can be *purified.*

◆ Build Grammar Skills

1. It was my father himself who questioned me about my dreams. The subordinate clause adds meaning to the main clause.
2. . . . he who touches the metal must be a priest or the son of a priest. The subordinate clause limits the subject, *he.*
3. When my father went into the house to search for the metal, I stood by the door . . . The subordinate clause adds information.
4. John entered the building because the dogs were chasing him. The subordinate clause develops the main idea.
5. After he ate and drank, he went to sleep. The subordinate clause answers the question *when.*

Grammar Reinforcement

For additional instruction and practice, use pp. 51–52 on Adjective and Adverb Clauses and p. 124 on Making Clear Connections in the *Writer's Solution Grammar Practice Book.*

Build Your Portfolio

Idea Bank

Writing

1. Postcard As John, write a detailed postcard to your family or a friend after a visit to the Place of the Gods. Describe this mysterious place.

2. Publicity Release Imagine that John visits locations among the People of the Hills and plans to speak about his recent experiences. Write a publicity release to be distributed before his speech. Include details that will interest people in him and his experiences.

3. Poem Write a poem John might compose to express his thoughts and feelings about what he experienced during his journey.

Speaking, Listening, and Viewing

4. Radio Interview With a partner, improvise a one-minute scene in which one of you plays the role of a radio news reporter and one plays the role of John, who has just arrived home from his journey. **[Performing Arts Link]**

5. Oral Presentation Prepare an oral presentation on a lost civilization. Find pictures of ruins of the civilization. Present a report to the class, using the pictures to illustrate your points. **[Social Studies Link]**

Researching and Representing

6. Tourism Poster Although New York City is in ruins in this story, it is one of the most vibrant, busy cities in the world. Create a tourism poster advertising some highlights of the "Big Apple."

7. Storyboard Choose a scene from this story and create a storyboard of it for the film version of "By the Waters of Babylon." **[Art Link]**

Online Activity www.phlit.phschool.com

Guided Writing Lesson

Description From Another Vantage Point

You learn about the Place of the Gods from John's thoughts, feelings, and experience. What if you were a fly on a wall and could see John enter a building in the Place of the Gods? Your vantage point, or perspective, would be vastly different from a person's because of your size and concerns about life.

Write a **description** of a familiar place from another vantage point. For example, you could describe your house from the perspective of your dog or your television set.

Writing Skills Focus: Consistent Point of View

Whether you're writing a description, a speech, or a short story, it is important to keep your point of view consistent. In "By the Waters of Babylon," Benét maintains a **consistent point of view**; throughout the story, he reveals only what John could know. In your description, you will reveal only what can be observed from the perspective of the animal or the object you choose to be.

Prewriting Look carefully at the place you are describing from your new vantage point. Jot down only what can be observed, not what you yourself know.

Drafting Describe the place in terms that your animal or object might use. For instance, if cars are zooming past, don't refer to them as cars, describe their sound, smell, and action. Include your reactions to your subject as well as your observations of it.

Revising Reread your draft, looking for places where you have included information you know rather than details that can be observed. Eliminate any details that interfere with a consistent point of view.

✓ ASSESSMENT OPTIONS

Formal Assessment, Selection Test, pp. 129–131, and Assessment Resources Software. The selection test is designed so that it can be easily customized to the performance levels of your students.

Alternative Assessment, p. 37, includes options for less advanced students, more advanced students, logical/mathematic learners, bodily/kinesthetic learners, and verbal/linguistic learners.

PORTFOLIO ASSESSMENT

Use the following rubrics in ***Alternative Assessment*** to assess student writing:

Postcard: Expression Rubric, p. 94
Publicity Release: Summary Rubric, p. 98
Poem: Poetry Rubric, p. 108
Guided Writing Lesson: Description Rubric, p. 97

Idea Bank

Customizing for
Performance Levels

Following are suggestions for matching Idea Bank topics with your students' performance levels:

Less Advanced Students: 1, 4, 7
Average Students: 2, 4, 6
More Advanced Students: 3, 5

Customizing for
Learning Modalities

Following are suggestions for matching Idea Bank topics with your students' learning modalities:

Verbal/Linguistic: 1, 2, 3, 4, 5
Bodily/Kinesthetic: 4
Visual/Spatial: 6, 7

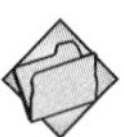

Guided Writing Lesson

Revision Strategy To help students finetune the vocabulary they create for this description, direct them to reenter their drafts, circling words that the animal or object may not know. Then, encourage students to revise these words.

For more prewriting, elaboration, and revision instruction, see *Prentice Hall Writing and Grammar.*

Writing and Language Transparencies Have students use the Comparison and Contrast organizer, pp. 95–97, to record differences between the original perspective and the vantage point of their description.

Writing Lab CD-ROM

Have students complete the tutorial on Description. Follow these steps:

1. Have students use the interactive instruction in using different organizational plans.
2. Students can use the annotated writing models to help them choose a specific point of view.
3. Students should draft their descriptions on computer.
4. Have them use the assessment criteria to help them revise their drafts.

LESSON OBJECTIVES

1. **To develop vocabulary and word identification skills**
   - Latin Word Roots: *-ver-*
   - Using the Word Bank: Context
   - Extending Word Study: Wide Reading (ATE)
2. **To use a variety of reading strategies to comprehend two short stories**
   - Connect Your Experience
   - Reading Strategy: Draw Inferences
   - Tips to Guide Reading (ATE)
   - Read to Discover Writing Models (ATE)
   - Idea Bank: Invitation
3. **To increase knowledge of other cultures and to connect common elements across cultures**
   - Connecting Themes Across Cultures (ATE)
   - Idea Bank: Roundtable Discussion
   - Speaking, Listening, and Viewing Mini-Lesson: Roundtable Discussion
4. **To express and support responses to the text**
   - Critical Thinking
   - Analyze Literary Criticism
   - Idea Bank: Journal Entry
5. **To analyze literary elements**
   - Literary Focus: Static and Dynamic Characters
   - Idea Bank: Story Ending
6. **To read in order to research self-selected and assigned topics**
   - Idea Bank: Period Presentation
   - Idea Bank: Multimedia Biography
   - Research Mini-Lesson (ATE)
7. **To use recursive writing processes to write a telephone conversation**
   - Guided Writing Lesson
8. **To increase knowledge of the rules of grammar and usage**
   - Build Grammar Skills: Restrictive and Nonrestrictive Adjective Clauses

Test Preparation

Critical Reading: Recognize Forms of Propaganda (ATE, p. 513) The teaching tips and sample test item in this workshop support the instruction and practice in the unit workshop:

Critical Reading: Recognize Forms of Propaganda; Distinguish Between Fact and Nonfact (SE, p. 565)

Guide for Reading

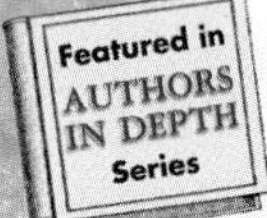

Anton Chekhov (1860–1904)

Anton Chekhov was born in the small coastal town of Taganrog in southern Russia. After the failure of his father's grocery business, his family moved to Moscow. Chekhov continued his schooling in Taganrog, then moved to Moscow to be with his family and to enroll in medical school. While a medical student, he wrote comic sketches and light short stories to earn money to help support his family. Although he suffered from tuberculosis, Chekhov continued to write until he died. *The Cherry Orchard,* one of his most famous plays, was written during the last year of his life.

Athough his reputation did not extend outside of Russia during his lifetime, since his death he has come to be regarded as one of the great short-story writers.

Mark Twain (1835–1910)

Like actors or musicians, writers sometimes take new names, called pen names. Mark Twain is the pen name of Samuel Langhorne Clemens, one of America's greatest writers. He was born in Florida, Missouri, and grew up in nearby Hannibal. He drew on his boyhood experiences for many of the characters and incidents that appear in his work.

Twain's formal education ended early. After he left school, he learned the printing trade. At various times, he worked as a printer and a riverboat pilot, prospected for gold, and gave lectures around the world. His pen name is from the cry of Mississippi River boatmen: "By the mark, twain!" measuring the river as two fathoms deep. His two most widely read novels are *The Adventures of Tom Sawyer* (1876) and *The Adventures of Huckleberry Finn* (1885).

◆ Build Vocabulary

LATIN WORD ROOTS: *-ver-*

The narrator of Mark Twain's "Luck" describes another character as a "man of strict *veracity.*" The word *veracity* means "truthfulness; honesty." Its root is *-ver-*, which comes from the Latin *verax,* meaning "speaking truly." The root *-ver-* is used in other words as well: to *verify* something is to see whether it's true. A *verdict* is a judgment that, ideally, reflects the truth.

USING THE WORD BANK

As you read, you will encounter the words on this list. Each word is defined on the page where it first appears. Preview the list before you read. With a partner, define any words or word parts that you already know.

taciturn
rheumatic
vestibule
zenith
countenance
veracity
guileless
prodigious
sublimity

◆ Build Grammar Skills

RESTRICTIVE AND NONRESTRICTIVE ADJECTIVE CLAUSES

Adjective clauses modify nouns or pronouns. An adjective clause is **restrictive** when it is necessary to complete the meaning of the noun or pronoun it modifies. It is not set off with a comma:

Orders were given *that no one was to be admitted.*

A **nonrestrictive clause** adds details that are not necessary to the meaning of the sentence, and it is set off with commas:

. . . and by the advice of kind-hearted Ivan Markovitch, his uncle, *who was taking his part,* he sat meekly in the hall by the door leading to the study . . .

Prentice Hall Literature Program Resources

REINFORCE / RETEACH / EXTEND

Selection Support Pages
Build Vocabulary: Word Roots: *-ver-*, p. 155
Build Grammar Skills: Restrictive and Nonrestrictive Adjective Clauses, p. 156
Reading Strategy: Make Inferences, p. 157
Literary Focus: Static and Dynamic Characters, p. 158

Strategies for Diverse Student Needs, p. 38

Beyond Literature
Humanities Connection: Personal Honor, p. 38

Formal Assessment Selection Test, pp. 132–134; Assessment Resources Software

Alternative Assessment, p. 38

Writing and Language Transparencies
Comparison and Contrast Organizer, pp. 95–98

Resource Pro CD-ROM

Listening to Literature Audiocassettes

A Problem ◆ Luck

◆ Literature and Your Life

Have you ever met a person who turned out to be different from what you had expected? A person's outside appearance often disguises the true feelings and thoughts of a person. In each of these stories, you may be surprised to find that what you see and hear does not always reflect what lies behind the actions and words of the main characters.

THEMATIC FOCUS: FACING THE CONSEQUENCES

After you've read these stories, you may have a new answer to the question "Do people make choices based on the potential consequences of their actions?

Journal Writing Jot down some notes about possible consequences you might experience as a result of a choice you make.

◆ Background for Understanding

CULTURE

People's lifestyles reflect their culture or country. The aristocracy (people born to ruling families) of England, where Mark Twain's "Luck" takes place, have more formal habits than English working people. The same situation existed in Russia, where Anton Chekhov lived and wrote, before the Communist revolution of 1917. For these groups of people, as well as for the wealthy business classes, appearance and honor often meant more than the truth of how each person felt, thought, and behaved.

◆ Literary Focus

STATIC AND DYNAMIC CHARACTERS

Characters are the people or animals who take part in the action of a work of fiction. Characters can be classified as either static or dynamic. **Static characters** do not change during the course of a story. They remain the same no matter what happens to them. **Dynamic characters** change and usually learn something as a result of the events of the story. The changes they undergo affect their attitudes, beliefs, or behavior.

◆ Reading Strategy

DRAW INFERENCES ABOUT CHARACTER

When you meet new people, you form opinions about them based on their words and actions and, sometimes, on what others tell you about them. When you put those clues together to form an idea about a person, you **draw inferences** about his or her personality, beliefs, or qualities. You get to know fictional characters in a similar way. Their actions and words provide clues from which you draw inferences about them. Use a graphic organizer like the one shown to draw inferences about the characters in these stories.

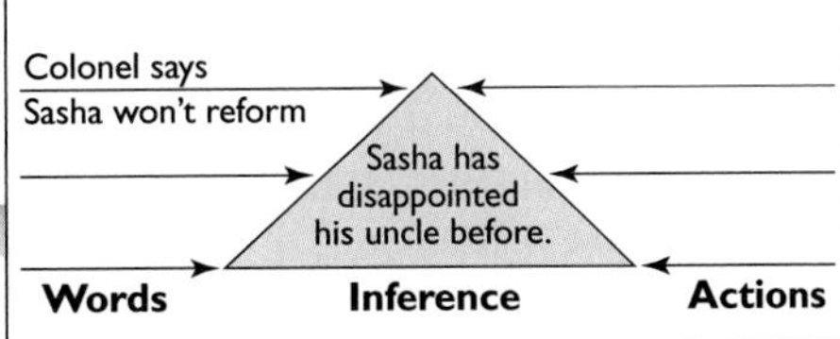

Have two students role-play a situation in which a customer gets too much change for a purchase. The customer then has to decide whether or not to return the money. Ask the class to respond to the skit and discuss the questions about honesty that it raises. Then tell them that each of these stories has important things to say about honesty, responsibility, and deception.

Connecting Themes Across Cultures

Point out that the consequences of actions can vary according to the rules of a person's culture. Tell students these stories feature characters who behave foolishly. Then, ask students to share their own knowledge of the consequences that would befall such actions in their own and other cultures.

Tips to Guide Reading

Silent Reading Encourage students to monitor their understanding of the reading strategy presented with these selections. In order to better draw inferences about characters, direct students to read silently while you walk around the room. Use the bracketed notes to help students analyze the characters' actions and ideas.

Customize for
Less Proficient Readers
Both stories contain long and complex sentences that may pose difficulty. Using examples from the stories, model how to break such sentences down into smaller parts. Remind students to use punctuation marks, as well as signal words such as *if, that,* and *so* as clues to the logic of the sentence.

Customize for
Pre-AP Students
Encourage Pre-AP students to contrast the two stories in terms of tone, style, and theme. Which writer's style did they prefer, and why?

Test Preparation Workshop

Critical Reading: Recognize Forms of Propaganda Standardized tests require students to read critically and analyze passages which contain elements of propaganda. Use this sample test item to give students practice with this skill.

> Twain's formal education ended early. After he left school, he embarked on a colorful mix of jobs—at various times, he worked as a printer and a riverboat pilot, prospected for gold and gave rousing lectures around the world.

The author tries to convince the reader of Twain's eccentricity by—?

A describing Twain's personality.
B questioning Twain's commitment.
C showing why Twain disliked his formal education.
D delineating Twain's varied career.

Guide students to see that *A, B,* and *C* are not supported by the passage. Only D accurately responds to the question.

Develop Understanding

One-Minute Insight In "A Problem," three uncles grapple with the question of what to do about their errant nephew Sasha. Instead of welcoming their decision to be lenient as an opportunity to mend his ways, however, Sasha seizes it as an opportunity to continue in his irresponsible habits, with just one difference—he has gained self-knowledge. He now sees how he can manipulate his relatives and avoid facing up to the consequences he deserves. The story raises important questions about forgiveness and responsibility.

◆ Critical Thinking

❶ **Analyze** What do these details suggest about the problem that the Uskov family faces? *They suggest the problem is a serious one; it could lead to embarrassment or shame for the entire family.*

▶ Critical Viewing ◀

❷ **Connect** *The posture of the man in the picture makes him look stiff and stern. The fact that his head is turned away from the viewer creates a cold and impersonal impression. Therefore, students may say they would not want to go to this man for help.*

Read to Discover Writing Models

Ask students to review the second paragraph of Chekhov's story. They should note that this is one compound sentence, garnished by many added phrases and clauses. Have students analyze the sentence and produce another which has the same structure.

A Problem

Anton Chekhov

Translated by Constance Garnett

The strictest measures were taken that the Uskovs' family secret might not leak out and become generally known. Half of the servants were sent off to the theater or the circus; the other half were sitting in the kitchen and not allowed to leave it. Orders were ❶ given that no one was to be admitted. The wife of the Colonel, her sister, and the governess, though they had been initiated into the secret, kept up a pretense of knowing nothing; they sat in the dining room and did not show themselves in the drawing room or the hall.

Sasha Uskov, the young man of twenty-five who was the cause of all the commotion, had arrived some time before, and by the advice of kind-hearted Ivan Markovitch, his uncle, who was taking his part, he sat meekly in the hall by the door leading to the study, and prepared himself to make an open, candid explanation.

The other side of the door, in the study, a family council was being

❷ ▶ **Critical Viewing** If you were in Sasha's situation, would you want to go to this man for help? Why or why not? **[Connect]**

Man on a Balcony, Boulevard Haussmann, 1880, Gustave Caillebotte, Art Resource

Block Scheduling Strategies

Consider these suggestions to take advantage of extended class time:

- Introduce the Literary Focus, Static and Dynamic Characters. Ask students to name familiar characters who exemplify both types. After reading the story, students can answer the Literary Focus questions on p. 525 and complete the Literary Focus page in ***Selection Support,*** p. 158.
- As students read, have them pay special attention to the Reading Strategy, Make Inferences About Character. Encourage them to use a chart such as the one on p. 513 to record and explain the inferences they make about the characters in the story.
- Have students listen to the stories on the audiocassette. Suggest that they listen for details that tell whether or not the main characters change as the stories unfold.
- Have students complete the Guided Writing Lesson on p. 526. As a prewriting activity, have a class discussion on the dialogue in "A Problem" and "Luck." Do students think the dialogue realistically reflects the way people talked in the late nineteenth century? How might they update some of the dialogue to reflect the way people talk today?
- Use the Humanities Connection: Personal Honor page in ***Beyond Literature,*** p. 38, to help students synthesize their response to the stories.

held. The subject under discussion was an exceedingly disagreeable and delicate one. Sasha Uskov had cashed at one of the banks a false promissory note,[1] and it had become due for payment three days before, and now his two paternal uncles and Ivan Markovitch, the brother of his dead mother, were deciding the question whether they should pay the money and save the family honor, or wash their hands of it and leave the case to go to trial.

To outsiders who have no personal interest in the matter such questions seem simple; for those who are so unfortunate as to have to decide them in earnest they are extremely difficult. The uncles had been talking for a long time, but the problem seemed no nearer decision.

"My friends!" said the uncle who was a colonel, and there was a note of exhaustion and bitterness in his voice. "Who says that family honor is a mere convention? I don't say that at all. I am only warning you against a false view; I am pointing out the possibility of an unpardonable mistake. How can you fail to see it? I am not speaking Chinese; I am speaking Russian!"

"My dear fellow, we do understand," Ivan Markovitch protested mildly.

"How can you understand if you say that I don't believe in family honor? I repeat once more; fa-mil-y ho-nor false-ly un-der-stood is a prejudice! Falsely understood! That's what I say: whatever may be the motives for screening a scoundrel, whoever he may be, and helping him to escape punishment, it is contrary to law and unworthy of a gentleman. It's not saving the family honor; it's civic cowardice! Take the army, for instance. . . . The honor of the army is more precious to us than any other honor, yet we don't screen our guilty members, but condemn them. And does the honor of the army suffer in consequence? Quite the opposite!"

The other paternal uncle, an official in the Treasury, a taciturn, dull-witted, and rheumatic man, sat silent, or spoke only of the fact that the Uskovs' name would get into the newspapers if the case went for trial. His opinion was that the case ought to be hushed up from the first and not become public property; but, apart from publicity in the newspapers, he advanced no other argument in support of this opinion. 5

The maternal uncle, kind-hearted Ivan Markovitch, spoke smoothly, softly, and with a tremor in his voice. He began with saying that youth has its rights and its peculiar temptations. Which of us has not been young, and who has not been led astray? To say nothing of ordinary mortals, even great men have not escaped errors and mistakes in their youth. Take, for instance, the biography of great writers. Did not every one of them gamble, drink, and draw down upon himself the anger of right-thinking people in his young days? If Sasha's error bordered upon crime, they must remember that Sasha had received practically no education; he had been expelled from the high school in the fifth class; he had lost his parents in early childhood, and so had been left at the tenderest age without guidance and good, benevolent influences. He was nervous, excitable, had no firm ground under his feet, and, above all, he had been unlucky. Even if he were guilty, anyway he deserved indulgence and the sympathy of all compassionate souls. He ought, of course, to be punished, but he was punished as it was by his conscience and the agonies he was enduring now while awaiting the sentence of his relations. The comparison with the army made by the Colonel was delightful, and did credit to his lofty intelligence; his appeal to their feeling of public

◆ Reading Strategy
What inferences can you make about Ivan Markovitch based on his speech? 6

◆ Build Vocabulary

taciturn (ta´ sə tərn) *adj.*: Preferring not to talk; uncommunicative; silent

rheumatic (rü ma´ tik) *adj.*: Suffering from a disease of the joints; able to move only with great pain

1. **promissory note:** Written promise to pay a certain sum of money on demand; an IOU.

Comprehension Check ☑

3 Have students explain in their own words what Sasha did to bring trouble upon himself and his family. *He forged an IOU and cashed it at a bank; if the money that he received is not paid back, he will be charged with a crime.*

◆ Build Grammar Skills

4 **Restrictive and Nonrestrictive Adjective Clauses** Point out the restrictive adjective clause *who was a colonel.* To show students why this clause is restrictive, have them read the sentence without it. Ask: Why is the clause necessary? *The clause identifies the particular uncle who is speaking.*

◆ Critical Thinking

5 **Contrast** Have students contrast the views of the two paternal uncles. How does each one's notion of family honor affect his opinion about how to treat Sasha? *The uncle who is with the treasury is concerned with family honor in the sense of keeping up appearances. The uncle who was a colonel regards this approach to family honor as a false and mistaken one—he believes that covering up another person's wrongdoing is dishonorable, no matter what the circumstances.*

◆ Reading Strategy

6 **Infer** Markovitch is kind-hearted and forgiving. His comments about Sasha show that he has an understanding, compassionate nature.

Humanities: Art

Man on a Balcony, Boulevard Haussman, 1880, by Gustave Caillebotte.

This man's posture appears stiff and stern, and his face is turned away from the viewer, depersonalizing the figure and creating an air of mystery.

Caillebotte is best known as an art patron and collector. During the late 1800's, he helped organize the exhibits that introduced the works of such Impressionists as Monet, Manet, and Renoir. Caillebotte's own works were also exhibited at some of these shows.

Use these questions for discussion:

1. In what ways does the setting in the painting reflect the setting of "A Problem"? *The man's elegant clothing and surroundings suggest that he is in an expensive home or apartment in town; "A Problem" takes place in the city home of an aristocratic family.*
2. Which character in the story does the figure in the painting resemble? Why? *The painting depicts an older man, apparently deep in thought. Students may say that he could be either the uncle who is a former colonel or Ivan Markovitch, Sasha's maternal uncle.*

Comprehension Check ☑

❶ What does Ivan Markovitch, Sasha's maternal uncle, think that the family should do about Sasha? *He feels that the family should forgive Sasha and repay the debt that he incurred.*

◆ Literary Focus

❷ **Static and Dynamic Characters** Remind students that a static character does not change during the course of a story. Then, have them identify Sasha's attitude toward his misdeed at this point. Encourage them to be aware of whether or not Sasha changes as the story progresses. *Students should note that at this point, Sasha feels neither ashamed nor guilty about cashing the false promissory note.*

◆ Literature and Your Life

❸ Students may say that they felt helpless and frustrated because they were not in control of what would happen to them; they may say they felt anxious and worried about what the other person would do or decide.

Extending Word Study

Wide Reading As students read the works of well-known and respected authors, encourage them to expand their own vocabulary by appreciating the author's selection of words. Encourage students to make a list of words that capture the essence of the story. They do not necessarily need to be unfamiliar words. Suggest that they note specific words such as Chekhov's choice of "purely anatomical peculiarities". Ask them to analyze the list to determine each word or phrase's effect and see why they were good choices for the author.

duty spoke for the chivalry of his soul, but they must not forget that in each individual the citizen is closely linked with the Christian. . . .

❶ "Shall we be false to civic duty," Ivan Markovitch exclaimed passionately, "if instead of punishing an erring boy we hold out to him a helping hand?"

Ivan Markovitch talked further of family honor. He had not the honor to belong to the Uskov family himself, but he knew their distinguished family went back to the thirteenth century; he did not forget for a minute, either, that his precious, beloved sister had been the wife of one of the representatives of that name. In short, the family was dear to him for many reasons, and he refused to admit the idea that, for the sake of a paltry fifteen hundred rubles,[2] a blot should be cast on the escutcheon[3] that was beyond all price. If all the motives he had brought forward were not sufficiently convincing, he, Ivan Markovitch, in conclusion, begged his listeners to ask themselves what was meant by crime? Crime is an immoral act founded upon ill-will. But is the will of man free? Philosophy has not yet given a positive answer to that question. Different views were held by the learned. The latest school of Lombroso,[4] for instance, denies the freedom of the will, and considers every crime as the product of the purely anatomical peculiarities of the individual.

"Ivan Markovitch," said the Colonel, in a voice of entreaty, "we are talking seriously about an important matter, and you bring in Lombroso, you clever fellow. Think a little, what are you saying all this for? Can you imagine that all your thunderings and rhetoric will furnish an answer to the question?"

❷ Sasha Uskov sat at the door and listened. He felt neither terror, shame, nor depression, but only weariness and inward emptiness. It seemed to him that it made absolutely no difference to him whether they forgave him or not; he had come here to hear his sentence and to explain himself simply because kind-hearted Ivan Markovitch had begged him to do so. He was not afraid of the future. It made no difference to him where he was: here in the hall, in prison, or in Siberia.

"If Siberia, then let it be Siberia, damn it all!"

He was sick of life and found it insufferably hard. He was inextricably involved in debt; he

> **◆ Literature and Your Life**
> Connect this story to a time in your life when your future was in someone else's hands. What was the dominant emotion you felt?

2. **rubles** (ro͞o′ bəlz) *n.*: Russian unit of currency.
3. **escutcheon** (is kə′ chən) *n.*: Shield on which a coat of arms is displayed.
4. **Lombroso:** Cesare Lombroso, (1836–1909), an Italian physician and criminologist who believed that a criminal was a distinct human type, with specific physical and mental deviations, and that a criminal tendency was the result of hereditary factors.

Beyond the Classroom

Career Connection: Criminology While arguing for leniency for Sasha, Ivan Markovitch brings up the latest theories of *criminology*—the scientific study of crime and criminal behavior. Although the particular ideas that this Chekhov character cites have long been out of fashion, criminology remains an important field of social science.

Among the questions that modern criminologists study are the causes of crime, the nature of criminal organizations, how to prevent crime, and how to rehabilitate convicted criminals. Criminologists may work within the criminal justice system, or they may teach and conduct studies within a college or university setting.

Have students gather more information on criminology and report their findings to the class. For example, students may focus on how the work of a criminologist differs from that of a *criminalist*—a person versed in criminal law or a psychiatrist dealing with criminality. They may also report on why some background in criminology is important for lawyers, judges, and others who work in the criminal justice system.

had not a farthing[5] in his pocket; his family had become detestable to him; he would have to part from his friends and his women sooner or later, as they had begun to be too contemptuous of his sponging on them. The future looked black.

Sasha was indifferent, and was only disturbed by one circumstance; the other side of the door they were calling him a scoundrel and a criminal. Every minute he was on the point of jumping up, bursting into the study and shouting in answer to the detestable metallic voice of the Colonel:

"You are lying!"

"Criminal" is a dreadful word—that is what murderers, thieves, robbers are; in fact, wicked and morally hopeless people. And Sasha was very far from being all that. . . . It was true he owed a great deal and did not pay his debts. But debt is not a crime, and it is unusual for a man not to be in debt. The Colonel and Ivan Markovitch were both in debt. . . .

"What have I done wrong besides?" Sasha wondered.

He had discounted a forged note. But all the young men he knew did the same. Handrikov and Von Burst always forged IOU's from their parents or friends when their allowances were not paid at the regular time, and then when they got their money from home they redeemed 4
them before they became due. Sasha had done the same, but had not redeemed the IOU because he had not got the money which Handrikov had promised to lend him. He was not to blame; it was the fault of circumstances. It was true that the use of another person's signature was considered reprehensible; but, still, it was not a crime but a generally accepted dodge, an ugly formality which injured no one and was quite harmless, for in forging the Colonel's signature Sasha had had no intention of causing anybody damage or loss.

"No, it doesn't mean that I am a criminal . . ." thought Sasha. "And it's not in my character to bring myself to commit a crime. I am soft, emotional. . . . When I have the money I help the poor. . . ."

Sasha was musing after this fashion while they went on talking the other side of the door.

"But, my friends, this is endless," the Colonel declared, getting excited. "Suppose we were to forgive him and pay the money. You know he would not give up leading a dissipated life, squandering money, making debts, going to our tailors and ordering suits in our names! Can you guarantee that this will be his last prank?

5. **farthing** (fär´ thing) *n.*: Coin of little value.

◀ **Critical Viewing** The ruble is the Russian monetary unit. How are these rubles similar to and different from other money, such as American dollars? **[Compare and Contrast]** 5

◆ Reading Strategy

4 Make Inferences About Character Encourage students to describe Sasha's line of reasoning in their own words. Then have them make inferences about his character and personality traits based on these thoughts. *Students should point out that Sasha makes numerous excuses for his behavior. They may infer that he generally does not take responsibility for his actions or that he does not have a basic sense of the difference between right and wrong.*

▶Critical Viewing◀

5 Compare and Contrast *Sample answer: The ruble is apparently more colorful and more ornate than American dollars.*

Customize for *Pre-AP Students*

Challenge students to work in small groups to do an in-depth analysis of the characters in the stories. Have each group member focus on one character in each story. Have them read aloud the character's words and lead the others in a discussion of the character's role, personality traits, and motives.

Customize for *Gifted/Talented Students*

Suggest to students that this story presents enough information for the eventual trial of Sasha. Ask one group of students to create an opening statement for the prosecution of Sasha, detailing the reasons he should be found guilty. Another group can create the opening statement for Sasha's defense. You may wish to allot time for the statements to be performed in class.

Analyze Literary Criticism

In the realm of world literature, Anton Chekhov greatly influenced the style of modern fiction writing and drama. His writing style captures the inner lives of his characters by focusing on their thoughts and the mood and atmosphere rather than just on plot and external action. James T. Farrell says of Chekhov's writing: "He developed the short story as a form of literary art to one of its highest peaks, and the translation of his stories into English has constituted one of the greatest single literary influences at work in the short story of America, England, and Ireland. This influence has been one of the factors encouraging the short-story writers of these nations to revolt against the conventional plot short story and seek in simple and realistic terms to make of the story a form that more seriously reflects life." Share this opinion with the students and then discuss questions such as the following:

1. Do you agree or disagree that Chekhov's writing has influenced modern short story style?
2. Does Chekhov provide realistic examples of life? Give examples from the selection.

◆ Literary Focus

❶ Static and Dynamic Characters Students should note the following: Neither the Colonel nor Ivan Markovitch shows changes in personality traits, attitudes, or beliefs. Neither seems to be learning or growing.

◆ Build Grammar Skills

❷ Restrictive and Nonrestrictive Adjective Clauses Point out the adjective clause *that were rolling down her cheeks,* which modifies the noun *tears.* Ask students if the clause is restrictive or nonrestrictive and have them explain their answers. *The clause is restrictive; it adds necessary information to the noun, and it is not set off by commas.*

◆ Build Grammar Skills

❸ Restrictive and Nonrestrictive Adjective Clauses Have students identify the restrictive adjective clause in this sentence. *The clause is "who had moved him to such wrath."* What noun does it modify? *It modifies* person.

As far as I am concerned, I have no faith whatever in his reforming!"

The official of the Treasury muttered something in reply; after him Ivan Markovitch began talking blandly and suavely again. The Colonel moved his chair impatiently and drowned the other's words with his detestable metallic voice. At last the door opened and Ivan Markovitch came out of the study; there were patches of red on his cleanshaven face.

"Come along," he said, taking Sasha by the hand. "Come and speak frankly from your heart. Without pride, my dear boy, humbly and from your heart."

> **◆ Literary Focus**
> ❶ Explain the ways in which the Colonel and Ivan Markovitch are static characters.

Sasha went into the study. The official of the Treasury was sitting down; the Colonel was standing before the table with one hand in his pocket and one knee on a chair. It was smoky and stifling in the study. Sasha did not look at the official or the Colonel; he felt suddenly ashamed and uncomfortable. He looked uneasily at Ivan Markovitch and muttered:

"I'll pay it . . . I'll give it back. . . ."

"What did you expect when you discounted the IOU?" he heard a metallic voice.

"I . . . Handrikov promised to lend me the money before now."

Sasha could say no more. He went out of the study and sat down again on the chair near the door. He would have been glad to go away altogether at once, but he was choking with hatred and he awfully wanted to remain, to tear the Colonel to pieces, to say something rude to him. He sat trying to think of something violent and effective to say to his hated uncle, and at that moment a woman's figure, shrouded in the twilight, appeared at the drawing room door. It was the Colonel's wife. She beckoned Sasha to her, and, wringing her hands, said, weeping:

"*Alexandre*, I know you don't like me, but . . . listen to me; listen, I beg you. . . . But, my dear, how can this have happened? Why, it's awful, awful! For goodness' sake, beg them, defend yourself, entreat them."

Sasha looked at her quivering shoulders, at the big tears that were rolling down her cheeks, heard behind his back the hollow, nervous voices of worried and exhausted people, and shrugged his shoulders. He had not in the least expected that his aristocratic relations would raise such a tempest over a paltry fifteen hundred rubles! He could not understand her tears nor the quiver of their voices.

An hour later he heard that the Colonel was getting the best of it; the uncles were finally inclining to let the case go for trial.

"The matter's settled," said the Colonel, sighing. "Enough."

After this decision all the uncles, even the emphatic Colonel, became noticeably depressed. A silence followed.

"Merciful Heavens!" signed Ivan Markovitch. "My poor sister!"

And he began saying in a subdued voice that most likely his sister, Sasha's mother, was present unseen in the study at that moment. He felt in his soul how the unhappy, saintly woman was weeping, grieving, and begging for her boy. For the sake of her peace beyond the grave, they ought to spare Sasha.

The sound of a muffled sob was heard. Ivan Markovitch was weeping and muttering something which it was impossible to catch through the door. The Colonel got up and paced from corner to corner. The long conversation began over again.

But then the clock in the drawing room struck two. The family council was over. To avoid seeing the person who had moved him to such wrath, the Colonel went from the study, not into the hall, but into the vestibule. . . . Ivan Markovitch came out into the hall. . . . He was agitated and rubbing his hands joyfully. His tear-stained eyes looked good-humored and his mouth was twisted into a smile.

"Capital," he said to Sasha. "Thank God! You can go home, my dear, and sleep tranquilly. We have decided to pay the sum, but on condition that you repent and come with me tomorrow

Speaking, Listening, and Viewing Mini-Lesson

Roundtable Discussion

This mini-lesson supports the Speaking, Listening, and Viewing activity in the Idea Bank on p. 526.

Introduce A roundtable discussion is an informal group discussion on a specific topic. While the group may or may not select a leader, you might encourage students to set an agenda so that all issues are discussed. Point out that students will discuss how the basic question raised in each story applies to our own times.

Develop Before students break into small groups, have them identify some of the specific questions and issues they might explore. Possibilities include:

- What choices does Sasha in "A Problem" make? What consequences might these choices lead to?
- How do the choices that the clergyman and Scoresby make in "Luck" differ? In what way does each character experience different consequences?
- What kind of person would be the modern equivalent of Sasha? Of the clergyman? Of Scoresby?

Apply Have students explore these and similar questions in groups, then present their summaries to the class.

Assess Have students evaluate their discussions on the basis of the following criteria:

- Was the summary clear?
- Was there evidence of reasoned discussion of the issue?
- Were specific applications made to modern times?

into the country and set to work."

A minute later Ivan Markovitch and Sasha in their greatcoats and caps were going down the stairs. The uncle was muttering something edifying. Sasha did not listen, but felt as though some uneasy weight were gradually slipping off his shoulders. They had forgiven him; he was free! A gust of joy sprang up within him and sent a sweet chill to his heart. He longed to breathe, to move swiftly, to live! Glancing at the street lamps and the black sky, he remembered that Von Burst was celebrating his name day[6] that evening at the "Bear," and again a rush of joy flooded his soul. . . .

"I am going!" he decided.

But then he remembered he had not a farthing, that the companions he was going to would despise him at once for his empty pockets. He must get hold of some money, come what may!

"Uncle, lend me a hundred rubles," he said to Ivan Markovitch.

His uncle, surprised, looked into his face and backed against a lamppost.

"Give it to me," said Sasha, shifting impatiently from one foot to the other and beginning to pant. "Uncle, I entreat you, give me a hundred rubles."

His face worked; he trembled, and seemed on the point of attacking his uncle. . . .

"Won't you?" he kept asking, seeing that his uncle was still amazed and did not understand. "Listen. If you don't, I'll give myself up tomorrow! I won't let you pay the IOU! I'll present another false note tomorrow!"

Petrified, muttering something incoherent in his horror, Ivan Markovitch took a hundred-ruble note out of his pocketbook and gave it to Sasha. The young man took it and walked rapidly away from him. . . . 5

Taking a sledge,[7] Sasha grew calmer, and felt a rush of joy within him again. The "rights of youth" of which kind-hearted Ivan Markovitch had spoken at the family council woke up and asserted themselves. Sasha pictured the drinking party before him, and, among the bottles, the women, and his friends, the thought flashed through his mind:

"Now I see that I am a criminal; yes, I am a criminal."

6. **name day:** Feast day of the saint after whom a person is named.

7. **sledge** (slej) *n.:* Strong, heavy sled.

◆ **Build Vocabulary**

vestibule (ves´ tə byül) *n.:* Small entrance hall or room

Guide for Responding

◆ Literature and Your Life

Reader's Response With whom in this story do you sympathize? Why?

Thematic Focus What point about choices and consequences is demonstrated by Sasha's experiences?

☑ Check Your Comprehension

1. Why does Sasha need help?
2. How does Uncle Ivan convince the other uncles to help Sasha?

◆ Critical Thinking

INTERPRET

1. Why do you think most of the relatives don't want to help Sasha? **[Speculate]**
2. Why do you think Sasha wrote a note he knew he could not honor? **[Infer]**

EVALUATE

3. Do you think Uncle Ivan's attitude helps or harms Sasha? Explain. **[Make a Judgment]**

APPLY

4. What would you have done if you were one of Sasha's uncles? **[Relate]**

4 **Clarification** Point out that Sasha remembers that his friend Von Burst is celebrating his *name day*—that is, the feast day of the saint after whom he was named. Explain that people in Russia and many other countries observe and celebrate name days in much the same way as we observe and celebrate birthdays.

◆ Critical Thinking

5 **Interpret** Ask students why Ivan Markovitch is horrified by Sasha's words. *He suddenly realizes that Sasha has no intention of repenting; he is shocked by Sasha's shamelessness and ingratitude.*

Reinforce and Extend

Answers

◆ Literature and Your Life

Reader's Response Some students may sympathize with Ivan Markovitch because his trust and kindness are betrayed by his nephew. Others may feel that Sasha is deeply troubled and needs help.

Thematic Focus Sasha has not been made to face the consequences of his actions and therefore will continue his "criminal" activity.

☑ Check Your Comprehension

1. Sasha needs help because he has cashed a false promissory note at the bank, and it has come due for payment. If his family doesn't cover the debt, Sasha will be tried in court, convicted, and probably sent to debtor's prison.
2. He reminds the other relatives that Sasha is young, uneducated, and an orphan, and should therefore be treated with leniency.

◆ Critical Thinking

1. Most of the relatives believe Sasha will never reform and will continue to disgrace the family name.
2. Sasha was playing financial roulette, believing he could cover one debt with another loan. He is behaving irresponsibly.
3. Some students may say that, ultimately, Uncle Ivan's kindness may help Sasha to reform; others will say that Uncle Ivan is simply enabling Sasha to continue his irresponsible ways.
4. Encourage students to think carefully about the effect their actions would have on Sasha. What will help Sasha more—letting him "off the hook" or forcing him to face the consequences of his actions?

Develop Understanding

One-Minute Insight In "Luck," a clergyman describes how he attempted to protect a military man from his own blundering ways—from the time the man was a cadet to his battlefield experience in the Crimean War. Due to luck, however, every situation in which the military man found himself seemed to work in his favor. Finally, the man became a renowned and highly decorated military leader. The reader has every reason to believe that the man will continue through life as the fortunate fool that he is.

◆ Build Grammar Skills

❶ Restrictive and Nonrestrictive Adjective Clauses Have students identify the restrictive adjective clause in the sentence beginning, "There sat the . . ." Ask: How is the clause punctuated? What noun does it modify? *The clause "whom I had heard of . . . that day" is essential to the meaning and would not have a comma in front of it if the nonessential phrase "in actual flesh" were deleted, together with its surrounding commas. The clause modifies man.*

◆ Critical Thinking

❷ Support Have students explain in their own words how the narrator feels about Scoresby. Encourage them to cite specific details or phrases in support of their answers. *Students should note that the narrator has enormous admiration for Scoresby; they may cite such phrases as "whom I had heard of so many thousand times," "forever celebrated," "that demigod," and so on.*

Luck

Mark Twain

It was at a banquet in London in honor of one of the two or three conspicuously illustrious[1] English military names of this generation. For reasons which will presently appear, I will withhold his real name and titles, and call him Lieutenant-General Lord Arthur Scoresby, V.C., K.C.B., etc., etc., etc. What a fascination there is in a renowned name! There sat the man, in actual flesh, whom I had heard of so many thousands of times since that day, thirty years before, when his name shot suddenly to the zenith from a Crimean battlefield,[2] to remain forever celebrated. ❶ It was food and drink ❷ to me to look, and look, and look at that demigod; scanning, searching, noting: the quietness, the reserve, the noble gravity of his countenance; the simple honesty that expressed itself all over him; the sweet unconsciousness of his greatness—unconsciousness of the hundreds of admiring eyes fastened upon him, unconsciousness of the deep, loving, sincere worship welling out of the breasts

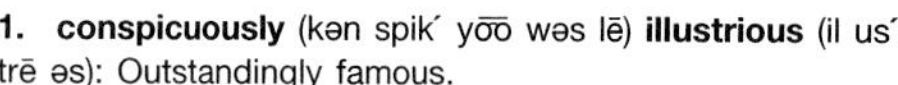

1. **conspicuously** (kən spik´ yo͞o wəs lē) **illustrious** (il us´ trē əs): Outstandingly famous.
2. **Crimean** (krī mē´ ən) **battlefield:** Place of battle during the Crimean War (1854–1856), in which Russia was defeated in trying to dominate southeastern Europe.

Scotland Forever, Elizabeth Butler, Leeds City Art Galleries

◆ Build Vocabulary

zenith (zē´ nith) *n.*: Highest point

countenance (koun´ tə nəns) *n.*: Expression on a person's face

veracity (və ras´ ə tē) *n.*: Truthfulness; honesty

Cross-Curricular Connection: Social Studies

Florence Nightingale Through a series of unlikely events Arthur Scoresby becomes a hero of the Crimean War, in which Great Britain, allied with France, Turkey, and the Italian kingdom of Sardinia, fought against Russia. Students may be interested to learn that a famous nineteenth-century woman—Florence Nightingale—was a real-life hero of that war.

In 1854, while Nightingale was working as the superintendent of a women's hospital in London, the Secretary of War asked her to travel to the Crimea and take charge of nursing for the allied troops. The conditions she found there were wretched and appalling, but she and her staff of nurses did much to improve army hospitals and save lives. As a result of her work, Nightingale became a world-famous expert on field medicine—the care of sick and wounded soldiers; several years later, during the American Civil War, she advised the United States on the operation and administration of military hospitals.

Have students do research to learn more about Florence Nightingale's life and her contributions to modern medicine.

of those people and flowing toward him.

The clergyman at my left was an old acquaintance of mine—clergyman now, but had spent the first half of his life in the camp and field, and as an instructor in the military school at Woolwich. Just at the moment I have been talking about, a veiled and singular light glimmered in his eyes, and he leaned down and muttered confidentially to me—indicating the hero of the banquet with a gesture:

"Privately—he's an absolute fool."

This verdict was a great surprise to me. If its subject had been Napoleon,[3] or Socrates,[4] or Solomon,[5] my astonishment could not have been greater. Two things I was well aware of: that the Reverend was a man of strict veracity,

▼ Critical Viewing Based on this painting, would you rather be a good soldier or a lucky one? Explain. **[Draw Conclusions]**

3. **Napoleon** (nə pō´ lē ən): Napoleon Bonaparte (1769–1821), French military leader and emperor of France from 1804 to 1815.
4. **Socrates** (säk´ rə tēz´): Athenian philosopher and teacher (470?–399 B.C.).
5. **Solomon** (säl´ ə mən): In the Bible, the King of Israel who built the first temple and was noted for his wisdom.

▶Critical Viewing◀

❸ Draw Conclusions *Students may prefer being a good soldier because there is more personal satisfaction in being good at something than being lucky; other students, however, may point out that lucky soldiers are not wounded or killed and may be rewarded for some things for which they did not have to work.*

Humanities: Art

Scotland Forever, 1881, by Elizabeth Butler.

Elizabeth Butler's vividly realistic and patriotic depictions of battle and military life made her one of the most successful painters in Victorian England. Queen Victoria herself was a great admirer of Butler's works and bought a Butler painting entitled *Calling the Roll After an Engagement, Crimea* for her own collection.

1. What elements in the painting convey a sense of movement and action? *Elements include the soldiers with raised swords in the foreground; the turbulent, rolling clouds and gunsmoke; and the point of view, in which the horses appear to charge directly toward the viewer.*
2. Which side of Scoresby does the painting reflect—the "public" Scoresby or the "real" Scoresby, known only by the clergyman and the narrator? Explain. *Students should note that the painting reflects the public Scoresby—that is, the one who is regarded as a brilliant military hero.*

◆ Reading Strategy

1 Make Inferences Have students use this passage to make inferences about the clergyman's character and his motives for helping young Scoresby. *Inferences may include: He is caring and soft-hearted; he helps Scoresby out of kindness.*

◆ Build Vocabulary

2 Word Roots: *-ver-* Point out that *veritably* contains the word root *-ver-*, which comes from the Latin *verax*, meaning "speaking truly." Have students use this information as well as context clues to determine the meaning of *veritably*. *It means truly.*

◆ Build Grammar Skills

3 Restrictive and Nonrestrictive Adjective Clauses Point out the nonrestrictive adjective clause *who knew a thousand times more than he.* Ask students what noun it modifies. How is it punctuated? *It modifies others; it is set off by commas.*

Comprehension Check 

4 How is Scoresby's performance on the mathematics exam similar to his performance on the history exam? *In both cases he did outstandingly well due to a "strangely lucky accident"—the questions that the clergyman drilled him on turned out to be the very ones that appeared on the exams.*

---

and that his judgment of men was good. Therefore I knew, beyond doubt or question, that the world was mistaken about this hero: he *was* a fool. So I meant to find out, at a convenient moment, how the Reverend, all solitary and alone, had discovered the secret.

Some days later the opportunity came, and this is what the Reverend told me:

About forty years ago I was an instructor in the military academy at Woolwich. I was present in one of the sections when young Scoresby underwent his preliminary examination. I was touched to the quick with pity; for the rest of the class answered up brightly and handsomely, while he—why, dear me, he didn't know *anything*, so to speak. He was evidently good, and sweet, and lovable, and guileless; and so it was exceedingly painful to see him
1 stand there, as serene as a graven image, and
2 deliver himself of answers which were veritably miraculous for stupidity and ignorance. All the compassion in me was aroused in his behalf. I said to myself, when he comes to be examined again, he will be flung over, of course; so it will be simply a harmless act of charity to ease his fall as much as I can. I took him aside, and found that he knew a little of Caesar's history;[6] and as he didn't know anything else, I went to work and drilled him like a galley slave on a certain line of stock questions concerning Caesar which I knew would be used. If you'll believe me, he went through with flying colors on examination day! He went through on that
3 purely superficial "cram," and got compliments too, while others, who knew a thousand times more than he, got plucked. By some strangely 3
lucky accident—an accident not likely to happen twice in a century—he was asked no question outside of the narrow limits of his drill.

It was stupefying. Well, all through his course I stood by him, with something of the sentiment which a mother feels for a crippled child; and he always saved himself—just by miracle, apparently.

Now of course the thing that would expose him and kill him at last was mathematics. I resolved to make his death as easy as I could; so I drilled him and crammed him, and crammed him and drilled him, just on the line of questions which the examiners would be most likely to use, and then launched him on his fate. Well, sir, try to conceive of the result: to my consternation he took the first prize! And with it he got a perfect ovation in the way of compliments.

Sleep? There was no more sleep for me for a week. My conscience tortured me day and night. What I had done I had done purely through charity, and only to ease the poor youth's fall—I never had dreamed of any such preposterous result as the thing that had happened. I felt as guilty and miserable as the creator of Frankenstein. Here was a woodenhead whom I had put in the way of glittering promotions and prodigious responsibilities, and but one thing could happen: he and his responsibilities would all go to ruin together at the first opportunity.

The Crimean War had just broken out. Of course there had to be a war, I said to myself: we couldn't have peace and give this donkey a chance to die before he is found out. I waited for the earthquake. It came. And it made me reel when it did come. He was actually gazetted[7] to a captaincy in a marching regiment! Better men grow old and gray in the service before they climb to a sublimity like that. And who could ever have foreseen that they would go and put such a load of responsibility on such green and inadequate shoulders?

6. **Caesar's** (sē′ zərz) **history:** Account of Julius Caesar (100?–44 B.C.), Roman emperor from 49 to 44 B.C.

7. **gazetted** (gə zet′ əd) *v.*: Officially promoted.

◆ Build Vocabulary

guileless (gīl′ lis) *adj.*: Without slyness or cunning; frank

prodigious (prə dij′ əs) *adj.*: Enormous

sublimity (sə blim′ ə tē) *n.*: A noble or exalted state

Research Skills Mini-Lesson

Using Text Organizers

This mini-lesson supports the Multimedia Biography project in the Idea Bank on p. 526.

Introduce Point out to students that, while researching, it is very helpful to use text organizers to locate and categorize information.

Develop Have students determine how they can best use maps and their organizers to locate where the author lived and worked. For example, after students have determined what country they wish to find, they may need to consult the index or table of contents of an atlas to locate the appropriate map. They may find it helpful to use key words or headings when researching on the Internet or in the library.

Apply Have students make use of text organizers to prepare a multimedia presentation. To reinforce the skill, ask students to keep a list of the text organizers they used.

Assess Ask students to present their research project to the class, including a brief description of their research experience. In addition to the quality of the presentation, assess students on their ability to use organizers successfully.

I could just barely have stood it if they had made him a cornet;[8] but a captain—think of it! I thought my hair would turn white.

Consider what I did—I who so loved repose and inaction. I said to myself, I am responsible to the country for this, and I must go along with him and protect the country against him as far as I can. So I took my poor little capital that I had saved up through years of work and grinding economy, and went with a sigh and bought a cornetcy in his regiment, and away we went to the field.

> ◆ **Literary Focus** How does the clergyman's observation indicate that Scoresby is a static character?

And there—oh dear, it was awful. Blunders?—why, he never did anything *but* blunder. But, you see, nobody was in the fellow's secret—everybody had him focused wrong, and necessarily misinterpreted his performance every time—consequently they took his idiotic blunders for inspirations of genius; they did, honestly! His mildest blunders were enough to make a man in his right mind cry; and they did make me cry—and rage and rave too, privately. And the thing that kept me always in a sweat of apprehension was the fact that every fresh blunder he made increased the luster of his reputation! I kept saying to myself, he'll get so high, that when discovery does finally come, it will be like the sun falling out of the sky.

He went right along up, from grade to grade, over the dead bodies of his superiors, until at last, in the hottest moment of the battle of * * * * down went our colonel, and my heart jumped into my mouth, for Scoresby was next in rank! Now for it, said I; we'll all land in Sheol[9] in ten minutes, sure.

The battle was awfully hot: the allies were steadily giving way all over the field. Our regiment occupied a position that was vital; a blunder now must be destruction. At this crucial moment, what does this immortal fool do but detach the regiment from its place and order a charge over a neighboring hill where

8. **cornet** (kôr net′) *n.*: British cavalry officer who carried his troop's flag.

9. **Sheol** (shē′ ol) *n.*: In the Bible, a place in the depths of the Earth where the dead are thought to dwell.

Hint to Modern Sculptors as an Ornament to a Future Square, Hand-colored etching by James Gillray, Victoria & Albert Museum Trustees

▲ Critical Viewing Does this man look like a good leader? Explain why or why not. **[Support]** 8

Humanities: Art

Hint to Modern Sculptors as an Ornament to a Future Square by James Gillray.

As its title indicates, this 200-year-old cartoon satirically depicts a statue that might adorn a future public square.

James Gillray (1757–1815) was a caricaturist—an artist who satirized the personalities and social mores of his day. Among Gillray's favorite targets were the English royal family and Napoleon I of France. He produced most of his work between 1780 and 1811.

Use these questions for discussion:

1. Based on the title and the picture, whom or what might the artist be satirizing? *Possibilities include a particular military leader of his time; the clichéd and unimaginative works of certain sculptors.*
2. Have students compare this artwork with *Scotland Forever*. Do they think that Gillray's cartoon reflects the public's image of Scoresby or the clergyman's image of him? *The cartoon reflects the clergyman's view of Scoresby.*

◆ Critical Thinking

5 Make a Judgment Have students identify the clergyman's reasons for going off to war with Scoresby. Then have them comment on his decision. Do they think it is wise or foolish? *Scoresby has been promoted, and the clergyman fears that his participation in the war will result in disaster. Some students may say that the clergyman's decision is wise and reasonable—he is the only one who knows the truth about Scoresby and thus can protect others from him. Other students may say that it is foolish—the clergyman should allow Scoresby to be exposed once and for all.*

◆ Literary Focus

6 Static and Dynamic Characters Scoresby did well in school by being lucky rather than intelligent. Now he is doing well in the army for the same reasons.

7 Clarification Students may wonder why Twain writes "the battle of * * * *" instead of naming the battle's location. Help them see that this device reinforces the narrator's claim that the events he is describing really took place, although he cannot reveal the identities of the people involved. Remind students that, at the beginning of the story, the narrator states, "For reasons which will presently appear, I will withhold his [Scoresby's] real name . . ."

▶Critical Viewing◀

8 Support *Students should note that the man looks too foppish and foolish to inspire confidence.*

Comprehension Check ☑

❶ In what way is the battle that the clergyman describes an example of another "lucky accident" in Scoresby's career? *The Russians mistake the English charge mindlessly led by Scoresby for a massive, well-planned attack.*

◆ Literary Focus

❷ **Static and Dynamic Characters** Ask students: Is Scoresby a static character or a dynamic character at this point? *Scoresby is static; he is still making mistakes that turn out right.*

◆ Critical Thinking

❸ **Analyze** Why does the clergyman tell the truth about Scoresby? *He can no longer hold in his sense of frustration and amazement.*

Reinforce and Extend

Answers

◆ *Literature and Your Life*

Reader's Response Some students may want to ask Scoresby to what he attributes his success.

Thematic Focus Ever since he chose to help Scoresby, he has felt responsible for him.

☑ Check Your Comprehension

1. He describes Scoresby as a fool.
2. He helps Scoresby with history and math, and joins Scoresby's regiment to help him in battle.
3. Scoresby is asked only questions to which he knows the answers on his examinations; he is made a captain in the army; his blunders in the war are taken for genius.
4. Scoresby wins a stunning military victory as a result of mistaking his right hand for his left.

◆ Critical Thinking

1. The narrator admires Scoresby; the clergyman thinks he is a fool.
2. He finds Scoresby "lovable," but pities him for being such a fool.
3. The clergyman feels that other people are his responsibility. Scoresby simply accepts his good fortune.
4. Students should include evidence from the story as support.
5. Both stories suggest that people may not necessarily learn from their errors.

---

there wasn't a suggestion of an enemy. "There you go!" I said to myself; "this *is* the end at last."

And away we did go, and were over the shoulder of the hill before the insane movement could be discovered and stopped. And what did we find? An entire and unsuspected Russian army in reserve! And what happened? We were eaten up? That is necessarily what would have happened in ninety-nine cases out of a hundred. But no, those Russians argued that no single regiment would come browsing around there at such a time. It must be the entire English army, and that the sly Russian game was detected ❶ and blocked; so they turned tail, and away they went, pell-mell, over the hill and down into the field, in wild confusion, and we after them; they themselves broke the solid Russian center in the field, and tore through, and in no time there was the most tremendous rout you ever saw, and the defeat of the allies was turned into a sweeping and splendid victory! Marshal Canrobert looked on, dizzy with astonishment, admiration, and delight; and sent right off for Scoresby, and hugged him, and decorated him on the field, in presence of all the armies!

❷ And what was Scoresby's blunder that time? Merely the mistaking his right hand for his left—that was all. An order had come to him to fall back and support our right; and instead, he fell *forward* and went over the hill to the left. But the name he won that day as a marvelous military genius filled the world with his glory, and that glory will never fade while history books last.

He is just as good and sweet and lovable and unpretending as a man can be, but he doesn't know enough to come in when it rains. Now that is absolutely true. He is the supremest fool in the universe; and until half an hour ago nobody knew it but himself and me. He has been pursued, day by day and year by year, by a most phenomenal and astonishing luckiness. He has been a shining soldier in all our wars for a generation; he has littered his whole military life with blunders, and yet has never committed one that didn't make him a knight or a baronet or a lord or something. Look at his breast; why, he is just clothed in domestic and foreign decorations. Well, sir, every one of them is the record of some shouting stupidity or other; and taken together, they are proof that the very best thing in all this world that can befall a man is to be born lucky. I say again, as I said at the banquet, Scoresby's an absolute fool.

Guide for Responding

◆ *Literature and Your Life*

Reader's Response If you could ask Scoresby about his experiences, what would you ask him?

Thematic Focus What is a consequence the clergyman experiences based on a choice he made when he was a teacher?

☑ Check Your Comprehension

1. How does the clergyman describe Scoresby?
2. Describe two things the clergyman does to help Scoresby.
3. Summarize the series of lucky events that put Scoresby in a position of leadership.
4. How does Scoresby achieve his "greatest victory"?

◆ Critical Thinking

INTERPRET

1. How does the narrator's first impression of Scoresby contrast with the view of him given by the clergyman? **[Distinguish]**
2. Why does the clergyman help Scoresby? **[Speculate]**
3. Compare and contrast Scoresby and the clergyman. **[Compare and Contrast]**
4. Do you agree with the clergyman that Scoresby is a fool? Explain your answer. In what way is the clergyman also a fool? **[Draw Conclusions]**

COMPARE LITERARY WORKS

5. Compare and contrast the points each story makes about choices and consequences. Support your ideas with examples. **[Compare and Contrast]**

Beyond the Selection

FURTHER READING

Other Works by the Authors

"The Duel," Anton Chekhov
"The Celebrated Jumping Frog of Calaveras County," Mark Twain

Other Works with the Theme of Choices and Consequences

"The Road Not Taken," Robert Frost
"The Necklace," Guy De Maupassant

We suggest that you preview these works before recommending them to students.

INTERNET

Students can visit the following Web sites to learn more about Chekhov and Twain.

For more on Chekhov, go to **http://www.winnipeg.Freenet.mb.ca/~vbu05/Anton_Chekhov.html**

For information about Twain's life and works, go to **http://www.literature.org/works/MarkTwain**

Please be aware, however, that sites may have changed since we published this information. We *strongly recommend* that you preview the sites before you send students to them.

Guide for Reponding (continued)

◆ Literary Focus

Static and Dynamic Characters

Some characters in stories can be classified as **static characters**—that is, characters that do not change during the course of the story. Others are **dynamic characters**—characters whose attitudes, beliefs, or personality traits change as a result of the story events. In these stories, both of the main characters are static.

1. Describe the behavior that led to Sasha Uskov's troubles in "A Problem." Describe the way he behaves at the end of the story.
2. Compare Arthur Scoresby's character traits at the beginning of "Luck" and at the end.
3. Explain why Scoresby and Sasha Uskov are both static characters.

◆ Build Vocabulary

Using the Latin Root *-ver-*

The root *-ver-* comes from the Latin *verax* and means "speaking truly." It forms the basis of a number of English words whose meaning relates to the idea of truth. On your paper, match each numbered word with its corresponding definition.

1. veritable	**a.** a truth
2. verisimilitude	**b.** the appearance of being true
3. verity	**c.** actual; in fact

Using the Word Bank: Context

On your paper, answer the following questions.

1. What's another word for the *zenith* of success?
2. What type of *countenance* does a clown typically display?
3. Should politicians have *veracity*? Why or why not?
4. How successful would a *guileless* burglar be?
5. True or false: The grasshopper is a *prodigious* creature.
6. Name a type of person who would be said to be in a position of *sublimity*.
7. Which career would most fit a *taciturn* person: violinist, teacher, or stand-up comedian?
8. Would a *rheumatic* person be good at sports? Why or why not?
9. What kind of furniture might fit in a *vestibule?*

◆ Reading Strategy

Draw Inferences About Character

You can apply logic to the evidence provided by each author to draw inferences about the personalities of characters in "Luck" and "A Problem." For example, when the Colonel in "A Problem" declares about his nephew, "I have no faith whatever in his reforming," you can infer that he has disappointed his family more than once.

1. What do you infer about Sasha's character when he asks his uncle for money at the end of the story?
2. What inferences can you draw about Scoresby based on the fact that all his advancements are a result of blunders?

◆ Build Grammar Skills

Restrictive and Nonrestrictive Adjective Clauses

A **restrictive adjective clause** is not set off by commas because it is necessary to complete the meaning of the noun or pronoun it modifies. A **nonrestrictive adjective clause** is set off by commas. It provides additional but not necessary information.

Practice Copy the following sentences in your notebook. Underline the adjective clause in each. Then tell whether it is restrictive or nonrestrictive.

1. "My friends!" said the uncle who was a colonel . . .
2. For reasons which will presently appear, I will withhold my name.
3. Others, who knew a thousand times more than he, got plucked.

Writing Application Write the following sentences in your notebook, supplying adjective clauses where there are blank spaces.

Sasha's uncle __?__ said he would help. He offered to pay the notes __?__ . Sasha wanted to go to the party __?__. He asked his uncle for money __?__. The uncle was shocked that his nephew __?__ would be so ungrateful.

Reteach

The difference between static and dynamic characters may be a difficult concept for some students to master. Have them select one of the stories and analyze its characters. Have them list all the characters in the story down one side of a piece of paper, leaving space between the characters' names. Then, have them fold the paper in an accordion fold so it has three columns. Ask students to take each character individually. In the first column, students should note the traits of each character at the start of the story. Students can skim the story for details that indicate whether the character changed or remained the same during the entire story. If the character changed, have students mark an X in the second fold, if not, have them mark the third fold. Ask students to defend their decisions.

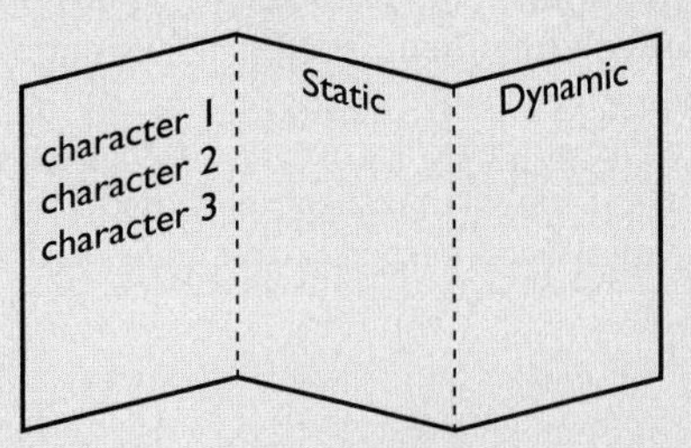

◆ Literary Focus

1. Sasha's recklessness and lack of responsibility lead to his troubles. At the end of the story, he recklessly betrays his uncle's trust.
2. Scoresby is the same lucky blunderer throughout.
3. Scoresby starts out and ends up a fool. Although Sasha's lack of morality is revealed at the end of the story, he has never had a sense of morality or responsibility.

◆ Build Vocabulary

Using the Latin Word Root *-ver-*

1. c 2. b 3. a

Using the Word Bank

1. Another word for *zenith* is height.
2. A clown usually displays a happy or comical *countenance*.
3. Politicians should have *veracity;* they should be honest.
4. A *guileless* burglar, without tricks, would be unsuccessful.
5. False; a grasshopper is small.
6. A happy and successful person would be in a position of *sublimity*.
7. A *taciturn* person would be more fit to be a violinist than a teacher or a comedian.
8. A *rheumatic* person would be stiff, rather than agile, and therefore not good at sports.

◆ Reading Strategy

1. Sasha has no moral sense.
2. Scoresby is lucky.

◆ Build Grammar Skills

1. "My friends!" said the uncle <u>who was a colonel</u> . . .; restrictive
2. For reasons <u>which will presently appear</u>, I will withhold my name; restrictive
3. Others, <u>who knew a thousand times more than he</u>, got plucked; nonrestrictive

Writing Application

Sample answers: Sasha's uncle, <u>who was sympathetic</u>, said he would help. He offered to pay the notes <u>that Sasha owed</u>. Sasha wanted to go to the party <u>that was being held that night</u>. He asked his uncle for money, <u>which he needed for the party</u>. The uncle was shocked that his nephew, <u>whom he had just helped</u>, would be so ungrateful.

Idea Bank

Following are suggestions for matching Idea Bank topics with your students' performance levels and learning modalities:

Customizing for Performance Levels

Less Advanced Students: 1, 4, 5
Average Students: 2, 4, 7
More Advanced Students: 3, 6

Customizing for Learning Modalities

Verbal/Linguistic: 1, 2, 3, 4, 6
Visual/Spatial: 5, 7

Guided Writing Lesson

Prewriting Strategy Before students begin writing their dialogues, have them use a cluster diagram to identify each speaker's characteristics and the realistic words and phrases that each character might use.

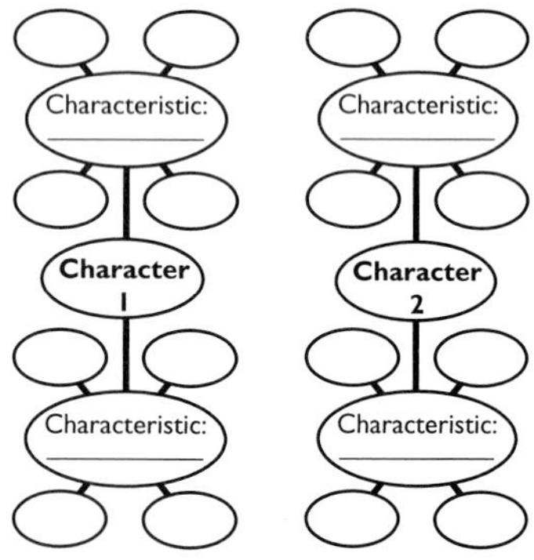

For more prewriting, elaboration, and revision strategies, see *Prentice Hall Writing and Grammar.*

Writing and Language Transparencies Students can use the Comparison and Contrast organizer, p. 97, to list points of agreement and disagreement in their conversations.

Writers at Work Videodisc

Have students view the videodisc segment from Chapter 2, featuring Maxine Hong Kingston, to see how she develops narrative elements.

Play frames 18612 to 19873

Writing Lab CD-ROM

Have students complete the tutorial on Creative Writing. Follow these steps:

1. Have students watch the video clip about gathering details.
2. Have students draft on computer.
3. Students can use the proofreading checklist for drama to guide revision.

Build Your Portfolio

Idea Bank

Writing

1. **Invitation** Write the invitation the narrator and clergyman from "Luck" might have received to attend the banquet in honor of Arthur Scoresby.
2. **Journal Entry** Write an entry in Sasha Uskov's journal from the day before his family met to discuss the promissory note he took out and failed to pay back on time.
3. **Story Ending** Write a new story ending for either "Luck" or "A Problem" that shows one major character changing as a result of the events in the original story.

Speaking, Listening, and Viewing

4. **Monologue** As the clergyman in "Luck," describe the character of Arthur Scoresby aloud to a partner. Base your description on details from the story.
5. **Period Presentation** Find pictures in books or specialty magazines that show how people dressed and lived in the mid- to late 1800's. Make a presentation of those pictures, or create your own drawings based on your research. **[Art Link; Social Studies Link]**

Researching and Representing

6. **Roundtable Discussion** With three other students, discuss how the messages about choices and consequences in these stories apply to modern times. Present a written summary of your conclusions to the rest of the class.
7. **Multimedia Biography** Create a multimedia biography of Twain or Chekhov. Use maps to show where they lived and the settings they wrote about. Record yourself reading a passage from the author's writing. **[Art Link; Social Studies Link]**

Online Activity www.phlit.phschool.com

Guided Writing Lesson

Telephone Conversation

Even though each of these stories takes place before the telephone was invented, it is possible to imagine updated versions of each story, in which the conversations take place on a telephone. When a person talks on a telephone, the language used reflects that person's unique personality.

Choose a subject from one of these stories, and write a **telephone conversation**. Use the kind of language contemporary people would use when talking on the phone.

Writing Skills: Realistic Dialogue

Realistic dialogue reflects the language people really use when they talk with one another. The dialogue in "Luck" and "A Problem" reflects the way people talked in the settings for those stories, the late nineteenth century. For your telephone conversation, choose and arrange words to convey the ideas and feelings each person might use in a real phone conversation.

Prewriting Once you decide on the two characters and subject of the telephone conversation, jot down specific quotations that reveal important characteristics or the speaking style of each speaker. Then list other words and phrases that each character might use.

Drafting Write the conversation, making it as believable as you can. Include the quotations and other phrases you wrote down for each speaker. You may even want to include stage directions in parentheses or brackets; for example: (*Coughs before answering*).

Revising Read your dialogue aloud with a partner. Listen to make sure each speaker responds to the other. If a sentence or word does not sound realistic, go back to your prewriting notes to find the appropriate language, or just rewrite it based on the way people speak.

✓ ASSESSMENT OPTIONS

Formal Assessment, Selection Test, pp. 132–134, and Assessment Resources Software. The selection test is designed so that it can be easily customized to the performance levels of your students.

Alternative Assessment, p. 38, includes options for less advanced students, more advanced students, visual/spatial learners, verbal/linguistic learners, musical/rhythmic learners, logical/mathematical, and interpersonal learners.

PORTFOLIO ASSESSMENT

Use the following rubrics in ***Alternative Assessment*** to assess student writing:
Invitation: General Rubric, p. 93
Journal Entry: Fictional Narrative Rubric, p. 95
Story Ending: Fictional Narrative Rubric, p. 95
Guided Writing Lesson: Drama Rubric, p. 109

Writing Process Workshop

Short Story

Short stories can be surprising, thrilling, thoughtful, or mysterious. However, short stories have certain elements in common: They create a single, powerful impression, have a limited number of characters and settings, and center on a conflict that is usually resolved by the story's end.

Write your own short story. The following skills, introduced in this section's Guided Writing Lessons, will help you write your story.

Writing Skills Focus

- **Use transitions to show time,** such as *later, next,* and *after that,* to keep the plot flowing smoothly. (See p. 476.)
- **Develop your plot so that it leads to a climax,** or high point of tension, and then have a resolution, in which the conflict is settled. (See p. 497.)
- **Bring your characters to life through realistic dialogue.** Read your dialogue aloud to see how it sounds. (See p. 526.)
- **Keep a consistent point of view**—either first person or third person—throughout the story. (See p. 511.)

In the following excerpt, the author uses these skills to heighten the conflict in the story.

Model From Literature

from *Leiningen Versus the Ants* by Carl Stephenson

"Unless they alter their course, and there's no reason why they should, they'll reach your plantation in two days at the latest." ①

Leiningen sucked placidly at a cigar about the size of a corn cob and for a few seconds ② gazed without answering the agitated District Commissioner. Then he took the cigar from his lips and leaned slightly forward. With his bristling gray hair, bulky nose, and lucid eyes, he had the look of an aging and shabby eagle. ③

"Decent of you," ④ he murmured, "paddling all this way just to give me the tip.

① The author wastes no time in setting up the story's conflict.

② The transition for a few seconds shows time passing.

③ The writer uses third-person point of view.

④ The dialogue is realistic and reveals the personalities of the characters.

Prepare and Engage

LESSON OBJECTIVES

- To use recursive writing processes to write a short story
- To demonstrate control over grammatical elements such as verb tense
- To demonstrate control over the conventions of written English as they apply to proper nouns

You may want to distribute the scoring rubric for a Fictional Narrative (p. 95 in ***Alternative Assessment***) to make students aware before they begin of the criteria on which they will be evaluated. See the suggestions on p. 529 for tips about customizing the rubric for this workshop.

Writers at Work Videodisc To introduce students to the key elements of a short story and learn how author Maxine Hong Kingston uses them in her writing, play the videodisc segment on Narration (Ch. 2). Have students discuss what Kingston says about how a story itself can shape a narrative.

Play frames 11644 to 20980

Writing Lab CD-ROM
If your students have access to computers, you may want to have them work on the tutorial on Narration to complete all or part of their short stories. Follow these steps:

1. Have students view the interactive model of a short story.
2. Suggest that students use a photo storyboard for plot ideas.
3. Have students draft on the computer.
4. Suggest students consult the screen on tightening suspense.
5. Have students consult the screen on punctuating dialogue.

Cross-Curricular Connection: Science

Science Fiction One of the most popular genres of fiction is science fiction, fiction that blends traditional narrative techniques with a fascination with the inventions, discoveries and world of science. Although many science fiction tales suffer from stiff prose that relegates them to second-rate status in the literary world, tales by authors such as Jules Verne, H. G. Wells, Isaac Asimov, and Ray Bradbury have been accepted into the greater canon of literature. Other authors such as Arthur C. Clarke, Ursula K. LeGuin, Frank Herbert, and Robert Heinlein have also achieved prestige in the literary world. You might encourage students with a predilection for math and/or science to take advantage of their interest in those fields and have them consider writing a science fiction story.

Develop Student Writing

Prewriting Strategy

Students who choose to develop the setting for their story before any other element may benefit from the blueprint technique. Use this blueprint of a house below as a model. As students sketch out the setting, the conflict and characters may come to mind.

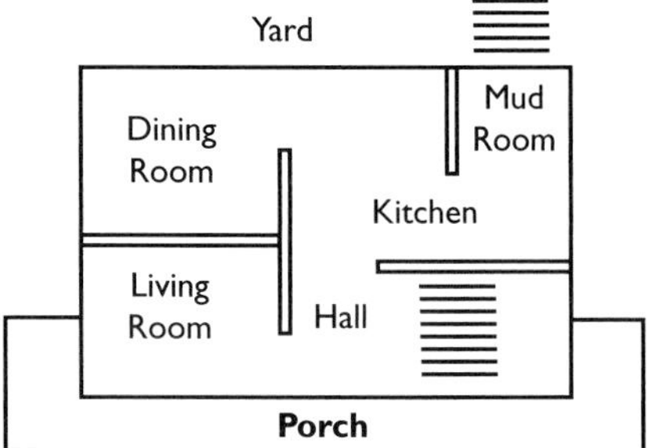

Customize for *English Language Learners*

These students may confuse homonyms such as *there* and *their*, and *to, too,* and *two*. Explain the differences among these words before the students begin drafting.

Customize for *Less Proficient Writers*

If these students are having difficulty thinking of a plot, encourage them to write about an incident in their own lives. Make sure they write in the third person.

Writing Lab CD-ROM

The Developing Narrative Elements section of the tutorial on Narration contains a Story Line diagram. Encourage students to use this screen to outline the plot elements of their stories, including exposition, inciting incident, rising action, climax, falling action, and resolution.

Elaboration Strategy

Suggest that students plan out their short stories, beginning with a dramatic opening incident and building to a high point or climax. Encourage them to draft without concern for grammatical or other errors. Once students have completed a draft, they can reenter their work to make extensive revisions.

Applying Language Skills: Verb Tense

Verbs have different forms to show time. These forms are called **tenses**. Use appropriate verb tenses when referring to different periods of time. For example, use the present tense for action in the present and use past tenses for actions that have already happened.

Wrong Tense:

Long before the detective met Mendoza, he hears about him.

Correct Tense:

Long before the detective met Mendoza, he had heard about him.

Practice On your paper, rewrite the following passage using correct verb tenses:

1. John remembers when covered bridges dot the countryside.
2. He continues to search for clues, since the mystery was still not solved.

Writing Application Check the tenses in your short story.

Writer's Solution Connection Writing Lab

For more examples of topics for short stories, see the Inspirations for Narration in the Narration tutorial in the Writing Lab.

Prewriting

Choose a Topic A good way to think of an idea for a short story is to create a Plot Word Bin like the one below. Make two lists, the first one containing potential main characters, the second containing potential conflicts. Mix and match the two until you come up with a suitable conflict.

Plot Word Bin

Characters	Conflicts
Detective	Missing diamond
Young doctor	Terminal illness
Recent immigrant	Crisis of conscience
Biologist	Environmental disaster
Reporter	Political scandal

Develop the Plot The plot is the sequence of events in your narrative. Begin the plot with an exposition that introduces the setting and characters. Then introduce the conflict. Develop the conflict with rising suspense and action until you reach the climax, or high point of tension. Finally, resolve the conflict and tie up any loose ends in the plot. Use a story line diagram like the one shown to help you plan the plot.

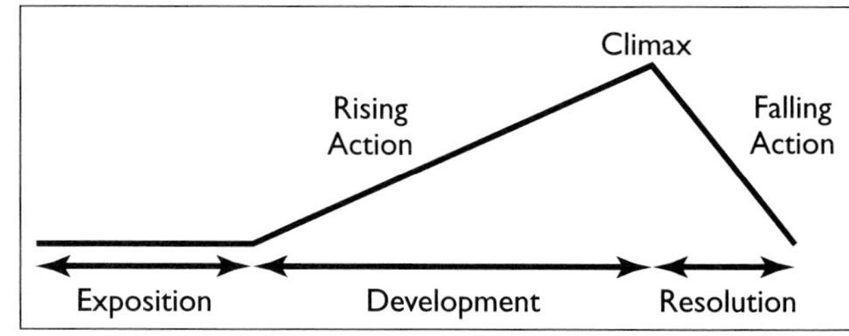

Drafting

Beginning Starting can be the hardest part of writing a short story. The simplest way to tell a story is to present the events in chronological order. You may want to start with a flashback, in the middle of the situation, and go back and fill in the details. You could also begin with a scene of dialogue that introduces the characters or conflict.

Ending A good ending to your narrative is as important as a good beginning. The ending should resolve the conflict, end the suspense, and tie up any loose strings in the plot. It should also be logically consistent with the preceding events.

Applying Language Skills

Verb Tense When writing short stories in particular, students may have trouble shifting between the present and past tenses. Remind them that they should probably use the past tense for most of the narration. Dialogue, of course, can be any tense. Remind them also to use the past perfect tense to describe a past action that occurred before another past action.

Answers

1. John remembers (*remembered* also acceptable) when covered bridges *dotted* the countryside.
2. He *continued* to search for clues, since the mystery *had* still not *been solved*. (*was still not solved* also acceptable)

Grammar Reinforcement

For additional instruction and practice, have students complete the **Language Lab CD-ROM** lesson on Verb Tense and the practice p. 67 in the *Writer's Solution Grammar Practice Book.*

Revising

Use a Checklist A first draft is not a final product. To make it into something wonderful, you need to trim, shape, and polish it. Use the following checklist to help you revise your writing.

- ▶ What can you do to make the plot or conflict clearer?
  Insert changes that would make the plot more logical or would help make the rising action more suspenseful. Add transitions where necessary.
- ▶ What can you do to make the characters more realistic?
  Add dialogue to bring them to life.
- ▶ Who is telling the story? Is this point of view consistent throughout the story?
- ▶ What language would make your writing more vivid or precise?
  Replace weak verbs with vivid ones and vague nouns with exact ones.
- ▶ What changes would vary the length and structure of your sentences?

Revision Model

① "P.L. Patterson, private investigator." #
~~"Hello?" she said.~~ "Mrs. Patterson, I'm glad I reached
② The voice on the line was
you." ~~said a~~ masculine and sophisticated ~~voice~~. "My name is Mr. Chamberlain. Some jewels belonging to my family were stolen last night. I'd like you to come by as soon as possible." ③

① The new dialogue reveals a direct, confident character.
② This change makes the sentence structure more interesting.
③ Here, the writer sets up the conflict.

Publishing

Consider a Live Audience Reading a short story aloud is a great way to share it with others. Keep the following points in mind when reading before others: Read slowly and clearly, make eye contact with your audience, vary your volume and tone for emphasis, and take on the personalities of your characters when you read dialogue.

Applying Language Skills: Proper Nouns

Proper nouns, which are always capitalized, name individual people, places, or things. Proper nouns are the most exact nouns.

Common Nouns:
author, lake, war, mountain

Proper Nouns:
Ernest Hemingway, Lake Malawi, World War II, Mt. Kenya

Practice On your paper, replace the following common nouns with proper nouns.

city	book
language	car
river	country
actress	politician
album	gem

Writing Application Review your short story. Look for places where replacing a common noun with a proper noun will make your story more vivid.

Writer's Solution Connection
Language Lab

For more practice with proper nouns, complete the Language Lab lesson on Types of Nouns.

Revision Strategy

Have students read their stories aloud to find awkward passages.

Writing Lab CD-ROM

Students can use the following tools for revising their short stories:

- Proofreading checklist
- Audio-annotated guides for revising dialogue
- Verb-tense checker
- Audio-annotated student model

Publishing

If students do not wish to share their short stories, suggest that they keep them for possible incorporation into a longer work.

Proper Nouns Remind students that proper nouns convey a sense of precision and exactness.

Suggested Answers

Bangkok	*Moby Dick*
Tamil	Corvette
the Amazon	Nepal
Meryl Streep	Bill Clinton
Abbey Road	the Hope Diamond

Grammar Reinforcement

Have students complete the **Language Lab CD-ROM** lesson on Types of Nouns and the practice p. 93 in the *Writer's Solution Grammar Practice Book.*

Reinforce and Extend

Prentice Hall Writing and Grammar For more prewriting, elaboration, and revision strategies, see *Prentice Hall Writing and Grammar.*

Connect to Literature Have students read and study some of the short stories in this book.

✓ ASSESSMENT		4	3	2	1
PORTFOLIO ASSESSMENT Use the rubric on Fictional Narrative in ***Alternative Assessment*** (p. 95) to assess the students' writing. Add these criteria to customize the rubric to this assignment.	**Verb Tense**	All verb tenses are used correctly. There are no shifts in tense.	There are a few shifts in verb tense.	There are noticeable shifts in verb tense.	There are so many shifts in verb tense that understanding is impaired.
	Transitions	Transitions are used effectively to keep the plot moving.	Transitions are used.	More transitions are needed.	Transitions are not used at all; the story suffers significantly as a result.

LESSON OBJECTIVES

- To use study strategies to better understand texts

Customize for
Pre-AP Students
Suggest that students choose a chapter from one of their content-area textbooks and read the chapter as many times as necessary to create their own study-guide questions for it. (They should first cover up any existing summaries, overviews, and questions.) They can then compare their own study-guide questions to the published ones in the textbook chapter. Discuss how creating one's own study guide can help learners focus on important ideas and stay focused while rereading.

Answers

1. Reading rapidly, or skimming, gives a general sense of the passage. Notes should include supporting details that are found by closer reading.
2. I. Lori Benson dreamed of foreign travel.
   II. She needed her parents' permission to travel and study abroad.
   III. Persuading her protective parents would be difficult.
3. Possible responses include: What does Lori Benson want? What problem does she face? Why does she have that problem?

Student Success Workshop

Study Skills — Using Study Strategies

Strategies for Success

Certain study strategies can enhance your comprehension and retention of assigned reading:

Skim and Scan To start reading a text, you can begin by skimming or scanning it. To skim, rapidly glance through the pages without reading every word. To scan, look through the pages in a broad, searching way to get a feel for the work's tone, subject matter, or purpose. Notice unfamiliar ideas, uses of language, or vocabulary.

Take Notes As you read, take notes. Write down the main ideas and any questions that come to mind. Jot down those unfamiliar words or ideas. Notes can help you clarify what you don't understand. Suppose, for example, an article refers to "flight pioneer Amelia Earhart." You might better understand the entire passage if you know more about Amelia Earhart. After making a note of her name, you can conduct some research.

Outline One way to make complex reading understandable is to create an outline that breaks down the text into topics and subtopics—or headings and subheadings. If you were reading an article about the artist Pablo Picasso, one topic heading might be "His Painting Career." Subheadings listed below might include: "Training," "First Exhibits," and "Cubist Style." By creating an outline, you can organize information so that it is easier to follow.

Use Study-Guide Questions Most textbooks include study-guide questions that can help you understand the text more fully. Study-guide questions for a science text might help you review the facts. Study-guide questions for a fictional story might help you concentrate on the author's point of view or on the development of a certain character.

Apply the Strategies

Look at the following passage, and apply the study strategies that follow.

> Visiting a foreign country had always been one of Lori Benson's dreams. As a girl growing up in the working-class neighborhoods of Pittsburgh, Lori seldom traveled any farther than the Maryland coast. When given the opportunity to travel abroad for six months with her classmates, it appeared that Lori's dream might come true. If only she could convince her parents to allow her to go on the trip. Working after school and on weekends, Lori had saved enough money to pay for the trip, but she knew she still needed her parents' permission. Ever since her brother Bobby had been injured in a car accident, Lori's parents were cautious about letting her travel. Lori knew she faced an uphill battle.

1. First, skim the text. Then, take notes. Are the ideas and details you recorded in your notes different from the ideas you got from skimming? Explain.
2. Create an outline of the passage. What are the main ideas in the text?
3. Write a set of study-guide questions that might help another reader to understand the text.

Here are some reading situations in which to use study strategies:

- *Reading an article about a complex science topic*
- *Gathering research information for a term paper*
- *Writing a review of a novel or a play*

Test Preparation Workshop

Reading Comprehension:
Identify the Main Idea Students can use study strategies to approach reading passages on standardized tests. Reading a test passage all the way through at a normal-to-fast rate and scanning, or running the eyes rapidly over the text to find particular names or terms, are useful test-taking techniques. Have students scan the passage quickly to answer the following question:

> Lori set out to convince her parents about the benefits of her European trip. She drafted a list of positive outcomes. She knew she would see the great art of Florence and visit the monuments of Paris and Rome. Suddenly, history would come alive for her!

What is the main idea of this passage?

A Lori needed to raise money for the trip. The trip was too expensive.
B Lori knew the trip had educational benefits.
C Lori was too young to travel.
D Lori's parents wanted her to continue her education.

Help students see that the best answer is B because the passage cites the educational benefits.

PART 2 Setting and Theme

Couple and Ship, Keith Lo Bue, Stock Illustration Source, Inc.

One-Minute Planning Guide

The selections in this part are stories that are strong in the elements of setting and theme. The part opens with Ray Bradbury's "There Will Come Soft Rains," in which the setting itself is the focus of the story. Italo Calvino's "The Garden of Stubborn Cats" also creates an unforgettable setting, in which cats face off against encroaching development. Pär Lagerkvist conveys a memorable theme about the burdens of responsibility in the fable-like "The Princess and All the Kingdom"; Luisa Valenzuela comments on the ills of oppressive regimes in "The Censors."

Customize for
Varying Student Needs

When assigning the selections in this part to your students, keep in mind the following factors:

"There Will Come Soft Rains"

- Some technical terms may pose problems for ESL Students.

"The Garden of Stubborn Cats"

- The plot may be difficult to follow for less proficient readers.

"The Princess and All the Kingdom"

- The point of the story is expressed so simply that some students may miss it.

"The Censors"

- The operations of the bureaucracy may be difficult for some students to understand.

Humanities: Art

Couple and Ship by Keith LoBue.

The style of this art recalls the art deco advertisements of the 1920's and 1930's; in addition, the clothing of the man and woman and their luggage evoke that period, when people who traveled overseas more typically traveled on ocean liners than on airplanes. Elicit the effect created by the artist's use of black, which sets off the heads of the man and woman as well as the upper part of the ship. Encourage students to discuss the effect of the artist's stylization here—the lack of detail, the solid blocks of color, as well as his rather theatrical (as opposed to naturalistic) use of light; the whole work is deliberately artificial, giving an air of glamour and mystery to the scene.

Help students link the artwork to the focus of this part, Setting and Theme, by answering the following questions:

1. If this art were used to illustrate a story, what ideas about travel might the picture suggest? *It might suggest that travel is exciting; that it is a diversion for wealthy people, since the couple is well-dressed; that people who travel entrust themselves to unknown and powerful forces, like the huge black ship.*
2. Suggest an idea for a story based on this artwork. *Sample answer: The couple are a pair of international spies who pose as a wealthy, leisured couple during the 1930's; they travel a great deal (the well-stamped suitcase). This time they are rushing to board a ship that will take them to China to look for a missing diplomat.*

Prepare and Engage

LESSON OBJECTIVES

1. **To develop vocabulary and word identification skills**
   - Word Origins: Words From Myths
   - Using the Word Bank: Context
   - Extending Word Study: Expand Vocabulary (ATE)
2. **To use a variety of reading strategies to comprehend two short stories**
   - Connect Your Experience
   - Reading Strategy: Clarify
   - Tips to Guide Reading: Sustained Reading (ATE)
   - Idea Bank: Schedule
   - Read to Be Entertained (ATE)
3. **To increase knowledge of other cultures and to connect common elements across cultures**
   - Connecting Themes Across Cultures (ATE)
4. **To express and support responses to the text**
   - Critical Thinking
   - Analyze Literary Criticism
   - Idea Bank: Sci-Fi Story
   - Idea Bank: Persuasive Argument
5. **To analyze literary elements**
   - Literary Focus: Setting
   - Idea Bank: Speculation
6. **To read in order to research self-selected and assigned topics**
   - Idea Bank: Presentation
   - Questions for Research
7. **To plan, prepare, organize, and present literary interpretations**
   - Idea Bank: Dialogue
   - Speaking, Listening, and Viewing: Dialogue
   - Idea Bank: Floor Plan
   - Viewing and Representing Mini-Lesson: Floor Plan (ATE)
8. **To use recursive writing processes to write an advertisement for a new technology**
   - Guided Writing Lesson
9. **To increase knowledge of the rules of grammar and usage**
   - Build Grammar Skills: Commonly Confused Words: *Lie and Lay*

Test Preparation

Critical Reading: Distinguish Between Fact and Nonfact (ATE, p. 533) The teaching tips and sample test item in this workshop support the instruction and practice in the unit workshop:

Critical Reading: Recognize Forms of Propaganda; Distinguish Between Fact and Nonfact (SE, p. 565)

Guide for Reading

Ray Bradbury *(1920–)*

Many of science-fiction writer Ray Bradbury's stories are set on Mars, but one of his books "lives" on the moon! Dandelion Crater on the moon is named for Bradbury's book *Dandelion Wine.*

Bradbury is one of the world's most celebrated science-fiction writers. He was born in Waukegan, Illinois, and grew up along the western shores of Lake Michigan. He began reading the stories of Edgar Allan Poe as a child and also developed a fascination with horror movies and fantasy—especially futuristic fantasy. In many of his stories, including "There Will Come Soft Rains," Bradbury explores the consequences of future technological growth.

Italo Calvino *(1923–1985)*

Italo Calvino was born in Cuba, but as a young boy, he moved with his family to Italy. He settled in Turin after fighting in the Italian Resistance during World War II. Two of his works of fiction, *The Path to the Nest of Spiders* and *Adam, One Afternoon,* were in fact inspired by his participation in the Resistance.

Calvino is best known for having edited a monumental collection of fables. According to his theory, the "fable formula," which involves a child in the woods or a knight fighting beasts, is the scheme for all human stories. One fable element that can be found in almost all of Calvino's fiction is the tension between character and environment. You will see this conflict between characters and environment in "The Garden of Stubborn Cats."

◆ Build Vocabulary

WORD ORIGINS: WORDS FROM MYTHS

In "There Will Come Soft Rains," Ray Bradbury describes "one *titanic* instant." *Titanic* comes from the classical myths of ancient Greece. The Titans were a race of giants who ruled the world long before the gods. They were overthrown by the Olympians, led by Zeus, who assumed dominion over the world after defeating the Titans. Because the Titans were giants with great strength, the word *titanic* describes something of great size or power. The "titanic instant" in this story is a powerful moment.

WORD BANK

Before you read, preview this list of words from the story. Write the words in two columns: words you know and words you need to learn.

warrens
titanic
paranoia
tremulous
psychopathic
supernal
itinerary
transoms
rank
scrimmage
indigence

◆ Build Grammar Skills

COMMONLY CONFUSED WORDS: *LIE* AND *LAY*

Because *lie* and *lay* seem similar, and because the past tense of *lie* is *lay,* these verbs are often confused. In fact, they have two different meanings and uses. *Lay* means "to put or set (something) down," and it usually takes a direct object. Its principal parts are *lay, laying, laid,* and *laid.*

dir. obj.
. . . he . . . *laid* his place among the packing-cases . . .

Lie means "to recline." Its principal parts are *lie, lying, lay,* and *lain. Lie* does not take a direct object.

. . . dry leaves *lay* everwhere under the boughs . . .

Prentice Hall Literature Program Resources

REINFORCE / RETEACH / EXTEND

Selection Support Pages
Build Vocabulary: Word Origins, p. 159
Build Grammar Skills: *Lie* and *Lay,* p. 160
Reading Strategy: Clarify, p. 161
Literary Focus: Setting, p. 162

Strategies for Diverse Student Needs, p. 39

Beyond Literature
Community Connection: Automation, p. 39

Formal Assessment Selection Test, pp. 135–137; Assessment Resources Software

Alternative Assessment, p. 39

Writing and Language Transparencies
Writing Process Model 7, pp. 45–51

Resource Pro CD-ROM

Listening to Literature Audiocassettes

◆ There Will Come Soft Rains ◆ The Garden of Stubborn Cats

◆ Literature and Your Life

Connect Your Experience

You've exchanged hundreds of e-mails with your best friend. Suddenly, something seems to be missing—your best friend. You're starting to forget what he or she looks and sounds like because all you have to do to communicate is press "send." Situations like this call your attention to the fact that advances in technology have disadvantages as well as advantages.

Thematic Focus: To the Future

These two stories highlight the need to examine the effects of progress as we move into the future.

Journal Writing Create a chart showing the pros and cons of a technological advance in this century, such as airplanes or transatlantic communication.

◆ Background for Understanding

Technology

Automation is the use of machines to perform tasks that require a decision. Some familiar uses of automation are thermostats that "decide" when to turn the heat on and off in a home and traffic lights that change based on the amount of traffic that passes through. Automation allows machines to perform tasks that are too boring or dangerous for people to do. The house of the future in "There Will Come Soft Rains" has an impressive level of automation. As more and more areas of business and personal life become automated, people continue to evaluate the effects of automation on society.

◆ Reading Strategy

Clarify

To avoid misunderstandings when you read, **clarify** any parts of the story you don't understand. The best way to do this is to read ahead for more information or read back to review what you have already learned. For example, you might want to review details of the setting, clarify the relationships among the characters, or look back at the details of a key event.

As both of these stories develop, you may come to places that are not completely clear. At these points, stop, look back or ahead, and put details together to clarify the events.

◆ Literary Focus

Setting

All stories have a **setting**—the time and place of the action—but authors sometimes emphasize a particular aspect of a setting to help bring out their theme. For example, time is of the greatest importance in "There Will Come Soft Rains" because everything that happens hinges on the fact that the story is set in the future.

In "The Garden of Stubborn Cats," place is the more important feature of the setting. Readers can join Marcovaldo, as he follows a cat around the city, getting a new perspective on familiar locations. Use a chart like the one shown to record details that help you identify and understand the setting of each story.

	Rains	Cats
Time Details		
Place Details		
Unusual Perspective Details		

Test Preparation Workshop

Critical Reading:
Distinguish Between Fact and Nonfact
As students prepare for standardized tests they need to be prepared to distinguish between fact and nonfact. To help students prepare, use this sample test item.

Automation is the use of machines to perform tasks that require a decision. Some familiar uses of automation are thermostats and traffic lights. Automation allows machines to perform tasks that are too boring or dangerous for people to do.

Which of the following is an OPINION stated in the passage? :

A Automation is the use of machines to perform tasks that require a decision.
B Some tasks are too boring for people to do.
C Automation is at work in thermostats.
D People don't have to do work that machines do,

A, B, and *C* are supported by the passage, but only *B* is an opinion.

Have students anticipate technological developments by describing a typical day in the life of someone living fifty years from now. For example, what kind of gadgets would be available for preparing breakfast and what kinds of transportation would take the person to work? Ask students to brainstorm for technological developments as you go through a day from morning to afternoon. Then tell them that each of these stories deals with the consequences of technology.

Connecting Themes Across Cultures

Each of these stories addresses technology's impact on the future. Certain cultures thriving today are strongly opposed to technology. For example, the Amish of Pennsylvania live in a society which bans the use of electricity and telephones. Ask students to share their knowledge of other cultures which have specific feelings about technology and the future.

Tips to Guide Reading

Sustained Reading Suggest that students enjoy the selections by reading in a sustained manner without stopping.

Customize for
Less Proficient Readers
These students may need help understanding what is happening in each story. Read the first pages aloud, and use the Reading Strategy prompts on pp. 536 and 543 to help students clarify what is going on.

Customize for
Pre-AP Students
Challenge these students to infer the message of the stories as they read. Have them compare and contrast the views of the two stories toward technological "progress."

Develop Understanding

One-Minute Insight With no human characters, this story is an ironic reflection on the strengths and weaknesses of human nature. It is also a warning about the limits and dangers of technology. The same technical wizardry that enables people of the future to create a fully automated house is also responsible for the creation of the nuclear weapons that destroy the human race. What use is all our cleverness, Bradbury seems to ask, without the wisdom to use it wisely and the humility to accept our vulnerable position in the universe?

Customize for *English Language Learners*

Before they begin reading, make sure students are familiar with words such as: *robot, electric eye,* and *radioactive* from the first selection, and *demolition, condominium, penthouses,* and *tabby* from the second.

Read to Be Entertained

Encourage students to set a purpose for reading to be entertained, particularly by Bradbury's highly popular science fiction writing. To help students enjoy Bradbury's house of the future, call attention to the variety of household activities his house is programmed to complete.

▶Critical Viewing◀

1 Predict *Students should recognize that fallout after a nuclear explosion contains a deadly, radioactive "soft rain." The story may take place at that future time.*

There Will Come Soft Rains

Ray Bradbury

1 ▲ Critical Viewing Based on the title of the story and this painting, make a prediction about the subject of the story. **[Predict]**

Block Scheduling Strategies

Consider these suggestions for taking advantage of extended class time:

- Introduce the literary element, Setting, by having students read the Literary Focus on p. 533. As students read, encourage them to be aware of the importance of setting in each story. After reading, they can answer the Literary Focus questions on p. 548 and complete the Literary Focus page in ***Selection Support,*** p. 162.
- Have students complete the Guided Writing Lesson (p. 549). Before they get started, have them study print ads for computers and other technological items in several different magazines. Have them discuss how the language and information in the ads are designed to appeal to different audiences.
- Introduce the Reading Strategy, Clarify. As students read, encourage them to look ahead and review what they have already read in order to clarify details of plot, character, and setting. Have them practice the strategy by answering the Reading Strategy questions on p. 548, and follow up with the Reading Strategy page in ***Selection Support,*** p. 161.
- As a follow-up activity, invite students to choose one of the projects on p. 549— Painting Presentation or Floor Plan.

Bikini, 1987, Vernon Fisher, Krannert Art Museum

In the living room the voice-clock sang, *Tick-tock, seven o'clock, time to get up, time to get up, seven o'clock!* as if it were afraid that nobody would. The morning house lay empty. The clock ticked on, repeating and repeating its sounds into the emptiness. *Seven-nine, breakfast time, seven-nine!* ❷

In the kitchen the breakfast stove gave a hissing sigh and ejected from its warm interior eight pieces of perfectly browned toast, eight eggs sunnyside up, sixteen slices of bacon, two coffees, and two cool glasses of milk.

"Today is August 4, 2026," said a second voice from the kitchen ceiling, "in the city of Allendale, California." It repeated the date three times for memory's sake. "Today is Mr. Featherstone's birthday. Today is the anniversary of Tilita's marriage. Insurance is payable, as are the water, gas, and light bills." ❸

Somewhere in the walls, relays clicked, memory tapes glided under electric eyes.

Eight-one, tick-tock, eight-one o'clock, off to school, off to work, run, run, eight one! But no doors slammed, no carpets took the soft tread of rubber heels. It was raining outside. The weather box on the front door sang quietly: "Rain, rain, go away; rubbers, raincoats for today . . ." And the rain tapped on the empty house, echoing.

Outside, the garage chimed and lifted its door to reveal the waiting car. After a long wait the door swung down again.

At eight-thirty the eggs were shriveled and the toast was like stone. An aluminum wedge scraped them into the sink, where hot water whirled them down a metal throat which digested and flushed them away to the distant sea. The dirty dishes were dropped into a hot washer and emerged twinkling dry.

Nine-fifteen, sang the clock, *time to clean.*

Out of warrens in the wall, tiny robot mice darted. The rooms were acrawl with the small cleaning animals, all rubber and metal. They thudded against chairs, whirling their mustached runners, kneading the rug nap, sucking gently at hidden dust. Then, like mysterious invaders, they popped into their burrows. Their pink electric eyes faded. The house was clean.

Ten o'clock. The sun came out from behind the rain. The

◆ Build Vocabulary

warrens (wôr′ ənz) *n.*: Mazelike passages

Analyze Literary Criticism

Ray Bradbury's writing is described by reviewer Christopher Jepsen in the following statement: "Depending on how you look at it, Ray Bradbury is either an expert creator of fiction and poetry, or a matchless stretcher of the truth. Either way, he is still a vital, respected, and well-loved literary giant ... He is thought of by many as the world's greatest living writer of science fiction and fantasy stories." Read Jepsen's evaluation of Bradbury's writing to the students and then use the following questions to stimulate discussion of his opinions.

1. Do you think that Bradbury is a master of creating science fiction, or a master of stretching the truth? *Students may say that Bradbury creates a programmable house that could be created today, thereby arguing that Bradbury simply stretches the truth.*
2. Find specific examples in "There Will Come Soft Rains" to support your answer to the first question.

◆ Reading Strategy

❷ **Clarify** Ask students why the house might be empty. What explanation can they offer for the phrase "as if it were afraid that nobody would"? *Students might speculate that the owners are away on vacation, have moved away, or have been called out on an emergency. The phrase suggests a more ominous explanation.*

◆ Literary Focus

❸ **Setting** Ask students if any details from this paragraph are familiar features of houses today. Then ask what all the details taken together might suggest about the time when the story takes place. *Although some people today have computerized calendars that remind them of important events, most do not have a talking house or stoves that automatically prepare meals. The details suggest that the story is set in the future.*

Humanities: Art

Bikini, 1987, by Vernon Fisher.

This photo shows the aftermath of a nuclear explosion on the Pacific island of Bikini, where the United States once tested its nuclear weapons. Vernon Fisher has worked as a photographer for newspapers in California and for magazines such as *Sports Illustrated, People,* and *Outside.* In his work he has covered breaking news stories, as well as sports events.

Use these questions for discussion:

1. What characteristic feature of a nuclear explosion can you see in the picture? *The mushroom cloud is characteristic of a nuclear explosion.*
2. What do you know about the immediate and long-term effects of a nuclear bomb? *Immediate effects include deadly firestorms; long-term effects include radioactive fallout, deadly particles that continue to fall from the sky days after the explosion.*
3. How might the title of this story refer to these effects? *The "soft rains" of the title might refer to radioactive fallout from a nuclear bomb.*

◆ Reading Strategy

❶ **Clarify** The details in this paragraph, taken together with those in the previous paragraph, suggest that the city has been destroyed by an atomic bomb or other nuclear weapon. The people who lived in the house were outside in their yard, caught unawares, when the bomb went off. Clues include "a city of rubble and ashes," "radioactive glow," the charring of the walls, and the radioactive silhouettes of the family members burned onto the walls of the house.

▶Critical Viewing◀

❷ **Compare and Contrast** *Like the house in the story, the one in the picture looks empty and desolate. It stands alone in an eerie red glow, similar to how students might imagine the last surviving house of a nuclear war to stand. Students may say the house is unlike the one they envision in the story because it looks old-fashioned, rather than futuristic. It does not look like a house that would be equipped with automated devices. The picture also does not show the charring and the radioactive silhouettes mentioned in the story.*

Customize for *Pre-AP Students*

Challenge students to find out more about the messages that Bradbury tried to convey in his science fiction stories, particularly about nuclear war. In addition to their own ideas, they may wish to investigate authoritative critiques of his work on the Internet or in the library.

Customize for *Gifted/Talented Students*

Listening to the tones and rhythms of the house's automated voice and robots will help these students imagine the setting of "There Will Come Soft Rains." Have these students weigh the positive and negative aspects of audiovisual technology as it may some day be applied in the home environment.

house stood alone in a city of rubble and ashes. This was the one house left standing. At night the ruined city gave off a radioactive glow which could be seen for miles.

Ten-fifteen. The garden sprinklers whirled up in golden founts, filling the soft morning air with scatterings of brightness. The water pelted windowpanes, running down the charred west side where the house had been burned evenly free of its white paint. The entire west face of the house was black, save for five places. Here the silhouette in paint of a man mowing a lawn. Here, as in a photograph, a woman bent to pick flowers. Still farther over, their images burned on wood in one titanic instant, a small boy, hands flung into the air; higher up, the image of a thrown ball, and opposite him a girl, hands raised to catch a ball which never came down.

❶ **◆ Reading Strategy** Use the details in this paragraph to clarify the situation of the story.

The five spots of paint—the man, the woman, the children, the ball—remained. The rest was a thin charcoaled layer.

The gentle-sprinkler rain filled the garden with falling light.

Until this day, how well the house had kept its peace. How carefully it had inquired, "Who goes there? What's the password?" and, getting no answer from lonely foxes and whining cats, it had shut up its windows and drawn shades in an old-maidenly preoccupation with self-protection which bordered on a mechanical paranoia.

It quivered at each sound, the house did. If a sparrow brushed a window, the shade snapped up. The bird, startled, flew off! No, not even a bird must touch the house!

The house was an altar with ten thousand attendants, big, small, servicing, attending, in choirs. But the gods had gone away, and the ritual of the religion continued senselessly, uselessly.

Twelve noon.

A dog whined, shivering, on the front porch.

The front door recognized the dog voice and opened. The dog, once huge and fleshy, but now gone to bone and covered with sores, moved in and through the house, tracking mud. Behind it whirred angry mice, angry at having to pick up mud, angry at inconvenience.

For not a leaf fragment blew under the door but what the wall panels flipped open and the

The Body of a House, #1 of 8, ©1993, Robert Beckman

▲ **Critical Viewing** How does the house in this picture compare with the house in the story? **[Compare and Contrast]** ❷

◆ Build Vocabulary

titanic (tī tan′ ik) *adj.*: Having great power

paranoia (par′ ə noi′ ə) *n.*: Mental disorder characterized by delusions of persecution

tremulous (trem′ yo͞o ləs) *adj.*: Trembling; quivering

Cross-Curricular Connection: Social Studies

Nuclear Weapons The world's first nuclear weapon was an atomic bomb developed by the United States. It was first tested by scientists in New Mexico in July of 1945, and a few weeks later it was used to bomb the Japanese cities of Hiroshima and Nagasaki, near the end of World War II. After the war, the United States and several other countries built thousands of nuclear weapons, many times more than enough to destroy each other. As these weapons proliferated, so did people's fears of a possible nuclear war. As tensions between the United States and the Soviet Union escalated during the Cold War, which lasted through the 1980's, American newspapers and magazines warned citizens of the dire consequences that might follow a nuclear attack. In this story, Bradbury projects the fears of his own time onto an indefinite future setting.

Have students discuss whether fears of nuclear war still play an important part in American life today. Ask what has happened since this story was written to increase or decrease such fears.

copper scrap rats flashed swiftly out. The offending dust, hair, or paper, seized in miniature steel jaws, was raced back to the burrows. There, down tubes which fed into the cellar, it was dropped into the sighing vent of an incinerator which sat like evil Baal[1] in a dark corner.

The dog ran upstairs, hysterically yelping to each door, at last realizing, as the house realized, that only silence was here.

It sniffed the air and scratched the kitchen door. Behind the door, the stove was making pancakes which filled the house with a rich baked odor and the scent of maple syrup.

The dog frothed at the mouth, lying at the door, sniffing, its eyes turned to fire. It ran wildly in circles, biting at its tail, spun in a frenzy, and died. It lay in the parlor for an hour.

Two o'clock, sang a voice.

Delicately sensing decay at last, the regiments of mice hummed out as softly as blown gray leaves in an electrical wind.

Two-fifteen.

The dog was gone.

In the cellar, the incinerator glowed suddenly and a whirl of sparks leaped up the chimney.

Two thirty-five.

Bridge tables sprouted from patio walls. Playing cards fluttered onto pads in a shower of pips. Glasses manifested on an oaken bench with egg-salad sandwiches. Music played.

But the tables were silent and the cards untouched.

At four o'clock the tables folded like great butterflies back through the paneled walls.

Four-thirty.

The nursery walls glowed.

Animals took shape: yellow giraffes, blue lions, pink antelopes, lilac panthers cavorting[2] in crystal substance. The walls were glass. They looked out upon color and fantasy. Hidden films clocked through well-oiled sprockets, and the walls lived. The nursery floor was woven to resemble a crisp, cereal meadow. Over this ran aluminum roaches and iron crickets, and in the hot still air butterflies of delicate red tissue wavered among the sharp aroma of animal spoors![3] There was the sound like a great matted yellow hive of bees within a dark bellows, the lazy bumble of a purring lion. And there was the patter of okapi[4] feet and the murmur of a fresh jungle rain, like other hoofs, falling upon the summer-starched grass. Now the walls dissolved into distances of parched weed, mile on mile, and warm endless sky. The animals drew away into thorn brakes and water holes.

It was the children's hour.

Five o'clock. The bath filled with clear hot water.

Six, seven, eight o'clock. The dinner dishes manipulated like magic tricks, and in the study a *click.* In the hearth a fire now blazed up warmly.

Nine o'clock. The beds warmed their hidden circuits, for nights were cool here.

Nine-five. A voice spoke from the study ceiling: "Mrs. McClellan, which poem would you like this evening?"

The house was silent.

The voice said at last, "Since you express no preference, I shall select a poem at random." Quiet music rose to back the voice. "Sara Teasdale. As I recall, your favorite. . . ."

There will come soft rains and the smell of the ground,
And swallows circling with their shimmering sound;

And frogs in the pools singing at night,
And wild plum trees in tremulous white;

Robins will wear their feathery fire,
Whistling their whims on a low fence-wire;

And not one will know of the war, not one
Will care at last when it is done.

◆ **Literary Focus** What do the details in this section tell you about the time period of the setting? 5

6

1. **Baal** (bā′ əl): An ancient Phoenician and Canaanite deity.
2. **cavorting** (kə vôrt′ ing) *v.*: Leaping or prancing about.
3. **spoors** (spōrz) *n.*: Droppings of wild animals.
4. **okapi** (ō kä′ pē) *n.*: African animal related to the giraffe but with a much shorter neck.

◆ Build Grammar Skills

3 Commonly Confused Words: *Lie* and *Lay* Ask students why the words *lying* and *lay* are correct in these two sentences. *Both words are principal parts of the verb* lie, *meaning "recline," the meaning needed here.* Lay, *in the second sentence, is used as the past tense of* lie, *rather than as the present tense of the verb* lay.

◆ Literature and Your Life

4 Ask students if they have any machines in their own homes that continue turning on and off even when no one is home. Then, ask why the house might prepare bridge tables and a lunch, even though no people are there. *Students are probably familiar with programmable devices such as VCRs, automated lighting systems, clock radios, and alarms. The house in the story has been programmed to provide certain functions at different times of day, to suit the usual routines of the people who once lived there.*

◆ Literary Focus

5 Setting The details suggest a future world in which the walls of a child's room are equipped with amazing multimedia equipment that can create the illusion of being in a jungle.

◆ Critical Thinking

6 Apply Ask students how the words of this poem can be applied to the story. *The title of the story is taken from the first line of the poem: "There will come soft rains." The poem describes the natural world continuing unawares, even after a war, much as the mechanical house continues functioning after a nuclear war.*

Humanities: Art

The Body of a House, #1 of 8, and The Body of a House, #6 of 8, 1993, by Robert Beckman.

The painting on p. 536 is the first of a series of eight large oil paintings depicting the successive stages of destruction of a house during a nuclear explosion. (Painting #6 of 8 is on p. 538.) The paintings are based on actual film footage shot during the test of a nuclear weapon in Nevada in 1953. The original paintings are eight feet long and nearly six feet high. The monumental size and stark realism of these paintings dramatize the destructiveness of a nuclear explosion.

Robert Beckman has worked with students as an artist in the schools in Nevada and has also completed murals for many buildings in Nevada and Colorado.

Use these questions for discussion:

1. Why does the house look so completely alone and uninhabited? *Students may say that there is no vegetation, no human or animal figures, no sign of a car, a road or driveway, no curtains in the windows.*
2. What effect would the other paintings have on the first of the series? (Students should look at painting #6 on the next page before they answer.) *Students might say that knowing the fate of the house adds drama to the first painting in the series.*
3. What destructive element does the painting #6 call to mind? *It suggests destruction by fire or a bomb.*

▶Critical Viewing◀

❶ **Connect** *Suggested response: The painting is dominated by wild splotches of red and black, suggesting the destructive effects of a fire or the firestorms associated with a nuclear explosion such as the one that occurred before this story begins.*

◆Critical Thinking

❷ **Make a Judgment** Ask students which lines of the poem could serve as the story's theme, or message. *"Not one would mind, neither bird nor tree/If mankind perished utterly."*

Comprehension Check ☑

❸ How does the fire start in the house? *The wind knocks a tree bough through the kitchen window. Flammable cleaning liquid spills over the stove and ignites. The fire is fed by the wind coming through the windows broken by the heat.*

Customize for *Logical/Mathematical Learners*

Ask these students to note the illogical details that contribute to the house's destruction. *Students should note that tree branches should be kept pruned away from windows and that cleaning solvents should never be stored near a stove.*

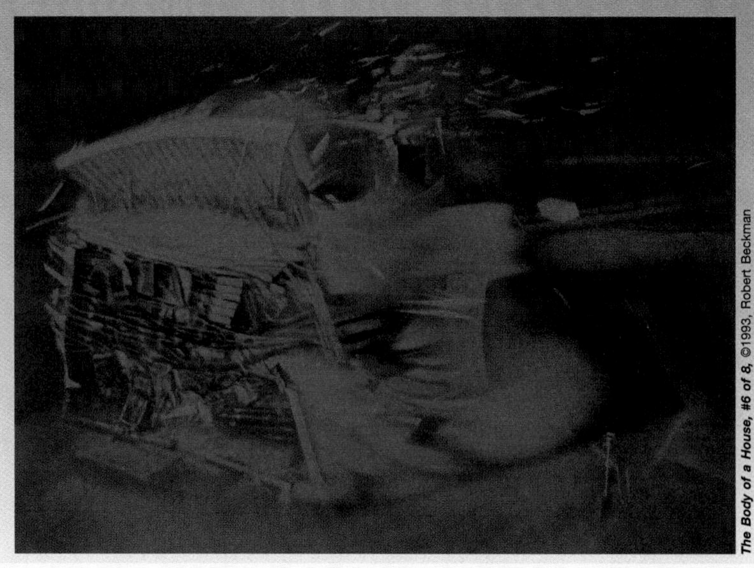

The Body of a House, #6 of 8, ©1993, Robert Beckman

❶ ▲ Critical Viewing Use the details in this picture to envision the events that occur before this story begins. **[Connect]**

❷ *Not one would mind, neither bird nor tree,*
If mankind perished utterly;

And Spring herself, when she woke at dawn
Would scarcely know that we were gone."

The fire burned on the stone hearth. The empty chairs faced each other between the silent walls, and the music played.

❸ At ten o'clock the house began to die.

The wind blew. A falling tree bough crashed through the kitchen window. Cleaning solvent, bottled, shattered over the stove. The room was ablaze in an instant!

"Fire!" screamed a voice. The house lights flashed, water pumps shot water from the ceilings. But the solvent spread on the linoleum, licking, eating, under the kitchen door, while the voices took it up in chorus: "Fire, fire, fire!"

The house tried to save itself. Doors sprang tightly shut, but the windows were broken by the heat and the wind blew and sucked upon the fire.

The house gave ground as the fire in ten billion angry sparks moved with flaming ease from room to room and then up the stairs. While scurrying water rats squeaked from the walls, pistoled their water, and ran for more. And the wall sprays let down showers of mechanical rain.

But too late. Somewhere, sighing, a pump shrugged to a stop. The quenching rain ceased. The reserve water supply which had filled baths and washed dishes for many quiet days was gone.

The fire crackled up the stairs. It fed upon Picassos and Matisses[5] in the upper halls, like delicacies, baking off the oily flesh, tenderly crisping the canvases into black shavings.

Now the fire lay in beds, stood in windows, changed the colors of drapes!

And then, reinforcements.

From attic trapdoors, blind robot faces peered down with faucet mouths gushing green chemical.

The fire backed off, as even an elephant must at the sight of a dead snake. Now there were twenty snakes whipping over the floor, killing the fire with a clear cold venom of green froth.

But the fire was clever. It had sent flame outside the house, up through the attic to the pumps there. An explosion! The attic brain which directed the pumps was shattered into bronze shrapnel on the beams.

The fire rushed back into every closet and felt of the clothes hung there.

The house shuddered, oak bone on bone, its bared skeleton cringing from the heat, its wire, its nerves revealed as if a surgeon had torn the skin off to let the red veins and capillaries quiver in the scalded air. Help, help! Fire! Run, run! Heat snapped mirrors like the first brittle winter

5. **Picassos** (pi kä´ sōz) **and Matisses** (mä tēs´ əz): Works by the painters Pablo Picasso and Henri Matisse.

Speaking, Listening, and Viewing Mini-Lesson

Inanimate Dialogue

This mini-lesson supports the Speaking, Listening, and Viewing activity in the Idea Bank on p. 549.

Introduce Tell students that a writer must try to imagine the attitudes and personalities of characters in order to write good dialogue.

Develop Before students begin their role-plays, have them work in pairs to list all the appliances in the story and choose two appliances that might have an interesting conversation. Then, have each partner quick-write a brief description of the interests and personality each appliance might have. To create well-rounded characters, students may enjoy identifying the pet peeves and personality quirks of the appliances they are describing.

Apply Have each pair of students choose a topic for their appliances to discuss and role-play what each appliance might have to say on this topic, as well as the feelings they might express for each other. Have different pairs of students perform their role-plays for the class.

Assess Have the class compare different interpretations of the same appliances and evaluate which role-play is most convincing. Students may use the Peer Assessment: Dramatic Performance page in ***Alternative Assessment,*** p. 120, to evaluate the performances.

ice. And the voices wailed Fire, fire, run, run, like a tragic nursery rhyme, a dozen voices, high, low, like children dying in a forest, alone, alone. And the voices fading as the wires popped their sheathings like hot chestnuts. One, two, three, four, five voices died.

In the nursery the jungle burned. Blue lions roared, purple giraffes bounded off. The panthers ran in circles, changing color, and ten million animals, running before the fire, vanished off toward a distant steaming river. . . .

Ten more voices died. In the last instant under the fire avalanche, other choruses, oblivious, could be heard announcing the time, playing music, cutting the lawn by remote-control mower, or setting an umbrella frantically out and in the slamming and opening front door, a thousand things happening, like a clock shop when each clock strikes the hour insanely before or after the other, a scene of maniac confusion, yet unity; singing, screaming, a few last cleaning mice darting bravely out to carry the horrid ashes away! And one voice, with sublime disregard for the situation, read poetry aloud in the fiery study, until all the film spools burned, until all the wires withered and the circuits cracked.

The fire burst the house and let it slam flat down, puffing out skirts of spark and smoke.

In the kitchen, an instant before the rain of fire and timber, the stove could be seen making breakfasts at a psychopathic rate, ten dozen eggs, six loaves of toast, twenty dozen bacon strips, which, eaten by fire, started the stove working again, hysterically hissing! 4

The crash. The attic smashing into kitchen and parlor. The parlor into cellar, cellar into subcellar. Deep freeze, armchair, film tapes, circuits, beds, and all like skeletons thrown in a cluttered mound deep under.

Smoke and silence. A great quantity of smoke.

Dawn showed faintly in the east. Among the ruins, one wall stood alone. Within the wall, a last voice said, over and over again and again, even as the sun rose to shine upon the heaped rubble and steam:

"Today is August 5, 2026, today is August 5, 2026, today is . . ."

◆ **Build Vocabulary**

psychopathic (sī´ kō path´ ik) *adj.*: With a dangerous mental disorder

Guide for Responding

◆ Literature and Your Life

Reader's Response Does the picture presented in this story fit with your idea of a future world? Why, or why not?

Thematic Focus Based on what you've read in this story, how do you think Bradbury views our culture's legacy to the future?

☑ **Check Your Comprehension**

1. List five functions the house performs.
2. What happened to the occupants of the house, and how do you know?
3. Describe the final hours of the house.

◆ Critical Thinking

INTERPRET

1. Why do you think Bradbury chose to have the house broadcast the poem? **[Speculate]**
2. Compare the house—both in its normal operations and in its final hours—to a human. **[Compare]**
3. Explain this story's message. **[Infer]**

APPLY

4. What qualities make this story different from others you know that deal with the future? **[Distinguish]**

EVALUATE

5. How possible do you think the future described in this story is? **[Make a Judgment]**

◆ Build Vocabulary

4 Word Origins: Words From Myths Tell students that the word *psychopathic* is derived from the Greek root *psyche*, meaning "breath," "life," or "soul." In Greek myth, Psyche was a beautiful maiden loved by the god Cupid. When Cupid abandoned her, Psyche searched the world over for her lost love. Ask students to list other words derived from the root *psyche*. *Responses may include* psychology, psychic, psychiatrist, psychosomatic.

Customize for
English Language Learners
Help these students to reread the story successfully by clarifying any words or technical terms with which they may be unfamiliar.

Reinforce and Extend

Answers

◆ Literature and Your Life

Reader's Response Some students may be more optimistic than Bradbury is in this story. Whatever their ideas of the future, encourage them to give reasons for their opinions.

Thematic Focus Some students may find Bradbury's view of our legacy to the future pessimistic. Others may see his story as a warning that we still have time to heed.

☑ **Check Your Comprehension**

1. The house announces each hour of the day, the date and special occasions that fall on it; opens and closes doors; self-cleans with robot mice; sets tables; and prepares food.
2. The family has been killed in a nuclear war or accident. Students should use the shapes on the side of the house and the dog's sores as clues.
3. The house tries to save itself by marshaling its firefighting apparatus, but the fire attacks the house's computerized brain. In the last instant before total collapse, every mechanism sounds at once.

◆ Critical Thinking

1. The poem explains the title of the story and also implies Bradbury's theme—that perhaps someone "would mind . . . /If mankind perished utterly."
2. The house, like a human, has a brain that controls its other functions. It carries on normal day-to-day activities according to a strict schedule and in an emergency uses all its resources for self-preservation.
3. Bradbury is asking readers to question the good of the most advanced technology if we use it to destroy ourselves.
4. Students may note that there are no characters in this story, except for the dying dog.
5. Students may find Bradbury's vision of the future exaggerated, now that the Cold War has ended. Encourage students to support their opinions with reasons and examples.

Develop Understanding

One-Minute Insight In this story, an Italian worker named Marcovaldo begins to become aware of cats and their pathways through a city. He discovers an old villa in a seedy garden where they congregate and resist the efforts of construction workers to build a new structure. For Calvino, the cats symbolize nature's mysterious, persistent presence even in a busy city. They also symbolize nature's resistance to human aims and designs.

◆ Reading Strategy

❶ Clarify Ask students what the author means by this opening sentence. Have them look ahead to find information about the setting that clarifies the meaning of the sentence. *From ". . . the streets are uninterruptedly overrun" through ". . . on the roof-tiles" describes the city of men; from "But in this vertical city . . ." to ". . . the ancient cat population still scurries" describes the city of cats. The two exist within the same boundaries, but are completely different; neither city is inhabitable by the population of the other.*

◆ Literary Focus

❷ Setting Ask students: Which details in this passage help you visualize the setting of the "city of men"? *Details include heavy traffic everywhere, apartment buildings and skyscrapers over every inch of land; there is no grass or gardens because the earth is covered with concrete.*

The Garden of Stubborn Cats

Italo Calvino Translated by William Weaver

❶ The city of cats and the city of men exist one inside the other, but they are not the same city. Few cats recall the time when there was no distinction: the streets and squares of men were also streets and squares of cats, and the lawns, courtyards, balconies, and fountains: you lived in a broad and various space. But for several generations now domestic felines have been prisoners of an uninhabitable city: the streets are uninterruptedly
❷ overrun by the mortal traffic of cat-crushing automobiles; in every square foot of terrain where once a garden extended or a vacant lot or the ruins of an old demolition, now condominiums loom up, welfare housing, brand-new skyscrapers; every entrance is crammed with parked cars; the courtyards, one by one, have been roofed by reinforced concrete and transformed into garages or movie houses or storerooms or workshops. And where a rolling plateau of low roofs once extended, copings,[1] terraces, water tanks, balconies, skylights, corrugated-iron sheds, now one general superstructure rises wherever structures can rise; the intermediate differences in height, between the low ground of the street and the supernal heaven of the penthouses, disappear; the cat of a recent litter seeks in vain the itinerary of its

1. **copings** (kō´ piŋz) *n.*: Top layers of masonry walls.

Humanities: Art

Cats in Art.

Because of their mysterious nature, their sensitivity to light and sound, and their skill as nighttime hunters, cats have been credited with supernatural powers in many cultures and have even been worshiped as gods in some. The ancient Egyptians, for example, produced many statues of cats in honor of their cat-goddess, Bastet. Later, cats were associated with witches in European cultures. Today, images of cats show our mixed feelings about these creatures. They are sometimes depicted as cute, cuddly balls of fluff and sometimes as mysterious, predatory hunters.

Use these questions for discussion:

1. How well do the pictures of cats shown in this selection reflect your own feelings about these animals? Explain. *Students who love cats' cozy furriness may prefer the images on pp. 540, 541, and 544; those who stress their mysterious, predatory natures may point to the art on p. 542.*
2. In your opinion, why are some people cat-lovers while others are dog-lovers? *Cats are independent, solitary hunters, while dogs may seem more friendly to and dependent on humans. People vary in their preferences for these qualities.*

fathers, the point from which to make the soft leap from balustrade to cornice to drainpipe, or for the quick climb on the roof-tiles.

But in this vertical city, in this compressed city where all voids tend to fill up and every block of cement tends to mingle with other blocks of cement, a kind of counter-city opens, a negative city, that consists of empty slices between wall and wall, of the minimal distances ordained by the building regulations between two constructions, between the rear of one construction and the rear of the next; it is a city of cavities, wells, air conduits, driveways, inner yards, accesses to basements, like a network of dry canals on a planet of stucco and tar, and it is through this network, grazing the walls, that the ancient cat population still scurries.

◆ Literary Focus
What details in this paragraph help you envision the setting?

On occasion, to pass the time, Marcovaldo would follow a cat. It was during the work-break, between noon and three, when all the personnel except Marcovaldo went home to eat, and he—who brought his lunch in his bag—laid his place among the packing-cases in the warehouse, chewed his snack, smoked a half-cigar, and wandered around, alone and idle, waiting for work to resume. In those hours, a cat that peeped in at a window was always welcome company, and a guide for new explorations. He had made friends with a tabby, well fed, a blue ribbon around its neck, surely living with some well-to-do family. This tabby shared with Marcovaldo the habit of an afternoon stroll right after lunch; and naturally a friendship sprang up.

Following his tabby friend, Marcovaldo had started looking at places as if through the round eyes of a cat and even if these places were the usual environs of his firm he saw them in a different light, as settings for cattish stories, with connections practicable only by light, velvety paws. Though from the outside the neighborhood seemed poor in cats, every day on his rounds Marcovaldo made the acquaintance of

some new face, and a miau, a hiss, a stiffening of fur on an arched back was enough for him to sense ties and intrigues and rivalries among them. At those moments he thought he had already penetrated the secrecy of the felines' society: and then he felt himself scrutinized by pupils that became slits, under the surveillance of the antennae of taut whiskers, and all the cats around him sat impassive as sphinxes, the pink triangles of their noses convergent on the black triangles of their lips, and the only things that moved were the tips of the ears, with a vibrant jerk like radar. They reached the end of a narrow passage, between squalid blank walls; and, looking around, Marcovaldo saw that the cats that had led him this far had vanished, all of them together, no telling in which direction, even his tabby friend, and they had left him alone. Their realm had territories, ceremonies, customs that it was not yet granted to him to discover.

On the other hand, from the cat city there opened unsuspected peepholes onto the city of men: and one day the same tabby led him to discover the great Biarritz Restaurant.

Anyone wishing to see the Biarritz Restaurant had only to assume the posture of a cat, that is, proceed on all fours. Cat and man, in this fashion, walked around a kind of dome, at whose foot some low, rectangular little windows opened. Following the tabby's example,

◆ Build Vocabulary

supernal (sə purn′ əl) *adj.*: Celestial or divine

itinerary (ī tin′ ər er′ ē) *n.*: Route

◆ Literary Focus

3 Setting Students may cite details such as "... every block of cement tends to mingle with other blocks of cement," "empty slices between wall and wall," "cavities, wells, air conduits, driveways, inner yards, accesses to basements," and the simile "like a network of dry canals on a planet of stucco and tar."

Comprehension Check ☑

4 Make sure students understand what is going on here and in the rest of the story: Marcovaldo, a warehouse worker, has three hours off for lunch—point out to students that in Italy and some other countries it is customary to take such a long break at midday and to return home—and he has decided to use the time to follow a cat around the city. If students need help, suggest they go back to the left column on this page to find details that clarify what Marcovaldo is doing.

◆ Build Vocabulary

5 Word Origins: Words From Myths Tell students that *sphinx* is a word derived from Greek mythology. In Greek myths the sphinx was a winged monster with a lion's body and the head of a woman. The sphinx killed anyone who could not answer its mysterious riddles. The word also came to be applied to ancient Egyptian statues with the body of a lion and the head of a man. Today the word *sphinx* is used to describe any unknowable, mysterious person or thing.

Art Transparency Before students read "The Garden of Stubborn Cats," display Art Transparency 5 and invite student comments. Discuss the surreal elements of Gary Kelley's painting and the contrast that it suggests between human civilization and the natural wilderness. After students read the story, use these questions for discussion:

1. How does the painting mirror the ideas that the narrator presents in the first two paragraphs of the story?
2. How does the painting work with the story to address the question "Whose World Is It, Anyway?"

◆ Literary Focus

❶ **Setting** Ask students which details helped them picture the setting of the fancy restaurant. *Students might cite gypsy violins, partridges and quails, silver dishes, white-gloved fingers, waiters in tailcoats, patent-leather shoes, gleaming parquet floor, potted palms, crystal and ice buckets with champagne bottles.*

▶Critical Viewing◀

❷ **Interpret** *The image captures the following qualities of cats: their mysteriousness, their sudden movements, their spookiness, their danger, their agility.*

Extending Word Study

Expand Vocabulary Students may find it easier to understand and appreciate the rich choice of words used by the authors if sample lines from each of the selections are read aloud. For example, note this passage from Calvino:

> But for several generations now domestic felines have been prisoners of an uninhabitable city: the streets are uninterruptedly overrun by the mortal traffic of cat-crushing automobiles . . .

Hold a class discussion to analyze how Calvino makes adjectives from noun and verb combinations and adverbs from adjectives. Then discuss how specific words and word combinations contribute to the overall effect of the story.

Marcovaldo looked down. They were transoms through which the luxurious hall received air and light. To the sound of gypsy violins, partridges and quails swirled by on silver dishes balanced by the white-gloved fingers of waiters in tailcoats. Or, more precisely, above the partridges and quails the dishes whirled, and above the dishes the white gloves, and poised on the waiters' patent-leather shoes, the gleaming parquet floor,[2] from which hung dwarf potted palms and tablecloths and crystal and buckets like bells with the champagne bottle for their clapper: everything was turned upside-down because Marcovaldo, for fear of being seen, wouldn't stick his head inside the window and confined himself to looking at the reversed reflection of the room in the tilted pane. ❶

But it was not so much the windows of the dining-room as those of the kitchens that interested the cat: looking through the former you saw, distant and somehow transfigured, what in the kitchens presented itself—quite concrete and within paw's reach—as a plucked bird or a fresh fish. And it was toward the kitchens, in fact, that the tabby wanted to lead Marcovaldo, either through a gesture of altruistic friendship or else because it counted on the man's help for one of its raids. Marcovaldo, however, was reluctant to leave his belvedere[3] over the main room: first as he was fascinated by the luxury of the place, and then because something down there had riveted his attention. To such an extent that, overcoming his fear of being seen, he kept peeking in, with his head in the transom.

In the midst of the room, directly under that pane, there was a little glass fish tank, a kind of aquarium, where some fat trout were swimming. A special customer approached, a man with a shiny bald pate, black suit, black beard. An old waiter in tailcoat followed him, carrying a little net as if he were going to catch butterflies. The gentleman in black looked at the trout with a grave, intent air; then he raised one hand and with a slow, solemn gesture singled out a fish. The waiter dipped the net into the tank, pursued the appointed trout, captured it, headed for the kitchens, holding out in front of him, like a lance, the net in which the fish wriggled. The gentleman in black, solemn as a magistrate who has handed down a capital sentence, went to take his seat and wait for the return of the trout, sauteed "à la meunière."[4]

If I found a way to drop a line from up here and make one of those trout bite, Marcovaldo thought, I couldn't be accused of theft; at worst, of fishing in an unauthorized place. And ignoring the miaus

2. **parquet** (pär kā′) **floor:** Floor with inlaid woodwork in geometric forms.

3. **belvedere** (bel′ və dir′) *n.*: Open, roofed gallery in an upper story, built for giving a view of the scenery.

4. **sauteed "à la meunière"** (sô tād′ à lä mə nyer′): Fish prepared by being rolled in flour, fried in butter, and sprinkled with lemon juice and chopped parsley.

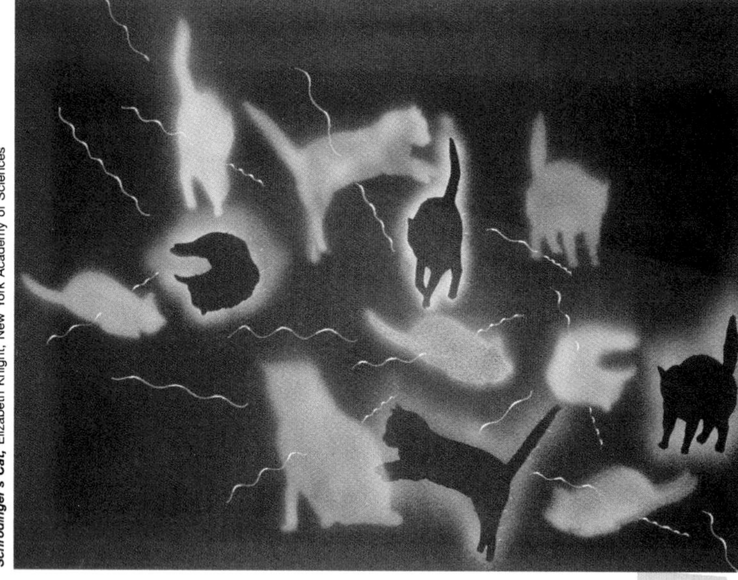

Schrodinger's Cat, Elizabeth Knight, New York Academy of Sciences

❷ ▲ Critical Viewing What qualities of cats are captured in this picture? **[Interpret]**

Beyond the Classroom

Career Connection

Urban Planning The situation in this story reflects the consequences of allowing developers to build wherever they wish, with no regard for the environmental impact of their construction. In many cities today, urban planners are responsible for balancing a community's need for progress and economic development with the need for a healthy environment that respects the natural world. Have students research this topic and find examples of cities that have successfully balanced these two opposing forces.

Community Connection

Visiting Animal Shelters In many cities and towns, the Society for the Prevention of Cruelty to Animals maintains animal shelters for abandoned pets, educates the public about pet ownership, and ensures the enforcement of laws protecting animals from cruel treatment. Have students visit a local animal shelter and report to the class on what is done in your community to ensure proper treatment of cats and other pets.

that called him toward the kitchens, he went to collect his fishing tackle.

Nobody in the crowded dining room of the Biarritz saw the long, fine line, armed with hook and bait, as it slowly dropped into the tank. The fish saw the bait, and flung themselves on it. In the fray one trout managed to bite the worm: and immediately it began to rise, rise, emerge from the water, a silvery flash, it darted up high, over the laid tables and the trolleys of hors d'oeuvres,[5] over the blue flames of the crêpes Suzette,[6] until it vanished into the heavens of the transom.

Marcovaldo had yanked the rod with the brisk snap of the expert fisherman, so the fish landed behind his back. The trout had barely touched the ground when the cat sprang. What little life the trout still had was lost between the tabby's teeth. Marcovaldo, who had abandoned his line at that moment to run and grab the fish, saw it snatched from under his nose, hook and all. He was quick to put one foot on the rod, but the snatch had been so strong that the rod was all the man had left, while the tabby ran off with the fish, pulling the line after it. Treacherous kitty! It had vanished.

But this time it wouldn't escape him: there was that long line trailing after him and showing the way he had taken. Though he had lost sight of the cat, Marcovaldo followed the end of the line: there it was, running along a wall; it climbed a parapet, wound through a doorway, was swallowed up by a basement . . . Marcovaldo, venturing into more and more cattish places, climbed roofs, straddled railings, always managed to catch a glimpse—perhaps only a second before it disappeared—of that moving trace that indicated a thief's path.

◆ Reading Strategy
What information in this paragraph helps you clarify the title of this story?

Now the line played out down a sidewalk, in the midst of the traffic, and Marcovaldo, running after it, almost managed to grab it. He flung himself down on his belly: there, he grabbed it! He managed to seize one end of the line before it slipped between the bars of a gate.

Beyond a half-rusted gate and two bits of wall buried under climbing plants, there was a little rank garden, with a small, abandoned-looking building at the far end of it. A carpet of dry leaves covered the path, and dry leaves lay everywhere under the boughs of the two plane-trees, forming actually some little mounds in the yard. A layer of leaves was yellowing in the green water of a pool. Enormous buildings rose 4
all around, skyscrapers with thousands of windows, like so many eyes trained disapprovingly on that little square patch with two trees, a few tiles, and all those yellow leaves, surviving right in the middle of an area of great traffic.

And in this garden, perched on the capitals and balustrades,[7] lying on the dry leaves of the flowerbeds, climbing on the trunks of the trees or on the drainpipes, motionless on their four paws, their tails making a question-mark, 5
seated to wash their faces, there were tiger cats, black cats, white cats, calico cats, tabbies, angoras, Persians, house cats and stray cats, perfumed cats and mangy cats. Marcovaldo realized he had finally reached the heart of the cats' realm, their secret island. And, in his emotion, he almost forgot his fish.

It had remained, that fish, hanging by the line from the branch of a tree, out of reach of the cats' leaps; it must have dropped from its kidnapper's mouth at some clumsy movement, perhaps as it was defended from the others, or perhaps displayed as an extraordinary prize. The line had got tangled, and Marcovaldo, tug as he would, couldn't manage to yank it loose. A furious battle had meanwhile been joined among the cats, to reach that unreachable fish, or rather, to win the right to try and reach 6
it. Each wanted to prevent the others from

5. **hors d'oeuvres** (ôr durvz′) *n.*: Appetizers served at the beginning of a meal.
6. **crêpes Suzette** (krāp′ soo zet′): Thin pancakes rolled or folded in a hot orange-flavored sauce and usually served in flaming brandy.
7. **capitals and balustrades** (bal′ əs trādz): Top parts of columns and railings, respectively.

◆ Build Vocabulary
transoms (tran′ səmz) *n.*: Small windows
rank (raŋk) *adj.*: Growing vigorously and coarsely

◆ Reading Strategy

3 Clarify The title mentions "stubborn cats"; the cat Marcovaldo is pursuing is stubborn in its refusal to yield the stolen trout.

◆ Literary Focus

4 Setting Ask students why the windows of the skyscrapers might seem to look "disapprovingly" on the little rank garden. *The garden is one of the few areas of the city where a little bit of nature still remains, unconquered by urban development.*

◆ Build Grammar Skills

5 Commonly Confused Words: *Lie* and *Lay* Ask students why the word *lying* is correct here. *The meaning of lie is "to recline," the meaning needed here. The word laying, on the other hand, means "putting or setting something down" and usually requires a direct object.*

◆ Build Vocabulary

6 Word Origins: Words From Mythology Tell students that the word *furious* is related to the word *fury*. In Greek mythology the Furies were avenging goddesses who inflicted plagues and other punishments on people. *Furious* means "angry," "intense," or "raging."

Viewing and Representing Mini-Lesson

Floor Plan

This mini-lesson supports the Researching and Representing project in the Idea Bank on p. 549.

Introduce If possible, show a variety of floor plans to the students from magazines or blueprint plans for a house-building project.

Develop Have students study the floor plans to determine how an architect draws the plan to scale and how symbols indicate stairwells, doors, and windows. Students may also wish to skim the selections to see what kind of house details are presented. They may also find it helpful to look through magazines or library materials to find house ideas that they like. Suggest that they make a list, categorizing their ideas by room and location.

Apply Students should use paper and pencil to sketch their plan roughly before they begin preparing a final plan drawn to scale. On their scaled drawing, they should use a ruler and make a symbol of the legend.

Assess Encourage students to display their completed floor plans to the class. Have students view the representations and critique them for neatness, completeness, and creativity.

◆ Reading Strategy

1 Clarify Ask students if they can guess to whom the two yellow, skinny hands belong. Encourage them to read the rest of this page to find out. *They belong to the Marchesa.*

Comprehension Check ☑

2 Why do the developers want the Marchesa's land? Why does she refuse to sell it? *The developers want to build modern skyscrapers on the land; it's very valuable because it's the last undeveloped space in the downtown area. The Marchesa wants to hold on to the land because she's old and doesn't want to give up her home.*

Listening to Literature Audiocassettes This is a good spot to play the audiocassette recording of the story. Students can listen to the neighbors' arguments about the fate of the Marchesa's land and decide for themselves which side of the argument sounds most convincing.

leaping: they hurled themselves on one another, they tangled in midair, they rolled around clutching each other, and finally a general war broke out in a whirl of dry, crackling leaves.

After many futile yanks, Marcovaldo now felt the line was free, but he took care not to pull it: the trout would have fallen right in the midst of that infuriated scrimmage of felines.

It was at this moment that, from the top of the walls of the gardens, a strange rain began to fall: fish-bones, heads, tails, even bits of lung and lights. Immediately the cats' attention was distracted from the suspended trout and they flung themselves on the new delicacies. To Marcovaldo, this seemed the right moment to pull the line and regain his fish. But, before he had time to act, from a blind of the little villa, two yellow, skinny hands darted out: one was
1 brandishing scissors; the other, a frying pan. The hand with the scissors was raised above the trout, the hand with the frying pan was thrust under it. The scissors cut the line, the trout fell into the pan; hands, scissors and pan withdrew, the blind closed: all in the space of a second. Marcovaldo was totally bewildered.

"Are you also a cat lover?" A voice at his back made him turn round. He was surrounded by little old women, some of them ancient, wearing old-fashioned hats on their heads; others, younger, but with the look of spinsters; and all were carrying in their hands or their bags packages of leftover meat or fish, and some even had little pans of milk. "Will you help me throw this package over the fence, for those poor creatures?"

All the ladies, cat lovers, gathered at this hour around the garden of dry leaves to take the food to their protégés.[8]

"Can you tell me why they are all here, these cats?" Marcovaldo inquired.

"Where else could they go? This garden is all they have left! Cats come here from other neighborhoods, too, from miles and miles around . . ."

"And birds, as well," another lady added. "They're forced to live by the hundreds and hundreds on these few trees . . ."

"And the frogs, they're all in that pool, and at night they never stop croaking . . . You can hear them even on the eighth floor of the buildings around here."

"Who does this villa belong to anyway?" Marcovaldo asked. Now, outside the gate, there weren't just the cat-loving ladies but also other people: the man from the gas pump opposite, the apprentices from a mechanic's shop, the postman, the grocer, some passers-by. And none of them, men and women, had to be asked twice: all wanted to have their say, as always when a mysterious and controversial subject comes up.

"It belongs to a Marchesa.[9] She lives there, but you never see her . . ."

"She's been offered millions and millions, by developers, for this little patch of land, but she won't sell . . ."

"What would she do with millions, an old woman all alone in the world? She wants to hold on to her house, even if it's falling to pieces, rather than be forced to move . . ."

"It's the only undeveloped bit of land in the downtown area . . . Its value goes up every year . . . They've made her offers—"

"Offers! That's not all. Threats, intimidation, persecution . . . You don't know the half of it! Those contractors!"

"But she holds out. She's held out for years . . ."

"She's a saint. Without her, where would those poor animals go?"

"A lot she cares about the animals, the old miser! Have you ever seen her give them anything to eat?"

"How can she feed the cats when she doesn't have food for herself? She's the last descendant of a ruined family!"

"She hates cats! I've seen her chasing them and hitting them with an umbrella!"

"Because they were tearing up her flowerbeds!"

8. **protégés** (prōt′ ə zhāz′) *n.*: Those guided and helped by another.

9. **Marchesa** (mär kā′ zä): Title of an Italian noblewoman.

Speaking, Listening, and Viewing Mini-Lesson

Persuasive Argument

This mini-lesson supports the Speaking, Listening, and Viewing activity in the Idea Bank on p. 549.

Introduce Tell students that the purpose of a persuasive argument is to influence the thoughts and actions of those who read or hear the argument. A persuasive argument should be well-reasoned and planned to appeal to a particular audience.

Develop Lead students to consider the following points:

- A persuasive argument uses reasons that appeal to the needs and concerns of the listener.
- Each reason is supported with evidence that the listener can understand.
- A persuasive argument should use words that are forceful, but not insulting to the listener.

Apply Have students make a list of reasons and facts they might use to appeal to the Marchesa. Then have them draft their arguments, using words that will present each reason as forcefully and respectfully as possible.

Assess Invite students to evaluate each others' arguments on the basis of how well they have supported each point. Use the Peer Assessment: Speaker/Speech page in ***Alternative Assessment,*** p. 118.

Connections to Today's World

It might surprise you to learn that Jim Davis, creator of Garfield—one of the world's most famous and beloved cats—has no cats. His wife is allergic to the furry felines!

When Davis created Garfield in 1978, he never imagined the phenomenal success that would follow. Garfield is the most widely syndicated Sunday comic in the United States, and worldwide it has more than 220 million daily readers. In addition to the daily and Sunday comics, Davis has written dozens of Garfield books, a CBS television series, and thirteen prime-time specials.

1. What qualities does Garfield have in common with the cats in "Garden of Stubborn Cats"?
2. Compare the way Calvino and Davis portray the relationship between humans and cats.
3. Why do you think this cartoon cat is so popular?

"What flowerbeds? I've never seen anything in this garden but a great crop of weeds!"

Marcovaldo realized that with regard to the old Marchesa opinions were sharply divided: some saw her as an angelic being, others as an egoist and a miser.

"It's the same with the birds; she never gives them a crumb!"

"She gives them hospitality. Isn't that plenty?"

"Like she gives the mosquitoes, you mean. They all come from here, from that pool. In the summertime the mosquitoes eat us alive, and it's all the fault of that Marchesa!"

"And the mice? This villa is a mine of mice. Under the dead leaves they have their burrows, and at night they come out . . ."

"As far as the mice go, the cats take care of them . . ."

"Oh, you and your cats! If we had to rely on them . . ."

"Why? Have you got something to say against cats?"

Here the discussion degenerated into a general quarrel.

"The authorities should do something: confiscate the villa!" one man cried.

"What gives them the right?" another protested.

"In a modern neighborhood like ours, a mouse-nest like this . . . it should be forbidden . . ." ❸

"Why, I picked my apartment precisely because it overlooked this little bit of green . . ."

"Green, hell! Think of the fine skyscraper they could build here!"

Marcovaldo would have liked to add something of his own, but he couldn't get a word in. Finally, all in one breath, he exclaimed: "The Marchesa stole a trout from me!"

The unexpected news supplied fresh ammunition to the old woman's enemies,

◆ Build Vocabulary
scrimmage (skrim´ ij) *n.*: Rough-and-tumble fight

Connections to Today's World

More About the Author
Jim Davis was born in Marion, Indiana, in 1945. He had asthma as a child and was forced to spend hours in bed. That is when he first began drawing cartoons. To find out more, students can visit the Garfield Web site at **http://www.garfield.com/paws/jimdavis.** Please be aware that sites may have changed since we published this information. Also, we *strongly recommend* that you preview sites before sending students to them.

Genre Connection

Ask students if they think cartoons, as well as stories, can communicate serious messages about such issues as the relationship between people and animals. Have them cite evidence from cartoons they have seen to support their point of view.

Customize for *Visual/Spatial Learners*

Have these students compare the image of Garfield the cat shown on this page with the photographs of cats shown throughout the story. How are the images similar? How are they different? *In both the cartoon and the photos, cats are shown as creatures with strong, independent, dominating personalities. The photos emphasize the mysterious implications of these qualities, while the cartoon emphasizes the amusing implications of them.*

◆ Critical Thinking

❸ Draw Conclusions Ask students what opposing forces the two groups of neighbors represent. What does each side want? *The two groups of neighbors represent the two opposing forces in the story—nature and technology. The neighbors who want the "little bit of green" to remain represent the force of nature; the ones who would rather have a skyscraper represent the force of "progress" and technology.*

Customize for
Less Proficient Readers

❶ Help these students define the words *exploited* and *indigence* by using context clues in this paragraph.

◆ Critical Thinking

❷ **Draw Conclusions** Ask which side, if any, the Marchesa is on—the side that wants to preserve the garden or the side that wants a skyscraper instead. *The Marchesa is not on either side. She doesn't care about the cats or the garden; she just wants to stay in her own house and not be bothered. She will complain only when either side affects her as an individual. Students may say she represents self-interest.*

◆ Literature and Your Life

❸ Students who prefer preserving the natural world over progress and development may cheer the cats on and be glad they are stopping the developers. Students who believe progress and development are important may feel that the cats should be removed.

◆ Build Vocabulary

❹ **Word Origins: Words From Myths** Tell students that the word *demon* is derived from the Greek *daimon* or *daemon*. In Greek mythology the daemons were supernatural beings with powers between those of gods and people. The word gradually came to mean "evil spirit."

❶ but her defenders exploited it as proof of the indigence to which the unfortunate noblewoman was reduced. Both sides agreed that Marcovaldo should go and knock at her door to demand an explanation.

It wasn't clear whether the gate was locked or unlocked; in any case, it opened, after a push, with a mournful creak. Marcovaldo picked his way among the leaves and cats, climbed the steps to the porch, knocked hard at the entrance.

At a window (the very one where the frying pan had appeared), the blind was raised slightly and in one corner a round, pale blue eye was seen, and a clump of hair dyed an undefinable color, and a dry skinny hand. A voice was heard, asking: "Who is it? Who's at the door?" the words accompanied by a cloud smelling of fried oil.

"It's me, Marchesa. The trout man," Marcovaldo explained. "I don't mean to trouble you. I only wanted to tell you, in case you didn't know, that the trout was stolen from me, by that cat, and I'm the one who caught it. In fact the line . . ."

"Those cats! It's always those cats . . . " the Marchesa said, from behind the shutter, with a shrill, somewhat nasal voice. "All my troubles come from the cats! Nobody knows what I go through! Prisoner night and day of those horrid beasts! And with all the refuse people throw over the walls, to spite me!"

"But my trout . . ."

❷ "Your trout! What am I supposed to know about your trout!" The Marchesa's voice became almost a scream, as if she wanted to drown out the sizzle of oil in the pan, which came through the window along with the aroma of fried fish. "How can I make sense of anything, with all the stuff that rains into my house?"

"I understand, but did you take the trout or didn't you?"

"When I think of all the damage I suffer because of the cats! Ah, fine state of affairs! I'm not responsible for anything! I can't tell you what I've lost! Thanks to those cats, who've occupied house and garden for years! My life at the mercy of those animals! Go and find the owners! Make them pay damages! Damages? A whole life destroyed! A prisoner here, unable to move a step!"

"Excuse me for asking: but who's forcing you to stay?"

From the crack in the blind there appeared sometimes a round, pale blue eye, sometimes a mouth with two protruding teeth; for a moment the whole face was visible, and to Marcovaldo it seemed, bewilderingly, the face of a cat.

"They keep me prisoner, they do, those cats! Oh, I'd be glad to leave! What wouldn't I give for a little apartment all my own, in a nice clean modern building! But I can't go out . . . They follow me, they block my path, they trip me up!" The voice became a whisper, as if to confide a secret. "They're afraid I'll sell the lot . . . They won't leave me . . . won't allow me . . . When the builders come to offer me a contract, you should see them, those cats! They get in the way, pull out their claws; they even chased a lawyer off! Once I had the contract right here, I was about to sign it, and they dived in through the window, knocked over the inkwell, tore up all the pages . . ."

All of a sudden Marcovaldo remembered the time, the shipping department, the boss. He tiptoed off over the dried leaves, as the voice continued to come through the slats of the blind, enfolded in that cloud apparently from the oil of a frying pan. "They even scratched me . . . I still have the scar . . . All alone here at the mercy of these demons . . ."

Winter came. A blossoming of white flakes decked the branches and capitals and the cats' tails. Under the snow, the dry leaves dissolved into mush. The cats were rarely seen, the cat

◆ Literature and Your Life

How do your opinions about progress and development affect your reaction to the cats' actions?

◆ Build Vocabulary

indigence (in´ di jəns) *n.*: Poverty

Reteach

Because it encourages self-monitored reading, a mastery of clarification techniques is important to a mastery of reading. As students read a passage or selection for the first time they may find they have missed details or facts. In addition, they may have formulated questions that need to be answered. They may find that rereading or reading ahead is the best strategy to supply the missing information. Have students use a chart like the one shown here to help them practice the skill externally. Suggest that students complete the chart as they read pp. 535–536 of "There Will Come Soft Rains". In the first column, have them list the details they need to clarify. Using one of the strategies, have them find the meaning and fill in the second column and then list which strategy they used in the third column.

Question	Answer	Strategy

lovers even less; the packages of fish-bones were consigned only to cats who came to the door. Nobody, for quite a while, had seen anything of the Marchesa. No smoke came now from the chimneypot of the villa.

One snowy day, the garden was again full of cats, who had returned as if it were spring, and they were miauing as if on a moonlight night. The neighbors realized that something had happened: they went and knocked at the Marchesa's door. She didn't answer: she was dead.

In the spring, instead of the garden, there was a huge building site that a contractor had set up. The steam shovels dug down to great depths to make room for the foundations, cement poured into the iron armatures, a very high crane passed beams to the workmen who were making the scaffoldings. But how could they get on with their work? Cats walked along all the planks, they made bricks fall and upset buckets of mortar, they fought in the midst of the piles of sand. When you started to raise an armature, you found a cat perched on top of it, hissing fiercely. More treacherous pusses climbed onto the masons' backs as if to purr, and there was no getting rid of them. And the birds continued making their nests in all the trestles,[10] the cab of the crane looked like an aviary . . . And you couldn't dip up a bucket of water that wasn't full of frogs, croaking and hopping . . . 5

10. **trestles** (tres′ əlz) *n.*: Frameworks of vertical or slanting beams and crosspieces.

Guide for Responding

◆ *Literature and Your Life*

Reader's Response What is your impression of the Marchesa's circumstances in this story? Was she trapped or not? Explain.

Thematic Focus Speculate on what will happen to street animals, such as the cats in the story, in the world of our future.

Questions for Research If you were to conduct some research about the effects of technology upon human, animal, and plant life, what questions might you hope to answer?

☑ Check Your Comprehension

1. What is the "negative city"? How is it created?
2. Why does Marcovaldo follow the cat?
3. Where does the tabby ultimately lead Marcovaldo, and what does Marcovaldo find there?
4. Describe the situation at the end of the story.

◆ Critical Thinking

INTERPRET

1. What do the developers represent in this story?
2. Explain why the Marchesa's supporters believe she is helping the cats and her critics think she is not. **[Infer; Compare and Contrast]**
3. What are the opposing forces in this story, and which prevails? Support your answer with evidence from the story. **[Draw Conclusions]**

EVALUATE

4. Evaluate Marcovaldo's thought, "I couldn't be accused of theft; at worst, of fishing in an unauthorized place." **[Assess]**

COMPARE LITERARY WORKS

5. Compare and contrast the views of Bradbury and Calvino concerning the forces of nature and the works of civilization. Support your ideas with evidence from each story. **[Compare and Contrast]**

Beyond the Selection

FURTHER READING

Other Works by the Authors

Dandelion Wine, Ray Bradbury
The Golden Apples of the Sun, Ray Bradbury
Something Wicked This Way Comes, Ray Bradbury
Marcovaldo or the Seasons in the City, Italo Calvino
Italian Folktales, Italo Calvino

Other Works About the Future

"The Fun They Had," Isaac Asimov

We suggest that you preview these works before recommending them to students.

INTERNET

For more on Bradbury, see: **http://www.on-ramp.com/johnston/bradbury.html; http://www.catch22.com/~espana/SFAuthors/SFB/Bradbury**

For Calvino, see: **http://userwww.service.emory.edu/~mpajare/calauto.html**

Sites may have changed since we published this information. We *strongly recommend* that you preview the sites before you send students to them.

◆ Critical Thinking

5 Predict Ask students if they predict the skyscraper will be finished. What seems to be happening? *Some students may say that nature will never stop the "wheels of progress"; others will say that in the end, nature is the stronger force and will prevail.*

Reinforce and Extend

Answers

◆ *Literature and Your Life*

Reader's Response According to the Marchesa, she is trapped because the cats thwart her attempts to sell or even to leave the villa.

Thematic Focus Some students may think they will be destroyed; others may agree with Calvino, that they will prevail.

Questions for Research Students may wish to ask specific questions such as, Is my life improved by modern technology? How?

☑ Check Your Comprehension

1. The "negative city" consists of the in-between spaces that the cats inhabit.
2. He follows the cat first out of curiosity; later he chases it to retrieve the trout.
3. The tabby leads him to the Garden of Stubborn Cats, where he finds the city's concentration of wildlife.
4. The wildlife of the garden is hampering the construction effort.

◆ Critical Thinking

1. They represent anti-natural forces.
2. Her supporters think she is helping the cats by preserving an area where they can live; her critics observe her adversarial relationship with the cats.
3. The opposing forces in the story are technology and nature. Nature prevails at the end, with animals subverting the builders' efforts.
4. Marcovaldo tells himself that he is not stealing the trout because the trout would voluntarily take his bait. Students may see Marcovaldo's reasoning as rationalization for stealing.
5. Some students may say that each writer believes that humans have the power to create valuable technology, but in the end this technology will lead to humanity's demise.

Guide for Responding *(continued)*

◆ Reading Strategy

CLARIFY

You may have felt confused by the events that occurred in either of the stories until you were able to **clarify**—make clear—the reasons particular events unfolded.

1. Identify two details of the situation in "There Will Come Soft Rains" that were unclear to you at the beginning of the story. Explain how you clarified these details.
2. How did the condition of the dog in "There Will Come Soft Rains" help you clarify the situation?
3. What was the final clue that allowed you to understand what had happened in "There Will Come Soft Rains"?
4. "The Garden of Stubborn Cats" opens with the statement "The city of cats and the city of men exist one inside the other, but they are not the same city." Identify three details that helped you clarify that statement.

◆ Literary Focus

SETTING

Both of these stories use **setting** as a significant element that contributes to their purposes. The events and the message in "There Will Come Soft Rains" are connected to the future. Time is the most important aspect of the setting.

Calvino presents his setting of a city within a city from an unusual perspective. Marcovaldo discovers places and things he wouldn't have known if he didn't follow his feline friends.

1. (a) Identify three details that alert you that "There Will Come Soft Rains" occurs in the future. (b) Why is this future setting essential to Bradbury's purpose?
2. Describe the future as it is presented in "There Will Come Soft Rains."
3. (a) Describe the city where Marcovaldo lives. (b) Why is this a good or a bad setting for cats and other animals?
4. (a) Contrast the city with the garden Marcovaldo discovers. (b) How does this contrast reinforce the message of the story?

◆ Build Vocabulary

USING WORDS FROM MYTHS

Look up each of the italicized words in a dictionary. On your paper, give the meaning of the word and explain how it relates to the mythological character from which it comes.

1. *tantalize:* from Tantalus, a Greek man for whom food and drink were always out of reach
2. *odyssey:* from Odysseus, a Greek hero who underwent a long and dangerous journey
3. *mercurial:* from Mercury, the speedy Roman messenger god

USING THE WORD BANK: Context

On your paper, write the word from the Word Bank suggested by each sentence.

1. You might use this word when planning a trip.
2. Rabbits live in these.
3. It would be tough to squeeze through one of these to escape a burning building.
4. Ending this is a societal problem.
5. Frequent run-ins with the law could give you this.
6. You'd use this word in astronomy.
7. An encounter with a bear would make you this.
8. This word describes weeds or an odor.
9. A thunderstorm is this.
10. People who are this are usually in hospitals.
11. You might get hurt in this activity.

◆ Build Grammar Skills

COMMONLY CONFUSED WORDS: *LIE* AND *LAY*

Lie means to rest or recline. Its principal parts are *lying, lay,* and *lain. Lay* means to set down, and its principal parts are *laying, laid,* and *laid.*

Practice Write the following sentences into your notebook, and circle the appropriate word.

1. The hungry dog is (lying, laying) at the door.
2. It (lies, lays) there waiting for someone to feed it.
3. Marcovaldo (lies, lays) the fish down.
4. When Marcovaldo arrived at the garden, cats were (lying, laying) everywhere.
5. The old woman of the house went to (lie, lay) down on her bed.

◆ Reading Strategy

1. Students may have been confused by the absence of people, the futuristic setting, and all the futuristic appliances. Once the narrator says "this was the one house left standing," the setting becomes clear.
2. The dog's sores indicate exposure to radioactivity.
3. Some students may find the final clue in the silhouettes of the family against the charred wall of the house; others will find the explanation in the poem by Sara Teasdale.
4. Examples include the "network" through which "the ancient cat population still scurries," the "territories, ceremonies, customs" that belong to the realm of cats, and the "unsuspected peepholes onto the city of men" used by the cats.

◆ Literary Focus

1. (a) Details that alert readers that "There Will Come Soft Rains" occurs in the future include the automated breakfast; the date, "August 4, 2026"; and the robot cleaning-mice. (b) Bradbury's purpose is to warn humans of what could happen if nuclear weapons are permitted to proliferate. To make his warning effective, he envisions a future as it could be if the warning goes unheeded.
2. Students should describe an automated world in which humans do little for themselves and are totally dependent on technology.
3. (a) Marcovaldo's city is so overpopulated and built up that practically no traces of nature are left. (b) The setting is bad for cats and other animals because their lives are endangered by threats such as "cat-crushing automobiles," but it is good for them because they can exist in their own "city of cats" where they live a life independent of humans.
4. (a) In the city, building and technology seem to have obliterated nature, while in the garden, nature seems to be going wild. (b) The wildness of the garden suggests that nature resists human effort to destroy it.

◆ Build Vocabulary

Words From Myths

1. *Tantalize* means "tempt": Tantalus was tempted by the food and drink he could not reach.
2. *Odyssey* means "long journey": Odysseus went on a long journey.
3. *Mercurial* means "unpredictable, quickly changing": Mercury traveled swiftly from one place to another.

Using the Word Bank

1. itinerary; 2. warrens;
3. transoms; 4. indigence;
5. paranoia; 6. supernal;
7. tremulous; 8. rank;
9. titanic; 10. psychopathic

◆ Build Grammar Skills

1. The hungry dog is lying at the door.
2. It lies there waiting for someone to feed it.
3. Marcovaldo lays the fish down, and the cat steals it.
4. When Marcovaldo arrived at the garden, cats were lying everywhere.
5. The old woman of the house went to lie down on her bed.

Grammar Reinforcement

For additional instruction and practice, use the page on Sixty Common Usage Problems (p. 91) in the *Writer's Solution Grammar Practice Book.*

Build Your Portfolio

Idea Bank

Writing

1. **Schedule** Write a schedule for the house in Bradbury's story. On it, record the house's duties for each of the twenty-four hours. Use duties from the story, and add some of your own.

2. **Speculation** Write three paragraphs in which you speculate what your life might be like in the year 2026, the year in which Bradbury's story ends.

3. **Science-Fiction Story** "The Garden of Stubborn Cats" shows how the cats have gained control of a small section of their city. Write a continuation of the story, in which the construction workers give up and the cats gain more control.

Speaking, Listening, and Viewing

4. **Inanimate Dialogue** Suppose the appliances in "There Will Come Soft Rains" could talk. Would they have similar interests? Role-play dialogue between two inanimate objects from the story.

5. **Persuasive Argument** As Marcovaldo, try to convince the Marchesa of the merits of staying in her villa and cultivating her garden. Support your argument with reasons. Present your argument to the class.

Researching and Representing

6. **Painting Presentation** Find out about the paintings of Picasso and Matisse—artists mentioned in Bradbury's story. Using books or photocopies, present your findings. **[Art Link]**

7. **Floor Plan** Draw a floor plan to scale—one inch for one yard—of your ideal house of the future. Briefly describe special features. **[Math Link]**

Online Activity www.phlit.phschool.com

Guided Writing Lesson

Advertisement for a New Technology

You've just discovered a great new technology, and you want to tell the world about it. It could be anything—from a way to grow tearless onions to a robot that interacts with human beings. The important thing is that you get your message across. Write an **advertisement** that describes the new technology, persuades your audience they need it, and provides ordering information.

Writing Skills Focus: Consider the Knowledge Level of Your Audience

Whether you're writing an advertisement, a short story, or a magazine article, you'll need to consider what your audience knows, Once you've determined the **knowledge level** of your audience, write for that level. For example, for an audience of people who've had no exposure to computers, define even simple computer terms. If you write at the knowledge level of your audience, you have a better chance of keeping their interest.

Prewriting Create and fill out a questionnaire to identify the characteristics of your audience. Provide information under headings such as Age Range, Education Level, Specialized Training, Technology, Buying Habits, and so on.

Drafting Write directly to your target audience—the people to whom you are trying to sell your product. They'll be more likely to buy your product if you address their needs in terms and language they can understand.

Revising Get feedback on your ad from someone whose knowledge level is close to that of your target audience. Define any technological terms that are unclear. Add any missing details about the function or advantages of your product.

✓ ASSESSMENT OPTIONS

Formal Assessment, Selection Test, pp. 135–137, and Assessment Resources Software. The selection test is designed so that it can be easily customized to the performance levels of your students. ***Alternative Assessment,*** p. 39, includes options for less advanced students, more advanced students, interpersonal learners, verbal/linguistic learners, musical/rhythmic learners, logical/mathematical learners and visual/spatial learners.

PORTFOLIO ASSESSMENT

Use the following rubrics in ***Alternative Assessment*** to assess student writing:
Schedule: Technical Description/Explanation Rubric, p. 115
Speculation: Expression Rubric, p. 94
Science-Fiction Story: Fictional Narrative Rubric, p. 95
Guided Writing Lesson: Persuasion Rubric, p. 105

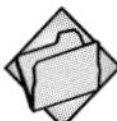

Idea Bank

Following are suggestions for matching Idea Bank topics with your students' performance levels and learning modalities:

Customizing for *Performance Levels*
Less Advanced Students: 1, 4, 7
Average Students: 2, 4, 6
More Advanced Students: 3, 5, 6

Customizing for *Learning Modalities*
Logical/Mathematical: 1, 2, 5, 7
Visual/Spatial: 6, 7
Verbal/Linguistic: 1, 2, 3, 4, 5

Guided Writing Lesson

Revision Strategy Analytic Talk will help students when their work is ready for final polishing. Form students into groups of five. Writers can read their advertisements, pause, and then read them again. During the second reading, listeners can take notes to help them remember technological terms that are unclear. Group members can comment and ask questions to help writers determine how they can better target their audience.

For more prewriting, elaboration, and revision strategies, see *Prentice Hall Writing and Grammar.*

Writing and Language Transparencies Use the Writing Process Model 7: Persuasive Essay, pp. 45–51, to guide students through the writing process.

Writers at Work Videodisc
Have students view the videodisc segment (Ch. 4) featuring Sayu Bhojwani to see how she uses persuasion in her work.

Play frames 33643 to 43235

Writing Lab CD-ROM
Have students complete the tutorial on Persuasion. Follow these steps:

1. Students can view the annotated model on supporting a persuasive argument.
2. Have students complete an Audience Profile.
3. Students should draft on computer.
4. Have them consider the tips for creating an ad when revising and editing their drafts.

Prepare and Engage

LESSON OBJECTIVES

1. **To develop vocabulary and word identification skills**
   - Latin Word Roots: *-ultra-*
   - Using the Word Bank: Synonyms
   - Extending Word Study: Context (ATE)
2. **To use a variety of reading strategies to comprehend short stories**
   - Connect Your Experience
   - Reading Strategy: Challenge the Writer's Message
   - Tips to Guide Reading (ATE)
3. **To increase knowledge of other cultures and to connect common elements across cultures**
   - Connecting Themes Across Cultures (ATE)
   - Cultural Connection (ATE)
   - Background for Understanding
   - Idea Bank: The Censor
4. **To express and support responses to the text**
   - Critical Thinking
5. **To analyze literary elements**
   - Literary Focus: Universal Themes
6. **To read in order to research self-selected and assigned topics**
   - Idea Bank: Music Collection
   - Idea Bank: Internet Research
7. **To plan, prepare, organize, and present literary interpretations**
   - Idea Bank: Princess With a Point of View
   - Idea Bank: Debate
   - Idea Bank: Speech
   - Speaking, Listening, and Viewing Mini-Lesson (ATE): Speech
8. **To use recursive writing processes to write a letter to an elected official**
   - Guided Writing Lesson
9. **To increase knowledge of the rules of grammar and usage**
   - Build Grammar Skills: *Who* and *Whom* in Adjective Clauses

Test Preparation

Critical Reading: Distinguish Between Fact and Nonfact (ATE, p. 551) The teaching tips and sample test item in this workshop support the instruction and practice in the unit workshop:

Critical Reading: Recognize Forms of Propaganda; Distinguish Between Fact and Nonfact (SE, p. 565)

Guide for Reading

Pär Lagerkvist *(1891–1974)*

Swedish writer Pär Lagerkvist (pär lä′ gər kvist′) did not achieve much public recognition until late in his career. Finally, however, when he was sixty, he won the most distinguished prize of all literary awards: the Nobel Prize.

Many Questions This Nobel Prize-winning writer was born the son of a railway worker. Unlike many of the inhabitants of his town, he received a university education, which led him to question many of his family's traditional beliefs. Because of his uncertainty, Lagerkvist's early work is pessimistic.

A Ray of Hope Although he continued to struggle with his beliefs, Lagerkvist's work gradually grew more optimistic. He reached a major turning point when he completed *The Triumph Over Life*, in which he expresses his growing faith in humanity.

Luisa Valenzuela *(1938–)*

Born in Buenos Aires, the capital of Argentina, Luisa Valenzuela has lived in places as diverse as New York City and Tepotzlán, Mexico, a little village with cobblestone streets where people still speak the ancient Aztec language. Because she was married to a French sailor, she lived for a time in Normandy and Paris. Valenzuela travels to extremes in some of her work as well. She changes spellings, creates new words and uses many puns.

Defender of Rights Like many other Latin American writers, Valenzuela writes novels and stories that are very political. Having lived through a repressive regime herself, she is a strong defender of human rights and an active member of several international human rights organizations. "The Censors" shows one aspect of the repressions she has experienced.

◆ Build Vocabulary

LATIN WORD ROOTS: *-ultra-*

In "The Censors," a young man with an *ulterior* motive applies for a job. *Ulterior* means "undisclosed; beyond what is stated." An ulterior motive, therefore, is a reason beyond the one that you tell others.

Ulterior comes from the Latin word *ultra*, which means "further; beyond." In English, *ultra* also takes the forms *ulter* and *ulti.* Other common words with this root include *ultrasonic*, "faster than (or "beyond") the speed of sound," and *ultimate*, "the farthest or last."

WORD BANK

As you read, you will encounter the words on this list. Each word is defined on the page where it first appears. Preview the list before you read, and look for the words in the story.

ardent
venerable
sordid
ulterior
staidness

◆ Build Grammar Skills

***WHO* AND *WHOM* IN ADJECTIVE CLAUSES**

Adjective clauses, also known as relative clauses, modify nouns or pronouns and begin with a relative pronoun. When choosing between the relative pronouns ***who*** and ***whom*** to introduce an adjective clause, use the following rules.

Use *who* if it is the subject of the clause:

subject
Mariana, *who* must finally feel safe there . . .

Use *whom* if it is a direct object or the object of a preposition in the clause.

dir. obj.
I have fought merely to win her *whom* I love, . . .

Prentice Hall Literature Program Resources

REINFORCE / RETEACH / EXTEND

Selection Support Pages
Build Vocabulary: Word Roots: *-ultra-*, p. 163
Build Grammar Skills: *Who* and *Whom* in Adjective Clauses, p. 164 Reading Strategy: Challenge the Writer's Message, p. 165
Literary Focus: Universal Themes, p. 166

Strategies for Diverse Student Needs, p. 40

Beyond Literature
Cross-Curricular Connection: Social Studies, p. 40

Formal Assessment Selection Test, pp. 138–140

Alternative Assessment, p. 40

Writing and Language Transparencies
Business Letter, pp. 61–64

Resource Pro CD-ROM

Listening to Literature Audiocassettes

The Princess and All the Kingdom ◆ The Censors ◆

◆ Literature and Your Life

CONNECT YOUR EXPERIENCE

Have you ever fought for something and then found out you got more than you had bargained for? Both of these stories are about people who believe they are pursuing noble intentions but find themselves in circumstances that are very different from those they had imagined.

Journal Writing Describe a situation in which your good intentions led to an unforeseen or even disastrous consequence.

THEMATIC FOCUS: FACING THE CONSEQUENCES

The events in these stories raise questions about how much control individuals have over the outcomes of their actions.

◆ Background for Understanding

HISTORY

Like the United States, Argentina, the setting of "The Censors," is a country with a high standard of living and a long tradition of immigration from all parts of the world. Unlike the United States, however, Argentina does not have a well-established tradition of democracy. Consequently, it has suffered for many years under colonialism and military dictatorships. In the 1970's, a military regime took power and brutally hunted down suspected political foes. Luisa Valenzuela spent many of those years in self-imposed exile. Although democracy has now been restored, many Argentines are still traumatized by the events of the "Dirty War" in which thousands of people lost their lives.

◆ Literary Focus

UNIVERSAL THEMES

From Argentina to Alaska, from Zurich to Zaire, it would be difficult to find a place where fairy tales are not told. One reason that fairy tales continue to be told to generation after generation of children around the world is that they deal with **universal themes**—messages that are relevant to people of almost any place or time—such as courage, love, and honor. "The Princess and All the Kingdom" uses a fairy-tale format to communicate a message about happiness and responsibility. The short story "The Censors" does not take the familiar fairy-tale form, but it does deal with the universal themes of power and fear.

◆ Reading Strategy

CHALLENGE THE WRITER'S MESSAGE

When you see a television commercial that implies you'll be able to jump as high as an NBA star if you just buy a particular brand of sneakers, do you go right out and buy a pair of the advertised footwear? If you're thinking critically, you'll **challenge the message** behind the advertisement.

Use the same critical strategy when you're reading. Look for the writer's message. Sometimes the writer states the message openly—either through the voice of a narrator or through one of the characters. In these cases, it's easy to recognize the message.

In other stories, the message is implied—often through the actions of the main character. In stories like these, try to state the message in your own words. Then ask yourself, "Does this message prove true in real life, or am I being sold a pair of magic sneakers?"

Test Preparation Workshop

Critical Reading: Distinguish Between Fact and Nonfact

Standardized tests require students to be able to recognize opinions and facts in a variety of texts. Use this sample test item.

> Valenzuela has lived in New York City and Mexico. Because she was married to a French sailor, she lived for a time in Normandy and Paris. Valenzuela travels to extremes in some of her work as well. She changes spellings, creates new words and uses many puns.

Which of the following is an OPINION expressed in the passage?

A As a writer, Valenzuela travels to extremes.
B She changes spellings.
C She creates new words.
D She has lived in a number of cities.

All responses are supported by the passage. However, *B* and *C* can be proven, and *D* is not stated directly. *A* is the only opinion expressed in the passage; it is the correct answer.

Develop Understanding

Have students look at the dramatic piece of art on p. 555 and read the title, "Restricted Man." Ask them to conjecture about the subject of the work. What is the artist's message? *The person appears trapped inside a cement box. The artist may be depicting political repression.* Ask students what kind of traps people find themselves in. Then have them predict what the theme might be in the stories they will read.

Connecting Themes Across Cultures

Censorship is a concept that has been found in other cultures as well as throughout history. Suggest that students list examples of censorship that they have encountered in their reading.

Tips to Guide Reading

Buddy Reading Students may find it helpful to apply to work with a partner to address tricky spots in these texts. Suggest that pairs use study strategies such as skimming and scanning to better understand their reading.

Customize for ***Less Proficient Readers***

To be sure these students comprehend the meaning, have them work in pairs to read the selections. Suggest they pause after each paragraph and take turns summarizing the content.

Customize for ***Pre-AP Students***

An important element in both stories is irony. Review the three main types of irony—verbal, situational, and dramatic—and determine which type of irony is most prevalent in each story. Students should support their choices with examples from each story.

Customize for ***English Language Learners***

These students can benefit from using the Story Map organizer in ***Writing and Language Transparencies,*** p. 84, to chart the events of the plots as they read.

Develop Understanding

One-Minute Insight There is a saying, "Be careful what you wish for, because you just might get it." These words of wisdom could apply to the main character in "The Princess and All the Kingdom." In this story, the prince yearns for the lovely princess and fights bravely to win her. To his surprise and initial dismay, he also wins the entire kingdom—with all its problems and responsibilities. The story suggests that even in our victorious moment, we cannot evade responsibility.

Humanities: Art

View of the Ile de la Cité, Paris, by Jehan Fouquet.

This piece of art illustrates a scene from a medieval kingdom. The stylized buildings with their turrets, towers, and banners evoke a fairy tale kingdom like the one in "The Princess and All the Kingdom."

Jehan Fouquet (c. 1420–1481) was probably the first French painter to win international renown. Having traveled to Rome in the mid-1400's, he learned Italian theories of perspective and architecture. When he returned to France, he became court painter to Louis XI. Best known for his miniatures and panel paintings, Fouquet demonstrated an appreciation of landscape and perspective.

▶Critical Viewing◀

❶ *Students should note that the work evokes tales of chivalry and knights in armor. They should be expecting to read a fairy tale or fantasy.*

Art Transparency Use Art Transparency 13 to further students' thinking about the topic of nobility. For example, encourage students to consider the responsibilities that Lagerkvist's prince had and what responsibilities the depicted nobles may have had. Students might speculate about whether the prince will come to function as well as in the scene depicted in *Feudal Nobility Outside Paris*. Invite students to express their reactions to that painting and/or Lagerkvist's story through a form of writing drama, music, or art of their own choosing.

The Princess and All the Kingdom

Pär Lagerkvist
Translated by Alan Blair

View of the Ile de la Cité, Paris, Jehan Fouquet, Bibliothèque Nationale, Paris

❶ ▲ Critical Viewing What clues does this painting give you about the style and content of the story you are about to read? **[Deduce]**

Block Scheduling Strategies

Consider these suggestions to take advantage of extended class time:

- Introduce the theme of wishes with the Daily Language Practice activities for Week 3, based on "The Three Wishes" of Folk and Fairy Tales, in ***Writing and Language Transparencies,*** p. 114.
- Encourage students to jot down their answers to the Critical Thinking questions on page 557 and then discuss their responses with partners.
- Have students work in discussion groups to answer the Reading Strategy questions on p. 558.
- Have students evaluate the improvised speeches in the Speaking, Listening, and Viewing activity on p. 559. They can use the Peer Assessment: Speaker/Speech, p. 118, in ***Alternative Assessment.***
- Have students work on the Guided Writing Lesson (p. 559). Suggest they brainstorm in a group about issues and appropriate elected officials. After students compose their letters, have them meet in small groups to receive feedback about the content of their letters before they revise them.

Once upon a time there was a prince, who went out to fight in order to win the princess whose beauty was greater than all others' and whom he loved above everything. He dared his life, he battled his way step by step through the country, ravaging it; nothing could stop him. He bled from his wounds but merely cast himself from one fight to the next, the most valiant nobleman to be seen and with a shield as pure as his own young features. At last he stood outside the city where the princess lived in her royal castle. It could not hold out against him and had to beg for mercy. The gates were thrown open; he rode in as conqueror.

When the princess saw how proud and handsome he was and thought of how he had dared his life for her sake, she could not withstand his power but gave him her hand. He knelt and covered it with ardent kisses. "Look, my bride, now I have won you!" he exclaimed, radiant with happiness. "Look, everything I have fought for, now I have won it!"

And he commanded that their wedding should take place this same day. The whole city decked itself out for the festival and the wedding was celebrated with rejoicing, pomp, and splendor.

When in the evening he went to enter the princess's bedchamber, he was met outside by the aged chancellor, a venerable man. Bowing his snow-white head, he tendered the keys of the kingdom and the crown of gold and precious stones to the young conqueror.

"Lord, here are the keys of the kingdom which open the treasuries where everything that now belongs to you is kept."

The prince frowned.

"What is that you say, old man? I do not want your keys. I have not fought for sordid gain. I have fought merely to win her whom I love, to win that which for me is the only costly thing on earth."

The old man replied, "This, too, you have won, lord. And you cannot set it aside. Now you must administer and look after it."

"Do you not understand what I say? Do you not understand that one can fight, can conquer, without asking any reward other than one's happiness—not fame and gold, not land and power on earth? Well, then, I have conquered but ask for nothing, only to live happily with what, for me, is the only thing of value in life." 4

"Yes, lord, you have conquered. You have fought your way forward as the bravest of the brave, you have shrunk from nothing, the land lies ravaged where you have passed by. You have won your happiness. But, lord, others have been robbed of theirs. You have conquered, and therefore everything now belongs to you. It is a big land, fertile and impoverished, mighty and laid waste, full of riches and need, full of joy and sorrow, and all is now yours. For he who has won the princess and happiness, to him also belongs this land where she was born; he shall govern and cherish it."

The prince stood there glowering and fingering the hilt of his sword uneasily.

"I am the prince of happiness, nothing else!" he burst out. "Don't want to be anything else. If you get in my way, then I have my trusty sword."

But the old man put out his hand soothingly and the young man's arm sank. He looked at him searchingly, with a wise man's calm. 5

"Lord, you are no longer a prince," he said gently. "You are a king." 6

And lifting the crown with his aged hands, he put it on the other's head.

When the young ruler felt it on his brow he stood silent and moved, more erect than before. And gravely, with his head crowned for power on earth, he went in to his beloved to share her bed. 7

> ◆ *Literature and Your Life*
>
> Contrast the prince's situation with a time when you acquired something you wanted only to find there were unforeseen conditions attached.

◆ Build Vocabulary

ardent (är′ dənt) *adj.*: Warm or intense in feeling

venerable (ven′ ər ə bəl) *adj.*: Worthy of respect by reason of age and dignity, character, or position

sordid (sôr′ did) *adj.*: Dirty; filthy

◆ Build Grammar Skills

2 *Who* and *Whom* in Adjective Clauses The opening sentence contains examples of both *who* and *whom* in adjective clauses. Have students explain why each relative pronoun is used correctly. *Who is the subject of the verb went. Whom is the direct object of the verb loved.*

◆ Literary Focus

3 Universal Themes In most fairy tales, an obstacle stands in the way of the prince and princess being united. Ask: What is the obstacle? *The passage suggests that the prince's new responsibilities are an obstacle.*

◆ Critical Thinking

4 Infer Ask students what they think is the real reason the prince doesn't want the keys. Is he really being noble, or is there another reason? *The prince thinks he is being noble, but he is really reacting to the chancellor's words, "Now you must administer and look after it." The prince wants to live "happily ever after" with the beautiful fairy-tale princess, but he doesn't want to face the responsibilities of running a real kingdom.*

◆ *Literature and Your Life*

5 Similar situations include the following: When students of driving age are allowed to use the family car, they are often asked to do family errands as well; students who have pets have to take care of them as well as play with them.

◆ Critical Thinking

6 Infer Ask: How does the chancellor feel toward the prince? Explain. *Responses can include: The chancellor feels compassion for the prince because he knows he is young and hasn't yet learned how difficult life can be; the chancellor knows he must be firm with the prince or he will never accept responsibility.*

◆ Reading Strategy

7 Challenge the Writer's Message Ask students: What does the crown symbolize? How does wearing the crown change the prince? *The crown symbolizes the responsibilities a king takes for his land and people. The prince is changed from a spoiled child to a mature young man.*

Speaking, Listening, and Viewing Mini-Lesson

Improvised Speech

This mini-lesson supports the Speaking, Listening, and Viewing activity in the Idea Bank on p. 559.

Introduce Remind students that an improvised speech is not written out in advance. However, the speechmaker should take a few moments to plan what she or he will say.

Develop Have students imagine themselves as the new king. Have them consider the following points before they speak:

- The land is fertile, full of riches and joy.
- The land is also laid waste, impoverished and full of sorrow.

Apply Students should think about what the waiting populace will want to hear; then, give their speeches in a voice with appropriate expression.

Assess Have students evaluate the speeches based on the following criteria:

- Did the speaker use a kingly tone?
- Were the points appropriate for the king to make?
- Was the speech well organized?

One-Minute Insight In "The Censors," Juan becomes a censor to reclaim a letter he himself had written, but in the process becomes obsessed with censorship. In his obsession, he seals his own fate in a way he never imagined. The story suggests that one's actions may have unintended consequences, for which one has to take responsibility.

◆ Critical Thinking

❶ **Analyze** The first paragraph contains a wealth of information about the main character. Ask: What do you know about Juan? *Juan is a worrier, almost to the point of obsession. He's such a worrier that he can't keep his mind on his job and he can't sleep.*

❷ **Clarification** The reference to the discount air fares indicates that the story is a contemporary one and perhaps is meant to add a little humor to what, in Juan's mind, is a very serious situation.

Comprehension Check ☑

❸ Why does Juan apply for a job in the censor's office? *He wants to intercept his letter to Mariana before someone in the censor's office reads it and finds either him or Mariana guilty of some imagined crime.*

Art Transparency Introduce "The Censors" by displaying Art Transparency 7. Have students describe the overall impression of Mary Cassatt's *The Letter* and speculate about the occasion that has prompted the woman to write. After students have read Valenzuela's story, display the transparency again. Have students contrast the painting's air of graciousness and freedom with the story's focus upon repression and bitter irony.

Extending Word Study

Context Suggest that students read "The Censors" carefully with an eye to what words or phrases would be cut if the story was censored for political reasons. People trying to send a hidden message past a censor often use words in an unusual context to send the meaning to their reader. In such an instance, context clues would give significant clues to an unusual meaning.

The Censors

Luisa Valenzuela
Translated by David Unger

❶ Poor Juan! One day they caught him with his guard down before he could even realize that what he had taken as a stroke of luck was really one of fate's dirty tricks. These things happen the minute you're careless, as one often is. Juancito let happiness—a feeling you can't trust—get the better of him when he received from a confidential source Mariana's new address in Paris and knew that she hadn't forgotten him. Without thinking twice, he sat down at his table and wrote her a letter. *The* letter that now keeps his mind off his job during the day and won't let him sleep at night (what had he scrawled, what had he put on that sheet of paper he sent to Mariana?).

Juan knows there won't be a problem with the letter's contents, that it's irreproachable, harmless. But what about the rest? He knows that they examine, sniff, feel, and read between the lines of each and every letter, and check its tiniest comma and most accidental stain. He knows that all letters pass from hand to hand and go through all sorts of tests in the huge censorship offices and that, in the end, very few continue on their way. Usually it takes months, even years, if there aren't any snags; all this time the freedom, maybe even the life, of both sender and receiver is in jeopardy. And that's why Juan's so troubled: thinking that something might happen to Mariana because ❷ of his letters. Of all people, Mariana, who must finally feel safe there where she always dreamt she'd live. But he knows that the *Censor's Secret Command* operates all over the world and cashes in on the discount in air fares; there's nothing to stop them from going as far as that hidden Paris neighborhood, kidnapping Mariana, and returning to their cozy homes, certain of having fulfilled their noble mission.

Well, you've got to beat them to the punch, do what everyone tries to do: sabotage the machinery, throw sand in its gears, get to the bottom of the problem so as to stop it.

❸ This was Juan's sound plan when he, like many others, applied for a censor's job—not because he had a calling or needed a job: no, he applied simply to intercept his own letter, a consoling albeit unoriginal idea. He was hired immediately, for each day more and more censors were needed and no one would bother to check on his references.

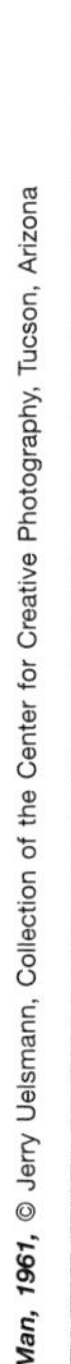
Restricted Man, 1961, © Jerry Uelsmann, Collection of the Center for Creative Photography, Tucson, Arizona

Cultural Connection

Argentina Even though "The Censors" could take place in any oppressive state, the author's nationality suggests that she probably intended the setting to be Argentina. The movie *Evita,* starring Madonna, brought a part of Argentina's history into the public eye. To begin a discussion about Argentina, you might draw on students' knowledge of the movie or the musical, and then direct the discussion into some of the geographical aspects of the country. For example, Argentina is the second largest country in South America, occupying most of the southern portion of the continent. Since it is so large, the landscape varies greatly, from the Andes Mountain regions to the barren plateau of Patagonia to the fertile plain called the Pampas. Ironically, Argentina's name comes from the Latin word for silver, but Argentina lacks the precious metal.

Interested students might like to form a small group to find out more about Argentina.

▲ **Critical Viewing** In what ways does this art suggest fear and repression? **[Analyze]**

Customize for
Less Proficient Readers

To be sure that students understand the basic plot of the story, have them identify who Juan and Mariana are and then invite them to summarize Juan's problem and his proposed solution.

Customize for
Logical/Mathematical Readers

Have these students create a chart that follows Juan's progress within the organization. In the first column, students can write his department; in the second column, they can record how his attitude changes with each promotion.

Customize for
Gifted/Talented Students

Ask students to select one of the stories and write a newspaper review of it, explaining why they would or would not recommend the selection to a friend. Then, have students exchange their reviews and act as a censor to the other's writing.

Insight From Pat Mora

Pat Mora offers the following insight. "Valenzuela has transformed the repression she and her country experienced into an experience for us, the readers. With some degree of fascination, we witness the transformation of the protagonist and, of course, we think about ourselves, about self-deception. The story is both psychological and political. We almost smack into the ending, those last two powerful sentences that remind us of the power of words. We are left uncomfortable, which is what I think Valenzuela wants. We are left wondering about our own definition of patriotism."

Humanities: Art

Restricted Man, 1961, by Jerry Uelsmann.

This photograph portrays how a man like Juan probably feels.

Photographer Jerry Uelsmann (1934–) received his M.F.A. from Indiana University in 1960 and immediately began teaching photography at the University of Florida. His work has been exhibited in more than 100 shows in the United States and around the world. He has published six books of photography and his work can be found on display in museums as diverse as the Metropolitan Museum of Art in New York and the Tokyo Metropolitan Museum of Photography.

Use these questions for discussion:

- What is the man in the photograph doing? *He is looking out through an opening in some stone.*
- What, do you think, does Uelsmann want you to know about the man? *The man has "tunnel" vision; he is as rigid and unmoving as the stone.*
- Why is this photograph appropriate for "The Censors"? *Juan has tunnel vision; he refuses to do anything not related to his job and becomes rigid in his quest to be the perfect censor.*

◆ Critical Thinking

❶ Analyze Ask: What do you know about Juan from his reaction when he is sent to Section K? *Students might say that Juan is losing touch with reality because he is so obsessed with worrying about his letter that he does not recognize the real danger in screening letters for explosives.*

◆ Critical Thinking

❷ Evaluate Draw students' attention to Juan's response to the union organizer. Ask: What are Juan's motives in reporting the man? Should Juan be proud of his promotion? Why or why not? *Juan reports the organizer to favorably impress his superiors. His words to himself as he leaves his boss's office tell the reader that Juan knows his motive was self-serving. Therefore, he should not be proud of his promotion, especially because the union organizer probably lost his job and perhaps his life.*

Comprehension Check ☑

❸ What was Juan's noble mission that is beginning to blur? *His noble mission was to intercept his letter to Mariana so that no harm would come to her. Now he is beginning to enjoy the work for its own sake.*

◆ Literary Focus

❹ Universal Themes Students may mention people who become so involved in a work project that they put its importance ahead of their families, or people who can't put the office behind them while they are on vacation, or people who lie or cheat to get ahead.

❺ Interpret Have students consider the sentence, "We don't know if this made him happy." Ask: How could the narrator, who seems to have known everything about Juan's innermost thoughts up until now, not know if promotion made Juan happy? *Perhaps the narrator is implying that Juan is acting less and less like a reasonable person, and so his state of mind can't be assessed.*

Listening to Literature Audiocassettes By listening to a reading of "The Censors," students will receive the full benefit of the storyteller's inflections, beginning with the opening words, "Poor Juan!"

Ulterior motives couldn't be overlooked by the *Censorship Division*, but they needn't be too strict with those who applied. They knew how hard it would be for the poor guys to find the letter they wanted and even if they did, what's a letter or two when the new censor would snap up so many others? That's how Juan managed to join the *Post Office's Censorship Division*, with a certain goal in mind.

The building had a festive air on the outside that contrasted with its inner staidness. Little by little, Juan was absorbed by his job, and he felt at peace since he was doing everything he could to get his letter for Mariana. He didn't even worry when, in his first month, he
❶ was sent to *Section K* where envelopes are very carefully screened for explosives.

> **Well, you've got to beat them to the punch, do what everyone tries to do: sabotage the machinery . . .**

It's true that on the third day, a fellow worker had his right hand blown off by a letter, but the division chief claimed it was sheer negligence on the victim's part. Juan and the other employees were allowed to go back to their work, though feeling less secure. After work, one of them tried to organize a strike to demand higher wages for unhealthy work, but Juan didn't join in; after thinking it over, he reported the man to his superiors and thus got promoted.

◆ Build Vocabulary

ulterior (ul tir´ ē ər) *adj.*: Undisclosed; beyond what is openly stated

staidness (stād´ nəs) *n.*: State of being settled or resistant to change

You don't form a habit by doing something once, he told himself as he left his boss's office. And when he was transferred to *Section F*, where letters are carefully checked for poison dust, he felt he had climbed a rung in the ladder.

By working hard, he quickly reached *Section E* where the job became more interesting, for he could now read and analyze the letters' contents. Here he could even hope to get hold of his letter, which, judging by the time that had elapsed, had gone through the other sections and was probably floating around in this one.

Soon his work became so absorbing that his noble mission blurred in his mind. Day after day he crossed out whole paragraphs in red ink, pitilessly chucking many letters into the censored basket. These were horrible days when he was shocked by the subtle and conniving ways employed by people to pass on subversive messages; his instincts were so sharp that he found behind a simple "the weather's unsettled" or "prices continue to soar" the wavering hand of someone secretly scheming to overthrow the Government.

> **◆ Literary Focus**
> The theme of someone's becoming so caught up in his work that he loses sight of his original mission is universal. Explain how.

His zeal brought him swift promotion. We don't know if this made him happy. Very few ❺
letters reached him in *Section B*—only a handful passed the other hurdles—so he read them over and over again, passed them under a

Beyond the Classroom

Career Connection

Postal Workers When Juan mailed his letter, it made a detour through his city's Post Office Censorship Division. Without such a detour, what would have happened to his letter? Although much of today's mail service is automated, postal workers are still needed to keep the mail flowing. Have interested students research United States Postal Service jobs and report their findings to the class. For example, students could investigate the following: educational requirements, application process, career opportunities, and pay and benefits.

Community Connection

Local Mail Service Where do students mail their letters? Where do they, or their parents, buy stamps? How do students receive their mail? The answers to these questions can vary greatly. Encourage students to do a survey that answers the three questions above. After students have compiled the results of their survey, they might like to discuss the results with someone who has lived in the community for more than ten or fifteen years to see how services have changed.

magnifying glass, searched for microprint with an electronic microscope, and tuned his sense of smell so that he was beat by the time he made it home. He'd barely manage to warm up his soup, eat some fruit, and fall into bed, satisfied with having done his duty. Only his darling mother worried, but she couldn't get him back on the right track. She'd say, though it wasn't always true: Lola called, she's at the bar with the girls, they miss you, they're waiting for you. Or else she'd leave a bottle of red wine on the table. But Juan wouldn't overdo it: any distraction could make him lose his edge, and the perfect censor had to be alert, keen, attentive, and sharp to nab cheats. He had a truly patriotic task, both self-denying and uplifting.

His basket for censored letters became the best fed as well as the most cunning basket in the whole *Censorship Division*. He was about to congratulate himself for having finally discovered his true mission, when his letter to Mariana reached his hands. Naturally, he censored it without regret. And just as naturally, he couldn't stop them from executing him the following morning, another victim of his devotion to his work. ❼

Guide for Responding

◆ Literature and Your Life

Reader's Response Do you think the prince's prize was worth the price in "The Princess and All the Kingdom"?

Thematic Focus In both of these stories, the universal theme of power shows the great responsibilities that come with power.

☑ Check Your Comprehension

1. In "The Princess and All the Kingdom," in addition to the princess's hand in marriage, what else does the prince receive?

2. In "The Censors," why does Juan seek a job as a censor?

3. What happens to Juan at the end of "The Censors"?

◆ Critical Thinking

INTERPRET

1. In "The Princess and All the Kingdom," why do you think the prince had to fight in order to win the princess? **[Speculate]**

2. In "The Princess and All the Kingdom," how do the attitudes of the aged chancellor and the prince contrast with each other? **[Compare and Contrast]**

3. In "The Censors," why does Juan's attitude change? **[Draw Conclusions]**

4. What is your opinion of Juan in "The Censors"? Support your opinion with examples from the story. **[Support]**

COMPARE LITERARY WORKS

5. To what types of situations in the real world do you think that the themes of these stories could be applied? **[Connect]**

Beyond the Selection

FURTHER READING

Other Works by the Authors
"A Hero's Death," Pär Lagerkvist
"Open Door," Luisa Valenzuela

Other Works With the Theme of Accepting Responsibility
We Are All Guilty, Kingsley Amis
One of the Boys, Scott Johnson

We suggest that you preview these works before recommending them to students.

INTERNET

The Internet provides opportunities for students to learn more about the authors.

For information and works by Pär Lagerkvist, go to **http://heml.passagen.se/iblis/lagrkvst.html**

For a review of Luisa Valenzuela's *Black Novel (With Argentines)*, go to **http://lenti.med.umn.edu/~ernesto/Criticas/Cri_BlackNovel.html**

Sites may have changed since we published this information. We *strongly recommend* that you preview the sites before students go to them.

▶Critical Thinking◀

❻ **Evaluate** Point out that Juan's attitude has been changing. Ask: How has Juan's attitude evolved? *Juan is so obsessed with his job, and he has become so paranoid, that he sees an evil intent in the most innocent messages.*

◆ Reading Strategy

❼ **Challenge the Writer's Message** The ending may have surprised students. Ask: Does the writer want you, the reader, to believe that Juan deserves what happens to him? Do you believe he deserves his fate? *Responses can include: Yes, Juan deserves to die for all the people whose letters he turned in; or No, Juan crosses the boundary to insanity when he censors his own letter, and so he does not deserve to die.*

Reinforce and Extend

Answers

◆ Literature and Your Life

Reader's Response Students may say that having power and responsibility is worth the price; others may argue that the burden of such responsibility will hinder him from experiencing carefree happiness.

Thematic Focus Students should give examples from each selection that support this statement.

☑ Check Your Comprehension

1. He receives the crown of king and the keys to the treasury.
2. Juan seeks to protect himself and Mariana from persecution.
3. Juan is executed as a traitor because in his zeal he has censored his own letter.

◆ Critical Thinking

1. The princess held the throne in her kingdom, so the prince needed to fight to win it.
2. The prince is carefree and irresponsible; the aged chancellor is wise and responsible.
3. Juan becomes caught up in the zeal of his work.
4. Students may consider Juan a fool, as they see that he has destroyed himself by his own actions.
5. "The Princess . . ." could apply to assuming the adult responsibilities of supporting oneself, paying taxes, and raising children.

Answers

◆ Reading Strategy

1. Teenagers are apt to view life in this way until they learn to accept the consequences of their actions.
2. Students may cite the stories of lottery winners who go bankrupt after spending their money.
3. Juan's pride in and devotion to his job causes him to forget his original purpose.
4. Some students may argue that Juan is too exaggerated to be a believable character. Others may observe that power is capable of making such changes in a person.

◆ Literary Focus

1. (a) Students may point to historical situations where a military victory forced the conquering nation to provide protection and rule for the vanquished. (b) Sample examples: Students who win elections must run their organizations; the suitor to the rich girl must spend money on her to keep her interest.
2. The simplicity of the plot and the uncomplicated nature of its characters make the fairy tale an effective vehicle for conveying a theme.
3. "The Censors" illustrates that power corrupts.
4. Sample response: In attempting to avenge a real wrong, people may take the law into their own hands.

◆ Build Vocabulary

Using the Latin Root *-ultra-*

1. c 2. a 3. b

Using the Word Bank

1. d 2. c 3. a 4. b 5. e

◆ Build Grammar Skills

1. who; 2. whom; 3. who; 4. who; 5. whom

Grammar Reinforcement

For additional instruction and practice, use the lesson in the **Language Lab CD-ROM** on Pronoun Case and the page on Special Problems With Pronouns (p. 79) in the *Writer's Solution Grammar Practice Book.*

Guide for Responding *(continued)*

◆ Reading Strategy

Challenge the Writer's Message

When you read critically, you **challenge the writer's message**—you test what the writer says or implies against your own experiences and opinions.

1. The prince wanted happiness without responsibility. Explain why you agree or disagree that some people approach life in a similar way.
2. Through the voice of the Chancellor, Lagerkvist states that happiness and responsibility are tied together, that every prize has a price. Explain why you agree or disagree with this idea.
3. In "The Censors," how does Juan's fast rise through the ranks of the Censorship Division relate to his downfall?
4. Did you find the changes in Juan's attitude believable or not? Explain.

◆ Literary Focus

Universal Themes

Though these two stories differ in style and subject matter, both have **universal themes**—timeless messages that apply to the lives of people all over the world.

1. (a) Explain how the message of "The Princess and All the Kingdom" could apply to a ruler of any country. (b) Explain how the message could apply to you and your friends.
2. What features of a fairy tale make it an effective form for communicating a theme?
3. State the theme of "The Censors" in your own words.
4. Juan sets out to beat the system of censorship that he feels is oppressive and unjust. In the end, he becomes one of the most aggressive censors. Describe another situation in which someone might become a part of a problem he or she originally tried to solve.

◆ Build Vocabulary

Using the Latin Root *-ultra-*

Many English words contain the root *-ultra-*, which means "further; beyond." On your paper, match each word with its correct definition.

1. ultraviolet — **a.** a final offer or demand
2. ultimatum — **b.** finally
3. ultimately — **c.** having wavelengths that are shorter than those of violet light

Using the Word Bank: Synonyms

On your paper, match each word from the Word Bank with its closest synonym.

1. ardent — **a.** filthy
2. venerable — **b.** hidden
3. sordid — **c.** revered
4. ulterior — **d.** zealous
5. staidness — **e.** stuffiness

◆ Build Grammar Skills

***Who* and *Whom* in Adjective Clauses**

In informal speech, some people may not distinguish between *who* and *whom*. In formal writing and speaking, however, it is important to use these words correctly.

Use **who** as the subject of a clause. Use **whom** as a direct or indirect object or as an object of a preposition.

Practice Write the following sentences on your paper, choosing the correct word from the parentheses.

1. There once was a prince (who, whom) fought to win the heart of a beautiful princess.
2. The prince did not care for riches; he wanted to be with the princess (who, whom) he loved so much.
3. The chancellor, (who, whom) was a patient man, informed the prince of his new responsibilities.
4. It was Juan (who, whom) became a censor for his own letter.
5. Juan knew (who, whom) the authorities wanted.

Reteach

To give students more practice identifying universal themes, use a chart like the one below. In one column, have students brainstorm a list of well-known stories and folk tales such as: "The Three Little Pigs" or "Cinderella". In the second column, have them list the universal theme that they believe is found in each well-known story. One strategy for recognizing a universal theme is for students to state the "message" that the story gives, or what they have learned about life from the story.

After students have analyzed well-known stories, have them add the selections, "The Princess and All the Kingdom" and "The Censors" to the chart. Students may wish to debate the message they believe each selection has to offer.

Name of Story	Message
The Three Little Pigs	Preparation pays off

Build Your Portfolio

Idea Bank

Writing

1. Letter to Juan All we know about the mysterious character Mariana in "The Censors" is that she is in Paris, perhaps to escape the dictatorship of her country. Write a letter from her to Juan, explaining her reasons for leaving her country.

2. The Censor Choose a partner and write each other a simple postcard, such as you would write while on vacation. Then, exchange cards and pretend that you are censors in a dictatorship. Based on what you've read in "The Censors," find three suspicious details and explain why you chose them.

3. Princess With a Point of View Write and perform a short monologue for the princess in "The Princess and All the Kingdom," in which she expresses *her* opinions on war, victory, love and responsibility. **[Performing Arts Link]**

Speaking, Listening, and Viewing

4. Debate Form two groups to debate both sides of a current censorship/free speech issue.

5. Improvised Speech As the prince who has just become a king, give your first speech to the crowd outside the palace. Consider how your facial expressions and gestures will be viewed by your audience, and try to make them "work" for you.

Researching and Representing

6. Music Collection Plan a CD based on the theme of freedom versus responsibility. List the names of popular songs you would include on the CD. **[Performing Arts Link]**

7. Internet Research Use the Internet to locate information on groups whose purpose is the advancement of human rights. Create a chart that shows your findings on at least two groups. **[Social Studies Link; Technology Link]**

Online Activity www.phlit.phschool.com

Guided Writing Lesson

Letter to an Elected Official

In "The Censors," Juan, like the author Luisa Valenzuela, had the misfortune of living under a dictatorship. In a democracy, government officials, who are often elected, must be responsive to the needs of the citizens. Conduct some research about a public issue that matters to you. Then write a letter to an elected official about it.

Writing Skills Focus: Correct Format

When you write a letter to a government official, you should use the format, or style, of a standard business letter.

Your Address
Date

Inside Address:
Name of Official
Department
Address

Greeting:

Body of letter

Closing,
Your Signature
Your Typed Name

Prewriting Find the information you need to complete the inside address. Then make notes on the points you have researched and want to discuss in your letter.

Drafting In the body of your letter, state the problem, summarize relevant information, and explain the action you want the official to take.

Revising Review your letter and eliminate any slang words or colloquial expressions. Check your spelling and grammar—especially your use of *who* and *whom*. For more on the correct use of *who* and *whom,* see pp. 550 and 558.

✓ ASSESSMENT OPTIONS

Formal Assessment, Selection Test, pp. 138–140, and Assessment Resources Software. The selection test is designed so that it can be easily customized to the performance levels of your students.

Alternative Assessment, p. 40, includes options for less advanced students, more advanced students, verbal/linguistic learners, visual/spatial learners, and intrapersonal learners.

PORTFOLIO ASSESSMENT

Use the following rubrics in ***Alternative Assessment*** to assess student writing:
Letter to Juan: Fictional Narrative Rubric, p. 95
The Censor: Evaluation/Review Rubric, p. 104
Princess With a Point of View: Expression Rubric, p. 94
Guided Writing Lesson: Persuasion Rubric, p. 105

Idea Bank

Following are suggestions for matching Idea Bank topics with your students' performance levels and learning modalities:

Customizing for *Performance Levels*
Less Advanced Students: 1, 4, 6, 7
Average Students: 2, 5, 6, 7
More Advanced Students: 3, 7

Customizing for *Learning Modalities*
Bodily/Kinesthetic: 3, 5
Verbal/Linguistic: 1, 2, 3, 4, 5
Musical/Rhythmic: 6
Logical/Mathematical: 2, 7

Guided Writing Lesson

Prewriting Strategy After students have identified the problem they will address, have them use hexagonal writing to clarify their point.

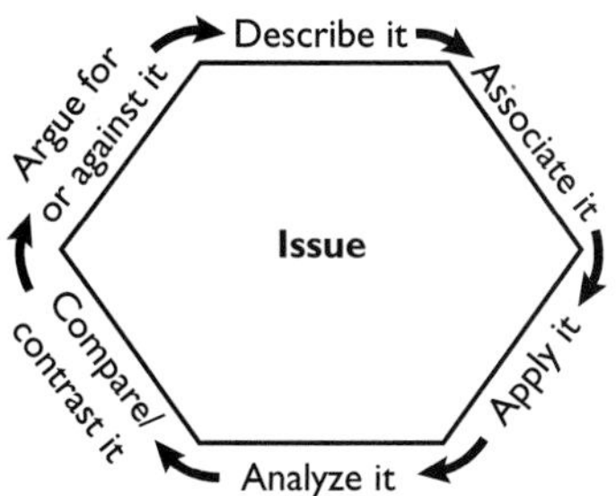

Use the model of a business letter in ***Writing and Language Transparencies,*** pp. 61–64, to guide students through the writing process.

For more prewriting, elaboration, and revision strategies, see *Prentice Hall Writing and Grammar.*

Writers at Work Videodisc

Have students view the videodisc segment (Ch. 4) featuring Sayu Bhojwani to see how she conveys information in writing proposals.

Play frames 39679 to 41420

Writing Lab CD-ROM

Have students complete the tutorial on Persuasion. Follow these steps:

1. Students can use the Pros and Cons Chart to evaluate their arguments.
2. Students should draft on computer.
3. Have them review the tips for including ideas in a letter.

Prepare and Engage

LESSON OBJECTIVES

- To use recursive writing processes to write a persuasive essay
- To recognize and and use appropriate sentence construction
- To demonstrate control over grammatical elements such as parallel structure

You may want to distribute the scoring rubric for Persuasion (p. 105 in ***Alternative Assessment***) to make students aware before they begin of the criteria on which they will be evaluated. See the suggestions on p. 562 for how you can customize the rubric to this workshop.

Writers at Work Videodisc
To introduce students to the key elements of persuasion and show them how Asia Society worker Sayu Bhojwani uses them in her proposal writing, play the videodisc segment on Persuasion (Ch. 4).

Play frames 33643 to 43235

Writing Lab CD-ROM
If your students have access to computers, you may want to have them work on the tutorial on Persuasion to complete all or part of their persuasive essays. Follow these steps:

1. Suggest that students review the interactive model of a persuasive essay.
2. Have students look at the examples of purposes for persuasive writing.
3. Students should draft on the computer.
4. For help revising drafts, students can use the screen Adding Supporting Details.
5. Suggest students use the Persuasion Word Bin to strengthen their drafts.

Persuasive Essay

Writing Process Workshop

You may have noticed one character persuading another in the short stories in this section. Persuasion can take place informally or formally. A **persuasive essay** is a formal opportunity to convince an audience to think or act in a certain way.

Develop a persuasive essay in which you convince readers to accept your position on an issue that is important to you. The following skills, introduced in this section's Guided Writing Lessons, will help you develop your persuasive essay.

Writing Skills Focus

- **Consider what your audience knows.** If you write at the knowledge level of your audience, you have a better chance of persuading them to accept your position. For instance, if your topic is state-to-state driving laws and your audience has little knowledge of them, make sure you let them know the facts. (See p. 549.)
- **Use the proper format.** A persuasive essay should first present your position, develop an argument with evidence to support that position, bring up counterarguments and then counter those arguments, and conclude with a summary or restatement. (See p. 559.)

The following excerpt from an article that recommends cycling and in-line skating at night demonstrates these skills.

MODEL

Most people automatically assume that bicycling at night is dangerous. After all, it's dark, and most decent people are safely off the streets.

① As it happens, most cars are also off the streets, which is one of the great attractions of night riding—or night in-line skating, for that matter. There are other appealing factors, too. ② You don't have to get up at 5 A.M. to get in a workout and you can enjoy the cool night air.

We are not, for obvious reasons, suggesting you go alone. Traveling with a buddy or two both increases your visibility and deters would-be harassers. . . . ③

① The writer mentions a possible problem with her argument and then offers reasons countering it.

② The writer backs up her original assertion with further examples.

③ The writer assumes that the audience has had experience cycling during the day but not at night, so she starts with a basic safety precaution.

Beyond the Classroom

Career Connection

Persuasive Writing Tell students that people in your community may routinely write persuasive essays as part of their work. Have students look for examples of persuasive essays in print and broadcast media. For example, they might find a letter to a newspaper editor stressing the need for road repair. Students can also find persuasive writing in advertisement posters on buses and trains, in political campaign messages, and on the Internet. Have students find a persuasive essay and analyze it, asking themselves whom the essay attempts to persuade, what its message is, and how successful they think it is.

Prewriting

Choose a Topic Think of issues that are important to you. You may want to browse through magazines and newspapers to look for ideas, or you may choose one of the following topics.

Topic Ideas

- School should be in session year-round
- Channel One should not have advertising
- Ticket brokers should be outlawed
- High-school newspapers should be censored

Anticipate Readers' Questions Once you've chosen your topic, clarify the position that you will present in your essay. Then list potential objections and questions about that position. For example, if your essay presents an argument that zoos are cruel and should be closed, you might list these questions as issues that your opponents would raise and that you must address:

- ▶ What will happen to the animals currently in zoos?
- ▶ What alternatives are there to educate people about animals?
- ▶ What arguments are there in favor of zoos?

Gather Strong Evidence Using the questions and objections you listed as a starting point, gather evidence—facts, statistics, and reasons—to support your argument. This may require research, either in the library or on the Internet.

Drafting

Appeal to Your Audience As you write, always keep your readers in mind. Use formal, respectful language, and address each concern you think your readers may have. Also, keep your audience's knowledge level in mind as you draft.

Present Strong Support for Your Argument Use the evidence you've gathered to support each point you make. Your argument is only as strong as the support you offer.

Use a Persuasive Tone Carefully choose your words and phrases to make readers eager to agree with your views. When discussing zoos, for example, you might mention the "cold iron bars" and the "harsh fluorescent light" of the cages.

Applying Language Skills: Types of Sentences

To enliven your writing, use different **types of sentences**, including simple sentences (a subject and verb), compound sentences (two independent clauses connected by a conjunction), and complex sentences (a main clause and one or more subordinate clauses).

Simple Sentence:

Seventy percent of the student body reads the school paper.

Compound Sentence:

The articles educate students on current events, and the columns entertain students and teachers alike.

Complex Sentence:

Because some people were upset by a few recent articles, they are calling for the paper to be censored.

Writing Application Make sure that your persuasive essay has a variety of sentence structures.

Writer's Solution Connection
Writing Lab

To tailor your writing for a specific audience, complete the Audience Profile in the Writing Lab tutorial on Persuasion.

Develop Student Writing

Prewriting Strategy

Once students have chosen a topic, introduce a graphic like the one below to help students study their topic in greater depth. On each point, students can provide information about the topic's causes, its effects, its predecessors and its opposites. Encourage students to use the information they gather to help flesh out their thinking and their writing.

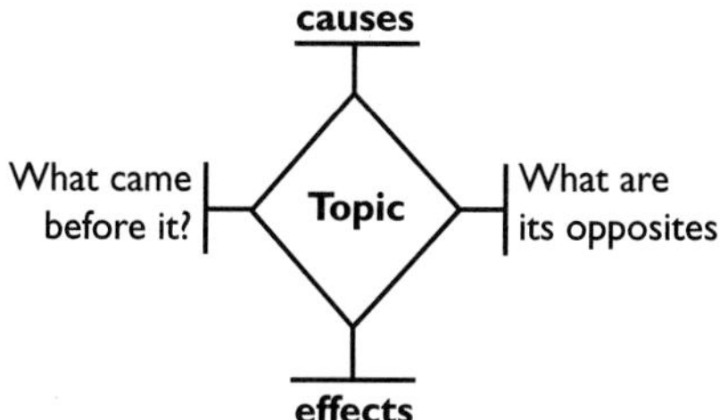

Writing Lab CD-ROM

Before students begin drafting, have them consult the screen on deciding what type of organization to use in the Organizing Details and Information section of the tutorial on Persuasion.

Elaboration Strategy

Encourage students to draft their persuasive essays in a single sitting, without pausing to labor over a single word or to correct a grammatical error. Once students have completed a draft, they'll have an opportunity to reenter their work and make extensive revisions.

Applying Language Skills

Types of Sentences Tell students that their essays will be much more interesting—and persuasive—if they vary their sentence types to include simple, compound, and complex sentences.

Grammar Reinforcement

For additional instruction and practice, have students complete the **Language Lab CD-ROM** lesson on Varying Sentence Structure and the practice pages 121–123 on Varying Your Sentences in the *Writer's Solution Grammar Practice Book.*

Applying Language Skills

Parallel Structure Tell students that using parallel structure will make their essays easier to read and therefore more persuasive.

Answers

Suggested response:
At Yellowstone you can ride a bike, or take a hike.

Grammar Reinforcement

Have students complete the **Language Lab CD-ROM** lesson on Eliminating Unnecessary Words and the practice pp. 64–65 on Faulty Parallelism in the *Writer's Solution Grammar Practice Book.*

Revision Strategy

Have the peer reviewer poke holes in the argument. The writer can then use these criticisms when revising the essay.

Writing Lab CD-ROM

The Revising and Editing section of the Writing Lab tutorial on Persuasion contains a Persuasion Word Bin. Have students consult this resource.

Publishing

Encourage students to discuss their essays with readers, especially those with different views.

Reinforce and Extend

Connection to Literature Unit 7, Nonfiction, contains two persuasive essays (p. 587 and p. 590).

Prentice Hall Writing and Grammar For more prewriting, elaboration, and revision strategies, see *Prentice Hall Writing and Grammar.*

Applying Language Skills: Parallel Structure

Use **parallel structure,** or similar grammatical form, to express similar ideas. The similarity in form helps readers recognize the similarity in content and makes the writing easier to remember.

Not Parallel:

In the Rocky Mountains, avalanches are one threat, and you also have to watch out for flash floods.

Parallel:

In the Rocky Mountains, avalanches are one threat, while flash floods are another.

Practice On your paper, correct the faulty parallelism in the following sentence.

At Yellowstone you can take a bike ride, and hiking is fun, too.

Writing Application Review your persuasive essay, and look for places where you can use parallel structure.

Writer's Solution Connection
Language Lab

For more practice with parallel structure, complete the Language Lab lesson on Varying Sentence Structure.

Revising

Hold a Peer Conference Share your draft with a classmate, and get some feedback. Use the comments as guidelines for revising your essay. Ask your peer these questions:

- Have I anticipated all my readers' questions?
- How well have I appealed to my audience?
- How persuasive is the tone in my writing?

Revision Model

What advantages would a student gain by working at a job after a day of school? ① ~~One disadvantage might be that the student would not be able to keep up with his or her school work. On the other hand, the~~ The student may feel more independent as a result of having ~~new~~ ② adult responsibilities and a little extra money. ③ On the whole, I believe the advantages outweigh the disadvantages.

① The writer deletes this line, which strays from his topic sentence.
② The writer replaces the word new with the more precise adult.
③ This sentence completes the essay.

Publishing

- **Classroom** Invite classmates to read your persuasive essay. Encourage them to share their opinions.
- **Newspaper** Send your essay to your school or local newspaper as a letter to the editor.
- **Internet** Post your essay on a bulletin board or class Web site. See what responses you receive.

ASSESSMENT		4	3	2	1
PORTFOLIO ASSESSMENT Use the rubric on Persuasion in ***Alternative Assessment*** (p. 105) to assess students' writing. Add these criteria to customize the rubric to this assignment.	**Sentence Variety**	A good mix of simple, compound, and complex sentences allows a natural flow from one point to the next.	There is a mix of simple, compound, and complex sentences. Essay flows from one point to the next.	Sentences vary occasionally; more variety is needed. Essay is slightly monotonous.	One type of sentence predominates, making the essay awkward and hindering the flow of ideas.
	Parallelism	Parallelism is used to help drive the important points home.	Parallelism is used occasionally.	Parallelism is not used; sentences are otherwise clear.	Parallelism is not used; sentences contain unnecessary words and phrases.

Student Success Workshop

Literary Response — Defending Your Response or Interpretation

Strategies for Success

You are entitled to your opinion. However, an opinion or an interpretation that is backed up with supporting information usually carries more weight. This can be especially true when you are asked to respond to or interpret something you have read. By reading carefully, you can gather information from the text to support your response or interpretation.

Use Text to Support Your Interpretation An interpretation includes your ideas about the meaning of a literary work—whether it is a poem, short story, novel, or biography. Look to the text itself to support your interpretation. For example, in a work of fiction, you might point to specific images, passages of dialogue, or plot events to clarify your interpretation of the significance of the setting, the motivation of a character, or the author's theme. In a biography, you might note how the language used by the author indicates the tone of the work.

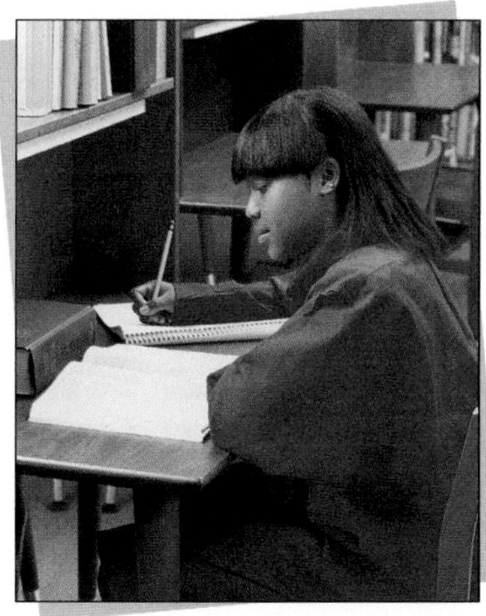

Use Text to Justify Your Response When you are asked your opinion of a literary text, find support for your opinion in the text. If you think the work is superficial, point out the lack of a theme. If you find the characters appealing, state which of their traits you admire. If you find a nonfiction text confusing, describe its lack of organization. If you are entertained by an autobiography, mention a few of the details that amuse you.

Apply the Strategies

Write a few paragraphs describing your response to or interpretation of two or more of the following types of texts. Support your response with references to elements in each text.

1. short story
2. magazine article
3. poem
4. lyrics of a popular song
5. newspaper editorial

Here are some situations in which using elements of text to support your interpretation or response can be helpful:

- Writing a book report
- Writing a review of a movie or play
- Evaluating the text of a political speech
- Answering a test question about a literary passage

LESSON OBJECTIVES

- To express and support responses to various types of texts, using elements of text to defend one's own responses and interpretations

Customize for
Less Advanced Students

Give students statements of opinion about literary texts, and together discuss how to offer specific and convincing support. Examples of opinion statements about literary texts:

- The main character in this story is just like a real person.
- The plot in this story is weak.
- The poet paints vivid pictures.
- The subject of this biography led an action-packed life.

Answers

1. Interpretations and judgments can be developed around the four literary elements of setting, plot, characterization, and theme.
2. Interpretations and judgments can be made about the subject of the article, the writer's craft, and the organization of ideas.
3. Interpretations and judgments of poetry should mention such features as imagery, figurative language, rhyme, rhythm, and repetition.
4. Interpretations and judgments of song lyrics can include features such as rhyme, rhythm, repetition, originality, and the songwriter's message.
5. Interpretations and judgments of persuasive writing should note the logic and effectiveness of the writer's support for a position, and possibly discuss viewpoint and bias.

Test Preparation Workshop

Evaluate and Make Judgments
Students can transfer the skill of defending a response to standardized tests. These tests frequently require students to make judgments that are supported by evidence from the passages. Use this sample test item to give students practice.

The latest brands of sports coolers are extremely popular among teenagers. However, there are several reasons that consumers should be wary of these new products. In addition to their prohibitive cost, they contain heavy artificial coloring that dyes the lips and tongue. The ecology-minded consumer will also find fault with the excess packaging.

Which word best describes the author's attitude toward the product being described?

A disdain
B amusement
C support
D embarrassment

The passage provides details which suggest the drink is not recommended. Therefore, the writer's attitude would best be described as disdain, A.

Prepare and Engage

LESSON OBJECTIVES

- To analyze verbal and nonverbal performance techniques
- To analyze and critique the significance of visual representations

Ask students to describe the work of a film critic, theater critic, art critic, music critic, or literary critic. During discussion, emphasize that *criticism* in this context does not have an unfavorable connotation. Help students to see that a critic is using knowledge and experience to make discriminating judgments about a performance or work of art.

Customize for
Logical/Mathematical Learners

This workshop mentions Shakespeare's *Romeo and Juliet* as the basis for *West Side Story.* Challenge students to find out more about interpretive works based on Shakespeare's plays. They may learn about the plays as sources of classical music, opera, ballet, modern dance, film, musicals, and more. They may also discover that onstage performances of the plays are not always "true" to the original. Suggest that students use their findings to compare and contrast two interpretations of the same work by Shakespeare.

Apply the Strategies

Critiques of the film versions of literary works should focus on the medium of film; encourage student critics to think about the original author's message and main ideas, rather than the details that inevitably differ when a story moves to film. How does the filmmaker try to capture the original message and main ideas?

For example, is *The Naked Jungle* as suspenseful as "Leiningen Versus the Ants?" Why or why not? Does the film *Fahrenheit 451* show the main character's growth and change as effectively as the novel? Why or why not?

Speaking, Listening, and Viewing Workshop

Evaluating Performance Techniques

"Thumbs up," "thumbs down" . . . almost everyone understands these ratings to judge a performance. However, to be an effective critic, you need to look closely at various elements of the performance.

Recognize Interpretations Performances that are based on another work are interpretations. Poetry readings are interpretations. So are retellings of old stories. Films based on novels or plays may be the most common kind of interpretation, but other types of performances are also based on original texts. For example, the ballet "Sleeping Beauty" is based on a fairy tale, and the Greek myth of Orpheus and Eurydice has been interpreted through modern dance.

Interpret the Original Work Before you can evaluate a performance based on another work, you need to know and interpret the original work yourself. For example, if you want to evaluate how successfully the film *West Side Story* interprets *Romeo and Juliet,* you need to begin by reading and forming your own interpretation of *Romeo and Juliet.*

Evaluate Verbal and Nonverbal Techniques Various techniques may be used in a performance to convey another person's interpretation of a work. Verbal techniques include intonation and pacing in oral reading, storytelling, and dramatic performance (on stage or film). Nonverbal techniques include facial expressions, gestures, and movement in musical performances, dance, or pantomime. Particularly in plays and films, nonverbal techniques include special effects created by lighting, camera angles, sequencing, and music. For example, a tense scene from a novel might be heightened dramatically in a movie through music and special camera angles. You can evaluate the effectiveness of specific verbal or nonverbal techniques by asking yourself:

- ▶ How effectively does this technique convey the author's original message?
- ▶ How does this technique affect the viewer's understanding of the original story?

As you evaluate the effectiveness of verbal and nonverbal techniques, try to decide how well you think they communicate a valid interpretation of the original work, and why.

Apply the Strategies

Be a critic, and evaluate one of the following films as an interpretation of another work. Analyze verbal and nonverbal performance techniques, special effects, camera angles, and music. Present your critique to your class or a small group.

1. *The Naked Jungle,* based on Carl Stephenson's short story "Leiningen Versus the Ants."
2. *Fahrenheit 451,* based on Ray Bradbury's novel of the same name.

Tips for Evaluating Performance Techniques

- ▶ Ask yourself questions about what you liked and disliked about the performance techniques.
- ▶ Avoid reading reviews of a performance before you see it, because they might influence your opinions of the performance techniques.

Cross-Curricular Connection: Music

Students may choose a particular performer, group, or musical genre and collect online and print reviews of recent performances. Reading and comparing their collected reviews, students can list the elements of a musical performance that a reviewer usually discusses. Students should also evaluate the strength of a reviewer's support for opinions.

Using a well-written review as a model, students can develop their own review of a musical performance. They may write their review; or they may present their ideas orally. Offer the option of "performing" a review with a partner.

Test Preparation Workshop

Critical Reading

Recognize Forms of Propaganda; Distinguish Between Fact and Nonfact

Strategies for Success

The reading sections of certain standardized tests require you to read a passage to recognize forms of propaganda. The tests also require you to distinguish between facts and nonfacts in a passage. Use the following strategies to help you answer test questions on these skills:

Recognize Propaganda Propaganda is information that may or may not be factual or accurate but which aims to persuade the public that it is. It may appear in speeches, brochures, advertisements, or editorials. As you read, try to determine what the writer hopes you will believe, what the writer's motives may be, and whether or not the information is factual or misleading.

For example, you might be asked to recognize propaganda in a passage such as the following:

> The mayor blames our factory for polluting the river. His new program will force us to report on how we are working to prevent industrial emissions from contaminating the air, ground, and water. If we don't comply, our company will face steep fines. The result? Predictably, workers will be laid off. The city can't afford to take this risk! We should all protest the mayor's plan.

You can tell from this that the author will

A work personally to reduce pollution.
B present the mayor's plan in a positive way.
C persuade readers not to support the mayor's program, despite its potential benefits to the environment.
D expose other businesses that are polluters.

The author does not speak of his or her own personal plans, so **A** is incorrect. **B** is incorrect, since the author does not praise the mayor's program. **D** is incorrect, since the author mentions no other businesses. The correct answer is **C**.

Distinguish Between Fact and Nonfact
Facts can be proved or checked. Nonfacts, or opinions, cannot be proved. Which of these statements about the mayor's plan is an opinion?

A The mayor blames our factory for polluting the river.
B The program will force us to report.
C The city can't afford to take this risk!
D If we don't comply, our company will face steep fines.

Answers **A**, **B**, and **D** are all facts that can be proven or checked. **C** is an opinion that cannot be proven and is the correct answer.

Apply the Strategies

Read the following passage from a political speech, and answer the questions.

> We are all aware of our schools' budget deficits. Yet the majority of taxpayers do not support a tax increase to help fund the schools. Many school programs have been eliminated or cut back over the last two years. I ask you to think about what our students' future will be if we don't help them today. A tax increase is the only answer. Please give our students hope for the future.

1 You can tell from the passage that the speaker
A is not telling the whole truth.
B is only trying to discredit an opponent.
C hopes to persuade the audience to take action.
D wants to convince the audience to vote.

2 Which of these is a fact stated in the passage?
A School programs have been cut back.
B Most taxpayers support a tax increase.
C A tax increase is the only answer.
D We are all aware of our schools' budget deficits.

Correlations to Standardized Tests

The reading comprehension skills reviewed in this workshop correspond to the following standardized test sections:
SAT Critical Reading
ACT Reading

Test Preparation

Each ATE workshop in Unit 6 supports the instruction here by providing teaching suggestions and a sample test item:

- **Recognize Forms of Propaganda** (ATE, p. 513)
- **Distinguish Between Fact and Nonfact** (ATE, pp. 469, 479, 499, 533, 551)

LESSON OBJECTIVES

- To evaluate the credibility of information sources
- To recognize modes of persuasion in texts

Answers

1. (C) hopes to persuade the audience to take action
2. (D) School programs have been cut back.

Test-Taking Tip

Notice Typography Tell students that test directions and questions may have a word or phrase highlighted with a different type style—capital letters, italics, bold, or underscored, for example. Display this test question as an example:

Which of the following statements expresses an OPINION?

Have students give ideas about why the word *opinion* is capitalized. (Test takers are supposed to pay attention to it and focus only on opinion statements in the answer choices.)

Display other questions with words that are commonly highlighted on tests, and discuss how typography helps the test takers. Examples:

- Which of these is NOT a cause?
- What is the BEST way to solve the problem?

Planning Instruction and Assessment

Unit Objectives

1. To read a variety of types of nonfiction
2. To apply a variety of reading strategies appropriate for reading nonfiction
3. To analyze literary elements
4. To use a variety of strategies to read unfamiliar words and to build vocabulary
5. To learn elements of grammar and usage
6. To use recursive writing processes to write in a variety of forms
7. To prepare, organize, and present literary presentations

Meeting the Objectives

With each selection, you will find instructional material and portfolio opportunities through which students can meet these objectives. Further, you will find additional practice pages for reading strategies, literary elements, vocabulary, and grammar in the ***Selection Support*** booklet in the ***Teaching Resources*** box.

Test Preparation

The end-of-unit workshop, **Comparing and Contrasting Texts; Analyzing Literary Language** (SE, p. 661), is supported by teaching tips and a sample test item in the ATE workshop with each selection grouping.

The following ATE workshops appear in this unit:

- **Comparing and Contrasting Texts** (ATE pp. 581, 625, 637, 647)
- **Analyze Literary Language** (ATE pp. 569, 595, 609)

The following additional workshops in the ATE give teaching tips and a sample test item for applying the skill taught in the Student Success Workshops:

- **Evaluating the Credibility of Information Sources** (ATE, p. 622)
- **Analyzing Text Structures** (ATE, p. 659)

The Last Painter on Earth, 1983, James Doolin, Koplin Gallery, Los Angeles, California

Humanities: Art

The Last Painter on Earth, 1983, by James Doolin.

The shadow represents a painter at his easel, and the landscape is meant to suggest a post-cataclysmic vision of Earth, an Earth more like the moon or Mars. The light looks as if the sun is setting, so the painter may be trying to catch the last light of day. Encourage students to recognize the futuristic or fantastic quality of the painting, in contrast to a standard self-portrait or landscape. Help students link the art to the focus of Unit 7, "Nonfiction," by answering the following questions:

1. In what ways is this painting like a persuasive essay? *By showing a barren Earth, the painting argues in favor of protecting the environment or against nuclear weapons.*
2. Why might "the last painter on Earth" continue to paint, and what might he be painting? *The last painter on Earth might continue to paint to take his mind off his loneliness; because he wants to leave a record of what he sees; because he might find this strange landscape compelling to paint; or because he has a memory of this eerily beautiful landscape.*

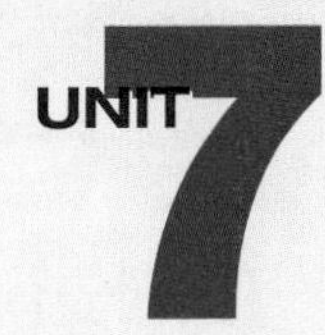

Nonfiction

Nonfiction introduces you to a wide variety of real people and places—some that are familiar to you and some that are far from your experience. Through the essays, biographies, and articles in this section, you can enjoy new experiences, consider new ideas, and learn new concepts.

Assessing Student Progress

The following tools are available to measure the degree to which students meet the unit objectives:

Informal Assessment

The questions on the Guide for Responding sections are a first level of response to the concepts and skills presented with the selection. Students' responses are a brief informal measure of their grasp of the material. Their responses on this level can indicate where further instruction and practice are needed. You may then follow up with the practice pages in the ***Selection Support*** booklet.

You will find literature and reading guides in the ***Alternative Assessment*** booklet, which you may give students on an individual basis for informal assessment of their performance.

Formal Assessment

In the ***Formal Assessment*** booklet, you will find selection tests and part tests.

Selection Tests The selection tests measure comprehension and skills acquisition for each selection or group of selections.

Part Tests Each part test applies the unit skills on a broader level. The Critical Reading section measures Unit Objectives 1, 2, and 3. The Vocabulary and Grammar section measures Objectives 4 and 5. The Essay section measures Objectives 1 and 6.

Alternative Assessment

Portfolios As you review individual pieces or the collected work in students' portfolios, you will find assessment sheets available in the portfolio section of the ***Alternative Assessment*** booklet.

Scoring Rubrics You will find scoring rubrics for writing modes in the ***Alternative Assessment*** booklet. You can apply these to Guided Writing Lessons and to Writing Process Workshop lessons.

Speaking, Listening, and Viewing The ***Alternative Assessment*** booklet contains assessment sheets for speaking, listening, and viewing activities.

Learning Modalities The ***Alternative Assessment*** contains activities that appeal to different learning styles. You may use these as an alternative measurement of students' growth.

Prepare and Engage

LESSON OBJECTIVES

1. **To develop vocabulary and word identification skills**
   - Latin suffixes: *-able*
   - Using the Word Bank: Synonym or Antonym?
   - Extending Word Study: Connotations (ATE)
2. **To use a variety of reading strategies to read and comprehend an expository essay**
   - Connect Your Experience
   - Reading for Success: Strategies for Reading Nonfiction
   - Tips to Guide Reading: Sustained Reading (ATE
   - Read to Appreciate Author's Craft (ATE)
3. **To increase knowledge of other cultures and to connect common elements across cultures**
   - Cultural Connection
4. **To express and support responses to the text**
   - Critical Thinking
   - Idea Bank: Letter
5. **To analyze literary elements**
   - Literary Focus: Expository Essay
   - Idea Bank: Cause-and-Effect Essay
6. **To read in order to research self-selected and assigned topics**
   - Research Skills Mini-Lesson: Researching Specific Information (ATE)
   - Idea Bank: Nature Report
7. **To plan, prepare, organize, and present literary interpretations**
   - Speaking, Listening, and Viewing Mini-Lesson: Poetry Reading (ATE)
8. **To use recursive writing processes to write a proposal**
   - Guided Writing Lesson
9. **To increase knowledge of the rules of grammar and usage**
   - Build Grammar Skills: Linking Verbs and Subject Complements

Test Preparation

Reading Comprehension: Analyzing Literary Language (ATE, p. 569) The teaching tips and sample test item in this workshop support the instruction and practice in the unit workshop.

Reading Comprehension: Comparing and Contrasting Texts; Analyzing Literary Language (SE, p. 661)

Guide for Reading

Rachel Carson *(1907–1964)*

Rachel Carson was successful in combining the two compelling interests of her life—nature and writing—into a career that spanned nearly a half century.

Nature's Inspiration Born in Springdale, Pennsylvania, Carson was a naturalist who specialized in marine biology—the study of sea life. Carson spent several summers during college at the Woods Hole Oceanographic Institution in Massachusetts. She later observed, "I am sure that the genesis of *The Sea Around Us* (1951) belongs to that first year at Woods Hole, when I began storing away facts about the sea—facts discovered in scientific literature or by personal observation and experience."

Environmental Crusader In her writing, Carson stressed the interrelation of all living things and the dependence of human welfare on natural processes.

In *Silent Spring* (1962), her most controversial book, Carson drew attention to the horrors and possible disaster resulting from wasteful and destructive uses of pesticides. *Silent Spring* caused such an uproar that it prompted President Kennedy to announce a federal investigation and helped launch the modern environmental movement.

Awards and Accolades Rachel Carson's writing helped lead to the establishment of the Environmental Protection Agency (EPA) in 1970 and to an overall environmental awareness. She received numerous honors and awards, including a National Book Award for *The Sea Around Us,* and honorary degrees in both science and literature.

At the time of her death in 1964, Carson was in the process of finishing her revisions of *The Sense of Wonder*, a book that enables children to share some of her love and enjoyment of nature.

◆ Build Vocabulary

LATIN SUFFIXES: *-able*

Rachel Carson calls the "marginal world"—the area where the land and sea meet—a *mutable* region. *Mutable* combines the Latin root *-mut-*, meaning "change," with the Latin suffix *-able*, meaning "that can or will be." A *mutable* region therefore is one that "can or is able to change." *Mutable* appropriately describes the edge of the sea, where the crashing surf and changing tides ensure that nothing remains in one state for long.

WORD BANK

Before you read, preview this list of words from the selection.

mutable
ephemeral
primeval
essence
marginal
subjectively
manifestations
cosmic

◆ Build Grammar Skills

LINKING VERBS AND SUBJECT COMPLEMENTS

In her descriptions of the "marginal world," Carson frequently uses sentences with linking verbs and subject complements. **Linking verbs** express a state of being rather than action. They link the subject with a **subject complement**—a noun, pronoun or adjective that identifies or elaborates on the subject.

s lv sc
The *edge* of the sea *is* a strange and beautiful *place*.

The link between a subject and a subject complement is so close that the sentence is like an equation: subject = complement. This pattern is effective for making descriptive statements.

Prentice Hall Literature Program Resources

REINFORCE / RETEACH / EXTEND

Selection Support Pages
Build Vocabulary: Suffixes: *-able,* p. 167
Build Grammar Skills: Linking Verbs and Subject Complements, p. 168
Reading for Success: Strategies for Reading Nonfiction, pp. 169–170
Literary Focus: Expository Essay, p. 171

Strategies for Diverse Student Needs, p. 41

Beyond Literature Cross Curricular Connection: *Science: Marine Biology,* p. 41

Formal Assessment Selection Test, pp. 145–147; Assessment Resources Software

Alternative Assessment, p. 41

Writing and Language Transparencies
Comparison-and-Contrast Organizer, pp. 96–98

Daily Language Practice
Week 20, p. 131

Resource Pro CD-ROM

Listening to Literature Audiocassettes

MODEL SELECTION

The Marginal World

◆ Literature and Your Life

Connect Your Experience

What place has special meaning for you? Perhaps a walk along the rocky shore holds fond memories of childhood vacations, or the local park in your town reminds you of good times with your friends. For Rachel Carson, the author of "The Marginal World," the edge of the sea is a special place of beauty and wonder.

Journal Writing Jot down your fondest memories of a place that has special meaning for you. What made it so special? What did you learn or gain from going there?

Thematic Focus: In Awe of Nature

As a scientist specializing in marine biology, Rachel Carson spent her life preserving our living Earth. Her essay provides some answers to the question, "Why should people care for the environment?"

◆ Background for Understanding

Science

In "The Marginal World," Rachel Carson describes the intertidal zone of the ocean—the zone between the high and low tide marks. Animals and organisms that live in this area must adapt to very changeable, and often harsh, conditions—periodic exposure to air and sun, changes in temperature, rain that dilutes salt water, evaporation that increases the salt level of tidal pools, and wave action.

Despite these changing conditions, many organisms thrive here because they adapt to the tidal actions by burrowing in sand, by living in tidal pools or crevices of rocks, or by living within a protective shell.

The adaptability and survival of these organisms is crucial to the survival of other sea-dwelling creatures—and even to human survival. This diverse food chain that begins with tiny microorganisms is a crucial system that acts as a lifeline for countless species.

◆ Literary Focus

Expository Essay

An **expository essay** is a piece of short nonfiction writing that informs by explaining, defining, or interpreting an idea, an event, or a process. Writers may develop expository essays in many ways, including analyzing, interpreting, or classifying information; giving illustrations; comparing and contrasting ideas; or presenting causes and effects.

In "The Marginal World," Rachel Carson uses examples to illustrate her points, classifies the different types of life found on the sea's edge, and explains the cause-and-effect relationships that affect the survival of these plants and animals. She organizes her observations by focusing on different places at different times of day.

Use a chart like the one shown to jot down details about each time and place.

Time and Place	Observations

Interest Grabber Have students look at the palms of their hands. To make the point that life exists on both visible and microscopic levels, show them a picture of skin cells from a science book or magazine. Suggest that looking at living things at a microscopic level can reveal whole new worlds. Rachel Carson uses this close focus to observe what happens in the place she calls "the marginal world"—that ever-changing sliver of space between land and sea. Where we might simply see a strip of sand, her close focus allows us to see that this limited space teems with animal and plant life.

Customize for *Less Proficient Readers*
Help these students to identify the main ideas of the first two paragraphs. Discuss how other ideas in the paragraphs relate to these main ideas. Encourage them to look for the link between main and supporting ideas in each paragraph of "The Marginal World."

Customize for *Pre-AP Students*
Ask students to assess the author's style as they read. What stylistic qualities differentiate this expository essay from other science writing they have read? What techniques does Carson borrow from poetry or fiction?

Customize for *English Language Learners*
Use maps, pictures, and diagrams to illustrate specialized vocabulary found in this selection. For instance, these students may need a visual reference for terms such as *sediments, continental margins, niche, basin, tentacle, flats,* and *cove.*

Customize for *Gifted/Talented Students*
Invite students to work together to create a classification chart of the animal and plant life in "The Marginal World." (For example, the phylum *Mollusca* includes the species lobster and ghost crab.) Encourage them to display their chart for classmates.

Test Preparation Workshop

Reading Comprehension: Analyzing Literary Language Some standardized tests include sections that assess students' reading ability. This type of question may require students to understand and analyze literary language. Provide students with the following sample question.

> The shore has a dual nature, changing with the swing of the tides, belonging now to the land, now to the sea. On the ebb tide it knows the harsh extremes of the land world, being exposed to heat and cold, to wind, to rain and drying sun. On the flood tide it is a water world, returning briefly to the relative stability of the open sea.

Which aspect of literary language best expresses the shore's dual nature?

A the repetition of phrases
B the descriptions of the harsh extremes of the land world
C the rhyming words within the sentences
D the descriptions of the conflict between land and water

Discuss repetition, description, and rhyme, and help students see that the correct answer is A.

Reading for Success

The Reading for Success page in each unit presents a set of problem-solving procedures to help readers understand authors' words and ideas on multiple levels. Good readers develop a bank of strategies from which they can draw as needed.

Unit 7 introduces strategies for reading nonfiction. These strategies give readers an approach for breaking down and understanding concepts, support, and structure in nonfiction text. By using these strategies as they read, students will be better able to analyze and evaluate the nonfiction material.

These strategies for reading nonfiction are modeled with "The Marginal World." Each green box shows an example of the thinking process involved in applying one of these strategies.

How to Use the Reading for Success Page

- Introduce the strategies for reading nonfiction, presenting each as a problem-solving procedure. Be sure students understand what each strategy involves and under what circumstances to apply it.
- Before students read the essay, have them preview it, looking at the annotations in the green boxes that model the strategies.
- To reinforce these strategies after students have read "The Marginal World," have students do the Reading for Success pages in ***Selection Support,*** pp. 169–170. This activity gives students an opportunity to read a selection and practice strategies for reading nonfiction by writing their own annotations.

Reading for Success

Strategies for Reading Nonfiction

Probably the majority of what you read is nonfiction—your textbooks, newspaper and magazine articles, information on the Internet. Reading nonfiction can open doors to new worlds, introduce you to interesting people, and help you to look at ideas and events in new ways. Because most nonfiction deals with information, concepts, or ideas, you will benefit from strategies that help you analyze it.

Recognize the writer's motivation.

Consider *why* the author is writing. What ideas or information does the author want to convey, or how does he or she want you to respond to this piece of writing? By being aware of the author's motivation, you can evaluate the credibility of the information you are being given, or you can be prepared to question what the writer is saying.

Identify the author's main points.

Sort out the main points the writer is making. If you're reading a textbook or news article, use the heads to help you identify the important points.

Identify support for the author's points.

Notice how the writer supports the points he or she makes. The author's reasoning and evidence should be believable and should lead you to understand and accept the points. If you find the support unsatisfactory, you may not accept the writer's ideas.

Recognize patterns of organization.

Noticing how the material is presented and developed can help you understand it. The writer may present material in a number of ways: explaining events chronologically, building up ideas in order of importance, comparing and contrasting ideas or things, showing the effects of causes, and so on.

Vary your reading rate.

You may read different kinds of nonfiction material at different rates, depending on your own purpose. When you're reading information that you need to remember, read slowly and attentively, perhaps even pausing to jot down notes. If you're looking for a fact or a single piece of information, you may want to skim very quickly, not trying to remember everything but looking only for the information you need.

As you read the following work of nonfiction by Rachel Carson, look at the notes in the boxes. These notes demonstrate how to apply the above strategies to a piece of literature.

Reading Strategies: Support and Reinforcement

Appropriate Reading Strategies Students are given a reading strategy to apply in reading each selection. All of the reading strategies in this unit apply to aspects of nonfiction. In other selections a strategy is suggested that is appropriate to the selection.

Reading Prompts To encourage application of the given reading strategy, there are occasional prompts, within green boxes, at appropriate and significant points. In addition, there are red boxes prompting application of the Literary Focus concept and maroon boxes prompting students to connect with their lives.

Using the Boxed Annotations and Prompts

The material in the green, red, and maroon boxes along the sides of selections is intended to help students apply the literary element and the reading strategy and to make a connection with their lives.

You may use the boxed material in these ways:

- Have students pause when they come to a box and respond to its prompt before they continue reading.
- Urge students to read through the selection ignoring the boxes. After they have read the selection completely, they may go back and review the selection, responding to the prompts.

breast was rosy with the light of the unrisen sun. The day was, after all, to be fair.

Later, as I stood above the tide near the entrance to the pool, the promise of that rosy light was sustained. From the base of the steep wall of rock on which I stood, a moss-covered ledge jutted seaward into deep water. In the surge at the rim of the ledge the dark fronds of oarweeds swayed, smooth and gleaming as leather. The projecting ledge was the path to the small hidden cave and its pool. Occasionally a swell, stronger than the rest, rolled smoothly over the rim and broke in foam against the cliff. But the intervals between such swells were long enough to admit me to the ledge and long enough for a glimpse of that fairy pool, so seldom and so briefly exposed.

And so I knelt on the wet carpet of sea moss and looked back into the dark cavern that held the pool in a shallow basin. The floor of the cave was only a few inches below the roof, and a mirror had been created in which all that grew on the ceiling was reflected in the still water below.

Under water that was clear as glass the pool was carpeted with green sponge. Gray patches of sea squirts[4] glistened on the ceiling and colonies of soft coral[5] were a pale apricot color. In the moment when I looked into the cave a little elfin starfish hung down, suspended by the merest thread, perhaps by only a single tube foot. It reached down to touch its own reflection, so perfectly delineated that there might have been, not one starfish, but two. The beauty of the reflected images and of the limpid[6] pool itself was the poignant[7] beauty of things that are ephemeral, existing only until the sea should return to fill the little cave.

Carson **supports her main point** by describing the strength and beauty of a starfish clinging to a ledge of the cave.

Whenever I go down into this magical zone of the low water of the spring tides, I look for the most delicately beautiful of all the shore's inhabitants—flowers that are not plant but animal, blooming on the threshold of the deeper sea. In that fairy cave I was not disappointed. Hanging from its roof were the pendent[8] flowers of the hydroid Tubularia, pale pink, fringed and delicate as the wind flower. Here were creatures so exquisitely fashioned that they seemed unreal, their beauty too fragile to exist in a world of crushing force. Yet every detail was functionally useful, every stalk and hydranth[9] and petallike tentacle fashioned for dealing with the realities of existence. I knew that they were merely waiting, in that moment of the tide's ebbing, for the return of the sea. Then in the rush of water, in the surge of surf and the pressure of the incoming tide, the delicate flower heads would stir with life. They would sway on their slender stalks, and their long tentacles would sweep the returning water, finding in it all that they needed for life.

With this example, Carson **supports her main point:** that the creatures at the edge of the sea have strength as well as beauty.

▲ **Critical Viewing** What characteristics of the crab have helped it survive living in the harsh sea? **[Analyze]** 4

And so in that enchanted place on the threshold of the sea the realities that possessed my mind were far from those of the land world I had left an hour before. In a different way the same sense of remoteness and of a world apart came to me in a twilight hour on a great beach on the coast of Georgia. I had come down after sunset and walked far out over sands that lay wet and gleaming, to the very 5

4. **sea squirts:** Sac-shaped water animals with tough outer coverings.
5. **coral** (kôr´ əl) *n.*: Animals with tentacles at the top of tubelike bodies.

6. **limpid** (lim´ pid) *adj.*: Clear.
7. **poignant** (poin´ yənt) *adj.*: Emotionally moving.
8. **pendent** (pen´ dənt) *adj.*: Hanging.
9. **hydranth** (hī´ dranth) *n.*: Feeding structure.

▶Critical Viewing◀

4 **Analyze** *Students may mention that the crab's hard outer shell protects it, and its legs move it across the rocky and sandy sea bottom.*

◆ Literary Focus

5 **Expository Essay** Point out the way in which Carson ends one description and moves directly into another. Ask: How does the author use comparison to make a transition in time and place in her essay? *She remarks that the same sense of remoteness came to her in both places, but in different ways.*

Extending Word Study

Connotations Draw students' attention to the word promise in the first sentence of the first full paragraph on this page. Discuss the connotation of "the promise of that rosy light," helping them to understand that in this sense, it means much more than a verbal promise that a person makes. Encourage them to describe the connotations of other words on this page, including "the *pressure* of the incoming tide," and "in that *enchanted* place."

Customize for
Musical/Rhythmic Learners
Carson's descriptions of the sea often call to mind aspects of music: *rush of water, surge of surf, pressure of incoming tides.* Suggest that these students find descriptions in the selection that remind them of music. In a small group, they can compare and contrast the sounds of the sea to music. They might also want to create their own musical descriptions of the sea.

Speaking, Listening, and Viewing Mini-Lesson

Poetry Reading

This mini-lesson supports the Speaking, Listening, and Viewing activity in the Idea Bank on p. 578.

Introduce Tell students that of all the forms of literature, poetry perhaps lends itself best to reading aloud because much of it uses musical devices such as rhythm and rhyme, alliteration, consonance and assonance. Successful poetry readers know how to pace reading, adjust their tone and emphasize certain words, phrases, or passages to bring out their musical qualities.

Develop Suggest that students find two or three poems about the ocean or the tides and then read them aloud to themselves to help determine which they would recite for the class. You might recommend "The Tide Rises, The Tide Falls" by Henry Wordsworth Longfellow or George Gordon, Lord Byron's "Apostrophe to the Ocean" from *Childe Harold's Pilgrimage.*

Apply Ask students to practice their recitation before delivering it to the class. Allow time for students to present their readings to the class.

Assess Have students evaluate their own readings by answering these questions: Did I speak clearly and fluently? Did I use my voice to bring out its emotion and musicality? You may also have students use the Peer Assessment sheet for Oral Interpretation, p. 119 in ***Alternative Assessment.***

◆ Reading for Success

❶ Identify Support for the Author's Points The author points out that the intertidal area seems distant from the adjoining land. Ask students: How does Carson use sensory details to support her point. *She mentions the wind, the sea, and the shore birds as the only sounds heard.*

▶Critical Viewing◀

❷ Connect *Students will probably say that it is clear that the photographer loves and respects these birds, and possibly all shore life, in the way that Carson does. He is probably interested in preserving the inhabitants of "the marginal world." Like Carson, the photographer shares his appreciation for nature with a wider audience.*

◆ Reading for Success

❸ Recognize the Author's Purpose Ask students to explain how they think the author wants readers to respond to the information in this passage. *This passage contains the information that a person can gain profound understanding of nature by close observation of the natural world. The author wants readers to respond to the passage by sharing her sense of awe at the wonders of nature, represented by the ghost crab.*

Read to Appreciate Author's Craft

Draw students' attention to the way the author combines scientific information with her personal response to nature. Have students look for passages that include this combination and choose one to write about in their journals.

edge of the retreating sea. Looking back across that immense flat, crossed by winding, waterfilled gullies and here and there holding shallow pools left by the tide, I was filled with awareness that this intertidal area, although abandoned briefly and rhythmically by the sea, is always reclaimed by the rising tide. There at the edge of low water the beach with its reminders of the land seemed far away. The only sounds were those of the wind and the sea and the
❶ birds. There was one sound of wind moving over water, and another of water sliding over the sand and tumbling down the faces of its own wave forms. The flats were astir with birds, and the voice of the willet[10] rang insistently. One of them stood at the edge of the water and gave its loud, urgent cry; an answer came from far up the beach and the two birds flew to join each other.

▲ ❷ Critical Viewing How might the photographer's purpose be similar to Carson's? **[Connect]**

The flats took on a mysterious quality as dusk approached and the last evening light was reflected from the scattered pools and creeks. Then birds became only dark shadows, with no color discernible. Sanderlings[11] scurried across the beach like little ghosts, and here and there the darker forms of the willets stood out. Often I could come very close to them before they would start up in alarm—the sanderlings running, the willets flying up, crying. Black skimmers[12] flew along the ocean's edge silhouetted against the dull, metallic gleam, or they went flitting above the sand like large, dimly seen moths. Sometimes they "skimmed" the winding creeks of tidal water, where little spreading surface ripples marked the presence of small fish.

Notice that Carson **organizes** her essay by describing different places at different times.

The shore at night is a different world, in which the very darkness that hides the distractions of daylight brings into sharper focus the elemental realities. Once, exploring the night beach, I surprised a small ghost crab in the searching beam of my torch. He was lying in a pit he had dug just above the surf, as though watching the sea and waiting. The blackness of the night possessed water, air, and beach. It was the darkness of an older world, before Man. There was no sound but the all-enveloping, primeval sounds of wind blowing over water and sand, and of waves crashing on the beach. There was no other visible life—just one small crab near the sea. I have seen hundreds of ghost crabs in other settings, but suddenly I was filled with the odd sensation that for the first time I knew the creature in its own world—that I understood, as never before, the essence of its being. In that moment time was suspended; the world to which I belonged did not exist and I might have been an onlooker from outer space. The little crab alone with the sea became a symbol that stood for life itself—for the delicate, destructible, yet incredibly vital force that somehow holds its place amid the harsh realities of the inorganic world.

These words reinforce that Carson's **motivation** is to share her feelings of awe with her readers.

The sense of creation comes with memories

10. willet (wil′ it) *n.*: Large, gray and white, long-legged wading bird.
11. Sanderlings: Small, gray and white birds found on sandy beaches.
12. skimmers: Long-winged sea birds.

Research Skills Mini-Lesson

Researching Specific Information

This mini-lesson supports the Beyond Literature activity on p. 576.

Introduce Have students read the information in the Cultural Connection box. Point out that while DDT and other pesticides got rid of harmful insects, they upset the balance of nature and caused damage to birds, frogs, and other animals that ate insects.

Develop Encourage students' research on why other countries use pesticides. Suggest, if necessary, that these chemicals protect crops from destructive insects and prevent disease-carrying insects from causing illness among people.

Apply Students may work in groups, each researching one country. Have them report why the country used pesticides and how the environmental movement worked to end this use.

Assess Suggest that students present the information both with visual aids and a written report. Evaluate based on the depth of research and the quality of presentation.

of a southern coast, where the sea and the mangroves,[13] working together, are building a wilderness of thousands of small islands off the southwestern coast of Florida, separated from each other by a tortuous[14] pattern of bays, lagoons, and narrow waterways, I remember a winter day when the sky was blue and drenched with sunlight; though there was no wind one was conscious of flowing air like cold clear crystal. I had landed on the surf-washed tip of one of those islands, and then worked my way around to the sheltered bay side. There I found the tide far out, exposing the broad mud flat of a cove bordered by the mangroves with their twisted branches, their glossy leaves, and their long prop roots reaching down, grasping and holding the mud, building the land out a little more, then again a little more.

> By **organizing** her essay around different examples of the edge of the sea at different times of day, Carson can share with readers the wide variety of life to be found at the edge of the sea.

The mud flats were strewn with the shells of that small, exquisitely colored mollusk,[15] the rose tellin, looking like scattered petals of pink roses. There must have been a colony nearby, living buried just under the surface of the mud. At first the only creature visible was a small heron in gray and rusty plumage—a reddish egret that waded across the flat with the stealthy, hesitant movements of its kind. But other land creatures had been there, for a line of fresh tracks wound in and out among the mangrove roots, marking the path of a raccoon feeding on the oysters that gripped the supporting roots with projections from their shells. Soon I found the tracks of a shore bird, probably a sanderling, and followed them a little; then they turned toward the water and were lost, for the tide had erased them and made them as though they had never been.

13. mangroves (maŋ´ grōvs) *n.*: Tropical trees that grow in swampy ground with spreading branches that send down roots and thus form more trunks.
14. tortuous (tôr´ cho͞o wəs) *adj.*: Full of twists and turns.
15. mollusk (mäl´ əsk) *n.*: One of a large group of soft-bodied animals with shells, including clams and snails.

Looking out over the cove I felt a strong sense of the interchangeability of land and sea in this marginal world of the shore, and of the links between the life of the two. There was also an awareness of the past and of the continuing flow of time, obliterating much that had gone before, as the sea had that morning washed away the tracks of the bird.

The sequence and meaning of the drift of time were quietly summarized in the existence of hundreds of small snails—the mangrove periwinkles—browsing on the branches and roots of the trees. Once their ancestors had been sea dwellers, bound to the salt waters by every tie of their life processes. Little by little over the thousands and millions of years the ties had been broken, the snails had adjusted themselves to life out of water, and now today they were living many feet above the tide to which they only occasionally returned. And perhaps, who could say how many ages hence, there would be in their descendants not even this gesture of remembrance for the sea. 6

> Here, Carson reinforces her **motivation**, to create in the reader a feeling of connection with nature.

The spiral shells of other snails—these quite minute[16]—left winding tracks on the mud as they moved about in search of food. They were horn shells, and when I saw them I had a nostalgic moment when I wished I might see what Audubon[17] saw, a century and more ago. For such little horn shells were the food of the flamingo, once so numerous on this coast, and when I half closed 7

16. minute (mī no͞ot´) *adj.*: Tiny.
17. Audubon (ôd´ ə bän´): John James Audubon (1785–1851), a famous ornithologist, naturalist, and painter famed for his paintings of North American birds.

◆ Build Vocabulary

primeval (prī mē´ vəl) *adj.*: Ancient or primitive
essence (es´ əns) *n.*: Real nature of something
marginal (mär´ jən əl) *adj.*: Occupying the borderland of a stable area

◆ Reading for Success

4 Identify Support for the Author's Points The author is explaining *how* the marginal world can remind us of creation. Ask how this description supports her main idea? *She shows how the mangroves build the land, creating it from the sea.*

◆ Reading for Success

5 Identify the Author's Main Points Have students summarize the main idea in this paragraph. Let them know that they will not find one sentence that states the main idea—they will have to pull the main idea from several sentences. *One of the things we can learn by studying the marginal world is that even when the shore looks empty and barren, close observation reveals that life exists there.*

◆ Critical Thinking

6 Generalize Ask students: What broader meaning about life does the author see in the snails' movement from sea to land? *The snails adaptation to a land environment over millions of years represents the force of evolution. It lets us know that we are connected to forms of life that came before us on the evolutionary scale and probably to life in the sea.*

7 Clarification Explain that Carson mentions Audubon here, not only because he lived a century ago when flamingos were more numerous than they are today, but also because he was known as a keen observer of nature. Ask: What do you suppose has happened to the flamingos? *They may have been run out of the groves by hunting, pollution, or many other causes.*

Reteach

Students who have difficulty following the descriptions in this essay may find it helpful to look for the author's pattern of organization. On the board, write headings that indicate three places she describes: the pool in the cave, the Georgia beach, and the Florida island. Have students suggest descriptive details to list under each heading.

Cave	Georgia beach	Florida island

Workplace Skills Mini-Lesson

Powers of Observation
The observational skills Carson applies to the world of tide pools are vital for a zoologist but useful for other workers as well.

Introduce Discuss what it means to have acute powers of observation: to notice details, to pay close attention, to be aware of things that others might miss.

Develop Review observations that students make in their lives; for example, observing details along an unfamiliar route or noticing that a friend got his or her hair trimmed.

Apply Have students list three summer jobs they might like to have and explain how powers of observation might help them to succeed in each one. For example, as a lifeguard, they would have to be very observant of all the people and activity in or near the water.

Assess Have volunteers share their ideas aloud. As a group, decide which of the described jobs requires the most acute powers of observation. Suggest that they write about several techniques they might use to improve their powers of observation before applying for such jobs.

▶Critical Viewing◀

❶ Compare and Contrast

Students might observe that the leaves appear more translucent than plants that grow on land, and that they are more delicate in both color and texture than land plants.

◆ Reading for Success

❷ Vary Your Reading Rate Suggest that students reread this sentence, slowing down to improve their understanding. Have them then paraphrase the author's statement. *Possible answer: The flamingos disappeared only a short while ago; sometimes a special occasion or place reminds us to think about the significance of time.*

◆ Reading for Success

❸ Identify the Author's Main Point Ask students to explain why this is an important sentence. How is it related to the author's main point? *Her main point is that we can learn much by studying the sea. This sentence states that the sea is more than beautiful—it is meaningful; that is, there is meaning to be gained from studying it.*

Reinforce and Extend

Answers

◆ Literature and Your Life

Reader's Response Students could name any aspect of nature—underwater life, stars and planets, woodland life. They should give reasons for their choices.

Thematic Focus Students might say that this essay deepened their understanding of the interrelatedness of life forms.

☑ Check Your Comprehension

1. She describes a pool in a cave at dawn.
2. She sees a starfish suspended from the ceiling and reflected in the pool.
3. She sees the edge of the low waters where many birds dwell; the shore at night and a single crab; an island off the southwest coast of Florida where she sees the mollusk, rose tellin.

❶ ▲ Critical Viewing How does this plant differ from plants that grow on land? **[Compare and Contrast]**

my eyes I could almost imagine a flock of these magnificent flame birds feeding in that cove, filling it with their color. It was a mere yesterday in the life of the earth that they were there; ❷ in nature, time and space are relative matters, perhaps most truly perceived subjectively in occasional flashes of insight, sparked by such a magical hour and place.

There is a common thread that links these scenes and memories—the spectacle of life in all its varied manifestations as it has appeared, evolved, and sometimes died out. Underlying the beauty of the spectacle there is meaning and significance. It is the elusiveness of that meaning that haunts us, that sends us again and again into the natural world where the key to the riddle is hidden. It sends us back to the edge of the sea, where the drama of life played its first scene on earth and perhaps even its prelude; where the forces of evolution are at work today, as they have been since the appearance of what we know as life; and where the spectacle of living creatures faced by the cosmic realities of their world is crystal clear.

◆ Build Vocabulary

subjectively (səb jek´ tiv lē) *adv.*: Personally

manifestations (man´ ə fes tā shənz) *n.*: Appearances or evidence

cosmic (käz´ mik) *adj.*: Relating to the universe

Guide for Responding

◆ Literature and Your Life

Reader's Response What aspects of nature intrigue you?

Thematic Focus What have you learned about nature from reading this essay?

Questions for Research Rachel Carson describes the fertility of the margins of the sea, but what about the depths? Generate research questions about the plant and animal life found in the deepest parts of the world's oceans.

☑ Check Your Comprehension

1. What time and special place does Carson describe first?
2. What special beauty does Carson find there?
3. Summarize the other times, places, and experiences Carson describes.

Beyond Literature

Cultural Connection

Pesticides Around the World Rachel Carson's book *Silent Spring* helped spark the environmental movement in this country. Through her work, the public learned about the way DDT and other pesticides can affect the broader environment. As a direct result, DDT was banned from general use in the United States by the early 1970's. DDT continued to be used in many nations, as are other pesticides no longer used here.

Activity Research the status of the environmental movement in another country, noting laws restricting the use of pesticides.

Beyond the Selection

FURTHER READING

Other Works by Rachel Carson

The Edge of the Sea
Silent Spring

Other Works With the Theme of Nature

Capturing Nature, John James Audubon
The Living Sea, Jacques-Yves Cousteau
Gentle Wilderness: The Sierra Nevada, John Muir

We suggest that you preview these works before recommending them to students.

INTERNET

We suggest the following sites on the Internet (all Web sites are subject to change)

For more about Rachel Carson, go to **http://www.teleport.com/~megaines/carson.htm**

An ecologically-minded newsletter based on Carson's life and work is located at **http://www.rachelcarson.org/newslett.html**

We *strongly recommend* that you preview the sites before you send students to them.

Guide for Responding (continued)

◆ Critical Thinking

INTERPRET

1. Explain Carson's statement, "The shore has a dual nature." **[Interpret]**
2. What broader meaning about life does the "marginal world" Carson describes help you to see? **[Interpret]**
3. Think of another title for this essay—one that states the meaning of the essay for you. **[Connect]**

EVALUATE

4. Compare the three different locations described in the essay. What are their similarities and differences? **[Compare and Contrast]**

APPLY

5. What other places could help you experience the interconnectedness of life? **[Relate]**

◆ Reading for Success

STRATEGIES FOR READING NONFICTION

Review the reading strategies and notes showing how to read nonfiction. Then apply those strategies to answer the following questions.

1. What is the author's main purpose in writing this essay?
2. (a) What three points does the author make about the sea and the creatures who inhabit it? (b) Explain how Carson supports each point.

◆ Literary Focus

EXPOSITORY ESSAY

An **expository essay** explains a concept, event, or process. In presenting information about life at the edge of the ocean, Carson explains the way plants and animals adapt to the changing environment.

1. Identify three reasons that Carson provides about why the level of the sea changes.
2. Explain the differences Carson identifies between the shore at night and the shore in daylight.
3. Summarize the main points Carson makes about the "marginal world."

◆ Build Vocabulary

USING THE LATIN SUFFIX *-able*

The Latin suffix *-able* means "capable of being." When added to the root of a word, it indicates the "ability" to do, provide, or be something.

On your paper, match each word ending in *-able* with the noun most closely associated with it.

1. perishable — a. truth
2. comfortable — b. couch
3. believable — c. food

USING THE WORD BANK: Synonym or Antonym?

For each of the following pairs of words, write *S* on your paper if the words are synonyms and *A* if they are antonyms.

1. essence, heart
2. manifestations, forms
3. marginal, borderline
4. mutable, solid
5. subjectively, disinterestedly
6. cosmic, earthly
7. ephemeral, short-lived
8. primeval, contemporary

◆ Build Grammar Skills

LINKING VERBS AND SUBJECT COMPLEMENTS

Rachel Carson uses **subject complements** following **linking verbs** to describe life where the earth and sea come together.

A **subject complement** is a noun, pronoun, or adjective that identifes or elaborates on the subject.

Practice Copy each sentence onto your paper. Label the linking verb in each sentence, then draw an arrow from the subject complement to the subject.

1. The projecting ledge was the path to the small hidden cave and its pool.
2. The shore is an ancient world . . .
3. For such little horn shells were the food of the flamingo . . .
4. . . . the moon was a luminous disc in the western sky . . .
5. . . . it is a world that keeps alive many creatures . . .

◆ Build Grammar Skills

Practice

1. The projecting ledge *was* the path to the small hidden cave and its pool.
2. The shore *is* an ancient world. . . .
3. For such little horns *were* the food of the flamingo.
4. the moon *was* a luminous disc in the western sky. . . .
5. . . . it *is* a world that keeps alive many creatures. . . .

Grammar Reinforcement

For additional instruction and practice, use the lesson in the **Language Lab CD-ROM** on Eight Parts of Speech to get information on linking verbs and p. 33 on Subject Complements in the *Writer's Solution Grammar Practice Book.*

Answers

◆ Critical Thinking

1. The shore is the meeting place between land and sea—its dual nature includes elements of both.
2. Carson communicates the broader meaning that all in nature is related—to each other and to past and future times.
3. Suggested titles: "Marine Life, Then and Now," "Changing Life on the Shore."
4. They are all part of shore life, but the locales and life they support differ: the cave pool has sponge, sea squirts, coral, and star fish; the beach in Georgia has willets, sanderlings, and other birds; the island off the coast of Florida has various kinds of mollusk.
5. Students might suggest forests, canyons, fields, or mountain areas.

◆ Reading for Success

1. Students might mention one of several possibilities: to show the interconnectedness of life forms, to communicate respect for shore life, to support her ideas as a conservationist.
2. Carson makes these points: (1) Life forms at the shore are enduring. Carson supports this with examples. (2) The shore is beautiful. Carson describes different locales at different times of day. (3) We can learn by studying the sea. Carson gives many examples of current and extinct species teaching us lessons about life.

◆ Literary Focus

1. The level of the sea rises and falls as glaciers melt or grow, as the ocean shifts, or as the earth's crust changes.
2. Whereas the daylight reveals different life forms and is filled with sounds of birds, the dark is quiet and so black that water, air, and beach seem to blend together.
3. The marginal world is beautiful; it teems with life that is strong and enduring; the forms of life support one another.

◆ Build Vocabulary

Using the Suffix *-able*

1. c 2. b 3. a

Using the Word Bank

1. s 2. s 3. s 4. a 5. a 6. a 7. s 8. a

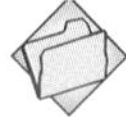

Idea Bank

Following are suggestions for matching Idea Bank topics with your students' performance levels and learning modalities:

Customizing for
Performance Levels

Less Advanced Students: 1, 4, 6
Average Students: 2, 5, 7
More Advanced Students: 3

Customizing for
Learning Modalities

Following are suggestions for matching Idea Bank topics with your students' learning modalities:
Visual/Spatial: 6, 7
Verbal/Linguistic: 4, 5
Rhythmic/Musical: 4
Logical/Mathematical: 3

Guided Writing Lesson

Elaboration Strategy As students describe a beautiful or exciting scene for their documentary proposals, they may find that they want more details. Have them draw a picture of the scene—if it is an outdoor nature scene, have them use an aerial view to capture the scene's details; if it is a microscopic look at nature, they can use a microscope's lens to enlarge the details.

For more prewriting, elaboration, and revision strategies, see *Prentice Hall Writing and Grammar.*

Writing and Language Transparencies Use the transparency for a Comparison-and-Contrast Organizer in ***Writing and Language Transparencies*** to help students identify comparisons in their proposals.

Writing Lab CD-ROM

Have students complete the tutorial on Description. Follow these steps:

1. Have students use the cluster diagram tool to connect details to the main idea of their proposals.
2. Suggest that students use the revision checker to find any vague or overused adjectives in the drafts of their proposals.

Build Your Portfolio

Idea Bank

Writing

1. **Letter** Imagine that you have been invited to accompany Rachel Carson on a nature excursion. Write a letter home to your family describing what you have seen and heard.
2. **Nature Report** Research at a library and write a report on an aspect of nature that you find interesting—a sunset, a blooming flower, a hawk's hunting habits. **[Science Link]**
3. **Cause-and-Effect Essay** Write a cause-and-effect essay on how the sea has eroded rocks and shorelines over the past thousands of years. **[Science Link]**

Speaking, Listening, and Viewing

4. **Poetry Reading** Oceans and rivers have long been an inspiration to writers and poets. Choose and recite a poem about the ocean or the tides to your class.
5. **Photo Essay** Environmental groups have used visual imagery, especially photographs, to great effect in building support for their positions. Collect a series of five photographs on environmental themes from magazines, brochures, or other sources, and create a photo essay.

Researching and Representing

6. **Art Exhibit** Create a classroom display with photographs and sketches that capture the magical or mysterious quality of the shore. Use a quotation from "The Marginal World" as a caption for each picture. **[Art Link]**
7. **The Living Sea** Use natural objects, photos, video, and music to give a multimedia presentation about the beauty of the ocean to your class. **[Science Link]**

Online Activity www.phlit.phschool.com

Guided Writing Lesson

Proposal for a Nature Documentary

The descriptive passages about the unpredictable sea in "The Marginal World" lend themselves to spectacular documentary footage! Write a **proposal** for a nature documentary for a science television program. Your documentary can be abo any element of nature that interests you. Your proposal will present your plan for the documentary, summarizing the content and pointing out any special features that it will include. You will probably want to make comparisons in your documentary. The following tip will help you to do that effective

Writing Skills Focus: Transitions to Show Comparisons

As you draft your proposal, use **transitional words**—such as *like, likewise, in contrast, similarly, nevertheless,* and *in the same way*—to show comparisons.

Rachel Carson uses a transition to compare bir to moths: "Black skimmers flew along the ocean's edge . . . *like* large, dimly seen moths."

Prewriting Decide on a topic for your documentary and then list all the elements you'll capture or film, including scenery and sounds. Jot down comparisons that you will use to show the similarities or differences between two items.

Drafting Use vivid descriptions to make your proposal appealing. Include a summary of an especially exciting or beautiful scene you plan to include. Indicate similarities between scenes and ideas with transitional words.

Revising Look over your proposal. Add transitio where necessary. Ask a partner to read your proposal to make sure it is clear and engaging.

✓ ASSESSMENT OPTIONS

Formal Assessment, Selection Test, pp. 145–147, and Assessment Resources Software. The selection test is designed so that it can be easily customized to the performance levels of your students.
Alternative Assessment, p. 41, includes options for less advanced students, more advanced students, verbal/linguistic learners, interpersonal learners, musical/rhythmic learners, and visual/spatial learners, logical/mathematical learners.

PORTFOLIO ASSESSMENT
Use the following rubrics in the ***Alternative Assessment*** booklet to assess student writing:
Letter: Description Rubric, p. 97
Nature Report: Research Report Rubric p. 106
Cause-and-Effect Essay: Cause-and-Effect Rubric p. 102

Part 1

Biographies and Personal Accounts

Cover, 1980, John Hall, Art Gallery of Hamilton, Canada

Humanities: Art

Cover, 1980, by John Hall.

Encourage students to appreciate the self-referential aspects of this painting, which is a little like a visual riddle or joke. Help them see that the painting is most likely a self-portrait, since the man above the word "COVER" seems to be working intently in what looks like an artist's studio—the central, square part of this painting is supposed to represent a protective cover for another painting that is wrapped up like a present to someone.

Students can link the artwork to the focus of Part 1, "Biographies and Personal Accounts":

1. If this is a self-portrait, what ideas about the artist does it give you? *It suggests that he is witty and likes to hide things, that he gets very caught up in his work and probably thinks his work is more important than he is.*
2. This is a painting that has very realistic details and almost looks like a photograph. In what ways might it be similar to a personal account of an actual event? *Students may suggest that this type of combined creativity and reality works with reality but does something personal and imaginative with it.*

One-Minute Planning Guide

The essays in Part 1 are all biographical or personal in content. They illustrate different types of essays. In "The Way to Rainy Mountain," Momaday reflects on the value of his grandmother's life and culture. Alexander Solzhenitsyn's Nobel Lecture makes a persuasive case for the solidarity of world writers against oppression, and Elie Wiesel in "Keep Memory Alive" makes a persuasive plea that readers not forget the horrors of the Holocaust. In "A Child's Christmas in Wales," Dylan Thomas remembers his childhood Christmas experiences. Langston Hughes offers a biographical portrait of the great opera singer Marian Anderson. In "Flood," a descriptive essay, Annie Dillard provides personal observations on a local flood.

Customizing for *Varying Student Needs*

The following factors may guide you in assigning the selections in this part.

"The Way to Rainy Mountain"

- Narrative, descriptive structure is accessible

Nobel Lecture; "Keep Memory Alive"

- The essays are brief, but concepts are more challenging

"A Child's Christmas in Wales"

- Somewhat complex descriptive language may challenge less proficient readers or ESL Students
- Humorous, narrative incidents make the essay appealing

"Marian Anderson: Famous Concert Singer"

- Short essay (four pages)
- Easily understandable language

"Flood"

- Language is straightforward, but the lack of narrative structure may make the essay hard for some students to follow.

Art Transparency Before you introduce Part 1, display Art Transparency 6. Call on volunteers to share anything they may know about George Washington Carver and his achievements—they might use the details in Johnson's painting for their responses. Discuss the "window" into events that biographical material can provide and the distinctions between biographies and personal accounts.

Prepare and Engage

LESSON OBJECTIVES

1. **To develop vocabulary and word identification skills**
   - Related Words: Forms of *reciprocity*
   - Using the Word Bank: Connotations
   - Extending Word Study: Thesaurus (ATE)
2. **To use a variety of reading strategies to read and comprehend an essay**
   - Connect Your Experience
   - Reading Strategy: Analyze the Author's Purpose
   - Read to Interpret (ATE)
3. **To increase knowledge of other cultures and to connect common elements across cultures**
   - Connecting Themes Across Cultures (ATE)
   - Cultural Connection (ATE)
4. **To express and support responses to the text**
   - Critical Thinking
   - Analyze a Musical Review (ATE)
   - Idea Bank: Letter
5. **To analyze literary elements**
   - Literary Focus: Reflective and Persuasive Essays
6. **To read in order to research self-selected and assigned topics**
   - Idea Bank: Report
   - Idea Bank: Native American Dances
   - Idea Bank: Writers-in-Prison
7. **To plan, prepare, organize, and present literary interpretations**
   - Speaking, Listening, and Viewing Mini-Lesson: Persuasive Speech (ATE)
8. **To use recursive writing processes to write an acceptance speech**
   - Guided Writing Lesson
9. **To increase knowledge of the rules of grammar and usage**
   - Build Grammar Skills: Capitalization of Proper Nouns and Adjectives

Test Preparation

Reading Comprehension: Comparing and Contrasting Texts (ATE, p. 581) The teaching tips and sample test item in this workshop support the instruction and practice in the unit workshop.

Reading Comprehension: Comparing and Contrasting Texts; Analyzing Literary Language (SE, p. 661)

Guide for Reading

N. Scott Momaday *(1934–)*

A Kiowa Indian, N. Scott Momaday's interest in Native American culture and history began as a child, when he lived on several Indian reservations where his parents taught. Momaday earned a doctoral degree from Stanford University, where he now teaches English. His first novel, *House Made of Dawn,* was awarded a Pulitzer Prize. *The Way to Rainy Mountain* includes his impressions of contemporary Kiowa culture and world view, as well as their history and legends.

Alexander Solzhenitsyn *(1918–)*

A dissident is one who departs from established opinion, and the Russian writer Alexander Solzhenitsyn has been a dissident his whole literary life. His first book, *A Day in the Life of Ivan Denisovitch*—the story of an inmate in a Soviet labor camp—was banned in the Soviet Union. Solzhenitsyn was tried for treason and exiled after the publication in Paris of parts of *The Gulag Archipelago*. Only since 1991 has his work been available to the people of his homeland. This excerpt from his Nobel lecture reflects on what it means to be part of a great world literature.

Elie Wiesel *(1928–)*

The Romanian-born teacher, philosopher, and writer Elie Wiesel was deported to the Nazi death camp at Auschwitz at age sixteen. His parents and sister were killed, and he was forced into slave labor at Buchenwald, another Nazi death camp. After surviving the war, Wiesel studied in France and moved to the United States in 1956. In his first book, *Night,* Wiesel recounts the horrors of his experiences at the hands of the Nazis.

Elie Wiesel has been awarded the Congressional Gold Medal of Achievement and the Nobel Peace Prize. He delivered the speech here in 1986, in acceptance of that prize.

◆ Build Vocabulary

RELATED WORDS: FORMS OF *RECIPROCITY*

"Today," Alexander Solzhenitsyn writes, "there is an almost instant *reciprocity*" between the writers of one country and the readers and writers of another. The word *reciprocity,* which means a "mutual action or dependence," has several forms. As the adjective *reciprocal,* it means "something done in response to something else" or simply, "mutual." As the verb *reciprocate,* it means "to do in return."

WORD BANK

Before you read, preview this list of words from the selections.

engender
tenuous
reciprocity
assimilate
inexorably
oratory
transcends

◆ Build Grammar Skills

CAPITALIZATION OF PROPER NOUNS AND ADJECTIVES

In these selections, you'll see many **proper nouns and adjectives**. All proper nouns and proper adjectives begin with capital letters. Proper nouns name specific places, people, and things.

Name of Place: Rainy Mountain
Name of Region: the West
Name of Group: the Kiowas
Name of Thing: Nobel Prize

Proper adjectives are adjectives made from proper nouns. For instance, the following examples come from the proper nouns the *West* and *Europe:*

Western writers
European writers

Prentice Hall Literature Program Resources

REINFORCE / RETEACH / EXTEND

Selection Support Pages
Build Vocabulary: Forms of *Reciprocity*, p. 172
Build Grammar Skills: Capitalization of Proper Nouns and Adjectives, p. 173
Reading Strategy: Author's Purpose, p. 174
Literary Focus: Reflective and Persuasive Essays, p. 175

Strategies for Diverse Student Needs, p. 42

Beyond Literature *Art*, p. 42

Formal Assessment Selection Test, pp. 148–150; Assessment Resources Software

Alternative Assessment, p. 42 material and customizable lesson plan

Resource Pro CD-ROM

Listening to Literature Audiocassettes

from The Way to Rainy Mountain ◆ from Nobel Lecture ◆ Keep Memory Alive ◆

◆ Literature and Your Life

Connect Your Experience

We all have memories, and we cherish those that are most important to us. Writers often relive their most vivid or important memories by recording them. These three works of literature are the records of three authors' recollections and reflections on important events in their lives.

Thematic Focus: From the Past

Memoirists and historic novelists, among others, reflect on the past in their writing. What do writers gain by reflecting on the past?

Journal Writing Jot down two or three memories that have stayed with you since childhood.

◆ Background for Understanding

Literature

One of the highest honors a writer can receive is to be awarded the Nobel Prize for Literature. The Nobel Prizes—which include awards in physics, chemistry, medicine, literature, and peace—were established by a Swede, Alfred Nobel, the inventor of dynamite. Wanting to be associated not with destruction but with peace, Nobel set up a fund to finance annual achievement and peace awards.

Both Alexander Solzhenitsyn and Elie Wiesel were awarded Nobel Prizes—Solzhenitsyn for literature and Wiesel for peace.

◆ Literary Focus

Reflective and Persuasive Essays

In a **reflective essay,** an author shares his or her thoughts about an idea or a personal experience. In the excerpt from *The Way to Rainy Mountain,* Momaday reflects on the death of his grandmother and the passing of the Kiowa culture.

A **persuasive essay** attempts to convince readers to adopt a particular opinion or course of action. Solzhenitsyn's and Wiesel's speeches use persuasive language and sound reasons to convince you that their ideas are worth embracing.

◆ Reading Strategy

Analyze the Author's Purpose

An **author's purpose** is the reason he or she is writing; for example, to inform or to entertain. N. Scott Momaday has a dual purpose in writing—to honor his grandmother's memory and to inform you about a culture that has been largely lost. The other two authors in this group, Solzhenitsyn and Wiesel, have the purpose of persuading you to adopt their opinion or point of view.

Each author's purpose comes with a set of criteria by which you can measure its success. For example, with a persuasive piece, ask yourself: Is it well-reasoned? Are the author's arguments supported by facts when appropriate? Does the author use persuasive language effectively?

Momaday's purpose is broader, and it can be analyzed according to each of its aims. Ask yourself: Have I gotten to know Momaday's grandmother in the way he intended? Did I gain interesting or useful information about the Kiowa Indian culture?

Answering questions like these will help you to formulate your own questions and make your own determination about the success of an author's purpose.

On the chalkboard, write the phrase "to bear witness." Then ask students to imagine the following scene: A strange-looking army comes in and abducts their entire class. Only one student escapes, and he or she returns to school a week later. Ask why it would be important for that student to explain what happened—to bear witness? Lead students to see that people who have experienced significant or harsh events need to inform others—both for their own sake and to try to prevent further atrocities. All the writers in this grouping have witnessed injustice: Momaday's Kiowa people have been oppressed, Wiesel fell victim to the Nazis, and Solzhenitsyn was a political prisoner. Writers who bear witness bring injustice to light.

Connecting Themes Across Cultures

N. Scott Momaday explains how his grandmother could describe the Black Hills, where she had never been, because she had heard about the place in stories. This is a common experience for all children. They may know details of their parents' or grandparents' past experiences. Invite students to share details of their own family's' pasts that they may have learned from stories.

Customize for *Less Proficient Readers*

Less proficient readers may benefit from hearing the two speeches read aloud. Play the recordings of Solzhenitsyn's Nobel Lecture and "Keep Memory Alive" as students read along in their texts.

Customize for *Pre-AP Students*

Suggest that students examine figurative language in "The Way to Rainy Mountain" and notice how Momaday uses it to evoke a vivid sense of place. They can jot down some examples in their journals and experiment with rewriting them or with using similar language in their own writing.

Test Preparation Workshop

Reading Comprehension: Comparing and Contrasting Texts

Standardized tests such as the SAT require students to compare and contrast aspects of two texts. These aspects may include themes, conflicts, and allusions. After students have read the selections, write this sample test question on the board.

What common theme appears in both "The Way to Rainy Mountain" and "Keep Memory Alive"?

A the meaningfulness of landscape
B the importance of remembering
C the tragedy of the destruction of a culture
D the horror of the death camps

Suggest that students begin by ruling out choices that apply to only one selection, such as A and D. Then help them recognize that C is not an accurate depiction of "Keep Memory Alive." B is the correct answer.

Develop Understanding

One-Minute Insight Like all the essays in this grouping, "The Way to Rainy Mountain" focuses on the importance of memory in understanding the lessons of the past. In this essay, N. Scott Momaday weaves together his love for tradition, nature, and community to give his message a particular essence—the spiritual essence of the Kiowa.

▶Critical Viewing◀

1 Relate *The body language of the Native American men in this painting expresses a variety of emotions: The man crouching on the right seems stern and serious; the man in the black hat next to him seems thoughtful; the pose of the older man in the center expresses resistance or stubbornness. Students might also note the man turning away in the background; perhaps he is indifferent. As a whole, this group seems serious.*

Customize for *English Language Learners*

Write these terms from "The Way to Rainy Mountain" on the chalkboard: *Rainy Mountain, Sun Dance Doll, land of Crows and Blackfeet.* Explain to students that Native American groups such as the Kiowa respect and often worship nature. As a mark of respect, they frequently name people, places, and things after animals and elements of nature.

from The Way to RAINY MOUNTAIN

N. Scott Momaday

Old Ones Talking, R. Brownell McGrew, Courtesy of the artist

1 ▲ **Critical Viewing** Describe three emotions or attitudes you see depicted in this painting. **[Relate]**

Block Scheduling Strategies

Consider these suggestions to take advantage of extended class time:

- Introduce types of essays, and indicate that these essays are examples of reflective and persuasive essays. Have students read the Literary Focus on p. 581 and, after reading the essays, answer the Literary Focus questions on p. 592.
- You may wish to break the class into three groups and assign each group to read and analyze one essay. Have groups prepare a brief presentation in which they "teach" their essay to the other groups, with special attention to the features of the essay type and the authors' purposes. Students can evaluate one another's presentations after reading all three essays.
- After students have read the selection, review the questions posed in the Reading Strategy feature on p. 581. Do students feel they now know Momaday's grandmother? Was the information on the Kiowa useful and significant? How would they describe Momaday's overall purpose in writing, and did he achieve his purpose?
- Direct students to work in discussion groups to answer the Critical Thinking questions on pp. 586, 589, and 591.
- Some students can develop the Report in the Idea Bank on p. 593. Encourage them to include information on other groups that suffered repression in the Soviet Union of the 1940's and 1950's.

A single knoll rises out of the plain in Oklahoma, north and west of the Wichita Range.[1] For my people, the Kiowas, it is an old landmark, and they gave it the name Rainy Mountain. The hardest weather in the world is there. Winter brings blizzards, hot tornadic winds arise in the spring, and in summer the prairie is an anvil's edge.[2] The grass turns brittle and brown, and it cracks beneath your feet. There are green belts along the rivers and creeks, linear groves of hickory and pecan, willow and witch hazel. At a distance in July or August the steaming foliage seems almost to writhe[3] in fire. Great green and yellow grasshoppers are everywhere in the tall grass, popping up like corn to sting the flesh, and tortoises crawl about on the red earth, going nowhere in the plenty of time. Loneliness is an aspect of the land. All things in the plain are isolate; there is no confusion of objects in the eye, but *one* hill or *one* tree or *one* man. To look upon that landscape in the early morning, with the sun at your back, is to lose the sense of proportion. Your imagination comes to life, and this, you think, is where Creation was begun.

I returned to Rainy Mountain in July. My grandmother had died in the spring, and I wanted to be at her grave. She had lived to be very old and at last infirm.[4] Her only living daughter was with her when she died, and I was told that in death her face was that of a child.

> ◆ **Reading Strategy**
> Why do you think Momaday included this detail?

I like to think of her as a child. When she was born, the Kiowas were living the last great moment of their history. For more than a hundred years they had controlled the open range from the Smoky Hill River to the Red, from the headwaters of the Canadian to the fork of the Arkansas and Cimarron. In alliance with the Comanches, they had ruled the whole of the southern Plains. War was their sacred business, and they were among the finest horsemen the world has ever known. But warfare for the Kiowas was preeminently a matter of disposition rather than of survival, and they never understood the grim, unrelenting advance of the U.S. Cavalry. When at last, divided and ill-provisioned, they were driven onto the Staked Plains in the cold rains of autumn, they fell into panic. In Palo Duro Canyon they abandoned their crucial stores to pillage[5] and had nothing then but their lives. In order to save themselves, they surrendered to the soldiers at Fort Sill and were imprisoned in the old stone corral that now stands as a military museum. My grandmother was spared the humiliation of those high gray walls by eight or ten years, but she must have known from birth the affliction of defeat, the dark brooding of old warriors.

Her name was Aho, and she belonged to the last culture to evolve in North America. Her forebears came down from the high country in western Montana nearly three centuries ago. They were a mountain people, a mysterious tribe of hunters whose language has never been positively classified in any major group. In the late seventeenth century they began a long migration to the south and east. ❺ It was a journey toward the dawn, and it led to a golden age. Along the way the Kiowas were befriended by the Crows, who gave them the culture and religion of the Plains. They acquired horses, and their ancient nomadic spirit was suddenly free of the ground. They acquired Tai-me, the sacred Sun Dance doll, from that moment the object and symbol of their worship, and so shared in the divinity of the sun. Not least, they acquired the sense of destiny, therefore courage and pride. When they entered upon the southern Plains they had been transformed. No longer were they slaves to the simple necessity of survival; they were a lordly and dangerous society of fighters and thieves, hunters and priests of the sun. According to their origin myth, they entered the world through a hollow log. From one point of view, their migration was the fruit of an old prophecy,

1. **Wichita** (wich ə tô´) **Range:** Mountain range in southwestern Oklahoma.
2. **anvil's edge:** Edge of the iron or steel block on which metal objects are hammered into shape.
3. **writhe** (rīth) *v.*: Twist in pain and agony.
4. **infirm** (in furm´) *adj.*: Weak; feeble.
5. **pillage** (pil´ ij) *n.*: Act of robbing and destroying, especially during wartime.

◆ Literary Focus

❷ **Reflective Essays** Ask: What characteristics in this paragraph indicate that it is part of a reflective essay? *The writer is describing a scene from his own past. His language is descriptive, and he includes his own thoughts and feelings about what he observes, as in "Loneliness is an aspect of the land."*

◆ Reading Strategy

❸ **Analyze the Author's Purpose** By saying that in death his grandmother's face was the face of a child, Momaday is revealing an aspect of her personality—her innocence—and arousing the reader's curiosity about his grandmother.

◆ Build Grammar Skills

❹ **Capitalization of Proper Nouns and Adjectives** Point out that the word *red*, which is not a proper adjective by itself, is capitalized in this sentence. Ask students to draw a conclusion about why *red* is capitalized here. *Students will probably guess that Red is part of the name of a place. This is correct; red becomes a proper adjective as part of the name Red River.*

◆ Reading Strategy

❺ **Analyze the Author's Purpose** Ask students why they think the author includes the information that the Kiowa's language has never been positively classified. *He is emphasizing the group's uniqueness to make it seem even more tragic that their traditions are fading away.*

Humanities: Art

Old Ones Talking by R. Brownell McGrew.

R. Brownell McGrew is a Native American artist who often focuses on Native American life as the subject of his paintings.

This painting depicts a group of Native American men gathered in the woods. The golden light of the sun through the trees illuminates the background and reflects off the colorful tones of the men's clothing, as it does off the ground and tree trunks, making the men seem a part of the natural surroundings and emphasizing the feeling of oneness with nature that comes forth in Momaday's piece.

Use these questions for discussion:

1. What specific aspects of their clothing suggest that the men in this painting are caught between native traditional and mainstream cultures? *Their jeans, shirts, and hats are items of contemporary western clothing, while their beads and jewelry and the hair of the man in the background are part of the customary dress of their American Indian tradition.*
2. How does the painting remind you of the description Momaday gives of the old warlords who visit his grandmother? *The men wear black hats and bright shirts; they have strips of cloth wound around their hair.*

◆ Reading Strategy

❶ Analyze the Author's Purpose Have students determine why the author includes this detail about the mountains in his essay. *It shows how much the Kiowa valued freedom; they preferred to be in an open environment where they could see the horizon, rather than enclosed by forests and mountains. This adds to the reader's knowledge about Momaday's people and their lives.*

◆ Literature and Your Life

❷ Ask students if there is a place in nature that makes them feel the "awful quiet" that Momaday mentions here. *Answers should focus on places that evoke a feeling of awe and a sense of the past.*

Extending Word Study

Thesaurus Momaday's descriptions paint vivid word pictures of the landscape. For instance, "the highland meadows are a stairway to the plain," "the earth unfolds," "the limit of the land recedes" are phrases that could have been written in a more basic style. Have students use a thesaurus to rephrase these descriptions. Then ask them to compare their phrases with Momaday's to increase their appreciation of vivid word choice.

Humanities: Art

Annie Old Crow by James Bama.

This painting of a Native American woman, done in the style of a portrait, seems to convey a quiet dignity. Have students note the jewelry and the decorative elements in the woman's braids and on her dress. You might have students discuss the strengths and weaknesses the portrait seems to reveal.

1. How are the struggles that the author's grandmother faced throughout her lifetime reflected in this woman's face? *The face shows many wrinkles, which seem to indicate a difficult life. Her expression seems to be one of acceptance or resignation.*
2. Are the traits shown in this painting similar to those demonstrated by the grandmother in the essay? *The woman in this painting shows strength, great age, and some sadness, but her bearing shows dignity. All of these qualities are those of the grandmother in the essay.*

for indeed they emerged from a sunless world.

Although my grandmother lived out her long life in the shadow of Rainy Mountain, the immense landscape of the continental interior lay like memory in her blood. She could tell of the Crows, whom she had never seen, and of the Black Hills, where she had never been. I wanted to see in reality what she had seen more perfectly in the mind's eye, and traveled fifteen hundred miles to begin my pilgrimage.

Yellowstone,[6] it seemed to me, was the top of the world, a region of deep lakes and dark timber, canyons and waterfalls. But, beautiful as it is, one might have the sense of confinement there. The skyline in all directions is close at hand, the high wall of the woods and deep cleavages of shade. There is a perfect freedom in the mountains, but it belongs to the eagle and the elk, the badger and the bear. ❶ The Kiowas reckoned their stature by the distance they could see, and they were bent and blind in the wilderness.

Descending eastward, the highland meadows are a stairway to the plain. In July the inland slope of the Rockies is luxuriant with flax and buckwheat, stonecrop and larkspur. The earth unfolds and the limit of the land recedes. Clusters of trees, and animals grazing far in the distance, cause the vision to reach away and wonder to build upon the mind. The sun follows a longer course in the day, and the sky is immense beyond all comparison. The great billowing clouds that sail upon it are shadows that move upon the brain like water, dividing light. Farther down, in the land of the Crows and Blackfeet, the plain is yellow. Sweet clover takes hold of the hills and bends upon itself to cover and seal the soil. There the Kiowas paused on their way; they had come to the place where they must change their lives. The sun is at home on the plains. Precisely there does it have the certain character of a god. When the Kiowas came to the land of the Crows, they could see the dark lees of the hills at dawn across the Bighorn River, the profusion of light on the grain shelves, the oldest deity ranging after the solstices. Not yet would they veer southward to the caldron[7] of the land that lay below; they must wean their blood from the northern winter and hold the mountains a while longer in their view. They bore Tai-me in procession to the east.

A dark mist lay over the Black Hills, and the land was like iron. At the top of a ridge I caught sight of Devil's Tower upthrust against the gray sky as if in the birth of time the core of the earth had broken through its crust and the motion of the world was begun. There are things in nature that engender an awful quiet in the heart of man; Devil's Tower is one of them. Two centuries ago, because they could not do otherwise, the Kiowas made a legend at the base of the rock. My grandmother said:

Eight children were there at play, seven sisters and their brother. Suddenly the boy was struck dumb; he trembled and began to run upon his hands and feet. His fingers became claws, and his body was covered with fur. Directly there was a bear where the boy had been. The sisters were terrified; they ran, and the bear after them. They came to the stump of a great tree, and the tree spoke to them. It bade them climb upon it, and as they did so it began to rise in the air. The bear came to kill them, but they were just beyond its reach. It reared against the tree and scored the bark all around with its claws. The seven sisters were borne into the sky, and they became the stars of the Big Dipper.

From that moment, and so long as the legend lives, the Kiowas have kinsmen in the night sky. Whatever they were in the mountains, they could be no more. However tenuous their well-being, however much they had suffered and would suffer again, they had found a way out of the wilderness.

My grandmother had a reverence for the sun, a holy regard that now is all but gone out of mankind. There was a wariness in her, and an

6. **Yellowstone:** Yellowstone National Park, mostly in northwestern Wyoming but including narrow strips in southern Montana and eastern Idaho.

7. **caldron** (kôl′ drən) *n.*: Heat like that of a boiling kettle.

Cross-Curricular Connection: Social Studies

The Kiowa Explain to students that the Kiowa Indians lived in the southern plains of North America. Buffalo hunters, they lived in lodges made of skin that they could transport easily from place to place. Like many Native Americans, their lifestyle was compromised as settlers discovered the vast open spaces of the plains. They vigorously protested white settlement in their territory and were hostile to settlers until 1875. After many Kiowa leaders were imprisoned and their horses taken, the Kiowa retreated to a reservation in southwestern Oklahoma.

Regional Native Americans Suggest that students research the history and influence of the Native Americans in your area. For instance, you may wish to point out that is likely that the local agricultural products that feed and support your community originated with the Native Americans' natural use of the land hundreds of years ago

Suggest that students consider what signs—such as place names, celebrations, or local art—suggest a Native American influence on the community? What was their relationship with white settlers in the area?

ancient awe. She was a Christian in her later years, but she had come a long way about, and she never forgot her birthright. As a child she had been to the Sun Dances; she had taken part in those annual rites, and by them she had learned the restoration of her people in the presence of Tai-me. She was about seven when the last Kiowa Sun Dance was held in 1887 on the Washita River above Rainy Mountain Creek. The buffalo were gone. In order to consummate the ancient sacrifice—to impale the head of a buffalo bull upon the medicine tree—a delegation of old men journeyed into Texas, there to beg and barter for an animal from the Goodnight herd. She was ten when the Kiowas came together for the last time as a living Sun Dance culture. They could find no buffalo; they had to hang an old hide from the sacred tree. Before the dance could begin, a company of soldiers rode out from Fort Sill under orders to disperse the tribe. Forbidden without cause the essential act of their faith, having seen the wild herds slaughtered and left to rot upon the ground, the Kiowas backed away forever from the medicine tree. That was July 20, 1890, at the great bend of the Washita. My grandmother was there. Without bitterness, and for as long as she lived, she bore a vision of deicide.[8]

Now that I can have her only in memory, I see my grandmother in the several postures that were peculiar to her: standing at the wood stove on a winter morning and turning meat in a great iron skillet; sitting at the south window, bent above her beadwork, and afterwards, when her vision failed, looking down for a long time into the fold of her hands; going out upon a cane, very slowly as she did when the weight of age came upon her; praying. I remember her most often at prayer. She made long, rambling prayers out of suffering and hope, having seen many things. I was never sure that I had the right to hear, so exclusive were they of all mere custom and company. The last time I saw her she prayed standing by the side of her bed at night, naked to the waist, the light of a kerosene lamp moving upon her dark skin. Her long, black hair, always drawn and braided in the day, lay upon her shoulders and against her breasts like a shawl. I do not speak Kiowa, and I never understood her prayers, but there was something inherently sad in the sound, some merest hesitation upon the syllables of sorrow. She began in a high and descending pitch, exhausting her breath to silence; then again and again—and always the same intensity of effort, of something that is, and is not, like urgency in the human voice. Transported so in the dancing light among the shadows of her room, she seemed beyond the reach of time. But that was illusion; I think I knew then that I should not see her again. 5 6

◆ Literary Focus
How do Momaday's recollections of his grandmother reflect his feelings for her?

Pouch, Kiowa ca. 1890–1910, New York State Historical Association, Cooperstown

Houses are like sentinels in the plain, old keepers of the weather watch. There, in a very little while, wood takes on the appearance of great age. All colors wear soon away in the wind and rain, and then the wood is burned gray and the grain appears and the nails turn red with rust. The windowpanes are black and opaque; you imagine there is nothing within, and indeed there are many ghosts, bones given up to the land. They stand here and there against the sky, and you approach them for a longer time than you expect. They belong in the distance; it is their domain.

Once there was a lot of sound in my grandmother's house, a lot of coming and going, feasting and talk. The summers there were full of excitement and reunion. The Kiowas are a summer people; they abide the cold and keep to themselves, but when the season turns and the land becomes warm and vital they cannot hold still; an old love of going returns upon them. The aged visitors who came to my grandmother's

8. **deicide** (dē′ ə sīd′) *n.*: Killing of a god.

◆ Build Vocabulary
engender (in jen′ dər) *v.* Bring about; cause; produce
tenuous (ten′ yōō əs) *adj.*: Slight; flimsy; not substantial or strong

◆ Critical Thinking

3 Infer Ask students how they think the ending of the Sun Dance affected Momaday and his grandmother. *His grandmother remembers it "Without bitterness," but the author appears to resent that the Kiowas were "Forbidden without cause the essential act of their faith, . . ."*

◆ Literary Focus

4 Reflective Essay The details Momaday chooses to describe his grandmother—such as her attention to her work and her prayers—indicate his respect and affection for her.

◆ Reading Strategy

5 Analyze the Author's Purpose Have students determine why the author reveals these details about his grandmother. *His strongest memories are of her at prayer. Her prayers reflected all the things she saw and suffered in her life; they were an essential part of her, and Momaday is showing respect for her privacy.*

◆ Critical Thinking

6 Interpret Ask students: What does Momaday mean by saying his grandmother ". . . seemed beyond the reach of time"? Why was that an illusion? *When she was praying, his grandmother seemed more like a symbol than an individual, and therefore as if she would not die; however, that was an illusion—she was mortal, and she did die.*

Customize for
Gifted/Talented Students
Let students know that M. Scott Momaday is also a poet. Suggest that students create poems describing the grandmother from the author's point of view. Ask students to share their poems with the class.

Cross-Curricular Connection: Art

Native American Beadwork Tell students that in the early 1800's, traders introduced glass beads to the Native Americans. Decorating in beads gradually replaced porcupine quill work. Women usually sewed beads onto buckskin clothing or bags, but some groups developed weaving techniques. The bead designs were mostly geometric, though around the turn of the century floral patterns became popular. The Cheyenne were known for creating sacred designs in beads; their decorations on cradle boards and moccasins symbolized protection and long life.

Interested students might enjoy finding out more about the meaning and technique of beadwork in different Native American groups, particularly the beadwork of the Kiowa. Suggest that students try some of the beadwork designs themselves. They can start by trying to work out a design on a T-shirt.

◆ Reading Strategy

1 Analyze the Author's Purpose Ask students: What is Momaday's purpose in reflecting back in this passage? *The author is comparing the liveliness and warmth of the meetings of elders to the silence and loneliness he now senses in his grandmother's rooms.*

◆ Literary Focus

2 Reflective Essay Ask students: Why does the author look back at his grandmother's grave? Why does he then come away? *The author feels he is breaking with his past, and he still feels drawn to it; he is able to come away because he realizes that he will always have the past in his memory.*

Reinforce and Extend

Answers

◆ *Literature and Your Life*

Reader's Response Students might be interested in exploring their cultural roots so that they can find out more about their personal identity.

Thematic Focus By reflecting on the past, students can put present-day events into perspective.

☑ Check Your Comprehension

1. They made up a legend to explain Devil's Tower.
2. Possible activities include feasting and talking, reminiscing, cooking, prayer meetings, the cousins playing together.

◆ Critical Thinking

1. Momaday is paying homage to the lost way of life of the Kiowa and specifically to the life of his grandmother.
2. Students might suggest that Momaday's reflection about the cricket could also apply to the Kiowa—that the spirit of the culture lives on in eternity.
3. Students should see that Momaday's life has bridged two cultures—Kiowa and mainstream contemporary American—much more than did his grandmother's life.

house when I was a child were made of lean and leather, and they bore themselves upright. They wore great black hats and bright ample shirts that shook in the wind. They rubbed fat upon their hair and wound their braids with strips of colored cloth. Some of them painted their faces and carried the scars of old and cherished enmities. They were an old council of warlords, come to remind and be reminded of who they were.
1 Their wives and daughters served them well. The women might indulge themselves; gossip was at once the mark and compensation of their servitude. They made loud and elaborate talk among themselves, full of jest and gesture, fright and false alarm. They went abroad in fringed and flowered shawls, bright beadwork and German silver. They were at home in the kitchen, and they prepared meals that were banquets.

There were frequent prayer meetings, and great nocturnal feasts. When I was a child I played with my cousins outside, where the lamplight fell upon the ground and the singing of the old people rose up around us and carried away into the darkness. There were a lot of good things to eat, a lot of laughter and surprise. And afterwards, when the quiet returned, I lay down with my grandmother and could hear the frogs away by the river and feel the motion of the air.

Now there is a funeral silence in the rooms, the endless wake of some final word. The walls have closed in upon my grandmother's house. When I returned to it in mourning, I saw for the first time in my life how small it was. It was late at night, and there was a white moon, nearly full. I sat for a long time on the stone steps by the kitchen door. From there I could see out across the land; I could see the long row of trees by the creek, the low light upon the rolling plains, and the stars of the Big Dipper. Once I looked at the moon and caught sight of a strange thing. A cricket had perched upon the handrail, only a few inches away from me. My line of vision was such that the creature filled the moon like a fossil. It had gone there, I thought, to live and die, for there, of all places, was its small definition made whole and eternal. A warm wind rose up and purled[9] like the longing within me.

The next morning I awoke at dawn and went out on the dirt road to Rainy Mountain. It was already hot, and the grasshoppers began to fill the air. Still, it was early in the morning, and the birds sang out of the shadows. The long yellow grass on the mountain shone in the bright light, and a scissortail[10] hied above the land. There, where it ought to be, at the end of a long and legendary way, was my grandmother's grave. Here and there on the dark **2**
stones were ancestral names. Looking back once, I saw the mountain and came away.

9. **purled** (purld) *v.*: Moved in ripples or with a murmuring sound; swirled.

10. **scissortail** (siz′ ər tāl′) *n.*: Pale gray and pink variety of flycatcher.

Guide for Responding

◆ *Literature and Your Life*

Reader's Response Would you be interested in searching out the roots of your culture in the way Momaday does? Explain.

Thematic Focus How can reflecting upon the past help you to understand yourself?

☑ Check Your Comprehension

1. What natural phenomenon did the Kiowa make up a legend to explain?
2. Describe two activities at Momaday's grandmother's house in the summer.

◆ Critical Thinking

INTERPRET

1. To what and to whom is Momaday paying homage in this piece? **[Infer]**
2. Describe the personality of Momaday's grandmother based on the details in the essay. **[Synthesize]**
3. What does the appearance of the cricket at the end of the essay signify about the Kiowa culture? **[Draw Conclusions]**

APPLY

4. How do you think Momaday's life differs from his grandmother's? **[Speculate]**

Cultural Connection

Community Feasts Momaday describes great nighttime feasts that his grandmother's friends held. Discuss with students what community feasts—Fourth of July picnics, church suppers, or feasts featuring the food of a particular cultural group—are held in their area. Talk about the reasons for such celebrations and why people enjoy them. Have students compare feasts in their community to the feasts the author describes.

To help them with their comparisons, use these questions:

1. What other activities take place at the community feasts you have attended or that you know about? What is the significance of these activities?
2. In what specific ways does the food served at these celebrations relate to the heritage of the people involved?

from Nobel Lecture

Alexander Solzhenitsyn

Translated by F. D. Reeve

I am, however, encouraged by a keen sense of WORLD LITERATURE as the one great heart that beats for the cares and misfortunes of our world, even though each corner sees and experiences them in a different way.

In past times, also, besides age-old national literatures there existed a concept of world literature as the link between the summits of national literatures and as the aggregate[1] of reciprocal literary influences. But there was a time lag: readers and writers came to know foreign writers only belatedly, sometimes centuries later, so that mutual influences were delayed and the network of national literary high points was visible not to contemporaries but to later generations.

Today, between writers of one country and the readers and writers of another, there is an almost instantaneous reciprocity as I myself know. My books, unpublished, alas, in my own country, despite hasty and often bad translations have quickly found a responsive world readership. Critical analysis of them has been undertaken by such leading Western writers as Heinrich Böll.[2] During all these recent years, **4**
when both my work and my freedom did not collapse, when against the laws of gravity they held on seemingly in thin air, seemingly ON NOTHING, on the invisible, mute surface tension of sympathetic people, with warm gratitude I learned, to my complete surprise, of the support of the world's writing fraternity. On my fiftieth birthday I was astounded to receive greetings from well-known European writers. No pressure put on me now passed unnoticed. During the dangerous weeks when I was being expelled from the Writers' Union,[3] THE PROTECTIVE WALL put forward by the prominent writers of the world saved me from worse persecution,

1. **aggregate** (ag´ rə git) *adj.*: Group of things gathered together and considered a whole.

2. **Heinrich Böll** (hīn riH böl): German novelist (1917–1985) and winner of the Nobel Prize for Literature.
3. **the Writers Union:** Official Soviet writers' organization.

◆ Build Vocabulary

reciprocity (res´ ə präs´ ə tē) *n.*: Mutual action; dependence

One-Minute Insight In this portion of Solzhenitsyn's Nobel Prize lecture, the great dissident writer reflects upon the importance of literature that bears witness—writers whose voices override lies and the readers who respond to and align with them. His speech celebrates the unity in the writing community—the solidarity that he describes as "one great heart."

◆ Critical Thinking

3 Interpret Ask students what the author means by saying that world literature is "one great heart." *He means that people from all over the world and from all cultures can share their experiences and gain understanding of each other through literature.*

4 Clarification Explain that Heinrich Böll was a writer who expressed controversial views without fear. He wrote on the horrors of war, criticized the government and religious institutions, and denounced nuclear weapons and human rights violations. After Solzhenitsyn was deported from the Soviet Union, Böll hosted him at his home.

Beyond the Classroom

Career Connection

Writer Alexander Solzhenitsyn describes the importance of a writer's role in linking people throughout the world. Discuss with students the different careers open to writers, such as journalist, playwright, novelist, screenwriter, and more specialized areas, such as technical writing. Talk about ways these careers brings people together through the medium of the written word.

Students might research careers in writing to find out what educational background and preparation helps young writers get started.

Publishing Remind students that Solzhenitsyn's work is now published in many languages throughout the world. In a way, writers and publishers collaborate to bring individual ideas to the world at large. Discuss career roles in publishing, such as newspaper, magazine, book, or Web site editor. Students might think about publishing support roles, such as salespeople and publicists. Invite students to consult career guides to publishing to find out more about the responsibilities of these jobs, as well as education, training, and experience that prepares people for them.

◆ Literary Focus

❶ **Persuasive Essay** Solzhenitsyn wants readers to accept that although repression still exists, the strength of world literature unites humans against it.

◆ Critical Thinking

❷ **Draw Conclusions** Ask students what the author means by saying that literature is a "sensitive and responsive" tool for unifying mankind. *Possible response: Literature brings together East and West, helping people of diverse cultures understand and care about one another.*

▶Critical Viewing◀

❸ **Draw Conclusions** *The pictures of writers on these stamps show that writers are important—they are highly regarded in their societies and even sometimes looked up to as national leaders.*

Read to Interpret

Ask students to consider why the author has such strong feelings about world literature. *Students may recognize that Solzhenitsyn knows he was protected from additional persecution in his homeland because of international pressure initiated by prominent writers around the world.*

▲ **Critical Viewing** These stamps from various countries honor writers. What do they suggest about the importance of writers? **[Draw Conclusions]**

and Norwegian writers and artists hospitably prepared shelter for me in the event that I was exiled from my country. Finally, my being nominated for a Nobel Prize was originated not in the land where I live and write but by François Mauriac[4] and his colleagues. Afterward, national writers' organizations expressed unanimous support for me.

As I have understood it and experienced it myself, world literature is no longer an abstraction or a generalized concept invented by literary critics, but a common body and common spirit, a living, heartfelt unity reflecting the growing spiritual unity of mankind. State borders still turn crimson, heated red-hot by electric fences and machine-gun fire; some ministries of internal affairs still suppose that literature is "an internal affair" of the countries under their jurisdiction; and newspaper headlines still herald, "They have no right to interfere in our internal affairs!" Meanwhile, no such thing as INTERNAL AFFAIRS remains on our crowded Earth. Mankind's salvation lies exclusively in everyone's making everything his business, in the people of the East being anything but indifferent to what is thought in the West, and in the people of the West being anything but indifferent to what happens in the East. Literature, one of the most sensitive and responsive tools of human existence, has been the first to pick up, adopt, and assimilate this sense of the growing unity of mankind. I therefore confidently turn to the world literature of the present, to hundreds of friends whom I have not met face to face and perhaps never will see.

> **◆ Literary Focus** ❶ What point does Solzhenitsyn want readers to support or accept?

My friends! Let us try to be helpful, if we are worth anything. In our own countries, torn by differences among parties, movements, castes, and groups, who for ages past has been not the dividing but the uniting force? This, essentially, is the position of writers, spokesmen of a national language, of the chief tie binding the nation, the very soil which the people inhabit, and, in fortunate circumstances, the nation's spirit too.

I think that world literature has the power in these frightening times to help mankind see itself accurately despite what is advocated by partisans[5] and by parties. It has the power to transmit the condensed experience of one region to another, so that different scales of values are combined, and so that one people accurately and concisely knows the true history of another with a power of recognition and acute awareness as if it had lived through that history itself—and could thus be spared repeating old mistakes. At the same time, perhaps we ourselves may succeed in developing our own

4. **François Mauriac** (frän swá´ mô ryák´): French novelist and essayist (1885–1970).

5. **partisans** (pärt´ ə zənz): Unreasoning; emotional supporters of a party or viewpoint.

◆ Build Vocabulary

assimilate (ə sim´ ə lāt´) *v.*: To absorb into a greater body

inexorably (in eks´ ə rə blē) *adv.*: Certainly

oratory (ôr´ ə tôr´ ē) *n.*: Skill in public speaking

Speaking, Listening, and Viewing Mini-Lesson

Persuasive Speech

This mini-lesson supports the Speaking, Listening, and Viewing activity in the Idea Bank on p. 593.

Introduce Have students talk about persuasive speeches they have heard or read. Point out that advertising is persuasion. Discuss techniques the speakers used to make their points—such as persuasive language and emphasizing their strongest points—and whether these techniques were effective.

Develop Have each student choose an issue to explore. Help them to think about effective ways to convince their audiences to share their opinions. Have them ask themselves these questions:

- What do I want to convince my audience to do or think?
- What reasons can I give my audience for agreeing with me?
- What objections might my audience raise?
- How can I counter these objections?

Apply Using the answers to the questions, students can write their speeches. Remind them to use language their audience will respond to and understand.

Assess You and the students can assess the effectiveness of the speeches with the Scoring Rubric for Persuasion and the Self and Peer Assessment sheets for a speech, pp. 105, 117, and 118 in ***Alternative Assessment.***

WORLDWIDE VIEW, like any man, with the center of the eye seeing what is nearby but the periphery[6] of vision taking in what is happening in the rest of the world. We will make correlations[7] and maintain worldwide standards.

Who, if not writers, are to condemn their own unsuccessful governments (in some states this is the easiest way to make a living; everyone who is not too lazy does it) as well as society itself, whether for its cowardly humiliation or for its self-satisfied weakness, or the lightheaded escapades of the young, or the youthful pirates brandishing knives?

We will be told: What can literature do against the pitiless onslaught of naked violence? Let us not forget that violence does not and cannot flourish by itself; it is inevitably intertwined with LYING. Between them there is the closest, the most profound and natural bond: nothing screens violence except lies, and the only way lies can hold out is by violence. Whoever has once announced violence as his METHOD must inexorably choose lying as his PRINCIPLE. At birth, violence behaves openly and even proudly. But as soon as it becomes stronger and firmly established, it senses the thinning of the air around it and cannot go on without befogging itself in lies, coating itself with lying's sugary oratory. It does not always or necessarily go straight for the gullet; usually it demands of its victims only allegiance to the lie, only complicity in the lie.

The simple act of an ordinary courageous man is not to take part, not to support lies! Let *that* come into the world and even reign over it, 4
but not through me. Writers and artists can do more: they can VANQUISH LIES! In the struggle against lies, art has always won and always will. Conspicuously, incontestably for everyone. Lies can stand up against much in the world, but not against art.

Once lies have been dispelled, the repulsive nakedness of violence will be exposed—and hollow violence will collapse.

That, my friends, is why I think we can help the world in its red-hot hour: not by the naysaying of having no armaments, not by abandoning oneself to the carefree life, but by going into battle!

In Russian, proverbs about TRUTH are favorites. They persistently express the considerable, bitter, grim experience of the people, often astonishingly:

ONE WORD OF TRUTH OUTWEIGHS THE WORLD.

On such a seemingly fantastic violation of the law of the conservation of mass and energy[8] are based both my own activities and my appeal to the writers of the whole world.

6. **periphery** (pə rif´ ə rē) *n.*: Boundary; perimeter.
7. **correlations** (kôr ə lā´ shənz) *n.*: Relationships; connections.

8. **the law of conservation of mass and energy:** This law states that in any physical or chemical change, neither mass nor energy can be lost.

Guide for Responding

◆ Literature and Your Life

Reader's Response Tell how a work of literature has helped you to understand the values and traditions of different people.

Thematic Focus How can reflecting on other people's experiences help you understand yourself?

☑ Check Your Comprehension

1. To what does the "one great heart" refer?
2. What does Solzhenitsyn believe writers and artists can do?

◆ Critical Thinking

INTERPRET

1. What connection does Solzhenitsyn see between lies and violence? **[Analyze]**
2. What is the meaning of the Russian proverb that Solzhenitsyn quotes? **[Interpret]**

APPLY

3. How well do you think Solzhenitsyn supports his statement that "no such thing as INTERNAL AFFAIRS remains on our crowded Earth"? **[Judge]**
4. Explain why you agree or disagree with the statement "Lies can stand up against much in the world, but not against art." **[Assess]**

Analyze Literary Criticism

In describing Solzhenitsyn's book "The Oak and the Calf," one reviewer writes, "As literature, it carries his unique eloquence. As memoir, it is a revealing expression of his personality and prejudices. And as a document, which all his books will remain, it provides additional testimony to the obtuse, cruel, and mediocre regime that rules from the Kremlin."

Read this passage to students, drawing attention to the elements mentioned:

- Solzhenitsyn's talent for literature
- Solzhenitsyn's personality and prejudices
- Solzhenitsyn's testimony against the Soviet regime.

Have students reread Solzhenitsyn's Nobel Lecture to find examples of each element. Discuss their interpretations of the review of Solzhenitsyn's work, based on what they find. Encourage them to use the examples to support their comments.

◆ Literary Focus

4 Persuasive Essay Ask students to put the author's argument in this passage in their own words. What techniques does the author use to persuade readers to accept his point of view? *The author's argument is that literature can help end violence by expressing and upholding truth, while exposing and dispelling lies. Persuasive techniques include that he emphasizes strong words and that he closes with a powerful last sentence that summarizes his thoughts. Students may also note Solzhenitsyn's eloquent style.*

Reinforce and Extend

Answers

◆ Literature and Your Life

Reader's Response Students might cite a work of literature from a culture different from their own and discuss how the author's background and reflections gave them special insights into that culture.

Thematic Focus Students might say that by picturing what they would do in someone else's situation they can learn more about themselves.

☑ Check Your Comprehension

1. The "one great heart" refers to world literature.
2. They can expose and dispel lies.

◆ Critical Thinking

1. Lies screen, or hide, violence.
2. "One word of truth outweighs the world" means that pure truth is rare and powerful.
3. Some students may say that although he mentions why we should make up for the fact that no INTERNAL AFFAIRS exists on the crowded earth (through literature), he does not support the quoted statement with evidence.
4. Students who agree might say that art has a universal power; those who disagree might think art is not strong enough or popular enough to expose lies.

Develop Understanding

One-Minute Insight Elie Wiesel's stirring speech reminds us of the urgent importance of remembering the Holocaust and the evil that drove it. Wiesel casts those who would remain silent in the role of perpetrator.

▶Critical Viewing◀

1 Connect *The boy in the picture looks apprehensive, or even frightened. If you combine the picture with the title "Keep Memory Alive," you wonder what the boy went through, and why it is important to remember the experience.*

Customize for
Less Proficient Readers
Prepare these students by explaining that Wiesel, the speaker, will hold an imaginary dialogue with himself as a youth. Ask students to identify movies or television programs they have seen in which this device has been used, and to describe the purpose or effect.

Reteach

Elie Wiesel writes modestly, as if he does not have "the right to represent the multitudes who have perished." Since students may not immediately recognize his persuasive techniques, have a student or students read the speech aloud. Ask students to describe how hearing the speech makes them feel. Then invite them to list details that make the speech persuasive. Record their suggestions on the board.

Keep Memory Alive

Elie Wiesel

1 ▲ Critical Viewing What emotion do you read on this boy's face? How does it relate to the title of this essay? **[Connect]**

Cross-Curricular Connection: Social Studies

Nazi Concentration Camps Explain that as early as 1933, Nazi leaders set up concentration camps where Jews, Communists, Gypsies, and others who the Nazi party felt did not exemplify pure Germans were imprisoned. By the time World War II started, more than 20,000 people were imprisoned in these camps. The numbers grew tremendously over the next six years. Inmates were worked to death; the sick were killed; Nazi doctors performed experiments on healthy individuals. Millions of camp victims were gassed or shot to death, and millions more died from sickness, overwork, starvation, and brutality.

Discuss with the class why Elie Wiesel feels it is so important to keep such horrifying memories alive. Why would it be wrong for people to put these terrible visions out of their minds? By remembering the horrors that human beings have committed against others, perhaps we can prevent such horrors from occurring in the present and future—or stand up in protest against violations of human rights when they do occur.

It is with a profound sense of humility that I accept the honor you have chosen to bestow upon me. I know: your choice transcends me. This both frightens and pleases me.

It frightens me because I wonder: do I have the right to represent the multitudes who have perished? Do I have the right to accept this great honor on their behalf? I do not. That would be presumptuous. No one may speak for the dead, no one may interpret their mutilated dreams and visions.

It pleases me because I may say that this honor belongs to all the survivors and their children, and through us, to the Jewish people with whose destiny I have always identified.

I remember: it happened yesterday or eternities ago. A young Jewish boy discovered the kingdom of night. I remember his bewilderment, I remember his anguish. It all happened so fast. The ghetto. The deportation.[1] The sealed cattle car. The fiery altar upon which the history of our people and the future of mankind were meant to be sacrificed.

I remember: he asked his father: "Can this be true? This is the 20th century, not the Middle Ages. Who would allow such crimes to be committed? How could the world remain silent?"

And now the boy is turning to me: "Tell me," he asks. "What have you done with my future? What have you done with your life?"

And I tell him that I have tried. That I have tried to keep memory alive, that I have tried to fight those who would forget. Because if we forget, we are guilty, we are accomplices. ❹

And then I explained to him how naive we were, that the world did know and remain silent. And that is why I swore never to be silent whenever and wherever human beings endure suffering and humiliation. We must always take sides. Neutrality helps the oppressor, never the victim. Silence encourages the tormentor, never the tormented.

1. **deportation** (dē′ pôr tā′ shən) *n.*: Expulsion from a country.

◆ Build Vocabulary

transcends (tran sendz′) *v.*: Surpasses; exceeds

Guide for Responding

◆ Literature and Your Life

Reader's Response Describe a situation today in which silently witnessing might do harm.

Thematic Focus Have you ever reflected on the past in order to keep a lesson in your mind? Explain.

Questions for Research Though the Holocaust was unique in many respects, it is also, sadly, not the only case of genocide in this century. Generate research questions about other cases of genocide.

☑ Check Your Comprehension

1. What right, or claim, does Wiesel question?
2. Why is the boy incredulous as he's being deported?
3. What does Wiesel call those who deliberately forget the Holocaust?

◆ Critical Thinking

INTERPRET

1. Why does Wiesel use the term "the fiery altar"? **[Interpret]**
2. What is Wiesel's purpose in having his boy self talk to his man self? **[Speculate; Synthesize]**
3. At the end of the piece, of what crime does Wiesel accuse the world, and how did this crime affect his future actions? **[Draw Conclusions]**

APPLY

4. Name two or three atrocities throughout history that were silently witnessed by some. **[Relate]**

EXTEND

5. What are some careers that might involve themselves with keeping historical memories alive? Explain your answer. **[Career Link]**

◆ Reading Strategy

❷ Analyze the Author's Purpose After clarifying that "survivors" refers to Holocaust survivors, ask students why the author mentions the Jewish people and Holocaust survivors. *He is accepting the Nobel Peace Prize on their behalf. The purpose of his speech is to keep the memory of what happened to his people alive.*

❸ Clarification Explain to students that during the war, many Jews were kept in ghettos, portions of town that were sealed off and guarded. At night, the Nazis would round up groups of Jews and take them to trains which transported them to concentration camps.

◆ Critical Thinking

❹ Infer Ask students how the voice of the boy affects the author. *The author feels a responsibility to his boyhood self to keep the memory of his family and the other Jews alive and to make a future where those crimes could never happen again.*

Reinforce and Extend

Answers

◆ Literature and Your Life

Reader's Response A possible situation might involve ignoring a person who is sick or in trouble because of the stigma of being associated with him or her.

Thematic Focus Students might say they have reflected on a particular past experience to keep from repeating a mistake.

☑ Check Your Comprehension

1. He questions the right to represent multitudes who have perished.
2. He can't believe this would happen in the twentieth century.
3. He calls them accomplices.

◆ Critical Thinking

1. Some students may say the term "fiery altar" is meant to refer to the death camp's crematoriums.
2. Students might guess that Wiesel used this device to dramatize the passing of time and to illustrate the Jew's accountability to his descendants.
3. He accuses the world of being a silent accomplice in the atrocities of the Holocaust. This silence caused Wiesel to commit himself to speaking the truth about the events.
4. Possible examples: Slaughter of Native North and Central American Indians, lynchings in the American South.
5. Possible careers include historian, documentary filmmaker, archivist or librarian, and cultural anthropologist.

Answers

◆ Reading Strategy

1. The strong family ties of the Kiowas is one of the reasons Momaday wants to memorialize his grandmother.
2. Knowing something about the oppressive Communist regime would help students to understand not only Solzhenitsyn's message, but his sense of urgency (or purpose) in writing it.

◆ Build Vocabulary

Using Forms of *Reciprocity*

1. reciprocal; 2. reciprocity; 3. reciprocate; 4. reciprocation

Using the Word Bank

1. tenuous; 2. assimilate; 3. reciprocity; 4. oratory; 5. transcends; 6. inexorably; 7. engender

◆ Literary Focus

1. (a) He loves and respects his grandmother; (b) He respects the Kiowa's unique culture and heritage and regrets their loss.
2. He uses the death of his grandmother as a metaphor for the death of the Kiowa's traditions and heritage.
3. Students should cite appropriate reasons supporting Solzhenitsyn's argument.
4. Allow time for students to compare and evaluate their choices.

◆ Build Grammar Skills

1. The last Sun Dance was held on the Washita River above Rainy Mountain Creek.
2. In July the inland slope of the Rockies is luxuriant.
3. The route stretched from Montana to the plains of Kansas and Oklahoma.
4. The Royal Swedish Academy of Sciences awarded the Jewish writer Elie Wiesel a Nobel Prize for his contributions to world peace.
5. The writer Solzhenitsyn was surprised to receive greetings from European writers.

Grammar Reinforcement

For practice, use the Problems with Capitalization lesson in the **Language Lab CD-ROM** and pp. 93–94 on Rules for Capitalization in the *Writer's Solution Grammar Practice Book.*

Guide for Responding *(continued)*

◆ Reading Strategy

ANALYZE THE AUTHOR'S PURPOSE

In these essays, Solzhenitsyn and Wiesel wrote to persuade and Momaday wrote to share his reflections on his grandmother and the culture of the Kiowas. Your own background knowledge and involvement in what you're reading can help you to understand an author's purpose.

1. Family ties among Kiowa Indians are very tight. How does this fact affect Momaday's purpose in writing?
2. Why would knowing some twentieth-century Russian history help you to understand Solzhenitsyn's purpose in writing?

◆ Build Vocabulary

USING FORMS OF *RECIPROCITY*

Words such as *reciprocity* have other forms—nouns, adjectives, adverbs, or verbs. On your paper, complete each sentence with a form of *reciprocity.*

a. reciprocity **c.** reciprocate
b. reciprocal **d.** reciprocation

1. Pen pals have a __?__ arrangement.
2. The worldwide response to Solzhenitsyn's writing demonstrates the __?__ between writers and readers.
3. Although his situation did not allow him to __?__, he appreciated the support of other writers.
4. Now, in __?__, he acknowledges their help in his acceptance speech.

USING THE WORD BANK: Connotations

On your paper, write the word from the Word Bank that is suggested by each song title.

1. *Hanging by a Thread*
2. *(You Know) I Fit Right In*
3. *Give and Take*
4. *Speaking for Myself*
5. *My Love Is Higher Than the Sky*
6. *Without a Doubt (It Has to Be)*
7. *You've Created This Feeling*

◆ Literary Focus

REFLECTIVE AND PERSUASIVE ESSAYS

Your own ideas, experiences, and opinions affect the way you respond to Momaday's reflections in the excerpt from *The Way to Rainy Mountain* and the arguments in the persuasive essays by Solzhenitsyn and Wiesel.

1. (a) How does Momaday feel about his grandmother? (b) How does he feel about Kiowa culture?
2. How do Momaday's reflections on the death of his grandmother help him communicate a message about his Kiowa culture?
3. Analyze how well Solzhenitsyn argues his premise that world literature belongs to the world and not to a single country. What reasons does he give?
4. In your opinion, what is the most persuasive sentence in "Keep Memory Alive"? Explain your choice.

◆ Build Grammar Skills

CAPITALIZATION OF PROPER NOUNS AND ADJECTIVES

All **proper nouns** and **proper adjectives** begin with capital letters.

Practice Rewrite the following sentences, capitalizing the proper nouns and adjectives in each.

1. The last sun dance was held on the washita river above rainy mountain creek.
2. In july the inland slope of the rockies is luxuriant.
3. The route stretched from montana to the plains of kansas and oklahoma.
4. The royal swedish academy of sciences awarded the jewish writer Elie Wiesel a nobel prize for his contributions to world peace.
5. The writer solzhenitsyn was surprised to receive greetings from european writers.

Writing Application Write a paragraph describing your achievements that would qualify you for a prize. Use at least two proper nouns and two proper adjectives.

Beyond the Selection

FURTHER READING

Other Works by the Authors

The Ancient Child, N. Scott Momaday
One Day in the Life of Ivan Denisovich, Alexander Solzhenitsyn
Night, Elie Wiesel

Other Works About the Past

The Diary of a Young Girl, Anne Frank
The Wall, John Hersey

We suggest that you preview these works before recommending them to students.

INTERNET

We suggest the following sites on the Internet (all Web sites are subject to change).

For N. Scott Momaday: **http://www.ipl.org/cgi/ref/native/browse.pl/A50**

For Alexander Solzhenitsyn: **http://www.empirenet.com/~rdaeley/authors/solzhenitsyn.html**

For Elie Wiesel: **http://members.aol.com/KatharenaE/private/Philo/Wiesel/wiesel.html**

We *strongly recommend* that you preview the sites before you send students to them.

Build Your Portfolio

Idea Bank

Writing

1. **Letter** Write a persuasive letter to convince a friend of the importance of remembering the Holocaust.

2. **Report** Write a two-page report on Communist Russia during the time Solzhenitsyn's work was being repressed, beginning in the 1940's. Emphasize the climate that resulted for writers.

3. **Creation Myth** The excerpt from *The Way to Rainy Mountain* includes a Kiowa myth that explains a rock formation in the Black Hills. Write a brief myth of your own to explain the origins of something—such as telling how the Big Dipper or another natural phenomenon came to be.

Speaking, Listening, and Viewing

4. **Persuasive Speech** Choose an issue, such as whether gyms should be open at night, and give a five-minute speech persuading your audience to feel as you do. **[Performing Arts Link]**

5. **Reviewing a Movie** Find a copy of the movie *Shoah* and view it. Then prepare a report for your classmates that describes the movie and offers your sense of what the film attempts. Also, tell whether you think it succeeds. **[History Link]**

Researching and Representing

6. **Native American Dances** In a small group, research the ritual dances of four Native American groups, including the Kiowa Sun Dance. Explain the dances to your class. **[Social Studies Link; Performing Arts Link]**

7. **Writers-in-Prison** Contact a human rights organization or search the Internet to find out about writers who, like Solzhenitsyn, have been imprisoned as a result of what they write. **[Social Studies Link]**

Online Activity www.phlit.phschool.com

Guided Writing Lesson

Acceptance Speech

The Nobel Prize remarks of Solzhenitsyn and Wiesel have been read by people around the world. Write an acceptance speech for the award of your dreams. The achievement is up to you, but this is your chance to address yourself to the largest possible audience. Organize your speech around a strong and meaningful main point.

Writing Skills Focus: Placement for Emphasis

In a speech or persuasive essay, the placement of ideas affects a reader's response to them. The last line of Elie Wiesel's speech—"Silence encourages the tormentor, never the tormented"—has tremendous staying power. Had he begun with this line, it might not have been as effective, because Wiesel needed to provide information to lead up to it. Arrange your ideas in an order that is clear and logical and that emphasizes the most important points. You may, like Wiesel, choose to place your most important points at the end of your speech to make a strong final impression.

Prewriting What will be your most important point? Write a list of possible points, then cross out points that seem weaker or difficult to handle in the form of a speech.

Drafting As you draft, keep in mind the final point you plan to make. Lead up to it with examples, facts, or relevant details.

Revising Read your speech aloud to yourself. Is your key point placed effectively? Make any necessary changes to improve the effectiveness of your speech. Check also that all proper nouns and adjectives are capitalized.

For more on capitalization of proper nouns and adjectives, see pp. 580 and 592.

✓ ASSESSMENT OPTIONS

Formal Assessment, Selection Test, pp. 148–150, and Assessment Resources Software. The selection test is designed so that it can be easily customized to the performance levels of your students.

Alternative Assessment, p. 42, includes options for less advanced students, more advanced students, verbal/linguistic learners, visual/spatial learners, and musical/rhythmic learners.

PORTFOLIO ASSESSMENT

Use the following rubrics in the ***Alternative Assessment*** booklet to assess student writing:
Letter: Persuasion Rubric, p. 105
Report: Research Report Rubric p. 106
Creation Myth: Fictional Narrative Rubric p. 95

Idea Bank

Following are suggestions for matching Idea Bank topics with your students' performance levels and learning modalities:

Customizing for *Performance Levels*

Less Advanced Students: 1, 4, 6
Average Students: 2, 5, 7
More Advanced Students: 3

Customizing for *Learning Modalities*

Visual/Spatial: 6, 7
Verbal/Linguistic: 4, 5
Rhythmic/Musical: 4
Logical/Mathematical: 3

Guided Writing Lesson

Prewriting Strategy Have students use cubing to organize ideas for their speeches and determine the order of importance of those ideas. Provide students with the pattern for a cube to direct analysis of their topics.

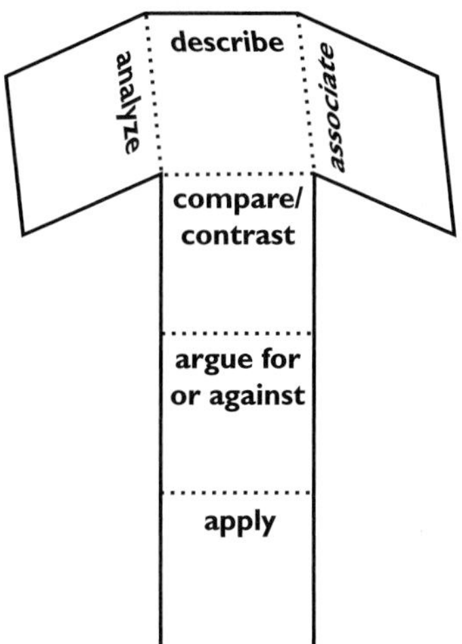

For more prewriting, elaboration, and revision strategies, see *Prentice Hall Writing and Grammar.*

Writing Lab CD-ROM

In writing their acceptance speeches, students should use persuasion. Have students complete the tutorial on Persuasion. Follow these steps:

1. Have students consult an annotated model on supporting a persuasive argument.
2. Suggest that students also go to the annotated example of exploiting an emotional reaction for ideas to give emotional appeal to a persuasive argument.
3. Ask students to use the notecard activity and drag cards into position in order to organize their ideas.

Prepare and Engage

LESSON OBJECTIVES

1. **To develop vocabulary and word identification skills**
   - Word Groups: Musical Words
   - Using the Word Bank: Connotations
   - Extending Word Study: Adjectives (ATE)
2. **To use a variety of reading strategies to read and comprehend biographies and autobiographies**
   - Connect Your Experience
   - Reading Strategy: Recognize the Author's Attitude
   - Tips to Guide Reading: Sustained Reading (ATE)
   - Read to Discover Models for Writing (ATE)
   - Idea Bank: Your Favorite Holiday
   - Idea Bank: Memory From Childhood
3. **To increase knowledge of other cultures and to connect common elements across cultures**
   - Cultural Connections (ATE)
4. **To express and support responses to the text**
   - Critical Thinking
5. **To analyze literary elements**
   - Literary Focus: Biography and Autobiography
   - Idea Bank: Biography
6. **To read in order to research self-selected and assigned topics**
   - Viewing and Representing Mini-Lesson: Multimedia Presentation (ATE)
   - Idea Bank: Visual Presentation
7. **To plan, prepare, organize, and present literary interpretations**
   - Idea Bank: Greeting Card
8. **To use recursive writing processes to write a letter**
   - Guided Writing Lesson
9. **To increase knowledge of the rules of grammar and usage**
   - Build Grammar Skills: Restrictive and Nonrestrictive Appositives

Test Preparation

Reading Comprehension: Analyzing Literary Language (ATE, p. 595) The teaching tips and sample test item in this workshop support the instruction and practice in the unit workshop.

Reading Comprehension: Comparing and Contrasting Texts; Analyzing Literary Language (SE, p. 661)

Guide for Reading

Dylan Thomas *(1914–1953)*

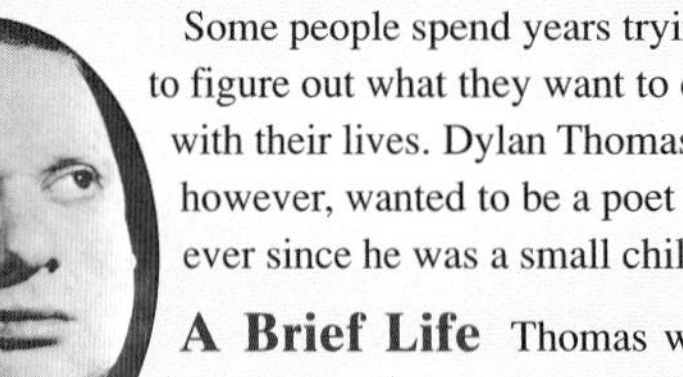

Some people spend years trying to figure out what they want to do with their lives. Dylan Thomas, however, wanted to be a poet ever since he was a small child.

A Brief Life Thomas was born in the picturesque seaside village of Swansea, Wales. In the poem "Fern Hill" (1946), he fondly evokes the memories of his early childhood.

Thomas's first book of poetry was published when he moved to London at the age of twenty. Recent research indicates that all his poems—at least the first drafts—were completed by the time he was twenty-one years old! His poetry readings in England and the United States brought him popular appeal, but little income. Poverty and a stormy private life took their toll, and Thomas died in New York at the age of thirty-nine.

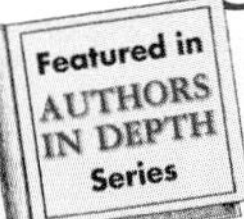

Langston Hughes *(1902–1967)*

Langston Hughes traveled to places as far and wide as Africa, Europe, the Soviet Union (now Russia), China, and Japan, and he lived in Paris and Italy.

Renaissance Man Although Hughes traveled widely, his work is associated mostly with the Harlem Renaissance —a period when some of America's finest writers, artists, and musicians centered in Harlem, New York, brought previously unrecognized aspects of the African American experience into the spotlight. Hughes, for instance, used the rhythm and mood of jazz and blues in his poetry. He has been called the poet laureate of the Harlem Renaissance, but he also wrote nonfiction, novels, and plays, as well as at least twenty scripts for opera, radio, and film.

◆ Build Vocabulary

WORD GROUPS: MUSICAL WORDS

The world of music has its own vocabulary of specific "musical" terms. One such word, which you will encounter in Hughes's account of Marian Anderson, is *aria*. An *aria* is a melody in an opera, usually for a solo voice with instrumental accompaniment. Another word he uses is *repertoire*, a French word that refers to a group of songs that a musician or singer knows well and is always ready to perform. Marian Anderson had a number of *arias* in her *repertoire*.

WORD BANK

Before you read, preview this list of words from the selections. Some may already be familiar to you. In your notebook, write all the words and jot down the meanings of those you know.

sidle
prey
wallowed
crocheted
brittle
trod
forlorn
arias
staunch
repertoire

◆ Build Grammar Skills

RESTRICTIVE AND NONRESTRICTIVE APPOSITIVES

An **appositive** is a noun or pronoun placed near another noun or pronoun to provide more information about it. An appositive phrase contains the appositive and any words that modify it.

Appositives are either restrictive or nonrestrictive. A **restrictive appositive** is essential to the meaning of the sentence and is not set off by commas.

> . . . I was in Mrs. Prothero's garden . . . with her son *Jim*.

The appositive *Jim* is restrictive. It is necessary to identify which son.

A **nonrestrictive appositive** is not essential and is set off by commas.

> . . . a famous group of Negro singers, *the Fisk Jubilee Singers*, had already carried the spirituals.

This appositive adds detail to the sentence, but it is not essential to the sentence's meaning.

Prentice Hall Literature Program Resources

REINFORCE / RETEACH / EXTEND

Selection Support Pages
Build Vocabulary: Musical Words, p. 176
Build Grammar Skills: Restrictive and Nonrestrictive Appositives, p. 177
Reading Strategy: Recognize Author's Attitude, p. 178

Literary Focus: Biography/Autobiography, p. 179

Strategies for Diverse Student Needs, p. 43

Beyond Literature Career Connection: Music, p. 43

Formal Assessment Selection Test, pp. 151–153; Assessment Resources Software

Alternative Assessment, p. 43

Writing and Language Transparencies Daily Language Practice, Week 16, p. 127

Art Transparency, 20

Resource Pro CD-ROM

Listening to Literature Audiocassettes

◆ A Child's Christmas in Wales ◆
Marian Anderson: Famous Concert Singer

◆ *Literature and Your Life*

CONNECT YOUR EXPERIENCE

Our remembrances take shape around people, places, and events from our past because they have a special significance. In "A Child's Christmas in Wales," Dylan Thomas shares memories of a holiday in his childhood home. Langston Hughes's account of Marion Anderson makes it possible for generations of readers to "remember" her.

THEMATIC FOCUS: FROM THE PAST

These two selections show two kinds of legacies—one personal, one public. What do you think is the value of reflecting on the past?

Journal Writing Write a short autobiographical account based on a person, place, or event that you remember fondly.

◆ Background for Understanding

HISTORY

That Marian Anderson (an African American woman living before the civil rights movements of the 1950's and 1960's) achieved the level of success she did is a remarkable achievement. Because of racial prejudice in the United States, Anderson and a number of other African American musicians and artists of the same era were unable to achieve the level of recognition of their white counterparts and went to Europe to find fame. Even after she achieved international recognition, Anderson was not permitted to sing in certain public places in the United States because of her race.

◆ Literary Focus

BIOGRAPHY AND AUTOBIOGRAPHY

A **biography** is an account of a person's life written by another individual. In many biographies, the major events and accomplishments of the subject's life are covered in chronological order. The biographer gathers information from sources such as letters, diaries, and interviews with the subject or people who knew the subject, and then weaves together and interprets the information.

An **autobiography,** on the other hand, is a person's own account of his or her life. The writer of an autobiography can share personal thoughts and feelings and may comment on the effects of certain events on his or her life. Dylan Thomas shares events from his life in his autobiographical account, "A Child's Christmas in Wales."

◆ Reading Strategy

RECOGNIZE THE AUTHOR'S ATTITUDE

Both biographers and autobiographers have a particular attitude toward their subjects. Once you recognize the **author's attitude** you'll be able to read with better understanding.

The author's attitude is the way he or she feels about the subject. This attitude is reflected in the way the author interprets the events of the subject's life. If the author admires and respects the subject, for example, then the author will present the details of the subject's life in such a way that you, the reader, will also admire and respect the subject.

In an autobiographical account, if the author remembers an event fondly or humorously or sadly, then you will feel that way too.

To recognize an author's attitude, notice the details and events the author chooses to present, and think about the message the author conveys—either directly or indirectly—through this information.

Test Preparation Workshop

Reading Comprehension: Analyzing Literary Language Literary language that students may be asked to analyze in order to answer reading questions on standardized tests may include evocative words, rhyme, repeated sounds, or rhythms. Have students read the first sentence of "A Child's Christmas in Wales," then answer this sample question.

How does the repetition of the "o" sound and the numbers six and twelve reveal the author's attitude toward his subject?

A It shows that he is in a hurry to share his memories.

B It shows that he remembers best when falling asleep.

C It shows how much he loves the snow.

D It shows that his childhood memories blur together.

The correct answer is D. The repetitious sounds contribute to his vague, but intense childhood memories.

To prepare students to read this pairing of remembrances, ask them to spend five minutes writing two kinds of memories. The first should be remembered sensations, such as of being caught in a storm. The second should be a recollection of information about their favorite performer or sports star. Discuss with students how the type of memory they write about affects the style and language of their writing. Let them know that they will see more clearly how subject matter can affect style in nonfiction when they read "A Child's Christmas in Wales" and "Marian Anderson: Famous Concert Singer."

Tips to Guide Reading

Sustained Reading Encourage students to read the selection all the way through in one sitting. They may want to vary their pace of reading in order to become accustomed to the author's use of language.

Customize for
Less Proficient Readers

Students may have difficulty comprehending Thomas's long, meandering sentences and poetic language. Have them follow along in their text as they listen to the **Listening to Literature Audiocassettes** recording of the selection. Stop the recording occasionally to give students a chance to summarize what they've read.

Customize for
Pre-AP Students

These students may enjoy performing an oral interpretation of "A Child's Christmas in Wales." Have them work together to analyze the feelings expressed in each section of the selection. Then they can decide on specific paragraphs for each student to interpret and read aloud.

Customize for
English Language Learners

These students might find some of the vocabulary in the narrative, as well as in the Word Bank, difficult to understand. To provide help with these words, give students context sentences; for example: On his way to school, Sam *trod* on the sidewalk.

Develop Understanding

One-Minute Insight "A Child's Christmas in Wales" evokes the enchantment that holiday celebrations hold for children. In this famous work, the voice of the adult Dylan Thomas describes childhood Christmases, blended and transfigured by the magic of memory. With fondness and nostalgia, he recalls the activities, sensory details, and people he associates with this holiday.

Customizing for
Intrapersonal Learners
These students may experience a sense of personal connection with the feelings and attitudes Thomas conveys in this autobiographical piece. As they read, encourage them to pause and reflect on events from their own past that arouse feelings similar to those that Thomas describes. They can record these feelings in their journals to later use them as a basis for their own remembrances.

◆ Critical Thinking

1 Interpret Let students know that Thomas is making the point that family stories tend to get exaggerated and mixed up. Ask students to explain why this might be so. *Events from the past tend to overlap in our memories and blur together; sometimes people exaggerate events to create a humorous or dramatic effect on listeners.*

A Child's Christmas in Wales

Dylan Thomas

1 One Christmas was so much like another, in those years around the sea-town corner now and out of all sound except the distant speaking of the voices I sometimes hear a moment before sleep, that I can never remember whether it snowed for six days and six nights when I was twelve or whether it snowed for twelve days and twelve nights when I was six. All the Christmases roll down toward the

Block Scheduling Strategies

Consider these suggestions to take advantage of extended class time:

- Introduce the concepts of biography and autobiography. After students have read these essays, have them answer the Literary Focus questions on p. 606. You may follow up with the Literary Focus page in ***Selection Support,*** p. 179.
- Have students listen to all or part of the selections on audiocassette. You may want to play "A Child's Christmas in Wales" in portions over several days to give students a chance to accustom themselves to the work's poetic language and improve their comprehension.
- Expand upon the Reading Strategy by encouraging volunteers to identify the authors' attitudes in literary works they have read recently, and to explain how they arrived at their conclusion.
- Use ***Daily Language Practice*** for Week 16. You may want to use the transparency on the overhead projector and have students write the sentences correctly, or you may dictate the sentences.
- Set aside class time for students' Visual and Multimedia Presentations from the Speaking, Listening, and Viewing activities and Researching and Representing activities in the Idea Bank on p. 607.

two-tongued sea, like a cold and headlong moon bundling down the sky that was our street; and they stop at the rim of the ice-edged, fish-freezing waves, and I plunge my hands in the snow and bring out whatever I can find. In goes my hand into that wool-white bell-tongued ball of holidays resting at the rim of the carol-singing seas, and out come Mrs. Prothero and the firemen.

It was on the afternoon of the day of Christmas Eve, and I was in Mrs. Prothero's garden, waiting for cats, with her son Jim. It was snowing. It was always snowing at Christmas. December, in my memory, is white as Lapland, though there were no reindeers. But there were cats. Patient, cold and callous, our hands wrapped in socks, we waited to snowball the cats. Sleek and long as jaguars and horrible-whiskered, spitting and snarling, they would slink and sidle over the white back-garden walls, and the lynx-eyed hunters, Jim and I, furcapped and moccasined trappers from Hudson Bay,[1] off Mumbles Road, would hurl our deadly snowballs at the green of their eyes. The wise cats never appeared. We were so still, Eskimo-footed arctic marksmen in the muffling silence of the eternal snows—eternal, ever since Wednesday—that we never heard Mrs. Prothero's first cry from her igloo at the bottom of the garden. Or, if we heard it at all, it was, to us, like the far-off challenge of our enemy and prey, the neighbor's polar cat. But soon the voice grew louder. "Fire!" cried Mrs. Prothero, and she beat the dinner-gong.

And we ran down the garden, with the snowballs in our arms, toward the house; and smoke, indeed, was pouring out of the dining room, and the gong was bombilating,[2] and Mrs. Prothero was announcing ruin like a town crier in Pompeii.[3] This was better than all the cats in Wales standing on the wall in a row. We bounded into the house, laden with snowballs, and stopped at the open door of the smoke-filled room.

Something was burning all right; perhaps it was Mr. Prothero, who always slept there after midday dinner with a newspaper over his face. But he was standing in the middle of the room, saying "A fine Christmas!" and smacking at the smoke with a slipper.

"Call the fire brigade," cried Mrs. Prothero as she beat the gong.

"They won't be there," said Mr. Prothero, "it's Christmas."

There was no fire to be seen, only clouds of smoke and Mr. Prothero standing in the middle of them, waving his slipper as though he were conducting.

"Do something," he said.

And we threw all our snowballs into the smoke—I think we missed Mr. Prothero—and ran out of the house to the telephone box.

"Let's call the police as well," Jim said.

"And the ambulance."

"And Ernie Jenkins, he likes fires."

But we only called the fire brigade, and soon the fire engine came and three tall men in helmets brought a hose into the house and Mr. Prothero got out just in time before they turned it on. Nobody could have had a noisier Christmas Eve. And when the firemen turned off the hose and were standing in the wet, smoky room, Jim's aunt, Miss Prothero, came downstairs and peered in at them. Jim and I waited, very quietly, to hear what she would say to them. She said the right thing, always. She looked at the three tall firemen in their shining helmets, standing among the smoke and cinders and dissolving snowballs, and she said: "Would you like anything to read?"

◆ Literary Focus Notice how Thomas reveals details in this passage that only someone who was present would know. ❻

Years and years and years ago, when I was a boy, when there were wolves in Wales, and birds the color of red-flannel petticoats whisked past the harp-shaped hills, when we sang and wallowed all night and day in caves that smelt

1. **Hudson Bay:** Inland sea in northeastern Canada.
2. **bombilating** (bäm′ bə lāt iŋ) *v.:* Making a buzzing, droning sound as though a bomb were approaching.
3. **Pompeii** (päm pā′): City in Italy that was destroyed by the eruption of Mount Vesuvius in A.D. 79.

◀ **Critical Viewing** Based on this picture, what kind of characters do you expect to find in Thomas's childhood memory? **[Draw Conclusions]**

◆ Build Vocabulary

sidle (sī′ dəl) *v.:* Move sideways in a sneaky manner

prey (prā) *n.:* Animal hunted and killed for food

wallowed (wäl′ ōd) *v.:* Enjoyed completely; took great pleasure

◆ Build Grammar Skills

❷ Restrictive and Nonrestrictive Appositives Ask students why the words *Jim and I* are set off by commas. What information do they add to the noun *hunters?* *The words Jim and I form a nonrestrictive appositive phrase. Because the appositive phrase is not essential, it is set off by commas. The phrase tells who the "lynx-eyed hunters" are.*

❸ Clarify If necessary, explain that Mrs. Prothero doesn't really live in an igloo. Thomas is describing events as the boys envisioned them in their imaginations, while they were pretending to be Eskimo hunters.

◆ Reading Strategy

❹ Recognize the Author's Attitude Ask students what attitude Thomas takes toward the fire in Mrs. Prothero's house. Then ask which details in the passage hint at his feelings. *Thomas is amused by the incident. Whimsical phrases such "bombilating," "like a town crier in Pompeii," and "better than all the cats in Wales standing on the wall in a row" suggest he finds the incidents funny and that he looks back fondly upon them.*

▶Critical Viewing◀

❺ Draw Conclusions Elicit responses such as the following: *Based on the expressions on the boys' faces, the memory might include boys who are mischievous and rambunctious.*

◆ Literary Focus

❻ Biography and Autobiography Point out the details, "three tall men in helmets," "Mr. Prothero got out just in time," and Miss Prothero's question "Would you like anything to read?"

Extending Word Study

Adjectives Encourage students to pay attention to the author's use of hyphenated words as adjectives, such as "the *ice-edged, fish-freezing* waves" and the "*carol-singing* seas." Discuss with them that the use of hyphens in compound words is a matter of changing style. In the case of compound modifiers, Thomas's use of hyphens in these adjectives does not follow the rules of hyphenation. However, you may wish to further discuss that in this case, the author's descriptive intent is clarified by the hyphens.

Cross-Curricular Connection: Social Studies

Wales A principality, Wales is located west of England. Along with England, Scotland, and Northern Ireland, it makes up the United Kingdom, or Great Britain. The Welsh have their own ancient language, but Welsh citizens are bilingual, speaking English as well.

Wales is bounded on the north by the Irish Sea, on the west by St. George's Channel (across which lies the country of Ireland), and on the south by the Bristol Channel. Wales has a maritime climate with heavy annual precipitation of rain and snow. Dylan Thomas was born in the southern seaport town of Swansea, a large industrial center where coal mined in the north is used in the manufacture of steel.

Have students discuss how living on the Welsh seacoast influenced Dylan Thomas's childhood experiences and memories.

Develop Understanding

❶ **Clarify** Explain that although Wales is part of the United Kingdom and governed by England, the Welsh have fought many battles throughout history to resist English rule.

Comprehension Check ☑

❷ Who might the small boy be? He might be a youngster who is listening while the narrator reminisces, or he might be a fantasized boy in the narrator's imagination.

◆ Critical Thinking

❸ **Infer** Ask students why the narrator tells the boy that the snows of his childhood were different from the snows of today. *Possible response: People tend to exaggerate memories from their childhood because the world seems more intense and extreme from a child's point of view.*

▶Critical Viewing◀

❹ **Assess** *Students should notice the relaxed body positions and facial expressions of the four figures. The soft light, the homey furnishings, and the sampler reading "GOD BLESS OUR HOME" create the comforting mood described in Thomas's piece.*

Read to Discover Models for Writing

Students may want to try some of the author's techniques in their own autobiographical writing. One technique is having the small boy interrupt the narrator and ask to hear about certain parts. Another technique is listing objects or feelings to create atmosphere. Thomas has long lists of foods, smells, and presents.

like Sunday afternoons in damp front farm-house parlors, and we chased, with the jaw-
❶ bones of deacons, the English and the bears, before the motor car, before the wheel, before the duchess-faced horse, when we rode the daft[4] and happy hills bareback, it snowed and it snowed. But here a small boy says: "It snowed last year, too. I made a snowman and my
❷ brother knocked it down and I knocked my brother down and then we had tea."

"But that was not the same snow," I say. "Our snow was not only shaken from whitewash buckets down the sky, it came shawling[5] out of the ground and swam and drifted out of the arms and hands
❸ and bodies of the trees; snow grew overnight on the roofs of the houses like a pure and grandfather moss, minutely white-ivied the walls and settled on the postman, opening the gate, like a dumb, numb thunder-storm of white, torn Christmas cards."

"Were there postmen then, too?"

"With sprinkling eyes and wind-cherried noses, on spread, frozen feet they crunched up to the doors and mittened on them manfully. But all that the children could hear was a ringing of bells."

"You mean that the postman went rat-a-tat-tat and the doors rang?"

"I mean that the bells that the children could hear were inside them."

"I only hear thunder sometimes, never bells."

"There were church bells, too."

"Inside them?"

"No, no, no, in the bat-black, snow-white belfries, tugged by bishops and storks. And they rang their tidings over the bandaged town, over the frozen foam of the powder and ice-cream hills, over the crackling sea. It seemed that all the churches boomed for joy under my window: and the weathercocks crew for Christmas, on our fence."

"Get back to the postmen."

"They were just ordinary postmen, fond of walking and dogs and Christmas and the snow. They knocked on the doors with blue knuckles. . . ."

"Ours has got a black knocker. . . ."

"And then they stood on the white Welcome mat in the little, drifted porches and huffed and puffed, making ghosts with their breath, and jogged from foot to foot like small boys wanting to go out."

The Aunts (tinted), Fritz Eichenberg etching, © Fritz Eichenberg Trust/Licensed by VAGA, New York, NY

▲ ❹ **Critical Viewing** How well does this picture capture the atmosphere of the holiday Thomas describes? **[Assess]**

"And then the presents?"

"And then the Presents, after the Christmas box. And the cold postman, with a rose on his button-nose, tingled down the tea-tray-slithered run of the chilly glinting hill. He went in his ice-bound boots like a man on fishmonger's slabs.[6] He wagged his bag like a frozen camel's hump, dizzily turned the corner on one foot, and was gone."

"Get back to the Presents."

"There were the Useful Presents: engulfing mufflers of the old coach days, and mittens made for giant sloths;[7] zebra scarfs of a

4. **daft:** Silly; foolish.
5. **shawling:** Draping like a shawl.

6. **fishmonger's slabs:** Flat, slimy surface on which fish are displayed for sale.
7. **sloths** (slôths) *n.:* Two-toed mammals that hang from trees.

◆ Build Vocabulary

crocheted (krō shād′) *v.:* Made with thread or yarn woven with hooked needles

Humanities: Art

The Whistle and **The Aunts** by Fritz Eichenberg.

The German artist Fritz Eichenberg has illustrated many classic children's books, including Jonathan Swift's *Gulliver's Travels* and the modern classic *Black Beauty,* by Anne Sewell. Born in Cologne, Germany, Eichenberg traveled as a young man and eventually settled in Tuckahoe, New York.

These highly rendered ink drawings depict two scenes described in Thomas's autobiographical work. In both illustrations, Eichenberg's cartoonish faces capture perfectly the boys and aunts Dylan describes—loving and cozy characters.

1. Why did the artist depict the two boys as looking exactly alike? *In the text Thomas says the other boy is "the spit of myself," meaning he looks the same. The physical resemblance also suggests the common cocky attitude the two boys share, as well as their similar Christmas experiences.*
2. Which aspects of the scene shown in "The Aunts" suggests a setting in the past? Which aspect of the scene might be the same as in a contemporary holiday illustration? *The clothing, hairstyles, and room furnishings suggest a past setting. The child playing among relatives is common to all times.*

substance like silky gum that could be tug-o'-warred down to the galoshes;[8] blinding tam-o'-shanters[9] like patchwork tea cozies[10] and bunny-suited busbies[11] and balaclavas[12] for victims of head-shrinking tribes; from aunts who always wore wool next to the skin there were mustached and rasping vests that made you wonder why the aunts had any skin left at all; and once I had a little crocheted nose bag from an aunt now, alas, no longer whinnying with us. And pictureless books in which small boys, though warned with quotations not to, *would* skate on Farmer Giles' pond and did and drowned; and books that told me everything about the wasp, except why."

"Go on to the Useless Presents."

"Bags of moist and many-colored jelly babies[13] and a folded flag and a false nose and a tram-conductor's cap[14] and a machine that punched tickets and rang a bell; never a catapult;[15] once, by mistake that no one could explain, a little hatchet; and a celluloid duck that made, when you pressed it, a most unducklike sound, a mewing moo that an ambitious cat might make who wished to be a cow; and a painting book in which I could make the grass, the trees, the sea and the animals any color I pleased, and still the dazzling sky-blue sheep are grazing in the red field under the rainbow-billed and peagreen birds. Hard-boileds, toffee, fudge and allsorts, crunches, cracknels, humbugs, glaciers, marzipan, and butterwelsh[16] for the Welsh. And troops of bright tin soldiers who, if they could not fight, could always run. And Snakes-and-Families and Happy Ladders.[17] And Easy Hobbi-Games for Little Engineers, complete with instructions. Oh, easy for Leonardo![18] And a whistle to make the dogs bark to wake up the old man next door to make him beat on the wall with his stick to shake our picture off the wall. And a packet of cigarettes: you put one in your mouth and you stood at the corner of the street and you waited for hours, in vain, for an old lady to scold you for smoking a cigarette, and then with a smirk you ate it. And then it was breakfast under the balloons."

◆ Reading Strategy
What is the author's attitude toward the Useful Presents? The Useless Presents? 5

"Were there Uncles, like in our house?"

"There are always Uncles at Christmas. The same Uncles. And on Christmas mornings, with dog-disturbing whistle and sugar fags,[19] I would scour the swatched town for the news of the little world, and find always a dead bird by the white Post Office or by the deserted swings; perhaps a robin, all but one of his fires out. Men and women wading or scooping back from chapel, with taproom noses and wind-bussed cheeks, all albinos,[20] huddled their stiff black jarring feathers against the irreligious snow. Mistletoe hung 6

The Aunts (detail and tint), Fritz Eichenberg etching, © Fritz Eichenberg Trust/Licensed by VAGA, New York, NY

8. **galoshes** (gə läsh′ əz) *n.:* Rubber overshoes or boots.
9. **tam-o'-shanters:** Scottish caps.
10. **tea cozies:** Knitted or padded covers placed over a teapot to keep the contents warm.
11. **busbies** (buz′ bēz): Tall fur hats worn as part of the full-dress uniforms of guardsmen in the British army.
12. **balaclavas** (bäl′ ə klä′ vəz): Knitted helmets with an opening for the nose and eyes.
13. **jelly babies:** Candies in the shape of babies.
14. **tram conductor's cap:** Streetcar or trolley car operator's cap.
15. **catapult** (kat′ ə pult′): Ancient military machine for throwing or shooting stones or spears; slingshot.
16. **hard-boileds . . . butterwelsh:** Various kinds of candy.
17. **Snakes-and-Families and Happy Ladders:** Games, the names of which Dylan Thomas mixes up on purpose. The games are actually Snakes-and-Ladders and Happy Families.
18. **Leonardo:** Leonardo da Vinci (1452–1519), an Italian painter, sculptor, architect, engineer, and scientist.
19. **sugar fags:** Candy cigarettes.
20. **albinos** (al bī′ nōz): People who because of a genetic factor have unusually pale skin and white hair.

◆ Reading Strategy

5 Recognize the Author's Attitude Elicit responses such as the following: *Like a child, Thomas still finds the "Useful Presents" uninteresting and silly. On the other hand, he still feels a sense of wonder, enchantment, and delight as he remembers the "Useless Presents," the favorite toys of his childhood.*

◆ Literary Focus

6 Biography and Autobiography Ask: In what ways do the details in this passage add to the autobiography? *The vivid details help readers to imagine exactly what life was like in Thomas's town at Christmas. The details enable readers to put themselves in the boy's place. They may also evoke readers' own memories of Christmas.*

Customize for *Visual Spatial Learners*
Encourage these students to compare the details of the pictures that accompany the text to the text itself. Tell students that because the pictures were created specifically for this story, they should be able to identify significant details in the pictures that reflect Thomas's recollections.

Art Transparency Use Art Transparency 20 to illustrate for students how an artist can uses images and impressions to create a sense of "memory." Ask students to identify the objects in the picture that are often associated with, or that suggest, memory or the past, such as mirrors, with their reflective properties, suggest looking back; the clock, as a timepiece, could represent the passage of time; the empty room suggests events that have passed or people that have left; and the train suggests moving on, leaving something behind. Then ask students to explain how these objects and the way they are represented might relate to the title. Finally, have students discuss how memory creates a sense of time transfixed, as in Thomas's recollection of Christmases past.

◆ Critical Thinking

❶ **Compare and Contrast** Ask students if the adults described in this passage share the children's sense of wonder and excitement about Christmas. Have them support their answers with details from the passage. *The adults do not seem to share the children's feelings. The uncles seem content but bored as they smoke their cigars. The aunts seem timid and uncomfortable.*

❷ **Clarification** Tell students that, in this context, the word *spit* means "an exact likeness." Students may have heard the related phrase "the spitting image."

◆ Literature and Your Life

❸ Students should note that specific sensory details help the reader see, hear, taste, smell, and feel the experience the author is recalling. Ask students to cite specific sensory details as examples.

◆ Reading Strategy

❹ **Recognize the Author's Attitude** Ask students what attitude the author seems to take toward the pretending games and pranks of his childhood. *He is delighted by them and seems to miss this imaginative, uninhibited time of his life.*

Customize for
Gifted/Talented Students
Students can design scenes that would appear if "A Child's Christmas in Wales" were performed as a play. They may want to create drawings, three-dimensional models, or role-play the scenes.

The Whistle (detail and tint), Fritz Eichenberg etching, © Fritz Eichenberg Trust/Licensed by VAGA, New York, NY

from the gas brackets[21] in all the front parlors; there was sherry and walnuts and bottled beer and crackers by the dessert-spoons; and cats in their fur-abouts watched the fires; and the high-heaped fire spat, all ready for the chestnuts and the mulling pokers. Some few large men sat in the front parlors, without their collars, Uncles almost certainly, trying their new cigars, holding them out judiciously at arms' length, returning them to their mouths, coughing, then holding them out again as though waiting for the explosion; and some few small aunts, not wanted in the kitchen, nor anywhere else for that matter, sat on the very edges of their chairs, poised and brittle, afraid to break, like faded cups and saucers."

❶

Not many those mornings trod the piling streets: an old man always, fawn-bowlered,[22] yellow-gloved and, at this time of year, with spats[23] of snow, would take his constitutional[24] to the white bowling green and back, as he would take it wet or fine on Christmas Day or Doomsday; sometimes two hale young men, with big pipes blazing, no overcoats and wind-blown scarfs, would trudge, unspeaking, down to the forlorn sea, to work up an appetite, to blow away the fumes, who knows, to walk into the waves until nothing of them was left but the two curling smoke clouds of their inextinguishable briars.[25] Then I would be slap-dashing home, the gravy smell of the dinners of others, the bird smell, the brandy, the pudding and mince, coiling up to my nostrils, when out of a snow-clogged side lane would come a boy the spit of myself, with a pink-tipped cigarette and the violet past of a black eye, cocky as a bullfinch, leering all to himself. I hated him on sight and sound, and would be about to put my dog whistle to my lips and blow him off the face of Christmas when suddenly he, with a violet wink, put *his* whistle to *his* lips and blew so stridently, so high, so exquisitely loud,

❷

21. **gas brackets:** Wall fixtures for gas lights.
22. **fawn-bowlered:** Tan-hatted.
23. **spats:** Coverings for the instep and ankle.
24. **constitutional:** Walk taken for one's health.
25. **briars:** Pipes.

that gobbling faces, their cheeks bulged with goose, would press against their tinseled windows, the whole length of the white echoing street. For dinner we had turkey and blazing pudding, and after dinner the Uncles sat in front of the fire, loosened all buttons, put their large moist hands over their watch chains, groaned a little and slept. Mothers, aunts and sisters scuttled to and fro, bearing tureens.[26] Auntie Bessie, who had already been frightened, twice, by a clock-work mouse, whimpered at the sideboard and had some elderberry wine. The dog was sick. Auntie Dosie had to have three aspirins, but Auntie Hannah, who liked port, stood in the middle of the snowbound back yard, singing like a big-bosomed thrush. I would blow up balloons to see how big they would blow up to; and, when they burst, which they all did, the Uncles jumped and rumbled. In the rich and heavy afternoon, the Uncles breathing like dolphins and the snow descending, I would sit among festoons[27] and Chinese lanterns and nibble dates and try to make a model man-o'-war[28] following the Instructions for Little Engineers, and produce what might be mistaken for a sea-going tramcar.

◆ *Literature and Your Life*
How does the author's use of sensory details intensify this memory for readers?

Or I would go out, my bright new boots squeaking, into the white world, on to the seaward hill, to call on Jim and Dan and Jack and to pad through the still streets, leaving huge deep footprints on the hidden pavements.

"I bet people will think there's been hippos."

"What would you do if you saw a hippo coming down our street?"

"I'd go like this, bang! I'd throw him over the railings and roll him down the hill and then I'd tickle him under the ear and he'd wag his tail."

"What would you do if you saw *two* hippos?"

Iron-flanked and bellowing he-hippos clanked and battered through the scudding snow toward us as we passed Mr. Daniel's house.

26. **tureens** (too̅ rēnz'): Deep dishes with covers.
27. **festoons:** Wreaths and garlands.
28. **man-o'-war:** Warship.

Cultural Connection

Winter Holidays Since ancient times many cultures around the world have celebrated holidays holidays during the months that fall during the middle of the winter season. Today in the United States, some of the best-known mid-winter holidays are Christmas, in which Christians celebrate the birth of the Infant Jesus; Hanukkah, in which Jews commemorate the rededication of the Temple of Jerusalem in ancient times; and Kwanzaa, a festival in which African Americans celebrate their African heritage.

Suggest that students compare traditional holidays from different cultures and religions by completing a chart of several different winter holidays. They can note facts under the following categories: Event Celebrated; Food; Dress; Customs (such as gift-giving); Decorations; and Games or Activities.

"Let's post Mr. Daniel a snowball through his letter box."

"Let's write things in the snow."

"Let's write, 'Mr. Daniel looks like a spaniel' all over his lawn."

Or we walked on the white shore. "Can the fishes see it's snowing?"

The silent one-clouded heavens drifted on to the sea. Now we were snow-blind travelers lost on the north hills, and vast dewlapped[29] dogs, with flasks round their necks, ambled and shambled up to us, baying "Excelsior."[30] We returned home through the poor streets where only a few children fumbled with bare red fingers in the wheel-rutted snow and cat-called after us, their voices fading away, as we trudged uphill, into the cries of the dock birds and the hooting of ships out in the whirling bay. And then, at tea the recovered Uncles would be jolly; and the ice cake loomed in the center of the table like a marble grave. Auntie Hannah laced her tea with rum, because it was only once a year.

Bring out the tall tales now that we told by the fire as the gaslight bubbled like a diver. Ghosts whooed like owls in the long nights when I dared not look over my shoulder; animals lurked in the cubbyhole under the stairs where the gas meter ticked. And I remember that we went singing carols once, when there wasn't the shaving of a moon to light the flying streets. At the end of a long road was a drive that led to a large house, and we stumbled up the darkness of the drive that night, each one of us afraid, each one holding a stone in his hand in case, and all of us too brave to say a word. The wind through the trees made noises as of old and unpleasant and maybe webfooted men wheezing in caves. We reached the black bulk of the house.

"What shall we give them? Hark the Herald?"

"No," Jack said, "Good King Wenceslas. I'll count three."

One, two, three, and we began to sing, our voices high and seemingly distant in the snow-felted darkness round the house that was occupied by nobody we knew. We stood close together, near the dark door.

Good King Wenceslas
looked out
On the Feast of Stephen . . . 6

And then a small, dry voice, like the voice of someone who has not spoken for a long time, joined our singing: a small, dry, eggshell voice from the other side of the door: a small dry voice through the keyhole. And when we stopped running we were outside *our* house; the front room was lovely; balloons floated under the hot-water-bottle-gulping gas; everything was good again and shone over the town.

"Perhaps it was a ghost," Jim said.

"Perhaps it was trolls,"[31] Dan said, who was always reading.

"Let's go in and see if there's any jelly left," Jack said. And we did that.

Always on Christmas night there was music. An uncle played the fiddle, a cousin sang "Cherry Ripe," and another uncle sang "Drake's Drum." It was very warm in the little house. Auntie Hannah, who had got on to the parsnip wine, sang a song about Bleeding Hearts and Death, and then another in which she said her heart was like a Bird's Nest; and then everybody laughed again; and then I went to bed. Looking through my bedroom window, out into the moonlight and the unending smoke-colored snow, I could see the lights in the windows of all the other houses on our hill and hear the music rising from them up the long, steadily falling night. I turned the gas down, I got into bed. I said some words to the close and holy darkness, 7
and then I slept.

The Whistle (detail and tint), Fritz Eichenberg etching, © Fritz Eichenberg Trust/Licensed by VAGA, New York, NY

29. **dewlapped:** Having loose folds of skin hanging from the throat.
30. **Excelsior** (ek sel′ sē ôr′): Latin phrase meaning "onward and upward."
31. **trolls:** Mythical Scandinavian beings.

◆ Build Vocabulary

brittle (brit′ əl) *adj.*: Stiff and unbending; easily broken or shattered
trod (träd) *v.*: Walked
forlorn (fər lôrn′) *adj.*: Abandoned; deserted

◆ *Literature and Your Life*

5 Ask students if families still tell each other ghost stories and other tall tales at holiday gatherings. Then ask what activities have often replaced such storytelling. *Many students will say that TV shows, videos, video games, and computer games have replaced storytelling at family gatherings.*

Customize for *English Language Learners*

6 Have students who are familiar with the customs of Christmas caroling explain these customs to those who are not. If they know the carols mentioned here, have them sing them or say their lyrics for English language learners in the class. In turn, these students can sing Christmas or holiday songs in their native languages.

◆ Critical Thinking

7 **Interpret** Ask students to describe the mood the last sentence of the selection conveys. *Students might describe a mood of contentment, peace, holiness, or mystery.*

Viewing and Representing Mini-Lesson

Multimedia Presentation

This mini-lesson supports the Researching and Representing activity on p. 607.

Introduce Students might research before they select a person to present. An area with which they are less familiar may provide interesting personalities who have participated and excelled in that area. Alternatively suggest that students choose a successful person in a field that they are interested in pursuing themselves.

Develop Students can use the Internet, periodical files in the library, reference books, and biographies as resources for their presentation research. When they feel that they have gathered adequate information, they will need to determine what media forms of multimedia best suit their subject.

Apply When their research and planning is complete, guide students to design and prepare their presentations, providing available equipment, as needed.

Assess Evaluate students based on their research and the appropriateness of their use of media in their presentations.

Develop Understanding

One-Minute Insight "Marian Anderson: Famous Concert Singer," by Langston Hughes, is an account of how the great African American singer overcame racial bias to become one of the world's most renowned and revered artists. Hughes's attitude toward his subject is one of admiration and esteem.

❶ **Clarification** Explain to students that, at the time this biographical account was written, the terms *Negro* and *colored* were the acceptable terms for *African Americans.* (You might want to lead a brief discussion about how the different terms reflect the social attitudes of their times.)

◆ Literary Focus

❷ **Biography and Autobiography** Ask students why Hughes includes this information about other African American performers in a biographical piece on Marian Anderson. *The information sets the scene by establishing the status and stereotypes of African American singers at the time Anderson was growing up. It also heightens the significance of her accomplishments.*

Marian Anderson: Famous Concert Singer

Langston Hughes

❶ When Marian Anderson was born in a little red brick house in Philadelphia, a famous group of Negro singers, the Fisk Jubilee Singers, had already carried the spirituals all over Europe. And a colored woman billed as "Black Patti" had become famous on variety programs as a singer of both folk songs and the classics. Both Negro and white minstrels had popularized American songs. The all-Negro musical comedies of Bert Williams and George Walker had been successful on Broadway. But no well-trained colored singers performing the great songs of Schubert, Handel, and the other masters, or the arias from famous operas, had become successful on the concert stage. And most people thought of Negro vocalists only in connection with spirituals. Roland Hayes[1] and Marian Anderson were the first to become famous enough to break this stereotype.

Marian Anderson's mother was a staunch church worker who loved to croon the hymns

1. **Roland Hayes** (1887–1977): Famous African American tenor in the United States.

Cross-Curricular Connection: Music

Vocal Music Spirituals are folk songs that were sung by enslaved African Americans, expressing their desire for freedom in terms of Christian images. The blues—from which rhythm and blues, jazz, and rock and roll were all derived—is another form of folk music that originated with African Americans. Classical music, on the other hand, is a European tradition of music in which individual composers wrote musical works according to formal rules. Professional writing and performing of this kind of music requires extensive training and education in musical notation and theory.

Marian Anderson was a skilled performer of classical as well as folk music. Share with students recordings of various types of vocal music from your library: spirituals, the blues, jazz, musicals, art songs, and opera. Have students compare and contrast performance styles and the emotional impact of the various types of vocal music.

of her faith about the house, as did the aunt who came to live with them when Marian's father died. Both parents were from Virginia. Marian's mother had been a schoolteacher there, and her father a farm boy. Shortly after they moved to Philadelphia where three daughters were born, the father died, and the mother went to work at Wanamaker's department store. But she saw to it that her children attended school and church regularly. The father had been an usher in the Union Baptist Church, so the congregation took an interest in his three little girls. Marian was the oldest and, before she was eight, singing in the Sunday school choir, she had already learned a great many hymns and spirituals by heart.

One day Marian saw an old violin in a pawnshop window marked $3.45. She set her mind on that violin, and began to save the nickels and dimes neighbors would give her for scrubbing their white front steps—the kind of stone steps so characteristic of Philadelphia and Baltimore houses—until she had $3.00. The pawnshop man let her take the violin at a reduced price. Marian never became very good on the violin. A few years later her mother bought a piano, so the child forgot all about it in favor of their newer instrument. By that time, too, her unusual singing voice had attracted the attention of her choir master, and at the age of fourteen she was promoted to a place in the main church choir. There she learned all four parts of all the hymns and anthems and could easily fill in anywhere from bass to soprano.

Sensing that she had exceptional musical talent, some of the church members began to raise money so that she might have singing lessons. But her first teacher, a colored woman, refused to accept any pay for instructing so talented a child. So the church folks put their money into a trust fund called "Marian Anderson's Future," banking it until the time came for her to have advanced training. Meanwhile, Marian attended South Philadelphia High School for Girls and took part in various group concerts, usually doing the solo parts. When she was fifteen she sang a group of songs alone at a Sunday School Convention in Harrisburg and word of her talent began to spread about the state. When she was graduated from high school, the Philadelphia Choral Society, a Negro group, sponsored her 6
further study and secured for her one of the best local teachers. Then in 1925 she journeyed to New York to take part, with three hundred other young singers, in the New York Philharmonic Competitions, where she won first place, and appeared with the orchestra at Lewisohn Stadium.

This appearance was given wide publicity, but very few lucrative engagements came in, so Marian continued to study. A Town Hall concert was arranged for her in New York, but it was unsuccessful. Meanwhile, she kept on singing with various choral groups, and herself gave concerts in churches and at some of the Negro colleges until, in 1930, a Rosenald Fellowship made European study possible. During her first year abroad she made her debut in Berlin. A prominent Scandinavian concert manager read of this concert, but was attracted more by the name, Anderson, than by what the critics said about her voice. "Ah," he said, "a Negro singer with a Swedish name! She is bound to be a success in Scandinavia." He sent two of his friends to Germany to hear her, one of them being Kosti Vehanen who shortly became her accompanist and remained with her for many years.

Sure enough, Marian Anderson did become a great success in the Scandinavian countries, where she learned to sing in both Finnish and Swedish, and her first concert tour of Europe 7
became a critical triumph. When she came back home to America, she gave several programs and appeared as soloist with the famous Hall Johnson Choir, but without financial success. However, the Scandinavian people, who had fallen in love with her, kept asking her to come back there. So, in 1933, she went again to Europe for 142 concerts in Norway, Sweden, Denmark, and Finland. She was decorated by the King of Denmark and the King of Sweden.

◀ **Critical Viewing** In what ways does this photograph illustrate the qualities Langston Hughes describes? **[Analyze]**

◆ Build Vocabulary

arias (är′ ē əz) *n.:* Melodies in an opera, especially for solo voice with instrumental accompaniment

staunch (stônch) *adj.:* Steadfast; loyal

◆ Reading Strategy

❸ Recognize the Author's Attitude Ask students: What attitude can you infer towards Anderson in this passage? Upon what evidence do you make your inference? *Hughes probably considers even her behavior as a child to be admirable. By using the phrase "she set her mind," Hughes conveys that Anderson was a determined person.*

◆ Build Vocabulary

❹ Musical Words Ask students who have sung in choruses to explain what the *bass* and *soprano* parts of choral music are. Then ask what a *solo* part is. *The bass part is the one with the lowest notes, sung by male singers; the soprano part has the highest notes and is usually sung by female singers. A solo part is one in which one singer performs alone. A solo is usually awarded to one of the best singers in the group.*

▶Critical Viewing◀

❺ Analyze Elicit responses such as the following: *The singer appears in a very dignified, confident pose worthy of admiration. The respectful look that the accompanist is giving Anderson echoes this attitude.*

◆ Build Grammar Skills

❻ Restrictive and Nonrestrictive Appositives Ask students why the phrase "a Negro group" is set off by commas. *It is a nonrestrictive appositive, giving further information about the Philadelphia Choral Society. Because the information in the appositive is not essential to the meaning of the sentence, it is set off with commas.*

◆ Critical Thinking

❼ Infer Ask students why they think Marian Anderson has to go to Europe to achieve her first major success. *Racial prejudice and stereotypes in the United States make it difficult for an American audience to accept an African American who sings classical music.*

Analyze Musical Criticism

Point out to students that just as there are specific elements they can analyze in works of literature, there are also specific elements they can analyze in a vocal performance. Appreciation and analysis of music does not require extensive musical training. Discuss musical elements that may be heard in a classical vocal performance:

- dynamic (volume) range: from loud to soft
- pitch range: from high notes to low notes
- emotional range: expression of sadness, happiness, as well as other emotions

Noted conductor Arturo Toscanini described Anderson's singing voice as one "heard once in a hundred years."

Have students listen to a Marian Anderson recording. Then suggest that they think about Toscanini's statement and musical elements as they analyze and discuss Anderson's performance.

1. Do you enjoy hearing her sing? *Some students may not appreciate the type of music she sings.*
2. Describe her voice as it sounds to you. *Students may note Anderson's powerful and emotional sound.*

◆ Literary Focus

❶ Biography and Autobiography Elicit responses such as the following: *Hughes chose to include this incident because it demonstrates admirable qualities in Marian Anderson's character: her courage, dignity, pride, and sense of responsibility to her audience.*

◆ Literary Focus

❷ Biography and Autobiography Ask students to identify possible sources of the facts in this paragraph and to explain why so many facts are included here. *Possible sources of the facts are newspapers, record companies, the singer herself, or her managers and publicity spokespeople. The facts are included to support the main idea of the paragraph: that Marian Anderson became one of the most popular and most honored singers in the nation and the world.*

◆ Reading Strategy

❸ Recognize the Author's Attitude Ask students why the author probably chose to describe these events. What can they infer is Hughes's attitude about the events he describes? *Hughes thought it was important for his readers to know that Anderson, despite her prominence, experienced racial prejudice. Students can infer that Hughes's attitude towards these injustices was one of anger or disgust.*

Reteach

Ask students what they think the author's attitude toward Marian Anderson is. Help them recognize that he admires both her talent and her courage in the face of adversity. He also appears to take pleasure in relating her triumphs as an artist. Have students choose passages from the selection that they think demonstrates the author's attitude and explain their choices.

Sibelius[2] dedicated a song to her. And the following spring she made her debut in Paris where she was so well received that she had to give three concerts that season at the Salle Gaveau.[3] Great successes followed in all the European capitals. In 1935 the famous conductor, Arturo Toscanini, listened to her sing at Salzburg.[4] He said, "What I heard today one is privileged to hear only once in a hundred years." It was in Europe that Marian Anderson began to be acclaimed by critics as "the greatest singer in the world."

When Marian Anderson again returned to America, she was a seasoned artist. News of her tremendous European successes had preceded her, so a big New York concert was planned. But a few days before she arrived at New York, in a storm on the liner crossing the Atlantic, Marian fell and broke her ankle. She refused to allow this to interfere with her concert, however, nor did she even want people to know about it. She wore a very long evening gown that night so that no one could see the plaster cast on her leg. She propped herself in a curve of the piano before the curtains parted, and gave her New York concert standing on one foot! The next day Howard Taubman wrote enthusiastically in *The New York Times*:

> ◆ Literary Focus
> ❶ Why do you think Hughes chose to include this incident in Marion Anderson's biography?

> Marian Anderson has returned to her native land one of the great singers of our time. . . . There is no doubt of it, she was mistress of all she surveyed. . . . It was music making that proved too deep for words.

A coast-to-coast American tour followed. And, from that season on, Marian Anderson has been one of our country's favorite singers, rated, according to *Variety*,[5] among the top ten of the concert stage who earn over $100,000 a year. Miss Anderson has sung with the great symphony orchestras, and appeared on all the major radio and television networks many times, being a particular favorite with the millions of listeners to the Ford Hour. During the years she has returned often to Europe for concerts, and among the numerous honors accorded her abroad was a request for a command performance before the King and Queen of England, and a decoration from the government of Finland. Her concerts in South America and Asia have been as successful as those elsewhere. Since 1935 she has averaged over one hundred programs a year in cities as far apart as Vienna, Buenos Aires, Moscow, and Tokyo. Her recordings have sold millions of copies around the world. She has been invited more than once to sing at the White House. She has appeared in concert at the Paris Opera and at the Metropolitan Opera House in New York. Several colleges have granted her honorary degrees, and in 1944 Smith College made her a Doctor of Music.

In spite of all this, as a Negro, Marian Anderson has not been immune from those aspects of racial segregation which affect most traveling artists of color in the United States. In his book, *Marian Anderson*, her longtime accompanist, Vehanen, tells of hotel accommodations being denied her, and service in dining rooms often refused. Once after a concert in a Southern city, Vehanen writes that some white friends drove Marian to the railroad station and took her into the main waiting room. But a policeman ran them out, since Negroes were not allowed in that part of the station. Then they went into the smaller waiting room marked, COLORED. But again they were ejected, because *white* people were not permitted in the cubby hole allotted to Negroes. So they all had to stand on the platform until the train arrived.

The most dramatic incident of prejudice in all Marian Anderson's career occurred in 1939 when the Daughters of the American Revolution, who own Constitution Hall in Washington, refused to allow her to sing there. The newspapers headlined this and many Americans were outraged. In protest a committee of prominent

---

2. **Sibelius** (si bä′ lē o͞os): Jean Sibelius (1865–1957), a Finnish composer.
3. **Salle Gaveau** (sal ga vō′): Concert hall in Paris, France.
4. **Salzburg:** City in Austria noted for its music festivals.
5. ***Variety*:** Show-business newspaper.

Beyond the Classroom

Career Connection

Music Langston Hughes's piece on Marian Anderson brings out that the great singer was accomplished in several musical genres, including spiritual and classical singing. Discuss with students the different roles open to those with musical talent and training, or ability and knowledge. These roles include performer, composer (one who creates music), lyricist (one who writes the lyrics for songs) arranger (one who resets music for different instruments or voices), producer (one who supervises the production of music), and sound engineer (one who manages the recording equipment). Lead students to see that several important fields use musicians in these roles, that they can be employed in the film, record, or advertising industries, as well as by companies who create multimedia products.

Interested students might research careers in music to find out what educational background and preparation is required for the roles discussed. Suggest that they contact a music department of a local college or search the Internet to get more information.

people, including a number of great artists and distinguished figures in the government, was formed. Through the efforts of this committee, Marian Anderson sang in Washington, anyway—before the statue of Abraham Lincoln—to one of the largest crowds ever to hear a singer at one time in the history of the world. Seventy-five thousand people stood in the open air on a cold clear Easter Sunday afternoon to hear her. And millions more listened to Marian Anderson that day over the radio or heard her in the newsreels that recorded the event. Harold Ickes, then Secretary of the Interior, presented Miss Anderson to that enormous audience standing in the plaza to pay honor, as he said, not only to a great singer, but to the basic ideals of democracy and equality.

In 1943 Marian Anderson married Orpheus H. Fisher, an architect, and settled down—between tours—in a beautiful country house in Connecticut where she rehearses new songs to add to her already vast repertoire. Sometimes her neighbors across the fields can hear the rich warm voice that covers three octaves singing in English, French, Finnish, or German. And sometimes they hear in the New England air that old Negro spiritual, "Honor, honor unto the dying Lamb. . . ."

Friends say that Marian Anderson has invested her money in real estate and in government bonds. Certainly, throughout her career, she has lived very simply, traveled without a maid or secretary, and carried her own sewing machine along by train, ship, or plane to mend her gowns. When in 1941 in Philadelphia she was awarded the coveted Bok Award for outstanding public service, the $10,000 that came with the medallion she used to establish a trust fund for "talented American artists without regard to race or creed." Now, each year from this fund promising young musicians receive scholarships.

◆ Reading Strategy
What attitude toward Marian Anderson is shown by the details given in this paragraph? 4

◆ **Build Vocabulary**

repertoire (rep´ ə twär) *n.*: Stock of songs that a singer knows and is ready to perform

Guide for Responding

◆ Literature and Your Life

Reader's Response If you could meet one person from Hughes's or Thomas's essay, whom would you choose? Why?

Thematic Focus How can something like Hughes's or Thomas's essay, which concentrate on the past, still be relevant in today's world?

☑ Check Your Comprehension

1. In "A Child's Christmas in Wales," how did Jim and Dylan respond to the fire at Prothero's house?

2. Decribe three events in Thomas's recollections of Christmas.

3. How did Marian Anderson's congregation help her?

4. What difficulties did Anderson face traveling in the United States?

◆ Critical Thinking

INTERPRET

1. What details indicate that "A Child's Christmas in Wales" is a childhood memory narrated by an adult? **[Analyze]**

2. In what ways was Christmas for the children different from Christmas for the adults? **[Contrast]**

3. Why was it so difficult for Marian Anderson to gain success in the United States? **[Interpret]**

4. What can you learn about Anderson from the way she chooses to spend the money given with the Bok Award? **[Draw Conclusions]**

APPLY

5. Why do people's memories tend to blend together and exaggerate the past? **[Relate]**

COMPARE LITERARY WORKS

6. These two writers are known as great poets. Do these pieces reflect a poet's sensibility and use of language? If so, in what ways? **[Connect]**

Beyond the Selection

FURTHER READING

Other Works by Dylan Thomas
"Fern Hill," "Poem in October"

Other Works by Langston Hughes
"Harriet Tubman: The Moses of Her People,"

Other Works About Special Memories
"A Christmas Memory," Truman Capote
"Women," Alice Walker

We suggest that you preview these works before recommending them to students.

INTERNET

Students can learn more at the following sites on the Internet. Please be aware that the sites may have changed since we published this information.

Dylan Thomas: **http://www.cord.edu./homepages/pjlerohl/DYLAN.html**

Black History Web site: **http://www.inter-log. com/~csteele/flavour.htmlz**

We *strongly recommend* that you preview the sites before you send students to them.

◆ Reading Strategy

4 Recognize the Author's Attitude Elicit responses such as the following: *The author shows admiration for Anderson's simplicity, humility, and generosity.*

Reinforce and Extend

Answers

◆ Literature and Your Life

Reader's Response Students might chose the character of Dylan Thomas as a boy or Marian Anderson. Both, in different ways, showed great spirit.

Thematic Focus Although people in the past had different kinds of experiences than they do today, they have basic human feelings in common.

☑ Check Your Comprehension

1. They ran to the house with their snowballs to put out the fire.
2. Possible events: getting Useful and Useless presents; eating turkey dinner; telling stories; caroling
3. They raised money to pay for her musical training.
4. Anderson encountered racial prejudice: She was sometimes refused rooms or service in hotels.

◆ Critical Thinking

1. In the first paragraph Thomas says he can never remember how long it snowed, indicating he's writing about a long time ago. All adventures of the "we" characters are adventures of little boys.
2. The children were excited and full of mischief; the adults were more disinterested and weary.
3. Her career in the United States was stalled by racial prejudice; people did not accept an African American who sang classical music.
4. Anderson was extremely generous in wanting young musicians to have an easier time than she had.
5. Memories blend and become exaggerated because time affects people's perceptions.
6. Sample response: Students may mention Thomas's poetic language and Hughes's appreciation of Anderson's artistic talent.

Guide for Responding *(continued)*

◆ Literary Focus

Biography and Autobiography

In an **autobiography,** the author may include details that would never be known through the research of a biographer. Dylan Thomas reveals details about his childhood that only he would know. In Langston Hughes's **biography** of Marion Anderson, he provides factual information about her life while emphasizing certain aspects of her character.

1. (a) Why do you think Thomas tells this memory of his childhood? (b) What details in "A Child's Christmas in Wales" support your opinion?
2. What incidents in "Marian Anderson: Famous Concert Singer" reveal Anderson's character?
3. (a) What aspects of Anderson's life has the author emphasized? (b) What has he left out?

◆ Build Vocabulary

Using Musical Words

Like law, medicine, and other disciplines, music has a vocabulary all its own. On your paper, match each of the following words with its definition.

1. soprano	**a.** sing in a soft, often sentimental, manner
2. croon	**b.** song of praise or devotion
3. anthem	**c.** highest vocal range for a woman or boy singer

Using the Word Bank: Connotations

On your paper, match each word from the Word Bank with the animal, person, or thing that is most closely associated with that word.

1. staunch	**a.** burglar
2. sidle	**b.** shoes
3. prey	**c.** lost child
4. wallowed	**d.** twigs
5. crocheted	**e.** sweater
6. brittle	**f.** pig
7. trod	**g.** friend
8. forlorn	**h.** hunter

◆ Reading Strategy

Recognize Author's Attitude

The **attitude** that a biographer or autobiographer has toward his or her subject is reflected in the way that the author presents information about that person.

1. (a) What is Dylan Thomas's attitude about the events in his childhood related in "A Child's Christmas in Wales"? (b) What details convey his attitude?
2. What details in "Marian Anderson: Famous Concert Singer" indicate that Hughes admires his subject?

◆ Build Grammar Skills

Restrictive and Nonrestrictive Appositives

Appositives and appositive phrases provide more information about the noun they are placed near. Appositives can be either restrictive or nonrestrictive. A **restrictive appositive** is essential to the meaning of the sentence and is not set off by commas. A **nonrestrictive appositive** is not essential and is set off by commas.

Practice Locate the appositive or appositive phrase in each sentence and identify it as restrictive or nonrestrictive.

1. I was in Mrs. Prothero's garden, waiting for cats, with her son Jim.
2. Jim's only aunt, Mabel, was staying with his family.
3. Marian Anderson's first teacher, an African American woman, refused to accept any pay for instructing so talented a child.
4. In 1943, Marian Anderson married the architect Orpheus H. Fisher and settled down in Connecticut.

Writing Application Rewrite each sentence on your paper, highlighting the appositive or appositve phrase and indicating whether it is restrictive or nonrestrictive. Include commas where necessary.

1. Marion Anderson beloved singer toured Europe.
2. The writer Langston Hughes admired Marion Anderson.
3. Dylan Thomas a famous writer shares his Christmas memories.

Answers

◆ Literary Focus

1. (a) Thomas wants to share his experience of a particular and warm childhood. (b) He remembers details such as the kinds of presents exchanged with great clarity.
2. Incidents that reveal Anderson's character include her saving money to buy the second-hand violin and her performing with a broken ankle.
3. (a) He has emphasized aspects of her career and the obstacles she met in achieving success. (b) He has left out mention of her personal life—her life outside music.

◆ Build Vocabulary

Using Musical Words

1. c 2. a 3. b

Using the Word Bank

1. g 2. a 3. h 4. f 5. e 6. d
7. b 8. c

◆ Reading Strategy

1. (a) Thomas finds many events in his childhood amusing. (b) He characterizes the people in his childhood in such a way as to make them seem humorous.
2. Hughes shows his admiration of Anderson by stressing her professionalism—such as performing with a broken ankle—and her generous nature—setting up a fund for young musicians.

◆ Build Grammar Skills

Practice

1. *Jim*—restrictive
2. *Mabel*—nonrestrictive
3. *an African American woman*—nonrestrictive
4. *Orpheus H. Fisher*—restrictive

Writing Application

1. Marion Anderson, beloved singer, toured Europe. (nonrestrictive)
2. The writer Langston Hughes admired Marian Anderson. (restrictive)
3. Dylan Thomas, a famous writer, shares his Christmas memories. (nonrestrictive)

Grammar Reinforcement

For additional instruction and practice, use the lesson in the **Language Lab CD-ROM** on Commas to get information on how to punctuate appositives and p. 40 on Appositives and Appositive Phrases in the *Writer's Solution Grammar Practice Book.*

Build Your Portfolio

Idea Bank

Writing

1. Your Favorite Holiday Write an essay about your favorite holiday. Describe how you typically spend this day and why it is so special to you.

2. Memory From Childhood Choose a memory from your childhood. Write down what you can recall, then interview others who are part of the memory. Write an account of the event, noting how others' recollections differ from yours.

3. Biography Write a biography of someone you know. Make a list of your subject's qualities and accomplishments. Then describe an incident from his or her life that best highlights those traits.

Speaking, Listening, and Viewing

4. Visual Presentation In the United States, Christmas is associated with winter, but millions of people in the Southern Hemisphere celebrate the holiday in their summer. Research the visual symbols of Christmas used in Latin America, and prepare a visual presentation for your classmates. **[Social Studies Link]**

5. Marian Anderson Recording Find one of Marian Anderson's recordings in a library and listen to it. Make a chart analyzing her singing. **[Music Link]**

Researching and Representing

6. Greeting Card Design a greeting card for a holiday that you celebrate. On the card, illustrate the customs and traditions common to that holiday. Inside, write a message that captures the spirit of the holiday. **[Art Link]**

7. Multimedia Presentation Choose an individual who has excelled in a field such as art or athletics. Give a multimedia presentation that shows the obstacles your subject had to overcome and how he or she has enriched that field.

Online Activity www.phlit.phschool.com

Guided Writing Lesson

Letter to Yourself in Twenty Years

Consider your life as an ongoing biography. It's easy to remember where you were and what you were doing a few years ago. It's far more challenging to think where you'll be and what you'll be doing twenty years from now. Perhaps you will be married and raising a family. You may be living in another city, or even another country. The possibilities are endless. Write a **letter to yourself**, to be opened in twenty years. In the letter, mention some of the high and low points of your life right now, and then discuss your dreams. Seal the letter and write on the envelope "To be opened in the year 20__."

Writing Skills Focus: Logical Organization

Choose a **logical method of organization** for your letter. You might organize it chronologically, starting in the present and gradually chronicling your projected achievements through the years. You might compare and contrast your life now with the life you would like twenty years from now. You might organize in order of importance, discussing what's most important to you now and what may seem less or more important as time passes.

Prewriting Make a two-column chart that shows your interests and abilities now (left column) and where these interests and abilities might lead you (right column). After creating your chart, choose an organization plan appropriate for your letter.

Drafting Use a personal, conversational tone for your letter—you are writing to yourself. Refer to your chart, including the details you think will most influence your future.

Revising Look back over your draft to see if there's anything you've left out. Make sure that you've been honest in your letter—remember, the only person you're trying to impress is yourself.

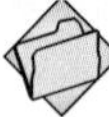

Idea Bank

Following are suggestions for matching Idea Bank topics with your students' performance levels and learning modalities:

Customizing for *Performance Levels*
Less Advanced Students: 1, 4, 6
Average Students: 2
More Advanced Students: 3, 5, 7

Customizing for *Learning Modalities*
Visual/Spatial: 6, 7
Verbal/Linguistic: 4,
Rhythmic/Musical: 4, 5

Guided Writing Lesson

Revision Strategy When students have finished drafting their letters, have them reenter their writing and analyze the organization they used. First have them use a colored pen or pencil to bracket each point they are making. Then have students list the points in the order in which they appear in their letters. Encourage them to analyze and evaluate the order and decide whether reordering the points, adding something that has been left out, or using a different method of organization will make their writing clearer when they open their letters in 20 years.

For more prewriting, elaboration, and revision strategies, see *Prentice Hall Writing and Grammar.*

Writing Lab CD-ROM
To develop their letters, have students complete the tutorial on Narration. Follow these steps:

1. Have students consult interactive tips for accomplishing a purpose.
2. Refer students to the Chain of Events tool to help them organize their letters to themselves in twenty years.
3. Have students use the Revision Checker for sentence length and passive voice.

✓ ASSESSMENT OPTIONS

Formal Assessment, Selection Test, pp. 151–153, and Assessment Resources Software. The selection test is designed so that it can be easily customized to the performance levels of your students.
Alternative Assessment, p. 43, includes options for less advanced students, more advanced students, verbal/linguistic learners, bodily/kinesthetic learners, visual/spatial learners, and musical/rhythmic learners.

PORTFOLIO ASSESSMENT
Use the following rubrics in the ***Alternative Assessment*** booklet to assess student writing:
Your Favorite Holiday: Description Rubric, p. 97
Memory From Childhood: Narrative Based on Personal Experience Rubric, p. 96
Biography: Description Rubric, p. 97

Prepare and Engage

LESSON OBJECTIVES

1. To develop vocabulary and word identification skills
- Latin prefixes: *mal-*
- Using the Word Bank: Antonyms
- Extending Word Study: Word Origins

2. To use a variety of reading strategies to read and comprehend an essay
- Connect Your Experience
- Reading Strategy: Recognize Facts and Impressions (ATE)
- Tips to Guide Reading: Sustained Reading (ATE)
- Read to Be Informed

3. To increase knowledge of other cultures and to connect common elements across cultures
- Connecting Themes Across Cultures (ATE)

4. To express and support responses to the text
- Critical Thinking
- Idea Bank: Storm Journal

5. To analyze literary elements
- Literary Focus: Descriptive Essay
- Idea Bank: Descriptive Paragraph

6. To read in order to research self-selected and assigned topics
- Research Skills Mini-Lesson: Researching Specific Information
- Idea Bank: Food-Chain Presentation
- Questions for Research

7. To plan, prepare, organize, and present literary interpretations
- Idea Bank: Fable

8. To speak clearly and effectively for a specific audience and purpose
- Idea Bank: Talk-Show Interview
- Speaking, Listening, and Viewing Mini-Lesson: Storm Report

9. To use recursive writing processes to write a radio transcript
- Guided Writing Lesson

10. To increase knowledge of the rules of grammar and usage
- Build Grammar Skills: Subject and Verb Agreement

Test Preparation

Reading Comprehension: Analyzing Literary Language (ATE, p. 609) The teaching tips and sample test item in this workshop support the instruction and practice in the unit workshop.

Reading Comprehension: Comparing and Contrasting Texts; Analyzing Literary Language (SE, p. 661)

Guide for Reading

Featured in AUTHORS IN DEPTH Series

Annie Dillard *(1945–)*

Life Near Tinker Creek Annie Dillard's romance with nature—observing it, learning from it, rejoicing in it—probably intensified during the four seasons she spent living near Tinker Creek, Virginia. An area of forests, creeks, and mountains, brimming with wildlife of all kinds, Tinker Creek so nurtured Dillard in her solitude that she began to write about it. She was twenty-nine when she wrote *Pilgrim at Tinker Creek*, a profound meditation on nature and religion that was awarded the Pulitzer Prize in 1975. "Flood," which recalls the effects of Hurricane Agnes in 1972, is set at Tinker Creek.

A Sustaining Childhood Annie Dillard grew up in Pittsburgh, Pennsylvania, the oldest of three daughters. Her affluent parents encouraged her to be creative and explore her surroundings, and they shared their knowledge of everything from plumbing to economics. Dillard reflected upon her childhood in her 1987 autobiography, *An American Childhood*. Her curiosity and exuberance is perhaps best exemplified in a description of her childhood attempts to fly.

> *I knew well that people could not fly—as well as anyone knows it—but I also knew that, with faith, all things are possible.*

From childhood on, it seems, Dillard's sense of awe set her apart from the doings of proper society around her.

Living by Literature Dillard continues to spend a great deal of time reading, writing, and teaching literature. She also teaches a course in nonfiction narrative writing. Her own books are devoted to the love of literature: *Living by Fiction* and *The Writing Life* were published in the 1980's.

◆ Build Vocabulary

LATIN PREFIXES: *mal-*

When some children capture a snapping turtle in "Flood," the animal makes a malevolent hiss. *Malevolent* contains the Latin prefix *mal-*, which means "bad, evil." A *malevolent* hiss would be one that shows ill will. You can also see *mal-* as a root in *dismal*, meaning "causing gloom or depression." During the flood, it rains all week—truly *dismal* weather.

WORD BANK

As you read this story, you will encounter the words in this list. Each word is defined on the page on which it first appears. Preview the list before you read.

obliterates
opacity
usurped
mauled
malevolent
repressed

◆ Build Grammar Skills

SUBJECT AND VERB AGREEMENT

In all writing, **subjects and verbs must agree** in number. When words intervene between the subject and verb, the correct agreement may not be immediately apparent. Consider this sentence from "Flood":

> s v
> Water that has picked up clay soils looks worse than other muddy waters...

The singular verb form *looks* agrees with its singular subject *water*, not with *soils*, even though *soils* is closer to the verb.

Annie Dillard writes a number of sentences like this one, with a modifying structure between the subject and the verb, yet she always makes the verb agree with its subject.

Prentice Hall Literature Program Resources

REINFORCE / RETEACH / EXTEND

Selection Support Pages
Build Vocabulary: Prefixes: *mal-*, p. 180
Build Grammar Skills: Subject-Verb Agreement, p. 181
Reading Strategy: Recognize Facts and Impressions, p. 182
Literary Focus: Descriptive Essay, p. 183

Strategies for Diverse Student Needs, p. 44

Beyond Literature
Community Connection: Flood Control, p. 44

Formal Assessment Selection Test, pp. 154–156; Assessment Resources Software

Alternative Assessment, p. 44

Resource Pro CD-ROM

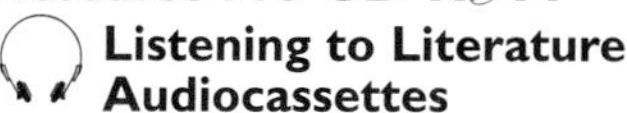

Flood

◆ Literature and Your Life

CONNECT YOUR EXPERIENCE

You walk outside and find that a freezing storm has left ice glittering everywhere you look—on tree branches, car roofs, and store awnings. When nature transforms our everyday sights into something extraordinary, as it does in "Flood," we have the chance to see the world anew. As Dillard describes the myriad aspects of a flood, think about what natural occurrences have transformed the world around you, if even for a moment.

THEMATIC FOCUS: NATURAL FORCES

Forces of nature can interrupt and even change our daily lives. What effects have the forces of nature had on you or people you know?

Journal Writing Write a paragraph describing in detail the effect of a natural force, such as a storm uprooting a tree.

◆ Background for Understanding

SCIENCE

The 1972 hurricane Agnes might have been downgraded to a tropical storm by the time it reached Annie Dillard's Tinker Creek, but it still produced the worst floods in Virginia's history. The low-lying basins of the Susquehanna, Allegheny, Chemung, Monongahela, Ohio, and James rivers were all struck by flash flooding from Hurricane Agnes. Dillard's home state of Pennsylvania was actually the worst hit by the floods.

Flash floods from hurricanes can destroy homes and ruin lives. They can leave fish swimming in people's basements, carry cars and furniture downstream, and erode riverbanks.

◆ Literary Focus

DESCRIPTIVE ESSAY

Reading "Flood" might make you feel that you're hip-high in rising creek water. You'll hear wind, feel rain, and see water rising and receding. That's because "Flood" succeeds as a **descriptive essay**, a short nonfiction work that contains details that show how something looks, feels, smells, sounds, or tastes. As you read, notice Dillard's use of language that appeals to your senses, like "knot of yellow, fleshy somethings" and "a high, windy sound more like air than water." These descriptions, which are visual, tactile, and auditory, have the effect of taking you off the page and into the flood.

◆ Reading Strategy

RECOGNIZE FACTS AND IMPRESSIONS

If you tell a friend that Dillard's essay describes the flooding of Tinker Creek in 1972, you are presenting a **fact**—information that can be proven. If you then say that the flood was really frightening, then you're giving your **impression**—a feeling or image retained from an experience.

Be aware when reading "Flood" that the facts you're reading about are verifiable. It can be proved, for example, that Tinker Creek flooded on June 21, 1972, or that the summer solstice is the longest day of the year. However, Dillard's impressions about the flood, such as that it was exciting, are personal; you might come away with different impressions.

Use a chart like this one to separate the facts and impressions in "Flood":

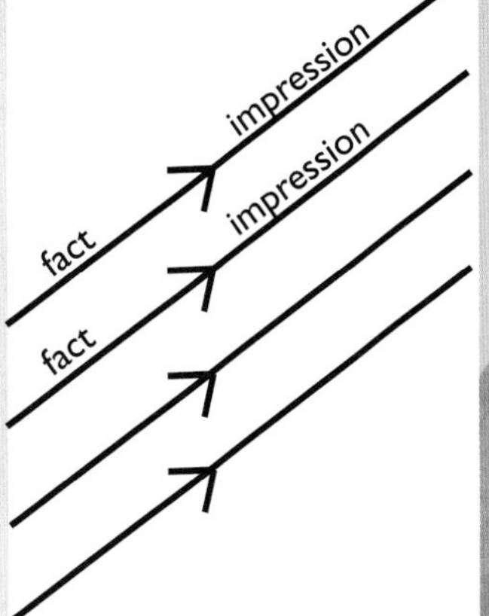

Test Preparation Workshop

Reading Comprehension: Analyzing Literary Language

To help students prepare to analyze literary language for standardized tests, share this passage from "Flood."

> Tinker Creek is out of oft four-foot banks, . . . The high creek doesn't look like our creek. . . . It looks like somebody else's creek that has usurped or eaten our creek and is roving frantically to escape, big and ugly, like a blacksnake caught in a kitchen drawer.

The words in this passage evoke the feeling—

A that something, or someone, is invading the author's home.
B that the creek is cold and wet.
C that everything is going to be all right.
D of happiness and joy that rains have come.

Draw students' attention to the simile "like a blacksnake in a kitchen drawer." Discuss with them what the impact of a trapped, or hiding snake might be. Then have them review the answer choices to determine that the correct answer is A.

Ask students to name and briefly describe any "disaster" movies—films that feature natural disasters such as earthquakes and tornadoes—they have seen recently. Why do they think these movies are so popular? (Students might respond that perhaps people like to feel shocked out of their everyday existence, that they "enjoy" being scared and then relieved when all comes to a happy conclusion.) Tell them that the selection they are about to read deals with a natural disaster. No special effects heighten this disaster; rather, the essayist Annie Dillard creates drama simply through telling the facts and giving her impressions.

Connecting Themes Across Cultures

Point out to students that there are myths about floods in many different cultures. Ask them to list possible reasons for this phenomenon.

Customize for *Less Proficient Readers*

In this selection, the author records the events of a flood in chronological order from before the flood to the time when the danger is past. Noting each event on a time line will help students keep track of the narrative.

Customize for *Pre-AP Students*

Although this is a prose selection, Dillard often uses poetic language, especially alliteration and simile. Have students examine and analyze her use of poetic language and imagery. They might rewrite several sentences without poetic language and compare them with the original.

Customize for *English Language Learners*

Help students to break down and interpret literally sentences that use figurative language, such as: *The water itself was an opaque pale green, like pulverized jade, still high and running fast, lightless, like no earthly water.* (The pale green water was the color of the precious stone jade if it had been broken up. The water was moving fast. It seemed as if it didn't hold light, and it looked like no water the author had seen before.)

Develop Understanding

One-Minute Insight Annie Dillard's recollection of the Tinker Creek flood is sparked by a watchful, uneasy feeling brought on by a June rain. As the account of the flood unfolds, tension rises. The landscape undergoes a dramatic change as a small creek becomes a roiling river that snatches everything in its path and transforms the landscape into an other-worldly waterscape—complete with waves and waterfalls. For the people in the area, the flood is frightening, but it also holds a certain fascination. When it is over and the waters begin to recede, people take up their normal lives once again. Dillard's account of the flood gives readers a glimpse of both nature's power and how people respond to its assault by helping one another.

Tips to Guide Reading

Sustained Reading Encourage students to read the essay all the way through at one sitting. Suggest that they mark details they want to return to later with sticky notes.

Customize for
Musical/Rhythmic Learners
Ask these students to describe how sound effects and background music contribute to their appreciation of movie scenes. Then, encourage these students to think of background music and sound effects as they read Dillard's vivid descriptions. Have students pause occasionally in their reading to explain the effects they would use in different sections and how these effects would enhance the scene.

FLOOD

Block Scheduling Strategies

Consider these suggestions to take advantage of extended class time:

- Introduce the descriptive essay. with the Literary Focus on p. 609. After reading "Flood," have students answer the Literary Focus questions on p. 617 and the Literary Focus page in ***Selection Support,*** p. 183.
- To help with the ***Beyond Literature*** activity (p. 44), Community Connection: *Flood Control.* Discuss with them dams they have seen or know about. To help them form opinions to answer the ***Beyond Literature*** questions, suggest that students research dams and flood control.
- Have students work together in small groups to discuss the Critical Thinking questions on p. 617.
- Have students read excerpts from *Pilgrim at Tinker Creek* to gain further insight about the area and Dillard's ties to it.
- Encourage students to work together to evaluate and enhance your school or community disaster-preparedness plan.
- At the prewriting stage of the Guided Writing Lesson on p. 618, have students work together to brainstorm for words and phrases that describe a hurricane. After they have drafted their transcripts, use the revision strategy on p. 618 of the ATE to help them with ratiocination.

It's summer. We had some deep spring sunshine about a month ago, in a drought; the nights were cold. It's been gray sporadically, but not oppressively, and rainy for a week, and I would think: When is the real hot stuff coming, the mind-melting weeding weather? It was rainy again this morning, the same spring rain, and then this afternoon a different rain came: a pounding, three-minute shower. And when it was over, the cloud dissolved to haze. I can't see Tinker Mountain. It's summer now: the heat is on. It's summer now all summer long. ❶

The season changed two hours ago. Will my life change as well? This is a time for resolutions, revolutions. The animals are going wild. I must have seen ten rabbits in as many minutes. Baltimore orioles are here; brown thrashers seem to be nesting down by Tinker Creek across the road. The coot is still around, big as a Thanksgiving turkey, and as careless; it doesn't even glance at a barking dog.

The creek's up. When the rain stopped today I walked across the road to the downed log by the steer crossing. The steers were across the creek, a black clot on a distant hill. High water had touched my log, the log I sit on, and dumped a smooth slope of muck in its lee. The water itself was an opaque pale green, like pulverized jade, still high and very fast, lightless, like no earthly water. A dog I've never seen before, thin as death, was flushing rabbits. ❷

A knot of yellow, fleshy somethings had grown up by the log. They didn't seem to have either proper stems or proper flowers, but instead only blind,

◀ Critical Viewing Do you think the physical damage or the emotional damage brought on by a natural disaster like this flood is harder to overcome? **[Support]** ❸

◆ *Literature and Your Life*

❶ Ask students what changes signal summer to them. What do they watch for as the season changes? *Students can share their ideas and observations. Encourage them to focus on sights, smells, sounds.*

◆ Literary Focus

❷ **Descriptive Essay** Ask students to identify the senses to which the author appeals in this passage. How do the sensory descriptions affect the mood in this passage? *The passage appeals to the senses of touch and sight. The sensory details "black clot," "a smooth slope of muck," "opaque pale green, like pulverized jade," "lightless, like no earthly water," and "thin as death" create an ominous mood.*

▶Critical Viewing◀

❸ **Support** *Students may say that the physical damage is shocking and immediate; the emotional damage may linger long after the physical damage is repaired, as people try to rebuild their lives and come to terms with what they have lost.*

Read to Be Informed

Students can learn many facts about what can happen during a flood. Invite them to note which events might occur in any flood, and which ones are unique to the Tinker Creek flood.

Research Skills Mini-Lesson

Researching Specific Information

This mini-lesson supports the Researching and Representing activity, Hurricane Chart, in the Idea Bank on p. 618.

Introduce Discuss with students why hurricanes can cause so much damage. You may want to helps students relate to another form of natural disaster that is appropriate to the area in which they live, such as earthquakes or tornadoes.

Develop Students can look for articles on hurricanes in the Readers' Guide to Periodical Literature in the library. They can also find information on the Internet. Guide their research by suggesting that they look for weather Web sites to provide statistics and facts.

Apply Once students have gathered the information, they will need to organize the material. Discuss with them they best chart design to present statistics and facts. Point out that inset maps might make it easier for those viewing their charts to better understand the relationship of hurricane locales.

Assess Evaluate students' charts based clarity and accuracy of the materials presented.

Develop Understanding

◆ Literary Focus

❶ **Descriptive Essay** Ask students which sensory details in this passage create an ominous feeling. *Students should note: "strangely empty," "so steamy I could barely see," "dead tan mud," "horny orange roots," "roots hung, an empty net in air, clutching an incongruous light bulb," "four jays flew around me very slowly, acting generally odd."*

◆ Literature and Your Life

❷ Point out that Dillard's apprehension is due in part to realizing that it is the anniversary of Hurricane Agnes. Ask students why anniversaries of memorable or devastating events are significant for people. *Students will probably realize that anniversaries of such events tend to bring the events to the forefront of people's minds. For some people, such anniversaries seem to suggest that the experience could be repeated.*

❸ **Clarification** If necessary, explain that hurricane season runs from May 15–November 30 each year. Hurricanes that occur during the season are named alphabetically.

◆ Reading Strategy

❹ **Recognize Facts and Impressions** Students should note the following: *That the creek is out of its four-foot banks is a verifiable fact. The rest of the information is based on Dillard's own impressions; for example, "The high creek doesn't look like our creek," "the high creek obliterates everything in flat opacity," and "It looks like somebody else's creek . . ." are personal impressions of the author that cannot be measured or verified.*

Extending Word Study

Word Origins Call students' attention to the word *opacity,* from the word bank, as Dillard uses it to describe the way that the water looks in the flooded creek. Guide them to use the dictionary to research its Latin word origin, *opacus,* meaning shady. Then ask them to do similar research of the Latin word origin of *obliterate.*

featureless growth, like etiolated[1] potato sprouts in a root cellar. I tried to dig one up from the crumbly soil, but they all apparently grew from a single, well-rooted corm, so I let them go.

Still, the day had an air of menace. A broken whiskey bottle by the log, the brown tip of a snake's tail disappearing between two rocks on the hill at my back, the rabbit the dog nearly caught, the rabies I knew was in the county, the bees who kept unaccountably fumbling at my forehead with their furred feet . . .

❶ I headed over to the new woods by the creek, the motorbike woods. They were strangely empty. The air was so steamy I could barely see. The ravine separating the woods from the field had filled during high water, and a dead tan mud clogged it now. The horny orange roots of one tree on the ravine's jagged bank had been stripped of soil; now the roots hung, an empty net in the air, clutching an incongruous light bulb stranded by receding waters. For the entire time that I walked in the woods, four jays flew around me very slowly, acting generally odd, and screaming on two held notes. There wasn't a breath of wind.

Coming out of the woods, I heard loud shots; they reverberated ominously in the damp air. But when I walked up the road, I saw what it was, and the dread quality of the whole afternoon vanished at once. It was a couple of garbage trucks, huge trash compacters humped like armadillos, and they were making their engines backfire to impress my neighbors' pretty daughters, high school girls who had just been let off the school bus. The long-haired girls strayed into giggling clumps at the corner of the road; the garbage trucks sped away gloriously, as if they had been the Tarleton twins on thoroughbreds cantering away from the gates of Tara.[2] In the distance a white vapor was rising from the waters of Carvin's Cove and catching in trailing tufts in the mountains' sides. I stood on my own porch, exhilarated, unwilling to go indoors.

❷ It was just this time last year that we had the flood. It was Hurricane Agnes, really, but by the time it got here, the weather bureau had demoted it to a tropical storm. ❸ I see by a clipping I saved that the date was June twenty-first, the solstice, midsummer's night, the longest daylight of the year; but I didn't notice it at the time. Everything was so exciting, and so very dark. All it did was rain. It rained, and the creek started to rise. The creek, naturally, rises every time it rains; this didn't seem any different. But it kept raining, and, that morning of the twenty-first, the creek kept rising.

That morning I'm standing at my kitchen window. Tinker Creek is out of its four-foot banks, way out, and it's still coming. The high creek doesn't look like our creek. Our creek splashes transparently over a jumble of rocks; the high creek obliterates everything in flat opacity. It looks like somebody else's creek that has usurped or eaten our creek and is roving frantically to escape, big and ugly, like a blacksnake caught in a kitchen drawer. The color is foul, a rusty cream. Water that has picked up clay soils looks worse than other muddy waters, because the particles of clay are so fine; they spread out and cloud the water so that you can't see light through even an inch of it in a drinking glass.

◆ **Reading Strategy** ❹ Is this a fact or an impression? How do you know?

Everything looks different. Where my eye is used to depth, I see the flat water, near, too

1. **etoliated** (ē′ tē ə lāt′ id) *adj.* Made pale and unhealthy.
2. **Tarleton twins . . . Tara:** Two suitors who try to win the love of Scarlett, the main character in *Gone With the Wind.*

◆ Build Vocabulary

obliterates (ə blit′ ə rāts′) *v.:* Destroys; erases without a trace

opacity (ō pas′ ə tē) *n.:* Quality of not letting light pass through

usurped (yo͞o surpt′) *v.:* Taken power over; held by force

Beyond the Classroom

Community Connection

Disaster Preparedness The efforts and expertise of many different people, agencies, and organizations come into play when a disaster strikes. Cooperation, quick response, and up-to-the-minute information is critical when coping with a disaster. Professionals and volunteers need to work together to implement safety measures, evacuate people in immediate danger, treat the injured, and orchestrate the clean-up. Smooth operation of these measures can mean the difference between life and death in the hours and days after a disaster occurs.

Have students find out about the people in their community who help ensure the safety of the population when a disaster hits: utility workers, fire fighters, police, volunteer ambulance drivers, paramedics, and so on. Interested students can collaborate to write a disaster short story or dramatic scene in which all these people work together successfully to respond to a large-scale emergency.

near. I see trees I never noticed before, the black verticals of their rainsoaked trunks standing out of the pale water like pilings for a rotted dock. The stillness of grassy banks and stony ledges is gone; I see rushing, a wild sweep and hurry in one direction, as swift and compelling as a waterfall. The Atkins kids are out in their tiny rain gear, staring at the monster creek. It's risen up to their gates; the neighbors are gathering; I go out.

I hear a roar, a high windy sound more like air than like water, like the run-together whaps of a helicopter's propeller after the engine is off, a high million rushings. The air smells damp and acrid, like fuel oil, or insecticide. It's raining.

I'm in no danger; my house is high. I hurry down the road to the bridge. Neighbors who have barely seen each other all winter are there, shaking their heads. Few have ever seen it before: the water is *over* the bridge. Even when I see the bridge now, which I do every day, I still can't believe it: the water was *over* the bridge, a foot or two over the bridge, which at normal times is eleven feet above the surface of the creek.

Now the water is receding slightly; someone has produced empty metal drums, which we roll to the bridge and set up in a square to keep cars from trying to cross. It takes a bit of nerve even to stand on the bridge; the flood has ripped away a wedge of concrete that buttressed the bridge on the bank. Now one corner of the bridge hangs apparently unsupported while water hurls in an arch just inches below.

It's hard to take it all in, it's all so new. I look at the creek at my feet. It smashes under the bridge like a fist, but there is no end to its force; it hurtles down as far as I can see till it lurches round the bend, filling the valley, flattening, mashing, pushed, wider and faster, till it fills my brain.

It's like a dragon. Maybe it's because the bridge we are on is chancy, but I notice that no one can help imagining himself washed overboard, and gauging his chances for survival. You couldn't live. Mark Spitz couldn't live. The water arches where the bridge's supports at the banks prevent its **8**

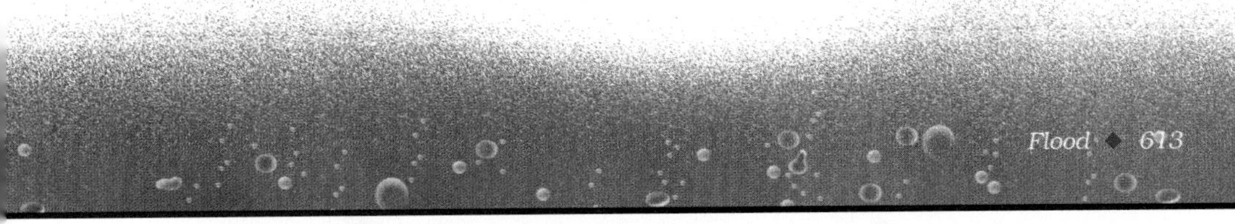

◆ Build Grammar Skills

5 Subject-Verb Agreement Ask students to identify the subject and verb in the clause, "The stillness of grassy banks and stony ledges is gone." Have them explain why the verb is singular. Discuss why the words "banks" and "ledges" might cause some confusion in determining subject-verb agreement. *Subject: stillness; verb: is. The verb is singular because it agrees with the singular subject "stillness." The plural nouns "banks" and "ledges" might confuse the issue because they are closer to the verb than the subject is.*

◆ Literary Focus

6 Descriptive Essay Have students identify the sensory images in the paragraph. *Dillard describes the sound of the water and the smell of the air.*

◆ Reading Strategy

7 Recognize Facts and Impressions Ask students to identify the facts in this passage and to explain how they can distinguish them from impressions. *These facts are in the paragraph: The neighbors are shaking their heads, the water is a foot or two over the bridge, the bridge is normally eleven feet above the surface of the creek. These facts can be verified by observation or measurement.*

8 Clarification Point out that U.S. swimmer Mark Spitz won seven gold medals at the 1972 Summer Olympics. Dillard's reference indicates that even the greatest swimmer could not survive.

Customize for
Visual/Spatial Learners
Encourage these students to compare the photograph on this page with Dillard's description of the effects of the flood at Tinker Creek. *Students might observe that the photo provides a broad aerial view, while Dillard's description focuses on details of nature and wildlife as they are affected by the flood.*

Speaking, Listening, and Viewing Mini-Lesson

Storm Report

This mini-lesson supports the Speaking, Listening, and Viewing activity in the Idea Bank on p. 618.

Introduce Discuss with students times when TV shows they were watching were interrupted by a winter storm warning, tornado watch, hurricane warning, or other extreme weather warning. Talk about the purpose of such warnings.

Develop Have students discuss the kinds of information that will be useful to local residents as the storm approaches, such as the expected severity of the storm, precautions residents should take, and community evacuation procedures, if necessary.

Apply Students can put together their two-minute broadcasts. Suggest that they focus on giving an initial report, updating information, or providing eyewitness coverage of the storm as it hits.

Assess Have students evaluate the broadcasts based on overall presentation and descriptive details. What made the most convincing reports successful?

◆ Literary Focus

❶ Descriptive Essay Students should note the following: *Dillard packs this passage with vivid visual images. For example, the floodwater looks "like dirty lace," the earth "moves backwards, rises and swells," the land looks "as though it were not solid and real at all, but painted on a scroll . . ."*

◆ Critical Thinking

❷ Analyze Ask students: Why do you think Dillard chose these particular objects to imagine floating down the creek? *Dillard made the objects as diverse as possible to create a bizarre impression.*

◆ Build Grammar Skills

❸ Subject-Verb Agreement Ask students to identify the subject and verb in this sentence and explain why the verb is singular even though the word "eggs" is plural. *Subject: hill; verb: is. The verb is singular to agree with the singular subject, "hill." The plural word "eggs" is not the subject, even though it is closer to the verb.*

Customize for
Interpersonal Learners
Allow time for these students to discuss Dillard's description and share their own impressions of floods based on experience or scenes from television news or movies. Encourage students to jot down details and ideas that help them envision the flood Dillard describes.

Customize for
Gifted/Talented Students
Students can draw and paint a picture showing details of the flooded creek. Encourage students to choose different passages to base their drawings on.

enormous volume from going wide, forcing it to go high; that arch drives down like a diving whale, and would butt you on the bottom. "You'd never know what hit you," one of the men says. But if you survived that part and managed to surface . . . ? How fast can you live? You'd need a windshield. You couldn't keep your head up; the water under the surface is fastest. You'd spin around like a sock in a clothes dryer. You couldn't grab onto a tree trunk without leaving that arm behind. No, you couldn't live. And if they ever found you, your gut would be solid red clay.

It's all I can do to stand. I feel dizzy, drawn, <u>mauled</u>. Below me the floodwater roils to a violent froth that looks like dirty lace, a lace that continuously explodes before my eyes. If I look away, the earth moves backwards, rises and swells, from the fixing of my eyes at one spot against the motion of the flood. All the familiar land looks as though it were not solid and real at all, but painted on a scroll like a backdrop, and that unrolled scroll has been shaken, so the earth sways and the air roars.

❶ **◆ Literary Focus** In what specific ways is this passage typical of a descriptive essay?

Everything imaginable is zipping by, almost too fast to see. If I stand on the bridge and look downstream, I get dizzy; but if I look upstream, I feel as though I am looking up the business end of an avalanche. There are dolls, split wood and kindling, dead fledgling songbirds, bottles, whole bushes and trees, rakes and garden gloves. Wooden, rough-hewn railroad ties charge by faster than any express. Lattice fencing bobs along, and a wooden picket gate. There are so many white plastic gallon milk jugs that when the flood ultimately recedes, they are left on the grassy banks looking from a distance like a flock of white geese.

I expect to see anything at all. In this one way, the creek is more like itself when it floods than at any other time: mediating, bringing things down. I wouldn't be at all surprised to see John Paul Jones coming round the bend, standing on the deck of the *Bon Homme Richard*, or Amelia Earhart waving gaily from the cockpit of her floating Lockheed. Why not a cello, a basket of breadfruit, a casket of antique coins? Here comes the Franklin expedition on snowshoes, and the three magi, plus camels, afloat on a canopied barge!

The whole world is in flood, the land as well as the water. Water streams down the trunks of trees, drips from hatbrims, courses across roads. The whole earth seems to slide like sand down a chute; water pouring over the least slope leaves the grass flattened, silver side up, pointing downstream. Everywhere windfall and flotsam twigs and leafy boughs, wood from woodpiles, bottles, and saturated straw spatter the ground or streak it in curving windrows. Tomatoes in flat gardens are literally floating in mud; they look as though they have been dropped whole into a boiling, brown-gravy stew. The level of the water table is at the top of the toe of my shoes. Pale muddy water lies on the flat so that it all but drowns the grass; it looks like a hideous parody of a light snow on the field, with only the dark tips of the grass blades visible.

When I look across the street, I can't believe my eyes. Right behind the road's shoulder are waves, waves whipped in rhythmically peaking scallops, racing downstream. The hill where I watched the praying mantis lay her eggs is a ❸
waterfall that splashes into a brown ocean. I can't even remember where the creek usually runs—it is everywhere now. My log is gone for sure, I think—but in fact, I discover later, it holds, rammed between growing trees. Only the cable suspending the steers' fence is visible,

◆ Build Vocabulary

mauled (môld) *adj.*: Roughly or clumsily handled

malevolent (mə lev′ ə lənt′) *adj.*: Intended as evil or harmful

repressed (ri prest′) Held back; restrained

Workplace Skills Mini-Lesson

Being Prepared

Introduce Make the point that people who have prepared for natural disasters by storing canned food and keeping flashlights and first-aid kits on hand are often able to get through a disaster with the least amount of trouble. Ask students how the habit of preparing in advance for problems in general could make an employee an especially valuable asset.

Develop Discuss the kinds of jobs for which advance preparation for problems would be important. For example, a baby sitter should have a list of emergency telephone numbers and information concerning where first-aid supplies can be found.

Apply Have students list two or three jobs for which being prepared is particularly important, then note specific measures they would take to be prepared in those jobs.

Assess Have students assess each other's lists on the basis of how appropriate each measure of preparation is to the job they listed. Which were the best preparation measures suggested, and why?

and not the fence itself; the steers' pasture is entirely in flood, a brown river. The river leaps its banks and smashes into the woods where the motorbikes go, devastating all but the sturdiest trees. The water is so deep and wide it seems as though you could navigate the *Queen Mary* in it, clear to Tinker Mountain.

What do animals do in these floods? I see a drowned muskrat go by like he's flying, but they all couldn't die; the water rises after every hard rain, and the creek is still full of muskrats. This flood is higher than their raised sleeping platforms in the banks; they must just race for high ground and hold on. Where do the fish go, and what do they do? Presumably their gills can filter oxygen out of this muck, but I don't know how. They must hide from the current behind any barriers they can find, and fast for a few days. They must: otherwise we'd have no fish; they'd all be in the Atlantic Ocean. What about herons and kingfishers, say? They can't see to eat. It usually seems to me that when I see any animal, its business is urgent enough that it couldn't easily be suspended for forty-eight hours. Crayfish, frogs, snails, rotifers? Most things must simply die. They couldn't live. Then I suppose that when the water goes down and clears, the survivors have a field day with no competition. But you'd think the bottom would be knocked out of the food chain—the whole pyramid would have no base plankton, and it would crumble, or crash with a thud. Maybe enough spores and larvae and eggs are constantly being borne down from slower upstream waters to repopulate . . . I don't know.

Some little children have discovered a snapping turtle as big as a tray. It's hard to believe that this creek could support a predator that size: its shell is a foot and a half across, and its head extends a good seven inches beyond the shell. When the children—in the company of a shrunken terrier—approach it on the bank, the snapper rears up on its thick front legs and hisses very impressively. I had read earlier that since turtles' shells are rigid, they don't have bellows lungs; they have to gulp for air. And, also since their shells are rigid, there's only room for so much inside, so when they are (6) frightened and planning a retreat, they have to expel air from their lungs to make room for head and feet—hence the malevolent hiss.

The next time I look, I see that the children have somehow maneuvered the snapper into a washtub. They're waving a broom handle at it in hopes that it will snap the wood like a matchstick, but the creature will not deign to oblige. The kids are crushed; all their lives they've heard that this is the one thing you do with a snapping turtle—you shove a broom handle near it, and it "snaps it like a matchstick." It's nature's way; it's sure-fire. But the turtle is having none of it. It avoids the broom handle with an air of patiently repressed rage. They let it go, and it beelines down the bank, dives unhesitatingly into the swirling floodwater, and that's the last we see of it.

A cheer comes up from the crowd on the bridge. The truck is here with a pump for the Bowerys' basement, hooray! We roll away the metal drums, the truck makes it over the bridge, to my amazement—the crowd cheers again. State police cruise by; everything's fine here; downstream people are in trouble. The bridge over by the Bings' on Tinker Creek looks like it's about to go. There's a tree trunk wedged against its railing, and a section of concrete is out. The Bings are away, and a young couple is living there, "taking care of the house." What can they do? The husband drove to work that morning as usual; a few hours later, his wife was evacuated from the front door in a *motorboat*.

I walk to the Bings'. Most of the people who are on our bridge eventually end up over there; it's just down the road. We straggle along in the rain, gathering a crowd. The men who work away from home are here, too; their wives have telephoned them at work this morning to say that the creek is rising fast,

◆ Literature and Your Life

4 Ask students how animals in their area would be affected by a natural disaster such as a severe storm or flood. What precautions could be taken to help protect pets and livestock? *Students might respond with an anecdote about how an animal was protected—or what happened to him or her—during a natural disaster they experienced or heard about.*

◆ Reading Strategy

5 Recognize Facts and Impressions Have students compare Dillard's impressions of the turtle with the facts that she relates about it. Which do they find clearer and more vivid? *Dillard describes the turtle as being as "big as a tray" before giving the actual dimensions of the turtle. Students may be divided on which is more vivid—the tray image or the measurement.*

◆ Literary Focus

6 Descriptive Essay Point out that the visual description is emphasized by Dillard's attention to specific even technical detail here, included in an almost off-hand fashion that nevertheless expands upon the image of the hissing turtle described earlier.

Reteach

Helps students distinguish facts and impressions in descriptions. Invite students to describe some of their own experiences to the class. They might relate stories about weather, travel, or surprise events, for example. Have the student-listeners list the facts and impressions in their classmates' stories. Write their suggestions on the board in a chart like the one shown here.

Facts	Impressions

Cross-Curricular Connection: Science

Flooding The devastation caused by flooding can be extreme, and the effect on the environment can be longterm. Common causes of river floods are too much rain at one time, as at Tinker Creek, and sudden melting of snow and ice. Under such conditions, rivers may receive more than ten times as much water as their beds can hold. Heavy rains produce flash floods if the rains cause small rivers or streams, such as Tinker Creek, to rise suddenly and overflow. Flash floods occur chiefly in mountainous areas and do not allow much time for people to be warned of danger.

Since 1936, a year of bad floods, the U.S. government has spent billions of dollars to prevent and control floods. Flood control involves building dams to store water and channels to allow it to flow quickly to the sea. It also involves various embankments to hold back river or sea waters, such as dikes, flood walls, and levees. These embankments help keep water off the land.

In addition, the National Weather Service has a network of river forecast centers and local district offices whose function it is to track the state of rivers and provide flood warnings, if necessary.

◆ *Literature and Your Life*

❶ Students may suggest that basic tasks, such as cutting down a tree, are made extraordinarily difficult by the flood waters.

◆ Critical Thinking

❷ **Interpret** In what way is this meeting representative of how people behave in crisis situations? *The narrator and the young man "pull together" so that each can pass on the narrow wall without falling. Once the problem has been solved, they continue on their separate ways. This represents the way people "pull together" and cooperate during an emergency, then go back to their usual, more isolated lives afterward.*

◆ Critical Thinking

❸ **Infer** What evidence does Dillard give to show that things are returning to normal? *Students should note that people are relaxing, children are playing, the atmosphere is not charged with dread and tension, as it was when the creek was rising.*

Reinforce and Extend

Answers

◆ *Literature and Your Life*

Reader's Response Some students might say their impression would be one of fear; others might say they would find the flood exhilarating.

Thematic Focus Encourage students to verify the facts they've learned by checking another source.

Questions for Research Students may suggest questions about the frequency or causes of floods, annual rainfall deviations, and flood control measures.

☑ **Check Your Comprehension**

1. It's out of its four-foot banks; the color is rusty.
2. The water's arches would knock people down; the water under the surface is so fast a person couldn't keep his/her head up.
3. Dolls, wood, bushes and trees, rakes, garden gloves, railroad ties, fencing, and plastic jugs rush by.
4. Dillard worries that they won't find food.
5. Dillard heads home because the water is going down and the danger is past.

and they'd better get home while the gettin's good.

There's a big crowd already there; everybody knows that the Bings' is low. The creek is coming in the recreation-room windows; it's halfway up the garage door. Later that day people will haul out everything salvageable and try to dry it: books, rugs, furniture—the lower level was filled from floor to ceiling. Now on this bridge a road crew is trying to chop away the wedged tree trunk with a long-handled ax. The handle isn't so long that they don't have to stand on the bridge, in Tinker Creek. I walk along a low brick wall that was built to retain the creek away from the house at high water. The wall holds just fine, but now that the creek's receding, it's retaining water around the house. On the wall I can walk right out into the flood and stand in the middle of it. Now on the return trip I meet a young man who's going in the opposite direction. The wall is one brick wide; we can't pass. So we clasp hands and lean out backwards over the turbulent water; our feet interlace like teeth on a zipper, we pull together, stand, and continue on our ways. The kids have spotted a rattlesnake draping itself out of harm's way in a bush; now they all want to walk over the brick wall to the bush, to get bitten by the snake.

> ❶ ◆ *Literature and Your Life*
> In what ways does the flood transform ordinary actions into extraordinary events?

The little Atkins kids are here, and they are hopping up and down. I wonder if I hopped up and down, would the bridge go? I could stand at the railing as at the railing of a steamboat, shouting deliriously, "Mark three! Quarter-less-three! Half twain! Quarter twain! . . ." as the current bore the broken bridge out of sight around the bend before she sank. . . .

Everyone else is standing around. Some of the women are carrying curious plastic umbrellas that look like diving bells—umbrellas they don't put up, but on; they don't get under, but in. They can see out dimly, like goldfish in bowls. Their voices from within sound distant, but with an underlying cheerfulness that plainly acknowledges, "Isn't this ridiculous?" Some of the men are wearing their fishing hats. Others duck their heads under folded newspapers held not very high in an effort to compromise between keeping their heads dry and letting rain run up their sleeves. Following some form of courtesy, I guess, they lower these newspapers when they speak with you, and squint politely into the rain.

Women are bringing coffee in mugs to the road crew. They've barely made a dent in the tree trunk, and they're giving up. It's a job for power tools; the water's going down anyway, and the danger is past. Some kid starts doing tricks on a skateboard; I head home. ❸

Guide for Responding

◆ *Literature and Your Life*

Reader's Response What do you think would have been your immediate impression on first seeing the flood? Explain.

Thematic Focus In what specific ways does this piece add to your knowledge about natural forces and their effects?

Questions for Research Generate research questions that would help you explore the subject of floods in countries around the world.

☑ **Check Your Comprehension**

1. What is different about Tinker Creek the morning before the flood?
2. What are some reasons that someone wouldn't survive in the flood waters?
3. What are some things that rush by in the water?
4. For what reason is Dillard concerned about the creatures who will survive the flood?
5. Why does Dillard eventually head home?

Beyond the Selection

FURTHER READING

Other Works by Annie Dillard

An American Childhood
The Living

Other Works About Natural Forces

The Johnstown Flood, David McCullough
The Sea Wolf, Jack London
K2, Triumph and Tragedy, Jim Curran

We suggest that you preview these works before recommending them to students.

INTERNET

Students can learn more about Annie Dillard and her work at the following Web sites. Please be aware that the sites may have changed.

http://www.well.com/USer/elliotts/smse_dillard.html

Students can find out more about floods and hurricanes at the following Web sites:

http://water.USgs.gov/
http://www.nhc.noaa.gov/index.html

We *strongly recommend* that you preview the sites before you send students to them.

Guide for Responding *(continued)*

◆ Critical Thinking

Interpret

1. What does the fact that Dillard stood on the bridge tell you about her character? Explain. **[Infer]**
2. Speculate about why Dillard lists the people and things she wouldn't be surprised to see floating down the creek. **[Speculate]**
3. What feelings about nature do you think Dillard wants you to take away from her piece? Explain. **[Draw Conclusions]**

Apply

4. Defend the following statement with examples from "Flood": Natural disasters bring people together. **[Defend]**

Extend

5. Describe the role of at least three kinds of professionals and volunteers who respond to natural disasters. **[Career Link]**

◆ Reading Strategy

Recognize Facts and Impressions

Recognizing a fact is a straightforward matter—a **fact** is provable. An **impression**, though, reflects an author's personal feelings.

1. Find evidence that Dillard's knowledge of history and religion contributed to her impressions of the flood.
2. Analyze this sentence in terms of fact and impression: "The steers were across the creek, a black clot on a distant hill."

◆ Literary Focus

Descriptive Essay

A **descriptive essay** is a short nonfiction work that provides concrete and sensory details so that you can clearly and easily envision the subject. A flood caused by a hurricane, while potentially horrible in real life, makes an excellent descriptive subject because it is full of sensory experiences.

1. Which of Dillard's descriptions best makes you feel you are at the flood? Why?
2. Find examples of language that appeals to each of the five senses.

◆ Build Vocabulary

Using the Latin Prefix *mal-*

The Latin prefix *mal-* means "bad, evil." On your paper, match each word with its appropriate definition.

1. malice **a.** criminal
2. malefactor **b.** to fail to work properly
3. malfunction **c.** desire to do harm to others

Using the Word Bank: Antonyms

On your paper, write the letter of the word that is the best antonym, or opposite, of the first word.

1. obliterates: (a) annihilates, (b) builds, (c) kills
2. usurped: (a) conquered, (b) swamped, (c) released
3. repressed: (a) freed, (b) oppressed, (c) bound
4. opacity: (a) depth, (b) translucence, (c) intelligence
5. mauled: (a) attacked, (b) smeared, (c) protected
6. malevolent: (a) corrupt, (b) injurious, (c) helpful

◆ Build Grammar Skills

Subject and Verb Agreement

Verbs must **agree** in number with their **subjects**, even when words intervene between the subject and verb. Don't be misled into making the verb agree with a noun that is closer but that is not the subject:

> When flood *waters* caused by a hurricane finally *recede* they can leave dead wildlife in their wake.

In this sentence, the plural verb form *recede* agrees with the plural subject *waters*. You should not make the verb agree with *hurricane*, even though *hurricane* is closer to the verb.

Practice Rewrite each of the following sentences so that their verbs agree in number with their subjects.

1. Neighbors who have barely seen each other all winter is there.
2. Most of the people who are on our bridge eventually ends up over there.
3. The hill where I watched the praying mantis lay her eggs are a waterfall that splashes.
4. The stillness of grassy banks and stony ledges are gone.

◆ Build Grammar Skills

Practice

1. Neighbors who have barely seen each other <u>are</u> there.
2. Most of the people who are on our bridge eventually <u>end</u> up over there.
3. The hill where I watched the praying mantis lay her eggs <u>is</u> a waterfall that splashes.
4. The stillness of grassy banks and stony ledges <u>is</u> gone.

Grammar Reinforcement

For additional instruction and practice, use the Subject-Verb Agreement lesson in the **Language Lab CD-ROM** and pp. 80–82 on Subject-Verb Agreement in the *Writer's Solution Grammar Practice Book.*

Answers

◆ Critical Thinking

1. Students should infer that Dillard is a brave person. Explanation should include description of dangers of standing on the failing bridge. She is also curious and interested in observing the flood's effects.
2. Dillard is probably trying to communicate the unusual power of the creek.
3. Dillard probably wants readers to feel a renewed respect for nature because she describes the flood and all it affected in such detail.
4. Examples: Neighbors who don't usually see one another are now helping one another; women bring mugs of coffee to the road crew; Dillard and the stranger clasp hands to pass over the wall.
5. Students may describe the work of paramedics, police or other rescue workers, helicopter pilots, road crews, firefighters.

◆ Reading Strategy

1. Students will probably point to Dillard's references to John Paul Jones, Amelia Earhart and the three magi.
2. Students should point out that while it was probably a provable fact that the steers were across the creek, that they looked like a black clot was Dillard's impression.

◆ Literary Focus

1. Students should recall a description, such as watching objects zip by on the river, and explain why it made them feel they were at the flood; for example: I could imagine things I own floating away.
2. Examples: The air smells damp and acrid—*smell;* a boiling brown gravy stew—*taste;* a violent froth that looks like dirty lace—*sight;* a high windy sound more like air than water—*hearing;* their shells are rigid—*touch.*

◆ Build Vocabulary

Using the Prefix *mal-*

1. c 2. a 3. b

Using the Word Bank

1. b 2. c 3. a 4. b 5. c 6. c

Idea Bank

Following are suggestions for matching Idea Bank topics with your students' performance levels and learning modalities:

Customizing for
Performance Levels
Less Advanced Students: 1
Average Students: 2, 4, 5
More Advanced Students: 3, 6

Customizing for
Learning Modalities
Visual/Spatial: 2
Verbal/Linguistic: 4, 5
Logical/Mathematical: 6, 7

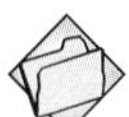

Guided Writing Lesson

Revision Strategy Have students reenter their writing and review their use of active and passive verbs. They can use a colored pen or pencil to circle all "to be" verbs which give their writing passive voice. Encourage them to rearrange the sentences where "to be" verbs appear or select strong, action verbs to replace them. Use the following sample to illustrate the process of creating active voice:

The rain was falling on the awning.
The rain fell on the awning.
The rain pelted the awning.

For more prewriting, elaboration, and revision strategies, see *Prentice Hall Writing and Grammar.*

Writing Lab CD-ROM

Have students complete the tutorial on Description. Follow these steps:

1. Suggest that students use the cluster diagram to record details of their impressions.
2. Encourage students to use the Sensory Word Bin to discover additional descriptive words.
3. Allow time for students to draft on the computer.
4. Have students use Revision Checker for vague or overused adjectives.

Build Your Portfolio

Idea Bank

Writing

1. **Descriptive Paragraph** What was the best food you ever tasted or the best song you ever heard? Using sensory language, write a paragraph describing a "best."
2. **Storm Journal** Write a three-paragraph factual or imaginary journal entry describing a major storm whipping through your neighborhood.
3. **Fable** Write a fable, set at the Tinker Creek flood, that features the animals and fish Dillard mentions. Remember, a fable is a brief story that usually has a moral.

Speaking, Listening, and Viewing

4. **Storm Report** A hurricane with 120-mile-an-hour winds is moving up the coast. As a broadcast meteorologist, give a two-minute warning and description of the storm.
5. **Talk-Show Interview** With a partner, prepare and present an interview between a television talk-show host and Annie Dillard about what it was like to be present at the flood at Tinker Creek.

Researching and Representing

6. **Hurricane Chart** Gather information on the worst hurricanes in history. Organize your findings (such as locale, deaths, and property damage toll) in a chart.
7. **Food-Chain Presentation** Dillard says that plankton, microscopic plants and animals, are the start of the food chain. Research information about the food chain at a creek. Organize your findings into a presentation in which you provide descriptions and pictures.

Online Activity www.phlit.phschool.com

Guided Writing Lesson

Radio Call-In Transcript

Write a **transcript** of a radio call-in show. A transcript is a written record of the dialogue. Here's your situation: A hurricane is traveling up the East Coast at sixteen miles an hour. Part of Florida is devastated. The hurricane just hit Georgia, and it's on its way to South Carolina. Write a transcript of a conversation between the show's host and a caller from each of these states. What they say is up to you, but make sure to convey their feelings and impressions.

Writing Skills Focus: Sensory Language

Describe the many sensory experiences of a hurricane so that others will feel they're on the scene. Use action verbs (*roar*) and figurative language (*looking from the distance like a flock of white geese*) that evoke the senses.

Prewriting Use a chart like this one to categorize words or phrases appropriate for describing a hurricane.

Visual	Auditory	Tactile	Olfactory (smell)	Taste

Drafting When writing, remember that the callers are likely to mention verifiable facts (amount of damage) along with their personal impressions of the storm. Include both in your transcript.

Revising Read your transcript aloud to a partner. Make sure that it flows naturally, as dialogue should. Also be sure that you have used sensory language in your transcript to convey the chaos and destruction caused by the hurricane.

ASSESSMENT OPTIONS

Formal Assessment, Selection Test, pp. 154–156, and Assessment Resources Software. The selection test is designed so that it can be easily customized to the performance levels of your students.

Alternative Assessment, p. 44 includes options for less advanced students, more advanced students, interpersonal learners, verbal/linguistic learners, logical/mathematical learners, and visual/spatial learners.

PORTFOLIO ASSESSMENT

Use the following rubrics in the ***Alternative Assessment*** booklet to assess student writing:
Descriptive Paragraph: Description Rubric, p. 97
Storm Journal: Description Rubric, p. 97
Fable: Fiction Narrative Rubric, p. 95
Guided Writing Lesson: Description Rubric, p. 97

Writing Process Workshop

Comparison-and-Contrast Essay

In the selections in this section, you probably saw similarities and differences in the ways in which writers view their identities, nature, jobs, and even movies.

A **comparison-and-contrast essay** is a brief written exploration of the similarities and differences between two (or more) things. Using the skills listed below—which were introduced in this section's Guided Writing Lessons—write a comparison-and-contrast essay on a topic that interests you.

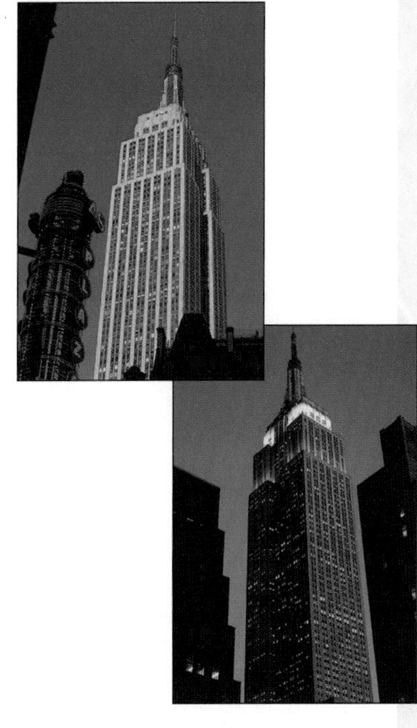

Writing Skills Focus

- **Choose a logical method of organization.** Decide whether your subject is best suited for point-by-point organization or subject-by-subject organization. (See p. 607.)
- **Use sensory language.** Words and phrases that appeal to one of the five senses help your readers vividly experience what you're comparing and contrasting. (See p. 618.)
- **Use transitions** such as *likewise, similarly, nevertheless,* and *in contrast* to indicate the relationships between ideas. (See p. 578.)

In the following excerpt, author Rachel Carson uses these skills to compare the shore under two different tides.

Model From Literature

from *The Marginal World* by Rachel Carson

The shore has a dual nature, changing with the swing of the tides, belonging now to the land, now to the sea. ① On the ebb tide it knows the harsh extremes of the land world, being exposed to the heat and cold, to wind, to rain, and drying sun. ② On the flood tide it is a water world, returning briefly to the stability of the open sea.

Only the most hardy and adaptable can survive in a region so mutable, ③ *yet* the area between the tides is crowded with plants and animals.

① Carson first describes the conditions at low tide, then she describes the conditions at high tide.

② The writer includes sensory details of *heat, cold, wind, rain and drying sun.*

③ The transition yet indicates the contrast between the lack of life one would expect in this harsh environment and the abundance of life forms that exists there.

Prepare and Engage

LESSON OBJECTIVES

- To use recursive writing processes to write a comparison-and-contrast essay
- To use commas appropriately
- To recognize and use forms of comparison

You may want to distribute the scoring rubric for Comparison/Contrast (p. 103 in ***Alternative Assessment***) to make students aware before they begin of the criteria on which they will be evaluated. See the suggestions on p. 621 for additional points with which you can customize the rubric for this workshop.

Refer students to the Writing Handbook for instruction in the writing process and for further information on comparison and contrast.

Writing Lab CD-ROM

If your students have access to computers, you may want to have them work on the tutorial on Exposition to complete all or part of their comparison-and-contrast essays. Follow these steps:

1. Have students view the interactive model of a comparison-and-contrast essay.
2. Suggest that students use a Venn diagram to organize their details.
3. Have students draft on the computer.
4. Have students use the screen Checking Your Paragraphs for organization.
5. Have students use the Proofreading checklist.

Connect to Literature Refer students to Rachel Carson's *The Marginal World* (p. 571). The essay contains examples of comparison and contrast.

Cross-Curricular Connection: Social Studies

Social Studies Comparisons and Contrasts Suggest that students look to other disciplines for a topic for a comparison-and-contrast essay. For example, scientifically inclined students can write essays comparing and contrasting the methods used to produce electricity, such as coal, hydroelectric, and nuclear. Students interested in social studies might compare the cultures of two nations or the reliance on public transportation in New York, Chicago, and Los Angeles. Students interested in physical education can compare the effects on the cardiovascular system of swimming, jogging, and cross-country skiing. Mechanically inclined students may want to compare and contrast the mechanical differences between automatic and manual transmissions.

Develop Student Writing

Prewriting Strategy

To help students determine the purpose of their essay, have them use a webbing technique to decide on their reasons for comparisons. They can explore the possibilities for three purposes and decide which is most appropriate for their personal ideas and thoughts on their topics.

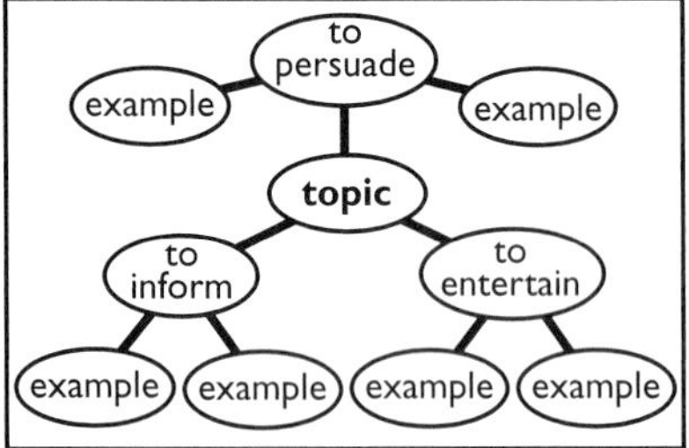

Customize for *English Language Learners*

Students may benefit from a review of comparative and superlative forms. Explain to them the differences between *more* and *most*, as well as *-er* and *-est*. Use the page on degrees of comparison, p. 86, in the *Writer's Solution Grammar Practice Book*.

Writing Lab CD-ROM

The Gathering Details and Organizing Details and Information sections of the tutorial on Exposition contain the following screens that will help students in writing their comparison-and-contrast essays:

- Answering topic questions
- Identifying important details
- Examples of details ordered by comparison and contrast
- Venn diagram

Writing and Language Transparencies Have students use the Comparison and Contrast Organizer, pp. 95–96, to develop and organize details for their essays.

Elaboration Strategy

Tell students that they should balance the details of comparison or contrast in their essays. For every detail that they present about item A, they should present a corresponding detail about item B. Details can be arranged in two ways:

- Each point about item A has a corresponding point about item B.
- Group all of the details about item A together and then all of those about item B.

Applying Language Skills: Commas

Use **commas** correctly in your essay. Too few commas cause confusion, while too many make writing choppy and slow. The following are some common uses of commas:

To Separate Items in a Series:
ghost crabs, herons, starfish . . .

To Set Off Interrupting Words:
The shore, however, . . .

To Separate Clauses in a Compound Sentence:
The tide is low, and I can reach the cave.

Practice On your paper, place commas correctly in the following sentences:

1. Parrotfish struggle to survive in the competitive environment of the coral reef but their strong jaws give them an advantage.
2. There are many life forms within the coral reef, including starfish coral sea squirts fronds and Tubularia.

Writing Application Review your use of commas in your essay. Revise when necessary.

Writer's Solution Connection
Writing Lab

For help organizing your essay, use the Organizing and Ordering Details section of the Exposition tutorial in the Writing Lab.

Prewriting

Brainstorm to Find a Topic With a small group of classmates, brainstorm to come up with possible topics. Consider topics such as actors, musicians, athletes, cities, television programs, and so on. List the ideas your group offers, then choose the topic that you find most interesting.

Decide on Your Purpose After choosing a topic, decide on the reason for your comparison. It might be one of the following reasons:

- **To inform** readers about your two subjects
- **To persuade** readers to accept a specific point of view related to the two subjects
- **To entertain** your audience by making an unlikely or unusual comparison

Once you've decided on your purpose, gather details that will help you achieve your purpose.

Keep Your Audience in Mind Identify your audience. Then keep the answers to questions such as these in mind as you gather details and write your essay:

- How old are my readers?
- What type of language will appeal to them?
- What might they already know about my topic?
- What might they not know that I should explain?

Organize Your Details Before you begin writing, use a Venn diagram like the one below to help organize your details. Write similarities in the space where the circles overlap, and note the differences in the outer sections of the circles.

Venn Diagram

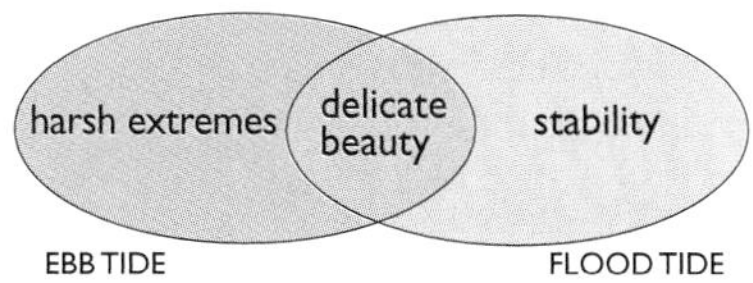

Drafting

Use Comparison-and-Contrast Organization There are two basic types of comparison-and-contrast organization: point-by-point and subject-by-subject. In point-by-point organization, each aspect of your subject is discussed in turn. For example, you might compare and contrast tape players and CD players in terms of cost, availability, and convenience of use.

In a subject-by-subject comparison, you would discuss all the features of one kind of player first and then discuss the features of the second kind.

Applying Language Skills

Commas Explain to students that while the use of commas may seem simple and self-evident, their importance should not be ignored. Too many, too few, or misplaced commas could result in misreading or confusion.

Answers

1. Parrotfish struggle to survive in the competitive environment of the coral reef, but their strong jaws give them an advantage.
2. There are many life forms within the coral reef, including starfish, coral, sea squirts, fronds, and Tubularia.

Grammar Reinforcement

For additional instruction and practice, have students complete the **Language Lab CD-ROM** lesson on Commas and practice pp. 99–101 on commas in the *Writer's Solution Grammar Practice Book*.

Give Specific Examples Be specific about the ways in which your subjects are alike and different. For example, if you are comparing and contrasting life in a desert region and life in a polar region, offer details showing how the climate specifically affects things such as shelter, diet, and general health. Also include similarities and differences in the sensory details.

Revising

Use a Checklist Refer to the Writing Skills Focus on p. 619, and use the items as a checklist to evaluate and revise your comparison-and-contrast essay. Ask yourself the following questions and make revisions as necessary.

- ▶ Have I used transitions to show comparisons?
- ▶ Have I organized my points logically?
- ▶ Have I used sensory language?

Revision Model

When you're choosing whether to buy cassettes or CDs①, you should consider several factors. Cassette tapes are cheap②er. Time and use, however, deteriorate the tape. CDs,③ on the other hand, will not deteriorate in quality.

① The writer adds a comma to make the sentence clear.
② This writer corrects this comparison.
③ The writer adds this transitional phrase to make the essay flow smoothly.

Publishing

Post Your Writing Electronically You can reach a large audience by posting your writing on the Internet for users interested in your subject. Consult with an experienced Internet user or visit Prentice Hall on the World Wide Web at http://phschool.com.

Give an Oral Presentation Arrange with a teacher or librarian for a time and place to give an oral reading of your paper. Then post a notice on a bulletin board, inviting people to attend the reading. In the notice, make the subject of your paper clear. During the reading, speak clearly and maintain eye contact with the audience. Leave time at the end for questions and answers.

Applying Language Skills: Forms of Comparison

Make sure you use the proper **forms of comparison** for adjectives and adverbs. Use the basic, or positive, form to modify another word, the comparative form to compare two things, and the superlative form to compare more than two things.

Positive Form:
slow, sunny, humid, bad

Comparative Form:
slower, sunnier, more humid, worse

Superlative Form:
slowest, sunniest, most humid, worst

Practice On your paper, correct the forms of comparison in the following sentences.

1. Of the two cars, Jack's was fastest.
2. Of all the cars, mine was the more colorful.

Writing Application Review your essay, checking that you have used the proper forms of comparison for all modifiers.

Writer's Solution Connection
Language Lab
For more practice with comparisons, complete the Language Lab lesson on Forms of Comparison.

Revision Strategy

Before students reenter their writing, have them review their prewriting notes to check that they have included the details they planned.

Writing Lab CD-ROM
Students can use the following tools in the Revising and Editing section of the tutorial on Exposition for revising their essays:

- Interactive Evaluation Checklists
- Revision Checkers for transition words and language variety
- Audio-annotated student model

Publishing

Students may wish to consider incorporating their comparison-and-contrast essay into a larger work, such as a persuasive speech or a visitor's guide. Discuss with students appropriate options based on their topics.

Reinforce and Extend

Applying Language Skills

Forms of Comparison Students will most likely use comparative and superlative forms frequently in their comparison-and-contrast essays. Make sure they understand the correct use and forms before drafting.

Answers

1. Of the two cars, Jack's was the *faster*.
2. Of all the cars, mine was the *most* colorful.

Grammar Reinforcement

For additional instruction and practice, have students complete the **Language Lab CD-ROM** lesson on Forms of Comparison and the practice p. 86 on Degrees of Comparison in the *Writer's Solution Grammar Practice Book*.

✓ Assessment

PORTFOLIO ASSESSMENT		4	3	2	1
Use the rubric on Comparison/Contrast in the ***Alternative Assessment*** booklet (p. 103) to assess students' writing. Add these criteria to customize the rubric to this assignment.	**Sensory Words**	Frequent, vivid sensory words significantly enrich the effectiveness of the essay.	Sensory words are used.	A few sensory words are used, but more are needed.	Sensory words are absent; the essay is dull and vague.
	Forms of Comparison	The comparative and superlative forms are used correctly.	Comparative and superlative forms are mostly correct.	There are a number of mistakes with the comparative and superlative forms.	Incorrect use of the comparative and superlative forms impairs understanding.

Prepare and Engage

LESSON OBJECTIVES

- To read critically to evaluate the credibility of information sources, including how the writer's motivation may affect that credibility

Customize for *Less Proficient Readers*

Have students imagine that they want to buy a used car. Display this list of sources (or display the actual sources, if possible): an automobile dealer's advertisement in the newspaper, an Internet site for a used-auto dealership, an article in a magazine about cars, reviews of used autos in a consumer magazine. Have students compare and contrast the sources. Then ask them to tell which sources are likely to have the most accurate information. Encourage them to give precise supporting reasons for their choice; they should recognize that consumers probably benefit most from unbiased expertise.

Answers

Possible answers:

As students evaluate the credibility of each information source, they may note these elements and more:

- the quantity and kinds of supporting evidence the writer offers
- the depth of the research
- the logic of the arguments
- the expertise of the writer and/or the people interviewed
- political affiliations
- the profit motive
- self-interest

Student Success Workshop

Real-World Reading Skills: Evaluating the Credibility of Information Sources

Strategies for Success

These days, thanks to the availability of research tools such as the Internet, it is possible to locate all kinds of information sources, on nearly any topic. But not all information sources are equally credible—that is, believable or accurate. Before you accept any piece of information as being true or factual, it is often wise to evaluate the credibility of the person or publication that is its source. For example, before you believe what a pamphlet says about what quantities of vitamins and minerals to take, you should know whether the author is medically qualified to give this advice. Do some research to check the credibility of your information sources.

Read Critically In order to evaluate the credibility of an information source, it helps to read critically:

- ▶ **Analyze "Facts" and Supporting "Evidence"** Any book, newspaper article, Web site, or magazine that intends to present "facts" about a topic must provide convincing supporting evidence in order to be considered believable. If the author has failed to do this, it may be worth taking time to analyze what he or she has presented. You can do some research. If you've read an account of UFO sightings, you can evaluate the credibility of the writer's "facts" and supporting "evidence" in the light of statistics gathered by scientific researchers. Consider all sides of an issue, rather than accepting one writer's version of the truth.
- ▶ **Evaluate the Author's Motivation** An important question to ask yourself when reading any article is whether the author is being objective, or unbiased—or whether he or she might be biased or trying to promote a certain point of view. For example, someone who works as a speechwriter or consultant for a political candidate might not be motivated to provide an unbiased or full report on the policies of that candidate's political opponent. Likewise, a writer hired to write an advertisement for a fast-food company is likely to downplay the health risks associated with high-fat foods.

Apply the Strategies

Locate and read two sources of information that present different viewpoints on the same topic. For example, you might read two magazine articles expressing opposite points of view on responsible forest management. Compare how credibly each side of the controversy—perhaps a timber company and a group of concerned forest rangers—presents its facts and supporting evidence. Make a list of the facts and supporting evidence each writer offers, and evaluate his or her motivation. Write several paragraphs evaluating the credibility of each information source.

Here are some situations in which to evaluate the credibility of an information source:

- ▶ *Reviewing sales information about a new product or service*
- ▶ *Reading a review of a particular work of art, such as a book, film, painting, or performance*
- ▶ *Evaluating an account of a controversial incident*
- ▶ *Reading an article about a new medical procedure*

Test Preparation Workshop

Evaluating the Credibility of Information Sources Standardized tests may ask students to analyze a writer's motivation or purpose, and to think critically about facts, opinions, and supporting evidence in reading selections. Students may see stems and questions like these on multiple-choice tests; discuss what kinds of answer choices are likely:

- The author provides evidence that . . .
- The author has made an assumption that . . .
- Which of the following best assesses the writer's credibility?

Give students this test question and answer choices for practice:

A good way to evaluate the credibility of an informational work is to

A look at the bibliography.
B read the publisher's description.
C decide whether the topic is controversial.
D see whether the author has a point of view.

Students should realize that a bibliography shows the depth of the author's research and may also suggest whether the sources used are themselves authoritative, therefore, A is the best answer.

PART 2 *Visual Essays and Workplace Writing*

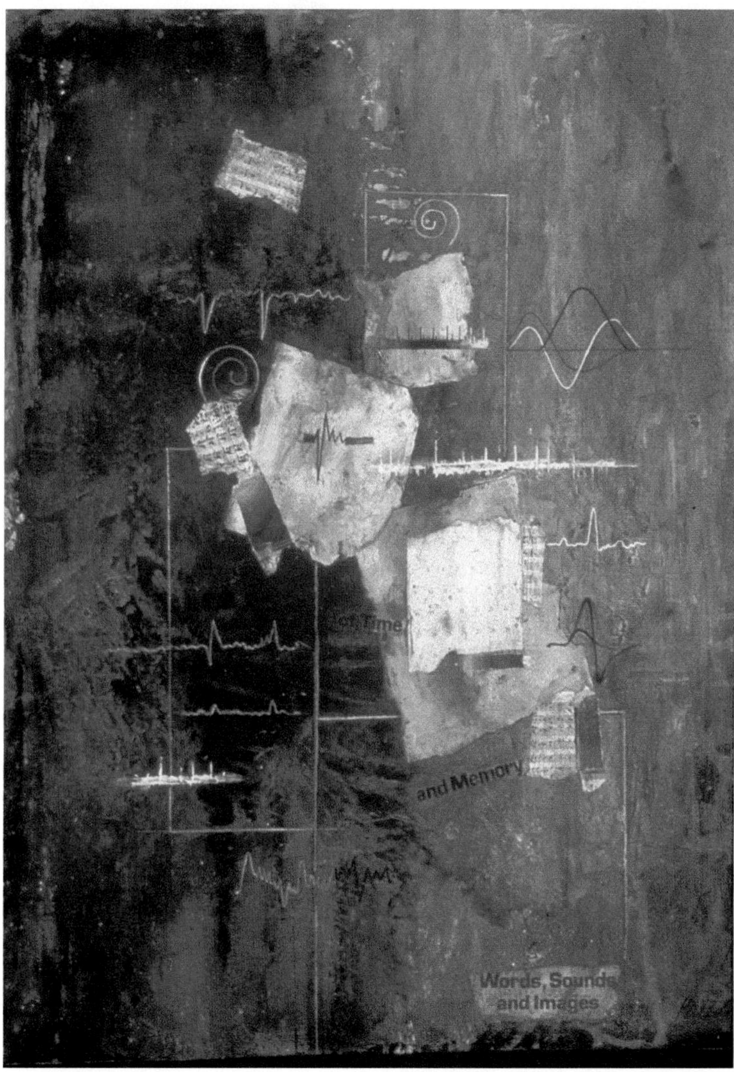

Time & Memory Series, Nydia Preede, Courtesy of the artist

One-Minute Planning Guide

The essays in this section represent the types of nonfiction students are likely to encounter in everyday reading. The two reviews of the *Star Wars* films appeared in newspapers. The visual essay "Mothers and Daughters" represents photographers' interpretations of relationships. "Imitating Nature's Mineral Artistry" explains a technical subject, with diagrams; it provides practice in reading scientific material. "Work That Counts" is a reflective description of work in the field of ornithology.

Customize for *Varying Student Needs*

When assigning the selections in this part, be aware of these factors:

Star Wars reviews
- Two brief, high interest

"Mothers and Daughters"
- Visual essay with engaging photographs
- The accompanying text includes some abstract concepts

"These Are Days"
- High-interest popular song

"Nature's Mineral Artistry"
- Contains technical descriptions, which may be challenging for some
- Diagrams may appeal to visual learners

"Work That Counts"
- Fairly easy reading
- Short

Humanities: Art

Time & Memory Series by Nydia Preede.

This work combines paint and collage, with scraps of paper glued to the canvas. Ask students to find elements that occur on the scraps of paper and also in the painted portions of the work (for ex-ample, the graph lines, the rectangular shapes). Ask them what words they can find in the work, such as *Words, Sounds, and Images* in the lower right; *Time* in the center; *and Memory* a few inches below. Explain that this is an abstract work, exploring the forms of things and how they look, rather than re-creating recognizable people, places, and things on canvas.

Help students link the artwork to the focus of Part 2, "Visual Essays and Workplace Writing," with the following questions:

1. What images in the artwork remind you of an office? *Students may suggest office images that include graphs, scraps of paper, and printed words.*
2. What idea about time and memory does this work help to communicate, and what elements of the work communicate this idea to you? *Sample answer: With its deep blue and green background, the artwork makes me think that memories are fragments, some clear, some unclear, floating in a kind of river of time.*

Prepare and Engage

LESSON OBJECTIVES

1. **To develop vocabulary and word identification skills**
   - Connotations
   - Using the Word Bank: Antonyms
   - Extending Word Study: Context and Origins (ATE)
2. **To use a variety of reading strategies to read and comprehend critical reviews**
   - Connect Your Experience
   - Reading Strategy : Identify Evidence
   - Read to Discover Models (ATE)
3. **To increase knowledge of other cultures and to connect common elements across cultures**
   - Connecting Themes Across Cultures (ATE)
4. **To express and support responses to the text**
   - Critical Thinking
   - Analyze a Film Review (ATE)
   - Idea Bank: Press Release
   - Idea Bank: Speech
   - Idea Bank: Interview
5. **To analyze literary elements**
   - Literary Focus: Critical Review
6. **To read in order to research self-selected and assigned topics**
   - Idea Bank: Movie Collage
   - Idea Bank: Science-Fiction Exhibit
7. **To speak clearly and effectively for a specific audience and purpose**
   - Speaking, Listening, and Viewing Mini-Lesson (ATE): *Star Wars* Recording
   - Speaking, Listening, and Viewing Mini-Lesson (ATE): Skit
8. **To use recursive writing processes to write a movie review**
   - Guided Writing Lesson
9. **To increase knowledge of the rules of grammar and usage**
   - Build Grammar Skills: Parenthetical Interrupters

Test Preparation

Reading Comprehension: Comparing and Contrasting Texts (ATE, p. 625) The teaching tips and sample test item in this workshop support the instruction and practice in the unit workshop.

Reading Comprehension: Comparing and Contrasting Texts; Analyzing Literary Language (SE, p. 661)

Guide for Reading

Vincent Canby *(1924–)*

If you were looking for all the news fit to print about movies between 1969 and 1993, you would have, no doubt, read the film reviews written by the lead film critic of *The New York Times*, Vincent Canby. In addition to theater and film reviews, he has also written the play *After All* (1981) and the novel *Unnatural Scenery* (1979). He continues to produce movie reviews as the Sunday drama critic for *The New York Times*.

Roger Ebert *(1942–)*

Thumbs up, thumbs down. These symbols for movies worth seeing or avoiding were made popular by the duo of Siskel and Ebert, Chicago-based movie reviewers and co-hosts of their own television program. Roger Ebert's reviews appear in the *Chicago Sun-Times* and two hundred other newspapers around the country. He has won two Pulitzer Prizes for his work. About movie viewing he has said: "The audience: In the dark, lined up facing the screen. The light comes from behind their heads—from back there where dreams come true."

◆ Build Vocabulary

CONNOTATIONS

In his review of the re-released 1997 version of *Star Wars*, Roger Ebert describes Han Solo, the character portrayed by Harrison Ford, as "laconic." The denotation, or dictionary definition, of *laconic* is "using few words to express thoughts." In this case, *laconic* has a connotation as well. A connotation is what a word suggests or implies. A *laconic* character is a person who not only uses few words, but usually does so almost impolitely because he or she understands the uselessness of idle chatter.

WORD BANK

As you read these reviews, you will encounter the words in this list. Each word is defined on the page where it first appears. Preview the list before you read, and look for each word as it appears in the reviews.

apotheosis
eclectic
facetiousness
adroit
piously
condescension
watershed
synthesis
fastidious
effete
laconic

◆ Build Grammar Skills

PARENTHETICAL INTERRUPTERS

As if they are having an informal conversation about a movie, reviewers add side remarks that interrupt the main flow of a sentence. These remarks are **parenthetical interrupters**—expressions that comment on or give additional information about the main part of a sentence. Because they interrupt the main idea, they are set off from the rest of the sentence with commas.

Look at these sentences from the movie reviews of *Star Wars* by Vincent Canby and Roger Ebert. The parenthetical interrupters are italicized:

> All of these works, *of course*, had earlier left their marks . . .
>
> Those who analyze its philosophy do so, *I imagine*, with a smile in their minds.

As you read these reviews, notice how such remarks make you feel that the reviewers are engaged in a conversation with you.

Prentice Hall Literature Program Resources

REINFORCE / RETEACH / EXTEND

Selection Support:
Build Vocabulary: Connotations, p. 184
Build Grammar Skills: Parenthetical Interrupters, p. 185
Reading Strategy: Identify Evidence, p. 186
Literary Focus: Critical Review, p. 187

Strategies for Diverse Students Needs, p. 45

Beyond Literature Media Connection: Classic Films, p. 45

Formal Assessment Selection Test, p. 157; Assessment Resources Software

Alternative Assessment, p. 45

Writing and Language Transparencies

Resource Pro CD-ROM

Listening to Literature Audiocassettes

Star Wars: A Trip to the Galaxy That's Fun and Funny . . .
◆ Star Wars: Breakthrough Film Still Has the Force ◆

◆ Literature and Your Life

Connect Your Experience

You're sitting in a crowded movie theater. The houselights dim. The audience, once chattering away, falls silent. As the projector cackles and the screen in front of you bursts into sight and sound, you feel a tinge of excitement and anticipation.

Sometimes a film is so bad that you feel that you've wasted both your time and money. Other times, you're pleasantly surprised. Occasionally, a film comes along that completely surpasses any expectations you may have had and redefines the movie-going experience for you. For millions of people, *Star Wars* was just such a film.

Thematic Focus: To the Future

What movie have you seen recently that you think will still be popular twenty years from now? Why?

Journal Writing Imagine that a Hollywood studio has given you an unlimited budget to produce and direct a film. What kind of film would you make, and why?

◆ Background for Understanding

Culture

If you travel down a long road, certain landmarks—say, a mountain, gorge, or building—will at once jump out at you and remain in your memory long after the trip has ended. These landmarks help define the road and put it in perspective. In a similar way, movies and other art forms become cultural landmarks for entire generations. From the moment in 1977 when *Star Wars* first opened, it became a landmark in the lives of people who were old enough to go see it at the movie theater. These reviews will help you understand why *Star Wars* is considered a landmark in cinema.

◆ Literary Focus

Critical Review

If you see a terrific movie, you might try to persuade a friend to go see it. Film critics provide this service for millions of newspaper readers every day. Reviewers, using evidence to support any claims, aim to convince you to follow their recommendation. They write **critical reviews** in which they discuss the various elements of a film and recommend that you see it—or not see it. Critical reviews tend to be persuasive.

◆ Reading Strategy

Identify Evidence

When you read a piece that is intended to persuade you, it is important that you identify the evidence the writer uses to support his or her claims. **Evidence** may be facts, statistics, observations, examples, and statements from authorities that support the writer's opinion.

Look to identify evidence that supports the claims each reviewer makes. You might use a chart like the one below. Then determine whether or not there is enough evidence to support the claim.

Claim	Evidence
	✓
	✓
	✓
	✓
	✓
	✓
	✓
	✓
	✓

Test Preparation Workshop

Reading Comprehension: Comparing and Contrasting Texts

Standardized tests such as the SAT require students to compare and contrast aspects of two texts. These aspects may include themes, conflicts, and allusions. After students have read both of the reviews in this selection grouping, write this sample test question on the board.

Both reviewers give their highest praise to—

A the quality of the acting
B the sophistication of the plot
C the fact that the movie is a classic
D the movie's special effects

By skimming over the reviews and noting main points, students will find that the best answer is D.

When taking tests, students may find it helpful to make notes about the main points of reading passages as they read them. They might underline or jot notes in the margin so they refer back to them when answering questions. Point out that they should make their notes brief and simple so the notes are helpful, rather than confusing.

If possible, show a brief clip from one of the *Star Wars* films. Point out that *Star Wars* has long been popular with movie fans of all ages, and that when it was re-released in theaters, twenty years after its original opening, it was a smash hit all over again. Tell the class that the following selections are reviews of this film twenty years apart. Two outstanding movie critics write about why this amazing film became such a success originally, and why, two decades later, *Star Wars* is considered a classic.

Connecting Themes Across Cultures

Vincent Canby compares the story of Stars Wars with elements of Superman, the Bible, and the legend of King Arthur and the knights of the Round Table. Roger Ebert tells us that George Lucas included aspects of basic myths in the screenplay. Ask students what myths or stories they might want to draw from if they were to create a film.

Customize for
Less Proficient Readers

Suggest to less proficient readers that they list the descriptive words and phrases that the reviewers use to evaluate the movie. When they've completed their lists, they can decide if the words and phrases are positive or negative.

Customize for
Pre-AP Students

Vincent Canby compares the movie Star Wars to a comic-book adventure. Encourage students to invent their own comic-book adventure, complete with a hero or heroine, the faithful sidekicks, a setting in a different time and place, and a simple plot of good against evil. Suggest that students work together to create the comic book.

Customize for
English Language Learners

Point out that the reviewers cite a number of other movies and works of literature in their reviews. Where possible, provide students with background information about these titles, or encourage other students who are familiar with the titles to do so.

Develop Understanding

One-Minute Insight In language that is exciting and enthusiastic, Vincent Canby reviews the first film in the *Star Wars* trilogy. He balances summary with evaluation, demonstrating for students the qualities of an effective review. In addition to offering an opinion on the movie itself, Canby analyzes the reasons why the characters and situations may be appealing to audiences.

Enrichment The almost human droids shown on this page are creations of George Lucas's imagination, but less sophisticated robots have long since emerged from science fiction into the real world. Point out to students other aspects of modern technology were "predicted" in fiction before they became a reality. Have interested students find out more about some of the inventions and innovations that appear in the work of Jules Verne and Edward Everett Hale.

Customize for
Gifted/Talented Students
Vincent Canby compares the movie Star Wars to a comic-book adventure. Encourage students to invent their own comic-book adventure, complete with a hero or heroine, the faithful sidekicks, a setting in a different time and place, and a simple plot of good against evil. Suggest that students work together to create the comic book.

Customize for
Visual/Spatial Learners
Suggest that students examine the photographs from the movie and evaluate the ways in which publicity photos like these might make people want to see a film.

STAR WARS —A TRIP TO A FAR GALAXY THAT'S FUN AND FUNNY . . .

Vincent Canby

from The New York Times, May 26, 1977

Block Scheduling Strategies

Consider these suggestions to take advantage of extended class time:

- Have students complete the journal activity in Literature and Your Life (p. 625), and form small groups to discuss what kinds of films they would choose to make, and why.
- Encourage students to prepare a Reading Strategy chart like the one on p. 625. Keeping a chart like this will help them answer the Reading Strategy questions on p. 634.
- Have students evaluate whether there is enough evidence to back up the reviewers' claims, and whether the evidence they present is persuasive.
- Have students work in discussion groups to answer the Critical Thinking questions (pp. 628 and 633).
- Have students look for and read other examples of film criticism, on the Internet or at the library, before or after they read the selection.
- Allow classtime for students to write their own movie reviews by completing the Guided Writing Lesson on p. 635.

"Star Wars," George Lucas's first film since his terrifically successful "American Graffiti," is the movie that the teen-agers in "American Graffiti" would have broken their necks to see. It's also the movie that's going to entertain a lot of contemporary folk who have a soft spot for the virtually ritualized manners of comic-book adventure.

"Star Wars," which opened yesterday[1] at the Astor Plaza, Orpheum and other theaters, is the most elaborate, most expensive, most beautiful movie serial ever made. It's both an apotheosis of "Flash Gordon" serials and a witty critique that makes associations with a variety of literature that is nothing if not eclectic: "Quo Vadis?", "Buck Rogers," "Ivanhoe," "Superman," "The Wizard of Oz," "The Gospel According to St. Matthew," the legend of King Arthur and the knights of the Round Table.

All of these works, of course, had earlier left their marks on the kind of science-fiction comic strips that Mr. Lucas, the writer as well as director of "Star Wars," here remembers with affection of such cheerfulness that he avoids facetiousness. The way definitely not to approach "Star Wars," though, is to expect a film of cosmic implications or to footnote it with so many references that one anticipates it as if it were a literary duty. It's fun and funny.

The time, according to the opening credit card, is "a long time ago" and the setting "a galaxy far far away," which gives Mr. Lucas and his associates total freedom to come up with their own landscapes, housing, vehicles, weapons, religion, politics—all of which are variations on the familiar.

When the film opens, dark times have fallen upon the galactal empire once ruled, we are given to believe, from a kind of space-age Camelot. Against these evil tyrants there is, in progress, a rebellion led by a certain Princess Leia Organa, a pretty round-faced young woman of old-fashioned pluck who, before you can catch your breath, has been captured by the guardians of the empire. Their object is to retrieve some secret plans that can be the empire's undoing.

That's about all the plot that anyone of voting age should be required to keep track of. The story of "Star Wars" could be written on the head of a pin and still leave room for the Bible. It is, rather, a breathless succession of escapes, pursuits, dangerous missions, unexpected encounters, with each one ending in some kind of defeat until the final one. 5

> ◆ Reading Strategy
> What evidence does Canby give to support his claim that the film is "fun and funny"?

These adventures involve, among others, an ever-optimistic young man named Luke Skywalker (Mark Hamill), who is innocent without being naive; Han Solo (Harrison Ford), a free-booting freelance, space-ship captain who goes where he can make the most money, and an old mystic named Ben Kenobi (Alec Guinness), one of the last of the Old Guard, a fellow in possession of what's called "the force," a mixture of what appears to be ESP and early Christian faith. 6

Accompanying these three as they set out to liberate the princess and restore justice to the empire are a pair of Laurel-and-Hardyish robots. 7 The thin one, who looks like a sort of brass woodman, talks in the polished phrases of a valet ("I'm adroit but I'm not very knowledgeable"), while the squat one, shaped like a portable washing machine, who is the one with the knowledge, simply squeaks and blinks his

1. **which opened yesterday:** Wednesday, May 25, 1977.

◀ **Critical Viewing** In what ways do R2-D2 and C-3PO remind you of Laurel and Hardy? **[Compare]**

◆ Build Vocabulary

apotheosis (ə päth′ ē ō′ sis) *n.*: Glorification of a person or thing; raising of something to the status of a god

eclectic (ek lek′ tik) *adj.*: Composed of material from various sources

facetiousness (fə sē′ shəs nəs) *n.*: Act of making jokes at an inappropriate time

adroit (ə droit′) *adj.*: Clever

Speaking, Listening, and Viewing Mini-Lesson

Star Wars Recording

This mini-lesson supports the Speaking, Listening, and Viewing activity in the Idea Bank on p. 635.

Introduce Lead a discussion in which the class analyzes the music in one scene from *Star Wars.* Then tell students they will be applying the same strategies in their presentations.

Develop Have students consider the following questions as they prepare their talks: What is the action and mood of the scene? How do the volume, pace, and rhythm of the music reflect the mood of that scene? Is the music used in other scenes in the film, and if so, what do the scenes have in common?

Apply Have students work in small groups to develop their talks. Suggest that they limit presentations to five minutes.

Assess Hold a discussion in which students talk about the effect of the presentations on their appreciation for this music and the film. Do they appreciate the score more since hearing the talks? Why or why not?

1 Clarification *Quo Vadis?* (1896) is a novel by Henryk Sienkiewicz about Rome under Emperor Nero. *Ivanhoe* (1817), by Sir Walter Scott, is a historical novel about the struggles between the Normans and Saxons in medieval England.

◆ Critical Thinking

2 Draw Conclusions Ask students what Canby seems to be saying about Star Wars by linking it to such a wide range of earlier film classics. *By tying Star Wars to film classics, Canby shows that it has a timeless quality and that it may well become a classic itself.*

◆ Build Vocabulary

3 Connotations Ask students to suggest connotations for the word *footnote,* and ask why Canby may have chosen the word. *Making footnotes is a scholarly activity. Canby implies that viewers should not approach the movie as though they were doing scholarly work.*

▶Critical Viewing◀

4 Make Comparisons *The physical contrast between the robots is reminiscent of Laurel and Hardy.*

◆ Reading Strategy

5 Identify Evidence Students can point to the following: *The links the author makes with such popular fiction serials as Flash Gordon and Buck Rogers, and with the comic book hero Superman. Students can also refer to the simple plot, the many action sequences, and the happy ending.*

Customize for *English Language Learners*

6 Point out that ESP stands for Extra-Sensory Perception, meaning the power to read minds and perceive things that cannot be detected by use of sight, hearing, or the other senses.

◆ Build Vocabulary

7 Connotations Ask students what the author wants to convey by using the term, *Laurel-and-Hardyish. By invoking Laurel and Hardy, a slapstick comedy team, Canby indicates that the robots are intended to be comic. This term definitely carries a connotation of funny or buffoonish.*

Develop Understanding

◆ Literary Focus

1 Critical Review Have students identify the persuasive language in this passage and point out Canby's supporting evidence. *Persuasive language includes stars, incredible, and fondness. Canby often supports his points with examples of the special effects and the elaborate settings.*

Reinforce and Extend

Answers

◆ Literature and Your Life

Reader's Response Most students would probably say they would enjoy it because Canby has made the movie seem very exciting.

Thematic Focus There are elements that evoke the past, such as princesses, and ones that suggest the future, such as androids.

☑ Check Your Comprehension

1. *Star Wars* was inspired by old-fashioned comic books and serial movies.
2. Princess Leia leads a rebellion against hostile forces in her galactic empire while the guardians of the empire try to retrieve some secret plan.
3. The true stars are the production designers and the special effects people.

◆ Critical Thinking

1. Young children will judge the film strictly on its entertainment value.
2. Yes, he says it is "fun and funny."
3. Canby rates special effects as most important, followed by plot. He considered acting least important.
4. Students might mention objectivity, a facility with language, and a wide knowledge of film.

lights. They are the year's best new comedy team.

In opposition to these good guys are the imperial forces led by someone called the Grand Moff Tarkin (Peter Cushing) and his executive assistant, Lord Darth Vader (David Prowse), a former student of Ben Kenobi who elected to leave heaven sometime before to join the evil ones.

1 The true stars of "Star Wars" are John Barry, who was responsible for the production design, and the people who were responsible for the incredible special effects—space ships, explosions of stars, space battles, hand-to-hand combat with what appear to be lethal neon swords. I have a particular fondness for the look of the interior of a gigantic satellite called the Death Star, a place full of the kind of waste space one finds today only in old Fifth Avenue mansions and public libraries.

There's also a very funny sequence in a low-life bar on a remote planet, a frontierlike establishment where they serve customers who look like turtles, apes, pythons and various amalgams of same, but draw the line at robots. Says the bartender piously: "We don't serve *their* kind here."

It's difficult to judge the performances in a film like this. I suspect that much of the time the actors had to perform with special effects that were later added in the laboratory. Yet everyone treats his material with the proper combination of solemnity and good humor that avoids condescension. One of Mr. Lucas's particular achievements is the manner in which he is able to recall the tackiness of the old comic strips and serials he loves without making a movie that is, itself, tacky. "Star Wars" is good enough to convince the most skeptical 8-year-old sci-fi buff, who is the toughest critic.

◆ Build Vocabulary

piously (pī´ əs lē) *adv.*: With actual or pretended religious devotion

condescension (kän´ di sen´ shən) *n.*: Looking down upon; regarding as below one's dignity

Guide for Responding

◆ Literature and Your Life

Reader's Response Do you think you would enjoy this movie based on Canby's review?

Thematic Focus How does *Star Wars* combine the past and the future?

☑ Check Your Comprehension

1. What are two sources that inspired *Star Wars?*
2. Summarize the plot elements of *Star Wars* that Canby identifies as all you "should be required to keep track of."
3. According to Canby, who are the "true stars" of *Star Wars?*

◆ Critical Thinking

INTERPRET

1. Why do you think Canby considers an "8-year-old sci-fi buff" the toughest critic of *Star Wars?* **[Speculate]**
2. Did Canby enjoy watching *Star Wars?* Explain. **[Infer]**
3. Explain how each of these elements affects Canby's evaluation of the film: acting, plot, special effects. **[Evaluate]**

EXTEND

4. What three skills do you think are important for a movie reviewer to have to judge movies well and to write interesting reviews? **[Career Link]**

Humanities: Film

At the end of the century, the American inventor Thomas Edison devised the *kinetoscope,* the first successful machine for showing motion pictures. In 1903, *The Great Train Robbery* appeared; it was the first movie with a plot—and the first western. Shot in New Jersey, it was three minutes long.

Movies quickly grew longer, more ambitious, and more popular. Until 1927, they were silent; theater musicians provided the only accompaniment. Instead of spoken dialogue, films had printed titles between scenes.

In 1927, the first film with a sound track made its debut: The *Jazz Singer,* starring Al Jolson. Overnight, the movies switched to sound, and many actors whose voices recorded poorly (or whose voices did not match their screen personalities) saw their careers come to abrupt ends.

Today, motion pictures are a huge worldwide industry, whose stars are often better known than heads of government.

Interested students can do further research about the history of films.

Star Wars

Breakthrough Film Still Has the Force

Roger Ebert

Of the *Chicago Sun-Times*

from *The Oakland Press*, Friday, January 31, 1997

To see "Star Wars" again after 20 years is to revisit a place in the mind. George Lucas' space epic has colonized our imaginations, and it is hard to stand back and see it simply as a motion picture because it has so completely become part of our memories. It's as goofy as a children's tale, as shallow as an
2 old Saturday afternoon serial, as corny as Kansas in August—and a masterpiece. Those who analyze its philosophy do so, I imagine, with a smile in their minds. May the Force be with them.

Like "Birth of a Nation" and "Citizen Kane," "Star Wars" was a technical <u>water-</u>
3 <u>shed</u> that influenced many of the movies that came after. These films have little in common, except for the way they came along at a crucial moment in cinema history, when new methods were ripe for <u>synthesis</u>. "Birth of a
4 Nation" brought together the developing language and shots and editing. "Citizen Kane" married special effects, advanced sound, a new photographic style and a freedom from linear storytelling. "Star Wars" combined a new generation of special effects with the high-energy action picture; it linked space opera and soap opera, fairy tales and legend, and packaged them as a wild visual ride.

"Star Wars" effectively brought to an end the golden era of early-1970s personal filmmaking and focused the industry on big-budget special effects blockbusters, blasting off a trend we are still living through. But you can't blame it for what it did; you can only observe how well it did it. In one way or another all the big studios have been trying to make another "Star Wars" ever since (pictures like "Raiders of the Lost Ark," "Jurassic Park" and "Independence Day" are its heirs). It located Hollywood's center of gravity at the intellectual and emotional level of a bright teenager.

> **◆ *Literature and Your Life***
> How does *Star Wars* compare and contrast with the types of films you enjoy? 5

It's possible, however, that as we grow older, we retain within the tastes of our ear- 6
lier selves. How else to explain how much fun "Star Wars" is, even for those who think they don't care for science fiction? It's a good-hearted film in every single frame, and shining through is the gift of a man who knew how to link state-of-the-art technology with a deceptively simple, really very powerful, story. It was not by accident that George Lucas worked with Joseph Campbell, an expert on the world's basic myths, in fashioning a screenplay that owes much to man's oldest stories.

By now the ritual of classic film revival is well established: an older classic is brought out from the studio vaults, restored frame by frame, re-released in the best theaters, and then re-launched on home video. With this "special edition" of the "Star Wars" trilogy (which includes new versions of "Return of the Jedi" and "The Empire Strikes Back"), Lucas has gone one step beyond. His special effects were so advanced in 1977 that they spun off an industry, including his own Industrial Light & Magic Co., the computer wizards who do many of today's best special effects.

Now Lucas has put IL&M to work touching up the effects, including some that his limited 1977 budget left him unsatisfied with. Most of

> **◆ Build Vocabulary**
> **watershed** (wô´ tər shed) *n.*: Moment or event after which nothing is the same
> **synthesis** (sin´ thə sis) *n.*: Whole made up of separate elements put together

Develop Understanding

Where Vincent Canby's original review of *Star Wars* foresaw a classic, Roger Ebert looks back twenty years later, upon the date of the film's 1997 re-release, to determine if indeed the film holds up to its status. To what extent are other science-fiction films of the past two decades in its debt? Ebert praises the film in an entirely different context than does Canby, for now it truly has become a classic.

◆ Literary Focus

2 Critical Review Ask students how they think the structure of this sentence contributes to the impression Roger Ebert wants to create of *Star Wars*. *Students may say that the adjectives "goofy," "shallow," and "corny" seem to belittle the movie. Abruptly, he calls it a masterpiece, and his final judgment appears even stronger in comparison with those adjectives.*

Comprehension Check ☑

3 Ask students what quality in *Star Wars* Ebert is singling out in this passage. *Star Wars successfully combines a number of relatively new film techniques for the first time.*

4 Clarification *Birth of a Nation* (1915), by D. W. Griffith, is a technical milestone in film—despite its content, which, especially on racial issues, is dated and offensive. *Citizen Kane* (1941), made by Orson Welles at age 23, is a movie classic.

◆ *Literature and Your Life*

5 Students fond of science fiction and other adventure films will probably find *Star Wars* very much to their liking; students with a taste for contemporary romances or other realistic films may say *Star Wars* is not the sort of film that interests them.

◆ Build Grammar Skills

6 Parenthetical Interrupters Ask students to identify the parenthetical interrupter in this sentence, and to explain how it comments on the main part of the sentence. *The interrupter is however, indicating this sentence represents a change in thinking from the sentence that preceded it.*

Beyond the Classroom

Career Connection

Motion Pictures and Television *Star Wars* is the product of a gigantic industry. In addition to their original home in Hollywood, California, film studios are now found all over the map, and every major city has TV stations with studios and offices.

Let students know that actors comprise only a small fraction of the movie and television work force. All studios have technical staffs: camera operators, electricians, carpenters, designers, and people skilled in lighting, sound, and editing. Major motion picture facilities employ specialists in areas such as wardrobe and properties, or props, such as futuristic weapons. In addition, special effects people are busy creating effects from exploding planets to Jabba the Hut. Special effects requires highly developed computer and electronic technology skills as well as imagination and design skills.

Encourage interested students to research careers in the film industry. They might select one or two movie-related jobs and find out what training and preparation would be most useful to someone planning such a career.

Develop Understanding

▶Critical Viewing◀

❶ **Analyze** *Students may point out that Han looks aggressive—like someone who can stand up for himself, even against the fearsome Jabba the Hut. Jabba's non-human look—his size, wrinkled skin, and reptilian face—make him look frightening and evil.*

❷ **Clarification** *2001: A Space Odyssey* is a science-fiction film that begins in the prehistoric past, and ends in the not-too-distant future. Like *Star Wars*, it was highly successful and influential.

◆Critical Thinking

❸ **Compare and Contrast** Ask students what qualities would make science fiction films seem dated when compared with these two movies. *Students may mention that films, especially older ones, with futuristic technology that is already obsolete would look dated. Films with primitive or cheaply-made special effects also fail to hold up over time.*

Read to Discover Models for Writing

Encourage students to compare the writing styles of Vincent Canby and Roger Ebert. Ask them whose style they prefer. Have students write opening paragraphs of their own movie reviews using one style or the other.

▲ Critical Viewing This scene between Han Solo and Jabba the Hut was added to the new version of *Star Wars*. What can you learn about these characters from this picture? **[Analyze]**

the changes are subtle: you'd need a side-by-side comparison to see that a new shot is a little better. There's about five minutes of new material, including a meeting between Han Solo and Jabba the Hut that was shot for the first version but not used. (We learn that Jabba is not immobile, but sloshes along in a kind of spongy undulation.) There's also an improved look to the city of Mos Eisley ("A wretched hive of scum and villainry," says Obi-Wan Kanobi). And the climactic battle scene against the Death Star has been rehabbed.[1]

The improvements are well done, but they point up how well the effects were done to begin with: If the changes are not obvious, that's because "Star Wars" got the look of the film so right in the first place. The obvious comparison is with Kubrick's "2001: A Space Odyssey," made 10 years earlier, in 1967, which also holds up perfectly well today. ❸ (One difference is that Kubrick went for realism, trying to imagine how his future world would really look, while Lucas cheerfully plundered the past; Han Solo's Millennium Falcon has a gun turret with a hand-operated weapon that would be at

1. **rehabbed** (rē´ hab´'d) *v.*: Rehabilitated.

Speaking, Listening, and Viewing Mini-Lesson

Skit

This mini-lesson supports the Speaking, Listening, and Viewing activity in the Idea Bank on p. 635.

Introduce Ask students if they have ever seen a TV show in which two film reviewers discuss new films, sometimes agreeing, sometimes not—a style of reviewing that was made popular by Roger Ebert and his late partner, Gene Siskel. Let students know they will pair off to improvise the same type of conversation, but as typical film-goers rather than critics.

Develop Have students brainstorm for specific topics they can bring up: plot, dialogue, acting, music, effects, costumes. Remind them that they should back up their opinions, positive or negative, with specific reasons and details.

Apply Students should think through their impression, and they might jot down points they plan to make before improvising their skits.

Assess Hold a class discussion in which students can evaluate how well each "critic" expressed his or her opinion and supported it with evidence.

home on a World War II bomber, but too slow to hit anything at space velocities.)

Two Lucas inspirations started the story
with a tease: He set the action not in the fu-
4 ture but "long ago," and jumped into the
middle of it with "Chapter 4: A New Hope."
These seemingly innocent touches were actually rather powerful; they gave the saga the aura of an ancient tale, and an ongoing one.

As if those two shocks were not enough for the movie's first moments, I learn from a review by Mark R. Leeper that this was the first film to pan the camera across a star field: "Space scenes had always been done with a fixed camera, and for a very good reason. It was more economical not to create a background of stars large enough to pan
through." As the camera tilts up, a vast
spaceship appears from the top of the screen
and moves overhead, an effect reinforced by
the surround sound. It is such a dramatic 5
opening that it's no wonder Lucas paid a fine
and resigned from the Directors' Guild rather
than obey its demand that he begin with
conventional opening credits.

The film has simple, well-defined characters, beginning with the robots R2D2 (childlike, easily hurt) and C3PO (fastidious, a

◆ Build Vocabulary

fastidious (fas tid′ ē əs) *adj.*: Not easy to please; discriminating

◆ Build Vocabulary

4 Connotations With students, consider the connotations of the word *inspirations*. Why did Ebert choose this particular word rather than ideas or notions? *The word* inspirations *connotes not simply ideas but brilliant or entirely unique ideas. Ebert is praising Lucas by using the word* inspirations.

◆ Literary Focus

5 Critical Review Have students identify the persuasive language in this passage. Ask them how Ebert supports his claim. *The phrase* dramatic opening *is persuasive. It tells potential viewers that they are in for something exciting right from the start. Ebert supports this claim by describing how the vast spaceship appears from the top of the screen, and telling that Lucas was willing to pay a fine and lose his membership in the Director's Guild in order to create this dramatic opening.*

Extending Word Study

Context Have students read the first full paragraph on p. 631. Draw their attention to the words *saga* and *aura* in the last sentence. Encourage students to define the words based on the context of the sentence. Then have them look up the words in the dictionary and find the meanings.

Customize for *Visual/Spatial Learners*

Play the portions of the *Star Wars* video that Ebert describes. Have these students evaluate his descriptions and opinions after viewing the scenes and settings themselves.

Analyze Film Reviews

Point out to students that each film reviewer has an emotional response to *Star Wars* that is part of his critical response. Vincent Canby appreciates the humor in the movie, and warns against taking its message too seriously. Roger Ebert, viewing the film as a classic, places it in its role in the historical of movie-making.

Offer students a choice of ways to examine these film reviews.

1. Have students write their own reviews of *Star Wars,* including comparisons of their responses with those of Canby and Ebert.
2. Have students search on the Internet to find other reviews of Star Wars, written either at its initial release or when it was re-released. They can compare these reviews with their own feelings or the reviews of Canby and Ebert.

▶Critical Viewing◀

❶ Speculate *Students might say that all three characters are attractive and courageous; Luke is noble and innocent; Princess Leia, independent and outspoken; Han Solo, a loner and a rebel. The characters' youth may make them appealing to young viewers, who can easily identify with them.*

◆Literary Focus

❷ Critical Review Have students go back to the beginning of the review to find appropriate words and phrases such as the following: *Ebert's use of "masterpiece," his statement that the film has become "part of our memories," and phrases such as "technical watershed." They can also cite Ebert's comparing the film with other great film classics such as* Birth of a Nation *and* Citizen Kane.

❸ Clarification Chesley Bonestell (1888–1986) was an artist who specialized in naturalistic paintings of other worlds, based on the most recent scientific data. He also worked on many science-fiction films, such as *War of the Worlds* and *Destination, Moon.*

Reteach

Students who have trouble with the concept of identifying evidence may recognize the idea of supporting details. Remind them that a film reviewer is stating his or her opinion, which is the main idea of the critical review. Like the main idea of an essay, the opinion must be supported by details. In the case of a film review, the details—or evidence— may be facts, observations, examples, and statements from authorities.

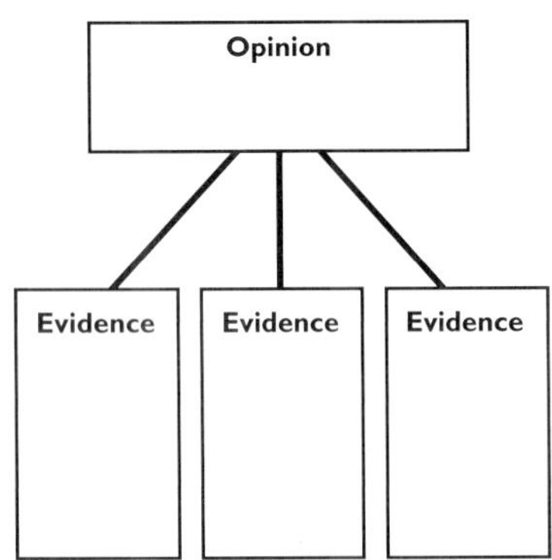

❶ ▲ Critical Viewing Which traits of the characters of "Star Wars" do you think helped to make them popular with viewers? **[Speculate]**

little effete). The evil Empire has all but triumphed in the galaxy, but rebel forces are preparing an assault on the Death Star. Princess Leia (pert, sassy Carrie Fisher) has information pinpointing the star's vulnerable point, and feeds it into R2D2's computer; when her ship is captured, the robots escape from the Death Star and find themselves on Luke Skywalker's planet, where soon Luke (Mark Hamill as an idealistic youngster) meets the wise, old, mysterious Ben Kanobi (Alec Guinness) and they hire the freelance space jockey Han Solo (Harrison Ford, already laconic) to carry them to Leia's rescue.

The story is advanced with spectacularly effective art design, set decoration and effects. Although the scene in the intergalactic bar is famous for the menagerie of alien drunks, there is another scene, when the two robots are thrown into a hold with other used droids, which equally fills the scene with fascinating throwaway details. And a scene in the Death Star's garbage bin (inhabited by a snake with head curiously shaped like E.T.'s) is also well done.

> **◆ Literary Focus** What words and phrases does Ebert use to advance his notion that *Star Wars* is a modern-day film classic?

Many of the planetscapes are startlingly beautiful, and owe something to Chesley Bonestell's imaginary drawings of other worlds. The final assault on the Death Star, when the fighter rockets speed between parallel walls, is a nod in the direction of "2001," with its light trip into another dimension: Kubrick showed, and Lucas learned, how to make the audience feel it is hurtling headlong through space.

Lucas fills his screen with loving touches.

Cross-Curricular Connection: Science

Robots The robots known as R2D2 and C3PO in *Star Wars* are historic and futuristic at the same time; they are yesterday's vision of what a robot looked like and what it could do.

The word *robot* originated in the Czech writer Karel Capek's 1921 play "R.U.R." (Rossum's Universal Robots). In that play, mechanical beings who were manufactured to be slaves for humanity stage a rebellion and kill their creators. Robots of early science fiction manifest people's fears that they will be overtaken by mechanization. The personalities of the *Star Wars* robots do not perpetuate that fear of the future. Today, it is difficult to distinguish robots from other forms of automation. However, robots are being used in some factories, and they are being developed to help people who have lost the use of their limbs.

Suggest that interested students research the modern application of robots in science, industry, and as a tool to help the physically challenged.

There are little alien rats hopping around the desert, and a chess game played with living creatures. Luke's weather-worn "Speeder" vehicle, which hovers over the sand, reminds me uncannily of a 1965 Mustang. And consider the details creating the presence, look and sound of Darth Vader, whose fanged face mask, black cape and hollow breathing are the setting for James Earl Jones's cold voice of doom. ❹

Seeing the film the first time, I was swept away, and have remained swept ever since. Seeing this restored version, I tried to be more objective, and noted that the gun battles on board the space ships go on a bit too long; it is remarkable that the empire marksmen never hit anyone important; and the fighter rain on the enemy ship now plays like the computer games it predicted. I wonder, too, if Lucas could have come up with a more challenging philosophy behind the Force. As Kenobi explains it, it's basically just going with the flow. What if Lucas had pushed a little further to include elements of nonviolence or ideas about intergalactic conservation? (It's a great waste of resources to blow up star systems.)

The films that will live forever are the simplest-seeming ones. They have profound depths, but their surfaces are as clear to an audience as a beloved old story. The way I know this is because the stories that seem immortal—the "Odyssey," the "Tale of Genji," ❺ "Don Quixote," "David Copperfield," "Huckleberry Finn"—are all the same: a brave but flawed hero, a quest, colorful people and places, sidekicks, the discovery of life's underlying truths. If I were asked to say with certainty which movies will still be widely known a century or two from now, I would list "2001," and "The Wizard of Oz," and Keaton and Chaplin, and Astaire and Rogers, and probably "Casablanca" . . . and "Star Wars," for sure. ❻

◆ **Build Vocabulary**

effete (e fēt′) *adj.*: Lacking vigor; overrefined

laconic (lə kän′ ik) *adj.*: Terse; using few words

Guide for Responding

◆ Literature and Your Life

Reader's Response What aspect of *Star Wars* did you find most interesting or surprising in either review?

Thematic Focus What are some ways in which Roger Ebert thinks of *Star Wars* as a film legacy for future movie viewers?

☑ Check Your Comprehension

1. According to Ebert, what quality does *Star Wars* as a film have in common with *Birth of a Nation* and *Citizen Kane?*
2. Give two examples of aspects of the newer version of the film that differ from the original.

◆ Critical Thinking

INTERPRET

1. The title of Ebert's review is "Breakthrough Film Still Has the Force." What makes *Star Wars* a breakthrough, original film? **[Analyze]**
2. In what ways does *Star Wars* fit Ebert's statement that "The films that will live forever are the simplest-seeming ones"?

EVALUATE

3. What movies do you think will be widely known a century or two from now? Explain why. **[Make a Judgment]**
4. Compare and contrast the two essays in terms of their purpose and tone. **[Compare and Contrast]**

◆ Build Vocabulary

❹ **Connotations** Ask students what words in this sentence suggest the evil nature of Darth Vader. *The adjective fanged connotes a deadly and immoral quality. The reference to James Earl Jones's cold voice of doom also carries an implication of menace.*

❺ **Clarification** Lady Murasaki Shikibus' *The Tale of Genji,* an eleventh-century A.D. novel, is thought to be one of the greatest works of Japanese literature. The hero, Prince Genji, exemplifies the virtues of courtliness and sensitivity to nature.

❻ **Clarification** Buster Keaton made some of the greatest silent film comedies. Charlie Chaplin created some of the greatest films ever, in both the silent and sound eras. Fred Astaire and Ginger Rogers were a song-and-dance team in movie musicals of the 1930's and 1940's. *Casablanca* (1942), with Humphrey Bogart and Ingrid Bergman, is one of the most popular movies ever made.

Reinforce and Extend

Answers

◆ Literature and Your Life

Reader's Response Some students may be most interested in reading about the special effects, while others will be interested in the plot or characterizations.

Thematic Response Ebert thinks everything about the technical production is so effective, and works so well with other film elements, that viewers in future generations will be influenced by it.

☑ Check Your Comprehension

1. Like these films, it was a technical watershed.
2. There's a meeting between Han Solo and Jabba the Hut that was not in the original version; an improved look at the city of Mos Eisely; and a rehabilitated climactic battle scene.

◆ Critical Thinking

1. Sample response: *Star Wars* was a breakthrough film because it effectively utilized new and invented technology, combining unprecedented special effects with an engaging plot and characters.
2. *Star Wars* meets the criteria Ebert expresses because it has simple, well-defined characters and because, more important, the philosophy behind it is strong and skillfully evoked.
3. Students should give reasons for their choices.
4. Vincent Canby portrays Star Wars as "fun and funny"—an entertaining movie with "incredible special effects." Roger Ebert treats the movie as a classic that changed the course of film history.

Answers

◆ Reading Strategy

1. He supports his claim particularly by citing the Laurel-and-Hardy quality of the two robots.
2. He cites similar types of stories with simple plots and powerful themes.
3. Students should cite Ebert's descriptions of R2D2 and C3PO.

◆ Build Vocabulary

Using Connotations

1. The slightly humorous connotation of the word *facetiousness* gives it an added dimension over *sarcasm*, which is more straightforward in meaning "harsh or bitter."
2. *Adroit* implies manual dexterity, while *cunning* is mental dexterity.

Using the Word Bank

1. b 2. c 3. a 4. a 5. c 6. c 7. b 8. a 9. c 10. b 11. a

◆ Literary Focus

1. His main points are that *Star Wars* combined new-generation special effects with high-energy action, linked space drama with human-scale drama, and made the whole experience a visual sensation.
2. Students might be particularly persuaded by Canby's final statement that the movie convinced a skeptical 8-year-old sci-fi buff.

◆ Build Grammar Skills

Practice

1. This film, I am sure, will survive technical innovations over the next decade.
2. *Star Wars,* in my opinion, is a classic movie.
3. The talents of the special effect crew, everyone can agree, are admirable.
4. Many people, of course, are familiar with characters from *Star Wars.*
5. *Star Wars* was the first film, interestingly, to pan the camera across a star field.

Grammar Reinforcement

For additional instruction and practice, use the Commas lesson in the **Language Lab CD-ROM** and pp. 99–101 on Commas in the *Writer's Solution Grammar Practice Book.*

Guide for Responding (continued)

◆ Reading Strategy

IDENTIFY EVIDENCE

As a conscientious and critical reader, you **identify the evidence** writers provide to support their opinions. The evidence may be facts, observations, examples, statements from authorities, or statistics.

When Roger Ebert praises the changes in special effects in the 1997 re-release of *Star Wars*, he cites examples of some of those changes, such as "an improved look to the city of Mos Eisley."

1. How does Vincent Canby support his claim that "The way definitely not to approach 'Star Wars,' though, is to expect a film of cosmic implications . . . It's fun and funny"?
2. What evidence does Roger Ebert give to support his claim that *Star Wars* presents a "deceptively simple, really very powerful, story"?
3. How does Roger Ebert support his claim that "the film has simple, well-defined characters"?

◆ Build Vocabulary

USING CONNOTATIONS

The connotation of a word is the thing or idea that the word suggests. The following pairs of words have similar meanings. On your paper, explain how the connotations of the words make them slightly different.

1. facetiousness, sarcasm
2. adroit, cunning

USING THE WORD BANK: Antonyms

On your paper, write the letter of the word that is the best antonym, or opposite, of the first word.

1. condescension: (a) criticism, (b) praise, (c)pride
2. eclectic: (a) varied, (b) boring, (c) consistent
3. apotheosis: (a) scorn, (b) acclaim, (c) flattery
4. laconic: (a) talkative, (b) quiet, (c) reticent
5. effete: (a) soft, (b) weak, (c) strong
6. fastidious: (a) finicky, (b) critical, (c) obliging
7. synthesis: (a) unification, (b) separation, (c) fusion
8. watershed: (a) trifle, (b) breakthrough, (c) river
9. piously: (a) religiously, (b) carelessly, (c) jokingly
10. adroit: (a) skillful, (b) clumsy, (c) practiced
11. facetiousness: (a) solemnity, (b) humor, (c) playfulness

◆ Literary Focus

CRITICAL REVIEW

In a **critical review**, the writer makes a recommendation and tries to persuade you to accept that recommendation.

Critical reviews, which frequently appear in newspapers or magazines, are a type of persuasive essay that helps people make informed choices about the movies on which to spend their entertainment dollars.

1. What are the main points that Roger Ebert uses to back up his assertion that *Star Wars* was a breakthrough film?
2. What is it about Vincent Canby's review that persuades you most—either positively or negatively—about *Star Wars?*

◆ Build Grammar Skills

PARENTHETICAL INTERRUPTERS

Parenthetical interrupters make Ebert's and Canby's reviews sound more conversational. Because parenthetical interrupters are not essential to the sentence, they are set off with commas.

Practice Rewrite each sentence, adding the parenthetical interrupter in parentheses. Remember to include commas.

1. This film will survive technical innovations over the next decade. (*I am sure*)
2. *Star Wars* is a classic movie. (*in my opinion*)
3. The talents of the special effects crew are admirable. (*everyone can agree*)
4. Many people are familiar with characters from *Star Wars.* (*of course*)
5. *Star Wars* was the first film to pan the camera across a star field. (*interestingly*)

Writing Application Write sentences using each of the following parenthetical interrupters.

1. after all
2. by the way
3. incidentally
4. I believe
5. in fact

Beyond the Selection

FURTHER READING

Other Works by the Authors

Roger Ebert's Book of Film, Roger Ebert
Unnatural Scenery, Vincent Canby

Other Film Criticism:

Agee on Film, James Agee
Kiss Kiss Bang Bang, Pauline Kael
When the Lights Go Down, by Pauline Kael

We suggest that you preview these works before recommending them to students.

INTERNET

Students can find more information about Roger Ebert and also read film reviews from other critics at the following Web sites. Please be aware that the sites may have changed since we published this information.

http://208.218.3.83/BuenaVista/SiskelAndEbert/Text/Biography_RogerEbertG.html

http://www.tisd.net/~pvp/MovieReviews.html

We *strongly recommend* that you preview the sites before you send students to them.

Build Your Portfolio

Idea Bank

Writing

1. **Press Release** Imagine that your school is going to have a special showing of *Star Wars.* Write a press release about the movie that explains why the film is worth seeing.

2. **Speech** Write a brief speech a person on the special effects crew of *Star Wars* might give upon winning an award for his or her work.

3. **Interview** Imagine that you could talk to Roger Ebert or Vincent Canby about reviewing movies. Write the interview questions and responses from that imaginary conversation.

Speaking, Listening, and Viewing

4. ***Star Wars* Recording** Play an excerpt from the *Star Wars* theme by composer John Williams. Then, give an explanation to your class about how the music enhances the mood of specific scenes from the movie.

5. **Skit** With a partner, improvise a skit in which two people come out of a theater after seeing the re-release of *Star Wars* and share their initial impressions. **[Performing Arts Link]**

Researching and Representing

6. **Movie Collage** Create a collage of quotations, images, and advertisements showing the types of movies you enjoy. Explain your collage to the class. **[Art Link]**

7. **Science-Fiction Exhibit** Design a *Star Wars* exhibit for a science-fiction museum. Create your own illustrations or use *Star Wars* souvenirs you might already have. Write display tags that explain or describe the items. Then organize them to exhibit for the class. **[Art Link]**

Online Activity **www.phlit.phschool.com**

Guided Writing Lesson

Movie Review

A **movie review** influences people's opinions and choices of movies to see. The title of a review and the first paragraph should hook the reader and promote the reviewer's point of view. The body of the review supports the opinion with summaries of the movie, facts, examples, and observations. The last paragraph repeats the initial opinions in a new and interesting way. Choose a movie you have recently seen and write a review to persuade a reader to see it—or not to see it.

Writing Skills Focus: Use Specific Examples

Include **specific examples** so that your readers will be able to picture aspects of the movie in their mind's eye. For each statement or claim you make about a movie, refer to a specific detail or scene to support your opinion. For instance, if you say, "This movie is guaranteed to make you cry," give an example of what happens in a sad scene or discuss background music that evokes a feeling of sorrow.

Prewriting Create an idea web to organize your ideas and find specific examples for your review. Start with your overall opinion. Then create branches for aspects of the movie that support that opinion. Cite specific examples for each aspect.

Drafting State your opinion at the beginning of the review, then support it with specific examples. You might include parenthetical interrupters to keep your tone conversational.

Revising Have a partner read your review for specific examples to back up your opinion. If necessary, you might include more examples or details to back up your opinion. Then check to see that your last paragraph interestingly restates your opinion.

✓ ASSESSMENT OPTIONS

Formal Assessment, Selection Test, pp. 157–159, and Assessment Resources Software. The selection test is designed so that it can be easily customized to the performance levels of your students.

Alternative Assessment, p. 45, includes options for less advanced students, more advanced students, musical/rhythmic learners, logical/mathematical learners, and bodily/kinesthetic learners.

PORTFOLIO ASSESSMENT

Use the following rubrics in the ***Alternative Assessment*** booklet to assess student writing:
Press Release: Persuasion Rubric, p. 105
Speech: Expression Rubric, p. 94
Interview: Fictional Narrative Rubric, p. 95

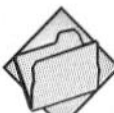

Idea Bank

Following are suggestions for matching Idea Bank topics with your students' performance levels and learning modalities:

Customizing for *Performance Levels*
Less Advanced Students: 6
Average Students: 2, 3, 4, 5
More Advanced Students: 7

Customizing for *Learning Modalities*
Visual/Spatial: 6
Verbal/Linguistic: 4, 5
Rhythmic/Musical: 4
Interpersonal: 5

Guided Writing Lesson

Prewriting Strategy Hold a class discussion and demonstrate webbing on the board.

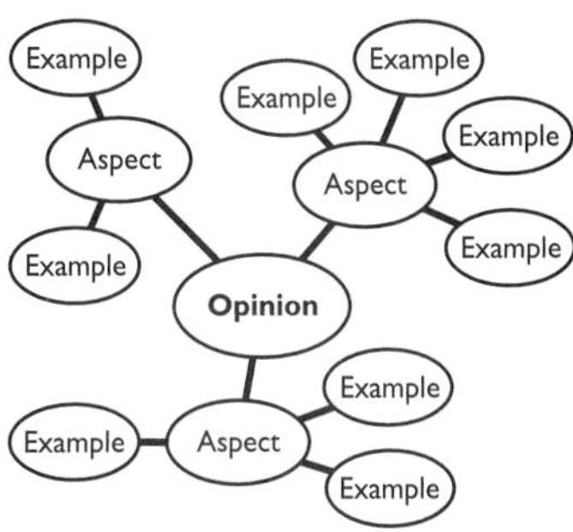

Point out to students that they may determine that there are more examples for some aspects of their opinions than others.

For more prewriting, elaboration, and revision strategies, see *Prentice Hall Writing and Grammar.*

Writers at Work Videodisc
Have students view the videodisc segment for Chapter 7 in which Miguel Algarín discusses the process of preparing a literary response.

Play frames 24470 to 26040

Writing Lab CD-ROM
Have students complete the tutorial on Response to Literature.

1. Students can use Response Wheels to explore combinations of literary elements and response methods to use in their movie reviews.
2. Students can use the Evaluation Word Bin to select from among adjective and adverb groups they might use in their movie reviews.

Prepare and Engage

LESSON OBJECTIVES

1. **To develop vocabulary and word identification skills**
   - Related Words: Words Describing Color
   - Using the Word Bank: Sentence Completions
   - Extending Word Study: Latin Prefix (ATE) *de-*
2. **To use a variety of reading strategies to read and comprehend a visual essay**
   - Connect Your Experience
   - Reading Strategy: Interpret Pictures
   - Read to Discover Models for Writing (ATE)
3. **To increase knowledge of other cultures and to connect common elements across cultures**
   - Connecting Themes Across Cultures (ATE)
4. **To express and support responses to the text**
   - Critical Thinking
   - Idea Bank: Descriptive Paragraph
   - Idea Bank: Interview
   - Idea Bank: Poem
5. **To analyze literary elements**
   - Literary Focus: Visual Essay
6. **To read in order to research self-selected and assigned topics**
   - Idea Bank: Parent-and-Child Encyclopedia
   - Viewing and Representing Mini-Lesson: Parent-and-Child Video (ATE)
7. **To speak clearly and effectively for a specific audience and purpose**
   - Speaking, Listening, and Viewing Mini-Lesson: Award Panel (ATE)
   - Idea Bank: Dramatic Reading
8. **To use recursive writing processes to write an introduction**
   - Guided Writing Lesson
9. **To increase knowledge of the rules of grammar and usage**
   - Build Grammar Skills: Semicolons in a Series

Test Preparation

Reading Comprehension: Comparing and Contrasting Texts (ATE, p. 637) The teaching tips and sample test item in this workshop support the instruction and practice in the unit workshop.

Reading Comprehension: Comparing and Contrasting Texts; Analyzing Literary Language (SE, p. 661)

Guide for Reading

Tillie Olsen *(1912–)*

Tillie Olsen knows about mothers and daughters as the mother of four daughters, one of whom is Julie Olsen Edwards, co-author of the essay from *Mothers & Daughters*. In addition to raising four daughters, Tillie Olsen has written fiction as well as nonfiction. She won the O. Henry first prize for her story "Tell Me a Riddle" in 1961. A well-known Canadian writer, Margaret Atwood, said about Tillie Olsen in a review: "Among women writers in the United States 'respect' is too pale a word: 'reverence' is more like it." Olsen's perceptive insights into the mother-daughter relationship have earned her such deserved praise by fellow women authors.

Estelle Jussim *(1927–)*

An expert on photography can help you understand or appreciate this art form. Estelle Jussim —a professor at Simmons College and an expert on photography, film, and popular imagery —is just such an expert and writer. Dr. Jussim is author of the award-winning books *Landscape as Photograph* (1985), *Slave to Beauty* (1981), *Frederic Remington, the Camera and the Old West* (1983), and *Visual Communication and the Graphic Arts* (1974). In her essay for the book *Mothers & Daughters*, Jussim conveys the unique relationships that mothers and daughters share.

◆ Build Vocabulary

RELATED WORDS: WORDS DESCRIBING COLOR

When Tillie Olsen uses the word *hue*, she is using just one of many words that refer to differences in a color. You can also refer to a color's *shade* or *tint*. *Hue* is a particular shade of a color that distinguishes it from other shades. The word *shade* refers to the degree of darkness of a particular color. A *tint* is a pale or delicate shade of a color.

WORD BANK

As you read the excerpt from *Mothers & Daughters*, you will encounter the words on this list. Each word is defined on the page where it first appears.

hue
sullenness
fervor
rapture
implicit

◆ Build Grammar Skills

SEMICOLONS IN A SERIES

In order to make long sentences clear, writers use **semicolons** to separate a series of items in which one or more of the items contain commas.

Notice that the semicolons in this sentence from *Mothers & Daughters* separate groups of words that already contain commas:

> Here are daughters and mothers of every shape and human hue; in every age and stage from mother and infant, to old daughter and old, old mother; and here is the family resemblance in face, expression, stance, body.

Prentice Hall Literature Program Resources

REINFORCE / RETEACH / EXTEND

Selection Support Pages
Build Vocabulary: Related Words: Words Describing Color, p. 188
Build Grammar Skills: Semicolons in a Series, p. 189
Reading Strategy: Interpret Pictures, p. 190
Literary Focus: Visual Essay, p. 191

Strategies for Diverse Student Needs, p. 46

Beyond Literature
Workplace Skills: *Effective Listening*, p. 46

Formal Assessment Selection Test, pp. 160-162; Assessment Resources Software

Alternative Assessment, p. 46

Resource Pro CD-ROM

Listening to Literature Audiocassettes

Mothers & Daughters

◆ Literature and Your Life

CONNECT YOUR EXPERIENCE

Countless films, books, and documentaries have offered glimpses into the relationship between mothers and daughters. You probably have formed your own ideas about the mother-daughter relationship from mothers and daughters you've known or from your own experiences. This essay will give you further insight into the unique relationship that mothers and daughters share.

THEMATIC FOCUS: LEGACIES

These mothers and daughters present a legacy for the future: The mothers will become grandmothers and the daughters will become mothers of a new generation of daughters.

Journal Writing Write what you think makes a good mother-daughter relationship.

◆ Background for Understanding

ART

One of the most exciting visual arts is also one of the newest—photography. Although the principles of photography were known for centuries, scientists and inventors produced the first portrait photographs in the 1820's. Americans took hold of this new visual art, and people like Mathew Brady amazed the world by photographically documenting historical events like the Civil War. By 1888, George Eastman produced a roll of paper film and a simple box camera for ordinary Americans to use—the Kodak camera and film. The photographs in *Mothers & Daughters* owe their existence to these early photography pioneers.

◆ Literary Focus

VISUAL ESSAY

Like a written essay, a **visual essay** presents information or makes a point about a subject, but a visual essay conveys its point through photographs or other visual forms as well as written text.

In *Mothers & Daughters,* Tillie Olsen and Estelle Jussim have combined written passages, from a variety of authors, with photographs to convey the relationship between mothers and daughters. The writers Tillie Olsen and her daughter Julie Olsen Edwards, Sage Sohier, Eudora Welty, and Estelle Jussim offer their insights on this relationship. Their words work with the photos to give different perspectives on a single theme.

◆ Reading Strategy

INTERPRET PICTURES

You've heard the saying that a picture is worth a thousand words. When you look at a picture, instead of reading words to get meaning, you **interpret** it by "reading" the elements of the picture.

In this visual essay, much of the message is communicated visually. To interpret these pictures, and to understand the relationship between the mothers and daughters, look at these elements in the pictures: the facial expressions and other body language, the closeness or distance between people, the backgrounds, and any other details in each photo that seem to give it particular meaning.

Test Preparation Workshop

Reading Comprehension: Comparing and Contrasting Texts Students will encounter questions that require them to compare and contrast aspects of two texts on standardized tests such as the SAT. Have them read the observations in this selection grouping on pp. 638 and 639. Then write this sample test question on the board.

What idea about taking photographs do both texts share?

A The photographer has only partial control over the result of the photograph.
B It is extremely difficult to take a portrait of two people together.
C A photograph is like a daughter.
D The mother-daughter relationship is fraught with cultural overtones.

Students should recognize that *B* and *D* refer only to the Olsen/Edwards passage, while *C* refers to the Sohier passage. Therefore, to satisfy the qualifier, *both,* in the question, *A* is the correct answer.

Raise students' interest in this selection with a quick journal-writing activity. Have them visualize their favorite family photograph. Each student should then write a description of that photo along with some thoughts on what makes it meaningful. Follow up by letting students know that photographs can reveal unique aspects of interpersonal relationships. In this visual essay, they will read, text and photographs collaborate to create brief (and yet full) portraits of mothers and daughters together.

Connecting Themes Across Cultures

Encourage students to find representations of relationships between mothers and daughters throughout history.

Customize for *Less Proficient Readers*

The stylistic variation among these texts may pose difficulties for less proficient readers. Guide these students to see that the texts represent different voices, just as the photographs represent different visions. Also encourage them to paraphrase the points that each writer makes.

Customize for *Pre-AP Students*

Encourage Pre-AP Students to evaluate and describe the texts and the photographs in terms of purpose and tone. For example, which works would they describe as intimate? Which are more formal? Which text is the most analytical? Students can gather in small groups to discuss their choices.

Customize for *English Language Learners*

This selection presents an opportunity to review a variety of verb tenses with students. Point out the present tense "the eye seeks deeper vision" from Olsen's piece; the past tense "I learned"; and the past-perfect tense "I'd (I had) got in my own bed" from Welty's piece. Help students to see why each tense was used.

Develop Understanding

One-Minute Insight The photographs and text in this visual essay combine to evoke the rich complexity of its theme. Five photographers and four writers explore the relationship between mothers and daughters from different perspectives. The overall multi-faceted approach is fitting for a relationship that cannot be summed up by a single image or statement—a relationship that is, in Tillie Olsen's words, "Multi, multiform."

◆ Build Grammar Skills

❶ Semicolons in a Series Call students' attention to the semicolons in this sentence. Encourage them to explain their function. *They separate items within the sentence that already contain commas.*

▶Critical Viewing◀

❷ Interpret *Some students may say that the photo shows "sullenness" and "estrangement"—they may cite the expressions on the people's faces and the distance between them. Others may say that it shows "admiration" and "wordless closeness," arguing that the daughters and mother feel secure enough within themselves to stand on their own.*

◆ Literary Focus

❸ Visual Essay Tillie Olsen's text refers to "a welter of images," and she calls these photographic images "Multi, multi-form." Ask students how Olsen's text is itself a multi-form welter of images describing the mother-daughter relationship. *Suggested responses: Olsen captures the "multiform" nature of the images by naming a wide variety of emotions, conditions, and circumstances; she conveys that every person and every mother-daughter relationship is unique.*

Customize for *Gifted/Talented Students*

Suggest that students write captions for each picture in this visual essay. Encourage them to consider these questions before writing: Who are these people? What are they doing? What do the details in each picture reveal about the people's lives?

Mothers & Daughters

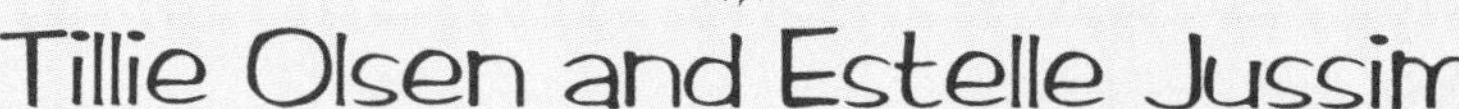

August, New Mexico, 1979, Danny Lyon, Magnum Photos, Inc.

Observations by Tillie Olsen and Julie Olsen Edwards

❶ Here are daughters and mothers of every shape and human hue; in every age and stage from mother and infant, to old daughter and old, old mother; and here is the family resemblance in face, expression, stance, body.

Here are mothers and daughters of lack and of privilege, in various dress, settings, environments; posing for photographs or (unconcerned with the camera) sharing tasks, ease, occasions, activities; holding, embracing, touching; or in terrible isolation.

Here is sullenness, anger or controlled anger, resentment; admiration, distaste; playfulness, pride; joy, joy, joy in each other; estrangement; wordless closeness or intense communion.

A welter[1] of images. Multi, multi-form. The eye seeks deeper vision. ❸

❷ ▲ **Critical Viewing** Which feelings described in the text do you think are shown in this photo? **[Interpret]**

1. **welter** (welʹ tər) *n.*: Hodge-podge; number of things tossed and tumbled about.

Block Scheduling Strategies

Consider these suggestions to take advantage of extended class time:

- Use the information in Background for Understanding (p. 637) as the basis of a class discussion on the history of photography. Then have students do research to learn more about one of the people or developments mentioned in the feature.
- Have students work in discussion groups to interpret the photos in this selection. Then have them answer the Reading Strategy questions on p. 644.
- Encourage interested students to do the Mood Palette activity in ***Alternative Assessment,*** p. 46. If necessary, explain that a painter's palette is a thin board used by painters for holding and mixing colors. Students can discuss the group of colors that convey the mood of each photo.
- Have students complete the Guided Writing Lesson (p. 645). Before students start, have a class discussion on the use of elaboration in the text with the photographs.

Observations by Sage Sohier

A photograph is a sort of daughter: conceived one hopes (but not necessarily) in rapture, it must come to life on its own.
4 One's relationship to it in the beginning largely consists of carting it around and having hopes for it. And *if* it is a successful one, it develops a personality, goes off alone, leads a life of which its mother might not be the best interpreter.

◆ Build Vocabulary

hue (hū) *n.*: Color; tint

sullenness (sul′ ən nəs) *n.*: Gloom; sadness

rapture (rap′chər) *n.*: State of being filled with joy

Untitled, Brookline, Massachusetts, 1986, Sage Sohier, Courtesy of the artist

5 ▲ Critical Viewing Why do you think the photographer chose to capture the mother hugging a cat instead of her daughter in this photograph? **[Infer]**

◆ Critical Thinking

4 Interpret After making sure that students understand that Sohier is comparing a photograph to a daughter, ask: What does it mean for a photograph to lead "a life of which its mother might not be the best interpreter"? *Suggested responses: The daughter becomes independent; she becomes "her own person." The photograph takes on meanings beyond those that the photographer intended or understood.*

▶Critical Viewing◀

5 Infer *Students may infer that the photographer wanted to capture a tense period in the mother and daughter's relationship. The two seem to be going through a conflict, and the mother finds it easier to express uncomplicated feelings toward the cat than complicated feelings toward her daughter.*

Read to Discover Models for Writing

Point out to students that the author uses a metaphor to describe the art of taking a photograph, by calling the photograph "a sort of daughter." Encourage students to come up with metaphors to describe themselves, their favorite activities, or something they observe.

Beyond the Classroom

Career Connection

Photography The photographs in this selection demonstrate that photography is a rich art form. Photography plays an important role in many fields, including fashion, real estate, medical and scientific research, advertising, and journalism.

Just as photographs are taken for a wide variety of purposes, photographers are employed in a wide variety of settings. These include magazines and news organizations, advertising agencies, tourist boards, and institutions such as museums and universities, which often employ staff photographers. Some photographers work on a freelance basis; they may work for several different companies, or they may make a living photographing weddings and other special events. In addition to photography skills, these professionals may use writing, marketing, and research skills in order to sell their work.

Have interested students identify and choose one specialized area of photography, such as wildlife photography, portrait photography, or news photography, to research and report on for the class.

Develop Understanding

◆ Literary Focus

❶ **Visual Essay** Have students contrast Welty's text with Olsen's. How do the two differ in perspective and focus? What purpose does each serve in the visual essay? *Students should note that Olsen's text deals with a broad subject—the many aspects of the mother-daughter relationship, while Welty's text offers an intimate look at one relationship—her own with her mother. They should also note that Olsen's text serves as an introduction to the essay, while Welty's text is one of the contributions to the essay.*

◆ Literature and Your Life

❷ What legacies does Welty acknowledge as she pays tribute to her mother? Do students think that these legacies are valuable in all parent-child relationships? *Students may say that Welty's mother taught her a love of reading and taught her about the power of love and emotion; both these legacies would be extremely important and valuable in any parent-child relationship.*

▶Critical Viewing◀

❸ **Analyze** *The mother's expression is proud, pleased, and forthright; she seems happy and comfortable about being photographed. The daughter's expression is more apprehensive and questioning. Students might note that the mother probably made their matching dresses and that the mother and daughter might feel differently about being photographed in them.*

Observations by Eudora Welty

I learned from the age of two or three that any room in our house, at any time of day, was there to read in, or to be read to. My mother read to me.
❶ She'd read to me in the big bedroom in the mornings, when we were in her rocker together, which ticked in rhythm as we rocked, as though we had a cricket accompanying the story. She'd read to me in the diningroom on winter afternoons in front of the coal fire, with our cuckoo clock ending the story with "Cuckoo," and at night when I'd got in my own bed. I must have given her no peace. Sometimes she'd read to me in the kitchen while she sat churning, and the churning sobbed along with *any* story. . . . She could still recite [the poems in McGuffey's Readers] in full when she was lying helpless and nearly blind, in her bed, an old lady. Reciting, her voice took on resonance and firmness, it rang with the old fervor, with ferocity even. She was
❷ teaching me one more, almost her last, lesson: emotions do not grow old. I knew that I would feel as she did, and I do.

Nellie G. Morgan and Tammie Pruitt Morgan, Bicentennial Celebration, Philadelphia, Mississippi, 1976, Roland Freeman, Courtesy of the artist

◆ Build Vocabulary

fervor (fur´ vər) *n.*: Passion; zeal

◀ **Critical Viewing** What word or words would you use to describe the mother's expression in this photograph? The daughter's? **[Analyze]** ❸

Beyond the Classroom

Community Connection

Local Artistry "Mothers and Daughters" showcases the work of distinguished photographers. Most communities offer places and opportunities for local artists to show their work.

In a class discussion, have students share information about any places they know of that exhibit or publicize the work of local artists. (Possibilities include schools, libraries, the Town Hall, restaurants, community centers, senior citizen centers, and churches and synagogues.)

Encourage students to follow up by consulting the events listings in your local newspaper and interviewing community members to learn more about local artists and art exhibits. Students can then share the information that they gathered by creating a guide to the art scene in their community.

Tang Chung, Lisa Lu, Lucia and Loretta, Los Angeles, California, 1986, Carla Weber, Courtesy of the artist

4 ▲ **Critical Viewing** Do you think this photograph was posed or taken by surprise? Explain your answer. **[Speculate]**

▶Critical Viewing◀

❹ **Speculate** *Students should note that the photograph was most likely taken by surprise. Although the two women are posing, they are posing for their mother's camera, and not that of the photographer who captured this family moment. They might also note that the older woman is aware the second photographer is taking a picture, but she does not quite seem to be posing.*

Customize for
Bodily/Kinesthetic Learners
Encourage these students to interpret the body language of the two young women being photographed. What do their poses reveal about their personalities and their relationship to each other? *Students might conclude from observing their somewhat stiff poses and careful grooming that the young women want to be perceived as proper or formal in some way; at the same time, their close poses and smiles indicate they are close and comfortable with each other.*

Reteach

Students may have trouble understanding the connections between the different written passages in this selection. Help them see that each passage has as its theme the relations of mothers and daughters. Encourage students to reread each passage and summarize it in their own words. Then discuss the range of ideas about mothers and daughters presented in this selection.

Speaking, Listening, and Viewing Mini-Lesson

Award Panel

This mini-lesson supports the Speaking, Listening, and Viewing activity in the Idea Bank on p. 645.

Introduce Explain to students that they will act as one judge on an award panel charged with choosing the best photograph of the year. Their task is to explain to fellow judges exactly why they think their choice should win the award.

Develop Have students choose a photograph to receive the award—one in this selection or they may find another they think deserves an award. Then have them identify presentation points:

- State their choice to receive the award
- Make a statement explaining and supporting their choice of the best photograph
- Elaborate by discussing in detail the reason for the choice. Point out the visual and emotional elements that make the photograph effective or powerful.

Apply Divide students into small groups of "judges." Each judge can use the tips in Develop Background to present and support his or her choice to the other judges.

Assess Have students evaluate the presentations. Were the judges' reasons clearly stated? Did their presentations help the other judges see the photos in a new light?

◆ Reading Strategy

❶ Interpret Pictures Ask students: What evidence in the picture on this page suggests that the two subjects are not caught in a "permanently ascribable" mood, but rather in just one mood in a moment of time? *Although the mother seems proud of her daughter's independence, this is not a "permanently ascribable mood." After the photograph is taken her mood might shift to one of protectiveness, anxiety, or something else. The daughter, who seems momentarily stunned in the photograph, is perhaps between moods; she might become joyous or fretful after the shutter has clicked.*

◆ Critical Thinking

❷ Support Ask students if they agree with Jussim's assertion that a photographer possesses a special "visual language." If so, what would they say are some of the elements of that language? *Students may cite the elements discussed in the Reading Strategy feature—namely, a special knack for capturing and understanding facial expressions, body language, the closeness or distance between people, the backgrounds, and other significant details.*

▶ Critical Viewing ◀

❸ Draw Conclusions *Students may say that the woman shows strength, self-confidence, poise, and determination.*

Extending Word Study

Latin Prefix *de-* Encourage students to determine the meaning of the word decoding using what they know of the Latin prefix de-. This prefix may mean a negation, removal, or reversal of the root word. Decoding means translating a coded message (in this case a photograph) into ordinary language.

Observations by Estelle Jussim

from "The Heart of the Ineffable"

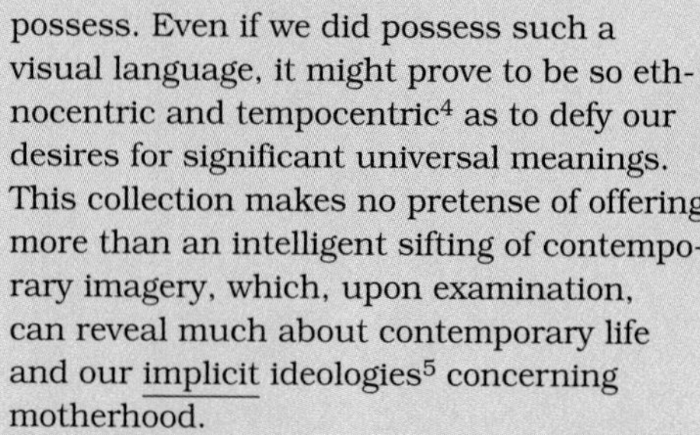

❶ It has been widely recognized that even the greatest portrait can capture only so much of an individual's personality and character, not all of that person's physical attributes, and certainly not a permanently ascribable[2] mood. An attempt by a photographer to convey not only one, but two persons and their relationship, might seem to be exceedingly difficult, if not impossible. To portray two persons defined as mother and daughter is to define a relationship fraught[3] with cultural and emotional overtones. Such intensity of meaning would seem to demand skillful decoding. Perhaps, also, it requires a grasp of visual language that not all of us possess. Even if we did possess such a visual language, it might prove to be so ethnocentric and tempocentric[4] as to defy our desires for significant universal meanings. ❷ This collection makes no pretense of offering more than an intelligent sifting of contemporary imagery, which, upon examination, can reveal much about contemporary life and our implicit ideologies[5] concerning motherhood.

2. **ascribable** (ə skrīb′ ə bəl) *adj.*: Assignable; attributable.
3. **fraught** (frôt) *v.*: Filled; loaded.
4. **ethnocentric** (eth′ nō sen′ trik) **and tempocentric** (tem′ pō sen′ trik): Excessively concerned with race and time.
5. **ideologies** (ī′ dē äl′ ə jēz) *n.*: Ways of thinking; doctrines.

◆ Build Vocabulary

implicit (im plis′ it) *adj.*: Essentially a part of; inherent

Untitled, Wilmington, Delaware, 1983, Bruce Horowitz, Courtesy of the artist

Beyond Literature

Career Connection

Careers in the Visual Arts There are many career opportunities available in the field of visual arts. Photographers may work for themselves or for magazines or advertising agencies. Other visual artists might create logos for products, design graphics for computer games, or design the layout of magazine pages. Media researchers find photos, video, and artwork, and they set up photo shoots for textbooks, advertising agencies, and magazines. What career in visual arts interests you most?

◀ **Critical Viewing** What does this woman's body language and expression suggest about her? **[Draw Conclusions]** ❸

Viewing and Representing Mini-Lesson

Parent-Child Video

This mini-lesson supports the Researching and Representing activity in the Idea Bank on p. 645.

Introduce To develop a video on parent-child relations, students may want to look for information from a variety of sources. They might interview health professionals, social workers, and individuals in families. They might also read reference books on the subject.

Develop Students can work together in groups to decide on a format for their videos. They might plan and film interviews, perform scenes as demonstrations, or use voice-overs while showing photographs.

Apply Suggest that students determine a running time for the video, such as 5 to 10 minutes. They can then decide on the length of time to spend on each segment or idea. Help students schedule use of equipment to prepare their videos

Assess Have students bring in their completed videotapes and share them with the class. Evaluate the videos based on how clearly they convey their messages.

CONNECTIONS TO TODAY'S WORLD

Some of our most vivid memories come from special times in our childhood. Perhaps your fondest memory is of building sand castles at the beach with your best friend or a special day shared with family. This song, like the photos in "Mothers & Daughters," captures special moments like these.

In the song "These Are Days," the speaker is reminding us that there are certain times in our lives that we will always remember. These precious memories will fill you "with laughter until you break" and make you feel "blessed and lucky." As you grow older, you'll encounter many more days you'll remember forever.

These Are Days

Robert Buck & Natalie Merchant

These are days you'll remember.
Never before and never since,
I promise, will the whole world be warm
as this.
And as you feel it, you'll know it's true
that you are blessed and lucky.
It's true that you are touched by something that will grow and bloom in you.

These are days you'll remember.
When May is rushing over you with desire
to be part of the miracle you see in every
hour.
You'll know it's true that you are blessed
and lucky.
It's true that you are touched by something that will grow and bloom in you.

These are days.

These are the days you might fill with
laughter until you break.
These days you might feel a shaft of light
make its way across your face.
And when you do you'll know how it was
meant to be.
See the signs and know their meaning.
It's true, you'll know how it was meant to
be.
Hear the signs and know they're speaking
to you, to you.

1. In what ways do the photographs in *Mothers & Daughters* recall days to remember?
2. What line from this song best describes a mother-daughter relationship?
3. Do you think this is an appropriate song to accompany these photos? Why or why not?

Guide for Responding

◆ Literature and Your Life

Reader's Response Which photograph do you like best? What is it that interested you most in it?

Thematic Focus Which photograph do you think best represents a future legacy? How and why?

☑ Check Your Comprehension

1. What fond childhood memory does Eudora Welty share?
2. To what does Sage Sohier compare a photograph?

Beyond the Selection

FURTHER READING

Other Works by the Authors

Silences, Tillie Olsen
Landscape as Photograph, Estelle Jussim

Other Works About Mothers and Daughters

The Joy Luck Club, Amy Tan
The Glass Menagerie, Tennessee Williams

We suggest that you preview these works before recommending them to students.

INTERNET

For more information about Tillie Olsen, go to: **http://mockingbird.creighton.edu/NCW/olsen.htm**

Please be aware that the sites may have changed since we published this information.

We *strongly recommend* that you preview the sites before you send students to them.

Connections to Today's World

As students read the words to "These Are Days," have them relate the words to the mothers and daughters in the photographs. Ask students how they remember memorable days or events.

About the Author Natalie Merchant, who co-wrote "These Are Days" with Robert Buck, is a contemporary singer and songwriter. Her hits include the album *Tigerlily* and the single "Jealousy."

Answers

1. Each photograph captures the special atmosphere, mood, and feelings that are associated with a particular time in the lives of mothers and daughters; in the years to come, the mothers and daughters will be able to look back at the photographs and recall how they looked and felt.
2. Students may cite the line "It's true that you are touched by something that will grow and bloom in you," saying that it expresses the legacy for the future that is part of every mother-daughter relationship.
3. Students may say that the song is appropriate, pointing out that both the song and the photos focus on relationships, emotions, and identity.

Reinforce and Extend

Answers

◆ Literature and Your Life

Reader's Response Students might choose photographs that feel personally meaningful to them; perhaps the setting or some aspect of a culture revealed in the photograph will particularly appeal to them.

Thematic Focus Students should choose a photograph in which they think something of permanent importance is passing between mother and daughter; for example in Bruce Horowitz's photograph the mother seems to be passing on a legacy of independence to her daughter.

☑ Check Your Comprehension

1. She shares the memory of her mother reading to her throughout her childhood.
2. Sage Sohier compares a photograph to a daughter.

Guide for Responding *(continued)*

◆ Critical Thinking

INTERPRET

1. How does "Tang Chung, Lisa Lu, Lucia, and Loretta" by Carla Weber, on p. 641 show what Tillie Olsen considers "A welter of images. Multi, multi-form"? **[Support]**

2. Sage Sohier says that a successful photograph, like a daughter, "develops a personality, goes off alone, leads a life of which its mother might not be the best interpreter." What kind of future relationship do you think the mother and daughter in Sohier's photograph on p. 639 will have? **[Interpret]**

EVALUATE

3. What do you think Estelle Jussim means by the "visual language" needed to portray a complex relationship? **[Interpret]**

EXTEND

4. In what careers could you use skill in photography? **[Career Link]**

◆ Reading Strategy

INTERPRET PICTURES

When you **interpret pictures**, you "read" their message from the elements within the pictures.

1. What do you think is the relationship between the mother and daughter in "Bicentennial Celebration" on p. 640?

2. What do you think is on the mother's mind in the photograph by Bruce Horowitz on p. 642?

3. Why do you think the oldest woman is smiling in "Tang Chung, Lisa Lu, Lucia, and Loretta" by Carla Weber on p. 641?

◆ Literary Focus

VISUAL ESSAY

A **visual essay** presents information on a subject through photographs or other visual forms along with written text.

1. Why do you need both the photography and writing to understand the relationships between mothers and daughters presented in this essay?

2. What details in Sage Sohier's text added to your understanding of her photograph? Explain.

◆ Build Vocabulary

USING COLORFUL WORDS

The words *hue, shade,* and *tint* have specific meanings related to color. On your paper, complete the following sentences using these words.

1. Many houses in Bermuda are painted in pastel __?__.

2. As night approached, the forest around them became darker and darker __?__ of green.

3. Dust particles in the air sometimes give the sunset a pinkish __?__.

USING THE WORD BANK: Sentence Completions

On your paper, write the word from the Word Bank that best completes each sentence.

1. Although the football team's skill was limited, its __?__ was enough to win the game.

2. The car commercial's __?__ message was that the car would make you popular.

3. The meat had a slightly greenish __?__, so I decided to throw it away.

4. The angry young boy could not hide his __?__ during his sister's recital.

5. The joyful woman's face filled with __?__ as she watched her son receive his diploma.

◆ Build Grammar Skills

SEMICOLONS IN A SERIES

Use **semicolons** to separate items in a series when the items already contain commas.

Practice On your paper, rewrite the following sentences, placing semicolons where needed to separate items in series.

1. Mothers and daughters can be happy, playful, joyous, they can be distraught, sad, forlorn, they can stare, stare, stare into the camera lens and still be a mystery.

2. This collection includes photographs by Sage Sohier, Nellie Morgan, and Tang Chung; observations by Tillie Olsen, Estelle Jussim, Sage Sohier, and Eudora Welty, and moments from the lives of several mothers and daughters.

Writing Application List your impressions of these photographs in several series. Use semicolons to separate the items in a series that already use commas.

Answers

◆ Critical Thinking

1. This photograph shows "A welter of images. Multi, multi-form" in that it seems to present two mother-daughter relationships (the older woman and the photographer; the photographer and her two daughters), and suggests various emotions and aspects of their relationships.
2. Some students might use the evidence of conflict between the mother and daughter to predict a future relationship of conflict; others will predict that the mother and daughter will resolve their conflict and go on to have a close future relationship.
3. Students might say that "visual language" means the ability to capture the poses and facial expressions that suggest deep or hidden parts of a relationship.
4. Students might mention journalism, advertising, or careers related to nature or the environment.

◆ Reading Strategy

1. It is possible that the girl is the mother's only daughter, since they are dressed alike and photographed alone.
2. Students might say that the mother is having proud thoughts about her daughter or that she is thinking about something entirely independent of their relationship.
3. She is probably amused that someone is taking a picture of the mother photographing the young women.

◆ Literary Focus

1. The text and the photographs each contribute a different kind of language to make a whole picture. The text is analytical, reflective, and metaphoric, while the photos capture revealing details about people's lives.
2. Sohier's detail about going off alone to lead a life of which the mother might not be the best interpreter might help students to understand the mood of disharmony in the photo.

◆ Build Vocabulary

Using Colorful Words

1. Many houses in Bermuda are painted in pastel <u>hues</u>.
2. As night approached, the forest around them became darker and darker <u>shades</u> of green.
3. Dust particles in the air sometimes give the sunset a pinkish <u>tint</u>.

Using the Word Bank

1. fervor; 2. implicit; 3. hue; 4. sullenness; 5. rapture

◆ Build Grammar Skills

Practice

1. Mothers and daughters can be happy, playful, joyous; they can be distraught, sad, forlorn; they can stare, stare, stare into the camera lens and still be a mystery.
2. This collection includes photographs by Sage Sohier, Nellie Morgan, and Tang Chung; observations by Tillie Olsen, Estelle Jussim, Sage Sohier, and Eudora Welty; and moments from the lives of several mothers and daughters.

Grammar Reinforcement

For additional instruction and practice, use the Semicolons, Colons, and Quotation Marks lesson in the **Language Lab CD-ROM** and pages 102–103 on Semicolons and Colons in the *Writer's Solution Grammar Practice Book.*

Build Your Portfolio

Idea Bank

Writing

1. **Descriptive Paragraph** Write a paragraph describing one of the photographs from *Mothers & Daughters*. Explain what may be happening and how the people feel.

2. **Interview** Write three questions and responses that are part of an interview between a magazine writer and a mother or daughter in one of the photos in this essay.

3. **Poem** Write a poem—with or without rhyme—that describes the mother-and-daughter relationship you observe in one of the photographs.

Speaking, Listening, and Viewing

4. **Award Panel** As a judge on a panel awarding a prize for best photograph of the year, state your choice for this prize and give your reasons.

5. **Dramatic Reading** Read aloud a poem or excerpt from a story about a mother and daughter. Tell how it relates to the relationships presented in this visual essay. **[Performing Arts Link]**

Researching and Representing

6. **Parent-and-Child Encyclopedia** Brainstorm for a list of terms related to relationships between parents and children. Write a brief entry for each term, and organize them alphabetically into a parent-and-child encyclopedia. **[Health Link]**

7. **Parent-and-Child Video** If a video camera is available, work with a group to develop a video on how children can better relate to parents and vice versa. You can use narration, dramatic scenes, and photographs. **[Art Link; Performing Arts Link]**

Online Activity www.phlit.phschool.com

Guided Writing Lesson

Introduction to an Art Exhibit

Certain kinds of programs, nonfiction books, or events may have an introduction that provides background or other information to give readers or viewers a context for what they are to read or see. For example, the passage by Tillie Olsen and Julie Olsen Edwards introduces the visual essay *Mothers & Daughters* by giving an overview of what readers will see in the essay. Write an **introduction** for a real or imagined art exhibit. The exhibit might be of work by art students in your school or by a group of local artists.

Writing Skills Focus: Elaboration

Elaboration is the development of details about an idea that will help readers see it or understand it fully. In your exhibit introduction, decide on the main points you want to make. Then think of details or personal information that will elaborate on these ideas so that your introduction is both engaging and helpful to those who attend the exhibit.

Prewriting In the left column of a two-column chart, list the main points you want to make in your introduction. In the right column, list the details you can use to elaborate each idea. Your details might include the reasons behind the purpose or goals of the exhibit, biographical details about the artists, details about the style of art or the medium, and anything else that will help exhibit-goers understand and enjoy the show.

Drafting Present each of your ideas in a topic sentence. Then elaborate on the idea using the relevant details from your chart.

Revising Have a writing partner read your introduction and give you feedback on your development of main ideas and details. Elaborate further on any ideas that are not developed enough.

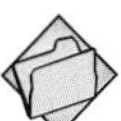

Idea Bank

Following are suggestions for matching Idea Bank topics with your students' performance levels and learning modalities:

Customizing for Performance Levels
Less Advanced Students: 1
Average Students: 2, 4, 3, 5, 6
More Advanced Students: 7

Customizing for Learning Modalities
Visual/Spatial: 7
Verbal/Linguistic: 4, 5
Logical/Mathematical: 6
Interpersonal: 2
Intrapersonal: 3

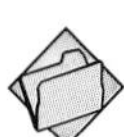

Guided Writing Lesson

Elaboration Strategy Guide students to layer their ideas using the **SEE** technique: making a **S**tatement, **E**xtending the statement, and **E**laborating on the statement. Model the **SEE** technique with the following example:
Statement: Art students exhibit their work.
Extension: Art students exhibit their works of mixed media.
Elaboration: Art students exhibit their collages, oil painting, charcoal sketches, and ceramic sculptures.

For more prewriting, elaboration, and revision strategies, see the *Prentice Hall Writing Program.*

Writing Lab CD-ROM
Have students complete the tutorial on exposition. Follow these steps:
1. Have students get interactive instruction on gathering details and then use a note cards activity to gather and order their details.
2. Suggest that students play the video tip in which writer N. Scott Momaday discusses paragraph organization, and main ideas and details.
3. Have students use an interactive self-evaluation checklist to help them evaluate and revise their introductions to an art exhibit.

✓ ASSESSMENT OPTIONS

Formal Assessment, Selection Test, pp. 160–162, and Assessment Resources Software. The selection test is designed so that it can be easily customized to the performance levels of your students.
Alternative Assessment, p.46, includes options for less advanced students, more advanced students, visual/spatial learners, intrapersonal learners, musical/rhythmic learners, and bodily/kinesthetic learners.

PORTFOLIO ASSESSMENT
Use the following rubrics in the ***Alternative Assessment*** booklet to assess student writing:
Descriptive Paragraph: Description Rubric, p. 97
Interview: Fictional Narrative Rubric, p. 95
Poem: Poetry Rubric, p. 108
Guided Writing Lesson: Definition/Classification Rubric, p. 99

Prepare and Engage

LESSON OBJECTIVES

1. **To develop vocabulary and word identification skills**
   - Greek Prefixes: *syn-*
   - Using the Word Bank: Analogies
   - Extending Word Study: Wide Reading
2. **To use a variety of reading strategies to read and comprehend technical articles**
   - Connect Your Experience
   - Reading Strategy: Relate Diagrams to Text
   - Read to Be Informed (ATE)
3. **To express and support responses to the text**
   - Critical Thinking
   - Idea Bank: Persuasive Letter
4. **To analyze literary elements**
   - Literary Focus: Technical Article
   - Idea Bank: Technical Article
5. **To read in order to research self-selected and assigned topics**
   - Idea Bank: Comparison-and-Contrast Essay
   - Idea Bank: Bird Shapes
   - Idea Bank: Conservation Update
   - Questions for Research
6. **To speak clearly and effectively for a specific audience and purpose**
   - Speaking, Listening, and Viewing Mini-Lesson (ATE): Oral Demonstration
7. **To use recursive writing processes to write a product description**
   - Guided Writing Lesson
8. **To increase knowledge of the rules of grammar and usage**
   - Build Grammar Skills: Varied Sentence Beginnings: Adverb Phrases

Test Preparation

Reading Comprehension: Comparing and Contrasting Texts (ATE, p. 647) The teaching tips and sample test item in this workshop support the instruction and practice in the unit workshop.

Reading Comprehension: Comparing and Contrasting Texts; Analyzing Literary Language (SE, p. 661)

Guide for Reading

Paul O'Neil *(1909–1988)*

After thirty years as a staff writer for the magazines *Time, Sports Illustrated,* and *Life,* Paul O'Neil became a freelance writer. He's the author of three volumes in the Time-Life series *The Old West*, and more recently wrote *Barnstormers and Speed Kings* in the *Epic of Flight* series. "Imitating Nature's Mineral Artistry" comes from the Time-Life book *Gemstones.*

Ernesto Ruelas Inzunza *(1968–   )*

Author of "Work That Counts," Ernesto Ruelas Inzunza is the executive director of Pronatura-Vera Cruz, a conservation organization in Vera Cruz, Mexico. Pronatura is raising money to meet a challenge grant from the National Fish and Wildlife Foundation and the Agency of International Development. The money will be used to build a nature center and bird observatory in Cardel, one of the monitoring stations mentioned in Inzunza's article. Contributors to this effort are dubbed "Friends of River of Raptors."

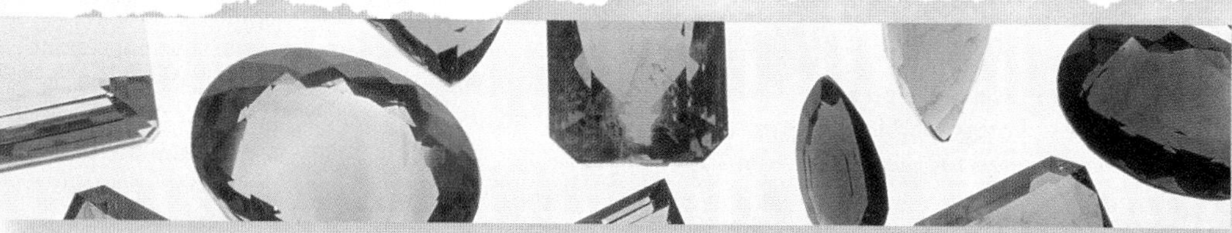

◆ Build Vocabulary

GREEK PREFIXES: *syn-*

In "Imitating Nature's Mineral Artistry," author Paul O'Neil describes the process used to make synthetic gems. *Synthetic* contains the prefix *syn-*, which comes from the Greek *syn* and means "together with." A *synthetic* gem is one that is produced by bringing parts together chemically as opposed to a gem that is formed naturally.

WORD BANK

As you read these essays, you will encounter the words on this list. Each word is defined on the page where it first appears. Preview the list before you read.

synthetic
constituents
synthesized
metamorphosis
divulge
saturated
fortuitous
vigilance
myriad
topography

◆ Build Grammar Skills

VARIED SENTENCE BEGINNINGS: ADVERB PHRASES

Good writing exhibits variety in sentence structure. To create variety and interest, writers sometimes begin their sentences with **adverb phrases**—prepositional phrases that modify a verb, adjective, or an adverb:

In laboratories and in factories, technicians can now create conditions . . .

In this example, two introductory prepositional phrases modify the verb *create. In laboratories* and *in factories* answer the question, Where can technicians create conditions?

Prentice Hall Literature Program Resources

REINFORCE / RETEACH / EXTEND

Selection Support Pages
Build Vocabulary: Prefixes: *syn-*, p. 192
Build Grammar Skills: Varied Sentence Beginnings: Adverb Phrases, p. 193
Reading Strategy: Relate Diagrams to Text, p. 194
Literary Focus: Technical Article, p. 195

Strategies for Diverse Student Needs, p. 47

Beyond Literature
Cross Curricular Connection: *Geography*, p. 47

Formal Assessment Selection Test, pp. 163–165; Assessment Resources Software

Alternative Assessment, p. 47

Writing and Language Transparencies
Cubing Organizer, pp. 87–89

Resource Pro CD-ROM

Listening to Literature Audiocassettes

Imitating Nature's Mineral Artistry
◆ Work That Counts ◆

◆ Literature and Your Life

Connect Your Experience

Have you ever tasted a tomato that came from a scientist's lab? Chemists, biogeneticists, and other scientists are experimenting to create products that until recently were found only in nature. When you read "Imitating Nature's Mineral Artistry," think about why people try to imitate nature and about the pros and cons of their ongoing effort.

Thematic Focus: Natural Forces

The chemists in "Imitating Nature's Mineral Artistry" try to imitate forces of nature to make diamonds and other gemstones. Do you think this is a worthwhile effort? Explain.

Journal Writing Write a paragraph describing something in nature you'd like to be able to produce yourself, and why.

◆ Background for Understanding

Math

One indicator of a gemstone's value—whether it is natural or synthetic (like those discussed in "Imitating Nature's Mineral Artistry")—is the number of carats (or karats). In ancient times, the word *carats* originally meant "seeds" or "beans," which were used in weighing precious stones. Today, one carat is equivalent to 200 milligrams.

The world's largest cut diamond, the Star of Africa, now in the royal scepter of the British crown jewels, weighs 530.2 carats. Perhaps the most famous cut diamond in the world, the Hope diamond, on view at the Smithsonian Institution in Washington D.C., weighs 44.5 carats.

◆ Literary Focus

Technical Article

"Imitating Nature's Mineral Artistry" and "Work That Counts" are **technical articles**—writing that explains procedures, provides instructions, or presents specialized information. Technical articles often use terms associated with a particular field of study. For example, the term *flux growth* relates to chemistry, while *raptors,* which means "birds of prey," is associated with ornithology, the study of birds.

To be as specific as possible in their explanations, technical articles often use visual aids to demonstrate their ideas.

◆ Reading Strategy

Relate Diagrams to Text

Artists aren't the only ones who think a picture is worth a thousand words. Many technical writers use **diagrams** to communicate their ideas and theories. Think of a diagram as a visual extension of the text. Rather than telling information, a diagram shows it. In "Imitating Nature's Mineral Artistry," the diagram of the flame-fusion growth of a ruby helps you to picture a complicated process. In so doing, it collaborates with the text to give you complete information. As you read, remember:

- A diagram is a drawing, plan, or outline of a thing or process.
- A diagram combines pictures, captions, and labels to present information visually.

Do not ignore or overlook diagrams. Use them as an aid to understanding.

Capture students interest by asking the question: Should people strive to imitate nature or to appreciate nature? Encourage students to take a position and support it with information they have learned in science class or on their own. Help them to see that scientists have long tried to imitate nature (early aviators tried to imitate the flight of a bird; recently scientists have cloned sheep). Other scientists have made a career out of preserving and appreciating nature. These two technical articles show ways in which nature is imitated—and simply appreciated.

Customize for
Less Proficient Readers

"Imitating Nature's Mineral Artistry" contains several highly technical and detailed passages. Work with less proficient readers to identify reading strategies that will help them deal with these passages, such as rereading, breaking down sentences, paraphrasing, identifying main ideas, and taking notes.

Customize for
Pre-AP Students

Encourage students to research and write explanatory notes for unfootnoted technical terms and references that appear within the articles. For example, students might explain what a *plankton sample* is or what *crystal* and *crystalline* mean in the context of geology.

Customize for
English Language Learners

Have students work in small groups made up of both English language learners and native speakers. Students can work together to determine the meanings of technical terms as well as of challenging nontechnical words such as *hallmarks, fortuitous,* and *funnel.*

Customize for
Gifted/Talented Students

Have students create their own diagrams that illustrate concepts related to geology, chemistry, or ornithology. Encourage students to present their work to the class.

Test Preparation Workshop

Reading Comprehension: Comparing and Contrasting Texts In order to answer questions on standardized tests, such as the SAT, which require students to compare and contrast aspects of two texts, students may need to determine which elements occur in just one selection, and which occur in both.

Have students read the technical articles in this selection grouping, and then write this sample test question on the board.

Which common element appears in both essays?

A a detailed explanation of how something is done
B a description of topography and atmospheric conditions
C the connection of history to the subject
D a description of bird migration

Through process of elimination, help students determine that the correct answer is *C*.

Develop Understanding

One-Minute Insight In "Imitating Nature's Mineral Artistry," author Paul O'Neil makes use of specialized terms, examples, comparisons, and numerical data as well as detailed diagrams to take readers on a guided tour of the high-tech world of gem synthesis.

◆ Reading Strategy

1 Relate Diagrams to Text Have students look at the diagram on p. 649. What key element helps readers to connect it to the concept that is introduced in this portion of the text? *The caption, which includes reference to "flame-fusion growth of ruby."*

◆ Critical Thinking

2 Identify Cause and Effect Have students explain in their own words why emeralds and certain other gems cannot be manufactured using the flame-fusion method. *Students should note that, unlike the flux growth method, the flame-fusion method involves extremely high temperatures. The ingredients that make up some gems are destroyed at such temperatures, while the ingredients that make up certain others fail to melt.*

▶Critical Viewing◀

3 Contrast *Students should note that the opal differs in color, in brilliance, or brightness, and in texture — whereas other gemstones have solid, smooth surfaces, the opal has a fragmented surface. Although it is solid, it resembles a sponge.*

◆ Reading Strategy

4 Relate Diagrams to Text Point out that the diagram on p. 649 that explains the flame-fusion method also provides information about what a *Verneuil furnace* and *boules* are. Have students refer to the diagram to explain these terms. *A Verneuil furnace is the device in which the chemical components of synthetic gems melt and then solidify; a boule is the solidified mass that forms when the melted chemicals cool down.*

Imitating Nature's Mineral Artistry

Paul O'Neil

In laboratories and factories, technicians can now create conditions of heat and chemical activity similar to those that give birth to gemstones deep within the earth. The result is synthetic gems, identical to their natural counterparts in chemistry and crystalline structure, and so similar in appearance that a microscope is often needed to tell them apart.

The chemical ingredients for a man-made gem are easy to obtain, since most gems consist of relatively common chemical compounds. The art of gem synthesis lies in the technique by which the gem material is liquefied, in a melt or a solution, and then allowed to crystallize slowly and evenly.

◆ **Reading Strategy** Here you're introduced to a concept that is further explained by a diagram.

1 The so-called flame-fusion method, based on melting and gradual cooling, has been used to grow crystals of about 100 minerals and gems, including ruby, sapphire and spinel.

2 But the ingredients of some gems decompose during the fierce heating needed to melt them, and others have extraordinarily high melting points. Such gems—among them emerald—are often manufactured by another process, called flux growth. In this process, the gem is crystallized from a solution of its constituents in a molten bath of a solvent, or flux—such as lead fluoride, boron oxide or lithium oxide.

Because of peculiarities in their internal structure, some gems cannot be synthesized by ordinary crystal growth. Opal, an orderly arrangement of minute, closely packed spheres of silica, is created in the laboratory by precipitating silica spheres through a chemical reaction, allowing them to settle to the bottom of the reaction vessel and then compressing and bonding them to form a compact and sturdy matrix.[1]

▲ **Critical Viewing** In what ways is the structure of this opal different from that of the emerald shown on p. 651? **[Contrast]** 3

Artful as they are, synthetic gems nevertheless bear hallmarks of their laboratory origin: an array of microscopic inclusions and growth marks that contrast tellingly with the blemishes and inclusions of natural gems.

One of the gaudier uses of the Verneuil furnace is to make synthetic rutile[2] by sifting pure titanium dioxide through the flame. The boules thus produced—black in color because of oxygen deficiency—are then reheated in a jet of oxygen. As the rutile grows hotter, it oxidizes and changes in color to deep blue followed by light blue, green and, finally, a pale yellow. The color metamorphosis can be stopped at any stage by removing the heat source. Sold since 1948 under a profusion of names, including astryl and titania, the gems are soft, with a hardness of 6 to 6.5, but are

1. **matrix** (mā´ triks) *n.*: Framework.
2. **rutile** (ro͞o´ təl) *n.*: Dark-red mineral.

Block Scheduling Strategies

Consider these suggestions to take advantage of extended class time:

- Have students complete the journal activity in Literature and Your Life (p. 647) and discuss their entries in small groups.
- Discuss the Reading Strategy on p. 647. Ask students to describe diagrams they have encountered in their science, math, or general reading. Follow up with the Reading Strategy page in ***Selection Support,*** p. 194.
- Have small groups of students answer the Critical Thinking questions on pp. 651 and 653.
- Use ***Alternative Assessment,*** p. 47, to assess the progress of students with varying performance levels or learning modalities.
- Have students complete the Guided Writing Lesson (p. 655). Use the Cubing Organizer, p. 87, in ***Writing and Language Transparencies*** to demonstrate how students might develop ideas to include in their product descriptions.

Verneuil Furnace Flame-Fusion Growth of Ruby

The chemical ingredients of ruby—aluminum oxide with a chromium coloring agent—sift from a hopper at the top of the apparatus shown above into a jet of oxygen. In a combustion chamber, the oxygen combines with hydrogen in a 4,000° F flame—hot enough to melt the powdered ingredients, which shower onto a ceramic rod at the base of the furnace. There the material solidifies and accumulates in a rounder crystalline mass known as a boule.

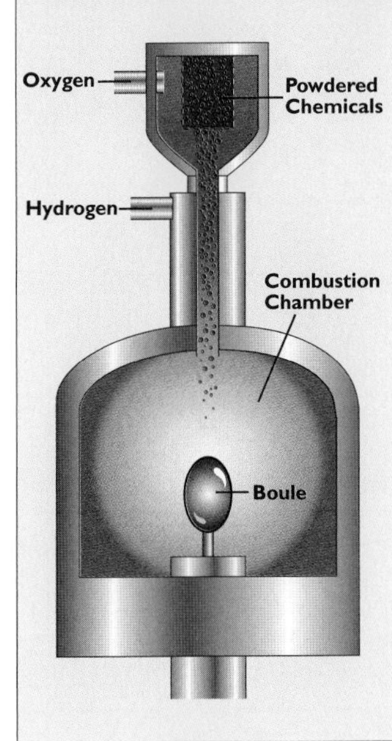

Diagram A

even flashier than strontium titanate, with seven times the fire of diamond.

Since diamonds consist of only one element, synthesizing them would seem to be relatively uncomplicated. The difficulty is one of technique, of creating—and containing—the enormous pressures and temperatures needed to pack carbon atoms tight enough to form diamond. Not surprisingly, many early attempts to synthesize diamond ended disastrously. Of the 80 experiments conducted in the late 19th Century by a Glasgow chemist named James Hannay, all but three were cut short by explosions, several of which wrecked the laboratory. Hannay was convinced that his pains had paid off: After several attempts, he discovered tiny flecks of diamond in his apparatus. But it is now thought that natural diamond dust from another of Hannay's projects had contaminated the experiment.

In the early 1950s, scientists at the General Electric Research Laboratories in Schenectady, New York, began experimenting with techniques for multiplying the force exerted by a hydraulic press. Using a pair of tapered pistons driven from opposite sides into the hole in a doughnut-shaped ring of tungsten carbide, they were able to subject the tiny intervening space to pressures of more than 1.5 million pounds per square inch. In a series of experiments directed by a chemist named H. Tracy Hall, the apparatus was loaded with a mixture of graphite powder and an iron compound, pressurized and 7
heated with an electric current to more than 4,800° F.—hot enough to melt the iron and dissolve some of the graphite. The dissolved carbon, scientists hoped, would then crystallize out of the molten iron as diamond. Finally, on December 16, 1954, Hall removed a sample from the press and broke it open along a plate of tantalum, a rare element used to conduct electric current. Hall later recalled the moment: "My hands began to tremble; my heart beat rapidly; my knees weakened and no longer gave support. My eyes had caught the flashing light from dozens of tiny triangular faces of octahedral crystals that were stuck to the tantalum and I knew that diamonds had finally been made by man."

Today, the same basic method that yielded Hall's initial success annually produces some 44,000 pounds of industrial diamonds—small 8
diamonds of no particular quality used as an industrial abrasive. Only a few minutes of high temperature and pressure are required to manufacture several hundred carats of

◆ Build Vocabulary

synthetic (sin thet′ ik) *adj.*: Artificially made

constituents (kən stich′ o͞o ənts) *n.*: Components; parts

synthesized (sin′ thə sīzd′) *v.*: Made by bringing together different elements

metamorphosis (met′ ə môr′ fə sis) *n.*: Change of form

◆ Literary Focus

5 Technical Article Point out that the word *element* refers to *a chemical element*—a substance that normally cannot be broken down into other substances. Have students point out another word distinctly related to chemistry and explain its significance within this passage. *Students should point out the word* carbon, *noting that this is the single element of which diamonds are made up.*

◆ Build Grammar Skills

6 Varied Sentence Beginnings: Adverb Phrases Have students identify the adverb phrase that begins this sentence. Also have them identify the word or words that it modifies. *The adverb phrase is "in the early 1950's"; it modifies* began.

◆ Literary Focus

7 Technical Article Point out that earlier in the article, O'Neil had stated that enormous pressures and temperatures are needed to synthesize diamonds. Scientists at G.E. produced a specially-designed hydraulic press to create the pressure. Have students identify the source of the temperatures in the experiments that O'Neil describes here. *The temperatures were produced by an electric current.*

◆ Critical Thinking

8 Apply Encourage students to use their general knowledge about the special qualities of diamonds to explain why the synthetic diamonds would make good industrial abrasives. *Based on prior knowledge, students may point out that diamonds are the hardest substance in nature.*

Extending Word Study

Wide Reading Scientific material often includes technical vocabulary that is specific to a nonfiction topic. Some words that are used in such a technical context, however, may also be used in other venues. Have students use dictionaries to study the meanings of *synthetic, constituents,* and *metamorphosis.* Ask them to write nonscientific sentences, using each of these words.

Beyond the Classroom

Career Connection

Geology As Paul O'Neil's article points out, nature's mineral artistry takes place deep within the earth, as heat and pressure act on various elements to produce precious gemstones.

Scientists who study gem formation and other earth processes are known as geologists. Many geologists apply their knowledge within various industries, studying and locating resources such as oil, gas, coal, precious minerals, and building stone. Others work in academic and research institutions, studying issues that range from predicting volcanic eruptions to determining the age of the earth.

Have interested students more about job-related applications of geology as well as scientific questions that geologists investigate. Encourage students to share their findings with the class.

◆ Reading Strategy

❶ **Relate Diagrams to Text** Point out that the process of emerald synthesis through flux growth is further explained in the diagram on this page. Ask students to study the diagram and its caption carefully, then identify the additional details that it provides. *The diagram names the chemical raw materials (beryllium, aluminum, and silicone) that are dissolved in the flux; it shows the electric furnace in which emeralds are synthesized; it specifies how (precipitation while cooling) and where (the bottom of the platinum crucible) the clusters of emeralds form.*

◆ Literary Focus

❷ **Technical Articles** Call students' attention to the specialized terms *specific gravity, refractive indices,* and *inclusions*. Have them use context clues to determine the approximate meanings of these terms. *Specific gravity and refractive indices—the plural of index—are standards or measures used to evaluate gems; inclusions in this context are bits of other minerals.* Also, have students explain where they might go to find the exact technical meanings of the terms. *Students might mention an encyclopedia, a book on gems and minerals, or Web sites devoted to gemology or geology.*

◆ Critical Thinking

❸ **Compare and Contrast** Have students draw on the details in this paragraph to name two differences between natural and synthetic rubies. *Natural rubies have straight growth lines, whereas synthetic rubies have curved ones; unlike natural rubies, synthetic rubies contain gas-filled bubbles.*

diamond grit from almost any carbon-containing material—paraffin, moth flakes, even sugar and peanuts. But the synthesis of gem-quality diamonds is another matter. In 1970, a painstaking variant of the General Electric method, using synthetic diamond grit as the feed material and maintaining the conditions of high temperature and pressure for stretches of a week, yielded a few gem-quality diamonds weighing up to a carat. But the cost of producing them was so high that it remains cheaper to mine gem diamonds.

Perhaps the finest products of humanity's age-old attempt to imitate nature in the creation of gemstones are synthetic emeralds. Beginning in the late 1930s, two pioneers, Carroll F. Chatham, a San Francisco chemist, and Pierre Gilson of France, succeeded in making emerald so close to the genuine article that it is worth several hundred dollars per carat—although that is still just 1/10 the price of natural emerald of similar quality. Chatham and Gilson did not divulge the details of their processes, but it is believed that both depend on a technique called flux growth, in which crystals are formed from raw materials dissolved in a flux—a substance that acts as a powerful solvent. In one type of flux growth, the chemical ingredients of emerald, in the form of natural beryl, are added to a 1,500° F. bath of flux to create a saturated solution, which circulates continuously through

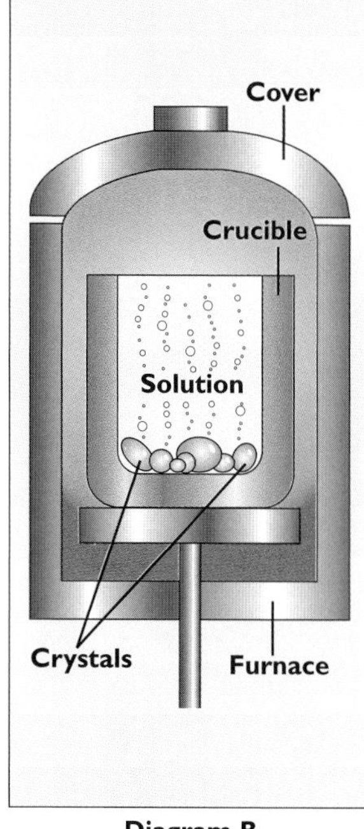

Diagram B

Flux Growth of Emerald

A saturated solution of emerald's chemical ingredients is produced by combining compounds of beryllium, aluminum, and silicone with a flux, or solvent, and heating the mixture to 1,500° F. in an electric furnace. As the mixture cools, gem crystals begin to precipitate out at the bottom of the platinum crucible containing the solution, eventually forming clusters of emeralds.

cooler parts of the container. There, the flux deposits crystals of emerald—so slowly that growth must continue for seven months to produce an emerald one quarter of an inch thick.

It is not easy to distinguish synthetic and natural emeralds, though the synthetic variety is often more transparent, richer in hue and in some ways more perfectly formed than natural emeralds. In addition, the synthetics have lower specific gravity and refractive indices. But the most telling test is usually a microscopic examination. Magnification of synthetic emeralds reveals fine, lacelike patterns formed by intersecting channels containing liquid flux. Natural emeralds, the fortuitous products of geologic turmoil, ordinarily display much coarser inclusions of pyrite, calcite, actinolite or other minerals. Another detection method is to expose the gems to ultraviolet light: The radiation has little effect on natural emeralds but causes Chatham emeralds to glow with a dull red fluorescence and Gilson synthetics to display an orange hue.

In synthetic rubies and sapphires, specific gravity and the refractive index are the same as in natural corundum. But visible under a microscope in natural gems are straight lines, called growth lines, set at definite angles. In Verneuil synthetics, the growth lines are curved, and spots, which are in

◆ Literary Focus
These precise details help you to clarify the difference between natural and synthetic rubies.

◆ Build Vocabulary

divulge (də vulj′) *v.*: Reveal

saturated (sach′ ə rāt′ id) *v.*: Completely filled; thoroughly soaked

fortuitous (fôr to͞o′ ə təs) *adj.*: Accidental and beneficial at the same time

vigilance (vij′ ə lens) *n.*: Watchfulness; alertness

Cross-Curricular Connection: Science

Geology and Gemology "Imitating Nature's Mineral Artistry" contains several terms used in the fields of gemology and geology. Groups of students can work together to research the meanings of these terms as well as explore and answer some basic questions related to these fields.

Suggest that students choose from among the following activities and questions.

- What is a rock? a mineral? a gem?
- What does *specific gravity* mean? What does *refractive index* (sometimes called *index of refraction*) mean?
- What is an *inclusion*? What are *growth marks* and *growth lines*?
- The author mentions that stones made from synthetic rutile have a hardness of 6 to 6.5. Find out the name of the scale that is used to measure the hardness of gems and minerals. Name three minerals that are harder than synthetic rutile and three that are softer.
- Compile a bibliography for classmates interested in learning more about gems.

Students can present their findings to the class, along with any diagram or visual aid that clarifies the concepts being discussed.

3 fact gas-filled bubbles, may be seen. Synthetic spinel, which masquerades as any of several species, can be detected by its differing refractive index.

Still, distinguishing between synthetic and natural gemstones calls for vigilance, and sometimes even experts lower their guard. One Manhattan dealer who specializes in colored gemstones, Abraham Nassi, was offered three large red rubies while on an expedition to Burma. "They looked good," he remembered later, and he was prepared to pay the equivalent of $160,000 for the lot. But before any money changed hands, a fourth ruby was offered.

"I had an idea that the four might be worth a half a million dollars," he said, "but wanted to have them in New York and give them a real inspection before I paid." Nassi suggested a total price of $300,000—but only if the stones could first be examined in New York.

The Burmese refused his condition. "That seemed funnier yet. I found a Bangkok dealer who had a microscope and began looking at the stones under magnification. Their color was wonderful but their crystal structure was peculiar. I spent $200 to telephone the Gemological Institute of America in New York and described what I had seen. They told me what I'd been looking at: This gang had somehow gotten their hands on synthetic Kashan rubies, made in Texas for about $100 a carat, taken them into the jungle and had almost sold them to me as the real thing."

▲ Critical Viewing How can you tell from this picture, and from clues in the text, that the emerald is real and not synthetic? **[Analyze]** 4

Guide for Responding

◆ Literature and Your Life

Reader's Response What are one or two techniques you know of that people have used to imitate nature? Explain.

Thematic Focus How would you determine if a natural product, such as oil or diamonds, was valuable?

Questions for Research Have men and women always valued gems? Generate research questions that would help explore the history of the human admiration of gemstones.

☑ Check Your Comprehension

1. What two kinds of natural gem-producing conditions have scientists learned to imitate?
2. What is the difference in appearance between a synthetic and a real emerald?
3. Contrast the process for making industrial diamonds with that of producing gem-quality diamonds.

◆ Critical Thinking

INTERPRET

1. a) What is the difference between flame-fusion and flux growth? b) Why are rubies made from the flame-fusion method, but emeralds from the flux growth method? **[Compare and Contrast]**
2. What is the major application today of G.E's 1954 experiment led by chemist H. Tracy Hall? **[Analyze]**
3. What characteristic of the diamond led early scientists to think that imitating it would be simple? **[Infer]**

APPLY

4. What might have happened if Abraham Nassi had bought the rubies from the Burmese? **[Speculate]**

EXTEND

5. What kind of knowledge is a gemologist likely to have? **[Career Link]**

Speaking, Listening, and Viewing Mini-Lesson

Oral Demonstration

This mini-lesson supports the Speaking, Listening, and Viewing activity in the Idea Bank on p. 655.

Introduce Tell students that in an oral demonstration, students can use words and actions to show a process or skill.

Develop Alert students to the criteria on which their oral demonstrations will be evaluated. Presentations should be clear, with appropriate visual aids or illustrations; steps should be presented in a logical order and connected with transitions such as first, then, until, after. Discuss these criteria with students and have them suggest other guidelines for what they think will contribute to an effective demonstration.

Apply Have students prepare and deliver their oral presentations.

Assess Use the criteria listed in the Develop Background section when evaluating students' presentations. In addition, you may wish to have students use the Self-Assessment: Speech form, p. 117, in the ***Alternative Assessment*** booklet.

▶Critical Viewing◀

4 Analyze *According to the article, the "imperfections" of this emerald would indicate it is real.*

Reinforce and Extend

Answers

◆ Literature and Your Life

Reader's Response Examples include virtual reality and cloning.

Thematic Focus Students might mention the concept of supply and demand, or they might talk about putting dollar values on beauty.

Questions for Research Students might begin their research by asking questions about which gems are considered most precious now; 100 years ago; 1000 years ago.

☑ Check Your Comprehension

1. Scientists have learned to create the (1) necessary temperatures and (2) chemical activity.
2. In general, synthetic gems have growth marks that natural gems don't have. In the case of emeralds, synthetic ones are often more transparent, richer in hue and more perfectly formed.
3. Industrial diamonds can be made from exposing any carbon-containing material to a few minutes of heat and pressure. For gem-quality diamonds, heat and pressure must be maintained for a week.

◆ Critical Thinking

1. (a) Flame fusion is based on melting and gradual cooling. In the flux growth method, a gem is crystallized from a solution of its constituents in a molten bath of solvent, or flux. (b) The chemical ingredients of rubies can take the 4,000° F heat, but the chemical ingredients of emeralds decompose during the heating needed to melt them. The temperature for flux growth is only 1,500 °F.
2. Hall's basic method is now used to make industrial diamonds.
3. It has only one element—carbon.
4. Possible response: He would have lost a lot of money.
5. Gemologists should know about the growth of natural gems, where they're found, their properties, and how to authenticate them.

Develop Understanding

One-Minute Insight In "Work That Counts," author Ernesto Ruelas Inzunza combines the elements of a technical article with his sense of enthusiasm for his field to give readers an exciting account of an important project in the field of wildlife biology.

◆ Build Grammar Skills

1 Varied Sentence Beginnings: Adverb Phrases Have students identify the adverb phrase that begins this sentence. *The phrase is* At eight this morning. What question does this prepositional phrase answer? *When were the Swainson's hawks taking off?*

◆ Literary Focus

2 Technical Articles Students should note that at the end of the next paragraph, the author explains that the topography and atmospheric conditions of the area provide the birds with winds and updrafts that help them in their migrations.

Read to Be Informed

Encourage students to record the information they learn from these technical articles. They can keep notes as they read. Have them draw a vertical line down the center of a sheet of paper. In the left-hand column, they can write down facts they learn from the reading. In the right-hand column, they can make comments of their own reactions or note connections with prior knowledge.

Insight From Pat Mora

Pat Mora offers this insight: "Students can be reminded of the value of taking the time to choose an effective title with this selection. Not all titles have a double meaning but noticing the technique can illustrate how such literary reverberations might strengthen a piece.

This author/ecologist not only conveys factual information. Through his writing, he also becomes an effective advocate. Question to ponder with students: Is it only birds that journey across the Americas? And what do we know about those human journeys?"

Work That Counts

Ernesto Ruelas Inzunza

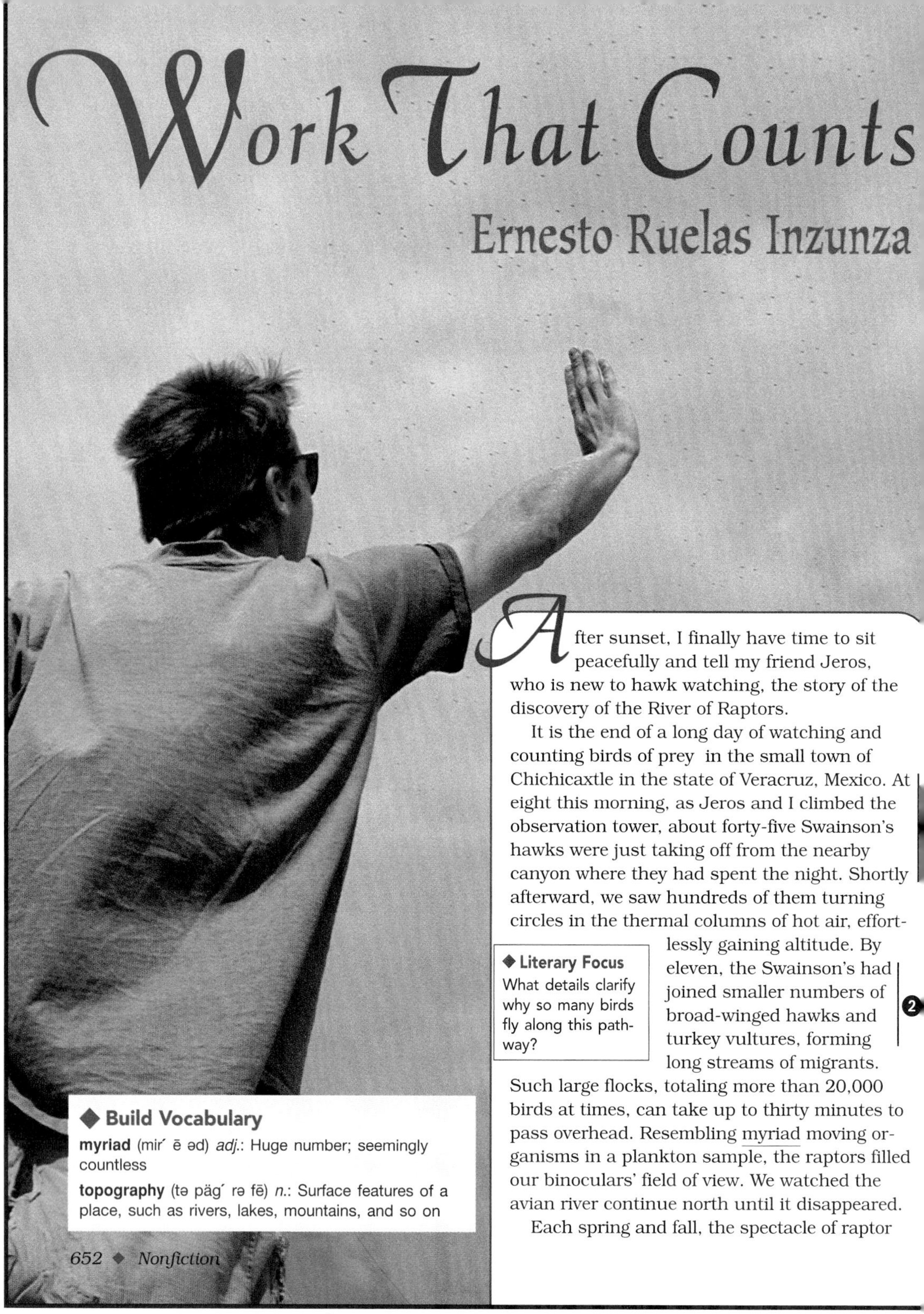

After sunset, I finally have time to sit peacefully and tell my friend Jeros, who is new to hawk watching, the story of the discovery of the River of Raptors.

It is the end of a long day of watching and counting birds of prey in the small town of Chichicaxtle in the state of Veracruz, Mexico. At eight this morning, as Jeros and I climbed the observation tower, about forty-five Swainson's hawks were just taking off from the nearby canyon where they had spent the night. Shortly afterward, we saw hundreds of them turning circles in the thermal columns of hot air, effortlessly gaining altitude. By eleven, the Swainson's had joined smaller numbers of broad-winged hawks and turkey vultures, forming long streams of migrants. 2 Such large flocks, totaling more than 20,000 birds at times, can take up to thirty minutes to pass overhead. Resembling myriad moving organisms in a plankton sample, the raptors filled our binoculars' field of view. We watched the avian river continue north until it disappeared.

Each spring and fall, the spectacle of raptor

> **◆ Literary Focus**
> What details clarify why so many birds fly along this pathway?

> **◆ Build Vocabulary**
> **myriad** (mir′ ē əd) *adj.*: Huge number; seemingly countless
> **topography** (tə päg′ rə fē) *n.*: Surface features of a place, such as rivers, lakes, mountains, and so on

Beyond the Classroom

Community Connection

Community Bird Counts In "Work That Counts," Ernesto Ruelas Inzunza quotes an 1897 account of the River of Raptors written by Frank M. Chapman. Chapman, who was curator of birds at the American Museum of Natural History, was also the founder of a bird count in which your students can participate—the annual Christmas Bird count, now sponsored by the National Audubon Society.

Every year, about 50,000 people take part in this nationwide event by spending one day be-tween December 17 and January 3 identifying and counting birds within a designated area. The participants report their findings to the Audubon Society, which analyzes and publishes the data and uses it for long-term research on birds.

Interested students can learn more about the Christmas Bird Count by contacting their local chapter of the Audubon Society.

migration fills the skies of Veracruz in eastern Mexico as the birds funnel through a narrow geographic corridor and above our monitoring stations at Chichicaxtle and Cardel. This bottleneck is formed where the Mexican central volcanic belt reaches the Gulf of Mexico and almost cuts the lowlands of the coastal plain in two. The topography and atmospheric conditions of the lowlands provide birds of prey and many other migrants with the conditions needed for migrating with the least expenditure of energy: tail winds and warm thermal updrafts.

Among the migrating raptors are turkey vultures; ospreys; swallow-tailed, Mississippi, and plumbeous kites; northern harriers; sharp-shinned, Cooper's, Harris's, red-shouldered, broad-winged, Swainson's, zone-tailed, and red-tailed hawks; and falcons, including kestrels, merlins, and peregrines. The migrations of a few other species—hook-billed kites, golden eagles and ferruginous hawks—are less well documented in Veracruz and are currently being studied. Five species of swallows, scissor-tailed flycatchers, white-winged and mourning doves, wood storks, white pelicans, cormorants, and white-faced and white ibises are also among the list of more than 220 species of migratory birds recorded at Veracruz. In fall, the count totals range between 2.5 million and 4 million birds, the highest count anywhere in the world, as birds journeying from eastern, central, and western North America converge here in Veracruz. ❹

After five in the evening, when the temperature dropped down to 82° F and the thermals ceased to form, the pace slowed. Now I can respond in more detail to Jeros's question about the discovery of the River of Raptors. I read him a paragraph written in the spring of 1897 by ornithologist Frank M. Chapman, of the American Museum of Natural History: "On April 6 and 16, flights of hawks—I was unable to determine the species—were observed passing northward, exceeding in number any migration of these birds I have before seen." Almost a hundred years passed before bird counts were organized at Veracruz and Chapman's statements were borne out. Yet as long as these lowlands have been inhabited, the migration must have been seen and accepted by the local inhabitants as an autumn phenomenon. I conclude by telling my friend that perhaps the River of Raptors has always been known. And, he adds, admired. ❺

Guide for Responding

◆ Literature and Your Life

Reader's Response Describe any bird migrations that you've observed. Where were you? What formation did the birds fly in? Could you identify the species?

Thematic Focus What observations have you made about the effect of natural forces, such as storms and droughts, upon birds?

☑ Check Your Comprehension

1. What is Inzunza's work as described in this article?
2. What conditions allow birds to migrate with the least expenditure of energy?
3. (a) Who discovered the River of Raptors? (b) Why was it unique at the time?

◆ Critical Thinking

INTERPRET

1. Explain how the title of this article has a double meaning. **[Analyze]**
2. Why do so many birds converge where the Mexican central volcanic belt reaches the Gulf of Mexico? **[Draw Conclusions]**
3. Why does Veracruz have the highest count of migrating birds of anywhere in the world? **[Analyze]**

APPLY

4. Why is Inzunza's job important? **[Synthesize]**

EXTEND

5. Birds of prey are carnivorous, or flesh eating. Name some other creatures that are carnivorous. Explain. **[Science Link]**

◆ Literary Focus

❸ Technical Article Encourage students to explain what *tail winds* are. *Tail winds are winds that blow in the same direction as the course of a flock of birds, a plane, a ship, and so on.* Then point out the term *thermal updrafts*—which means rising columns of warm air. Ask students what sources they could access to learn more about these phenomena. *Possibilities include printed or online encyclopedia; meteorology books, or Web sites dealing with meteorology.*

◆ Critical Thinking

❹ Support Have students cite one or more details in this passage to support the conclusion that the observatory in Veracruz is important to areas well beyond Veracruz. *The observatory is linked to bird life throughout North America; the author states that migrating birds from eastern, central and western North America converge in Veracruz.*

◆ Critical Thinking

❺ Interpret What point do students think that the author is making in the last sentence? *Possible responses: He shows that the River of Raptors has a significance that is more than purely scientific; he is expressing the idea that people have an innate connection to nature.*

Reteach

Some students may have difficulty understanding the explanations that accompany the diagrams. Suggest that they work in pairs to decipher the text and rewrite it in their own words.

Reinforce and Extend

Answers

◆ Literature and Your Life

Reader's Response Sample response: I was in the local park and I saw a flock of Canada geese flying in a V-formation.

Thematic Focus Students may have observed birds temporarily disappear in a storm or die off in a severe drought.

☑ Check Your Comprehension

1. He observes and counts birds of prey for a conservation organization.
2. Tail winds and warm thermal updrafts allow them to migrate with less energy.
3. (a) Frank M. Chapman discovered it (b) The number of birds migrating far exceeded any Chapman had seen.

◆ Critical Thinking

1. The title is literal: counting birds; and figurative: work that is meaningful.
2. Birds converge there because the topographic and atmospheric conditions are ideal for easy migrating.
3. Students will probably say that Veracruz has such a high number of migrating birds because birds from eastern, central, and western North America converge there.
4. By counting and tracking the of birds migrating each year scientists know which species might be endangered.
5. Possible examples of carnivorous creatures are sharks, people, bears, insectivorous plants.

Answers

◆ Reading Strategy

1. Powdered chemical ingredients of a gem sift from a hopper into a combustion chamber where the chemicals are melted. The melted powder falls onto a ceramic rod at the base of the chamber and accumulate into the mass known as a boule.
2. A solution of emeralds' chemical ingredients is produced by combining a chemical compound with a flux; the solution is heated in an electric furnace; gem crystals precipitate out as they cool.
3. Students' diagrams should use arrows to show tail winds and warm thermal updrafts.

◆ Literary Focus

1. Examples include synthetic diamonds, emeralds and rubies.
2. Sample response: A raptor is a bird of prey; students could check a dictionary or ornithology text to find out about a raptor.
3. Inzunza compares the large migration of birds to moving organisms in a plankton sample.

◆ Build Vocabulary

Using the Prefix *syn-*

1. b 2. a 3. c

Using the Word Bank

1. divulge
2. myriad
3. vigilance
4. constituents
5. synthetic
6. topography
7. fortuitous
8. saturated
9. metamorphosis
10. synthesized

◆ Build Grammar Skills

Writing Application

1. *After sunset*, I finally have time to tell my friend the story of the River of Raptors.
2. *At the monitoring station*, hawk counting is serious business.
3. *Shortly afterward*, we saw hundreds of Swainson's hawks climbing the thermals.
4. *In the strong tailwinds and warm thermals*, the hawks fly easily.

Grammar Reinforcement

For additional instruction and practice, use the Varying Sentence Structure lesson in the **Language Lab CD-ROM** and pp. 121–123, Varying Your Sentences, *Writer's Solution Grammar Practice Book*.

Guide for Responding *(continued)*

◆ Reading Strategy

RELATE DIAGRAMS TO TEXT

Because diagrams can explain something visually, they have many different applications. Working with text, diagrams are often included in instructions and manuals and in articles explaining a process. In "Imitating Nature's Mineral Artistry," O'Neil uses both text and diagrams to give a clear picture of how synthetic gems are formed.

1. Using Diagram A, explain, in sequential order, the process by which powdered chemicals become a boule, such as a ruby boule.
2. Use Diagram B to identify the stages of flux growth.
3. Create a simple diagram that shows how the geographic bottleneck described in "Work That Counts" creates favorable flight conditions. Use a map of Mexico to locate the central volcanic belt, the Gulf of Mexico, and the lowlands of the coastal plain.

◆ Literary Focus

TECHNICAL ARTICLES

These two technical articles differ in the complexity of their ideas and in the way these ideas are demonstrated, but—like all technical articles—they both explain a process.

O'Neil includes diagrams with "Imitating Nature's Mineral Artistry" to help explain visually the complex process of creating synthetic gems. He also uses examples to demonstrate the processes he explains. In "Work That Counts," Inzunza uses comparisons and statistics to clarify his points.

1. Identify an example that O'Neil uses to demonstrate the synthetic creation of gems in "Imitating Nature's Mineral Artistry."
2. Give two examples of specialized language in "Work That Counts." Tell what the terms mean or where you could go to find out.
3. Explain the comparison Inzunza uses in "Work That Counts" to clarify the enormous number of birds that have been counted traveling past the monitoring stations at Chichicaxtle and Cardel.

◆ Build Vocabulary

USING THE GREEK PREFIX *syn-*

The Greek prefix *syn-* means "together with." On your paper, match each word with its corresponding definition.

1. synchronize **a.** number of symptoms occurring together
2. syndrome **b.** to move at the same time
3. synthesize **c.** make by putting parts together

USING THE WORD BANK: Analogies

On your paper, complete each analogy using the words from the Word Bank.

1. *Hide* is to *conceal* as ___?___ is to *tell.*
2. *Scarcity* is to *one* as ___?___ is to *one million.*
3. *Concentration* is to *relaxation* as ___?___ is to *sleep.*
4. *Ingredients* is to *recipe* as ___?___ is to *whole.*
5. *Nature* is to *natural* as ___?___ is to *man-made.*
6. *Nose* is to *face* as *mountain* is to ___?___.
7. *Unlucky* is to *accident* as ___?___ is to *bonus.*
8. *Sold out* is to *concert* as ___?___ is to *solution.*
9. *Oxidation* is to *decay* as *heat* is to ___?___.
10. *Grow* is to *plant* as ___?___ is to *form.*

◆ Build Grammar Skills

VARIED SENTENCE BEGINNINGS: ADVERB PHRASES

Adverb phrases are prepositional phrases that modify a verb, adjective, or another adverb. Placing an adverb phrase at the beginning of a sentence is one way to achieve sentence variety.

Writing Application Identify the adverb phrase in the following sentences. Then, on your paper, rewrite each sentence moving the adverb phrase to the beginning. Make any other adjustments required in the sentence.

1. I finally have time after sunset to tell my friend the story of the River of Raptors.
2. Hawk counting at the monitoring station is serious business.
3. We saw hundreds of Swainson's hawks shortly afterward climbing the thermals.
4. The hawks fly easily in the strong tailwinds and warm thermals.

Beyond the Selection

FURTHER READING

Other Works by Paul O'Neil

Gemstones
Barnstormers and Speed Kings

Other Works About Imitating Natural Forces

Rappacini's Daughter, Nathaniel Hawthorne
Frankenstein, Mary Shelley

We suggest that you preview these works before recommending them to students.

INTERNET

We recommend the following Internet sites (all Web sites are subject to change).

For more about natural and synthetic gems: **http://micro.magnet.fsu.edu/micro/gallery/presious/precious.html**

To find out more about hawks and birds of prey, go to: **http://www.execpc.con/~laurag/raptor/raptor.html**

We *strongly recommend* that you preview the sites before you send students to them.

Build Your Portfolio

Idea Bank

Writing

1. **Persuasive Letter** Suppose you're Ernesto Inzunza, and you're raising money to continue your work. Write a three-paragraph introductory letter to a funding source describing the importance of studying and protecting birds.

2. **Comparison-and-Contrast Essay** Choose two species of raptor, such as osprey and turkey vulture. Write one or two pages comparing their eating, migratory, and nesting habits.

3. **Technical Article** Write a detailed explanation of a process that you take for granted, such as making toast or opening your locker. Create diagrams that clarify your explanation.

Speaking, Listening, and Viewing

4. **Bird Shapes** Ernesto Ruelas Inzunza probably learned to identify so many different raptors by viewing charts with bird drawings or silhouettes. Create your own poster that would help a novice ornithologist identify several raptors. **[Science Link]**

5. **Oral Demonstration** In detailed steps, explain and demonstrate for the class a process with which you're especially familiar, such as how to play your favorite computer game. **[Speech Link]**

Researching and Representing

6. **Conservation Update** Using pictures and research material from books or the Internet, prepare an update on efforts to preserve the status of endangered birds worldwide. **[Science Link]**

7. **Diamond Weighing** You know the Star of Africa weighs 530.2 mg. and the Hope diamond weighs 44.5. mg. Using an equivalency table for U.S. and metric measurements, calculate the weight in ounces of these diamonds. **[Math Link]**

Online Activity www.phlit.phschool.com

Guided Writing Lesson

Product Description

Product descriptions are important pieces of writing because they introduce a particular product to consumers who will decide whether or not to purchase the product. Write a two-page description of the product of your choice for a consumer magazine. Include important information such as price and color choice, and technical details such as measurements and operating requirements.

Writing Skills Focus: Precise Details

In describing your product, give **precise details.** Instead of saying, "Cruiser has great safety features," say: "Cruiser has dual air bags and two three-point safety belts in the front, two in the rear. The front shoulder mounts have a height adjustment. All doors come equipped with child safety locks."

Prewriting Make a chart labeling the categories your product description will cover. Under each category, jot down precise details.

Design	Safety	Maneuverability
1.	1.	1.
2.	2.	2.

Drafting You might want to organize your report according to the categories you've chosen. If so, devote a paragraph to each category. Make a general statement or a point about each category and then support it with details from your chart. Make sure all details relate to the category.

Revising Review your description by asking yourself: What more would I need to know if I were buying this product? Is every detail specific and completely accurate? Add any further details needed to make your description complete.

✓ ASSESSMENT OPTIONS

Formal Assessment, Selection Test, pp. 163–165, and Assessment Resources Software. The selection test is designed so that it can be easily customized to the performance levels of your students.

Alternative Assessment, p. 47, includes options for less advanced students, more advanced students, intrapersonal learners, logical/mathematical learners, verbal/linguistic learners, and visual/spatial learners.

PORTFOLIO ASSESSMENT

Use the following rubrics in the ***Alternative Assessment*** booklet to assess student writing:
Persuasive Letter: Persuasion Rubric, p. 105
Comparison-and-Contrast Essay: Comparison-and-Contrast Rubric, p. 103
Technical Article: Technical Description/ Explanation Rubric, p. 115

Idea Bank

Following are suggestions for matching Idea Bank topics with your students' performance levels and learning modalities:

Customizing for *Performance Levels*
Less Advanced Students: 1, 4
Average Students: 2, 5, 6, 7
More Advanced Students: 3

Customizing for *Learning Modalities*
Visual/Spatial: 6
Verbal/Linguistic: 4, 5
Logical/Mathematical: 5, 7

Guided Writing Lesson

Revision Strategy Have students reenter their writing and highlight each detail. The ask them to review each detail and determine whether it is accurate and specific enough to allow readers to understand and see the product. If not, students should rewrite parts of the description to be more precise.

For more prewriting, elaboration, and revision strategies, see *Prentice Hall Writing and Grammar.*

Writing and Language Transparencies Use the Cubing Organizer transparency (p. 87) to demonstrate a way students can develop details for their product descriptions.

Writers at Work Videodisc
Have students view the videodisc segment for Chapter 1 in which Colleen McElroy talks about her strategy for gathering details. Discuss how her strategy may be applied to all forms or descriptive writing.

Play frames 3324 to 4292

Writing Lab CD-ROM
Have students complete the tutorial on description. Follow these steps:

1. Have students consult an audio-annotated student model of a first draft of a student's description. The student comments on the choices she made in drafting the piece.
2. Suggest that students refer to tips for peer editors to learn about peer review strategies for improving a description.

Prepare and Engage

LESSON OBJECTIVES

1. To use recursive writing processes to write a response to literature
2. To recognize and avoid unnecessary words
3. To recognize and use infinitives and infinitive phrases correctly

You may want to distribute the scoring rubric for Response to Literature (p. 110 in ***Alternative Assessment***) to make students aware of the criteria on which their work will be evaluated. For suggestions on how you can customize the rubric, see p. 206.

Writers at Work Videodisc

Play the videodisc segment in which Miguel Algarín discusses the process of preparing a literary response. Encourage students to consider why an experienced teacher and poet like Algarín records his reactions to a work.

Play frames 26321 to 29738

Writing Lab CD-ROM

If your students have access to computers, they may work on the tutorial on Response to Literature to complete their persuasive essays. Have students follow these steps:

1. Review the audio-annotated Literary Models to see example of six different kinds of literary response.
2. Use the tips for using quotations in the Drafting section to see how statements are more effective when they include a supporting quotation from the work.
3. Draft on the computer.
4. Use the video tip from Miguel Algarín to hear a professional writer's views on revising a draft.
5. Use the tips for creating an interesting title in the Publishing and Presenting section.

Responding to Literature on an Essay Test

Writing Process Workshop

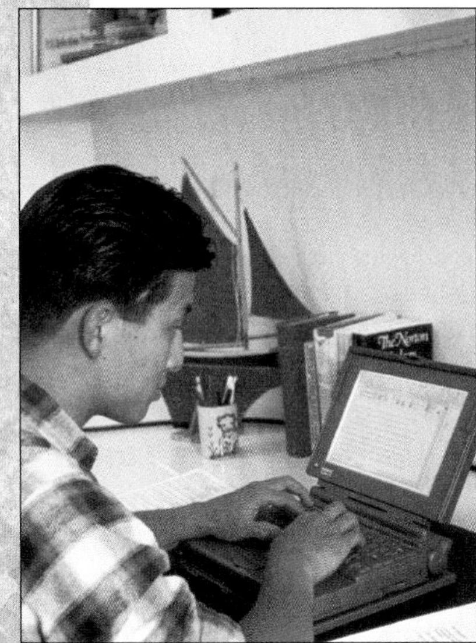

In class, you are frequently asked to think about and discuss a particular sentence or passage in a literary work. Similarly, in an essay test, you may be asked to respond to a question or idea based on a particular literary passage that you've read. The test is designed to assess your writing ability, so be sure you respond fully and directly to the test question. Organize your ideas and supporting details clearly and logically, to make your writing interesting. Stay focused on your purpose for writing so that your sentences all contribute to the whole.

The following skills, introduced in this section's Guided Writing Lessons, will help you write an essay responding to literature:

- **Give specific examples.** If you state that prominent writers worldwide saved Solzhenitsyn from worse persecution, include the example that Norwegian writers and artists offered him shelter. (See page 635.)
- **Elaborate,** or develop details so that the reader can clearly picture what you are saying. (See page 645.)
- **Give precise details.** Instead of saying, "Our class has helped many people," say "The 150 residents of the local nursing home have enjoyed our weekly concerts." (See page 655.)

The following excerpt from an essay about "Mothers & Daughters" demonstrates these skills:

① The writer gives a specific example of a long-lasting mother-and-daughter relationship.
② The writer elaborates on the many types of relationships by describing the variety of emotions and social situations presented.
③ The writer provides a precise detail about one photographer's unique perspective.

Writing Model

Relationships come in all shapes and sizes. It is clear when you read the photo essay "Mothers & Daughters" that these relationships are unique and are not limited to the early years of life. ① Eudora Welty's mother, for example, shared lessons about a love of reading from the time Eudora was two or three until she was an adult. ② The essay includes observations of mothers and daughters who are happy, sullen, wealthy, and poor. ③ One photographer compares the mothers and daughters in the pictures she takes.

Prewriting

Choose a Position In his Nobel lecture, Alexander Solzhenitsyn shares his view that "mankind's salvation lies exclusively in everyone's making everything his business. . . ." Write an essay explaining your reaction to this idea.

Reread the selection to understand how Solzhenitsyn supports his belief. Decide whether or not you share his view, and support your position with examples from the selection and from your own experiences. Remember, it was Solzhenitsyn's own personal experiences that led him to share his opinion. In choosing your position, you too should consider your own experiences.

Gather Details After forming your opinion, review Solzhenitsyn's lecture, looking for supporting evidence. Focus on the lecture to gather details. Your essay should refer often and specifically to the selection. If you share Solzhenitsyn's point of view, you'll want to cite examples from his speech. If you disagree with his view, support your opinion with passages from the selection, as well as examples from your own experiences.

Drafting

Engage Your Audience Experienced writers know that they need to grab readers' attention at the beginning. Don't just repeat the test question in your first sentence. Instead, try one of these approaches:

- Start with a quotation from Solzhenitsyn's speech that highlights your position.
- Begin with a startling example from current events that supports your position.
- Cite an example from personal experience to introduce your point of view.

Use Transition Words To strengthen your essay, add transition words to show how your ideas work together. Choose words from the Transition Word Bin below:

Transition Word Bin

Spatial	Cause and Effect	Compare and Contrast
behind	because	identically
at the center	as a result	in the same way
alongside	consequently	different from
within	side effect	more, less, most
on top of	outcome	similarly, equally

Applying Language Skills: Eliminating Unnecessary Words

Needless words weigh down your writing and may confuse your readers. **Eliminate unnecessary words** in your essay.

Wordy: The Sierra 2000 is more or less a pretty decent value in those fun things we love to call cameras. As a matter of fact, I believe that I'll hop right on down to the store and buy one for my little old self.

Streamlined: The Sierra 2000 is such a decent value in camera equipment, I think I'll buy one for myself.

Practice Eliminate unnecessary words in the following:

Past history shows that just when you think that the camera can't possibly be improved or made easier to use by professionals and amateurs alike, some smart inventor comes along and does just that.

Writing Application Make sure that your essay has no unnecessary words.

Writer's Solution Connection
Language Lab

For more practice streamlining your sentences, complete the Language Lab lesson on Eliminating Unnecessary Words.

Prewriting Strategy

Have students review the process of hexagonal writing to use for a literature response essay that they may be asked to write for an essay test.

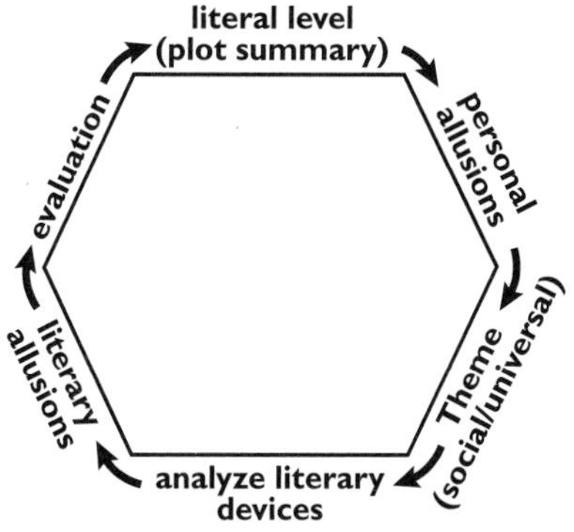

Customize for
English Language Learners

Students with English as a second language may have difficulty identifying unnecessary words. You may wish to have them mark their writing with a colored pen or pencil and then review their assessment of what which words are necessary, giving them feedback, as is appropriate.

Writing Lab CD-ROM

To prepare students for responding to literature on an essay test, have them use the Response Wheels in Focusing Your Response section of the tutorial on Response to Literature so they can explore combinations of literary elements and response methods to focus a response.

Elaboration Strategy

As students draft for essay tests, encourage them to create simple cluster diagrams to use transition words to keep their writing focused and to help them follow through with the position they chose.

Applying Language Skills

Eliminating Unnecessary Words Remind students that needless words will confuse readers; redundant ones bore them.

Answer

Possible response:

History shows that computers get more powerful and less expensive with each passing year.

Grammar Reinforcement

For additional instruction and practice, have students complete the **Language Lab CD-ROM** lesson on Eliminating Unnecessary Words and the practice page (p. 119) on Using Words Concisely in the *Writer's Solution Grammar Practice Book*.

Revision Strategy

It is important, as students reenter their writing when writing for an essay test, to verify that they have responded directly to the test question. Encourage them to refer back to the original question and carefully reread what it asked for. Keeping the parameters of an essay question in mind will help direct their revision process.

Prentice Hall Writing and Grammar For more prewriting, elaboration, and revision strategies, see *Prentice Hall Writing and Grammar.*

Publishing

You might suggest that students keep their essay responses to review before taking future essay tests. They might find it helpful to jot notes of what they would do differently when taking another test.

Reinforce and Extend

Applying Language Skills

Infinitives and Infinitive Phrases

Suggested Answer

To record music from CDs is this tape deck's main function.

For additional instruction and practice, have students complete the practice p. 46 on Infinitives and Infinitive Phrases in the *Writer's Solution Grammar Practice Book.* Have students reflect on the critical evaluation skills they developed in doing a consumer review. They might discuss or write in their journals in what other situations they might apply these skills.

APPLYING LANGUAGE SKILLS: Infinitives and Infinitive Phrases

An **infinitive** is the base form of a verb, usually preceded by *to;* it can be used as a noun, an adjective, or an adverb. An **infinitive phrase** contains an infinitive and all the words that go with it.

Infinitive: To connect is this author's goal.

Infinitive Phrase: To connect with people around the world is this author's goal.

Practice On your paper, change the following sentence into one with an infinitive:

> Expressing the common experiences of people around the world is one goal of good literature.

Writing Application Review your essay. Add infinitives where they would make your sentence structure more interesting.

Writer's Solution Connection Writing Lab

To help you revise your essay, see the Revising and Editing screen of the Writing Lab Tutorial for Response to Literature.

Revising

Use a Checklist Use the following checklist to improve your essay:

- Did I respond directly to the test question?
- What appropriate details and quotations from the literature can I add to strengthen my point of view?
- Have I used precise language and correct spelling, grammar, and usage?
- Is my organization clear and easy to follow?
- Have I elaborated on my points to make them clear to the reader?

REVISION MODEL

The observations in "Mothers & Daughters" show many ① Tillie Olsen and Julie Olsen Edwards give examples of a wide range of relationships, while Eudora Welty focuses on a single relationship with her own mother. viewpoints. The photographs and text work together to explain this unique ~~and amazing~~ ② relationship. In understanding this essay, "reading" the photographs is just as ~~important~~ crucial ③ as reading the text, as Estelle Jussim points out in her observation, "it requires a grasp of visual language." ④

① The writer adds this detail to specify the types of relationships discussed in the essay.
② The writer eliminates an unnecessary word.
③ The writer changes a word to clarify meaning.
④ The writer elaborates on the last sentence to support it with a detail.

Publishing

Submit Your Essay to Be Scored If you are satisfied with your essay's content, read it through one last time to check for errors. Then submit it to your teacher.

✓ ASSESSMENT

PORTFOLIO ASSESSMENT

Use these criteria rubric to assess students' writing.

	4	3	2	1
Organization and Style	The essay is very well organized and all assertions are supported.	The essay is organized and most assertions are supported.	Organization needs some improvement. Few points are supported.	The essay is poorly organized and support for points is lacking.
Grammar, Usage, and Mechanics	There are few or no errors in grammar, usage, or mechanics.	There are some, but not significant, errors in grammar, usage, or mechanics.	Significant errors in grammar, usage, or mechanics that interfere with the reading.	There are many serious errors in grammar, usage, or mechanics.

Student Success Workshop

Real-World Reading Skills

Analyzing Text Structures

Strategies for Success

Every text has a structure. Consider the basic structure of an essay: introduction, elaboration, and conclusion. In nonfiction, the text structure may be organized on a principle of comparison and contrast, cause and effect, or some type of order, such as chronological order. As you analyze a text structure, you may want to create a graphic organizer, such as a chart, diagram, or timeline, to help make sense of the information.

Comparison and Contrast If the author's purpose is to compare and contrast, the structure of the text will point out similarities and differences between things or ideas. For example, an article might compare and contrast two car models. A chart that compares and contrasts the features of each car might be included.

Cause and Effect Nonfiction texts often show cause-and-effect relationships between pieces of information. A magazine article on a space shuttle flight may include a paragraph explaining how bad weather forced the shuttle to land somewhere other than the planned spot and how that change delayed the launching of a communications satellite. You can use a graphic organizer like this chart to list causes and effects:

Cause	Effect
Bad weather	Unplanned landing site
Unplanned landing site	Satellite launch rescheduled

Chronological Order Text is sometimes structured in chronological order, which means the order in which events occurred. To analyze the chronological order of those events, draw up a timeline, listing dates and corresponding events in the order in which they occurred.

Apply the Strategies

Read the text that follows. Then answer the questions.

In 1970, the average commercial fisherman on Cape Island Bay pulled in three tons of fish each week. As more people bought boats and became fishermen, the quantity of cod each person caught began to shrink. By 1990, the average commercial fisherman on Cape Island Bay was catching less than one ton of fish per week. Yet, as boats became more expensive, fishermen fished for longer periods, hoping to catch enough fish to pay for their boats. By 1998, cod stocks had dwindled. Many fishermen have had to sell their boats and seek other types of work.

1. Identify the text structure in the passage above, and explain how it helps you understand the author's information. Create a graphic organizer based on the text structure.
2. Analyze the text structures of a newspaper article and an editorial. Then create graphic organizers to represent the text structure of each.

Here are some situations in which it may be important to analyze text structures with the help of graphic organizers:

- Reading a scientific report
- Reading about computer technology to find out which products you want or need
- Reading a novel or story in which the events are arranged in the order in which a character thinks about them

Test Preparation Workshop

Analyzing Text Structures
Informational reading passages on standardized tests often have one or more of the organizational patterns discussed in this workshop. Thinking about how the text is structured, and even sketching a graphic organizer if time allows, can help test takers focus on the most important information and connections.

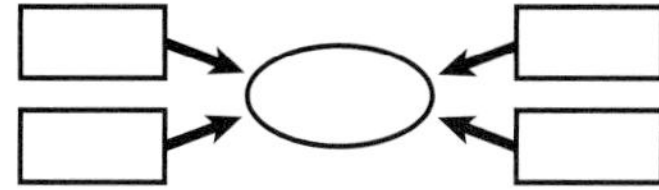

With which of these texts would you use the graphic organizer shown?

A a short biography of James Madison
B a summary of the U.S. Bill of Rights
C a textbook chapter about the causes of the American Revolution
D a review of four books about the Founders of the United States

Have students tell why the graphic organizer works best with choice C, a text that discusses causes leading to a single effect.

Prepare and Engage

LESSON OBJECTIVES

- To construct images such as graphic organizers based on text descriptions and text structures
- To analyze text structures such as compare and contrast, cause and effect, and chronological ordering for how they influence understanding

Customize for
English Language Learners
Help students to recognize text structures. Provide a list of words that signal each structure named in the workshop; students may focus on the appropriate structure by using the words in oral or written sentences:

- Comparison and Contrast: same, like, different, on the other hand, in contrast
- Cause and Effect: because, since, therefore, so, as a result
- Chronological Order: before, after, during, finally, first, next, later that day

Answers

1. The main text structure is cause and effect. The writer is explaining how each event led to another over a period of about 20 years.

   In a two-column chart, items under the heading Causes are
   - Increased number of fishermen
   - Increased costs of boats
   - Increased length of fishing time
   - Dwindling cod stocks

   Corresponding items under the heading Effects are
   - Reduced per-person catches of cod
   - Increased length of fishing time
   - Dwindling cod stocks
   - Boats sold and jobs lost
2. A news story told as a narrative may have text structured in chronological order: beginning, middle, end. A news story discussing issues may be organized around a chain of causes and effects. An editorial may have a main-idea/supporting details structure: an opinion supported by evidence, examples, and reasons.

Prepare and Engage

LESSON OBJECTIVES

1. To recognize genres such as nightly news, newsmagazines, and documentaries and identify the unique properties of each

Have students tell whether they have ever experienced or witnessed an event that was later reported on the television news. Did the reporter cover the event fully? fairly? Discuss reactions to the report.

Customize for
Logical/Mathematical Learners

A criticism of TV news is that important stories are covered superficially. Students can gather data that support or disprove this idea. Suggest that they survey news reports each evening for at least a week, count the minutes spent on each topic, and present their conclusions with a graph.

Apply the Strategies

1. Students critiquing a wildlife documentary may note that its purpose is to make viewers sensitive to the natural world and to persuade them to respect the depicted animals and their habitat. If the focus of the viewer's attention is a predator, the narrative and images combine to win the viewer's support—the viewer roots for a successful hunt. If the focus is a prey animal, however, the viewer roots for a successful getaway.
2. Students may observe many persuasive techniques in television newsmagazines—extreme close-ups of interviewees, for example, by the selection of excerpts from interviews, and by fast-cutting techniques that point out contradictions or contrasts.
3. Students should select a national or international news event. To compare and contrast the treatment, they should take notes to document the sources (television, newspaper, Web site) and to summarize the facts provided.

Speaking, Listening, and Viewing Workshop

Analyzing a Media Presentation

One of the quickest ways to find out about current events is to turn on a television set. However, don't be in a hurry to accept all you see. Think of a media presentation as a product; analyze and critique it for quality before accepting it. Consider all the elements that contribute to the way information is presented.

Recognize the Genre Identify the type of media presentation you are viewing. Be aware that each genre has its own style, and adjust your response to its message accordingly.

Straightforward news reports, such as the nightly news, are meant to recount information factually and objectively—that is, without stating the newscaster's or the station's opinion. For example, a report on a political campaign would present the results of popularity polls, but not the reporters' opinions about the candidates.

Documentaries offer an in-depth, factual exploration of a topic and may or may not reveal the personal slant of the filmmaker. They often include visual and sound techniques, such as special editing effects, camera angles, music, and sequencing, which convey additional messages to the viewer.

Television newsmagazines offer in-depth exploration of a topic, often with a less objective slant. In either genre, a focus on overcrowding in homeless shelters might include interviews with homeless people or a tour of a shelter, as well as facts and statistics.

Editorials offer an opinion, often persuasively and usually on a controversial topic. They are usually accompanied by an announcement that the views presented are the opinions of one individual. An editorial that proposes raising the speed limit might offer personal opinions supported by facts and statistics.

Recognize Persuasive Techniques Be on the lookout for any visual symbols in a media message. Listen closely to the language used. Broad generalizations, statements that may not be completely logical, and emotional words may be intended to persuade you to think a certain way or change your point of view. Notice how different word choices can completely change the effect of a news report:

> A wild grizzly terrorized a group of unsuspecting Boy Scouts camping in the wilderness.
>
> A group of Boy Scouts were surprised by an unexpected visitor to their campsite—a grizzly!

Apply the Strategies

Choose one or more of these activities. Apply the strategies for critically viewing media presentations.

1. Watch a media presentation on television. Identify the genre of the presentation. Explain its basic message. Then critique the presentation. Note and evaluate any persuasive techniques that influence your response.
2. Watch a documentary or newsmagazine on television. Critique and evaluate how its use of visual and sound techniques conveys messages.
3. Compare and contrast the media coverage of the same event on television, in a newspaper, and on the Internet.

Tips for Analyzing Media Presentations

- *Identify the type of report you are seeing.*
- *Separate the main idea of the media message from any persuasive techniques.*
- *Pay attention to language and word choice that might cause you to react in a certain way.*

Beyond the Classroom

Community Connection

Local Access The local access cable channel is available for community use. Students may survey the program offerings and critique one or more targeted to young people their age. Issues to consider: purpose or message, quality of production, and value to the community. They may also investigate what "public access" means—how is it decided who can present a program? Students who have been involved with local access productions can report on their experiences.

Workplace Skills

Critical Evaluation Point out to students that the ability to review and analyze a media presentation is beneficial in almost many workplace situations. Workplace responsibilities may call on employees to review proposal presentations, news reports. Being able to evaluate quality, purpose, and possible bias—for instance a client's advertising proposal—gives insight into what's behind it and enables them to adjust their approach and response to it.

Test Preparation Workshop

Reading Comprehension

Comparing and Contrasting Texts; Analyzing Literary Language

Strategies for Success

The reading sections of standardized tests often require you to compare and contrast aspects—such as themes, conflicts, and allusions—of two texts. The tests may also require you to analyze the literary language.

Compare and Contrast Aspects of Texts

To compare and contrast, read each passage carefully and analyze the literary elements. If a test asks you to compare and contrast the themes of two passages, think about the similarities or differences between the main ideas or messages of the texts. Look at the following example:

Read the passages, and answer the question:

Passage A:

The first settlers in the Western Hemisphere were faced with a world that was strange and unknown to them. They encountered unfamiliar lands, animals, and weather conditions. They had to learn to survive in a climate that could turn deadly in an instant.

Passage B:

The members of the Concordia space station had entered an uncharted universe. All of their most technically advanced equipment was useless to them. Alien life forces surrounded their ship. Intelligence experts on board raced to figure out who these forces were and what they wanted.

1 What theme is shared by both passages?

A Space travel
B Frontier life
C Entering unknown worlds
D Fighting off enemies

Only one passage deals with space travel, so **A** is wrong. Only one deals with frontier life, so **B** is wrong. Although there are dangers in both, **D** is not correct. The theme of both passages, although presented differently, is **C**.

Analyze Melodies of Literary Language

Writers often create "melodies" in the language of their work with evocative words, rhyme, repeated sounds, or rhythms. On a reading test, "listen" to the sound effects and think about what they express. Read the passage that follows, and answer the questions.

Let others cheer the winning man,
There's one I hold worthwhile;
'Tis he who does the best he can,
Then loses with a smile.
Beaten he is, but not to stay
Down with rank and file;
That man will win some other day,
Who loses with a smile.

2 How are evocative words and rhythms used to create a kind of melody in the poem?

A Evocative words express happiness.
B No melody is present in the poem.
C The poem's regular rhythm and rhyme create an upbeat kind of melody.
D The poem's words and rhythms sing a song of a man shamed by defeat.

The correct answer is **C**.

Apply the Strategies

Reread the poetry, and answer the questions:

1 What is the theme of the poem?

A Winning is everything.
B It's hard to smile when you lose.
C The real winner can smile in defeat.
D Don't ever accept defeat.

2 In what way is the word "smile" an example of evocative literary language?

A It conveys the idea that competition is fun.
B It conveys a spirit of joy.
C It conveys two different emotions in the lines where it is used: first, good sportsmanship; second, the happiness of victory.
D It is used here sarcastically.

Correlations to Standardized Tests

The reading comprehension skills reviewed in this Workshop correspond to the following standardized test sections:

SAT Critical Reading
ACT Reading

Test Preparation

Each ATE workshop in Unit 1 supports the instruction here by providing teaching suggestions and a sample test item:

Analyze Literary Language (ATE, pp. 569, 595, 609)
Comparing and Contrasting Texts (ATE, pp. 581, 625, 637, 647)

LESSON OBJECTIVES

- To compare and contrast varying aspects of text such as themes, conflicts, and allusions
- To analyze the melodies of literary language, including its use of evocative words and rhythms

Answers

1. (C) The real winner can smile in defeat.
2. (C) It conveys two different emotions in the lines where it is used; first, good sportsmanship; second, the happiness of victory.

Test-Taking Tip

Look Back and Predict Advise students to follow these steps when looking for answers to multiple-choice questions about reading passages. The steps should be followed after the first normal-to-fast reading of the passage: First, scan the passage to find the particular term or phrase in the question. Then predict an answer to the question. Finally, read the answer choices to see which one is the best match with your prediction.

Have students reread question 2, "In what way is the word 'smile' an example of evocative literary language?" Have them find the word *smile* in the poem, reread the lines that surround it, and then tell what the word suggests. Students should recognize that in the context of the poem, the word *smile* suggests a goodhearted acceptance of defeat, cheerfulness, and hope for a future win. Of the four answer choices, *A* and *B* are too much alike and seem incomplete, and *D* is clearly wrong—answer choice *C* comes closest to the prediction. Point out to students that knowing the correct answer before they review the answer choices may prevent them from becoming misled by any of the choices.

Planning Instruction and Assessment

Unit Objectives

1. To read plays that exemplify classic Greek drama and Shakespearean drama
2. To apply a variety of reading strategies, particularly strategies for reading drama, appropriate for reading these plays
3. To analyze literary elements
4. To use a variety of strategies to read unfamiliar words and to build vocabulary
5. To learn elements of grammar, usage, and style
6. To use recursive writing processes to write in a variety of forms
7. To express and support responses to various types of texts
8. To prepare, organize, and present literary interpretation

Meeting the Objectives
With each selection, you will find instructional material and portfolio opportunities through which students can meet these objectives. Further, you will find additional practice pages for reading strategies, literary elements, vocabulary, and grammar in the ***Selection Support*** booklet in the ***Teaching Resources*** box.

Test Preparation

The unit workshop, **Reading Comprehension: Characteristics of Text** (SE, p. 809), is supported by teaching tips and a sample test item in the ATE workshop with each selection grouping.

- **Identify Patterns of Organization** (ATE, pp. 669, 711, 733, 789)
- **Notice Word Choice** (ATE, pp. 685, 751, 773)

The following additional workshops in the ATE give teaching tips and a sample test item for applying the skill taught in the Student Success Workshop:

- **Locating Information on the Internet** (ATE, p. 704)
- **Find Supporting Evidence** (ATE, p. 809)

Humanities: Art

Commedia dell'Arte by Andre Rouillard.

Although the title of this painting indicates a specific dramatic form, the figures show gestures, expressions, and costumes. The masked figures have exaggerated comic costumes and features. The harlequin is a comic character well known in drama. The man in the hat wears a mask with a fake-nose caricature. The man and the woman on the left of the stage are more realistic types. The young man sitting center stage wears a mask, but with a subtle expression of sorrow.

Have students link this painting with drama.

1. How might these characters be similar to those in a television situation comedy? *The actors play fixed characters in situations that basically do not change.*
2. Why do you think the artist portrayed a group performing with only one person watching? *With the single viewer in the darkened window the artist suggests that while performance is often judged based on audience reaction, the performance has a value that is separate from the audience reaction. In other words, it's what we do that counts, not what others think of it.*

UNIT 8

Commedia dell'arte, Andre Rouillard

Drama

Drama is one of our earliest literary forms. Ancient people would act out great triumphs, deep fears, or heartfelt wishes in religious rites. Since then, drama has evolved into its modern forms, which range from lively musicals to biting satires. It is the doing or acting quality that makes drama unique in literature. As you read the dramas in this unit, see and hear the action being performed on the stage in your mind.

Assessing Student Progress

The following tools are available to measure the degree to which students meet the unit objectives:

Informal Assessment

The questions on the Guide for Responding sections are a first level of response to the concepts and skills presented with the selection. Students' responses are a brief informal measure of their grasp of the material. Their responses on this level can indicate where further instruction and practice are needed. You may then follow up with the practice pages in the ***Selection Support*** booklet.

You will find literature and reading guides in the ***Alternative Assessment*** booklet, which you may give students on an individual basis for informal assessment of their performance.

Formal Assessment

In the ***Formal Assessment*** booklet, you will find selection tests and a unit test.

Selection Tests The selection tests measure comprehension and skills acquisition for each selection or group of selections.

Unit Test The unit test applies the unit skills on a broader level. The Critical Reading section measures Unit Objectives 1, 2, and 3. The Vocabulary and Grammar section measures Objectives 4 and 5. The Essay section measures Objectives 1 and 6.

Alternative Assessment

Portfolios As you review individual pieces or the collected work in students' portfolios, you will find assessment sheets available in the portfolio section of the ***Alternative Assessment*** booklet.

Scoring Rubrics You will find scoring rubrics for writing modes in the ***Alternative Assessment*** booklet. You can apply these to Guided Writing Lessons and to Writing Process Workshop lessons.

Speaking, Listening, and Viewing The ***Alternative Assessment*** booklet contains assessment sheets for speaking, listening, and viewing activities.

Learning Modalities The ***Alternative Assessment*** booklet contains activities that appeal to different learning styles. You may use these too as an alternative measurement of students' growth.

Reading for Success

The Reading for Success page in each unit presents a set of problem-solving procedures to help readers understand authors' words and ideas on multiple levels. Good readers develop a bank of strategies from which they can draw as needed and apply to a variety of reading situations.

Unit 8 presents strategies for reading drama. Students will have encountered most of these strategies earlier. Here, however, they apply them to a very specific situation: reading plays.

How to Use the Reading for Success Pages

- Have students preview the Reading for Success page, identifying which strategies they have used before and which are new to students. Then present each strategy as a problem-solving procedure as it applies to drama. For instance, most students have envisioned the action of short stories. Using stage directions to envision the action, however, is a specific way to apply this strategy to drama. Be sure students understand what each strategy involves and under what circumstances to apply it.
- Before reading, have students preview these plays, looking at the annotations in the green boxes that model the strategies.

Reading for Success

Strategies for Reading Drama

While plays share many elements with prose, fiction, and poetry, the greatest difference is that a drama is designed to be acted out on a stage before an audience. The story is told mostly through dialogue and action. Stage directions indicate when and how the actors move and sometimes suggest sound and lighting effects. When you read a play, you are reading a script; you must always keep in mind that it was written to be performed.

The following strategies will help you interact with the text of a drama and imagine the action and characters in performance.

Envision the action.

Reading a play without envisioning the action is like watching a movie with your eyes shut. Use the stage directions and other details to create the scene in your mind. How and where do the actors move? What do they sound like? What goes on between the characters?

Predict.

As the action develops, make predictions about what you think will happen. Look for hints in the dialogue or action that seem to suggest a certain outcome. As you read on, you will see whether your predictions are correct.

Question.

Note the questions that come to mind as you read. For example, why do the characters act as they do? What causes events to happen? Why does the author include certain information? Look for answers to your questions as you read.

Connect the play to its historical context.

When does the action of the drama occur? What conditions exist during the times? If the drama takes place in a historical or foreign setting, you may have to consider that customs and accepted conduct may differ from that to which you are accustomed.

Summarize.

Dramas are often broken into acts or scenes. These natural breaks give you an opportunity to review the action. What is the conflict? What happens to move it toward its resolution? Put the characters' actions and words together as you summarize.

When you read the plays in this unit, use these general strategies, as well as those specifically suggested with each drama. They will help you understand the conflict and resolution of the dramas and gain insight into the themes.

Reading Strategies: Support and Reinforcement

Appropriate Reading Strategies Students are given a reading strategy to apply in each act of the plays. Each reading strategy is appropriate to the content of the act.

Reading Prompts To encourage application of the given strategy, there are occasional prompts, within green boxes, at appropriate and significant points.

In addition, there are red boxes prompting application of the Literary Focus concept and maroon boxes prompting students to connect with their lives.

Using the Boxed Annotations and Prompts The material in the green, red, and maroon boxes along the sides of selections is intended to help students apply the literary element and the reading strategy and to make a connection with their lives.

You may use the boxed material in several ways:

- When you introduce the Literary Focus, Reading Strategy, or the Literature and Your Life connection, have students preview the appropriate prompts in the selection to get an overview of how the skill or concept will be developed.
- Have students pause when they come to a box and respond to its prompt before they continue reading. If your students keep reading journals, encourage them to record in the journal the page number, the question or idea proposed in the prompt, and their response.

Part 1 *Dramatic Beginnings*

Theatre of Herodes Atticus, Acropolis, Odeon, Athens, Greece

One-Minute Planning Guide

The two sections of *Antigone* in this unit present a range of emotions, characters, and dramatic techniques and elements that will help students understand the classic beauty of ancient Greek drama. The special feature on the Greek theater gives students background on how plays were presented as well as providing information about the Oedipus myth, which will be vital to their understanding of *Antigone*. Part 1 of *Antigone* introduces two tragic characters making decisions and taking stands that will have profound consequences. Part 2 explores Greek beliefs on the balance between fate and individual choice.

Customize for
Varying Student Needs

When assigning the selections in Part 1 to your students, keep in mind the following factors:

- Without an understanding of the Oedipus myth, students will be confused by frequent references to characters and events from the myth.
- The formal, stylized language may be problematic for your less proficient readers or for students learning English.
- Pre-AP students will appreciate the footnotes that give more detail about allusions to other Greek myths and historical events.

Humanities: Art

Theatre of Herodes Atticus, Acropolis—Odeon, Athens, Greece.

This photograph shows a theater built on the Acropolis in Athens, near the site of the older Theater of Dionysos, where *Antigone* and the other plays of Sophocles were originally performed. The theater shown here was built in A.D. 161 by Herodes Atticus, a wealthy Roman who constructed the theater in memory of his dead wife; it follows the classical Roman rather than the Greek model and seats about 5,000 spectators (the Theater of Dionysos could seat about 14,000). Herodes Atticus' Theater is now used for an annual summer festival of music and drama.

Have students link the painting to the focus of Part 1, "Dramatic Beginnings," by answering the following question:

Ancient Greek drama used such nonrealistic elements as masks and a chorus, a group of people who spoke in unison. Why might this type of drama be better suited to this theater than a contemporary realistic play, with naturalistic sets and costumes? *Most students will probably say that it would be difficult to create the illusion of a closed, realistic space in an open theater like this.*

Enrichment

Greek Tragedy A Greek tragedy is usually centered on the suffering of a major character and ends in disaster. The origins of tragedy are obscure, but by the time Sophocles wrote, tragedy was a highly developed dramatic form, strongly linked with both religious ritual and artistic performance. It used poetic language, as well as song, and never completely abandoned its sacred origins.

Students living in secular societies will have some difficulty understanding the degree to which religion informed daily life in ancient Greece. The Greeks believed that the good will of the gods determined the city's welfare. Reverence, the fulfillment of religious duty, and patriotism were often synonymous.

Characters had human traits but were actually larger than life. Students accustomed to characters with personality and used to seeing cameras focus in on minute revealing muscular twitches on the faces of tragic characters will miss these aspects in Greek drama. Although characters have their assigned traits, these characteristics are so universal that the personages represent examples or types rather than unique personalities.

Finally, tragedies were usually presented as part of a trilogy. Much of the content was based on myths familiar to the ancient Greeks. This inherited and familiar cultural background made it possible for the playwright to include pungent and subtle allusions whose importance could be understood by ancient Greek audiences without the benefit of explanation.

Art Transparency As students read "The Greek Theater," they should note that the plays of the classical world differed from modern drama in many ways. Discuss the distinctives of Greek drama, emphasizing the fact that today's readers still respond to many of the plays, such as *Antigone,* because the plays deal with universal concepts. Display Art Transparency 14 and draw students' attention to the details of the mosaic in *Actors Preparing for a Performance.* At some point during the reading of *Antigone,* students might enjoy bringing the mosaic to life by taking the parts of the actors and discussing the play from their perspective.

THE GREEK THEATER

Theater was a celebration in ancient Greece. The Athenians of the fifth century B.C. held festivals to honor Dionysos (dī´ ə nī səs), their god of wine. During these holidays, citizens gathered to watch competitions between playwrights, who presented plays derived from well-known myths. These plays depicted events that exposed arrogance and that emphasized reverence for the gods.

Thousands of Athenians saw the plays. In an outdoor theater like the one shown on page 667, seats rose away in a semicircle from a level orchestral area. The plays performed in these theaters had limited numbers of characters, and scenes were interspersed with songs. There were no curtains to allow for changes of scenery between acts. No violence or irreverence was depicted on stage, although such matters were central to the plots of many plays. Such events occurred offstage and were reported in dialogue.

THE PRESENTATION OF THE PLAYS

Ancient Greek playwrights used a consistent format for most of their productions. Plays opened with a prologue, or exposition, which presented the background to situate the conflict. The entering chorus then sang a parados (par´ əd əs), or opening song. This was followed by the first scene. The chorus's song, called an ode, divided scenes, thus serving the same purpose as a curtain does in modern theater.

The Chorus. The role of the chorus was central to the production and important in interpreting the meaning of the plays. During the odes, a leader called the choragos (kō rā´ gəs) might exchange thoughts with the group in a dialogue. During that recital, the group rotated first from right to left, singing the strophe (strō´ fē). Then the chorus members moved in the opposite direction during the antistrophe. An epode was included in some odes as a sort of final stanza. At the conclusion, there was a paean (pē´ ən) of thanksgiving to Dionysos and an exodos (ek´ sə dəs), or final exiting scene. Clearly, the chorus played an essential part in any play's success.

THE OEDIPUS MYTH

Sophocles wrote three tragedies about the royal family of Thebes, a city in northeastern Greece. Called the Theban plays, these tragedies were *Oedipus the King, Oedipus at Colonus,* and *Antigone.* The stories of these plays were as familiar to the audience as the story of Noah and the Ark or Jonah and the Whale is to many people today.

Abandoned at Birth. Oedipus (ed´ ə pəs) was abandoned at birth by his parents, the Theban king Laios (lā´ yəs) and his wife, Iocaste (yō kas´ tə). A fortuneteller proclaimed in an oracle that the infant would kill his father and marry his mother. Wishing to avoid that fate, the couple had Oedipus taken off to be abandoned on a mountaintop by a servant who was to ensure the baby's death. The parents assumed that this mission was completed. In fact, however, the servant pitied the newborn and gave him to a childless couple in a distant city who raised the boy without ever mentioning his adoption.

A Famous Riddle. When Oedipus left that city to start his adult life, he still did not know that his real father was Laios and that his mother was Iocaste. His travels took him toward Thebes, where he killed a man without knowing it was Laios. Oedipus' fame grew

Drama and the Dionysian Festivals

In Athens, dramatic competitions were held at festivals honoring Dionysos, the Greek god of wine and fertile crops. (Theatrical competitions were never held at festivals honoring other gods.) Of the four annual festivals, the festival City Dionysia was the most prestigious. It was an elaborate festival, extending over several days, at which Athens showed off its wealth and culture to attendees from all over ancient Greece.

Before a festival officially began, the playwrights appeared before public officials and the sponsors of the plays and announced the subjects of their plays. Processions and sacrifices marked the official opening of the festival, after which five days were devoted to performances. Tragedies, comedies, and satyr plays (bawdy comedies that often lampooned the stories of gods and heroes) were performed. In addition, choral recitations were performed and judged.

▲ Critical Viewing What might be some advantages and disadvantages to watching a performance in a theater like this one? **[Assess]**

after he confronted the Sphinx, a monster that killed those unable to answer its riddle. The riddle was this: What creature walks on four legs at dawn, two legs at noon, and three legs in the evening? Oedipus answered that the creature was man, a being who crawls as an infant on all fours, walks erect in midlife, and uses a third leg in the form of a cane during old age. The Sphinx leaped into the sea after Oedipus gave the correct answer, and Oedipus was received in the city as a hero.

A Royal Marriage. Iocaste, now a widow, agreed to marry the unknown champion. The couple lived happily for years and raised four children of their own. Then a plague befell the city. The priests claimed the plague was punishment for some unknown sin. During an investigation of his own background, Oedipus learned the facts of his birth. In horror at this revelation, Iocaste committed suicide and Oedipus blinded himself. Iocaste's brother, Creon (krē än), took control of the city and allowed one of Oedipus' children, Antigone (an tig´ ə nē), to lead Oedipus into exile where he died.

A Daughter Mourns. After her return to Thebes, Antigone was deeply troubled by her experience. Her sister, Ismene (is mē´ nē), and brothers, Eteocles (ē tē´ ə klēz) and Polyneices (päl´ ə nī´ sēz) were also burdened by their family background. They were haunted by the curse that caused their father to fulfill his own prophecy and condemned his sons to kill each other for the control of Thebes.

Order Restored. By the time *Antigone* opens, Creon has restored some order to Thebes. The civil war between the brothers has just ended. Eteocles and Polyneices have killed each other in combat. Eteocles had supported Creon's established order and was buried with honors. Polyneices had rebelled with the forces of Argos against Thebes, and Creon ordered that his corpse be left to rot. Antigone's decision to disobey that command is central to the play.

▶Critical Viewing◀

Assess The majestic mountains surrounding the theater make a natural backdrop that enhances the power of the drama. Some students may enjoy watching a performance in the fresh air. Others may express concern over whether the actors could be seen or heard.

Enrichment

The Big Three The main contenders for the tragedy prize at the dramatic competitions were Aeschylus, Euripedes, and Sophocles. Our knowledge of Greek tragedy is based mainly on the work of these three playwrights of the fifth century.

The oldest, Aeschylus, was born to an aristocratic family. As a young man, he earned fame as a soldier fighting against the Persians. He won his first prize for tragedy at approximately forty years of age. (He had been writing for sixteen years.) He won his last prize for tragedy when he was past sixty, with the *Orestia,* a trilogy considered by many to be his masterpiece. Although Aeschylus wrote ninety plays, only seven of them have survived to the present day.

At the age of twenty-seven, Sophocles defeated Aeschylus in the playwright's contest with his first tragedy. Like Aeschylus, Sophocles had served in the military. He held political positions as well, and was a priest of Asclepius, the Greek god of healing. He was the most conservative of the three great tragedians, both socially and religiously.

Euripedes, the youngest of the three, had surprisingly modern attitudes. His characters had greater psychological depth and were more human than the characters of the other two tragedians. In addition, his language was simpler and more colloquial. He disapproved of the prevailing Greek attitudes that subordinated women and glorified war. These beliefs, embedded in the social criticism in his plays, may account for the limited popularity of his plays in ancient Greece. (He won only four prizes in his lifetime.) Today, he is acknowledged as one of the most powerful dramatists in history.

The Development of Actors

Until the fifth century, tragic dramatists acted their own works—alone—with only the chorus to back them up. Early in his career, Aeschylus introduced a second actor. Dialogue could now occur between two characters. Playwrights continued to act in their own tragedies, however, until the early part of fourth century B.C., when Sophocles introduced a third actor. He did not act in his own plays, and eventually, other playwrights followed his example. When awards for actors were introduced into the competitions (approximately 450 B.C.), the separation between actor and playwright was complete. The number of actors remained fixed at three, requiring a single actor to play many roles. The logistics of some plays even required that the same role be played by different actors in different scenes. Elaborate masks and costumes helped the audience identify each character, no matter which actor played the role.

Prepare and Engage

LESSON OBJECTIVES

1. **To develop vocabulary and word identification skills**
   - Latin Prefixes: *trans-*
   - Using the Word Bank: Definitions
   - Extending Word Study: Word Parts
2. **To use a variety of reading strategies to comprehend a Greek drama**
   - Connect Your Experience
   - Reading Strategy: Question the Characters' Motives
   - Tips to Guide Reading (ATE)
   - Read to Discover (ATE)
   - Idea Bank: Newspaper Article
3. **To increase knowledge of other cultures and to connect common elements across cultures**
   - Connecting Themes Across Cultures (ATE)
   - Cultural Connection (ATE)
4. **To express and support responses to the text**
   - Critical Thinking
   - Idea Bank: Letter
   - Analyze Literary Criticism
5. **To analyze literary elements**
   - Literary Focus: Protagonist and Antagonist
   - Background for Understanding
6. **To plan, prepare, organize, and present literary interpretations**
   - Idea Bank: Readers Theatre
   - Speaking, Listening, and Viewing Mini-Lesson: Readers Theatre (ATE)
7. **To increase knowledge of the rules of grammar and usage**
   - Build Grammar Skills: Coordinating Conjunctions

Test Preparation

Reading Comprehension: Identify Patterns of Organization (ATE, p. 669) The teaching tips and sample test item in this workshop support the instruction and practice in the unit workshop:
Reading Comprehension: Characteristics of Text (SE, p. 809)

Guide for Reading

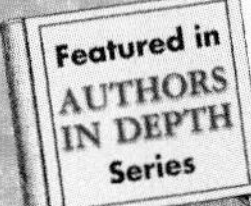

Featured in AUTHORS IN DEPTH Series

Sophocles *(c. 496–406 B.C.)*

The ancient Greek dramatist Sophocles (säf´ ə klēz) wrote one hundred plays, but only seven remain in existence. His most famous are the three dealing with Oedipus and his children: *Oedipus Rex* (Oedipus the King), *Oedipus at Colonus*, and *Antigone*. This trilogy was written over a span of forty years.

Born in Kolonos, near Athens, Sophocles was one of the most respected Greek dramatists of his time. He was admired not only for his poetic and dramatic skills but also for his good looks and musical talent. Sophocles frequently won first place in the competitions of plays performed in the Dionysian festivals. With his first tragedy, written at age twenty-seven, he defeated the highly respected Aeschylus (es´ kə ləs). Sophocles made some changes to the traditions of Greek theater. One of the most important changes was to increase the size of the chorus.

In his dramas, Sophocles was mainly concerned with the search for truth and self-understanding—even when the search leads to tragedy. His ability to see current values in old myths thrilled his contemporaries. Audiences since have continued to appreciate the freshness and vitality of his world view.

In *Antigone*, King Creon reaches an understanding of his own faults only after paying a very high price.

◆ Build Vocabulary

LATIN PREFIXES: *trans-*

In Act I of *Antigone,* the chorus asks, "What mortal arrogance *transcends* the wrath of Zeus?" The Latin prefix *trans-,* which means "through," "across," or "over," will help you to define *transcends* as "to go above or beyond limits." As you read *Antigone,* you will be *transported* to another time and place.

WORD BANK

As you read this drama, you will encounter the words on this list. Each word is defined on the page where it first appears. Preview the list before you read. Though you may not know the words, you may still be able to identify the part of speech of each word, which will give you a clue to the word's use. In your notebook, write the words and their parts of speech.

sated
anarchists
sententiously
sultry
transcends

◆ Build Grammar Skills

COORDINATING CONJUNCTIONS

A **coordinating conjunction** links two or more words or groups of words of equal importance. Many sentences in *Antigone* consist of two clauses of equal rank joined by a coordinating conjunction. The conjunction not only joins the clauses but shows the relationship between the ideas in the clauses. Look at these examples from *Antigone.*

The conjunction *and* shows addition:

Our temples shall be sweet with hymns of praise,
And the long night shall echo with our chorus.

The conjunctions *but* and *yet* show contrast or exception:

No one values friendship more highly than I; *but* we must remember . . .

The conjunction *or* shows alternatives:

Find that man, bring him here to me, *or* your death / Will be the least of your problems. . . .

Prentice Hall Literature Program Resources

REINFORCE / RETEACH / EXTEND

Selection Support Pages
Build Vocabulary: Prefixes: *trans-*, p. 196
Build Grammar Skills: Conjunctions, p. 197
Reading Strategy: Characters' Motives, p. 198
Literary Focus: Protagonist and Antagonist, p. 199

Strategies for Diverse Students' Needs, p. 48
Beyond Literature, The Greek Theater, p. 48
Daily Language Practice Week 11, Greek Drama, p. 26
Formal Assessment Selection Test, pp. 170–172; Assessment Resources Software
Alternative Assessment, p. 48

Resource Pro CD-ROM
Listening to Literature Audiocassettes
Literature CD-ROM

Antigone

◆ Literature and Your Life

Connect Your Experience

History is full of instances where political situations create family conflicts. In American history, the Civil War is often noted for pitting brother against brother. In this play, a young woman must decide whether to act on loyalty to her family or to follow the law of the land.

Thematic Focus: Choices and Consequences

Not every conflict has a clear winner and loser. Notice the ways in which Creon and Antigone, the main characters in this play, experience both victory and defeat.

Journal Entry Jot down a list of issues on which you would be willing to take a stand. Next to each issue, write down under what circumstances, if any, you might choose *not* to take a stand.

◆ Background for Understanding

Literature

The chorus is an essential element of Greek drama. This group comments on and may explain the action of the play. Sometimes the chorus speaks in a single voice as a group, sometimes in dialogue between two sections of the group.

In an opening song—the *parados* (parˊ əd əs), the chorus explains the central conflict of the play. Between scenes, the chorus recites an *ode*. During the ode, the group moves from right to left, singing the *strophe* (strōˊ fē). Then the chorus members move in the opposite direction during the *antistrophe*.

◆ Literary Focus

Protagonist and Antagonist

When you describe a movie to a friend, you probably relate the story in terms of the main character and what happens to him or her. A movie is usually written so that you side with one of the characters more than the others and hope that he or she succeeds. In a literary work, the main character is called the **protagonist**. The protagonist is the main character, the one at the center of the action. The **antagonist** is the character or force in conflict with the protagonist.

In this play, Antigone is the protagonist; she is in conflict with the antagonist, her uncle—Creon the king.

◆ Reading Strategy

Question the Characters' Motives

When you decide to do something, what causes you to act? The inner drive or impulse that makes you act is called your motive. When you read about a character like Antigone, you wonder why she acts the way she does and makes the decisions she does. To understand the conflict and resolution in any play, **question the characters' motives.**

At the beginning of the play, Antigone says to her sister, Ismene:

> And now you can prove
> what you are:
> A true sister, or a traitor to
> your family.

What do you think is Antigone's motive in confronting her sister so harshly? Is Antigone a strong, ethical character testing her sister's strength or is she too proud, too willful, too full of her own self-worth? Your questioning of her motives and the motives of the king, Creon, will help you better understand and appreciate the forces at work in the play.

Test Preparation Workshop

Reading Comprehension: Identify Patterns of Organization

As students prepare for standardized tests, they need to refine their abilities to analyze the characteristics of clearly written texts. Use this sample test item to give students practice with this comprehension skill.

> Locaste, now a widow, agreed to marry the unknown champion. The couple lived happily for years and raised four children of their own. Then a plague befell the city.

What pattern of organization is used in this passage?

A compare/contrast
B chronological
C flashback
D point-by-point

Words like *now, for years,* and *then,* indicated that this narrative paragraph describes events in the order in which they happened. B is the correct response.

Write the word *tragedy* in large capital letters on the chalkboard. Encourage students to jot down a list of current events they would describe as tragedies. Then explain the definition of tragedy as it applies to drama: A person of importance, such as a king or princess, moves from happiness to disaster (and often to death) through some character flaw or error in judgment, or through the forces of fate. Lead a discussion in which students analyze their original suggestions of tragedies in light of this more specific definition. Then tell them that this play, *Antigone,* is a famous Greek tragedy.

Connecting Themes Across Cultures

Antigone believes so strongly in her brother's right to a burial that she is willing to put her life in danger—by her actions, she makes the choice to face the consequences. Challenge students to name heroes from recent history who make such a bold move. *Students may note civil rights leaders such as Martin Luther King, Jr., and Nelson Mandela.*

Tips to Guide Reading

Shared Reading Students may find it easier to comprehend this drama if you read a good part of it together with them. Once students become accustomed to the style, you may encourage them to read silently on their own.

Customize for ***Less Proficient Readers***

Unfamiliar Greek character names may be difficult for some students. Introduce the cast list, character identification information, and pronunciation guide on p. 670.

Customize for ***Pre-AP Students***

A tragic character flaw that can lead to a hero's downfall is *hubris,* or excessive pride. As students read, encourage them to analyze actions in the play to determine which characters exhibit this flaw and how it affects the plot.

Develop Understanding

One-Minute Insight In the first part of this play Sophocles establishes the main characters and the conflict. Proud and reckless, the fiery princess of Thebes, Antigone, breaks the law to bury her brother, who has been labeled a traitor by the king, her uncle. By so doing, she embarks on a course toward her own destruction and the destruction of those around her. As the play opens, the audience is invited to contrast Antigone with her sister, Ismene, who begs Antigone to be reasonable and accept the law. This contrast is a major thread that runs throughout the play.

When Antigone argues her actions with Creon, her uncle and the king, the conflict between human law and divine law is firmly established.

Customize for *English Language Learners*
Explain stage directions in simpler terms. Paraphrase "a platform that extends the length of the facade" as an acting platform as wide as the front of the king's palace.

❶ **Clarification** Point out to students that these stage directions were not written by Sophocles, but were added by the translators to help modern audiences envision and understand the action. The "assault on Thebes," which is given as a time reference, would have been a historic battle familiar to Greeks watching this play in the fifth century.

◆ **Background for Understanding**

❷ Explain that the prologue to a Greek tragedy is an introductory scene, which may be a monologue or a dialogue. In the prologue, the playwright sets up the situation. In this case, the prologue alerts readers that the sisters have lost two brothers who fought on opposite sides in a battle. One brother has been buried with honors, and the other is left unburied by the king's orders.

ANTIGONE

PROLOGUE THROUGH SCENE 2

Sophocles

Translated by Dudley Fitts and Robert Fitzgerald

❶ ***Scene.*** *Before the palace of* CREON, *King of Thebes. A central double door, and two lateral doors. A platform extends the length of the facade, and from this platform three steps lead down into the "orchestra," or chorus-ground.*

Time. *Dawn of the day after the repulse of the Argive*[1] *army from the assault on Thebes.*

❷ **Prologue**

[ANTIGONE *and* ISMENE *enter from the central door of the Palace.*]

ANTIGONE. Ismene, dear sister.
You would think that we had already suffered enough
For the curse on Oedipus:[2]

1. **Argive** (är′ gīv): From Argos, the capital of a section of ancient Greece.
2. **curse on Oedipus:** This curse refers to the fate of Oedipus, who was doomed by a decree of the gods to kill his father and marry his mother while ignorant of their true identities.

PERSONS REPRESENTED

ANTIGONE (an tig′ ə nē′), daughter of Oedipus, former King of Thebes
ISMENE (is mē′ nē), another daughter of Oedipus
EURYDICE (yoo rid′ ə sē′), wife of Creon
CREON (krē′ än), King of Thebes, uncle of Antigone and Ismene
HAIMON (hī′ mən), Creon's son, engaged to Antigone
TEIRESIAS (tī rē′ sē əs), a blind prophet
A SENTRY
A MESSENGER
CHORUS
CHORAGOS (kō rā′ gəs), leader of the chorus
A BOY, who leads Teiresias
GUARDS
SERVANTS

▲ ❸ **Critical Viewing** What does this temple, dedicated to Poseidon, the god of the sea, suggest about the importance of the gods in Greek life? **[Draw Conclusions]**

Block Scheduling Strategies

Consider these suggestions to take advantage of extended class time:

- Introduce students to the conventions of Greek theater with the Looking at Literature Videodisc, Chapter 8.
- Have students read Background for Understanding (p. 669) for information about the role of the chorus in Greek drama. Discuss what students know about modern play structure—acts, scenes, and so on.
- Use Daily Language Practice for Week 11. You may either use the transparency on the overhead and have students write the passages correctly, or you may dictate the passages and have students write them.
- Use ***Listening to Literature Audiocassettes*** to play portions of the play aloud.
- Suggest that students work in groups to brainstorm for a list of words containing the root *trans-*. Point out that *trans-* is often used as a prefix. Then have them complete the Build Grammar Skills page on the Word Root *trans-*, p. 196 in ***Selection Support.***

Antigone 671

▶Critical Viewing◀

❸ The temple appears majestic and important. It indicates that the gods were important and honored at the time this temple was built.

Read to Discover

Remind students that the drama was written more than 2,000 years ago. As they read, ask them to set a purpose for reading: Why has this play stood the test of time? What does it say to audiences of countless generations? *Although Antigone is a tragedy, students may argue that its youthful heroine makes a brave and exciting choice, the tension level is dramatically high, and there is an important lesson to be learned from the story.*

Customize for *Logical/Mathematical Learners*

These students especially will benefit from creating a family tree that indicates the relationships between Oedipus, Creon, Antigone, Ismene, the dead brothers, and Locaste. Students can annotate the tree as they discover new information. For instance, later in the story, students will learn that Antigone accompanied her father, Oedipus, into exile. Students can add a note next to Antigone's name that indicates this aspect of the relationship.

Humanities: Art

Temple of Poseidon at Sounion.

This photograph shows the Temple of Poseidon at Sounion. Built around 440 B.C., the temple sits on a promontory overlooking the sea and visible by the ships that passed beneath. It is a ruin now, but once it had six columns at each end, and thirteen on each side. Archaeologists have found fragments of sculpture near the site that suggest the front of the temple was decorated with a carved frieze depicting a battle against the Centaurs—wild mythical creatures that had the body of a horse and the arms, chest, and head of a man.

Explain to students that Greek temples fall into three categories based on how the capitals, or tops, of their columns were designed. This temple of Poseidon is *Doric;* that is, each column has a flat rectangular slab on top. Other temples are *Ionic,* with capitals carved in a ram's-horn design, while a third type, *Corinthian,* has capitals carved with a leaf or floral design.

Encourage interested students to do further research to find out more about Greek art and architecture.

◆ Literary Focus

❶ **Protagonist and Antagonist** Antigone sets the action in motion and shows love for her brothers by wanting them both to receive the honors of burial. Because she instigates the action and elicits readers, sympathy through her determination to "do the right thing," students can begin to identify her as the protagonist.

❷ **Clarification** Antigone's strong statement may be clearer to students if they understand that the Greeks believed that the dead had to be buried before the soul could be at rest. If Ismene won't help bury her brother, she is condemning him to eternal unrest.

◆ Reading Strategy

❸ Ask students how this statement helps clarify Antigone's motives. *Although Antigone is motivated by her desire to honor divine law, her love for her brother is also a powerful motive.*

◆ Critical Thinking

❹ **Speculate** Have students speculate what Creon might do to the women if they disobey his edict. *Some students may suggest that he will have them stoned according to the penalty that has been announced. Others may feel that his family relationship with the women will lead him to be more lenient.*

❺ **Clarification** In this statement, Antigone is exhibiting hubris—excessive pride that will contribute to her downfall.

Customize for
Gifted/Talented Students
Challenge students to write a news article about the story told in the drama. Remind students that they need to find details in the play that answer the questions: Who, What, When, Where and Why.

I cannot imagine any grief
That you and I have not gone through.
And now—
Have they told you of the new decree of our King Creon?

ISMENE. I have heard nothing: I know
That two sisters lost two brothers, a double death
In a single hour; and I know that the Argive army
Fled in the night; but beyond this, nothing.

ANTIGONE. I thought so. And that is why I wanted you
To come out here with me. There is something we must do.

ISMENE. Why do you speak so strangely?

ANTIGONE. Listen, Ismene:
Creon buried our brother Eteocles
With military honors, gave him a soldier's funeral,
And it was right that he should;
but Polyneices,
Who fought as bravely
and died as miserably,—
They say that Creon has sworn
No one shall bury him,
no one mourn for him,
But his body must lie in the fields, a sweet treasure
For carrion birds[3] to find as they search for food.
That is what they say, and our good Creon is coming here
To announce it publicly; and the penalty—
Stoning to death in the public square!
There it is,
And now you can prove what you are:
A true sister, or a traitor to your family. ❷

> ◆ **Literary Focus**
> What qualities does Antigone show here that help you identify her as the **protagonist?**

ISMENE. Antigone, you are mad! What could I possibly do?

ANTIGONE. You must decide whether you will help me or not.

ISMENE. I do not understand you. Help you in what?

ANTIGONE. Ismene, I am going to bury him. Will you come?

ISMENE. Bury him! You have just said the new law forbids it.

ANTIGONE. He is my brother. And he is your brother, too.

ISMENE. But think of the danger! Think what Creon will do!

ANTIGONE. Creon is not strong enough to stand in my way. ❺

ISMENE. Ah sister!
Oedipus died, everyone hating him ❻

3. **carrion** (kar´ ē ən) **birds**: Scavenger birds, such as vultures, that eat the decaying leftovers of another animal's kill.

Analyze Literary Criticism

High school students are frequently asked to read Sophocles' tragedy, *Antigone* and write critical papers expressing opinions about the work and its universal themes. Statements made by students often differ, so your classes may find it interesting to compare their thoughts and opinions with those of others. Share the following two statements written by high school students with the class:

"Conflict is one of the main themes in Sophocles' *Antigone*. The conflict between the state and the individual is the controlling factor in the plot of the play."

"The actions of the characters in Sophocles' play are essentially selfish. Antigone's seemingly selfless actions are driven by the more selfish desires for praise and eternal life."

To generate class discussion and analysis, ask students the following questions:

1. Do you agree with either student? Why or why not?
2. Why do you think the two students analyze the drama in such a different manner?

For what his own search brought to light, his eyes
Ripped out by his own hand; and Iocaste died,
His mother and wife at once: she twisted the cords
That strangled her life; and our two brothers died,
Each killed by the other's sword. And we are left:
But oh, Antigone,
Think how much more terrible than these
Our own death would be if we should go against Creon
And do what he has forbidden! We are only women,
We cannot fight with men, Antigone!
The law is strong, we must give in to the law
In this thing, and in worse. I beg the Dead
To forgive me, but I am helpless: I must yield
To those in authority. And I think it is dangerous business
To be always meddling.

ANTIGONE. If that is what you think,
I should not want you, even if you asked to come.
You have made your choice and you can be what you want to be.
But I will bury him; and if I must die,
I say that this crime is holy: I shall lie down
With him in death, and I shall be as dear
To him as he to me. It is the dead,
Not the living, who make the longest demands:
We die for ever . . .
You may do as you like,
Since apparently the laws of the gods mean nothing to you.

> ◆ **Reading Strategy**
> What is Antigone's motive for wanting to bury her brother?

ISMENE. They mean a great deal to me; but I have no strength
To break laws that were made for the public good.

ANTIGONE. That must be your excuse, I suppose. But as for me,
I will bury the brother I love.

ISMENE. Antigone,
I am so afraid for you!

ANTIGONE. You need not be:
You have yourself to consider, after all.

ISMENE. But no one must hear of this, you must tell no one!
I will keep it a secret, I promise!

ANTIGONE. Oh tell it! Tell everyone!
Think how they'll hate you when it all comes out
If they learn that you knew about it all the time!

ISMENE. So fiery! You should be cold with fear.

ANTIGONE. Perhaps. But I am doing only what I must.

ISMENE. But can you do it? I say that you cannot.

ANTIGONE. Very well: when my strength gives out, I shall do no more. ⑩

ISMENE. Impossible things should not be tried at all.

ANTIGONE. Go away, Ismene:
I shall be hating you soon, and the dead will too,
For your words are hateful. Leave me my foolish plan:
I am not afraid of the danger; if it means death,
It will not be the worst of deaths—death without honor.

ISMENE. Go then, if you feel that you must.
You are unwise.
But a loyal friend indeed to those who love you.

[Exit into the Palace. ANTIGONE *goes off, left. Enter the* CHORUS.]

Parodos

CHORUS. [STROPHE 1]

Now the long blade of the sun, lying

❻ **Clarification** Tell students that the story of Oedipus, Locaste, and their sons would have been so familiar to Greek audiences that these brief references would have been easily understood. Contemporary readers, however, may need some background information. Refer students to pp. 666 and 667 for background on Oedipus.

◆ Critical Thinking

❼ **Analyze** Invite students to identify personality traits Ismene reveals in this speech. *She is fearful of death, she believes women are weak and subordinate to men, and she is frightened of authority.*

◆ Build Grammar Skills

❽ **Coordinating Conjunctions** Have students identify the conjunctions in this passage and identify the relationships between the clauses joined by the conjunctions. *The conjunction* and *joins the clauses "You have made your choice," "you can be what you want to be." It adds one idea to another. The conjunction* but *shows the contrast between what Ismene might do or be ("you can be what you want to be") and what Antigone will do ("I will bury him.")*

◆ Reading Strategy

❾ **Question the Characters' Motives** Students may suggest that Antigone wants to bury her brother out of family loyalty. She loved Polyneices and wants his body to have an honorable burial. Students should note Antigone's words, "this crime is holy," and her reference to "the laws of the gods." Divine law is also one of her motives.

◆ Critical Thinking

❿ **Contrast** Based on this exchange, have students identify the fundamental difference between Ismene and Antigone. *Antigone is active—she tries to affect events through her actions, even when it seems futile. Ismene is passive. She allows circumstances to rule her actions.*

Cross-Curricular Connection: History

Seven Against Thebes The battle known as "Seven Against Thebes" is renowned in legend and forms the basis for plays by Aeschylus and Euripedes. According to legend, Oedipus' sons had agreed to occupy the throne on alternate years. To get around the agreement, during his year of reign, Eteocles banished his brother to Argos, where Polyneices married the daughter of the king. He gathered an army, which he led with six Argive heroes and returned to attack Thebes.

Each of the seven Argive leaders stationed himself at one of the seven gates that led to Thebes. In response, Eteocles sent six generals to man each of six gates, while he himself went to the the the gate where Polyneices waited. In the ensuing battle, six of the seven against Thebes were slain, including Polyneices, who killed his brother before succumbing himself.

Customize for *Less Proficient Readers*

Ask students to summarize what they have learned from the Prologue. *Antigone and Ismene had two brothers who killed each other in battle. One was buried with honors, but their uncle, King Creon, will not allow the other to be buried. Antigone wants to bury him herself, but her sister, Ismene, is afraid to break the law.*

◆ Critical Thinking

❶ **Analyze** Sophocles uses a metaphor to characterize Polyneices in battle. Discuss the metaphor, and ask students to explain how the image helps them imagine the kind of leader Polyneices was. Then ask students why Sophocles might have portrayed Polyneices this way. *An eagle is usually associated with freedom, nobility, strength, and bold action. These qualities can help students recognize the qualities in Polyneices that made him a fearless and inspirational leader. By portraying Polyneices this way, Sophocles makes Creon look worse for not allowing his burial.*

◆ Critical Thinking

❷ **Connect** The Chorus explains that the bragging and swaggering of the seemingly triumphant troops with Polyneices led the gods to turn against them and bring about their defeat. Encourage students to connect this fact to the current action of the play. *The Chorus's explanation reveals the Greek belief that excessive pride would bring on the wrath of the gods and lead to a reversal of fortune. Students should keep this in mind as they read on, looking for evidence of excessive pride in both Antigone and Creon.*

Customize for *Pre-AP Students*

❸ Ask these students to explain the irony of Antistrophe 2. *The chorus is announcing the beginning of an era of peace and prosperity. In fact, even more catastrophes are about to occur.*

Level east to west, touches with glory
Thebes of the Seven Gates.[4] Open,
unlidded
Eye of golden day! O marching light
Across the eddy and rush of Dirce's
stream,[5]
Striking the white shields of the enemy
Thrown headlong backward from the blaze
of morning!

CHORAGOS. Polyneices their commander
Roused them with windy phrases,
❶ He the wild eagle screaming
Insults above our land,
His wings their shields of snow,
His crest their marshalled helms.

CHORUS. [ANTISTROPHE 1]
Against our seven gates in a yawning ring
The famished spears came onward in the
night;
But before his jaws were sated with our
blood,
Or pinefire took the garland of our towers,
He was thrown back; and as he turned,
great Thebes—
No tender victim for his noisy power—
Rose like a dragon behind him, shouting
war.

CHORAGOS. For God hates utterly
The bray of bragging tongues;
❷ And when he beheld their smiling,
Their swagger of golden helms,
The frown of his thunder blasted
Their first man from our walls.

CHORUS. [STROPHE 2]
We heard his shout of triumph high in the
air
Turn to a scream; far out in a flaming arc
He fell with his windy torch, and the earth
struck him.
And others storming in fury no less than
his
Found shock of death in the dusty joy of
battle.

CHORAGOS. Seven captains at seven gates
Yielded their clanging arms to the god
That bends the battle-line and breaks it.
These two only, brothers in blood,
Face to face in matchless rage,
Mirroring each the other's death,
Clashed in long combat.

CHORUS. [ANTISTROPHE 2]
But now in the beautiful morning of
victory
Let Thebes of the many chariots sing for
joy!
With hearts for dancing we'll take leave of
war:
Our temples shall be sweet with hymns of
praise,
And the long night shall echo with our
chorus.

Scene 1

CHORAGOS. But now at last our new King is
coming:
Creon of Thebes, Menoikeus'[6] son.
In this auspicious dawn of his reign
What are the new complexities
That shifting Fate has woven for him?
What is his counsel? Why has he
summoned
The old men to hear him?

[Enter CREON *from the Palace, center. He addresses the* CHORUS *from the top step.]*

CREON. Gentlemen: I have the honor to inform you that our Ship of State, which recent storms have threatened to destroy, has come safely to harbor at last, guided by the merciful wisdom of Heaven. I have summoned you here this morning because I know that I can depend upon you: your devotion to King Laïos was absolute; you never hesitated in your duty to our late ruler Oedipus; and when Oedipus died, your loyalty was transferred to his children. Unfortunately, as you know, his two sons,

4. **Seven Gates:** The city of Thebes was defended by walls containing seven entrances.
5. **Dirce's** (dur′ sēz) **stream:** Small river near Thebes into which the body of Dirce, one of the city's early queens, was thrown after her murder.
6. **Menoikeus** (me noi′ kē əs)

◆ Build Vocabulary

sated (sāt′ əd) : Satisfied or pleased

Humanities: Literature

Aristotle's Definition of Tragedy

Aristotle was a Greek philosopher. Born two decades after Socrates' death, he developed an aesthetic, or artistic, philosophy that set up a definition for tragedy and rules that dramatists should follow when writing tragedies.

According to Aristotle's definition, tragedy is an "imitation of an action that is serious, complete, and has sufficient size, in a language that is made sweet . . . exciting pity and fear, bringing about the catharsis of such emotions" (trans. Gudeman). In other words, tragedy is drama about a serious and lofty subject, written in poetic language. Its purpose is to elicit a strong, purifying, emotional response on the part of the audience.

Every tragedy, according to Aristotle, must have six elements: plot, character, thought, diction, music, and spectacle. Furthermore, a tragedy must reflect unity of action and time. In other words, the action should be continuous, with no time lapses or secondary plots. It must take place within a single day.

Challenge students to show how *Antigone* exemplifies Aristotle's elements of tragedy.

the princes Eteocles and Polyneices, have killed each other in battle; and I, as the next in blood, have succeeded to the full power of the throne.

I am aware, of course, that no Ruler can expect complete loyalty from his subjects until he has been tested in office. Nevertheless, I say to you at the very outset that I have nothing but contempt for the kind of Governor who is afraid, for whatever reason, to follow the course that he knows is best for the State; and as for the man who sets private friendship above the public welfare—I have no use for him, ❹ either. I call God to witness that if I saw my country headed for ruin, I should not be afraid to speak out plainly; and I need hardly remind you that I would never have any dealings with an enemy of the people. No one values friendship more highly than I; but we must remember that friends made at the risk of wrecking our Ship are not real friends at all.

These are my principles, at any rate, and that is why I have made the following decision concerning the sons of Oedipus: Eteocles, who died as a man should die, fighting for his country, is to be buried with full military honors, with all the ❺ ceremony that is usual when the greatest heroes die; but his brother Polyneices, who broke his exile to come back with fire and sword against his native city and the shrines of his fathers' gods, whose one idea was to spill the blood of his blood and sell his own people into slavery—Polyneices, I say, is to have no burial: no man is to touch him or say the least prayer for him; he shall lie on the plain, unburied; and the birds and the scavenging dogs can do with him whatever they like. This is my command and you can see the wisdom behind it. As long as I am King, no traitor is going to be honored with the loyal man. But whoever shows by word and deed that he is on the side of the State—he shall have my respect while he is living, and my reverence when he is dead.

> ◆ **Literary Focus**
> ❻ How do Creon's words reveal him as the **antagonist** in this play?

CHORAGOS. If that is your will, Creon son of Menoikeus, You have the right to enforce it: we are yours.

CREON. That is my will. Take care that you do your part.

CHORAGOS. We are old men: let the younger ones carry it out.

CREON. I do not mean that: the sentries have been appointed.

CHORAGOS. Then what is it that you would have us do?

CREON. You will give no support to whoever breaks this law.

CHORAGOS. Only a crazy man is in love with death!

CREON. And death it is; yet money talks, and the wisest Have sometimes been known to count a few coins too many. ❼

[*Enter* SENTRY *from left.*]

SENTRY. I'll not say that I'm out of breath from running, King, because every time I stopped to think about what I have to tell you, I felt like going back. And all the time a voice kept saying, "You fool, don't you know you're walking straight into trouble?"; and then another voice: "Yes, but if you let somebody else get the news to Creon first, it will be even worse than that for you!" But good sense won out, at least I hope it was good sense, and here I am with a story that makes no sense at all; but I'll tell it anyhow, because, as they say, what's going to happen's going to happen, and— ❽

CREON. Come to the point. What have you to say?

SENTRY. I did not do it. I did not see who did it. You must not punish me for what someone else has done.

CREON. A comprehensive defense! More

◆ Critical Thinking

❹ **Predict** Based on these words, how do students predict Creon will react to Antigone's disobedience? *Most students will probably predict that Creon will treat Antigone as harshly as he would any other disobedient subject. His words "the man who sets private friendship above the public welfare—I have no use for him" and "friends made at the risk of wrecking our Ship are not real friends at all" are indications that he does not allow his personal relationships to influence his official decisions.*

◆ Reading Strategy

❺ **Question the Characters' Motives** What motives does Creon reveal in this speech? *Some students may say that Creon is concerned with the public good; others may feel that he is only trying to strengthen his power by making an example of Polyneices and creating fear in those who would oppose him.*

◆ Literary Focus

❻ **Protagonist and Antagonist** Creon's cold words put him in opposition to Antigone, with whom most readers will sympathize because of her noble ideals and love for her brother.

◆ Critical Thinking

❼ **Analyze** What do these words reveal about Creon's character? *Creon's first thought is that someone might disobey him for financial gain. He does not even consider that someone might be motivated by love, honor, or respect for religious law. This reveals that his character is not very noble.*

◆ Background for Understanding

❽ **Literature** Explain to students that another convention of theater in ancient Greece was that much of the action was imagined to have occurred offstage and was reported through dialogue. This led to extensive use of messengers like this sentry. Although the sentry is a minor role, he plays an important function in the play.

Cultural Connection

The Golden Age of Greece

Sophocles lived during the "Golden Age of Greece" (461–431 B.C.). During this time, Athens was Greece's cultural center and its most powerful state. Many Athenians were wealthy and had leisure time to pursue interests such as philosophy and the arts. Many of the great art treasures created during this period may still be seen in museums throughout the world.

The Athenian political structure was based on the city state, or *polis*. The governing body consisted of nine rulers called *archons*, ten generals, a citizen assembly, and ten executive committees. People's law courts administered justice.

In 431 B.C., surrounding city-states led by Sparta, challenged Athenian power. The resulting conflict, the Peloponnesian Wars, resulted in the defeat of Athens. Sparta became Greece's most powerful city-state, but Athens remained Greece's intellectual center.

Discuss with students which cities are the intellectual and cultural centers in the United States and Europe. Suggest they choose cities to research.

◆ Critical Thinking

❶ Draw Conclusions Ask students why Creon assumes that a man has defied him. *Students should recall Ismene's earlier words about the weakness of women. These words will help them draw the conclusion that the subordinate position of women in ancient Greece leads Creon to assume that only a man would have the courage or strength to commit an act of defiance against him.*

❷ Clarification Here, Sophocles restates the Greek belief that the soul cannot rest when the body remains unburied. Having the sentry describe the burial in terms of the ghost's peace reinforces the conflict between Creon's law and divine law.

◆ Critical Thinking

❸ Infer What can you infer from the drastic action the soldiers are willing to take to prove they did not bury Polyneices? *Students can infer that the soldiers fear the wrath of Creon; Creon's threats are not idle.*

◆ Literature and Your Life

❹ Suggested responses: It is difficult to admit that a position you've strongly defended could be wrong because it means the courage or sacrifice involved in taking the stand was for nothing. Some students may suggest that it's difficult to admit an error because it is embarrassing.

◆ Reading Strategy

❺ Question the Characters' Motives What does Creon reveal in this speech about his motives? *In this speech, Creon reveals that he fears plots against him. This may be a motive for his inflexible stand against anyone burying Polyneices: Creon is trying to intimidate any others who would rise against him.*

Customize for *Verbal/Linguistic Learners*

As they would when reading poetry, students should pay attention to the punctuation clues in the play. Punctuation will help them known when a thought begins and ends. Demonstrate reading one of Antigone's speeches to students, showing how it can be read aloud in sentence form.

effective, perhaps,
If I knew its purpose. Come: what is it?

SENTRY. A dreadful thing . . . I don't know
how to put it—

CREON. Out with it!

SENTRY. Well, then;
The dead man—
Polyneices—

[*Pause. The* SENTRY *is overcome, fumbles for words.* CREON *waits impassively.*]

out there—
someone,—
New dust on the slimy flesh!

[*Pause. No sign from* CREON.]

Someone has given it burial that way, and
Gone . . .

[*Long pause.* CREON *finally speaks with deadly control.*]

❶ **CREON.** And the man who dared do this?

SENTRY. I swear I
Do not know! You must believe me!
Listen:
The ground was dry, not a sign of digging, no,
Not a wheeltrack in the dust, no trace of anyone.
It was when they relieved us this morning: and one of them,
The corporal, pointed to it.
There it was,
The strangest—
Look:
The body, just mounded over with light dust: you see?
❷ Not buried really, but as if they'd covered it
Just enough for the ghost's peace. And no sign
Of dogs or any wild animal that had been there.
And then what a scene there was! Every man of us
Accusing the other: we all proved the other man did it,
We all had proof that we could not have done it.
We were ready to take hot iron in our hands,
Walk through fire, swear by all the gods,
It was not I!
I do not know who it was, but it was not I!

[CREON'S *rage has been mounting steadily, but the* SENTRY *is too intent upon his story to notice it.*]

And then, when this came to nothing, someone said
A thing that silenced us and made us stare
Down at the ground: you had to be told the news,
And one of us had to do it! We threw the dice,
And the bad luck fell to me. So here I am,
No happier to be here than you are to have me:
Nobody likes the man who brings bad news.

CHORAGOS. I have been wondering, King: can it be that the gods have done this?

CREON. [*Furiously*] Stop!
Must you doddering wrecks
Go out of your heads entirely? "The gods!"
Intolerable!
The gods favor this corpse? Why? How had he served them?
Tried to loot their temples, burn their images,
Yes, and the whole State, and its laws with it!
Is it your senile opinion that the gods love to honor bad men?
A pious thought!—
No, from the very beginning
There have been those who have whispered together,

> ◆ *Literature and Your Life*
> Why is it difficult to accept that a stand you've taken could be wrong?

◆ Build Vocabulary

anarchists (an′ ər kists) *n.*: Those who disrespect laws or rules

sententiously (sen ten′ shəs lē) *adv.*: Pointed; expressing much in few words

Beyond the Classroom

Career Connection

Sentry A sentry's job is to keep watch and to prevent unauthorized persons from passing. It is a job that still exists in the military, and it has many parallels in civilian life as well. Have students explain the role of sentries, or security guards, in department stores, in retirement communities, at busy intersections, and in public parks. Students may be able to suggest other places where sentries are used.

Community Connection

Cemeteries Different cultures have different ways of honoring and housing the dead. At one time, it was customary to bury people on their own property, but now most communities have special places where the dead are buried or entombed. Many of these cemeteries are affiliated with particular religions. Students may use the Yellow Pages or a local map to determine how many such sites exist in their community.

Stiff-necked anarchists, putting their heads together,
Scheming against me in alleys. These are the men,
And they have bribed my own guard to do this thing.
Money! [*Sententiously*]
There's nothing in the world so demoralizing as money.
Down go your cities,
Homes gone, men gone, honest hearts corrupted,
Crookedness of all kinds, and all for money!

[*To* SENTRY]

But you—!

I swear by God and by the throne of God,
The man who has done this thing shall pay for it!
Find that man, bring him here to me, or your death
Will be the least of your problems: I'll string you up
Alive, and there will be certain ways to make you
Discover your employer before you die;
And the process may teach you a lesson you seem to have missed:
The dearest profit is sometimes all too dear:
That depends on the source. Do you understand me?
A fortune won is often misfortune.

SENTRY. King, may I speak?

CREON. Your very voice distresses me.

SENTRY. Are you sure that it is my voice, and not your conscience? [8]

CREON. By God, he wants to analyze me now!

SENTRY. It is not what I say, but what has been done, that hurts you.

CREON. You talk too much.

SENTRY. Maybe; but I've done nothing.

CREON. Sold your soul for some silver: that's all you've done.

SENTRY. How dreadful it is when the right judge judges wrong! [9]

CREON. Your figures of speech
May entertain you now; but unless you bring me the man,
You will get little profit from them in the end.

[*Exit* CREON *into the Palace.*]

SENTRY. "Bring me the man"—!
I'd like nothing better than bringing him the man!
But bring him or not, you have seen the last of me here.
At any rate, I am safe!

[*Exit* SENTRY.]

Ode 1

CHORUS. [STROPHE 1]

Numberless are the world's wonders, but none
More wonderful than man; the stormgray sea
Yields to his prows, the huge crests bear him high;
Earth, holy and inexhaustible, is graven
With shining furrows where his plows have gone

6 Clarification Explain that in ancient Greek mythology, a group of gods ruled heaven and earth, which is why the sentry swears by all the gods. When characters speak of a single "God," they mean Zeus, king of the gods.

◆ Critical Thinking

7 Relate Ask students to explain why people sometimes blame the messenger for the bad news he or she brings, as Creon does here. *Because Creon cannot punish the person who actually did the burying, he takes out his anger on the messenger. A rational man would realize that the messenger would not report his own disobedience. Encourage students to give examples from books, movies, television programs, or personal experience when a messenger was blamed for his or her message.*

◆ Literary Focus

8 Protagonist and Antagonist Ask students how the sentry's question reinforces Creon's character as the antagonist. *The sentry's question, as well as the chorus's earlier version of the same question, indicates that the public sides with the person who buried Polyneices*

◆ Critical Thinking

9 Analyze What is significant about the sentry's statement? *The sentry's statement captures the heart of the conflict; it also lends support to Creon as a tragic figure. Although he is usually a "right judge," or rational man, he is allowing his fear and pride to lead him into rash decisions.*

Extending Word Study

Word Parts: *-arch* Point out the word *anarchist*, defined for students on p. 676. Explain to students that the word part *-arch* means ruler or leader. Students may be familiar with the terms *monarch, monarchy*, or *anarchy*. Asks students to use their knowledge of the word part to determine the meaning of *oligarchy* *rule by a few* and *hierarchy* *rule by a system of graded ranks.*

Speaking, Listening, and Viewing Mini-Lesson

Readers Theatre

This mini-lesson supports the Speaking, Listening, and Viewing activity in the Idea Bank on p. 683.

Introduce Explain that in a Readers Theatre presentation, dialogue is read rather than memorized, and the physical action is not staged.

Develop Have students brainstorm for a list of qualities that make an oral presentation impressive. These might include expressive voices, clear diction, and dramatic facial expressions.

Apply Help groups assign roles, and let any extras act as the chorus. Provide time for students to rehearse their scenes. You may choose to have the chorus's lines assigned to individual chorus members, rather than have them read in unison.

Assess Once groups have presented their scenes, ask students to assess one another's scenes on the basis of clear speech and dramatic presentation. You may want to use the Peer Assessment guidelines for Oral Interpretation in ***Alternative Assessment,*** p. 119.

Customize for *Less Proficient Readers*

❶ Help these students recognize that the chorus's ode does not advance the action, but is a speech in honor of humans' superiority over the world of nature. Clarify the achievements listed: People sail over the seas, they use the earth and animals to fulfill their needs, and, above all, they have reason and intellect.

Customize for *Pre-AP Students*

❷ Have these students add some modern achievements to the chorus's ode. Then encourage students to discuss the achievements and the cost. How is the ancient Greek view of humans' relationship to the natural world similar to and different from a contemporary view?

◆ Critical Thinking

❸ **Analyze** Ask students to name the character who would most agree with this sentiment on the part of the chorus and to explain their answers. *Creon would agree with these words. He is the leader of the state and, above all, upholds the state and its laws. To Creon, breaking the law is an act of anarchy, the worst possible crime.*

◆ Reading Strategy

❹ **Question the Characters' Motives** Ask students what Antigone's motive might be for burying Polyneices a second time. *Her motive for burying him the first time was sisterly love; she wanted his soul to rest. When her work was undone, the same motives drove her to rebury him.*

Customize for *Bodily/Kinesthetic Learners*

The Greek tragedies have inspired other artists through the ages. Students who excel at dance might like to choose a scene from the play to choreograph and perform (with or without words or music) for the class.

Year after year, the timeless labor of stallions.

[ANTISTROPHE 1]

The lightboned birds and beasts that cling to cover,
The lithe fish lighting their reaches of dim water,
All are taken, tamed in the net of his mind;
The lion on the hill, the wild horse
❶ windy-maned,
❷ Resign to him; and his blunt yoke has broken
The sultry shoulders of the mountain bull.

[STROPHE 2]

Words also, and thought as rapid as air,
He fashions to his good use; statecraft is his,
And his the skill that deflects the arrows of snow,
The spears of winter rain: from every wind
He has made himself secure—from all but one:
In the late wind of death he cannot stand.

[ANTISTROPHE 2]

O clear intelligence, force beyond all measure!
O fate of man, working both good and evil!
When the laws are kept, how proudly his city stands!
When the laws are broken, what of his city then?
❸ Never may the anarchic man find rest at my hearth,
Never be it said that my thoughts are his thoughts.

Scene 2

[*Re-enter* SENTRY *leading* ANTIGONE.]

CHORAGOS. What does this mean? Surely this captive woman
Is the Princess, Antigone. Why should she be taken?

❹ **SENTRY.** Here is the one who did it! We caught her
In the very act of burying him.—Where is Creon?

CHORAGOS. Just coming from the house.

[*Enter* CREON, *center.*]

CREON. What has happened?
Why have you come back so soon?

SENTRY. [*Expansively*] O King,
A man should never be too sure of anything:
I would have sworn
That you'd not see me here again: your anger
Frightened me so, and the things you threatened me with;
But how could I tell then
That I'd be able to solve the case so soon?
No dice-throwing this time: I was only too glad to come!

Here is this woman. She is the guilty one:
We found her trying to bury him.
Take her, then; question her; judge her as you will.
I am through with the whole thing now, and glad of it.

CREON. But this is Antigone! Why have you brought her here?

SENTRY. She was burying him, I tell you!

CREON. [*Severely*] Is this the truth?

SENTRY. I saw her with my own eyes. Can I say more?

CREON. The details: come, tell me quickly!

SENTRY. It was like this:
After those terrible threats of yours, King,
We went back and brushed the dust away from the body.
The flesh was soft by now, and stinking,
So we sat on a hill to windward and kept guard.
No napping this time! We kept each other awake.
But nothing happened until the white round sun
Whirled in the center of the round sky over us:
Then, suddenly,
A storm of dust roared up from the earth, and the sky
Went out, the plain vanished with all its trees

◆ Build Vocabulary

sultry (sul´ trē) *adj.*: Oppressively hot or moist; inflamed

Humanities: Performing Arts

The Greek Theater Remind students that all the characters they have met so far would have been played by only three actors (all men) in the original ancient Greek performances. Have students review the play to this point and realize that, excepting the chorus, there are usually only two characters on stage at a time. Encourage students to examine the play to see how the parts might have been broken up. For instance, point out that the actor who plays Antigone cannot also play Creon, since they are on stage at the same time. For more on Greek theater, use the page on Greek theater in ***Beyond Literature,*** p. 48. You can also use the Literature CD-ROM ***How to Read and Understand Drama,*** Feature 4 on the Greek chorus. Suggest that interested students find out more about the history of Greek drama and the types of costumes, masks, and stage settings that were often used.

In the stinging dark. We closed our eyes and endured it.
5 The whirlwind lasted a long time, but it passed;
And then we looked, and there was Antigone!
I have seen
A mother bird come back to a stripped nest, heard
Her crying bitterly a broken note or two
For the young ones stolen. Just so, when this girl
Found the bare corpse, and all her love's work wasted,
She wept, and cried on heaven to damm the hands
That had done this thing.
And then she brought more dust
And sprinkled wine three times for her brother's ghost.
We ran and took her at once. She was not afraid,
Not even when we charged her with what she had done.
She denied nothing.
And this was a comfort to me,
And some uneasiness: for it is a good thing
To escape from death, but it is no great pleasure
To bring death to a friend.
Yet I always say
There is nothing so comfortable as your own safe skin!

CREON. [*Slowly, dangerously*] And you, Antigone,
You with your head hanging,—do you confess this thing?

ANTIGONE. I do. I deny nothing.

CREON. [*To* SENTRY] You may go.

[*Exit* SENTRY.]

[TO ANTIGONE] Tell me, tell me briefly:
Had you heard my proclamation touching this matter?

ANTIGONE. It was public. Could I help hearing it?

CREON. And yet you dared defy the law.

ANTIGONE. I dared.
It was not God's proclamation. That final Justice
That rules the world below makes no such laws.
Your edict, King, was strong,
But all your strength is weakness itself against
The immortal unrecorded laws of God.
They are not merely now: they were, and shall be,
Operative forever, beyond man utterly.

I knew I must die, even without your decree:
I am only mortal. And if I must die
Now, before it is my time to die,
Surely this is no hardship: can anyone
Living, as I live, with evil all about me,
Think Death less than a friend? This death of mine
Is of no importance; but if I had left my brother
Lying in death unburied, I should have suffered.
Now I do not.
You smile at me. Ah Creon,
Think me a fool, if you like; but it may well be 9
That a fool convicts me of folly.

CHORAGOS. Like father, like daughter: both headstrong, deaf to reason!
She has never learned to yield.

CREON. She has much to learn.
The inflexible heart breaks first, the toughest iron
Cracks first, and the wildest horses bend their necks.
At the pull of the smallest curb.
Pride? In a slave? 10
This girl is guilty of a double insolence,
Breaking the given laws and boasting of it.
Who is the man here,
She or I, if this crime goes unpunished?
Sister's child, or more than sister's child,
Or closer yet in blood—she and her sister
Win bitter death for this!

[TO SERVANTS] Go, some of you,

◆ Literary Focus

5 Protagonist and Antagonist Ask students why Sophocles might have included this detail. *The whirlwind that raises dust and hides Antigone suggests that even the gods are on her side.*

◆ Reading Strategy

6 Question the Characters' Motives What does this description indicate about Antigone's motives? *Antigone's crying like a mother bird reinforces that Antigone's motive is love for her brother. The fact that she repeats the religious ritual indicates that she is also motivated by loyalty to divine law.*

◆ Reading Strategy

7 Question the Characters' Motives Why doesn't Antigone deny what she has done? *Her integrity and conviction that she has done the right thing won't allow her to deny it. It isn't enough that she does it; she must also stand by her decision.*

8 Question the Characters' Motives Ask students why Creon asks this question. What is he hoping to hear? What side of Creon's personality do we get a small glimpse of in this line? *Creon may be hoping that Antigone will say she has not heard the proclamation. Then he will not have to punish her. Creon is showing a gentler side than we have seen.*

◆ Literary Focus

9 Protagonist and Antagonist With this line, Sophocles indirectly poses a question to the audience: Who is the fool? Who is right and who is wrong? Have students give and support their opinions. *Some may agree that the law of the gods takes precedence; others, the law of the state. Students should ask themselves what would happen if people placed the laws of their religions over secular law in our society today before they took positions.*

◆ Reading Strategy

10 Question the Characters' Motives Ask students: Why does Creon feel he must punish his niece? *Not only has Antigone broken the law, but she has shown no remorse. Creon will be perceived as a weak leader if he does not punish her.*

Beyond the Classroom

Life and Work Skills

Decision Making Point out to students that in some ways, the chorus is like a jury, weighing both sides of the conflict between Creon and Antigone and offering an opinion. While the chorus is not required to come to a final decision (as a jury is), they do analyze the actions and statements of the characters. Point out to students that analyzing all sides of an issue, weighing evidence, and coming to a decision are important decision-making skills in many aspects of life and work.

Lead students to brainstorm for a number of life situations in which they might have to "weigh the evidence." Suggest situations such as listening to a salesperson's pitch, deciding whether to contribute money to a charity, or supporting one political candidate over another. Ask students to identify the kinds of information they would want to know or the evidence they would need to weigh in each situation in order to make a judgment. How would they judge if some of that information were unavailable?

◆ Critical Thinking

❶ **Infer** Ask students: What is Creon's main worry here and why is he so determined to get the Choragos to understand his turmoil. *Creon is now more upset by Antigone's public defiance than he is by her crime. He may be beginning to have doubts that lead him to seek the approval or corroboration of others.*

◆ Critical Thinking

❷ **Interpret** Why does Creon think Antigone's death will give him everything? *Creon feels that her death will show he is stronger, and it will eliminate the challenge to his authority. Tell students to keep Creon's statement in mind as events unfold so that they will appreciate the irony that Antigone's death actually causes Creon to lose everything.*

◆ Build Grammar Skills

❸ **Coordinating Conjunctions** Challenge students to analyze why the coordinating conjunction *but* is a better choice here than *and*. *Antigone is saying that the people agree with her; however, they are afraid to speak up. She is contrasting the ideas expressed in the two clauses. The coordinating conjunction* and *would simply add one clause to the other, but would not contrast them.*

◆ Critical Thinking

❹ **Evaluate** Allow time for students to debate the merits of Creon's and Antigone's arguments.

Customize for
Logical/Mathematical Learners

Have these students order the events leading up to Antigone's arrest and sentencing on a timeline. Remind students that even events that occur offstage must be included.

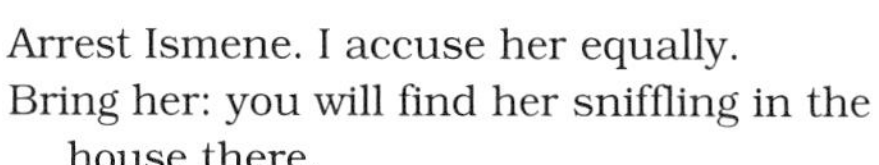

Arrest Ismene. I accuse her equally.
Bring her: you will find her sniffling in the house there.

❶ Her mind's a traitor: crimes kept in the dark
Cry for light, and the guardian brain shudders;
But how much worse than this
Is brazen boasting of barefaced anarchy!

ANTIGONE. Creon, what more do you want than my death?

❷ **CREON.** Nothing.
That gives me everything.

ANTIGONE. Then I beg you: kill me.
This talking is a great weariness: your words
Are distasteful to me, and I am sure that mine
Seem so to you. And yet they should not seem so:
I should have praise and honor for what I have done.
All these men here would praise me
Were their lips not frozen shut with fear of you.

[*Bitterly*]
Ah the good fortune of kings,
Licensed to say and do whatever they please!

CREON. You are alone here in that opinion.

❸ **ANTIGONE.** No, they are with me. But they keep their tongues in leash.

CREON. Maybe. But you are guilty, and they are not.

ANTIGONE. There is no guilt in reverence for the dead.

CREON. But Eteocles—was he not your brother too?

ANTIGONE. My brother too.

CREON. And you insult his memory?

ANTIGONE. [*Softly*] The dead man would not say that I insult it.

CREON. He would: for you honor a traitor as much as him.

ANTIGONE. His own brother, traitor or not, and equal in blood.

CREON. He made war on his country. Eteocles defended it.

ANTIGONE. Nevertheless, there are honors due all the dead.

CREON. But not the same for the wicked as for the just.

ANTIGONE. Ah Creon, Creon,
Which of us can say what the gods hold wicked?

CREON. An enemy is an enemy, even dead.

ANTIGONE. It is my nature to join in love, not hate.

CREON. [*Finally losing patience*] Go join them, then; if you must have your love,
Find it in hell!

CHORAGOS. But see, Ismene comes:

[*Enter* ISMENE, *guarded*.]

Humanities: Architecture

Amphitheater Sophocles' tragedies were formally performed in *amphitheaters,* open-air structures built expressly for public performances. (See the photograph on p. 667.) *Amphi-* means "on both sides," or "around," and an amphitheater is designed to place the audience on tiers of seats around the action of a play. The bowl-like structure of Greek amphitheaters resulted in remarkable acoustic properties; audiences could hear the actors' voices clearly, even when they spoke quietly.

A typical amphitheater might seat the audience in a semicircle facing the *proscenium,* or the front of the stage. At either side between audience and stage would be a corridor called a *parodos,* through which the chorus might enter.

The most famous amphitheater in the world, the Coliseum, is Roman, not Greek. Roman amphitheaters were often built to house gladiatorial contests rather than dramas. The stages of Roman amphitheaters were raised above the level on which the chorus performed; those of Greek theaters were set at the same level as the chorus's acting area, or *orchestra.*

Have students describe any experiences they have had with outdoor performances, either dramatic or musical.

Those tears are sisterly, the cloud
That shadows her eyes rains down gentle sorrow.

CREON. You too, Ismene,
Snake in my ordered house, sucking my blood
Stealthily—and all the time I never knew
❺ That these two sisters were aiming at my throne!
Ismene,
Do you confess your share in this crime, or deny it?
Answer me.

ISMENE. Yes, if she will let me say so. I am guilty.

❻ **ANTIGONE.** [*Coldly*] No, Ismene. You have no right to say so.
You would not help me, and I will not have you help me.

❼ **ISMENE.** But now I know what you meant; and I am here
To join you, to take my share of punishment.

ANTIGONE. The dead man and the gods who rule the dead
Know whose act this was. Words are not friends.

ISMENE. Do you refuse me, Antigone? I want to die with you:
I too have a duty that I must discharge to the dead.

ANTIGONE. You shall not lessen my death by sharing it.

ISMENE. What do I care for life when you are dead?

ANTIGONE. Ask Creon. You're always hanging on his opinions.

ISMENE. You are laughing at me. Why, Antigone?

ANTIGONE. It's a joyless laughter, Ismene.

ISMENE. But can I do nothing?

ANTIGONE. Yes. Save yourself. I shall not envy you.
There are those who will praise you; I shall have honor, too.

ISMENE. But we are equally guilty!

ANTIGONE. No more, Ismene.
You are alive, but I belong to Death.

❽ **CREON.** [*To the* CHORUS] Gentlemen, I beg you to observe these girls:
One has just now lost her mind; the other,
It seems, has never had a mind at all.

ISMENE. Grief teaches the steadiest minds to waver, King.

CREON. Yours certainly did, when you assumed guilt with the guilty!

ISMENE. But how could I go on living without her?

CREON. You are.
She is already dead.

ISMENE. But your own son's bride!

CREON. There are places enough for him to push his plow.
I want no wicked women for my sons!

ISMENE. O dearest Haimon, how your father wrongs you!

CREON. I've had enough of your childish talk of marriage!

CHORAGOS. Do you really intend to steal this girl from your son?

CREON. No; Death will do that for me.

CHORAGOS. Then she must die?

CREON. [*Ironically*] You dazzle me.
—But enough of this talk!
❾ [*To* GUARDS] You, there, take them away and guard them well:
For they are but women, and even brave men run
When they see Death coming.

[*Exit* ISMENE, ANTIGONE, *and* GUARDS.]

◆ Literary Focus

❺ Protagonist and Antagonist Ask students why Creon thinks Antigone and Ismene have betrayed him. *He thinks they are trying to take power away from him.*

◆ Reading Strategy

❻ Question the Characters' Motives Have students speculate on the possible reasons that Antigone will not allow Ismene to help her. *Students may say that Antigone is offended because Ismene is offering her help too late, that Antigone wants to protect Ismene, or that Antigone wants all the glory of defiance for herself.*

◆ Reading Strategy

❼ Question the Characters' Motives Ismene feared death earlier in the play. Discuss with students why, now, she wants to die, even though she is innocent of any crime against the state. *Students may say that Ismene feels guilty for not supporting her sister, or perhaps she feels guilty for not obeying the law of the gods.*

◆ Critical Thinking

❽ Interpret Which of the sisters does Creon think "lost her mind"? Which "never had a mind"? *Suggested answer: Creon is saying that Ismene has just lost her mind when she decided to join Antigone. To Creon, Antigone's actions have been mad all along, so she "never had a mind."*

◆ Critical Thinking

❾ Make Judgments Creon feels that the women require guarding because they will naturally try to escape their fate. Ask students: How accurate is Creon's assessment of Antigone and Ismene? *He may be right about Ismene, but Antigone has no fear of death; she is braver than the "brave men" Creon mentions.*

Humanities: Literature

Tragedy Then and Now While Sophocles fulfilled the requirements for tragedy set forth by Aristotle in his *Poetics,* drama evolved and changed over history, so that modern dramatists do not now feel they must remain within the confines of Aristotle's famous definition. Willy Loman in Arthur Miller's *Death of a Salesman,* and Blanche Dubois in Tennessee Williams's *A Streetcar Named Desire,* for example, are neither of noble birth nor character. They are, on the other hand, very ordinary characters with whom the audience can more easily identify.

Two other requirements for tragedy, however, do survive in modern drama: that the audience be made to feel "pity and terror," and that at the end, a "catharsis," a cleansing, purification, or purging of the emotions, takes place. In other words, the audience sympathizes with and fears for the protagonist, and then feels emotionally drained or exhausted at the end of the play.

Lead students to identify the sources of pity, terror, and catharsis in tragic plots of movies they have seen, and in *Antigone,* as they progress through the play.

Reinforce and Extend

Answers

◆ ***Literature and Your Life***

Reader's Response Those students who agree with Antigone might respond that to bury a beloved brother is only decent and natural, regardless of the consequences. Those who agree with Ismene may say that nothing is accomplished by disobeying Creon's order.

Thematic Focus Although students will recall that the proclaimed punishment was stoning, they may feel there is still time for Creon to relent. Most students will probably feel that Antigone's courage will enable her to face whatever consequences Creon chooses.

☑ **Check Your Comprehension**

1. Polyneices fought as bravely as his honored brother, Eteocles. Antigone feels that burying him would be a holy crime, obeying the supreme authority of the gods.
2. Creon reacts in a violent rage.

◆ Critical Thinking

1. Ismene means that women are not as physically strong as men, nor are they trained as soldiers. In addition, her words reflect that women were seen as lower than men in ancient Greek society.
2. While some students may understand Ismene's fear, others may feel that for some beliefs, no price is too high.
3. This statement shows Creon's inflexibility and lack of judgment as a new ruler. To demonstrate his power, he is willing to punish someone even after the person is dead. Some students may argue that the dead can have no enemies.
4. In Thebes, Creon governed by his will, whether it be good or ill. A modern (democratic) government is set up with laws to restrain and balance the powers that affect its citizens.

Ode II

CHORUS. [STROPHE 1]

Fortunate is the man who has never tasted
 God's vengeance!
Where once the anger of heaven has struck,
 that house is shaken
Forever: damnation rises behind each child
Like a wave cresting out of the black
 northeast,
When the long darkness undersea roars up
And bursts drumming death upon the
 windwhipped sand.

[ANTISTROPHE 1]

I have seen this gathering sorrow from time
 long past
Loom upon Oedipus' children: generation
 from generation
Takes the compulsive rage of the enemy
 god.
So lately this last flower of Oedipus' line
Drank the sunlight! but now a passionate
 word
And a handful of dust have closed up all its
 beauty.

[STROPHE 2]

 What mortal arrogance
 Transcends the wrath of Zeus?[7]
Sleep cannot lull him, nor the effortless
 long months
Of the timeless gods: but he is young
 forever,
And his house is the shining day of high
 Olympos.[8]
 All that is and shall be,
 And all the past, is his.
No pride on earth is free of the curse of
 heaven.

[ANTISTROPHE 2]

 The straying dreams of men
 May bring them ghosts of joy:
But as they drowse, the waking embers
 burn them;
Or they walk with fixed eyes, as blind men
 walk.
But the ancient wisdom speaks for our
 own time:
 Fate works most for woe
 With Folly's fairest show.
Man's little pleasure is the spring of sorrow.

7. Zeus (zo͞os): King of all Greek gods, he was believed to throw lightning bolts when angry.
8. Olympos (ō lim´ pəs): Mountain in Greece, also known as Olympus, where the gods were believed to live in ease and splendor.

◆ Build Vocabulary

transcends (tran sendz´) *v.*: Goes above or beyond limits; exceeds

Guide for Responding

◆ *Literature and Your Life*

Reader's Response Antigone and Ismene disagree over the burial of Polyneices. With whom do you agree?

Thematic Focus Antigone chooses to do what she thinks is right, rather than give in to Creon's law. What consequences do you think she will face as a result of her choices?

☑ **Check Your Comprehension**

1. Why does Antigone feel that her brother should get a proper burial?
2. How does Creon react to the news of Polyneices' burial?

◆ Critical Thinking

INTERPRET

1. Explain what Ismene means when she says, "We are only women, / We cannot fight with men, Antigone!" **[Interpret]**
2. How might Ismene's advice to her sister seem cowardly to some readers? **[Analyze]**
3. In his argument with Antigone, Creon declares "An enemy is an enemy, even dead." What does he mean? Do you agree? **[Interpret]**

EXTEND

4. Compare and contrast the government of Creon in Thebes with a modern-day government. **[Social Studies Link]**

Reteach

To reinforce the reading strategy, questioning the characters' motives, you may choose to rephrase the technique. Ask students to analyze what makes each character behave the way he or she does. Suggest that students draw two-column charts to analyze characters' motives.

Character	Motive

Have them review the character list on p. 670 and list the main characters. Then suggest that they review the play up to this point to analyze the motives for each character. Suggest that students ask themselves questions such as these:

- Why does the character take certain actions?
- If I put myself in the character's place, what actions might I take and why?

Questioning the motives of the characters will enhance understanding of the plot and conflict found in the drama.

Guide for Responding (continued)

◆ Reading Strategy

QUESTION THE CHARACTERS' MOTIVES

To fully understand the action of the play, **question the characters' motives.**

1. What was Ismene's motive for not going along with Antigone at first?
2. What is Antigone's motive for burying Polyneices?
3. What is Creon's motive for insisting on Antigone's death?

◆ Literary Focus

PROTAGONIST AND ANTAGONIST

A **protagonist** is the main character of a literary work, and an **antagonist** is a character or force in conflict with the main character.

1. Describe the conflict between Antigone and Creon.
2. What qualities of each character contribute to the conflict?
3. Give examples of actions and feelings that show that Antigone is the protagonist and Creon is the antagonist.

◆ Build Vocabulary

USING THE LATIN PREFIX *trans-*

Knowing that the Latin prefix *trans-* means "through," "above," or "across" will help you define other words that contain *trans-*. On your paper, match each word with its appropriate definition.

1. transparent	**a.** send through the air
2. transmit	**b.** lift up and move
3. transplant	**c.** pierce through
4. transfix	**d.** lets light shine through

USING THE WORD BANK: Definitions

Copy the words from Column A into your notebook. Next to each word, write the letter of its definition from Column B.

Column A	Column B
1. sated	**a.** pointedly
2. anarchists	**b.** oppressively hot or moist
3. sententiously	**c.** go above or beyond the limit
4. sultry	**d.** satisfied or pleased
5. transcend	**e.** those who disrespect rules

◆ Build Grammar Skills

COORDINATING CONJUNCTIONS

A **coordinating conjunction** links two words or grammatical structures of equal importance.

Practice Rewrite each pair of sentences as one sentence, with the coordinating conjunction *but, for, or,* or *and.* Choose the conjunction based on the way ideas are linked.

1. Antigone wants to bury her brother. Ismene is afraid to break the law that Creon decreed.
2. Oedipus learned the truth of what he had done. Antigone accompanied her father into exile.
3. Both Antigone and Ismene grieved. Their brothers killed each other during battle.
4. Ismene could choose to stand up to Creon. She could accept scorn from her sister, Antigone.

Writing Application Write a summary of *Antigone* from the Prologue through Scene 2. Combine clauses using each of the following coordinating conjunctions at least once: *yet, for, and,* and *but.*

Idea Bank

Writing

1. Newspaper Article Write a brief newspaper article with a headline that would have appeared in a Thebes newspaper (if newspapers existed then) the day after Polyneices was buried. Answer the questions *who? what? where? when? why?* in your article.

2. Letter Imagine that you are Ismene. Write a letter to your sister, Antigone, before her arrest by the sentry. What would you tell her about her plans to bury Polyneices? How would you present this delicate situation?

Speaking, Listening, and Viewing

3. Readers Theatre With a small group, rehearse and present a scene from *Antigone* in a Readers Theatre performance for your class. Have a group of students perform as the chorus and assign individuals for the other roles. **[Performing Arts Link]**

Answers

◆ Reading Strategy

1. Ismene's motive is fear for her life.
2. Antigone's motives are love for her brother, honor and loyalty to the gods, and a belief in divine law.
3. As a new ruler he must establish himself as all powerful.

◆ Literary Focus

1. The conflict centers on which is more important: human, civil law or divine law and family loyalty.
2. Antigone's loyalty to her brother, her strong character, and her refusal to compromise her ideals contribute to her conflict with Creon, who is inflexible, proud, and fearful of any challenge to his authority.
3. Antigone is a sympathetic character who readers want to see succeed because her actions seem admirable and noble. Creon's character is not sympathetic because his actions seem cruel and self-promoting.

◆ Build Vocabulary

Using the Latin Prefix *trans-*
1. d. 2. a. 3. b. 4. c.

Using the Word Bank
1. d. 2. e. 3. a. 4. b. 5. c.

◆ Build Grammar Skills

Practice

1. Antigone wants to bury her brother, *but* Ismene is afraid to break the law that Creon decreed.
2. Oedipus learned the truth of what he had done, *and* Antigone accompanied her father into exile.
3. Both Antigone and Ismene grieved, *for* their brothers killed each other during battle.
4. Ismene could choose to stand up to Creon, *or* she could accept scorn from her sister, Antigone.

Idea Bank

Customizing for *Performance Levels*

Following are suggestions for matching Idea Bank topics with your students' performance levels:
Less Advanced: 2
Average: 1
More Advanced: 1, 3

Customizing for *Learning Modalities*

Following are the suggestions for matching Idea Bank topics with your students' learning modalities:
Verbal/Linguistic: 1, 2, 3
Interpersonal: 1, 2
Intrapersonal: 3

✓ ASSESSMENT OPTIONS

Formal Assessment Selection Test, pp. 170–172, Assessment Resources Software. The selection test is designed so that it can be easily customized to the ability levels of your students.

PORTFOLIO ASSESSMENT

Use the following rubrics in ***Alternative Assessment*** to assess student writing:
Newspaper Article: Summary Rubric
Letter: Expression Rubric

Grammar Reinforcement

For additional instruction and practice, use the lesson in the **Writing Lab CD-ROM** on Eight Parts of Speech, and p. 22 on Conjunctions and Interjections and p. 120 on Sentence Combining in *Writer's Solution Grammar Practice Book.*

Prepare and Engage

LESSON OBJECTIVES

1. **To develop vocabulary and word identification skills**
   - Greek Roots: *-chor-*
   - Using the Word Bank: Synonyms
   - Extending Word Study: Use Reference Materials (ATE)
2. **To use a variety of reading strategies to comprehend a Greek drama**
   - Connect Your Experience
   - Reading Strategy: Identify With a Character
   - Tips to Guide Reading (ATE)
   - Read to Appreciate an Author's Craft (ATE)
   - Idea Bank: Final Speech
3. **To increase knowledge of other cultures and to connect common elements across cultures**
   - Connecting Themes Across Cultures (ATE)
   - Beyond Literature: Cultural Connection
4. **To express and support responses to the text**
   - Critical Thinking
   - Idea Bank: Introduction
   - Idea Bank: Editorial
   - Idea Bank: Film Response
5. **To analyze literary elements**
   - Literary Focus: Tragic Character
6. **To read in order to research self-selected and assigned topics**
   - Idea Bank: Multimedia Presentation
   - Viewing and Representing Mini-Lesson (ATE)
   - Research Skills Mini-Lesson (ATE)
7. **To plan, prepare, organize, and present literary interpretations**
   - Idea Bank: Mock Trial
8. **To use recursive writing processes to write a scene of conflict**
   - Guided Writing Lesson
9. **To increase knowledge of the rules of grammar and usage**
   - Build Grammar Skills: Pronoun Case in Incomplete Clauses

Test Preparation

Reading Comprehension: Notice Word Choice (ATE, p. 685) The teaching tips and sample test item in this workshop support the instruction and practice in the unit workshop:

Reading Comprehension: Characteristics of Text (SE, p. 809)

Guide for Reading

◆ Review and Anticipate

In Scenes 1 and 2, Antigone decides to give her brother Polyneices a proper burial, defying the orders of her uncle Creon, the ruler of Thebes. When Creon finds out, he orders her put to death, claiming that he cannot allow her to disobey him just because she is his niece. Both Creon and Antigone seem locked in a course of action by circumstances and their beliefs. As Scene 2 ends, the Chorus sings, "*Fate works most for woe / With Folly's fairest show. /* Man's little pleasure is the spring of sorrow." Notice how the events in the remainder of the play carry out the statement that Fate works most for woe.

◆ Literary Focus

Tragic Character

In this play, two strong-willed people, Creon and Antigone, can both be seen as tragic. A **tragic character** is a significant person who experiences a reversal of fortune as a result of fate or a flaw or weakness in his or her character. Critics debate who the tragic hero is in *Antigone*. Some claim Creon fits the definition better, although Antigone's name has been used in the title. The exchanges between Creon and Antigone lead to an irreversible point from which Creon's pride will not allow him to retreat. His actions bring about the tragic events that follow. Others see the flaw in Antigone. To them, her determination is a form of pride, which makes her unyielding and leads to her doom.

◆ Build Grammar Skills

Pronoun Case in Incomplete Clauses

In certain kinds of English constructions, some words are omitted because they are understood. When a pronoun occurs in an **incomplete clause,** its case is what it would be if the construction were complete. Clauses beginning with *than* or *as* are often incomplete. Look at this line from Scene 3:

Let's lose to a man, at least! Is a woman stronger than we?

The understood word in this line is *are*. The completed clause therefore would be "Is a woman stronger than *we are*?" When you complete the clause, you can see that *we* is the correct pronoun; you would not say, "Is a woman stronger than *us are*?"

◆ Reading Strategy

Identify With a Character

When you **identify with a character**, you put yourself in the character's place. Because you take on his or her feelings or issues, and you experience what he or she does, you sympathize with that character. You may even feel as if you *are* that character. For example, you may suffer with Antigone as she struggles to do what she thinks is right, or you may feel Ismene's fear of punishment. Putting yourself in a character's place can give you greater insight into that character's motives and the events of the play.

◆ Build Vocabulary

Greek Roots: *-chor-*

An important feature of Greek tragedy is the chorus; a member of the chorus is called a *chorister*. The root of *chorister* and *chorus* is *-chor-*, which comes from Terpsichore (terp sik′ ə rē), the Greek Muse of dance and song.

Word Bank

Before you read, preview this list of words from the play.

deference
vile
piety
blasphemy
lamentation
chorister

Prentice Hall Literature Program Resources

REINFORCE / RETEACH / EXTEND

Selection Support
Build Vocabulary: Word Roots: *-chor-*, p. 200
Build Grammar Skills: Pronoun Case, p. 201
Reading Strategy: Identify With a Character, p. 202
Literary Focus: Tragic Character, p. 203

Strategies for Diverse Students Needs, p. 49

Beyond Literature
Government in Ancient Greece, p. 49

Daily Language Practice Week 12, Greek Theater, p. 28

Formal Assessment Selection Test, pp. 173–175; Assessment Resources Software

Alternative Assessment, p. 49

Writing and Language Transparencies
Daily Language Practice, Week 12, p. 123

Art Transparencies
Transparency 15

Resource Pro CD-ROM

Listening to Literature Audiocassettes

ANTIGONE

SCENES 3 THROUGH 5

Sophocles

Translated by Dudley Fitts and Robert Fitzgerald

Scene 3

CHORAGOS. But here is Haimon, King, the last of all your sons.
Is it grief for Antigone that brings him here,
And bitterness at being robbed of his bride?

[*Enter* HAIMON.]

CREON. We shall soon see, and no need of diviners.[1]
—Son,
You have heard my final judgment on that girl:
Have you come here hating me, or have you come
With deference and with love, whatever I do?

HAIMON. I am your son, father. You are my guide.
You make things clear for me, and I obey you.
No marriage means more to me than your continuing wisdom. ❶

CREON. Good. That is the way to behave: subordinate
Everything else, my son, to your father's will.
This is what a man prays for, that he may get
Sons attentive and dutiful in his house, ❷
Each one hating his father's enemies,
Honoring his father's friends. But if his sons
Fail him, if they turn out unprofitably,
What has he fathered but trouble for himself
And amusement for the malicious? ❸
So you are right
Not to lose your head over this woman.
Your pleasure with her would soon grow cold, Haimon,
And then you'd have a hellcat in bed and elsewhere.
Let her find her husband in Hell!
Of all the people in this city, only she
Has had contempt for my law and broken it.

Do you want me to show myself weak before the people?
Or to break my sworn word? No, and I will not.
The woman dies.
I suppose she'll plead "family ties." Well, let her. ❹

1. **diviners** (də vin′ ərz): Those who forecast the future.

◆ Build Vocabulary

deference (def′ ər əns) *n.*: Yielding in thought

Develop Understanding

One-Minute Insight As the events in the second part of *Antigone* unfold, we watch Creon and Antigone move inexorably toward their respective fates. The events set in motion through their own strong-willed choices seem fated to lead each character to his or her downfall.

Customize for
Less Proficient Readers and English Language Learners
To help these students continue through the second part of the play, review with them the list of characters' names and the relationships between the characters.

◆ Reading Strategy

❶ **Identify With a Character** Ask students if they think that Haimon really means what he says. Why does he say this? *Students may say that Haimon, hoping that Creon might be persuaded to spare Antigone, is being careful not to antagonize or goad his father.*

◆ Critical Thinking

❷ **Predict** Invite students to predict whether Haimon will continue to be the kind of son his father praises. How will Creon feel if Haimon ceases to be "attentive and dutiful"? *Students may predict that Haimon will oppose his father. Creon places tremendous importance on the dutiful qualities in a son, and therefore will be emotionally devastated later.*

◆ Reading Strategy

❸ **Identify With a Character** Invite students to suggest what motives, personal or political, might lie behind this statement. *Creon wants his son to see things his way. Also, his authority as king could be weakened if Haimon were seen to oppose him.*

◆ Critical Thinking

❹ **Analyze** Ask students how Creon's present circumstances as a ruler might affect the attitude he takes in this passage. *Creon is intent on not showing any sign of weakness that could undermine his authority in Thebes.*

Test Preparation Workshop

Reading Comprehension: Notice Word Choice To help students prepare for standardized tests, offer them practice in analyzing the characteristics of texts. Use this sample test item to help students notice the effect of word choice.

Antigone is a stubborn young woman who will not give into the law of the land. Her sister Ismene begs desperately with her to change her mind, but Antigone will have none of her sister's pleading.

In this passage, the word *stubborn*—

A shows the writer's attitude toward Antigone
B provides a fact about Antigone
C shows how Antigone felt about herself
D shows how Ismene felt about Antigone

Since the word *stubborn* reveals bias, students should consider answers *A, C,* and *D*. There is not enough information in the passage to support *C* or *D*. Answer *A* is the best choice.

◆ Literary Focus

❶ **Tragic Character** Ask students to identify a quality in Creon's character, suggested in this passage, that might drive him into a conflict that cannot be resolved. *Lead students to point out Creon's rigidity and tendency to see any deviation from submission to his will as "anarchy," and a threat to the state.*

◆ Reading Strategy

❷ **Identify With a Character** Ask students to put themselves in Haimon's place and indicate, based on what they know of his character, what they think his concerns are as he speaks, and to explain their answers. Is he more concerned with Antigone or with public opinion toward his father? *Haimon seems more concerned about his father's reputation. However, he is probably using this argument to achieve his real purpose—saving Antigone.*

◆ Literary Focus

❸ **Tragic Character** Haimon points out that Creon has a temper and that he is not willing to listen rationally to the opinions of others.

Tips to Guide Reading

Sustained Reading Students will find it easier to follow the details of the plot if they read the play in a sustained manner without stopping.

Customize for *Pre-AP Students*

Suggest that students analyze the entire play and choose what they consider to be the best part and the worst part. Have them write short explanations citing the reasons they chose each part. Students can then exchange ideas with classmates in small group discussions.

Customize for *Gifted/Talented Students*

Have students evaluate the play and decide what Creon might have done that would have been fairer and brought about a happier ending. Suggest that they write their "happy" ending in a screenplay format.

If I permit my own family to rebel,
How shall I earn the world's obedience?
Show me the man who keeps his house in hand,
He's fit for public authority.
I'll have no dealings
❶ With lawbreakers, critics of the government:
Whoever is chosen to govern should be obeyed—
Must be obeyed, in all things, great and small,
Just and unjust! O Haimon,
The man who knows how to obey, and that man only,
Knows how to give commands when the time comes.
You can depend on him, no matter how fast
The spears come: he's a good soldier, he'll stick it out.

Anarchy, anarchy! Show me a greater evil!
This is why cities tumble and the great houses rain down,
This is what scatters armies!

No, no: good lives are made so by discipline.
We keep the laws then, and the lawmakers,
And no woman shall seduce us. If we must lose,
Let's lose to a man, at least! Is a woman stronger than we?

CHORAGOS. Unless time has rusted my wits,
What you say, King, is said with point and dignity.

HAIMON. [*Boyishly earnest*] Father:
Reason is God's crowning gift to man, and you are right
To warn me against losing mine. I cannot say—
❷ I hope that I shall never want to say!—that you
Have reasoned badly. Yet there are other men
Who can reason, too; and their opinions might be helpful.
You are not in a position to know everything
That people say or do, or what they feel:
Your temper terrifies them—everyone
Will tell you only what you like to hear.
But I, at any rate, can listen; and I have heard them
Muttering and whispering in the dark about this girl.
They say no woman has ever, so unreasonably,
Died so shameful a death for a generous act:
"She covered her brother's body. Is this indecent?
She kept him from dogs and vultures. Is this a crime?
Death?—She should have all the honor that we can give her!"

This is the way they talk out there in the city.

You must believe me:
Nothing is closer to me than your happiness.
What could be closer? Must not any son
Value his father's fortune as his father does his?
I beg you, do not be unchangeable:
Do not believe that you alone can be right.
The man who thinks that,
The man who maintains that only he has the power
To reason correctly, the gift to speak, the soul—
A man like that, when you know him, turns out empty.

It is not reason never to yield to reason!

In flood time you can see how some trees bend,
And because they bend, even their twigs are safe,
While stubborn trees are torn up, roots and all.
And the same thing happens in sailing:
Make your sheet fast, never slacken—and

> **◆ Literary Focus**
> What traits does Haimon point out to Creon that make the king a tragic character?

◆ Build Vocabulary

vile (vīl) *adj.*: Extremely disgusting

Block Scheduling Strategies

Consider these suggestions to take advantage of extended class time:

- Invite students to listen to part or all of the selection recording. Hold a discussion in which they explain how hearing the dialogue spoken aloud enhanced their appreciation of the drama.
- Allow time for students to visit an electronic museum exhibit of life in ancient Greece. For Internet address, see p. 699.
- Use Daily Language Practice for Week 12. You may put the transparency on an overhead projector and have students write the passages correctly or you may dictate the passages to students.
- As a class, complete the Literary Focus page on tragic character in ***Selection Support***, p. 203. After students have read the selection, allow them to meet in groups to complete the Literary Focus questions on p. 699.
- Organize discussion groups in which students can explore the strengths and weaknesses of Haimon's and Creon's arguments.

over you go,
Head over heels and under: and there's your voyage.
Forget you are angry! Let yourself be moved!
I know I am young; but please let me say this:
The ideal condition
Would be, I admit, that men should be right by instinct;
But since we are all too likely to go astray,
The reasonable thing is to learn from those who can teach.

CHORAGOS. You will do well to listen to him, King,
If what he says is sensible. And you, Haimon,
Must listen to your father.—Both speak well.

CREON. You consider it right for a man of my years and experience
To go to school to a boy?

HAIMON. It is not right
If I am wrong. But if I am young, and right,
What does my age matter?

CREON. You think it right to stand up for an anarchist?

HAIMON. Not at all. I pay no respect to criminals.

CREON. Then she is not a criminal?

HAIMON. The City would deny it, to a man.

CREON. And the City proposes to teach me how to rule?

HAIMON. Ah. Who is it that's talking like a boy now?

CREON. My voice is the one voice giving orders in this City!

HAIMON. It is no City if it takes orders from one voice.

CREON. The State is the King!

HAIMON. Yes, if the State is a desert.

[*Pause*]

CREON. This boy, it seems, has sold out to a woman.

HAIMON. If you are a woman: my concern is only for you.

CREON. So? Your "concern"! In a public brawl with your father!

HAIMON. How about you, in a public brawl with justice?

CREON. With justice, when all that I do is within my rights? **6**

HAIMON. You have no right to trample on God's right.

CREON. [*Completely out of control*] Fool, adolescent fool! Taken in by a woman!

HAIMON. You'll never see me taken in by anything vile.

CREON. Every word you say is for her!

HAIMON. [*quietly, darkly*] And for you.
And for me. And for the gods under the earth.

CREON. You'll never marry her while she lives.

HAIMON. Then she must die.—But her death will cause another. **7**

CREON. Another?
Have you lost your senses? Is this an open threat?

HAIMON. There is no threat in speaking to emptiness.

CREON. I swear you'll regret this superior tone of yours!
You are the empty one!

HAIMON. If you were not my father,
I'd say you were perverse.

CREON. You girlstruck fool, don't play at words with me! **8**

HAIMON. I am sorry. You prefer silence.

> ◆ **Reading Strategy**
> In what ways can you identify with Haimon in this scene?

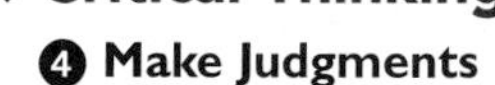

◆ Critical Thinking

4 Make Judgments Invite students to summarize Creon's and Haimon's arguments in this passage. Then present them with a choice: Who presents the more convincing argument? *Creon implies that a man's judgment will always be better than a boy's. Then he argues that Antigone broke the law; she is a criminal, and therefore Haimon should not stand up for her. Haimon argues that age is immaterial; what counts is who is right. He then implies that, if most people in the city deny that Antigone is a criminal, she must not be one. Students should note that, while Haimon makes a good point about the irrelevance of age in an argument, Creon's argument against Antigone is stronger than Haimon's argument in her favor.*

◆ Critical Thinking

5 Compare and Contrast Ask students to compare the political positions expressed by Creon and Haimon. *Students may say that Creon represents a tyrannical position—that a city must be ruled by one person. Haimon believes that no one person can rule without the consent of his or her subjects.*

◆ Critical Thinking

6 Compare and Contrast Ask students to indicate what concepts of "justice" Creon and Haimon argue for. *Elicit answers to the effect that Creon speaks of "justice" in purely legal or civic terms, while Haimon claims to represent divine justice, that set down by the gods.*

◆ Critical Thinking

7 Interpret Ask students to explain how Creon has interpreted Haimon's previous statement. *Students should explain that Creon sees the statement that Antigone's "death will cause another" as a threat on Haimon's part; that Haimon will take Creon's life.*

◆ Reading Strategy

8 Identify With a Character Students will probably identify with the frustration Haimon feels at being unable to reason with his father; this has led him to abandon attempts at persuasion and fall into name-calling.

Cultural Connection

Enrichment: The Library of Alexandria
Besides *Antigone*, six other tragedies by Sophocles survive today, as well as seven by Aeschylus, and eighteen by Euripides. But historical records cite many other plays by these and other playwrights. Where are these plays? What happened to them?

In the early third century B.C., Ptolemy I, ruler of Egypt, built in the city of Alexandria a library to house all of Greek literature, or as much as could be found. He and Ptolemy II collected approximately 700,000 works over the years. The library at Alexandria was the first important library in the world and remained a center for scholars until 47 B.C.

In that year, the library burned, and most of its collection was lost. Some think that Roman soldiers under Octavius Caesar may have been guilty, but the fire might have been accidental. In addition to this great loss, some Greek literature, including dramas, was destroyed by officials of Roman libraries because they were deemed unfit to be saved for posterity. As a result, only a small fraction of the total output of the great Greek dramatists survives.

◆ Literary Focus

❶ Tragic Character Have students discuss what they think Creon hopes to achieve if he carries out this threat. Do they think his motive is revenge and anger or something else? Remind students to base their answers on what they know of Creon. *Based on what students have learned about Creon, they should say that Creon needs to show the city of Thebes that no act against the state will go unpunished. He is making an example of Antigone. His pride and stubbornness blind him to the potential consequences Haimon warns him against.*

◆ Critical Thinking

❷ Evaluate Encourage students to evaluate the significance of providing food to the condemned person. *Students should recognize that in a society as bound by ritual and convention as ancient Greek society is, the providing of food is a symbol that indicates that the state did not actually kill the condemned person, but that some other force intervened. This is consistent with the Greek concept of fate.*

Customize for *Interpersonal Learners*

Ask students to work in small groups and discuss whether they would prefer to have Antigone or Ismene for a friend. Which qualities in each would make that person a more valuable friend? Then ask students which character they would prefer to have as a sister. If their response is different, ask students why they might look for qualities in a friend different from the qualities they would value in a close relative.

CREON. Now, by God—!
I swear, by all the gods in heaven above us,
You'll watch it, I swear you shall!

❶ [*To the* SERVANTS] Bring her out!
Bring the woman out! Let her die before
his eyes!
Here, this instant, with her bridegroom
beside her!

HAIMON. Not here, no; she will not die here,
King.
And you will never see my face again.
Go on raving as long as you've a friend to
endure you.

[*Exit* HAIMON.]

CHORAGOS. Gone, gone.
Creon,a young man in a rage is dangerous!

CREON. Let him do, or dream to do, more
than a man can.
He shall not save these girls from death.

CHORAGOS. These girls?
You have sentenced them both?

CREON. No, you are right.
I will not kill the one whose hands are
clean.

CHORAGOS. But Antigone?

CREON. [*Somberly*] I will carry her far away
Out there in the wilderness, and lock her
❷ Living in a vault of stone. She shall have
food,
As the custom is, to absolve the State of her
death.
And there let her pray to the gods of hell:
They are her only gods:
Perhaps they will show her an escape from
death,
Or she may learn,
though late,
That piety shown the dead is pity in vain.

[*Exit* CREON.]

Ode III

CHORUS. [STROPHE]
Love, unconquerable
Waster of rich men, keeper
Of warm lights and all-night vigil
In the soft face of a girl:
Sea-wanderer, forest-visitor!
Even the pure Immortals cannot escape
you,
And mortal man, in his one day's dusk,
Trembles before your glory.

[ANTISTROPHE]
Surely you swerve upon ruin
The just man's consenting heart,
As here you have made bright anger
Strike between father and son—
And none has conquered but Love!
A girl's glance working the will of heaven:
Pleasure to her alone who mocks us,
Merciless Aphrodite.[2]

---

2. **Aphrodite** (af rə dit′ ē): Goddess of beauty and love, who is sometimes vengeful in her retaliation for offenses.

◆ Build Vocabulary

piety (pī′ ə tē) *n.*: Holiness; respect for the divine

blasphemy (blas′ fə mē) *n.*: Disrespectful action or speech against a deity

Research Skills Mini-Lesson

Select a Specific Topic

Introduce Many assignments for the school curriculum require students to conduct research. Although often an assignment will be specific, sometimes the subject is broad. In those cases, students need to narrow the scope of the topic before they begin.

Develop Ask students to consider a very general assignment such as the following: "Write a 200-word report about *Sophocles.*" Point out that pages and pages have been devoted to scholarly writings about Sophocles. The topic as given in this assignment is not specific enough to be researched unless it is narrowed.

Apply Have students work in pairs to develop a list of questions designed to narrow the broad topic down to a specific one. They may come up with questions such as:

- What do I want to know about Sophocles?
- Should I cover his life or his writings?
- Do I want to use examples of his plays?

Hold a class discussion to pool the lists of questions and brainstorm a class tip list on how best to narrow a broad assignment topic into a manageable project Finally ask students to produce a narrow topic that suits the following assignment: "Write a 200-word report on *Antigone.*"

Assess Assess students on their ability to produce a manageable research question. Use the class tips to guide assessment.

Scene 4

CHORAGOS. [*As* ANTIGONE *enters guarded*] But
I can no longer stand in awe of this,
Nor, seeing what I see, keep back my tears.
Here is Antigone, passing to that chamber
Where all find sleep at last.

ANTIGONE. [STROPHE 1]
Look upon me, friends, and pity me
Turning back at the night's edge to say
Good-by to the sun that shines for me no longer;
❸ Now sleepy Death
Summons me down to Acheron,[3] that cold shore:
There is no bridesong there, nor any music.

CHORUS. Yet not unpraised, not without a kind of honor,
You walk at last into the underworld;
❹ Untouched by sickness, broken by no sword.
What woman has ever found your way to death?

ANTIGONE. [ANTISTROPHE 1]
How often I have heard the story of Niobe,[4]
Tantalos'[5] wretched daughter, how the stone
Clung fast about her, ivy-close: and they say
The rain falls endlessly
And sifting soft snow; her tears are never done.
I feel the loneliness of her death in mine.

CHORUS. But she was born of heaven, and you
Are woman, woman-born. If her death is yours,
A mortal woman's, is this not for you
Glory in our world and in the world beyond?

ANTIGONE. [STROPHE 2]
You laugh at me. Ah, friends, friends,
Can you not wait until I am dead? O Thebes,
O men many-charioted, in love with Fortune,
Dear springs of Dirce, sacred Theban grove,
Be witnesses for me, denied all pity,
Unjustly judged! and think a word of love
For her whose path turns
Under dark earth, where there are no more tears.

CHORUS. You have passed beyond human daring and come at last
Into a place of stone where Justice sits. ❺
I cannot tell
What shape of your father's guilt appears in this.

ANTIGONE. [ANTISTROPHE 2]
You have touched it at last: that bridal bed
Unspeakable, horror of son and mother mingling:
Their crime, infection of all our family!
O Oedipus, father and brother!
Your marriage strikes from the grave to murder mine.
I have been a stranger here in my own land:
All my life
The blasphemy of my birth has followed me.

CHORUS. Reverence is a virtue, but strength
Lives in established law: that must prevail.
You have made your choice,
Your death is the doing of your conscious hand.

> ◆ **Literary Focus** ❻
> What flaw in Antigone does the chorus point out?

ANTIGONE. [EPODE]
Then let me go, since all your words are bitter,
And the very light of the sun is cold to me.

3. **Acheron** (ak′ ər än′): River in the underworld over which the dead are ferried.
4. **Niobe** (nī ə bē′): A queen of Thebes who was turned to stone while weeping for her slain children. Her seven sons and seven daughters were killed by Artemis and Apollo, the divine twins of Leto. These gods ruined Niobe after Leto complained that Niobe insulted her by bragging of maternal superiority. It was Zeus who turned the bereaved Niobe to stone, but her lament continued and her tears created a stream.
5. **Tantalos** (tan′ tə ləs): Niobe's father, who was condemned to eternal frustration in the underworld because he revealed the secrets of the gods. Tantalos was tormented by being kept just out of reach of the water and food that was near him but which he could never reach to enjoy.

Humanities: Mythology

Tantalus and Niobe Antigone's reference to Niobe would have been very familiar to ancient Greek audiences. They would have known that Niobe was the daughter of Tantalus, who tried to humiliate the gods. As punishment, the gods placed Tantalus in a pool of water he could never drink in the midst of fruit trees he could never reach. Because he offended the gods so seriously, Tantalus' descendants were cursed as well. Niobe, Tantalus' daughter ruled Thebes with her husband Amphion. When she, like her father, challenged the gods, the gods struck down her seven children. In her grief, Niobe is said to have turned to stone—a stone forever wet with her tears.

Ask students to identify the connections between the stories of Tantalus and Niobe and Antigone. *Students should notice that Niobe ruled Thebes, where Antigone lives. Like Niobe and her children, Antigone belongs to a cursed family. Excessive pride plays a role in both stories as well.*

◆ Reading Strategy

❸ Identify With a Character Have students try to imagine themselves in Antigone's position in this scene and to interpret her feelings. Then ask them why they think Antigone makes no attempt to escape or rally public opinion to her side to oppose Creon's death sentence. *Basing their thoughts on what they have already learned about Antigone, students may infer that she wants to be a martyr.*

Comprehension Check ☑

❹ Ask students to paraphrase what the chorus says to Antigone in this passage. *Lead students to respond that the chorus points out that for Antigone, a mortal woman, to suffer the same fate as Niobe, who was descended from a god, raises Antigone to a more exalted stature.*

◆ Literary Focus

❺ Tragic Character Ask students what the Chorus implies about the character of Antigone when they say that she has "passed beyond human daring . . . into a place of stone where Justice sits." *Students may say that the chorus sees Antigone's resolve and determination as far greater than that of most people, but she must still be subject to the laws of the state.*

◆ Literary Focus

❻ Tragic Character The Chorus points out that although reverence for the dead is admirable, Antigone made her choice when she opposed human law. Her unwillingness to recognize human law leads to her downfall.

Read to Appreciate Author's Craft

Classical works such as Sophocles' *Antigone* provide students with an excellent opportunity to read with the purpose of appreciating an author's craft. Ask students to analyze the role of the Chorus and whether Sophocles has created a likable "character" in this group of speakers.

▶Critical Viewing◀

❶ Infer The fact that a battle scene is used as decoration for an object meant to be both beautiful and useful suggests that war is a significant facet of life in Greek city-states.

◆ Reading Strategy

❷ Identify With a Character Ask students to put themselves in Creon's place and explain why he is motivated to say what he does in this passage. *Students can note that Creon will be responsible for Antigone's death, even if he does not kill her with his own hands; he is paying only lip service to the law of the gods, who may or may not approve of his actions. He still places his own law above divine law.*

◆ Reading Strategy

❸ Identify With a Character Ask students to explain Antigone's feelings at this point. *While she is certain she is right and feels justified as she goes to her death, she can't help wishing that Creon will be punished for what he is doing to her.*

◆ Literary Focus

❹ Tragic Character In what way is having a passionate, unyielding heart a fatal flaw? *Antigone's passion and unwillingness to compromise draw her into the conflict that results in her death.*

Art Transparency As students have read in "The Greek Theater" (SE, p. 666), the plays of the classical world differed from modern drama in many ways. Review some distinguishing characteristics of Greek drama, emphasizing the fact that today's readers still respond to many of the plays—like *Antigone*—because the plays deal with universal concepts. Display Art Transparency 15, *Actors Preparing for a Performance.* Have students comment about details in the mosaic that suggest elements of Greek drama. At some point during the reading of *Antigone*, students might enjoy bringing the mosaic to life by taking the parts of the actors and discussing the play from their perspective.

Etruscan Amphora, black-figured, pontic fighting soldiers, white dove on shield, National Museum, Warsaw, Poland

❶ ▲ Critical Viewing What does the art on this vessel indicate about the significance of warfare in ancient Greece? **[Infer]**

Lead me to my vigil, where I must have
Neither love nor lamentation; no song, but silence.

[CREON *interrupts impatiently.*]

CREON. If dirges and planned lamentations could put off death,
Men would be singing forever.

[*To the* SERVANTS] Take her, go!
❷ You know your orders: take her to the vault
And leave her alone there. And if she lives or dies,
That's her affair, not ours: our hands are clean.

ANTIGONE. O tomb, vaulted bride-bed in eternal rock,
Soon I shall be with my own again
Where Persephone[6] welcomes the thin ghosts underground:
And I shall see my father again, and you, mother,
And dearest Polyneices—
dearest indeed
To me, since it was my hand
That washed him clean and poured the ritual wine:
And my reward is death before my time!

❸ And yet, as men's hearts know, I have done no wrong,
I have not sinned before God. Or if I have,
I shall know the truth in death. But if the guilt
Lies upon Creon who judged me, then, I pray,
May his punishment equal my own.

❹ **CHORAGOS.** O passionate heart,
Unyielding, tormented still by the same winds!

CREON. Her guards shall have good cause to regret their delaying.

ANTIGONE. Ah! That voice is like the voice of death!

CREON. I can give you no reason to think you are mistaken.

ANTIGONE. Thebes, and you my fathers' gods,
And rulers of Thebes, you see me now, the last
Unhappy daughter of a line of kings,
Your kings, led away to death. You will remember
What things I suffer, and at what men's hands,
Because I would not transgress the laws of heaven.

[*To the* GUARDS, *simply*]

Come: let us wait no longer.

[*Exit* ANTIGONE, *left, guarded.*]

◆ Build Vocabulary

lamentation (lam′ ən tā′ shən) *n.*: An expression of grief; weeping

6. **Persephone** (pər sef′ ə nē): Queen of the underworld.

Humanities: Art

Etruscan Amphora Most of the ancient Greek painting that survives today is found on vases. The vase itself is made of red clay. The artist then covered sections with a black glaze to create the figures and patterns. Vase painters captured the myths, legends, wars, Olympic games, and domestic affairs of ancient Greece. One of the most popular vessels artists chose to paint on was the amphora—a two handled jar such as the one seen here. Help students connect the art to the play with the following questions:

1. What events from *Antigone* might the scene on this vase portray? *The scene could be showing the battle in which Antigone's two brothers were killed.*
2. Why might an artist choose to capture a scene such as this one? *Battles and heroic deeds were important to the ancient Greeks; capturing them in a painting was one way to tell the stories and preserve their history.*

Ode IV

CHORUS. [STROPHE 1]

All Danae's beauty[7] was locked away
In a brazen cell where the sunlight could not come:
A small room, still as any grave, enclosed her.
Yet she was a princess too,
And Zeus in a rain of gold poured love upon her.
O child, child,
No power in wealth or war
Or tough sea-blackened ships
Can prevail against untiring Destiny!

[ANTISTROPHE 1]

And Dryas' son[8] also, that furious king,
Bore the god's prisoning anger for his pride:
Sealed up by Dionysos[9] in deaf stone,
His madness died among echoes.
So at the last he learned what dreadful power
His tongue had mocked:
For he had profaned the revels,
And fired the wrath of the nine
Implacable Sisters[10] that love the sound of the flute.

[STROPHE 2]

And old men tell a half-remembered tale
Of horror done where a dark ledge splits the sea
And a double surf beats on the gray shores:
How a king's new woman, sick
With hatred for the queen he had imprisoned,
Ripped out his two sons' eyes with her bloody hands
While grinning Ares[11] watched the shuttle plunge
Four times: four blind wounds crying for revenge,

[ANTISTROPHE 2]

Crying, tears and blood mingled. —Piteously born,
Those sons whose mother was of heavenly birth!
Her father was the god of the North Wind
And she was cradled by gales,
She raced with young colts on the glittering hills
And walked untrammeled in the open light:
But in her marriage deathless Fate found means
To build a tomb like yours for all her joy.

Scene 5

[Enter blind TEIRESIAS, *led by a boy. The opening speeches of* TEIRESIAS *should be in singsong contrast to the realistic lines of* CREON.*]*

TEIRESIAS. This is the way the blind man comes, Princes, Princes,
Lock-step, two heads lit by the eyes of one.

CREON. What new thing have you to tell us, old Teiresias?

TEIRESIAS. I have much to tell you: listen to the prophet, Creon.

CREON. I am not aware that I have ever failed to listen.

TEIRESIAS. Then you have done wisely, King, and ruled well.

CREON. I admit my debt to you.[12] But what have you to say?

---

7. **Danae's** (dan´ ā ēz´) **beauty:** Danae was imprisoned in a brazen, dark tower when it was foretold that she would mother a son who would kill her father. Her beauty attracted Zeus, who visited her in the form of a shower of gold. Perseus was born of the union, and Danae was exiled with the child over stormy seas from which Zeus saved them. Years later, as prophesied, the boy did kill the man he failed to recognize as his grandfather.
8. **Dryas'** (drī´ əs) **son:** Lycorgos (lī kur´ gəs), whose opposition to the worship of Dionysos was severely punished by the gods. He drove the followers of the god from Thrace and was driven insane for having done so. Lycorgos recovered from his madness while imprisoned in a cave, but he was later blinded by Zeus as additional punishment for his offense.
9. **Dionysos** (dī ə nī´ səs): God of wine, in whose honor the Greek plays were performed.
10. **nine Implacable Sisters:** Nine muses, or goddesses, of science and literature. They are the daughters of Zeus and Mnemosyne (ne mas´ ə nē´)—Memory—who inspired invention and influenced the production of art. They are called implacable (im plak´ ə bəl) because they were unforgiving and denied inspiration to anyone who offended them.
11. **Ares** (er´ ēz): God of war.
12. **my debt to you:** Creon is here admitting that he would not have acquired the throne if Teiresias had not moved the former king, Oedipus, to an investigation of his own background that led eventually to his downfall. The news of his personal history, uncovered with help from Teiresias, forced Oedipus into exile.

◆ Critical Thinking

5 Make Inferences Ask students to explain why the power of Fate is shown to be especially strong in the cases of Danae and Antigone. *Both Danae and Antigone were princesses of royal blood, whose high station did not shield them from their fates. Lead students to see the similarity in all the tales told by the Chorus in this strophe and antistrophe.*

◆ Background for Understanding

6 The Chorus refers to the story of King Phineus of Salmydessus in Thrace. Phineus imprisoned his first wife, Cleopatra (not the Egyptian Queen) after marrying a second wife, Idaea. Out of jealousy, Idaea made false accusations of treachery against Cleopatra's sons, Plexippus and Pandion, and put out their eyes with a weaver's shuttle. Remind students that Oedipus' eyes were put out by his own hand.

Extending Word Study

Use Reference Materials
Challenge students to skim through Ode IV looking for words that they might not encounter in a drama written today. For instance, students might list the words *brazen*, *profaned*, and *implacable*. Have students prepare a list of these words and use reference materials to determine the precise meaning as intended by Sophocles when he wrote them years ago.

Speaking, Listening, and Viewing Mini-Lesson

Mock Trial

This mini-lesson supports the Speaking, Listening, and Viewing activity in the Idea Bank on p. 700.

Introduce Explain that a mock trial is like a play. Students play the parts of Antigone, attorneys, witnesses, judge, and jury. As in a true trial, it is the lawyer's responsibility to prove a case.

Develop The defense attorney and "Antigone" should plan their testimony while the prosecutor meets with witnesses to take depositions from each. Both lawyers should prepare opening statements that outline their arguments.

Apply The trial should begin with the opening statements, then testimony and cross-examination, and the lawyers' final arguments. Then the jury can convene and vote. Students should speak clearly and use standard English.

Assess Have students use Peer Assessment: Dramatic Performance in ***Alternative Assessment,*** p. 120.

◆ Background for Understanding

❶ Burnt offerings were traditional in many religions. Either whole animals or particular parts of animals were placed on an altar fire and burnt as a gift to please a god. If the offering did not burn it was taken as a sign that the god in question was angry at some offense.

◆ Literary Focus

❷ Ask students to identify how Creon and Antigone are guilty of the crime of pride. *Creon's pride leads him to ignore the will of the gods; it blinds him to the will of the people. Antigone's pride leads her to isolate herself from her sister and defy civil law.*

◆ Reading Strategy

❸ Identify With a Character
Creon reveals that he has been misled by unscrupulous fortunetellers before. This makes him suspicious of Tereisias' motives.

Customize for
Less Proficient Readers
Help these students to understand the exchange between Creon and Teiresias by dividing it into two parts. First, have students identify what Teiresias did and saw before he encountered Creon. Then, have students describe the conflict between Creon and Teiresias. *Before Teiresias encounters Creon, he is disturbed by the fighting of the temple birds. Then, his offering to the gods fails. During the conflict between Creon and Teiresias, Teiresias claims that the bad signs indicate disaster brought on by Creon's actions. He accuses Creon of acting out of pride and advises him to be more flexible. Creon says he will no longer be manipulated by fortunetellers. Teiresias loses his temper and predicts tragedy for Creon's family.*

TEIRESIAS. This, Creon: you stand once more on the edge of fate.

CREON. What do you mean? Your words are a kind of dread.

TEIRESIAS. Listen, Creon:
I was sitting in my chair of augury,[13] at the place
Where the birds gather about me. They were all a-chatter,
As is their habit, when suddenly I heard
A strange note in their jangling, a scream, a
Whirring fury; I knew that they were fighting,
Tearing each other, dying
In a whirlwind of wings clashing. And I was afraid.
I began the rites of burnt-offering at the altar,
But Hephaistos[14] failed me: instead of bright flame,
There was only the sputtering slime of the fat thigh-flesh
❶ Melting: the entrails dissolved in gray smoke,
The bare bone burst from the welter. And no blaze!

This was a sign from heaven. My boy described it,
Seeing for me as I see for others.

I tell you, Creon, you yourself have brought
This new calamity upon us. Our hearths and altars
Are stained with the corruption of dogs and carrion birds
That glut themselves on the corpse of Oedipus' son.
The gods are deaf when we pray to them, their fire
Recoils from our offering, their birds of omen
Have no cry of comfort, for they are gorged
With the thick blood of the dead.
O my son,
These are no trifles! Think: all men make mistakes,
But a good man yields when he knows his course is wrong,
And repairs the evil. The only crime is pride.

Give in to the dead man, then: do not fight with a corpse—
What glory is it to kill a man who is dead?
Think, I beg you:
It is for your own good that I speak as I do.
You should be able to yield for your own good.

CREON. It seems that prophets have made me their especial province.
All my life long
I have been a kind of butt for the dull arrows ❸
Of doddering fortunetellers!
No, Teiresias:

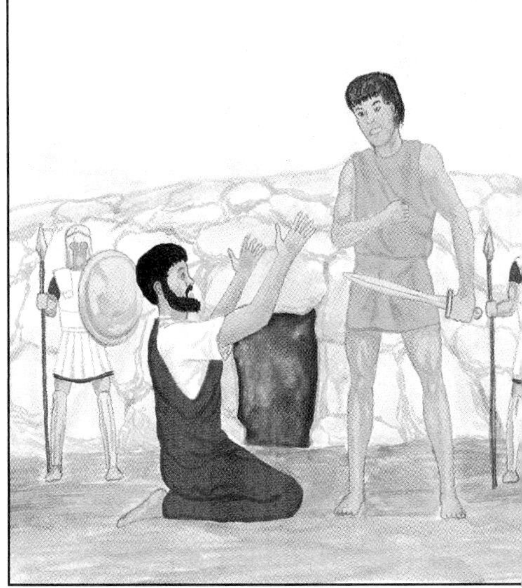

If your birds—if the great eagles of God himself
Should carry him stinking bit by bit to heaven,
I would not yield. I am not afraid of pollution:

13. **chair of augury:** The seat near the temple from which Teiresias would deliver his predictions about the future. Augury was the skill of telling such fortunes from a consideration of omens, like the flight of birds or the position of stars.
14. **Hephaistos** (he fes´ təs): God of fire and the forge. He would be invoked, as he is here by Teiresias, for aid in the starting of ceremonial fires.

Humanities: Theater

Greek Theater
Following is a glossary of terms from classical Greek theater. Students might be interested in learning some of them and identifying parts of *Antigone* to which they could be applied:

Catharsis (ka thär´ sis): emotional relief or purification that an audience was supposed to experience upon watching a Greek tragedy.

Exodos (eks´ ə dəs): the departure of the chorus from the stage at the end of a Greek tragedy.

Hamartia (he mär´ she): the tragic flaw that causes the downfall of a tragic hero or heroine

Hubris (hyo͞o´ bris): Excessive pride on the part of a character; a common form of *hamartia.*

Orchestra (ôr´ kis trə): the circular space in front of the stage of a Greek theater in which the chorus performed.

Parodos (pa´ rə dəs): the initial entrance of the chorus in a Greek tragedy; their entrance song.

Peripeteia (pe ri pi tā´ a): a sudden change of fortune, like Creon's in *Antigone*

Skene (skē´ nāy): the stage of a Greek theater, where the actors (but not the chorus) performed.

Stychomythia (stik ə mith´ yä): the dialogue pattern in Greek drama. Actors begin scenes with long speeches to state positions. As conflict increases and tension builds, the speeches become shorter.

No man can defile the gods.
Do what you will,
Go into business, make money, speculate
In India gold or that synthetic gold from Sardis,[15]
Get rich otherwise than by my consent to bury him.
Teiresias, it is a sorry thing when a wise man
Sells his wisdom, lets out his words for hire!

TEIRESIAS. Ah Creon! Is there no man left in the world—

CREON. To do what?—Come, let's have the aphorism![16]

TEIRESIAS. No man who knows that wisdom outweighs any wealth?

CREON. As surely as bribes are baser than any baseness.

TEIRESIAS. You are sick, Creon! You are deathly sick!

CREON. As you say: it is not my place to challenge a prophet.

TEIRESIAS. Yet you have said my prophecy is for sale.

CREON. The generation of prophets has always loved gold.

TEIRESIAS. The generation of kings has always loved brass.

CREON. You forget yourself! You are speaking to your King.

TEIRESIAS. I know it. You are a king because of me.

CREON. You have a certain skill; but you have sold out.

TEIRESIAS. King, you will drive me to words that—

CREON. Say them, say them!
Only remember: I will not pay you for them.

TEIRESIAS. No, you will find them too costly.

CREON. No doubt. Speak:
Whatever you say, you will not change my will.

TEIRESIAS. Then take this, and take it to heart!
The time is not far off when you shall pay back
Corpse for corpse, flesh of your own flesh.
You have thrust the child of this world into living night,
You have kept from the gods below the child that is theirs:
The one in a grave before her death, the other,
Dead, denied the grave. This is your crime:
And the Furies[17] and the dark gods of Hell
Are swift with terrible punishment for you.

Do you want to buy me now, Creon?

Not many days,
And your house will be full of men and women weeping,
And curses will be hurled at you from far
Cities grieving for sons unburied, left to rot
Before the walls of Thebes.

These are my arrows, Creon: they are all for you.

But come, child: lead me home. [*To* BOY]
Let him waste his fine anger upon younger men.
Maybe he will learn at last
To control a wiser tongue in a better head.

[*Exit* TEIRESIAS.]

CHORAGOS. The old man has gone, King, but his words
Remain to plague us. I am old, too,
But I cannot remember
that he was ever false.

CREON. That is true. . . . It troubles me.
Oh it is hard to give in! but it is worse

◆ **Reading Strategy** What details help you identify with Creon's refusal to yield?

15. **Sardis** (sär′ dis): Capital of ancient Lydia, which produced the first coins made from an alloy of gold and silver.

16. **aphorism** (af′ ə riz′ əm): Brief, insightful saying. Creon is taunting the prophet and suggesting that the old man is capable only of relying on trite, meaningless expressions instead of any original thinking.

17. **Furies** (fyo͞or′ ēz): Goddesses of vengence, who made insane those whose crimes were unpunished, especially those who had sinned against their own families.

◆ Literary Focus

❹ **Tragic Character** Ask students what character trait this statement reveals in Creon, and how it might lead him to disaster. *Creon shows himself here to be both rigid and extreme in his position. When logic fails, he falls back on his authority as king.*

◆ Critical Thinking

❺ **Analyze** Ask students what Creon's insistence that Teiresias has been corrupted suggests about Creon's thinking. *Students may say that Creon is not capable of considering any viewpoint opposed to his, and will entertain even a far-fetched rationale to discredit it. Students may also recall that Creon first suspected even Antigone of acting for money rather than principles.*

Comprehension Check ☑

❻ What does Teiresias mean, "Corpse for corpse, flesh of your own flesh"? Who is the "child of this world"? Who is the child that Creon has "kept from the gods below"? *Teiresias means that by sentencing Antigone to death, Creon will also cause his son's death. The "child of this world" is Antigone, whom Creon has entombed; the other child is Polyneices, whom Creon refused proper burial.*

◆ Reading Strategy

❼ **Identify With a Character** Ask students to imagine themselves in Creon's place, and suggest a motive for Creon's change of attitude toward Teiresias. *Elicit answers to the effect that Creon has committed himself so totally to his course of action regarding Antigone that he cannot bring himself to change his mind, and must try to discredit the prophet instead.*

Humanities: Theater

Greek Theater Students may be interested in the ways Greek theater differs from modern theater. Point out these differences:

- The ancient Greeks used little scenery. Scenes were painted on the three sides of pyramid-shaped structures called *periaktoi* (pe rē av′ toi). These structures could be swiveled around by "stage hands" to show changes of setting.
- Since no violence was supposed to appear on stage, if a character was killed, a "tableau," or wheeled platform with an actor playing the part of the dead character, would be pushed forward onto the stage.
- In some Greek dramas, gods appeared "flying" in baskets hung from cranes called *machina* (mä′ ke nä), or "machines."
- All actors were male, with boys playing female roles. Actors wore masks with voice amplifiers, like small megaphones, built into the mouth openings. Some wore platform shoes called *kothurnoi* to make them look taller and more imposing.

Encourage students to apply these facts to *Antigone,* where appropriate. For example, tableaus would have been used in the scene in which Eurydice kills herself; the actor playing Creon might have worn *kothurnoi* to indicate Creon's importance; Antigone would have been played by a boy.

◆ Critical Thinking

❶ **Make Judgments** Ask students why they think Creon finds it so hard to give in now, even though he is clearly wavering. *Students might explain that Creon has made his position regarding Antigone's punishment a symbol of his authority in Thebes. He believes that to give ground in any way would raise doubts about his effectiveness as a ruler.*

◆ Reading Strategy

❷ **Identify With a Character** Ask students to put themselves in Creon's place at this moment in the play, and to suggest reasons, based on the events of the play and on what they know of him, for his sudden change of heart. *Students might say that Creon has always feared what the gods can do to those who offend them. That is why he had claimed that Antigone's death would not be his fault. When the Choragos reminds him that Teiresias is never wrong about such matters, Creon suddenly senses that he might be in serious trouble.*

To risk everything for stubborn pride.

❶ CHORAGOS. Creon: take my advice.

CREON. What shall I do?

❷ CHORAGOS. Go quickly: free Antigone from her vault
And build a tomb for the body of Polyneices.

CREON. You would have me do this?

CHORAGOS. Creon, yes!
And it must be done at once: God moves
Swiftly to cancel the folly of stubborn men.

CREON. It is hard to deny the heart! But I
Will do it: I will not fight with destiny.

CHORAGOS. You must go yourself, you cannot leave it to others.

CREON. I will go.
—Bring axes, servants:
Come with me to the tomb. I buried her, I
Will set her free.
Oh quickly!
My mind misgives—
The laws of the gods are mighty, and a man must serve them
To the last day of his life!

[*Exit* CREON.]

Pæan

CHORAGOS. [STROPHE 1]
God of many names

CHORUS. O Iacchos[18]
son
of Kadmeian Semele[19]
O born of the Thunder!
Guardian of the West
Regent
of Eleusis' plain[20]
O Prince of maenad Thebes[21]
and the Dragon Field by rippling
Ismenos:[22]

CHORAGOS. [ANTISTROPHE 1]
God of many names

CHORUS. the flame of torches
flares on our hills
the nymphs of Iacchos
dance at the spring of Castalia:[23]

from the vine-close mountain
come ah come in ivy:
Evohe evohe![24] sings through the streets of Thebes

CHORAGOS. [STROPHE 2]
God of many names

CHORUS. Iacchos of Thebes
heavenly Child
of Semele bride of the Thunderer!
The shadow of plague is upon us:
come
with clement feet[25]
oh come from Parnasos[26]
down the long slopes
across the lamenting water

CHORAGOS. [ANTISTROPHE 2]
Io[27] Fire! Chorister of the throbbing stars!

---

18. **Iacchos** (ē´ ə kəs): One of several alternate names for Dionysos.
19. **Kadmeian Semele** (sem´ ə lē´): Semele was a mortal and the mother of Dionysos. She was the daughter of Thebes' founder, Kadmos.
20. **Eleusis'** (i lo͞o´ sis) **plain:** Located north of Athens, this plain was a site of worship for Dionysos and Demeter, gods who protected the harvests of grapes and corn, respectively.
21. **maenad** (mē´ nad) **Thebes:** The city is here compared to a maenad, one of Dionysos' female worshipers. Such a follower would be thought of as uncontrolled or disturbed, much as Thebes was while being upset by the civil war.
22. **Dragon Field . . . Ismenos** (is mē´ nəs): The Dragon Field was located by the banks of Ismenos, a river sacred to Apollo that flows near Thebes. The Dragon Field was where Kadmos miraculously created warriors by sowing the teeth of the dragon he killed there. Those men helped him establish the city.
23. **Castalia** (kas tā´ lē ə): Location of a site sacred to Apollo, where his followers would worship.
24. **Evohe** (ē vō´ ē): Triumphant shout of affirmation (like "Amen") used at ceremonies dedicated to Dionysos.
25. **clement feet:** *Clement* means "kind" or "favorable." The chorus is here asking Dionysos to step gently into the troubled path and to intervene in a healing manner.
26. **Parnasos** (pär nas´ əs): Mountain that was sacred to both Dionysos and Apollo, located in central Greece.
27. **Io** (ē´ ō): Greek word for "Behold" or "Hail."

◆ Build Vocabulary

chorister (kôr´ is tər) *n.*: Member of a chorus

Viewing and Representing Mini-Lesson

Multimedia Presentation

This mini-lesson supports the Research and Representing project in the Idea Bank on p. 700.

Introduce Make arrangements to have the class go to the school auditorium and tour the stage, backstage, and seating area. Point out to students that ancient plays were not only written differently, the physical arrangement of modern theaters is quite different from ancient Greek theaters.

Develop As students plan their multimedia presentation, suggest that they consider the ways they will develop the presentation and what technologies they will use. Encourage students to employ videos, maps, diagrams, recordings, and photographs.

Apply Have students conduct their research and prepare their presentations. You may wish to have small groups of students work together to develop a presentation.

Assess Students should share their presentation with the class. Use the Multimedia Report rubric, p. 107 in ***Alternative Assessment,*** to evaluate students' work.

O purest among the voices of the night!
Thou son of God, blaze for us!

CHORUS. Come with choric rapture of circling Maenads
Who cry *Io Iacche!*[28]
God of many names!

Exodus

[*Enter* MESSENGER, *left.*]

MESSENGER. Men of the line of Kadmos,[29] you who live
Near Amphion's citadel:[30]
I cannot say
❸ Of any condition of human life "This is fixed,
This is clearly good, or bad." Fate raises up,
And Fate casts down the happy and unhappy alike:
No man can foretell his Fate.
Take the case of Creon:
Creon was happy once, as I count happiness:
Victorious in battle, sole governor of the land,
Fortunate father of children nobly born.
And now it has all gone from him! Who can say
That a man is still alive when his life's joy fails?
He is a walking dead man. Grant him rich,
Let him live like a king in his great house:
If his pleasure is gone, I would not give
So much as the shadow of smoke for all he owns.

CHORAGOS. Your words hint at sorrow: what is your news for us?

MESSENGER. They are dead. The living are guilty of their death.

CHORAGOS. Who is guilty? Who is dead? Speak!

MESSENGER. Haimon.
Haimon is dead; and the hand that killed him
Is his own hand.

CHORAGOS. His father's? or his own?

MESSENGER. His own, driven mad by the murder his father had done.

CHORAGOS. Teiresias, Teiresias, how clearly you saw it all!

MESSENGER. This is my news: you must draw what conclusions you can from it.

CHORAGOS. But look: Eurydice, our Queen:
Has she overheard us?

[*Enter* EURYDICE *from the Palace, center.*]

EURYDICE. I have heard something, friends:
As I was unlocking the gate of Pallas'[31] shrine,
For I needed her help today, I heard a voice
Telling of some new sorrow. And I fainted
There at the temple with all my maidens about me.
But speak again: whatever it is, I can bear it:
Grief and I are no strangers.

MESSENGER. Dearest Lady,
I will tell you plainly all that I have seen.
I shall not try to comfort you: what is the use,
Since comfort could lie only in what is not true?
The truth is always best.
I went with Creon
To the outer plain where Polyneices was lying,
No friend to pity him, his body shredded by dogs.
We made our prayers in that place to Hecate[32]
And Pluto,[33] that they would be merciful.
And we bathed
The corpse with holy water, and we brought
Fresh-broken branches to burn what was

---

28. ***Io Iacche*** (ē ō ē´ ə ke): Cry of celebration used by Dionysian worshipers.
29. **Kadmos** (kad´ məs): Founder of the city of Thebes, whose daughter, Semele, gave birth to Dionysos.
30. **Amphion's** (am fī´ ənz) **citadel:** Amphion was a king of Thebes credited with erecting the walls of the fortress, or citadel, by using his lyre so magically that its music caused the stones to move themselves into proper place.
31. **Pallas** (pal´ əs): Pallas Athena, the goddess of wisdom.
32. **Hecate** (hek´ ə tē): Goddess of the underworld.
33. **Pluto** (plo͞ot´ ō): God of the underworld who managed the souls of the departed.

◆ Critical Thinking

❸ Interpret Ask students to explain the significance of a person's wealth or social status in determining his or her happiness, according to what the Messenger says. *The Messenger says that a person's wealth or social status has no bearing at all on what finally becomes of him or her.*

◆ Critical Thinking

❹ Make Inferences Ask students to infer what has happened, based on the Messenger's words. *By saying that happiness "has all gone from" Creon, and that "life's joy fails," the Messenger implies that Antigone is dead, and probably Haimon as well.*

Customize for *Less Proficient Readers*

Help these students to summarize what has happened. They should understand that Antigone is dead and that Haimon has killed himself.

Cross-Curricular Connection: Social Studies

The Olympic Games The Greek legacy to the Western World comprises a great deal more than drama. Every four years, athletes from around the world meet to participate in the Olympic games which originated in Greece in 776 B.C. Greek ideas about law, freedom, justice, and government have influenced political thinking to the present day. In the arts and sciences, Greek works became a standard of excellence for the later people of Europe. In fact, the word *museum* literally means "house of the Muses." (The Muses were nine Greek goddesses who presided over the arts and sciences.) The achievements of the Greeks were especially remarkable because they were produced by a scattering of tiny city-states whose bitter rivalries eventually cost them their freedom. Suggest that interested students do research to find out more about the history of the Olympic Games and how the current games compare to those that were held originally. Have them prepare an oral or written report to share the information they find.

◆ Background for Understanding

❶ The ancient Greeks performed elaborate rituals over dead bodies. The Messenger here gives a brief description of the rite that Creon had earlier refused to allow for Polyneices.

◆ Reading Strategy

❷ **Identify With a Character** Ask students to put themselves in Creon's place, and to suggest why Creon asks if he is now a prophet. *Students may say that Creon had been afraid that he would find something awful at Antigone's vault, and he now fears that his misgivings will be justified.*

◆ Critical Thinking

❸ **Analyze** Ask students to imagine why Antigone might have hanged herself. *Students may suggest that she preferred to die quickly by her own hand rather than gradually starve to death.*

◆ Reading Strategy

❹ **Identify With a Character** Although it is difficult to identify with a character in such a tragic situation, encourage students to try to identify with Haimon. Then have them explain why Haimon cannot forgive his father, even though Creon begs his forgiveness. *Suggested response: Haimon is mad with grief over the death of Antigone, and he sees his father as her murderer. What Creon has done is beyond forgiveness.*

left of it,
❶ And upon the urn we heaped up a towering barrow
Of the earth of his own land.
When we were done, we ran
To the vault where Antigone lay on her couch of stone.
One of the servants had gone ahead,
And while he was yet far off he heard a voice
Grieving within the chamber, and he came back
And told Creon. And as the King went closer,
The air was full of wailing, the words lost,
❷ And he begged us to make all haste. "Am I a prophet?"
He said, weeping, "And must I walk this road,
The saddest of all that I have gone before?
My son's voice calls me on. Oh quickly, quickly!
Look through the crevice there, and tell me
If it is Haimon, or some deception of the gods!"

We obeyed; and in the cavern's farthest corner
We saw her lying:
She had made a noose of her fine linen veil
❸ And hanged herself. Haimon lay beside her,
His arms about her waist, lamenting her,
His love lost underground, crying out
That his father had stolen her away from him.

When Creon saw him the tears rushed to his eyes
And he called to him: "What have you done, child? Speak to me.
What are you thinking that makes your eyes so strange?
❹ O my son, my son, I come to you on my knees!"
But Haimon spat in his face. He said not a word,
Staring—
And suddenly drew his sword
And lunged. Creon shrank back, the blade missed; and the boy,
Desperate against himself, drove it half its length
Into his own side, and fell. And as he died
He gathered Antigone close in his arms again,
Choking, his blood bright red on her white cheek.
And now he lies dead with the dead, and she is his
At last, his bride in the houses of the dead.

[*Exit* EURYDICE *into the Palace.*]

CHORAGOS. She has left us without a word. What can this mean?

MESSENGER. It troubles me, too; yet she knows what is best,
Her grief is too great for public lamentation,
And doubtless she has gone to her chamber to weep
For her dead son, leading her maidens in his dirge.

CHORAGOS. It may be so: but I fear this deep silence.

[*Pause*]

MESSENGER. I will see what she is doing. I will go in.

[*Exit* MESSENGER *into the Palace.*]

[*Enter* CREON *with attendants, bearing* HAIMON'S *body.*]

CHORAGOS. But here is the King himself: oh look at him,
Bearing his own damnation in his arms.

CREON. Nothing you say can touch me any more.
My own blind heart has brought me
From darkness to final darkness. Here you see
The father murdering, the murdered son—
And all my civic wisdom!

Haimon my son, so young, so young to die,
I was the fool, not you; and you died for me.

Workplace Skills Mini-Lesson

Appropriate Disagreement

This mini-lesson will develop students' ability to assert themselves in a manner appropriate for the workplace.

Introduce Ask students to describe Antigone's personality. Elicit that she speaks her mind, even in the face of strong opposition. Tell students that in the course of any job, they may find themselves disagreeing with a person in authority. When it is appropriate for them to voice their disagreement, they should do so in a respectful manner.

Develop As a group, brainstorm for a list of issues over which employees and managers might disagree. Guide students to see that issues such as scheduling, dress code, procedure, and morale are potential trouble spots. Discuss specific situations in which it is appropriate for a student employee to voice disagreement and situations in which it probably isn't appropriate.

Apply Allow time for pairs of students to role-play several of the situations. Have class members offer suggestions, then allow the partners to improve their technique.

Assess Evaluate students on the following points:

- ability to distinguish appropriate situations
- ability to put forth a position clearly
- ability to express disagreement calmly and respectfully

CHORAGOS. That is the truth; but you were late in learning it.

CREON. This truth is hard to bear. Surely a god
Has crushed me beneath the hugest weight of heaven,
And driven me headlong a barbaric way
To trample out the thing I held most dear.

The pains that men will take to come to pain!

[*Enter* MESSENGER *from the Palace.*]

MESSENGER. The burden you carry in your hands is heavy,
But it is not all: you will find more in your house.

CREON. What burden worse than this shall I find there?

MESSENGER. The Queen is dead.

CREON. O port of death, deaf world,
Is there no pity for me? And you, Angel of evil,
I was dead, and your words are death again.
Is it true, boy? Can it be true?
Is my wife dead? Has death bred death?

MESSENGER. You can see for yourself.

[*The doors are opened, and the body of* EURYDICE *is disclosed within.*]

CREON. Oh pity!
All true, all true, and more than I can bear!
O my wife, my son!

MESSENGER. She stood before the altar, and her heart
Welcomed the knife her own hand guided,
And a great cry burst from her lips for Megareus[34] dead,
And for Haimon dead, her sons; and her last breath
Was a curse for their father, the murderer of her sons.
And she fell, and the dark flowed in through her closing eyes.

CREON. O God, I am sick with fear.
Are there no swords here? Has no one a blow for me?

MESSENGER. Her curse is upon you for the deaths of both.

CREON. It is right that it should be. I alone am guilty.
I know it, and I say it. Lead me in,
Quickly, friends.
I have neither life nor substance. Lead me in. ❻

CHORAGOS. You are right, if there can be right in so much wrong.
The briefest way is best in a world of sorrow.

34. Megareus (mə gā´ rē əs): Oldest son of Creon and Eurydice, who was killed in the civil war by Argive forces invading Thebes.

◆ Critical Thinking

❺ **Analyze** Ask students to suggest what burden Creon is now carrying, beyond the death of his son. *Students' responses should include Creon's awareness that his own behavior and willfulness caused Haimon's death, even though he thought to have acted for the good of the city. Some students may predict that the Chorus will suggest other misfortunes are about to be revealed.*

◆ Reading Strategy

❻ **Identify With a Character** Ask students whether they, if in Creon's place, would agree that all the guilt for what has happened should be placed on his head alone. Ask them to explain their reasoning. *Students may agree that Creon is wholly at fault because of his rigid and repressive mentality. On the other hand, they might find that other circumstances may have played a part as well: Antigone's stubbornness or fate, for example.*

Customize for *Visual/Spatial Learners*

Help these students organize the information on these pages by using a Timeline or Chain-of-Events Organizer. This visual representation will help them understand the relationships between the many events that are revealed in quick succession.

Reteach

The reading strategy urges students to identify with a character. Ask students to consider whether or not they enjoy their favorite television shows because they feel as if they can identify with the characters and find themselves in similar situations. The same process can be applied to reading a drama. Encourage students to apply this empathetic attitude toward the young Antigone. Suggest that students complete a chart like the one here to help elucidate their reactions to each character.

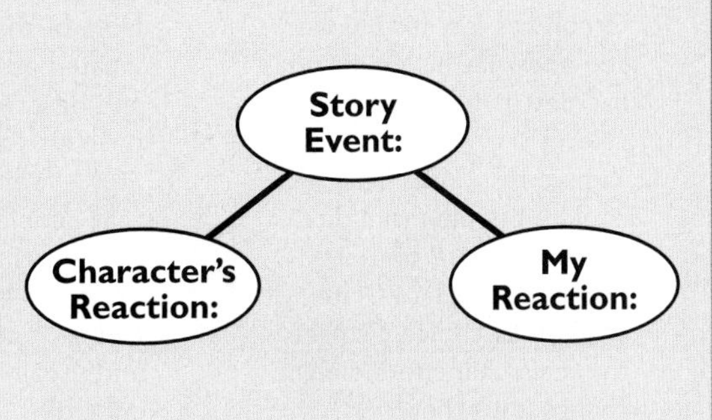

CREON. Let it come,
Let death come quickly, and be kind to me.
I would not ever see the sun again.

CHORAGOS. All that will come when it will; but we, meanwhile,
Have much to do. Leave the future to itself.

CREON. All my heart was in that prayer!

CHORAGOS. Then do not pray any more: the sky is deaf.

❶ **CREON.** Lead me away. I have been rash and foolish.
I have killed my son and my wife.
I look for comfort; my comfort lies here dead.
Whatever my hands have touched has come to nothing.
Fate has brought all my pride to a thought of dust.

[As CREON *is being led into the house, the* CHORAGOS *advances and speaks directly to the audience.]*

CHORAGOS. There is no happiness where there is no wisdom;
No wisdom but in submission to the gods.
Big words are always punished,
And proud men in old age learn to be wise.

Guide for Responding

◆ Literature and Your Life

Reader's Response In Scene 3, Creon and Haimon express sharply different points of view. With which character do you most agree? Why?

Thematic Focus What choices do Creon and Antigone make that lead to their downfall?

Journal Activity List the reasons you think Creon should or should not have changed his mind. Explain which reason you feel is most compelling.

✓ Check Your Comprehension

1. Why do Creon and Haimon argue?
2. According to Teiresias, what terrible punishment awaits Creon?
3. What action does Creon take after Teiresias's prophecy?
4. What does the Messenger tell Eurydice before she leaves the stage during the Exodos?
5. What finally happens to Antigone? Haimon? Eurydice?

◆ Critical Thinking

INTERPRET

1. Explain the conflicts that drive Haimon to take extreme measures. Does he seem more concerned with divine law, to which Antigone turns for her justification, or with human law? Support your answer. **[Analyze]**
2. Why does Creon say "I have neither life nor substance" in the Exodus? **[Infer]**
3. How great a role do you think fate plays in dictating the outcome of the story? **[Support]**

EVALUATE

4. Both Antigone and Creon are unwilling to appear weak. How could this trait influence a person's outlook on life? **[Evaluate]**

APPLY

5. Explain how this play demonstrates the tension that sometimes exists between individual conscience and designated authority. **[Analyze]**
6. Near the end of the play, Creon says, "The pains that men will take to come to pain!" How do his words apply to contemporary society? **[Relate]**

◆ Literary Focus

❶ **Tragic Character** Ask students whether they believe that Creon or Antigone is the more tragic figure in this drama, and to explain their choices. *Students may choose Antigone because she appears more blameless and sympathetic, having acted in accordance with the principles of divine justice. They may choose Creon because of the way in which a flaw in his character has brought him down from such a height to such a depth of loss and despair.*

Reinforce and Extend

Answers

◆ Literature and Your Life

Reader's Response Some students might point out that Creon will seem weak if he backs down, yet many will agree with Haimon, who maintains that his father will lose the respect of the entire city if he remains inflexible, and that "It is not reason never to yield to reason!"

Thematic Focus They choose to remain rigid in their beliefs, are unwilling to appear weak, and refuse to reason or compromise.

✓ Check Your Comprehension

1. Haimon thinks his father's judgment is too rash.
2. Teiresias predicts that Creon's house will be full of tears and that his own flesh (Haimon) shall pay back "corpse for corpse."
3. Creon sets out to bury Polyneices and free Antigone.
4. The Messenger tells Eurydice that Creon was too late to save Antigone, and that her son, Haimon, is dead.
5. Antigone hangs herself. In his raging grief, Haimon tries to kill his father, misses, but then mortally wounds himself, dying next to Antigone. Cursing her husband, Eurydice kills herself.

◆ Critical Thinking

1. Haimon is more concerned with divine law. He listens to the people, and overhears their sympathy for Antigone—that what she did for her brother was no crime, but a decent act. He begs his father to listen to reason, "God's crowning gift to man," and exclaims that Creon has "no right to trample on God's right."
2. Creon has lost his beloved son and wife; his rigid pride has destroyed his power to rule.
3. Sample responses: The choices people make dictate the course of their own lives, not fate—fate changes as choice changes; the main characters didn't change, thus they were stuck with their fate. Others may say that fate is fixed from birth, the sum total of innate pattern of behavior and destiny, which we are unable to alter.
4. Students might respond that people who are afraid of appearing to be weak, indeed are; they resort to trying to control others and usually end up out of control.
5. Suggested response: The entire play is based on the tension between individual, divine conscience (Antigone), and civil, human authority (Creon), with the potential for human reason (Haimon) to save the day.
6. Students can offer examples from contemporary literature, television programs, and current movies in addition to real-life examples.

Guide for Responding (continued)

◆ Literary Focus

Tragic Character

A **tragic character** is one who suffers a downfall. This character is marked with a tragic flaw that contributes to his or her doom.

1. (a) In your opinion, who is brought down most completely at the conclusion of the action? (b) Give evidence to support your answer.
2. (a) What is this character's tragic flaw? (b) How does this flaw lead to the character's downfall?
3. What role, if any, does fate play in leading to the downfall?

◆ Reading Strategy

Identify With a Character

When you **identify with a character** in a drama, you sympathize with his or her struggles or experiences.

1. With which character did you most identify? Why?
2. Which actions, events, or lines in the play led you to identify with that character?
3. How did your identification with a character draw you into the action of the play?

Beyond Literature

Cultural Connection

Burial Customs Different societies and cultures have different "burial" customs, some of which are not burials at all! Antigone "buries" her brother by sprinkling his corpse with wine and dust. The Vikings placed kings and great warriors on barges and then set them on fire. Some Aborigines in Australia leave bodies in trees. In Tibet a sky burial returns the body to nature by exposing it to birds and the elements on a high mountain. **Activity** Find out more about a burial custom and write a brief explanation of how it reflects the needs and beliefs of a culture.

◆ Build Grammar Skills

Pronoun Case in Incomplete Clauses

In **incomplete clauses** introduced by *than* or *as*, a pronoun takes the case that it would have if the understood words were present.

Practice On your paper, write the correct pronoun to complete each sentence. Then write the words that are needed to complete each sentence.

1. The Chorus members see all; no one sees more than (*they/them*) __?__.
2. When Haimon heard of Antigone's sentence, no one was more enraged than (*he/him*) __?__.
3. The rest of the group was as certain as (*I/me*) __?__ about the outcome of the play.
4. Though Ismene avoids her sister's fate, most people believe that Antigone is a much stronger character than (*she/her*) __?__.
5. Although the details of her problems are different, Antigone faces some of the same issues as ____. (*we/us*)

◆ Build Vocabulary

Using the Greek Root *-chor-*

The Greek root *-chor-* comes from Terpsichore, the Muse of dance and song. Match each of the words in Column A with its definition in Column B.

Column A	Column B
1. choral	**a.** creating dance
2. choir	**b.** group of singers
3. choreography	**c.** sung or performed by a chorus

Using the Word Bank: Synonyms

On your paper, write the letter of the word that is the best synonym of the first word.

1. deference: (a) indignity, (b) respect, (c) irony
2. vile: (a) corrupt, (b) honorable, (c) edible
3. piety: (a) atheism, (b) reverence, (c) solitude
4. blasphemy: (a) violence, (b) vandalism, (c) disrespect
5. lamentation: (a) mourning, (b) cheer, (c) glee
6. chorister: (a) warden, (b) singer, (c) lawgiver

Beyond the Selection

FURTHER READING

Other Ancient Greek Tragedies

Oedipus Rex, Sophocles
The Seven Against Thebes, Aeschylus

Other Books About Ancient Greek Myths

The Greek Way, Edith Hamilton
Hercules, My Shipmate, Robert Graves

We suggest that you preview these works before recommending them to students.

INTERNET

Students can find information about *Antigone* and ancient Greece at the following Web sites:

http://www.temple.edu/classics/antigone.html

http://www.museum_upenn.edu/Greek_World/Intro.html

Please be aware that addresses may have changed since we published this information. We *strongly recommend* that you preview the sites before you send students to them.

Answers

◆ Literary Focus

1. Sample response: (a) Creon. (b) He lost everything that matters in life: his wife, his son, and the respect of his people.
2. (a) Creon has intense pride, will not listen to reason, and is inflexible. (b) By not using reason, he sets up a no-win situation; everyone loses.
3. Sample response: The consequences of fate were brought before Creon by Teiresias to no avail, because he would not listen or use reason. Without reason, fate took its natural course.

◆ Reading Strategy

1. Sample response: Haimon. For the love of his father and Antigone, he tried to guide his father with a wisdom that was beyond his years; he would have made a wise king. We understand Haimon, for we feel frustrated by situations in which negative consequences could have been avoided, if only our advice had been heeded.
2. Students should offer reasons why the lines or actions hold particular meaning for them.
3. Students may respond that they felt as though they could be the character, that it made the situation very real for them, instead of remote and distant.

◆ Build Grammar Skills

1. The Chorus members see all; no one sees more than *they*.
2. When Haimon heard of Antigone's sentence, no one was more enraged than *he*.
3. The rest of the group was as certain as *I* about the outcome of the play.
4. Though Ismene avoids her sister's fate, most people believe that Antigone is a much stronger character than *she*.
5. Although the details of her problems are different, Antigone faces some of the same issues as *we*.

◆ Build Vocabulary

Using the Root *-chor-*

1. c 2. b 3. a

Using the Word Bank

1. b 2. a 3. b 4. c
5. a 6. b

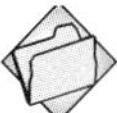

Idea Bank

Customizing for
Performance Levels

Following are suggestions for matching Idea Bank topics with your students' ability levels:
Less Advanced: 1, 5
Average: 2, 4, 5, 6
More Advanced: 3, 4, 6

Customizing for
Learning Modalities

Following are suggestions for matching Idea Bank topics with your students' learning modalities:
Interpersonal: 4, 5
Visual/Spatial: 5, 6
Bodily /Kinesthetic: 4

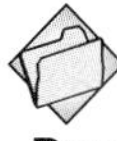

Guided Writing Lesson

Prewriting Strategy Draw the hexagonal on the board and label it as shown to give students a heuristic for analyzing the confrontation for which they will write a screenplay.

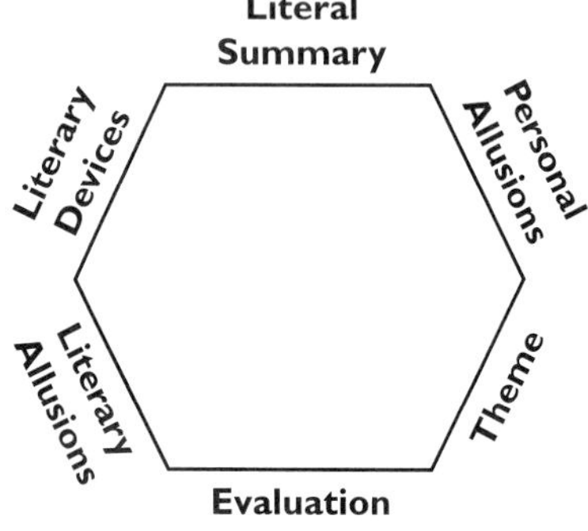

For more on the hexagonal heuristic, and additional strategies for prewriting, elaboration, and revision, see *Prentice Hall Writing and Grammar.*

Writing Lab CD-ROM

Have students complete the tutorial on Creative Writing. Follow these steps:

1. Use the instruction on formatting a script.
2. Use the stage directions Word Bin to get ideas for how characters will move, sound, and act.
3. Use the revision guidelines for making dialogue realistic.

Build Your Portfolio

Idea Bank

Writing

1. **Introduction** Imagine that you are the director of a student theater group in your school. Write a brief introduction to present to an audience before they see a performance of *Antigone*.

2. **Final Speech** Create a brief final speech in which the messenger has one last chance to comment on the action. You might begin with the line "I shall go now over the world's paths to tell the sad story of . . ."

3. **Editorial** Imagine that you are an editor for a Thebes newspaper. Write an editorial on whether Creon's response to Antigone's action was appropriate. **[Career Link]**

Speaking, Listening, and Viewing

4. **Mock Trial** Hold a mock trial in which both sides of Antigone's case are argued before the class. Have the class act as a jury to determine which argument is more convincing.

5. **Film Response** If possible, see a video version of a few scenes of *Antigone*. With other classmates, compare and contrast your ideas about the characters from reading the play with the interpretations on the video.

Researching and Representing

6. **Multimedia Presentation** Create a multimedia presentation on ancient Greek theater. Include illustrations or labeled diagrams, tape recordings of excerpts from *Antigone*, historical maps, timelines, and other items. **[Social Studies Link; Media Link]**

Online Activity www.phlit.phschool.com

Guided Writing Lesson

Scene of Conflict

In Scene 2, as the Sentry hands over to Creon the person arrested for burying Polyneices, Creon exclaims: "But this is Antigone! Why have you brought her here?" That moment captures the major conflict in the play. Think of a conflict from a story, play, or novel that would make a gripping scene for a movie. Who are the characters? What is the reason for their confrontation? Focus on this moment and use it to write a **scene of conflict** for a screenplay.

Writing Skills Focus: Format

The **format** for a screenplay is similar to that of other kinds of drama. The characters' words are set in blocks following the characters' names and special directions are printed in italics, often enclosed in parentheses. Use the format for *Antigone* as a model. Your directions will include information about lights, sound, and camera angles, which are obviously not a part of this ancient Greek script.

Prewriting Draw a picture to get a sense of the setting of the scene for which you will give directions. Indicate where the characters will be seen, and jot down notes about how they might move or what kind of background music to play.

Drafting Write out what the characters say and do as they act out their conflict. Include directions about character movement, camera shots, and background sounds or music within parentheses, separate from the dialogue.

Revising Ask a partner to read your scene and tell you whether your conflict conveys suspense or tension. Your partner may help you sharpen the characters' lines or clarify and expand descriptions that help the reader envision the background.

✓ ASSESSMENT OPTIONS

Formal Assessment, Selection Test, pp. 173–174, and Assessment Resources Software. The selection test is designed so that it can be easily customized to the ability levels of your students.
Alternative Assessment, p. 49, includes options for less advanced students, more advanced students, logical /mathematical learners, bodily/kinesthetic learners, and visual/spatial learners.

PORTFOLIO ASSESSMENT

Use the following rubrics in the ***Alternative Assessment*** booklet to assess student writing:
Introduction: Expression Rubric, p. 94
Final Speech: Summary Rubric, p. 98
Editorial: Persuasion Rubric, p. 105
Guided Writing Lesson: Drama Rubric, p. 109

Writing Process Workshop

Video Script

When you watch actors in a movie or television show, have you ever wondered how they know what to say and when to say it? They work from a **video script,** which has all the lines with directions for how to say them and how to move. Write a video script for a scene for a contemporary version of *Antigone*. In addition to the dialogue, include the directions for actors' movements, sound, lighting, and camera angles.

The following skills, introduced in this section's Guided Writing Lessons, will help you write a video script.

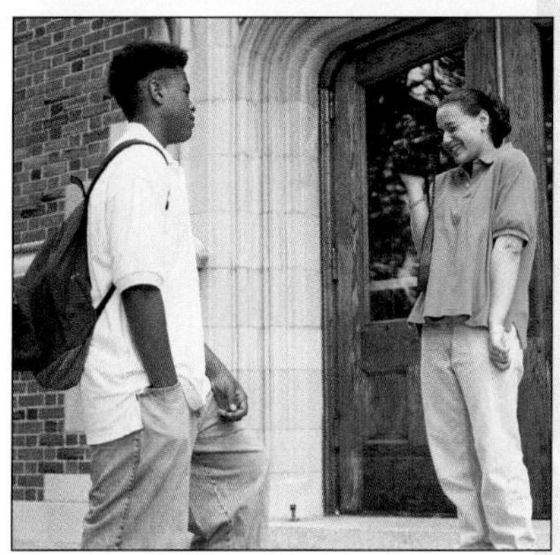

Writing Skills Focus

- ▶ **Use the proper format** to make your video script easy to understand. The characters' words should be set in blocks following the characters' names. Directions should be in italics, if you are working on a computer; otherwise, enclose them in parentheses. (Use the format for *Antigone* as a model.) In the directions, include information about lights, sound, and camera angles. (See p. 700.)
- ▶ **Concentrate on dialogue.** Dialogue is the heart of a drama. It is what breathes life into the characters. Your first priority should be to make your dialogue realistic and interesting.

The following excerpt from *Antigone* shows some of the features of the format for drama.

Model From Literature

from *Antigone* by Sophocles

① **Scene 5**

② [Enter blind ③ TEIRESIAS, led by a boy. The opening speeches of TEIRESIAS should be in singsong in contrast to the lines of CREON.]

TEIRESIAS. This is the way the blind man comes, Princes, Princes,
Lock step, two heads lit by the eyes of one.

CREON. What new thing have you to tell us, old Teiresias?

TEIRESIAS. ④ I have much to tell you: listen to the prophet Creon.

① Indicate the scene number.

② Stage directions and camera directions are set off with brackets or parentheses

③ Names of characters are printed in capitals—even in the stage directions. This way, actors can easily find any dialogue or directions that relate to them.

④ Each character's lines follow the character's name.

Prepare and Engage

LESSON OBJECTIVES

- To use recursive writing processes to write a video script
- To demonstrate control over the varieties of language
- To demonstrate control over grammatical elements such as punctuation of direct address

You may distribute copies of the Scoring Rubric for Drama (p. 109) in ***Alternative Assessment*** to make students aware before they begin of the criteria on which they will be evaluated. See the suggestions on p. 703 for ways to customize the rubric for this workshop.

Writing Lab CD-ROM
If your students have access to computers, you may want to have them work on the tutorial on Creative Writing to complete all or part of their video script. Follow these steps:

1. Have students use the interactive model of a dramatic scene.
2. Encourage students to use the word bins for drama and view the video clips about gathering details for drama.
3. Have students draft on the computer.
4. Suggest that students review the audio-annotated writing models for drama before they complete their drafts.
5. Have pairs of students complete the peer evaluation checklists for plays.

Beyond the Classroom

Career Connection As they write their scripts, students will make a variety of decisions that would be made by a number of different people in the theater or movie business. Although only a few students may be interested in pursuing careers as script writers, students can use this assignment as a springboard to consider which aspects of the entertainment industry do interest them. Remind students that movie and video studios employ electricians as well as lighting designers, administrative assistants as well as directors, tailors as well as costume designers, and personal trainers as well as dancers. For every production, a medical technician is hired to provide on-the-spot health care and caterers are hired to feed the actors and crew. Have students make a list of the many tasks besides acting that would need to be done if their video scripts were really being produced.

Develop Student Writing

Prewriting Strategy
You can use the Grid Organizer to help your students develop character traits. Place the organizer on the overhead projector. Write the character's name in the vertical box on the left. List the categories of traits in the first column of boxes. Then ask students to suggest details to fill in the appropriate boxes for each category.

Customize for
English Language Learners
Rephrase the character trait categories as questions for these students to answer. For instance, instead of listing "appearance" ask "What does the character look like?" Then, make sure these students understand the meaning of drama-related terms and expressions, such as dialogue, stage directions, character development, costume, sound effects, and others.

Customize for
Less Proficient Writers
These students especially will benefit from using the Character Trait Word Bin or brainstorming in a group for character traits before beginning to draft.

Customize for
Pre-AP Students
Challenge these students to relate their updated characters to famous political or entertainment figures who have qualities and issues similar to those of Creon and Antigone. Ask students to include an explanation of the parallels between their characters and the celebrities that served as character models.

Customize for
Bodily/Kinesthetic Learners
These students can role-play the scene before writing their contemporary dialogues. The acting out of the scene and the "trying on" of the role will help these students find updated language for these ancient characters.

APPLYING LANGUAGE SKILLS: Spoken and Written Language

Spoken language is usually more casual and conversational than **written language**. When you write dialogue—the words characters speak—you should use words and expressions that imitate natural speech and that reveal the personality of the character speaking.

from *Antigone*:

ISMENE. Antigone, you are mad! What could I possibly do?

ANTIGONE. You must decide whether you will help me or not.

ISMENE. I do not understand you. Help you in what?

ANTIGONE. Ismene, I am going to bury him. Will you come?

ISMENE. Bury him! You have just said the new law forbids it.

Practice Write a short conversation that you and a friend might have.

Writer's Solution Connection
Writing Lab

To help you write dialogue that reflects the personalities of your characters, use the section on Developing Characters and Plots in the Creative Writing Tutorial on the Writer's Solution Writing Lab.

Prewriting

Choose a Conflict At the heart of every drama is a conflict. Choose a moment of conflict from the play to use as the basis for your video script.

Develop Character Traits In a dramatic scene, you reveal the personalities of the characters through their dialogue and actions, as well as through the comments and behavior of other characters. Gather details about your characters from the text of *Antigone* to bring them to life. Review the play and update details. For example, a contemporary Antigone might wear jeans; a contemporary Haimon's goal might be to sing in a band. Fill in a chart like the one below to identify and describe important character traits for each of your characters. Use these details to help you imagine how your characters will look, sound, and act.

Character's		
	Appearance	
	Personality Traits	
	Habits and Abilities	
	Goals	

Drafting

Write the Dialogue Review the format of the dialogue in *Antigone*, and use it as the model for formatting your dialogue.

Use the dialogue itself, rather than the stage directions, to advance the action. For example, when Eurydice kills herself, have another character describe what happened, rather than describing it in the stage directions as something that the audience will see.

Use contemporary language in your updated scene. Give the dialogue a modern-day feel by using words, phrases, and expressions such as you and your friends might use.

Use Stage Directions How will the actors in your video scene know how to speak particular lines? How will they know when to move or stand still? Provide stage directions that give a clear and complete picture to performers and to people who are reading the play.

Writing Lab CD-ROM
If possible, have students use the interactive Character Traits Word Bin of the Creative Writing tutorial. Students can print the list of words they select and refer the list during drafting.

Elaboration Strategy
Encourage students to refer to their lists or charts of character traits while they are drafting. Students should choose words and use expressions that will reveal these traits through dialogue. Remind students, however, that they should not labor over word choice at this point. If a particular section is giving them difficulty, they should draft the rest of the scene and return later to the difficult portion.

Applying Language Skills
Spoken and Written Language
If time permits, encourage students to prepare for writing their dialogues by spending a day paying special attention to the way they speak. Students should jot down notes for a day on expressions and phrasings that they hear that they think they might use to give the sense of spoken language to their dialogues.

Revising

Use a Revision Checklist Use the following checklist to help you revise your video script.

- ▶ What is your scene's main conflict? How might it be possible to make this conflict stronger?
- ▶ How well does dialogue develop your characters? How can you improve the way the dialogue reveals the personalities of your characters? How can you make the dialogue sound more like natural speech?
- ▶ How thorough and clear are your stage directions? What can you add or change that will make the action even clearer to a reader or an actor?

Revision Model

ISMENE: ①I'm ~~I am~~ not sure what I can do, Antigone.
②It's crazy! ~~It is not wise.~~

ANTIGONE: ③Choose! ~~Won't you please help me?~~

ISMENE: ①I'm ~~I am~~ confused. ④What can I do? ~~In what way would you like me to help you?~~

① The writer changes *I am* to the contraction *I'm* to make the dialogue sound more conversational.
② The writer replaces this formally written sentence with a colloquial expression that reflects natural speech.
③ The writer makes Antigone's words more forceful to reflect the strength of her character.
④ The writer changes Ismene's question to sound more natural.

Publishing

Perform Your Scene Using the dialogue and stage directions in your video script, stage a performance of your scene. Have the actors rehearse the scene, and review any parts of the script that seem difficult or confusing. Appoint a technical director to take care of things such as lighting, sound, and camera angles.

Applying Language Skills: Punctuating Words of Direct Address

When one character speaks directly to another using the listener's name or other identifier, the speaker is using *direct address.* Nouns of direct address should be set off with commas, as in the following examples:

Everything else, my son, to your father's will.

Antigone, are you mad?

Practice Add a character's name or other identifier to indicate to whom each character is speaking.

1. You must decide. (Antigone to Ismene)
2. What can I do? (Ismene to Antigone)

Writing Application Add nouns of direct address to some of your dialogue. Set off words of direct address with commas.

Writer's Solution Connection Language Lab

For more on nouns of direct address, see the lesson on Commas in the Writer's Solution Language Lab.

Revision Strategy

Have students reenter their writing to compare their scripts to the Character Traits Grid they created in prewriting. Encourage students to use colored pencils to mark off words that describe each category: appearance; personality traits; habits and abilities; and goals.

Revision Model You might have students work in pairs to discuss the Revision Model on this page and suggest similar revisions to each other's work. After reading the scenes aloud together, students can use the revision guidelines to revise their own work and to offer constructive criticism of their partner's work.

Writing Lab CD-ROM
Students can view the video tips for peer editors and use peer evaluation checklists on-line. The proofreading section also offers an audio-annotated literary model for formatting a play.

Publishing

If students choose to perform their scenes, they can evaluate one another using the Peer Assessment for a Dramatic Performance on p. 120 in ***Alternative Assessment.***

Reinforce and Extend

Applying Language Skills

Point out to students that nouns of direct address can sometimes be used to add emphasis or urgency to a character's words. In other cases, they can create a personal, immediate tone.

Suggested answers:
1. Ismene, you must decide.
2. What can I do, sister?

✓ Assessment

PORTFOLIO ASSESSMENT		4	3	2	1
Use the rubric for Drama in ***Alternative Assessment*** (p. 109) to assess students' writing. Use these criteria to customize the rubric to the assignment.	**Spoken and Written Language**	All dialogue reflects the patterns and expressions of natural speech.	Most dialogue reflects the patterns and expressions of natural speech.	Some dialogue reflects the patterns and expressions of natural speech.	Little or no dialogue reflects the patterns and expressions of natural speech.
	Punctuating Words of Direct Address	Words of direct address are used effectively and always punctuated correctly.	Words of direct address are used and usually punctuated correctly.	Words of direct address are seldom punctuated correctly.	Words of direct address are not used or punctuated correctly.

Prepare and Engage

LESSON OBJECTIVES
- To research self-selected and assigned topics

Customize for
Interpersonal Learners
Some searching methods (the use of a plus symbol corresponding to the Boolean operator AND, for example) are widely used. Other methods for narrowing a topic are unique to each Internet search engine. Student partners or small teams can explore the Help section of each search engine to develop a "Guide to Searching" useful to classmates doing Internet research.

Answers

Possible answers for researching an author, Ray Bradbury, are given:

1. The key words *Ray Bradbury* were suitable.
2. Two search engines, Altavista and Infoseek, both yielded thousands of Web sites. The first ten or twenty were the best matches. Links appeared in each Web site, mainly to others given by the search engine.
3. The most complete Web site, with a biography and many useful links, was the Ray Bradbury Page at www.BrookingsBook.com, a site for a commercial bookseller. Some Web sites were selling books and games, rather than providing information; others were no longer being maintained.
4. The most accurate sources are newspaper articles, interviews, a study guide, and Web sites that are continually updated with contributions and corrections submitted by fans of Ray Bradbury's works.

Student Success Workshop

Research Skills — Locating Information on the Internet

Strategies for Success

Tools like the Internet can make conducting research less time-consuming than it once was. Sometimes, however, finding specific information on the Internet can be difficult. For instance, if you search for information about the 1998 Winter Olympic Games in Nagano, Japan, you might find thousands of pages of information—from biographies of athletes to the history of the Olympics, along with details about individual sports. How do you find exactly what you want?

Rev Up Your Search Engines Search engines such as Yahoo, Lycos, or Excite can help you find your way through the maze of Internet information. They search for Internet "links" to Web pages and deliver them to Internet users. Search engines invite you to use "key words." If you're looking for information about your favorite NFL football team, you might type "Dallas Cowboys" or "NFL Football" into the blank key-word space provided by the search engine.

Narrow Your Topic To save time and reduce the risk of reaching a dead end, be as specific as possible in indicating what you're looking for. Say you want to learn more about a particular musician. The key word *music* might eventually get you to information about that musician, but it could take a long time. Typing in the person's name as the key word—or the kind of music he or she performs—will more quickly lead you to information you want.

Select Reliable Sources Anyone with a computer and Internet access can set up an Internet Web page. To get accurate information, search for sites from individuals or organizations with credentials. For example, if you are planning a trip to New York City, you will most likely find more complete, accurate, and up-to-date information on a Web site produced by an official New York City tourism agency than by a private citizen offering information about his favorite restaurants. You must evaluate the credibility and accuracy of information sources you consult.

Apply the Strategies

Use the Internet to gather information on the history of your home state, a recipe for a favorite meal, the author of a book you enjoyed, or a topic of your own. Then answer these questions:

1. How did you narrow down your search topic? Were your key words too broad, too narrow, or just right?
2. Which search engine did you use? Did one search engine provide more useful information than others? Explain how "links" worked to help you in your search.
3. Describe some characteristics of Web sites you visited. Which were helpful? Which characteristics were unnecessary?
4. Which information sources did you consider most accurate? Why?

Here are situations in which you may want to locate information on the Internet:
- ▶ Comparing different product brands
- ▶ Researching information about colleges
- ▶ Needing a long-range weather forecast
- ▶ Learning about groups that interest you
- ▶ Researching a city, state, or country
- ▶ Searching for a text in an out-of-town library

Test Preparation Workshop

Locating Information on the Internet Point out that the concept of key words is not new to the Internet; key words are valuable tools for finding information anwhere— in card catalogs, in the bound volumes or on-line version of an encyclopedia, in a periodicals database, and more. Provide the following sample test question:

To find information about wildlife preserves in the Central American country of Costa Rica, what key words are probably most useful and efficient?

A "Central American wildlife preserves"
B Costa Rica + wildlife
C conservation > wildlife preserves
D Central America - Costa Rican wildlife

Discuss the use of quotation marks (to keep a phrase together), the plus symbol (to limit the search to documents with both terms), the "greater than" symbol (to find a narrower subject within a category), and the minus symbol (to search for a term excluding the subtracted subcategory). Students should recognize that the key words in B are likeliest to lead directly to the needed information.

Part 2 History and Tradition

Roman senators at the Imperial Court,
Museo Nazionale Romano delle Terme, Rome, Italy

One-Minute Planning Guide

The acts in this play cover a variety of dramatic elements that will give students insight into the history and tradition of the theater—especially the work of William Shakespeare. Each of the five acts in *The Tragedy of Julius Caesar* develops an aspect of drama or tragedy while exploring the consequences of each character's actions. Act I introduces a power struggle—a theme so timeless that directors have used *The Tragedy of Julius Caesar* to portray the political situations of many countries and ages. In Act II, students watch Caesar ignore warnings and signs as he walks into the assassination trap. In Act III, in some of the most stirring and memorable soliloquies in drama, Brutus and Antony expound on the choices made.

Act IV develops Brutus' internal conflict through his external conflict with Cassius, a character whose base motives highlight Brutus' noble ones. Act V brings the action to a close with a battle. Antony's triumph in this battle brings about the resolution of all individual, public, and political conflicts.

Customize for *Varying Student Needs*

When assigning this play to your students, keep in mind the following factors:

Act I
- The list of unfamiliar character names may intimidate some students.
- Glosses in a text may be unfamiliar to many students.

Act II
- Some students may have difficulty reading blank verse for meaning.

Act III
- Pre-AP Students will enjoy reading the full text of the famous soliloquies in this act.
- Some students may need help understanding the irony in Antony's persuasive speech to the crowd.

Act IV
- This act focuses much more on dialogue than action. Events are referred to or implied rather than described. Students may need help with reading between the lines.

Act V
- The action in this act is fast-paced and students may need help to identify changes in location.

Humanities: Art

Roman Senators at the Imperial Court.

During the five centuries of the Roman republic, the Senate was the most powerful body in the government; made up largely of aristocrats, it is today considered a model of orderly government. The republic was destroyed by the civil war that followed the assassination of Julius Caesar. When the republic was finally replaced by empire during the reign of Augustus, the Senate was kept on, like the other institutions of government, but it became the tool of the emperor, not the independent body that had ruled during the days of the republic.

Help students link this art with the focus of Part 2, "History and Tradition," by answering the following question:

How does art help society preserve history and tradition? *Art often reflects or comments on important issues or people. Art like this sculpture provides a concrete clue about people who lived thousands of years ago.*

Enrichment

Shakespeare's Globe Theater

Most of Shakespeare's masterpieces were performed at the Globe theater. It was built by Richard and Cuthbert Burbage, sons of James Burbage, who had constructed London's first theater (named, simply, The Theater). Theater people occupied an odd position in London society. Although the city fathers looked down on actors, the common people clamored to see them perform in plays. Men like Shakespeare and the Burbages enjoyed a reputation somewhat like that of a rock star today.

The popularity of plays meant that Shakespeare's Globe, while small enough to allow actors to be heard, had to house audiences as large as 2,500 to 3,000 people. These "packed" houses must have been quite uncomfortable at times, especially when you consider that people didn't bathe or change their clothes very often. Those who paid an admission price of a penny stood throughout the performance. The second most expensive seats in the house were located in a gallery behind the performers. Although these audience members could see only the actors' backs and probably couldn't hear very well, they were willing to pay the extra price to ensure that they themselves would be seen by the rest of the audience.

Modern technology such as lighting and special sound effects was not available to Shakespeare and his contemporaries. For this reason, indications of light, sound, and setting, were often written into the script. Characters are likely to announce "'Tis dark!" as they enter a scene.

The first Globe burned to the ground in 1613, when a cannon fired in a performance of *Henry VIII* ignited the theater's thatched roof. The theater was rebuilt, and it is the foundation of this second Globe that was discovered in 1990.

The SHAKESPEAREAN

The Globe Theater

The Tragedy of Julius Caesar, like most of Shakespeare's plays, was produced in a public theater. Public theaters were built around roofless courtyards having no artificial light. Performances, therefore, were given only during daylight hours. Surrounding the courtyard were three levels of galleries with benches where wealthier playgoers sat. Poorer spectators, called groundlings, stood and watched a play from the courtyard, which was called the pit.

Most of Shakespeare's plays were performed in the Globe theater. No one is certain exactly what the Globe looked like, though Shakespeare tells us it was round or octagonal. We know that it was open to the sky and that it held between 2,500 and 3,000 people. (This knowledge was the basis for the reconstruction of the Globe theater that began in 1988.) Its foundation was discovered in 1990; its excavation has revealed clues about the plays, the actors, and the audience. The tiny part of the foundation initially uncovered yielded a great number of hazelnut shells. Hazelnuts were Elizabethan "popcorn"; people munched on them all during a performance.

The stage was a platform that extended into the pit. Actors entered and left the stage from doors located behind the platform. The portion of the galleries behind and above the stage was used primarily as dressing and storage rooms. The second-level gallery right above the stage, however, was used as an upper stage.

There was no scenery in the theaters of Shakespeare's day. Settings were indicated by references in the dialogue. As a result, one scene could follow another in rapid succession. The actors wore elaborate clothing—typical Elizabethan clothing, not costuming.

▲ The new Globe Theater under construction.

▼ Below, visitors enjoy the newly constructed Globe at the International Shakespeare Globe Centre in Southwark, England.

Thus, the plays produced in Shakespeare's day were fast-paced, colorful productions that usually lasted two hours.

An important difference between Shakespeare's theater and theater of today is that acting companies of the sixteenth century were made up only of men and boys. Women did not perform on the stage, as it was not considered proper. Boys aged eleven, twelve, or thirteen—before their voices changed—performed the female roles.

Reconstructing the Globe

In 1988, on April 23 (believed to be Shakespeare's birthday), years of fund-raising and effort resulted in a remarkable birthday present for the playwright. Work began on a reconstruction of his Globe theater. The design is based on archaeological evidence and a drawing by Wendeslas Hollar. A contract drawn up in 1600 for the Fortune playhouse (built by the same carpenter who built the Globe) provides additional details.

The new Globe, like the first two, is made of wood. Traditional sixteenth-century carpentry techniques were used for much of the construction. A thatched roof protects the stage and galleries and lime plaster covers the walls. After long years of fund-raising and construction, the theater opened to its first full season on June 8, 1997, with a production of *Henry V.*

▼ This drawing shows the features of the Globe theater. Notice the stage, the doors through which actors enter and exit, the "upper stage," the galleries where wealthy people sit, and the pit where the groundlings stand.

Enrichment

The Globe Today London's new Globe theater is considered a remarkable replica of Shakespeare's original. Located on the Thames, a short distance from the site of the original, it retains the characteristics of the original—including the circular shape, open center, and thatched roof. Since few details of the original remain, the builders relied on the building contracts, which are extant, for the rival theaters, the Rose and the Fortune. These theaters were built by the same carpenter as the Globe.

The new Globe seats 1,000. Because the seats curve around the stage, everyone has a different view of the action; for some, the view is blocked by pillars, but no audience member is more than fifty feet from the stage. The yard, or pit, has room for 450 groundlings, some of whom rest their arms on the edge of the stage. As in Elizabethan times, the audience tends to join in the proceedings, commenting on the action.

Plays are performed as they would have been in Shakespeare's time, with little or no scenery, people moving around in the yard, and vendors circulating to sell refreshments. The experience is a contrast to performances in modern theaters—even performances of Shakespeare's plays—which take place in a darkened, quiet theater with an attentive and respectful audience.

Customize for *Bodily/Kinesthetic Learners*

Encourage these students to construct a model of the Globe or an Elizabethan theater. They may use the sketch on this page or do research to discover further details about the theater's construction.

Customize for *Visual/Spatial Learners*

Encourage these students to refer to the diagram as they read *The Tragedy of Julius Caesar,* determining where various parts of the action would best be staged.

Internet

For additional information, see *Shakespeare and the Globe: Then and Now* on the Internet at this address: **http://shakespeare.eb.com/shakespeare/index2.html**

We recommend that you preview this site before sending students to it. Be aware that addresses may have changed since we published this information.

The site includes biographies, videos, articles, and images related to the works of Shakespeare and the reconstructed Globe theater.

More About the Author

Shakespeare lived in the intellectual world of the Renaissance, the religious world of the Reformation, and the widening geographic world of the Age of Exploration. Although Shakespeare and his contemporaries did not apply these labels to their time, they were profoundly influenced by the climate of change and adventure.

Ironically, the more that boundaries and traditions were challenged, the more fiercely Elizabethans clung to them. For this reason, rank, social status, and rules of propriety were extremely important to the people of Shakespeare's day. So fanatic were the Elizabethans about social order that Clothing Acts were passed—clothing laws that specified the clothing that could be worn by different classes of people. Not surprisingly, the Clothing Acts were largely ignored, but they reflect the sentiment of the times. Students will notice at the opening of Act I of *The Tragedy of Julius Caesar* that the working class are chided for going about in public without the proper attire that indicates their station and function.

Literature CD-ROM To acquaint students with William Shakespeare's life, use *The Time, Life, and Works of Shakespeare* CD-ROM. In Feature 2, students can learn about Shakespeare's early life. Shakespeare's career as an actor is described in Feature 3. Feature 4 documents Shakespeare's rise as a playwright. Feature 5 focuses on the historical context that shaped Shakespeare's later work, and includes information about the Essex rebellion, the ascent to the throne of James I, other major dramatists of Shakespeare's day, and the publication of the first folio of Shakespeare's plays.

To build background on drama, use the CD-ROM *How to Read and Understand Drama,* Feature 3. This feature focuses on the ways in which stage directions suggest dramatic elements, how scenery and lighting indicate transitions in time and place, and how stage devices and conventions help to reveal a character's inner thoughts.

Guide for Reading

William Shakespeare

(1564–1616)

William Shakespeare is regarded as the greatest writer in the English language. Nearly 400 years after his death, Shakespeare's plays continue to be read widely and produced throughout the world. They have the same powerful impact on today's audiences as they had when they were first staged.

What's Past Is Prologue Based on records showing that Shakespeare was baptized on April 26, 1564, scholars estimate the date of his birth as April 23 of the same year. He was born in Stratford-on-Avon, northwest of London. Shakespeare's father, John, was a successful glove maker and businessman. He was a respected man and a leader in the community. Shakespeare's mother, whose maiden name was Mary Arden, was the daughter of his father's landlord. No written evidence of Shakespeare's boyhood exists, but given his father's status, it is probable that young Will attended the Stratford Grammar School, where he acquired a knowledge of Latin. In addition to Latin grammar, Shakespeare and his classmates would have read Latin dramas by Plautus and Terence, Latin poetry by Ovid, Horace, and Virgil, and studied logic, history, natural history, and some Greek. When Shakespeare left school, he had a solid foundation of classical literature and other subjects.

In late November or early December 1582, Shakespeare married Anne Hathaway. Records show that she was twenty-six and he was eighteen. The couple had a daughter, Susanna, in 1583, and twins, Judith and Hamnet, in 1585. Some scholars believe that for a brief time after his marriage, Shakespeare served as a country schoolmaster.

All the World's a Stage It's uncertain how Shakespeare came to be connected with the theater in the 1580's. Perhaps he was influenced by seeing the traveling performers who stopped and performed in Stratford on their way to London. At the age of eighteen or nineteen, he is believed to have been acting in plays in London. Friends in London helped him financially and professionally. Soon, he was well established in social and theatrical circles. By 1594, he was part owner and principal playwright of the Lord Chamberlain's Men, one of the most successful theater companies in London.

In 1599, the company built the famous Globe theater, where most of Shakespeare's plays were performed. When James I became king in 1603, following the death of Elizabeth I, he took control of the Lord Chamberlain's Men and renamed the company The King's Men. A major stockholder in the company, Shakespeare continued to write for and act with this company.

Parting Is Such Sweet Sorrow

In about 1610, Shakespeare retired to Stratford, a prosperous middle-class man, having profited from his share in a successful theater company. He moved into the second largest house in Stratford, invested in grain and farmland, and continued to write plays.

Shakespeare wrote his will on March 25, 1616. He left the bulk of his property to his oldest daughter Susanna, and a smaller sum to his other daughter Judith. (Hamnet had died in 1596.) According to the laws of the time, his widow automatically received a lifetime income from one-third of his estate. Although Susanna and Judith both had children, none lived to have children of their own. For this reason, Shakespeare has no living descendants. On April 23 (his birthday, if scholars are correct), 1616, Shakespeare died.

The Tragedy of Julius Caesar

from *Shakespeare Alive!*
Joseph Papp and Elizabeth Kirkland

Joseph Papp, the founder and producer of the New York Shakespeare festival, devoted his life to making Shakespeare accessible to all. In Shakespeare Alive! *he recreates the England in which Shakespeare lived and worked.*

Pounds of flesh in Venice; ambitious king-killers in Scotland; star-crossed lovers in Verona; daughterly ingratitude in ancient Britain; whimsical courtships in the Forest of Arden; sultry love and stern politics in ancient Egypt—Shakespeare's imagination appears to have cornered the market on exciting, inventive plot making. It seems there's no story he hasn't thought of. But how could all of these intriguing plots and stirring adventures possibly come from a single brain?

The answer is simple—they didn't. When it came to plots, Shakespeare was a borrower, not an inventor. It is astonishing to realize that not a single one of the stories in his plays was his own creation. Rather than growing his plots himself, he plucked them from the plentiful orchards of other authors.

Yet before we start suspecting Shakespeare of plagiarism, we'd better take a look at what everyone else was doing in the literary world. Although this business of outright lifting from other writers' work might seem dubious to us, it wasn't unusual in Shakespeare's time. Without copyright laws to protect an author's works,the business of writing and publishing was truly a "free trade" affair, and everyone's works were saleable commodities. Furthermore, the authors' originality just wasn't an issue; in fact, they were openly encouraged to imitate certain writing styles and literary models, especially, but not exclusively, the classical ones. The upshot of all this was that sixteenth-century authors and playwrights regularly raided both their predecessors and their colleagues, without giving it a second thought; one contemporary of Shakespeare's boasts proudly, "I have so written, as I have read."

In his far-flung borrowing, then, Shakespeare was a product of his times; and yet in this, as in so much else, he flew high above his contemporaries. Shakespeare's ultimate source was the broad spirit of the age, which he drew on in his own unique fashion. The great literary works available in the Elizabethan time mingled in his mind with cheap ballads and penny-pamphlets on sale in Saint Paul's Churchyard, with tavern jokes, church sermons, and the constant influx of new information about foreign lands.All of this jostled up against the phrases and sounds of the everyday work and play of tanners, alehouse keepers, sailors, merchants, constables, nobles, and foreigners in London. Shakespeare imbibed the rich Elizabethan atmosphere as he walked the streets of London, and it was this atmosphere that he converted magically into theater.

Familiar Expressions from Shakespeare

You've probably quoted Shakespeare without even realizing it! Look for familiar expressions and phrases in the following list. You may be surprised at how much Shakespeare you already know!

"Eaten out of house and home," *Henry IV Part 2*, Act 2, Scene 1
"Cruel to be kind," *Hamlet,* Act 3, Scene 4
"Knock,/ knock! Who's there?" *Macbeth,* Act 2, Scene 3
"Too much of a good thing," *As You Like It,* Act 4, Scene 1
"Neither a borrower nor a lender be," *Hamlet,* Act 1, Scene 3
"Something wicked this way comes," *Macbeth,* Act 4, Scene 1
"To thine own self be true," *Hamlet,* Act 1, Scene 3
"A tower of strength," *Richard III,* Act 5, Scene 3

◆ Background for Understanding

The Tragedy of Julius Caesar in Performance In 1988, Joseph Papp's New York Shakespeare Festival produced *The Tragedy of Julius Caesar.* The performance starred Al Pacino as Mark Antony and Martin Sheen as Brutus. This was not the first time popular actors played these prestigious roles. Marlon Brando played Mark Antony in Metro-Goldwyn-Mayer's 1953 movie production of the play. Both Papp's and Metro's productions were traditional interpretations, with classic settings and period costumes. Others, however, have used the political themes in the play as a comment on contemporary social and political issues. In 1937, Orson Welles staged a production in which Antony's "Friends, Romans, countrymen" funeral oration was delivered amidst searchlights and symbols suggesting a Nazi rally. A 1993 production portrays Cassius as an ambitious businessman and Mark Antony as a contemporary military leader. One of the first plays to be performed at the newly constructed Globe theater in 1599, *The Tragedy of Julius Caesar* has remained a vital and relevant production piece for more than four centuries.

Enrichment Shakespeare's plays have not only had a powerful impact on audiences over the centuries, but they have also had a powerful impact on everyday contemporary English. Dozens of familiar words and phrases were invented by Shakespeare—"catch cold," "laugh it off," "disgraceful conduct," "fair play," and the slang word "lousy," to name just a few. As critic Christopher Morley has written, "Everyone is a Shakespeare scholar unconsciously. You yourself have probably quoted him today."

Humanities: Performing Arts

Playwrights Like Hollywood screenwriters, playwrights of the sixteenth century were subject in large part to the whims of the public. Plays were not judged successful based on their literary merit; they were assessed on the size of the audience they drew. And, like movie theaters, sixteenth-century theaters were constantly changing their offerings. This demand for fresh, new material in short order is part of what earned playwrights their reputations as hacks. With a demand for quick turnover, the playwrights couldn't afford to be particularly careful about creating perfect plays. Like today's entertainment industry, sixteenth- century drama was a ratings game.

After a theater company bought a play from the playwright, they registered it with the office of the Master of Revels. Originally set up to organize court entertainment, the office of the Master of Revels became a powerful department through which government regulations were carried out. This power extended to censorship; in 1589 the Master of Revels was given power to "strike out such part and matters as they shall find unfit and undecent to be handled in plays."

Prepare and Engage

LESSON OBJECTIVES

1. **To develop vocabulary and word identification skills**
   - Related Words: Forms of *Portent*
   - Using the Word Bank: Synonyms
   - Extending Word Study: Puns
2. **To use a variety of reading strategies to read and comprehend an essay**
   - Connect Your Experience
   - Reading Strategy: Use Text Aids
   - Tips to Guide Reading
   - Read to Appreciate Author's Craft
3. **To increase knowledge of other cultures and to connect common elements across cultures**
   - Connecting Themes Across Cultures (ATE)
4. **To express and support responses to the text**
   - Critical Thinking
   - Idea Bank: Journal Entry
   - Idea Bank: Speech
   - Analyze Literary Criticism
5. **To analyze literary elements**
   - Literary Focus: Exposition in Drama
6. **To read in order to research self-selected and assigned topics**
   - Idea Bank: Roman Symbols
   - Speaking, Listening, and Viewing Mini-Lesson
7. **To increase knowledge of the rules of grammar and usage**
   - Build Grammar Skills: The Subjunctive Mood

Test Preparation

Reading Comprehension: Identify Patterns of Organization (ATE, p. 711) The teaching tips and sample test item in this workshop support the instruction and practice in the unit workshop: **Reading Comprehension: Characteristics of Text** (SE, p. 809)

Guide for Reading

◆ Background for Understanding

HISTORY

In 60 B.C., Gaius Julius Caesar joined forces with Marcus Licinius Crassus and Gnaeus Pompey to rule Rome as the First Triumvirate. Although he was trained as a politician, Caesar demonstrated his skill as a warrior with military victories in Gaul and Britain. When his growing strength and popularity began to make Pompey nervous, Pompey allied himself with Caesar's conservative rivals and ordered Caesar to give up his army. Caesar's response was fast and forceful. With his army, he led his troops against Pompey, forcing Pompey and the conservatives to flee to the Balkans. Within sixty days, Caesar became master of Italy. He continued to war with and pursue Pompey, following him to Egypt, where Caesar discovered Pompey had been murdered.

Pompey's forces reorganized after the death of their leader. Caesar defeated these forces once and for all in Spain, where he triumphed over the sons of Pompey. (It is from this final battle that Caesar is returning at the opening of the play.) Soon after, Julius Caesar was assassinated by a group of aristocrats led by Marcus Junius Brutus and Caius Cassius.

The characters in this play are real people who acted in the real-life drama of this episode in Roman history. Marcus Brutus lived from 85–45 B.C. He was a quiet, idealistic man. He had fought against Caesar in support of Pompey, but when Pompey was defeated, Caesar pardoned Brutus and the two resumed the friendship they had before the conflict. Brutus' father-in-law, however, killed himself rather than submit to Caesar's rule. Cassius, who was married to Brutus' sister Junia, also had supported Pompey and was pardoned when Pompey was defeated. These details from history helped set the stage for the hidden resentments and suspicions that fill *The Tragedy of Julius Caesar.*

LITERATURE

Julius Caesar was a great general, a gifted speaker, and a popular ruler—so why would anyone want to kill him? Shakespeare didn't make up this tragic tale of power and betrayal. He based his play on real people and real events. Shakespeare read about Caesar (and his friends and enemies) in the chronicles of Plutarch, a Greek biographer who delved into the psychological as well as the factual details of his subjects' lives. Shakespeare and other people of his time were able to read Plutarch's *Lives of the Noble Greeks and Romans* translated from Latin into English by Sir Thomas North.

Some Common Elizabethan Words

The English language was somewhat different during Shakespeare's time. As you read *The Tragedy of Julius Caesar*, most of the unfamiliar words and phrases you will encounter are explained in footnotes. The following, however, appear so frequently that learning them will make your reading of the play easier.

anon: Soon
aye: Yes
betimes: Right now
e'en: Even
e'er: Ever
hence: Away, from here
hie: Hurry
hither: Here
marry: Indeed
prithee: Pray thee
sooth: Truly
withal: In addition
wont: Accustomed

Prentice Hall Literature Program Resources

REINFORCE / RETEACH / EXTEND

Selection Support Pages
Build Vocabulary: Forms of *Portent*, p. 204
Build Grammar Skills: Subjunctive Mood, p. 205
Reading Strategy: Use Text Aids, p. 206
Literary Focus: Exposition in Drama, p. 207

Strategies for Diverse Student Needs, p. 50

Beyond Literature The Globe Theater, p. 51

Formal Assessment Selection Test, pp. 176–178; Assessment Resources Software

Alternative Assessment, p. 50

Writing and Language Transparencies

Daily Language Practice, Week 13, p. 124
Context Chart, pp. 59–64

Resource Pro CD-ROM

Listening to Literature Audiocassettes

Literature CD-ROM

The Tragedy of Julius Caesar, Act I

◆ Literature and Your Life

Connect Your Experience

Have you ever persuaded someone to do or believe something by the way you spoke and what you said, or been persuaded by someone else? The art of persuasion plays an important role early in this play.

Journal Writing List three things you have recently been persuaded to do, or ideas you have been persuaded to consider valid. For each, explain how you were persuaded.

Thematic Focus: Facing the Consequences

Although political powers sometimes try to persuade one another with words, often they try to "persuade" one another by force. Why do you think political forces so often go to war rather than settle differences through peaceful means?

◆ Literary Focus

Exposition in Drama

The **exposition** of a drama is the opening part of the work that introduces the characters, the setting, the situation, and any other details crucial to an understanding of the work. For example, in the opening of *The Tragedy of Julius Caesar,* a man in the crowd states, "We make holiday to see Caesar and to rejoice in his triumph." The response of the tribunes indicates that they fear Caesar's growing power. In just a few lines of dialogue, Shakespeare has revealed the basic situation: Caesar is returning victorious, the public loves him, and some in the government resent him. The scenes that follow build on the information presented in the exposition.

◆ Build Grammar Skills

The Subjunctive Mood

The **subjunctive mood** of a verb is used in two situations. It is used to express a condition that is contrary to fact:

If I *were* Brutus now, and he *were* Cassius . . .

In this situation, the verb form is always *were.*

The subjunctive mood is also used in clauses beginning with *that* to express indirectly a demand, recommendation, suggestion, or statement of necessity.

Antony requested that Caesar *take* the crown.

Here, the verb is always the base form. It does not change, regardless of the subject.

◆ Reading Strategy

Use Text Aids

Playwrights provide **text aids** for actors, which can help readers as well. The stage directions that tell actors where and how to move can help you to picture what is happening on the stage. Pay attention to the stage directions (enclosed in brackets in the text) to help you follow the stage action.

Elizabethan plays prepared for a modern reading audience provide another aid: Notes and glosses along the sides of text lines explain the meanings of words and phrases that are no longer in use. Refer to these notes to clarify unfamiliar language.

◆ Build Vocabulary

Related Words: Forms of *Portent*

In Act I, much is made of the *portentous* signs that something bad is about to happen. The adjective *portentous* comes from the verb *portend,* which means "to be an omen or warning of." The noun form is *portent.* There will be many *portents* in the acts that follow.

Word Bank

Before you read, preview this list of words from the selection.

replication
spare
infirmity
surly
portentous
prodigious

Develop Understanding

One-Minute Insight Based on historical events in ancient Rome, Shakespeare's *The Tragedy of Julius Caesar* is a brilliant study of character and conflict set in a political arena. Much of the plot hinges on the character and internal conflicts of Caesar's friend Brutus, who is drawn, at first reluctantly, into an assassination conspiracy against Caesar. The choices Brutus makes—and the consequences of these choices—make for a rich portrait of the conflicts between loyalty and ambition; between friendship and what Brutus comes to perceive as his patriotic duty.

Customize for
Less Proficient Readers
To familiarize these students with the plot and characters of the play before they begin reading, you may want to play the portion of a video version through the events in Act I. The version featuring Marlon Brando as Antony is available in most video stores.

Customize for
Pre-AP Students
Suggest that students form a discussion group to analyze the conflicts introduced in Act I of the play: the external conflict between the conspirators and Caesar and the internal conflict within Brutus. Suggest that they watch how these conflicts change and develop throughout the play.

Customize for
English Language Learners
These students will have the most difficulty with Shakespeare's language. You may want to summarize the act for them and have them read only selected key speeches, focusing on the exposition of the plot and the techniques Cassius uses to persuade Brutus to join his conspiracy.

Customize for
Gifted/Talented Students
Encourage students to meet in groups to interpret the behavior of the major characters after reading each scene. Each member of the group could choose a different character to role-play or defend during the meetings.

Test Preparation Workshop

Reading Comprehension: Identify Patterns of Organization Many national standardized tests require students to analyze the characteristics of a text, including identifying patterns of organization. Use this sample test item to help students with this reading skill.

> Although this business of outright lifting from other writers' work might seem dubious to us, it wasn't unusual in Shakespeare's time. Without copyright laws to protect an author's works, the business of writing and publishing was truly a free trade affair.

The author makes a connection to the publishing world of today in order to—

A show a comparison
B show a contrast
C persuade
D entertain

Guide students to see that the author is showing a difference, or contrast between two time periods. The correct answer is B.

▶Critical Viewing◀

Infer *The man standing is looking down at the other two men who have to raise their eyes to see him. The way the men are positioned suggests that the standing man is figuratively as well as literally elevated above the others.*

Humanities: Film

On stage, an actor is usually separated from even the closest members of the audience by a space of at least five feet. In many theaters, the stage is raised from two to five feet above the seating area as well. For this reason, subtle facial expressions and small gestures are not the most effective means of communicating a character's emotions. In a movie, however, every twitch of an actor's eyebrow is visible to the audience. The smallest motion of an actor's hand can be used to indicate purpose, indecision, or tension. For instance, close-ups in the MGM version of *Julius Caesar* show the anxiety the conspirators feel before the assassination attempt. In addition to close-ups, camera angles and techniques can be used to enhance the mood of a scene. Ask students to answer the following questions about this still from the MGM version of *Julius Caesar*:

1. How does the camera angle contribute to the sense of Caesar's authority over the kneeling men? *By shooting from over Caesar's shoulder, the director highlights Caesar's physical position over the men.*
2. Describe the expressions on the faces of the characters. *Caesar's expression is calm and confident. He is unaware of the plot against him. The expressions of the kneeling men betray some of their nervousness. Cassius, kneeling at center, wears an expression of repressed anticipation.*

The Tragedy of JULIUS CAESAR

William Shakespeare

▲ Critical Viewing How can you tell that the man standing is a man of power? **[Infer]**

Block Scheduling Strategies

Consider these suggestions to take advantage of extended class time:

- Invite students to view Feature 2 on the CD-ROM, *The Time, Life, and Works of Shakespeare.* This feature focuses on Shakespeare's early life and Elizabethan London.
- As an alternative to a silent reading of the play, assign roles and have groups act out selected scenes. Encourage students to act the stage directions.
- Make the audiocassette available to students who would like to listen to all or part of the selection.
- Have students work individually or in groups to complete the Critical Thinking questions on p. 730.
- Have students complete Reading Strategy: *Use Text Aids* in ***Selection Support,*** p. 206.

CHARACTERS

Julius Caesar		**A Soothsayer**	
Octavius Caesar **Marcus Antonius** **M. Aemilius Lepidus**	triumvirs* after the death of Julius Caesar	**Cinna,** a poet	
Cicero **Publius** **Popilius Lena**	senators	**Another Poet**	
Marcus Brutus **Cassius** **Casca** **Trebonius** **Ligarius** **Decius Brutus** **Metellus Cimber** **Cinna**	conspirators against Julius Caesar	**Lucilius** **Titinius** **Messala** **Young Cato** **Volumnius**	friends to Brutus and Cassius
Flavius **Marullus**	tribunes	**Varro** **Clitus** **Claudius** **Strato** **Lucius** **Dardanius**	servants to Brutus
Artemidorus of Cnidos, a teacher of rhetoric		**Pindarus,** servant to Cassius	
		Calpurnia, wife to Caesar	
		Portia, wife to Brutus	
		Senators, Citizens, Guards, Attendants, and so on	

Scene: During most of the play, at Rome; afterward near Sardis, and near Philippi.

***triumvirs** (trī um′ vərz) *n.*: In ancient Rome, a group of three rulers who share authority equally.

Act I

Scene i. *Rome. A street.*

[*Enter* FLAVIUS, MARULLUS, *and certain* COMMONERS[1] *over the stage.*]

FLAVIUS. Hence! Home, you idle creatures, get you home!
2 Is this a holiday? What, know you not,
Being mechanical,[2] you ought not walk
Upon a laboring day without the sign
Of your profession?[3] Speak, what trade art thou?

CARPENTER. Why, sir, a carpenter.

1. **commoners** (kam′ ən ərz) *n.*: People not of the nobility or upper classes.

2. **mechanical:** Of the working class.

3. **sign/Of your profession:** Work clothes and tools.

Customize for
Less Proficient Readers
Assure students who find assimilating all the names on the *Characters* list daunting that, as they read, they will associate the characters with their names. In the meanwhile, help them make flash cards, each with the name of a character on one side and his relationship to Caesar or another character on the back. For example, you might write "Casca" on the front and "conspirator against Caesar" on the back; or "Lucius" on the front of a card and "servant to Brutus" on the back.

◆ Literary Focus

2 Exposition in Drama Pose the question of why Shakespeare would begin a serious play such as this one with such a seemingly lighthearted opening scene. *Lead students to predict that the opening scene will serve the purpose of exposition—of "announcing" to the audience the main topic of the play.*

Humanities: Performing Arts

Staging This opening scene and Caesar's entrance have been staged in a variety of ways to set the scene for a variety of directors' interpretations of the play. The MGM film has Caesar entering in a military procession being cheered by a crowd larger than any theater would accommodate. The emphasis is on pomp and pageantry. In a later production, mounted by the Royal Shakespeare company in England, Caesar is strikingly silhouetted against a simple background of pillars, lending dignity and stature to his character. Trevor Nunn (who also directed *Cats* and *Les Miserables*) dressed Caesar in black leather and had him enter on a red carpet, flanked by soldiers dressed in gray uniforms. Ask students how each of these entrances might affect their feelings at the beginning of the play. Students should recognize that the choice a director makes about Caesar's entrance will create an emotional response in the audience. The audience's emotional response to Caesar will affect their view of all subsequent events in the play.

◆ Reading Strategy

❶ **Use Text Aids** Direct students to *gloss* 5 and explain how the two different meanings of the word *cobbler* lead to a misunderstanding between Marullus and the cobbler. *Marullus thinks the tradesman is describing himself as a clumsy worker, when in fact the man is identifying his trade as a mender of shoes.*

◆ Literary Focus

❷ **Exposition in Drama** Marullus' speech reveals that, recently, the common people were loyal to Pompey, the general defeated by Caesar, and celebrated his triumphs. Now that Pompey has been defeated by Caesar, the people have abruptly shifted their loyalty to Caesar.

Customize for *English Language Learners*
Guide these students to understand the figurative language "you blocks, you stones" and "hard hearts" in Marullus' address to the crowd.

Extending Word Study

Notice Word Choice Draw students' attention to the puns the Cobbler makes when answering the Tribunes. In addition to the ones noted, *soles* in line 15 is a play on *souls.* Encourage students to look for puns, which Shakespeare uses frequently, as they read the play.

MARULLUS. Where is thy leather apron and thy rule?
What dost thou with thy best apparel on?
You, sir, what trade are you?

COBBLER. Truly, sir, in respect of a fine workman,[4] I am but, as you would say, a cobbler.[5]

❶ **MARULLUS.** But what trade art thou? Answer me directly.

COBBLER. A trade, sir, that, I hope, I may use with a safe conscience, which is indeed, sir, a mender of bad soles.

FLAVIUS. What trade, thou knave?[6] Thou naughty knave what trade?

COBBLER. Nay, I beseech you, sir, be not out with me: yet, if you be out,[7] sir, I can mend you.[8]

MARULLUS. What mean'st thou by that? Mend me, thou saucy fellow?

COBBLER. Why, sir, cobble you.

FLAVIUS. Thou art a cobbler, art thou?

COBBLER. Truly, sir, all that I live by is with the awl:[9] I meddle with no tradesman's matters, nor women's matters; but withal, I am indeed, sir, a surgeon to old shoes: when they are in great danger, I recover them. As proper men as ever trod upon neat's leather[10] have gone upon my handiwork.

FLAVIUS. But wherefore art not in thy shop today?
Why dost thou lead these men about the streets?

COBBLER. Truly, sir, to wear out their shoes, to get myself into more work. But indeed, sir, we make holiday to see Caesar and to rejoice in his triumph.[11]

MARULLUS. Wherefore rejoice? What conquest brings he home?
What tributaries[12] follow him to Rome,
To grace in captive bonds his chariot wheels?
You blocks, you stones, you worse than senseless things!
O you hard hearts, you cruel men of Rome,
Knew you not Pompey?[13] Many a time and oft
Have you climbed up to walls and battlements,
To tow'rs and windows, yea, to chimney tops,

4. **in respect of a fine workman:** In relation to a skilled worker.
5. **cobbler:** Mender of shoes or a clumsy, bungling worker.

6. **knave** (nāv) *n.*: Tricky rascal; rogue.

7. **be not out . . . if you be out:** Be not angry . . . if you have worn-out shoes.
8. **mend you:** Mend your shoes or improve your disposition.

9. **awl** (ôl) *n.*: Small, pointed tool for making holes in leather.

10. **neat's leather:** Leather made from the hides of cattle.

11. **triumph** (trī´ əmf) *n.*: In ancient Rome, a procession celebrating the return of a victorious general and his army.
12. **tributaries** (trib´ yoo ter´ ēz) *n.*: Captives.

> **◆ Literary Focus** ❷
> What background do you learn from Marullus' speech?

13. **Pompey** (päm´ pē): A Roman general and triumvir defeated by Caesar in 48 B.C. and later murdered.

Cross-Curricular Connection: History

Pompey the Great Marullus asks the mob, "Knew you not Pompey?" He is referring to the Roman general Pompey the Great (106–48 B.C.), once an ally of Caesar, and later, the last obstacle Caesar had to overcome in his rise to power.

Pompey grew up in a wealthy Roman family, in a time of warfare between two generals, Gaius Marius and Lucius Sulla. Still in his twenties, he raised an army of three legions, allied himself with Sulla, and beat Marius. The Senate sent him to Spain, where he defeated Marius' followers.

A string of victories made Pompey a hero to the public but a threat to the Senate, which feared that they could not control such a hero. In 60 B.C., Pompey, Julius Caesar, and Marcus Crassus, formed what became known as the First Triumvirate, to resist the Senate's antimilitarism.

Pompey started to worry about Caesar's growing power and broke with him, leading to civil war. Pompey's army lost two battles to Caesar. After the second, in 48 B.C., Pompey escaped to Egypt, but was killed by order of the Roman-dominated Egyptian government.

Your infants in your arms, and there have sat
The livelong day, with patient expectation,
To see great Pompey pass the streets of Rome.
And when you saw his chariot but appear,
Have you not made an universal shout,
That Tiber[14] trembled underneath her banks
To hear the replication of your sounds
Made in her concave shores?[15]
And do you now put on your best attire?
And do you now cull out[16] a holiday?
And do you now strew flowers in his way
That comes in triumph over Pompey's blood?[17]
Be gone!
Run to your houses, fall upon your knees,
Pray to the gods to intermit the plague[18]
That needs must light on this ingratitude.

FLAVIUS. Go, go, good countrymen, and, for this fault,
Assemble all the poor men of your sort;
Draw them to Tiber banks and weep your tears
Into the channel, till the lowest stream
Do kiss the most exalted shores of all.[19]

(3) *[All the* COMMONERS *exit.]*

See, whe'r their basest mettle[20] be not moved,
They vanish tongue-tied in their guiltiness.
Go you down that way toward the Capitol;
This way will I. Disrobe the images,
If you do find them decked with ceremonies.[21]

MARULLUS. May we do so?
You know it is the feast of Lupercal.[22]

FLAVIUS. It is no matter; let no images
Be hung with Caesar's trophies. I'll about
And drive away the vulgar[23] from the streets;
So do you too, where you perceive them thick.
(4) These growing feathers plucked from Caesar's wing
Will make him fly an ordinary pitch,[24]
Who else would soar above the view of men
And keep us all in servile fearfulness. *[Exit]*

Scene ii. *A public place.*

[Enter CAESAR, ANTONY *(for the course),*[1] CALPURNIA, PORTIA, DECIUS, CICERO, BRUTUS, CASSIUS, CASCA, *a* SOOTHSAYER; *after them,* MARULLUS *and* FLAVIUS.]

14. Tiber (tī´ bər): River that flows through Rome.

15. concave shores: Hollowed-out banks; overhanging banks.

16. cull out: Pick out; select.

17. Pompey's blood: Pompey's sons, whom Caesar has just defeated.

18. intermit the plague (plāg): Stop the calamity or trouble.

19. the most exalted shores of all: The highest banks.

20. whe'r their basest mettle: Whether the most inferior material of which they are made.

21. Disrobe the images . . . decked with ceremonies: Strip the statues . . . covered with decorations.

22. feast of Lupercal (lo͞o´ pər kal): Ancient Roman festival celebrated on February 15.

23. vulgar (vul´ gər) *n.*: Common people.

24. pitch: Upward flight of a hawk.

1. for the course: Ready for the foot race that was part of the Lupercal festivities.

◆ Build Vocabulary

replication (rep´ lə kā´ shən) *n.*: Echo or reverberation

◆ Reading Strategy

(3) **Use Text Aids** Students should note when Flavius stops addressing the crowd and begins speaking to Marullus. Ask how they can tell when this change occurs. *He begins addressing Marullus in line 62. Students can tell when the change begins because the stage directions after line 61 indicate that the Commoners exit the stage at that point and Marullus is the only other person left on stage.*

◆ Literary Focus

(4) **Exposition in Drama** Lead students to identify the reason Flavius gives for removing Caesar's trophies from public places. What information does this passage provide about Caesar? *Flavius is afraid that all the tributes will make Caesar feel too powerful and encourage him to be tyrannical. The passage introduces Caesar as potentially dangerous to the Roman republic and its citizens.*

Writing and Language Transparencies Use the Context Chart, pp. 107–109, in ***Writing and Language Transparencies.*** The chart offers suggestions for several ways the chart can be used to enhance your students' understanding of the play.

Literature CD-ROM *The Life, Time, and Works of Shakespeare* Use feature 5 to support students' exploration of the historical and social context in which this play was written.

Reteach

Students may have trouble understanding the exposition of Scene i. Help them by reviewing the following ideas:

- At this time Rome was a republic, which meant that it was a state ruled by elected leaders rather than by a monarch.
- In Rome the tribunes, such as Marullus and Flavius, were elected officials whose job was to protect the rights and interests of the common people.
- The tribunes, like many others in the government, did not want Caesar to be so powerful. They saw his power as a threat to the freedom they enjoyed as citizens of a republic.

In the first scene it appears that the tribunes feel they have to convince the commoners that Julius Caesar's victory over Pompey is not in their interest.

❶ Clarification Explain that a soothsayer is a fortune-teller and that in ancient Rome such prophets were taken very seriously. Soothsayers were believed to receive special signs of coming events from the gods. They often advised leaders about whether to go to war and about the best time for constructing buildings or passing important laws.

◆ Reading Strategy

❷ Use Text Aids Students should explain how the glosses helped them understand the unfamiliar language. For instance, without gloss 4, students might not have known whether the ides of March were things like winds, animals, or frogs, or a specific date, as the note clarifies.

Customize for *Interpersonal Learners*

Have two interpersonal learners read aloud the important dialogue between Cassius and Brutus that begins here with line 25 and continues through line 177. Stop them occasionally and ask them to explain to the class how Cassius is trying to win Brutus over to his point of view and how Brutus is responding.

CAESAR. Calpurnia!

CASCA. Peace, ho! Caesar speaks.

CAESAR. Calpurnia!

CALPURNIA. Here, my lord.

CAESAR. Stand you directly in Antonius' way
When he doth run his course. Antonius!

ANTONY. Caesar, my lord?

CAESAR. Forget not in your speed, Antonius,
To touch Calpurnia; for our elders say
The barren, touchèd in this holy chase,
Shake off their sterile curse.[2]

ANTONY. I shall remember:
When Caesar says "Do this," it is performed.

CAESAR. Set on, and leave no ceremony out.

SOOTHSAYER. Caesar!

CAESAR. Ha! Who calls?

CASCA. Bid every noise be still; peace yet again!

CAESAR. Who is it in the press[3] that calls on me?
I hear a tongue, shriller than all the music,
Cry "Caesar." Speak; Caesar is turned to hear.

SOOTHSAYER. Beware the ides of March.[4]

CAESAR. What man is that?

BRUTUS. A soothsayer bids you beware the ides of March.

CAESAR. Set him before me; let me see his face.

CASSIUS. Fellow, come from the throng; look upon Caesar.

CAESAR. What say'st thou to me now? Speak once again.

SOOTHSAYER. Beware the ides of March.

CAESAR. He is a dreamer, let us leave him. Pass.

[A trumpet sounds. Exit all but BRUTUS *and* CASSIUS.*]*

CASSIUS. Will you go see the order of the course?[5]

BRUTUS. Not I.

CASSIUS. I pray you do.

BRUTUS. I am not gamesome:[6] I do lack some part
Of that quick spirit[7] that is in Antony.

2. barren . . . sterile curse: It was believed that women who were unable to bear children (such as Calpurnia), if touched by a runner during this race, would then be able to bear children.

3. press *n.*: Crowd.

4. ides (īdz) **of March:** March 15.

◆ Reading Strategy Which glosses on this page did you use to clarify unfamiliar language?

5. order of the course: The race.

6. gamesome (gām´ səm) *adj.*: Having a liking for sports.

7. quick spirit: Lively disposition.

Cross-Curricular Connection: History

Calendars Caesar is warned to beware "the ides of March." Explain that the *ides* came near the middle of each month in the old Roman calendar.

The earliest known Roman calendar consisted of ten months and a 304-day year. The ten months were called Martius, Aprilis, Maius, Junius, Quintilis, Sextilis, September, October, November, and December. The last six names were taken from the Latin words for the numbers five through ten.

By the time of Julius Caesar, about 700 years later, the calendar was about three months ahead of the natural cycle of seasons. In 46 B.C., Julius Caesar asked an astronomer to create a more accurate calendar. A 365-day year was divided into twelve months of thirty-one or thirty days each, except for February, which had only twenty-nine days. Every fourth year, it would have thirty days. Quintilius was renamed July to honor Julius Caesar. Sextilis was later renamed August to honor the emperor Augustus. Tradition has it that Augustus moved a day from February to August to make his month as long as Caesar's.

Have students research our current Gregorian calendar and compare it to the Roman calendar.

▲ **Critical Viewing** At what or whom do you think Caesar and Antony are looking? **[Speculate]**

Let me not hinder, Cassius, your desires;
I'll leave you.

CASSIUS. Brutus, I do observe you now of late;
I have not from your eyes that gentleness
And show of love as I was wont[8] to have;
You bear too stubborn and too strange a hand[9]
Over your friend that loves you.

BRUTUS. Cassius,
Be not deceived: if I have veiled my look,
I turn the trouble of my countenance
Merely upon myself.[10] Vexèd I am
Of late with passions[11] of some difference,[12]
Conceptions only proper to myself,[13]
Which give some soil,[14] perhaps, to my behaviors;
But let not therefore my good friends be grieved

8. wont (wōnt): Accustomed.

9. bear . . . hand: Treat too harshly and too like a stranger.

10. if I . . . upon myself: If I have been less open, my troubled face is due entirely to personal matters.

11. passions: Feelings; emotions.

12. of some difference: In conflict.

13. Conceptions . . . myself: Thoughts that concern only me.

14. soil: Blemish.

▶Critical Viewing◀

❸ Speculate *The guarded expressions and alert body language of Caesar and Antony suggest that they are looking at someone or something they do not completely like or trust. Students may suggest that this is one or more of the conspirators, people in the crowd, or a statue from which Caesar's trophies have been removed.*

◆Critical Thinking

❹ Analyze Guide students to use the side notes for this passage to paraphrase what Brutus is saying about himself. Then ask what kind of conflict Brutus might be feeling as his friend Caesar rises to power. *Brutus is saying that he has been experiencing inner conflict lately. Because he has been so preoccupied with his own thoughts, he has not been paying much attention to his friends. Students may speculate that Brutus is torn by his feelings of love for Caesar and his fears that Caesar is becoming too powerful.*

Comprehension Check ☑

❶ What does Cassius mean when he asks if Brutus can see his own face and his own shadow? *He is suggesting that Brutus cannot see his own inner self, the noble qualities that other people can see in him.*

❷ **Clarification** Explain that *glass* is another word for mirror. By offering to be Brutus' "glass," Cassius is saying that he will help Brutus see himself more clearly, that he will reveal Brutus' noble qualities, which Brutus himself seems not to see.

◆ ***Literature and Your Life***

❸ *Some students may suggest that they appreciate the insights these friends are able to give them. Others may say that it's annoying to have someone presume they know how you think or feel.*

(Among which number, Cassius, be you one)
Nor construe any further my neglect
Than that poor Brutus, with himself at war,
Forgets the shows of love to other men.

CASSIUS. Then, Brutus, I have much mistook your passion;
By means whereof this breast of mine hath buried[15]
Thoughts of great value, worthy cogitations.[16]
Tell me, good Brutus, can you see your face?

BRUTUS. No, Cassius; for the eye sees not itself
But by reflection, by some other things.

CASSIUS. 'Tis just.[17]
❶ And it is very much lamented,[18] Brutus,
That you have no such mirrors as will turn
Your hidden worthiness into your eye,
That you might see your shadow.[19] I have heard
Where many of the best respect[20] in Rome
(Except immortal Caesar), speaking of Brutus,
And groaning underneath this age's yoke,[21]
Have wished that noble Brutus had his eyes.

BRUTUS. Into what dangers would you lead me, Cassius,
That you would have me seek into myself
For that which is not in me?

CASSIUS. Therefore, good Brutus, be prepared to hear;
And since you know you cannot see yourself
❷ So well as by reflection, I, your glass
Will modestly discover to yourself
That of yourself which you yet know not of.[22]
And be not jealous on[23] me, gentle Brutus:
Were I a common laughter,[24] or did use
To stale with ordinary oaths my love
To every new protester;[25] if you know
That I do fawn on men and hug them hard,
And after scandal[26] them; or if you know
That I profess myself in banqueting
To all the rout,[27] then hold me dangerous.

[*Flourish of trumpets and shout*]

BRUTUS. What means this shouting? I do fear the people
Choose Caesar for their king.

CASSIUS. Ay, do you fear it?
Then must I think you would not have it so.

BRUTUS. I would not, Cassius, yet I love him well.

15. By means . . . buried: Because of which I have kept to myself.
16. cogitations (kaj ə tā′ shənz) *n.*: Thoughts.
17. 'Tis just: It is true.
18. lamented (lə men′ t'd) *v.*: Regretted.
19. turn . . . shadow: Reflect your hidden noble qualities so you could see their image.
20. the best respect: Most respected people.
21. this age's yoke: The tyranny of Caesar.

◆ ***Literature and Your Life***
Cassius claims to know Brutus better than Brutus knows himself. How do you deal with friends who think they know what you want or what you think? ❸

22. Will modestly . . . know not of: Will without exaggeration make known to you the qualities you have that you are unaware of.
23. be not jealous on: Do not be suspicious of.
24. common laughter: Object of ridicule.
25. To stale . . . new protester: To make cheap my friendship to anyone who promises to be my friend.
26. scandal: Slander; gossip about.
27. profess myself . . . rout: Declare my friendship to the common crowd.

Cross-Curricular Connection: Social Studies

Roman Government The Roman Republic was founded in 509 B.C. when the harsh Etruscan king Tarquinius Superbus was overthrown. Until 27 B.C., Rome remained a republic; that is, there was no king or emperor. Two consuls, elected each year by an assembly called the *Comitia Centuriata,* governed as chief executives, each having the right to veto decisions of the other. The Senate consisted of 300 senators chosen for life by the consuls. Because the *patricians,* or nobility, controlled the Comitia Centuriata, the *plebeians,* or common people, set up their own assembly, the *Concilium Plebis.* In addition, there were *praetors,* or judicial officials, *quaestors,* or financial officials, and *censors,* supervisors of public morals.

Invite students to find parallels between the structure of the Roman republic and our own government.

But wherefore do you hold me here so long?
What is it that you would impart to me?
If it be aught toward the general good,[28]
Set honor in one eye and death i' th' other,
And I will look on both indifferently;[29]
For let the gods so speed[30] me, as I love
The name of honor more than I fear death.

CASSIUS. I know that virtue to be in you, Brutus,
As well as I do know your outward favor.[31]
Well, honor is the subject of my story.
I cannot tell what you and other men
Think of this life, but for my single self,
I had as lief not be,[32] as live to be
In awe of such a thing as I myself.[33]
I was born free as Caesar; so were you:
We both have fed as well, and we can both
Endure the winter's cold as well as he:
For once, upon a raw and gusty day,
The troubled Tiber chafing with[34] her shores,
Caesar said to me "Darest thou, Cassius, now
Leap in with me into this angry flood,
And swim to yonder point?" Upon the word,
Accout'red[35] as I was, I plungèd in
And bade him follow: so indeed he did.
❹ The torrent roared, and we did buffet[36] it
With lusty sinews,[37] throwing it aside
And stemming it with hearts of controversy.[38]
But ere we could arrive the point proposed,
Caesar cried "Help me, Cassius, or I sink!"
I, as Aeneas,[39] our Great ancestor,
Did from the flames of Troy upon his shoulder
The old Anchises bear, so from the waves of Tiber
❺ Did I the tired Caesar. And this man
Is now become a god, and Cassius is
A wretched creature, and must bend his body
If Caesar carelessly but nod on him.
He had a fever when he was in Spain,
And when the fit was on him, I did mark
How he did shake: 'tis true, this god did shake.
His coward lips did from their color fly,[40]
❻ And that same eye whose bend[41] doth awe the world
did lose his[42] luster: I did hear him groan;
Ay, and that tongue of his, that bade the Romans
Mark him and write his speeches in their books,

28. aught . . . good: Anything to do with the public welfare.
29. indifferently: Without preference or concern.
30. speed: Give good fortune to.
31. favor: Face; appearance.
32. as lief not be: Just as soon not exist.
33. such a thing as I myself: Another human being (Caesar).
34. chafing with: Raging against.
35. Accout'red: Dressed in armor.
36. buffet (buf′ it) *v.*: Struggle against.
37. lusty sinews (sin′ yo͞oz): Strong muscles.
38. stemming it . . . controversy: Making progress against it with our intense rivalry.
39. Aeneas (ē nē′ əs): Trojan hero of the poet Virgil's epic poem *Aeneid,* who carried his old father, Anchises, from the burning city of Troy and later founded Rome.
40. His coward lips . . . fly: Color fled from his lips, which were like cowardly soldiers fleeing from a battle.
41. bend *n.*: Glance.
42. his: Its.

◆ Critical Thinking

❹ Make Judgments Ask students to judge whether Cassius provides compelling reasons to convince Brutus. *Students may feel that the weakness Cassius describes here is a reason Brutus should help him overthrow Caesar's ambition. Some students may suggest that while Cassius offers reasons why Caesar should not rule, he does not make a convincing argument for assassination.*

◆ Reading Strategy

❺ Use Text Aids Ask students what gloss 39 adds to their understanding of this passage. *The gloss explains the comparison Cassius is making. Without the text aid, students would not understand the connection between Anchises and Caesar.*

◆ Critical Thinking

❻ Connect Ask student how this example connects to the earlier example of swimming in the river. *Both examples are meant to demonstrate to Brutus that Caesar is too weak to rule. They also serve to demonstrate that Cassius is not a loyal friend; he uses two instances when he helped Caesar against him.*

Customize for
Less Proficient Readers
Help these students understand that Cassius is describing past events to illustrate his assertions about Caesar's character. Ask students to identify the two events Cassius describes. *The first example describes when Caesar challenged Cassius to a swimming race but Cassius had to save the panicking Caesar from the river. The second example describes a time in Spain, when Caesar suffered from a fever. He showed no courage or fortitude but cried out for water.*

◆ Reading Strategy

1 Use Text Aids Ask students what important information they get from the stage directions in this section. *The stage directions indicate a shout from the crowd and a flourish of trumpets. This, along with the dialogue, allows students to infer that some honor is being offered to Caesar.*

Comprehension Check ☑

2 Who or what does Cassius say is to blame for the tyrannical rule that Romans are suffering? *He says that the people themselves are to blame for putting up with Caesar and not fighting back.*

◆ Literature and Your Life

3 Cassius uses flattery to try to win Brutus over to his side. Ask students if they think flattery and compliments are usually effective in persuading people to do something. Do students tend to trust people who flatter them? *Students should note the importance of distinguishing between flattery as a persuasive tool and a sincere compliment.*

Connecting Themes Across Cultures

Point out the reference to a great flood in line 152. This flood was a part of Greek mythology. Have students read footnote 53 to learn more. Then ask students to name other flood stories they know. *Some students may be familiar with the story of Noah's Ark.* You may wish to discuss the role of flooding in different cultures.

Alas, it cried, "Give me some drink, Titinius,"
As a sick girl. Ye gods! It doth amaze me,
A man of such a feeble temper[43] should
So get the start of[44] the majestic world,
And bear the palm[45] alone.

[*Shout. Flourish of trumpets*]

BRUTUS. Another general shout?
I do believe that these applauses are
For some new honors that are heaped on Caesar.

CASSIUS. Why, man, he doth bestride the narrow world
Like a Colossus,[46] and we petty men
Walk under his huge legs and peep about
To find ourselves dishonorable[47] graves.
Men at some time are masters of their fates:
The fault, dear Brutus, is not in our stars,[48]
But in ourselves, that we are underlings.[49]
Brutus and Caesar: what should be in that "Caesar"?
Why should that name be sounded[50] more than
  yours?
Write them together, yours is as fair a name;
Sound them, it doth become the mouth as well;
Weigh them, it is as heavy; conjure[51] with 'em,
"Brutus" will start[52] a spirit as soon as "Caesar."
Now, in the names of all the gods at once,
Upon what meat doth this our Caesar feed,
That he is grown so great? Age, thou art shamed!
Rome, thou hast lost the breed of noble bloods!
When went there by an age, since the great flood,[53]
But it was famed with[54] more than with one man?
When could they say (till now) that talked of Rome,
That her wide walks encompassed but one man?
Now is it Rome indeed, and room enough,
When there is in it but one only man.
O, you and I have heard our fathers say,
There was a Brutus[55] once that would have brooked[56]
Th' eternal devil to keep his state in Rome
As easily as a king.

BRUTUS. That you do love me, I am nothing jealous;[57]
What you would work me to,[58] I have some aim;[59]
How I have thought of this, and of these times,
I shall recount hereafter. For this present,
I would not so (with love I might entreat you)
Be any further moved. What you have said
I will consider; what you have to say

43. feeble temper: Weak physical constitution.
44. get the start of: Become the leader of.
45. palm: Symbol of victory; victor's prize.

46. Colossus (kə läs´ əs) *n.*: Gigantic statue of Apollo, a god of Greek and Roman mythology, which was set at the entrance to the harbor of Rhodes about 280 B.C. and was included among the seven wonders of the ancient world.
47. dishonorable (dis än´ ər ə b'l) *adj.*: Shameful (because they will not be of free men).
48. stars: Destinies. The stars were thought to control people's lives.
49. underlings: Inferior people.
50. sounded: Spoken or announced by trumpets.
51. conjure (kän jər) *v.*: Summon a spirit by a magic spell.
52. start: Raise.
53. great flood: In Greek mythology, a flood that drowned everyone except Deucalion and his wife Pyrrha who were saved by the god Zeus because of their virtue.
54. But it was famed with: Without the age being made famous by.
55. Brutus: Lucius Junius Brutus had helped expel the last king of Rome and had helped found the Republic in 509 B.C.
56. brooked: Put up with.
57. nothing jealous: Not at all doubting.
58. work me to: Persuade me of.
59. aim: Idea.

I will with patience hear, and find a time
Both meet to hear and answer such high things.
Till then, my noble friend, chew upon[60] this:
Brutus had rather be a villager
Than to repute himself a son of Rome
Under these hard conditions as this time
Is like to lay upon us.

CASSIUS. I am glad
That my weak words have struck but thus much show
Of fire from Brutus.

[*Enter* CAESAR *and his* TRAIN.]

BRUTUS. The games are done, and Caesar is returning.

CASSIUS. As they pass by, pluck Casca by the sleeve,
And he will (after his sour fashion) tell you
What hath proceeded worthy note today.

BRUTUS. I will do so. But look you, Cassius,
The angry spot doth glow on Caesar's brow,
And all the rest look like a chidden train:[61]
Calpurnia's cheek is pale, and Cicero
Looks with such ferret[62] and such fiery eyes
❺ As we have seen him in the Capitol,
Being crossed in conference[63] by some senators.

CASSIUS. Casca will tell us what the matter is.

CAESAR. Antonius.

ANTONY. Caesar?

CAESAR. Let me have men about me that are fat,
Sleek-headed men, and such as sleep a-nights.
❻ Yond Cassius has a lean and hungry look;
He thinks too much: such men are dangerous.

ANTONY. Fear him not, Caesar, he's not dangerous;
He is a noble Roman, and well given.[64]

CAESAR. Would he were fatter! But I fear him not.
Yet if my name were liable to fear,
I do not know the man I should avoid
So soon as that spare Cassius. He reads much,
He is a great observer, and he looks
quite through the deeds of men.[65] He loves no plays,
As thou dost, Antony; he hears no music;
Seldom he smiles, and smiles in such a sort[66]

60. chew upon: Think about.

◆ Reading Strategy
How do the stage directions here help you understand the action? ❹

61. chidden train: Scolded attendants.

62. ferret (fer′ it) *n.*: Small animal, like a weasel, with reddish eyes.

63. crossed in conference: Opposed in debate.

64. well given: Well disposed.

65. looks . . . deeds of men: Sees through people's actions to their motives.

66. sort: Way.

◆ Build Vocabulary

spare (sper) *adj.*: Lean or thin

◆ Reading Strategy

❹ Suggested response: The stage directions help readers visualize what is happening on stage. Knowing that Caesar and all his followers are entering at this point explains why the conversation between Brutus and Cassius is cut off so abruptly.

◆ Reading Strategy

❺ **Use Text Aids** Direct students to side note 62, asking them how knowing what a ferret looks like helps them understand Brutus' description of Cicero. *The comparison to a weasel with reddish eyes helps readers understand that Brutus is describing Cicero as a crafty, sneaky, looking fellow.*

◆ Critical Thinking

❻ **Interpret** Direct students' attention to the famous line, "Cassius has a lean and hungry look." Ask them what Caesar means by this line and what else Caesar has to say about Cassius in this passage. *He means that Cassius is unsatisfied and hungry for power. Cassius knows how to read people's characters and manipulate them; he is single-minded, having no outside interests to distract him from his serious ambitions.*

Customizing for *English Language Learners*

Help these students identify and interpret the clues that indicate that Caesar and his followers are angry and upset. Point out phrases with which they may be unfamiliar and help them paraphrase them in simpler language. *Clues include "angry spot" (line 183; angry expression), "Looks with such ferret and such fiery eyes" (line 186; narrow and threatening), "Being crossed in conference" (line 188; disagreed with).*

Cross-Curricular Connection: History

The Roman Empire The year 27 B.C. marked the end of the Roman republic. In that year, Octavius became princeps, or ruler, of Rome, and took the name Augustus. After that, supreme authority rested with the emperor, who was aided and advised by the Senate. The emperor was chosen either by his predecessor or by the army. As time went on, the Senate lost power, and Rome became an absolute monarchy. Rome controlled many provinces; in fact, in A.D. 117, the Roman empire stretched from northern Britain to the shores of the Red Sea and the Persian Gulf. It included Hibernia (Scotland), Britannia (England), Gallia (France), Hispania (Spain), Achaia (Greece), and Aegyptus (Egypt), among many others. The provinces were governed by Roman governors, aided by a staff of military assistants. Local officials, however, were allowed to manage local affairs.

▶Critical Viewing◀

❶ **Infer** *Cassius, in the picture, has very lean, angular features and Caesar says he distrusts a man with a "lean and hungry look." Also, Cassius' facial expression is unfriendly and threatening.*

◆Critical Thinking

❷ **Make Judgments** Have students evaluate how accurate they find Caesar's view of Cassius as a threat. *Caesar has a very clear idea of Cassius' motives for opposing him.*

Writing and Language Transparencies Use Daily Language Practice for Week 13. You can display the sentences on the overhead projector and have students make corrections or you can dictate the sentences and have students write them correctly.

◀ Critical Viewing What details of Cassius' appearance can you see in this picture that might make Caesar distrust him? **[Infer]**

As if he mocked himself, and scorned his spirit
That could be moved to smile at anything.
Such men as he be never at heart's ease
Whiles they behold a greater than themselves,
❷ And therefore are they very dangerous.
I rather tell thee what is to be feared
Than what I fear; for always I am Caesar.
Come on my right hand, for this ear is deaf,
And tell me truly what thou think'st of him.

[*A trumpet sounds.* CAESAR *and his* TRAIN *exit.*]

CASCA. You pulled me by the cloak; would you speak
with me?

Humanities: Literature

Cassius Plutarch, a Greek biographer, wrote biographies of famous Greek and Roman statesmen and generals. Shakespeare's characterizations of the principals in *Julius Caesar* are based largely on what he learned from reading Plutarch's *The Lives of the Noble Grecians and Romans*. The following excerpt from the Dryden translation gives a clear indication of the character of the real-life Cassius: "Cassius, a man of fierce disposition, and one that out of private malice, rather than love of public, hated Caesar, not the tyrant, continually fired and stirred him up. Brutus felt the rule an oppression, but Cassius hated the ruler; and among other reasons on which he grounded his quarrel against Caesar, the loss of his lions which he had procured . . . for Caesar, finding these . . . seized them for himself."

Ask students the following questions:

1. How well does Shakespeare's portrayal of Cassius fit with this description? *Shakespeare's characterization is consistent with Plutarch's description.*
2. How does this description affect your interpretation of Cassius' stories about Caesar? *This insight into Cassius' character will lead most students to question his motives in plotting against Caesar.*

BRUTUS. Ay, Casca; tell us what hath chanced[67] today, That Caesar looks so sad.

CASCA. Why, you were with him, were you not?

BRUTUS. I should not then ask Casca what had chanced.

❸ **CASCA.** Why, there was a crown offered him; and being offered him, he put it by[68] with the back of his hand, thus; and then the people fell a-shouting.

BRUTUS. What was the second noise for?

CASCA. Why, for that too.

CASSIUS. They shouted thrice; what was the last cry for?

CASCA. Why, for that too.

BRUTUS. Was the crown offered him thrice?

CASCA. Ay, marry, was't, and he put it by thrice, every time gentler than other; and at every putting-by mine honest neighbors shouted.

CASSIUS. Who offered him the crown?

CASCA. Why, Antony.

BRUTUS. Tell us the manner of it, gentle Casca.

CASCA. I can as well be hanged as tell the manner of it: it was mere foolery; I did not mark it. I saw Mark Antony offer him a crown—yet 'twas not a crown neither, 'twas one of these coronets[69]—and, as I told you, he put it by once; but for all that, to my thinking, he would fain[70] have had it. Then he offered it to him again; then he put it by again; but to my thinking, he was very loath to lay his fingers off it. And then he offered it the third time. He put it the third time by; and still as he refused it, the rabblement[71] hooted, and clapped their chopt[72] hands, and threw up their sweaty nightcaps,[73] and uttered such a deal of stinking breath because Caesar refused the crown, that it had, almost, choked Caesar; for he swounded[74] and fell down at it. And for mine own part, I durst not laugh, for fear of opening my lips and receiving the bad air.

CASSIUS. But, soft,[75] I pray you; what, did Caesar swound?

CASCA. He fell down in the market place, and foamed at mouth, and was speechless.

67. hath chanced: Has happened.

68. put it by: Pushed it away.

69. coronets (kôr´ ə nets´) *n.*: Ornamental bands used as crowns.

70. fain (fān) *adv.*: Gladly.

71. rabblement (răb´ əl mənt) *n.*: Mob.

72. chopt (chäpt) *adj.*: Chapped.

73. nightcaps: Workers' caps.

74. swounded: Swooned; fainted.

75. soft: Slowly.

◆ **Literary Focus**
How does this dialogue develop the situation set up in the exposition? ❹

◆ Literary Focus

❸ **Exposition in Drama** The passage (lines 220–222) describes in detail what was referred to in more general terms earlier in the scene.

◆ Literary Focus

❹ **Exposition in Drama** This dialogue develops the public's love for Caesar, which was revealed in the exposition.

Customize for *Bodily/Kinesthetic Learners*

Have these students act out the offering of the crown, the refusals, and the reactions of the crowd each time. Tell students to use slightly exaggerated body language and facial expressions to indicate the characters' emotions.

Tips to Guide Reading

Sustained Reading Encourage students to read the entire passage in which Casca describes what happened to upset Caesar. While students may need to reread the text in order to understand all the events, they can get a feeling for the conversation by reading it straight through.

Speaking, Listening, and Viewing Mini-Lesson

Roman Symbols

This mini-lesson supports the Speaking, Listening, and Viewing activity in the Idea Bank on p. 731.

Introduce Discuss Roman history of this period with students. Since Rome had been a republic for 500 years, it is not surprising that some citizens objected to the idea that Julius Caesar would be named emperor. Point out that symbols, such as those seen on United States currency often convey an idea or feeling about the government they represent.

Develop Students may find several symbols of Rome's republican era and its imperial era in reference books or on the Internet. Have them work in groups to choose a symbol for each period.

Apply Have each group reproduce the symbols through drawing or collage. Students can display the symbols along with explanations for their choices.

Assess Students' work may be evaluated based on the selection and explanation of the symbol.

◆ Reading Strategy

❶ Use Text Aids Ask students how notes 76 and 77 clarify what Brutus and Cassius are saying. *Brutus and Cassius use the term falling sickness in two very different ways, which readers might not be able to figure out. Brutus is referring to a physical illness that Caesar might have. Cassius uses the term metaphorically to describe the humiliating position of the Roman people under Caesar's rule.*

Comprehension Check ☑

❷ Why was Caesar sad and angry after the people offered him the crown three times? *His act of refusing the crown did not work out the way he planned: Instead of continuing to beg him to accept it, the crowd was happy that he refused and they stopped asking him. Caesar now feels betrayed by the people.*

❸ Clarification Ask students if they are familiar with the expression "It was Greek to me," meaning that something was incomprehensible.

◆ Literary Focus

❹ Exposition in Drama Ask students what important information is revealed here about increasing tensions between Caesar and other Roman leaders. *The tribunes Marullus and Flavius have been exiled or killed by Caesar, which will increase the fear and resentment that other Roman leaders feel toward Caesar.*

BRUTUS. 'Tis very like he hath the falling-sickness.[76]

❶ **CASSIUS.** No, Caesar hath it not; but you, and I,
And honest Casca, we have the falling-sickness.[77]

CASCA. I know not what you mean by that, but I am sure Caesar fell down. If the tag-rag people[78] did not clap him and hiss him, according as he pleased and displeased them, as they use[79] to do the players in the theater, I am no true man.

BRUTUS. What said he when he came unto himself?

CASCA. Marry, before he fell down, when he perceived the common herd was glad he refused the crown, he plucked me ope his doublet[80] and offered them his throat to cut. An I had been a man of any occupation,[81] if I would not have taken him at a word, I would I might go to hell among the rogues. And so he ❷ fell. When he came to himself again, he said, if he had done or said anything amiss, he desired their worships to think it was his infirmity.[82] Three or four wenches,[83] where I stood, cried "Alas, good soul!" and forgave him with all their hearts; but there's no heed to be taken of them; if Caesar had stabbed their mothers, they would have done no less.

BRUTUS. And after that, he came thus sad away?

CASCA. Ay.

CASSIUS. Did Cicero say anything?

CASCA. Ay, he spoke Greek.

CASSIUS. To what effect?

CASCA. Nay, an I tell you that, I'll ne'er look you i' th' face again. But those that understood him smiled at one ❸ another and shook their heads; but for mine own part, it was Greek to me. I could tell you more news too: Marullus and Flavius, for pulling scarfs off Cae- ❹ sar's images, are put to silence.[84] Fare you well. There was more foolery yet, if I could remember it.

CASSIUS. Will you sup with me tonight, Casca?

CASCA. No, I am promised forth.[85]

CASSIUS. Will you dine with me tomorrow?

CASCA. Ay, if I be alive, and your mind hold,[86] and your dinner worth the eating.

76. falling-sickness: Epilepsy.

77. We have the falling-sickness: We are becoming helpless under Caesar's rule.

78. tag-rag people: The rabble.

79. use: Are accustomed.

80. doublet (dub′ lit) *n.*: Close-fitting jacket.

81. An I . . . occupation: If I had been a working-man (or a man of action).

82. infirmity *n.*: Caesar's illness is epilepsy.

83. wenches (wench′ əz) *n.*: Young women.

84. for pulling . . . silence: For taking decorations off statues of Caesar, have been silenced (by being forbidden to take part in public affairs, exiled, or perhaps even executed).

85. am promised forth: Have a previous engagement.

86. hold: Does not change.

◆ Build Vocabulary

infirmity (in fur′ mə tē) *n.*: Illness; physical defect

Cross-Curricular Connection: Science

Epilepsy Some historical sources claim that Julius Caesar suffered from epilepsy, the condition to which Brutus refers as "the falling sickness" (line 254). Epilepsy is a general term used to cover a variety of chronic neurological disorders. Epileptics can suffer from seizures that involve muscle spasms and loss of consciousness. Some forms of epilepsy are known to be caused by injury or infection of the brain, while the cause of other forms is unknown. Today, epileptic seizures can be controlled by drugs and sometimes by diet.

Have students contact a local medical center for more information on epilepsy and other chronic disorders of the brain and nervous system.

CASSIUS. Good; I will expect you.

CASCA. Do so. Farewell, both. [*Exit*]

BRUTUS. What a blunt[87] fellow is this grown to be!
He was quick mettle[88] when he went to school.

CASSIUS. So is he now in execution[89]
Of any bold or noble enterprise,
However he puts on this tardy form.[90]
This rudeness is a sauce to his good wit,[91]
Which gives men stomach to disgest[92] his words
With better appetite.

BRUTUS. And so it is. For this time I will leave you.
Tomorrow, if you please to speak with me,
I will come home to you; or if you will,
Come home to me, and I will wait for you.

CASSIUS. I will do so. Till then, think of the world.[93]

[*Exit* BRUTUS.]

Well, Brutus, thou art noble; yet I see
Thy honorable mettle may be wrought
From that it is disposed;[94] therefore it is meet
That noble minds keep ever with their likes;
For who so firm that cannot be seduced?
Caesar doth bear me hard,[95] but he loves Brutus.
If I were Brutus now, and he were Cassius,
❻ He should not humor me.[96] I will this night,
In several hands,[97] in at his windows throw,
As if they came from several citizens,
Writings, all tending to the great opinion[98]
That Rome holds of his name; wherein obscurely
Caesar's ambition shall be glancèd at.[99]
And after this, let Caesar seat him sure;[100]
For we will shake him, or worse days endure. [*Exit*]

Scene iii. *A street.*

[*Thunder and lightning. Enter from opposite sides,* CASCA *and* CICERO.]

CICERO. Good even, Casca; brought you Caesar home?
Why are you breathless? And why stare you so?

CASCA. Are not you moved, when all the sway of earth[1]

87. blunt: Dull; not sharp.
88. quick mettle: Of a lively disposition.
89. execution (ek´ sə kyoo͞´shən) *n.*: Carrying out; doing.
90. tardy form: Sluggish appearance.
91. wit: Intelligence.
92. disgest: Digest.

93. the world: Present state of affairs.

◆ **Reading Strategy**
Use the glosses to clarify unfamiliar terms. Then explain what Cassius means in lines 308–310. ❺

94. wrought . . . is disposed: Shaped (like iron) in a way different from its usual form.
95. bear me hard: Dislikes me.
96. humor me: Win me over.
97. several hands: Different handwritings.
98. tending to the great opinion: Pointing out the great respect.
99. glancèd at: Hinted at.
100. seat him sure: Establish himself securely.

1. all the sway of earth: The stable order of Earth.

◆ Reading Strategy

❺ **Use Text Aids** The gloss, side note 94, helps students understand the pun of *mettle* and *metal.* Without the text aid explaining how metal is wrought, students might comprehend only the literal meaning of Cassius' words.

Comprehension Check ☑

❻ How does Cassius plan to use Brutus' concern for the public welfare to win Brutus over to the conspiracy against Caesar? *He plans to write phony letters to Brutus, supposedly from concerned citizens worried about the effects of Caesar's rule.*

Customize for *Verbal/Linguistic Learners*

Have these students draft a brief note they might write if they were Cassius. Encourage them to choose the details they will include based on what they have learned about Brutus and how he might be influenced. Tell students they can compare their notes to Cassius' in the beginning of Act II.

Analyze Literary Criticism

One critic has written, "Shakespeare has scarcely created anything more splendid than the relation in which he has placed Cassius to Brutus." According to this writer, Cassius is "the clever, politic revolutionist opposed" to Brutus, "the man of noble soul and moral nature."

Share this critique with students. Ask them to consider this viewpoint as they read the play. They may want to keep notes in their journals, concerning both Cassius' and Brutus' motives for the assassination. When students finish reading, have them compare their views of Brutus and Cassius with this reviewer's.

◆ Reading Strategy

❶ **Use Text Aids** Note 2 helps students envision the trees splitting in two. Notes 9 and 10 help students envision the women. Note 11 clarifies what kind of bird students should picture in their minds.

◆ Build Vocabulary

❷ **Forms of *Portent*** Challenge students to analyze the word *portentous*. What is the noun form of the word, and what does it mean? What is the suffix, and what is its function? Then ask why Casca describes the strange sights he has seen as "portentous things." *The noun form is portent, which means "omen" or "warning." The suffix is -ous, which changes a noun to an adjective. Casca believes the strange sights are signs or warnings from the gods that something bad is about to happen.*

◆ Literary Focus

❸ **Exposition in Drama** Ask students what important information is developed in Cicero's words. *Students may say that the speech is included to remind readers or audience members that Caesar is coming to the Capitol the next day. The reminder builds suspense as it supplies information.*

Read to Appreciate Author's Craft

Draw students' attention to Cicero's response to Casca's fears. In lines 34 and 35 Cicero implies that a person might create his own explanation for the strange events, just as Cassius will do on the following page. Guide students to see that Cicero's lines prepare the audience for Cassius' statements.

Shakes like a thing unfirm? O Cicero,
I have seen tempests, when the scolding winds
Have rived[2] the knotty oaks, and I have seen
Th' ambitious ocean swell and rage and foam,
To be exalted with[3] the threat'ning clouds;
But never till tonight, never till now,
Did I go through a tempest dropping fire.
Either there is a civil strife in heaven,
Or else the world, too saucy[4] with the gods,
Incenses[5] them to send destruction.

CICERO. Why, saw you anything more wonderful?

CASCA. A common slave—you know him well by sight—
Held up his left hand, which did flame and burn
Like twenty torches joined, and yet his hand,
Not sensible of[6] fire, remained unscorched.
Besides—I ha' not since put up my sword—
Against[7] the Capitol I met a lion,
Who glazed[8] upon me and went surly by
Without annoying me. And there were drawn
Upon a heap[9] a hundred ghastly[10] women,
Transformèd with their fear, who swore they saw
Men, all in fire, walk up and down the streets.
And yesterday the bird of night[11] did sit
Even at noonday upon the market place,
Hooting and shrieking. When these prodigies[12]
Do so conjointly meet,[13] let not men say,
"These are their reasons, they are natural,"
❷ For I believe they are portentous things
Unto the climate that they point upon.[14]

❸ CICERO. Indeed, it is a strange-disposèd[15] time:
But men may construe things after their fashion,[16]
Clean from the purpose[17] of the things themselves.
Comes Caesar to the Capitol tomorrow?

CASCA. He doth; for he did bid Antonius
Send word to you he would be there tomorrow.

CICERO. Good night then, Casca; this disturbèd sky
Is not to walk in.

CASCA. Farewell, Cicero. [*Exit* CICERO.]

[*Enter* CASSIUS.]

CASSIUS. Who's there?

CASCA. A Roman.

2. Have rived: Have split.

3. exalted with: Lifted up to.

4. saucy: Rude; impudent.

5. Incenses: Enrages.

◆ Reading Strategy

Which notes helped you envision Casca's experiences? ❶

6. sensible of: Sensitive to.

7. Against: Opposite or near.

8. glazed: Stared.

9. were drawn . . . heap: Huddled together.

10. ghastly (gast´ lē) *adj.*: Ghostlike; pale.

11. bird of night: Owl.

12. prodigies (präd´ ə jēz) *n.*: Extraordinary happenings.

13. conjointly meet: Occur at the same time and place.

14. portentous (pôr ten´ təs) **. . . upon:** Bad omens for the country they point to.

15. strange-disposèd: Abnormal.

16. construe . . . fashion: Explain in their own way.

17. Clean from the purpose: Different from the real meaning.

Viewing and Representing Mini-Lesson

Visual Images

This mini-lesson suggests an activity drawn from Casca's description of the unusual sights he has seen this night.

Introduce Shakespeare is known for his abundance of visual images, many based on the natural world. In this case the images are supernatural.

Develop Have students work in pairs to reread Casca's speech, lines 15–32. Each pair can make a list of the images they find in the passage.

Apply Students can decide on a way to illustrate the scene Casca describes, whether as a drawing, a diorama, or some other medium. Encourage students to include the images that most appeal to them.

Assess Evaluate the artwork based on how closely students read and interpreted Casca's speech.

CASSIUS. Casca, by your voice.

CASCA. Your ear is good. Cassius, what night is this?

CASSIUS. A very pleasing night to honest men.

CASCA. Who ever knew the heavens menace so?

CASSIUS. Those that have known the earth so full of faults.
For my part, I have walked about the streets,
Submitting me unto the perilous night,
❹ And thus unbracèd,[18] Casca, as you see,
Have bared my bosom to the thunder-stone;[19]
And when the cross[20] blue lightning seemed to open
The breast of heaven, I did present myself
Even in the aim and very flash of it.

CASCA. But wherefore did you so much tempt the heavens?
It is the part[21] of men to fear and tremble
When the most mighty gods by tokens send
Such dreadful heralds to astonish[22] us.

CASSIUS. You are dull, Casca, and those sparks of life
That should be in a Roman you do want,[23]
Or else you use not. You look pale, and gaze,
And put on fear, and cast yourself in wonder,[24]
To see the strange impatience of the heavens;
But if you would consider the true cause
Why all these fires, why all these gliding ghosts,
Why birds and beasts from quality and kind,[25]
Why old men, fools, and children calculate,[26]
Why all these things change from their ordinance,[27]
❺ Their natures and preformèd faculties,
To monstrous quality,[28] why, you shall find
That heaven hath infused them with these spirits[29]
To make them instruments of fear and warning
Unto some monstrous state.[30]
Now could I, Casca, name to thee a man
Most like this dreadful night,
That thunders, lightens, opens graves, and roars
❻ As doth the lion in the Capitol;
A man no mightier than thyself, or me,
In personal action, yet prodigious grown
And fearful,[31] as these strange eruptions are.

CASCA. 'Tis Caesar that you mean, is it not, Cassius?

18. unbracèd: With jacket open.
19. thunder-stone: Thunderbolt.
20. cross: Zigzag.
21. part: Role.
22. by tokens . . . to astonish: By portentous signs send such awful announcements to frighten and stun.
23. want: Lack.
24. put on . . . in wonder: Show fear and are amazed.
25. from quality and kind: Acting contrary to their nature.
26. calculate: Make predictions.
27. ordinance: Regular behavior.
28. preformèd . . . quality: Established function to unnatural behavior.
29. infused . . . spirits: Filled them with supernatural powers.
30. monstrous state: Abnormal condition of government.
31. fearful: Causing fear.

◆ Build Vocabulary

surly (sur´ lē) *adv.*: In a proud, commanding way

portentous (pôr ten´ təs) *adj.*: Foreboding; full of unspecified meaning

prodigious (prə dij´ əs) *adj.*: Impressively forceful

◆ Critical Thinking

❹ Evaluate Ask students what qualities Cassius reveals by his behavior during the storm. Do they find his behavior admirable or foolish? *Some students may say that Cassius' behavior shows his courage and is admirable. Others may say that Cassius is a show-off and braggart who foolishly goes looking for trouble and seeking out danger.*

Comprehension Check ☑

❺ According to Cassius, how is Caesar like the stormy night? *Like a dangerous storm, Caesar has become very powerful and is using his power to frighten people into submission.*

◆ Critical Thinking

❻ Interpret Cassius claims that the storms are a result of Caesar's revolt against the order. Ask students to suggest another explanation based on Elizabethan beliefs. *The conspirators' plot against their ruler would be seen as a revolt against political order.*

Humanities: Literature

Shakespeare's "Ghostwriters"
Shakespeare wrote in a time when plagiarism was not as well defined as it is today. Playwrights and authors freely borrowed from one another's works and often adapted classic works. This loose attitude toward intellectual ownership has led some scholars to suggest that Shakespeare is not the sole author of all the works attributed to him. Although this theory is no longer widely accepted, students should be familiar with the theory and the reasons for it. The following Elizabethan men of letters have been considered as potential "ghostwriters" of the plays we now call Shakespeare's:

Christopher Marlowe is thought to have died in a tavern brawl in 1594—but perhaps he did not. He may have survived and written the plays we attribute to Shakespeare.

Francis Bacon, scientist and philosopher, was a prolific writer. His advocates argue that he might have been embarrassed to admit to writing such frivolous material as plays, and arranged to credit them to Shakespeare.

Lord Oxford was a nobleman in Queen Elizabeth's court. It would have been beneath Oxford's dignity to write for the theater. He would have sought out an obscure, lower-born person to take credit of authorship—someone like Shakespeare.

Have students find out more about Shakespeare's contemporaries and the theories surrounding an alternative authorship of some plays.

◆ Reading Strategy

❶ **Use Text Aids** Direct students' attention to the side notes to help them paraphrase how Cassius responds to the news that Caesar will be crowned king the next day. *Cassius says he would rather kill himself than live under Caesar's tyranny.*

◆ Build Grammar Skills

❷ **The Subjunctive Mood** Tell students that in this sentence the word *if* is implied. The sentence could be paraphrased this way in modern English: "*If* the Romans *were* not as weak and timid as deer, then Caesar would not be as fierce as a lion." By using the subjunctive mood, Cassius is indicating a condition contrary to fact. In other words, he believes that the Romans *are* weak.

Comprehension Check ☑

❸ What fear does Cassius express here? How does Casca reassure him? *Cassius expresses the fear that he is criticizing Caesar to someone who remains loyal to Caesar and will betray the plot against Caesar. Casca answers that he is not loyal to Caesar and will support Cassius in his plot.*

CASSIUS. Let it be who it is; for Romans now
Have thews[32] and limbs like to their ancestors;
But, woe the while![33] Our fathers' minds are dead,
And we are governed with our mothers' spirits;
Our yoke and sufferance[34] show us womanish.

CASCA. Indeed, they say the senators tomorrow
Mean to establish Caesar as a king;
And he shall wear his crown by sea and land,
In every place save here in Italy.

CASSIUS. I know where I will wear this dagger then;
Cassius from bondage will deliver[35] Cassius.
Therein,[36] ye gods, you make the weak most strong;
Therein, ye gods, you tyrants do defeat.
Nor stony tower, nor walls of beaten brass,
Nor airless dungeon, nor strong links of iron,
❶ Can be retentive to[37] the strength of spirit;
But life, being weary of these worldly bars,
Never lacks power to dismiss itself.
If I know this, know all the world besides,
That part of tyranny that I do bear
I can shake off at pleasure. *[Thunder still]*

CASCA. So can I;
So every bondman in his own hand bears
The power to cancel his captivity.

CASSIUS. And why should Caesar be a tyrant then?
Poor man, I know he would not be a wolf
But that he sees the Romans are but sheep;
❷ He were no lion, were not Romans hinds.[38]
Those that with haste will make a mighty fire
Begin it with weak straws. What trash is Rome,
What rubbish and what offal,[39] when it serves
For the base matter[40] to illuminate
So vile a thing as Caesar! But, O grief,
Where hast thou led me? I, perhaps, speak this
Before a willing bondman; then I know
My answer must be made.[41] But I am armed,
And dangers are to me indifferent.

❸ **CASCA.** You speak to Casca, and to such a man
That is no fleering tell-tale.[42] Hold, my hand.
Be factious[43] for redress of all these griefs,[44]
And I will set this foot of mine as far
As who goes farthest. *[They clasp hands.]*

32. thews (thyo͞oz) *n.*: Muscles or sinews; strength.
33. woe the while: Alas for the times.
34. yoke and sufferance: Slavery and meek acceptance of it.
35. will deliver: Will set free.
36. Therein: In that way (by using his dagger on himself).
37. be retentive to: Confine.
38. hinds (hīndz) *n.*: Female deer; peasants; servants.
39. offal (ôf´ əl) *n.*: Garbage.
40. base matter: Inferior or low material; foundation materials.
41. speak this . . . answer must be made: Say this before a willing servant of Caesar's; then I know I will have to answer for my words.
42. fleering tell-tale: Sneering tattletale.
43. factious (fak´ shəs) *adj.*: Active in forming a faction or a political party.
44. redress (rē´ dres) **of all these griefs:** Setting

◆ Literary Focus
Explain how Cassius' speech echoes the sentiments expressed by the tribunes in the exposition in Scene i.

Cultural Connection

Hierarchy Hierarchy and order were very important in Elizabethan times. Animals, the planets, angels, and society were all organized according to rigid rules of rank and classification. The same applied to the political organization of a country. The king or queen was at the top of the ladder, and very definite strata were set below the ruler. The Elizabethan educational system focused on order and obedience. Any break in the natural, social, religious, or political order was unthinkable. Elizabethans believed that such a transgression set off violent disturbances in the heavens and in nature. This belief is manifested in the storms and unusual events described by Casca in this scene. Some break in order has brought on storms and unnatural events.

CASSIUS. There's a bargain made.
Now know you, Casca, I have moved already
Some certain of the noblest-minded Romans
To undergo[45] with me an enterprise
Of honorable dangerous consequence;[46]
And I do know, by this[47] they stay for me
In Pompey's porch;[48] for now, this fearful night,
There is no stir or walking in the streets,
And the complexion of the element[49]
In favor's like[50] the work we have in hand,
Most bloody, fiery, and most terrible.

[*Enter* CINNA.]

CASCA. Stand close[51] awhile, for here comes one in haste.

CASSIUS. 'Tis Cinna; I do know him by his gait;[52]
He is a friend. Cinna, where haste you so?

CINNA. To find out you. Who's that? Metellus Cimber?

CASSIUS. No, it is Casca, one incorporate[53]
To our attempts. Am I not stayed[54] for, Cinna?

CINNA. I am glad on't.[55] What a fearful night is this!
There's two or three of us have seen strange sights.

CASSIUS. Am I not stayed for? Tell me.

CINNA. Yes, you are.
O Cassius, if you could
But win the noble Brutus to our party—

CASSIUS. Be you content. Good Cinna, take this paper,
And look you lay it in the praetor's chair,[56]
Where Brutus may but find it;[57] and throw this
In at his window: set this up with wax
Upon old Brutus'[58] statue. All this done,
Repair to Pompey's porch, where you shall find us.
Is Decius Brutus and Trebonius there?

CINNA. All but Metellus Cimber, and he's gone
To seek you at your house. Well, I will hie,
And so bestow these papers as you bade me.

CASSIUS. That done, repair to Pompey's Theater.

[*Exit* CINNA.]

Come, Casca, you and I will yet ere day

right all these grievances.
45. undergo: Undertake.
46. consequence (kän′ sə kwens′) *n.*: Importance.
47. by this: By this time.
48. Pompey's porch: Portico of Pompey's Theater.
49. complexion of the element: Condition of the sky; weather.
50. In favor's like: In appearance is like.
51. close: Hidden.
52. gait (gāt) *n.*: Way of moving.
53. incorporate (in kôr′ pər it) *adj.*: United.
54. stayed: Waited.
55. on't: Of it.
56. praetor's (prē′ tərz) **chair:** Roman magistrate's (or judge's) chair.
57. Where . . . find it: Where only Brutus (as the chief magistrate) will find it.
58. old Brutus': Lucius Junius Brutus, the founder of Rome.

◆ Literary Focus

4 Exposition in Drama Ask students how Cassius' plan connects to the public sentiment revealed in the exposition. *In the exposition, readers learn that the public loves Caesar. This love does not support Cassius' plan and will make it more difficult for him to convince Brutus that Caesar should not rule. Therefore, he is setting in motion a plan to make Brutus believe that public sentiment has changed.*

Customize for *Less Proficient Readers*

Help these students to paraphrase Cassius' words to Casca. Then ask for volunteers to read the speech aloud with appropriate portentous expression.

Customize for *English Language Learners*

Help these students match up the names of every character mentioned on this page with their names in the character list at the start of the act. Lead them to establish that every character on the page is loyal to Cassius and not to Caesar.

Humanities: Architecture

Roman Architecture Horace, the Roman poet, proclaimed, "Conquered Greece led the conqueror captive." He was referring to the fact that when Rome conquered Greece, shiploads of Greek statues were brought to Rome, and, when the supply was exhausted, Roman copies were made. Later, Rome developed its own styles of art and architecture.

Graceful paintings decorated the walls of wealthy Roman homes; the basilica, which provided the basic form for later Christian churches, was developed; the Roman arch made it possible to enclose vast areas of space under one roof. Have students research and report on Rome's achievements in art and architecture.

You might suggest they look up famous Roman structures such as the Colosseum, the Arch of Titus, the Baths of Caracalla, and the Pantheon. A good art history book will provide photographs of Roman statues such as the Bust of Hadrian, the Emperor Augustus Addressing His Army, and the reliefs from Trajan's Column.

◆ Critical Thinking

❶ **Interpret** Ask students to explain Casca's reason for wanting Brutus to join the conspiracy. *Because the common people love and trust Brutus, they will support the overthrow of Caesar if Brutus says it is the right thing to do.*

Customize for
Less Proficient Readers
Help these students identify the most significant information in each scene.

Reinforce and Extend

Answers

Reader's Response Students will probably respond to the frightening, ominous nature of the sights.

Thematic Focus Responses include Caesar's decision to refuse the crown, Brutus' decision to consider Cassius' proposal, and Cassius' decision to approach the other conspirators.

1. The tribunes are contemptuous of the common people because they are fickle in their allegiance.
2. (a) The soothsayer warns, "Beware the ides of March." (b) Caesar dismisses the warning, calling the soothsayer a dreamer.
3. Casca reports that Julius Caesar was offered the crown three times, and each time (though more and more reluctantly) Caesar refused it. As the people cheered his refusal, Caesar swooned and fell.
4. During a severe thunderstorm, Casca is frightened by a man whose hand is on fire and the reports of men walking burning through the streets.
5. Casca and Cassius are going to see Brutus.

See Brutus at his house; three parts of him
Is ours already, and the man entire
Upon the next encounter yields him ours.

CASCA. O, he sits high in all the people's hearts;
And that which would appear offense[59] in us,
❶ His countenance,[60] like richest alchemy,[61]
Will change to virtue and to worthiness.

CASSIUS. Him, and his worth, and our great need of him,
You have right well conceited.[62] Let us go,
For it is after midnight, and ere day
We will awake him and be sure of him. [*Exit*]

59. offense (ə fens′) *n.*: Crime.
60. countenance (koun′ tə nəns) *n.*: Support.
61. alchemy (al′ kə mē) *n.*: An early form of chemistry in which the goal was to change metals of little value into gold.
62. conceited (kən sēt′ id): Understood.

Guide for Responding

◆ *Literature and Your Life*

Reader's Response What is your reaction to the sight that Cassius, Casca, and Cinna observe during a stormy night in Scene iii?

Thematic Focus Several characters make choices during this act. Which do you think is the most important? Explain.

☑ Check Your Comprehension

1. Explain why the tribunes have only contempt for the common people of Rome.
2. (a) What warning does the soothsayer give? (b) What is Caesar's reaction to this warning?
3. Summarize Casca's report of what happened at the games.
4. What frightens Casca before he meets Cassius at night?
5. Where are Casca and Cassius going as the act closes?

◆ Critical Thinking

INTERPRET

1. (a) How does Cassius feel about Caesar? (b) Why does Caesar fear Cassius? **[Infer]**
2. In what important ways is Brutus different from Cassius? **[Compare and Contrast]**
3. Why is Brutus' participation in the plot essential to Cassius? **[Draw Conclusions]**

APPLY

4. Explain how Brutus, Cassius and Caesar represent qualities that can be found in people of any time period.
5. The philosopher Jeremy Bentham has written, "Tyranny and anarchy are never far asunder." Explain the meaning of this quotation. Then explain how it relates to this play. **[Synthesize]**

COMPARE LITERARY WORKS

6. Reread Teiresias' auguries in Scene V of *Antigone,* and look for parallels between that situation and the situation surrounding Cassius' description of "the strange impatience of the heavens" in Act I, Scene iii, of *The Tragedy of Julius Caesar.* **[Connect]**

◆ Critical Thinking

1. (a) Cassius is envious of Caesar and bitter about his success. (b) Caesar fears that Cassius has a "lean and hungry look"; Cassius thinks too much and Caesar believes such men are dangerous.
2. Brutus is different from Cassius because he is honorable and is trusted by his noble peers.
3. Brutus' participation will sway others to accept the assassination.
4. Brutus represents honor and integrity; Cassius represents envy and discord; Caesar represents ambition and power.
5. Suggested response: Lawlessness and disorder (anarchy) may be resolved by adopting a harsh, restrictive, oppressive form of government (tyranny). A system of law is needed to avoid both.
6. Sample answer: Teiresias pays attention to unusual signs from the natural world and draws the conclusion that Creon must allow the burial of Polyneices. Cassius' interpretation of the strange signs is that they are caused by Caesar's grasping for power. In both situations, the cause of the disturbing portents is the misbehavior of the ruler.

Guide for Responding (continued)

◆ Reading Strategy

Use Text Aids

Notes and stage directions help you to understand the action in *The Tragedy of Julius Caesar*. For example, the directions at the opening of Act I help you to envision the vitality and frenzy of the crowd scene that opens the act. The side notes help you understand that a "mechanical" is not a robot, but a common working man.

1. What information is provided in the side note for Act I, Scene i, line 11, that helps readers to understand the dialogue that follows?
2. The stage directions in Act I, Scene ii, indicate a flourish of trumpets and shouts offstage during the conversation between Brutus and Cassius. Why is it necessary that readers know about these offstage noises?

◆ Literary Focus

Exposition in Drama

The **exposition** is the part of the plot (usually the beginning) that lays the groundwork for the rest of the drama by revealing information about the basic situation.

1. What important information does Marullus reveal in Act I, Scene i, in his speech beginning with line 33?
2. How do you learn that some in the government are resentful of Caesar?

◆ Build Grammar Skills

The Subjunctive Mood

The subjunctive mood expresses either a condition that is contrary to fact or a wish, suggestion, demand, or request.

Practice In your notebook, rewrite each sentence to express the subjunctive mood.

1. If only I was king, things would be different.
2. He spoke as though he was the only one to tell the truth.
3. The curtain stirred as if it was a ghost moving on stage.
4. Caesar orders that Antony touches Calpurnia during the race.
5. Cassius requests that Brutus joins the conspirators.

◆ Build Vocabulary

Related Words: Forms of *Portent*

Complete the following sentences in your notebook, using *portend, portent,* or *portentous.*

1. I fear these to be __?__ dreams.
2. The __?__ Casca spoke of frightened him.
3. The storms __?__ that something terrible will happen.

Using the Word Bank: Synonyms

Copy each of the following words in your notebook, and write the letter of the word that is its synonym next to it.

1. replication: (a) original, (b) copy, (c) absence of sound
2. spare: (a) frightened, (b) thin, (c) muscular
3. infirmity: (a)strength, (b) weakness, (c) temper
4. surly: (a) bold, (b) timid, (c) polite
5. portentous: (a) optimistic, (b) unclear, (c) foreboding
6. prodigious: (a) passive, (b) forceful, (c) awkward

Idea Bank

Writing

1. **Journal Entry** Write a journal entry that Caesar might have written following the afternoon at the races during which Antony presented him with a crown three times.

2. **Speech** As Cassius, write an interior monologue—the words that might go through his mind—if Caesar did accept the crown that Anthony offered.

Speaking, Listening, and Viewing

3. **Roman Symbols** Julius Caesar's career brought Rome to the crossroads between its earlier republican era and its later imperial era. Research the art and visual symbols of both eras, and choose a symbol that captures the spirit of each. **[History Link]**

◆ Reading Strategy

1. The entire dialogue cleverly revolves around double meaning. The side note about the dual usages of *cobbler* illuminates this.
2. The offstage noises indicate that something significant and official is occurring offstage.

◆ Literary Focus

1. Marullus introduces the fact that not everyone is rejoicing over Caesar's power and popularity.
2. Through statements made in conversations between characters, readers learn that Marullus, Flavius, Cassius, Brutus, and Casca resent (in varying degrees) Caesar's rise to power.

◆ Build Grammar Skills

1. If only I *were* king, things would be different.
2. He spoke as though he *were* the only one to tell the truth.
3. The curtain stirred as if it *were* a ghost moving on stage.
4. Caesar orders that Antony *touch* Calpurnia during the race.
5. Cassius requests that Brutus *join* the conspirators.

◆ Build Vocabulary

Related Words: Forms of *Portent*

1. I fear these to be *portentous* dreams.
2. The *portent* Casca spoke of frightened him.
3. The storms *portend* that something terrible will happen.

Using the Word Bank

1. b 2. b 3. b 4. a 5. c 6. b

Idea Bank

Customizing for *Performance Levels*

Following are suggestions for matching Idea Bank topics with your students' ability levels:

Less Advanced: 1
Average: 2, 3
More Advanced: 2

Customizing for *Learning Modalities:*

Following are suggestions for matching Idea Bank topics with your students' learning modalities:

Intrapersonal: 1
Interpersonal: 3
Verbal/Linguistic: 1, 2, 3
Bodily/Kinesthetic: 3

✓ ASSESSMENT OPTIONS

Formal Assessment, Selection Test, pp. 176–178 and Assessment Resources Software. The selection test is designed so that it can be easily customized to the ability levels of your students

PORTFOLIO ASSESSMENT

Use the following rubrics in ***Alternative Assessment*** to assess student writing:

Journal Entry: Expression Rubric, p. 94
Speech: Expression Rubric, p. 94

Prepare and Engage

LESSON OBJECTIVES

1. **To develop vocabulary and word identification skills**
   - Latin Roots: *-spir-*
   - Using the Word Bank: Definitions
   - Extending Word Study: Context
2. **To use a variety of reading strategies to read and comprehend an essay**
   - Connect Your Experience
   - Reading Strategy: Read Blank Verse
   - Tips to Guide Reading
   - Read to Be Informed
3. **To increase knowledge of other cultures and to connect common elements across cultures**
   - Connecting Themes Across Cultures (ATE)
4. **To express and support responses to the text**
   - Critical Thinking
   - Idea Bank: Editorial
   - Idea Bank: Monologue
   - Idea Bank: Debate
   - Speaking, Listening, and Viewing Mini-Lesson: Debate
5. **To analyze literary elements**
   - Literary Focus: Blank Verse
6. **To increase knowledge of the rules of grammar and usage**
   - Build Grammar Skills: Commonly Confused Words: *Affect* and *Effect*

Test Preparation

Reading Comprehension: Identify Patterns of Organization (ATE, p. 733) The teaching tips and sample test item in this workshop support the instruction and practice in the unit workshop:
Reading Comprehension: Characteristics of Text (SE, p. 809)

Ask students to suggest reasons why a political leader's enemies might form a conspiracy against him or her. Have students record their suggestions in their journals and refer to them—and add to them—as they read this act.

Guide for Reading, Act II

◆ Review and Anticipate

As Caesar returns triumphantly from his war against Pompey's sons, he dismisses a warning to "beware the ides of March." The common people have turned their loyalty from Pompey to Caesar, and they cry out for Caesar to accept the emperor's crown. Although Caesar refuses three times, some still doubt his sincerity. Cassius, whom Caesar distrusts because of his "lean and hungry look," persuades Casca to join a conspiracy against Caesar. Brutus, although he is Caesar's friend, worries about Caesar's ambition. The conspirators plant letters that they hope will bring Brutus to their side. As Act II opens, on the eve of the ides of March, Brutus receives both the letters and a visit from Casca and Cassius. As the act progresses, notice the warnings that Caesar ignores and the shift of power within the group of conspirators.

◆ Literary Focus

Blank Verse

Blank verse is a poetic unrhymed iambic pentameter. **Iambic** means that an unaccented or unstressed syllable is followed by an accented or stressed one. **Pentameter** means that there are five feet per line. (A foot is one set in the pattern of accented and unaccented syllables. In this case, a foot is one iamb.)

By̆ áll | thĕ góds | thăt Ró|măns bów | bĕfóre,
Ĭ hére | dĭscárd | mȳ síck|nĕss! Sóul | ŏf Róme,

The Tragedy of Julius Caesar is written mainly in blank verse. Shakespeare uses blank verse for important or aristocratic characters, but his minor characters speak in ordinary prose.

◆ Build Grammar Skills

Commonly Confused Words: *Affect* and *Effect*

When Portia says "Hoping it was but an effect of humor, Which sometime hath his hour with every man," she uses a word that is frequently misused: *effect*. Most often, as in this sentence, *effect* is a noun meaning "the result." *Effect* can also be a verb meaning "to bring about" or "to cause." *Affect* is always a verb meaning "to influence." Look at these examples:

Cassius' letters *affected* Brutus' decision.
The *effect* of the letters was significant.

◆ Reading Strategy

Read Blank Verse

The blank verse structure of Shakespeare's plays should not stand in the way of your understanding. In reading *The Tragedy of Julius Caesar*, don't confuse a line with a sentence. A sentence may continue through several lines. Each line may begin with a capital letter, but that is a poetic convention. A capital letter at the beginning of a line doesn't necessarily indicate the beginning of a sentence. To read for meaning, read in sentences. Though you may pause over a comma at the end of a line, don't stop until you come to a period.

◆ Build Vocabulary

Latin Roots: *-spir-*

In Act II of *The Tragedy of Julius Caesar,* a number of Romans *conspire* to overthrow Caesar. The Latin word root *-spir-* means "to breathe"; thus, *conspire* means "to breathe together" or, in other words, "to unite." The root *-spir* is also the root of *conspiracy*, a secret agreement to perform together a treacherous act.

Word Bank

Before you read, preview this list of words from this act.

augmented
entreated
conspiracy
resolution
exploit
imminent

Prentice Hall Literature Program Resources

REINFORCE / RETEACH / EXTEND

Selection Support Pages
Build Vocabulary: Word Roots: *-spir-*, p. 208
Build Grammar Skills: Commonly Confused Words: *Affect* and *Effect*, p. 209
Reading Strategy: Read Blank Verse, p. 210
Literary Focus: Blank Verse, p.211

Strategies for Diverse Student Needs, p. 51

Beyond Literature
Multicultural Connection: Omens and Portents, p. 51

Formal Assessment Selection Test, pp. 179–181; Assessment Resources Software

Alternative Assessment, p. 51

Resource Pro CD-ROM

Listening to Literature Audiocassettes

Literature CD-ROM

The Tragedy of

JULIUS CAESAR

William Shakespeare

Act II

Scene i. *Rome.*

[*Enter* BRUTUS *in his orchard.*]

BRUTUS. What, Lucius, ho!
I cannot, by the progress of the stars,
Give guess how near to day. Lucius, I say!
I would it were my fault to sleep so soundly.
When, Lucius, when? Awake, I say! What, Lucius!

[*Enter* LUCIUS.]

LUCIUS. Called you, my lord?

BRUTUS. Get me a taper in my study, Lucius.
When it is lighted, come and call me here.

LUCIUS. I will, my lord. [*Exit*]

BRUTUS. It must be by his death; and for my part,
I know no personal cause to spurn at[1] him,
But for the general.[2] He would be crowned.
How that might change his nature, there's the question.
It is the bright day that brings forth the adder,[3]
And that craves[4] wary walking. Crown him that,
And then I grant we put a sting in him
That at his will he may do danger with.
Th' abuse of greatness is when it disjoins
Remorse from power;[5] and, to speak truth of Caesar,
I have not known when his affections swayed[6]
More than his reason. But 'tis a common proof[7]
That lowliness[8] is young ambition's ladder,
Whereto the climber upward turns his face;
But when he once attains the upmost round,
He then unto the ladder turns his back,
Looks in the clouds, scorning the base degrees[9]
By which he did ascend. So Caesar may;
Then lest he may, prevent.[10] And, since the quarrel
Will bear no color[11] for the thing he is,

◆ Literary Focus
Read lines 10–20 of Brutus' speech aloud to hear the stressed and unstressed syllables of the iambs.

1. **spurn at:** Kick against; rebel.
2. **the general:** The public good.
3. **adder** (ad′ ər) *n.*: Poisonous snake.
4. **craves:** Requires.
5. **disjoins . . . power:** Separates mercy from power.
6. **affections swayed:** Emotions ruled.
7. **proof:** Experience.
8. **lowliness:** Humility.
9. **base degrees:** Low steps or people in lower positions.
10. **lest . . . prevent:** In case he may, we must stop him.
11. **the quarrel . . . no color:** Our complaint cannot be justified in view of what he now is.

Test Preparation Workshop

Reading Comprehension: Identify Patterns of Organization
Many standardized tests require students to analyze the characteristics of a text. Use this sample test item to help students with this skill.

"Cowards die many times before their deaths;
The valiant never taste of death but once."

What pattern of organization is used in this passage?

A Flashback
B Chronological order
C Cause and effect
D Comparison and contrast

Students may note that the pattern is comparison and contrast, because the speaker indicates the different ways cowards and the brave view the idea of death. The correct response is D.

Develop Understanding

One-Minute Insight Act II of *The Tragedy of Julius Caesar* focuses on Brutus' internal conflict. His intense self-examination and struggle with himself over issues of duty, honor, and loyalty are a sharp contrast to Caesar's lack of awareness. Caesar misses the subtle indications and the outright warnings that he is in danger. In this act, an inexorable shift in power (both public and among the conspirators) begins.

Connecting Themes Across Cultures

Invite students to make comparisons between the issues Brutus considers in his struggle over proper government and those that were considered by those who fought the American Revolution.

Customize for ***Musical/Rhythmic Learners***

Have these students lead groups in tapping out the iambic pentameter of the poetry in this act and finding the exceptions to the rule. You may wish to suggest specific passages, such as Brutus' first monologue beginning on p. 733, or the dialogue between Brutus and Cassius in lines 86–89.

◆ Literary Focus

1 Blank Verse Begin the act by having students scan a few lines spoken by Brutus and the lines spoken by Lucius. How do they differ, and why? *Brutus speaks in blank verse, except in the first line, in which he calls his servant. Lucius speaks in brief answers that are not in blank verse. Shakespeare uses blank verse for aristocratic or important characters, whereas servants and minor characters usually speak in prose. (Emphasize "usually," as Lucius' speech, lines 35–38, is in blank verse.)*

◆ Literary Focus

2 Blank Verse Remind students that iambic pentameter reflects the natural rhythm of speech. While they should exaggerate the stresses to identify the rhythm, Shakespeare did not intend for the lines to be spoken in a sing-song pattern.

◆ Critical Thinking

❶ **Interpret** Lead students to consider why Brutus compares Caesar to a serpent's egg, rather than to a serpent or snake. *Brutus doesn't compare Caesar to a snake, because Caesar hasn't actually done any harm yet. Like a snake's egg, though, Caesar has the potential to become something dangerous.*

Customize for
Less Proficient Readers

❷ Remind students who are confused by this passage that in Act I Caesar is advised by the soothsayer to beware the ides of March. Help them recall that the ides fall on the fifteenth of the month.

◆ Critical Thinking

❸ **Make Inferences** Ask students why they think Brutus interprets this portion of the letter as he does. *He is looking for a reason to support his inclination to join the conspirators.*

Listening to Literature Audiocassettes Play this portion of the recording while students follow the text. Listening while reading will help them reinforce the two speakers of the dialogue. It will also help students hear the natural pauses that occur as Brutus reads the letter and thinks about its ramifications.

Customize for
Gifted/Talented Students

Have students construct a scenario of events that have occurred since Act I ended. Ask them to include the amount of time that has passed and what Cassius and Brutus apparently have been doing.

Customize for
Pre-AP Students

Ask these students to identify dialogue in which a line of iambic pentameter is begun by one character and completed by another. You can show students examples in lines 76–77 and lines 95–98.

Fashion it[12] thus: that what he is, augmented
Would run to these and these extremities;[13]
❶ And therefore think him as a serpent's egg
Which hatched, would as his kind grow mischievous,
And kill him in the shell.

[*Enter* LUCIUS.]

LUCIUS. The taper burneth in your closet,[14] sir.
Searching the window for a flint,[15] I found
This paper thus sealed up, and I am sure
It did not lie there when I went to bed.
[*Gives him the letter*]

BRUTUS. Get you to bed again; it is not day.
Is not tomorrow, boy, the ides of March?

❷ **LUCIUS.** I know not, sir.

BRUTUS. Look in the calendar and bring me word.

LUCIUS. I will, sir. [*Exit*]

BRUTUS. The exhalations[16] whizzing in the air
Give so much light that I may read by them.
[*Opens the letter and reads*]

"Brutus, thou sleep'st; awake, and see thyself.
Shall Rome, &c.[17] Speak, strike, redress.
Brutus, thou sleep'st; awake."

Such instigations[18] have been often dropped
Where I have took them up.
"Shall Rome, &c." Thus must I piece it out:[19]
❸ Shall Rome stand under one man's awe?[20] What, Rome?
My ancestors did from the streets of Rome
The Tarquin[21] drive, when he was called a king.
"Speak, strike, redress." Am I entreated
To speak and strike? O Rome, I make thee promise,
If the redress will follow, thou receivest
Thy full petition at the hand of[22] Brutus!

[*Enter* LUCIUS.]

LUCIUS. Sir, March is wasted fifteen days. [*Knock within*]

BRUTUS. 'Tis good. Go to the gate; somebody knocks.
[*Exit* LUCIUS.]

Since Cassius first did whet[23] me against Caesar,
I have not slept.
Between the acting of a dreadful thing
And the first motion,[24] all the interim is

12. Fashion it: State the case.
13. extremities (ek strem´ ə tēz) *n.*: Extremes (of tyranny).
14. closet: Study.
15. flint: Stone used to start a fire.
16. exhalations (eks´ hə lā´ shənz) *n.*: Meteors.
17. &c.: *et cetera*, Latin for "and so forth."
18. instigations (in´ stə gā´ shənz) *n.*: Urgings, incitements, or spurs to act.
19. piece it out: Figure out the meaning.
20. under one man's awe: In fearful reverence of one man.
21. Tarquin (tär´ kwin): King of Rome driven out by Lucius Junius Brutus, Brutus' ancestor.
22. Thy full . . . hand of: All you ask from.
23. whet (hwet) *v.*: Sharpen; incite.
24. motion: Idea; suggestion.

Block Scheduling Strategies

Consider these suggestions to take advantage of extended class time:

- Invite students to view Feature 2 on the CD-ROM *The Time, Life, and Works of Shakespeare.* This feature focuses on the Elizabethan Age and Elizabethan theater.
- Students can work in small groups to read portions of the play aloud. Encourage them to note the rhythm of the blank verse as they read.
- After completing the Reader's Response question on p. 748 of the Guide for Responding, students may enjoy holding a debate between those who would have joined the conspiracy and those who would not.
- Have students complete the Literary Focus page on blank verse in ***Selection Support,*** p. 211.
- Students may work individually or in groups to answer the Critical Thinking questions on p. 748.
- Have students work in pairs to complete the Monologue in the Idea Bank on p. 749 and read their monologues aloud to the class.

Like a phantasma,[25] or a hideous dream.
The genius and the mortal instruments[26]
Are then in council, and the state of a man,
Like to a little kingdom, suffers then
The nature of an insurrection.[27]

[*Enter* LUCIUS.]

LUCIUS. Sir, 'tis your brother[28] Cassius at the door,
Who doth desire to see you.

BRUTUS. Is he alone?

LUCIUS. No, sir, there are moe[29] with him.

BRUTUS. Do you know them?

LUCIUS. No, sir; their hats are plucked about their ears,
And half their faces buried in their cloaks,
That by no means I may discover them
By any mark of favor.[30]

BRUTUS. Let 'em enter. [*Exit* LUCIUS.]
They are the faction. O conspiracy,
❹ Sham'st thou to show thy dang'rous brow by night,
When evils are most free? O, then by day
Where wilt thou find a cavern dark enough
To mask thy monstrous visage? Seek none, conspiracy;
Hide it in smiles and affability:
For if thou path, thy native semblance on,[31]
Not Erebus[32] itself were dim enough
To hide thee from prevention.[33]

[*Enter the conspirators,* CASSIUS, CASCA, DECIUS, CINNA, METELLUS CIMBER, *and* TREBONIUS.]

CASSIUS. I think we are too bold upon[34] your rest.
Good morrow, Brutus; do we trouble you?

BRUTUS. I have been up this hour, awake all night.
Know I these men that come along with you?

❻
CASSIUS. Yes, every man of them; and no man here
But honors you; and every one doth wish
You had but that opinion of yourself
Which every noble Roman bears of you.
This is Trebonius.

BRUTUS. He is welcome hither.

CASSIUS. This, Decius Brutus.

BRUTUS. He is welcome too.

25. **all the . . . a phantasma:** All the time between seems like a nightmare.
26. **mortal instruments:** Bodily powers.
27. **insurrection** (in′ sə rek′ shən) *n.*: Revolt.
28. **brother:** Brother-in-law (Cassius was married to Brutus' sister).
29. **moe:** More.
30. **discover . . . favor:** Identify them by their appearance.

◆ **Literary Focus**
What exclamation does Shakespeare include that helps him maintain the iambic pentameter of lines 77 and 79? ❺

31. **path . . . semblance on:** Walk looking as you normally do.
32. **Erebus** (er′ ə bəs): Dark place between Earth and Hades.
33. **prevention:** Being discovered and stopped.
34. **upon:** In interfering with.

◆ Build Vocabulary

augmented (ôg ment′ id) *v.*: Made greater

entreated (in trēt′ id) *v.*: Begged; pleaded with

conspiracy (kən spir′ ə sē) *n.*: Group plotting a harmful act or the plot itself

◆ Reading Strategy

❹ Read Blank Verse Have students determine how many sentences these six lines, starting with "Let 'em enter" and ending with "visage," contain. Then ask a student to read the lines aloud, pausing only where the sentences end. *The lines contain four sentences, ending with "enter," "faction," "free," and "visage."*

◆ Literary Focus

❺ Blank Verse The exclamation "O" is used twice and it helps to maintain the rhythm of lines 77 and 79.

◆ Critical Thinking

❻ Draw Conclusions Guide students to consider why Cassius speaks to Brutus in this flattering way. What does Cassius hope to achieve? *He is flattering Brutus, hoping to draw him into the conspiracy.*

Customize for
English Language Learners
Students whose first language is not English may be confused by the use of the words *thee*, *thy*, and *thou*. Explain that these are old ways of saying *you* (*thee* and *thou*) and *your* (*thy*).

Extending Word Study

Context Encourage students to determine the meaning of *visage*, line 81, by using context clues. Then have them look it up in the dictionary to find the definition.

Research Skills Mini-Lesson

Thesis Statements

This mini-lesson is designed to help students who are conducting a research project of any kind.

Introduce When students conduct research of any topic, they are likely to get to a point when they have narrowed a topic and are ready to begin writing. A thesis statement identifies the main idea of a research paper. Remind students that developing a thesis statement is part of the research process.

Develop Before drafting thesis statements, students should carefully review all the notes they have taken. They should determine the most important ideas they've gathered, eliminate information that does not support the ideas they wish to pursue, and then summarize the notes that are left. By polishing this summary into a single coherent sentence, students will have created a thesis statement.

Apply Ask students to share their thinking as they create thesis statements from their research. Alternatively, you may choose to create a set of "notes" for students to apply the skills of this lesson.

Assess Evaluate thesis statements on their ability to focus a topic, and to reflect the research that has been gathered.

❶ Clarification Explain to students that Casca is drawing an analogy between the sun and Caesar. He points out that just as the sun will change its course as the year progresses, so will Caesar change as his power increases.

❷ Enrichment Point out to students that Casca's knowledge of astronomy would have been based on theories of Hipparchus and other Greeks, who claimed that the planets and sun circled the Earth. Shakespeare, however, would have been acquainted with the ideas of Copernicus, who believed that the planets traveled around the sun. Copernicus also developed the theory of axle tilt, which explained the change in seasons by changes in the angle of the Earth's tilt toward the sun—an idea that Casca mentions here.

Comprehension Check ☑

❸ Why doesn't Brutus want to swear an oath? *He wants to believe that he and the other conspirators are such honorable men that their lives are already sworn to truthfulness; an oath would be unnecessary.*

CASSIUS. This, Casca; this, Cinna; and this, Metellus
Cimber.

BRUTUS. They are all welcome.
What watchful cares do interpose themselves
Betwixt your eyes and night?[35]

CASSIUS. Shall I entreat[36] a word? [*They whisper.*]

DECIUS. Here lies the east; doth not the day break here?

CASCA. No.

CINNA. O, pardon, sir, it doth; and yon gray lines
❶ That fret[37] the clouds are messengers of day.

CASCA. You shall confess that you are both deceived.
❷ Here, as I point my sword, the sun arises,
Which is a great way growing on[38] the south,
Weighing[39] the youthful season of the year.
Some two months hence, up higher toward the north
He first presents his fire; and the high[40] east
Stands as the Capitol, directly here.

BRUTUS. Give me your hands all over, one by one.

CASSIUS. And let us swear our resolution.

❸ **BRUTUS.** No, not an oath. If not the face of men,
The sufferance of our souls, the time's abuse[41]—
If these be motives weak, break off betimes,[42]
And every man hence to his idle bed.
So let high-sighted[43] tyranny range on
Till each man drop by lottery.[44] But if these
(As I am sure they do) bear fire enough
To kindle cowards and to steel with valor
The melting spirits of women, then, countrymen,
What need we any spur but our own cause
To prick us to redress?[45] What other bond
Than secret Romans, that have spoke the word,
And will not palter?[46] And what other oath
Than honesty to honesty engaged[47]
That this shall be, or we will fall for it?
Swear priests and cowards and men cautelous,[48]
Old feeble carrions[49] and such suffering souls
That welcome wrongs; unto bad causes swear
Such creatures as men doubt; but do not stain
The even[50] virtue of our enterprise,
Nor th' insuppressive mettle[51] of our spirits,
To think that or our cause or[52] our performance
Did need an oath; when every drop of blood
That every Roman bears, and nobly bears,

35. watchful . . . night: Worries that keep you from sleep.
36. entreat (in trēt′) *v.*: Speak.
37. fret (fret) *v.*: Decorate with a pattern.
38. growing on: Tending toward.
39. Weighing: Considering.
40. high: Due.
41. the face . . . time's abuse: The sadness on men's faces, the suffering of our souls, the present abuses.
42. betimes: Quickly.
43. high-sighted: Arrogant (as a hawk about to swoop down on its prey).
44. by lottery: By chance or in his turn.
45. prick us to redress: Goad or spur us on to correct these evils.
46. palter (pôl′ tər): Talk insincerely.
47. honesty engaged: Personal honor pledged.
48. cautelous: Cautious.
49. carrions (kar′ ē ənz) *n.*: Decaying flesh.
50. even: Constant.
51. insuppressive mettle: Uncrushable courage.
52. or . . . or: Either our cause or.

◆ Build Vocabulary

resolution (rez′ ə lo͞o′ shən) *n.*: Strong determination

Cultural Connection

Greek/Roman Gods Brutus says that "not Erebus itself were dim enough" (Scene 1, line 84) to hide the conspiracy to assassinate Caesar. Explain to students that Erebus was, in Greek mythology, the part of the underworld (Hades) through which the dead first pass. By the time of Julius Caesar, the Romans had taken for their own many of the gods of the Greeks, but given them Roman names. Hermes, messenger of the gods, was called Mercury; Aphrodite, goddess of love and beauty, Venus; Hera, queen of the gods, Juno; and the king of the Gods, Zeus, was called Jupiter by the Romans. Interested students might list the Roman names of other Greek gods such as Hades (Pluto), Athena (Minerva), Poseidon (Neptune), and Artemis (Diana).

4 ▲ **Critical Viewing** What do you think the group is saying to Brutus here? **[Speculate]**

Is guilty of a several bastardy[53]
If he do break the smallest particle
Of any promise that hath passed from him.

CASSIUS. But what of Cicero? Shall we sound him?[54]
I think he will stand very strong with us.

CASCA. Let us not leave him out.

CINNA. No, by no means.

METELLUS. O, let us have him, for his silver hairs
Will purchase us a good opinion,
And buy men's voices to commend our deeds.
It shall be said his judgment ruled our hands;
Our youths and wildness shall no whit[55] appear,
But all be buried in his gravity.

5 **BRUTUS.** O, name him not! Let us not break with him;[56]
For he will never follow anything
That other men begin.

CASSIUS. Then leave him out.

CASCA. Indeed, he is not fit.

DECIUS. Shall no man else be touched but only Caesar?

CASSIUS. Decius, well urged. I think it is not meet

53. guilty . . . bastardy: Is no true Roman.

54. sound him: Find out his opinion.

◆ ***Literature and Your Life***

Metellus is saying that Cicero's age and reputation for wisdom will lead people to accept the actions of the conspirators more rapidly. Explain why you think people should or should not be judged by the company they keep. 6

55. no whit (hwit) *n.*: Not the least bit.

56. break with him: Confide in him.

▶Critical Viewing◀

4 Speculate Logical answers include the greetings beginning with line 86, the discussion of the sunrise beginning with line 100. Some students may suggest that Brutus is speaking to the others, delivering his monologue beginning with line 114.

◆Critical Thinking

5 Make Inferences Ask students to suggest another reason Brutus might have for not wanting to include Cicero. *He may not want to confide in Cicero because he knows Cicero's honor and will not go along with the plot. He may also fear that Cicero will betray them.*

◆*Literature and Your Life*

6 Encourage students to support their individual responses with examples from literature, movies, television programs, and, if they wish, from personal experience.

Cross-Curricular Connection: History

Cicero Tell students that Marcus Tullius Cicero was one of the great speakers and writers of Rome. He studied philosophy and rhetoric in Greece, and after returning to Rome was elected praetor (an administrator of civil justice) in 66 B.C., and then consul in 63 B.C.

Cicero, who believed in a republican form of government, supported Pompey in the struggle between Pompey and Caesar, and approved of Caesar's murder. In 43 B.C., when Caesar's supporters Octavius (later the emperor Augustus), Mark Antony, and Marcus Aemilius Lepidus came to power as the Second Triumvirate, Cicero was one of many they condemned to death. He was slain trying to escape from his home in Tuscany.

Cicero's prose became the model for literary expression in Europe, and his orations are still among the most commonly studied Latin works.

◆ Build Vocabulary

❶ Word Roots: *-spir-* Students can easily locate the word root *-spir-* in this passage. Challenge them to define the word *spirit,* using the meaning of the word root ("to breathe"). *Spirit means "breath of life."*

◆ Critical Thinking

❷ Analyze Have students determine why it is important to Brutus that Caesar be killed "boldly, but not wrathfully." *For Brutus, it would be dishonorable if Caesar were killed in anger.*

Literature CD-ROM Use the Literature CD-ROM feature 4 to give students background on Elizabethan staging conventions. After using the feature, lead a class discussion applying what students have learned to *The Tragedy of Julius Caesar.*

Tips to Guide Reading

Whisper Reading Encourage students to whisper read Brutus's speech in which he refuses to allow Antony to be killed. This will help them feel the rhythm of the play's language.

Mark Antony, so well beloved of Caesar,
Should outlive Caesar; we shall find of[57] him
A shrewd contriver;[58] and you know, his means,
If he improve[59] them, may well stretch so far
As to annoy[60] us all; which to prevent,
Let Antony and Caesar fall together.

BRUTUS. Our course will seem too bloody, Caius Cassius,
To cut the head off and then hack the limbs,
Like wrath in death and envy afterwards;[61]
For Antony is but a limb of Caesar.
Let's be sacrificers, but not butchers, Caius.
❶ We all stand up against the spirit of Caesar,
And in the spirit of men there is no blood.
O, that we then could come by Caesar's spirit,[62]
And not dismember Caesar! But, alas,
Caesar must bleed for it. And, gentle[63] friends,
Let's kill him boldly, but not wrathfully;
Let's carve him as a dish fit for the gods,
Not hew him as a carcass fit for hounds.
And let our hearts, as subtle masters do,
Stir up their servants[64] to an act of rage,
❷ And after seem to chide 'em.[65] This shall make
Our purpose necessary, and not envious;
Which so appearing to the common eyes,
We shall be called purgers,[66] not murderers.
And for Mark Antony, think not of him;
For he can do no more than Caesar's arm
When Caesar's head is off.

CASSIUS. Yet I fear him;
For in the ingrafted[67] love he bears to Caesar—

BRUTUS. Alas, good Cassius, do not think of him.
If he love Caesar, all that he can do
Is to himself—take thought[68] and die for Caesar.
And that were much he should,[69] for he is given
To sports, to wildness, and much company.

TREBONIUS. There is no fear in him; let him not die,
For he will live and laugh at this hereafter.

[*Clock strikes.*]

BRUTUS. Peace! Count the clock.

CASSIUS. The clock hath stricken three.

TREBONIUS. 'Tis time to part.

CASSIUS. But it is doubtful yet
Whether Caesar will come forth today or no;

57. of: In.
58. contriver (kən triv´ ər) *n.*: Schemer.
59. improve: Increase.
60. annoy: Harm.
61. Like . . . envy afterwards: As if we were killing in anger with hatred afterward.
62. come by Caesar's spirit: Get hold of the principles of tyranny for which Caesar stands.
63. gentle: Honorable; noble.
64. servants: Their hands.
65. chide 'em: Scold them.
66. purgers: Healers.
67. ingrafted: Deeply rooted.
68. take thought: Become melancholy.
69. that were much he should: It is unlikely he would do that.

Humanities: Literature

Plutarch's *Lives* Much of the information that Shakespeare used to create *The Tragedy of Julius Caesar* came from one source, familiarly known as Plutarch's *Lives,* written by the Greek writer Plutarch (A.D. 46?–A.D. 120?).

The book contains a series of paired biographies, each pair comparing one Greek and one Roman statesman. Shakespeare, like other playwrights of his time, used translations of Plutarch by Sir Thomas North when writing about Greece or Rome.

Every character in *Julius Caesar* is found in Plutarch, except for Brutus' servant Lucius. Even details such as Cassius' leanness, Brutus' studiousness, and Caesar's "falling sickness" are found in Plutarch's work.

Let students know that Shakespeare didn't plagiarize or steal Plutarch's work. He just used Plutarch as a springboard for his own creative genius.

Ask students to name contemporary novels or movies that are based on the lives of real people. What sources do students think contemporary writers might use to find background on their real-life characters? *Students will probably suggest that information can be found in magazines, newspapers, on the Internet, and for some people, in biographies or autobiographies.*

For he is superstitious grown of late,
Quite from the main[70] opinion he held once
Of fantasy, of dreams, and ceremonies.[71]
It may be these apparent prodigies,
The unaccustomed terror of this night,
And the persuasion of his augurers[72]
May hold him from the Capitol today.

DECIUS. Never fear that. If he be so resolved,
I can o'ersway him;[73] for he loves to hear
That unicorns may be betrayed with trees,[74]
And bears with glasses,[75] elephants with holes,[76]
Lions with toils,[77] and men with flatterers;
But when I tell him he hates flatterers
He says he does, being then most flatterèd.
Let me work;
For I can give his humor the true bent,[78]
And I will bring him to the Capitol.

CASSIUS. Nay, we will all of us be there to fetch him.

BRUTUS. By the eighth hour; is that the uttermost?[79]

CINNA. Be that the uttermost, and fail not then.

METELLUS. Caius Ligarius doth bear Caesar hard,[80]
Who rated[81] him for speaking well of Pompey.
I wonder none of you have thought of him.

BRUTUS. Now, good Metellus, go along by him.
He loves me well, and I have given him reasons;
Send him but hither, and I'll fashion[82] him.

CASSIUS. The morning comes upon 's; we'll leave you, Brutus.
And, friends, disperse yourselves; but all remember
What you have said, and show yourselves true Romans.

BRUTUS. Good gentlemen, look fresh and merrily.
Let not our looks put on[83] our purposes,
But bear it[84] as our Roman actors do,
With untired spirits and formal constancy.[85]
And so good morrow to you every one.

[*Exit all but* BRUTUS.]

Boy! Lucius! Fast asleep? It is no matter;
Enjoy the honey-heavy dew of slumber.
Thou hast no figures nor no fantasies
Which busy care draws in the brains of men;
Therefore thou sleep'st so sound.

70. Quite from the main: Quite changed from the strong.
71. ceremonies: Omens.
72. augurers (ô´ gər ərz) *n.*: Officials who interpreted omens to decide if they were favorable or unfavorable for an undertaking.
73. I can o'ersway him: I can change his mind.
74. unicorns . . . trees: Story that tells how standing in front of a tree and stepping aside at the last moment cause a charging unicorn to bury his horn in the tree and be caught.
75. glasses: Mirrors.
76. holes: Pitfalls.
77. toils: Nets; snares.
78. give his humor the true bent: Bend his feelings in the right direction.
79. uttermost: Latest.
80. doth bear Caesar hard: Has a grudge against Caesar.
81. rated: Berated.
82. fashion: Mold.
83. put on: Show.
84. bear it: Carry it off.
85. formal constancy: Consistent dignity.

◆ Literary Focus

3 Blank Verse Students should be able to locate the line in Decius' speech that is not in iambic pentameter. Invite them to conjecture about why Shakespeare included the short line "Let me work." *It is important that Decius convince Caesar to come to the Capitol—his "work" is a vital part of the plot. Therefore, it is reasonable to conjecture that Shakespeare set the statement off to call attention to it.*

4 Clarification Remind students of the struggle between Caesar and Pompey. Caius Ligarius is one who supported Pompey; therefore, he and Caesar have been enemies since the revolt.

Customize for *Bodily/Kinesthetic Learners*

Allow these students to act out the conversation beginning on p. 737 with line 141, in which the conspirators discuss the potential participants and the nature of the assassination. Encourage them to use body language, gestures, and facial expressions to indicate the feelings and attitudes of each character.

Beyond the Classroom

Community Connection

Local Government Explain to students that the Roman government was, at this time, run by a group of senators who made the laws for Rome. Have students talk about how their community is governed. Is there a town or city council? Is it run by a mayor, a town supervisor, or a group of council persons? Encourage them to find out how local rules and regulations are made, and discuss with them how power is divided so no one person is all-powerful.

◆ Reading Strategy

❶ Read Blank Verse *There are seven complete sentences in Portia's speech. Remind students that a semicolon separates two independent clauses. Pausing at the semicolon will help students identify the ideas expressed in the longer sentences in this speech.*

◆ Reading Strategy

❷ Read Blank Verse With students, determine where a reader should pause in Scene i, lines 245–251. Analyze the passage for meaning. Then ask a volunteer to read the passage aloud. *There are pauses: after "insisted," "not," "you," "did," "enkindled," and "humor." Read for meaning, the passage could be restated as follows: I insisted (that you tell me your problem), but instead of answering, you waved me away with your hand. I left, not wanting to make you even more impatient, and hoping that your impatience with me was just the result of an ordinary bad mood.*

Comprehension Check ☑

❸ Does Portia believe Brutus' explanation? What does she think is wrong with him? *No, she knows he is not sick. She believes he is troubled in his mind.*

[*Enter* PORTIA.]

PORTIA. Brutus, my lord.

BRUTUS. Portia, what mean you? Wherefore rise you now
It is not for your health thus to commit
Your weak condition to the raw cold morning.

PORTIA. Nor for yours neither. Y'have ungently, Brutus,
Stole from my bed; and yesternight at supper
You suddenly arose and walked about,
Musing and sighing, with your arms across;
And when I asked you what the matter was,
You stared upon me with ungentle looks.
I urged you further; then you scratched your head,
And too impatiently stamped with your foot.
Yet I insisted, yet you answered not,
But with an angry wafter[86] of your hand
❷ Gave sign for me to leave you. So I did,
Fearing to strengthen that impatience
Which seemed too much enkindled, and withal
Hoping it was but an effect of humor,
Which sometime hath his[87] hour with every man.
It will not let you eat, nor talk, nor sleep,
And could it work so much upon your shape
As it hath much prevailed on your condition,[88]
I should not know you[89] Brutus. Dear my lord,
Make me acquainted with your cause of grief.

BRUTUS. I am not well in health, and that is all.

PORTIA. Brutus is wise and, were he not in health,
He would embrace the means to come by it.

BRUTUS. Why, so I do. Good Portia, go to bed.

PORTIA. Is Brutus sick, and is it physical[90]
❸ To walk unbracèd and suck up the humors[91]
Of the dank morning? What, is Brutus sick,
And will he steal out of his wholesome bed,
To dare the vile contagion of the night,
And tempt the rheumy and unpurgèd air[92]
To add unto his sickness? No, my Brutus:
You have some sick offense[93] within your mind.
Which by the right and virtue of my place
I ought to know of; and upon my knees
I charm[94] you, by my once commended[95] beauty,
By all your vows of love, and that great vow[96]
Which did incorporate and make us one,
That you unfold to me, your self, your half,
Why you are heavy,[97] and what men tonight

◆ **Reading Strategy** ❶ How many complete sentences are in Portia's speech?

86. wafter: Waving.

87. his: Its.

88. condition: Disposition.

89. I should not know you: I would not recognize you as.

90. physical: Healthy.

91. humors: Dampness.

92. tempt . . . air: Risk exposing himself to the air that is likely to cause rheumatism and air that has not been purified by the sun.

93. sick offense: Harmful sickness.

94. charm: Beg.

95. commended: Praised.

96. great vow: Marriage vow.

97. heavy: Sorrowful.

Cross-Curricular Connection: History

Julius Caesar's Life

Julius Caesar is dead before the play that bears his name is even half over. For those who are curious to know more about this great leader, share the following information. Interested students may want to research a particular period in Caesar's life or read some of his writings and speeches.

Gaius Julius Caesar (100?–44 B.C.), a Roman general and statesman, was a brilliant military leader who helped make Rome the center of an empire that stretched across Europe. Caesar also won fame as an orator, politician, and writer. He began his political career as director of public works and games in 65 B.C. In 62, he became *praetor,* the office next in rank to consul, and in 60, joined with Marcus Licinius Crassus and Gaeus Pompey in the *First Triumvirate,* an alliance that ruled Rome. The three took power when Caesar was elected consul in 59, the same year in which he married Calpurnia. Also that year, Pompey married Caesar's daughter, Julia (from Caesar's first marriage, to Cornelia, who had died about ten years earlier). In 58, knowing he needed military fame and a loyal army in order to gain more power, Caesar began a campaign to conquer Gaul (France). A military genius, Caesar drove the Germans out of Gaul and invaded Britain twice, in 55 and 54.

(continues on page 741)

Have had resort to you; for here have been
Some six or seven, who did hide their faces
Even from darkness.

BRUTUS. Kneel not, gentle Portia.

PORTIA. I should not need, if you were gentle Brutus.
Within the bond of marriage, tell me, Brutus,
Is it excepted[98] I should know no secrets
That appertain[99] to you? Am I your self
But, as it were, in sort or limitation,[100]
To keep with you at meals, comfort your bed,
And talk to you sometimes? Dwell I but in the
suburbs[101]
Of your good pleasure? If it be no more,
Portia is Brutus' harlot, not his wife.

BRUTUS. You are my true and honorable wife,
As dear to me as are the ruddy drops[102]
❹ That visit my sad heart.

PORTIA. If this were true, then should I know this secret.
I grant I am a woman; but withal
A woman that Lord Brutus took to wife.
I grant I am a woman; but withal
A woman well reputed, Cato's daughter.[103]
Think you I am no stronger than my sex,
Being so fathered and so husbanded?
Tell me your counsels,[104] I will not disclose 'em.
I have made strong proof of my constancy,
Giving myself a voluntary wound
Here in the thigh; can I bear that with patience,
And not my husband's secrets?

BRUTUS. O ye gods,
❺ Render[105] me worthy of this noble wife! *[Knock]*
Hark, hark! One knocks. Portia, go in a while,
And by and by thy bosom shall partake
The secrets of my heart.
All my engagements[106] I will construe to thee,
All the charactery of my sad brows.[107]
Leave me with haste. *[Exit* PORTIA.*]*

❻ *[Enter* LUCIUS *and* CAIUS LIGARIUS.*]*

Lucius, who's that knocks?

LUCIUS. Here is a sick man that would speak with you.

BRUTUS. Caius Ligarius, that Metellus spake of.
Boy, stand aside. Caius Ligarius! How?

CAIUS. Vouchsafe good morrow from a feeble tongue.

98. excepted: Made an exception.
99. appertain (ap´ ər tān´) *v.*: Belong.
100. in sort or limitation: Within a limited way.
101. suburbs: Outskirts.
102. ruddy drops: Blood.
103. Cato's daughter: Marcus Porcius Cato had been an ally of Pompey and enemy of Caesar. He killed himself rather than be captured by Caesar.
104. counsels: Secrets.
105. Render (ren´ dər) *v.*: Make.
106. engagements: Commitments.
107. All the charactery of my sad brows: All that is written on my face.

◆ *Literature and Your Life*

❹ Ask students how they feel when they know someone like a friend or family member is keeping a secret from them. How do they feel when they know they have to keep a secret? Lead a discussion in which students apply their own feelings to Portia's position. After students have analyzed the situation, have them offer opinions on whether or not Brutus should or should not have told Portia what's going on.

◆ Critical Thinking

❺ **Analyze** Draw students' attention to Scene i, line 303: "Render me worthy of this noble wife!" Ask students what Brutus' words reveal about his character. *Brutus admires the qualities of loyalty, discretion, courage, and strength that Portia displays. His admiration for these qualities reinforces that he is, essentially, an honorable man.*

◆ Literary Focus

❻ **Blank Verse** Call students' attention to line 309. Point out that the line continues after the stage directions for characters to exit and enter. Brutus would not pause, but would continue speaking as actors moved around him.

Read to Be Informed

Portia appears only briefly in the play, but she is a presence throughout. Ask students to read pp. 740–741 to learn more about the character of Portia. They may also want to compare her with Calpurnia, the wife of Julius Caesar.

(continued)

In 49, Pompey, alarmed and jealous at Caesar's huge success, allied himself with a group who ordered Caesar to give up his army. Rather than comply, Caesar led 5,000 men against Pompey, whose troops surrendered, forcing Pompey and his cohorts to flee Rome. He again defeated Pompey's army in Greece and followed him to Egypt, to find that Pompey had been murdered. In Egypt, Caesar met and fell in love with Cleopatra, and before returning to Rome, won a war that made her ruler of Egypt. After winning two more battles against Pompey's forces, Caesar became the unrivaled ruler of the Roman empire. He pardoned the followers of Pompey, and was granted the powers of dictator for ten years by the Roman people. Later, he was made dictator for life. At a public festival, Mark Antony tested popular feeling by offering Caesar the crown of a king. Because the Romans hated kings, Caesar refused the crown.

Comprehension Check ☑

❶ What piece of work does Brutus mean? Why will it make sick men whole? *Brutus refers to the killing of Caesar, which will make Rome whole again, after being sick with Caesar's tyranny.*

◆ Critical Thinking

❷ **Interpret** In this passage, Caesar's words are aimed at two different people. Have a volunteer read the lines so that it is clear that Caesar is first talking to himself, then calling to a servant to ask who is there. *The reader should change her or his tone of voice before addressing the servant. She or he might choose to pause before "Who's within?" or to make these words follow "They murder Caesar!" very quickly, as if he had been startled by the sound of a possible intruder.*

◆ Literary Focus

❸ **Blank Verse** *The first two lines technically have an extra syllable. In line 1, however, the rhythm leads "heaven" to be pronounced as one syllable (heav'n) while in line 2, the last two syllables of "Calpurnia" slide together, as if they were one unstressed syllable. (cal purn´ yä)*

BRUTUS. O, what a time have you chose out,[108] brave Caius,
To wear a kerchief![109] Would you were not sick!

CAIUS. I am not sick, if Brutus have in hand
Any exploit worthy the name of honor.

BRUTUS. Such an exploit have I in hand, Ligarius,
Had you a healthful ear to hear of it.

CAIUS. By all the gods that Romans bow before,
I here discard my sickness! Soul of Rome,
Brave son, derived from honorable loins,[110]
Thou, like an exorcist,[111] hast conjured up
My mortifièd spirit.[112] Now bid me run,
And I will strive with things impossible.
Yea, get the better of them. What's to do?

❶ BRUTUS. A piece of work that will make sick men whole.

CAIUS. But are not some whole that we must make sick?

BRUTUS. That must we also. What it is, my Caius,
I shall unfold[113] to thee, as we are going
To whom it must be done.

CAIUS. Set on[114] your foot,
And with a heart new-fired I follow you,
To do I know not what; but it sufficeth[115]
That Brutus leads me on. *[Thunder]*

BRUTUS. Follow me, then. *[Exit]*

Scene ii. *Caesar's house.*

[Thunder and lightning. Enter JULIUS CAESAR *in his nightgown.]*

❷ CAESAR. Nor heaven nor earth have been at peace tonight:
Thrice hath Calpurnia in her sleep cried out,
"Help, ho! They murder Caesar!" Who's within?

[Enter a SERVANT.*]*

SERVANT. My lord?

CAESAR. Go bid the priests do present[1] sacrifice,
And bring me their opinions of success.

SERVANT. I will, my lord. *[Exit]*

[Enter CALPURNIA.*]*

CALPURNIA. What mean you, Caesar? Think you to walk forth?
You shall not stir out of your house today.

108. chose out: Picked out.

109. To wear a kerchief: Caius wears a scarf to protect him from drafts because he is sick.

110. derived from honorable loins: Descended from Lucius Junius Brutus, founder of Rome.

111. exorcist (ek´ sôr sist) *n.*: One who calls up spirits.

112. mortifièd spirit: Paralyzed, as if dead, spirit.

113. unfold: Disclose.

114. Set on: Advance.

115. sufficeth (sə fis´ eth) *v.*: Is enough.

◆ Literary Focus ❸
Which of these lines (1–4) have an extra unaccented syllable? Why doesn't the extra syllable disrupt the rhythm of the iambs?

1. present: Immediate.

◆ Build Vocabulary
exploit (eks´ ploit) *n.*: Act or deed, especially a heroic achievement

Beyond the Classroom

Workplace Skills

Cutting Costs Students who know that movies made today have budgets that run into many millions may be surprised to learn that the MGM film of *Julius Caesar* was produced with a budget of only 1.7 million. This included the salaries of several big stars (John Gielgud, Marlon Brando, Deborah Kerr, and Greer Garson) as well as costumes, sets, lighting, salaries for the crew, feeding the cast and crew during production, and insurance. To stay within this budget, which was tight even by 1950's standards, sets and costumes from another movie were used! Togas, armor, and columns from *Quo Vadis*, another MGM film set in Rome during Nero's reign, were recycled in this film about Caesar's reign. Point out to students that the producers of *Julius Caesar* probably made this decision by balancing the cost of the costumes against the importance of having big stars. Encourage students to find out as much as possible about the budget of a recent blockbuster film. Encourage them to discuss the information with others in class and to suggest realistic cost-saving measures.

CAESAR. Caesar shall forth. The things that threatened me
Ne'er looked but on my back; when they shall see
The face of Caesar, they are vanishèd.

❹ **CALPURNIA.** Caesar, I never stood on ceremonies,[2]
Yet now they fright me. There is one within,
Besides the things that we have heard and seen,
Recounts most horrid sights seen by the watch.[3]
A lioness hath whelpèd[4] in the streets,
And graves have yawned, and yielded up their dead;
Fierce fiery warriors fought upon the clouds
In ranks and squadrons and right form of war,[5]
❺ Which drizzled blood upon the Capitol;
The noise of battle hurtled[6] in the air,
Horses did neigh and dying men did groan,
And ghosts did shriek and squeal about the street.
O Caesar, these things are beyond all use,[7]
And I do fear them.

❻ **CAESAR.** What can be avoided
Whose end is purposed[8] by the mighty gods?
Yet Caesar shall go forth; for these predictions
Are to the world in general as to Caesar.[9]

CALPURNIA. When beggars die, there are no comets seen;
The heavens themselves blaze forth[10] the death of princes.

❼ **CAESAR.** Cowards die many times before their deaths;
The valiant never taste of death but once.
Of all the wonders that I yet have heard,
It seems to me most strange that men should fear,
Seeing that death, a necessary end,
Will come when it will come.

[*Enter a* SERVANT.]

What say the augurers?

SERVANT. They would not have you to stir forth today.
Plucking the entrails of an offering forth,[11]
They could not find a heart within the beast.

CAESAR. The gods do this in shame of[12] cowardice:
Caesar should be a beast without a heart
If he should stay at home today for fear.
No, Caesar shall not; Danger knows full well
That Caesar is more dangerous than he.
We are two lions littered[13] in one day,
And I the elder and more terrible,
And Caesar shall go forth.

2. **stood on ceremonies:** Paid attention to omens.
3. **Recounts . . . watch:** Tells about the awful sights seen by the watchman.
4. **whelpèd:** Given birth.
5. **right form of war:** Proper military formation of war.
6. **hurtled:** (hurt´ əld) *v.*: Clashed together.
7. **beyond all use:** Contrary to all experience.
8. **is purposed:** Is intended.
9. **for these . . . as to Caesar:** Because these predictions apply to the rest of the world as much as they apply to Caesar.
10. **blaze forth:** Proclaim with meteors and comets.
11. **Plucking . . . forth:** Pulling out the insides of a sacrificed animal.
12. **in shame of:** In order to shame.
13. **littered:** Born.

❹ **Clarification** "I never stood on ceremonies" is another of Shakespeare's phrases that has become a common modern expression. "Don't stand on ceremony" has come to mean "Don't be so formal; don't feel as if you have to follow social conventions." At this point, you may want to discuss with students other expressions from Shakespeare. You can begin your discussion with the ones listed on p. 708.

◆ Critical Thinking

❺ **Connect** Have students explain the significance of these events based on their connection to the events that frightened Casca in Act I. *Like Casca, Calpurnia is frightened by unnatural events that indicate a break in the order.*

◆ Critical Thinking

❻ **Evaluate** Have students evaluate the validity of Caesar's argument. *Although students have the luxury of knowing the portents do, in fact, apply to Caesar, he makes a valid point. The portents could apply to someone else. As Calpurnia points out, however, he overstates the case when he says such portents are to the world at large. Only a serious break in order—a threat to someone of importance—would create such a disturbance in nature.*

Comprehension Check ☑

❼ What does Caesar mean when he says that cowards die many times before their death? *He means that people who fear death suffer from imagining and fearing their end.*

Cross-Curricular Connection: Social Studies

Soothsayers Explain to students that, in the fourth century B.C., the Romans overcame the Etruscans, who had ruled Rome along with most of what is now Italy. The Romans retained some features of the Etruscan religion, which placed a great deal of importance upon prophesy and divination. Soothsayers predicted the future by studying the flight of birds and the intestines of animals.

When Caesar asks, "What say the augurers?" (Scene ii, line 38), and the reply is, "Plucking the entrails of an offering forth,/ They could not find a heart within the beast," Shakespeare is referring to such soothsayers' rituals, adapted by the Romans from the older Etruscan religion.

Suggest that interested students research the history of the Etruscans and the influence of their culture on Rome.

◆ Reading Strategy

❶ **Read Blank Verse** With students, determine where a reader would pause in Calpurnia's speech. Then have a volunteer read the passage aloud. *There should be pauses after "confidence," "today," "own," "House," "today." There should be no pause after "fear." It is the last word in a line, but the sense of the lines would not indicate a pause.*

◆ Critical Thinking

❷ **Interpret** Ask students why Caesar changes his mind and won't let Decius give illness as a reason for Caesar's not going to the Senate House. *He does not want to lie in front of Decius. It would make him seem weak. A powerful person doesn't have to make excuses.*

◆ Critical Thinking

❸ **Analyze** Remind students that Decius is one of the conspirators. What is his motive for interpreting Caesar's dream in a positive way? On what need of Caesar's is he playing? *Decius is trying to get Caesar to go to the Senate House because that is where the conspirators plan to kill him. Decius knows that Caesar needs to feel powerful. He knows his interpretation of the dream will appeal to this need.*

CALPURNIA. Alas, my lord,
Your wisdom is consumed in confidence.[14]
Do not go forth today. Call it my fear
❶ That keeps you in the house and not your own.
We'll send Mark Antony to the Senate House,
And he shall say you are not well today.
Let me, upon my knee, prevail in this.

CAESAR. Mark Antony shall say I am not well,
And for thy humor,[15] I will stay at home.

[*Enter* DECIUS.]

Here's Decius Brutus, he shall tell them so.

DECIUS. Caesar, all hail! Good morrow, worthy Caesar;
I come to fetch you to the Senate House.

CAESAR. And you are come in very happy time[16]
❷ To bear my greeting to the senators,
And tell them that I will not come today.
Cannot, is false; and that I dare not, falser:
I will not come today. Tell them so, Decius.

CALPURNIA. Say he is sick.

CAESAR. Shall Caesar send a lie?
Have I in conquest stretched mine arm so far
To be afeard to tell graybeards[17] the truth?
Decius, go tell them Caesar will not come.

DECIUS. Most mighty Caesar, let me know some cause,
Lest I be laughed at when I tell them so.

CAESAR. The cause is in my will: I will not come.
That is enough to satisfy the Senate.
But for your private satisfaction,
Because I love you, I will let you know.
Calpurnia here, my wife, stays me at home.
She dreamt tonight she saw my statue,
Which, like a fountain with an hundred spouts,
Did run pure blood, and many lusty Romans
Came smiling and did bathe their hands in it.
And these does she apply for[18] warnings and
portents
And evils imminent, and on her knee
Hath begged that I will stay at home today.

DECIUS. This dream is all amiss interpreted;
It was a vision fair and fortunate:
❸ Your statue spouting blood in many pipes,
In which so many smiling Romans bathed,
Signifies that from you great Rome shall suck

14. confidence: Overconfidence.

15. humor: Whim.

16. in very happy time: At just the right moment.

17. afeard to tell graybeards: Afraid to tell old men (the senators).

◆ Literary Focus
What is the pattern of stressed and unstressed syllables in lines 71–75?

18. apply for: Consider to be.

◆ Build Vocabulary
imminent (im´ ə nənt) *adj.*: About to happen

❸ Reviving blood, and that great men shall press
For tinctures, stains, relics, and cognizance.[19]
This by Calpurnia's dream is signified.

CAESAR. And this way have you well expounded[20] it.

DECIUS. I have, when you have heard what I can say;
And know it now, the Senate have concluded
To give this day a crown to mighty Caesar.
If you shall send them word you will not come,
Their minds may change. Besides, it were a mock
❹ Apt to be rendered,[21] for someone to say
"Break up the Senate till another time,
❺ When Caesar's wife shall meet with better dreams."
If Caesar hide himself, shall they not whisper
"Lo, Caesar is afraid"?
Pardon me, Caesar, for my dear dear love
To your proceeding[22] bids me tell you this,
And reason to my love is liable.[23]

CAESAR. How foolish do your fears seem now, Calpurnia!
I am ashamèd I did yield to them.
Give me my robe,[24] for I will go.

[*Enter* BRUTUS, LIGARIUS, METELLUS CIMBER, CASCA, TREBONIUS, CINNA, *and* PUBLIUS.]

And look where Publius is come to fetch me.

PUBLIUS. Good morrow, Caesar.

CAESAR. Welcome, Publius.
What, Brutus, are you stirred so early too?
Good morrow, Casca. Caius Ligarius.
Caesar was ne'er so much your enemy[25]
As that same ague[26] which hath made you lean.
What is't o'clock?

BRUTUS. Caesar, 'tis strucken eight.

CAESAR. I thank you for your pains and courtesy.

[*Enter* ANTONY.]

See! Antony, that revels[27] long a-nights,
Is notwithstanding up. Good morrow, Antony.

ANTONY. So to most noble Caesar.

CAESAR. Bid them prepare[28] within.
I am to blame to be thus waited for.
Now, Cinna; now, Metellus; what Trebonius,
I have an hour's talk in store for you;
Remember that you call on me today;

19. shall press . . . cognizance: Decius interprets Calpurnia's dream with a double meaning. To Caesar he suggests that people will beg for badges to show they are Caesar's servants. To the audience, that people will seek remembrances of his death.

20. expounded (ik spound′ əd) *v.*: Interpreted; explained.

21. mock . . . rendered: Jeering comment likely to be made.

22. proceeding: Advancing in your career.

23. reason . . . liable: My judgment is not as strong as my affection for you is.

24. robe: Toga.

25. Caius Ligarius . . . your enemy: Caesar had recently pardoned Ligarius for supporting Pompey during the civil war.

26. ague (ā gyo͞o) *n.*: Fever.

27. revels (rev′ əlz) *v.*: Makes merry.

28. prepare: Set out refreshments.

◆ Critical Thinking

❹ Interpret Invite volunteers to try saying Decius' speech in contemporary, informal English. *Sample answer: Hey Caesar, the Senate was going to give you a crown today, but they'll probably change their minds if you're too chicken to go because of a silly dream your wife had. Too bad, Caesar. Chicken!*

◆ Reading Strategy

❺ Read Blank Verse Ask volunteers to read lines 92–104, emphasizing the iambic pentameter; then read as they think the lines should be read on a stage. *The first reading will have a sing-song sound; the second should sound natural, yet bring out the underlying meter of the verse.*

Workplace Skills Mini-Lesson

Leadership

Introduce The characters of Caesar, Cassius, Brutus, and Antony display a variety of leadership qualities. Tell students to identify and evaluate the qualities of each character and describe ways in which a contemporary person might demonstrate the qualities.

Develop Have students meet in groups to identify two or three leadership qualities for each of the four characters. Remind students that the different personalities of the characters will mean that they will possess different leadership qualities.

Apply Have students use an Analysis Map to explore each quality they've identified. The examples section of the map will help students identify current situations in which a person might display the leadership quality or skill. You will find the Analysis Map, and instructions for its use, on pp. 71–73 of ***Transparencies for Writing.*** After students have completed the Maps, have students share their conclusions with the class.

Assess You may want to collect the Analysis Maps to evaluate the extent to which students explored each quality.

▶Critical Viewing◀

❶ **Connect** *The men are merely pretending to be loyal; they actually intend to kill Caesar.*

Comprehension Check ☑

❷ What does Trebonius mean when he says "your best friends shall wish I had been further"? *He means that he will be close enough to Caesar to aid in his murder. When the deed is done, any friends of Caesar's will wish Trebonius and the other assassins had not stood so close.*

◆ Literary Focus

❸ **Blank Verse** Point out that Artemidorus' note to Caesar is not in blank verse. Ask students why they think the playwright made this choice. *The uneven rhythm of the note gives it added importance; the sharp, emphatic sound of the warnings strikes the listener or reader more strongly than it would in blank verse.*

❶ ▲ Critical Viewing Based on what you've read so far, how sincere do you think these men are in kneeling before Caesar? **[Connect]**

Be near me, that I may remember you.

❷ TREBONIUS. Caesar, I will [*aside*] and so near will I be,
That your best friends shall wish I had been further.

CAESAR. Good friends, go in and taste some wine with me,
And we (like friends) will straightway go together.

BRUTUS. [*Aside*] That every like is not the same,[29] O Caesar,
The heart of Brutus earns[30] to think upon. [*Exit*]

29. That every like . . . the same: That everyone who seems to be a friend may actually be an enemy.
30. earns: Sorrows.

Scene iii. *A street near the Capitol, close to Brutus' house.*

[*Enter* ARTEMIDORUS, *reading a paper.*]

❸ ARTEMIDORUS. "Caesar, beware of Brutus; take heed of Cassius; come not near Casca; have an eye to Cinna; trust not Trebonius; mark well Metellus Cimber; Decius Brutus loves thee not; thou hast wronged Caius Ligarius. There is but one mind in all these men, and it is bent against Caesar. If thou beest not immortal, look about you: security gives way to conspiracy.[1] The mighty gods defend thee!
Thy lover,[2] ARTEMIDORUS."
Here will I stand till Caesar pass along,
And as a suitor[3] will I give him this.

1. security . . . conspiracy: Overconfident carelessness allows the conspiracy to proceed.
2. lover: Devoted friend.
3. suitor (so͞ot´ ər) *n.*: Person who requests, petitions, or entreats.

Speaking, Listening, and Viewing Mini-Lesson

Debate

This mini-lesson supports the Speaking, Listening, and Viewing activity in the Idea Bank on p. 749.

Introduce Review that, in a debate, each of two teams supports the pro or con side of a statement. In this case, students will consider the statement "Brutus is an honorable man." Team members will alternate giving arguments, and at the end, have a chance to answer, or *rebut,* the opposing arguments.

Develop Students should review Brutus' words and actions to support the position the groups will argue. Suggest that students consider the following in preparing their arguments:

- Brutus' feelings about Caesar
- his feelings about himself
- his feelings on the conspiracy and his part in it

Apply Once they have collected evidence, encourage students to draft persuasive speeches to argue their side. In addition, remind each group to anticipate the arguments of the opposition and to be prepared to rebut them. Groups can take turns holding their debates before the rest of the class.

Assess Evaluate students' debates based on the relevance of the examples students choose, the consistency of the position they take, and the effectiveness of the delivery.

My heart laments that virtue cannot live
Out of the teeth of emulation.
❹ If thou read this, O Caesar, thou mayest live;
If not, the Fates with traitors do contrive.[4] [*Exit*]

4. **contrive:** Conspire.

Scene iv. *Another part of the street.*

[*Enter* PORTIA *and* LUCIUS.]

❺ **PORTIA.** I prithee, boy, run to the Senate House;
Stay not to answer me, but get thee gone.
Why dost thou stay?

LUCIUS. To know my errand, madam.

PORTIA. I would have had thee there and here again
Ere I can tell thee what thou shouldst do there.
O constancy,[1] be strong upon my side;
Set a huge mountain 'tween my heart and tongue!
I have a man's mind, but a woman's might.[2]
How hard it is for women to keep counsel![3]
Art thou here yet?

LUCIUS. Madam, what should I do?
Run to the Capitol, and nothing else?
And so return to you, and nothing else?

PORTIA. Yes, bring me word, boy, if thy lord look well,
For he went sickly forth; and take good note
What Caesar doth, what suitors press to him.
Hark, boy, what noise is that?

LUCIUS. I hear none, madam.

PORTIA. Prithee, listen well.
I heard a bustling rumor like a fray,[4]
And the wind brings it from the Capitol.

LUCIUS. Sooth, madam, I hear nothing.

[*Enter the* SOOTHSAYER.]

PORTIA. Come hither, fellow. Which way hast thou been?

SOOTHSAYER. At mine own house, good lady.

PORTIA. What is't o'clock?

SOOTHSAYER. About the ninth hour, lady.

PORTIA. Is Caesar yet gone to the Capitol?

SOOTHSAYER. Madam, not yet; I go to take my stand,
To see him pass on the Capitol.

❼ **PORTIA.** Thou hast some suit[5] to Caesar, hast thou not?

1. **constancy** (kän′ stən sē) *n.*: Firmness of mind or purpose; resoluteness.
2. **might:** Strength.
3. **counsel:** Secret.

◆ **Reading Strategy**
Where should you pause when reading these lines? Why? ❻

4. **fray** (frā) *n.*: Fight or brawl.

5. **suit** (so͞ot) *n.*: Petition.

❹ **Clarification** Explain that the Fates were three goddesses who controlled human life. One spun the web of life, one measured it, and one cut it at the end.

◆ Critical Thinking

❺ **Relate** Portia's anxiety makes her talk to herself and give partial instructions to the boy Lucius. Ask students to suggest other ways that anxiety can affect a person's behavior. *Anxiety or nervousness might cause someone to behave impatiently, to cry, or to perform poorly on a test or in a sport.*

◆ Reading Strategy

❻ **Read Blank Verse** *The punctuation indicates that the reader should pause after "Yes," "well," "forth," "doth," and "him" to communicate the sense of Portia's words. Point out to students that a less emphatic pause might be used to set off the two uses of direct address, "boy."*

◆ Critical Thinking

❼ **Draw Conclusions** What can students conclude that Portia is trying to discover through her questions? *Based on Portia's discussion with Brutus, students can conclude that she is trying to discover anything to do with Caesar that might involve Brutus.*

Reteach

You may wish to show students the pattern of iambic pentameter as shown in the scanned lines here. To help students to read blank verse, read the lines aloud, demonstrating that the reader does not stop at the end of the line but follows punctuation. Stress that the rhythm of the blank verse underlies the speeches, but does not interfere with the content.

'Tis time to part.
But it is doubtful yet
Whether Caesar will come forth today or no;

Point out that even when lines are divided between speakers they usually maintain the five foot rhythm. Encourage students to read parts of the play aloud.

◆ Critical Thinking

❶ **Predict** Have students predict what the soothsayer will tell Caesar and, based on his reaction to Calpurnia's dream, how Caesar will respond. *The soothsayer will predict Caesar's death, but Caesar, not wanting to appear superstitious or weak, will probably ignore the warning.*

Customize for
Pre-AP Students
Discuss with students the fact that the delivery of Shakespeare's blank verse has been a source of controversy in modern times. Some actors and critics feel that the poetry is the most important aspect of the work, and that the lines should be "classically declaimed," with a strong emphasis on the rhythm and line length (sometimes at the expense of "realism"). Many actors in modern times, however, deliver Shakespeare's lines completely for sense, leading to a prose reading. Encourage students to read reviews of performances by contemporary actors, such as Mel Gibson, Tracy Ullman, Glenn Close, James Earl Jones, and look for comments on the way each actor chooses to deliver the lines.

SOOTHSAYER. That I have, lady; if it will please Caesar
To be so good to Caesar as to hear me,
I shall beseech him to befriend himself.

PORTIA. Why, know'st thou any harm's intended towards him?

SOOTHSAYER. None that I know will be, much that I fear may chance.
Good morrow to you. Here the street is narrow;
The throng that follows Caesar at the heels,.
❶ Of senators, of praetors, common suitors,
Will crowd a feeble man almost to death.
I'll get me to a place more void,[6] and there
Speak to great Caesar as he comes along. [*Exit*]

PORTIA. I must go in. Ay me, how weak a thing
The heart of woman is! O Brutus,
The heavens speed[7] thee in thine enterprise![8]
Sure, the boy heard me—Brutus hath a suit
That Caesar will not grant—O, I grow faint.
Run, Lucius, and commend me[9] to my lord;
Say I am merry; come to me again,
And bring me word what he doth say to thee.

[*Exit separately*]

6. **void:** Empty.

7. **speed:** Prosper.
8. **enterprise** (en´ tər prīz´) *n.*: Undertaking; project.

9. **commend me** (kə mend´) *v.*: Give my kind regards.

Guide for Responding

◆ Literature and Your Life

Reader's Response If you had been a Roman citizen, would you have joined the conspirators? Why or why not?

Thematic Focus Whose choices in this act do you think will have the most significant consequences?

☑ Check Your Comprehension

1. In Scene i, lines 10–28, what reasons does Brutus give for killing Caesar?
2. Why is a meeting held at Brutus' house, and who attends the meeting?
3. Explain the two changes in the assassination plan that Brutus recommends.
4. What reasons does Calpurnia, Caesar's wife, give for wanting him to stay home?
5. Who persuades Caesar to go to the Capitol and how?

◆ Critical Thinking

INTERPRET

1. (a) Why do you think the writer leaves gaps in the letter that Lucius finds? (b) What inferences do you draw from the way Brutus fills in these gaps? **[Infer]**
2. Brutus justifies his actions by comparing Caesar to a serpent's egg in Scene i, lines 32–34. Explain how this is an example of a false analogy (a comparison that is not logical). **[Analyze]**
3. (a) Why does Brutus decide to go along with the conspirators? (b) Explain whether you think his decision proves him honorable. **[Support]**

EVALUATE

4. Which of Brutus' reasons for joining the conspirators do you find most convincing? Explain. **[Assess]**

APPLY

5. How might unwillingness to seem weak lead people to take unnecessary risks? **[Relate]**

Reinforce and Extend

Answers

◆ Literature and Your Life

Reader's Response Students should base their decision upon the times and what they would stand to gain or lose.

Thematic Focus Examples: Caesar's choice avoids or risks death; Brutus' choice will safeguard the republic of Rome or affect his reputation and honor.

☑ Check Your Comprehension

1. Brutus fears that once Caesar is crowned, he will abuse his power.
2. Cassius, Casca, Decius, Cinna, Metellus Cimber, and Trebonius meet at Brutus' house to plan Caesar's assassination.
3. Brutus recommends that Caesar should be killed boldly, but not wrathfully, and that Mark Antony should not be killed.
4. Calpurnia tells Caesar about the unnatural omens seen by the guards, and of her dream in which a statue of Caesar was bleeding.
5. Decius convinces Caesar to go to the Capitol by convincing him that Calpurnia's dream was a sign of Caesar's power and popularity.

◆ Critical Thinking

1. (a) Brutus' own misgivings about Caesar fill in the gaps more effectively than anything the writer could have invented. (b) A reader can infer that Brutus feels honor-bound to strike and redress the injustice of Caesar's supreme power.
2. A snake's egg cannot hatch into anything but a snake. Caesar as ruler may develop in any number of ways; the outcome is not as certain as it is with a snake's egg.
3. (a) Brutus fears Caesar will abuse his power and, because of the letter he reads, believes that the public opposes Caesar's rule. (b) His decision may be seen as that of an honorable man struggling to do something that is difficult to achieve, a public good; or it may be seen as the ignoble betrayal of a disloyal friend.
4. Remind students that they must identify one of Brutus' reasons. Encourage students to explain how Brutus' reasons fit into their own philosophy.
5. Students should be able to relate their answers to this question to the issue of peer pressure.

Guide for Responding (continued)

◆ Literary Focus

Blank Verse

Blank verse is written in iambic pentameter—ten-syllable lines in which every second syllable is stressed. Shakespeare often departs from the pattern to avoid monotony, to imitate the rhythms of real speech, or to vary the "music" of the verse. You might see such a departure in this exercise.

Copy the following passages on a separate piece of paper, and indicate the pattern of unaccented and accented syllables. Using the ˘ mark for an unaccented syllable and the mark ´ for an accented one.

1. Act II, Scene i, lines 162–165
2. Act II, Scene ii, lines 33–37

◆ Build Grammar Skills

Commonly Confused Words: *Affect* and *Effect*

In Act II, the *effect* of Cassius' letters is that Brutus, who is deeply *affected* by them, agrees to help overthrow Caesar.

Practice Copy these sentences and add the correct form of *affect* or *effect* in the space provided.

1. Calpurnia's dreams __?__ her deeply.
2. The __?__ of Decius' interpretation of Portia's dream is that Caesar decides to go out.
3. The soothsayer's remarks to the __?__ that Caesar was in danger worried Portia.
4. How will Caesar's assassination __?__ the people of Rome?

◆ Reading Strategy

Read Blank Verse

In reading Shakespearean verse, let the sentence structure rather than the lines guide you to meaning.

1. Read lines 162–174 in Act II, Scene i. How many sentences are in this passage?
2. Copy lines 162–174 as a paragraph. Read your paragraph aloud and mark it to indicate where it is natural to take a breath or pause.

◆ Build Vocabulary

Using the Latin Root *-spir-*

You will recognize the Latin word root *-spir-*, meaning "to breathe," in the following words: *inspire, expire, spirit,* and *respiration*. Use these words to complete the following sentences on your paper.

1. To __?__ is to breathe one's last breath.
2. To __?__ is to breathe confidence into another.
3. __?__ is the act of breathing.
4. The __?__ of patriotism breathes patriotic feelings into people.

Using the Word Bank: Definitions

Copy the words from Column A into your notebook. Next to each word, write the letter of its definition from Column B.

Column A	Column B
1. augmented	a. heroic or difficult deed
2. entreated	b. plot
3. conspiracy	c. about to happen
4. resolution	d. begged
5. exploit	e. made greater
6. imminent	f. determination

Idea Bank

Writing

1. **Editorial** As one of the tribunes, write a letter to the editor of *The Roman Times* expressing your feelings about the changing loyalties of the common people.

2. **Monologue** Write a brief monologue in contemporary language that Brutus might give, expressing his mixed feelings about Caesar.

Speaking, Listening, and Viewing

3. **Debate** As a group, debate the following question: Is Brutus an honorable man?

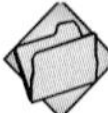

Idea Bank

Following are suggestions for matching Idea Bank topics with students' performance levels and learning modalities:

Customizing for *Performance Levels*

Less Advanced: 1
Average: 3
More Advanced: 2

Customizing for *Learning Modalities*

Intrapersonal Learners: 2
Interpersonal Learners: 3
Verbal/Linguistic Learners: 1, 2

✓ ASSESSMENT OPTIONS

Formal Assessment, Selection Test, pp. 179–181, and Assessment Resources Software. The selection test is designed so that it can be easily customized to the ability levels of your students.

PORTFOLIO ASSESSMENT

Use the following rubrics in ***Alternative Assessment*** to assess students' writing:
Editorial: Persuasion Rubric, p. 105
Monologue: Expression Rubric, p. 94

Answers

◆ Literary Focus

1. **Brutus.** Our course will seem too bloody, Caius Cassius,
   To cut the head off and then hack the limbs,
   Like wrath in death and envy afterwards;
   For Antony is but a limb of Caesar.
2. **Caesar.** Cowards die many times before their deaths;
   The valiant never taste of death but once.
   Of all the wonders that I yet have heard,
   It seems to me most strange that men should fear,
   Seeing that death, a necessary end,
   Will come when it will come.

◆ Build Grammar Skills

1. affect; 2. effect; 3. effect; 4. affect

◆ Reading Strategy

1. There are six sentences.
2. Suggested answer: Our course will seem too bloody,/Caius Cassius,/to cut the head off and then hack the limbs, like wrath in death and envy afterwards;/for Antony is but a limb of Caesar./Let's be sacrificers, but not butchers, Caius./We all stand up against the spirit of Caesar, and in the spirit of men there is no blood./O, that we could come by Caesar's spirit, and not dismember Caesar!/But, alas, Caesar must bleed for it./And, gentle friends, let's kill him boldly, but not wrathfully;/let's carve him as a dish fit for the gods, not hew him as a carcass fit for hounds.

◆ Build Vocabulary

Using the Latin Root *-spir-*

1. To *expire* is to breathe one's last breath.
2. To *inspire* is to breathe confidence into another.
3. *Respiration* is the act of breathing.
4. The *spirit* of patriotism breathes patriotic feelings into people.

Using the Word Bank

1. e 2. d 3. b 4. f 5. a 6. c

Prepare and Engage

LESSON OBJECTIVES

1. **To develop vocabulary and word identification skills**
   - Latin Roots: *-ora-*
   - Using the Word Bank: Analogies
2. **To use a variety of reading strategies to read and comprehend an essay**
   - Connect Your Experience
   - Reading Strategy: Paraphrase
   - Tips to Guide Reading
   - Idea Bank: Obituary
   - Read to Appreciate Author's Craft
3. **To express and support responses to the text**
   - Critical Thinking
   - Analyze Literary Criticism
   - Idea Bank: Reaction to Speeches
4. **To analyze literary elements**
   - Literary Focus: Dramatic Speeches
5. **To plan, prepare, organize, and present literary interpretations**
   - Idea Bank: Background Music
   - Speaking, Listening, and Viewing Mini-Lesson: Background Music
6. **To increase knowledge of the rules of grammar and usage**
   - Build Grammar Skills: Parallel Structure

Test Preparation

Reading Comprehension: Notice Word Choice (ATE, p. 751) The teaching tips and sample test item in this workshop support the instruction and practice in the unit workshop:
Reading Comprehension: Characteristics of Text (SE, p. 809)

Guide for Reading, Act III

◆ Review and Anticipate

Having ignored the warnings of both the soothsayer in Act I and of his wife, Calpurnia, in Act II, Caesar proceeds to the capitol on the ides of March. Decius has told him that the Senate has decided this day to confer a crown upon Caesar, in effect making him the emperor. Accompanying Caesar to the capitol are the conspirators, led by Cassius and Brutus, as well as Caesar's friend Mark Antony.

As the events in this act unfold, more warnings are ignored and the common people, accused in Act I of being fickle, once again show how easily their loyalties are swayed. This act is the turning point that sets irreversible wheels in motion.

◆ Literary Focus

DRAMATIC SPEECHES

In Shakespearean drama, characters often make special kinds of speeches. An **aside** is a brief comment a character makes that reveals his or her thoughts to the audience or another character. An aside is heard only by the audience or the character to whom it is directed. A **soliloquy** is a longer speech in which a character speaks as if to himself or herself. During a soliloquy, the speaker is usually alone onstage, but even if other characters are on stage, they do not hear the character speaking. Cassius' speech in Act I, Scene ii, lines 308–322, is an example of a soliloquy. Similar to a soliloquy is a monologue. A **monologue** is a long, uninterrupted speech by one character. Antony's famous speech in Act III, Scene ii, beginning with "Friends, Romans, countrymen . . ." is a monologue.

◆ Build Grammar Skills

PARALLEL STRUCTURE

Parallel structure is the use of similar grammatical forms to express similar ideas. The similarity in form emphasizes the similarity in content. Speakers often use parallel structure to make their speeches rhythmic and memorable. In Brutus' speech in Act III, Scene ii, he uses parallel clauses and sentence patterns.

> As Caesar loved me, I weep for him; as he was fortunate, I rejoice at it; as he was valiant, I honor him; but as he was ambitious, I slew him.

The repetition of *as . . . I . . .* builds up to an effective climax, making Brutus' reasons for slaying Caesar readily apparent.

◆ Reading Strategy

PARAPHRASE

To modern readers, Shakespeare's writing can appear dense and difficult to understand. One way to approach Shakespeare's passages is to **paraphrase,** or restate, them in your own words.

Shakespeare's Version

> Yet in the number I do know but one / That unassailable holds on his rank, / Unshaked of motion; and that I am he . . .

Paraphrased Version

> I'm the only person I know who can neither be harmed nor moved by others' desires.

As you read, paraphrase any difficult passages you encounter.

◆ Build Vocabulary

LATIN ROOTS: *-ora-*

Act III of *The Tragedy of Julius Caesar* is noted for its orations. An oration is a speech given at a formal ceremony, such as a graduation or a funeral. *Oration* has as its root the Latin verb *orare,* which means "to speak."

WORD BANK

Before you read, preview this list of words from Act III.

suit
spurn
confounded
mutiny
malice
oration
discourse
vile

Prentice Hall Literature Program Resources

REINFORCE / RETEACH / EXTEND

Selection Support Pages
Build Vocabulary: Word Roots: *-ora-*, p. 212
Build Grammar Skills: Parallel Structure, p. 201
Reading Strategy: Paraphrase, p. 214
Literary Focus: Dramatic Speeches, p. 215

Strategies for Diverse Student Needs, p. 52
Beyond Literature Community Connection: Eulogies, p. 52
Formal Assessment Selection Test, p. 182, Assessment Resources Software
Alternative Assessment, p. 52

Writing and Language Transparencies Cause-and-Effect Organizer, p. 99
Resource Pro CD-ROM
Listening to Literature Audiocassettes
Literature CD-ROM

The Tragedy of

JULIUS CAESAR

William Shakespeare

Act III

Scene i. *Rome. Before the Capitol.*

[*Flourish of trumpets. Enter* CAESAR, BRUTUS, CASSIUS, CASCA, DECIUS, METELLUS CIMBER, TREBONIUS, CINNA, ANTONY, LEPIDUS, ARTEMIDORUS, PUBLIUS, POPILIUS, *and the* SOOTHSAYER.]

CAESAR. The ides of March are come.

SOOTHSAYER. Ay, Caesar, but not gone.

ARTEMIDORUS. Hail, Caesar! Read this schedule.[1]

DECIUS. Trebonius doth desire you to o'er-read,
At your best leisure, this his humble suit.

ARTEMIDORUS. O Caesar, read mine first; for mine's a suit
❶ That touches Caesar nearer. Read it, great Caesar.

CAESAR. What touches us ourself shall be last served.

ARTEMIDORUS. Delay not, Caesar; read it instantly.

CAESAR. What, is the fellow mad?

PUBLIUS. Sirrah, give place.[2]

CASSIUS. What, urge you your petitions in the street?
Come to the Capitol.

[CAESAR *goes to the Capitol, the rest following.*]

POPILIUS. I wish your enterprise today may thrive.

CASSIUS. What enterprise, Popilius?

POPILIUS. Fare you well.
[*Advances to* CAESAR]

BRUTUS. What said Popilius Lena?

CASSIUS. He wished today our enterprise might thrive.
I fear our purpose is discoverèd.

BRUTUS. Look how he makes to[3] Caesar; mark him.

CASSIUS. Casca, be sudden,[4] for we fear prevention.
Brutus, what shall be done? If this be known,
Cassius or Caesar never shall turn back,[5]
For I will slay myself.

1. **schedule** (skej´ o͞ol) *n.*: Paper.

2. **give place:** Get out of the way.

3. **makes to:** Approaches.

4. **be sudden:** Be quick.

5. **Cassius . . . back:** Either Cassius or Caesar will not return alive.

◆ Build Vocabulary

suit (so͞ot) *n.*: Old word meaning "petition"

Test Preparation Workshop

Reading Comprehension: Notice Word Choice Standardized tests often require students to analyze the characteristics of a text. Help students to practice the skill of analyzing a writer's word choice by introducing the following sample test item.

Low-crooked curtsies, and base spaniel fawning
Thy brother by decree is banished
If thou dost bend and pray and fawn for him,
I spurn thee like a cur out of my way.

The words base, cur and spurn reveal the speaker's—

A anger toward his audience
B love for his audience
C bewilderment by his audience
D jealousy of his audience

Guide students to see that the speaker speaks with disdain about people who bow and pray before him. The correct response is *A*.

Develop Understanding

One-Minute Insight The ides of March have arrived, Caesar makes his way to the Capitol, and the conspirators strike him down as planned. The conspirators' triumph does not last long, however; in a misguided effort at reconciliation, Brutus allows Mark Antony to take center stage at Caesar's funeral. Mark Antony turns out to be not only a loyal follower of Caesar, but also a brilliantly manipulative speaker who subtly coaxes the people of Rome into a frenzy. Rather than hailing the return of liberty and freedom, the crowd vows revenge and sends the conspirators fleeing in terror.

Customize for
English Language Learners
Paraphrasing will be more difficult for these students than for native speakers. To help English language learners with this reading strategy, provide as many opportunities as possible for them to work closely with a partner or a small group of classmates. Encourage the students to identify difficult passages and help one another restate them in contemporary English.

Comprehension Check ☑

❶ Ask students what is in the paper that Artemidorus unsuccessfully urges Caesar to read. If necessary, have them look back at Act II, Scene iii. *The paper contains a detailed warning about the conspiracy.*

Customize for
Pre-AP Students
Encourage students to analyze the speeches of Artemidorus and Popilius. Students may remember the teacher Artemidorus preparing his letter in Act II. Have them look back to the character list on p. 713 to find that Popilius is a senator. Ask students to consider why Shakespeare included Artemidorus' failed effort to warn Caesar and Popilius' comment implying he was aware of the conspiracy.

◆ Reading Strategy

(1) Paraphrase Ask students to paraphrase the exchange that takes place as the conspirators prepare for the assassination. *Suggested paraphrase:*

CASSIUS: Trebonius knows what to do. Look, Brutus—he's getting Mark Antony out of the way.

DECIUS: Where is Metellus Cimber? It's time for him to present his petition to Caesar.

BRUTUS: He's ready. Stay with him and back him up.

CINNA: Casca, you will strike first.

◆ Reading Strategy

(2) Paraphrase Caesar says that others, who are not as strong as he is, might be influenced by flattery and pleading. Caesar is so strong, though, that his mind will not be changed so easily and he has only contempt for people who think he would be.

◆ Critical Thinking

(3) Analyze Point out to students that in order to get into position, the conspirators quickly follow one after the other in their petitions for Publius Cimber, in effect, "ganging up" on Caesar. This emotional tactic foreshadows the physical ganging up that is soon to occur.

Customize for *Gifted/Talented Students*

Invite students to dramatize the scene in which the conspirators pretend to petition Caesar and then kill him. Encourage them to create the scene in silence, using only movements and expressions to reveal the action.

BRUTUS. Cassius, be constant.[6]
Popilius Lena speaks not of our purposes;
For look, he smiles, and Caesar doth not change.[7]
CASSIUS. Trebonius knows his time; for look you, Brutus,
He draws Mark Antony out of the way.
[*Exit* ANTONY *and* TREBONIUS.]

(1)
DECIUS. Where is Metellus Cimber? Let him go
And presently prefer his suit[8] to Caesar.

BRUTUS. He is addressed.[9] Press near and second[10] him.

CINNA. Casca, you are the first that rears your hand.

CAESAR. Are we all ready? What is now amiss
That Caesar and his Senate must redress?[11]

METELLUS. Most high, most mighty, and most puissant[12] Caesar,
Metellus Cimber throws before thy seat
An humble heart. [*Kneeling*]

CAESAR. I must prevent thee, Cimber.
These couchings and these lowly courtesies[13]
Might fire the blood of ordinary men,
And turn preordinance and first decree
Into the law of children.[14] Be not fond[15]
To think that Caesar bears such rebel blood
That will be thawed from the true quality[16]
(2) With that which melteth fools—I mean sweet words,
Low-crookèd curtsies, and base spaniel fawning.[17]
Thy brother by decree is banishèd.
If thou dost bend and pray and fawn for him,
I spurn thee like a cur out of my way.
Know, Caesar doth not wrong, nor without cause
Will he be satisfied.

METELLUS. Is there no voice more worthy than my own,
To sound more sweetly in great Caesar's ear
For the repealing of my banished brother?

BRUTUS. I kiss thy hand, but not in flattery, Caesar,
Desiring thee that Publius Cimber may
Have an immediate freedom of repeal.

CAESAR. What, Brutus?

(3)
CASSIUS. Pardon, Caesar; Caesar, pardon!
As low as to thy foot doth Cassius fall
To beg enfranchisement[18] for Publius Cimber.

CAESAR. I could be well moved, if I were as you;
If I could pray to move,[19] prayers would move me;
But I am constant as the Northern Star,

6. **constant:** Firm; calm.

7. **change:** Change the expression on his face.

8. **presently prefer his suit:** Immediately present his petition.

9. **addressed:** Ready.

10. **second:** Support.

11. **amiss . . . redress:** Wrong that Caesar and his Senate must correct.

12. **puissant** (pyōō´ i sənt) *adj.*: Powerful.

13. **couchings . . . courtesies:** Low bowings and humble gestures of reverence.

14. **And turn . . . law of children:** And change what has already been decided as children might change their minds.

15. **fond** *adj.*: Foolish.

16. **rebel . . . quality:** Unstable disposition that will be changed from firmness.

17. **base spaniel fawning:** Low doglike cringing.

18. **enfranchisement** (en fran´ chiz mənt) *n.*: Freedom.

19. **pray to move:** Beg others to change their minds.

◆ **Reading Strategy**
Paraphrase Caesar's disdainful words to Metellus.

Block Scheduling Strategies

Consider these suggestions to take advantage of extended class time:

- Suggest that students view feature 4 of the CD-ROM *The Time, Life, and Works of Shakespeare*. They will learn more about Shakespeare's later life, Shakespeare's Stratford, and the Globe theater.
- Use a video of the movie *Julius Caesar* and the **Listening to Literature Audiocassette** recording to support the text. Encourage students to identify how each approach enhanced their appreciation of a particular scene.
- Have students work with partners to find examples of parallel structure in Act III; then have them complete the Practice activity in Build Grammar Skills (p. 771).
- Students can choose and complete one of the writing assignments in the Idea Bank (p. 771).
- Ask students to complete Literary Focus: Dramatic Speeches in ***Selection Support,*** p. 215.

Of whose true-fixed and resting[20] quality
There is no fellow[21] in the firmament.[22]
The skies are painted with unnumb'red sparks,
They are all fire and every one doth shine;
But there's but one in all doth hold his[23] place.
So in the world; 'tis furnished well with men,
And men are flesh and blood, and apprehensive;[24]
❹ Yet in the number I do know but one
That unassailable holds on his rank,[25]
Unshaked of motion;[26] and that I am he,
Let me a little show it, even in this—
That I was constant. Cimber should be banished,
And constant do remain to keep him so.

CINNA. O Caesar—

CAESAR. Hence! Wilt thou lift up Olympus?[27]

DECIUS. Great Caesar—

CAESAR. Doth not Brutus bootless[28] kneel?

CASCA. Speak hands for me! [*They stab* CAESAR.]

CAESAR. *Et tu, Brutè?*[29] Then fall, Caesar. [*Dies*]

CINNA. Liberty! Freedom! Tyranny is dead!
Run hence, proclaim, cry it about the streets.

CASSIUS. Some to the common pulpits,[30] and cry out
"Liberty, freedom, and enfranchisement!"

BRUTUS. People, and senators, be not affrighted.
Fly not; stand still; ambition's debt is paid.[31]

CASCA. Go to the pulpit, Brutus.

DECIUS. And Cassius too.

BRUTUS. Where's Publius?

CINNA. Here, quite confounded with this mutiny.

METELLUS. Stand fast together, lest some friend of Caesar's
Should chance—

BRUTUS. Talk not of standing. Publius, good cheer;
There is no harm intended to your person,
Nor to no Roman else. So tell them, Publius.

CASSIUS. And leave us, Publius, lest that the people
Rushing on us should do your age some mischief.

BRUTUS. Do so; and let no man abide[32] this deed
But we the doers.

[*Enter* TREBONIUS.]

CASSIUS. Where is Antony?

20. **resting:** Immovable.

21. **fellow:** Equal.

22. **firmament** (fur´ mə mənt) *n.*: Sky.

23. **his:** Its.

24. **apprehensive** (ap´ rə hen´ siv) *adj.*: Able to understand.

25. **unassailable . . . rank:** Unattackable maintains his position.

26. **Unshaked of motion:** Unmoved by his own or others' impulses.

27. **Olympus** (ō lim´ pəs): Mountain in northern Greece that was, in Greek mythology, the home of the gods.

28. **bootless:** Uselessly.

29. ***Et tu, Brutè?*:** Latin for *And you, Brutus?*

30. **pulpits** (po͝ol´ pits) *n.*: Speakers' platforms.

31. **ambition's . . . paid:** Ambition received what it deserved.

32. **let no man abide:** Let no man take responsibility for.

◆ Build Vocabulary

spurn (spurn) *v.*: Old word meaning "to kick disdainfully"

confounded (kən found´ id) *adj.*: Confused

mutiny (myo͞ot´ ən ē) *n.*: Open rebellion against authority

◆ Reading Strategy

❹ Paraphrase Challenge students to paraphrase these lines, in which Caesar continues to compare himself to the Northern Star. *Suggested paraphrase: "This is also how it is in the world. The world is full of men, and they all show signs of life; but there is only one that cannot be knocked out of place."* You might then encourage students to comment on what the speech reveals about Caesar. *Students may say that it confirms some of the conspirators' beliefs. Caesar shows himself to be haughty and inflexible; he holds himself above others.*

Customize for *Less Proficient Readers*

Point out that a play's stage directions, which appear within brackets and in italics, contain essential information for both actors and readers. Have students identify the critical action named in the stage directions that accompany lines 76 and 77. *The conspirators stab Caesar; Caesar dies.*

Cross-Curricular Connection: Science

Astronomy: The North Star When Caesar insists that he cannot be moved by prayers or entreaties as other men can, he compares himself to the North Star:

> But I am constant as the Northern Star,
> Of whose true-fixed and resting quality
> There is no fellow in the firmament.
> (Scene i, lines 60–63)

Invite a group of students to prepare a brief presentation in which they explain the scientific significance behind this image. In their presentations, students can use a globe, diagrams, or other visual aids to help answer the following questions:

- Why does the North Star appear "constant," or stationary, throughout the year?
- Why do other stars seem to move through the sky during the course of a year?
- What is another name for the North Star? Will this star always be the North Star, or will it eventually be replaced by another?

▶Critical Viewing◀

❶ **Analyze** The conspirators' actions make them seem submissive to Caesar and intimidated by him. They appear to be honoring Caesar but, in fact, are getting in position to kill him.

◆ Reading Strategy

❷ **Paraphrase** Sample paraphrase: We have done Caesar a favor, because everyone fears death, and now Caesar won't have to fear it any longer.

Customize for Less Proficient Readers

Work with these students to begin identifying the causes and effects of Caesar's assassination. Use the page on Cause and Effect, ***Strategies for Diverse Needs,*** p. 52.

Customize for Visual/Spatial Learners

These students might benefit from using the Cause-and-Effect organizer found in ***Writing and Language Transparencies,*** pp. 99–101.

❶ ▲ Critical Viewing Explain how this picture captures the deception of the conspirators. **[Analyze]**

TREBONIUS. Fled to his house amazed.[33]
Men, wives, and children stare, cry out and run,
As[34] it were doomsday.

BRUTUS. Fates, we will know your pleasures.
That we shall die, we know; 'tis but the time,
And drawing days out, that men stand upon.[35]

CASCA. Why, he that cuts off twenty years of life
Cuts off so many years of fearing death.

BRUTUS. Grant that, and then is death a benefit.
So are we Caesar's friends, that have abridged
His time of fearing death. Stoop, Romans, stoop,
And let us bathe our hands in Caesar's blood
Up to the elbows, and besmear our swords.
Then walk we forth, even to the market place,
And waving our red weapons o'er our heads,
Let's all cry "Peace, freedom, and liberty!"

33. **amazed:** Astounded.

34. **As:** As if.

35. **drawing . . . upon:** Prolonging life that people care about.

◆ **Reading Strategy** Paraphrase Brutus' justifications for killing Caesar. ❷

Speaking, Listening, and Viewing Mini-Lesson

Background Music

This mini-lesson supports the Speaking, Listening, and Viewing activity in the Idea Bank on p. 771.

Introduce Have students discuss movies, television shows, or plays in which background music was an effective enhancement. Invite them to list moods that background music can suggest.

Develop Have groups of students talk about the assassination scene and the moods the music should support.

- What is the mood of the opening?
- What kind of music would emphasize the horror of the assassination?
- How would the crowd react after the assassination, and what music might be most effective in emphasizing their mood?

Apply Allow students time to select their music, and, if possible, to tape it. One member of each group can explain what is happening in the scene as the music plays.

Assess After each presentation, the class may evaluate the choice of music on the basis of how well students felt the music enhanced the scene.

❸ **CASSIUS.** Stoop then, and wash. How many ages hence
Shall this our lofty scene be acted over
In states unborn and accents yet unknown!

BRUTUS. How many times shall Caesar bleed in sport,[36]
That now on Pompey's basis lies along[37]
No worthier than the dust!

CASSIUS. So oft as that shall be,
So often shall the knot[38] of us be called
The men that gave their country liberty.

DECIUS. What, shall we forth?

CASSIUS. Ay, every man away.
Brutus shall lead, and we will grace his heels[39]
With the most boldest and best hearts of Rome.

[*Enter a* SERVANT.]

BRUTUS. Soft, who comes here? A friend of Antony's.

SERVANT. Thus, Brutus, did my master bid me kneel;
Thus did Mark Antony bid me fall down;
And, being prostrate, thus he bade me say:
❹ Brutus is noble, wise, valiant, and honest;
Caesar was mighty, bold, royal, and loving.
Say I love Brutus and I honor him;
Say I feared Caesar, honored him, and loved him.
If Brutus will vouchsafe that Antony
❺ May safely come to him and be resolved[40]
How Caesar hath deserved to lie in death,
Mark Antony shall not love Caesar dead
So well as Brutus living; but will follow
The fortunes and affairs of noble Brutus
Thorough the hazards of this untrod state[41]
With all true faith. So says my master Antony.

BRUTUS. Thy master is a wise and valiant Roman;
I never thought him worse.
Tell him, so[42] please him come unto this place,
He shall be satisfied and, by my honor,
Depart untouched.

SERVANT. I'll fetch him presently.

[*Exit* SERVANT]

BRUTUS. I know that we shall have him well to friend.[43]

❻ **CASSIUS.** I wish we may. But yet have I a mind
That fears him much; and my misgiving still
Falls shrewdly to the purpose.[44]

[*Enter* ANTONY.]

BRUTUS. But here comes Antony. Welcome, Mark Antony.

36. in sport: In plays.

37. on Pompey's basis lies along: By the pedestal of Pompey's statue lies stretched out.

38. knot: Group.

39. grace his heels: Honor him by following him.

◆ Reading Strategy
The servant carries a message from Mark Antony to Brutus. Paraphrase the message only.

40. be resolved: Have it explained.

41. Thorough . . . state: Through the dangers of this new state of affairs.

42. so: If it should.

43. to friend: As a friend.

44. my misgiving . . . to the purpose: My doubts always turn out to be justified.

Comprehension Check ☑

❸ Invite students to summarize the thoughts that Cassius and Brutus express in these lines. *They will go down in history as liberators of Rome.*

◆ Build Grammar Skills

❹ **Parallel Structure** Point out the parallel elements in lines 126–127 and 128–129. Encourage students to explain the purpose that these parallel elements serve within the servant's speech. *They are meant to express Mark Antony's dual feelings and loyalties; they emphasize that Mark Antony does not honor Caesar more than he honors Brutus.*

◆ Reading Strategy

❺ **Paraphrase** Students may paraphrase the message in the following way: Antony says that he honors both Brutus and Caesar. Antony would like to come to Brutus to hear his reasons for killing Caesar, but Antony wants to be assured of his own safety. If Brutus' reasons seem sound to Antony, he will cooperate with Brutus in all future endeavors.

◆ Critical Thinking

❻ **Contrast** Ask students the following question: How does Brutus' attitude toward Mark Antony contrast with Cassius' attitude? Then encourage students to explain how this contrast helps create suspense within the scene. *Students should note that Brutus is inclined to trust Mark Antony, while Cassius strongly distrusts him. This contrast creates suspense because it is yet to be revealed which of the two is right.*

Comprehension Check ☑

❶ In his first speech to Antony, what does Brutus acknowledge about the conspirators' act? How does he go on to justify it? *He acknowledges that it was bloody and cruel but insists that the conspirators acted for the general good of Rome.*

◆ Literary Focus

❷ **Dramatic Speeches** Point out that in this long speech, Antony addresses first the conspirators and then Caesar's corpse. Then ask students if they would classify the speech as a soliloquy or a monologue. *Students should identify it as a monologue, since it is addressed to other onstage performers.*

ANTONY. O mighty Caesar! Dost thou lie so low?
Are all thy conquests, glories, triumphs, spoils,
Shrunk to this little measure? Fare thee well.
I know not, gentlemen, what you intend,
Who else must be let blood,[45] who else is rank.[46]
If I myself, there is no hour so fit
As Caesar's death's hour, nor no instrument
Of half that worth as those your swords, made rich
With the most noble blood of all this world.
I do beseech ye, if you bear me hard,[47]
Now, whilst your purpled hands[48] do reek and smoke,
Fulfill your pleasure. Live[49] a thousand years,
I shall not find myself so apt[50] to die;
No place will please me so, no mean of death,[51]
As here by Caesar, and by you cut off,
The choice and master spirits of this age.

BRUTUS. O Antony, beg not your death of us!
Though now we must appear bloody and cruel,
As by our hands and this our present act
You see we do, yet see you but our hands
And this the bleeding business they have done.
Our hearts you see not; they are pitiful;[52]
And pity to the general wrong of Rome—
❶ As fire drives out fire, so pity pity[53]—
Hath done this deed on Caesar. For your part,
To you our swords have leaden[54] points, Mark
Antony:
Our arms in strength of malice, and our hearts
Of brothers' temper,[55] do receive you in
With all kind love, good thoughts, and reverence.

CASSIUS. Your voice[56] shall be as strong as any man's
In the disposing of new dignities.[57]

BRUTUS. Only be patient till we have appeased
The multitude, beside themselves with fear,
And then we will deliver[58] you the cause
Why I, that did love Caesar when I struck him,
Have thus proceeded.

ANTONY. I doubt not of your wisdom.
Let each man render me his bloody hand.
First, Marcus Brutus, will I shake with you;
Next, Caius Cassius, do I take your hand;
❷ Now, Decius Brutus, yours; now yours, Metellus;
Yours, Cinna; and, my valiant Casca, yours;
Though last, not least in love, yours, good Trebonius.
Gentlemen all—alas, what shall I say?
My credit[59] now stands on such slippery ground

45. be let blood: Be killed.
46. rank: Too powerful; in need of bloodletting.
47. bear me hard: Have a grudge against me.
48. purpled hands: Bloody hands.
49. Live: If I live.
50. apt: Ready.
51. mean of death: Way of dying.
52. pitiful: Full of pity.
53. pity pity: Pity for Rome drove out pity for Caesar.
54. leaden: Dull; blunt.
55. Of brothers' temper: Filled with brotherly feelings.
56. voice: Vote.
57. dignities: Offices.
58. deliver: Tell to.
59. credit: Reputation.

◆ Build Vocabulary

malice (mal′ is) *n.*: Desire to harm or see harm done to others

Cross-Curricular Connection: Social Studies

Assassinations The word *assassination* usually means the murder of a politically prominent person. The word comes from *Hashshashun* ("hemp-eaters"), a band of Muslims in Persia and Asia Minor in the 1100's. They smoked a drug called *hashish,* which is made from the hemp plant, and killed their enemies while under its influence.

History is dotted with other assassinations in addition to that of Julius Caesar. Saint Thomas à Becket was murdered in Canterbury Cathedral in 1170. The assassination of Archduke Ferdinand of Austria in 1914 was one cause of World War I. The series of assassinations committed by the Black Dragon Society in Japan during the 1930's threw control of the government into the hands of the Japanese army. Four Presidents of the United States have been assassinated: Lincoln in 1865, Garfield in 1881, McKinley in 1901, and Kennedy in 1963.

Suggest that students research the assassination of a politically prominent person in history.

That one of two bad ways you must conceit[60] me,
Either a coward or a flatterer.
That I did love thee, Caesar, O, 'tis true!
If then thy spirit look upon us now,
Shall it not grieve thee dearer[61] than thy death
To see thy Antony making his peace,
Shaking the bloody fingers of thy foes,
Most noble, in the presence of thy corse?[62]
Had I as many eyes as thou hast wounds,
Weeping as fast as they stream forth thy blood,
❷ It would become me better than to close[63]
In terms of friendship with thine enemies.
Pardon me, Julius! Here wast thou bayed,[64] brave
hart;[65]
Here didst thou fall, and here thy hunters stand,
Signed in thy spoil[66] and crimsoned in thy Lethe.[67]
O world, thou wast the forest to this hart;
And this indeed, O world, the heart of thee.
How like a deer, stroken[68] by many princes,
Dost thou here lie!

CASSIUS. Mark Antony—

ANTONY. Pardon me, Caius Cassius.
The enemies of Caesar shall say this;
Then, in a friend, it is cold modesty.[69]

CASSIUS. I blame you not for praising Caesar so;
But what compact[70] mean you to have with us?
Will you be pricked[71] in number of our friends,
Or shall we on,[72] and not depend on you?

❸ **ANTONY.** Therefore I took your hands, but was indeed
Swayed from the point by looking down on Caesar.
Friends am I with you all, and love you all,
Upon this hope, that you shall give me reasons
Why, and wherein, Caesar was dangerous.

BRUTUS. Or else were this a savage spectacle.
Our reasons are so full of good regard[73]
That were you, Antony, the son of Caesar,
You should be satisfied.

ANTONY. That's all I seek;
And am moreover suitor that I may
Produce[74] his body to the market place,
And in the pulpit, as becomes a friend,
Speak in the order[75] of his funeral.

BRUTUS. You shall, Mark Antony.

❹ **CASSIUS.** Brutus, a word with you.
[*Aside to* BRUTUS] You know not what you do; do not

60. conceit (kən sēt′) v.: Think of.

61. dearer: More deeply.

62. corse: Corpse.

63. close (clōz) *v.*: Reach an agreement.

64. bayed: Cornered.

65. hart (härt) *n.*: Deer.

66. Signed in thy spoil: Marked by signs of your decaying parts.

67. Lethe (lēth′ ē): River in Hades, but in this case a river of blood.

68. stroken: Struck down.

69. cold modesty: Calm, moderate speech.

70. compact (käm′ pakt) *n.*: Agreement.

71. pricked: Marked.

72. on: Proceed.

73. so full of good regard: So carefully considered.

74. Produce: Bring forth.

75. order: Course of the ceremonies.

❹ **◆ Literary Focus**
Why doesn't Cassius want the other characters to hear what he says to Brutus in this aside?

◆ Reading Strategy

❸ **Paraphrase** Encourage students to paraphrase Cassius' questions and Antony's reply. *Suggested paraphrase:*

CASSIUS: How do you see yourself in relation to us? Can we count on you as a friend or not?

ANTONY: As a friend—that's why I shook hands with each of you, but then I got carried away because of Caesar's corpse. I will be friends with you all and love you all on the condition that you explain to me why Caesar was dangerous.

◆ Literary Focus

❹ **Dramatic Speeches** *Cassius does not want Antony to hear what he has to say because he doesn't want to destroy the illusion of trust between Antony and the conspirators. Although Brutus is convinced of Antony's good intentions, Cassius remains suspicious.*

◆ Critical Thinking

❶ Contrast Point out that once again Brutus and Cassius show different views of Mark Antony. Invite students to identify their contrasting opinions as well as the reasons behind them. *Students should note that Cassius believes that it would be a great mistake to allow Antony to speak at Caesar's funeral because he is liable to turn public opinion against the conspirators. Brutus, on the other hand, continues to believe that Mark Antony poses no threat; in fact, he believes that Antony's presence at the funeral will strengthen the conspirators' position and help bring about reconciliation.*

◆ Literary Focus

❷ Dramatic Speeches Antony reveals that he intends to avenge Caesar's death.

◆ Critical Thinking

❸ Draw Conclusions Encourage students to draw conclusions about Mark Antony based on this speech. For example: How does it help to explain his behavior earlier in this scene? Does it confirm Brutus' or Cassius' view of Antony? *Students should note that in this speech Antony reveals his true self and true motives; his efforts to win the trust of the conspirators were part of a plot for revenge. As it turns out, Cassius was right to suspect him of deceit.*

◆ Literary Focus

❹ Dramatic Speeches Would students classify this speech as an aside, a soliloquy, or a monologue? Encourage them to explain their answers. *The speech is a soliloquy—it is a long speech, and Antony is alone on stage.*

consent
That Antony speak in his funeral.
Know you how much the people may be moved
By that which he will utter?

BRUTUS. By your pardon:
I will myself into the pulpit first,
And show the reason of our Caesar's death.
What Antony shall speak, I will protest[76]
He speaks by leave and by permission,
And that we are contented Caesar shall
Have all true rites and lawful ceremonies.
It shall advantage more than do us wrong.[77]

CASSIUS. I know not what may fall;[78] I like it not.

BRUTUS. Mark Antony, here, take you Caesar's body.
You shall not in your funeral speech blame us,
But speak all good you can devise of Caesar,
❶ And say you do't by our permission;
Else shall you not have any hand at all
About his funeral. And you shall speak
In the same pulpit whereto I am going,
After my speech is ended.

ANTONY. Be it so;
I do desire no more.

BRUTUS. Prepare the body then, and follow us.

[*Exit all but* ANTONY.]

ANTONY. O pardon me, thou bleeding piece of earth,
That I am meek and gentle with these butchers!
Thou art the ruins of the noblest man
That ever livèd in the tide of times.[79]
Woe to the hand that shed this costly blood!
Over thy wounds now do I prophesy
(Which like dumb mouths do ope their ruby lips
To beg the voice and utterance of my tongue),
A curse shall light upon the limbs of men;
❸ Domestic fury and fierce civil strife
❹ Shall cumber[80] all the parts of Italy;
Blood and destruction shall be so in use,[81]
And dreadful objects so familiar,
That mothers shall but smile when they behold
Their infants quartered with the hands of war,
All pity choked with custom of fell deeds;[82]
And Caesar's spirit, ranging[83] for revenge,
With Ate[84] by his side come hot from hell,
Shall in these confines[85] with a monarch's voice
Cry "Havoc,"[86] and let slip[87] the dogs of war,

76. protest: Declare.

77. advantage . . . wrong: Benefit us more than hurt us.

78. what may fall: What may happen.

79. tide of times: Course of all history.

80. cumber (kum´ bər) *v.*: Distress; burden.

81. in use: Customary.

82. fell deeds: Cruel acts.

83. ranging: Roaming like a wild beast in search of prey.

84. Ate (ā´ tē): Greek goddess personifying reckless ambition in man.

85. confines (kän´ finz) *n.*: Boundaries.

◆ Literary Focus
What does Antony's soliloquy reveal that other characters do not know? ❷

86. Havoc: Latin for *no quarter,* signal for general slaughter.

87. slip: Loose.

◆ Build Vocabulary

oration (ô rā´ shən) *n.*: Formal speech, especially one given at a state occasion, ceremony, or funeral

discourse (dis kôrs´) *v.*: Speak formally and at length

That this foul deed shall smell above the earth
With carrion[88] men, groaning for burial.

[*Enter* OCTAVIUS' SERVANT.]

You serve Octavius Caesar, do you not?

SERVANT. I do, Mark Antony.

ANTONY. Caesar did write for him to come to Rome.

SERVANT. He did receive his letters and is coming,
And bid me say to you by word of mouth—
O Caesar! [*Seeing the body*]

ANTONY. Thy heart is big;[89] get thee apart and weep.
Passion, I see, is catching, for mine eyes,
Seeing those beads of sorrow stand in thine,
Began to water. Is thy master coming?

SERVANT. He lies tonight within seven leagues[90] of Rome.

ANTONY. Post[91] back with speed, and tell him what hath chanced.[92]
Here is a mourning Rome, a dangerous Rome,
No Rome of safety for Octavius yet.
Hie hence and tell him so. Yet stay awhile;
Thou shalt not back till I have borne this corse
Into the market place; there shall I try[93]
In my oration how the people take
The cruel issue[94] of these bloody men;
According to the which, thou shalt discourse
To young Octavius of the state of things.
Lend me your hand. [*Exit*]

88. **carrion** (kar′ ē ən) *adj.*: Dead and rotting.

89. **big:** Swollen with grief.

90. **lies . . . seven leagues:** Is camped tonight within twenty-one miles.

91. **Post:** Hasten.

92. **hath chanced:** Has happened.

93. **try:** Test.

94. **cruel issue:** Outcome of the cruelty.

Scene ii. *The Forum*

[*Enter* BRUTUS *and goes into the pulpit, and* CASSIUS, *with the* PLEBEIANS.[1]]

PLEBEIANS. We will be satisfied![2] Let us be satisfied!

BRUTUS. Then follow me, and give me audience, friends.
Cassius, go you into the other street
And part the numbers.[3]
Those that will hear me speak, let 'em stay here;
Those that will follow Cassius, go with him;
And public reasons shall be renderèd
Of Caesar's death.

FIRST PLEBEIAN. I will hear Brutus speak.

SECOND PLEBEIAN. I will hear Cassius, and compare their reasons,
When severally[4] we hear them renderèd.

[*Exit* CASSIUS, *with some of the* PLEBEIANS.]

1. **Plebeians** (plē bē′ ənz) *n.*: Commoners; members of the lower class.

2. **be satisfied:** Get an explanation.

3. **part the numbers:** Divide the crowd.

4. **severally** (sev′ ər əl ē) *adv.*: Separately.

◆ Critical Thinking

5 Interpret Ask students what Antony's message to Octavius reveals about his true political plans. *Allied with Octavius, he will oppose the conspirators when the time is right.*

◆ Build Grammar Skills

6 Parallel Structure Call students' attention to the parallel structure in Brutus' directions. The structure makes the choices clear and equal: Listen to Brutus or listen to Cassius.

Customize for *Less Proficient Readers*

Help these students use the stage directions on these pages to identify when characters enter and leave the stage. Have students explain who is hearing what is said at each point. *Cassius and Antony hear Brutus say that Antony can speak at the funeral. Only Brutus hears Cassius's suspicions about Antony. Antony is alone on stage when he speaks to Caesar's corpse. Octavius' servant enters. No one hears the conversation between the servant and Antony.*

Cross-Curricular Connection: History

Rome Shakespeare has the assassination of Caesar take place at the Capitol, in the area called the *Roman Forum* (though the killing actually happened in the Senate House). Mark Antony delivers his funeral oration at the same site. This is apt, because the Roman Forum was Rome's administrative and legal center. The word *forum* originally meant "marketplace," and Rome had several such areas. But the Roman Forum was the true center of the city, and the Roman world. Among the buildings there were the Senate House or *Curia*, the Temples of Saturn and Concord, and the *Tabularium* (Hall of Records).

Because most Roman streets were narrow, the Forum, with its open space, was an ideal setting for important official events, like triumphal processions for victorious generals. Often, it was the occurrences of major consequence, such as the crowning of Octavius Caesar as the first Roman emperor, Augustus.

Archaeologists have excavated much of the Forum, allowing modern visitors to see the remains of several imposing structures and get a sense of the grandeur of ancient Rome.

▶Critical Viewing◀

1 Connect *Point out to students that Antony is probably speaking his soliloquy in this picture. The text for his speech appears on p. 762. Based on his stance and gestures, Antony is probably near the end of his soliloquy when he incites the crowd to action.*

◆ Build Grammar Skills

2 Parallel Structure Point out that Brutus uses parallel structure at several points in this speech. Encourage students to point out each instance. *Students should point out parallel elements in the following sections: . . . hear me...that you may better judge; As Caesar loved me, . . . I slew him; There is tears, . . . for his ambition; Who is here so base, . . . for him I have offended.* Also encourage students to describe the effect of the parallel elements within the speech. *Responses may include: They make the speech more powerful and memorable; they help Brutus to hold the audience's attention.*

◆ Literary Focus

3 *Brutus is trying to convince the crowd that he loved Caesar but that there was a higher duty than his loyalty to Caesar. He knows that if he starts off by denigrating Caesar, the crowd will not listen to anything else he says. By saying he loves Caesar, he draws the crowd in so that they will listen to his reasons.*

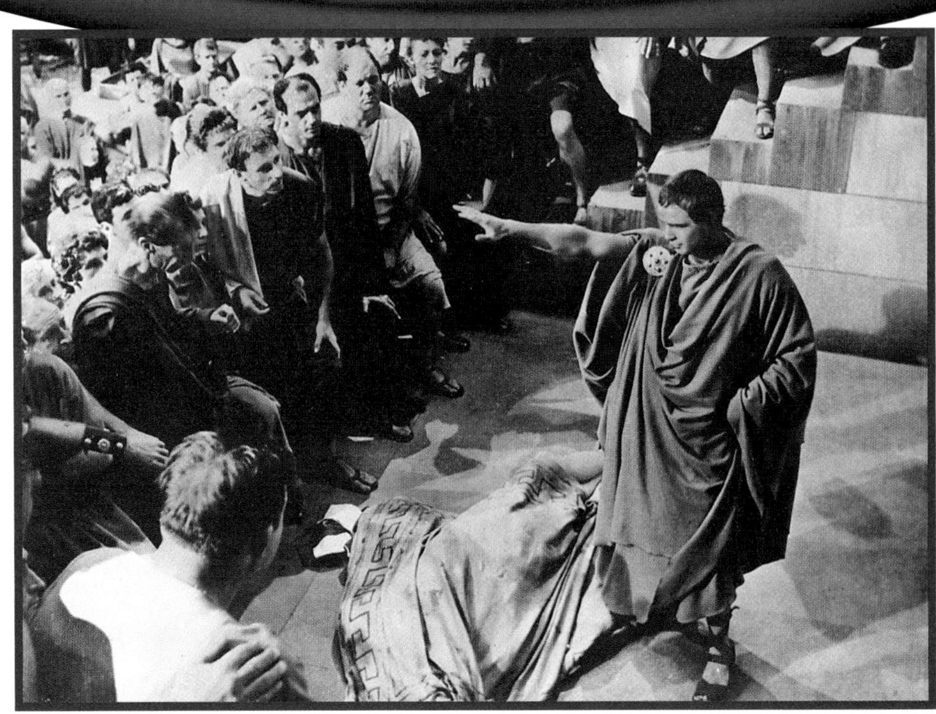

1 ▲ **Critical Viewing** Based on his stance and his gestures, which words of his speech do you think Antony is speaking? **[Connect]**

THIRD PLEBEIAN. The noble Brutus is ascended. Silence!

BRUTUS. Be patient till the last.

Romans, countrymen, and lovers,[5] hear me for my cause, and be silent, that you may hear. Believe me for mine honor, and have respect to mine honor, that you may believe. Censure[6] me in your wisdom, and awake your senses,[7] that you may the better judge. If there be any in this assembly, any dear friend of Caesar's, to him I say that Brutus' love to Caesar was no less than his. If then that friend demand why Brutus rose against Caesar, this is my answer: Not 2 that I loved Caesar less, but that I loved Rome more. Had you rather Caesar were living, and die all slaves, than that Caesar were dead, to live all free men? As Caesar loved me, I weep for him; as he was fortunate, I rejoice at it; as he was valiant, I honor him; but, as he was ambitious, I slew him. There is tears, for his love; joy, for his fortune; honor, for his valor; and death, for his ambition. Who is here so base,[8] that would be a bondman?[9] If any, speak; for him have I offended. Who is here so rude,[10] that would not be a Roman? If any, speak; for him have I offended. Who is

5. **lovers:** Dear friends.

6. **Censure** (sen′ shər) *v.*: Condemn as wrong; criticize.

7. **senses:** Powers of reason.

◆ Literary Focus
What is Brutus trying to accomplish with this monologue? 3

8. **base:** Low.

9. **bondman:** Slave.

10. **rude:** Ignorant.

here so vile, that will not love his country? If any, speak; for him have I offended. I pause for a reply.

ALL. None, Brutus, none!

BRUTUS. Then none have I offended. I have done no more to Caesar than you shall do to Brutus. The question of his death is enrolled in the Capitol;[11] his glory not extenuated,[12] wherein he was worthy, nor his offenses enforced,[13] for which he suffered death.

[*Enter* MARK ANTONY, *with* CAESAR'S *body.*]

❹ Here comes his body, mourned by Mark Antony, who, though he had no hand in his death, shall receive the benefit of his dying, a place in the commonwealth, as which of you shall not? With this I depart, that, as I slew my best lover for the good of Rome, I have the same dagger for myself, when it shall please my country to need my death.

ALL. Live, Brutus! Live, live!

❺

FIRST PLEBEIAN. Bring him with triumph home unto his house.

SECOND PLEBEIAN. Give him a statue with his ancestors.

THIRD PLEBEIAN. Let him be Caesar.

FOURTH PLEBEIAN. Caesar's better parts[14]
Shall be crowned in Brutus.

FIRST PLEBEIAN. We'll bring him to his house with shouts and clamors.

BRUTUS. My countrymen—

SECOND PLEBEIAN. Peace! Silence! Brutus speaks.

FIRST PLEBEIAN. Peace, ho!

BRUTUS. Good countrymen, let me depart alone,
And, for my sake, stay here with Antony.
Do grace to Caesar's corpse, and grace his speech
Tending to Caesar's glories,[15] which Mark Antony
By our permission, is allowed to make.
I do entreat you, not a man depart,
Save I alone, till Antony have spoke. [*Exit*]

FIRST PLEBEIAN. Stay, ho! And let us hear Mark Antony.

THIRD PLEBEIAN. Let him go up into the public chair;
We'll hear him. Noble Antony, go up.

ANTONY. For Brutus' sake, I am beholding[16] to you.

FOURTH PLEBEIAN. What does he say of Brutus?

THIRD PLEBEIAN. He says, for Brutus' sake,
He finds himself beholding to us all.

11. The question . . . in the Capitol: The whole matter of his death is on record in the Capitol.
12. extenuated (ik sten´ yo͞o wāt id) *v.*: Underrated.
13. enforced (en fôrsd´) *v.*: Given force to.

14. parts: Qualities.

15. Do grace . . . glories: Honor Caesar's body and the speech telling of Caesar's achievements.

16. beholding: Indebted.

◆ **Build Vocabulary**
vile (vīl) *adj.*: Depraved; ignoble

Comprehension Check ☑

❹ What does Brutus mean when he says that all of those present will receive "a place in the commonwealth" as a result of Caesar's death? *Caesar's ambition to become a godlike emperor has been put down; the new government will serve and represent all Romans, including the plebeians.*

◆ Critical Thinking

❺ **Connect** Ask students to connect the plebeians' behavior to the behavior of the tradesmen in Act I. What does this indicate about the common people? *Like the mechanicals in the opening scene, these plebeians are quick to change their loyalty from one leader to another. This fickleness indicates that they are easily swayed and their loyalty can be manipulated.*

Customize for
English Language Learners
Help these students restate the formal, stylized language in these passages in simpler English. For instance, Mark Antony's entrance as announced by Brutus could be rephrased as "Here comes Antony carrying Caesar's body. He didn't help kill him, but he will benefit from his death. You all will."

Beyond the Classroom

Community Connection

Public Forums The main events of Act III take place at the *Forum,* a large public square that was the seat of the Roman government. Among the buildings clustered there were several temples; the *Tabularium,* or Hall of Records; and the Capitol, or Senate House, where Caesar's assassination occurs. Many illustrious speakers addressed the citizens of Rome from a permanent platform that faced the center of the square.

In a class discussion, have students identify buildings in your community that serve public functions and/or serve as public gathering places. Students might then do research to learn more about the roles that these buildings play. For example, students might focus on such questions as: What types of records are kept at your Town or City Hall? Where would someone go to look up a local law or ordinance? What community-wide events are held at local schools or libraries?

Comprehension Check ☑

❶ How did Brutus' speeches affect the crowd of plebeians? *Brutus has won them over—they are convinced that Caesar was a tyrant and deserved to die.*

◆ Build Grammar Skills

❷ **Parallel Structure** Point out the repeated statements within Antony's speech. *Brutus is an honorable man; Brutus says he (Caesar) was ambitious.* Encourage students to comment on the effect that this repetition creates. *Students may say that it helps make the speech rhythmic and compelling. They may also point out that through the rest of his words, Mark Antony casts increasing doubt on both these statements with each repetition.*

◆ Literary Focus

❸ **Dramatic Speeches** Would students classify this speech as a soliloquy or a monologue? Why? *Monologue—in this speech, Mark Antony addresses other characters.*

◆ Literary Focus

❹ **Dramatic Speeches** Both men begin by asking for the audience's attention in almost the same way; both use the technique of asking the audience questions (rhetorical questions); both mention Caesar's ambition. Antony's speech, however, is meant to achieve the opposite effect of Brutus'.

◆ Reading Strategy

❺ **Paraphrase** *Sample paraphrase: I am so overcome with sorrow at Caesar's death that I can't speak.*

Tips to Guide Reading

Sustained Reading Encourage students to read all of Mark Antony's speech through p. 768 at one time. Have them try to imagine Antony speaking to the crowd and various plebeians making responses. Ask students how Antony affects the crowd during the course of this speech.

FOURTH PLEBEIAN. 'Twere best he speak no harm of Brutus here!

FIRST PLEBEIAN. This Caesar was a tyrant.

THIRD PLEBEIAN. Nay, that's certain.
We are blest that Rome is rid of him.

SECOND PLEBEIAN. Peace! Let us hear what Antony can say.

ANTONY. You gentle Romans—

ALL. Peace, ho! Let us hear him.

ANTONY. Friends, Romans, countrymen, lend me your ears;
I come to bury Caesar, not to praise him.
The evil that men do lives after them,
The good is oft interrèd with their bones;
So let it be with Caesar. The noble Brutus
Hath told you Caesar was ambitious.
If it were so, it was a grievous fault,
And grievously hath Caesar answered[17] it.
Here, under leave of Brutus and the rest
(For Brutus is an honorable man,
So are they all, all honorable men),
Come I to speak in Caesar's funeral.
He was my friend, faithful and just to me;
But Brutus says he was ambitious,
And Brutus is an honorable man.
He hath brought many captives home to Rome,
Whose ransoms did the general coffers fill;
Did this in Caesar seem ambitious?
When that the poor have cried, Caesar hath wept;
Ambition should be made of sterner stuff.
Yet Brutus says he was ambitious;
And Brutus is an honorable man.
You all did see that on the Lupercal
I thrice presented him a kingly crown,
Which he did thrice refuse. Was this ambition?
Yet Brutus says he was ambitious;
And sure he is an honorable man.
I speak not to disprove what Brutus spoke,
But here I am to speak what I do know.
You all did love him once, not without cause;
What cause withholds you then to mourn for him?
O judgment, thou art fled to brutish beasts,
And men have lost their reason! Bear with me;
My heart is in the coffin there with Caesar,
And I must pause till it come back to me.

17. **answered:** Paid the penalty for.

◆ Literary Focus
Notice how Antony's monologue reflects the style and structure of Brutus' monologue. ❹

◆ Reading Strategy
Paraphrase the reason Antony gives for pausing in his speech. ❺

Humanities: Performing Arts

Rhetoric If students look back at the cast of characters at the beginning of the play, they will see that Artemidorus, the citizen who tries to warn Caesar of danger in Scene i, lines 3–8, is identified as a teacher of rhetoric—the art of public speaking. Artemidorus' profession, along with Brutus' and Mark Antony's eloquent speeches before the crowd of plebeians, illustrates the importance of rhetoric in ancient Rome. The Romans learned a great deal about rhetoric from the Greeks, whose most famous orators and teachers of rhetoric included Pericles, Demosthenes, and Aristotle. In both ancient Greece and Rome, post-secondary education emphasized rhetoric in order to prepare young men for careers in law and politics.

As students read Act III, have them discuss whether they think Brutus or Mark Antony is the better orator and why.

FIRST PLEBEIAN. Methinks there is much reason in his sayings.

SECOND PLEBEIAN. If thou consider rightly of the matter,
Caesar has had great wrong.

THIRD PLEBEIAN. Has he, masters?
I fear there will a worse come in his place.

FOURTH PLEBEIAN. Marked ye his words? He would not take the crown,
6 Therefore 'tis certain he was not ambitious.

7 FIRST PLEBEIAN. If it be found so, some will dear abide it.[18]

SECOND PLEBEIAN. Poor soul, his eyes are red as fire with weeping.

THIRD PLEBEIAN. There's not a nobler man in Rome than Antony.

FOURTH PLEBEIAN. Now mark him, he begins again to speak.

ANTONY. But yesterday the word of Caesar might
Have stood against the world; now lies he there,
And none so poor to[19] do him reverence.

18. **dear abide/it:** Pay dearly for it.

19. **to:** As to.

◀ Critical Viewing How does this actor portray Antony's passion in delivering Caesar's eulogy? **[Connect]** 8

◆ Critical Thinking

6 Connect Call students' attention to the fact that, as in the opening scene and during Brutus' speech, the plebeians are changing their minds again. Now, they are turning against Brutus and doubting his claim that Caesar was ambitious. Moments ago, they wanted to erect a monument to Brutus.

Customize for *Logical/Mathematical Learners*

7 After Brutus' and Antony's monologues have been read, allow your logical/mathematical learners to conduct a survey or hold a class vote about which of the two men makes a more convincing case. Students may represent the results on a graph. Follow up with a discussion on the reasons why students (and plebeians) might be swayed by the words of these men.

▶ Critical Viewing ◀

8 Connect *His tense body language and intense facial expression convey his passion.*

Listening to Literature Audiocassettes Play the audiocassette recording of Brutus' and Antony's monologues. Encourage students to listen without following the text. Have students discuss the difference between reading the speeches and hearing them.

Beyond the Classroom

Workplace Skills

Public Speaking Discuss with students that many careers involve some form of public speaking. Some jobs may involve presenting an idea, demonstrating a product, or reporting results to a large group. Other jobs may use public speaking skills on a smaller scale, for instance, in conducting a meeting. Even a telephone conversation involves some public speaking skills! In life, students may use public speaking skills when they attend town council meetings or other group situations in which attendees are encouraged to voice their opinion.

Outline for students the qualities of an effective speaker: projection, diction, eye contact, and variety. Have them practice these skills by delivering a short portion of either of the monologues. For more information on public speaking skills, refer to the Speaking, Listening, and Viewing Handbook on p. 1027.

◆ Literary Focus

❶ **Dramatic Speeches** Have students explain what Mark Antony does to manipulate the crowd as he continues his address. *Responses may include these: He speaks with double meanings—that is, he suggests that he does not want to stir up "mutiny and rage" while that is precisely what he means to do; he says that he does not intend to read Caesar's will, knowing that his words will only heighten the crowd's interest.*

Connections to Today's World

The granddaughter of Yitzhak Rabin, the slain Israeli leader, delivers a eulogy for her grandfather. Noa Ben Artzi-Pelossof's eulogy is no funeral oration like Mark Antony's for Caesar, but it is every bit as moving, as she says a final farewell to the man she simply called *Saba,* the Hebrew word for grandfather.

Genre Connection

Traditionally, the eulogy, or funeral speech, is an opportunity for the family and loved ones of the deceased to talk publicly about the person's good, admirable, or lovable qualities.

Discuss with students whether there are more similarities or more differences between Antony's funeral oration for Caesar and this moving speech. Are there more similarities or more differences between the feelings of the speaker for the person who was killed?

Thematic Connection

Ask students to state the theme of each speech—Antony's funeral oration for Caesar and Noa Ben Artzi-Pelossof's eulogy for her grandfather Yitzhak Rabin. What part does revenge play in either speech?

O masters! If I were disposed to stir
Your hearts and minds to mutiny and rage,
I should do Brutus wrong and Cassius wrong,
Who, you all know, are honorable men.
I will not do them wrong; I rather choose
To wrong the dead, to wrong myself and you,
Than I will wrong such honorable men.
But here's a parchment with the seal of Caesar;
❶ I found it in his closet; 'tis his will.
Let but the commons[20] hear this testament,
Which, pardon me, I do not mean to read,
And they would go and kiss dead Caesar's wounds,
And dip their napkins[21] in his sacred blood;
Yea, beg a hair of him for memory,
And dying, mention it within their wills,
Bequeathing it as a rich legacy
Unto their issue.[22]

FOURTH PLEBEIAN. We'll hear the will; read it, Mark Antony.

ALL. The will, the will! We will hear Caesar's will!

ANTONY. Have patience, gentle friends, I must not read it.

20. **commons:** Plebeians; commoners.

21. **napkins:** Handkerchiefs.

22. **issue:** Heirs.

Connections to Today's World

All leaders live in some danger of violence against them by groups or individuals who do not agree with their policies. Like Caesar, Yitzhak Rabin's life was cut short by an assassination.

Noa Ben Artzi-Pelossof (1977–) is the granddaughter of Yitzhak Rabin, the Prime Minister of Israel from 1974 to 1977 and 1993 to 1995. A celebrated soldier and statesman, he was the first Prime Minister born in Israel. In 1994, Rabin received the Nobel Peace Prize for his efforts toward peace. He was assassinated on November 5, 1995.

In her eulogy at his funeral, Artzi-Pelossof expressed her personal feelings about this public man.

Eulogy for a Fallen Leader— Yitzhak Rabin

Noa Ben Artzi-Pelossof

"Grandfather, you were the pillar of fire in front of the camp and now we are left in the camp alone, in the dark; and we are so cold and so sad.

"I know that people talk in terms of a national tragedy, and of comforting an entire nation, but we feel the huge void that remains in your absence when grandmother doesn't stop crying.

"Few people really knew you. Now they will talk about you for quite some time, but I feel that they really don't know just how great the pain is, how great the tragedy is; something has been destroyed.

"Grandfather, you were and still are our hero. I want you

It is not meet you know how Caesar loved you.
You are not wood, you are not stones, but men;
And being men, hearing the will of Caesar,
It will inflame you, it will make you mad.
'Tis good you know not that you are his heirs;
For if you should, O, what would come of it?

FOURTH PLEBEIAN. Read the will! We'll hear it, Antony!
You shall read us the will, Caesar's will!

ANTONY. Will you be patient? Will you stay awhile?
I have o'ershot myself[23] to tell you of it.
I fear I wrong the honorable men
Whose daggers have stabbed Caesar; I do fear it.

FOURTH PLEBEIAN. They were traitors. Honorable men!

ALL. The will! The testament!

SECOND PLEBEIAN. They were villains, murderers! The will! Read the will!

❷

ANTONY. You will compel me then to read the will?
Then make a ring about the corpse of Caesar,
And let me show you him that made the will.
Shall I descend? And will you give me leave?

23. o'ershot myself: Gone too far.

to know that every time I did anything, I saw you in front of me.

"Your appreciation and your love accompanied us every step down the road, and our lives were always shaped by your values. You, who never abandoned anything, are now abandoned. And here you are, my ever-present hero, cold, alone, and I cannot do anything to save you. You are missed so much.

"Others greater than I have already eulogized you, but none of them ever had the pleasure I had to feel the caresses of your arms, your soft hands, to merit your warm embrace that was reserved only for us, to see your half-smile that always told me so much, that same smile which is no longer, frozen in the grave with you.

"I have no feelings of revenge because my pain and feelings of loss are so large, too large. The ground has been swept out from below us, and we are groping now, trying to wander about in this empty void, without any success so far.

"I am not able to finish this; left with no alternative, I say goodbye to you, hero, and ask you to rest in peace, and think about us, and miss us, as down here we love you so very much. I imagine angels are accompanying you now, and I ask them to take care of you because you deserve their protection.

"We will love you, Saba, forever."

1. Compare and contrast the message of Noa Ben Artzi-Pelossof's eulogy for her grandfather with Antony's eulogy for Caesar.
2. (a)How does Artzi-Pelossof help her listeners know her grandfather? (b) How does Antony help his listeners know Caesar?
3. Why do you think some people choose violence to express their disagreement with a leader's policies?

◆ Critical Thinking

❷ **Interpret** Point out that the common people, who had just moments ago cheered and supported Brutus, now call the conspirators "traitors," "villains," and "murderers." Have students identify the immediate cause of the crowd's change of heart. Also encourage students to comment on what the people's behavior reveals about their traits and motives.

Students should note that the plebeians turn against the conspirators upon hearing about Caesar's will. They may conclude that the plebeians are fickle and unpredictable in their loyalties and that they are motivated by greed and self-interest.

Read to Appreciate Author's Craft

Encourage students to look for ways Antony's speech manipulates the audience. Point out that one method is his repetition of the phrase "Brutus is an honorable man." Students may note Antony's "proof" that Caesar was not ambitious, as well as his pointing out the wounds on Caesar's body.

Answers to Connections to Today's World

1. Both speakers admire their subjects but Antony uses irony to make his points about Caesar's death. Artzi-Pelossof speaks in a more straightforward manner about her feelings. Both speakers express sorrow at the loss of the subject. Antony uses his eulogy to place blame and stir up a conflict. Artzi-Pelossof does not have feelings of revenge.
2. (a) She describes the kind of man he was in terms of their personal relationship. (b) He describes the public good Caesar achieved.
3. People who are unable or unwilling to go through peaceful, public means to express their disagreement with a leader may feel they need to use violence to make a point. In their answers, students should identify some of the peaceful means a person might use to express his or her disagreement.

Customize for
Bodily/Kinesthetic Learners

❶ Have a volunteer perform Antony's speech, lines 170–198, using appropriate gestures and a coat or jacket to represent Caesar's body and toga. Ask other members of the class to act out the plebeians' reactions by reading aloud lines 199–206. Afterward, discuss what makes Antony's speech so effective. Lead students to see that by vividly describing Caesar's death, Antony appeals to the people's emotions; he portrays the assassination as a crime against an individual rather than as an abstract political act.

◆ Reading Strategy

❷ **Paraphrase** One paraphrase might be "If you have any feelings, you will be moved by what you are about to see and hear. You all recognize Caesar's cloak—I'll never forget the first time he wore it."

ALL. Come down.

SECOND PLEBEIAN. Descend. [ANTONY *comes down.*]

THIRD PLEBEIAN. You shall have leave.

FOURTH PLEBEIAN. A ring! Stand round.

FIRST PLEBEIAN. Stand from the hearse,[24] stand from the body!

SECOND PLEBEIAN. Room for Antony, most noble Antony!

ANTONY. Nay, press not so upon me; stand far off.

ALL. Stand back! Room! Bear back.

ANTONY. If you have tears, prepare to shed them now.
You all do know this mantle;[25] I remember
The first time ever Caesar put it on:
'Twas on a summer's evening, in his tent,
That day he overcame the Nervii.
Look, in this place ran Cassius' dagger through;
See what a rent[26] the envious[27] Casca made;
Through this the well-belovèd Brutus stabbed,
And as he plucked his cursèd steel away,
Mark how the blood of Caesar followed it,
As[28] rushing out of doors, to be resolved[29]
If Brutus so unkindly knocked, or no;
For Brutus, as you know, was Caesar's angel.
Judge, O you gods, how dearly Caesar loved him!
This was the most unkindest cut of all;
For when the noble Caesar saw him stab,
Ingratitude, more strong than traitors' arms,
Quite vanquished him. Then burst his mighty heart;
And, in his mantle muffling up his face,
Even at the base of Pompey's statue
(Which all the while ran blood) great Caesar fell.
O, what a fall was there, my countrymen!
Then I, and you, and all of us fell down,
Whilst bloody treason flourished[30] over us.
O, now you weep, and I perceive you feel
The dint[31] of pity; these are gracious drops.
Kind souls, what[32] weep you when you but behold
Our Caesar's vesture[33] wounded? Look you here,
Here is himself, marred as you see with[34] traitors.

FIRST PLEBEIAN. O piteous spectacle!

SECOND PLEBEIAN. O noble Caesar!

THIRD PLEBEIAN. O woeful day!

FOURTH PLEBEIAN. O traitors, villains!

24. hearse (hurs) *n.*: Coffin.

25. mantle (man' təl) *n.*: Cloak; toga.

26. rent (rent) *n.*: Torn place.

27. envious (en' vē əs) *adj.*: Spiteful.

28. As: As if.

29. to be resolved: To learn for certain.

◆ Reading Strategy
Paraphrase Antony's words to the crowd. ❷

30. flourished (flur' ishd) *v.*: Grew; triumphed.

31. dint (dint) *n.*: Force.

32. what: Why.

33. vesture (ves' chər) *n.*: Clothing.

34. with: By.

Analyze Literary Criticism

Shakespearean scholar G. B Harrison writes that Mark Antony overcomes Brutus by his "superior knowledge of human nature" when he makes the funeral speech over Caesar's body. "He understands crowds, and Brutus does not. Brutus thinks that it is only necessary to tell the crowd why he killed Caesar and they will at once fall into orderly democratic ways. Antony knows better, and by a magnificent piece of oratory he so turns the crowd against the conspirators that they flee for their lives."

Share this critique with students. Ask them to read all of Antony's speech, paying attention to the responses of the crowd. Then have them compare their own feeling about the speech with Harrison's comments. To help students write this comparison, ask a few questions:

- Is Brutus truly an honorable man?
- Is Antony an honorable man? Is he being honest in the speech?
- Was Caesar ambitious? Is it likely he would have become emperor?
- Why does Antony make the speech?

FIRST PLEBEIAN. O most bloody sight!

SECOND PLEBEIAN. We will be revenged.

ALL. Revenge! About![35] Seek! Burn! Fire! Kill! Slay!
Let not a traitor live!

ANTONY. Stay, countrymen.

FIRST PEBEIAN. Peace there! Hear the noble Antony.

SECOND PLEBEIAN. We'll hear him, we'll follow him, we'll die with him!

ANTONY. Good friends, sweet friends, let me not stir you up
To such a sudden flood of mutiny.
They that have done this deed are honorable.
What private griefs[36] they have, alas, I know not,
That made them do it. They are wise and honorable,
And will, no doubt, with reasons answer you.
I come not, friends, to steal away your hearts;
I am no orator, as Brutus is;
But (as you know me all) a plain blunt man
❸ That love my friend, and that they know full well
❹ That gave me public leave[37] to speak of him.
For I have neither writ, nor words, nor worth,
❺ Action, or utterance,[38] nor the power of speech
To stir men's blood; I only speak right on.[39]
I tell you that which you yourselves do know,
Show you sweet Caesar's wounds, poor poor dumb mouths,
And bid them speak for me. But were I Brutus,
And Brutus Antony, there were an Antony
Would ruffle up your spirits, and put a tongue
In every wound of Caesar's that should move
The stones of Rome to rise and mutiny.

ALL. We'll mutiny.

FIRST PLEBEIAN. We'll burn the house of Brutus.

THIRD PLEBEIAN. Away, then! Come, seek the conspirators.

ANTONY. Yet hear me, countrymen. Yet hear me speak.

ALL. Peace, ho! Hear Antony, most noble Antony!

ANTONY. Why, friends, you go to do you know not what:
Wherein hath Caesar thus deserved your loves?
Alas, you know not; I must tell you then:
You have forgot the will I told you of.

ALL. Most true, the will! Let's stay and hear the will.

ANTONY. Here is the will, and under Caesar's seal.
To every Roman citizen he gives,
To every several man, seventy-five drachmas.

35. **About:** Let's go.

36. **griefs** (grēfs) *n.*: Grievances.

37. **leave:** Permission.

38. **neither writ . . . utterance** (ut´ ər əns): Neither written speech, nor fluency, nor reputation, nor gestures, nor style of speaking.

39. **right on:** Directly.

◆ Literary Focus

❸ **Dramatic Speeches** Encourage students to comment on the tactics that Antony uses as he continues to address and manipulate the crowd. *Students may point out the following: He cleverly plants the idea of mutiny in people's minds when he says that he does not want to stir up mutiny; he casts doubt on the reasons behind the assassination by saying that they are a mystery to him; he swears that his only motive is to speak his mind.*

Customize for *Pre-AP Students*

❹ Point out that Mark Antony's speech is brimming with ironies. Encourage students to cite specific lines and explain the sources of irony within them. For example, what would students say is ironic about Antony's statement that "I have neither writ, nor words . . . /. . . nor the power of speech/To stir men's blood" (lines 222–224)?

◆ Build Vocabulary

❺ **Word Roots: *-ora-*** Point out that *orator* (line 218) contains the word root *-ora-*, which comes from the Latin verb *orare*, which means "to speak." Have students determine the meaning of *orator*. *Students should connect the word root ora—having to do with speaking—with the suffix -tor- one who does or performs an action, and determine that "orator" means a speaker—in particular, a public speaker.*

Cross-Curricular Connection: Social Studies

Roman Society Roman society was divided into two main groups: citizens and noncitizens. About ten percent of people in Rome were citizens. This group included the ruling class, or *aristocracy;* wealthy businessmen; and *plebeians,* or the lower classes. People from all over the Roman empire were granted Roman citizenship. Noncitizens included foreigners who had not become Roman citizens and slaves, who might be prisoners of war, children sold by needy parents, or condemned criminals. Slaves, who ranged from cultured Greek teachers to uneducated laborers, had no rights whatsoever. Some slaves, however, were able to buy their freedom, or were granted it by their owners.

Roman women had no legal rights, although they were held in high esteem, and encouraged to attend public functions, unlike their counterparts in Greece. However, they could not vote.

Children began their education at home. The sons of wealthy families were sent to school from the age of six, and took on the responsibilities of adults at about sixteen. The education of most girls was limited to domestic concerns. Once they had reached sixteen, they were considered to be ready for marriage.

◆ Literary Focus

❶ Dramatic Speeches Suggested response: In this brief speech, Antony reveals his thoughts to the audience. By the word "mischief," the audience knows that Antony meant to subvert the conspirators' plot.

◆ Critical Thinking

❷ Predict Have students predict what Antony wants to discuss with Octavius. *Based on Antony's actions, and his earlier discussion with Octavius' servant, Antony probably wants to discuss an alliance formed for the purpose of driving out the conspirators.*

Customize for *English Language Learners*

❸ The archaic language in this section may pose difficulties for students acquiring proficiency in English. Preview words like *afoot, thither, rid, beliked,* and help students discover contemporary synonyms.

SECOND PLEBEIAN. Most noble Caesar! We'll revenge his death!

THIRD PLEBEIAN. O royal Caesar!

ANTONY. Hear me with patience.

ALL. Peace, ho!

ANTONY. Moreover, he hath left you all his walks,
His private arbors, and new-planted orchards,[40]
On this side Tiber; he hath left them you,
And to your heirs forever: common pleasures,[41]
To walk abroad and recreate yourselves.
Here was a Caesar! When comes such another?

FIRST PLEBEIAN. Never, never! Come, away, away!
We'll burn his body in the holy place,
And with the brands[42] fire the traitors' houses.
Take up the body.

SECOND PLEBEIAN. Go fetch fire.

THIRD PLEBEIAN. Pluck down benches.

FOURTH PLEBEIAN. Pluck down forms, windows, anything!

[*Exit* PLEBEIANS *with the body.*]

ANTONY. Now let it work: Mischief, thou art afoot,
Take thou what course thou wilt.

[*Enter* SERVANT.]

How now, fellow?

SERVANT. Sir, Octavius is already come to Rome.

ANTONY. Where is he?

❷ ❸ SERVANT. He and Lepidus are at Caesar's house.

ANTONY. And thither[43] will I straight to visit him;
He comes upon a wish. Fortune is merry,
And in this mood will give us anything.

SERVANT. I heard him say, Brutus and Cassius
Are rid[44] like madmen through the gates of Rome.

ANTONY. Belike[45] they had some notice of the people,[46]
How I had moved them. Bring me to Octavius. [*Exit*]

Scene iii. *A street.*

[*Enter* CINNA THE POET, *and after him the* PLEBEIANS.]

CINNA. I dreamt tonight that I did feast with Caesar,
And things unluckily charge my fantasy.[1]
I have no will to wander forth of doors,[2]
Yet something leads me forth?

40. walks . . . orchards: Parks, his private trees, and newly planted gardens.
41. common pleasures: Public places of recreation.
42. brands: Torches.

> **◆ Literary Focus**
> How does this aside indicate the true intentions behind Antony's monologue? ❶

43. thither: There.
44. Are rid: Have ridden.
45. Belike: Probably.
46. notice of the people: Word about the mood of the people.

1. things . . . fantasy: The events that have happened weigh heavily on my imagination.
2. of doors: Outdoors.

Cross-Curricular Connection: History

The Emperors of Rome In 27 B.C., Octavius, with whom Antony hopes to join forces in the third act, took the name of Augustus and became the first emperor of Rome. Rome was then no longer a republic, but a monarchy, as Brutus, Cassius, and the other conspirators had feared. The reign of Augustus, however, marked the beginning of the *Pax Romana* (Roman peace), which lasted for 200 years, during which commerce flourished and the standard of living rose.

Among other emperors of this period were Tiberius (14–37 A.D.), Caligula (37–41), Claudius (41–54), Nero (54–68), Trajan (98–117), Hadrian, and Marcus Aurelius (161–180). Suggest that students choose one of these Roman emperors to research, and report on the emperor's life and events in Rome during his reign.

4 ▲ **Critical Viewing** Why do you think ancient Roman sculptors portrayed political scenes such as this one? **[Speculate]**

FIRST PLEBEIAN. What is your name?

SECOND PLEBEIAN. Whither are you going?

THIRD PLEBEIAN. Where do you dwell?

FOURTH PLEBEIAN. Are you a married man or a bachelor?

5 **SECOND PLEBEIAN.** Answer every man directly.

FIRST PLEBEIAN. Ay, and briefly.

FOURTH PLEBEIAN. Ay, and wisely.

THIRD PLEBEIAN. Ay, and truly, you were best.

CINNA. What is my name? Whither am I going? Where do I dwell? Am I a married man or a bachelor? Then, to answer every man directly and briefly, wisely and truly: wisely I say, I am a bachelor.

SECOND PLEBEIAN. That's as much as to say, they are fools that marry; you'll bear me a bang[3] for that, I fear. Proceed directly.

CINNA. Directly, I am going to Caesar's funeral.

FIRST PLEBEIAN. As a friend or an enemy?

CINNA. As a friend.

SECOND PLEBEIAN. That matter is answered directly.

3. **bear me a bang:** Get a blow from me.

▶Critical Viewing◀

4 **Speculate** *As events in this play illustrate, Romans were very involved in the workings of their political system and followed the activities of their leaders closely.*

Customize for
Musical/Rhythmic Learners

5 This passage (lines 5–12), with its short, repetitive question-and-response lines, might be fun for these students to read aloud. Encourage them to experiment with different voices, accents, tones, and so on. If possible, make a cassette recorder available so they can tape their readings and decide which they like best.

Reteach

Help students understand dramatic speeches by pointing out models from the play.

- **Aside** Cassius speaks in an aside to Brutus in Act III, scene i, lines 231–235, warning Brutus not to trust Antony. This is an aside because the three men are standing together, and Cassius speaks privately to Brutus.
- **Soliloquy** In the same scene, lines 254–275, Antony has a soliloquy. He speaks alone on stage, addressing his words to the dead Caesar.
- **Monologue** Brutus gives a monologue in scene ii, beginning at line 12, when he makes his speech to the crowd. Though he is interrupted by plebeians at times, he is the primary speaker.

Encourage students to look for other examples throughout the play. Students can complete a chart like the one shown here, identifying character, act, scene, and line numbers.

Aside	Soliloquy	Monologue

Comprehension Check ☑

❶ Ask students: What does the crowd's attack on Cinna and the exclamations that follow reveal about the situation in Rome as Act III ends? *The plebeians have become irrational and bloodthirsty as a result of Antony's speeches; they mean to riot and take revenge on the conspirators.*

Listening to Literature Audiocassettes Now that students have read Act III, you might have them listen to some or all of the scenes within it on the **Listening to Literature Audiocassettes.**

Reinforce and Extend

Answers

◆ *Literature and Your Life*

Reader's Response To activate students' thinking, have them isolate words or phrases that make a strong impression on them. Then ask them to focus on these impressions as they answer the questions.

Thematic Focus Sample response: Even though Caesar was warned about his fate and he had a choice, his egotistical character actually made the prediction come true. Fate and character seemed to be linked.

☑ Check Your Comprehension

1. Trebonius presents Caesar with a petition and Artemidorus presents him with a letter of warning, but Caesar does not read either.
2. Brutus tells the people that his love for Rome caused him to turn against Caesar.
3. Antony repeatedly refers to Brutus as an "honorable" man.
4. Antony's speech enrages the common people.

◆ Critical Thinking

1. Antony befriends the conspirators to protect himself, to determine who are the assassins, and to position himself to speak at Caesar's funeral.
2. Brutus allows Antony to speak at Caesar's funeral because Brutus plans to speak first and because he mistakenly believes Antony's speaking will be more an advantage than a disadvantage.
3. The contents of Caesar's will enrage the citizens even more against the conspirators.

FOURTH PLEBEIAN. For your dwelling, briefly.

CINNA. Briefly, I dwell by the Capitol.

THIRD PLEBEIAN. Your name, sir, truly.

CINNA. Truly, my name is Cinna.

FIRST PLEBEIAN. Tear him to pieces! He's a conspirator.

❶ **CINNA.** I am Cinna the poet! I am Cinna the poet!

FOURTH PLEBEIAN. Tear him for his bad verses! Tear him for his bad verses!

CINNA. I am not Cinna the conspirator.

FOURTH PLEBEIAN. It is no matter, his name's Cinna; pluck but his name out of his heart, and turn him going.[4]

THIRD PLEBEIAN. Tear him, tear him! [*They attack him.*] Come, brands, ho! Firebrands![5] To Brutus', to Cassius'! Burn all! Some to Decius' house, and some to Casca's; some to Ligarius'! Away, go!

[*Exit all the* PLEBEIANS *with* CINNA.]

4. **turn him/going:** Send him on his way.

5. **Firebrands:** People who stir up others to revolt.

Guide for Responding

◆ *Literature and Your Life*

Reader's Response If you had been in the crowd at Caesar's funeral in Scene ii, how would you have responded to Antony's speech?

Thematic Focus What role do you think fate plays in the death of Caesar? What role do you think Caesar's own character plays?

☑ Check Your Comprehension

1. What petition is presented to Caesar, and how does he respond to it?
2. What justification for Caesar's assassination does Brutus give to the people?
3. How does Antony repeatedly refer to Brutus during the funeral oration?
4. What effect does Antony's oration have on the common people?

◆ Critical Thinking

INTERPRET

1. Why does Antony befriend the conspirators immediately after the assassination? **[Interpret]**
2. Why does Brutus allow Antony to speak at Caesar's funeral? **[Analyze]**
3. How does Caesar's will affect the people? **[Interpret]**

APPLY

4. Antony convinces the crowd to accept his view of Caesar and the conspirators. Think of a modern leader who tries to influence public opinion. What techniques does he or she use? **[Relate]**

COMPARE LITERARY WORKS

5. Compare and contrast the role of the Plebeians in *Julius Caesar* with the role of the Chorus in *Antigone*. **[Compare and Contrast]**

4. Sample responses: Persuasive speakers use repetition and parallel structure; use simple, memorable themes; choose words carefully; build to a conclusive conviction; and connect to their audience.
5. The plebeians are easily swayed by spectacle or powerful oratory. They respond to the actions of the main characters. The Chorus comments on and explains the action of the play, analyzing it and offering an opinion.

◆ Build Grammar Skills

1. Caesar is described with parallel superlative adjectives, all starting with *most.*
2. Brutus is described with four adjectives; then Caesar is described with the same number.
3. Brutus uses parallel clauses.
4. Antony speaks with two parallel infinitive phrases.
5. Brutus poses two parallel questions.

◆ Build Vocabulary

Using the Latin Root *-ora-*

1. c 2. a 3. b

Using the Word Bank

1. mutiny
2. oration
3. vile
4. malice
5. suit
6. discourse
7. spurn
8. confounded

Guide for Responding *(continued)*

◆ Reading Strategy

PARAPHRASE

Paraphrasing, or restating in your own words, is an effective way to clarify and understand Shakespeare's verse.

On your paper, paraphrase the following passages from Act III.

1. Caesar's speech, Scene i, lines 58–73.
2. The servant's speech, Scene i, lines 123–137.
3. Mark Antony's speech, Scene ii, lines 74–108.

◆ Literary Focus

DRAMATIC SPEECHES

Dramatic speeches, such as asides, soliloquys, and monologues, are some of the most famous and memorable parts of Shakespearean dramas.

1. Contrast what Antony says to the other characters in Act III, Scene i, lines 218–222, with what he says in his soliloquy, lines 254–275.
2. Examine Brutus' monologue in Act III, Scene ii, lines 12–34. Do you think Brutus is speaking his true feelings? Explain.
3. What does Antony's aside in Act III, Scene iii, lines 262–263, reveal about the true purpose of his speech to the crowd?

◆ Build Grammar Skills

PARALLEL STRUCTURE

Parallel structure, the expression of similar ideas in similar grammatical form, can make ordinary prose more poetic and a speech more powerful.

Practice In your notebook, identify and explain the parallel elements in each of the following examples.

1. Most high, most mighty, most puissant, Caesar . . .
2. Brutus is noble, wise, valiant, and honest; / Caesar was mighty, bold, royal, and loving.
3. Not that I loved Caesar less, but that I loved Rome more.
4. I come to bury Caesar, not to praise him.
5. Who is here so base, that/would be a bondman? . . .Who is here so rude, that would not be a/Roman?

◆ Build Vocabulary

USING THE LATIN ROOT *-ora-*

The Latin root *-ora-,* meaning "to speak," is found in a number of English words. In Act III of *The Tragedy of Julius Caesar*, when Mark Antony claims, "I am no *orator,* as Brutus is," do you believe him?

On your paper, match each of the following words, with *-ora-* as a root, with its definition.

1. oral — **a.** a skilled speaker
2. orator — **b.** skill in public speaking
3. oratory — **c.** spoken

USING THE WORD BANK: Analogies

On your paper, complete each analogy using the words from the Word Bank.

1. *Riot* is to *prison* as ___?___ is to *ship.*
2. *Eulogy* is to *funeral* as ___?___ is to *graduation.*
3. *Helpful* is to *nurse* as ___?___ is to *liar.*
4. *Goodwill* is to *volunteer* as ___?___ is to *murderer.*
5. *Application* is to *job* as ___?___ is to *favor.*
6. *Running* is to *motion* as ___?___ is to *communication.*
7. *Punch* is to *fight* as ___?___ is to *insult.*
8. *Wise* is to *enlightened* as ___?___ is to *ignorant.*

Idea Bank

Writing

1. Obituary Write a newspaper obituary to announce Caesar's death. An obituary contains facts about a person's life and the circumstances of his or her death. Use details about Caesar from Acts I–III to write the obituary.

2. Reaction to Speeches Imagine that you are a visitor to Rome who has just heard both Brutus' and Mark Antony's speeches. Write a commentary in which you explain which is more persuasive and why.

Speaking, Listening, and Viewing

3. Background Music Select a piece of background music that would be appropriate for the assassination scene. Play the music for the class and explain why you chose it. **[Music Link]**

◆ Reading Strategy

1. I am not easily swayed to change my mind—I am unmoved and I maintain my position. Cimber stays banished.
2. Brutus, Mark Antony told me to humble myself before you and tell you that Antony admires and respects you and feared Caesar. Will you allow Antony to come here safely, so you can explain why you killed Caesar? Antony shall not mourn Caesar, but will faithfully follow Brutus through the dangers of this new state of affairs.
3. Listen: I'm here to bury Caesar, not to praise him. Let's just forget about Caesar's good deeds. Brutus says Caesar was ambitious. If that's so, Caesar was wrong, and he has paid the price. Brutus and the rest gave me permission to speak here. Caesar was my friend but if Brutus says Caesar was ambitious, I guess he was. Caesar made money for all of us and cried over the needs of the poor, but Brutus wouldn't say he was ambitious if he weren't. I tried to give Caesar the crown, but he turned it down. I don't mean to contradict Brutus, but Caesar can't have been all bad: You loved him once; what happened? This is crazy. I can't talk anymore; I'm too upset.

◆ Literary Focus

1. Antony tells the conspirators that they are his friends. In his soliloquy, Antony mourns Caesar and calls the conspirators butchers.
2. Brutus frankly explains his part in Caesar's death when he says that he loved Caesar, but he loved the Roman people more. He is probably sincere. There are many earlier examples of Brutus' love for Caesar, and his concern for Rome.
3. Antony wished to set the crowd against Brutus and the conspirators.

Idea Bank

Customizing for
Learning Modalities
Verbal/Linguistic: 1, 2
Musical/Rhythmic: 3
Interpersonal: 2

Customizing for
Performance Levels
Less Advanced: 2
Average: 1, 2, 3
More Advanced: 1

✓ ASSESSMENT OPTIONS

Formal Assessment Selection Test, pp. 182–184, and Assessment Resources Software. The selection test is designed so that it can be easily customized to the ability levels of your students.

PORTFOLIO ASSESSMENT
Use the following rubrics in ***Alternative Assessment*** to assess student writing:
Obituary: Description Rubric, p. 97
Reaction to Speeches: Response to Literature Rubric, p. 110

Prepare and Engage

LESSON OBJECTIVES

1. To develop vocabulary and word identification skills
- Greek Roots: *-phil-*
- Using the Word Bank: Sentence Completions
- Extending Word Study: Figurative Language

2. To use a variety of reading strategies to read and comprehend an essay
- Connect Your Experience
- Reading Strategy: Read Between the Lines
- Tips to Guide Reading
- Read to Appreciate Author's Craft

3. To increase knowledge of other cultures and to connect common elements across cultures
- Connecting Themes Across Cultures (ATE)

4. To express and support responses to the text
- Critical Thinking
- Idea Bank: Character Profile
- Idea Bank: Rewrite a Scene

5. To analyze literary elements
- Literary Focus: Conflict in Drama

6. To read in order to research self-selected and assigned topics
- Idea Bank: Presentation
- Speaking, Listening, and Viewing: Presentation

7. To increase knowledge of the rules of grammar and usage
- Build Grammar Skills: Noun Clauses

Test Preparation

Reading Comprehension: Notice Word Choice (ATE, p. 773) The teaching tips and sample test item in this workshop support the instruction and practice in the unit workshop:
Reading Comprehension: Characteristics of Text (SE, p. 809)

Guide for Reading, Act IV

◆ Review and Anticipate

After the conspirators assassinate Caesar, both Brutus and Mark Antony give funeral speeches. Brutus, using logic and reason, explains to the crowd that Caesar's death was necessary to keep all Romans free. The crowd at first wholeheartedly accepts Brutus' speech. Then, Mark Antony takes the stage and persuades the crowd that Caesar was a great man and Brutus is a traitor. The crowd, having been worked to a frenzy, rushes off to find and destroy the conspirators.

As Act IV opens, Antony, Lepidus (a general), and Octavius Caesar (Julius Caesar's nephew) are planning which of their political opponents must be killed. The remainder of the act reveals the growing conflict between Cassius and Brutus. As the act closes, a mysterious visitor foreshadows Brutus' fate.

◆ Literary Focus

Conflict in Drama

Conflict, the struggle between two forces, is what creates drama. The conflict may be **external**—between two characters or groups—or it can be **internal**—involving a character's struggle to decide between two opposing ideas or values. The climax of the play is the point at which the internal and external conflicts are greatest. Usually the action rises to the climax—the moment of highest tension—and then falls as the conflicts are resolved.

What makes conflicts in drama especially compelling is that often the audience can see the outcome of events before the characters themselves can. In Act IV, as the conflict between the two armies nears, it becomes more and more obvious to the audience how the battle will turn out. There is a grisly fascination in watching the characters move inevitably toward their fates.

◆ Build Grammar Skills

Noun Clauses

A **noun clause** is a subordinate clause (a group of words with a subject and verb that cannot stand alone as a sentence) that functions as a noun in a sentence. It may act as a subject, direct or indirect object, or object of a preposition.

Subject: *That you have wronged me* doth appear in this.
Direct Object: You know *that you are Brutus that speaks this.*
Object of Preposition: The common people are swayed by *whoever speaks most persuasively.*

◆ Reading Strategy

Read Between the Lines

People and situations in drama—as in life—are not always what they appear to be on the surface. Though you must read line by line to follow the action, by **reading between the lines** you can discover a deeper or different meaning to a character's words or actions.

For example, at the opening of Act IV, Mark Antony describes Lepidus as "meet to be sent on errands." The implication is that Lepidus is capable of little more. You must read between the lines to understand Octavius' reply as well. Octavius points out that Antony "took his voice who should be pricked to die." By this, Octavius is implying that he thought that Antony valued Lepidus' judgment.

◆ Build Vocabulary

Greek Roots: *-phil-*

In Act IV, a tragedy befalls Brutus, and he finds his philosophy fails to comfort him. A *philosophy* is a system of principles or beliefs. The root of the word is the Greek *-phil-*, which means "love." A related meaning of *philosophy* is "love of wisdom."

Word Bank

Before you read, preview this list of words from Act IV.

legacies
slanderous
covert
chastisement
philosophy

Prentice Hall Literature Program Resources

REINFORCE / RETEACH / EXTEND

Selection Support Pages
Build Vocabulary: Word Roots: *-phil-*, p. 216
Build Grammar Skills: Noun Clauses, p. 217
Reading Strategy: Read Between the Lines, p. 218
Literary Focus: Conflict in Drama, p. 219

Strategies for Diverse Student Needs, p. 53

Beyond Literature
Career Connection: Political Science, p. 53

Formal Assessment Selection Test, pp. 185–187; Assessment Resources Software

Alternative Assessment, p. 53

Resource Pro CD-ROM

Listening to Literature Audiocassettes

The Tragedy of JULIUS CAESAR

William Shakespeare

Act IV

Scene i. *A house in Rome.*

[*Enter* ANTONY, OCTAVIUS, *and* LEPIDUS.]

ANTONY. These many then shall die; their names are pricked.

OCTAVIUS. Your brother too must die; consent you, Lepidus?

LEPIDUS. I do consent—

OCTAVIUS. Prick him down, Antony.

❶ **LEPIDUS.** Upon condition Publius shall not live,
Who is your sister's son, Mark Antony.

ANTONY. He shall not live; look, with a spot I damn him.[1]
But, Lepidus, go you to Caesar's house;
Fetch the will hither, and we shall determine
How to cut off some charge in legacies.

LEPIDUS. What, shall I find you here?

OCTAVIUS. Or[2] here or at the Capitol. [*Exit* LEPIDUS.]

ANTONY. This is a slight unmeritable[3] man,
Meet to be sent on errands; is it fit,
The threefold world[4] divided, he should stand
One of the three to share it?

OCTAVIUS. So you thought him,
And took his voice[5] who should be pricked to die
In our black sentence and proscription.[6]

❷ **ANTONY.** Octavius, I have seen more days[7] than you;
❸ And though we lay these honors on this man,
To ease ourselves of divers sland'rous loads,[8]
He shall but bear them as the ass bears gold,
To groan and sweat under the business,
Either led or driven, as we point the way;
And having brought our treasure where we will,
Then take we down his load, and turn him off,
(Like to the empty ass) to shake his ears
And graze in commons.[9]

1. **with a spot . . . him:** With a mark on the tablet, I condemn him.
2. **Or:** Either.
3. **slight unmeritable:** Insignificant and without merit.
4. **threefold world:** Three areas of the Roman empire—Europe, Asia, and Africa.
5. **voice:** Vote; opinion.
6. **proscription:** List of those sentenced to death or exile.
7. **have seen more days:** Am older.
8. **divers sland'rous loads:** Various burdens of blame.
9. **in commons:** On public pasture.

◆ Build Vocabulary

legacies (leg′ ə sēz) *n.*: Money, property, or position left in a will to someone

slanderous (slan′ dər əs) *adj.*: Damaging to a person's reputation

Test Preparation Workshop

Reading Comprehension: Notice Word Choice Several national standardized tests require students to analyze the characteristics of a text, including noting how word choice helps to establish an author's point of view. Read this speech by Octavius to students, then ask them to write a short answer to the question.

"Let us do so; for we are at the stake,
And bayed about with many enemies;
And some that smile have in their hearts, I fear,
Millions of mischiefs."

What do the words "bayed," "stake," and "enemies" reveal most about the speaker?

A He feels he is at a crossroads.
B He feels he will be set aflame.
C He plans an attack.
D He feels he is in jeopardy.

Guide students to see that the speaker uses figurative language to describe his situation. The correct response is D.

Develop Understanding

One-Minute Insight Act IV takes place as the triumvirate (Antony, Octavius, and Lepidus) and the conspirators (Cassius and Brutus) prepare for battle. In this act Shakespeare gives us a new perspective on the principal characters. Antony's cold, calculating side is revealed as he expresses his plan to divide power between himself and Octavius, leaving Lepidus out. Brutus' emotional side is shown as he lashes out at Cassius, then apologizes, citing as an excuse his grief at Portia's death.

Connecting Themes Across Cultures

In this act, the ghost of Caesar appears to Brutus. Ghosts appear in literature in different cultures, from Japanese fairy tales to Native American legends. Some foretell death, as in this play, while others help the living. Ask students to name other stories that use ghosts and to explain the function of it.

◆ Background for Understanding

❶ Students might be interested to know that Shakespeare compressed time in order to make his play work. Octavius did not arrive in Rome until six weeks after Caesar's death, and he did not ally himself with Antony and Lepidus until eighteen months later.

◆ Literary Focus

❷ **Conflict in Drama** Ask students to summarize the conflict between Antony and Octavius. Is the conflict internal or external? *Antony speaks to Octavius behind Lepidus' back, plotting to leave Lepidus out, should they win the battle, but letting him remain for the present to share any blame. Octavius argues in favor of Lepidus. The conflict is external.*

◆ Critical Thinking

❸ **Make Inferences** Encourage students to think about the new character traits Shakespeare reveals about Antony and Octavius. *Readers learn that Antony has a deceitful side, and that Octavius is more loyal and honest than Antony.*

▶Critical Viewing◀

❶ **Draw Conclusions** *Students can draw the conclusion that these are powerful, important men by noticing the elegant clothing, the sumptuous food, the confident postures and expressions.*

◆Critical Thinking

❷ **Make Inferences** Antony and Octavius disagreed about Lepidus, but now move on to more important matters. Ask: What can you infer about both Antony and Octavius from this abrupt change of topic? *The two men are intelligent and practical. They recognize the need to put aside their personal differences and focus on how best to counteract the threat from Cassius and Brutus.*

Customize for *Less Proficient Readers and English Language Learners*

These students may need assistance in recognizing that the discussion between Octavius and Antony concerns the man who just left the room. Help students to understand that Antony compares Lepidus to a horse to highlight Lepidus' inability and unworthiness to think and act as one of the triumvirate.

Customize for *Pre-AP Students*

Suggest that advanced students choose a passage in which reading between the lines is necessary to get the speaker's full meaning. Suggest they rewrite the passage in "plain English"—words that explicitly express its meaning. Invite students to contrast the two versions and discuss why Shakespeare chose language that required more of an effort on the part of the reader.

❶ ▲ Critical Viewing What details in this picture indicate that these are important, powerful men? **[Draw Conclusions]**

OCTAVIUS. You may do your will;
But he's a tried and valiant soldier.

ANTONY. So is my horse, Octavius, and for that
I do appoint him store of provender.[10]
It is a creature that I teach to fight,
To wind,[11] to stop, to run directly on,
His corporal motion governed by my spirit.[12]
And, in some taste,[13] is Lepidus but so.
He must be taught, and trained, and bid go forth.
A barren-spirited[14] fellow; one that feeds
On objects, arts, and imitations,[15]
Which, out of use and staled[16] by other men,
Begin his fashion.[17] Do not talk of him
But as a property. And now, Octavius,
Listen great things. Brutus and Cassius
Are levying powers;[18] we must straight make head.[19]
Therefore let our alliance be combined,
Our best friends made, our means stretched;[20]
And let us presently go sit in council
❷ How covert matters may be best disclosed,
And open perils surest answerèd.[21]

OCTAVIUS. Let us do so; for we are at the stake,[22]
And bayed about with many enemies;
And some that smile have in their hearts, I fear,
Millions of mischiefs.[23] *[Exit]*

10. appoint . . . provender: Give him a supply of food.
11. wind (wīnd) *v.:* Turn.
12. His . . . spirit: His body movements governed by my mind.
13. taste: Degree.
14. barren-spirited: Without ideas of his own.
15. feeds/On objects, arts, and imitations: Enjoys curiosities, arts, and styles.
16. staled: Cheapened.
17. Begin his fashion: He begins to use. (He is hopelessly behind the times.)
18. levying powers: Enlisting troops.
19. straight make head: Quickly gather soldiers.
20. stretched: Used to the fullest advantage.
21. How . . . answerèd: How secrets may be discovered and dangers met.
22. at the stake: Like a bear tied to a stake and set upon by many dogs.
23. mischiefs: Plans to injure us.

Block Scheduling Strategies

Consider these suggestions to take advantage of extended class time:

- Students may enjoy viewing feature 5 of the CD-ROM *The Time, Life, and Works of Shakespeare.* They will be introduced to other Elizabethan dramatists.
- As a class, analyze the internal and external conflicts Brutus faces. Then have students complete Literary Focus: Conflict in Drama in ***Selection Support***, p. 219.
- Invite students to listen to Act IV of the play on audiocassette. Then discuss how the actors' presentation affected students' understanding of the conflicts between Antony and Octavius and between Brutus and Cassius.
- Suggest that students work in small groups to complete the Critical Thinking questions (p. 786).
- Encourage students to choose an idea from the Idea Bank (p. 787). After students complete their writing, suggest they trade papers with partners and evaluate each other's writing on the basis of how well they have interpreted the characters of Brutus or Portia.

Scene ii. *Camp near Sardis.*

[*Drum. Enter* BRUTUS, LUCILIUS, LUCIUS, *and the* ARMY. TITINIUS *and* PINDARUS *meet them.*]

BRUTUS. Stand ho!

LUCILIUS. Give the word, ho! and stand.

BRUTUS. What now, Lucilius, is Cassius near?

LUCILIUS. He is at hand, and Pindarus is come
To do you salutation[1] from his master.

❸ **BRUTUS.** He greets me well. Your master, Pindarus,
In his own change, or by ill officers,
Hath given me some worthy cause to wish
Things done undone;[2] but if he be at hand,
I shall be satisfied.

PINDARUS. I do not doubt
But that my noble master will appear
Such as he is, full of regard and honor.

BRUTUS. He is not doubted. A word, Lucilius,
How he received you; let me be resolved.[3]

❹ **LUCILIUS.** With courtesy and with respect enough,
But not with such familiar instances,[4]
Nor with such free and friendly conference[5]
As he hath used of old.

BRUTUS. Thou hast described
A hot friend cooling. Ever note, Lucilius,
When love begins to sicken and decay
It useth an enforcèd ceremony.[6]
There are no tricks in plain and simple faith;
But hollow[7] men, like horses hot at hand,[8]
Make gallant show and promise of their mettle;

[*Low march within*]

But when they should endure the bloody spur,
They fall their crests, and like deceitful jades
Sink in the trial.[9] Comes his army on?

LUCILIUS. They mean this night in Sardis to be
quartered;
The greater part, the horse in general,[10]
Are come with Cassius.

[*Enter* CASSIUS *and his Powers.*]

BRUTUS. Hark! He is arrived.
March gently[11] on to meet him.

CASSIUS. Stand, ho!

◆ Literary Focus
How does the greeting between Brutus and Lucilius indicate the increasing tension of the conflict?

1. **To do you salutation:** To bring you greetings.

2. **In his own . . . done undone:** Has changed in his feelings toward me or has received bad advice from subordinates and has made me wish we had not done what we did.

3. **resolved:** Fully informed.

4. **familiar instances:** Marks of friendship.

5. **conference:** Conversation.

6. **enforcèd ceremony:** Forced formality.

7. **hollow:** Insincere.

8. **hot at hand:** Full of spirit when reined in.

9. **They fall . . . the trial:** They drop their necks, and like worn-out worthless horses, fail the test.

10. **horse in general:** Cavalry.

11. **gently:** Slowly.

◆ Build Vocabulary

covert (kuv´ ərt) *adj.*: Hidden; secret

◆ Literary Focus

❸ Conflict in Drama Make sure students understand that Brutus speaks first to his own servant, Lucilius, about Cassius' servant, Pindarus ("*He* greets me well"). Then he speaks directly to Pindarus, referring to Cassius ("*Your master . . .*") Ask: What does Brutus suspect Cassius of doing? What is the source of Brutus' internal conflict? *The line "In his own change, or by ill officers" implies that Brutus suspects Cassius of being involved in some sort of corruption. Because Brutus can justify his own part in the conspiracy only if he believes that each conspirator was honorable, he is deeply disturbed by his suspicions about Cassius.*

◆ Reading Strategy

❹ Read Between the Lines Ask: By reading between the lines in this passage, what can you infer about the relationship between Brutus and Cassius? *The relationship is not as strong as it once was. Brutus has already told Lucilius that he suspects Cassius of dishonesty. What he interprets as coolness on the part of Cassius makes him think either that Cassius is angry with him or that Cassius has something to hide.*

Customize for *Gifted/Talented Students*

Write the following job description on the chalk board.
Wanted: Strong leader for battle. Must be willing to die and to lead others into death. Position offers no job security and co-workers cannot be trusted.
Discuss with students whether they would take such an undesirable position. Then point out to students that this job description outlines the situation in which Brutus finds himself in Act IV. You may wish to have students write brief job descriptions for other main characters to identify their situations as the act opens.

◆ Reading Strategy

❶ Read Between the Lines Remind students that if they read between the lines, they can often learn how characters perceive themselves. Ask: How does Brutus view himself? *Brutus perceives himself as one who is fair to everyone, even to his enemies.*

◆ Reading Strategy

❷ Read Between the Lines Suggest that, by reading between the lines, students can find Brutus' reason for wanting to speak with Cassius privately, where the troops cannot hear. *Brutus says that the armies "should perceive nothing but love" between himself and Cassius because he understands the demands of leadership. Good leaders should present a united front to their subordinates.*

◆ Literary Focus

❸ Conflict in Drama This passage (lines 1–12) explains Cassius' ill-feeling toward Brutus. Have students work with partners, using the notes in the text, to paraphrase it. *Sample answer:*
CASSIUS: The reason I'm angry is that you denounced Lucius for taking bribes, even though I had written you a letter in his defense.
BRUTUS: You shouldn't have written a letter defending a dishonest man.
CASSIUS: At a time like this, you shouldn't be so critical of every little thing.
BRUTUS: You, yourself, have a reputation for taking bribes.

◆ Reading Strategy

❹ Read Between the Lines Ask students what they can determine about Cassius' personality by reading between the lines. *Responses can include this: Cassius is saying that if others besides Brutus accused him of dishonesty he would kill them. These are the words of a hot-tempered, aggressive man.*

BRUTUS. Stand, ho! Speak the word along.

FIRST SOLDIER. Stand!

SECOND SOLDIER. Stand!

THIRD SOLDIER. Stand!

CASSIUS. Most noble brother, you have done me wrong.

❶ **BRUTUS.** Judge me, you gods! Wrong I mine enemies?
And if not so, how should I wrong a brother?

CASSIUS. Brutus, this sober form[12] of yours hides
wrongs;
And when you do them—

BRUTUS. Cassius, be content.[13]
Speak your griefs softly; I do know you well.
Before the eyes of both our armies here
❷ (Which should perceive nothing but love from us)
Let us not wrangle. Bid them move away;
Then in my tent, Cassius, enlarge[14] your griefs,
And I will give you audience.

CASSIUS. Pindarus,
Bid our commanders lead their charges[15] off
A little from this ground.

BRUTUS. Lucilius, do you the like, and let no man
Come to our tent till we have done our conference.
Let Lucius and Titinius guard our door.

[*Exit all but* BRUTUS *and* CASSIUS]

Scene iii. *Brutus' tent.*

CASSIUS. That you have wronged me doth appear in this:
You have condemned and noted[1] Lucius Pella
For taking bribes here of the Sardians;
Wherein my letters, praying on his side,[2]
Because I knew the man, was slighted off.[3]

BRUTUS. You wronged yourself to write in such a case.

❸ **CASSIUS.** In such a time as this it is not meet
That every nice offense should bear his comment.[4]

BRUTUS. Let me tell you, Cassius, you yourself
Are much condemned to have an itching palm,[5]
To sell and mart[6] your offices for gold
To undeservers.

CASSIUS. I an itching palm?
❹ You know that you are Brutus that speaks this,
Or, by the gods, this speech were else your last.

BRUTUS. The name of Cassius honors[7] this corruption,

12. sober form: Serious manner.

13. be content: Be patient.

14. enlarge: Freely express.

15. charges: Troops.

1. noted: Publicly denounced.

2. praying on his side: Pleading on his behalf.

3. slighted off: Disregarded.

4. every . . . comment: Every petty fault should receive its criticism.

5. condemned . . . palm: Accused of having a hand eager to accept bribes.

6. mart: Trade.

7. honors: Gives respectability to.

And chastisement doth therefore hide his head.

CASSIUS. Chastisement!

BRUTUS. Remember March, the ides of March remember.
Did not great Julius bleed for justice' sake?
What villain touched his body, that did stab,
And not[8] for justice? What, shall one of us,
That struck the foremost man of all this world
❺ But for supporting robbers,[9] shall we now
Contaminate our fingers with base bribes,
And sell the mighty space of our large honors[10]
For so much trash[11] as may be grasped thus?
I had rather be a dog, and bay[12] the moon,
Than such a Roman.

CASSIUS. Brutus, bait[13] not me;
I'll not endure it. You forget yourself
❻ To hedge me in.[14] I am a soldier, I,
Older in practice, abler than yourself
To make conditions.[15]

❼ **BRUTUS.** Go to! You are not, Cassius.

CASSIUS. I am.

BRUTUS. I say you are not.

CASSIUS. Urge[16] me no more, I shall forget myself;
Have mind upon your health;[17] tempt me no farther.

BRUTUS. Away, slight[18] man!

❽ **CASSIUS.** Is't possible?

BRUTUS. Hear me, for I will speak.
Must I give way and room to your rash choler?[19]
Shall I be frighted when a madman stares?

CASSIUS. O ye gods, ye gods! Must I endure all this?

BRUTUS. All this? Ay, more: fret till your proud heart break.
Go show your slaves how choleric[20] you are,
And make your bondmen tremble. Must I budge?[21]
Must I observe you?[22] Must I stand and crouch
Under your testy humor?[23] By the gods,
You shall digest the venom of your spleen,[24]
Though it do split you; for, from this day forth,
I'll use you for my mirth,[25] yea, for my laughter,
When you are waspish.[26]

CASSIUS. Is it come to this?

BRUTUS. You say you are a better soldier:
Let it appear so; make your vaunting[27] true,

8. **And not:** Except.

9. **But . . . robbers:** Here Brutus says, for the first time, that Caesar's officials were also involved in taking bribes and that this was a motive in his assassination.

10. **honors:** Offices.

11. **trash:** Dirty money.

12. **bay:** Howl at.

13. **bait:** Harass (as a bear tied to a stake is harassed by dogs).

14. **hedge me in:** Restrict my actions.

15. **conditions:** Decisions.

16. **Urge:** Drive.

17. **health:** Safety.

18. **slight:** Insignificant.

19. **choler** (käl′ ər) *n.*: Anger.

20. **choleric** (käl′ ər ik) *adj.*: Quick-tempered.

21. **budge:** Flinch away from you.

22. **observe you:** Show reverence toward you.

23. **testy humor:** Irritability.

24. **digest . . . spleen:** Eat the poison of your spleen. (The spleen was thought to be the source of anger.)

25. **mirth:** Amusement.

26. **waspish:** Bad-tempered.

27. **vaunting** (vônt′ iŋ) *n.*: Boasting.

◆ Build Vocabulary

chastisement (chas tīz′ mənt) *n.*: Punishment; severe criticism

Comprehension Check ✓

❺ Challenge students to summarize Brutus' speech in their own words. If they have difficulty, suggest they work with partners or in groups. *Suggested response: Caesar was the greatest man in the world except for one thing—he allowed his followers to be corrupt ("But for supporting robbers . . ."). Now Cassius, who took part in killing Caesar, is accepting bribes, himself. Cassius' corruption turns Caesar's assassination into a hypocritical act rather than an honorable one.*

❻ **Clarification** Shakespeare alludes to a bear tied to a stake, harassed by dogs. Bear baiting was a favorite spectator sport in Elizabethan times.

❼ **Clarification** Be sure students notice the comma between the words "not" and "Cassius." Brutus is not saying, "You are not Cassius." He is saying, "You are not abler than I am, Cassius," in reference to Cassius' preceding speech.

◆ Reading Strategy

❽ **Read Between the Lines**
Remind students of Cassius' previous warning to Brutus (lines 14–15). Here he threatens Brutus again. Ask students to interpret Cassius' threat and to suggest what Brutus reveals about his personality in his response to Cassius. *Sample answer: I'm not afraid of you. Go threaten your slaves if you want to scare someone. I swear you'll be sorry for what you said! Brutus, too, is aggressive and not easily frightened.*

◆ Build Grammar Skills

❶ **Noun Clauses** Have students identify the noun clause in line 64 and explain its function. *The clause is "that I shall be sorry for"; it is the direct object of the verb phrase "may do" and answers the question "may do what?"*

◆ Reading Strategy

❷ **Read Between the Lines** Cassius' strong reaction to Brutus' accusations suggests that he is very sensitive about being thought weak or cowardly. He has a similar reaction when he is accused of taking bribes. Students can read between the lines that Brutus is probably not the first person to accuse him of weakness and dishonesty.

◆ Literary Focus

❸ **Conflict in Drama** Suggested response: In addition to accusing Cassius of accepting bribes, Brutus expresses anger at Cassius for refusing to help with gold to pay his legions.

Customize for *Gifted/Talented Students*

Have students work in pairs to dramatize the characters of Brutus and Cassius in conflict. Suggest that students try different ways to show the conflict, such as speaking the actual dialogue, improvising a scene, or choreographing a mime or dance. Each pair can perform for the class.

And it shall please me well. For mine own part,
I shall be glad to learn of[28] noble men.

CASSIUS. You wrong me every way; you wrong me, Brutus;
I said, an elder soldier, not a better.
Did I say, better?

BRUTUS. If you did, I care not.

CASSIUS. When Caesar lived, he durst not thus have moved[29] me.

BRUTUS. Peace, peace, you durst not so have tempted him.

CASSIUS. I durst not?

BRUTUS. No.

CASSIUS. What? Durst not tempt him?

BRUTUS. For your life you durst not.

CASSIUS. Do not presume too much upon my love;
❶ I may do that I shall be sorry for.

BRUTUS. You have done that you should be sorry for.
There is no terror, Cassius, in your threats;
For I am armed so strong in honesty
That they pass by me as the idle wind,
Which I respect not. I did send to you
For certain sums of gold, which you denied me;
For I can raise no money by vile means.
By heaven, I had rather coin my heart
And drop my blood for drachmas than to wring
From the hard hands of peasants their vile trash
By any indirection.[30] I did send
To you for gold to pay my legions,
Which you denied me. Was that done like Cassius?
Should I have answered Caius Cassius so?
When Marcus Brutus grows so covetous[31]
To lock such rascal counters[32] from his friends,
Be ready, gods, with all your thunderbolts,
Dash him to pieces!

CASSIUS. I denied you not.

BRUTUS. You did.

CASSIUS. I did not. He was but a fool
That brought my answer back. Brutus hath rived[33] my heart.
A friend should bear his friend's infirmities;

28. **learn of:** Hear about; learn from.

29. **moved:** Irritated.

> **◆ Reading Strategy**
> What can you read between the lines that would help you explain why Cassius is so offended by Brutus' words? ❷

> **◆ Literary Focus**
> How does this conflict between Brutus and Cassius reflect Brutus' internal conflict over his participation in the conspiracy? ❸

30. **indirection:** Irregular methods.

31. **covetous** (kuv´ it əs) *adj.*: Greedy.

32. **rascal counters:** Worthless coins.

33. **rived** (rīv'd) *v.*: Broken.

Beyond the Classroom

Workplace Skills

Expressing Disagreement In the heat of the moment, Brutus and Cassius express their disagreement with each other in very hostile terms. If they had expressed their disagreement differently, the conflict between them may have been avoided. Tell students that there are appropriate and constructive ways to express disagreement in life and in the workplace. As a class, come up with some guidelines for expressing disagreement.

Elicit from students the following points:

- Use a calm, respectful tone.
- Present your reasons and offer evidence.
- Listen to what the other person has to say and consider his or her point of view before responding.

For more instruction and activities that will develop students' ability to express disagreement effectively and appropriately, use the Speaking, Listening, and Viewing Workshop on p. 298.

But Brutus makes mine greater than they are.

BRUTUS. I do not, till you practice them on me.

CASSIUS. You love me not.

BRUTUS. I do not like your faults.

CASSIUS. A friendly eye could never see such faults.

BRUTUS. A flatterer's would not, though they do appear
As huge as high Olympus.

CASSIUS. Come, Antony, and young Octavius, come,
Revenge yourselves alone[34] on Cassius,
For Cassius is aweary of the world:
Hated by one he loves; braved[35] by his brother;
Checked like a bondman;[36] all his faults observed,
Set in a notebook, learned and conned by rote[37]
To cast into my teeth. O, I could weep
My spirit from mine eyes! There is my dagger,
And here my naked breast; within, a heart
Dearer than Pluto's mine,[38] richer than gold;
If that thou be'st a Roman, take it forth.
❹ I, that denied thee gold, will give my heart.
Strike as thou didst at Caesar; for I know,
When thou didst hate him worst, thou lovedst him
better
Than ever thou lovedst Cassius.

BRUTUS. Sheathe your dagger.
Be angry when you will, it shall have scope.[39]
Do what you will, dishonor shall be humor.[40]
O Cassius, you are yokèd[41] with a lamb
That carries anger as the flint bears fire,
Who, much enforcèd,[42] shows a hasty spark,
And straight is cold again.

CASSIUS. Hath Cassius lived
To be but mirth and laughter to his Brutus
When grief and blood ill-tempered vexeth him?

❺ **BRUTUS.** When I spoke that, I was ill-tempered too.

CASSIUS. Do you confess so much? Give me your hand.

BRUTUS. And my heart too.

CASSIUS. O Brutus!

BRUTUS. What's the matter?

CASSIUS. Have not you love enough to bear with me
When that rash humor which my mother gave me
Makes me forgetful?

34. alone: Only.

35. braved: Bullied.

36. Checked like a bondman: Scolded like a slave.

37. conned by rote: Memorized.

38. Pluto's mine: Mythological Roman god of the underworld and of riches symbolized by his mine.

39. scope: Free play.

40. dishonor . . . humor: Any dishonorable acts will be considered just your irritable disposition.

41. yokèd: In partnership.

42. enforcèd: Provoked.

◆ Reading Strategy

❹ Read Between the Lines Cassius makes a dramatic gesture in this passage, offering Brutus his dagger to kill him. Ask students whether or not they believe Cassius is wholly sincere. If not, why does he make the gesture? *Students may say that both Cassius and Brutus know that the dagger will not be accepted. If Cassius thought it would, he would not have offered it. He is trying to end the argument because he needs Brutus, and he wants to take Brutus' mind off the bribery issue.*

◆ Reading Strategy

❺ Read Between the Lines You may want to point out that although this play was written almost 500 years ago, Cassius and Brutus both make use of what have become standard contemporary excuses. See if students can identify these excuses for hurting someone's feelings. *Cassius offers being "ill tempered" as an excuse (I was in a bad mood). Brutus offers the same excuse (". . . I was ill-tempered too"). Then Cassius adds that his mother gave him his "rash humor" (I can't help it; it's in my genes).*

Tips to Guide Reading

Sustained Reading Encourage students to practice sustained reading to follow the conflict between Brutus and Cassius, starting with Scene ii and continuing to line 161, Scene iii. Then have students explain what the quarrel is about in their own words.

▶Critical Viewing◀

❶ **Analyze** *Suggested answer: The two men are looking directly at each other, standing very erect, and scowling. Cassius' hand is on his dagger.*

◆Reading Strategy

❷ **Read Between the Lines** Ask students to venture guesses about the purpose of this passage. Why did Shakespeare include it? *Students may say that it draws Brutus and Cassius together after their argument. Now they can both take out their anger on the poet!*

Read to Appreciate Author's Craft

Remind students that Act IV, scene iii marks the second time a poet wanders into a scene. The first occurred at the end of Act III, when Cinna the Poet is mistaken for a conspirator and is attacked by a group of plebeians. The poet in Act IV, scene iii tries to mend the quarrel between Brutus and Cassius, only to be insulted and told to leave. Ask students to brainstorm for reasons poets appear as comic characters in this play.

◀ Critical Viewing How do the expressions and body language of these actors playing Brutus and Cassius indicate conflict? **[Analyze]** ❶

BRUTUS. Yes, Cassius, and from henceforth,
When you are overearnest with your Brutus,
He'll think your mother chides, and leave you so.[43]

[*Enter a* POET, *followed by* LUCILIUS, TITINIUS, *and* LUCIUS.]

POET. Let me go in to see the generals;
There is some grudge between 'em; 'tis not meet
They be alone.

LUCILIUS. You shall not come to them.

POET. Nothing but death shall stay me.

CASSIUS. How now? What's the matter?

POET. For shame, you generals! What do you mean?
Love, and be friends, as two such men should be;
❷ For I have seen more years, I'm sure, than ye.

CASSIUS. Ha, ha! How vilely doth this cynic[44] rhyme!

BRUTUS. Get you hence, sirrah! Saucy fellow, hence!

CASSIUS. Bear with him, Brutus, 'tis his fashion.

BRUTUS. I'll know his humor when he knows his time.[45]
What should the wars do with these jigging[46] fools?
Companion,[47] hence!

CASSIUS. Away, away, be gone! [*Exit* POET.]

43. your mother . . . so: It is just your inherited disposition and let it go at that.

44. cynic: Rude fellow.

45. I'll know . . . time: I'll accept his eccentricity when he chooses a proper time to exhibit it.
46. jigging: Rhyming.
47. Companion: Fellow (used to show contempt).

Beyond the Classroom

Career Connection

Poet Toward the end of Scene iii, a poet appears. No one seems to pay much attention to him, and we might wonder why Shakespeare, himself a poet, included this minor character.

Some students in the class may read and/or write poetry, or even aspire to becoming poets. Lead students to recognize that most poets have jobs, often as English teachers or college professors, in addition to writing poetry—at least when they start out. Encourage interested students to investigate the "second" professions of poets whom they admire. Suggest that they also investigate how a student interested in poetry writing can get training and practice, and how a beginning poet gets his or her poems published. Young poets in your class might enjoy getting together to read and discuss one another's poems. They could form a poetry club at school to lend one another support.

BRUTUS. Lucilius and Titinius, bid the commanders
Prepare to lodge their companies tonight.

CASSIUS. And come yourselves, and bring Messala with
you
Immediately to us. [*Exit* LUCILIUS *and* TITINIUS.]

BRUTUS. Lucius, a bowl of wine. [*Exit* LUCIUS.]

3 **CASSIUS.** I did not think you could have been so angry.

BRUTUS. O Cassius, I am sick of many griefs.

CASSIUS. Of your philosophy you make no use,
If you give place to accidental evils.[48]

BRUTUS. No man bears sorrow better. Portia is dead.

CASSIUS. Ha? Portia?

BRUTUS. She is dead.

CASSIUS. How scaped I killing when I crossed you so?[49]
O insupportable and touching loss!
Upon[50] what sickness?

BRUTUS. Impatient of my absence,
And grief that young Octavius with Mark Antony
4 Have made themselves so strong—for with her death
That tidings[51] came—with this she fell distract,[52]
And (her attendants absent) swallowed fire.

CASSIUS. And died so?

BRUTUS. Even so.

5 **CASSIUS.** O ye immortal gods!

[*Enter* LUCIUS, *with wine and tapers.*]

BRUTUS. Speak no more of her. Give me a bowl of wine
In this I bury all unkindness, Cassius. [*Drinks*]

CASSIUS. My heart is thirsty for that noble pledge.
Fill, Lucius, till the wine o'erswell the cup;
I cannot drink too much of Brutus' love.

[*Drinks. Exit* LUCIUS.]

[*Enter* TITINIUS *and* MESSALA.]

BRUTUS. Come in, Titinius! Welcome, good Messala.
Now sit we close about this taper here,
And call in question[53] our necessities.

CASSIUS. Portia, art thou gone?

BRUTUS. No more, I pray you.
Messala, I have here receivèd letters

◆ Literary Focus
With what internal conflicts is Brutus struggling?

48. Of your philosophy . . . accidental evils: Brutus' philosophy was Stoicism. As a Stoic he believed that nothing evil would happen to a good man.

49. How scaped . . . you so?: How did I escape being killed when I opposed you so?

50. Upon: As a result of.

51. tidings: News.

52. fell distract: Became distraught.

53. call in question: Examine.

◆ Build Vocabulary
philosophy (fil äs´ ə fē) *n.*: System of principles or beliefs

◆ Build Grammar Skills

3 Noun Clauses Draw students' attention to Cassius' words. Ask them to identify the noun clause and its function in the sentence. *The clause is "you could have been so angry"; it is the direct object of "did think."* You may want to point out that the relative pronoun *that* has been omitted.

4 Clarification According to the Roman historian Plutarch, Portia committed suicide by swallowing burning coals.

◆ Critical Thinking

5 Compare and Contrast Invite discussion about how this scene might have been different if Brutus had informed Cassius of Portia's death at the beginning. *Possible responses: Cassius would have been less likely to speak his mind because he would not have wanted to upset Brutus; Cassius would have blamed Brutus' anger on the death of Portia and might not have taken Brutus' insulting words seriously.*

Speaking, Listening, and Viewing Mini-Lesson

Presentation

This mini-lesson supports the Speaking, Listening, and Viewing activity on p. 787.

Introduce Stoicism was developed by the Greek philosopher Zeno of Citium, who lived from 340–265 B.C. His teachings included the idea that people should not be moved by either joy or sorrow.

Develop Review the elements of a successful presentation with students, encouraging them to consider these points:

- In presenting information, students should consider what their audience already knows about the subject.
- Presenters should have prepared comments. However, they should not read directly from notes.
- Eye contact and interaction with the audience enhance a presentation.

Apply To help students prepare their presentations, suggest that they plan a visual that will guide their talk. For example, students may prepare a chart to outline the main ideas of stoicism; then they may connect characters' words and actions with these ideas.

Assess Evaluate students on their ability to make a coherent and animated presentation, on the thoroughness of their research, and on the supporting evidence they give for their choice.

◆ Background for Understanding

❶ Tell students that Cicero was a distinguished Roman orator and statesman. Because he believed in a republican form of government, he was one of the many Antony, Octavius, and Lepidus condemned to death. He was killed trying to escape from his home. (For more information on Cicero, see Cross-Curricular Connection note in Act II, p. 737.)

❷ **Clarification** Some scholars believe that Shakespeare meant to delete either Messala's telling Brutus of Portia's death or Brutus' telling Cassius previously of her death. Otherwise, it appears that either Brutus is pretending not to know of Portia's death, or that Shakespeare made a mistake.

◆ Reading Strategy

❸ **Read Between the Lines**
Suggested response: *Brutus shows little emotion in front of his friend Messala, but his reaction was quite different with Cassius. Perhaps this is because, in this passage, he really knows about her death already, and so is not shocked.*

◆ Critical Thinking

❹ **Make Inferences** Students have seen Antony and Octavius putting aside personal matters to discuss matters of war. Ask students which character is like Antony and Octavius in this respect. Have them contrast Cassius with Brutus. *Brutus is able to stop thinking about his wife's death to concentrate on the impending battle ("our work alive"). Cassius says he would not be able to suppress his feelings as Brutus does ("... my nature could not bear it so").*

That young Octavius and Mark Antony
Come down upon us with a mighty power,[54]
Bending their expedition toward Philippi.[55]

MESSALA. Myself have letters of the selfsame tenure.[56]

BRUTUS. With what addition?

MESSALA. That by proscription and bills of outlawry
Octavius, Antony, and Lepidus
Have put to death an hundred senators.

BRUTUS. Therein our letters do not well agree.
Mine speak of seventy senators that died
By their proscriptions, Cicero being one.

❶ CASSIUS. Cicero one?

MESSALA. Cicero is dead,
And by that order of proscription.
Had you your letters from your wife, my lord?

BRUTUS. No, Messala.

MESSALA. Nor nothing in your letters writ of her?

BRUTUS. Nothing, Messala.

MESSALA. That methinks is strange.

BRUTUS. Why ask you? Hear you aught[57] of her in yours?

MESSALA. No, my lord.

BRUTUS. Now as you are a Roman, tell me true.

❷ MESSALA. Then like a Roman bear the truth I tell,
For certain she is dead, and by strange manner.

BRUTUS. Why, farewell, Portia. We must die, Messala.
With meditating that she must die once,
I have the patience to endure it now.

MESSALA. Even so great men great losses should endure.

CASSIUS. I have as much of this in art[58] as you,
But yet my nature could not bear it so.

❹ BRUTUS. Well, to our work alive.[59] What do you think
Of marching to Philippi presently?

CASSIUS. I do not think it good.

BRUTUS. Your reason?

CASSIUS. This it is:
'Tis better that the enemy seek us;
So shall he waste his means, weary his soldiers,
Doing himself offense,[60] whilst we, lying still,

54. power: Army.

55. Bending . . . Philippi (fi lip′ ī): Directing their rapid march toward Philippi.

56. selfsame tenure: Same message.

57. aught (ôt) *n.*: Anything at all.

◆ **Reading Strategy** ❸
What can you learn about Brutus' feelings for Portia by reading between the lines?

58. have . . . art: Have as much Stoicism in theory.

59. to our work alive: Let us go about the work we have to do as living men.

60. offense: Harm.

Are full of rest, defense, and nimbleness.

BRUTUS. Good reasons must of force[61] give place to better.
The people 'twixt Philippi and this ground
Do stand but in a forced affection;[62]
For they have grudged us contribution.[63]
The enemy, marching along by them,
By them shall make a fuller number up,[64]
Come on refreshed, new-added[65] and encouraged;
From which advantage shall we cut him off
If at Philippi we do face him there,
These people at our back.

❺ **CASSIUS.** Hear me, good brother.

BRUTUS. Under your pardon.[66] You must note beside
That we have tried the utmost of our friends,
Our legions are brimful, our cause is ripe.
The enemy increaseth every day;
We, at the height, are ready to decline.
There is a tide in the affairs of men
Which, taken at the flood, leads on to fortune;
Omitted,[67] all the voyage of their life
Is bound[68] in shallows and in miseries.
On such a full sea are we now afloat,
And we must take the current when it serves,
Or lose our ventures.

❻ **CASSIUS.** Then, with your will,[69] go on;
We'll along ourselves and meet them at Philippi.

BRUTUS. The deep of night is crept upon our talk,
And nature must obey necessity,
Which we will niggard with a little rest.[70]
There is no more to say?

CASSIUS. No more. Good night.
Early tomorrow will we rise and hence.[71]

[*Enter* LUCIUS.]

BRUTUS. Lucius, my gown.[72] [*Exit* LUCIUS.]
Farewell, good Messala.
Good night, Titinius. Noble, noble Cassius,
Good night, and good repose.

CASSIUS. O my dear brother,
This was an ill beginning of the night.
Never come[73] such division 'tween our souls!
Let it not, Brutus.

[*Enter* LUCIUS, *with the gown.*]

61. of force: Of necessity.

62. Do stand . . . affection: Support us only by fear of force.

63. grudged us contribution: Given us aid and supplies grudgingly.

64. shall make . . . up: Will add more to their numbers.

65. new-added: Reinforced.

66. Under your pardon: Excuse me.

67. Omitted: Neglected.

68. bound: Confined.

69. with your will: As you wish.

70. niggard . . . rest: Satisfy stingily with a short sleep.

71. hence: Leave.

72. gown: Nightgown.

73. Never come: May there never come.

Customize for *Less Proficient Readers*

❺ Help these students summarize Cassius' plan for battle, and then Brutus' plan. *Cassius suggests that they should stay where they are and be fresh for battle, while the enemy will be tired from marching. Brutus thinks they should march to Philippi because the enemy may pick up more forces as they are on the march.* Encourage discussion about which plan is best. Direct them to lines 223–224 to find out which plan will be adopted.

◆ Reading Strategy

❻ Read Between the Lines
Encourage students to find out what they can determine about the relationship between Cassius and Brutus by reading between the lines as they argue their points about different battle strategies. *Students might say that, because Cassius gives in to Brutus, Brutus has more power in the relationship.*

Extending Word Study

Figurative Language Have students read lines 217–223 of Brutus' speech, in which he is using figurative language to compare a person's life with a ship at sea. Encourage students to paraphrase the lines. Have them explain the meaning of the different images. Then ask students to comment on the power of the comparison.

Workplace Skills Mini-Lesson

Providing Input for Decisions

Introduce Refer students to Brutus' and Cassius' conversation on this page about the merits of attacking at Philippi or waiting to be attacked. Draw attention to the manner in which each man presents his points for consideration.

Develop Let students know that in the business world, decisions are frequently made after several people have offered their opinion. Note also that as the level of responsibility of a person increases, so will the rate at which he or she will be asked to express opinions that will affect important decisions. Discuss ways to express opinions in such a situation. Lead students to consider these points:

- When stating an opinion, always have strong reasons that support the opinion.
- Speak in a respectful and rational tone of voice.

Apply Present this scenario: You work for a small store. Your boss tells you she is considering opening on Sundays. She asks for your opinion. Have students work in small groups to provide input into the decision.

Assess Students should evaluate one another on the strength of their opinion, supporting facts, and tone.

◆ Reading Strategy

❶ Read Between the Lines This passage reveals the complexity of Brutus' personality. Have students explain the complexity. *Only a short time ago, Brutus was the man who could put his wife's death out of his mind to discuss a battle plan. In this passage, we see a kinder, gentler side of Brutus' personality.*

Customize for Less Proficient Readers

These students may benefit from acting out portions of these scenes with students taking individual parts. Use the ***Strategies for Diverse Student Needs*** page on Preparing a Reader's Theater, p. 53, to assist these students in preparing.

Customize for Pre-AP Students

Have these students improvise a monologue or write a journal entry that captures Brutus' thoughts and feelings at this point in the play. Encourage students to reference details from the play that affect his situation and his feelings about it.

BRUTUS. Everything is well.

CASSIUS. Good night, my lord.

BRUTUS. Good night, good brother.

TITINIUS, MESSALA. Good night, Lord Brutus.

BRUTUS. Farewell, every one.

[*Exit*]

Give me the gown. Where is thy instrument?[74]

LUCIUS. Here in the tent.

BRUTUS. What, thou speak'st drowsily?
Poor knave,[75] I blame thee not; thou art
❶ o'erwatched.[76]
Call Claudius and some other of my men;
I'll have them sleep on cushions in my tent.

LUCIUS. Varro and Claudius!

[*Enter* VARRO *and* CLAUDIUS.]

VARRO. Calls my lord?

BRUTUS. I pray you, sirs, lie in my tent and sleep.
It may be I shall raise[77] you by and by
On business to my brother Cassius.

VARRO. So please you, we will stand and watch your pleasure.

BRUTUS. I will not have it so; lie down, good sirs;
It may be I shall otherwise bethink me.[78]

[VARRO *and* CLAUDIUS *lie down.*]

Look. Lucius, here's the book I sought for so;
I put it in the pocket of my gown.

LUCIUS. I was sure your lordship did not give it me.

BRUTUS. Bear with me, good boy, I am much forgetful.
Canst thou hold up thy heavy eyes awhile,
And touch[79] thy instrument a strain or two?

LUCIUS. Ay, my lord, an't[80] please you.

BRUTUS. It does, my boy.
I trouble thee too much, but thou art willing.

LUCIUS. It is my duty, sir.

BRUTUS. I should not urge thy duty past thy might;
I know young bloods[81] look for a time of rest.

74. **instrument:** Lute (probably).

75. **knave** (nāv) *n.*: Servant.

76. **o'erwatched:** Weary with too much watchfulness.

77. **raise:** Wake.

78. **otherwise bethink me:** Change my mind.

79. **touch:** Play.

80. **an't:** If it.

81. **young bloods:** Young bodies.

Reteach

Use a graphic like the one shown here to help students understand that a character's internal conflict may affect the external conflict in the plot. In this play, Brutus is torn between his belief that he had to stop Caesar's rise to power and his guilt at having killed him. Since he is an honest man, Brutus is disturbed by what he perceives as Cassius' dishonesty, leading to an external conflict. Encourage students to record other internal and external conflicts throughout the play.

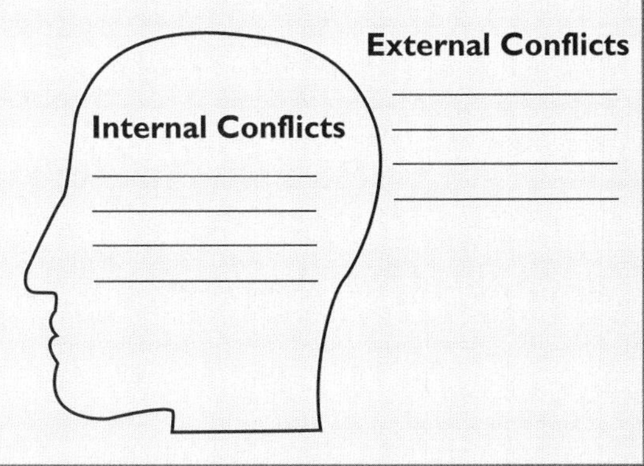

LUCIUS. I have slept, my lord, already.

BRUTUS. It was well done, and thou shalt sleep again;
I will not hold thee long. If I do live,
I will be good to thee.

[*Music, and a song*]

This is a sleepy tune. O murd'rous[82] slumber!
Layest thou thy leaden mace[83] upon my boy,
That plays thee music? Gentle knave, good night;
I will not do thee so much wrong to wake thee.
If thou dost nod, thou break'st thy instrument;
I'll take it from thee; and, good boy, good night.
Let me see, let me see; is not the leaf[84] turned down
Where I left reading? Here it is, I think.

[*Enter the* GHOST OF CAESAR.]

❷ How ill this taper burns. Ha! Who comes here?
I think it is the weakness of mine eyes
That shapes this monstrous apparition.[85]
It comes upon[86] me. Art thou anything?
Art thou some god, some angel, or some devil,
That mak'st my blood cold, and my hair to stare?[87]
Speak to me what thou art.

GHOST. Thy evil spirit, Brutus.

BRUTUS. Why com'st thou?

GHOST. To tell thee thou shalt see me at Philippi.

BRUTUS. Well; then I shall see thee again?

GHOST. Ay, at Philippi.

❹ BRUTUS. Why, I will see thee at Philippi then.

[*Exit* GHOST.]

Now I have taken heart thou vanishest.
Ill spirit, I would hold more talk with thee.
Boy! Lucius! Varro! Claudius! Sirs, awake!
Claudius!

LUCIUS. The strings, my lord, are false.[88]

BRUTUS. He thinks he still is at his instrument.
Lucius, awake!

LUCIUS. My lord?

BRUTUS. Didst thou dream, Lucius, that thou so criedst
out?

82. **murd'rous:** Deathlike.

83. **mace** (mās) *n.*: Staff of office (an allusion to the practice of tapping a person on the shoulder with a mace when arresting him).

84. **leaf:** Page.

85. **monstrous apparition:** Ominous ghost.

86. **upon:** Toward.

87. **stare:** Stand on end.

88. **false:** Out of tune.

◆ **Reading Strategy**
What warning can you discover by reading between the lines? ❸

❷ **Clarification** Brutus remarks that the candle burns "ill." Explain that candles were thought to dim in the presence of ghosts.

◆ Critical Thinking

❸ **Make Inferences** The ghost of Caesar appears to Brutus. Ask: Why does the ghost appear to Brutus? Do you think that Brutus understands the ghost's message? *The ghost is telling Brutus that disaster awaits him at Philippi. Students may suggest that Brutus does not understand the message at first because his response ("Why, I will see thee at Philippi then") seems matter-of-fact. When the ghost vanishes, Brutus realizes that he should have asked for an explanation.*

◆ Reading Strategy

❹ **Read Between the Lines**
Suggested response: *The ghost warns of a meeting at Philippi. This suggests that Brutus may die there.*

Customize for
Visual/Spatial Learners
Encourage these students to consider how best to represent the ghost on stage. Invite them to share their ideas with classmates.

Beyond the Classroom

Career Connection

Music Careers Students who are interested in careers in music should explore the many "backstage" roles in the industry. Sound technicians, electricians, agents, business managers, and others who perform behind the scenes are able to work in an exciting field that interests them, even if they can't sing or play an instrument. Have interested students do research and create a chart showing the many opportunities available in the music industry.

Political Science The events in this play give a negative view of politics and politicians. Point out to students, however, that many people seek public office to do good—to change policy or improve the quality of life in their area. Under our system of government, however, these people can't just take an office; they must be elected or appointed. Have students do research to find the political positions available at the local, state, and national level. Follow up with the Career Connection: Political Science, p. 53, in ***Beyond Literature.***

Reinforce and Extend

Answers

◆ *Literature and Your Life*

Reader's Response Ask students if there is anything about either man that elicits sympathy. Is either one kind, considerate, compassionate, merciful, or worthy of sympathy?

Thematic Focus Example: Brutus will most likely die.

☑ Check Your Comprehension

1. Antony, Octavius, and Lepidus are in control of Rome after the death of Caesar. Antony is the oldest and the strongest personality; Octavius is his right-hand man; Lepidus is only fit for running errands.
2. Cassius is angry because Brutus has condemned Lucius Pella. Cassius defends himself by telling Brutus to kill him, thus putting himself at Brutus' mercy.
3. Portia commits suicide. Brutus accepts her death fatalistically, but Cassius expresses grief.
4. The candle dims, and the ghost of Julius Caesar appears and speaks to Brutus. Brutus speaks with the ghost and asks it not to leave because he wants to talk to it more.

◆ Critical Thinking

1. The argument between Brutus and Cassius is much more emotional in tone than the argument between Octavius and Antony.
2. Brutus may not want Cassius' pity to cloud their discussion, or he may not want to let Cassius know that he is mourning and potentially more vulnerable than usual.
3. The ghost of Caesar is portending the death of Brutus.
4. Students should base their predictions on events that have occurred so far as well as on character traits.
5. Although students may not agree with the actions of each character, they may be able to recognize the leadership qualities in each. Have students explain the qualities that led them to make their choice.

LUCIUS. My lord, I do not know that I did cry.

BRUTUS. Yes, that thou didst. Didst thou see anything?

LUCIUS. Nothing, my lord.

BRUTUS. Sleep again, Lucius. Sirrah Claudius!
[*To* VARRO] Fellow thou, awake!

VARRO. My lord?

CLAUDIUS. My lord?

BOTH. Why did you so cry out, sirs, in your sleep?

BRUTUS. Did we, my lord?

BRUTUS. Ay. Saw you anything?

VARRO. No, my lord, I saw nothing.

CLAUDIUS. Nor I, my lord.

BRUTUS. Go and commend me[89] to my brother Cassius;
Bid him set on his pow'rs betimes before,[90]
And we will follow.

BOTH. It shall be done, my lord. [*Exit*]

89. commend me: Carry my greetings.
90. set on . . . before: Advance his troops.

Guide for Responding

◆ *Literature and Your Life*

Reader's Response With whom do you sympathize more in Act IV—Brutus or Cassius? Why?

Thematic Focus What consequences do you think Brutus will face for the choices he has made?

☑ Check Your Comprehension

1. What three men rule Rome after Caesar's death? Describe each of them.
2. What is the immediate cause of the quarrel between Brutus and Cassius? How does Cassius defend himself?
3. How does Portia die? Describe Brutus' and Cassius' reactions to the death.
4. What supernatural event occurs at the end of the act? Describe Brutus' reaction to the event.

◆ Critical Thinking

INTERPRET

1. How is the argument between Brutus and Cassius different from the one between Octavius and Antony in Scene i? **[Contrast]**
2. Why do you think Brutus delays telling Cassius of Portia's death? **[Infer]**
3. What does the ghost mean when he says to Brutus, "Thou shalt see me at Philippi"? **[Draw Conclusions]**
4. Who do you think will be the victor in the upcoming battle? Explain. **[Speculate]**

EVALUATE

5. Which character in this act do you feel would make the best leader for Rome? Explain. **[Assess]**

☑ ASSESSMENT OPTIONS

Formal Assessment, Selection Test, pp. 185–187, and Assessment Resources Software. The selection test is designed so that it can be easily customized to the ability levels of your students.

PORTFOLIO ASSESSMENT
Use the following rubrics in ***Alternative Assessment*** to assess student writing.
Character Profile: Description Rubric, p. 97
Rewrite a Scene: Drama Rubric, p. 109

Guide for Responding *(continued)*

◆ Reading Strategy

Read Between the Lines

Shakespeare provides clues that indicate a deeper meaning to some lines—but you have to **read between the lines** to find the clues.

For instance, in the middle of the act, when Brutus and Cassius are arguing, Brutus says, "Remember March, the ides of March remember." What he is really referring to is the assassination of Caesar, though he does not say so explicitly in this line.

1. In Scene iii, Brutus says to Cassius, "You yourself / Are much condemned to have an itching palm, / To sell and mart your offices for gold / To undeservers." What is Brutus saying about Cassius' character?

2. By reading between the lines of the conversations between Brutus and Cassius, what hints can you find that they will probably be defeated at Philippi?

◆ Build Vocabulary

Using the Greek Root *-phil-*

The Greek root *-phil-* means "love." It is a common root of English words. On your paper, write the word with the root *-phil-* that correctly completes each sentence.

1. __?__ could be called a "love of wisdom."

2. A __?__ is a person who donates money to one or more charitable organizations.

3. __?__ is a city whose name means "city of brotherly love."

Using the Word Bank: Sentence Completions

Copy the following sentences into your notebook, and complete each sentence with a word from the Word Bank.

1. In an atmosphere of suspicion, Antony and Octavius make __?__ plans.

2. Cassius denies the __?__ accusations that Brutus reports have been made against Cassius.

3. Antony requests to see Caesar's will to begin sorting and carrying out Caesar's __?__.

4. Stoicism was the __?__ Brutus followed.

5. Brutus' __?__ of Cassius for allowing bribery leads to a bitter argument.

◆ Literary Focus

Conflict in Drama

As Brutus and Cassius prepare for battle, it becomes increasingly clear that their efforts are doomed. The outcome of the battle will resolve the **conflict** between the two political forces.

1. What have you known about Cassius that Brutus just begins to realize in this act?

2. How does the conflict between Cassius and Brutus heighten the tension of the larger conflict to come?

◆ Build Grammar Skills

Noun Clauses

A **noun clause** is a subordinate clause used as a noun. It can function as a subject, predicate noun, direct object, indirect object, or object of a preposition.

Practice On your paper write these sentences and underline the noun clause in each one. Then identify its function in the sentence.

1. Brutus says that he is Caesar's friend.

2. What he does is shocking to Caesar.

3. Do what you will.

4. You must note beside / That we have tried the utmost of our friends.

Idea Bank

Writing

1. Character Profile Write a profile of Brutus as if for a magazine-style news program. Include interviews with friends, "coworkers," and family members.

2. Rewrite a Scene Write another scene for Act IV, in which Portia's ghost confronts Brutus.

Speaking, Listening, and Viewing

3. Presentation Use an encyclopedia to research the philosophical movement called Stoicism, and determine which character in the play best embodies its teachings. Explain your choice in a class presentation. **[History Link]**

◆ Reading Strategy

1. He is saying that Cassius has a reputation for taking bribes. Students might read between the lines that Brutus is inclined to believe what he has heard.
2. The unstated message that students can read between the lines is that the public doesn't support the two men, that each of the men has doubts about their ability to succeed, that the men have doubts about each other that will make it difficult for them to present a united front.

◆ Build Vocabulary

Using the Greek Root *-phil-*

1. Philosophy could be called a love of wisdom.
2. A philanthropist is a person who donates money to one or more charitable organizations.
3. Philadelphia is a city whose name means "city of brotherly love."

Using the Word Bank

1. covert
2. slanderous
3. legacies
4. philosophy
5. chastisement

◆ Literary Focus

1. Students probably recognized long before Brutus did that Cassius is not noble; he is a devious man motivated by self-promotion and preservation.
2. The conflict between Cassius and Brutus heightens the sense that everything is falling apart. Even the conspirators are fighting with one another.

◆ Build Grammar Skills

1. that he is Caesar's friend: direct object
2. What he does: subject
3. What you will: direct object
4. That we have tried: direct object

Idea Bank

Customizing for
Learning Modalities

The following suggestions will help you match Idea Bank topics to your students' learning modalities:
Musical Rhythmic: 3
Verbal/Linguistic: 1, 2
Interpersonal: 1

Customizing for
Performance Levels

Following are suggestions for matching Idea Bank topics with your students' performance levels:
Less Advanced: 1, 3
Average: 1, 2, 3
More Advanced: 2

Prepare and Engage

LESSON OBJECTIVES

1. **To develop vocabulary and word identification skills**
   - Anglo-Saxon Prefixes: *mis-*
   - Using the Word Bank: Synonyms
   - Extending Word Study: Context
2. **To use a variety of reading strategies to read and comprehend an essay**
   - Connect Your Experience
   - Reading Strategy: Identify Cause and Effect
   - Read to Be Informed
3. **To increase knowledge of other cultures and to connect common elements across cultures**
   - Cultural Connection: The World's Shakespeare
4. **To express and support responses to the text**
   - Critical Thinking
   - Idea Bank: Epitaph
   - Idea Bank: Take a Side
   - Idea Bank: View a Play
5. **To analyze literary elements**
   - Literary Focus: Tragedy
6. **To read in order to research self-selected and assigned topics**
   - Idea Bank: Model of the Globe
   - Idea Bank: Elizabethan Faire
   - Research Skills Mini-Lesson: Elizabethan Faire
7. **To plan, prepare, organize, and present literary interpretations**
   - Idea Bank: Response
   - Idea Bank: Sound Effects
   - Speaking, Listening, and Viewing Mini-Lesson: Sound Effects
8. **To use recursive writing processes to write a speech**
   - Guided Writing Lesson
9. **To increase knowledge of the rules of grammar and usage**
   - Build Grammar Skills: Words of Direct Address

Test Preparation

Reading Comprehension: Identify Patterns of Organization (ATE, p. 789) The teaching tips and sample test item in this workshop support the instruction and practice in the unit workshop:

Reading Comprehension: Characteristics of Text (SE, p. 809)

Guide for Reading, Act V

◆ Review and Anticipate

In Act IV, the alliance between Brutus and Cassius begins to fall apart. Brutus accuses Cassius of accepting bribes, and Cassius criticizes Brutus' abilities as a leader in war. After they resolve their differences, Brutus is visited by Caesar's ghost, who promises he will see him at Philippi.

Act V opens on the plains of Philippi with the armies of Octavius and Antony amassed against those of Brutus and Cassius. As the defenders of Caesar's legacy prepare to battle his assassins, nothing less than the future of Rome is at stake.

◆ Literary Focus

TRAGEDY

Tragedy is a dramatic form that was first defined around 330 B.C. by the Greek philosopher Aristotle. The main character in a tragedy is involved in a struggle that ends in disaster. This character is always a person of high rank whose ruin is caused by a tragic flaw or weakness. The tragic flaw may be excessive ambition, pride, jealousy, or some other common human frailty. The flaw inevitably leads to the character's downfall. As this play unfolds, Brutus' blindness to the true motives of the other conspirators leads him into disastrous alliances and actions. His downfall is tragic because he is a noble man (as stated by Antony at the end of this act) who did the wrong thing for the right reason.

◆ Build Grammar Skills

WORDS OF DIRECT ADDRESS

Dialogue is the backbone of any drama: With the exceptions of asides and soliloquies, the characters are always speaking to one another. When the playwright wants to emphasize to whom a character is speaking, he or she will set off these **words of direct address** with commas and occasionally an exclamation point. Look at these examples from Act V:

Now, *Antony,* our hopes are answered . . .

Stand fast, *Titinius,* we must out and talk . . .

Villains! You did not do so, when your vile daggers / Hacked . . .

Notice the words of direct address that clarify to whom a character is speaking.

◆ Reading Strategy

IDENTIFY CAUSE AND EFFECT

Dramatic situations have both causes and effects. A **cause** is what makes something occur; an **effect** is the result. Plays are carefully constructed with a chain of causes and effects that lead to the final tragic outcome.

Caesar's actions, which Brutus perceives as showing too much ambition, are the cause of Brutus' decision to join the conspiracy. The effect is Caesar's death.

You can track interlocking causes and effects in *The Tragedy of Julius Caesar* with a graphic organizer like the following:

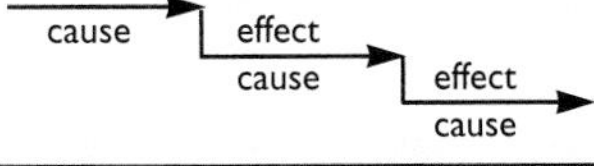

◆ Build Vocabulary

ANGLO-SAXON PREFIXES: *mis-*

In this act you will encounter the word *misconstrue,* which contains the Anglo-Saxon prefix *mis-,* meaning "wrong" or "bad." *Misconstrue* means "make the wrong interpretation."

WORD BANK

Before you read, preview this list of words from Act V.

presage
ensign
consorted
demeanor
disconsolate
misconstrued
envy

Prentice Hall Literature Program Resources

REINFORCE / RETEACH / EXTEND

Selection Support Pages
Build Vocabulary: Prefixes: *mis-*, p. 220
Build Grammar Skills: Words of Direct Address, p. 221
Reading Strategy: Identify Cause and Effect, p. 222
Literary Focus: Tragedy, p. 223

Strategies for Diverse Student Needs, p. 54

Beyond Literature
Workplace Connection: Leadership Skills, p. 54

Formal Assessment Selection Test, pp. 188–189; Assessment Resources Software

Alternative Assessment, p. 54

Resource Pro CD-ROM

Listening to Literature Audiocassettes

The Tragedy of

JULIUS CAESAR

William Shakespeare

Act V

Scene i. *The plains of Philippi.*

[*Enter* OCTAVIUS, ANTONY, *and their Army.*]

❶

OCTAVIUS. Now, Antony, our hopes are answerèd;
You said the enemy would not come down,
But keep the hills and upper regions.
It proves not so; their battles[1] are at hand;
They mean to warn[2] us at Philippi here,
Answering before we do demand of them.[3]

ANTONY. Tut, I am in their bosoms,[4] and I know
Wherefore[5] they do it. They could be content
To visit other places, and come down
With fearful bravery,[6] thinking by this face[7]
To fasten in our thoughts[8] that they have courage;
But 'tis not so.

1. **battles:** Armies.
2. **warn:** Challenge.
3. **Answering . . . of them:** Appearing in opposition to us before we challenge them.
4. **am in their bosoms:** Know what they are thinking.
5. **Wherefore:** Why.
6. **fearful bravery:** Awesome show of bravery covering up their fear.
7. **face**: Appearance.
8. **fasten in our thoughts:** Convince us.

❷ ▼ Critical Viewing What details in this sculpture indicate that the subjects are preparing for battle? **[Analyze]**

Relief of Domitius Ahenobarbus, Louvre, Paris, France

Develop Understanding

Act V of *Julius Caesar* resolves the conflict between the triumvirate (Octavius Caesar, Antony, and Lepidus) and Brutus and Cassius at the battle of Philippi. Although his tragic flaw—poor judgment—leads to his downfall, Brutus maintains his nobility and courage to the end.

Customize for
Less Proficient Readers

Many new minor characters are introduced in this final act. Keeping all the names straight may be challenging for these students. Suggest that they make an alphabetical "Cast of Characters" to keep as they read.

Customize for
English Language Learners

Have these students listen to Act V on the recording, as they follow along in the text. Help them summarize the action in each scene.

Listening to Literature Audiocassettes

◆ Critical Thinking

❶ **Make Judgments** Based on this passage, who do students now think was right about the plan of attack—Cassius or Brutus? How do students think the battle will turn out? *Because Octavius says "our hopes are answered," and Antony says that he knows what Cassius and Brutus are thinking, one can assume that Brutus' plan—the one they adopted—was wrong. Antony and Octavius will probably win the battle.*

▶Critical Viewing◀

❷ **Analyze** *Suggested response: The shields, swords, armor, and helmets suggest preparation for battle.*

Test Preparation Workshop

Reading Comprehension: Identify Patterns of Organization

Standardized tests often require students to analyze the characteristics of a text. Help students be aware of words that offer clues to a passage's pattern of organization by introducing the following sample test item:

> The main character of a tragedy is always a person of high rank whose ruin is caused by a tragic flaw such as ambition, pride, jealousy. As this play unfolds, Brutus' blindness leads him into disastrous alliances.

Which pattern of organization does the passage demonstrate?

A Cause and effect
B General to specific
C Chronological
D Specific to general

Guide students to see that a reference to Brutus' flaw serves as an example of the first sentence. The correct response is *A*.

◆ Build Grammar Skills

❶ **Words of Direct Address** Ask students: To whom is the messenger speaking? How do you know? *The messenger is addressing the generals. Readers know this because the word "generals," set off by commas, is included in the sentence.*

◆ Literary Focus

❷ **Tragedy** Sample answer: Brutus' words are tragic because he did not use words with Caesar; Antony heightens the tragedy by reminding Brutus how Caesar trusted his loving and loyal words.

◆ Critical Thinking

❸ **Infer** Discuss with the class how Antony feels toward Brutus and why he feel this way. *Anthony is angry with Brutus for his part in assassinating Caesar. He points out the fatal hypocrisy of Brutus, who appeared to honor Caesar right up to the moment he stabbed him.*

Customize for *Pre-AP Students*

Have students analyze the exchange between the opposing generals. Ask them to describe the various insults, boasts, and threats the four men make to one another.

[*Enter a* MESSENGER.]

❶ MESSENGER. Prepare you, generals,
The enemy comes on in gallant show;
Their bloody sign[9] of battle is hung out,
And something to be done immediately.

ANTONY. Octavius, lead your battle softly[10] on
Upon the left hand of the even[11] field.

OCTAVIUS. Upon the right hand I; keep thou the left.

ANTONY. Why do you cross me in this exigent?[12]

OCTAVIUS. I do not cross you; but I will do so. [*March*]

[*Drum. Enter* BRUTUS, CASSIUS, *and their Army;* LUCILIUS, TITINIUS, MESSALA, *and others.*]

BRUTUS. They stand, and would have parley.[13]

CASSIUS. Stand fast, Titinius, we must out and talk.

OCTAVIUS. Mark Antony, shall we give sign of battle?

ANTONY. No, Caesar, we will answer on their charge.[14]
Make forth;[15] the generals would have some words.

OCTAVIUS. Stir not until the signal.

BRUTUS. Words before blows; is it so, countrymen?

OCTAVIUS. Not that we love words better, as you do.

BRUTUS. Good words are better than bad strokes, Octavius.

❸ ANTONY. In your bad strokes, Brutus, you give good words;
Witness the hole you made in Caesar's heart,
Crying "Long live! Hail, Caesar!"

CASSIUS. Antony,
The posture[16] of your blows are yet unknown;
But for your words, they rob the Hybla bees,[17]
And leave them honeyless.

ANTONY. Not stingless too.

BRUTUS. O, yes, and soundless too;
For you have stol'n their buzzing, Antony,
And very wisely threat before you sting.

ANTONY. Villains! You did not so, when your vile daggers
Hacked one another in the sides of Caesar.
You showed your teeth[18] like apes, and fawned like hounds,

9. **bloody sign:** Red flag.

10. **softly:** Slowly.

11. **even:** Level.

12. **exigent:** Critical situation.

13. **parley:** Conference between enemies.

14. **answer on their charge:** Meet their advance.

15. **Make forth:** Go forward.

◆ **Literary Focus** Why are Brutus' words in line 29 tragic? How does Antony's reply highlight the tragedy? ❷

16. **posture:** Quality.

17. **Hybla bees:** Bees, from the town of Hybla in Sicily, noted for their sweet honey.

18. **showed your teeth:** Grinned.

Block Scheduling Strategies

Consider these suggestions to take advantage of extended class time:

- Treat students to readings from Shakespeare's sonnets and plays included in Feature 3 on the CD-ROM *The Time, Life, and Works of Shakespeare.*
- Have students research Shakespeare on the Internet either before or after they complete the play. See pp. 707 and 800 for an Internet address they can access.
- Students can pair up to complete the Build Grammar Skills lesson on p. 802.
- A group can listen to all or part of this act on the audiocassette. Suggest that students discuss how hearing the play performed affected their appreciation and their ability to follow the language of the play.

And bowed like bondmen, kissing Caesar's feet;
Whilst damnèd Casca, like a cur, behind
Struck Caesar on the neck. O you flatterers!

❹ **CASSIUS.** Flatterers! Now, Brutus, thank yourself;
This tongue had not offended so today,
❺ If Cassius might have ruled.[19]

❻ **OCTAVIUS.** Come, come, the cause.[20] If arguing make us sweat,
The proof[21] of it will turn to redder drops.
Look,
I draw a sword against conspirators.
When think you that the sword goes up[22] again?
Never, till Caesar's three and thirty wounds
Be well avenged; or till another Caesar
Have added slaughter to the sword of traitors.[23]

❼ **BRUTUS.** Caesar, thou canst not die by traitors' hands,
Unless thou bring'st them with thee.

OCTAVIUS. So I hope.
I was not born to die on Brutus' sword.

BRUTUS. O, if thou wert the noblest of thy strain,[24]
Young man, thou couldst not die more honorable.

CASSIUS. A peevish[25] schoolboy, worthless of such honor,
Joined with a masker and a reveler.[26]

ANTONY. Old Cassius still!

OCTAVIUS. Come, Antony; away!
Defiance, traitors, hurl we in your teeth.
If you dare fight today, come to the field;
If not, when you have stomachs.[27]

[*Exit* OCTAVIUS, ANTONY, *and Army.*]

CASSIUS. Why, now blow wind, swell billow, and swim bark![28]
The storm is up, and all is on the hazard.[29]

BRUTUS. Ho, Lucilius, hark, a word with you.

[LUCILIUS *and* MESSALA *stand forth.*]

LUCILIUS. My lord?

[BRUTUS *and* LUCILIUS *converse apart.*]

CASSIUS. Messala.

MESSALA. What says my general?

19. If Cassius might have ruled: If Cassius had had his way when he urged that Antony be killed.
20. cause: Business at hand.
21. proof: Test.

22. goes up: Goes into its scabbard.

23. till another Caesar . . . traitors: Until I, another Caesar, have also been killed by you.

24. noblest of thy strain: Best of your family.

25. peevish: Silly.

26. a masker and a reveler: One who takes part in masquerades and festivities.

27. stomachs: Appetites for battle.

28. bark: Ship.

29. on the hazard: At stake.

◆ Reading Strategy

❹ **Identify Cause and Effect** Recall with students Brutus' earlier decision not to kill Antony as well as Caesar. Invite them to conjecture how the opposite decision would have changed the course of events. *The effect of not killing Antony is the battle that is about to be fought. If the conspirators had gotten Antony out of the way, they may have "gotten away" with killing Caesar.*

◆ Literary Focus

❺ **Tragedy** Lead students to contrast Brutus with Cassius. What difference in their personalities led Cassius to suggest killing Antony, while Brutus would not agree? Why is Brutus considered a tragic hero, but not Cassius? *By contrast with Cassius, Brutus is more honorable and noble, and therefore more tragic. Brutus' acceptance of Cassius is a sign of Brutus' tragic flaw—he is blind to Cassius' envious and self-serving nature.*

Comprehension Check ☑

❻ What does Octavius mean by these lines? *"Let's get to the point. If arguing makes us sweat, fighting it out will make us bleed."*

◆ Literary Focus

❼ **Tragedy** Help students understand the significance of these lines, in which Brutus says that Octavius cannot be killed by a traitor because neither Brutus nor Cassius is a traitor. Discuss with students why Shakespeare keeps reminding readers that Brutus does not consider himself a traitor. *If Brutus had killed Caesar for any other but a patriotic reason, he would not stand up as a tragic hero. He would be a traitor and a murderer.*

Viewing and Representing Mini-Lesson

Model of the Globe

This mini-lesson supports the first Researching and Representing activity in the Idea Bank on p. 803.

Introduce Students may know that most of Shakespeare's plays were produced in the Globe theater, which was very different from modern theaters. There were no lights and no scenery, making it necessary for changes in setting to be indicated by characters' words.

Develop Encourage students to begin research by reading pp. 706–707 of their textbooks. They can find more information on the Internet, in encyclopedias, and in books on theater. Suggest they look for details on how actors entered the stage and where the audience sat.

Apply As students build a model of the Globe, encourage them to imagine scenes in Julius Caesar being performed. They can write a description of one scene as it might have appeared on the stage.

Assess Evaluate students' work based on accuracy of the model.

Customize for *English Language Learners*

❶ Guide students to see that Cassius is using metaphors—literary comparisons—to suggest the fierce battle to come. Be sure students understand that his words are not to be taken literally. Students may wish to share some metaphors or idioms from their native languages.

◆ Reading Strategy

❷ **Identify Cause and Effect** Sample answer: Cassius is nervous because he has seen a bad omen. Students may suggest that the effects of his nervousness include his conflict with Brutus and a potentially poor performance on the battlefield.

◆ Build Grammar Skills

❸ **Words of Direct Address** Ask students: To whom is Cassius speaking? How do the commas help you know how to read the lines aloud? *Cassius is speaking to Brutus. The commas signal a pause before and after "most noble Brutus."*

❹ **Clarification** Explain that Brutus is saying he does not believe in taking his own life, rather than waiting for death as ordained by fate. However, if the only alternative is to walk back to Rome as a captive, he would take his life.

❺ **Clarification** Explain that Cato (Portia's father) was on Pompey's side during the civil war between Caesar and Pompey. Cato committed suicide at the battle of Utica in 46 B.C. rather than fall into captivity.

CASSIUS. Messala,
This is my birthday; as this very day
Was Cassius born. Give me thy hand, Messala:
Be thou my witness that against my will
(As Pompey was)[30] am I compelled to set[31]
Upon one battle all our liberties.
You know that I held Epicurus strong,[32]
And his opinion; now I change my mind,
And partly credit things that do presage.
❶ Coming from Sardis, on our former[33] ensign
Two mighty eagles fell,[34] and there they perched,
Gorging and feeding from our soldiers' hands,
Who to Philippi here consorted us.
This morning are they fled away and gone,
And in their steads do ravens, crows, and kites[35]
Fly o'er our heads and downward look on us
As we were sickly prey; their shadows seem
A canopy most fatal,[36] under which
Our army lies, ready to give up the ghost.

MESSALA. Believe not so.

CASSIUS. I but believe it partly,
For I am fresh of spirit and resolved
To meet all perils very constantly.[37]

BRUTUS. Even so, Lucilius.

CASSIUS. Now, most noble Brutus,
❸ The gods today stand friendly, that we may,
Lovers in peace, lead on our days to age!
But since the affairs of men rest still incertain,[38]
Let's reason with the worst that may befall.[39]
If we do lose this battle, then is this
The very last time we shall speak together.
What are you then determinèd to do?

BRUTUS. Even by the rule of that philosophy
By which I did blame Cato for the death
Which he did give himself; I know not how,
❹ But I do find it cowardly and vile,
❺ For fear of what might fall, so to prevent
The time of life,[40] arming myself with patience
To stay the providence[41] of some high powers
That govern us below.

CASSIUS. Then, if we lose this battle,
You are contented to be led in triumph[42]
Thorough[43] the streets of Rome?

BRUTUS. No, Cassius, no; think not, thou noble Roman,

30. As Pompey was: Against his own judgment, Pompey was urged to do battle against Caesar. The battle resulted in Pompey's defeat and murder.
31. set: Stake.
32. held Epicurus strong: Believed in Epicurus' philosophy that the gods do not interest themselves in human affairs and that omens are merely superstitions.
33. former: Foremost.
34. fell: Swooped down.

◆ **Reading Strategy** What is the cause of Cassius' nervousness? What might its effect be? ❷

35. ravens . . . kites: Birds that are bad omens.
36. A canopy most fatal: A rooflike covering foretelling death.
37. very constantly: Most resolutely.
38. rest still incertain: Always remain uncertain.
39. befall: Happen.

40. so to prevent . . . life: Thus to anticipate the natural end of life.
41. stay the providence: Await the ordained fate.
42. in triumph: As a captive in the victor's procession.
43. Thorough: Through.

That ever Brutus will go bound to Rome;
He bears too great a mind. But this same day
Must end that work the ides of March begun;
And whether we shall meet again I know not.
Therefore our everlasting farewell take.
Forever, and forever, farewell, Cassius!
If we do meet again, why, we shall smile;
If not, why then this parting was well made.

CASSIUS. Forever, and forever, farewell, Brutus!
If we do meet again, we'll smile indeed;
If not, 'tis true this parting was well made.

BRUTUS. Why then, lead on. O, that a man might know
The end of this day's business ere it come!
But it sufficeth that the day will end,
And then the end is known. Come, ho! Away! [*Exit*]

◆ *Literature and Your Life*
Do you think people should prepare for the worst or expect the best? ❻

Scene ii. *The field of battle.*

[*Call to arms sounds. Enter* BRUTUS *and* MESSALA.]

BRUTUS. Ride, ride, Messala, ride, and give these bills[1]
Unto the legions on the other side.[2]
[*Loud call to arms*]
Let them set on at once; for I perceive
But cold demeanor[3] in Octavius' wing,
And sudden push gives them the overthrow,[4]
Ride, ride, Messala! Let them all come down.[5] [*Exit*]

1. **bills:** Written orders.
2. **other side:** Wing of the army commanded by Cassius.
3. **cold demeanor:** (di mēn′ ər): Lack of spirit in their conduct.
4. **sudden push . . . overthrow:** Sudden attack will defeat them.
5. **Let . . . down:** Attack all at once.

Scene iii. *The field of battle.*

[*Calls to arms sound. Enter* CASSIUS *and* TITINIUS.]

CASSIUS. O, look, Titinius, look, the villains[1] fly!
Myself have to mine own turned enemy.[2]
This ensign here of mine was turning back;
I slew the coward, and did take it[3] from him.

TITINIUS. O Cassius, Brutus gave the word too early,
Who, having some advantage on Octavius,
Took it too eagerly; his soldiers fell to spoil,[4] ❼
Whilst we by Antony are all enclosed.

[*Enter* PINDARUS.]

PINDARUS. Fly further off, my lord, fly further off!
Mark Antony is in your tents, my lord.
Fly, therefore, noble Cassius, fly far off!

CASSIUS. This hill is far enough. Look, look, Titinius!
Are those my tents where I perceive the fire?

TITINIUS. They are, my lord.

1. **villains:** His own men.
2. **Myself . . . enemy:** I have become an enemy to my own soldiers.
3. **it:** Banner or standard.
4. **fell to spoil:** Began to loot.

◆ Build Vocabulary

presage (prē sāj′) *v.*: Warn of a future event

ensign (en′ s'n) *n.*: Old word for a standard bearer; one who carries a flag

consorted (kän sôr tid) *v.*: Joined; accompanied

demeanor (di mēn ər) *n.*: Behavior

◆ *Literature and Your Life*

❻ Encourage students to support their answers with examples from movies, literature, and life. Some students may not be comfortable sharing personal details. Make clear to students that they can use examples from fiction.

Comprehension Check ☑

❼ What mistake did Brutus make? *Brutus gave the victory signal to his men too soon. Having overcome Octavius, they began plundering the enemy camp instead of coming to the aid of Cassius' men when they were surrounded by Antony's forces.*

Extending Word Study

Context Have students determine the meaning of *sufficeth,* line 124, by using context clues. Ask them what the modern spelling of the word is.

Customize for *Gifted/Talented Students*

Remind students that a play is meant to be seen. Readers who cannot view the action may have trouble keeping track of who is—and is not—on stage at any given time. Suggest to students that they can sketch simple diagrams indicating the placement and movement of onstage characters.

Cross-Curricular Connection: History

Pompey Early in *Julius Caesar,* Marullus asks a mob, "Knew you not Pompey?" He means the Roman general Pompey the Great (106-48 B.C.), once an ally of Caesar, and later, the last obstacle Caesar had to overcome in his rise to power.

Pompey grew up in a wealthy Roman family, in a time of warfare between two generals, Gaius Marius and Lucius Sulla. Still in his twenties, he raised an army of three legions, allied himself with Sulla, and beat Marius. The Senate sent him to Spain, where he defeated Marius' followers.

A string of victories made Pompey a hero to the public, but a threat to the Senate, which feared that they could not control such a hero. In 60 B.C., Pompey, Julius Caesar, and Marcus Crassus formed what became known as the First Triumvirate, to resist the Senate's antimilitarism.

Pompey started to worry about Caesar's growing power and broke with him, leading to civil war. Pompey's army lost two battles to Caesar. After the second, in 48 B.C., Pompey escaped to Egypt, but was killed by order of the Roman-dominated Egyptian government.

◆ Critical Thinking

1 Interpret Ask students to explain the point Cassius is making in this short speech. *Cassius says that he is going to die on his birthday. He compares his life to a journey at the end of which he has returned to the spot where he began. The image of a journey is strengthened by Brutus' mention of a compass.*

◆ Reading Strategy

2 Identify Cause and Effect Have students explain what causes Cassius to order Pindarus to kill him. *Cassius believes he has caused his friend Titinius to be captured by Antony's legions.*

◆ Literary Focus

3 Tragedy Invite students to discuss why they do, or do not, view Cassius' death as tragic. *Students should note that Cassius' death is not tragic because Cassius is not a tragic figure. In Act IV, Shakespeare deliberately shows that he was involved in shady dealings, and earlier in the play he was shown as being scheming and envious. His nature is not noble enough for his death to be considered tragic.*

CASSIUS. Titinius, if thou lovest me,
Mount thou my horse and hide[5] thy spurs in him
Till he have brought thee up to yonder troops
And here again, that I may rest assured
Whether yond troops are friend or enemy.

TITINIUS. I will be here again even with a thought.[6] [*Exit*]

CASSIUS. Go, Pindarus, get higher on that hill;
My sight was ever thick.[7] Regard[8] Titinius,
And tell me what thou not'st about the field.

[*Exit* PINDARUS.]

1 This day I breathèd first. Time is come round,
And where I did begin, there shall I end.
My life is run his compass.[9] Sirrah, what news?

PINDARUS. [*Above*] O my lord!

CASSIUS. What news?

PINDARUS. [*Above*] Titinius is enclosèd round about
With horsemen that make to him on the spur;[10]
Yet he spurs on. Now they are almost on him.
Now, Titinius! Now some light.[11] O, he lights too!
He's ta'en![12] [*Shout*] And, hark! They shout for joy.

CASSIUS. Come down; behold no more.
O, coward that I am, to live so long,
To see my best friend ta'en before my face!

[*Enter* PINDARUS.]

Come hither, sirrah.
In Parthia did I take thee prisoner;
And then I swore thee, saving of thy life,
That whatsoever I did bid thee do,
Thou shouldst attempt it. Come now, keep thine oath.
3 Now be a freeman, and with this good sword,
That ran through Caesar's bowels, search[13] this bosom.
Stand not[14] to answer. Here, take thou the hilts,
And when my face is covered, as 'tis now,
Guide thou the sword—Caesar, thou art revenged,
Even with the sword that killed thee. [*Dies*]

PINDARUS. So, I am free; yet would not so have been,
Durst I have done my will. O Cassius!
Far from this country Pindarus shall run,
Where never Roman shall take note of him. [*Exit*]

5. **hide:** Sink.
6. **even with a thought:** As quick as a thought.
7. **thick:** Dim.
8. **Regard:** Observe.
9. **his compass:** Its full course.
10. **make . . . spur:** Ride toward him at top speed.
11. **light:** Dismount from their horses.
12. **ta'en:** Taken; captured.
13. **search:** Penetrate.
14. **Stand not:** Do not wait.

◆ Reading Strategy What is the cause of Cassius' request? What might be some effects of Pindarus fulfilling the request? 2

Speaking, Listening, and Viewing Mini-Lesson

Sound Effects
This mini-lesson supports the Speaking, Listening, and Viewing activity in Idea Bank on p. 803.

Introduce Lead students to note that sound effects add color and realism to a scene, but should not distract the audience's attention from the dialogue, or drown out dialogue.

Develop Invite discussion about how sound effects add to enjoyment and appreciation of a performance.

Students can consider these questions:

- Where can the text use sound effects?
- How will each sound effect be created?

Apply Students can experiment with sound effects while other students read portions of the play aloud. For presentations, sound effects may be live or recorded on tape. If possible, record all readings with sound effects.

Assess Have students evaluate how well the sound effects enhanced the scenes. They should point out places where the effects distracted from or drowned out the reading.

4 5 ▲ **Critical Viewing** This battle is the outcome of events that were set in motion earlier in the play. What is the original cause that leads to this battle? **[Analyze]**

[*Enter* TITINIUS *and* MESSALA.]

MESSALA. It is but change,[15] Titinius; for Octavius
Is overthrown by noble Brutus' power,
As Cassius' legions are by Antony.

6 TITINIUS. These tidings will well comfort Cassius.

MESSALA. Where did you leave him?

TITINIUS. All disconsolate,
With Pindarus his bondman, on this hill.

15. **change:** An exchange.

◆ **Build Vocabulary**

disconsolate (dis kän′ sə lit) *adj.*: So unhappy that nothing will comfort

▶Critical Viewing◀

4 **Analyze** *Suggested response: The ultimate cause of the battle is the conflict between two factions: those who believe in the republic and those who were in favor of making Caesar emperor.*

Customize for *Visual/Spatial Learners*

5 Use the picture on this page to help visual/spatial learners understand what a confusing scene a battle is and how Cassius misinterpreted the action he viewed. Ask students if they can tell who is winning the battle pictured here. *Most students will not be able to find details to support the claim that either side is winning. They should be able to relate their own confusion to Cassius' misinterpretation of events.*

Comprehension Check ☑

6 How was Pindarus' report false? *Titinius has returned; therefore, there was no reason for Cassius to die.*

Read to Be Informed

Ask students what they learn from Messala's speech. *Cassius and Brutus are not fully defeated, as Cassius fears.*

Cross-Curricular Connection: History

Octavius Caesar Julius Caesar failed to become the first Roman emperor; that honor fell to his chosen heir, *Octavius Caesar* (63 B.C.–A.D. 14), in 27 B.C. He took the name *Augustus* (Latin for "The Exalted").

When Julius was assassinated in 44 B.C., Octavius, nineteen, hurried to Rome to assert his rights as Julius' heir. He joined forces with Julius' former chief lieutenant, Mark Antony, who had taken control of Rome after the assassination.

They ruled with general Marcus Lepidus as a triumvirate, which controlled Rome after their forces beat those of Brutus and Cassius in 42 B.C.

The triumvirate fell apart. Lepidus was made to retire. Antony, who ruled Rome's eastern provinces, joined with the queen of Egypt, Cleopatra, to fight Octavius for domination of Rome, but their fleet was sunk in 31 B.C., in the Battle of Actium, leaving Octavius in complete control.

As Emperor Augustus, Octavius was an energetic ruler, who expanded the empire, strengthened the army, and built up the city of Rome. He himself said, "I found Rome brick and left it marble."

◆ Build Vocabulary

❶ Prefixes: *mis-* Point out that *mistrust* contains the prefix *mis-*. Ask students: What does this prefix add to your understanding of the meaning of the word *mistrust*? *Added to the root "trust," "mistrust" means "do not trust," as in "I mistrust (do not trust) him."*

◆ Reading Strategy

❷ Identify Cause and Effect Ask students to predict what effect Pindarus' false report might have on Titinius. *Pindarus' report that Titinius had been captured caused Cassius to kill himself, believing Titinius' capture to be his fault. Students may say that Cassius' death, in turn may cause Titinius to kill himself, knowing that Cassius died for his sake.*

◆ Build Grammar Skills

❸ Words of Direct Address Ask students: What dual purpose does the direct address "brave Cassius" serve? *The phrase identifies the person to whom Titinius is speaking and emphasizes how Titinius regards Cassius.*

MESSALA. Is not that he that lies upon the ground?

TITINIUS. He lies not like the living. O my heart!

MESSALA. Is not that he?

TITINIUS. No, this was he, Messala,
But Cassius is no more. O setting sun,
As in thy red rays thou dost sink to night,
So in his red blood Cassius' day is set.
The sun of Rome is set. Our day is gone;
Clouds, dews, and dangers come; our deeds are done!
Mistrust of my success[16] hath done this deed.

❶ MESSALA. Mistrust of good success hath done this deed.
O hateful Error, Melancholy's child,[17]
Why dost thou show to the apt thoughts of men
The things that are not?[18] O Error, soon conceived,[19]
Thou never com'st unto a happy birth,
But kill'st the mother that engend'red thee![20]

TITINIUS. What, Pindarus! Where art thou, Pindarus?

MESSALA. Seek him, Titinius, whilst I go to meet
The noble Brutus, thrusting this report
Into his ears. I may say "thrusting" it;
❷ For piercing steel and darts envenomèd[21]
Shall be as welcome to the ears of Brutus
As tidings of this sight.

TITINIUS. Hie you, Messala,
And I will seek for Pindarus the while. [*Exit* MESSALA.]
Why didst thou send me forth, brave[22] Cassius?
❸ Did I not meet thy friends, and did not they
Put on my brows this wreath of victory,
And bid me give it thee? Didst thou not hear their
shouts?
Alas, thou hast misconstrued everything!
But hold thee,[23] take this garland on thy brow;
Thy Brutus bid me give it thee, and I
Will do his bidding. Brutus, come apace,[24]
And see how I regarded[25] Caius Cassius.
By your leave,[26] gods. This is a Roman's part:[27]
Come, Cassius' sword, and find Titinius' heart. [*Dies*]

[*Call to arms sounds. Enter* BRUTUS, MESSALA, YOUNG CATO, STRATO, VOLUMNIUS, *and* LUCILIUS.]

BRUTUS. Where, where, Messala, doth his body lie?

MESSALA. Lo, yonder, and Titinius mourning it.

BRUTUS. Titinius' face is upward.

16. Mistrust . . . success: Fear that I would not succeed.

17. Melancholy's child: One of despondent temperament.

18. Why dost . . . are not?: Why do you (despondent temperament) fill easily impressed men's thoughts with imagined fears?

19. conceived: Created.

20. mother . . . thee: Cassius (in this case), who conceived the error.

21. envenomèd: Poisoned.

22. brave: Noble.

23. hold thee: Wait a moment.

24. apace: Quickly.

25. regarded: Honored.

26. By your leave: With your permission.

27. part: Role; duty.

◆ Build Vocabulary

misconstrued (mis kän strood′) *v.*: Misunderstood; misinterpreted

Research Skills Mini-Lesson

Elizabethan Faire

This mini-lesson supports the second Researching and Representing activity in the Idea Bank on p. 803.

Introduce Students may like to know what the audience at one of Shakespeare's plays would have been wearing, what food they would have eaten, and what music and art they appreciated.

Develop Students can work in groups to research the different aspects of this project. They will need to research fashion, musical instruments and recordings of Renaissance music, the art in England at that time, and the food of the day.

Apply Students in each group can develop a plan for displaying what they have learned. They may present sketches or models of clothing, reproductions of art and music, and offer dishes common to Shakespeare's time.

Assess If possible, invite other classes to the Elizabethan Faire. Evaluate students' work based on the depth of their research.

CATO. He is slain.

BRUTUS. O Julius Caesar, thou art mighty yet!
Thy spirit walks abroad, and turns our swords
In our own proper entrails.[28] [*Low calls to arms*]

CATO. Brave Titinius!
Look, whe'r[29] he have not crowned dead Cassius.

BRUTUS. Are yet two Romans living such as these?
The last of all the Romans, fare thee well!
It is impossible that ever Rome
Should breed thy fellow.[30] Friends, I owe moe tears
To this dead man than you shall see me pay.
I shall find time, Cassius; I shall find time.
Come, therefore, and to Thasos[31] send his body;
His funerals shall not be in our camp,
Lest it discomfort us.[32] Lucilius, come,
And come, young Cato; let us to the field.
Labeo and Flavius set our battles[33] on.
'Tis three o'clock; and, Romans, yet ere night
We shall try fortune in a second fight. [*Exit*]

28. own proper entrails: Very own inner organs.
29. whe'r: Whether.
30. fellow: Equal.
31. Thasos: An island not far from Philippi.
32. discomfort us: Discourage our soldiers.
33. battles: Armies.

Scene iv. *The field of battle.*

[*Call to arms sounds. Enter* BRUTUS, MESSALA, YOUNG CATO, LUCILIUS, *and* FLAVIUS.]

BRUTUS. Yet, countrymen, O, yet hold up your heads!

[*Exit, with followers*]

CATO. What bastard[1] doth not? Who will go with me?
I will proclaim my name about the field.
I am the son of Marcus Cato,[2] ho!
A foe to tyrants, and my country's friend.
I am the son of Marcus Cato, ho!

[*Enter* SOLDIERS *and fight.*]

LUCILIUS. And I am Brutus, Marcus Brutus, I;
Brutus, my country's friend; know me for Brutus![3]

[YOUNG CATO *falls.*]

O young and noble Cato, art thou down?
Why, now thou diest as bravely as Titinius,
And mayst be honored, being Cato's son.

FIRST SOLDIER. Yield, or thou diest.

LUCILIUS. Only I yield to die.[4]
There is so much that thou wilt kill me straight;[5]
Kill Brutus, and be honored in his death.

FIRST SOLDIER. We must not. A noble prisoner!

1. bastard: Person who is not a true Roman.
2. Marcus Cato: Brutus' wife's father.
3. And I am . . . Brutus: Lucilius impersonates Brutus in order to protect him and confuse the enemy.
4. Only . . . die: I will surrender only to die.
5. much . . . straight: Much honor in it that you will kill me immediately.

Customize for
Verbal/Linguistic Learners
Invite these students to summarize Brutus' eulogy of Cassius and deliver their summaries to the class. *Students should make the following points: Rome will never again see Cassius' equal; I will make the time to give Cassius the tribute he deserves; we will hold Cassius' funeral in Thasos so our soldiers are not discouraged.*

Customize for
Musical/Rhythmic Readers
Invite these students to share a piece of music that captures the mood of this scene. Have the rest of the class analyze the music and explain its suitability.

◆ **Reading Strategy**

❶ **Identify Cause and Effect**
Sample answer: Antony respects Brutus, and therefore Lucilius, because he is Brutus' friend. He does not want to make an enemy of Lucilius.

Comprehension Check ☑

❷ What does Brutus want Clitus and Dardanius to do? Why? *Brutus wants his men to kill him so he will not be taken prisoner.*

◆ **Reading Strategy**

❸ **Identify Cause and Effect**
Students may identify several causes of Brutus' despair including his almost certain defeat to come in the battle, his death predicted by Caesar's ghost, a realization that he aligned himself with dishonorable men, or the fact that he killed Caesar, a man who trusted him.

[*Enter* ANTONY.]

SECOND SOLDIER. Room, ho! Tell Antony, Brutus is ta'en.

FIRST SOLDIER. I'll tell thee news. Here comes the general.
Brutus is ta'en, Brutus is ta'en, my lord.

ANTONY. Where is he?

LUCILIUS. Safe, Antony; Brutus is safe enough.
I dare assure thee that no enemy
Shall ever take alive the noble Brutus.
The gods defend him from so great a shame!
When you do find him, or alive or dead,
He will be found like Brutus, like himself.[6]

ANTONY. This is not Brutus, friend, but, I assure you,
A prize no less in worth. Keep this man safe;
Give him all kindness. I had rather have
Such men my friends than enemies. Go on,
And see whe'r Brutus be alive or dead,
And bring us word unto[7] Octavius' tent
How everything is chanced.[8] [*Exit*]

6. like himself: Behaving in a noble way.

◆ **Reading Strategy**
Identify why Antony treats Lucilius the way he does. ❶

7. unto: In.
8. is chanced: Has happened.

Scene v. *The field of battle.*

[*Enter* BRUTUS, DARDANIUS, CLITUS, STRATO, *and* VOLUMNIUS.]

BRUTUS. Come, poor remains[1] of friends, rest on this rock.

CLITUS. Statilius showed the torchlight,[2] but, my lord,
He came not back; he is or ta'en or slain.

BRUTUS. Sit thee down, Clitus. Slaying is the word;
It is a deed in fashion. Hark thee, Clitus. [*Whispers*]

❷ **CLITUS.** What, I, my lord? No, not for all the world!

BRUTUS. Peace then, no words.

CLITUS. I'll rather kill myself.

BRUTUS. Hark thee, Dardanius. [*Whispers*]

DARDANIUS. Shall I do such a deed?

CLITUS. O Dardanius!

DARDANIUS. O Clitus!

CLITUS. What ill request did Brutus make to thee?

DARDANIUS. To kill him, Clitus. Look, he meditates.

CLITUS. Now is that noble vessel[3] full of grief,
That it runs over even at his eyes.

1. poor remains: Pitiful survivors.

2. showed the torchlight: Signaled with a torch.

◆ **Reading Strategy**
What is the cause of Brutus' despair? What is the effect? ❸

3. vessel: Human being.

Beyond the Classroom

Career Connection

Military Careers Military battles play important roles in Shakespeare's tragedies, *Julius Caesar, Antony and Cleopatra, Macbeth*, and *Hamlet*. While the United States has not been involved in a major war for decades, more than 500,000 U.S. Army personnel are on active duty today. Women as well as men pursue careers in the army, navy, marines, and air force. Have students find out about career opportunities in the military, including training, education, pay, benefits, and years of service required.

Community Connection

War Memorials Monuments have been erected around the world to honor war heroes. Encourage students to survey their town to find memorials to local war heroes. Students can then search town records to find out more about each soldier's life and death.

BRUTUS. Come hither, good Volumnius; list[4] a word.

VOLUMNIUS. What says my lord?

BRUTUS. Why, this, Volumnius:
The ghost of Caesar hath appeared to me
Two several[5] times by night; at Sardis once,
And this last night here in Philippi fields.
I know my hour is come.

❹ **VOLUMNIUS.** Not so, my lord.

❺ **BRUTUS.** Nay, I am sure it is, Volumnius.
Thou seest the world, Volumnius, how it goes;
Our enemies have beat us to the pit.[6]

[*Low calls to arms*]

It is more worthy to leap in ourselves
Than tarry till they push us.[7] Good Volumnius,
Thou know'st that we two went to school together;
Even for that our love of old, I prithee
Hold thou my sword-hilts whilst I run on it.

VOLUMNIUS. That's not an office[8] for a friend, my lord.

[*Call to arms still*]

CLITUS. Fly, fly, my lord, there is no tarrying here.

BRUTUS. Farewell to you; and you; and you, Volumnius.
Strato, thou hast been all this while asleep;
Farewell to thee too, Strato. Countrymen,
My heart doth joy that yet in all my life
❻ I found no man but he was true to me.
I shall have glory by this losing day
More than Octavius and Mark Antony
By this vile conquest shall attain unto.[9]
So fare you well at once, for Brutus' tongue
Hath almost ended his life's history.
Night hangs upon mine eyes; my bones would rest,
That have but labored to attain this hour.[10]

[*Call to arms sounds. Cry within,* "Fly, fly, fly!"]

CLITUS. Fly, my lord, fly!

BRUTUS. Hence! I will follow.

[*Exit* CLITUS, DARDANIUS, *and* VOLUMNIUS.]

I prithee, Strato, stay thou by thy lord,
Thou art a fellow of a good respect.[11]
Thy life hath had some smatch[12] of honor in it;
Hold then my sword, and turn away thy face,
While I do run upon it. Wilt thou, Strato?

4. list: Hear.

5. several: Separate.

6. pit: Trap or grave.

7. tarry . . . us: Wait until they kill us.

8. office: Task.

9. By this . . . unto: By this evil victory shall gain. (Brutus sees the victory of Octavius and Antony as causing the downfall of Roman freedom.)

10. this hour: Time of death.

11. respect: Reputation.

12. smatch: Smack or taste.

◆ Build Grammar Skills

❹ **Words of Direct Address** Ask students: To whom is Brutus speaking? How can you tell from the words of direct address that Brutus trusts Volumnius to help him? *Brutus is talking to Volumnius, as indicated by the several times he uses Volumnius' name. Brutus' trust is shown by the word "good."*

◆ Reading Strategy

❺ **Cause and Effect** Encourage students to speculate about the cause of this defeat. Ask them whose decision it was to meet the enemy at Philippi in the first place. Have them recall Cassius' words in Act IV, Scene iii, which explain his reasons for not marching to Philippi, but waiting for the enemy at Sardis instead. How might the battle have gone differently if Brutus had accepted Cassius' decision? *In Act IV, Scene iii, Cassius says, "Tis better that the enemy seek us./So shall he waste his means, weary his soldiers,/Doing himself offence; whilst we, lying still,/Are full of rest, defence, and nimbleness." If Brutus had listened to Cassius, they may have won the battle.*

◆ Literary Focus

❻ **Tragedy** Direct students' attention to the line "I found no man but he was true to me." Ask: To what qualities of the tragic hero does this fact point in Brutus? *It points to his nobility. Brutus, like others who attract loyal friends and followers, is a good leader and an honorable person.*

Customize for *Pre-AP Students*

Challenge Pre-AP students to make a plot diagram showing how the events in the play led to Brutus' death.

Reteach

Discuss the idea of tragedy with students. A main character faces either an internal or external conflict—or both—and is ruined by a personal flaw or weakness. Even though the title indicates the main character is Julius Caesar, most people consider Brutus the character who brings about his own ruin. Ask students to describe how Brutus allows himself to commit an act that causes his downfall. In what ways is he good, and how does he go wrong?

You may also want students to look at Julius Caesar as a character destroyed by a tragic flaw. How did Caesar bring about his own demise? What could he have done to avoid it?

▶Critical Viewing◀

❶ Analyze *Conflict is indicated by the drawn sword and the war helmet. Triumph may be indicated by the expression on the face of the man wearing the helmet, by the fact that he is still wearing his helmet, and by the fact that his head is placed above the other man's. Defeat may be indicated by the missing helmet, by the pained expression of the man with the sword, and by the fact that he seems almost to be sinking out of the picture.*

◆ Critical Thinking

❷ Interpret Invite interpretation of Brutus' final words. How do they reveal his essential nobility? *By saying that he is more ready to die than he was to murder Caesar, Brutus shows that he did not want to kill Caesar for selfish reasons.*

◆ Reading Strategy

❸ Identify Cause and Effect Guide the class in tracing the chain of causes and effects that begins with the conspirators' plan to kill Caesar and ends with Brutus' death. Have students note how each effect became a cause for the next effect. *Brutus, Cassius, and the other conspirators kill Caesar; Antony and Octavius, who supported Caesar, oppose Brutus and Cassius in the battle of Philippi; Octavius' legions defeat Brutus'; Brutus takes his own life.*

◆ Literary Focus

❹ Tragic Hero *Some students may identify Caesar as the tragic hero while others will identify Brutus as the tragic hero.*

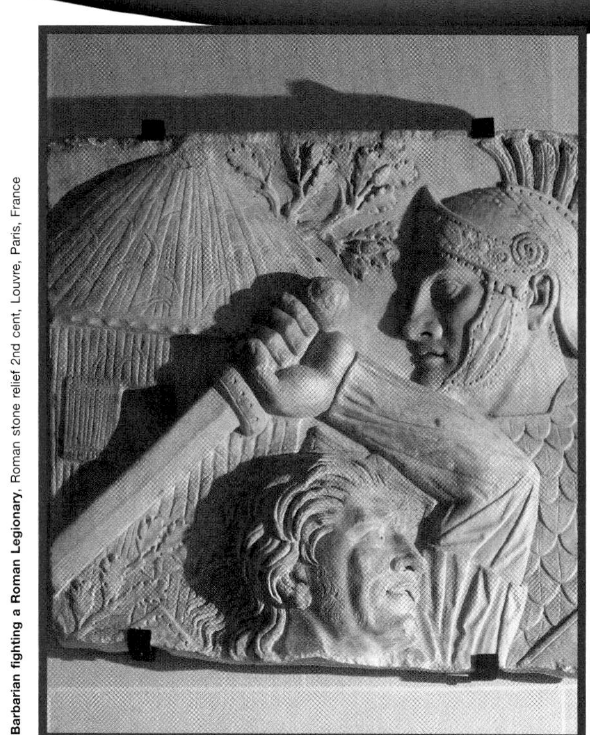

Barbarian fighting a Roman Legionary. Roman stone relief 2nd cent, Louvre, Paris, France

◀ Critical Viewing What details in this sculpture indicate conflict, triumph, and defeat? **[Analyze]** ❶

STRATO. Give me your hand first. Fare you well, my lord.

❷ BRUTUS. Farewell, good Strato—Caesar, now be still;
❸ I killed not thee with half so good a will. [*Dies*]

[*Call to arms sounds. Retreat sounds. Enter* ANTONY, OCTAVIUS, MESSALA, LUCILIUS, *and the Army.*]

◆ **Literary Focus** Considering Antony's words, ask yourself who the real tragic hero in this play is. ❹

OCTAVIUS. What man is that?

MESSALA. My master's man.[13] Strato, where is thy master?

STRATO. Free from the bondage you are in, Messala;
The conquerors can but make a fire of him
For Brutus only overcame himself,
And no man else hath honor[14] by his death.

LUCILIUS. So Brutus should be found. I thank thee, Brutus,
That thou hast proved Lucilius' saying[15] true.

OCTAVIUS. All that served Brutus, I will entertain them.[16]
Fellow, wilt thou bestow[17] thy time with me?

STRATO. Ay, if Messala will prefer[18] me to you.

13. **man:** Servant.

14. **no man else hath honor:** No other man gains honor.

15. **Lucilius' saying:** See Act V, Scene iv, line 25.

16. **entertain them:** Take them into my service.

17. **bestow:** Spend.

18. **prefer:** Recommend.

Beyond the Selection

FURTHER READING

Other Works by William Shakespeare

The Tragedy of Hamlet, Prince Of Denmark
The Tragedy of Othello
The Comedy of Errors

Other Works About Choices and Consequences

For Whom the Bell Tolls, Ernest Hemingway
Catch-22, Joseph Heller
The Red Badge of Courage, Stephen Crane

INTERNET

For information about the complete works of William Shakespeare, the Globe theater, and the Elizabethan era, go to **http://pc1.fhs.weber.k12.ut.us/academ/English/marler/shakes/william.htm**

Please be aware, however, that sites may have changed from the time we published this information. We *strongly recommend* that you preview sites before you send students to them.

OCTAVIUS. Do so, good Messala.

MESSALA. How died my master, Strato?

STRATO. I held the sword, and he did run on it.

MESSALA. Octavius, then take him to follow thee,
That did the latest service to my master.

ANTONY. This was the noblest Roman of them all.
All the conspirators save[19] only he
Did that[20] they did in envy of great Caesar;
He, only in a general honest thought
5 And common good to all, made one of them.[21]
His life was gentle,[22] and the elements
So mixed[23] in him that Nature might stand up
And say to all the world, "This was a man!"

OCTAVIUS. According to his virtue,[24] let us use[25] him
With all respect and rites of burial.
Within my tent his bones tonight shall lie,
6 Most like a soldier ordered honorably.[26]
So call the field[27] to rest, and let's away
To part[28] the glories of this happy day. [*Exit all.*]

19. save: Except.
20. that: What.
21. made one of them: Became one of the conspirators.
22. gentle: Noble.
23. so mixed: Well balanced.
24. virtue: Excellence.
25. use: Treat.
26. ordered honorably: Treated with honor.
27. field: Army.
28. part: Share.

◆ Build Vocabulary

envy (en′ vē) *n.*: Feeling of desire for another's possessions or qualities and jealousy at not having them

Guide for Responding

◆ Literature and Your Life

Reader's Response What insights did you gain from the play?

Thematic Focus Explain how the choices some characters made in this act were the inevitable consequences of events that occurred much earlier in the play.

Questions for Research How accurate is Shakespeare's version of the deaths of Cassius and Brutus? Generate research questions about the historical Battle of Phillipi.

☑ Check Your Comprehension

1. On whose birthday does the battle take place, and how does that person feel about the battle?
2. Explain the misunderstanding that leads to Cassius' death.
3. Why does Brutus think it is time to die?
4. Who does Antony say is the noblest Roman of all?

◆ Critical Thinking

INTERPRET

1. What does Cassius mean in Act V, Scene i, lines 45–47? **[Analyze]**
2. What does Brutus mean by his final words, "Caesar, now be still; / I killed not thee with half so good a will"? **[Interpret]**
3. How and why does Antony's attitude toward Brutus change during this act? **[Infer]**

APPLY

4. Now that Octavius and Antony have triumphed, what do you think will become of the Roman republic? Do you think this is a good or bad thing? **[Speculate]**

EXTEND

5. Compare another defeated leader from history to Brutus. Explain how the circumstances, possible motives, and outcomes are similar and different. **[Social Studies Link]**

◆ Critical Thinking

1. Cassius says that Antony would not be able to speak such insults if Brutus had listened to Cassius' advice to kill Antony.
2. Brutus is more ready to die than he was to murder Caesar.
3. At the beginning of Act V, Antony see Brutus as a villain for his part in the assassination of Caesar. At the end, Antony finally realizes that Brutus was the only conspirator who killed out of an honest concern for the common good, not for envy or power.
4. Sample response: The Roman republic will die, but the people helped to let it happen. They, too, made a choice and must suffer the consequences.
5. Example: Robert E. Lee would be an example of a noble leader who, because of his deep sense of honor, aligned himself with the wrong side and was defeated.

◆ Critical Thinking

5 Infer Ask students: Why does Antony praise his enemy, Brutus? *Antony has come to see Brutus as a truly honorable man. He realizes that Brutus thought he was acting for the good of Rome, not for personal gain.*

◆ Critical Thinking

6 Speculate Lead a discussion about Rome's future following the action of the play. What does the phrase "part the glories of this happy day" suggest? *Students may suggest that "happy day" suggests a hopeful future—at least for Antony and Octavius. Since Antony and Octavius were battling those who fought to save the republic (Brutus and Cassius), students might predict that Rome will become a monarchy.*

Reinforce and Extend

Answers

◆ Literature and Your Life

Reader's Response Students may respond: If a good person does something wrong for the right reason, it still turns out badly. Beware of whose company you keep. Watch out for flatterers. Never underestimate your enemy.

Thematic Focus Suggested answer: Brutus' defeat is the inevitable consequence of his joining men with selfish motives.

Questions for Research Suggested responses: When did the battle of Phillipi occur? How did Brutus die/ How did Cassius die?

☑ Check Your Comprehension

1. The battle takes place on Cassius' birthday, and he feels it is one of many bad omens.
2. When Cassius saw Titinius unseated from his horse, he assumed that everything was lost.
3. Brutus thinks it is time to die because he feels that the victory of Antony and Octavius marks the end of Roman freedom.
4. Anthony says that Brutus is the noblest Roman of all.

◆ Reading Strategy

1. The effects that result in this act from Caesar's assassination include the battle, which in conjunction with other events causes the deaths of Cassius and Brutus. Antony and Octavius become rulers of Rome.
2. Brutus committed suicide because the threat of defeat and surrender meant he would be led bound through the streets of Rome in disgrace. The effect of his suicide is that the fighting will stop and Brutus will have an honorable funeral.

◆ Literary Focus

1. Example: Brutus' tragic flaw is error in judgment—he misjudged Cassius, Antony, and the Roman people.
2. Once Brutus joined the conspirators, he could not turn back, because even if he turned them in, he would be accused of being part of the plot, lose the trust of Caesar, and still lose the republic.
3. Examples: In V, v, lines 36–38, Brutus states, "I shall have glory by losing day/More the Octavius and Mark Antony/By this vile conquest shall attain unto." In lines 50–51, Brutus says, ". . . Caesar, now be still;/I killed not thee with half so good a will." In V, v, lines 13–14, Clitus says of Brutus: "Now is that noble vessel full of grief,/That it runs over even at his eyes."

◆ Build Vocabulary

Using the Anglo-Saxon Prefix *mis-*

1. b 2. a 3. c

Using the Word Bank

1. a 2. c 3. c 4. b
5. b 6. a 7. b

◆ Build Grammar Skills

Practice

1. Prepare, you generals, the enemy comes on in a gallant show.
2. Octavius, lead your battle softly on.
3. In your bad strokes, Brutus, you give good words.
4. Young man, thou couldst not die more honorable.
5. Mark Antony, shall we give sign of battle?
6. No Caesar, we will answer on their charge.

Guide for Responding (continued)

◆ Reading Strategy

IDENTIFY CAUSE AND EFFECT

When you **identify the causes and effects** of actions in this drama, you see the relationships between events that bring about the ultimate tragedy.

1. List three effects of Caesar's death that occur in Act V. Explain the chain of events that lead to the final result.
2. What is the immediate cause of Brutus' suicide? What do you think its effect will be?

◆ Literary Focus

TRAGEDY

The last act of *The Tragedy of Julius Caesar* depicts the downfall of Brutus. His death is the inevitable consequence of a chain of events set in motion when he joined the conspirators in Act I.

1. In your own words, what is Brutus' tragic flaw?
2. Once Brutus has joined the conspirators, can he turn back? Why or why not?
3. Find two passages that show that Brutus is essentially a noble man.

Beyond Literature

Cultural Connection

The World's Shakespeare Ben Jonson, Shakespeare's contemporary, said that Shakespeare "was not of an age, but was for all time." He might have added: for all the world. Even in the first decades of the 1600's, Shakespeare's plays were being translated and performed in other languages. (*Hamlet,* translated into German, may have been first.) Today, translations of his plays exist in many languages, including Chinese, Greek, and Japanese. Themes from the plays have provided the bases for operas, ballets, musical comedies, and contemporary movies.

Activity View one of the Japanese films by Akira Kurasawa that is based on a Shakespearean work: *Throne of Blood,* an adaptation of *Macbeth,* or *Ran,* an adaptation of *King Lear.* Write a brief assessment of how the themes work in the context of another culture.

◆ Build Vocabulary

USING THE ANGLO-SAXON PREFIX ***mis-***

The Anglo-Saxon prefix *mis-* means "wrong" or "bad." On your paper, match each word that begins with *mis-* with its definition.

1. misnomer	**a.** one who thinks badly of people
2. misanthrope	**b.** a wrong name
3. misconduct	**c.** bad behavior

USING THE WORD BANK: Synonyms

On your paper, write the letter of the word that is a synonym for the word from the Word Bank.

1. misconstrued: (a) confused, (b) angered, (c) understood
2. presage: (a) help, (b) review, (c) predict
3. disconsolate: (a) joyful, (b) angry, (c) cheerless
4. consorted: (a) abandoned, (b) accompanied, (c) served
5. demeanor: (a) feelings, (b) behavior, (c) anger
6. ensign: (a) flag-bearer, (b) signature, (c) janitor
7. envy: (a) sympathy, (b) jealousy, (c) sadness

◆ Build Grammar Skills

WORDS OF DIRECT ADDRESS

Writers set off **words of direct address** with commas and occasionally an exclamation point.

Practice On your paper, write the following passages. Underline the word or words of direct address and insert the proper punctuation.

1. Prepare you generals the enemy comes on in a gallant show.
2. Octavius lead your battle softly on.
3. In your bad strokes Brutus you give good words.
4. Young man thou couldst not die more honorable.
5. Mark Antony shall we give sign of battle?
6. No Caesar we will answer on their charge.

Writing Application Write a brief dialogue between two or more characters that could be part of a play. In the dialogue, have the characters address each other directly. Punctuate their words of direct address properly.

Writing Application

Sample Response:

Adam, you and I have to talk when I come home over the holidays.

I'll be working most days, Jennifer, but we'll figure something out.

Build Your Portfolio

Idea Bank

Writing

1. **Epitaph** Write an epitaph for Brutus. An epitaph is brief, gives birth and death dates, and often includes an appropriate inspiring verse.
2. **Response** In Act V, Scene i, lines 39–44, Antony launches a bitter verbal attack against Brutus and Cassius. Brutus makes no attempt to respond. Write a short speech in which Brutus *does* respond to Antony's criticism.
3. **Take a Side** Throughout the play, Brutus gives his reasons for killing Caesar. Antony just as eloquently states why Caesar should not have been killed. With whom do you agree? Write a position paper taking either Brutus' or Antony's side. Support any assertions you make.

Speaking, Listening, and Viewing

4. **Sound Effects** With classmates, create sound effects for the final act of the play. Make a recording of the effects and play them for the class.
5. **View a Play** If you can, attend a local production of one of Shakespeare's plays or rent a video of one. After viewing, read sections of the play in a small group, comparing your own treatment to that in the full production.

Researching and Representing

6. **Model of the Globe** Research to find out more about the Globe theater. Create a model of the theater to better understand how plays like *The Tragedy of Julius Caesar* were performed during Shakespeare's day.
7. **Elizabethan Faire** With a group, organize an "Elizabethan Faire," incorporating costumes, music, art, and, if possible, food to give your classmates a flavor of the period in which Shakespeare lived and wrote.

Online Activity www.phlit.phschool.com

Guided Writing Lesson

Speech

When Antony presented the crown to Caesar, he probably spoke to the spectators with a prepared talk, or speech. Most likely, he said something at the beginning of the speech to grab the attention of the listeners. Then he probably presented supporting facts and anecdotes to show why Caesar was worthy of the crown. Write your own speech to honor a special person or event.

Writing Skills Focus: Connotation

Shakespeare chose carefully the words he put into the mouths of his characters. He was aware that words carry **connotations**—associations that give them deeper meaning than their literal definitions. For instance, the word *valiant* has associations that are not communicated by simply saying *brave*. The word *integrity* paints a more vivid picture of a person's character than *honesty* does. Use words with positive connotations to lend power to your speech.

Prewriting Brainstorm for qualities and impressions of the person or event that is the subject of your speech. Using a dictionary or thesaurus, make a list of words that have both a literal and connotative meaning that will help you express these ideas.

Drafting Use lively, specific verbs in your speech. Choose verbs connotative for their meanings. A word like *sizzle* literally means "extremely hot." Its connotation, however, suggests more—someone or something that is very exciting and energetic.

Revising Read your speech aloud to a small group. Does your first sentence grab their attention? Are your verbs lively and energetic with connotative as well as literal meanings? Ask the group for suggestions and make revisions you feel will improve your speech.

Idea Bank

Following are suggestions for matching Idea Bank topics with your students' performance levels and learning modalities.

Customizing for *Performance Levels*
Less Advanced: 1, 4
Average: 2, 5, 7
More Advanced: 3, 5, 6, 7

Customizing for *Learning Modalities*
Musical/Rhythmic: 4
Interpersonal: 5, 7
Bodily/Kinesthetic: 6, 7
Visual/Spatial: 6, 7

Guided Writing Lesson

Revision Strategy When students begin ratiocination of their speeches, have them reenter their writing and draw on the following list of codes to revise their papers:

To be active writers, circle "to be" verbs.
Words that are repeated, draw a wavy line under repeated words.
Underline each sentence.
[Bracket] sentence beginnings.
In each sentence, draw an arrow from subject to predicate.
Draw a line around cliches.
Checkmark words that might be imprecise.
Cross out the word very.
Draw lines next to anything that needs developing. =
Draw a triangle around the word it.

For more prewriting, elaboration, and revision strategies, see *Prentice Hall Writing and Grammar*.

Writing Lab CD-ROM
Have students write their speeches using the tutorial on Persuasion. Follow these steps:
1. Use the note cards activity to organize ideas.
2. Have students draft on the computer.
3. Use the revision checker for double comparisons.

ASSESSMENT OPTIONS

Formal Assessment, Selection Test, pp. 188–189, Assessment Resources Software. The selection test is designed so that it can be easily customized to the ability levels of your students.
Alternative Assessment, p. 54, includes options for less advanced students and more advanced students.

PORTFOLIO ASSESSMENT
Use the following rubrics in the ***Alternative Assessment*** booklet to assess student writing:
Epitaph: Response to Literature Rubric. p.110
Response: Expression Rubric, p. 94
Take a Side: Persuasion Rubric, p. 105
Guided Writing Lesson: Persuasion Rubric, p. 105

Prepare and Engage

LESSON OBJECTIVES

- To use recursive writing processes to write a critical evaluation
- To recognize and use correct placement of quotation marks and underlining
- To recognize and use correct capitalization

You may distribute copies of the Scoring Rubric for Response to Literature (p. 110) in ***Alternative Assessment*** to make students aware before they begin of the criteria on which they will be evaluated. See the suggestions on p. 806 for ways you can customize the rubric for this workshop.

Writers at Work Videodisc
Play the videodisc segment on Response to Literature (Ch. 7) in which Miguel Algarín discusses the process of preparing a literary response.

Play frames 24470 to 26040

Writing Lab CD-ROM
If your students have access to computers, you may want to have them work on the tutorial on Response to Literature to complete all or part of their critical reviews. Follow these steps:

1. Encourage students to use the Response Wheel activity in the Prewriting section.
2. Suggest that students write to the purpose by completing an audience profile and then using the instruction on writing for different purposes.
3. Have students draft on computer.
4. Tell students to use the revision checkers for varied language and for pronoun and antecedents.
5. Have students review the instruction on punctuating literary titles.

Critical Evaluation Writing Process Workshop

When you're deciding whether or not to see a new movie, you may look at television or newspaper reviews of the movie to see what the critics think. A movie review is one type of critical evaluation—a written or spoken examination of what is and is not effective in a literary work, television program, or movie. Most often, a critical evaluation includes a brief summary of the work, comments upon its merits or weaknesses, and recommendations to readers or viewers.

Write a critical evaluation of *The Tragedy of Julius Caesar* or another literary work you've read. The following skills, introduced in this section's Guided Writing Lesson, will help you.

Writing Skills Focus

- **Choose words with appropriate connotations.** Choosing words that have strong connotations—feelings and ideas associated with them—will give your evaluation more punch. (See p. 803.)
- **Provide examples** from the text for support. For example, if you say, "Antony is a skilled orator," follow that with a sentence such as, "In Act III, Scene ii, he stirs up the crowd with his 'Friends, Romans, countrymen . . .' speech."

The following is an excerpt from Ben Okri's critical evaluation of *Clear Light of Day*, a novel by Anita Desai.

Model From Literature

① Silence is clarity and white heat in Anita Desai's *Clear Light of Day*, a novel about a family reunion, its unease, and the ② disturbing remembrances that accompany it. Tara, now married to a diplomat, revisits her childhood home in Old Delhi and finds that, on the ③ shabby surface, nothing has changed.

① The writer offers an opinion about the effect of silence in Desai's novel.

② The writer gives an indication of the mood of the book.

③ The writer uses a word with connotations that create an image in readers' minds.

Prewriting

Choose a Topic To which selection in this book have you had the strongest reaction? That selection will make the best subject for a critical evaluation. Scan the table of contents, or flip through the book to spark your memory.

Clarify Your Opinions Once you've chosen your selection, collect your thoughts about it. Create a chart like this one, listing what you liked about the selection and what you didn't like about it.

What I Liked	What I Didn't Like

Identify Your Purpose Review your list of likes and dislikes. Decide whether you will or will not recommend the work to other readers.

Summarize Your Opinions Begin by jotting down a brief summary of the selection. Then list your opinions about various aspects of the work, as well as the work as a whole. Next, jot down details from the story that will help support each opinion.

Drafting

Follow a Format Using the details you've gathered, draft your evaluation. Start with a paragraph that reveals your general opinion of the selection. Follow with a brief summary of the key details. Then elaborate on your opinion of the work, providing examples and details for support. End with a recommendation to readers.

Use Evaluative Modifiers Present your opinions forcefully and clearly by using precise adjectives to either praise or criticize the work. Look at these examples:

Precise Adjectives

Mild Praise	High Praise	Mild Disapproval	Strong Disapproval
readable	imaginative	dull	awful
expressive	hilarious	unfocused	tactless
solid	inspired	vague	tedious
mildly amusing	stimulating	inconsistent	painfully boring
informative	original	melodramatic	useless

Applying Language Skills: Quotation Marks and Underlining

Place quotation marks around any examples that you quote directly from the text. If you are evaluating a poem or short story, place its title in quotation marks. If you are evaluating a novel or play, underline the title (if you are writing by hand) or enter it in italics (if you are working on a computer).

Plays and Novels:

The Tragedy of Julius Caesar

The Catcher in the Rye

Poems and Short Stories:

"Reapers"

"The Monkey's Paw"

Practice On your paper, write the following passage, placing quotation marks or underlining where necessary.

> In Shakespeare's play Hamlet, the famous lines To be or not to be show Prince Hamlet's classic moment of indecision.

Writer's Solution Connection
Language Lab

For more practice with quotation marks, complete the Language Lab lesson on Semicolons, Colons, and Quotation Marks.

Develop Student Writing

Prewriting Strategy

To help students choose a topic, you might suggest that they brainstorm in groups for a list of literary works they have read recently. Tell them to jot down notes as they share ideas. They can use their notes to choose a literary work about which to write.

Literary Work	Description of the Work	My Reaction to the Work
1.		
2.		
3.		
4.		

Customize for *English Language Learners*

Students learning English may have trouble using a variety of evaluative words. Help these students make lists of synonyms for words such as *like, dislike, good,* and *bad* that they can use to add variety to their critical evaluations.

Customize for *Less Proficient Writers*

These students might need some guidance in choosing details to put into their critical evaluations. Work with them to create a set of questions that can guide them as they draft, such as "What was the best feature of this literary work? What specific examples of this feature do you find in the work?"

Customize for *Pre-AP Students*

Challenge these students to write about a longer work, and to incorporate specific literary terms in their critical reviews.

Writing Lab CD-ROM

The Gathering Details section of the Response to Literature tutorial contains a Word Bin of evaluation words. Have students use this activity to generate ideas for different words they can use to express their assessment of a work.

Elaboration Strategy

Encourage students to draft their critical evaluations in a single sitting, getting all their ideas down on paper without laboring over word choice. Once students have completed a draft, they can reenter their work and look for places where they can elaborate with examples.

Applying Language Skills

Quotation Marks and Underlining Remind students that in an analysis evaluating a literary work, and possibly comparing it to others, it will be especially important for students to use quotation marks and underlining correctly.

Answer

In Shakespeare's play, *Hamlet,* the famous lines "To be or not to be" show Prince Hamlet's classic moment of indecision.

Grammar Reinforcement

For additional practice, use the **Language Lab CD-ROM** on Semicolons, Colons, and Quotation Marks.

Revision Strategy

Have students check their work for variety in evaluation words and for supporting examples. If they feel they need more supporting examples, encourage them to go back into the story to find some before creating a final draft.

Writing Lab CD-ROM

The revising screen contains information on going back to the selection for more information. Have students review this screen before creating a final draft.

For more prewriting, elaboration, and revision strategies, see *Prentice Hall Writing and Grammar.*

Reinforce and Extend

Applying Language Skills

Practice Answer In the end, perhaps, it is Caesar's belief in his own immortality that proves to be his downfall: Just before he dies he tells the senators, "But I am constant as the Northern Star."

APPLYING LANGUAGE SKILLS: Capitalization

Observe the following rules of capitalization of sentence beginnings:

1. Capitalize the first word of a direct quotation that can stand alone as a sentence:
   The soothsayer says to Caesar, "Beware the ides of March."
2. Capitalize the first word of a sentence in parentheses if that sentence stands alone:
   Caesar made a show of refusing the crown. (In fact, he had arranged with Brutus to offer it to him.)
3. Capitalize the first word of a sentence after a colon:
   Brutus has a quality that makes Antony admire him: He is honest.

Practice In your notebook, capitalize the proper words in the following sentence.

In the end, perhaps, it is caesar's belief in his own immortality that proves to be his downfall: just before he dies, he tells the senators, "but I am constant as the northern star."

Writer's Solution Connection
Writing Lab

For more help using quotations in your literary analysis, see Using Quotations in the Writing Lab tutorial on Response to Literature.

Offer Precise Details It's not enough to simply say that you found a story humorous; you must back up your opinions. Explain *why* you found the story humorous, and cite specific examples of details that contributed to the humor.

Revising

Use a Checklist Use this checklist to guide your revision.

- ▶ Have you summarized the selection in a way that will enable readers to follow what you're saying?
- ▶ Have you clearly expressed your opinion of the work?
- ▶ Do your evaluative modifiers express the appropriate degree of praise or disappointment?
- ▶ What can you do to strengthen your support for your opinion?

Use a Model Look at the revisions made in this paragraph from a review of Shakespeare's poem *The Tragedy of Julius Caesar.*

REVISION MODEL

In the ①"Tragedy of Julius Caesar," Cassius is one of the conspirators against Caesar. Cassius believes that the gods do not interest themselves in human affairs ②and that omens are merely superstitions. Now he credits his fate to bad omens. He thinks that when eagles follow their armies to Philippi, it is a good sign. However, when the eagles are replaced by ravens and crows, this foreshadows death to him. ③"Their shadows seem a canopy most fatal," says Cassius.

① The writer changes the quotation marks to underscore because a play is a full-length work.
② The writer adds information that clarifies her point.
③ This quotation from the text supports the writer's point.

Publishing

- ▶ **Create a Class Publication** With some classmates, create a class magazine of critical reviews.
- ▶ **Create a Book Group on the Internet** Post your critical evaluation on a bulletin board. Invite other readers to share their responses to your evaluation and to share evaluations of books they have enjoyed.

ASSESSMENT

PORTFOLIO ASSESSMENT
Use the rubric on Response to Literature in the ***Alternative Assessment*** booklet (p. 110) to assess students' writing. Add these criteria to customize the rubric to this assignment.

	4	3	2	1
Choose words with appropriate connotations	All words used convey connotations appropriate to purpose.	Most words used convey connotations appropriate to purpose.	Some words do not have appropriate connotations.	Few, if any, words have appropriate connotations.
Provide examples	All assertions are supported with examples.	Most assertions are supported with examples.	Some of the examples do not directly support the assertion being made.	Few appropriate examples are used.

Student Success Workshop

Research Skills — Conducting a Research Project

Strategies for Success

Research assignments require you to use various strategies to locate and categorize information. Text organizers—such as overviews, headings, and graphic features—can guide you in your search. You can gather your information in various ways: by taking notes, by creating an outline, or by writing up a summary. As you write your report, keep your audience in mind and direct your final report to that audience. In your report, state your conclusions clearly, supporting them with facts.

Use Text Organizers The first challenge every researcher faces is figuring out where to find helpful information. Fortunately, many texts include organizing features—such as a table of contents, section titles, and chapter titles—that can point you in the right direction. For instance, a biography of William Shakespeare might be divided by sections and chapters that allow you to locate and categorize information about his life, poems, and plays.

Report to Your Audience The tone and style in which you report the findings of your research should be appropriate for your audience. Think about arranging and presenting your research findings in a way that is most engaging to that particular audience. For example, a report to middle-grade students about Shakespeare's play *Julius Caesar* might rely heavily on illustrations and other graphic features to convey information. A report on the same subject presented to college students might include quotations from the play and from research sources, plus maps and a timeline.

Draw Conclusions Conducting research is a lot like piecing together a puzzle or solving a mystery. As you gather more and more information about your topic, a clearer picture emerges. Finally, you are able to draw some conclusions based on the information you've gathered. Your research into the life and work of William Shakespeare, for example, might lead you to draw conclusions about why he wrote about what he did and how audiences of his time may have responded to his work. When you present your conclusions, support them with evidence from your research.

Apply the Strategies

Choose one of the topics listed below, and research it fully using the strategies you've learned.

1. Compare the historical life and death of Julius Caesar with the details presented in Shakespeare's play.
2. Find out what life was like for an actor in Shakespeare's day.
3. Write a biographical portrait of another playwright who wrote during the time of Shakespeare.
4. Report on the activities of a modern-day Shakespeare company.

Here are some situations in which you need to know how to conduct research:

- *Writing a term paper*
- *Comparing opinions on a controversial topic*
- *Presenting a review of competing products or services*
- *Writing a newspaper or magazine article*

Prepare and Engage

LESSON OBJECTIVES

- To research self-selected and assigned topics, using text organizers such as overviews, headings, and graphic features to locate and categorize information
- To produce reports and research projects in varying forms for audiences
- To locate facts and details

Customize for
Less Advanced Students
Build on students' interests to offer alternative Shakespeare-related topics for research. Among the possibilities: an illustrated report on costume design, a research paper on varied film versions of a particular play, a booklet on the meanings and sources of well-known quotations.

Apply the Strategies

Answers

1. Students' research-based conclusions might have to do with Shakespeare's source of information (Plutarch), his compression of time for dramatic purposes, or his possibly unrealistic depiction of Caesar's character.
2. Students' research may lead them to describe the system of patronage and the likelihood that Shakespeare himself was among the Lord Chamberlain's company of actors.
3. Elizabethan and Jacobean playwrights to investigate include Ben Johnson, Christopher Marlowe, John Webster, George Chapman, John Heywood, Thomas Kyd, and John Ford.
4. Students should use Internet search engines and periodicals databases to choose a Shakespearean company to study.

Test Preparation Workshop

Locate Facts and Details
Learning how to locate information efficiently will help students perform successfully on reading comprehension sections that require them to locate specific facts and details within a given passage. Use the passage in the student edition and the following sample test item to demonstrate.

When did the stockpiling of nuclear weapons begin to slow down?

A After World War II
B When the Soviet Union embraces communism
C By the 1980's
D Before World War II

Students should be able to locate the answer by looking for dates and keywords. After students have read the sentences they find, they should recognize C as the correct answer.

Prepare and Engage

LESSON OBJECTIVES

- To prepare, organize, plan, and perform a dramatic scene

Ask students to define "great acting." What actors, in their opinion, have superior skills? What makes them superior? List the characteristics that students suggest.

Customize for
English Language Learners

Encourage participation at the level at which students feel comfortable. Some students may want to try a small speaking role in one of the workshop activities. Others may prefer to portray a character through nonverbal strategies. Still others may prepare an original dramatic work in their native language, using all the strategies discussed in the workshop.

Apply the Strategies

Answers

1. A parody might depict celebrities or competitors in the news today. Issues of power and betrayal can be caricatured. Shakespeare's language and drama should still be recognizable.
2. Characters in modern dress and in a contemporary setting should speak Shakespeare's lines as written.
3. Challenge students to retell the story without using the device of a narrator. The words and actions of the characters should enable the audience to follow the narrative.

Speaking, Listening, and Viewing Workshop

Performing a Dramatic Scene

Any dramatic performance—a play, a satirical skit, or an improvisation—involves exciting challenges of self-expression. Most dramatic performances, especially those based on literary works, involve interpretation.

Get Into It Your first step in a dramatic performance based on a literary work is to become familiar with the text itself. Read the original work several times; talking it over with friends can help you decide how you'll interpret it. If you are portraying a specific character, get to know who you are. Think about your character's mood, motivation, and personality.

Know Your Audience You need to know your audience, too. Will you be performing for your entire class or for a small group? As you prepare, keep in mind where your audience will be. You will need to keep your body turned toward them.

Use Your Voice Your voice and how you use it will determine how effective your performance will be. Practice ways of using the pitch and intonation of your voice to convey your interpretation of your character's mood and personality. Think about timing: Your pauses can be as important as your words. Remember to project your voice at a level that everyone can hear—even if your character seems to be whispering or saying something quietly.

Use Body Language Don't forget to use nonverbal strategies. Your facial expressions, gestures, and posture all work to communicate your interpretation of the character you are portraying. When deciding how to use body language, consider your character's age, background, and gender.

Apply the Strategies

Choose one or two of the following activities, and apply the strategies for performing a dramatic scene.

1. Prepare a parody of a scene from *Julius Caesar* for your class.
2. In a small group, choose a scene from *Julius Caesar* and produce a modern adaptation of it for your class.
3. Prepare an original dramatic work based on a myth, true story, fable, fairy tale, or poem, and present it to your friends and family members.

Tips on Learning Your Lines

Use these tricks for memorizing your lines:

- Audiotape your performance, and listen to the recording again and again.
- Repeat your lines while you're doing other things, like cleaning your room.
- Become familiar with other characters' lines, so you will recognize your cues to speak.

Cross-Curricular Connection: Art

Architecture Shakespeare's Julius Caesar is set in the Rome of 45 B.C. Students can look for examples of art, sculpture, and architecture of the period or depicting the period. Books, museums, and Web sites are among the sources they can consult. In addition, they might research the sets and set decoration used in Roman Empire movies, such as *Julius Caesar.* They might also research the different kinds of columns that originated with Roman architecture.

By selecting recognizable images, students can create an artwork for a production of the play. They might choose to design a program, for example, a backdrop, or an entire set.

Test Preparation Workshop

Reading Comprehension — Characteristics of Text

Strategies for Success

The reading sections of standardized tests often require you to analyze the characteristics of clear texts, including patterns of organization and word choice. Use the following strategies to help you answer test questions on these skills:

Identify Patterns of Organization The organization of information within a text affects the meaning of the text. Writers may organize information to compare or contrast things, to establish chronological order, or to show a cause-and-effect relationship. As you read, identify these patterns of organization. Read the following sample passage, and write your answer to the question on a separate piece of paper.

> The use of automobiles has increased around the world. Twenty years ago, you could travel to many places without encountering a noisy, exhaust-spewing car. As global trade and world economies have expanded, more people have purchased cars. Environmentalists contend that this increase is not a healthy trend. In parts of China today, it is nearly impossible to breathe because of the glut of unnecessary cars on the roads. Twenty years ago, those same roads were filled with nonpolluting bicycles.

What patterns of organization are used in this passage? Support your answer.

Sample answer: Chronology is used in speaking of the number of cars twenty years ago and today. Comparison is used in comparing these two time periods. Cause and effect is used in mentioning the effects of expanded trade and the polluting effects of cars.

Notice Word Choice The words that a writer chooses help to establish the writer's point of view or opinion. On a separate sheet of paper, write an answer to the following question:

> Explain how key words in the previous passage on the use of automobiles express the writer's point of view. Support your answer.

Sample answer: The writer has a negative opinion of cars: The words "noisy, exhaust-spewing" and "unnecessary" show that the writer doesn't favor cars.

Apply the Strategies

Read the following passage, and write short answers to the questions.

> At the end of World War II, the United States and the Soviet Union distrusted each other. The two superpowers competed to influence other nations. The Soviet Union supported a brutal system called communism. The United States embraced democracy for its freedom-loving people. Tensions mounted as each country built nuclear weapons. As a result, each side stockpiled enough weapons to destroy each other—and the world. Then the two countries began to reduce their arms. By the 1980's, the reduction of nuclear weapons had resulted in decreased world tensions.

1 Explain how the writer has used patterns of organization. Support your answer.

2 Explain how the writer's choice of certain words reveals his or her point of view. Support your answer.

Test-Taking Tip

Find Supporting Evidence
When asked for written responses to questions about a reading selection, test takers are often told to support their answer. Tell students that supporting your answer means "offer supporting evidence from the selection"—and the more evidence, the better. Supporting evidence often takes the form of direct quotations from the selection, along with paraphrases. Have students write responses to this question about the sample passage at the end of the workshop:

> According to the writer, what would have been the worst outcome of the competition between the two superpowers? Support your answer.

Have volunteers display their responses, which should include a quotation from the passage. Sample: The writer believes that the worst outcome would have been the destruction of the world. Each superpower "stockpiled enough weapons to destroy each other—and the world."

Correlations to Standardized Tests

The reading comprehension skills reviewed in this Workshop correspond to the following standardized test section:
SAT Critical Reading

Test Preparation

Each ATE workshop in Unit 8 supports the instruction here by providing teaching suggestions and a sample test item:

- **Identify Patterns of Organization** (ATE, pp. 669, 711, 733, 789)
- **Notice Word Choice** (ATE, pp. 685, 751, 773)

LESSON OBJECTIVES

- To comprehend selections using a variety of strategies, including analyzing text structures such as compare and contrast, cause and effect, and chronological ordering for how they influence understanding

Answers

1. The main pattern of organization is chronological. The passage begins with the end of World War II and ends with the 1980's. Comparison/contrast is used to point out differences between the Soviet Union and the United States. Cause-and-effect is shown with the reason for the buildup of nuclear weapons.
2. The writer's anti-Soviet, pro-American point of view is revealed in the words "brutal system called communism," which contrasts with the favorable words "embraced democracy for its freedom-loving people."

Planning Instruction and Assessment

Unit Objectives

1. To read a variety of poems
2. To apply a variety of reading strategies appropriate for reading poetry
3. To analyze literary elements in poetry
4. To use a variety of strategies to read unfamiliar words and to build vocabulary
5. To learn elements of grammar, usage, and style
6. To use recursive writing processes to write in a variety of forms
7. To express and support responses to various types of texts
8. To prepare, organize, and present literary interpretations

Meeting the Objectives With each selection, you will find instructional material and portfolio opportunities through which students can meet these objectives. Further, you will find additional practice pages for reading strategies, literary elements, vocabulary, and grammar in the ***Selection Support*** booklet in the ***Teaching Resources*** box.

Test Preparation

The unit workshop, **Critical Reading: Analyzing an Author's Meaning and Style** (SE, p. 877), is supported by a teaching tip and sample test item in the ATE workshop with each selection grouping: **Analyzing an Author's Meaning and Style (**ATE, pp. 813, 823, 833, 847, 855, 865)

The following additional workshops in the ATE give teaching tips and a sample test item for applying the skill taught in the Student Sucess Workshop: **Distinguishing Between Connotation and Denotation** (SE, p. 844) **Analyzing Characteristics of Texts** (SE, p. 875)

Awaiting Spring, Scott Burdick

Humanities: Art

Awaiting Spring by Scott Burdick.

Call attention to the elements of balance in this painting. Students might note the two figures poised at either end of the staircase. Help them see the balance between the heavily carved staircase and the delicate bare tree and cloudy sky above it. There is also the balance between what is fixed—the carved figure and staircase—and what can change—the living woman, the tree about to bud, and the sky about to rain.

Have students link this painting with the focus of Unit 9, Poetry, with the following questions:

1. Poems are memorable for their images and figures of speech. What description or figure of speech (imaginative comparison) would you use to describe this painting? *Students might say that the sky looks like a smoky blue marble or the tree reaches its arms to the stone angel.*
2. If you were to write a poem about this painting, what would it express, and what images in the painting contribute to that idea or emotion? *Sample answer: My poem would be melancholy; the cloudy sky and the woman whose face is turned away contribute to that emotion.*

Poetry

There are almost as many definitions of poetry as there are poets. Poetry can appear in neat stanzas, or it can look almost like prose on a page. Sometimes, it might even form a picture with the words. It can tell a story, express an idea, define a character, convey an emotion, describe a setting, or examine a situation. The poems in this unit will give you a sense of the wide range of literature that we call poetry.

Assessing Student Progress

The following tools are available to measure the degree to which students meet the unit objectives:

Informal Assessment

The questions on the Guide for Responding sections are a first level of response to the concepts and skills presented with the selection. Students' responses are a brief informal measure of their grasp of the material. Their responses on this level can indicate where further instruction and practice are needed. You may then follow up with the practice pages in the ***Selection Support*** booklet. You will find literature and reading guides in the ***Alternative Assessment*** booklet, which you may give students on an individual basis for informal assessment of their performance.

Formal Assessment

In the ***Formal Assessment*** booklet, you will find selection tests and a unit test.

Selection Tests The selection tests measure comprehension and skills acquisition for each selection or group of selections.

Unit Test The unit test, which calls on students to read a passage of literature they have not previously seen, applies the unit skills on a broader level. The Critical Reading section measures Unit Objectives 1, 2, and 3. The Vocabulary and Grammar section measures Objectives 4 and 5. The Essay section measures Objectives 1 and 6. Both the Critical Reading and Vocabulary and Grammar sections use formats similar to those found on many standardized tests, including the SAT.

Alternative Assessment

Portfolios As you review individual pieces or the collected work in students' portfolios, you will find assessment sheets available in the portfolio section of the ***Alternative Assessment*** booklet.

Scoring Rubrics You will find scoring rubrics for writing modes in the ***Alternative Assessment*** booklet. You can apply these to Guided Writing Lessons and to Writing Process Workshop lessons.

Speaking, Listening, and Viewing The ***Alternative Assessment*** booklet contains assessment sheets for speaking, listening, and Viewing activities.

Learning Modalities The ***Alternative Assessment*** contains activities that appeal to different learning styles. You may use these to as an alternative measurement of students' growth

Prepare and Engage

LESSON OBJECTIVES

1. **To develop vocabulary and word identification skills**
   - Words With Multiple Meanings
   - Using the Word Bank: Elaboration
   - Extending Word Study: Use Reference Materials (ATE)
2. **To use a variety of reading strategies to comprehend a world literature poem**
   - Connect Your Experience
   - Reading for Success: Strategies for Reading Poetry
   - Tips to Guide Reading: Recall (ATE)
   - Read to Be Entertained (ATE)
3. **To increase knowledge of other cultures and to connect common elements across cultures**
   - Background for Understanding
   - Idea Bank: Reading World Literature
4. **To express and support responses to the text**
   - Critical Thinking
   - Idea Bank: Journal Entry
   - Idea Bank: Editorial
5. **To analyze literary elements**
   - Literary Focus: Atmosphere
   - Idea Bank: Alternate Chorus
6. **To read in order to research self-selected and assigned topics**
   - Idea Bank: Encyclopedia of Folklore
   - Idea Bank: Irish Writers Timeline
7. **To plan, prepare, organize, and present literary interpretations**
   - Speaking, Listening, and Viewing Mini-Lesson: Folk Music (ATE)
8. **To use recursive writing processes to write a report**
   - Guided Writing Lesson
9. **To increase knowledge of the rules of grammar and usage**
   - Build Grammar Skills: Inverted Word Order

Test Preparation

Critical Reading: Analyzing an Author's Meaning and Style (ATE, p. 813) The teaching tips and sample test item in this workshop support the instruction and practice in the unit workshop:

Critical Reading: Analyzing an Author's Meaning and Style (SE, p. 877)

Guide for Reading

William Butler Yeats

(1865–1939)

A father who believes in the "religion of art" can leave an unusual legacy for a son inclined to be an artist. William Butler Yeats was the son of John Butler Yeats, a well-known Irish painter. William studied painting for three years, and art remained one of the three main concerns of his life. The other two were Irish nationalism and the study of the supernatural. These concerns are central issues in much of Yeats's poetry and drama. "The Stolen Child" reflects his fascination with Irish folklore, a source he used frequently in his early work.

The "First Irish Poet" Yeats's poetry broke new ground. His writing was simple, natural, and more closely linked to the voice of Irish people, their folklore traditions, and their national concerns than that of previous Irish poets. His interest in Irish politics and nationalism led him to help found the Irish National Theater in 1899.

For a time, Yeats moved to England because of political conflicts between people in Ireland of English and Irish ancestry. (His father was of English ancestry, and his mother was of Irish ancestry.) When he returned, he resided in Thoor Ballylee, a countryside tower that became an important symbol in his later poems. Yeats is considered one of the greatest twentieth-century poets in the English language.

Yeats was awarded the Nobel Prize for Literature in 1922. In one of his most famous poems, "Under Ben Bulben," he provides his own epitaph in the last lines of the poem. These lines are carved on Yeats's tombstone:

Cast a cold eye
On life, on death,
Horseman, pass by!

◆ Build Vocabulary

WORDS WITH MULTIPLE MEANINGS

When Yeats says, "Where the wave of moonlight *glosses* / The dim grey sands with light," he is describing the moonlight shining or polishing each grain of sand with its rays of light. *Gloss* is one of many words in English that has multiple meanings. In this poem, it means "to shine; make lustrous"; *gloss* can also be a noun meaning an explanation inserted in a text to make it more understandable, similar to an annotation or a footnote.

herons glosses slumbering

WORD BANK

Before you read, preview this list of words from the poem.

◆ Build Grammar Skills

INVERTED WORD ORDER

"The Stolen Child" begins with the line "Where dips the rocky highland . . ." What makes the clause sound unusual is the **inverted word order.** Usually, English word order falls into a subject-verb-complement pattern. In the clause from Yeats's poem, the verb, *dips,* precedes the subject, *the rocky highland.* Yeats intentionally uses inverted word order to give a mysterious, chantlike quality to his poem. When you see other instances of inverted word order, read the sentence in normal order for sense.

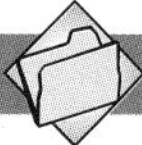

Prentice Hall Literature Program Resources

REINFORCE / RETEACH / EXTEND

Selection Support Pages
Build Vocabulary: Words With Multiple Meanings, p. 224
Build Grammar Skills: Inverted Word Order, p. 225
Reading for Success: Strategies for Reading Poetry, pp. 226–227
Literary Focus: Atmosphere, p. 228

Strategies for Diverse Student Needs, p. 55

Beyond Literature
Cultural Connection: *Celtic Folklore*, p. 55

Formal Assessment Selection Test, pp. 195–197; Assessment Resources Software

Alternative Assessment, p. 55

Resource Pro CD-ROM

Listening to Literature Audiocassettes

Literature CD-ROM

MODEL SELECTION

The Stolen Child

◆ Literature and Your Life

CONNECT YOUR EXPERIENCE

In almost any culture around the world, you can hear tales of little people who, through their supernatural powers, can make a person rich, beautiful, or powerful. Fairies, elves, sprites, pixies—these are just a few of the names by which these magical folk are known. As you may know from fairy tales, getting their help is not always as easy as it seems. There's usually a hidden price to pay. "The Stolen Child" tells the story of fairies who offer a world of pleasant delights—but at a very high price.

Journal Writing Jot down what you know about fairies and other magical little people from folklore and fairy tales.

THEMATIC FOCUS: MAKING CHOICES

The fairies in "The Stolen Child" offer compelling reasons for the child to follow them. At the end of the poem, notice the suggestion of what is lost in exchange for this choice. Next time you face a choice, you may ask yourself not only what you will gain, but what you may lose.

◆ Background for Understanding

CULTURE

Some call them pixies or sprites, others call them fairies; each of these creatures comes from folklore and legend. They are human in shape with magical powers. In Irish, or Celtic, folklore, these spirit creatures are called fairies. They live in a place called Avalon, which means "place of apples."

According to folklore, if you find a circle of dark green grass or a circle of mushrooms, you may have stumbled onto a fairy ring—a place where fairies have danced. If you see a glow come from decaying wood, it is believed you have seen a fairy spark. In reality, the first phenomenon is created by fungus and the second from phosphorous (which glows) produced in decaying wood.

◆ Literary Focus

ATMOSPHERE

Picture the following setting as the first scene in a movie: Nightfall. Large birds flap their long wings, creating shadows on a lonely lake. Water rats wake from sleep and begin to scamper in circles. The dew glistens in the moonlight.

These images create a tranquil, slightly mysterious or even magical atmosphere. **Atmosphere** is the mood or the overall feeling that a story or poem conveys. A writer establishes atmosphere through details of the setting or action. In poetry, rhyme, meter, and other sound devices can also create atmosphere. Together, all these elements create the effect the poet wants.

The following lines from "The Stolen Child" create a mysterious, mystical atmosphere in which a meeting takes place between fairies and a human child.

Where the wave of moonlight
  glosses
The dim grey sands with light,
Far off by the furthest Rosses . . .

Tell students that this poem describes a choice between the reality of the human world and an escape to a magical world. On the chalkboard, create a pros and cons chart exploring the advantages and disadvantages of escaping reality. In the pro column, you might list "no responsibility." In the con column, you might list "losing friends and family." Have students brainstorm for other pros and cons. Leave the list on the chalkboard while students read the poem so that they can compare their ideas with the ideas expressed in the poem.

Tips to Guide Reading

Recall Students may find it helpful to stop and recall details from the poems at several points during their reading in order to appreciate the atmosphere of the poem.

Customize for
Less Proficient Readers
Less proficient readers may benefit from paraphrasing each stanza of the poem as they read. Encourage them to keep in mind the fairies' purpose—to tempt a human child away from human life.

Customize for
Pre-AP Students
Challenge students to identify and distinguish between the characteristics of the various types of figurative language used throughout the poems. Encourage them to explain why they think each type of figurative language is, or isn't, effective.

Customize for
English Language Learners
Students whose first language is not English may be confused by the inverted word order in the first and fourth stanzas. Help them restate the lines, placing the words in standard order.

Customize for
Gifted/Talented Students
Ask students to hypothesize about what the poem would be like if the author had expressed it as a story, a drama, or even a painting. Have them compare and contrast the different methods of expression.

Test Preparation Workshop

Critical Reading:
Analyzing an Author's Meaning and Style

Students preparing to take standardized tests such as the PSAT need to be reminded of the importance of determining what the author is implying when answering questions on a critical reading selection. For additional practice in using this skill, have students read the poem "The Stolen Child."

Consider the following question. Which of the choices best describes the author's opinion?

A Fairies will take good care of the child.
B The human child will sacrifice little by going with the fairies.
C The fairy's theft of the child will cause pain and sadness in the human world.
D The fairy world is superior.

Suggest that students quickly eliminate answer choices that are not suggested in the poem. They should be able to determine that although the poem is told from the point of view of the fairies, the human child will still be in a world that is not his own and his loss will cause suffering. Therefore, answer C is best.

Reading for Success

The Reading for Success page in each unit presents a set of problem-solving procedures to help readers understand authors' words and ideas on multiple levels. Good readers develop a bank of strategies from which they can draw as needed.

Unit 9 introduces strategies for reading poetry. These strategies give readers an approach to understand poetry through its distinguishing qualities, including figurative language, images, and sound elements. By using these strategies as they read, students will be better able to analyze the material presented in this selection.

These strategies for reading poetry are modeled with "The Stolen Child." Each green box shows an example of the thinking process involved in applying one of these strategies.

How to Use the Reading for Success Page

- Introduce the strategies for reading poetry, presenting each as a problem-solving procedure. Be sure students understand what each strategy involves and under what circumstances to apply it.
- Before students read the poem, have them preview it, looking at the annotations in the green boxes that model the strategies.
- To reinforce these strategies after students have read "The Stolen Child," have students do the Reading for Success pages in ***Selection Support,*** pp. 226–227. This activity gives students an opportunity to read a selection and practice strategies for reading poetry by writing their own annotations.

Reading for Success

Strategies for Reading Poetry

Poetry is a very distinctive kind of writing. It differs from other forms of writing in its appearance, its use of language, and its sound. Poets' imaginative use of language can sometimes make a poem seem complex or hard to understand. Here are strategies to help you read poetry successfully and enjoy it as well.

Identify the speaker.

When you read a poem, you are hearing the voice of the poem's speaker. The speaker is not necessarily the poet, although it can be or it can be a part of the poet's personality. The speaker may be a character created by the poet. Determine who you think is "telling" the poem, and try to determine his or her perspective on the situation in the poem. Recognizing the speaker and his or her perspective will give you an insight into the meaning of the poem.

Envision images and figures of speech.

Use your senses to experience the pleasures of a poem. For instance, see the dim gray sands bathed in moonlight; feel the frothy bubbles of the trout stream; hear the mooing of the cows on the nearby hillside.

Read according to punctuation.

Keep in mind that even if a poem is shaped to fit a particular rhythm and rhyme, a poem's words are put together and punctuated as sentences. For example, when you read "The Stolen Child," notice that each stanza is a complete sentence, expressing a complete thought. When you read a poem, don't stop at the end of each line unless a punctuation mark (period, comma, colon, semicolon, or dash) stops you.

Listen to the poem.

One of the things that distinguishes poetry from prose is its sound. Poetry is meant to be read aloud; only by doing so will you hear the music of the poet's words.

Paraphrase.

Restate the speaker's experiences and feelings in your own words. Restating the lines or stanzas will help you clarify their meaning.

Respond to what you read.

Think about what the speaker has said. How do the images in the poem affect you? What does the poem say to you?

As you read "The Stolen Child," look at the notes in the boxes. These notes demonstrate how to apply these strategies to a poem.

Reading Strategies: Support and Reinforcement

Appropriate Reading Strategies Students are given a reading strategy to apply in reading each selection. Each reading strategy in this unit will help them gain insight into the poems to which they apply it.

Reading Prompts To encourage application of the given reading strategy, there are occasional prompts, within green boxes, at appropriate and significant points.

In addition, there are red boxes prompting application of the Literary Focus concept and maroon boxes prompting students to connect with their lives.

Using the Boxed Annotations and Prompts
The material in the green, red, and maroon boxes along the sides of selections is intended to help students apply the literary element and the reading strategy and to make a connection with their lives.

You may use the boxed material in these ways:

- Have students pause when they come to a box and respond to its prompt before they continue reading.
- Urge students to read through the selection ignoring the boxes. After they have read the selection completely, they may go back and review the selection, responding to the prompts.

MODEL

THE STOLEN CHILD

WILLIAM BUTLER YEATS

Notice that the **speakers** of this poem are the fairies. Their point of view affects your view of events.

Where dips the rocky highland
Of Sleuth Wood in the lake,
There lies a leafy island
Where flapping herons wake
The drowsy water rats;
There we've hid our faery[1] vats,
Full of berries
And of reddest stolen cherries.
Come away, O human child!
To the waters and the wild
With a faery, hand in hand,
For the world's more full of weeping than you can understand. ❶

Use your senses to envision the grains of sand glowing in the moonlight.

Where the wave of moonlight glosses
The dim grey sands with light,
Far off by furthest Rosses[2]

1. **faery:** A different spelling of fairy.
2. **Rosses:** Marshes.

◆ Build Vocabulary

herons (her´ ənz) *n.*: Birds with long necks, legs, and bills that live along riverbanks and marshes

glosses (glôs´ əs) *v.*: Shines

◀ Critical Viewing In what way does this picture contribute to the dreamlike atmosphere of "The Stolen Child"? **[Infer]** ❷

Block Scheduling Strategies

Consider these suggestions to take advantage of extended class time:

- Have students view Feature 2 on the **Literature CD-ROM.** This section discusses the definition of poetry and oral tradition.
- Introduce the strategies for reading poetry on p. 811. Have students review the application of these strategies in the boxed annotations. After they have read the poem, have them answer the Reading for Success questions on p. 819.
- Have students work in small groups to discuss and answer the questions in the Connections to Today's World feature on p. 817. Then, have the groups present their answers to the class.
- Ask small groups of students to complete the Alternate Chorus writing activity in the Idea Bank on p. 820. Then groups can read the poem and their choruses into a tape recorder and play the recording for the class.
- Students who are interested in the Irish Writers Timeline in the Idea Bank on p. 820 might enjoy creating an Irish History Timeline showing the historical events that influenced Yeats and his writing.

Develop Understanding

In this poem, fairies are tempting a child to come away from his life as a human, with all its attendant suffering, and join them in a fairyland where nature is friendly and benign. In the last stanza, however, the fairies reveal that the child will also leave the good things in human life and go to the unknown, the wild world of the fairies. Readers are left to contemplate the price that must be paid for escaping the trials and responsibilities of the real world.

◆ Reading for Success

❶ **Identify the Speaker** Ask students who the speakers are and what word or words reveal the speakers' identity. *The speakers are fairies, and the words "we've" and "our" together with their descriptions reveal their identity.*

▶Critical Viewing◀

❷ **Infer** *This misty photograph of a forest contributes to the magical, dreamlike tone of Yeats's poem; it's easy to imagine the fairies leaping "to and fro" and chasing bubbles in this scene.*

Art Transparency Display Art Transparency 16 and encourage student comments. As you discuss "The Stolen Child," have students summarize the argument that the fairies make to lure the child away from the world. Call students' attention to what Carrington's painting may suggest about the boundary between fantasy and reality and why they think the child in the poem chose the world of fantasy.

Literature CD-ROM To introduce students to poetry you might use the **Literature CD-ROM**, Feature 4, which introduces poetry, discusses reader response to poetry, and provides quotations from several well-known poets.

◆ Build Vocabulary

❶ Words With Multiple Meanings Ask students what the word *foot* can mean as both a noun and a verb. *Foot as a noun is a body part; foot as a verb means to move quickly or dance.* Which meaning of the word is used here? *Foot here means to move quickly or dance.*

◆ Reading for Success

❷ Envision Images and Figures of Speech Ask students to describe the image they envision when they read the lines, "While the world is full of troubles/And is anxious in its sleep." To what does Yeats compare "the world"? *Students should envision the world as a person tossing and turning in his or her sleep.*

◆ Reading for Success

❸ Listen to the Poem; Respond Have volunteers read aloud the chorus of the poem. Ask students how this part of the poem affects them. *Students may indicate that the chorus makes them feel uneasy, or that they find it magical and appealing.*

◆ Literary Focus

❹ Atmosphere Ask students to describe the atmosphere that is created by the repetition of this chorus. *The chantlike quality of the chorus and the images in it create a magical, mysterious atmosphere.*

◆ Reading for Success

❺ Paraphrase Have students restate this portion of the stanza in their own words. *Where the water runs from the hills above Glen-Car, we whisper in the ears of sleeping fish and make them uneasy.*

◆ Reading for Success

❻ Read According to Punctuation Have students read this stanza aloud, pausing where punctuation indicates, rather than at the ends of lines. *Students should pause after going "solemn-eyed" and "breast."*

Read to Be Entertained

Students should set a reading purpose to be entertained by the poetry and the author's use of atmosphere, rich vocabulary, and description.

---

❶ We foot it all the night,
Weaving olden dances
Mingling hands and mingling glances
Till the moon has taken flight;
To and fro we leap
❷ And chase the frothy bubbles,
While the world is full of troubles
And is anxious in its sleep.
Come away, O human child!
To the waters and the wild
❸ *With a faery, hand in hand,*
❹ *For the world's more full of weeping*
than you can understand.

Where the wandering water gushes
From the hills above Glen-Car,
In pools among the rushes
❺ That scarce could bathe a star,
We seek for slumbering trout
And whispering in their ears
Give them unquiet dreams;
Leaning softly out
From ferns that drop their tears
Over the young streams.
Come away, O human child!
To the waters and the wild
With a faery, hand in hand,
For the world's more full of weeping
than you can understand.

Away with us he's going,
The solemn-eyed:
He'll hear no more the lowing[3]
Of the calves on the warm hillside ❻
Or the kettle on the hob[4]
Sing peace into his breast,
Or see the brown mice bob
Round and round the oatmeal chest.

For he comes, the human child,
To the waters and the wild
With a faery, hand in hand,
From a world more full of weeping
than he can understand.

Respond by identifying your feelings about the fairies' triumph.

◆ Build Vocabulary

slumbering (slum′ bər iŋ) *v.*: Sleeping

3. **lowing** (lō′ iŋ) *n.*: Mooing.
4. **hob** (häb) *n.*: Ledge on a fireplace used for keeping a kettle or pan warm.

Guide for Responding

◆ *Literature and Your Life*

Reader's Response Do you agree with the line repeated in "The Stolen Child" that "the world's more full of weeping than you can understand"? Why or why not?

Thematic Focus What do you think will be the consequence of a human child choosing to go with fairies rather than staying with humans?

☑ Check Your Comprehension

1. Who is the speaker of this poem?
2. Where have the fairies hidden vats full of berries?
3. Why do the fairies say the human child should go with them?
4. Summarize what happens in the poem.

Reinforce and Extend

Answers

◆ *Literature and Your Life*

Reader's Response Students' answers will depend upon their personal experience, but they should support their opinion with examples or evidence.

Thematic Focus Some students might indicate that the child's human nature will arise and cause conflicts; others might indicate that the child will betray the earthly world.

☑ Check Your Comprehension

1. A fairy (or group of fairies) is the speaker of the poem.
2. They have hidden the vats of berries on a lake island.
3. They say the child should come with them because the world is full of sadness.
4. Fairies try to lure a child to come with them; they tempt it with berries and descriptions of carefree, mischievous activities. In the end, the child goes with the fairies, leaving behind the earthly world.

Connections to Today's World

"The Stolen Child" tells of a child lost through fairies' magical powers. "Cat's in the Cradle" tells of a lost childhood. Not until the child is grown does the father realize all the precious moments he has lost.

An artist in the American folk tradition of Woody Guthrie and Bob Dylan, Harry Chapin wrote songs that are essentially short stories set to music. A true humanitarian, over the course of his career he raised more than five million dollars for various causes. He died in 1981 in a car crash, while on the way to perform at a benefit concert.

Cat's in the Cradle

Harry Chapin and Sandy Chapin

My child arrived just the other day,
He came to the world in the usual way.
But there were planes to catch, and bills
to pay.
He learned to walk while I was away.
And he was talking 'fore I knew it, and
as he grew,
He'd say, "I'm gonna be like you, Dad.
You know I'm gonna be like you."

And the cat's in the cradle and the silver
spoon,
Little boy blue and the man in the moon.
"When you coming home, Dad?" "I don't
know when,
But we'll get together then.
You know we'll have a good time then."

My son turned ten just the other day.
He said, "Thanks for the ball, Dad, come
on let's play.
Can you teach me to throw?" I said, "Not
today,
I got a lot to do." He said, "That's ok."
And he walked away but his smile,
lemme tell you,
Said, "I'm gonna be like him, yeah.
You know, I'm gonna be like him."

And the cat's in the cradle and the silver
spoon,
Little boy blue and the man in the moon.
"When you coming home, Dad?" "I don't
know when,
But we'll get together then.
You know we'll have a good time then."

Well, he came from college just the other
day,
So much like a man I just had to say,
"Son, I'm proud of you. Can you sit for a
while?"
He shook his head, and he said with a
smile,
"What I'd really like, Dad, is to borrow
the car keys.
See you later. Can I have them please?"

Connections to Today's World

Like "The Stolen Child," Harry Chapin's song "Cat's in the Cradle" tells the story of a lost child. The child in the song, however, is not lost through magical means. The everyday cares and worries of the real word eventually create a void between father and son that cannot be crossed.

More About the Author
Singer/songwriter Harry Chapin (1942–1981) was a social activist as well as an artist. He committed time and money to the cause of ending world hunger, founding World Hunger Year in 1975. Besides being a songwriter, Chapin was a filmmaker (nominated for an Academy Award) and the author of a musical play (nominated for two Tony Awards). Chapin died in a car accident on July 16, 1981.

Customize for
English Laanguage Learners
Students whose first language is not English may not be familiar with the nursery rhymes from which these lines are taken. Have volunteers recite the rhymes and discuss why the writer chose to include them.

Thematic Connection
Ask students how the child in Chapin's song is learning to realize that the world is "full of weeping," just as it is for the stolen child. *As he asks for his father's company and is denied, he learns to adjust to not having his father's companionship.*

Customize for
Pre-AP Students
Advanced readers can be challenged to explain how the narrative turns around in the third verse. In what way has the son become like his father?

Speaking, Listening, and Viewing Mini-Lesson

Folk Music
This mini-lesson supports the Speaking, Listening, and Viewing activity in the Idea Bank on p. 820.

Introduce Many folk songs tell stories. Because these songs come from cultures all over the world, many have references that listeners may not understand. If students choose songs from unfamiliar cultures, they may have to research in order to understand and explain such references.

Develop When looking for songs, students should consider these questions:

- From which culture does the song come?
- On what story is the song based?
- What references will have to be explained?
- Does the song differ from, or add to, the story?

Apply Many libraries are sources for song books and recordings of folk songs. Students should take notes on the stories, list and research their references, then give their presentations.

Assess Students should answer the questions in Develop Background. Assess presentations based on how thoroughly each question is addressed.

Extending Word Study

Reference Materials Students will find it helpful to determine precise meanings of words in the poem that may have multiple definitions They can use reference materials such as the dictionary or thesaurus. Suggest that students list each unfamiliar word on an index card with the multiple definitions, so that they can review the cards as needed to increase their vocabulary.

◆ Critical Thinking

Compare and Contrast Ask students how this song and Yeats's poem are similar and how they are different. *They both use rhythm and rhyme and both include a verse/refrain, or chorus. They treat the theme of loss and the troubles faced in the real world. In Yeats's poem, a child is lost when he leaves the real world. In Chapin's song, a child is lost when he becomes part of the real world.*

◆ Critical Thinking

Draw Conclusions The father and the son in the picture, unlike the father and the son in the song, are spending time together on an activity they are enjoying. They find time to "escape" from the trials of the world together; they are forming an emotional bond.

▶Critical Viewing◀

1 Draw Conclusions *The man in the poem does not have time for his son, while the boy and the man in the painting are spending quality time together.*

Answers

1. Students may point out that the theme (demanding modern life swallowing up people's time), language ("my new job's a hassle") and details (college, car keys) of Chapin's song could all make it a modern version of the story in Yeats's poem.
2. Yeats's poem and Chapin's song are both told in stanzas that alternate between pieces of a story in progress and a chorus, or refrain.
3. The moral to this song might be "Enjoy the people you love before it's too late."
4. Sample advice: (a) Devote some attention to your son before it's too late; (b) Be forgiving toward your father even though he was not always there for you.

Reteach

Students who experience difficulty analyzing the atmosphere and setting of a poem should be encouraged to make a list of the author's words that appeal to the senses. Then discuss with them how the imagery establishes the poem's setting and contributes to its atmosphere.

Connections to Today's World

▲ Critical Viewing What details in this picture indicate that this father and son are closer to each other than the father and son in "Cat's in the Cradle"? **[Draw Conclusions]** **1**

And the cat's in the cradle and the silver
spoon,
Little boy blue and the man in the moon.
"When you coming home, son?" "I don't
know when,
But we'll get together then, Dad.
You know we'll have a good time then."

I've long since retired and my son's
moved away.
I called him up just the other day.
I said, "I'd like to see you if you don't
mind."
He said, "I'd love to, Dad, if I could
find the time.
You see, my new job's a hassle and
the kid's got the flu,
But it's sure nice talking to you,
Dad.
It's been sure nice talking to you."
And as I hung up the phone, it occurred
to me,
He'd grown up just like me.
My boy was just like me.

And the cat's in the cradle and the silver
spoon,
Little boy blue and the man in the moon.
"When you coming home, son?" "I don't
know when,
But we'll get together then, Dad.
You know we'll have a good time
then."

1. In what way is the story told in "Cat's in the Cradle" a modern version of "The Stolen Child"?
2. Explain how the structure of "The Stolen Child" is similar to the structure of this song.
3. If there were a moral to this song, what would it be?
4. (a) What advice would you give to the father in this song? (b) What advice would you give to the son?

Beyond the Selection

FURTHER READING

Other Works by the Authors

Collected Poems, by William Butler Yeats
Collected Plays, by William Butler Yeats
Heads and Tails, by Harry Chapin
Short Stories, by Harry Chapin

Other Works With the Theme of Choices and Consequences

"The Road Not Taken," by Robert Frost
"anyone lived in a pretty how town," by E. E. Cummings
"Richard Corey," by Edward Arlington Robinson

INTERNET

We suggest the following sites on the Internet (all Web sites are subject to change).

For more information on William Butler Yeats's life and works:
http://www.nadn.navy.mil/EnglishDept/ILV/yeats.htm

For more about Harry Chapin and his work:
http://www.littlejason.com/chapin/index.html

We *strongly recommend* that you preview the sites before you send students to them.

Guide for Responding (continued)

◆ Critical Thinking

Interpret

1. What details in the setting of this poem create a sense of mystery and magic? **[Analyze]**

2. (a)Which events in the poem could occur in real life? (b) Which could occur only in fantasy stories? **[Classify]**

Evaluate

3. The fairies list the features of the human world that the child must leave behind. Do you think the fairies promise enough to make such a sacrifice worthwhile? **[Assess]**

Extend

4. Which art form—film, theater, music, dance, painting, photography, or sculpture—do you think would be the best to interpret this poem? Explain. **[Career Link]**

◆ Reading for Success

Strategies for Reading Poetry

Review the reading strategies and the notes describing how to read poetry. Then apply these strategies to answer the following questions.

1. How does knowing the speaker of the poem help you understand what is happening?

2. Which sense(s) do you use most in reading this poem? Explain your answer.

3. Paraphrase the following lines from the fifth stanza: "We seek for slumbering trout/And whispering in their ears/Give them unquiet dreams."

4. Explain how reading each stanza as a sentence helps you understand the story in the poem.

◆ Literary Focus

Atmosphere

Atmosphere is the feeling created by a story or poem. Descriptive details, word choice, and the rhythm and rhyme create the atmosphere in "The Stolen Child."

1. What is the atmosphere of this poem? Which words, images, or techniques establish this atmosphere?

2. In what way does the atmosphere affect your expectations of how the poem will turn out?

◆ Build Vocabulary

Using Words With Multiple Meanings

Many words in English, such as *gloss,* have different meanings. Read the following sentence sets. Identify the word in each set that is used with different meanings. In your notebook, explain the different meanings.

1. The glosses helped me understand the play.
The sunlight glosses the trees with gold.

2. The small plane climbed until it was just a dot in the sky.
My mother used a plane to level the top of the door.
The haughty woman thought she existed on a higher plane than the common people.

3. We caught more than one hundred fish in our net.
You must calculate your budget on your net income.

Using the Word Bank: Elaboration

On your paper, answer each question.

1. Where would you expect to see a heron?

2. What kind of item from your home would you gloss?

3. Would you want to drive a truck while slumbering? Why or why not?

◆ Build Grammar Skills

Inverted Word Order

Poets sometimes use **inverted word order** to emphasize words or to make their writing fit a rhyme or rhythm pattern. In the line, "Where dips the rocky highland," Yeats inverts the word order to create a sense of otherworldliness—of creatures who do not speak in the same speech patterns as people do.

Inverted word order changes the usual subject-verb-complement pattern of word order in English.

Practice Find three other examples of inverted word order in "The Stolen Child." Identify the pattern of each. Then, in each case, explain the effect Yeats created by inverting word order.

Answers
◆ Critical Thinking

1. Mysterious or magical setting details include the leafy island waves of moonlight gray sands and dripping ferns.
2. (a) Some events that could occur in real life are flapping herons waking water rats, calves lowing on a hillside, and mice running around the oatmeal chest; (b) fantasy events include fairies dancing in the moonlight and whispering in the ears of fish.
3. Students may think the fairies' promises are too ambiguous to take the risk.
4. Some students may mention dance because the poem features an evocative moonlight dance.

◆ Reading for Success

1. Knowing that the speaker of the poem is a fairy or group of fairies helps to highlight the choice between magic and reality.
2. Students will probably say they use the sense of sight the most because there are many vivid set images they can mentally picture.
3. Example: We look for sleeping fish and whisper disturbing thoughts in their ears so they will sleep poorly.
4. Reading each stanza as a sentence helps to clarify complete thoughts.

◆ Literary Focus

1. Sample response: The poem has a magical, mysterious atmosphere, supported by images such as *wave of moonlight; dim gray sands with light* and *bathe a star.*
2. Students might say the magical atmosphere of the poem suggests that the child might be taken off by the fairies, which in fact happens.

◆ Build Vocabulary

Words With Multiple Meanings

1. First sentence: *glosses* means "a marginal explanation"; second sentence: *glosses* means "to put a shine upon."
2. First sentence: *plane* means airplane; second sentence: *plane* means a "woodworking instrument used for paring and smoothing"; third sentence: *plane* means a level of dignity.
3. First sentence: *net* means "a fabric with an open mesh"; second sentence: *Net* means "remaining after deductions, as for expenses."

Using the Word Bank

1. You might expect to see a heron near water.
2. You might gloss a tabletop or a mirror.
3. You would not want to drive a truck while slumbering, or sleeping, because you could get into an accident.

◆ Build Grammar Skills

Examples: (1) "To and fro we leap" is a adverb/subject/verb structure which creates a dance-like effect; (2) "Where the wandering water gushes" is an adverb/subject/verb structure, a repeated construction in the poem that creates a musical effect; (3) "Away with us he's going" is a complement/subject/verb structure, creating a musical, jaunty effect.

Grammar Reinforcement

For practice, use the **Language Lab CD-ROM** Special Problems in Agreement lesson and p. 121, Varying Your Sentences, in *Writer's Solution Grammar Practice Book.*

Idea Bank

Following are suggestions for matching Idea Bank topics with your students' performance levels and learning modalities:

Customizing for *Performance Levels*
Less Advanced Students: 1, 4
Average Students: 2, 3, 5, 6,
More Advanced Students: 7

Customizing for *Learning Modalities*
Verbal/Linguistic: 4, 5
Interpersonal: 4
Visual/Spatial: 7
Musical/Rhythmic 3, 4, 5

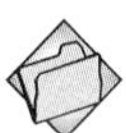

Guided Writing Lesson

Prewriting Strategy The reporter's formula will provide students with the investigative means to begin their crime reports. Have students create a chart to gather their details before they create their drawings. They can use the chart as a guide to reviewing the poem.

Who?
What?
Where?
Why?
When?
How?

For more prewriting, elaboration, and revision strategies, see *Prentice Hall Writing and Grammar.*

Writers at Work Videodisc
Have students view the videodisc segment for Chapter 8 in which Larry Cataldo talks about the importance of gathering precise details for practical writing.

Play frames 35100 to 37293

Writing Lab CD-ROM
Have students complete the tutorial on Practical and Technical Writing:

1. Have students answer Purpose Profile questions aimed at helping to achieve an intended purpose.
2. Encourage students to use Transition Word bins to select words that suggest chronological and spatial relationships that they can use in their crime report.
3. Have students use a Proofreading Checklist to pinpoint possible errors in their drafts.

Build Your Portfolio

Idea Bank

Writing

1. **Journal Entry** Imagine that you are the child the fairies stole. Write a postcard home. Tell your family what life with the fairies is like.
2. **Editorial** Imagine that you live in the area where the child was stolen by fairies. Write an editorial for the local newspaper. In it share your opinion on what happened and how the community should respond to the kidnapping.
3. **Alternate Chorus** Write lyrics for a chorus that a group of humans might whisper to the child to persuade him to remain in the human world. You may use rhythm and rhyme similar to that in "The Stolen Child."

Speaking, Listening, and Viewing

4. **Reading World Literature** The pixies, sprites, and faeries of Irish folklore have equivalents in folklore from other cultures. Explore the folklore or fairy tales of Africa or Asia and select a story to read to your class that reflects the theme of "The Stolen Child."
5. **Folk Music** Choose a song that tells a story from folklore. Learn the story on which the song is based. Play the song for your class, and explain the references they don't understand. **[Music Link]**

Researching and Representing

6. **Irish Writers Timeline** Create a timeline that shows Yeats's place in the spectrum of Irish authors. Annotate the timeline to indicate any authors who influenced or were influenced by Yeats.
7. **Encyclopedia of Folklore** Research how other cultures besides the Irish perceive the magical people in folklore. Create a mini-encyclopedia. Include an explanation and illustration for each culture. **[Social Studies Link]**

Online Activity **www.phlit.phschool.com**

Guided Writing Lesson

Crime Report

What W. B. Yeats describes in "The Stolen Child" is a kidnapping. Imagine that you are a detective who investigates the crime of the child stolen. Write a **crime report** describing what you found at a crime scene, including evidence or possible clues for solving the crime. In your crime report, you would include interviews with witnesses to the crime as well as people who may have seen or heard anything out of the ordinary on the night of the crime.

Writing Skills Focus: Clear, Consistent Purpose

Your purpose determines the details, tone, and language you use when writing. A crime report has a **clear, consistent purpose:** to describe all information available about a crime in an orderly, logical fashion with as much detail as possible so that the crime can eventually be solved. Keep this purpose in mind as you write. Be thorough, but don't wander off in directions that have no bearing on the case.

Prewriting Review the poem to gather details about the fairies' habits and the setting. Use these details to create a diagram of the crime scene, using labels to identify each important object. As you draw, you may think of more details about the crime scene to include in your report. Refer to the diagram as you draft.

Drafting Use exact nouns and vivid verbs to help readers picture the scene the way you encountered it. If you include information from eyewitnesses, use direct quotations from them.

Revising Show your crime scene diagram and report draft to a classmate. Ask your classmate to match the labeled objects in the sketch with details in your report. This will help you identify any details that need to be added to your report.

✓ ASSESSMENT OPTIONS

Formal Assessment, Selection Test, pp. 195–197, and Assessment Resources Software. The selection test is designed so that it can be easily customized to the performance levels of your students.

Alternative Assessment, p. 55, includes options for less advanced students, more advanced students, musical/rhythmic learners, visual/spatial learners, interpersonal learners, and verbal/linguistic learners.

PORTFOLIO ASSESSMENT
Use the following rubrics in the ***Alternative Assessment*** booklet to assess student writing:
Journal Entry: Description Rubric, p. 97
Editorial: Persuasion Rubric, p. 105
Alternate Chorus: Poetry Rubric, p. 108
Guided Writing Lesson: Technical Description/ Explanation Rubric, p. 115

PART 1 *Meaning and Sound*

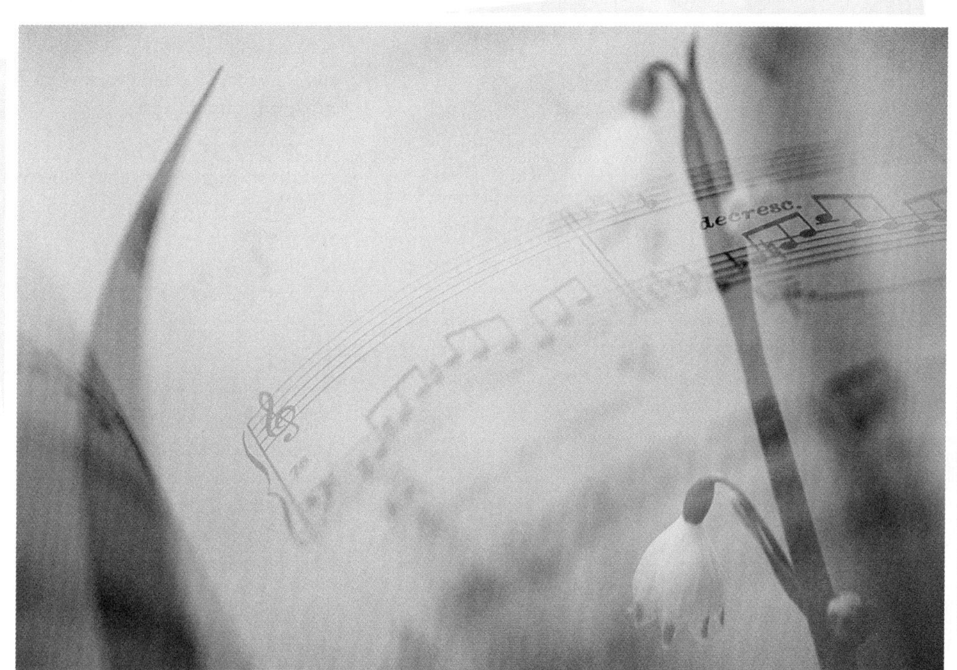

Untitled, O. S. Eguchi

One-Minute Planning Guide

Part I focuses on the language of poetry—the way that poets create meaning and effects through words. The poems provide examples of musical devices and figures of speech. The first group of poems—ranging from formal, structured poems, like Robert Browning's "Meeting at Night" to traditional chants like the Navajo "Prayer of First Dancers"—illustrates sound devices. The second group, illustrating simile, metaphor, and personification, includes classic poems by Emily Dickinson and Eve Merriam and contemporary poems by Yehuda Amichai and Philip Fried.

Customize for
Varying Student Needs

When assigning the poems in this part, keep in mind these factors:

- All of the poems except "Prayer of First Dancers" are very short.
- The following poems contain vocabulary that may challenge less proficient readers or ESL Students:
  "The Kraken"
  "Right Hand"
- The following poems contain abstract concepts:
  "A Pace Like That"
  "Right Hand"
- Students will benefit from having a context for "Prayer of First Dancers," a longer poem with much repetition
- The following poems contain sharp, accessible images:
  "Reapers"
  "Metaphor"
- Dickinson's irregularities of capitalization and punctuation in "The Wind—tapped like a tired Man" may confuse some readers

Humanities: Art

Untitled by O. S. Eguchi.

This untitled photograph superimposes a stalk of flowers on a page of sheet music. Explain to students that the photographer develops two separate negatives on the same sheet of paper to achieve this effect. Combining the images in this way suggests a relationship between them. Use the following questions to link the painting to the focus of Part 1, "Meaning and Sound."

1. What relationship between a flower and a song might the photographer be suggesting? *The photographer might be suggesting that songs, like flowers, have a certain symmetry, that the beauty in both seems simple but is actually quite complex, and perhaps that both increase in beauty upon reflection.*
2. Poetry is the type of literature that most people perceive to be closest to music. What are songlike features in poetry? *Songlike features in poetry include rhythm, the sounds of various words, the use of rhyme, the use of repeated patterns of sound.*

Prepare and Engage

LESSON OBJECTIVES

1. **To develop vocabulary and word identification skills**
   - Latin Prefixes: *mil-*
   - Using the Word Bank: Context
   - Extending Word Study: Wide Reading (ATE)
2. **To use a variety of reading strategies to comprehend poems**
   - Connect Your Experience
   - Reading Strategy: Listen
   - Tips to Guide Reading: Use Punctuation (ATE)
   - Read to Appreciate an Author's Craft (ATE)
3. **To express and support responses to the text**
   - Critical Thinking
   - Idea Bank: Letter to Editor
4. **To analyze literary elements**
   - Literary Focus: Musical Devices
   - Idea Bank: City Chant
   - Idea Bank: Musical Devices
5. **To read in order to research self-selected and assigned topics**
   - Speaking, Listening, and Viewing Mini-Lesson: Oral Report (ATE)
   - Viewing and Representing Mini-Lesson: Creatures Across Cultures (ATE)
   - Idea Bank: World War I
6. **To use recursive writing processes to write a proposal**
   - Guided Writing Lesson
7. **To increase knowledge of the rules of grammar and usage**
   - Build Grammar Skills: Concrete and Abstract Nouns

Test Preparation

Critical Reading: Analyzing an Author's Meaning and Style (ATE, p. 823) The teaching tips and sample test item in this workshop support the instruction and practice in the unit workshop.

Critical Reading: Analyzing an Author's Meaning and Style (SE, p. 877)

Guide for Reading

John McCrae *(1872–1918)*

A physician working as a medical officer in France during World War I, McCrae saw first-hand the war about which he wrote. "In Flanders Fields" was published by the British magazine *Punch* in 1915. The poem was reprinted in the United States to boost the morale of soldiers and to encourage civilians to join the service.

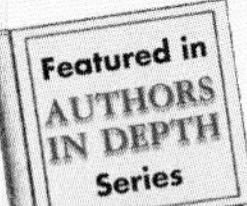

Alfred, Lord Tennyson *(1809–1892)*

No artist can ever know how time will view his or her achievements. The most popular English poet of the nineteenth century and the first English writer ever to be made a baron, Alfred, Lord Tennyson lost favor with the public shortly after his death. Today, however, he is again known as the greatest Victorian poet and perhaps the most lyrical poet in the history of the English language.

Jean Toomer *(1894–1967)*

French, Dutch, Welsh, German, Jewish, African, and Indian: Jean Toomer was descended from all these ethnicities and races. "Because of these," he said, "my position in America has been a curious one." In 1923, Toomer became famous at a young age with the publication of his book *Cane*, which includes short stories, poems, and a short novel.

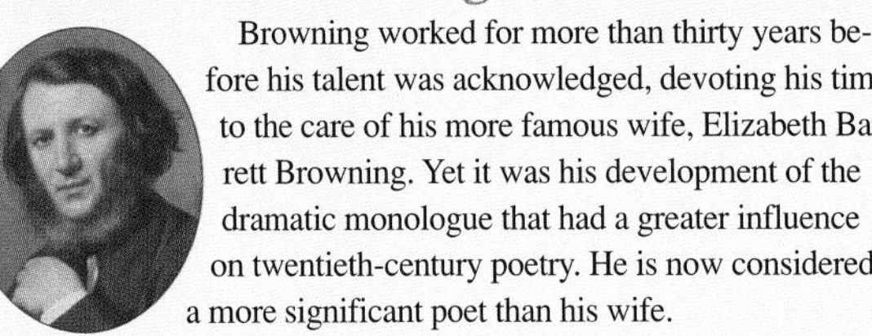

Robert Browning *(1812–1889)*

Browning worked for more than thirty years before his talent was acknowledged, devoting his time to the care of his more famous wife, Elizabeth Barrett Browning. Yet it was his development of the dramatic monologue that had a greater influence on twentieth-century poetry. He is now considered a more significant poet than his wife.

Navajo

The Navajo today constitute the largest Native American tribe in the United States. Chants and sand paintings are part of a the Navajo's complex system of ceremonials. "Prayer of First Dancers" from *The Night Chant* comes from that tradition of holy ceremonies.

◆ Build Vocabulary

LATIN PREFIXES: *mil-*

When Alfred, Lord Tennyson wants to emphasize the incredible size and age of the Kraken and its surroundings, he describes the "Huge sponges of *millennial* growth and height" that surround it. *Millennial*, which means "of or relating to a thousand-year period," contains the prefix *mil-* and comes from the Latin *mille*, which means "one thousand." The sponges in Tennyson's poem, therefore, are so old that they've been growing for literally a thousand years.

WORD BANK

Before you read, preview these words from the poems.

abysmal
millennial

◆ Build Grammar Skills

CONCRETE AND ABSTRACT NOUNS

A **concrete noun** names something physical that can be directly perceived by one of the five senses, while an **abstract noun** names an idea, belief, quality or concept—something that cannot be seen, heard, smelled, tasted, or touched.

You can see, touch, and smell the *poppies* (a concrete noun) in "In Flanders Fields," but you cannot directly perceive *speed* (an abstract noun) in "Meeting at Night."

Poets rely on concrete nouns to create sensory images. You will notice far more concrete nouns in these and other poems than abstract nouns.

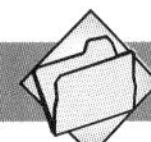

Prentice Hall Literature Program Resources

REINFORCE / RETEACH / EXTEND

Selection Support Pages
Build Vocabulary: Prefixes: *mil-*, p. 229
Build Grammar Skills: Abstract Nouns, p. 230
Reading Strategy: Listen, p. 231
Literary Focus: Musical Devices, p. 232

Strategies for Diverse Student Needs, p. 56

Beyond Literature *Art,* p. 56

Formal Assessment Selection Test, pp. 198–200; Assessment Resources Software

Alternative Assessment, p. 56

Resource Pro CD-ROM

Listening to Literature Audiocassettes

Literature CD-ROM

In Flanders Fields ◆ The Kraken
Reapers ◆ Meeting at Night ◆ Prayer of First Dancers

◆ Literature and Your Life

CONNECT YOUR EXPERIENCE

A story read aloud, a moving speech, a dramatic proclamation: When you hear any of these, you may have the impression that you are hearing music. Similarly, when you read poetry, your inner voice can turn the lines into a song in your head. Think about the songs you like, and what it is about them that appeals to you. As you read these poems, try to hear them as songs.

Journal Writing Write down the lyrics to one of your favorite songs, and read the lyrics aloud without music. Do the words themselves suggest music? Why or why not?

THEMATIC FOCUS: FROM THE PAST

Poets and songwriters are influenced by the poems and songs of previous generations. Think about how the poems and songs you know relate in structure and subject matter to the poems in this group.

◆ Background for Understanding

HISTORY

Many factors led to World War I (1914–1918), the backdrop of John McCrae's poem "In Flanders Fields." Principal among them were the territorial and economic rivalries between Russia, France, and Great Britain on one side and Germany and Austria-Hungary on the other. These conflicts had been brewing since the late nineteenth century. Flanders, a region in northern France and western Belgium, was a chief battlefield of the war. Many towns were destroyed, and once-productive farmland was blighted with miles of bomb craters, trenches—and bodies.

◆ Reading Strategy

LISTEN

Listening is an important skill for appreciating all literature, but especially for poetry, which is created for the ear, as well as for the eye. To appreciate the sound of a poem, listen to it as it is read aloud. Listen to the rhythm of the lines, and pay attention to rhymes and other repeated sounds. For example, the first four lines of "The Kraken" end with alternating rhymes. Often, the rhythms and sounds of a poem suggest a mood or reflect an idea. "In Flanders Fields" has a regular repetitive beat, suggesting the regularity of rows of grave markers repeating and repeating. Notice the effect when the regular rhythm is broken, and how the broken rhythm calls attention to certain lines.

◆ Literary Focus

MUSICAL DEVICES

One of the things that distinguishes poetry from prose is the former's use of **musical devices,** the tools of language that a poet uses to make a poem sound a certain way.

Alliteration is the repetition of the first sound of several words. In "Reapers," for instance, the men "start their silent swinging." Each repetition of the *s* sound echoes the swish of the blades.

Onomatopoeia is the use of words to imitate actual sounds—*bang, tap,* and *swish* sound like what they mean.

Assonance is the repetition of similar vowel sounds. In "The Kraken," Tennyson repeats the long *e* sound in a number of words: *deep, beneath, dreamless, sleep,* and *see.*

Consonance is the repetition of similar consonant sounds at the end of accented syllables. In "Meeting at Night," notice the repeated *t* and *ch* sounds in "blue spurt of a lighted match." This repetition strengthens the impression these words create.

Meter is the formal organization of rhythms in a poem. You can hear the pattern of alternating stressed and unstressed syllables in the first two lines of "In Flanders Fields."

Repetition and **rhyme** also give a poem the sound of a song.

Test Preparation Workshop

Critical Reading: Analyzing an Author's Meaning and Style

As students prepare for standardized tests such as ACT and SAT, they need to be prepared to paraphrase words and phrases in a poem in order to better interpret the writer's meaning. To help students prepare, ask them to read the poem "In Flanders Fields" on p. 824 and use the imagery and details of the poem to support their choice, which answer best completes the sentence.

The author's attitude toward war and death is most accurately described as—

A patriotism **C** pride
B pain **D** disrespect

Suggest that students briefly paraphrase the poem in their own words and then read quickly to eliminate choices, based on details of the poem, that they recognize as incorrect. They may also use their own experience to eliminate answers. Using this strategy they should recognize that answer B is the best interpretation because the speaker of the poem mourns the lives of those who have died.

Interest Grabber To capture students' interest in these five musical poems, ask them to name their favorite songs, and write the five most popular on the chalkboard. Then ask students to identify the major mood of each of these songs—for example, wistful, defiant, or inspiring. Encourage students to think of situations in which songs or music are used to stir people's emotions. (Students may suggest religious ceremonies, celebrations, patriotic events, or movies.) Let them know that they will be reading five poems that also use "music"—the sounds and feelings of words—to create emotion.

Tips to Guide Reading

Use Punctuation Students will find it easier to understand the poems if they read following the punctuation markings.

Customize for
Less Proficient Readers and English Language Learners
To help readers understand the difficult vocabulary and complicated images expressed in the poems, invite them to listen to the recording of the selections as they follow along in the text.

Customize for
Pre-AP Students
Challenge Pre-AP Students to write in their journals a comparison of the different views of religion and nature suggested in "Prayer of First Dancers" and "The Kraken."

Customize for
Gifted/Talented Students
Suggest that students select one of the poems and create a musical interpretation or dance. If they wish, they may create simple scenery and costumes to enhance their interpretation.

Literature CD-ROM Use the CD-ROM Features 8 and 9. These features discuss the relationship between content and form of poetry and discuss rhythm, rhyme, and alliteration.

Develop Understanding

One-Minute Insight This poem, in its stark simplicity, calls on the living to acknowledge our bond with the dead—and our debt to those who gave their lives. The dead, the speakers of the poem, call upon us to take up the fight for a better world.

◆ Build Grammar Skills

❶ Concrete and Abstract Nouns Ask students to identify the nouns in this passage and to tell whether they are concrete or abstract. *The following nouns are all concrete:* fields, poppies, crosses, row. Invite students to speculate about why the poet has chosen only concrete nouns. *Concrete nouns can be perceived with the senses, so they create vivid, sensory images.*

◆ Critical Thinking

❷ Interpret Ask students what the torch in this passage represents. *Suggested response: The torch represents the cause for which the soldiers fought.*

▶Critical Viewing◀

❸ Speculate *The poet seems to like simple things, as evidenced by the poem's simple, straightforward language. He would probably like this simple marker.*

Humanities: Art

Nineteenth-century wood engraving of a Kraken.

This wood engraving shows the Scandinavian sea monster, Kraken, attacking a ship. The illustration presents the Kraken as a threatening and destructive creature. The rough lines indicating turmoil in the scene contribute to a mood of fear and horror.

Discuss these ideas:

1. Does the picture of the Kraken match the mental image you formed from reading Tennyson's poem? Explain. *Some students may say that the Kraken in the picture does match their mental images; others may find the Kraken in the picture too stylized and even graceful.*
2. According to the last line of the poem, what should happen to the Kraken in the picture? *The Kraken should die.*

In Flanders Fields

John McCrae

❶ In Flanders fields the poppies blow
Between the crosses, row on row,
That mark our place; and in the sky
The larks, still bravely singing, fly
Scarce heard amid the guns below.

We are the Dead. Short days ago
We lived, felt dawn, saw sunset glow,
Loved and were loved, and now we lie
In Flanders fields.

Take up our quarrel with the foe:
❷ To you from failing hands we throw
The torch; be yours to hold it high.
If ye break faith with us who die
We shall not sleep, though poppies grow
In Flanders fields.

❸ ▲ **Critical Viewing** How do you think the poet would feel about this simple marker? **[Speculate]**

Block Scheduling Strategies

Consider these suggestions to take advantage of extended class time:

- Have students view the **Literature CD-ROM,** Features 8 and 9, focusing on poets' use of rhythm, rhyme, and alliteration.
- Have groups of students work together to create a combined presentation of the Letter to the Editor writing activity and the World War I researching and representing activities.
- Suggest that students complete the journal activity in Literature and Your Life (p. 823).
- Introduce the Literary Focus musical devices. Have students answer the Literary Focus questions on p. 830; follow up with the Literary Focus page in ***Selection Support,*** p. 231.
- Have students complete the Writing Application in the Build Grammar Skills activity on p. 830. Partners can underline the concrete nouns and circle the abstract nouns in each other's paragraphs. Students can also complete the Build Grammar Skills page on Concrete and Abstract Nouns in ***Selection Support,*** p. 230.

THE KRAKEN

Alfred, Lord Tennyson

Below the thunders of the upper deep;
❹ Far, far beneath in the abysmal sea,
His ancient, dreamless, uninvaded sleep
The Kraken[1] sleepeth: faintest sunlights flee
About his shadowy sides: above him swell
❺ Huge sponges of millennial growth and height;
And far away into the sickly light,
From many a wondrous grot[2] and secret cell
Unnumbered and enormous polypi[3]
Winnow[4] with giant arms the slumbering green.
There hath he lain for ages and will lie
Battening[5] upon huge seaworms in his sleep,
❻ Until the latter fire[6] shall heat the deep;
Then once by man and angels to be seen,
In roaring he shall rise and on the surface die.

1. **Kraken** (krä′ kən) *n.*: Sea monster resembling a giant squid; from Scandinavian folklore.
2. **grot** (grät) *n.*: Grotto; an underwater cave.
3. **polypi** (päl′ ip ē) *n.*: Corallike creatures with long, waving tentacles.
4. **winnow** (win′ ō) *v.*: To fan; to move wings or tentacles.
5. **Battening** (bat′ən iŋ) *v.*: Feeding on; growing fat on.
6. **the latter fire:** The apocalypse.

◆ **Build Vocabulary**

abysmal (ə biz′ məl) *adj.:* Bottomless; too deep for measurement; profoundly deep

millennial (mi len′ ē əl) *adj.:* Lasting one thousand years

Critical Viewing
How does this rendition of the Kraken compare and contrast with the impression of the Kraken in Tennyson's poem? **[Compare and Contrast]**

Develop Understanding

One-Minute Insight The poet's imagination is captured by the mythical sea monster that lives at the bottom of the ocean. An elemental force of nature, the Kraken dies only when the world ends. Like all creations of the imagination, the Kraken thrives in an unexplored world, but loses its power when brought to light and examined.

◆ Literary Focus

❹ **Musical Devices** Ask students to identify the use of repetition and rhyme. *Students should see that "far" and forms of "sleep" are repeated; there are rhymes between "deep" and "sleep," "sea" and "flee."*

◆ Build Vocabulary

❺ **The Prefix *mil-*** Point out that millennial contains the prefix *mil-*. Ask what the prefix and the word mean. Then ask how this particular word adds to the effect of the poem. *Students should know that mil- means "one thousand," and that millennial means "lasting one thousand years." The word contributes to the image of an ancient creature.*

◆ Literary Focus

❻ **Musical Devices** Invite students to identify the musical device here. *Students should identify assonance: in the single-syllable words deep and seen, the vowel sounds are repeated but followed by different consonants.*

▶Critical Viewing◀

❼ **Compare and Contrast** *Students may say that the many arms reflect the Kraken's "unnumbered polypi" and that the partially seen creature is mysterious like the Kraken.*

Read to
Appreciate Author's Craft
As students read to appreciate an author's craft encourage them to listen to the sound of the author's words and rhythm read aloud.

Viewing and Representing Mini-Lesson

Creatures Across Cultures
This mini-lesson supports the Researching and Representing activity in the Idea Bank on p. 831.

Introduce Ask students to reread the poem on p. 825 and envision the Kraken from the descriptive words used by Tennyson.

Develop When preparing their representations of mythological creatures, encourage students to be creative. Students may wish to prepare a multimedia display, a computerized project, or locate artwork or photographs that illustrate a mythological creature. Have them find creatures and monsters described by cultures from around the world and decide which they wish to illustrate and how they plan to represent it.

Apply Have students prepare their representation. In addition, they may wish to provide information about the creature. They may find that some of the creatures are not just legend, but well-known with a long history of "sightings," for example, Big Foot and the Loch Ness monster.

Assess Have students display their representations for the class and assess them based on creativity and research.

Develop Understanding

One-Minute Insight The reapers in this poem are too busy to notice the field rat injured by the blade of one of their mowers. Or, perhaps the impersonal, repetitive nature of their job has dulled their sense of pity for a small animal.

◆ Literary Focus

❶ **Musical Devices** Ask students to identify the musical devices in these lines. *Students should note the alliteration of* start, silent, *and* swinging, *as well as of* thing, that's *and* their. *They should also note the rhyme of the end-of-line words* done *and* one.

▶Critical Viewing◀

❷ **Connect** *The farmer is dwarfed by the land and the animals: birds, sky, clouds, and furrows all appear large and looming. Students could generalize from this picture that the land is the master of farmers.*

Extending Word Study

Descriptive Words Because poets often use rich, descriptive words, students will find that reading poetry provides an excellent opportunity for them to expand their vocabulary. Suggest that students skim through the poems in the selection and make a list of the words they wish to use in their own writing and speaking.

Humanities: Art

Ploughing by Nancy Smith.

All the major forms in this bold and graphic representation of a man ploughing a field—the birds flying helter skelter, the farmer, the draft horses—are rendered in silhouette, accenting the starkness of the vast country landscape.

Use this question for discussion. What line from "Reapers" does this picture most closely illustrate? Why? *Students might cite the line "Black horses drive a mower through the weeds," because this, and not the reapers with scythes, is closest to what is shown.*

Reapers

Jean Toomer

Black reapers with the sound of steel on stones
Are sharpening scythes. I see them place the hones[1]
❶ In their hip-pockets as a thing that's done,
And start their silent swinging, one by one.
Black horses drive a mower through the weeds,
And there, a field rat, startled, squealing bleeds,
His belly close to ground. I see the blade,
Blood-stained, continue cutting weeds and shade.

1. **hones** (hōnz) *n.*: Hard stones used to sharpen cutting tools.

The Countryman has to live by faith.

Ploughing, Nancy Smith, Stapleton Collection

❷ ▶ **Critical Viewing** Based on this picture, describe the relationship between farmers and the land. **[Connect]**

Speaking, Listening, and Viewing Mini-Lesson

Oral Report

This mini-lesson supports the Speaking, Listening, and Viewing activity in the Idea Bank on p. 831.

Introduce An oral report is a brief oral presentation that conveys information. In a good oral report, the speaker uses clear, simple language, speaks audibly and with expression at an even pace, and occasionally uses visual aids to help listeners understand and remember what they hear.

Develop Help students identify resources where they can find both mythical creatures and the beliefs people have had about their existence. Tell students that ideally, both "believers" and "nonbelievers" should feel the student's report was fair and complete.

Apply Students' reports should include a description of the creature, its history, and the beliefs about it. Remind students to use a lively, engaging tone of voice and to use visual aids to add needed information or enhance their reports.

Assess Assess students' reports based on content, organization, and presentation. Students might use the Peer Assessment: Speaker/Speech form, pp. 118 and 119 in ***Alternative Assessment.***

Meeting at Night

Robert Browning

1

The gray sea and the long black land;
And the yellow half-moon large and low;
And the startled little waves that leap
In fiery ringlets from their sleep,
As I gain the cove with pushing prow,
And quench its speed i' the slushy sand.

2

Then a mile of warm sea-scented beach;
Three fields to cross till a farm appears;
A tap at the pane, the quick sharp scratch
And blue spurt of a lighted match,
And a voice less loud, through its joys and fears,
Than the two hearts beating each to each!

Atlantic Moon, Jane Wilson, Fischbach Gallery, New York

❸ ▶ Critical Viewing Identify the elements of this picture that reflect the setting and atmosphere of "Meeting at Night." **[Support]**

Guide for Responding

◆ Literature and Your Life

Reader's Response Which of these four poems seems most relevant to your life? Why?

Thematic Focus Which of these poems do you think focuses the most on handing down something from the past? Explain.

☑ Check Your Comprehension

1. In "The Kraken," what is the Kraken doing, and how do you know?
2. Who are the speakers of "In Flanders Fields"? How do you know?
3. In "Reapers," what do the reapers do before they start swinging their scythes?
4. Describe the journey of the speaker of "Meeting at Night."

◆ Critical Thinking

INTERPRET

1. What would be the far-reaching effect of "the latter fire" that could cause the Kraken's death? **[Analyze]**
2. The speakers of "In Flanders Fields" deliver an urgent message to the poem's audience. What is this message? **[Interpret]**
3. What is the central message of "The Reapers"? **[Speculate]**
4. At the end of "Meeting at Night," what is the reason for the "tap at the pane"?

COMPARE LITERARY WORKS

5. Look for the pattern of rhymes in each of the poems in this section. Compare those patterns and their effect on the mood of each poem. **[Compare]**

◆ Critical Thinking

1. An apocalypse ("the latter fire") would end the world.
2. The urgent message the speakers deliver is that their deaths will be in vain unless their successors, the audience of the poem, fight for the same principles they did. "If ye break faith with us who die" indicates a moral pact between soldiers dead and alive.
3. Students might say that the central message is that even death or pain cannot stop the forward movement of progress.
4. The tap on the window pane announces to one lover the arrival of the other.
5. Students may suggest that the repeating rhymes that skip lines as they do in "The Kraken" make the poem more suspenseful.

Develop Understanding

One-Minute Insight Two lovers meet on a warm, moonlit night. The suspense and romance of this event is heightened by Browning's use of music, rhythm, and vivid imagery.

▶Critical Viewing◀

❸ **Support** *Students should point out that, as in the poem, the picture portrays the sea meeting the shore, lit only by the moon.*

Reinforce and Extend

Answers

◆ Literature and Your Life

Reader's Response Students might cite "Meeting at Night," which features a romance.

Thematic Focus "In Flanders Fields" is the most explicit poem about handing down a legacy—in this case from the dead to the living.

☑ Check Your Comprehension

1. The Kraken is sleeping. Evidence includes "dreamless, uninvaded sleep," "The Kraken sleepeth," and "Battening upon huge seaworms in his sleep."
2. "In Flanders Fields" is spoken by the war dead. "We are the Dead" supports this.
3. They sharpen their scythes.
4. The speaker travels over water, a mile of beach, and three fields to reach a farmhouse.

Humanities: Art

Atlantic Moon by Jane Wilson.

American painter Jane Wilson was born in Iowa in 1924. Her work is exhibited in art galleries and museums across the country.

Use this question for discussion: Would you change this picture to make it more representative of the poem? Explain. *Some students might say that they would not change the picture because it represents the mood of the poem, if not its images. Other students might wish for a more detailed representation.*

Develop Understanding

One-Minute Insight "Prayer of First Dancers" conveys the Navajo people's profound sense of connection with nature. Like all chants, this one relies on the rhythmical repetition of phrases; it produces an effect of gathering momentum in praise and a request for spiritual and physical healing.

◆ Literary Focus

❶ **Musical Devices** Invite students to identify the musical device in these lines. Then ask what impact this device has. *Students may say that repetition induces a prayerful, reverent attitude; that it conveys a sense of wonder; or that it creates a strong rhythm for dancing.*

◆ Reading Strategy

❷ **Listen** Remind students of the poem's traditional uses as a chant and a prayer. Ask one or two students to read the passage aloud, reminding them that they are addressing "he-rain." Then discuss the differences between reading the poem silently and hearing it read aloud. *Students will probably say that hearing the poem makes its repetition more powerful and conveys its emotion more fully.*

▶Critical Viewing◀

❸ **Connect** *Suggested response: Both the painting and the poem use repetition.*

◆ Build Grammar Skills

❹ **Concrete and Abstract Nouns** Ask students to identify the concrete nouns in this passage. Then ask students to describe the effect of so many concrete with no abstract nouns. *Concrete nouns are rainbow, head, darkness, cloud, ends, wings, he-rain, mist, she-rain. Students should realize that the poem celebrates nature—the concrete, material world that can be experienced with the senses. The poem is not concerned with ideas or abstractions.*

PRAYER OF FIRST DANCERS

from The Night Chant

Our Home and Native Land, 1983, Dannielle B. Hayes

Navajo

In Tse'gíhi,
In the house made of the dawn,
In the house made of the evening twilight,
❶ In the house made of the dark cloud,
In the house made of the he-rain,
In the house made of the dark mist,
In the house made of the she-rain,
In the house made of pollen,
In the house made of grasshoppers,
Where the dark mist curtains the doorway,
The path to which is on the rainbow,
Where the zigzag lightning stands high on top,
Where the he-rain stands high on top,
Oh, male divinity!
With your moccasins of dark cloud, come to us.
With your leggings of dark cloud, come to us.
With your shirt of dark cloud, come to us.
❷ With your head-dress of dark cloud, come to us.
With your mind enveloped in dark cloud, come to us.
With the dark thunder above you, come to us soaring.
With the shapen cloud at your feet, come to us soaring.
With the far darkness made of the dark cloud over your head, come to us soaring.
With the far darkness made of the he-rain over your head, come to us soaring.
With the far darkness made of the dark mist over your head, come to us soaring.
With the far darkness made of the she-rain over your head, come to us soaring.
With the zigzag lightning flung out on high over your head, come to us soaring.
With the rainbow hanging high over your head, come to us soaring.
With the far darkness made of the dark cloud on the ends of your wings, come to us soaring.
With the far darkness made of the he-rain on the ends of your wings, come to us soaring.
With the far darkness made of the dark mist on the ends of your wings, come to us soaring.
With the far darkness made of the she-rain on the ends of your wings, come to us soaring.
With the zigzag lightning flung out on high on the ends of your wings, come to us soaring.
With the rainbow hanging high on the ends of your wings, come to us soaring.
With the near darkness made of the dark

❹ ▲ **Critical Viewing** What technique used in this picture reflects a technique in "Prayer of First Dancers"? Explain. **[Connect]**

Humanities: Art

Our Home and Native Land, 1983, by Danielle Hayes.

This gouache and pencil work emphasizes repetition both in the way the six Native American figures seem to echo one another and in its use of color—bright orange—repeated in various parts of the picture. Discuss with students the reasons that poets, musical composers, painters, and other artists might choose to use repetition in the works they create.

Use the following questions for discussion:

1. How does the repetition in the poem and the painting emphasize aspects of both works? *Students may say it indicates respect, importance, or a pleasing aspect of the ceremony.*
2. Both the poem and the dance portrayed here use repetition. Why do you think repetition is an important part of this religious ceremony? *Students may say that repetition in dance conveys a sense that all are working in unison to celebrate nature. Repetition in the poem is a way of celebrating each aspect of nature.*

cloud, of the he-rain, of the dark mist
and of the she-rain, come to us.
With the darkness on the earth, come to
us.
With these I wish the foam floating on
the flowing water over the roots of the
great corn.
I have made your sacrifice.
I have prepared a smoke for you.
My feet restore for me.
❺ My limbs restore for me.
My body restore for me.
My mind restore for me.
My voice restore for me.

* * * *

Happily the old men will regard you.
Happily the old women will regard you.
Happily the young men will regard you.
Happily the young women will regard you.
Happily the boys will regard you.
Happily the girls will regard you.
Happily the children will regard you.
Happily the chiefs will regard you.
Happily, as they scatter in different
directions, they will regard you.
Happily, as they approach their homes,
they will regard you.
Happily may their roads home be on the
trail of pollen.
Happily may they all get back.
In beauty I walk.
With beauty before me, I walk.
With beauty behind me, I walk.
With beauty below me, I walk.
With beauty above me, I walk. ❻
With beauty all around me, I walk.
It is finished again in beauty,
It is finished in beauty,
It is finished in beauty,
It is finished in beauty.

Guide for Responding

◆ *Literature and Your Life*

Reader's Response Which elements of this poem did you find most musical? Why?

Thematic Focus Based on your reading of "Prayer of First Dancers," what important legacy do you think the Navajo have handed down to their children? Explain.

☑ Check Your Comprehension

1. Identify three images from nature that are repeated throughout "Prayer of First Dancers."
2. What is the speaker's request?

◆ Critical Thinking

INTERPRET

1. What attitude does the speaker of "Prayer of First Dancers" have toward the "you" being addressed in the chant? **[Draw Conclusions]**
2. What details indicate a strong sense of community? **[Support]**

APPLY

3. What does "Prayer of First Dancers" reveal about the Navajos' attitude toward nature? **[Generalize]**
4. Identify a contemporary song that contains images and ideas similar to those found in "Prayer of First Dancers." **[Relate]**

Beyond the Selection

FURTHER READING

Other Works by the Authors

In Flanders Fields, and Other Poems, John McCrae
"Ulysses," Alfred, Lord Tennyson
Cane, Jean Toomer
"My Last Duchess," Robert Browning

Other Works With the Theme of "From the Past"

Spoon River Anthology, Edgar Lee Masters
"Kubla Khan," Samuel Taylor Coleridge

INTERNET

We suggest the following sites, which are subject to change.
For information on McCrae:
http://www.IAEhv.np/users/robr/poppies.html
On Tennyson:
http://tqd.advanced.org/3187/tennyson.html
On Toomer:
http://micket.la.psu.edu/~jselzer/burke/toom.doc
On Browning:
http://mirrors.org.sg./victorian/rb/rbbio.html

We *strongly recommend* that you preview these sites before you send students to them.

◆ Critical Thinking

❺ **Infer** Ask students what the speaker doing? What does the speaker ask for in return? *The speaker is preparing a sacrifice in honor of the divinity. In return, he asks for health.*

◆ Critical Thinking

❻ **Draw Conclusions** Ask students why the speaker refers to beauty so often in this passage. *Students should see that the speaker loves the beauty of nature and is able to appreciate it now that the sacrifice and the ceremony have been performed*

Reteach

Use of literary musical devices by poets is a difference between prose and poetry that students should be able to identify. Suggest that students make a chart of the devices listed on p. 823. Then, challenge them to find at least one example of each in this selection. You may wish to have students continue using their chart later in the unit.

Reinforce and Extend

Answers

◆ *Literature and Your Life*

Reader's Response Students might mention the repetition, which contributes to its lulling, chant-like quality.

Thematic Focus Students are likely to mention a deep reverence for nature.

☑ Check Your Comprehension

1. Three images are the darkness, a rainbow, and lightning.
2. The speaker's request is for the divinity to restore his health.

◆ Critical Thinking

1. The attitude of the speaker toward "you" is one of reverence.
2. The constant repetition of the pronoun us indicates a community feeling; the refrain beginning *Happily* includes mention of all different group members of the community.
3. The Navajos hold nature in high esteem and feel humble before it.
4. Students should mention a song that conveys nature's power.

Reinforce and Extend

Answers

◆ Reading Strategy

1. There are ten syllables in each line of "The Kraken." Rhyming word pairs include deep/sleep; sea/flee; swell/cell; height/light; lie/die; green/seen.
2. "In Flanders Fields" breaks the rhythm and creates a jolting effect which pulls the reader's focus to these lines.
3. Alliteration is the sound effect of the first two lines in "Reapers"; the sound reflects the swishing motion of the blades through the grass.
4. Repetition is the principal sound effect in "Prayer of First Dancers," and it creates the rhythm of a chant.

◆ Literary Focus

1. The combination of assonance and consonance creates a feeling of depth and mystery.
2. The meter of "In Flanders Field" has the quality of a march, and the poem stresses the importance of marching on.
3. Alliteration is the most prominent musical device: sound/steel/stones/sharpening/scythes/silent/swinging/startled/squealing/shades; close/continued/cutting
4. Alliteration: long/land/large/low/leap; Onomatopoeia: quench; slushy; scratch; Consonance: beach; scratch
5. (a) Repetition is most prominent. (b) The repetition makes it perfect for a chant, which is characterized by repetition and a lulling rhythm.

◆ Build Vocabulary

Using the Prefix *mil-*

1. b 2. c 3. d 4. a

Using the Word Bank

1. It would be very difficult because the pool would be too deep for measurement.
2. You would have to wait one thousand years.

Guide for Responding *(continued)*

◆ Reading Strategy

LISTEN

Listening to the sounds and rhythms of these poems is part of the poetic experience. The sound of a poem gives you insight into the poet's intent.

1. Listen to the rhyme and rhythm of "The Kraken." How many syllables are in each line? Identify three pairs of rhyming words.
2. The rhythm of "In Flanders Fields" is a regular beat that occasionally breaks. Identify the lines where the rhythm is broken, and explain how it affects the way you listen to those lines.
3. What sound do you hear repeated in the first two lines of "Reapers"? What action from the poem does this sound reflect?
4. (a) What sounds and rhythms do you hear in "Prayer of First Dancers"? (b) What effect do these sounds create?

◆ Literary Focus

MUSICAL DEVICES

Just as a composer of music must know harmony and melody in order to create the effects he or she desires, poets use various language tools, or **musical devices,** to create effects in their poems.

1. In the first five lines of "The Kraken," Tennyson combines both assonance and consonance. What is the effect of this combination of musical devices?
2. How does the meter of "In Flanders Fields" relate to the purpose of the poem?
3. What musical device is most prominent in "Reapers"? Give examples.
4. Cite an example of alliteration, onomatopoeia, and consonance in "Meeting at Night."
5. (a) What musical device is most prominent in "Prayer of First Dancers"? (b) How does this device lend itself to the way in which the poem is traditionally used?

◆ Build Vocabulary

USING THE LATIN PREFIX *mil-*

The prefix *mil-* comes from the Latin *mille*, meaning "one thousand." On your paper, match each word beginning with *mil-* with its definition.

1. millennium **a.** one thousand thousands
2. millipede **b.** a period of one thousand years
3. millimeter **c.** an insect with many legs
4. million **d.** one one-thousandth of a meter

USING THE WORD BANK: Context

On your paper, answer the following questions.

1. If a pool were *abysmal*, how easy would it be for you to retrieve your sunglasses if you dropped them in it? Explain.
2. If you planted *millennial* roses, how long would you have to wait to see them bloom?

◆ Build Grammar Skills

CONCRETE AND ABSTRACT NOUNS

Concrete nouns name specific things that can be perceived by the senses. **Abstract nouns** name ideas or concepts that cannot be seen, heard, felt, tasted, or smelled. The word *moccasins* from "Prayer of First Dancers" is a concrete noun because it names something you can see and feel. *Beauty,* on the other hand, is a concept that cannot be directly perceived by the senses. It is an abstract noun.

Practice On your paper, identify each noun as *concrete* or *abstract.*

1. poppies	**5.** ringlets	**9.** rainbow
2. hope	**6.** joy	**10.** beauty
3. dawn	**7.** voice	**11.** conflict
4. scythes	**8.** fears	**12.** hearts

Writing Application On your paper, write a paragraph about these poems from the point of view of an enthusiastic critic. Use at least four of the following abstract and concrete nouns: *beauty, battleground, mountains, clouds, spirituality, seaworms, thrill, faith, scythes, herbs,* and *sea.* Underline the concrete nouns, and circle the abstract nouns.

◆ Build Grammar Skills

Practice

Concrete Nouns: 1. poppies; 3. dawn; 4. scythes; 5. ringlets; 7. voice; 9. rainbow; 12. hearts

Abstract Nouns: 2. hope; 6. joy; 8. fears; 10. beauty; 11. conflict

Grammar Reinforcement

For additional instruction and practice, use the Types of Nouns lesson in the **Language Lab CD-ROM** and p. 5 on Nouns in the *Writer's Solution Grammar Practice Book.*

Build Your Portfolio

Idea Bank

Writing

1. Letter to the Editor It is 1917, and World War I is raging. You've just read "In Flanders Fields." Write a letter to the editor saying why you do or don't agree with the poem.

2. City Chant "Prayer of First Dancers" praises many aspects of nature. Write a chant (with variations on a repeated phrase) in which you praise aspects of a city or town.

3. Musical Devices Compare two of these poems in terms of the musical devices used in them.

Speaking, Listening, and Viewing

4. Visual Presentation Jean Toomer does not romanticize the image of farming in his poem, but many artists have presented idealized visions of agricultural life. Research pastoral and landscape painting, and prepare a visual presentation of such images. **[Art Link]**

5. Oral Report Find out more about mythical creatures like the Kraken, such as the Yeti or the Loch Ness monster. Give an oral report explaining the reasons some people think these creatures exist and the reasons some people don't. **[Science Link]**

Researching and Representing

6. Creatures Across Cultures Create a poster or other visual presentation showing mythological monsters, such as the Kraken, from various cultures. Provide pictures and detailed descriptions. **[Social Studies Link]**

7. World War I Up until World War II broke out, World War I was known as "The Great War." Why is this? Research the death toll from each country participating in World War I. Present your statistics in a table. **[Math Link]**

Online Activity www.phlit.phschool.com

Guided Writing Lesson

Proposal for a Poetry Anthology

Because many poems are fairly short, poetry is a form of literature well suited to anthologies. An anthology is a collection of works that have something in common, either in form or theme. Write a **proposal for a poetry anthology** that you would like to create. Choose a number of poems that you feel belong together. You can arrange them by form, such as an anthology of sonnets or haiku; by theme, such as love, individuality, or hope; or by poetic element.

Writing Skills Focus: Specific Examples

Once you've decided on the common element that will link the poems in your anthology, make sure that you give **specific examples** of each in your proposal. For example, if you plan to organize your anthology by musical devices, show examples of alliteration, consonance, and repetition in the poems you suggest.

Prewriting Think of how you would like to arrange your poems. For example, if you're going to make an anthology based on musical devices, you might make a chart like this one:

Musical Device	Title	Example
Alliteration	"Reapers"	*S*teel on *s*tones
Onomatopoeia	"Meeting . . ."	Slushy sand

Drafting Begin by explaining the concept or organization of the anthology you propose. Then introduce the specific examples you have chosen.

Revising Ask a friend to review your proposal. Have you included specific examples of each form or genre of poem? Is it clear why you want to include each poem? If not, revise your proposal to make it more complete and clear.

✓ ASSESSMENT OPTIONS

Formal Assessment, Selection Test, pp. 198–200, and Assessment Resources Software. The selection test is designed so that it can be easily customized to the performance levels of your students.

Alternative Assessment, p. 56, includes options for less advanced students, more advanced students, verbal/linguistic learners and bodily/kinesthetic learners.

PORTFOLIO ASSESSMENT

Use the following rubrics in the ***Alternative Assessment*** booklet to assess student writing:
Letter to Editor: Persuasion Rubric, p. 105
City Chant: Poetry Rubric, p. 108
Musical Devices: Comparison/Contrast Rubric, p. 103
Guided Writing Lesson: Description Rubric, p. 97

Idea Bank

Following are suggestions for matching Idea Bank topics with your students' performance levels and learning modalities:

Customizing for *Performance Levels*
Less Advanced Students: 1, 4
Average Students: 2, 3, 5, 6,
More Advanced Students: 7

Customizing for *Learning Modalities*
Musical/Rhythmic: 2, 3
Verbal/Linguistic: 4, 5
Logical/Mathematical: 7
Visual/Spatial: 6

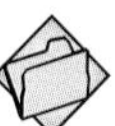

Guided Writing Lesson

Elaboration Strategy Guide students to explain the concept of the anthology they are proposing by using the **SEE** technique: Making a **S**tatement, **E**xtending the statement, and **E**laborating on the statement. Model the **SEE** technique with the following example:

Statement: Poems with musical devices belong together in an anthology.

Extension: Poems with musical devices such as alliteration and onomatopoeia belong together in an anthology.

Elaboration: Poems with musical devices such as "Reapers" which uses alliteration and "Meeting at Night" which uses onomatopoeia belong together in an anthology.

For more prewriting, elaboration, and revision strategies, see the new *Prentice Hall Writing and Grammar Program.*

Writing Lab CD-ROM

Have students complete the tutorial on Descriptive Writing. Follow these steps:

- Encourage students to complete the Audience Profile to help them focus on their intended audience.
- Have students use the interactive instruction on ways they can organize their proposal.
- Tell students to use the revision checkers for vague or overused adjectives before completing their final revision.

Prepare and Engage

LESSON OBJECTIVES

1. **To develop vocabulary and word identification skills**
   - Latin Word Roots: *-tac-*
   - Using the Word Bank: Word Choice
   - Extending Word Study: Expand Vocabulary Through Discussion (ATE)
2. **To use a variety of reading strategies to comprehend poems**
   - Connect Your Experience
   - Reading Strategy: Paraphrase
   - Tips to Guide Reading: Whisper Reading (ATE)
   - Read to Appreciate Author's Craft (ATE)
3. **To increase knowledge of other cultures and to connect common elements across cultures**
   - Connecting Themes Across Cultures (ATE) 9A
   - Background for Understanding
   - Idea Bank: Most Admired
   - Idea Bank: Metaphor Poem
4. **To express and support responses to the text**
   - Critical Thinking
   - Analyze Literary Criticism
5. **To analyze literary elements**
   - Literary Focus: Figurative Language
6. **To read in order to research self-selected and assigned topics**
   - Research Skills Mini-Lesson: Using Anthologies
   - Idea Bank: Visual Biography
   - Idea Bank: Hurricane Statistics TAAS 5
7. **To plan, prepare, organize, and present literary interpretations**
   - Speaking, Listening, and Viewing Mini-Lesson: Dialogue
   - Idea Bank: Wind Interview
8. **To use recursive writing processes to develop a character**
   - Guided Writing Lesson
9. **To increase knowledge of the rules of grammar and usage**
   - Build Grammar Skills: Elliptical Clauses

Test Preparation

Critical Reading: Analyzing an Author's Meaning and Style (ATE, p. 833) The teaching tips and sample test item in this workshop support the instruction and practice in the unit workshop.

Critical Reading: Analyzing an Author's Meaning and Style (SE, p. 877)

Guide for Reading

Emily Dickinson *(1830–1886)*

Emily Dickinson was born in Amherst, Massachusetts. As she grew older, she rarely left her house. In fact, during the last ten years of her life, she dressed only in white and would not allow anyone to see her. When her health failed, she permitted her doctor to examine her only by observing her from a distance. In 1886, Emily Dickinson died in the house in which she was born. (To learn more about Emily Dickinson, see pp. 414 and 415.)

Yehuda Amichai *(1924–)*

Although born in Germany, Yehuda Amichai (yə ho͞o´ də ä´ mi khī) emigrated with his family to Palestine, the region that became Israel in 1948. He was a soldier in the Israeli defense forces and fought in several wars.

In addition to poetry, Amichai has also written short stories, a novel, and a play. He writes in Hebrew, using this ancient language to write about timeless themes and contemporary topics. Amichai's poetry has been translated into more than thirty languages.

Eve Merriam *(1916–1992)*

Eve Merriam was born in Philadelphia. Because her family was always interested in books and reading, Merriam began her lifelong fascination with poetry at an early age. She has written books of poetry for children, including *There Is No Rhyme for Silver,* and adults, including *Family Circle.* Merriam calls poetry the most immediate and richest form of communication.

Philip Fried *(1945–)*

Philip Fried, a poet and editor, is the founder of *The Manhattan Review*, an international poetry journal, as well as the author of two collections of poetry, *Mutual Trespasses* and *Quantum Genesis. The Manhattan Review* features interviews with poets from around the world as well as translations of their work. Fried has also collaborated with his wife, photographer Lynn Saville, on *Acquainted With the Night,* a collection of poems selected by him and photographs taken by her.

◆ Build Vocabulary

LATIN WORD ROOTS: *-tac-*

In "Right Hand," the speaker recalls watching his grandfather iron "countless *taciturn* trousers."

Taciturn has as its root *-tac-*. This Latin root and its variation *-tic-* mean "silent." *Taciturn* means "silent; uncommunicative." A *tacit* agreement is one that is understood; it does not need to be spoken.

WORD BANK

Before you read, preview this list of words from the poems.

countenance
tremulous
flurriedly
decipher
taciturn
eloquent
guttural
diffused
garrulity

◆ Build Grammar Skills

ELLIPTICAL CLAUSES

In an **elliptical clause,** one or more words are omitted because they are understood. Often, in adjective clauses, the relative pronoun *that* is not written or spoken.

I'm looking at the lemon tree *[that] I planted.*

The complete clause is *that I planted,* but the word *that* is understood.

Elliptical clauses in which the relative pronoun is not stated have an informal, conversational tone.

Prentice Hall Literature Program Resources

REINFORCE / RETEACH / EXTEND

Selection Support Pages
Build Vocabulary: Word Roots: *-tac-*, p. 233
Build Grammar Skills: Elliptical Clauses, p. 234
Reading Strategy: Paraphrase, p. 235
Literary Focus: Figurative Language, p. 236

Strategies for Diverse Student Needs, p. 57

Beyond Literature Workplace Connection: Time Management Skills, p. 57

Formal Assessment Selection Test, pp. 201–203; and Assessment Resources Software

Alternative Assessment, p. 57

Resource Pro CD-ROM

Listening to Literature Audiocassettes

The Wind—tapped like a tired Man
A Pace Like That ◆ Metaphor ◆ Right Hand ◆

◆ Literature and Your Life

Connect Your Experience

Some days just don't go the way we'd like. Fortunately, there is always a new day to make a fresh start and right a wrong or accomplish a goal. If you appreciate the possibilities of each new day, you'll be surprised how much you can accomplish!

Thematic Focus: From the Past

The speakers in these poems realize the importance of each day and the effect of the large and small choices they make.

Journal Writing Jot down choices that you are currently facing in your life—such as what classes to take or whether to take an after-school job. Indicate the hopes for and concerns about the outcomes of your choices.

◆ Background for Understanding

Culture

In "A Pace Like That," Amichai makes a comparison to a Torah scroll. A Torah scroll is a long, rolled parchment. On this parchment, the first five books of the Bible are written in Hebrew. The Torah relates centuries of Jewish history. Particular readings from the Torah are assigned to each day; the entire cycle of readings takes a year to complete.

◆ Literary Focus

Figurative Language

Figurative language is writing or speech not meant to be interpreted literally. Writers use a variety of figures of speech to help readers see things in new ways.

A **simile** compares unlike things using the word *like* or *as*. In "Right Hand," Fried uses a simile when he says his grandfather's hand moves "back and forth *like* a Greek chorus." A **metaphor** also makes a comparison, by writing or speaking about one thing as if it were another. In her poem "Metaphor," Merriam writes about a day as if it were a sheet of paper. **Personification** is a figure of speech in which an object, animal, or idea is described as if it had human characteristics. For instance, "The Wind—tapped like a tired Man" describes the wind as a guest in a home.

◆ Reading Strategy

Paraphrase

A poet's style and word choice are intended to create a particular mood or convey a feeling in a poem, but because of the concise nature of poetry, you may not see the intended meaning right away. It's helpful to **paraphrase** the lines of a poem, using your own words to restate what the lines say. When you read these poems, pause occasionally to paraphrase complicated lines or stanzas. If the poet makes a comparison, express the similarities in your own words. For example, after you read the first four lines of Amichai's poem "A Pace Like That," you can paraphrase them like this:

> I realized when I was looking at the lemon tree I planted last year that I'd like to slow down. I'd like to take the time to appreciate things like the tree growing in my yard.

Keep a chart on which you paraphrase passages from the poems.

Poet's Words	Paraphrase

Before students read, have them share the lyrics of favorite songs they think express important messages about life. Help students to recognize any figurative language in the lyrics. If necessary, remind them that figurative expressions are imaginative comparisons used to describe a person, place, or idea. Tell students that, like song lyrics, these poems use imaginative comparisons to make a point.

Connecting Themes Across Cultures

Point out to students that making hard choices and decisions is an issue that has been faced by persons from all cultures throughout history.

Tips to Guide Reading

Whisper Read Have students whisper read the poems. Listen to their reading—encouraging and explaining poetry phrasing, as needed, with individual students.

Customize for
Less Proficient Readers

You can help these students understand figurative language by discussing such common expressions as "This job is a piece of cake" (metaphor), "He was as fast as lightning" (simile), and "The wind is howling outside my window" (personification).

Customize for
Pre-AP Students

Suggest that students work in small groups to discuss their analyses and interpretations of the poems on a chart which asks the questions: What is the theme? What is the tone? What is the speaker's attitude?

Customize for
English Language Learners

Invite these students to share colloquial expressions and sayings about life from their native languages. If possible, have them write the sayings on the board, translate them into English, and point out any examples of similes, metaphors, and personification.

Test Preparation Workshop

Critical Reading: Analyzing an Author's Meaning and Style As students prepare to take standardized tests, they may need further instruction on using critical reading as well as writing skills. Interpreting phrases by analyzing an author's meaning and style is a skill that will be helpful to students in their own writing if the test question gives a writing prompt. Use the following sample question.

> Read the poem "The Wind—tapped like a tired Man" on p. 834 and respond to the following writing prompt:
>
> What impression of the wind does Emily Dickinson create in her poem?

A response to this prompt should (1) include an appropriate thesis statement, developed with supporting details that respond to the theme of Dickinson's poem; (2) be clearly organized; and (3) be written with appropriate sentence construction and punctuation.

Remind students that a writing prompt requires them to provide more than just their opinion—details, examples, and impressions from the poem are part of the scoring criteria.

Develop Understanding

One-Minute Insight

By personifying a gentle wind blowing through the speaker's room, Emily Dickinson conveys a sense of connection with nature and the importance of the everyday events of the natural world. In "A Pace Like That," Yehuda Amichai expresses this same sense of connection and stresses the importance of taking time to enjoy each day.

◆ Literary Focus

❶ **Figurative Language** This line contains two types of figurative language. Ask students to identify them. *Simile—the wind is being compared to a man; personification—in "tapping," the wind is taking on human characteristics.*

◆ Literary Focus

❷ **Figurative Language** Ask students what human characteristics the speaker gives to the wind to personify it. *She says the wind has speech, a countenance (face), and fingers.*

◆ Critical Thinking

❸ **Interpret** Ask students what simile in this stanza helps convey the speaker's impression of the wind in her room. Then ask what impression the simile conveys. *She says the wind is "like a timid Man," suggesting that the wind is a gentle, tentative visitor that doesn't stay long. Perhaps the speaker wants the wind to stay, since she says she "became alone."*

▶ Critical Viewing ◀

❹ **Relate** *The picture seems to relate to "The Wind—tapped like a tired Man" since it pictures a window and room that is a likely setting for the poem.*

The Wind—tapped like a tired Ma

Emily Dickins

❶ The Wind—tapped like a tired Man—
And like a Host—"Come in"
I boldly answered—entered then
My Residence within

A Rapid—footless Guest—
To offer whom a Chair
Were as impossible as hand
A Sofa to the Air—

No Bone had He to bind Him—
His Speech was like the Push
❷ Of numerous Humming Birds at once
From a superior Bush—

His Countenance—a Billow—
His Fingers, as He passed
Let go a music—as of tunes
Blown tremulous in Glass—

He visited—still flitting—
Then like a timid Man
❸ Again, He tapped—'twas flurriedly—
And I became alone—

▲ Critical Viewing Explain to which poem you think this picture best relates. **[Relate]** ❹

◆ Build Vocabulary

countenance (koun´ tə nəns) *n.*: The face; facial features

tremulous (trem´ yo͞o ləs) *adj.*: Trembling; quivering

flurriedly (flʉr´ əd lē) *adv.*: In a flustered, agitated way

Block Scheduling Strategies

Consider these suggestions to take advantage of extended class time:

- Introduce or review the types of figurative language presented in the Literary Focus on p. 833. Reinforce students' understanding of figurative language by having them suggest similes and metaphors based on the images accompanying these selections.
- Introduce elliptical clauses. Have students read the explanation in Build Grammar Skills on p. 832 and complete the exercise on p. 839. You may also have students complete Build Grammar Skills in ***Selection Support,*** p. 234.
- Direct students to gather into small groups to discuss and then answer the Critical Thinking questions on pp. 835, 837, and 838.
- Provide the discussion or presentation found in ***Alternative Assessment*** to assess students' understanding and progress, based on their varying performance levels or learning modalities.

A PACE LIKE THAT

Yehuda Amichai

I'm looking at the lemon tree I planted.
A year ago. I'd need a different pace, a slower one,
to observe the growth of its branches, its leaves as they open.
I want a pace like that.
Not like reading a newspaper
but the way a child learns to read,
5 or the way you quietly decipher the inscription
on an ancient tombstone.

And what a Torah scroll takes an entire year to do
as it rolls its way from Genesis to the death of Moses,
6 I do each day in haste
or in sleepless nights, rolling over from side to side.

The longer you live, the more people there are
who comment on your actions. Like a worker
in a manhole: at the opening above him
7 people stand around giving free advice
and yelling instructions,
but he's all alone down there in his depths.

◆ **Build Vocabulary**

decipher (dē sī′ fər) *v.*: Translate; make out the meaning

Guide for Responding

◆ Literature and Your Life

Reader's Response What kind of pace would you like to keep in your own life?

Thematic Focus Each of these poems reflects its poet's perspective on life by showing a response to day-to-day events. What "day-to-day" choices have you made that indicate your approach to life?

☑ Check Your Comprehension

1. In "The Wind—tapped like a tired Man," who is the "Guest" who enters the speaker's residence?
2. What does the speaker in "A Pace Like That" say happens more the longer you live?

◆ Critical Thinking

INTERPRET

1. What impression of the wind does Emily Dickinson present through her poem? **[Interpret]**
2. In "A Pace Like That," why might the speaker want a slower pace in which to live? **[Infer]**
3. Why is the Torah scroll a good image for a slow pace? **[Support]**

APPLY

4. Describe the pace at which you think life should be lived. **[Relate]**

COMPARE LITERARY WORKS

5. In what way do the images of nature in these poems reflect similar attitudes toward the natural world? **[Compare and Contrast]**

Analyze Literary Criticism

It has been said of Emily Dickinson's poetry, "Emily was original and innovative in her poetry. Many of her poems were not completed and written on scraps of paper, such as old grocery lists. Eventually when her poetry was published, editors arranged her works with titles, rearranged the syntax, and standardized Dickinson's grammar. Fortunately in 1955, Thomas Johnson published Dickinson's poems in their original formats, thus displaying the creative genius and peculiarity of her poetry."

Read this analysis of Emily Dickinson's poetry and discuss students' reactions.

1. Do you agree that Dickinson's solitary lifestyle is reflected in her writing? *Yes, her writing seems lonely because her work is introspective.*
2. Find examples of grammar or mechanics in her writing style which an editor might have wished to change or standardize. *In her first four lines, most editors would not capitalize the common nouns, others might object to her use of em dashes.*
3. Do you think her writing is creative and peculiar? *Possible answer: Yes, because she chooses unusual words such as flurriedly.*

◆ Build Grammar Skills

5 Elliptical Clauses Have students identify the two elliptical clauses in this passage and tell what missing word is understood in each clause. *Line 6 contains the clause "a child learns to read." Lines 7–8 include the clause "you quietly decipher the inscription on an ancient tombstone." The relative pronoun "that" is understood.*

◆ Reading Strategy

6 Paraphrase To help students paraphrase these lines, point out that the Torah helps people understand their place in life. Then ask students to restate the entire stanza. *I struggle all the time to find quick answers about my life, instead of slowing down and exploring these questions.*

◆ Literary Focus

7 Figurative Language Ask students what two things are compared in the simile in the last stanza. *The simile compares a person who has lived a long time with a worker in a manhole.*

Reinforce and Extend

Answers

◆ Literature and Your Life

Reader's Response Some students may wish for a slow, meditative pace, but most students will probably want to meet the fast pace of life.

Thematic Focus Possible response: I don't try out for another sport because I don't want too much pressure.

☑ Check Your Comprehension

1. The guest is the wind.
2. The longer you live, the more advice you get.

◆ Critical Thinking

1. She offers the impression of a nervous, timid character.
2. The speaker wants a slower pace to appreciate life more and to analyze things with more care.
3. It is a good image because it takes a year to read the Torah scroll, but the year-long reading repays the reader with insights.
4. Students might describe a pace that alternates busy activity with time for reflection.
5. All the poems show a deep respect and reverence for nature.

Develop Understanding

One-Minute Insight Through an extended metaphor comparing each new morning to a blank sheet of paper, Eve Merriam conveys an optimistic view of life: that each new day is important because it brings an opportunity for a fresh start.

◆ Literary Focus

❶ Figurative Language Ask students to identify the figurative expression in this stanza and explain the figurative language. *"Morning is/a new sheet of paper" is a metaphor—a new sheet of paper and a new day each offer a fresh start.*

◆ Critical Thinking

❷ Interpret Ask students what the used "sheet of paper" might represent and where it might be filed away each day. *Suggested response: The used sheet of paper is the person's experience that day. The consequences of that experience are filed away in the person's memory, as a resource to be mined in the future.*

▶Critical Viewing◀

❸ Analyze *The photograph may have been chosen because the colors of dawn and the freshness of the scene emphasize the newness of morning. Also, the climbing figure suggests the effort and accomplishment that are possible with each new day.*

Read to
Appreciate Author's Craft
As students read poetry they will find it meaningful to study the styles of writing. Poets offer detail, rhythm, punctuation, and word choice to create a mood and tell a story.

Customize for
Gifted/Talented Students
Suggest that students imagine that it is first thing in the morning and their journals are a "new sheet of paper". Have them write something that reflects a sense of freshness—it might be a brief poem, a scene from a story, or a description of an insight they had recently.

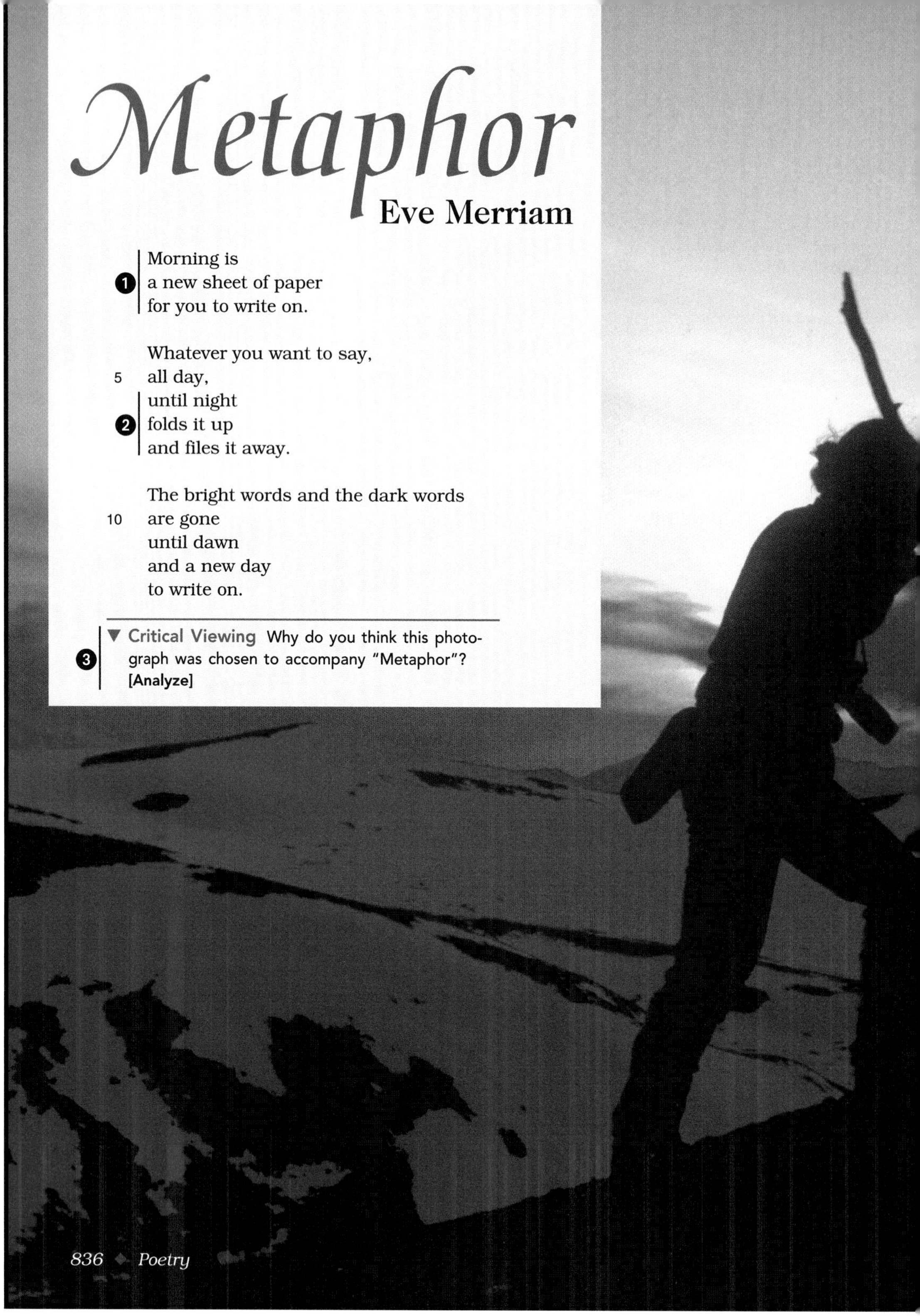

Metaphor

Eve Merriam

❶ Morning is
a new sheet of paper
for you to write on.

Whatever you want to say,
all day,
until night
❷ folds it up
and files it away.

The bright words and the dark words
are gone
until dawn
and a new day
to write on.

❸ ▼ Critical Viewing Why do you think this photograph was chosen to accompany "Metaphor"? **[Analyze]**

Workplace Skills Mini-Lesson

Being Focused
Observing the slow growth of a lemon tree and studying the Torah, two activities Amichai refers to in his poem, require that a person be focused, a skill that is important in many jobs.

Introduce Discuss what it means to be focused: applying close attention to the task at hand, the ability to cancel out distractions, the desire to carry a project through to completion.

Develop Review some ways in which students apply focus in their own lives; for example, concentrating on learning the complete rules of a new game, studying for an important test in the middle of a bustling room, or exceeding their personal best in a track sport.

Apply Have students list three jobs or careers they would be interested in, and explain how the ability to focus might help them succeed in each one.

Assess Have individuals share their ideas aloud. Assess based on how well students demonstrate the need for focus in the jobs they list.

Guide for Responding

◆ Literature and Your Life

Reader's Response To what would you compare the morning? Why?

Thematic Focus Each new day provides an opportunity to make choices that will have positive consequences. What are some possible effects of a positive approach to each new day?

Journal Writing Jot down a few sentences about a choice you made that did not have the results you wanted. What might you do differently if given the same choice again?

☑ Check Your Comprehension

1. To what is morning compared?
2. What does dawn bring?

◆ Critical Thinking

INTERPRET

1. What does "files it away" in line 8 suggest? **[Infer]**
2. What do you think the poet means by "The bright words and the dark words" in line 9? **[Interpret]**

EVALUATE

3. What makes this metaphor so effective? **[Evaluate]**

Extending Word Study

Metaphors Discussing metaphors is an excellent way for students to expand their vocabulary. Challenge students to brainstorm for as many metaphors as they can for a new day; for example, "morning is a seedling sprouting out of fertile soil." Encourage them to be creative and use a thesaurus or dictionary if they wish.

Reteach

Understanding figurative language is a skill that will help students comprehend and enjoy poetry. Have students that need additional practice draw a three column chart on a piece of paper and head each column with: Simile, Metaphor, and Personification. Have them choose one of the poems and analyze the author's words to see which column they might fit into.

Reinforce and Extend

Answers

◆ Literature and Your Life

Reader's Response Sample response: I would compare the morning to a child's first steps because it is a time of day to be moved into slowly.

Thematic Focus A positive approach to each new day will lead people to accept new challenges and gather exciting or important new experience.

☑ Check Your Comprehension

1. Morning is compared to a new sheet of paper.
2. Dawn brings a new day.

◆ Critical Thinking

1. "Files it away" suggests storing it (experience) for future use.
2. "The bright words and the dark words" might represent good and bad feelings, moods, and experiences that people accumulate throughout the day.
3. Comparing morning to a new sheet of paper is an effective metaphor because it holds up to all of Merriam's examples; morning is like new paper because it gets used, stored away, and replaced by a new, fresh opportunity.

Speaking, Listening, and Viewing Mini-Lesson

Dialogue

This mini-lesson supports the Speaking, Listening, and Viewing activity in the Idea Bank on p. 840.

Introduce A dialogue is a conversation reflecting the personalities and ideas of the characters involved, in this case, the speakers of two poems. Students should prepare by analyzing the poems for clues to the speakers' ideas and attitudes.

Develop Have partners choose speakers to portray, and to explore, their speakers' characters. Lead students to consider these questions:

- What is each character's attitude toward life?
- How would the character react to being stuck in an elevator?
- What insights can each speaker offer the other?

Apply After answering the questions above, students should outline their elevator conversations. Allow them to rehearse and then present their role-played conversations to the class.

Assess Evaluate each role play, based on how well it reflects the differing personalities and points of view of the two speakers.

Develop Understanding

One-Minute Insight In this poem, the speaker honors his grandfather, a Jewish immigrant whose right hand—seamed, eloquent, and self-assured—reveals his character and the quality of his days. In this characterization, Fried celebrates the importance of an "ordinary" (yet extraordinary) man.

◆ Literary Focus

❶ **Figurative Language** Ask students to identify the personification in these lines. *The hand is compared to a smiling person.*

❷ **Clarification** Yiddish is a language that was spoken by many Eastern European Jews. They brought the language with them when they immigrated to the United States. The language, a variation of German, has original words of its own and many guttural, rasping sounds. Although Yiddish influences can be found with some English speakers, the language is not fluently spoken in this country today.

❸ **Clarification** A Greek chorus was a group of actors or singers used to comment from the sidelines on the significance of the action in an ancient Greek play. The chorus moved first to one side of the stage and then to the other as they recited their lines.

◆ Reading Strategy

❹ **Paraphrase** Ask students to explain this line's meaning in their own words. *Sample answer: Although Grandpa hadn't said much in a long time, his hand was very expressive.*

Art Transparency Display Art Transparency 11. Ask for descriptions of the scene. After students have read "Right Hand," call on volunteers to describe the character of Grandfather. Invite students to compare the "magic" that comes from the magician's right hand as he performs before a crowd with the influence of Grandfather's right hand, as he lives his heritage before his family.

RIGHT HAND

Philip Fried

Grandfather carried his voice in the seamed
palm of his right hand, the one
that had ironed countless taciturn trousers.

❶ What an eloquent hand, it broke into grins
and self-assured narration whenever
it opened—how could a hand carry nothing,
bear away nothing from its nation?
When it entered a room, even the corners
❷ mumbled in Yiddish, the very dust
had sifted from consonants' guttural rubbing.

The poems this hand had proclaimed to shirts
as it moved back and forth like a Greek chorus
❸ across the stage of the ironing board—
these poems had diffused in clouds of steam.

Grandpa himself had long been struck dumb
❹ by the garrulity of this hand,
but sometimes he'd thrust it deep in his pocket
and, straightening up, display an uncanny
knack for spelling English words.

◆ Build Vocabulary

taciturn (tas´ ə tʉrn) *adj.*: Silent; uncommunicative

eloquent (el´ ə kwənt) *adj.*: Vividly expressive

guttural (gut´ ər əl) *adj.*: Produced from the throat; harsh; rasping

diffused (di fyo͞ozd´) *v.*: Spread out; dispersed

garrulity (gə ro͞o´ lə tē) *n.*: Talkativeness

Guide for Responding

◆ Literature and Your Life

Reader's Response Would you like to spend time with the man described in this poem? Why or why not?

Thematic Focus What are some significant choices the grandfather has made in his life?

☑ Check Your Comprehension

1. What does Grandfather's hand do as it irons shirts?
2. Describe two ways in which Grandfather's hand expresses itself.

◆ Critical Thinking

INTERPRET

1. Explain the contrast between Grandfather's hand and Grandfather himself. **[Analyze]**
2. Why do you think Grandfather puts his hand in his pocket when he spells English words? **[Infer]**
3. Explain the meaning of the lines "When it entered a room, even the corners/mumbled in Yiddish . . ."

APPLY

4. Describe a friend's personality through his or her hands, eyes, or smile. **[Relate]**

Reinforce and Extend

Answers

◆ Literature and Your Life

Reader's Response Students might feel they would not be able to communicate with him, while others will be intrigued by his unique character.

Thematic Focus He chose to come to the U.S.; he chose to keep to himself rather than talk much to others.

☑ Check Your Comprehension

1. It "speaks" to the shirts.
2. It "broke into grins/and self-assured narration" and "proclaimed poems."

◆ Critical Thinking

1. Grandfather's hand is eloquent and garrulous, while he is as taciturn as the trousers he presses.
2. He is self-conscious; he does not want his Yiddish self (the hand) to emerge.
3. These lines indicate that the Grandfather's hand is a strong presence—people are drawn to its Yiddish influence, and respond in "Yiddish" ways.
4. Sample response: His eyes dart all around, quickly, trying to keep pace with the flow of his ideas.

Guide for Responding (continued)

◆ Reading Strategy

Paraphrase

Paraphrasing—restating in your own words—is one way to clarify the meaning of complex or abstract lines or sections of these poems.

1. Paraphrase the first and last stanzas of "The Wind—tapped like a tired Man."
2. (a) Choose words that describe the speed of each event or activity in the first two stanzas of "A Pace Like That." (b) Use these words to paraphrase what Amichai says about the kind of pace he wants to achieve.
3. The poem "Metaphor" is written in three sentences. Paraphrase each sentence.
4. (a) Identify two words Fried uses to describe his grandfather's hand, and give a synonym for each. (b) Paraphrase the description using the synonyms you have chosen.

◆ Literary Focus

Figurative Language

Figurative language is speech or writing that presents ideas in a way not meant to be interpreted literally. Specific types of figurative language are called figures of speech. Common figures of speech are **simile, metaphor,** and **personification**. Poets and other writers use figurative language to create vivid word pictures, to make their writing emotionally intense and concentrated, and to state their ideas in new and unusual ways.

1. (a) What simile does Amichai use in "A Pace Like That" to describe the way people comment on his actions? (b) Explain how this comparison clarifies his meaning.
2. What qualities of the wind might lead Emily Dickinson to describe it as a rapid, footless guest?
3. Identify the simile Fried uses in "Right Hand" to describe the movement of his grandfather's hand ironing shirts.
4. Explain the metaphor in "Metaphor."
5. Which poem uses the most vivid personification? Use examples to support your answer.

◆ Build Vocabulary

Using the Latin Root *-tac-*

Knowing that the Latin root *-tac-* and its variant *-tic-* mean "silent," describe the following people or things in your notebook.

1. taciturn judge
2. reticent witness
3. tacit understanding

Using the Word Bank: Word Choice

In your notebook, respond to each of the numbered items using words from the Word Bank. Use each word only once.

1. List four words that deal with speech or speaking.
2. Write one adjective and one adverb that could be used to describe the actions or attitude of a high-strung, excited person.
3. Write a synonym for the word *face*.
4. Write the word that names what a shade or thin curtain does to light shining through it.
5. Identify the word you would most likely find in a story about a secret code.

◆ Build Grammar Skills

Elliptical Clauses

In an **elliptical clause,** words that are understood or implied are omitted.

Practice Copy the following sentences in your notebook. Underline the elliptical clause in each; then write the omitted word or words.

1. I don't understand the way you decipher the inscription.
2. I admire the way he writes.
3. Do you remember the year he came to live here?
4. He is the one I need to help me.
5. The poems this hand had proclaimed to shirts . . .

Beyond the Selection

FURTHER READING

Other Works by the Poets

"A Light Exists in Spring," Emily Dickinson
"This Is My Mother's House," Yehuda Amichai
Family Circle, Eve Merriam
"Sunday," Philip Fried

Other Works About Daily Choices

"Ballad of the Morning Streets," Amiri Baraka
"Reveille," A. E. Housman

We suggest that you preview these works before recommending them to students.

INTERNET

Students can visit the following Web sites for more information. Please be aware that sites may have changed since we published this information.

Dickinson: **http://www.learner.org/channel/previews/multimedia.html**

Merriam: **http://mbhs.bergtraum.k12.ny.us/cybereng/poetry/eatpoem.html**

We *strongly recommend* that you preview sites before you send students to them.

Answers

◆ Reading Strategy

1. (1) The Wind came to my window and I boldly invited It in, so the Wind entered. (2) It visited but then It nervously asked to be excused, after which I was left alone.
2. (a) Sample response: Looking at the lemon tree—leisurely; sleeping and dreaming—hurriedly. (b) He wants to observe things in a leisurely way.
3. Morning is a new opportunity. You choose what to do with it and in the evening it's all filed away. A new day brings new opportunities.
4. (a) eloquent: expressive; garrulity: talkativeness; (b) My grandfather's hand was expressive and talkative.

◆ Literary Focus

1. (a) He says they're like people standing around a manhole yelling down advice. (b) This comparison conveys the speaker's sense of being observed.
2. The wind is stealthy and quick; it doesn't leave a trace.
3. It moved back and forth like a Greek Chorus moves across a stage.
4. A clean sheet of paper is a new start; so is a new day.
5. Sample response: "The Wind" because it makes the wind seem just like a quick, nervous person.

◆ Build Vocabulary

Using the Latin Word Root *-tac-*

1. one who doesn't talk much
2. a witness who is reluctant to speak
3. an unspoken understanding

Using the Word Bank

1. taciturn, eloquent, guttural, garrulity; 2. tremulous, flurriedly; 3. countenance; 4. diffused; 5. decipher

◆ Build Grammar Skills

1. I don't understand the way (that) you decipher the inscription.
2. I admire the way (that) he writes.
3. Do you remember the year (that) I came to live here?
4. He is the one (who) I need to help me.
5. The poems (that) this hand had proclaimed to shirts.

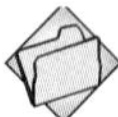

Idea Bank

Following are suggestions for matching Idea Bank topics with your students' performance levels and learning modalities:

Customizing for *Performance Levels*

Less Advanced Students: 1, 6
Average Students: 2, 4, 5
More Advanced Students: 3, 7

Customizing for *Learning Modalities*

Interpersonal: 4, 5
Verbal/Linguistic: 3, 4, 5
Logical/Mathematical: 7
Visual/Spatial: 6

Guided Writing Lesson

Prewriting Strategy Use a pentad to help students focus their character creations. Have students draw a five-pointed star, writing the name of an object in the center. Then they can quickly label each point of the star with one quality of the object.

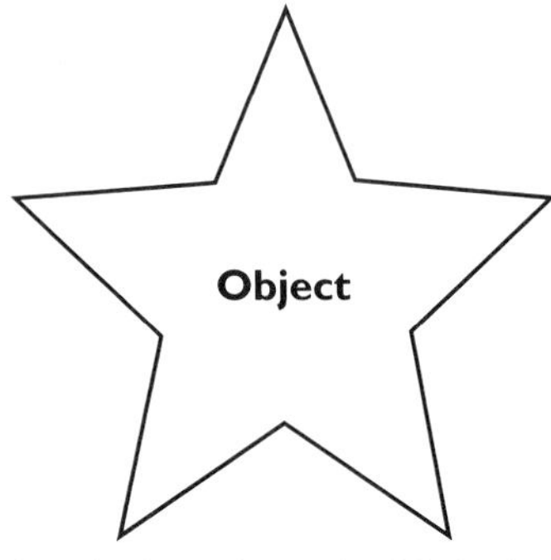

After thinking about the labels they have attached, ask students to commit to one point on the star and freewrite to that focus. They can use the ideas and details generated from this freewriting to begin their drafts.

For more prewriting, elaboration, and revision strategies, see *Prentice Hall Writing and Grammar.*

Writing Lab CD-ROM

Students can use these steps for the tutorial on Descriptive Writing:

1. Have students use a Character Trait Word Bin for examples of words that might be used to create characters. Allow time for students to draft on computer.
2. Encourage students to use Revision Checkers to find any overused or vague adjectives in their descriptions.

Build Your Portfolio

Idea Bank

Writing Ideas

1. **Most Admired** "Right Hand" is a celebration of a person the poet admires. Write a paragraph about someone you admire. Describe his or her admirable qualities and physical features.
2. **Perfect Day Directions** The poem "Metaphor" describes a day as a sheet of paper on which you can write anything you choose. Write the "directions" for your perfect day.
3. **Metaphor Poem** Eve Merriam uses the metaphor of a sheet of paper to describe the possibilities of each new day. Write a brief poem in which you use one central metaphor to describe "choices."

Speaking, Listening, and Viewing

4. **Wind Interview** With a partner, prepare and act out an interview with the speaker of "The Wind—tapped like a tired Man."
5. **Dialogue** Imagine that the speakers of "A Pace Like That" and "Metaphor" have been stuck on an elevator together for three hours. Role-play the conversation that might be taking place between them as they head into hour four.

Researching and Representing

6. **Visual Biography** Fried associates ironing, Yiddish, and spelling with his grandfather. Create a collage biography of a relative or friend. Arrange pictures and objects on a paper to show the things you associate with this person. **[Art Link]**
7. **Hurricane Statistics** The wind in Dickinson's poem is a much friendlier wind than one you'd encounter in a hurricane. Find statistics about hurricanes' wind speeds, frequency, and duration. Present your findings to the class using charts and graphs. **[Math Link; Science Link]**

Online Activity www.phlit.phschool.com

Guided Writing Lesson

Character Creation

In "The Wind—tapped like a tired Man," Emily Dickinson brings the wind to life with personification; she describes the wind's movements as the actions of a person. Use techniques similar to Dickinson's to create a character from an object (such as a computer), a plant (such as a tree outside your window), or a weather condition (such as rain). Write a description of how this character acts and sounds, giving the subject of your description human qualities.

Writing Focus: Consistent Focus

In describing your character, keep a **consistent focus.** If you begin by characterizing an object as an energetic three-year-old, use comparisons that suggest this image throughout your description. In "The Wind—tapped like a tired Man," Dickinson keeps a consistent focus; all her comparisons and details create a unified image of the nervous movements of a "tremulous," "flitting" visitor.

Prewriting Begin by listing the qualities of the thing you are describing. Ask yourself questions about how your subject moves, looks, and sounds. Based on these details, determine the type of character your subject is. The details may suggest a gentle elderly person or a cranky child.

Drafting Organize your description around a specific moment. For instance, Emily Dickinson describes a moment when the wind blows through her house. You might describe a moment when a tree is scratching on your window or your computer is "waking up."

Revising Ask a partner to read your description and tell you the general impression he or she gets from it. Together, look for any details that do not contribute to the general impression or central focus. Revise to create a more unified picture of your subject.

ASSESSMENT OPTIONS

Formal Assessment, Selection Test, pp. 201–203, and Assessment Resources Software. The selection test is designed so that it can be easily customized to the performance levels of your students.

Alternative Assessment, p. 57, includes options for less advanced students, more advanced students, interpersonal learners, verbal/linguistic learners and visual/spatial learners.

PORTFOLIO ASSESSMENT

Use the following rubrics in the ***Alternative Assessment*** booklet to assess student writing:
Most Admired: Description Rubric, p. 97
Perfect Day Directions: How-to/Explanation Rubric, p. 100
Metaphor Poem: Poetry Rubric, p. 108
Guided Writing Lesson: Description, p. 97

Writing Process Workshop

Literary Analysis

Have you ever seen a movie with a friend and then afterwards had a deep discussion in which you picked apart every aspect of the film? Literary critics, teachers, and students do the same with a work of literature when they write a literary analysis.

Write a **literary analysis** of one of the works in this section. Closely examine the work of literature by taking it apart and discussing its various elements. A literary analysis provides the opportunity for you to explain how the author has used particular literary elements and how those elements work together to convey the author's message.

The following skills will help you write a keen literary analysis.

Ploughing (detail), Nancy Smith, Stapleton Collection

Writing Skills Focus

- **Be consistent in your purpose.** For example, if your purpose is to explain the use of nature words in haiku, then don't discuss sound devices. (See p. 820.)
- **Use specific examples.** Every time you make an assertion about the work, back it up with an example from the text. (See p. 831.)
- **Paraphrase** specific passages to further describe images or explain details.

The following excerpt from a literary analysis about imagery in haiku shows these skills.

Writing Model

Haiku by Issa

A gentle spring rain.
Look, a rat is lapping
Sumida River. ①

Issa, the writer of this haiku, knew well how important it is to use seasonal words in haiku. Although this haiku contains a scarce 15 syllables, because of the poet's choice of words it conveys a lasting image of a peaceful scene of a creature by a river in the rain.

By briefly describing a riverside scene in a soft spring rain, ② Issa creates a clear image in our minds. "Lapping" further clarifies that image. ③ We are reminded . . .

① The writer uses a specific example of a haiku.

② The writer paraphrases to describe the image.

③ The writer sticks to the purpose: to explain the importance of imagery in haiku.

Prepare and Engage

Lesson Objectives

1. To use recursive writing processes to write a literary analysis
2. To recognize and and avoid run-on sentences
3. To recognize and use adjective clauses appropriately

Before students begin, you may want to share with them the Scoring Rubric for Literary Analysis/Interpretation (p. 112 in ***Alternative Assessment***) so students see the criteria by which they will be evaluated. Suggestions on p. 843 customize the rubric to this workshop.

Writing and Language Transparencies You may wish to use Writing Process Model 8: Interpreting a Work of Literature (pp. 53–59) to model the writing process and to provide students with a model literary analysis.

Writers at Work Videodisc
To introduce students to the key elements of a literary response and to let them hear teacher and poet Miguel Algarín discuss response to literature, play the videodisc segment on Response to Literature (Ch. 7).

Play frames 22209 to 31154

Writing Lab CD-ROM
If students have access to computers, have them work in the tutorial on Response to Literature to complete all or part of their literary analysis. Follow these steps:

1. Students can review the interactive model of a response to literature.
2. Have students use the Response Wheels to focus their response.
3. Have students use the Evaluation Word Bins to improve word choice.
4. After drafting, students can use the Interactive Self-Evaluation Checklist to guide revision.

Beyond the Classroom

Workplace Skills

Scientific Analyses Explain to students that literary analysis and scientific analysis share similar critical thinking processes. When medical researchers write up their findings, their technical reports must withstand the critical analysis of the worldwide scientific community. While readers analyze literary works in terms of their literary elements and how they fit together, readers analyze technical reports in terms of scientific method, validity in comparison with other scientific data, and possible flaws in studies, procedures, and documentation of results.

Discuss with students the similarities and differences between the uses and effects of literary and scientific studies. For instance, encourage students to recognize that literary critiques may affect whether readers buy and/or read books; scientific analyses may determine a medical procedure to be successful or render it unusable.

Develop Student Writing

Prewriting Strategy

Once students have selected a literary work to analyze, have them use hexagonal writing to move their response to an elaborated text analysis. Thoroughly examining and evaluating the literature will allow them to elaborate on their central idea effectively.

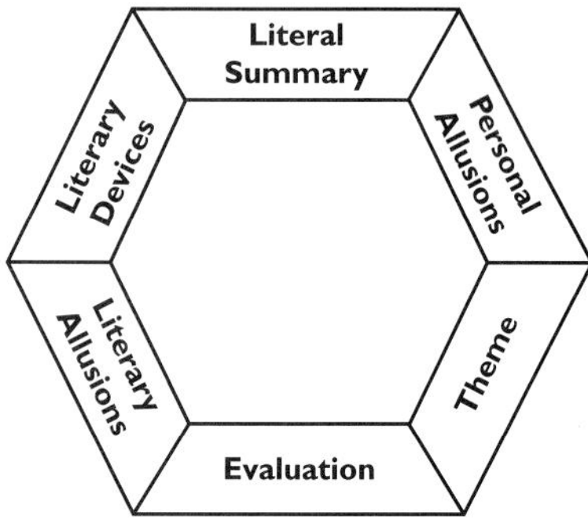

Customize for
ESL Students

Because these students may not have yet developed a wide range of evaluative words, work with them to create a list of precise descriptors.

Elaboration Strategy

Remind students that to support the main idea of a literary analysis they must use specific details, including quoted phrases and sentences, from the literary work.

Applying Language Skills

Run-on Sentences A literary analysis aims to show clear relationships among the literary elements a writer uses. Run-on sentences, however, run ideas together, blurring the relationships the analysis should establish.

Answers

Suggested response: Repetition is a common sound device, and the Navajo often used it in their poetry. It gives the poetry a ceremonial, almost sacred feeling.

Grammar Reinforcement

For additional instruction, use the **Language Lab CD-ROM** lesson on Fragments and Run-on Sentences and the practice page on Fragments and Run-ons, p. 59, in the *Writer's Solution Grammar Practice Book.*

Applying Language Skills: Run-on Sentences

Avoid run-on sentences—sentences that have two main clauses not separated by adequate punctuation.

Run-on Sentence:

Emily Dickinson frequently punctuates her poems with dashes, they give the poems a unique feel and style.

Corrected With a Conjunction:

Emily Dickinson frequently punctuates her poems with dashes, and they give the poems a unique feel and style.

Corrected With a Semicolon:

Emily Dickinson frequently punctuates her poems with dashes; they give the poems a unique feel and style.

Practice On your paper, correct the following run-on sentence.

> Repetition is a common sound device, the Navajo often used it in their poetry, it gives the poetry a ceremonial, almost sacred feeling.

Writer's Solution Connection
Language Lab

For more practice correcting run-on sentences, complete the Language Lab lesson on Run-on Sentences and Fragments.

Prewriting

Interview Yourself Review works of literature you've read during the past year. Then answer the following questions:

- What were the most enjoyable, interesting, and frustrating literary works I encountered this year?
- Why did the works strike me this way?
- What was especially memorable about the subjects or stories?
- Which characters come to mind in an especially vivid way?
- What was special about any of the settings of the works or about the author's use of language?
- Would I want to reread any of these literary works? Why or why not?

Take notes as you conduct your self-interview, and use these notes to help you choose a topic for a literary analysis.

Consider the Meaning If you're writing a literary analysis of a poem, ask yourself how the poet used language to get his or her message across. Think about the use of figurative language. What images has the poet created to convey ideas to the reader? If you are analyzing a lyric poem, look for details the poet uses to suggest mood or feeling.

Focus Your Topic Explore your reactions to the work you've chosen. You won't be able to include everything you think and feel about the work, so concentrate on one of its literary elements—setting, theme, or mood, for example. Make a chart like the following one to further help you focus your topic:

Literary Work	Broad Topic	Focused Topic
"The Monkey's Paw"	Suspense	The author's use of foreshadowing to build suspense
Julius Caesar	Soliloquy	Cassius' speech in Act I, ii, 308–322
"Meeting at Night"	Sound Devices	How alliteration and onomatopoeia add to the poem's meaning

Drafting

Write the Introduction Your introduction is the place to capture your readers' attention and tell them the purpose of your paper. Include the title and author of the work you'll be evaluating. Open with a statement that will intrigue your readers. Then clearly state your main idea.

Research Skills Mini-Lesson

Using Resources

Introduce When researching poets, students may have difficulty locating appropriate information. They may have access to reference materials, but not be able to find what they are looking for because they do not use text organizers efficiently.

Develop Provide a sampling of reference books including poetry anthologies and literature collections. Have students examine the books to see how text organizers, such as headings, graphic organizers, tables of contents, indexes, and text features organize the books' materials.

Apply Have students select one of the poets represented in Unit 9 and use the resources you have made available to locate information to write brief reports. They should include biographical information about the poets they are researching and an example or listing of the poet's work. Have students provide a bibliography which identifies where resource materials were found.

Assess Have students present their reports to the class by explaining how they located the information they found. Assess their work on the basis of providing the required information.

Write the Body and Conclusion Develop your main idea in the **body** of your analysis. Present each main idea in a **separate paragraph,** and include specific details to support each main idea. In the **conclusion,** restate your main idea and make a final, compelling point.

Revising

Use a Checklist The following checklist will help you revise your literary analysis:

- Do you grab the reader's attention in the first paragraph?
- Is your main idea clearly presented? Does the body of your analysis support and develop your main idea?
- Are your introduction, body, and conclusion clearly organized?
- Do you use specific examples and quotations?

Revision Model

In "Meeting at Night," Robert Browning uses ~~lots of musical devices~~ ① alliteration and onomatopoeia to make the poem more vivid. When the ~~narrator is in the boat, you can~~ ② the terms "pushing prow" and "slushy sand" let the reader feel his exertion. Also, ~~when he knocks on the window it sounds really vivid.~~ ② In the second stanza, the words "Tap at the pane" are themselves like a hand striking a window.

① *Alliteration and onomatopoeia are more specific than lots of musical devices.*

② *The writer replaces vague statements with direct quotations from the text.*

Publishing

Create a Library Display With your classmates and the librarian, create a library display of your literary analyses.

- Set up the display so that it attracts students' attention.
- Bind and mount the analyses to make them accessible and attractive.
- Use posters, photos, or other illustrations to make the display visually appealing.

Applying Language Skills: Adjective Clauses

An adjective clause is a subordinate clause (a clause that contains a subject and a verb, but cannot stand alone as a sentence) that modifies a noun or pronoun in a sentence's main clause. The following words commonly introduce adjective clauses:

that, which, who, whom, whose, whoever, where, when

The adjective clause in the following sentence modifies *figurative device*:

Simile is the figurative device that Tennyson uses most.

Practice On your paper, identify the adjective clauses in the following sentences and indicate which word in the main clause it modifies.

1. The object to which Emily Dickinson compares the wind is a tired man.
2. The man who wrote that poem lived a long time ago.

Writer's Solution Connection Writing Lab

For more help using quotations in your literary analysis, see Using Quotations in the Writing Lab tutorial on Response to Literature.

Revision Strategy

After discussing the Revision Model, use the Revision Overlay for Writing Process Model 8: Interpreting a Work of Literature, p. 55, ***Writing and Language Transparencies,*** to further model the revision process.

Prentice Hall Writing and Grammar For more prewriting, elaboration, and revision strategies, see *Prentice Hall Writing and Grammar.*

Publishing

Remind students that literary analyses are often published in newspapers and magazines as well as on the Internet. They may want to pursue these sources of publishing.

Reinforce and Extend

Applying Language Skills

Adjective Clauses Discuss with students how they can, by using adjective clauses, combine short, choppy sentences into more mature sentences. You might model this process for them.

Answers

1. The adjective clause *to which Emily Dickinson compares the wind* modifies *object.*
2. The adjective clause *who wrote that poem* modifies *man.*

Grammar Reinforcement

For additional instruction, use Adjective Clauses, p. 51, in the *Writer's Solution Grammar Practice Book.*

Connect to Literature Unit 7, Nonfiction, includes two examples of critical reviews: Vincent Canby's "Star Wars—A Trip to a Far Galaxy That's Fun and Funny" (p. 631) and Roger Ebert's "Star Wars: Breakthrough Film Still Has the Force" (p. 626).

✓ ASSESSMENT		4	3	2	1
PORTFOLIO ASSESSMENT Use the rubric on Literary Analysis/Interpretation (p. 112) to assess students' writing. Add these criteria to customize the rubric to this assignment.	**Reference to Specific Literary Elements**	All significant literary elements and the author's purpose for using them are addressed.	Literary elements and the author's purpose for using them are addressed only in part.	Few of the literary elements are addressed; the purpose for them is only addressed in part.	Few of the literary elements are addressed; the purpose for using them is not addressed.
	Sentence Structure	The writer uses a variety of sentence structures, including complex sentences with adjective clauses.	The writer varies sentence structure but there is limited use of complex sentences.	The writer uses some sentence variety but no complex sentences.	The writer uses no sentence variety.

Prepare and Engage

LESSON OBJECTIVES

- To discriminate between connotative and denotative meanings and interpret the connotative power of words

Customize for
Less Advanced Students

As some students may have difficulty distinguishing between connotation and denotation, have pairs or small groups use verses from some popular ballads with which they are familiar and identify words or phrases with denotative and connotative meanings. Have students discuss how the connotative associations contribute to the power of the lyrics.

Answers

1. Paragraphs might indicate that the verse uses strong connotative and denotative meanings to persuade the reader that aging should not be passive. The words *burn, rave,* and *rage* use their denotative meanings; coupled with the connotative associations of the phrases *close of day,* and *dying of the light,* they make a powerful statement to argue that aging should be strong, active, and alive.
2. Responses should indicate an understanding of how connotative associations are chosen to form a mood, opinion, or argument within a poem.

Student Success Workshop

Vocabulary Development

Distinguishing Between Connotation and Denotation

Strategies for Success

A common challenge faced by readers of literature—especially of poetry—is understanding the difference between the denotations and connotations of language the author has used. The words or expressions that you read may mean one thing when taken literally, but the author may have used them to convey other, indirect meanings as well. Here are some strategies that can help you distinguish between connotation and denotation:

Define Denotation The denotation of a word or phrase is its exact or literal definition. With the help of a dictionary, you can easily determine and understand a denotation. There is no need to interpret it. For instance, in the sentence "The doctor performed an operation on Consuelo's heart," the word *heart* has the same meaning as its dictionary definition. Its denotation is "the organ of the body that pumps blood."

Interpret Connotation The connotation of a word or phrase is its implied, or suggested, meaning. Connotations cannot always be easily defined, and they do require interpretation. To figure out the connotation of a word or phrase, notice its context—the sense or ideas expressed in the rest of the sentence, paragraph, line, or verse. If you are reading a poem that includes the line "He would do anything to win Consuelo's heart," you would guess that the poet intends you to understand more than the dictionary definition of the word *heart.* In order to understand the line, you might interpret the connotation of the word *heart* as "love."

Sometimes the connotation of a word or phrase more broadly suggests ideas, attitudes, or other associations with the word or phrase. For example, when you read the word *limousine,* you probably think of more than just a long car. You might think of things the limousine has come to symbolize—such as wealth, fame, or status. These are connotations of the word *limousine.*

Apply the Strategies

1 Read the following verse from Dylan Thomas's poem "Do Not Go Gentle Into That Good Night." List the denotations and connotations of the words and phrases in italics. Then write a paragraph interpreting the verse. Support your ideas with references to the denotations and connotations of the italicized words and phrases in the text.

Do not *go gentle* into *that good night,*
Old age should *burn* and *rave* at *close of day;*
Rage, rage against the *dying of the light.*

2 Choose another poem from this section. Find a passage in which the words have especially strong connotations. Then write a paragraph in which you explain how the connotations of the various words contribute to the overall meaning of the passage.

Here are situations in which it is often important to distinguish between denotations and connotations:

- When interpreting poetry
- When presenting a storytelling or poetry reading
- When reading advertisements
- When reading sports reports of an athlete's accomplishments

Test Preparation Workshop

Distinguishing Between Connotation and Denotation

Vocabulary development will help students perform well on any standardized test. By becoming familiar with connotative and denotative meanings, students will more easily answer analogy items on standardized tests.

Explain to students that once they recognize the connotative meanings of *limousine,* they can use that knowledge to more quickly answer a test item on analogies such as the following:

limousine : car ::

A chauffeur : passenger
B milk : cow
C board : train
D private jet : plane

Guide students to understand that by recognizing that a limousine is a luxurious type of car, with its own connotative meanings, they can more easily spot the correct answer, D, which uses a similar connotative association.

Part 2 Structure

Helicon Desk, Cathleen Toelke

One-Minute Planning Guide

The poems in this section illustrate the art of poetry. Structure, or verbal design, provides a framework within which poets work. These poems illustrate categories of poetry—narrative, dramatic, and lyric—and tightly structured forms—sonnet, villanelle, tanka, and haiku.

Customize for *Varying Student Needs*

- All of the poems, except "La Belle Dame sans Merci" are short. "La Belle Dame sans Merci" is two pages.
- The following poems contain vocabulary that may challenge less proficient readers or ESL Students.

Sonnet 18

"Danny Deever" (dialect)

- The following poems contain simple language and clear images and messages:

"Making a Fist"

"Jade Flower Palace"

"The Moon at the Fortified Pass"

"What Are Friends For"

Tanka

Haiku

- Students may be intrigued by the clever arrangement of words in "Some Like Poetry"

Humanities: Art

Helicon Desk by Cathleen Toelke.

Explain that "Helicon" has several meanings, but the most likely one for this painting comes from Greek mythology, in which the Helicon Mountains were the home of the Muses, the divine figures who inspired writers, artists, and performers. Help students see how a writing desk could be compared to the home of the Muses. The whole painting invites the imagination to play with associations. Call attention to the way the items in the painting resemble folded pieces of paper, like origami—the folding screen, the sharp-edged shadows, and the oddly jutting desk. Help students link this art with the focus of Part 2, "Structure," by discussing their responses to the following questions:

1. What kind of poetry do you think this artist would write? *Students may feel that the angular, structured images in the painting indicate that the artist would write highly structured poetry.*
2. A poem is an arrangement of words structured to arouse emotion and convey meaning. Look at the way the items in this painting are arranged. Which item do you think the artist wants you to notice first, and what has she done to draw your attention to it? *Students' responses will vary, but they should explain whether the item they choose has other items pointing at it, or is a brighter color, or is placed at a focal point.*

Prepare and Engage

LESSON OBJECTIVES

1. **To develop vocabulary and word identification skills**
   - Word Roots: *-journ-*
   - Using the Word Bank: Sentence Completions
   - Extending Word Study: Use Reference Materials (ATE)
2. **To use a variety of reading strategies to comprehend poems**
   - Connect Your Experience
   - Reading Strategy: Identifying Speaker
   - Tips to Guide Reading: Sustained Reading (ATE)
   - Read to Be Entertained (ATE)
3. **To increase knowledge of other cultures and to connect common elements across cultures**
   - Background for Understanding
   - Idea Bank: Diary Entry
4. **To express and support responses to the text**
   - Critical Thinking
   - Idea Bank: Letter to the Knight
   - Idea Bank: Art
5. **To analyze literary elements**
   - Literary Focus: Narrative and Dramatic Poetry
   - Idea Bank: Mock Narrative
6. **To read in order to research self-selected and assigned topics**
   - Idea Bank: Dialect Chart
7. **To plan, prepare, organize, and present literary interpretations**
   - Speaking, Listening, and Viewing Mini-Lesson: Story in Music (ATE)
   - Idea Bank: Oral Reading
8. **To use recursive writing processes to write a news bulletin**
   - Guided Writing Lesson
9. **To increase knowledge of the rules of grammar and usage**
   - Build Grammar Skills: Hyphens

Test Preparation

Critical Reading: Analyzing an Author's Meaning and Style (ATE, p. 847) The teaching tips and sample test item in this workshop support the instruction and practice in the unit workshop.

Critical Reading: Analyzing an Author's Meaning and Style (SE, p. 877)

Guide for Reading

John Keats *(1795–1821)*

John Keats was born in England. Both of his parents died while he was still a boy, and his guardian sent Keats to school in London. Later, Keats studied surgery. He decided, however, to devote his life to writing poetry.

In 1816, Keats met Leigh Hunt, an editor who published Keats's first sonnet, "On First Looking Into Chapman's Homer." Hunt also introduced Keats to Shelley and Wordsworth. Like them, he emphasized feeling and imagination over reason and logic in his poetry.

Although he died young, Keats left a surprisingly large body of work. His poems, including the narrative poem "La Belle Dame sans Merci," communicate an appreciation of beauty and a sadness at its impermanence.

Rudyard Kipling *(1865–1936)*

Rudyard Kipling was born in India to English parents. He grew up speaking both Hindustani and English until the age of six, when he was sent to England for a formal education.

Returning to India at eighteen, Kipling worked as a journalist. Many of his early poems and stories first appeared in newspapers. "Danny Deever" was included in a collection of Kipling's poems called *Barracks Room Ballads*.

In 1907, he became the first English author to win the Nobel Prize for Literature. He produced a vast body of work, including stories, poems, and novels.

◆ Build Vocabulary

WORD ROOTS: *-journ-*

In "La Belle Dame sans Merci," the speaker laments "And this is why I *sojourn* here . . ." The word *sojourn* contains the root *-journ-*, which comes from the Latin *diurnalis,* meaning "day." It's easy to understand how the current meaning of *sojourn,* "stay temporarily," could evolve from "a day's stay."

Other words that contain the root, such as *journal* and *adjourn*, also have meanings that have evolved from the meaning of "day."

WORD BANK

As you read these poems, you will encounter the words on this list. Each word is defined on the page where it first appears. Preview the list before you read.

sedge
thrall
sojourn
whimpers
quickstep

◆ Build Grammar Skills

HYPHENS

These poems contain examples of **hyphens**—used to connect two or more words that function as a single word. Notice the use of hyphens in the following examples from the poems:

Pale Warriors, *death-pale* were they all

"What makes that *front-rank* man fall down?"

The hyphens used in these lines from the poems form compound modifiers. Hyphens are not used in compound modifiers that include words ending in *-ly* (*poorly* trusted, for example) or with compound proper adjectives. (*Native American* customs for instance). Hyphens are used, however, in many compound nouns, such as mother-in-law.

Prentice Hall Literature Program Resources

REINFORCE / RETEACH / EXTEND

Selection Support Pages
Build Vocabulary: Word Roots: *-journ-*, p. 237
Build Grammar Skills: Hyphens, p. 238
Reading Strategy: Identify the Speaker, p. 239
Literary Focus: Narrative and Dramatic Poetry, p. 240

Strategies for Diverse Student Needs, p. 58

Beyond Literature *The Military*, p. 58

Formal Assessment Selection Test, pp. 204–206; and Assessment Resources Software

Alternative Assessment, p. 58

Writing and Language Transparencies

Graphic Organizer: Story Map, pp. 83–86

Resource Pro CD-ROM

Listening to Literature Audiocassettes

Literature CD-ROM

La Belle Dame sans Merci
◆ Danny Deever ◆

◆ Literature and Your Life

Connect Your Experience

Our choices in life are based on what we want and need. Sometimes, we want what we can't have. "La Belle Dame sans Merci" relates the tale of a knight who cannot have the love of the beautiful woman he serves. "Danny Deever" shows the consequences of one man's rash action, but it does not reveal the wants or needs that led to his choice.

Thematic Focus: Facing the Consequences

In both "La Belle Dame sans Merci" and "Danny Deever," characters must face the consequences of choices they have made. Think about whether the price they pay is too high.

Journal Writing Outline the standards on which you make choices.

◆ Background for Understanding

History

In "La Belle Dame sans Merci," a knight pines for a beautiful woman who is forever out of his reach. This unattainable desire is at the heart of courtly love, a medieval code of attitudes and conduct followed by noble lords and ladies, especially knights.

In the tradition of courtly love, a knight focuses his adoration on a beautiful, intelligent, high-minded woman. Whether or not the woman loves him is immaterial. This love is believed too noble and pure to be corrupted by physical affection. The knight performs great deeds to honor the lady, but he suffers terribly in the knowledge that his affection can never be returned.

◆ Literary Focus

Narrative and Dramatic Poetry

A **narrative poem** tells a story and is usually longer than other types of poems. Like any story, a narrative poem has one or more characters, a setting, a conflict, and a series of events that come to a conclusion. Most narrative poems are divided into stanzas—or groups of lines that have the same pattern of rhythm and rhyme.

Dramatic poetry is poetry in which one or more characters speak. By using the words of one or more speakers to tell directly what is happening, dramatic poetry creates the illusion that the reader is actually witnessing a dramatic event.

◆ Reading Strategy

Identify the Speaker

Whenever you read a poem, **identify its speaker** as an important first step in gaining insight into the poem. The speaker of the poem may be the poet or a fictitious character created by the poet. Even when a poet uses the pronoun *I* in a poem, the speaker may be fictional and not the poet himself or herself.

For example, in "La Belle Dame sans Merci," Keats uses the characters themselves as the speakers, and by doing so, is able to delve deeply into the characters' minds. We are able to feel the knight's anguish and emotions.

Like other fictional characters, the speaker in a narrative poem may reveal information about himself or herself directly, through forthright statements, or indirectly, through hints and implications.

Test Preparation Workshop

Critical Reading: Analyzing an Author's Meaning and Style

A standardized test may require students to analyze an author's style and meaning in order to answer test items. Use the following sample question for students' preparation and practice:

Read the poem "La Belle Dame sans Merci" on pp. 848–849. What idea does the author suggest or imply in this poem?

A The knight is happy.

B The knight is lonely and sad.

C The autumn setting reflects the knight's good fortune.

D The beautiful lady was a good fairy.

In order to select the best answer choice, suggest that students paraphrase the poem in a sentence or two, using their own words. This strategy will help them determine the author's main idea and implications. Lead students to notice that the author does not imply answers *A*, *C*, or *D* in the poem. Therefore, by process of elimination, students will find that B is the best answer choice.

Write on the chalkboard the headings *choices* and *consequences*. Under *choices*, write "stayed up all night watching an old movie." Under *consequences*, write, "slept through next morning's neighborhood soccer game." Encourage students to add to some common choices and consequences to the list. Then explain that many unwise choices are minor and their consequences short-lived. The poor choices the characters in these poems make, however, lead to more serious consequences.

Tips to Guide Reading

Sustained Reading Students will find that reading narrative and dramatic poetry in an uninterrupted, sustained manner will enhance their understanding and enjoyment.

Customize for
Less Proficient Readers and English Language Learners

Some students may have trouble with the vocabulary in "La Belle Dame sans Merci." Remind them to use the text footnotes. Explain that the when the Cockney dialect in "Danny Deever" is written, the letters "h" at the beginning of a word and "g" in "ing" words are often dropped, which makes the words look difficult to read.

Customize for
Pre-AP Students

These students may enjoy finding out more about the rules of courtly love. Encourage them to consider how the knight in "La Belle Dame sans Merci" follows or deviates from the rules.

Customize for
Gifted/Talented Students

Suggest that students evaluate the rhythmic qualities of "Danny Deever" which seem to underscore the military theme. Have students find out about military music—music composed to inspire soldiers. If possible, find recordings to share with classmates.

Literature CD-ROM Use Feature 4 on the **Literature CD-ROM:** *How to Read and Understand Poetry.* This segment can serve as an introduction to narrative poetry.

Develop Understanding

One-Minute Insight

"La Belle Dame sans Merci" (literally, "The Beautiful Woman Without Pity") is a character who appears in world literature under different names—Circe or Morgan le Fay, for example. In English, she is the *beldame*, a word for a woman who takes pleasure in destroying the unlucky men whom she enthralls. In this poem, a young man comes under her spell, only to find his life drained away after an enchanted night. Students might relate to the broader theme of this poem—things that seem attractive can sometimes disappoint or even endanger a person.

▶Critical Viewing◀

❶ **Support** *Suggested response: She is pulling him toward her by tugging at a wrapping about his neck; she looks relaxed and he is not resisting her.*

◆ Literary Focus

❷ **Narrative and Dramatic Poetry** Ask students to identify the setting and character introduced in the first stanza. *The setting is on the withered grass by a lake; the knight-at-arms is the character.*

❸ **Clarification** Explain to students that the lily and the fading rose both suggest death. At the time he wrote this poem, Keats was nursing his brother, who was dying of tuberculosis.

◆ Reading Strategy

❹ **Identify the Speaker** In these stanzas a new speaker is established. Ask students to identify the speaker of the first stanza, the one here, and to predict which will be the main character in the story that is about to unfold. *The first speaker is a minor character who finds the knight by the lake. The second speaker is the knight. Students should note that the knight is the main character; he tells his story.*

Read to Appreciate a Writer's Craft

Point out that both of these poems use rhythm and rhyme to narrate stories. Discuss with students how these literary devices add interest to the narratives.

La Belle Dame sans Merci[1]

John Keats

La Belle Dame sans Merci, John W. Waterhouse, Hessisches Landes Museum, Darmstadt

❶ ▲ Critical Viewing What evidence indicates that the lady has the knight "in thrall"? **[Support]**

O what can ail thee, knight-at-arms,
  Alone and palely loitering?
The sedge has withered from the lake,
  And no birds sing.

O what can ail thee, knight-at-arms,
  So haggard and so woe-begone?
The squirrel's granary is full,
  And the harvest's done.

I see a lily on thy brow,
  With anguish moist and fever dew,
And on thy cheeks a fading rose
  Fast withereth too.

I met a lady in the meads,[2]
  Full beautiful—a faery's child,
Her hair was long, her foot was light,
  And her eyes were wild.

I made a garland for her head,
  And bracelets too, and fragrant zone;[3]
She looked at me as she did love,
  And made sweet moan.

I set her on my pacing steed,
  And nothing else saw all day long,
For sidelong would she bend, and sing
  A faery's song.

1. **La Belle Dame sans Merci:** "The Beautiful Lady Without Pity" (French).
2. **meads** (mēdz) *n.:* Old-fashioned form of meadow.
3. **fragrant zone:** Sweet-smelling plant.

Block Scheduling Strategies

Consider these suggestions to take advantage of extended class time:

- Invite students to view Feature 4 on the CD-ROM, which features narrative poetry.
- Interested students can do further research on the subject of courtly love and the Middle Ages, discussed in Background for Understanding on p. 847. They might find books such as the following useful: *The Art of Courtly Love* by Andreas Cappellanus and *French Chivalry* by Sidney Painter.
- After discussing narrative and dramatic poetry, have students work in small groups to answer the Literary Focus questions on p. 852 and complete Literary Focus: Narrative and Dramatic Poetry in ***Selection Support***, p. 240.
- Allow time for students to work in groups, reading the poems aloud. The have them listen to the **Listening to Literature Audiocassette** recordings of the poems. Students can analyze and evaluate the recorded readings as well as their own.

She found me roots of relish sweet,
   And honey wild, and manna dew,[4]
And sure in language strange she said—
   'I love thee true.'

She took me to her elfin grot,[5]
   And there she wept, and sighed full sore,
And there I shut her wild wild eyes
   With kisses four.

And there she lullèd me asleep,
   And there I dreamed—Ah! woe betide!
The latest dream I ever dreamed
   On the cold hill's side.

❺

I saw pale kings and princes too,
   Pale warriors, death-pale were they all;
They cried—'La Belle Dame sans Merci
   Hath thee in thrall!'

I saw their starved lips in the gloam,
   With horrid warning gapèd wide,
And I awoke and found me here,
   On the cold hill's side.

And this is why I sojourn here,
   Alone and palely loitering,
Though the sedge has withered from the lake,
   And no birds sing.

❻

4. **manna** (man′ ə) **dew** (doo): Sweet substance obtained from the bark of certain ash trees.
5. **elfin** (el′ fən) **grot:** Cave belonging to a fairy.

◆ Build Vocabulary

sedge (sej) *n.*: Grassy plant that grows in wet areas

thrall (thrôl) *n.*: Complete control; slavery

sojourn (sō′ jurn) *v.*: Stay temporarily

Guide for Responding

◆ Literature and Your Life

Reader's Response What word or words would you use to describe the knight? Explain your answer.

Thematic Focus What choices did the knight make that brought about his current condition?

Contemporary Connection Romantic poets, like Keats, sometimes sought refuge from the everyday world in an imagined world. With a group, discuss this reaction and whether there are parallels in contemporary culture.

☑ Check Your Comprehension

1. What is the setting of the poem?
2. Describe the lady the knight meets.
3. Describe the knight's dream.

◆ Critical Thinking

INTERPRET

1. Explain how the people in the knight's dream relate to his present condition. **[Analyze]**
2. Why is the knight "alone and palely loitering"? **[Draw Conclusions]**
3. In what way does the autumn setting reinforce the meaning and the mood of the poem? **[Connect]**

APPLY

4. In ancient myths, the fertility of the land is tied to the health of a heroic figure. The land can be bountiful again only when the spell put on the heroic figure is broken. Explain how "La Belle Dame sans Merci" incorporates elements of a myth. **[Apply]**

Humanities: Art

La Belle Dame sans Merci by John W. Waterhouse.

English painter John William Waterhouse (1849–1917) was inspired by the poetry of Keats and Tennyson. His distinctive style—dreamy and romantic—perfectly captures the mood of Keats's poem.

This painting sets "La Belle Dame" and the knight in a dark and mysterious forest. The rich detail of the painting shows the flowers of the forest and the patterns and textures of the woman's clothing and the knight's armor. Her luminous skin and appealing face draw the knight to her.

Use this question for discussion:

1. How would you compare the lady in the picture to the one described in Keats's poem, "La Belle Dam sans Merci"? *Students might observe the lady is similar because she has long hair, a mysterious air, and an intent expression.*

◆ Critical Thinking

❺ **Infer** Ask students what the knight's dream is telling him about his own fate. *His dream is telling him that he too will become a victim of La Belle Dame.*

◆ Literary Focus

❻ **Narrative Poetry** Have students explain the resolution of the conflict. *The knight is doomed to pine away for the lady until he dies.*

Reinforce and Extend

Answers

◆ Literature and Your Life

Reader's Response Some students may describe the knight as weak or lacking in valor because he allows himself to be taken in.

Thematic Focus He lets himself fall in love with the lady, and he lets her lead him into the elfin grot.

Contemporary Connection Have students analyze the aspects of Keats' writing that cause him to be considered a romantic poet.

☑ Check Your Comprehension

1. The setting is the countryside, by a lake, in late autumn.
2. The lady is beautiful, with long hair, a light step, and wild eyes.
3. The knight dreams of death-pale kings, princes, and warriors warning him that La Belle Dame sans Merci has him in her thrall.

◆ Critical Thinking

1. The people in the knight's dream had all fallen victim to La Belle Dame in the past.
2. The knight has now lost his vigor and sense of purpose.
3. The late autumn setting reinforces the meaning and mood of the poem because in late autumn nature is barren and depleted of vigor in much the way the lady has left the knight.
4. The repetition of the phrase "the sedge has withered from the lake" reinforces the notion that the land, like the heroic knight, has fallen weak. This connection between fertility of land and health of hero is a concept borrowed from myth.

Develop Understanding

One-Minute Insight In Kipling's poem, young soldiers about to witness the hanging of one of their ranks are "dreadin'" what they've "got to watch." Kipling never reveals the reasons behind Danny's crime. Instead he focuses on the reactions of the men who lived, worked, ate, and drank with him.

Listening to Literature Audiocassettes "Danny Deever" is a rhythmic poem spoken in dialect. Students might enjoy listening to the audiocassette as they read the poem so they can hear the sound of the dialect for themselves.

◆ Reading Strategy

❶ Identify the Speaker Ask students to identify the two speakers of this dramatic poem. *Files-on-Parade and Color-Sergeant are the speakers.*

◆ Build Grammar Skills

❷ Hyphens Ask students to identify the part of speech of each hyphenated word in lines 9–11. Ask why the words are hyphenated. *Rear-rank—noun; Files-on-Parade—noun; front-rank— adjective; Color-Sergeant—noun. They connect two or more words that function as a single word.*

◆ Literary Focus

❸ Narrative and Dramatic Poetry Ask how this passage helps readers feel they are actually witnessing the events being described? *Sample response: The conversation creates a sense of immediacy, as if the reader were standing near the two speakers hearing them.*

Extending Word Study

Reference Materials In addition to discussing Word Bank selections, have students expand their vocabulary by using reference materials to look up the meanings of unfamiliar words.

Reteach

Students will benefit from a class discussion to identify the speaker in each of the poems.

Danny Deever

Rudyard Kipling

❶ "What are the bugles blowin' for?" said Files-on-Parade.[1]
"To turn you out, to turn you out," the Color-Sergeant[2] said.
"What makes you look so white, so white?" said Files-on-Parade.
"I'm dreadin' what I've got to watch," the Color-Sergeant said.
For they're hangin' Danny Deever, you can hear the Dead March play,
The regiment's in 'ollow square[3] —they're hangin' him today;
They've taken of his buttons off an' cut his stripes away,
An' they're hangin' Danny Deever in the mornin'.

❷ "What makes the rear-rank breathe so 'ard?" said Files-on-Parade.
"It's bitter cold, it's bitter cold," the Color-Sergeant said.
"What makes that front-rank man fall down?" says Files-on-Parade.
"A touch o' sun, a touch o' sun," the Color-Sergeant said.
They are hangin' Danny Deever, they are marchin' of 'im round,
They 'ave 'alted Danny Deever by 'is coffin on the ground;
An' 'e'll swing in 'arf a minute for a sneakin' shootin' hound—
O they're hangin' Danny Deever in the mornin'!

"'Is cot was right-'and cot to mine," said Files-on-Parade.
"'E's sleepin' out an' far tonight," the Color-Sergeant said.
"I've drunk 'is beer a score o' times," said Files-on-Parade.
"'E's drinkin' bitter beer alone," the Color-Sergeant said.
❸ They are hangin' Danny Deever, you must mark 'im to 'is place,
For 'e shot a comrade sleepin'—you must look 'im in the face;
Nine 'undred of 'is county an' the regiment's disgrace,
While they're hangin' Danny Deever in the mornin'.

"What's that so black agin the sun?" said Files-on-Parade.
"It's Danny fightin' 'ard for life," the Color-Sergeant said.
"What's that that whimpers over'ead?" said Files-on-Parade.
"It's Danny's soul that's passin' now," the Color-Sergeant said.
For they're done with Danny Deever, you can 'ear the quickstep play,
The regiment's in column, an' they're marchin' us away;
Ho! the young recruits are shakin', an' they'll want their beer to-day,
After hangin' Danny Deever in the mornin'.

1. **Files-on-Parade:** Soldier who directs marching formation.
2. **Color-Sergeant:** Flag-bearer.
3. **'ollow square:** For a hanging, soldiers' ranks form three sides of a square; the fourth side is the gallows.

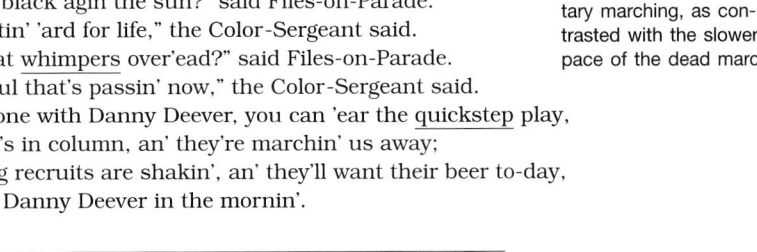

◆ Build Vocabulary

whimpers (hwim′ pərz) *v.*: Makes a low, whining sound, as in crying or fear

quickstep (kwik′ step′) *n.*: Pace used in normal military marching, as contrasted with the slower pace of the dead march

Speaking, Listening, and Viewing Mini-Lesson

Story in Music

This mini-lesson supports the Speaking, Listening, and Viewing activity in the Idea Bank on p. 853.

Introduce Explain to students that they will choose songs that tell a story from each of three musical genres. In each case, they will explain the song's storytelling techniques, such as using a narrator, or employing a rhythmical pattern.

Develop Ballads, country music, folk songs, and the blues often tell stories. Have students consider these questions as they choose their songs.

- What is the story's plot? Who are the characters? Describe the setting.
- Does the song have a refrain or chorus? Does it contain a strong rhythm? Does it rhyme?

Apply Students can introduce and play the songs they have chosen, explaining what each is about and the techniques that help make it effective, and answering questions their classmates may have.

Assess Evaluate students' work on preparation and clarity, or use the Peer Assessment: Speaker/Speech form, p. 118, in ***Alternative Assessment***.

The Battle of Bunker Hill, Howard Pyle, Delaware Art Museum

▲ Critical Viewing Compare the method of fighting depicted in this painting with the way battles are fought today. **[Analyze]** 4

Guide for Responding

◆ Literature and Your Life

Reader's Response If you were in the regiment, how would you feel about having to watch the hanging? Explain.

Thematic Focus What might lead someone like Danny Deever to make a choice that he must have known would result in his execution?

Journal Entry Write a journal entry exploring your response to this poem.

☑ Check Your Comprehension

1. Describe the setting of "Danny Deever."
2. Who are the two soldiers who relate the event through their dialogue?
3. Of the two speakers in the poem, which has some prior experience with military executions?
4. For what crime is Danny Deever being executed?

◆ Critical Thinking

INTERPRET

1. What does Files-on-Parade mean when he says, "I've drunk 'is beer a score o' times"? **[Infer]**
2. Compare and contrast Files-on-Parade and the Color-Sergeant. **[Compare and Contrast]**
3. The Color-Sergeant explains one soldier's hard breathing by saying it is "bitter cold." He explains another soldier's fainting as the result of a "touch o' sun." Are these conflicting explanations believable? What really accounts for the physical problems of the men? **[Draw Conclusions]**

EVALUATE

4. The poem gives few facts about Danny Deever or his crime. Explain whether this lack of information makes you more or less sympathetic to him. **[Evaluate]**

Humanities: Art

The Battle of Bunker Hill by Howard Pyle.

A writer as well as an artist, Howard Pyle (1853–1911) is particularly well-known for his magnificent illustrations of such children's classics as *The Merry Adventures of Robin Hood*. His consistent use of rich color created a dramatic lifelike world.

Use these questions for discussion:

1. Which of the painting's details are similar to the poem's? Which details are different? *Possible similarities: The army is marching in formation. The uniforms suggest a historical setting. Possible differences: There is no flag bearer in the painting. In Pyle's picture the battle is raging, although there's no indication this is the case in the poem.*
2. Does the illustration glorify war? *Some students may say that the painting suggests that war is heroic and noble; others may say that the dead bodies indicate the horrible reality of any war.*

▶Critical Viewing◀

4 **Analyze** *Sample answer: The soldiers in the painting are marching in straight lines with muskets as their weapons. If they met an enemy, they would fight face-to-face. Today, much fighting is done at a distance. Weapons are more sophisticated, and land soldiers rarely march.*

Reinforce and Extend

Answers

◆ Literature and Your Life

Reader's Response Students are likely to respond that they would find it painful or uncomfortable to watch the hanging; some might also say they would identify with Danny Deever and feel afraid.

Thematic Response Students might respond that Danny Deever was a reckless person who did not consider consequences before acting.

☑ Check Your Comprehension

1. "Danny Deever" is set on a battlefield or on the way to a battlefield; the regiment is marching.
2. The Color-Sergeant and Files-on-Parade relate the events.
3. The Color-Sergeant has experience with military executions.
4. Danny Deever killed a comrade who was sleeping.

◆ Critical Thinking

1. He means that he and Danny Deever were friends—or at least they had drinks together many times.
2. The Color-Sergeant seems wiser, and perhaps more hardened, to the ways of the military; Files-on-Parade is more naive and innocent.
3. The conflicting explanations are not believable; it's obvious that the Color-Sergeant is covering up the soldiers' horrified reaction at the brutal act they are witnessing—the hanging of Danny Deever.
4. Many students will say that the lack of information makes them more sympathetic to Deever because Deever's side of the story is never heard, and he might be unjustly accused.

Reading Strategy

1. He reveals that the lady is a beautiful lady without pity, and suggests that she cast a spell on him. A speaker who had not had direct experience with the lady could not have revealed this.
2. Students might say that "Danny Deever" would have been more effective if told exclusively by the speakers because their dialogue is already effective, and it seems as if they have the perspective to tell the whole story.

Literary Focus

1. The first two stanzas reveal the setting and introduce the main character, a knight-at-arms.
2. The speaker in stanzas 1–3 is someone who encounters the knight and asks him what's wrong. From stanza 4 on, the knight tells his story of what has happened to him. This shift from one speaker to another sets up the flashback into the knight's story.
3. The last stanza ties the story together because it makes it clear that the knight has answered the first speaker's question.
4. The dialect in "Danny Deever" creates the effect of authenticity.
5. Students might say another soldier is speaking because the dialect is the same and because he says "you can 'ear the quickstep play," as if he were present on the scene.

Build Vocabulary

Using the Word Root *-journ-*

1. adjourned; 2. journal; 3. journalist

Using the Word Bank

1. sedge
2. quickstep
3. sojourn
4. thrall
5. whimpers

Build Grammar Skills

The British army was based on well-built traditions and rock-solid rules that would not allow for leniency for Danny Deever. Files-on-Parade had the cot on the left-hand side of Deever.

Grammar Reinforcement

For additional practice, use p. 109 on Hyphens in the *Writer's Solution Grammar Practice Book.*

Guide for Responding *(continued)*

Reading Strategy

Identify the Speaker

The **speaker** is the voice of a poem. The speaker may be the poet, or it may be a fictional character or even an inanimate object. It is up to you, the reader, to identify the speaker in a poem.

1. What does the speaker of "La Belle Dame sans Merci" reveal about the lady? How would this poem be different if Keats had used a different speaker?
2. Tell whether you think "Danny Deever" would have been more effective if all the action had been revealed through the words of Files-on-Parade and the Color-Sergeant. Explain your answer.

Literary Focus

Narrative and Dramatic Poetry

"La Belle Dame sans Merci" is a **narrative poem**—a poem that tells a story. Like a short story, it has a plot, characters, and a setting.

"Danny Deever" is a **dramatic poem**—a poem in which one or more characters tell what is happening through dialogue.

1. In "La Belle Dames sans Merci," which stanzas describe the setting and introduce the main character?
2. The speaker from stanza 4 to the end of "La Belle Dame sans Merci" is different from the speaker of stanzas 1–3. How does this shift help communicate what is happening in the story?
3. How does the last stanza of "La Belle Dame sans Merci" tie the story together?
4. In "Danny Deever," what effect is created by having Files-on-Parade and the Color-Sergeant speak in dialect?
5. The last half of each stanza of "Danny Deever" employs the same distinctive speech patterns used by Files-on-Parade and the Color-Sergeant. These lines, however, are not enclosed in quotation marks. Who do you think is speaking those words—another soldier, the poet, or some other observer?

Build Vocabulary

Using the Root *-journ-*

Knowing that the root *-journ-* means "day," fill in each blank with a word that contains the root.

1. At the end of the day, the meeting was __?__.
2. Each day, I write my thoughts and impressions in my __?__.
3. One aspect of the career of __?__ is gathering facts about and reporting on the day's events.

Using the Word Bank: Sentence Completions

Practice Copy the following sentences in your notebook, and fill in the blanks with the appropriate word from the Word Bank.

1. The ground near the pond was covered with __?__.
2. The kindergarten class drew laughs from the crowd as they marched on stage in __?__.
3. While in London, we had a __?__ at a quaint bed-and-breakfast.
4. The beautiful woman held the enchanted knight in __?__.
5. We could hear the __?__ of the child who had been scolded and sent to his room.

Build Grammar Skills

Hyphens

Hyphens are used to separate the parts of some compound nouns and adjectives. Hyphens are not used in compound modifiers that include words ending in *-ly* or with compound proper adjectives. Hyphens are used, however, in many compound nouns.

Practice Copy the paragraph below into your notebook. Insert hyphens where necessary.

The British army was based on well built traditions and rock solid rules that would not allow for leniency for Danny Deever. Files on Parade had the cot on the left hand side of Deever.

Beyond the Selection

FURTHER READING

Other Works by the Authors

"Ode on a Grecian Urn," John Keats
Barrack-Room Ballads, Kim, Rudyard Kipling

Other Works About Choices and Consequences

"Ozymandias," Percy Bysshe Shelley
"Lucy Grey," William Wordsworth

We suggest that you preview these works before recommending them.

INTERNET

You and your students may learn more about Keats and Kipling at the following Web sites. Please be aware that the sites may have changed since we published this information.

Keats: **http://utl1.library.utoronto.ca/utel/rp/authors/keats.html**

Kipling: **http://www.kipling.org.uk/rudyard.htm**

We *strongly recommend* that you preview the sites before you send students to them.

Build Your Portfolio

Idea Bank

Writing

1. **Diary Entry** As Files-on-Parade or the Color-Sergeant, write a diary entry relating your reactions to the events of the day.
2. **Letter to the Knight** As an advice columnist, respond to a letter from the knight in "La Belle Dame sans Merci." Tell him whether you think his "courtly love" is worth the price he's paying and what you think he should do. **[Career Link]**
3. **Mock Narrative** Write a mock narrative poem about a silly or insignificant event. Use rhythm and repetition as Kipling does in"Danny Deever."

Speaking, Listening, and Viewing

4. **Oral Reading** In small groups, practice reading "Danny Deever" aloud, experimenting with ways of making each speaker sound natural but different from the other. When you are ready, give a reading of "Danny Deever" for your class.
5. **Story in Music** Like poems, the lyrics of songs often tell a story. Stories can be found in a wide variety of musical styles, including ballads, country, pop, rap, and the blues. Choose an example from each of three styles. Play them for the class and explain the techniques, such as rhythm and repetition, that each uses. **[Music Link]**

Researching and Representing

6. **Dialect Chart** Create a chart that would help readers of "Danny Deever" understand the dialect and special language. Show how some words and expressions, such as "'arf a minute" and "score o' times" would be expressed by you and your friends. **[Social Studies Link]**
7. **Art** Depict either of the poems in art form. Use any medium to capture the mood of the poem and represent your interpretation. **[Art Link]**

Online Activity www.phlit.phschool.com

Guided Writing Lesson

News Bulletin Based on Poem

Imagine that you are a news reporter present at the hanging of Danny Deever. Your job is to get the story on Deever and be ready to go on the air live from the scene. Write a **news bulletin** that will inform your listeners about the circumstances leading up to the hanging and the mood of the soldiers.

Writing Skills Focus: Climax and Resolution

In a news bulletin, the **climax**—or high point of conflict—is usually mentioned right away to grab the viewers' or listeners' attention. For instance, in your report about Danny Deever, you might lead with "Just moments ago, an execution took place here at Rudyard Kipling army base." Once your listeners are hooked, you can fill in the details. Report on the **resolution** (Danny's death) and the events that follow the resolution.

Prewriting Review the poem to gather details about the mood of the soldiers. Look also for statements in the poem by Files-on-Parade and the Color-Sergeant that could be used as quotations in your report.

Drafting Begin your broadcast with a sensational lead-in, guaranteed to "hook" the viewers. Then, start at the beginning of the story, and lead listeners through the series of events that led to the climax you reported at the opening of your report. Conclude with a description of the atmosphere following the event.

Revising Read over your report and identify the exciting lead-in, the sequence of events leading to the climax, quotations from observers, and a wrap-up. If you cannot identify any one of these parts, revise your report to include it.

✓ ASSESSMENT OPTIONS

Formal Assessment, Selection Test, pp. 204–206, and Assessment Resources Software. The selection test is designed so that it can be easily customized to the performance levels of your students.

Alternative Assessment, p. 58, includes options for less advanced students, more advanced students, musical/rhythmic learners, logical/mathematical learners, visual/spatial learners, intrapersonal learners, and verbal/linguistic learners.

PORTFOLIO ASSESSMENT

Use the following rubrics in ***Alternative Assessment*** to assess student writing:
Diary Entry: Expression Rubric, p. 94
Letter to the Knight: Problem-Solution Rubric, p. 101
Mock Narrative: Poetry Rubric, p. 108
Guided Writing Lesson: Summary Rubric, p. 98

Idea Bank

Following are suggestions for matching Idea Bank topics with your students' performance levels and learning modalities:

Customizing for *Performance Levels*
Less Advanced Students: 1, 4
Average Students: 2, 5, 6, 7
More Advanced Students: 3

Customizing for *Learning Modalities*
Musical/Rhythmic: 5
Verbal/Linguistic: 4, 5
Logical/Mathematical: 6
Visual/Spatial: 7

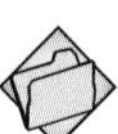

Guided Writing Lesson

Prewriting Strategy Give students six notecards apiece to implement the reporter's formula as they review the poem and gather details.

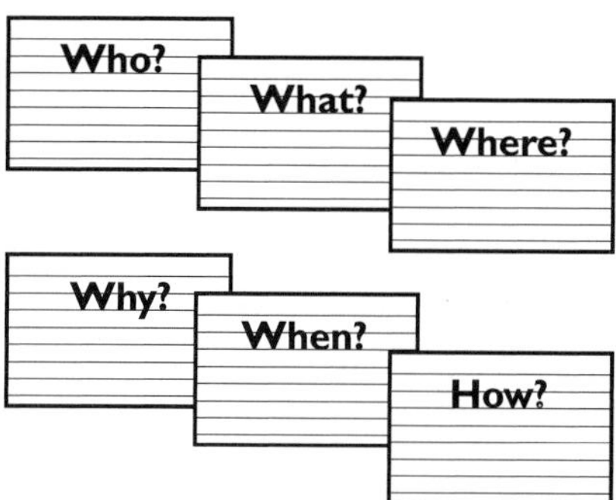

When they have gathered details on their cards, they can try various arrangements of the cards to determine the "hook" and the climax (and the details and events that lead to it).

For more prewriting, elaboration, and revision strategies, see *Prentice Hall Writing and Grammar.*

Writing and Language Transparencies You might have students use the Story Map, pp. 83–86, to work out the climax and resolution in their news bulletins.

Writing Lab CD-ROM
Have students complete the tutorial on Narrative Writing. Follow these steps:

1. Have students use a Chain of Events chart to map out the sequence of events for their news bulletins describing what led up to Danny Deever's hanging.
2. Encourage students to consult interactive tips on better word choice to learn how to revise dull statements by adding strong verbs and precise nouns.

Prepare and Engage

LESSON OBJECTIVES

1. **To develop vocabulary and word identification skills**
   - Greek Roots: *-path-*
   - Using the Word Bank: Word Choice
   - Extending Word Study: Word Roots (ATE)
2. **To use a variety of reading strategies to comprehend poems**
   - Connect Your Experience
   - Reading Strategy: Read in Sentences
   - Tips to Guide Reading: Whisper Read (ATE)
   - Read to Discover Writing Models (ATE)
3. **To increase knowledge of other cultures and to connect common elements across cultures**
   - Connecting Themes Across Cultures (ATE)
   - Cultural Connection (ATE)
   - Background for Understanding
   - Beyond Literature: Poetry and Politics
4. **To express and support responses to the text**
   - Critical Thinking
   - Idea Bank: Remembrance
   - Idea Bank: Statement Poem
   - Idea Bank: Story
   - Idea Bank: Painting/Drawing
5. **To analyze literary elements**
   - Literary Focus: Lyric Poetry
6. **To read in order to research self-selected and assigned topics**
   - Idea Bank: Profile of a People
   - Viewing and Representing Mini-Lesson: Visual Presentation (ATE)
7. **To plan, prepare, organize, and present literary interpretations**
   - Idea Bank: Reading to Music
8. **To use recursive writing processes to write a Lyric Poem**
   - Guided Writing Lesson
9. **To increase knowledge of the rules of grammar and usage**
   - Build Grammar Skills: Adjectival Modifiers

Test Preparation

Critical Reading: Analyzing an Author's Meaning and Style (ATE, p. 855) The teaching tips and sample test item in this workshop support the instruction and practice in the unit workshop.

Critical Reading: Analyzing an Author's Meaning and Style (SE, p. 877)

Guide for Reading

Federico García Lorca *(1898–1936)*

Federico García Lorca wrote many of his poems shortly after World War I, a culturally vibrant time in his homeland of rural Andalusia, outside Granada, Spain. Although García Lorca didn't intend his work to be political, Nationalist forces found it offensive, and they assassinated him at the beginning of the Spanish Civil War.

Naomi Shihab Nye *(1952–)*

Poet, songwriter, short-story writer, and children's book author, Naomi Shihab Nye now lives in San Antonio, Texas. Her perception, imaginative sense of language, and ability to keep you close to an experience are evident in "Making a Fist."

Tu Fu *(712–770)*

Chinese poet Tu Fu of the Tang Dynasty was little known and for the most part unappreciated during his lifetime. Today, however, he is regarded as a supreme craftsman. His poems are admired as much for their form as for their content. Tu Fu's poems celebrate nature, condemn the senselessness of war, and, as in "Jade Flower Palace," lament the passage of time.

Li Po *(702–762)*

A major Chinese classical poet of the Tang Dynasty, Li Po was a romantic who wrote about the joys of nature, love, friendship, and solitude. Although he was influenced by Taoist thought, he did not embrace the simple lifestyle this philosophy encouraged.

Rosellen Brown *(1939–)*

Besides being a poet, Rosellen Brown is an accomplished novelist and short-story writer. Her novel *Tender Mercies* was a national bestseller and became a major motion picture. Her latest book of poetry, *Cora Frye's Pillow Book,* was published in 1994.

Wisława Szymborska *(1923–)*

The author of sixteen collections of poetry, Wisława Szymborska of Poland has said, "No questions are of such significance as those that are naive." Her poetry asks direct questions about the meaning of life and death. Upon granting her the 1996 Nobel Prize for Literature, the Swedish Academy called her the "Mozart of poetry."

◆ Build Vocabulary

GREEK ROOTS: *-path-*

As the ancient poet sits and views the even more ancient ruins in Tu Fu's "Jade Flower Palace," the pathos of the scene overcomes him. *Pathos* contains the Greek root *-path-* which means "feelings; suffering." *Pathos* itself describes the quality in an object or situation that evokes stong feelings of sorrow, compassion, or sym*pathy*.

WORD BANK

Before you read, preview this list of words from the poems.

monotonously
pathos
wistful

◆ Build Grammar Skills

ADJECTIVAL MODIFIERS

Several types of structures act as adjectives. Among the structures that may be **adjectival modifiers** are prepositional phrases, participial phrases, and adjective clauses. Here are examples from these poems:

Prepositional Phrase:

Now begins the cry / *Of the guitar*

The prepositional phrase *of the guitar* modifies *cry*.

Participial Phrase:

I felt the life *sliding out of me*

The participial phrase *sliding out of me* modifies *life*.

Adjectival Clause:

I *who did not die*

The adjectival clause *who did not die* modifies the pronoun *I*.

Prentice Hall Literature Program Resources

REINFORCE / RETEACH / EXTEND

Selection Support Pages
Build Vocabulary: Greek Roots: *-path-*, p. 241
Build Grammar Skills: Adjectival Modifiers, p. 242
Reading Strategy: Read in Sentences, p. 243
Literary Focus: Lyric Poetry, p. 244

Strategies for Diverse Student Needs, p. 59

Beyond Literature
Cross-Curricular Connection: Social Studies: *The Great Wall of China,* p. 59

Formal Assessment Selection Test, pp. 207–209; Assessment Resources Software

Alternative Assessment, p. 59

Resource Pro CD-ROM

Listening to Literature Audiocassettes

The Guitar ◆ Making a Fist
Jade Flower Palace ◆ The Moon at the Fortified Pass
What Are Friends For ◆ Some Like Poetry

◆ Literature and Your Life

Connect Your Experience

If you've ever reflected upon the meaning of friendship, beauty, war, or death, you already have something in common with these poets. Questioning issues such as these is often where poetry begins.

Look for important themes in these poems, and compare the poets' reflections with your own.

Journal Writing Jot down several themes that you might want to explore in a poem. Note several of your reflections on each theme.

Thematic Focus: To the Future

The poems in this group span the time from the eighth through the twentieth centuries. Because the poets' thoughts are timeless, people of future generations can read the poems and reflect on them, just as you are doing.

◆ Background for Understanding

Literature

Certain poems are classified as "lyric" poems because of their highly musical qualities. Originally, in ancient Greece, poems were recited or sung to the accompaniment of a lyre, a small stringed, harp-like instrument. Even today, lyrics are associated with music: The words to songs are called lyrics.

◆ Literary Focus

Lyric Poetry

Lyric poetry is poetry expressing the observations and feelings of a single speaker. It was originally written to be accompanied by music; its musicality is one of its distinctive features.

A lyric poem may follow a traditional form, such as a sonnet, or it may be written in *free verse*—verse not written in a formal rhythmical pattern. "Making a Fist" and "What Are Friends For" are written in free verse.

While reading, you'll notice that a lyric poem, unlike a narrative poem, never tells a full story. Rather, it zeros in on an experience or creates and explores a single effect. Use an organizer like the one shown to explore how the details in each poem contribute to the main effect.

◆ Reading Strategy

Read in Sentences

One way that poetry is different from prose is that poetry is written in lines and stanzas, while prose is written in sentences and paragraphs. Yet poetry, like prose, achieves its meaning through sentences. In poetry, a sentence may extend over several lines or it may even end in the middle of a line.

To get the literal meaning of a poem, **read** it **according to its sentences,** not its lines. Don't stop at the end of a line unless there is a period, comma, colon, semicolon, or dash. Notice where the stops are in the following lines from Federico García Lorca's "The Guitar":

Now begins the cry
Of the guitar,
Breaking down the vaults
Of dawn.
Now begins the cry
Of the guitar.

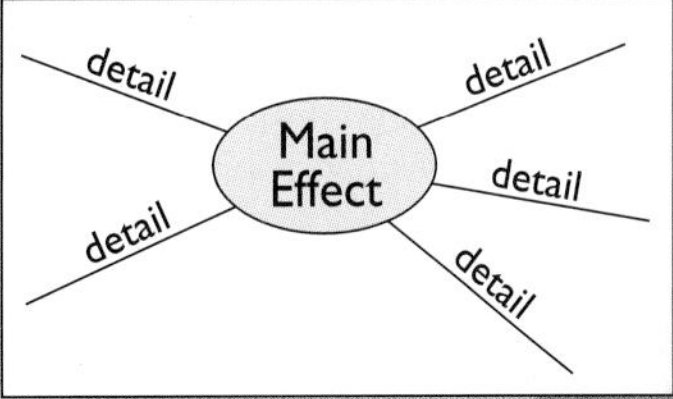

Write the word *poetry* in large block letters at the center of the chalkboard. Around it, write the words *Friendship, Beauty, Sadness, War,* and *Death.* Circle each word, and connect it to the word *poetry.* Let students know this is a cluster diagram showing some major themes of lyric poetry. Invite students to suggest words and phrases of their own, such as love, youth, age, growing up, and nature. Emphasize that a lyric poem can express anything a human being feels or observes. Tell students that they are going to read six lyric poems on six different themes, and that each one is like a snapshot of the poet's feelings at a certain time. Urge students to "see" this snapshot as they read each poem.

Connecting Themes Across Cultures

Ask students what style of poetic writing they think appeals to readers today; have them predict what will appeal in future years.

Tips to Guide Reading

Whisper Read Have students whisper read while you listen to hear whether they are picking up the musical quality of the lyric poems.

Customize for *Less Proficient Readers*

Ask students to state the main idea of each poem in one sentence. If students have trouble, suggest that they look again at the cluster diagram on the chalkboard for clues.

Customize for *Pre-AP Students*

Invite students to describe the setting of each poem and analyze how it affects the poem's mood, or atmosphere.

Customize for *English Language Learners*

Ask students to skim the poems and write down easy as well as difficult words or phrases. Encourage students to explain the easy words; then work with them to find the meaning of the more difficult ones using such aids as cognates and picture clues from accompanying illustrations.

Test Preparation Workshop

Critical Reading: Analyzing an Author's Meaning and Style When completing test items that pertain to a critical reading passage on the SAT test, students need to be prepared to understand an author's implications. Have them read "What Are Friends For," p. 860, and answer the following sample test question:

Which of the following statements would the author most likely agree with:

A Friends are worth nothing.

B New friends are best.

C Friendship is a lost art.

D Friends are there when you need them.

Guide students to read the choices quickly and eliminate any that are completely incorrect: *B* and *C* are not supported by the poem's details. Then students need only to analyze the opinions expressed in the poem to determine whether *A* or *D* is the most likely opinion of the author. Because the author says "friends fill you with music," *D* is the choice with which the author would most likely agree.

Develop Understanding

One-Minute Insight In "The Guitar," the speaker compares the mournful notes of a guitar to a wounded heart. A fist becomes the central image in "Making a Fist"; the speaker's mother answers her fearful question about death by saying that you know you are going to die "when you can no longer make a fist." These poems are united in their use of single powerful images to encompass strong and complicated emotions.

Insight From Pat Mora

Pat Mora offers the following insight. "I return again and again to Lorca's *Poema del Cante Jondo: Poem of the Deep Song,* the book that contains "La Guitarra." Lorca and Neruda are two of my favorite poets. Students (and all of us) can learn much from them. Both create music on the page. When Lorca spent time in New York, he was fascinated by jazz. In his own country, he worked to preserve the tradition of the deep song, the plaintive sadness we hear in his poem."

▶Critical Viewing◀

1 Infer *The position of the man's head, the expression on his face, and the dark colors indicate that he is probably playing a mournful song.*

◆Critical Thinking

2 Interpret Ask students to identify the mood of the poem and to cite specific words that convey that mood. *The mood of the poem is sad or mournful. The repetition of the words* cry *and* weeps *convey that mood.*

◆Build Grammar Skills

3 Adjectival Modifiers Ask students to identify the adjectival modifier in line 21 to identify its structure and to identify the noun it modifies. *"Without a target" is a prepositional phrase modifying the noun "arrow."*

▶Critical Viewing◀

4 Make a Judgment *Students who appreciate impressionistic artwork will probably find the painting effective because it shows both open hands and fists.*

The Guitar

Federico García Lorca
Translated by Elizabeth du Gué Trapier

The Old Guitarist, 1903, Pablo Picasso, Art Institute of Chicago

1 ▲ Critical Viewing What kind of song do you think the man in this painting is playing? Explain your answer. **[Infer]**

Now begins the cry
Of the guitar,
Breaking the vaults
Of dawn.
Now begins the cry
Of the guitar.
Useless
To still it.
Impossible
To still it.
It weeps monotonously
As weeps the water,
As weeps the wind
Over snow.
Impossible
To still it.
It weeps
For distant things,
Warm southern sands
Desiring white camellias.[1]
It mourns the arrow without a
target,
The evening without morning.
And the first bird dead
Upon a branch.
O guitar!
A wounded heart,
Wounded by five swords.

1. **camellias** (kə mēl´ yəz): Flowers of the camellia, a type of evergreen tree and shrub that grows mainly in the Far East.

◆ Build Vocabulary

monotonously (mə nät´ən əs lē) *adv.:* Going on and on without variation

Humanities: Art

The Old Guitarist, 1903, by Pablo Picasso
Spanish-born Pablo Picasso (1881–1973) is generally considered one of the most important visual artists of the twentieth century. During his career, Picasso went through numerous periods. In his Blue Period he painted figures in a dark, sorrowful, and pessimistic mood—epitomized by *The Old Guitarist.*

How do you think author Garcia Lorca would have responded to Picasso's painting? *He would probably have liked it as it expresses in visual medium much of what he was expressing in words.*

Impressions of Hands, 1969, by Antoni Tapies
Antoni Tapies (1923–) was born and raised in Barcelona, Spain. Largely self-taught, he was influential in the development of relief-like paint surfaces. In some of his work he scratches into earth-colored layers of paint to which texture has been added.

Compare and contrast the feeling you get from the opened hands and closed fist in the picture. *The fist portrays a feeling of threat and the opened hand a sense of freedom.*

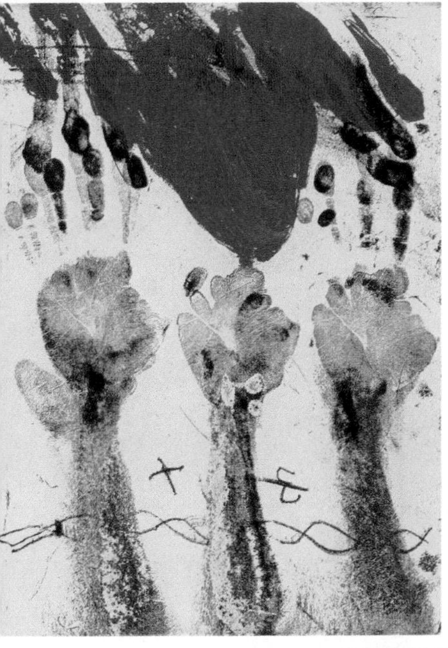

ressions of Hands, 1969, Antoni Tapies, Museum of Modern Art, New York

▲ Critical Viewing Do you think this is an effective painting to accompany this poem? Why or why not? **[Make a Judgment]**

Making a Fist

Naomi Shihab Nye

For the first time, on the road north of Tampico,[1]
I felt the life sliding out of me,
a drum in the desert, harder and harder to hear.
I was seven, I lay in the car
watching palm trees swirl a sickening pattern
past the glass.
My stomach was a melon split wide inside my skin.

"How do you know if you are going to die?"
I begged my mother.
We had been traveling for days.
With strange confidence she answered,
"When you can no longer make a fist."

Years later I smile to think of that journey,
the borders we must cross separately,
stamped with our unanswerable woes.
I who did not die, who am still living,
still lying in the backseat behind all my questions,
clenching and opening one small hand. ❻

1. **Tampico** (tam pē kō′): Seaport in eastern Mexico.

Guide for Responding

◆ Literature and Your Life

Reader's Response What single image in these two poems did you find most striking? Why?

Thematic Focus Which of these poems would you include in a time capsule? Why?

☑ Check Your Comprehension

1. To what does García Lorca compare the weeping of the guitar?
2. (a) What does the speaker ask in "Making a Fist"? (b) What answer does the mother give?

◆ Critical Thinking

INTERPRET

1. What emotions does García Lorca give the guitar in his poem? **[Infer]**
2. What does the poet's childhood journey represent in "Making a Fist"? **[Interpret]**

EVALUATE

3. Which of these poems more effectively communicates the speaker's reaction to a single event? Explain. **[Criticize]**

EXTEND

4. What musical instrument seems most like a person to you? Why? **[Music Link]**

◆ Reading Strategy

❺ **Read in Sentences** Invite a volunteer to read the second stanza aloud in sentence form, stopping in the appropriate places in order to make it sound natural.

◆ Literary Focus

❻ **Lyric Poetry** Lyric poetry zeroes in on an experience in order to express feelings. What feelings are reflected in these lines? *Suggested response: As an adult, the speaker is still like a child with a painful curiosity about (and fear of) death.*

Read to Discover Models for Writing

When reading lyric poetry, students should take note of poets' writing styles they might emulate in their own writing.

Reinforce and Extend

Answers

◆ Literature and Your Life

Reader's Response Encourage students to cite details that contribute to the strength of the impression.

Thematic Focus Sample response: "The Guitar," because it expresses a representative and universal feeling of mourning and loss.

☑ Check Your Comprehension

1. He compares it to the weeping sound of water and wind.
2. (a) The speaker asks, "How do you know when you are going to die?" (b) The mother answers, "When you can no longer make a fist."

◆ Critical Thinking

1. He gives it sorrow and longing.
2. Possible response: The childhood journey in "Making a Fist" stands for the journey of life.
3. Students might respond that "Making a Fist" more effectively communicates the speaker's reaction to a single event because the "event"—personalizing death for the first time—is made more explicit in that poem.
4. Sample response: A piano seems most like a person because it can express many moods.

Viewing and Representing Mini-Lesson

Visual Presentation

This mini-lesson supports the Visual Presentation activity in the Idea Bank on p. 863.

Introduce Before they begin researching, ask students to envision the Jade Flower Palace from the descriptive words used by the author.

Develop Have students look for information, photographs, illustrations, and artwork that depicts Chinese architecture. After they have located information, suggest that they formulate a multimedia presentation by making use of video, or photographs to represent their findings. If students have access to digital cameras or scanning equipment, they may wish to create a web page or computerized presentation.

Apply Challenge students to work in small groups to formulate their representation of Chinese architecture. Suggest that they find appropriate Chinese music as an accompaniment.

Assess Use the Multimedia Report rubric, p. 107, in **Alternative Assessment** to evaluate students' presentations.

Develop Understanding

One-Minute Insight "Jade Flower Palace" is a lyric poem that expresses the speaker's feeling about the impermanence of power and glory. The setting includes images of scurrying rats, ruins, and ghost fires that convey the message that power and glory are fleeting. In contrast, the setting of "The Moon at the Fortified Pass" is an active kingdom—its people alive and its armies on the move. Yet it is in a lonely moment in time in the mountain setting that the speaker portrays the soldiers' homesickness and fear of death in order to emphasize the senselessness of war.

◆ Reading Strategy

❶ **Read in Sentences** Ask a student to read from "The stream . . ." to "tiles" in order to notice the stops and to emphasize the short, simple sentences.

◆ Build Grammar Skills

❷ **Adjectival Modifiers** Ask students to find a participial phrase used as an adjectival modifier in lines 4–5. What noun does it modify? *"Standing in ruins" is a participial phrase modifying the noun "palace."*

◆ Critical Thinking

❸ **Infer** Ask students which images in this passage convey the idea that things are not permanent. *The images of ghost fires and shattered pavements that are all washed away convey the idea of impermanence.*

◆ Reading Strategy

❹ **Read in Sentences** Point out that the word "Only" (line 14) begins a sentence that crosses a stanza break. Ask a volunteer to read the sentence aloud.

◆ Literary Focus

❺ **Lyric Poetry** Encourage students to suggest what feelings the speaker in this lyric poem expresses. *Suggested answers: This speaker expresses the feelings of sadness, wistfulness, loneliness, and perhaps a sense of resignation.*

Jade Flower Palace

Tu Fu

Translated by
Kenneth Rexroth

❶ The stream swirls. The wind moans in
The pines. Gray rats scurry over
Broken tiles. What prince, long ago,
❷ Built this palace, standing in
Ruins beside the cliffs? There are
❸ Green ghost fires in the black rooms.
The shattered pavements are all
Washed away. Ten thousand organ
Pipes whistle and roar. The storm
Scatters the red autumn leaves.
His dancing girls are yellow dust.
Their painted cheeks have crumbled
Away. His gold chariots
❹ And courtiers are gone. Only

A stone horse is left of his
❺ Glory. I sit on the grass and
Start a poem, but the pathos of
It overcomes me. The future
Slips imperceptibly away.
Who can say what the years will bring?

◆ Build Vocabulary

pathos (pā´ thäs) *n.*: Quality in something experienced or observed that arouses feelings of pity, sorrow, sympathy, or compassion

wistful (wist´ fəl) *adj.*: Expressing longing

Block Scheduling Strategies

Consider these suggestions to take advantage of extended class time:

- Have students complete the journal activity in Literature and Your Life (p. 855). After they read the poems, ask them to search for ways in which the poems illuminate the themes they jotted down.
- Allow time for students to look for other poems that deal with the themes addressed in these two poems. Have students share poems they've found with the rest of the class.
- Invite students to prepare and present the Visual Presentation activity, in the Idea Bank on p. 863. Use the Viewing and Representing Mini-Lesson on p. 859, to get students started.
- Have students complete the Guided Writing Lesson, p. 863. Use the instruction on p. 863 of the ATE to help them draft their poems.

The Moon at the Fortified Pass

Li Po
Translated by
Lin Yutang

The bright moon lifts from the Mountain of Heaven
In an infinite haze of cloud and sea,
And the wind, that has come a thousand miles, ❻
Beats at the Jade Pass[1] basements. . . .
China marches its men down Po-teng Road
While Tartar[2] troops peer across blue waters of the bay. . . . ❼
And since not one battle famous in history
Sent all its fighters back again,
The soldiers turn round, looking toward the border,
And think of home, with wistful eyes, ❽
And of those tonight in the upper chambers
Who toss and sigh and cannot rest.

1. **Jade Pass:** Gap in the Great Wall in northeastern China.
2. **Tartar** (tär′ tər): Tartars were nomadic tribes who originally lived in Mongolia, Manchuria, and Siberia. From A.D. 200 through 400, the Tartars were almost constantly at war with the Chinese. A thousand years later, under the leadership of Genghis Khan, the Tartars conquered China as well as a number of European and Asian countries.

◀ **Critical Viewing** Imagine this picture as a setting for "The Moon at the Fortified Pass." What might make the soldiers "wistful"? **[Analyze]** ❾

◆ Build Grammar Skills

❻ **Adjectival Modifiers** Challenge students to identify the adjectival modifiers for "haze" (line 2) and "wind" (line 3) and to state what type each is. *The prepositional phrase "of cloud and sea" modifies the noun "haze." The adjective clause "that has come a thousand miles" modifies the noun "wind."*

◆ Literary Focus

❼ **Lyric Poetry** Point out that since this is a lyric poem, its historical situation is described in only two lines. In a narrative poem, much more about the history of this conflict would have been explained. Ask students to describe the setting for this event. *Sample answer: The place is the Jade Pass, a fortified gap in the Great Wall in northeastern China. The setting is moonlit, hazy, windy, and far from home.*

◆ Critical Thinking

❽ **Infer** What descriptive words in this passage indicate the soldiers' feeling, and what is that feeling? *The phrases "looking toward the border," "And think of home," reflect the soldiers' feeling, which is one of homesickness.*

▶Critical Viewing◀

❾ **Analyze** *Suggested response: These aspects of the setting would make the soldiers wistful: the darkness of night; the beauty of the moon; the loneliness of the mountains; the distance from home.*

Customize for
Gifted/Talented Students
These students might be interested in expressing the theme and spirit of one of these poems in a different form; for example, a journal entry, a brief musical interpretation, a painting, or a dance. Suggest that they begin by jotting down the theme, then decide which art form would best express the feelings they associate with that theme.

Cultural Connection

Community Gathering Places The speaker in Rosellen Brown's poem suggests that friends make life more enjoyable. Many communities and different cultures host events where people gather to share friendship and good times. Holiday activities, parades, block parties, town picnics, and concerts in the park are just a few types of gatherings that are sponsored by communities.

Challenge students to generate a list of places around the world where friends gather—they can research, as needed. In France, outdoor cafes are popular summertime gathering places; in Greece, the town square; in other locations it might be church or the community hall. What events or gathering places does your own community offer?

Discuss with them how community gathering places may have changed over time. What might have caused changes? Encourage them to consider the impact of technological advances such as cars, TV, air conditioning, and so forth. Ask them to speculate about future gathering places.

Develop Understanding

One-Minute Insight "What Are Friends For" examines a contrast of opinions about friendship. The speaker presents her mother's cynical view of friendship. The daughter, in contrast, expresses the positive attitude that friends offer emotional support, not material things. In "Some Like Poetry," the speaker expresses her feelings about poetry. Each stanza of the poem examines one of the words in the title: *Some, Like,* and *Poetry*. In the end, the reader discovers that for the poet *like* is a vast understatement.

◆ Critical Thinking

❶ **Speculate** Ask students what occurrences might have contributed to the mother's pessimistic view of friendship. *Suggested response: In the past friends have forgotten duties, failed to visit, and not baked a casserole for a sick friend. The mother has experienced other disappointments from friends, too. Someone "has just made her bitter."*

◆ Critical Thinking

❷ **Analyze** Ask students to express the speaker's view of friendship. *Friends are extremely important for emotional reasons (they "touch" you and "fill you with music"). The speaker may be suggesting that if friends occasionally disappoint by not fulfilling small obligations, they are "there" in the most meaningful ways—they give of themselves.*

▶Critical Viewing◀

❸ **Analyze** *Suggested answer: The artist has captured the qualities of closeness and trust, and the feeling of sharing an experience.*

Extending Word Study

Word Roots Challenge students to find all the words in the poems that contain the Greek root *-path-*. Have them make a chart of the words and use reference materials to find the precise meaning as it is used in the poem. Additionally, students may wish to examine words in the dictionary to find the root *-path-*.

What Are Friends For

Rosellen Brown

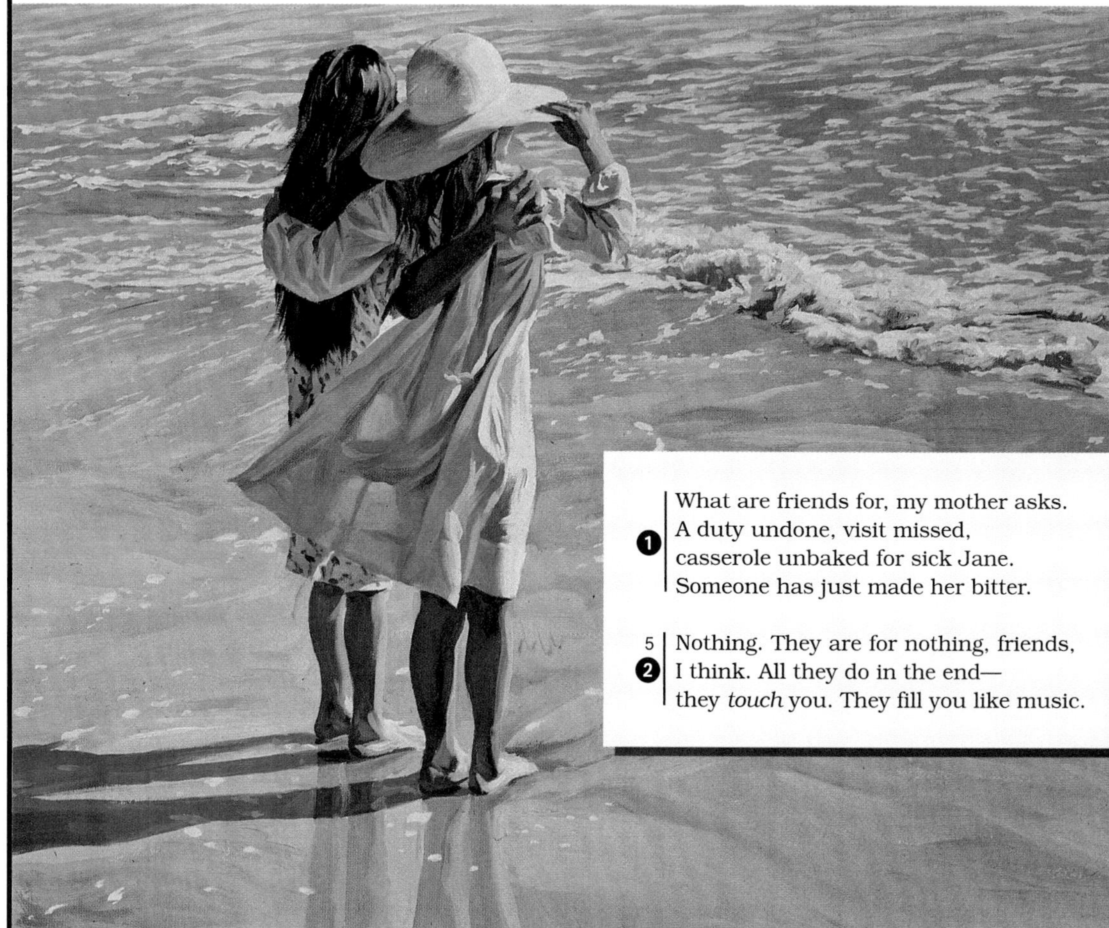

❶
What are friends for, my mother asks.
A duty undone, visit missed,
casserole unbaked for sick Jane.
Someone has just made her bitter.

❷
Nothing. They are for nothing, friends,
I think. All they do in the end—
they *touch* you. They fill you like music.

Best Friends, Craig Nelson/Bernstein & Andriulli, Inc.

❸ ▲ **Critical Viewing** What qualities of friendship has the artist captured? **[Analyze]**

Workplace Skills Mini-Lesson

Developing a Positive Attitude

Introduce Having a positive attitude toward co-workers and tasks is important in almost any job.

Develop Let students know that they can develop strategies for a positive attitude about tasks for which they have negative feelings:

- Keep in mind the long view. Find something to be gained by completing the task—proving one's self responsible to complete tasks that may be more interesting; earning the trust and respect of others.
- Emphasize positive aspects of the task. For example, it may be a source of satisfaction to complete an unpleasant task well and speedily.

Apply Ask students to think of a job or task that they dislike. On the left side of a two-column chart, they can list three things they do not like about the task. On the right side they should identify a believable positive strategy to counteract each negative thought.

Assess Encourage students to assess their own work based on the strategies they discussed.

Some Like Poetry

Wisława Szymborska

Translated by Joanna Trzeciak

Some—
that means not all.
Not even the majority of all but the minority. ❹
Not counting school, where one must,
and poets themselves,
there will be perhaps two in a thousand.

Like—
but one also likes chicken-noodle soup,
one likes compliments and the color blue,
one likes an old scarf,
one likes to prove one's point,
one likes to pet a dog.

Poetry—
but what sort of thing is poetry?
More than one shaky answer ❺
has been given to this question.
But I do not know and do not know and clutch on to it,
as to a saving bannister.

Guide for Responding

◆ Literature and Your Life

Reader's Response With which speaker would you most like to have a conversation? Why?

Thematic Focus What do these poems draw from the past?

☑ Check Your Comprehension

1. Where does the speaker of "Jade Flower Palace" sit, and what does he do?
2. Identify the event on which Li Po focuses in "The Moon at the Fortified Pass."
3. What answer is given by the speaker to the title question, "What Are Friends For"?
4. Identify two examples in "Some Like Poetry" of different meanings of the word *like*.

◆ Critical Thinking

INTERPRET

1. Explain the statement in "Jade Flower Palace," "The future/slips imperceptively away." **[Draw Conclusions]**
2. How does Li Po feel toward the soldiers going into battle? **[Interpret]**
3. In "What Are Friends For," how do the speaker's feelings contrast with her mother's? **[Contrast]**
4. What is the speaker's point in "Some Like Poetry"? **[Interpret]**

EXTEND

5. Name another work of literature that deals with war and compare its central message with that of "The Moon at the Fortified Pass." **[Literature Link]**

◆ Critical Thinking

❹ **Interpret** Ask students what statement the speaker is making about "some" in relation to poetry. *Sample answer: Poetry is not to everyone's taste; only some people like it.*

◆ Literary Focus

❺ **Lyric Poetry** Ask students to summarize the speaker's feelings about poetry. *For the speaker, poetry is lifesaving.*

Reinforce and Extend

Answers

◆ Literature and Your Life

Reader's Response Sample response: I would most like to have a conversation with the speaker of "What Are Friends For" because she clearly respects people.

Thematic Focus These poems draw upon feelings and experiences of the poets' pasts.

☑ Check Your Comprehension

1. He sits on the grass and begins to write a poem.
2. The event is a confrontation between the Tartars and the Chinese.
3. Friends fill an emotional need.
4. Examples: One likes chicken soup; one likes to pet a dog.

◆ Critical Thinking

1. The future will become the past and slip away.
2. Li Po knows the soldiers might not come back from battle, and he seems to sympathize with them.
3. The mother's feelings are cynical; the speaker's feelings are generous and optimistic.
4. Her point is that it is hard to evaluate who likes poetry and how much they like it, but that she places an ultimate value on poetry.
5. Students might mention such works as "In Flanders Fields," "Conscientious Objector," "Desert Exile," or "There Will Come Soft Rains."

Beyond the Selection

FURTHER READING

Other Works by the Poets

The Poet in New York, Lorca; *Words Under the Words*, Nye; *A Rosellen Brown Reader*, Brown; *View with a Grain of Sand*, Szymborska

Other Works About Legacies

"Ozymandias" Percy Bysshe Shelley

Leaves of Grass, Walt Whitman

We suggest that you preview these works before recommending them to students.

INTERNET

Students can learn more about the poets at the following Web site. Be aware that the sites may have changed since we published this information.

Naomi Shaib Nye: **http://www.mme.wsu.edu/~lau**

Tu Fu: **http://mirrors.org.sg/hyperhistory...n2/ people_n2/persons4_n2/tufu.html**

For a news release reporting Szymborska's Nobel Prize go to **http://www.poland.net/siec.polska/03**

We *strongly recommend* that you preview sites.

Guide for Responding *(continued)*

◆ Reading Strategy

Read in Sentences

Reading poetry in sentences, not necessarily by line, can guide you through a poem's structure and help you understand its meaning.

1. The second sentence in "The Guitar" is a repetition of part of the first sentence. Explain how the punctuation leads you to read the two sentences differently.
2. Contrast the sentences in "Jade Flower Palace" and "The Moon at the Fortified Pass" based on the use of commas and periods.
3. "Some Like Poetry" interrupts one short sentence with elaboration about each word. What is the brief sentence "hidden" in Szymborska's poem?

◆ Literary Focus

Lyric Poetry

A **lyric poem** takes a sharp-eyed and concentrated look at a single incident or experience, and in doing so, reveals the feelings of the poem's speaker. Some of these lyric poems suggest a story beneath the surface, but they don't actually tell that story.

1. What would you say is the central emotion conveyed in "The Guitar"?
2. (a) On what single subject does "Some Like Poetry" focus? (b) What is the speaker's personal feeling about the subject?

Beyond Literature

Cultural Connection

Poetry and Politics Federico García Lorca was assassinated by Nationalist forces during the Spanish Civil War. In assassinating a poet, the Nationalists signified the power of the poet. Many governments, too, have noted this power and either sought to silence poets or to cultivate relations with them.

Activity Research the role of America's poet laureate. How does the office bring the power of the poet into service of the nation today?

◆ Build Vocabulary

Using the Greek Root *-path-*

The Greek root *-path-* means "feeling; suffering." On your paper, write the word you would most closely associate with the person or thing in each numbered item.

1. A very sad movie: (a) pathology, (b) pathos, (c) antipathy
2. A medical researcher: (a) pathos, (b) sympathy, (c) pathology
3. An enemy: (a) sympathy, (b) antipathy, (c) empathy
4. A suffering animal: (a) empathy, (b) sympathy, (c) pathos
5. A very close friend: (a) antipathy, (b) pathology, (c) empathy

Using the Word Bank: Word Choice

On your paper, write the word from the Word Bank suggested by each book title.

1. *A Film Critic's Guide to the 100 Saddest Movies of All Time*
2. *The Odyssey*
3. *Games to Play on Long Car Trips*

◆ Build Grammar Skills

Adjectival Modifiers

These poems use several different types of word groups as **adjectival modifiers** to describe or limit the meaning of nouns or pronouns.

Practice Copy each of the following items in your notebook. Underline the modifier in each, and draw a line to the word that it modifies.

1. It mourns the arrow without a target.
2. The soldiers turn round, looking toward the border.
3. And the wind, that has come a thousand miles . . .
4. . . . While Tartar troops peer across blue waters of the bay.
5. . . . Warm southern sands/Desiring white camellias.

Answers

◆ Reading Strategy

1. The reader pauses at the comma on the first sentence, then reads a further description. The second sentence is read as a simple statement, ending with a period.
2. The short sentences of "Jade Flower Palace" give the poem a staccato rhythm, while "The Moon at the Fortified Pass" has longer sentences, marked by commas and ellipses, that create a more flowing rhythm.
3. The brief sentence is "Some like poetry."

◆ Literary Focus

1. The central emotion is one of melancholy or mournfulness.
2. (a) It focuses on how people feel about poetry. (b) The speaker has a passionate and life-sustaining love for poetry.

◆ Build Vocabulary

Use the Root *-path-*

1. (b) pathos; 2. (c) pathology; 3. (b) antipathy; 4. (b) sympathy; 5. (c) empathy

Using the Word Bank

1. wistful; 2. pathos; 3. monotonously

◆ Build Grammar Skills

Practice

1. It mourns the **arrow** without a target.
2. The **soldiers** turn around, looking toward the border.
3. And the **wind**, that has come a thousand miles.
4. . . .While Tartar **troops** peer across blue waters of the bay.
5. . . . .Warm southern **sands**/Desiring white camellias.

Grammar Reinforcement

For additional instruction and practice, use p. 51 on Adjective Clauses in the *Writer's Solution Grammar Practice Book*.

Reteach

Students may not find the entire thoughts of sentences in poetry. Remind them that the poet's punctuation choices are important. It may be easier for students to recognize a poem's sentences if they copy it onto a piece of paper without printed line breaks; then use a highlighter to mark the punctuation. They also might note pauses and sentence phrasing on their handwritten copies with marks of their own choosing. Suggest that students make a chart that has punctuation in one column and the action it signals in the other.

Punctuation	Action

If students need a review, remind them that a comma says to slow down and a period says to stop. Have students explore the poems' punctuation and place it on their chart.

Build Your Portfolio

Idea Bank

Writing

1. Remembrance In "Making a Fist," Naomi Shihab Nye focuses on an emotionally powerful moment. Write a paragraph describing such a moment experienced by a character in a book or movie you enjoyed.

2. Statement Poem Each section of "Some Like Poetry" elaborates on one of the three words in the poem's title. Write a simple three- or four-word statement, and create a poem around the words using Szymborska's poem as a model.

3. Story Write a short story using the mother and speaker of "What Are Friends For" as your main characters. Create a plot, conflict, and resolution.

Speaking, Listening, and Viewing

4. Reading to Music Find and play for the class a recording of classical Spanish guitar music. Play the recording a second time, softly, as you read "The Guitar." Explain why you chose the music you did. **[Performing Arts Link]**

5. Visual Presentation What would the Jade Flower Palace have looked like? Research Chinese architecture, and collect images of palaces from Tu Fu's era to present to your class along with a brief explanation of the subject. **[Art Link]**

Researching and Representing

6. Painting/Drawing Imagine that the speaker of "Jade Flower Palace" sits on the grass to paint rather than to write. In your favorite medium, draw or paint what the speaker sees. **[Art Link]**

7. Profile of a People Who were the Tartars? Research their role in history and their conflict with the Chinese. Present your findings to the class in a report with illustrations. **[Social Studies Link]**

Online Activity www.phlit.phschool.com

Guided Writing Lesson

Lyric Poem

Think about an experience or moment in time that left a particularly strong impression on you. Watching the ocean during a storm, the first time you heard the song that became your favorite, the sight of a shooting star streaking across the night sky—the possibilities are limitless. Write a **lyric poem** in which you enable your readers to experience the moment as you did.

Writing Skills Focus: Setting and Mood

A poem's **setting,** the time and place in which the experience occurred, and its **mood,** the feeling you get while reading, are often closely related. In "Jade Flower Palace," the setting of the forsaken and decrepit palace creates a desolate mood. Focus on a setting that will create a distinct mood.

Prewriting Where did your memorable moment occur? What did the place look like, and what feelings did it give you? Before you write, use a chart like this to organize your information:

Place	Descriptive Words	Feelings I Got
Lake at night	Clear, cool, mysterious	Calm, awe, delight

Drafting Write your impressions and feelings using vivid descriptive language to capture the mood of the setting. Although you may use partial sentences or break sentences over several lines, use punctuation to indicate pauses and stops.

Revising It's useful to read a poem aloud to yourself when you're revising it. Trust your ear to pick up any awkward rhythms or clunky word choices, then revise to correct these problems. Add modifiers where more detail is needed to describe the setting or create a mood. For more on adjectival modifiers, see pp. 854 and 862.

✓ ASSESSMENT OPTIONS

Formal Assessment, Selection Test, pp. 207–209, and Assessment Resources Software. The selection test is designed so that it can be easily customized to the performance levels of your students.

Alternative Assessment, p. 59, includes options for less advanced students, more advanced students, verbal/linguistic learners, interpersonal learners, logical/mathematical learners, intrapersonal learners, musical/rhythmical learners and bodily/kinesthetic learners.

PORTFOLIO ASSESSMENT

Use the following rubrics in the ***Alternative Assessment*** booklet to assess student writing:
Remembrance: Description Rubric, p. 97
Statement Poem: Poetry Rubric, p. 108
Story: Fictional Narrative Rubric, p. 95
Lyric Poem: Poetry Rubric, p. 108

Idea Bank

Following are suggestions for matching Idea Bank topics with your students' performance levels:

Customizing for *Performance Levels*
Less Advanced Students: 1, 4
Average Students: 2, 3, 6
More Advanced Students: 5, 7

Customizing for *Learning Modalities*
Musical/Rhythmic: 4
Verbal/Linguistic: 4, 5
Visual/Spatial: 6

Guided Writing Lesson

Elaboration Strategy To help students move from prewriting to drafting their poems, offer the following list of suggestions:

- Make the first line interesting—start in the middle of things.
- Don't erase (it's gone); cross out or circle (you might change your mind).
- When you want to change something, try playing with the syntax before you change the words.
- Use strong, vivid verbs.
- Consider each and every word.
- Don't use more words than you need.

For more prewriting, elaboration, and revision strategies, see *Prentice Hall Writing and Grammar.*

Writers at Work Videodisc
Have students view the videodisc segment for Chapter 6 in which Naomi Shihab Nye talks about gathering details for creative writing.

Play frames 20514 to 20978

Writing Lab CD-ROM
Have students complete the tutorial on Creative Writing. Follow these steps:

1. Ask students to use Word Bins for Poetry to see words or phrases they might use in their poems. These word bins feature rhyming words, sensory details, colors, and places.
2. Have students select a video tip from Naomi Shihab Nye to hear her thoughts on revising a draft.
3. Ask students to go to Guide for Publishing and Presenting where they will follow checklists designed to help them plan a class poetry reading.

Prepare and Engage

LESSON OBJECTIVES

1. To develop vocabulary and word identification skills
- Related Words: Forms of *Temperate*
- Using the Word Bank: Analogies
- Extending Word Study: Dictionary (ATE)

2. To use a variety of reading strategies to comprehend poems
- Connect Your Experience
- Reading Strategy: Envision the Imagery
- Tips to Guide Reading: Interpret (ATE)
- Read to Discover Models (ATE)

3. To increase knowledge of other cultures and to connect common elements across cultures
- Connecting Themes Across Cultures (ATE)
- Beyond Literature: Haiku Competitions

4. To express and support responses to the text
- Critical Thinking
- Analyze Literary Criticism (ATE)

5. To analyze literary elements
- Literary Focus: Poetic Forms
- Idea Bank: Villanelle Opener
- Idea Bank: Haiku
- Idea Bank: Essay

6. To read in order to research self-selected and assigned topics
- Research Skills Mini-Lesson: Locate Specific Information (ATE)
- Idea Bank: Japanese Poetry

7. To plan, prepare, organize, and present literary interpretations
- Idea Bank: Oral Report
- Idea Bank: Viewing Poets Corner

8. To use recursive writing processes to write a report
- Guided Writing Lesson

9. To increase knowledge of the rules of grammar and usage
- Build Grammar Skills: Noun Clauses

Test Preparation

Critical Reading: Analyzing an Author's Meaning and Style (ATE, p. 865) The teaching tips and sample test item in this workshop support the instruction and practice in the unit workshop.

Critical Reading: Analyzing an Author's Meaning and Style (SE, p. 877)

Guide for Reading

William Shakespeare *(1564–1616)*

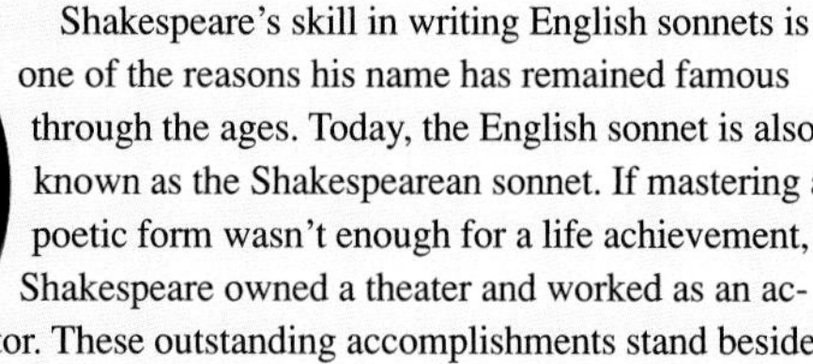

Shakespeare's skill in writing English sonnets is one of the reasons his name has remained famous through the ages. Today, the English sonnet is also known as the Shakespearean sonnet. If mastering a poetic form wasn't enough for a life achievement, Shakespeare owned a theater and worked as an actor. These outstanding accomplishments stand beside the thirty-eight plays he wrote within about twenty years. (To learn more about Shakespeare, turn to pp. 710 and 711.)

Theodore Roethke *(1908–1963)*

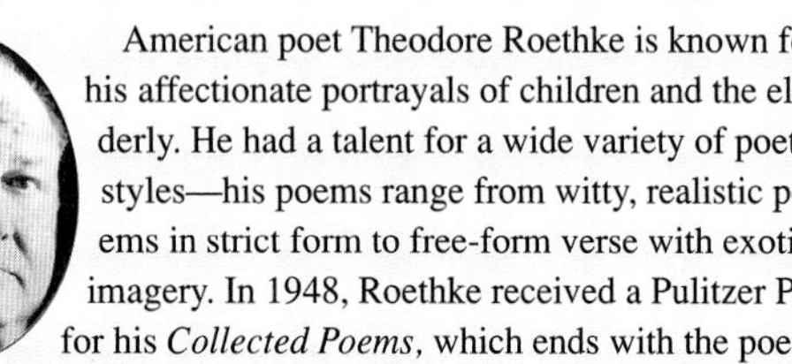

American poet Theodore Roethke is known for his affectionate portrayals of children and the elderly. He had a talent for a wide variety of poetic styles—his poems range from witty, realistic poems in strict form to free-form verse with exotic imagery. In 1948, Roethke received a Pulitzer Prize for his *Collected Poems,* which ends with the poem "The Waking."

Ki no Tsurayuki *(872–945)*

Ki no Tsurayuki (kē nō tso͞o rä yo͞o kē) was the chief aide to Emperor Daigo and one of the leading poets, critics, and diarists of his time. He helped assemble, and wrote the preface to, the *Kōkin Wakashū*—a major anthology of Japanese poetry of the time.

Priest Jakuren *(1139?–1202)*

Jakuren entered the Buddhist priesthood at the age of twenty-three. He spent his time traveling the countryside, writing poetry, and seeking spiritual fulfillment.

Matsuo Bashō *(1644–1694)*

Matsuo Bashō was a master of *renga,* a type of collaborative poem. Haiku evolved from the starting verse of this type of poem. A master of poetic forms, Bashō traveled the countryside teaching others.

Kobayashi Issa *(1762–1826)*

Banished from his rural home as a teenager, Kobayashi Issa (kō bä yä shē ē sä) lived his life in urban poverty. His difficult circumstances created in him an appreciation for the fleeting lives of small creatures.

◆ Build Vocabulary

RELATED WORDS: FORMS OF *TEMPERATE*

You will encounter the word *temperate,* which means "not extreme," in Sonnet 18. Other forms of the word *temperate* also indicate moderation. For instance, *temperance* is "restrained or moderate behavior." To *temper* something is "to bring it to the right consistency—to remove its extremes."

WORD BANK

Before reading, preview these words from the poems.

temperate
eternal

◆ Build Grammar Skills

NOUN CLAUSES

A **noun clause** is a subordinate clause used as a noun in a sentence. (A subordinate clause is a group of words that contains a subject and a verb but cannot stand alone as a sentence.) Like a noun, a noun clause can function as a subject, object, or a predicate noun.

Subject:

What falls away is always.

Direct Object:

One cannot ask loneliness / *How or where it starts.*

Object of a Preposition:

I feel my fate in *what I cannot fear.*

Predicate Noun:

Japanese poets' belief was *that poems should be brief.*

Prentice Hall Literature Program Resources

REINFORCE / RETEACH / EXTEND

Selection Support Pages
Build Vocabulary: Related Words: Forms of *Temperate,* p. 245
Build Grammar Skills: Noun Clauses, p. 246
Reading Strategy: Envision the Imagery, p. 247
Literary Focus: Poetic Forms, p. 248

Strategies for Diverse Student Needs, p. 60

Beyond Literature Science, p. 60

Formal Assessment Selection Test, pp. 210–212; Assessment Resources Software

Alternative Assessment, p. 60

Writing and Language Transparencies
Daily Language Practice: Week 24, p. 135.

Literature CD-ROM

Resource Pro CD-ROM

Listening to Literature Audiocassettes

◆ Literature and Your Life

Connect Your Experience

When you participate in a sport or play a game, you agree to follow certain rules. The rules exist, in part, to create a challenge—to test a player's skill. In the same way, the rules governing certain forms of poetry challenge the poets' skills. Some poets choose to "play the game" of the sonnet, the haiku, or the villanelle.

Thematic Focus: Humans and Nature

The many images from nature in these poems may lead you to ask: Why do poets frequently focus on nature?

Journal Writing Jot down an image from nature that you might use as the basis for a poem.

◆ Background for Understanding

Literature

Poetry has many forms. For centuries, the tanka was the only form used by Japanese poets. The popularity of the tanka and the haiku shows the Japanese preference for simplicity and for suggestion over elaboration.

Sonnets developed from Italian songs in the Middle Ages. (The word *sonnet* comes from the Italian word *sonetto,* which means "little sound or song.") Villanelles originated in the "round" songs of medieval French farm workers. The repetition that comes from the round songs is a major feature of villanelles.

◆ Literary Focus

Poetic Forms

To express their ideas, poets can choose from a variety of **poetic forms,** or structures. The following are a few examples.

A **haiku** is a lyric, unrhymed poem of three lines of five, seven, and five syllables. A **tanka** consists of five unrhymed lines of five, seven, five, seven, seven syllables. Both forms include simple, straightforward images. Traditionally, a haiku always includes an image from nature.

A **sonnet** is a fourteen-line poem written in iambic pentameter (five unaccented syllables each followed by an accented one). There are two types, Shakespearean (English) and Petrarchan (Italian). A Shakespearean sonnet contains three quatrains (which rhyme *abab cdcd efef*) followed by a rhymed couplet (*gg*).

A **villanelle** is a lyric poem written in three-line stanzas, ending with a four-line stanza. It has two refrains formed by repeating line 1 in lines 6, 12, and 18 and line 3 in lines 9, 15, and 19.

◆ Reading Strategy

Envision the Imagery

To appreciate the images that the poets use, create a mental picture. When you **envision,** you use your memory and imagination to *see, feel, hear, smell,* and *taste* what the poets describe. For example, when you read Tsurayuki's image of a winter night, feel the bitter wind blowing off the river and hear the birds' mournful calls. Use associations to help you. For example, although you may have never heard a plover cry, you have probably heard some bird that makes a sad sound. Comparisons will also help you. Shakespeare compares the qualities of a particular woman to those of a summer day. Envisioning the summer day helps you appreciate some of the feelings Shakespeare associates with the woman of his sonnet.

Use a graphic organizer like the one shown to help you envision the imagery in these poems.

Image	Association
"Darling buds of May"	Warm sun Bright colors
Spring rain	Freshness Renewal

Test Preparation Workshop

Critical Reading: Analyzing an Author's Meaning and Style As students prepare for standardized tests such as the SAT, it will help them to practice analyzing an author's meaning and style to understand the writer's message. Ask students to read "Sonnet 18" on p. 866, noting the details of the poem.

According to the author, the speaker's love—

A is like the wind

B is ever changing like nature

C will live as long as men breathe

D is always changing

Suggest that students analyze the answer choices and review the poem to determine which one answer best supports the author's meaning: he compares his love to many things, but believes it will live eternally—*C* is the best answer among the choices offered.

To prepare students to envision the imagery of the poems, bring in posters or magazine photos that depict different seasons and moods of nature. You might also play an audiotape of natural sounds such as wind, water, and bird songs. Have students discuss the feelings and memories they have when they see each photo and hear each sound. Then encourage them to make similar associations as they read the poetry.

Connecting Themes Across Cultures

Nature is a theme found in examples of literature from around the world. Challenge students to find examples of nature poems from other cultures.

Tips to Guide Reading

Interpret Encourage students to read to interpret the author's meaning, particularly the short poems on pp. 868–869.

Customize for
English Language Learners and Less Proficient Readers
Help students paraphrase each poem, encouraging them to use their own words, in order to better understand the author's meaning.

Customize for
Pre-AP Students
Challenge students to write original poems illustrating each of the poetic forms introduced in the selection.

Customize for
Gifted/Talented Students
To enhance the reading of tanka and haiku, suggest that students go to the library and find examples of Japanese art like the illustration on p. 868. Suggest that they find a painting that reflects the mood and imagery of one of the short poems. Alternatively, they might wish to find Japanese music as an accompaniment.

Literature CD-ROM Use Feature 10 of *How to Read and Understand Poetry,* which looks at how all the separate elements of poetry come together to form an overall impression. This segment examines the sonnet as an example of unity of poetic elements.

Develop Understanding

One-Minute Insight Shakespeare's famous sonnet begins by praising the beauty and temperance of his beloved as surpassing those of a summer day. It ends by testifying to the power of poetry to immortalize the person the poet loves.

"The Waking" reflects upon our daily process of waking up—literally and figuratively—the process of becoming "awake" to the world of nature and the meaning of life.

◆ Literary Focus

1 Poetic Forms Ask students to identify the end rhymes that help unify the sonnet. *The end rhymes "day" and "May" (lines 1 and 3) and "temperate" and "date" (lines 2 and 4) unify the first four lines, giving them an abab rhyme scheme. The rhyme scheme for the rest of the poem is cdcd, efef, gg.*

Comprehension Check 

2 Be sure students understand the meaning of "the eye of heaven." *It is the sun.*

◆ Critical Thinking

3 Interpret Ask students why the beloved's "eternal summer" (beauty) will never fade, unlike the beauty of an actual summer day. *The beloved's "eternal summer" will never fade because it will be kept alive by those who read Shakespeare's sonnet.*

▶Critical Viewing◀

4 Compare and Contrast
Students should include details of hairstyles, clothing, and jewelry.

Humanities: Art

Frances Howard by Isaac Oliver.

Isaac Oliver (1564–1617) was one of the chief portrait miniaturists at the courts of Elizabeth I and James I in England. A miniaturist is an artist who paints very small, detailed paintings. Ask students: What objective does Oliver's portrait share with Shakespeare's Sonnet 18? *Suggested response: Isaac Oliver's miniature portrait attempts to do in paint what Shakespeare's sonnet does in words—to commit its subject, a young woman, to immortality.*

Sonnet 18

William Shakespeare

Frances Howard, Isaac Oliver, Victoria and Albert Museum

Shall I compare thee to a summer's day?
Thou art more lovely and more temperate:
Rough winds do shake the darling buds of May,
And summer's lease hath all too short a date:
Sometime too hot the eye of heaven shines,
And often is his gold complexion dimmed;
And every fair from fair sometime declines,
By chance or nature's changing course untrimmed;[1]
But thy eternal summer shall not fade,
Nor lose possession of that fair thou owest;[2]
Nor shall Death brag thou wander'st in his shade,
When in eternal lines to time thou grow'st:
    So long as men can breathe, or eyes can see,
    So long lives this, and this gives life to thee.

▲ **Critical Viewing** Notice the formal pose of this late sixteenth- century portrait. In what ways have fashions and perceptions of beauty changed since this portrait was painted? **[Compare and Contrast]**

1. **untrimmed:** (un trimd´) *v.*: Not made or kept neat; disordered.
2. **owest:** (ō´ ist) *v.*: Own.

◆ Build Vocabulary

temperate (tem´ pər it) *adj.*: Moderate in degree or quality

Block Scheduling Strategies

Consider these suggestions to take advantage of extended class time:

- Lead a class discussion based on the Thematic Focus question in Literature and Your Life: "Why do poets frequently focus on nature?" Help students understand that urban environments are also affected by elements of nature, including seasons and weather conditions.
- Use Analyze Literary Criticism, p. 867, to expand students' appreciation and understanding of Shakespeare's poetry.
- Before students write their haiku from the Idea Bank (p. 871), have them divide into small groups to brainstorm for themes and scenes from nature that would be suitable to the haiku form. Group members can read their haiku aloud to one another.
- Use Daily Language Practice for Week 24. You may display the practice sentences on an overhead projector and have students write them correctly, or you may dictate the sentences to students.

The Waking

Theodore Roethke

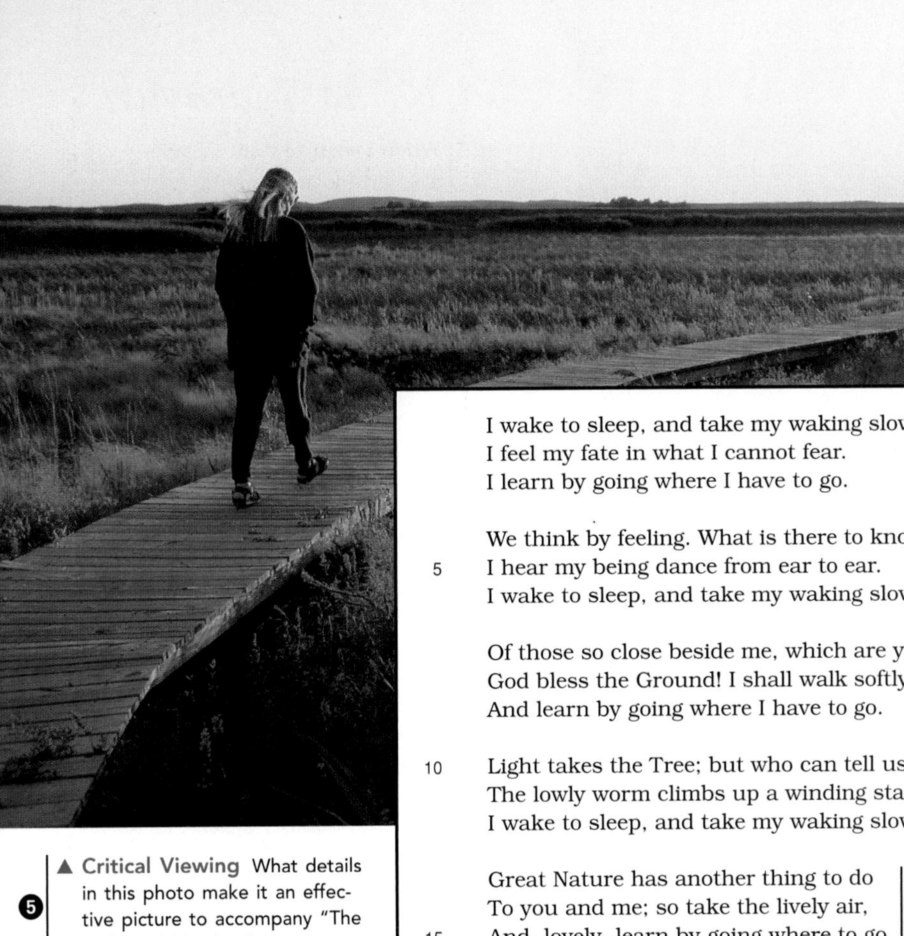

I wake to sleep, and take my waking slow.
I feel my fate in what I cannot fear.
I learn by going where I have to go.

We think by feeling. What is there to know?
I hear my being dance from ear to ear.
I wake to sleep, and take my waking slow.

Of those so close beside me, which are you?
God bless the Ground! I shall walk softly there,
And learn by going where I have to go.

Light takes the Tree; but who can tell us how? (6)
The lowly worm climbs up a winding stair;
I wake to sleep, and take my waking slow.

Great Nature has another thing to do (7)
To you and me; so take the lively air,
And, lovely, learn by going where to go.

This shaking keeps me steady. I should know.
What falls away is always. And is near.
I wake to sleep, and take my waking slow. (8)
I learn by going where I have to go.

(5) ▲ **Critical Viewing** What details in this photo make it an effective picture to accompany "The Waking"? **[Analyze]**

Analyze Literary Criticism

William Shakespeare's writings have always been popular, and he is often considered one of the world's greatest authors. Share the following literary opinion with the students:

"People want to know more about Shakespeare's private life. They have searched his plays for hints, with little result. However, he left 154 sonnets, published, probably against his wishes, in 1609. Many readers believe that these reveal an important part of his life. The sonnets he wrote have attracted more attention than anything else he wrote except "Hamlet." As poetry they are superb. However, people are more interested in them because they may tell a true story. The story is hinted at, rather than told."

Use the following questions for class discussion:

1. Do you agree with the opinion that Shakespeare was revealing his private life in this sonnet? Give examples from the poem. *Students may think his descriptive words such as* lovely *indicate a personal attitude.*
2. What person might Shakespeare have been writing about? *Shakespeare was probably writing about a special person in his life.*

▶Critical Viewing◀

5 Analyze *Possible response: The woman appears to take her waking slowly; she seems contemplative, and she is possibly appreciating nature.*

◆ Reading Strategy

6 Envision the Imagery To help students envision the imagery in this stanza, have them close their eyes and imagine morning sunlight shining on a tree that they know well. Encourage them to imagine as many details as possible, and ask for volunteers to describe what they envision.

◆ Critical Thinking

7 Interpret Ask students what is meant by the lines "Great Nature has another thing to do / To you and me: so take the lively air." *Students may say these lines are asking us to be aware of our feelings because nature teaches us to appreciate the beauty of life; "another thing to do / to you and me" may refer to death; the advice of these lines may be to appreciate nature in the present.*

◆ Literary Focus

8 Poetic Forms Point out the scheme of stanzas and refrains in a villanelle as described on page 865. Ask students to find where these two refrain lines appear earlier in the poem. Then ask why Roethke might have chosen these two lines as the refrain. *The refrain lines appear in lines 1, 3, 6, and 12. Variations on them appear in lines 9 and 15. These lines express the central meaning of the poem: that waking up to life and learning about life represent a gradual process that cannot be rushed or planned.*

Read to Discover Models for Writing

Students will find it helpful to set a purpose to read to discover writing models using various poetic forms introduced in the Literary Focus on p. 865.

Extending Word Study

Dictionary When reading poetry, it is likely that students will encounter unfamiliar words. Encourage them to use the dictionary to find precise meanings of words within the contexts of the poetry that they read.

Develop Understanding

One-Minute Insight These four Japanese poems reflect a traditional Buddhist emphasis on contemplation of nature as a path to wisdom and understanding of life. Vivid, fleeting images from nature express ideas and feelings about human experience.

◆ Critical Thinking

❶ **Interpret** Ask students to explain the connection between the winter scene, the girl, and the writer's feelings. *Suggested response: The description of the cold winter night and the crying plover suggests that the girl has been coldhearted or unfriendly to the writer, and as a result, he feels sad.*

◆ Literature and Your Life

❷ Ask students to remember a fall evening from their own experience and jot down sensory details and feelings it brings to mind.

▶Critical Viewing◀

❸ **Compare and Contrast** *Possible response: The painting conveys a lonely nighttime feeling like the mood of the two tankas; a peaceful feeling of quiet contentment and solitude, unlike the lonely feelings of the poems.*

Humanities: Art

The Monkey Bridge in Koshu Province, 1841, by Hiroshige Hitsu.

The Japanese artist and printmaker Hiroshige Hitsu (1797–1858) is widely admired, and his many works are collected all over the world today. Hiroshige was a great master of Japanese wood block printing. His restful, reflective landscapes were very popular in Japan during his lifetime and influenced western artists Whistler, Cezanne, and Van Gogh. Capturing the mysterious and profound moods of nature, Hiroshige often made prints to illustrate haiku.

Many of Hitsu's paintings and prints feature bridges like the one in this picture. Why do you think Hitsu was interested in bridges as a painting subject? *Students might point out that bridges are an evocative symbol because they enable people to go from one part of nature to another.*

The Monkey Bridge in Koshu Province, 1841, Hiroshige Hitsu, Christie's, New York

Tanka

Translated by Geoffrey Bownas

Ki no Tsurayuki

❶
When I went to visit
The girl I love so much,
That winter night
The river blew so cold
That the plovers[1] were crying.

1. **plovers** (pluv´ ərz) *n.*: Wading shore birds with short tails, long, pointed wings, and short, stout beaks.

Priest Jakuren

❷
One cannot ask loneliness
How or where it starts.
On the cypress-mountain,[1]
Autumn evening.

1. **cypress-mountain:** Cypress trees are cone-bearing evergreen trees, native to North America, Europe, and Asia.

❸ ◀ Critical Viewing Compare the mood of this painting with the mood or feelings evoked in these tankas. **[Compare and Contrast]**

Research Skills Mini-Lesson

Locate Specific Information

Introduce A difficult aspect of research is finding specific information. Pose the following research problem: While writing a research paper, they remember the lines from a sonnet, "Shall I compare thee to a summer's day? . . ." and want to directly quote the sonnet. However, they can't remember the source or author. How would they find it?

Develop As a class, brainstorm for a list of possible resources. Set a time limit and challenge students to find the quotation in as many locations other than their text as possible.

Apply As students work, have them make a list of the places they look and whether or not the location was helpful and easy to use.

Assess Hold a class discussion to evaluate the resources students found. For example, they may conclude that the Internet led them to nonspecific information, and was therefore inefficient. If they don't know the author's identity, poetry anthologies might not help. Quotation books might contain the quotation, but students would need to carefully use the index and topic headings in order to locate it.

Translated by
Daniel C. Buchanan

4 落ちざまに
水こぼしけり
花椿

Bashō

Falling upon earth,
Pure water spills from the cup
Of the camellia.

Issa

5 A gentle spring rain.
Look, a rat is lapping
Sumida River.

春雨や
鼠のなめる
隅田川 6

Beyond Literature

Cultural Connection

Haiku Competitions You may not think of poetry as a national pastime, but for many people in Japan haiku is as popular as baseball or football is here. Japanese children learn to compose the 5-7-5 poems in elementary school. Many of them develop a love for the simple yet profound form. Every year, at New Year's, a poetry exhibition called the *utakai* is held. Thousands of people, from the emperor on down, submit poems that are then read before a national television audience.

Guide for Responding

◆ Literature and Your Life

Reader's Response Which poetic form did you like most? What about it did you most enjoy?

Thematic Focus Which poetic form would you like to write in? What would be the form's advantages and disadvantages?

Questions for Research How old is the haiku, and who were its earliest practitioners? Generate research questions about the origins and development of haiku.

☑ Check Your Comprehension

1. To what does the speaker of Sonnet 18 refer that "shall not fade"?
2. What dances "from ear to ear" in "The Waking"?
3. (a) What does Bashō describe in his haiku? (b) What creature is the subject of Issa's haiku?
4. What real-life situation makes the plovers cry in the tanka by Ki no Tsurayuki?
5. What does the word "it" refer to in the line by Priest Jakuren, "How or where it starts"?

◆ Critical Thinking

Interpret

1. In Sonnet 18, does the beloved fare better or worse than a summer's day? Explain how you know. **[Draw Conclusions]**
2. What does the speaker of "The Waking" mean by, "I wake to sleep, and take my waking slow"? **[Interpret]**
3. What is the connection between loneliness and the cypress-mountain in the tanka by Priest Jakuren? **[Connect]**
4. To which senses do the haiku appeal? **[Analyze]**

Apply

5. Choose one of these poems, and explain how you might experience the ideas and feelings in it if the poem were not written in its particular form. **[Speculate]**

Compare Literary Works

6. Which form do you think is most challenging for a poet to use? Explain. **[Compare]**

◆ Reading Strategy

4 Envision the Imagery Have students recall a moment when they took the time to observe a flower closely. Ask how and when a flower might be like a cup of "pure water." Then ask what feelings this mental image of a flower conveys to them. *Sample answers: A flower is like pure water when dew or rain collects on its petals. The image conveys a feeling of freshness and new beginnings.*

5 Clarification In traditional Japanese culture, animals symbolize specific qualities. The rat is thought to be small, quiet, and gentle. Thus the rat symbolizes the gentleness described in this fleeting scene.

6 Clarification Make sure students understand that the characters next to each haiku are the original Japanese texts of the poems. Point out that each Japanese character is itself a small picture, or image, that conveys certain associations.

Reteach

Have students make a chart to record sensory details as they read and envision.

Reinforce and Extend

Answers

◆ Literature and Your Life

Reader's Response I enjoyed haiku the most because it expresses so much in so few words.

Thematic Focus The Shakespearean sonnet would be challenging because the rhythm and rhyme scheme would be hard to achieve while still conveying fresh meaning and feeling.

Questions for Research Students might use the definition of haiku on p. 959 to help them start.

☑ Check Your Comprehension

1. "Thy eternal summer" (the subject's beauty) shall not fade.
2. The speaker's being dances from ear to ear.
3. (a) Bashō describes rain or dew drops falling on the ground from a camellia that has fallen. (b) Issa writes about a rat.
4. The cold winds off the river made the plovers cry.
5. The pronoun *it* refers to loneliness.

◆ Critical Thinking

1. The beloved fares better, because unlike the summer day she is not shaken by rough winds, the hot sun does not dim her complexion and, most of all, the beloved's summer does not die as the season's does.
2. The speaker probably means that he is asleep when awake in that he is still meditative, admitting the morning slowly.
3. The origins of both loneliness and the cypress mountain would be difficult to pinpoint or explain.
4. Bashō appeals to the sense of sight (falling upon earth, camellia) and also taste and touch (pure water); Issa appeals to taste and touch (a rat is lapping / Sumida River).
5. Example response: In the haiku by Ki no Tsurayuki, the feelings of being rejected by a beloved are connected to the plovers crying. Written in another form, this comparison might not be as effective or as subtle.
6. Students might say the Shakespearean sonnet is the most challenging because the restrictions of its form are the most demanding.

Develop Understanding

Answers

◆ Reading Strategy

1. Students might associate these sensory details with hot summer days in which the temperature was very hot and the sky was hazy rather than bright.
2. Students might feel anticipation or curiosity.
3. Answers may include the following images: the plovers crying; the cypress mountain; water spilling from a camellia; rat lapping river water.

◆ Literary Focus

1. The message is that the beloved is fairer than a summer's day.
2. The first "fair" refers to one who is attractive, and the second "fair" refers to a temporary condition.
3. The third quatrain contrasts the woman's fairness with summer by saying her fairness will not fade. The earlier quatrains identified similar ties.
4. "Eternal lines" refers to immortality.
5. "This" refers to the poem.
6. The final couplet states that all the good qualities listed will live forever in this poem.
7. "I wake to sleep and take my waking slow" and "I learn by going where I have to go."
8. Both the tanka and the haiku include simple, straightforward images that relate to nature.

◆ Build Vocabulary

Using Forms of *Temperate*

1. temperate; 2. temperance; 3. intemperate; 4. tempered

Using the Word Bank

1. intemperate; 2. eternal; 3. moderate; 4. eternity

◆ Build Grammar Skills

1. whoever was interested (indirect object)
2. what I cannot fear. (object of preposition)
3. Whoever reads these poems (subject)
4. thou wander'st in his shade. (direct object)
5. that the refrain must repeat in a particular line (predicate noun)

Guide for Responding *(continued)*

◆ Reading Strategy

ENVISION THE IMAGERY

Associations and details help you **envision the imagery** in these poems. The imagery, in turn, helps you understand the poet's message.

1. In Sonnet 18, what sensory details do you associate with "Sometime too hot the eye of heaven shines, / And often is his gold complexion dimmed"?

2. What feelings do you experience when you envision the "winding stair" in Roethke's "The Waking"?

3. Identify one image from each tanka and haiku.

◆ Literary Focus

POETIC FORMS

The poets in this section wrote in a variety of **poetic forms,** each using rules to structure poems with certain patterns of lines, syllables, rhythms, and rhymes. These poems are examples of sonnet, villanelle, tanka, and haiku.

The Shakespearean sonnet contains four quatrains (four-line groups) followed by one rhymed couplet (a two-line group). Usually, each quatrain explores a different aspect of the poem's idea. The couplet sums up the poem or comments on what is said in the quatrains.

1. What is the message of the first two quatrains of Sonnet 18?

2. To what does the first "fair," in line 7 refer? The second?

3. How does the third quatrain relate to the first two?

4. What are the "eternal lines" of line 12?

5. To what does "this" refer in the final line?

6. How does the final couplet sum up Sonnet 18?

7. What are the two refrain lines in "The Waking"?

8. Because a Japanese word may have a different number of syllables in English, haiku and tanka do not always have the standard number of syllables or lines in their English translations. Even in translation, however, the poems retain other features of the form. Explain how the tanka and haiku in this section fit the form.

◆ Build Vocabulary

USING FORMS OF *TEMPERATE*

Copy the following sentences in your notebook. Complete each sentence with one of these words: *tempered, temperate, intemperate, temperance.*

1. Priest Jakuren lived a __?__ life.

2. He practiced __?__ in his activities.

3. A rash, __?__, act would be unthinkable for him.

4. Like metal that has been __?__ in a furnace, his character was strengthened by his simple life.

USING THE WORD BANK: Analogies

Notice the relationship between the first pair of words in each numbered item. In your notebook, complete the second pair of words by supplying a word that indicates a similar relationship.

1. *Foolish* is to *thoughtful* as __?__ is to *temperate.*

2. *Mortal* is to __?__ as *solar* is to *lunar.*

3. *Compassionate* is to *kind* as __?__ is to *temperate.*

4. *Earth* is to *earthly* as __?__ is to *eternal.*

◆ Build Grammar Skills

NOUN CLAUSES

A **noun clause** is a subordinate clause that functions as a noun. A noun clause can be a subject, predicate noun, direct object, indirect object, or object of a preposition.

Practice Copy the following sentences in your notebook. Underline the noun clause in each, and identify how it is used (subject, predicate noun, direct object, indirect object, or object of a preposition).

1. Bashō taught whoever was interested the form of *renga.*

2. "I feel my fate in what I cannot fear."

3. Whoever reads these poems will be enriched.

4. "Nor shall Death brag thou wander'st in his shade, . . ."

5. One difficulty of writing a villanelle is that the refrain must repeat in a particular line.

Beyond the Selection

FURTHER READING

Other Works by the Poets

"Sonnet 29," William Shakespeare
"Child on Top of a Greenhouse," Theodore Roethke; "Autumn," Matsuo Bashō

Other Works About Nature

"Spring Is Like a Perhaps Hand," E.E. Cummings
"Wind and Water and Stone," Octavio Paz
"After Apple Picking" and "Birches," Robert Frost

We suggest that you preview these works before recommending them to students.

INTERNET

Students can learn more about these poets and forms of poetry at the following Web sites. Please be aware that the sites may have changed since we published this information.

To learn more about haiku, go to **http:// awaweb.co.jp/~kunikiyo/ indexj.html**

To learn more about Bashō, go to **http://www. stonebridge.com/basho.html**

We *strongly recommend* that you preview these sites before you send students to them.

Build Your Portfolio

Idea Bank

Writing

1. Villanelle Opener Write a three-line stanza to begin a villanelle, using "The Waking" as a model. In the first and third lines, express ideas you would want to repeat throughout the poem.

2. Haiku Choose a theme or scene from nature and write a haiku. Follow the 5-7-5 syllable pattern of haikus.

3. Essay Write a "how-to" essay explaining how to tell the difference between a sonnet and a villanelle. Use "The Waking" and Sonnet 18 as examples.

Speaking, Listening, and Viewing

4. Rhyme Scheme With a partner, read aloud Sonnet 18 or "The Waking." Experiment with alternating and combining your voices. Perform your reading for the class. **[Performing Arts Link]**

5. Viewing Poet's Corner The British pay tribute to many of their best-loved poets, like Shakespeare, by including memorials to them in the Poet's Corner of Westminster Abbey. Look at photos of the Poet's Corner and write a brief description of the site.

Researching and Representing

6. Oral Report Find out more about William Shakespeare. Present your findings in an oral report to the class. Include a reading of a sonnet other than Sonnet 18. **[Performing Arts Link]**

7. Japanese Poetry Create a poster that would spark student interest in Japanese poetry. Present information about major poetic forms, old and new. Include poems or excerpts from poems. **[Social Studies Link]**

Online Activity www.phlit.phschool.com

Guided Writing Lesson

Consumer Report of Poetic Forms

A consumer report outlines the features of a product or service. The report focuses on the subject's strengths and weaknesses. The information is presented in such a way that a consumer or "shopper" can decide for himself or herself. Imagine that your classmates are shopping for a poetic form to read. Write a **consumer report** of the poetic forms in this section. In your report, discuss the advantages and disadvantages of each form and conclude with a recommendation.

Writing Skills: Grab Readers' Attention

In order to capture and keep the attention of readers, introduce your report with a lively statement that tells an important finding or conclusion. That is how you **grab a reader's attention.** You can use a direct quotation from a survey, an image, or a bold statement. For example, a consumer report about haiku might begin: "Haiku delivers images strong enough to last three centuries."

Prewriting Use a three-column chart to categorize the features of each form as advantages and disadvantages. Focus on the high and low points for a reader. For instance, you might see the length of a haiku as a drawback—"not much poem for your money."

Drafting Be specific about what you see as noteworthy in each poetic form. Support the claims you make by including examples from the poems in this section.

Revising Try out your introductory sentence on a partner. Does it grab his or her attention? Is the rest of your report clearly written and accurate? Consider your partner's suggestions, and make the necessary revisions.

Idea Bank

Following are suggestions for matching Idea Bank topics with your students' performance levels and learning modalities:

Customizing for *Performance Levels*

Less Advanced Students: 1, 4
Average Students: 2, 5, 6, 7
More Advanced Students: 3

Customizing for *Learning Modalities*

Intrapersonal: 2
Verbal/Linguistic: 4, 5, 6
Visual/Spatial: 7

Guided Writing Lesson

Prewriting Strategy Draw a hexagon on the board and label it as shown to give students a hexagonal heuristic for writing their consumer reports.

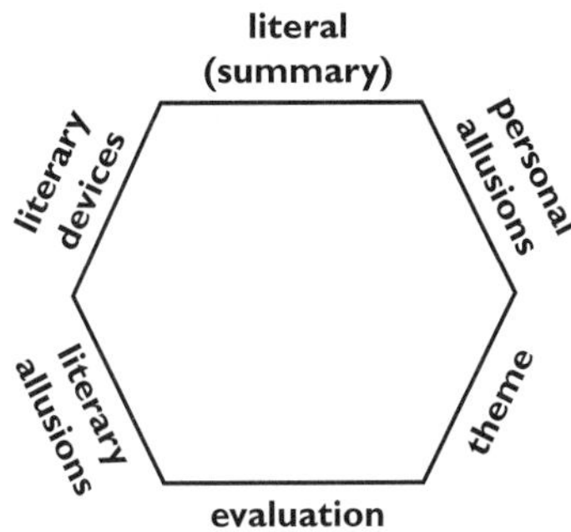

For more prewriting, elaboration, and revision strategies, see the *Prentice Hall Writing and Grammar.*

Writing Lab CD-ROM

Have students complete the tutorial on Exposition. Follow these steps:

1. Have students view a video clip and see an example of a comparison-and-contrast essay and a product evaluation. Have them discuss how these essays include techniques that they might apply to their consumer report of poetic forms.
2. Suggest that students use the notecard activity to help them organize their ideas for their consumer report.

ASSESSMENT OPTIONS

Formal Assessment, Selection Test, pp. 210–212, and Assessment Resources Software. The selection test is designed so that it can be easily customized to the performance levels of your students.

Alternative Assessment, p. 60, includes options for less advanced students, more advanced students, logical/mathematical learners, visual/spatial learners, and interpersonal learners.

PORTFOLIO ASSESSMENT

Use the following rubrics in the ***Alternative Assessment*** booklet to assess student writing:
Villanelle Opener: Poetry Rubric, p. 108
Haiku: Poetry Rubric, p. 108
Essay: How-to/Process Explanation Rubric, p. 100
Guided Writing Lesson: Comparison/Contrast Rubric, p. 103; Technical Description/Explanation Rubric, p. 115

Prepare and Engage

LESSON OBJECTIVES

1. To use recursive writing processes to write a narrative poem
2. To recognize and use punctuation appropriately in poetry
3. To recognize and avoid problems with modifiers

Before students begin, you may want to share with them the Scoring Rubric for Poetry (p. 108 in ***Alternative Assessment***) so that students see the criteria by which they will be evaluated. Suggestions on p. 874 customize the rubric to this workshop.

Writers at Work Videodisc
To introduce students to the key elements of poetry and to show how poet Naomi Shihab Nye uses them, play the videodisc segment on Creative Writing (Ch. 6).

Play frames 11043 to 20512

Writing Lab CD-ROM
If students have access to computers, have them work in the tutorial on Creative Writing to complete all or part of their narrative poems. Follow these steps:

1. Students can review the interactive model of a poem.
2. To help students choose a topic, have them watch the author video to learn how poet Nye finds ideas for poems.
3. Students can draft their narrative poems on computer.
4. Have students use the Audio-annotated Student Model to compare the first draft with a revision to see how and why one writer revised his poem.

Narrative Poem
Writing Process Workshop

La Belle Dame sans Merci, John W. Waterhouse, Hessisches Landes Museum, Darmstadt

One of the poems in this section is a narrative poem. A **narrative poem** tells a story; it is usually longer than other types of poems. Like a story, a narrative poem has one or more characters, a conflict, and a series of events that come to a conclusion. Most narrative poems are divided into stanzas, or groups of lines that have the same rhyme pattern.

Write a narrative poem. The following skills, introduced in this unit's Guided Writing Lessons, will help you write a narrative poem.

Writing Skills Focus

- **Grab the reader's attention.** Begin your poem with a dramatic statement or scene. Next, introduce a conflict. Build up that conflict to a **climax,** and then end the poem with the resolution of the climax. (See pp. 853 and 871.)
- **Use musical devices** such as alliteration, onomatopoeia, and consonance to give your narrative poem a musical quality.
- **Pay attention to setting and mood.** Establish a setting that lets your reader envision the action. Use vivid verbs, adjectives, adverbs, and exact nouns to set the proper mood. (See p. 863.)

The following stanzas from John Keats's narrative poem show these skills at work.

MODEL FROM LITERATURE

from "La Belle Dame sans Merci" by John Keats

O what can ail thee, knight-at-arms,
Alone and palely loitering? ①
The sedge has withered from the lake,
And no birds sing. ②

* * *

I met a lady in the meads,
Full beautiful—a faery's child,
Her hair was long, her foot was light,
And her eyes were wild.

* * *

She took me to her elfin grot,
③ And there she wept, and sighed full sore,
And there I shut her wild wild eyes
With kisses four. . .

① The poet grabs the reader's attention with a mysterious question.
② The poet creates a somber mood with these images.
③ The poet uses alliteration in this stanza, repeating the *s* and *sh* sounds with *She . . . she . . . sighed . . . sore . . . shut.*

Beyond the Classroom

Workplace Skill

Elements of Advertising Although the advertising world rarely uses narrative poems, the elements employed in writing them are widely applied. Advertisers must grab the audience's attention and introduce some element with which the viewer or listener can identify, such as a problem: how to stay trim, which car to buy, or where to find the best bargains. Musical devices, especially rhyme and rhythm, help audiences remember the message long after seeing, hearing, or reading the advertisement. Finally, the setting and mood of a visual ad also convey a strong message. Ask students to analyze a print ad from a magazine in terms of the elements of a narrative poem. Use these questions to help students think about the literary aspects of the ad:

- Which nonvisual elements are strongest?
- Do the visual elements match the literary elements of the text appropriately?
- How would you change the text to make it stronger?
- What is most memorable about the ad?

Prewriting

Choose a Topic A narrative poem tells a story. Think of a story that will be the basis for your poem. You can use your imagination or you can write about a real-life event or experience. Use the following suggestions to help you come up with a story for your narrative poem:

- **Examine photos, newspapers, or magazines.** Most pictures and articles have a story behind them. Look for those that will stimulate your imagination.
- **Create a Conflict Word Bin.** Create two lists, like the ones below. The first should have main characters; the second, a person, group, force, or problem that the main character must face. Mix and match the two columns until you find a suitable combination for your narrative poem.

Conflict Word Bin	
Character	***Conflict***
A knight	searching for an answer
A teenager	struggling with a decision
A detective	preparing for a challenge
An athlete	searching for a criminal

- **Use sensory images**—words that appeal to the senses of sight, sound, smell, taste, and touch—to make your narrative poem more vivid. Before drafting, make a list of words relevant to your narrative that appeal to each of these senses. Refer to this list as you write.
- **Think of a climax and resolution.** The plot of your narrative poem must eventually lead to a climax, the high point of the action. After the conflict, the action falls and a resolution is reached, in which the conflict is settled and loose ends are tied up.

Drafting

Use Musical Devices In poetry, sound is often as important as meaning. Use one or all of the following musical devices to enhance the mood and meaning of your poem:

Rhyme is the most commonly used sound device:

This darksome burn, horseback brown,
His rollrock highroad roaring down . . .

APPLYING LANGUAGE SKILLS: Punctuating Poetry

Use commas, semicolons, quotation marks, and end punctuation according to the same rules you use for prose. You will notice that lines of some poems begin with a capital letter, regardless of the punctuation at the end of the previous line. Place punctuation at the end of a line only if you want to indicate a pause or a stop.

From "La Belle Dame sans Merci":

I saw pale kings and princes too,
Pale warriors, death pale were they all;
They cried—'La Belle Dame sans Merci
Hath thee in thrall!'

Writing Application Identify places in your narrative poem where punctuation should be used to indicate pauses.

Writer's Solution Connection Writing Lab

To help you with your story line, refer to the Story Line Diagram in the Writing Lab tutorial on Creative Writing.

Develop Student Writing

Prewriting Strategy

Students may find it helpful to create visual metaphors for their poetry, using drawing as a prewriting strategy. This will allow them to represent ordinary ideas, things, events, and people in extraordinary ways. Their visual representations will provide a basis for finding words to express their poetic thoughts.

Writing and Language Transparencies Since a narrative poem tells a story, you may want students to use a Story Map graphic organizer (***Writing and Language Transparencies,*** p. 83) to organize the elements of their narration.

Customize for *Pre-AP Students*

Have students concentrate on a story that introduces symbolic meaning. Suggest that they choose some object, such as an item from nature, a utensil, or an article of clothing, that will play a symbolic role in the story-poem.

Writing Lab CD-ROM

A Poetry Topic Wheel and a Conflict Wheel are included in the Choosing a Topic section of the tutorial on Creative Writing. Students can use these to select a topic for a narrative poem and save the activities to their Activity Drawer.

Elaboration Strategy

After students have gathered their poetic thoughts with drawing, have them use a pentad to organize the ideas and find ways to elaborate on the narrative that they are telling. Have them focus on the action of the narrative and jot notes derived from their drawing at each point of the pentad.

plying Language Skills

nctuating Poetry Suggest to students that they te the poem as prose in order to punctuate accu- ly. That process will help them avoid rote end-of- punctuation.

Grammar Reinforcement

For additional explanation and examples of poetic devices and narrative elements, use the On-line Writing Handbook on the **Language Lab CD-ROM.**

Revision Strategy

You may want to have students work with a three-member editorial board to revise their narrative poems. One board member should respond to the story line; another to the musical devices; another to the punctuation.

Prentice Hall Writing and Grammar For more prewriting, elaboration, and revision strategies, see *Prentice Hall Writing and Grammar.*

Writing Lab CD-ROM

The Interactive Self-Evaluation Checklists in the Revision section of the tutorial on Creative Writing will help students judge the subject, images, form, and sound devices in their narrative poems.

Publishing

Remind students that the dramatic readings and performances can be done live or on audio- or videotape.

Reinforce and Extend

Applying Language Skills

Problems with Modifiers

Remind students that problems with modifiers can alter meaning in writing, including in a narrative poem.

Connect to Literature Refer students to Alexander Pushkin's narrative poem "The Bridegroom" (p. 54) in Unit 1. Have students review the poem for characterization and conflict.

Applying Language Skills: Problems With Modifiers

Avoid the following **problems with modifiers** as you draft your poem:

Double Negative:
There weren't no stars out.

Double Comparison:
Bullet was a more faster horse.

Improper Use of *Here*:
This here car is my favorite.

Confusing Adjective and Adverb:
That cat moves slow.
(correct: slowly)

Practice On your paper, correct the problems with modifiers in the following poem.

And as I stared
The most greatest beast
Leaped quick to my side
"Don't fear nothing!"
I said to myself . . .

Writing Application Review your narrative poem and correct any problems with modifiers.

Writer's Solution Connection
Language Lab

For more practice with modifiers, complete the Language Lab lesson on Problems With Modifiers.

Rhythm and Meter Rhythm is the pattern of accented and unaccented syllables in a line of poetry. Meter is the number of beats per line. Experiment with different rhythms and meters to create different moods.

Alliteration is the repetition of consonant sounds at the beginning of words:

The *l*ong *l*ight shakes across the *l*akes . . .

Onomatopoeia is the use of words that imitate the sounds they name. Examples include *whirr, buzz* and *bang.*

Revising

Have a Peer Check Your Work Use the following checklist with a peer to help you revise your narrative poem.

- Is the story easy to follow? How can the writer clarify what happens?
- Are the images striking and vivid? How might the images be made more effective?
- Does the author use musical devices?

Revision Model

As I recall, the night was clear,

And scarcely a whisper could I ~~discern~~ ① hear,

From the people on the street below,

~~Walking around~~ ② Shuffling about in the evening snow.

① *The writer changes this word to preserve the rhyme and meter.*

② *Shuffling is more descriptive and onomatopoetic than walking.*

Publishing

- **Give a Dramatic Reading** With a group of classmates, arrange to have a reading of your narrative poems. You might wish to have another student serve as host of the reading and introduce each poet. When you present your poem, speak clearly and with emotion.
- **Perform Your Poem** Stage a performance of your narrative poem. Act as the director, and use classmates as actors.

ASSESSMENT		4	3	2	1
PORTFOLIO ASSESSMENT Use the rubric on Poetry in ***Alternative Assessment*** (p. 108) to assess students' writing. Add these criteria to customize the rubric to this assignment.	**Narrative Element: Character**	The writer develops a character who is consistent in what he says and does.	The writer develops a character who shows somewhat consistent behavior.	The writer develops a character who behaves somewhat inconsistently.	The writer develops a totally inconsistent character.
	Narrative Element: Conflict and Resolution	The poem builds a series of conflicts and reaches a resolution of all of them.	The poem builds a series of conflicts and reaches a partial resolution of them.	The poem builds few conflicts but resolves them.	The poem builds few or no conflicts and resolves none of them.

Student Success Workshop

Real-World Reading Skills — Analyzing Characteristics of Texts

Strategies for Success

Writers make careful choices about how they use and organize words. Their choices can be especially obvious in poetry, where a writer may create a certain rhythm or "melody" of words in a particular sequence or pattern. In fiction, nonfiction, drama, and poetry, writers often use words that evoke a specific emotion, mood, or association. Being aware of the characteristics of texts will help you get more from the literature you read.

Analyze Patterns of Organization Different types of writing are organized differently. For example, poems are often organized into stanzas, or groups of poetic lines. Fiction and nonfiction are usually organized by paragraphs and chapters; nonfiction is sometimes organized by sections. Notice how the text you read is organized. Its pattern of organization makes its content easier to follow.

Analyze Syntax and Word Choice Syntax is the order in which a word or words, acting as different parts of speech, are used or arranged in a piece of writing. In a given passage, a particular word may be used as a subject, object, verb, or adjective—and it's important to distinguish which. In poetry, syntax can range from obviously "correct" or traditional styles, such as that of Robert Frost, to nontraditional styles that experiment with grammar and punctuation, such as the work of E.E. Cummings.

In Frost's poem, "Stopping by Woods on a Snowy Evening," the last stanza reads:

The woods are lovely, dark, and deep,
But I have promises to keep,
And miles to go before I sleep,
And miles to go before I sleep.

If you were analyzing the word choice and syntax of this passage, you might point out that the poet repeats the third line to reinforce and deepen its meaning. You might argue that his choice of the word *sleep* can have two meanings—the **denotative,** or literal, meaning of sleep and the **connotative,** or metaphorical, implication of death.

Analyze Sounds In poems, words within or at the ends of lines may rhyme, but they don't have to. Whether or not they rhyme, all words have rhythms, and the sequence of their sounds creates patterns that evoke a particular feeling. In Frost's poem, he writes of woods that are "lovely, dark, and deep." Despite the contradictory connotations of the word *lovely* and the words *dark* and *deep,* notice the pleasing rhythm and sounds of these words used together. A certain mood is created. These woods are different from woods that are "beautiful, dim, and thick." Specific words and syntax create rhythms and melodic sounds, which in turn evoke meanings.

Apply the Strategies

Choose a poem from Unit 9, and write several paragraphs analyzing the following elements:

1. Patterns of organization
2. Syntax
3. Word choice
4. Sounds, including rhyme and rhythm

Here are some situations in which it is important to analyze the characteristics of texts:

- When reading dialogue in a play
- When listening to a political speech
- When evaluating song lyrics

Prepare and Engage

LESSON OBJECTIVES

- To analyze the texts, including the patterns of organization, syntax, and word choice
- To analyze literary language

Apply the Strategies

Customize for
Interpersonal Learners

Provide copies of some of Shakespeare's sonnets, such as numbers 18, 65, and 116, and have pairs or small groups discuss the characteristics of each poem, including organization, syntax, and sounds. Encourage students to compare and contrast the characteristics of the sonnets.

Answers

1. Responses should describe the stanzas of the poem chosen.
2. Responses should indicate an understanding of the poet's use of traditional or nontraditional syntax.
3. Responses should highlight examples of effective or unusual word choice in the poem.
4. Examples of sound devices in the poem should be given.

Test Preparation Workshop

Analyzing Characteristics of Texts Applying the skills used in analyzing characteristics of text will help students perform well on any standardized test. The reading comprehension and vocabulary sections of tests often require students to be able to find information quickly, and recognize an author's intentions and choices. Write the following two lines of Robert Frost's poem on the board, along with the following sample test item.

The only other sound's the sweep
Of easy wind and downy flake.

Which of the following is the best meaning of the word flake as it is used in the poem?

A A thin piece or layer
B To chip off
C A small crystal of snow
D To fleck

Guide students to recognize that C is the best answer because it fits clearly with the title and context of the poem. Discuss why Frost might have made this choice.

Prepare and Engage

LESSON OBJECTIVES

1. To make interpret literature
2. To use verbal and nonverbal performance techniques

Discuss with students how they communicate without speaking or writing—through looks, gestures, posture, and facial expressions—and why nonverbal forms of communication can be so "telling." Some nonverbal techniques can be broad and read by all, while others may be more subtle and meant for just one person.

Customize for
Musical/Rhythmic Learners

Choosing a musical piece to accompany a nonverbal interpretation can help students determine the rhythm and mood. Explain that the music should probably match the literary work in some ways, such as the tempo, mood, or how the interpretation will "flow." Encourage students to try out more than one piece of music while working on their interpretations.

Apply the Strategies

Remind students that they should be prepared to explain why they chose certain nonverbal techniques. Experimenting with different techniques as they plan will help students make and justify their choices, and will aid them in becoming more familiar with the work.

Speaking, Listening, and Viewing Workshop

Presenting a Nonverbal Interpretation

Moviegoers roared with laughter while watching Charlie Chaplin perform, though he never said a word! The work of actors in silent films, such as Chaplin, Mary Pickford, and Buster Keaton, has endured over time. Pantomime, dance, and instrumental music are all creative means of expressing ideas nonverbally. When interpreting a literary work, you may choose nonverbal techniques—and prove that actions can speak louder than words.

Think About It When selecting a work to interpret, consider your own interests. Your audience won't feel excited about your performance if you aren't. Once you've chosen a text, you will need to decide exactly what you have to say about it. Your nonverbal performance should express your own unique interpretation of the entire work or a specific aspect of it. Will you focus on the theme of the play, the moral of the story, the plot of the epic, or the feelings of the poem's speaker? Remember that your interpretation should be valid—in other words, you should be able to defend it by pointing to the text.

Plan Your Performance Don't forget who your audience will be. Your performance for an audience of young children should differ from a performance before your classmates. Your classmates may instantly associate the action of a mime raising a hand with the action of a student offering to answer a teacher's question, but a group of preschool children might not. Consider also how some nonverbal actions may be universally understood, while others might "speak" only to specific groups.

Experiment Your body movements, gestures, and facial expressions are your tools: Find out what effects you can get. Remember that timing is another of your tools—and one of the most important. Based on what you want to communicate, try varying the speed of your movements. Short pauses and prolonged stillness "speak," too. Classic pantomime artists, like Marcel Marceau, often seem to move in slow motion, so don't rush through your performance unless your interpretation demands it.

Rehearse Again and Again Nonverbal performances take time to perfect. Practicing in front of a mirror will help you see what's working. Ask friends and family members to give you feedback. If you can, videotape a rehearsal. Make sure your performance communicates your ideas as obviously as possible. Rehearse until you feel comfortable and confident.

Apply the Strategies

Alone or with a partner, choose a poem from this unit to pantomime for your class. Use the strategies presented here, and plan your performance as a nonverbal interpretation of the text. Afterwards, invite questions from your audience. Explain why you selected your nonverbal performance techniques, based on your analysis and interpretation of the poem.

Tips for Performing Nonverbally

When planning a nonverbal performance of a literary text, use these techniques:

- Practice in front of a mirror to see what your expressions, body language, and gestures are "saying." As you evaluate what you see, pretend you're an audience member.
- Experiment with using actions in different "sizes." Does exaggerating a movement change your message?

Beyond the Classroom

Workplace Skills Mini-Lesson

Using Body Language Body language, often called nonverbal communication, plays a large role in the workplace. For example, the personnel director watches an interviewee's body language during a job interview; the boss watches an employee's body language during a briefing; employees watch the boss's body language during job reviews. Likewise, salespeople watch customers' body language for reactions to products or services.

Whether a worker is interacting with a potential client, a difficult customer, or a new co-worker, nonverbal communication contributes to the interactive tone. At times, people intentionally use nonverbal techniques in the workplace to communicate. Sometimes, nonverbal communication may say more than the speaker really intends—or it can be misread.

Have students brainstorm for a list of workplace situations in which nonverbal communication plays an important role. Then students role-play some of the situations. Afterward, have students discuss how nonverbal communication contributed to the situation.

Test Preparation Workshop

Critical Reading: Analyzing an Author's Meaning and Style

Strategies for Success

The reading sections of some standardized tests require you to read a passage to understand an author's ideas and to decide what an author suggests or implies.

Interpret Phrases First, read the passage to be sure you understand the context. Then restate the phrase in your own words. Read this passage, and answer the question:

During the 1980's, marine scientists noticed that huge stretches of coral reefs, normally a vast array of shades and hues, had begun turning white. Scientists eventually discovered the cause. The reefs had discharged the populations of microscopic, single-celled organisms that gave the reefs their color. The bleaching has so far been linked both to natural environmental events and to interference from humans. While some tracts have repaired themselves over time, scientists have continued to monitor the bleached reefs, searching for answers.

1 "A vast array of shades and hues" means
A a huge experiment in color.
B a large room for creating color.
C a wide range of colors.
D colors worth studying.

To arrive at **C**—the correct answer—you could paraphrase this phrase as "many (vast array) different colors (shades and hues)."

Determine What an Author Implies To infer an author's implication or suggestion, select an answer based on information in the passage and your own knowledge. Eliminate answer choices that relate to something not suggested in the passage or that draw a conclusion that is too general. For example, consider the question that follows about the passage on coral reefs:

2 With which of the following statements might the author agree?
A The bleaching of coral reefs will probably be attributed to industrial pollutants.
B Further scientific study is needed to determine what role humans have played in the bleaching of coral reefs.
C Scientists will probably discover in the near future the causes of bleaching.
D The phenomenon has probably been occurring for some time.

A is too far-reaching, so it can be eliminated. **C** and **D** are not logical extensions of the information presented in the passage. **B** is correct.

Apply the Strategies

Read the passage, and answer the questions:

The current trend toward reducing fat in our diets is an idea that requires careful examination. Fats are integral to proper body function; they serve to protect and support our organs, and fat is a primary source of insulation. Our bodies need fat as a source of energy and to absorb vitamins. A balanced diet is composed of the recommended proportions of carbohydrates, proteins, vitamins, minerals, and fats. This should be the goal toward which we work.

1 "Integral to proper body function" means that fat
A is a part of the body.
B helps the body works.
C is a key to the digestive system.
D is needed to help our bodies work.

2 With which statement might the author agree?
A The end usually justifies the means.
B An extreme position leads to problems.
C Foolish people get what they deserve.
D Ignore the "experts"; trust your instincts.

Correlations to Standardized Tests

The reading comprehension skills reviewed in this Workshop correspond to the following standardized test sections:
SAT Critical Reading
ACT Reading

Test Preparation

Each ATE workshop in Unit I supports the instruction here by providing teaching suggestions and a sample test item:
Analyzing an Author's Meaning and Style
(ATE, pp. 813, 823, 833, 847, 855, 865)

LESSON OBJECTIVES

- To analyze the characteristics of clearly written texts, including the patterns of organization, syntax, and word choice

Answers

1. (D) is needed to help our bodies work.
2. (B) An extreme position leads to problems.

Test-Taking Tip

Test the Answer Choices

Explain to students that when they answer standardized test items that use words with which they are not familiar, a good strategy is to try each answer choice where the unfamiliar word appears in the text. For example, if a student is unsure of the meaning of *integral,* substituting each answer choice for the phrase "are ______ to proper body function" will help determine which choice makes the most sense. While *B* might seem to be an accurate choice, when read in the context of the text, it is clear that it is not a strong enough statement. *D* makes the stronger statement, so it is the correct answer.

Remind students that they will always need to read the sentences of the test items *carefully*—details cannot be ignored (they are often a clue to the correct answer).

Planning Instruction and Assessment

Unit Objectives

1. To read epic and legendary stories from around the world
2. To apply a variety of reading strategies appropriate for reading these selections.
3. To analyze literary elements
4. To use a variety of strategies to read unfamiliar words and to build vocabulary
5. To learn elements of grammar, usage, and style
6. To use recursive writing processes to write in a variety of forms
7. To express and support responses to various types of texts
8. To prepare, organize, and present literary interpretations

Meeting the Objectives With each selection, you will find instructional material and portfolio opportunities through which students can meet these objectives. Further, you will find additional practice pages for reading strategies, literary elements, vocabulary, and grammar in the ***Selection Support*** booklet in the ***Teaching Resources*** box.

Test Preparation

The end-of-unit workshop **Writing Skills: Strategy, Organization, and Style** (SE, p. 951) is supported by a teaching tip and sample test item in the ATE workshop with each selection grouping:

- **Strategy** (ATE, p. 883)
- **Organization** (ATE, p. 923)
- **Style** (ATE, pp. 893, 933)

The following additional workshops in the ATE give teaching tips and a sample test item for applying the skill taught in the Student Success Workshops:

- **Reading Silently With Comprehension** (ATE, p. 920)
- **Reading a Map** (ATE, p. 949)

Knights About to Depart on the Quest for the Holy Grail, Tapestry designed by Sir E. Burne-Jones, woven by William Morris & Co., Birmingham Museums and Art Gallery

Humanities: Art

Knights About to Depart on the Quest for the Holy Grail, designed by Sir Edward Burne-Jones, tapestry woven by William Morris and Company.

This tapestry represents the collaborative effort of two great Victorian artists: Edward Coley Burne-Jones (1833–1898) and William Morris (1834–1896). The two men met at Oxford, where they were both divinity students. Burne-Jones was a painter and designer; Morris, besides being a painter, wrote brilliant poetry and designed furniture and wallpaper.

The subject of King Arthur and his knights exerted a strong hold over the imaginations of the Victorians, inspiring many beautiful works of art. The lady with the crown on the left is probably Queen Guinevere, who appears to be handing a shield to King Arthur, her husband.

Use this question for discussion:

Why do you think stories about legendary figures like King Arthur continue to hold such an attraction for people? *Such stories contain exciting adventures; the heroes they tell about embody qualities that are widely admired.*

UNIT 10

Epics and Legends

Great legends develop in every culture, reflecting the history and beliefs of the people who create them. These stories serve two purposes: They explain important events in the history of a people, and they shape these events into a heroic and memorable form. The various tales of different cultures have become identifying marks of these cultures; other people can read these stories and sense how the culture was shaped and what figures and issues are central to its history.

Within each of these stories, the customs, folklore, and history of a particular culture are revealed, sometimes in an entertaining manner.

Assessing Student Progress

The following tools are available to measure the degree to which students meet the unit objectives:

Informal Assessment

The questions on the Guide for Responding sections are a first level of response to the concepts and skills presented with the selection. Students' responses are a brief informal measure of their grasp of the material. Their responses on this level can indicate where further instruction and practice are needed. You may then follow up with the practice pages in the ***Selection Support*** booklet. You will find literature and reading guides in the ***Alternative Assessment*** booklet, which you may give students on an individual basis for informal assessment of their performance.

Formal Assessment

In the ***Formal Assessment*** booklet, you will find selection tests and a unit test.

Selection Tests The selection tests measure comprehension and skills acquisition for each selection or group of selections.

Unit Test The unit test, which calls on students to read a passage of literature they have not previously seen, applies the unit skills on a broader level. The Critical Reading section measures Unit Objectives 1, 2, and 3. The Vocabulary and Grammar section measures Objectives 4 and 5. The Essay section measures Objectives 1 and 6. Both the Critical Reading and Vocabulary and Grammar sections use formats similar to those found on many standardized tests, including the SAT.

Art Transparency Have students read the introductory information about the importance of folk literature, then explain that folk art serves a similar purpose. Display Art Transparency 9, inviting students to describe the details in the painting and their overall impressions of it. To extend the discussion, you might turn the classroom into an art gallery and have students display drawings, paintings, or photographs that express the customs or history of their heritage.

Alternative Assessment

Portfolios As you review individual pieces or the collected work in students' portfolios, you will find assessment sheets available in the portfolio section of the ***Alternative Assessment*** booklet.

Scoring Rubrics You will find scoring rubrics for writing modes in the ***Alternative Assessment*** booklet. You can apply these to Guided Writing Lessons and to Writing Process Workshop lessons.

Speaking, Listening, and Viewing The ***Alternative Assessment*** booklet contains assessment sheets for speaking, listening, and viewing activities.

Learning Modalities The ***Alternative Assessment*** booklet contains activities that appeal to different learning styles. You may use these as an alternative measurement of students' growth.

Reading for Success

The Reading for Success page in each unit presents a set of problem-solving procedures to help readers understand authors' words and ideas on multiple levels. Good readers develop a bank of strategies from which they can draw as needed and apply in a variety of reading situations.

Unit 10 presents strategies for reading epics and legends. Students will have encountered these strategies earlier. Here, however, they apply them to a specific kind of literature.

How to Use the Reading for Success Page

- Introduce the strategies for reading epics and legends, presenting each as a problem-solving procedure. Be sure students understand what each strategy involves and under what circumstances to apply it.
- Before students read the selections in this unit, point out that these selections represent legendary stories from a variety of world cultures. They should be open to the cultural context; they may encounter attitudes and customs different from what they might expect. Accepting these differences is an important part of the reading process.

Reading for Success

Strategies for Reading Epics and Legends

Every culture has its epics and legends—stories of heroes who embody the values, strengths, and traditions of that culture. While the legends may differ from culture to culture, the feature they have in common is a hero who achieves fame through great deeds. Because the legendary stories in this unit come from widely different time periods and cultures, you need to be open to differences in style and structure. The following strategies will help you read epics and legends effectively.

Reread or read ahead.

If you don't understand a passage, reread it, looking for connections among the words or sentences. It might also help you to read ahead, because a word or idea may be clarified further on. Try to follow the plot line.

Summarize.

As you read, pause periodically to restate in your own words what you have read. By doing this in your mind, you can check your understanding of the key events and their significance.

Be aware of the historical and cultural context.

The heroic tales in this unit took place long ago and far away. Customs and attitudes are very different from those that you know, and places may be unfamiliar. It's important to be open to these differences and not to impose preset expectations. Before you begin the following selections, familiarize yourself with the names of the characters.

Look for the writer's purpose and attitude.

Most epics and legends were passed on from generation to generation to preserve the history and values of a culture. The stories you will read here have other purposes as well. For instance, the purpose of *Don Quixote* is to poke fun at the values of the culture in which Cervantes lived. The writer's purpose in *Arthur Becomes King of Britain* is to bring some humanity and humor to the legendary hero.

You will read heroic tales more effectively if you actively use these strategies. You will be better able to follow the plot and apply your understanding to your own world.

Reading Strategies: Support and Reinforcement

Appropriate Reading Strategies Students are given a reading strategy to apply with each selection. Applying the strategies will give them insight into each selection.

Reading Prompts To encourage application of the given reading strategy, there are occasional prompts, within green boxes, at appropriate and significant points.

In addition, there are red boxes prompting application of the Literary Focus concept and maroon boxes prompting students to connect with their lives.

Using the Boxed Annotations and Prompts

The material in the green, red, and maroon boxes along the sides of selections is intended to help students apply the literary element and the reading strategy and to make a connection with their lives. You may use the boxed material in several ways:

- Have students pause when they come to a box and respond to its prompt before they continue reading.
- Urge students to read through the selection ignoring the boxes. After they have read the selection completely, they may go back and review the selection, responding to the prompts.

Part 1 *European Traditions*

Sir Galahad, George Frederic Watts, The Fogg Art Museum, Harvard University

One-Minute Planning Guide

The first part of Unit 10 begins with an excerpt from *Don Quixote* that mocks the medieval romance. Tennyson's "Morte d'Arthur" tells the story of Arthur's death and the return of Excalibur to the Lady of the Lake. In his elegant poetry, Tennyson captures the grandeur of this classic legend. The excerpt from T. H. White's *The Once and Future King*, "Arthur Becomes King of Britain," takes a less reverent tone as it tells how young Arthur became king. White's gently comic prose version of the Arthurian legend was the inspiration for the stage and movie musical *Camelot*.

Customize for *Varying Student Needs*

When assigning the selections in this part, keep in mind these factors:

from *Don Quixote*

- Students who are less proficient in reading may be put off at first by the elaborate style. Have them preview the picture on page 887 and be sure they know that Cervantes was making fun of flowery books about knights and their adventures.

"Morte d'Arthur"

- ESL Students may have trouble deciphering Tennyson's meaning. Summarize passages for them and then play the section of the audiocassette where the passage is read.

"Arthur Becomes King of Britain"

- The story may seem so foreign to less advanced students that they may not at first catch its humorous tone. Before they read it, tell them the "straight" version of the same events.

Humanities: Art

Sir Galahad by George Frederic Watts.

George Frederic Watts (1817–1904) was a successful English painter and sculptor. He studied at the Royal Academy and then spent some time in Italy, where he was influenced by the work of the great Italian Renaissance painter Titian.

Tell students that Sir Galahad was the son of Sir Lancelot and surpassed his father in virtue; in some versions of the Arthurian legend, Galahad is the only truly pure knight, and he succeeds in finding the Holy Grail. Then use these questions for discussion:

1. The knight who fights for justice and virtue has been the prime hero in the European tradition for centuries. Modern versions include the cowboy and good soldier. What has the painter done to make Galahad look heroic in this painting? *He has painted Galahad with an ideal beauty and strength, in brilliantly gleaming armor, accompanied by a beautiful white horse. Galahad's head is surrounded by a halo-like cloud.*
2. What would a contemporary Galahad look like? In particular, how would this person differ from the hero shown in this painting? *Students may propose figures who resemble such heroes as Luke Skywalker or Batman. They should explain what the hero would be wearing, what—if any—weapons he or she carries, and what animal or vehicle—if any—he or she rides.*

Prepare and Engage

LESSON OBJECTIVES

1. **To develop vocabulary and word identification skills**
   - Latin Word Roots: *-son-*
   - Using the Word Bank: Synonyms
   - Extending Word Study: Dictionary
2. **To use a variety of reading strategies to comprehend epics and legends**
   - Connect Your Experience
   - Reading Strategy: Compare and Contrast
   - Tips to Guide Reading: Sustained Reading (ATE)
   - Read to Appreciate Author's Craft (ATE)
3. **To increase knowledge of other cultures and to connect common elements across cultures**
   - Background for Understanding
   - Connecting Themes Across Cultures
4. **To express and support responses to the text**
   - Critical Thinking
   - Idea Bank: Cartoon
   - Idea Bank: Don Quixote in America
   - Idea Bank: Create a Scene
   - Idea Bank: Definition of a Hero
5. **To analyze literary elements**
   - Literary Focus: Parody
6. **To plan, prepare, organize, and present literary interpretations**
   - Idea Bank: Musical Drama
   - Idea Bank: Visual Essay
7. **To speak clearly and effectively for a specific audience and purpose**
   - Speaking, Listening, and Viewing Mini-Lesson: Role Play (ATE)
8. **To use recursive writing processes to write a character sketch**
   - Guided Writing Lesson
9. **To increase knowledge of the rules of grammar and usage**
   - Build Grammar Skills: Gerunds and Gerund Phrases

Test Preparation

Writing Skills: Strategy (ATE, p. 883) The teaching tips and sample test item in this workshop support the instruction and practice in the unit workshop:
Writing Skills: Strategy, Organization, and Style (SE, p. 951)

Guide for Reading

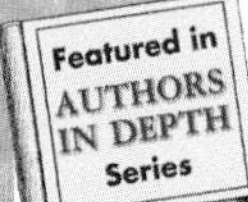

Miguel de Cervantes

(1547–1616)

As the creative genius behind *Don Quixote*, Miguel de Cervantes is counted among the world's greatest writers. His masterpiece *Don Quixote* has been translated into more than sixty languages and continues to be studied, critiqued, and debated even today. A poet and playwright as well as a novelist, Cervantes was born in a small town outside Madrid, Spain. Little is known about the author's early life—except the misfortunes he experienced.

A Life Full of Adventure As a young soldier in Turkey, Cervantes was wounded and permanently lost the use of his left arm and hand. Sailing home from the war, he was captured and enslaved by pirates. They took him to Algiers, where he was held prisoner for five years. Finally, he was freed when the Trinitarian friars paid a five-hundred-ducat ransom for him.

Settling Down Back in Spain, Cervantes married and took a job as a purchasing agent for the navy. His misfortunes continued, however; problems with work and finances resulted in fines and imprisonment. His luck finally turned when he published the first part of *Don Quixote*. He settled in Madrid and devoted his last years to writing. Wildly popular when it was first published, *Don Quixote* later became the model for a new type of fiction: that of the hero who does not conform to his times.

◆ Build Vocabulary

Latin Word Roots: *-son-*

In this selection, Don Quixote decides to name his horse Rocinante because he believes it is a "lofty, sonorous name." *Sonorous* has the Latin root *-son-,* which comes from the Latin *sonorus*, meaning "a sound." Knowing this root helps you to see that *sonorous* means "having a powerful, rich sound." You can also see this root in words such as *sonic*, which means "having to do with sound."

Word Bank

As you read this story, you will encounter the words in this list. Each word is defined on the page where it first appears. Preview the list before you read.

lucidity
adulation
interminable
affable
sallying
requisite
sonorous
veracious
vanquish
extolled

◆ Build Grammar Skills

Gerunds and Gerund Phrases

As you read *Don Quixote*, look for examples of gerunds and gerund phrases. A **gerund** is a verb form ending in *-ing* that acts as a noun. A **gerund phrase** includes all the words that go with a gerund. Like nouns, gerunds and gerund phrases can perform all the roles of a noun in a sentence: subject, direct or indirect object, object of a preposition, and appositive. In this example, the gerund *hunting* is used as the object of the preposition *of:*

> Don Quixote was an early riser and fond of *hunting.*

In the following example, the gerund phrase *reading books of chivalry* acts as the object of the preposition *to:*

> . . . the above named gentleman devoted his leisure . . . to *reading books of chivalry* . . .

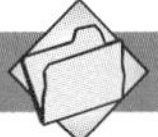

Prentice Hall Literature Program Resources

REINFORCE / RETEACH / EXTEND

Selection Support Pages
Build Vocabulary: Word Roots: *-son-*, p. 249
Build Grammar Skills: Gerund Phrases, p. 250
Reading Strategy: Compare and Contrast, p. 251
Literary Focus: Parody, p. 252

Strategies for Diverse Student Needs, p. 61

Beyond Literature
Cultural Connection: *Spain's Golden Age*, p. 61

Daily Language Practice
Weeks 31 and 32, pp. 66–69

Formal Assessment Selection Test, pp. 217–219; Assessment Resources Software

Alternative Assessment, p. 61

Writing and Language Transparencies
Daily Language Practice, Weeks 31 and 32, pp. 142 and 143

Resource Pro CD-ROM

Listening to Literature Audiocassettes

from Don Quixote

◆ Literature and Your Life

Connect Your Experience

You're reading the latest suspense or adventure novel and have encountered a devious villain. As the conflict intensifies, you find yourself silently shouting at the pages. You know they're just words on the page, but in the excitement of the tale you get a little carried away. The main character in *Don Quixote* gets carried away by the excitement of the romantic stories he reads about knights and battles. His overactive imagination creates some humorous scenes and situations.

Journal Writing Briefly describe the last book, movie, or video game that "carried you away."

Thematic Focus: Overcoming Obstacles

Don Quixote's imagination is a powerful force. You may wonder, as you follow his adventures, whether his imagination helps him or hurts him.

◆ Background for Understanding

Culture

Cervantes was born at the peak of Spain's Golden Age, a time when Spanish power and influence in Europe and the Western Hemisphere were greater than ever before or since. By the time Cervantes wrote *Don Quixote*, however, Spain's fortunes were fast declining because of a series of disastrous wars, bad economic policies, and the stunning defeat of the Spanish Armada by the British Navy in 1588. This last event signaled the end of Spain's rule of the seas and the beginning of England's. To some extent, Spain's transition from great confidence to deep despair is echoed in the novel, as Don Quixote takes refuge in chivalry from the realities of an unfriendly world.

◆ Literary Focus

Parody

A **parody** is a comical piece of writing that mocks the characteristics of a specific literary form. By exaggerating or humorously imitating the ideas, language, tone, or action in a work of literature, a parody calls attention to the ridiculous qualities of its subject. A parody works best when the object of its ridicule is a usually serious topic. *Don Quixote* is a parody that ridicules knights and the literature of chivalry. By exaggerating Don Quixote's behavior, Cervantes entertains his audience while making fun of the traditional "knight in shining armor."

◆ Reading Strategy

Compare and Contrast

Much of the humor in *Don Quixote* comes from the sharp difference between the ideal knight and Don Quixote's version of a knight. **Comparing and contrasting** the two versions will highlight the humor of Don Quixote, a mock "knight in shining armor." To help you identify the similarities and differences between Don Quixote and an "ideal knight," make a chart with three columns. In the first column, list the qualities or things that you associate with real knights—a war horse, armor, a squire, a lady love, bold adventures, and so on. Label the second column, "Ideal Knight" and list details about the ideal knight's horse, armor, and so on. Label the third column Don Quixote. Then, as you read the selection, jot down details that compare and contrast Don Quixote's knightly attributes and possessions with the ideal.

Qualities or Things	Ideal Knight	Don Quixote
armor		
squire		
war horse		
adventures		
opponents		
motivation		

Test Preparation Workshop

Writing Skills: Strategy

Standardized tests, such as ACT, ask students to demonstrate their knowledge of writing skills. Strategy questions may ask whether an addtion to the passage is appropriate in the context of the writing. Give students this sample test item.

> Writing of Don Quixote, Cervantes says that he became so absorbed in his books and spent so much time reading stories of knights and their deeds that his brain was damaged and he lost his mind.

Suppose that Cervantes wanted to say more about the dangers of reading all the time. The most suitable addition is—

A Don Quixote lost touch with reality.

B Don Quixote sold off his land to buy books.

C Don Quixote used all his time for reading.

D Don Quixote read about one subject only.

The statements in *A, C,* and *D* are already implied or stated in the passage. B is the correct answer.

Ask students to describe some of the superheroes they've seen in films. Then invite them to brainstorm for episodes in a film that makes fun of superheroes. Encourage them to use exaggeration and distortion to heighten the humor of their invented scenes. Finally, point out that they are using techniques similar to those that Cervantes uses in his parody.

Tips to Guide Reading

Sustained Reading Stress that the purpose for reading this selection is enjoyment and that students can enhance their enjoyment by using the Reading Strategy for this selection. Suggest to them that they keep the contrast between Don Quixote's real and imagined behavior in mind as they read through to the conclusion.

Connecting Themes Across Cultures

Don Quixote is a cultural icon around the world—the idea of "chasing windmills" appears in other literature, films and TV. Discuss with students the similarities and differences between going after giants that are really windmills and going after dreams for achievement.

Customize for
English Language Learners and Less Proficient Readers

Students may have difficulty filling in the Reading Strategy chart that compares and contrasts Don Quixote with an "ideal knight." Model the process by helping students identify relevant passages. Then encourage them to jot down details that apply to each of the headings—*Ideal Knight; Don Quixote.*

Customize for
Pre-AP Students

Encourage students to distinguish the words and phrases that identify this selection as a parody. Students might then use the tale of Don Quixote as a basis to examine the qualities of parody in general, identifying other familiar literary works as parodies.

Develop Understanding

One-Minute Insight "... enchantments, quarrels, battles, challenges, wounds, wooings, loves, agonies. . . ." This list summarizes the "impossible nonsense" found in the stories of knights that Cervantes parodies. His main character is Don Quixote, an old gentleman who has gone crazy reading books of chivalry and now tries to emulate the knights of former times. He dons rusty armor, mounts a tired old horse, and calls a farm-girl his Lady. Later, he attacks a windmill he believes is a giant, ignoring the warnings of his "squire," Sancho Panza. Through Quixote, Cervantes humorously and touchingly contrasts romantic ideals with life's realities.

▶Critical Viewing◀

1 Evaluate *Don Quixote's heroic qualities are shown through his upright posture—he is prepared to do heroic battle should the need arise; his emaciated horse and the fact that he is pictured without a face seem ridiculous.*

◆Critical Thinking

2 Infer Have students draw conclusions about Quixote. *He is an impoverished gentleman who must spend all of his income to maintain an upper-class lifestyle.*

◆Critical Thinking

3 Evaluate Ask students why these remarks are humorous. *Cervantes adds an element of humor and irony by seeming to take his fictional hero seriously.*

Insight From Pat Mora

Pat Mora offers the following insight. "I often tell students how much I regret never finding work by the Spanish or Latin Americans or U.S. Latinos in my English textbooks when I was in school. This master work of world literature by Cervantes can be the occasion for discussing the richness of the above literary traditions in the Americas. Using lofty language, Cervantes makes us smile, reminding us that humor need not be limited to cartoons and sitcoms. Humor can be a literary endeavor, and certain students would enjoy the challenge of this style."

The First Part of The Ingenious Gentleman Don Quixote of La Mancha[1]

from Don Quixote

Miguel de Cervantes

Translated by John Ormsby

Don Quixote, Honoré Daumier, Neue Pinakothek, Munich

1 ▲ **Critical Viewing** What heroic qualities of Don Quixote are captured in this picture? What ridiculous qualities? **[Evaluate]**

CHAPTER I

Which Treats of the Character and Pursuits of the Famous Gentleman Don Quixote of La Mancha

In a village of La Mancha, which I prefer to leave unnamed, there lived not long ago one of those gentlemen that keep a lance in the lance-rack, an old shield, a lean hack, and a greyhound for hunting. A stew of rather more beef than mutton, hash on most nights, bacon and eggs on Saturdays, lentils on Fridays, and a pigeon or so extra on Sundays consumed three quarters of his income. The rest went for a coat of fine cloth and velvet breeches and shoes to match for holidays, while on weekdays he cut a fine figure in his best homespun. He had in his house a housekeeper past forty, a niece under twenty, and a lad for the field and marketplace, who saddled the hack as well as handled the pruning knife. The age of this gentleman of ours was bordering on fifty. He was of a hardy constitution, spare, gaunt-featured, a very early riser, and fond of hunting. Some say that his surname was Quixada or Quesada (for there is no unanimity among those who write on the subject), although reasonable conjectures tend to show that he was called Quexana. But this scarcely affects our story; it will be enough not to stray a hair's breadth from the truth in telling it.

1. **La Mancha:** Province in south central Spain.

Block Scheduling Strategies

Consider these suggestions to take advantage of extended class time:

- Use the information and examples in Build Grammar Skills (p. 882) to introduce gerunds. Suggest that students review their own writing for more examples of gerunds and gerund phrases. Have students do the Build Grammar Skills exercise on p. 890.
- Introduce the concept of parody in the Literary Focus on p. 883. You may wish to use the Literary Focus page on parody in ***Selection Support***, p. 252, for further instruction. Then have students answer the Literary Focus questions on p. 890.
- Display the sentences from Daily Language Practice for Weeks 31 and 32 on an overhead projector and have students write them correctly. Or dictate the sentences to students.
- Arrange for students to watch a video performance or listen to the soundtrack of the musical *Man of La Mancha*. The viewing or listening experience will help students complete one of the Speaking, Listening, and Viewing projects in the Idea Bank (p. 891).

You must know that the above-named gentleman devoted his leisure (which was mostly all the year round) to reading books of chivalry—and with such ardor and avidity that he almost entirely abandoned the chase and even the management of his property. To such a pitch did his eagerness and infatuation go that he sold many an acre of tillage land to buy books of chivalry to read, bringing home all he could find.

But there were none he liked so well as those written by the famous Feliciano de Silva, for their lucidity of style and complicated conceits[2] were as pearls in his sight, particularly when in his reading he came upon outpourings of adulation and courtly challenges. There he often found passages like *"the reason of the unreason with which my reason is afflicted so weakens my reason that with reason I complain of your beauty"*; or again, *"the high heavens, that of your divinity divinely fortify you with the stars, render you deserving of the desert your greatness deserves."*

> **◆ Literary Focus**
> Read this italicized passage aloud. What qualities of writing does it appear to mock?

Over this sort of folderol[3] the poor gentleman lost his wits, and he used to lie awake striving to understand it and worm out its meaning; though Aristotle[4] himself could have made out or extracted nothing, had he come back to life for that special purpose. He was rather uneasy about the wounds which Don Belianís gave and received, because it seemed to him that, however skilled the surgeons who had cured him, he must have had his face and body covered all over with seams and scars. He commended, however, the author's way of ending his book, with a promise to go on with that interminable adventure, and many a time he felt the urge to take up his pen and finish it just as its author had promised. He would no doubt have done so, and succeeded with it too, had he not been occupied with greater and more absorbing thoughts.

Many an argument did he have with the priest of his village (a learned man, and a graduate of Sigüenza[5]) as to which had been the better knight, Palmerín of England or Amadís of Gaul. Master Nicolás, the village barber, however, used to say that neither of them came up to the Knight of Phœbus, and that if there was any that could compare with *him* it was Don Galaor, the brother of Amadís of Gaul, because he had a spirit equal to every occasion, and was no wishy-washy knight or a crybaby like his brother, while in valor he was not a whit behind him. ❻

In short, he became so absorbed in his books that he spent his nights from sunset to sunrise, and his days from dawn to dark, poring over them; and what with little sleep and much reading his brain shriveled up and he lost his wits. His imagination was stuffed with all he read in his books about enchantments, quarrels, battles, challenges, wounds, wooings, loves, agonies, and all sorts of impossible nonsense. It became so firmly planted in his mind that the whole fabric of invention and fancy he read about was true, that to him no history in the world was better substantiated. He used to say the Cid Ruy Díaz[6] was a very good knight but that he was not to be compared with the Knight of the Burning Sword who with one backstroke cut in half two fierce and monstrous giants. ❼ He thought more of Bernardo del Carpio because at Roncesvalles he slew Roland in spite of enchantments, availing himself of Hercules' trick when he strangled Antæus the son of Terra in his arms. He approved highly of the giant Morgante, because, although of the giant breed which is always arrogant and

---

2. **conceits** (kən sēts′) *n.*: Elaborate comparisons or metaphors.
3. **folderol** (fäl′ də räl′) *n.*: Mere nonsense.
4. **Aristotle** (ar′ is tät′əl): Ancient Greek philosopher.
5. **Sigüenza** (sē gwän′ sä): One of a group of "minor universities" granting degrees that were often laughed at by Spanish humorists.
6. **Cid Ruy Díaz** (sēd ro͞o′ē dē′ äs): Famous Spanish soldier Ruy Diaz de Vivar: called the Cid, a derivation of the Arabic word for lord.

◆ Build Vocabulary

lucidity (lo͞o sid′ ə tē) *n.*: Clarity; ability to be understood

adulation (a′ jo͞o lā′ shən) *n.*: Excessive praise or admiration

interminable (in tʉr′ mi nə bəl) *adj.*: Lasting, or seeming to last forever

◆ Critical Thinking

❹ **Draw Conclusions** Based on this passage, what conclusions can students draw about Don Quixote's interest in books of chivalry? *Suggested responses: It is taking over his life; it is making him neglect his responsibilities.*

◆ Literary Focus

❺ **Parody** Students should note the mock loftiness of the passage and the absurd repetitions within it. They may say that Cervantes is using exaggeration to ridicule the artificiality and triteness of the typical heroic novel.

◆ Reading Strategy

❻ **Compare and Contrast** Point out that in this passage Cervantes pokes fun at certain customs and attitudes of his day. Have students identify those customs and attitudes. *Suggested responses: Cervantes might be mocking people's preoccupation with books of chivalry and their heroes.* Ask students to identify conventions of our culture that compare to the ones Cervantes mocks in this passage. *Students might observe that many people talk about film, television, and pop stars in the same way as these characters talk about knights.*

◆ Critical Thinking

❼ **Interpret** Have students express in their own words the main idea that this passage conveys. *Responses may include the following: Don Quixote can no longer distinguish between fantasy and reality; he talks about fictional characters as if they were real people.*

Read to Appreciate Author's Craft

Cervantes understood Don Quixote's passionate desire to be something that he could not be. Most people have feelings like this and can identify with his hero. All through his life, Cervantes wanted to be a great poet. He wrote twenty to thirty plays in verse in the years immediately following 1585, but he was not pleased with any of them. By the time he wrote *Don Quixote,* he had realized that he lacked poetic gifts. The absurdity and appeal of this great character at the center of a masterpiece derive not only from Cervantes's graceful style but also from his identification with his hero.

Humanities: Art

Don Quixote by Honoré Daumier.

The caricaturist, painter, and sculptor Honoré Daumier (1808–1879) is best known for his cartoons satirizing the politics and society of nineteenth century France. He found a wide audience for his cartoons attacking certain public figures and aspects of society. After 1850 Daumier produced a series of works based on *Don Quixote.* This image of Don Quixote on his horse is very loosely rendered and almost appears incomplete when compared to earlier, more detailed versions of the painting. Nevertheless, his lively use of line and texture captures the essence of the gentleman of La Mancha. Use these questions for discussion:

1. Why do you think Daumier painted Don Quixote as a faceless figure? *Sample response: In reality, Don Quixote was simply masquerading as a knight. By painting him as faceless Daumier revealed the truth about him.*
2. If you were painting a portrait of Don Quixote on his horse, how would your painting compare to this one? *Students might exaggerate details to show Quixote's foolishness, or paint Quixote as he saw himself—a regal and heroic figure.*

◆ Build Grammar Skills

1 Gerund Phrases Have students identify the gerund phrase in this sentence. *Students should identify the phrase* kicking at that traitor of a Ganelon. Then have them explain its function in the sentence. *It is the object of the preposition* of.

◆ Literary Focus

2 Parody Have students use this passage to describe the author's attitude toward his "hero," Don Quixote. Encourage them to cite specific phrases to support their responses. *Students may say that the author views Don Quixote as an outlandish, deluded, and somewhat pitiful character. In support, they may cite such phrases as "his wits being quite gone," "strangest notion," "madman," and "poor man."*

◆ Reading Strategy

3 Compare and Contrast Students may note that a traditional knight's helmet is polished, impressive-looking, fully closed, and able to withstand cuts and blows. Don Quixote's helmet, on the other hand, is a crude and improvised piece of old armor, with "a kind of half-helmet of pasteboard."

Comprehension Check 

4 Suggest that students carefully reread this difficult sentence. Then have them explain what Cervantes is saying about Don Quixote and his horse. *Although the horse is in reality a broken-down and pitiful-looking creature, in Don Quixote's eyes, it is more magnificent than the most celebrated horses from history.*

◆ Critical Thinking

5 Connect Ask: In what ways is Don Quixote's approach to naming his horse similar to his approach to outfitting himself with armor? *Elicit the following: In both cases, he uses his imagination to transform something shabby into something heroic; in both cases, he does all he can to model himself on the famous knights whom he admires.*

ill-mannered, he alone was affable and well-bred. But above all he admired Reinaldos of Montalbán, especially when he saw him sallying forth from his castle and robbing everyone he met, and when beyond the seas he stole that image of Mohammed which, as his history says, was entirely of gold. 1 To have a bout of kicking at that traitor of a Ganelon he would have given his housekeeper, and his niece into the bargain.

2 In a word, his wits being quite gone, he hit upon the strangest notion that ever madman in this world hit upon. He fancied it was right and requisite, no less for his own greater renown than in the service of his country, that he should make a knight-errant of himself, roaming the world over in full armor and on horseback in quest of adventures. He would put into practice all that he had read of as being the usual practices of knights-errant: righting every kind of wrong, and exposing himself to peril and danger from which he would emerge to reap eternal fame and glory. Already the poor man saw himself crowned by the might of his arm Emperor of Trebizond[7] at least. And so, carried away by the intense enjoyment he found in these pleasant fancies, he began at once to put his scheme into execution.

The first thing he did was to clean up some armor that had belonged to his ancestors and had for ages been lying forgotten in a corner, covered with rust and mildew. He scoured and polished it as best he could, but the one great defect he saw in it was that it had no closed helmet, nothing but a simple morion.[8] This deficiency, however, his ingenuity made good, for he contrived a kind of half-helmet of pasteboard which, fitted on to the morion, looked like a whole one. It is true that, in order to see if it was strong and fit to withstand a cut, he drew his sword and gave it a couple of slashes, the first of which undid in an instant what had taken him a week to do. The ease with which he had knocked it to pieces disconcerted him somewhat, and to guard against the danger he set to work again, fixing bars of iron on the inside until he was satisfied with its strength. Then, not caring to try any more experiments with it, he accepted and commissioned it as a helmet of the most perfect construction.

3 ◆ **Reading Strategy** Compare and contrast Don Quixote's armor with that of a traditional knight's.

He next proceeded to inspect his nag, which, with its cracked hoofs and more blemishes than the steed of Gonela, that "*tantum pellis et ossa fruit*,"[9] surpassed in his eyes the Bucephalus of Alexander or the Babieca of the Cid.[10] Four days were spent in thinking what name to give him, because (as he said to himself) it was not right that a horse belonging to a knight so famous, and one with such merits of its own, should be without some distinctive name. He strove to find something that would indicate what it had been before belonging to a knight-errant, and what it had now become. It was only reasonable that it should be given a new name to match the new career adopted by its master, and that the name should be a distinguished and full-sounding one, befitting the new order and calling it was about to follow. And so, after having composed, struck out, rejected, added to, unmade, and remade a multitude of names out of his memory and fancy, he decided upon calling it Rocinante. To his thinking this was a lofty, sonorous name that nevertheless indicated what the hack's[11]

7. **Trebizond** (treb´ i zänd´): In medieval times, a Greek empire off the southeast coast of the Black Sea.
8. **morion** (mōr´ ē än´) *n.*: Old-fashioned soldier's helmet with a brim, covering the top part of the head.

9. ***"tantum pellis et ossa fruit"*** (tän´ tum pel´ is et äs´ ə froo´ it): "It was nothing but skin and bones" (Latin).
10. **Bucephalus** (byoo sef´ ə ləs) **of Alexander or the Babieca** (bäb ē ā´ kä) **of the Cid:** Bucephalus was Alexander the Great's war horse; Babieca was the Cid's war horse.
11. **hack's:** Horse's.

◆ Build Vocabulary

affable (af´ ə bəl) *adj.*: Pleasant; friendly
sallying (sal´ ē iŋ) *v.*: Rushing forth suddenly
requisite (rek´ wə zit) *adj.*: Required by circumstances
sonorous (sə nôr´ əs) *adj.*: Having a powerful, impressive sound
veracious (və rā´ shəs) *adj.*: Truthful; accurate
vanquish (vaŋ´ kwish) *v.*: Conquer; force into submission
extolled (eks tōld´) *adj.*: Praised

Cross-Curricular Connection: History

History of Armor The first thing that Don Quixote does after deciding to become a knight-errant is to clean up some old and rusty armor that had belonged to his ancestors. The outfit that he restores would have dated from the period in which the manufacturing and use of armor reached its peak in Europe—the 1300's to the mid-1500's. After this time, gunpowder was increasingly used in battle and the production of armor, useful in hand-to-hand combat, declined.

Have students describe Don Quixote's armor, and discuss how the description reinforces his identity as a hero who does not conform to his times. You might also have groups of students research and then report on the use and design of armor in various periods and cultures, ranging from ancient Greece to Spain of the 1500's. Encourage them to provide pictures of the various types of armor when they present their reports to the class.

status had been before it became what now it was, the first and foremost of all the hacks in the world.

Having got a name for his horse so much to his taste, he was anxious to get one for himself, and he spent eight days more pondering over this point. At last he made up his mind to call himself Don Quixote—which, as stated above, led the authors of this veracious history to infer that his name quite assuredly must have been Quixada, and not Quesada as others would have it. It occurred to him, however, that the valiant Amadís was not content to call himself Amadís and nothing more but added the name of his kingdom and country to make it famous and called himself Amadís of Gaul. So he, like a good knight, resolved to add on the name of his own region and style himself Don Quixote of La Mancha. He believed that this accurately described his origin and country, and that he did it honor by taking its name for his own.

So then, his armor being furbished, his morion turned into a helmet, his hack christened, and he himself confirmed, he came to the conclusion that nothing more was needed now but to look for a lady to be in love with, for a knight-errant without love was like a tree without leaves or fruit, or a body without a soul. 6

"If, for my sins, or by my good fortune," he said to himself, "I come across some giant hereabouts, a common occurrence with knights-errant, and knock him to the ground in one onslaught, or cleave him asunder at the waist, or, in short, vanquish and subdue him, will it not be well to have someone I may send him to as a present, that he may come in and fall on his knees before my sweet lady, and in a humble, submissive voice say, 'I am the giant Caraculiambro, lord of the island of Malindrania, vanquished in single combat by the never sufficiently extolled knight Don Quixote of La Mancha, who has commanded me to present myself before your grace, that your highness may dispose of me at your pleasure'?" 7

Oh, how our good gentleman enjoyed the delivery of this speech, especially when he had thought of someone to call his lady! There was, so the story goes, in a village near his own a very good-looking farm-girl with whom he had been at one time in love, though, so far as is

Don Quixote and the Windmill, c.1900, Francisco J. Torrome

▲ **Critical Viewing** How does this picture illustrate the effects of the "shriveled brain" of the hero? **[Connect]** 8

Humanities: Art

Don Quixote and the Windmill, 1900, by Francisco J. Torrome.

This artwork by Francisco J. Torrome captures the decisive moment in the "Terrible and Undreamed-of Adventure of the Windmills." Torrome captures the comedy of this episode. Don Quixote loses his battle with the windmill and is dashed to the ground while a dismayed Sancho Panza clutches his head in the distance. The downward slant of the blades of the windmill emphasize the forward thrust of the man and the horse as they fall. The idyllic landscape behind Sancho contrasts with the chaotic scene in the foreground.

Use this question for discussion:

How does this illustration contrast Don Quixote and Sancho Panza? *Quixote perceives the windmills as monsters, while Panza—a realist—sees them for what they are. Quixote pays for his folly, while Panza is dismayed but unharmed.*

Customize for *Less Proficient Readers*

6 Point out that the author provides a brief summary at this point in the tale. Invite students to expand upon this summary by making their own general statements about Don Quixote and his actions so far. *Possible summary: Obsessed by romantic tales of chivalry, Don Quixote, a man who had led a quiet and ordinary life, prepares to embark upon new adventures as a knight-errant.*

◆ Literary Focus

7 **Parody** Encourage students to identify and discuss ways in which Cervantes parodies tales of chivalry in this passage. *Responses may include: Quixote refers to encounters with giants as "common occurrences" within such tales; he imitates the absurdly flowery style of speech in these tales when he recounts the words of the giant Caraculiambro, and he finds a pretext to refer to himself immodestly and ridiculously as "the never sufficiently extolled knight Don Quixote of La Mancha."*

►Critical Viewing◄

8 **Connect** *Students should connect the question to the earlier passage in which Cervantes reveals that the main effect of Don Quixote's "shriveled brain" is a failure to distinguish between fantasy and reality.*

Customize for *English Language Learners*

Recognizing and using gerund phrases can significantly increase fluency understanding, since gerunds can perform all the functions in sentences that nouns can. Provide English language learners with extra instruction in this skill. Then have them complete Build Grammar Skills: Gerund Phrases, p. 250 in ***Selection Support***.

Customize for *Gifted/Talented Students*

Draw a parallel between parodies and caricature, exaggerated depictions of people to create a humorous effect. Most students will know caricature from political cartoons. Have these students find examples of caricatures by classic or contemporary artists. Invite them to write short parodistic sketches based on the caricatures. Then they can show the caricature to the class and read their parodies.

◆ Literary Focus

❶ **Parody** Students may note that the object of a knight's love is traditionally a princess, queen, or other noble lady. Don Quixote's love, however, is described as a "farm-girl."

◆ Critical Thinking

❷ **Compare and Contrast** Encourage students to point out the differences between Sancho Panza and Don Quixote that are brought out in this passage. *Students may describe Sancho Panza as realistic, practical, or straightforward; Don Quixote by contrast, may be described as unrealistic, overly romantic, or totally deluded.*

◆ Reading Strategy

❸ **Compare and Contrast** In what way is the outcome of Don Quixote's battle different from the outcome a "real" knight would experience? *Students should note that Don Quixote comes away defeated and humiliated; a traditional knight would fight capably against a real foe.*

Comprehension Check ☑

❹ Point out that the "sage Freston" to whom Don Quixote refers was introduced in a chapter that precedes this episode. Then encourage students to use context clues to explain who this person is. *He is an evil magician and Don Quixote's enemy.*

◆ Build Grammar Skills

❺ **Gerund Phrases** Have students identify the gerund phrase in this passage. *Students should identify the phrase vanquishing them.* What is its function in the sentence in which it appears? *It is the object of the preposition of.*

Extending Word Study

Dictionary Don Quixote's name has entered the language as an adjective, *quixotic,* which describes behavior like the knight's. Have students use a dictionary to search for other adjectives based on proper names (and no longer capitalized), such as *oedipal, platonic, gargantuan,* and *mercurial.*

> ◆ **Literary Focus**
> ❶ How is Don Quixote's lady love a parody of the traditional fair maiden that is the object of a knight's love?

known, she never knew it nor gave a thought to the matter. Her name was Aldonza Lorenzo, and upon her he thought fit to confer the title of Lady of his Thoughts. Searching for a name not too remote from her own, yet which would aim at and bring to mind that of a princess and great lady, he decided upon calling her Dulcinea del Toboso, since she was a native of El Toboso. To his way of thinking, the name was musical, uncommon, and significant, like all those he had bestowed upon himself and his belongings.

CHAPTER VIII
Of the Good Fortune Which the Valiant Don Quixote Had in the Terrible and Undreamed-of Adventure of the Windmills, With Other Occurrences Worthy to Be Fitly Recorded

At this point they came in sight of thirty or forty windmills that are on that plain.

"Fortune," said Don Quixote to his squire, as soon as he had seen them, "is arranging matters for us better than we could have hoped. Look there, friend Sancho Panza,[12] where thirty or more monstrous giants rise up, all of whom I mean to engage in battle and slay, and with whose spoils we shall begin to make our fortunes. For this is righteous warfare, and it is God's good service to sweep so evil a breed from off the face of the earth."

"What giants?" said Sancho Panza.

"Those you see there," answered his master, "with the long arms, and some have them nearly two leagues[13] long."

❷ "Look, your worship," said Sancho. "What we see there are not giants but windmills, and what seem to be their arms are the vanes that turned by the wind make the millstone go."

"It is easy to see," replied Don Quixote, "that you are not used to this business of adventures. Those are giants, and if you are afraid, away with you out of here and betake yourself to prayer, while I engage them in fierce and unequal combat."

So saying, he gave the spur to his steed Rocinante, heedless of the cries his squire Sancho sent after him, warning him that most certainly they were windmills and not giants he was going to attack. He, however, was so positive they were giants that he neither heard the cries of Sancho, nor perceived, near as he was, what they were.

"Fly not, cowards and vile beings," he shouted, "for a single knight attacks you."

A slight breeze at this moment sprang up, and the great vanes began to move.

"Though ye flourish more arms than the giant Briareus, ye have to reckon with me!" exclaimed Don Quixote, when he saw this.

So saying, he commended himself with all his heart to his lady Dulcinea, imploring her to support him in such a peril. With lance braced and covered by his shield, he charged at Rocinante's fullest gallop and attacked the first mill that stood in front of him. But as he drove his lance-point into the sail, the wind whirled it around with such force that it shivered the lance to pieces. It swept away with it horse and rider, and they were sent rolling over the plain, in sad condition indeed.

Sancho hastened to his assistance as fast as the animal could go. When he came up he found Don Quixote unable to move, with such an impact had Rocinante fallen with him.

"God bless me!" said Sancho. "Did I not tell your worship to watch what you were doing, because they were only windmills? No one could have made any mistake about it unless he had something of the same kind in his head."

"Silence, friend Sancho," replied Don Quixote. "The fortunes of war more than any other are liable to frequent fluctuations. Moreover I think, and it is the truth, that that same sage Frestón who carried off my study and books, has turned these giants into mills in order to rob me of the glory of vanquishing them, such is the enmity he bears me. But in the end his wicked arts will avail but little against my good sword."

12. Sancho Panza: A simple country man whom Don Quixote takes as his squire. In contrast to Don Quixote, Panza is practical and has common sense.
13. leagues: A league is about three miles.

Speaking, Listening, and Viewing Mini-Lesson

Role Play

This mini-lesson supports the Speaking, Listening, and Viewing activity in the Idea Bank on p. 891.

Introduce Don Quixote and Sancho Panza go in quest of adventures together, but the two have very different views of the world—as indicated by the scene in which Sancho tries to talk Don Quixote out of attacking the windmills.

Develop Have students analyze the conversation that occurs before Don Quixote charges the windmills. They can identify the main points each character makes as well as the traits each shows.

Apply Have students work in pairs to prepare their role plays. Suggest that partners create their own versions of the scene by elaborating on the points and traits they identified. Encourage them also to use both facial expressions and gestures to help communicate the personality traits of the characters.

Assess Let students evaluate their own and their classmate's work. After each performance you might ask: Did the scene bring out the contrasts between the two characters? How did it show these contrasts?

"God's will be done," said Sancho Panza, and helping him to rise got him up again on Rocinante, whose shoulder was half dislocated. Then, discussing the adventure, they followed the road to Puerto Lápice, for there, said Don Quixote, they could not fail to find adventures in abundance and variety, as it was a well-traveled thoroughfare. For all that, he was much grieved at the loss of his lance, and said so to his squire.

> ◆ *Literature and Your Life*
> How has Don Quixote let his books "go to his head"? Can you relate to his feelings?

"I remember having read," he added, "how a Spanish knight, Diego Pérez de Vargas by name, having broken his sword in battle, tore from an oak a ponderous bough or branch. With it he did such things that day, and pounded so many Moors, that he got the surname of Machuca, and he and his descendants from that day forth were called Vargas y Machuca. I mention this because from the first oak I see I mean to tear such a branch, large and stout. I am determined and resolved to do such deeds with it that you may deem yourself very fortunate in being found worthy to see them and be an eyewitness of things that will scarcely be believed."

"Be that as God wills," said Sancho, "I believe it all as your worship says it. But straighten yourself a little, for you seem to be leaning to one side, maybe from the shaking you got when you fell."

"That is the truth," said Don Quixote, "and if I make no complaint of the pain it is because knights-errant are not permitted to complain of any wound, even though their bowels be coming out through it."

"If so," said Sancho, "I have nothing to say. But God knows I would rather your worship complained when anything ailed you. For my part, I confess I must complain however small the ache may be, unless this rule about not complaining applies to the squires of knights-errant also." 7

Don Quixote could not help laughing at his squire's simplicity, and assured him he might complain whenever and however he chose, just as he liked. So far he had never read of anything to the contrary in the order of knighthood.

Sancho reminded him it was dinner time, to which his master answered that he wanted nothing himself just then, but that Sancho might eat when he had a mind. With this permission Sancho settled himself as comfortably as he could on his beast, and taking out of the saddlebags what he had stowed away in them, he jogged along behind his master munching slowly. From time to time he took a pull at the wineskin with all the enjoyment that the thirstiest tavernkeeper in Málaga might have envied. And while he went on in this way, between gulps, he never gave a thought to any of the promises his master had made him, nor did he rate it as hardship but rather as recreation going in quest of adventures, however dangerous they might be.

Guide for Responding

◆ *Literature and Your Life*

Reader's Response Which aspect of Don Quixote's appearance or behavior do you think is most ridiculous? Why?

Thematic Focus How does Don Quixote's imagination both create obstacles and help him overcome them?

☑ Check Your Comprehension

1. What sorts of books does Don Quixote read?
2. What unusual decision does Don Quixote make as a result of his reading?
3. What sent Don Quixote and his horse rolling across the plain?

Beyond the Selection

FURTHER READING

Other Works by Miguel de Cervantes

La Galatea
Exemplary Novels
Eight Comedies and Eight Entremeses

Other Works About the Power of Imagination

"The Secret Life of Walter Mitty," James Thurber
"Ode on a Grecian Urn," John Keats
"The Legend of Sleepy Hollow," Washington Irving

We suggest that you preview these works before recommending them to students.

INTERNET

We recommend the following site on the Internet (all Web sites are subject to change).

For background information on Don Quixote, a "tour" of historic editions, and a collection of illustrations, go to: **http://milton.mse.jhu.edu:8003/quixote/index/html**

We *strongly recommend* that you preview this site before you send students to it.

◆ *Literature and Your Life*

6 Students may say that Don Quixote has let his books "go to his head" to the point that he models his life on them. They may be able to relate to his fascination with an idealized fictional world and its heroes but not to the extremes to which he goes.

◆ Critical Thinking

7 **Infer** Encourage students to use this passage to make inferences about Sancho Panza. *Inferences may include these: He is a realist; he has no illusions about being heroic or extraordinary; he is a down-to-earth person; he is sympathetic and respectful toward Don Quixote.*

Reteach

The contrast between Don Quixote's ideals and reality is strong. Students who find Cervantes's irony difficult to grasp, as well as visual/spatial learners, may benefit from the use of a Venn diagram. The overlap of the diagram's two circles will show what the ideals and reality have in common.

Reinforce and Extend

Answers

◆ *Literature and Your Life*

Reader's Response Students might find it most ridiculous when Don Quixote confuses the windmills for monsters that must be vanquished, and he charges at them.

Thematic Focus On the one hand, Quixote's imagination causes him to imagine unreal threats, making windmills into monsters. However, he overcomes "obstacles" with imaginative explanations as when he says sage Freston (the magician) turned the monsters into windmills to humiliate him.

☑ Check Your Comprehension

1. He reads tales of chivalry.
2. He decides to become a knight-errant.
3. He pierced a windmill sail with his lance and the wind whirled it around with such force that Don Quixote and his horse went flying.

Answers
◆ Critical Thinking

1. Reading books about chivalry has filled Don Quixote's mind with delusions about himself.
2. By using special names for people and things Don Quixote inflates their status.
3. He sees the windmills as giants because he is delusional and his need to perform a chivalrous act is so great.
4. Seeing things as they are, he keeps his master from even greater danger.
5. This approach enables one to be happy in one's own world, however, it is also unrealistic and dangerous.
6. Students are likely to refer to career guides, course catalogues, books or Web sites that focus on a particular field.

◆ Reading Strategy

1. Sample response: In his own mind, Quixote was like the knights of old in that he was well-bred, honorable, and adventurous.
2. Don Quixote is older, more pretentious, and certainly less sane than his idealized image of a knight.
3. The contrast tells us that Cervantes took an ironic and cynical view of chivalry—he probably thought it a pompous and outdated medieval convention.

◆ Literary Focus

1. Through his detailed description of Don Quixote dressing in rusty armor, Cervantes pokes fun at the way knights dressed.
2. It is an example of parody because it shows how a real knight would attack a real monster, but the effort becomes a mockery when the monster turns out to be a windmill.
3. Cervantes parodies knights' names by having Don Quixote call himself Don Quixote of la Mancha; he parodies knights' fine horses by giving the delusional Quixote an emaciated nag; he parodies the social status of knights' ladies by making Quixote's lady a farm-girl; he parodies knights' battles by putting Quixote in battle with a windmill.

Guide for Responding (continued)

◆ Critical Thinking

Interpret

1. How has reading books about chivalry affected Don Quixote's mind? **[Analyze]**
2. Why does Don Quixote like to use special names for people and things? **[Infer]**
3. What makes Don Quixote see the windmills as giant monsters? **[Speculate]**
4. Why is Sancho Panza a particularly helpful squire to Don Quixote? **[Deduce]**

Evaluate

5. Don Quixote makes the world fit his illusions. What are the advantages and dangers of such an approach to life? **[Evaluate]**

Extend

6. Don Quixote tries to learn about being a knight from reading romantic, fictional accounts. What sources would you use to find out about a career that interested you? **[Career Link]**

◆ Reading Strategy

Compare and Contrast

To see the humor of *Don Quixote*, **compare and contrast** the elements of the parody with the original. Look for similarities and differences between Don Quixote and the "ideal knight."

1. In what ways is Don Quixote, at least in his own mind, similar to the knights of old?
2. In what general ways does Don Quixote contrast with his idealized image of a knight?
3. What does this contrast tell us about Cervantes's view of chivalry?

◆ Literary Focus

Parody

Cervantes creates a **parody** of the literature of chivalry by ridiculing the behavior of knights and suggesting that chivalrous ideals are pure illusion.

1. How does Cervantes poke fun at the way knights dressed?
2. How is the incident with the windmills an example of parody?
3. What specific aspects of chivalry does Cervantes parody? Give examples.

◆ Build Vocabulary

Using the Latin Root *-son-*

Knowing that the Latin root *-son-* means "hearing or sound," match each word with its definition. On your paper, write the correct definition next to each numbered word.

1. sonic	**a.** unity of sound
2. consonance	**b.** not in harmony
3. dissonant	**c.** having to do with sound
4. unison	**d.** harmony of musical tones

Using the Word Bank: Synonyms

On your paper, write the word from the Word Bank whose meaning is closest to that of the words below.

1. necessary	**6.** unending
2. dashing forth	**7.** honest
3. friendly	**8.** conquer
4. resonant	**9.** clearness
5. praised	**10.** excessive praise

◆ Build Grammar Skills

Gerunds and Gerund Phrases

A **gerund** is a verb form ending in *-ing* used as a noun. A **gerund phrase** includes all the words that go with the gerund. Gerunds and gerund phrases perform all the same roles in a sentence that a noun does: subject, direct or indirect object, object of preposition, and appositive.

Practice Copy the following sentences in your notebook. Underline the gerunds or gerund phrases. Identify the function of each gerund or gerund phrase in the sentence.

1. It will be enough not to stray from the truth in telling it.
2. He commends the author's way of ending his books.
3. He follows the usual practice of knights: righting wrongs and exposing himself to all kinds of danger.
4. On his journey, Don Quixote tries attacking windmills.
5. Eating is one of Sancho's greatest pleasures.

◆ Build Vocabulary

Using the Latin Root *-son-*

1. c 2. d 3. b 4. a

Using the Word Bank

1. requisite	6. interminable
2. sallying	7. veracious
3. affable	8. vanquish
4. sonorous	9. lucidity
5. extolled	10. adulation

◆ Build Grammar Skills

1. It will be enough not to stray from the truth in telling it. (object of preposition *in*)
2. He commends the author's way of ending his books. (object of preposition *of*)
3. He follows the usual practice of knights: righting wrongs and exposing himself to all kinds of danger. (appositive—further explains "the usual practice of knights")
4. On his journey, Don Quixote tries attacking windmills. (direct object)
5. Eating is one of Sancho's greatest pleasures. (subject)

Grammar Reinforcement

For additional instruction, use pp. 44–45 on Gerunds and Gerund Phrases in the *Writer's Solution Grammar Practice Book.*

Build Your Portfolio

Idea Bank

Writing

1. Definition of a Hero Write a definition of a modern hero. Include the qualities that you think people of today admire. Give examples from movies, sports, or entertainment to illustrate your points.

2. Don Quixote in America Suppose Don Quixote were to wander into your community for his next adventure. Write one or two paragraphs describing problems he might encounter.

3. Create a Scene In another scene from the novel, Don Quixote decides a flock of sheep is an enemy army and charges! Write the dialogue Don Quixote and Sancho might have had before or after the charge.

Speaking, Listening, and Viewing

4. Role Play Role-play the scene in which Sancho tries to talk Don Quixote out of attacking the windmills. **[Performing Arts Link]**

5. Musical Drama The musical *Man of La Mancha* is based on the character Don Quixote. Watch a video performance, noting how the story's theme is portrayed visually. Then discuss what the songs reveal about the hero's infatuation with romantic ideals. Share your conclusions with the class. **[Music Link]**

Researching and Representing

6. Cartoon Reread the description of Don Quixote's armor and horse. Then draw a cartoon of the forlorn-looking knight astride Rocinante as they joust the windmill. **[Art Link]**

7. Visual Essay Create a visual essay on the theme of heroes. Use photos from magazines and newspapers. Write captions that illustrate how your examples and opinions relate to a central message about heroes. **[Social Studies Link]**

Online Activity www.phlit.phschool.com

Guided Writing Lesson

Sketch of a Comic Hero

The typical hero of a work of literature—whether warrior, political leader, great athlete, or something else—usually has one defining characteristic: He or she is very serious. The quest or challenge that the hero undertakes is also one of the gravest import. Cervantes, however, turned the entire genre of the heroic tale on its head when he created his comic hero Don Quixote. In the spirit of Cervantes, create a comic hero and write a **sketch** of that hero. Describe your hero's character traits and achievements.

Writing Skills Focus: Clear and Logical Organization

To present your hero in a sketch, you'll need a **clear and logical organization**. For instance, you might want to describe the hero's life and exploits chronologically. Or you may discuss your hero's attributes in order of importance, starting from the least important and moving to the most. Whatever method you choose, use it consistently for the entire sketch.

Prewriting Start by creating a character chart like the one below, using it to categorize the various character traits of your hero. Underneath each trait, give an example that you can use in your draft.

Trait:	Example:
Nearsighted	Attempts to slay windmills
Absorbed in heroic books	Thinks of himself as a great hero

Drafting Begin your profile with a catchy introduction, such as a quotation, question, or anecdote that illustrates a humorous quality of your hero. Then discuss qualities of your hero and give examples of each.

Revising Ask a peer whether your sketch conveys the comic qualities of your hero. If not, add further details to show those qualities.

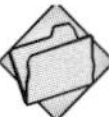

Idea Bank

Following are suggestions for matching Idea Bank topics with your students' performance levels and learning modalities:

Customizing for Performance Levels

Less Advanced Students: 1, 4
Average Students: 2, 5, 6
More Advanced Students: 3, 7

Customizing for Learning Modalities

Following are suggestions for matching Idea Bank topics with your students' learning modalities:
Musical/Rhythmic: 5
Verbal/Linguistic: 1, 2, 3, 4, 5
Visual/Spatial: 6, 7

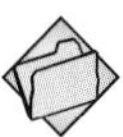

Guided Writing Lesson

Prewriting Strategy Help students organize their character sketches in a clear and logical manner, by giving them 4–5 notecards on which to write character traits. Have students list one attribute per card; they might also jot down their examples on the cards. They can then arrange and rearrange the cards to determine the most logical organization for their sketches, as well as deciding which attribute can be described as the catchiest introduction.

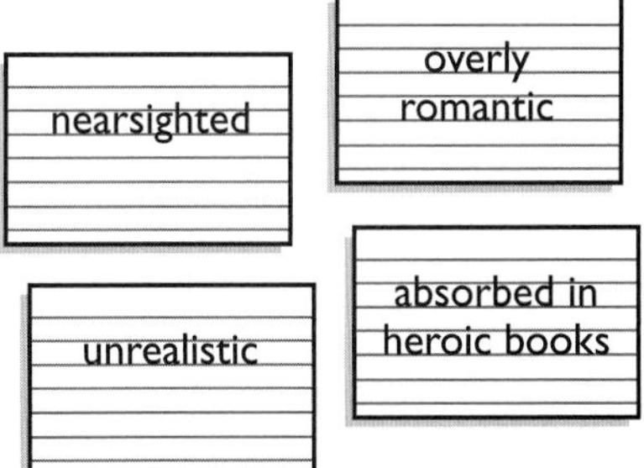

For more prewriting, elaboration, and revision strategies, see *Prentice Hall Writing and Grammar.*

Writing Lab CD-ROM

Students can use these steps to complete the Descriptive Writing tutorial:

1. Have students use the Word Bins activity to see examples of character trait words they might use in their sketch of a comic hero.
2. Have students compose their sketches on the computer.
3. Have students refer to the peer review guidelines and checklist during peer review.

✓ ASSESSMENT OPTIONS

Formal Assessment, Selection Test, pp. 217–219, and Assessment Resources Software. The selection test is designed so that it can be easily customized to the performance levels of your students.

Alternative Assessment, p. 61, includes options for less advanced students, more advanced students, intrapersonal learners and verbal/linguistic learners.

PORTFOLIO ASSESSMENT

Use the following rubrics in the ***Alternative Assessment*** booklet to assess student writing:
Definition of a Hero: Definition/Classification Rubric, p. 99
Don Quixote in America: Problem-Solution Rubric, p. 101
Create a Scene: Fictional Narrative Rubric, p. 95
Guided Writing Lesson: Description Rubric, p. 97

Prepare and Engage

LESSON OBJECTIVES

1. To develop vocabulary and word identification skills
- Latin Suffixes: *-ous*
- Using the Word Bank: Synonyms
- Extending Word Study: Dictionary (ATE)

2. To use a variety of reading strategies to comprehend epics and legends
- Connect Your Experience
- Reading Strategy: Recognize an Author's Attitude
- Tips to Guide Reading: Whisper Read (ATE)
- Read to Be Entertained (ATE)
- Idea Bank: List

3. To increase knowledge of other cultures and to connect common elements across cultures
- Connecting Themes Across Cultures (ATE)
- Background for Understanding

4. To express and support responses to the text
- Critical Thinking
- Analyze Literary Criticism
- Idea Bank: Music
- Idea Bank: Local Legends

5. To analyze literary elements
- Literary Focus: Legends

6. To read in order to research self-selected and assigned topics
- Questions for Research
- Viewing and Representing Mini-Lesson: Feudalism Chart (ATE)
- Research Skills Mini-Lesson: Evaluating Sources (ATE)

7. To plan, prepare, organize, and present literary interpretations
- Idea Bank: Art
- Speaking, Listening, and Viewing: Oral Reading

8. To use recursive writing processes to write a letter
- Guided Writing Lesson

9. To increase knowledge of the rules of grammar and usage
- Build Grammar Skills: Subjunctive Mood

Test Preparation

Writing Skills: Style (ATE, p. 893) The teaching tips and sample test item in this workshop support the instruction and practice in the unit workshop:

Writing Skills: Strategy, Organization, and Style (SE, p. 951)

Guide for Reading

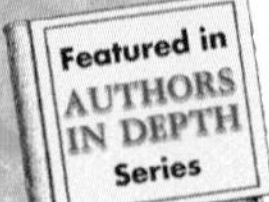

Alfred, Lord Tennyson *(1809–1892)*

The fourth son of twelve children, Tennyson was born in Lincolnshire, England. After preparing for college at his clergyman father's home, he attended Cambridge University for a few years, but strained family finances forced him to withdraw before receiving a degree. Living at home, he perfected his craft as a poet, experimenting with different poetic forms. From 1850 to his death, he enjoyed a popular and enthusiastic following for his exquisite short lyrics and powerful longer works. The subjects of his poems are widely drawn from the biblical and classical eras as well as events of his time. The "Morte d'Arthur" is the most famous excerpt from his epic *Idylls of the King*, a set of twelve narrative poems based on the Arthurian legends.

T. H. White *(1906–1964)*

Terence Hanbury White's interesting life began in Bombay, India. At the age of thirty, he resigned his teaching position to devote himself to his many interests. These included flying airplanes, deep-sea diving, falconry, knitting, jumping horses, and, of course, writing. Many of these skills and hobbies later found their way into his writing. His most famous work, from which "Arthur Becomes King of Britain" is taken, is the four-part novel *The Once and Future King* (1958), a comic retelling of the Arthurian legends originally written down 500 years earlier by Sir Thomas Malory. *The Once and Future King* inspired the musical *Camelot* (1960) as well as the movie *Monty Python and the Holy Grail* (1974).

◆ Build Vocabulary

Latin Suffixes: *-ous*

In "Arthur Becomes King of Britain," one of the characters, a young man named Kay, in his preparations to be knighted, takes a *sumptuous* bath. *Sumptuous* combines the Latin word *sumptus*, meaning "expense," with the suffix *-ous*, which means "like" or "pertaining to." *Sumptuous*, which means "magnificent; splendid," pertains to the expense of something. There are dozens of other words with the Latin suffix *-ous*, such as *slanderous* (relating to slander) and *adventurous* (relating to adventure).

Word Bank

As you read these selections, you will encounter the words in this list. Each word is defined on the page where it first appears. Preview the list before you read.

lamentation
swarthy
stickler
sumptuous
palfrey

◆ Build Grammar Skills

Subjunctive Mood

As you read "Arthur Becomes King of Britain" and "Morte d'Arthur," you'll see examples of verbs in the **subjunctive mood**. The subjunctive mood has two purposes. The first is to state a wish or condition that is contrary to fact, usually in clauses beginning with *if*, *as if*, or *as though*.

The past subjunctive of the verb *be* is always *were*, not *was*, regardless of the subject:

The Wart went as pale as Sir Kay was, and looked as if he *were* going to strike him.

The subjunctive mood is also used in clauses beginning with *that* to express, indirectly, a demand, recommendation, suggestion, or statement of necessity:

To prove his worth, it was required that Wart *remove* the sword.

Here, the verb is always the base form. It does not change, regardless of the subject.

Prentice Hall Literature Program Resources

REINFORCE / RETEACH / EXTEND

Selection Support Pages
Build Vocabulary: Suffixes *-ous*, p. 253
Build Grammar Skills: Subjunctive Mood, p. 254
Reading Strategy: Author's Attitude, p. 255
Literary Focus: Legend, p. 256

Strategies for Diverse Student Needs
"Morte d'Arthur," "Arthur Becomes King," p. 62

Beyond Literature
Courage, Honesty, and Compassion, p. 62

Formal Assessment Selection Test, pp. 220–222; Assessment Resources Software

Alternative Assessment, p. 62

Writing and Language Transparencies
Writing Process Model 9: Business Letter, pp. 61–64

Resource Pro CD-ROM

Listening to Literature Audiocassettes

Morte d'Arthur ◆ Arthur Becomes King of Britain

◆ Literature and Your Life

Connect Your Experience

The heroes you admire reveal a great deal about what's important to you. Arthur's legend has made him a hero to many people to whom courage, honesty, and compassion are important.

Journal Writing List three people you see as heroes. Give at least two reasons why you consider each a hero.

Thematic Focus: From the Past

According to the legend, before Arthur formed the Round Table, knights went around fighting for the sake of fighting. The Arthurian tradition has given following generations a model for using strength for a good cause.

◆ Background for Understanding

History

The real King Arthur was most likely a British chieftain who defeated the Saxons in a decisive battle in A.D. 518. For years afterward, bards across England and Wales sang about his exploits. In 1138, Geoffrey of Monmouth celebrated Arthur's real and imagined triumphs in his *History of the Kings of Britain*. Around the same time, French troubadours elaborated on the tales by adding Lady Guinevere and the Knights of the Round Table. The enriched legends then returned to England, where Thomas Malory (1400–1471) reworked them in his *Le Morte d'Arthur* (French for "The Death of Arthur").

◆ Literary Focus

Legend

A **legend** is a popular story handed down for generations. Most legends have some basis in historical fact, which usually has become obscured or lost through centuries of retelling and embellishment. Artists, poets, screenwriters, and novelists often turn to legends for inspiration. T. H. White, for example, based his novel *The Once and Future King* on the Arthurian legends, and Alfred, Lord Tennyson uses the same source for his epic poem *The Idylls of the King*.

◆ Reading Strategy

Recognize an Author's Attitude

All writers have a particular attitude toward their subjects. Recognizing the **author's attitude** will give you an insight into the work.

The author's attitude is the way he or she feels about the subject. This attitude is reflected in the way the author interprets and presents characters and events. If the author admires and respects the subject, for example, then the author will present the details in such a way that you, the reader, will also admire and respect the subject.

To recognize an author's attitude, notice the details and events the author chooses to present, and think about the message the author conveys—either directly or indirectly—through this information.

As you read "Morte d'Arthur" look for clues that show the author's serious and respectful attitude toward his subject. Then, as you read "Arthur Becomes King of Britain" consider how White's attitude is quite different.

Test Preparation Workshop

Writing Skills: Style

Standardized tests often ask students to demonstrate their knowledge of writing skills. Style questions focus on appropriate and effective use of language. Give students this sample test question.

If thou shouldst never see my face again,
Pray for my soul. More things are wrought by prayer
Than this world dreams of. Wherefore, let thy voice
Rise like a fountain for me night and day.

Tennyson's tone in this speech by Arthur to Sir Bedivere is best described as—

A sentimental **C** stern
B pessimistic **D** exalted

Guide students to see that D is the correct answer here. The dying Arthur is not speaking sternly, *C*, but with exaltation, *D*, to say that Sir Bedivere should pray; Arthur does not face death with pessimism, *B*. There is nothing sentimental, *A*, about this particular expression of belief, even if one disagrees with it.

If possible, show a portion of *Monty Python and the Holy Grail* followed by a scene from *Camelot*. Ask students to compare and contrast the versions. Students will notice that plot details and language differ, and the writers have different attitudes toward the subject. Point out that this comically irreverent movie and romantic musical share the same source as Tennyson's formal and elegant "Morte d'Arthur." and T.H. White's "Arthur Becomes King of Britain."

Tips to Guide Reading

Whisper Read Have students whisper read "Morte d'Arthur" as you listen for their understanding of the narrative quality of the epic poem.

Connecting Themes Across Cultures

Throughout the Victorian period in England, many people longed for an older, pre-industrial period, when (they thought) people's lives had more meaning and spirituality. This longing resulted in an intense interest in everything medieval. Have students identify contemporary groups who would like to see a return to older times and earlier values.

Customize for *Less Proficient Readers*

Suggest to students that "Morte d'Arthur" needs special attention because of its stylized language. Direct them to read the vocabulary notes before reading a passage, keep a running summary of the poem and a list of puzzling words and phrases as they read (with the numbers of the lines where they appear) to review after they have finished the legend.

Customize for *Pre-AP Students*

These selections relate elements of the same legend from divergent viewpoints and attitudes. Have students think about how White and Tennyson might have responded to each other's material. Which elements might have been useful to them in creating their own work, and which elements might they have responded to negatively?

Develop Understanding

One-Minute Insight A legend works on many levels. Readers may see the story of King Arthur as a saga of knights and battles or as a fantasy of wizards and magic. Tennyson stressed the affirmation of ageless moral principals such as goodness, honor, loyalty, honesty, and bravery. He lived when scientific speculation had cast doubts on religious matters. To him, it was important that Arthur shine forth as a beacon of moral goodness in an increasingly skeptical world.

He ties this ancient legend to his world by telling a story within a story: Several friends, while sitting around the fire on Christmas Eve, prevail upon the poet in the group to share his retelling of the Arthur legend. The poet finally agrees to share one portion of the story. He then tells the story of Arthur's death, and Sir Bedivere's obedience to the dying king's last request. Like the men around the fire, Bedivere mourns the passing of an age, the death of all that seems noble and true. As the tale winds to a close, Arthur's funeral barge floats away and the friends are roused from their rapt involvement in the tale. Tennyson ends on an optimistic note, with bells singing out a return of Arthur and what he represented.

❶ **Clarification** The author frames the telling of "Morte d'Arthur" in his own era. The poem opens late on Christmas Eve after the festivities are done. A group of friends is sad that in modern times the serious aspects of Christmas are neglected in favor of games and lighter interests. The friends include the narrator (Tennyson), Francis (Frank) Allen (the host), Holmes (a parson), and Everard Hall (the poet who will read his tale of King Arthur).

Comprehension Check ✓

❷ What reason does Hall give for thinking his books are of little value? *Styles and forms in poetry change over time, just as the creations of nature do. Hall thinks that his poems are old-fashioned and therefore not worth saving.*

Morte d'Arthur

Alfred, Lord Tennyson

The Epic

At Francis Allen's on the Christmas eve—
The game of forfeits[1] done—the girls all kissed
Beneath the sacred bush[2] and passed away—
The parson Holmes, the poet Everard Hall,
❶ The host, and I sat round the wassail bowl,[3]
Then halfway ebbed; and there we held a talk,
How all the old honor had from Christmas gone,
Or gone or dwindled down to some odd games
In some odd nooks like this; till I, tired out
With cutting eights[4] that day upon the pond,
Where, three times slipping from the outer edge,
I bumped the ice into three several stars,
Fell in a doze; and half-awake I heard
The parson taking wide and wider sweeps,
Now harping on the church commissioners,
Now hawking at geology and schism;[5]
Until I woke, and found him settled down
Upon the general decay of faith
Right through the world: "at home was little left,
And none abroad; there was no anchor, none,
To hold by." Francis, laughing, clapped his hand
On Everard's shoulder, with "I hold by him."
"And I," quoth Everard, "by the wassail-bowl."
"Why yes," I said, "we knew your gift that way
At college; but another which you had—
I mean of verse (for so we held it then),
What came of that?" "You know," said Frank, "he burnt
His epic, his King Arthur, some twelve books"—
And then to me demanding why: "O, sir,
He thought that nothing new was said, or else
Something so said 'twas nothing—that a truth
Looks freshest in the fashion of the day;
God knows; he has a mint of reasons; ask.
It pleased *me* well enough." "Nay, nay," said Hall,
"Why take the style of those heroic times?
For nature brings not back the mastodon,[6]
❷ Nor we those times; and why should any man
Remodel models? these twelve books of mine

1. **forfeits** (fôr′ fits) *n.*: Game in which something is taken away as a penalty for making a mistake.
2. **sacred bush:** Mistletoe.
3. **wassail bowl** (wäs′ əl bōl′) *n.*: Punch bowl.
4. **cutting eights:** Ice-skating so that skates cut figure eights in the ice.
5. **schism** (siz′ əm) *n.*: Division within an organization, especially a church, because of a difference of opinion.
6. **mastodon** (mas′ tə dän′) *n.*: Extinct animal resembling the elephant but larger.

Block Scheduling Strategies

Consider these suggestions to take advantage of extended class time:

- Before students read, have discussion groups exchange ideas on a hero's attributes. Then have them work on the Journal Writing activity in Literature and Your Life (p. 893). Encourage them to think of ways in which heroes are similar.
- Suggest that students apply the Reading Strategy, Recognize an Author's Attitude, to these pages. Have them answer the Reading Strategy questions on p. 915 and follow up with the Reading Strategy page in ***Selection Support***, p. 255.
- Show portions of *A Connecticut Yankee in King Arthur's Court, Camelot,* and *Monty Python and the Holy Grail.* Encourage students to compare plot details and authors' attitudes.
- Have students writer letters of recommendation, using the Guided Writing Lesson on p. 916. Provide them with an elaboration strategy, using the instruction notes on p. 916 of the ATE.

The Dream of Arthur in Avalon (detail), Sir Edward Burne-Jones, The Museo de Arte de Ponce, The Luis A. Ferré Foundation, Inc. Ponce, Puerto Rico

3 ▲ Critical Viewing What does this picture tell you about the circumstances of Arthur's death? **[Infer]**

▶Critical Viewing◀

3 Infer Elicit responses such as the following: *Arthur is mourned by several stately women, several of whom wear royal crowns. Their positions and expressions show grief, but they are formal, rather than natural. Arthur's passing appears as a ritual.*

Customize for *Pre-AP Students*

Ask students to analyze lines 13–22 and suggest why a mid-nineteenth century parson might tie "geology" to a "decay of faith." *Students should recognize that geology represents science, which is often, but not necessarily, seen as being in opposition to religion and faith.*

Customize for *English Language Learners*

Both of these pieces could be challenging for these students. Tennyson uses old language forms, such as the second person singular pronouns and verbs, as in *thou wouldst,* as well as old-fashioned words. White's characters speak everything from Cockney dialect ("Nah then, one-two, special mourning for 'is lite majesty, lower awai on all the standards…") to upper-class chitchat. Have English language learners work with students proficient in English to identify unfamiliar turns of phrase and speech patterns; they should write what these phrases state as well as what they imply.

Customize for *Gifted/Talented Students*

Have these students follow the example of Everard Hall in Tennyson's poem and write a brief passage of unrhymed blank verse (iambic pentameter) describing some historical moment that other students will recognize. Challenge them to use *thou* and *thee* with the correct verb forms. Have them read their verses to the students for discussion and peer evaluation.

Humanities: Art

The Dream of Arthur in Avalon by Sir Edward Burne-Jones.

It is not surprising that the British Pre-Raphaelite painter Sir Edward Coley Burne-Jones (1833–1898) chose this scene from Arthurian legend as a painting subject—he was known for his enthusiasm for the medieval. The subject of this painting is taken from Malory's *Morte d'Arthur*.

Burne-Jones's dreamy, romantic "literary" style, executed in a flat technique, was effective not only in painting but in stained glass, tapestry, mosaic, and relief—all media that interested medieval artists as well.

Use this question for discussion:

What seems to be happening to King Arthur in this picture? How do you know? *Students might say that King Arthur is on his death bed. His dream might be of paradise.*

Comprehension Check ☑

❶ Ask students to paraphrase this passage. *At the narrator's request Francis, the host, gets Hall's poem. Hall is persuaded to read his work aloud. After expressing doubt on the quality, Hall reads in a clear, resonant voice.*

◆ Reading Strategy

❷ **Recognize an Author's Attitude** Suggested response: The formal language and dramatic images seem to indicate that Tennyson's attitude toward this subject is reverent and respectful. The image of the broken cross in a ruined chapel is the author's way of creating the feeling that Arthur's defeat is also the defeat of goodness and virtue.

◆ Critical Thinking

❸ **Speculate** Invite students to conjecture why Arthur doubts that there shall be no "talk of knightly deeds" in the future. *All of Arthur's knights have been killed except for Sir Bedivere. With Arthur himself mortally wounded, the ways of preserving a world of brave and noble acts are about to vanish.*

◆ Critical Thinking

❹ **Evaluate** Invite students to consider how the use of modern words, like "wounded" and "helmet" in place of old-fashioned words such as "smitten" and "helm," would have affected this passage. *Suggested response: The old-fashioned words stress the gulf in time between the story of King Arthur and today. This kind of language gives the poem a solemn, serious tone.*

Were faint Homeric echoes,[7] nothing-worth,
Mere chaff and draff,[8] much better burnt." "But I,"
Said Francis, "picked the eleventh from this hearth,
And have it; keep a thing, its use will come.
I hoard it as a sugarplum for Holmes."
He laughed, and I, though sleepy, like a horse
That hears the corn-bin open, pricked my ears;
For I remembered Everard's college fame
When we were Freshmen. Then at my request
He brought it; and the poet, little urged,
❶ But with some prelude of disparagement,
Read, mouthing out his hollow o's and a's,
Deep-chested music, and to this result.

Morte d'Arthur

So all day long the noise of battle rolled
Among the mountains by the winter sea,
Until King Arthur's table, man by man,
Had fallen in Lyonnesse[9] about their lord,
King Arthur; then, because his wound was deep,
The bold Sir Bedivere uplifted him,
Sir Bedivere, the last of all his knights,
And bore him to a chapel nigh the field,
A broken chancel[10] with a broken cross,
That stood on a dark strait of barren land.
On one side lay the ocean, and on one
Lay a great water, and the moon was full.
Then spake King Arthur to Sir Bedivere:
"The sequel of today unsolders[11] all
The goodliest fellowship of famous knights
❸ Whereof this world holds record. Such a sleep
They sleep—the men I loved. I think that we
Shall never more, at any future time,
Delight our souls with talk of knightly deeds,
Walking about the gardens and the halls
Of Camelot, as in the days that were.
I perish by this people which I made—
Though Merlin sware that I should come again
To rule once more—but let what will be be,
I am so deeply smitten through the helm[12]
That without help I cannot last till morn.
❹ Thou therefore take my brand[13] Excalibur,
Which was my pride; for thou rememberest how
In those old days, one summer noon, an arm
Rose up from out the bosom of the lake,
Clothed in white samite,[14] mystic, wonderful,
Holding the sword—and how I rowed across
And took it, and have worn it, like a king;
And, wheresoever I am sung or told

7. Homeric echoes (hō mer′ ik ek′ ōs): Imitations of the poems of the Greek poet Homer (of about the eighth century B.C.).

8. chaff and draff: Anything worthless; dregs.

❷ **◆ Reading Strategy** What is Tennyson's attitude toward his subject? How can you tell?

9. Lyonnesse (lī′ ə nes′): Legendary country off the southwestern coast of England, supposed to have sunk beneath the sea.

10. chancel (chan′ səl) *n.*: Part of a church around the altar.

11. unsolders (un säd′ ərs) *v.*: Separates.

12. helm: Helmet.

13. brand: Sword.

14. samite (sam′ īt) *n.*: Heavy silk fabric.

Speaking, Listening, and Viewing Mini-Lesson

Oral Report

This mini-lesson supports the Speaking, Listening, and Viewing activity in the Idea Bank on p. 916.

Introduce Ask students to describe their impressions of poetry read aloud. Discuss elements that make it effective. Have students select a passage from "Morte d'Arthur" to read orally.

Develop To help students develop their oral readings, suggest that they do the following:

- Work by themselves in front of a mirror to polish gestures and expressions.
- Record themselves to listen for awkward spots to be improved for their final presentations.
- Practice with partners, making suggestions to improve the presentations.

Apply Have students present their readings. You might record the readings on audiotape so that students may listen to their own work and that of other class members.

Assess Students can assess the readings by using the Peer Assessment: Oral Interpretation form, p. 119, in the ***Alternative Assessment*** booklet.

In aftertime, this also shall be known.
But now delay not; take Excalibur,
And fling him far into the middle mere;[15]
Watch what thou seest, and lightly[16] bring me word."
To him replied the bold Sir Bedivere:
"It is not meet,[17] Sir King, to leave thee thus,
Aidless, alone, and smitten through the helm.
A little thing may harm a wounded man.
Yet I thy hest will all perform at full,[18]
Watch what I see, and lightly bring thee word."
So saying, from the ruined shrine he stepped
And in the moon athwart the place of tombs,
Where lay the mighty bones of ancient men,
Old knights, and over them the sea wind sang
Shrill, chill, with flakes of foam. He, stepping down
By zigzag paths and juts of pointed rock,
Came on the shining levels of the lake.
There drew he forth the brand Excalibur,
And o'er him, drawing it, the winter moon,
Brightening the skirts of a long cloud, ran forth
And sparkled keen with frost against the hilt;
For all the haft[19] twinkled with diamond sparks,
Myriads[20] of topaz lights, and jacinth work[21]
Of subtlest jewelry. He gazed so long
That both his eyes were dazzled, as he stood,
6 This way and that dividing the swift mind,
In act to throw; but at the last it seemed
Better to leave Excalibur concealed
There in the many-knotted water flags,[22]
That whistled still and dry about the marge.[23]
So strode he back slow to the wounded king.
Then spake King Arthur to Sir Bedivere:
"Hast thou performed my mission which I gave?
What is it thou hast seen, or what hast heard?"
And answer made the bold Sir Bedivere:
"I heard the ripple washing in the reeds,
And the wild water lapping on the crag."
To whom replied King Arthur, faint and pale:
7 "Thou hast betrayed thy nature and thy name,
Not rendering[24] true answer, as beseemed[25]
Thy fealty, nor like a noble knight;
For surer sign had followed, either hand,
Or voice, or else a motion of the mere.
This is a shameful thing for men to lie.
Yet now, I charge thee, quickly go again
As thou art lief and dear, and do the thing
I bade thee, watch, and lightly bring me word."
Then went Sir Bedivere the second time
Across the ridge, and paced beside the mere,

15. **mere** (mir) *n.*: Lake.
16. **lightly** *adv.*: Quickly.

> ◆ **Literary Focus**
> 5 How does Arthur's command add mystery to the legend?

17. **meet** *adj.*: Proper.
18. **I thy hest will all perform at full:** I will carry out your order completely.
19. **haft** *n.*: Handle or hilt of a sword.
20. **myriads** (mir´ e ədz) *n.*: Large numbers.
21. **topaz** (tō´ paz) . . . **work:** Yellow and reddish-orange jewels.
22. **water flags:** Marsh plants.
23. **marge** (marj) *n.*: Edge.
24. **rendering** (ren´ dər iŋ) *v.*: Giving.
25. **beseemed** (bi sēmd´) *v.*: Was suitable to.

◆ Literary Focus

5 **Suggested response:** *Arthur commands that he be told what happens after the sword is thrown into the lake. Readers' interest is heightened because his command indicates something unusual might happen.*

◆ Critical Thinking

6 **Infer** Ask students what quality of Excalibur the author focuses on in this passage and what effect that quality has on Sir Bedivere. *Tennyson focuses on the bright colors of the jewels on the handle of the sword and describes the hypnotic effect the jewels have on Sir Bedivere.*

7 **Clarification** King Arthur makes a play on words here. The name "Bedivere" means "of truth," or "truthful." Thus when Sir Bedivere lies about what he did with the sword, Arthur accuses him of betraying his name.

Customize for *English Language Learners*

These students will need assistance with the style and wording of this poem. Help these students discover unfamiliar words that are repeated throughout the poem, such as *hast, wouldst, thou,* and *thee.* Lead students to use context clues and similarities to known words to recognize that that these words mean *has, would,* and *you.*

Extending Word Study

Dictionary Arthur refers to Sir Bedivere as "lief and dear." Have students check a dictionary to find the meaning of *lief* and other unusual words in the poem not defined in the student book.

Cross-Curricular Connection: History

Chivalry in Medieval Times King Arthur and his retinue are thought of as advocates of *chivalry*—the code of behavior that was supposed to govern the actions of knights and nobles in the Middle Ages. The word comes from the French *chevalerie*, or mounted soldiers. The English word *cavalry* is derived from the same root.

The primary sources on the nature of chivalry are poems by eleventh- and twelfth-century minstrels in England and Europe. These epics celebrated the deeds and character of idealized heroes. These heroes were deeply devout and ever ready to defend their faith, even with their lives. They protected the weak and helpless and fought evil and injustice. Most were devoted to particular women, in whose names they performed their gallantries.

Have students research the code of chivalry by which King Arthur and his knights lived. Then have them rewrite and update that code to fit our times. Suggest to students that their revised codes of chivalry encompass the noblest human characteristics while also reflecting the realities of the time and place in which students live.

◆ Critical Thinking

❶ Compare and Contrast Have students explain how Bedivere's rationale for disobeying King Arthur's command differs from his previous one. *Previously Sir Bedivere had been too dazzled by the jeweled sword to speak at all. This time he can speak and says that it would be wrong to deprive the world of such a splendid object as Excalibur.*

◆ Build Grammar Skills

❷ Subjunctive Mood Ask students how many examples of the subjunctive mood occur in this passage (lines 143–147), what verb is used, and why the subjunctive mood is employed in each case. *There are three uses of the subjunctive mood: "if this were done," "Were it well to obey," "if a king demand." The first two uses describe situations that are contrary to fact; the third use expresses a demand.*

◆ Literature and Your Life

❸ Suggested response: *Societies preserve things that belonged to a hero as a way of cherishing his or her memory. People like to see things that belonged to heroes because it gives them a sense of being close to, or touched by, heroism themselves.*

◆ Literary Focus

❹ Legend Ask students if they have heard a different account of how Arthur acquired Excalibur. Then have them explain why the details of a legend may vary in different tellings. *Many students will have heard that the young Arthur discovered the sword lodged in a stone. Students should recognize that as legends are passed along, often orally, each new teller changes the story to one degree or another. If a story is told throught the generations, one area may end up with a version that is very different from the version in another area.*

Counting the dewy pebbles, fixed in thought;
But when he saw the wonder of the hilt,
How curiously and strangely chased,[26] he smote
His palms together, and he cried aloud:
    "And if indeed I cast the brand away;
Surely a precious thing, one worthy note,
❶ Should thus be lost forever from the earth,
Which might have pleased the eyes of many men.
What good should follow this, if this were done?
What harm, undone? deep harm to disobey,
❷ Seeing obedience is the bond of rule.
Were it well to obey then, if a king demand
An act unprofitable, against himself?
The king is sick, and knows not what he does.
What record, or what relic of my lord
Should be to aftertime, but empty breath
And rumors of a doubt? but were this kept,
Stored in some treasure-house of mighty kings,
Some one might show it at a joust of arms,
Saying, 'King Arthur's sword, Excalibur,
Wrought by the lonely maiden of the lake;
❹ Nine years she wrought it, sitting in the deeps
Upon the hidden bases of the hills.'
So might some old man speak in the aftertime
To all the people, winning reverence;
But now much honor and much fame were lost."
    So spake he, clouded with his own conceit,
And hid Excalibur the second time,
And so strode back slow to the wounded king.
    Then spoke King Arthur, breathing heavily:
"What is it thou hast seen, or what hast heard?"
    And answer made the bold Sir Bedivere:
"I heard the water lapping on the crag,
And the long ripple washing in the reeds."
    To whom replied King Arthur, much in wrath:
"Ah, miserable and unkind, untrue,
Unknightly, traitor-hearted! Woe is me!
Authority forgets a dying king,
Laid widowed of the power in his eye
That bowed the will. I see thee what thou art,
For thou, the latest-left of all my knights,
In whom should meet the offices[27] of all,
❺ Thou wouldst betray me for the precious hilt;
Either from lust of gold, or like a girl
Valuing the giddy pleasure of the eyes.
Yet, for a man may fail in duty twice,
And the third time may prosper, get thee hence;
But, if thou spare to fling Excalibur,
I will arise and slay thee with my hands."

26. chased *v.*: Decorated by engraving or embossing.

27. offices *n.*: Duties.

❸ **◆ *Literature and Your Life***

Why do you think societies preserve the things that belong to a hero? Why do people like to see things that belonged to their heroes?

Humanities: Literature

The *Round Table* is a name that is used both as a designation for King Arthur's court and for a table where Arthur would sit with his knights. The earliest reference to this table is in a twelfth-century historical chronicle in verse, *Le Roman de Brut*, by Wace, a Norman poet. He wrote that the king wanted the table to be round to prevent fighting among the knights for the seats of highest honor. At a round table, all seats were equal in prestige.

A description of the Round Table by an English priest, Layamon, says that it could seat 1,600 men and could be folded up and carried on horseback. Another version says that the table sat twelve and that one seat, the *siege perilous* (*siege* is French for "seat") was left empty. It was reserved for a knight who was pure enough to find the Holy Grail, the cup used by Jesus at the Last Supper. Suddenly, this legend has it, the name of Sir Galahad appeared on this chair, and he occupied it from then on. Galahad was one of the three knights who found the Grail. The others were Sir Bors and Sir Perceval (also known as Parsifal) Students might enjoy researching one of these men and reporting their findings to the class.

Then quickly rose Sir Bedivere, and ran,
And, leaping down the ridges lightly, plunged
Among the bulrush beds,[28] and clutched the sword,
And strongly wheeled and threw it. The great brand
Made lightnings in the splendor of the moon,
And flashing round and round, and whirled in an arch,
Shot like a streamer of the northern morn,[29]
Seen where the moving isles of winter shock[30]
By night, with noises of the northern sea.
So flashed and fell the brand Excalibur;
But ere he dipped the surface, rose an arm
Clothed in white samite, mystic, wonderful,
And caught him by the hilt, and brandished him
Three times, and drew him under in the mere.
And lightly went the other to the king.
Then spoke King Arthur, drawing thicker breath:
"Now see I by thine eyes that this is done.
Speak out; what is it thou hast heard, or seen?"
And answer made the bold Sir Bedivere:
"Sir King, I closed mine eyelids, lest the gems
Should blind my purpose, for I never saw,
Nor shall see, here or elsewhere, till I die,
Not though I live three lives of mortal men,
So great a miracle as yonder hilt.
Then with both hands I flung him, wheeling him;
But when I looked again, behold an arm,
Clothed in white samite, mystic, wonderful,
❼ That caught him by the hilt, and brandished him
Three times, and drew him under in the mere."
And answer made King Arthur, breathing hard:
"My end draws nigh; 'tis time that I were gone.
Make broad thy shoulders to receive my weight,
And bear me to the margin,[31] yet I fear
My wound hath taken cold, and I shall die."
So saying, from the pavement he half rose,
Slowly, with pain, reclining on his arm,
And looking wistfully with wide blue eyes
As in a picture. Him Sir Bedivere
Remorsefully regarded through his tears,
And would have spoken, but he found not words,
Then took with care, and kneeling on one knee,
O'er both his shoulders drew the languid hands,
And rising bore him through the place of tombs.
But, as he walked, King Arthur panted hard,
Like one that feels a nightmare on his bed
When all the house is mute. So sighed the king,
Muttering and murmuring at his ear, "Quick, quick!
I fear it is too late, and I shall die."
But the other swiftly strode from ridge to ridge,

28. bulrush (bo͝ol′ rush) **beds:** Growth of marsh plants.

29. a streamer of the northern morn: Northern lights; the aurora borealis.

30. the moving isles of winter shock: Icebergs crash.

31. margin (mar′ jən) *n.:* Edge.

❻ ◆ **Literary Focus** What aspects of Sir Bedivere's act are typical of legends?

◆ Reading Strategy

❺ **Recognize an Author's Attitude** Ask students to explain Tennyson's attitude toward Arthur in this passage. *Tennyson shows that Arthur, even in death, is not a pathetic figure. He maintains his nobility and even flashes of his strength, as shown here.*

◆ Literary Focus

❻ **Legends** Suggested response: *Sir Bedivere twice fails to carry out Arthur's command before finally obeying. He gives the same reply, virtually word for word, when Arthur questions him after his two failures to obey. This repetition of events heightens the suspense, stresses the magical qualities of Excalibur, and is typical of legend.*

◆ Critical Thinking

❼ **Make Judgments** Point out that Sir Bedivere repeats almost word for word the narrator's account of the mysterious arm taking Excalibur into the lake. Ask students to suggest a possible reason for Tennyson's use of repetition. *Suggested response: Repetition is a means of pointing out the artificial and old-fashioned style of this poem. By using devices associated with literature of an earlier period, Tennyson stresses the idea that this story, together with its underlying values, is ageless.*

Analyze Literary Criticism

Tennyson's poetry reflects the moral and aesthetic values of the Victorian social class, and he became the favorite target of younger poets rebelling against these same values. The end of the 1800's saw an important change in the aims and ambitions of many poets. Whereas Tennyson never questioned his obligation to write poetry that was accessible and enjoyable to the public, modern poets have tended to impose their own standards on readers with intellectually tough and often obscure poems. One of the great modern poets, W. H. Auden, expressed his dismay over Tennyson, calling him "stupid," praising his gift for beautiful language and powerful imagery but ridiculing his intellectual powers. He referred to *The Idylls of the King* as "charades of the Middle Ages." Today, critics still praise Tennyson's great metrical skill and beautiful imagery but complain about his sentimentality and intellectual shallowness.

Discuss with students whether or not they agree with Tennyson's modern critics. Then have them write a journal entry, answering the following question: Does a poet have an obligation to write poems that many people can understand and enjoy? *Some students may state that they would like reading poetry better if the poet made his or her poems easier to understand. Others may say that poetry is personal expression for which poets have freedom to write what they want to write.*

◆ Literary Focus

❶ Legend How do these details reflect Arthur's legendary status? *These mysterious women on a barge that appears on the lake from which Excalibur came create a sense of mystery and wonder must have some magical power to know of Arthur's death. His affiliation with these magical women makes Arthur seem larger than life.*

◆ Build Grammar Skills

❷ Subjunctive Mood Ask students which verb in this passage (lines 251–253) indicates the use of the subjunctive mood and why the mood is employed here. *The verb is* were. *The subjunctive mood states a condition that is contrary to fact. "As it were one voice" should be understood as "As if it were one voice, but it isn't."*

Customize for *Visual/Spatial Learners*

❸ The passage that describes King Arthur being placed in the barge with three queens to attend him uses many phrases, including "his brow / striped with dark blood; his face was white / And colorless, and like the withered moon" that appeal to the sense of sight. Have students create notes for a film version of this scene, describing camera angles, lighting, and other efftects to heighten the visual effects of the scene.

◆ Critical Thinking

❹ Connect Ask students to connect Sir Bedivere's lament to the conversation between the friends at the opening of the poem. *The friends at the beginning of the poem complain that the times have changed, that nothing is sacred anymore. Bedivere mourns the passing away of a noble, honorable time. He feels that all that is good and true has died with Arthur.*

Clothed with his breath, and looking, as he walked,
Larger than human on the frozen hills.
He heard the deep behind him, and a cry
Before. His own thought drove him like a goad.[32]
Dry clashed his harness[33] in the icy caves
And barren chasms, and all to left and right
The bare black cliff clanged round him, as he based
His feet on juts of slippery crag that rang
Sharp-smitten with the dint of armèd heels—
And on a sudden, lo! the level lake,
And the long glories of the winter moon.
  Then saw they how there hove a dusky barge,
Dark as a funeral scarf from stem to stern,
Beneath them; and descending they were ware
❶ That all the decks were dense with stately forms
Black-stoled,[34] black-hooded, like a dream—by these
Three queens with crowns of gold—and from them rose
A cry that shivered to the tingling stars,
And, as it were one voice, an agony
❷ Of lamentation, like a wind that shrills
All night in a waste land, where no one comes,
Or hath come, since the making of the world.
  Then murmured Arthur, "Place me in the barge,"
And to the barge they came. There those three queens
Put forth their hands, and took the king, and wept.
But she that rose the tallest of them all
And fairest laid his head upon her lap,
And loosed the shattered casque,[35] and chafed his hands,
And called him by his name, complaining loud,
And dropping bitter tears against his brow
Striped with dark blood; for all his face was white
And colorless, and like the withered moon
Smote by the fresh beam of the springing east;
❸ And all his greaves and cuisses dashed with drops
Of onset;[36] and the light and lustrous curls—
That made his forehead like a rising sun
High from the dais-throne—were parched with dust;
Or, clotted into points and hanging loose,
Mixed with the knightly growth that fringed his lips.
So like a shattered column lay the king;
Not like that Arthur who, with lance in rest,
From spur to plume a star of tournament,
Shot through the lists at Camelot, and charged
Before the eyes of ladies and of kings.
  Then loudly cried the bold Sir Bedivere:
"Ah! my Lord Arthur, whither shall I go?
❹ Where shall I hide my forehead and my eyes?
For now I see the true old times are dead,
When every morning brought a noble chance,

32. goad (gōd) *n.*: Sharp pointed stick used to drive oxen.

33. harness (har´ nis) *n.*: Armor.

34. black-stoled: Wearing long black scarves around their shoulders.

35. casque (kask) *n.*: Helmet.

36. greaves (grevz) **and cuisses** (kwis´ əs) **. . . onset:** Armor for the legs below the knee and for the thigh spattered with blood from the battle.

◆ Build Vocabulary

lamentation (lam´ ən tā´ shən) *n.*: Mourning

Humanities: Art

Coats of Arms In the eleventh century, around the time when the Arthurian legend is supposed to have taken place, knights and nobles began to display coats of arms on shields and flags. These were symbolic identifications of themselves and their families. The original purpose of these coats of arms was to allow the knights' followers to identify them in battle. Holding a shield in front of himself for protection, he would also display it prominently so a would-be attacker would quickly recognize a friend or foe.

Coats of arms often carried mottoes in addition to symbols and were handed down over generations, developing into an elaborate system. The study of coats of arms is called heraldry because it was the heralds, originally message bearers, who regulated and registered coats of arms in huge books called armorials. No two families could use the same design. Britain is the only country still to make use of these designs today, though a family's history often can be traced to a particular coat of arms.

Interested students might want to make a chart comparing coats of arms of some prominent medieval families. They can chart such information as the meaning of the symbols used, the mottoes carried, the colors used, arrangement of visual elements, and ways in which the coats of arms were personally connected to the families they identified. Encourage students to research their own families' coats of arms, or to create their own coats of arms with symbols and colors that reflect their talents and abilities.

How Sir Bedivere Cast the Sword Excalibur Into the Water, Aubrey Beardsley, Houghton Library, Harvard University

5 ▲ **Critical Viewing** This illustration depicts a significant moment in the Arthurian legend. What symbolic details does the illustrator include? What is their significance? **[Interpret]**

▶Critical Viewing◀

5 Interpret Elicit responses such as the following: *The illustration depicts the silk-clad arm taking the sword Excalibur into the lake. Sir Bedivere stands in a formal posture with his arm raised in a farewell salute. The darkness surrounding the scene suggests the serious and somber nature of this mysterious event.*

Customize for
Bodily/Kinesthetic Learners

The rigors of knighthood were intense. Besides the skill required for swordfighting and jousting, the knights spent a great deal of time on horseback and carried the weight of their armor. Have students research the type and amount of physical training required for a knight in medieval times, and present their findings to the class.

Humanities: Art

How Sir Bedivere Cast the Sword Excalibur Into the Water by Aubrey Beardsley.

Aubrey Beardsley (1872–1898) was a major figure in the 1890's art movement *Art Nouveau,* which was marked by the use of an elegant style, featuring flowing curves and elaborate decorative elements. Beardsley had a strong influence on this movement, a particularly high achievement considering he died of tuberculosis at the age of 25. This illustration is one of 500 drawings by Beardsley for an edition of Sir Thomas Malory's fifteenth-century book, *Le Morte D'Arthur,* the source used by Tennyson for *The Idylls of the King.* Use the following question for discussion:

How does this picture contrast with Tennyson's description of the event? *Students may say that Tennyson emphasizes action and movement while the illustration presents a stylized, motionless scene. Also Tennyson's setting seems wilder, colder, and more barren than Beardsley's quiet lake surrounded by reeds and plants.*

◆ Critical Thinking

❶ **Infer** Invite students to suggest explanations for Sir Bedivere's gloomy forecast of his future. *Suggested response: Sir Bedivere had been part of a fellowship. Now that he is the last remaining Knight of the Round Table, he doubts that he can maintain their values and way of life by himself. He fears that he will be isolated in a world whose beliefs are foreign to him.*

◆ Critical Thinking

❷ **Interpret** Ask: What does Arthur's answer mean, particularly the line "Lest one good custom should corrupt the world"? *Arthur sees that God has many ways of guiding people to a good, virtuous life. ". . .Lest one good custom should corrupt the world" means that God recognizes that even by following a good custom, people would get stuck and become unable to grow.*

◆ Critical Thinking

❸ **Interpret** Challenge students to interpret Arthur's words to Sir Bedivere. What does Arthur believe that Sir Bedivere should do in times to come? *Arthur advises Sir Bedivere to continue to practice the beliefs that the Round Table stood for by praying for his own soul and for those of his friends. This desire to pray is what distinguishes human beings from beasts.*

◆ Build Vocabulary

❹ **Latin Suffixes *-ous*** Ask students how they would determine the meaning of the word "grievous." *The root of "grievous" is related to the word "grief." The suffix -ous means "like" or "pertaining to." Therefore, "grievous" means "pertaining to grief."*

◆ Literary Focus

❺ **Legend** Elicit responses like the following: *Like other legendary paradises, Avilion offers an escape from daily worries and pain; it is a place where all is fair and mild, a nurturing environment free of conflict.*

❻ **Clarification** The poet Everard Hall's retelling of the King Arthur legend ends here. The narrator switches to the original Christmas Eve setting at the beginning of the poem.

And every chance brought out a noble knight.
Such times have been not since the light that led
The holy Elders with the gift of myrrh.[37]
But now the whole ROUND TABLE is dissolved
Which was an image of the mighty world;
❶ And I, the last, go forth companionless,
And the days darken round me, and the years,
Among new men, strange faces, other minds."
And slowly answered Arthur from the barge:
"The old order changeth, yielding place to new,
❷ And God fulfills himself in many ways,
Lest one good custom should corrupt the world.
Comfort thyself: what comfort is in me?
I have lived my life, and that which I have done
May He within himself make pure! but thou,
If thou shouldst never see my face again,
Pray for my soul. More things are wrought by prayer
Than this world dreams of. Wherefore, let thy voice
Rise like a fountain for me night and day.
For what are men better than sheep or goats
❸ That nourish a blind life within the brain,
If, knowing God, they lift not hands of prayer
Both for themselves and those who call them friend?
For so the whole round earth is every way
Bound by gold chains about the feet of God.
But now farewell. I am going a long way
With these thou seest—if indeed I go—
For all my mind is clouded with a doubt—
To the island-valley of Avilion;[38]
Where falls not hail, or rain, or any snow,
Nor ever wind blows loudly, but it lies
Deep-meadowed, happy, fair with orchard lawns
And bowery[39] hollows crowned with summer sea,
❹ Where I will heal me of my grievous wound."
So said he, and the barge with oar and sail
Moved from the brink, like some full-breasted swan
that, fluting a wild carol ere her death,
Ruffles her pure cold plume, takes the flood
With swarthy webs. Long stood Sir Bedivere
Revolving many memories, till the hull
Looked one black dot against the verge of dawn,
And on the mere the wailing died away.

❻ Here ended Hall, and our last light, that long
Had winked and threatened darkness, flared and fell;
At which the parson, sent to sleep with sound,
And waked with silence, grunted "Good!" but we
Sat rapt:[40] it was the tone with which he read—
Perhaps some modern touches here and there

37. the light . . . of myrrh (mur): Star that guided the three Kings (the holy Elders) with their gift of incense (myrrh) to Bethlehem at the birth of Jesus.

38. island-valley of Avilion: Island paradise of Avalon where heroes were taken after death, according to Celtic mythology and medieval romances.

❺ 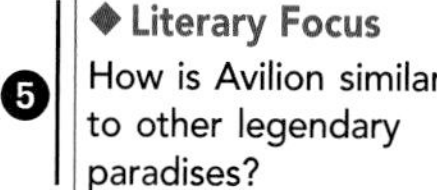
◆ Literary Focus
How is Avilion similar to other legendary paradises?

39. bowery (bou´ ər ē) *adj.*: Enclosed by overhanging boughs of trees or by vines.

40. rapt *adj.*: Completely absorbed; engrossed.

◆ Build Vocabulary

swarthy (swôr´ thē) *adj.*: Having a dark complexion

Cross-Curricular Connection: History

Battle Protection During the Middle Ages, types of armor changed as different kinds of warfare developed. In the twelfth century, the time of King Arthur, a knight's main protection was chain mail, or tiny metal rings, linked together. A coat of chain mail deflected arrows, swords, and lances. Metal helmets protected the head and face.

Chain mail, however, was vulnerable to thirteenth-century weapons like longbows, maces, crossbows, and battle-axes. As a result, plate armor was introduced. It was designed to cover the entire body and included armored *gauntlets*, or gloves, and *sollerets*, or shoes. Although full-plate armor was secure, it had disadvantages. It severely limited movement. It was very expensive, costing as much as a farm. It was also heavy; a knight in full armor had to be hoisted onto his horse by a machine.

The invention of guns made plate armor obsolete. By the sixteenth century, only breastplates and helmets were worn. Students might further research the progression of battle protection.

Redeemed[41] it from the charge of nothingness—
Or else we loved the man, and prized his work;
I know not; but we sitting, as I said,
The cock crew loud, as at that time of year
The lusty bird takes every hour for dawn.
Then Francis, muttering, like a man ill-used,
"There now—that's nothing!" drew a little back,
And drove his heel into the smoldered log,
That sent a blast of sparkles up the flue.
And so to bed, where yet in sleep I seemed
To sail with Arthur under looming shores,
Point after point; till on to dawn, when dreams
Begin to feel the truth and stir of day,
7 To me, methought, who waited with the crowd,
There came a bark that, blowing forward, bore
King Arthur; like a modern gentleman
Of stateliest port;[42] and all the people cried,
"Arthur is come again: he cannot die."
Then those that stood upon the hills behind
Repeated—"Come again, and thrice as fair";
And, further inland, voices echoed—"Come
With all good things, and war shall be no more."
At this a hundred bells began to peal,
That with the sound I woke, and heard indeed
The clear church bells ring in the Christmas morn.

41. **Redeemed** (ri dēmd′) *v.*: Rescued or saved.

42. **of stateliest port:** Who carried himself in a most majestic or dignified manner.

8 ◆ **Reading Strategy**
Hall's story ends on Christmas morning. What does this tell you about Tennyson's attitude toward Arthur?

Guide for Responding

◆ *Literature and Your Life*

Reader's Response What is your opinion of Sir Bedivere's actions in response to Arthur's request? Explain.

Thematic Focus How do Arthur's actions in his final hours create a legacy of courage and honor for the generations that follow?

☑ Check Your Comprehension

1. What occasion is being celebrated at the start of the poem?
2. In the poem within the poem, what has happened to King Arthur?
3. What does Arthur specifically request of Sir Bedivere? How does Bedivere react?
4. Describe Arthur's departure.

◆ Critical Thinking

INTERPRET

1. What does Arthur say will soon be lost forever? How, in lines 277–289, does Sir Bedivere echo Arthur's feelings? **[Connect]**
2. What are Sir Bedivere's reasons for not throwing Excalibur into the lake? **[Interpret]**
3. Interpret Arthur's final words to Sir Bedivere. **[Interpret]**

EVALUATE

4. Would this selection have a different effect if it had been written in prose? Explain. **[Assess]**

APPLY

5. The modern novelist F. Scott Fitzgerald has written, "Show me a hero and I will write you a tragedy." Do you think that the Arthurian legend is a tragedy? Explain your answer. **[Define]**

◆ Literary Focus

7 Legend Ask students what quality of a legendary figure is brought out in this passage. *Students may point out that a legendary hero like King Arthur is timeless and his virtues (goodness, loyalty, honor, honesty, bravery) never die. These virtues also appeal to contemporary people.*

◆ Reading Strategy

8 Recognize an Author's Attitude Suggested response: *There is a connection between the ringing of bells on Christmas morning to celebrate the coming of Christ and the arrival of King Arthur in the narrator's dream. Tennyson seems to see Arthur as an embodiment of Christian values. Thus Tennyson's attitude toward Arthur may be summed up as admiring, and very respectful.*

Reinforce and Extend

Answers

◆ *Literature and Your Life*

Reader's Response Students might respond that Sir Bedivere did not act in a knightly manner.

Thematic Focus King Arthur's final actions showed that it is noble to surrender oneself to the ever-changing times—to respect change as necessary rather than try to stop time or control fate.

☑ Check Your Comprehension

1. Christmas Eve is being celebrated.
2. King Arthur has been mortally wounded in battle.
3. King Arthur requests that Sir Bedivere fling his brand (sword) Excalibur into the lake, from where he first obtained it.
4. King Arthur is taken on a barge where he dies, to be transported after death to Avilion, the island paradise.

◆ Critical Thinking

1. Arthur says that knightly deeds will be lost forever, and Sir Bedivere later echoes that by saying the whole Round Table is lost and worrying what is to become of him.
2. Sir Bedivere is dazzled by the material splendor of Excalibur and the glory it represents.
3. Sample answer: King Arthur is saying that destiny is wrapped up with God's will, that humans must pray to Him for themselves and each other in order to live richly and meaningfully.
4. This selection would have created a different effect if written in prose; poetry devices such as repetition and figurative language create a vivid mood and setting.
5. Some students might find it a tragedy because King Arthur is killed in battle and chivalry dies with him, while others might say it is not a tragedy because Arthur has influenced his subjects wisely.

Develop Understanding

One-Minute Insight Legends are very adaptable. Where Tennyson sees Arthur as a heroic embodiment of ancient goodness and virtue, T.H. White views young Arthur in a more accessible way. Even figures of legend, he seems to say, are recognizably human. The characters in White's version of the Arthurian story are not stiff figures in an old-fashioned, still-life tableau. They live, breathe, and blunder. In fact, this excerpt from "The Once and Future King" tells how Arthur became king becasue Sir Kay forgot his sword.

◆ Reading Strategy

❶ Recognize an Author's Attitude Recognizing the speech styles of the characters will help understand White's attitude toward them and toward his subject. Some of White's characters have speech patterns that reflect mannerisms of provincial English nobles of modern times, especially those with little education or culture. King Pellinore's constant use of "what" as an interjection is one example. Another is Sir Ector's habit of dropping the final *g* in words like "comin'" or "anythin'." White seems to be poking fun at these characters.

❷ Clarification King Pellinore is the king of a northern part of Britain. He is describing the death of the renowned King Uther Pendragon, the Conqueror (Arthur's father and predecessor as King of England). The boy Wart is the young Arthur. Sir Ector is one of Uther's knights, and Sir Kay is his son.

Customize for
English Language Learners
Assist students in translating the Sergeant's dialect: "Nah" (Now), "fer" (for), "'is" (his), "lite" (late, or recently deceased), "awai" (away).

Arthur Becomes King of Britain

from The Once and Future King

T. H. White

King Pellinore arrived for the important weekend in a high state of flurry.

"I say," he exclaimed, "do you know? Have you heard? Is it a secret, what?"

❶ "Is what a secret, what?" they asked him.

"Why, the King," cried his majesty. "You know, about the King?"

"What's the matter with the King?" inquired Sir Ector. "You don't say he's comin' down to hunt with those darned hounds of his or anythin' like that?"

"He's dead," cried King Pellinore tragically. ❷ "He's dead, poor fellah, and can't hunt any more."

Sir Grummore stood up respectfully and took off his cap.

"The King is dead," he said. "Long live the King."

Everybody else felt they ought to stand up too, and the boys' nurse burst into tears.

"There, there," she sobbed. "His loyal highness dead and gone, and him such a respectful gentleman. Many's the illuminated picture I've cut out of him, from the Illustrated Missals, aye, and stuck up over the mantel. From the time when he was in swaddling bands,[1] right through them world towers till he was a-visiting the dispersed areas as the world's Prince Charming, there wasn't a picture of 'im but I had it out, aye, and give 'im a last thought o' nights."

"Compose yourself, Nannie," said Sir Ector.

"It is solemn, isn't it?" said King Pellinore, "what? Uther the Conqueror, 1066 to 1216."

"A solemn moment," said Sir Grummore. "The King is dead. Long live the King."

"We ought to pull down the curtains," said Kay, who was always a stickler for good form, "or half-mast[2] the banners."

"That's right," said Sir Ector. "Somebody go and tell the sergeant-at-arms."

It was obviously the Wart's duty to execute this command, for he was now the junior nobleman present, so he ran out cheerfully to find the sergeant. Soon those who were left in the solar[3] could hear a voice crying out, "Nah then, one-two, special mourning fer 'is lite majesty, lower awai on the command Two!" and then the flapping of all the standards, banners, pennons, pennoncells, banderolls, guidons, streamers and cognizances[4] which made gay the

1. **swaddling bands:** Long, narrows bands of cloths wrapped around a newborn baby in former times.

2. **half-mast** (haf mast´) *v.*: Hang a flag at half-mast.
3. **solar** (sō´ lər) *n.*: Here, sun room. Solar is often used as an adjective.
4. **standards . . . cognizances** (käg´ nə zən´ səz) *n.*: Banners or flags.

◆ Build Vocabulary

stickler (stik´ lər) *n.*: Person who insists uncompromisingly on the observance of something specified

Cross-Curricular Connection: History

Knights and Squires During the Middle Ages, if a young boy of good family wished to be a *knight* (boys of the lower classes could not hope for this honor), he left home at the age of seven to serve in another noble household as a *page*. He studied the rules of knightly behavior and the use of small weapons. At the age of fifteen, he became a *squire* (Arthur is Sir Kay's squire), serving as a knight's valet and learning to fight on horseback. He would accompany his knight into battle and fight by his side. After five years, the squire would be eligible for knighthood.

Knighthood could be conferred by any knight. There was little ceremony involved at first. The knight helped the squire into his armor and proclaimed his new status. The ceremony later grew more elaborate. Two knights took part, and a new knight was tapped on the back with a sword. Later still, knighthood took on more of a religious character, and knights-to-be had to keep an all-night vigil in church, fasting and praying, and swearing to follow the dictates of the Church.

Invite students to research the modern-day ceremonial customs of knighthood.

The Crowning of Arthur, Royal MS, by permission of the British Library

snowy turrets of the Forest Sauvage.

"How did you hear?" asked Sir Ector.

"I was pricking through the purlieus[5] of the forest after that Beast, you know, when I met with a solemn friar of orders gray, and he told me. It's the very latest news."

"Poor old Pendragon," said Sir Ector.

"The King is dead," said Sir Grummore solemnly. "Long live the King."

"It is all very well for you to keep on mentioning that, my dear Grummore," exclaimed King Pellinore petulantly, "but who is this King, what, that is to live so long, what, accordin' to you?"

"Well, his heir," said Sir Grummore, rather taken aback.

"Our blessed monarch," said the Nurse tearfully, "never had no hair. Anybody that studied the loyal family knowed that."

"Good gracious!" exclaimed Sir Ector. "But he must have had a next-of-kin?"

"That's just it," cried King Pellinore in high excitement. "That's the excitin' part of it, what? No hair and no next of skin, and who's to succeed to the throne? That's what my friar was so excited about, what, and why he was asking who could succeed to what, what? What?"

"Do you mean to tell me," exclaimed Sir Grummore indignantly, "that there ain't no King of Gramarye?" ❻

▲ **Critical Viewing** Based on what you've read so far, how do you think T. H. White would feel about the formality and ceremony of this coronation scene? **[Draw Conclusions]** ❹

◆ **Reading Strategy** What does Pellinore's way of speaking tell you about the author's attitude toward him? ❺

5. **purlieus** (pur′ lo͞oz) *n.*: Outlying part of a forest, exempted from forest laws.

❸ **Clarification** "Pricking" is an archaic word meaning "riding."

▶Critical Viewing◀

❹ **Draw Conclusions** Suggested response: *Judging from T.H. White's attitude towards the formality of court life to this point, which he mocks by giving events an absurd twist, he would probably poke fun of the stateliness of the occasion.*

◆ Reading Strategy

❺ **Recognize an Author's Attitude** First, be sure that students are aware of malapropisms like "hair" (for heir) and "next of skin" (for next of kin) and the confusion caused by the constant interjection of "what." Then elicit responses such as the following: *The comic use of language suggests that White has a humorous attitude and does not take his subject terribly seriously at this point.*

❻ **Clarification** "Gramarye" is another name for England.

Customize for *Gifted/Talented Students*

These students may be the first to grasp the humor of the nurse's collection of pictures of the king she has cut out of hand-illustrated, or illuminated, manuscripts. These documents would have been valuable in medieval times; today they would be nearly priceless. Have students make a photocopy of a reproduction of a manuscript illumination and write a short text telling what it represents. Discourage any clipping of illustrations.

Humanities: Art

The Crowning of Arthur (Royal MS).

This page of an illuminated manuscript shows Arthur being crowned. Although the drawing style is simple, even somewhat cartoonish, the illustration depicts a stately occasion. The most important figure, next to Arthur himself, is a Bishop. The Bishop is recognized by his pointed headdress, or miter, and his robes. Thus, one important aspect of the coronation is that it is approved by the Church. Arthur holds a scepter, which symbolizes his authority over worldly affairs. The other onlookers represent the acceptance of Arthur by his new subjects. Use this question for discussion:

Does this illustration show what you would expect to see at a coronation ritual? Why or why not? *Students might respond that they would expect to see more luxurious clothing and jewels at a coronation, but the ritual of the Bishop placing the crown upon the king, who is holding a scepter, and the expressions of the eager onlookers would all probably be what students would expect to see.*

1 Clarification Characters sometimes lapse into old-fashioned, stylized language, like "signs and wonders of no mean might." This suggests that King Pellinore may be repeating something he has heard from someone else, possibly from a "solemn friar of orders grey." This formal language suggests the importance of the news.

◆ Reading Strategy

2 Recognize an Author's Attitude Ask students how this description of the sword in the stone shows the author's attitude toward King Pellinore. *Suggested response: Pellinore's muddled description is a sign that the author wants to portray Pellinore as a comic character, somewhat limited in brain power.*

◆ Critical Thinking

3 Infer Invite students to suggest what the effect is of Sir Grummore's reaction to the description of the sword in the stone. *Sir Grummore's indignant response—that the appearance of the sword is possibly the work of "agitators"—is a humorous device that gently pokes fun at the image of Excalibur, which is usually shown in a more solemn way.*

◆ Build Vocabulary

4 Latin Suffixes *-ous* Challenge students to explain how they would figure out the meaning of the word piteously. *First drop the second suffix -ly (they will add it again at the end). Then note that the root of the word is pity. The suffix -ous means "like" or "pertaining to." Thus "piteous" means "pertaining to pity," or "pathetic," and "piteously" means "pathetically."*

◆ Literary Focus

5 Legend Suggested response: *The formal, old-fashioned language points up the ancient origin of the legend, and creates an amusing contrast to the everyday, comic world that most of the characters inhabit.*

"Not a scrap of one," cried King Pellinore,
1 feeling important. "And there have been signs and wonders of no mean might."

"I think it's a scandal," said Sir Grummore. "God knows what the dear old country is comin' to."

"What sort of signs and wonders?" asked Sir Ector.

"Well, there has appeared a sort of sword in a stone, what, in a sort of a church. Not
2 in the church, if you see what I mean, and not in the stone, but that sort of thing, what, like you might say."

"I don't know what the Church is coming to," said Sir Grummore.

"It's in an anvil,"[6] explained the King.

"The Church?"

"No, the sword."

"But I thought you said the sword was in the stone?"

"No," said King Pellinore. "The stone is outside the Church."

"Look here, Pellinore," said Sir Ector. "You have a bit of a rest, old boy, and start again. Here, drink up this horn of mead[7] and take it easy."

"The sword," said King Pellinore, "is stuck through an anvil which stands on a stone. It goes right through the anvil and into the stone. The anvil is stuck to the stone. The stone stands outside a church. Give me some more mead."

"I don't think that's much of a wonder," remarked Sir Grummore. "What I wonder at
3 is that they should allow such things to happen. But you can't tell nowadays, what with all these Saxon agitators."[8]

"My dear fellah," cried Pellinore, getting excited again, "it's not where the stone is, what, that I'm trying to tell you, but what is written on it, what, where it is."

"What?"

"Why, on its pommel."[9]

"Come on, Pellinore," said Sir Ector. "You just sit quite still with your face to the wall for a minute, and then tell us what you are talkin' about. Take it easy, old boy. No need for hurryin'. You sit still and look at the wall, there's a good chap, and talk as slow as you can."

"There are words written on this sword in this stone outside this church," cried King
Pellinore piteously, "and these words are as follows. Oh, do try to listen to me, you two, instead of interruptin' all the time about nothing for it makes a man's head go ever so." 4

"What are these words?" asked Kay.

"These words say this," said King Pellinore, "so far as I can understand from that old friar of orders gray."

"Go on, do," said Kay, for the King had come to a halt.

"Go on," said Sir Ector, "what do these words on this sword in this anvil in this stone outside this church, say?"

King Pellinore closed his eyes tight, extended his arms in both directions, and announced in capital letters, "Whoso Pulleth Out This Sword of this Stone and Anvil, is Rightwise King Born of All England."

> **◆ Literary Focus**
> What do formal words like these contribute to the legend? 5

"Who said that?" asked Sir Grummore.

"But the sword said it, like I tell you."

"Talkative weapon," remarked Sir Grummore skeptically.

"It was written on it," cried the King angrily. "Written on it in letters of gold."

"Why didn't you pull it out then?" asked Sir Grummore.

"But I tell you that I wasn't there. All this that I am telling you was told to me by that friar I was telling you of, like I tell you."

---

6. **anvil** (an′ vəl) *n.*: Iron or steel block.
7. **mead** (mēd) *n.*: Drink made of fermented honey and water, often with spices or fruit added.
8. **Saxon** (sak′ sən) **agitators:** Ancient Germanic people who conquered parts of England.
9. **pommel** (pum′ əl) *n.*: Round knob on the end of the hilt of some swords.

Humanities: Literature

The Legend of King Arthur The first known reference to King Arthur appeared in *Gododdin*, a seventh-century Welsh poem. The reference was noted by Nennius, a Welsh chronicler, in his *Historia Britonum* (A.D. 900). In the next few centuries, Arthur became a popular figure in Britain and Brittany in France. His stature grew in French Breton tales until he was seen as a great ruler and warlord. By the twelfth century, Britain had made him a national folk hero.

In Geoffrey of Monmouth's *Historia regum Britanniae* (1137), Arthur is shown as the master of a great empire. Tales of Arthur and his court spread all over Europe. A French poet, Chretien de Troyes, wrote romances focusing on Sir Lancelot and Sir Perceval. German poets added more Arthurian literature. Wolfram von Eschenbach wrote *Parzifal*, and Gottfried von Strassburg created the story of Tristan and Isolde.

In writing *Le Morte D'Arthur*, Sir Thomas Malory used these different stories to create the first comprehensive account of the legend in English. Malory's work has served as the basis for most Arthurian literature since that time.

"Has this sword with this inscription been pulled out?" inquired Sir Ector.

"No," whispered King Pellinore dramatically. "That's where the whole excitement comes in. They can't pull this sword out at all, although they have all been tryin' like fun, and so they have had to proclaim a tournament all over England, for New Year's Day, so that the man who comes to the tournament and pulls out the sword can be King of all England forever, what, I say."

"Oh, father," cried Kay. "The man who pulls the sword out of the stone will be the King of England. Can't we go to the tournament, father, and have a shot?"

"Couldn't think of it," said Sir Ector.

"Long way to London," said Sir Grummore, shaking his head.

"My father went there once," said King Pellinore.

Kay said, "Oh, surely we could go? When I am knighted I shall have to go to a tournament somewhere, and this one happens at just the right date. All the best people will be there, and we should see the famous knights and great kings. It does not matter about the sword, of course, but think of the tournament, probably the greatest there has ever been in Gramarye, and all the things we should see and do. Dear father, let me go to this tourney, if you love me, so that I may bear away the prize of all, in my maiden fight."

"But, Kay," said Sir Ector, "I have never been to London."

"All the more reason to go. I believe that anybody who does not go for a tournament like this will be proving that he has no noble blood in his veins. Think what people will say about us, if we do not go and have a shot at that sword. They will say that Sir Ector's family was too vulgar and knew it had no chance."

"We all know the family has no chance," said Sir Ector, "that is, for the sword."

"Lot of people in London," remarked Sir Grummore, with a wild surmise. "So they say."

He took a deep breath and goggled at his host with eyes like marbles.

"And shops," added King Pellinore suddenly, also beginning to breathe heavily.

"Dang it!" cried Sir Ector, bumping his horn mug on the table so that it spilled. "Let's all go to London, then, and see the new King!"

They rose up as one man.

"Why shouldn't I be as good a man as my father?" exclaimed King Pellinore.

"Dash it all," cried Sir Grummore. "After all, it is the capital!"

"Hurray!" shouted Kay.

"Lord have mercy," said the nurse.

At this moment the Wart came in with Merlyn, and everybody was too excited to notice that, if he had not been grown up now, he would have been on the verge of tears.

"Oh, Wart," cried Kay, forgetting for the moment that he was only addressing his squire, and slipping back into the familiarity of their boyhood. "What do you think? We are all going to London for a great tournament on New Year's Day!"

"Are we?"

"Yes, and you will carry my shield and spears for the jousts, and I shall win the palm[10] of everybody and be a great knight!"

"Well, I am glad we are going," said the Wart, "for Merlyn is leaving us too."

"Oh, we shan't need Merlyn."

"He is leaving us," repeated the Wart.

"Leavin' us?" asked Sir Ector. "I thought it was we that were leavin'?"

"He is going away from the Forest Sauvage."

Sir Ector said, "Come now, Merlyn, what's all this about? I don't understand all this a bit."

"I have come to say Goodbye, Sir Ector,"

10. **win the palm:** Be the winner. A palm leaf is a symbol of victory.

◆ Critical Thinking

6 Speculate Have students speculate about why Kay is so eager to go to the tournament. *Sample answer: All the great knights of the kingdom will go. Fighting in this tournament will provide the newly-knighted Sir Kay with two possibilities for the future: (1) a once-in-a-lifetime chance to test his strength against the best opponents and (2) the opportunity to gain instant fame as a fighter.*

◆ Reading Strategy

7 Recognize an Author's Attitude Ask students to suggest why the author makes these characters seem to be so in awe of London. *Suggested response: Earlier the author ridiculed Pellinore, Ector, and Grummore for their lack of intelligence. Here he also wants to make it clear that they are unsophisticated local people, without any experience of the world beyond their immediate community.*

◆ Literary Focus

8 Legend Ask students to share what they know about Merlyn's role in the Arthurian legend. *Students may offer different explanations. Point out that these differences are a feature of legends. Retelling a story varies the details from version to version.*

Customize for *Pre-AP Students*

Have students pay attention to White's mixture of modern idioms with medieval scenes that call for Tennyson's deliberately old-fashioned language. Kay asks his father if they can go to the tournament so that they can "have a shot" at it. When Pellinore decides to go to the tournament he says, "Dang it!" Have these students suggest more traditional responses to the situations in the story, such as "try our courage" and "Zounds!"

Viewing and Representing Mini-Lesson

Feudalism Chart

This Mini-Lesson supports the Researching and Representing activity in the Idea Bank on p. 916

Introduce Explain to students that a feudalism chart is a sort of vertical flowchart of fealty that shows the social, religious, and political hierarchy of the feudalistic system. It resembles a family tree, but it isn't chronological. Typically, a Western feudalism chart would have the Pope or the Holy Roman Emperor at the top, the peasants at the bottom, and everyone else placed somewhere in between.

Develop Have students research participants in the feudal system: knights, squires, yeomen, and so on. Tell students they must decide how comprehensive their charts will be. Will they include the clergy? Where will they place certain offices, such as bishops?

Apply Encourage students to make their charts visually appealing with relevant heraldry and symbols of office. Chess players may contribute some good ideas based on the board placement and assigned movements of chess pieces, which are based on and represent the medieval feudal system.

Assess Evaluate students' feudalism charts first on accurate organization: Is everyone in his or her right place? Then consider the artistic qualities of the charts: Have students made an effort to match visually appealing symbols with stations?

◆ Critical Thinking

❶ **Infer** Have students explain why they think White has Sir Ector suggest that Merlyn remain and become a librarian. *Sample answer: Ector is shown to be shallow because he cannot appreciate Merlyn's unusual powers. Thus he suggests that Merlyn take up a limited clerical job.*

▶Critical Viewing◀

❷ **Infer** *Suggested response: The responses of the surrounding people, pointing and raising their hands in surprise, indicate the young man is performing an amazing feat.*

Read to Be Entertained

Much of the pleasure to be derived from earlier parts of *The Sword in the Stone* (1939) comes from the broad humor with which T. H. White satirizes 20th-century English manners and mores by depicting the Middle Ages as a sort of bogus version of his own period. This is analogous to W. S. Gilbert's libretto for *The Mikado,* the operetta with Japanese characters that pokes fun at English manners and snobbery. White was also reacting to the solemnity with which the Victorians regarded the Middle Ages. If the English can be viewed as xenophobic, superior, or snobbish, they also enjoy better than anyone making fun of themselves. With all the humor provided by this piece, the absurd conclusion is genuinely moving. Significantly, the later books in *The Once and Future King, The Witch in the Wood* (1940), *The Ill-Made Knight* (1941), and *The Candle in the Wind* (1942), are less entertaining, perhaps reflecting White's anxiety over England's entry into World War II.

Gallahad's Sword in Stone, Royal MS, by permission of the British Library

▲ **Critical Viewing** How can you tell that the young man in this picture is performing an amazing feat? **[Infer]** ❷

said the old magician. "Tomorrow my pupil Kay will be knighted, and the next week my other pupil will go away as his squire. I have outlived my usefulness here, and it is time to go."

"Now, now, don't say that," said Sir Ector. "I think you're a jolly useful chap whatever
❶ happens. You just stay and teach me, or be the librarian or something. Don't you leave an old man alone, after the children have flown."

"We shall all meet again," said Merlyn. "There is no cause to be sad."

"Don't go," said Kay.

"I must go," replied their tutor. "We have had a good time while we were young, but it

Humanities: Art

Gallahad's Sword in Stone (Royal MS).

This illuminated, meaning "decorated," manuscript page shows the act of pulling a sword from a stone, one element of the legendary story. In the selection, Arthur becomes King after he removes the sword from the stone. Therefore, students may wonder why Galahad is portrayed here as removing the sword. In legend, Galahad (Lancelot's son) successfully repeated Arthur's feat. The circumstances were slightly different for Galahad's attempt, as the stone was floating in a river when he removed the sword. The drama of the moment is highlighted by an attentive audience, including a king and queen. Use this question for discussion:

Does the character pulling the sword from the stone seem aware of the magnitude of his feat? What features of this picture help you to answer this question? *Students might observe that the character has a mild, even casual expression on his face, indicating he is not aware of the magnitude of his feat. Although he is pulling the sword with both hands, he does not appear to be expending huge amounts of strength or energy.*

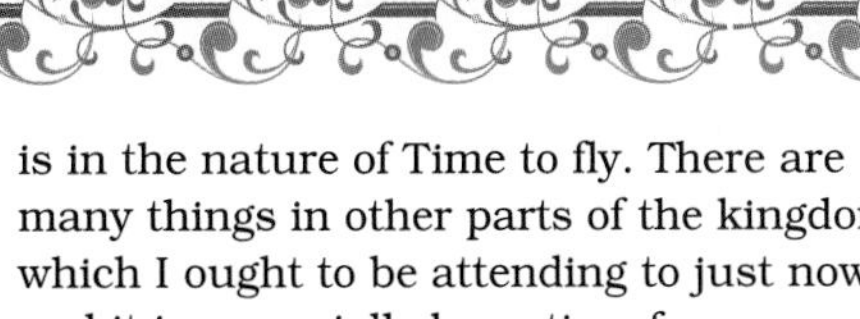

is in the nature of Time to fly. There are many things in other parts of the kingdom which I ought to be attending to just now, and it is a specially busy time for me. Come, Archimedes, say Goodbye to the company.'

"Goodbye," said Archimedes tenderly to the Wart.

"Goodbye," said the Wart without looking up at all.

"But you can't go," cried Sir Ector, "not without a month's notice."

"Can't I?" replied Merlyn, taking up the position always used by philosophers who propose to dematerialize. He stood on his toes, while Archimedes held tight to his shoulder—began to spin on them slowly like a top—spun faster and faster till he was only a blur of grayish light— and in a few seconds there was no one there at all.

"Goodbye, Wart," cried two faint voices outside the solar window.

"Goodbye," said the Wart for the last time—and the poor fellow went quickly out of the room.

> ◆ *Literature and Your Life*
> What qualities do you admire in Wart? What qualities do you not admire?

The knighting took place in a whirl of preparations. Kay's sumptuous bath had to be set up in the box room, between two towel-horses and an old box of selected games which contained a worn-out straw dart-board—it was called fléchette in those days—because all the other rooms were full of packing. The nurse spent the whole time constructing new warm pants for everybody, on the principle that the climate of any place outside the Forest
5 Sauvage must be treacherous to the extreme, and, as for the sergeant, he polished all the armor till it was quite brittle and sharpened the swords till they were almost worn away.

At last it was time to set out.

Perhaps, if you happen not to have lived in the Old England of the twelfth century, or whenever it was, and in a remote castle on the borders of the Marshes at that, you will find it difficult to imagine the wonders of their journey.

The road, or track, ran most of the time along the high ridges of the hills or downs, and they could look down on either side of them upon the desolate marshes where the snowy reeds sighed, and the ice crackled, and the duck in the red sunsets quacked loud on the winter air. The whole country was like that. Perhaps there would be a moory marsh on one side of the ridge, and a forest of a hundred thousand acres on the other, with all the great branches weighted in white. They could sometimes see a wisp of smoke among the trees, or a huddle of buildings far out among the impassable reeds, and twice they came to quite respectable towns which had several inns to boast of, but on the whole it was an England without civilization. The better roads were cleared of cover for a bow-shot on either side of them, lest the traveler should be slain by hidden thieves.

They slept where they could, sometimes in the hut of some cottager who was prepared to welcome them, sometimes in the castle of a brother knight who invited them to refresh themselves, sometimes in the firelight and fleas of a dirty little hovel with a bush tied to a pole outside it—this was the signboard used at that time by inns— 6
and once or twice on the open ground, all huddled together for warmth between their grazing chargers. Wherever they went and wherever they slept, the east wind whistled in the reeds, and the geese went over high in the starlight, honking at the stars.

> ◆ **Build Vocabulary**
> **sumptuous** (sump´ cho͞o əs) *adj.*: Magnificent

◆ Reading Strategy

3 Recognize an Author's Attitude Invite students to describe the author's attitude toward Merlyn in this passage. *Suggested response: Even though Merlyn shows his magical powers by vanishing, the author downplays Merlyn's feat as if it were an everyday occurrence. His attitude toward Merlyn seems distant and matter-of-fact.*

◆ *Literature and Your Life*

4 Some students may admire Wart's sensitivity, others may see it as a sign of weakness. Encourage students to identify Wart's goodbye to Merlyn with a difficult parting they have experienced.

◆ Build Vocabulary

5 Latin Suffixes *-ous* Challenge students to explain how they can determine the definition of the word *treacherous*. *The word root is related to the word treachery. The suffix -ous means "like," or "pertaining to." "Treacherous," then, means "pertaining to treachery," or, in this context, "untrustworthy."*

◆ Reading Strategy

6 Recognize an Author's Attitude What attitude is revealed by this description of the places where the travelers stayed? *An author may show his or her attitude toward a subject through contrast. Here there is a huge contrast between images commonly associated with a group of nobles on a journey, such as luxurious housing and fine food and the barren, scruffy, even squalid images the author presents. The contrast makes it clear that the author is making fun of the crude conditions that he sees as common in the provinces of Britain of that time.*

Cross-Curricular Connection: History

Castles At the time when the story of King Arthur takes place, kings lived in *castles*, fortified structures that housed the king and his advisers, stored food and arms, served as a prison, and protected the local population from attack.

A castle sat on high ground. If the land was flat, an artificial hill, or *motte*, was built. It was ringed by a *moat*, a water-filled ditch, crossed by a *drawbridge* that could be raised from inside the castle. The high stone walls were up to thirty feet thick, with platforms from which defenders could fight off attackers. Inside the wall was a courtyard, or *bailey*. Within the bailey stood a tall tower known as a *keep*, or *donjon*—the strongest point.

Attackers might attempt a *siege* and starve a castle's occupants into surrender. They could try to tunnel under the walls or knock the heavy wooden doors down with a battering ram. Tall wooden towers might be pushed against the castle walls to enable soldiers to swarm onto the platforms. A stone castle was nearly invulnerable to attack, however, until the appearance of guns during the 1400's, at which point stone fortifications ceased to be effective.

❶ **Clarification** Tournaments were held in outlying areas of the kingdom, just as in London. In a poor and remote area such as King Pellinore's realm, however, there would not have been a permanent site for tournaments. An area would be cleared and the necessary facilities set up on a temporary basis.

◆ Reading Strategy

❷ **Recognize an Author's Attitude** Have students suggest an explanation for the vivid and striking description the author gives of the tournament grounds. What is White implying about his characters with this description? *Students should bear in mind that Ector, Pellinore, and the others are familiar only with their place of birth. By using these dazzling details, the author shows how the place must look through their eyes. It is another way in which he pokes fun at their inexperience and lack of culture.*

Comprehension Check ☑

❸ Why do Sir Kay's actions make the Wart so angry? *Sample answer: The Wart has been Kay's close companion for a long time. Now that Kay is a knight, Wart thinks Kay is being disrespectful. He is treating Wart as a servant who does errands for payment, rather than as an old friend.*

London was full to the brim. If Sir Ector had not been lucky enough to own a little land in Pie Street, on which there stood a respectable inn, they would have been hard put to it to find a lodging. But he did own it, and as a matter of fact drew most of his dividends from that source, so they were able to get three beds between the five of them. They thought themselves fortunate.

On the first day of the tournament, Sir Kay managed to get them on the way to the lists at least an hour before the jousts could possibly begin. He had lain awake all night, imagining how he was going to beat the best barons in England, and he had not been able to eat his breakfast. Now he rode at the front of the cavalcade, with pale cheeks, and Wart wished there was something he could do to calm him down.

❶ For country people, who only knew the dismantled tilting ground[11] of Sir Ector's castle, the scene which met their eyes was ravishing. It was a huge green pit in the earth, about as big as the arena of a football match. It lay ten feet lower than the surrounding country, with sloping banks, and the snow had been swept off it. It had been kept warm with straw, which had been cleared off that morning, and now the close-worn grass sparkled green in the white landscape. Round the arena there was a world of color so dazzling and moving and twinkling as to make one blink one's eyes. ❷ The wooden grandstands were painted in scarlet and white. The silk pavilions of famous people, pitched on every side, were azure and green and saffron and checkered. The pennons and pennoncells which floated everywhere in the sharp wind were flapping with every color of the rainbow, as they strained and slapped at their flagpoles, and the barrier down the middle of the arena itself was done in chessboard squares of black and white. Most of the combatants and their friends had not yet arrived, but one could see from those few who had come how the very people would turn the scene into a bank of flowers, and how the armor would flash, and the scalloped sleeves of the heralds jig in the wind, as they raised their brazen trumpets to their lips to shake the fleecy clouds of winter with joyances[12] and fanfares.

"Good heavens!" cried Sir Kay. "I have left my sword at home."

"Can't joust without a sword," said Sir Grummore. "Quite irregular."

"Better go and fetch it," said Sir Ector. "You have time."

"My squire will do," said Sir Kay. "What an awful mistake to make! Here, squire, ride hard back to the inn and fetch my sword. You shall have a shilling[13] if you fetch it in time."

The Wart went as pale as Sir Kay was, and looked as if he were going to strike him. Then he said, "It shall be done, master," and turned his ambling palfrey against the stream of newcomers. He began to push his way toward their hostelry[14] as best he might.

❸ "To offer me money!" cried the Wart to himself. "To look down at this beastly little donkey-affair off his great charger and to call me Squire! Oh, Merlyn, give me patience with the brute, and stop me from throwing his filthy shilling in his face."

When he got to the inn it was closed. Everybody had thronged to see the famous tournament, and the entire household had followed after the mob. Those were lawless days and it was not safe to leave your house—or even to go to sleep in it—unless you were certain that it was impregnable.[15]

11. **tilting ground:** Ground on which a joust takes place.

12. **joyances** (joiˊ əns iz) *n.*: Old word for *rejoicing*.
13. **shilling** (shilˊ in) *n.*: British silver coin.
14. **hostelry** (hasˊ təl rē) *n.*: Inn.
15. **impregnable** (im pregˊ nə bəl) *adj.*: Not capable of being entered by force.

Cross-Curricular Connection: History

Tournaments A tournament such as the one to which Arthur and his companions go in this story is quite different from the tournaments staged by knights in the 1100's. In these events, a large number of knights would form two "armies" that would fight each other, often for several days, and over large expanses of territory. Often, large sums of money were wagered on the outcome.

Kings grew to dislike these tournaments; when a number of armed knights gathered together, there was always a possibility of rebellion. Also, such mock battles usually resulted in the destruction of property, and people might be injured or even killed.

By the 1200's, milder tournaments evolved, like the one in which Sir Kay hopes to compete. Knights would *joust*, or fight with blunted weapons. They also engaged in *tilting*. In this competition, two mounted knights with lances would charge each other in narrow lanes, or *lists*, on either side of a wooden barrier and attempt to knock each other from their horses. Injuries and deaths might occur, but the newer form of tournament proved to be very popular, and considerably safer.

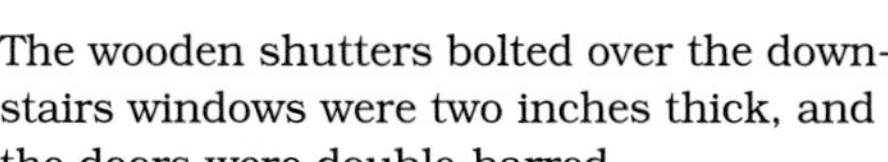

The wooden shutters bolted over the downstairs windows were two inches thick, and the doors were double-barred.

"Now what do I do," asked the Wart, "to earn my shilling?"

He looked ruefully at the blind little inn, and began to laugh.

"Poor Kay," he said. "All that shilling stuff was only because he was scared and miserable, and now he has good cause to be. Well, he shall have a sword of some sort if I have to break into the Tower of London.

"How does one get hold of a sword?" he continued. "Where can I steal one? Could I waylay some knight even if I am mounted on an ambling pad, and take his weapons by force? There must be some swordsmith or armorer in a great town like this, whose shop would be still open."

He turned his mount and cantered off along the street. There was a quiet churchyard at the end of it, with a kind of square in front of the church door. In the middle of the square there was a heavy stone with an anvil on it, and a fine new sword was stuck through the anvil.

"Well," said the Wart, "I suppose it is some sort of war memorial, but it will have to do. I am sure nobody would grudge Kay a war memorial, if they knew his desperate straits"

He tied his reins round a post of the lych gate,[16] strode up the gravel path, and took hold of the sword.

"Come, sword," he said. "I must cry your mercy and take you for a better cause.

"This is extraordinary," said the Wart. "I feel strange when I have hold of this sword, and I notice everything much more clearly. Look at the beautiful gargoyles[17] of the church, and of the monastery which it belongs to. See how splendidly all the famous banners in the aisle are waving. How nobly that yew[18] holds up the red flakes of its timbers to worship God. How clean the snow is. I can smell something like sweet briar—and is it music that I hear?"

It was music, whether of pan-pipes or of recorders, and the light in the churchyard was so clear, without being dazzling, that one could have picked a pin out twenty yards away.

"There is something in this place," said the Wart. "There are people. Oh, people, what do you want?" 6

Nobody answered him, but the music was loud and the light beautiful.

"People," cried the Wart, "I must take this sword. It is not for me, but for Kay. I will bring it back."

There was still no answer, and Wart turned back to the anvil. He saw the golden letters, which he did not read, and the jewels on the pommel, flashing in the lovely light.

"Come, sword," said the Wart.

He took hold of the handles with both hands, and strained against the stone. There was a melodious consort[19] on the recorders, but nothing moved. 7

The Wart let go of the handles, when they were beginning to bite into the palms of his hands, and stepped back, seeing stars.

"It is well fixed," he said.

He took hold of it again and pulled with all his might. The music played more strongly, and the light all about the churchyard glowed like amethysts; but the sword still stuck. 8

"Oh, Merlyn," cried the Wart, "help me to get this weapon."

16. **lych** (lich) **gate:** Roofed gate at the entrance to a churchyard.

17. **gargoyles** (gar′ goilz) *n.*: Gotesquely carved animals or fantastic creatures, on a building.
18. **yew** (yo͞o) *n.*: Type of evergreen tree with red cones.
19. **consort** (kan′ sort) *n.*: Harmony of sounds.

◆ Build Vocabulary

palfrey (pôl′ frē) *n.*: Saddle horse, especially one for a woman

4 Clarification "Pad" in this context is a derogatory word for a horse that is old, infirm, or otherwise unimpressive.

◆ Critical Thinking

5 Infer Ask students what Wart's feelings when he holds the sword suggest about the sword itself. *Suggested response: Wart's feeling strange and noticing everything more clearly suggests that the sword has some kind of extraordinary power.*

◆ Critical Thinking

6 Interpret Invite students' explanations for the presence of the people who do not answer and the otherworldly music in this passage. *Suggested response: The people's not answering Wart may suggest that they are not flesh-and-blood onlookers, but possibly ghosts or magicians. The music, which comes from nowhere, is not made by human beings. Something mysterious and magical is taking place.*

◆ Build Vocabulary

7 Latin Suffixes *-ous* Ask students how they would determine the meaning of the word "melodious." *Students should see that the root of the word is related to melody. The suffix -ous means "like" or "pertaining to." Therefore, melodious means "pertaining to, or like, melody."*

◆ Literary Focus

8 Legend Ask students how anyone but Wart could know what sounds were heard at that moment. Why would the author include these details? *Students should recognize that these details cannot be verified by witnesses, but were probably added to enhance the significance of this legendary moment.*

Research Skills Mini-Lesson

Evaluating Sources

Introduce Tell students that when they have gathered their sources for a research project or paper, they must evaluate them to make sure they are worthwhile.

Develop Suggest to students that it is helpful to make source cards as they gather information. Then explain the following strategies for evaluating sources:

- Check the table of contents and the index to see whether the book contains information directly related to your topic.
- If your topic is in a field of rapid change or growth, make sure the material is not too old to be useful. This means checking the publication dates of the material.
- Try to evaluate the author's knowledge and the reputation of the publication.
- Look through chapters or articles for relevant information.

Apply Give students plenty of time to evaluate their sources. They will do this with ease when they know the process.

Assess Check to make sure that students have followed the four strategies above. They should have weeded out some of their sources in the process.

❶ **Clarification** Students should know that in an earlier section of *The Once and Future King*, Merlyn had used his powers to temporarily transform young Arthur into various animals, including a fish and a bird, so that he could learn their wisdom and communicate with them. These animals make a reappearance here and repeat advice that they had given him previously.

◆ Critical Thinking

❷ **Infer** Have students explain how the love that the animals have for Arthur helps him pull out the sword. How does the presence of the animals add to the occasion? *Suggested response: Because of the special bond Arthur has with these animals, he is aware of a "power" within him. The presence of the animals adds to the mystery and magic of the occasion.*

▶Critical Viewing◀

❸ **Infer** Elicit responses such as the following: *By representing the Round Table and its knights and the Holy Grail in such detail, art such as this helps the viewer to create a mental image of important scenes from legends, thus preserving them in the viewer's mind.*

❹ **Clarification** A merlin is a variety of hawk. Hawks depend on the gripping power of their taloned feet to capture prey. The merlin offers Arthur advice on how to grip the sword. Like the advice of the other animals, it is based on its own experience. The name of the wizard, here given as "Merlyn," is also spelled "Merlin," and he may be named after the bird.

The Round Table and the Holy Grail, Musee Conde, Chantilly, France

▲ **Critical Viewing** Explain how art, like the painting shown here, can preserve a legend visually. **[Infer]** 3

These was a kind of rushing noise, and a long chord played along with it. All round the churchyard there were hundreds of old friends. They rose over the church wall all together, like the Punch-and-Judy[20] ghosts of remembered days, and there were badgers and nightingales and vulgar crows and 1 hares and wild geese and falcons and fishes and dogs and dainty unicorns and solitary wasps and hedgehogs and griffins and the thousand other animals he had met. They loomed round the church wall, the lovers and helpers of the Wart, and they all spoke solemnly in turn. Some of them had come from the banners in the church, where they were painted in heraldry, some from the wa- 2 ters and the sky and the fields about—but all, down to the smallest shrew mouse, had come to help on account of love. Wart felt his power grow.

"Put your back into it," said a luce (or pike) off one of the heraldic banners, "as you once did when I was going to snap you up. Remember that power springs from the nape of the neck."

"What about those forearms," asked a badger gravely, "that are held together by a chest? Come along, my dear embryo,[21] and find your tool."

A merlin sitting at the top of the yew tree cried out, "Now then, Captain Wart, what is the first law of the foot? I thought I once 4 heard something about never letting go."

"Don't work like a stalling woodpecker," urged a tawny owl affectionately. "Keep up

20. **Punch-and-Judy:** Puppets of the quarrelsome Punch and his wife, Judy, who constantly fight in a comical way.

21. **embryo:** (em′ brē ō) *n.*: Anything in an early stage of development.

Humanities: Art

The Round Table and the Holy Grail.

This illustration shows the round table, twelve knights in various positions and rooms near the table, and the Holy Grail, the cup believed to have been used by Jesus at the Last Supper.

Use this question for discussion:

How is the style of this illustration different from the ones on pages 905 and 908? *Students should recognize that this illustration is more colorful and shows more detail than the others; it also features motifs of flowers, handwriting from what is probably an illuminated manuscript, and other details and symbols meaningful to the legend. Students may also notice that there are other frames partially shown. This artwork probably tells a story in the same way a comic strip or storyboard might.*

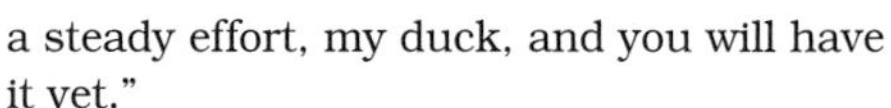

a steady effort, my duck, and you will have it yet."

A white-front said. "Now, Wart, if you were once able to fly the great North Sea, surely you can coordinate a few little wing-muscles here and there? Fold your powers together, with the spirit of your mind, and it will come out like butter. Come along, Homo sapiens,[22] for all we humble friends of yours are waiting here to cheer."

The Wart walked up to the great sword for the third time. He put out his right hand softly and drew it out as gently as from a scabbard.

There was a lot of cheering, a noise like a hurdy-gurdy[23] which went on and on. In the middle of this noise, after a long time, he saw Kay and gave him the sword. The people at the tournament were making a frightful row.

"But this is not my sword," said Sir Kay.

"It was the only one I could get," said the Wart. "The inn was locked."

"It is a nice-looking sword. Where did you get it?"

"I found it stuck in a stone, outside a church."

Sir Kay had been watching the tilting nervously, waiting for his turn. He had not paid much attention to his squire.

"That is a funny place to find one," he said.

"Yes, it was stuck through an anvil."

"What?" cried Sir Kay, suddenly rounding upon him. "Did you just say this sword was stuck in a stone?"

"It was," said the Wart. "It was a sort of war memorial."

Sir Kay stared at him for several seconds in amazement, opened his mouth, shut it again, licked his lips, then turned his back and plunged through the crowd. He was looking for Sir Ector, and the Wart followed after him.

"Father," cried Sir Kay, "come here a moment."

"Yes, my boy," said Sir Ector. "Splendid falls these professional chaps do manage. Why, what's the matter, Kay? You look as white as a sheet."

"Do you remember that sword which the King of England would pull out?"

"Yes."

"Well, here it is. I have it. It is in my hand. I pulled it out." 6

Sir Ector did not say anything silly. He looked at Kay and he looked at the Wart. Then he stared at Kay again, long and lovingly, and said, "We will go back to the church."

"Now then, Kay," he said, when they were at the church door. He looked at his first-born kindly, but straight between the eyes. "Here is the stone, and you have the sword. It will make you the King of England. You are my son that I am proud of, and always will be, whatever you do. Will you promise me that you took it out by your own might?" 7

Kay looked at his father. He also looked at the Wart and at the sword.

Then he handed the sword to the Wart quite quietly.

He said, "I am a liar. Wart pulled it out." 8

As far as the Wart was concerned, there was a time after this in which Sir Ector kept telling him to put the sword back into the stone—which he did—and in which Sir Ector and Kay then vainly tried to take it out. The Wart took it out for them, and stuck it back again once or twice. After this, there was another time which was more painful.

He saw that his dear guardian was looking quite old and powerless, and that he was kneeling down with difficulty on a gouty[24] knee.

"Sir," said Sir Ector, without looking up, although he was speaking to his own boy.

---

22. Homo sapiens (hō´ mō sā´ pē ənz´): Human being.

23. hurdy-gurdy (hur´ dē gur´ dē) *n.*: Musical instrument, like a barrel organ, played by turning a crank.

24. gouty (gout´ ē) *adj.*: Having gout, a disease causing swelling and severe pain in the joints.

◆ Literary Focus

5 Legend Why do you think talking animals have been introduced into the Arthurian legend? *The presence of talking animals underscores the magical quality of this moment and of what Arthur is about to accomplish.*

◆ Critical Thinking

6 Analyze Encourage students to offer ideas as to what characteristic in Sir Kay is brought out in this passage. *Students may recall that Sir Kay's ambition for fame and accomplishment had been established when he urged his father to take him to the great tournament. Faced with an opportunity to claim the throne of England, Sir Kay's automatic response reflects that ambition.*

◆ Reading Strategy

7 Recognize an Author's Attitude Ask students for their opinions on the author's attitude toward Sir Ector in this passage. *Students may observe a different attitude at work here. The author has Sir Ector speak clearly and grammatically and show himself to be a loving and honorable man. It is one place where the author brings out some of Sir Ector's virtues and treats him with respect.*

◆ Critical Thinking

8 Analyze Have students explain Sir Kay's abrupt change of heart and confession. *Suggested response: Sir Kay cannot lie to his father now that he has had the chance to consider the implications of what he had claimed. He is showing that he is an honorable man.*

Reteach

Point out to students the difference between Tennyson and White in their attitudes toward the Arthurian legends. Guide students to understand this difference by showing a graphic representation of the authors' attitudes. Use this graphic organizer to help students isolate details and events the authors choose to present and think about the messages the authors convey—either directly or indirectly—through this information.

details or events	message conveyed	author's attitude
King Author asks Sir Bedivere whether he has performed his mission.	Arthur rules England with seriousness and authority.	serious respect
The Wart does not want Sir Ector to kneel before him.	Arthur is unsure of what pulling the sword from the stone means.	newfound respect

◆ Critical Thinking

❶ Infer Ask students why Wart reacts as he does to the last developments in the story. *Suggested response: The relationships between Wart and those he has thought of as his family have abruptly changed. Deprived of these family ties, Wart may suddenly feel isolated, and fearful of a strange and unlooked-for future.*

Reinforce and Extend

Answers

◆ Literature and Your Life

Reader's Response Students might say young Arthur (or Wart) because he is sensible and honorable and, as revealed by the final scene, very human.

Thematic Focus Students might say that perhaps Wart is a new kind of hero—one who is softer and who pays attention to the needs of others rather than placing ultimate emphasis on showing his prowess.

Question for Research There are many sources of information on King Arthur, from standard reference works to individual books. Have students check library card catalogs or databases.

1. He brings the news that the King is dead.
2. Whoever can pull the sword out of the anvil and the stone will be the next King of England.
3. Sir Kay left his sword at home.
4. He removes the sword from the anvil and stone.
5. They realize that he pulled the sword from the stone, which was the object of the tournament.

◆ Critical Thinking

1. Magical forces of nature seem to unite to help Wart draw the sword from the stone; talking animals coax him to success.
2. His explanations, at first, reveal that he is shallow and ambitious.
3. Wart is ambivalent about becoming King; he seems fearful and does not want to rise above his friends.
4. Sample response: White's dialogue for his characters is crude and unbecoming of knights; he uses malapropisms like "next of skin"; he puts the knights in undignified situations, such as how he describes their lodging in London.
5. Possible response: Sir Bedivere's lament is nostalgic, full of respect, despair, and loneliness. In contrast, Sir Grummore speaks irreverently about the absence of a monarch.

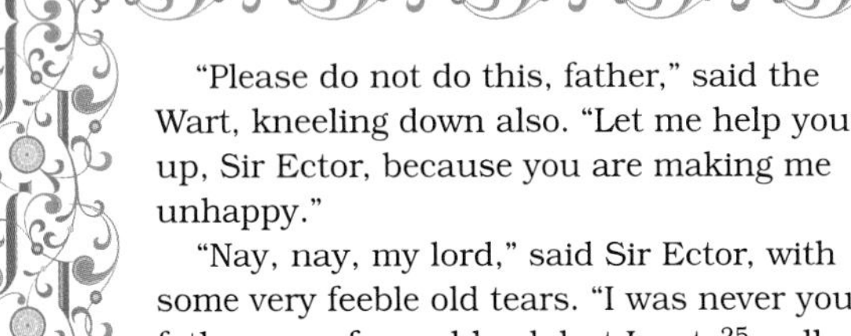

"Please do not do this, father," said the Wart, kneeling down also. "Let me help you up, Sir Ector, because you are making me unhappy."

"Nay, nay, my lord," said Sir Ector, with some very feeble old tears. "I was never your father nor of your blood, but I wote[25] well ye are of an higher blood than I wend[26] ye were."

"Plenty of people have told me you are not my father," said the Wart, "but it does not matter a bit."

"Sir," said Sir Ector humbly, "will ye be my good and gracious lord when ye are King?"

"Don't!" said the Wart.

"Sir," said Sir Ector, "I will ask no more of you but that you will make my son, your foster-brother, Sir Kay, seneschal[27] of all your lands."

Kay was kneeling down too, and it was more than the Wart could bear.

"Oh, do stop," he cried. "Of course he can be seneschal, if I have got to be this King, and, oh, father, don't kneel down like that, because it breaks my heart. Please get up, Sir Ector, and don't make everything so horrible. Oh, dear, oh, dear, I wish I had never seen that filthy sword at all."

And the Wart also burst into tears.

25. **wote** (wot) *v.*: Old word meaning know.
26. **wend** (wend) *v.*: Here, old word meaning *thought*.
27. **seneschal** (sen´ ə shəl) *n.*: Steward in the house of a medieval noble.

Guide for Responding

◆ Literature and Your Life

Reader's Response Which character is your favorite? Why?

Thematic Focus Is the Wart the type of courageous hero you expect to meet in a traditional tale of heroism? What qualities might a humble character like the Wart model for future generations?

Questions for Research T. H. White's deep knowledge of Arthurian legends is apparent in *The Once and Future King*. Generate research questions about the sources that are available to learn of the legendary reign of King Arthur.

☑ Check Your Comprehension

1. What significant news does King Pellinore bring?
2. Explain how the new king of England is to be chosen.
3. Why does Sir Kay ask the Wart to hurry back to the inn from the arena?
4. What extraordinary feat does the Wart perform in the churchyard?
5. What do Sir Ector and Sir Kay realize when the Wart returns to the arena?

◆ Critical Thinking

INTERPRET

1. In what ways is the Wart's drawing of the sword from the stone a moment of magic and mystery? **[Support]**
2. What do Sir Kay's explanations to Sir Ector about pulling the sword reveal about Sir Kay's character? **[Analyze]**
3. How does the Wart feel about becoming king? **[Draw Conclusions]**

EVALUATE

4. Give some examples of how T. H. White pokes fun at the Arthurian legends with a light and humorous attitude. **[Evaluate]**

COMPARE LITERARY WORKS

5. Compare the tone of Sir Bedivere's lament over King Arthur's death in Tennyson's poem (lines 277–289) with Sir Grummore's complaints about the state of Church and country at the death of King Pendragon (page 906). **[Compare and Contrast]**

Guide for Responding (continued)

◆ Reading Strategy

Recognize an Author's Attitude

Recognizing an **author's attitude** toward his or her subject will help you appreciate a piece of writing. Authors T. H. White and Alfred, Lord Tennyson, have strikingly different attitudes toward their common subject, Arthur.

1. Find three examples of words, phrases, and situations in "Arthur Becomes King of Britain" that show T. H. White's light and humorous attitude toward the Arthurian legends.
2. (a) What is Tennyson's attitude toward his subject? (b) Cite three passages in "Morte d'Arthur" that show Tennyson's attitude.

◆ Literary Focus

Legend

A **legend** is an imaginative story handed down for generations and believed, but not proved, to have a historical basis. Legends also provide information about the culture that created them.

1. Do you think warfare was a common occurrence during this period? Support your opinion.
2. What values or qualities do the Arthurian legends illustrate that indicate that the legend will continue through future generations?
3. Why do you think the details of a legend, such as how Arthur acquires Excalibur, differ from version to version?

Beyond Literature

Cultural Connection

Political Legends Like King Arthur, most great leaders spawn legends. Consider George Washington. It was understood at the time of its founding that the new nation needed powerful examples of legitimacy in order to survive and that Washington's very real personal integrity would be the example to use. Mason Weems wrote a biography of Washington that underscored this trait by including sheer fabrications. Hence, generations of schoolchildren learned a story (about Washington and a cherry tree) that never happened.

◆ Build Vocabulary

Using the Latin Suffix *-ous*

The common Latin suffix *-ous* means "like" or "pertaining to." On your paper, write the word from the following list that best completes each sentence.

a. sumptuous **b.** adventurous **c.** slanderous

1. To hurt his reputation, his opponents spread __?__ stories about him.
2. White and Tennyson both tell __?__ tales.
3. The king prepared a __?__ banquet for his guests.

Using the Word Bank: Definitions

On your paper, write the word from the Word Bank that best defines each statement.

1. Sounds of this are heard at funerals.
2. Things that are this are usually expensive as well.
3. You'd better practice before riding one of these.
4. A fastidious person is probably this also.
5. Spending too much time in the sun will make your skin look this way.

◆ Build Grammar Skills

Subjunctive Mood

Writers use the **subjunctive mood** of the verb to state a condition that is contrary to fact, usually in clauses beginning with *if, as if,* or *as though*, or to express indirectly a demand, suggestion, or statement of necessity. The most commonly used subjunctive form is the past subjunctive of *be*, which is always *were*.

Practice In your notebook, correct each sentence by writing the correct subjunctive form.

1. Sir Bedivere acted as if Excalibur was more important than Arthur's command.
2. My end draws nigh; 'tis time that I am gone.
3. What heroes would be in Avilion, if there really was such a place?
4. If King Arthur was to come again, would war really end?
5. Arthur demanded that Bedivere should cast Excalibur into the lake.

Answers

◆ Reading Strategy

1. Sample response: "Compose yourself, Nanny"; all of Sir Gramarye's dialogue; lines such as "Can't joust without a sword. Quite irregular."
2. (a) Tennyson's attitude is respectful and reverent toward Arthur and admiring toward Bedivere. (b) His respectful attitude is indicated in lines 50 and 51; his admiration for Sir Bedivere shows in lines 56–59; and his attitude of awe and reverence shows in lines 350–354.

◆ Literary Focus

1. The swords, armor, and jousts, or war games, in these works seem to indicate that warfare was common.
2. Qualities such as courage and honesty are paid tribute in the tales; these qualities will still be respected in future generations.
3 Legends are passed down through the generations along different channels. Each storyteller adds something or changes something that he or she feels enhances the tale.

◆ Build Vocabulary

Using the Latin Suffix *-ous*
1. c 2. b 3. a

Using the Word Bank
1. lamentation; 2. sumptuous; 3. palfrey; 4. stickler; 5. swarthy

◆ Build Grammar Skills

1. Sire Bedivere acted as if Excalibur were more important than Arthur's command.
2. My end draws nigh; 'tis time that I go.
3. What heroes would be in Avilion, if there really were such a place?
4. If King Arthur were to come again, would war really end?
5. Arthur demanded that Bedivere cast Excalibur into the lake.

Beyond the Selection

FURTHER READING

The complete book *The Once and Future King.*

More Books by T. H. White

The Book of Merlyn (the end of the Arthur story)
The Book of Beasts

Other Books About King Arthur

The Acts of King Arthur and His Noble Knights, John Steinbeck
A Connecticut Yankee in King Arthur's Court, Mark Twain

We suggest that you preview these works.

INTERNET

We suggest the following sites on the Internet (all Web sites are subject to change).

For more information about Alfred, Lord Tennyson, go to **http://charon. sfus.edu/TENNYSON/tennyson.html**

For more information about T.H. White, go to **http://www2.netdoor.com/~moulder/thwhite.html**

We *strongly recommend* that you preview these sites before you send students to them.

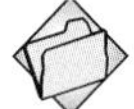

Idea Bank

Following are suggestions for matching Idea Bank topics with your students' performance levels and learning modalities:

Customizing for
Performance Levels
Less Advanced Students: 1, 5
Average Students: 2, 4, 6
More Advanced Students: 3, 7

Customizing for
Learning Modalities
Following are suggestions for matching Idea Bank topics with your students' learning modalities:
Musical/Rhythmic: 4
Verbal/Linguistic: 4, 5
Bodily/Kinesthetic: 5
Visual/Spatial: 6
Logical/Mathematical: 7

Guided Writing Lesson

Elaboration Strategy Students can use the **SEE** technique to support their claims: make a Statement, Extend the statement, and Elaborate on the statement. Model the **SEE** technique with the following example.

Statement: Luke Skywalker should be knighted.

Extension: Luke Skywalker is a hero who should be knighted.

Elaboration: Luke Skywalker is a hero who has performed noble deeds such as saving others, and he should be knighted.

Writing and Language Transparencies Use the set of transparencies for Writing Process Model 9: Business Letter, pp. 61–64, to provide a model of a business letter and to guide students through the writing and revising process.

Writing Lab CD-ROM
Have students complete the tutorial on practical and technical writing. Follow these steps:

1. Refer students to the Purpose Profile, where they can answer a series of questions to help them achieve their intended purpose.
2. Suggest that students use the Letter Shell to help them correctly format their letter of recommendation.
3. Have students use a Revision Checker for Vague Language. This tool will help them replace vague terms with more precise ones.

Build Your Portfolio

Idea Bank

Writing

1. **List** Based on these two selections, make a list of Arthur's heroic qualities. Explain which actions or words indicate each quality.

2. **Epic Essay** Write an essay analyzing the qualities of "Morte d'Arthur" that make it an epic. Mention the values expressed in the selection, the qualities that make Arthur a hero, and the ways in which the actions and events are larger than life.

3. **Local Legends** Choose a legend with which you are familiar and write a short scene that might be used in a stage or screen version of the legend.

Speaking, Listening, and Viewing

4. **Music** The musical *Camelot* is based on *The Once and Future King*. With several classmates, watch a videotape or listen to the soundtrack of *Camelot*. As a panel, discuss how the film or lyrics depict the Arthurian legend. Each panel member can present a different aspect. **[Music Link]**

5. **Oral Report** Like Britain, Japan had a feudal era with warring *daimyo* (lords) and unifying *shoguns* (rulers). Research the subject of feudal Japan to find a leader like Arthur, and prepare a brief oral report on his accomplishments. **[History Link]**

Researching and Representing

6. **Art** Create a painting or drawing to illustrate an important event in "Arthur Becomes King of Britain." **[Art Link]**

7. **Feudalism Chart** Feudalism was an economic, political, and social system in medieval England. Feudalism was also practiced in Japan and other European countries. Research feudalism at the library. Make a chart to compare and contrast the practice of feudalism in different countries. **[Social Studies Link]**

Online Activity www.phlit.phschool.com

Guided Writing Lesson

Letter of Recommendation

Is there someone from history, from fiction, or from your own life who deserves the title "Sir" in the grand land of Camelot? Write a **letter of recommendation** to King Arthur. Explain how this person meets the qualifications for knighthood and describe the talents or abilities he or she would contribute to Arthur's court.

As you plan and write the letter of recommendation, keep this point in mind:

Writing Skills Focus: Clear and Consistent Purpose

Open with a **clear statement of your purpose**, telling your recommendation for knighthood and your reasons. In the body of your letter, you must develop your purpose-setting statement in a clear and consistent way. That means each detail or example you give should show why your candidate is fit to sit at the Round Table.

Prewriting Write the name of your candidate and list as many facts, details, and examples about his or her life as you can recall. Choose the information that most supports your claim that he or she is qualified for knighthood; for example, honorable, brave, honest, and trustworthy.

Drafting As you write your letter, use the information you have listed. You may want to organize your points by order of importance, leading up to the most important.

Revising Reread your draft. Does every detail support your purpose in a clear and consistent way? Have you made clear how your candidate meets the qualifications? Have you followed the correct form for a business letter? Revise to strengthen your letter's content, consistency, and format.

✓ ASSESSMENT OPTIONS

Formal Assessment, Selection Test, pp. 220–222, and Assessment Resources Software. The selection test is designed so that it can be easily customized to the performance levels of your students.

Alternative Assessment, p. 62, includes options for less advanced students, more advanced students, visual/spatial learners, bodily/kinesthetic learners, and interpersonal learners.

PORTFOLIO ASSESSMENT
Use the following rubrics in the ***Alternative Assessment*** booklet to assess student writing:
List: Definition/Classification Rubric, p. 99
Epic Essay: Response to Literature Rubric, p. 110
Local Legends: Fictional Narrative Rubric, p. 95
Guided Writing Lesson: Business Letter/Memo Rubric, p. 113

Writing Process Workshop

Research Paper

When you present factual information on a topic you've researched—such as the Arthurian legends—you're writing a **research paper.** A research paper usually includes an introduction that states the main idea, a body that develops and elaborates on the main idea, and a conclusion that summarizes the points you have made. When you refer to information you've found through your research, you need to give credit to the source in a footnote or parenthetical citation. At the end of the paper, include a bibliography that lists all the sources you used.

Write a research paper on a topic that interests you. The following skills, introduced in this section's Guided Writing Lessons, will help.

Writing Skills Focus

- **Use clear and logical organization** for your paper. Whether you choose order of importance, chronological, or compare-and-contrast, stick with that method of organization for the body of your research paper. (See p. 891.)
- **Have a clear, consistent purpose** for your research paper. State your purpose in your opening paragraph, and develop it in the body of the paper. (See p. 916.)

The following introduction from a paper on the effect of CDs on the music industry shows these skills at work.

Writing Model

① CDs have had a dramatic impact on the music industry. Although music has always been big business, CDs have made it even more so.

Since the 1983 introduction of CD technology, the music industry has increased sales by $100 million annually. The new technology created consumer demand in nearly every category. From pop to jazz to rock to rap, the instant popularity of CDs created a revolution in how music is delivered. ②

① The purpose of this report is to describe the influence of CDs on the music industry. The writer sticks to this point in his introduction.

② The writer uses point-by-point organization: He makes an observation or comment about CDs and then backs it up with an example.

Prepare and Engage

LESSON OBJECTIVES

- To use recursive writing processes to write a research paper
- To generate and support a topic sentence
- To cite sources appropriately

Before students begin, you may want to share with them the Scoring Rubric for Research Report/Paper (page 106 in ***Alternative Assessment***) so that students see the criteria by which they will be evaluated. Suggestions on page 919 customize the rubric to this workshop.

Connect to Literature Unit 7, Nonfiction, contains material that can serve as primary and secondary sources for a research paper. Explain to students that if they writing about Marian Anderson, for example, then Langston Hughes's "Marian Anderson: Famous Concert Singer" is a secondary source, written about Anderson, not by her. However, if they were investigating Hughes's writing style, the Anderson article is a primary source. Good research includes both. Ask students, in groups, to skim Unit 7 and decide which pieces could be primary and which secondary sources.

Writers at Work Videodisc
Play the Research Writing videodisc segment, Ch. 5, for students to hear N. Scott Momaday discuss research.

Play frames 3 to 9933

Writing Lab CD-ROM
Students can work in the tutorial on Research Writing to complete all or part of their research paper. Follow these steps:

1. Students can review the interactive models of five types of research writing.
2. Have students use a Topic Web and consult tips to narrow their topics.
3. Have students use the audio-annotated instruction on organization.
4. The Transition Word Bin will help students refine idea connections.

Develop Student Writing

Prewriting Strategy
Use an advanced-level research loop to guide students as they begin their research papers.

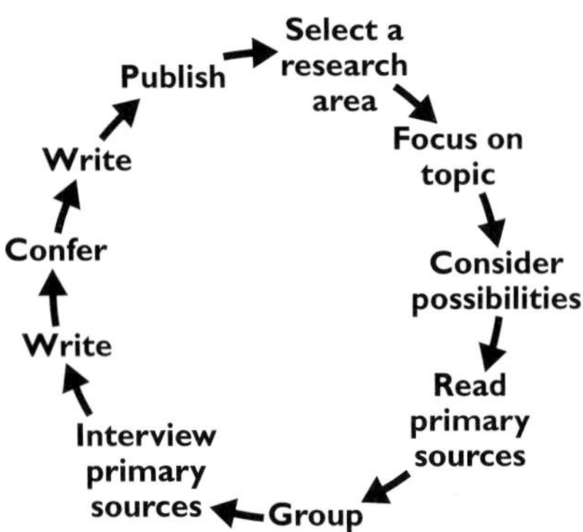

Customize for
Visual/Spatial Learners
Encourage students to use visuals in their research papers: graphs, charts, maps, photographs, and diagrams.

Writing Lab CD-ROM
The Gathering Information section in the Research Writing tutorial gives tips for using library resources, using on-line services, and taking notes.

Elaboration Strategy
You may want to designate the documentation form you prefer students use—parenthetical, footnote, or endnote—but remind them that all three forms are valid means of citing sources. Remind students that every supporting detail will have come from some source and therefore must be documented.

Applying Language Skills
Topic Sentence and Support
Remind students that every paragraph has a topic sentence; together, the topic sentences equal the thesis statement. If students prepare an outline, each lettered item in the outline (A, B, C, etc.) should be reflected in a topic sentence and, therefore, a paragraph.

Answer
Suggested response: Fiber-rich foods contribute to good health.

Grammar Reinforcement

For additional instruction and practice, use "Understanding Research Papers," and "Writing a Research Paper," pp. 135–136, in the *Writer's Solution Grammar Practice Book.*

APPLYING LANGUAGE SKILLS: Topic Sentence and Support

Each of your paragraphs has a main idea that is stated in a **topic sentence.** The **supporting sentences** further develop the main idea with details, explanations, and examples. Notice the topic sentence (the first sentence) and supporting sentences in the following paragraph:

A medieval feast was designed to appeal to the senses. The dishes were colorful, such as green eel stew, and highly spiced, such as rabbit seasoned with ginger and nutmeg. Regarding flavor, most dishes were a bit sour and salty.

Practice On your paper, add a topic sentence to the following paragraph.

One of the ways in which fiber-rich foods help is by reducing the risk of heart disease. Another is by cleansing the digestive system of infection.

Writer's Solution Connection
Language Lab
For more help writing effective topic sentences, complete the Language Lab lesson on Topic Sentence and Support.

Prewriting

Choose a Topic To choose a topic for your research paper, ask a question that is interesting, relevant, and for which there is plenty of information available. If you can't think of a topic, consider one of the topic ideas listed here.

Topic Ideas
- A famous writer
- An endangered animal or plant
- A recent invention or discovery
- The source of a famous myth or legend

Find Appropriate Sources In a library, locate the resources that will help you. These may include history books, newspapers, magazines, databases, and the Internet. Use the most up-to-date resources, because they may contain information not included in older materials.

Take Accurate Notes Use note cards and source cards to record your information. Here are some tips:

Note Cards
- Enter only one piece of information on each card.
- Include the page number from which you obtained the information.
- Write a head at the top of each card telling on which aspect of your topic the note focuses.

Source Cards
- Create one source card for each source you use.
- List all the information you will need for crediting the source: author, title, publisher, date, and so on.

Drafting

Organize Your Ideas Write a thesis statement, which indicates the main point you want to make about your topic. All of the information in your paper should support your thesis statement. Include your thesis statement in your introduction. Follow with a series of body paragraphs, each focusing on a single subpoint and providing supporting details. End with a conclusion that drives home your main idea.

Work With Your Notes Use your note cards as you draft your research paper. Work the information from your notes into your draft. Copy facts and page references accurately, but draw your own conclusions from that information.

Cross-Curricular Connection: Science

Scientific Research Explain to students that research is the backbone of the scientific community. However, instead of beginning with a thesis sentence, scientists begin with a hypothesis that they prove or disprove. Scientists write in scientific language, beginning with a review of the scientific literature that has already been written on the topic. They they turn to primary research, discussing control and experimental groups, variables, and results. Scientific writing must be precise, accurate and thorough in order to communicate the topic to other scientists. Because scientists rely on one another's work to determine future hypotheses, the work must be documented so that anyone who uses the material can find all of the sources available on the topic. A scientist like any other academic, must document his or her findings and credit sources. Have students check scientific journals for examples of scientific writing.

Document Your Sources You are required to document, or give credit to, your sources in the following situations:

- When you use another person's exact words
- When you use another person's idea, even if you rephrase it in your own words

Failure to do so is called plagiarism—presenting someone else's ideas as your own. Plagiarism is a serious offense.

Quote Your Sources Accurately At some points in your paper, you will wish to quote a source directly. Be sure that you record those passages word for word.

Revising

Use a Checklist The following checklist will help you revise.

- ▶ Do all the body paragraphs support my thesis statement?
  As you revise, make sure that you've actually made a point about your topic in each paragraph, rather than just restating information you've gathered. For example, if you're writing a paper about Peter the Great, you wouldn't simply state the facts of his life, you'd want to draw some conclusions about why he was a great leader.
- ▶ Is my information accurate?
  Invite a peer to read your draft. If the reader questions the accuracy of any information, go back to your notes and check them.
- ▶ Have I accurately cited my sources of information?
  Make sure that every source that you rephrase and every passage that you quote directly are marked with a footnote or a parenthetical citation. If you have omitted one, use your note cards to identify the source. Then add a citation.
- ▶ Is my paper clearly organized?
  Read through your paper from start to finish, looking for any places where it seems to jump around or where one idea doesn't seem to flow logically from the previous one. Rearrange your ideas to make the organization clear, and add transitions to make connections from one idea to the next.

Publishing

- ▶ **Classroom** Share your research paper by presenting it to classmates as a special news report.
- ▶ **Audio Corner** Make a recording of your report. Create a classroom corner where classmates can listen to your recording.

APPLYING LANGUAGE SKILLS: Citing Sources

When you quote a passage directly and when you paraphrase an idea from a source, **cite the source** in a parenthetical citation or in a footnote. A parenthetical citation immediately follows the quoted information. A footnote appears at the bottom of the page.

Parenthetical Citation:

Astronomers suspected that supernovas "might serve as stellar forges." (Murdin 119)

Footnote:

1. Paul Murdin, *Supernovae* (Cambridge: Cambridge University Press, 1985), 119.

Writing Application Add quotations to your research paper. Then document those quotations.

Writer's Solution Connection
Writing Lab

For additional help in crediting sources, use the Citing and Crediting Sources section of the Writing Lab tutorial on Research Writing.

Revision Strategy

When students reenter their writing, suggest that they review it, using a highlighting marker to indicate sentences and passages of their research paper that need clarification. Then they can refer to the topic sentences of each paragraph that has been highlighted to determine whether what they have written adequately supports the topic sentences, needs revision, or needs to be replaced.

Prentice Hall Writing and Grammar For more prewriting, elaboration, and revision strategies, see *Prentice Hall Writing and Grammar.*

Publishing

If students interviewed someone in preparation for completing the research paper, they may want to send the interviewee a completed copy.

Reinforce and Extend

Applying Language Skills

Citing Sources

Remind students that to use someone else's ideas or words is to commit plagiarism. Thus, to avoid literary theft, they must cite sources for paraphrased as well as quoted ideas.

Applying Knowledge

After students have completed their papers, ask them to discuss the logical processes involved in gathering, organizing, and presenting information. Ask how these logical processes apply to other kinds of writing.

✓ ASSESSMENT		4	3	2	1
PORTFOLIO ASSESSMENT Use the rubric on Description in ***Alternative Assessment*** (p. 106) to assess students' writing. Add these criteria to customize the rubric to this assignment.	**Topic Sentences**	The research paper includes and supports a topic sentence in every paragraph.	The research paper includes and supports a topic sentence in most paragraphs.	The research paper supports topic sentences.	The research paper includes few topic sentences and little or no support.
	Research Process	The writer completed the research process using exemplary sources evidenced by exemplary note cards.	The writer completed the research process using adequate sources evidenced by adequate note cards.	The writer partly completed the research process using some sources evidenced by some note cards.	The writer did not complete the research process.

Prepare and Engage

LESSON OBJECTIVES

- To read silently with comprehension for a sustained period of time

Customize for
Intrapersonal Learners

Have students create a sustained silent reading log to help them learn more about their reading and comprehension skills. The log should note the date, starting and ending times, and setting of the readings, what was read, and the key concepts or ideas about the text. Encourage students to also note how they felt about the actual reading experience—was it enjoyable? Was the setting too distracting? Have students review their logs as time goes on to better understand what variables seem to work best for them.

Answers

Students should note the time spent reading, the name of the selection, and where and when the reading took place. When testing themselves for comprehension, students should include what criteria they used.

Student Success Workshop

Real-World Reading Skills

Reading Silently With Comprehension

Strategies for Success

One mark of a good reader is being able to comprehend and remember information while reading silently for a long period of time. This skill is not as simple as it sounds, but you can learn to apply concentration when you're reading.

Recognize Your Purpose for Reading Do you ever find that when you read for pleasure you retain nearly every detail of information, but when you read to "learn," you suddenly have trouble concentrating? Tell yourself that no matter what you are reading, you are reading for pleasure—and that you are always learning, no matter what you read.

Know Your Limits If reading silently for comprehension is something you don't do often, it may take you a while to develop your powers of concentration. In that case, set realistic goals for yourself. Don't expect to silently read and comprehend an entire novel in one night. Set time or page limits for yourself. It's better to understand fully and remember one chapter of a book than it is to race through the whole text and come away with nothing.

Get Comfortable There is a great feeling to finding a special spot where you can "lose yourself" in a book. Seek out such a place when you are reading silently for comprehension. Look for a quiet space with good lighting. If you find that you're becoming *too* comfortable and are getting drowsy, move to a chair that helps you sit up straighter and stay awake.

Avoid Interruptions Everyone has experienced what it's like to be interrupted and to lose concentration. If you find that happening, take a short break and come back to the text in a few minutes. You may want to move to a quieter, more private, or less distracting reading space where you can concentrate better.

Check Up on Yourself Get in the habit of giving yourself short quizzes about what you're reading. Review the main ideas of the text. Go back and figure out the relationships between the characters. Create a graphic organizer, such as a chart or diagram, to remind yourself of an important aspect of what you've read so far.

Apply the Strategies

Choose a selection to read silently for a sustained period of time. Follow the strategies, and test yourself for comprehension.

Here are some situations in which you should read silently with comprehension for a sustained period of time:

- Studying for a test
- Taking a comprehension test
- Reading a complex text
- Trying to follow complicated written instructions
- Reviewing the terms of a contract or agreement

Test Preparation Workshop

Reading Silently With Comprehension

The ability to read silently and comprehend the text is key to performing well on the reading sections of standardized tests such as the SAT. By developing concentration and checking up on themselves, students will be better prepared to answer test items that follow reading passages on standardized tests.

Remind students that when they write their own papers, they are expected to provide details to explain, support, or challenge their main points. As they read silently to prepare for standardized tests, they will want to pay close attention to the author's details—those details will explain, support and challenge the author's main points of the passage. Test questions may require them to analyze the main points and/or the details.

You may wish to select a passage from one of the epics or legends in Unit 10 for students to read silently. Have students create their own practice multiple-choice comprehension questions for the passage.

PART 2 World Heroes

Rama and Lakshman Confer With the Animal Armies, from the *Adventures of Rama*, Freer Gallery of Art, Smithsonian Institution, Washington, D.C.

Dipankara Buddha, 17th Century A.D., Nepal, Asian Art Museum of San Francisco, The Avery Brundage Collection

One-Minute Planning Guide

In Part 2, students will meet heroes from India and old Mali, as well as some modern movie characters who will help them understand that epics tell timeless tales in any age. In "Rama's Initiation," the adventures of the young epic hero Rama provide an exciting story and provides students with a context to understand Indian cultural beliefs. "Sundiata: An Epic of Old Mali" is a classic tale of an underdog. Based on a historical figure, it relates how the physically disabled boy Mari Djata overcomes obstacles to become a powerful and respected hero. The elements of epics are connected to modern culture in the high-interest essay "Star Wars: An Epic for Today." The author shows how the writer of the Star Wars trilogy incorporates storytelling techniques that have been used since before people had a written history.

Customize for *Varying Student Needs*

When assigning the selections in this part, keep in mind these factors.

"Rama's Initiation"

- The unfamiliar names of characters may prove difficult for less advanced readers.
- Most students will need assistance appreciating the cultural details.
- The vocabulary is challenging.

from *Sundiata*

- Less advanced students and ESL Students will need assistance with the unusual and formal diction.
- Some characters have more than one name, which may confuse some students.
- Cultural references will need to be explained.

Humanities: Art

Rama and Lakshman Confer With the Animal Armies, from *Adventures of Rama.*

Rama, hero of the Indian epic *The Ramayana,* was the human form of the god Vishnu. He is usually portrayed with dark skin (here blue); Lakshman is his half-brother.

Dipankara Buddha (17th-century Nepal). Dipankara, also called Atisa, was an Indian Buddhist whose traveled to Tibet and whose reforms became the basis for a Tibetan Buddhist sect.

Figure of a drummer seated on a folding stool, Ashanti brass.

The Ashanti people live in the west African countries of Ghana, Togo, and the Ivory Coast. This brass figure is used for weighing quantities of gold.

Help students link this art with the focus of Part 2, "World Heroes," by answering the following question:

Imagine a truly global hero, for a united Earth. What problems might such a hero combat and what qualities would he or she need? *Students are likely to envision the hero battling problems such as an alien invasion or environmental crisis. The hero might need such traditional qualities as bravery and intelligence, as well as less traditional skills, such as the ability to adapt to bizarre or rapidly changing situations and to unite very different allies.*

Prepare and Engage

LESSON OBJECTIVES

1. **To develop vocabulary and word identification skills**
   - Latin Word Roots: *-min-*
   - Using the Word Bank: Synonyms
   - Extending Word Study: Thesaurus (ATE)
2. **To use a variety of reading strategies to comprehend a personal narrative**
   - Connect Your Experience
   - Reading Strategy: Draw Inferences About Culture
   - Read to Be Informed (ATE)
   - Tips to Guide Reading: Sustained Reading (ATE)
   - Idea Bank: Letter
   - Idea Bank: Opening Argument
3. **To increase knowledge of other cultures and to connect common elements across cultures**
   - Connecting Themes Across Cultures (ATE)
   - Background for Understanding
   - Cultural Connection (ATE)
   - Idea Bank: Personal Narrative
4. **To express and support responses to the text**
   - Critical Thinking
5. **To analyze literary elements**
   - Literary Focus: Epic Hero
6. **To read in order to research self-selected and assigned topics**
   - Questions for Research
7. **To plan, prepare, organize, and present literary interpretations**
   - Speaking, Listening, and Viewing Mini-Lesson: Oral Tales (ATE)
   - Idea Bank: Poster
   - Idea Bank: Painting
   - Idea Bank: Dance
8. **To use recursive writing processes to write a screenplay proposal**
   - Guided Writing Lesson
9. **To increase knowledge of the rules of grammar and usage**
   - Build Grammar Skills: Restrictive and Nonrestrictive Appositives

Test Preparation

Writing Skills: Organization (ATE, p. 923) The teaching tips and sample test item in this workshop support the instruction and practice in the unit workshop:

Writing Skills: Strategy, Organization, and Style (SE, p. 951)

Guide for Reading

About the *Ramayana*

The great Indian epic, the *Ramayana,* written by the poet Valmike, consists of twenty-four thousand stanzas. Parts of the *Ramayana* date from 500 B.C.

The epic tells how Prince Rama wins his bride, Sita, by proving his strength. Just as he is about to inherit the throne, evil plots result in his banishment from the kingdom. For fourteen years, he wanders in exile with his wife, Sita, and his brother, Lakshmana. Sita is kidnapped, and Rama rescues her with the help of Manuman, the monkey god. After the rescue, Rama is welcomed back to the kingdom.

The excerpt you are about to read tells of adventures from Rama's childhood, before his banishment. Even as boys, Rama and his brother Lakshmana show extraordinary strength and ability.

R. K. Narayan *(1906–)*

For the writer R. K. Narayan (nə rī´ en), the *Ramayana* and *Mahabharata* played a significant role in fostering a love for literature. He often cites the importance of oral literature in traditional Indian society: "The storyteller who has studied the epics, the *Ramayana* and the *Mahabharata,* may take up any of the thousand episodes in them, create a narrative with his individual stamp on it, and hold the attention of an audience, numbering thousands, for hours."

Born into the Hindu Brahmin caste, Narayan spoke Tamil at home, used English at school, and was taught traditional Indian melodies and prayers in Sanskrit, India's ancient classical language. In addition to his contemporary versions of Indian epics, R. K. Narayan has published dozens of novels and short story collections.

◆ Build Vocabulary

Latin Word Roots: *-min-*

The character Agasthya in this episode from the *Ramayana* is referred to as *diminutive.* The Latin root *-min-* in *diminutive* comes from the Latin *minutus,* meaning "small." Therefore, when Agasthya is described as being *diminutive,* it means he is tiny in size.

Word Bank

As you read "Rama's Initiation" from the *Ramayana,* you will encounter the words on this list. Each word will be defined on the page where it first appears. Before you read, list in your notebook any words or word parts that you think you recognize. Then, as you read, check whether the words mean what you thought they did.

austerities
decrepitude
sublime
august
secular
obeisance
exuberance
diminutive
esoteric

◆ Build Grammar Skills

Restrictive and Nonrestrictive Appositives

An appositive is a noun or pronoun placed next to another noun or pronoun to identify, rename, or explain it. An appositive phrase is a noun or pronoun with modifiers, placed next to a noun or pronoun to add information or details. An appositive is **restrictive** when it is necessary to clarify or identify the noun to which it refers. Commas are not used with restrictive appositives.

Restrictive: Send your son *Rama* with me.

Since the king has more than one son, the appositive *Rama* is necessary to identify which son.

An appositive is **nonrestrictive** if it provides additional, but not necessary, information. Nonrestrictive appositives are set off with commas.

Nonrestrictive: This Thataka is more dreadful than Yama, *the god of death,* who takes a life only when the time is ripe.

Since there is only one Yama, the appositive phrase adds information, but it is not necessary.

Prentice Hall Literature Program Resources

REINFORCE / RETEACH / EXTEND

Selection Support Pages
Build Vocabulary: Word Roots: *-min-,* p. 257
Build Grammar Skills: Restrictive and Nonrestrictive Appositives, p. 258
Reading Strategy: Make Inferences About Culture, p. 259
Literary Focus: The Epic Hero, p. 260

Strategies for Diverse Student Needs, p. 63

Beyond Literature
Cultural Connection: *Hinduism in India,* p. 63

Formal Assessment Selection Test, pp. 223–225, Assessment Resources Software

Alternative Assessment, p. 63

Writing and Language Transparencies Art Transparency 14

Resource Pro CD-ROM

Listening to Literature Audiocassettes

Rama's Initiation *from the Ramayana*

◆ Literature and Your Life

CONNECT YOUR EXPERIENCE

What qualities do you think a hero possesses? As you read this episode from the *Ramayana,* you might be surprised to note that ancient heroes have much in common with contemporary superheroes; heroes have always combatted evil, and as you'll see in the *Ramayana,* they have respected the land that nurtures all people.

Journal Writing All over the world, young people prove their mental, spiritual, and physical strength to themselves, to their peers, and to adults. Choose a young person who you believe has heroic qualities. In your journal, jot down some notes upon which you could base an epic focusing on this person.

THEMATIC FOCUS: FROM THE PAST

The *Ramayana* has influenced nearly every aspect of Indian culture —from children's bedtime stories to religious studies. Ask yourself what Rama's adventures reveal about Indian culture.

◆ Background for Understanding

CULTURE

Hinduism, one of the oldest living religions in the world, is the major religion of India. While it has no single book that outlines all its doctrines and beliefs, there are many sacred writings. These include the *Vedas,* which contain prayers, hymns, explanations, and philosophy; the *Puranas,* which tell the tales of Hindu gods and goddesses; the Hindu epics *Mahabharata* and the *Ramayana* and the *Manu-Smitri,* a code of religious and social law. The *Ramayana* tells of Prince Rama, believed by many to be another incarnation of the Hindu god Krishna.

◆ Literary Focus

THE EPIC HERO

The **epic hero** possesses certain qualities—bravery, great strength, and a desire to achieve immortality through heroic deeds. The hero is based on a legendary or historic person who travels on a long and challenging journey, during which he proves his heroic qualities: He fights evil, falls in love, protects his honor, and rescues people in distress.

This episode from the *Ramayana* puts Rama in a situation in which he must prove some of his heroic qualities.

◆ Reading Strategy

DRAW INFERENCES ABOUT CULTURE

You can use information revealed in sources such as epics to **draw inferences about a culture.** Chances are, you don't know a great deal about life in India 2,000 years ago. However, if you combine the details in the *Ramayana* with your own experiences, you can draw some strong inferences about this ancient culture. In particular, the experiences of the hero Rama will reveal the customs and values of his culture.

To help you draw inferences about a culture, use a chart like the one below to jot down cultural details from the epic, details from your own background and experience, and the resulting cultural inferences.

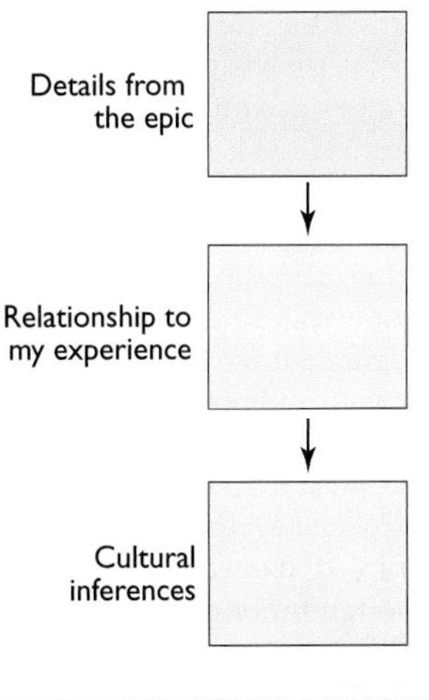

Make the statement: "Superheroes from all times and cultures possess certain traits in common." Then have students generate a representative list of superheroes from ancient to present times—for example, Zeus, King Arthur, Robin Hood, and Xena, Warrior Princess. Discuss with students the characteristics that some of these heroes hold in common, such as courage, bravery, loyalty, and integrity. Let them know that in reading this selection about a young Indian boy, they will get an opportunity to witness the making of a hero.

Tips to Guide Reading

Sustained Reading This text, with its long names and portentous pronouncements, will challenge students' concentration. Suggest that students use the comprehension strategies on the Student Success Workshop page (p. 920) to help them "stick with it."

Connecting Themes Across Cultures

Have students think about their readings in literature and history to identify other literary works that define a culture as the *Ramayana* defines India's.

Customize for
Less Proficient Readers

To avoid confusion, draw attention to p. 927, "Thataka's Story." Explain that a story within a story is a common narrative technique in epics.

Customize for
Pre-AP Students

The *Ramayana,* like Homer's epic poems, was recited from memory for centuries before being written down. Suggest that students search for passages that they can render into verse by changing as few words as possible in this prose translation.

Customize for
English Language Learners

So that students will not spend too much time on the pronunciation of characters' names at the expense of fluency, pronounce the names of the main characters: King Dasaratha and his sons Rama and Lakshmana; Viswamithra; Vasishtha; and Thataka, using the phonetic spellings on pp. 924, 925, and 926 to pronounce the names for students.

Test Preparation Workshop

Writing Skills: Organization The ACT requires that students choose the most logical sequence of ideas or decide whether a sentence should be added, deleted, or moved. To give students practice in organization, use the following test item.

(1) King Dasaratha watched apprehensively as his son Rama left the palace. (2) Viswamithra had made it clear that he wanted Rama to go with him. (3) Vasishtha suggested that it would be a good idea to send Rama along with Viswamithra. (4) Rama and his brother left the limits of the city. (5) Viswamithra was the sort of man who knew what he wanted.

Choose the sequence of sentence numbers that will make the structure most logical.

A No change
B 2, 1, 3, 4, 5
C 1, 4, 2, 3, 5
D 5, 2, 3, 1, 4

The correct answer is *D*. Because a series of events or actions is taking place, the best organization for this information is chronological.

Develop Understanding

One-Minute Insight In "Rama's Initiation," the young man Rama accepts his calling to help defend a sage and perform a sacrifice in a far-away sacred place. He proves himself by defeating a demon and thus begins his adventures as an epic hero. His adventures demonstrate the importance of bravery, strength, and respect for wisdom in Indian culture.

◆ Critical Thinking

❶ Infer The writer states that Viswamithra was a dreaded name. Ask students what they can infer about Viswamithra's actions as king. *Suggested response: He was probably feared because he is described as a conqueror and as quick-tempered.*

▶ Critical Viewing ◀

❷ Speculate *Suggested response: The meeting might be about something that involves the whole community.*

Humanities: Art

Persian translation of the Ramayana of Valmiki (detail).

This piece, by an unknown artist, illustrates a scene from the *Ramayana*. The picture plane is divided by the architectural elements of the columns, a device often used in Indian painting to suggest depth.

Ask students what might be the difference between the people sitting on the canopied platform and those in the foreground of the picture. *Students might speculate that the people on the platform belong to a ruling or governing class. They might comment on the distance between the platform and the people surrounding it, and observe that it might symbolize the distance between two classes.*

Art Transparency After students read the introductory information about the *Ramayana*, display Art Transparency 14. Invite student comments, discussing a basic connection to the Hindu epic. Leave the transparency on the overhead as students read "Rama's Initiation"; then follow up with discussion or student writing about the nature of heroism.

Rama's Initiation

from the Ramayana

R. K. Narayan

The new assembly hall, Dasaratha's[1] latest pride, was crowded all day with visiting dignitaries, royal emissaries, and citizens coming in with representations or appeals for justice. The King was always accessible, and fulfilled his duties as the ruler of Kosala without grudging the hours spent in public service.

On a certain afternoon, messengers at the gate came running in to announce, "Sage Viswamithra."[2] When the message was relayed to the King, he got up and hurried forward to receive the visitor. ❶ Viswamithra, once a king, a conqueror, and a dreaded name until he renounced his kingly role and chose to become a sage (which he accomplished through severe austerities), combined in himself the sage's eminence and the king's authority and was quick tempered and positive. Dasaratha led him to a proper seat and said, "This is a day of glory for us; your gracious presence is most welcome. You must have come from afar. Would you first rest?"

"No need," the sage replied simply. He had complete mastery over his bodily needs through inner discipline and austerities, and was above the effects of heat, cold, hunger, fatigue, and even decrepitude. The King later asked politely, "Is there anything I can do?" Viswamithra looked steadily at the King and answered, "Yes. I am here to ask of you a favor. I wish to perform, before the next full moon, a

▲ Critical Viewing What do you think is the topic of this public meeting? [Speculate] ❷

1. **Dasaratha's** (dä sä rä´ täz)
2. **Viswamithra** (vish wä´ mē trä): Teacher of Rama, the main character of the Ramayana.

Block Scheduling Strategies

Consider these suggestions to take advantage of extended class time.

- Allow time for students to share other stories that tell the adventures of a hero. Use these examples to help students construct a definition of an epic hero.
- Introduce the concept of making inferences about a culture with the Reading Strategy feature (p. 923). Lead students to see how they can combine the notes they write in the first two boxes on the chart to come up with general inferences about a culture. Then direct students to complete the Reading Strategy questions on p. 930.
- Both researching and representing activities in the Idea Bank (p. 931) involve the arts. You might want to plan ahead so that students can use class time to work on their projects. Students choosing the art project will need to bring their supplies with them. Students choosing the dance project will need to select their music in advance.

yagna[3] at Sidhasrama[4]. Doubtless you know where it is?"

"I have passed that sacred ground beyond the Ganges[5] many times."

The sage interrupted. "But there are creatures hovering about waiting to disturb every holy undertaking there, who must be overcome in the same manner as one has to conquer the five-fold evils[6] within before one can realize holiness. Those evil creatures are endowed with immeasurable powers of destruction. But it is our duty to pursue our aims undeterred. The yagna I propose to perform will strengthen the beneficial forces of this world, and please the gods above."

"It is my duty to protect your sublime effort. Tell me when, and I will be there."

The sage said, "No need to disturb your august self. Send your son Rama with me, and he will help me. He can."

"Rama!" cried the King, surprised, "When I am here to serve you."

Viswamithra's temper was already stirring. "I know your greatness," he said, cutting the King short. "But I want Rama to go with me. If you are not willing, you may say so."

The air became suddenly tense. The assembly, the ministers and officials, watched in solemn silence. The King looked miserable. "Rama is still a child, still learning the arts and practicing the use of arms." His sentences never seemed to conclude, but trailed away as he tried to explain. "He is a boy, a child, he is too young and tender to contend with demons."

"But I know Rama," was all that Viswamithra said in reply.

"I can send you an army, or myself lead an army to guard your performance. What can a stripling[7] like Rama do against those terrible forces . . .? I will help you just as I helped Indra[8] once when he was harassed and deprived of his kingdom."

Viswamithra ignored his speech and rose to leave. "If you cannot send Rama, I need none else." He started to move down the passage.

The King was too stricken to move. When Viswamithra had gone half way, he realized that the visitor was leaving unceremoniously and was not even shown the courtesy of being escorted to the door. Vasishtha,[9] the King's priest and guide, whispered to Dasaratha, "Follow him and call him back," and hurried forward even before the King could grasp what he was saying. He almost ran as Viswamithra had reached the end of the hall and, blocking his way, said, "The King is coming; please don't go. He did not mean . . ." ❻

A wry smile played on Viswamithra's face as he said without any trace of bitterness, "Why are you or anyone agitated? I came here for a purpose; it has failed: no reason to prolong my stay."

"Oh, eminent one, you were yourself a king once."

"What has that to do with us now?" asked Viswamithra, rather irked, since he hated all

3. **yagna** (yäg nä´) *n.*: Sacrifice.
4. **Sidhasrama** (sēd häs rä´ mä)
5. **Ganges** (gan´ jēz): River in northern India.
6. **five-fold evils:** Lust, anger, miserliness, egoism, and envy.

7. **stripling** (strip´ liŋ) *n.*: Young boy passing into manhood.
8. **Indra** (in´ drə): Hindu god associated with rain and thunderclouds.
9. **Vasishtha** (vä sē´ sh tä): King's priest and guide.

◆ Build Vocabulary

austerities (ô ster´ ə tēz) *n.*: Self-denials

decrepitude (dē krep´ ə to͞od) *n.*: State of being worn out by old age or illness

sublime (sə blīm´) *adj.*: Noble; admirable

august (ô gust´) *adj.*: Worthy of respect because of age and dignity

◆ Reading Strategy

❸ Make Inferences About Culture Ask: What inference can you make from this passage about the ancient Indians' view of evil? *The ancient Indians viewed evil as being both internal and external. The evils within a person are lust, anger, miserliness, egoism, and envy. Evil in the world was believed to be caused by external forces—non-human creatures or powerful demons.*

◆ Critical Thinking

❹ Infer Ask students why they think Viswamithra is unwilling to accept the king's aid. *Suggested answer: Since Viswamithra is a holy man and a sage, he probably knows something about Rama that the king does not.*

◆ Reading Strategy

❺ Make Inferences About Culture In this passage, what personal value is King Dasaratha displaying? *The King is demonstrating the family value of protecting a young child from danger and evil.*

◆ Build Grammar Skills

❻ Restrictive and Nonrestrictive Appositives Have students identify the appositive phrase in the sentence and explain its function. *"the King's priest and guide" is a nonrestrictive appositive that is not necessary to the meaning of the sentence. Vasishtha is already identified by the use of his name. This phrase adds further information about who Vasishtha is.*

Writing and Language Transparencies To give students more insight into Hinduism, use Art Transparency 14. You will find accompanying instruction and activities related to *The Ramayana* on pp. 59–62.

Extending Word Study

Thesaurus Have students look for synonyms for the words from the word bank on pp. 924, and 925: *austerities, decrepitude, sublime,* and *august.* They can use a thesaurus or another synonym-finding reference. Ask them to write sentences using the original words and the synonyms that they find. Discuss with them how the synonyms give subtly different meanings to the sentences.

Speaking, Listening, and Viewing Mini-Lesson

Oral Tales

This mini-lesson supports the Speaking, Listening, and Viewing activity in the Idea Bank on p. 931.

Introduce In ancient times, oral tales, or epics, were the means by which a culture's history and values were handed down from generation to generation. Often there was a designated storyteller who remembered and recited the epics.

Develop Suggest the following steps to help students prepare their versions of the *Ramayana.*

- Reread the story and then try to tell it from memory. They can take notes to fill in the gaps.
- Practice effective delivery by varying the volume, the pace, and the tone of their voices.

Apply Have students create their versions of the epic and practice telling them to partners, applying the points listed above, before recording them.

Assess Students assess the readings by using the Peer Assessment: Oral Interpretation form, p. 119, in the ***Alternative Assessment*** booklet.

Comprehension Check ☑

❶ King Dasaratha does not want to send Rama on a dangerous mission. How does Vasishtha explain the King's reluctance to the sage Viswamithra? *Dasaratha waited a long time for his firstborn son. Thus he is reluctant to allow him to be exposed to danger.*

❷ **Clarification** Point out that Vasishtha recognizes that a divine purpose is probably at work here. Explain that Vishnu, one of the Hindu gods, is known as the Preserver, or god of life. Hindus believe that Vishnu has appeared in nine forms, or *avatars*. One of these avatars is Rama.

◆ Literary Focus

❸ **The Epic Hero** Lead students to the following answer: *One of the "requirements" of an epic hero is that he go on a long and challenging journey in which he demonstrates his heroic qualities. Viswamithra wants to take Rama on a journey to a distant place where he will vanquish evil creatures.*

❹ **Clarification** Tell students that the Hindu religion has many gods and thus is called *polytheistic*. Three of the most important gods are Brahma (the Creator), Vishnu (the Preserver), and Shiva (the Destroyer). Ask students to explain the significance of the arrival of Rama at the place where Shiva meditated. *Rama is an avatar (form) of Vishnu, the Preserver of life, whereas Shiva is the Destroyer of life. The stage seems set for some kind of battle.*

Customize for
Interpersonal Learners
Allow groups of these students to read the story aloud, with a different student taking each part and one student acting as narrator. After reading, students can discuss what their characters may have been thinking and feeling at various points.

Customize for
Gifted/Talented Students
After the students have read about how Thataka created the desert that Viswamithra, Rama, and Lakshmana must cross, have them devise a mythic origin for a natural phenomenon, such as the Grand Canyon. Encourage them to write it as an episode in an epic and read it to the class.

reference to his secular past and wanted always to be known as a Brahma Rishi.[10]

❶ Vasishtha answered mildly, "Only to remind you of an ordinary man's feelings, especially a man like Dasaratha who had been childless and had to pray hard for an issue . . ."

"Well, it may be so, great one; I still say that I came on a mission and wish to leave, since it has failed."

"It has not failed," said Vasishtha, and just then the King came up to join them in the passage; the assembly was on its feet.

Dasaratha made a deep obeisance and said, "Come back to your seat, Your Holiness."

"For what purpose, Your Majesty?" Viswamithra asked.

"Easier to talk seated . . ."

"I don't believe in any talk," said Viswamithra; but Vasishtha pleaded with him until he returned to his seat.

❷ When they were all seated again, Vasishtha addressed the King: "There must be a divine purpose working through this seer, who may know but will not explain. It is a privilege that Rama's help should be sought. Do not bar his way. Let him go with the sage."

❸ ◆ **Literary Focus** Explain how this speech of Vasishtha relates to Rama's status as an epic hero.

"When, oh when?" the King asked anxiously.

"Now," said Viswamithra.

The King looked woebegone and desperate, and the sage relented enough to utter a word of comfort. "You cannot count on the physical proximity of someone you love, all the time. A seed that sprouts at the foot of its parent tree remains stunted until it is transplanted. Rama will be in my care, and he will be quite well. But ultimately, he will leave me too. Every human being, when the time comes, has to depart and seek his fulfillment in his own way."

"Sidhasrama is far away . . .?" began the King.

"I'll ease his path for him, no need for a chariot to take us there," said Viswamithra reading his mind.

"Rama has never been separated from his brother Lakshmana.[11] May he also go with him?" pleaded the King, and he looked relieved when he heard Viswamithra say, "Yes, I will look after both, though their mission will be to look after me. Let them get ready to follow me; let them select their favorite weapons and prepare to leave."

Dasaratha, with the look of one delivering hostages into the hand of an enemy, turned to his minister and said, "Fetch my sons."

Following the footsteps of their master like his shadows, Rama and Lakshmana went past the limits of the city and reached the Sarayu River, which bounded the capital on the north. When night fell, they rested at a wooded grove and at dawn crossed the river. When the sun came over the mountain peak, they reached a pleasant grove over which hung, like a canopy, fragrant smoke from numerous sacrificial fires. Viswamithra explained to Rama, "This is where God Shiva[12] meditated once upon a time and reduced to ashes the god of love when he attempted to spoil his meditation. From time immemorial saints praying to Shiva come here to perform their sacrifices, and the pall of smoke you notice is from their sacrificial fires." ❹

A group of hermits emerged from their seclusion, received Viswamithra, and invited him and his two disciples to stay with them for the night. Viswamithra resumed his journey at dawn and reached a desert region at midday. The mere expression "desert" hardly conveys the absolute aridity of this land. Under a relentless sun, all vegetation had dried and turned to dust, stone and rock crumbled into powdery sand, which lay in vast dunes, stretching away to the horizon.

10. **Brahma Rishi** (brä′ mä rī′ shē): Enlightened sage.

11. **Lakshmana** (läks mä′ nä)

12. **God Shiva** (shē′ və): Hindu god of destruction.

Cross-Curricular Connection: Social Studies

Hinduism The major religion of India, Hinduism, is the oldest religion in the world. One of the important teachings of Hinduism is reincarnation. Hindus believe that when the body dies, the soul is reborn in a continuous process. The soul of someone who lives a good personal life and performs pious deeds will be reborn into a higher status, possibly one of wealth and high standing in society. The soul of a person who lives a bad personal life and performs evil deeds will be reborn into a lower condition, such as that of a pig or a cockroach.

Another major aspect of Hinduism in the past was the *caste system,* a strict system of hereditary social classes. Members of one caste could not mix with members of the other castes. In recent times, however, different castes do intermingle. These are four traditional castes: the *Brahmans,* or priests; the *Kishatryas,* nobles and military leaders; the *Vaisyas,* business people and landowners; and the *Sudras,* farmers, workers, and servants. *Untouchables* were considered so low that they were outside the caste system. "Untouchability" was outlawed in 1950.

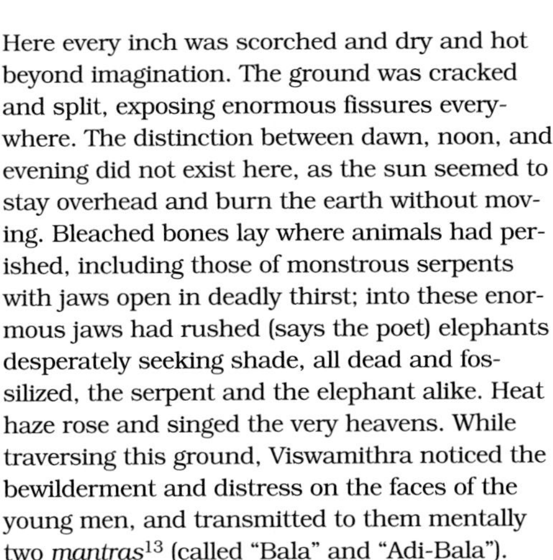

Here every inch was scorched and dry and hot beyond imagination. The ground was cracked and split, exposing enormous fissures everywhere. The distinction between dawn, noon, and evening did not exist here, as the sun seemed to stay overhead and burn the earth without moving. Bleached bones lay where animals had perished, including those of monstrous serpents with jaws open in deadly thirst; into these enormous jaws had rushed (says the poet) elephants desperately seeking shade, all dead and fossilized, the serpent and the elephant alike. Heat haze rose and singed the very heavens. While traversing this ground, Viswamithra noticed the bewilderment and distress on the faces of the young men, and transmitted to them mentally two *mantras*[13] (called "Bala" and "Adi-Bala"). When they meditated on and recited these incantations, the arid atmosphere was transformed for the rest of their passage and they felt as if they were wading through a cool stream with a southern summer breeze blowing in their faces. Rama, ever curious to know the country he was passing through, asked, "Why is this land so terrible? Why does it seem accursed?"

> ◆ **Reading Strategy**
> What inferences can you make about the role of meditation and incantations in Indian culture and religion?

"You will learn the answer if you listen to this story—of a woman fierce, ruthless, eating and digesting all living creatures, possessing the strength of a thousand mad elephants."

13. ***mantras*** (män′träz): Sacred syllables.

◆ Build Vocabulary

secular (sek′ yə lər) *adj.*: Not sacred or religious

obeisance (ō bā′ səns) *n.*: Gesture of respect

exuberance (eg zo͞o′ bər əns) *n.*: State of high spirits and good health

diminutive (də min′ yo͞o tiv) *adj.*: Smaller than average

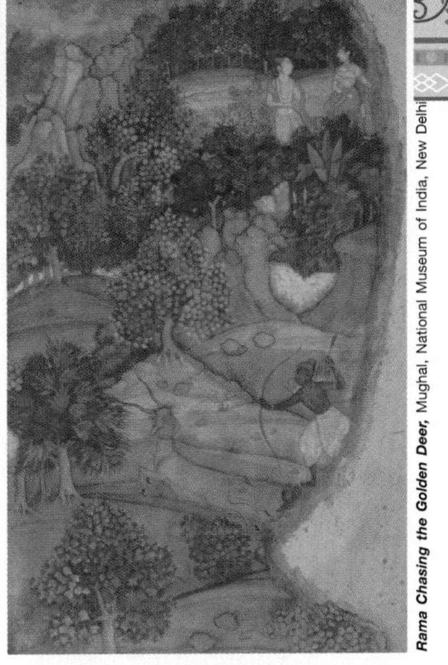

Rama Chasing the Golden Deer, Mughal, National Museum of India, New Delhi

▲ **Critical Viewing** What details in this painting support inferences you've made from reading this epic? **[Connect; Support]** 

Thataka's Story

The woman I speak of was the daughter of Suketha[14] a *yaksha,* a demigod of great valor, might, and purity. She was beautiful and full of wild energy. When she grew up she was married to a chieftain named Sunda. Two sons were born to them—Mareecha and Subahu[15]—who were endowed with enormous supernatural powers in addition to physical strength; and in their conceit and exuberance they laid waste their surroundings. Their father, delighted at their pranks and infected by their mood, joined in their activities. He pulled out ancient trees by their roots and flung them about, and he slaughtered all creatures that came his way. This depredation came to the notice of the great savant Agasthya[16] (the diminutive saint who 9

14. **Suketha** (so͞o kā′ tä)
15. **Mareecha** (mä′ rē chä) **and Subahu** (sä bä′ ho͞o)
16. **savant** (sə vänt′) **Agasthya** (ä gus tē yä′): Learned man named Agasthya.

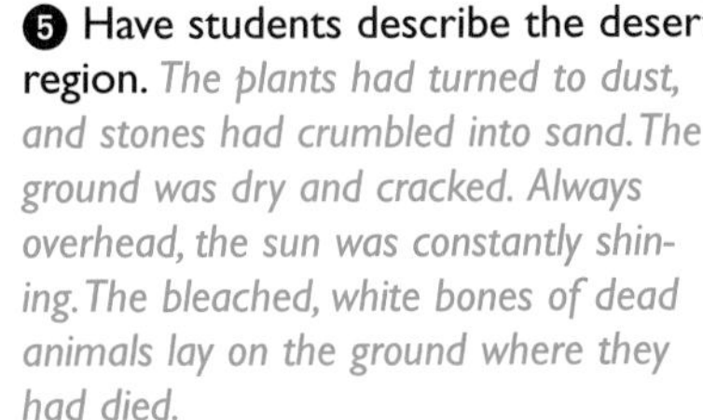

Comprehension Check ☑

❺ Have students describe the desert region. *The plants had turned to dust, and stones had crumbled into sand. The ground was dry and cracked. Always overhead, the sun was constantly shining. The bleached, white bones of dead animals lay on the ground where they had died.*

◆ Reading Strategy

❻ **Make Inferences About Culture** Elicit responses such as the following: *Sample answer: The Indian people use meditation and incantations to help free the human spirit to rise beyond the demands and discomforts of the human body.*

◆ Reading Strategy

❼ **Make Inferences About Culture** Rama asks Viswamithra why the land is so terrible. What two inferences can students make about ancient Indian culture from Viswamithra's response? *(1) Storytelling is an important way to impart history or lessons. (2) Humans—or rather demigods and demons in human form—can possess supernatural powers.*

▶Critical Viewing◀

❽ **Connect; Support** Suggested response: Students might comment that the scene shows that Rama is brave and adventurous, and that Lakshmana helps Rama in his endeavors.

◆ Build Grammar Skills

❾ **Restrictive and Nonrestrictive Appositives** Have students identify the appositive here, say whether it is restrictive or nonrestrictive, and why. *The appositive is Agasthya. It is restrictive because it is necessary to the meaning of the sentence. Otherwise, the audience would not know to which savant Viswamithra is referring.*

Cultural Connection

Language History The *Sanskrit language* is considered part of the Indo-European family of languages, which includes English, German, Latin, and Farsi (spoken in ancient Persia and modern Iran). The beginnings of Sanskrit can be traced to approximately 1500 B.C. when the Aryans invaded India, bringing their language with them. This language evolved into Vedic Sanskrit, the language of the Indian upper classes. Gradually, Vedic Sanskrit fell out of use as a spoken language but became a standard form of written language, referred to now as classical Sanskrit. The Sanskrit literature began orally and was passed down through many generations before the stories were written down. Two of the most important works of classical Sanskrit are the *Ramayana* and the *Mahabharata.*

Encourage interested students to learn more about the Sanskrit language and literature. For example, students might find out about the sacred syllable "om." (It is a word of assent comparable to the English "amen.") "Om" is used as a way to help meditation. Students might be interested in finding out the meaning of other Sanskrit words that are commonly used in yogic practice.

Rama Chases a Demon Disguised as a Golden Deer, Fazl, Freer Gallery of Art, Smithsonian Institution, Washington, D.C.

1 ▲ Critical Viewing What details in this painting indicate Rama's importance? **[Analyze]**

once, when certain demoniac beings hid themselves at the bottom of the sea and Indra appealed for his help to track them, had sipped off the waters of the ocean). Agasthya had his hermitage in this forest, and when he noticed the destruction around, he cursed the perpetrator of this deed and Sunda fell dead. When his wife learned of his death, she and her sons stormed in, roaring revenge on the saint. He met their challenge by cursing them. "Since you are destroyers of life, may you become *asuras*[17] and dwell in the nether worlds." (Till now they had been demigods. Now they were degraded to demonhood.) The three at once underwent a transformation; their features and stature became forbidding, and their natures changed to match. The sons left to seek the company of superdemons. The mother was left alone and lives on here, breathing fire and wishing everything ill. Nothing flourishes here; only heat and sand remain. She is a scorcher. She carries a trident with spikes; a cobra entwined on her arm is her armlet. The name of this fearsome creature is Thataka.[18] Just as the presence of a little *loba* (meanness) dries up and disfigures a whole human personality, so does the presence of this monster turn into desert a region which was once fertile. In her restlessness she constantly harasses the hermits at their prayers; she gobbles up anything that moves and sends it down her entrails.

Touching the bow slung on his shoulder, Rama asked. "Where is she to be found?"

Before Viswamithra could answer, she arrived, the ground rocking under her feet and a storm preceding her. She loomed over them with her eyes spitting fire, her fangs bared, her lips parted revealing a cavernous mouth; and her brows twitching in rage. She raised her trident and roared, "In this my kingdom, I have crushed out the minutest womb of life and you have been sent down so that I may not remain hungry."

Rama hesitated; for all her evil, she was still a woman. How could he kill her? Reading his thoughts, Viswamithra said, "You shall not consider her a woman at all. Such a monster must receive no consideration. Her strength, ruthlessness, appearance, rule her out of that category. Formerly God Vishnu himself killed Kyathi, the wife of Brigu,[19] who harbored the

17. ***asuras*** (ä so͞o´ räz)

18. **Thataka** (tä tä´ kä)

19. **Vishnu** (vēsh´ no͞o) . . . **Kyathi** (kyä´ tē) . . . **Brigu** (brē´go͞o)

◆ Build Vocabulary

esoteric (es´ ə ter´ ik) *adj.*: Beyond the understanding of most people

▶Critical Viewing◀

1 Analyze Sample answer: *In this piece of art, Rama is admired for his prowess as a hunter.*

◆Critical Thinking

2 Synthesize Draw attention to the physical change in Thataka and her sons. Ask how this change is related to their actions. *Sample answer: They were superior beings, or demigods. However, they did not use their great powers to do good; instead they behaved worse than wild animals. Their changed appearance reflects the evil ways in which they acted.*

◆Build Vocabulary

3 Latin Word Roots: *-min-* Have students identify the word with the root *-min-* and ask them what it means in this context. *The word is* minutest, *meaning "small." Thataka is saying that she has gotten rid of everything—even the smallest bit of life.*

◆Critical Thinking

4 Draw Conclusions Point out that Rama hesitates to kill Thataka when she confronts him. Ask students what they can conclude about Rama. *Possible response: Apparently Rama has been taught to respect women and not to harm them.*

◆Build Grammar Skills

5 Restrictive and Nonrestrictive Appositives Have students identify the appositive phrase and explain whether it is restrictive or nonrestrictive. *"The god of death" is the appositive. It is nonrestrictive because it is not necessary to the meaning of the sentence but gives added information about Yama.*

Read to Be Informed

If students have not read any of the *Ramayana* or the *Mahabharata,* this excerpt provides a good introduction to the Indian epics. The literary elements of epics make this story interesting and exciting: the fatherly reluctance of King Dasaratha to let his son leave home at such an early age; Thataka's instant appearance to the three men after Viswamithra relates her history; Rama's natural courage and sensitivity—the marks of an epic hero.

Humanities: Art

Rama Chases a Demon Disguised as a Golden Deer.

This visual interpretation of a scene from the *Ramayana* is in the collection of the Freer Gallery, a gift made to the nation by Charles Lang Freer (1856–1919), a United States financier and art collector with a particular interest in Asian art. Use these questions for discussion:

1. How might Rama know that the golden deer he is hunting is actually a demon? *Students might respond that since ancient Indians believed that the body could be transformed and forces of evil could assume other physical identities, the prospect of a demonic force disguising itself as an innocent animal was one that Rama was free to consider.*
2. For what purpose might Rama be hunting the golden deer? *He might be hunting it for the purpose of killing it, and thus ridding the empire of an evil force.*

asuras fleeing his wrath, when she refused to yield them. Mandorai,[20] a woman bent upon destroying all the worlds, was vanquished by Indra and he earned the gratitude of humanity. These are but two instances. A woman of demoniac tendencies loses all consideration to be treated as a woman. This Thataka is more dreadful than Yama, the god of death, who takes a life only when the time is ripe. But this monster, at the very scent of a living creature, craves to kill and eat. Do not picture her as a woman at all. You must rid this world of her. It is your duty."

Rama said, "I will carry out your wish."

Thataka threw her three-pronged spear at Rama. As it came flaming, Rama strung his bow and sent an arrow which broke it into fragments. Next she raised a hail of stones under which to crush her adversaries. Rama sent up his arrows, which shielded them from the attack. Finally Rama's arrow pierced her throat and ended her career; thereby also inaugurating Rama's life's mission of destroying evil and demonry in this world. The gods assembled in the sky and expressed their joy and relief and enjoined Viswamithra, "Oh, adept and master of weapons, impart without any reserve all your knowledge and powers to this lad. He is a savior." Viswamithra obeyed this injunction and taught Rama all the esoteric techniques in weaponry. Thereafter the presiding deities of various weapons, *asthras*,[21] appeared before Rama submissively and declared, "Now we are yours: command us night or day."

> ◆ *Literature and Your Life*
> How does Rama compare to most contemporary superheros? **6**

20. **Mandorai** (mänd rä´ ē)

21. ***asthras*** (äs´ träz)

Guide for Responding

◆ *Literature and Your Life*

Reader's Response Do you think Viswamithra did the right thing by persuading Rama to overcome his hesitation about killing Thataka? Why or why not?

Thematic Focus At the time Viswamithra asked for Rama, Dasaratha was still trying to pass down to his son the qualities that would equip him to be a hero. If you had been in Dasaratha's place, would you have let Rama go? Explain your answer.

Questions for Research The *Ramayana* has a long, glorious history, but is it still central to Hindu culture? Generate research questions about the place of the *Ramayana* in current Indian society.

☑ Check Your Comprehension

1. Why does the sage Viswamithra want Rama to accompany him to Sidhasrama?
2. Why is King Dasaratha at first reluctant to grant the sage's request?
3. Why is the region through which Rama, Lakshmana, and Viswamithra pass so inhospitable?
4. (a) Why is Rama reluctant to fight Thataka at first? (b) How does Viswamithra persuade him to fight?
5. What are the outcomes of Rama's first battle?

Beyond the Selection

FURTHER READING

Other Works by R. K. Narayan
Under the Banyan Tree and Other Stories, *Grandmother's Tale*, *Waiting for the Mahatma*

Other Works About Heroes of the Past
The *Odyssey*, Homer
The *Aeneid*, Virgil
Idylls of the King, Alfred, Lord Tennyson
Poetic Edda (Unknown)

We suggest that you preview these works before recommending them to students.

INTERNET

We suggest the following sites on the Internet (all Web sites are subject to change).

For a lesson plan on the *Ramayana* accompanied by the story and a teaching guide, go to: **http://www. askasia.org/frclasrom/lessplan/1000054.htm**

For more information on R.K. Narayan, go to: **http:// members.aol.com/mohangk/narayan.htm**

We *strongly recommend* that you preview the sites before you send students to them.

◆ *Literature and Your Life*

6 *Possible response: Rama and today's superheroes show strength, courage, and a commitment to conquering evil.*

Customize for
Verbal/Linguistic Learners
On p. 926, Viswamithra uses the metaphor of a tree and its seedlings to explain why Rama must leave the home of his father. Now that Rama has defeated Thataka, challenge students to create a metaphor that describes his accomplishment.

Reinforce and Extend

Answers

◆ *Literature and Your Life*

Reader's Response Possible response: Yes, because he was teaching him not to accept things at face value.

Thematic Focus Some students will say no, while others will say they would have let Rama go because he was destined to serve his culture and prove his heroism.

Questions for Research Students might suggest questions about how and when people in India study the *Ramayana*.

☑ Check Your Comprehension

1. He wants Rama to help him perform a sacrifice at Sudhasrama.
2. King Dasaratha says that his son is still a child, he is not ready for such a mission.
3. The region is parched, littered with bleached animal bones, and there is no distinction between night and day.
4. (a) Rama is reluctant to fight Thataka because she is a woman. (b) Viswamithra explains who she is and says "a woman of demonic tendencies loses all consideration to be treated as a woman."
5. Rama's arrow pierces Thataka's throat, killing her and initiating Rama into his mission of destroying evil.

Reteach

For students who need additional practice or assistance in making inferences about a culture, you may wish to refer them to p. 63 in ***Strategies for Diverse Student Needs.***

Answers

◆ Critical Thinking

1. Viswamithra, a sage, knew that by challenging Rama in this way he would help the boy to prove his prowess and heroic qualities.
2. He has found enlightenment and probably wants no reminder of his worldly ways and, perhaps, of his past failings.
3. They undergo physical transformation as a result of Agasthya's curse so that their appearance will reflect their internal evil.
4. Viswamithra is wise, worldly, and self-disciplined, and he can impart valuable lessons to Rama about the difference between how things appear and their true nature.
5. A child could be compared to a seed in any time period because the principle still applies: like a seed growing into a tree, a child is small and needs nurturing to develop into a healthy adult.
6. Students might compare Rama with a superhero from a comic book, science-fiction series, or a film in which the hero exhibits prowess to vanquish evil.

◆ Literary Focus

1. Rama's journey with Viswamithra, on which he is introduced to the workings of evil, begin his passage from childhood to adulthood.
2. Rama shows his heroic powers by overcoming his reservations and killing Thataka, an evil force.
3. The people recognized Rama's heroism and asked Viswamithra to prepare him to lead them in all they would do.

◆ Reading Strategy

1. The *Ramayana* shows that the wisdom and spiritual powers of the sage can overcome worldly trials.
2. The *Ramayana* reveals that kings had great respect for sages in ancient India; they accepted their counsel and followed their recommendations.
3. Readers can infer that ancient Indians honored and protected women.

◆ Build Vocabulary

Using the Latin Root *-min-*

1. minimum—small amount; 2. minority—smaller number of two parts; 3. small or brief amount of time; 4. diminish—to make smaller

Using the Word Bank

1.deprivations; 2. weariness; 3. pleasant; 4. dignified; 5. nonreligious; 6. respect; 7. excitement; 8. little; 9. mysterious

◆ Build Grammar Skills

1. Viswamithra, a sage of great understanding, entered the king's assembly hall.
2. King Dasaratha, the father of two young sons, greeted the sage warmly.
3. "Send your son Rama with me, and he will help me," said the sage.
4. Vasishtha, the king's priest and guide, urged Dasaratha to agree to the sage's demand.
5. In the end the brothers Rama and Lakshmana accompanied the holy man on his quest.

Grammar Reinforcement

For additional instruction and practice, use the Commas lesson in the **Language Lab CD-ROM** and page 40 on Appositive and Appositive Phrases in the *Writer's Solution Grammar Practice Book*.

Guide for Responding *(continued)*

◆ Critical Thinking

INTERPRET

1. Explain why Viswamithra chose the young and inexperienced Rama to help him perform such a dangerous task. **[Infer]**
2. Why do you think Viswamithra dislikes all references to his nonreligious past? **[Interpret]**
3. Why do you think Thataka and her two sons undergo a physical transformation as one result of Agasthya's curse? **[Draw Conclusions]**
4. Explain why Viswamithra is a worthy teacher to Rama in his quest to be a hero. **[Interpret]**

APPLY

5. Explain how Viswamithra's comparison of a child to a seed could apply in any time period. **[Relate]**

EXTEND

6. Compare and contrast Rama with a popular superhero in a story, book, or film with which you are familiar. **[Literature Link]**

◆ Literary Focus

THE EPIC HERO

The **epic hero** is the central character of an epic. In his adventures, the hero demonstrates extraordinary skills and special qualities.

1. How does Rama begin the passage from childhood to adulthood?
2. How does Rama show his heroic powers?
3. How do the events that follow Rama's battle with Thataka indicate that Rama is an epic hero?

◆ Reading Strategy

DRAW INFERENCES ABOUT CULTURE

The *Ramayana* presents a picture of Indian culture 2,000 years ago. From the stories told and the details given, you can **infer** beliefs, values, and customs of the period.

1. How does the *Ramayana* show the importance of the sage in Indian culture?
2. What does the *Ramayana* reveal about the relationship between kings and sages in ancient India?
3. Rama hesitates before killing Thataka because she is a woman. What can you infer from this about Indian culture and society?

◆ Build Vocabulary

USING THE LATIN ROOT *-min-*

The Latin root *-min-* means "small." Use this knowledge to help you define each of the following words:

1. minimum **2.** minority **3.** minute **4.** diminish

USING THE WORD BANK: Synonyms

On your paper, write the word whose meaning is closest to that of the first word.

1. austerities: (a) savings, (b) deprivations, (c) blows
2. decrepitude: (a) weariness, (b) unconcern, (c) fear
3. sublime: (a) pleasant, (b) tragic, (c) noble
4. august: (a) overheated, (b) dignified, (c) confused
5. secular: (a) nonreligious, (b) expansive, (c) serious
6. obeisance: (a) anger, (b) shallowness, (c) respect
7. exuberance: (a) excitement, (b) gloom, (c) conceit
8. diminutive: (a) foolish, (b) little, (c) showy
9. esoteric: (a) mysterious, (b) accessible, (c) haughty

◆ Build Grammar Skills

RESTRICTIVE AND NONRESTRICTIVE APPOSITIVES

Restrictive appositives and appositive phrases are essential to the meaning of the sentence; they are not set off by commas. **Nonrestrictive** appositives are not essential to the sentence's meaning; these are set off with commas.

Practice In your notebook, write the following sentences. Underline the appositive or appositive phrase in each. If the appositive is nonrestrictive, set it off with commas.

1. Viswamithra a sage of great understanding entered the king's assembly hall.
2. King Dasaratha the father of two young sons greeted the sage warmly.
3. "Send your son Rama with me, and he will help me," said the sage.
4. Vasishtha the king's priest and guide urged Dasaratha to agree to the sage's demand.
5. In the end, the brothers Rama and Lakshmana accompanied the holy man on his quest.

Build Your Portfolio

Idea Bank

Writing

1. Letter As Viswamithra, write a letter to Dasaratha asking permission for Rama to accompany you on a dangerous mission. Explain why the mission will be a growth experience.

2. Personal Narrative Rama's initiation into adulthood was characteristic for an epic hero. What experience has helped prepare you for adulthood? Write a brief personal narrative relating this experience and its impact on you.

3. Opening Argument You are a lawyer called upon to defend Thataka. Write an opening argument in which you detail how you will prove that Thataka was grossly misjudged. Your objective is to restore Thataka to her status as a demigod.

Speaking, Listening, and Viewing

4. Oral Tales Prepare a version of this episode for an audience of young children. Make an audiotape to give to young relatives or friends. **[Performing Arts Link]**

5. Poster Rama is believed to be just one of the *avatars,* or incarnations, of the Hindu god Vishnu. Create a poster that shows Vishnu in some of his other forms, using classical Hindu imagery. Include text that explains any symbolism present in the image.

Researching and Representing

6. Painting Reread the description of the devouring creature Thataka and the desert domain she inhabited. Create a painting that expresses the terrifying mood of this scene. **[Art Link]**

7. Dance With a group of classmates, reenact the heroic journey and battle of Rama as a dance. Incorporate classical Indian music into your performance. **[Performing Arts Link]**

Online Activity www.phlit.phschool.com

Guided Writing Lesson

Script Treatment Proposal

The *Ramayana* has all the ingredients for a summer blockbuster—exotic settings, a fearless superhero, an old sage with magical powers. Think what a special effects artist could do with an evil creature like Thataka! Write a **script treatment** outlining how you propose to tell the story, cast the film, and use special effects and music to create a box-office success.

Writing Skills Focus: Appropriate Language for Your Purpose

Your script treatment has to show its readers that you're onto a great film idea. To do this, you'll have to make every word count. Use vivid words and phrases to express the excitement and suspense of key scenes. Also, use **language** that appeals to the emotions, such as a *stirring* scene, and *sympathetic* and *inspiring* characters.

Prewriting Before you begin writing, envision your film in your mind. To help you plan your script treatment, make an outline with headings such as story events, cast, special effects, and music. For each heading, list ideas and suggestions that you think will keep the attention of a large audience.

Events	Cast	Special Effects	Music

Drafting As you draft your treatment, draw on the information in your outline. Add to it as you envision new and better scene ideas. Use vivid and precise terms and language that will appeal to your readers' emotions.

Revising Reread your draft. Ask: Have I left out any information the backers of the film will want to know? Is my persuasive language convincing and emotional? Is it *too* emotional? Revise accordingly.

Idea Bank

Following are suggestions for matching Idea Bank topics with your students' performance levels and learning modalities:

Customizing for Performance Levels

Less Advanced Students: 1, 4
Average Students: 2, 5, 6, 7
More Advanced Students: 3

Customizing for Learning Modalities

Musical/Rhythmic: 5
Verbal/Linguistic: 4, 5
Bodily/Kinesthetic: 7
Visual/Spatial: 6
Logical/Mathematical: 3

Guided Writing Lesson

Prewriting Strategy Guide students to envision their films by having them begin with the cubing strategy. Students can create a cube as a manipulative to think about all aspects of their films before they outline their script treatments.

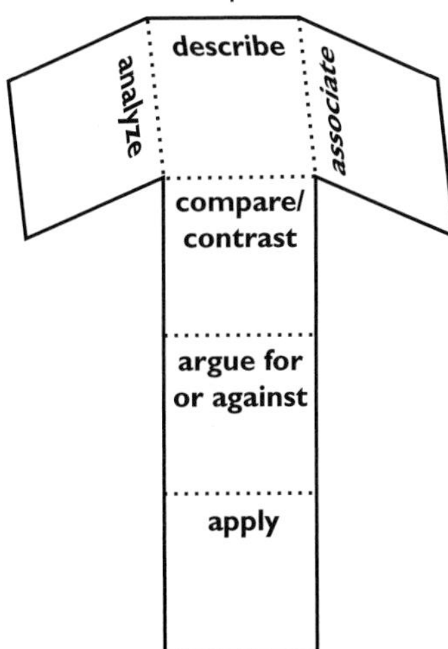

For more prewriting, elaboration, and revision strategies, see *Prentice Hall Writing and Grammar.*

Writing Lab CD-ROM

Have students complete the tutorial on Exposition. Follow these steps:

1. Have students use the Note Cards activity to organize details of setting, characters, and special effects.
2. Have students view the screen on Audience and Purpose.
3. Allow time for students to draft on the computer.
4. Suggest that students use the Transitions Word Bin for ideas on words that will help show the relationships between ideas.
5. Have students use Revision Checker for Homophones before completing their final revision.

✓ ASSESSMENT OPTIONS

Formal Assessment, Selection Test, pp. 223–225, and Assessment Resources Software. The selection test is designed so that it can be easily customized to the performance levels of your students.

Alternative Assessment, p. 63, includes options for less advanced students, more advanced students, logical/mathematical learners, musical/rhythmic learners, intrapersonal learners, bodily/kinesthetic learners, and interpersonal learners.

PORTFOLIO ASSESSMENT

Use the following rubrics in the ***Alternative Assessment*** booklet to assess student writing:
Letter: Persuasion Rubric, p. 105
Personal Narrative: Narrative Based on Personal Experience Rubric, p. 96
Opening Argument: Persuasion Rubric, p. 105
Guided Writing Lesson: Description Rubric, p. 97

Prepare and Engage

LESSON OBJECTIVES

1. **To develop vocabulary and word identification skills**
   - Latin Word Roots: *-firm-*
   - Using the Word Bank: Synonyms
   - Extending Word Study: Dictionary (ATE)
2. **To use a variety of reading strategies to comprehend a personal narrative**
   - Connect Your Experience
   - Reading Strategy: Storyteller's Purpose
   - Tips to Guide Reading: Sustained Reading (ATE)
   - Read to Be Informed (ATE)
   - Idea Bank: News Article
3. **To increase knowledge of other cultures and to connect common elements across cultures**
   - Connecting Themes Across Cultures (ATE)
   - Background for Understanding
4. **To express and support responses to the text**
   - Critical Thinking
   - Idea Bank: Role Play
   - Idea Bank: Writing in the Heroic Tradition
   - Analyze Film Criticism (ATE)
5. **To analyze literary elements**
   - Literary Focus: Epic Conflict
   - Idea Bank: Critical Evaluation
6. **To read in order to research self-selected and assigned topics**
   - Idea Bank: Documentary
   - Research Skills Mini-Lesson: Taking Notes From Sources (ATE)
   - Viewing and Representing Mini-Lesson: Chart (ATE)
7. **To speak clearly and effectively for a specific audience and purpose**
   - Speaking, Listening, and Viewing Mini-Lesson: Oral Tales
8. **To use recursive writing processes to write storytelling notes**
   - Guided Writing Lesson
9. **To increase knowledge of the rules of grammar and usage**
   - Build Grammar Skills: Sentence Variety

Test Preparation

Writing Skills: Style (ATE, p. 933) The teaching tips and sample test item in this workshop support the instruction and practice in the unit workshop:

Writing Skills: Strategy, Organization, and Style (SE, p. 951)

Guide for Reading

Sundiata

Although the original author is not known, the story of Sundiata has been told by the storytellers, or griots (grē´ ōz), of Mali—an African republic—for many centuries. Many African ethnic groups rely on the memories of their griots, rather than on written accounts, to preserve a record of the past.

Griots are both storytellers and historians. They call themselves the memory of the people, and they travel from village to village, teaching the history and legends of their ancestors to the new generations. Thus, the griots preserve their history and culture orally.

D. T. Niane

After listening to the stories told by Mamadou Kouyate (mä´ mä do͞o ko͞o ya´ te), a griot of the Keita clan, Djibril Tamsir Niane (dyē´ bril täm´ sēr nī´ yan) wrote *Sundiata: An Epic of Old Mali* in his Malinke language. Niane's work was translated into English and other languages, and now people all over the world profit from the griot's wisdom.

Niane's own ancestors were griots. In addition to *Sundiata,* D. T. Niane has collected and retold many other ancient legends of Mali. His translations of the ancient oral histories is one way he affirms their value. A noted historian, his specific area of interest is medieval African empires. This expertise has helped him to create the background for *Sundiata* and other works.

◆ Build Vocabulary

Latin Word Roots: *-firm-*

The hero in this selection, Mari Djata, is said to have an *infirmity.* The root *-firm-* is derived from the Latin word *firmare,* "to strengthen." By combining this meaning with the meaning of the prefix *in-,* "lacking" or "without," you can figure out that *infirmity* means "without strength" or "physical weakness."

Word Bank

As you read this selection from *Sundiata,* you will encounter the words on this list. Each word is defined on the page where it first appears.

With a partner, read the words aloud. Share the meaning of any of the words you already know.

fathom
taciturn
malicious
infirmity
innuendo
diabolical
estranged
affront

◆ Build Grammar Skills

Sentence Variety

Writers use **sentence variety** to create an interesting rhythm in their writing. They vary their sentences in several ways. D. T. Niane uses a mix of sentence lengths and structures. He also varies his sentence types, using declarative, interrogative, and exclamatory sentences:

Declarative: *Malicious tongues began to blab.*
Interrogative: *What three-year-old has not yet taken his first steps?*
Exclamatory: *How impatient man is!*

Using different sentence beginnings also adds variety:

Begins With an Adverb: *Now* he was resting on nothing . . .
Begins With a Prepositional Phrase: *At the age of three* he still crawled along on all-fours . . .
Begins With a Participial Phrase: *Having become all-powerful,* Sassouma Bérété persecuted Sogolon . . .

As you read from *Sundiata,* notice the effect of the sentence variety.

Prentice Hall Literature Program Resources

REINFORCE / RETEACH / EXTEND

Selection Support Pages
Build Vocabulary: Word Roots: *-firm-*, p. 261
Build Grammar Skills: Sentence Variety, p. 262
Reading Strategy: Storyteller's Purpose, p. 263
Literary Focus: Epic Conflict, p. 264

Strategies for Diverse Student Needs, p. 64

Beyond Literature
Cross Curricular Connection: *Geography*, p. 64

Formal Assessment Selection Test, pp. 226–228; Assessment Resources Software

Alternative Assessment, p. 64

Writing and Language Transparencies
Week 28, p. 139

Resource Pro CD-ROM

Listening to Literature Audiocassettes

from Sundiata: An Epic of Old Mali

◆ Literature and Your Life

Connect Your Experience

If you've ever been ridiculed—even over something as trivial as a bad haircut or a botched basketball shot—you know that the temptation to strike back can be strong. While it may not always be appropriate to strike back, often there are other ways to put a stop to ridicule. In this episode, the much-belittled Mari Djata finds a noble way to not only stop the ridicule, but also to become a hero.

Journal Writing Write about a time when, like Mari Djata in this story, you were unfairly compared with another. Describe the situation and how you felt.

Thematic Focus: From the Past

Ideally, the legacy handed down from king to king encompasses wisdom, prudence, courage, and great strength. What are the results when one of these qualities is absent? How do people respond? Think about these questions as you read this selection.

◆ Background for Understanding

History

Almost 1,000 years ago, the area of west Africa that includes present-day Ghana and Mali was highly unstable. Rival kings fought for control of the salt and gold caravan trade that passed through their territory. Eventually, Sumanguru, a warrior king of Ghana, gained control of the region and cruelly oppressed the Mandinka people of Mali. Although weak and scattered, the Mandinka rebelled against Sumanguru. Just when Mali needed a leader most, against all odds, the hero Sogolon-Diata rose to power. (In rapidly spoken Mandinka, "Sogolon-Diata" became "Sundiata.") A member of the Keita clan which had ruled Mali for centuries, Sundiata united his people, fought off Sumanguru, and ushered in a glorious period of peace and prosperity.

◆ Literary Focus

Epic Conflict

At the heart of any epic is an **epic conflict**—a situation in which the hero struggles against an obstacle or set of obstacles. Part of an epic conflict may be a difficult situation in childhood. In the traditional epic, the hero surmounts difficulties, conquers enemies, and finally emerges triumphant. Through these struggles, the hero passes from childhood to adulthood, proving his wisdom, bravery, and power.

As you read from the folk epic *Sundiata*, take note of the obstacles that confront Mari Djata, blocking his path on the way to achieving heroism.

◆ Reading Strategy

Storyteller's Purpose

Griots have a **purpose,** or reason for relating their stories. The griots who told and retold the story of Sundiata for centuries had several purposes. First, they wanted to inform their people about important historical events. In addition, they intended to entertain their listeners with an exciting account of a hero's adventures. Further, by recounting the positive and negative results of various actions, the griots instructed the people in appropriate or expected behavior. Thinking about these different purposes will give you greater insight into the epic *Sundiata*.

To help you keep track of the storyteller's purposes, make a chart like the one shown. As you read the selection, list events, passages, or other aspects of the epic that illustrate each of the purposes.

Inform	Entertain	Persuade

Most good political leaders use brain, not brawn, to settle most problems. Action heroes, however, often use more brawn than brain to fight evil. Ask students for examples of each—politicians who think out problems, and fictional superheroes who use extraordinary physical powers to make their impact on the world. Then let students know that the storytellers, or griots, of Mali told of political leaders that were like action heroes. The excerpt from *Sundiata* they will read describes a person who is both is a great leader and the possessor of superhuman powers.

Connecting Themes Across Cultures

Most of the legends in this unit are about hereditary rulers or people who come to power. Have students brainstorm about how leaders become legends in a democracy, where leaders are elected.

Customize for *Less Proficient Readers*

Ask students to pause at the end of each page to ask themselves: "What is Mari Djata's (Sogolon's son's) problem? What might happen to solve that problem?" When they finish reading, have them go back and review their predictions to see which were most nearly correct.

Customize for *Pre-AP Students*

Have these students compare the epic conflict in this legend with that in the other legends in the unit. Does this story have the qualities of an epic? Have students categorize this story in a genre and defend their choices. Is it a tall tale or a legend, or does it rise to the level of an epic?

Customize for *English Language Learners*

Remind students that the hero Sundiata is also called Sogolon's son, Sogolon Djata, and Mari Djata. Write these names on the chalkboard, along with their pronunciations, for these students to refer to as they read. This quick-reference chart will help them keep track of Sundiata's actions throughout the epic.

Test Preparation Workshop

Writing Skills: Style The SAT tests verbal skills in various ways. Style questions focus on understanding the writer's point of view based on his or her effective use of language. The following passage and question will help students assess their understanding of style.

> Malicious tongues began to blab. What three-year-old has not yet taken his first steps? What three-year-old is not the despair of his parents through his whims and shifts of mood? What three-year-old is not the joy of his circle through his backwardness in talking?

Which of the following best replaces the word *malicious?*

A inappropriate
B unkind
C friendly
D deficient

The tone of the passage reflects the frustration of the child's mother. By process of elimination, students should determine that the attitude of others is *unkind,* answer B.

Develop Understanding

One-Minute Insight

In this translation of an African legend, future king Mari Djata (also known as Sogolon Djata and as Sundiata), seems a most unlikely hero, with his huge head and his inability to stand upright. How Mari Djata overcomes his infirmity and regains his honor is an exciting and instructive tale.

Tips to Guide Reading

Sustained Reading Before students begin to read, you may wish to review the strategies already used in this unit to encourage sustained reading with comprehension. The cast of characters, with all the unfamiliar names at the beginning of the selection, will solve the biggest obstacle to ongoing reading. Assure students that quickly referring to the list while they are reading is not an unreasonable interruption if it helps them to distinguish among the characters.

Customize for *Pre-AP Students*

These students might enjoy creating an epic that tells the (fictionalized) tale of an American leader. Have them pattern their epic after this one by providing a problem and its solution, supporting characters who create obstacles to the hero's success, and a hero who is able to overcome those obstacles.

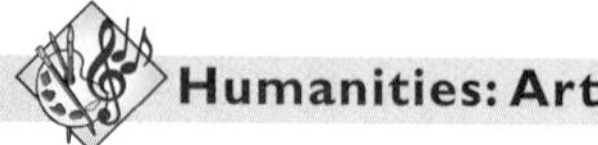

Humanities: Art

Senegalese Glass Painting.

In urban areas of modern Senegal, painting on glass is a popular art form. What originally began as a way to make inexpensive and durable advertising signs for businesses and trucks has become an art form with striking results.

This work is painted in vivid primary colors that are flatly applied. The artist makes little attempt to show depth with gradations of color or shadows. The result is a bright pattern that is bold and decorative in the manner of African fabric.

from Sundiata: An Epic of Old Mali

D. T. Niane

Senegalese Glass Painting Used on Sundiata, collection of Professor Donal Cruise-O'Brien, Courtesy of Longman International Education

CHARACTERS IN *SUNDIATA*

Balla Fasséké (bä´ lä fä sä´ kä): Griot and counselor of Sundiata.

Boukari (bo͞o kä´ rē): Son of the king and Namandjé, one of his wives; also called Manding (män´ diŋ) Boukari.

Dankaran Touman (dän´ kä rän to͞o´ män): Son of the king and his first wife, Sassouma, who is also called Sassouma Bérété.

Djamarou (jä mä´ ro͞o): Daughter of Sogolon and the king; sister of Sundiata and Kolonkan.

Farakourou (fä rä ko͞o´ ro͞o): Master of the forges.

Gnankouman Doua (nän ko͞o´ män do͞o´ ə) The king's griot; also called simply, Doua.

Kolonkan (kō lōn´ kən): Sundiata's eldest sister.

Namandjé (nä män´ jē): One of the king's wives.

Naré Maghan (nä´ rā mäg´ hän): Sundiata's father.

Nounfaïri (no͞on´ fä ē´ rē): Soothsayer and smith; father of Farakourou.

Sassouma Bérété (sä so͞o´ mä be´ re te): The king's first wife.

Sogolon (sô gô lōn´): Sundiata's mother; also called Sogolon Kedjou (kā´ jo͞o).

Sundiata (so͞on dyä´ tä): Legendary king of Mali; referred to as Djata (dyä´ tä) and Sogolon Djata, which means "son of Sogolon." Sundiata is also called Mari (mä´ rē) Djata.

Block Scheduling Strategies

Consider these suggestions to take advantage of extended class time:

- Ask students to work in groups to brainstorm for a list of words containing the root *-firm-* introduced in Build Vocabulary on p. 932. Allow time for groups to compare their lists.
- As you review the information in Background for Understanding (p. 933), display a map and have students share facts about West Africa that they have learned in social studies classes.
- Introduce the Reading Strategy: Storyteller's Purpose on p. 933. Have students fill out a chart as they read the story and then answer the Reading Strategy questions on p. 940. You may follow up with the Reading Strategy page in ***Selection Support,*** p. 263.
- Students may work in small groups to answer the Critical Thinking questions on p. 940. Reconvene the class to discuss the answers.
- Use the recording of *Sundiata* to explore the difference between reading and hearing a story. Discuss the fact that the art of the griots was in taking a historic event and rendering it as oral history with a dramatic flair.

CHILDHOOD

God has his mysteries which none can fathom. You, perhaps, will be a king. You can do nothing about it. You, on the other hand, will be unlucky, but you can do nothing about that either. Each man finds his way already marked out for him and he can change nothing of it.

Sogolon's son had a slow and difficult childhood. At the age of three he still crawled along on all-fours while children of the same age were already walking. He had nothing of the great beauty of his father Naré Maghan. He had a head so big that he seemed unable to support it; he also had large eyes which would open wide whenever anyone entered his mother's house. He was taciturn and used to spend the whole day just sitting in the middle of the house. Whenever his mother went out he would crawl on all-fours to rummage about in the calabashes[1] in search of food, for he was very greedy.

Malicious tongues began to blab. What three-year-old has not yet taken his first steps? What three-year-old is not the despair of his parents through his whims and shifts of mood? What three-year-old is not the joy of his circle through his backwardness in talking? Sogolon Djata (for it was thus that they called him, prefixing his mother's name to his), Sogolon Djata, then, was very different from others of his own age. He spoke little and his severe face never relaxed into a smile. You would have thought that he was already thinking, and what amused children of his age bored him. Often Sogolon would make some of them come to him to keep him company. These children were already walking and she hoped that Djata, seeing his companions walking, would be tempted to do likewise. But nothing came of it. Besides, Sogolon Djata would brain the poor little things with his already strong arms and none of them would come near him any more.

The king's first wife was the first to rejoice at Sogolon Djata's infirmity. Her own son, Dankaran Touman, was already eleven. He was a fine and lively boy, who spent the day running about the village with those of his own age. He had even begun his initiation in the bush.[2] The king had had a bow made for him and he used to go behind the town to practice archery with his companions. Sassouma was quite happy and snapped her fingers at Sogolon, whose child was still crawling on the ground. Whenever the latter happened to pass by her house, she would say, "Come, my son, walk, jump, leap about. The jinn[3] didn't promise you anything out of the ordinary, but I prefer a son who walks on his two legs to a lion that crawls on the ground." She spoke thus whenever Sogolon went by her door. The innuendo would go straight home and then she would burst into laughter, that diabolical laughter which a jealous woman knows how to use so well.

Her son's infirmity weighed heavily upon Sogolon Kedjou; she had resorted to all her talent as a sorceress to give strength to her son's legs, but the rarest herbs had been useless. The king himself lost hope.

How impatient man is! Naré Maghan became imperceptibly estranged but Gnankouman

1. **calabashes** (kal´ ə bash´ iz) *n.*: Dried, hollow shells of gourds, used as bowls.

2. **initiation in the bush:** Education in tribal lore given to twelve-year-old West African boys so they can become full members of the tribe.

3. **jinn** (jin) *n.*: Supernatural beings that influence human affairs. Their promise was that the son of Sogolon would make Mali a great empire.

◀ **Critical Viewing** How does the artist show which is the most important character in this painting? **[Analyze]**

◆ Build Vocabulary

fathom (fath´ əm) *v.*: Understand thoroughly
taciturn (tas´ ə turn) *adj.*: Uncommunicative
malicious (mə lish´ əs) *adj.*: Intentionally harmful
infirmity (in fur´ mə tē) *n.*: Physical weakness
innuendo (in´ yo͞o en´ dō) *n.*: Insinuation
diabolical (dī ə bäl´ ik əl) *adj.*: Wicked; cruel
estranged (e strānjd´) *adv.*: Removed from; at a distance

◆ Reading Strategy

1 Storyteller's Purpose Point out the use of the pronoun *you* in this opening paragraph. Ask what the storyteller's purpose is in this section. *His purpose is to teach each person a lesson. By using the pronoun you, the storyteller makes direct contact with the listener.*

◆ Build Grammar Skills

2 Sentence Variety Have students notice the rhythm created by the storyteller's use of questions here. Ask students to consider how the use of questions gets listeners involved in the story. *Suggested response: The questions allow listeners to respond directly to the story.*

▶Critical Viewing◀

3 Analyze *The artist places one figure at the center of the painting and makes him larger than the others. This man is also shown to have more elaborate clothing than the others. He also holds a staff, which often indicates a ruler or wise man. The attention of all the other figures is focused on the central figure. In these ways, the artist indicates that this character is the most important one in the painting.*

◆ Reading Strategy

4 Storyteller's Purpose What is the storyteller's purpose in telling you this? What does he want you to believe about Sogolon? *The storyteller's purpose is to emphasize the extent of the infirmity that Mari Djata (Sogolon Djata) must overcome. He also wants people to understand how cruel Sassouma, Mari Djata's enemy, can be.*

Humanities: Literature

Oral Tradition Long before there were books and libraries, people shared their history and stories through oral literature. Information was passed from generation to generation in song, poem, or story form. These oral histories recounted the culture of a people through plots and characters that everyone could understand and remember. The themes of oral literature centered on the beginning of the world, love, and tragedy. Oral histories included epic tales of heroism, ballads, folk tales, fables, and proverbs. These oral tales often followed people as they moved from place to place, telling the stories they knew. That is why we find stories of a great flood in the literature of many different cultures, and why certain fairy tales with the same character(s) reappear. Much later, when written works became more common, many of these oral tales were recorded in writing. That is how *The Epic of Gilgamesh*, Greek myths, the *Ramayana*, and *Sundiata* remain with us today.

Students may enjoy speculating on how the electronic age might further change the nature of the passage of literature from one generation to the next.

❶ **Clarification** Students should know that earlier in the *Sundiata*, a soothsayer (fortune teller) had told King Naré Maghan that his son by Sogolon would have a glorious future.

◆ Reading Strategy

❷ **Storyteller's Purpose** Storytellers often use metaphor to teach a lesson. What is the metaphor, or comparison, that the Griot Doua is using here? What lesson is he teaching? *Sample answer: Doua is comparing Mari Djata (Sogolon's son) to a silk cotton tree. The tree emerges from a tiny seed (as a baby does) and develops slowly and with difficulty (like the boy Mari Djata). The lesson is to have patience. While a boy may develop slowly and with infirmities, in time he will grow up to be a strong man.*

◆ Literary Focus

❸ **Epic Conflict** In this paragraph, the storyteller foreshadows the struggle to follow. Ask students what three things mentioned here appear to stand in the way of Mari Djata's success? *The obstacles that stand in the way of Mari Djata's success are his failure to walk, the fact that the king is aging and will no longer be able to protect him, and the growth of the son of his enemy, Sassouma.*

◆ Build Grammar Skills

❹ **Sentence Variety** The author changes the rhythm of his words when the old king speaks. Ask students how sentence variety makes the king's speech sound impressive. *Suggested response: (1) He uses long sentences to list the griots of his family, to tell what Mari Djata will learn, and to say what he will inherit. (2) To emphasize his power as king, he injects two imperative sentences: "Be inseparable . . ." and "May your destiny be. . . ." (3) To add a poetic quality to his words, the king starts some sentences with prepositional phrases: "In Mali . . ." and "From his mouth. . . ." (4) He begins several sentences with "I" to highlight what he personally has done as king.*

Comprehension Check ☑

❺ Be sure students know who "the lion" represents. *It is Mari Djata. In one of her insults, Sassouma called him "a lion that crawls on the ground."*

Doua never ceased reminding him of the hunter's words. Sogolon became pregnant again. The king hoped for a son, but it was a daughter called Kolonkan. She resembled her mother and had nothing of her father's beauty. The disheartened king debarred Sogolon from his house and she lived in semi-disgrace for a while. Naré Maghan married the daughter of one of his allies, the king of the Kamaras. She was called Namandjé and her beauty was legendary. A year later she brought a boy into the world. When the king consulted soothsayers[4] on the destiny of this son, he received the reply that Namandjé's child would be the right hand of some mighty king. The king gave the newly-born the name of Boukari. He was to be called Manding Boukari or Manding Bory later on.

❶ Naré Maghan was very perplexed. Could it be that the stiff jointed son of Sogolon was the one the hunter soothsayer had foretold?

"The Almighty has his mysteries," Gnankouman Doua would say and, taking up the hunter's words, added, "The silk cotton tree emerges from a tiny seed."

❷ One day Naré Maghan came along to the house of Nounfaïri, the blacksmith seer of Niani. He was an old, blind man. He received the king in the anteroom which served as his workshop. To the king's question he replied, "When the seed germinates growth is not always easy; great trees grow slowly but they plunge their roots deep into the ground."

"But has the seed really germinated?" said the king.

"Of course," replied the blind seer. "Only the growth is not as quick as you would like it; how impatient man is."

This interview and Doua's confidence gave the king some assurance. To the great displeasure of Sassouma Bérété the king restored Sogolon to favor and soon another daughter was born to her. She was given the name of Djamarou.

❸ However, all Niani talked of nothing else but the stiff-legged son of Sogolon. He was now seven and he still crawled to get about. In spite of all the king's affection, Sogolon was in despair. Naré Maghan aged and he felt his time coming to an end. Dankaran Touman, the son of Sassouma Bérété, was now a fine youth.

❹ One day Naré Maghan made Mari Djata come to him and he spoke to the child as one speaks to an adult. "Mari Djata, I am growing old and soon I shall be no more among you, but before death takes me off I am going to give you the present each king gives his successor. In Mali every prince has his own griot. Doua's father was my father's griot, Doua is mine and the son of Doua, Balla Fasséké here, will be your griot. Be inseparable friends from this day forward. From his mouth you will hear the history of your ancestors, you will learn the art of governing Mali according to the principles which our ancestors have bequeathed to us. I have served my term and done my duty too. I have done everything which a king of Mali ought to do. I am handing an enlarged kingdom over to you and I leave you sure allies. May your destiny be accomplished, but never forget that Niani is your capital and Mali the cradle of your ancestors."

The child, as if he had understood the whole meaning of the king's words, beckoned Balla Fasséké to approach. He made room for him on the hide he was sitting on and then said, "Balla, you will be my griot."

"Yes, son of Sogolon, if it pleases God," replied Balla Fasséké.

The king and Doua exchanged glances that radiated confidence.

The Lion's Awakening ❺

A short while after this interview between Naré Maghan and his son the king died. Sogolon's son was no more than seven years old. The council of elders met in the king's palace. It was no use Doua's defending the king's will which reserved the throne for Mari Djata, for the council took no account of Naré Maghan's wish. With the help of Sassouma Bérété's intrigues, Dankaran Touman was proclaimed king and a regency council was formed in which the queen mother was all-powerful. A short time after, Doua died.

As men have short memories, Sogolon's son

4. **soothsayers** (sōōth′ sā′ ərz) *n.*: People who can foretell the future.

Viewing and Representing Mini-Lesson

Chart

This Mini-Lesson supports the researching and representing activity in the Idea Bank on p. 941.

Introduce Ask students if they have seen posters that show families of various fruits and vegetables. You may want to obtain one to show students.

Develop Discuss with students that people have used herbs for medicinal and other purposes for millennia. Distinguishing one herb from another and knowing its effects is important when using herbs. Have students consult general reference books for pictures of herbs and descriptions of their uses. They might want to limit their charts to herbs for specific purposes, such as flavoring or medicine. Their charts should include a suitable name, visual representations, common and scientific names, and uses of the herb plant.

Apply Supply students with a variety of art materials with which to create their charts.

Assess Assess students on the accuracy of their charts. Make sure they have limited their charts to certain kinds of herbs. Discuss with students the artistic decisions that have been made on their classmates' charts.

was spoken of with nothing but irony and scorn. People had seen one-eyed kings, one-armed kings, and lame kings, but a stiff-legged king had never been heard tell of. No matter how great the destiny promised for Mari Djata might be, the throne could not be given to someone who had no power in his legs; if the jinn loved him, let them begin by giving him the use of his legs. Such were the remarks that Sogolon heard every day. The queen mother, Sassouma Bérété, was the source of all this gossip.

Having become all-powerful, Sassouma Bérété persecuted Sogolon because the late Naré Maghan had preferred her. She banished Sogolon and her son to a back yard of the palace. Mari Djata's mother now occupied an old hut which had served as a lumber-room of Sassouma's.

The wicked queen mother allowed free passage to all those inquisitive people who wanted to see the child that still crawled at the age of seven. Nearly all the inhabitants of Niani filed into the palace and the poor Sogolon wept to see herself thus given over to public ridicule. Mari Djata took on a ferocious look in front of the crowd of sightseers. Sogolon found a little consolation only in the love of her eldest daughter, Kolonkan. She was four and she could walk. She seemed to understand all her mother's miseries and already she helped her with the housework. Sometimes, when Sogolon was attending to the chores, it was she who stayed beside her sister Djamarou, quite small as yet.

> ◆ *Literature and Your Life*
> Why do you think people ridicule others even when they know the pain and hurt it causes?

Sogolon Kedjou and her children lived on the queen mother's leftovers, but she kept a little garden in the open ground behind the village. It was there that she passed her brightest moments looking after her onions and gnougous.[5] One day she happened to be short of condiments and went to the queen mother to beg a little baobab leaf.[6]

"Look you," said the malicious Sassouma, "I have a calabash full. Help yourself, you poor woman. As for me, my son knew how to walk at seven and it was he who went and picked these baobab leaves. Take them then, since your son is unequal to mine." Then she laughed derisively with that fierce laughter which cuts through your flesh and penetrates right to the bone.

Sogolon Kedjou was dumbfounded. She had never imagined that hate could be so strong in a human being. With a lump in her throat she left Sassouma's. Outside her hut Mari Djata, sitting on his useless legs, was blandly eating out of a calabash. Unable to contain herself any longer, Sogolon burst into sobs and seizing a piece of wood, hit her son.

5. **gnougous** (nōō′ gōōz′) *n.*: Root vegetables.
6. **baobab** (bā′ ō bab′) leaf *n.*: Baobab is a thick-trunked tree; its leaves are used to flavor foods.

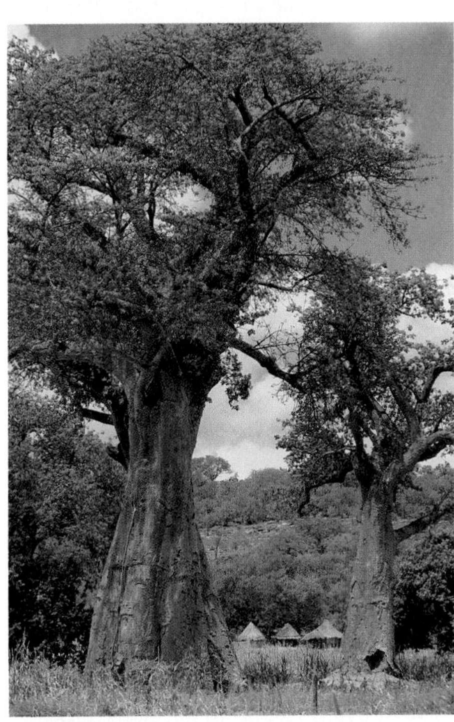

▲ **Critical Viewing** What skills might be needed to gather leaves from these baobab trees? **[Infer]** 8

◆ *Literature and Your Life*

6 To help students respond to this question, point out that one of the purposes of this legend is to teach a lesson. *Sample answer: Some people ridicule others to cover up their own insecurities.*

◆ Critical Thinking

7 **Interpret** Point out that Sassouma, who has mercilessly ridiculed Sogolon and her Mari Djata, allows them to eat her leftovers. Ask: What does this fact say about Sassouma? *Most students will recognize that by feeding Sogolon and Mari Djata leftovers, Sassouma has found yet another way to humiliate them.*

▶Critical Viewing◀

8 **Infer** Sample answer: *To gather leaves from the baobab trees, one would need to be a good climber, and to be strong and agile.*

Read to Be Informed

Most legendary figures combine intelligence, rectitude, and physical strength to achieve their status. There are those, however, who show a great concentration of one quality. Solomon was celebrated for his wisdom. Don Quixote is famous for being wildly idealistic. Sundiata is legendary for his brute strength. In this selection we get little or no evidence of the leadership qualities which made him a legend in Mali. The reader is left to assume that strength is enough.

Extending Word Study

Dictionary In the last paragraph on p. 937, Sogolon Kedjou is *dumbfounded.* Prior knowledge and/or context will probably provide students with a sense of what the word means. However, they may be interested in discovering the precise meaning of this portmanteau word—a word that combines two other words in form and meaning—by using a dictionary.

Cross-Curricular Connection: Social Studies

Mali The empire of Mali, which Sundiata formed in the thirteenth century, is in the region now known as the Republic of Mali. It is the largest country in West Africa.

This empire was a very rich state and one of the world's major producers of gold, but it has a history of instability. It was taken over in the fifteenth century by the Songhai empire, but that empire declined rapidly, and the region became a jumble of small states. In the nineteenth century, Mali became part of the French empire. It broke from the French in 1960 under the leadership of Modibo Keita, a man from the same Keita tribe as Sundiata. Keita became the first president of the republic, but he was overthrown in 1968 by General Moussa Traoré, who in turn was overthrown in 1991.

Locate Mali on a map and discuss with students how its location made it an important crossroads in Sundiata's times.

◆ Literary Focus

❶ **Epic Conflict** Sample response: *Because Sogolon's great humiliation has led her to attack her son, Mari Djata is suddenly awakened to the obstacles he needs to overcome to create a better life for his mother and to fulfill his potential. This realization heightens the epic conflict.*

◆ Critical Thinking

❷ **Infer** Have students explain how they can tell that the smith and the griot know why Mari Djata wants the iron bar. *They refer to this as "the great day." In addition, the smith is identified as a soothsayer, or fortuneteller, who would know what the future will bring.*

◆ Reading Strategy

❸ **Storyteller's Purpose** Have students determine whether the purpose of this passage is to instruct or to entertain. What technique does the griot use to keep the audience interested? *Some students will suggest that the use of suspense indicates the storyteller's wish to entertain. Others may feel that by focusing on Sundiata's strenuous effort, the storyteller is teaching a lesson about determination.*

Reteach

There are two kinds of conflict in this legend: regular conflict and epic conflict. The regular conflict, which students will readily understand, is the rather unpleasant one between the two mothers, Sogolon and Sassouma. The epic conflict is between Mari Djata and the obstacles he must overcome to achieve legendary status. You may want to use the following graphic organizer to make this more abstract conflict obvious.

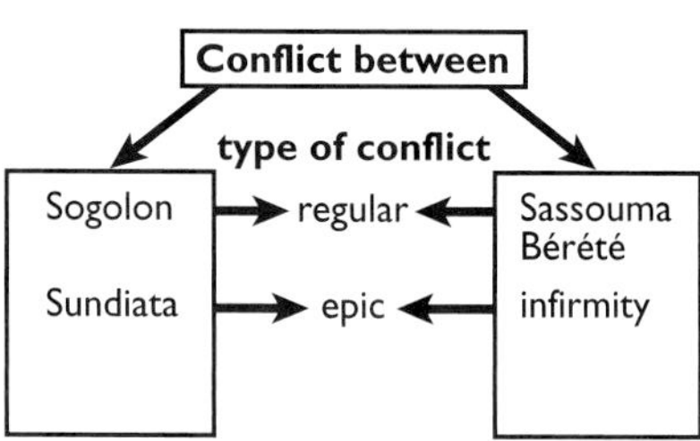

"Oh son of misfortune, will you never walk? Through your fault I have just suffered the greatest <u>affront</u> of my life! What have I done, God, for you to punish me in this way?"

Mari Djata seized the piece of wood and, looking at his mother, said, "Mother, what's the matter?"

"Shut up, nothing can ever wash me clean of this insult."

"But what then?"

"Sassouma has just humiliated me over a matter of a baobab leaf. At your age her own son could walk and used to bring his mother baobab leaves."

"Cheer up, Mother, cheer up."

"No. It's too much. I can't."

"Very well then, I am going to walk today," said Mari Djata. "Go and tell my father's smiths to make me the heaviest possible iron rod. Mother, do you want just the leaves of the baobab or would you rather I brought you the whole tree?"

❶ **◆ Literary Focus** In what way does this event contribute to the epic conflict?

"Ah, my son, to wipe out this insult I want the tree and its roots at my feet outside my hut."

Balla Fasséké, who was present, ran to the master smith, Farakourou, to order an iron rod.

Sogolon had sat down in front of her hut. She was weeping softly and holding her head between her two hands. Mari Djata went calmly back to his calabash of rice and began eating again as if nothing had happened. From time to time he looked up discreetly at his mother, who was murmuring in a low voice, "I want the whole tree, in front of my hut, the whole tree."

All of a sudden a voice burst into laughter behind the hut. It was the wicked Sassouma telling one of her serving women about the scene of humiliation and she was laughing loudly so that Sogolon could hear. Sogolon fled into the hut and hid her face under the blankets so as not to have before her eyes this heedless boy, who was more preoccupied with eating than with anything else. With her head buried in the bedclothes Sogolon wept and her body shook violently. Her daughter, Sogolon Djamarou, had come and sat down beside her and she said, "Mother, Mother, don't cry. Why are you crying?"

Mari Djata had finished eating and, dragging himself along on his legs, he came and sat under the wall of the hut for the sun was scorching. What was he thinking about? He alone knew.

The royal forges were situated outside the walls and over a hundred smiths worked there. The bows, spears, arrows and shields of Niani's warriors came from there. When Balla Fasséké came to order the iron rod, Farakourou said to him, "The great day has arrived then?"

"Yes. Today is a day like any other, but it will see what no other day has seen."

The master of the forges, Farakourou, was the son of the old Nounfaïri, and he was a soothsayer like his father. In his workshops there was an enormous iron bar wrought by his father, Nounfaïri. Everybody wondered what this bar was destined to be used for. Farakourou called six of his apprentices and told them to carry the iron bar to Sogolon's house.

When the smiths put the gigantic iron bar down in front of the hut the noise was so frightening that Sogolon, who was lying down, jumped up with a start. Then Balla Fasséké, son of Gnankouman Doua, spoke.

"Here is the great day, Mari Djata. I am speaking to you, Maghan, son of Sogolon. The waters of the Niger can efface the stain from the body, but they cannot wipe out an insult. Arise, young lion, roar, and may the bush know that from henceforth it has a master."

The apprentice smiths were still there, Sogolon had come out, and everyone was watching Mari Djata. He crept on all-fours and came to the iron bar. Supporting himself on his knees and one hand, with the other hand he picked up the iron bar without any effort and stood it up vertically. Now he was resting on nothing but his knees and held the bar with both his hands. A deathly silence had gripped all those present. Sogolon Djata closed his eyes, held tight, the muscles in his arms tensed. With a violent jerk he threw his weight on to it and his knees left the ground. Sogolon Kedjou was all eyes and watched her son's legs,

Speaking, Listening, and Viewing Mini-Lesson

Oral Tales

This mini-lesson supports the Speaking, Listening, and Viewing activity in the Idea Bank on p. 941.

Introduce A family's oral tale might be the story of how they came to live where they do, how they got into a business for which they are known, or how they achieved something special in their lives.

Develop Point out that many oral tales provide details in chronological order. Students might make outlines or timelines to help them organize their thoughts. They should consider the use of suspense and humor to hold the audience's attention. Remind students that by using sentence variety in their oral tales, they will help engage listeners.

Apply Have students practice their tales by recording them, listening, and then revising them. Suggest that they use an appropriate tone of voice when relating suspenseful or humorous events. Have them deliver the polished tales to the class.

Assess Evaluate students' work for clarity, use of sentence variety, appropriate tone of voice, and ability to hold an audience.

which were trembling as though from an electric shock. Djata was sweating and the sweat ran from his brow. In a great effort he straightened up and was on his feet at one go—but the great bar of iron was twisted and had taken the form of a bow!

Then Balla Fasséké sang out the "Hymn to the Bow," striking up with his powerful voice:

"Take your bow, Simbon.
Take your bow and let us go.
Take your bow, Sogolon Djata."

When Sogolon saw her son standing she stood dumb for a moment, then suddenly she sang these words of thanks to God, who had given her son the use of his legs:

"Oh day, what a beautiful day,
Oh day, day of joy;
Allah[7] Almighty, you never created a finer day.
So my son is going to walk!"

Standing in the position of a soldier at ease, Sogolon Djata, supported by his enormous rod, was sweating great beads of sweat. Balla Fasséké's song had alerted the whole palace and people came running from all over to see what had happened, and each stood bewildered before Sogolon's son. The queen mother had rushed there and when she saw Mari Djata standing up she trembled from head to foot. After recovering his breath Sogolon's son dropped the bar and the crowd stood to one side. His first steps were those of a giant. Balla Fasséké fell into step and pointing his finger at Djata, he cried:

> ◆ **Reading Strategy**
> For what purposes might the griot have included songs in this story?

"Room, room, make room!
The lion has walked;
Hide antelopes,
Get out of his way."

Behind Niani there was a young baobab tree and it was there that the children of the town came to pick leaves for their mothers. With all his might the son of Sogolon tore up the tree and put it on his shoulders and went back to his mother. He threw the tree in front of the hut and said, "Mother, here are some baobab leaves for you. From henceforth it will be outside your hut that the women of Niani will come to stock up."

7. **Allah** (al' ə): Muslim name for God.

◆ **Build Vocabulary**

affront (ə frunt') *n.*: Intentional insult

Guide for Responding

◆ Literature and Your Life

Reader's Response Were you surprised when Sogolon struck Mari Djata toward the end of the epic? Explain why you were or were not surprised.

Thematic Focus As part of his legacy, King Naré Maghan passed down to Mari Djata "an enlarged kingdom" and "sure allies." Do you think Mari Djata is qualified to build upon that legacy? Explain.

Group Discussion Discuss the qualities that make a hero. Does Mari Djata possess those qualities? Why or why not?

☑ Check Your Comprehension

1. What is the attitude of Sassouma Bérété and other people in the kingdom toward Mari Djata?
2. What prediction does the soothsayer make about the king's son?
3. What happens to Sogolon and her son after the king dies?
4. What surprising announcement does Mari Djata make after Sassouma Bérété insults his mother?
5. What extraordinary feat does seven-year-old Mari Djata accomplish?

Beyond the Selection

FURTHER READING

Another Work by D.T. Niane

Africa From the Twelfth to the Sixteenth Century

Other Works About Heroic Struggles

"The Labors of Hercules," *Handbook of Greek Mythology*, H.J. Rose
"David and Goliath" I Samuel 17, the Bible
The War of the Worlds, H.G. Wells
The Eyes of the Dragon, Stephen King

We suggest that you preview these works before recommending them to students.

INTERNET

The Internet provides an opportunity to learn more about *Sundiata* at the following Web site (all Web sites are subject to change).

To read the story of the *Sundiata* and learn more about Mali culture and about griots, go to: **http://artsedge.kennedy-center.org/aoi/html/mali.html**

We *strongly recommend* that you preview this site before you send students to it.

◆ Literary Focus

❹ **Epic Conflict** The great iron bar might have been twisted into a variety of shapes. Have students speculate on why the storyteller insists that it formed the shape of a bow. *The bow represents Mari Djata's strength and his ability to fight against his enemies.*

◆ Reading Strategy

❺ **Storyteller's Purpose** Suggested response: One role of griots was to pass along their wisdom and knowledge in the form of song. Here the griot sings songs of praise: they herald the phenomenal rise of King Sogolon Djata (Mari Djata), who has overthrown his enemies and, most of all, overcome obstacles that would have daunted most men.

Reinforce and Extend

Customize for
Verbal/Linguistic Learners

Today we would call Mari Djata an "underdog." The underdog as hero is a common theme in modern times. Have students discuss movies about underdogs who ultimately triumph over obstacles.

Answers

◆ Literature and Your Life

Reader's Response Some students might have been surprised that Sogolon struck the son whom she loved and protected, but others will not be surprised that mounting pressures caused Sogolon to resort to this unjust act.

Thematic Focus Students might say that Mari Djata's ingenuity and spectacular rise at the end of the epic show he has the strength and character to build upon his father's legacy.

☑ Check Your Comprehension

1. They gossip about him, belittle him, and are completely unsupportive.
2. The soothsayer says the king's son, Namandjé's child, will be the right hand to some mighty king.
3. They occupy an old hut on Sassouma's property.
4. He says, "I am going to walk today."
5. He pulled a baobab tree up from the roots and presented it to his mother.

Guide for Responding (continued)

◆ Critical Thinking

INTERPRET

1. What does the soothsayer mean when he tells the king, "great trees grow slowly"? **[Interpret]**
2. Why doesn't Mari Djata respond to the crowds who torment and tease him? **[Infer]**
3. In what specific ways does this epic illustrate the importance of honor? **[Support]**

COMPARE LITERARY WORKS

4. In "Rama's Initiation," you learn that Viswamithra became an important sage through "great austerities." Is there any parallel in Sundiata's rise to greatness? Explain. **[Connect]**

◆ Reading Strategy

STORYTELLER'S PURPOSE

The griots of ancient Mali had different purposes in mind as they retold the story of Sundiata.

1. What do you think was the storyteller's main purpose for telling this epic? Explain.
2. Why do you think the storyteller includes praises to Allah at the end of the epic?

◆ Literary Focus

EPIC CONFLICT

Mari Djata's confrontation of his physical disability creates the **epic conflict** in this tale.

1. How does Mari Djata respond to the way people react to his disability?
2. In what specific ways does Mari Djata's disability contribute to his effectiveness as a leader?

Beyond Literature

Community Connection

Preserving History Through Stories

Most cultures owe a great deal of their preserved history to storytellers. The *griots* of Mali preserved the epic tale of Sundiata. Celtic history was passed on by the *bards;* their Anglo-Saxon counterparts were called *scops.* Storytellers captured attitudes and customs of a time and preserved the names of important historical figures. Find out more about the function of storytellers in a culture that interests you. Share what you learn with your class.

◆ Build Vocabulary

USING THE LATIN ROOT *-firm-*

The Latin root *-firm-* means "to strengthen." Incorporate the meaning of "strengthen" in the definitions of each of the following words:

1. confirm **2.** affirm **3.** firmament

USING THE WORD BANK: Synonyms

On your paper, write the word whose meaning is closest to that of the first word.

1. fathom: (a) confuse, (b) understand, (c) remove
2. taciturn: (a) angry, (b) gracious, (c) tight-lipped
3. malicious: (a) mournful, (b) harmful, (c) changeable
4. infirmity: (a) sadness, (b) illness, (c) fear
5. innuendo: (a) style, (b) hint, (c) allowance
6. diabolical: (a) evil, (b) passionate, (c) extreme
7. estranged: (a) removed, (b) indecent, (c) plentiful
8. affront: (a) coverup, (b) accident, (c) insult

◆ Build Grammar Skills

SENTENCE VARIETY

It's important to vary the structure and kinds of sentences you use. **Sentence variety** means more than using sentences of different length. Beginning sentences with different constructions is also an effective way to achieve sentence variety.

Practice In your notebook, rewrite the following sentences so that each begins with either an adverb, prepositional phrase, participial phrase (Verb form, acting as an adjective, along with the words that complete it), or subordinate clause (A group of words, containing a subject and a verb, that cannot stand alone as a sentence).

1. Sogolon tried in vain to heal her son using potions and herbs.
2. The stiff-legged son of Sogolon still crawled about although he was now seven.
3. The young prince slowly straightened up and was on his feet in one go.
4. Mari Djata tore up the tree with all his might and went back to his hut.
5. Sogolon wept with her head buried in the bedclothes, and her body shook violently.

Answers

◆ Critical Thinking

1. The soothsayer means that it takes a long time to nurture the qualities of greatness; Mari Djata is growing slowly now to become great later.
2. Some students might say that Mari Djata seems to be above insult, while others will respond that he knows he will eventually prove his superiority over the crowds.
3. Through the triumph of Mari Djata, the epic shows that cruel words and deeds must not be allowed free rein, and that those with honor must protect those with little power; in a good world, honor will prevail.
4. Students might compare this monarchy with that of King Arthur's court or the court of King Dasaratha from the *Ramayana.*

◆ Reading Strategy

1. The storyteller's main purpose in telling this epic was probably to prove that qualities of greatness can be found anywhere, including within those people society sees as infirm.
2. It is part of the Muslim culture to praise Allah, or God, who is regarded as responsible for shaping events.

◆ Literary Focus

1. Mari Djata seems unruffled by people's reaction to his disability. On one occasion he "brains" other children who are walking near him.
2. Mari Djata's disability has enabled him to see people for what they truly are. He knows people as both loyal and cruel, and insight into people will make him an effective leader.

◆ Build Vocabulary

Using the Latin Root *-firm-*

1. to strongly establish; 2. to say with strength that sometime is true; 3. expanse of the heavens

Using the Word Bank

1. understand; 2. tight-lipped; 3. harmful; 4. illness; 5. hint; 6. evil; 7. removed; 8. insult

◆ Build Grammar Skills

Example sentences:

1. Using potions and herbs, Sogolon tried in vain to heal her son.
2. Although he was now seven, the stiff-legged son of Sogolon still crawled about.
3. In one go, the young prince slowly straightened up and was on his feet.
4. With all his might, Mari Djata tore up the tree, and then he went back to his hunt.
5. With her head buried in the bedclothes, Sologon wept and her body shook violently.

Grammar Reinforcement

For additional instruction and practice, use the Varying Sentence Structure and Varying Sentence Lengths and Structures lessons in the **Language Lab CD-ROM.** You may also use pages 121–123 on Varying Your Sentences in the *Writer's Solution Grammar Practice Book.*

Build Your Portfolio

Idea Bank

Writing

1. **News Article** You are an eyewitness to Mari Djata's extraordinary feat. Write an account of this event for a newspaper. Answer the questions *who? what? when? where? why?* and *how?*

2. **Writing in the Heroic Tradition** Write a brief episode in the later life of Mari Djata. Show how he fulfills the heroic tradition. Include cultural details revealed in *Sundiata.*

3. **Critical Evaluation** In an essay, evaluate the central conflict in *Sundiata.* Keeping in mind the characteristics of an epic, is the conflict believable and engaging? Support your points with examples from the epic.

Speaking, Listening, and Viewing

4. **Oral Tales** Many families keep their histories alive in the same way that Mali villages do. Share a family story that focuses on your family's origins or on a milestone, such as a birth, death, or a special achievement. **[Social Studies Link]**

5. **Role Play** Imagine that Sogolon and Sassouma Bérété meet each other right after Sundiata tears up the baobab tree. Role-play a conversation between them. **[Performing Arts Link]**

Researching and Representing

6. **Documentary** Do research to learn about the arts in the country of Mali. Present your findings to the class in the form of a mini-documentary. **[Art Link; Social Studies Link]**

7. **Herb Research** Sogolon used the rarest herbs in an effort to cure her son. Write a research report on the different ways herbs have been used as healing agents in ancient and current times. **[Science Link; Social Studies Link]**

Online Activity www.phlit.phschool.com

Guided Writing Lesson

Storytelling Notes

Although the griots of ancient Mali presented epics from memory, a modern storyteller might want to work from a good set of notes. Combine the old and the new to write the outline for a storytelling of the *Sundiata* epic today. The following tip will help you write effective notes.

Writing Skills Focus: Audience Knowledge

Considering your **audience's knowledge** is an important part of storytelling. You can't assume, for example, that your listeners know where Mali is. They may not know what a baobab, a calabash, or even a soothsayer is either. In your notes, be sure to identify and define the terms with which a general audience may be unfamiliar.

Prewriting Make a chart that lists the characters and events you will include. Under each heading, jot down ideas for what might best enrich your telling of the story. Remember, you don't have to develop a finished piece of writing, only notes.

Drafting In your draft, elaborate on the thoughts and notes you compiled in prewriting. Account for all the parts of a story: an introduction to characters and setting, a conflict, a climax, and a resolution. Also, make sure you consider the knowledge level of your audience. For example, for a general audience of any age, define unfamiliar terms. You might also want to compare ancient practices with contemporary ones.

Revising Read through your notes to be sure they will serve you well when you go to tell your story. Ask: Did I account for all parts of the story? Did I provide enough background information to keep my audience informed?

ASSESSMENT OPTIONS

Formal Assessment, Selection Test, pp. 226–228, and Assessment Resources Software. The selection test is designed so that it can be easily customized to the performance levels of your students.

Alternative Assessment, p. 64, includes options for less advanced students, more advanced students, verbal/linguistic learner, visual/spatial learners, and logical/mathematical learners.

PORTFOLIO ASSESSMENT

Use the following rubrics in the ***Alternative Assessment*** booklet to assess student writing:
News Article: Summary Rubric, p. 98
Writing in the Heroic Tradition: Fictional Narrative Rubric, p. 95
Critical Evaluation: Evaluation/Review Rubric, p. 104
Guided Writing Lesson: Fictional Narrative Rubric, p. 95

Idea Bank

Following are suggestions for matching Idea Bank topics with your students' performance levels and learning modalities:

Customizing for *Performance Levels*

Less Advanced Students: 4, 5
Average Students: 1, 2, 6
More Advanced Students: 3, 7

Customizing for *Learning Modalities*

Following are suggestions for matching Idea Bank topics with your students' learning modalities:
Verbal/Linguistic: 4, 5
Interpersonal: 5
Visual/Spatial: 6

Guided Writing Lesson

Elaboration Strategy Have students use the events and details of the *Sundiata* epic, combined with the events and ideas they want to use in their storytellings, to visually plot their stories on maps. Their maps might look something like this.

For more prewriting, elaboration, and revision strategies, see *Prentice Hall Writing and Grammar.*

Writing Lab CD-ROM

Have students complete the tutorial on Narration. Follow these steps:

1. Have students use a Story Line Diagram. This will enable them to visually map out stages of the plot that they can then record in their storytelling notes.
2. Suggest that students use the note-card activity to work out the order of their notes.

Connections to Today's World

The movie trilogy known as *Star Wars* is a modern epic. It is the tale of a young hero and his battle to overcome obstacles and to fight evil. As Mari Djata had to learn leadership skills from his griot and his father, young Luke Skywalker learns the skills he will need to save the universe from the Jedi knights (from Obi-Wan Kenobi, in particular).

In this selection, the origins of the names of the characters in the *Star Wars* epic are explained. Students will see that the sound and the background of each name help reflect the personality and the role of the character.

Extension Many students will have seen one or all of the *Star Wars* films, but the details of the film may not be fresh in their minds. As an optional activity, you may wish to have interested students rent and watch the *Star Wars* videos and then present a report to the class in which they identify and explain the elements of *Star Wars* that are characteristic an epic.

Customize for
Pre-AP Students
Have these students find out more about some of the references used in this essay, such as J.R.R. Tolkien's *Lord of the Rings,* the John Carter of Mars tales by Edgar Rice Burroughs, and Frank Herbert's *Dune*. Students can present relevant information to the class to enhance their understanding of this essay.

Connections to Today's World

The epics in this section reflect the values and traditions of the cultures from which they come. In "Star Wars: An Epic for Today," Eric Nash explores the ways in which the *Star Wars* trilogy brings together elements of contemporary American society with references to epics of the world.

George Lucas's science-fiction *Star Wars* trilogy includes *Star Wars* (1977), *The Empire Strikes Back* (1980), and *Return of the Jedi* (1983). These films were so popular that upon re-release in 1996, they drew larger crowds than any other films released at the same time.

Star Wars is widely viewed as a modern epic. It contains many of the elements of a classic epic: It chronicles the adventures of a hero; it vividly describes battles between good and evil; and it reflects the values of a culture.

Star Wars: An Epic for Today

Eric P. Nash

Twenty years ago, the film maker George Lucas expanded everybody's notion of how fast a movie could really move with the first installment of his "Star Wars" trilogy. A new generation of moviegoers will be introduced to "Star Wars" on Friday, when the film returns to the big screen with a digitally remastered soundtrack, new scenes (including a meeting between Han Solo and the gelatinous Jabba the Hutt) and some visually enhanced effects. Part of what makes the "Star Wars" universe such fun is that the characters seem to emerge from their own complex cultures. Then there is the ear-tickling felicity of the names. It's hard to resist saying Boba Fett, Bounty Hunter, out loud just to try it on the lips. Just where did George Lucas come up with all these weird names?

"Basically, I developed the names for the characters phonetically," Mr. Lucas

Humanities: Literature

Epics and Legends Influenced by the heroes of epics and legends, George Lucas set a traditional hero tale in a futuristic setting. In the *Star Wars* saga, Lucas traces the adventures of Luke Skywalker, using traditional aspects of a hero. Pitting the young Skywalker against the experienced Darth Vader and the conflict between the small rebel force and the powerful Empire are examples of the battle between the underdog and the bully.

Like other epic heroes, Skywalker has his weaknesses as well as his strengths. He has to overcome the fears and disadvantages that come with being an ordinary human, as well as a hero. The hero's origin is often marked by an unusual circumstance, such as Sundiata's slow progress in walking. Skywalker, like King Arthur, is raised by foster parents, not knowing his true heritage.

Skywalker does not journey alone. In the tradition of other heroes, he has his trustworthy companions, Han Solo, Princess Leia, Chewbacca, C-3PO, and R2D2. Skywalker receives the gifts of the Force from his spiritual guide, Obi-Wan Kenobi. Students may draw parallels to King Arthur and Merlyn.

As often happens in epics, Skywalker is separated from his companions. Alone, he must seek out a spiritual teacher on a long journey or quest. When he returns, he is prepared to confront the forces and temptations that would defeat an ordinary man. Therefore, when he confronts Darth Vader, who is both enemy and father, Skywalker is strong enough to suffer serious injury rather than give up the struggle for his cause.

1 ▲ **Critical Viewing** What details make the subject of this picture look like a legendary hero? **[Analyze]**

said. "I obviously wanted to telegraph a bit of the character in the name. The names needed to sound unusual but not spacey. I wanted to stay away from the kind of science fiction names like Zenon and Zorba. They had to sound indigenous and have consistency between their names and their culture."

Much has been made of the director's use of world myths from Joseph Campbell's "Hero With a Thousand Faces," but "Star Wars" is also a synthesis of the treasure trove of American pop culture—everything from comic strips, pulp fiction and films ranging from John Ford's "Searchers" to Victor Fleming's "Wizard of Oz" to Akira Kurosawa's "Hidden Fortress."

"Star Wars" in turn has spawned a galaxy of sub-industries—more than two dozen novels, trading cards, action figures, role-playing games, scores of websites and guides specializing in intergalactic arcana—many of which

▶Critical Viewing◀

1 Analyze Students might cite the hooded cloak, the serious and thoughtful facial expression, the magical weapon, and the stature of the figure.

Customize for *Visual/Spatial Learners*

Guide students to translate their visual impressions of the images presented with this piece on *Star Wars,* along with their knowledge of the movies, into verbal descriptions. You may wish to suggest words and phrases with which they can free-associate to come up with descriptions, such as "glowing saber," and "legendary hero."

Research Skills Mini-Lesson

Taking Notes From Sources

Introduce Tell students that when they are taking notes from sources, they must decide in what forms they wish to use material in their papers or projects. They can choose either direct quotations or paraphrases.

Develop Explain that a direct quotation reproduces the exact words of the source. Direct quotations are valuable when the author expresses something as well as it can be expressed. Also, authors with great reputations in their fields merit direct quotation. Tell them that a paraphrase is a restatement in their own words of the ideas in a passage. Students must accurately convey the message of the original text without plagiarizing it.

Apply Have students practice taking notes from sources. Make sure they observe the mechanical forms for direct quotations, such as double and single quotation marks and ellipsis points. Tell them that these sources must be credited whether they have been quoted directly or paraphrased.

Assess Evaluate the students' notes for accuracy of copying, in the case of direct quotations. Check to make sure that their paraphrases do not misrepresent the original ideas of the sources.

▶Critical Viewing◀

❶ **Relate** *Students might cite King Kong or the yeti.*

◆Critical Thinking

❷ **Infer** Characters' names may reflect their personalities and may telegraph their roles in a story. Ask students why they think the name Darth Vader is appropriate and what his role is in the epic. *Sample answer: The origin of the name Darth Vader from the Dutch "Dark Father" suits Darth Vader who is a wicked person. He represents the forces of evil that Luke must overcome.*

◆Critical Thinking

❸ **Relate** Have students explain how the origin of Luke Skywalker's name relates to his role in the epic. *Suggested response: Luke comes from the Greek "leukos" meaning light. Skywalker is the name of Loki, the Norse god of fire. Thus Luke Skywalker will be the hero who uses the power of "the Force" (fire) to fight on the side of good (light) against the evil represented by Darth Vader.*

CONNECTIONS TO TODAY'S WORLD

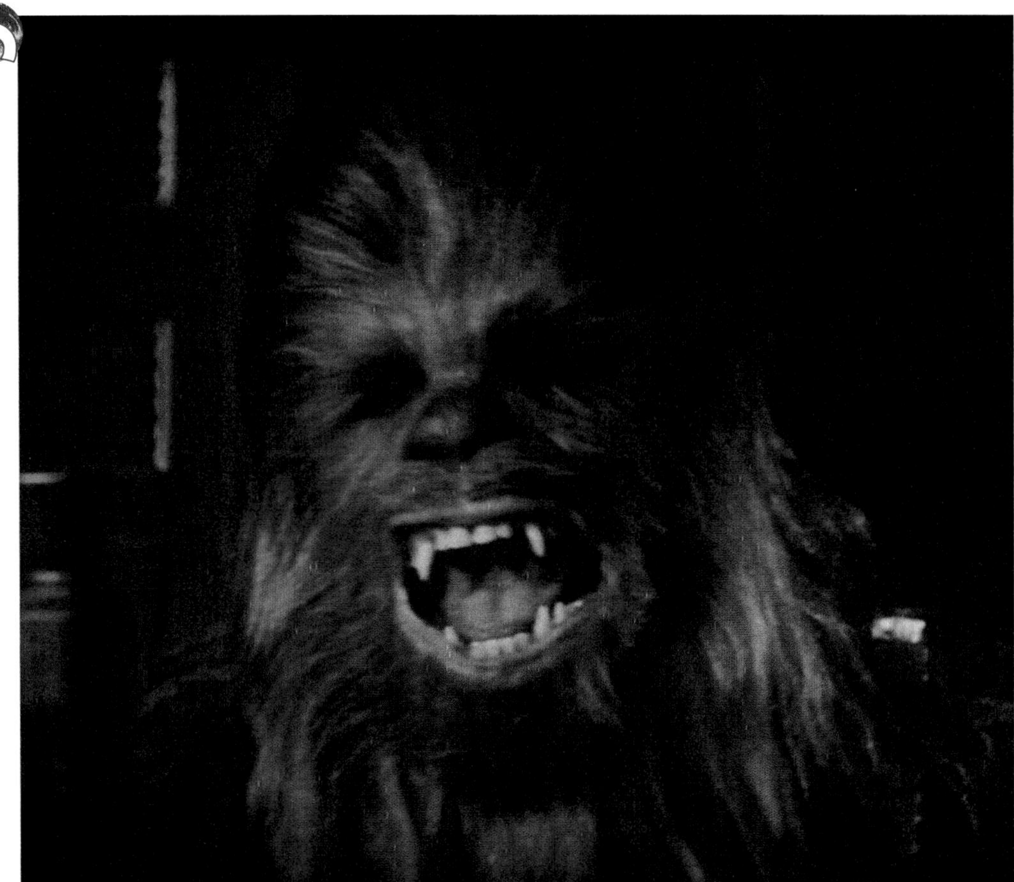

❶ ▲ **Critical Viewing** What other mythical creatures does this Wookiee bring to mind? **[Relate]**

have been consulted in preparing this interstellar who's who.

❷ **Darth Vader:** Mr. Lucas went back to the Dutch root for father to arrive at a name that approximates "Dark Father." Vader's original name is Anakin Skywalker. Anakin is a variation on a race of giants in Genesis, and Skywalker is an appellation for Loki, the Norse god of fire and mischief. The inspiration for Vader's face mask was in all likelihood the grille of a '56 Chevy.

❸ **Luke Skywalker:** The name of the character played by Mark Hamill derives from the Greek leukos, or light, an interesting contrast to Darth Vader. Luke of the Gospels was a gentile who converted to Christianity, an appropriate name for a boy who discovers the power of the Force.

Tatooine is the name of Luke's home planet, derived from the town of Tataouine in Tunisia, the country where the desert scenes in "Star Wars" were filmed. An early draft of the script was called "The Adventures of Luke Starkiller." It's easy to read Luke S. as a stand-in for Lucas.

Princess Leia Organa (Carrie Fisher) has braids that resemble dinner rolls, but her name evokes the lovely Dejah Thoris in the

Analyze Film Criticism

The commercial success of *Star Wars,* the first in George Lucas's saga, surprised everyone, including its producers, who watched the advance "rushes" with dismay. Most critics conceded that the movie was fun but warned moviegoers to "check your brains at the door." A typical reaction to the movie was that of film critic David Pirie:

> Hollywood began as an amusement arcade, so it's appropriate that its most profitable film should be as formally enchanting and psychologically sterile as a . . . pinball machine.

This reaction epitomizes many film critics' predicament. They are writing reviews of a form of mass entertainment. Yet, when a movie like *Star Wars* comes along and breaks box office records, they often complain that the popularity—and the money—hasn't gone to some fine, deserving filmmaker who makes probing, "intelligent" or "art" films. Of course, many of these films never make money. An art film used to be described by film producers as "ahead of its time."

Invite students to discuss the commercial movie vs. art film debate—do they think movies intended for mass audiences can ever appeal to those who have loftier film standards, and vice versa?

John Carter of Mars tales by Edgar Rice Burroughs, as well as Lady Galadriel of Lothlorien in J. R. Tolkien's "Lord of the Rings." The surname Organa reflects the conflict of nature and technology seen in the forest-dwelling heroes pitted against the machines of the Empire, according to Lucas's biographer, Dale Pollock.

The name **Han Solo** (Harrison Ford) capitalizes on the archaic sound of Han, a variation of John, to set us in a mythical world. The name Solo addresses his key character issue. Solo is a lone gun who must learn to trust others and identify with a greater cause. The swashbuckler's name also recalls one of the great pop culture adventurers, Napoleon Solo, "The Man from U.N.C.L.E." Napoleon Solo, by the way, first appeared as a minor hood in the James Bond novel "Goldfinger."

R2-D2 According to Mr. Lucas, the robot who resembles a whistling Hoover vacuum cleaner got his name from a sound editor's shorthand for "Reel Two, Dialogue Two" during the making of his earlier hit, "American Graffiti."

Chewbacca, the towering Wookiee, was a name inspired by Indiana, Mr. Lucas's rambunctious malamute. (The dog also lent his name to the hero of the film maker's Indiana Jones series.) Wookiee comes from an ad lib in "THX 1138," the film maker's first feature film: "I think I ran over a Wookiee back there."

Jedi, the name of the ancient knighthood, is a tip of the hat to Burroughs's Barsoom, where lords bear the title of Jed or Jeddak.

Obi-Wan Kenobi (Alec Guinness), also known as old Ben Kenobi, is revealed to us as a Jedi knight and introduces Luke to the power of the Force. Obi is the Japanese word for the sash used to tie a kimono; it may connote the Jedi knight's status as a martial arts master. Similarly, Wan sounds like the Japanese honorific suffix san. "OB" is also short for Old Ben, but there is chatter on the Internet that his name is really OB-1, a cryptic reference to Mr. Lucas's much anticipated history of the Clone Wars in future "Star Wars" installments.

Ewoks, those almost unbearably cute, highly marketable teddy-bear characters who saved the day in "The Return of the Jedi" inhabit the forest moon of Endor (the witch in the Book of Samuel hailed from a similarly named locale). Their name may sound like a variant of Wookiee, but it is taken from Miwok, the Indian tribe indigenous to San Rafael, California, the location of Mr. Lucas's Skywalker ranch.

Boba Fett, at least according to one fan on the World Wide Web, is a sly reference to another hotshot jockey, Bob Falfa, the drag racer played by none other than Mr. Ford in "American Graffiti."

Banthas, the shaggy, screw-horned mounts of the honking **Sand People,** are a variation on banth, a beast found on Barsoom. The Sand People bear similarities to nomadic tribes in the science fiction writer Frank Herbert's desert classic "Dune." The diminutive **Jawas,** who chatter like the cartoon chipmunks Chip 'n Dale, call to mind Indonesian Islam. Their name is perhaps echoic of Moroccan Gnawa trance music.

1. Why do you think George Lucas looked to world myths, literature, and popular culture for the characters' names for *Star Wars*?
2. Name three sources Lucas used for names and explain how the names and their sources are significant in terms of world cultures.
3. What does *Star Wars* reveal about contemporary American culture?
4. In what ways is the *Star Wars* trilogy a modern-day epic?

4 Literature Connection
George Lucas borrowed freely from many other works of fantasy and science fiction. Have students who have read *Lord of the Rings* explain how it fits into the epic genre. *It is the tale of an unlikely hero and an epic conflict between good and evil.*

◆ Critical Thinking

5 Make Judgments Han Solo's last name recalls Napoleon Solo from the popular espionage series *The Man From U.N.C.L.E.*, and R2-D2's name came from a movie sound editor's words. Ask: How do these two names reflect what the writer George Lucas thinks about contemporary American culture? *Suggested response: These names point out the important role of television and movies in creating the heroes of contemporary culture.*

6 Literature Connection The Jedi knights are reminiscent of warriors in a number of epics and legends. Ask students to name famous knights from literature. *Students will probably mention knights of the Round Table, such as Lancelot, Tristram, Gawain, and Galahad.*

◆ Critical Thinking

7 Infer Invite students to consider how Obi-Wan Kenobi's name reflects his role in *Star Wars*. *Suggested response: The word obi brings to mind a martial arts master and wan sounds like a Japanese title of honor. Thus, Obi-Wan Kenobi is an honored person who teaches Luke Skywalker how to battle using the power of "the Force."*

Answers

1. He may have looked to world myths and literature to connect his epic tale to the epic tradition. He may have included elements of popular culture because he knew that all epics reflect aspects of the culture from which they come.
2. Lucas uses names from Norse mythology, which connects his characters to world myths; he uses biblical references that tie to the religious beliefs of much of the Western world; he uses Moroccan Gnawan music, which ties his story to Eastern cultures.
3. The Millenium Falcon's resemblance to a souped-up car reflects an admiration for an enterprising mind, the plot reflects an appreciation for pure adventure, and the unusual characters and names reflect diversity.
4. The epic qualities of *Star Wars* include a hero overcoming enormous odds, a hero with special abilities and powers, and a reflection of the culture from which it comes.

Prepare and Engage

LESSON OBJECTIVES

1. To use a range of techniques to plan and create a multimedia presentation to communicate with others
2. To use recursive writing processes to prepare the written portion of a multimedia presentation
3. To use semicolons and colons appropriately
4. To recognize and use concise language

Before students begin, you may want to share with them the Scoring Rubric for Multimedia Report (p. 107 in ***Alternative Assessment***) so students see the criteria by which they will be evaluated. Suggestions on p. 948 customize the rubric to this workshop.

Connect to Literature You might refer students to the selection from "Rare Air: Michael on Michael" (p. 359) in Unit 4. Have students discuss the multimedia presentation that could spring from it.

Writing Lab CD-ROM

If students have access to computers, have them work in the Research Writing tutorial, the multimedia presentation segments, to complete all or part of their presentations. Follow these steps:

1. Students can see an audio-annotated model of a multimedia presentation.
2. Have students study video tips from writers about how audience shapes a presentation.
3. Have students study writing tips for using maps, charts, and graphs.

Multimedia Presentation Writing Process Workshop

When epics and legends were told in ancient times, the storytellers had only their voices to bring the tales to life for their audiences. You have many other resources available for presentations. Create a **multimedia presentation** on a subject that interests you. A multimedia presentation supplies information through a variety of media. Among the media you may use are written materials, slides, videos, music, maps, charts, graphs, photos, drawings, and fine art reproductions.

The following skills from this section's Guided Writing Lessons will help you make an interesting multimedia presentation.

Writing Skills Focus

- **Use an appropriate medium** for the subject. For instance, if you're discussing the effect of television on how we get the news, include video clips.
- **Use language appropriate for your purpose.** For example, if your purpose is to share the beauty and excitement of diving, use words such as *exhilarating* or *graceful* to help your audience envision the experience. (See p. 931.)
- **Consider audience knowledge.** Don't "talk down" to your audience but do define technical terms that may be unfamiliar. Use visual aids to help them understand aspects of your topic that are outside their experience. (See p. 941.)

The following excerpt from the written portion of a multimedia presentation on scuba diving shows these skills.

WRITING MODEL

When I first arrived in scuba class, I was frightened and had second thoughts. My teacher, however, dispelled those fears when she showed me how the regulator, or breathing device, ① worked. (*Listen to this part of an interview with her as she describes the concept of the regulator.*)

Diving exposed me to a larger world than I could ever have imagined. For instance, seeing a stingray on a dive is an exhilarating ② and slightly frightening experience. Here is some video footage of some stingrays that we had the pleasure of diving with. ③

① Since the audience consists of classmates who may not have done scuba diving before, the presenter explains what a regulator is.

② The writer uses language that helps convey her feelings about the dive.

③ Since the most prominent sensations experienced in diving are visual ones, the presenter uses photographs and video in her presentation.

Beyond the Classroom

Workplace Skills

Multimedia in the Workplace The workplace relies heavily on multimedia for presentations. Multimedia in the workplace, however, often refers to computer technology and sophisticated video technology.

Discuss with students various forms of multimedia presentations that they encounter on a regular basis. For instance, they may not think of advertisements and news programs in relation to the type of multimedia presentations they are preparing. However, you might suggest that they pay attention to these types of presentations, looking for ideas and methods that they might be able to incorporate on a smaller scale, with the technology and visuals to which they have access.

Point out that many businesses use presentation software to communicate to clients and groups of employees, in addition to standard charts and graphs. This type of presentation allows the presenter to use full color, sound, and motion along with text and visual displays. If students have access to this type of technology, suggest they consider using it for their own multimedia presentation.

Prewriting

Use a Topic Web If you're not assigned a topic, choose one that interests you and that you can develop with multimedia. You can use a topic web like the one shown to help narrow your topic.

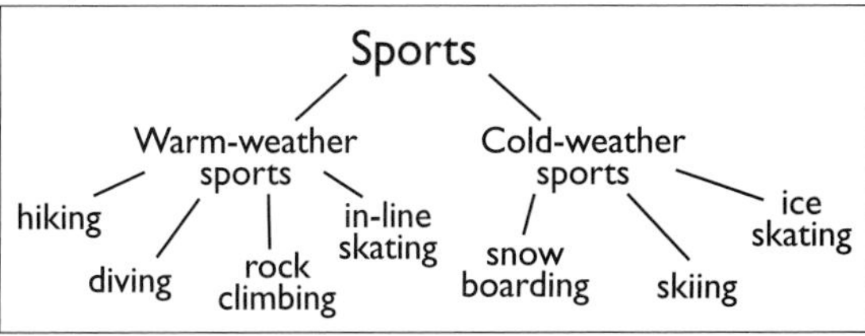

Find Multimedia Support Visual aids and other types of media will significantly enliven your presentation. Indicate how the media will enhance your audience's understanding of the topic. For instance, your written report may indicate that readers should press "play" to hear a recording of music from a particular country. If you are giving an oral presentation, explain why you are showing a visual.

Maps can clarify historical or geographical information.
Graphs and Charts can make complicated information easier to understand.
Pictures can illustrate objects, scenes, and other details.
Diagrams can show the relationships of parts to a whole.
Audio and Video can bring your subject to life for your audience.

Drafting

Write a Strong Introduction A strong introduction grabs the audience's attention and tells them what to expect in your multimedia presentation. To make the topic clear, include your main idea in the introduction. To capture your audience's interest, you might open with a question, an anecdote, a quotation from an expert, a startling fact, or a piece of media. Use the following introduction as an example:

"Good morning, Chicagoans. The temperature on this January morning is a lovely 75 degrees. Traffic's blocked up due to a burst dike on the lake. There's also a monsoon warning for this afternoon . . . "

A scene from a sci-fi thriller? Hardly. As this graph shows, this could be a typical forecast from fifty years in the future if we continue to deplete the ozone layer at current levels . . .

Applying Language Skills: Semicolons and Colons

In the written portion of your report, use a **semicolon** to form a compound sentence when the two ideas being joined are closely related and are not joined by a conjunction:

The palace of Versailles is near Paris; it was built by Louis XIV.

Also use semicolons to separate items on a list that already contain commas:

Attractions in and around Paris include churches like Notre Dame; the palace at Versailles, just outside Paris; and the Louvre, an art museum.

You might also need to create lists or cite long quotations. Use **colons** to introduce a list of items after words like *the following* or a long, block-indented quotation.

Notre Dame's architectural details include the following: flying buttresses, two lofty towers, and numerous gargoyles.

Writer's Solution Connection
Language Lab

For more practice with colons and semicolons, complete the Language Lab lesson on Semicolons, Colons, and Quotation Marks.

Develop Student Writing

Prewriting Strategy

As they plan their multimedia presentations, have students use index cards to represent the various media effects they will use. By having a concrete representation of the media, they arrange and rearrange placement, as well as keep better track of what media they are using.

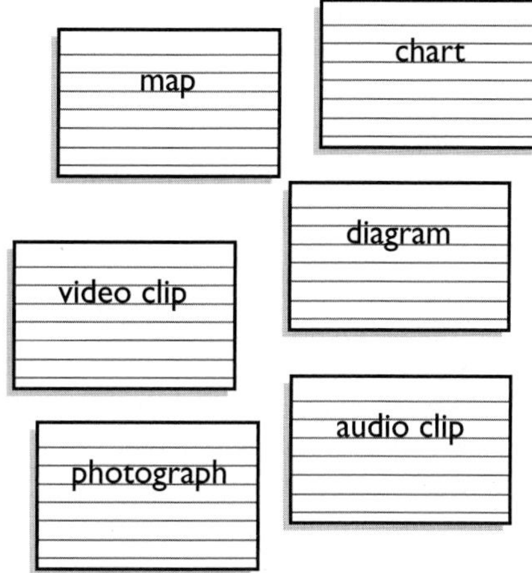

Customize for
Less Proficient Writers
Multimedia presentations offer students with less-developed writing skills an opportunity to communicate their specific messages to others without the constraint of preparing the messages in writing. Pair or group these students with more proficient writers, and encourage them to use a variety of forms and technologies, such as videos, photographs, and so forth, to communicate their messages.

Writing Lab CD-ROM
Have students who work best in groups use the Group Projects in the Inspirations in the Research Writing tutorial to find topics for their multimedia presentations.

Elaboration Strategy

As they prepare, plan, write, and create their multimedia presentations, encourage students to explore the range of visual and audio representations available to them. Remind them that the many literary devices they have studied can be effectively applied to a multimedia presentation: alliteration, personification, analogy, symbolism, foreshadowing, flashback, and so on. Students might benefit from a class brainstorming session for ways to translate these devices into multimedia formats.

Applying Language Skills

Semicolons and Colons
Remind students that as they show more mature writing style, they will use phrases and clauses to enhance sentence structures. Semicolons and colons will thus become essential to their writing accuracy.

Grammar Reinforcement

For additional explanation and practice on semicolons and colons, use the Semicolons and Colons worksheet, p. 102, in the *Writer's Solution Grammar Practice Book.*

Writing and Language Transparencies You may want students to use a Herringbone Organizer (p. 76) to organize their thoughts and connect the various media to a central idea.

Revision Strategy

You may want to have peer editors work in groups made up of multiple learning styles. Visual learners can respond to visuals; verbal/linguistic learners to auditory and text. A fourth member of the group—perhaps a logical/mathematical learner—should focus on how the pieces fit together.

Prentice Hall Writing and Grammar For more prewriting, elaboration, and revision strategies, see *Prentice Hall Writing and Grammar.*

Writing Lab CD-ROM

Students can use the Organization Outliner tool in the Revising and Editing section of the Research Writing tutorial to help them highlight the relationships among the parts in the presentations.

They can then use the Revision Checker for Unity and Coherence to refine the text portion of the presentation.

Publishing

You may want to suggest that students save their multimedia reports for their job portfolios.

Reinforce and Extend

Applying Language Skills

Concise Language

Remind students that the most powerful language springs from specific nouns and verbs, not a series of adjectives and adverbs.

Answer

Possible revision: As I descended through the crystal-clear water, hundreds of fish swam below.

Applying Language Skills: Concise Language

Use **concise language**—exact nouns, vivid verbs, the right adjectives and adverbs (as opposed to many adjectives and adverbs). Eliminate unnecessary words and phrases.

Vague and Wordy:

As you may or may not know, the coral reef has many colors and hues. An immense number and lots of different kinds of various fish and food live in and around one small piece of the reef.

Concise:

The coral reef is an explosion of color. A single section of reef can support more than 200 varieties of fish.

Practice In your notebook, make the following sentence concise.

As I descended through the blue clear, bright, and rather warm water, I saw a whole bunch of fish moving below me somewhere.

Writer's Solution Connection Writing Lab

For more help on giving your presentation, see Tips on Presenting Work Orally in the Publishing and Presenting section of the Writing Lab tutorial on Research.

Write the Body Develop your main idea in the body of the written portion of your presentation. Back up assertions with solid facts. Use multimedia examples to illustrate points or observations that you make.

Write an Effective Conclusion A strong conclusion underscores your main points and encourages the audience to keep thinking about your presentation. Consider ending your presentation with an entertaining or startling fact or quotation. Accompany it with a visual or audio segment that will remain in the audience's mind after your presentation has ended.

Revising

Use a Checklist The following checklist will help you revise your multimedia presentation:

- Do you use the appropriate language for your audience?
- Do you use the appropriate medium or media for your subject?
- Is there a clear connection between your words and the visuals you use?
- Is your language concise?

Revision Model

On a dive, we used a special camera to take underwater photos. ~~Listen to my teacher talking about the camera.~~ ① Here is a picture of such a camera. We also had to use a BCD ② , or buoyancy control device, to keep us from sinking to the bottom or rising to the surface too quickly.

① The presenter changes the medium from audio to a picture to better illustrate an underwater camera.

② Because the audience may be unfamiliar with the term BCD, the presenter defines it.

Publishing

- **Present Your Report** Present your multimedia presentation to the class. Make sure that you arrange beforehand for any equipment that you will need, such as an overhead projector or television and VCR. During the presentation, remember to speak loudly and clearly.

✓ ASSESSMENT

PORTFOLIO ASSESSMENT

Use the rubric on Multimedia Report in ***Alternative Assessment*** (p. 107) to assess student writing. Add these criteria to customize the rubric to this assignment.

	4	3	2	1
Introduction	The multimedia presentation opens with a vibrant attention getter.	The presentation opens with an attention getter.	The presentation opens with an attempt at gaining audience attention.	The presentation omits any introductory attention getter.
Concise Language	The verbal portions of the multimedia presentation exhibit consistently concise language.	The verbal portions usually exhibit concise language.	The verbal portions sometimes exhibit concise language.	The verbal portions rarely exhibit concise language.

Student Success Workshop

Real-World Reading Skills — Reading a Map

Strategies for Success

Imagine that you went to a new city alone and the only thing you had to guide you was a map. You'd soon know how important it is to be able to read maps! To navigate your way through a city or town, you would use a street map. Street maps of cities often show buildings, parks, and other landmarks besides streets.

Identify Your Purpose First, clarify why you're looking at a street map. Are you looking for a particular street, or do you want an overall layout of a neighborhood? Do you want to visit a specific landmark or museum? Sometimes a specific section, such as the downtown area of a big city, will be blown up in a separate, more detailed box. If you are looking for a location in this section, you can find it more easily if you use the detailed map.

Get an Overview After you identify your purpose, determine whether the street map meets your needs.

- Does it show the entire area or a section?
- Are all streets shown or just major ones?
- Which way is north on the map?
- What is the scale of centimeters or inches to a kilometer or a mile?
- Does the map include landmarks and buildings?

Read the Map Start by finding your location on the map. Next, locate your destination. Finally, plan a route from your location to your destination by identifying the direction you need to travel, the streets you need to take, and the places where you will need to make turns.

Apply the Strategies

You're staying in a hotel on Page Street. Use the map of London to answer the questions.

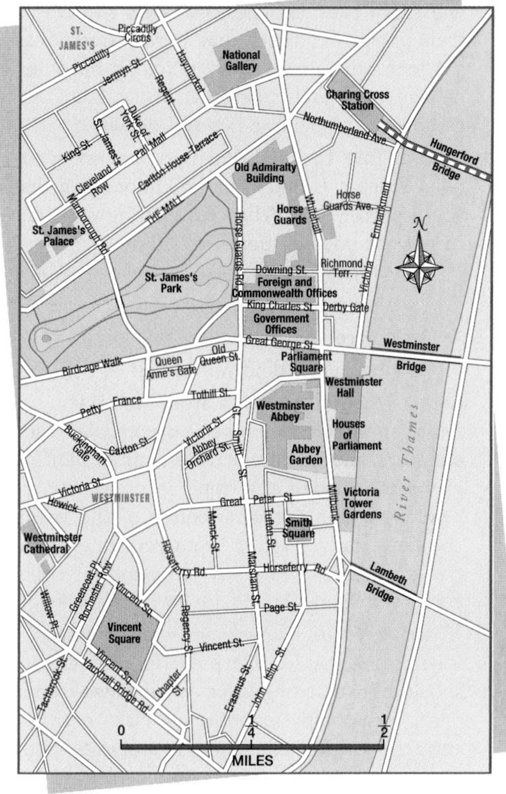

1. What direction must you travel to get from Page Street to Westminster Cathedral?
2. What is the most direct route from Westminster Cathedral to the entrance of St. James's Park on King Charles Street?
3. In what order would you visit Westminster Cathedral, St. James's Park, and Parliament Square, starting from where you are staying? Why?

Prepare and Engage

LESSON OBJECTIVES

- To interpret and use graphic sources of information

Point out to students that reading a map is an essential skill for both personal and business life. You may also want to point out that some automobiles now come equipped with computerized maps that pinpoint the car's location and give directions from there to a specific destination. Likewise, maps on the Internet pinpoint directions to virtually any address in the United States.

Apply the Strategies

Customize for
Bodily/Kinesthetic Learners
Explain to these students that they may better be able to follow a map if they hold the map to correspond to the direction they are facing.

Have students study the map carefully. You may want to suggest that they reposition the map as they make left or right turns.

Answers

1. You must travel northwest to get from Page Street to Westminster Cathedral.
2. The most direct route is Victoria Street to Smith Street to King Charles Street.
3. Suggested answers: the best order is either Parliament Square, St. James Park, and then Westminster Cathedral or Westminster Cathedral, St. James Park, and Parliament Square. Both these routes avoid backtracking.

Test Preparation Workshop

Reading a Map
In addition to questions about text, standardized tests may require students to interpret information presented in graphic representations, such as a map. Point out to students that visual—like text—information provides the basis for drawing conclusions and making inferences.

Using the map of London on p. 949 of their textbooks, give students the following sample test item.

The Foreign and Commonwealth Offices are located closest to—

A St. James's Palace **C** Lambreth Bridge
B Vincent Square **D** Westminster Cathedral

Students will need to identify all of the locations and draw conclusions about the location of the Foreign and Commonwealth Offices in relation to the answer-choice locations. Point out that knowing the actual distances between locations is not necessary to determine that A, St. James's Palace, is the closest location.

Prepare and Engage

LESSON OBJECTIVES

- To plan, prepare, and present an interpretation of literature by telling a story

Discuss with students the many ways they tell stories in their lives, such as passing on a joke or humorous event or recounting a trip or an embarrassing moment. Invite students to offer examples of friends or relatives who they feel are good storytellers. Ask students to explain the qualities that make their stories a success.

Customize for *Bodily/Kinesthetic Learners*

Encourage students to experiment with different body movements when they tell a story. They might feel more comfortable standing and moving, or the story might be more effective when told quietly in an intimate setting. Becoming familiar with the story and its tone will help students determine an effective mode of telling it.

Explain that giving constructive criticism allows both the performer and the viewer an opportunity to learn. When critiquing performances, remind viewers to ask why the performer made a certain choice, rather than simply stating why they liked or disliked a particular aspect.

Speaking, Listening, and Viewing Workshop

Telling a Story

The story of Cinderella has been told and retold in countries and cultures around the world, with each storyteller interpreting and retelling the tale in his or her own way. Legends, fairy tales, tall tales, and epics all have their origins in ancient oral literary traditions. Yet each time an old story is told, it becomes new again, as each storyteller brings a unique perspective to familiar fictional details.

Find a Tale to Tell When you are going to tell a story, it is important to choose one that you especially like. When considering what tale to tell, ask yourself these questions:

- Who will my audience be? What kind of tale will this particular audience enjoy?
- Where will I be telling the story?
- How much time will I have?

Learn It You can't tell a story well if you forget an important event in the middle! Learn the story, and be comfortable with its plot elements, including the rising action, climax, and resolution. Give special attention to the ending and how you will tell it: From your interpretation of the story, what do you want your audience to feel, understand, or go away thinking?

Make It Yours Experiment with different ways to tell the story. A powerful character should have a strong voice, while a weak one might speak softly or hesitantly. Make each character's voice unique and appropriate. Use a dialect only if it is necessary and only if you can perform it convincingly—otherwise, it will be a distraction to your audience. Consider creative ways of using your voice to suggest sounds and details of setting, such as a howling wind or an echo in a canyon. Remember that the way you use your body—through movement and gestures—is often as important as the way you use your voice. It's your interpretation, so make the story your own.

Add Some Extras You might consider using some simple props or costume parts in your storytelling. If they are significant in the story, these kinds of visual elements can strengthen your performance. Using percussion instruments or objects to create more sounds (of a door opening, footsteps descending a staircase, hooves galloping away) can be effective, too.

Try It Out Rehearsing the storytelling for an audience is the best way to find out how you're doing. Tell the story to a few friends or family members first. Ask them for comments and suggestions, and consider their feedback carefully. Be sure to find out what they especially liked about the story or the way you told it.

Apply the Strategies

Choose a legend, myth, or epic tale to retell to a small group or the whole class. Plan, prepare, and practice your performance. Afterwards, invite your audience to evaluate and ask questions about your performance. Defend your storytelling on the basis of your interpretation of the legend, myth, or epic.

Storytelling Tips

When retelling a story, these tips can help:

- *Experiment to find the most effective ways to get the story's point across to the audience.*
- *Vary the sounds of your voice to indicate changes—of characters, moods, and scenes.*
- *Practice telling the story while you're doing other things, like cleaning your room.*

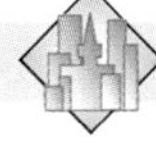

Beyond the Classroom

Community Connection

Attend a Storytelling Storytellers are popular in many parts of the community. Libraries often present professional storytellers; they may be featured in community theater events, and even a keynote speaker at a function such as a fund-raiser or sports banquet is a storyteller.

Have students attend a storytelling event and write a review. Students should note what parts of the performance they found especially effective—or not—and why. Encourage them to be aware of verbal (pitch, tone of voice) and nonverbal (posture and eye contact) performance techniques. Invite students who attend the same event to hold a panel review of the performance.

Test Preparation Workshop

Writing Skills: Strategy, Organization, and Style

Strategies for Success

Some standardized tests ask you to demonstrate your knowledge of writing skills. The test questions often ask about organization or sequence of sentences, the choice of words, and the overall style and tone of a passage. Some questions may ask you to evaluate the author's strategy.

Strategy Questions Strategy questions ask whether a given revision in the passage is appropriate in the context of the essay. For example:

> Many lake areas now have signs placed by the Environmental Protection Agency warning against doing harm to wetlands.

Suppose that the writer wanted to say more about the warnings to protect wetlands. Which of these additions is most suitable?

A Violations could result in a serious fine.
B Many people like to tramp through wetlands.
C People have developed organizations aimed at saving wetlands.
D Wetlands are threatened by development.

While **B, C,** and **D** provide additional information about wetlands and the people who protect or abuse them, only **A** provides additional information about the warnings. **A** is correct.

Organization Questions These questions ask you to choose the most logical sequence of ideas or to decide whether a sentence should be added, deleted, or moved. For example:

> (1) Drivers are compelled to wear seat belts or be in violation of the law. (2) As more people have worn seat belts, the number of automobile deaths has dropped. (3) Many states now have seat-belt laws. (4) More states should consider enacting seat-belt laws as a way of saving lives. (5) Drivers who violate the law are given hefty fines.

1 Choose the sequence of sentence numbers that will make the structure most logical:

A NO CHANGE	**C** 3, 1, 5, 2, 4
B 5, 4, 3, 1, 2	**D** 1, 4, 2, 3, 5

The correct answer is **C.** Any arrangement of sentences provides information, but the one in **C** makes the passage most logical.

Style Questions These questions focus on conveying the writer's point of view and the use of appropriate and effective language for the intended audience. Reread the passage about seat belts, and answer the question that follows.

2 The tone may best be described as:

A persuasive.	**C** matter-of-fact.
B emotional.	**D** whimsical.

The correct answer is **A.** Reread sentence 4. Any time a sentence tells you what "should" be done, the writer is using persuasion.

Apply the Strategies

Read this passage, and answer the questions.

> (1) It's time for all cities to realize that these laws make sense. (2) Several cities have enacted laws prohibiting bicycle riding on sidewalks. (3) When will people realize that bicycles should not be allowed on sidewalks? (4) Such laws have prevented injuries to pedestrians. (5) Many city sidewalks are clogged with cyclists competing for space with pedestrians.

1 Choose the sequence that will make the paragraph's structure most logical:

A 3, 5, 2, 4, 1	**C** 5, 3, 1, 2, 4
B 1, 2, 3, 5, 4	**D** 4, 2, 1, 3, 5

2 The tone of this passage may best be described as:

A emotional.	**C** funny.
B persuasive.	**D** gloomy.

Correlations to Standardized Tests

The writing skills reviewed in this Workshop correspond to the following standardized test section:
ACT Writing Skills

Test Preparation

Each ATE workshop in Unit I supports the instruction here by providing teaching suggestions and a sample test item:
Strategy (ATE, p. 883)
Organization (ATE, p. 923)
Style (ATE, pp. 893, 933)

LESSON OBJECTIVES

- To analyze the characteristics of clearly written texts, including the patterns of organization, syntax, and word choice
- To recognize logical, deceptive, and/or faulty modes of persuasion in texts

Answers

1. (A) 3, 5, 2, 4, 1
2. (B) persuasive

Test-Taking Tip

Process of Elimination
Point out to students that often they can answer questions more efficiently on a standardized test by using the process of elimination. For example, question 1 in Apply the Strategies asks which sentence sequence will make the paragraph's structure most logical. Explain to students that they need only check each choice—they should not try to create the most logical structure themselves, and then check to see if that structure is one of the answer choices. They can eliminate quickly any choice that begins the sequence with a sentence that would not logically begin a paragraph. Answers *B* and *D* can be eliminated, as they start with sentences that include phrases such as "these laws" and "such laws." By following the same strategy, students will identify *A* as the correct answer.

How to Use Analyzing Real-World Texts

The Analyzing Real-World Texts section contains ten nonfiction selections from real-world sources, such as Web sites, newspaper editorials, and journals. The instruction for each selection introduces a reading strategy, such as analyzing characteristics of texts. Questions requiring students to apply the strategy follow the selection. In addition, each real-world selection is thematically linked to a selection in the body of the book. Questions linking the two works appear at the end of the real-world selection.

You can use the Analyzing Real-World Texts selections individually to expose students to material from varied sources. Engaging with the real-world reading strategies can help students develop life skills, such as locating information or evaluating the credibility of information sources. You can also use the selections to help students develop skills, such as recognizing an author's purpose, tested for on standardized tests such as the SAT and TAAS.

By teaching each selection in conjunction with the selection to which it is thematically linked, you can help students develop reading comprehension skills such as the ability to recognize themes.

LESSON OBJECTIVES

1. **To read for different purposes in varied sources**
   - Selection: Diary Entry
   - Reading Strategy
2. **To use a variety of reading strategies to comprehend a diary entry**
   - Reading Strategy
3. **To analyze literary elements**
   - Compare Literary Forms

Analyzing Real-World Texts

About the Author

Like other Jews, **Anne Frank** (1929–1945) and her family faced persecution in Nazi-ruled Germany. They fled to Holland in 1933, but in 1942 the Nazis invaded their new homeland. The Franks hid but were eventually arrested. Anne died in a concentration camp in 1945.

◆Reading Strategy

Establish a Purpose for Reading To guide you through a text, **establish a purpose for reading.**

You might read Anne's *Diary* to learn about the fate of European Jews. In that case, you will spend time with her list of anti-Jewish laws. If instead you are reading for insight into her character, you will muse over her self-descriptions. You might also read to appreciate the writer's craft, to be entertained, or to find models for your writing.

Use a graphic organizer like the one below to list details from the *Diary* that fit your purpose in reading.

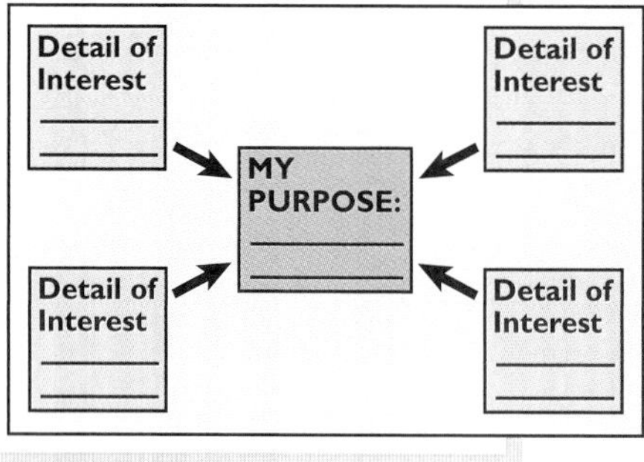

from The Diary of a Young Girl

Anne Frank

20 June, 1942

I haven't written for a few days, because I wanted first of all to think about my diary. It's an odd idea for someone like me to keep a diary; not only because I have never done so before, but because it seems to me that neither I—nor for that matter anyone else—will be interested in the [confessions] of a thirteen-year-old schoolgirl. Still, what does that matter? I want to write, but more than that, I want to bring out all kinds of things that lie buried deep in my heart.

There is a saying that "paper is more patient than man"; it came back to me on one of my slightly melancholy days, while I sat chin in hand, feeling too bored and limp even to make up my mind whether to go out or stay at home. Yes, there is no doubt that paper is patient and as I don't intend to show this cardboard-covered notebook, bearing the proud name of "diary," to anyone, unless I find a real friend, boy or girl, probably nobody cares. And now I come to the root of the matter, the reason for my starting a diary: it is that I have no such real friend.

Let me put it more clearly, since no one will believe that a girl of thirteen feels herself quite alone in the world, nor is it so. I have darling parents and a sister of sixteen. I know about thirty people whom one might call friends—I have strings of boy friends, anxious to catch a glimpse of me and who, failing that, peep at me through mirrors in class. I have relations, aunts and uncles, who are darlings too, a good home, no—I don't seem to lack anything, [save "the" friend]. But it's the same with all my friends, just fun and joking, nothing more. I can never bring myself to talk of anything outside the common round. We don't seem to be able to get any closer, that is the root of the trouble. Perhaps I lack confidence, but anyway, there it is, a stubborn fact and I don't seem to be able to do anything about it.

Hence, this diary. In order to enhance in my mind's

Connecting to "Two Friends," Guy de Maupassant, p. 96

To connect Anne Frank's diary entry to de Maupassant's short story "Two Friends," ask students to describe what friends need from each other. *Possible responses: Companionship; sympathy; understanding; help toward a common goal; fun.* Explain that Anne Frank's diary entry and de Maupassant's short story, both set during wartime, demonstrate the importance of friendship. Friendship means something different, though, in each selection.

Have students read or review "Two Friends" and Anne Frank's diary entry, paying special attention to the kind of friendship each describes. Then, have them answer the "Compare Literary Forms" questions, p. 953.

eye the picture of the friend for whom I have waited so long, I don't want to set down a series of bald facts in a diary like most people do, but I want this diary itself to be my friend, and I shall call my friend Kitty. No one will grasp what I'm talking about if I begin my letters to Kitty just out of the blue, so, albeit unwillingly, I will start by sketching in brief the story of my life.

My father was thirty-six when he married my mother, who was then twenty-five. My sister Margot was born in 1926 in Frankfort-on-Main, I followed on June 12, 1929, and, as we are Jewish, we emigrated to Holland in 1933,[1] where my father was appointed Managing Director of Travies N.V. This firm is in close relationship with the firm of Kolen & Co. in the same building, of which my father is a partner.

The rest of our family, however, felt the full impact of Hitler's anti-Jewish laws, so life was filled with anxiety. In 1938 after the pogroms,[2] my two uncles (my mother's brothers) escaped to the U.S.A. My old grandmother came to us, she was then seventy-three. After May 1940 good times rapidly fled: first the war, then the capitulation,[3] followed by the arrival of the Germans, which is when the sufferings of us Jews really began. Anti-Jewish decrees followed each other in quick succession. Jews must wear a yellow star, Jews must hand in their bicycles, Jews are banned from trams and are forbidden to drive, Jews are only allowed to do their shopping between three and five o'clock and then only in shops which bear the placard "Jewish shop." Jews must be indoors by eight o'clock and cannot even sit in their own gardens after that hour. Jews are forbidden to visit theaters, cinemas, and other places of entertainment. Jews may not take part in public sports. Swimming baths, tennis courts, hockey fields, and other sports grounds are all prohibited to them. Jews may not visit Christians. Jews must go to Jewish schools, and many more restrictions of a similar kind.

So we could not do this and were forbidden to do that. But life went on in spite of it all. Jopie used to say to me, "You're scared to do anything, because it may be forbidden." Our freedom was strictly limited. Yet things were still bearable.

Granny died in January 1942; no one will ever know how much she is present in my thoughts and how much I love her still.

In 1934 I went to school at the Montessori Kindergarten[4] and continued there. It was at the end of the school year, I was in form 6B, when I had to say good-by to Mrs. K. We both wept, it was very sad. In 1941 I went, with my sister Margot, to the Jewish Secondary School, she into the fourth form and I into the first.

So far everything is all right with the four of us and here I come to the present day.

1. **1933:** The year the Nazis came to power in Germany.
2. **pogroms** (pō grämz´) *n.*: Organized massacres.
3. **the capitulation** (kə pich´ yoo lā´ shən): The Netherlands surrendered to the invading Germans in May 1940.
4. **Montessori Kindergarten:** School founded on the liberal educational ideas of Maria Montessori (1870–1952).

◆ Apply the Reading Strategy

1. Cite three details in Anne's diary entry on which you would focus if your purpose were to learn more about the history of Jews in Nazi-occupied Europe.
2. Cite three details from the entry of special interest if your purpose were to learn more about Anne's character.
3. Which of these two purposes does the diary entry better serve? Explain.

◆ Compare Literary Forms

1. Read or review Guy de Maupassant's short story "Two Friends," p. 96. Citing details from this story and from Anne Frank's diary, explain ways in which war can dramatize the importance of friendship.
2. The friends in "Two Friends" barely say anything to each other; Anne wants to tell her "friend" everything. What conclusions about friendship can you draw from this contrast?

Answers

◆ Apply the Reading Strategy

1. For the purpose of learning more about the history of the Jews in Nazi-occupied Europe, students should focus on Anne's account of her family's fate, on her description of anti-Jewish laws, on the fact that Germany introduced anti-Jewish laws into the countries, such as Holland, that it occupied during the war, and on Anne's judgment that, despite these laws, "things were still bearable."
2. For the purpose of learning more about Anne's character, readers should focus on her lack of a "true friend," her desire to talk about things "outside the common round" but her inability to do so with those she knows, the matter-of-fact tone in which she reports the family history, and the imagination she shows in writing a diary in the form of letters to an imaginary friend.
3. Students may note that, while Anne's account of her family reveals something about the fate of Jews during the war, it is incomplete. The diary entry may better serve the purpose of learning about Anne's character, since in it she clearly describes one of her deepest concerns.

◆ Compare Literary Forms

1. In the de Maupassant story, war shows how strong friendship can be: the simple friendship of the two men helps them stand up to their Prussian interrogator. Against the background of war, their simple, dignified farewell—each calls the other by the formal "Monsieur" just before they are shot—shows that what is unexpressed in friendship may be its greatest strength. In Anne's diary entry, war emphasizes how basic a need friendship is; even in time of war, Anne's foremost preoccupation is her desire for a true friend.
2. Answers include: the needs a friend fulfills differ radically from one friendship to the next; both self-expression and a silent, easy "just being together" are aspects of friendship.

Prepare and Engage

LESSON OBJECTIVES

1. **To read for different purposes in varied sources**
   - Selection: Letters
2. **To analyze literary elements**
   - Reading Strategy
3. **To analyze literary elements**
   - Compare Literary Forms

Answers

◆ Apply the Reading Strategy

(a), (b) The following facts and feelings, evident in Mandela's letters, reflect his historical circumstances: Mandela's loneliness and isolation from his friends and family are the result of his imprisonment, reflecting the struggle in South Africa for an end to apartheid; the infrequency of letters and visitors may reflect oppressive policies by the government toward political prisoners; Mandela's wife has also been "detained," further increasing his worry and the infrequency of her letters; Mandela's joy at receiving a letter reflects the isolation of prison life; his sadness at the thought that his wife does not receive his letters reflects uncertainty created by the government's repressive measures.

◆ Compare Literary Forms

(a) The speaker in Diop's poem first reflects that he has never seen the Africa of "proud warriors" (l. 2), but that history has drenched the land in blood (ll. 6–8); he expresses outrage and frustration at the thought that Africa is "the back that bends" (l. 13) in servitude. The voice that answers counsels patience and a stern kind of hope in the comparison of Africa to a "young and sturdy tree" (l. 18) whose fruits will "grow to have / The bitter taste of liberty" (l. 23–24). (b) All three feelings—pride in Africa's past, before white domination; outrage at injustice toward blacks; and patient hope for future liberation—might have helped Mandela endure over two decades in prison.

Analyzing Real-World Texts

About the Author

Nelson Mandela (1918–) spent twenty-seven years in prison for his opposition to the white-dominated South African government. Apartheid ended in 1991, and in 1994 Mandela became the first black president of South Africa.

◆ Reading Strategy

Connect Literature to Historical Context By connecting a work to its **historical context**—the beliefs, trends, and events that shaped people's lives at the time—you can better understand it. Your knowledge of Nelson Mandela will help answer questions you may have about his prison letters. For example, knowing that prison authorities routinely read his mail helps you understand why he does not ask his wife Winnie for political news.

Read "About the Author." Then, as you read the letters, list each sign of the historical context that you find, using a graphic organizer like the one below.

Fact About Historical Context	How Reflected in Letters
Mandela was an enemy of the former white South African government. His mail was screened by authorities.	He writes about his feelings, memories, and the visits he has received—not about politics.

Letters From Nelson Mandela

Written from prison to his wife

26 October 1976

I have been fairly successful in putting on a mask behind which I have pined for the family, alone, never rushing for the post when it comes until somebody calls out my name. I also never linger after visits although sometimes the urge to do so becomes quite terrible. I am struggling to suppress my emotions as I write this letter.

I have received only one letter since you were detained, that one dated 22 August. I do not know anything about family affairs, such as payment of rent, telephone bills, care of children and their expenses, whether you will get a job when released. As long as I don't hear from you, I will remain worried and dry like a desert.

I recall the Karoo I crossed on several occasions. I saw the desert again in Botswana on my way to and from Africa—endless pits of sand and not a drop of water. I have not had a letter from you. I feel dry like a desert.

Letters from you and the family are like the arrival of summer rains and spring that liven my life and make it enjoyable.

Whenever I write you, I feel that inside physical warmth, that makes me forget all my problems. I become full of love.

26 May 1978

I feel sad that I write letters to you and you never receive them.

◆ Apply the Reading Strategy

(a) Cite three facts or feelings that reflect the historical circumstances in which Mandela was writing. (b) For each, explain how it reflects the circumstances.

◆ Compare Literary Forms

Read or review David Diop's "Africa," p. 202. (a) Summarize the speaker's feelings for Africa. (b) Explain how such feelings help to explain Mandela's endurance of prison.

Connecting to "Africa," David Diop, p. 202.

To connect these prison letters from Nelson Mandela to David Diop's poem "Africa," ask students to discuss the feelings that attach people to their country. *Possible responses: Pride; love; patriotism; loyalty; gratitude.* Point out that various countries throughout history have been ruled by other countries or by unjust governments. Ask students how such a situation might affect a person's feelings for his or her country. *Possible responses: The person might feel frustration or sorrow for the condition of his or her country and anger or hatred for those ruling it; alternatively, a person might feel gratitude to a ruling country for the help it gives his or her country.* Explain to students that both Nelson Mandela and David Diop respond to political injustice in Africa with strong feeling. Ask students to keep this background in mind as they read or review David Diop's "Africa" and Nelson Mandela's "Letters." Then, have them answer the "Compare Literary Forms" question, p. 954.

About the Author

A historian of American culture, **Ann Douglas** (1942–) teaches at Columbia University.

◆ Reading Strategy

Evaluate Credibility of Information Sources To **evaluate sources,** determine the authors' purpose. If they wish to persuade, they may not provide accurate details. However, if the authors are experts in the field, they will be careful with the facts, if only to protect their reputations.

"It's Be-bop, Man!" is from *The New York Times*, an established, trustworthy source. The author is a cultural historian whose purpose is to give general historical background on be-bop. Therefore, you can trust her information on history, but you might be cautious with her remarks on music theory.

Using a graphic organizer like this one, rate the article's credibility in each category listed.

	Example	Credibility	My Reasoning
[Na]mes, Places, [Da]tes	1964: Monk defines jazz as "New York."	High credibility	The *Times* could easily check this date; the author is a scholar accustomed to fact-checking.
[Ac]curate [Qu]otations			
[Hi]storical [Ev]ents			
[Bi]ographical [De]tails			
[Ge]neralizations [Ab]out History [of J]azz			

Feel the City's Pulse? It's Be-bop, Man!

Ann Douglas

Newspaper feature, *The New York Times,* August 28, 1998

In 1964, Thelonious Monk, one of the pioneers of be-bop and perhaps jazz's greatest composer, was asked by an interviewer to define jazz. Though Monk disliked questions and usually ignored them, this time he didn't miss a beat: "New York, man. You can feel it. It's around in the air."

. . .

Be-bop (bop for short) was sometimes labeled "New York Jazz," and it is, in fact, the only major school of jazz to which the city can lay proprietary claim. Jazz of the 20's, dominated by Louis Armstrong, originated in New Orleans, migrating to New York only after a formative detour in Chicago. Armstrong inspired 30's swing, the music of the big bands led by Benny Goodman, Artie Shaw, Glenn Miller, Count Basie and Duke Ellington, the "mother bands," as Gillespie[1] called them, whose music the be-boppers both emulated and revolutionized.

. . . Bop's wide-ranging allusiveness, its quicksilver expressivity, angular dissonance[2] and shockingly extended palette of pitches and rhythms echoed the international mix, the fluidity and speed of New York life.

Jamming After Hours

Bop began at roughly the same time as World War II, in 1940 when Monk, then 23, was hired to play with Kenny (Klook) Clarke, the man who transformed jazz drumming, at Minton's Playhouse in Harlem.

1. **Gillespie** (1917–1993): John Birks "Dizzy" Gillespie, jazz trumpeter. He was a pioneer of be-bop and Afro-Cuban jazz.
2. **dissonance** (dis´ ə nəns): Lack of harmony; combination of pitches that creates tension, leading to another, resolving combination.

Prepare and Engage

LESSON OBJECTIVES

1. **To read for different purposes in varied sources**
   - Selection: Newspaper Feature
2. **To read critically to evaluate texts**
   - Reading Strategy
3. **To analyze literary elements**
   - Compare Literary Forms

Connecting to "Jazz Fantasia," Carl Sandburg, p. 247

To connect this newspaper feature to Carl Sandburg's poem "Jazz Fantasia," ask students to name a form of music and then describe the qualities that define it. *Answers will vary.* Ask students how easy it is to describe music in words. *Answers will vary. Students may note that it is easier to sing, hum, or make noises imitating music than it is to describe it in words.* Explain that both Carl Sandburg and Ann Douglas have taken on the difficult task of describing music in words. Have students read or review Sandburg's "Jazz Fantasia" and Ann Douglas's newspaper feature "Feel the City's Pulse?", paying special attention to the writers' descriptions of music. Next, have students answer the "Compare Literary Forms" questions, p. 956.

Answers

◆ Apply the Reading Strategy

1. The article is fairly credible as a source for explaining the rise in popularity of be-bop over swing. The author is a cultural historian, who can be expected to report basic social facts and trends correctly. However, since her purpose is to provide general background on the subject, she may not be as careful in her analysis as she would be if defending it in a professional article on history.
2. The article is not entirely credible as a source of theoretical explanations of music. The author's specialty is history, not music; her purpose is to provide general background, not technical information. However, she has probably looked at some credible sources for this information.
3. Douglas's enthusiasm for be-bop might suggest a bias that would lead her to conceal unflattering facts about the music and its performers. However, it is also possible that her enthusiasm has moved her to study the subject thoroughly, enhancing the overall credibility of this newspaper feature.

◆ Compare Literary Forms

1. (a) Students may contrast the "sob" of "long cool winding saxophones" (l. 2), the trombones that "ooze," the "husha- / husha-hush" of the drums (ll. 5, 6), and the "moan" and "cry" of the band (ll. 7–8) in Sandburg's poem with the "quicksilver expressivity, angular dissonance," "side-sliding harmonies and whirlwind pace" of be-bop in Douglas's descriptions. (b) It is unlikely that Sandburg is describing the same music that Douglas is. In her description, be-bop is fast, intellectually challenging, and geometrical music; Sandburg is describing an earthy, sensuous kind of jazz.
2. Students may respond that the poem best captures the sound and spirit of a music, since it uses a range of concentrated, expressive images and onomatopoetic word-sounds. Others may note that, by adding history and biography to descriptions of the music, the newspaper feature creates a more realistic picture to associate with the music than the poem does.

Sites of Bop's Triumphs and Tragedies

1. **Savoy Ballroom,** Lenox Avenue and 140th Street, Harlem. Charlie Parker played in this legendary jazz and dance hall with the Jay McShann Orchestra in his early days in New York.
2. **Minton's Playhouse,** 210 West 118th Street, Morningside Heights. Charlie Christian, Kenny Clarke, Thelonious Monk, Parker, and Gillespie made musical history here in the early 1940's.
3. **St. Peter's Church,** 54th Street and Lexington Avenue, Manhattan (also its current site). Monk's funeral took place here on Feb. 22, 1982, with musicians playing for three hours.
4. **52d Street,** between Fifth and Sixth Avenues, known as "The Street." A magical block of jazz clubs, including the Onyx, Spotlite, Three Deuces, and Kelly's Stable.
5. **Birdland,** 1678 Broadway, at 53d Street, Manhattan. It opened on Dec. 15, 1949, with dozens of (caged) birds on view and Charlie (Bird) Parker presiding.
6. **216 West 19th Street.** Eager to become "a New York musician," Gillespie lived here with his brother when he first came to town from Philadelphia in 1937, eating for 25 cents a day.

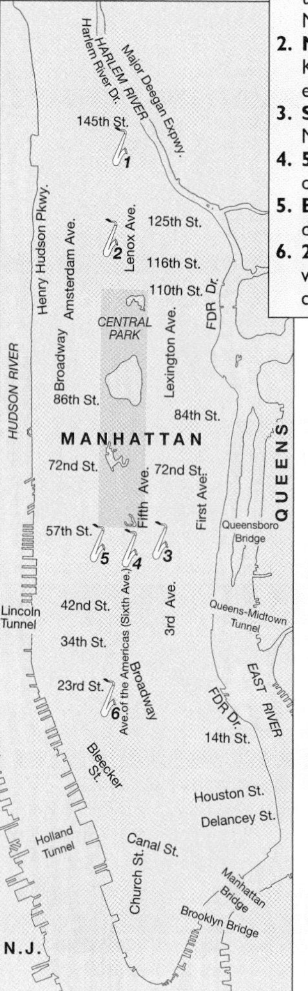

Gillespie jammed with them after his regular engagement, and Parker[3] joined them a year later. When Minton's closed for the night, they adjourned to Clark Monroe's Uptown House, an after-hours club where an extraordinary teen-age drummer named Max Roach played in the band.

The nation's entrance into the war in late 1941 imposed gas rationing, entertainment taxes and curfews, sharply restricting travel. The swing bands were touring bands, and some of them continued to tour, but now everyone was looking for a long-term base in a big city, easily accessible by public transit.

What hurt swing helped be-bop. The expense and risks of touring (especially down South) had been far greater for black musicians than for white. The cramped quarters of many city clubs suited the young bop musicians, eager to work with the small ensembles that maximized opportunities for experimentation.

. . .

The word "be-bop," which both Monk and Gillespie claimed to have coined, described the music's unconventional stop-and-start form, especially Gillespie and Parker's witty eighth-note pair conclusions. The purpose of bop's irregular phrasings, side-sliding harmonies and whirlwind pace, was, in Kenny Clarke's words, to "raise the standards of musicianship," to tell people, "Whatever you go into, go into it intelligently." The be-boppers were the real New York intellectuals, the hippest, smartest men in town.

3. **Parker** (1920–1955): Charlie Parker, nicknamed "Bird"; influential, virtuoso jazz saxophonist and pioneer of be-bop.

◆ Apply the Reading Strategy

1. How credible is the article as a source for explanations of be-bop's rise in popularity over swing?
2. How credible is the article as a source of theoretical explanations of music, such as the reference to the "extended palette of pitches"?
3. Douglas's descriptions of be-bop are enthusiastic. Does this make them more or less credible? Explain.

◆ Compare Literary Forms

1. Read or review Carl Sandburg's poem "Jazz Fantasia," p. 247. (a) Compare one of his descriptions of the sound of jazz with one of Douglas's descriptions. (b) On the basis of this comparison, how likely is it that Sandburg is describing be-bop?
2. Which form better captures the spirit of a music: the poem or the newpaper feature?

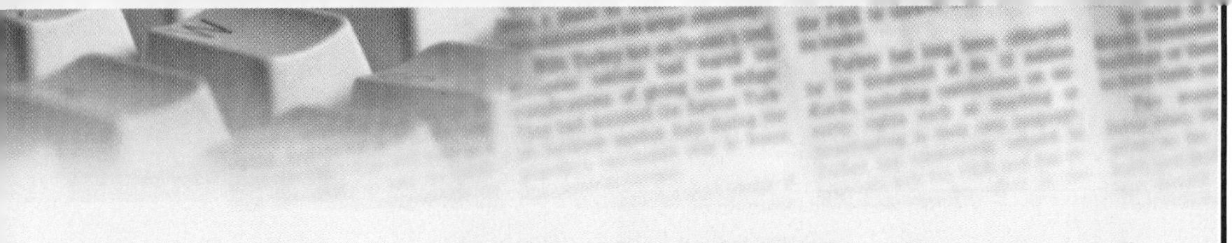

65-MPH Speed Limit Is Saving Lives

Charles Lave

Consumers' Research Magazine, September 1977

Despite opposition from many national safety groups, in November 1995 Congress gave the states permission to raise speed limits. Opponents had testified that raising speed limits would cause an additional 4,400 to 6,000 deaths per year. Fortunately, it didn't work out that way.

Fatalities did not increase. They did not rise by the 10% to 14% expected by the opponents of the change, nor even by the 2% to 3% that would be expected from recent trends. Instead, fatalities fell by 0.7%. This surprising outcome was not the result of a decline in travel: Total vehicle miles rose 1.8% between 1995 and 1996.

Although Congress gave permission to raise speed limits in November 1995, it took the states a while to create and pass new legislation, and only half of those that did react had done so by May 1996.

A drop in fatalities following an increase in speed limits is not unprecedented.[1] The 1987 change in speed limits produced similar results. In 1987 Congress gave the states permission to raise speed limits on portions of their Interstate highways. Some states raised speed limits, some did not. Comparing the subsequent fatality rates across these groups, holding constant a number of other factors, the states that raised speed limits experienced a 3.4% to 5.1% drop in fatality rates compared to the states that did not raise speed limits.

Why didn't fatalities increase in 1987 and 1996 as had been widely expected? My research cited three possible factors. Part of the answer is contained in testimony given to Congress by senior highway-patrol administrators. They said

1. **unprecedented** (un pres´ ə den´ tid) *adj.*: Without prior example; surprising.

About the Author

Charles Lave (1938–) is the Chairman of the Department of Economics of the University of California, Irvine.

◆ Reading Strategy

Recognize Logical Modes of Persuasion: Induction and Deduction The article "65-MPH Speed Limit Is Saving Lives" uses both **deductive and inductive modes of persuasion. Deductive reasoning** proves a conclusion by applying a principle to a specific case:

Deduction Diagram

[Pri]nciple:	If speed limits over 55 mph are unsafe, traffic deaths will go up when the speed limit is raised.
[Sp]ecific [Ca]se:	The speed limit was raised to 65 mph, but fatalities did not increase.
[Co]nclusion:	Speed limits over 55 mph are not inherently unsafe.

Inductive reasoning leads from a number of cases to a generalization:

Induction Diagram

[Ca]ses:	In 1987 and in 1986, the speed limit was raised.
[Pa]ttern:	In each case, fatalities declined.
[Ge]neralization:	Raising speed limits does not increase fatalities.

Using graphic organizers like the ones above, analyze each argument in the article, identifying it as an induction or a deduction.

Prepare and Engage

LESSON OBJECTIVES

1. **To read for different purposes in varied sources**
   - Selection: Scientific Text
2. **To read critically to evaluate texts**
   - Reading Strategy
3. **To use a variety of reading strategies to comprehend scientific text**
   - Reading Strategy
4. **To analyze literary elements**
   - Compare Literary Forms

Connecting to "Auto Wreck," Karl Shapiro, p. 367

To connect this statistical study with Karl Shapiro's poem "Auto Wreck," suggest to students that people can respond in many different ways to surprising or important events in life. Ask students to describe how a fan might respond when the home team clinches a championship. What would a television producer do in response to the key play? What might a public official do in response to the victory? *Answers include: Fans in the stands will erupt in a cheer. Television producers will run replays of the decisive moments in the game, showing them from different angles and interviewing experts to explain the nature of each play. The mayor of the town or city may hold a parade.* Explain that this statistical study and Karl Shapiro's poem "Auto Wreck" are both responses to the tragedy of automobile accidents. Just as a fan's cheer and an instant replay are different responses to the clinching moment in a game, so the poem and the statistical study are different reactions to the fact of traffic accidents.

Ask students to read or review Shapiro's "Auto Wreck" and Charles Lave's "65-MPH Speed Limit Is Saving Lives," focusing on the different perspective each takes on traffic accidents. Then, have them answer the "Compare Literary Forms" question, p. 958.

Answers

◆ Apply the Reading Strategy

1. The argument is a deduction. It starts from the principle that "Certain police activities are more effective at promoting safety than the enforcement of the speed limit is." It then applies the principle to a specific case: "When the speed limit was raised, the states devoted fewer resources to enforcing the speed limit." The conclusion is that "When the speed limit was raised, the police were able to promote safety more effectively."
2. To prove that there was a "reallocation" of traffic—that more motorists used the interstate highways rather than local roads after the speed limit was raised—the author would have to examine the number of vehicles traveling both kinds of roads before and after the speed limit was raised. He would then make a generalization from these figures. The argument would be an induction, since it would move from specific cases (represented by the numbers) to a generalization about "reallocation of traffic."
3. In arguing that lower "speed variance" leads to fewer fatalities, the writer assumes that speed variance "produces more overtaking and passing and hence more chances for collisions." In suggesting that lower speed variance resulted from raising the speed limit, he assumes that many drivers want to go faster than 55 mph, but that many of these drivers are content to drive at 65 or under.

◆ Compare Literary Forms

The article presents truths about actual patterns in highway accidents and explains factors affecting the fatality rates. It presents such accidents in the mass, as numbers and statistics, so the truth of the horror and physical details of an actual accident do not appear. Karl Shapiro's "Auto Wreck" creates a vivid picture of the aftermath of a wreck, conveys the reactions of survivors in lines such as "Our throats were tight as tourniquets" (l. 22), and reflects on the larger implications of this form of death, which "spatters all we knew of denouement / Across the expedient and wicked stones" (ll. 38, 39)—a death without sense. The poem shows truths of human experience; it does not reflect on the causes of such accidents, though, or on policies that may prevent them.

Analyzing Real-World Texts

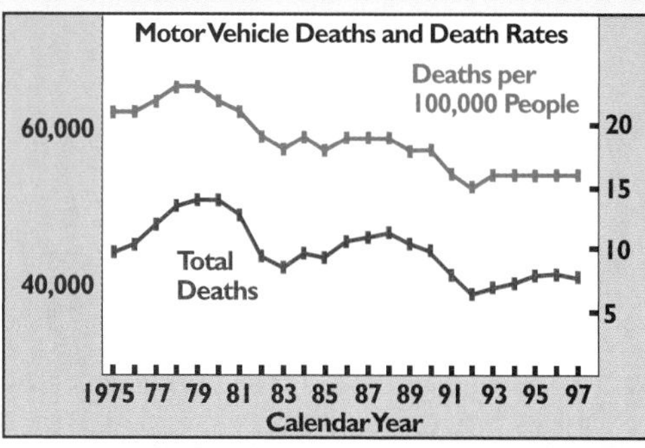

that pressure from the federal government to enforce compliance with a 55-mph limit had forced them to take patrol officers away from other safety activities and move them to the task of speed-limit enforcement on Interstate highways, even though they did not believe that action was the best use of their patrol resources. This opinion was widely shared among the state highway-patrol chiefs. In 1988 their national organization passed a resolution that stated: "[Federal demands to enforce the 55-mph limit] force the over-concentration of limited resources for the express purpose of attaining compliance rather than application of resources in a manner most effectively enhancing total highway safety."

Thus relaxing the speed laws eased the highway patrols' enforcement burden, allowing them to reallocate[2] patrol resources to activities they considered more important for promoting safety.

There might also have been a reallocation of traffic when speed limits were raised. Previously, if a driver wanted to go faster than the limit on the heavily policed Interstate highways, he might have moved to one of the parallel two-lane roads. Though much more dangerous, these roads had very little speed enforcement. Raising speed limits would lure such drivers back to the Interstates, thus reallocating traffic from dangerous roads to safe ones.

Finally, speed variance among cars may have decreased when speed limits were raised. Speed variance is highly dangerous because it produces more overtaking and passing and hence more chances for collisions. Thus when setting speed limits, it is critical to choose a limit that drivers are willing to obey. Suppose most drivers wanted to go faster than 55 mph: Some obeyed the limit, some ignored it. Raising the limit would give the law-abiding drivers a chance to speed up, hence reducing speed variance and increasing safety.

These results do not imply that we should raise speed limits even further as a quick and easy way to increase highway safety. But it should be clear that the conventional wisdom — "speed kills" — is not a complete picture of the world. Highway safety is a much more complex matter, and should be analyzed as the outcome of a system of interdependent[3] behaviors.

2. **reallocate** (rē al´ ō kāt) *v.*: To change the distribution of.

3. **interdependent** (in´ tər dē pen´ dənt) *adj.*: Dependent on each other, so that changing one changes the others.

◆ Apply the Reading Strategy

1. The writer argues that a higher speed limit lets the police promote safety more effectively. Break this argument into steps. Explain whether it is a deduction or an induction.
2. What kind of argument—deductive or inductive—would the author need to prove that there was a "reallocation" of traffic?
3. In arguing that lower "speed variance" leads to fewer fatalities, what assumption does he make?

◆ Compare Literary Forms

Read or review Karl Shapiro's poem "Auto Wreck," p. 367. Contrast the perspective of the article on highway accidents with the perspective of the poem. What truths emerge and what truths are not expressed in each?

About the Author

The Nature Company publishes popular reference books on a variety of scientific subjects in addition to selling scientific equipment.

◆ Reading Strategy

Analyze Text Structures: Cause and Effect **Cause and effect** is a structure that shows the connection between events. A cause is an event or force that brings about another event (its effect). The effect of one event can also be the cause of another event.

In "Lightning and Thunder," the writer explains how the attraction between charges in a cloud and charges in the ground causes an effect—the flow of negative charges from the cloud to the earth below. This event is one in the series that causes lightning.

Use a graphic organizer like the one below to list three causes and their effects as described in the article.

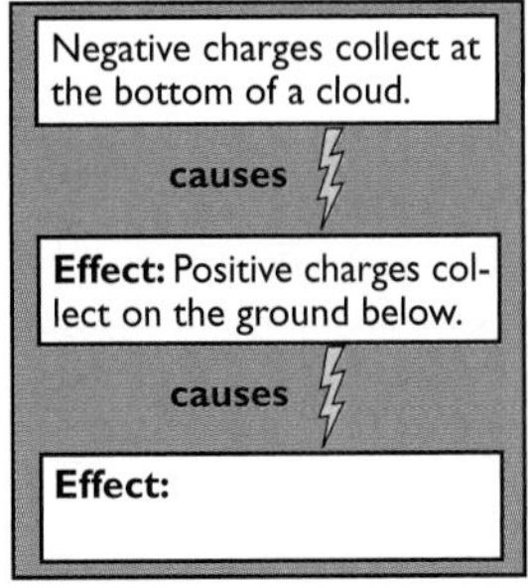

Lightning and Thunder

Science text from *The Nature Company Guides: Weather*

Lightning is the result of a build-up of opposite electrical charges within a cumulonimbus cloud.[1] Exactly how this happens is not yet clear, but it seems that ice crystals, which form in the upper part of the cloud, are generally positively charged while water droplets, which tend to sink to the bottom of the cloud, are normally negatively charged. It may be that updrafts carry the positive charges up and downdrafts[2] drag the negative charges down.

As this build-up occurs, a positive charge also forms near the ground under the cloud and moves with the cloud.

Opposites Attract

The opposing electrical charges are strongly attracted to each other. Eventually, the insulating[3] layer of air between the charges cannot keep them apart any longer and a discharge takes place. Negative charges move toward positive charges in an invisible, jagged, zigzag pattern, called a stepped leader. When the negative charge meets the positive charge, a massive electrical current—the lightning bolt—is created and then sustained[4] by a return positive charge back to the cloud. This positive charge travels extremely quickly—about 60,000 miles per second (96,000 kps).

All of this can be repeated rapidly in the same lightning bolt, which gives the lightning its flickering appearance. The process continues until all the charges in the cloud have dissipated.[5]

Most discharges take place within a cloud, between clouds, or between a cloud and the air if there is sufficient charge in the air. Only about one in four lightning bolts

---

1. **cumulonimbus** (kyo͞o´ myo͞o lō nim´ bəs) **cloud:** Dense, puffy cloud stretching for a considerable vertical distance.
2. **updrafts . . . downdrafts**: Air currents blowing up and down, respectively.
3. **insulating** (in´ sə lāt´ iŋ) *adj.*: Not allowing the passage of electric current.
4. **sustained** (sə stānd´) *v.*: Kept in existence.
5. **dissipated** (dis´ ə pāt´ id) *v.*: Disappeared; become scattered.

Prepare and Engage

LESSON OBJECTIVES

1. **To read for different purposes in varied sources**
   - Selection: Scientific Text
2. **To use a variety of reading strategies to comprehend a scientific text**
   - Reading Strategy
3. **To analyze literary elements**
   - Compare Literary Forms

Connecting to "A Storm in the Mountains" Alexander Solzhenitsyn, p. 450

To connect this science text to Alexander Solzhenitsyn's reflective essay "A Storm in the Mountains," have students collaborate in describing a storm, each adding details in turn. *Details include: rumbling thunder; a sudden breeze before the raindrops begin to fall; flickering lightning.* Ask them whether they have explained the storm or merely described it. *Suggested response: They have only described it.* Then, ask them if they have dramatized the storm—made it seem vividly real, and so captured the essential experience of being in the storm. *Suggested response: Again, they have only described it.* Explain to the class that "Lightning and Thunder" offers an explanation of a storm, while Solzhenitsyn's "A Storm in the Mountains" presents a dramatization. Have students read or review the two selections, paying particular attention to the differences between the selections and a simple description. Then, have students answer the "Compare Literary Forms" questions, p. 960.

Answers

◆ Apply the Reading Strategy

1. Cause-and-effect relationships in the article include: (1) Drafts (cause) carry positively charged ice crystals in a cloud upward and carry negatively charged water droplets downward (effect); (2) the build-up of negative charges at the bottom of the cloud (cause) causes a positive charge to form near the ground under the cloud (effect); (3) these opposing charges attract each other (cause), leading negative charges to move toward the ground in a stepped leader (effect); (4) when the negative charges meet the positive charges below (cause), a huge electrical current is created in which positive charges flow upward from the earth (effect); (5) the repetition of this process (cause) creates the flickering of lightning (effect); (6) the process stops (effect) when all the charges in the cloud have become spread out (cause); (7) a lightning bolt superheats the air (cause), causing the air to expand and then contract rapidly (effect); (8) this rapid expansion and contraction (cause) creates the sound waves we hear as thunder (effect); (9) light waves travel faster than sound waves (cause), so we see lightning before we hear the thunder (effect); (10) when the build-up of opposite charges is insufficient to create a true lightning bolt (cause), a mass of sparks may appear above the ground (effect).
2. See answer to 1 above, items (1) through (6).
3. Distance between the observer and the storm "causes" the difference between forked and sheet lightning; an observer close by will see the lightning as forked, while one farther away will see sheets of lightning.

◆ Compare Literary Forms

1. Solzhenitsyn's "A Storm in the Mountains" captures the experience of an intense lightning storm—the disorienting alternation between blinding light and utter darkness, the manner in which the storm encompasses the whole landscape (thunder drowning the rivers, lightning making the mountains appear and disappear), and the paradoxical feeling of calm a large storm can cause. By contrast, the article does not spend any time with the response of people to storms—either disorientation or wonder. Unlike Solzhenitsyn's piece, the scientific text explains the physical causes and processes at work in thunder and lightning.
2. Students may answer that a scientific explanation presents a deeper truth than a poetic description, since the facts in an explanation remain the same, regardless of who experiences the storm, while a poetic description depends on the perspective of the writer and the reader for its truth. Others may respond: the poetic description is deeper, since it captures the experience of the storm (what it is like to live through it) instead of reporting facts that lack human significance. Others may respond: both the explanation and the description have validity in their own, distinct spheres.

Analyzing Real-World Texts

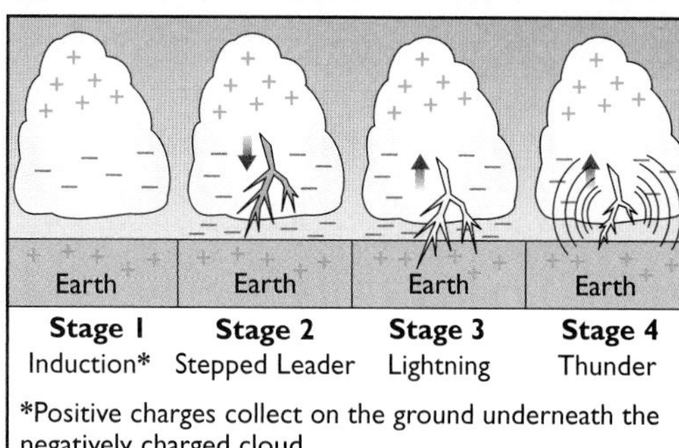

*Positive charges collect on the ground underneath the negatively charged cloud.

strikes the ground. When this happens, the descending leader attracts ground-level positive charges upward, usually from an elevated object such as a tree or building. A lightning bolt that travels all the way from the top of a cloud to negatively charged ground outside the area beneath the cloud is known as a positive flash.

All forms of lightning may appear as forked, sheet, or streaked lightning, depending on how far the observer is from the charge.

The Sound and the Fury

The temperature of a lightning bolt exceeds 40,000° F (22,000° C). When a bolt forms, the air around it is superheated, which causes the air to expand then contract rapidly. This creates sound waves that we hear as thunder. Because light waves travel much faster than sound waves, we see the lightning before hearing the thunder. It takes about 5 seconds for thunder to travel 1 mile (3 seconds/km), so it's possible to calculate how far away a storm is by counting the seconds between seeing the lightning flash and hearing the thunder, and dividing by five, for miles (or three, for km). Generally, thunder is inaudible farther than 20 miles (32 km) away.

Sparks May Fly

There are two other types of atmospheric electricity. A rare form, known as ball lightning, occurs when some of the charge from a cloud-to-ground strike forms a small, round ball. This ball of light may roll along the ground or climb objects until it either explodes or dissipates.

Sometimes, when the build-up of opposite charges is insufficient for a lightning bolt to form, a mass of sparks appears high above the ground in the vicinity of the thunderstorm. This phenomenon was first noted at the top of ships' masts and was subsequently named St. Elmo's fire, after the patron saint of sailors.

◆ Apply the Reading Strategy

1. Cite three cause-and-effect relationships described in the article.
2. Outline each step leading to the creation of a normal lightning flash between cloud and earth.
3. What factor causes the difference between forked and sheet lightning?

◆ Compare Literary Forms

1. Read or review Alexander Solzhenitsyn's "A Storm in the Mountains," p. 450. What aspect of a thunderstorm does his description capture that this article does not? What does this article show that Solzhenitsyn's piece does not?
2. Which do you think presents a deeper truth: a scientific explanation of lightning or a poetic description of a storm? Explain your response.

Egyptology Web

Background

Cambridge University, the host of this Web site, was founded around 1209 in the city of Cambridge, near London, England. It is one of the world's oldest universities.

◆ **Reading Strategy**

Use Reference Material

You may occasionally meet unfamiliar words, phrases, or concepts. To answer questions you may have, use reference material, such as encyclopedias and Internet resources.

For instance, you can find information about the study of ancient Egypt through this Egyptology Web page. As with many Web pages, the main links offered by the site are laid out in a sidebar. Scan the sidebar to determine where to find information. Be aware that many sites offer a "Search" feature and site index to help you locate information quickly.

In a graphic organizer like the one below, list each link, and note the kind of information you expect to find through it.

Link	Information I Expect to Find
News & Gossip	Information about recent discoveries, as well as professional news that only archaeologists would be interested in

Popular local items
News & Gossip
Announcements
Bulletin Board
Email addresses
Commercial stuff
Tomb of Senneferi (TT99)
Beinlich Wordlist
Wilbour Library Acquisitions

Main pages
Local resources
Essential resources elsewhere
Institutions
Museums

This page is set up with the kind assistance of the Newton Institute in the University of Cambridge to provide a World Wide Web resource for Egyptological information. The pages are not a publication of the Newton Institute, and all matters concerning them (e.g. comments, criticisms, and suggestions for items to include) should be sent to Nigel Strudwick.

Click here for guidelines on the format of material.

HISTORY: Egyptology Resources was set up in 1994 and was the first web page set up specifically for the benefit of those interested in Egyptology, whether laymen or professionals. The links you can go to from here are grouped into hopefully helpful divisions, with those which have their homes on this site separated at the top.

◆ **Apply the Reading Strategy**

1. Where can users click to learn more about the people who put together the site?
2. What link should users click to find a good Egyptian exhibit near them?

◆ **Compare Literary Forms**

Read or review "By the Waters of Babylon," p. 500. Compare John's attitude toward a past civilization with that represented by this site.

Prepare and Engage

LESSON OBJECTIVES

1. **To read for different purposes in varied sources**
   - Selection: Web Site
2. **To read in order to research self-selected and assigned topics**
   - Reading Strategy
3. **To analyze literary elements**
   - Compare Literary Forms

Answers

◆ **Apply the Reading Strategy**

1. Users can click on the name "Nigel Strudwick," which is highlighted in the main text, to learn more about the probable author of the page. (They may also find out more about those responsible under "Announcements" and "Bulletin Board.")
2. Users who wish to find an Egyptian exhibit near them should click on "Museums" in the sidebar, and possibly on "Institutions" as well.

◆ **Compare Literary Forms**

In "By the Waters of Babylon," John's attitude toward the past civilization begins as one of awe, curiosity, and reverence. He ends with the sobering realization that the wonders of the past were created—and destroyed—by men and women just like himself. By contrast, this site treats the past as a territory to be researched in cooperation with others in the present day. There is less sense of the mystery of the past, of the way it intrudes on or is cordoned off from the present, or of the balancing realization that the people of the past shared much in common with those of the present.

Connecting to "By the Waters of Babylon," Stephen Vincent Benét, p. 500

To connect this Web page to Stephen Vincent Benét's "By the Waters of Babylon," ask students to offer images suggesting the distant past. *Possible responses: The pyramids; cave paintings; ruined columns; fossils; museum reconstructions of historic sites.* Then, ask them to think over their answers and explain whether there is a sense in which the past can be located in a specific place. *Possible responses: Yes. While the past itself no longer exists, the signs of the past may be concentrated in special places, such as ruins, museums, and so on.* Explain to students that both Benét's story and this Web site situate the past in a special "place." One places the past in a distant, dangerous zone; the other makes the past accessible through a computer. Have students read or review "By the Waters of Babylon" and look over the Egyptology Web, focusing on the way each "places" the past. Then, have them answer the "Compare Literary Forms" question on this page.

Prepare and Engage

LESSON OBJECTIVES

1. **To read for different purposes in varied sources**
   - Selection: Book Review
2. **To read critically to evaluate texts**
   - Reading Strategy
3. **To analyze literary elements**
   - Compare Literary Forms

Connecting to "The Marginal World," Rachel Carson, p. 571

To connect this review of Rachel Carson's *Silent Spring* with her essay "The Marginal World," ask students to discuss various attitudes people take regarding the environment and technology, and the words in which they express these attitudes. For instance, some people might view the wilderness before the arrival of human beings as essentially pure. They might use the phrase "pristine wilderness" to describe this condition. Others might emphasize the benefits that technological progress offers to people. They might use the phrase "strides in technology," suggesting that technological progress is a journey on which it is important to get ahead.

Have students read or review Rachel Carson's "The Marginal World" and this review of *Silent Spring*, paying special attention to the attitude toward the environment or technology presented by each. Then, have students answer the "Compare Literary Forms" question, p. 963.

About the Authors

Bruce N. Ames (1928–) and **Thomas Jukes** (1906–) are science professors at the University of California, Berkeley.

◆ Reading Strategy

Recognize Faulty Modes of Persuasion Language that arouses strong reactions without reasoned support is known as **loaded language.** This review suggests that environmentalism considers itself a "holy cause" and so justifies biased writing. No evidence is provided—"holy cause" is loaded language.

A **non sequitur** is a conclusion that does not follow from prior statements. The reviewers conclude that pesticides lower cancer rates because the vegetables they protect prevent cancer—a non sequitur, since pesticides may still cause cancer.

In a chart like the one below, list examples of loaded language and non sequiturs in this review.

	Loaded Language	Non Sequitur
Example 1	"Holy cause"	Pesticides save vegetables, so "pesticides lead to lower cancer rates."
Explanation of Example 1	Implies that environmentalists are fanatics who distort facts—an unsupported generalization	Vegetables may prevent cancer, but pesticides might still drive up cancer rates.
Example 2		
Explanation of Example 2		

Silent Spring

Bruce N. Ames; Thomas Jukes

Book review, *Reason*, December 1993

Rachel Carson's *Silent Spring* (1962) became the inspiration for the environmental movement. Its elegant prose expressed passionate outrage at the ravaging of beautiful, unspoiled nature by man. Its frightening message was that we are all being injured by deadly poisons (DDT[1] and other pesticides) put out by a callous[2] chemical industry. This message was snapped up by intellectuals, and the book sold over a million copies. Many organizations have sprung up to spread Carson's message.

Rachel Carson set the style for environmentalism. Exaggeration and omission of pertinent[3] contradictory evidence are acceptable for the holy cause.

The book starts with a romanticized vision of a world in harmony, followed by a horror story of an "evil spell that settled on the community: mysterious maladies swept the flocks of chickens; the cattle and sheep sickened and died. . . . Children . . . would be stricken and die within a few hours. . . . The few birds seen anywhere were moribund[4] . . . and could not fly. . . . [A] white granular powder . . . had fallen like snow upon the roofs and the lawns, the fields and the streams."

The powder was DDT, which actually saved tens of millions of lives, more than any substance in history, with the possible exception of antibiotics. The benefits of DDT were omitted from the book. *Silent Spring* said the American robin was "on the verge of extinction," yet Roger Tory Peterson (the dean of American ornithologists[5]) said it was the most numerous bird on the continent. DDT was highly toxic to mosquitoes but of very low toxicity to honey bees and higher animals. In the Third World, DDT saved the lives of millions of children who otherwise would

1. **DDT:** Acronym for dichloro-diphenyl-trichloroethane, a powerful chemical first used as a pesticide in 1939. Its use was restricted by the United States government in 1972.
2. **callous** (kal′ əs) *adj.*: Without feeling.
3. **pertinent** (pur′ tə nənt) *adj.*: Relevant; to the point.
4. **moribund** (môr′ i bund′) *adj.*: Dying.
5. **ornithologists** (ôr′ nə thäl′ ə jists) *n.*: Scientists who study birds.

have been exposed to malaria[6] and other insect-borne diseases.

DDT displaced the more toxic and persistent lead arsenate. DDT was the first of a series of synthetic agricultural chemicals that have advanced public health by increasing the supply and reducing the price of fruits and vegetables. People who eat few fruits and vegetables, compared to those who eat about four or five portions a day, have about double the cancer rate for most types of cancer and run an increased risk of heart disease and cataracts[7] as well. Thus, pesticides lead to lower cancer rates and improved health. Life expectancy has steadily increased in our era of pesticides. Pesticide residues in food are trivial in terms of cancer causation or toxicity. There has never been any convincing evidence that DDT (or pesticide residues in food) has ever caused cancer in man or that DDT had a significant impact on the population of our eagles or other birds.

Carson's fundamental misconception was: "For the first time in the history of the world, every human being is now subjected to contact with dangerous chemicals, from the moment of conception until death." This is nonsense: Every chemical is dangerous if the concentration is too high. Moreover, 99.9 percent of the chemicals humans ingest are natural. For example, 99.99 percent of the pesticides humans eat are natural pesticides produced by plants to kill off predators. About half of all natural chemicals tested at high dose, including natural pesticides, cause cancer in rodents. People determined to rid the world of synthetic chemicals refuse to face these facts. Risk assessment methods build in huge safety factors[8] for synthetic chemicals, while natural chemicals are ignored. Current policy diverts enormous resources from important to unimportant risks.

6. **malaria** (mə ler′ ē ə) *n.*: Disease causing fever and chills, transmitted by mosquitoes.
7. **cataracts** (kat′ ə rakts′) *n.*: Cloudy areas in the lens of the eye that cause blindness.

8. **risk assessment . . . safety factors:** That is, in defining how much of a chemical must be present before it is dangerous, scientists intentionally overestimate the danger.

◆ Apply the Reading Strategy

1. Cite two examples of loaded language and two non sequiturs in the review.
2. Is it a non sequitur to claim that DDT saved the lives of millions, given the fact that it kills disease-bearing insects? Explain.
3. Explain whether the phrase "enormous resources" is an example of loaded language.

◆ Compare Literary Forms

Read or review Rachel Carson's essay "The Marginal World," p. 571. Find an example in her writing that might fit the description given by these reviewers. Then, explain whether you agree with their evaluation.

Answers

◆ Apply the Reading Strategy

1. Uses of loaded language include: "intellectuals" (which has pejorative connotations here; used to describe Carson's audience), "holy cause" (used to describe environmentalism); "romanticized" (used to describe Carson's account of nature before the use of DDT); "trivial" (used to describe the effects of pesticide residues in food); "refuse to face these facts" (used to describe the attitude of those who oppose the use of pesticides); "huge" (used to describe the safety factors used in risk assessment methods); "enormous" (used to describe the amount of resources devoted to the risks of synthetic chemicals). Non sequiturs include: "DDT replaced the more toxic and persistent lead arsenate" (insofar as this suggests that its use is acceptable); pesticides reduce cancer by increasing the availability of cancer-preventing fruits and vegetables; 99.9 percent of the pesticides ingested by people are natural, therefore it is wrong to think of artificial pesticides as a special danger.
2. It is not a non sequitur to claim that DDT saved the lives of millions by killing off disease-carrying insects, since it is clear that reducing the number of these insects could reduce the spread of disease. (Students may note, however, that the writers do not present evidence, such as statistics or a causal analysis, for this point.)
3. "Enormous resources" is loaded language, since it encourages a negative response in the reader but does not support this suggestion with reasons or proof.

◆ Compare Literary Forms

As an example of Carson's "romanticized vision of a world in harmony," students may cite passages from "The Marginal World" such as the following: "Underlying the beauty of the spectacle there is meaning and significance. It is the elusiveness of that meaning that haunts us, that sends us again and again into the natural world where the key to the riddle is hidden" (p. 576).

Prepare and Engage

LESSON OBJECTIVES

1. **To read for different purposes in varied sources**
   - Selection: Critical Commentary
2. **To use a variety of reading strategies to comprehend a critical commentary**
   - Reading Strategy
3. **To analyze literary elements**
   - Compare Literary Forms

Connecting to *Antigone,* Sophocles, p. 670

To connect Aristotle's critical commentary to Sophocles's tragedy *Antigone,* ask students to construct a definition of a tragedy, using examples from plays with which they are familiar. *Possible response: A play involves the presentation of events through the actions of actors; a tragedy is a play with an unhappy ending, such as* Romeo and Juliet, *in which the main characters die.* Then, explain that Aristotle lived in ancient Greece, in the era when the world's first tragedies were still performed in their traditional form. When Aristotle set about defining tragedy, he looked to these plays for examples.

Have students read or review Sophocles' *Antigone*. Then, have them read this selection from Aristotle's *Poetics* and answer the "Compare Literary Forms" questions, p. 965.

About the Author

Aristotle (384–322 B.C.), an ancient Greek thinker, has had an enormous influence on Western ideas. For centuries, Europeans and Arabs have studied his works on astronomy, logic, psychology, metaphysics, and other subjects. He lived at a time when tragedy was still produced in its traditional form.

◆Reading Strategy

Analyze Text Structures: Definitions and Examples

To capture an idea, writers move between **definitions**—statements that apply to many cases—and **examples**—cases that illustrate the definition.

Aristotle defines a reversal as "a change from one state of affairs to its opposite, one which conforms . . . to probability or necessity." This definition applies to a number of tragedies. He next illustrates the definition with examples, including the messenger's arrival in *Oedipus*.

Using a graphic organizer like the one below, list each definition and example in this piece.

Term Defined	Definition	Examples
Reversal	"A change from one state of affairs to its opposite, one which conforms . . . to probability or necessity"	**1.** In *Oedipus*, the arrival of the messenger, who thinks he brings good news but actually brings disaster **2.**

On Tragedy (from *The Poetics*)

Aristotle

Critical commentary

A Description of Tragedy

. . .

Tragedy . . . is a representation of an action that is worth serious attention, complete in itself, and of some amplitude;[1] in language enriched by a variety of artistic devices appropriate to the several parts of the play; presented in the form of action, not narration; by means of pity and fear bringing about the purgation[2] of such emotions. By language that is enriched I refer to language possessing rhythm, and music or song; and by artistic devices appropriate to the several parts I mean that some are produced by the medium of verse alone, and others again with the help of song.

. . .

Reversal, Discovery, and Calamity

As has already been noted, a reversal is a change from one state of affairs to its opposite, one which conforms, as I have said, to probability or necessity. In *Oedipus,*[3] for example, the Messenger who came to cheer Oedipus and relieve him of his fear about his mother did the very opposite by revealing to him who he was. In the *Lynceus*, again, Lynceus is being led off to execution, followed by Danaus[4] who is to kill him, when, as a result of events that occurred earlier, it comes about that he is saved and it is Danaus who is put to death.

As the word itself indicates, a discovery is a change from ignorance to knowledge, and it leads either to love

1. **amplitude** (am′ plə to͞od′) *n.*: Fullness; scope.
2. **purgation** (pʉr gā′ shən) *n.*: Cleansing.
3. ***Oedipus*** (ed′ i pəs) *n.*: *Oedipus Rex,* a tragedy by Sophocles (säf′ ə klēz′) (*c.* 496–406). Oedipus, king of Thebes, mistakenly kills his father and marries his mother, learning of his crime years later.
4. ***Lynceus*** (link′ ā əs) **. . . Danaus** (dan′ ā əs): In Greek mythology, Danaus, King of Argos, instructed his daughters, the Danaïds, to kill their husbands; only Lynceus survived. *Lynceus* is a lost play.

or to hatred between persons destined for good or ill fortune. The most effective form of discovery is that which is accompanied by reversals, like the one in *Oedipus*. There are of course other forms of discovery, for what I have described may happen in relation to inanimate and trifling objects, and moreover it is possible to discover whether a person has done something or not. But the form of discovery most essentially related to the plot and action of the play is the one described above, for a discovery of this kind in combination with a reversal will carry with it either pity or fear, and it is such actions as these that, according to my definition, tragedy represents; and further, such a combination is likely to lead to a happy or an unhappy ending.

As it is persons who are involved in the discovery, it may be that only one person's identity is revealed to another, that of the second being already known. Sometimes, however, a natural recognition of two parties is necessary, as for example, when the identity of Iphigenia was made known to Orestes[5] by the sending of the letter, and a second discovery was required to make him known to Iphigenia.

Two elements of plot, then, reversal and discovery, turn upon such incidents as these. A third is suffering, or calamity. Of these three, reversal and discovery have already been defined. A calamity is an action of a destructive or painful nature, such as death openly represented, excessive suffering, wounding, and the like.

Tragic Action

. . .

We saw that the structure of tragedy at its best should be complex, not simple, and that it should represent actions capable of awakening fear and pity—for this is a characteristic function of representations of this type. It follows in the first place that good men should not be shown passing from prosperity to misery, for this does not inspire fear or pity, it merely disgusts us. Nor should evil men be shown progressing from misery to prosperity. This is the most untragic of all plots, for it has none of the requisites of tragedy; it does not appeal to our humanity, or awaken pity or fear in us. Nor again should an utterly worthless man be seen falling from prosperity into misery. Such a course might indeed play upon our humane feelings, but it would not arouse either pity or fear; for our pity is awakened by undeserved misfortune, and our fear by that of someone just like ourselves—pity for the undeserving sufferer and fear for the man like ourselves—so that the situation in question would have nothing in it either pitiful or fearful.

There remains a mean between these extremes. This is the sort of man who is not conspicuous for virtue and justice, and whose fall into misery is not due to vice and depravity, but rather to some error, a man who enjoys prosperity and a high reputation, like Oedipus and Thyestes[6] and other famous members of families like theirs.

5. **Iphigenia** (if´ ə jə nē´ ə) . . . **Orestes** (or es´ tēz´): Daughter and son of King Agamemnon and Clytemnestra. In *Iphiginea Among the Taurians*, by Euripides (yōō rip´ i dēz´) (*c.* 484–406 B.C.), Orestes is captured and sent to Iphiginea to be sacrificed; she recognizes him and they escape.

6. **Thyestes** (thī es´ tēz´): In Greek mythology, ruler of Mycenae (mī sē´ nē); he, his brother Atreus (ā´ trē əs), and Atreus' descendants (the House of Atreus), committed terrible crimes and met terrible ends.

◆ Apply the Reading Strategy

1. Cite four definitions Aristotle makes. Also cite the example, if any, that illustrates each.
2. Explain the way in which Aristotle uses his definition of tragedy to support a judgment about good tragic plots.

◆ Compare Literary Forms

1. Read or review Sophocles' play *Antigone*, p. 670. Explain whether it contains a reversal, discovery, or calamity as Aristotle defines the terms.
2. Compare your response to the play to Aristotle's definition of the effect of tragedy on viewers.

Answers

◆ Apply the Reading Strategy

1. Aristotle defines *tragedy* as "a representation of an action [series of events] that is worth serious attention, complete in itself, and of some amplitude; in language enriched by a variety of artistic devices . . . presented in the form of action . . . ; [and] by means of pity and fear bringing about the purgation of such emotions." In the course of this text, he gives several examples, including *Oedipus* and *Lynceus*. He defines a *reversal* as "a change from one state of affairs to its opposite, one which conforms . . . to probability or necessity" (that is, a change that is plausible). His examples include the arrival of the Messenger in *Oedipus* and the rescue of Lynceus and execution of Danaus in *Lynceus*. He defines *discovery* as " a change from ignorance to knowledge, [leading] either to love or to hatred between persons destined for good or ill fortune." He gives as examples Oedipus' discovery of his true identity and crime in *Oedipus* and Orestes' and Iphigenia's recognition of each other in *Iphigenia Among the Taurians*. He defines a *calamity* as "an action of a destructive or painful nature." He gives the examples of "death openly represented, excessive suffering, [and] wounding," but no specific textual examples appear.
2. Aristotle defines a tragedy in part as a play that inspires pity and fear, leading to the "purgation" of these emotions. This definition enables him to judge among various plots to single out those that will in fact inspire these emotions. He decides that only a play involving the fall of a man "not conspicuous for virtue and justice," a fall brought about by error is suited to inspire fear and pity. Using this definition, he can judge between good and bad tragedies—plays that do not have this kind of plot are bad tragedies.

◆ Compare Literary Forms

1. Examples of reversal include Creon's transformation from a proud king to a crushed man—a change "from one state of affairs to its opposite" that is plausible. Examples of a discovery include the discovery that Antigone has been burying her brother Polyneices' body and Creon's realization that "Whatever my hands have touched has come to nothing." (Exodus, ll. 137)—both are changes "from ignorance to knowledge, [leading] either to love or hatred between persons destined for good or ill fortune." Examples of calamity include the suicides of Haimon and Eurydice, and Creon's despair at the news—these are "actions of a destructive or painful nature."
2. Answers will vary. Some students may answer that Creon's fall from powerful king to "a walking dead man" (Exodus, l. 12) moved them to pity, since Creon acts in the name of justice, and even to fear, since his mistake might happen to any well-intentioned person. Others may say that his unwillingness to compromise kept them from pitying him. Students may or may not agree that they were "purged" of these emotions.

Prepare and Engage

LESSON OBJECTIVES

1. **To read for different purposes in varied sources**
   - Selection: Historical Essay
2. **To read critically to evaluate texts**
   - Reading Strategy
3. **To analyze literary elements**
   - Compare Literary Forms

Connecting to "The Guitar," Federico García Lorca, p. 856

To connect this historical essay to Federico García Lorca's poem "The Guitar," ask students to identify musical instruments strongly connected with a specific national or ethnic identity. *Suggested responses: The bagpipes are typically associated with Scotland; the pennywhistle with Ireland; the balalaika with Russia; the mandolin with Italy.* Then, explain that the guitar has held an important place in Spanish folk culture for centuries. Beginning in the 1930's, a Spanish classical guitarist named Andrés Segovia brought the guitar new prominence as a "serious" instrument in classical music. Explain that the importance of the guitar for Spain appears both in Lorca's poem and in Hill's historical essay.

Have students read or review Lorca's "The Guitar." Then, have them read Hill's "The History of the Guitar" and answer the "Compare Literary Forms" question, p. 967.

About the Author

Thomas A. Hill (1954–) has pursued a variety of occupations—farming, magazine writing, cabinetmaking. He has also played the guitar on tour as a folk singer.

◆ Reading Strategy

Analyze Characteristics of Texts: Patterns of Organization Writers can organize information in a variety of ways. **Patterns of organization** include chronological order, spatial order, order of importance, and point-by-point comparisons.

In "The History of the Guitar," the author orders much of his information chronologically, starting with the guitar's earliest ancestors and then moving to later instruments. He also compares instruments point-by-point.

Using a graphic organizer like the one below, note an example of items that are ordered chronologically (one example has been provided). Complete the example of a point-by-point comparison. Then, find another example of this pattern.

Pattern of Organization	Examples
Chronological Order	*Topic 1.* Greeks had stringed instruments with sound boxes. *Topic 2.* These instruments influenced English gitterns and Spanish vihuelas.
Point-by-Point Comparison	*Topic 1.* Gittern and vihuela *versus* guitar: body shape *Topic 2.* ______ ______

The History of the Guitar

Thomas A. Hill

Historical essay

. . .

When we attempt to pinpoint the origins of deliberately produced, carefully designed instruments, we run into problems, because the very first instrument makers were not very concerned with posterity. They did not leave written records. One approach we might try, in an effort to find out where the guitar came from, would be an examination of languages.

The ancient Assyrians,[1] four thousand years ago, had an instrument that they called a *chetarah.* We know little more about it other than that it was a stringed instrument with a sound-box, but the name is intriguing. The ancient Hebrews had their *kinnura,* the Chaldeans[2] their *qitra,* and the Greeks their *cithara* and *citharis*—which Greek writers of the day were careful to emphasize were *not* the same instrument. It is with the Greeks, in fact, that the first clear history of the evolution of an instrument begins; some of this history can again be traced with purely linguistic devices. The cithara and citharis were members of a family of musical instruments called *fides*—a word that is ancient Greek for "strings." From the *fides* family it is easy to draw lines to the medieval French *vielle,* the German *fiedel,* the English *fithele* or *fiddle,* and the *vihuela,* national instrument of medieval Spain. Significantly, much of the music for the vihuela (of which a great deal survives to the present day) can easily be transcribed[3] for the guitar.

In England, the influences of the cithara and citharis led to the evolution of such instruments as the *cither, zither, cittern,* and *gittern,* with which instrument the linguistic parallel we seek is fairly easy to draw.

1. **Assyrians** (ə sir′ ē ənz): Founders of an ancient empire in the Middle East, flourishing in the seventh century B.C.
2. **Chaldeans** (kal dē′ ənz): A people that rose to power in Babylon, an ancient empire of the Middle East, during the sixth century B.C.
3. **transcribed** (tran skrībd′) *v.*: Adapted a piece of music for an instrument other than the one for which it was written.

Gitterns dating back to 1330 can be seen in the British Museum. In Spain, there is music for the vihuela that dates back at least that far.

What did these instruments look like? Superficially, they bore a substantial resemblance to the guitar as we know it today, although the sides seldom curved in as far as do the sides of the modern guitar. They were usually strung with *pairs* of strings, or *courses*, much like a modern twelve-string guitar. The two strings of each course were tuned either in unison or an octave[4] apart. For a while, there seemed to be no standard for the number of courses an instrument should have; there are both vihuelas and gitterns with as few as four courses and as many as seven. By the fifteenth century, the vihuela seems to have settled on six as the standard number of courses. . . . In England, the gittern settled down to four courses. . . . Historians of this period do note the existence in Spain of an instrument called the *guitarra*. . . . But no music was being written for this instrument, and nobody seems to have been paying much attention to it.

Meanwhile, in Africa, the Arabs had been playing an instrument that they called *al-ud*, or "the wood," for centuries. When the Moors crossed the Straits of Gibraltar[5] in the twelfth century to conquer Spain, they brought this instrument with them. It quickly became popular, and by the time anybody who spoke English was talking about it, al-ud had become *lute*. The lute's main contribution to the evolution of the guitar as we know it today seems to have been the fret, a metal bar on the fingerboard. Until the arrival of the lute, the European forerunners of the guitar had no frets at all. Since the fret made it a little easier to play the same tune the same way more than once, and helped to standardize tunings, it was a resounding success. The first Arabic lutes in Europe had movable frets, tied to the neck, usually about eight in number. Consequently, the first vihuelas to which frets were added also had movable ones.

The lute—or rather the people who brought it to Europe—made another important contribution. The Moorish artistic influence, blowing the cobwebs away from stodgy Spanish art and society, created an artistic climate that encouraged music to flourish. And so the instruments on which the music was played flourished as well, and continued to evolve and improve. This is a contribution that cannot be overestimated.

If any general lines can be drawn, perhaps it can be said that descendants of the original al-ud, crossing the Straits of Gibraltar, collided in Spain with the descendants of the Greek cithara and citharis. Sprinkled with a little bit of gittern influence from England, the result led ultimately to what we know today as the guitar.

4. **unison** (yo͞on′ ə sən) . . . **octave** (äk′ tiv): A unison consists of two tones of the same pitch. An octave consists of two tones that are eight notes apart in the scale. The pitches in an octave sound "the same" and are named by the same note.

5. **Moors** (mo͝orz) . . . **Gibraltar** (ji brôl′ tər): Groups of Moors, an Arab people of north Africa, invaded Spain at various times, starting in the eighth century A.D. The Straits of Gibraltar are waters dividing Spain from Africa.

◆ Apply the Reading Strategy

1. What pattern of organization does Hill use when he discusses the Assyrians before he discusses Greek instruments?

2. What pattern of organization leads Hill to discuss the Arabian al-ud after describing the English gittern and Spanish vihuela?

◆ Compare Literary Forms

Read or review Federico García Lorca's poem "The Guitar," p. 856. Explain whether Hill's essay helps you to understand the special place of the guitar in the heart of a Spaniard such as Lorca.

Answers

◆ Apply the Reading Strategy

1. In discussing the Assyrians before discussing the Greeks, Hill is following chronological order: Assyrian civilization pre-dates Greek civilization. He also follows order of importance: the Greeks leave the first clear record of guitar-like instruments, so they are more important to his discussion than the Assyrians.
2. Hill discusses the al-lud after describing the gittern and the vihuela for chronological reasons—the al-lud influenced the vihuela after vihuelas had existed for some time. He is also using a kind of spatial order, breaking down the parts of the guitar and comparing them with these early instruments. He has already discussed the strings and body shape of the vihuela and gittern. Next, he discusses frets, which were added to these instruments as a result of the influence of the al-lud.

◆ Compare Literary Forms

Hill's essay shows that the guitar and its predecessors were important in Spanish culture for centuries. He also suggests that, along with technical innovations contributing to the guitar, the Moors brought new cultural energy to Spanish music. Traces of this exciting influence, interwoven with Spanish identity, may be embodied in the guitar in Spanish culture. In Lorca's poem, the guitar is so deeply embedded in life that its song seems to inhabit the water, the wind, (ll. 11-13) and those desires that are for what is distant or impossible (ll. 17-24).

Prepare and Engage

LESSON OBJECTIVES

1. **To read for different purposes in varied sources**
   - Selection: Atlas Entry
2. **To use a variety of reading strategies to comprehend an atlas entry**
   - Reading Strategy

Connecting to the Sundiata, p. 934

To connect this atlas entry for Mali to the *Sundiata,* an epic of Mali, explain to students that epics are part of an oral tradition—literature passed from one storyteller to another, but not written down. Such literature has a strong link with a particular people in a particular place. In the heroic deeds they narrate, epics express the central values of a culture and so create an image of a people for itself.

Have students skim the atlas entry of Mali, and then have them speculate on the life people may have led there in the past. *Suggested response: Though much of Mali is desert, the River Niger brings water to the central and southwestern regions. People may have farmed and traded along the river.*

Next, have students scan the introductory material to the *Sundiata,* pp. 932–933 for information on the people who created the epic, their name, and their way of life. Then, have students answer the "Compare Literary Forms" question, p. 969.

Analyzing Real-World Texts

Background

The maps in an atlas show physical features of the world, such as cities, mountains, rivers, and roads. They may also provide information on climate, population, and political systems. The Dorling Kindersley atlas combines the two kinds of information in one visual display.

◆ Reading Strategy

Skimming and Scanning

By **skimming** a text, you can get an idea of the organization and scope of a work before reading it. Read quickly, taking in groups of words. Stop for headings and other set-off text, such as bold, italicized, or oversized.

By **scanning,** you can locate specific information fast. Let your eyes move quickly over the page. Look for words related to the information you are seeking. Stop and read the sections where they are found.

Skim this entry from an atlas. Use a graphic organizer such as the one below to record each kind of information you can find.

Subjects Covered	How I Know
Politics of Mali	Heading
Languages spoken in Mali	Icon of person with dialogue balloon

Mali

Adapted from the Dorling Kindersley *World Reference Atlas*

MALI

Official Name: Republic of Mali
Capital: Bamako
Population: 10.8 million
Currency: CFA franc
Official Language: French

Mali is landlocked in the heart of West Africa. Its mostly flat terrain comprises virtually uninhabited Saharan plains in the north and more fertile savanna land in the south, where most of the population live. The River Niger irrigates the central and southwestern regions of the country. Following independence in 1960, Mali experienced a long period of largely single-party rule. It became a multiparty democracy in 1992.

CLIMATE

In the south, intensely hot, dry weather precedes the westerly rains. Mali's northern half is almost rainless.

TRANSPORTATION

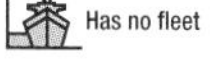

Mali is linked by rail with the port of Dakar in Senegal, and by good roads to the port of Abidjan in Ivory Coast.

TOURISM

Tourism is largely safari-oriented, although the historic cities of Djénné, Gao and Mopti, lying on the banks of the River Niger, also attract visitors. A national domestic airline began operating in 1990.

PEOPLE

Mali's most significant ethnic group, the Bambara, is also politically dominant. The Bambara speak the *lingua franca* of the River Niger, which is shared with other groups including the Malinke. The relationship between the Bambara–Malinke majority and the Tuareg nomads of the Saharan north is often tense and sometimes violent. As with elsewhere in Africa, the extended family, often based around the village, is a vital social security system and a link between the urban and rural poor. There are a few powerful women in Mali but, in general, women have little status.

POLITICS

The successful transition to multiparty politics in 1992 followed the overthrow in the previous year of Moussa Traoré, Mali's dictator for 23 years. The army's role was crucial in leading the coup, while Colonel Touré, who acted as interim president, was responsible for the swift return to civilian rule in less than a year. The change marks Mali's first experience of multipartyism. Maintaining good relations with the Tuaregs, after a peace agreement in 1991, is a key issue. However, the main challenge facing President Alpha Oumar Konaré's government is to alleviate poverty while placating the opposition, which feels that the luxury of multipartyism is something that Mali cannot afford. As Konaré's austerity measures have begun to take effect, opposition to his policies has increased.

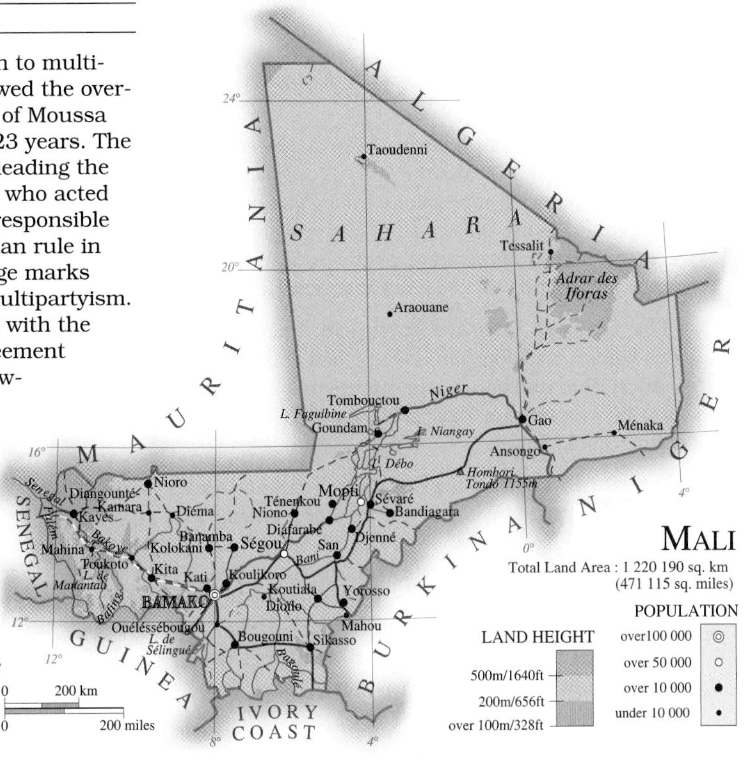

◆ Apply the Reading Strategy

1. Name three different kinds of information you can find in this entry. For each, explain whether you discovered it by skimming or by scanning.
2. Referring to this entry, explain an important change to the political system of Mali in the 1990's. How did you find this information?
3. Scan the map to locate the capital of Mali. Explain how you found it.

◆ Compare Literary Forms

Scan the introductory material to the *Sundiata,* an epic of Old Mali, pp. 932–933. Then, refer to this atlas to determine whether the ethnic group that told the story of Sundiata is the most dominant group in Mali.

Answers

◆ Apply the Reading Strategy

1. Students may note that they can find information on Mali's climate, transportation, tourism industry, people, politics, languages, population density, capital city, currency, and geography. They can discover the presence of each of these various kinds of information by skimming and stopping for large-type heads or distinctive icons. (The presence of the map itself shows that information on geography is available.) Scanning is useful for finding particular pieces of information, not for determining the kinds of information available.
2. According to this entry, the country changed from a dictatorship to a multiparty system in 1992. Students may say that they found this information by skimming the text, and then scanning under the heading "Politics," stopping for numbers and words such as "1992," "multiparty," and "dictator."
3. Students may note that the name of the capital of Mali, Bamako, appears in capital letters in a special font in the map. While skimming the page, they may have also discovered the name of the capital, which appears set off at the beginning of the entry.

◆ Compare Literary Forms

By skimming, then scanning under the head "People," students will find that the Bambara are the dominant group of Mali. By skimming the introductory pages to the *Sundiata,* then scanning the section on the author and the "Background for Understanding" (pp. 932, 933), students will discover that the epic is from from the Mandinka people, not the Bambara.

Prepare and Engage

LESSON OBJECTIVES

To read world literature in order to understand different cultures and the common elements across cultures, to respond to the texts, and to analyze literary elements within the texts
- Critical Thinking

How to Use Literature in Translation

This section contains seven selections, each presented in its original Spanish and in an English translation. These bilingual selections are organized in groups, according to literary or cultural affinities. Each of these smaller sections is accompanied by:
- an introduction containing background information on the author or authors and, for every section but one, a relevant cultural or literary note
- a follow-up consisting of critical thinking questions and one or more questions requiring students to compare a Spanish original with its English translation.

Following are strategies for using Literature in Translation:
- Have students read and discuss The Art of Translation, p. 970. Ask them to discuss their own previous ideas about translation.
- Have students who do not speak or read Spanish increase their knowledge of Spanish culture and literature by reading The Art of Translation, the introductory material for each section, and the English translations. Also have them answer the follow-up questions, including those that ask them to compare a translation with its original.
- Have students who speak and read Spanish read the Spanish originals aloud to the class and serve as experts in evaluating answers to questions comparing English and Spanish texts.
- Pair a Spanish-speaker with a student who does not speak Spanish, and have them alternate reading the Spanish original and the translation aloud to the class. Then have students work on the questions individually or in groups.
- Pair a Spanish-speaker with a student who does not speak Spanish, and have them read the selections together and answer the questions.
- Have a Spanish-speaker and a student who does not speak Spanish collaborate on a retranslation of one or more lines from a selection. Then have them discuss their translation with the class, comparing and contrasting it with the translation in the book.

You will probably devise your own additional strategies for using Literature in Translation.

Literature in Translation
Paired Readings in English and Spanish

The Art of Translation

This section contains literary works that were written in Spanish, and it shows the Spanish originals together with English translations. Even if you do not read Spanish, the use of both languages will give you a greater awareness of literature written in Spanish and a greater appreciation for the work that translators do.

The Spanish Literary Tradition Spanish has a rich literary tradition, both in Spain and in the Americas. That tradition is well represented here, with works by writers from Mexico, El Salvador, Chile, Peru, and the United States.

Translation Seeing the original and its translation together will remind you that a translator worked hard to create a faithful English version of the Spanish text. Translation *is* hard work because no language corresponds exactly to another. Translators must therefore make many choices as they create a version of the original in another language, and qualified translators can disagree about these choices. That is why translation is an art, not a science.

About the Authors

Octavio Paz [ôk tä´ vyô päs] (1914–1998) traveled around the world as a diplomat for his native Mexico. In addition to his imaginative poetry, he wrote literary criticism and essays. Paz was awarded the Nobel Prize for Literature in 1990.

Gabriela Mistral [gä brē e´ lä mē sträl´] (1889–1957) grew up in northern Chile and had a many-sided career as an educator, cultural minister, diplomat, and poet. In 1945, she became the first Latin American woman to win the Nobel Prize for Literature.

Literary Note

Each of these poets explores the theme of personal identity—*who am I?*— in a different way. Paz experiments with summarizing the whole meaning of his life in a few words ("Epitaph for No Stone"). Mistral reenacts the way in which we lose the world and ourselves every night ("Night").

Epitaph for No Stone

Octavio Paz
Translated by Eliot Weinberger

Mixcoac was my village: three nocturnal syllables,
a half-mask of shadow across a face of sun.
Our Lady, Mother Dustcloud, came,
came and ate it. I went out in the world.
My words were my house, air my tomb.

Epitafio sobre ninguna piedra

Octavio Paz

Mixcoac fue mi pueblo: tres sílabas nocturnas,
un antifaz de sombra sobre un rostro solar.
Vino Nuestra Señora, la Tolvanera Madre.
Vino y se lo comió. Yo andaba por el mundo.
Mi casa fueron mis palabras, mi tumba el aire.

Traducción de literatura

Lecturas en Inglés y Español en pareja

Night

Gabriela Mistral
Translated by Doris Dana

Mountain ranges dissolve,
cattle wander astray,
the sun returns to its forge,
all the world slips away.

Orchard and garden are fading,
the farmhouse already immersed.
My mountains submerge their crests
and their living cry.

All creatures are sliding aslant
down toward forgetfulness and sleep.
You and I, also, my baby,
tumble down toward night's keep.

Noche

Gabriela Mistral

Las montañas se deshacen,
el ganado se ha perdido;
el sol regresa a su fragua:
todo el mundo se va huido.

Se va borrando la huerta,
la granja se ha sumergido
y mi cordillera sume
su cumbre y su grito vivo.

Las criaturas resbalan
de soslayo hacia el olvido,
y también los dos rodamos
hacia la noche, mi niño.

Critical Thinking

1. What do you think Paz means in "Epitaph for No Stone" when he says that "Mother Dustcloud. . . ate" his village? **[Interpret]**
2. In "Epitaph for No Stone," how could "words" have been Paz's "house"? **[Interpret]**
3. What feeling does "Night" convey about the loss of identity in "forgetfulness and sleep"? Explain. **[Analyze]**
4. Sum up who you are in a brief paragraph for your school yearbook. **[Relate]**

Compare English and Spanish Texts

5. Compare the first lines of the Spanish original and the English translation of "Epitaph for No Stone." What are the Spanish counterparts for the English words *village, three, nocturnal,* and *syllables?* **[Compare and Contrast]**
6. Look at the final words in each line of the Spanish and English texts of "Night." Does the English translation exactly reproduce the rhyme scheme of the Spanish original? Explain. **[Compare and Contrast]**

Beyond the Selection

INTERNET
Students can learn more at the following Web sites. Please be aware, however, that this site may have changed from the time we published this information.

For background information on Octavio Paz, go to: **http://nobelprizes.com/nobel/literature/1990a.html**

For background information on Gabriela Mistral, go to: **http://nobelprizes.com/nobel/literature/1945a.html**

We *strongly recommend* that you preview the sites before you send students to them.

More About the Authors
For more information on and selections by Octavio Paz and Gabriela Mistral, see pp. 86–89.

Answers

◆ Critical Thinking

1. This question will challenge students. They might interpret the line to mean that the village, for some reason, became part of the earth again. It might have been destroyed by natural forces or by human builders clearing it away to make room for other structures.
2. In a sense, an author "lives" in the words he or she writes. Those words, rather than a real house, are the author's dwelling place, especially after the author dies.
3. Students might respond that because the poem seems like a lullaby, it conveys the feeling that the temporary loss of identity in sleep is a good thing.
4. Students should briefly list and explain their most important qualities, attitudes, and beliefs.

◆ Compare English and Spanish Texts

5. The Spanish counterparts are as follows:

village	pueblo
three	tres
nocturnal	nocturnas
syllables	silabas

6. The English version does not exactly reproduce the rhyme scheme of the Spanish version. In the Spanish original, the second and fourth lines of all three stanzas rhyme. However, in the translation, the second and fourth lines rhyme only in the first and last stanzas.

Prepare and Engage

LESSON OBJECTIVES

To read world literature in order to understand different cultures and the common elements across cultures, to respond to the texts, and to analyze literary elements within the texts

- Critical Thinking

About the Authors

César Vallejo [sā′ zär və yā′ hō] (1892–1938), from a small town in northern Peru, is now recognized as one of the greatest poets of the twentieth century. Among his important books are *Trilce* and *Human Poems.* Robert Bly wrote that Vallejo "had a tremendous feeling for... his family."

Tino Villanueva [tē′ nō vi yä nwā′ və] (1941–), who comes from San Marcos, Texas, teaches Spanish at Boston University. His book of poems *Scene from the Movie "Giant,"* one of four books of poetry he has written, won a 1994 American Book Award.

To My Brother Miguel

in memoriam

César Vallejo
Translated by John Knoepfle and James Wright

Brother, today I sit on the brick bench outside the house,
where you make a bottomless emptiness.
I remember we used to play at this hour of the day, and mama
would calm us: "There now, boys . . ."

Now I go hide
as before, from all these evening
prayers, and I hope that you will not find me.
In the parlor, the entrance hall, the corridors.
Later, you hide, and I do not find you.
I remember we made each other cry,
brother, in that game.

Miguel, you hid yourself
one night in August, nearly at daybreak,
but instead of laughing when you hid, you were sad.
And your other heart of those dead afternoons
is tired of looking and not finding you. And now
shadows fall on the soul.

Listen, brother, don't be too late
coming out. All right? Mama might worry.

A mi hermano Miguel

in memoriam

César Vallejo

Hermano, hoy estoy en el poyo de la casa,
donde nos haces una falta sin fondo!
Me acuerdo que jugábamos esta hora, y que mamá
nos acariciaba: "Pero, hijos . . ."

Ahora yo me escondo,
como antes, todas estas oraciones
vespertinas, y espero que tú no des conmigo.
Por la sala, el zaguán, los corredores.
Después, te ocultas tú, y yo no doy contigo.
Me acuerdo que nos hacíamos llorar,
hermano, en aquel juego.

Miguel, tú te escondiste
una noche de agosto, al alborear;
pero, en vez de ocultarte riendo, estabas triste.
Y tu gemelo corazón de esas tardes
extintas se ha aburrido de no encontrarte. Y ya
cae sombra en el alma.

Oye hermano, no tardes
en salir. ¿Bueno? Puede inquietarse mamá.

Traducción de literatura
Lecturas en Inglés y Español en pareja

I Only Know That Now

Tino Villanueva
Translated by James Hoggard

In memory,
that moving wind,
I'm the muted places
where I've been,
I'm the suns
that stunned me,
the fatigue I felt as a child
and the diminishment that came with it.
And maybe
this solidarity of words
is inadequate
to tell all that
and, as is true in understanding time,
it's not enough
to understand
how soul measures past.
I only know
that now that I see myself
in the path I've made
I'm at home with myself and all that
    means,
I recognize
how much of all I've been
waits in memory.
And I could never walk away from
anything behind this story.

Sólo sé que ahora

Tino Villanueva

En el viento móvil
del recuerdo
soy los lugares apagados
donde he estado,
los soles
que me dejaron azonzado,
los cansancios infantiles
y su negación acorde.
Y pienso que quizás esta
solidaridad de palabras
no sea suficiente
para contar
tal y como entiendo el tiempo,
no sea suficiente
para entender
cómo el alma mide el tiempo atrás.
Sólo sé
que ahora que me veo
en la vereda que he formado
estoy conmigo y con mi todo,
reconozco
que todo cuanto he sido
espera en la memoria.
Las razones de esta historia
jamás podré abdicar.

Critical Thinking

1. In "To My Brother Miguel," why do you think the brothers "made each other cry" in the game of hide-and-seek? **[Infer]**
2. In what way is Miguel "hiding" as Vallejo writes the poem? **[Interpret]**
3. What specific passages in "To My Brother Miguel" suggest Vallejo's love for his brother? Explain. **[Support]**
4. In "I Only Know That Now," does Villanueva suggest positive or negative experiences in talking about his past? Explain. **[Classify]**
5. What passage in "I Only Know That Now" indicates that Villanueva has accepted everything that has happened to him? Explain. **[Support]**
6. In what way would human life be different if memory extended back only a single year? **[Hypothesize]**

Compare English and Spanish Texts

7. Using the English translation of "To My Brother Miguel," identify the Spanish word for *brother* and find where it appears in the Spanish original. **[Compare and Contrast]**

Answers

◆ Critical Thinking

1. Students may respond that each brother caused the other to cry by hiding so well that he could not be found.
2. Students will probably see that, at the time Vallejo writes, his brother is "hiding" in death.
3. Students will probably realize that Vallejo suggests his love for his brother by stressing the sadness of his absence (he calls it "a bottomless emptiness"). He also expresses tenderness by addressing his brother directly as "Brother" and "Miguel."
4. Students may respond that Villanueva suggests negative experiences in talking about his past. He says that "suns . . . stunned" him and he felt "fatigue." Being stunned and feeling tired are negative experiences.
5. Students may observe that line 20 of the poem—"I'm at home with myself and all that means"—indicates that Villanueva has accepted what has happened. To feel "at home with" oneself means not to deny one's past experiences. This is confirmed in lines 24–25, in which he says, "And I could never walk away from / anything behind this story." He won't deny his past.
6. Most students will realize that such a limitation would result in a curtailment of personal affection and loyalty, which are based on memory. This limitation might also affect people's ability to formulate long-term goals, an ability which also requires memory.

◆ Compare English and Spanish Texts

7. The Spanish word for *brother* is *hermano,* and it can be most easily spotted in the title. It also appears in lines 1 and 18 of the Spanish original.

Prepare and Engage

LESSON OBJECTIVES

To read world literature in order to understand different cultures and the common elements across cultures, to respond to the texts, and to analyze literary elements within the texts

- Critical Thinking

More About the Author

For more information about Federico García Lorca, see p. 854. For a translation of his poem "The Guitar," see p. 856.

Literature in Translation

Paired Readings in English and Spanish

About the Authors

Federico García Lorca [fe de *r*ē´ kô gä*r* *th*ē´ ä lô*r*´ kä] (1898–1936) drew inspiration for his poetry from the diverse cultures of his native Andalusia [an´ da lo͞o´ zha] in southern Spain. He was especially influenced by the songs and dances of gypsies.

Pablo Neruda [pä´ blô ne *r*o͞o´ *th*ä] (1904–1973) was a Chilean poet and Nobel Prize-winner who had a deep feeling for his country and its people. In 1948, he had to flee from the secret police of the Chilean dictator González Videla. Neruda wrote "It Was the Grape's Autumn" to honor one of the men who helped save his life by hiding him.

Cultural Note

The Aztec were the dominant Native American group when the Spanish arrived in what is now Mexico. As the Aztec myth "The Sun and the Moon" indicates, the Aztec believed that the gods had to sacrifice themselves to create the universe.

Literary Note

The selections in this group show that poetry and legend help readers look at the natural world with fresh eyes. The poets help readers appreciate the hypnotic beauty of the Moon ("The Moon Rising") and a way of life in touch with the Earth ("It Was the Grape's Autumn"). The Mexican legend gives an imaginative explanation for the origin of the sun and the moon.

The Moon Rising

Federico García Lorca
Translated by Lysander Kemp

When the moon rises,
the bells hang silent,
and impenetrable footpaths
appear.

When the moon rises,
the sea covers the land,
and the heart feels
like an island in infinity.

Nobody eats oranges
under the full moon.
One must eat fruit
that is green and cold.

When the moon rises,
moon of a hundred equal faces,
the silver coinage
sobs in the pocket.

La luna asoma

Federico García Lorca

Cuando sale la luna
se pierden las campanas
y aparecen las sendas
impenetrables.

Cuando sale la luna,
el mar cubre la tierra
y el corazón se siente
isla en el infinito.

Nadie come naranjas
bajo la luna llena.
Es preciso comer
fruta verde y helada.

Cuando sale la luna
de cien rostros iguales,
la moneda de plata
solloza en el bolsillo.

Traducción de literatura

Lecturas en Inglés y Español en pareja

"It Was the Grape's Autumn"

Pablo Neruda
Translated by James Wright and Robert Bly

It was the grape's autumn.
The dense vinefield shivered.
The white clusters, half-hidden,
found their mild fingers cold,
and the black grapes were filling
their tiny stout udders
from a round and secret river.
The man of the house, an artisan
with a hawk's face, read to me
the pale earth book
about the darkening days.
His kindliness saw deep into the fruit,
the trunk of the vine, and the work
of the pruning knife, which lets the tree keep
its simple goblet shape.
He talked to his horses
as if to immense boys: behind him
the five cats trailed,
and the dogs of that household,
some arched and slow moving,
others running crazily
under the cold peach trees.
He knew each branch,
each scar on his trees,
and his ancient voice taught me
while it was stroking his horses.

"Era el otoño de las uvas"

Pablo Neruda

Era el otoño de las uvas.
Temblaba el parral numeroso.
Los racimos blancos, velados,
escarchaban sus dulces dedos,
y las negras uvas llenaban
sus pequeñas ubres repletas
de un secreto río redondo.
El dueño de casa, artesano
de magro rostro, me leía
el pálido libro terrestre
de los días crepusculares.
Su bondad conocía el fruto,
la rama troncal y el trabajo
de la poda que deja al árbol
su desnuda forma de copa.
A los caballos conversaba
como a inmensos niños: seguían
detrás de él los cinco gatos
y los perros de aquella casa,
unos enarcados y lentos,
otros corriendo locamente
bajo los fríos durazneros.
Él conocía cada rama,
cada cicatriz de los árboles,
y su antigua voz me enseñaba
acariciando a los caballos.

The Sun and the Moon

Retold by Genevieve Barlow and William N. Stivers

Before there was light in the world, the gods of Teotihuacan [tā ō tē wä kän′, city of the gods near Mexico City] were talking among themselves, trying to decide who was going to give light to the world. All the gods were in a large room in one of the many temples. They asked, "Who among us are willing to give light to the world?" All of them knew that to give light to the world was not an easy task. It was going to cost the lives of those who decided to do it, for they would have to throw themselves into a great fire.

No one answered at first. Then, one of the youngest of the gods, Tecuciztecatl, spoke and said in a loud voice, "I am willing to throw myself into the fire." Everyone said together, "The god Tecuciztecatl is a great god! We all congratulate him."

But there had to be two gods and there was no one else among them brave enough to accompany Tecuciztecatl. He made fun of the others saying, "Where is there a god as brave as I in the whole region? Isn't there anyone willing to sacrifice his life to give light to the world?"

No one answered. All of them kept silent for a few minutes and then they began to talk among themselves. During this discussion, there was so much noise and such moving about that no one noticed that a very old god got up slowly and stood in front of them all.

The old god was poor and humble. His clothing was not elegant. All the others wanted to know why he had stood up.

"What does he want?" some said.

"Who does he think he is?" others commented.

El sol y la luna

Narración: Genevieve Barlow y William N. Stivers

Antes de que hubiera luz en el mundo, los dioses de Teotihuacán hablaron entre sí para decidir quiénes iban a dar luz al mundo. Todos los dioses estaban en un salón grande de uno de los muchos templos. Preguntaron:

—¿Quiénes de nosotros van a dar luz al mundo?

Todos sabían que dar luz al mundo no era una tarea fácil. Iba a costar la vida de los que decidieran hacerlo, pues tenían que echarse en una gran hoguera.

Nadie contestó al principio. Luego uno de los más jóvenes de los dioses, Tecuciztécatl, habló y dijo en voz alta:

—Yo estoy dispuesto a echarme al fuego.

Todos a una voz dijeron: —¡El dios Tecuciztécatl es un gran dios! Todos te felicitamos.

Pero necesitaban dos dioses y no había otro dios lo suficientemente valiente para acompañar a Tecuciztécatl. Él se burló de los otros diciendo:

—¿Dónde hay un dios tan valiente como yo en toda la región? ¿Nadie se atreve a ofrecer su vida para dar luz al mundo?

Nadie contestó. Todos guardaron silencio por unos minutos y luego comenzaron a discutir entre sí. Durante la discusión el ruido era tan grande y el movimiento tanto que no se dieron cuenta de que un dios viejito se levantó lentamente y se puso delante de todos ellos.

El viejito era pobre y humilde. Su ropa no era elegante. Los otros quisieron saber por qué él se había levantado.

—¿Qué quiere él? —dijeron algunos.

—¿Quién cree él que es? —dijeron otros.

English

"We do not have time for the old now," the younger gods said.

"He is not brave enough," some of the gods shouted.

"How can an old god want to give up his life?" the chiefs of the gods said.

But the old god, raising his hand, asked for silence and said, "I am Nanoatzin, and I am old indeed, but I am willing to give my life. The world needs light. And, since there are no other volunteers, I want to offer what is left of my life to give light to the world."

After a moment of silence they all shouted, "Great is Nanoatzin!" If the congratulations given to Tecuciztecatl were many, those given to Nanoatzin were even more.

Then, they all began to make the necessary garments for the ceremony. They were truly beautiful, made of very fine cotton, with gold, silver, and bird feathers of every color.

For a whole week no one ate anything. All of them meditated, because giving the world light was very important.

When the day arrived, a great fire was lit in the center of the room. The light illuminated everything.

Tecuciztecatl was the first to approach the fire, but the heat was so intense that he moved back. Four times he tried to enter, but he was never brave enough.

Then Nanoatzin, the old god, got up and walked toward the fire. He entered the fire and lay down calmly.

"Oh!" everyone said reverently. And everyone repeated in a whisper, "Great is Nanoatzin!"

Then it was Tecuciztecatl's turn. He was ashamed. The old god was not afraid, but he was. So he threw himself into the fire too.

All the gods waited and when there was no longer any fire, all of them got up and left the room to wait for the light.

Español

—No tenemos tiempo para los viejitos ahora—dijeron los más jóvenes.

—Él no es lo suficientemente valiente—gritaron unos de los dioses.

—¿Cómo puede querer un viejito dar su vida?—dijeron los principales de entre los dioses.

Pero el viejito, levantando la mano, pidiendo silencio, dijo:

—Y soy Nanoatzín, viejo sí, pero dispuesto a dar mi vida. El mundo necesita luz. Como no hay otros voluntarios, quiero ofrecer lo que queda de mi vida para dar luz al mundo.

Después de un momento de silencio, —Grande es Nanoatzín—gritaron todos. Si las felicitaciones dadas a Tecuciztécatl fueron muchas, las dadas a Nanoatzín fueron mayores.

Luego todos se pusieron a hacer la ropa necesaria para la ceremonia. Era muy bonita, de algodón muy fino, con oro, plata y plumas de aves de todos colores.

Durante toda una semana nadie comió. Todos estaban en estado de meditación porque dar luz al mundo era muy importante.

Cuando llegó el día, encendieron una gran hoguera en el centro del salón. La luz iluminó todo.

Tecuciztécatl fue el primero que se acercó al fuego, pero el calor era tanto que él se retiró. Cuatro veces trató de entrar, pero él no se atrevía.

Luego Nanoatzín, el viejito, se levantó y caminó hacia la hoguera. Él entró en el fuego y se acostó tranquilamante.

—¡Ay!—dijeron todos con mucha reverencia. Y en voz baja todos repitieron: ¡Grande es Nanoatzín!

Después le tocó a Tecuciztécatl. Él tenía vergüenza. El viejito no tenía miedo y él sí. Así que él se echó al fuego también.

Todos los dioses esperaron y, cuando ya no había fuego, todos se levantaron y salieron del salón para esperar las luces.

Answers

◆ Critical Thinking

1. Students may respond that in the first stanza, the rising moon mysteriously seems to silence the bells and make "impenetrable footpaths / appear"; in the second stanza, the rising moon mysteriously influences the tides and makes the heart feel the mystery of "infinity"; in the last stanza, the rising moon causes silver coins to sob mysteriously in one's pocket.
2. Perceptive students may suggest that the guitar, an instrument often used to accompany gypsy music, would be suitable for such a song.
3. Students can choose from among these examples: The man reads "the pale earth book," indicating that he knows about the changing hours of light; "His kindliness saw deep into the fruit," indicating that he understands growing things; "He talked to his horses / as if to immense boys," indicating that he accepts his animals almost as if they are part of his family; "the five cats trailed," indicating they feel close to him; and "He knew each branch, / each scar on his trees," indicating again his knowledge of plants.
4. The life of the gods is not one of pleasure and ease because the gods (or two of them, at least) must sacrifice themselves to create the sun and the moon.

◆ Compare English and Spanish Texts

5. In the Spanish original, the verb precedes the subject: *"sale* la luna / *se pierden* las campanas / y *aparecen* las sendas . . ."
6. (a) In "It Was the Grape's Autumn": *horses* (lines 16 and 26, both versions) are *los caballos*; *cats* (line 18, both versions) are *los gatos*; *dogs* (line 19, both versions) are *los perros*. (b) The Spanish word *gatos* is most closely related to its English counterpart: *cats*. However, students who understand the relationship of the words *cavalier* and *cavalry* to *horses* will see a link with *caballos*.

Literature in Translation
Paired Readings in English and Spanish

English

They did not know from which direction the light would appear, nor how it would appear. Suddenly, a ray of sun appeared in the east, then the full sun. It was very brilliant and everyone knew that it was Nanoatzin because he had entered the fire first.

Then, after some time, another light appeared. It was the moon, and it was as brilliant as the sun.

One of the gods then said, "We should not have two lights that are the same. Nanoatzin entered first. He should have the brighter light. We should darken the second light a little."

Then, another god took a rabbit and threw it into the sky, hitting the moon.

To this day, the sun is brighter than the moon and if one looks carefully at the moon, one can see the tracks of the rabbit.

Español

No sabían de qué dirección ni cómo iba a llegar la luz. De repente, un rayo de sol apareció en el este; luego, el sol entero. Era muy brillante y todos sabían que era Nanoatzín porque él entró en el fuego primero.

Después de algún tiempo, salió también otra luz. Era la luna, y era tan brillante como el sol.

Uno de los dioses luego dijo:

—No debemos tener dos luces iguales. Nanoatzín entró primero. Él debe tener la luz más fuerte. Debemos oscurecer un poco la segunda luz.

Y otro de los dioses agarró un conejo y lo arrojó al cielo, pegándole a la luna.

Hasta el día de hoy, el sol es más brillante que la luna; y si uno se fija bien en la luna, puede ver las huellas del conejo.

Critical Thinking

1. Explain three ways in which "The Moon Rising" suggests the mystery of the moon. **[Support]**
2. What instrument or instruments would provide the best accompaniment for a song based on "The Moon Rising"? Why? **[Music Link]**
3. Find three passages in "It Was the Grape's Autumn" that show the closeness of the "man of the house" and the natural world, and explain your choices. **[Support]**
4. Explain how, in "The Sun and the Moon," the life of the gods is not simply one of pleasure and ease. **[Analyze]**

Compare English and Spanish Texts

5. Compare the first stanzas of the Spanish original and the translation of Federico García Lorca's "The Moon Rising." How does the position of the verb in the sentence differ in the Spanish original and in the English translation? (Hint: Does it go before or after the noun?) **[Compare and Contrast]**
6. (a) By comparing the Spanish and English texts of "It Was the Grape's Autumn," identify the Spanish words for *horses, cats,* and *dogs.* (b) Which Spanish word is most closely related to its English counterpart? **[Compare and Contrast]**

Suggestions for Sustained Reading

Sustained Reading and Its Benefits Novels, plays, short-story collections, and full-length nonfiction works all provide a great opportunity for sustained reading—reading that takes place over an extended period of time. Through any of these types of writing, you can travel to new and distant worlds, follow a character's life from birth through adulthood, and experience events unlike anything that happens in your everyday life.

The Keys to Successful Sustained Reading Reading longer works can be more challenging than reading brief pieces because longer works usually involve more characters and plot events and because it is unlikely that you will read a longer work in a single sitting. Following are a few of the keys to successful sustained reading:

- **Set aside extended periods of time.** It is very hard to follow a longer work if you read it in short intervals of a few minutes at a time. Read in periods of a half hour or more. Do not allow yourself to be distracted by the television set or the telephone.
- **Make yourself comfortable.** You'll concentrate better if you make yourself comfortable each time you sit down to read. Choose a comfortable chair in a place you like.
- **Take notes as you read.** Jot down details of the settings, note information about the characters, and record important events.
- **Hold book-circle discussions.** Get together with classmates who are reading the same work. Share your reactions. Discuss what you learn about the characters, and try to analyze the message the writer is trying to convey.

The Prentice Hall Literature Library The Prentice Hall Literature Library includes many longer works that fit in well with the literature included in this book. Your teacher can provide you with access to many of these titles. In addition, you can find an unlimited array of other extended reading possibilities in bookstores and in your local libraries.

Suggested Works and Connections to Unit Themes Following are some suggestions for longer works that will give you the opportunity to experience the fun of sustained reading. Each of the suggestions further explores one of the themes in this book. Many of the titles are included in the Prentice Hall Literature Library.

Planning Students' Sustained Reading

The works listed here are good choices for extending the themes explored in each thematic unit (Units 1–5). Included are descriptions of the books, tips for teaching them, and a guide to the related materials available for each. Use this information to help you decide which books to teach or to recommend to your students.

Literature Study Guides

Literature study guides are available for the titles listed below. These guides include section summaries, discussion questions, writing assignments, and activity ideas. They also provide helpful information about the author and the historical background of each book.

- *Lord of the Flies*
- *Literature From Around the World*
- *Silas Marner*
- *The Red Badge of Courage*
- *Cry, the Beloved Country*
- *Animal Farm*
- *Latino Literature*
- *Of Mice and Men*
- *Things Fall Apart*
- *African American Literature*

Resources for Teaching Novels, Plays, and Literature Collections

This booklet includes graphic organizers, teaching strategies, and transparencies that will be useful in teaching any of these works. In addition, it includes formal tests for many of the selections.

Customize for
Varying Student Needs

When assigning the selections for each unit, keep in mind the following factors:

Unit 1

- *Lord of the Flies* is a contemporary classic with a high interest level. It contains the sensitive issues noted below:
- *The Man Eater of Malgudi* makes a good introduction to the culture of India.
- *Watership Down* is another high-interest contemporary classic.

Unit 2

- *Literature From Around the World* contains a variety of selections of different lengths in translation.
- *Wouldn't Take Nothing for My Journey Now* is divided into short, manageable chapters and will be of special interest to female students.
- *Silas Marner* is a long Victorian classic that might require a number of weeks to teach.

Unit 3

- Though the novel is short, the language used in *The Red Badge of Courage* is challenging.
- *Cry, the Beloved Country* is a long novel that will require a long time commitment.
- *Animal Farm* can supplement students' learning about the Russian Revolution.

Suggested Titles Related to Thematic Units

Unit One

Lord of the Flies
William Golding

William Golding's exciting and terrifying story has been a favorite of high-school and college students since it was first published in 1954. A plane crashes on a tropical island in the Pacific, stranding a group of six- to twelve-year-old boys from a private school. The boys' society quickly degenerates into a nightmarish power struggle brought on by their own darkest fears and impulses. Vivid yet compact, the story moves swiftly to its fiery conclusion.

The Man Eater of Malgudi
R. K. Narayan

Like many of Narayan's stories, this tale takes place in the fictional Indian town of Malgudi. Nataraj, the main character, owns a small printing press in the town and has never had any enemies. Things change abruptly when an unruly taxidermist named Vasu moves into his attic, bringing with him a jungle's worth of stuffed animals. In the end, Nataraj dares to confront his intimidating tenant. Share the suspense as Nataraj waits to see the results of his daring decision.

Watership Down
Richard Adams

This is the exciting story of the journey of a group of rabbits forced to leave their home and search for a new warren amid the scenic and beautiful English countryside. Their journey is fraught with danger from foxes, weasels, humans, and other rabbits. Hardly a children's story, Richard Adams's tale shows us the world from a rabbit's point of view. At the same time, he makes keen observations about humans and our relationship to each other and to nature.

Unit Two

Literature From Around the World
Prentice Hall Collection

A collection of short stories, poems, and essays, this anthology includes the most respected writers of the twentieth century and the past. Works of authors from around the world deal with the universal themes of success, personal challenges, and overcoming obstacles. The book features works from all regions, including Europe, Asia, Africa, South America, and the Middle East.

Wouldn't Take Nothing for My Journey Now
Maya Angelou

A collection of inspirational essays, *Wouldn't Take Nothing for My Journey Now* celebrates life and discusses developing one's full potential in today's world. In the personal, informal tone of an autobiography, Maya Angelou discusses her own experiences and then draws universal lessons from them.

Silas Marner
George Eliot

The hero of George Eliot's story is an extremely near-sighted linen weaver in nineteenth-century England. Accused unjustly of theft, Marner becomes a recluse for fifteen years, hoarding the gold that he earns from his trade. When circumstances deprive him of that as well, Marner must end his long reclusiveness. Having lost everything he once held dear, he finds all of his chances for redemption hinge on a little orphan girl with golden hair.

Unit Three

The Red Badge of Courage
Stephen Crane

Stephen Crane's classic about the Civil War ushered in a new era of war stories: Rather than narrating an epic about victory and defeat in battle, *The Red Badge of Courage* follows the personal reactions of one soldier, a young, idealistic farm boy named Henry Fleming. Swept suddenly into the heat of battle, Henry must confront his own fears and make a decision between cowardice and courage that may well cost him his life.

Cry, the Beloved Country
Alan Paton

This story, considered the

Sensitive Issues

Some of these works contain potentially sensitive issues such as the ones below. You might consider these issues when deciding what to teach.

- *Lord of the Flies* contains some violence which results in death. It also contains some religious and sexual imagery.
- *Silas Marner* rejects many traditional religious teachings.
- *Cry, the Beloved Country* addresses the pain caused by apartheid in South Africa.

Suggested Titles Related to Thematic Units (continued)

greatest novel ever to come out of South Africa, concerns the unlikely relationship that develops between two men. A black pastor from a rural village, who journeys to the city of Johannesburg to find his sister and son, and a coldhearted white man find themselves on the opposite sides of a tragic event. The two men discover their races and families have more in common than they ever could have imagined.

Animal Farm
George Orwell

A simple tale with a powerful message about revolution, *Animal Farm* tells the story of the beasts of Manor Farm. Suffering hunger and neglect at the hands of Mr. Jones, the animals rebel, drive the farmer and his wife off the land, and set up their own society where "All animals are equal." Equality, however, means different things to different animals. To their dismay, the animals soon find that "some animals are more equal than others."

Unit Four

Latino Literature
Prentice Hall Collection

This collection includes the finest essays, poems, and fiction by modern Latino authors. Gary Soto, Sandra Cisneros, Pat Mora, Richard Rodriguez, Rudolfo Anaya, and Julia Alvarez, among others, share their works that deal with life's challenges and choices.

Of Mice and Men
John Steinbeck

John Steinbeck's classic story tells of the unforgettable friendship between two California migrant workers: Lenny, a simple-minded kind-hearted man, and George, a headstrong determined man who is also devoted to protecting Lenny. The two friends set out to acquire a farm of their own, but a tragic turn of events brings an unexpected end to their dreams.

Things Fall Apart
Chinua Achebe

This story by one of Africa's most famous and respected novelists tells the tale of Okonkwo, a wealthy and powerful man from a rural Nigerian village named Umuofia. From the first sentence of the novel, Achebe envelops us in the sights and sounds of the traditional African village. Achebe's voice is both loving and critical of the traditional culture—a culture that starts to fall apart when it runs headlong into European colonialism.

Unit Five

Annie John
Jamaica Kincaid

Annie John is a series of eight short stories that describe the title character's childhood and adolescence on the Caribbean island of Antigua. Told in the hypnotic voice of the young schoolgirl, the stories vividly describe the mischief of her childhood, the tension of her adolescence, and the eventual separation from her homeland.

Oliver Twist
Charles Dickens

Oliver Twist depicts the poverty, crime, and working conditions of nineteenth-century London. The hero of the tale is a young orphan named Oliver Twist who, for the grave crime of asking for more porridge, is expelled from the workhouse in which he was born. Kidnapped by a gang of thugs and forced to take part in a burglary, Oliver experiences many close brushes with the dark criminal underbelly of London before being rescued by the wealthy Mr. Brownlow.

African American Literature
Prentice Hall Collection

This collection of poems, short stories, and essays will introduce you to the finest African American literature—from folk tales to contemporary fiction. Organized chronologically, the book features such authors as Maya Angelou, Langston Hughes, Paul Laurence Dunbar, Alice Walker, Rita Dove, and Richard Wright. Each of these African American authors explores the ways in which people expand their horizons.

Customize for *Varying Student Needs*

When assigning the selections for each unit, keep in mind the following factors:

Unit 4

- The anthology *Latino Literature* contains a wide array of works of various lengths and levels by contemporary Latino authors.
- *Of Mice and Men* is a short classic with a high level of interest.
- *Things Fall Apart* is a high-interest work and is considered the most famous contemporary African novel.

Unit 5

- *Annie John* is an example of what it means to grow up in the Caribbean.
- *Oliver Twist* reveals the sordid details of the underworld of the slums of London in the late nineteenth century.
- The anthology *African American Literature* contains works of varying lengths and levels of accessibility.

Sensitive Issues

Some of these works contain potentially sensitive issues such as the ones below. You might consider these issues when deciding what to teach.

- *Things Fall Apart* contains some frank conversations about sexual matters. Also the treatment of Ibo and Christian religions might be troublesome to some students who hold strong Christian beliefs.
- *Annie John* explores a young person's experiences with death, separation, emotional illness, and parent-child conflict.

Prentice Hall Literature Library

The Prentice Hall Literature Library offers a wide variety of classic and contemporary works from around the world. You may choose to study these works with your class or to recommend them to students for individual reading.

Using the Test Practice Bank

These tests provide practice test items in reading comprehension and writing skills, which correlate to standardized test objectives in content and formats. For each Test Preparation Workshop that appears in the book, you will find here a page of extra test items that focus on the same skill. In addition, several tests provide practice in a combination of skills, along with writing prompts.

You may choose to have your students use this practice bank from time to time in conjunction with the Test Preparation Workshops; alternatively, you may want students to spend a block of time working on the entire practice bank during a standardized test preparation period.

Correlations to Standardized Tests

The reading comprehension practice items on this page correspond to the following standardized test section:

ACT Reading

Answers

1 (B) Using the dates as context clues one can determine that *posthumous* means "after death."
2 (A) The line "other soldiers stole the money and blamed Flipper" provides a context clue indicating that *fabricated* means "invented."
3 (D) The words "but he was found guilty" suggest that *acquitted* means the opposite—"found to be not guilty."
4 (C) In the context of the sentence, *hatred* is the logical answer.
5 (B) That a Henry Flipper award is presented each year suggests that *revered* means "respected."
6 (A) The context of the entire passage indicates that *adversity* means "difficulties."

Test Practice Bank

Reading Comprehension

Using Context Clues to Determine Word Meanings

Read the passage, and then answer the questions that follow. Mark the letter of your answer on a bubble sheet if your teacher provides one; otherwise, number from 1 to 6 on a separate sheet of paper, and write the letter of the correct answer next to each number.

> In February 1999, President William Clinton gave a posthumous pardon to Henry O. Flipper, a West Point graduate who died in 1940. Flipper, the first African American graduate of the army military academy, was court-martialed in 1881 on apparently fabricated charges. Flipper commanded the "Buffalo Soldier" unit of the 10th Cavalry. While in charge of funds at Fort Davis, Texas, he was charged with stealing $2,500. He was acquitted of the theft, but he was found guilty of conduct unbecoming an officer. Historical research revealed that other soldiers stole the money and blamed Flipper out of racial animosity.
>
> Flipper is revered in army history. The annual Henry Flipper award is presented to a West Point cadet who overcomes adversity.

1 The word posthumous in this passage means—
A before death
B after death
C during service
D after birth

2 The word fabricated in this passage means—
A invented
B truthful
C extravagant
D sincere

3 In this passage, the word acquitted means—
A blamed for other crimes
B discharged from duty
C found to be guilty
D found to be not guilty

4 The word animosity in this passage means—
A distrust
B indifference
C hatred
D warmth

5 In this passage, the word revered means—
A forgotten
B respected
C belittled
D forgiven

6 The word adversity in this passage means—
A difficulties
B gossip
C poverty
D wrongdoing

See the Test Preparation Workshop on page 113 for tips on answering questions about using context clues.

Reading Comprehension

Recognize Facts, Details, and Sequence

Read the passage, and then answer the questions that follow. Mark the letter of your answer on a bubble sheet if your teacher provides one; otherwise, number from 1 to 6 on a separate sheet of paper, and write the letter of the correct answer next to each number.

During the Civil War, many Texans wanted to secede from the United States. However, the state's governor fought hard to keep Texas in the Union and to sidestep a bloody war. After the Secession Convention voted to withdraw from the Union in 1861, Governor Sam Houston put the question before a statewide vote, but Texas voters also chose secession. Houston then sought a compromise, arguing that Texas could become a republic—as it had been before joining the United States—and thus avoid being drawn into the war; this measure also failed.

To prevent Union sympathizers from holding power, the Secession Convention declared that elected officials must swear allegiance to the Confederacy. Houston refused. Although President Abraham Lincoln offered to keep Houston in power with federal troops, the governor feared such action would cause a war among Texans. Instead of accepting Lincoln's support, he resigned from office.

1 Which of the following was an obstacle to Texas's secession?
A Governor Sam Houston
B Secession Convention
C Texas voters
D troops sent by Lincoln

2 When did Sam Houston put secession to a statewide vote?
A after hearing the Secession Convention's decision
B after refusing Lincoln's offer
C before attempting compromise
D after resigning from office

3 Sam Houston refused President Lincoln's offer because he—
A feared for his life
B respected the voters' decision
C wanted to avoid a Texas civil war
D approved of the Secession Convention's decision

4 Why did the Secession Convention demand that all elected officials swear an oath of allegiance?
A to promote Union ideals
B to remove Union sympathizers
C to identify Confederate officers
D to protect Governor Houston

5 Why did President Lincoln offer to send federal troops to Texas?
A to begin the Civil War
B to form a republic
C to keep Texas in the Union
D to keep Houston in office

6 Why did Governor Houston resign?
A to avoid compromise
B to avoid swearing allegiance to the Confederacy
C to join the Union army
D to seek another office

See the Test Preparation Workshop on page 215 for tips on answering questions about facts, details, and sequence.

Correlations to Standardized Tests

The reading comprehension practice items on this page correspond to the following standardized test section:
ACT Reading

Answers

1 (A) The first sentence says that the state's governor fought hard to keep Texas in the Union.
2 (A) The second sentence states that Sam Houston put secession to a statewide vote after the vote of the Secession Convention.
3 (C) The second sentence from the end states that Houston feared that his being kept in power by federal troops would cause a war among Texans.
4 (B) The first sentence of the second paragraph states that the Secession Convention demanded an oath of allegiance to prevent Union sympathizers from holding power.
5 (D) The second sentence from the end states that Lincoln offered to keep Houston in power with federal troops.
6 (B) The second paragraph states that Houston refused to sign the oath of allegiance and then resigned from office.

Correlations to Standardized Tests

The reading comprehension practice items on this page correspond to the following standardized test section:
ACT Reading

Answers

1 (D) The main idea, that residential landscapes use much water, is found in the first sentence of the first paragraph.
2 (C) By referring to the use of 10,000 gallons of water as "extravagant," the writer implies that water should be conserved.
3 (C) The main idea, that use of native plants is increasing, is found in the last sentence of the paragraph and supported by preceding information.
4 (D) In describing attempts by people to conserve water by using drought-tolerant plants, the writer implies that water is a limited resource.
5 (A) The writer's mention of the growth in municipal water demand implies that growing cities will use more water.
6 (A) In discussing the "extravagant" use of water for landscaping in the first paragraph, the writer implies the need for conservation and, in the second paragraph, provides a solution in his descriptions of drought-tolerant native plants.

Reading Comprehension

Stated and Implied Main Ideas

Read the passage, and then answer the questions that follow. Mark the letter of your answer on a bubble sheet if your teacher provides one; otherwise, number from 1 to 6 on a separate sheet of paper, and write the letter of the correct answer next to each number.

Up to one half of a city's water supply might be used on residential landscapes in the summer. A lawn of St. Augustine grass can demand 50 inches of rain per year, which is more than the average rainfall of many dry areas. A typical yard of tropical grass can use an extravagant 10,000 gallons of water in a year.

Increasingly, people in dry areas are using native, drought-tolerant plants in their landscaping. For example, buffalo grass requires only 20 inches of rain yearly. Hardy trees such as mountain laurel and redbud require little water and are beautiful as well. As municipal water demand grows and aquifers are depleted, more people are turning to native plants to conserve water.

1 What is the stated main idea of the first paragraph?
A Some people waste water.
B St. Augustine grass is beautiful.
C People should not water lawns.
D Landscaping uses much water.

2 What is the implied main idea of the first paragraph?
A Lawns should be abolished.
B Cities need more water.
C Water should be conserved.
D City water should be rationed.

3 What is the stated main idea of the second paragraph?
A People should buy buffalo grass.
B Redbud trees are hardy.
C Use of native plants is increasing.
D Tropical grasses use much water.

4 What is the implied main idea of the second paragraph?
A Water is expensive.
B Mountain laurels will be popular.
C Buffalo grass is attractive.
D Water is a limited resource.

5 In the second paragraph, the author implies that
A growing cities will use more water.
B most areas receive 20 inches of annual rain.
C summer water use is high.
D aquifers are not being depleted.

6 What is the implied main idea of the passage?
A People should conserve water by using more native plants.
B Cities charge too much for water.
C More buffalo grass is needed.
D Native plants are attractive.

See the Test Preparation Workshop on page 299 for tips on answering questions about main ideas.

Reading Comprehension

Recognizing Cause and Effect; Predicting Outcomes

Read the passage, and then answer the questions that follow. Mark the letter of your answer on a bubble sheet if your teacher provides one; otherwise, number from 1 to 6 on a separate sheet of paper, and write the letter of the correct answer next to each number.

Joyce's trip to the airport was a disaster. She had planned to pick up her friend from Ohio. However, Hal's flight was delayed because of bad weather, and he missed his final connection. He was too busy to call Joyce and tell her his schedule had changed; he was trying to make sure his checked bags would be transferred correctly. Besides, he told himself, Joyce was such an experienced traveler, she would certainly confirm his schedule and discover the delay.

When Joyce arrived at the airport, she discovered that Hal's plane wouldn't land for two hours. She knew she should have checked on the status of his flight, but she had assumed that the flight would be on time. As a result, she had to wait and was annoyed with herself for her carelessness. Eventually, though, her impatience vanished as she looked forward to seeing her friend. Although the delay wasn't Hal's fault, he worried that Joyce would be inconvenienced. He didn't want to waste his good friend's time.

1 How did the weather affect Hal's trip?
A He lost his luggage.
B His flight was canceled.
C He was two hours late.
D Joyce was angry with him.

2 Why did Joyce have to wait at the airport?
A She thought Hal would call her.
B She had not checked the flight's schedule.
C Hal was always late.
D She drove through bad weather.

3 Why didn't Hal call Joyce to tell her he would arrive late?
A He forgot to call her.
B She was already at the airport.
C He was busy taking care of his luggage.
D He lost her phone number.

4 How might Hal react to Joyce when the plane finally arrives?
A He will ask her to carry his luggage.
B He will be angry with her.
C He will laugh at her mistake.
D He will apologize for the delay.

5 How might Joyce respond when Hal steps off the plane?
A She might be annoyed.
B She might be relieved.
C She will be happy to see him.
D She will probably be angry.

6 What can you predict about Joyce's next trip to the airport?
A She will ask Hal to pick her up.
B She will check the flight's status.
C She will expect a long wait.
D She will not check her bags.

See the Test Preparation Workshop on page 377 for tips on answering questions about recognizing cause and effect and predicting outcomes.

Correlations to Standardized Tests

The reading comprehension practice items on this page correspond to the following standardized test section:
ACT Reading

Answers

1 (C) The first sentence of the second paragraph states that Joyce discovered that Hal's plane would not land for two hours.
2 (B) The second sentence of the second paragraph states that Joyce should have checked on the status of the flight.
3 (C) The fourth sentence of the first paragraph states that Hal was too busy to call.
4 (D) Because Hal was worried that Joyce would be inconvenienced, one can predict that he will apologize for the delay.
5 (C) Since Joyce's impatience vanished and she was looking forward to seeing Hal, one can predict that she will be happy to see him.
6 (B) One can predict that Joyce will check a flight's schedule in order to avoid another possible long wait at the airport.

Correlations to Standardized Tests

The reading comprehension practice items on this page correspond to the following standardized test section:
ACT Reading

Answers

1 (A) The population of London did not surpass that of Venice until 1600.
2 (B) The bars for both London and Naples are even, ending at the same point just below the 300,000 line.
3 (C) From 1600 to 1750 the population bar for Venice remains constant at just below 200,000.
4 (B) Beginning in 1470, the population of Paris was more than twice that of London; by 1750, the population of London was 100,000 greater than that of Paris.
5 (C) Between 1600 and 1650, the population of Naples dropped from 300,000 to just above 200,000.
6 (C) In 1650, the population of Paris was nearly 500,000, whereas that of London was just 400,000. By 1700 the populations of the two cities were the same.

Test Practice Bank

Reading Comprehension

Interpret Graphic Aids; Evaluate and Make Judgments

Look at the graph, read the passage, and then answer the questions that follow. Mark the letter of your answer on a bubble sheet if your teacher provides one; otherwise, number from 1 to 6 on a separate sheet of paper, and write the letter of the correct answer next to each number.

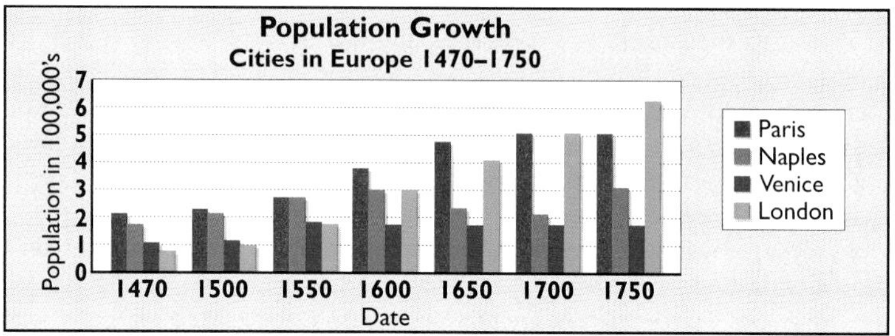

The bar graph shows the growth of four cities in Europe from 1470 to 1750.

1 During which years was the population of Venice greater than the population of London?
A 1470–1550
B 1550–1600
C 1650–1750
D 1700–1750

2 In the year 1550, the population of—
A London declined from the previous measurement.
B Paris and Naples were the same.
C Venice doubled from the previous measurement.
D Paris was greater than Naples.

3 From 1600 to 1750, the population of what city remained unchanged?
A Paris
B Naples
C Venice
D London

4 Based on information in the bar graph, which of these statements is true?
A Paris was Europe's largest city.
B London grew larger than Paris.
C Naples grew steadily in size.
D Venice's population declined.

5 During which years did Naples's population decline from the previous measurement?
A 1500 and 1550
B 1550 and 1600
C 1600 and 1650
D 1650 and 1700

6 What was the last year in which Paris was larger than London?
A 1600
B 1650
C 1700
D 1750

See the Test Preparation Workshop on page 465 for tips on answering questions about interpreting graphic aids and evaluating and making judgments.

Critical Reading

Recognize Forms of Propaganda; Distinguish Between Fact and Nonfact

Read the passage, and then answer the questions that follow. Mark the letter of your answer on a bubble sheet if your teacher provides one; otherwise, number from 1 to 6 on a separate sheet of paper, and write the letter of the correct answer next to each number.

Austin, Texas, city officials have stated that neighborhood swimming pools must close by August 31. In Texas, however, the temperature can remain in the 90's until almost October! The city declares that it does not have the money to staff all neighborhood pools and that people who wish to swim can go to the main municipal pool. The main municipal pool is not convenient for children, and it could not accommodate all the people who now use neighborhood pools.

Neighborhood pools contribute greatly to our community. They keep children busy and out of trouble. In hot weather, they are a necessity! Help Neighborhood Pools (HNP) urges you to contact your city council members, circulate petitions, and help us raise the money necessary to keep pools open for another five weeks. Our children and our neighborhood deserve to have access to this valuable resource.

1 You can tell from this passage that the author intends to—
A go to the main municipal pool
B stop swimming on August 31
C persuade readers to support neighborhood pools
D give children swimming lessons

2 Which of these statements about neighborhood pools is an opinion?
A Pools help the community.
B Extended staffing for pools will cost extra money.
C Pools must close by August 31.
D Children often use pools in hot weather.

3 You can tell that the speaker is—
A supporting HNP
B exaggerating the situation
C trying to discredit city officials
D attempting to win readers' votes

4 Which of these statements about neighborhood pools is a fact?
A They are a necessity.
B They keep children out of trouble.
C The main pool is not convenient.
D Fall weather in Texas can be hot.

5 You can tell from the passage that city officials—
A oppose neighborhood pools
B need money to extend pool hours
C favor the main municipal pool
D dislike neighborhood groups

6 The author indicates that the best way to extend pool hours is to—
A make demands of the mayor
B contact city council members
C write letters to the newspaper
D volunteer to staff the pool

See the Test Preparation Workshop on page 565 for tips on answering questions about forms of propaganda and fact and nonfact.

Correlations to Standardized Tests

The reading comprehension practice items on this page correspond to the following standardized test section:
ACT Reading

Answers

1 (C) In the first paragraph the writer describes a problem; in the second paragraph he urges readers to take action to solve the problem.
2 (A) No proof is given to show that pools help the community.
3 (A) The writer asks that readers help raise money for HNP. The writer is not attempting to win votes because no election is being held.
4 (D) This statement is supported by the fact that the temperature can remain in the 90's until almost October.
5 (B) The third sentence in the first paragraph states that the city declares that it does not have the money to staff the pools.
6 (B) In the second sentence from the end, the writer urges readers to contact their city council members.

Correlations to Standardized Tests

The reading comprehension practice items on this page correspond to the following standardized test sections:

SAT Critical Reading
ACT Reading

Answers

1 (B) Passage A refers to Lawrence's participation in the Arab revolt; Passage B refers to Jones's series of adventures.
2 (C) Both men were archaeologists working in desert areas; only Jones was fictional.
4 (A) "Tenderly" and "fragile" evoke feelings of romance—not betrayal, humor, or suspicion.
5 (D) The even iambic rhythm is soothing, and words such as "deep-hearted" and "love song" evoke romantic feelings.
6 (B) The romantic wistfulness of the first verse changes to sarcasm as the poet writes, "just my luck." The effect is comic.

Test Practice Bank

Reading Comprehension

Comparing and Contrasting Texts; Analyzing Literary Language

Read the passages, and then answer the questions that follow. Mark the letter of your answer on a bubble sheet if your teacher provides one; otherwise, number from 1 to 6 on a separate sheet of paper, and write the letter of the correct answer next to each number.

Passage A:

The British adventurer T. E. Lawrence worked as an archaeologist in the Middle East. He used his knowledge of Arabic language and culture to advise Arab leaders in an uprising against the Ottoman Empire in 1917 and 1918. His participation in the Arab revolt made him the romantic hero known as "Lawrence of Arabia."

Passage B:

In the movie "Raiders of the Lost Ark," an American archaeologist named Indiana Jones has a series of adventures while searching for an ancient treasure. His search is complicated by both romance and run-ins with enemy soldiers. The character Indiana Jones performs courageous deeds in a romantic desert setting.

1 What theme is shared by both passages?
A Love
B Adventure
C Hardship
D Literature

2 What is the biggest difference between the subjects of the passages?
A Jones was in the desert.
B Lawrence was in Arabia.
C Jones was a fictional character.
D Lawrence was an archaeologist.

A single flow'r he sent me, since we met.
  All tenderly his messenger he chose.
Deep-hearted, pure, with scented dew still wet—
  One perfect rose.
I knew the language of the floweret;
  "My fragile leaves," it said, "his heart enclose."
Love long has taken for his amulet
  One perfect rose.
Why is it no one ever sent me yet
  One perfect limousine, do you suppose?
Ah no, it's always just my luck to get
  One perfect rose.

3 What feelings do the words "tenderly" and "fragile" evoke?
A romance
B betrayal
C humor
D suspicion

4 What kind of mood is set by the poem's rhythm and language?
A abrupt
B harsh
C upbeat and happy
D soothing and romantic

5 What change occurs in the poem's last stanza?
A The poet's love abandons her.
B The language changes for comic effect.
C The poet ends with a lovely image.
D The poet receives an unusual present.

See the Test Preparation Workshop on page 661 for tips on questions about comparing and contrasting texts and analyzing literary language.

Reading Comprehension

Characteristics of Text

Writers may organize information to compare or contrast things, to establish chronological order, or to show cause-and-effect relationships. As you read, identify these patterns of organization. Read the following passage, and then answer the questions that follow. Write your answers to the questions on a separate sheet of paper.

> The kingdom of Great Britain is changing in ways that would leave Americans dizzy. Since the sixteenth century, England, Scotland, and Wales have been ruled together. Now, both Scotland and Wales have voted for self-government. Imagine the states of Texas and Florida becoming independent from the United States! British currency may change from the British pound to the euro of the European Union. Can you think of buying lunch with anything but dollars and cents? Even the flag is changing—from the blue and red British union jack to the simple red and white St. George's Cross of England. Would a flag other than the United States stars and stripes seem odd to you?
>
> In some countries, all these changes might seem like a frightening, revolutionary upheaval. Yet the English seem to be focusing on the idea of change rather than on a sense of loss. Their adaptability seems to echo the words of the writer George Orwell, who hoped that there would always be an England with "the power to change out of recognition and yet remain the same."

1 What patterns of organization are used in this passage? Support your answer.

2 The words that a writer chooses help to establish the writer's point of view or opinion. On a separate sheet of paper, write an answer to the following question: Explain how key words in the passage on Great Britain express the writer's point of view. Support your answer.

See the Test Preparation Workshop on page 809 for tips on answering questions about characteristics of text.

Correlations to Standardized Tests

The reading comprehension practice items on this page correspond to the following standardized test sections:

SAT Critical Reading
ACT Reading

Answers

1 *Possible response:*
Students may respond that the passage uses a comparison-contrast pattern of organization, since the author imagines how the changes in Great Britain might appear to a reader in the United States. Students also may mention that the passage uses chronology, since it mentions how the country's organization has changed over four hundred years.

2 *Possible response:*
The author indicates that such changes might be disruptive or "revolutionary." However, the tone of phrases such as "leave Americans dizzy" indicates that the author is not alarmed. The final quote indicates a mood of hope.

Correlations to Standardized Tests

The reading comprehension practice items on this page correspond to the following standardized test sections:

SAT Critical Reading
ACT Reading

Answers

1 (D) "Soggy" suggests "wet," and "flyaway" suggests "dry."
2 (B) The first paragraph states that resort operators cannot trust their investments to chance, and that machines can provide almost-perfect snow.
3 (A) Depending only on the weather, resort operators could lose money when conditions for skiing are poor.
4 (C) In snow science, computers are used to help "produce perfect snow in imperfect conditions."
5 (A) The author states that snow science "requires a great deal of skill."
6 (B) The implication is that snowmaking has grown as ski resort business has grown.

Test Practice Bank

Reading Comprehension

Analyzing an Author's Meaning and Style

Read the passage, and then answer the questions that follow. Mark the letter of your answer on a bubble sheet if your teacher provides one; otherwise, number from 1 to 6 on a separate sheet of paper, and write the letter of the correct answer next to each number.

Ski resorts once depended upon nature to provide adequate snow. However, skiing is a business, and resort operators cannot trust their investments to chance. Instead, they have made snowmaking a science. Machines can provide trails with almost-perfect snow in all types of weather. The trick is to atomize water with compressed air, sending it out to freeze into tiny ice pellets.

This snow science, which now calculates snowflakes with computers, requires a great deal of skill to produce perfect snow in imperfect conditions. The water pipes in snow machines are inclined to freeze. Magnificent snow will melt when it comes into contact with barely frozen ground. Variations in temperature and humidity must be taken into account or a machine will produce soggy sludge or flyaway snow that is useless for skiing.

1 In this passage, the phrase "soggy sludge or flyaway snow" means—
A snow that is dirty
B snow that is blown away
C snow that is perfect for skiing
D snow that is too wet or too dry

2 With which of the following statements might the author agree?
A Snow machines always produce perfect snow in all conditions.
B Snow machines help increase the skiing business.
C Computers are essential for perfect skiing.
D Resort operators should depend on natural snow.

3 The phrase "cannot trust their investments to chance" means—
A resorts can't depend on weather
B natural snow is inferior
C resorts ignore weather reports
D skiers demand adequate snow

4 The phrase "calculates snowflakes with computers" means computers—
A measure snowfall
B design snowflakes
C help produce artificial snow
D cannot produce perfect snow

5 The author might agree that—
A it is difficult to manufacture snow
B anyone can make perfect snow
C weather is unimportant
D wet snow is somewhat useful

6 The passage implies that—
A artificial snow is beautiful
B artificial snow is big business
C artificial snow is not a challenge
D artificial snow melts quickly

See the Test Preparation Workshop on page 877 for tips on answering questions about an author's meaning and style.

Combined Skills

Reading Comprehension and Critical Reading

Read the passage, and then answer the questions that follow. Mark the letter of your answer on a bubble sheet if your teacher provides one; otherwise, number from 1 to 9 on a separate sheet of paper, and write the letter of the correct answer next to each number.

In 1973, a young Italian student went to the South Pacific to implement a life-long dream. After preparing himself by reading all the available materials, Giancarlo Scoditti set out for the island of Kitawa. This tiny island north of New Guinea became his life's work, and, as he wrote down details of the inhabitants' culture, the anthropologist became known as "the man who remembers."

Kitawa islanders are famous for their canoes, which are decorated with beautifully carved boards on the prow, the front of the boat. Yet, until Scoditti arrived, even the most complete accounts of the canoes were secondhand. During his many visits, Scoditti studied with artisans, learning the techniques and engineering required for creating the traditional canoes. A master craftsman named Towitara, a wise, aged repository of tradition and lore, taught him the symbolism of the carvings and even shared with him the chant recited during the carver's initiation ceremony. Scoditti translated the chant, which reads in part:

My mind, enveloped, creates images,
Lost in dreams will create images—
Images for our companions.
You are transformed into me.
You are transformed into me, Towitara.

After living on the island for about a year, Scoditti was included in a ritual called the Kula Ring. In this social ritual, men travel by canoe to other islands—traveling east in the spring and west in the fall—to exchange ceremonial gifts. The ceremony is a test of skill and endurance that proves the men can recognize ocean currents and navigate by the stars.

Although the Kitawa islanders possess no written language, they have passed along details about their religion and legends for hundreds of years. However, as modern society encroaches on the island, many of the traditional stories and methods are in danger of being lost. As children go away to school, they return with Western values and desires. Many young people now refuse to participate in traditional dances or village gatherings.

Ironically, "the man who remembers" may know more about some aspects of Kitawa culture than many of the islanders. After all, he has been writing down his observations, recording conversations, and filming traditional dances for more than twenty-five years. Even his teacher, the master carver, encouraged Scoditti to return to his home and record his observations about this South Pacific island people.

1 In the passage, the word repository means
A reference book
B storehouse
C lost work
D deposit

2 Which of the following did Scoditti do first?
A He filmed traditional dances.
B He studied with artisans.
C He traveled to Kitawa in 1973.
D He read about Kitawa.

Correlations to Standardized Tests

The reading comprehension and critical reading practice items on these two pages correspond to the following standardized test sections:
SAT Critical Reading
ACT Reading

Answers

1 (B) Because Towitara was wise and taught Scoditti, one can determine that *repository* probably means "storehouse."
2 (D) The first paragraph states that Scoditti read all available materials before setting out for Kitawa.

Answers *(continued)*

3 (D) The paragraph states that traditional stories and methods are in danger of being lost as modern society encroaches.

4 (A) The master carver would be pleased because he had encouraged Scoditti to record his observations.

5 (C) Because the Kitawa islanders go west in the fall, they would most likely travel first to Kiriwina Island.

6 (A) Whether or not something is beautiful is almost always an opinion.

7 (B) Repetition is a musical device that can create melody in a poem.

8 (C) Having to prove each year that they can recognize ocean currents and navigate by the stars, the men demonstrate that ocean travel is a necessary skill.

9 The passage is organized primarily chronologically. Students may observe that traditional culture is contrasted with modern culture.

3 What is the implied main idea of the fourth paragraph?

A Scoditti should teach children how to carve canoe prows.
B Children should stay on the island of Kitawa.
C The Kitawa have no written language.
D Contact with Western ideas can change traditional cultures.

4 How might the master carver respond to Scoditti's twenty-five-year study of Kitawa?

A He would be pleased that the island's culture was so carefully recorded.
B He would be curious as to why fewer people learned to carve prow boards.
C He would be proud that young people had learned more about Western ideas.
D He would be angry at Scoditti's interference.

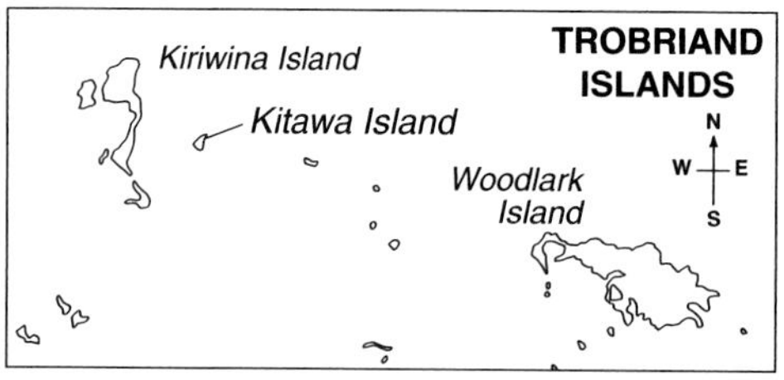

5 Refer to the map and to the sample passage. Then answer the following question: In the fall, Kitawa islanders participating in the Kula Ring would likely travel first to what island?

A Woodlark Island
B the Trobriand islands
C Kiriwina Island
D New Guinea

6 Which of the following statements about Kitawa Island is an opinion?

A The canoes made on the island are beautiful.
B Scoditti began visiting the island in 1973.
C Some Kitawa children now travel to other islands to go to school.
D Kitawa has no written language.

7 How are evocative words and rhythms in the carver's initiation chant used to create a kind of melody in the poem?

A There are no rhyming words or melodies in the chant.
B The repetition of the word "images" and of the last two lines give the chant a regular rhythm.
C The chant is abrupt and irregular.
D The poet details what he will carve into the prow of a canoe.

8 The phrase "proves the men can recognize ocean currents and navigate by the stars" means—

A travel by canoe is no longer valued
B Kitawa men once knew how to travel by the ocean's currents
C ocean travel is a necessary skill for the people of Kitawa
D navigation must be taught to children on other islands

9 On a separate sheet of paper, explain the patterns of organization used in this passage. Support your answer.

Test Practice Bank

Writing Skills

Strategy, Organization, and Style

Read the passages, and then answer the questions that follow. Mark the letter of your answer on a bubble sheet if your teacher provides one; otherwise, number from 1 to 4 on a separate sheet of paper, and write the letter of the correct answer next to each number.

As the U.S. population ages, more people are moving to retirement communities. Now, though, retirement communities are being advertised not just as places to pass the time as you watch yourself grow older. Retirement was once thought of as a sedentary time. Now, advertisements for retirement resorts describe retirement as an action-packed time of personal growth, exploration, and, most of all, enjoyment.

1 Suppose the writer wanted to say more about the aging of the U.S. population. Which of the following additions is most suitable?
- **A** The U.S. population is choosing to ignore that it is growing older.
- **B** Baby boomers are, by their sheer numbers, affecting retirement.
- **C** Because of economics, more people are delaying retirement.
- **D** Many baby boomers are still caring for their aging parents.

2 Suppose the writer wanted to say more about the growth of retirement resorts. Which of the following additions is most suitable?
- **A** Retirement communities provide a useful service for aging adults.
- **B** Retirement communities have outstanding golf courses.
- **C** It is in the best interests of retirement communities to make the "golden years" look good.
- **D** With more people retiring, many jobs should be opening up for younger people.

(1) In the mid-nineteenth century, three million people in Ireland subsisted almost entirely on potatoes and buttermilk. (2) More than one million people perished from starvation and disease; another million and a half people emigrated. (3) When potatoes were imported from America, they became a necessary food source. (4) The potato blight, which raged between 1845 and 1851, turned this vital source of food into rotting slime. (5) The famine also took its toll on Irish culture: With the population decimated, the Irish language declined as well.

3 Choose the sequence of sentence numbers that will make the paragraph's structure most logical:
- **A** NO CHANGE
- **B** 5, 4, 3, 2, 1
- **C** 4, 3, 1, 2, 5
- **D** 3, 1, 4, 2, 5

4 The tone of this passage may best be described as—
- **A** persuasive
- **B** emotional
- **C** matter-of-fact
- **D** whimsical

See the Test Preparation Workshop on page 951 for tips on answering questions about strategy, organization, and style.

Correlations to Standardized Tests

The writing skills practice items on this page correspond to the following standardized test section:
ACT English: Rhetorical Skills

Answers

1 (B) This statement is most suitable because the focus of the paragraph is on changes in attitudes toward retirement.
2 (C) This statement supports the line about advertisements for retirement resorts.
3 (D) This sequence begins with a general statement about potatoes and then goes on to give a chronological account of Ireland's loss of its vital food source and the consequences.
4 (C) The content of the passage is serious, but the facts are given in an unemotional, matter-of-fact tone.

Correlations to Standardized Tests

The writing skills practice items on this page correspond to the following standardized test section:

ACT English: Usage/Mechanics

Answers

1 (D) *Its* should not have an apostrophe because it is a pronoun, not a contraction.

2 (C) A serial comma is needed after *water.*

3 (A) No change is needed; the singular verb form *spends* agrees with the singular subject *one.*

4 (B) The singular verb form *thinks* is needed to agree with the singular subject *he* and to maintain the present tense in which the passage is written.

5 (C) This choice correctly eliminates a fragment by turning "Discouraging everyone" into a complete sentence.

Test Practice Bank

Writing Skills

Punctuation; Grammar and Usage; Sentence Structure

Read the passage, and then answer the questions that follow. Mark the letter of your answer on a bubble sheet if your teacher provides one; otherwise, number from 1 to 5 on a separate sheet of paper, and write the letter of the correct answer next to each number.

(1) The cookbook recipe appears to be extremely fussy about it's requirements for a basic loaf of bread. (2) Henry complains, "The author makes a combination of water flour, salt, and yeast seem too complicated." (3) Only one of his friends spends enough time in the kitchen to tackle such a recipe. (4) An enthusiastic amateur baker, he think that everyone should enjoy making fresh bread. (5) He says, "Complicated instructions are a mistake. Discouraging everyone."

1 Which of the following corrections is correct for sentence 1?
A NO CHANGE
B The cookbook recipe appears to be extremely fussy about it's requirements, for a basic loaf of bread.
C The cookbooks' recipe appears to be extremely fussy about it's requirements for a basic loaf of bread.
D The cookbook recipe appears to be extremely fussy about its requirements for a basic loaf of bread.

2 Which of the following selections is correct for sentence 2?
A NO CHANGE
B Henry complains, "The author makes a combination of water flour, salt, and yeast, seem too complicated."
C Henry complains, "The author makes a combination of water, flour, salt, and yeast seem too complicated."
D Henry complains "The author makes a combination of water flour, salt, and yeast seem too complicated."

3 Correct the underlined word in sentence 3:
A NO CHANGE
B spend
C are spending
D were spending

4 Correct the underlined word in sentence 4:
A NO CHANGE
B thinks
C thought
D were thinking

5 Correct the underlined words in sentence 5:
A NO CHANGE
B mistake; discouraging
C mistake. They discourage
D mistake, they discourage

Writing Skills

Spelling, Capitalization, and Punctuation

Read the passage, and decide which type of error, if any, appears in each underlined section. Mark the letter of your answer on a bubble sheet if your teacher provides one; otherwise, number from 1 to 6 on a separate sheet of paper, and write the letter of the correct answer next to each number.

The History Club will be showing a special film in honor of veterans day. (1) Because we have been studying World War II (2) in our history class, we will watch a classic movie about veterans' who return from that war. (3) The film is called *The Best Years of Our Lives* and it won several (4) Academy Awards when it was released. The film, which follows the lives of several soldiers, shows the difficultys of returning to (5) civilian life. Our teacher, Ms. Cornwell, said, The scene that shows (6) dozens of scrapped, rusting airplanes illustrates how useless many of the returning veterans felt."

1 **A** Spelling error
B Capitalization error
C Punctuation error
D No error

2 **A** Spelling error
B Capitalization error
C Punctuation error
D No error

3 **A** Spelling error
B Capitalization error
C Punctuation error
D No error

4 **A** Spelling error
B Capitalization error
C Punctuation error
D No error

5 **A** Spelling error
B Capitalization error
C Punctuation error
D No error

6 **A** Spelling error
B Capitalization error
C Punctuation error
D No error

Correlations to Standardized Tests

The writing skills practice items on this page correspond to the following standardized test section:
ACT English: Usage/Mechanics

Answers

1 (B) *Veterans Day* should be capitalized.
2 (D)
3 (C) *Veterans* should not have an apostrophe.
4 (C) A comma is needed after *Lives* to join the two independent clauses correctly.
5 (A) *Difficulties* is spelled incorrectly.
6 (C) Opening quotation marks are needed before *The*.

Correlations to Standardized Tests

The writing skills practice items on this page correspond to the following standardized test section:

ACT English: Usage/Mechanics

Answers

1 (A) A semicolon correctly joins two independent clauses of a compound sentence.

2 (C) This choice corrects the fragment beginning with "For example," turning it into a complete sentence.

3 (B) This choice correctly combines a simple sentence and a fragment to form a compound sentence joined by a comma and *and.* It also eliminates the incorrect comma after *cooks.*

Test Practice Bank

Writing Skills

Construction, Usage, and Editing Skills

Read the passage. Some sections are underlined. The underlined sections may be one of the following: incomplete sentences, run-on sentences, correctly written sentences that should be combined, correctly written sentences that do not need to be rewritten. Mark the letter of your answer on a bubble sheet if your teacher provides one; otherwise, number from 1 to 4 on a separate sheet of paper, and write the letter of the correct answer next to each number.

> A small town just south of here has not yet been swallowed up by the big city, it still stands on its own. (1) It's not hip, or restored, or historically significant. Perhaps its charm is that it remains decidedly uncool. For example, dinner at the volunteer fire department. (2)
>
> Few establishments are brave enough to put cheese on Chinese entrees. The cooks, must figure you didn't come for elegant cuisine. Don't insult you with pretend sophistication. (3)

1 **A** A small town just south of here has not yet been swallowed up by the big city; it still stands on its own.
B A small town just south of here has not yet been swallowed up by the big city, but it still stands on its own.
C A small town just south of here has not yet been swallowed up by the big city, however, it still stands on its own.
D Correct as is

2 **A** Perhaps its charm is that it remains decidedly uncool. Dinner at the volunteer fire department.
B Perhaps its charm is that it remains decidedly uncool, for example. In offering dinner at the volunteer fire department.
C Perhaps its charm is that it remains decidedly uncool. For example, dinner is served at the volunteer fire department.
D Correct as is

3 **A** The cooks, they must figure. You didn't come for elegant cuisine, and they don't insult you with pretend sophistication.
B The cooks must figure you didn't come for elegant cuisine, and they don't insult you with pretend sophistication.
C The cooks must figure you didn't come for elegant cuisine, they don't insult you with pretend sophistication.
D Correct as is

Test Practice Bank

Writing Skills

Usage

Read the passage and choose the word or group of words that belongs in each space. Mark the letter of your answer on a bubble sheet if your teacher provides one; otherwise, number from 1 to 6 on a separate sheet of paper, and write the letter of the correct answer next to each number.

I think that the new apartment building being planned in New York City __(1)__! To begin with, the edifice will be __(2)__ than all the buildings around it. It will loom over all of __(3)__. The city zoning officials have interpreted city codes much too __(4)__. People __(5)__ time to protest the building permit. When people become more aware of the building proposal, they certainly __(6)__ their objections known.

1 **A** had been dreadful
B will be dreadful
C has been dreadful
D should have been dreadful

2 **A** much taller
B tallest
C more taller
D most tallest

3 **A** it
B those
C them
D they

4 **A** losing
B lose
C loose
D loosely

5 **A** haven't had no
B haven't had
C ain't had any
D hadn't no

6 **A** will make
B will have made
C made
D will have been making

Writing Prompts: Persuasive Letters

Some people believe that students should be required to participate in volunteer work before being allowed to graduate from high school. What is your position on this issue? Write a letter to your local school board stating your position and supporting it with convincing reasons. Be sure to explain your reasons in detail.

Imagine that you could have a safety feature on your computer that would protect your personal data, such as your social security number and financial information, from being misused. However, the safety feature also would allow people to record your use of the Internet. Would you give up some of your privacy in exchange for this safety feature? Write a letter to the editor of your local newspaper stating your position and supporting it with convincing reasons.

Correlations to Standardized Tests

The writing skills practice items and writing prompts on this page correspond to the following standardized test section:

ACT English: Usage

Answers

1 (B) The future tense is needed because the building is not yet built; it is only being planned.
2 (A) *Much taller* is the correct comparative form.
3 (C) *Them* is the objective pronoun that correctly agrees with its antecedent, *buildings*.
4 (D) The adverb *loosely* is needed to modify the verb *interpreted*.
5 (B) *Haven't had* is the correct negative; the other choices are incorrect double negatives.
6 (A) Only the simple future tense is needed.

Rubric for Writing Prompts

0	1	2	3	4
ff topic ank paper reign language egible, incoherent ot enough content to ore	Incorrect purpose, mode, or audience Brief, vague Unelaborated Rambling Lack of language control Poor organization	Correct purpose, mode, audience Some elaboration Some details Gaps in organization Limited language control	Correct purpose, mode, audience Moderately well elaborated Clear, effective language Organized (perhaps with brief digressions)	Correct purpose, mode, audience Effective elaboration Consistent organization Sense of completeness, fluency

Correlations to Standardized Tests

The writing skills practice items on this page correspond to the following standardized test section:

ACT English: Usage/Mechanics

Answers

1 (B) This choice correctly combines the two sentences, placing "a small town in North Texas" in apposition to "place."

2 (C) A comma is needed after "Panhandle" to finish setting off the appositive phrase.

3 (D) An apostrophe is needed to make *McMurtry's* possessive.

4 (A) A serial comma is needed after "Poetry."

Test Practice Bank

Writing Skills

Revising and Editing

Read the passage, and then answer the questions that follow. Mark the letter of your answer on a bubble sheet if your teacher provides one; otherwise, number from 1 to 4 on a separate sheet of paper, and write the letter of the correct answer next to each number.

One of the best used-book stores around is emerging in an out-of-the way place. This out-of-the-way place is a small town in North Texas. Larry McMurtry, the author of Lonesome Dove, an epic novel about a Texas cattle drive, and The Last Picture Show, a novel about modern life in the Texas Panhandle is bringing used books to Archer City. A lot of them. He plans for his store, called Booked Up, eventually to have a million books.

Closed-up buildings in Archer City have provided ample room for housing McMurtrys collection, which now fills up four storefronts. A former car dealership provides the most space. Poetry fiction, and literature in translation are spread out over three stores across the street. Some of the store's treasures could be expected—loads of mysteries, children's books, and biographies. Others are a charming surprise.

1 What is the **BEST** way to combine the two sentences in lines 1–2? (*"One of . . . North Texas."*)

A In a small town in North Texas, one of the best used-book stores around is emerging in an out-of-the way place.

B One of the best used-book stores around is emerging in an out-of-the way place, a small town in North Texas.

C One of the best used-book stores around is emerging, and it is emerging in an out-of-the way place—a small town in North Texas.

D One of the best used-book stores around is emerging in an out-of-the way place, but this out-of-the-way place is a small town in North Texas.

2 What is the **BEST** change, if any, to make in the sentence in lines 2–5? (*"Larry McMurtry . . . Archer City."*)

A change **Last Picture Show** to **"Last Picture Show"**

B Delete the comma after ***drive***

C Insert a comma after ***Panhandle***

D Make no change

3 What is the **BEST** change to make in the sentence in lines 7–8 (*"Closed-up . . . four storefronts."*)

A Delete the comma after ***collection***

B Change ***fills*** to **fill**

C Change ***housing*** to **houses**

D Change ***McMurtrys*** to **McMurtry's**

4 What is the **BEST** change to make in the sentence in lines 9–10 (*"Poetry fiction . . .the street."*)

A Insert a comma after ***Poetry***

B Insert a comma after ***literature***

C Change ***translation*** to **translate**

D Make no change

Reading Comprehension and Writing Tasks

Read the passage, and then answer the questions that follow. Mark the letter of your answer on a bubble sheet if your teacher provides one; otherwise, number from 1 to 9 on a separate sheet of paper, and write the letter of the correct answer next to each number.

Wheat Field With Kayak

1 If one must be present for an act of severe weather, I recommend the relatively well-mannered type of flood I once witnessed. Floods can be violent, dangerous, and destructive. They trap people in houses, forcing them onto roofs and into rescue boats. They whisk people out of their cars, leaving them clinging to the tops of trees. My flood wasn't like that. It was destructive, yes, but leisurely enough to allow time for reflection.

2 When I went to bed that evening, no one appeared at all worried about the creek that ran past our farm. It had been raining all day, and raining upstream even harder, but Turkey Creek hadn't flooded in years. Well, it occasionally came out of its banks and plopped mud on the alfalfa field, but that didn't hurt much. When I woke up in the middle of the night, I hadn't a clue why there were so many people around. The neighbors had come to help move machinery to higher ground and to move furniture out of the basement. They advised us that a soggy mattress weighs several hundred pounds and that we really wanted to move beds while they were dry.

3 Rearranging furniture at midnight was a novelty, and I cheerfully contributed my part. Still, the preparations for our flood seemed rather casual. No, we didn't need to move all the equipment, my father said. Surely the water won't get that high. The neighbors took their leave and went home to their houses on the hill. After a time, my mother suggested that we should leave, too. I said I couldn't possibly go without ironing my clothes for school the next day. In the time it took for my parents to get the car from the garage, a wall of water rolled across the driveway. As we watched from the porch, the water over the road became too high to drive through even in the pickup. Sixth grade would have to wait.

4 Even at this point, our flood remained interesting rather than threatening. (The prospect of missing school was interesting, indeed.) At some point, the electricity went out, and we used the emergency kerosene lamps that were stored in the kitchen cabinet. I watched them glow in the bedroom mirror as I listened to the sound of water pouring in the basement window and lapping against the walls. My father was listening, too, and at some point he cleared the stairs to the attic, just in case.

Correlations to Standardized Tests

The reading comprehension and writing skills practice items on these three pages correspond to the following standardized test section:

ACT Reading

5 He could have saved himself the trouble. The water crested at the end of the sidewalk, just at the bottom of our front porch stairs. It kindly left our house dry, but when we rose the next morning, we saw how it had transformed our farm. My father stood on the front porch, looking at the muddy brown water flowing over our yard, and he recited his version of a line from Whittier's "Snowbound": "I looked out on a world unknown / A world I could not call my own."

1 The narrator's family prepares for a flood by—
A moving furniture and equipment
B moving livestock
C leaving for higher ground
D repairing kayaks

2 The problem shown in Paragraph 2 is that—
A water has entered the narrator's house
B cattle are stranded
C rain has been falling all day
D furniture has been destroyed

3 The family's neighbors arrive to—
A take them to safety
B help them move property
C take shelter from the flood
D discuss the change in weather

4 The main idea of Paragraph 3 is that the family—
A managed to save all their belongings
B scoffed at their neighbors' warnings
C were panicked by the rushing water
D waited too long to leave their home

5 From Paragraph 3, the reader can tell that the narrator's father is NOT easily—
A embarrassed
B worried
C angered
D pleased

6 From Paragraph 4, the reader can tell that the narrator is treating the events of the flood as—
A a tragedy
B a comedy
C an adventure
D a catastrophe

7 The actions of the narrator's father in Paragraph 4 show that he is—
A lackadaisical concerning the flood
B vigilant about preparing for the flood
C nervous about his valuable property
D prepared to move his family to safety

8 In Paragraph 5, the narrator's father uses figurative language to describe
A the foolhardiness of human beings
B nature's power
C the gift of friendship
D the wisdom of animals

9 Which of these is a theme for this essay?
A Nature's power can be fascinating when viewed from a safe distance.
B Nature's power can be cruel and brutal.
C Nature's power can be random and unpredictable.
D Nature's power can be gentle and beautiful.

Answers

1 (A) Paragraph 2 states that neighbors had come to help move machinery and furniture.
2 (C) Although the rain had not entered the narrator's house, it had been falling all day and threatened a flood.
3 (B) Paragraph 2 states that neighbors had come to help move machinery and furniture.
4 (D) Because the water was already pouring in the basement window and the father cleared the stairs to the attic, the writer implies that the family waited too long to leave their home.
5 (B) The father seems not to be easily worried because the atmosphere in the house is calm, and although he cleared the stairs to the attic, he did it "at some point," apparently without making a fuss about it.
6 (C) The narrator states that the flood remained interesting rather than threatening, and she liked the prospect of missing school.
7 (D) By clearing the stairs, the father shows he is ready to move his family to safety.
8 ((B) The father refers to their farm as a "world unknown" because it has been transformed by the power of nature.
9 (C) The theme is expressed in the father's version of the line from Whittier: He could not call the world his own because of the randomness and unpredictability of nature's power.

Test Practice Bank

Writing Tasks

The following activity is designed to assess your writing ability. The prompts will ask you to explain something. You may think of your audience as being any reader other than yourself.

> Explain how the actions of the narrator's father give you insight into his character. Support your answer with evidence from the essay.

> The author states that the flood "was destructive, yes, but leisurely enough to allow time for reflection." Write a short essay discussing the ways in which the author supports this statement.

> How does a potential crisis, such as the flood in this essay, tend to bring out the best in people? Find instances in the essay of people being good-natured. Then write your own essay, using real or made-up examples, describing how people come together in a time of need.

> In "Wheat Field With Kayak," the narrator witnesses a potentially devastating flood that causes her to reflect on forces beyond her control and her own family's good fortune.
>
> Write an essay explaining how high-school students deal with forces beyond their control. You may use examples from real life, the selection you just read, books, movies, music, or television shows.

Rubric for Writing Prompts

0	1	2	3	4
f topic nk paper reign language gible, incoherent ot enough content to ore	Incorrect purpose, mode, or audience Brief, vague Unelaborated Rambling Lack of language control Poor organization	Correct purpose, mode, audience Some elaboration Some details Gaps in organization Limited language control	Correct purpose, mode, audience Moderately well elaborated Clear, effective language Organized (perhaps with brief digressions)	Correct purpose, mode, audience Effective elaboration Consistent organization Sense of completeness, fluency

GLOSSARY

abashed (ə bashd′) *adj.*: Embarrassed

adept (ə dept′) *adj.*: Expert; highly skilled

admonition (ad′ mə nish′ ən) *n.*: Warning; mild reprimand

adroit (ə droit′) *adj.*: Clever

aggrieved (ə grēvd′) *v.*: Wronged

alluvium (ə lo͞o′ vē əm) *n.*: Material such as sand or gravel deposited by moving water

amenable (ə mē′ nə bəl) *adj.*: Responsive; open

amiably (ā′ mē ə blē) *adv.*: In a cheerful, friendly way

anarchists (an′ ər kists) *n.*: Those who disrespect laws or rules

annals (an′ əlz) *n.*: Historical records or chronicles; history

apotheosis (ə päth′ ē ō′ sis) *n.*: Glorification of a person or thing; raising of something to the status of a god

apprenticed (ə pren′ tist) *v.*: Assigned to work a specified length of time in a craft or trade in return for instruction

appurtenances (ə purt′ ən əns əz) *n.*: Accessories

arabesque (ar′ ə besk′) *adj.*: Elaborately designed

arable (ar′ ə bəl) *adj.*: Suitable for growing crops

ardent (är′ dənt) *adj.*: Warm or intense in feeling

arias (är′ ē əz) *n.*: Melodies in an opera, especially for solo voice with instrumental accompaniment

assailed (ə sāld′) *v.*: Attacked physically

assimilate (ə sim′ ə lāt′) *v.*: To absorb into a greater body

assuage (ə swāj′) *v.*: Calm; pacify

asunder (ə sun′ dər) *adv.*: Into pieces or parts

audaciously (ô dā′ shəs lē) *adv.*: In a bold way

august (ô gust′) *adj.*: Imposing and magnificent

austere (ô stir′) *adj.*: Severe; stern

avaricious (av′ ə rish′ əs) *adj.*: Greedy for riches

banal (bā′ nəl) *adj.*: Dull or stale because of overuse

belay (bi lā′) *n.*: Rope support

blasphemy (blas′ fə mē) *n.*: Disrespectful action or speech against a deity

bough (bou) *n.*: Tree branch

bouquet (bo͞o kā′) *n.*: Fragrance

bowels (bou′ əlz) *n.*: Intestines; guts

brittle (brit′ əl) *adj.*: Stiff and unbending; easily broken or shattered

centenarian (sen′ tə ner′ ē ən) *n.*: Person who is at least one hundred years old

cessation (se sā′ shən) *n.*: Stopping, either forever or for some time

chastisement (chas tiz′ mənt) *n.*: Punishment; severe criticism

choleric (käl′ ər ik) *adj.*: Quick-tempered

chorister (kôr′ is tər) *n.*: Member of a chorus

clarity (klar′ ə tē) *n.*: The quality or condition of being clear

commiserate (kə miz′ ər āt′) *v.*: Sympathize; share suffering

communal (käm yo͞o′ nəl) *adj.*: Shared by the community

compelled (kəm peld′) *v.*: Forced to do something

condescension (kän′ di sen′ shən) *n.*: Looking down upon; regarding as below one's dignity

conferred (kən furd′) *v.*: Granted or bestowed

confounded (kən found′ id) *adj.*: Confused

consorted (kän sôr′ tid) *v.*: Joined; accompanied

conspicuous (kən spik′ yo͞o əs) *adj.*: Easy to see

constituents (kən stich′ o͞o ənts) *n.*: Components; parts

contagious (kən tā′ jəs) *adj.*: Spread by direct or indirect contact

contemplation (kän′ tem plā′ shən) *n.*: Thoughtful inspection; study

contemplatively (kən tem′ plā tiv lē) *adv.*: In a thoughtful or studious way

contention (kən ten′ shən) *n.*: Statement that one argues for

contrition (kən trish′ ən) *n.*: Feeling of remorse for having done something wrong

convalescents (kän′ və les′ ənts) *n.*: People who are recovering from illness

conviction (kən vik′ shən) *n.*: Strong belief

convoluted (kän′ və lo͞ot′ id) *adj.*: Intricate; twisted

convulsive (kən vul′ siv) *adj.*: Marked by an involuntary muscular contraction

cosmic (käz′ mik) *adj.*: Relating to the universe

countenance (koun′ tə nəns) *n.*: Expression on a person's face

counterfeiting (koun′ tər fit′ iŋ) *v.*: Making imitation money to pass off as real money

covert (kuv′ ərt) *adj.*: Hidden; secret

credulity (krə do͞o′ lə tē) *n.*: Tendency to believe too readily

crocheted (krō shād′) *v.*: Made with thread or yarn woven with hooked needles

cursory (kur′ sə rē) *adj.*: Superficial; done rapidly with little attention to detail

deference (def′ ər əns) *n.*: Yielding in thought

deftness (deft′ nis) *n.*: Skillfulness

demeanor (di mēn′ ər) *n.*: Behavior

deranged (də rānjd′) *adj.*: Unsettled

destitute (des′ tə to͞ot′) *adj.*: Poverty stricken; in great need

destitute (des′ tə to͞ot) *n.*: Those living in poverty

detained (dē tānd′) *v.*: Kept in custody

dilapidated (di lap′ ə dāt′ id) *adj.*: Fallen into a shabby and neglected state

dire (dīr) *adj.*: Calling for quick action; urgent

disapprobation (dis ap′ rə bā′ shən) *n.*: Disapproval

discernible (di zurn′ i bəl′) *adj.*: Recognizable; noticeable

disconsolate (dis kän′ sə lit) *adj.*: So unhappy that nothing will comfort

discourse (dis kôrs′) *v.*: Speak formally and at length

disparaged (di spar′ ijd) *v.*: Spoke slightly of; belittled

disparaging (di spar′ ij iŋ) *adj.*: Belittling; showing contempt for

disreputable (dis rep′ yo͞o tə bəl) *adj.*: Not respectable

divulge (də vulj′) *v.*: Reveal

doddering (däd′ ər iŋ) *adj.*: Shaky, tottering, or senile

doughty (dout′ ē) *adj.*: Brave; valiant

eclectic (ek lek′ tik) *adj.*: Composed of material from various sources

edifice (ed′ i fis) *n.*: Building

effete (e fēt′) *adj.*: Lacking vigor; overrefined

emanating (em′ ə nāt′ iŋ) *v.*: Coming forth

encroaching (en krōch′ iŋ) *v.*: Trespassing or intruding

engender (in jen′ dər) *v.* Bring about; cause; produce

ensign (en′ sən) *n.*: Old word for a standard bearer; one who carries a flag

enthralls (en thrôlz′) *v.*: Captivates; fascinates

envy (en′ vē) *n.*: Feeling of desire for another's possessions or qualities and jealousy at not having them

ephemeral (i fem′ ə rəl) *adj.*: Passing quickly

epitaph (ep′ ə taf) *n.*: Inscription on a tomb or gravestone

essence (es′ əns) *n.*: Crucial element or basis

euphemism (yo͞o′ fə miz′ əm) *n.*: Word or phrase substituted for a more offensive word or phrase

expedient (ek spē′ dē′ ənt) *adj.*: Convenient

expedition (eks′ pə dish′ ən) *n.*: Journey or voyage for a definite purpose

exploit (eks′ ploit) *n.*: Act or deed, especially a heroic achievement

expound (eks pound′) *v.*: Explain in detail

exquisite (eks′ kwi zit) *adj.*: Delicately beautiful

facetiousness (fə sē′ shəs nəs) *n.*: Act of making jokes at an inappropriate time

fallow (fal′ ō) *adj.*: Plowed but not planted

fastidious (fas tid′ ē əs) *adj.*: Not easy to

please; discriminating

fervor (fur´ vər) *n.*: Passion; zeal

fettered (fet´ ərd) *adj.*: Restrained, as with a chain

flout (flout) *v.*: Show open contempt

fomentation (fō men tā´ shən) *n.*: Incitement; a stirring up

fomentations (fō´ mən tā´ shənz) *n.*: Applications of warm, moist substances in the treatment of an injury

forbore (fôr bôr´) *v.*: Refrained from

ford (fôrd) *n.*: Shallow place in a stream or river where people can cross

foreboding (fôr bōd´ iŋ) *n.*: Feeling that something bad will happen

forestalled (fôr stôld´) *v.*: Prevented by having done something ahead of time

forlorn (fər lôrn´) *adj.*: Abandoned; deserted

fortuitous (fôr to͞o´ ə təs) *adj.*: Accidental and beneficial at the same time

frond (fränd) *n.*: Leaflike shoot of seaweed

furtively (fur´ tiv lē) *adv.*: Secretly; stealthily

fusillade (fyo͞o´ sə lād´) *n.*: Something that is like the rapid firing of many firearms

gibe (jīb) *v.*: Jeer; taunt

gout (gout) *n.*: Spurt; splash; glob

grimace (gri´ məs) *n.*: Twisted facial expression

grimacing (grim´ əs iŋ) *v.*: Making a twisted or distorted facial expression

guileless (gīl´ lis) *adj.*: Without slyness or cunning; frank

habiliments (hə bil´ ə mənts) *n.*: Clothing

hindrances (hin´ drəns əz) *n.*: People or things in the way; obstacles

hue (hū) *n.*: Color; tint

imminent (im´ ə nənt) *adj.*: About to happen

immutable (im myo͞ot´ ə bəl) *adj.*: Unchangeable

impediments (im pĕd´ ə məntz) *n.*: Something standing in the way of something else

impending (im pen´ diŋ) *adj.*: About to happen

imperceptibly (im pər sep´ tə blē) *adv.*: In such a slight way as to be almost unnoticeable

imperious (im pir´ ē əs) *adj.*: Commanding; powerful

imperiously (im pir´ ē əs lē´) *adv.*: Arrogantly

impertinence (im purt´ ən əns) *n.*: Inappropriate, rude action

impetuous (im pech´ o͞o əs) *adj.*: Impulsive; passionate

implicit (im plis´ it) *adj.*: Essentially a part of; inherent

imploring (im plôr´ iŋ) *v.*: Asking or begging

importunity (im´ pôr to͞on´ i tē) *n.*: Persistence in requesting or demanding

impregnable (im preg´ nə bəl) *adj.*: Unconquerable; not able to be captured

incessantly (in ses´ ənt lē´) *adv.*: Endlessly; constantly

incredulity (in´ krə do͞o´ lə tē) *n.*: Unwillingness or inability to believe

indigence (in´ di jəns) *n.*: Poverty

indignant (in dig´ nənt) *adj.*: Feeling or expressing anger or scorn, especially at an injustice

indignantly (in dig´ nənt lē) *adv.*: Feeling anger as a reaction to ungratefulness

indomitable (in däm´ it ə bəl) *adj.*: Not easily defeated

induced (in do͞ost´) *v.*: Caused

indulgence (in dul´ jəns) *n.*: Leniency; forgiveness

inert (i nurt´) *adj.*: Lacking the power to move; inactive

inestimable (in es´ tə mə bəl) *adj.*: Priceless; beyond measure

inexorably (in eks´ ə rə blē) *adv.*: Certainly

infested (in fest´ id) *adj.*: Overrun by

infirmity (in fur´ mə tē) *n.*: Illness; physical defect

influx (in´ fluks) *n.*: A coming in

ingratiating (in grā´ shē āt´ iŋ) *adj.*: Bringing into favor

inherent (in hir´ ənt) *adj.*: Inborn; existing in naturally and inseparably

insatiable (in sā´ shə bəl) *adj.*: Cannot be satisfied; constantly wanting more

interminable (in tur´ mi nə bəl) *adj.*: Seemingly endless

irascible (i ras´ ə bəl) *adj.*: Easily angered; quick-tempered

itinerary (ī tin´ ər er´ ē) *n.*: Route

jangle (jaŋ´ gəl) *n.*: Discord; harsh sounds

jauntiness (jônt´ ē nis) *n.*: Carefree attitude

jovial (jō´ vē əl) *adj.*: Full of good humor

judicious (jo͞o dish´ əs) *adj.*: Showing good judgment; wise and careful

laborious (lə bôr´ ē əs) *adj.*: Involving or calling for much hard work; difficult

labyrinth (lab´ ə rinth) *n.*: Maze

laconic (lə kän´ ik) *adj.*: Terse; using few words

lacquered (lak´ ərd) *adj.*: Coated with varnish made from shellac or resin

lamentation (la mən tā´ shən) *n.*: Act of crying out in grief; wailing

legacies (leg´ ə sēz) *n.*: Money, property, or position left in a will to someone

lifeless (līf´ lis) *adj.*: Without life

limpid (lim´ pid) *adj.*: Perfectly clear; transparent

litany (lit´ ən ē) *n.*: Series of responsive religious readings

loomed (lo͞omd) *v.*: Appeared in a large or threatening form

luminous (lo͞o´ mə nəs) *adj.*: Giving off light

malevolent (mə lev´ ə lənt´) *adj.*: Intended as evil or harmful

malice (mal´ is) *n.*: Desire to harm or see harm done to others

maligned (mə līnd´) *adj.*: Spoken ill of

manifestation (man´ ə fes tā´ shən) *n.*: Something that is made clear or plainly revealed

manifestations (man´ ə fes tā´ shənz) *n.*: Appearances or evidence

marginal (mär´ jən əl) *adj.*: Occupying the borderland of a stable area

mauled (môld) *adj.*: Roughly or clumsily handled

melancholy (mel´ ən käl´ ē) *adj.*: Sad and depressed

metamorphosis (met´ ə môr´ fə sis) *n.*: Change of form

misconstrued (mis kän stro͞od´) *v.*: Misunderstood; misinterpreted

monosyllabic (mon´ ō si lab´ ik) *adj.*: Having only one syllable

moreover (môr ō´ vər) *adv.*: In addition to; further

mottled (mät´ əld) *adj.*: Marked with spots of different shades

mutable (myo͞ot´ ə bəl) *adj.*: Capable of change

mutiny (myo͞ot´ ən ē) *n.*: Open rebellion against authority

myriad (mir´ ē əd) *adj.*: Huge number; seemingly countless

nevertheless (nev´ ər thə les´) *adv.*: In spite of that; however

nonchalantly (nän´ shə länt´ lē) *adv.*: Casually; indifferently

obliterates (ə blit´ ə rāts´) *v.*: Destroys; erases without a trace

officious (ə fish´ əs) *adj.*: Overly ready to serve

opacity (ō pas´ ə tē) *n.*: Quality of not letting light pass through

oration (ô rā´ shən) *n.*: Formal speech, especially one given at a state occasion, ceremony, or funeral

oratory (ôr´ ə tôr´ ē) *n.*: Skill in public speaking

paddocks (pad´ əks) *n.*: Small enclosed fields

pallor (pal´ ər) *n.*: Lack of color; unnatural paleness

paranoia (par´ ə noi´ ə) *n.*: Mental disorder characterized by delusions of persecution

peons (pē´ änz) *n.*: Laborers

pervaded (pər vād´ id) *v.*: Spread throughout; filled

philosophy (fil äs´ ə fē) *n.*: System of principles or beliefs

piety (pī´ ə tē) *n.*: Holiness; respect for the divine

piously (pī´ əs lē) *adv.*: With actual or pretended religious devotion

piquancy (pē´ kən sē) *n.*: Pleasantly sharp quality

piqued (pēkt) *v.*: Offended

plausibility (plô´ zə bil´ ə tē) *n.*: Believability

poignant (poin´ yənt) *adj.*: Emotionally moving

portentous (pôr ten´ təs) *adj.*: Foreboding; full of unspecified meaning

portentously (pôr ten´ təs lē) *adv.*: Ominously; scarily

potency (pōt´ ən sē) *n.*: Power

precarious (prē ker´ ē əs) *adj.*: Dangerously lacking in security or stability

precipitous (prē sip´ ə təs) *adj.*: Steep

presage (prē sāj') *v.*: Warn of a future event

prey (prā) *n.*: Animal hunted and killed for food

primeval (prī mē' vəl) *adj.*: Ancient or primitive

procession (prō sesh' ən) *n.*: Number of persons or things moving forward in an orderly or formal way

prodigious (prə dij' əs) *adj.*: Enormous

proficiency (prō fish' ən sē) *n.*: Expertise

profound (prō found') *adj.*: Deep

promontories (präm' ən tôr' ēz) *n.*: High places extending out over a body of water

prosaic (prō zā' ik) *adj.*: Commonplace; ordinary

protagonist (prō tag' ə nist') *n.*: Main character; person who plays a leading part

provender (präv' ən dər) *n.*: Food

psychopathic (sī' kō path' ik) *adj.*: With a dangerous mental disorder

purified (pyoor' ə fīd) *v.*: Cleansed; made pure.

raked (rākd) *v.*: Scratched or scraped, as with a rake

rank (raŋk) *adj.*: Growing vigorously and coarsely

rapture (rap'chər) *n.*: State of being filled with joy

reap (rēp) *v.*: Gather

reciprocity (res' ə präs' ə tē) *n.*: Mutual action; dependence

refuse (ref' yo͞oz) *n.*: Anything thrown away as useless

relish (rel' ish) *n.*: Pleasure and enjoyment

repertoire (rep' ə twär) *n.*: Stock of songs that a singer knows and is ready to perform

replication (rep' lə kā' shən) *n.*: Echo or reverberation

repressed (ri presd') *v.:* Held back or restrained

resolution (rez' ə lo͞o' shən) *n.*: Strong determination

reveling (rev' əl iŋ) *v.*: Taking great pleasure

revere (ri vir') *v.:* Regard with deep respect and love

rheumatic (rü ma' tik) *adj.*: Suffering from a disease of the joints; able to move only with great pain

sagacity (sə gas' ə tē) *n.*: Wisdom

sated (sāt' əd) : Satisfied or pleased

satiated (sā' shē ā tid) *adj.*: Having had enough; full

saturated (sach' ə rāt' id) *v.*: Completely filled; thoroughly soaked

scrimmage (skrim' ij) *n.*: Rough-and-tumble fight

scrutinized (skro͞ot' ən īzd') *v.*: Looked at carefully; examined closely

sententiously (sen ten' shəs lē) *adv.*: Pointed; expressing much in few words

sheaf (shēf) *n.*: Bundle of grain

shirked (shûrkt) *v.*: Neglected or avoided

sidle (sī' dəl) *v.*: Move sideways in a sneaky way

slanderous (slan' dər əs) *adj.*: Damaging to a person's reputation

sordid (sôr' did) *adj.*: Dirty; filthy

sovereigns (säv' rənz) *n.*: British gold coins worth one pound each

spare (sper) *adj.*: Lean or thin

spurn (spurn) *v.*: Old word meaning "to kick disdainfully"

staidness (stād' nəs) *n.*: State of being settled or resistant to change

stark (stärk) *adj.*: Bare; plain

staunch (stônch) *adj.*: Steadfast; loyal

stifle (stī' fəl) *v.*: Hold back

stupefied (sto͞o' pə fīd') *adj.*: Dazed; stunned

stupor (sto͞o' per) *n.*: Mental dullness, as if drugged

subjectively (səb jek' tiv lē) *adv.*: Personally

sublimity (sə blim' ə tē) *n.*: A noble or exalted state

sullen (sul' ən) *adj.*: Gloomy; sad

sullenness (sul' ən nəs) *n.*: Gloom; sadness

sultry (sul' trē) *adj.*: Oppressively hot and moist; sweltering

supernal (sə purn' əl) *adj.*: Celestial or divine

supplication (sup' lə kā' shən) *n.*: The act of asking humbly and earnestly

surly (sur' lē) *adv.*: In a proud, commanding way

surpassed (sər past') *v.*: Went beyond; excelled

syndrome (sin' drōm) *n.*: Group of signs that occur together and may form a pattern

synthesis (sin' thə sis) *n.*: Whole made up of separate elements put together

synthesized (sin' thə sīzd') *v.*: Made by bringing together different elements

synthetic (sin thet' ik) *adj.*: Artificially made

taciturn (ta' sə tərn) *adj.*: Preferring not to talk; uncommunicative; silent

taut (tôt) *adj.*: High-strung; tense

tempering (tem' pə riŋ) *adj.*: Modifying or adjusting

tenuous (ten' yoo wəs) *adj.*: Slight; flimsy; not substantial or strong

terra firma (ter' ə fur' mə): Latin for "solid earth."

thrall (thrôl) *n.*: Servant; slave

timorous (tim' ər es) *adj.*: Full of fear; timid

titanic (tī tan' ik) *adj.*: Huge and powerful

topography (tə päg' rə fē) *n.*: Surface features of a place, such as rivers, lakes, mountains, and so on

transcends (tran sendz') *v.*: Goes above or beyond limits; exceeds

transoms (tran' səmz) *n.*: Small windows

tremulous (trem' yo͞o ləs) *adj.*: Trembling; quivering

trod (träd) *v.*: Walked

trough (trôf) *n.*: Long, shallow V-shaped container from which farm animals drink water or eat feed

tumult (to͞o' mult) *n.*: Noisy commotion

ulterior (ul tir' ē ər) *adj.*: Undisclosed; beyond what is openly stated

undulations (un' dyo͞o lā' shənz) *n.*: Waves

unwieldy (un wēl' dē) *adj.*: Hard to manage because of shape or weight

usurped (yo͞o surpt') *v.*: Taken power over; held by force

venerable (ven' ər ə bəl) *adj.*: Worthy of respect by reason of age and dignity, character, or position

ventured (ven' chərd) *v.*: Took a risk

veracity (və ras' ə tē) *n.*: Truthfulness; honesty

vernal (vurn' əl) *adj.*: Springlike

vertigo (vur' ti gō) *n.*: Dizzy, confused state of mind

vestibule (ves' tə byül) *n.*: Small entrance hall or room

vigilance (vij' ə lens) *n.*: Watchfulness; alertness

vile (vīl) *adj.*: Extremely disgusting

vociferous (vō sif' ər əs) *adj.*: Loud; noisy

volition (vō lish' ən) *n.*: The act of using the will

wallowed (wäl' ōd) *v.*: Enjoyed completely; took great pleasure

warrens (wôr' ənz) *n.*: Mazelike passages

watershed (wô' tər shed) *n.*: Moment or event after which nothing is the same

weir (wēr) *n.*: Low dam

zenith (zē' nith) *n.*: Highest point

Literary Terms Handbook

ACT *See* Drama.

ALLITERATION *Alliteration* is the repetition of initial consonant sounds. Writers use alliteration to give emphasis to words, to imitate sounds, and to create musical effects. Notice, in the following lines from Jean Toomer's "Reapers," how the *s* sounds suggest the sound of the blades sliding against stones to be sharpened.

> Black reapers with the sound of steel on stones/Are sharpening scythes . . .

See also Assonance, Consonance, *and* Rhyme.

ALLUSION An *allusion* is a reference to a well-known person, place, event, literary work, or work of art. Writers often make allusions to famous works such as the Bible or William Shakespeare's plays. They also make allusions to mythology, politics, or current events. For example, the title of Stephen Vincent Benét's story "By the Waters of Babylon," p. 500, is an allusion to Psalm 137 in the Bible.

ANECDOTE An *anecdote* is a brief story about an interesting, amusing, or strange event. Anecdotes are told to entertain or to make a point. James Thurber, for example, fills "The Dog That Bit People," p. 234, with humorous anecdotes about his family and their dog, Muggs.

See also Narrative.

ANTAGONIST The *antagonist* of a work is the character who opposes the protagonist (the character whom readers want to see succeed). Creon is the antagonist in the play *Antigone*, p. 670.

See also Character *and* Protagonist.

ANTICLIMAX Like a climax, an *anticlimax* is the turning point in a story. However, an anticlimax is always a letdown. It's the point at which you learn that the story will not turn out the way you'd expected.

APHORISM An *aphorism* is a brief, memorable saying that expresses a basic truth. Many cultures pass on wisdom in the form of aphorisms, such as the aphorisms from Confucius' *The Analects*, p. 204.

ASIDE An *aside* is a short speech delivered by an actor in a play, expressing the character's thoughts.

In his autobiography, *Rare Air: Michael on Michael*, Michael Jordan shares his experiences through words and photographs.

Traditionally, the aside is directed to the audience and is presumed to be inaudible to the other actors.

ASSONANCE *Assonance* is the repetition of vowel sounds followed by different consonants in two or more stressed syllables. In "The Kraken," p. 825, Tennyson repeats the long e sound in the following lines:

> Below the thunders of the upper *deep*;
> Far, far beneath in the abysmal *sea*,
> His ancient, dreamless, uninvaded *sleep*
> The Kraken sleepeth: faintest sunlights *flee*

See also Consonance.

ATMOSPHERE *Atmosphere*, or *mood*, is the feeling created in a reader by a literary work or passage. The atmosphere is often suggested by descriptive details. The following lines from "The Stolen Child," p. 815, create a mysterious, mystical atmosphere in which a meeting takes place between fairies and a human child:

> Where the wave of moonlight glosses
> The dim grey sands with light

AUTOBIOGRAPHY An *autobiography* is a form of nonfiction in which a person tells his or her own life story. An autobiography may tell about the person's whole life or only a part of it. "A Child's Christmas in Wales," p. 596, is an autobiographical incident from the life of writer Dylan Thomas.

See also Biography *and* Nonfiction.

BIOGRAPHY A *biography* is a form of nonfiction in which a writer tells the life story of another person. Biographies have been written about many famous people, historical and contemporary, but they can also be written about "ordinary" people. "Marion Anderson: Famous Concert Singer," p. 602, is a brief biography by Langston Hughes.

See also Autobiography and Nonfiction.

BLANK VERSE *Blank verse* is poetry written in unrhymed iambic pentameter lines. This verse form was widely used by Elizabethan dramatists like William Shakespeare. *The Tragedy of Julius Caesar,* p. 712, is written mostly in blank verse.

See also Meter.

CHARACTER A *character* is a person or an animal who takes part in the action of a literary work. The *main character,* or *protagonist,* is the most important character in a story. This character often changes in some important way as a result of the story's events.

The *antagonist* opposes the main character. Characters are sometimes classified as round or flat, dynamic or static. A round character shows many different traits—faults as well as virtues. Annie John's mother in *A Walk to the Jetty* is an example of a round character. At times, she is kind and loving to Annie; at other times, she is stern and overbearing. Annie's father is a flat character. We see him only as a quiet, nonconfrontational man. A dynamic character develops and grows during the course of the story, as does Tom Benecke in Jack Finney's "Contents of the Dead Man's Pocket," on p. 5. A static character does not change. Scoresby in Mark Twain's "Luck," p. 520, is a static character.

See also Antagonist, Characterization, Motivation, *and* Protagonist.

CHARACTERIZATION *Characterization* is the act of creating and developing a character. In *direct characterization,* the author directly states a character's traits. For example, in William Melvin Kelley's "A Visit to Grandmother," on p. 166, GL is described as "part con man, part practical joker and part Don Juan." A writer uses *indirect characterization* when showing a character's personality through his or her actions, thoughts, feelings, words, and appearance or through another character's observations and reactions. In the same story, Kelley presents Chig's observations and memories of his father. Kelley also shows the actions and words of Chig's father during the emotional scene with Chig's grandmother. Such indirect characterization relies on the reader to put together the clues that will designate the character's personality.

See also Character.

CLIMAX The *climax* of a story, novel, or play is the high point of interest or suspense. The events that make up the rising action lead up to the climax. The events that make up the falling action follow the climax. The climax of "Damon and Pythias," p. 102, occurs when the deadline has been reached and Pythias has not yet returned.

See also Conflict, Plot, *and* Anticlimax.

CONFLICT A *conflict* is a struggle between opposing forces. Characters in conflict form the basis of stories, novels, and plays.

There are two kinds of conflict: external and internal. In an *external conflict,* the main character struggles against an outside force, as in Carl Stephenson's "Leiningen Versus the Ants," p. 480, in which Leiningen and his men struggle against an army of ants. The outside force may be nature itself, in a person-against-nature conflict. Edmund Hillary and Tenzing Norgay face such a conflict in "The Final Assault."

An *internal conflict* involves a character in conflict with himself or herself. For example, in Doris Lessing's "Through the Tunnel," p. 221, Jerry faces a struggle between his desire to swim through the tunnel and his fear of the danger involved.

A story may have more than one conflict. In addition to his internal conflict, Jerry also faces external conflicts—the tunnel's length and the oppressive water pressure.

See also Plot.

CONNOTATION The *connotation* of a word is the set of ideas associated with it in addition to its explicit meaning. For example, the title "The Bean Eaters" refers literally to people who eat beans. The phrase connotes simplicity and poverty.

The connotation of a word can be personal, based on individual experiences, but more often, cultural connotations—those recognizable by most people in a group—determine a writer's word choices.

See also Denotation.

CONSONANCE *Consonance* is the repetition of similar consonant sounds at the end of accented syllables. In "Meeting at Night," p. 827, the repeated *t* and *ch* sounds in "the spurt of a lighted match" create consonance. Consonance is used to create musical effects, to link ideas, and to emphasize particular words.

See also Assonance.

COUPLET A *couplet* is a pair of rhyming lines, usually of the same length and meter. A couplet generally expresses a single idea. Shakespeare's Sonnet 18, on p. 866, ends with the following couplet:

> So long as men can breathe, or eyes can see
> So long lives this, and this gives life to thee.

See also Stanza.

CRITICAL REVIEW A *critical review* offers one person's judgment of a movie, play, or other performance. In the review, the reviewer discusses the various elements of the performance and makes a recommendation. Critical reviews tend to be persuasive.

See also Persuasion.

DENOTATION The *denotation* of a word is its dictionary meaning, independent of other associations that the word may have. The denotation of the word *lake*, for example, is an inland body of water.

See also Connotation.

DENOUEMENT See Plot.

DESCRIPTION A *description* is a portrait in words of a person, place, or object. Descriptive writing uses sensory details—those that appeal to the senses: sight, hearing, taste, smell, and touch. Description can be found in all types of writing. Annie Dillard's essay "Flood," on p. 610, contains descriptive passages.

DEVELOPMENT See Plot.

DIALECT *Dialect* is the form of language spoken by people in a particular region or group. Pronunciation, vocabulary, and sentence structure are affected by dialect. Writers use dialect to make their characters sound realistic and to create local color. In Chinua Achebe's "Civil Peace," on p. 396, some of the characters speak in a Nigerian dialect of English.

DIALOGUE A *dialogue* is a conversation between characters. Writers use dialogue to reveal character, to present events, to add variety to a narrative, and to interest readers.

DICTION *Diction* is word choice. To discuss a writer's diction is to consider the vocabulary used, the appropriateness of the words, and the vividness of the language. Both the *denotation*, or literal meaning, and the *connotation*, or associations, of words contribute to the overall effect. Diction can be formal, as in this excerpt from Edgar Allan Poe's "The Masque of the Red Death," which begins on p. 78:

> It was a voluptuous scene, that masquerade. But first let me tell of the rooms in which it was held. There were seven—an imperial suite.

Diction can also be informal and conversational, as in these lines from "Flood" by Annie Dillard, on p. 610:

> Women are bringing coffee in mugs to the road crew . . . Some kid starts doing tricks on a skateboard; I head home.

See also Connotation *and* Denotation.

DIRECT CHARACTERIZATION
See Characterization.

DRAMA A *drama* is a story written to be performed by actors. The script of a drama is made up of dialogue—the words the actors say—and stage directions, which are comments on how and where action occurs.

The drama's setting is the place where the action occurs. It is indicated by one or more sets that suggest interior or exterior scenes. Props are objects, such as a sword or a cup of tea, that are used onstage.

At the beginning of most plays, a brief exposition gives the audience some background information about the characters and the situation. Just as in a story or novel, the plot of a drama is built around characters in conflict.

Dramas are divided into large units called *acts* and into smaller units called *scenes*. A long play may include many sets that change with the scenes or it may indicate a change of scene with lighting.

See also Genre, Stage Directions, *and* Tragedy.

DRAMATIC IRONY See Irony.

DRAMATIC POETRY *Dramatic poetry* is poetry that uses the techniques of drama. A dramatic poem is a verse that presents the speech of one or more characters. Dramatic poems are like little plays and usually involve many narrative elements, such as setting, conflict, and plot. Such elements may be found in Rudyard Kipling's "Danny Deever," on p. 850.

EPIC An *epic* is a long narrative or narrative poem about the deeds of gods or heroes. Because of its length and its loftiness of theme, an epic usually presents a telling portrait of the culture in which it was produced. The ancient *folk epics* like the *Ramayana* and *Sundiata* were recited aloud as entertainment at feasts and were not written down until long after they were composed.

See also Narrative Poem.

ESSAY An *essay* is a short nonfiction work about a particular subject. In an *analytical essay*, the author breaks down a large idea into parts. By explaining how the parts of a concept or an object fit together, the essay helps readers understand the whole idea or thing.

A *descriptive* essay seeks to convey an impression about a person, place, or object. In "Flood," p. 610, Annie Dillard describes the effects of a terrible storm.

An *expository* essay gives information, discusses ideas, or explains a process. In Rachel Carson's "The Marginal World," p. 571, the author presents examples and facts that share information about the mysterious sea in a personal and entertaining way.

A *humorous essay* presents the author's thoughts on a subject in an amusing way that is intended to make readers laugh. James Thurber's "The Dog That Bit People," p. 234, is a humorous essay.

A *narrative essay* tells a true story. In the narrative essay from "Speak, Memory," on p. 305, Nabokov tells a true story from his childhood.

In a *reflective essay*, a writer shares his or her thoughts about and impressions of an idea or experience. In the excerpt from *The Way to Rainy Mountain*, p. 582, N. Scott Momaday reflects on the death of his grandmother.

A *persuasive essay* attempts to convince readers to adopt a particular opinion or course of action. The excerpt from Solzhenitsyn's Nobel lecture, p. 587, and "Keep Memory Alive," p. 591, are persuasive essays.

A *visual essay* presents information or makes a point about a subject through photographs and other visual forms as well as through text. One of the visual essays in this book is "Mothers & Daughters," p. 638.

This classification of essays is loose at best. Most essays contain passages that could be classified differently from the essay as a whole. For example, a descriptive passage may be found in a narrative essay, or a factual, expository section may be used to support a persuasive argument.

See also Description, Exposition, Genre, Narration, Nonfiction, *and* Persuasion.

EXPOSITION *Exposition* is writing or speech that explains a process or presents information. In the plot of a story or drama, the exposition is the part of the work that introduces the characters, the setting, and the basic situation.

EXTENDED METAPHOR In an *extended metaphor*, as in a regular metaphor, a subject is spoken or written of as though it were something else. However, an extended metaphor differs from a regular metaphor in that several comparisons are made. All extended metaphors sustain the comparison for several lines or for an entire poem. Eve Merriam uses an extended metaphor in her poem "Metaphor," on p. 836, to compare morning to "a new sheet of paper."

See also Figurative Language *and* Metaphor.

FALLING ACTION See Plot.

FANTASY A *fantasy* is highly imaginative writing that contains elements not found in real life. Examples of fantasy include stories that involve supernatural elements, stories that resemble fairy tales, and stories that deal with imaginary places and creatures. Many science-fiction stories, such as Ray Bradbury's "There Will Come Soft Rains," on p. 534, contain elements of fantasy.

See also Science Fiction.

FICTION *Fiction* is prose writing that tells about imaginary characters and events. The term is usually used for novels and short stories, but it also applies to dramas and narrative poetry. Some writers rely on their imaginations alone to create their works of fiction. Others base their fiction on actual events and people, to which they add invented characters, dialogue, and plot situations.

See also Genre, Narrative, *and* Nonfiction.

FIGURATIVE LANGUAGE *Figurative language* is writing or speech not meant to be interpreted literally.

Figurative language is often used to create vivid impressions by setting up comparisons between dissimilar things.

Look, for example, at this description from Emily Dickinson's "The Wind tapped like a tired Man":

> His Countenance—a Billow—
> His Fingers, as He passed
> Let go a music—as of tunes
> Blown tremulous in Glass—

Some frequently used figures of speech are *metaphors, similes,* and *personification.*

See also Literal Language, Metaphors, Personification, *and* Similes.

FOOT See Meter.

FORESHADOWING *Foreshadowing* is the use in a literary work of clues that suggest events that have yet to occur. Use of this technique helps to create suspense, keeping readers wondering and speculating about what will happen next. There are many instances of foreshadowing in W. W. Jacobs's "The Monkey's Paw," on p. 46. For example, Mr. White's son says that he bets he never will see the money wished for by his father. This proves true and foreshadows his death.

See also Suspense.

FREE VERSE *Free verse* is poetry not written in a regular rhythmical pattern, or meter. Free verse seeks to capture the rhythms of speech. It is the dominant form of contemporary poetry. "What Are Friends For" by Rosellen Brown, p. 857, and "Making a Fist" by Naomi Shihab Nye, p. 860, are examples of free verse.

See also Meter.

GENRE A *genre* is a category or type of literature. Literature is commonly divided into three major genres: poetry, prose, and drama. Each major genre is in turn divided into smaller genres, as follows:

1. Poetry: Lyric Poetry, Concrete Poetry, Dramatic Poetry, Narrative Poetry, and Epic Poetry
2. Prose: Fiction (Novels and Short Stories) and Nonfiction (Biography, Autobiography, Letters, Essays, and Reports)
3. Drama: Serious Drama and Tragedy, Comic Drama, Melodrama, and Farce

See also Drama, Poetry, *and* Prose.

HAIKU The *haiku* is a three-line verse form. The first and third lines of a haiku each have five syllables. The second line has seven syllables. A haiku seeks to convey a single vivid emotion by means of images from nature. The poems on p. 869 are haiku.

Translators of Japanese haiku try to maintain the syllabic requirements. Western writers, however, sometimes use the form more loosely.

IAMB *See* Meter.

IMAGE An *image* is a word or phrase that appeals to one or more of the five senses—sight, hearing, touch, taste, or smell. Writers use images to re-create sensory experiences in words.

See also Description.

IMAGERY *Imagery* is the descriptive or figurative language used in literature to create word pictures for the reader. These pictures, or images, are created by details of sight, sound, taste, touch, smell, or movement.

INDIRECT CHARACTERIZATION *See* Characterization.

IRONY *Irony* is the general term for literary techniques that portray differences between appearance and reality, expectation and result, or meaning and intention. In *verbal irony,* words are used to suggest the opposite of what is meant. In *dramatic irony,* there is a contradiction between what a character thinks and what the reader or audience knows to be true. In *irony of situation,* an event occurs that directly contradicts the expectations of the characters, the reader, or the audience.

During the funeral in William Shakespeare's *The Tragedy of Julius Caesar,* p. 712, Antony calls Brutus "an honorable man" when, in fact, he wants the people to think just the opposite. This is an example of verbal irony.

In the same play, dramatic irony occurs when the audience, knowing that Caesar will be assassinated, watches him set out on the ides of March.

In W. W. Jacobs's "The Monkey's Paw," p. 46, the Whites expect the paw to bring them happiness; instead, it brings them nothing but grief. This is an example of irony of situation.

LEGEND A *legend* is a widely told story about the past that may or may not have a foundation in fact. One example, retold in many versions, is the legend of King Arthur. A legend often reflects a people's identity or cultural values. It generally has more historical truth and less emphasis on the supernatural than does a myth.

See also Myth.

LITERAL LANGUAGE *Literal language* uses words in their ordinary senses. It is the opposite of *figurative language.* If you tell someone standing on a diving board to jump in, you are speaking literally. If you tell someone standing on a street corner to jump in a lake, you are speaking figuratively.

See also Figurative Language.

LYRIC POEM A *lyric poem* is a highly musical verse that expresses the observations and feelings of a single speaker. In ancient times, lyric poems were sung to the accompaniment of the lyre, a type of stringed instrument. Modern lyric poems are not usually sung. However, they still have a musical quality that is achieved through rhythm and such other devices as alliteration and rhyme. Federico García Lorca's "The Guitar," on p. 856, is a lyric poem expressing the wailing and crying sound of a guitar.

METAPHOR A *metaphor* is a figure of speech in which one thing is spoken of as though it were something else. Unlike a simile, which compares two things using *like* or *as,* a metaphor implies a comparison between them. In "Making a Fist," on p. 857, Naomi Shihab Nye uses this metaphor:

My stomach was a melon
split wide inside my skin.

See also Extended Metaphor *and* Figurative Language.

METER The *meter* of a poem is its rhythmical

Mark Antony's "Friends, Romans, countrymen . . ." monologue from *The Tragedy of Julius Caesar* is one of the most famous dramatic speeches in literature.

pattern. This pattern is determined by the number and types of stresses, or beats, in each line. To describe the meter of a poem, you must scan its lines. *Scanning* involves marking the stressed and unstressed syllables. Each strong stress is marked with a slanted accent mark (´) and each unstressed syllable with a curved accent mark (˘). The stressed and unstressed syllables are then divided by vertical lines (|) into groups called *feet.* The following types of feet are common in English poetry:

1. *Iamb:* a foot with one unstressed syllable followed by a stressed syllable, as in the word "again"
2. *Trochee:* a foot with a stressed syllable followed by an unstressed syllable, as in the word "wonder"
3. *Anapest:* a foot with two unstressed syllables followed by one strong stress, as in the phrase "on the beach"
4. *Dactyl:* a foot with one strong stress followed by two unstressed syllables, as in the word "wonderful"
5. *Spondee:* a foot with two strong stresses, as in the word "spacewalk"

Depending on the type of foot that is most common in them, lines of poetry are described as *iambic, trochaic, anapestic,* and so forth.

Lines are also described in terms of the number of feet that occur in them, as follows:

1. *Monometer:* one foot
   Aľl thíngs
   Áre ă
   Bĕcómiňg.
2. *Dimeter:*
   Ă búyĕr | fŏr thém
   Ă hándsŏme | yoŭng mán
   —"The Bridegroom," p. 54
3. Trimeter:
   Sŭccéss iš | cóuntĕd | swéetĕst
   Bў thóse| whŏ ne´er | sŭccéed.
   —"Success is counted sweetest," p. 148
4. *Tetrameter:* verse written in four-foot lines
5. *Pentameter:* verse written in five-foot lines
6. *Hexameter:* verse written in six-foot lines
7. *Heptameter:* verse written in seven-foot lines

Blank verse is poetry written in unrhymed iambic pentameter. Poetry that does not have a regular meter is called *free verse.*

MONOLOGUE A *monologue* is a speech by one character in a play, story, or poem. A monologue may be addressed to another character or to the audience, or it may be a *soliloquy*—a speech that presents the character's thoughts as though the character were overheard when alone. In Act II, Scene i, of *The Tragedy of Julius Caesar,* p. 712, Brutus delivers an impassioned monologue citing reasons to assassinate Caesar.

See also Drama *and* Soliloquy.

MOOD *See* Atmosphere.

MORAL A *moral* is a lesson taught by a literary work. A fable usually ends with a moral that is directly stated.

MOTIVATION *Motivation* is a reason that explains or partially explains why a character thinks, feels, acts, or behaves in a certain way. Motivation results from a combination of the character's personality and the situation that confronts the character.

See also Character *and* Characterization.

MYTH A *myth* is a fictional tale that explains the actions of gods or the causes of natural phenomena. Unlike legends, myths have little historical truth and involve supernatural elements. Every culture has its collection of myths. Among the most familiar are the myths of the ancient Greeks and Romans. "Damon and Pythias," on p. 102, is a classic Greek myth about the unbreakable bond of friendship.

See also Oral Tradition.

NARRATION *Narration* is writing that tells a story. The act of telling a story in speech is also called narration. Novels and short stories are fictional narratives. Nonfiction works such as news stories, biographies, and autobiographies are also narratives. A narrative poem tells a story in verse.

See also Anecdote, Essay, Narrative Poem, Nonfiction, Novel, *and* Short Story.

NARRATIVE A *narrative* is a story told in fiction, nonfiction, poetry, or drama.

See also Narration.

NARRATIVE POEM A *narrative poem* is one that tells a story. "La Belle Dame sans Merci," on p. 842, is an example of a narrative poem. It tells the story of a knight driven to despair because he loves a pitiless woman.

See also Dramatic Poetry, Epic, *and* Narration.

NARRATOR A *narrator* is a speaker or character who tells a story. The narrator may be either a character in the story or an outside observer. The writer's choice of narrator determines the story's *point of view,* which in turn determines the type and amount of information the writer can reveal.

See also Speaker *and* Point of View.

NONFICTION *Nonfiction* is prose writing that presents and explains ideas or that tells about real people, places, objects, or events. Nonfiction narratives are about actual people, places, and events, unlike fictional narratives, which present imaginary characters and events. To be classed as nonfiction, a work must be true.

Among nonfiction forms are essays, newspaper and magazine articles, journals, travelogues, biographies, and autobiographies. Historical, scientific, technical, political, and philosophical writings are also nonfiction.

See also Autobiography, Biography, *and* Essay.

NOVEL A *novel* is a long work of fiction. Like a short story, a novel has a plot that explores characters in conflict. However, a novel is much longer than a short story and may have one or more subplots, or minor stories, and several themes.

OCTAVE See Stanza.

ONOMATOPOEIA *Onomatopoeia* is the use of words that imitate sounds. *Whirr, thud, sizzle,* and *hiss* are typical examples. Writers can deliberately choose words that contribute to a desired sound effect.

ORAL TRADITION The *oral tradition* is the passing of songs, stories, and poems from generation to generation by word of mouth. Many folk songs, ballads, fairy tales, legends, and myths originated in the oral tradition.

See also Myth.

PARABLE A *parable* is a simple, brief narrative that teaches a lesson by using characters and events to stand for abstract ideas. The parable "How Much Land Does a Man Need?" p. 130, teaches a lesson about greed.

PARODY A *parody* is a comical piece of writing that mocks the characteristics of a specific literary form. Through exaggeration of the types of ideas, language, tone, or action in a type of literature or a specific work, a parody calls attention to the ridiculous aspects of its subject. The excerpt from *Don Quixote*, p. 884, is a parody of the romantic literature that was popular in the late sixteenth century.

PENTAMETER See Meter.

PERSONIFICATION *Personification* is a type of figurative language in which a nonhuman subject is given human characteristics. Emily Dickinson personifies the wind when she describes it as tapping like a tired man.

See also Figurative Language.

PERSUASION *Persuasion* is writing or speech that attempts to convince the reader to adopt a particular opinion or course of action. A newspaper editorial that says a city council decision was wrong is an example of persuasive writing attempting to mold opinion. Critical reviews, such as the reviews of the movie *Star Wars*, pp. 626 and 629, are a form of persuasive writing.

See also Critical Review *and* Essay.

PLOT *Plot* is the sequence of events in a literary work. In most novels, dramas, short stories, and narrative poems, the plot involves both characters and a central conflict. The plot usually begins with an *exposition* that introduces the setting, the characters, and the basic situation. This is followed by the *inciting incident,* which introduces the central conflict. The conflict then increases during the *development* until it reaches a high point of interest or suspense, the *climax.* All the events leading up to the climax make up the *rising action.* The climax is followed by the *falling action,* which leads to the *resolution,* or end, of the central conflict. Any events that occur after the resolution make up the *denouement.*

POETRY *Poetry* is one of the three major types of literature; the others are prose and drama. Most poems make use of highly concise, musical, and emotionally charged language. Many also make use of imagery, figurative language, and special devices of sound such as rhyme. Poems are often divided into lines and stanzas and often employ regular rhythmical patterns, or meters. However, some poems are written out just like prose, and some poems are written in free verse.

See also Free Verse, Genre, Meter, Rhyme, *and* Rhythm.

POINT OF VIEW The *point of view* is the perspective, or vantage point, from which the story is told. If the narrator is part of the action, the story is told from the *first-person* point of view. We see and know only what the character telling the story knows. "By the Waters of Babylon," p. 500, is told from the first-person point of view. In a story told by a *third person,* the narrator is someone outside the action. An *omniscient third-person* narrator is all-knowing; the narrator knows more about the characters and events than any one character can know. The third-person omniscient narrator of "The Street of the Cañon," on p. 440, reveals the thoughts and feelings of several characters. A *limited third-person* narrator tells only the thoughts and feelings of one character. "A Visit to Grandmother," p. 166, is told by a third-person limited narrator.

See also Narrator.

PROSE *Prose* is the ordinary form of written language. Most writing that is not poetry, drama, or song is considered prose. Prose, one of the major genres of literature, occurs in two forms: fiction and nonfiction.

See also Fiction, Genre, *and* Nonfiction.

PROTAGONIST The main character in a work of fiction—the character readers would like to see succeed—is the *protagonist.* Antigone is the protagonist of the play *Antigone.*

See also Antagonist *and* Character.

REPETITION *Repetition* is the use of any element of language—a sound, a word, a phrase, a clause, or a sentence—more than once. In "Prayer of First Dancers" from *The Night Chant,* on p. 828, the words "in the house made" are repeated eight times, each time in connection with a different image.

Poets use many kinds of repetition. Alliteration, assonance, rhyme, and rhythm are repetitions of certain sounds and sound patterns.

A refrain is a repeated line or group of lines. In both prose and poetry, repetition is used for musical effects and for emphasis.

See also Alliteration, Assonance, Consonance, Rhyme, *and* Rhythm.

RESOLUTION See Plot.

RHYME *Rhyme* is the repetition of sounds at the ends of words. *End rhyme* occurs when the rhyming words come at the ends of lines, as in "The Kraken," by Alfred, Lord Tennyson, p. 825:

> Below the thunders of the upper *deep;*
> Far, far beneath in the abysmal **sea,**
> His ancient, dreamless, uninvaded *sleep*
> The Kraken sleepeth: faintest sunlights **flee**

Internal rhyme occurs when the rhyming words fall within a line.

See also Repetition *and* Rhyme Scheme.

RHYME SCHEME A *rhyme scheme* is a regular pattern of rhyming words in a poem. The rhyme scheme of a poem is indicated by using different letters of the alphabet for each new rhyme. In an *aabb* stanza, for example, line 1 rhymes with line 2 and line 3 rhymes with line 4.

Many poems use the same pattern of rhymes, though not the same rhymes, in each stanza.

See also Rhyme.

RHYTHM *Rhythm* is the pattern of *beats,* or stresses, in spoken or written language. Some poems have a very specific pattern, or meter, whereas prose and free verse use the natural rhythms of everyday speech.

See also Meter.

RISING ACTION See Plot.

SCENE See Drama.

SCIENCE FICTION *Science fiction* is writing that tells about imaginary events that involve science or technology. Many science-fiction stories are set in the future. The setting can be on Earth, in space, on other planets, or in a totally imaginary place. Ray Bradbury's "There Will Come Soft Rains," on p. 534, is an example of science fiction.

See also Fantasy.

SENSORY LANGUAGE Sensory language is writing or speech that appeals to one or more of the senses.

See also Image.

SESTET See Stanza.

SETTING The *setting* of a literary work is the time

and place of the action. Time can include not only the historical period—past, present, or future—but also a specific year, season, or time of day. Place may involve not only the geographical place—a region, country, state, or town—but also the social, economic, or cultural environment.

In some stories, setting serves merely as a backdrop for action, a context in which the characters move and speak. In others, however, setting is a crucial element. The setting functions as the "main character" in Ray Bradbury's "There Will Come Soft Rains," on p. 534.

Description of the setting often helps establish the mood of a story. For example, in Edgar Allan Poe's "The Masque of the Red Death," on p. 78, the setting contributes to the growing horror.

See also Mood.

SHORT STORY A *short story* is a brief work of fiction. The short story resembles the longer novel but generally has a simpler plot and setting. In addition, the short story tends to reveal character at a crucial moment rather than to develop it through many incidents. For example, Doris Lessing's "Through the Tunnel," p. 221, concentrates on what happens as Jerry learns to swim through the tunnel.

See also Fiction, Genre, *and* Novel.

SIMILE A *simile* is a figure of speech in which *like* or *as* is used to make a comparison between two basically unlike ideas. "Alexandra is as bright as Jason" is a comparison, not a simile. "Alexandra is as bright as a bulb" is a simile.

Poets often use similes. The following example from Philip Fried's "Right Hand," on p. 838, compares a hand to a Greek chorus:

> . . . as it moved back and forth like a Greek chorus
> across the stage of the ironing board

By drawing together different elements, effective similes make vivid and meaningful comparisons that enrich what the writer has to say.

See also Figurative Language.

SOLILOQUY A *soliloquy* is a long speech expressing the thoughts of a character alone on stage. In William Shakespeare's *The Tragedy of Julius Caesar*, p. 712, Brutus begins a soliloquy while he is alone in his orchard. This soliloquy reveals Brutus' fears about how Caesar might change were he crowned king.

See also Monologue.

SONNET A *sonnet* is a fourteen-line lyric poem, usually written in rhymed iambic pentameter. The *English*, or *Shakespearean, sonnet* consists of three quatrains (four-line stanzas) and a couplet (two lines), usually rhyming *abab cdcd efef gg.*

The couplet usually comments on the ideas contained in the preceding twelve lines. The sonnet is usually not printed with the stanzas divided, but a reader can see distinct ideas in each. See Sonnet 18 by William Shakespeare on p. 866.

The *Italian*, or *Petrarchan, sonnet* consists of an octave (eight-line stanza) and a sestet (six-line stanza). Often the octave rhymes *abbaabba* and the sestet rhymes *cdecde*. The octave states a theme or asks a question. The sestet comments on or answers the question.

The Petrarchan sonnet took its name from Petrarch, a fourteenth-century Italian poet. Once the form was introduced in England, it underwent changes. The Shakespearean sonnet is, of course, named after William Shakespeare.

See also Lyric Poem, Meter, *and* Stanza.

SPEAKER The *speaker* is the imaginary voice assumed by the writer of a poem. In many poems, the speaker is not identified by name. When reading a poem, remember that the speaker within the poem may be a person, an animal, a thing, or an abstraction. The speaker in Gabriela Mistral's "Fear," on p. 889, is a woman who fears for her daughter's future.

STAGE DIRECTIONS *Stage directions* are notes included in a drama to describe how the work is to be performed or staged. These instructions are printed in italics and are not spoken aloud. They are used to describe sets, lighting, sound effects, and the appearance, personalities, and movements of characters.

See also Drama.

STANZA A *stanza* is a formal division of lines in a poem, considered as a unit. Often the stanzas in a poem are separated by spaces.

Stanzas are sometimes named according to the number of lines found in them. A *couplet*, for example, is a two-line stanza. A *tercet* is a stanza with three lines. Other types of stanzas include the following:

1. *Quatrain*: four-line stanza
2. *Cinquain*: five-line stanza
3. *Sestet*: six-line stanza
4. *Heptastich*: seven-line stanza
5. *Octave*: eight-line stanza

Sonnets, limericks, and haiku all have distinct stanza forms. A *sonnet* is a fourteen-line poem that is made up either of three quatrains and a couplet or of an octave followed by a sestet. A *limerick* consists of a single five-line stanza with a particular pattern of rhymes. A *haiku* is made up of a single three-line stanza.

See also Haiku *and* Sonnet.

SURPRISE ENDING A *surprise ending* is a conclusion that violates the expectations of the reader but in a way that is both logical and believable. O. Henry's "Hearts and Hands," on p. 264, and Saki's "The Open Window," on p. 471, have surprise endings. Both authors were masters of this form.

SUSPENSE *Suspense* is a feeling of curiosity or uncertainty about the outcome of events in a literary work. Writers create suspense by raising questions in the minds of their readers.

SYMBOL A *symbol* is anything that stands for or represents something else. An object that serves as a symbol has its own meaning, but it also represents abstract ideas. Marks on paper can symbolize spoken words. A flag symbolizes a country. A flashy car may symbolize wealth. Writers sometimes use such conventional symbols in their work, but sometimes they also create symbols of their own through emphasis or repetition.

In Edgar Allan Poe's "The Masque of the Red Death," on p. 78, the masked figure symbolizes death and the clock symbolizes the passage of time.

TANKA A tanka consists of five unrhymed lines with a pattern of five, seven, five, seven, seven syllables. Tankas appear on p. 868.

TECHNICAL ARTICLE A *technical article* is a type of expository writing that explains a procedure, provides instructions, or represents specialized information. Often, specialized vocabulary is used. Sometimes, diagrams or charts illustrate complicated structures or steps. The technical article "Imitating Nature's Mineral Artistry," p. 648, explains how technology is used to create synthetic gems.

TETRAMETER See Meter.

THEME A *theme* is a central message or insight into life revealed through a literary work. The theme is not a condensed summary of the plot. Instead, it is a generalization about people or about life that is communicated through the literary work.

The theme of a literary work may be stated directly or implied. In "The Princess and All the Kingdom," on p. 552, the moral is clearly and simply stated by the old chancellor, who explains to the prince that his conquests have brought him new responsibilities. In "The Censors," on p. 554, a powerful message is also delivered, but no one states exactly what it is. The theme of Valenzuela's short story is not stated—it's implied.

When the theme of a work is *implied*, readers think about what the work seems to say about the nature of people or about life. The story or poem can be viewed as a specific example of the generalization the writer is trying to communicate.

Note that there is usually no single correct statement of a work's theme, though there can be incorrect ones. Also, a long work, like a novel or a full-length play, may have several themes. Finally, not all literary works have themes. A work meant only to entertain may have no theme at all.

TONE The *tone* of a literary work is the writer's attitude toward his or her audience and subject. The tone can often be described by a single adjective, such as *formal* or *informal*, *serious* or *playful*, *bitter* or *ironic*. Rachel Carson's awed and respectful tone in "The Marginal World," on p. 571, expresses her intensity as she seeks the meaning behind the beauty of the natural world.

TRAGEDY A *tragedy* is a work of literature, especially a play, that results in a catastrophe for the main character. In ancient Greek drama, the main character was always a significant person, a king or a hero, and the cause of the tragedy was a tragic flaw, or weakness, in his or her character. In modern drama, the main character can be an ordinary person and the cause of the tragedy can be some evil in society itself. The purpose of tragedy is not only to arouse fear and pity in the audience, but also, in some cases, to convey a sense of the grandeur and nobility of the human spirit.

Shakespeare's *The Tragedy of Julius Caesar*, on p. 714, is a tragedy. Brutus is a brave and noble figure whose tragic flaw is assuming that honorable ends justify dishonorable means.

See also Drama.

TRIMETER See Meter.

VERBAL IRONY See Irony.

VILLANELLE A *villanelle* is a lyric poem written in three-line stanzas, ending with a four-line stanza. It has two refrain lines that appear initially in the first and third lines of the first stanza; then they appear alternately as the third line of subsequent stanzas, and finally, as the last two lines of the poem. Theodore Roethke's "The Waking," on p. 867, is an example of a villanelle.

The Writing Process

A polished piece of writing can seem to have been effortlessly created, but most good writing is the result of a process of writing, rethinking, and rewriting. The process can roughly be divided into a series of stages: prewriting, drafting, revising, editing, proofreading, and publishing.

It's important to remember that the writing process is one that moves backward as well as forward. Even while you are moving forward in the creation of your composition, you may still return to a previous stage—to rethink or rewrite.

Following are stages of the writing process, with key points to address during each stage.

Prewriting

In this stage, you plan out the work to be done. You prepare to write by exploring ideas, gathering information, and working out an organization. Following are the key steps to take at this stage.

Step 1: Analyze the writing situation. Start by clarifying your assignment, so that you know exactly what you are supposed to do.

- *Focus your topic.* If necessary, narrow the topic—the subject you are writing about—so that you can write about it fully in the space you have.
- *Know your purpose.* What is your goal for this paper? What do you want to accomplish? Your purpose will determine what you include in it.
- *Know your audience.* Who will read your paper influences what you say and how you say it.

Step 2: Gather ideas and information. You can do this in a number of ways:

- *Brainstorm.* When you brainstorm, either alone or with others, you come up with possible ideas to use in your paper. Not all of your brainstormed ideas will be useful or suitable. You'll need to evaluate them later.
- *Consult other people about your subject.* Speaking informally with others may suggest an idea or approach you did not see at first.
- *Make a list of questions about your topic.* When your list is complete, find the answers to your questions.
- *Do research.* Your topic may require information that you don't have, so you will need to go to other sources to find information. There are numerous ways to find information on a topic. See the Research Handbook on p. 1029 for suggestions.

The ideas and information you gather will become the content of your paper. Not all of the information you gather will be needed. As you develop and revise your paper, you will make further decisions about what to include and what to leave out.

Step 3: Organize. First, make a rough plan for the way you want to present your information. Sort your ideas and notes; decide what goes with what and which points are the most important. You can make an outline to show the order of ideas, or you can use some other organizing plan that works for you.

There are many ways in which you can organize and develop your material. Use a method that works for your topic. Following are common methods of organizing information in the development of a paper:

- *Chronological Order* In this method, events are presented in the order in which they occurred. This organization works best for presenting narrative material or explaining in a "how to."
- *Spatial Order* In spatial order, details are presented as seen in space; for example, from left to right or from foreground to background. This order is good for descriptive writing.
- *Order of Importance* This order helps readers see the relative importance of ideas. You present ideas from most to least important or from least to most important.
- *Main Idea and Details* This logical organization works well to support an idea or opinion.

Drafting

When you draft, you put down your ideas on paper in rough form. Working from your prewriting notes and your outline or plan, you develop and present your ideas in sentences and paragraphs.

Don't worry about getting everything perfect at the drafting stage. Concentrate on getting your ideas down.

Draft in a way that works for you. Some writers work best by writing a quick draft—putting down all their ideas without stopping to evaluate them. Other writers prefer to develop each paragraph carefully and thoughtfully, making sure that each main idea is supported by details.

As you are developing a draft, keep in mind your purpose and your audience. These determine what you say and how you say it.

Don't be afraid to change your original plans during drafting. Some of the best ideas are those that were not planned at the beginning. Write as many drafts as you like. You can draft over and over until you've got it the way you like.

Most papers, regardless of the topic, are developed with an introduction, a body, and a conclusion. Here are tips for developing these parts:

Introduction In the introduction to a paper, you want to engage your readers' attention and let them know the purpose of your paper. You may use the following strategies in your introduction:

- State your main idea.
- Use an anecdote.
- Startle your readers.
- Take a stand.
- Quote someone.

Body of the paper In the body of your paper, you present your information and make your points. Your **organization** is an important factor in leading readers through your ideas. Your elaboration on your main ideas is also important. **Elaboration** is the development of ideas to make your written work precise and complete. You can use the following kinds of details to elaborate your main ideas:

- Facts and statistics
- Sensory details
- Explanation and definition
- Anecdotes
- Examples
- Quotations

Conclusion The ending of your paper is the final impression you leave with your readers. Your conclusion should give readers the sense that you have pulled everything together. Following are some effective ways to end your paper:

- Summarize and restate.
- State an opinion.
- Call for action.
- Ask a question.
- Tell an anecdote.

Revising

Once you have a draft, you can look at it critically or have others review it. This is the time to make changes—on many levels. Revising is the process of reworking what you have written to make it as good as it can be. You may change some details so that your ideas flow smoothly and are clearly supported. You may discover that some details don't work, and you'll need to discard them. Two strategies may help you start the revising process:

1. Read your work aloud. This is an excellent way to catch any ideas or details that have been left out and to notice errors in logic.
2. Ask someone else to read your work. Choose someone who can point out its strengths and suggest how to improve it.

How do you know what to look for and what to change? Here is a checklist of major writing issues. If the answer to any of these questions is no, then that is an area that needs revision.

1. Does the writing achieve your purpose?
2. Does the paper have unity? That is, does it have a single focus, with all details and information contributing to that focus?
3. Is the arrangement of information clear and logical?
4. Have you elaborated enough to give your audience adequate information?

Editing

When you edit, you look more closely at the language you have used, so that the way you express your ideas is most effective.

- Replace dull language with vivid, precise words.
- Cut or change redundant expressions (unnecessary repetition).
- Cut empty words and phrases—those that do not add anything to the writing.
- Check passive voice. Usually active voice is more effective.
- Replace wordy expressions with shorter, more precise ones.

Proofreading

After you finish your final draft, the last step is to proofread the draft to make it ready for a reader. You may do this on your own or with the help of a partner.

It's useful to have both a dictionary and a usage handbook to help you check for correctness. Here are the tasks in proofreading:

- Correct errors in grammar and usage.
- Correct errors in punctuation and capitalization.
- Correct errors in spelling.

The Modes of Writing

Description

Description is writing that creates a vivid picture for readers, draws readers into a scene, and makes readers feel as if they are meeting a character or experiencing an event firsthand. A description may stand on its own or be part of a longer work, such as a short story.

When you write a description, bring it to life with sensory details, which tell how your subject looks, smells, sounds, tastes, or feels. You'll want to choose your details carefully so that you create a single main impression of your subject. Avoid language and details that don't contribute to this main impression. Keep these guidelines in mind whenever you are assigned one of the following types of description:

Observation In an observation, you describe an event that you have witnessed firsthand, often over an extended period of time. You may focus on an aspect of daily life or on a scientific phenomenon, such as a storm or an eclipse.

Remembrance When you write a remembrance, you use vivid, descriptive details to bring to life memorable people, places, or events from your past.

Description of a Place Often used to set the scene in a story or drama, your description of a place should convey the physical look and atmosphere of a scene—either interior or exterior.

Character Profile In a character profile, you capture a person's appearance and personality traits and reveal information about his or her life. Your subject may be a real person or a fictional character.

Narration

Whenever writers tell any type of story, they are using **narration.** While there are many kinds of narration, most narratives share certain elements—characters, a setting, a sequence of events (or plot, in fiction), and, often, a theme. You might be asked to try your hand at one of these types of narration:

Anecdote An anecdote, which may be oral or written, is a brief and often humorous narrative that is true or based on the truth. You may use an anecdote both to entertain and to make a general point about life.

Personal Narrative A personal narrative is a true story about a memorable experience or period in your life. In a personal narrative, your feelings about events shape the way you tell the story—even the way you describe people and places.

Firsthand Biography A firsthand biography tells about the life (or a period in the life) of a person whom you know personally. You can use your close relationship with the person to help you include personal insights not found in biographies based solely on research.

Short Story Short stories are short fictional, or made-up, narratives in which a main character faces a conflict that is resolved by the end of the story. In planning a short story, you focus on developing the plot, the setting, and the characters. You must also decide on a point of view: Will your story be told by a character who participates in the action or by someone who describes the action as an outside observer?

Exposition

Exposition is writing that informs or explains. The information you include in expository writing is factual or (when you're expressing an opinion) based on fact.

Your expository writing should reflect a well-thought-out organization—one that includes a clear introduction, body, and conclusion and is appropriate for the type of exposition you are writing. Here are some types of exposition you may be asked to write:

Cause-and-Effect Essay In a cause-and-effect essay, you consider the reasons something did happen or might happen. You may examine several causes of a single effect or several effects of a single cause.

Comparison-and-Contrast Essay When you write a comparison-and-contrast essay, you consider the similarities and differences between two or more subjects. You may organize your essay point by point—discussing each aspect of your subject in turn—or subject by subject—discussing all the qualities of one subject first and then the qualities of the next subject.

Problem-and-Solution Essay In a problem-and-solution essay, you identify a conflict or problem and offer a resolution. Begin with a clear statement of the problem and follow with a reasoned path to a solution.

Summary To write a summary or synopsis of an event or a literary work, you include only the details that your readers will need in order to understand the key features of the event or the literary work. Omit any personal opinions; include only factual details.

How-to Instructions You use how-to instructions

to explain the steps involved in doing a particular task. In writing instructions, it is also important to anticipate and answer questions the reader may have about why a particular procedure is being recommended.

Persuasion

Persuasion is writing or speaking that attempts to convince people to agree with a position or to take a desired action. When used effectively, persuasive writing has the power to change people's lives. As a reader and a writer, you will find yourself engaged in many forms of persuasion. Here are a few of them:

Persuasive Essay In writing a persuasive essay, you build an argument, supporting your opinions with a variety of evidence: facts, statistics, examples, statements from experts. You also anticipate and develop counter-arguments to opposing opinions.

Advertisement When you write an advertisement, you present information in an appealing way to make the product or service seem desirable.

Position Paper In a position paper, you try to persuade readers to accept your views on a controversial issue. Most often, your audience will consist of people who have some power to shape policy related to the issue. Your views in a position paper should be supported with evidence.

Persuasive Speech A persuasive speech is a piece of persuasion that you present orally instead of in writing. As a persuasive speaker, you use a variety of techniques, such as repetition of key points, to capture your audience's interest and to add force to your argument.

Letter to the Editor When you write a letter to the editor, you may be responding to an article or an editorial published earlier or you may be writing to express concern on an issue of importance to the community. Your letter should describe the issue briefly, present your views supported with evidence, and state any action you think should be taken.

Research Writing

Writers often use outside research to gather information and explore subjects of interest. The product of that research is called **research writing.** In connection with your reading, you may occasionally be assigned one of the following types of research writing:

Biographical Report In a biographical report, you examine a person's life and achievements. You include the dates and details of the main events in the person's life and, at times, make educated guesses about the reasons behind those events. For your biographical report, you may need to research not only the life of an individual but also the times in which he or she lived.

Research Paper A research paper uses information gathered from a variety of outside sources to explore a topic. In your research paper, you will usually include an introduction, in which your thesis, or main point, is stated; a body, in which you present support for the thesis; and a conclusion that summarizes, or restates, your main points. You should credit the sources of information, using footnotes or other types of citation, and include a bibliography, or general list of sources, at the end.

Multimedia Presentation In preparing a multimedia presentation, you will gather and organize information in a variety of media, or means of communication. You may use written materials, slides, videos, audiocassettes, sound effects, art, photographs, models, charts, and diagrams.

Creative Writing

Creative writing blends imagination, ideas, and emotions and allows you to present your own unique view of the world. Poems, plays, short stories, dramas, and even some cartoons are examples of creative writing. All are represented in this anthology and may provide inspiration for you to produce your own creative works, such as the following:

Lyric Poem In a lyric poem, you use sensory images, figurative language, and sound devices to express deep thoughts and feelings about a subject. To give your lyric poem a musical quality, employ sound devices, such as rhyme, rhythm, alliteration, and onomatopoeia.

Narrative Poem Writing a narrative poem is similar to writing a short story, with a plot, characters, and a theme. However, your narrative poem, unlike a story, will be divided into stanzas (groups of lines that form a unit) usually composed of rhyming lines that have a definite rhythm, or beat.

Song Lyrics In writing lyrics, or words, for a song, you use many elements of poetry—rhyme, rhythm, repetition, and imagery. In addition, your song lyrics should convey emotions, as well as interesting ideas.

Drama When you write a drama or a dramatic scene, you are writing a story that is intended to be performed. Since a drama consists almost entirely of the words and actions of the characters, be sure to write dialogue that clearly shows the characters' personalities, thoughts, and emotions, and stage directions that convey your ideas about sets, props, sound effects, and the speaking style and movements of the characters.

Response to Literature

In a **response to literature,** you express your thoughts and feelings about a work and often, in so doing, gain a better understanding of what the work is all about. Your response to literature can take many forms—oral or written, formal or informal. During the course of your reading, you may be asked to respond to a work of literature in one of these forms:

Literary Analysis In a literary analysis, you take a critical look at various important elements in the work. You then attempt to explain how the author has used those elements and how they work together to convey the author's message.

Retelling of a Fairy Tale Most fairy tales—stories about good and evil characters, giants, and magic deeds—have been handed down from generation to generation, and often the original authors are unknown. When you retell a fairy tale in your own way, you can add to the original or change it. For example, you might set it in another place or time period or write it as a poem or a drama.

Reader's Response Journal Entry Your reader's response journal is a record of your thoughts and feelings about works you have read. Use it to remind yourself of writers and works that you particularly liked or disliked or to provide a source of writing ideas.

Letter to an Author People sometimes respond to a work of literature by writing a letter to the author. You can praise the work, ask questions, or offer constructive criticism.

Critical Review In a critical review of a literary work, you discuss various elements in the work and offer opinions about them. You may also give a summary of the work and a recommendation to readers.

Practical and Technical Writing

Practical writing is fact-based writing that people do in the workplace or in their day-to-day lives. Business letters, memos, school forms, and job applications are examples of practical writing. **Technical writing,** which is also based on facts, explains procedures, provides instructions, or presents specialized information. You encounter technical writing every time you read a manual or a set of instructions.

In the following descriptions, you'll find tips for tackling several types of practical and technical writing:

Letter Requesting Information In a letter requesting information, you state the information you're searching for and ask any specific questions you have. In your letter, include your name and address so that you can receive a response. Include the date, which can help you or the recipient keep track of correspondence. It is also customary to include the address of the party to whom you are writing. Use a formal greeting followed by a colon. Keep the body of the letter as brief and clear as possible. Use a polite closing, and remember to sign as well as type or print your name.

News Release News releases announce factual information about upcoming events. Also called press releases, they are usually sent to local newspapers, local radio stations, and other media. When you write a news release, use this format: Position your name and phone number in the upper right corner. Then capture your main point in a centered headline, which will allow the recipient to see at a glance what the news release is about. In the body, present factual information in a concise way. You may begin with an opening location tag that tells in which town or city the news release originated. The numeral 30 or number signs (###) customarily indicate the end of the news release.

Guidelines When you write guidelines, you give information about how people should act or you provide tips on how to do something. List guidelines one by one, using somewhat formal language. Your guidelines may or may not be numbered. In addition to factual information, which should be complete and accurate, guidelines may contain your opinions.

Process Explanation In a process explanation, you offer a step-by-step explanation of how to do something. Your explanation should be specific, using headings, labels, or numbers to make the process clear. You may also include diagrams or other illustrations to further clarify the process.

Grammar and Mechanics Handbook

Nouns A **noun** is the name of a person, place, or thing. A **common noun** names any one of a class of people, places, or things. A **proper noun** names a specific person, place, or thing.

Common Noun	Proper Noun
city	Washington, D.C.

Pronouns A **pronoun** is a word that stands for a noun or for a word that takes the place of a noun.

A **personal pronoun** refers to (1) the person speaking, (2) the person spoken to, or (3) the person, place, or thing spoken about.

	Singular	Plural
First Person	I, me, my, mine	we, us, our, ours
Second Person	you, your, yours	you, your, yours
Third Person	he, him, his, she, her, hers, it, its	they, them, their, theirs

A **reflexive pronoun** ends in *-self* or *-selves* and adds information to a sentence by pointing back to a noun or a pronoun earlier in the sentence.

> I was saying to *myself,* "Ed, my boy, this Everest—you've got to push it a bit harder!"
>
> —"The Final Assault," Edmund Hillary, p. 29

An **intensive pronoun** ends in *-self* or *-selves* and simply adds emphasis to a noun or a pronoun in the same sentence.

> After a time, I *myself* was allowed to go into the dead houses and search for metal.
>
> —"By the Waters of Babylon," Stephen Vincent Benét, p. 500

A **demonstrative pronoun** directs attention to a specific person, place, or thing.

this *these* *that* *those*

These are the juiciest pears I've ever tasted.

A **relative pronoun** begins a subordinate (relative) clause and connects it to another idea in the sentence.

The poet *who* wrote "Fear" is Gabriela Mistral.

An **indefinite pronoun** refers to a person, place, or thing, often without specifying which one.

> And then, for a moment, *all* is still, . . .
>
> —"The Masque of the Red Death," Edgar Allan Poe, p. 81

Verbs A **verb** is a word that expresses time while showing an action, a condition, or the fact that something exists.

An **action verb** indicates the action of someone or something.

An action verb is **transitive** if it directs action toward someone or something named in the same sentence.

> He *dusted* his hands, muttering.
>
> —"Contents of the Dead Man's Pocket," Jack Finney, p. 5

An action verb is **intransitive** if it does not direct action toward something or someone named in the same sentence.

> I *waved* and *shouted,* then as suddenly *stopped* as I realized my foolishness.
>
> —"The Final Assault," Edmund Hillary, p. 31

A **linking verb** is a verb that connects the subject of a sentence with a noun or pronoun that renames or describes the subject. All linking verbs are intransitive.

> Romance at short notice *was* her specialty.
>
> —"The Open Window," Saki, p. 474

A **helping verb** is a verb that can be added to another verb to make a verb phrase.

Nor *did* I suspect that these experiences could be part of a novel's meaning.

Adjectives An **adjective** describes a noun or a pronoun or gives a noun or a pronoun a more specific meaning. Adjectives answer these questions:

What kind?	*blue* lamp, *large* tree
Which one?	*this* table, *those* books
How many?	*five* stars, *several* buses
How much?	*less* money, *enough* votes

The articles *the, a,* and *an* are adjectives. *An* is used before a word beginning with a vowel sound.

A noun may sometimes be used as an adjective.

diamond necklace *summer* vacation

Adverbs An **adverb** modifies a verb, an adjective, or another adverb. Adverbs answer the questions *where, when, in what way,* or *to what extent.*

He could stand *there.* (modifies verb *stand*)
He was *blissfully* happy. (modifies adjective *happy*)
It ended *too* soon. (modifies adverb *soon*)

Prepositions A **preposition** relates a noun or a pronoun that appears with it to another word in the sentence.

before the end *near* me *inside* our fence

Conjunctions A **conjunction** connects other words or groups of words.

A **coordinating conjunction** connects similar kinds or groups of words.

mother *and* father simple *yet* stylish

Correlative conjunctions are used in pairs to connect similar words or groups of words.

both Sue *and* Meg *neither* he *nor* I

A **subordinating conjunction** connects two complete ideas by placing one idea below the other in rank or importance.

You would know him *if* you saw him.

Sentences A **sentence** is a group of words with a subject and a predicate. Together, these parts express a complete thought.

A **fragment** is a group of words that does not express a complete thought.

Subject and Verb Agreement To make a subject and verb agree, make sure that both are singular or both are plural.

Many *storms are* the cause of beach erosion.
Either the *cats* or the *dog is* hungry.
Neither *Angie* nor her *sisters were* present.
The *conductor,* as well as the soloists, *was applauded.*

Phrase A **phrase** is a group of words, without a subject and a verb, that functions in a sentence as one part of speech.

A **prepositional phrase** is a group of words that includes a preposition and a noun or a pronoun that is the object of the preposition.

outside my window below the counter

An **adjective phrase** is a prepositional phrase that modifies a noun or a pronoun by telling *what kind* or *which one.*

The wooden gates *of that lane* stood open.

An **adverb phrase** is a prepositional phrase that modifies a verb, an adjective, or an adverb by pointing out *where, when, in what way,* or *to what extent.*

On a sudden impulse, he got to his feet.
—"Contents of the Dead Man's Pocket,"
Jack Finney, p. 8

An **appositive phrase** is a noun or a pronoun with modifiers, placed next to a noun or a pronoun to identify it or add information and details.

M. Morissot, *watchmaker by trade but local militiaman for the time being,* stopped short . . .

—"Two Friends," Guy de Maupassant, p. 96

A **participial phrase** is a participle with its modifiers or complements. The entire phrase acts as an adjective.

Choosing such a tide, I hoped for a glimpse of the pool.

—"The Marginal World," Rachel Carson, p. 572

A **gerund phrase** is a gerund with modifiers or a complement, all acting together as a noun.

. . . *moving along the ledge* was quite as easy as he thought it would be.
—"Contents of the Dead Man's Pocket,"
Jack Finney, p. 9

An **infinitive phrase** is an infinitive with modifiers, complements, or a subject, all acting together as a single part of speech.

To be alive to hear this song is a victory . . .

—"Old Song," Traditional, p. 202

Clauses A **clause** is a group of words with a subject and a verb.

An **independent clause** has a subject and a verb and can stand by itself as a complete sentence.

A **subordinate clause** has a subject and a verb but cannot stand by itself as a complete sentence; it can only be part of a sentence.

An **adjective clause** is a subordinate clause that modifies a noun or a pronoun by telling *what kind* or *which one.*

For country people, *who only knew the dismantled tilting ground of Sir Ector's castle,* the scene which met their eyes was ravishing.

—"Arthur Becomes King of Britain,"
T. H. White, p. 910

An **adverb clause** modifies a verb, an adjective, an adverb, or a verbal by telling *where, when, in what way, to what extent, under what condition,* or *why.*

She took up that magazine *when her daughter-in-law came in . . .*

—"The Good Deed," Pearl S. Buck, p. 342

A **noun clause** is a subordinate clause that acts as a noun.

That you have wronged me doth appear in this.

—*The Tragedy of Julius Caesar,* William Shakespeare, p. 228

Summary of Capitalization and Punctuation

Capitalization

Capitalize the first word of a sentence and also the first word in a quotation if the quotation is a complete sentence.

"Mummy," he said, "I can stay under water for two minutes—. . ."

—"Through the Tunnel," Doris Lessing, p. 281

Capitalize all proper nouns and adjectives.

W. W. Jacobs   Flanders Fields   African writers

Capitalize a person's title when it is followed by the person's name or when it is used in direct address.

Reverend Tallboys   Mrs. Prothero   Major Moberly

Capitalize titles showing family relationships when they refer to a specific person, unless they are preceded by a possessive noun or pronoun.

Grandmother   his father

Capitalize the first word and all other key words in the titles of books, periodicals, poems, stories, plays, paintings, and other works of art.

The Way to Rainy Mountain   "Spring and All"

Punctuation

End Marks Use a **period** to end a declarative sentence, an imperative sentence, an indirect question, and most abbreviations.

She broke off with a little shudder.

—"The Open Window," Saki, p. 472

Use a **question mark** to end a direct question, an incomplete question, or a statement that is intended as a question.

"Monkey's paw?" said Mrs. White curiously.

—"The Monkey's Paw," W. W. Jacobs, p. 48

Use an **exclamation mark** after a statement showing strong emotion, an urgent imperative sentence, or an interjection expressing strong emotion.

"Bring him in! Bring him in now!"

—"The Dog That Bit People," James Thurber, p. 238

Commas Use a **comma** before the coordinating conjunction to separate two independent clauses in a compound sentence.

His arms had begun to tremble from the steady strain of clinging to his narrow perch, and he did not know what to do now . . .

—"Contents of the Dead Man's Pocket," Jack Finney, p. 16

Use commas to separate three or more words, phrases, or clauses in a series.

Animals took shape: yellow giraffes, blue lions, pink antelopes, lilac panthers cavorting in crystal substance.

—"There Will Come Soft Rains," Ray Bradbury, p. 537

Use commas to separate adjectives of equal rank. Do not use commas to separate adjectives that must stay in a specific order.

I was immediately transported to the foot of mountains, with narrow defiles twisting in and out amongst their *towering, arid* peaks.

—"The Cabuliwallah," Rabindranath Tagore, p. 287

Use a comma after an introductory word, phrase, or clause.

When Marian Anderson again returned to America, she was a seasoned artist.

—"Marian Anderson: Famous Concert Singer," Langston Hughes, p. 604

Use commas to set off parenthetical and nonessential expressions.

All of these works, *of course*, had earlier left their marks . . .

—"Star Wars: A Trip to a Galaxy . . . ," Vincent Canby, p. 626

Use commas with places, dates, and titles.

Poe was raised in Richmond, Virginia.
August 4, 2026
Alfred, Lord Tennyson

Use a comma to indicate words left out of an elliptical sentence, to set off a direct quotation, and to prevent a sentence from being misunderstood.

> Vincent Canby writes for *The New York Times;* Roger Ebert, for the *Chicago Sun Times.*

Semicolons Use a **semicolon** to join independent clauses that are not already joined by a conjunction.

> They could find no buffalo; *they had to hang an old hide from the sacred tree.*
>
> —*The Way to Rainy Mountain,* N. Scott Momaday, p. 585

Use a semicolon to join independent clauses separated by either a conjunctive adverb or a transitional expression.

> James Thurber wrote many books; moreover, he was a cartoonist and a journalist.

Use semicolons to avoid confusion when independent clauses or items in a series already contain commas.

> There were the Useful Presents: engulfing mufflers of the old coach days, and mittens made for giant sloths; zebra scarfs of a substance like silky gum that could be tug-o'-warred down to the galoshes; . . .
>
> —"A Child's Christmas in Wales," Dylan Thomas, p. 598

Colons Use a **colon** in order to introduce a list of items following an independent clause.

> The authors we are reading include a number of poets: Robert Frost, Octavio Paz, and Emily Dickinson.

Use a colon to introduce a formal quotation.

> The next day Howard Taubman wrote enthusiastically in *The New York Times:*
> Marian Anderson has returned to her native land one of the great singers of our time . . .
>
> —"Marian Anderson: Famous Concert Singer," Langston Hughes, p. 604

Quotation Marks A **direct quotation** represents a person's exact speech or thoughts and is enclosed in quotation marks.

> "Clara, my mind is made up."
>
> —"With All Flags Flying," Anne Tyler, p. 472

An **indirect quotation** reports only the general meaning of what a person said or thought and does not require quotation marks.

> She rattled on cheerfully about the shooting and the scarcity of birds, . . .
>
> —"The Open Window," Saki, p. 472

Always place a comma or a period inside the final quotation mark.

> "There are ceremonies going on," I said, "and I am busy."
>
> —"The Cabuliwallah," Rabindranath Tagore, p. 290

Place a question mark or an exclamation mark inside the final quotation mark if the end mark is part of the quotation; if it is not part of the quotation, place it outside the final quotation mark.

> "If you only cleared the house, you'd be quite happy, wouldn't you?"
>
> —"The Monkey's Paw," W. W. Jacobs, p. 49
>
> Have you ever read the poem "Africa"?

Use single quotation marks for a quotation within a quotation.

Use quotation marks around the titles of short written works, episodes in a series, songs, and titles of works mentioned as parts of a collection.

"Making a Fist" "These Are Days"

Underline or italicize titles of longer works, such as plays, movies, or novels.

Dashes Use **dashes** to indicate an abrupt change of thought, a dramatic interrupting idea, or a summary statement.

> It made her so mad to see Muggs lying there, oblivious of the mice—they came running up to her—that she slapped him and he slashed at her, but he didn't make it.
>
> —"The Dog That Bit People," James Thurber, p. 236

Parentheses Use **parentheses** to set off asides and explanations only when the material is not essential or when it consists of one or more sentences.

> Automatically I looked at our pressure gauges—just over 2,900 pounds (2,900 pounds was just over 700 liters; 180 into 700 was about 4). . .
>
> —"The Final Assault," Edmund Hillary, p. 31

Hyphens Use a **hyphen** with certain numbers, after certain prefixes, with two or more words used as one word, and with a compound modifier coming before a noun.

fifty-two greenish-blue water

Apostrophes Add an **apostrophe** and -*s* to show the possessive case of most singular nouns.

Prospero's castle the playwright's craft

Add an apostrophe to show the possessive case of plural nouns ending in -*s* and -*es*.

the sailors' ships the babies' mothers

Add an apostrophe and -*s* to show the possessive case of plural nouns that do not end in -*s* or -*es*.

the children's games the people's friend

Use an apostrophe in a contraction to indicate the position of the missing letter or letters.

I *didn't* love any one of you more than the other.

—"A Visit to Grandmother,"
William Melvin Kelley, p. 174

GLOSSARY OF COMMON USAGE

among, between

Among is usually used with three or more items. *Between* is generally used with only two items.

Among the poems we read this year, Eve Merriam's "Metaphor" was my favorite.

"Like the Sun" tells of one man's conflict *between* telling the truth and telling white lies.

amount, number

Amount refers to a mass or a unit, whereas *number* refers to individual items that can be counted. Therefore, *amount* generally appears with a singular noun, and *number* appears with a plural noun.

Being able to climb Mount Everest requires a huge *amount* of training.

In his story "The Masque of the Red Death," Poe uses a *number* of intriguing symbols.

any, all

Any should not be used in place of *any other* or *all*.

Rajika liked Anne Tyler's "With All Flags Flying" better than *any other* short story.

Of *all* W. W. Jacobs's short stories, "The Monkey's Paw" is the most famous.

around

In formal writing, *around* should not be used to mean *approximately* or *about*. These usages are allowable, however, in informal writing or in colloquial dialogue.

Shakespeare's *Romeo and Juliet* had its first performance in *approximately* 1595.

Shakespeare was *about* thirty when he wrote this play.

as, because, like, as to

The word *as* has several meanings and can function as several parts of speech. To avoid confusion, use *because* rather than *as* when you want to indicate cause and effect.

Because Cyril was interested in the history of African American poetry, he decided to write his report on Langston Hughes.

Do not use the preposition *like* to introduce a clause that requires the conjunction *as*.

James Thurber conversed *as* he wrote—wittily.

The use of *as to* for *about* is awkward and should be avoided.

Rosa has an interesting theory *about* Edgar Allan Poe's choice of subject matter.

bad, badly

Use the predicate adjective *bad* after linking verbs such as *feel*, *look*, and *seem*. Use *badly* whenever an adverb is required.

Sara Teasdale's poem "There Will Come Soft Rains" shows clearly that the author felt *bad* about the destruction of the war.

In "Through the Tunnel," Jerry *badly* wants to be able to swim the length of the tunnel.

because of, due to

Use *due to* if it can logically replace the phrase *caused by*. In introductory phrases, however, *because of* is better usage than *due to*.

The popularity of the mystery is largely *due to* the works of Edgar Allan Poe.

Because of lack of oxygen, Edmund Hillary and

Tenzing Norgay moved more and more lethargically as they made their way up Everest.

being as, being that

Avoid these expressions. Use *because* or *since* instead.

Because the protagonist of Anton Chekhov's "A Problem" is a static character, he changes little in the course of the story.

Since there was a question about who reached the summit of Everest first, Tenzing Norgay decided to answer that question once and for all in his biography.

beside, besides

Beside is a preposition meaning "at the side of" or "close to." Do not confuse *beside* with *besides*, which means "in addition to." *Besides* can be a preposition or an adverb.

As the three men cross the lawn and approach the open window, a brown spaniel trots *beside* them.

There are many other Indian oral epics *besides* the *Ramayana*.

can, may

The verb *can* generally refers to the ability to do something. The verb *may* generally refers to permission to do something.

Dylan Thomas describes his childhood Christmases so vividly that most readers *can* visualize the scene.

Creon's edict states that no one *may* bury Polyneices.

different from, different than

The preferred usage is *different from*.

The structure and rhyme scheme of a Shakespearean sonnet are *different from* the organization of a Petrarchan sonnet.

farther, further

Use *farther* when you refer to distance. Use *further* when you mean "to a greater degree" or "additional."

The *farther* the ants travel, the more ominous and destructive they seem.

The storm at the end of Act I of *The Tragedy of Julius Caesar further* hints at the ominous deeds to come.

fewer, less

Use *fewer* for things that can be counted. Use *less* for amounts or quantities that cannot be counted.

Poetry often uses *fewer* words than prose to convey ideas and images.

It takes *less* time to perform a Greek tragedy than to perform a Shakespearean play.

good, well

Use the adjective *good* after linking verbs such as *feel, look, smell, taste,* and *seem*. Use *well* whenever you need an adverb or as an adjective describing health.

Caesar remarks that Cassius does not look *good*; on the contrary, his appearance is "lean" and "hungry."

Twain wrote especially *well* when he described eccentric characters.

hopefully

You should not attach this adverb to a sentence loosely, as in "*Hopefully*, the rain will stop by noon." Rewrite the sentence so that *hopefully* modifies a specific verb. Other possible ways of revising such sentences include using the adjective *hopeful* or a phrase such as *everyone hopes that*.

Dr. Martin Luther King, Jr., wrote and spoke *hopefully* about his dream of racial harmony.

Mr. White was *hopeful* that the monkey's paw would bring him good fortune.

Everyone *hopes* that the class production of *Antigone* will be a big success.

its, it's

Do not confuse the possessive pronoun *its* with the contraction *it's*, used in place of "it is" or "it has."

In *its* very first lines, "The Stolen Child" establishes an eerie mood.

In "The Street of the Cañon," Pepe knows that *it's* dangerous to attend Don Roméo's party.

just, only

When you use *just* as an adverb meaning "no more than," be sure you place it directly before the word it logically modifies. Likewise, be sure you place *only* before the word it logically modifies.

Just one wish changed the Whites' lives forever.

A short story can usually develop *only* a few characters, whereas a novel can include many.

kind of, sort of

In formal writing, you should not use these colloquial expressions. Instead, use a word such as *rather* or *somewhat*.

Poe portrays Prince Prospero as *rather* arrogant.

The tone of Tenzig Norgay's biography is *somewhat* defensive.

lay, lie

Do not confuse these verbs. *Lay* is a transitive verb meaning "to set or put something down." Its principal parts are *lay, laying, laid, laid. Lie* is an intransitive verb meaning "to recline." Its principal parts are *lie, lying, lay, lain.*

The monkey's paw *lay* on the table in the living room for a while before anyone dared to pick it up.

La belle dame sans merci enchants the knight as he *lies* in her "elfin grot."

leave, let

Be careful not to confuse these verbs. *Leave* means "to go away" or "to allow to remain." *Let* means "to permit."

Threatening *Antigone* not to disobey his orders, Creon angrily *leaves* the stage.

At first Mr. Carpenter's family does not want to *let* him enter the retirement home.

raise, rise

Raise is a transitive verb that usually takes a direct object. *Rise* is an intransitive verb and never takes a direct object.

In his speech, Antony unexpectedly *raises* the subject of Caesar's will.

When the Cabuliwallah comes to call, Mini *rises* from her chair and runs to greet him.

set, sit

Do not confuse these verbs. *Set* is a transitive verb meaning "to put (something) in a certain place." Its principal parts are *set, setting, set, set. Sit* is an intransitive verb meaning "to be seated." Its principal parts are *sit, sitting, sat, sat.*

Antigone's conduct *sets* a high standard for all those who believe that conscience must be our ultimate guide.

Jerry's mother *sits* in her beach chair while Jerry swims in the ocean.

so, so that

Be careful not to use the coordinating conjunction *so* when your context requires *so that. So* means "accordingly" or "therefore" and expresses a cause-and-effect relationship. *So that* expresses purpose.

He wanted to do well on the test, *so* he read *The Tragedy of Julius Caesar* again.

Antony uses eloquent rhetoric to stir up the people *so that* they will turn against the conspirators.

than, then

The conjunction *than* is used to connect the two parts of a comparison. Do not confuse *than* with the adverb *then,* which usually refers to time.

I enjoyed "The Marginal World" more *than* "The Flood."

Marian Anderson gave a triumphant singing recital in New York that evening, and she *then* embarked on a coast-to-coast American tour.

that, which, who

Use the relative pronoun *that* to refer to things or people. Use *which* only for things and *who* only for people.

The poem *that* Cheryl liked the most was "The street."

Haiku, *which* consists of only seventeen syllables, is often built around one or two vivid images.

The assassin *who* strikes Caesar first is Casca.

unique

Because *unique* means "one of a kind," you should not use it carelessly to mean "interesting" or "unusual." Avoid such illogical expressions as "most unique," "very unique," and "extremely unique."

Emily Dickinson's unconventional themes and bold experiments with form make her *unique* in the history of nineteenth-century American poetry.

when, where

Do not directly follow a linking verb with *when* or *where.* Be careful not to use *where* when your context requires *that.*

Faulty: The exposition is *when* an author provides the reader with important background information.

Revised: In the exposition, an author provides the reader with important background information.

Faulty: Madras, India, is *where* R. K. Narayan was born.

Revised: R. K. Narayan was born in Madras, India.

Speaking, Listening, and Viewing Handbook

Language—such as the literature in this book—is often written down. But even more often, it is communicated orally or visually. Oral and visual forms of communication involve speaking, listening, and viewing.

Having strong speaking, listening, and viewing skills will benefit you both in and out of school. Many of the assignments accompanying the literature in this textbook involve speaking, listening, and viewing skills. The terms in this handbook will give you a better understanding of the many elements that are part of oral and visual communication.

Oral and Visual Communication

You use oral and visual forms of communication in many types of situations every day. You use them in conversations as well as in class discussions, speeches, interviews, debates, performances, and media presentations. When you communicate face to face or before an audience, you may use more than spoken words to get your message across. When you speak on the phone, you rely on numerous verbal and listening skills.

The following terms will give you a better understanding of the many elements that are part of oral and visual communication:

ARTICULATION is the process of forming sounds into words by using the tongue, teeth, lower jaw, and soft palate to produce speech sounds.

BODY LANGUAGE refers to the use of facial expressions, eye contact, gestures, posture, and movement to communicate a feeling or an idea.

CONNOTATION is the set of associations a word calls to mind. The connotations of the words you choose influence the message you send. For example, most people respond more favorably to being described as "slim" rather than as "skinny." The connotation of *slim* is more appealing than that of *skinny.*

EYE CONTACT is direct visual contact with another person's eyes.

FEEDBACK is the set of verbal and nonverbal reactions that indicate to a speaker that a message has been received and understood.

GESTURES are the movements made with arms, hands, face, and fingers to communicate.

INFLECTION refers to the rise and fall in the pitch of the voice in speaking; it is also called **intonation.**

LISTENING is understanding and interpreting sound in a meaningful way. You listen differently for different purposes.

Listening for key information: For example, when a teacher gives an assignment, or when someone gives you directions to a place, you listen for key information.

Listening for main points: In a classroom exchange of ideas or information, or while watching a television documentary, you listen for main points.

Listening critically: When you evaluate a performance, song, or a persuasive or political speech, you listen critically, questioning and judging the speaker's message.

NONVERBAL COMMUNICATION is communication without the use of words. People communicate nonverbally through gestures, facial expressions, posture, and body movements. Sign language is an entire language based on nonverbal communication.

PROJECTION is speaking in such a way that the voice carries clearly to an audience. It's important to project your voice when speaking in a large space like a classroom or an auditorium.

VOCAL DELIVERY is the way in which you present a message. Your vocal delivery involves all of the following elements:

Volume: the loudness or quietness of your voice
Pitch: the high or low quality of your voice
Rate: the speed at which you speak; also called pace
Stress: the amount of emphasis placed on different syllables in a word or on different words in a sentence

All of these elements, individually and together, contribute to the meaning of a spoken message.

Speaking, Listening, and Viewing

The following terms apply to speaking, listening, and viewing presentations and productions:

AUDIENCE Your audience in any situation is the person or people to whom you direct your message. An audience can be a group of people sitting in a classroom or an auditorium observing a performance or just one person to whom you address a question or a comment. When preparing for any speaking situation, it's useful to analyze your audience, learning what you can about their background, interests, and attitudes so that you can tailor your message to them.

DEBATE A debate is a formal public-speaking situation in which participants prepare and present arguments on opposing sides of a question, stated as a **proposition.** The proposition must be controversial: It must concern an issue that may be solved in two different, valid ways.

The two sides in a debate are the *affirmative* (pro) and the *negative* (con). The affirmative side argues in favor of the proposition, while the negative side argues against it. The affirmative side begins the debate, since it is seeking a change in a belief or policy. The opposing sides take turns presenting their arguments, and each side has an opportunity for *rebuttal,* in which they may challenge or question the other side's argument.

DOCUMENTARY A documentary is a film that presents in-depth, factual information on a given topic. The topic may be about people, places, or events. Through visual and sound techniques, the documentary may communicate the filmmaker's analysis of the topic.

INTERVIEW An interview is a form of interaction in which one person, the interviewer, asks questions of another person, the interviewee. Interviews may take place for many purposes: to obtain information, to discover a person's suitability for a job or a college, or to inform the public of a notable person's opinions.

MEDIA PRESENTATION Media presentations convey information to viewers and listeners by means of radio, TV, films, videos, still photography, Internet Web pages, newspapers, magazines, animation, and other forms of visual art.

NEWSMAGAZINE refers to a television program that offers news about current topics. The newsmagazine is usually less objective, or strictly factual, than a **news report,** because it may include interviews, opinions, and viewer responses.

ORAL INTERPRETATION is the reading or speaking of a work of literature aloud for an audience. Oral interpretation involves explaining the ideas, meaning, or structure of a work of literature. The speaker interprets the work through his or her vocal delivery. **Poetry reading** and **storytelling,** in which a speaker reads a poem or tells a story expressively, are forms of oral interpretation.

PANEL DISCUSSION is a group discussion on a topic of interest common to all members of a panel and to a listening audience. A panel is usually composed of four to six experts on a particular topic who are brought together to share information and opinions.

PANTOMIME is a form of nonverbal communication in which an idea or a story is communicated completely through the use of gestures, body language, and facial expressions, without any words at all.

READERS THEATRE is a dramatic reading of a work of literature in which participants take parts from a story or play and read them aloud in expressive voices. Unlike a play, however, sets and costumes are not part of the performance, and the participants remain seated or standing as they deliver their lines.

ROLE PLAY To role-play is to take the role of a person or character and, as that character, act out a given situation, speaking, acting, and responding in the manner of the character.

SPECIAL EFFECTS are used in media presentations to communicate various types of things to viewers and listeners. They include artificial sounds and images. Special **visual and sound techniques,** often used to communicate in films, include unusual camera angles, reaction shots, sequencing, and music.

SPEECH A speech is a talk or an address given to an audience. A speech may be **impromptu**—delivered on the spur of the moment with no preparation—or formally prepared and delivered for a specific purpose or occasion.

- *Purposes:* The most common purposes of speeches are to persuade (for example, political speeches), to entertain, to explain, and to inform.
- *Occasions:* Different occasions call for different types of speeches. Speeches given on these occasions could be persuasive, entertaining, or informative, as appropriate. The following are common occasions for speeches.
  Introduction: Introducing a speaker or presenter at a meeting or assembly
  Presentation: Giving an award or acknowledging the contributions of someone
  Acceptance: Accepting an award or a tribute
  Keynote: Giving an inspirational address at a large meeting or convention
  Commencement: Honoring the graduates of a school or university

VISUAL REPRESENTATION Visual representations include informative texts, entertaining texts, and advertisements. They use elements of design—such as shape, line, color, and texture—to communicate.

Research Handbook

Many of the assignments and activities in this literature book require you to find out more about your topic. Whenever you need ideas, details, or information, you must conduct research. You can find information by using library resources and computer resources, as well as by interviewing experts in a field.

Before you begin, create a research plan that lists the questions you want answered about your topic. Then decide which sources will best provide answers to those questions. When gathering information, it is important to use a variety of sources and not to rely on one main source of information. It is also important to document where you find different pieces of information you use so that you can cite those sources in your work.

The suggestions that follow can help you locate your sources.

Library Resources

Libraries contain many sources of information in both print and electronic form. You'll save time if you plan your research before actually going to the library. Make a list of the information you think you will need, and for each item list possible sources for the information. Here are some sources to consider:

NONFICTION BOOKS An excellent starting point for researching your topic, nonfiction books can provide either broad coverage or specific details, depending on the book. To find appropriate nonfiction books, use the library catalog, which may be in card files or in electronic form on computers. In either case, you can search by author, title, or subject; in a computer catalog, you can also search by key word. When you find the listing for a book you want, print it out or copy down the title, author, and call number. The call number, which also appears on the book's spine, will help you locate the book in the library.

NEWSPAPERS AND MAGAZINES Books are often not the best places for finding up-to-the-minute information. Instead, you might try newspapers and magazines. To find information about an event that occurred on a specific date, go directly to newspapers and magazines for that date. To find articles on a particular topic, use indexes like the *Readers' Guide to Periodical Literature*, which lists magazine articles under subject headings. For each article that you want, jot down the title, author (if given), page number or numbers, and the name and date of the magazine in which the article appears. If your library does not have the magazine you need, either as a separate issue or on microfilm, you may still be able to obtain photocopies of the article through an interlibrary loan.

REFERENCE WORKS The following important reference materials can also help you with your research.

- ***General encyclopedias*** have articles on thousands of topics and are a good starting point for your research, although they shouldn't be used as primary sources.
- ***Specialized encyclopedias*** contain articles in particular subject areas, such as science, music, or art.
- ***Biographical dictionaries and indexes*** contain brief articles on people and often suggest where to find more information.
- ***Almanacs*** provide statistics and data on current events and act as a calendar for the upcoming year.
- ***Atlases***, or books of maps, usually include geographical facts and may also include information like population and weather statistics.
- ***Indexes and bibliographies***, such as the *Readers' Guide to Periodical Literature*, tell you in what publications you can find specific information, articles, or shorter works (such as poems or essays).
- ***Vertical files*** (drawers in file cabinets) hold pamphlets, booklets, and government publications that often provide current information.

Computer Research

The Internet Use the Internet to get up-to-the-minute information on virtually any topic. The Internet provides access to a multitude of resource-rich sources such as news media, museums, colleges and universities, and government institutions. There are a number of indexes and directories organized by subject to help you locate information on the Internet, including Yahoo!, the World Wide Web Virtual Library, the Kids Web, and the Webcrawler. These indexes and directories will help you find direct links to information related to your topic.

Internet Sources and Addresses

- *Yahoo! Directory* allows you to do word searches or link directly to your topic by clicking on such subjects as the arts, computers, entertainment, or government.
  http://www.yahoo.com
- *World Wide Web Virtual Library* is a comprehensive and easy-to-use subject catalog that provides direct links to academic subjects in alphabetical order.
  http://celtic.stanford.edu/vlib/Overview.html
- *Kids Web* supplies links to reference materials, such as dictionaries, *Bartlett's Familiar Quotations*, a thesaurus, and a world fact book.
  http://www.npac.syr.edu/textbook/kidsweb/
- *Webcrawler* helps you to find links to information about your topic that are available on the Internet when you type in a concise term or key word.
  http://www.webcrawler.com

CD-ROM References

Other sources that you can access using a computer are available on CD-ROM. The Wilson Disk, Newsquest, the *Readers' Guide to Periodical Literature*, and many other useful indexes are available on CD-ROM, as are encyclopedias, almanacs, atlases, and other reference works. Check your library to see which are available.

Interviews as Research Sources

People who are experts in their field or who have experience or knowledge relevant to your topic are excellent sources for your research. If such people are available to you, the way to obtain information from them is through an interview. Follow these guidelines to make your interview successful and productive:

- Make an appointment at a time convenient to the person you want to interview, and arrange to meet in a place where he or she will feel comfortable talking freely.
- If necessary, do research in advance to help you prepare the questions you will ask.
- Before the interview, list the questions you will ask, wording them so that they encourage specific answers. Avoid questions that can be answered simply with *yes* or *no*.
- Make an audiotape or videotape of the interview, if possible. If not, write down the answers as accurately as you can.
- Include the date of the interview at the top of your notes or on the tape.
- Follow up with a thank-you note or phone call to the person you interviewed.

Sources for a Multimedia Presentation

When preparing a multimedia presentation, keep in mind that you'll need to use some of your research findings to illustrate or support your main ideas when you actually give the presentation. Do research to find media support, such as visuals, CDs, and so on—in addition to those media you might create yourself. Here are some media that may be useful as both sources and illustrations:

- Musical recordings on audiocassette or compact disk (CD), often available at libraries
- Videos that you prepare yourself
- Fine art reproductions, often available at libraries and museums
- Photographs that you or others have taken
- Computer presentations using slide shows, graphics, and so on
- Video- or audiocassette recordings of interviews that you conduct

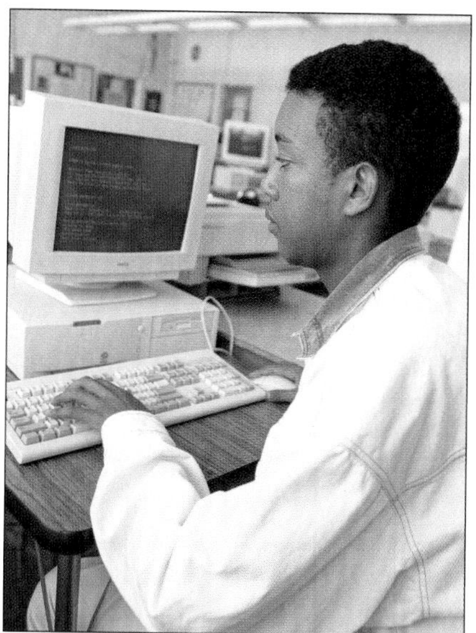

*I*NDEX OF *A*UTHORS AND *T*ITLES

Page numbers in *italics* refer to biographical information.

Index of Skills

LITERARY TERMS

READING STRATEGIES

GRAMMAR, USAGE, AND MECHANICS

VOCABULARY

CRITICAL THINKING AND VIEWING

WRITING

Writing Opportunities

Writing Skills

SPEAKING, LISTENING, AND VIEWING

LIFE AND WORK SKILLS

RESEARCHING AND REPRESENTING

ACKNOWLEDGMENTS (CONTINUED)

Chana Bloch "Pride" by Dahlia Ravikovitch, translated by Chana Bloch and Ariel Bloch from *The Window,* Sheep Meadow Press, 1989. Reprinted by permission of Chana Bloch.
Robert Bly "It Was the Grape's Autumn" by Pablo Neruda, translated by Robert Bly and James Wright, and "To My Brother Miguel" by César Vallejo, translated by John Knoepfle and James Wright, from *Neruda and Vallejo: Selected Poems,* edited by Robert Bly. Copyright © 1971 by Robert Bly.
Brandt & Brandt Literary Agents, Inc. "By the Waters of Babylon" by Stephen Vincent Benét, from *The Selected Works of Stephen Vincent Benét,* Holt, Rinehart & Winston, Inc. Copyright 1937 by Stephen Vincent Benét. Copyright renewed © 1964 by Thomas C. Benét, Stephanie B. Mahin and Rachel Benét Lewis. Reprinted by permission of Brandt & Brandt Literary Agents, Inc.
Curtis Brown Ltd. Excerpts from *Higher Than Hope: The Authorized Biography of Nelson Mandela* by Fatima Meer. Copyright © 1988 by Fatima Meer.
Knox Burger Associates, LTD. From *The Guitar: An Introduction to the Instrument* by Thomas A. Hill. Copyright © 1973 by Thomas A. Hill. Reprinted by permission of Knox Burger Associates, Ltd.
Don Congdon Associates, Inc. "Contents of the Dead Man's Pocket" by Jack Finney, published in *Collier's,* 1956. Copyright © 1957 by Crowell Collier Publishing, renewed 1984 by Jack Finney. "There Will Come Soft Rains" by Ray Bradbury, published in *Collier's Weekly,* 1950. Copyright © 1950 by Crowell-Collier Publishing, renewed 1977 by Ray Bradbury. Reprinted by permission of Don Congdon Associates, Inc.
Crown Publishers, Inc., a division of Random House, Inc. "Damon and Pythias" from *Classic Myths to Read Aloud* by William Russell. Copyright © 1988 by William F. Russell. Reprinted by permission of Crown Publishers, Inc.
Curbstone Press "Mirror Image"/"Espejeos" by Claribel Alegría from *Fugues,* translated by D. J. Flakoll. Copyright © 1993 by Claribel Alegría. Translation © 1993 by D. J. Flakoll. Reprinted with permission of Curbstone Press.
Darhansoff & Verrill Literary Agency "I Am Not One of Those Who Left the Land" by Anna Akhmatova from *Poems of Akhmatova,* selected, translated and introduced by Stanley Kunitz and Max Hayward, Copyright © 1973. Reprinted by permission of Darhansoff & Verrill Literary Agency.
Doubleday, a division of Bantam Doubleday Dell Publishing Group, Inc. "Shakespeare's Reading List" from *Shakespeare Alive!* by Joseph Papp and Elizabeth Kirkland. Copyright © 1988 by New York Shakespeare Festival. "A Visit to Grandmother," copyright © 1964 by William Melvin Kelley, from *Dancers on the Shore* by William Melvin Kelley. "The Bridge" by Leopold Staff, from *Postwar Polish Poetry,* selected and translated by Czeslaw Milosz. Translation copyright 1965 by Czeslaw Milosz. "The Waking," copyright 1953 by Theodore Roethke, from *The Collected Poems of Theodore Roethke* by Theodore Roethke. Used by permission of Doubleday, a division of Bantam Doubleday Dell Publishing Group, Inc.
Doubleday, a division of Bantam Doubleday Dell Publishing Group, Inc., and Harold Ober Associates, Inc. "Civil Peace" from *Girls at War and Other Stories* by Chinua Achebe. Copyright © 1972, 1973 by Chinua Achebe. Used by permission of Doubleday, a division of Bantam Doubleday Dell Publishing Group, Inc., and Harold Ober Associates, Inc.
Doubleday, a Division of Bantam Doubleday Dell Publishing Group, Inc., and Penguin Books Ltd. From *The Diary of Anne Frank.* Copyright © 1986 by Anne Frank-Fonds, Basle/Switzerland. English translation Copyright © 1989 by Doubleday, a Division of Bantam Doubleday Dell Publishing Group, Inc., and by Penguin Books, Ltd.
Roger Ebert "'Star Wars' Breakthrough Film Still Has the Force" by Roger Ebert. First published in January 1997, *Chicago Sun Times.* © 1977 The Ebert Co., Ltd. Used by permission of the author.
Editions Robert Laffont From *In the Name of Sorrow and Hope* by Noa Ben Artzi-Pelossof. Copyright © 1996 by Editions Robert Laffont.
Ann Elmo Agency, Inc. "Leiningen Versus the Ants" by Carl Stephenson. Reprinted by permission of Ann Elmo Agency, Inc., 60 East 42nd Street, New York, NY 10165.
EMI Blackwood Music Inc. "Yesterday," words and music by John Lennon and Paul McCartney. Copyright © 1965, 1966, Renewed 1993, 1994 Sony/ATV Songs LLC. Administered by EMI Blackwood Music Inc. (BMI). All rights reserved. International Copyright Secured. Used by Permission.
Farrar, Straus & Giroux, Inc. "What Are Friends For" by Rosellen Brown. From *Cora Fry's pillow book* by Rosellen Brown. Copyright © 1994. "A Walk to the Jetty" from *Annie John* by Jamaica Kincaid. Copyright © 1985 by Jamaica Kincaid. "The Fish" from *The Complete Poems 1927–1979* by Elizabeth Bishop. Copyright © 1979, 1983 by Alice Helen Methfessel. Excerpt from *Nobel Lecture* by Alexander Solzhenitsyn, translated by F. D. Reeve. Copyright © 1972 by the Nobel Foundation. Translation copyright © 1972 by Farrar, Straus & Giroux, Inc. "A Storm in the Mountains" from *Stories and Prose Poems* by Alexander Solzhenitsyn, translated by Michael Glenny. Translation copyright © 1971 by Michael Glenny. Reprinted by permission of Farrar, Straus & Giroux, Inc.
Frankfurt, Garbus, Klein & Selz Lyrics from "Cats in the Cradle" by Sandy and Harry Chapin. Copyright © 1974 Story Songs Ltd. Used with permission. All Rights Reserved.
Harcourt Brace & Company "Jazz Fantasia" from *Smoke and Steel* by Carl Sandburg, copyright 1920 by Harcourt Brace & Company and renewed 1948 by Carl Sandburg. "How to React to Familiar Faces" from *How to Travel With a Salmon & Other Essays* by Umberto Eco, copyright © Gruppo Editoriale Fabbri, Bompiani, Sonzogno, Estas S.p.A., English translation by William Weaver, copyright © 1994 by Harcourt Brace & Company. "Antigone" from *Sophocles: The Oedipus Cycle,* An English Version by Dudley Fitts and Robert Fitzgerald, copyright 1939 by Harcourt Brace & Company and renewed 1967 by Dudley Fitts and Robert Fitzgerald. CAUTION: All rights, including professional, amateur, motion picture, recitation, lecturing, performance, public reading, radio broadcasting, and television are strictly reserved. Inquiries on all rights should be addressed to Harcourt Brace & Company, Permissions Department, Orlando, FL 32887-6777. Reprinted by permission of Harcourt Brace & Company.
Harcourt Brace and Company, The Executors of the Estate of Virginia Woolf, and The Hogarth Press, an imprint of Random House UK. "The Widow and the Parrot" from *The Complete Shorter Fiction of Virginia Woolf,* copyright © 1985 by Quentin Bell and Angelica Garnett. Reprinted by permission.
Harcourt Brace and Company, and The Wylie Agency, Inc. "The Garden of Stubborn Cats" from *Marcovaldo or the Seasons in the City* by Italo Calvino, English translation copyright © 1983 by Harcourt Brace & Company and Martin Secker & Warburg, Ltd. Reprinted by permission.
HarperCollins Publishers, Inc. Excerpts from *Rare Air* by

Michael Jordan. Photographs by Walter Iooss, Jr. Edited by Mark Vancil. Copyright © 1993 Rare Air, Ltd. Text © 1993 Michael Jordan. Photos © 1993 Walter Iooss, Jr. "Flood" from *Pilgrim At Tinker Creek* by Annie Dillard. Copyright © 1974 by Annie Dillard. Reprinted by permission of HarperCollins Publishers, Inc.
HarperCollins Publishers Inc., and Jonathan Clowes Ltd. "Through the Tunnel" from *The Habit of Loving* by Doris Lessing. Copyright © 1955 by Doris Lessing. Originally appeared in *The New Yorker.* Copyright renewed. Reprinted by kind permission of HarperCollins Publishers, Inc., and Jonathan Clowes Ltd., London, on behalf of Doris Lessing.
HarperCollins Publishers Ltd. From *The Analects of Confucius,* translated by Arthur Waley. Reprinted by permission of HarperCollins Publishers Ltd.
Harvard University Press Excerpts from *One Writer's Beginnings* by Eudora Welty. Reprinted by permission of the publisher, Cambridge, Mass.: Harvard University Press, Copyright © 1983, 1984 by Eudora Welty.
Harvard University Press and the Trustees of Amherst College "The Wind—tapped like a tired Man" (#436), "I dwell in Possibility—" (#657), and "Success is counted sweetest" (poem #67) by Emily Dickinson. Reprinted by permission of the publishers and the Trustees of Amherst College from *The Poems of Emily Dickinson,* Thomas J. Johnson, ed., Cambridge, Mass.: The Belknap Press of Harvard University Press, Copyright © 1951, 1955, 1979, 1983 by the President and Fellows of Harvard College.
Hill and Wang, a division of Farrar, Straus & Giroux, Inc., and Albert Bonniers Forlag AB "The Princess and All the Kingdom" from *The Marriage Feast* by Pär Lagerkvist, translated by Alan Blair. Translation copyright © 1954 by Random House. Reprinted by permission of Hill and Wang, a division of Farrar, Straus & Giroux, Inc., and Albert Bonniers Forlag AB.
Hispanic Society of America "The Guitar" by Federico García Lorca from *Translations From Hispanic Poets,* edited by Elizabeth du Gue Trapier. Reprinted by permission of the Hispanic Society of America.
Hodder and Stoughton Limited "The Final Assault" from *High Adventure* by Edmund Hillary. Copyright 1955. Reproduced by permission of Hodder and Stoughton Limited.
Henry Holt & Co. "Mowing" and "After Apple Picking" from *The Poetry of Robert Frost,* edited by Edward Connery Lathem. Published by Holt, Rinehart and Winston.
Houghton Mifflin Company "The Marginal World" from *The Edge of the Sea* by Rachel Carson. Copyright © 1955 by Rachel L. Carson, © renewed 1983 by Roger Christie. Reprinted by permission of Houghton Mifflin Company. All rights reserved.
Japan Publications, Inc. "Falling upon earth" by Bashō and "A gentle spring rain" by Issa, reprinted from *One Hundred Famous Haiku,* translated by Daniel C. Buchanan, with permission from Japan Publications, Inc., ©1973
John Johnson Ltd., and Penguin Books Ltd. "The Bridegroom," from *The Bronze Horseman and Other Poems* by Alexander Pushkin, translated by D. M. Thomas (Penguin Books 1982). Translation copyright © D. M. Thomas, 1982. Reprinted by permission of John Johnson (Authors' Agent) Limited, and Penguin Books Ltd.
The Johns Hopkins University Press "Night"/"Noche" and "Fear" from *Selected Poems of Gabriela Mistral,* translated and edited by Doris Dana. Copyright © 1961, 1964, 1970, 1971 by Doris Dana. Reprinted by permission of The Johns Hopkins University Press.
Alfred A. Knopf, Inc. "The Apple Tree" from *The Scrapbook of Katherine Mansfield* by Katherine Mansfield, edit., J. Middleton Murry. Copyright 1939 by Alfred A. Knopf, Inc., and renewed 1967 by Mrs. Mary Middleton Murry. "The Weary Blues" from *Selected Poems* by Langston Hughes. Copyright 1926 by Alfred A. Knopf, Inc., and renewed 1954 by Langston Hughes. Reprinted by permission of the publisher.
Jon Krakauer From "Into Thin Air" by Jon Krakauer from the September 1996 issue of *Outside Magazine.* Reprinted by permission of the author.
John Landau Management "These Are Days" by Natalie Merchant, from *Our Time in Eden,* copyright © 1992 ASCAP. Reprinted by permission of John Landau Management.
Charles Lave "65 MPH speed limit is saving lives" by Charles Lave, reprinted from *Access,* U.C. Berkeley Transportation Center's magazine in *Consumers' Research Magazine,* Sept. 1997. Copyright 1997 Consumers' Research Inc. Reprinted by permission of the author.
Library of America "Prayer of First Dancers," Navajo, from *The Night Chant,* by permission of the Library of America.
Liveright Publishing Corporation "Reapers" from *Cane* by Jean Toomer. Copyright 1923 by Boni & Liveright, renewed 1951 by Jean Toomer. Reprinted by permission of Liveright Publishing Corporation.
Martin Secker & Warburg, Ltd. Excerpt from *My Left Foot* by Christy Brown. Copyright © 1954 by Christy Brown. Reprinted by permission of Martin Secker & Warburg, Ltd.
Natural History Magazine "Work That Counts" by Ernest Ruelas Inzunza from *Natural History,* October 1996, Volume 105, Number 10. Copyright © the American Museum of Natural History, 1996. Reprinted by permission of *Natural History* Magazine.
NAL Penguin, a division of Penguin Books USA Inc. From *The Tragedy of Julius Caesar* by William Shakespeare, edited by William and Barbara Rosen. Copyright © 1963 by William and Barbara Rosen.
NBA Properties, Inc., and Frank Deford "NBA: The Greatest Ever" by Frank DeFord which aired on NBC, November 2, 1996. Reprinted with the permission of NBA Properties, Inc., and Frank Deford.
New Directions Publishing Corp. "A Tree Telling of Orpheus" by Denise Levertov, from *Poems 1968–1972.* Copyright © 1970 by Denise Levertov. "The Street" by Octavio Paz, from *Selected Poems.* Copyright © 1973 by Octavio Paz and Muriel Rukeyser. "Spring and All" by William Carlos Williams, from *Collected Poems: 1909–1939, Volume I.* Copyright © 1938 by New Directions Publishing Corp. "Jade Blossom Palace" by Tu Fu, translated by David Hinton, from *The Selected Poems of Tu Fu.* Copyright © 1989 by David Hinton. "Epitaph for No Stone" by Octavio Paz, translated by Eliot Weinberger from *Collected Poems 1957–1987.* Copyright © 1986 by Octavio Paz and Eliot Weinberger. "The Moon Rising" by Federico García Lorca, translated by Lysander Kemp, from *The Selected Poems of Federico García Lorca.* Copyright © 1955 by New Directions Publishing Corporation. Reprinted by permission of New Directions Publishing Corp.
New Directions Publishing Corporation, and David Higham Associates Ltd. Dylan Thomas, *A Child's Christmas in Wales.* Copyright © 1952 by Dylan Thomas; Copyright © 1954 New Directions Publishing Corporation. Reprinted by permission of New Directions Publishing Corporation, and David Higham Associates Ltd.
New Orleans Poetry Journal Press, Inc. "Columbus

Dying" from *Adam's Footprint* by Vassar Miller, Copyright © 1956 by Vassar Miller. Reprinted by permission of New Orleans Poetry Journal Press, Inc.

The New York Times Co. "Star Wars: An Epic For Today" ("The Names Came From Earth") by Eric Nash, published in *The New York Times,* January 26, 1997. Copyright © 1997 by The New York Times Company. "Star Wars—A Trip to a Far Galaxy" by Vincent Canby, published in *The New York Times,* May 16, 1977. Copyright © 1977 by The New York Times Co. Reprinted by permission of The New York Times Co.

The Nobel Foundation "Keep Memory Alive," excerpt from Elie Wiesel's Nobel Prize Acceptance Speech. Copyright © 1986 by the Nobel Foundation. Used by permission of the Nobel Foundation, Oslo, Norway.

North Point Press, a division of Farrar Straus & Giroux, Inc. "All" by Bei Dao, translated by Donald Finkel and Xueliang Chen, and "Also All" by Shu Ting, translated by Donald Finkel and Jinsheng Yi, from *A Splintered Mirror: Chinese Poetry from the Democracy Movement,* translated by Donald Finkel. Translation copyright © 1991 by Donald Finkel. Reprinted by permission of North Point Press, a division of Farrar, Straus & Giroux.

W. W. Norton & Company, Inc. From *Don Quixote,* A Norton Critical Edition, The Ormbsby Translation, Revised by Miguel de Cervantes, edited by Joseph Jones & Kenneth Douglas. Copyright © 1981 by W. W. Norton & Company, Inc. Reprinted by permission of W. W. Norton & Company, Inc.

NTC/Contemporary Publishing Group, Inc. "The Sun and the Moon"/"El sol y la luna" from *Legends from Mexico/ Leyendas de Mexico* by Genevieve Barlow and William N. Stivers. Copyright © 1995 by NTC Publishing Group. Used with permission of NTC/Contemporary Publishing Group, Inc.

Naomi Shihab Nye "Making a Fist" from *Hugging the Jukebox* by Naomi Shihab Nye. Copyright © Naomi Shihab Nye, 1982. Reprinted by permission of the author.

Harold Ober Associates, Inc. "The Good Deed" by Pearl S. Buck. Copyright 1953 by Pearl S. Buck. Copyright renewed 1981. "Marian Anderson: Famous Concert Singer" by Langston Hughes. Copyright © 1954 by Langston Hughes, renewed 1982 by George Houston Bass. Reprinted by permission of Harold Ober Associates, Incorporated.

Peter Owen Ltd. "A Man" by Nina Cassian, translated by Roy MacGregor-Hastie. Reprinted by permission of Peter Owen Ltd, London.

Pantheon Books, a division of Random House, Inc. "The Orphan Boy and the Elk Dog," from *American Indian Myths and Legends* by Richard Erdoes and Alfonso Ortiz, editors. Copyright © 1984 by Richard Erdoes and Alfonso Ortiz. Reprinted by permission of Pantheon Books, a division of Random House, Inc.

Penguin Books Ltd. "One cannot ask loneliness" by Priest Jakuren, from *The Penguin Book of Japanese Verse* edited and translated by Geoffrey Bownas and Anthony Thwaite (Penguin Books, 1964). Translation copyright © Geoffrey Bownas and Anthony Thwaite, 1964. Reprinted by permission of Penguin Books Ltd.

Présence Africaine "Africa" from *Coups de Pilon* by David Diop, published by Présence Africaine, 1956. "Childhood" and "The Lion's Awakening" from *Sundiata: An Epic of Old Mali* by D. T. Niane, translated by G. D. Pickett. © Présence Africaine 1960 (original French version: *Soundjata, ou L'Epopée Mandingue*). © Longman Group Ltd. (English Version) 1965. Reprinted by permission of Présence Africaine.

Reynolds Price "What's in a Picture," retitled "A Picture From the Past" by Reynolds Price from the September/October 1996 issue of *Civilization Magazine,* copyright © 1996. Reprinted by permission of the author.

The Putnam Publishing Group "In Flanders Fields" reprinted by permission of The Putnam Publishing Group from *In Flanders Fields* by John McCrae. Copyright © 1919 by G. P. Putnam's Sons, Renewed.

The Putnam Publishing Group, and David Higham Associates "Arthur Becomes King" from *The Once and Future King* by T. H. White. Copyright © 1939, 1940 by T. H. White; Renewed © 1958 by T. H. White Proprietor. Reprinted by permission of The Putnam Publishing Group, and David Higham Associates.

Random House, Inc. "The Moon at the Fortified Pass" by Li Po, translated by Wytter Bynner, from *The Wisdom of China and India* edited by Lin Yutang. Copyright 1942 and renewed 1970 by Random House, Inc. "At Harvest Time" and "Style" from *Wouldn't Take Nothing For My Journey Now* by Maya Angelou. Copyright © 1993 by Maya Angelou. Reprinted by permission of Random House, Inc.

Real World Music and Lipservices "Biko" by Peter Gabriel. © 1980 by Real World Music Ltd. Reproduced with kind permission of Real World Music and Lipservices. All Rights Reserved. International Copyright Secured.

Reason Magazine Book review of Rachel Carson's *Silent Spring* by Bruce N. Ames and Thomas Jukes is reprinted with permission from the December 1993 issue of *Reason* Magazine. Copyright 1999 by the Reason Foundation, 3415 S. Sepulveda Blvd., Los Angeles, CA 90034. www.reason.com.

Marian Reiner "Metaphor" from *It Doesn't Always Have to Rhyme* by Eve Merriam. Copyright © 1964 by Eve Merriam. Copyright renewed 1992 Eve Merriam. Reprinted by permission of Marian Reiner.

Russell & Volkening "Uncoiling" from *Daughters of the Fifth Sun* by Pat Mora. Copyright © 1995 by Pat Mora. Published by Riverside Books. "With All Flags Flying" by Anne Tyler, published by *Redbook Magazine,* June 1971. Copyright © 1971 by Anne Tyler. Reprinted by the permission of Russell & Volkening as agents for the authors.

Schocken Books, distributed by Pantheon Books, a division of Random House, Inc. "Before the Law," from *Franz Kafka: The Complete Stories* by Franz Kafka, edited by Nahum N. Glatzer. Copyright © 1946, 1947, 1948, 1949, 1954, 1958, 1971 by Schocken Books, Inc. Reprinted by permission of Schocken Books, distributed by Pantheon Books, a division of Random House, Inc.

Simon & Schuster Inc. and A. P. Watt "The Stolen Child" reprinted with permission of Simon & Schuster from *The Collected Poems of W. B. Yeats, Volume I: The Poems,* Revised and edited by Richard J. Finneran. Copyright 1906 by Macmillan Publishing Company, renewed 1934 by William Butler Yeats.

The Society of Authors as the literary representative of the Estate of W. W. Jacobs "The Monkey's Paw" from *The Lady of the Barge* by W. W. Jacobs. Reprinted by permission.

Sage Sohier Sage Sohier, *Untitled,* text and photograph © Sage Sohier, Brookline, Massachusetts, 1986. Published in *Mothers & Daughters* by Tillie Olsen with Julie Olsen Edwards and Estelle Jussim. Reprinted by permission of the author.

The Estate of Rabindranath Tagore "The Cabuliwallah" from *A Tagore Reader* by Rabindranath Tagore, copyright © 1945.

Third World Press "The Bean Eaters" from *Blacks* by Gwendolyn Brooks. Copyright © 1991 by Gwendolyn Brooks. Reprinted by permission of the publisher, Third World Press, Chicago, IL

Rosemary A. Thurber "The Dog That Bit People," copyright

1933, © 1961 by James Thurber. From *My Life and Hard Times,* published by Harper & Row. Reprinted by permission of Rosemary A. Thurber.

Time-Life Books, Inc. "Imitating Nature's Mineral Artistry" from *Planet Earth: Gemstones* by Paul O'Neil and the Editors of Time-Life Books. Copyright © 1983 Time-Life Books Inc. Reprinted by permission of Time-Life Books, Inc.

Joanna Trzeciak "Some Like Poetry" by Wislawa Szymborska, translated by Joanna Trzeciak, first appeared in *The New Yorker,* October 1996. © 1996 Wislawa Szymborska. All rights reserved. Used by permission of the translator.

The University of California Press "A Pace Like That" translated by Chana Bloch, from *The Selected Poetry of Yehuda Amichai,* edited and translated by Chana Bloch and Stephen Mitchell. Copyright © 1996 The Regents of the University of California. Reprinted by permission of The University of California Press.

University of New Mexico Press Reprinted from *The Way to Rainy Mountain* by N. Scott Momaday. First published in *The Reporter,* January 26, 1967. © 1969 The University of New Mexico Press and reprinted with their permission.

The University of North Carolina Press "The Street of the Cañon" from *Mexican Village* by Josephina Niggli. Copyright 1945 The University of North Carolina Press. Reprinted by permission of the publisher.

Viking Penguin, a division of Penguin Books USA Inc. "Like the Sun" from *Under the Banyan Tree* by R. K. Narayan. Copyright © 1985 by R. K. Narayan. From *What Makes a Degas a Degas* by Richard Muhlberger. Copyright © 1993 by The Metropolitan Museum of Art. Used by permission of Viking Penguin, a division of Penguin Books USA Inc. "The Open Window" from *The Complete Short Stories of Saki* (H. H. Munro), published by Viking Press, Inc.

Tino Villanueva "I Only Know That Now"/"Solo sé que ahora" by Tino Villanueva, first appeared in *Crónica de mis años peores.* Copyright 1987 by Tino Villanueva. Reprinted by permission of the author.

Vintage Books, a division of Random House, Inc. From *Speak, Memory* by Vladimir Nabokov. Copyright © 1966 by Vladimir Nabokov. Reprinted by permission of Vintage Books, a Division of Random House, Inc.

Wallace Literary Agency for R. K. Narayan "Rama's Initiation" from *The Ramayana: A Shortened Modern Prose Version of the Indian Epic* by R. K. Narayan. Published by Penguin Books. Copyright © 1972 by R. K. Narayan. Reprinted by permission of the author.

A. P. Watt Ltd. From *A Problem* by Anton Chekhov, translated from Russian by Constance Garnett. Reprinted by permission of A. P. Watt Ltd. on behalf of The Executors of the Estate of Constance Garnett.

Weldon Owen Publishing "Understanding Lightning and Thunder" (originally titled "Electrical Phenomena"), an extract from *The Nature Company Guides: Weather* by William J. Burroughs, Bob Crowder, Ted Robertson, Eleanor Vallier-Talbot, Richard Whitaker. © 1996 Weldon Owen Pty Limited. Reprinted by permission of Weldon Owen Publishing.

Wieser & Wieser, Inc. "Auto Wreck" from *Collected Poems 1940–1978* by Karl Shapiro. Copyright 1942 and renewed 1970 by Karl Shapiro. Reprinted by permission of Wieser & Wieser, Inc.

Zohar Press Grateful acknowledgment to Zohar Press for permission to reprint "Right Hand" by Philip Fried from his book *Quantum Genesis and Other Poems* (Zohar, 1997).

Note: Every effort has been made to locate the copyright owner of material reprinted in this book. Omissions brought to our attention will be corrected in subsequent editions.

Art Credits

Cover and Title Page: Hideo Kurihara/Tony Stone Images; **vi:** (top) Guido A. Rossi/The Image Bank; **vii:** *Traditional Yam Harvest*, John Mainga, LAMU, The Gallery of Contemporary African Art, photo by John Lei/Omni-Photo Communications, Inc.; **viii:** Corbis-Bettmann; **vix:** UPI/Corbis-Bettmann; **x:** *The Color of Sun*, Howard Terpning, oil, 26" x 26", The Greenwich Workshop Inc.; **xi:** (top) © Kenneth H. Thomas/Photo Researchers, Inc.; (bottom) *The Body of a House #6 of 8*, © 1993, Robert Beckman, oil on canvas, 69"x 96 1/2", photo by Tony Scodwell; **xii:** (top) Stephen J. Krasemann/DRK Photo; (bottom) courtesy of the photographer; **xiii:** Photofest; **xiv:** *Best Friends*, Craig Nelson/Bernstein & Andriulli, Inc.; **xvi:** (top) By permission of the Houghton Library, Harvard University; (bottom) Photofest; **1:** *Guardrail/Ocean*, 1985, Woody Gwyn, Egg tempera on wood panel, 12" x 12"; **3:** The Granger Collection, New York; **5:** Joseph Nettis/Stock, Boston; **9:** Ken Karp Photography; **12–13:** Joseph Nettis/Stock, Boston; **21:** *Le Modèle Vivant*, René Magritte, Christie's ImagesSuperstock, © 1997 C. Herscovici, Brussels/Artists Rights Society (ARS), New York; **22:** (left) UPI/Corbis-Bettmann; (right) AP/Wide World Photos; **24–25:** Fotopic/Omni-Photo Communications, Inc.; **28–29:** Paul Keel/Photo Researchers, Inc.; **31:** UPI/Corbis-Bettmann; **32:** Fotopic/Omni-Photo Communications, Inc.; **33:** NASA; **36:** The Granger Collection, New York; **37:** Guido A. Rossi/The Image Bank; **38:** Paul Keel/Photo Researchers, Inc.; **40:** Fotopic/Omni-Photo Communications, Inc.; **44:** (left) UPI/Corbis-Bettmann; (right) Scala/Art Resource, NY; **55:** *The Lights of Marriage* (detail), Marc Chagall, Kunsthaus, Zurich, © 1997 Artists Rights Society (ARS), New York/ADAGP, Paris; **60:** Photo by Sigrid Estrada; **63:** *San Antonio de Oriente* (detail), 1954, José Antonio Velásquez, oil on canvas, Museum of Modern Art of Latin America, Washington, D.C.; **65:** *Port de la Saline, Haiti*, n.d., Lois Mailou Jones, Courtesy of the artist; **71:** Ken Karp Photography; **75:** Rob Day/Stock Illustration Source, Inc.; **76:** Corbis-Bettmann; **82:** *Les Masques et la Mort 1897*, James Ensor, © Estate of James Ensor, Giraudon/Art Resource, New York; **86:** (top) UPI/Corbis-Bettmann; (center) AP/Wide World Photos; (bottom) The National Portrait Gallery, Smithsonian Institution, Washington, D.C./Art Resource, NY; **88:** *Woman With Child*, Pablo Picasso, Museo Picasso, Barcelona, Spain, Scala/Art Resource, NY, © 1997 Estate of Pablo Picasso/Artists Rights Society (ARS), New York; **90–91:** *Untitled*, © 1996 David Gaz Studio/Soodak Represents; **94:** Corbis-Bettmann; **97:** *The Anglers, Study for "La Grande Jatte,"* 1883, Georges Seurat, oil on panel, 16 x 25 cm. Musée Nat. d'Art Moderne, Troyes, France, Giraudon/Art Resource, NY; **98:** *Les Maisons Cabassud à la Ville d'Avray*, Jean Baptiste Camille Corot, The Louvre, Paris, Scala/Art Resource, New York; **103:** Culver Pictures, Inc.; **108:** © Kee Van den Berg/Photo Researchers, Inc.; **111:** Corel Professional Photos CD-ROM™; **112:** Ken Karp Photography; **114–115:** *Steps to the Steps*, Brad Holland, courtesy of the artist; **116:** Prentice Hall; **120:** *Orion, 1984*, Martin Wong, Acrylic on canvas, 36" diameter, courtesy of Exit Art Gallery, New York; **123:** Steve Dunwell/The Image Bank; **127:** *Earth and Sky Puzzle*, Curtis Parker/SIS; **128:** *L. N. Tolstoi*, I. E. Repin, Sovfoto/Eastfoto; **130:** *Rest During the Harvest*, Alexander Morosov, Tretyakov Gallery, Moscow, Russia, Scala/Art Resource, NY; **130–135:** (background) Corel Professional Photos CD-ROM™; **135:** (center) *Cornfield at Ewell* (detail), c.1846, William Holman Hunt, oil on board, 20.2 cm x 31.8 cm. Tate Gallery, London, Great Britain/Art Resource, NY; **136–137:** (background) Corel Professional Photos CD-ROM™; **137:** (center) *The Hay Harvest*, Boris Kustodiev, Scala/Art Resource, NY; **138–139:** (background) Corel Professional Photos CD-ROM™; **140:** (center) D. Brookover/Photonica; **140–143:** (background) Corel Professional Photos CD-ROM™; **146:** (top) The Granger Collection, New York; (center) Arte Público Press; (bottom) photo by Maud Lipscomb; **148:** *The Terrace at Meric*, 1867, Frédéric Bazille, 21 3/4" x 36", Cincinnati Museum of Art, oil on canvas, gift of Mark P. Herschede, 1976; **150–151:** Steve Bronstein/The Image Bank; **154:** Rod Tuach/Globe Photos; **157 & 159:** Photofest; **166–167:** *Springtime Rain*, 1975, Ogden M. Pleissner, Ogden M. Pleissner Estate Marion G. Pleissner Trust, Bankers Trust Company. photo by Grace Davies/Omni-Photo Communications, Inc.; **169:** courtesy of the artist; **172:** *Spring Fever, 1978* From the Profile Part I: The Twenties series (Mecklenburg County), collage on board, 7" x 9 3/8" private collection, © Romare Bearden Foundation/Licensed by VAGA, NY; **177:** Corel Professional Photos CD-ROM™; **181:** *Untitled*, Bart Forbes; **182:** (left) Dimitri Kessel/Life Magazine; (right) Henry McGee/Globe Photos; **183:** Corel Professional Photos CD-ROM™; **185:** (center) *The Mowers*, by Sir George Clausen (1852–1944), Usher Gallery, Lincoln/Bridgeman Art Library London/New York **186–187:** (background) Corel Professional Photos CD-ROM™; **188:** *Wind on the Water*, bronze, 8 1/2' x 8' x 4', Richard McDermott Miller; **189:** *Daphne*, Mary Frank, ceramic in eight parts, overall 39 by 38 by 5 1/2 in., Photo Courtesy DC Moore Gallery, New York; **192:** Corbis-Bettmann; **193:** *Apple Plenty*, 1970, Herbert Shuptrine. Private collection, courtesy New York Graphic Society; **194:** *Orchard With Flowering Fruit Trees, Springtime, Pontoise*, 1877, Camille Pissarro, Musée d'Orsay, Paris; **195:** *Apple Plenty*, 1970, Herbert Shuptrine. Private collection, courtesy New York Graphic Society; **197:** Corel Professional Photos CD-ROM™; **200:** (top) AP/Wide World Photos; (bottom) & (center) Dorothy Alexander; **202:** *Traditional Yam Harvest*, John Mainga, LAMU, The Gallery of Contemporary African Art, photo by John Lei/Omni-Photo Communications, Inc.; **203:** NASA; **204:** AP/Wide World Photos; **206:** *Old Trees by Cold Waterfall, 1470–1559*, Wen Zhengming, The Los Angeles County Museum of Art, Ernest Larsen Blancok Memorial Fund; **210:** Ken Karp Photography; **213:** Ken Karp Photography; **214:** Bob Daemmrich/PNI; **216–217:** *The Deluge*, 1920, Winifred Knights, Tate Gallery, London, Great Britain, Art Resource, NY; **218:** Thomas Victor; **221:** © 1995 Yukimasa Hirota/Photonica; **222–223:** *The Beach Treat* (detail), Suzanne Nagler, photograph © Stephen Tucker, collection of Mr. and Mrs. X. Daniel Kafcas; **225:** *The Diver*, Dennis Angel, oil on panel, 40" x 32"; **227:** *Coast Scene, Isles of Shoals, 1901*, Childe Hassam, The Metropolitan Museum of Art, gift of George A. Hearn, 1909, © 1987 by The Metropolitan Museum of Art; **231:** *Woman Dragging Key to Keyhole*, Brad Holland; **232:** UPI/Corbis-Bettmann; **233, 235, & 237:** ©1933 by James Thurber. © 1961 renewed by Helen Thurber and Rosemary A. Thurber. Reprinted by arrangement with Rosemary A. Thurber and The Barbara Hogenson Agency; **242:** (top) *Edna St. Vincent Millay* (detail), Charles Ellis, The National Portrait Gallery, Smithsonian Institution, Washington, D. C./Art Resource, New York; (center) *Langston Hughes* (detail), c. 1925, Winold Reiss, The National Portrait Gallery, Smithsonian Institution, Washington, D. C./Art Resource, New York; (bottom) *Carl Sandburg*, Miriam Svet, The National Portrait Gallery, Smithsonian Institution, Washington, D.C./Art Resource, New York; **243:** Corel Professional Photos CD-ROM™; **244–245:** Frank Siteman/Omni-Photo Communications, Inc.; **246:** (tr) *Solo/Interval, 1987*, Romare Bearden, collage on board, 11"x14", © 1997 Romare Bearden Foundation/Licensed by VAGA, NY; (bl) © Frank Driggs Collection/Archive Photos; **247:** *Autumn Lamp (Guitar Player), 1983*, Romare Bearden, from the Mecklenburg Autumn Series, Oil with collage, 40" x 31", private collection, © 1997 Romare Bearden Foundation/Licensed by VAGA, NY; **250:** AP/Wide World Photos; **253:** *Face in the Sun*, Hal Lose/Stock Illustration Source, Inc.; **257:** Will Faller © 1995; **261:** Gerald Bustomante/Stock Illustration Source, Inc.; **262:** (left) UPI/Corbis-Bettmann; (right) Thomas Victor; **267:** Kenneth Redding/The Image Bank; **270:** (right) R. Dominguec/Globe Photos; **273:** *Mess Line: Noon at Manzanar*, Ansel Adams, Courtesy of the Library of Congress, copywork by Grace Davies; **274:** Corbis-Bettmann; **276:** Culver Pictures, Inc.; **282:** The Granger Collection, New York; **284–285:** P. & G. Bowater/The Image Bank; **288:** NASA; **289 & 294:** Corel Professional Photos CD-ROM™; **297:** Kopstein/Monkmeyer; **298:** Ken Karp Photography; **300–301:** *Summer Breeze*, 1995, Alice Dalton Brown, oil on canvas, 50" x 72", Courtesy Fischbach Gallery, NY, photo: Peter Jacobs; **302:** Sovfoto/Eastfoto; **303:** Family archives, the Estate of Vladimir Nabokov; **306:** Tina Merandon/Photonica; **311:** *Untitled*, David Wilcox, The Newborn Group; **312:** photo by Diana Walker; **314–315:** *Route 6, Eastham*, 1941, Edward Hopper, oil on canvas, 27" x 38". Collection of the Sheldon Swope Art Museum, Terre Haute, Indiana; **316:** Bill Aron/Photo Researchers, Inc.; **319:** *Stairway*, 1949, Edward Hopper, oil on wood, 16" x 11 7/8" (40.6cm x 30.2cm), collection of Whitney Museum of American Art, Josephine N. Hopper Bequest, 70.1265, Photograph © 1997: Whitney Museum of American Art; **324:** (top) & (center) The Granger Collection, New York; (bottom) © Archive Photos; **327:** Frank Siteman/Omni-Photo Communications, Inc.; **328:** Art Zamur/Liaison International; **329:** © Archive Photos; **333:** Corel Professional Photos CD-ROM™; **337:** © James Endicott/Stock Illustration Source, Inc.; **338:** *Pearl S. Buck* (detail), Vita Solomon, National Portrait Gallery, Smithsonian Institution, Washington, D. C./Art Resource, New York; **340–341:** *Mother and Daughter: Leaf from a Manchu family album,* unidentified artist, ink and color on paper, 13 1/8" x 14 1/8". The Metropolitan Museum of Art, anonymous gift, 1952. (52.209.3j) © 1980 by the Metropolitan Museum of Art; **348 & 352:** Ken Karp Photography; **356:** (background) NASA; (top) Adam Scull/Globe Photos; (bottom) John Barrett/Globe Photos; **358:** (top) and (bottom) Andrew D. Bernstein/NBA photos; **359:** Focus On Sports, Inc.; **360:** UPI/Corbis-Bettmann; **361:** NASA; **362:** (top) and (bottom) AP/Wide World Photos; **362–363:** *Peacefulness*, Tran Nguyen Dan, Indochina Arts Project; **366:** G. R. Roberts/Omni-Photo Communications, Inc.; **368:** *Enigma of the Hour*, 1912, Giorgio de Chirico, Coll. Mattioli, Milan, Italy, Scala/Art Resource, NY, © Foundation Georgio de Chirico/Licensed by VAGA, New York, NY; **372:** Tina Merandon/Photonica; **376:** Ken Karp Photography; **378–379:** *Torn in Transit*, 1890–95, oil on canvas, 13 1/2" x 17", John Haberle, Collection of the Brandywine River Museum, gift of Amanda K. Berls. Photograph by Richard Carter, 1988; **380:** The Granger Collection, New York; **381:** Corel Professional Photos CD-ROM™; **383:** © Jeanne White/Photo Researchers, Inc.; **386–387:** Corel Professional Photos CD-ROM™; **388 & 389:** Image © 1997 PhotoDisc, Inc.; **393:** *Mingling*, Diana Ong, Superstock; **394:** AP/Wide World Photos; **396–397:** Betty Press/Woodfin Camp & Associates; **399:** © The Stock Market/John Curtis; **404:** (left) UPI/Corbis-Bettmann; (right) J. P. Gauthier/Globe Photos; **405:** Gifford/Liaison International; **406:** (bl) Grace Davies/Omni-Photo Communications, Inc.; (br) Barrie Fanton/Omni-Photo Communications, Inc.; **407:** NASA; **408:** Gifford/Liaison International; **412:** AP/Wide World Photos; **413:** Prentice Hall; **414:** The Granger Collection, New York; **417:** *Dancers, Pink and Green*, Edgar Degas, oil on canvas, 32 3/8" x 29 3/4" (82.2 x 75.6 cm), signed (lower right): Degas. The Metropolitan Museum of Art, Bequest of Mrs. H. O. Havemeyer, 1929. The H. O. Havemeyer Collection. (29.100.42). Photograph © 1980 by The Metropolitan Museum of Art; **418:** *Carriage at the Races*, 1872, Edgar Degas, oil on canvas 14 3/8" x 22" (36.5 cm x 55.9 cm) 1931 Purchase Fund, courtesy of Museum of Fine Arts, Boston; **424:** Myrleen Ferguson/PhotoEdit; **425:** *Waiting for Will, 1986,* Janet Fish; **426:** Dann Coffey/The Image Bank; **427:** *Following the Buffalo Run*, Charles M. Russell, Amon Carter Museum, Forth Worth; **428:** *The Color of Sun*, Howard Terpning, oil, 26" x 26", The Greenwich Workshop Inc.; **431:** *Crow Lodge of Twenty-five Buffalo Skins, 1832–33,* George Catlin, National Museum of American Art, Washington, D. C./Art Resource, NY; **432:** *Wild Horses at Play*, 1834–37, George Catlin, National Museum of American Art, Washington, D. C./Art Resource, NY; **440–441:** The Daughters of the Republic of Texas Library, Gift of the Yanaguana Society, 1947; **443:** Esbin/Anderson/Omni-Photo Communications, Inc.; **448:** (top) Sovfoto/Eastfoto; (center) The Granger Collection, New York; (bottom) Courtesy of New Directions Publishing Corporation; **450:** John Foster/Science Source/Photo Researchers, Inc.; **451–457:** Corel Professional Photos CD-ROM™; **460:** ©1993 Capital Cities/ABC, Inc.; **464:** Paul Conklin/Photo Edit; **466–467:** *Final Departure*, oil on canvas, 42" x 70", Lisa Learner; **468:** The Granger Collection, New York; **471:** Superstock; **473:** *The Hunters*, Gari Melchers, mid-1920s, oil on canvas, 53 3/8" x 50 1/4", Belmont, The Gari Melehers Estate & Memorial Gallery, Mary Washington College, Fredericksburg, VA; **477:** Paul Mici-ch/The Image Bank; **478:** © Andrew Syred/Science Photo Library/Photo Researchers, Inc.; **480:** © Kenneth H. Thomas/Photo Researchers, Inc.; **482–495** (border) © Kenneth H. Thomas/Photo Researchers, Inc.; **483, 486, 493:** Photofest; **498:** AP/Wide World Photos; **501:** *City Night*, 1926, Georgia O'Keeffe, Minneapolis Institute of Arts, Photo by Malcolm Varon, N.Y.C., © 1997 The Georgia O'Keeffe Foundation/Artists Rights Society (ARS), New York; **505:** *Red Hills and Bones*, 1941, Georgia O'Keeffe, Philadelphia Museum of Art, The Alfred Stieglitz Collection, © 1997 The Georgia O'Keeffe Foundation/Artists Rights Society (ARS), New York; **512:** (left) Corbis-Bettmann; (right) *Samuel Langhorne Clemens (Mark Twain)*, (detail), 1935, Frank Edwin Larson, National Portrait Gallery, Smithsonian Institution, Washington, D. C./Art Resource, New York; **514:** Erich Lessing/Art Resource, NY. private collection, Switzerland; **516–517:** Corel Professional Photos CD-ROM™; **520–521:** *Scotland Forever*, Elizabeth Butler, Leeds City Art Galleries; **523:** *Hint to Modern Sculptors as an Ornament to a Future Square*, James Gillray, hand-colored etching, Victoria and Albert Museum Trustees/Art Resource, NY; **527:** Photofest; **531:** © Keith LoBue/Stock Illustration Source, Inc. **532:** (left) Thomas Victor; (right) Sovfoto/Eastfoto; **534–535:** *Bikini*, 1987, Vernon Fisher, collection of the Krannert Art Museum and Kinkead Pavilion, University of Illinois, Champaign-Urbana; **536:** *The Body of a House #1 of 8.* © Robert Beckman 1993, oil on canvas, 69" x 96 1/2", photo by Tony Scodwell; **538:** *The Body of a House #6 of 8*, © 1993, Robert Beckman, oil on canvas, 69" x 96 1/2", Photo by Tony Scodwell; **540:** (tc) Joel Greenstein/ Omni-Photo Communications, Inc.; **541:** (tr) Frank Siteman/Stock, Boston; (bottom) Joan Slatkin/Omni-Photo Communications, Inc.; **542:** *Schrodinger's Cat*, 1989, Elizabeth Knight, New York Academy of Sciences; **544:** Catrina Genovese/Omni-Photo Communications, Inc.; **545:** (background) NASA; (center) Garfield © 1993 Paws, Inc., Dist. by Universal Press Syndicate. Reprinted with permission. All rights reserved; **546:** Joan Slatkin/Omni-Photo Communications, Inc.; **550:** The Granger Collection, New York; **552:** *Chronicles of St. Denis: Death of Clotharl/View of the Ile de la Cité, Paris,* Jehan Fouquet, Bibliothèque Nationale, Paris/Bridgeman Art Library, London/Superstock, Inc.; **554–555:** *Restricted Man, 1961,* © Jerry Uelsmann, collection of the Center for Creative Photography; **560:** David Young-Wolff/PhotoEdit; **563:** Ken Karp Photography; **566–567:** *The Last Painter on Earth*, 1983, oil on canvas, 72" x 120", James Doolin, courtesy of Koplin Gallery, Los Angeles, California; **568:** UPI/Corbis-Bettmann; **569:** Richard J. Green/Photo Researchers, Inc.; **571:** (background) Richard J. Green/Photo Researchers, Inc.; (top) Gregory Ochocki/Photo Researchers, Inc.; (bottom) © Fred Winner/Jacana/Photo Researchers, Inc.; **572:** (tr) Gregory Ochocki/Photo Researchers, Inc.; **572–573:** (background) Andrew J. Martinez/Photo Researchers, Inc.; **573:** (center) Stephen J. Krasemann/DRK Photo; **574:** (top) Mark Goebel/Omni-Photo Communications, Inc.; **574–575:** (background) Gregory Ochocki/Photo Researchers, Inc.; **575:** (center) Lawrence Migdale/Stock, Boston; **576:** (background) Gregory Ochocki/Photo Researchers, Inc.; (tl) Andrew J. Martinez/Photo Researchers, Inc.; **579:** *Cover, 1980,* John Hall, acrylic on canvas, 111.5 cm x 111.5 cm. Art Gallery of Hamilton, Canada, gift of Lillian and Leroy Page Charitable Foundation, Estate of E. L. Steiner, estate of Mabel Waldon Thompson, and the Canada Council Art Bank, 1981; **580:** (top) Thomas Victor; (center) © Sergey Tetrin/Archive Photos; (bottom) AP/Wide World Photos; **582:** (top & bottom) Kiowa arrows, F. H. Cushing, wood, feathers, fiber, pigment, L: 26 1/2", The Brooklyn Museum of Art, 30.780.1-6, estate of Stewart Culin, Museum Purchase; (center) *Old Ones Talking*, R. Brownell McGrew, Courtesy of the artist; **583:** Fan, Kiowa, c. 1900, eagle feathers, beads, cotton, leather H: 28 1/2" x W: 7 1/2". Gift of University of Tulsa, Bright Roddy Collection, Philbrook Art Center, Tulsa, Oklahoma, 1995.25.10; **584:** *Annie Old Crow*, James Bama, courtesy of the artist; **585:** Pouch, ca. 1890–1910, Kiowa hide, native pigment, glass and metal beads and silk binding. H: 6" x W: 4 1/2", T328, Thaw Collection, Fenimore House Museum, New York State Historical Association, Cooperstown. Photo by John Bigelow Taylor, N.Y.C.; **590:** Photofest; **594:** (left) Corbis-Bettmann; (right) *Langston Hughes* (detail), c.1925, Winold Reiss, The National Portrait Gallery, Smithsonian Institution, Washington, D. C./Art Resource, New York; **596, 598, 599, 600, 601:** © 1997 Estate of Fritz Eichenberg/Licensed by VAGA, New York, NY; **602:** UPI/Corbis-Bettmann; **608:** Thomas Victor; **610–611 & 613:** Steve Proehl/The Image Bank; **619:** (top) Lisa Quinones/Black Star/PNI; (bottom) Hiroyuki Matsumoto/Black Star/PNI; **623:** Courtesy of the artist; **624:** (left) © Frank Capri/Saga/Archive Photos; (right) Lisa Rose/ Globe Photos; **626, 630–631, 632:** Photofest; **638:** Danny Lyon/Magnum Photos, Inc.; **639:** *Brookline, Massachusetts*, 1986, Photograph by Sage Sohier © 1986; **640:** (left) *Nellie G. Morgan and Tammie Pruitt Morgan, Bicentennial Celebration, Philadelphia, Mississippi, 1976.* Photo © 1997, Roland L. Freeman; **640–641 & 642:** Courtesy of the photographer; **646:** (left) Ralph Morese/Life Magazine © Time Inc.; (center) Andy Caulfield/The

Image Bank; (right) Photo by Scott Weidensaul; **648:** (rc) © Photo Researchers, Inc.; **648–649 & 650–651:** (background) Andy Caulfield/ The Image Bank; **651:** (rc) © Carl Frank/Photo Researchers, Inc.; **652:** Scott Weidensaul; **656:** David Young-Wolff/PhotoEdit; **662-663:** Superstock; **665:** Richard Barnet/Omni-Photo Communications, Inc.; **667:** © Uniphoto, Inc. **668:** Vatican Museum/Scala/Art Resource, NY; **670-671:** (background) Fotopic/Omni-Photo Communications, Inc.; **685:** (background) Fotopic/Omni-Photo Communications, Inc.; **690:** Etruscan Amphora, Black-figured, pontic fighting soldiers, white dove on shield, National Museum, Warsaw, Poland, Erich Lessing/Art Resource, NY; **701:** Ken Karp Photography; **705:** *Roman Senators at the Imperial Court*, Roman relief. Museo Nazionale Romano delle Terme, Rome, Italy, Alinari/Art Resource, NY; **706:** (top) & (bottom) Robert Harding Picture Library; **707:** Illustration by Hugh Dixon from "Shakespeare in Performance," courtesy of Salamander Books, London; **708:** *William Shakespeare* (detail), Artist Unknown, courtesy of the National Portrait Gallery, London; **710:** © Michael Holford/ Collection of the British Museum; **712:** Culver Pictures, Inc.; **717 & 722:** Photofest; **737 & 746:** Culver Pictures, Inc.; **754, 760, 763:** Photofest; **764 & 765:** (background) NASA; **769:** Extispicium Relief (inspection of entrails) from the Forum of Trajan, Rome. Early Hadrianic. Louvre, Paris, France, Alinari/Art Resource, NY; **774 & 780:** Photofest; **789:** Relief of *Domitius Ahenobarbus*, scene of a census, Louvre, Paris, France, Erich Lessing/Art Resource, NY; **795:** Photofest; **800:** Erich Lessing/Art Resource, NY; **804:** Photofest; **808:** Tony Freeman/Photo Edit; **810–811:** *Awaiting Spring*, Scott Burdick, watercolor, 20"x 30", courtesy of the artist; **812:** The Granger Collection, New York; **815 & 816:** Corel Professional Photos CD-ROM™; **817 & 818:** (background) NASA; (top) Michael W. Nelson/PNI; **821:** O. S. Eguchi/Photonica; **822:** (top) & (bottom) The Granger Collection, New York; (tc) *Alfred, Lord Tennyson*, c.1840, S. Laurence, courtesy of the National Portrait Gallery, London; (bc) *Jean Toomer* (detail), c.1925, Winold Reiss, gift of Laurence A. Fleischman and Howard Garfinkle with a matching grant from the National Endowment of the Arts, National Portrait Gallery, Smithsonian Institution, Washington, D. C./Art Resource, New York; **824:** Lorette Moureau; **825:** The Granger Collection, New York; **826:** *Ploughing*, transport poster, Nancy Smith (fl.1940–50) Stapleton Collection/The Bridgeman Art Library International Ltd., London/New York; **827:** *Atlantic Moon*, Jane Wilson, oil on linen 18" x 18", courtesy Fischbach Gallery, New York; **828:** *Our Home and Native Land, 1983*, Dannielle B. Hayes, work print, gouache and pencil, 22" x 30", Omni-Photo Communications, Inc.; **832:** (tl) The Granger Collection, New York; (tr) Photo by Bachrach; (bl) Inge Morath/Magnum Photos, Inc.; (br) Photo by Lynn Saville; **834:** Catherine Karnow/ Woodfin Camp & Associates; **836–837:** Corel Professional Photos CD-ROM™; **841:** *Ploughing*, transport poster, Nancy Smith (fl.1940–50) Stapleton Collection/The Bridgeman Art Library International Ltd., London/New York; **845:** © 1989 Cathleen Toelke; **846:** (left) The Granger Collection, New York; (right) *Rudyard Kipling* (detail), 1899, P. Burne-Jones, courtesy of the National Portrait Gallery, London; **848:** *La Belle Dame sans Merci*, John W. Waterhouse, Hessiches Landes Museum, Darmstadt, Germany; **850:** Corel Professional Photos CD-ROM™; **851:** *The Battle of Bunker Hill*, Howard Pyle, Delaware Art Museum, Howard Pyle Collection; **854:** (top) By permission of the heirs of Federico García Lorca, Rogelio Robelis Saavedra and Courtney Jose Choin Castro; (center) photo by Michael Nye; (bottom) AP/Wide World Photos; **856:** *The Old Guitarist*, 1903, Pablo Picasso, Spanish, 1881–1973, oil on panel 112.9 cm x 82.6 cm, Helen Birch Bartlett Memorial Collection, 1926.253 photograph courtesy of The Art Institute of Chicago. All rights reserved, © 1997 estate of Pablo Picasso/Artists Rights Society (ARS), New York; **857:** *The Hands (Les Mains)*, 1969, Antoni Tapies, Soft ground etching, printed in black and aquatint, printed in medium red brown, plate: 19 9/16 x 15 1/2" (49.7 x 39.4 cm). The Museum of Modern Art, New York. Donald Karshan Fund. Photograph ©1999 The Museum of Modern Art, New York. ©1998 Artists Rights Society (ARS), New York/ADAGP, Paris **858–859:** Corel Professional Photos CD-ROM™; **860:** *Best Friends*, Craig Nelson/ Bernstein & Andriulli, Inc.; **864:** (top) *William Shakespeare* (detail), artist unknown, Courtesy of the National Portrait Gallery, London; (bottom) AP/Wide World Photos; **866:** *Frances Howard*, Isaac Oliver, Victoria and Albert Museum/Art Resource, NY; **867:** Frank Siteman/Stock, Boston; **868:** *The Monkey Bridge in Koshu Province*, 1841, Hiroshige Hitsu, Christie's, New York; **872:** *La Belle Dame sans Merci*, John W. Waterhouse, Hessiches Landes Museum, Darmstadt, Germany; **878–879:** *Knights About to Depart on the Quest for the Holy Grail*, Tapestry designed by Sir E. Burne-Jones, woven by William Morris & Co., (129'07) Birmingham Museums and Art Gallery; **881:** *Sir Galahad*, by George Frederick Watts (1817–1904), The Fogg Art Museum, Harvard University/ Bridgeman Art Library International Ltd., London/New York; **882:** The Granger Collection, New York; **884:** *Don Quixote*, Honoré Daumier, Neue Pinakothek, Munich, Giraudon/Art Resource, New York; **887:** *Don Quixote and the Windmill*, c. 1900, Francisco J. Torrome, Bonhams, London/Bridgeman Art Library International, London/New York; **892:** (left) *Alfred, Lord Tennyson*, c.1840, S. Laurence, courtesy of the National Portrait Gallery, London; (right) Thomas Victor; **895:** *The Dream of Arthur in Avalon*, detail, Sir Edward Burne-Jones, The Museo de Arte de Ponce, The Luis A. Ferré Foundation, Inc., Ponce, Puerto Rico; **901:** By permission of the Houghton Library, Harvard University; **905:** *The Crowning of Arthur*, Royal MS, By permission of the British Library; **908:** *Gallahad's Sword in the Stone*, Royal MS, by permission of the British Library; **912:** *The Round Table and the Holy Grail*, miniature from the *Romand de Tristan.* Ms. 645–647/315–317 v.3 fol. 1, 2nd half of 15th c., Musée Condée, Chantilly, France. Giraudon/Art Resource, NY; **917 & 921:** (tr) The Granger Collection, New York; (lc) *Rama and Lakshman Confer With the Animal Armies*, from *The Adventures of Rama*, courtesy of the Freer Gallery of Art, Smithsonian Institution, Washington, D.C., fol. 194v, full view; (br) *Dipankara Buddha*, gilt copper repoussé, 17th century A.D., 27 1/2" x 9 3/4", Asian Art Museum of San Francisco, The Avery Brundage Collection; **922:** AP/Wide World Photos; **924:** Persian translation of the *Ramayana of Valmiki* (detail), Mughal, school of Akbar, late 16th century, Indian manuscript, miniatures in opaque colors and gold: average leaf—27.5 cm x 15.2 cm, courtesy of the Freer Gallery of Art, Smithsonian Institution, Washington, D. C., 07.271 24r; **927:** *Rama Chasing the Golden Deer*, from the *Ramayana*, Sanskrit text on the reverse, 1600, Mughal, National Museum of India, New Delhi/The Bridgeman Art Library International Ltd., London/New York; **928:** *Rama Chases a Demon Disguised as a Golden Deer*, Fazl, courtesy of the Freer Gallery of Art, Smithsonian Institution, Washington, D. C., fol. 128v; **932 & 934:** Senegalese glass painting used on *Sundiata*, from the collection of Professor Donal Cruise-O'Brien, Courtesy of Longman International Education; **937:** Michael Melford/The Image Bank; **942:** (background) NASA; **943 & 944:** (top) Photofest; **944–945:** (background) NASA; **946:** © The Stock Market/Norbert Wu 1996; **961:** Nigel Strudwick/Cambridge University; **969:** Dorling Kindersley; **1005:** UPI/Corbis-Bettmann; **1010:** Photofest, Mary Kate Denny/Photo Edit.